OXFORD

ESSENTIAL WORLD ATLAS

The editors are grateful to the following for acting as specialist geography consultants on "*The World in Focus*" front section:

Professor D. Brunsden, Kings College, University of London, UK
Dr C. Clarke, Oxford University, UK
Dr I. S. Evans, Durham University, UK
Professor P. Haggett, University of Bristol, UK
Professor K. McLachlan, University of London, UK
Professor M. Monmonier, Syracuse University, New York, USA
Professor M-L. Hsu, University of Minnesota, Minnesota, USA
Professor M. J. Tooley, University of St Andrews, UK
Dr T. Unwin, Royal Holloway, University of London, UK

THE WORLD IN FOCUS
Cartography by Philip's

Picture Acknowledgements
NASA/GSFC page 14

Illustrations: Stefan Chabluk

WORLD CITIES
Cartography by Philip's

Page 10, Dublin: The town plan of Dublin is based on Ordnance Survey Ireland by permission of the Government Permit Number 8186. © Ordnance Survey Ireland and Government of Ireland.

Ordnance Survey **Page 11, Edinburgh, and page 15, London:**
This product includes mapping data licensed from Ordnance Survey® with the permission of the Controller of Her Majesty's Stationery Office. © Crown copyright 2007. All rights reserved. Licence number 100011710.

Vector data courtesy of Gräfe and Unser Verlag GmbH, München, Germany
(city-center maps of Bangkok, Beijing, Cape Town, Jerusalem, Mexico City, Moscow, Singapore, Sydney, Tokyo and Washington D.C.)
The following city maps utilize base data supplied courtesy of MapQuest.com, Inc. (© MapQuest)
(Las Vegas, New Orleans, Orlando)

All satellite images in this section courtesy of NPA Group, Edenbridge, Kent (www.satmaps.com)

Updated reprint 2007

Philip's, a division of
Octopus Publishing Group Limited,
2–4 Heron Quays, London E14 4JP
An Hachette Livre UK Company

Published in North America by
Oxford University Press, Inc.,
198 Madison Avenue,
New York, N.Y. 10016

www.oup.com/us/atlas

OXFORD UNIVERSITY PRESS Oxford is a registered trademark of Oxford University Press

Library of Congress Cataloging-in-Publication Data available

ISBN 13 978–0–19–531322–2
ISBN 10 0–19–531322–4

Printing (last digit):
9 8 7 6 5 4 3 2

Printed in Hong Kong

OXFORD

ESSENTIAL WORLD ATLAS

FOURTH EDITION

Contents

World Statistics

Countries vi
Physical Dimensions vii
User Guide viii

The World in Focus

Planet Earth 2–3
Restless Earth 4–5
Landforms 6–7
Oceans 8–9
Climate 10–11
Water and Vegetation 12–13
Environment 14–15
Population 16–17
The Human Family 18–19
Wealth 20–21
Quality of Life 22–23
Energy 24–25
Production 26–27
Trade 28–29
Travel and Tourism 30–31

World Cities

Amsterdam 2
Athens 2
Atlanta 3
Baghdad 3
Bangkok 3
Barcelona 4
Beijing 4
Berlin 5
Boston 6
Brussels 6
Budapest 7
Buenos Aires 7
Cairo 7
Cape Town 8
Copenhagen 8
Chicago 9
Delhi 10
Dublin 10
Edinburgh 11
Guangzhou 11
Helsinki 11
Hong Kong 12
Istanbul 12
Jakarta 12
Jerusalem 13
Johannesburg 13
Karachi 13
Kolkata 14
Lagos 14
Las Vegas 14
Lima 14
London 15
Lisbon 16
Los Angeles 16
Madrid 17
Manila 17
Melbourne 18
Mexico City 18
Miami 18
Milan 19
Moscow 19
Montréal 20
Mumbai 20
Munich 21
New Orleans 21
New York 22
Orlando 23
Osaka 23
Oslo 23
Paris 24
Prague 25
Rio de Janeiro 25
Rome 26
San Francisco 26
St Petersburg 27
Santiago 27
São Paulo 27
Seoul 27
Shanghai 28
Singapore 28
Stockholm 29
Sydney 29
Tokyo 30
Tehran 31
Toronto 31
Vienna 32
Warsaw 32
Washington 33
Wellington 33
Index to City Maps 34–39
World Cities Satellite Images 40–48

World Maps

Map Symbols 1

The World: Political 1:95 000 000 2–3

Arctic Ocean 1:35 000 000 4

Antarctica 1:35 000 000 5

Europe

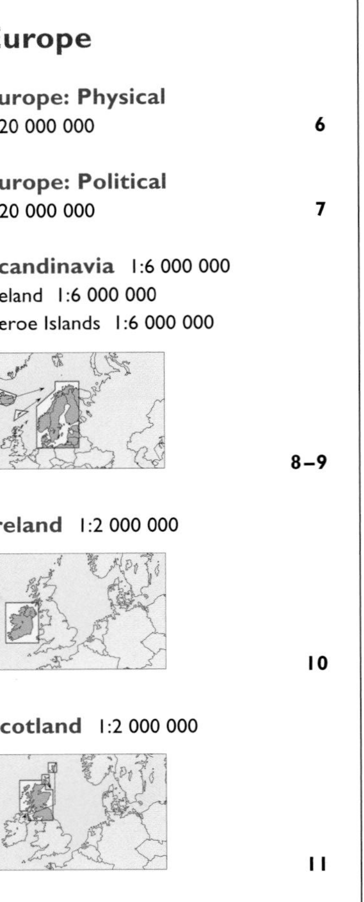

Europe: Physical 1:20 000 000 6

Europe: Political 1:20 000 000 7

Scandinavia 1:6 000 000
Iceland 1:6 000 000
Færoe Islands 1:6 000 000 8–9

Ireland 1:2 000 000 10

Scotland 1:2 000 000 11

England and Wales 1:2 000 000 12–13

British Isles 1:5 000 000 14

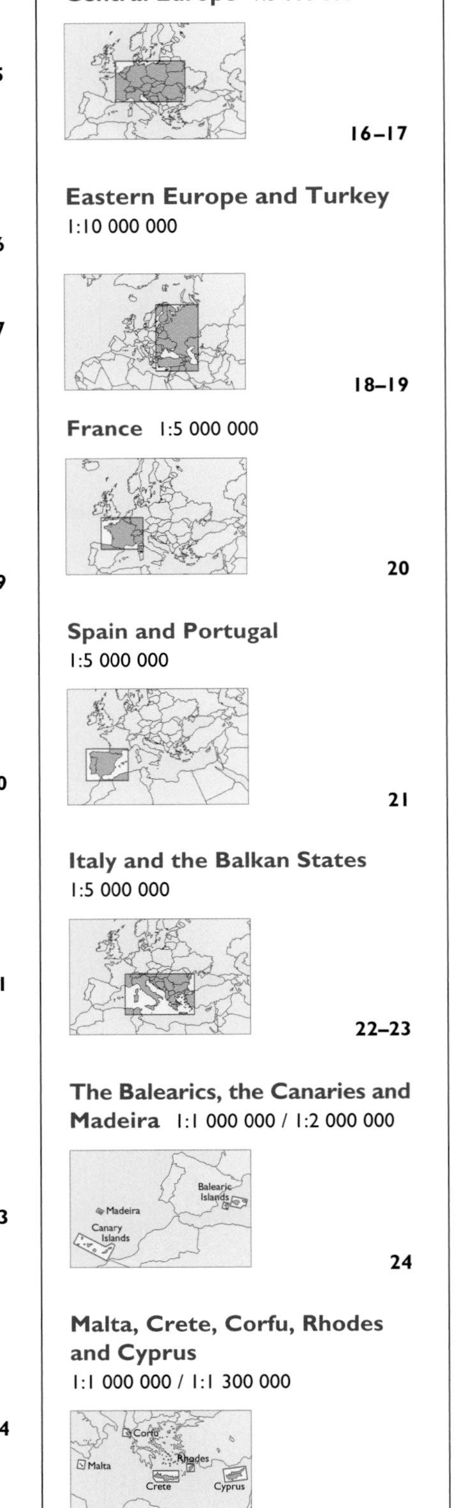

Netherlands, Belgium and Luxembourg 1:2 500 000 15

Central Europe 1:5 000 000 16–17

Eastern Europe and Turkey 1:10 000 000 18–19

France 1:5 000 000 20

Spain and Portugal 1:5 000 000 21

Italy and the Balkan States 1:5 000 000 22–23

The Balearics, the Canaries and Madeira 1:1 000 000 / 1:2 000 000 24

Malta, Crete, Corfu, Rhodes and Cyprus 1:1 000 000 / 1:1 300 000 25

Asia

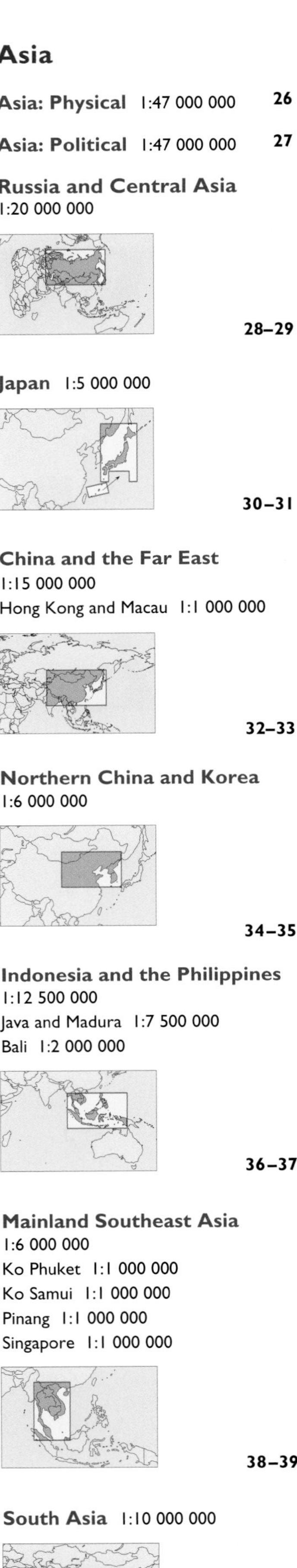

Asia: Physical 1:47 000 000 26

Asia: Political 1:47 000 000 27

Russia and Central Asia 1:20 000 000 28–29

Japan 1:5 000 000 30–31

China and the Far East 1:15 000 000
Hong Kong and Macau 1:1 000 000 32–33

Northern China and Korea 1:6 000 000 34–35

Indonesia and the Philippines 1:12 500 000
Java and Madura 1:7 500 000
Bali 1:2 000 000 36–37

Mainland Southeast Asia 1:6 000 000
Ko Phuket 1:1 000 000
Ko Samui 1:1 000 000
Pinang 1:1 000 000
Singapore 1:1 000 000 38–39

South Asia 1:10 000 000 40–41

Northern India, Pakistan and Nepal
1:6 000 000
Jammu and Kashmir 1:6 000 000

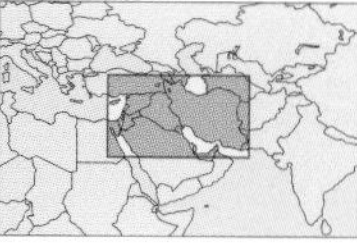

42–43

The Middle East
1:7 000 000

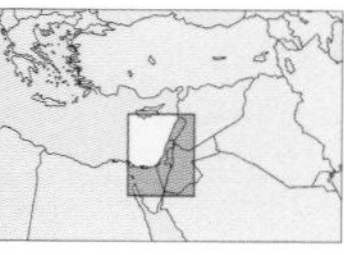

44–45

The Near East 1:2 500 000

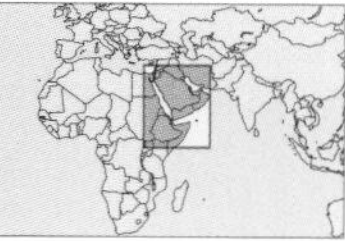

46

Arabia and the Horn of Africa 1:15 000 000

47

Africa

Africa: Physical
:42 000 000 48

Africa: Political
:42 000 000 49

Northern Africa
:15 000 000
Azores 1:15 000 000
Cape Verde Islands 1:10 000 000

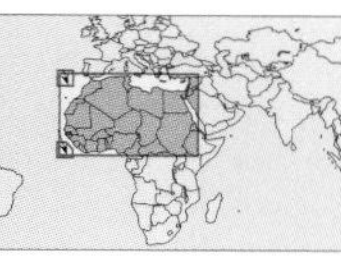

50–51

Central and Southern Africa
:15 000 000
Seychelles 1:2 500 000
Réunion 1:2 500 000
Mauritius 1:2 500 000
Comoros 1:8 000 000

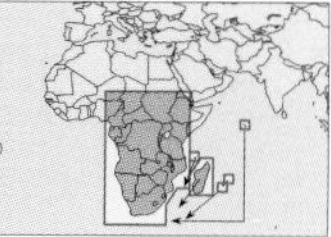

52–53

East Africa 1:8 000 000

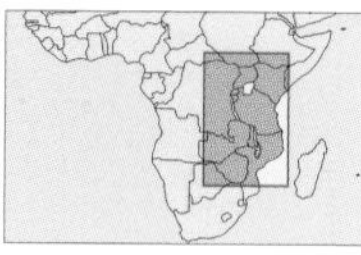

54–55

Southern Africa
1:8 000 000
Madagascar 1:8 000 000

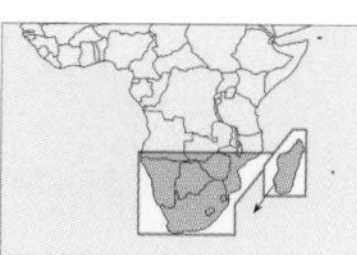

56–57

Australia and Oceania

Australia and Oceania: Physical and Political
1:50 000 000 58

New Zealand 1:6 000 000
Samoan Islands 1:6 000 000
Fiji 1:6 000 000
Tonga 1:6 000 000
Tahiti and Moorea 1:1 000 000

59

Western Australia
1:8 000 000

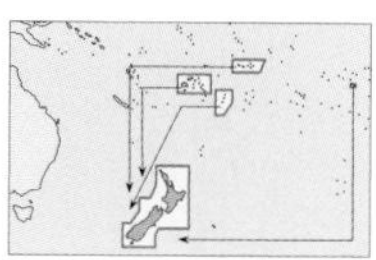

60–61

Eastern Australia
1:8 000 000
Whitsunday Islands 1:2 500 000
Tasmania 1:8 000 000

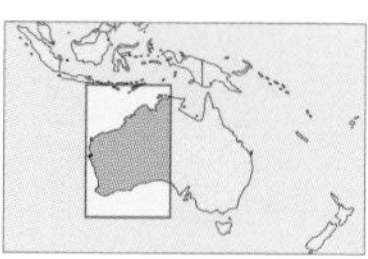

62–63

Pacific Ocean
1:54 000 000 64–65

North America

North America: Physical
1:35 000 000 66

North America: Political
1:35 000 000 67

Canada 1:15 000 000

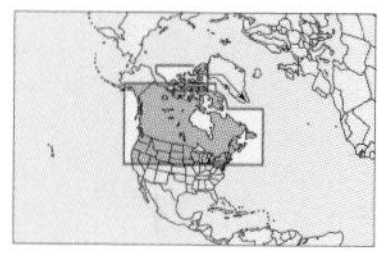

68–69

Western Canada 1:7 000 000

70–71

Eastern Canada 1:7 000 000

72–73

United States 1:12 000 000
Hawai'i 1:10 000 000
Alaska 1:30 000 000

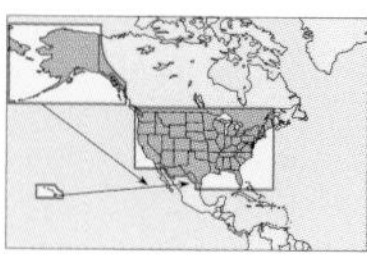

74–75

United States – West
1:6 700 000

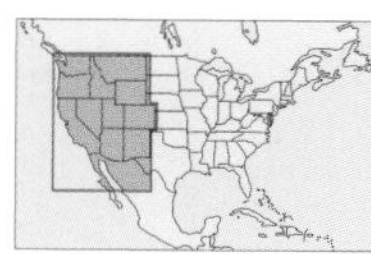

76–77

Central and Southern California and Western Washington
1:2 500 000

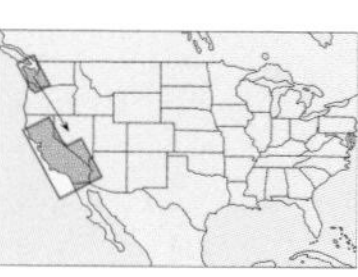

78–79

United States – Midwest and Northeast
1:6 700 000

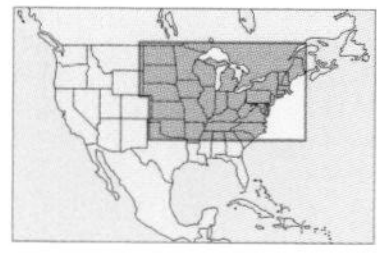

80–81

Northeastern United States
1:2 500 000

82–83

United States – South
1:6 700 000

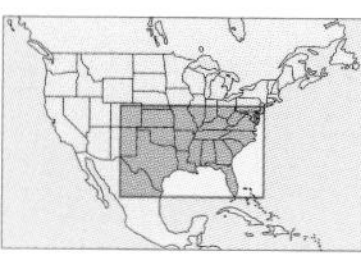

84–85

Mexico 1:8 000 000

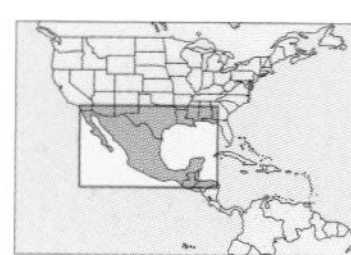

86–87

Central America and the West Indies 1:8 000 000
Jamaica 1:3 000 000
Guadeloupe 1:2 000 000
Martinique 1:2 000 000
Puerto Rico 1:3 000 000
Virgin Islands 1:2 000 000
St Lucia 1:2 000 000
Barbados 1:2 000 000

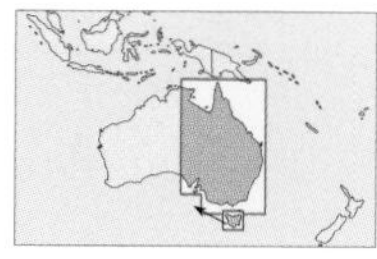

88–89

South America

South America: Physical
1:35 000 000 90

South America: Political
1:35 000 000 91

South America – North
1:16 000 000
Trinidad and Tobago 1:2 500 000

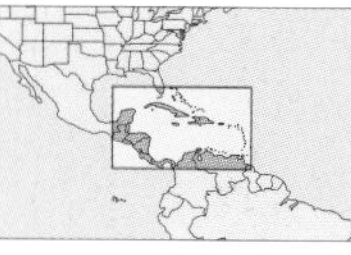

92–93

Central South America
1:8 000 000

94–95

South America – South
1:16 000 000

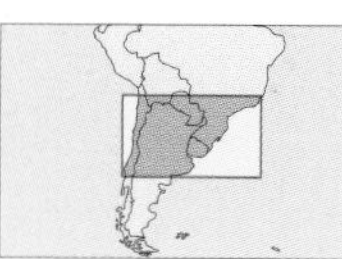

96

Index to World Maps
97–176

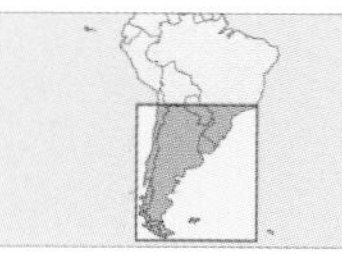

World Statistics: Countries

This alphabetical list includes the principal countries and territories of the world. If a territory is not completely independent, the country it is associated with is named. The area figures give the total area of land, inland water, and ice. The population figures are 2006 estimates where available. The annual income is the Gross Domestic Product per capita in US dollars. The figures are the latest available, usually 2006 estimates.

Country/Territory	Area km² Thousands	Area miles² Thousands	Population Thousands	Capital	Annual Income US $
Afghanistan	652	252	31,057	Kabul	800
Albania	28.7	11.1	3,582	Tirana	5,600
Algeria	2,382	920	32,930	Algiers	7,700
American Samoa (US)	0.20	0.08	58	Pago Pago	5,800
Andorra	0.47	0.18	71	Andorra La Vella	38,800
Angola	1,247	481	12,127	Luanda	4,300
Anguilla (UK)	0.10	0.04	13	The Valley	8,800
Antigua & Barbuda	0.44	0.17	69	St John's	10,900
Argentina	2,780	1,074	39,922	Buenos Aires	15,000
Armenia	29.8	11.5	2,976	Yerevan	5,400
Aruba (Netherlands)	0.19	0.07	72	Oranjestad	21,800
Australia	7,741	2,989	20,264	Canberra	32,900
Austria	83.9	32.4	8,193	Vienna	35,500
Azerbaijan	86.6	33.4	7,962	Baku	7,300
Azores (Portugal)	2.2	0.86	236	Ponta Delgada	15,000
Bahamas	13.9	5.4	304	Nassau	21,300
Bahrain	0.69	0.27	699	Manama	25,300
Bangladesh	144	55.6	147,365	Dhaka	2,200
Barbados	0.43	0.17	280	Bridgetown	18,200
Belarus	208	80.2	10,293	Minsk	7,800
Belgium	30.5	11.8	10,379	Brussels	31,800
Belize	23.0	8.9	288	Belmopan	8,400
Benin	113	43.5	7,863	Porto-Novo	1,100
Bermuda (UK)	0.05	0.02	66	Hamilton	69,900
Bhutan	47.0	18.1	2,280	Thimphu	1,400
Bolivia	1,099	424	8,989	La Paz/Sucre	3,000
Bosnia-Herzegovina	51.2	19.8	4,499	Sarajevo	5,500
Botswana	582	225	1,640	Gaborone	11,400
Brazil	8,514	3,287	188,078	Brasília	8,600
Brunei	5.8	2.2	379	Bandar Seri Begawan	25,600
Bulgaria	111	42.8	7,385	Sofia	10,400
Burkina Faso	274	106	13,903	Ouagadougou	1,300
Burma (Myanmar)	677	261	47,383	Rangoon/Naypyidaw	1,800
Burundi	27.8	10.7	8,090	Bujumbura	700
Cambodia	181	69.9	13,881	Phnom Penh	2,600
Cameroon	475	184	17,341	Yaoundé	2,400
Canada	9,971	3,850	33,099	Ottawa	35,200
Canary Is. (Spain)	7.2	2.8	1,682	Las Palmas/Santa Cruz	19,900
Cape Verde Is.	4.0	1.6	421	Praia	6,000
Cayman Is. (UK)	0.26	0.10	45	George Town	43,800
Central African Republic	623	241	4,303	Bangui	1,100
Chad	1,284	496	9,944	Ndjaména	1,500
Chile	757	292	16,134	Santiago	12,700
China	9,597	3,705	1,313,974	Beijing	7,600
Colombia	1,139	440	43,593	Bogotá	8,400
Comoros	2.2	0.86	691	Moroni	600
Congo	342	132	3,702	Brazzaville	1,300
Congo (Dem. Rep. of the)	2,345	905	62,661	Kinshasa	700
Cook Is. (NZ)	0.24	0.09	21	Avarua	9,100
Costa Rica	51.1	19.7	4,075	San José	12,000
Croatia	56.5	21.8	4,495	Zagreb	13,200
Cuba	111	42.8	11,383	Havana	3,900
Cyprus	9.3	3.6	784	Nicosia	22,700
Czech Republic	78.9	30.5	10,235	Prague	21,600
Denmark	43.1	16.6	5,451	Copenhagen	37,000
Djibouti	23.2	9.0	487	Djibouti	1,000
Dominica	0.75	0.29	69	Roseau	3,800
Dominican Republic	48.5	18.7	9,184	Santo Domingo	8,000
East Timor	14.9	5.7	1,063	Dili	800
Ecuador	284	109	13,548	Quito	4,500
Egypt	1,001	387	78,887	Cairo	4,200
El Salvador	21.0	8.1	6,822	San Salvador	4,900
Equatorial Guinea	28.1	10.8	540	Malabo	5,200
Eritrea	118	45.4	4,787	Asmara	1,000
Estonia	45.1	17.4	1,324	Tallinn	19,600
Ethiopia	1,104	426	74,778	Addis Ababa	1,000
Faroe Is. (Denmark)	1.4	0.54	47	Tórshavn	31,000
Fiji	18.3	7.1	906	Suva	6,100
Finland	338	131	5,231	Helsinki	32,800
France	552	213	60,876	Paris	30,100
French Guiana (France)	90.0	34.7	200	Cayenne	8,300
French Polynesia (France)	4.0	1.5	275	Papeete	17,500
Gabon	268	103	1,425	Libreville	7,200
Gambia, The	11.3	4.4	1,642	Banjul	2,000
Gaza Strip (OPT)*	0.36	0.14	1,429	–	1,500
Georgia	69.7	26.9	4,661	Tbilisi	3,800
Germany	357	138	82,422	Berlin	31,400
Ghana	239	92.1	22,410	Accra	2,600
Gibraltar (UK)	0.006	0.002	28	Gibraltar Town	27,900
Greece	132	50.9	10,668	Athens	23,500
Greenland (Denmark)	2,176	840	56	Nuuk	20,000
Grenada	0.34	0.13	90	St George's	3,900
Guadeloupe (France)	1.7	0.66	453	Basse-Terre	7,900
Guam (US)	0.55	0.21	171	Agana	15,000
Guatemala	109	42.0	12,294	Guatemala City	4,900
Guinea	246	94.9	9,690	Conakry	2,000
Guinea-Bissau	36.1	13.9	1,442	Bissau	900
Guyana	215	83.0	767	Georgetown	4,700
Haiti	27.8	10.7	8,309	Port-au-Prince	1,800
Honduras	112	43.3	7,326	Tegucigalpa	3,000
Hungary	93.0	35.9	9,981	Budapest	17,300
Iceland	103	39.8	299	Reykjavik	38,100
India	3,287	1,269	1,095,352	New Delhi	3,700
Indonesia	1,905	735	245,453	Jakarta	3,800
Iran	1,648	636	68,688	Tehran	8,900
Iraq	438	169	26,783	Baghdad	2,900
Ireland	70.3	27.1	4,062	Dublin	43,600
Israel	20.6	8.0	6,352	Jerusalem	26,200
Italy	301	116	58,134	Rome	29,700
Ivory Coast (Côte d'Ivoire)	322	125	17,655	Yamoussoukro	1,600
Jamaica	11.0	4.2	2,758	Kingston	4,600
Japan	378	146	127,464	Tokyo	33,100
Jordan	89.3	34.5	5,907	Amman	4,900
Kazakhstan	2,725	1,052	15,233	Astana	9,100
Kenya	580	224	34,708	Nairobi	1,200
Kiribati	0.73	0.28	105	Tarawa	2,700
Korea, North	121	46.5	23,113	Pyŏngyang	1,800
Korea, South	99.3	38.3	48,847	Seoul	24,200
Kuwait	17.8	6.9	2,418	Kuwait City	21,600
Kyrgyzstan	200	77.2	5,214	Bishkek	2,000
Laos	237	91.4	6,368	Vientiane	2,100
Latvia	64.6	24.9	2,275	Riga	15,400
Lebanon	10.4	4.0	3,874	Beirut	5,500
Lesotho	30.4	11.7	2,022	Maseru	2,600
Liberia	111	43.0	3,042	Monrovia	1,000
Libya	1,760	679	5,901	Tripoli	12,700
Liechtenstein	0.16	0.06	34	Vaduz	25,000
Lithuania	65.2	25.2	3,586	Vilnius	15,100
Luxembourg	2.6	1.0	474	Luxembourg	68,800
Macedonia (FYROM)	25.7	9.9	2,051	Skopje	8,200
Madagascar	587	227	18,595	Antananarivo	900
Madeira (Portugal)	0.78	0.30	241	Funchal	22,700
Malawi	118	45.7	13,014	Lilongwe	600
Malaysia	330	127	24,386	Kuala Lumpur/Putrajaya	12,700
Maldives	0.30	0.12	359	Malé	3,900
Mali	1,240	479	11,717	Bamako	1,200
Malta	0.32	0.12	400	Valletta	20,300
Marshall Is.	0.18	0.07	60	Majuro	2,900
Martinique (France)	1.1	0.43	436	Fort-de-France	14,400
Mauritania	1,026	396	3,177	Nouakchott	2,600
Mauritius	2.0	0.79	1,241	Port Louis	13,500
Mayotte (France)	0.37	0.14	201	Mamoundzou	4,900
Mexico	1,958	756	107,450	Mexico City	10,600
Micronesia, Fed. States of	0.70	0.27	108	Palikir	2,300
Moldova	33.9	13.1	4,467	Chişinău	2,000
Monaco	0.001	0.0004	33	Monaco	30,000
Mongolia	1,567	605	2,832	Ulan Bator	2,000
Montenegro	14.0	5.4	631	Podgorica	3,800
Montserrat (UK)	0.10	0.04	9	Plymouth	3,400
Morocco	447	172	33,241	Rabat	4,400
Mozambique	802	309	19,687	Maputo	1,500
Namibia	824	318	2,044	Windhoek	7,400
Nauru	0.02	0.008	13	Yaren District	5,000
Nepal	147	56.8	28,287	Katmandu	1,500
Netherlands	41.5	16.0	16,491	Amsterdam/The Hague	31,700
Netherlands Antilles (Neths)	0.80	0.31	222	Willemstad	16,000
New Caledonia (France)	18.6	7.2	219	Nouméa	15,000
New Zealand	271	104	4,076	Wellington	26,000
Nicaragua	130	50.2	5,570	Managua	3,000
Niger	1,267	489	12,525	Niamey	1,000
Nigeria	924	357	131,860	Abuja	1,400
Northern Mariana Is. (US)	0.46	0.18	82	Saipan	12,500
Norway	324	125	4,611	Oslo	47,800
Oman	310	119	3,102	Muscat	14,100
Pakistan	796	307	165,804	Islamabad	2,600
Palau	0.46	0.18	21	Koror	7,600
Panama	75.5	29.2	3,191	Panamá	7,900
Papua New Guinea	463	179	5,671	Port Moresby	2,700
Paraguay	407	157	6,506	Asunción	4,700
Peru	1,285	496	28,303	Lima	6,400
Philippines	300	116	89,469	Manila	5,000
Poland	323	125	38,537	Warsaw	14,100
Portugal	88.8	34.3	10,606	Lisbon	19,100
Puerto Rico (US)	8.9	3.4	3,927	San Juan	19,100
Qatar	11.0	4.2	885	Doha	29,400
Réunion (France)	2.5	0.97	788	St-Denis	6,200
Romania	238	92.0	22,304	Bucharest	8,800
Russia	17,075	6,593	142,894	Moscow	12,100
Rwanda	26.3	10.2	8,648	Kigali	1,600
St Kitts & Nevis	0.26	0.10	39	Basseterre	8,200
St Lucia	0.54	0.21	168	Castries	4,800
St Vincent & Grenadines	0.39	0.15	118	Kingstown	3,600
Samoa	2.8	1.1	177	Apia	2,100
San Marino	0.06	0.02	29	San Marino	34,100
São Tomé & Príncipe	0.96	0.37	193	São Tomé	1,200
Saudi Arabia	2,150	830	27,020	Riyadh	13,800
Senegal	197	76.0	11,987	Dakar	1,800
Serbia	88.4	34.1	9,396	Belgrade	4,400
Seychelles	0.46	0.18	82	Victoria	7,800
Sierra Leone	71.7	27.7	6,005	Freetown	900
Singapore	0.68	0.26	4,492	Singapore City	30,900
Slovak Republic	49.0	18.9	5,439	Bratislava	17,700
Slovenia	20.3	7.8	2,010	Ljubljana	23,400
Solomon Is.	28.9	11.2	552	Honiara	600
Somalia	638	246	8,863	Mogadishu	600
South Africa	1,221	471	44,188	Cape Town/Pretoria	13,000
Spain	498	192	40,398	Madrid	27,000
Sri Lanka	65.6	25.3	20,222	Colombo	4,600
Sudan	2,506	967	41,236	Khartoum	2,300
Suriname	163	63.0	439	Paramaribo	7,100
Swaziland	17.4	6.7	1,136	Mbabane	5,500
Sweden	450	174	9,017	Stockholm	31,600
Switzerland	41.3	15.9	7,524	Bern	33,600
Syria	185	71.5	18,881	Damascus	4,000
Taiwan	36.0	13.9	23,036	Taipei	29,000
Tajikistan	143	55.3	7,321	Dushanbe	1,300
Tanzania	945	365	37,445	Dodoma	800
Thailand	513	198	64,632	Bangkok	9,100
Togo	56.8	21.9	5,549	Lomé	1,700
Tonga	0.65	0.25	115	Nuku'alofa	2,200
Trinidad & Tobago	5.1	2.0	1,066	Port of Spain	19,700
Tunisia	164	63.2	10,175	Tunis	8,600
Turkey	775	299	70,414	Ankara	8,900
Turkmenistan	488	188	5,043	Ashkhabad	8,900
Turks & Caicos Is. (UK)	0.43	0.17	21	Cockburn Town	11,500
Tuvalu	0.03	0.01	12	Fongafale	1,600
Uganda	241	93.1	28,196	Kampala	1,800
Ukraine	604	233	46,711	Kiev	7,600
United Arab Emirates	83.6	32.3	2,603	Abu Dhabi	49,700
United Kingdom	242	93.4	60,609	London	31,400
United States of America	9,629	3,718	301,139	Washington, DC	43,500
Uruguay	175	67.6	3,432	Montevideo	10,700
Uzbekistan	447	173	27,307	Tashkent	2,000
Vanuatu	12.2	4.7	209	Port-Vila	2,900
Venezuela	912	352	25,730	Caracas	6,900
Vietnam	332	128	84,403	Hanoi	3,100
Virgin Is. (UK)	0.15	0.06	23	Road Town	38,500
Virgin Is. (US)	0.35	0.13	109	Charlotte Amalie	14,500
Wallis & Futuna Is. (France)	0.20	0.08	16	Mata-Utu	3,800
West Bank (OPT)*	5.9	2.3	2,460	–	1,500
Western Sahara	266	103	273	El Aaiún	N/A
Yemen	528	204	21,456	Sana'	900
Zambia	753	291	11,502	Lusaka	1,000
Zimbabwe	391	151	12,237	Harare	2,000

*OPT = Occupied Palestinian Territory N/A = Not available

World Statistics: Physical Dimensions

Each topic list is divided into continents and within a continent the items are listed in order of size. The bottom part of many of the lists is selective in order to give examples from as many different countries as possible. The order of the continents is the same as in the atlas, beginning with Europe and ending with South America. The figures are rounded as appropriate.

World, Continents, Oceans

	km²	miles²	%
The World	509,450,000	196,672,000	–
Land	149,450,000	57,688,000	29.3
Water	360,000,000	138,984,000	70.7
Asia	44,500,000	17,177,000	29.8
Africa	30,302,000	11,697,000	20.3
North America	24,241,000	9,357,000	16.2
South America	17,793,000	6,868,000	11.9
Antarctica	14,100,000	5,443,000	9.4
Europe	9,957,000	3,843,000	6.7
Australia & Oceania	8,557,000	3,303,000	5.7
Pacific Ocean	155,557,000	60,061,000	46.4
Atlantic Ocean	76,762,000	29,638,000	22.9
Indian Ocean	68,556,000	26,470,000	20.4
Southern Ocean	20,327,000	7,848,000	6.1
Arctic Ocean	14,056,000	5,427,000	4.2

Ocean Depths

Atlantic Ocean	m	ft
Puerto Rico (Milwaukee) Deep	9,220	30,249
Cayman Trench	7,680	25,197
Gulf of Mexico	5,203	17,070
Mediterranean Sea	5,121	16,801
Black Sea	2,211	7,254
North Sea	660	2,165
Indian Ocean	**m**	**ft**
Java Trench	7,450	24,442
Red Sea	2,635	8,454
Pacific Ocean	**m**	**ft**
Mariana Trench	11,022	36,161
Tonga Trench	10,882	35,702
Japan Trench	10,554	34,626
Kuril Trench	10,542	34,587
Arctic Ocean	**m**	**ft**
Molloy Deep	5,608	18,399
Southern Ocean	**m**	**ft**
South Sandwich Trench	7,235	23,737

Mountains

Europe		m	ft
Elbrus	*Russia*	5,642	18,510
Mont Blanc	*France/Italy*	4,808	15,774
Monte Rosa	*Italy/Switzerland*	4,634	15,203
Dom	*Switzerland*	4,545	14,911
Liskamm	*Switzerland*	4,527	14,852
Weisshorn	*Switzerland*	4,505	14,780
Taschorn	*Switzerland*	4,490	14,730
Matterhorn/Cervino	*Italy/Switzerland*	4,478	14,691
Mont Maudit	*France/Italy*	4,465	14,649
Dent Blanche	*Switzerland*	4,356	14,291
Nadelhorn	*Switzerland*	4,327	14,196
Grandes Jorasses	*France/Italy*	4,208	13,806
Jungfrau	*Switzerland*	4,158	13,642
Grossglockner	*Austria*	3,797	12,457
Mulhacén	*Spain*	3,478	11,411
Zugspitze	*Germany*	2,962	9,718
Olympus	*Greece*	2,917	9,570
Triglav	*Slovenia*	2,863	9,393
Gerlachovka	*Slovak Republic*	2,655	8,711
Galdhøpiggen	*Norway*	2,469	8,100
Ben Nevis	*UK*	1,342	4,403
Asia		**m**	**ft**
Everest	*China/Nepal*	8,850	29,035
K2 (Godwin Austen)	*China/Kashmir*	8,611	28,251
Kanchenjunga	*India/Nepal*	8,598	28,208
Lhotse	*China/Nepal*	8,516	27,939
Makalu	*China/Nepal*	8,481	27,824
Cho Oyu	*China/Nepal*	8,201	26,906
Dhaulagiri	*Nepal*	8,167	26,795
Manaslu	*Nepal*	8,156	26,758
Nanga Parbat	*Kashmir*	8,126	26,660
Annapurna	*Nepal*	8,078	26,502
Gasherbrum	*China/Kashmir*	8,068	26,469
Broad Peak	*China/Kashmir*	8,051	26,414
Xixabangma	*China*	8,012	26,286
Kangbachen	*Nepal*	7,858	25,781
Trivor	*Pakistan*	7,720	25,328
Pik Imeni Ismail Samani	*Tajikistan*	7,495	24,590
Demavend	*Iran*	5,604	18,386
Ararat	*Turkey*	5,165	16,945
Gunong Kinabalu	*Malaysia (Borneo)*	4,101	13,455
Fuji-San	*Japan*	3,776	12,388
Africa		**m**	**ft**
Kilimanjaro	*Tanzania*	5,895	19,340
Mt Kenya	*Kenya*	5,199	17,057
Ruwenzori (Margherita)	*Ug./Congo (D.R.)*	5,109	16,762
Meru	*Tanzania*	4,565	14,977
Ras Dashen	*Ethiopia*	4,533	14,872
Karisimbi	*Rwanda/Congo (D.R.)*	4,507	14,787
Mt Elgon	*Kenya/Uganda*	4,321	14,176
Batu	*Ethiopia*	4,307	14,130
Toubkal	*Morocco*	4,165	13,665
Mt Cameroun	*Cameroon*	4,070	13,353
Oceania		**m**	**ft**
Puncak Jaya	*Indonesia*	5,029	16,499
Puncak Trikora	*Indonesia*	4,730	15,518
Puncak Mandala	*Indonesia*	4,702	15,427
Mt Wilhelm	*Papua New Guinea*	4,508	14,790
Mauna Kea	*USA (Hawai'i)*	4,205	13,796
Mauna Loa	*USA (Hawai'i)*	4,169	13,681
Aoraki Mt Cook	*New Zealand*	3,753	12,313
Mt Kosciuszko	*Australia*	2,230	7,316
North America		**m**	**ft**
Mt McKinley (Denali)	*USA (Alaska)*	6,194	20,321
Mt Logan	*Canada*	5,959	19,551
Pico de Orizaba	*Mexico*	5,610	18,405
Mt St Elias	*USA/Canada*	5,489	18,008
Popocatépetl	*Mexico*	5,452	17,887
Mt Foraker	*USA (Alaska)*	5,304	17,401
Iztaccihuatl	*Mexico*	5,286	17,343
Mt Lucania	*Canada*	5,226	17,146
Mt Steele	*Canada*	5,073	16,644
Mt Bona	*USA (Alaska)*	5,005	16,420
Mt Whitney	*USA*	4,418	14,495
Tajumulco	*Guatemala*	4,220	13,845
Chirripó Grande	*Costa Rica*	3,837	12,589
Pico Duarte	*Dominican Rep.*	3,175	10,417
South America		**m**	**ft**
Aconcagua	*Argentina*	6,962	22,841
Bonete	*Argentina*	6,872	22,546
Ojos del Salado	*Argentina/Chile*	6,863	22,516
Pissis	*Argentina*	6,779	22,241
Mercedario	*Argentina/Chile*	6,770	22,211
Huascarán	*Peru*	6,768	22,204
Llullaillaco	*Argentina/Chile*	6,723	22,057
Nudo de Cachi	*Argentina*	6,720	22,047
Yerupaja	*Peru*	6,632	21,758
Sajama	*Bolivia*	6,520	21,391
Chimborazo	*Ecuador*	6,267	20,561
Pico Cristóbal Colón	*Colombia*	5,800	19,029
Pico Bolivar	*Venezuela*	5,007	16,427
Antarctica		**m**	**ft**
Vinson Massif		4,897	16,066
Mt Kirkpatrick		4,528	14,855

Rivers

Europe		km	miles
Volga	*Caspian Sea*	3,700	2,300
Danube	*Black Sea*	2,850	1,770
Ural	*Caspian Sea*	2,535	1,575
Dnepr (Dnipro)	*Black Sea*	2,285	1,420
Kama	*Volga*	2,030	1,260
Don	*Black Sea*	1,990	1,240
Petchora	*Arctic Ocean*	1,790	1,110
Oka	*Volga*	1,480	920
Dnister (Dniester)	*Black Sea*	1,400	870
Vyatka	*Kama*	1,370	850
Rhine	*North Sea*	1,320	820
N. Dvina	*Arctic Ocean*	1,290	800
Elbe	*North Sea*	1,145	710
Asia		**km**	**miles**
Yangtze	*Pacific Ocean*	6,380	3,960
Yenisey–Angara	*Arctic Ocean*	5,550	3,445
Huang He	*Pacific Ocean*	5,464	3,395
Ob–Irtysh	*Arctic Ocean*	5,410	3,360
Mekong	*Pacific Ocean*	4,500	2,795
Amur	*Pacific Ocean*	4,442	2,760
Lena	*Arctic Ocean*	4,402	2,735
Irtysh	*Ob*	4,250	2,640
Yenisey	*Arctic Ocean*	4,090	2,540
Ob	*Arctic Ocean*	3,680	2,285
Indus	*Indian Ocean*	3,100	1,925
Brahmaputra	*Indian Ocean*	2,900	1,800
Syrdarya	*Aral Sea*	2,860	1,775
Salween	*Indian Ocean*	2,800	1,740
Euphrates	*Indian Ocean*	2,700	1,675
Amudarya	*Aral Sea*	2,540	1,575
Africa		**km**	**miles**
Nile	*Mediterranean*	6,695	4,180
Congo	*Atlantic Ocean*	4,670	2,900
Niger	*Atlantic Ocean*	4,180	2,595
Zambezi	*Indian Ocean*	3,540	2,200
Oubangi/Uele	*Congo (D.R.)*	2,250	1,400
Kasai	*Congo (D.R.)*	1,950	1,210
Shaballe	*Indian Ocean*	1,930	1,200
Orange	*Atlantic Ocean*	1,860	1,155
Cubango	*Okavango Delta*	1,800	1,120
Limpopo	*Indian Ocean*	1,770	1,100
Senegal	*Atlantic Ocean*	1,640	1,020
Australia		**km**	**miles**
Murray–Darling	*Southern Ocean*	3,750	2,330
Darling	*Murray*	3,070	1,905
Murray	*Southern Ocean*	2,575	1,600
Murrumbidgee	*Murray*	1,690	1,050
North America		**km**	**miles**
Mississippi–Missouri	*Gulf of Mexico*	5,971	3,710
Mackenzie	*Arctic Ocean*	4,240	2,630
Missouri	*Mississippi*	4,088	2,540
Mississippi	*Gulf of Mexico*	3,782	2,350
Yukon	*Pacific Ocean*	3,185	1,980
Rio Grande	*Gulf of Mexico*	3,030	1,880
Arkansas	*Mississippi*	2,340	1,450
Colorado	*Pacific Ocean*	2,330	1,445
Red	*Mississippi*	2,040	1,270
Columbia	*Pacific Ocean*	1,950	1,210
Saskatchewan	*Lake Winnipeg*	1,940	1,205
South America		**km**	**miles**
Amazon	*Atlantic Ocean*	6,450	4,010
Paraná–Plate	*Atlantic Ocean*	4,500	2,800
Purus	*Amazon*	3,350	2,080
Madeira	*Amazon*	3,200	1,990
São Francisco	*Atlantic Ocean*	2,900	1,800
Paraná	*Plate*	2,800	1,740
Tocantins	*Atlantic Ocean*	2,750	1,710
Orinoco	*Atlantic Ocean*	2,740	1,700
Paraguay	*Paraná*	2,550	1,580
Pilcomayo	*Paraná*	2,500	1,550
Araguaia	*Tocantins*	2,250	1,400

Lakes

Europe		km²	miles²
Lake Ladoga	*Russia*	17,700	6,800
Lake Onega	*Russia*	9,700	3,700
Saimaa system	*Finland*	8,000	3,100
Vänern	*Sweden*	5,500	2,100
Asia		**km²**	**miles²**
Caspian Sea	*Asia*	371,000	143,000
Lake Baikal	*Russia*	30,500	11,780
Tonlé Sap	*Cambodia*	20,000	7,700
Lake Balqash	*Kazakhstan*	18,500	7,100
Aral Sea	*Kazakhstan/Uzbekistan*	17,160	6,625
Africa		**km²**	**miles²**
Lake Victoria	*East Africa*	68,000	26,300
Lake Tanganyika	*Central Africa*	33,000	13,000
Lake Malawi/Nyasa	*East Africa*	29,600	11,430
Lake Chad	*Central Africa*	25,000	9,700
Lake Bangweulu	*Zambia*	9,840	3,800
Lake Turkana	*Ethiopia/Kenya*	8,500	3,290
Australia		**km²**	**miles²**
Lake Eyre	*Australia*	8,900	3,400
Lake Torrens	*Australia*	5,800	2,200
Lake Gairdner	*Australia*	4,800	1,900
North America		**km²**	**miles²**
Lake Superior	*Canada/USA*	82,350	31,800
Lake Huron	*Canada/USA*	59,600	23,010
Lake Michigan	*USA*	58,000	22,400
Great Bear Lake	*Canada*	31,800	12,280
Great Slave Lake	*Canada*	28,500	11,000
Lake Erie	*Canada/USA*	25,700	9,900
Lake Winnipeg	*Canada*	24,400	9,400
Lake Ontario	*Canada/USA*	19,500	7,500
Lake Nicaragua	*Nicaragua*	8,200	3,200
South America		**km²**	**miles²**
Lake Titicaca	*Bolivia/Peru*	8,300	3,200
Lake Poopo	*Bolivia*	2,800	1,100

Islands

Europe		km²	miles²
Great Britain	*UK*	229,880	88,700
Iceland	*Atlantic Ocean*	103,000	39,800
Ireland	*Ireland/UK*	84,400	32,600
Novaya Zemlya (N.)	*Russia*	48,200	18,600
Sicily	*Italy*	25,500	9,800
Corsica	*France*	8,700	3,400
Asia		**km²**	**miles²**
Borneo	*Southeast Asia*	744,360	287,400
Sumatra	*Indonesia*	473,600	182,860
Honshu	*Japan*	230,500	88,980
Sulawesi (Celebes)	*Indonesia*	189,000	73,000
Java	*Indonesia*	126,700	48,900
Luzon	*Philippines*	104,700	40,400
Hokkaido	*Japan*	78,400	30,300
Africa		**km²**	**miles²**
Madagascar	*Indian Ocean*	587,040	226,660
Socotra	*Indian Ocean*	3,600	1,400
Réunion	*Indian Ocean*	2,500	965
Oceania		**km²**	**miles²**
New Guinea	*Indonesia/Papua NG*	821,030	317,000
New Zealand (S.)	*Pacific Ocean*	150,500	58,100
New Zealand (N.)	*Pacific Ocean*	114,700	44,300
Tasmania	*Australia*	67,800	26,200
Hawai'i	*Pacific Ocean*	10,450	4,000
North America		**km²**	**miles²**
Greenland	*Atlantic Ocean*	2,175,600	839,800
Baffin Is.	*Canada*	508,000	196,100
Victoria Is.	*Canada*	212,200	81,900
Ellesmere Is.	*Canada*	212,000	81,800
Cuba	*Caribbean Sea*	110,860	42,800
Hispaniola	*Dominican Rep./Haiti*	76,200	29,400
Jamaica	*Caribbean Sea*	11,400	4,400
Puerto Rico	*Atlantic Ocean*	8,900	3,400
South America		**km²**	**miles²**
Tierra del Fuego	*Argentina/Chile*	47,000	18,100
Falkland Is. (E.)	*Atlantic Ocean*	6,800	2,600

User Guide

The reference maps which form the main body of this atlas have been prepared in accordance with the highest standards of international cartography to provide an accurate and detailed representation of the Earth. The scales and projections used have been carefully chosen to give balanced coverage of the world, while emphasizing the most densely populated and economically significant regions. A hallmark of Philip's mapping is the use of hill shading and relief coloring to create a graphic impression of landforms: this makes the maps exceptionally easy to read. However, knowledge of the key features employed in the construction and presentation of the maps will enable the reader to derive the fullest benefit from the atlas.

Map sequence

The atlas covers the Earth continent by continent: first Europe; then its land neighbor Asia (mapped north before south, in a clockwise sequence), then Africa, Australia and Oceania, North America, and South America. This is the classic arrangement adopted by most cartographers since the 16th century. For each continent, there are maps at a variety of scales. First, physical relief and political maps of the whole continent; then a series of larger-scale maps of the regions within the continent, each followed, where required, by still larger-scale maps of the most important or densely populated areas. The governing principle is that by turning the pages of the atlas, the reader moves steadily from north to south through each continent, with each map overlapping its neighbors.

Map presentation

With very few exceptions (for example, for the Arctic and Antarctica), the maps are drawn with north at the top, regardless of whether they are presented upright or sideways on the page. In the borders will be found the map title; a locator diagram showing the area covered; continuation arrows showing the page numbers for maps of adjacent areas; the scale; the projection used; the degrees of latitude and longitude; and the letters and figures used in the index for locating place names and geographical features. Physical relief maps also have a height reference panel identifying the colors used for each layer of contouring.

Map symbols

Each map contains a vast amount of detail which can only be conveyed clearly and accurately by the use of symbols. Points and circles of varying sizes locate and identify the relative importance of towns and cities; different styles of type are employed for administrative, geographical, and regional place names. A variety of pictorial symbols denote features such as glaciers and marshes, as well as man-made structures including roads, railroads, airports, and canals.

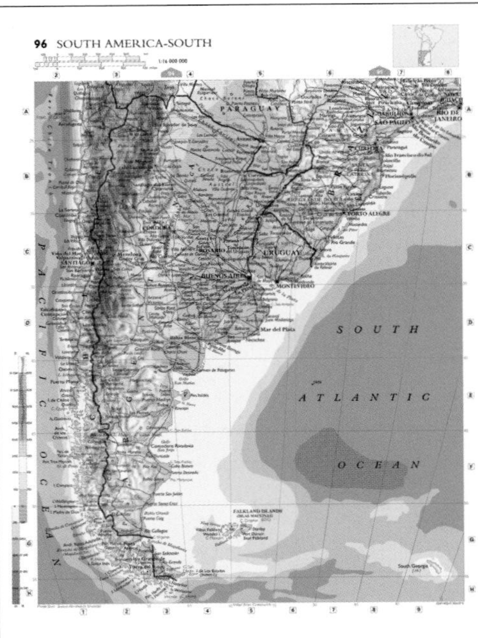

International borders are shown by red lines. Where neighboring countries are in dispute, for example in the Middle East, the maps show the *de facto* boundary between nations, regardless of the legal or historical situation. The symbols are explained on the first page of the World Maps section of the atlas.

Map scales

The scale of each map is given in the numerical form known as the "representative fraction." The first figure is always one, signifying one unit of distance on the map; the second figure, usually in millions, is the number by which the map unit must be multiplied to give the equivalent distance on the Earth's surface. Calculations can easily be made in centimeters and kilometers, by dividing the Earth units figure by 100 000 (i.e. deleting the last five 0s). Thus 1:1 000 000 means 1 cm = 10 km. The calculation for inches and miles is more laborious, but 1 000 000 divided by 63 360 (the number of inches in a mile) shows that the ratio 1:1 000 000 means approximately 1 inch = 16 miles. The table below provides distance equivalents for scales down to 1:50 000 000.

LARGE SCALE		
1:1 000 000	1 cm = 10 km	1 inch = 16 miles
1:2 500 000	1 cm = 25 km	1 inch = 39.5 miles
1:5 000 000	1 cm = 50 km	1 inch = 79 miles
1:6 000 000	1 cm = 60 km	1 inch = 95 miles
1:8 000 000	1 cm = 80 km	1 inch = 126 miles
1:10 000 000	1 cm = 100 km	1 inch = 158 miles
1:15 000 000	1 cm = 150 km	1 inch = 237 miles
1:20 000 000	1 cm = 200 km	1 inch = 316 miles
1:50 000 000	1 cm = 500 km	1 inch = 790 miles
SMALL SCALE		

Measuring distances

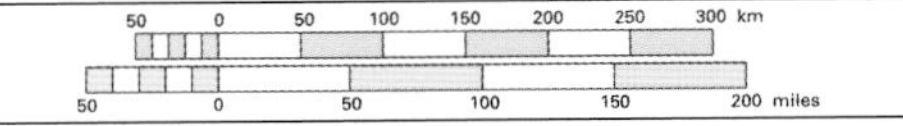

Although each map is accompanied by a scale bar, distances cannot always be measured with confidence because of the distortions involved in portraying the curved surface of the Earth on a flat page. As a general rule, the larger the map scale (i.e. the lower the number of Earth units in the representative fraction), the more accurate and reliable will be the distance measured. On small-scale maps such as those of the world and of entire continents, measurement may only be accurate along the "standard parallels," or central axes, and should not be attempted without considering the map projection.

Latitude and longitude

Accurate positioning of individual points on the Earth's surface is made possible by reference to the geometrical system of latitude and longitude. Latitude *parallels* are drawn west–east around the Earth and numbered by degrees north and south of the Equator, which is designated 0° of latitude. Longitude *meridians* are drawn north–south and numbered by degrees east and west of the *prime meridian*, 0° of longitude, which passes through Greenwich in England. By referring to these coordinates and their subdivisions of minutes (1/60th of a degree) and seconds (1/60th of a minute), any place on Earth can be located to within a few hundred meters. Latitude and longitude are indicated by blue lines on the maps; they are straight or curved according to the projection employed. Reference to these lines is the easiest way of determining the relative positions of places on different maps, and for plotting compass directions.

Name forms

For ease of reference, both English and local name forms appear in the atlas. Oceans, seas, and countries are shown in English throughout the atlas; country names may be abbreviated to their commonly accepted form (for example, Germany, not The Federal Republic of Germany). Conventional English forms are also used for place names on the smaller-scale maps of the continents. However, local name forms are used on all large-scale and regional maps, with the English form given in brackets only for important cities – the large-scale map of Russia and Central Asia thus shows Moskva (Moscow). For countries which do not use a Roman script, place names have been transcribed according to the systems adopted by the British and US Geographic Names Authorities. For China, the Pin Yin system has been used, with some more widely known forms appearing in brackets, as with Beijing (Peking). Both English and local names appear in the index, the English form being cross-referenced to the local form.

THE WORLD IN FOCUS

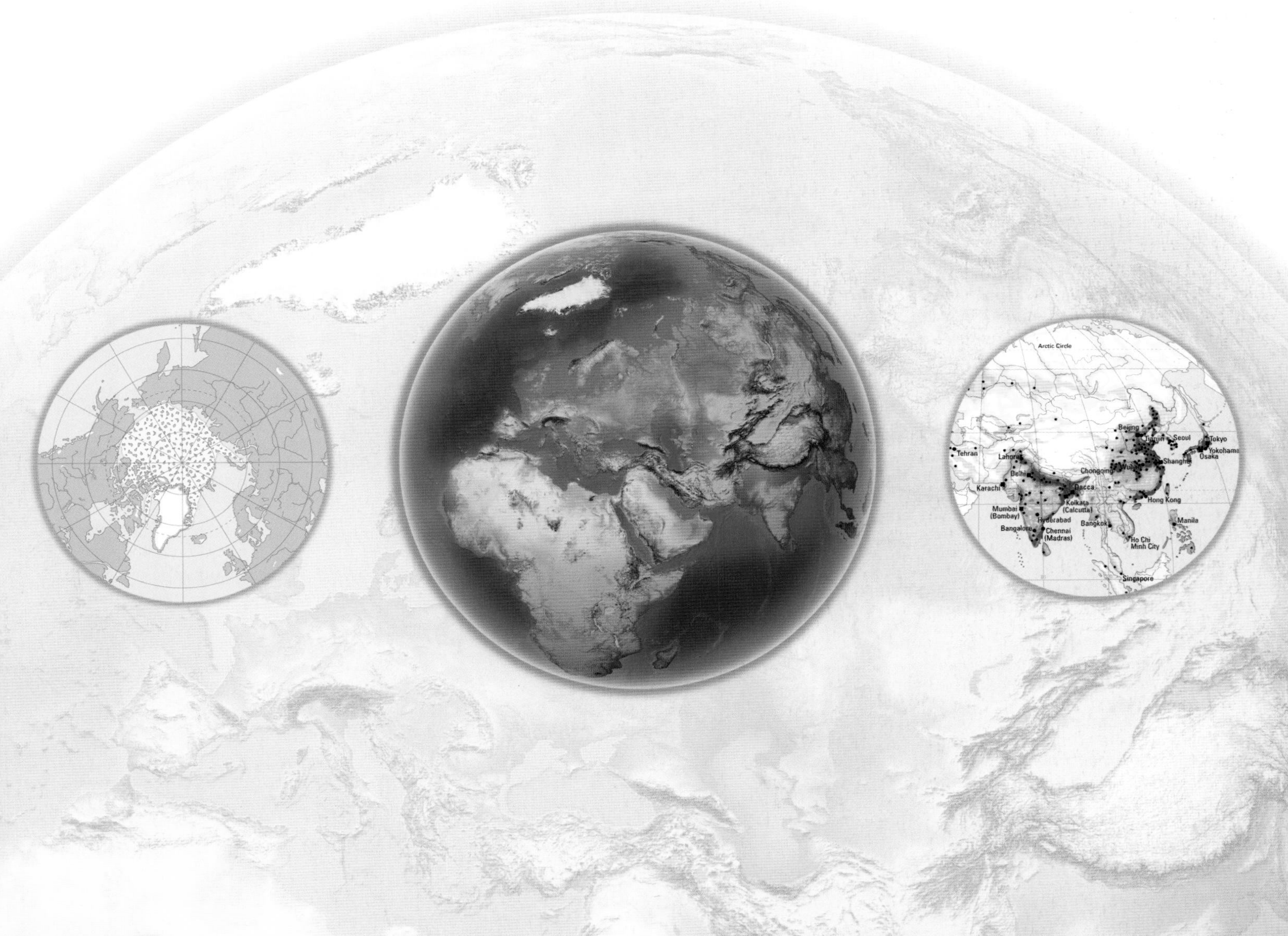

Planet Earth	2	Water & Vegetation	12	Quality of Life	22
Restless Earth	4	Environment	14	Energy	24
Landforms	6	Population	16	Production	26
Oceans	8	The Human Family	18	Trade	28
Climate	10	Wealth	20	Travel & Tourism	30

Planet Earth

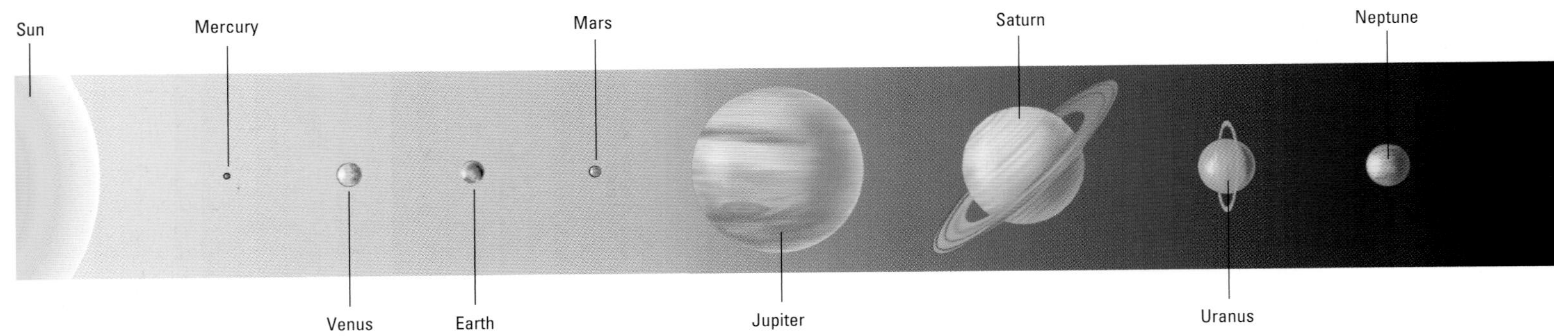

The Solar System

A minute part of one of the billions of galaxies (collections of stars) that populate the Universe, the Solar System lies about 26,000 light-years from the center of our own galaxy, the "Milky Way." Thought to be about 5 billion years old, it consists of a central Sun with eight planets and their moons revolving around it, attracted by its gravitational pull. The planets orbit the Sun in the same direction – counterclockwise when viewed from above the Sun's north pole – and almost in the same plane. Their orbital distances, however, vary enormously.

The Sun's diameter is 109 times that of the Earth, and the temperature at its core – caused by continuous thermonuclear fusions of hydrogen into helium – is estimated to be 27 million degrees Fahrenheit. It is the Solar System's only source of light and heat.

Profile of the Planets

	Mean distance from Sun (million miles)	Mass (Earth = 1)	Period of orbit (Earth days/years)	Period of rotation (Earth days)	Equatorial diameter (miles)	Number of known satellites*
Mercury	36.0	0.06	87.97 days	58.65	3,032	0
Venus	67.2	0.82	224.7 days	243.02	7,521	0
Earth	93.0	1.00	365.3 days	1.00	7,926	1
Mars	141.6	0.11	687.0 days	1.029	4,220	2
Jupiter	483.7	317.8	11.86 years	0.411	88,848	63
Saturn	886.6	95.2	29.45 years	0.428	74,900	59
Uranus	1,784	14.5	84.02 years	0.720	31,764	27
Neptune	2,795	17.2	164.8 years	0.673	30,776	13

** Number of known satellites at mid-2007*

All planetary orbits are elliptical in form, but only Mercury follows a path that deviates noticeably from a circular one. In 2006, Pluto was demoted from its former status as a planet and is now regarded as a member of the Kuiper Belt of icy bodies at the fringes of the Solar System.

The Seasons

Seasons occur because the Earth's axis is tilted at an angle of approximately 23½°. When the northern hemisphere is tilted to a maximum extent toward the Sun, on June 21, the Sun is overhead at the Tropic of Cancer (latitude 23½° North). This is midsummer, or the summer solstice, in the northern hemisphere.

On September 22 or 23, the Sun is overhead at the equator, and day and night are of equal length throughout the world. This is the autumnal equinox in the northern hemisphere. On December 21 or 22, the Sun is overhead at the Tropic of Capricorn (23½° South), the winter solstice in the northern hemisphere. The overhead Sun then tracks north until, on March 21, it is overhead at the equator. This is the spring (vernal) equinox in the northern hemisphere.

In the southern hemisphere, the seasons are the reverse of those in the north.

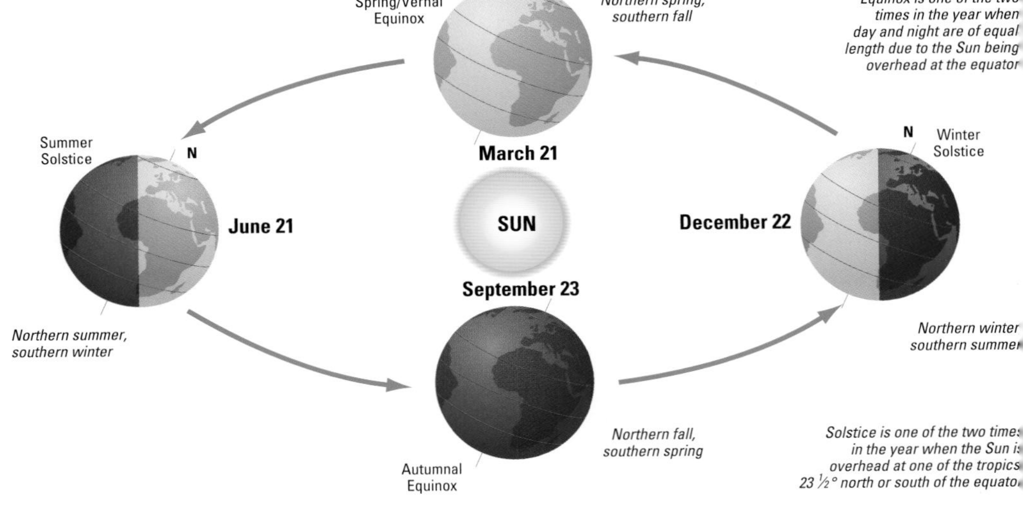

Day and Night

The Sun appears to rise in the east, reach its highest point at noon, and then set in the west, to be followed by night. In reality, it is not the Sun that is moving but the Earth rotating from west to east. The moment when the Sun's upper limb first appears above the horizon is termed sunrise; the moment when the Sun's upper limb disappears below the horizon is sunset.

At the summer solstice in the northern hemisphere (June 21), the Arctic has total daylight and the Antarctic total darkness. The opposite occurs at the winter solstice (December 21 or 22). At the equator, the length of day and night are almost equal all year.

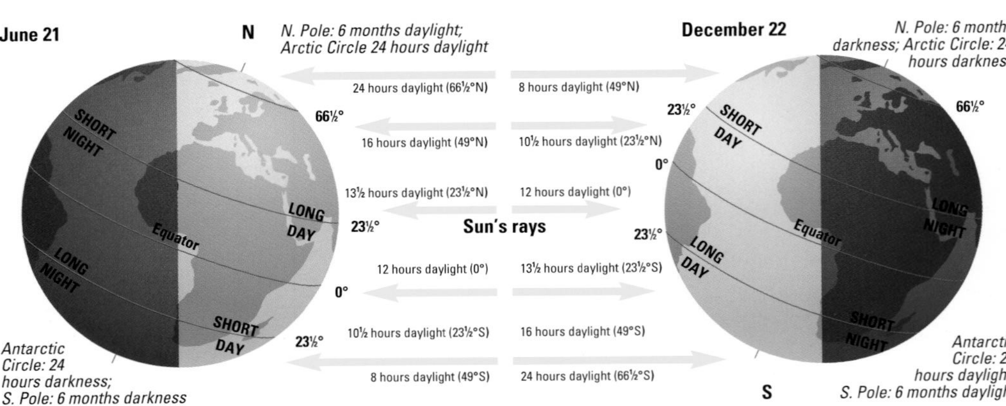

Time

Year: The time taken by the Earth to revolve around the Sun, or 365.24 days.

Leap Year: A calendar year of 366 days, February 29 being the additional day. It offsets the difference between the calendar and the solar year.

Month: The 12 calendar months of the year are approximately equal in length to a lunar month.

Week: An artificial period of 7 days, not based on astronomical time.

Day: The time taken by the Earth to complete one rotation on its axis.

Hour: 24 hours make one day. The day is divided into hours a.m. (ante meridiem or before noon) and p.m. (post meridiem or after noon), although most timetables now use the 24-hour system, from midnight to midnight.

Sunrise

Spring Equinox
Autumnal Equinox
Hours AM
Latitude
9 8 7 6 5 4 3 2
60°N
40°N
20°N
0°(Equator)
20°S
40°S
60°S
J F M A M J J A S O N D
Months of the year

Sunset

Spring Equinox
Autumnal Equinox
Hours PM
Latitude
21 20 19 18 17 16 15 14
60°S
40°S
20°S
0°(Equator)
20°N
40°N
60°N
J F M A M J J A S O N D
Months of the year

The Moon

Phases of the Moon

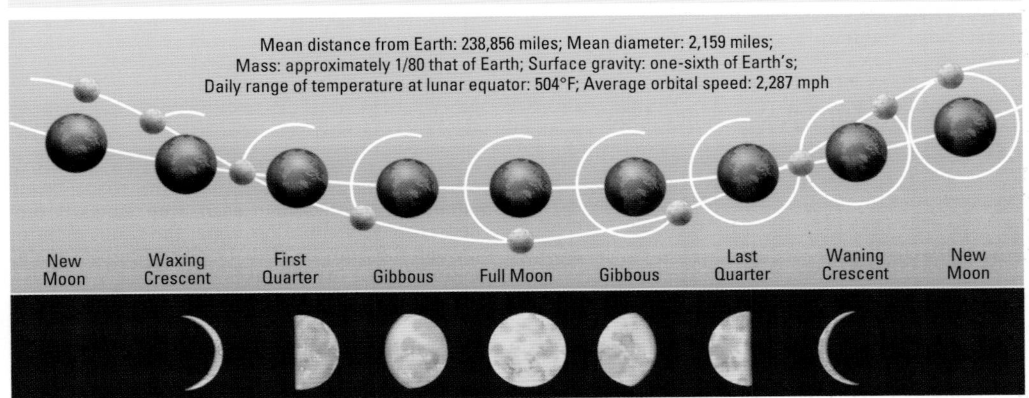

The Moon rotates more slowly than the Earth, taking just over 27 days to make one complete rotation on its axis. Since this corresponds to the Moon's orbital period around the Earth, the Moon always presents the same hemisphere toward us, and we never see the far side. The interval between one New Moon and the next is 29½ days – this is called a lunation, or lunar month. The Moon shines only by reflected sunlight, and emits no light of its own. During each lunation the Moon displays a complete cycle of phases, caused by the changing angle of illumination from the Sun.

Eclipses

When the Moon passes between the Sun and the Earth, the Sun becomes partially eclipsed (1). A partial eclipse can become a total eclipse if the Moon covers the Sun completely (2) and the dark central part of the lunar shadow touches the Earth. The broad geographical zone covered by the Moon's outer shadow (P) has only a very small central area (often less than 62 miles wide) that experiences totality. Totality can never last for more than 7½ minutes, and it is usually briefer than this. Lunar eclipses take place when the Moon moves through the shadow of the Earth, and can also be partial or total. Any single location on Earth can experience a maximum of four solar and three lunar eclipses in any single year, while a total solar eclipse occurs an average of once every 360 years for any given location.

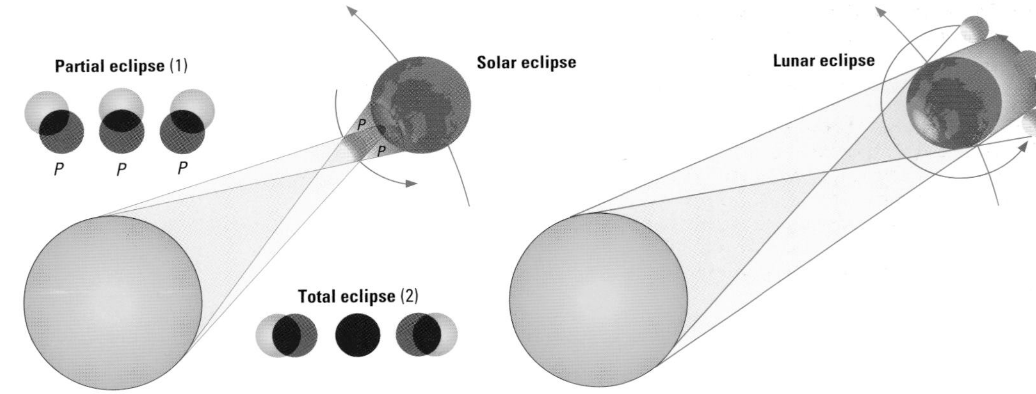

Tides

The daily rise and fall of the ocean's tides are the result of the gravitational pull of the Moon and that of the Sun, though the effect of the latter is not as strong as that of the Moon. This effect is greatest on the hemisphere facing the Moon and causes a tidal "bulge."

When the Sun, Earth, and Moon are in line, spring tides occur: high tide reaches the highest values, and low tide falls to low levels. When lunar and solar forces are least coincidental with the Sun and Moon at an angle (near the Moon's first and third quarters), neap tides occur, which have a small tidal range.

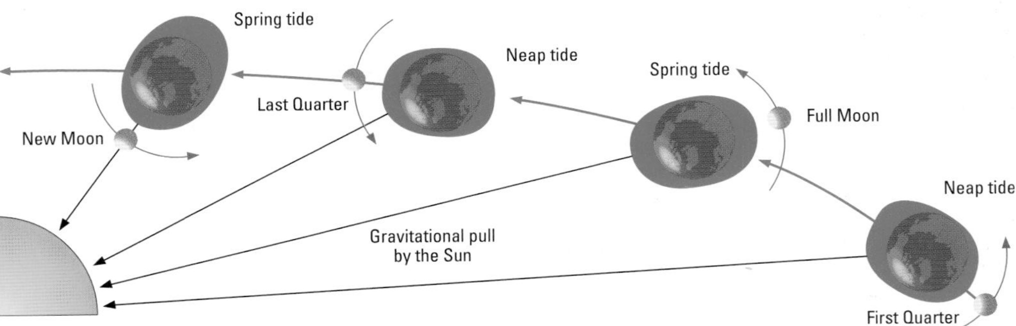

Restless Earth

The Earth's Structure

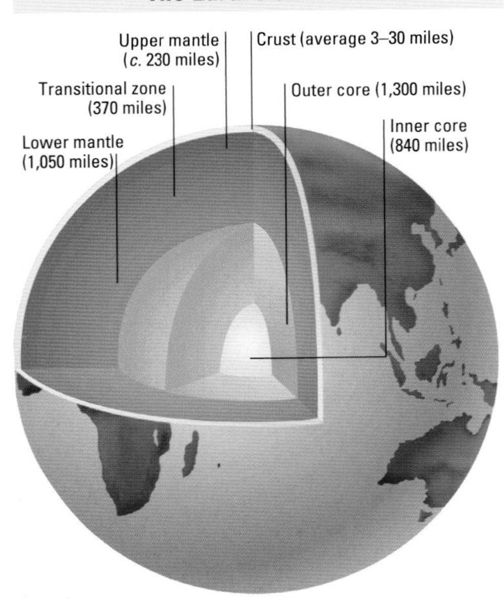

Continental Drift

About 200 million years ago the original Pangaea land mass began to split into two continental groups, which further separated over time to produce the present-day configuration.

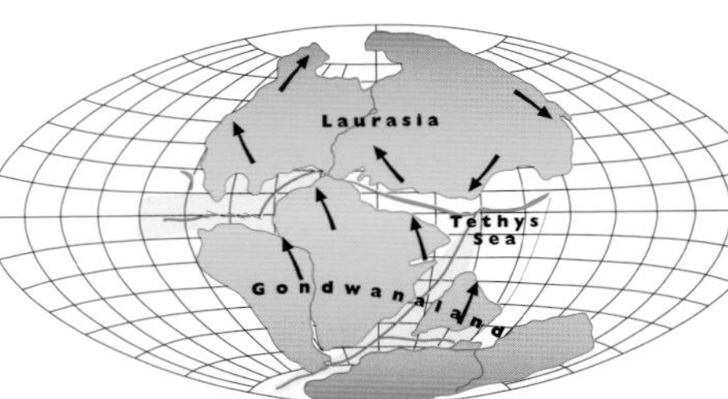

180 million years ago

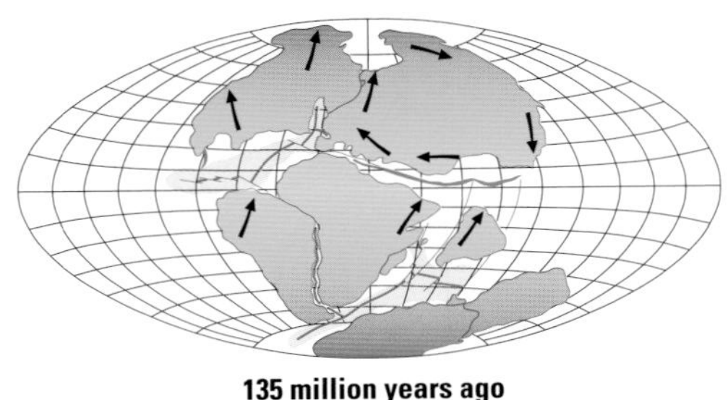

135 million years ago

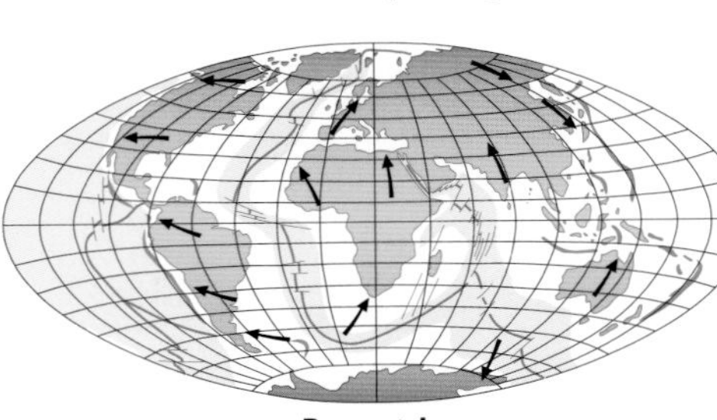

Present day

Trench
Rift
New ocean floor
Zones of slippage

Notable Earthquakes Since 1900

Year	Location	Richter Scale	Deaths
1906	San Francisco, USA	8.3	3,000
1906	Valparaiso, Chile	8.6	22,000
1908	Messina, Italy	7.5	83,000
1915	Avezzano, Italy	7.5	30,000
1920	Gansu (Kansu), China	8.6	180,000
1923	Yokohama, Japan	8.3	143,000
1927	Nan Shan, China	8.3	200,000
1932	Gansu (Kansu), China	7.6	70,000
1933	Sanriku, Japan	8.9	2,990
1934	Bihar, India/Nepal	8.4	10,700
1935	Quetta, India (*now* Pakistan)	7.5	60,000
1939	Chillan, Chile	8.3	28,000
1939	Erzincan, Turkey	7.9	30,000
1960	S. W. Chile	9.5	2,200
1960	Agadir, Morocco	5.8	12,000
1962	Khorasan, Iran	7.1	12,230
1964	Anchorage, USA	9.2	125
1968	N. E. Iran	7.4	12,000
1970	N. Peru	7.8	70,000
1972	Managua, Nicaragua	6.2	5,000
1974	N. Pakistan	6.3	5,200
1976	Guatemala	7.5	22,500
1976	Tangshan, China	8.2	255,000
1978	Tabas, Iran	7.7	25,000
1980	El Asnam, Algeria	7.3	20,000
1980	S. Italy	7.2	4,800
1985	Mexico City, Mexico	8.1	4,200
1988	N.W. Armenia	6.8	55,000
1990	N. Iran	7.7	36,000
1992	Flores, Indonesia	6.8	1,895
1993	Maharashtra, India	6.4	30,000
1994	Los Angeles, USA	6.6	51
1995	Kobe, Japan	7.2	5,000
1995	Sakhalin Is., Russia	7.5	2,000
1996	Yunnan, China	7.0	240
1997	N. E. Iran	7.1	2,400
1998	Takhar, Afghanistan	6.1	4,200
1998	Rostaq, Afghanistan	7.0	5,000
1999	Izmit, Turkey	7.4	15,000
1999	Taipei, Taiwan	7.6	1,700
2001	Gujarat, India	7.7	14,000
2002	Baghlan, Afghanistan	6.1	1,000
2003	Boumerdes, Algeria	6.8	2,200
2003	Bam, Iran	6.6	30,000
2004	Sumatra, Indonesia	9.0	250,000
2005	N. Pakistan	7.6	74,000
2006	Java, Indonesia	6.4	6,200

Earthquakes

Earthquake magnitude is usually rated according to either the Richter or the Modified Mercalli scale, both devised by seismologists in the 1930s. The Richter scale measures absolute earthquake power with mathematical precision: each step upward represents a tenfold increase in shockwave amplitude. Theoretically, there is no upper limit, but most of the largest earthquakes measured have been rated at between 8.8 and 8.9. The 12-point Mercalli scale, based on observed effects, is often more meaningful, ranging from I (earthquakes noticed only by seismographs) to XII (total destruction); intermediate points include V (people awakened at night; unstable objects overturned), VII (collapse of ordinary buildings, chimneys and monuments fall), and IX (conspicuous cracks in ground; serious damage to reservoirs).

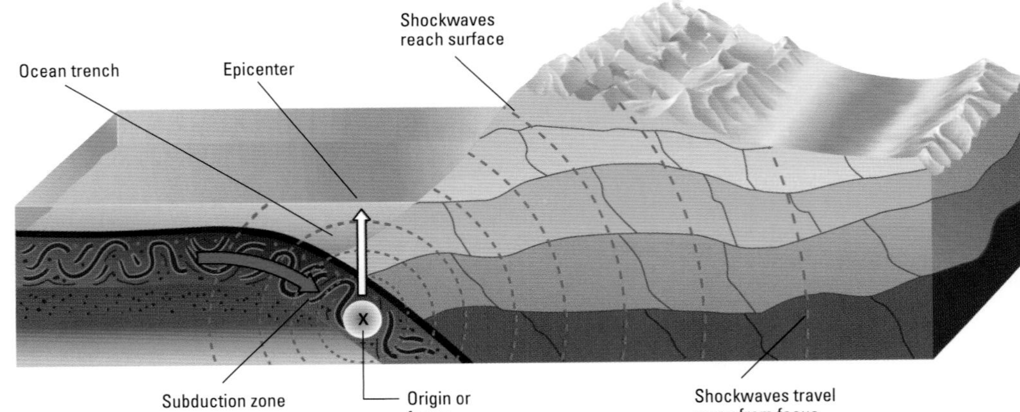

Structure and Earthquakes

Mobile land areas
Submarine zones of mobile land areas
Stable land platforms
Submarine extensions of stable land platforms
Mid-oceanic volcanic ridges
Oceanic platforms

1976 Principal earthquakes and dates (since 1900)

Earthquakes are a series of rapid vibrations originating from the slipping or faulting of parts of the Earth's crust when stresses within build up to breaking point. They usually happen at depths varying from 5 miles to 20 miles. Severe earthquakes cause extensive damage when they take place in populated areas, destroying structures and severing communications. Most initial loss of life occurs due to secondary causes such as falling masonry, fires, and flooding.

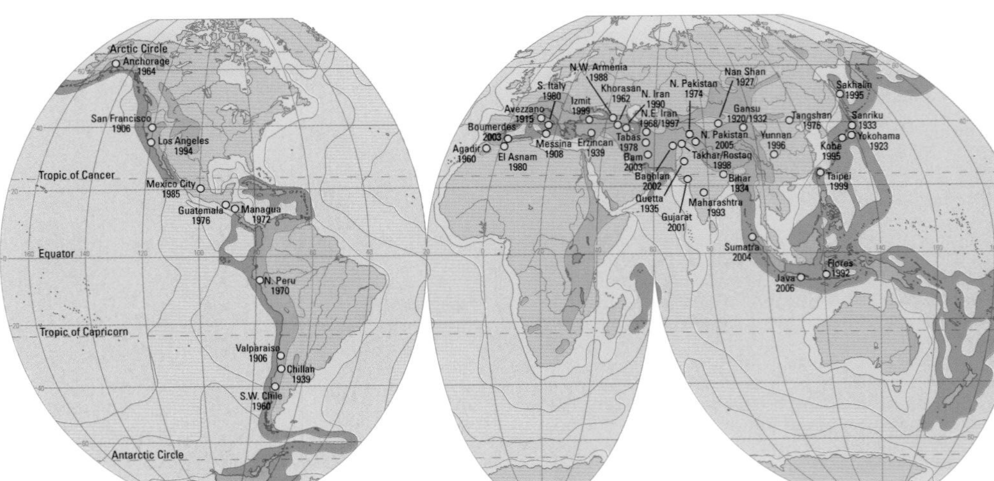

Plate Tectonics

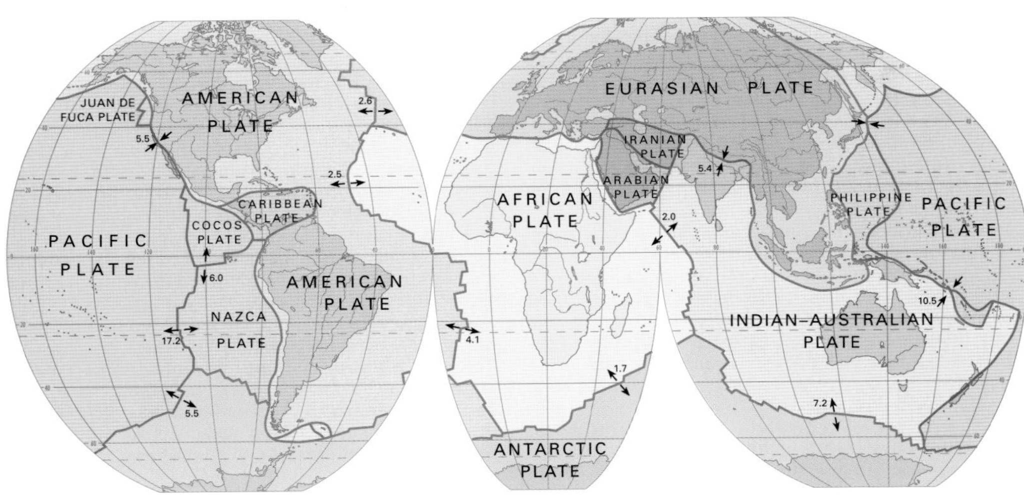

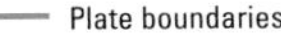

The drifting of the continents is a feature that is unique to Planet Earth. The complementary, almost jigsaw-puzzle fit of the coastlines on each side of the Atlantic Ocean inspired Alfred Wegener's theory of continental drift in 1915. The theory suggested that the ancient super-continent, which Wegener named Pangaea, incorporated all of the Earth's land masses and gradually split up to form today's continents.

The original debate about continental drift was a prelude to a more radical idea: plate tectonics. The basic theory is that the Earth's crust is made up of a series of rigid plates which float on a soft layer of the mantle and are moved about by continental convection currents within the Earth's interior. These plates diverge and converge along margins marked by seismic activity. Plates diverge from mid-ocean ridges where molten lava pushes upward and forces the plates apart at rates of up to 1.6 inches [40 mm] a year.

The three diagrams, left, give some examples of plate boundaries from around the world. Diagram (a) shows sea-floor spreading at the Mid-Atlantic Ridge as the American and African plates slowly diverge. The same thing is happening in (b) where sea-floor spreading at the Mid-Indian Ocean Ridge is forcing the Indian–Australian plate to collide into the Eurasian plate. In (c) oceanic crust (sima) is being subducted beneath lighter continental crust (sial).

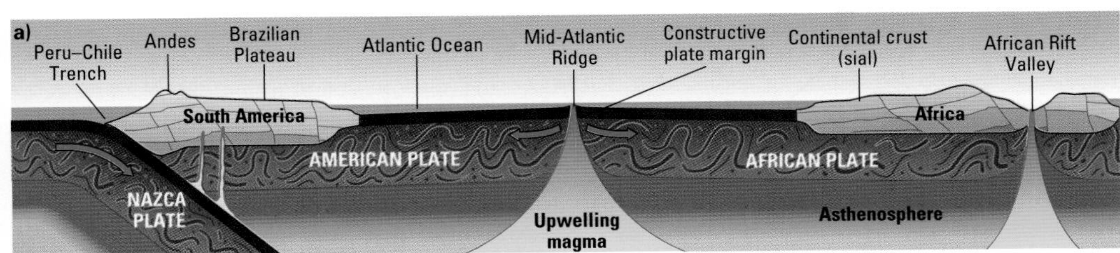

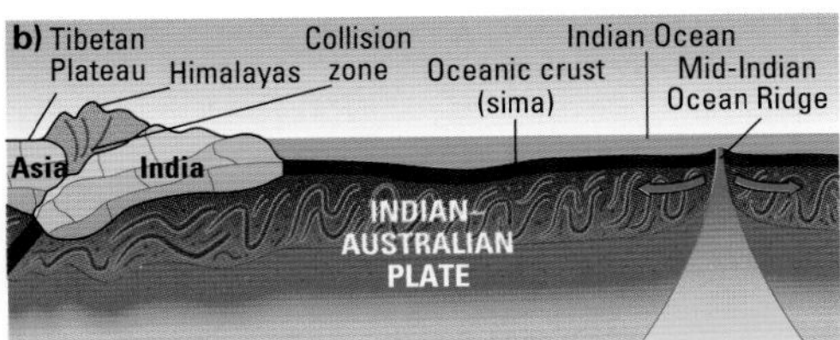

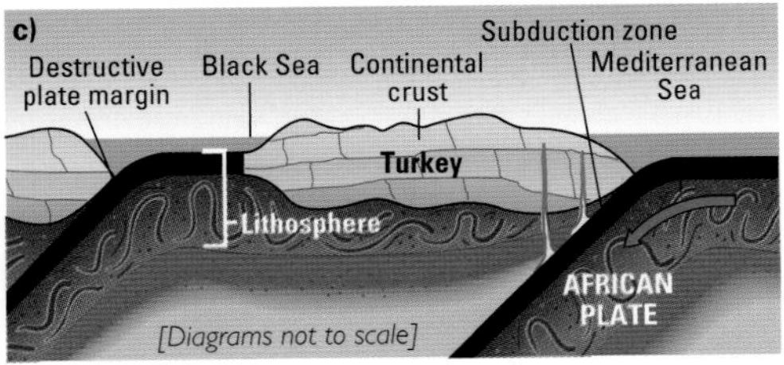

Volcanoes

Volcanoes occur when hot liquefied rock beneath the Earth's crust is pushed up by pressure to the surface as molten lava. Some volcanoes erupt in an explosive way, throwing out rocks and ash, whilst others are effusive and lava flows out of the vent. There are volcanoes which are both, such as Mount Fuji. An accumulation of lava and cinders creates cones of variable size and shape. As a result of many eruptions over centuries, Mount Etna in Sicily has a circumference of more than 75 miles [120 km].

Climatologists believe that volcanic ash, if ejected high into the atmosphere, can influence temperature and weather for several years afterward. The 1991 eruption of Mount Pinatubo in the Philippines ejected more than 20 million tons of dust and ash 20 miles [32 km] into the atmosphere and is believed to have accelerated ozone depletion over a large part of the globe.

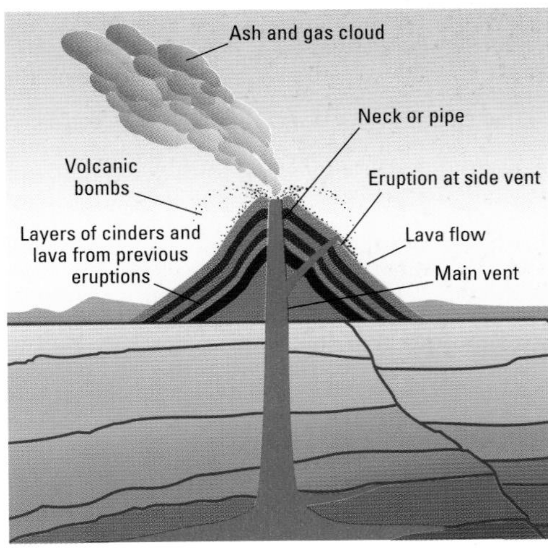

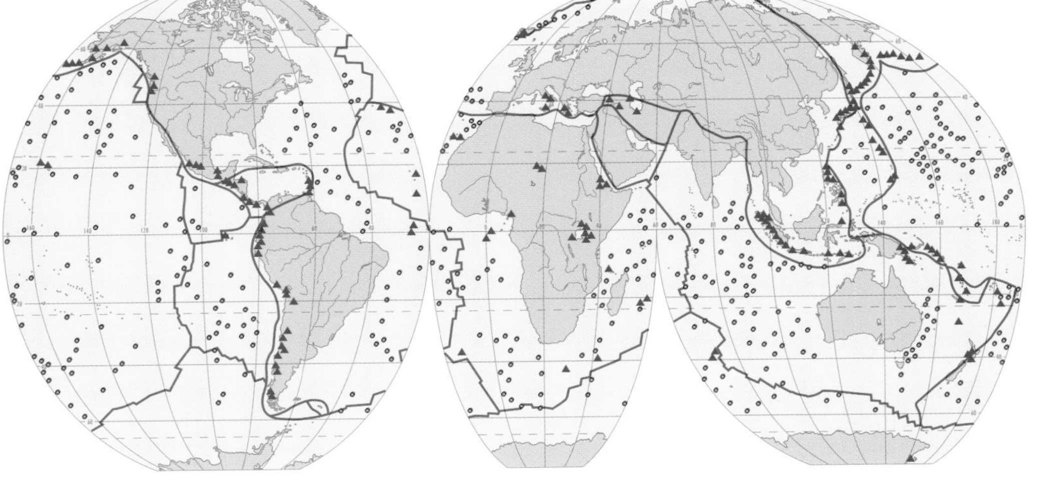

Distribution of Volcanoes

Volcanoes today may be the subject of considerable scientific study but they remain both dramatic and unpredictable: in 1991 Mount Pinatubo, 62 miles [100 km] north of the Philippines capital Manila, suddenly burst into life after lying dormant for more than six centuries. Most of the world's active volcanoes occur in a belt around the Pacific Ocean, on the edge of the Pacific plate, called the "ring of fire." Indonesia has the greatest concentration with 90 volcanoes, 12 of which are active. The most famous, Krakatoa, erupted in 1883 with such force that the resulting tidal wave killed 36,000 people and tremors were felt as far away as Australia.

○ Submarine volcanoes

▲ Land volcanoes active since 1700

— Boundaries of tectonic plates

Landforms

The Rock Cycle

James Hutton first proposed the rock cycle in the late 1700s after he observed the slow but steady effects of erosion.

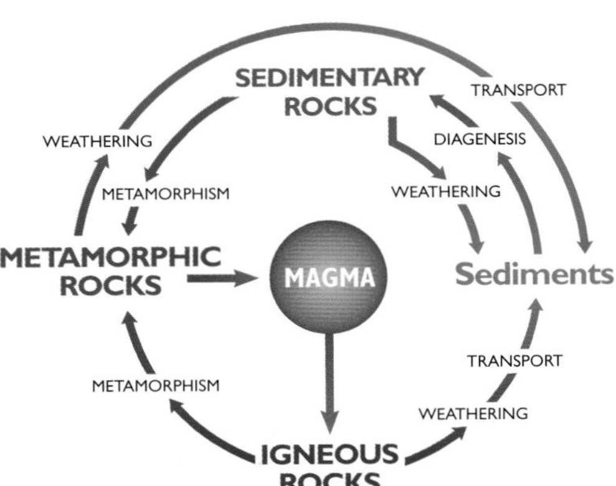

Above and below the surface of the oceans, the features of the Earth's crust are constantly changing. The phenomenal forces generated by convection currents in the molten core of our planet carry the vast segments or "plates" of the crust across the globe in an endless cycle of creation and destruction. A continent may travel little more than 1 inch [25 mm] per year, yet in the vast span of geological time this process throws up giant mountain ranges and creates new land.

Destruction of the landscape, however, begins as soon as it is formed. Wind, water, ice, and sea, the main agents of erosion, mount a constant assault that even the most resistant rocks cannot withstand. Mountain peaks may dwindle by as little as a few fractions of an inch each year, but if they are not uplifted by further movements of the crust they will eventually be reduced to rubble and transported away.

Water is the most powerful agent of erosion – it has been estimated that 100 billion tons of sediment are washed into the oceans every year. Three Asian rivers account for 20% of this total; the Huang He, in China, and the Brahmaputra and Ganges in Bangladesh.

Rivers and glaciers, like the sea itself, generate much of their effect through abrasion – pounding the land with the debris they carry with them. But as well as destroying they also create new landforms, many of them spectacular: vast deltas like those of the Mississippi and the Nile, or the deep fjords cut by glaciers in British Columbia, Norway, and New Zealand.

Geologists once considered that landscapes evolved from "young," newly uplifted mountainous areas, through a "mature" hilly stage, to an "old age" stage when the land was reduced to an almost flat plain, or peneplain. This theory, called the "cycle of erosion," fell into disuse when it became evident that so many factors, including the effects of plate tectonics and climatic change, constantly interrupt the cycle, which takes no account of the highly complex interactions that shape the surface of our planet.

Mountain Building

Mountains are formed when pressures on the Earth's crust caused by continental drift become so intense that the surface buckles or cracks. This happens where oceanic crust is subducted by continental crust or, more dramatically, where two tectonic plates collide: the Rockies, Andes, Alps, Urals, and Himalayas resulted from such impacts. These are all known as fold mountains because they were formed by the compression of the rocks, forcing the surface to bend and fold like a crumpled rug. The Himalayas are formed from the folded former sediments of the Tethys Sea which was trapped in the collision zone between the Indian and Eurasian plates.

The other main mountain-building process occurs when the crust fractures to create faults, allowing rock to be forced upward in large blocks; or when the pressure of magma within the crust forces the surface to bulge into a dome, or erupts to form a volcano. Large mountain ranges may reveal a combination of these features; the Alps, for example, have been compressed so violently that the folds are fragmented by numerous faults and intrusions of molten igneous rock.

Over millions of years, even the greatest mountain ranges can be reduced by the agents of erosion (most notably rivers) to a low rugged landscape known as a peneplain.

Types of faults: Faults occur where the crust is being stretched or compressed so violently that the rock strata break in a horizontal or vertical movement. They are classified by the direction in which the blocks of rock have moved. A normal fault results when a vertical movement causes the surface to break apart; compression causes a reverse fault. Horizontal movement causes shearing, known as a strike-slip fault. When the rock breaks in two places, the central block may be pushed up in a horst fault, or sink (creating a rift valley) in a graben fault.

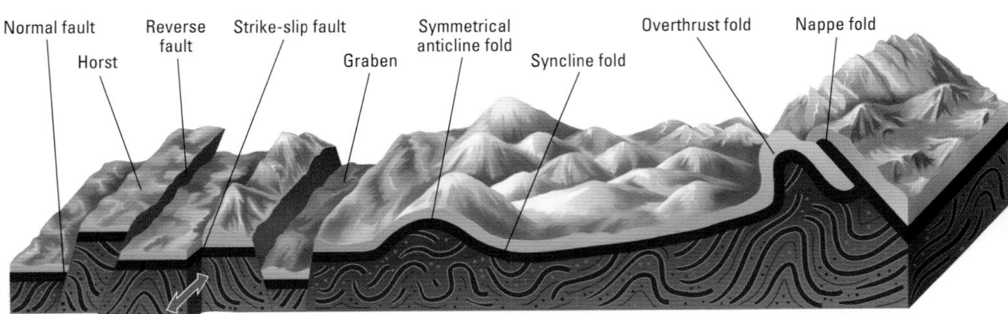

Types of fold: Folds occur when rock strata are squeezed and compressed. They are common, therefore, at destructive plate margins and where plates have collided, forcing the rocks to buckle into mountain ranges. Geographers give different names to the degrees of fold that result from continuing pressure on the rock. A simple fold may be symmetric, with even slopes on either side, but as the pressure builds up, one slope becomes steeper and the fold becomes asymmetric. Later, the ridge or "anticline" at the top of the fold may slide over the lower ground or "syncline" to form a recumbent fold. Eventually, the rock strata may break under the pressure to form an overthrust and finally a nappe fold.

Continental Glaciation

Ice sheets were at their greatest extent about 200,000 years ago. The maximum advance of the last Ice Age was about 18,000 years ago, when ice covered virtually all of Canada and reached as far south as the Bristol Channel in Britain.

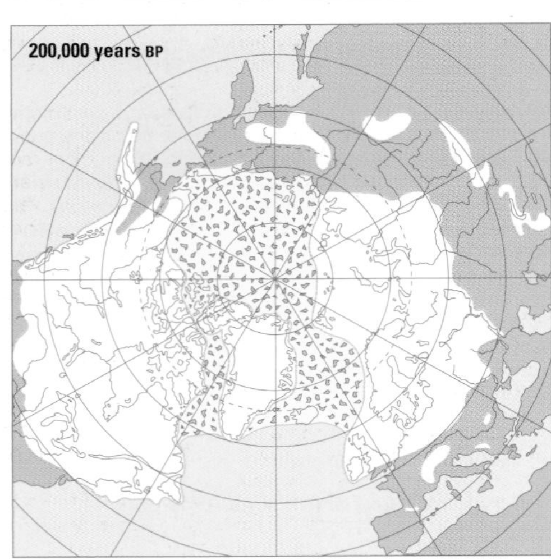

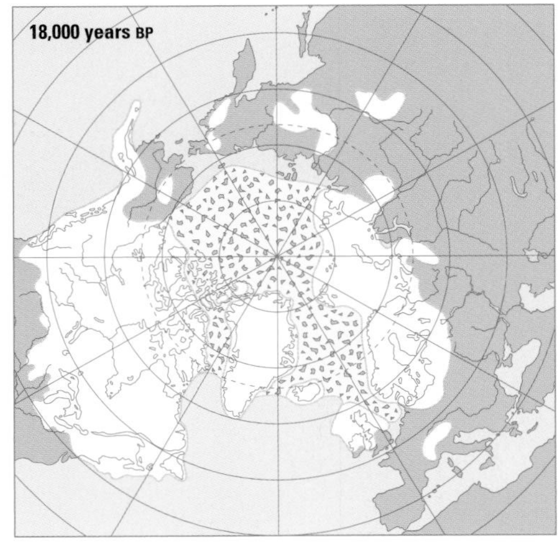

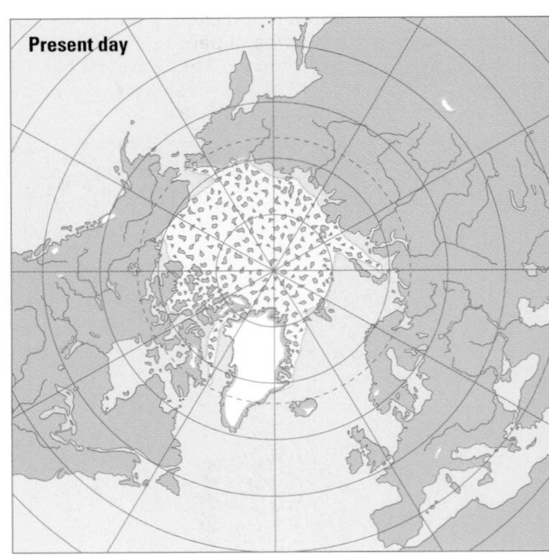

Natural Landforms

A stylized diagram to show a selection of landforms found in the mid-latitudes.

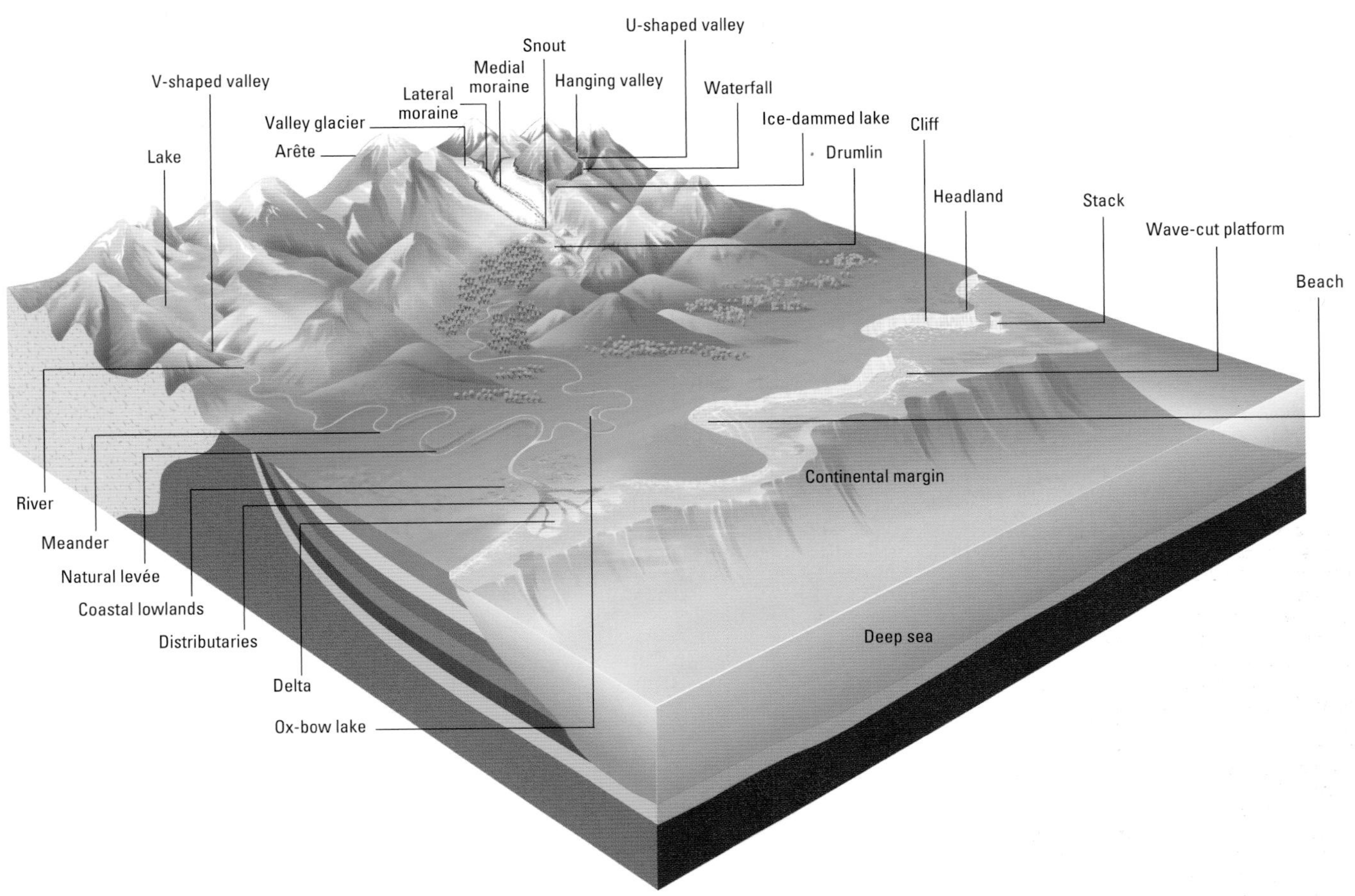

Desert Landscapes

The popular image that deserts are all huge expanses of sand is wrong. Despite harsh conditions, deserts contain some of the most varied and interesting landscapes in the world. They are also one of the most extensive environments – the hot and cold deserts together cover almost 40% of the Earth's surface.

The three types of hot desert are known by their Arabic names: sand desert, called *erg*, covers only about one-fifth of the world's desert; the rest is divided between *hammada* (areas of bare rock) and *reg* (broad plains covered by loose gravel or pebbles).

In areas of *erg*, such as the Namib Desert, the shape of the dunes reflects the character of local winds. Where winds are constant in direction, crescent-shaped *barchan* dunes form. In areas of bare rock, wind-blown sand is a major agent of erosion. The erosion is mainly confined to within 6.5 ft [2 m] of the surface, producing characteristic mushroom-shaped rocks.

Surface Processes

Catastrophic changes to natural landforms are periodically caused by such phenomena as avalanches, landslides, and volcanic eruptions, but most of the processes that shape the Earth's surface operate extremely slowly in human terms. One estimate, based on a study in the United States, suggested that 3 ft [1 m] of land was removed from the entire surface of the country, on average, every 29,500 years. However, the time-scale varies from 1,300 years to 154,200 years depending on the terrain and climate.

In hot, dry climates, mechanical weathering, a result of rapid temperature changes, causes the outer layers of rock to peel away, while in cold mountainous regions, boulders are prised apart when water freezes in cracks in rocks. Chemical weathering, at its greatest in warm, humid regions, is responsible for hollowing out limestone caves and decomposing granites.

The erosion of soil and rock is greatest on sloping land and the steeper the slope, the greater the tendency for mass wasting – the movement of soil and rock downhill under the influence of gravity. The mechanisms of mass wasting (ranging from very slow to very rapid) vary with the type of material, but the presence of water as a lubricant is usually an important factor.

Running water is the world's leading agent of erosion and transportation. The energy of a river depends on several factors, including its velocity and volume, and its erosive power is at its peak when it is in full flood. Sea waves also exert tremendous erosive power during storms when they hurl pebbles against the shore, undercutting cliffs and hollowing out caves.

Glacier ice forms in mountain hollows and spills out to form valley glaciers, which transport rocks shattered by frost action. As glaciers move, rocks embedded into the ice erode steep-sided, U-shaped valleys. Evidence of glaciation in mountain regions includes cirques, knife-edged ridges, or arêtes, and pyramidal peaks.

Oceans

The Great Oceans

Relative sizes of the world's oceans

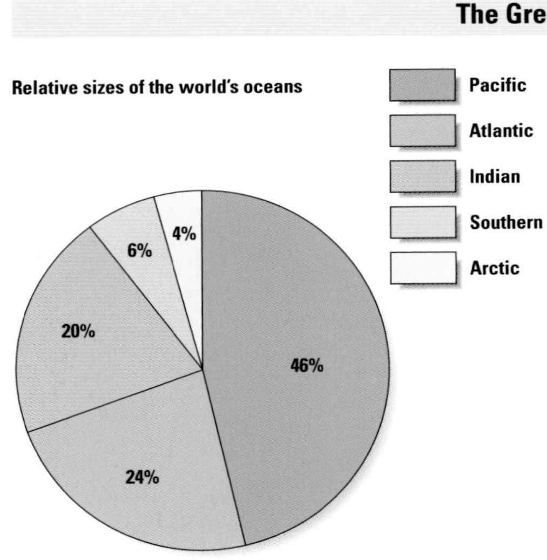

From ancient times to about the 15th century, the legendary "Seven Seas" comprised the Red Sea, Mediterranean Sea, Persian Gulf, Black Sea, Adriatic Sea, Caspian Sea, and Indian Sea.

The Earth is a watery planet: more than 70% of its surface – over 140,000,000 sq miles [360,000,000 sq km] – is covered by the oceans and seas. The mighty Pacific alone accounts for nearly 36% of the total, and more than 46% of the sea area. Gravity holds in around 320 million cu. miles [1,400 million cu. km] of water, of which over 97% is saline.

The vast underwater world starts in the shallows of the seaside and plunges to depths of more than 36,000 ft [11,000 m]. The continental shelf, part of the land mass, drops gently to around 650 ft [200 m]; here the seabed falls away suddenly at an angle of 3° to 6° – the continental slope. The third stage, called the continental rise, is more gradual with gradients varying from 1 in 100 to 1 in 700. At an average depth of 16,500 ft [5,000 m] there begins the aptly-named abyssal plain – massive submarine depths where sunlight fails to penetrate and few creatures can survive.

From these plains rise volcanoes which, taken from base to top, rival and even surpass the tallest continental mountains in height. Mauna Kea, on Hawai'i, reaches a total of 33,400 ft [10,203 m], some 4,500 ft [1,355 m] more than Mount Everest, though scarcely 40% is visible above sea level.

In addition, there are underwater mountain chains up to 600 miles [1,000 km] across, whose peaks sometimes appear above sea level as islands, such as Iceland and Tristan da Cunha.

The Ocean Depths

Average and maximum depths of the world's great oceans, in feet

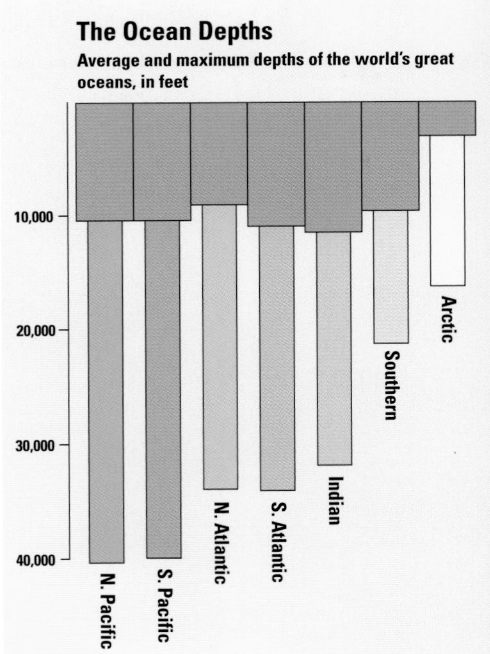

Ocean Currents

January ocean currents

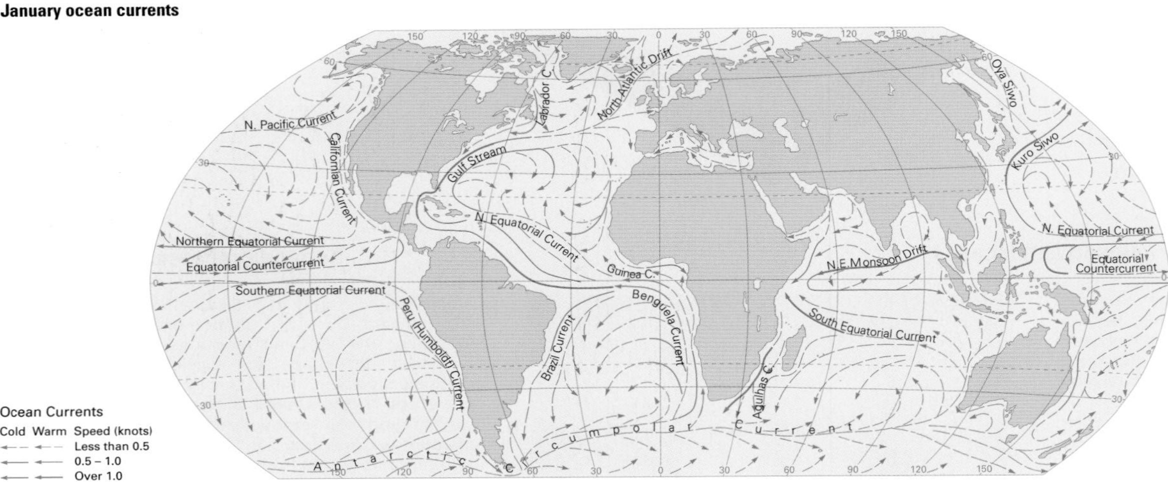

July ocean currents

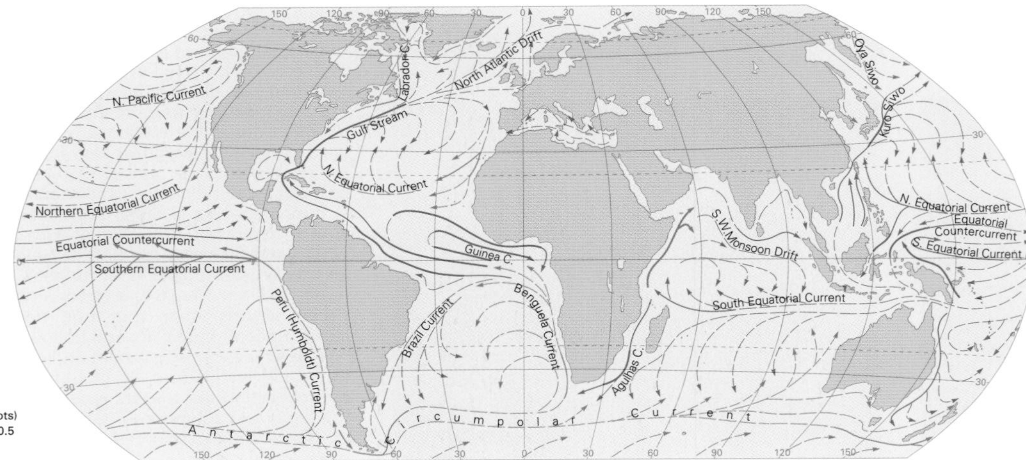

Moving immense quantities of energy as well as billions of tons of water every hour, the ocean currents are a vital part of the great heat engine that drives the Earth's climate. They themselves are produced by a twofold mechanism. At the surface, winds push huge masses of water before them; in the deep ocean, below an abrupt temperature gradient that separates the churning surface waters from the still depths, density variations cause slow vertical movements.

The pattern of circulation of the great surface currents is determined by the displacement known as the Coriolis effect. As the Earth turns beneath a moving object – whether it is a tennis ball or a vast mass of water – it appears to be deflected to one side. The deflection is most obvious near the Equator, where the Earth's surface is spinning eastward at 1,050 mph [1,700 km/h]; currents moving poleward are curved clockwise in the northern hemisphere and counterclockwise in the southern.

The result is a system of spinning circles known as gyres. The Coriolis effect piles up water on the left of each gyre, creating a narrow, fast-moving stream that is matched by a slower, broader returning current on the right. North and south of the Equator, the fastest currents are located in the west and in the east respectively. In each case, warm water moves from the Equator and cold water returns to it. Cold currents often bring an upwelling of nutrients with them, supporting the world's most economically important fisheries.

Depending on the prevailing winds, some currents on or near the Equator may reverse their direction in the course of the year – a seasonal variation on which Asian monsoon rains depend, and whose occasional failure can bring disaster to millions.

World Fishing Areas

Main commercial fishing areas (numbered FAO regions)

Catch by top marine fishing areas, million tons (2004)

1.	Pacific, NW	[61]	21.6	22.7%
2.	Pacific, SE	[87]	15.5	16.3%
3.	Pacific, WC	[71]	11.0	11.6%
4.	Atlantic, NE	[27]	10.0	10.5%
5.	Indian, E	[57]	5.6	5.9%
6.	Indian, W	[51]	4.1	4.3%
7.	Atlantic, EC	[34]	3.4	3.6%
8.	Pacific, NE	[67]	3.1	3.3%
9.	Atlantic, NW	[21]	2.4	2.5%
10.	Atlantic, WC	[31]	2.1	2.2%

Principal fishing areas

Leading fishing nations

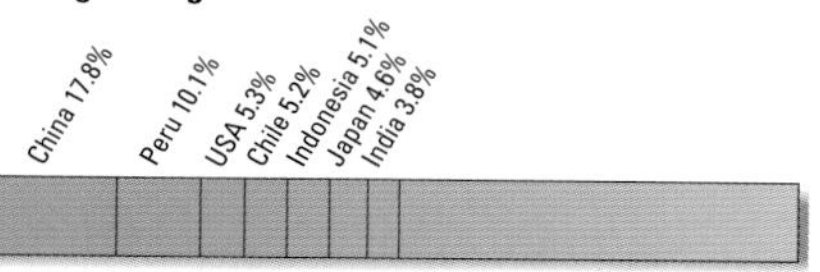

World total (2004): 95,000,000 tons
(Marine catch 90.3% Inland catch 9.7%)

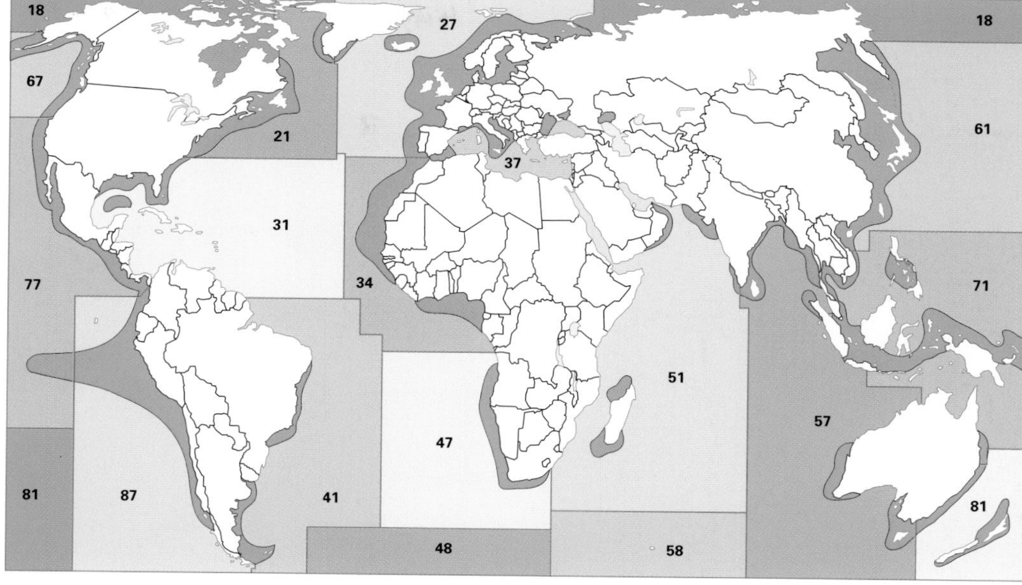

Marine Pollution

Sources of marine oil pollution

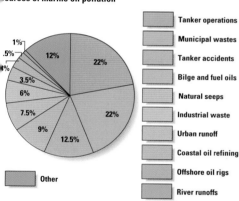

Oil Spills

Major oil spills from tankers and combined carriers

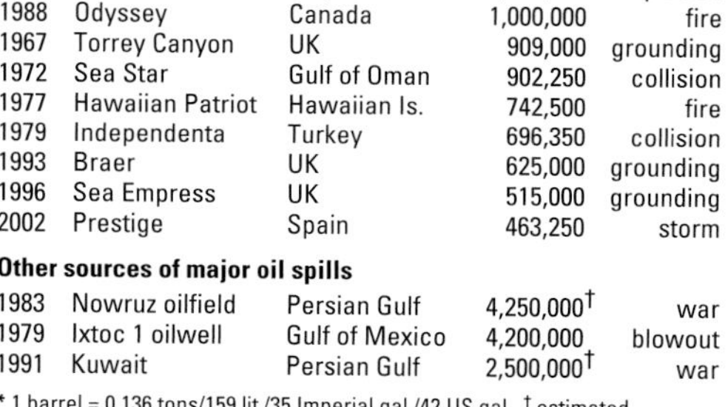

Year	Vessel	Location	Spill (barrels) *	Cause
1979	Atlantic Empress	West Indies	1,890,000	collision
1983	Castillo De Bellver	South Africa	1,760,000	fire
1978	Amoco Cadiz	France	1,628,000	grounding
1991	Haven	Italy	1,029,000	explosion
1988	Odyssey	Canada	1,000,000	fire
1967	Torrey Canyon	UK	909,000	grounding
1972	Sea Star	Gulf of Oman	902,250	collision
1977	Hawaiian Patriot	Hawaiian Is.	742,500	fire
1979	Independenta	Turkey	696,350	collision
1993	Braer	UK	625,000	grounding
1996	Sea Empress	UK	515,000	grounding
2002	Prestige	Spain	463,250	storm
Other sources of major oil spills				
1983	Nowruz oilfield	Persian Gulf	4,250,000†	war
1979	Ixtoc 1 oilwell	Gulf of Mexico	4,200,000	blowout
1991	Kuwait	Persian Gulf	2,500,000†	war

* 1 barrel = 0.136 tons/159 lit./35 Imperial gal./42 US gal. † estimated

River Pollution

Sources of river pollution, USA

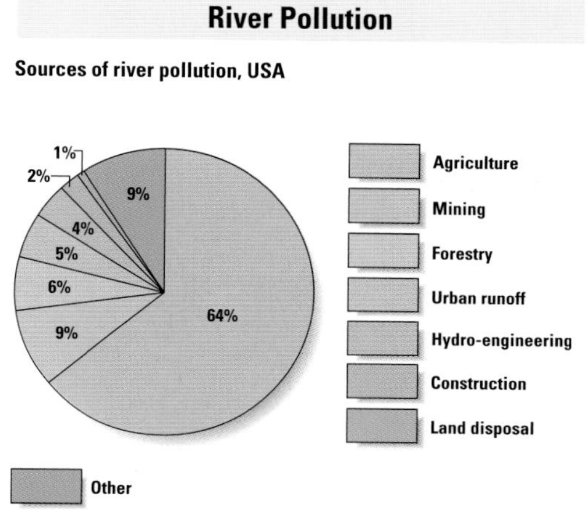

Water Pollution

Severely polluted sea areas and lakes

Polluted sea areas and lakes

Areas of frequent oil pollution by shipping

Major oil tanker spills

Major oil rig blowouts

Offshore dumpsites for industrial and municipal waste

Severely polluted rivers and estuaries

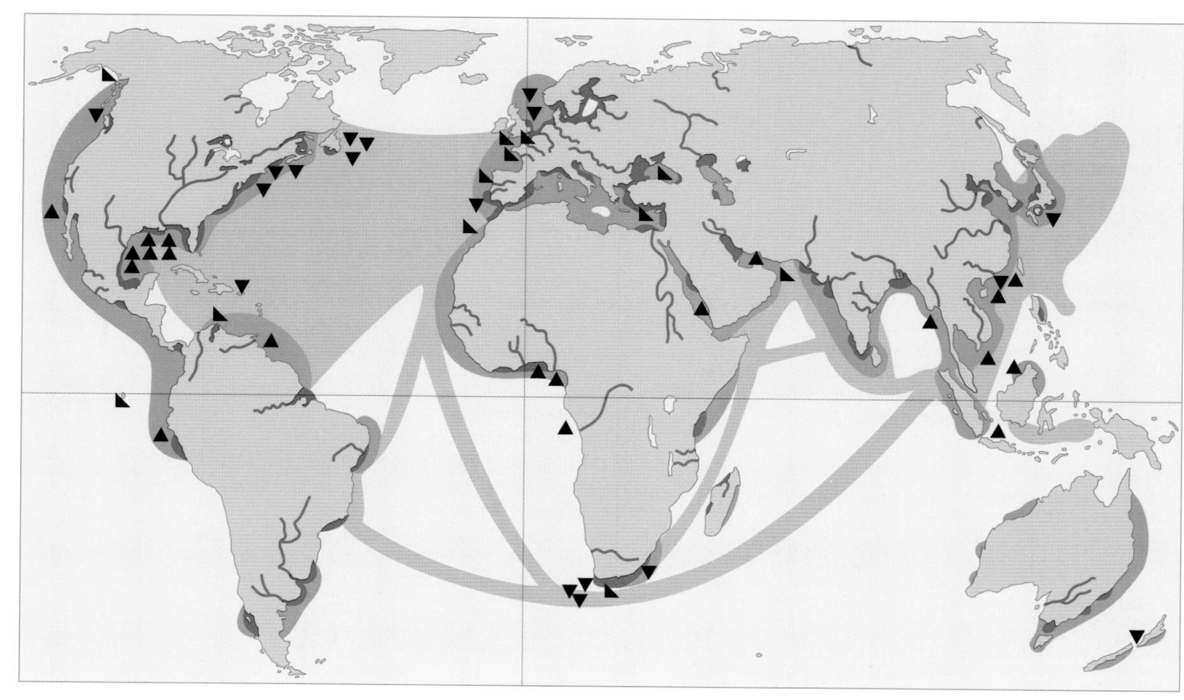

he most notorious tanker spillage of the 980s occurred when the *Exxon Valdez* ran ground in Prince William Sound, Alaska, 1989, spilling 267,000 barrels of crude oil lose to shore in a sensitive ecological area. his rates as the world's 28th worst spill in rms of volume.

Climate

Climatic Regions

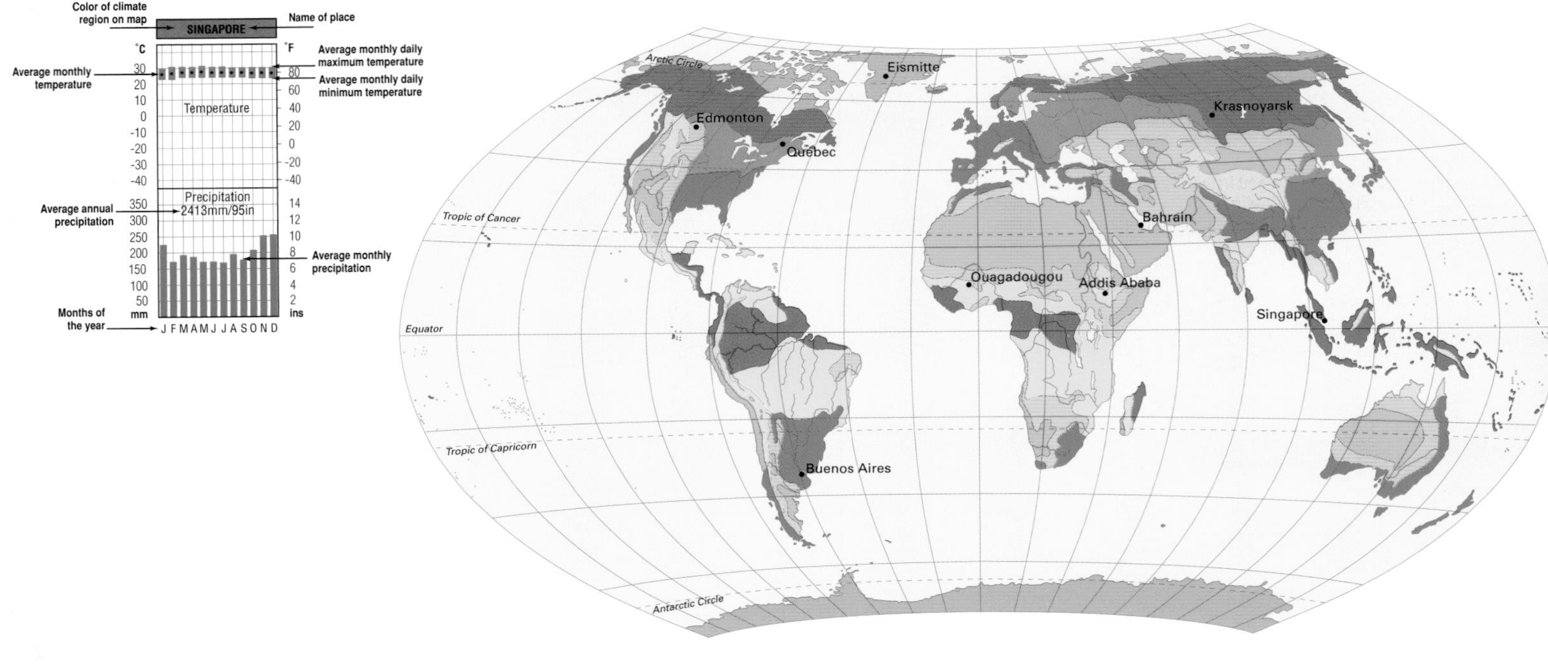

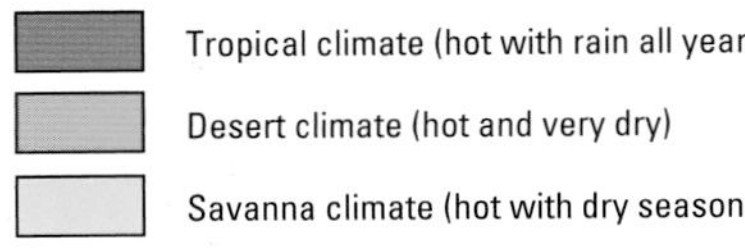

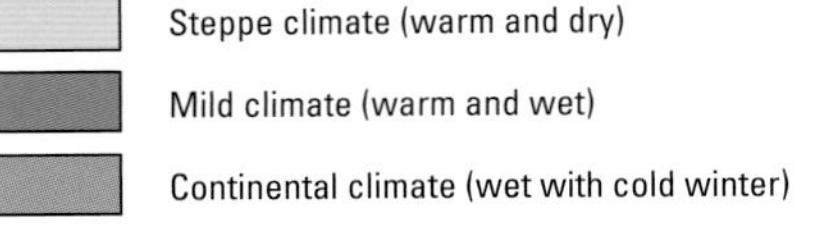

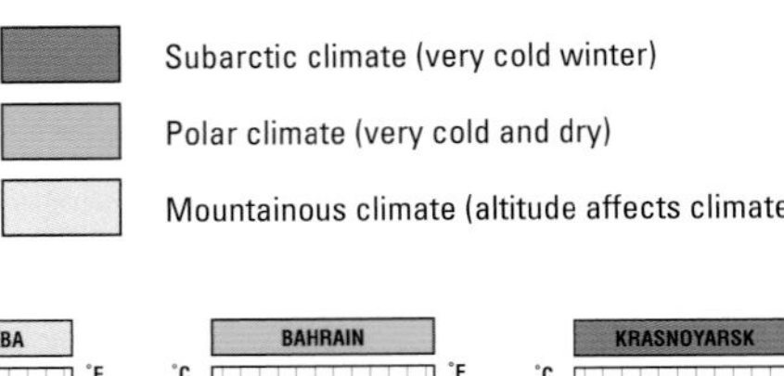

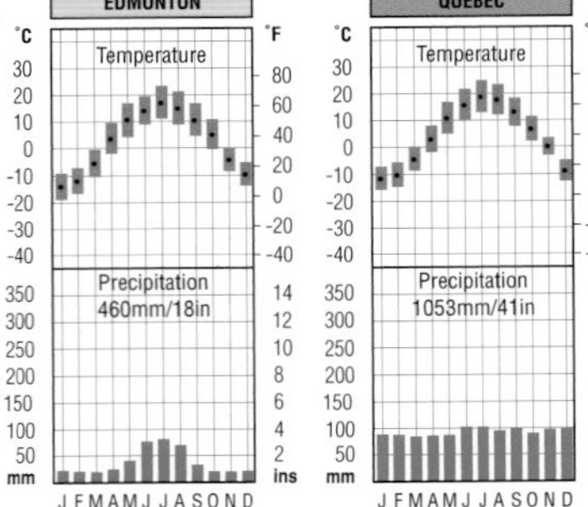

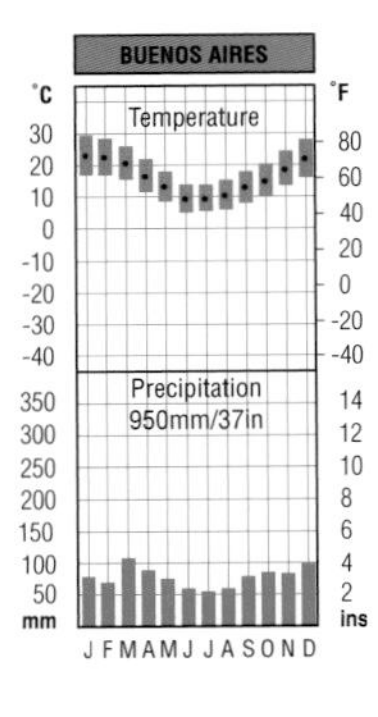

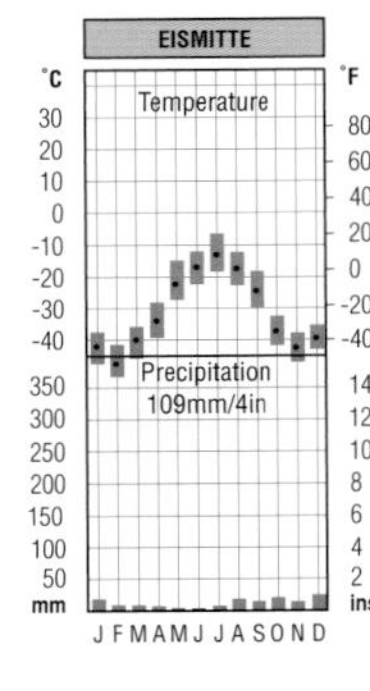

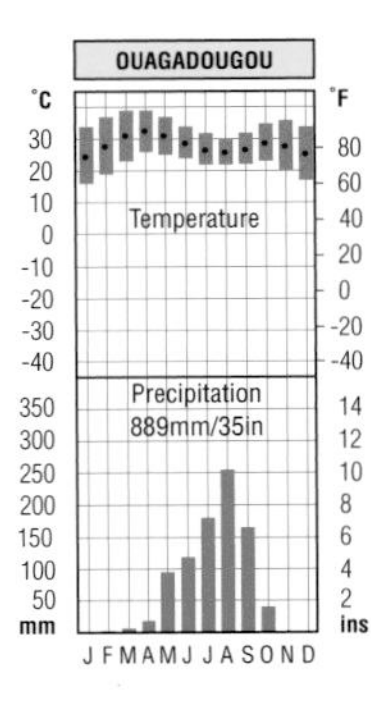

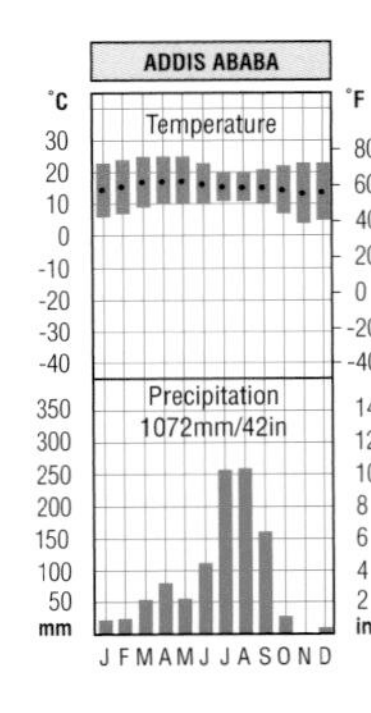

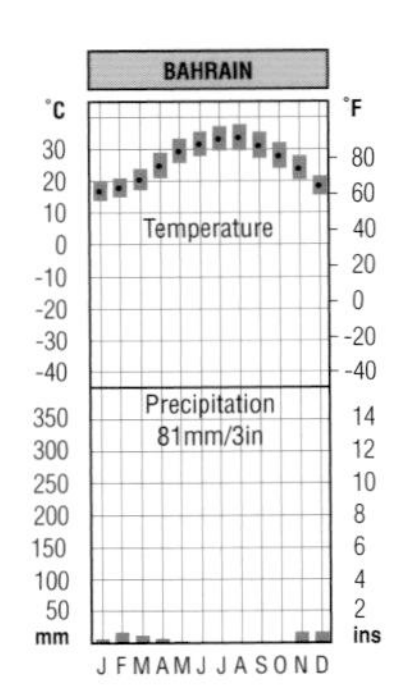

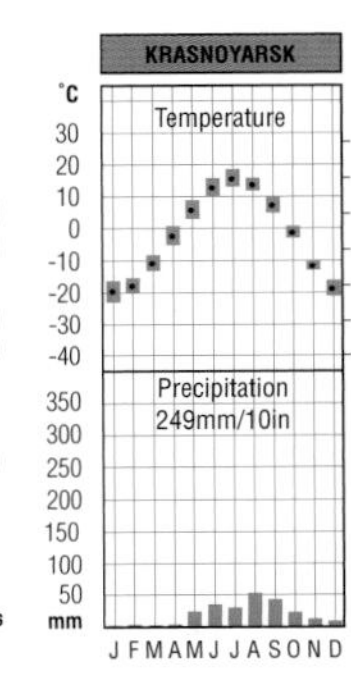

Climate Records

Temperature

Highest recorded shade temperature: Al Aziziyah, Libya, 135.9°F [57.7°C], September 13, 1922.

Highest mean annual temperature: Dallol, Ethiopia, 94°F [34.4°C], 1960–66.

Longest heatwave: Marble Bar, W. Australia, 162 days over 100°F [38°C], October 23, 1923, to April 7, 1924.

Lowest recorded temperature (outside poles): Verkhoyansk, Siberia, –93.6°F [–69.8°C], February 7, 1892.

Lowest mean annual temperature: Polus Nedostupnosti, Pole of Cold, Antarctica, –72°F [–57.8°C].

Precipitation

Driest place: Quillagua, Chile, mean annual rainfall 0.02 inches [0.5 mm], 1964–2001.

Wettest place (12 months): Cherrapunji, Meghalaya, N. E. India, 1,042 inches [26,461 mm], August 1860 to July 1861. Cherrapunji also holds the record for the most rainfall in one month: 115 inches [2,930 mm], July 1861.

Wettest place (average): Mt Wai-ale-ale, Hawai'i, USA, mean annual rainfall 459.8 inches [11,680 mm].

Wettest place (24 hours): Fac Fac, Réunion, Indian Ocean, 71.9 inches [1,825 mm], March 15–16, 1952.

Heaviest hailstones: Gopalganj, Bangladesh, up to 2.25 lb [1.02 kg], April 14, 1986 (killed 92 people).

Heaviest snowfall (continuous): Bessans, Savoie, France, 68 inches [1,730 mm] in 19 hours, April 5–6, 1969.

Heaviest snowfall (season/year): Mt Baker, Washington, USA, 28,956 mm [1,140 in], June 1998 to June 1999.

Pressure and winds

Highest barometric pressure: Agata, Siberia (at 862 ft [262 m] altitude), 1,083.8 mb, December 31, 1968.

Lowest barometric pressure: Typhoon Tip, Guam, Pacific Ocean, 870 mb, October 12, 1979.

Highest recorded wind speed: Mt Washington, New Hampshire, USA, 231 mph [371 km/h], April 12, 1934. This is three times as strong as hurricane force on the Beaufort Scale.

Windiest place: Commonwealth Bay, Antarctica, where gales frequently reach over 200 mph [320 km/h].

Climate

Climate is weather in the long term: the seasonal pattern of hot and cold, wet and dry, averaged over time (usually 30 years). At the simplest level, it is caused by the uneven heating of the Earth. Surplus heat at the Equator passes toward the poles, leveling out the energy differential. Its passage is marked by a ceaseless churning of the atmosphere and the oceans, further agitated by the Earth's diurnal spin and the motion it imparts to moving air and water. The heat's means of transport – by winds and ocean currents, by the continual evaporation and recondensation of water molecules – is the weather itself. There are four basic types of climate, each of which can be further subdivided: tropical, desert (dry), temperate, and polar.

Composition of Dry Air

Nitrogen	78.09%	Sulfur dioxide	trace
Oxygen	20.95%	Nitrogen oxide	trace
Argon	0.93%	Methane	trace
Water vapor	0.2–4.0%	Dust	trace
Carbon dioxide	0.03%	Helium	trace
Ozone	0.00006%	Neon	trace

El Niño

In a normal year, southeasterly trade winds drive surface waters westward off the coast of South America, drawing cold, nutrient-rich water up from below. In an El Niño year (which occurs every 2–7 years), warm water from the west Pacific suppresses upwelling in the east, depriving the region of nutrients. The water is warmed by as much as 12°F [7°C], disturbing the tropical atmospheric circulation. During an intense El Niño, the southeast trade winds change direction and become equatorial westerlies, resulting in climatic extremes in many regions of the world, such as drought in parts of Australia and India, and heavy rainfall in southeastern USA. An intense El Niño occurred in 1997–8, with resultant freak weather conditions across the entire Pacific region.

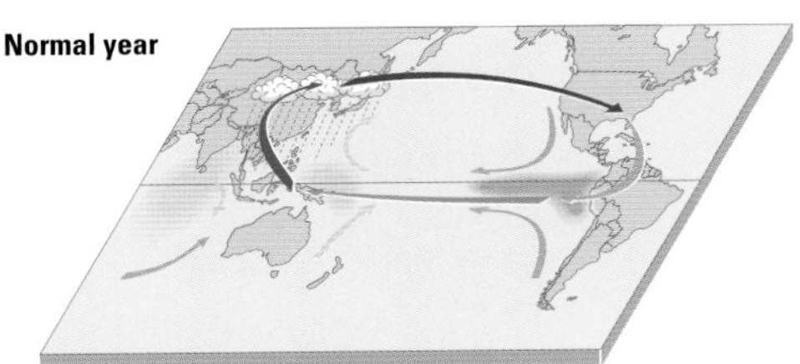

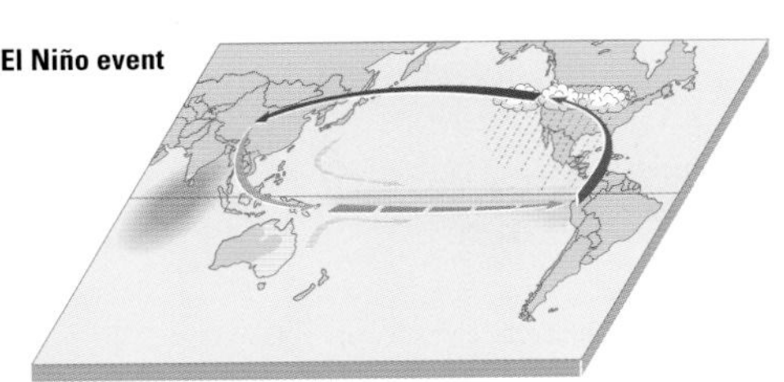

Beaufort Wind Scale

Named after the 19th-century British naval officer who devised it, the Beaufort Scale assesses wind speed according to its effects. It was originally designed as an aid for sailors, but has since been adapted for use on the land.

Scale	Wind speed mph	km/h	Effect
0	0–1	0–1	**Calm** Smoke rises vertically
1	1–3	1–5	**Light air** Wind direction shown only by smoke drift
2	4–7	6–11	**Light breeze** Wind felt on face; leaves rustle; vanes moved by wind
3	8–12	12–19	**Gentle breeze** Leaves and small twigs in constant motion; wind extends small flag
4	13–18	20–28	**Moderate** Raises dust and loose paper; small branches move
5	19–24	29–38	**Fresh** Small trees in leaf sway; wavelets on inland waters
6	25–31	39–49	**Strong** Large branches move; difficult to use umbrellas
7	32–38	50–61	**Near gale** Whole trees in motion; difficult to walk against wind
8	39–46	62–74	**Gale** Twigs break from trees; walking very difficult
9	47–54	75–88	**Strong gale** Slight structural damage
10	55–63	89–102	**Storm** Trees uprooted; serious structural damage
11	64–72	103–117	**Violent storm** Widespread damage
12	73+	118+	**Hurricane**

Conversions

°C = (°F − 32) × 5/9; °F = (°C × 9/5) + 32; 0°C = 32°F
1 in = 25.4 mm; 1 mm = 0.0394 in; 100 mm = 3.94 in

Temperature

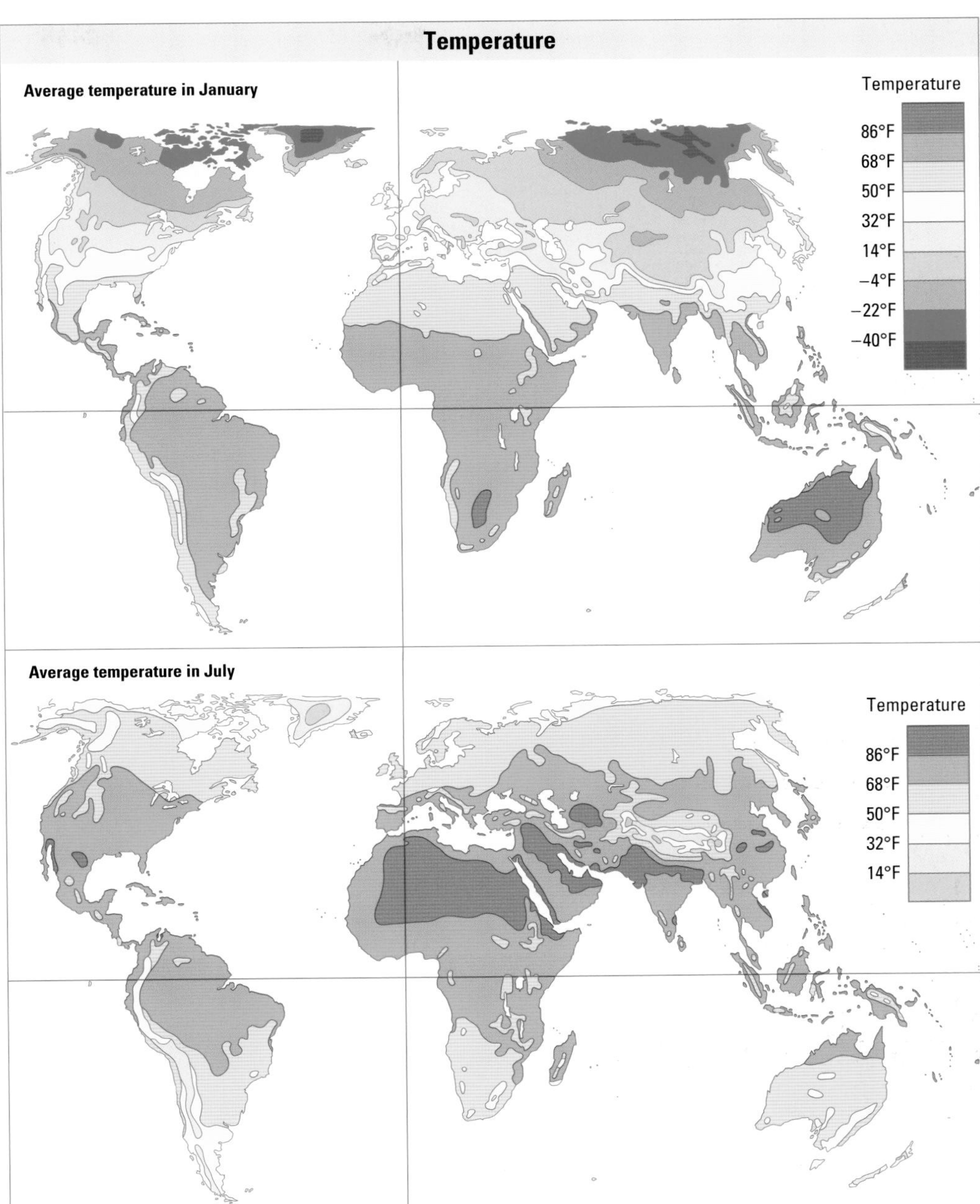

Precipitation

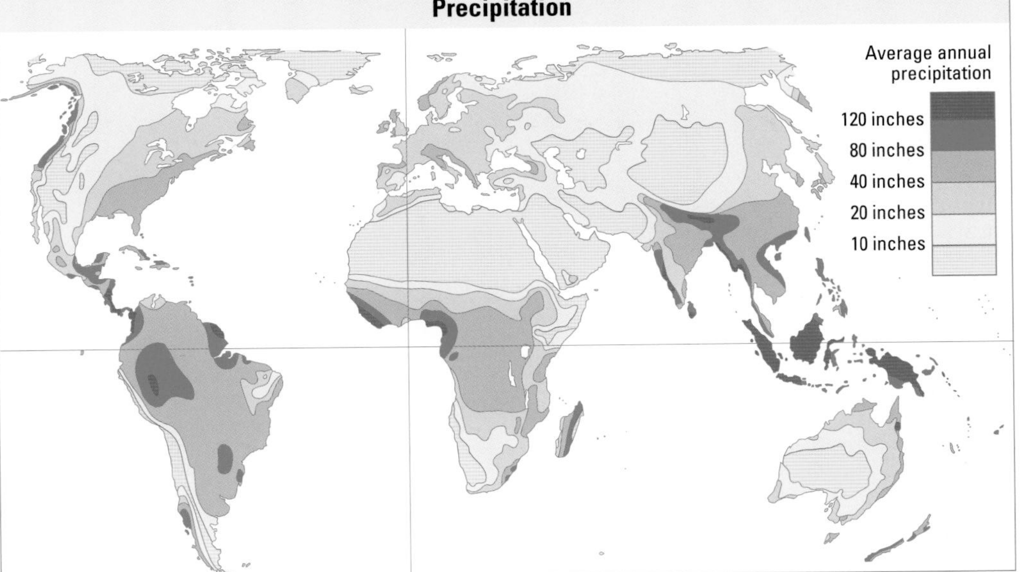

Water and Vegetation

The Hydrological Cycle

The world's water balance is regulated by the constant recycling of water between the oceans, atmosphere and land. The movement of water between these three reservoirs is known as the hydrological cycle. The oceans play a vital role in the hydrological cycle: 74% of the total precipitation falls over the oceans and 84% of the total evaporation comes from the oceans.

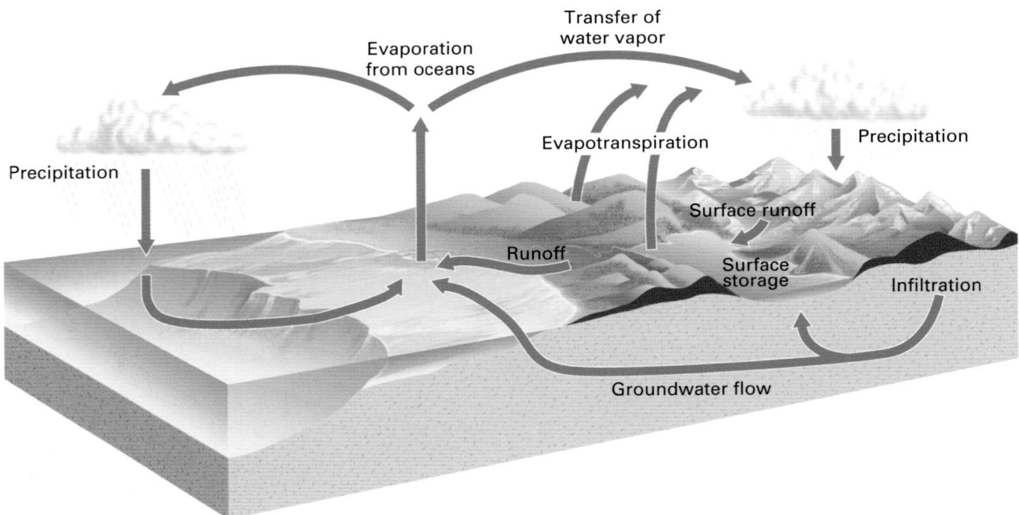

Water Distribution

The distribution of planetary water, by percentage. Oceans and ice caps together account for more than 99% of the total; the breakdown of the remainder is estimated.

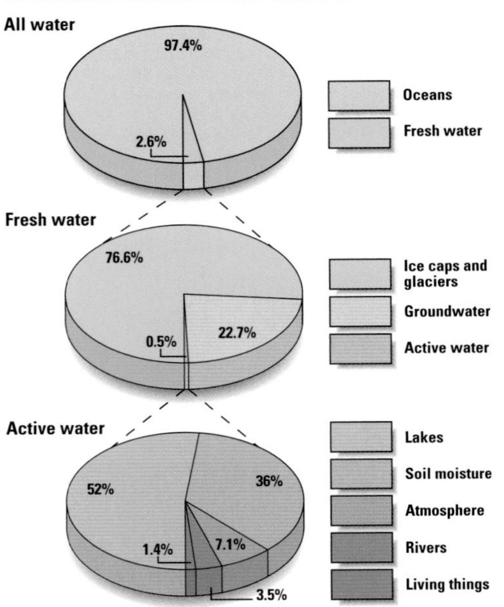

Water Utilization

Domestic | Industrial | Agriculture

The percentage breakdown of water usage by sector, selected countries (2002)

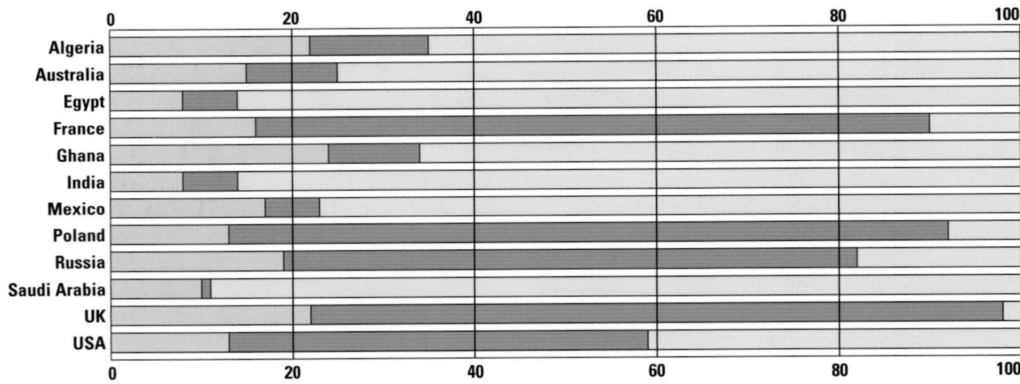

Water Usage

Almost all the world's water is 3,000 million years old, and all of it cycles endlessly through the hydrosphere, though at different rates. Water vapor circulates over days, even hours, deep ocean water circulates over millennia, and ice-cap water remains solid for millions of years.

Fresh water is essential to all terrestrial life. Humans cannot survive more than a few days without it, and even the hardiest desert plants and animals could not exist without some water. Agriculture requires huge quantities of fresh water: without large-scale irrigation most of the world's people would starve. In the USA, agriculture uses 41% and industry 46% of all water withdrawals.

According to the latest figures, the average North American uses 1.3 million liters per year. This is more than six times the average African, who uses just 186,000 liters of water each year. Europeans and Australians use 694,000 liters per year.

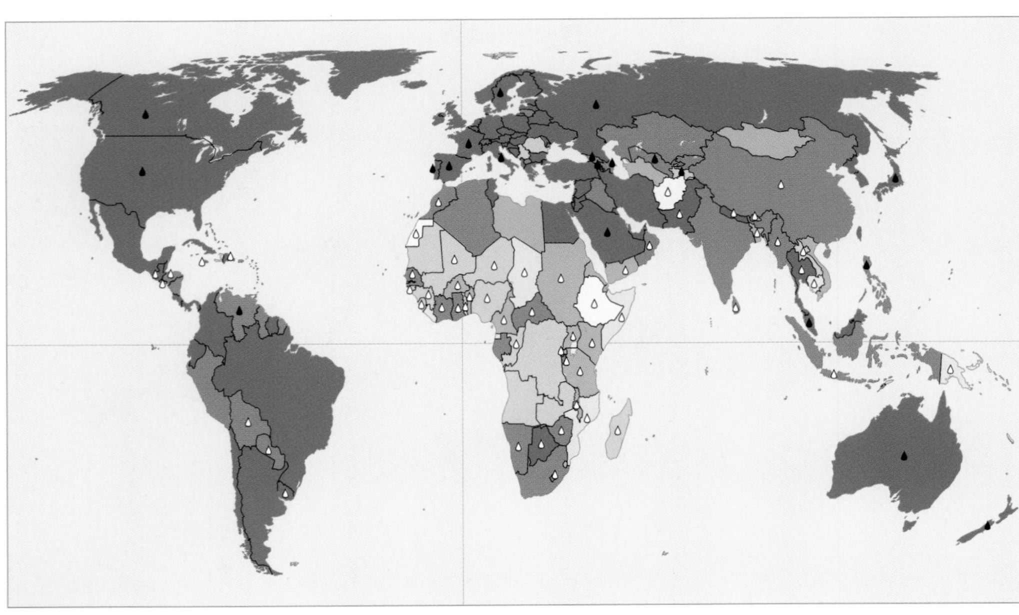

Water Supply

Percentage of total population with access to safe drinking water (2004)

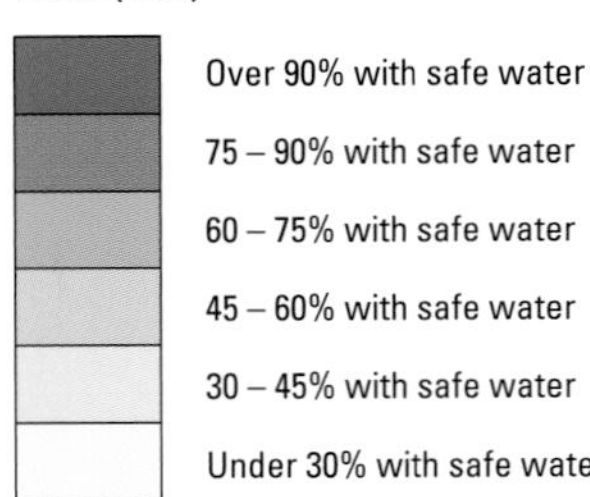

Over 90% with safe water

75 – 90% with safe water

60 – 75% with safe water

45 – 60% with safe water

30 – 45% with safe water

Under 30% with safe water

Under 80 liters per person per day domestic water consumption

Over 320 liters per person per day domestic water consumption

NB: 80 liters of water a day is considered necessary for a reasonable quality of life.

Least well-provided countries

Afghanistan	13%	Papua New Guinea	39%
Ethiopia	22%	Cambodia	41%
Western Sahara	26%	Somalia	42%

Natural Vegetation

Regional variation in vegetation

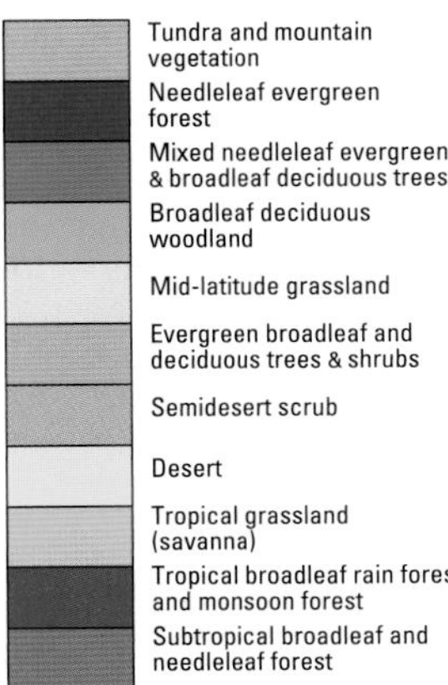

The map shows the natural "climax vegetation" of regions, as dictated by climate and topography. In most cases, however, agricultural activity has drastically altered the vegetation pattern. Western Europe, for example, lost most of its broadleaf forest many centuries ago, while irrigation has turned some natural semidesert into productive land.

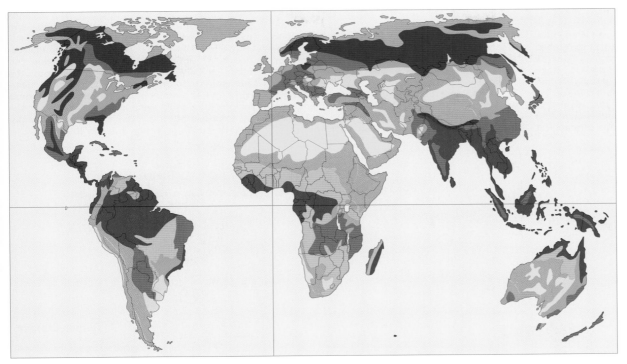

Land Use by Continent (2004)

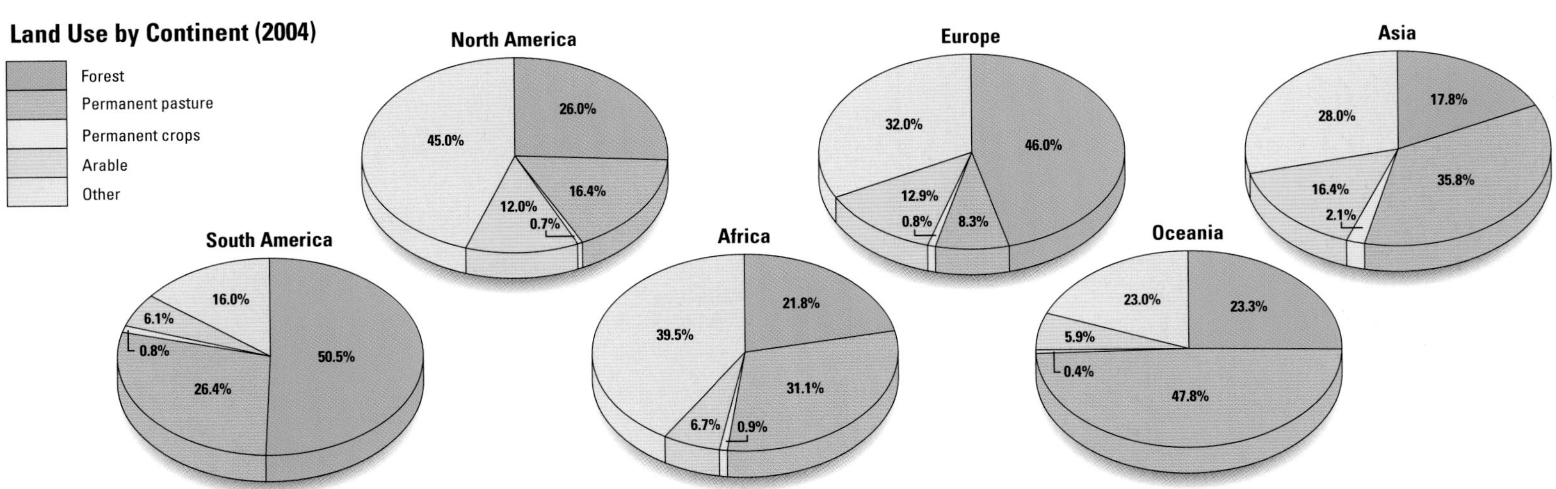

Forestry: Production

Forest and woodland (million hectares)		Annual production (2005, million cubic meters) Fuelwood	Industrial roundwood*
World	***3,869.5***	***1,792.1***	***1710.6***
Europe	1,039.3	117.3	544.0
S. America	885.6	192.8	186.7
Africa	649.9	563.3	69.4
N. & C. America	549.3	130.2	623.6
Asia	547.8	779.5	237.5
Oceania	197.6	9.0	49.4

Paper and Board
Top producers (2005)**

USA	81,437
China	53,463
Japan	29,295
Germany	21,679
Canada	19,673

Top exporters (2005)**

Canada	15,731
Germany	12,205
Finland	11,155
Sweden	10,593
USA	9,610

* roundwood is timber as it is felled
** in thousand tons

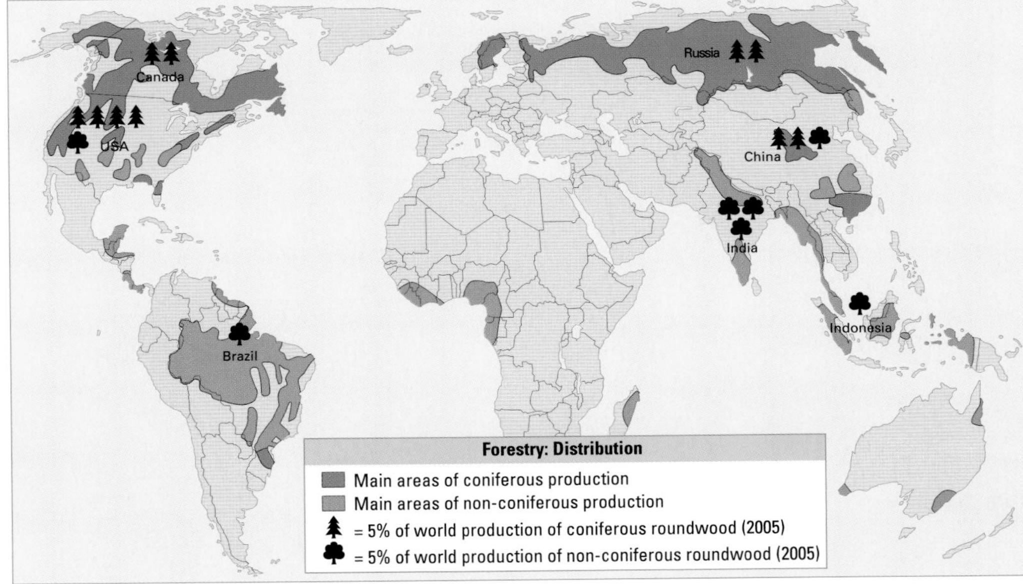

Environment

Humans have always had a dramatic effect on their environment, at least since the development of agriculture almost 10,000 years ago. Generally, the Earth has accepted human interference without obvious ill effects: the complex systems that regulate the global environment have been able to absorb substantial damage while maintaining a stable and comfortable home for the planet's trillions of lifeforms. But advancing human technology and the rapidly-expanding populations it supports are now threatening to overwhelm the Earth's ability to compensate.

Industrial wastes, acid rainfall, desertification, and large-scale deforestation all combine to create environmental change at a rate far faster than the great slow cycles of planetary evolution can accommodate. As a result of overcultivation, overgrazing, and overcutting of groundcover for firewood, desertification is affecting as much as 60% of the world's croplands. In addition, with fire and chainsaws, humans are destroying more forest in a day than their ancestors could have done in a century, upsetting the balance between plant and animal, carbon dioxide and oxygen, on which all life ultimately depends.

The fossil fuels that power industrial civilization have pumped enough carbon dioxide and other so-called greenhouse gases into the atmosphere to make climatic change a near-certainty. As a result of the combination of these factors, the Earth's average temperature has risen by approximately 1°F [0.5°C] since the beginning of the 20th century, and it is still rising.

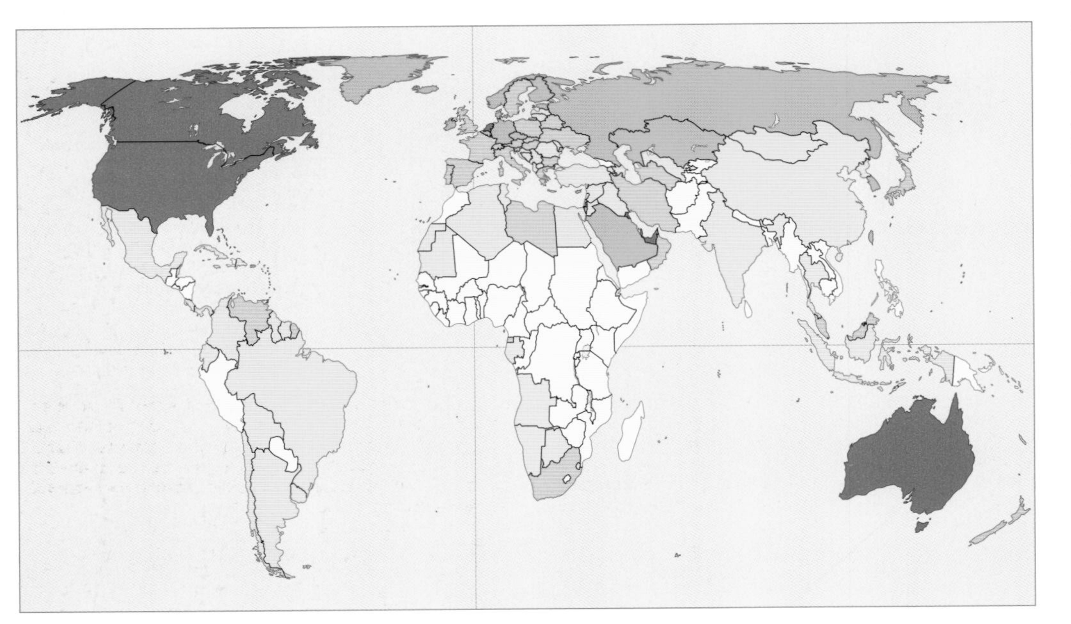

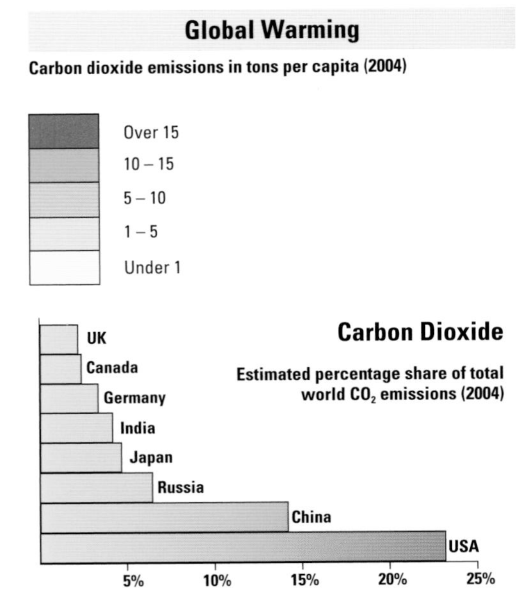

Temperature Rise

PROJECTED CHANGE IN GLOBAL WARMING

F°: +38, +36, +34, +32, +31

1950, 1970, 1990, 2010, 2030, 2050

Rise in average temperatures assuming present trends in CO_2 emissions continue

Assuming some cuts are made in emissions

Assuming drastic cuts are made in emissions

Sea Level Rise

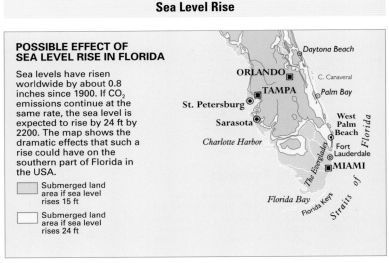

POSSIBLE EFFECT OF SEA LEVEL RISE IN FLORIDA

Sea levels have risen worldwide by about 0.8 inches since 1900. If CO_2 emissions continue at the same rate, the sea level is expected to rise by 24 ft by 2200. The map shows the dramatic effects that such a rise could have on the southern part of Florida in the USA.

Submerged land area if sea level rises 15 ft

Submerged land area if sea level rises 24 ft

Daytona Beach, ORLANDO, C. Canaveral, TAMPA, Palm Bay, St. Petersburg, Sarasota, West Palm Beach, Charlotte Harbor, Fort Lauderdale, MIAMI, The Everglades, Florida Bay, Florida Keys, Straits of Florida

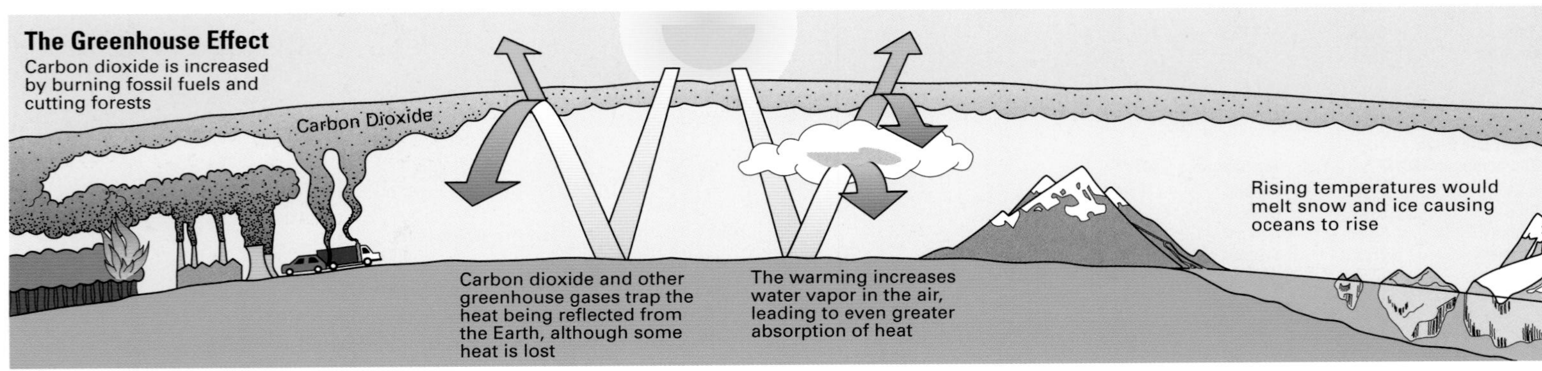

The Greenhouse Effect
Carbon dioxide is increased by burning fossil fuels and cutting forests
Carbon Dioxide
Carbon dioxide and other greenhouse gases trap the heat being reflected from the Earth, although some heat is lost
The warming increases water vapor in the air, leading to even greater absorption of heat
Rising temperatures would melt snow and ice causing oceans to rise

Desertification

Existing deserts

Areas with a high risk of desertification

Areas with a moderate risk of desertification

Former areas of rain forest

Existing rain forest

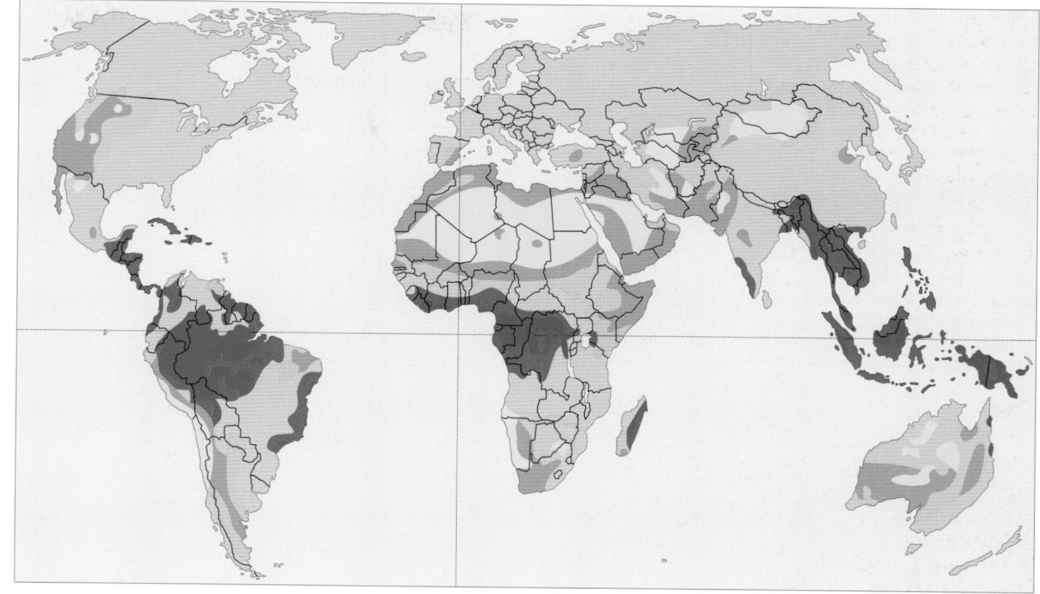

Forest Clearance

Thousands of hectares of forest cleared annually, tropical countries surveyed 1980–85, 1990–95 and 2000–05. Loss as a percentage of remaining stocks is shown in figures on each column. Gain is indicated as a minus figure.

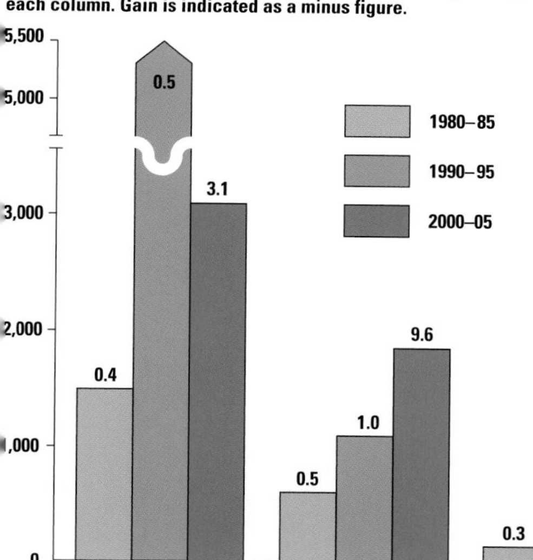

Deforestation

The Earth's remaining forests are under attack from three directions: expanding agriculture, logging, and growing consumption of fuelwood, often in combination. Sometimes deforestation is the direct result of government policy, as in the efforts made to resettle the urban poor in some parts of Brazil; just as often, it comes about despite state attempts at conservation. Loggers, licensed or unlicensed, blaze a trail into virgin forest, often destroying twice as many trees as they harvest. Landless farmers follow, burning away most of what remains to plant their crops, completing the destruction. Some countries such as Vietnam and Costa Rica have successfully implemented reafforestation programs.

Ozone Depletion

he ozone layer, 15–18 miles [25–30 km] above sea level, acts as barrier to most of the Sun's harmful ultra-violet radiation, proecting us from the ionizing radiation that can cause skin cancer nd cataracts. In recent years, however, two holes in the ozone ayer have been observed during winter: one over the Arctic and e other, the size of the USA, over Antarctica. By 1996, ozone ad been reduced to around a half of its 1970 amount. The ozone $_3$) is broken down by chlorine released into the atmosphere as FCs (chlorofluorocarbons) – chemicals used in refrigerators, ackaging, and aerosols.

Air Pollution

Sulfur dioxide is the main pollutant associated with industrial cities. According to the World Health Organization, at least 600 million people live in urban areas where sulfur dioxide concentrations regularly reach damaging levels. One of the world's most dangerously polluted urban areas is Mexico City, due to a combination of its enclosed valley location, 3 million cars and 60,000 factories. In May 1998, this lethal cocktail was added to by nearby forest fires and the resultant air pollution led to over 20% of the population (3 million people) complaining of respiratory problems.

Acid Rain

Killing trees, poisoning lakes and rivers, and eating away buildings, acid rain is mostly produced by sulfur dioxide emissions from industry and volcanic eruptions. By the mid 1990s, acid rain had sterilized 4,000 or more of Sweden's lakes and left 45% of Switzerland's alpine conifers dead or dying, while the monuments of Greece were dissolving in Athens' smog. Prevailing wind patterns mean that the acids often fall many hundred miles from where the original pollutants were discharged. In parts of Europe acid deposition has slightly decreased, following reductions in emissions, but not by enough.

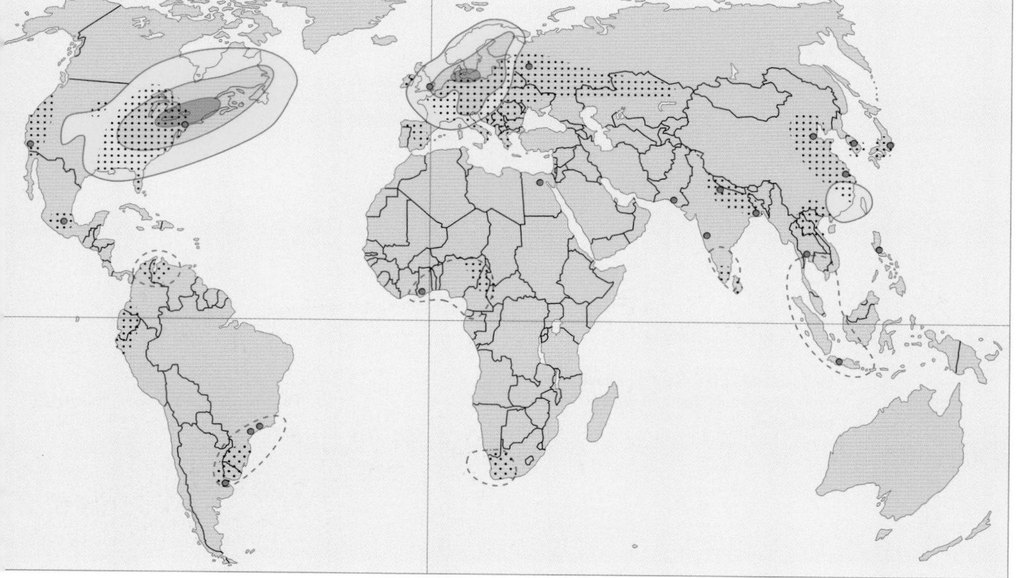

World Pollution

Acid rain and sources of acidic emissions (latest available year)

Acid rain is caused by high levels of sulfur and nitrogen in the atmosphere. They combine with water vapor and oxygen to form acids (H_2SO_4 and HNO_3) which fall as precipitation.

Regions where sulfur and nitrogen oxides are released in high concentrations, mainly from fossil fuel combustion

Major cities with high levels of air pollution (including nitrogen and sulfur emissions)

Areas of heavy acid deposition

pH numbers indicate acidity, decreasing from a neutral 7. Normal rain, slightly acid from dissolved carbon dioxide, never exceeds a pH of 5.6.

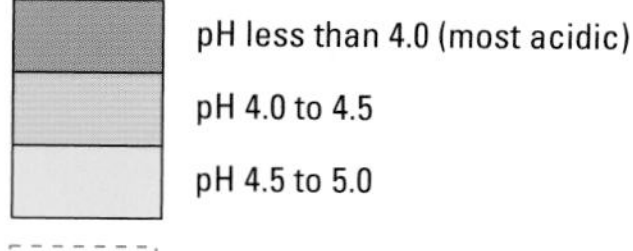

Areas where acid rain is a potential problem

Population

Demographic Profiles

Developed nations such as the UK have populations evenly spread across the age groups and, usually, a growing proportion of elderly people. The great majority of the people in developing nations, however, are in the younger age groups, about to enter their most fertile years. In time, these population profiles should resemble the world profile (even Nigeria has made recent progress by reducing its birth rate), but the transition will come about only after a few more generations of rapid population growth.

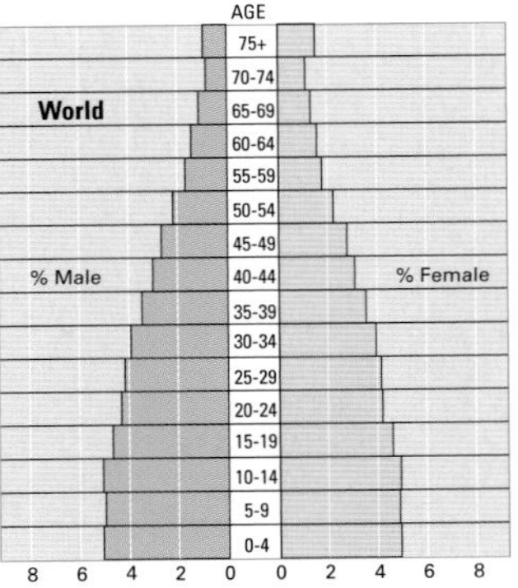

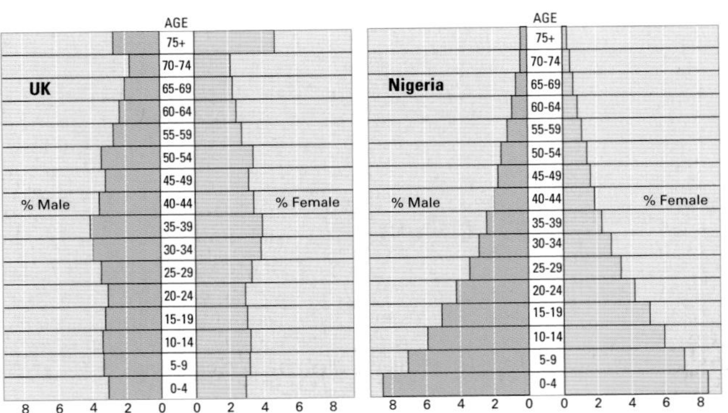

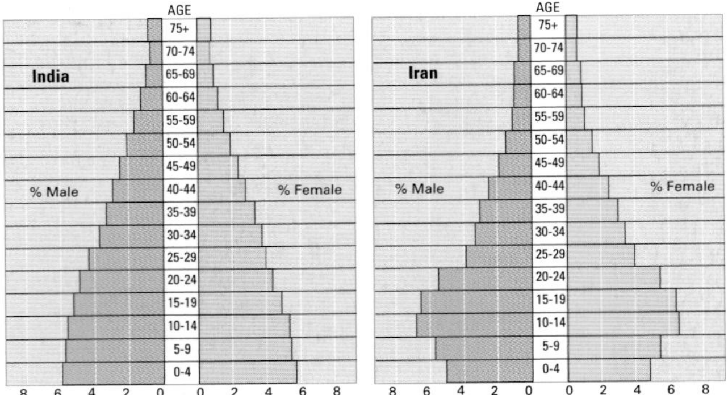

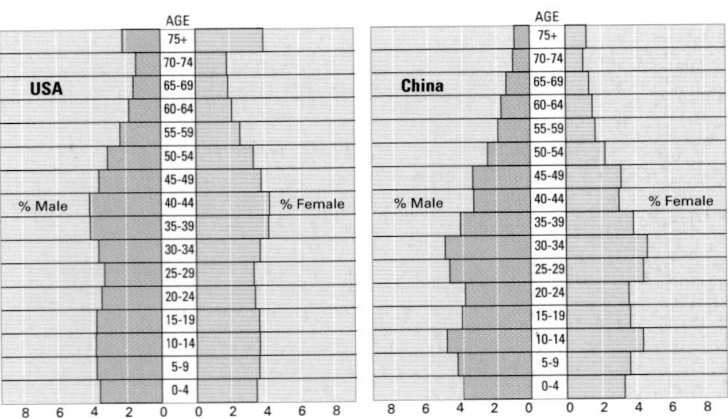

Most Populous Nations, in millions (2006 estimates)

Rank	Country	Millions	Rank	Country	Millions	Rank	Country	Millions
1.	China	1,314	9.	Nigeria	132	17.	Turkey	70
2.	India	1,095	10.	Japan	127	18.	Iran	69
3.	USA	301	11.	Mexico	107	19.	Thailand	65
4.	Indonesia	245	12.	Philippines	89	20.	Congo (Dem. Rep.)	63
5.	Brazil	188	13.	Vietnam	84	21.	France	61
6.	Pakistan	166	14.	Germany	82	22.	UK	61
7.	Bangladesh	147	15.	Egypt	79	23.	Italy	58
8.	Russia	143	16.	Ethiopia	75	24.	South Korea	49

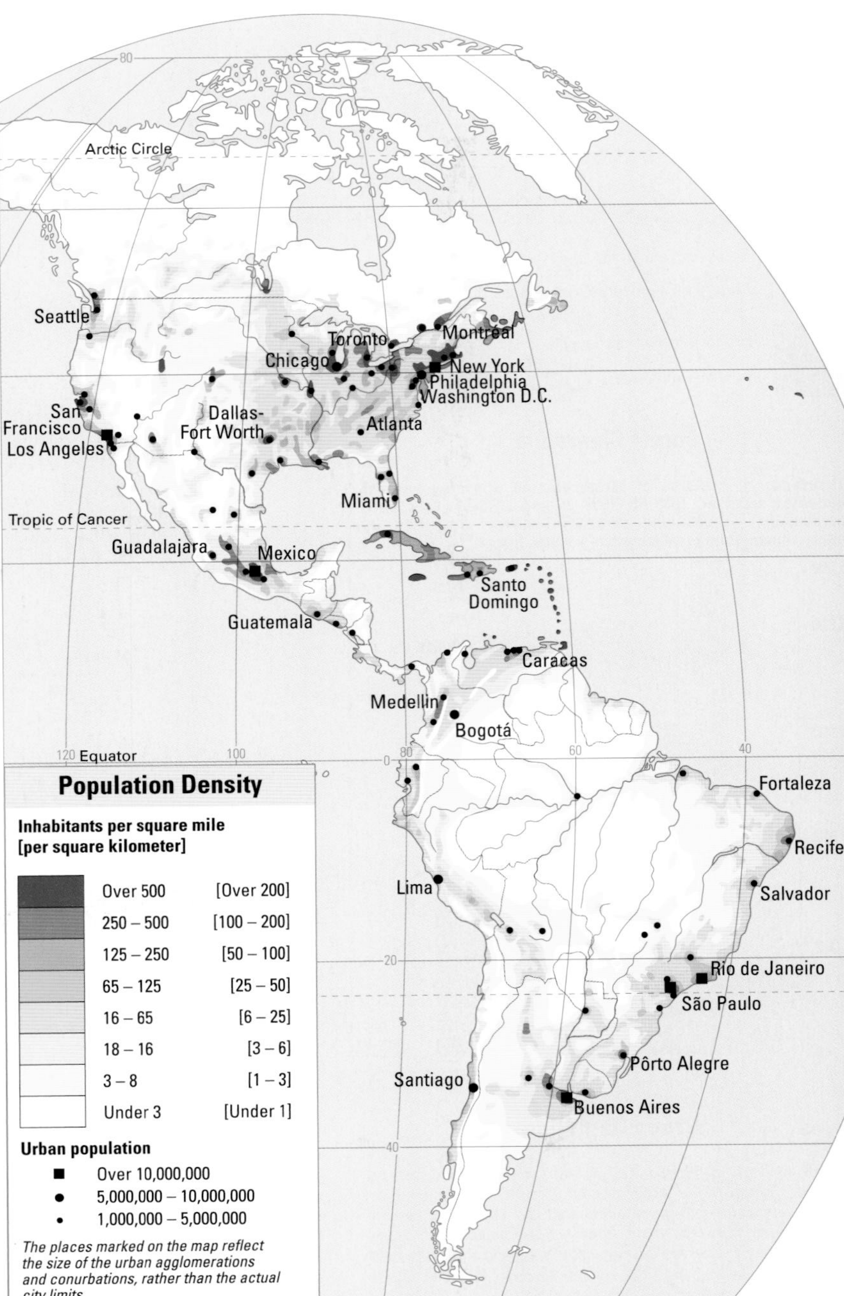

Continental Comparisons

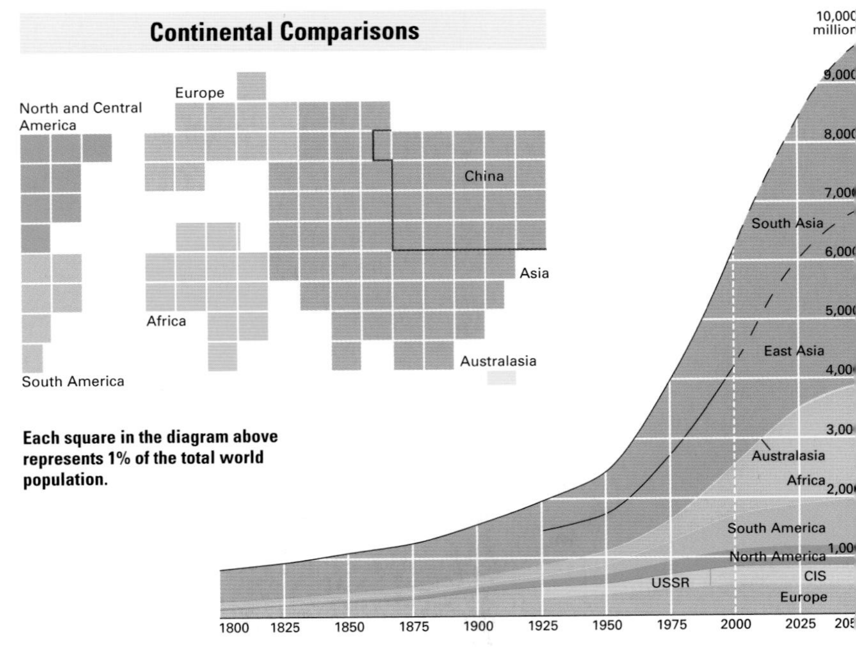

Each square in the diagram above represents 1% of the total world population.

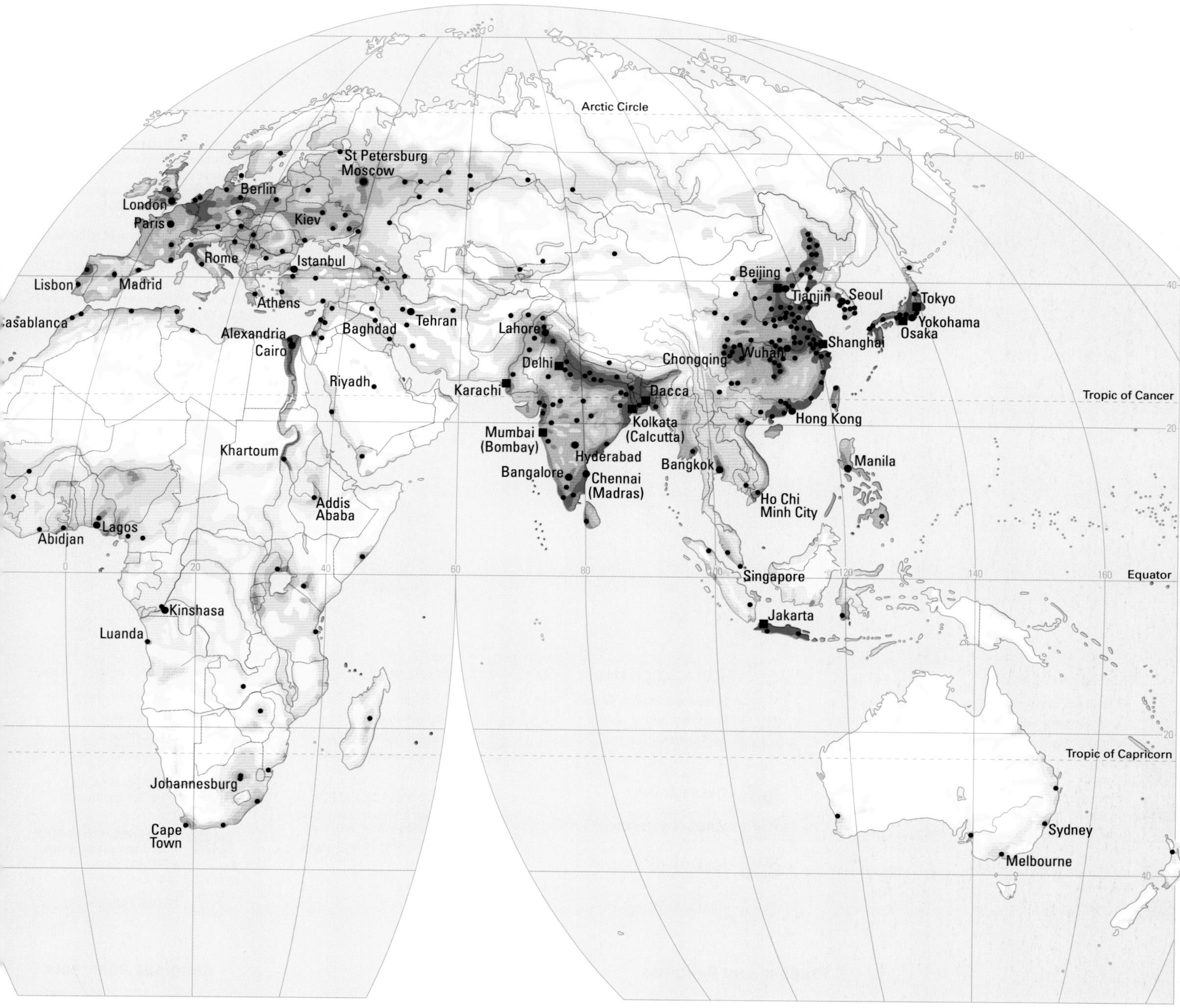

Arctic Circle
St Petersburg
Moscow
Berlin
London
Paris
Kiev
Rome
Istanbul
Lisbon
Madrid
Athens
asablanca
Alexandria
Cairo
Baghdad
Tehran
Riyadh
Lahore
Delhi
Karachi
Beijing
Tianjin
Seoul
Tokyo
Yokohama
Osaka
Shanghai
Wuhan
Chongqing
Dacca
Kolkata
(Calcutta)
Hong Kong
Tropic of Cancer
Mumbai
(Bombay)
Hyderabad
Bangalore
Chennai
(Madras)
Bangkok
Manila
Ho Chi
Minh City
Khartoum
Addis
Ababa
Abidjan
Lagos
Singapore
Equator
Kinshasa
Luanda
Jakarta
Tropic of Capricorn
Johannesburg
Cape
Town
Sydney
Melbourne

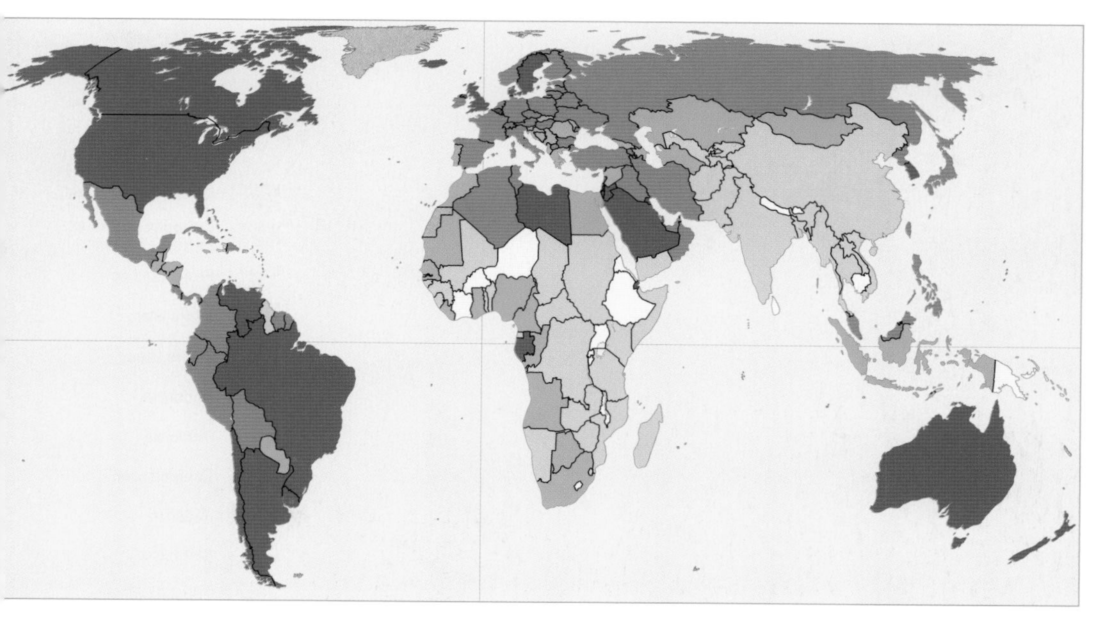

Urban Population

Percentage of total population living in towns and cities (2004)

- Over 80%
- 60 – 80%
- 40 – 60%
- 20 – 40%
- Under 20%
- No data available

Most urbanized

Singapore 100%
Kuwait 97%
Belgium 97%
Bahrain 96%
Qatar 95%

Least urbanized

Burundi 10%
Bhutan 11%
Trinidad & Tobago ..12%
Uganda 13%
Papua New Guinea .13%

The Human Family

Predominant Languages

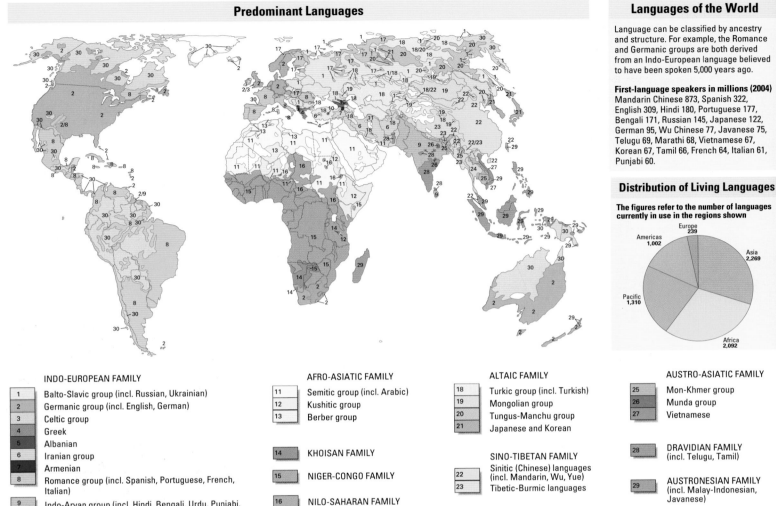

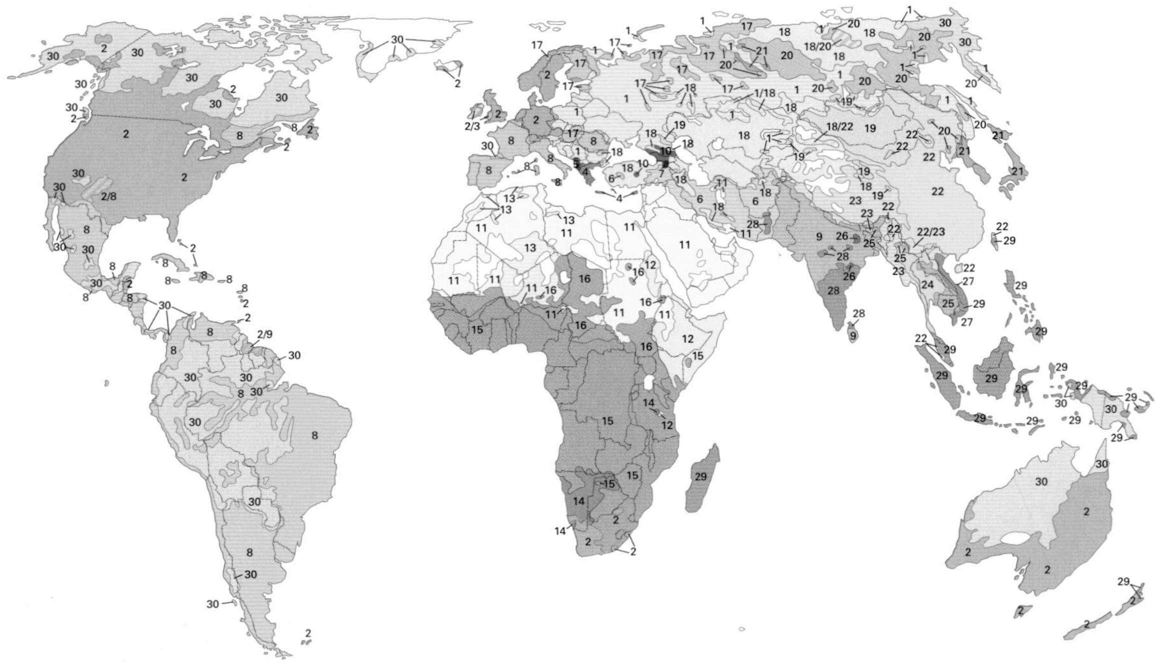

INDO-EUROPEAN FAMILY

- 1 Balto-Slavic group (incl. Russian, Ukrainian)
- 2 Germanic group (incl. English, German)
- 3 Celtic group
- 4 Greek
- 5 Albanian
- 6 Iranian group
- 7 Armenian
- 8 Romance group (incl. Spanish, Portuguese, French, Italian)
- 9 Indo-Aryan group (incl. Hindi, Bengali, Urdu, Punjabi, Marathi)

10 CAUCASIAN FAMILY

AFRO-ASIATIC FAMILY

- 11 Semitic group (incl. Arabic)
- 12 Kushitic group
- 13 Berber group

14 KHOISAN FAMILY

15 NIGER-CONGO FAMILY

16 NILO-SAHARAN FAMILY

17 URALIC FAMILY

ALTAIC FAMILY

- 18 Turkic group (incl. Turkish)
- 19 Mongolian group
- 20 Tungus-Manchu group
- 21 Japanese and Korean

SINO-TIBETAN FAMILY

- 22 Sinitic (Chinese) languages (incl. Mandarin, Wu, Yue)
- 23 Tibetic-Burmic languages

24 TAI FAMILY

AUSTRO-ASIATIC FAMILY

- 25 Mon-Khmer group
- 26 Munda group
- 27 Vietnamese

28 DRAVIDIAN FAMILY (incl. Telugu, Tamil)

29 AUSTRONESIAN FAMILY (incl. Malay-Indonesian, Javanese)

30 OTHER LANGUAGES

Languages of the World

Language can be classified by ancestry and structure. For example, the Romance and Germanic groups are both derived from an Indo-European language believed to have been spoken 5,000 years ago.

First-language speakers in millions (2004)
Mandarin Chinese 873, Spanish 322, English 309, Hindi 180, Portuguese 177, Bengali 171, Russian 145, Japanese 122, German 95, Wu Chinese 77, Javanese 75, Telugu 69, Marathi 68, Vietnamese 67, Korean 67, Tamil 66, French 64, Italian 61, Punjabi 60.

Distribution of Living Languages

The figures refer to the number of languages currently in use in the regions shown

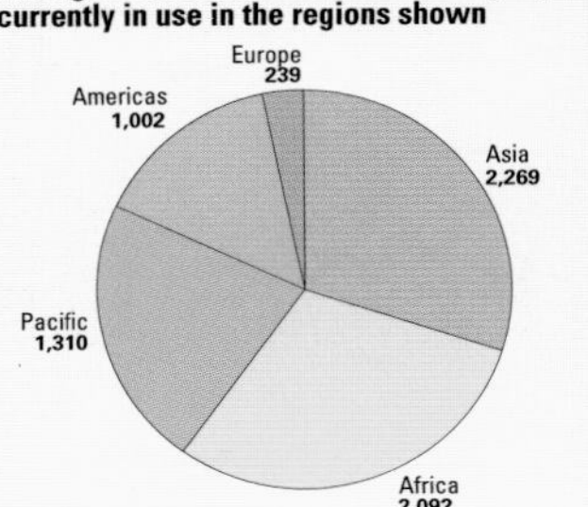

Predominant Religions

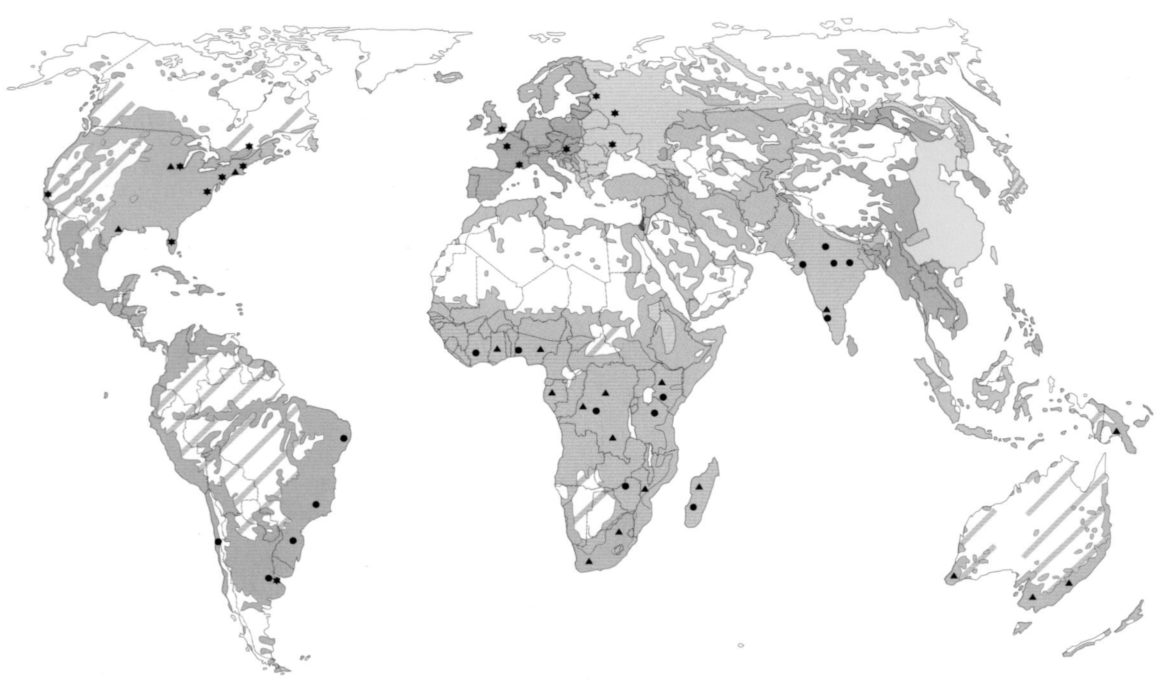

- Roman Catholicism
- Orthodox and other Eastern Churches
- Protestantism
- Sunni Islam
- Shi'ite Islam
- Buddhism
- Hinduism
- Confucianism
- Judaism
- Shintoism
- Tribal Religions

Religious Adherents

Religious adherents in millions (2005)

Religion	Millions	Religion	Millions
Christianity	2,100	Hindu	832
Roman Catholic	*1,050*	Chinese folk	394
Protestant	*396*	Buddhism	329
Orthodox	*240*	Ethnic religions	300
Anglican	*73*	New religions	103
Others	*341*	Sikhism	23
Islam	1,070	Judaism	15
Sunni	*940*	Spiritism	12
Shi'ite	*120*	Baha'i	6
Others	*10*	Confucianism	6
Non-religious/		Jainism	5
Agnostic/Atheist	1,100	Shintoism	3

United Nations

Created in 1945 to promote peace and cooperation and based in New York, the United Nations is the world's largest international organization, with 192 members and an annual budget of US $1.9 billion (2006). Each member of the General Assembly has one vote, while the five permanent members of the 15-nation Security Council – China, France, Russia, UK, and USA – hold a veto. The Secretariat is the UN's principal administrative arm. The 54 members of the Economic and Social Council are responsible for economic, social, cultural, educational, health, and related matters. The UN has 16 specialized agencies – based in Canada, France, Switzerland, and Italy, as well as the USA – which help members in fields such as education (UNESCO), agriculture (FAO), medicine (WHO), and finance (IFC). By the end of 1994, all the original 11 trust territories of the Trusteeship Council had become independent.

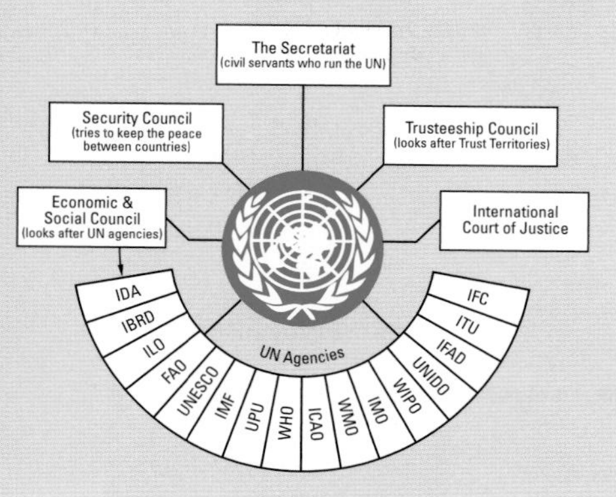

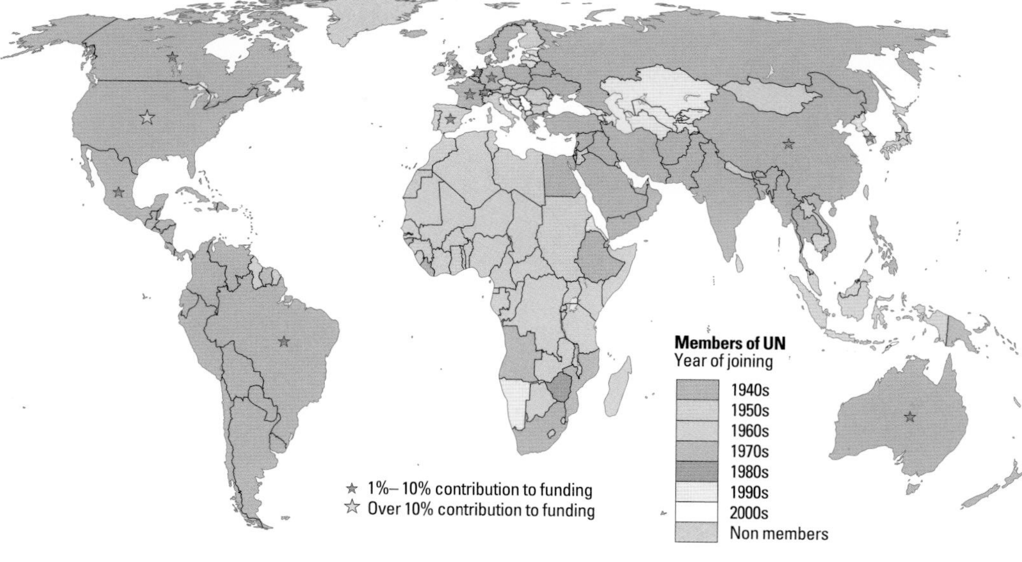

MEMBERSHIP OF THE UN In 1945 there were 51 members; by the end of 2006 membership had increased to 192 following the admission of East Timor, Switzerland, and Montenegro. There are 2 independent states which are not members of the UN – Taiwan and the Vatican City. All the successor states of the former USSR had joined by the end of 1992. The official languages of the UN are Chinese, English, French, Russian, Spanish, and Arabic.

FUNDING The UN regular budget for 2006 was US$1.9 billion. Contributions are assessed by the members' ability to pay, with the maximum 22% of the total (USA's share), the minimum 0.01%. The European Union pays over 37% of the budget.

PEACEKEEPING The UN has been involved in 61 peacekeeping operations worldwide since 1948.

International Organizations

CP African-Caribbean-Pacific (formed in 1963). Members have economic ties with the EU.
PEC Asia-Pacific Economic Cooperation (formed in 1989). It aims to enhance economic growth and rosperity for the region and to strengthen the Asia-Pacific community. APEC is the only intergovernmental rouping in the world operating on the basis of non-binding commitments, open dialogue, and equal espect for the views of all participants. There are 21 member economies.
RAB LEAGUE (formed in 1945). The League's aim is to promote economic, social, political, and military ooperation. There are 22 member nations.
SEAN Association of Southeast Asian Nations (formed in 1967). Cambodia joined in 1999.
U The African Union replaced the Organization of African Unity (formed in 1963) in 2002. Its 53 members epresent over 94% of Africa's population. Arabic, French, Portuguese, and English are recognized as orking languages.
OLOMBO PLAN (formed in 1951). Its 25 members aim to promote economic and social development in sia and the Pacific.
OMMONWEALTH The Commonwealth of Nations evolved from the British Empire. Pakistan was uspended in 1999, and Zimbabwe in 2002. In response to its continued suspension, Zimbabwe left the ommonwealth in December 2003. Pakistan was reinstated in 2004, but Fiji Islands was suspended in ecember 2006 following a military coup. It now comprises 16 Queen's realms, 31 republics and 6 digenous monarchies, giving a total of 53 member states.
U European Union (evolved from the European Community in 1993). Cyprus, the Czech Republic, Estonia, ungary, Latvia, Lithuania, Malta, Poland, the Slovak Republic, and Slovenia joined the EU in May 2004; Bulgaria nd Romania joined in January 2007. The other members are Austria, Belgium, Denmark, Finland, France, ermany, Greece, Ireland, Italy, Luxembourg, Netherlands, Portugal, Spain, Sweden, and the UK – together ese 27 countries aim to integrate economies, coordinate social developments, and bring about political union.
IA Latin American Integration Association (1980). Its aim is to promote freer regional trade.
ATO North Atlantic Treaty Organization (formed in 1949). It continues after 1991 despite the winding up of e Warsaw Pact. Bulgaria, Estonia, Latvia, Lithuania, Romania, the Slovak Republic, and Slovenia became embers in 2004.

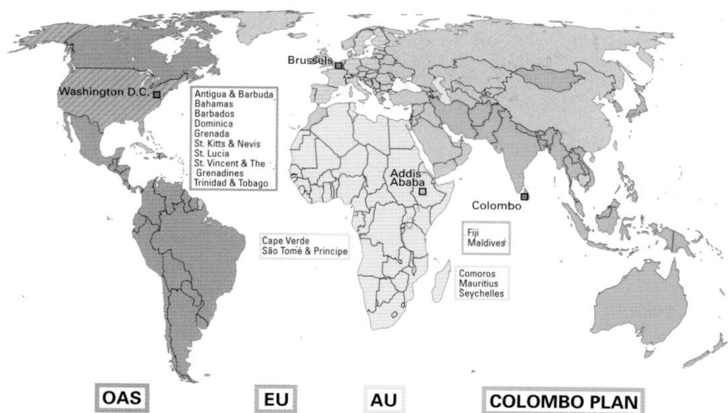

OAS Organization of American States (formed in 1948). It aims to promote social and economic cooperation between developed countries of North America and developing nations of Latin America.
OECD Organization for Economic Cooperation and Development (formed in 1961). It comprises 30 major free-market economies. Poland, Hungary, and South Korea joined in 1996, and the Slovak Republic in 2000. 'G8' is its 'inner group' of leading industrial nations, comprising Canada, France, Germany, Italy, Japan, Russia, UK, and USA.
OPEC Organization of Petroleum Exporting Countries (formed in 1960). It controls about three-quarters of the world's oil supply. Gabon left the organization in 1996.

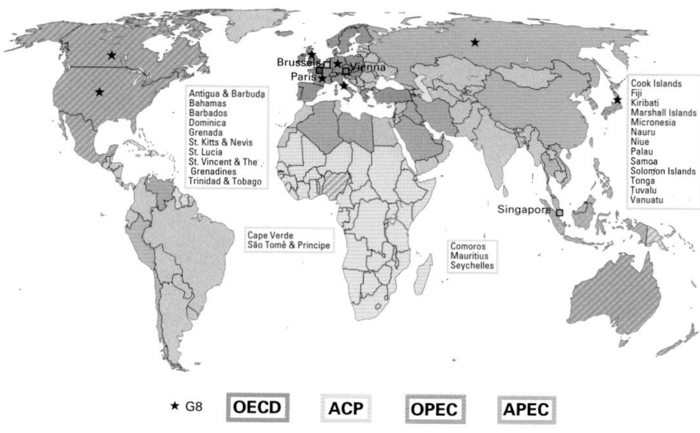

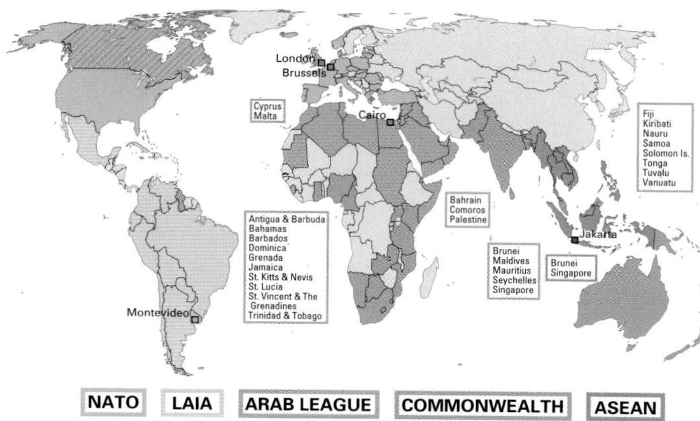

Wealth

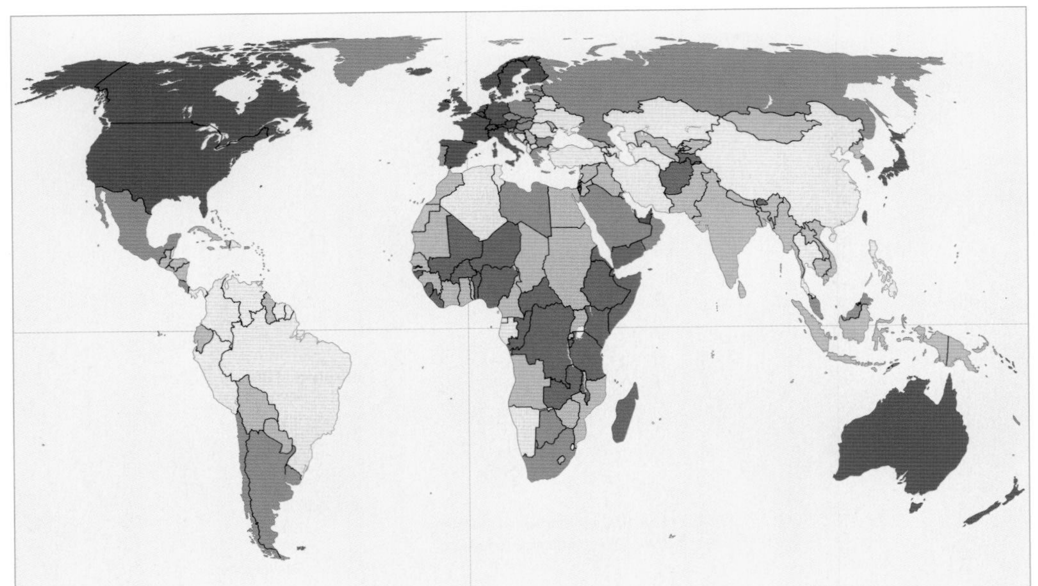

Levels of Income

Gross Domestic Product per capita: the annual value of goods and services divided by the population, using purchasing power parity (PPP) (2006)

Over 250% of world average

100% – 250% of world average

[World average per person US$10,000]

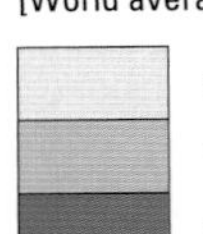

50% – 100% of world average

15% – 50% of world average

Under 15% of world average

No data available

Wealth Creation

The Gross Domestic Product (GDP) of the world's largest economies, US$ million (2006)

1.	USA	12,980,000	23.	Poland	543,000
2.	China	10,000,000	24.	Netherlands	512,000
3.	Japan	4,220,000	25.	Philippines	443,000
4.	India	4,042,000	26.	Pakistan	427,000
5.	Germany	2,585,000	27.	Saudi Arabia	374,000
6.	UK	1,903,000	28.	Colombia	367,000
7.	France	1,871,000	29.	Ukraine	356,000
8.	Italy	1,727,000	30.	Bangladesh	331,000
9.	Russia	1,723,000	31.	Belgium	330,000
10.	Brazil	1,616,000	32.	Egypt	328,000
11.	South Korea	1,180,000	33.	Malaysia	309,000
12.	Canada	1,165,000	34.	Sweden	285,000
13.	Mexico	1,134,000	35.	Austria	280,000
14.	Spain	1,070,000	36.	Vietnam	259,000
15.	Indonesia	935,000	37.	Algeria	253,000
16.	Taiwan	686,000	38.	Hong Kong	253,000
17.	Australia	666,000	39.	Switzerland	253,000
18.	Turkey	627,000	40.	Greece	252,000
19.	Iran	610,000	41.	Czech Republic	221,000
20.	Argentina	599,000	42.	Norway	207,000
21.	Thailand	586,000	43.	Portugal	203,000
22.	South Africa	576,000	44.	Chile	203,000

The Wealth Gap

The world's richest and poorest countries, by Gross Domestic Product per capita in US $ (2006)

Richest countries		Poorest countries	
1. Luxembourg	68,800	1. Somalia	600
2. UAE	49,700	2. Malawi	600
3. Norway	47,800	3. Comoros	600
4. Ireland	43,600	4. Congo (Dem. Rep.)	700
5. USA	43,500	5. Burundi	700
6. Andorra	38,800	6. Tanzania	800
7. Iceland	38,100	7. East Timor	800
8. Denmark	37,000	8. Afghanistan	800
9. Hong Kong (China)	36,500	9. Yemen	900
10. Austria	35,500	10. Sierra Leone	900
11. Canada	35,200	11. Madagascar	900
12. San Marino	34,100	12. Guinea-Bissau	900
13. Switzerland	33,600	13. Zambia	1,000
14. Japan	33,100	14. Niger	1,000
15. Australia	32,900	15. Liberia	1,000
16. Finland	32,800	16. Ethiopia	1,000
17. Belgium	31,800	17. Eritrea	1,000
18. Netherlands	31,700	18. Djibouti	1,000
19. Sweden	31,600	19. Central African Rep.	1,100
20. Germany	31,400	20. Benin	1,100
21. UK	31,400	21. Mali	1,200

Continental Shares

Shares of population and of wealth (GNI) by continent

Population

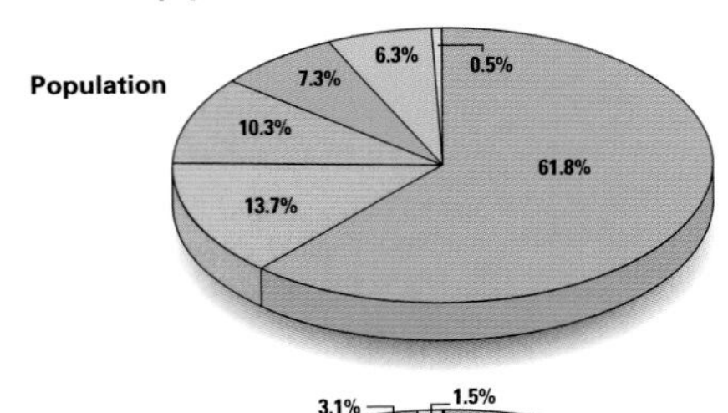

GNI

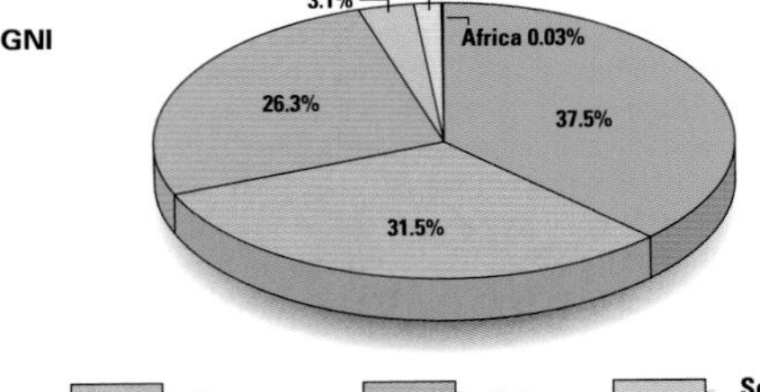

Inflation

Average annual rate of inflation (2006)

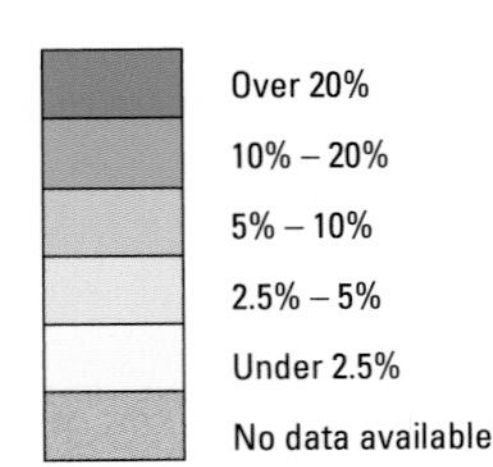

Over 20%

10% – 20%

5% – 10%

2.5% – 5%

Under 2.5%

No data available

Highest inflation

Zimbabwe 976%
Iraq 65%
Guinea 29%
Burma (Myanmar) . .21%
Congo (Dem. Rep.) . .18%

Lowest inflation

Nauru . . . .–3.6%
Vanuatu . . . .–1.6%
San Marino . . . . . .–1.5%
Barbados . . . .–0.5%
Dominica . . . .–0.1%

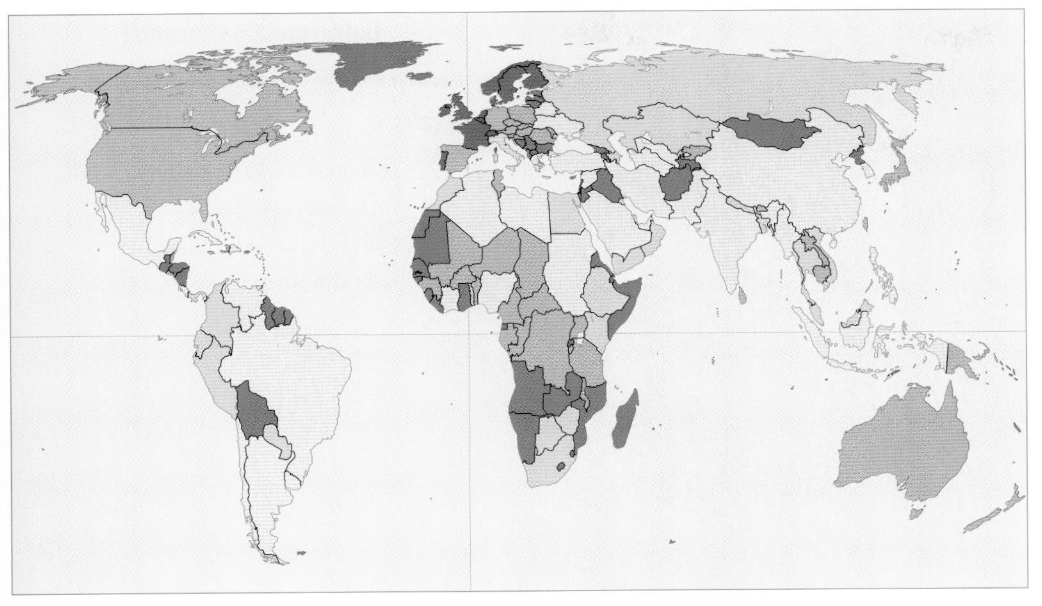

International Aid

Official Development Assistance (ODA) provided and received, per capita (2004)

Providers:
- Over $100 per person
- $50 – $100 per person
- $20 – $50 per person

Receivers:
- Under $10 per person
- $10 – $25 per person
- $25 – $50 per person
- Over $50 per person

No data available

Debt and Aid

International debtors and the aid they receive

Although aid grants make a vital contribution to many of the world's poorer countries, they are usually dwarfed by the burden of debt that the developing economies are expected to repay. It is estimated that the total debt burden of developing countries is US$523 billion.

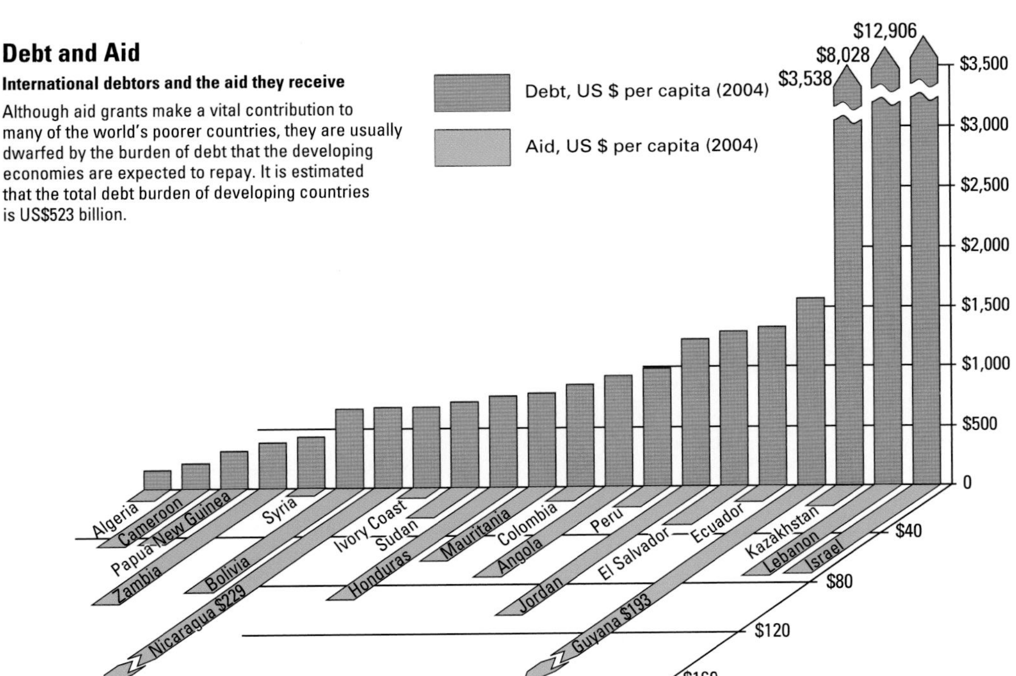

Distribution of Spending

Percentage share of household spending, selected countries

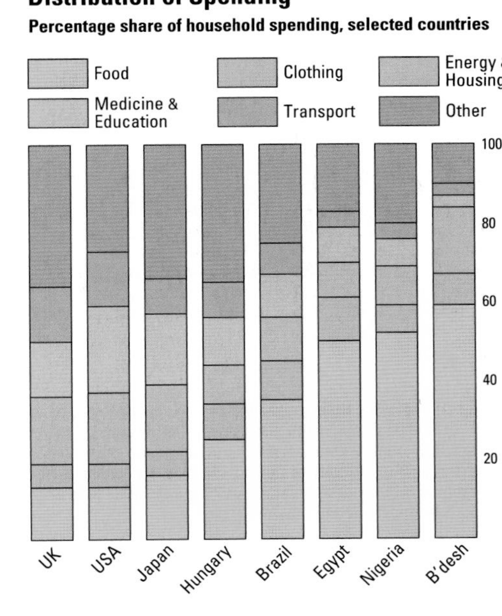

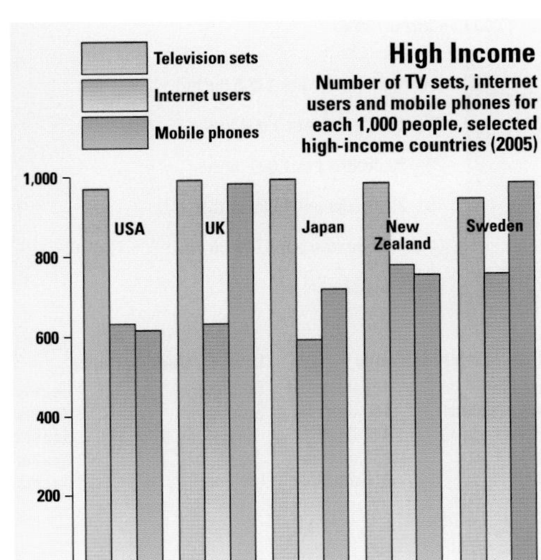

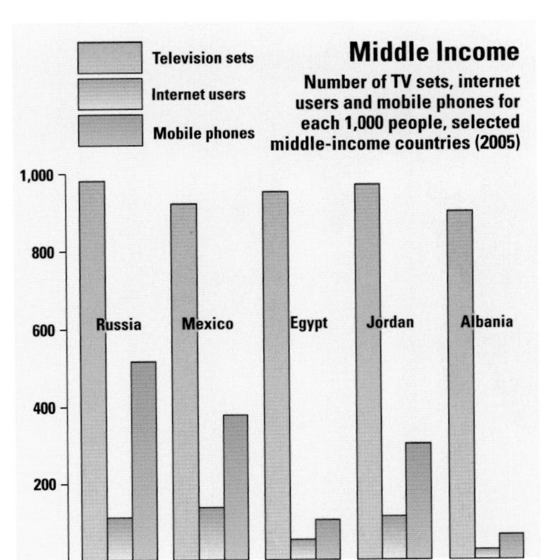

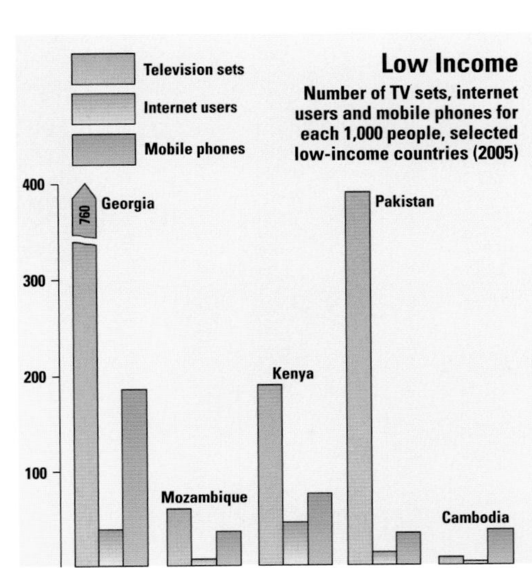

Quality of Life

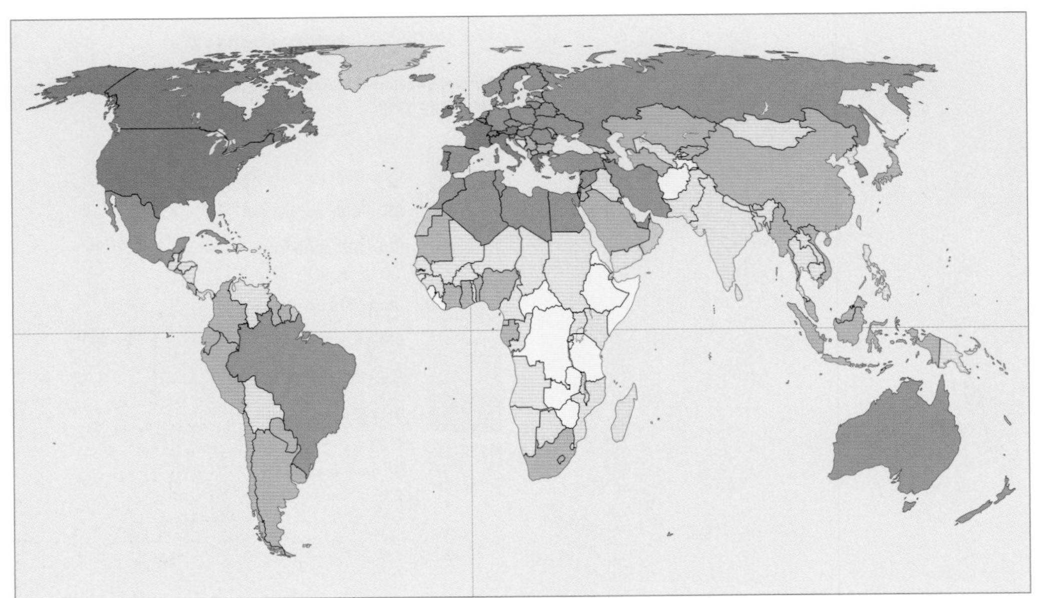

Daily Food Consumption

Average daily food intake in calories per person (2003)

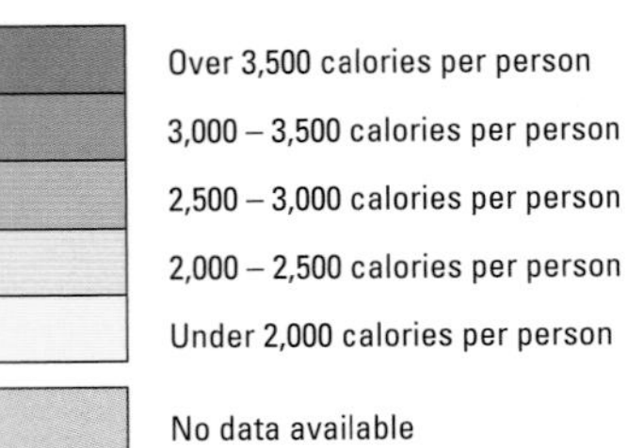

Hospital Capacity

Hospital beds available for each 1,000 people (2003)

Highest capacity		Lowest capacity	
Monaco	19.6	Nepal	0.2
Japan	14.7	Bangladesh	0.3
North Korea	13.6	Somalia	0.4
Niue	13.0	Afghanistan	0.4
Belarus	11.3	Guatemala	0.5
Russia	10.5	Cambodia	0.5
Germany	8.9	Yemen	0.6
Ukraine	8.8	Burma (Myanmar)	0.6
Lithuania	8.7	Sudan	0.7
Czech Republic	8.6	Pakistan	0.7

Although the ratio of people to hospital beds gives a good approximation of a country's health provision, it is not an absolute indicator. Raw numbers may mask inefficiency and other weaknesses: the high availability of beds in Belarus, for example, has not prevented infant mortality rates over three times as high as in the United Kingdom and the United States.

Life Expectancy

Years of life expectancy at birth, selected countries (2005)

The chart shows combined data for both sexes. On average, women live longer than men worldwide, even in developing countries with high maternal mortality rates. Overall, life expectancy is steadily rising, though the difference between rich and poor nations remains dramatic.

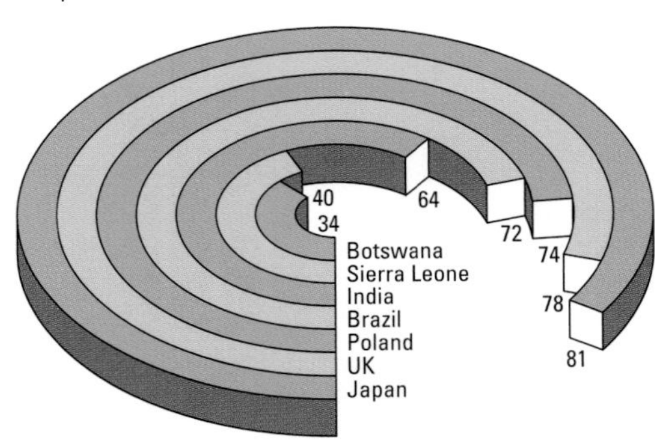

Causes of Death

Causes of death for selected countries by percentage

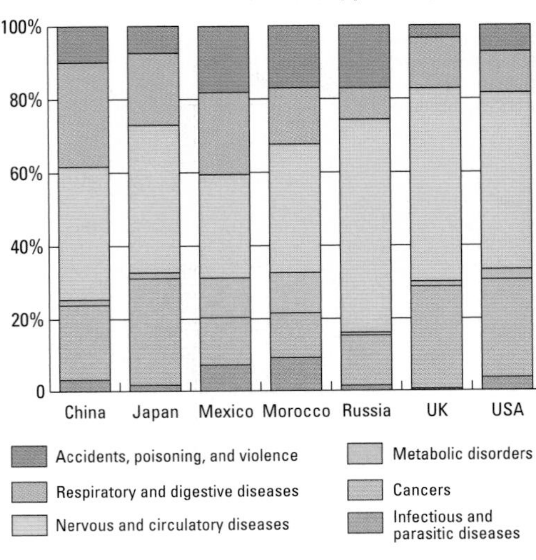

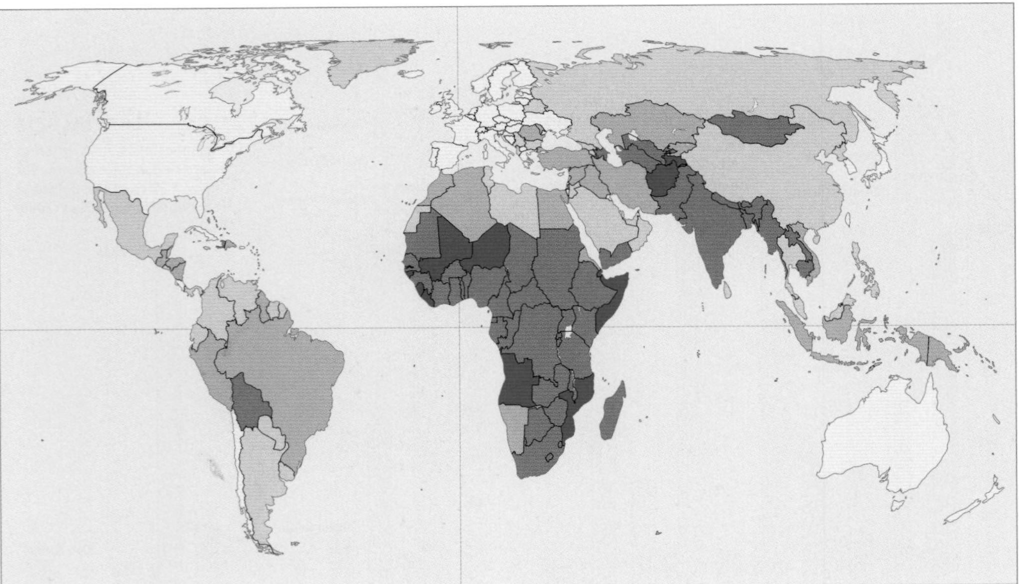

Infant Mortality

Number of babies who died under the age of one, per 1,000 live births (2006)

Highest infant mortality		Lowest infant mortality	
Angola	185 deaths	Singapore	2 deaths
Sierra Leone	160 deaths	Sweden	3 deaths
Afghanistan	160 deaths	Hong Kong (China)	3 deaths
Liberia	156 deaths	Japan	3 deaths
Niger	118 deaths	Iceland	3 deaths

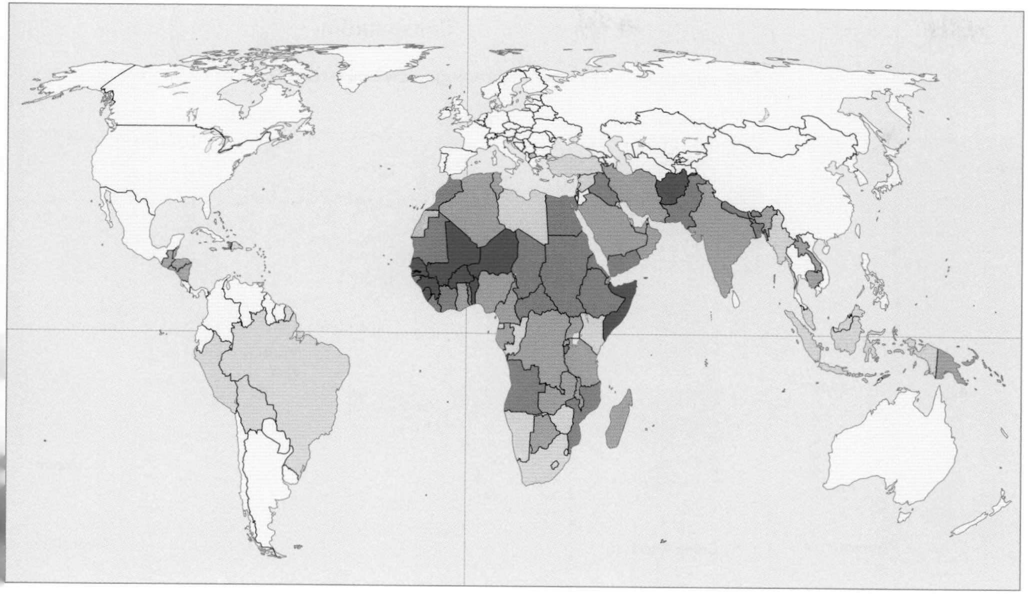

Illiteracy

Percentage of the total adult population unable to read or write (2004)

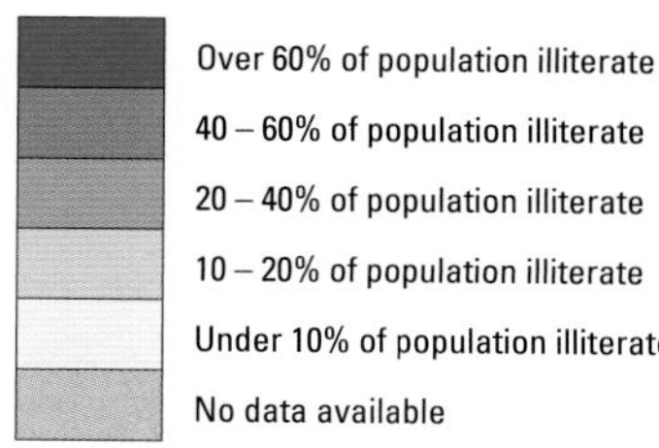

Countries with the highest and lowest illiteracy rates

Highest		Lowest	
Burkina Faso	87	Australia	0
Niger	83	Denmark	0
Mali	81	Finland	0
Sierra Leone	69	Liechtenstein	0
Guinea	64	Luxembourg	0

Fertility and Education

Fertility rates compared with female education, selected countries (2000–05)

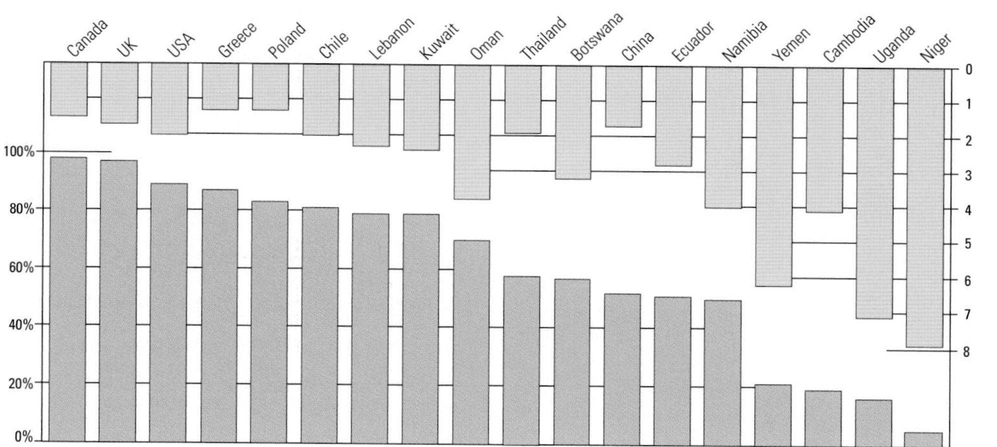

Living Standards

At first sight, most international contrasts in living standards are swamped by differences in wealth. The rich not only have more money, they have more of everything, including years of life. Those with only a little money are obliged to spend most of it on food and clothing, the basic maintenance costs of their existence; air travel and tourism are unlikely to feature on their expenditure lists. However, poverty and wealth are both relative: slum dwellers living on social security payments in an affluent industrial country have far more resources at their disposal than an average African peasant, but feel their own poverty nonetheless. A middle-class Indian lawyer cannot command a fraction of the earnings of a counterpart living in New York, London, or Rome; nevertheless, he rightly sees himself as prosperous.

The rich not only live longer, on average, than the poor, they also die from different causes. Infectious and parasitic diseases, all but eliminated in the developed world, remain a scourge in the developing nations. On the other hand, more than two-thirds of the populations of OECD nations eventually succumb to cancer or circulatory disease.

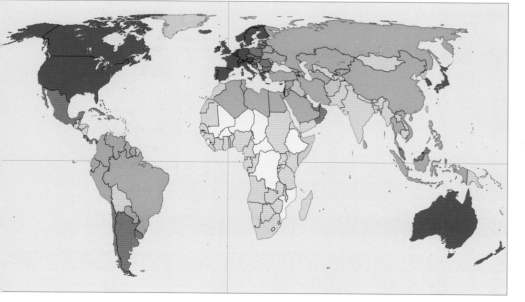

Human Development Index

The Human Development Index (HDI), calculated by the UN Development Program, gives a value to countries using indicators of life expectancy, education, and standards of living (2004). Higher values show more developed countries.

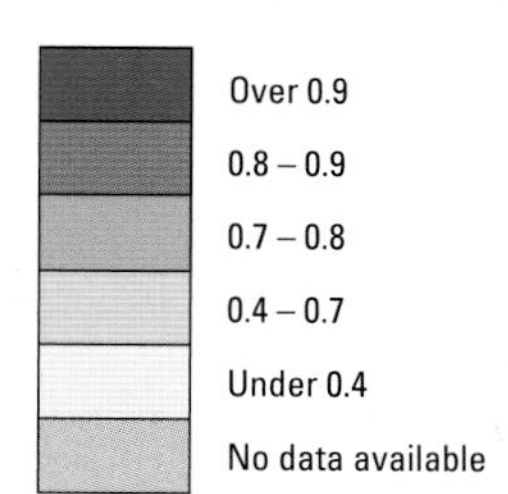

Highest values		Lowest values	
Norway	0.965	Niger	0.311
Iceland	0.960	Sierra Leone	0.335
Australia	0.957	Mali	0.338
Ireland	0.956	Burkina Faso	0.342
Sweden	0.951	Guinea-Bissau	0.349

Energy

Production

Each square represents 1% of world energy production (2005)

Consumption

Each square represents 1% of world energy consumption (2005)

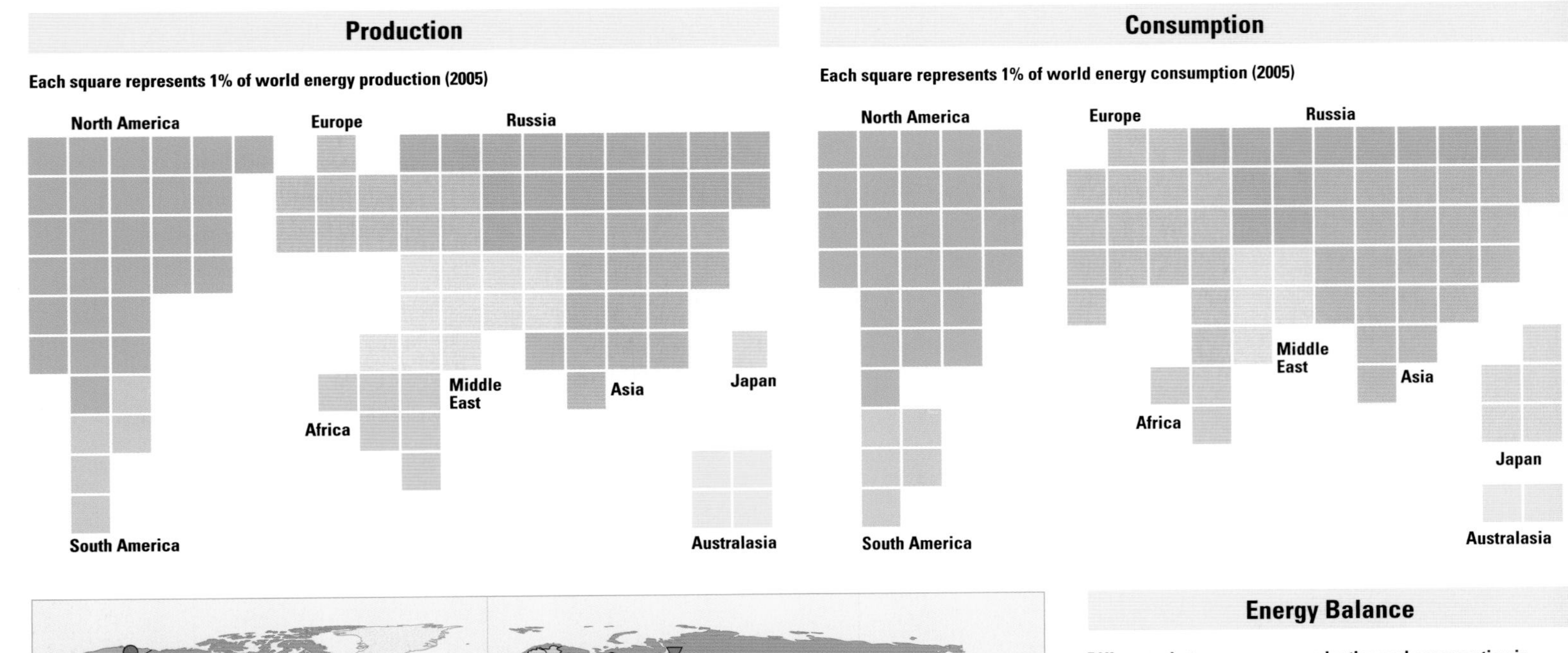

Energy Balance

Difference between energy production and consumption in millions of tons of oil equivalent (MtOe) (2004)

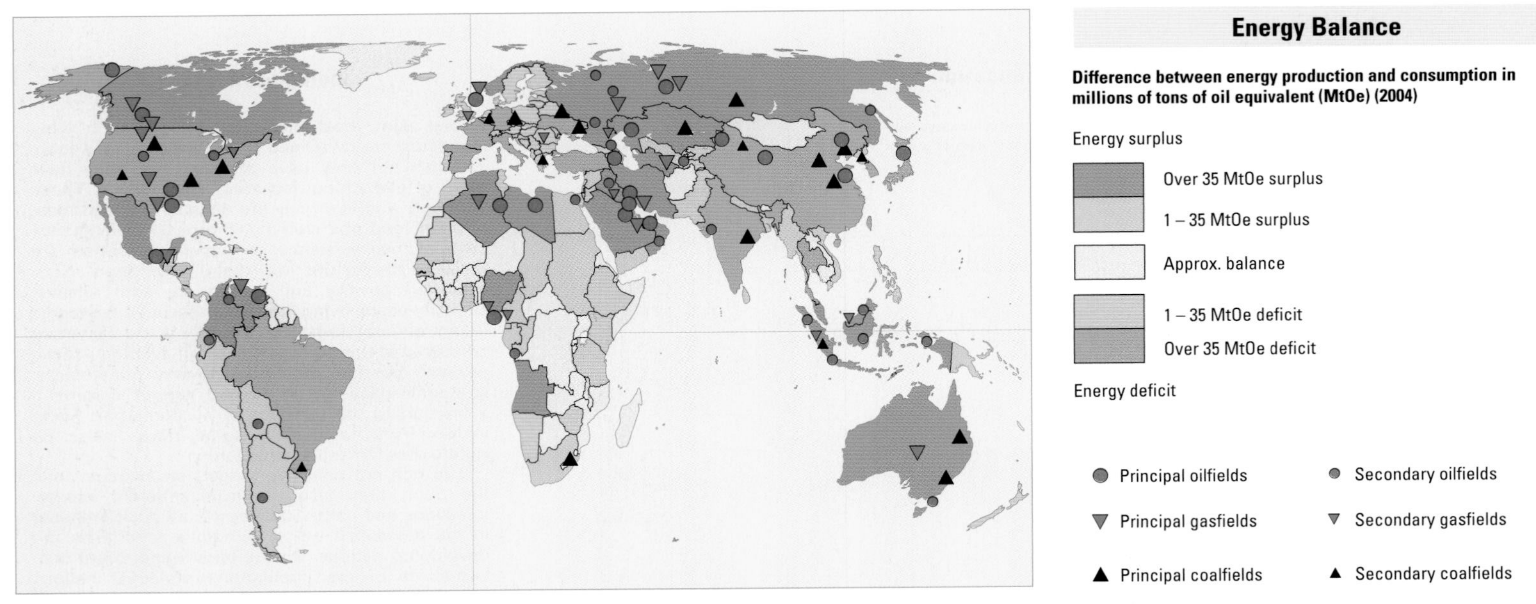

World Energy Consumption

Energy consumed by world regions, measured in million tons of oil equivalent in 2005. Total world consumption was 10,537 MtOe. Only energy from oil, gas, coal, nuclear, and hydroelectric sources are included. Excluded are fuels such as wood, peat, animal waste, wind, solar, and geothermal which, though important in some countries, are unreliably documented in terms of consumption statistics.

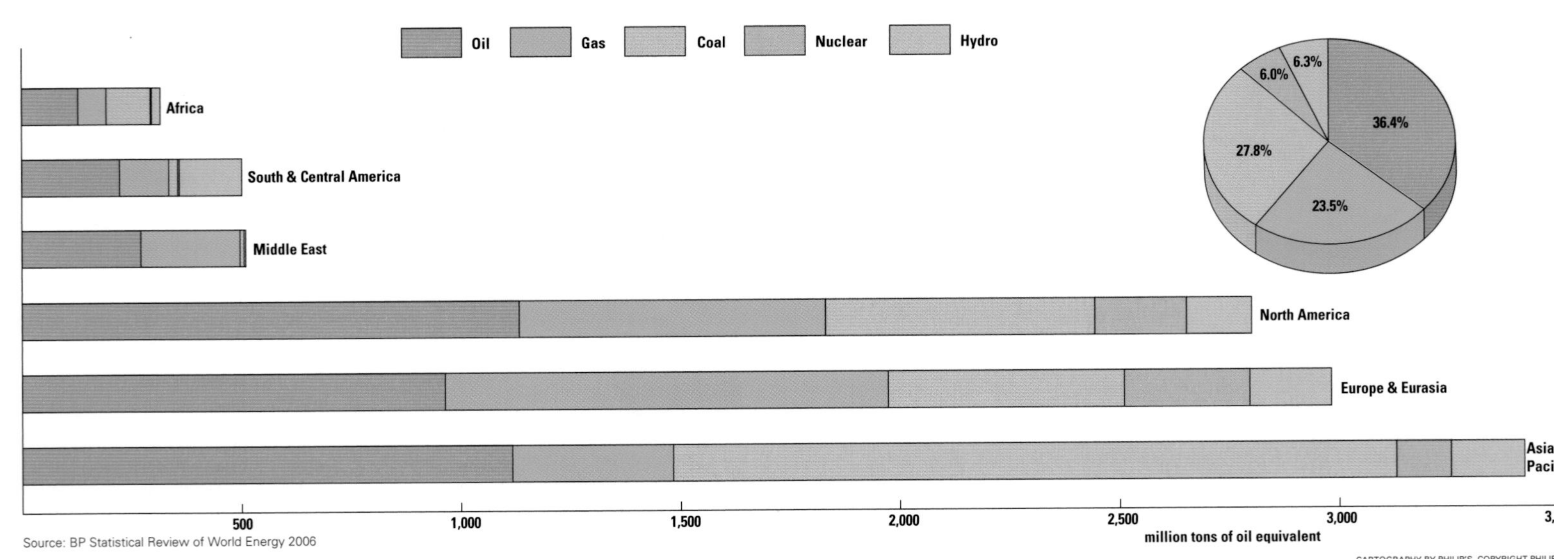

Source: BP Statistical Review of World Energy 2006

Energy

Energy is used to keep us warm or cool, fuel our industries and our transport systems, and even feed us; high-intensity agriculture, with its use of fertilizers, pesticides, and machinery, is heavily energy-dependent. Although we live in a high-energy society, there are vast discrepancies between rich and poor; for example, a North American consumes 13 times as much energy as a Chinese person. But even developing nations have more power at their disposal than was imaginable a century ago.

The distribution of energy supplies, most importantly fossil fuels (coal, oil, and natural gas), is very uneven. In addition, the diagrams and map opposite show that the largest producers of energy are not necessarily the largest consumers. The movement of energy supplies around the world is therefore an important component of international trade. In 2005, total world movements in oil amounted to 2,462 million tons.

As the finite reserves of fossil fuels are depleted, renewable energy sources, such as solar, hydro-thermal, wind, tidal, and biomass, will become increasingly important around the world.

Nuclear Power

Major producers by percentage of world total and by percentage of domestic electricity generation (2004)

Country	% of world total production	Country	% of nuclear as proportion of domestic electricity
1. USA	30.1%	1. Lithuania	80.6%
2. France	16.3%	2. France	78.8%
3. Japan	10.4%	3. Belgium	57.1%
4. Germany	6.1%	4. Slovak Rep.	56.2%
5. Russia	5.2%	5. Sweden	58.8%
6. South Korea	4.7%	6. Ukraine	45.9%
7. Canada	3.3%	7. Switzerland	41.3%
8. Ukraine	3.2%	8. Armenia	38.6%
9. UK	2.8%	9. Bulgaria	37.2%
= Sweden	2.8%	10. South Korea	36.0%

Although the 1980s were a bad time for the nuclear power industry (major projects ran over budget and fears of long-term environmental damage were heavily reinforced by the 1986 disaster at Chernobyl), the industry picked up in the early 1990s. Whilst the number of reactors is still increasing, however, orders for new plants have shrunk. Sixteen countries currently rely on nuclear power to supply over 25% of their electricity requirements.

Hydroelectricity

Major producers by percentage of world total and by percentage of domestic electricity generation (2004)

Country	% of world total production	Country	% of hydroelectric as proportion of domestic electricity
1. Canada	12.2%	1. Bhutan	100%
2. China	11.9%	= Paraguay	100%
3. Brazil	11.6%	= Lesotho	100%
4. USA	9.8%	4. Mozambique	99.8%
5. Russia	6.0%	5. Congo	99.7%
6. Norway	3.9%	= Congo (Dem. Rep.)	99.7%
7. Japan	3.4%	= Uganda	99.7%
8. India	3.0%	8. Nepal	99.6%
9. Sweden	2.3%	9. Zambia	99.5%
10. France	2.2%	10. Norway	98.8%

Countries heavily reliant on hydroelectricity are usually small and non-industrial: a high proportion of hydroelectric power more often reflects a modest energy budget than vast hydroelectric resources. The USA, for instance, produces only 6.7% of its power requirements from hydroelectricity; yet that 6.7% amounts to more than seven times the hydropower generated by most of Africa.

Fuel Exports

Fuels as a percentage of total value of exports (2004)

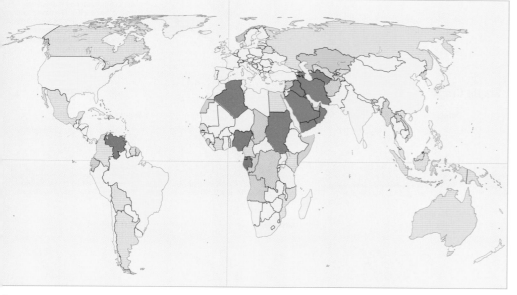

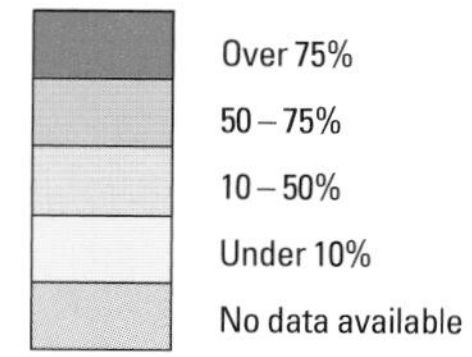

In the 1970s, oil exports became a political issue when OPEC sought to increase the influence of developing countries in world affairs by raising oil prices and restricting production. But its power was short-lived, following a fall in demand for oil in the 1980s, due to an increase in energy efficiency and development of alternative resources. However, with the heavy energy demands of the Asian economies early in the 21st century, both oil and gas prices have risen sharply.

Measurements

For historical reasons, oil is traded in "barrels." The weight and volume equivalents (shown right) are all based on average-density "Arabian light" crude oil.

The energy equivalents given for a ton of oil are also somewhat imprecise: oil and coal of different qualities will have varying energy contents, a fact usually reflected in their price on world markets.

Conversion Rates

1 barrel = 0.136 tons or 159 liters or 35 Imperial gallons or 42 US gallons

1 ton = 7.33 barrels or 1,185 liters or 256 Imperial gallons or 261 US gallons

1 ton oil = 1.5 tons hard coal or 3.0 tons lignite or 12,000 kWh

1 Imperial gallon = 1.201 US gallons or 4.546 liters or 277.4 cubic inches

World Coal Reserves

World coal reserves (including lignite) by region and country, thousand million tons (2005)

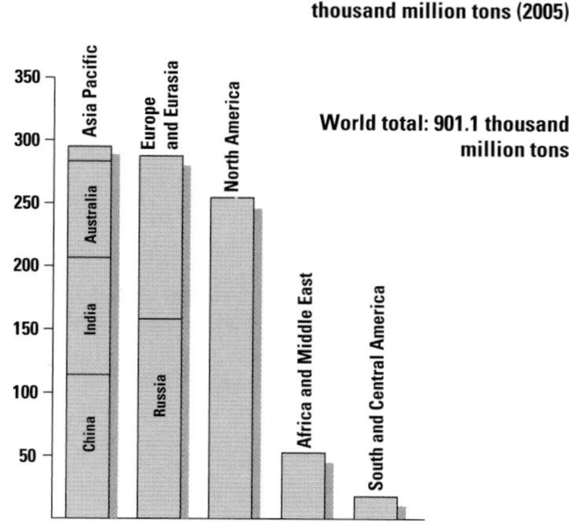

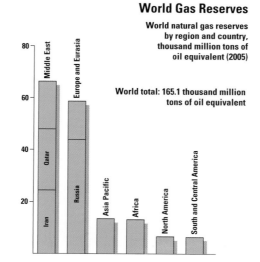

World Gas Reserves

World natural gas reserves by region and country, thousand million tons of oil equivalent (2005)

World total: 165.1 thousand million tons of oil equivalent

80
60
40
20
Middle East
Qatar
Iran
Europe and Eurasia
Russia
Asia Pacific
Africa
North America
South and Central America

World Oil Reserves

World oil reserves by region and country, thousand million tons (2005)

World total: 163.6 thousand million tons

100
75
50
25
Middle East
Iraq
Iran
Saudi Arabia
Europe and Eurasia
South and Central America
Africa
North America
Asia Pacific

Production

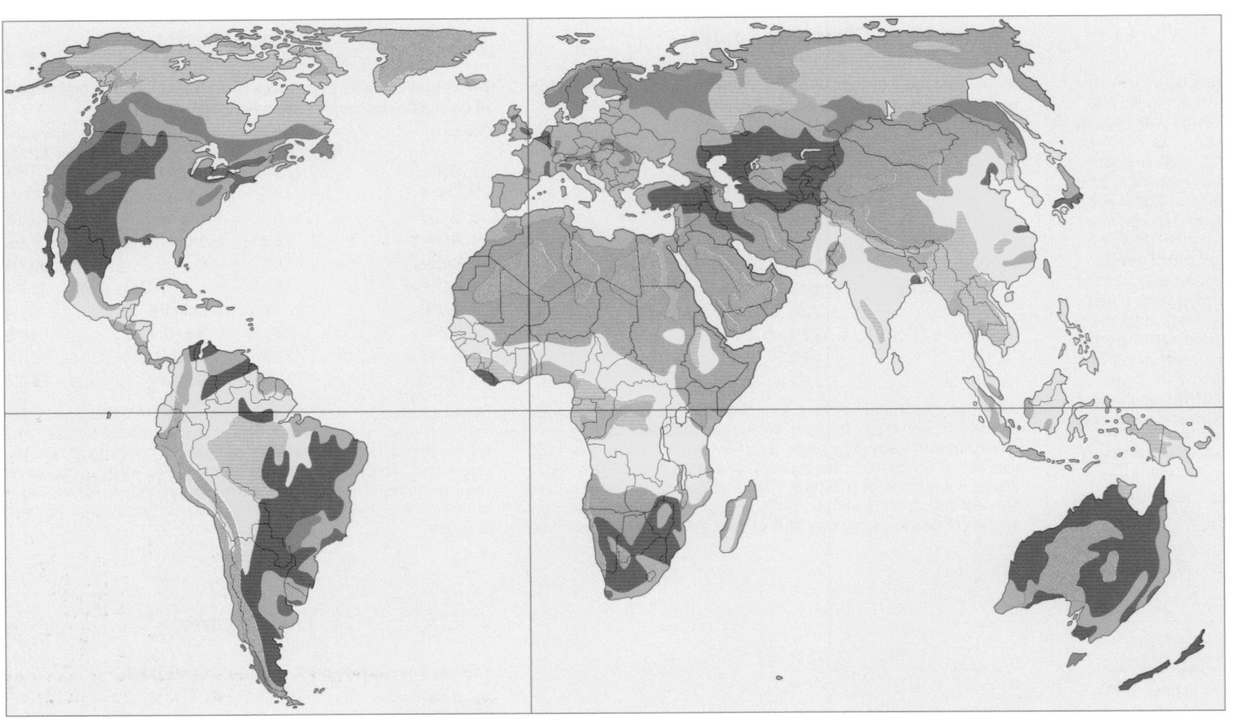

Agriculture

Predominant type of farming or land use

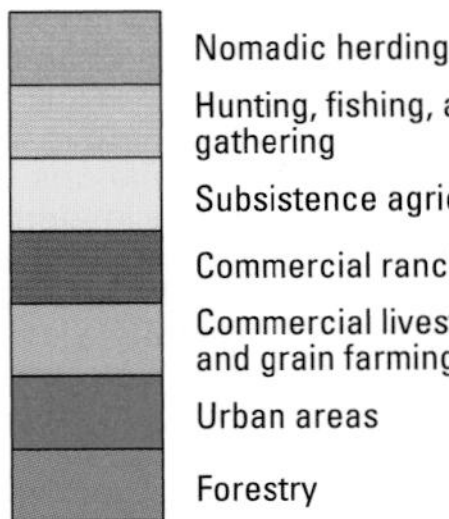

The development of agriculture has transformed human existence more than any other. The whole business of farming is constantly developing: due mainly to the new varieties of rice and wheat, world grain production has more than doubled since 1965. New machinery and modern agricultural techniques enable relatively few farmers to produce enough food for the world's 6 billion or so people.

Staple Crops

Sugars

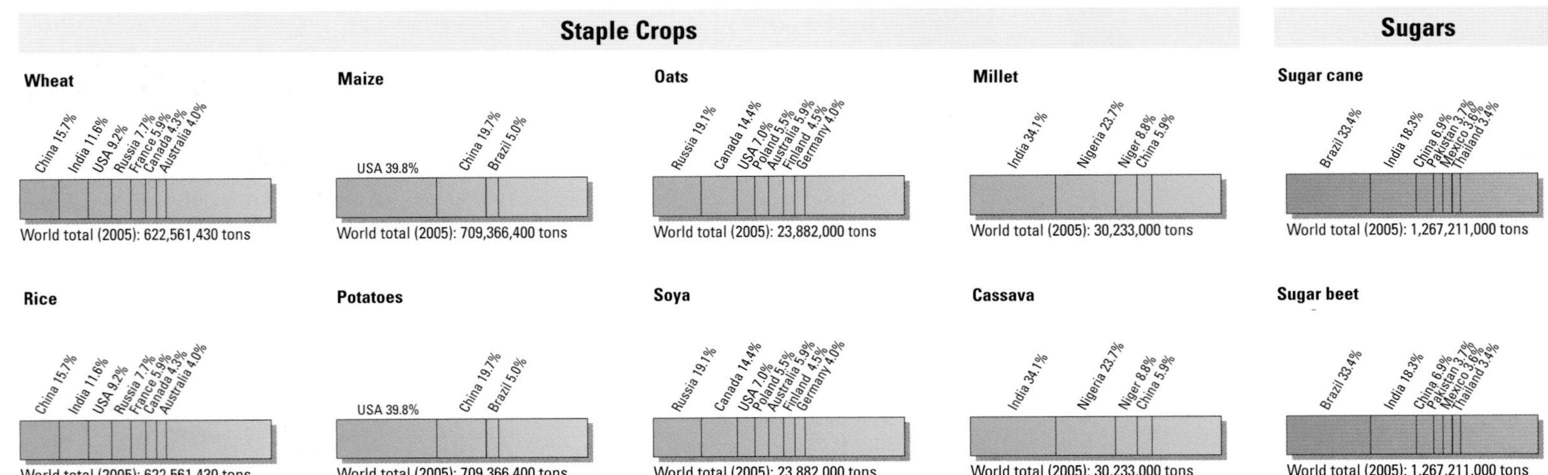

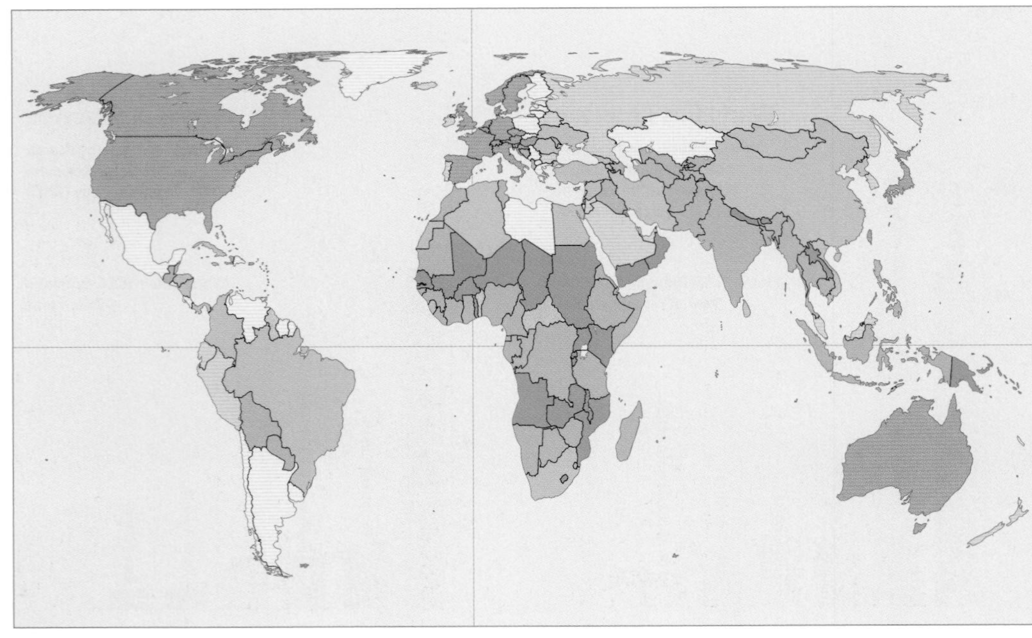

Employment

The number of workers employed in manufacturing for every 100 workers engaged in agriculture (2005)

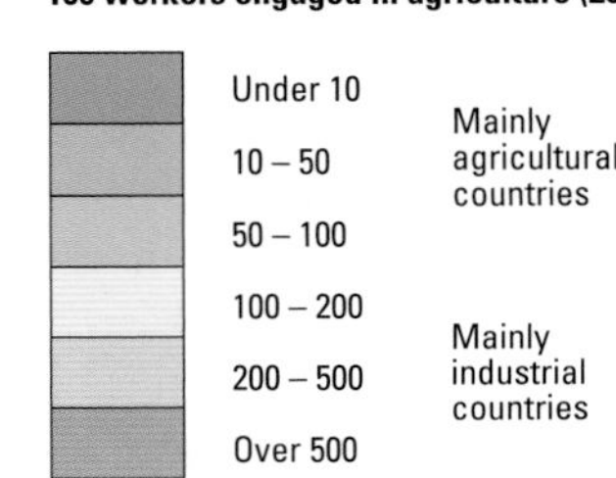

Countries with the highest and lowest number of workers employed in manufacturing per 100 workers engaged in agriculture (2005)

Highest		Lowest	
Bahrain	7,900	Burundi	2.5
San Marino	4,200	Yemen	5.0
Micronesia	3,822	Oman	5.0
USA	3,271	Rwanda	5.6
Liechtenstein	2,350	Malawi	5.6

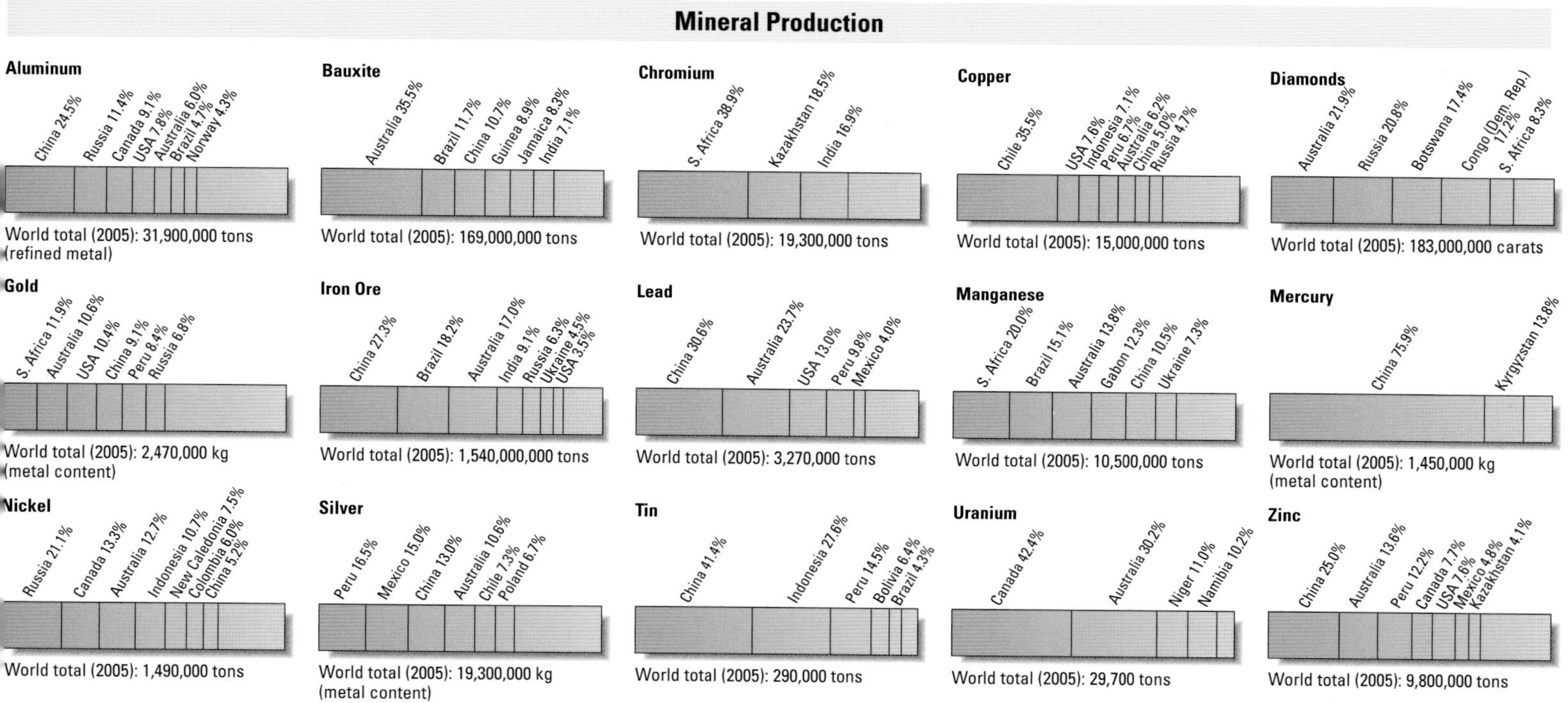

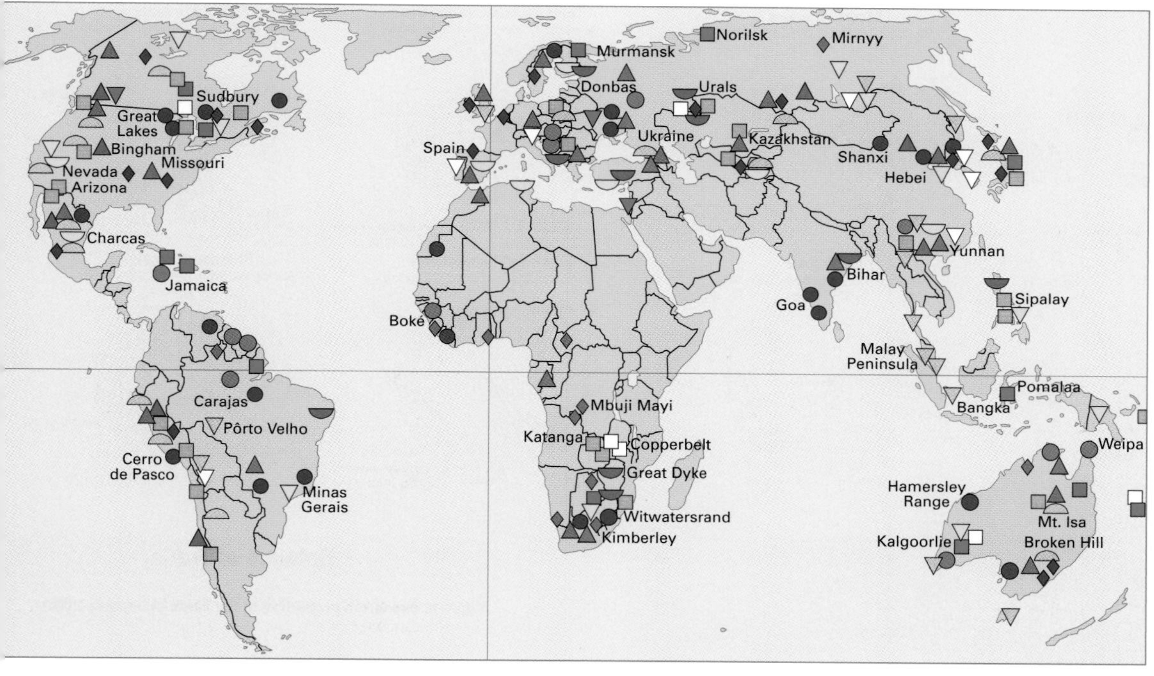

Mineral Distribution

The map shows the richest sources of the most important minerals (major mineral locations are named)

- Bauxite
- Chromium
- Cobalt
- Copper
- Diamonds
- Gold
- Iron ore
- Lead
- Manganese
- Mercury
- Molybdenum
- Nickel
- Potash
- Silver
- Tin
- Tungsten
- Zinc

The map does not show undersea deposits, most of which are considered inaccessible.

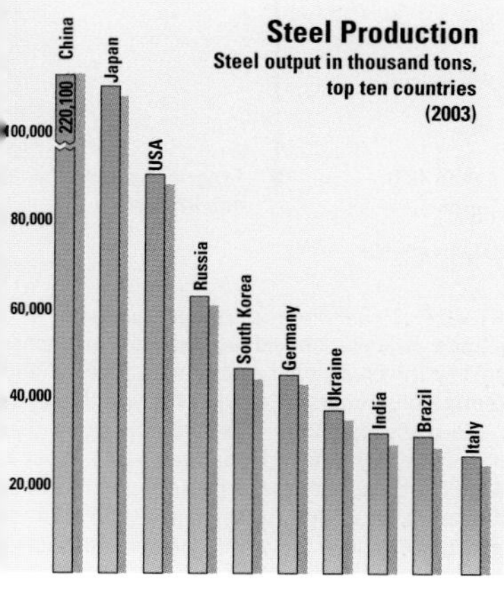

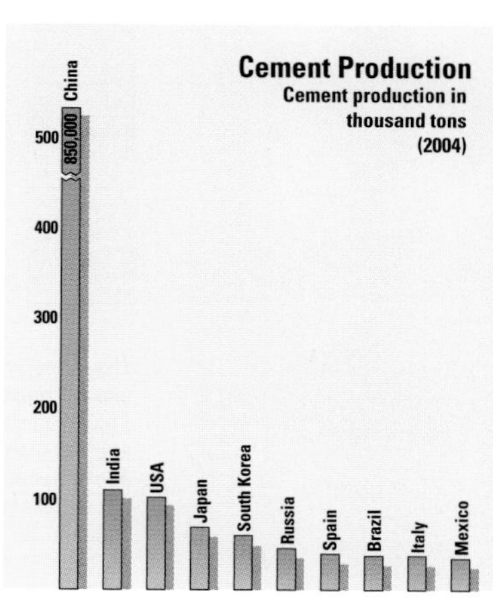

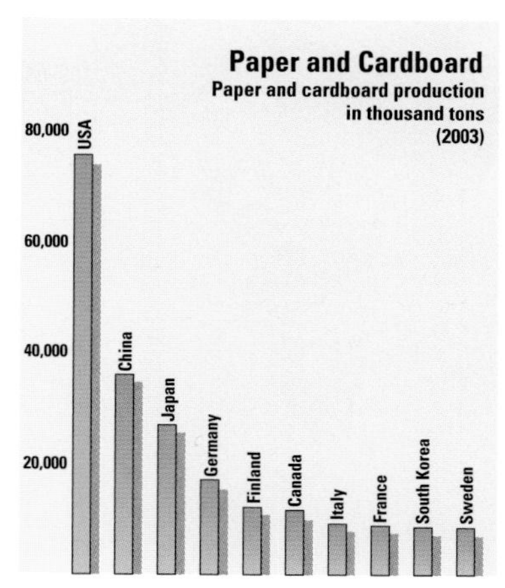

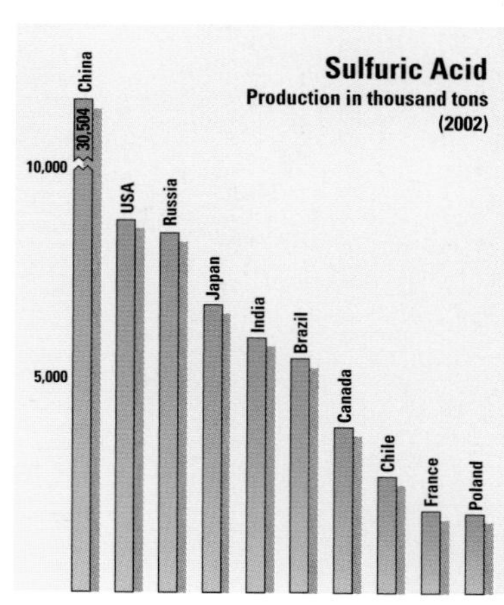

Trade

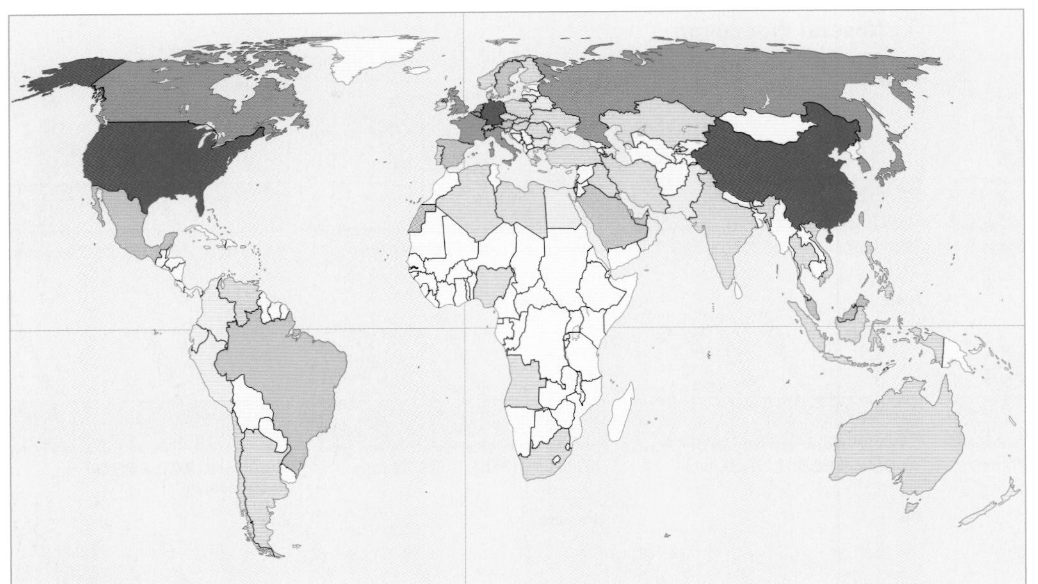

Share of World Trade

Percentage share of total world exports by value (2006)

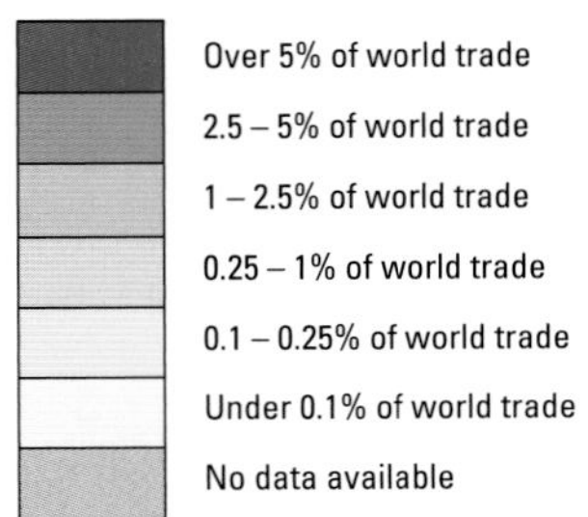

Largest share of world trade		Smallest share of world trade	
Germany	9.1%	East Timor	0.0%
USA	8.2%	Eritrea	0.0%
China	7.8%	Burundi	0.0%
Hong Kong (China)	4.9%	Rwanda	0.0%
Japan	4.8%	Guinea-Bissau	0.0%

The Main Trading Nations

The imports and exports of the top ten trading nations as a percentage of world trade (2006). Each country's trade in manufactured goods is shown in dark blue

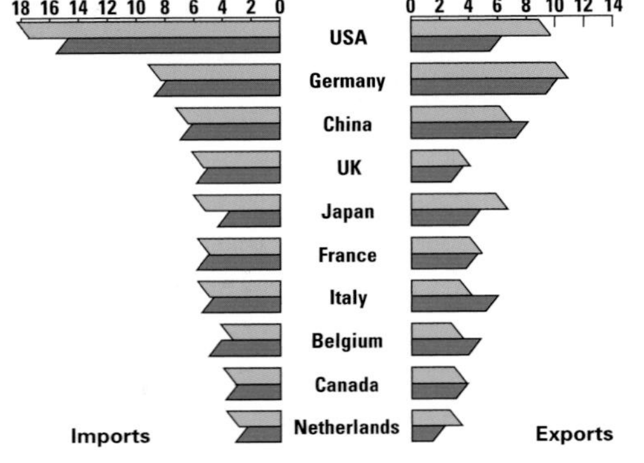

Major exports

Leading manufactured items and their exporters (2004)

Motor Vehicles
World total (2004): US$ 265,898 million

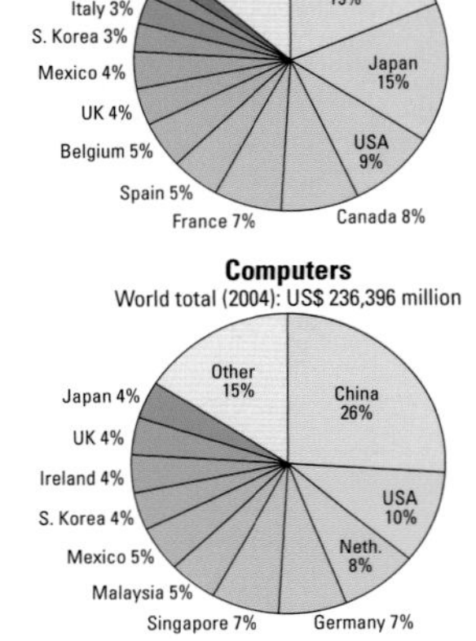

Telecommunications Gear
World total (2004): US$ 405,989 million

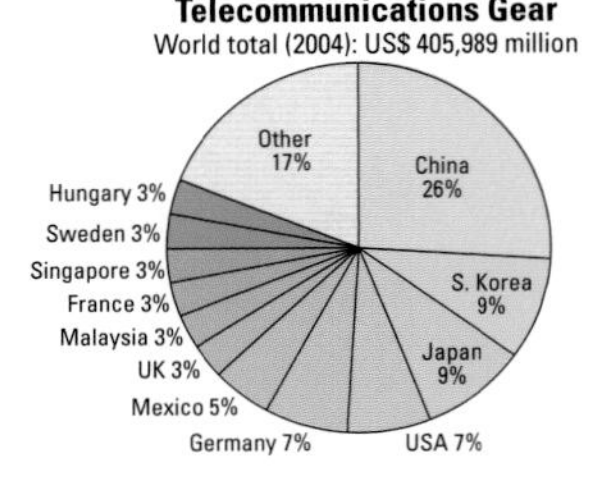

Electrical Components
World total (2004): US$ 838,552 million

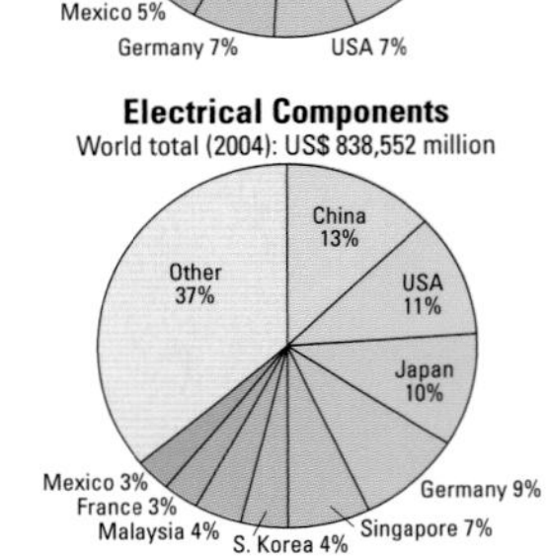

Petrol Products
World total (2004): US$ 496,092 million

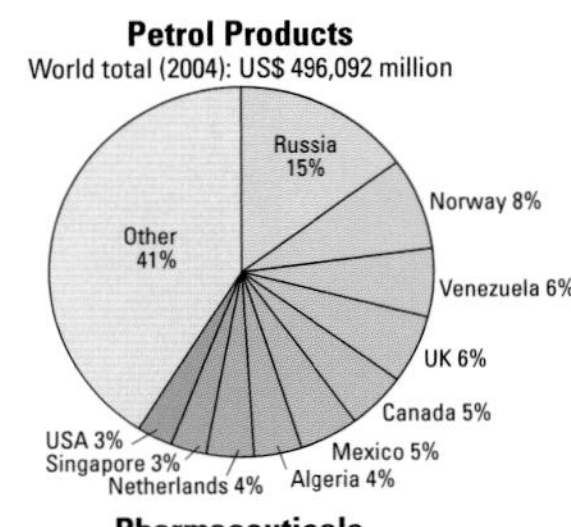

Pharmaceuticals
World total (2004): US$ 311,399 million

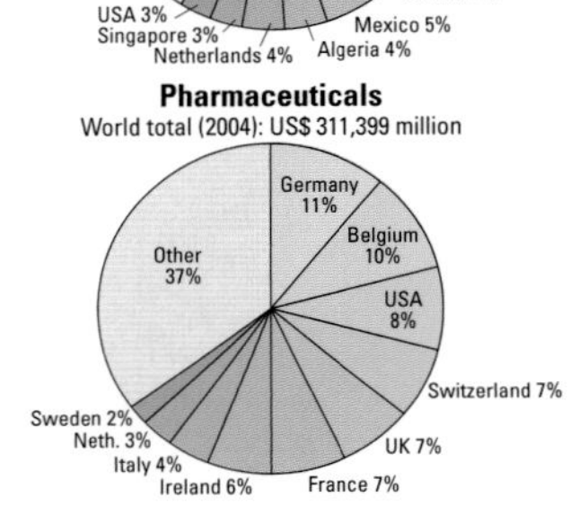

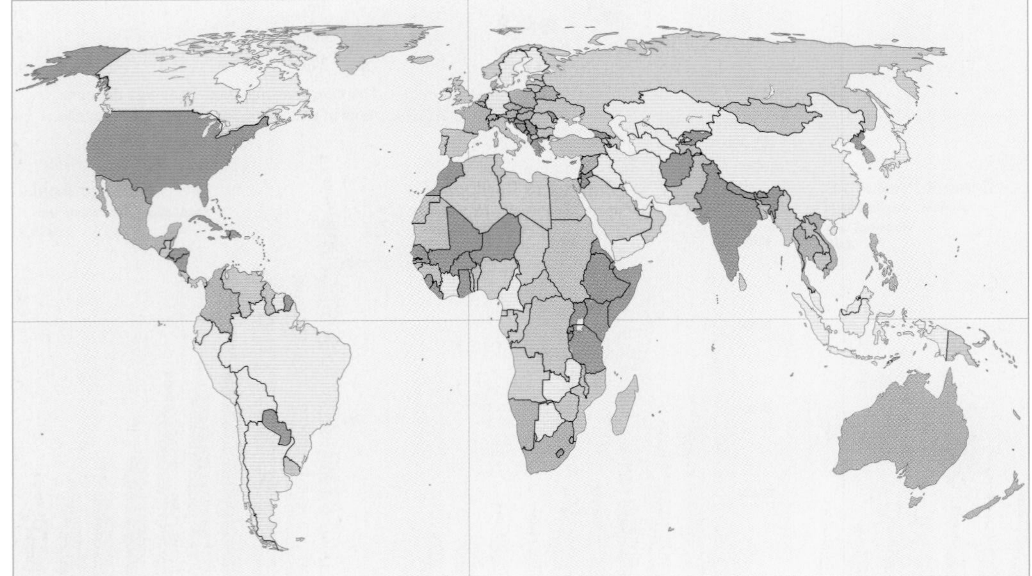

Balance of Trade

Value of exports in proportion to the value of imports (2006)

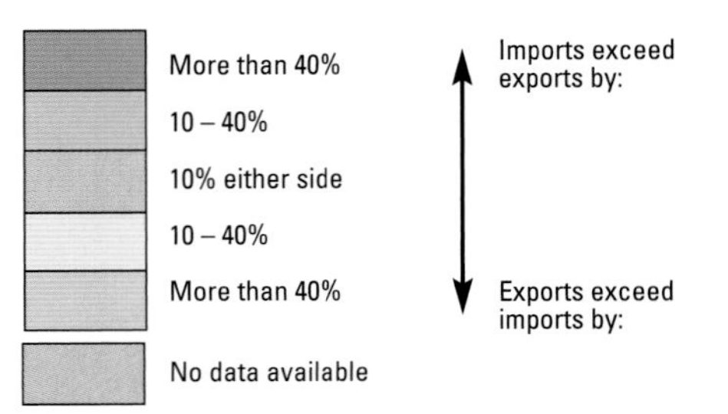

The total world trade balance should amount to zero, since exports must equal imports on a global scale. In practice, at least $100 billion in exports go unrecorded, leaving the world with an apparent deficit and many countries in a better position than public accounting reveals. However, a favorable trade balance is not necessarily a sign of prosperity: many poorer countries must maintain a high surplus in order to service debts, and do so by restricting imports below the levels needed to sustain successful economies.

Trade in Primary Exports

Primary exports as a percentage of total export value (2004)

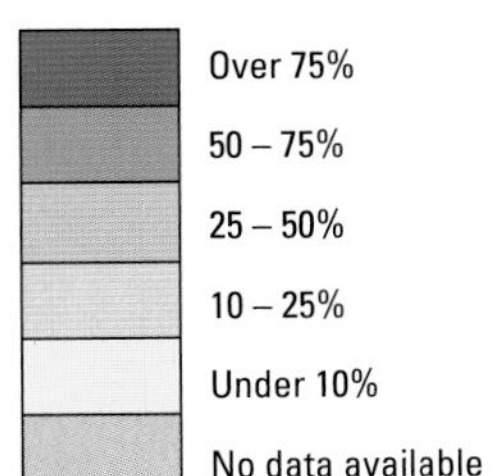

Primary exports are raw materials or partly processed products that form the basis for manufacturing. They are the necessary requirements of industries and include agricultural products, minerals, fuels, and timber, as well as many semimanufactured goods such as cotton, which has been spun but not woven, wood pulp, or flour. Many developed countries have few natural resources and rely on imports for the majority of their primary products. The countries of Southeast Asia export hardwoods to the rest of the world, while many South American countries are heavily dependent on coffee exports.

Merchant Fleets

Merchant fleets in thousand gross registered tonnage (2006). Although a large number of vessels are registered in Liberia and Panama, they are not part of the national fleet

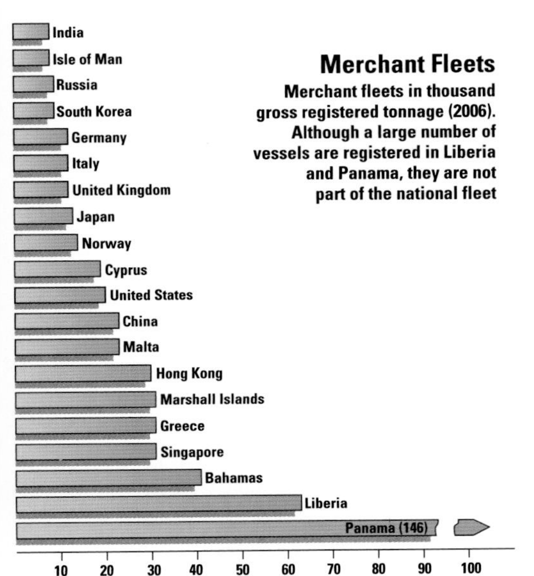

Top Ten Ports

Total container traffic, in million TEU (2004)
("TEU" stands for Twenty-foot Equivalent Unit, the equivalent of a standard container)

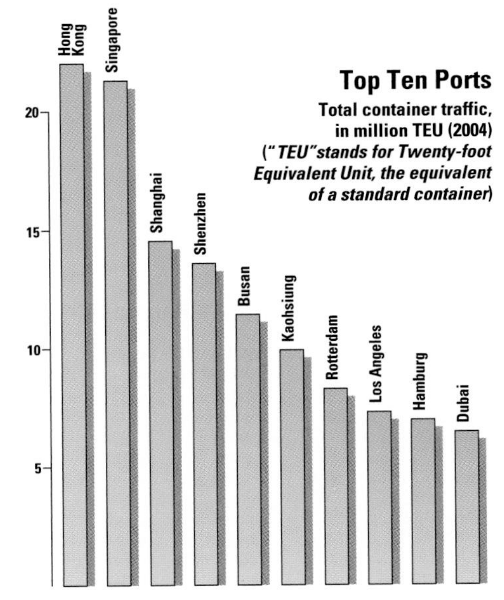

Types of Vessels

World fleet by type of vessel (2006)

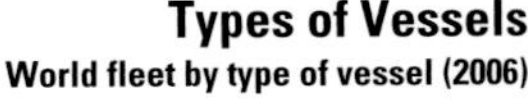

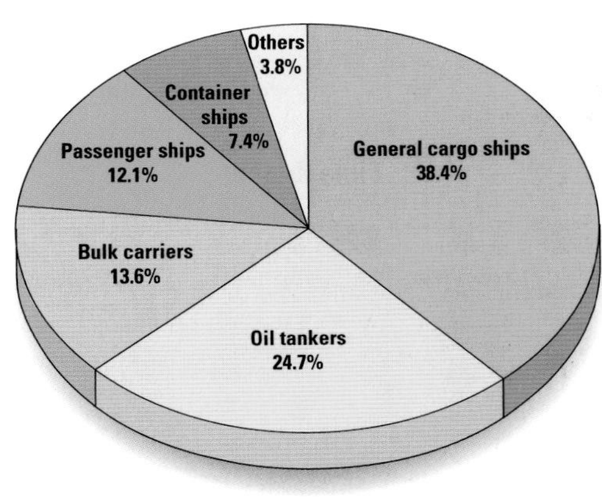

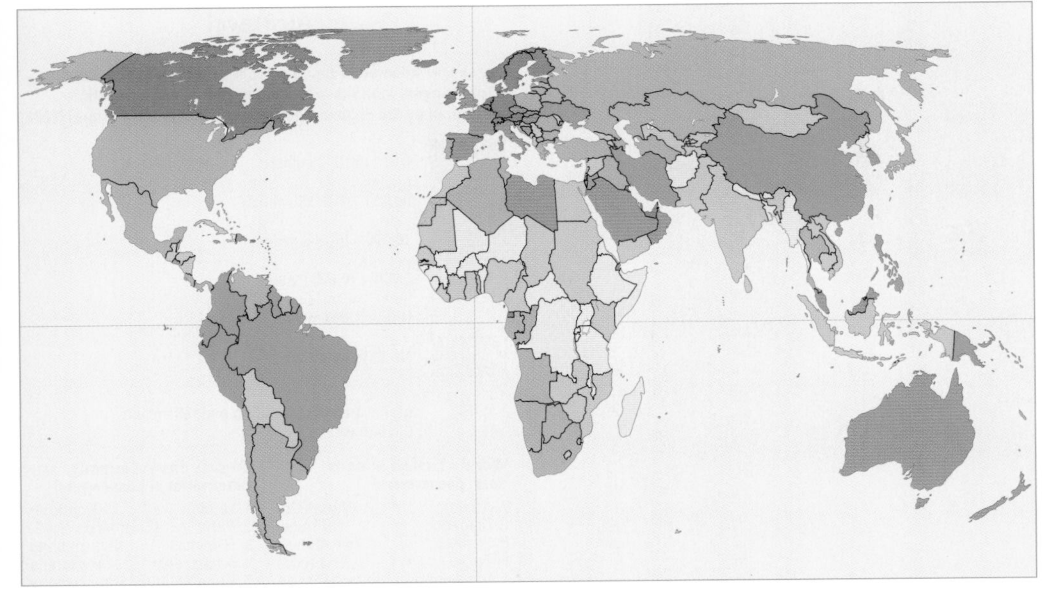

Exports Per Capita

Value of exports in US $, divided by total population (2006)

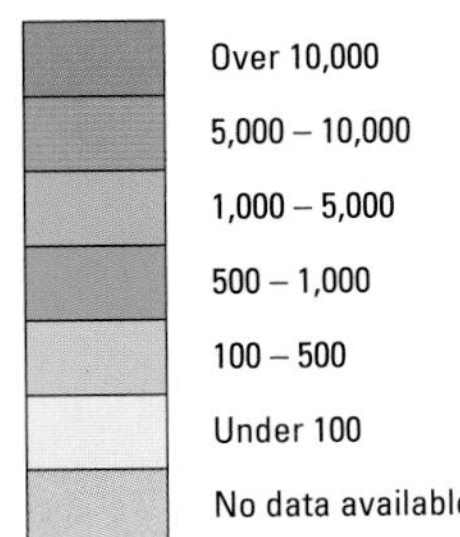

Highest per capita

Hong Kong	$88,121
Liechtenstein	$72,675
Singapore	$63,132
United Arab Emirates	$52,676
Luxembourg	$41,209

Travel and Tourism

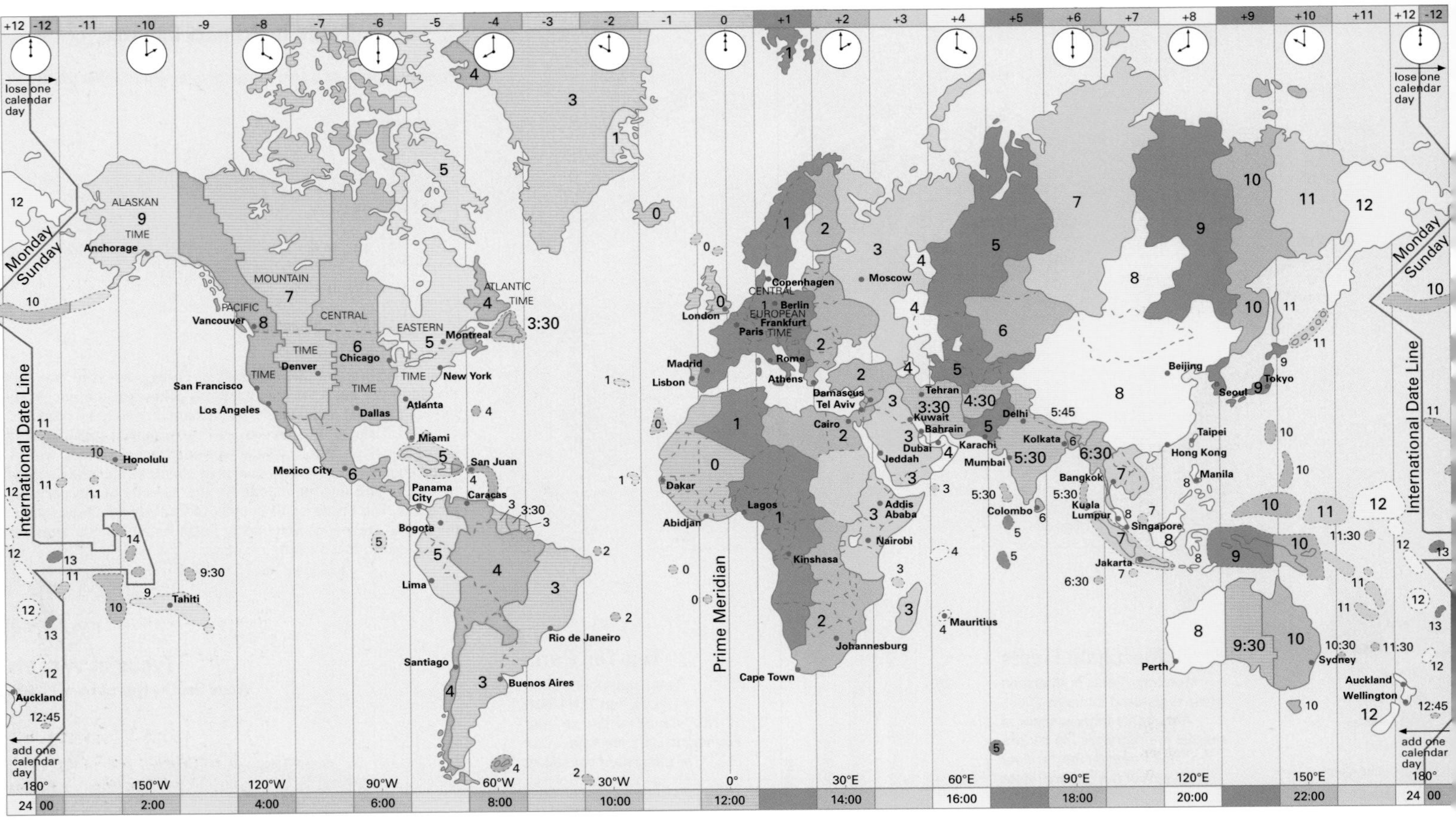

Projection: Mercator

Time Zones

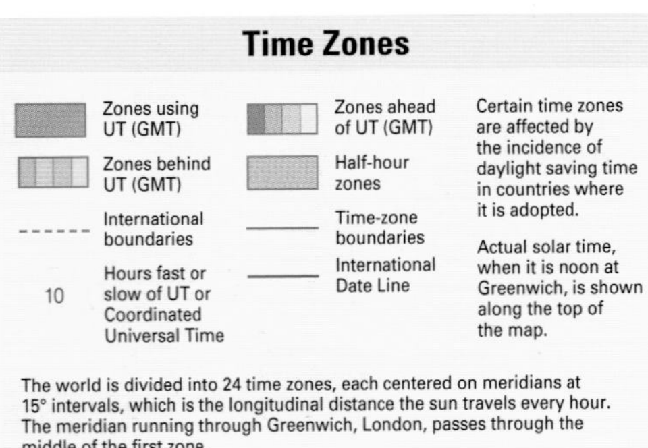

The world is divided into 24 time zones, each centered on meridians at 15° intervals, which is the longitudinal distance the sun travels every hour. The meridian running through Greenwich, London, passes through the middle of the first zone.

Rail and Road: The Leading Nations

	Total rail network ('000 km)	Passenger km per head per year	Total road network ('000 km)	Vehicle km per head per year	Number of vehicles per km of roads
1.	USA 233.8	Japan 1,891	USA 6,378.3	USA 12,505	Hong Kong 287
2.	Russia 85.5	Switzerland 1,751	India 3,319.6	Luxembourg 7,989	Qatar 284
3.	Canada 73.2	Belarus 1,334	China 1,765.2	Kuwait 7,251	UAE 232
4.	India 63.1	France 1,203	Brazil 1,724.9	France 7,142	Germany 195
5.	China 60.5	Ukraine 1,100	Canada 1,408.8	Sweden 6,991	Lebanon 191
6.	Germany 36.1	Russia 1,080	Japan 1,171.4	Germany 6,806	Macau 172
7.	Argentina 34.2	Austria 1,008	France 893.1	Denmark 6,764	Singapore 167
8.	France 29.3	Denmark 999	Australia 811.6	Austria 6,518	South Korea 160
9.	Mexico 26.5	Netherlands 855	Spain 664.9	Netherlands 5,984	Kuwait 156
10.	South Africa 22.7	Germany 842	Russia 537.3	UK 5,738	Taiwan 150
11.	Brazil 22.1	Italy 811	Italy 479.7	Canada 5,493	Israel 111
12.	Ukraine 22.1	Belgium 795	UK 371.9	Italy 4,852	Malta 110

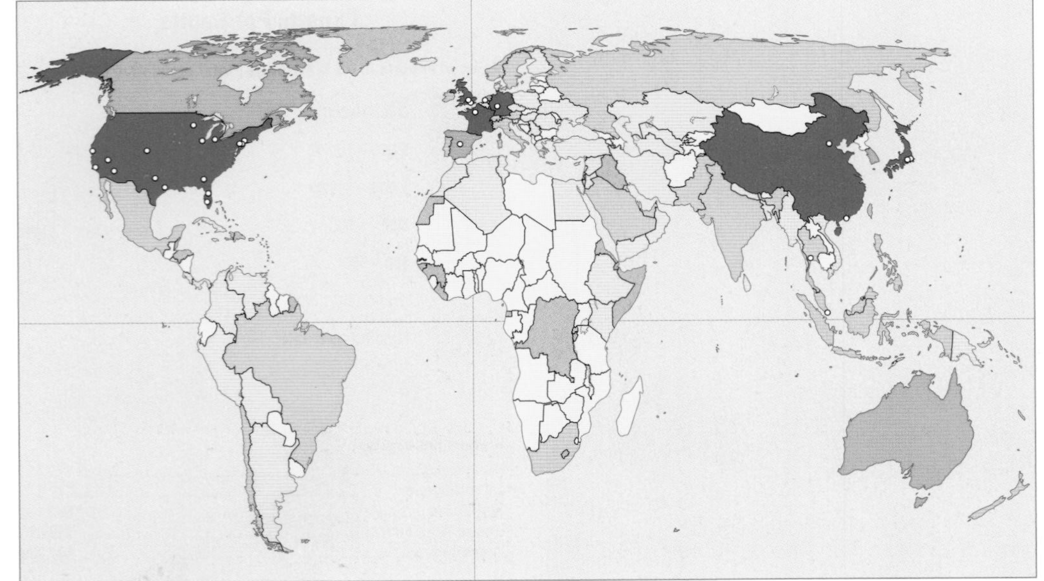

Air Travel

Passenger kilometers flown on scheduled flights (the number of passengers in thousands – international and domestic – multiplied by the distance flown from the airport of origin) (2002)

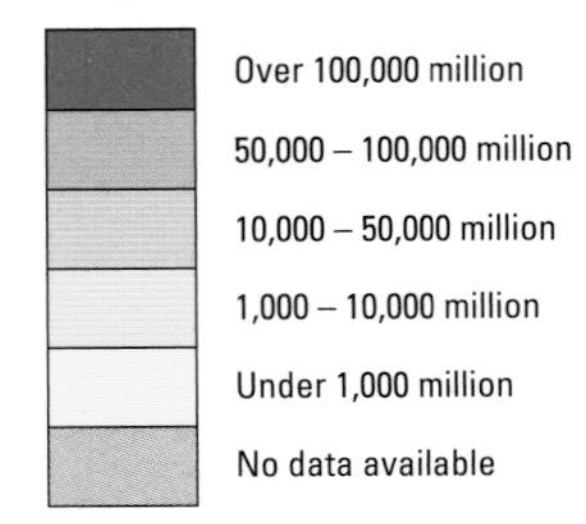

Major airports (handling over 30 million passengers)

World's busiest airports (total passengers)

1. Atlanta (Hartsfield)
2. Chicago (O'Hare)
3. London (Heathrow)
4. Tokyo (Haneda)
5. Los Angeles (International)

World's busiest airports (international passengers)

1. London (Heathrow)
2. Paris (Charles de Gaulle)
3. Frankfurt (International)
4. Amsterdam (Schipol)
5. Hong Kong (International)

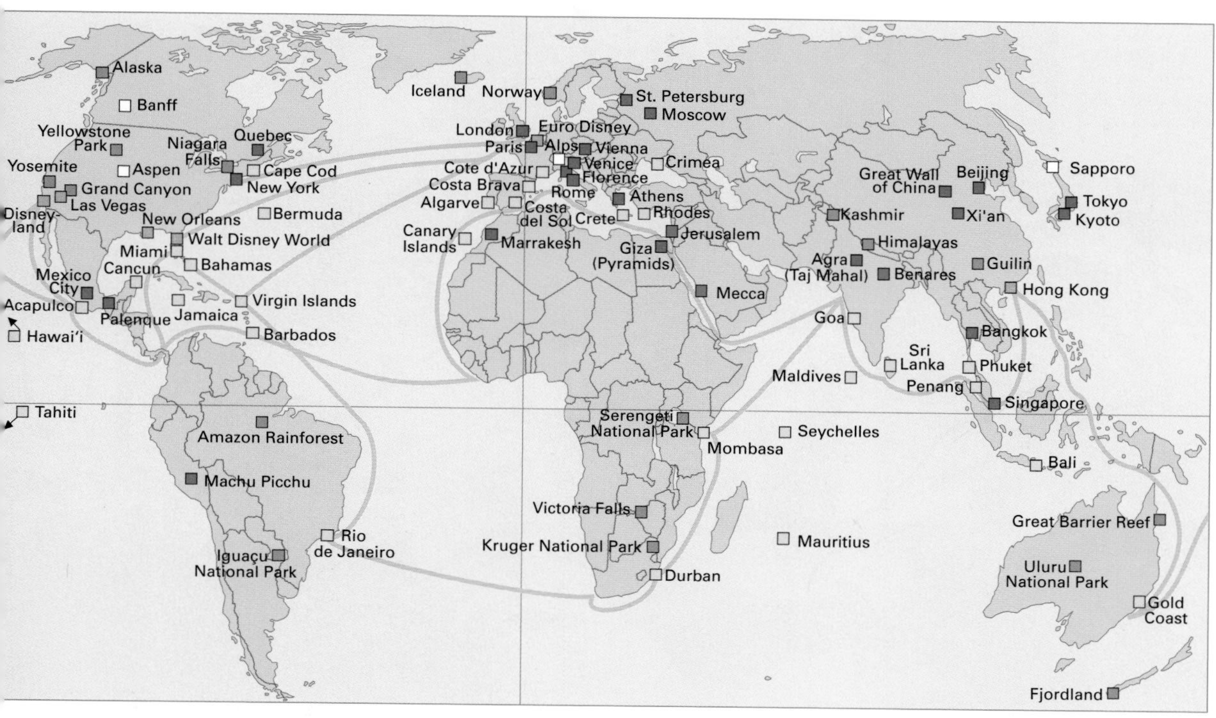

Destinations

- Cultural and historical centers
- Coastal resorts
- Ski resorts
- Centres of entertainment
- Places of pilgrimage
- Places of great natural beauty
- Popular holiday cruise routes

Visitors to the USA

Overseas arrivals to the USA, in thousands (2004)

1. Canada	13,849
2. UK	4,302
3. Mexico	3,993
4. Japan	3,748
5. Germany	1,319
6. France	775
7. South Korea	627
8. Australia	520
9. Italy	470
10. Netherlands	424

Tourist Spending

Countries spending the most on overseas tourism, US$ million (2004)

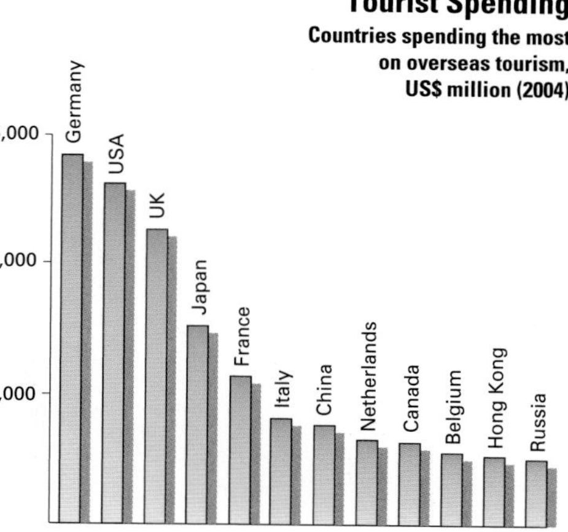

Importance of Tourism

		Arrivals from abroad (2004)	% of world total (2004)
1.	France	75,121,000	9.9%
2.	Spain	53,599,000	7.1%
3.	USA	46,077,000	6.1%
4.	China	41,761,000	5.5%
5.	Italy	37,071,000	4.9%
6.	UK	27,755,000	3.7%
7.	Hong Kong	21,811,000	2.9%
8.	Mexico	20,618,000	2.7%
9.	Germany	20,137,000	2.7%
10.	Austria	19,373,000	2.6%
11.	Canada	19,150,000	2.5%
12.	Turkey	16,826,000	2.2%

After 3 years of stagnant growth, international tourist arrivals reached an all-time record of 763 million in 2004, almost 11% more than in 2003. Growth was common to all regions, but particularly strong in Asia and the Pacific, and in the Middle East.

Tourist Earnings

Countries receiving the most from overseas tourism, US$ million (2004)

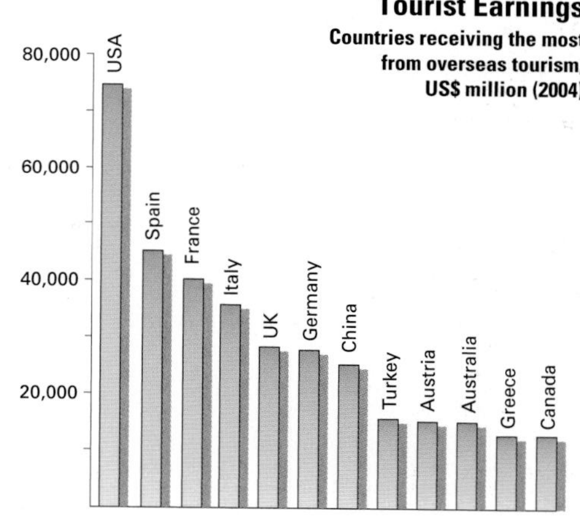

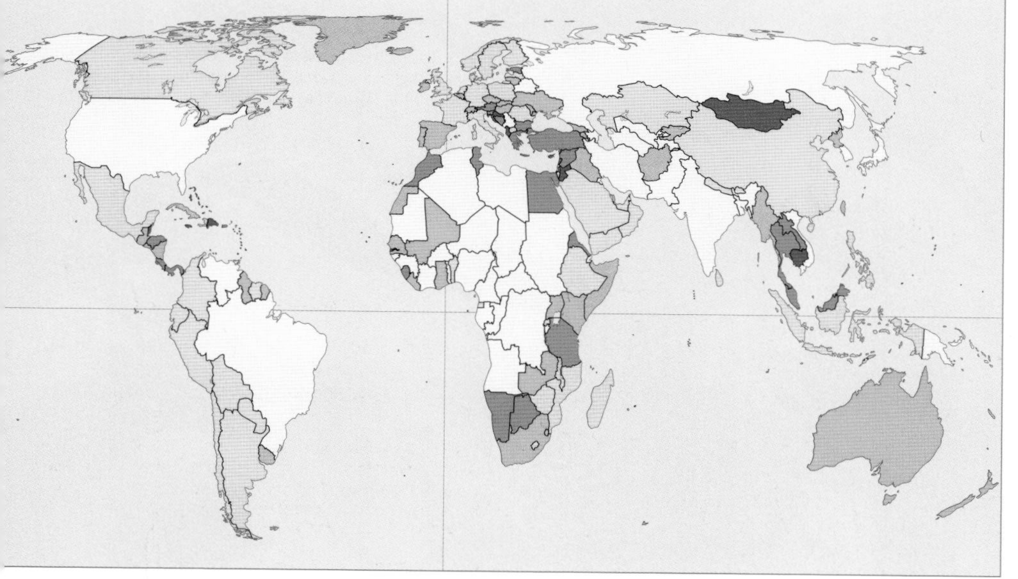

Tourism

Tourism receipts as a percentage of Gross National Income (2005)

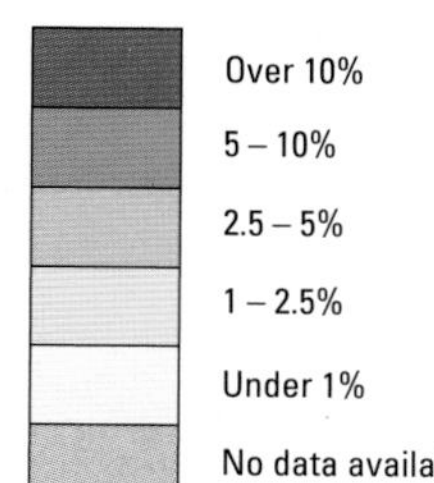

Percentage change in tourist arrivals from 2004 to 2005 (top six countries in total number of arrivals)

France	+1.2%
Spain	+3.7%
USA	+0.02%
China	+8.5%
Italy	–1.5%
UK	+8.0%

– Mt Everest, China/Nepal –

Part of the Himalaya range, Mt Everest – the highest mountain in the world at 29,035 ft (8,850 m) – lies just north of center in this image. The two arms of the Rongbuk glacier flow away from the triangular shaded north wall, with the Kangshung glacier due east. The international boundary between China and Nepal bisects the peak, which was first climbed on May 28, 1953.

WORLD CITIES

Amsterdam 2
Athens 2
Atlanta 3
Baghdad 3
Bangkok 3
Barcelona 4
Beijing 4
Berlin 5
Boston 6
Brussels 6
Budapest 7
Buenos Aires 7
Cairo 7
Cape Town 8
Copenhagen 8
Chicago 9
Delhi 10
Dublin 10
Edinburgh 11
Guangzhou 11
Helsinki 11
Hong Kong 12
Istanbul 12
Jakarta 12
Jerusalem 13
Johannesburg 13
Karachi 13
Kolkata 14
Lagos 14
Las Vegas 14
Lima 14
London 15
Los Angeles 16
Lisbon 16
Madrid 17
Manila 17
Melbourne 18
Mexico City 18
Miami 18
Milan 19
Moscow 19
Montréal 20
Mumbai 20
Munich 21
New Orleans 21
New York 22
Orlando 23
Osaka 23
Oslo 23
Paris 24
Prague 25
Rio de Janeiro 25
Rome 26
San Francisco 26
St Petersburg 27
Santiago 27
São Paulo 27
Seoul 27
Shanghai 28
Singapore 28
Stockholm 29
Sydney 29
Tokyo 30
Tehran 31
Toronto 31
Vienna 32
Warsaw 32
Washington 33
Wellington 33

Index 34–39

WORLD CITIES SATELLITE IMAGES

Cape Town 40
Chicago 41
Karachi 42
London 43
New York 44
San Francisco 45
Santiago 46
Sydney 47
Tokyo 48

CITY MAPS

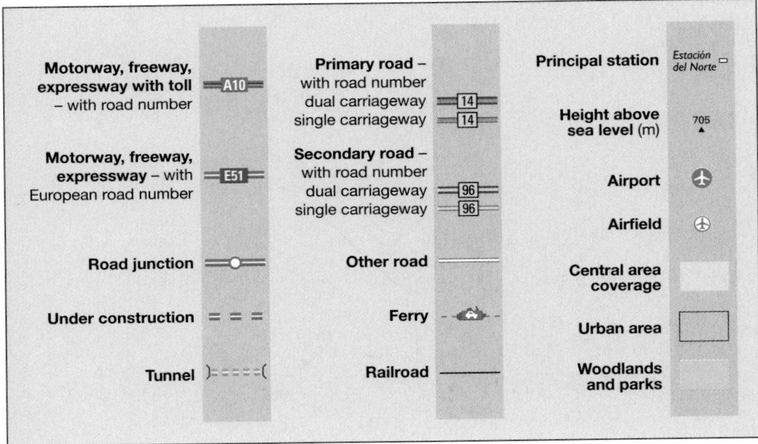

CENTRAL AREA MAPS

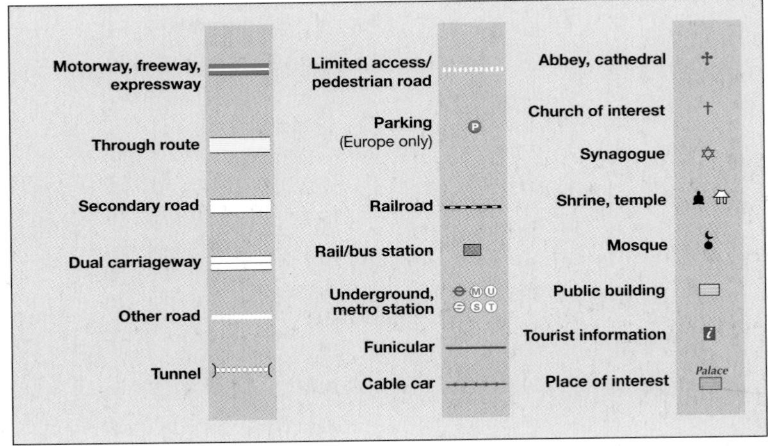

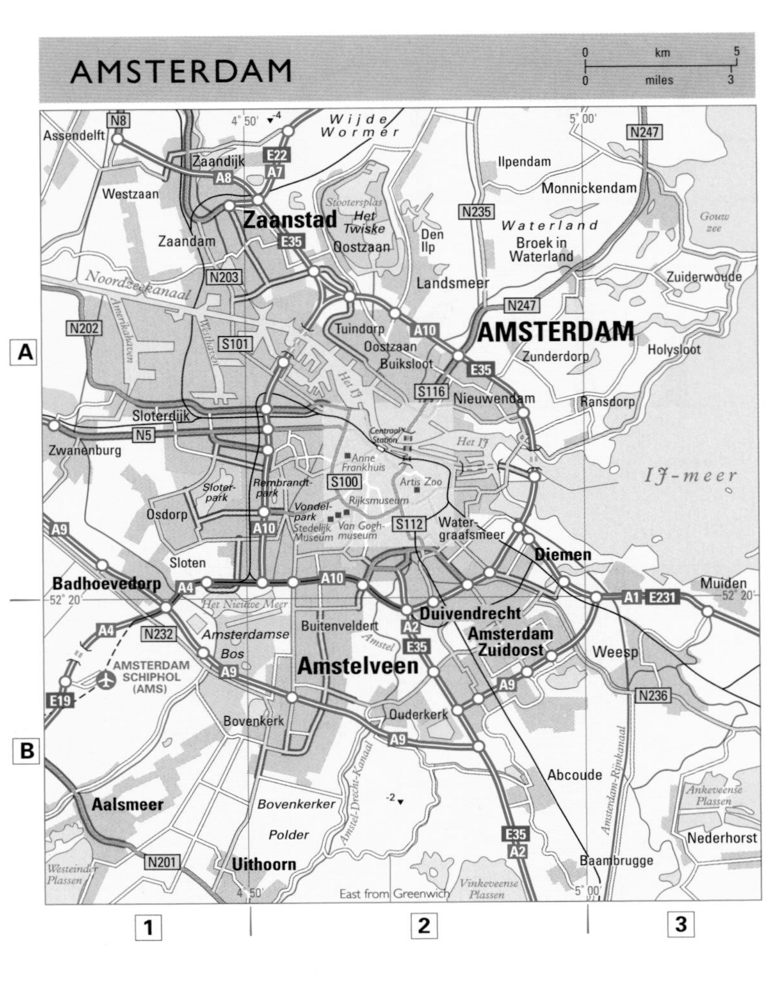
AMSTERDAM
0 km 5
0 miles 3
Assendelft
Wijde Wormer
Ilpendam
Monnickendam
Westzaan
Zaandijk
Zaanstad
Zaandam
Het Twiske
Oostzaan
Den Ilp
Waterland
Broek in Waterland
Gouw zee
Noordzeekanaal
Landsmeer
Zuiderwoude
Tuindorp Oostzaan
Buiksloot
AMSTERDAM
Zunderdorp
Holysloot
Nieuwendam
Ransdorp
Sloterdijk
Zwanenburg
IJ-meer
Osdorp
Sloterpark
Rembrandt-park
Vondelpark
Rijksmuseum
Artis Zoo
Watergraafsmeer
Diemen
Badhoevedorp
Sloten
Muiden
Amsterdamse Bos
Buitenveldert
Duivendrecht
Amsterdam Zuidoost
Weesp
AMSTERDAM SCHIPHOL (AMS)
Amstelveen
Bovenkerk
Ouderkerk
Abcoude
Aalsmeer
Bovenkerker Polder
Ankeveense Plassen
Nederhorst
Uithoorn
Baambrugge
Westeinder Plassen
Vinkeveense Plassen
East from Greenwich
A
B
1
2
3

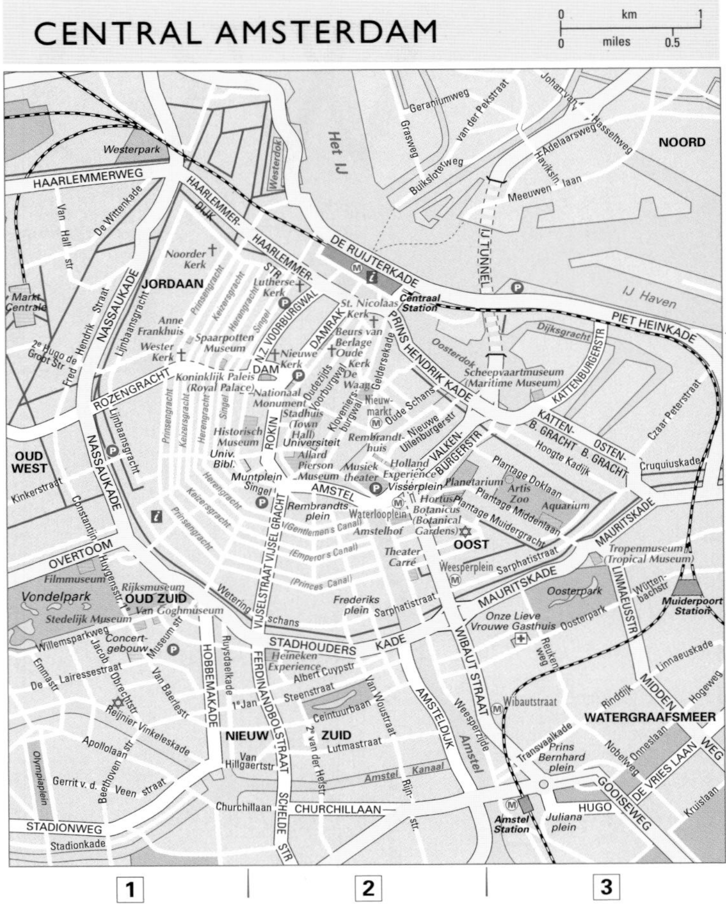
CENTRAL AMSTERDAM
0 km 1
0 miles 0.5
Westerpark
HAARLEMMERWEG
Het IJ
NOORD
IJ Haven
DE RUIJTERKADE
Centraal Station
PIET HEINKADE
JORDAAN
Noorder Kerk
Anne Frankhuis
Wester Kerk
DAM
Koninklijk Paleis (Royal Palace)
Nationaal Monument
Historisch Museum
Scheepvaartmuseum (Maritime Museum)
ROZENGRACHT
OUD WEST
Muntplein
Rembrandtsplein
Waterlooplein
AMSTEL
OOST
Plantage
Artis Zoo
Hortus Botanicus (Botanical Gardens)
Tropenmuseum (Tropical Museum)
Muiderpoort Station
OVERTOOM
Vondelpark
Rijksmuseum
Van Goghmuseum
Stedelijk Museum
OUD ZUID
Concertgebouw
Heineken Experience
Albert Cuypstr
Frederiks plein
Theater Carré
Onze Lieve Vrouwe Gasthuis
STADHOUDERSKADE
WATERGRAAFSMEER
NIEUW ZUID
CHURCHILLAAN
Amstel Station
Julianaplein
STADIONWEG
1
2
3

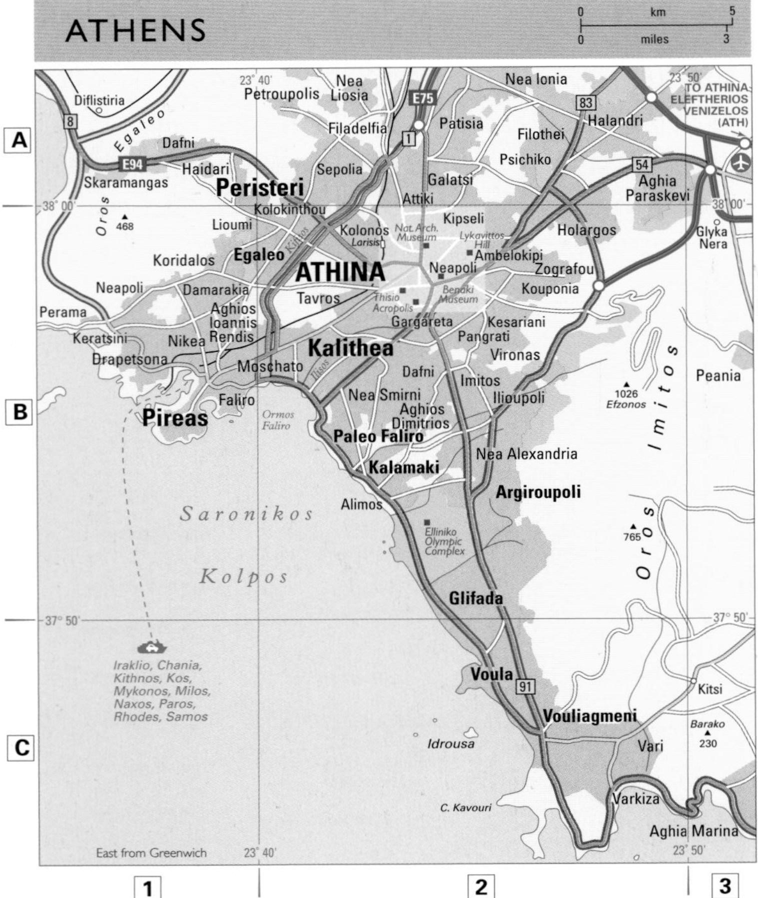
ATHENS
0 km 5
0 miles 3
Diflistiria
Petroupolis
Nea Liosia
Nea Ionia
TO ATHINA ELEFTHERIOS VENIZELOS (ATH)
Halandri
Filothei
Patisia
Filadelfia
Psichiko
Dafni
Haidari
Skaramangas
Sepolia
Galatsi
Aghia Paraskevi
Peristeri
Kolokinthou
Liomi
Kolonos
Kipseli
Holargos
Glyka Nera
Koridalos
Egaleo
ATHINA
Ambelokipi
Zografou
Neapoli
Damarakia
Tavros
Kouponia
Perama
Aghios Ioannis Rendis
Keratsini
Nikea
Gargareta
Kesariani
Drapetsona
Moschato
Kalithea
Pangrati
Vironas
Dafni
Imitos
Ilioupoli
Peania
Pireas
Faliro
Nea Smirni
Aghios Dimitrios
Paleo Faliro
Kalamaki
Nea Alexandria
Imitos
Saronikos Kolpos
Alimos
Argiroupoli
Ellinikó Olympic Complex
Oros
Glifada
Iraklio, Chania, Kithnos, Kos, Mykonos, Milos, Naxos, Paros, Rhodes, Samos
Voula
Kitsi
Vouliagmeni
Idrousa
Vari
Varkiza
C. Kavouri
Aghia Marina
East from Greenwich
A
B
C
1
2
3

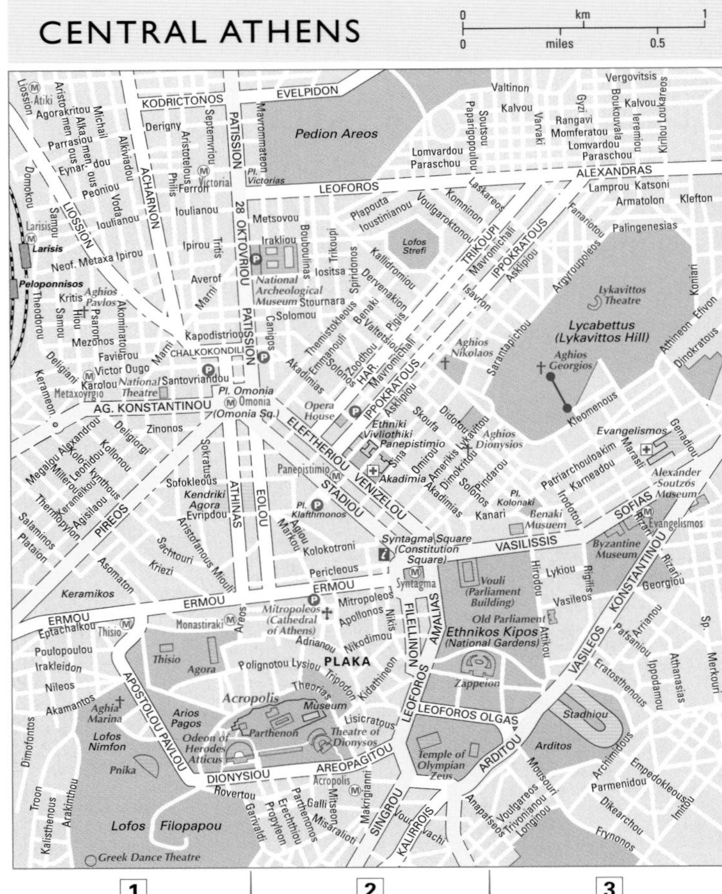
CENTRAL ATHENS
0 km 1
0 miles 0.5
KODRICTONOS
EVELPIDON
Pedion Areos
ALEXANDRAS
LEOFOROS
Larisis
Peloponnisos
ACHARNON
28 OKTOVRIOU
PATISSION
National Archeological Museum
Lofos Strefi
Lykavittos Theatre
Lycabettus (Lykavittos Hill)
Aghios Georgios
Aghios Nikolaos
Kapodistriou
CHALKOKONDILI
Pl. Omonia (Omonia Sq.)
AG. KONSTANTINOU
National Theatre
Opera House
ELEFTHERIOU VENIZELOU
PANEPISTIMIOU
STADIOU
ATHINAS
EOLOU
PIREOS
Kendriki Agora
Pl. Klafthmonos
Syntagma Square (Constitution Square)
VASILISSIS
Benaki Museum
Byzantine Museum
Vouli (Parliament Building)
ERMOU
Monastiraki
Mitropoleos (Cathedral of Athens)
Thisio
Agora
PLAKA
Old Parliament
Ethnikos Kipos (National Gardens)
Zappeion
Acropolis
Parthenon
Odeon of Herodes Atticus
Theatre of Dionysos
Temple of Olympian Zeus
LEOFOROS OLGAS
Stadhiou
Arditos
AREOPAGITOU
DIONYSIOU
APOSTOLOU PAVLOU
Lofos Nimfon
Pnika
Lofos Filopapou
Greek Dance Theatre
SINGROU
1
2
3

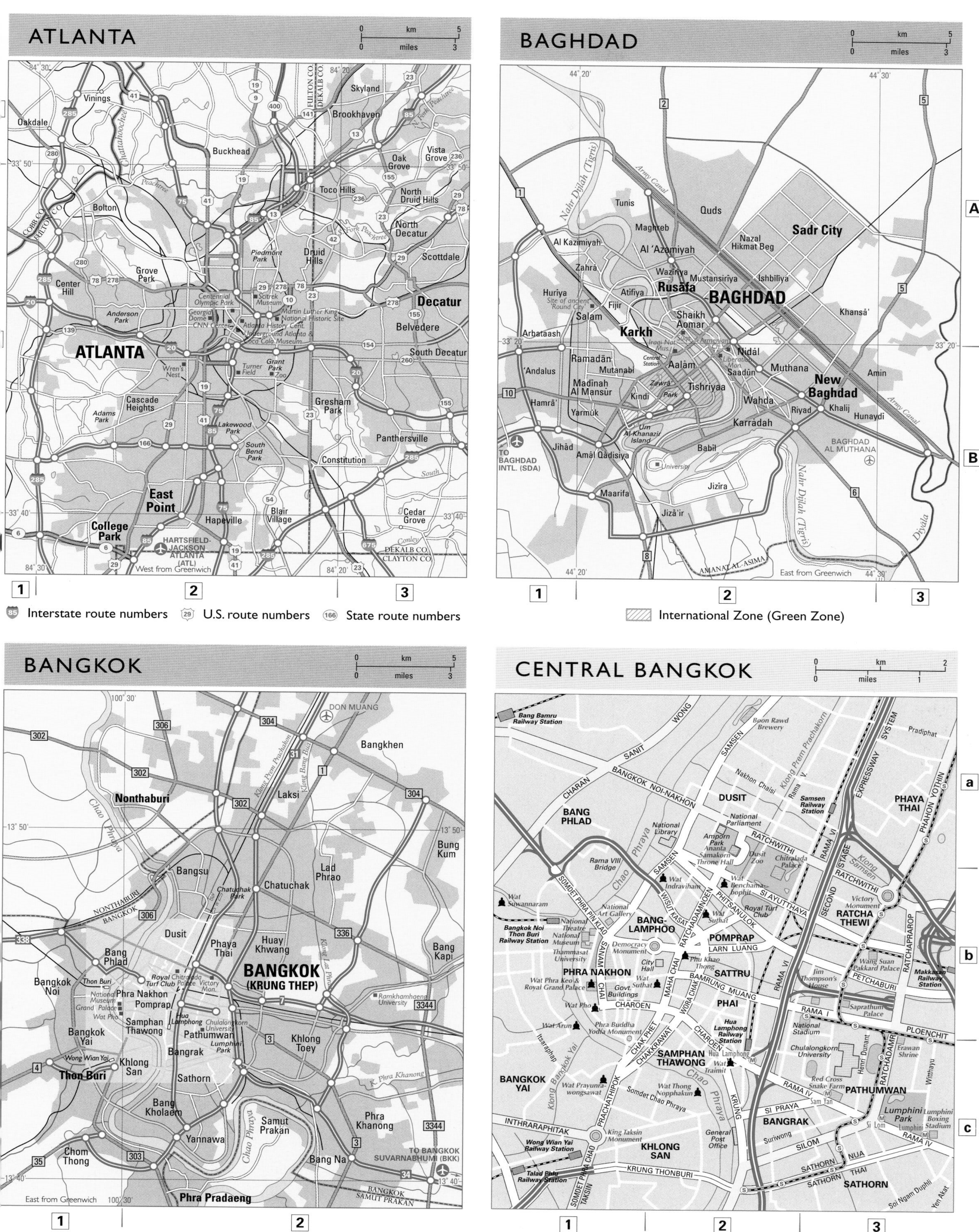
ATLANTA
0 km 5
0 miles 3
Vinings
Oakdale
Skyland
Brookhaven
Buckhead
Oak Grove
Vista Grove
Toco Hills
North Druid Hills
Bolton
North Decatur
Piedmont Park
Druid Hills
Scottdale
Grove Park
Center Hill
Centennial Olympic Park
Scitrek Museum
Martin Luther King National Historic Site
Decatur
Anderson Park
Georgia Dome
CNN Center
Atlanta History Cent.
Underground Atlanta & Coca Cola Museum
Belvedere
ATLANTA
Wren's Nest
Turner Field
Grant Park
Zoo
South Decatur
Cascade Heights
Adams Park
Gresham Park
Lakewood Park
South Bend Park
Panthersville
Constitution
East Point
Hapeville
Blair Village
Cedar Grove
College Park
HARTSFIELD-JACKSON ATLANTA (ATL)
West from Greenwich
FULTON CO.
DEKALB CO.
COBB CO.
CLAYTON CO.
Chattahoochee
Peachtree
Interstate route numbers
U.S. route numbers
State route numbers
BAGHDAD
0 km 5
0 miles 3
Army Canal
Tunis
Quds
Maghreb
Nazal Hikmat Beg
Sadr City
Al Kazimiyah
Al 'Azamiyah
Zahra
Waziriya
Mustansiriya
Ishbiliya
Atifiya
Rusafa
Huriya
Site of ancient Round City
Fijir
Salam
BAGHDAD
Shaikh Aomar
Khansa'
Arbataash
Karkh
Iraqi Nat. Mus.
Nidal
Ramadan
Mutanabi
Central Station
Aalam
Liberation Mon.
Saadun
Muthana
'Andalus
Madinah Al Mansur
Zawra' Park
Tishriyaa
New Baghdad
Amin
Hamra'
Yarmuk
Kindi
Wahda
Riyad
Khalij
Hunaydi
Um Al-Khanazir Island
Karradah
Jihad
Amal Qadisiya
Babil
BAGHDAD AL MUTHANA
TO BAGHDAD INTL. (SDA)
University
Jizira
Maarifa
Jiza'ir
Nahr Dijlah (Tigris)
Diyala
AMANAT AL-ASIMA
East from Greenwich
International Zone (Green Zone)
BANGKOK
0 km 5
0 miles 3
DON MUANG
Bangkhen
Nonthaburi
Laksi
Chao Phraya
Bung Kum
Lad Phrao
Bangsu
Chatuchak
Chatuchak Park
NONTHABURI
BANGKOK
Dusit
Bang Kapi
Phaya Thai
Huay Khwang
Bang Phlad
BANGKOK (KRUNG THEP)
Bangkok Noi
Thon Buri
Royal Turf Club
Chitralada Palace
Victory Mon.
National Museum
Grand Palace
Wat Pho
Phra Nakhon
Pomprap
Ramkhamhaeng University
Samphan Thawong
Hua Lamphong
Chulalongkorn University
Bangkok Yai
Pathumwan
Lumphini Park
Khlong Toey
Wong Wian Yai
Khlong San
Bangrak
Sathorn
K. Phra Khanong
Bang Kholaem
Phra Khanong
Samut Prakan
Yannawa
Chom Thong
Bang Na
TO BANGKOK SUVARNABHUMI (BKK)
BANGKOK SAMUT PRAKAN
Phra Pradaeng
East from Greenwich
CENTRAL BANGKOK
0 km 2
0 miles 1
Bang Bamru Railway Station
Boon Rawd Brewery
Pradiphat
SAMSEN
SANIT
WONG
BANGKOK NOI-NAKHON
CHARAN
DUSIT
Samsen Railway Station
EXPRESSWAY SYSTEM
PHAYA THAI
PHAHON YOTHIN
BANG PHLAD
National Parliament
National Library
Ampорn Park
Ananta Samakorn Throne Hall
Dusit Zoo
Chitralada Palace
RATCHWITHI
Rama VIII Bridge
Wat Indraviharn
Wat Benchamabophit
SI AYUTTHAYA
Victory Monument
RATCHA THEWI
Wat Suwannaram
National Art Gallery
Royal Turf Club
Bangkok Noi Thon Buri Railway Station
National Theatre
National Museum
Thammasat University
BANG LAMPHOO
Democracy Monument
POMPRAP
LARN LUANG
Wat Suthat
Jim Thompson's House
Wang Suan Pakkard Palace
PETCHABURI
Makkasan Railway Station
PHRA NAKHON
Wat Phra Keo & Royal Grand Palace
City Hall
Govt. Buildings
SATTRU
BAMRUNG MUANG
PHAI
Wat Pho
CHAROEN
RAMA I
Sapathum Palace
PLOENCHIT
Wat Arun
Phra Buddha Yodfa Monument
Hua Lamphong Railway Station
National Stadium
Chulalongkorn University
Erawan Shrine
SAMPHAN THAWONG
BANGKOK YAI
Wat Prayunrawongsawat
Wat Thong Nopphakun
Somdet Chao Phraya
Wat Traimit
Red Cross Snake Farm
RAMA IV
PATHUMWAN
Lumphini Park
Lumphini Boxing Stadium
SI PRAYA
BANGRAK
INTHRAPHITAK
King Taksin Monument
General Post Office
Wong Wian Yai Railway Station
KHLONG SAN
SILOM
Suriwong
SATHORN
Talad Phlu Railway Station
KRUNG THONBURI
SATHORN
Soi Ngam Duphli
Yen Akat
Skytrain

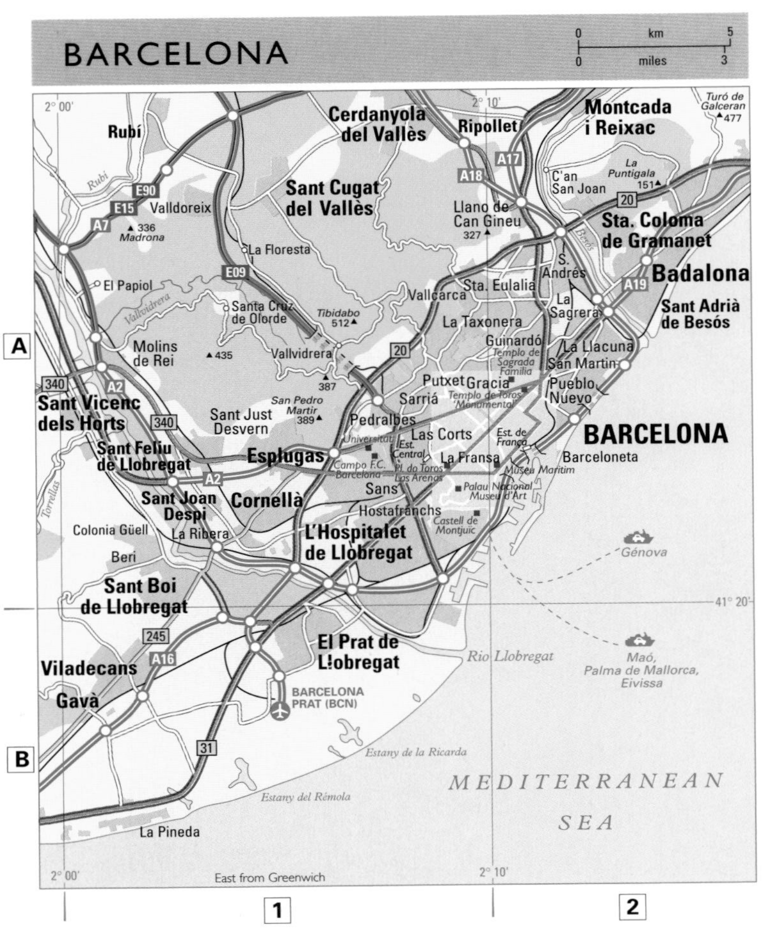

BARCELONA
0 km 5
0 miles 3
2° 00'
2° 10'
Turó de Galceran 477
Rubí
Cerdanyola del Vallès
Ripollet
Montcada i Reixac
A17
A18
C'an San Joan
La Puntigala 151
E90
E15
A7
Valldoreix
336 Madrona
Sant Cugat del Vallès
Llano de Can Gineu 327
Sta. Coloma de Gramanet
La Floresta
E09
Badalona
El Papiol
Santa Cruz de Olorde
Tibidabo 512
Vallcarca
Sta. Eulalia
S. Andrés
La Sagrera
A19
Sant Adrià de Besós
La Taxonera
Guinardó
Molins de Rei
435
Vallvidrera
387
La Llacuna
San Martin
20
340
A2
Sant Vicenç dels Horts
Sant Just Desvern
San Pedro Martir 389
Putxet
Gràcia
Sarriá
Pueblo Nuevo
Pedralbes
Las Corts
BARCELONA
Sant Feliu de Llobregat
Esplugas
La Fransa
Barceloneta
Sant Joan Despi
Cornellà
Sans
Hostafranchs
Colonia Güell
La Ribera
L'Hospitalet de Llobregat
Beri
Gènova
Sant Boi de Llobregat
41° 20'
245
El Prat de Llobregat
Riu Llobregat
A16
Maó, Palma de Mallorca, Eivissa
Viladecans
BARCELONA PRAT (BCN)
Gavà
31
Estany de la Ricarda
Estany del Remola
MEDITERRANEAN SEA
La Pineda
East from Greenwich
A
B
1
2

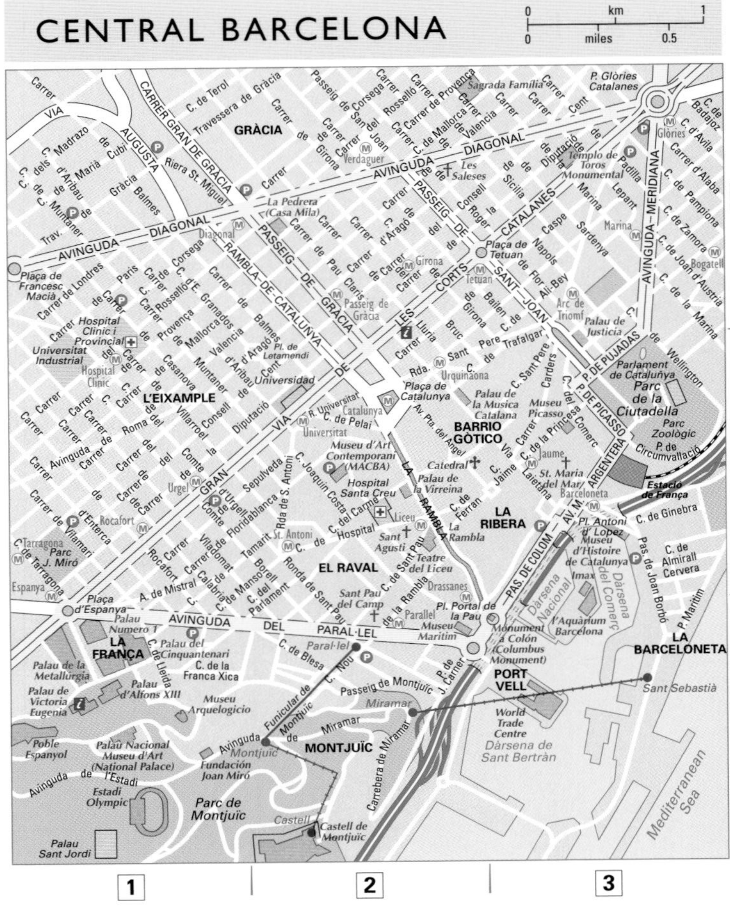

CENTRAL BARCELONA
0 km 1
0 miles 0.5
GRÀCIA
AVINGUDA DIAGONAL
PASSEIG DE GRÀCIA
RAMBLA DE CATALUNYA
La Pedrera (Casa Mila)
Sagrada Familia
P. Glòries Catalanes
Plaça de Francesc Macià
Hospital Clinic i Provincial
Universitat Industrial
L'EIXAMPLE
Universidad
Plaça de Catalunya
BARRIO GÒTICO
Palau de la Musica Catalana
Museu Picasso
Parc de la Ciutadella
Parc Zoològic
Catedral
LA RIBERA
Estació de França
Museu d'Art Contemporani (MACBA)
Hospital Santa Creu
LA RAMBLA
Palau de la Virreina
EL RAVAL
Teatre del Liceu
Drassanes
Plaça d'Espanya
AVINGUDA DEL PARAL·LEL
LA FRANÇA
Monument a Colón (Columbus Monument)
L'Aquàrium Barcelona
LA BARCELONETA
PORT VELL
World Trade Centre
Dàrsena de Sant Bertràn
Sant Sebastià
Palau Nacional Museu d'Art (National Palace)
Fundación Joan Miró
Museu Arquelogicio
Poble Espanyol
MONTJUÏC
Parc de Montjuïc
Estadi Olympic
Castell de Montjuïc
Palau Sant Jordi
Mediterranean Sea
1
2
3

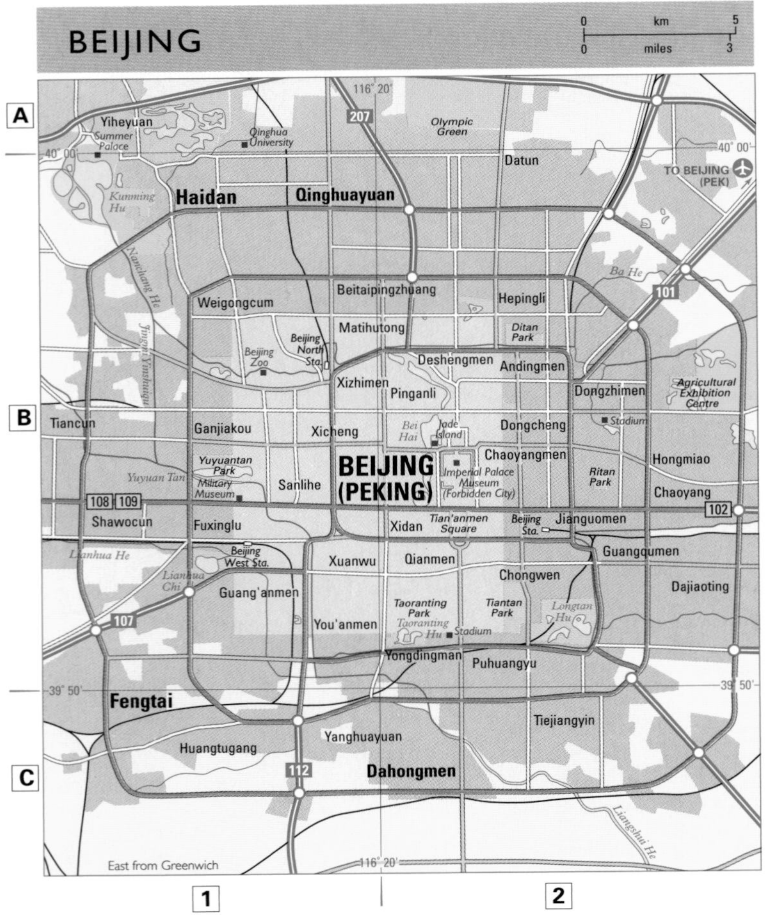

BEIJING
0 km 5
0 miles 3
116° 20'
40° 00'
39° 50'
Yiheyuan
Summer Palace
Qinghua University
207
Olympic Green
Datun
TO BEIJING (PEK)
Kunming Hu
Haidan
Qinghuayuan
Ba He
101
Beitaipingzhuang
Weigongcum
Hepingli
Matihutong
Ditan Park
Beijing Zoo
Beijing North Sta.
Deshengmen
Andingmen
Xizhimen
Pinganli
Dongzhimen
Agricultural Exhibition Centre
Tiancun
Ganjiakou
Xicheng
Bei Hai
Jade Island
Dongcheng
Stadium
Yuyuantan Park
Military Museum
BEIJING (PEKING)
Imperial Palace Museum (Forbidden City)
Chaoyangmen
Ritan Park
Hongmiao
Sanlihe
108
109
Chaoyang
102
Shawocun
Fuxinglu
Xidan
Tian'anmen Square
Beijing Sta.
Jianguomen
Lianhua He
Beijing West Sta.
Xuanwu
Qianmen
Guangqumen
Guang'anmen
Chongwen
Dajiaoting
107
Taoranting Park
Tiantan Park
Longtan Hu
You'anmen
Stadium
Yongdingmen
Puhuangyu
Fengtai
Yanghuayuan
Tiejiangyin
Huangtugang
112
Dahongmen
Liangshui He
East from Greenwich
A
B
C
1
2

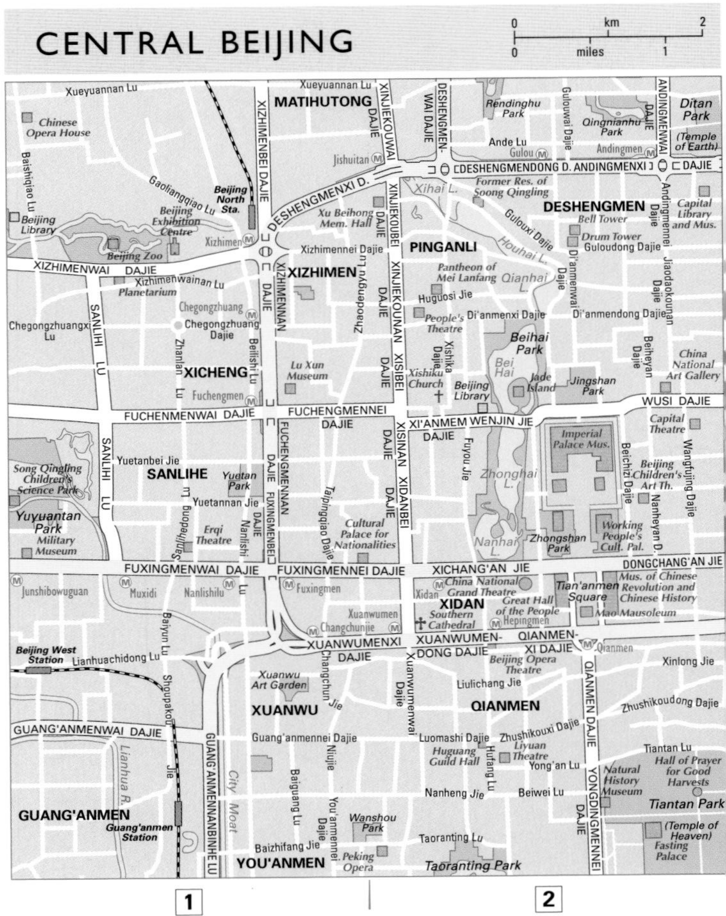

CENTRAL BEIJING
0 km 2
0 miles 1
Xueyuannan Lu
MATIHUTONG
Ditan Park
Chinese Opera House
Beijing North Sta.
DESHENGMENDONG D. ANDINGMENXI D. DAJIE
Former Res. of Soong Qingling
DESHENGMEN
Xu Beihong Mem. Hall
Beijing Library
Beijing Exhibition Centre
Beijing Zoo
XIZHIMENWAI DAJIE
XIZHIMEN
PINGANLI
Beijing Planetarium
Pantheon of Mei Lanfang
Chegongzhuang
Beihai Park
XICHENG
Lu Xun Museum
Jade Island
Jingshan Park
China National Art Gallery
FUCHENMENWAI DAJIE
FUCHENGMENNEI DAJIE
XI'ANMEN WENJIN JIE
WUSI DAJIE
Capital Theatre
Imperial Palace Mus.
Song Qingling Children's Science Park
SANLIHE
Yuetan Park
Yuyuantan Park
Military Museum
Cultural Palace for Nationalities
Zhongshan Park
Working People's Cult. Pal.
FUXINGMENWAI DAJIE
FUXINGMENNEI DAJIE
XICHANG'AN JIE
DONGCHANG'AN JIE
China National Grand Theatre
XIDAN
Tian'anmen Square
Great Hall of the People
Mus. of Chinese Revolution and Chinese History
Mao Mausoleum
Beijing West Station
XUANWUMENXI DAJIE
XUANWUMEN-DONG DAJIE
QIANMEN-XI DAJIE
Xinlong Jie
Xuanwu Art Garden
Beijing Opera Theatre
XUANWU
QIANMEN
GUANG'ANMENWAI DAJIE
Huguang Guild Hall
Natural History Museum
Tiantan Park
(Temple of Heaven)
Fasting Palace
GUANG'ANMEN
Guang'anmen Station
Wanshou Park
YOU'ANMEN
Taoranting Park
1
2

BERLIN

0 km 5
0 miles 3

Hennigsdorf
Schönwalde
Nieder Neuendorf
Siedlung Schönwalde
Alter Finkenkrug
Hermsdorf
Schulzendorf
Heiligensee
Lübars
Waidmannslust
Blankenfelde
Bucholz
Schwanebeck
Neu Buch
Birkholz
Birkholzaue
Löhme
Werneuchen
Rudolfshöhe
Seefeld
Karow
Neu Lindenberg
Lindenberg
Blumberg
Krummensee
Wegendorf
Konradshöhe
Tegel
Wittenau
Rosenthal
Niederschönhausen
Blankenburg
Malchow
Ahrensfelde
Mehrow
Paulshof
Trappenfelde
Neuhönow
Altlandsberg Nord
Altlandsberg
Waldheim
Falkensee
Falkenhagen
Finkenkrug
Seegefeld
Johannesstift
Tegelort
Scharfenberg
Reinickendorf
Pankow
Heinersdorf
Wartenberg
Falkenberg
Eiche
Eiche Süd
Hönow
Seeberg
Friedrichslust
Fredersdorf Nord
Haselhorst
BERLIN-TEGEL (TXL)
Wedding
Weissensee
Hohenschönhausen
Marzahn
Hellersdorf
Neuenhagen
Fredersdorf
Spandau
Zitadelle
Volkspark Jungfernheide
Siemensstadt
Prenzlauerberg
Döberitz
Dallgow
Staaken
Charlottenburg
Schlossgarten
Schloss Charlottenburg
Olympia Stadion
Deutsche Oper
Tiergarten
Mitte
Volkspark Friedrichshain
Friedrichshain
Lichtenburg
Wuhlgarten
Birkenstein
Seeburg
Universität
Zoo
Berlin Dom
Brandenburger Tor
BERLIN
Kreuzberg
Friedrichsfelde
Biesdorf
Kaulsdorf
Mahlsdorf
Dahlwitz-Hoppegarten
Bollensdorf
Vogelsdorf
Teufelsberg
Gatow
Grunewald
Wilmersdorf
Landwehr kanal
Schöneberg
Neukölln
Treptow
Karlshorst
Münchehofe
Heidemühle
Waldesruh
Kleinschönebeck
Schöneiche
Gross Glienicke
Schmargendorf
BERLIN-TEMPELHOF (THF)
Dahlem
Friedenau
Tempelhof
Oberschöneweide
Niederschöneweide
Gratzwalde
Fichtenau
Schönblick
Krampnitz
Kladow
Steglitz
Friedrichshagen
Woltersdorf
Neu Fahrland
Schwanenwerder
Zehlendorf
Britz
Köpenick
Grosse Müggelsee
Wilhelmshagen
Springeberg
Nedlitz
Sacrow
Pfaueninsel
Nikolassee
Mariendorf
Johannisthal
Aldershof
Rahnsdorf
Wannsee
Lichterfelde
Lankwitz
Buckow
Rudow
Altglienicke
Grünau
Wendenschloss
Müggelberge
Müggelheim
Erkner
Neu Buchhorst
Schloss Cecilienhof
Schloss Babelsberg
Potsdam
Dreilinden
Kleinmachnow
Marienfelde
Seehof
Osdorf
Teltow
Grossziethen
Bohnsdorf
BERLIN-SCHÖNEFELD (SXF)
Karolinenhof
Gosen
Sanssouci
Potsdam Museum
Klein Gleinicke
East from Greenwich

A
B
1 2 3 4 5

CENTRAL BERLIN

0 km 1
0 miles 0.5

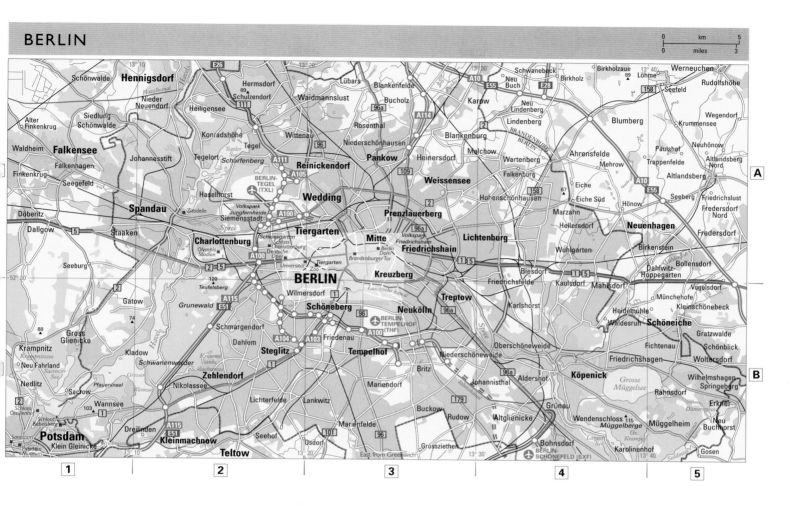

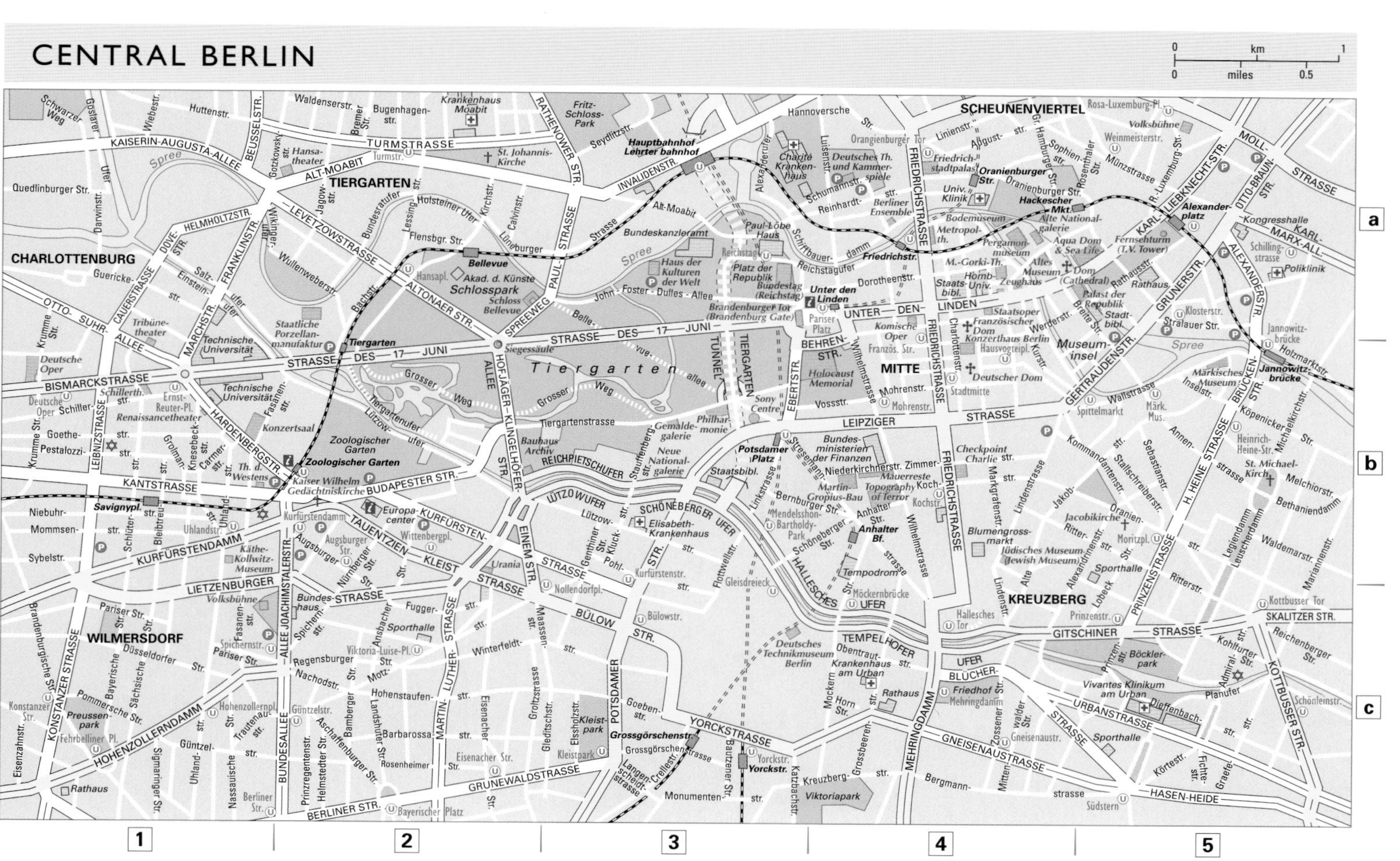

a
b
c
1 2 3 4 5

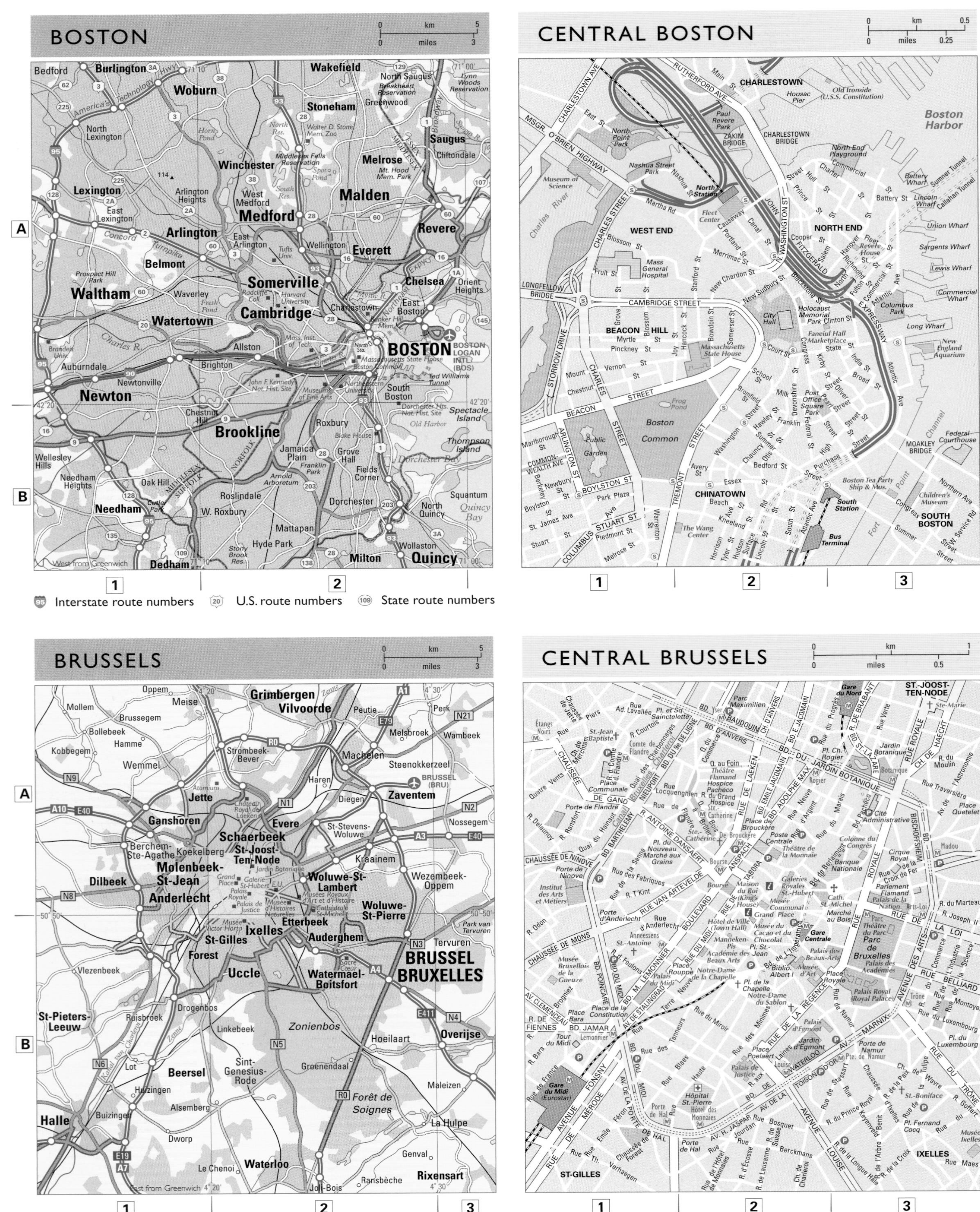
BOSTON
km 0 5
miles 0 3
Bedford
Burlington
Woburn
Wakefield
North Saugus
Breakheart Reservation
Lynn Woods Reservation
Stoneham
Greenwood
North Lexington
Walter D. Stone Mem. Zoo
Saugus
Winchester
Middlesex Fells Reservation
Melrose
Mt. Hood Mem. Park
Cliftondale
Lexington
Arlington Heights
West Medford
Malden
East Lexington
Medford
Revere
Arlington
East Arlington
Wellington
Everett
Belmont
Tufts Univ.
Chelsea
Orient Heights
Prospect Hill Park
Waltham
Waverley
Somerville
Harvard University
East Boston
Cambridge
Charlestown
Bunker Hill Mem.
Watertown
Mass. Inst. of Tech.
Charles R.
Allston
BOSTON
BOSTON LOGAN INTL. (BOS)
Auburndale
Brighton
Massachusetts State House
Boston Common
Ted Williams Tunnel
Newtonville
John F. Kennedy Nat. Hist. Site
Museum of Fine Arts
Northeastern University
South Boston
Newton
Chestnut Hill
Dorchester Hts. Nat. Hist. Site
Spectacle Island
Old Harbor
Roxbury
Brookline
Blake House
Thompson Island
Wellesley Hills
Jamaica Plain
Grove Hall
Franklin Park
Dorchester Bay
Needham Heights
Oak Hill
Arnold Arboretum
Fields Corner
Roslindale
Squantum
Needham
Cutler Park
W. Roxbury
Dorchester
North Quincy
Quincy Bay
Mattapan
Hyde Park
Stony Brook Res.
Wollaston
Dedham
Milton
Quincy
West from Greenwich
Interstate route numbers
U.S. route numbers
State route numbers
CENTRAL BOSTON
km 0 0.5
miles 0 0.25
CHARLESTOWN
Old Ironside (U.S.S. Constitution)
Hoosac Pier
Paul Revere Park
Boston Harbor
North Point Park
ZAKIM BRIDGE
CHARLESTOWN BRIDGE
North End Playground
Museum of Science
Nashua Street Park
North Station
Battery Wharf
Lincoln Wharf
Fleet Center
WEST END
NORTH END
Union Wharf
Sargents Wharf
Mass General Hospital
Lewis Wharf
Commercial Wharf
Paul Revere House
Columbus Park
LONGFELLOW BRIDGE
CAMBRIDGE STREET
City Hall
Holocaust Memorial
Long Wharf
BEACON HILL
Faneuil Hall Marketplace
Massachusetts State House
New England Aquarium
STORROW DRIVE
Frog Pond
Boston Common
Public Garden
Post Office Square Park
Federal Courthouse
MOAKLEY BRIDGE
CHINATOWN
Boston Tea Party Ship & Mus.
Children's Museum
South Station
SOUTH BOSTON
The Wang Center
Bus Terminal
BRUSSELS
km 0 5
miles 0 3
Oppem
Meise
Grimbergen
Vilvoorde
Mollem
Brussegem
Peutie
Perk
Bollebeek
Hamme
Melsbroek
Wambeek
Kobbegem
Strombeek-Bever
Machelen
Steenokkerzeel
Wemmel
BRUSSEL (BRU)
Haren
Atomium
Jette
Diegem
Zaventem
Ganshoren
Evere
Nossegem
St-Stevens-Woluwe
Schaerbeek
Berchem-Ste-Agathe
Koekelberg
St-Joost-Ten-Node
Kraainem
Molenbeek-St-Jean
Jardin Botanique
Woluwe-St-Lambert
Wezembeek-Oppem
Dilbeek
Anderlecht
Woluwe-St-Pierre
Etterbeek
Park van Tervuren
Ixelles
St-Gilles
Auderghem
Tervuren
Forest
BRUSSEL BRUXELLES
Vlezenbeek
Uccle
Watermael-Boitsfort
St-Pieters-Leeuw
Drogenbos
Ruisbroek
Linkebeek
Zonienbos
Overijse
Hoeilaart
Lot
Sint-Genesius-Rode
Groenendaal
Beersel
Maleizen
Huizingen
Forêt de Soignes
Halle
Buizingen
Alsemberg
La Hulpe
Dworp
Genval
Waterloo
Le Chenoi
Rixensart
Joli-Bois
Ransbèche
East from Greenwich
CENTRAL BRUSSELS
km 0 1
miles 0 0.5
Gare du Nord
ST.-JOOST-TEN-NODE
Parc Maximilien
Jardin Botanique
Place Rogier
Rue Neuve
Place de Brouckère
Théâtre de la Monnaie
Cité Administrative
Colonne du Congrès
Banque Nationale
Cirque Royal
Parlement Flamand
Palais de la Nation
Galeries Royales St.-Hubert
Cath. St.-Michel
Bourse
Maison du Roi (King's House)
Grand Place
Hôtel de Ville (Town Hall)
Musée du Cacao et du Chocolat
Manneken-Pis
Gare Centrale
Parc de Bruxelles
Palais des Académies
Palais des Beaux-Arts
Place Royale
Palais Royal (Royal Palace)
Notre-Dame de la Chapelle
Notre-Dame du Sablon
Place Poelaert
Palais de Justice
Jardin d'Egmont
Porte de Namur
Tour du Midi
Gare du Midi (Eurostar)
Porte de Hal
Hôpital St.-Pierre
ST-GILLES
IXELLES
Musée Ixelles

BUDAPEST

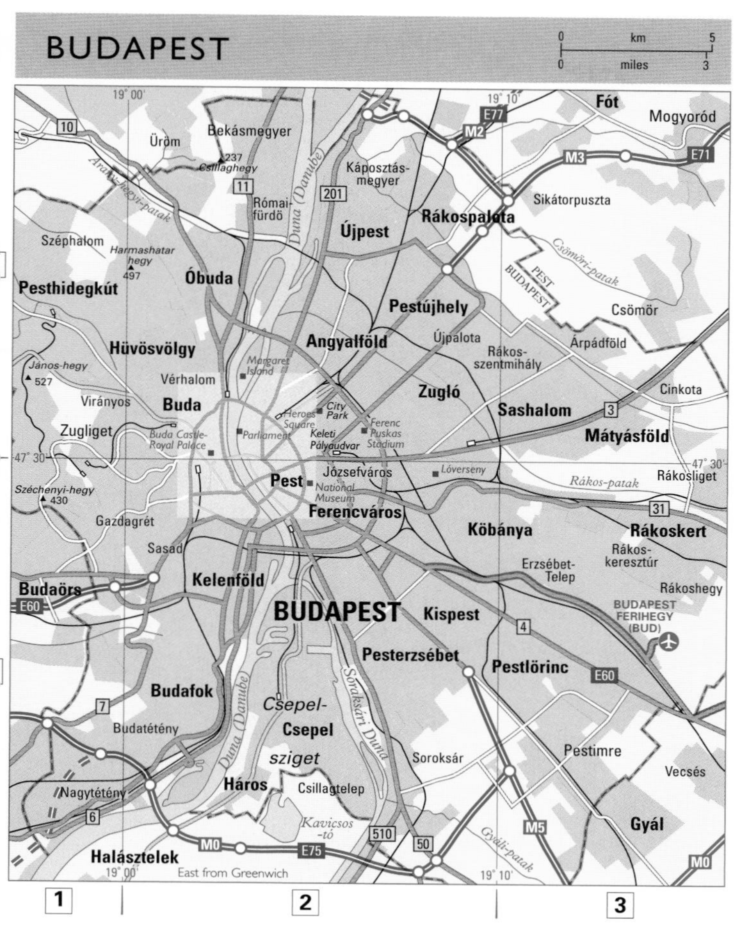

CENTRAL BUDAPEST

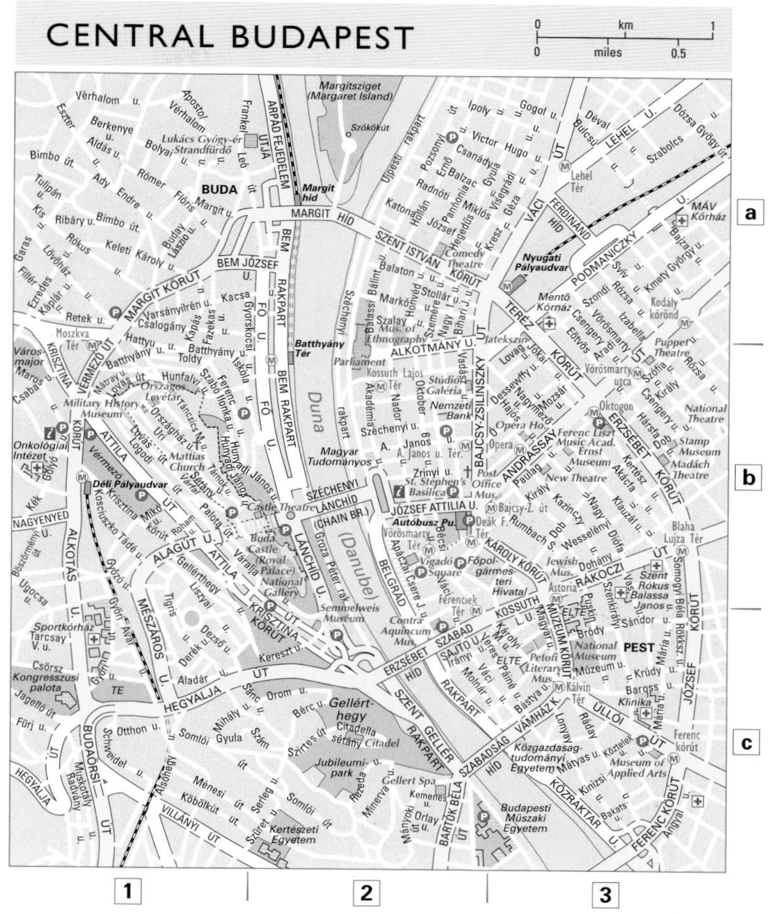

BUENOS AIRES

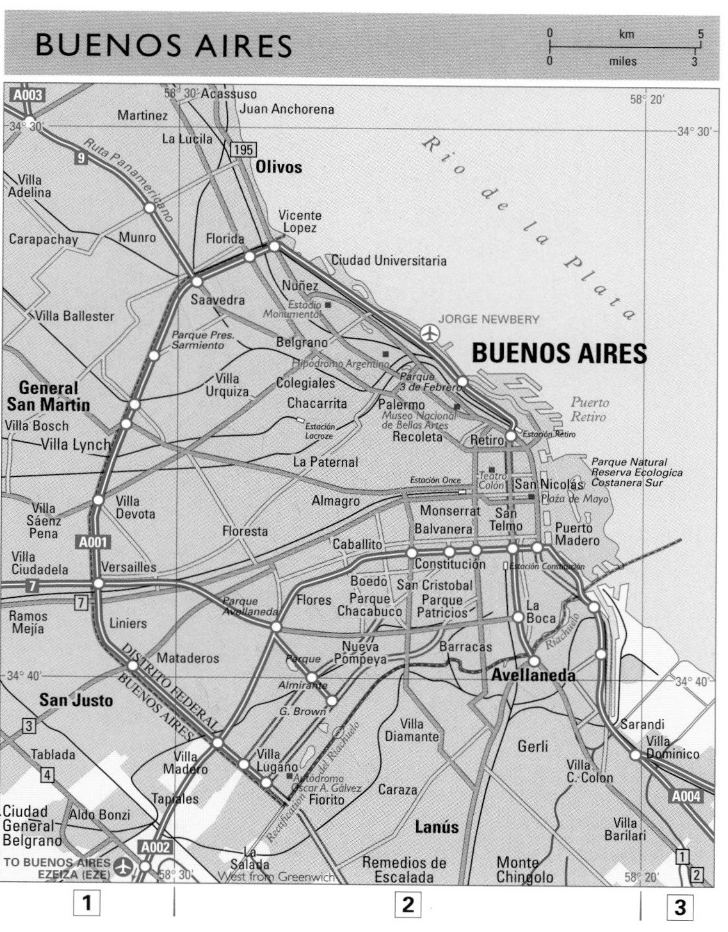

CAIRO

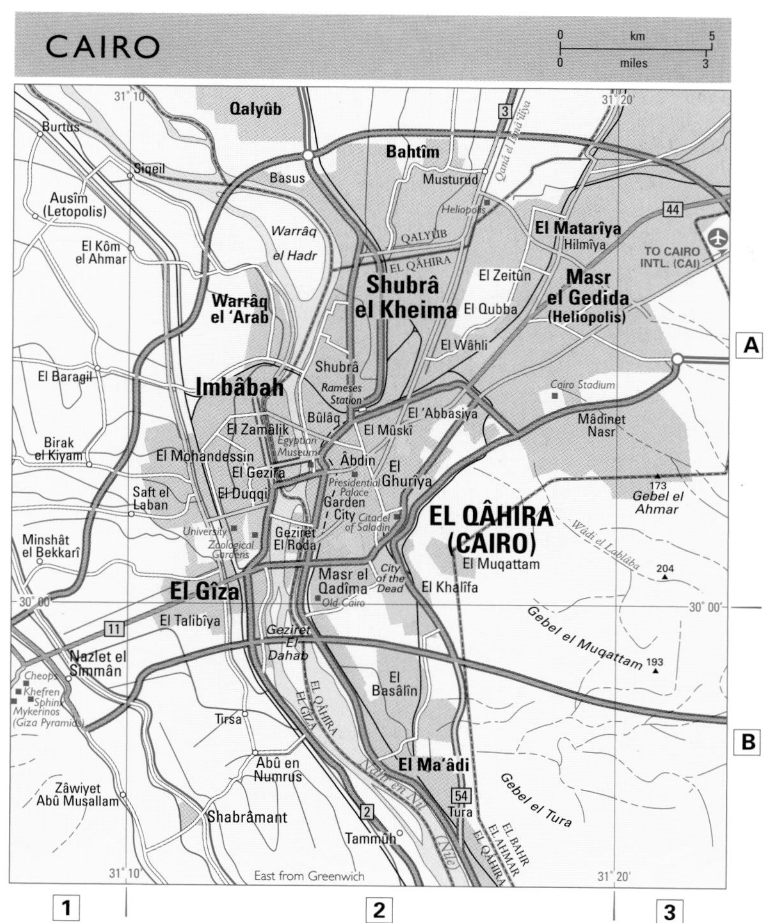

CAPE TOWN

0 km 5
0 miles 3

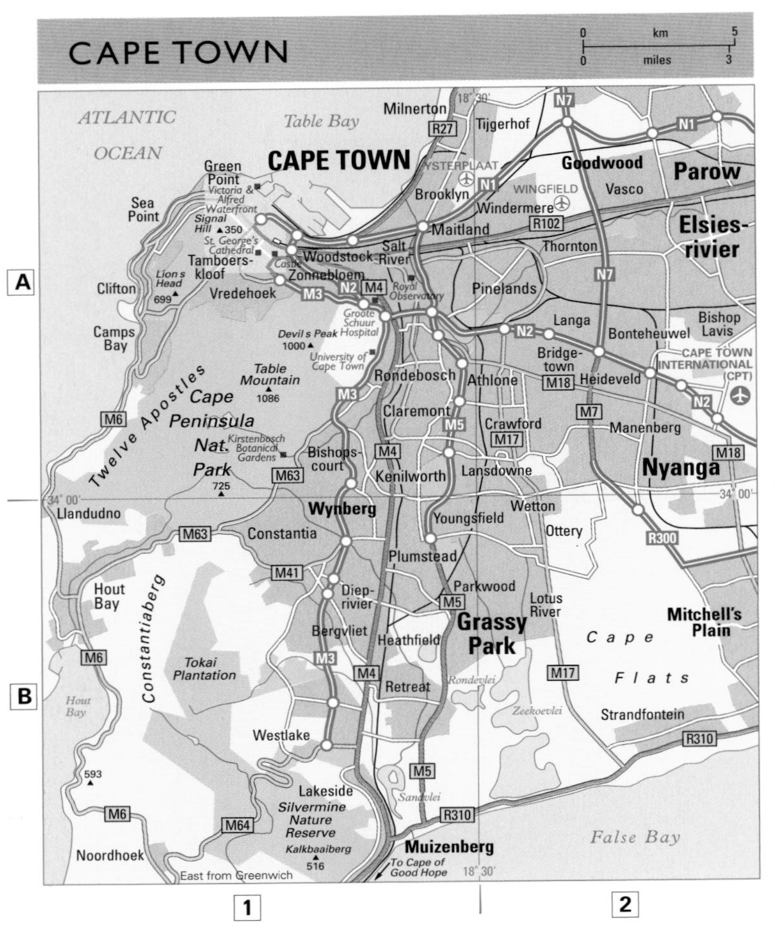

CENTRAL CAPE TOWN

0 km 0.5
0 miles 0.25

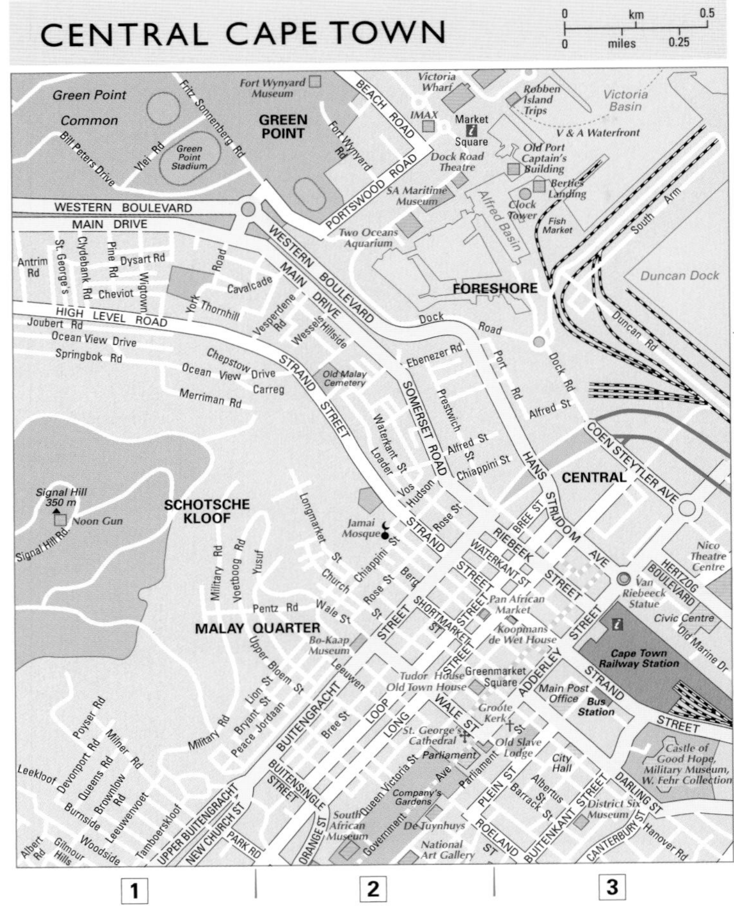

COPENHAGEN

0 km 5
0 miles 3

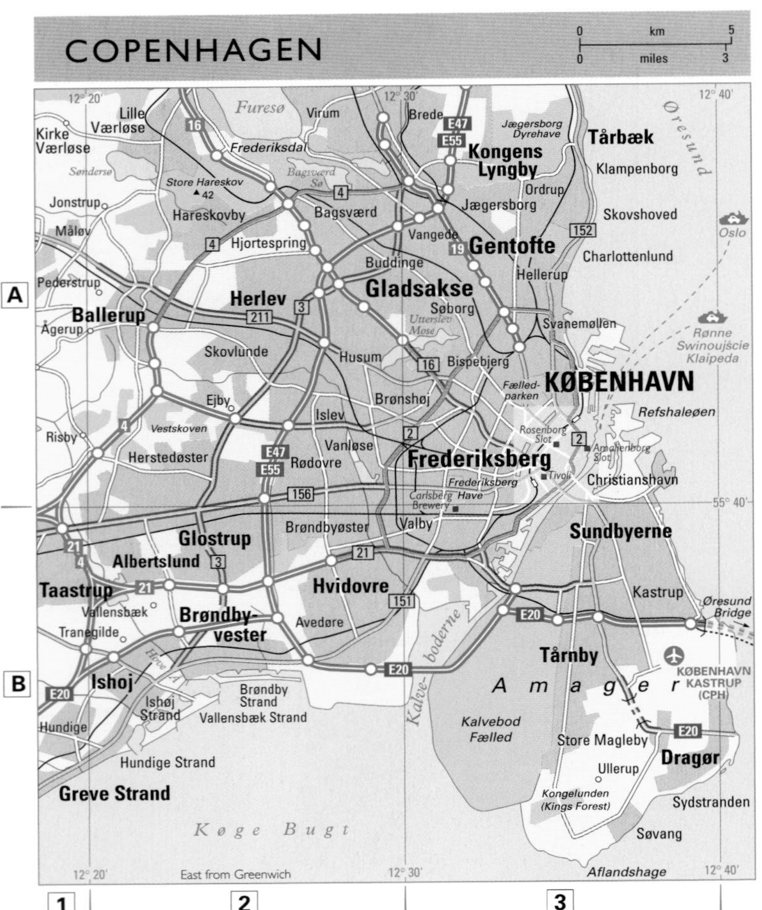

CENTRAL COPENHAGEN

0 km 0.5
0 miles 0.25

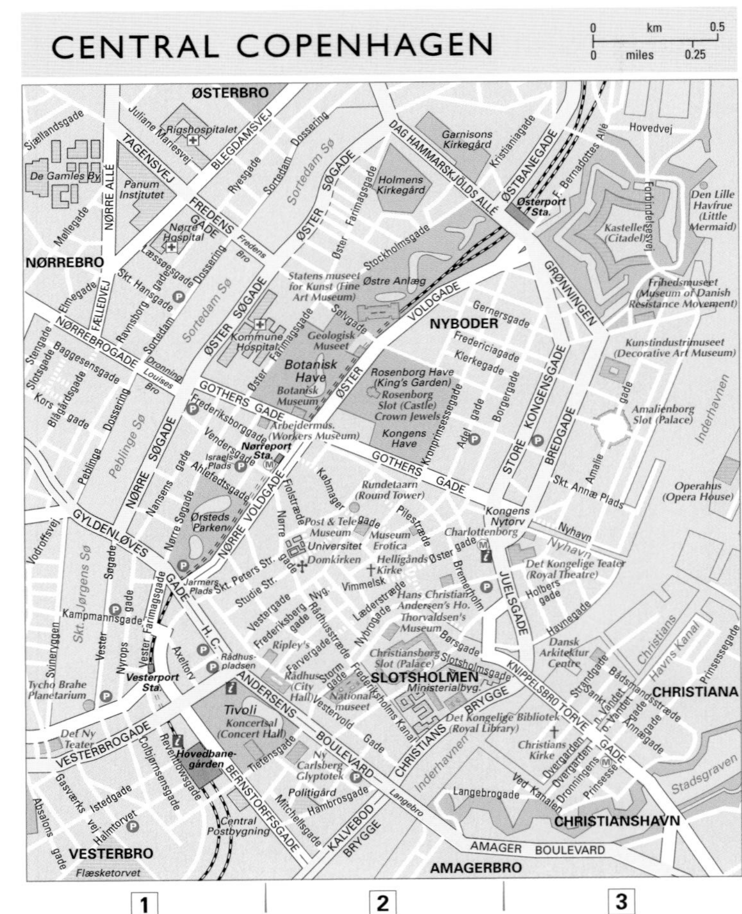

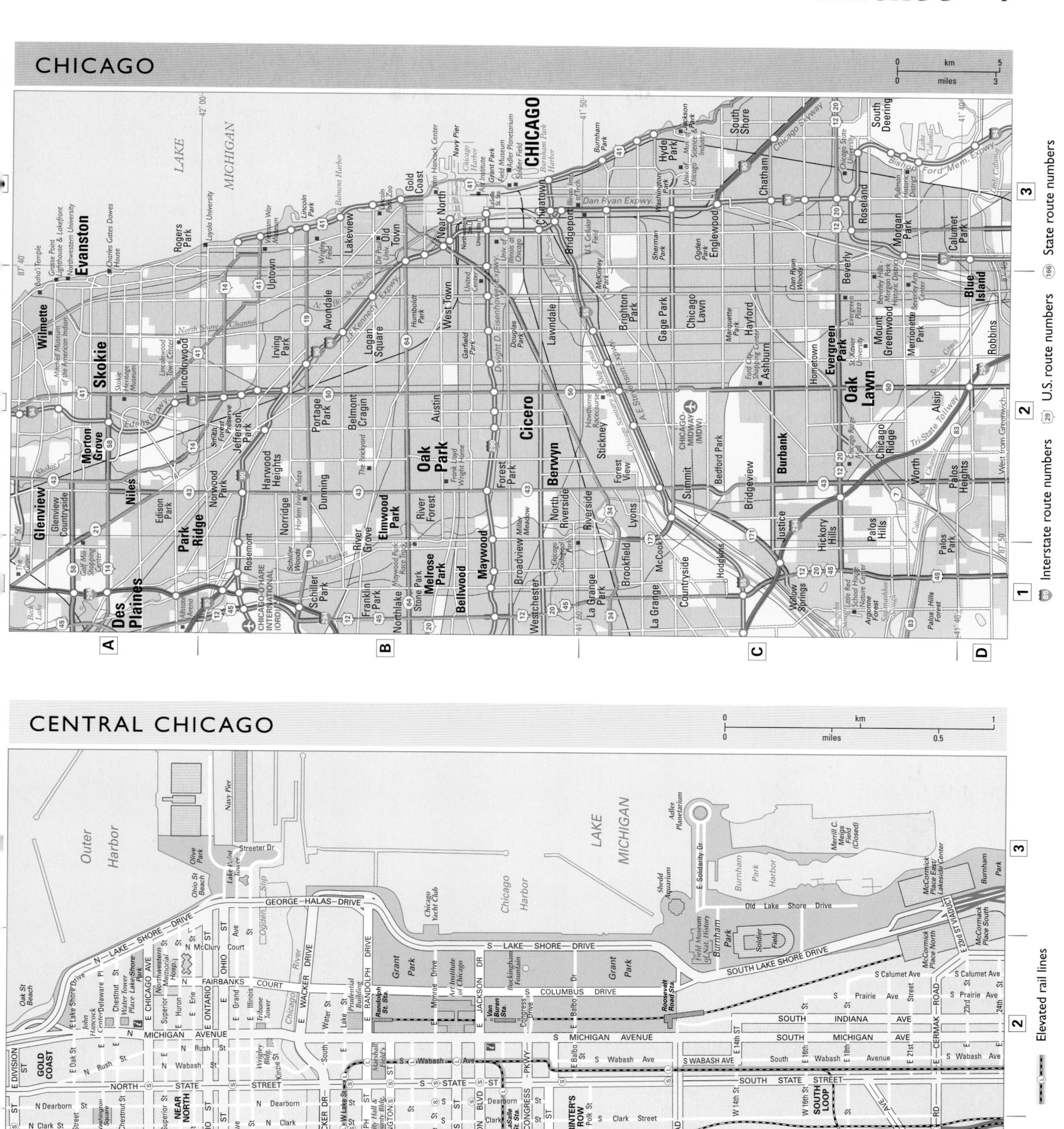
CHICAGO
km
miles
LAKE MICHIGAN
CHICAGO
Des Plaines
Park Ridge
Niles
Skokie
Evanston
Wilmette
Morton Grove
Glenview
Lincolnwood
Rogers Park
Uptown
Lakeview
Lincoln Park
Gold Coast
Near North
Old Town
West Town
Logan Square
Avondale
Irving Park
Portage Park
Jefferson Park
Norwood Park
Edison Park
Harwood Heights
Norridge
Dunning
Belmont Cragin
Austin
Oak Park
River Forest
Elmwood Park
River Grove
Franklin Park
Schiller Park
Rosemont
Melrose Park
Stone Park
Northlake
Bellwood
Maywood
Forest Park
Broadview
Westchester
Berwyn
Cicero
North Riverside
Riverside
Lyons
Brookfield
La Grange Park
La Grange
McCook
Countryside
Hodgkins
Summit
Stickney
Forest View
Lawndale
Bridgeport
Chinatown
Brighton Park
Gage Park
Chicago Lawn
Ashburn
Hayford
Bedford Park
Bridgeview
Burbank
Justice
Hickory Hills
Willow Springs
Palos Hills
Palos Park
Palos Heights
Worth
Chicago Ridge
Oak Lawn
Hometown
Evergreen Park
Beverly
Mount Greenwood
Morgan Park
Blue Island
Robbins
Alsip
Merrionette Park
Calumet Park
Roseland
Chatham
Englewood
Hyde Park
South Shore
South Deering
CHICAGO-O'HARE INTERNATIONAL (ORD)
CHICAGO-MIDWAY (MDW)
Interstate route numbers
U.S. route numbers
State route numbers
CENTRAL CHICAGO
km
miles
LAKE MICHIGAN
Outer Harbor
Chicago Harbor
Navy Pier
Grant Park
Burnham Park
Soldier Field
Shedd Aquarium
Adler Planetarium
GOLD COAST
NEAR NORTH
RIVER NORTH
THE LOOP
PRINTER'S ROW
SOUTH LOOP
CHINATOWN
N LAKE SHORE DRIVE
S LAKE SHORE DRIVE
MICHIGAN AVENUE
NORTH STATE STREET
SOUTH STATE STREET
W ROOSEVELT ROAD
Chicago River
Elevated rail lines

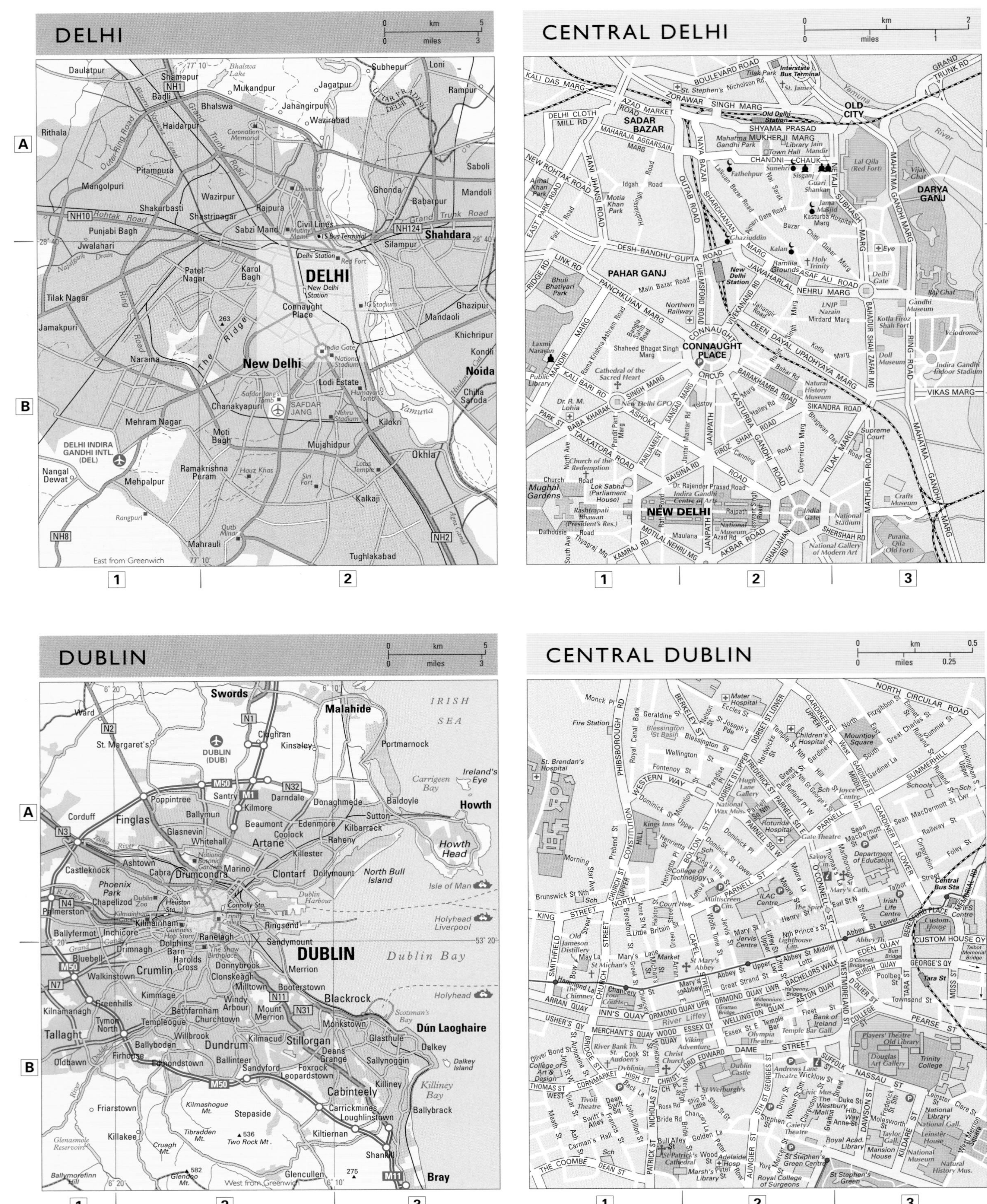
DELHI
0 km 5
0 miles 3
Daulatpur
Shamapur
Mukandpur
Jagatpur
Subhepur
Loni
Rampur
Badli
Bhalswa
Jahangirpuri
Wazirabad
Rithala
Haidarpur
Coronation Memorial
Outer Ring Road
Grand Trunk Road
Pitampura
Saboli
Mangolpuri
University
Ghonda
Mandoli
Wazirpur
Babarpur
Shakurbasti
Rajpura
Shastrinagar
Civil Lines
Rohtak Road
Punjabi Bagh
Sabzi Mand
I.S.Bus Terminal
Silampur
Shahdara
Jwalahari
Delhi Station
Red Fort
Patel Nagar
Karol Bagh
DELHI
New Delhi Station
Tilak Nagar
Connaught Place
IG Stadium
Ghazipur
Mandaoli
Jamakpuri
The Ridge
Khichripur
India Gate
National Stadium
Kondli
Naraina
New Delhi
Noida
Lodi Estate
Safdar Jang's Tomb
Humayun's Tomb
Chanakyapuri
SAFDAR JANG
Chilla Saroda
Mehram Nagar
Nehru Stadium
Yamuna
Kilokri
Moti Bagh
DELHI INDIRA GANDHI INTL. (DEL)
Mujahidpur
Okhla
Nangal Dewat
Ramakrishna Puram
Hauz Khas
Lotus Temple
Mehpalpur
Siri Fort
Kalkaji
Rangpuri
Qutb Minar
Mahrauli
Agra Canal
East from Greenwich
Tughlakabad
NH1
NH10
NH124
NH8
NH2
77° 10'
28° 40'
263
CENTRAL DELHI
0 km 2
0 miles 1
KALI DAS MARG
BOULEVARD ROAD
Tilak Park
Interstate Bus Terminal
St. Stephen's
Nicholson Rd
St. James
GRAND TRUNK RD
ZORAWAR SINGH MARG
AZAD MARKET ROAD
SADAR BAZAR
Old Delhi Station
OLD CITY
DELHI CLOTH MILL RD
MAHARAJA AGGARSAIN MARG
SHYAMA PRASAD MUKHERJI MARG
Mahatma Gandhi Park
Library
Jain Mandir
Town Hall
CHANDNI CHAUK
Lal Qila (Red Fort)
Vijay Ghat
NEW ROHTAK ROAD
RANI JHANSI ROAD
QUTAB ROAD
NAYA BAZAR
Fathehpur
Sunehri
Sisganj
Gauri Shankar
Jama Masjid
Kasturba Hospital
DARYA GANJ
Ajmal Khan Park
Idgah Road
Motia Khan Park
SHARDHANAN
Ajmeri Gate Road
NETAJI SUBHASH MARG
MAHATMA GANDHI MARG
EAST PARK ROAD
Ghaziuddin
Kalan
Eye
DESH-BANDHU-GUPTA ROAD
Ramlila Grounds
Holy Trinity
ASAF ALI ROAD
Delhi Gate
LINK RD
PAHAR GANJ
New Delhi Station
JAWAHARLAL NEHRU MARG
Raj Ghat
RIDGE RD
Bhuli Bhatiyari Park
Main Bazar Road
CHELMSFORD ROAD
LNJP Narain Mirdard Marg
Gandhi Museum
PANCHKUIAN MARG
Northern Railway
VIVEKANAND RD
Kotla Firoz Shah Fort
Velodrome
DEEN DAYAL UPADHYAYA MARG
Laxmi Narayan
Shaheed Bhagat Singh Marg
CONNAUGHT PLACE
Doll Museum
RING ROAD
Cathedral of the Sacred Heart
CIRCUS
BARAKHAMBA ROAD
Indira Gandhi Indoor Stadium
Public Library
MANDIR MARG
KALI BARI RD
SINGH MARG
Natural History Museum
VIKAS MARG
Dr. R. M. Lohia
New Delhi GPO
ASHOKA
Tolstoy
KASTURBA
Hailey Rd
SIKANDRA ROAD
PARK ST
BABA KHARAK
SANSAD MARG
JANPATH
Supreme Court
TALKATORA ROAD
Pandit Pant Marg
PARLIAMENT ST
Jantar Mantar Rd
FIROZ SHAH ROAD
Copernicus Marg
TILAK MARG
MATHURA ROAD
North Ave
Church of the Redemption
Church Road
RAISINA RD
Dr. Rajender Prasad Road
Indira Gandhi Centre of Arts
Crafts Museum
Mughal Gardens
Lok Sabha (Parliament House)
NEW DELHI
Rajpath
India Gate
National Stadium
Rashtrapati Bhawan (President's Res.)
National Museum
Dalhousie Road
Maulana Azad Rd
SHERSHAH RD
Purana Qila (Old Fort)
South Ave
Thyagraj Mg
KAMRAJ RD
MOTILAL NEHRU MG
AKBAR ROAD
SHAHJAHAN RD
National Gallery of Modern Art
DUBLIN
0 km 5
0 miles 3
Swords
IRISH SEA
Ward
Malahide
N1
N2
Cloghran
St. Margaret's
DUBLIN (DUB)
Kinsaley
Portmarnock
M50
N32
M1
Santry
Ireland's Eye
Carrigeen Bay
Poppintree
Darndale
Kilmore
Donaghmede
Baldoyle
Howth
Corduff
Ballymun
Sutton
Finglas
Beaumont
Edenmore
Kilbarrack
N3
Glasnevin
Coolock
Whitehall
Artane
Raheny
Howth Head
Tolka River
National Botanic Gardens
Killester
Castleknock
Ashtown
Marino
Cabra
Drumcondra
Clontarf
Dollymount
North Bull Island
Phoenix Park
Isle of Man
Chapelizod
Dublin Zoo
Dublin Harbour
N4
R. Liffey
Palmerston
Heuston Sta.
Connolly Sta.
Trinity College
Holyhead
Liverpool
Kilmainham
Ringsend
Ballyfermot
Inchicore
Ranelagh
Sandymount
Guinness Hop Store
53° 20'
Drimnagh
Dolphins Barn
The Shaw Birthplace
DUBLIN
Dublin Bay
Bluebell
Harolds Cross
M50
Donnybrook
Crumlin
Merrion
Walkinstown
Clonskeagh
N7
Milltown
Booterstown
Kimmage
N11
Kilnamanagh
Greenhills
Windy Arbour
N31
Blackrock
Bathfarnham
Mount Merrion
Scotsman's Bay
Templeogue
Churchtown
Monkstown
Dún Laoghaire
Tymon North
Tallaght
Willbrook
Glasthule
Ballyboden
Dundrum
Kilmacud
Stillorgan
Dalkey
Firhouse
Deans Grange
Oldbawn
Edmondstown
Ballinteer
Sallynoggin
Dalkey Island
Sandyford
Foxrock
Leopardstown
Killiney
Cabinteely
Killiney Bay
Friarstown
Kilmashogue Mt.
Stepaside
Carrickmines
Ballybrack
Loughlinstown
Glenasmole Reservoir
Killakee
Tibradden Mt.
536 Two Rock Mt.
Kiltiernan
Cruagh Mt.
Shankill
582 Glendoo Mt.
Ballymorefinn Hill
Glencullen
275
West from Greenwich
M11
Bray
6° 20'
6° 10'
CENTRAL DUBLIN
0 km 0.5
0 miles 0.25
NORTH CIRCULAR ROAD
Mater Hospital
Monck Pl
Geraldine St
Eccles St
St Joseph's Pde
Fire Station
Blessington St Basin
Children's Hospital
Mountjoy Square
PHIBSBOROUGH RD
Royal Canal Bank
BERKELEY ST
DORSET ST LOWER
GARDINER ST UPPER
Blessington St
Wellington St
St. Brendan's Hospital
Fontenoy St
Great Charles St
SUMMERHILL
WESTERN WAY
Hugh Lane Gallery
Great Denmark St
Sch
Joyce Centre
Schools
National Wax Mus.
Parnell Sq Nth
Rotunda Hospital
Sean MacDermott St
Railway St
CONSTITUTION HILL
King's Inns
Gate Theatre
PARNELL ST
Department of Education
Foley St
Morning Star Ave
College of Technology
Central Bus Sta
Talbot St
Brunswick St Nth
CHURCH ST
NORTH KING STREET
Court Hse
Multiscreen Cin.
ILAC Centre
The Spire
Irish Life Centre
IFS Centre
Custom House
BERESFORD PLACE
MEMORIAL RD
SMITHFIELD
Old Jameson Distillery
Henry St
Nth Prince's St
Abbey Th.
CUSTOM HOUSE QY
Little Britain St
Mary St
Jervis Centre
Lighthouse Cin.
Abbey St Middle
EDEN QUAY
Butt Bridge
Talbot Memorial Bridge
Mary's Lane
Market
St Mary's Abbey
O'Connell Bridge
BURGH QUAY
GEORGE'S QY
St Michan's
Great Strand St
BACHELORS WALK
Poolbeg St
Tara St
The Chimney
Chancery
Four Courts
Ha'penny Bridge
ASTON QUAY
Townsend St
ARRAN QUAY
ORMOND QUAY UPR
ORMOND QUAY LWR
Millennium Bridge
Grattan Bridge
Fleet St
Bank of Ireland
PEARSE ST
USHER'S QY
INN'S QUAY
River Liffey
ESSEX QY
WELLINGTON QUAY
Temple Bar
COLLEGE ST
MERCHANT'S QUAY
WOOD QUAY
Olympia Theatre
Temple Bar Gall.
Players' Theatre
Old Library
Oliver Bond St
River Bank Th.
St. Audoen's
Cook St
Viking Adventure
DAME STREET
Dublinia
Christ Church
LORD EDWARD
Dublin Castle
Douglas Hyde Art Gallery
Trinity College
College of Art & Design
HIGH ST
CORNMARKET
Andrews Lane Theatre
Wicklow St
NASSAU ST
THOMAS ST WEST
St Werburgh's
Tivoli Theatre
Civic Mus.
The Westbury
Leinster St
Clare St
Swift's Alley
Dean Swift Sq
Ross Rd
Bride Rd
Ship St Little
Stephen St
Hib. Way
National Library
National Gall.
Gaiety Theatre
Mansion House
Leinster House
Molesworth St
Royal Acad. Library
Taylor Gall.
National Museum
Natural History Mus.
West Merrion Square
St. Patrick's Cathedral
Bull Alley
Golden La
Adelaide Hosp
Marsh's Library
St Stephen's Green Centre
St Stephen's Green
Royal College of Surgeons
THE COOMBE
DEAN ST
PATRICK ST
NICHOLAS ST
AUNGIER ST
DAWSON ST
KILDARE ST
GRAFTON ST
Light Rail (LUAS)

EDINBURGH

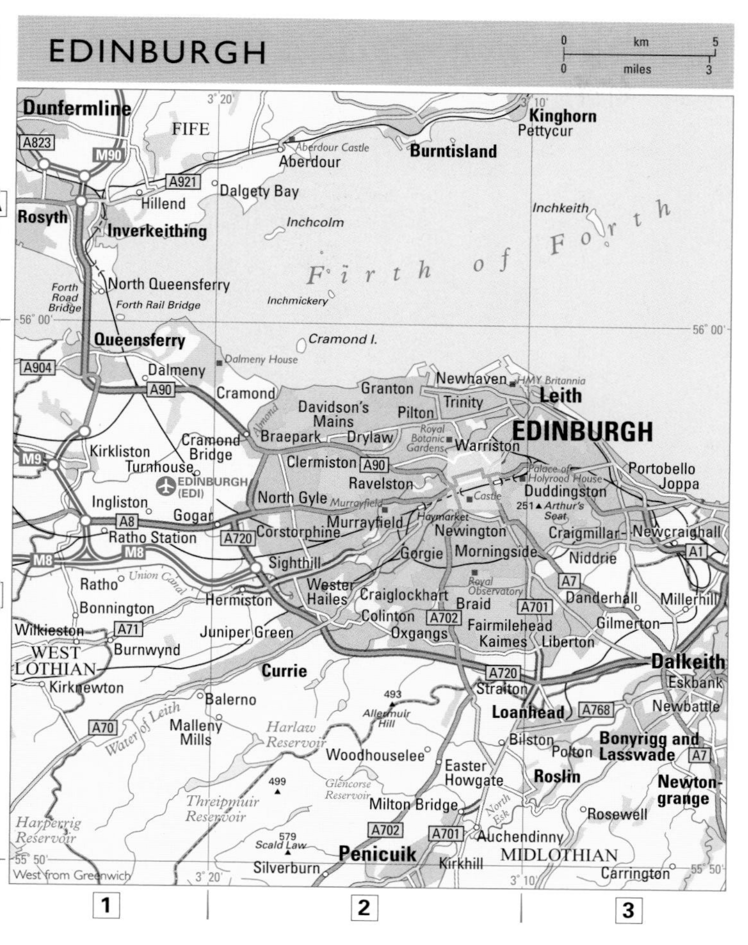

CENTRAL EDINBURGH

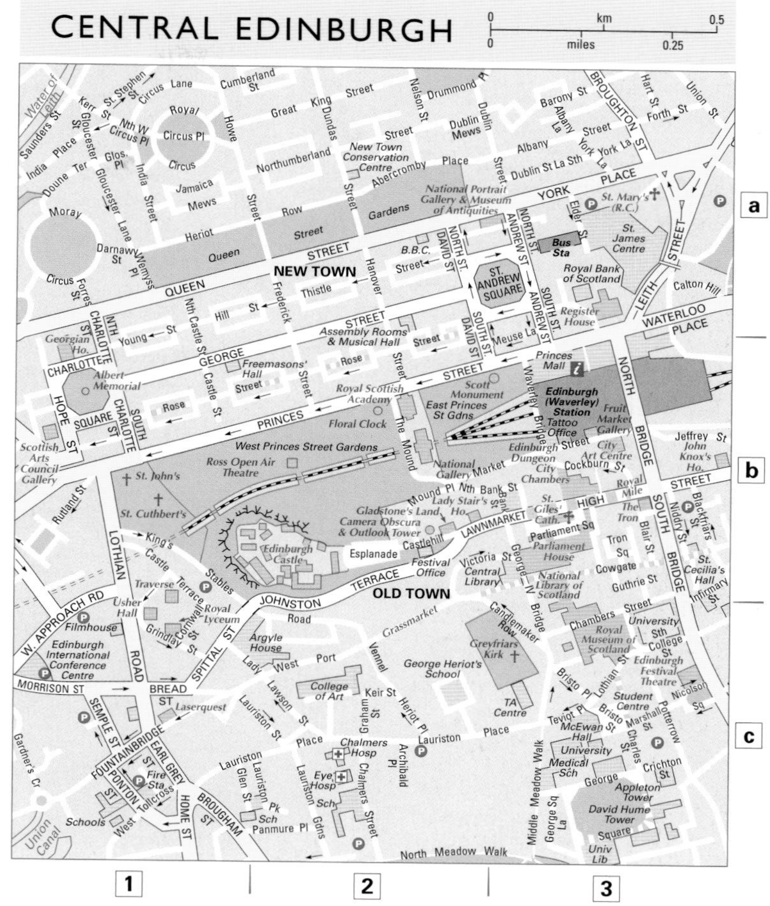

GUANGZHOU

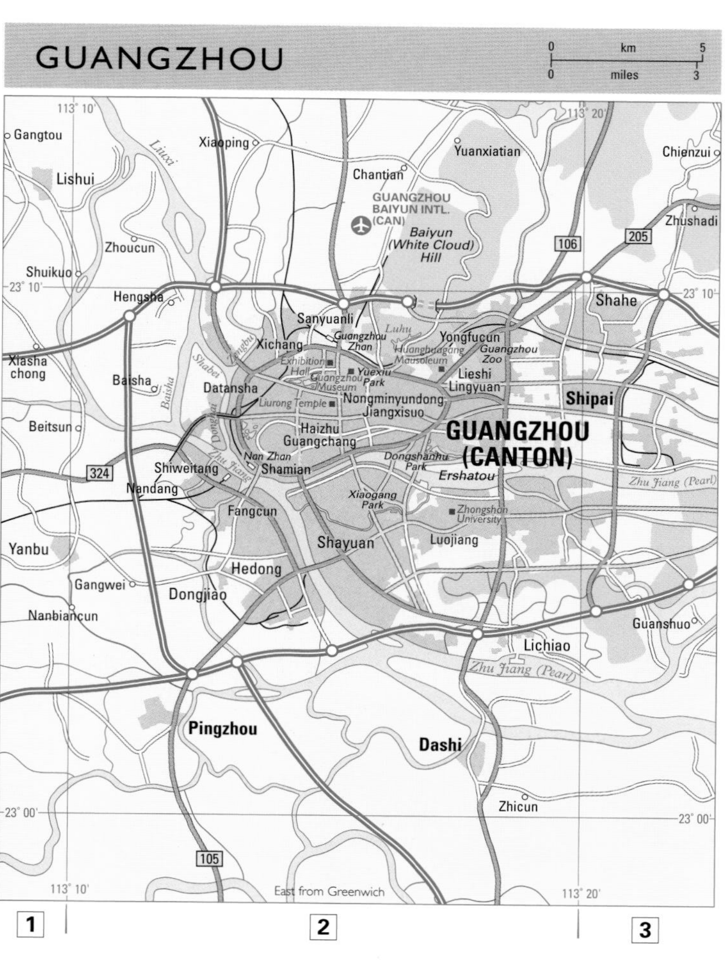

HELSINKI

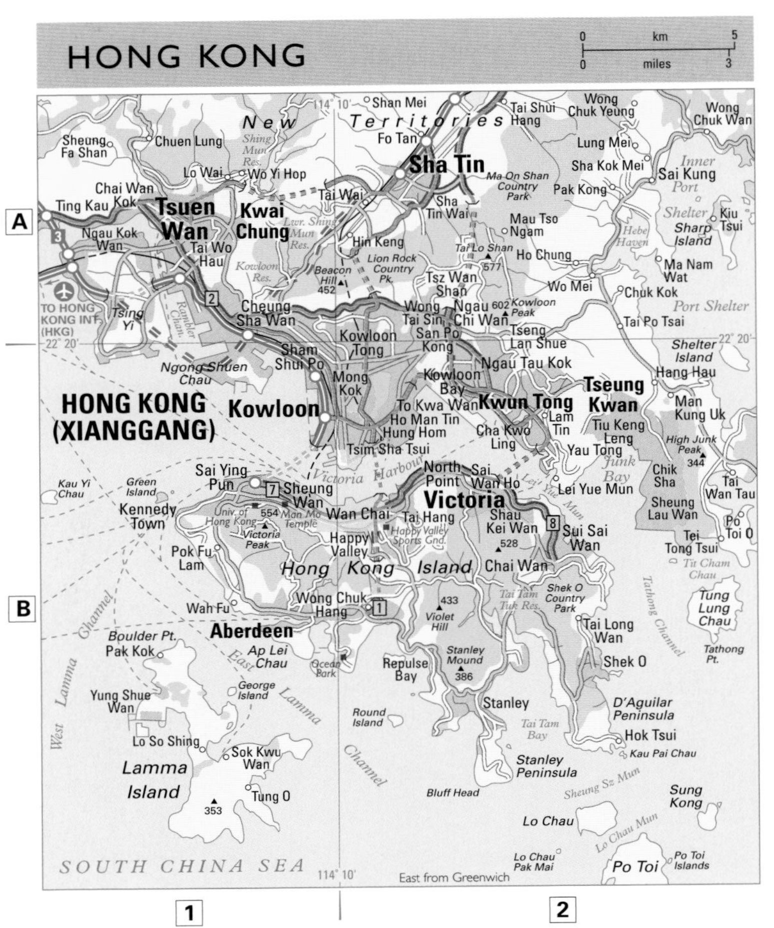
HONG KONG
0 km 5
0 miles 3
New Territories
Shan Mei
Tai Shui Hang
Wong Chuk Yeung
Wong Chuk Wan
Sheung Fa Shan
Chuen Lung
Shing Mun Res.
Fo Tan
Sha Tin
Luk Mei
Sha Kok Mei
Inner Port Shelter
Sai Kung
Lo Wai
Wo Yi Hop
Ma On Shan Country Park
Pak Kong
Chai Wan Kok
Ting Kau
Tsuen Wan
Kwai Chung
Tai Wai
Sha Tin Wai
Mau Tso Ngam
Kiu Tsui
Sharp Island
Ngau Kok Wan
Tai Wo Hau
Hin Keng
Lion Rock Country Pk.
Tai Lo Shan
Ho Chung
Hebe Haven
Ma Nam Wat
Kowloon Res.
Beacon Hill 452
Tsz Wan Shan
Wo Mei
Chuk Kok
Port Shelter
TO HONG KONG INT. (HKG)
Tsing Yi
Cheung Sha Wan
Wong Tai Sin
Ngau Chi Wan
Kowloon Peak 602
Tai Po Tsai
San Po Kong
Tseng Lan Shue
Shelter Island
Sham Shui Po
Kowloon Tong
Ngau Tau Kok
Ngong Shuen Chau
Mong Kok
Kowloon Bay
Tseung Kwan
Hang Hau
HONG KONG (XIANGGANG)
Kowloon
To Kwa Wan
Kwun Tong
Man Kung Uk
Ho Man Tin
Hung Hom
Cha Kwo Ling
Lam Tin
Tiu Keng Leng
Tsim Sha Tsui
Yau Tong
Junk Bay
High Junk Peak 344
Sai Ying Pun
North Point
Sai Wan Ho
Chik Sha
Tai Wan Tau
Kau Yi Chau
Green Island
Sheung Wan
Victoria Harbour
Victoria
Lei Yue Mun
Kennedy Town
Wan Chai
Tai Hang
Shau Kei Wan
Sheung Lau Wan
Po Toi O
Victoria Peak 554
Happy Valley
Sui Sai Wan
Tei Tong Tsui
Pok Fu Lam
Hong Kong Island
Chai Wan
Tit Cham Chau
Wah Fu
Wong Chuk Hang
433
Violet Hill
Shek O Country Park
Tung Lung Chau
Boulder Pt.
Pak Kok
Aberdeen
Ap Lei Chau
Ocean Park
Tai Long Wan
Tathong Pt.
Repulse Bay
Stanley Mound 386
Shek O
Yung Shue Wan
George Island
Stanley
D'Aguilar Peninsula
Round Island
Tai Tam Bay
Hok Tsui
Lo So Shing
Sok Kwu Wan
Stanley Peninsula
Kau Pai Chau
Lamma Island
Tung O
353
Bluff Head
Sung Kong
Lo Chau
Lo Chau Pak Mai
Po Toi
Po Toi Islands
SOUTH CHINA SEA
West Lamma Channel
East Lamma Channel
Tathong Channel
114° 10'
22° 20'
East from Greenwich
A
B
1
2

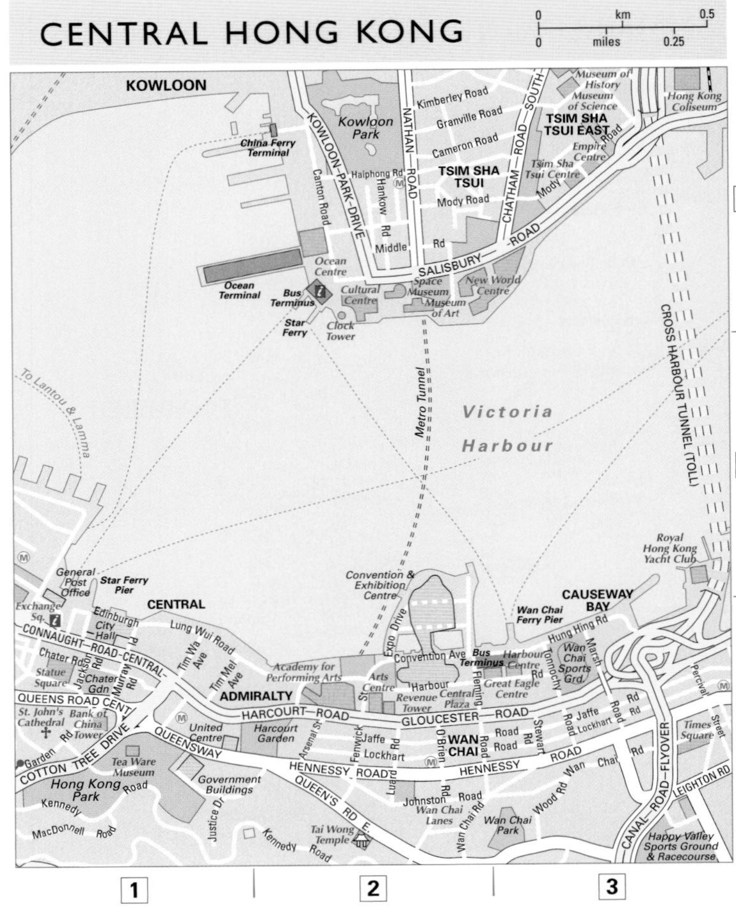
CENTRAL HONG KONG
0 km 0.5
0 miles 0.25
KOWLOON
Kowloon Park
China Ferry Terminal
Kimberley Road
Granville Road
Cameron Road
Museum of History
Museum of Science
Hong Kong Coliseum
TSIM SHA TSUI EAST
TSIM SHA TSUI
Mody Road
Tsim Sha Tsui Centre
Empire Centre
Haiphong Rd
Canton Road
KOWLOON PARK DRIVE
NATHAN ROAD
CHATHAM ROAD SOUTH
SALISBURY ROAD
Middle Rd
Ocean Centre
Ocean Terminal
Bus Terminus
Cultural Centre
Space Museum
Museum of Art
New World Centre
Star Ferry
Clock Tower
CROSS HARBOUR TUNNEL (TOLL)
Metro Tunnel
Victoria Harbour
To Lantau & Lamma
Royal Hong Kong Yacht Club
General Post Office
Star Ferry Pier
Convention & Exhibition Centre
CAUSEWAY BAY
Wan Chai Ferry Pier
CENTRAL
Exchange Sq.
Edinburgh
City Hall
Chater Rd
Statue Square
Chater Gdn
CONNAUGHT ROAD CENTRAL
Lung Wui Road
Tim Wa Ave
Tim Mei Ave
Academy for Performing Arts
Arts Centre
Harbour Centre
Great Eagle Centre
Wan Chai Sports Grd.
ADMIRALTY
QUEENS ROAD CENT
St. John's Cathedral
Bank of China Tower
HARCOURT ROAD
GLOUCESTER ROAD
United Centre
Harcourt Garden
Lockhart
WAN CHAI
Times Square
COTTON TREE DRIVE
QUEENSWAY
Tea Ware Museum
HENNESSY ROAD
Hong Kong Park
Government Buildings
Johnston Road
Wan Chai Lanes
Wan Chai Park
Kennedy Road
MacDonnell Road
Justice Dr
Tai Wong Temple
CANAL ROAD FLYOVER
Happy Valley Sports Ground & Racecourse
1
2
3

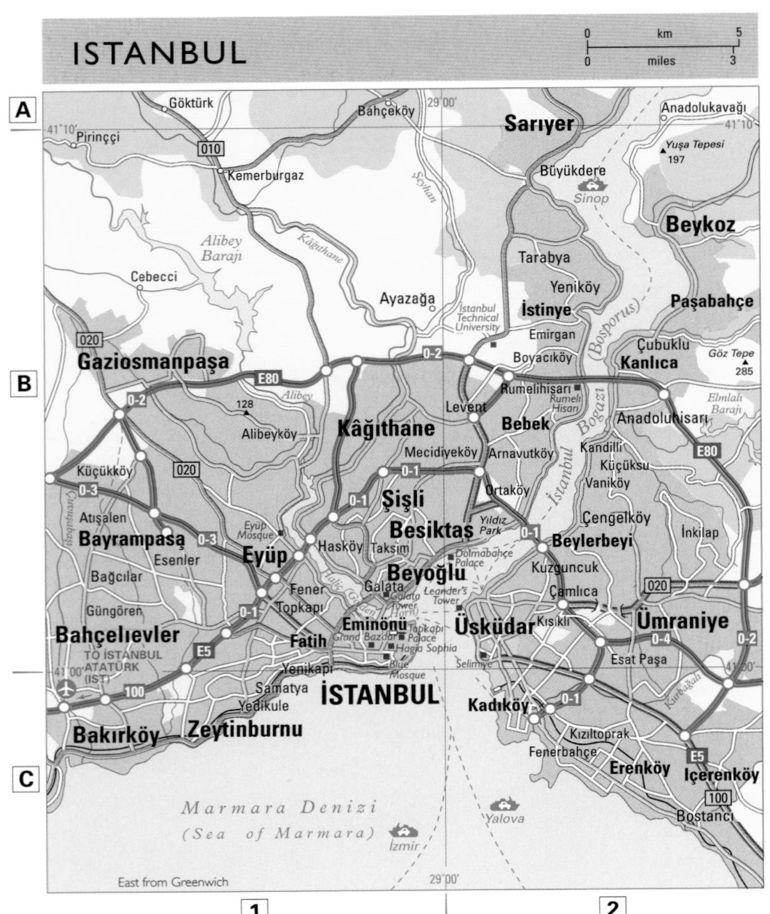
ISTANBUL
0 km 5
0 miles 3
A
B
C
Göktürk
Bahçeköy
Sarıyer
Anadolukavağı
Pirinççi
010
Kemerburgaz
Yuşa Tepesi 197
Büyükdere
Sinop
Beykoz
Alibey Barajı
Kâğıthane
Tarabya
Cebecci
Yeniköy
Ayazağa
İstanbul Technical University
İstinye
Paşabahçe
Emirgan
020
Gaziosmanpaşa
Boyacıköy
Çubuklu
Kanlıca
Göz Tepe 285
E80
Rumelihisarı
Levent
Bebek
Anadoluhisarı
Alibeyköy
Kâğıthane
Kandilli
Küçükköy
Mecidiyeköy
Arnavutköy
Küçüksu
Vaniköy
Ortaköy
Şişli
Besiktaş
Yıldız Park
Çengelköy
Atışalen
Bayrampaşa
Eyüp
Hasköy
Taksim
Beylerbeyi
İnkilap
Esenler
Bağcılar
Beyoğlu
Dolmabahçe Palace
Kuzguncuk
Fener
Galata
Leander's Tower
Çamlıca
Güngören
Topkapı
Bahçelıevler
Eminönü
Grand Bazaar
Topkapı Palace
Üsküdar
Kısıklı
Ümraniye
Fatih
Hagia Sophia
Esat Paşa
TO İSTANBUL ATATÜRK (IST)
Yenikapı
Samatya
İSTANBUL
Kadıköy
Yedikule
Bakırköy
Zeytinburnu
Kızıltoprak
Fenerbahçe
Erenköy
İçerenköy
Marmara Denizi (Sea of Marmara)
İzmir
Yalova
Bostancı
İstanbul Boğazı (Bosporus)
East from Greenwich
29° 00'
41° 10'
1
2

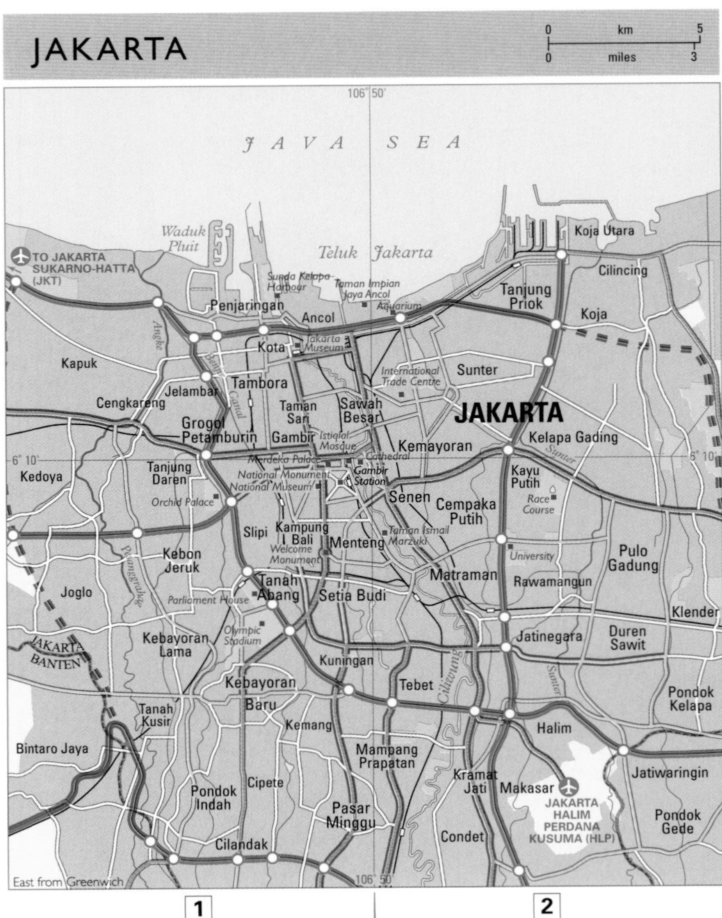
JAKARTA
0 km 5
0 miles 3
106° 50'
JAVA SEA
Waduk Pluit
Teluk Jakarta
Koja Utara
TO JAKARTA SUKARNO-HATTA (JKT)
Sunda Kelapa Harbour
Taman Impian Jaya Ancol
Cilincing
Penjaringan
Ancol
Aquarium
Tanjung Priok
Koja
Kota
Jakarta Museum
Kapuk
International Trade Centre
Sunter
Tambora
Jelambar
Cengkareng
Taman Sari
Sawah Besar
JAKARTA
Grogol Petamburin
Gambir
Istiqlal Mosque
Kelapa Gading
Kemayoran
Merdeka Palace
Cathedral
Tanjung Duren
National Monument
National Museum
Gambir Station
Kayu Putih
Kedoya
Orchid Palace
Senen
Cempaka Putih
Race Course
Slipi
Kampung Bali
Menteng
Taman Ismail Marzuki
Welcome Monument
Kebon Jeruk
University
Pulo Gadung
Matraman
Joglo
Tanah Abang
Parliament House
Setia Budi
Rawamangun
Klender
Kebayoran Lama
Olympic Stadium
Jatinegara
Duren Sawit
Kuningan
Tebet
Kebayoran Baru
Pondok Kelapa
Tanah Kusir
Kemang
Halim
Bintaro Jaya
Mampang Prapatan
Kramat Jati
Makasar
Jatiwaringin
Pondok Indah
Cipete
JAKARTA HALIM PERDANA KUSUMA (HLP)
Pasar Minggu
Pondok Gede
Condet
Cilandak
East from Greenwich
6° 10'
1
2

JERUSALEM

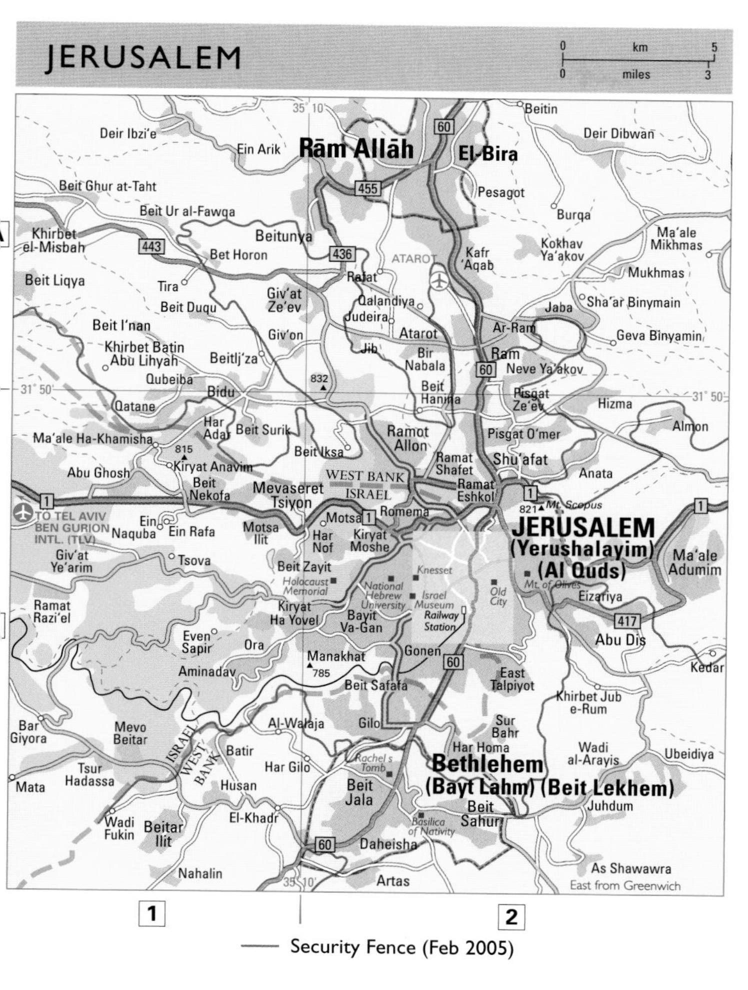

Security Fence (Feb 2005)

CENTRAL JERUSALEM

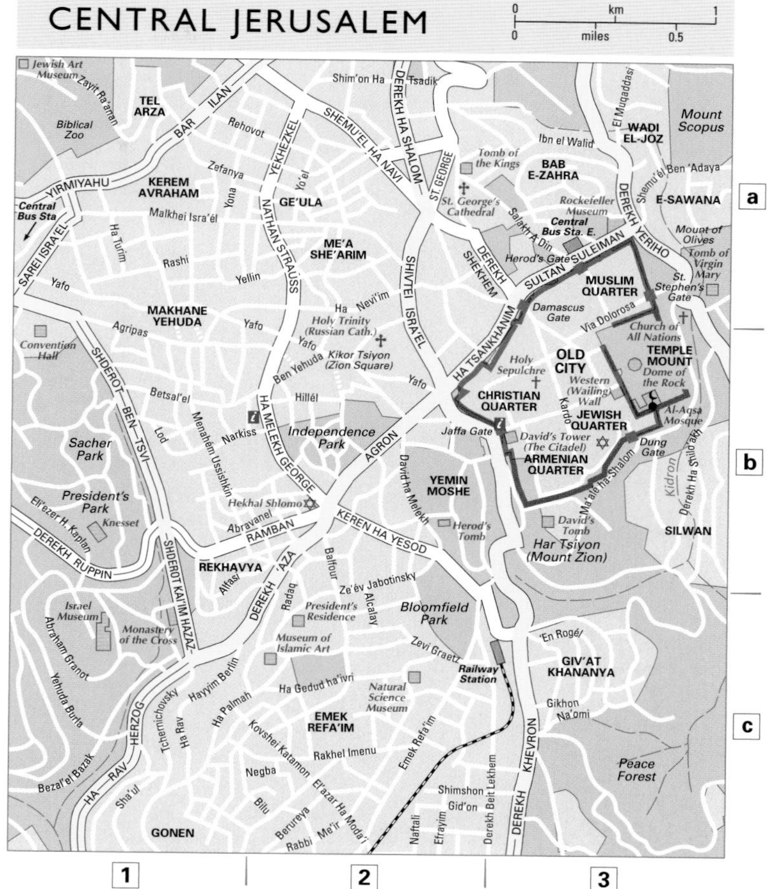

JOHANNESBURG

KARACHI

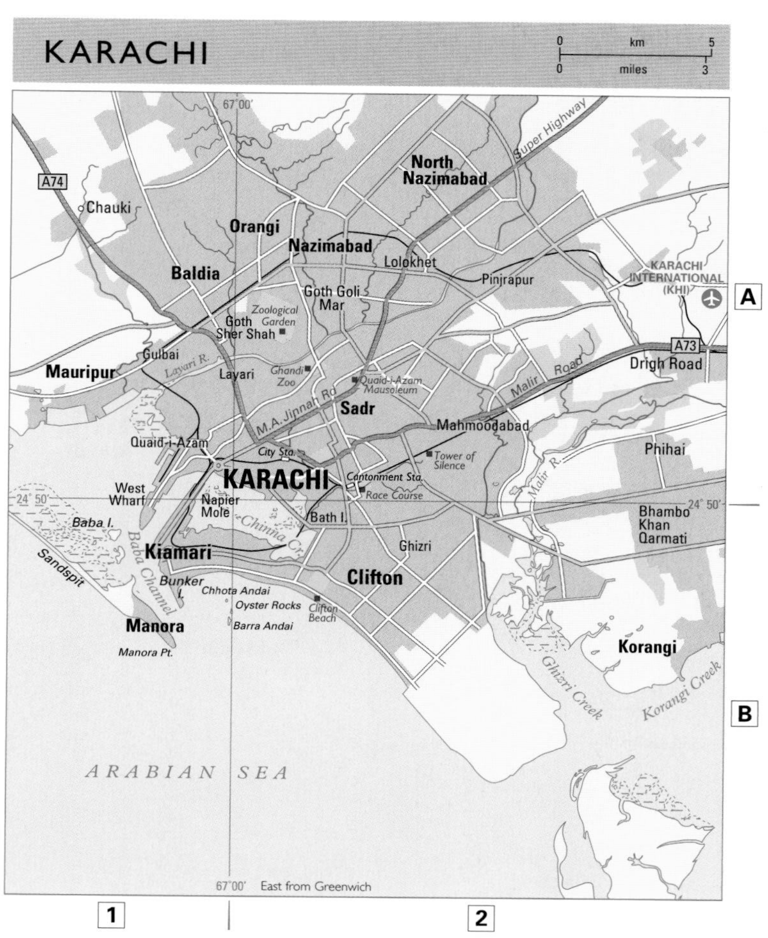

KOLKATA

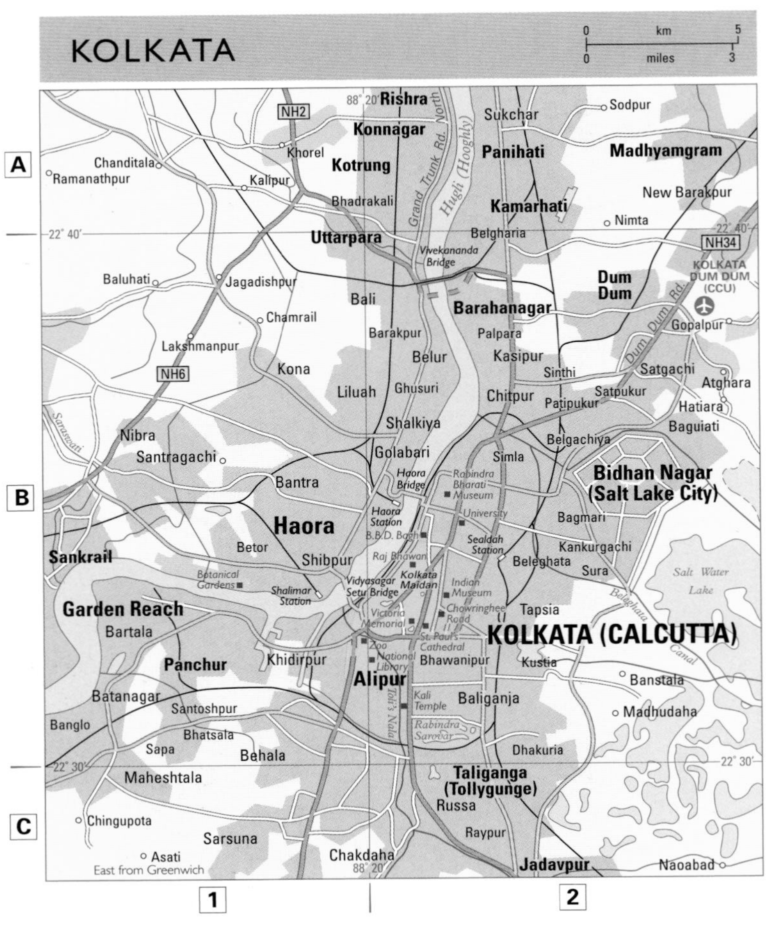

LAGOS

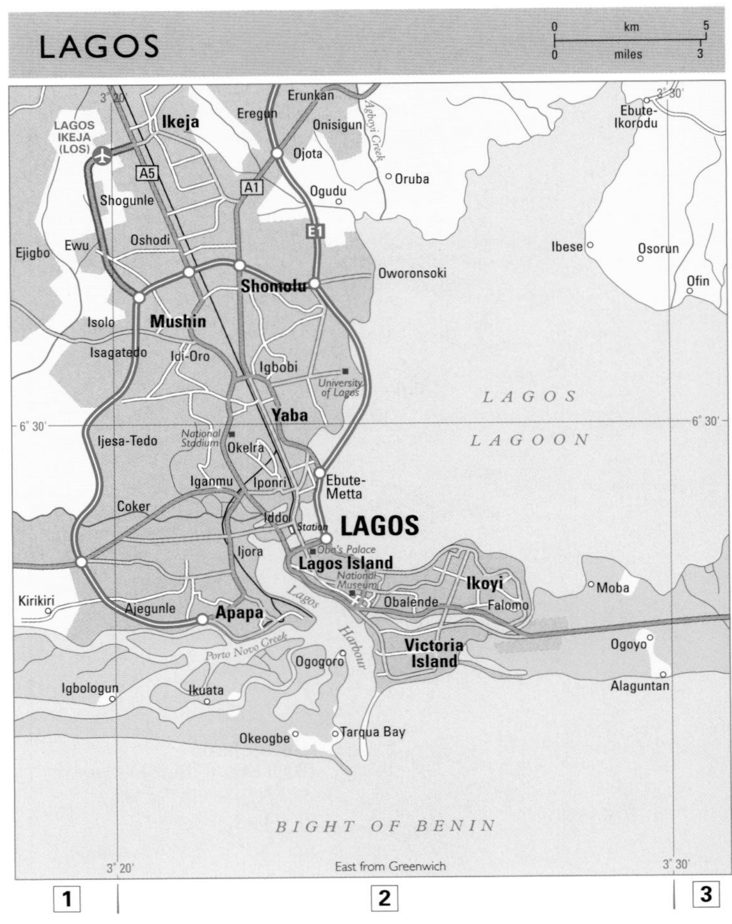

LAS VEGAS

Interstate route numbers   U.S. route numbers   State route numbers

LIMA

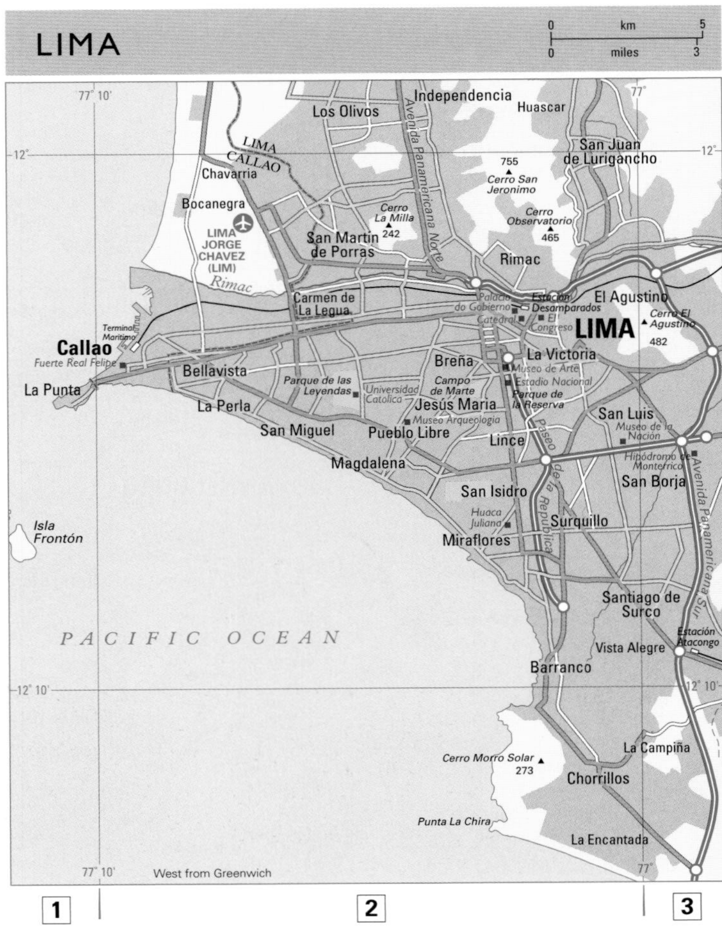

LONDON

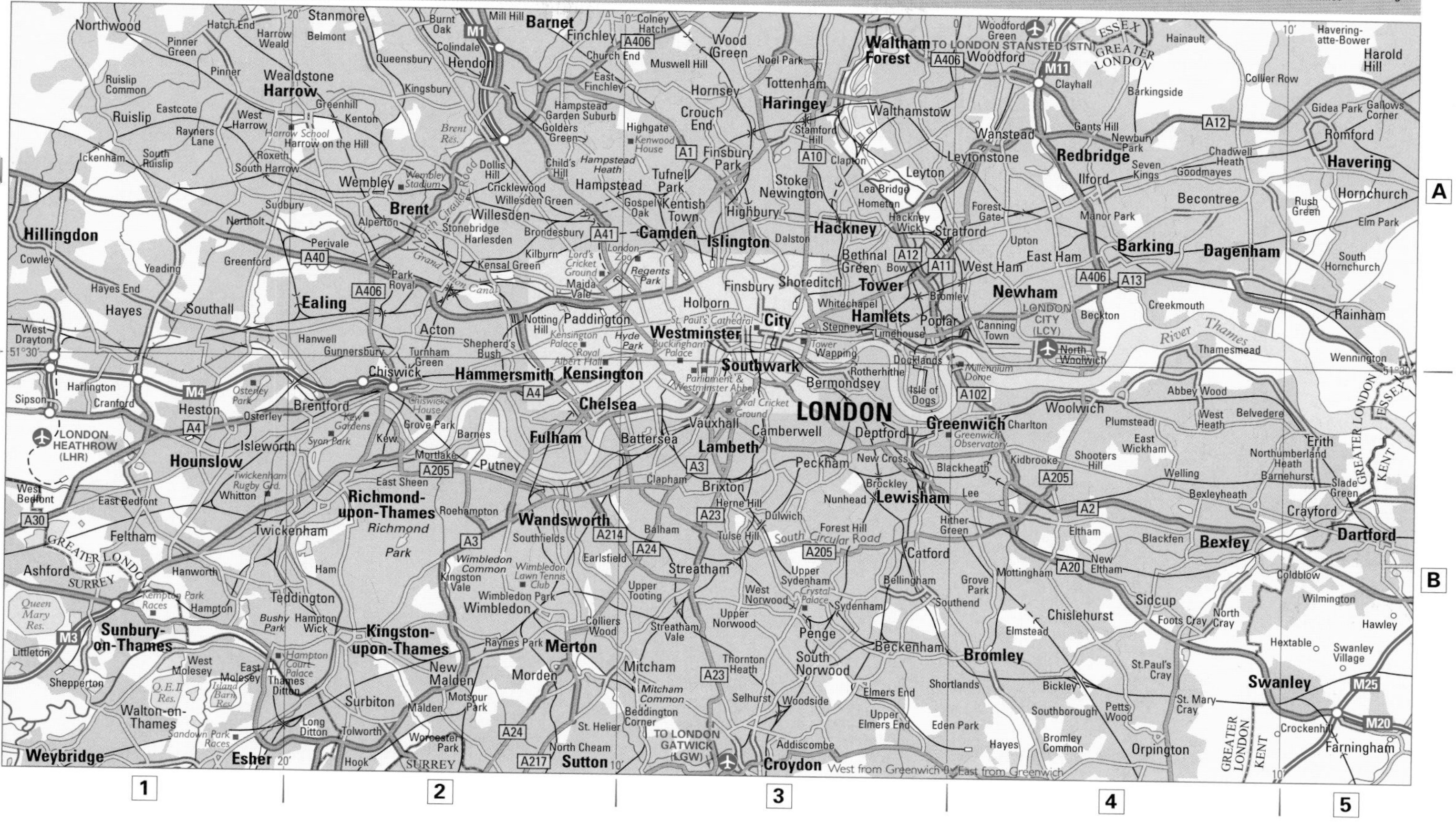

0 km 5
0 miles 3

A
B

1 2 3 4 5

CENTRAL LONDON

0 km 2
0 miles 1

a
b
c

1 2 3 4 5

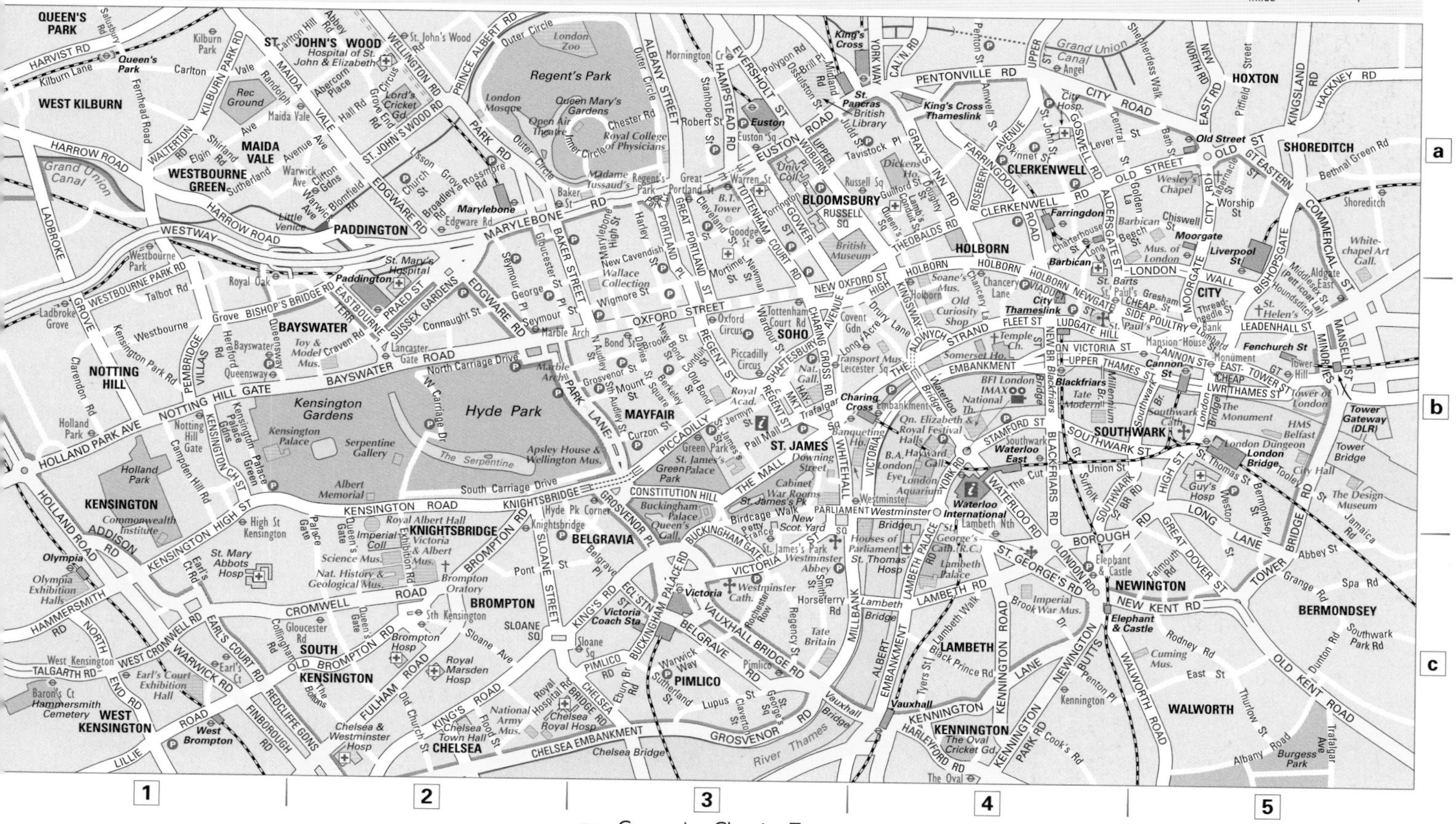

Congestion Charging Zone

LISBON

0 km 5
0 miles 3

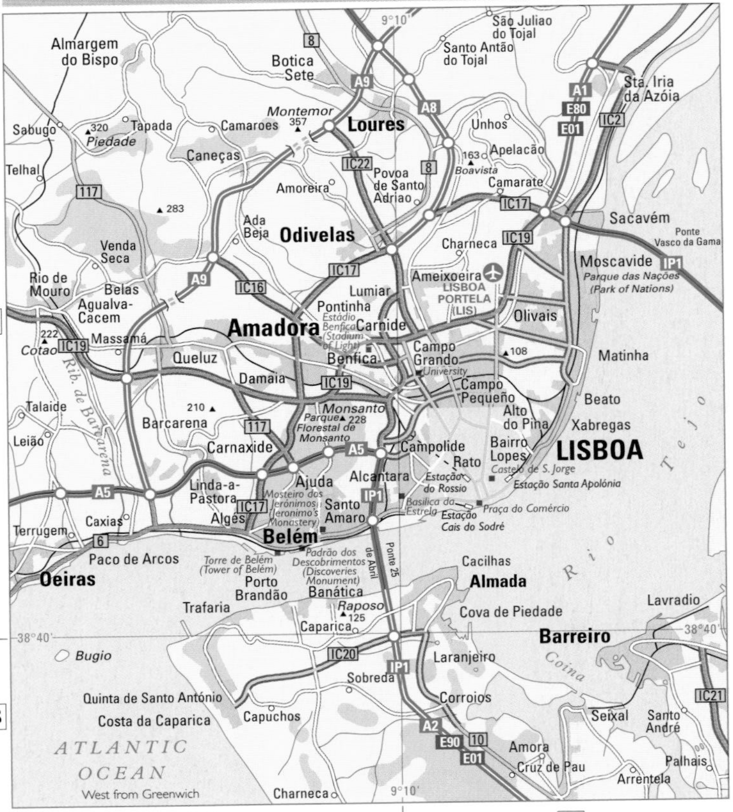

West from Greenwich

CENTRAL LISBON

0 km 1
0 miles 0.5

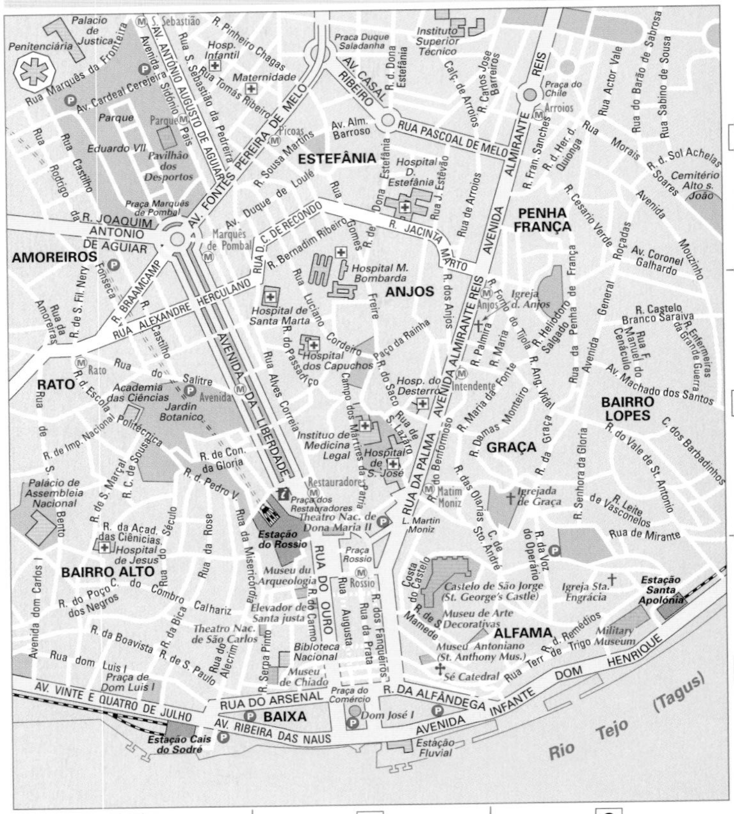

LOS ANGELES

0 km 5
0 miles 3

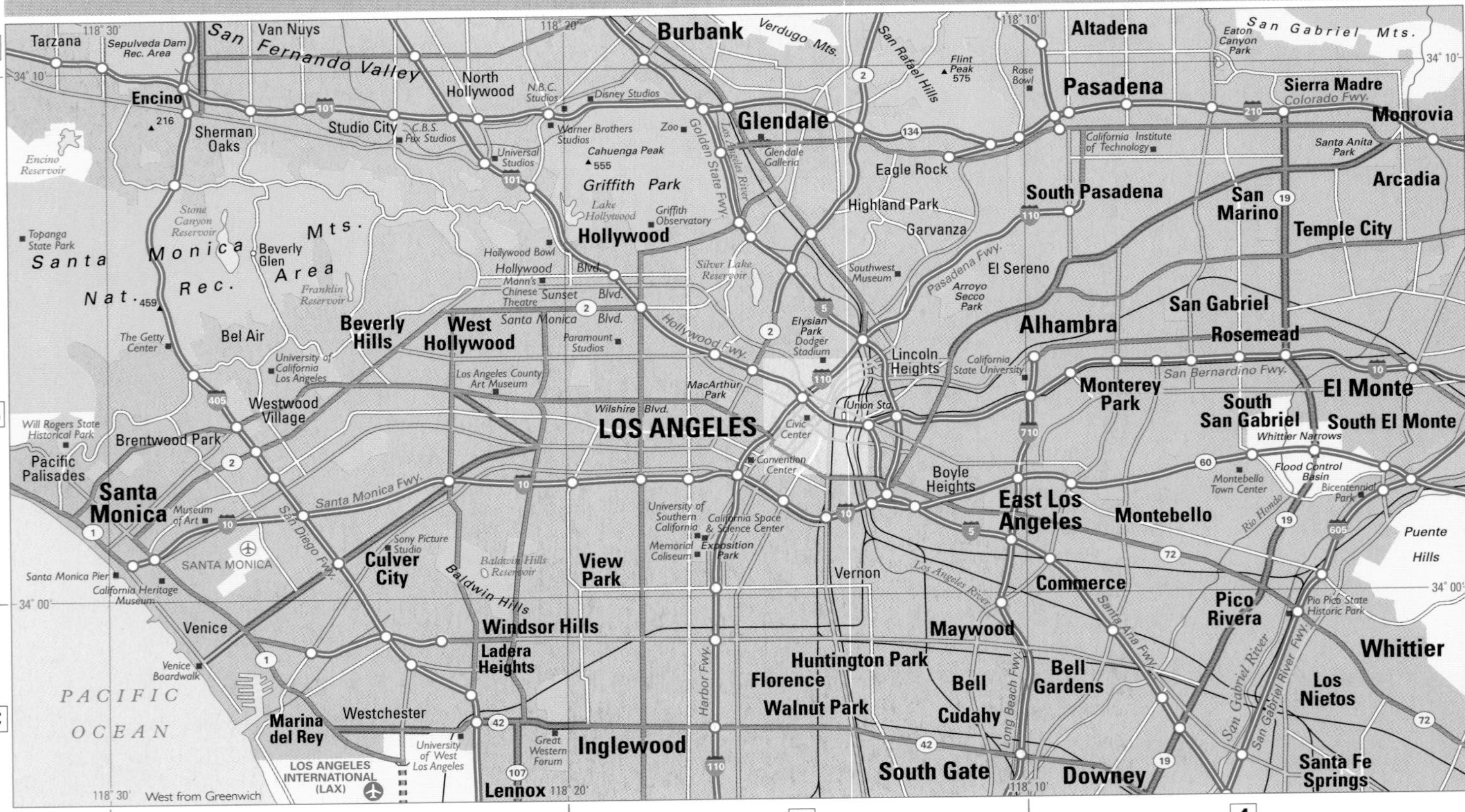

West from Greenwich

Interstate route numbers State route numbers

MADRID

0 km 5
0 miles 3

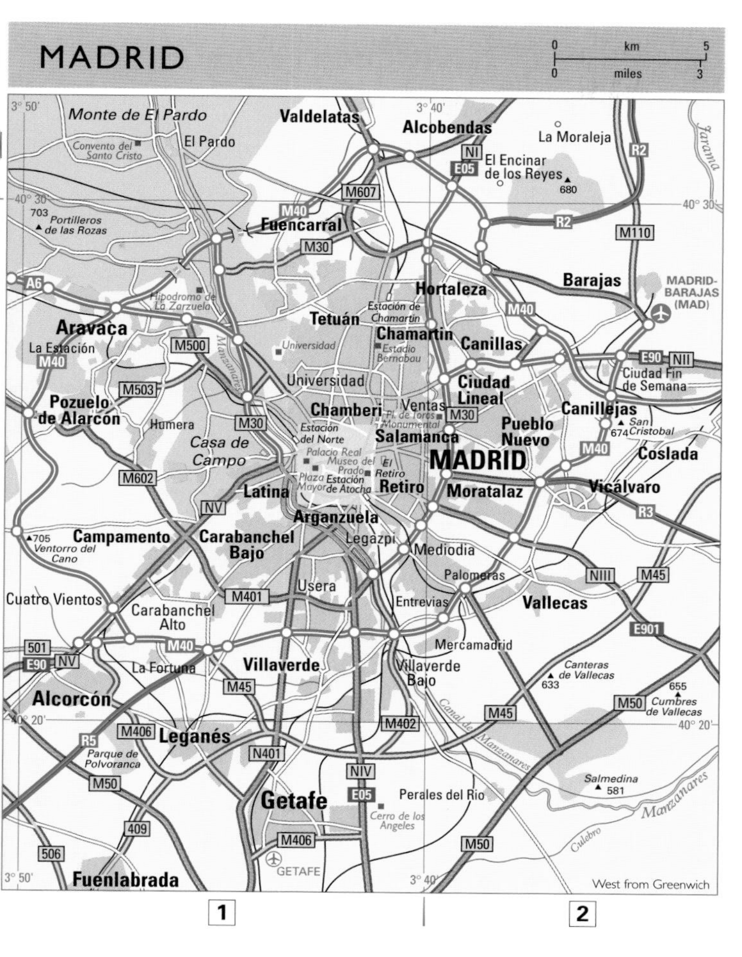

1 2

CENTRAL MADRID

0 km 1
0 miles 0.5

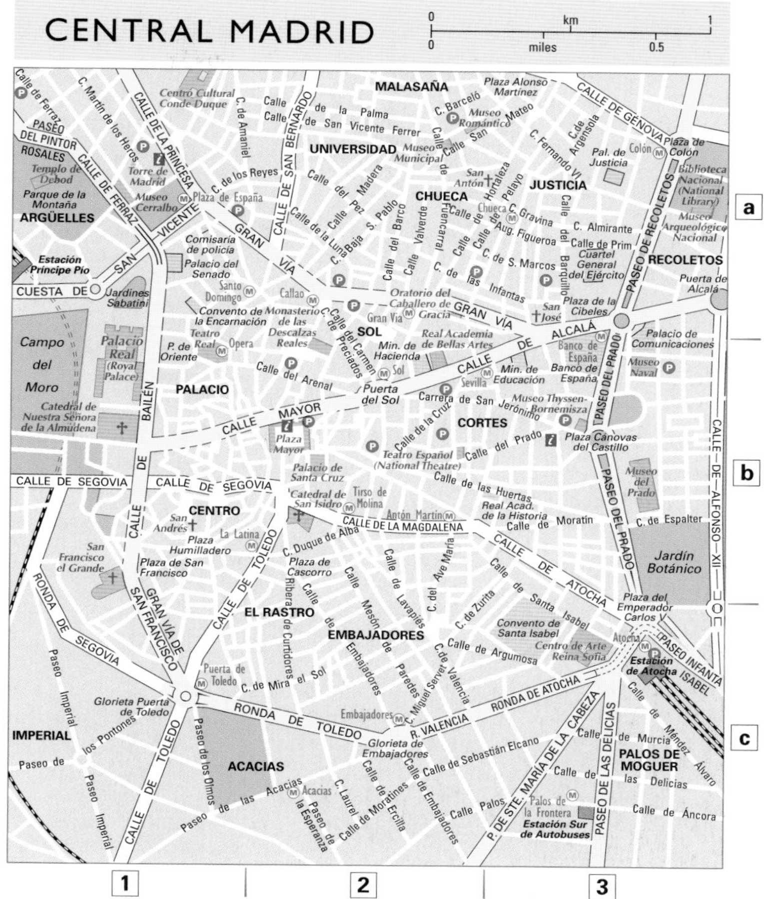

1 2 3

CENTRAL LOS ANGELES

0 km 1
0 miles 0.5

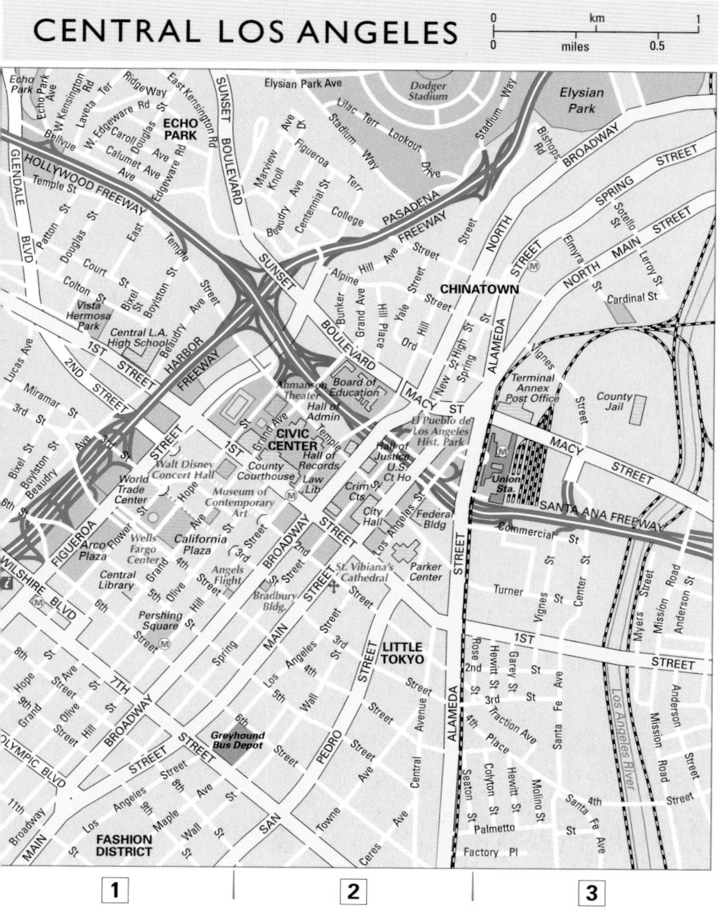

1 2 3

MANILA

0 km 5
0 miles 3

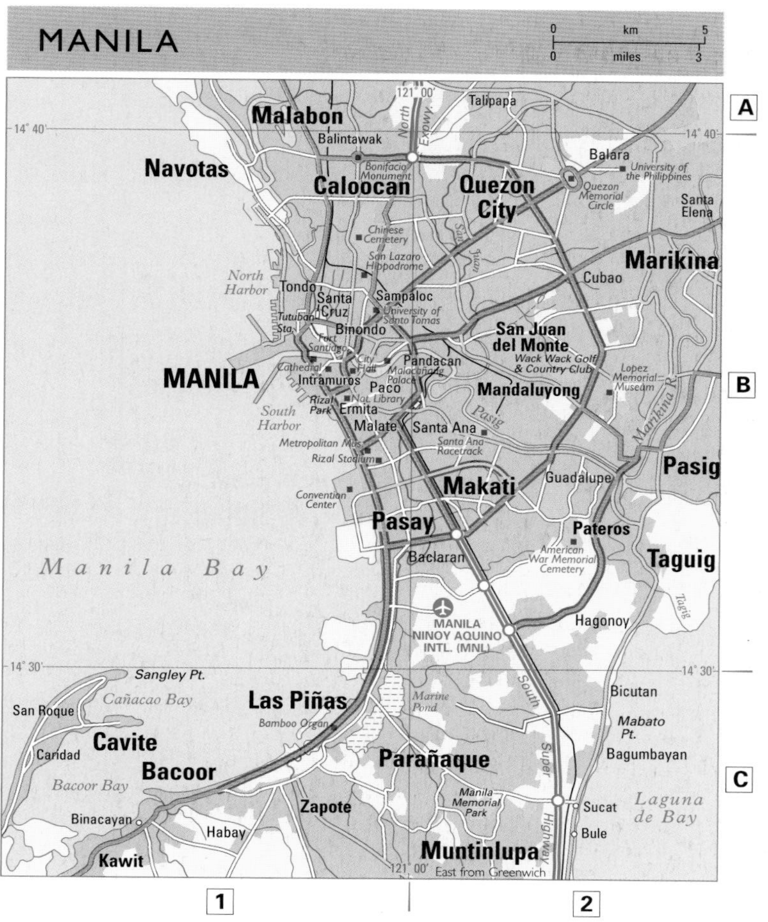

1 2

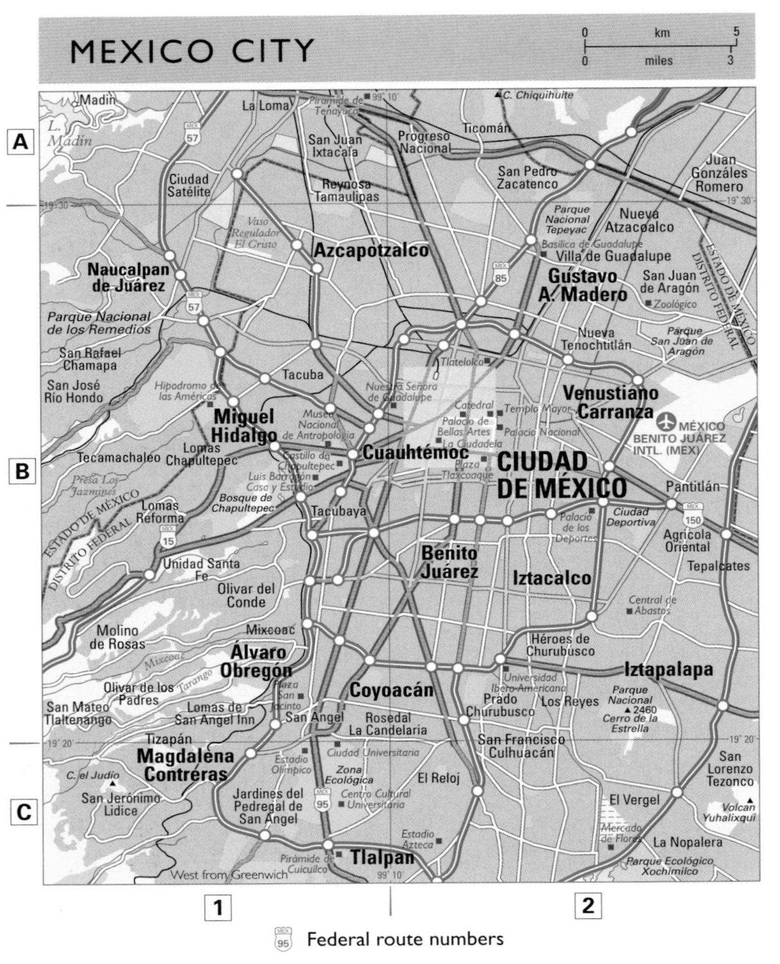

Federal route numbers

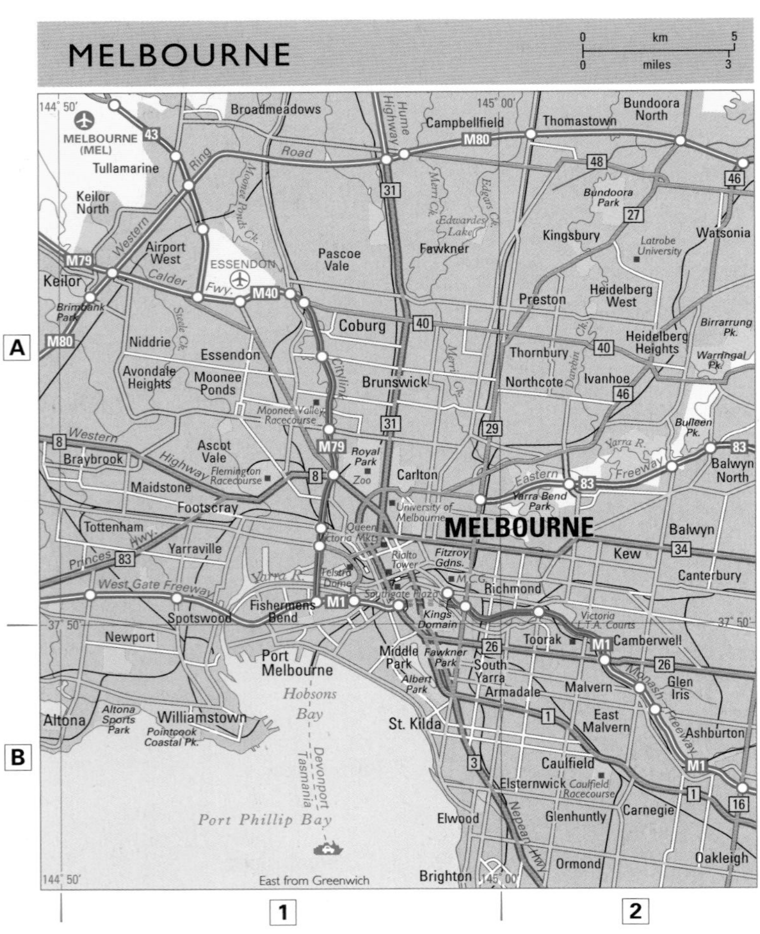

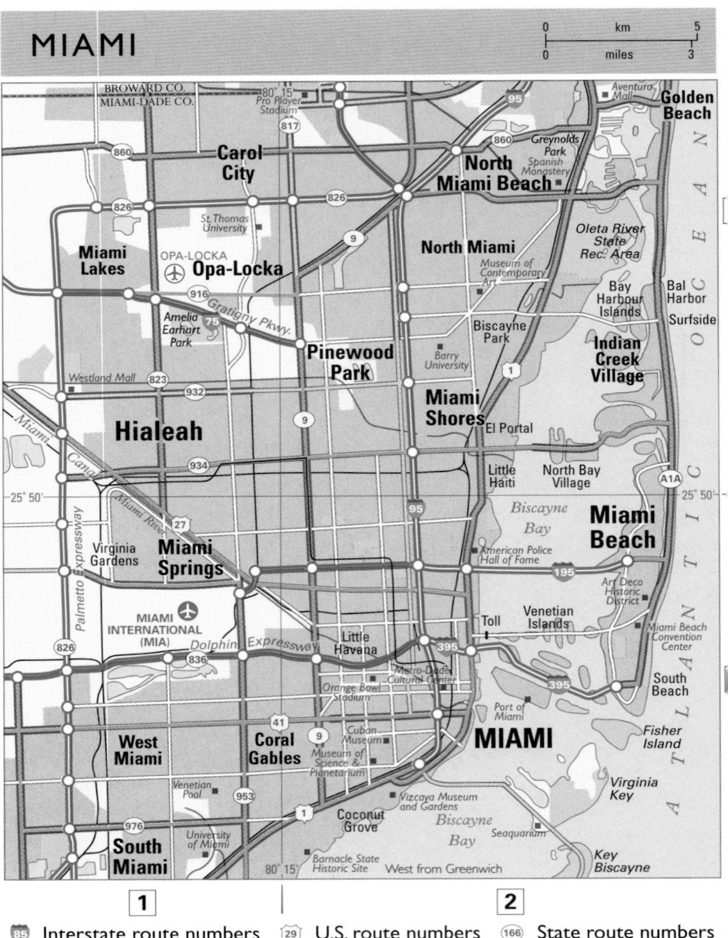

Interstate route numbers | U.S. route numbers | State route numbers

MILAN

0 km 5
0 miles 3

CENTRAL MOSCOW

0 km 1
0 miles 0.5

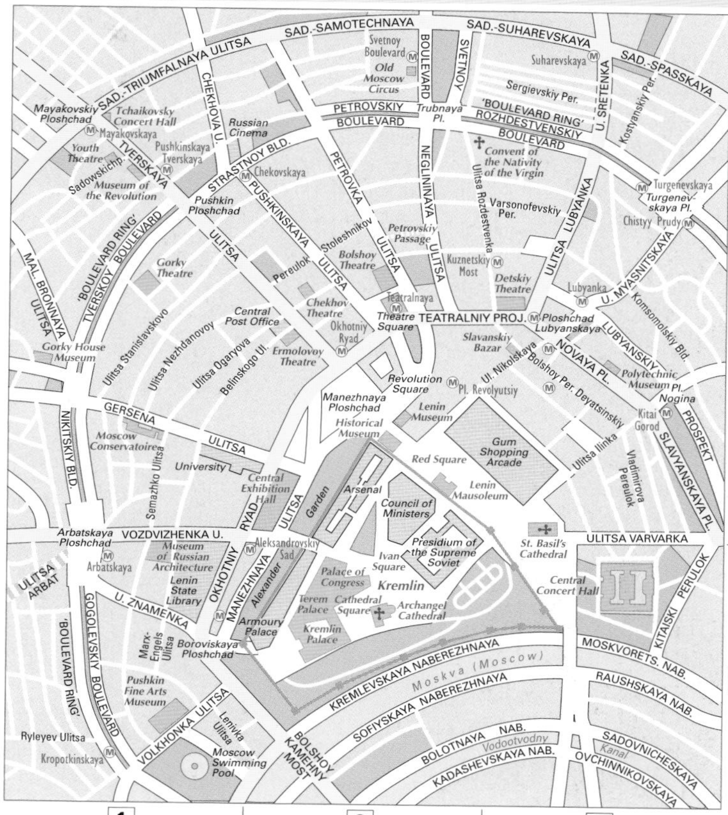

MOSCOW

0 km 5
0 miles 3

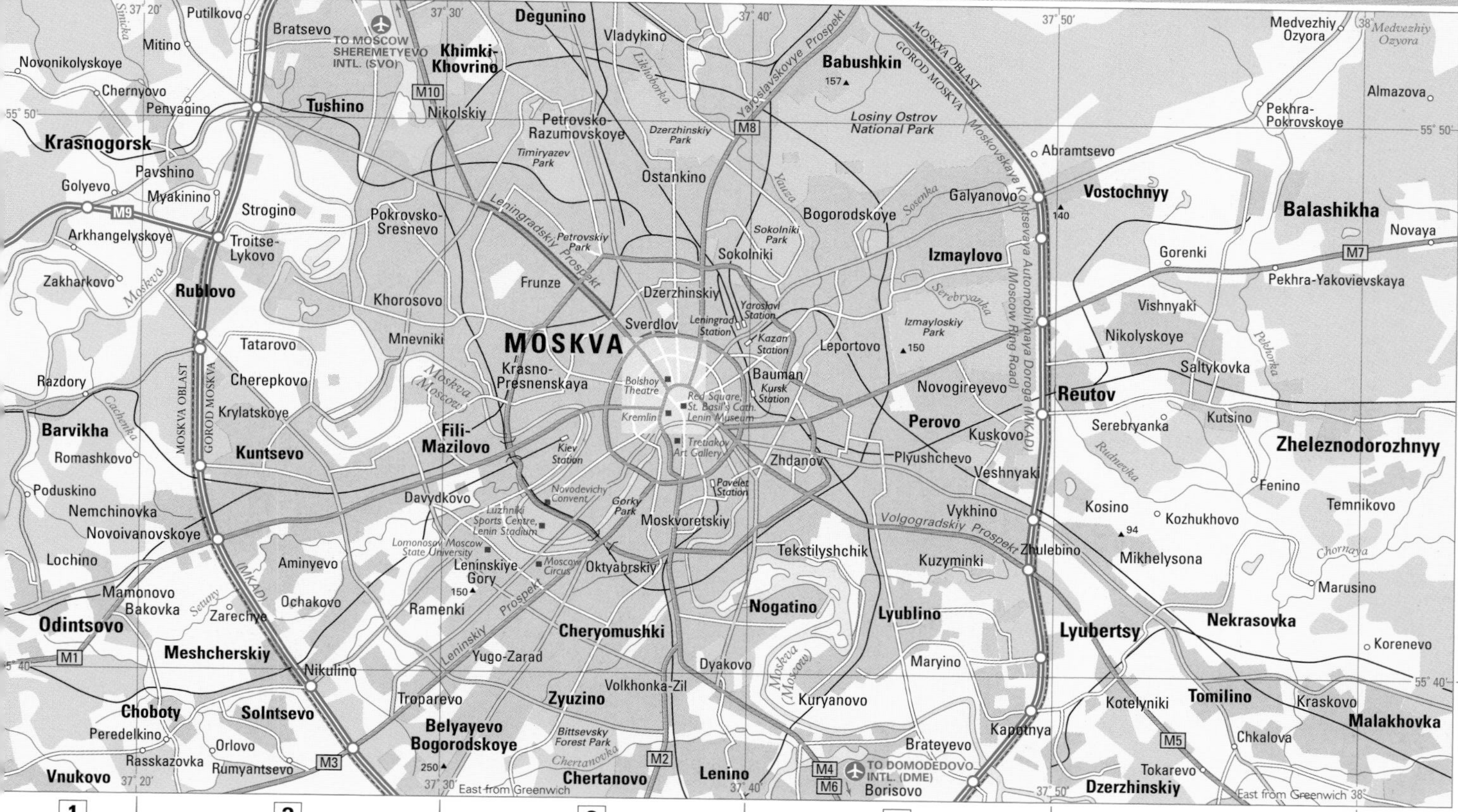

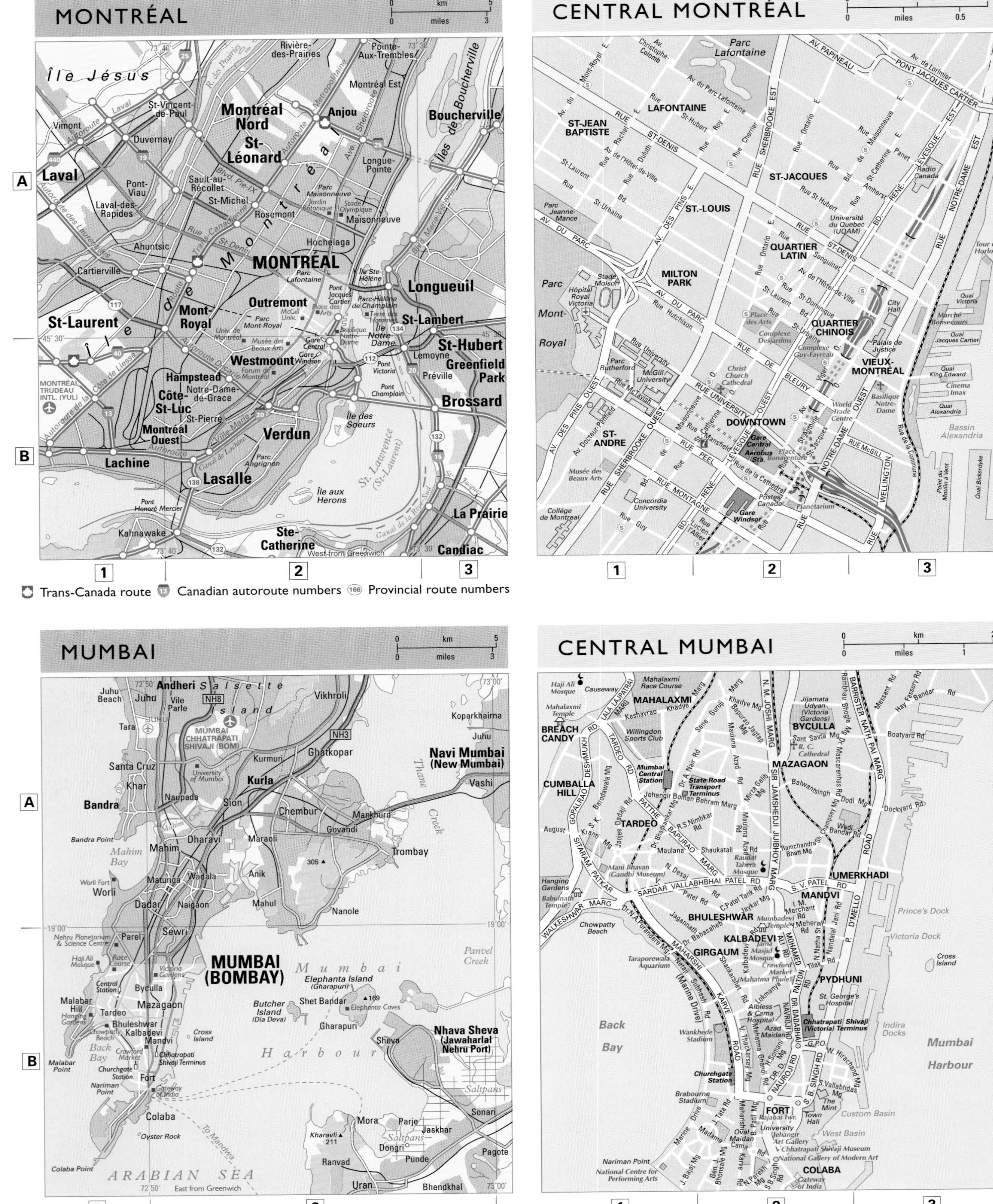
MONTRÉAL
km
miles
Île Jésus
Rivière-des-Prairies
Pointe-Aux-Trembles
Montréal Est
Montréal Nord
Anjou
Boucherville
St-Vincent-de-Paul
Vimont
Duvernay
St-Léonard
Longue-Pointe
Laval
Pont-Viau
Sault-au-Récollet
St-Michel
Laval-des-Rapides
Rosemont
Maisonneuve
Hochelaga
Ahuntsic
Cartierville
MONTRÉAL
Longueuil
Outremont
St-Laurent
Mont-Royal
St-Lambert
Westmount
St-Hubert
Greenfield Park
Lemoyne
Préville
Hampstead
Notre-Dame-de-Grace
Côte-St-Luc
St-Pierre
Brossard
Montréal Ouest
Verdun
Lachine
Lasalle
Île des Soeurs
Île aux Herons
La Prairie
Kahnawake
Ste-Catherine
Candiac
West from Greenwich
MONTRÉAL TRUDEAU INTL. (YUL)
Trans-Canada route
Canadian autoroute numbers
Provincial route numbers
CENTRAL MONTRÉAL
Parc Lafontaine
LAFONTAINE
ST-JEAN BAPTISTE
ST-JACQUES
ST.-LOUIS
QUARTIER LATIN
MILTON PARK
Parc Mont-Royal
QUARTIER CHINOIS
VIEUX-MONTRÉAL
DOWNTOWN
ST-ANDRE
Gare Centrale
Gare Windsor
Concordia University
McGill University
Université du Quebec (UQAM)
Radio Canada
Bassin Alexandria
MUMBAI
Andheri
Salsette Island
Juhu Beach
Juhu
Vile Parle
Vikhroli
Koparkhairna
Tara
MUMBAI CHHATRAPATI SHIVAJI (BOM)
Ghatkopar
Navi Mumbai (New Mumbai)
Santa Cruz
Kurla
Vashi
Khar
Bandra
Sion
Chembur
Mankhurd
Bandra Point
Mahim Bay
Mahim
Dharavi
Trombay
Worli
Matunga
Wadala
Anik
Dadar
Naigaon
Mahul
Nanole
Parel
Sewri
MUMBAI (BOMBAY)
Mumbai Harbour
Elephanta Island (Gharapuri)
Panvel Creek
Malabar Hill
Byculla
Mazagaon
Tardeo
Butcher Island (Dia Deva)
Shet Bandar
Bhuleshwar
Kalbadevi
Mandvi
Cross Island
Gharapuri
Sheva
Nhava Sheva (Jawaharlal Nehru Port)
Malabar Point
Fort
Colaba
Oyster Rock
Colaba Point
ARABIAN SEA
Mora
Sonari
Jaskhar
Dongri
Punde
Pagote
Ranvad
Uran
Bhendkhal
East from Greenwich
CENTRAL MUMBAI
MAHALAXMI
BYCULLA
BREACH CANDY
MAZAGAON
CUMBALLA HILL
TARDEO
UMERKHADI
MANDVI
BHULESHWAR
KALBADEVI
GIRGAUM
PYDHUNI
Back Bay
Mumbai Harbour
Churchgate Station
Chhatrapati Shivaji (Victoria) Terminus
FORT
COLABA
Gateway of India

MUNICH

CENTRAL MUNICH

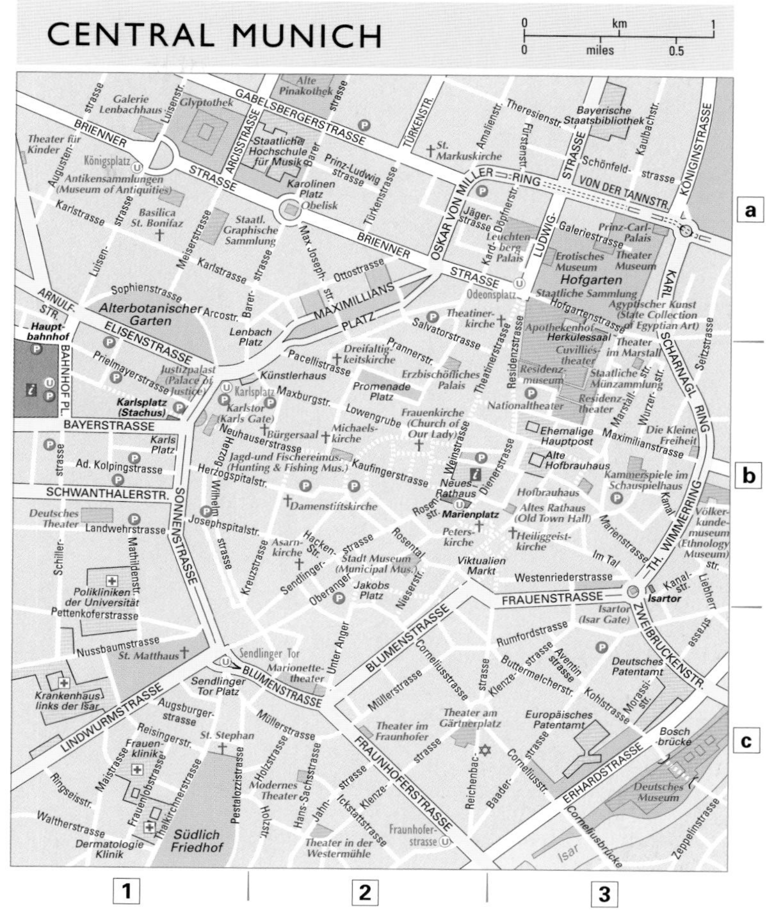

NEW ORLEANS

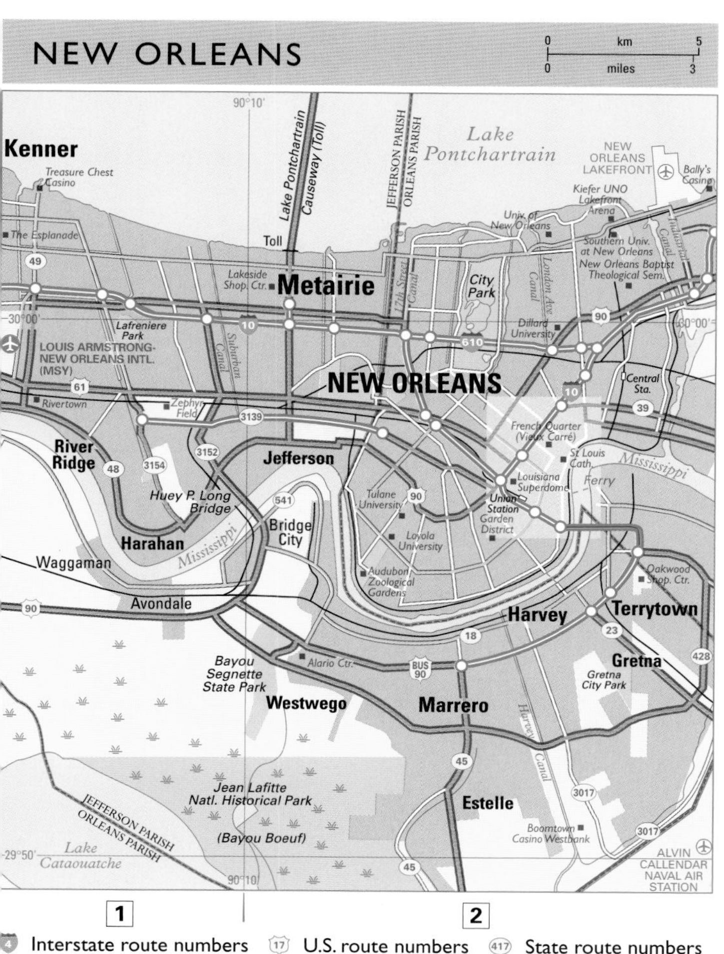

Interstate route numbers U.S. route numbers State route numbers

CENTRAL NEW ORLEANS

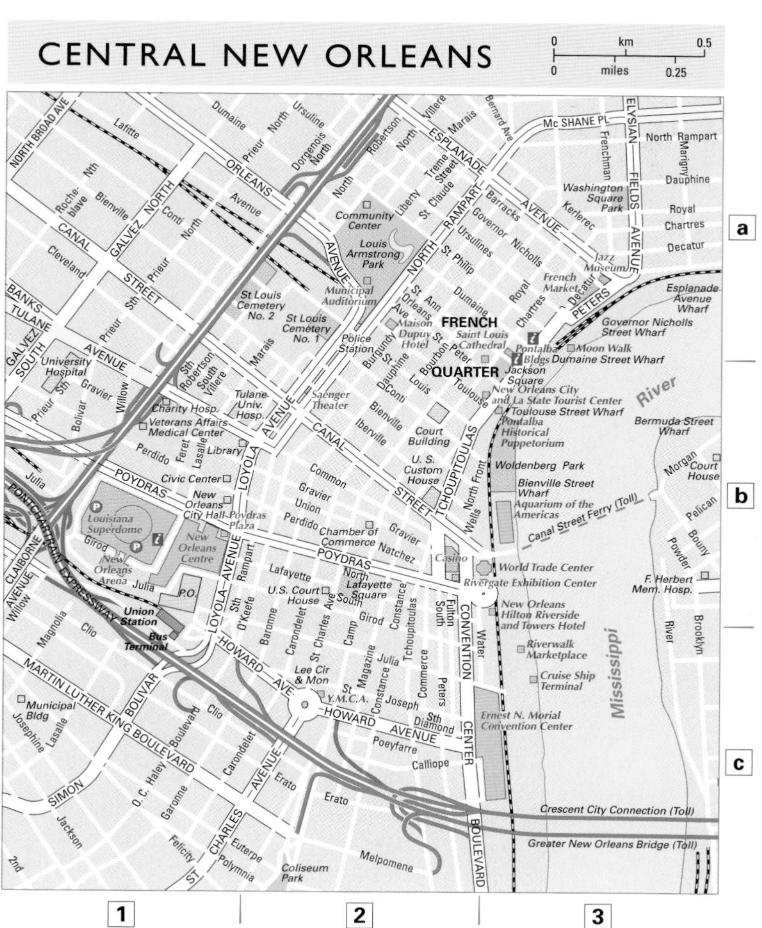

NEW YORK

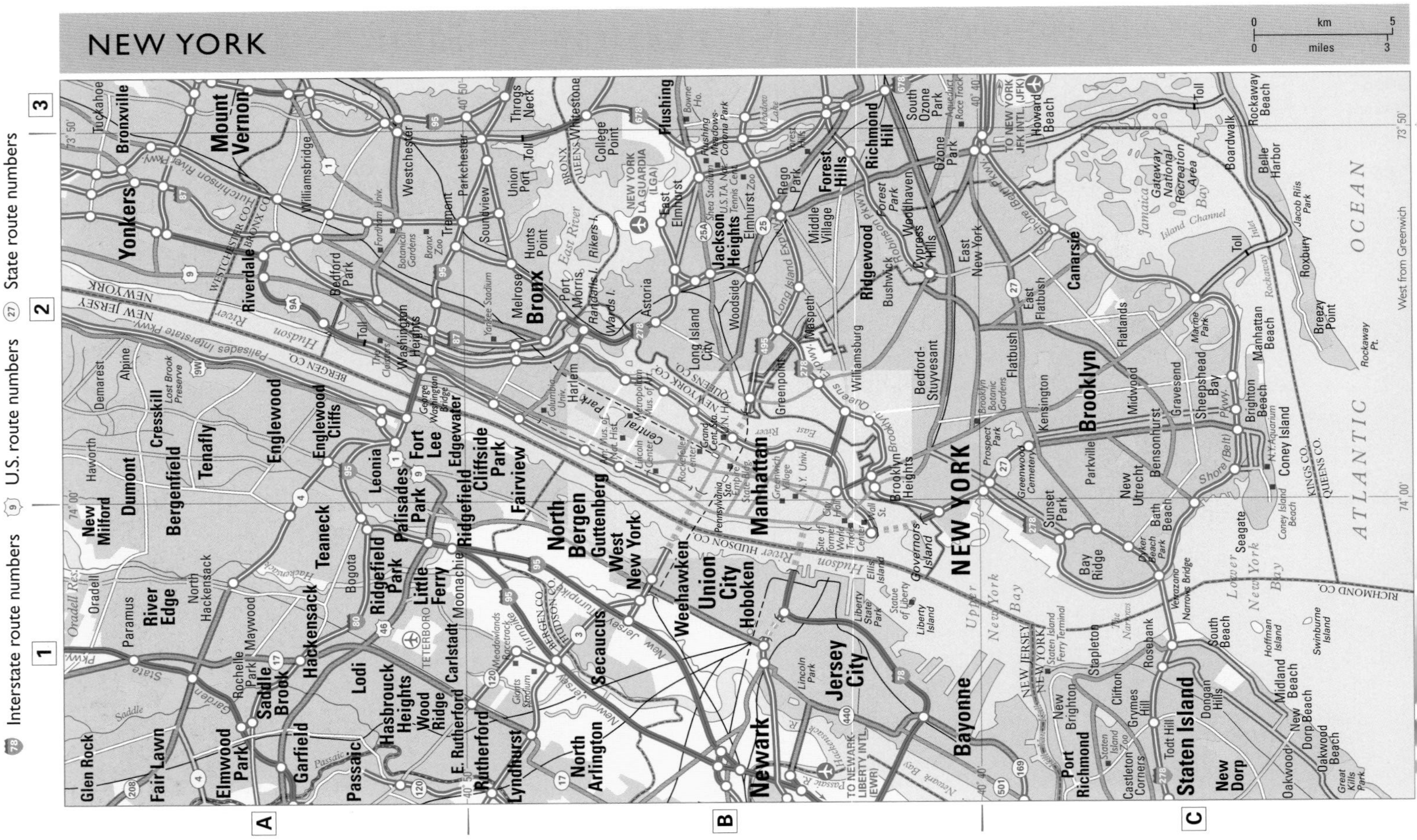

78 Interstate route numbers

9 U.S. route numbers

27 State route numbers

0 km 5

0 miles 3

CENTRAL NEW YORK

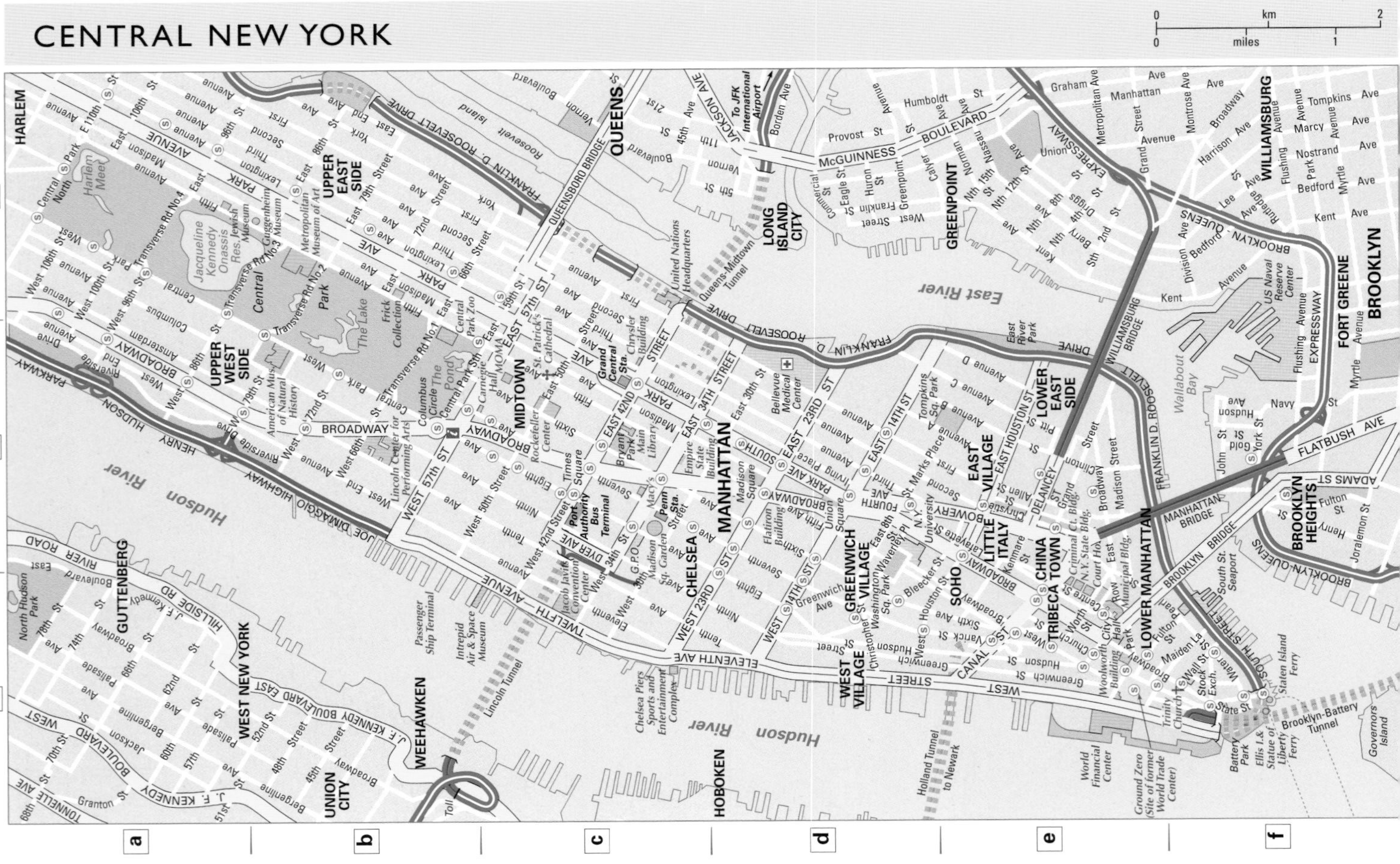

0 km 2

0 miles 1

ORLANDO

Interstate route numbers · U.S. route numbers · State route numbers

OSAKA

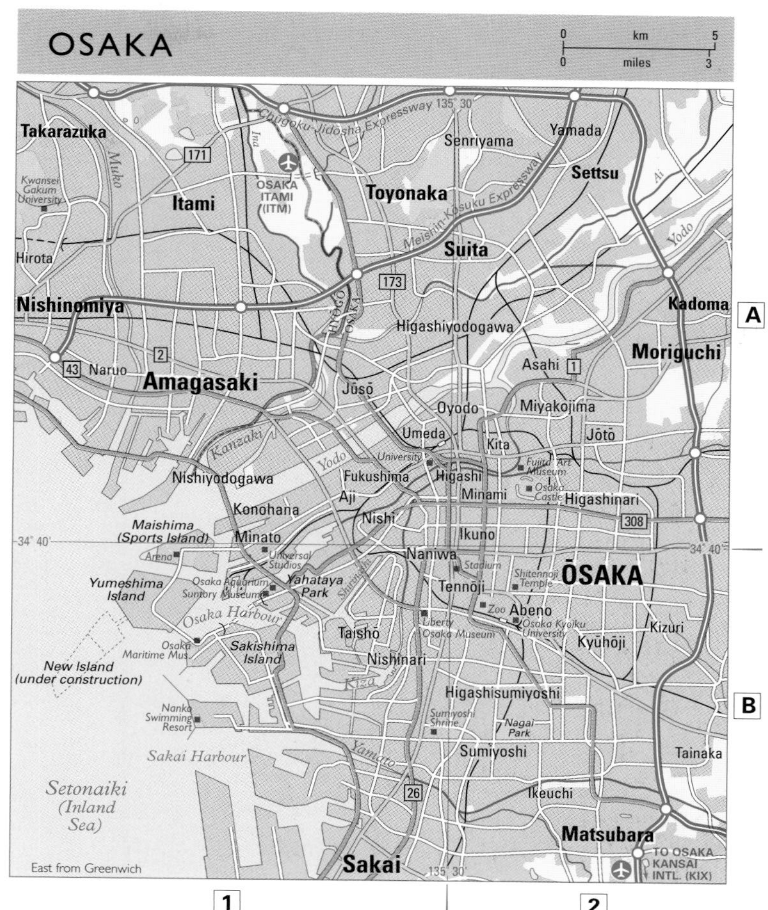

OSLO

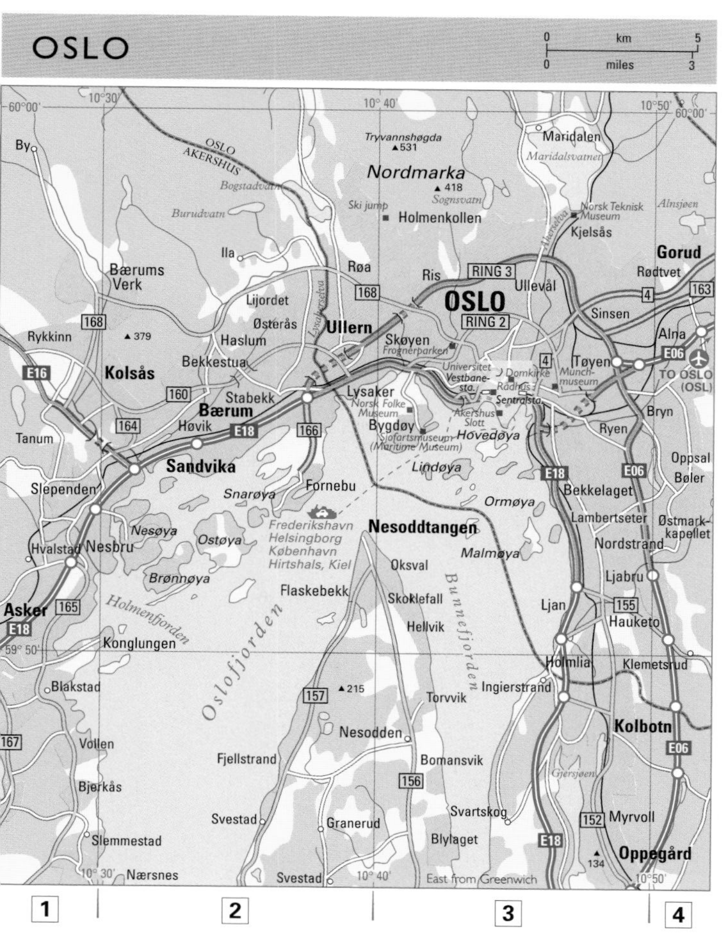

CENTRAL OSLO

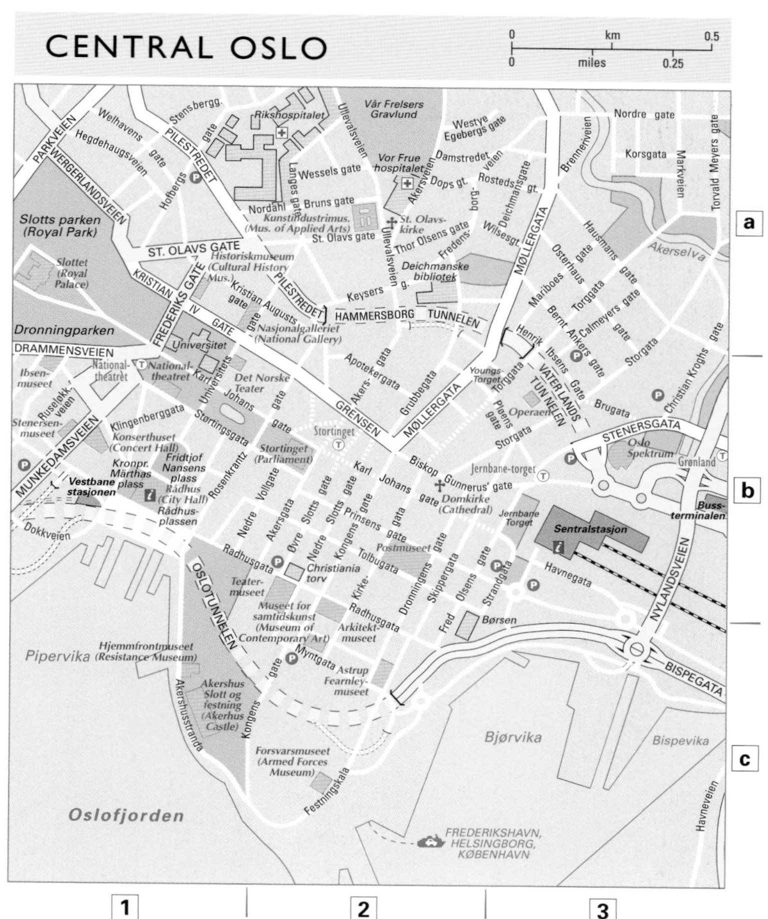

PARIS

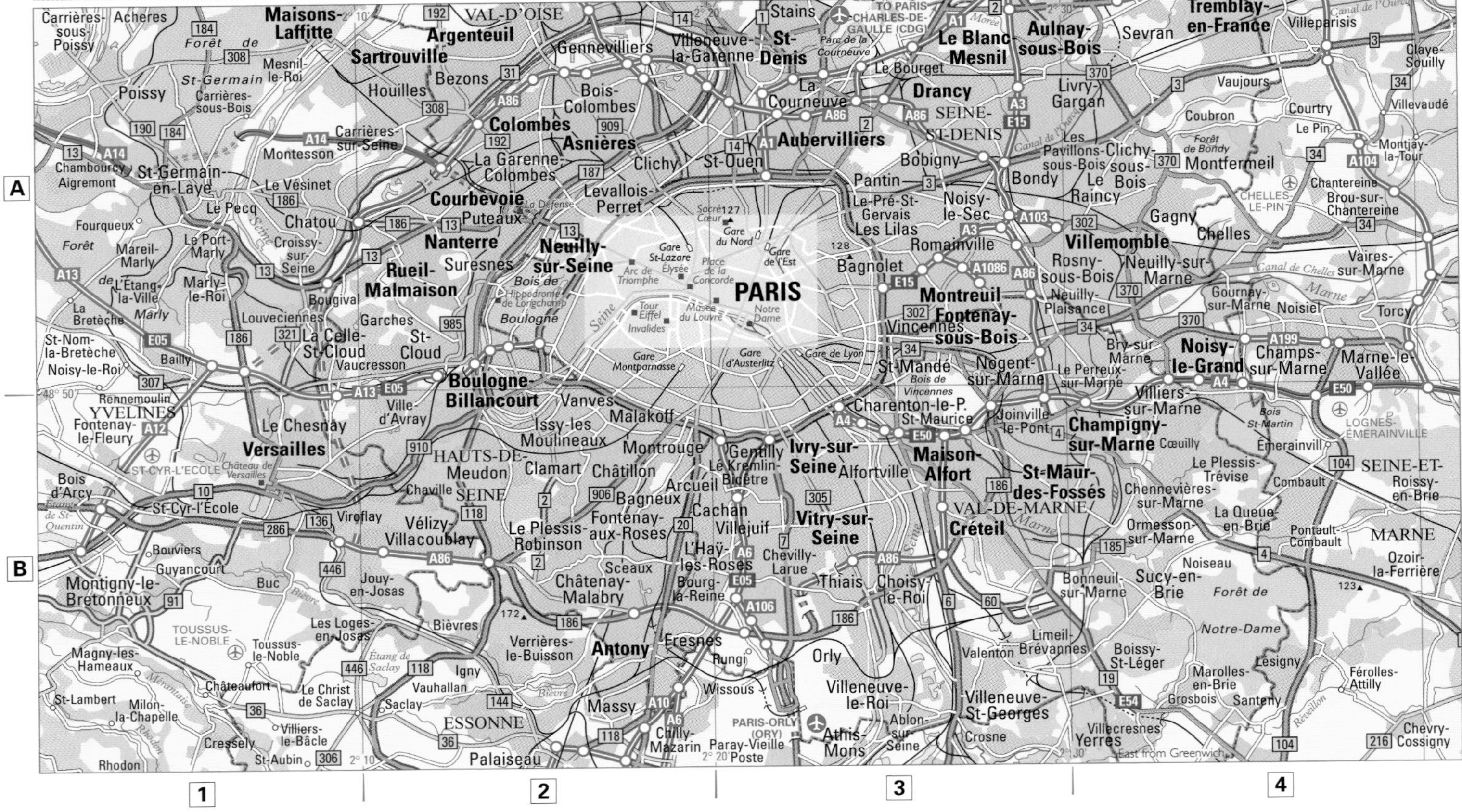

0 km 5
0 miles 3

Maisons-Laffitte
Argenteuil
Sartrouville
Gennevilliers
Villeneuve-la-Garenne
St-Denis
Le Blanc Mesnil
Aulnay-sous-Bois
Tremblay-en-France
Colombes
Asnières
Aubervilliers
Drancy
Courbevoie
Nanterre
Neuilly-sur-Seine
Rueil-Malmaison
PARIS
Villemomble
Montreuil
Fontenay-sous-Bois
Noisy-le-Grand
Champigny-sur-Marne
Boulogne-Billancourt
Versailles
Ivry-sur-Seine
Maison-Alfort
St-Maur-des-Fossés
Vitry-sur-Seine
Créteil
Antony

A B

1 2 3 4

CENTRAL PARIS

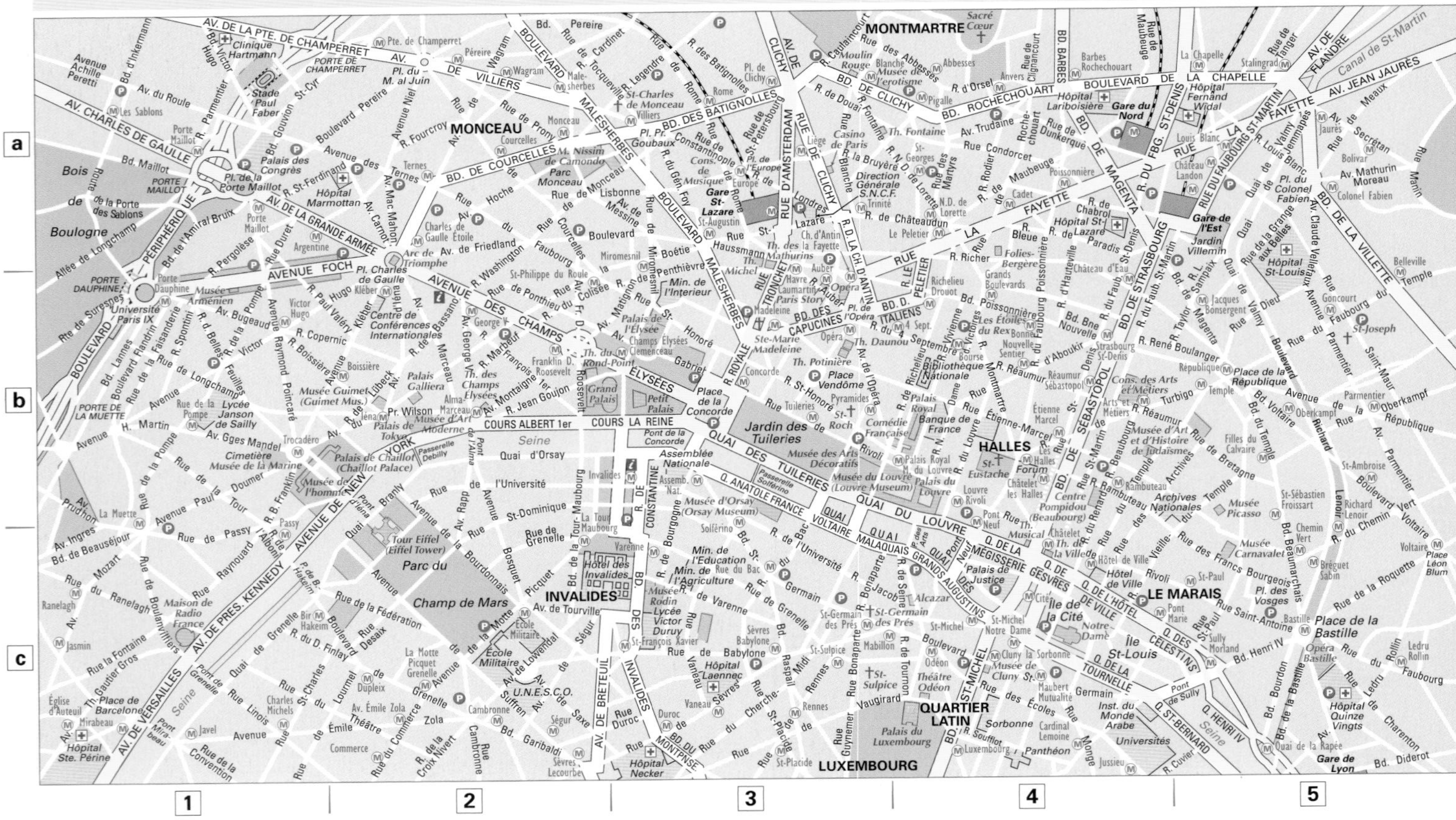

0 km 1
0 miles 0.5

MONTMARTRE
MONCEAU
HALLES
INVALIDES
LE MARAIS
QUARTIER LATIN
LUXEMBOURG

a b c

1 2 3 4 5

PRAGUE

0 km 5
0 miles 3

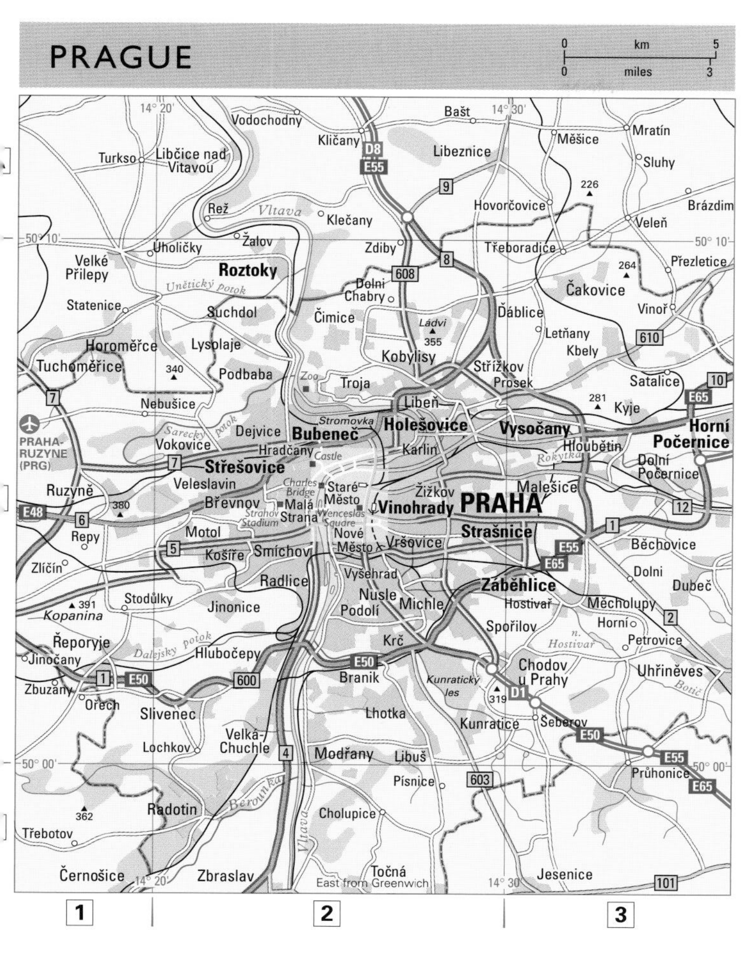

1 2 3

CENTRAL PRAGUE

0 km 1
0 miles 0.5

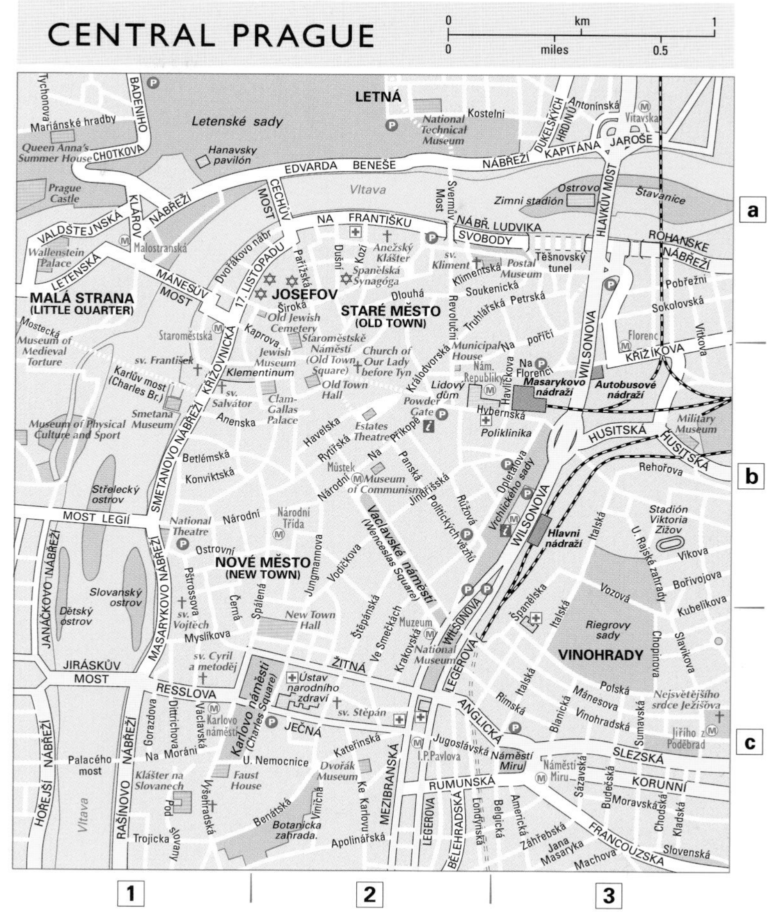

1 2 3

RIO DE JANEIRO

0 km 5
0 miles 3

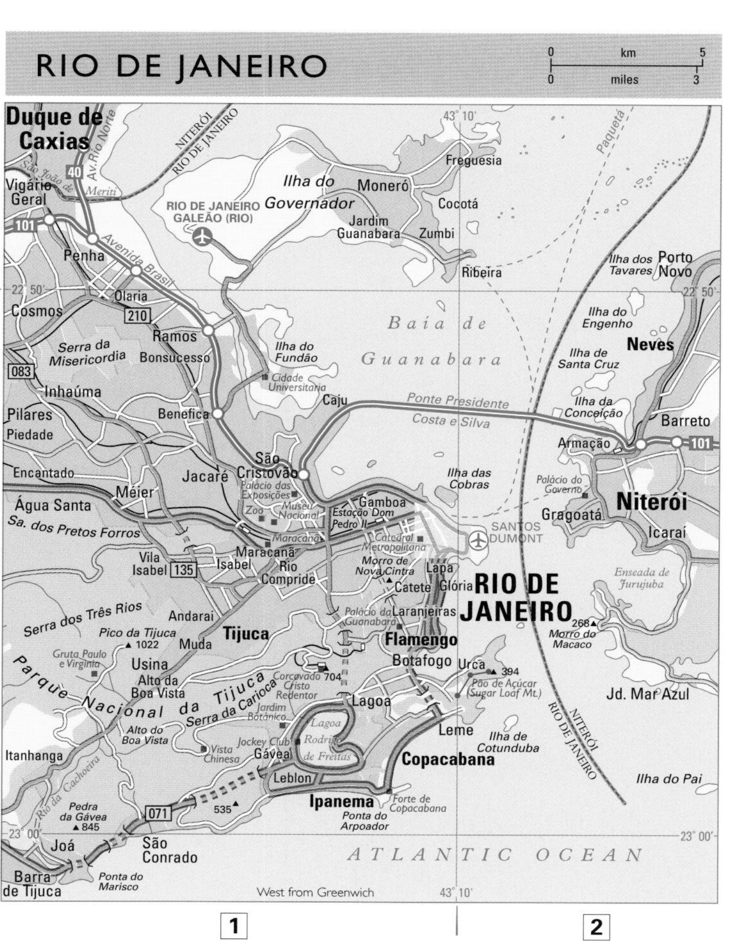

1 2

CENTRAL RIO DE JANEIRO

0 km 0.25
0 miles 0.125

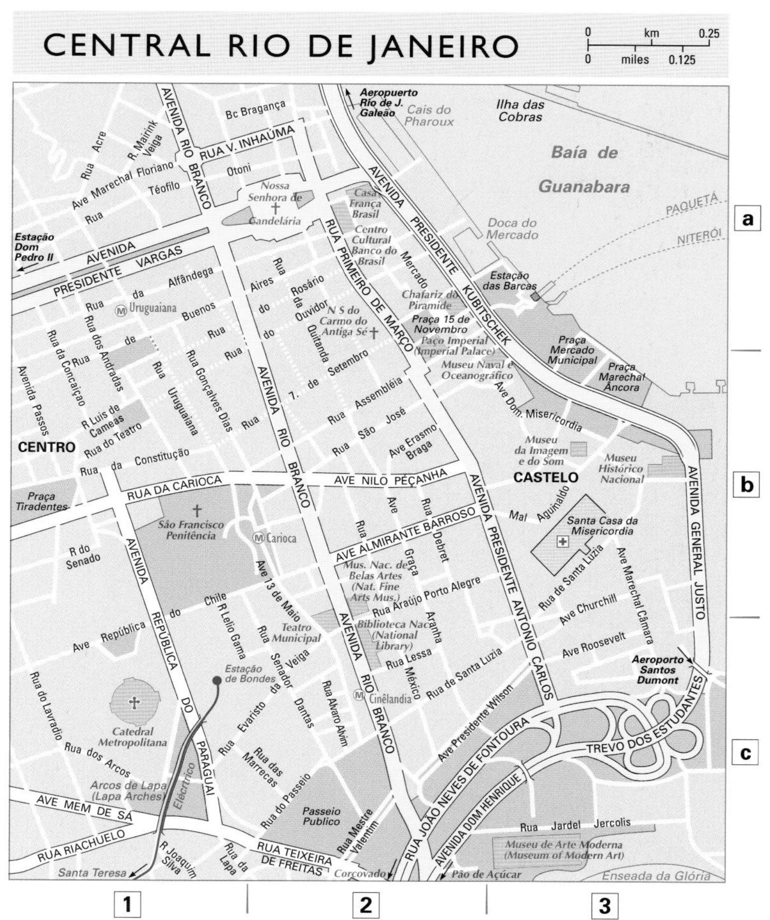

1 2 3

ROME

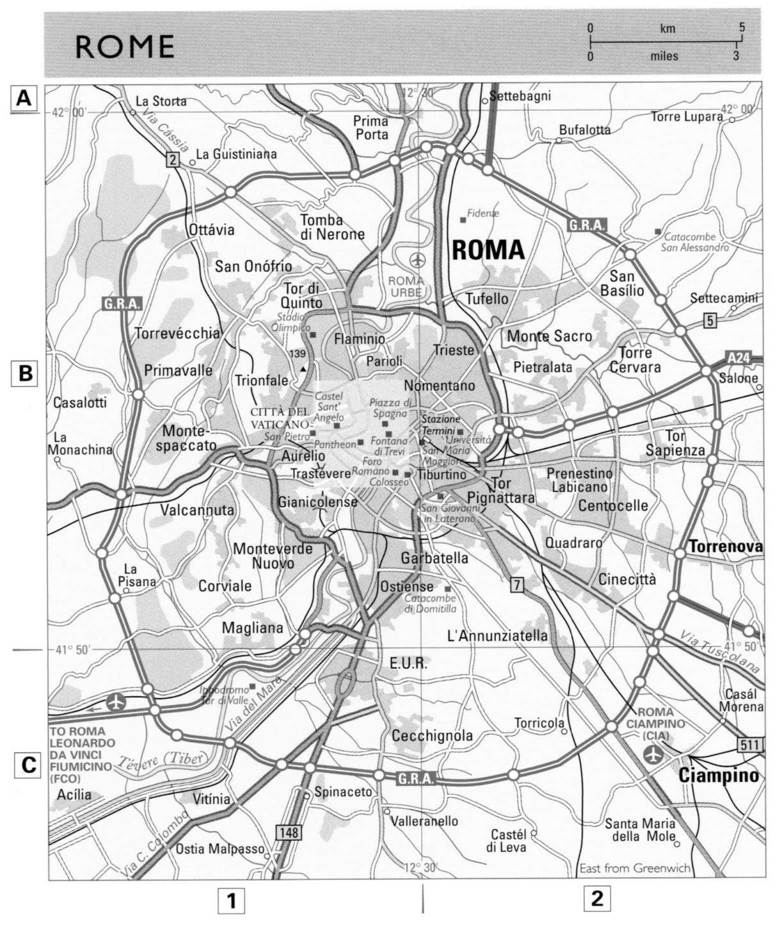

CENTRAL ROME

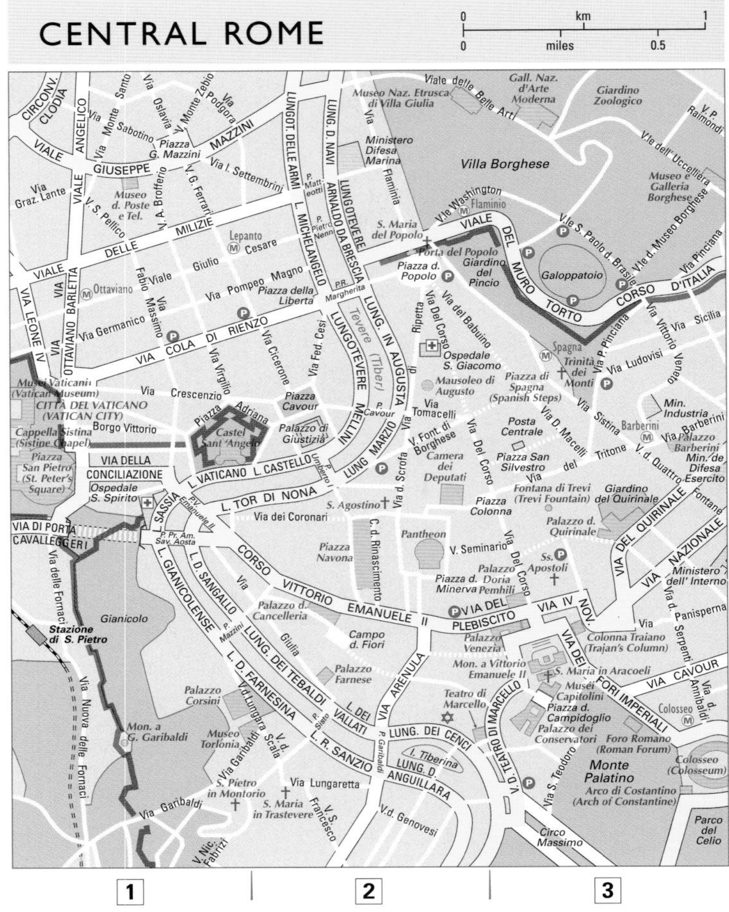

SAN FRANCISCO

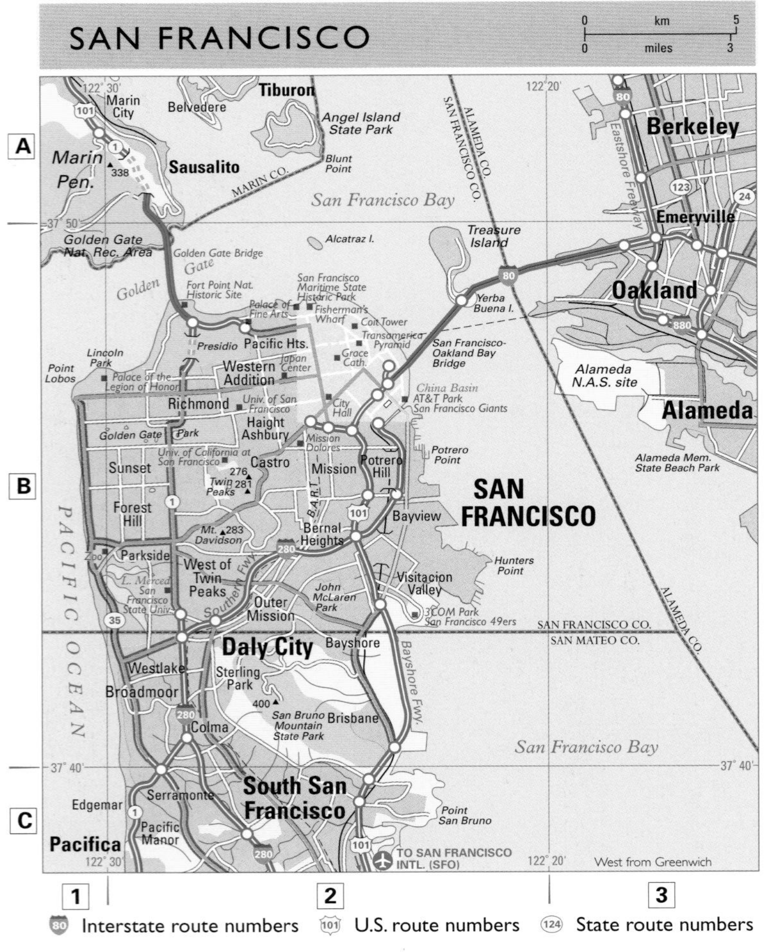

CENTRAL SAN FRANCISCO

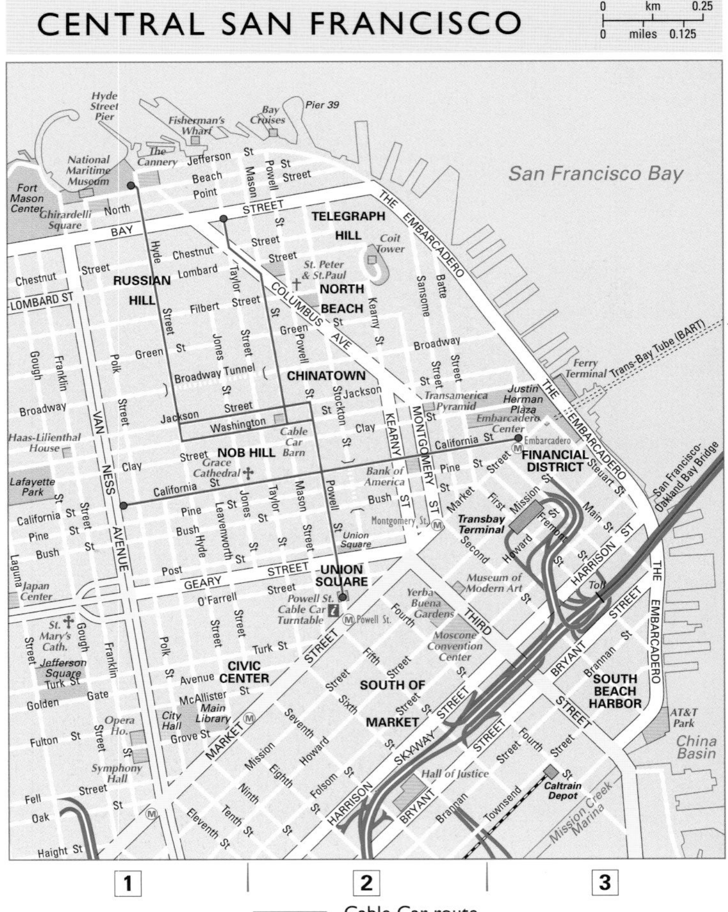

80 Interstate route numbers   101 U.S. route numbers   124 State route numbers

Cable Car route

ST PETERSBURG

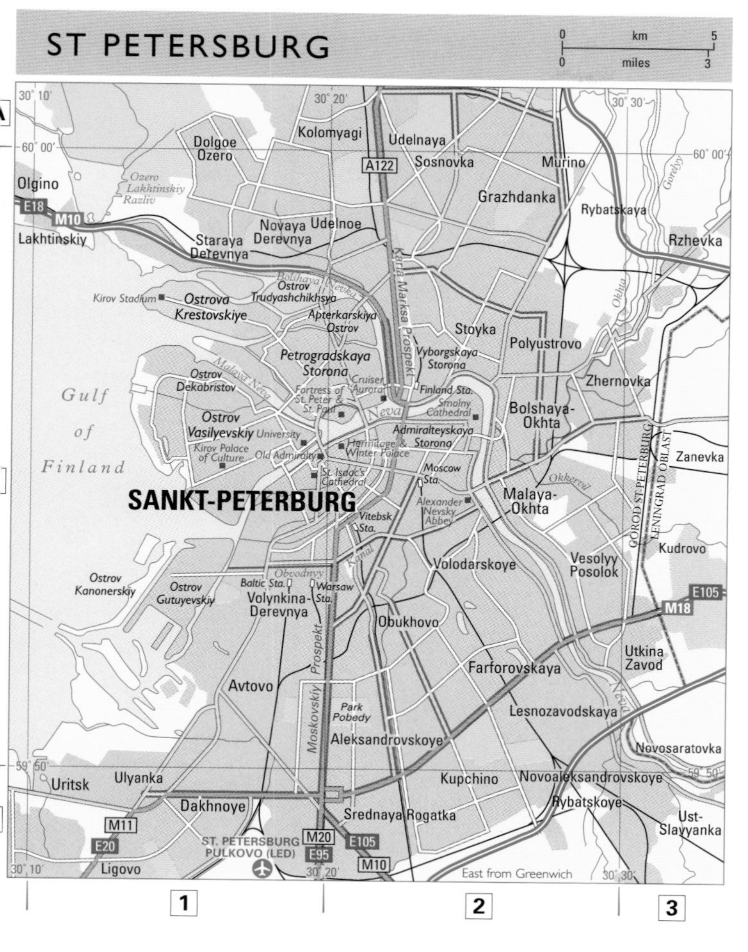

SANTIAGO

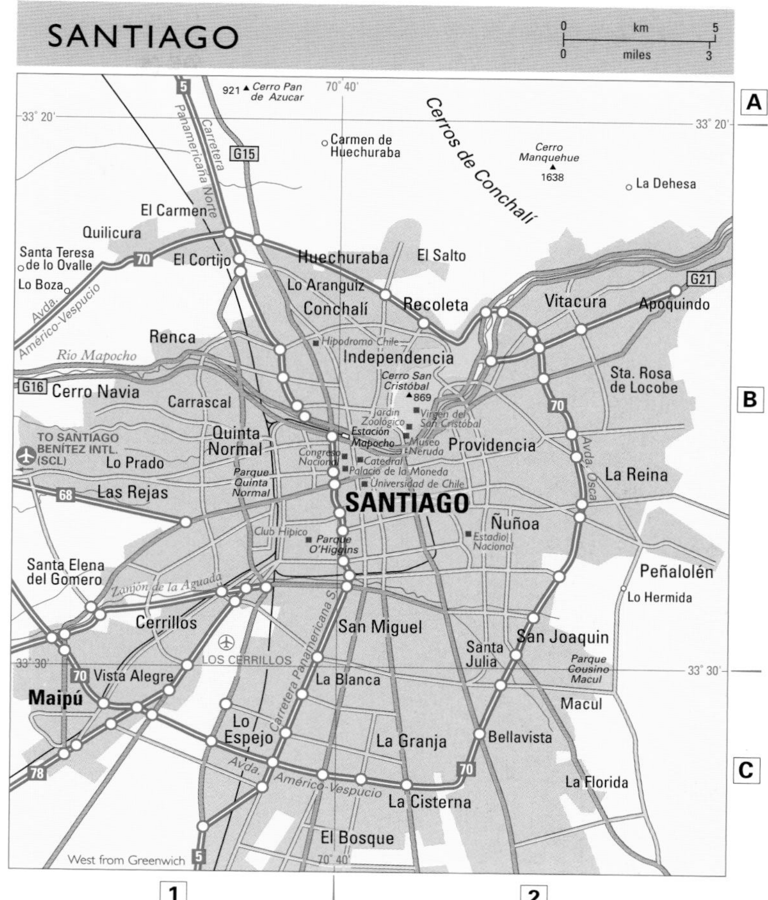

SÃO PAULO

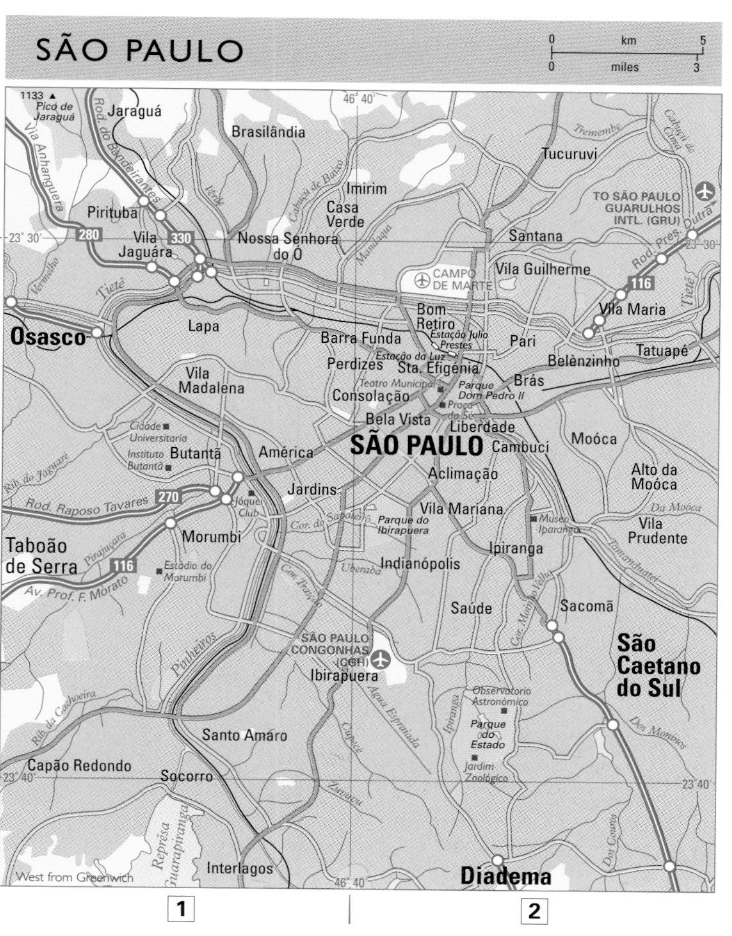

SEOUL

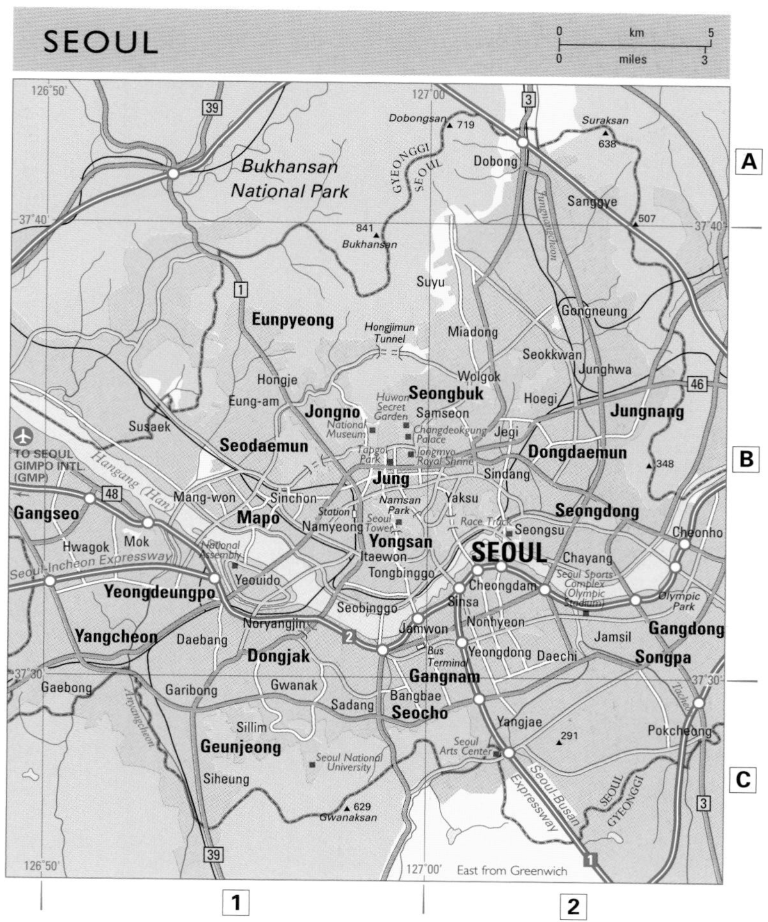

SHANGHAI

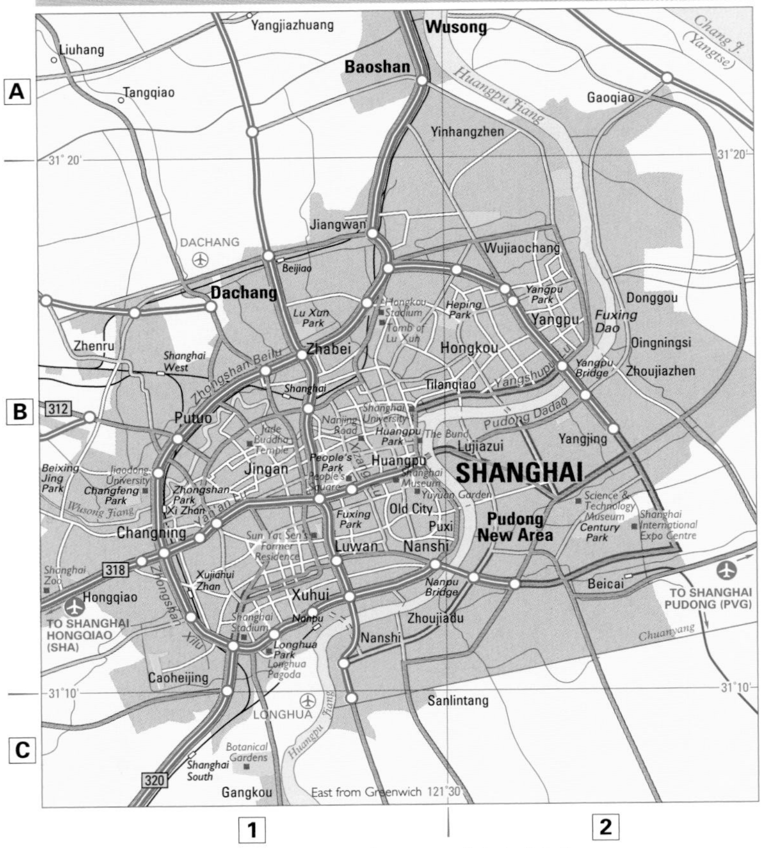

0 km 5
0 miles 3

East from Greenwich 121°30'

— Magnetic Levitation (Maglev) Railway

CENTRAL SINGAPORE

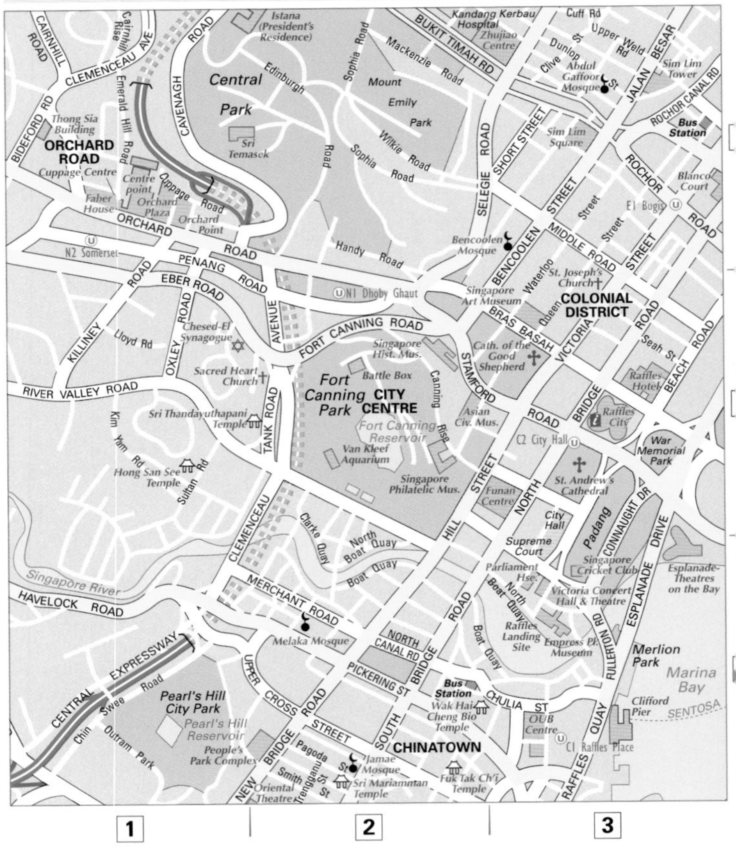

0 km 1
0 miles 0.5

SINGAPORE

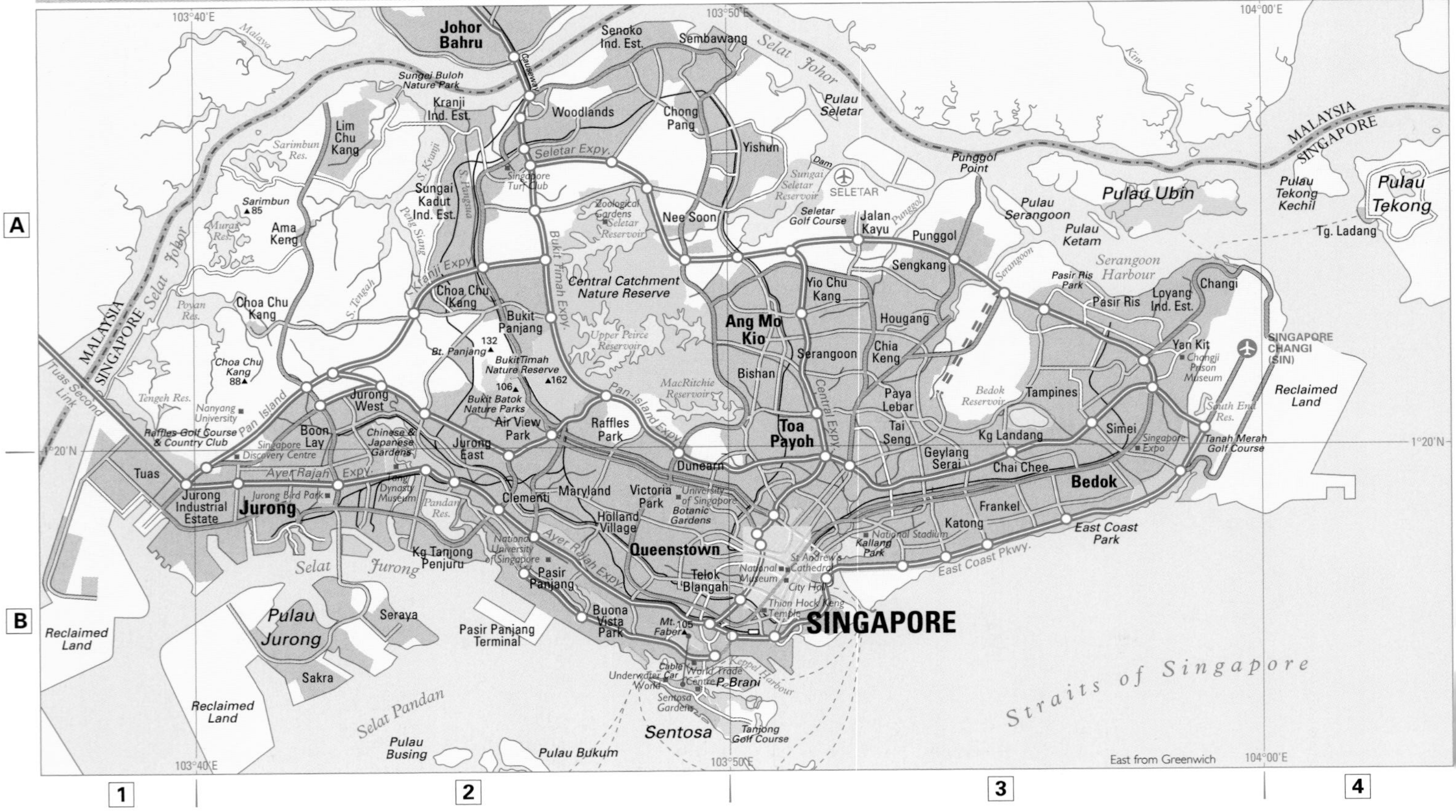

0 km 5
0 miles 3

East from Greenwich

STOCKHOLM

CENTRAL STOCKHOLM

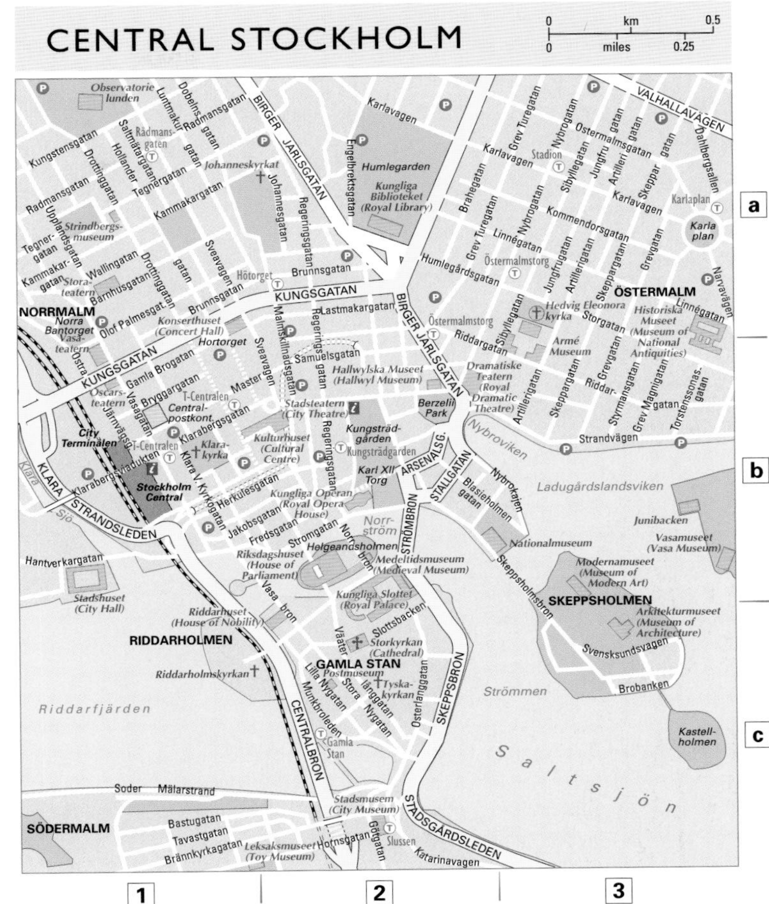

SYDNEY

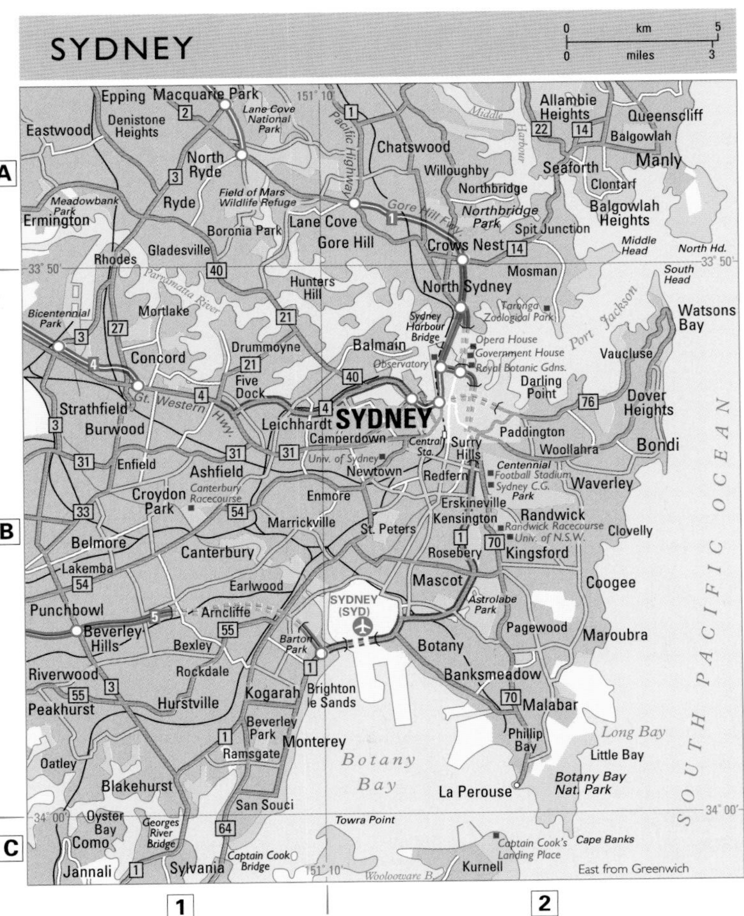

CENTRAL SYDNEY

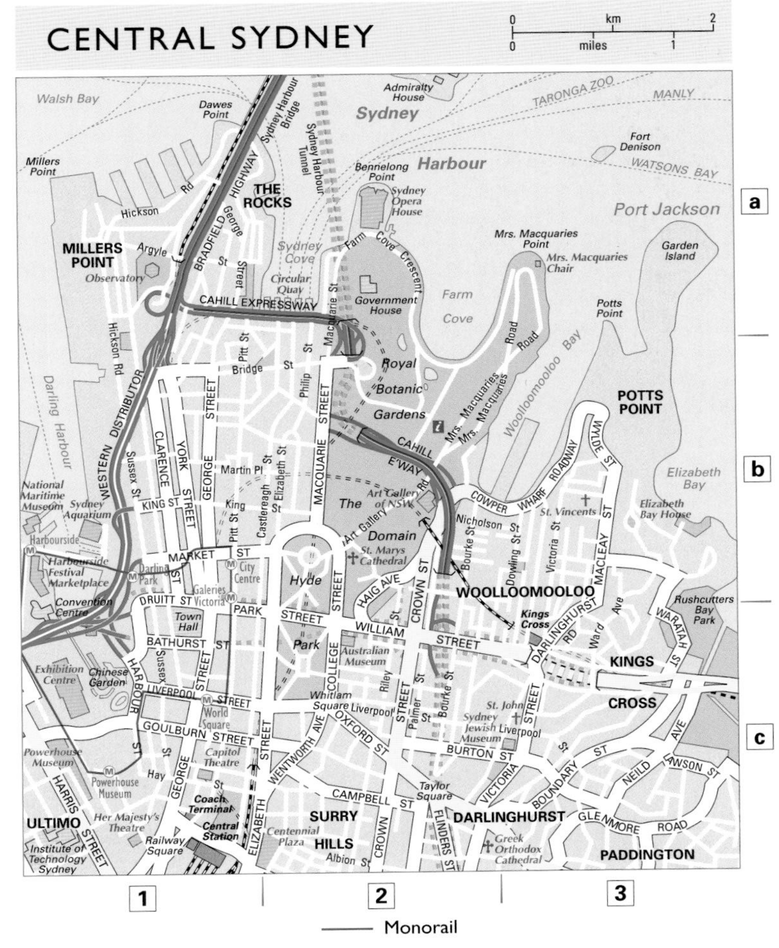

Monorail

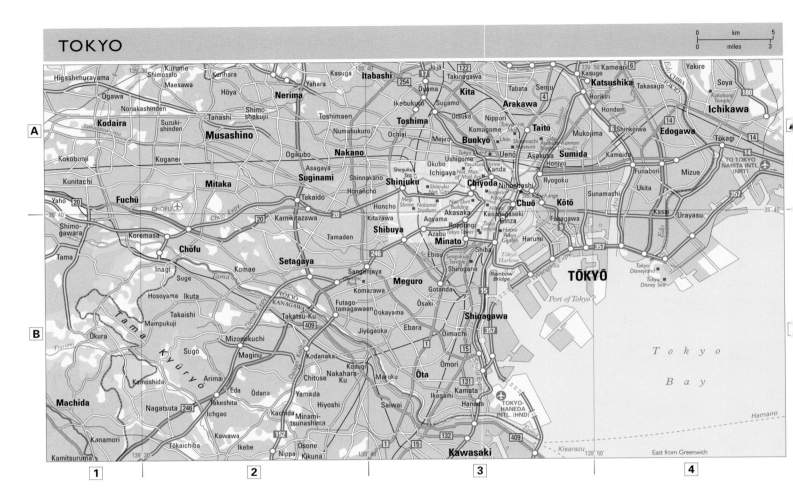

TOKYO

0 km 5
0 miles 3

East from Greenwich

1 2 3 4

A B

CENTRAL TOKYO

0 km 0.5
0 miles 0.25

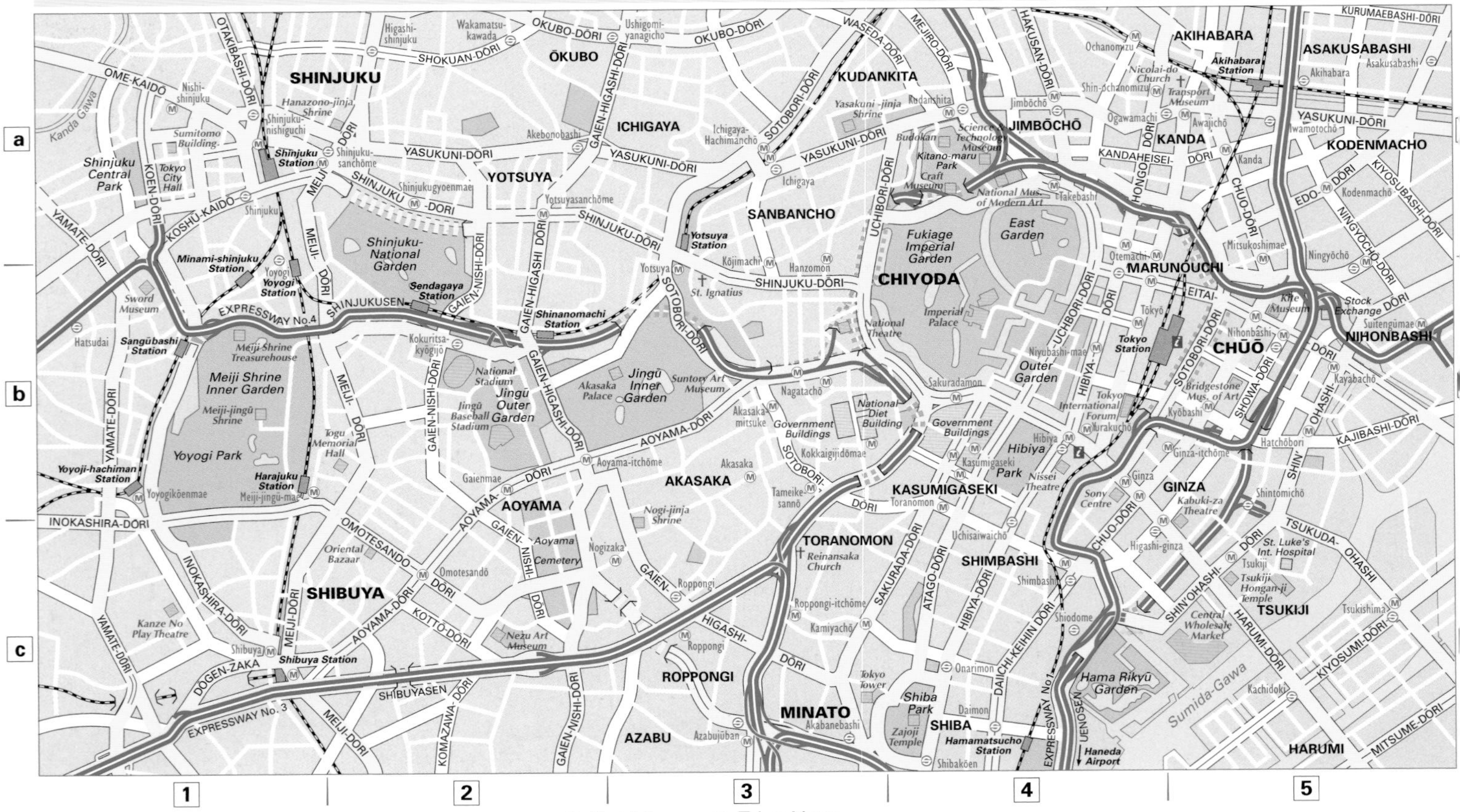

1 2 3 4 5

a b c

Toei Subway Tokyo Metro

TEHRAN

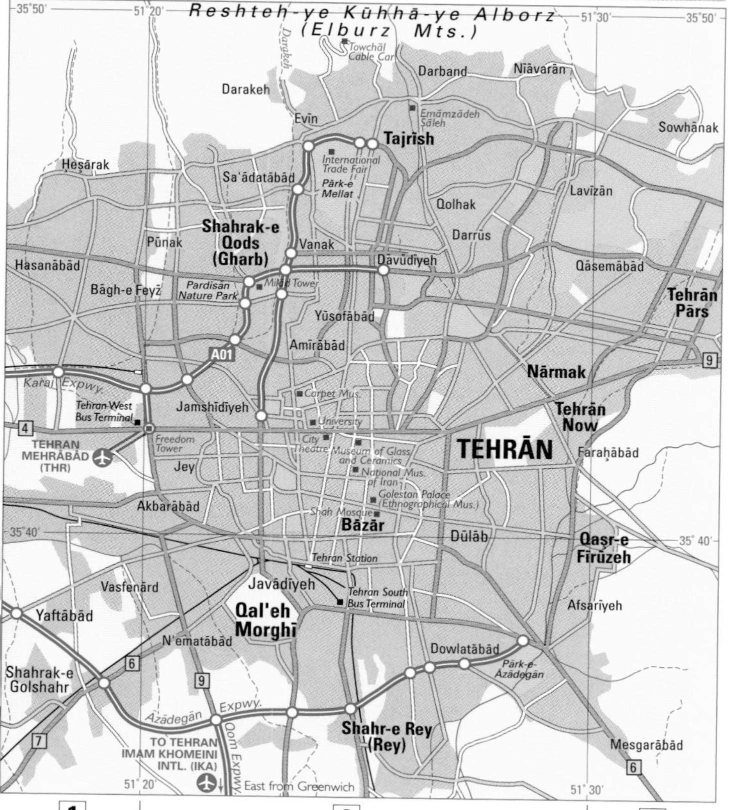

0 km 5
0 miles 3

Reshteh-ye Kūhhā-ye Alborz (Elburz Mts.)
Towchāl Cable Car
Darband
Nīāvarān
Darakeh
Evīn
Emāmzādeh Sāleh
Tajrīsh
Sowhānak
Hesārak
International Trade Fair
Sa'ādatābād
Pārk-e Mellat
Lavīzān
Qolhak
Shahrak-e Qods (Gharb)
Pūnak
Darrūs
Vanak
Hasanābād
Dāvūdīyeh
Qāsemābād
Bāgh-e Feyz
Pardisān Nature Park
Milād Tower
Tehrān Pārs
Yūsofābād
Amīrābād
A01
Nārmak
Karaj Expwy.
Tehran West Bus Terminal
Jamshīdīyeh
Carpet Mus.
University
Tehrān Now
TEHRAN MEHRĀBĀD (THR)
Freedom Tower
Jey
City Theatre
Museum of Glass and Ceramics
National Mus. of Iran
TEHRĀN
Farahābād
Akbarābād
Golestān Palace Ethnographical Mus.
Shah Mosque
Bāzār
Dūlāb
Qasr-e Fīrūzeh
Tehran Station
Javādīyeh
Vasfenārd
Tehran South Bus Terminal
Yaftābād
Qal'eh Morghī
Afsarīyeh
N'ematābād
Dowlatābād
Pārk-e Āzādegān
Shahrak-e Golshahr
Āzādegān Expwy.
Qom Expwy.
Shahr-e Rey (Rey)
TO TEHRAN IMAM KHOMEINI INTL. (IKA)
Mesgarābād
East from Greenwich
35°50′ 51°20′ 51°30′ 35°40′
1 2 3

CENTRAL TORONTO

0 km 0.5
0 miles 0.25

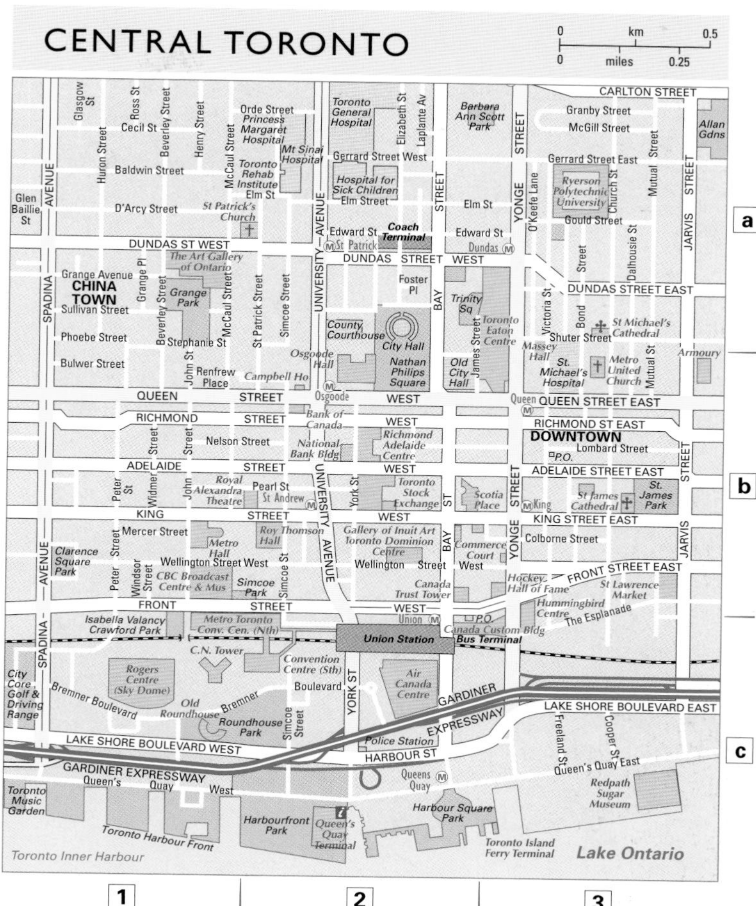

TORONTO

0 km 5
0 miles 3

79°40′ 79°30′ 79°20′ 79°10′
Boyd Conservation Area
Humber
East Humber
Vaughan
Thornhill
The Promenade
Concord
East Don
Markham
Metro Toronto Zoo
Rouge
Little Rouge
Fairport
Brown
Rouge Hill
Glen Rouge Park
West Rouge
Pine Grove
Edgeley
Newtonbrook
Woodbridge
Fisherville
G. Ross Lord Park
Willowdale
East Don Parkland
Fairview Mall
Agincourt
Malvern
Highland Creek
Port Union
Northmount
Black Creek Pioneer Village
York University
Morningside Park
Humber Summit
Lansing
Scarborough Town Centre
Woburn
West Hill
Beaumonte Heights
North York
Highland
Bendale
Eastpoint Park
York Mills
East Don
Armour Heights
Northwood Park
Black Creek
Wexford
Hague Park
Creek
Claireville Reservoir
Thistletown
DOWNSVIEW C.A.F.B.
Scarborough
Massey
Humberwood Park
Kipling Heights
Downsview
Lawrence Heights
Don Mills
Cliffside
Woodbine Centre
Rexdale
Humberlea
Yorkdale Shopping Centre
York Univ.
Wilket Creek Park
Sunnybrook Health Science Centre
Malton
Woodbine Race Track
Weston
Forest Hill
Ontario Science Centre
Thorncliffe
Danforth
Leaside
Bluffers Park
TORONTO LESTER B. PEARSON INTL. (YYZ)
Cedarvale Park
Dentonia Park
York
Don Valley Pkwy
East York
Scarborough Bluffs
Birch Cliff
Humber Valley Village
Mount Dennis
Casa Loma
Kew Gardens
Royal Ontario Museum
Riverdale Park
43°40′
Etobicoke
Mimico Creek
Lambton Mills
Swansea
University of Toronto
Parliament Buildings
Ashbridge's Bay Park
Hanlon
Old City Hall
Union Sta.
Gardiner Expy.
Islington
High Park
C.N. Tower & Rogers Centre
Kingsway
Old Fort York
TORONTO
Markland Wood
Humber Bay
Humber
Parkdale
Exhibition Place
TORONTO CITY CENTRE (ISLAND)
Burnhamthorpe
Humber Bay
Ontario Place
Toronto Harbour
Tommy Thompson Park
Summerville
Humber Bay Park
Toronto Islands
Island Park
LAKE ONTARIO
Elizabeth Way
Mimico
Gibraltar Point
Dixie Mall
Queen
New Toronto
Square One
Humber College
Samuel Smith Park
Cooksville
Mississauga
Long Branch
West from Greenwich
A
B
1 2 3 4

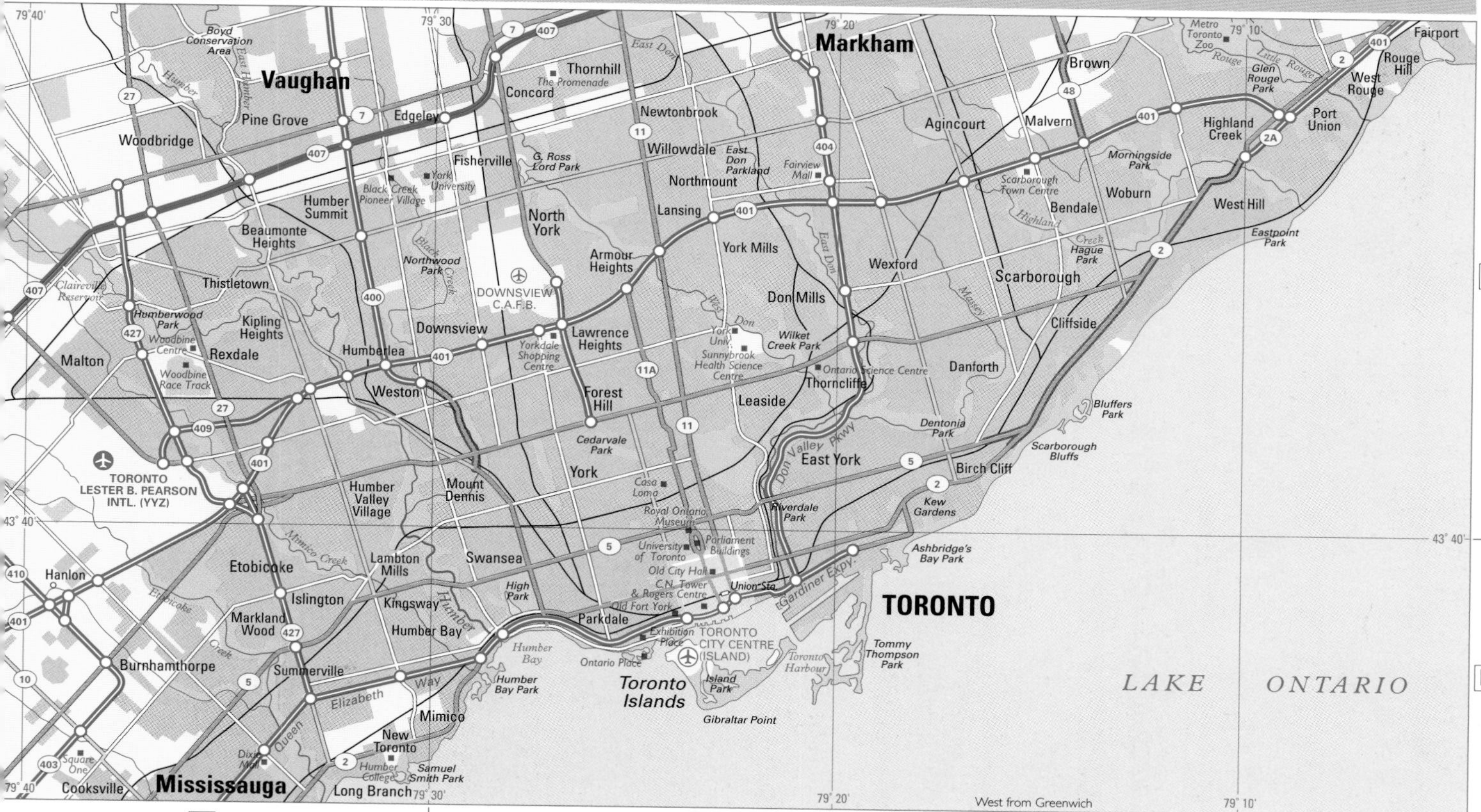

(427) Provincial route numbers

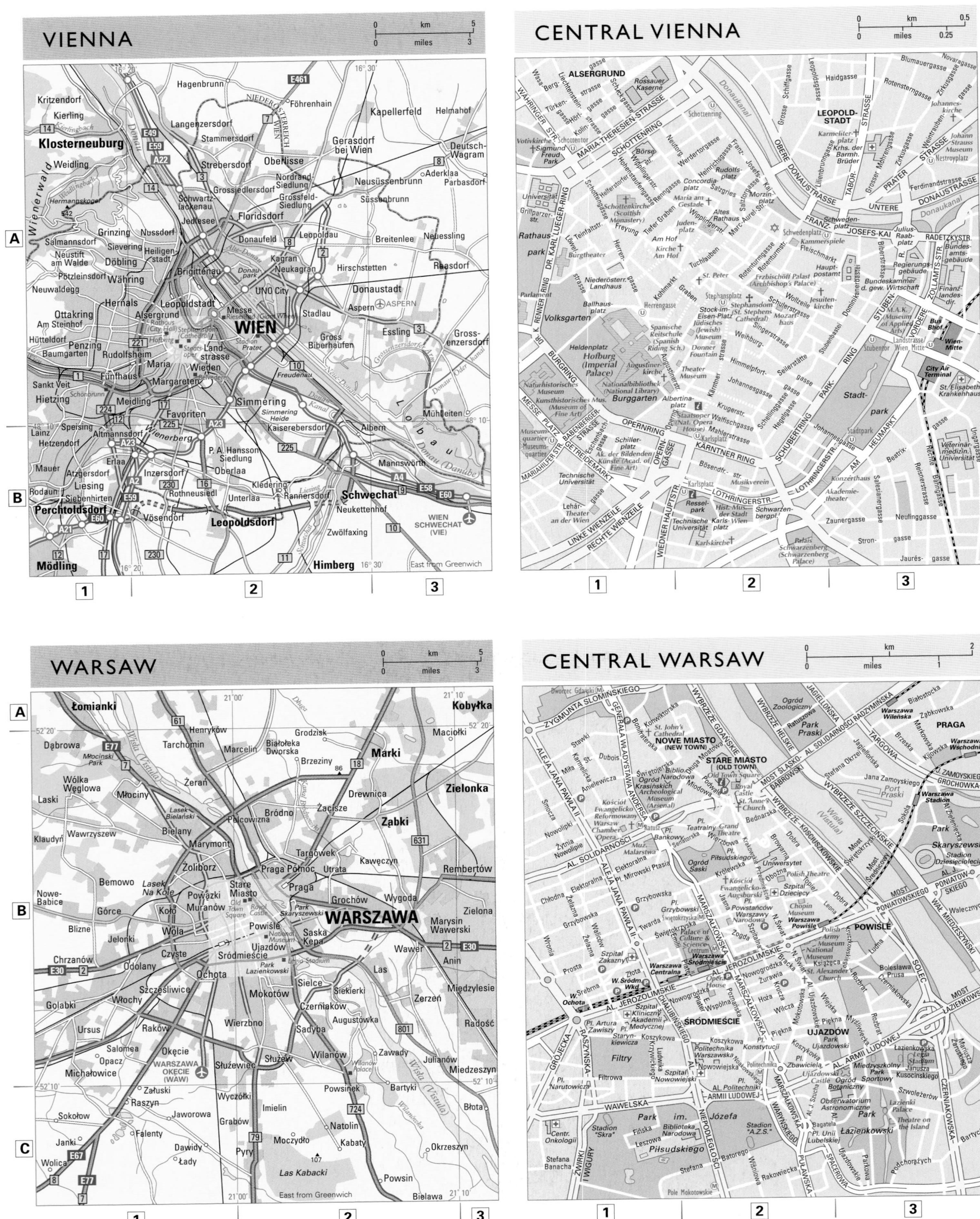
VIENNA
CENTRAL VIENNA
WARSAW
CENTRAL WARSAW
km
miles
East from Greenwich

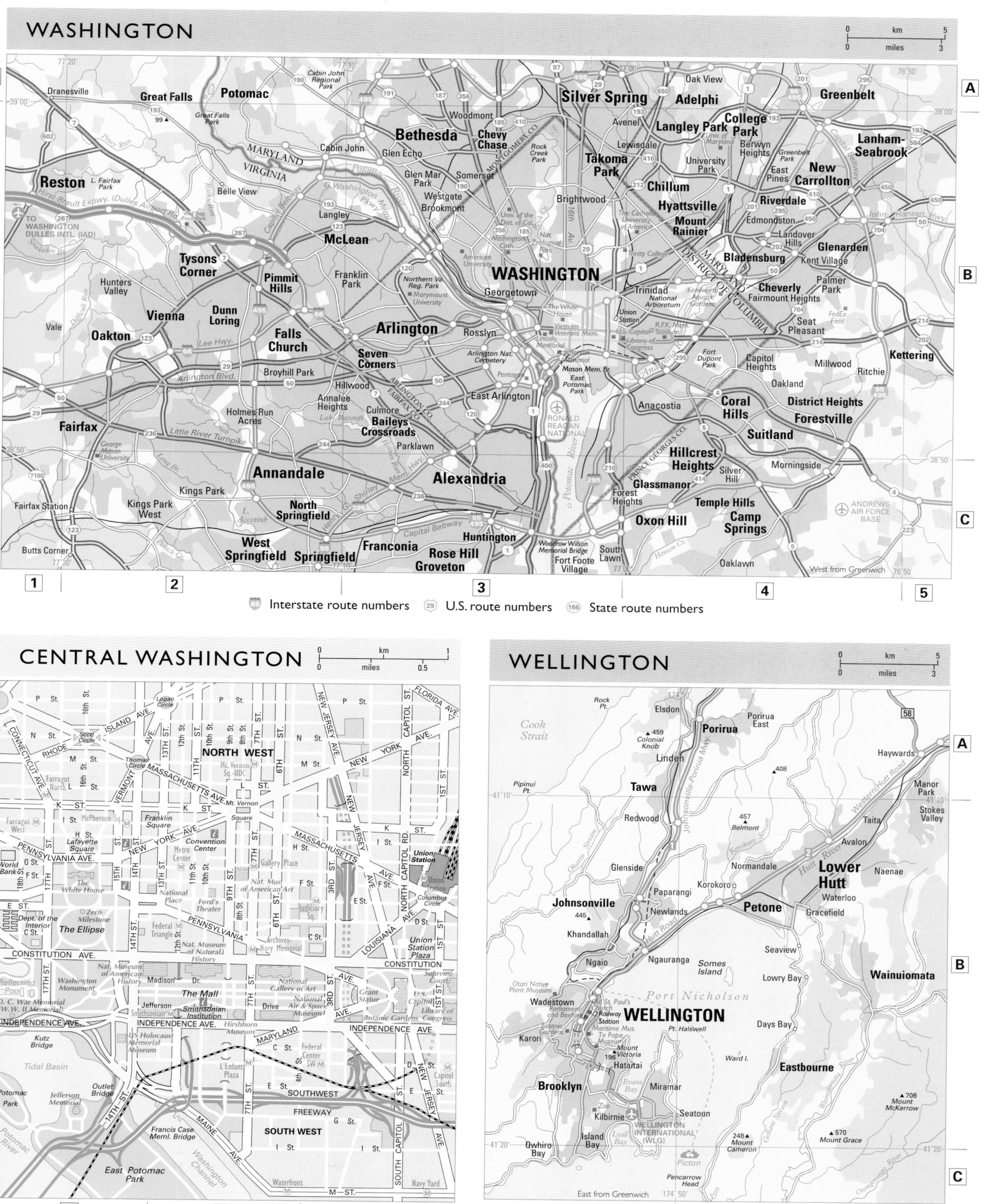
WASHINGTON
km 0 5
miles 0 3
Dranesville
Great Falls
Potomac
Great Falls Park
Cabin John Regional Park
Silver Spring
Oak View
Adelphi
Greenbelt
Woodmont
Bethesda
Chevy Chase
Avenel
Langley Park
College Park
Lanham-Seabrook
Cabin John
Glen Echo
Rock Creek Park
Lewisdale
Berwyn Heights
Greenbelt Park
Takoma Park
University Park
East Pines
New Carrollton
MARYLAND
VIRGINIA
Glen Mar Park
Somerset
Reston
L. Fairfax Park
Belle View
Westgate
Brookmont
Brightwood
Chillum
Hyattsville
Riverdale
TO WASHINGTON DULLES INTL. (IAD)
Langley
Mount Rainier
Edmondston
Landover Hills
McLean
Glenarden
Tysons Corner
Hunters Valley
Pimmit Hills
Franklin Park
Northern Va. Reg. Park
Marymount University
WASHINGTON
Trinidad
National Arboretum
Bladensburg
Kent Village
Palmer Park
Cheverly
Fairmount Heights
Georgetown
Vienna
Dunn Loring
Vale
Oakton
Falls Church
Arlington
Rosslyn
The White House
Union Station
Seat Pleasant
Seven Corners
Arlington Nat. Cemetery
Lincoln Memorial
Vietnam Veterans Mem.
U.S. Capitol
Library of Congress
R.F.K. Mem. Stadium
Kettering
Broyhill Park
Jefferson Memorial
Mason Mem. Br.
Fort Dupont Park
Capitol Heights
Millwood
Ritchie
Pentagon
East Potomac Park
Oakland
Hillwood
East Arlington
Anacostia
Coral Hills
District Heights
Annalee Heights
Fairfax
Holmes Run Acres
Culmore
Baileys Crossroads
Forestville
Suitland
Little River Turnpike
Lake Barcroft
RONALD REAGAN NATIONAL
George Mason University
Parklawn
Hillcrest Heights
Morningside
Silver Hill
Annandale
Alexandria
Glassmanor
Kings Park
Forest Heights
Fairfax Station
Kings Park West
North Springfield
Temple Hills
Camp Springs
Oxon Hill
ANDREWS AIR FORCE BASE
West Springfield
Springfield
Franconia
Huntington
Rose Hill
Woodrow Wilson Memorial Bridge
Fort Foote Village
South Lawn
Butts Corner
Groveton
Oaklawn
West from Greenwich
1 2 3 4 5
A B C
Interstate route numbers
U.S. route numbers
State route numbers
CENTRAL WASHINGTON
km 0 1
miles 0 0.5
NORTH WEST
Logan Circle
Scott Circle
Thomas Circle
Mt. Vernon Sq.-UDC
Farragut North
Mt. Vernon Square
Franklin Square
McPherson Sq.
Farragut West
Lafayette Square
Convention Center
Metro Center
Union Station
Gallery Place
Nat. Mus. of American Art
The White House
National Place
Ford's Theater
Judiciary Sq.
Columbus Circle
Zero Milestone
Dept. of the Interior
The Ellipse
Federal Triangle
Nat. Museum of Natural History
Archives-Navy Memorial
Union Station Plaza
CONSTITUTION AVE.
Nat. Museum of American History
National Gallery of Art
Supreme Court
Reflecting Pool
Washington Monument
The Mall
National Air & Space Museum
Grant Statue
U.S. Capitol
Library of Congress
D. C. War Memorial (W.W. II Memorial)
Smithsonian Institution
Botanic Gardens
INDEPENDENCE AVE.
Hirshhorn Museum
Kutz Bridge
US Holocaust Memorial Museum
Federal Center SW
Tidal Basin
L'Enfant Plaza
Capitol South
Potomac Park
Jefferson Memorial
Outlet Bridge
SOUTHWEST FREEWAY
Francis Case Meml. Bridge
SOUTH WEST
Potomac River
Washington Channel
East Potomac Park
Waterfront
Navy Yard
1 2 3
WELLINGTON
km 0 5
miles 0 3
Rock Pt.
Elsdon
Porirua East
Cook Strait
459 Colonial Knob
Porirua
Linden
Haywards
Pipinui Pt.
Tawa
408
Manor Park
Stokes Valley
Redwood
457 Belmont
Taita
Avalon
Glenside
Normandale
Lower Hutt
Naenae
Paparangi
Korokoro
Johnsonville
Newlands
Petone
Waterloo
Gracefield
445
Khandallah
Seaview
Ngaio
Ngauranga
Somes Island
Lowry Bay
Wainuiomata
Otari Native Plant Museum
Port Nicholson
Wadestown
WELLINGTON
Parliament and Beehive
Railway Station
Botanic Gardens
Maritime Mus.
Te Papa Museum
Pt. Halswell
Days Bay
Karori
196 Mount Victoria
Hataitai
Ward I.
Eastbourne
Brooklyn
Evans Bay
Miramar
Zoo
Kilbirnie
Seatoun
WELLINGTON INTERNATIONAL (WLG)
706 Mount McKerrow
Owhiro Bay
Island Bay
Lyall Bay
248 Mount Cameron
570 Mount Grace
Picton
Pencarrow Head
East from Greenwich
1 2
A B C

INDEX TO CITY MAPS

The index contains the names of all the principal places and features shown on the City Maps. Each name is followed by an additional entry in italics giving the name of the City Map within which it is located.

The number in bold type which follows each name refers to the number of the City Map page where that feature or place will be found.

The letter and figure which are immediately after the page number give the grid square on the map within which the feature or place is situated.

The letter represents the latitude and the figure the longitude. The ful geographic reference is provided in the border of the City Maps.

The location given is the centre of the city, suburb or feature and is no necessarily the name. Rivers, canals and roads are indexed to their name Rivers carry the symbol → after their name.

An explanation of the alphabetical order rules and a list of the abbrevia- tions used are to be found at the beginning of the World Map Index.

A

Aalām *Baghdad* **3** B2
Abbey Wood *London* **15** B4
Abcoude *Amsterdam* **2** B2
Âbdin *Cairo* **7** A2
Abeno *Osaka* **23** B2
Aberdeen *Hong Kong* **12** B1
Aberdour *Edinburgh* **11** A2
Aberdour Castle *Edinburgh* **11** A2
Abfanggraben → *Munich* **21** A3
Ablon-sur-Seine *Paris* **24** B3
Abramtsevo *Moscow* **19** B3
Abu Dis *Jerusalem* **13** B2
Abû en Numrus *Cairo* **7** B2
Abu Ghosh *Jerusalem* **13** B1
Acassuso *Buenos Aires* **7** A1
Accotink, L. *Washington* **33** C2
Accotink Cr. → *Washington* **33** B2
Achères *Paris* **24** A1
Acília *Rome* **26** C1
Aclimação *São Paulo* **27** B2
Acropolis *Athens* **2** B2
Acton *London* **15** A2
Açúcar, Pão de *Rio de Janeiro* **25** B2
Ada Beja *Lisbon* **16** A1
Adams Park *Atlanta* **3** B2
Addiscombe *London* **15** B3
Adelphi *Washington* **33** A4
Aderklaa *Vienna* **32** A3
Adler Planetarium *Chicago* **9** B3
Admiralteyskaya Storona *St. Petersburg* **27** B2
Áffori *Milan* **19** A2
Aflandshage *Copenhagen* **8** B3
Afsarīyeh *Tehran* **31** B2
Agboyi Cr. → *Lagos* **14** A2
Ågerup *Copenhagen* **8** A1
Ågesta *Stockholm* **29** B2
Aghia Marina *Athens* **2** C3
Aghia Paraskevi *Athens* **2** A2
Aghios Dimitrios *Athens* **2** B2
Aghios Ioannis Rendis *Athens* **2** B1
Agincourt *Toronto* **31** A3
Agra Canal *Delhi* **10** B2
Agricola Oriental *Mexico City* **18** B2
Agua Espraiada → *São Paulo* **27** B2
Agualva-Cacem *Lisbon* **16** A1
Agustino, Cerro El *Lima* **14** B3
Ahrensfelde *Berlin* **5** A4
Ahuntsic *Montreal* **20** A1
Ai → *Osaka* **23** A2
Aigremont *Paris* **24** A1
Air View Park *Singapore* **28** A2
Airport West *Melbourne* **18** A1
Ajegunle *Lagos* **14** B2
Aji *Osaka* **23** A1
Ajuda *Lisbon* **16** A1
Akalla *Stockholm* **29** A1
Akasaka *Tokyo* **30** A3
Akbarābād *Tehran* **31** A2
Akershus Castle = Akershus Slott *Oslo* **23** A3
Akershus Slott *Oslo* **23** A3
Al 'Aẓamīyah *Baghdad* **3** A2
Al Quds = Jerusalem *Jerusalem* **13** B2
Al-Walaja *Jerusalem* **13** B1
Alaguntan *Lagos* **14** B2
Alameda *San Francisco* **26** B3
Alameda Memorial State Beach Park *San Francisco* **26** B3
Albern *Vienna* **32** B2
Albert Park *Melbourne* **18** B1
Alberton *Johannesburg* **13** B2
Albertslund *Copenhagen* **8** B2
Albysjön *Stockholm* **29** B1
Alcantara *Lisbon* **16** A1
Alcatraz I. *San Francisco* **26** B2
Alcobendas *Madrid* **17** A2
Alcorcón *Madrid* **17** B1
Aldershof *Berlin* **5** B4
Aldo Bonzi *Buenos Aires* **7** C1
Aleksandrovskoye *St. Petersburg* **27** B2
Alexander Nevsky Abbey *St. Petersburg* **27** B2
Alexandra *Johannesburg* **13** A2
Alexandra *Singapore* **28** B2
Alexandria *Washington* **33** C3
Alfortville *Paris* **24** B3
Algés *Lisbon* **16** A1
Alhambra *Los Angeles* **16** B4
Alibey → *Istanbul* **12** B1
Alibey Barajı *Istanbul* **12** B1
Alibeyköy *Istanbul* **12** B1
Alimos *Athens* **2** B2
Alipur *Kolkata* **14** B1
Allach *Munich* **21** A1
Allambie Heights *Sydney* **29** A2
Allermuir Hill *Edinburgh* **11** B2
Allstate Arena *Chicago* **9** A1
Allston *Boston* **6** A2
Almada *Lisbon* **16** A2
Almagro *Buenos Aires* **7** B2
Almargem do Bispo *Lisbon* **16** A1
Almirante G. Brown, Parque *Buenos Aires* **7** C2
Almon *Jerusalem* **13** B2
Almond → *Edinburgh* **11** B2
Alna *Oslo* **23** A4
Alnsjøen *Oslo* **23** A4
Alperton *London* **15** A2
Alpine *New York* **22** A2
Alrode *Johannesburg* **13** B2
Alsemberg *Brussels* **6** B1
Alsergrund *Vienna* **32** A2
Alsip *Chicago* **9** C2
Ålsten *Stockholm* **29** B1
Älta *Stockholm* **29** B3
Altadena *Los Angeles* **16** A4
Alte-Donau → *Vienna* **32** A2
Alter Finkenkrug *Berlin* **5** A1
Altes Rathaus *Munich* **21** B2
Altglienicke *Berlin* **5** B4
Altlandsberg *Berlin* **5** A5
Altlandsberg Nord *Berlin* **5** A5
Altmannsdorf *Vienna* **32** B1
Alto da Boa Vista *Rio de Janeiro* **25** B1
Alto da Moóca *São Paulo* **27** B2
Alto do Pina *Lisbon* **16** A2
Altona *Melbourne* **18** B1
Alvik *Stockholm* **29** B1
Älvsjo *Stockholm* **29** B2
Älvvik *Stockholm* **29** A3
Am Hasenbergl *Munich* **21** A2
Am Steinhof *Vienna* **32** A1
Am Wald *Munich* **21** B2
Ama Keng *Singapore* **28** A2
Amadora *Lisbon* **16** A1
Amagasaki *Osaka* **23** A1
Amager *Copenhagen* **8** B3
Amāl Qādisiya *Baghdad* **3** B2
Amalienborg Slot *Copenhagen* **8** A3
Amata *Milan* **19** A1
Ambelokipi *Athens* **2** B2
Ameixoeira *Lisbon* **16** A2
América *São Paulo* **27** B1
American Police Hall of Fame *Miami* **18** B2
American University *Washington* **33** B3
Amin *Baghdad* **3** B2
Aminadav *Jerusalem* **13** B1
Amīrābād *Tehran* **31** A2
Amora *Lisbon* **16** B2
Amoreira *Lisbon* **16** A1
Amper → *Munich* **21** A1
Amstel-Drecht-Kanaal *Amsterdam* **2** B2
Amstelveen *Amsterdam* **2** B2
Amsterdam *Amsterdam* **2** A2
Amsterdam ✈ **(AMS)** *Amsterdam* **2** B1
Amsterdam-Rijnkanaal *Amsterdam* **2** B3
Amsterdam Zuidoost *Amsterdam* **2** B2
Amsterdamse Bos *Amsterdam* **2** B1
Anacosta → *Washington* **33** B4
Anacostia *Washington* **33** B4
Anadoluhisarı *Istanbul* **12** B2
Anadolukavağı *Istanbul* **12** A2
Anata *Jerusalem* **13** B2
Ancol *Jakarta* **12** A1
'Andalus *Baghdad* **3** B1
Andaraí *Rio de Janeiro* **25** B1
Anderlecht *Brussels* **6** A1
Anderson Park *Atlanta* **3** B2
Andingmen *Beijing* **4** B2
Ang Mo Kio *Singapore* **28** A3
Ängby *Stockholm* **29** A1
Angel I. *San Francisco* **26** A2
Angel Island State Park ⌓ *San Francisco* **26** A2
Angke, Kali → *Jakarta* **12** A1
Angyalföld *Budapest* **7** A2
Anik *Mumbai* **20** A2
Anin *Warsaw* **32** B2
Anjou *Montreal* **20** A2
Annalee Heights *Washington* **33** B2
Annandale *Washington* **33** C2
Anne Frankhuis *Amsterdam* **2** A2
Antony *Paris* **24** B2
Aoyama *Tokyo* **30** B3
Ap Lei Chau *Hong Kong* **12** B1
Apapa *Lagos* **14** B2
Apelacão *Lisbon* **16** A2
Apopka, L. *Orlando* **23** A1
Apoquindo *Santiago* **27** B2
Apterkarskiy Ostrov *St. Petersburg* **27** B2
Ar Kazimiyah *Baghdad* **3** B1
Ar Ram *Jerusalem* **13** A2
Ara → *Tokyo* **30** A4
Arakawa *Tokyo* **30** A3
Arany-hegyi-patak → *Budapest* **7** A2
Aravaca *Madrid* **17** B1
Arbataash *Baghdad* **3** A1
Arc de Triomphe *Paris* **24** A2
Arcadia *Los Angeles* **16** B4
Arcueil *Paris* **24** B2
Arese *Milan* **19** A1
Arganzuela *Madrid* **17** B1
Argenteuil *Paris* **24** A2
Argiroupoli *Athens* **2** B2
Argonne Forest *Chicago* **9** C1
Arima *Tokyo* **30** B2
Arlanda ✈ **(ARN)** *Stockholm* **29** A1
Arlington *Boston* **6** A1
Arlington *Washington* **33** B3
Arlington Heights *Boston* **6** A1
Arlington Nat. Cemetery *Washington* **33** B3
Armação *Rio de Janeiro* **25** B2
Armadale *Melbourne* **18** B2
Armour Heights *Toronto* **31** A2
Arncliffe *Sydney* **29** B1
Arnold Arboretum *Boston* **6** B2
Árpádföld *Budapest* **7** A3
Arrentela *Lisbon* **16** B2
Arroyo Seco Park *Los Angeles* **16** B3
Årsta *Stockholm* **29** B2
Art Institute *Chicago* **9** B3
Artane *Dublin* **10** A2
Artas *Jerusalem* **13** B2
Arthur's Seat *Edinburgh* **11** B3
Arts, Place des *Montreal* **20** A2
As Shawawra *Jerusalem* **13** B2
Asagaya *Tokyo* **30** A2
Asahi *Osaka* **23** A2
Asakusa *Tokyo* **30** A3
Asati *Kolkata* **14** C1
Aschheim *Munich* **21** A3
Ascot Vale *Melbourne* **18** A1
Ashbridge's Bay Park *Toronto* **31** B3
Ashburn *Chicago* **9** C2
Ashburton *Melbourne* **18** B2
Ashfield *Sydney* **29** B1
Ashford *London* **15** B1
Ashtown *Dublin* **10** A2
Askisto *Helsinki* **11** B1
Askrikefjärden *Stockholm* **29** A3
Asnières *Paris* **24** A2
Aspern *Vienna* **32** A2
Aspern ✈ *Vienna* **32** A3
Assago *Milan* **19** B1
Assendelft *Amsterdam* **2** A1
Assiano *Milan* **19** B1
Astoria *New York* **22** B2
Astrolabe Park *Sydney* **29** B2
Atarot *Jerusalem* **13** A2
Atarot ✈ *Jerusalem* **13** A2
Atghara *Kolkata* **14** B2
Athens = Athina *Athens* **2** B2
Athina *Athens* **2** B2
Athina ✈ **(ATH)** *Athens* **2** A3
Athínai = Athina *Athens* **2** B2
Athis-Mons *Paris* **24** B3
Athlone *Cape Town* **8** A2
Atholl *Johannesburg* **13** A2
Atīfiya *Baghdad* **3** A2
Atişalen *Istanbul* **12** B1
Atlanta *Atlanta* **3** B2
Atlanta Hartsfield Int. ✈ **(ATL)** *Atlanta* **3** C2
Atlanta Zoo *Atlanta* **3** B2
Atomium *Brussels* **6** A2
Attiki *Athens* **2** A2
Atzgersdorf *Vienna* **32** B1
Aubervilliers *Paris* **24** A3
Aubing *Munich* **21** B1
Auburndale *Boston* **6** A1
Auchendinny *Edinburgh* **11** B2
Auckland Park *Johannesburg* **13** B2
Auderghem *Brussels* **6** B2
Augustówka *Warsaw* **32** B2
Aulnay-sous-Bois *Paris* **24** A3
Aurelio *Rome* **26** B1
Ausîm *Cairo* **7** A1
Austerlitz, Gare d' *Paris* **24** A3
Austin *Chicago* **9** B2
Avalon *Wellington* **33** B2
Avedøre *Copenhagen* **8** B2
Avellaneda *Buenos Aires* **7** C2
Avenel *Washington* **33** B4
Avondale *Chicago* **9** B2
Avondale Heights *Melbourne* **18** A1
Avtovo *St. Petersburg* **27** B1
Ayazağa *Istanbul* **12** B1
Ayer Chawan, Pulau *Singapore* **28** B2
Ayer Merbau, Pulau *Singapore* **28** B2
Azabu *Tokyo* **30** B3
Azcapotzalco *Mexico City* **18** B1
Azteca, Estadia *Mexico City* **18** C2
Azucar, Cerro Pan de *Santiago* **27** A1

B

Baambrugge *Amsterdam* **2** B2
Baba Ch. *Karachi* **13** B1
Baba I. *Karachi* **13** B1
Babarpur *Delhi* **10** A2
Babushkin *Moscow* **19** A3
Back B. *Mumbai* **20** B1
Baclaran *Manila* **17** B2
Bacoor *Manila* **17** C1
Bacoor B. *Manila* **17** C1
Badalona *Barcelona* **4** A2
Badhoevedorp *Amsterdam* **2** A1
Badli *Delhi* **10** A1
Bærum *Oslo* **23** A2
Bağcılar *Istanbul* **12** B1
Bággio *Milan* **19** B1
Bāgh-e-Feyz *Tehran* **31** A1
Baghdād *Baghdad* **3** A2
Baghdad al Muthana ✈ *Baghdad* **3** B2
Baghdad Int. ✈ **(SDA)** *Baghdad* **3** B1
Bagmari *Kolkata* **14** B2
Bagneux *Paris* **24** B2
Bagnolet *Paris* **24** A3
Bagsværd *Copenhagen* **8** A2
Bagsværd Sø *Copenhagen* **8** A2
Baguiati *Kolkata* **14** B2
Bagumbayan *Manila* **17** C2
Baha'i Temple *Chicago* **9** A2
Bahçeköy *Istanbul* **12** A1
Bahçelıevler *Istanbul* **12** B1
Bahtîm *Cairo* **7** A2
Baile Atha Cliath = Dublin *Dublin* **10** A2
Baileys Crossroads *Washington* **33** B3
Bailly *Paris* **24** A1
Bairro Lopes *Lisbon* **16** A2
Baisha *Guangzhou* **11** B2
Baiyun Hill *Guangzhou* **11** B2
Baiyun Int. ✈ **(CAN)** *Guangzhou* **11** A2
Bakırköy *Istanbul* **12** C1
Bal Harbor *Miami* **18** A2
Balara *Manila* **17** B2
Baldia *Karachi* **13** A1
Baldoyle *Dublin* **10** A3
Baldwin, L. *Orlando* **23** A3
Baldwin Hills *Los Angeles* **16** B2
Baldwin Hills Res. *Los Angeles* **16** B2
Balgowlah *Sydney* **29** A2
Balgowlah Heights *Sydney* **29** A2
Balham *London* **15** B3
Bali *Kolkata* **14** B1
Baliganja *Kolkata* **14** B2
Balingsnäs *Stockholm* **29** B2
Balingsta *Stockholm* **29** B2
Balintawak *Manila* **17** B1
Ballerup *Copenhagen* **8** A2
Ballinteer *Dublin* **10** B2
Ballyboden *Dublin* **10** B2
Ballybrack *Dublin* **10** B3
Ballyfermot *Dublin* **10** A1
Ballymorefinn Hill *Dublin* **10** B1
Ballymun *Dublin* **10** A2
Balmain *Sydney* **29** B2
Baluhati *Kolkata* **14** B1
Balvanera *Buenos Aires* **7** B2
Balwyn *Melbourne* **18** A2
Balwyn North *Melbourne* **18** A2
Banática *Lisbon* **16** A1
Bandra *Mumbai* **20** A1
Bandra Pt. *Mumbai* **20** A1
Bang Kapi *Bangkok* **3** B2
Bang Na *Bangkok* **3** B2
Bangbae *Seoul* **27** C1
Bangkhen *Bangkok* **3** A2
Bangkok *Bangkok* **3** B2
Bangkok Noi *Bangkok* **3** B1
Bangkok Yai *Bangkok* **3** B1
Banglo *Kolkata* **14** B1
Bangrak *Bangkok* **3** B2
Bangsu *Bangkok* **3** B2
Banks, C. *Sydney* **29** C2
Banksmeadow *Sydney* **29** B2
Banstala *Kolkata* **14** B2
Bantra *Kolkata* **14** B1
Baoshan *Shanghai* **28** A1
Bar Giyora *Jerusalem* **13** B1
Barahanagar *Kolkata* **14** B2
Barajas *Madrid* **17** B2
Barajas, Madrid ✈ **(MAD)** *Madrid* **17** B2
Barakpur *Kolkata* **14** A2
Barcarena *Lisbon* **16** A1
Barcarena, Rib. de → *Lisbon* **16** A1
Barcelona *Barcelona* **4** A2
Barcelona-Prat ✈ **(BCN)** *Barcelona* **4** B1
Barceloneta *Barcelona* **4** A2
Barcroft, L. *Washington* **33** B3
Barking *London* **15** A4
Barkingside *London* **15** A4
Barnes *London* **15** B2
Barnet *London* **15** A2
Barra Andai *Karachi* **13** B2
Barra Funda *São Paulo* **27** B2
Barracas *Buenos Aires* **7** B2
Barrackpur = Barakpur *Kolkata* **14** A2
Barranco *Lima* **14** B2
Barreiro *Lisbon* **16** B2
Barreto *Rio de Janeiro* **25** B2
Bartala *Kolkata* **14** B1
Barton Park *Sydney* **29** B1
Bartyki *Warsaw* **32** C2
Basus *Cairo* **7** A2
Batanagar *Kolkata* **14** B1
Bath Beach *New York* **22** C1
Bath I. *Karachi* **13** B2
Batir *Jerusalem* **13** B1
Batok, Bukit *Singapore* **28** A2
Battersea *London* **15** B3
Bauman *Moscow* **19** B3
Baumgarten *Vienna* **32** A1
Bay, L. *Orlando* **23** A2
Bay Harbour Islands *Miami* **18** A2
Bay Hill *Orlando* **23** B1
Bay Ridge *New York* **22** C1
Bayit Va-Gan *Jerusalem* **13** B2
Bayonne *New York* **22** B1
Bayrampaşa *Istanbul* **12** B1
Bayshore *San Francisco* **26** B2
Bayt Lahm *Jerusalem* **13** B2
Bayview *San Francisco* **26** B2
Bāzār *Tehran* **31** A2
Beacon Hill *Hong Kong* **12** A2
Beato *Lisbon* **16** A2
Beaumont *Dublin* **10** A2
Beaumonte Heights *Toronto* **31** A1
Bebek *Istanbul* **12** B2
Běchovice *Prague* **25** B3
Beck L. *Chicago* **9** A1
Beckenham *London* **15** B3
Beckton *London* **15** A4
Becontree *London* **15** A4
Beddington Corner *London* **15** B3
Bedford *Boston* **6** A1
Bedford Park *Chicago* **9** C2
Bedford Park *New York* **22** A2
Bedford Stuyvesant *New York* **22** B2
Bedford View *Johannesburg* **13** B2
Bedok *Singapore* **28** B3
Bedok, Res. *Singapore* **28** A3
Beersel *Brussels* **6** B1
Behala *Kolkata* **14** B1
Bei Hai *Beijing* **4** B2
Beicai *Shanghai* **28** B2
Beijing *Beijing* **4** B1
Beit Duqu *Jerusalem* **13** A1
Beit Ghur at-Taht *Jerusalem* **13** A1
Beit Ghur el-Fawqa *Jerusalem* **13** A1
Beit Hanina *Jerusalem* **13** B2
Beit Ij'za *Jerusalem* **13** A1
Beit Iksa *Jerusalem* **13** B2
Beit I'nan *Jerusalem* **13** A1
Beit Jala *Jerusalem* **13** B2
Beit Lekhem = Bayt Lahm *Jerusalem* **13** B2
Beit Liqya *Jerusalem* **13** A1
Beit Nekofa *Jerusalem* **13** B1
Beit Sahur *Jerusalem* **13** B2
Beit Sofafa *Jerusalem* **13** B2
Beit Surik *Jerusalem* **13** B1
Beit Ur al-Fawqa *Jerusalem* **13** A1
Beit Zayit *Jerusalem* **13** B1
Beitaipingzhuan *Beijing* **4** B1
Beitar Ilit *Jerusalem* **13** B1
Beitin *Jerusalem* **13** A2
Beitsun *Guangzhou* **11** B2
Beitunya *Jerusalem* **13** A2
Beixing Jing Park *Shanghai* **28** B1
Békásmegyer *Budapest* **7** A2
Bekkelaget *Oslo* **23** A3
Bekkestua *Oslo* **23** A2
Bel Air *Los Angeles* **16** B2
Bela Vista *São Paulo* **27** B2
Bélanger *Montreal* **20** A1
Belas *Lisbon* **16** A1
Beleghata *Kolkata* **14** B2
Belém *Lisbon* **16** A1
Belém, Torre de *Lisbon* **16** A1
Belènzinho *São Paulo* **27** B2
Belgachiya *Kolkata* **14** B2
Belgharia *Kolkata* **14** B2
Belgrano *Buenos Aires* **7** B2
Bell *Los Angeles* **16** C3
Bell Gardens *Los Angeles* **16** C4
Bellavista *Lima* **14** B2
Bellavista *Santiago* **27** C2
Belle Harbor *New York* **22** C2
Belle Isle *Orlando* **23** B2
Belle View *Washington* **33** B2
Bellingham *London* **15** B3
Bellwood *Chicago* **9** B1
Belmont *Boston* **6** A1
Belmont *London* **15** A2
Belmont, Mt. *Wellington* **33** B2
Belmont Cragin *Chicago* **9** B2
Belmont Harbor *Chicago* **9** B3
Belmore *Sydney* **29** B1
Belur *Kolkata* **14** B2
Belvedere *Atlanta* **3** B3
Belvedere *London* **15** B4
Belvedere *San Francisco* **26** A2
Belyayevo Bogorodskoye *Moscow* **19** C2
Bemowo *Warsaw* **32** B1
Benaki Museum *Athens* **2** B2
Bendale *Toronto* **31** A3
Benefica *Rio de Janeiro* **25** B1
Benfica *Lisbon* **16** A1
Benito Juárez *Mexico City* **18** B2
Benito Juárez, Int. ✈ **(MEX)** *Mexico City* **18** B2
Bensonhurst *New York* **22** C2
Berchem-Ste-Agathe *Brussels* **6** A1
Berg am Laim *Munich* **21** B2
Bergenfield *New York* **22** A2
Bergham *Munich* **21** B2
Bergvliet *Cape Town* **8** B1
Beri *Barcelona* **4** A1
Berkeley *San Francisco* **26** A3
Berlin *Berlin* **5** A3
Berlin Dom *Berlin* **5** A3
Berlin Tegel ✈ **(TXL)** *Berlin* **5** A2
Berlin Tempelhof ✈ **(THF)** *Berlin* **5** B3
Bermondsey *London* **15** B3
Bernabeu, Estadio *Madrid* **17** B1
Bernal Heights *San Francisco* **26** B2
Berwyn *Chicago* **9** B2
Berwyn Heights *Washington* **33** B4
Besiktas *Istanbul* **12** B2
Besós → *Barcelona* **4** A2
Bessie, L. *Orlando* **23** B1
Bet Horon *Jerusalem* **13** A1
Bethesda *Washington* **33** B3
Bethlehem = Bayt Lahm *Jerusalem* **13** B2
Bethnal Green *London* **15** A3
Betor *Kolkata* **14** B1
Beulah *Orlando* **23** A1
Beulah, L. *Orlando* **23** A1
Beverley Hills *Sydney* **29** B1
Beverley Park *Sydney* **29** B1
Beverly *Chicago* **9** C3
Beverly Arts Center *Chicago* **9** C2
Beverly Glen *Los Angeles* **16** B2
Beverly Hills *Los Angeles* **16** B2
Beverly Hills -Morgan Park Historic District *Chicago* **9** C2
Bexley *Sydney* **29** B1
Bexley □ *London* **15** B4
Bexleyheath *London* **15** B4
Beykoz *Istanbul* **12** B2
Beylerbeyi *Istanbul* **12** B2
Beyoğlu *Istanbul* **12** B1
Bezons *Paris* **24** A2
Bezuidenhout Park *Johannesburg* **13** B2
Bhadrakali *Kolkata* **14** A2
Bhalswa *Delhi* **10** A2
Bhambo Khan Qarmati *Karachi* **13** B2
Bhatsala *Kolkata* **14** B1
Bhawanipur *Kolkata* **14** B2
Bhendkhal *Mumbai* **20** B2
Bhuleshwar *Mumbai* **20** B1
Białołeka Dworska *Warsaw* **32** B2
Bicentennial Park *Los Angeles* **16** B4
Bicentennial Park *Sydney* **29** B1
Bickley *London* **15** B4
Bicutan *Manila* **17** C2
Bidhan Nagar *Kolkata* **14** B2
Bidu *Jerusalem* **13** B1
Bielany *Warsaw* **32** B1
Bielawa *Warsaw* **32** C2
Biesdorf *Berlin* **5** A4
Bièvre → *Paris* **24** B1
Bièvres *Paris* **24** B2
Big Sand Lake *Orlando* **23** B2
Bilston *Edinburgh* **11** B2
Binacayan *Manila* **17** C1
Binondo *Manila* **17** B1
Bintaro Jaya *Jakarta* **12** B1
Bir Nabala *Jerusalem* **13** A2
Birak el Kiyam *Cairo* **7** A1
Birch Cliff *Toronto* **31** A3
Birkenstein *Berlin* **5** A5
Birkholz *Berlin* **5** A4
Birkholzaue *Berlin* **5** A4
Birrarrung Park *Melbourne* **18** A2
Biscayne Park *Miami* **18** A2
Bishop Lavis *Cape Town* **8** A2
Bishopscourt *Cape Town* **8** A1
Bispebjerg *Copenhagen* **8** A3
Bittsevsky Forest Park *Moscow* **19** C2
Björknas *Stockholm* **29** B3
Black Cr. → *Toronto* **31** A2
Black Creek Pioneer Village *Toronto* **31** A1
Blackfen *London* **15** B4
Blackheath *London* **15** B4
Blackrock *Dublin* **10** B2
Bladensburg *Washington* **33** B4
Blair Village *Atlanta* **3** C2
Blairgowrie *Johannesburg* **13** A2
Blake House *Boston* **6** B2
Blakehurst *Sydney* **29** B1
Blakstad *Oslo* **23** B1
Blanche, L. *Orlando* **23** B1
Blankenburg *Berlin* **5** A3
Blankenfelde *Berlin* **5** A3
Blizne *Warsaw* **32** B1
Błota *Warsaw* **32** C3
Blue Island *Chicago* **9** D2
Blue Mosque = Sultanahme Camil *Istanbul* **12** B1
Bluebell *Dublin* **10** B1
Bluff Hd. *Hong Kong* **12** B2
Bluffers Park *Toronto* **31** A3
Blumberg *Berlin* **5** A4
Blunt Pt. *San Francisco* **26** A2
Blutenberg *Munich* **21** B1
Blylaget *Oslo* **23** B3
Boa Vista, Alto do *Rio de Janeiro* **25** B1
Boardwalk *New York* **22** C3
Boavista *Lisbon* **16** A2
Bobigny *Paris* **24** A3
Bocanegra *Lima* **14** B2
Boedo *Buenos Aires* **7** B2
Bogenhausen *Munich* **21** B2
Boggy Creek Swamp *Orlando* **23** B2
Bogorodskoye *Moscow* **19** B3
Bogota *New York* **22** A1
Bogstadvatnet *Oslo* **23** A2
Bohnsdorf *Berlin* **5** B4
Bois-Colombes *Paris* **24** A2
Bois-d'Arcy *Paris* **24** B1
Boissy-St-Léger *Paris* **24** B4
Boldinasco *Milan* **19** B1
Bøler *Oslo* **23** A4
Bollate *Milan* **19** A1
Bollebeek *Brussels* **6** A1
Bollensdorf *Berlin* **5** A5
Bollmora *Stockholm* **29** B3
Bolshaya Okhta *St. Petersburg* **27** B2
Bolton *Atlanta* **3** B2
Bom Retiro *São Paulo* **27** B2
Bombay = Mumbai *Mumbai* **20** B2
Bondi *Sydney* **29** B2
Bondy *Paris* **24** A3
Bondy, Forêt de *Paris* **24** A4
Bonifacio Monument *Manila* **17** B1
Bonneuil-sur-Marne *Paris* **24** B4
Bonnington *Edinburgh* **11** B1
Bonnyrigg and Lasswade *Edinburgh* **11** B3
Bonsucesso *Rio de Janeiro* **25** B1
Bonteheuwel *Cape Town* **8** A2
Boo *Stockholm* **29** A3
Booterstown *Dublin* **10** B2
Borisovo *Moscow* **19** C3
Borle *Mumbai* **20** A2
Boronia Park *Sydney* **29** A1
Bosmont *Johannesburg* **13** B1
Bosön *Stockholm* **29** A3
Bosporus = İstanbul Boğazı *Istanbul* **12** B2
Bostancı *Istanbul* **12** C2
Boston *Boston* **6** A2
Boston Common *Boston* **6** A2
Boston Logan Int. ✈ **(BOS)** *Boston* **6** A2
Botafogo *Rio de Janeiro* **25** B1
Botany *Sydney* **29** B2
Botany B. *Sydney* **29** B2
Botany Bay Nat. Park △ *Sydney* **29** B2
Botič → *Prague* **25** B3
Botica Sete *Lisbon* **16** A1
Boucherville *Montreal* **20** A3
Boucherville, Îs. de *Montreal* **20** A3
Bougival *Paris* **24** A1
Boulder Pt. *Hong Kong* **12** B1
Boulogne, Bois de *Paris* **24** A2
Boulogne-Billancourt *Paris* **24** A2
Bourg-la-Reine *Paris* **24** B2
Bouviers *Paris* **24** B1
Bovenkerk *Amsterdam* **2** B2
Bovenkerker Polder *Amsterdam* **2** B2
Bovisa *Milan* **19** A2
Bow *London* **15** A3
Boyacıköy *Istanbul* **12** B2
Boyd Conservation Area *Toronto* **31** A1
Boyle Heights *Los Angeles* **16** B3
Braepark *Edinburgh* **11** B2
Braid *Edinburgh* **11** B2
Bramley *Johannesburg* **13** A2
Brandeis University *Boston* **6** A1
Brandenburger Tor *Berlin* **5** A3
Brani, Pulau *Singapore* **28** B3
Branik *Prague* **25** B2
Brännkyrka *Stockholm* **29** B2
Brás *São Paulo* **27** B2
Brasilândia *São Paulo* **27** A1
Brateyevo *Moscow* **19** C3
Braybrook *Melbourne* **18** A1
Brázdim *Prague* **25** A3
Breakheart Reservation *Boston* **6** A2
Brede *Copenhagen* **8** A3
Breezy Point *New York* **22** C2
Breitenlee *Vienna* **32** A3
Breña *Lima* **14** B2
Brent □ *London* **15** A2
Brent Res. *London* **15** A2
Brentford *London* **15** B2
Brentwood Park *Los Angeles* **16** B2
Brera *Milan* **19** B2
Bresso *Milan* **19** A2
Brevik *Stockholm* **29** A3
Břevnov *Prague* **25** B2
Brickyard, The *Chicago* **9** B2
Bridgeport *Chicago* **9** B3
Bridgetown *Cape Town* **8** A2
Bridgeview *Chicago* **9** C2
Brighton *Boston* **6** A2
Brighton *Melbourne* **18** B1
Brighton Beach *New York* **22** C2
Brighton le Sands *Sydney* **29** B1
Brighton Park *Chicago* **9** C2
Brightwood *Washington* **33** B3
Brigittenau *Vienna* **32** A2
Brimbank Park *Melbourne* **18** A1
Brisbane *San Francisco* **26** B2
Britz *Berlin* **5** B3
Brixton *London* **15** B3
Broadmeadows *Melbourne* **18** A1
Broadmoor *San Francisco* **26** B2
Broadview *Chicago* **9** B1
Brockley *London* **15** B3
Bródno *Warsaw* **32** B2
Bródnowski, Kanal *Warsaw* **32** B2
Broek *Amsterdam* **2** A2
Bromley □ *London* **15** B4
Bromley Common *London* **15** B4
Bromma *Stockholm* **29** A1
Bromma ✈ *Stockholm* **29** A1
Brøndby Strand *Copenhagen* **8** B2
Brøndbyøster *Copenhagen* **8** B2
Brøndbyvester *Copenhagen* **8** B2
Brondesbury *London* **15** A2
Brønnøya *Oslo* **23** A2
Brønshøj *Copenhagen* **8** A2
Bronxville *New York* **22** A3
Brookfield *Chicago* **9** C1
Brookhaven *Atlanta* **3** A2
Brookline *Boston* **6** B2
Brooklyn *Cape Town* **8** A1
Brooklyn *New York* **22** C2
Brooklyn *Wellington* **33** B1
Brooklyn Heights *New York* **22** B2
Brookmont *Washington* **33** B3
Brossard *Montreal* **20** B3
Brou-sur-Chantereine *Paris* **24** A4
Brown *Toronto* **31** A3
Broyhill Park *Washington* **33** B2
Brughério *Milan* **19** A2
Brunswick *Melbourne* **18** A1
Brussegem *Brussels* **6** A1
Brussel *Brussels* **6** A2
Brussel ✈ **(BRU)** *Brussels* **6** A2
Brussels = Brussel *Brussels* **6** A
Bruxelles = Brussel *Brussels* **6** A
Bruzzano *Milan* **19** A2
Bry-sur-Marne *Paris* **24** A4
Bryan, L. *Orlando* **23** B2
Bryanston *Johannesburg* **13** A1
Bryn *Oslo* **23** A1
Brzeziny *Warsaw* **32** B2
Bubeneč *Prague* **25** B2
Buc *Paris* **24** B1
Buchenhain *Munich* **21** B1
Buchholz *Berlin* **5** A3
Buckhead *Atlanta* **3** A2
Buckingham Palace *London* **15** A3
Buckow *Berlin* **5** B3
Buda *Budapest* **7** A2
Buda Castle = Budavári palota *Budapest* **7**
Budafok *Budapest* **7** B2
Budaörs *Budapest* **7** B1
Budapest *Budapest* **7** B2
Budapest ✈ **(BUD)** *Budapest* **7**
Budatétény *Budapest* **7** B2
Budavári palota *Budapest* **7** A2
Budding *Copenhagen* **8** A3
Buena Ventura Lakes *Orlando* **23** B2
Buena Vista *San Francisco* **26** B
Buenos Aires *Buenos Aires* **7** B
Bufalotta *Rome* **26** B2
Bugio *Lisbon* **16** B1
Buiksloot *Amsterdam* **2** A2
Buitenveldert *Amsterdam* **2** B2
Buizingen *Brussels* **6** B1
Bukhansan *Seoul* **27** B1
Bukit Panjang Nature Reserve *Singapore* **28** A2
Bukit Timah Nature Reserve *Singapore* **28** A2
Bukum, Pulau *Singapore* **28** B
Bûlâq *Cairo* **7** A2
Bule *Manila* **17** C2
Bulim *Singapore* **28** A2
Bullen Park *Melbourne* **18** A2
Bund, The *Shanghai* **28** B1
Bundoora North *Melbourne* **1**
Bundoora Park *Melbourne* **18**
Bunker Hill Memorial *Boston* **6** A2
Bunker I. *Karachi* **13** B1
Bunkyō *Tokyo* **30** A3
Bunnefjorden *Oslo* **23** A3
Buona Vista Park *Singapore* **2**
Burbank *Chicago* **9** C2
Burbank *Los Angeles* **16** A3
Burden, L. *Orlando* **23** B1
Burlington *Boston* **6** A1
Burnham Park *Chicago* **9** C3
Burnham Park Harbor *Chicago* **9** B3
Burnhamthorpe *Toronto* **31** B
Burnt Oak *London* **15** A2
Burntisland *Edinburgh* **11** A2
Burnwynd *Edinburgh* **11** B1
Burqa *Jerusalem* **13** A2
Burtus *Cairo* **7** A1
Burudvatn *Oslo* **23** A2
Burwood *Sydney* **29** B1
Bushwick *New York* **22** B2
Bushy Park *London* **15** B1
Butantã *São Paulo* **27** B1
Butcher I. *Mumbai* **20** B2
Butler, L. *Orlando* **23** B1
Butts Corner *Washington* **33** C
Büyükdere *Istanbul* **12** B2
Byculla *Mumbai* **20** B2
Bygdøy *Oslo* **23** A3

C

C.B.S. Fox Studios *Los Angeles* **16** B2
C.N.N. Center *Atlanta* **3** B2
C.N. Tower *Toronto* **31** B2
Caballito *Buenos Aires* **7** B2
Cabin John *Washington* **33** B2
Cabin John Regional Park ⌓ *Washington* **33** A2
Cabinteely *Dublin* **10** B3
Cabra *Dublin* **10** A2
Cabuçú de Baixo → *São Paulo* **27** A1
Cabuçú de Cima → *São Paulo* **27** A2
Cachan *Paris* **24** B2
Cachoeira, Rib. da → *São Paulo* **27** B1
Cacilhas *Lisbon* **16** A2
Cahuenga Park *Los Angeles*
Cain, L. *Orlando* **23** B2
Cairo = El Qâhira *Cairo* **7** A2
Cairo Int. ✈ **(CAI)** *Cairo* **7** A3
Caju *Rio de Janeiro* **25** B1
Čakovice *Prague* **25** B3
Calcutta = Kolkata *Kolkata*
California Inst. of Tech. *Los Angeles* **16** B4
California Los Angeles, University of *Los Angeles* **1**
California State University *Los Angeles* **16**
Callao *Lima* **14** B2
Caloocan *Manila* **17** B1
Calumet L. *Chicago* **9** C3
Calumet Park *Chicago* **9** C3

alumet Sag Channel ⛴
Chicago 9 C2
alvairate Milan 19 B2
amarate Lisbon 16 A2
amaroes Lisbon 16 A1
amberwell London 15 B3
amberwell Melbourne 18 B2
ambridge Boston 6 A2
ambuci São Paulo 27 B2
amden □ London 15 A3
ameron, Mt. Wellington 33 B2
amlıca Istanbul 12 B2
amp Springs Washington 33 C4
ampamento Madrid 17 B1
ampbellfield Melbourne 18 A1
amperdown Sydney 29 B2
ampo, Casa de Madrid 17 B1
ampo F.C. Barcelona
Barcelona 4 A1
ampo Grando Lisbon 16 A2
ampo Pequeño Lisbon 16 A2
ampolide Lisbon 16 A2
amps Bay Cape Town 8 A1
an San Joan Barcelona 4 A2
añacao B. Manila 17 C1
anarsie New York 22 C2
andiac Montreal 20 B3
aneças Lisbon 16 A1
anillas Madrid 17 B2
anillejas Madrid 17 B2
anning Town London 15 A4
anteras de Vallecas
Madrid 17 B2
anterbury Melbourne 18 A2
anterbury Sydney 29 B1
anton = Guangzhou
Guangzhou 11 B2
oheijing Shanghai 28 B1
apão Redondo São Paulo 27 B1
aparica Lisbon 16 A2
aparica, Costa da Lisbon 16 B1
ape Flats Cape Town 8 B2
ape Peninsula △
Cape Town 8 A1
ape Town Cape Town 8 A1
ape Town Int. ✈ (CPT)
Cape Town 8 A2
apitol Heights Washington 33 B4
aptain Cook Bridge
Sydney 29 C1
aptain Cook Landing
Place Park Sydney 29 C2
apuchos Lisbon 16 B1
arabanchel Alto Madrid 17 B1
arabanchel Bajo Madrid 17 B1
arapachay Buenos Aires 7 B1
araza Buenos Aires 7 C2
aridad Manila 17 C1
arioca, Sa. da
Rio de Janeiro 25 B1
arlstadt New York 22 A1
arlton Melbourne 18 A1
armen de Huechuraba
Santiago 27 B1
armen de la Legua Lima 14 B2
arnaxide Lisbon 16 A1
arnegie Melbourne 18 B2
arnide Lisbon 16 A1
arol City Miami 18 A1
arrascal Santiago 27 B1
arrickmines Dublin 10 B3
arrières-sous-Bois Paris 24 A1
arrières-sous-Poissy Paris 24 A1
arrières-sur-Seine Paris 24 A2
arrigeen B. Dublin 10 A3
artierville Montreal 20 A1
a Loma Toronto 31 A2
a Verde São Paulo 27 A1
asil Morena Rome 26 C2
asalotti Rome 26 B1
asade Heights Atlanta 3 B2
astel di Leva Rome 26 C2
astel Sant'Angelo Rome 26 B1
astleknock Dublin 10 A1
astleton Corners
New York 22 C1
ate Rio de Janeiro 25 B1
ford London 15 B3
aerine, L. Orlando 23 B2
afield Melbourne 18 B2
ate Manila 17 C1
as Lisbon 16 A1
ecci Istanbul 12 B1
achignola Rome 26 C2
alienhof, Schloss Berlin 5 B1
ar Grove Atlanta 3 C3
arvale Park Toronto 31 A2
apaka Putih Jakarta 12 B2
agelköy Istanbul 12 B2
agkareng Jakarta 12 A1
atennial Olympic Park
Atlanta 3 B2
atennial Park Sydney 29 B2
ater Hill Atlanta 3 B2
atocelle Rome 26 B2
atral, Gare Montreal 20 B2
atral Park New York 22 B2
anyola del Vallès
arcelona 4 A1
alos Santiago 27 B1
ao de la Estrella,
arque Nacional △
exico City 18 B2
ao de los Ángeles
adrid 17 C1
ao Navia Santiago 27 B1
ano Boscone Milan 19 B1
ate Milan 19 B1
Kwo Ling Hong Kong 12 B2
aarrita Buenos Aires 7 B2
adwell Heath London 15 A4
Chee Singapore 28 B3
Wan Hong Kong 12 B2
Wan Kok Hong Kong 12 A1
akdaha Kolkata 14 C1
amartin Madrid 17 B1
anberi Madrid 17 B1
anbourcy Paris 24 A1
ampigny-sur-Marne
aris 24 B4
amplain, Pont Montreal 20 B2
amps-sur-Marne Paris 24 A4
anrail Kolkata 14 B1
aakyapuri Delhi 10 B2
aditala Kolkata 14 A1
angfeng Park Shanghai 28 B1
anghai = Shanghai
anghai 28 B2
angi Singapore 28 A3
angi, Singapore ✈
N) Singapore 28 A3
angning Shanghai 28 B1
atereine Paris 24 A4
atian Guangzhou 11 A2
ayang Beijing 4 B2
ayangmen Beijing 4 B2
aelizod Dublin 10 A1
aultepec, Bosque de
exico City 18 B1
aultepec, Castillo de
exico City 18 B1

Charenton-le-Pont Paris 24 B3
Charleroi, Kanal de ⛴
Brussels 6 B1
Charles Bridge = Karlův
most Prague 25 B2
Charles Gates Dawes
House Chicago 9 A2
Charlestown Boston 6 A2
Charlottenburg Berlin 5 A2
Charlottenburg, Schloss
Berlin 5 A2
Charlottenlund Copenhagen 8 A3
Charlton London 15 B4
Charneca Lisbon 16 A2
Chase, L. Orlando 23 B1
Châteaufort Paris 24 B1
Châtenay-Malabry Paris 24 B2
Chatham Chicago 9 C3
Chatillon Paris 24 B2
Chatou Paris 24 A1
Chatpur Kolkata 14 B2
Chatswood Sydney 29 A2
Chatuchak Bangkok 3 B2
Chatuchak Park Bangkok 3 B2
Chauki Karachi 13 A1
Chavarria Lima 14 B2
Chaville Paris 24 B2
Chayang Seoul 27 B2
Chelles Paris 24 A4
Chelles, Canal de Paris 24 A4
Chells-le-Pin ✈ Paris 24 A4
Chelsea Boston 6 A2
Chelsea London 15 B2
Chembur Mumbai 20 A2
Chennevières-sur-Marne
Paris 24 B4
Cheongdam Seoul 27 B2
Cheonho Seoul 27 B2
Cheops Cairo 7 B1
Chertanovka ⛴ Moscow 19 C2
Chertanovo Moscow 19 C2
Cheryomushki Moscow 19 B2
Chestnut Hill Boston 6 B1
Cheung Sha Wan
Hong Kong 12 A1
Cheverly Washington 33 B4
Chevilly-Larue Paris 24 B3
Chevry-Cossigny Paris 24 B4
Chevy Chase Washington 33 B3
Chhatrapati Shivaji,
Mumbai ✈ (BOM)
Mumbai 20 A2
Chia Keng Singapore 28 A3
Chiaravalle Milanese
Milan 19 B2
Chicago Chicago 9 B3
Chicago, University of
Chicago 9 C3
Chicago Harbor Chicago 9 B3
Chicago Lawn Chicago 9 C2
Chicago-Midway ✈
(MDW) Chicago 9 C2
Chicago O'Hare Int. ✈
(ORD) Chicago 9 B1
Chicago Ridge Chicago 9 C2
Chicago River, North
Branch ⛴ Chicago 9 B2
Chicago Sanitary and
Ship Canal Chicago 9 C2
Chicago State University
Chicago 9 C3
Chicago Zoo Chicago 9 B1
Chienzui Guangzhou 11 A3
Chik Sha Hong Kong 12 B2
Child's Hill London 15 A2
Chilla Saroda Delhi 10 B2
Chillum Washington 33 B4
Chilly-Mazarin Paris 24 B2
China Basin San Francisco 26 B2
Chingupota Kolkata 14 C1
Chinna Cr. ⛴ Karachi 13 B2
Chiquihuite, Cerro
Mexico City 18 A2
Chislehurst London 15 B4
Chiswick London 15 B2
Chiswick House London 15 B2
Chitose Tokyo 30 B2
Chitralada Palace Bangkok 3 B2
Chiyoda Tokyo 30 A3
Choa Chu Kang Singapore 28 A2
Chodov u Prahy Prague 25 B3
Chōfu Tokyo 30 B2
Choisy-le-Roi Paris 24 B3
Cholupice Prague 25 C2
Chom Thong Bangkok 3 B1
Chong Pang Singapore 28 A2
Chongwen Beijing 4 B2
Chorrillos Lima 14 C2
Chowpatty Beach Mumbai 20 B1
Christianshavn Copenhagen 8 A3
Chrzanów Warsaw 32 B1
Chuen Lung Hong Kong 12 A1
Chuk Kok Hong Kong 12 A2
Chulalongkom Univ.
Bangkok 3 B2
Chuō Tokyo 30 A3
Church End London 15 A2
Churchtown Dublin 10 B2
Ciampino Rome 26 C2
Ciampino ✈ Rome 26 C2
Cicero Chicago 9 B2
Cilandak Jakarta 12 B1
Cilincing Jakarta 12 A2
Ciliwung ⛴ Jakarta 12 B2
Čimice Prague 25 B2
Cinecittà Rome 26 B2
Cinisello Balsamo Milan 19 A2
Cinkota Budapest 7 A3
Cipete Jakarta 12 B1
Città degli Studi Milan 19 B2
Città del Vaticano =
Vatican City ■ Rome 26 B1
City, The London 15 A3
City of the Dead Cairo 7 A2
Ciudad de México
Mexico City 18 B2
Ciudad Deportiva
Mexico City 18 B2
Ciudad Fin de Semana
Madrid 17 B2
Ciudad General Belgrano
Buenos Aires 7 C1
Ciudad Lineál Madrid 17 B2
Ciudad Satélite Mexico City 18 A1
Ciudad Universitaria
Buenos Aires 7 B2
Ciudad Universitaria
Mexico City 18 C1
Claireville Res. Toronto 31 A1
Clamart Paris 24 B2
Clapham London 15 B3
Clapton London 15 A3
Claremont Cape Town 8 A1
Clayhall London 15 A4
Clear, L. Orlando 23 A2
Clermiston Edinburgh 11 B2
Clichy Paris 24 A2
Clichy-sous-Bois Paris 24 A4
Cliffside Toronto 31 A3
Cliffside Park New York 22 B2
Clifton Cape Town 8 A1

Clifton Karachi 13 B2
Clifton New York 22 C1
Clifton Beach Karachi 13 B2
Cliftondale Boston 6 A2
Cloghran Dublin 10 A2
Clonskeagh Dublin 10 B2
Clontarf Dublin 10 A2
Clontarf Sydney 29 A2
Clovelly Sydney 29 B2
Cobras, I. das Rio de Janeiro 25 B2
Coburg Melbourne 18 A1
Cocotá Rio de Janeiro 25 A1
Cœuilly Paris 24 B4
Coina Lisbon 16 B2
Coker Lagos 14 B2
Colaba Mumbai 20 B1
Colaba Pt. Mumbai 20 B1
Colegiales Buenos Aires 7 B2
Colindale London 15 A2
Colinton Edinburgh 11 B2
College Park Atlanta 3 C2
College Park Washington 33 B4
College Point New York 22 B2
Collégien Paris 24 A4
Collier Row London 15 A4
Colliers Wood London 15 B2
Colma San Francisco 26 B2
Colney Hatch London 15 A3
Cologno Monzese Milan 19 A2
Colombes Paris 24 A2
Colonia Güell Barcelona 4 A1
Colonial Knob Wellington 33 A1
Colosseo Rome 26 B1
Colosseum = Colosseo
Rome 26 B1
Combault Paris 24 B4
Comércio, Praça do Lisbon 16 A2
Commerce Los Angeles 16 B4
Como Sydney 29 C1
Conceição, I. da
Rio de Janeiro 25 B2
Conchali Santiago 27 B2
Concord Sydney 29 B1
Concord Toronto 31 A2
Concorde, Place de la Paris 24 A2
Concorezzo Milan 19 A2
Condet Jakarta 12 A2
Coney Island New York 22 C2
Congonhas São Paulo ✈
(CGH) São Paulo 27 B2
Conley ⛴ Atlanta 3 C3
Connaught Place Delhi 10 B2
Consolação São Paulo 27 B2
Constantia Cape Town 8 B1
Constitución Buenos Aires 7 B2
Constitution Atlanta 3 B2
Convention Center
Los Angeles 16 B3
Conway Orlando 23 B2
Conway, L. Orlando 23 B2
Coogee Sydney 29 B2
Cooksville Toronto 31 B1
Coolock Dublin 10 A2
Copacabana Rio de Janeiro 25 B1
Copenhagen =
København Copenhagen 8 A2
Coral Gables Miami 18 B2
Coral Hills Washington 33 B4
Corcovado, Cristo
Redentor Rio de Janeiro 25 B1
Corduff Dublin 10 A1
Cormano Milan 19 A2
Cornaredo Milan 19 A1
Córsico Milan 19 B1
Corstorphine Edinburgh 11 B2
Corviale Rome 26 B1
Coslada Madrid 17 B2
Cossigny Paris 24 B4
Cotao Lisbon 16 A1
Côte-St-Luc Montreal 20 B2
Cotunduba, I. de
Rio de Janeiro 25 B2
Coubron Paris 24 A4
Countryside Chicago 9 C1
County Art Museum
Los Angeles 16 B2
Courbevoie Paris 24 A2
Courtry Paris 24 A4
Cowley London 15 A1
Coyoacán Mexico City 18 B2
Craighall Park
Johannesburg 13 A2
Craiglockhart Edinburgh 11 B2
Craigmillar Edinburgh 11 B3
Cramond Edinburgh 11 B2
Cramond Bridge Edinburgh 11 B1
Cramond I. Edinburgh 11 B2
Cranford London 15 B1
Crawford Cape Town 8 A2
Crayford London 15 B5
Creekmouth London 15 A4
Crescent, L. Orlando 23 A1
Crescenzago Milan 19 A2
Cressely Paris 24 B1
Cresskill New York 22 A2
Créteil Paris 24 B3
Cricklewood London 15 A2
Cristo Redentor, Estatua
do Rio de Janeiro 25 B1
Crockenhill London 15 B4
Croissy-Beaubourg Paris 24 B4
Croissy-sur-Seine Paris 24 A1
Crosby Johannesburg 13 B1
Crosne Paris 24 B3
Cross I. Mumbai 20 B2
Crouch End London 15 A3
Crown Mine Johannesburg 13 B1
Crows Nest Sydney 29 A2
Croydon London 15 B3
Croydon Park Sydney 29 B1
Cruagh Mt. Dublin 10 B2
Crumlin Dublin 10 B2
Cruz de Pau Lisbon 16 B2
Crystal Palace London 15 B3
Csepel Budapest 7 B2
Csepelsziget Budapest 7 B2
Csillaghegy Budapest 7 A2
Csillagtelep Budapest 7 B2
Csömör Budapest 7 A3
Csömöri-patak ⛴ Budapest 7 A3
Cuatro Vientos Madrid 17 B1
Cuauhtémoc Mexico City 18 B2
Cuban Museum Miami 18 B2
Cubao Manila 17 B2
Çubuklu Istanbul 12 B2
Cudahy Los Angeles 16 C3
Cuicuilco, Pirámido de
Mexico City 18 C1
Culmore Washington 33 B3
Culver City Los Angeles 16 B2
Cumbres de Vallecas
Madrid 17 B2
Cupecé São Paulo 27 B1
Currie Edinburgh 11 B2
Cusago Milan 19 B1
Cusano Milanino Milan 19 A2
Cutler Park Boston 6 B1
Çuvuşabaşi ⛴ Istanbul 12 B1
Cypress Hills New York 22 B2
Czerniaków Warsaw 32 B2
Czyste Warsaw 32 B1

D

Da Moóca ⛴ São Paulo 27 B2
Ďáblice Prague 25 B2
Dąbrowa Warsaw 32 B1
Dachang Shanghai 28 B1
Dachang ✈ Shanghai 28 B1
Dachau Munich 21 A1
Dachau-Ost Munich 21 A1
Dachauer Moos Munich 21 A1
Dadar Mumbai 20 A1
Daebang Seoul 27 B1
Daechi Seoul 27 B2
Dafni Athens 2 B2
Dagenham London 15 A4
Daglfing Munich 21 B2
Dahab, Gezîret el Cairo 7 B2
Daheisha Jerusalem 13 B2
Dahlem Berlin 5 B2
Dahlwitz-Hoppegarten
Berlin 5 A5
Dahongmen Beijing 4 C2
Dajiaoting Beijing 4 B2
Dakhnoye St. Petersburg 27 C1
Dalejsky potok ⛴ Prague 25 B2
Dalgety Bay Edinburgh 11 A1
Dalkeith Edinburgh 11 B3
Dalkey Dublin 10 B3
Dalkey I. Dublin 10 B3
Dallgow Berlin 5 A1
Dalmeny Edinburgh 11 B1
Dalston London 15 A3
Daly City San Francisco 26 B2
Damaia Lisbon 16 A1
Damarakia Athens 2 B1
Dämeritzsee Berlin 5 B5
Dan Ryan Woods Chicago 9 C2
Danderhall Edinburgh 11 B3
Danderyd Stockholm 29 A2
Danforth Toronto 31 A3
Darakeh Tehran 31 A2
Darband Tehran 31 A2
Darling Point Sydney 29 B2
Darndale Dublin 10 A2
Darrüs Tehran 31 A2
Dartford London 15 B5
Dashi Guangzhou 11 B2
Datansha Guangzhou 11 B2
Datun Beijing 4 B2
Daulatpur Delhi 10 A1
Davidson, Mt.
San Francisco 26 B2
Davidson's Mains
Edinburgh 11 B2
Dāvūdiyeh Tehran 31 A2
Davydkovo Moscow 19 B1
Dawidy Warsaw 32 C1
Days Bay Wellington 33 B2
Decatur Atlanta 3 B3
Dedham Boston 6 B1
Degunino Moscow 19 A2
Deir Dibwan Jerusalem 13 A2
Deir Ibzi'e Jerusalem 13 A1
Dejvice Prague 25 B2
Dekabristov, Ostrov
St. Petersburg 27 B1
Delhi Delhi 10 B2
Demarest New York 22 A2
Den Ilp Amsterdam 2 A2
Denistone Heights Sydney 29 A1
Dentonia Park Toronto 31 A3
DePaul University Chicago 9 B3
Deptford London 15 B3
Des Plaines Chicago 9 A1
Deshengmen Beijing 4 B2
Deutsch-Wagram Vienna 32 A3
Deutsche Oper Berlin 5 A2
Deutscher Museum
Munich 21 B2
Devil's Peak Cape Town 8 A1
Dhakuria Kolkata 14 B2
Dharavi Mumbai 20 A2
Diadema São Paulo 27 C2
Diegen Brussels 6 A2
Diemen Amsterdam 2 A2
Diepkloof Johannesburg 13 B1
Dieprivier Cape Town 8 B1
Difficult Run ⛴
Washington 33 B2
Dilbeek Brussels 6 A1
Dilli = Delhi Delhi 10 B2
Dirnismaning Munich 21 A2
Disney-M.G.M. Studios
Orlando 23 B1
Disney Studios Los Angeles 16 B3
District Heights
Washington 33 B4
Djakarta = Jakarta Jakarta 12 A2
Djursholm Stockholm 29 A2
Döberitz Berlin 5 A1
Döbling Vienna 32 A2
Dobong Seoul 27 B2
Dobongsan Seoul 27 A2
Docklands London 15 A3
Doctor Phillips Orlando 23 B2
Dodder ⛴ Dublin 10 B1
Dodger Stadium
Los Angeles 16 B3
Dogs, Isle of London 15 B3
Dolgoe Ozero St. Petersburg 27 A1
Dollis Hill London 15 A2
Dollymount Dublin 10 A2
Dolni Prague 25 B3
Dolni Chabry Prague 25 B2
Dolni Počernice Prague 25 B3
Dolphins Barn Dublin 10 B2
Dom Pedro II, Parque
São Paulo 27 B2
Don Mills Toronto 31 A2
Don Muang Int. ✈ (BKK)
Bangkok 3 A2
Donaghmede Dublin 10 A3
Donau-Oder Kanal Vienna 32 A3
Donaufeld Vienna 32 A2
Donaupark Vienna 32 A2
Donaustadt Vienna 32 A2
Dongan Hills New York 22 C1
Dongcheng Beijing 4 B2
Dongdaemung Seoul 27 B2
Donggou Shanghai 28 B2
Dongjak Seoul 27 B1
Dongjiao Guangzhou 11 B2
Dongri Mumbai 20 B2
Dongshanhu Park
Guangzhou 11 B2
Dongzhimen Beijing 4 B2
Donnybrook Dublin 10 B2
Doornfontein Johannesburg 13 B2
Dorchester Boston 6 B2
Dorchester B. Boston 6 B2
Dorchester Heights Nat.
Historical Site △ Boston 6 B2
Dornach Munich 21 B3
Dorval Int., Montréal ✈
(YUL) Montreal 20 B1
Dos Couros ⛴ São Paulo 27 C2
Dos Moninos ⛴ São Paulo 27 C2
Douglas Park Chicago 9 B2
Dover Heights Sydney 29 B2

Dowlatābād Tehran 31 B2
Down, L. Orlando 23 A1
Downey Los Angeles 16 C4
Downsview Toronto 31 A1
Downsview C.A.F.B. ✈
Toronto 31 A2
Dragør Copenhagen 8 B3
Drancy Paris 24 A3
Dranesville Washington 33 A1
Drapetsona Athens 2 B1
Dreilinden Berlin 5 B2
Drewnica Warsaw 32 B2
Drigh Road Karachi 13 A2
Drimnagh Dublin 10 B2
Drogenbos Brussels 6 B1
Druid Hills Atlanta 3 B2
Drumcondra Dublin 10 A2
Drummoyne Sydney 29 B1
Drylaw Edinburgh 11 B2
Dubeč Prague 25 B3
Dublin Dublin 10 A2
Dublin ✈ (DUB) Dublin 10 A2
Dublin B. Dublin 10 B3
Dublin Harbour Dublin 10 A2
Duddingston Edinburgh 11 B3
Dugnano Milan 19 A2
Duivendrecht Amsterdam 2 B2
Dūlāb Tehran 31 B2
Dulwich London 15 B3
Dum Dum Kolkata 14 B2
Dum Dum Int. ✈ (CCU)
Kolkata 14 B2
Dumont New York 22 A2
Dún Laoghaire Dublin 10 B3
Dundrum Dublin 10 B2
Dunearn Singapore 28 B2
Dúnleary = Dún
Laoghaire Dublin 10 B3
Dunn Loring Washington 33 B2
Dunning Chicago 9 B2
Dunvegan Johannesburg 13 A2
Duomo Milan 19 B2
Duque de Caxias
Rio de Janeiro 25 A1
Duren Sawit Jakarta 12 A2
Dusit Bangkok 3 B2
Dworp Brussels 6 B1
Dyakovo Moscow 19 B2
Dyker Beach Park
New York 22 C1
Dzerzhinskiy Moscow 19 B2
Dzerzhinskiy Park Moscow 19 B2

E

E.U.R. = Esposizione
Universale di Roma
Rome 26 C1
Eagle Rock Los Angeles 16 B3
Ealing □ London 15 A2
Earlsfield London 15 B2
Earlwood Sydney 29 B1
East Arlington Boston 6 A2
East Arlington Washington 33 B3
East Bedfont London 15 B1
East Boston Boston 6 A2
East Don ⛴ Toronto 31 A2
East Don Parkland Toronto 31 A2
East Elmhurst New York 22 B2
East Finchley London 15 A2
East Flatbush New York 22 C2
East Ham London 15 A4
East Humber ⛴ Toronto 31 A1
East Lamma Channel
Hong Kong 12 B1
East Lexington Boston 6 A1
East Los Angeles
Los Angeles 16 B3
East Molesey London 15 B1
East New York New York 22 B2
East Pines Washington 33 B4
East Point Atlanta 3 B2
East Potomac Park
Washington 33 B3
East River ⛴ New York 22 B2
East Rutherford New York 22 A1
East Sheen London 15 B2
East Talpiyot Jerusalem 13 B2
East Wickham London 15 B4
East York Toronto 31 A2
Eastbourne Wellington 33 B2
Eastcote London 15 A1
Easter Howgate Edinburgh 11 B2
Eastpoint Park Toronto 31 A4
Eastwood Sydney 29 A1
Eaton Canyon Park
Los Angeles 16 A4
Ebara Tokyo 30 B3
Ebisu Tokyo 30 B3
Ebute-Ikorodu Lagos 14 A2
Ebute-Metta Lagos 14 B2
Eda Tokyo 30 B2
Edendale Johannesburg 13 A2
Edenmore Dublin 10 A2
Edgars Cr. ⛴ Melbourne 18 A1
Edgeley Toronto 31 A1
Edgemar San Francisco 26 C2
Edgewater New York 22 B2
Edgewood Orlando 23 B2
Edinburgh Edinburgh 11 B2
Edinburgh ✈ (EDI)
Edinburgh 11 B1
Edinburgh Castle
Edinburgh 11 B2
Edison Park Chicago 9 A2
Edmondston Washington 33 B4
Edmondstown Dublin 10 B2
Edo ⛴ Tokyo 30 B4
Edogawa Tokyo 30 A4
Edsberg Stockholm 29 A1
Edwards L. Melbourne 18 A1
Efzonos Athens 2 B2
Egaleo Athens 2 B2
Egaleo, Oros Athens 2 B1
Eiche Berlin 5 A4
Eiche Sud Berlin 5 A4
Eiffel, Tour Paris 24 A2
Ein Arik Jerusalem 13 A1
Ein Naquba Jerusalem 13 B1
Ein Rafa Jerusalem 13 B1
Eizariya Jerusalem 13 B2
Ejby Copenhagen 8 A2
Ejigbo Lagos 14 A1
Ekeberg Oslo 23 A3
Eknäs Stockholm 29 B3
El 'Abbasiya Cairo 7 A2
El Agustino Lima 14 B2
El Baragil Cairo 7 A1
El Basâtîn Cairo 7 B2
El Bira Jerusalem 13 A2
El Bosque Santiago 27 C2
El Carmen Santiago 27 B1
El Cortijo Santiago 27 B1
El Cristo, Vaso Regulador
Mexico City 18 B1
El Duqqi Cairo 7 A2
El Encinar de los Reyes
Madrid 17 A2
El Gezira Cairo 7 A2

El Ghuriya Cairo 7 A2
El Giza Cairo 7 A2
El Khadr Jerusalem 13 B1
El Khalîfa Cairo 7 A2
El Kôm el Ahmar Cairo 7 A2
El Ma'âdi Cairo 7 B2
El Matariya Cairo 7 A2
El Mohandessin Cairo 7 A2
El Monte Los Angeles 16 B4
El Muqattam Cairo 7 A2
El Mûskî Cairo 7 A2
El Pardo Madrid 17 A1
El Portal Miami 18 A2
El Prat de Llobregat
Barcelona 4 B1
El Qâhira Cairo 7 A2
El Qubba Cairo 7 A2
El Reloj Mexico City 18 C2
El Retiro Madrid 17 B1
El Salto Santiago 27 B2
El Sereno Los Angeles 16 B3
El Talibiya Cairo 7 B2
El Vergel Mexico City 18 C2
El Wâhli Cairo 7 A2
El Zamâlik Cairo 7 A2
El Zeitûn Cairo 7 A2
Elephanta Caves Mumbai 20 B2
Elephanta I. Mumbai 20 B2
Ellboda Stockholm 29 A3
Ellenor, L. Orlando 23 B2
Elliniko Olympic Complex
Athens 2 B2
Ellis I. New York 22 B1
Elm Park London 15 A5
Elmers End London 15 B3
Elmhurst New York 22 B2
Elmstead London 15 B4
Elmwood Park Chicago 9 B2
Elmwood Park New York 22 A1
Elsdon Wellington 33 A1
Elsiesrivier Cape Town 8 A2
Elsternwick Melbourne 18 B2
Eltham London 15 B4
Elwood Melbourne 18 B1
Élysée Paris 24 A2
Elysian Park Los Angeles 16 B3
Emāmzādeh Sāleh Tehran 31 A2
Émerainville Paris 24 B4
Emeryville San Francisco 26 A3
Eminönü Istanbul 12 B1
Emirgan Istanbul 12 B2
Emmarentia Johannesburg 13 A2
Empire State Building
New York 22 B2
Encantado Rio de Janeiro 25 B1
Encino Los Angeles 16 B2
Encino Res. Los Angeles 16 B1
Enebyberg Stockholm 29 A1
Enfield Sydney 29 B1
Engenho, I. do
Rio de Janeiro 25 B2
Englewood Chicago 9 C3
Englewood New York 22 A2
Englewood Cliffs New York 22 A2
Enmore Sydney 29 B2
Enskede Stockholm 29 B2
Entrevias Madrid 17 B1
Epcot Orlando 23 B1
Epping Sydney 29 A1
Eregun Lagos 14 A2
Erenköy Istanbul 12 C2
Erith London 15 B5
Erlaa Vienna 32 B1
Ermington Sydney 29 A1
Ermita Manila 17 B1
Ershatou Guangzhou 11 B2
Erskineville Sydney 29 B2
Erunkan Lagos 14 A2
Erzsébet-Telep Budapest 7 B3
Eschenried Munich 21 A1
Esenler Istanbul 12 B1
Esher London 15 B1
Eskbank Edinburgh 11 B3
Esplugas Barcelona 4 A1
Esposizione Universale di
Roma Rome 26 C1
Essendon Melbourne 18 A1
Essendon ✈ (MEB)
Melbourne 18 A1
Essingen Stockholm 29 B1
Essling Vienna 32 A3
Est, Gare de l' Paris 24 A3
Estado, Parque do
São Paulo 27 B2
Estrela, Basilica da Lisbon 16 A2
Etobicoke Toronto 31 B1
Etobicoke Cr. ⛴ Toronto 31 B1
Etterbeek Brussels 6 B2
Eung-am Seoul 27 B1
Eunpyeong Seoul 27 B1
Evanston Chicago 9 A2
Even Sapir Jerusalem 13 B1
Evere Brussels 6 A2
Everett Boston 6 A2
Evergreen Park Chicago 9 C2
Evin Tehran 31 A2
Ewu Lagos 14 A1
Exhibition Place Toronto 31 B2
Exposições, Palácio das
Rio de Janeiro 25 B1
Eyüp Istanbul 12 B1
Ezeiza ✈ (EZE) Buenos Aires 7 B2

F

Fabour, Mt. Singapore 28 B2
Fælledparken Copenhagen 8 A3
Fågelön Stockholm 29 B1
Fagersjö Stockholm 29 B2
Fair Lawn New York 22 A1
Fairfax Washington 33 B2
Fairfax Station Washington 33 C2
Fairland Johannesburg 13 A1
Fairmilehead Edinburgh 11 B2
Fairmount Heights
Washington 33 B4
Fairport Toronto 31 A4
Fairview New York 22 B2
Fairview, L. Orlando 23 A2
Falenty Warsaw 32 C1
Faliro Athens 2 B1
Faliro, Ormos Athens 2 B2
Falkenburg Berlin 5 A4
Falkenhagen Berlin 5 A1
Falkensee Berlin 5 A1
Falls Church Washington 33 B2
Falomo Lagos 14 B2
False Bay Cape Town 8 B2
Fangcun Guangzhou 11 B2
Farahābād Tehran 31 A2
Farforovskaya
St. Petersburg 27 B2
Farningham London 15 B5
Farsta Stockholm 29 B2
Fasanerie-Nord Munich 21 A2
Fasangarten Munich 21 B2
Fatih Istanbul 12 B1
Favoriten Vienna 32 B2
Fawkner Melbourne 18 A1
Fawkner Park Melbourne 18 B1

FedEx Stadium Washington 33 B4
Feijó Lisbon 16 B2
Feldkirchen Munich 21 B3
Feldmoching Munich 21 A2
Feltham London 15 B1
Fener Istanbul 12 B1
Fenerbahçe Istanbul 12 C2
Fengtai Beijing 4 C1
Ferencváros Budapest 7 B2
Ferihegy, Budapest ✈
(BUD) Budapest 7 B3
Ferndale Johannesburg 13 A2
Férolles-Attilly Paris 24 B4
Fichtenau Berlin 5 B5
Field Museum of Natural
History Chicago 9 B3
Fields Corner Boston 6 B2
Fiera Camp Milan 19 B1
Figino Milan 19 B1
Fijir Baghdad 3 A2
Filadelfia Athens 2 A2
Fili-Mazilovo Moscow 19 B1
Filothei Athens 2 A2
Finchley London 15 A2
Fine Arts, Museum of
Boston 6 A2
Finglas Dublin 10 A2
Finsbury London 15 A3
Finsbury Park London 15 A3
Fiorito Buenos Aires 7 C2
Firhouse Dublin 10 B2
Fischerhäuser Munich 21 A3
Fisher Island Miami 18 B2
Fishermans Bend
Melbourne 18 A1
Fisherville Toronto 31 A2
Fisksätra Stockholm 29 B3
Fitzroy Gardens Melbourne 18 A1
Five Dock Sydney 29 B1
Fjellstrand Oslo 23 B2
Flamengo Rio de Janeiro 25 B1
Flamingo Orlando 23 B2
Flaminio Rome 26 B1
Flaskebekk Oslo 23 A2
Flatbush New York 22 C2
Flaten Stockholm 29 B2
Flatlands New York 22 C2
Flemington Racecourse
Melbourne 18 A1
Flint Pk. Los Angeles 16 B3
Florence Los Angeles 16 C3
Florence Bloom Bird
Sanctuary △
Johannesburg 13 A2
Florentia Johannesburg 13 B2
Flores Buenos Aires 7 B2
Flores, Mercado de
Mexico City 18 C2
Floresta Buenos Aires 7 B2
Florida Buenos Aires 7 B2
Florida Johannesburg 13 B1
Floridsdorf Vienna 32 A2
Flushing New York 22 B3
Flushing Meadows
Corona Park New York 22 B2
Flysta Stockholm 29 A1
Fo Tan Hong Kong 12 A2
Föhrenhain Vienna 32 A2
Fontainebleau Johannesburg 13 A1
Fontenay-aux-Roses Paris 24 B2
Fontenay-le-Fleury Paris 24 B1
Fontenay-sous-Bois Paris 24 A3
Foots Cray London 15 B4
Footscray Melbourne 18 A1
Forbidden City = Imperial
Palace Museum Beijing 4 B2
Forest Brussels 6 B1
Forest Gate London 15 A4
Forest Heights Washington 33 C3
Forest Hill London 15 B3
Forest Hill Toronto 31 A2
Forest Hills New York 22 B2
Forest Park Chicago 9 B2
Forest Park New York 22 B2
Forest View Chicago 9 C2
Forestville Washington 33 B4
Fornebu Oslo 23 A2
Foro Romano Rome 26 B1
Forstenried Munich 21 B1
Forstenrieder Park Munich 21 B1
Fort Mumbai 20 B1
Fort Dupont Park
Washington 33 B4
Fort Foote Village
Washington 33 C3
Fort Lee New York 22 A2
Forth, Firth of Edinburgh 11 A2
Forth Rail Bridge Edinburgh 11 A1
Forth Road Bridge
Edinburgh 11 A1
Fót Budapest 7 A3
Fourqueux Paris 24 A1
Foxrock Dublin 10 B2
Franconia Washington 33 C3
Frank Lloyd Wright
Home Chicago 9 B2
Frankel Singapore 28 B3
Franklin Park Boston 6 B2
Franklin Park Chicago 9 B1
Franklin Park Washington 33 B3
Franklin Res. Los Angeles 16 B2
Frauenkirche Munich 21 B2
Frederiksberg Copenhagen 8 A3
Frederiksdal Copenhagen 8 A2
Fredersdorf Berlin 5 A5
Freguesia Rio de Janeiro 25 A1
Freidrichshain,
Volkspark Berlin 5 A3
Freiham Munich 21 B1
Freimann Munich 21 A2
French Quarter
New Orleans 21 B2
Fresh Pond Boston 6 A2
Fresnes Paris 24 B2
Freudenau Vienna 32 A2
Friarstown Dublin 10 B1
Friedenau Berlin 5 B3
Friedrichsfelde Berlin 5 B4
Friedrichshagen Berlin 5 B4
Friedrichshain Berlin 5 A3
Friedrichslust Berlin 5 A5
Friherrs Helsinki 11 B1
Frilufts Museum Helsinki 11 B2
Frontón, I. Lima 14 B1
Frunze Moscow 19 B2
Fūchū Tokyo 30 A1
Fuencarral Madrid 17 B1
Fuenlabrada Madrid 17 C1
Fukagawa Tokyo 30 B3
Fukushima Osaka 23 A1
Fulham London 15 B2
Fundão, I. do Rio de Janeiro 25 B1
Fünfhaus Vienna 32 A2
Fureso Copenhagen 8 A2
Fürth Munich 21 B2
Futago-tamagawaen
Tokyo 30 B2
Fuxing Dao Shanghai 28 B2
Fuxing Park Shanghai 28 B1
Fuxinglu Beijing 4 B1

G

G. Ross Lord Park Toronto 31 A2
Gaebong Seoul 27 C1
Gage Park Chicago 9 C2
Gagny Paris 24 A4
Galata Istanbul 12 B1
Galata Tower Istanbul 12 B1
Galatsi Athens 2 A2
Galeão, Int. de ✈ (GIG)
Rio de Janeiro 25 A1
Galyanovo Moscow 19 B3
Gambir Jakarta 12 A1
Gamboa Rio de Janeiro 25 B1
Gamboloita Milan 19 B2
Gamlebyen Oslo 23 A3
Gangdong Seoul 27 B2
Gangnam Seoul 27 B1
Gangseo Seoul 27 B1
Gangtou Guangzhou 11 A1
Gangwei Guangzhou 11 B2
Ganjiakou Beijing 4 B1
Ganshoren Brussels 6 A1
Gants Hill London 15 A4
Gaoqiao Shanghai 28 A2
Garbagnate Milanese
Milan 19 A1
Garbatella Rome 26 B2
Garches Paris 24 A2
Garching Munich 21 A3
Garden City Cairo 7 A2
Garden Reach Kolkata 14 B1
Garder Oslo 23 B2
Garfield New York 22 A1
Garfield Park Chicago 9 B2
Gargareta Athens 2 B2
Garibong Seoul 27 C1
Garvanza Los Angeles 16 B3
Gåshaga Stockholm 29 A3
Gateway △ New York 22 C2
Gateway of India Mumbai 20 B2
Gatow Berlin 5 B1
Gavà Barcelona 4 B1
Gávea Rio de Janeiro 25 B1
Gávea, Pedra da
Rio de Janeiro 25 B1
Gazdagrét Budapest 7 B1
Gaziosmanpaşa Istanbul 12 B1
Gebel el Ahmar Cairo 7 A3
Gebel el Muqattam Cairo 7 A2
Gebel el Tura Cairo 7 B2
Geiselgasteig Munich 21 B2
General San Martin
Buenos Aires 7 B1
Gennevilliers Paris 24 A2
Gentilly Paris 24 B3
Gentofte Copenhagen 8 A3
Genval Brussels 6 B2
George I. Hong Kong 12 B1
Georges River Bridge
Sydney 29 C1
Georgetown Washington 33 B3
Georgia Dome Atlanta 3 B2
Gerasdorf bei Wien Vienna 32 A2
Gerberau Munich 21 A1
Gerli Buenos Aires 7 C2
Germiston Johannesburg 13 B2
Gernich Munich 21 B2
Getafe Madrid 17 C1
Getty Center, The
Los Angeles 16 B2
Geunjeong Seoul 27 C1
Geva Binyamin Jerusalem 13 A2
Geylang Serai Singapore 28 B3
Gharapuri Mumbai 20 B2
Gharb = Shahrak-e Qods
Tehran 31 A2
Ghatkopar Mumbai 20 A2
Ghazipur Delhi 10 B2
Ghizri Karachi 13 B2
Ghizri Cr. ⛴ Karachi 13 B2
Ghonda Delhi 10 A2
Ghusuri Kolkata 14 B2
Gianicolense Rome 26 B1
Giant Wheel = Riesenrad
Vienna 32 A2
Gibraltar Pt. Toronto 31 B2
Gidea Park London 15 A5
Giesing Munich 21 B2
Gilmerton Edinburgh 11 B3
Gilo Jerusalem 13 B2
Gimmersta Stockholm 29 B3
Ginza Tokyo 30 B3
Giv'at Ram Jerusalem 13 B2
Giv'at Ye'arim Jerusalem 13 B1
Giv'at Ze'ev Jerusalem 13 A2
Giv'on Jerusalem 13 A1
Giza = El Gîza Cairo 7 A2
Giza Pyramids Cairo 7 B1
Gjersjøen Oslo 23 B3
Gladesville Sydney 29 B1
Gladsakse Copenhagen 8 A2
Glasnevin Dublin 10 A2
Glassmanor Washington 33 C4
Glasthule Dublin 10 B3
Glen Iris Melbourne 18 B2
Glen Mar Park Washington 33 B3
Glen Rock New York 22 A1
Glen Rouge Park Toronto 31 A4
Glenarden Washington 33 B4
Glenasmole Reservoirs
Dublin 10 B1
Glencorse Res. Edinburgh 11 B2
Glencullen Dublin 10 B2
Glendale Los Angeles 16 B3
Glendoo Mt. Dublin 10 B2
Glenhuntly Melbourne 18 B2
Glenside Wellington 33 B1
Glenview Chicago 9 A2
Glenview Countryside
Chicago 9 A2
Glenvista Johannesburg 13 B2
Glifada Athens 2 B2
Glömsta Stockholm 29 B1
Glostrup Copenhagen 8 B2
Gogar Edinburgh 11 B2
Göktürk Istanbul 12 A1
Golabari Kolkata 14 B2
Golabki Warsaw 32 B1
Gold Coast Chicago 9 B3
Golden Gate San Francisco 26 B2
Golden Gate △
San Francisco 26 A2
Golden Gate Bridge
San Francisco 26 B2
Golden Gate Park
San Francisco 26 B2
Golden Horn = Haliç
Istanbul 12 B1
Golders Green London 15 A2
Golestan Palace Tehran 31 A2
Gollans Stream ⛴
Wellington 33 B2
Gonen Jerusalem 13 B2
Gongneung Seoul 27 B2
Goodmayes London 15 A4
Goodwood Cape Town 8 A2
Gopalpur Kolkata 14 B2
Górce Warsaw 32 B1
Gore Hill Sydney 29 A2

Gorelyy → St. Petersburg 27 A3
Gorgie Edinburgh 11 B2
Gorky Park Moscow 19 B2
Gosen Berlin 5 B5
Gosener kanal Berlin 5 B5
Gospel Oak London 15 A3
Gotanda Tokyo 30 B3
Goth Goli Mar Karachi 13 A2
Goth Sher Shah Karachi 13 A1
Gotha Orlando 23 A1
Gournay-sur-Marne Paris 24 A4
Governador, I. do Rio de Janeiro 25 A1
Governors I. New York 22 B1
Grabów Warsaw 32 C1
Grace, Mt. Wellington 33 B2
Gracefield Wellington 33 B2
Gracia Barcelona 4 A2
Gräfelfing Munich 21 B1
Gragoatá Rio de Janeiro 25 B2
Grand Bazaar = Kapali Carsi Istanbul 12 B1
Grand Central Station New York 22 B2
Grand Palace Bangkok 3 B1
Grande Place Brussels 6 A2
Grankulla = Kauniainen Helsinki 11 B1
Grant Park Chicago 9 B3
Granton Edinburgh 11 B2
Grassy Park Cape Town 8 B2
Gratosóglio Milan 19 B2
Gratzwalde Berlin 5 B5
Gravesend New York 22 C2
Grazhdanka St. Petersburg 27 B2
Great Falls Washington 33 B2
Great Falls Park Washington 33 B2
Great Western Forum Los Angeles 16 C2
Greco Milan 19 A2
Green I. Hong Kong 12 B1
Green Point Cape Town 8 A1
Greenbelt Washington 33 A4
Greenbelt Park Washington 33 B4
Greenfield Park Montreal 20 B3
Greenford London 15 A1
Greenhill London 15 A2
Greenhills Dublin 10 B1
Greenpoint New York 22 B2
Greenwich ☐ London 15 B3
Greenwich Observatory London 15 B3
Greenwich Village New York 22 B2
Greenwood Boston 6 A2
Grefsen Oslo 23 A3
Gresham Park Atlanta 3 B2
Greve Strand Copenhagen 8 B1
Griebnitzsee Berlin 5 B1
Griffith Park Los Angeles 16 B3
Grimbergen Brussels 6 A2
Grinzing Vienna 32 A2
Gröbenried Munich 21 A1
Grochów Warsaw 32 B2
Grodzisk Warsaw 32 B2
Groenendaal Brussels 6 B2
Grogol Petamburin Jakarta 12 A1
Gronsdorf Munich 21 B3
Grorud Oslo 23 A4
Gross-Glienicke Berlin 5 B1
Gross-Hadern Munich 21 B1
Gross-Lappen Munich 21 A2
Grosse Krampe Berlin 5 B5
Grosse Müggelsee Berlin 5 B4
Grosse Point Lighthouse Chicago 9 A2
Grossenzersdorf Vienna 32 A3
Grossenzersdorfer Arm → Vienna 32 A3
Grosser Biberhaufen Vienna 32 A2
Grosser Wannsee Berlin 5 B2
Grossfeld-Siedlung Vienna 32 A2
Grosshesselohe Munich 21 B2
Grossjedlersdorf Vienna 32 A2
Grossziethen Berlin 5 B3
Ground Zero New York 22 B1
Grove, The Chicago 9 A1
Grove Hall Boston 6 B2
Grove Park Atlanta 3 B2
Grove Park Hounslow, London 15 B2
Grove Park Lewisham, London 15 B4
Groveton Washington 33 C3
Grünau Berlin 5 B4
Grunewald Berlin 5 B2
Grünwald Munich 21 B2
Grünwalder Forst Munich 21 B2
Grymes Hill New York 22 C1
Guadalupe Manila 17 B2
Guadalupe, Basilica de Mexico City 18 B2
Guanabara, B. de Rio de Janeiro 25 B1
Guanabara, Jardim Rio de Janeiro 25 A1
Guanabara, Palácio da Rio de Janeiro 25 B1
Guang'anmen Beijing 4 B1
Guangqumen Beijing 4 B2
Guangzhou Guangzhou 11 B2
Guanshuo Guangzhou 11 B3
Gudö Stockholm 29 B3
Güell, Parque de Barcelona 4 A2
Guinardó Barcelona 4 A2
Gulbai Karachi 13 A1
Güngören Istanbul 12 B1
Gunnersbury London 15 B2
Gustavo A. Madero Mexico City 18 B2
Guttenberg New York 22 B1
Gutuyevskiy, Ostrov St. Petersburg 27 B1
Guyancourt Paris 24 B1
Gwanak Seoul 27 C1
Gwanaksan Seoul 27 C1
Gyál Budapest 7 B3
Gyáli-patak → Budapest 7 B2

H

Haaga Helsinki 11 B2
Haar Munich 21 B3
Habay Manila 17 C1
Hackbridge London 15 B3
Hackensack New York 22 A1
Hackensack → New York 22 B1
Hackney ☐ London 15 A3
Hackney Wick London 15 A3
Hadr, Warrâq el Cairo 7 A2
Haga Stockholm 29 A2
Hagenbrunn Vienna 32 A2
Hägersten Stockholm 29 B1
Häggvik Stockholm 29 A1
Hagonoy Manila 17 B2
Hague Park Toronto 31 A3
Haidan Beijing 4 B1
Haidari Athens 2 A1
Haidarpur Delhi 10 A1
Haidhausen Munich 21 B2
Haight-Ashbury San Francisco 26 B2
Hainault London 15 A4
Haizhu Guangchang Guangzhou 11 B2
Hakunila Helsinki 11 B3
Halandri Athens 2 A2
Halásztelek Budapest 7 B1
Haliç Istanbul 12 B1
Halim Perdana Kusuma Int. ✕ (HLP) Jakarta 12 B2
Halle Brussels 6 B1
Haltiala Helsinki 11 B2
Haltiavuori Helsinki 11 B2
Ham London 15 B2
Hämeenkylä Helsinki 11 B1
Hammarby Stockholm 29 B2
Hamme Brussels 6 A1
Hammersmith London 15 B2
Hampstead London 15 A2
Hampstead Montreal 20 B2
Hampstead Garden Suburb London 15 A2
Hampstead Heath London 15 A2
Hampton London 15 B1
Hampton Court Palace London 15 B1
Hampton Wick London 15 B2
Hamrā' Baghdad 3 B1
Hanala Helsinki 11 A3
Haneda Tokyo 30 B3
Haneda, Tōkyō ✕ (HND) Tokyo 30 B3
Hang Hau Hong Kong 12 B2
Hanging Gardens Mumbai 20 B1
Hanlon Toronto 31 B1
Hanwell London 15 A1
Hanworth London 15 B1
Haora Kolkata 14 B1
Hapeville Atlanta 3 C2
Happy Valley Hong Kong 12 B2
Har Adar Jerusalem 13 B1
Har Gilo Jerusalem 13 B2
Har Homa Jerusalem 13 B2
Har Nof Jerusalem 13 B2
Haren Brussels 6 A2
Hareskovby Copenhagen 8 A2
Haringey ☐ London 15 A3
Harjusuo Helsinki 11 B3
Harlaching Munich 21 B2
Harlaw Res. Edinburgh 11 B2
Harlem New York 22 B2
Harlesden London 15 A2
Harlington London 15 B1
Harmaja Helsinki 11 C2
Harmashatar hegy Budapest 7 A2
Harolds Cross Dublin 10 B2
Háros Budapest 7 B2
Harperrig Res. Edinburgh 11 B1
Harrow ☐ London 15 A1
Harrow on the Hill London 15 A1
Harrow School London 15 A1
Harrow Weald London 15 A1
Hartsfield-Atlanta Int. ✕ (ATL) Atlanta 3 C2
Harumi Tokyo 30 B3
Harvard University Boston 6 A2
Harwood Heights Chicago 9 B2
Ḥasanābād Tehran 31 A1
Hasbrouck Heights New York 22 A1
Haselhorst Berlin 5 A2
Hasköy Istanbul 12 B1
Hasle Oslo 23 B2
Haslum Oslo 23 A2
Hästhagen Stockholm 29 B2
Hataitai Wellington 33 B1
Hatch End London 15 A1
Hatiara Kolkata 14 B2
Hauketo Oslo 23 A3
Hauz Khas Delhi 10 B2
Havel → Berlin 5 A2
Havelkanal Berlin 5 A2
Havering ☐ London 15 A5
Havering-atte-Bower London 15 A5
Haworth New York 22 A2
Hawthorne Racecourse Chicago 9 C2
Hayes Bromley, London 15 B4
Hayes Hillingdon, London 15 A1
Hayes End London 15 A1
Hayford Chicago 9 C2
Haywards Wellington 33 A2
Heathfield Cape Town 8 A2
Heathrow, London ✕ (LHR) London 15 B1
Hebe Haven Hong Kong 12 A2
Hedong Guangzhou 11 B2
Heidelberg Heights Melbourne 18 A2
Heidelberg West Melbourne 18 A2
Heidemühle Berlin 5 B5
Heideveld Cape Town 8 A2
Heiligensee Berlin 5 A2
Heiligenstadt Vienna 32 A2
Heinersdorf Berlin 5 A3
Hélène de Champlain, Parc ⌂ Montreal 20 A2
Helenelund Stockholm 29 A1
Heliopolis = Masr el Gedida Cairo 7 A2
Hellersdorf Berlin 5 A4
Hellerup Copenhagen 8 A3
Helmahof Vienna 32 A3
Helsingfors = Helsinki Helsinki 11 B2
Helsinki Helsinki 11 B2
Helsinki-Vantaa ✕ (HEL) Helsinki 11 B2
Hendon London 15 A2
Hengsha Guangzhou 11 B2
Hennigsdorf Berlin 5 A2
Henryków Warsaw 32 B1
Henson Cr. → Washington 33 C4
Henttaa Helsinki 11 B1
Heping Park Shanghai 28 B2
Hepingli Beijing 4 B2
Herlev Copenhagen 8 A2
Herman Eckstein Park Johannesburg 13 A2
Hermannskogel Vienna 32 A1
Hermiston Edinburgh 11 B2
Hermitage and Winter Palace St. Petersburg 27 B1
Hermsdorf Berlin 5 A2
Hernals Vienna 32 A2
Herne Hill London 15 B3
Héroes de Churubusco Mexico City 18 B2
Herons, Î. aux Montreal 20 B2
Herstedøster Copenhagen 8 A2
Herttoniemi Helsinki 11 B3
Ḥeşārak Tehran 31 A1
Heston London 15 B1
Hetzendorf Vienna 32 B1
Hextable London 15 B5
Hialeah Miami 18 A1
Hiawassa, L. Orlando 23 A2
Hickory Hills Chicago 9 C2
Hiekkaharju Helsinki 11 B3
Hietaniemi Helsinki 11 B2
Hietzing Vienna 32 A1
Higashi Osaka 23 A2
Higashimurayama Tokyo 30 A1
Higashinari Osaka 23 A2
Higashisumiyoshi Osaka 23 B2
Higashiyodogawa Osaka 23 A1
High Park Toronto 31 B2
Highbury London 15 A3
Highgate London 15 A3
Highland Cr. → Toronto 31 A3
Highland Creek Toronto 31 A3
Highland Park Los Angeles 16 B3
Highlands North Johannesburg 13 A2
Hillcrest Heights Washington 33 C4
Hillend Edinburgh 11 A1
Hillingdon ☐ London 15 A1
Hillwood Washington 33 B3
Hilmīya Cairo 7 A2
Hin Keng Hong Kong 12 A2
Hirota Osaka 23 A1
Hirschstetten Vienna 32 A2
History Center Atlanta 3 B2
Hither Green London 15 B3
Hiyoshi Tokyo 30 B2
Hizma Jerusalem 13 B2
Hjortekær Copenhagen 8 A3
Hjortespring Copenhagen 8 A2
Hlubočepy Prague 25 B2
Ho Chung Hong Kong 12 A2
Ho Man Tin Hong Kong 12 B2
Hoboken New York 22 B1
Hobsons B. Melbourne 18 B1
Hochbrück Munich 21 A2
Hochelaga Montreal 20 A2
Hodgkins Chicago 9 C1
Hoegi Seoul 27 B2
Hoeilaart Brussels 6 B2
Hofburg Vienna 32 A2
Hoffman I. New York 22 C1
Hohenbrunn Munich 21 B3
Hohenschönhausen Berlin 5 A4
Holargos Athens 2 B2
Holborn London 15 A3
Holden, L. Orlando 23 B2
Holešovice Prague 25 B2
Holland Village Singapore 28 B2
Höllriegelskreuth Munich 21 B1
Hollywood Los Angeles 16 B3
Hollywood Bowl Los Angeles 16 B2
Holmenkollen Oslo 23 A3
Holmes Run Acres Washington 33 B2
Holmgård Stockholm 29 B1
Holmlia Oslo 23 B3
Holocaust Memorial Jerusalem 13 B2
Holyrood House, Palace of Edinburgh 11 B3
Holysloot Amsterdam 2 A3
Homerton London 15 A3
Hometown Chicago 9 C2
Hōnanchō Tokyo 30 A2
Honcho Tokyo 30 A3
Honden Tokyo 30 A4
Hondo, Rio → Los Angeles 16 B4
Hong Kong Hong Kong 12 B1
Hong Kong, Univ. of Hong Kong 12 B1
Hong Kong I. Hong Kong 12 B2
Hongje Seoul 27 B1
Hongjimun Tunnel Seoul 27 B1
Hongkou Shanghai 28 B1
Hongmiao Beijing 4 B2
Hongqiao Shanghai 28 B1
Honjyo Tokyo 30 A3
Honoré Mercier, Pont Montreal 20 B1
Hönow Berlin 5 A4
Hook London 15 B2
Horikiri Tokyo 30 A4
Horn Pond Boston 6 A1
Hornchurch London 15 A5
Horni Prague 25 B3
Horni Počernice Prague 25 B3
Hornsey London 15 A3
Horoměřice Prague 25 B1
Hortaleza Madrid 17 B2
Hosoyama Tokyo 30 B2
Hostafrancs Barcelona 4 A1
Hostivař Prague 25 B3
Houbětin Prague 25 B3
Houghton Johannesburg 13 B2
Houilles Paris 24 A2
Hounslow ☐ London 15 B1
Hout Bay Cape Town 8 B1
Hove Å → Copenhagen 8 A1
Hovedøya Oslo 23 A3
Høvik Oslo 23 A2
Hovorčovice Prague 25 A3
Howard Beach New York 22 C2
Howrah = Haora Kolkata 14 B1
Howth Dublin 10 A3
Howth Hd. Dublin 10 A3
Hōya Tokyo 30 A2
Hradčany Prague 25 B2
Huanghuagang Mausoleum Guangzhou 11 B2
Huangpu Shanghai 28 B2
Huangpu Jiang → Shanghai 28 B1
Huangpu Park Shanghai 28 B1
Huangtugang Beijing 4 C1
Huascar Lima 14 A2
Huay Khwang Bangkok 3 B2
Huddinge Stockholm 29 B2
Huechuraba Santiago 27 B1
Huertas de San Beltran Barcelona 4 A1
Huizingen Brussels 6 B1
Humayun's Tomb Delhi 10 B2
Humber → Toronto 31 A1
Humber B. Toronto 31 B2
Humber Bay Toronto 31 B2
Humber Bay Park Toronto 31 B2
Humber College Toronto 31 B1
Humber Summit Toronto 31 A1
Humber Valley Village Toronto 31 A1
Humberlea Toronto 31 A1
Humberwood Park Toronto 31 A1
Humboldt Park Chicago 9 B2
Humera Madrid 17 B1
Hunaydī Baghdad 3 B2
Hundige Copenhagen 8 B1
Hundige Strand Copenhagen 8 B2
Hung Hom Hong Kong 12 B2
Hunters Hill Sydney 29 B1
Hunters Pt. San Francisco 26 B2
Hunters Valley Washington 33 B2
Huntington Washington 33 C3
Huntington Park Los Angeles 16 C3
Hurīya Baghdad 3 A1
Hurstville Sydney 29 B1
Husan Jerusalem 13 B1
Husby Stockholm 29 A1
Husum Copenhagen 8 A2
Hutt → Wellington 33 B2
Hütteldorf Vienna 32 A1
Hűvösvölgy Budapest 7 A2
Huwon Secret Garden Seoul 27 B1
Hvalstad Oslo 23 A1
Hvalstrand Oslo 23 A2
Hvidovre Copenhagen 8 B2
Hwagok Seoul 27 B1
Hyattsville Washington 33 B4
Hyde Park Boston 6 B2
Hyde Park Chicago 9 C3
Hyde Park Johannesburg 13 A2
Hyde Park London 15 A2
Hyde Park Sydney 29 B2

I

Ibese Lagos 14 A2
Ibirapuera São Paulo 27 B1
Ibirapuera, Parque do São Paulo 27 B2
Icarai Rio de Janeiro 25 B2
Içerenköy Istanbul 12 C2
Ichgao Tokyo 30 B2
Ichigaya Tokyo 30 A3
Ichikawa Tokyo 30 A4
Ickenham London 15 A1
Iddo Lagos 14 B2
Idi-Oro Lagos 14 A2
Iganmu Lagos 14 B2
Igbobi Lagos 14 A2
Igbologun Lagos 14 B1
Igny Paris 24 B2
IJ, Het → Amsterdam 2 A2
IJ-meer Amsterdam 2 A3
Ijesa-Tedo Lagos 14 B1
Ijora Lagos 14 B2
Ikebe Tokyo 30 B2
Ikebukuro Tokyo 30 A3
Ikegami Tokyo 30 B3
Ikeja Lagos 14 A2
Ikenchi Osaka 23 B2
Ikoyi Lagos 14 B2
Ikuata Lagos 14 B2
Ikuno Osaka 23 A2
Ikuta Tokyo 30 B2
Ila Oslo 23 A2
Ilford London 15 A4
Ilioupoli Athens 2 B2
Illinois at Chicago, University of Chicago 9 B3
Illinois Institute of Technology Chicago 9 B3
Ilpendam Amsterdam 2 A2
Ilsos → Athens 2 B2
Imbâbah Cairo 7 A2
Imielin Warsaw 32 C2
Imirim São Paulo 27 A2
Imitos Athens 2 B2
Imitos, Oros Athens 2 B2
Imperial Palace Museum Beijing 4 B2
Inagi Tokyo 30 B2
Inchcolm Edinburgh 11 A2
Inchicore Dublin 10 A1
Inchkeith Edinburgh 11 A3
Inchmickery Edinburgh 11 A2
Incirano Milan 19 A1
Independencia Lima 14 A2
Independencia Santiago 27 B2
India Gate Delhi 10 B2
Indian Creek Village Miami 18 A2
Indianópolis São Paulo 27 B2
Indira Gandhi Int. ✕ (DEL) Delhi 10 B1
Industria Johannesburg 13 B1
Ingierstrand Oslo 23 B3
Inglewood Los Angeles 16 C3
Ingliston Edinburgh 11 B1
Inhaúma Rio de Janeiro 25 B1
Inner Port Shelter Hong Kong 12 A2
Interlagos São Paulo 27 C1
Intramuros Manila 17 B1
Invalides Paris 24 A2
Inverkeithing Edinburgh 11 A1
Inzersdorf Vienna 32 B2
Ipanema Rio de Janeiro 25 B1
Ipiranga São Paulo 27 B2
Ipiranga → São Paulo 27 B2
Iponri Lagos 14 B2
Ireland's Eye Dublin 10 A3
Irving Park Chicago 9 B2
Isabel Rio de Janeiro 25 B1
Isagatedo Lagos 14 A1
Isar → Munich 21 A3
Ishbiliya Baghdad 3 A2
Ishøj Strand Copenhagen 8 B2
Island Bay Wellington 33 B1
Island Park Toronto 31 B2
Islev Copenhagen 8 A2
Isleworth London 15 B2
Islington Toronto 31 B1
Islington ☐ London 15 A3
Ismaning Munich 21 A3
Ismayloskiy Park Moscow 19 B3
Isolo Lagos 14 B1
Issy-les-Moulineaux Paris 24 B2
İstanbul Istanbul 12 C1
İstanbul Boğazı Istanbul 12 B2
Istinye Istanbul 12 B2
Itä Hakkila Helsinki 11 B3
Itaewon Seoul 27 B1
Itami Osaka 23 A1
Itanhanga Rio de Janeiro 25 B1
Ivanhoe Melbourne 18 A2
Ivry-sur-Seine Paris 24 B3
Ixelles Brussels 6 B2
Izmaylovo Moscow 19 B3
Iztacalco Mexico City 18 B2
Iztapalapa Mexico City 18 B2

J

Jaba Jerusalem 13 A2
Jacaré Rio de Janeiro 25 B1
Jackson Heights New York 22 B2
Jackson Park Chicago 9 C3
Jacques-Cartier Montreal 20 A3
Jacques-Cartier, Pont Montreal 20 A2
Jadavpur Kolkata 14 C2
Jade Buddha Temple Shanghai 28 B1
Jægersborg Copenhagen 8 A3
Jægersborg Dyrehave Copenhagen 8 A3
Jagadishpur Kolkata 14 B1
Jagatpur Delhi 10 A2
Jaguaré, Rib. do → São Paulo 27 B1
Jahangirpur Delhi 10 A2
Jakarta Jakarta 12 A2
Jakarta, Teluk Jakarta 12 A1
Jalan Kayu Singapore 28 A3
Jamaica B. New York 22 C3
Jamaica Plain Boston 6 B2
Jamakpuri Delhi 10 B1
Jamshīdīyeh Tehran 31 A2
Jamsil Seoul 27 B2
Jamwon Seoul 27 B2
Janki Warsaw 32 C1
Jannali Sydney 29 C1
Jaraguá São Paulo 27 A1
Jaraguá, Pico de São Paulo 27 A1
Jardim Paulista São Paulo 27 B1
Järvatältet Stockholm 29 A1
Jaskhar Mumbai 20 B2
Jatinegara Jakarta 12 B2
Javādīyeh Tehran 31 B2
Jaworowa Warsaw 32 C1
Jedlesee Vienna 32 A2
Jefferson Memorial Washington 33 B3
Jefferson Park Chicago 9 B2
Jegi Seoul 27 B2
Jelambar Jakarta 12 A1
Jelonki Warsaw 32 B1
Jerónimos, Mosteiro dos Lisbon 16 A1
Jersey City New York 22 B1
Jerusalem Jerusalem 13 B2
Jessamine, L. Orlando 23 B2
Jésus, Î. Montreal 20 A1
Jesús Maria Lima 14 B2
Jette Brussels 6 A1
Jey Tehran 31 B2
Jianguomen Beijing 4 B2
Jiangwan Shanghai 28 B1
Jib Jerusalem 13 A2
Jihād Baghdad 3 B1
Jingan Shanghai 28 B1
Jinočany Prague 25 B1
Jinonice Prague 25 B2
Jiulong = Kowloon Hong Kong 12 B1
Jiyūgaoka Tokyo 30 B3
Jizā'ir Baghdad 3 B2
Jizīra Baghdad 3 B2
Joglo Jakarta 12 B1
Johannesburg Johannesburg 13 B2
Johannesburg, Univ. of Johannesburg 13 B2
Johanneskirchen Munich 21 A2
Johannesstift Berlin 5 A2
Johannisthal Berlin 5 B4
John F. Kennedy Nat. Historic Site ⌂ Boston 6 A2
John McLaren Park San Francisco 26 B2
Johnsonville Wellington 33 B1
Joinville-le-Pont Paris 24 B3
Joli-Bois Brussels 6 B2
Jollas Helsinki 11 B3
Jongmyo Royal Shrine Seoul 27 B1
Jongno Seoul 27 B1
Jonstrup Copenhagen 8 A2
Joppa Edinburgh 11 B3
Jorge Chavez, Int. ✕ (LIM) Lima 14 B2
Jorge Newbery ✕ Buenos Aires 7 B2
Józefa Piłsudskiego Park Warsaw 32 B1
Jōtō Osaka 23 A2
Jouy-en-Josas Paris 24 B2
Juan Anchorena Buenos Aires 7 A2
Juan González Romero Mexico City 18 A2
Juárez Int. ✕ (MEX) Mexico City 18 B2
Judeira Jerusalem 13 A2
Juhdum Jerusalem 13 B2
Juhu Mumbai 20 A2
Jūjā Tokyo 30 A3
Jukskeirivier → Johannesburg 13 A2
Julianów Warsaw 32 B2
Jung Seoul 27 B1
Jungfernheide, Volkspark Berlin 5 A2
Jungfernsee Berlin 5 B1
Junghwa Seoul 27 B2
Jungnang Seoul 27 B2
Jungnangcheon → Seoul 27 B1
Juniper Green Edinburgh 11 B2
Junk B. Hong Kong 12 B2
Jurong Singapore 28 B2
Jurong, Selat Singapore 28 B2
Jurong Industrial Estate Singapore 28 B1
Jurujuba, Enseada de Rio de Janeiro 25 B2
Jūsō Osaka 23 A1
Justice Chicago 9 C2
Jwalahari Delhi 10 B1

K

Kaapstad = Cape Town Cape Town 8 A1
Kabaty Warsaw 32 C2
Kadıköy Istanbul 12 C2
Kadoma Osaka 23 A2
Kafr 'Aqab Jerusalem 13 A2
Kâğıthane Istanbul 12 B1
Kâğıthane → Istanbul 12 B1
Kagran Vienna 32 A2
Kahnawake Montreal 20 B1
Kaimes Edinburgh 11 B2
Kaiserebersdorf Vienna 32 B2
Kaivoksela Helsinki 11 B2
Kalamaki Athens 2 B2
Kalbadevi Mumbai 20 B1
Kalipur Kolkata 14 A1
Kalithea Athens 2 B2
Kalkaji Delhi 10 B2
Kalvebod Fælled Copenhagen 8 B3
Kalveboderne Copenhagen 8 B3
Kamarhati Kolkata 14 A2
Kamata Tokyo 30 B3
Kameari Tokyo 30 A4
Kameido Tokyo 30 A4
Kami-Itabashi Tokyo 30 A3
Kamikitazawa Tokyo 30 B2
Kamitsuruma Tokyo 30 B1
Kamoshida Tokyo 30 B2
Kampong Landang Singapore 28 A3
Kampong Tanjong Penjuru Singapore 28 B2
Kampung Bali Jakarta 12 B1
Kanamori Tokyo 30 B1
Kanda Tokyo 30 A3
Kandilli Istanbul 12 B2
Kankurgachi Kolkata 14 B2
Kanlıca Istanbul 12 B2
Kanonerskiy, Ostrov St. Petersburg 27 B1
Kanzaki → Osaka 23 A1
Kapali Carsi Istanbul 12 B1
Kapellerfeld Vienna 32 A2
Káposztásmegyer Budapest 7 A2
Kapotnya Moscow 19 C3
Käppala Stockholm 29 A3
Kapuk Jakarta 12 A1
Käpylä Helsinki 11 B2
Karachi Karachi 13 A2
Karachi Int. ✕ (KHI) Karachi 13 A2
Karkh Baghdad 3 A2
Karlin Prague 25 B2
Karlsfeld Munich 21 A1
Karlshorst Berlin 5 B4
Karlův most Prague 25 B2
Karol Bagh Delhi 10 B2
Karolinenhof Berlin 5 B4
Karori Wellington 33 B1
Karow Berlin 5 A3
Karrādah Baghdad 3 B2
Kärsön Stockholm 29 B1
Kasai Tokyo 30 B4
Kasipur Kolkata 14 B2
Kastrup Copenhagen 8 B3
Kastrup, København ✕ (CPH) Copenhagen 8 B3
Kasuga Tokyo 30 A2
Kasuge Tokyo 30 A3
Kasumigaseki Tokyo 30 B3
Katong Singapore 28 B3
Katrineberg Stockholm 29 B1
Katsushika Tokyo 30 A4
Kau Pai Chau Hong Kong 12 B2
Kau Yi Chau Hong Kong 12 B1
Kaulsdorf Berlin 5 B4
Kauniainen Helsinki 11 B1
Kawasaki Tokyo 30 B3
Kawawa Tokyo 30 B2
Kawęczyn Warsaw 32 B2
Kayu Putih Jakarta 12 B2
Kbely Prague 25 B3
Kebayoran Baru Jakarta 12 B1
Kebayoran Lama Jakarta 12 B1
Kebon Jeruk Jakarta 12 B1
Kedar Jerusalem 13 B2
Kedoya Jakarta 12 B1
Keilor Melbourne 18 A1
Keilor North Melbourne 18 A1
Keimola Helsinki 11 A1
Kelapa Gading Jakarta 12 A2
Kelenföld Budapest 7 B2
Kelvin Johannesburg 13 A2
Kemang Jakarta 12 B1
Kemayoran Jakarta 12 B2
Kemerburgaz Istanbul 12 B1
Kempton Park Races London 15 B1
Kenilworth Cape Town 8 A1
Kennedy Town Hong Kong 12 B1
Kensal Green London 15 A2
Kensington Johannesburg 13 B2
Kensington London 15 A2
Kensington New York 22 C2
Kensington Sydney 29 B2
Kensington Palace London 15 A2
Kent Village Washington 33 B4
Kentish Town London 15 A3
Kenton London 15 A2
Kenwood House London 15 A3
Kepa Warsaw 32 B2
Keppel Harbour Singapore 28 B2
Kesariani Athens 2 B2
Kettering Washington 33 B5
Kew London 15 B2
Kew Melbourne 18 A2
Kew Gardens London 15 B2
Kew Gardens Toronto 31 A3
Key Biscayne Miami 18 B2
Khalīj Baghdad 3 B2
Khandallah Wellington 33 B1
Khansā' Baghdad 3 A2
Kharavli Mumbai 20 B2
Khefren Cairo 7 B1
Khichripur Delhi 10 B2
Khidirpur Kolkata 14 B1
Khimki-Khovrino Moscow 19 A2
Khirbet Batin Abu Lihyah Jerusalem 13 A1
Khirbet el-Misbah Jerusalem 13 A1
Khirbet Jub e-Rum Jerusalem 13 B2
Khlong San Bangkok 3 B2
Khlong Toey Bangkok 3 B2
Khorel Kolkata 14 A1
Khorosovo Moscow 19 B1
Kiamari Karachi 13 B1
Kierling Vienna 32 A1
Kierlingbach → Vienna 32 A1
Kifisos → Athens 2 B2
Kikuna Tokyo 30 B2
Kilbarrack Dublin 10 A3
Kilbirnie Wellington 33 B1
Kilburn London 15 A2
Killester Dublin 10 B2
Killiney Dublin 10 B3
Killiney B. Dublin 10 B3
Kilmacud Dublin 10 B2
Kilmainham Dublin 10 A2
Kilmainham Gaol Dublin 10 A2
Kilmashogue Mt. Dublin 10 B2
Kilmore Dublin 10 A2
Kilnamanagh Dublin 10 B1
Kilo Helsinki 11 B1
Kilokri Delhi 10 B2
Kiltiernan Dublin 10 B2
Kimmage Dublin 10 B2
Kindi Baghdad 3 B2
Kinghorn Edinburgh 11 A2
Kings Domain Melbourne 18 A1
Kings Forest = Kongelunden Copenhagen 8 B3
Kings Park Washington 33 C2
Kings Park West Washington 33 C2
Kingsbury London 15 A2
Kingsbury Melbourne 18 A2
Kingsford Sydney 29 B2
Kingsford Smith, Sydney ✕ (SYD) Sydney 29 B2
Kingston-upon-Thames ☐ London 15 B2
Kingston Vale London 15 B2
Kingsway Toronto 31 B1
Kinsaley Dublin 10 A2
Kipling Heights Toronto 31 A1
Kipseli Athens 2 B2
Kirchstockbach Munich 21 B3
Kirchtrudering Munich 21 B3
Kirikiri Lagos 14 B1
Kirke Værløse Copenhagen 8 A1
Kirkhill Edinburgh 11 B2
Kirkliston Edinburgh 11 B1
Kirknewton Edinburgh 11 B1
Kirov Palace of Culture St. Petersburg 27 B1
Kiryat Anavim Jerusalem 13 B1
Kiryat Ha Yovel Jerusalem 13 B1
Kısıklı Istanbul 12 B2
Kispest Budapest 7 B2
Kista Stockholm 29 A1
Kita Osaka 23 A2
Kita Tokyo 30 A3
Kitazawa Tokyo 30 B3
Kiu Tsiu Hong Kong 12 A2
Kivistö Helsinki 11 B2
Kızıltoprak Istanbul 12 C2
Kizuri Osaka 23 B2
Kjelsås Oslo 23 A3
Kladow Berlin 5 B1
Klampenborg Copenhagen 8 A3
Klaudyń Warsaw 32 B1
Klečany Prague 25 A2
Kledering Vienna 32 B2
Klein Jukskei → Johannesburg 13 A1
Kleinmachnow Berlin 5 B2
Kleinschönebeck Berlin 5 B5
Klemetsrud Oslo 23 A4
Klender Jakarta 12 A2
Klíčany Prague 25 A2
Klipriviersberg Nature Reserve Johannesburg 13 B2
Klosterneuburg Vienna 32 A1
Kőbánya Budapest 7 B2
Kobbegem Brussels 6 A1
København Copenhagen 8 A2
København ✕ (CPH) Copenhagen 8 B3
Kobylisy Prague 25 B2
Kobyłka Warsaw 32 A3
Kodaira Tokyo 30 A1
Kodanaka Tokyo 30 B2
Koekelberg Brussels 6 A1
Koganei Tokyo 30 A2
Kogarah Sydney 29 B1
Koivupää Helsinki 11 B2
Koja Jakarta 12 A2
Koja Utara Jakarta 12 A2
Kokhav Ya'akov Jerusalem 13 A2
Kokobunji Tokyo 30 A1
Kokobunji-Temple Tokyo 30 A4
Kolarängen Stockholm 29 B3
Kolbotn Oslo 23 B3
Kolkata Kolkata 14 B2
Kolkata Dum Dum Int. ✕ (CCU) Kolkata 14 B2
Kolkata Maidan Kolkata 14 B1
Kolo Warsaw 32 B1
Kolokinthou Athens 2 B2
Kolomyagi St. Petersburg 27 A1
Kolonos Athens 2 B2
Kolsås Oslo 23 A2
Komae Tokyo 30 B2
Komagome Tokyo 30 A3
Komazawa Tokyo 30 B3
Kona Kolkata 14 B1
Konala Helsinki 11 B2
Kondli Delhi 10 B2
Kongelunden Copenhagen 8 B3
Kongens Lyngby Copenhagen 8 A3
Kongo Helsinki 11 A1
Konnagar Kolkata 14 A2
Konohana Osaka 23 A1
Konradshöhe Berlin 5 A2
Kopanina Prague 25 B1
Koparkhairna Mumbai 20 A2
Köpenick Berlin 5 B4
Korangi Karachi 13 B2
Koremasa Tokyo 30 B1
Koridalos Athens 2 B1
Korokoro Wellington 33 B2
Korokoro Stream → Wellington 33 B2
Kosino Moscow 19 B4
Kosugi Tokyo 30 B2
Kota Jakarta 12 A1
Kōtō Tokyo 30 A3
Kotrung Kolkata 14 A2
Kouponia Athens 2 B2
Kowloon Hong Kong 12 B1
Kowloon Peak Hong Kong 12 A2
Kowloon Res. Hong Kong 12 A1
Kowloon Tong Hong Kong 12 A2
Kraainem Brussels 6 A2
Krailling Munich 21 B1
Krampnitz Berlin 5 B1
Krampnitzsee Berlin 5 B1
Kranji, Sungei → Singapore 28 A2
Kranji Industrial Estate Singapore 28 A2
Krasno-Presnenskaya Moscow 19 B2
Krč Prague 25 B2
Kremlin Moscow 19 B2
Krestovskiye, Ostrov St. Petersburg 27 B1
Kreuzberg Berlin 5 A3
Kritzendorf Vienna 32 A1
Krumme Lanke Berlin 5 B2
Krummensee Berlin 5 A5
Krung Thep = Bangkok Bangkok 3 B2
Krusboda Stockholm 29 B3
Kuangchou = Guangzhou Guangzhou 11 B2
Küçükköy Istanbul 12 B1
Küçüksu Istanbul 12 B2
Kudrovo St. Petersburg 27 B3
Kulosaari Helsinki 11 B3
Kumla Stockholm 29 B3
Kungens kurva Stockholm 29 B1
Kungliga Slottet Stockholm 29 B2
Kungshatt Stockholm 29 B1
Kungsholmen Stockholm 29 A2
Kuningan Jakarta 12 B1
Kunitachi Tokyo 30 A1
Kunming Hu Beijing 4 B1
Kunratice Prague 25 B2
Kupchino St. Petersburg 27 B2
Kurbağalı → Istanbul 12 C2
Kurihara Tokyo 30 A2
Kurla Mumbai 20 A2
Kurmuri Mumbai 20 A2
Kurume Tokyo 30 A2
Kuryanovo Moscow 19 C3
Kuskovo Moscow 19 B3
Kustia Kolkata 14 B2
Kuzguncuk Istanbul 12 B2
Kuzyminki Moscow 19 B3
Kwai Chung Hong Kong 12 A1
Kwangchow = Guangzhou Guangzhou 11 B2
Kwun Tong Hong Kong 12 B2
Kyje Prague 25 B3
Kyūhōji Osaka 23 B2

L

La Blanca Santiago 27 C2
La Boca Buenos Aires 7 B2
La Bretèche Paris 24 A1
La Campiña Lima 14 C2
La Celle-St-Cloud Paris 24 A1
La Cisterna Santiago 27 C2
La Courneuve Paris 24 A3
La Dehesa Santiago 27 B2
La Encantada Lima 14 C2
La Estación Madrid 17 B1
La Floresta Barcelona 4 A1
La Florida Santiago 27 C2
La Fortuna Madrid 17 B1
La Fransa Barcelona 4 A1
La Garenne-Colombes Paris 24 A2
La Giustiniana Rome 26 B1
La Grange Chicago 9 C1
La Grange Park Chicago 9 C1
La Granja Santiago 27 B2
La Guardia, New York ✕ (LGA) New York 22 B2
La Hulpe Brussels 6 B2
La Llacuna Barcelona 4 A2
La Loma Mexico City 18 A1
La Lucila Buenos Aires 7 B2
La Maladrerie Paris 24 A1
La Milla, Cerro Lima 14 B2
La Monachina Rome 26 B1
La Moraleja Madrid 17 A2
La Nopalera Mexico City 18 C2
La Paternal Buenos Aires 7 B2
La Perla Lima 14 B2
La Perouse Sydney 29 B2
La Pineda Barcelona 4 B1
La Pisana Rome 26 B1
La Prairie Montreal 20 B3
La Punta Lima 14 B1
La Puntigala Barcelona 4 A2
La Queue-en-Brie Paris 24 B4
La Reina Santiago 27 B2
La Ribera Barcelona 4 A1
La Sagrera Barcelona 4 A2
La Salada Buenos Aires 7 C2
La Scala Milan 19 B2
La Storta Rome 26 A1
La Taxonera Barcelona 4 A2
La Victoria Lima 14 B2
Laajalahti Helsinki 11 B1
Laajasalo Helsinki 11 B3
Laaksolahti Helsinki 11 B1
Lablâba, W. el → Cairo 7 A2
Lachine Montreal 20 B1
Lachine, Canal de Montreal 20
Lad Phrao Bangkok 3 B2
Ladera Heights Los Angeles 16
Ládví Prague 25 B2
Lady Warsaw 32 C1
Lafontaine, Parc Montreal 20 A
Lagoa Rio de Janeiro 25 B1
Lagos Lagos 14 B2
Lagos Harbour Lagos 14 B2
Lagos-Ikeja ✕ (LOS) Lagos 14
Lagos Island Lagos 14 B2
Lagos Lagoon Lagos 14 B2
Laguna de B. Manila 17 C2
Laim Munich 21 B2
Lainate Milan 19 A1
Lainz Vienna 32 B1
Lake Buena Vista Orlando 23 B
Lake Cain Hills Orlando 23 B2
Lake Fairfax Park Washington 33 B2
Lakemba Sydney 29 B1
Lakeside Cape Town 8 B1
Lakeside Johannesburg 13 A2
Lakeview Chicago 9 B3
Lakewood Park Atlanta 3 B2
Lakhtinskiy St. Petersburg 27 B
Lakhtinskiy Razliv, Oz. St. Petersburg 27 B1
Lakshmanpur Kolkata 14 B1
Laksi Bangkok 3 A2
Lal Qila Delhi 10 B2
Lam Tin Hong Kong 12 B2
Lambert Oslo 23 A3
Lambeth ☐ London 15 B3
Lambrate Milan 19 B2
Lambro, Parco Milan 19 B2
Lambton Mills Toronto 31 B1
Lamma I. Hong Kong 12 B1
Landover Hills Washington 33
Landsmeer Amsterdam 2 A2
Landstrasse Vienna 32 A2
Landwehr kanal Berlin 5 B3
Lane Cove Sydney 29 A1
Lane Cove National Park ⌂ Sydney 29 A1
Langa Cape Town 8 A2
Langenzersdorf Vienna 32 A2
Langer See Berlin 5 B4
Langley Washington 33 B2
Langley Park Washington 33 B
Langwald Munich 21 A1
Lanham Washington 33 B4
Lankwitz Berlin 5 B3
L'Annunziatella Rome 26 C2
Lansdowne Cape Town 8 A2
Lansing Toronto 31 A2
Lanus Buenos Aires 7 C2
Lapa Rio de Janeiro 25 B1
Laranjeiras Rio de Janeiro 25 B
Las Warsaw 32 B2
Las Corts Barcelona 4 A1
Las Kabacki Warsaw 32 C2
Las Pinas Manila 17 C1
Las Rejas Santiago 27 B1
Lasalle Montreal 20 B2
LaSalle Street Station Chicago 9 B3
Lasek Bielański Warsaw 32 B
Lasek Na Kole Warsaw 32 B1
Laski Warsaw 32 B1
Latina Madrid 17 B1
Lattasaari Helsinki 11 C2
Laval-des-Rapides Montreal 2
Lavīzān Tehran 31 A2
Lavradio Lisbon 16 A2
Lawndale Chicago 9 B2
Lawne L. Orlando 23 A2
Lawrence Heights Toronto 31
Layari Karachi 13 A1
Layari → Karachi 13 A1
Łazienkowski Park Warsaw 32 B2
Le Blanc-Mesnil Paris 24 A3
Le Bourget Paris 24 A3
Le Chenoi Brussels 6 B2
Le Chesnay Paris 24 B1
Le Christ de Saclay Paris 24 B
Le Kremlin-Bicêtre Paris 24 B
Le Mesnil-le-Roi Paris 24 A1
Le Pecq Paris 24 A1
Le Perreux Paris 24 A3
Le Pin Paris 24 A4
Le Plessis-Robinson Paris 24
Le Plessis-Trévise Paris 24 B4
Le Port-Marly Paris 24 A1
Le Pré-St-Gervais Paris 24 A3
Le Raincy Paris 24 A4
Le Vésinet Paris 24 A1
Lea Bridge London 15 A3
Leaside Toronto 31 A2
Leblon Rio de Janeiro 25 B1
Lee London 15 B4
Leganés Madrid 17 C1
Legazpi Madrid 17 B1
Lehtisaari Helsinki 11 B2
Lei Yue Mun Hong Kong 12 B
Leião Lisbon 16 A1

eichhardt Sydney 29 B1
eith Edinburgh 11 B3
eme Rio de Janeiro 25 B1
emoyne Montreal 20 B3
enin Moscow 19 B2
enino Moscow 19 C2
eninskiye Gory Moscow 19 B2
ennox Los Angeles 16 C2
eonia New York 22 A2
eopardstown Dublin 10 B2
eopoldau Vienna 32 A2
eopoldsdorf Vienna 32 B2
eopoldstadt Vienna 32 A2
eportovo Moscow 19 B3
eppävaara Helsinki 11 B1
es Lilas Paris 24 A3
es Loges-en-Josas Paris 24 B1
es Pavillons-sous-Bois
Paris 24 A4
esigny Paris 24 B4
esnozavodskaya
St. Petersburg 27 B2
ester B. Pearson Int.,
Toronto ✕ (YYZ) Toronto 31 A1
Étang-la-Ville Paris 24 A1
etňany Prague 25 B3
topolis = Ausîm Cairo 7 A1
vallois-Perret Paris 24 A2
vent Istanbul 12 B2
wisdale Washington 33 B4
wisham □ London 15 B3
xington Boston 6 A1
yton London 15 A3
ytonstone London 15 A4
Hay-les-Roses Paris 24 B3
Hospitalet de Llobregat
Barcelona 4 A1
otka Prague 25 B2
angshui He → Beijing 4 C2
anhua Chi Beijing 4 B1
anhua He → Beijing 4 B1
ěčice nad Vitavou Prague 25 A2
beň Prague 25 B2
berdade São Paulo 27 B2
berton Edinburgh 11 B3
berty I. New York 22 B1
berty Osaka Museum
Osaka 23 B1
berty State Park △
New York 22 B1
beznice Prague 25 A2
buš Prague 25 B2
chiao Guangzhou 11 B2
chtenburg Berlin 5 A4
chterfelde Berlin 5 B2
dingö Stockholm 29 A2
shi Lingyuan Guangzhou 11 B2
sing Vienna 32 B1
sing → Vienna 32 B2
ovo St. Petersburg 27 C1
ordet Oslo 23 A2
hoborka → Moscow 19 A2
a Vårtan Stockholm 29 A3
e Værløse Copenhagen 8 A2
ah Kolkata 14 B1
a Chu Kang Singapore 28 A2
a Lima 14 B2
abiate Milan 19 A1
ehouse London 15 A3
il-Brévannes Paris 24 B3
ate, Milano ✕ (LIN)
Milan 19 B2
bropark Johannesburg 13 A2
coln Center for
Performing Arts
New York 22 B2
coln Heights Los Angeles 16 B3
coln Memorial
Washington 33 B3
coln Park Chicago 9 B3
coln Park New York 22 B1
coln Park San Francisco 26 B1
coln Park Zoo Chicago 9 B3
colnwood Chicago 9 A2
la-a-Pastora Lisbon 16 A1
den Johannesburg 13 A2
den Wellington 33 A1
denberg Berlin 5 A4
loya Oslo 23 A3
ers Buenos Aires 7 B1
kebeek Brussels 6 B2
ksfield Johannesburg 13 A2
meyer Johannesburg 13 B2
na Helsinki 11 A2
uvaara Helsinki 11 B1
a Rock Country
ark △ Hong Kong 12 A2
's Head Cape Town 8 A1
mi Athens 2 B2
oa Lisbon 16 A2
oa ✕ (LIS) Lisbon 16 A2
on = Lisboa Lisbon 16 A2
ui Guangzhou 11 A1
e B. Sydney 29 B2
e Calumet → Chicago 9 D3
e Ferry New York 22 A1
e Lake Conway
lando 23 B2
e Red School House
ature Center Chicago 9 C1
e Rouge → Toronto 31 A4
ang Shanghai 28 A1
ong Temple Guangzhou 11 B2
y-Gargan Paris 24 A4
Oslo 23 A3
o de Can Gineu
rcelona 4 A2
ranguiz Santiago 27 B2
oza Santiago 27 B1
hau Hong Kong 12 B2
hau Pak Mai
ng Kong 12 B2
spejo Santiago 27 C1
ermida Santiago 27 B2
rado Santiago 27 B1
o Shing Hong Kong 12 B1
ai Hong Kong 12 A1
head Edinburgh 11 B3
u Vienna 32 A3
s. Pt. San Francisco 26 B1
am Munich 21 B1
kov Prague 25 B2
hausen Munich 21 A1
k New York 22 A1
Estate Delhi 10 B2
n Int., Boston ✕
OS) Boston 6 A2
n Square Chicago 9 B2
es-Émerainville ✕
is 24 B4
ne Berlin 5 A5
chet Karachi 13 A2
as Chapultepec
xico City 18 B1
as de San Angel Inn
xico City 18 B1
ardy East
annesburg 13 A2
anki Warsaw 32 A1
s Reforma
xico City 18 B1
London London 15 B3
London City ✕ (LCY)
London 15 A4
London Heathrow ✕
(LHR) London 15 B1
London Zoo London 15 A3
Long B. Sydney 29 B2
Long Branch Toronto 31 B1
Long Brook → Washington 33 C2
Long Ditton London 15 B2
Long Island City New York 22 B2
Longchamp, Hippodrome
de Paris 24 A2
Longhua Pagoda Shanghai 28 B1
Longhua Park Shanghai 28 B1
Longjohn Slough Chicago 9 C1
Longtan Hu → Beijing 4 B2
Longue-Pointe Montreal 20 A2
Longueuil Montreal 20 A3
Longueuil-St-Hubert =
St-Hubert Montreal 20 B3
Loni Delhi 10 A2
Loop, The Chicago 9 B3
Lord's Cricket Ground
London 15 A2
Loreto Milan 19 B2
Los Angeles Los Angeles 16 B3
Los Angeles Int. ✕ (LAX)
Los Angeles 16 C2
Los Cerrillos ✕ (ULC)
Santiago 27 B1
Los Nietos Los Angeles 16 C4
Los Olivos Lima 14 A2
Los Reyes Mexico City 18 B2
Losiny Ostrov △ Moscow 19 A3
Lot Brussels 6 B1
Lotus River Cape Town 8 B2
Lotus Temple Delhi 10 B2
Loughlinstown Dublin 10 B3
Louise, L. Orlando 23 B1
Louisiana Superdome
New Orleans 21 B2
Loures Lisbon 16 A1
Louveciennes Paris 24 A1
Louvre, Musée du Paris 24 A3
Lower B. New York 22 C1
Lower Hutt Wellington 33 B2
Lower New York B. =
Lower B. New York 22 C1
Lower Shing Mun Res.
Hong Kong 12 A1
Lowry Bay Wellington 33 B2
Loyola University Chicago 9 B3
Lu Xun, Tomb of Shanghai 28 B1
Lu Xun Park Shanghai 28 B1
Lübars Berlin 5 A3
Lucy, L. Orlando 23 A2
Ludwigsfeld Munich 21 A1
Luhu Guangzhou 11 B2
Lumiar Lisbon 16 A2
Lundtofte Copenhagen 8 A3
Lung Mei Hong Kong 12 A2
Luojiang Guangzhou 11 B2
Lustheim Munich 21 A2
Luwan Shanghai 28 B1
Luzhniki Sports Centre
Moscow 19 B2
Lyndhurst New York 22 B1
Lynn Woods Res. Boston 6 A2
Lyon, Gare de Paris 24 A3
Lyons Chicago 9 C2
Lysaker Oslo 23 A2
Lysakerselva → Oslo 23 A2
Lysolaje Prague 25 B2
Lyublino Moscow 19 B3

M

Ma Nam Wat Hong Kong 12 A2
Ma On Shan Country
Park △ Hong Kong 12 A2
Ma'ale Adumim Jerusalem 13 B2
Ma'ale Ha Khamisha
Jerusalem 13 B1
Ma'ale Mikhmas Jerusalem 13 A2
Maantiekylä Helsinki 11 A3
Maarifa Baghdad 3 B2
Mabato Pt. Manila 17 C2
Mabel, L. Orlando 23 B1
Macaco, Morro do
Rio de Janeiro 25 B2
McCook Chicago 9 C2
McGill University Montreal 20 A2
Machelen Brussels 6 A2
Machida Tokyo 30 B1
Maciołki Warsaw 32 B2
McKerrow, Mt. Wellington 33 B2
McKinley Park Chicago 9 C2
McLean Washington 33 B2
Macopocho → Santiago 27 B1
MacRitchie Res. Singapore 28 A2
Macul Santiago 27 C2
Madhudaha Kolkata 14 B2
Madhyamgram Kolkata 14 A2
Madin Mexico City 18 A1
Madin, L. Mexico City 18 A1
Madīnah Al Mansūr
Baghdad 3 B2
Mādinet Nasr Cairo 7 A2
Madrid Madrid 17 B1
Madrid Barajas ✕ (MAD)
Madrid 17 B2
Madrona Barcelona 4 A1
Maesawa Tokyo 30 A2
Magdalena Lima 14 B2
Magdalena Contreras
Mexico City 18 C1
Maghreb Baghdad 3 A2
Maginu Tokyo 30 B2
Magliana Rome 26 B1
Magny-les-Hameaux Paris 24 B1
Maheshtala Kolkata 14 C1
Mahim Mumbai 20 A2
Mahim B. Mumbai 20 A1
Mahlsdorf Berlin 5 A4
Mahmoodabad Karachi 13 A2
Mahrauli Delhi 10 B2
Mahul Mumbai 20 A2
Maida Vale London 15 A2
Maidstone Melbourne 18 A1
Maipú Santiago 27 C1
Maisonneuve, Parc
Montreal 20 A2
Maisons-Alfort Paris 24 B3
Maisons-Laffitte Paris 24 A1
Maissonneuve Montreal 20 A2
Maitland Cape Town 8 A1
Makasar Jakarta 12 A2
Makati Manila 17 B2
Mäkiniitty Helsinki 11 A2
Malá Strana Prague 25 B2
Malabar Sydney 29 B2
Malabar Hill Mumbai 20 B1
Malabar Pt. Mumbai 20 B1
Malabon Manila 17 B1
Malacañang Palace Manila 17 B1
Malahide Dublin 10 A3
Malakoff Paris 24 B2
Mälarhöjaen Stockholm 29 B1
Malate Manila 17 B1
Malaya Neva St. Petersburg 27 B1
Malaya Okhta
St. Petersburg 27 B2
Malchow Berlin 5 A3
Malden Boston 6 A2
Malden London 15 B2
Maleizen Brussels 6 B3
Malešice Prague 25 B3
Malir → Karachi 13 B2
Malleny Mills Edinburgh 11 B2
Malmi Helsinki 11 B2
Malmøya Oslo 23 A3
Måløv Copenhagen 8 A2
Malton Toronto 31 A1
Malvern Johannesburg 13 B2
Malvern Melbourne 18 B2
Malvern Toronto 31 A3
Mampang Prapatan
Jakarta 12 B1
Mampukuji Tokyo 30 B2
Man Budrukh Mumbai 20 A2
Man Khurd Mumbai 20 A2
Manakhat Jerusalem 13 B2
Mandaluyong Manila 17 B2
Mandaoli Delhi 10 B2
Mandaqui → São Paulo 27 A2
Mandoli Delhi 10 A2
Mandvi Mumbai 20 B2
Manenberg Cape Town 8 A2
Mang Kung Uk Hong Kong 12 B2
Mang-won Seoul 27 B1
Mangolpuri Delhi 10 A1
Manguinhos ✕
Rio de Janeiro 25 B1
Manhattan New York 22 B2
Manhattan Beach
New York 22 C2
Manila Manila 17 B1
Manila Ninoy Aquino
Int. ✕ (MNL) Manila 17 B2
Mankkaa Helsinki 11 B1
Manly Sydney 29 A2
Mann, L. Orlando 23 A2
Mann's Chinese Theatre
Los Angeles 16 B2
Mannswörth Vienna 32 B3
Manor Park London 15 A4
Manor Park Wellington 33 A2
Manora Karachi 13 B1
Manora Pt. Karachi 13 B1
Manquehue, Cerro
Santiago 27 B2
Manzanares, Canal de
Madrid 17 C2
Mapo Seoul 27 B1
Maracanã Rio de Janeiro 25 B1
Maraoli Mumbai 20 A2
Marcelin Warsaw 32 B1
Mareil-Marly Paris 24 A1
Margareten Vienna 32 A2
Maria Vienna 32 A2
Maridalen Oslo 23 A3
Maridalsvatnet Oslo 23 A3
Mariendorf Berlin 5 B3
Marienfelde Berlin 5 B3
Marikina Manila 17 B2
Marikina → Manila 17 B2
Marin City San Francisco 26 A1
Marin Pen. San Francisco 26 A1
Marina del Rey Los Angeles 16 C2
Marino Dublin 10 A2
Marisco, Ponta do
Rio de Janeiro 25 C1
Markham Toronto 31 A2
Marki Warsaw 32 B2
Markland Wood Toronto 31 B1
Marly, Forêt de Paris 24 A1
Marly-le-Roi Paris 24 A1
Marne-la-Vallée Paris 24 A4
Marolles-en-Brie Paris 24 B4
Maroubra Sydney 29 B2
Marquette Park Chicago 9 C2
Marrickville Sydney 29 B1
Marsfield Sydney 29 A1
Marsha, L. Orlando 23 B2
Marte, Campo de São Paulo 27 B2
Martesana, Naviglio della
Milan 19 A2
Martin Luther King Nat.
Historic Site △ Atlanta 3 B2
Martinez Buenos Aires 7 A1
Martinkylä Helsinki 11 B2
Martinsried Munich 21 B1
Maruko Tokyo 30 B3
Maryino Moscow 19 B3
Maryland Singapore 28 B2
Marymont Warsaw 32 B1
Marysin Wawerski
Warsaw 32 B2
Marzahn Berlin 5 A4
Mascot Sydney 29 B2
Masmo Stockholm 29 B1
Maspeth New York 22 B2
Masr el Gedida Cairo 7 A2
Masr el Qadîma Cairo 7 A2
Massachusetts Inst. of
Tech. Boston 6 A2
Massamá Lisbon 16 A1
Massey → Toronto 31 A3
Massy Paris 24 B2
Mata Jerusalem 13 B1
Matihutong Beijing 4 B1
Matinha Lisbon 16 A2
Matramam Jakarta 12 B2
Matsubara Osaka 23 B2
Mattapan Boston 6 B2
Mátyásföld Budapest 7 A3
Mau Tso Ngam Hong Kong 12 A2
Mauer Vienna 32 B1
Mauripur Karachi 13 A1
Maxhof Munich 21 B1
Mayfair Johannesburg 13 B2
Mayor, Plaza Madrid 17 B1
Maywood Chicago 9 B1
Maywood Los Angeles 16 C3
Maywood New York 22 A1
Maywood Park Race
Track Chicago 9 B1
Mazagaon Mumbai 20 B2
Meadowbank Park Sydney 29 A1
Měcholupy Prague 25 B2
Měčice Prague 25 A3
Mecidiyeköy Istanbul 12 B2
Medford Boston 6 A2
Mediodia Madrid 17 B2
Meguro Tokyo 30 B3
Meguro → Tokyo 30 B3
Mehpalpur Delhi 10 B1
Mehrābād ✕ (THR) Tehran 31 A1
Mehram Nagar Delhi 10 B1
Mehrow Berlin 5 A4
Meidling Vienna 32 A2
Méier Rio de Janeiro 25 B1
Meiji Shrine Tokyo 30 A3
Meise Brussels 6 A1
Mejiro Tokyo 30 A3
Melbourne Melbourne 18 A1
Melbourne ✕ (MEL)
Melbourne 18 A1
Melkki Helsinki 11 C2
Mellunkylä Helsinki 11 B3
Mellunmäki Helsinki 11 B3
Melrose Boston 6 A2
Melrose New York 22 B2
Melrose Park Chicago 9 B1
Melsbroek Brussels 6 A2
Melville Johannesburg 13 B2
Menteng Jakarta 12 B1
Mérantaise → Paris 24 B1
Mercamadrid Madrid 17 B2
Merced, L. San Francisco 26 B2
Meredale Johannesburg 13 B1
Merlimau, Pulau Singapore 28 B2
Merri Cr. → Melbourne 18 A1
Merrion Dublin 10 B2
Merrionette Park Chicago 9 C2
Merton □ London 15 B2
Mesgarābād Tehran 31 B3
Messe Vienna 32 A2
Metanópoli Milan 19 B2
Metro-Dade Cultural
Centre Miami 18 B2
Metro Toronto Zoo Toronto 31 A3
Metropolitan Museum of
Art New York 22 B2
Meudon Paris 24 B2
Mevaseret Tsiyon
Jerusalem 13 B1
Mevo Beitar Jerusalem 13 B1
México Mexico City 18 B2
México, Ciudad de
Mexico City 18 B2
Mexico City Int. ✕ (MEX)
Mexico City 18 B2
Meyersdal Johannesburg 13 B2
Mezzate Milan 19 B2
Miadong Seoul 27 B2
Miami Miami 18 B2
Miami Beach Miami 18 B2
Miami Canal Miami 18 A1
Miami Int. ✕ (MIA) Miami 18 B1
Miami Shores Miami 18 A2
Miami Springs Miami 18 B1
Miasto Warsaw 32 B2
Michałowice Warsaw 32 B1
Michle Prague 25 B2
Middle Harbour Sydney 29 A2
Middle Hd. Sydney 29 A2
Middle Park Melbourne 18 B1
Middle Village New York 22 B2
Middlesex Fells
Reservation Boston 6 A2
Midland Beach New York 22 C1
Midwood New York 22 C2
Miedzeszyn Warsaw 32 B3
Międzylesie Warsaw 32 B3
Miessaari Helsinki 11 C1
Miguel Hidalgo Mexico City 18 B1
Milan = Milano Milan 19 B1
Milanese, Parco
Regionale △ Milan 19 A1
Milano Milan 19 B1
Milano Due Milan 19 B2
Milano Linate ✕ (LIN)
Milan 19 B2
Milano San Felice Milan 19 B2
Milbertshofen Munich 21 A2
Mill Hill London 15 A2
Millennium Dome London 15 A4
Miller Meadow Chicago 9 B2
Millerhill Edinburgh 11 B3
Milltown Dublin 10 B2
Millwood Washington 33 B4
Milnerton Cape Town 8 A1
Milon-la-Chapelle Paris 24 B1
Milton Boston 6 B2
Milton Bridge Edinburgh 11 B2
Mimico Toronto 31 B2
Mimico Creek → Toronto 31 B1
Minami Osaka 23 A2
Minamitsunashima Tokyo 30 B2
Minato Osaka 23 B1
Minato Tokyo 30 B3
Minshât el Bekkarî Cairo 7 A1
Miraflores Lima 14 B2
Miramar Wellington 33 B1
Misericordia, Sa. da
Rio de Janeiro 25 B1
Mission San Francisco 26 B2
Mississauga Toronto 31 B1
Mitaka Tokyo 30 A2
Mitcham London 15 B2
Mitcham Common London 15 B3
Mitchell Museum of the
American Indian Chicago 9 A2
Mitchell's Plain Cape Town 8 B2
Mitte Berlin 5 A3
Mittel Isarkanal →
Munich 21 A3
Mixcoac Mexico City 18 B1
Miyakojima Osaka 23 A2
Mizonokuchi Tokyo 30 B2
Mizue Tokyo 30 A4
Młocinski Park Warsaw 32 B1
Młociny Warsaw 32 B1
Mnevniki Moscow 19 B1
Moba Lagos 14 B2
Moczydło Warsaw 32 C2
Modderfontein
Johannesburg 13 A2
Modřany Prague 25 B2
Mogyoród Budapest 7 A3
Moinho Velho, Cor. →
São Paulo 27 B2
Mok Seoul 27 B1
Mokotów Warsaw 32 B2
Molenbeek-St-Jean Brussels 6 A1
Molino de Rosas
Mexico City 18 B1
Mollem Brussels 6 A1
Mollins de Rey Barcelona 4 A1
Mondeor Johannesburg 13 B2
Moneda, Palacio de la
Santiago 27 B2
Moneró Rio de Janeiro 25 A1
Mong Kok Hong Kong 12 B2
Monkstown Dublin 10 B3
Monnickendam Amsterdam 2 A3
Monrovia Los Angeles 16 B4
Monsanto Lisbon 16 A1
Monsanto, Parque
Florestal de Lisbon 16 A1
Mont-Royal Montreal 20 A2
Mont-Royal, Parc Montreal 20 A2
Montana de Montjuich
Barcelona 4 A1
Montcada i Reixac
Barcelona 4 A2
Monte Chingolo
Buenos Aires 7 C2
Montebello Los Angeles 16 B4
Montemor Lisbon 16 A1
Monterey Park Los Angeles 16 B4
Montespaccato Rome 26 B1
Montesson Paris 24 A1
Monteverde Nuovo Rome 26 B1
Montfermeil Paris 24 A4
Montigny-le-Bretonneux
Paris 24 B1
Montjay-la-Tour Paris 24 A4
Montparnasse, Gare Paris 24 A2
Montréal Montreal 20 A2
Montréal, Î. de Montreal 20 A2
Montréal, Université de
Montreal 20 B2
Montréal Est Montreal 20 A2
Montréal-Nord Montreal 20 A2
Montréal-Ouest Montreal 20 B1
Montréal Trudeau Int. ✕
(YUL) Montreal 20 B1
Montreuil Paris 24 A3
Montrouge Paris 24 B2
Montserrat Buenos Aires 7 B2
Monza Milan 19 A2
Monzoro Milan 19 B1
Moóca São Paulo 27 B2
Moonachie New York 22 B1
Moonee Ponds Melbourne 18 A1
Moonee Valley
Racecourse Melbourne 18 A1
Moosach Munich 21 A2
Mora Mumbai 20 B2
Moratalaz Madrid 17 B2
Mörby Stockholm 29 A2
Morden London 15 B2
Morée → Paris 24 A3
Morgan Park Chicago 9 C3
Moriguchi Osaka 23 A2
Morivione Milan 19 B2
Morningside Edinburgh 11 B2
Morningside Johannesburg 13 A2
Morningside Washington 33 C4
Morningside Park Orlando 23 B2
Morningside Park Toronto 31 A3
Morro Solar, Cerro Lima 14 C2
Mortlake London 15 B2
Mortlake Sydney 29 B1
Morton Grove Chicago 9 A2
Morumbi São Paulo 27 B1
Moscavide Lisbon 16 A2
Moschato Athens 2 B2
Moscow = Moskva
Moscow 19 B2
Moskva Moscow 19 B2
Moskvoretskiy Moscow 19 B2
Mosman Sydney 29 A2
Móstoles Madrid 17 C1
Moti Bagh Delhi 10 B2
Motol Prague 25 B1
Motsa Jerusalem 13 B2
Motsa Ilit Jerusalem 13 B1
Motspur Park London 15 B2
Mottingham London 15 B4
Mount Dennis Toronto 31 A2
Mount Greenwood Chicago 9 C2
Mount Hood Memorial
Park △ Boston 6 A2
Mount Merrion Dublin 10 B2
Mount Rainier Washington 33 B4
Mount Vernon New York 22 A3
Müggelberge Berlin 5 B4
Müggelheim Berlin 5 B5
Muggiò Milan 19 A2
Mühleiten Vienna 32 A3
Mühlenfliess → Berlin 5 A5
Muiden Amsterdam 2 A3
Muizenberg Cape Town 8 B1
Mujahidpur Delhi 10 B2
Mukandpur Delhi 10 A2
Mukhmas Jerusalem 13 A2
Muko → Osaka 23 A1
Mukojima Tokyo 30 A3
Mulbarton Johannesburg 13 B2
Mumbai Mumbai 20 B2
Mumbai Chhatrapati
Shivaji Int. ✕ (BOM)
Mumbai 20 A2
Mumbai Harbour Mumbai 20 B2
Munch Museum Oslo 23 A3
Münchehofe Berlin 5 B5
München Munich 21 B2
München Franz Josef
Strauss ✕ (MUC) Munich 21 A2
Munich = München
Munich 21 B2
Munkkiniemi Helsinki 11 B2
Munro Buenos Aires 7 B1
Muntinlupa Manila 17 C2
Murai Res. Singapore 28 A2
Muranów Warsaw 32 B1
Murino St. Petersburg 27 B2
Murrayfield Edinburgh 11 B2
Musashino Tokyo 30 A2
Museu Nacional
Rio de Janeiro 25 B1
Mushin Lagos 14 A2
Musocco Milan 19 B1
Mustansiriya Baghdad 3 A2
Musturud Cairo 7 A2
Muswell Hill London 15 A3
Mutanabi Baghdad 3 B2
Muthana Baghdad 3 B2
Mykerinos Cairo 7 B1
Myllypuro Helsinki 11 B3
Mystic → Boston 6 A2

N

Nacka Stockholm 29 B3
Naenae Wellington 33 B2
Næsnes Oslo 23 B1
Nagatsuta Tokyo 30 B2
Nagytétény Budapest 7 B1
Nahalin Jerusalem 13 B1
Najafgarh Drain → Delhi 10 B1
Nakahara Tokyo 30 B2
Nakano Tokyo 30 A3
Namsan Park Seoul 27 B1
Namyeong Seoul 27 B1
Nanbiancun Guangzhou 11 B1
Nanchang He → Beijing 4 B1
Nandang Guangzhou 11 B2
Nangal Dewat Delhi 10 B1
Naniwa Osaka 23 B1
Nanole Mumbai 20 A2
Nanpu Bridge Shanghai 28 B2
Nanshi Shanghai 28 B1
Nanterre Paris 24 A2
Naoabad Kolkata 14 C2
Napier Mole Karachi 13 B1
Naraina Delhi 10 B1
Nariman Point Mumbai 20 B1
Nariman Pt. Mumbai 20 B1
Nārmak Tehran 31 A2
Naruo Osaka 23 A1
Näsby Stockholm 29 A2
Näsbypark Stockholm 29 A2
National Arboretum
Washington 33 B3
National Zoological Park
Washington 33 B3
Nativity, Basilica of
Jerusalem 13 B2
Natolin Warsaw 32 C2
Naucalpan de Juárez
Mexico City 18 B1
Naupada Mumbai 20 A2
Navi Mumbai Mumbai 20 A2
Naviglio di Pavia Milan 19 B1
Naviglio Grande Milan 19 B1
Navotas Manila 17 B1
Navy Pier Chicago 9 B3
Nazal Hikmat Beg Baghdad 3 A2
Nazimabad Karachi 13 A2
Nazlet el Simmân Cairo 7 B1
Nea Alexandria Athens 2 B2
Nea Ionia Athens 2 A2
Nea Liosia Athens 2 A2
Nea Smirni Athens 2 B2
Neapoli Athens 2 B2
Near North Chicago 9 B3
Nebušice Prague 25 B1
Nederhorst Amsterdam 2 B3
Nedlitz Berlin 5 B1
Nee Soon Singapore 28 A2
Needham Boston 6 B1
Needham Heights Boston 6 B1
N'ematābād Tehran 31 B2
Nerima Tokyo 30 A3
Nesodden Oslo 23 B3
Nesoddtangen Oslo 23 A3
Nesøya Oslo 23 A2
Neu Aubing Munich 21 B1
Neu Buch Berlin 5 A4
Neu Buchhorst Berlin 5 B5
Neu Fahrland Berlin 5 B1
Neu Lindenberg Berlin 5 A4
Neubiberg Munich 21 B3
Neuenhagen Berlin 5 A4
Neuessling Vienna 32 A3
Neuhausen Munich 21 B2
Neuherberg Munich 21 A2
Neuhönow Berlin 5 A5
Neuilly-Plaisance Paris 24 A4
Neuilly-sur-Marne Paris 24 A4
Neuilly-sur-Seine Paris 24 A2
Neukagran Vienna 32 A2
Neukettenhof Vienna 32 B2
Neukölln Berlin 5 B3
Neuperlach Munich 21 B2
Neuried Munich 21 B1
Neustift am Walde Vienna 32 A1
Neusüssenbrunn Vienna 32 A2
Neuwaldegg Vienna 32 A1
Neve Ya'akov Jerusalem 13 A2
Neves Rio de Janeiro 25 B2
New Baghdād Baghdad 3 B2
New Barakpur Kolkata 14 A2
New Brighton New York 22 C1
New Canada Johannesburg 13 B1
New Canada Dam
Johannesburg 13 B1
New Carrollton Washington 33 B4
New Cross London 15 B3
New Delhi Delhi 10 B2
New Dorp New York 22 C1
New Dorp Beach New York 22 C1
New Malden London 15 B2
New Milford New York 22 A1
New Mumbai = Navi
Mumbai Mumbai 20 A2
New Territories Hong Kong 12 A1
New Toronto Toronto 31 B1
New Utrecht New York 22 C2
New York New York 22 B3
New York La Guardia ✕
(LGA) New York 22 B2
Newark B. New York 22 B1
Newbattle Edinburgh 11 B3
Newbury Park London 15 A4
Newcraighall Edinburgh 11 B3
Newham □ London 15 A4
Newhaven Edinburgh 11 B2
Newington Edinburgh 11 B2
Newlands Johannesburg 13 B1
Newlands Wellington 33 B1
Newport Melbourne 18 B1
Newton Boston 6 B1
Newtonbrook Toronto 31 A2
Newtongrange Edinburgh 11 B3
Newtonville Boston 6 A1
Newtown Sydney 29 B2
Ngaio Wellington 33 B1
Ngau Chi Wan Hong Kong 12 A2
Ngau Tau Kok Hong Kong 12 B2
Ngauranga Wellington 33 B1
Ngong Shuen Chau
Hong Kong 12 B1
Ngua Kok Wan Hong Kong 12 A1
Nhava Sheva Mumbai 20 B2
Niāvarān Tehran 31 A2
Nibra Kolkata 14 B1
Nīdāl Baghdad 3 B2
Niddrie Edinburgh 11 B3
Niddrie Melbourne 18 A1
Nieder Neuendorf Berlin 5 A2
Niederschöneweide Berlin 5 B3
Niederschönhausen Berlin 5 A3
Niemeyer Rio de Janeiro 25 B1
Nieuwendam Amsterdam 2 A2
Nihonbashi Tokyo 30 A3
Niipperi Helsinki 11 B1
Nikea Athens 2 B1
Nikolassee Berlin 5 B2
Nikolskoy Moscow 19 B1
Niles Chicago 9 A2
Nimta Kolkata 14 A2
Ninoy Aquino Int. ✕
(MNL) Manila 17 B2
Nippa Tokyo 30 B2
Nippori Tokyo 30 A3
Nishi Osaka 23 A1
Nishinari Osaka 23 B1
Nishinomiya Osaka 23 A1
Nishiyodogawa Osaka 23 A1
Niterói Rio de Janeiro 25 B2
Nockeby Stockholm 29 B1
Noel Park London 15 A3
Nogatino Moscow 19 B3
Nogent-sur-Marne Paris 24 A3
Noida Delhi 10 B2
Noiseau Paris 24 B4
Noisiel Paris 24 A4
Noisy-le-Grand Paris 24 A4
Noisy-le-Roi Paris 24 A1
Noisy-le-Sec Paris 24 A3
Nokkala Helsinki 11 C1
Nomentano Rome 26 B2
Nonakashinden Tokyo 30 A2
Nongminyundong
Jiangxisuo Guangzhou 11 B2
Nonhyeon Seoul 27 B2
Nonthaburi Bangkok 3 A1
Noordgesig Johannesburg 13 B1
Noordzeekanaal Amsterdam 2 A1
Nord, Gare du Paris 24 A3
Nordmarka Oslo 23 A3
Nordrand-Siedlung Vienna 32 A2
Nordstrand Oslo 23 A3
Normandale Wellington 33 B2
Norridge Chicago 9 B2
Norrmalm Stockholm 29 A2
North Arlington New York 22 B1
North Bay Village Miami 18 A2
North Bergen New York 22 B1
North Bull I. Dublin 10 A3
North Cheam London 15 B2
North Cray London 15 B4
North Decatur Atlanta 3 B3
North Druid Hills Atlanta 3 B3
North Esk → Edinburgh 11 B2
North Gyle Edinburgh 11 B2
North Hackensack
New York 22 A1
North Harbor Manila 17 B1
North Hd. Sydney 29 A2
North Hollywood
Los Angeles 16 B2
North Lexington Boston 6 A1
North Miami Miami 18 A2
North Miami Beach Miami 18 A2
North Nazimabad Karachi 13 A2
North Pt. Hong Kong 12 B2
North Queensferry
Edinburgh 11 A1
North Quincy Boston 6 B2
North Res. Boston 6 A2
North Riverside Chicago 9 B2
North Saugus Boston 6 A2
North Shore Channel →
Chicago 9 B2
North Springfield
Washington 33 C2
North Station Boston 6 A2
North Sydney Sydney 29 B2
North Woolwich London 15 A4
North York Toronto 31 A2
Northbridge Sydney 29 A2
Northbridge Park Sydney 29 A2
Northcliff Johannesburg 13 A1
Northcote Melbourne 18 A2
Northeastern University
Boston 6 A2
Northern Virginia
Regional Park △
Washington 33 B3
Northlake Chicago 9 B1
Northmount Toronto 31 A2
Northolt London 15 A1
Northumberland Heath
London 15 B5
Northwestern Station
Chicago 9 B3
Northwestern University
Chicago 9 A2
Northwood London 15 A1
Northwood Park Toronto 31 A1
Norwood Johannesburg 13 A2
Norwood Park Chicago 9 B2
Noryangjin Seoul 27 B1
Nossa Senhora do Ó
São Paulo 27 B1
Nossegem Brussels 6 A3
Notre-Dame Paris 24 A3
Notre-Dame, Basilique
Montreal 20 B2
Notre-Dame, Bois Paris 24 B4
Notre-Dame-de-Grace
Montreal 20 B2
Notting Hill London 15 A2
Nova Milanese Milan 19 A2
Novate Milanese Milan 19 A1
Novaya Derevnya
St. Petersburg 27 A1
Nové Město Prague 25 B2
Novoalekssandrovskoye
St. Petersburg 27 B2
Novodevichy Convent
Moscow 19 B2
Novogireyevo Moscow 19 B3
Novosaratovka
St. Petersburg 27 B3
Nowe-Babice Warsaw 32 B1
Nowe Miasto Warsaw 32 B2
Nöykkiö Helsinki 11 B1
Nueva Atzacoalco
Mexico City 18 B2
Nueva Pompeya
Buenos Aires 7 C2
Nueva Tenochtitlán
Mexico City 18 B2
Nuijala Helsinki 11 B1
Numabukuro Tokyo 30 A2
Nuñez Buenos Aires 7 B2
Nunhead London 15 B3
Ñuñoa Santiago 27 B2
Nusle Prague 25 B2
Nussdorf Vienna 32 A2
Nyanga Cape Town 8 A2
Nymphenburg Munich 21 B2
Nymphenburg, Schloss
Munich 21 B2

O

O. R. Tambo Int. ✕ (JNB)
Johannesburg 13 A2
Oak Grove Atlanta 3 A3
Oak Hill Boston 6 B1
Oak Lawn Chicago 9 C2
Oak Park Chicago 9 B2
Oak View Washington 33 A4
Oakdale Atlanta 3 A2
Oakland San Francisco 26 B3
Oakland Washington 33 B4
Oaklawn Washington 33 C4
Oakleigh Melbourne 18 B2
Oakton Washington 33 B2
Oakwood Beach New York 22 C1
Oatley Sydney 29 B1
Obalende Lagos 14 B2
Oba's Palace Lagos 14 B2
Oberföhring Munich 21 B2
Oberhaching Munich 21 B2
Oberlaa Vienna 32 B2
Oberlisse Vienna 32 A2
Obermenzing Munich 21 A1
Obermoos Schwaige
Munich 21 A1
Oberschleissheim Munich 21 A2
Oberschöneweide Berlin 5 B4
Observatory Johannesburg 13 B2
Óbuda Budapest 7 A2
Obukhovo St. Petersburg 27 B2
Obvodnyy Kanal
St. Petersburg 27 B1
Ocean Park Hong Kong 12 B2
Ochota Warsaw 32 B1
Ocoee Orlando 23 A1
Ōdana Tokyo 30 B2
Öden-Stockach Munich 21 B3
Odilampi Helsinki 11 B1
Odivelas Lisbon 16 A1
Odolany Warsaw 32 B1
Oeiras Lisbon 16 A1
Ofin Lagos 14 B3
Ogawa Tokyo 30 A1
Ogden Park Chicago 9 C2
Ogikubo Tokyo 30 A2
Ogogoro Lagos 14 B2
Ogoyo Lagos 14 B2
Ogudu Lagos 14 A2
O'Hare Int., Chicago ✕
(ORD) Chicago 9 B1
Ohariu Stream →
Wellington 33 B1
O'Higgins, Parque Santiago 27 B2
Ōimachi Tokyo 30 B3
Ojota Lagos 14 A2
Okęcie Warsaw 32 B1
Okęcie, Warszawa ✕
(WAW) Warsaw 32 B1
Okelra Lagos 14 B2
Okeogbe Lagos 14 B2
Okhla Delhi 10 B2
Okhta → St. Petersburg 27 B2
Okkervil → St. Petersburg 27 B2
Okrzeszyn Warsaw 32 C2
Oksval Oslo 23 A3
Oktyabrskiy Moscow 19 B2
Okubo Tokyo 30 A3
Ōkura Tokyo 30 B1
Olari Helsinki 11 B1
Olaria Rio de Janeiro 25 B1
Old Admiralty
St. Petersburg 27 B1
Old City Jerusalem 13 B2
Old City Shanghai 28 B1
Old City Hall Toronto 31 B2
Old Fort York Toronto 31 B2
Old Harbor Boston 6 B2
Old Town Chicago 9 B3
Old Town Hall = Altes
Rathaus Munich 21 B2
Oldbawn Dublin 10 B1
Olgino St. Petersburg 27 A1
Olimpico, Estadio
Mexico City 18 C1
Olivais Lisbon 16 A2
Olivar de los Padres
Mexico City 18 B1
Olivar del Conde
Mexico City 18 B1
Olives, Mt. of Jerusalem 13 B2
Olivia, L. Orlando 23 B1
Olivos Buenos Aires 7 B2
Olona → Milan 19 B1
Olympia, L. Orlando 23 A1
Olympic Stadium =
Turner Field Atlanta 3 B2
Olympic Stadium Helsinki 11 B2
Olympique, Stade Montreal 20 A2
Ōmori Tokyo 30 B3
Onisigun Lagos 14 A2
Ontario Science Centre
Toronto 31 A2
Ōokayama Tokyo 30 B3
Oostzaan Amsterdam 2 A2
Opa-Locka Miami 18 A1
Opa-Locka ✕ (OPF) Miami 18 A1
Opacz Warsaw 32 B1
Ophirton Johannesburg 13 B2
Oppegård Oslo 23 B3
Oppem Brussels 6 A1
Oppsal Oslo 23 A4
Ora Jerusalem 13 B1
Oradell New York 22 A1
Oradell Res. New York 22 A1
Orange Bowl Stadium
Miami 18 B2
Orangi Karachi 13 A2
Ordrup Copenhagen 8 A3
Orech Prague 25 B1
Orient Heights Boston 6 A3
Orlando Orlando 23 B1
Orlando Dam Johannesburg 13 B1
Orlando East Johannesburg 13 B1
Orlando Executive ✕
Orlando 23 A2
Orlando Int. ✕ (MCO)
Orlando 23 B3
Orlovista Orlando 23 A2
Orly Paris 24 B3
Orly, Paris ✕ (ORY) Paris 24 B3
Ormesson-sur-Marne
Paris 24 B4
Ormond Melbourne 18 B2
Ormøya Oslo 23 A3
Orpington London 15 B4
Ortaköy Istanbul 12 B2
Ortica Milan 19 B2
Oruba Lagos 14 A2
Ōsaka Osaka 23 B2
Ōsaka Castle Osaka 23 A2
Ōsaka Harbour Osaka 23 B1
Ōsaka Itami Int. ✕ (ITM)
Osaka 23 A1
Ōsaka Kansai ✕ (KIX)
Osaka 23 B2
Ōsaki Tokyo 30 B3
Osasco São Paulo 27 B1
Osdorf Berlin 5 B3
Osdorp Amsterdam 2 A1
Oshodi Lagos 14 A2
Oslo Oslo 23 A3
Oslo ✕ (OSL) Oslo 23 A4
Ōsone Tokyo 30 B2
Osorun Lagos 14 A2
Ospiate Milan 19 A1
Ostankino Moscow 19 B2
Osterley London 15 B1
Osterley Park London 15 B1
Östermalm Stockholm 29 A2
Österskär Stockholm 29 A3
Ostia Malpasso Rome 26 C1
Ostiense Rome 26 B1
Østmarkkapellet Oslo 23 A4
Østøya Oslo 23 B2
Østre Aker Oslo 23 A3
Ōta Tokyo 30 B3
Otaniemi Helsinki 11 B1
Otari Open Air Museum
Wellington 33 B1
Otsuka Tokyo 30 A3
Ottakring Vienna 32 A1
Ottávia Rome 26 B1
Ottery Cape Town 8 B2
Ottobrunn Munich 21 B3
Ouderkerk Amsterdam 2 B2
Oulunkylä Helsinki 11 B2
Ourcq, Canal de l' Paris 24 A3
Outer Mission
San Francisco 26 B2
Outremont Montreal 20 A2
Overijse Brussels 6 B3
Owhiro Bay Wellington 33 C1
Oworonsoki Lagos 14 A2
Oxgangs Edinburgh 11 B2
Oxon Hill Washington 33 C4
Oyodo Osaka 23 A1
Oyster B. Sydney 29 C1
Oyster Rock Mumbai 20 B1
Oyster Rocks Karachi 13 B2
Ozoir-la-Ferrière Paris 24 B4
Ozone Park New York 22 B2

P

Pacific Heights
San Francisco 26 B2
Pacific Manor San Francisco 26 C2
Pacific Palisades
Los Angeles 16 B1
Pacifica San Francisco 26 C2
Paco Manila 17 B1
Paco de Arcos Lisbon 16 A1
Paddington London 15 A2

Paddington *Sydney* 29 B2
Paderno *Milan* 19 A1
Pagewood *Sydney* 29 B2
Pagote *Mumbai* 20 B2
Pai, I. do *Rio de Janeiro* 25 B2
Pak Kok *Hong Kong* 12 B1
Pak Kong *Hong Kong* 12 A2
Pakila *Helsinki* 11 B2
Palacio Real *Madrid* 17 B1
Palaiseau *Paris* 24 B2
Palazzolo *Milan* 19 A1
Paleo Faliro *Athens* 2 B2
Palermo *Buenos Aires* 7 B2
Palhais *Lisbon* 16 B2
Palisades Park *New York* 22 A1
Palmer Park *Washington* 33 B4
Palmerston *Dublin* 10 A1
Paloheinä *Helsinki* 11 B2
Palomeras *Madrid* 17 B2
Palos Heights *Chicago* 9 D2
Palos Hills *Chicago* 9 C2
Palos Hills Forest *Chicago* 9 C1
Palos Park *Chicago* 9 C1
Palpara *Kolkata* 14 B2
Panchur *Kolkata* 14 B1
Pandacan *Manila* 17 B2
Pandan, Selat *Singapore* 28 B2
Pandan Res. *Singapore* 28 B2
Pangrati *Athens* 2 B2
Pangsua, Sungei → *Singapore* 28 A2
Panihati *Kolkata* 14 A2
Panjang, Bukit *Singapore* 28 A2
Panke → *Berlin* 5 A3
Pankow *Berlin* 5 A3
Pantheon *Rome* 26 B1
Panthersville *Atlanta* 3 B3
Pantin *Paris* 24 A3
Pantitlán *Mexico City* 18 B2
Panvel Cr. → *Mumbai* 20 B2
Paparangi *Wellington* 33 B1
Papiol *Barcelona* 4 A1
Paramount Studios *Los Angeles* 16 B3
Paramus *New York* 22 A1
Paranaque *Manila* 17 B1
Paray-Vieille-Poste *Paris* 24 B3
Pardisān Nature Park *Tehran* 31 A2
Parel *Mumbai* 20 B1
Pari *São Paulo* 27 B2
Parioli *Rome* 26 B1
Paris *Paris* 24 A3
Paris Orly ✈ (ORY) *Paris* 24 B3
Parje *Mumbai* 20 B2
Pārk-e Āzādegān *Tehran* 31 B2
Pārk-e Mellat *Tehran* 31 A2
Park Ridge *Chicago* 9 A1
Park Royal *London* 15 A2
Parkchester *New York* 22 B2
Parkdale *Toronto* 31 B2
Parkhurst *Johannesburg* 13 A2
Parklawn *Washington* 33 B3
Parkmore *Johannesburg* 13 A2
Parkside *San Francisco* 26 B2
Parktown *Johannesburg* 13 B2
Parkview *Johannesburg* 13 A2
Parkville *New York* 22 C2
Parkwood *Cape Town* 8 B1
Parkwood *Johannesburg* 13 A2
Parow *Cape Town* 8 A2
Parque Chacabuco *Buenos Aires* 7 B2
Parque Patricios *Buenos Aires* 7 B2
Parramatta → *Sydney* 29 A1
Paşabahçe *Istanbul* 12 B2
Pasadena *Los Angeles* 16 B4
Pasar Minggu *Jakarta* 12 B1
Pasay *Manila* 17 B1
Pascoe Vale *Melbourne* 18 A1
Pasig *Manila* 17 B2
Pasig → *Manila* 17 B2
Pasila *Helsinki* 11 B2
Pasing *Munich* 21 B1
Pasir Panjang *Singapore* 28 B2
Pasir Ris *Singapore* 28 A3
Passaic *New York* 22 A1
Passaic → *New York* 22 B1
Passirana *Milan* 19 A1
Patel Nagar *Delhi* 10 B1
Pateros *Manila* 17 B2
Pathumwan *Bangkok* 3 B2
Patipukur *Kolkata* 14 B2
Patisia *Athens* 2 A2
Paulo E. Virginia, Gruta *Rio de Janeiro* 25 B1
Paulshof *Berlin* 5 A5
Paya Lebar *Singapore* 28 A3
Peakhurst *Sydney* 29 B1
Peania *Athens* 2 B3
Pearson Int. Toronto ✈ (YYZ) *Toronto* 31 A1
Peckham *London* 15 B3
Pederstrup *Copenhagen* 8 A2
Pedralbes *Barcelona* 4 A1
Pedregal de San Angel, Jardines del *Mexico City* 18 C1
Peip'ing = Beijing *Beijing* 4 B1
Peking = Beijing *Beijing* 4 B1
Pelcowizna *Warsaw* 32 B2
Peñalolén *Santiago* 27 B2
Pencarrow Hd. *Wellington* 33 C2
Peng Siang → *Singapore* 28 A2
Penge *London* 15 B3
Penha *Rio de Janeiro* 25 A1
Penicuik *Edinburgh* 11 B2
Penjaringan *Jakarta* 12 A1
Pentagon *Washington* 33 B3
Penzing *Vienna* 32 A1
People's Park *Shanghai* 28 B1
People's Square *Shanghai* 28 B1
Perales del Rio *Madrid* 17 C2
Perchtoldsdorf *Vienna* 32 B1
Perdizes *São Paulo* 27 B2
Peristeri *Athens* 2 A2
Perivale *London* 15 A2
Perk *Brussels* 6 A2
Perlach *Munich* 21 B2
Perlacher Forst *Munich* 21 B2
Pero *Milan* 19 A1
Peropok, Bukit *Singapore* 28 B2
Perovo *Moscow* 19 B3
Pertusella *Milan* 19 A1
Pesagot *Jerusalem* 13 A2
Pesanggrahag, Kali → *Jakarta* 12 B1
Peschiera Borromeo *Milan* 19 B2
Pesek, Pulau *Singapore* 28 B2
Pest *Budapest* 7 B2
Pesterzsébet *Budapest* 7 B2
Pesthidegkút *Budapest* 7 A1
Pestimre *Budapest* 7 B3
Pestlőrinc *Budapest* 7 B3
Pestújhely *Budapest* 7 A2
Petas *Helsinki* 11 B2
Petone *Wellington* 33 B2
Petrogradskaya Storona *St. Petersburg* 27 B2
Petroupoli *Athens* 2 A2
Petrovice *Prague* 25 B3
Petrovskiy Park *Moscow* 19 B2
Petrovsko-Razumovskoye *Moscow* 19 B2
Pettycur *Edinburgh* 11 A2
Peutie *Brussels* 6 A2
Pfaueninsel *Berlin* 5 B1
Phaya Thai *Bangkok* 3 B2
Phihai *Karachi* 13 A2
Phillip B. *Sydney* 29 B2
Phoenix Park *Dublin* 10 A2
Phra Khanong *Bangkok* 3 B2
Phra Nakhon *Bangkok* 3 B2
Phra Pradaeng *Bangkok* 3 C2
Phranakhon *Bangkok* 3 B1
Pico Rivera *Los Angeles* 16 C4
Piedade *Lisbon* 16 A1
Piedade *Rio de Janeiro* 25 B1
Piedade, Cova da *Lisbon* 16 A2
Piedmont Park *Atlanta* 3 B2
Pierre Elliott Trudeau ✈ (YUL) *Montreal* 20 B1
Pietralata *Rome* 26 B2
Pihlajamäki *Helsinki* 11 B2
Pihlajasaari *Helsinki* 11 C2
Pilares *Rio de Janeiro* 25 B1
Pilton *Edinburgh* 11 B2
Pimmit Hills *Washington* 33 B2
Pine Castle *Orlando* 23 B2
Pine Grove *Toronto* 31 A1
Pine Hills *Orlando* 23 A2
Pinewood Park *Miami* 18 A2
Piney Run → *Washington* 33 B2
Pinganli *Beijing* 4 B2
Pingzhou *Guangzhou* 11 B2
Pinheiros → *São Paulo* 27 B1
Pinjrapur *Karachi* 13 A2
Pinner *London* 15 A1
Pinner Green *London* 15 A1
Pioltello *Milan* 19 A2
Pipinui Pt. *Wellington* 33 A1
Piræus = Pireas *Athens* 2 B1
Piraiévs = Pireas *Athens* 2 B1
Pirajuçara → *São Paulo* 27 B1
Pireas *Athens* 2 B1
Pirinççi *Istanbul* 12 B1
Pirituba *São Paulo* 27 A1
Pirkkola *Helsinki* 11 B2
Pisgat O'mer *Jerusalem* 13 B2
Pisgat Ze'ev *Jerusalem* 13 B2
Pisnice *Prague* 25 C2
Pitampura *Delhi* 10 A1
Pitkäjärvi *Helsinki* 11 B1
Planegg *Munich* 21 B1
Pleasure Island *Orlando* 23 B1
Plumstead *Cape Town* 8 B1
Plumstead *London* 15 B4
Plyushchevo *Moscow* 19 B3
Po Toi *Hong Kong* 12 B2
Po Toi O *Hong Kong* 12 B2
Poasco *Milan* 19 B2
Podbaba *Prague* 25 B2
Podoli *Prague* 25 B2
Pohick Creek → *Washington* 33 C2
Pointe-Aux-Trembles *Montreal* 20 A2
Poissy *Paris* 24 A1
Pok Fu Lam *Hong Kong* 12 B1
Pokcheong *Seoul* 27 C2
Pokrovsko-Sresnevo *Moscow* 19 B1
Polton *Edinburgh* 11 B3
Polvoranca, Parque de *Madrid* 17 C1
Polyustrovo *St. Petersburg* 27 B2
Pomprap *Bangkok* 3 B2
Pondok Gede *Jakarta* 12 A2
Pondok Indah *Jakarta* 12 B1
Pont-Viau *Montreal* 20 A1
Pontault-Combault *Paris* 24 B4
Pontinha *Lisbon* 16 A1
Poplar *London* 15 A3
Poppintree *Dublin* 10 A2
Porirua *Wellington* 33 A2
Porirua East *Wellington* 33 A2
Port Melbourne *Melbourne* 18 B1
Port Nicholson *Wellington* 33 B2
Port Richmond *New York* 22 C1
Port Shelter *Hong Kong* 12 A2
Port Union *Toronto* 31 A4
Portage Park *Chicago* 9 B2
Portela, Lisboa ✈ (LIS) *Lisbon* 16 A2
Porter, L. *Orlando* 23 A3
Portmarnock *Dublin* 10 A3
Porto Brandão *Lisbon* 16 A1
Pôrto Novo *Rio de Janeiro* 25 A2
Porto Novo Cr. → *Lagos* 14 B2
Portobello *Edinburgh* 11 B3
Portrero *San Francisco* 26 B3
Potomac *Washington* 33 A2
Potrero Pt. *San Francisco* 26 B2
Potsdam *Berlin* 5 B1
Potzham *Munich* 21 B2
Pötzleinsdorf *Vienna* 32 A1
Povoa de Santo Adriao *Lisbon* 16 A2
Powązki *Warsaw* 32 B1
Powiśle *Warsaw* 32 B2
Powsin *Warsaw* 32 C2
Powsinek *Warsaw* 32 C2
Poyan Res. *Singapore* 28 A2
Pozuelo de Alarcón *Madrid* 17 B1
Prado, Museo del *Madrid* 17 B1
Prado Churubusco *Mexico City* 18 B2
Praga *Warsaw* 32 B2
Prague = Praha *Prague* 25 B2
Praha *Prague* 25 B2
Praha ✈ (PRG) *Prague* 25 B1
Praires, R. des → *Montreal* 20 A2
Prater *Vienna* 32 A2
Precotto *Milan* 19 A2
Prenestino Labicano *Rome* 26 B2
Prenzlauerberg *Berlin* 5 A3
Preston *Melbourne* 18 A1
Pretos Forros, Sa. dos *Rio de Janeiro* 25 B1
Préville *Montreal* 20 B3
Přezletice *Prague* 25 B3
Prima Porta *Rome* 26 B1
Primavalle *Rome* 26 B1
Primrose *Johannesburg* 13 B2
Progreso Nacional *Mexico City* 18 A2
Prosek *Prague* 25 B3
Prospect Hill Park *Boston* 6 A1
Providencia *Santiago* 27 B2
Průhonice *Prague* 25 C3
Psichiko *Athens* 2 A2
Pudong New Area *Shanghai* 28 B2
Pueblo Libre *Lima* 14 B2
Pueblo Nuevo *Barcelona* 4 A2
Pueblo Nuevo *Madrid* 17 B2
Puerto Madero *Buenos Aires* 7 B2
Puhuangyu *Beijing* 4 B2
Puistola *Helsinki* 11 B3
Pukinmäki *Helsinki* 11 B2
Pulkovo Int. ✈ (LED) *St. Petersburg* 27 C1
Pullach *Munich* 21 B1
Pullman Historic District *Chicago* 9 C3
Pulo Gadung *Jakarta* 12 B2
Pūnak *Tehran* 31 A2
Punchbowl *Sydney* 29 B1
Punde *Mumbai* 20 B2
Punggol *Singapore* 28 A3
Punggol, Sungei → *Singapore* 28 A3
Punggol Pt. *Singapore* 28 A3
Punjabi Bagh *Delhi* 10 A1
Puotila *Helsinki* 11 B3
Puteaux *Paris* 24 A2
Putney *London* 15 B2
Putuo *Shanghai* 28 B1
Putxet *Barcelona* 4 A1
Puxi *Shanghai* 28 B1
Pyramids *Cairo* 7 B1
Pyry *Warsaw* 32 C1

Q

Qalandiya *Jerusalem* 13 A2
Qal'eh Morghī *Tehran* 31 B2
Qanâ el Ismâ'ilîya *Cairo* 7 A2
Qāsemābād *Tehran* 31 A3
Qasr-e Fīrūzeh *Tehran* 31 B3
Qatane *Jerusalem* 13 B1
Qianmen *Beijing* 4 B2
Qinghuayuan *Beijing* 4 B1
Qingningsi *Shanghai* 28 B2
Qolhak *Tehran* 31 A2
Quadraro *Rome* 26 B2
Quaid-i-Azam *Karachi* 13 A1
Quartiere Zingone *Milan* 19 B1
Qubeiba *Jerusalem* 13 A1
Quds *Baghdad* 3 A2
Queen Mary Res. *London* 15 B1
Queen Victoria Market *Melbourne* 18 A1
Queensbury *London* 15 A2
Queenscliffe *Sydney* 29 A2
Queensferry *Edinburgh* 11 B1
Queenstown *Singapore* 28 B2
Quellerina *Johannesburg* 13 A1
Queluz *Lisbon* 16 A1
Quezon City *Manila* 17 B2
Quilicura *Santiago* 27 B1
Quincy *Boston* 6 B2
Quincy B. *Boston* 6 B3
Quinta Normal *Santiago* 27 B1
Quinto de Stampi *Milan* 19 B2
Quinto Romano *Milan* 19 B1
Quirinale *Rome* 26 B1

R

R.F.K. Memorial Stadium *Washington* 33 B4
Raasdorf *Vienna* 32 A3
Radcliffe College *Boston* 6 A2
Rådhus *Oslo* 23 A3
Radlice *Prague* 25 B2
Radość *Warsaw* 32 B3
Radotin *Prague* 25 C2
Rafat *Jerusalem* 13 A2
Raffles Park *Singapore* 28 B2
Raheny *Dublin* 10 A3
Rahnsdorf *Berlin* 5 B5
Rainham *London* 15 A5
Rajakylä *Helsinki* 11 B3
Rajpura *Delhi* 10 A2
Rákos-patak → *Budapest* 7 B3
Rákoshegy *Budapest* 7 B3
Rákoskeresztúr *Budapest* 7 B3
Rákoskert *Budapest* 7 B3
Rákosliget *Budapest* 7 B3
Rákospalota *Budapest* 7 A2
Rákosszentmihály *Budapest* 7 A2
Raków *Warsaw* 32 B1
Ram *Jerusalem* 13 A2
Rām Allāh *Jerusalem* 13 A2
Ramadān *Baghdad* 3 B2
Ramakrishna Puram *Delhi* 10 B1
Ramallah = Rām Allāh *Jerusalem* 13 A2
Ramanathpur *Kolkata* 14 A1
Ramat Allon *Jerusalem* 13 B2
Ramat Eshkol *Jerusalem* 13 B2
Ramat Razi'el *Jerusalem* 13 B1
Ramat Shafet *Jerusalem* 13 B2
Rambler Channel *Hong Kong* 12 A1
Ramenki *Moscow* 19 B1
Ramersdorf *Munich* 21 B2
Rameses Station *Cairo* 7 A2
Ramos *Rio de Janeiro* 25 B1
Ramos Mejia *Buenos Aires* 7 B1
Ramot *Jerusalem* 13 B2
Rampur *Delhi* 10 A2
Ramsgate *Sydney* 29 B1
Rand ✈ (QRA) *Johannesburg* 13 B2
Randalls I. *New York* 22 B2
Randburg *Johannesburg* 13 A1
Randhart *Johannesburg* 13 B2
Randpark Ridge *Johannesburg* 13 A1
Randwick *Sydney* 29 B2
Ranelagh *Dublin* 10 A2
Rangpuri *Delhi* 10 B1
Rannersdorf *Vienna* 32 B2
Ransbèche *Brussels* 6 B2
Ransdorp *Amsterdam* 2 A2
Ranvad *Mumbai* 20 B2
Raposo *Lisbon* 16 A1
Rastaala *Helsinki* 11 B1
Rastila *Helsinki* 11 B3
Raszyn *Warsaw* 32 C1
Rathfarnham *Dublin* 10 B2
Ratho *Edinburgh* 11 B1
Ratho Station *Edinburgh* 11 B1
Rato *Lisbon* 16 A2
Ravelston *Edinburgh* 11 B2
Rawamangun *Jakarta* 12 B2
Rayners Lane *London* 15 A1
Raynes Park *London* 15 B2
Raypur *Kolkata* 14 C2
Real Felipe, Fuerte *Lima* 14 B2
Reams, L. *Orlando* 23 B1
Recoleta *Buenos Aires* 7 B2
Recoleta *Santiago* 27 B2
Red Fort = Lal Qila *Delhi* 10 B2
Red Square *Moscow* 19 B2
Redbridge □ *London* 15 A4
Redfern *Sydney* 29 B2
Redwood *Wellington* 33 B1
Refshaleøen *Copenhagen* 8 A3
Regents Park *Johannesburg* 13 B2
Regent's Park *London* 15 A3
Rego Park *New York* 22 B2
Reinickendorf *Berlin* 5 A3
Rekola *Helsinki* 11 B3
Rembertów *Warsaw* 32 B2
Rembrandtpark *Amsterdam* 2 A2
Remedios, Parque Nacional de los △ *Mexico City* 18 B1
Remedios de Escalada *Buenos Aires* 7 C2
Rémola, Estany del *Barcelona* 4 B1
Renca *Santiago* 27 B1
Rennemoulin *Paris* 24 A1
Řeporyje *Prague* 25 B1
Repulse Bay *Hong Kong* 12 B2
Repy *Prague* 25 B1
Residenz *Munich* 21 B2
Reston *Washington* 33 B2
Retiro *Buenos Aires* 7 B2
Retiro *Madrid* 17 B1
Retiro, Puerto *Buenos Aires* 7 B2
Retreat *Cape Town* 8 B1
Reutov *Moscow* 19 B4
Réveillon → *Paris* 24 B4
Revere *Boston* 6 A2
Rexdale *Toronto* 31 A1
Reynosa Tamaulipas *Mexico City* 18 A1
Rho *Milan* 19 A1
Rhodes *Sydney* 29 A1
Rhodon *Paris* 24 B1
Rhodon → *Paris* 24 B1
Rialto Towers *Melbourne* 18 A1
Ribeira *Rio de Janeiro* 25 A1
Ricarda, Estany de la *Barcelona* 4 B1
Richmond *Melbourne* 18 A2
Richmond *San Francisco* 26 B2
Richmond Hill *New York* 22 B2
Richmond Park *London* 15 B2
Richmond-upon-Thames □ *London* 15 B2
Ridge, The *Delhi* 10 B2
Ridgefield *New York* 22 B1
Ridgefield Park *New York* 22 A1
Ridgewood *New York* 22 B2
Riem *Munich* 21 B3
Riesenrad *Vienna* 32 A2
Rijksmuseum *Amsterdam* 2 A2
Rikers I. *New York* 22 B2
Rimac *Lima* 14 B2
Ringsend *Dublin* 10 A2
Rinkeby *Stockholm* 29 A1
Rio Comprido *Rio de Janeiro* 25 B1
Rio de Janeiro *Rio de Janeiro* 25 B1
Rio de Janeiro Galeão ✈ (GIG) *Rio de Janeiro* 25 A1
Rio de Mouro *Lisbon* 16 A1
Ripollet *Barcelona* 4 A1
Ris *Oslo* 23 A3
Risby *Copenhagen* 8 A1
Rishra *Kolkata* 14 A2
Ritchie *Washington* 33 B4
Rithala *Delhi* 10 A1
Rive Sud, Canal de la *Montreal* 20 B2
River Edge *New York* 22 A1
River Forest *Chicago* 9 B2
River Grove *Chicago* 9 B1
Riverdale *New York* 22 A2
Riverdale *Washington* 33 B4
Riverdale Park *Toronto* 31 A2
Riverlea *Johannesburg* 13 B1
Riverside *Chicago* 9 C2
Riverwood *Sydney* 29 B1
Rivière-des-Praires *Montreal* 20 A2
Rixensart *Brussels* 6 B3
Riyad *Baghdad* 3 B2
Rizal Park *Manila* 17 B1
Rizal Stadium *Manila* 17 B1
Røa *Oslo* 23 A2
Robbins *Chicago* 9 D2
Robertsham *Johannesburg* 13 B2
Rochelle Park *New York* 22 A1
Rock Cr. → *Washington* 33 B3
Rock Creek Park *Washington* 33 B3
Rock Pt. *Wellington* 33 A1
Rockaway Beach *New York* 22 C3
Rockaway Pt. *New York* 22 C2
Rockdale *Sydney* 29 B1
Rockefeller Center *New York* 22 B2
Rocky Run → *Washington* 33 B2
Roda, Gezîret el *Cairo* 7 A2
Roda I. = Roda, Gezîret el *Cairo* 7 A2
Rodaon *Vienna* 32 B1
Rødovre *Copenhagen* 8 A2
Rodrigo de Freitas, L. *Rio de Janeiro* 25 B1
Roehampton *London* 15 B2
Rogers Park *Chicago* 9 A3
Roihuvuori *Helsinki* 11 B3
Roissy-en-Brie *Paris* 24 B4
Rokytka → *Prague* 25 B3
Roma *Rome* 26 B1
Roma Urbe ✈ *Rome* 26 B1
Római-Fürdő *Budapest* 7 A2
Romainville *Paris* 24 A3
Roman Forum = Foro Romano *Rome* 26 B1
Romano Banco *Milan* 19 B1
Rome = Roma *Rome* 26 B1
Romema *Jerusalem* 13 B2
Romford *London* 15 A5
Ronald Reagan National, Washington ✈ (DCA) *Washington* 33 B3
Rondebosch *Cape Town* 8 A1
Roppongi *Tokyo* 30 B3
Rose, L. *Orlando* 23 A1
Rose Bowl *Los Angeles* 16 B4
Rose Hill *Washington* 33 C3
Rosebank *Johannesburg* 13 A2
Rosebank *New York* 22 C1
Rosebery *Sydney* 29 B2
Rosedal La Candelaria *Mexico City* 18 B2
Roseland *Chicago* 9 C3
Rosemead *Los Angeles* 16 B4
Rosemont *Chicago* 9 B1
Rosemont *Montreal* 20 A2
Rosenborg Slot *Copenhagen* 8 A3
Rosenthal *Berlin* 5 A3
Rosettenville *Johannesburg* 13 B2
Rosewell *Edinburgh* 11 B3
Rosherville Dam *Johannesburg* 13 B2
Rösjön *Stockholm* 29 A2
Roslags-Näsby *Stockholm* 29 A2
Roslin *Edinburgh* 11 B3
Roslindale *Boston* 6 B2
Rosny-sous-Bois *Paris* 24 A4
Rosslyn *Washington* 33 B3
Rosyth *Edinburgh* 11 A1
Rotherhithe *London* 15 B3
Rothneusiedl *Vienna* 32 B2
Rothschmaige *Munich* 21 A1
Rouge Hill *Toronto* 31 A4
Round I. *Hong Kong* 12 B2
Roxbury *Boston* 6 B2
Roxeth *London* 15 A1
Royal Botanic Gardens *Edinburgh* 11 B2
Royal Observatory *Edinburgh* 11 B2
Royal Palace = Kungliga Slottet *Stockholm* 29 B2
Royal Park *Melbourne* 18 A1
Röylä *Helsinki* 11 B1
Rozas, Portilleros de las *Madrid* 17 B1
Roztoky *Prague* 25 B2
Rozzano *Milan* 19 B1
Rubí → *Barcelona* 4 A1
Rudolfsheim *Vienna* 32 A2
Rudolfshöhe *Berlin* 5 A5
Rudow *Berlin* 5 B3
Rueil-Malmaison *Paris* 24 A2
Ruisbroek *Brussels* 6 B1
Ruislip *London* 15 A1
Rumelihisarı *Istanbul* 12 B2
Rungis *Paris* 24 B3
Rusāfa *Baghdad* 3 A2
Rush Green *London* 15 A5
Russa *Kolkata* 14 C2
Rutherford *New York* 22 B1
Ruzyně *Prague* 25 B1
Ruzyne, Praha ✈ (PRG) *Prague* 25 B1
Rybatskaya *St. Petersburg* 27 B2
Rydboholm *Stockholm* 29 A3
Ryde *Sydney* 29 A1
Ryogoku *Tokyo* 30 A3
Rzhevka *St. Petersburg* 27 B3

S

Sa'ādatābād *Tehran* 31 A2
Saadūn *Baghdad* 3 B2
Saavedra *Buenos Aires* 7 B2
Saboli *Delhi* 10 A2
Sabugo *Lisbon* 16 A1
Sabzi Mand *Delhi* 10 A2
Sacavém *Lisbon* 16 A2
Saclay *Paris* 24 B2
Saclay, Étang de *Paris* 24 B1
Sacomã *São Paulo* 27 B2
Sacré Cœur *Paris* 24 A3
Sacrow *Berlin* 5 B1
Sacrower See *Berlin* 5 B1
Sadang *Seoul* 27 C1
Saddle → *New York* 22 A1
Saddle Brook *New York* 22 A1
Sadr *Karachi* 13 A2
Sadr City *Baghdad* 3 A2
Sadyba *Warsaw* 32 B2
Safdar Jang's Tomb *Delhi* 10 B2
Saft el Laban *Cairo* 7 A2
Saganashkee Slough *Chicago* 9 C1
Sagene *Oslo* 23 A3
Sagrada Familia, Templo de *Barcelona* 4 A2
Sahar, Mumbai ✈ (BOM) *Mumbai* 20 A2
Sai Kung *Hong Kong* 12 A2
Sai Wan Ho *Hong Kong* 12 B2
Sai Ying Pun *Hong Kong* 12 B1
St-Aubin *Paris* 24 B1
St-Cloud *Paris* 24 A2
St-Cyr-l'École *Paris* 24 B1
St-Cyr-l'École ✈ *Paris* 24 B1
St-Denis *Paris* 24 A3
St-Germain, Forêt de *Paris* 24 A1
St-Germain-en-Laye *Paris* 24 A1
St-Gilles *Brussels* 6 B2
St. Helier *London* 15 B2
St-Hubert *Montreal* 20 B3
St. Hubert, Galeries Royales *Brussels* 6 A2
St. Isaac's Cathedral *St. Petersburg* 27 B1
St-Jacques → *Montreal* 20 B3
St-Joost-Ten-Node *Brussels* 6 A2
St. Kilda *Melbourne* 18 B1
St-Lambert *Montreal* 20 A3
St-Lambert *Paris* 24 B1
St-Laurent *Montreal* 20 A1
St-Léonard *Montreal* 20 A2
St. Magelungen *Stockholm* 29 B2
St-Mandé *Paris* 24 A3
St. Margaret's *Dublin* 10 A2
St-Martin, Bois *Paris* 24 B4
St. Mary Cray *London* 15 B4
St-Maur-des-Fossés *Paris* 24 B3
St-Maurice *Paris* 24 B3
St-Michel *Montreal* 20 A2
St. Nikolaus-Kirken *Prague* 25 B2
St-Ouen *Paris* 24 A3
St. Paul's Cray *London* 15 B4
St. Peters *Sydney* 29 B2
St. Petersburg = Sankt-Peterburg *St. Petersburg* 27 B1
St-Pierre *Montreal* 20 B2
St-Pieters Leew *Brussels* 6 B1
St-Quentin, Étang de *Paris* 24 B1
St-Stevens-Woluwe *Brussels* 6 A2
St-Vincent-de-Paul *Montreal* 20 A2
St. Xavier University *Chicago* 9 C2
Ste-Catherine *Montreal* 20 B2
Ste-Hélène, Î. *Montreal* 20 A2
Saiwai *Tokyo* 30 B3
Sakai *Osaka* 23 B1
Sakai Harbour *Osaka* 23 B1
Sakra, Pulau *Singapore* 28 B2
Salam *Baghdad* 3 A2
Salamanca *Madrid* 17 B1
Sallynoggin *Dublin* 10 B3
Salmannsdorf *Vienna* 32 A1
Salmedina *Madrid* 17 C2
Salomea *Warsaw* 32 B1
Salsette I. *Mumbai* 20 A2
Salt Lake City = Bidhan Nagar *Kolkata* 14 B2
Salt River *Cape Town* 8 A1
Salt Water L. *Kolkata* 14 B2
Saltsjö-Duvnäs *Stockholm* 29 B3
Samatya *Istanbul* 12 C1
Sampaloc *Manila* 17 B1
Samphan Thawong *Bangkok* 3 B2
Samseon *Seoul* 27 B2
Samuel Smith Park *Toronto* 31 B1
Samut Prakan *Bangkok* 3 B2
San Andrés *Barcelona* 4 A2
San Angel *Mexico City* 18 B1
San Basilio *Rome* 26 B2
San Borja *Lima* 14 B3
San Bóvio *Milan* 19 B2
San Bruno, Pt. *San Francisco* 26 C2
San Bruno Mountain State Park ⌂ *San Francisco* 26 B2
San Cristobal *Buenos Aires* 7 B2
San Cristobal *Madrid* 17 B2
San Cristóbal, Cerro *Santiago* 27 B2
San Cristoforo *Milan* 19 B1
San Donato Milanese *Milan* 19 B2
San Francisco *San Francisco* 26 B2
San Francisco B. *San Francisco* 26 B3
San Francisco Culhuacán *Mexico City* 18 C2
San Fruttuoso *Milan* 19 A2
San Gabriel *Los Angeles* 16 B4
San Gabriel → *Los Angeles* 16 C4
San Giuliano Milanese *Milan* 19 B2
San Isidro *Lima* 14 B2
San Jerónimo Lídice *Mexico City* 18 C1
San Joaquin *Santiago* 27 B2
San José Río Hondo *Mexico City* 18 B1
San Juan → *Manila* 17 B2
San Juan de Aragón *Mexico City* 18 B2
San Juan de Aragón, Parque *Mexico City* 18 B2
San Juan de Lurigancho *Lima* 14 A2
San Juan del Monte *Manila* 17 B2
San Juan Ixtacala *Mexico City* 18 A1
San Just Desvern *Barcelona* 4 A1
San Justo *Buenos Aires* 7 C1
San Lorenzo Tezonco *Mexico City* 18 C2
San Luis *Lima* 14 B2
San Marino *Los Angeles* 16 B4
San Martin *Barcelona* 4 A2
San Martin de Porras *Lima* 14 B2
San Mateo Tlaltenango *Mexico City* 18 B1
San Miguel *Lima* 14 B2
San Miguel *Santiago* 27 B2
San Nicolás *Buenos Aires* 7 B2
San Onófrio *Rome* 26 B1
San Pedro Martir *Barcelona* 4 A1
San Pedro Zacatenco *Mexico City* 18 A2
San Pietro, Piazza *Rome* 26 B1
San Po Kong *Hong Kong* 12 A2
San Rafael Chamapa *Mexico City* 18 B1
San Rafael Hills *Los Angeles* 16 A3
San Roque *Manila* 17 B2
San Siro *Milan* 19 B1
San Souci *Sydney* 29 B1
San Telmo *Buenos Aires* 7 B2
San Vicenc dels Horts *Barcelona* 4 A1
Sandown *Johannesburg* 13 A2
Sandown Park Races *London* 15 B1
Sandton *Johannesburg* 13 A2
Sandvika *Oslo* 23 A2
Sandyford *Dublin* 10 B2
Sandymount *Dublin* 10 B2
Sangenjaya *Tokyo* 30 B2
Sanggye *Seoul* 27 B2
Sangley Pt. *Manila* 17 C1
Sankrail *Kolkata* 14 B1
Sankt-Peterburg *St. Petersburg* 27 B1
Sankt Veit *Vienna* 32 A1
Sanlihe *Beijing* 4 B1
Sanlintang *Shanghai* 28 C1
Sans *Barcelona* 4 A1
Sanssouci *Berlin* 5 B1
Sant Ambrogio, Basilica di *Milan* 19 B2
Sant Boi de Llobregat *Barcelona* 4 A1
Sant Cugat *Barcelona* 4 A1
Sant Feliu de Llobregat *Barcelona* 4 A1
Sant Joan Despi *Barcelona* 4 A1
Santa Ana *Manila* 17 B2
Santa Anita Park *Los Angeles* 16 B4
Santa Coloma de Gramenet *Barcelona* 4 A2
Santa Cruz *Manila* 17 B1
Santa Cruz *Mumbai* 20 A1
Santa Cruz, I. de *Rio de Janeiro* 25 B2
Santa Cruz de Olorde *Barcelona* 4 A1
Santa Efigênia *São Paulo* 27 B2
Santa Elena *Manila* 17 B2
Santa Elena del Gomero *Santiago* 27 B1
Santa Eulàlia *Barcelona* 4 A2
Santa Fe Springs *Los Angeles* 16 C4
Santa Iria da Azóia *Lisbon* 16 A2
Santa Julia *Santiago* 27 C2
Santa Monica *Los Angeles* 16 B2
Santa Monica Mts. *Los Angeles* 16 B2
Santa Rosa de Locobe *Santiago* 27 B2
Santa Teresa de la Ovalle *Santiago* 27 B1
Santahamina *Helsinki* 11 C3
Santana *São Paulo* 27 A2
Santeny *Paris* 24 B4
Santiago *Santiago* 27 B2
Santiago Benitez ✈ (SCL) *Santiago* 27 B1
Santiago de Surco *Lima* 14 B2
Santo Amaro *Lisbon* 16 A1
Santo Amaro *São Paulo* 27 B1
Santo Andre *Lisbon* 16 B2
Santo Antão do Tojal *Lisbon* 16 A2
Santo Antônio, Qta. de *Lisbon* 16 B1
Santo Tomas, Univ. of *Manila* 17 B1
Santos Dumont ✈ (SDU) *Rio de Janeiro* 25 B2
Santoshpur *Kolkata* 14 B1
Santragachi *Kolkata* 14 B1
Santry *Dublin* 10 A2
Sanyuanli *Guangzhou* 11 B2
São Caetano do Sul *São Paulo* 27 B2
São Conrado *Rio de Janeiro* 25 C1
São Cristóvão *Rio de Janeiro* 25 B1
São Jorge, Castelo de *Lisbon* 16 A2
São Julião do Tojal *Lisbon* 16 A2
São Paulo *São Paulo* 27 B2
São Paulo Congonhas ✈ (CGH) *São Paulo* 27 B2
Sapa *Kolkata* 14 B1
Sapateiro, Cor. do → *São Paulo* 27 B1
Sarandi *Buenos Aires* 7 C2
Saraswati → *Kolkata* 14 A1
Sarecky potok → *Prague* 25 B2
Sarimbun *Singapore* 28 A2
Sarimbun Res. *Singapore* 28 A2
Sarıyer *Istanbul* 12 A2
Sarriá *Barcelona* 4 A1
Sarsuna *Kolkata* 14 C1
Sartrouville *Paris* 24 A2
Sasad *Budapest* 7 B2
Sashalom *Budapest* 7 A3
Saska *Warsaw* 32 B2
Satalice *Prague* 25 B3
Satgachi *Kolkata* 14 B2
Satpukur *Kolkata* 14 B2
Sätra *Stockholm* 29 B1
Saúde *São Paulo* 27 B2
Saugus *Boston* 6 A2
Saugus → *Boston* 6 A2
Sault-au-Récollet *Montreal* 20 A2
Sausalito *San Francisco* 26 A2
Sawah Besar *Jakarta* 12 A1
Scald Law *Edinburgh* 11 B2
Scarborough *Toronto* 31 A3
Scarborough Bluffs *Toronto* 31 A3
Sceaux *Paris* 24 B2
Schaerbeek *Brussels* 6 A2
Scharfenberg *Berlin* 5 A2
Schiller Park *Chicago* 9 B1
Schiller Woods *Chicago* 9 B1
Schiphol, Amsterdam ✈ (AMS) *Amsterdam* 2 B1
Schlachtensee *Berlin* 5 B2
Schlossgarten *Berlin* 5 A2
Schmargendorf *Berlin* 5 B2
Schönblick *Berlin* 5 B5
Schönbrunn *Vienna* 32 A1
Schöneberg *Berlin* 5 B3
Schönefeld *Berlin* 5 B4
Schöneiche *Berlin* 5 B5
Schönwalde *Berlin* 5 A1
Schulzendorf *Berlin* 5 A2
Schwabing *Munich* 21 B2
Schwanebeck *Berlin* 5 A4
Schwanenwerder *Berlin* 5 B2
Schwarzlackenau *Vienna* 32 A2
Schwechat *Vienna* 32 B2
Schwechat, Wien ✈ (VIE) *Vienna* 32 B3
Science and Industry, Museum of *Chicago* 9 C3
Scitrek Museum *Atlanta* 3 B2
Scopus, Mt. *Jerusalem* 13 B2
Scottdale *Atlanta* 3 B3
Scutari = Üsküdar *Istanbul* 12 B2
Sea Point *Cape Town* 8 A1
Seabrook *Washington* 33 B5
Seacliff *San Francisco* 26 B2
Seaforth *Sydney* 29 A2
Seagate *New York* 22 C1
Seat Pleasant *Washington* 33 B4
Seaview *Wellington* 33 B2
SeaWorld *Orlando* 23 B2
Šeberov *Prague* 25 B3
Secaucus *New York* 22 B1
Seddinsee *Berlin* 5 B5
Seeberg *Berlin* 5 A5
Seeburg *Berlin* 5 A1
Seefeld *Berlin* 5 A5
Seegefeld *Berlin* 5 A1
Seehof *Berlin* 5 B2
Segeltorp *Stockholm* 29 B1
Segrate *Milan* 19 B2
Seguro *Milan* 19 B1
Seixal *Lisbon* 16 B2
Selby *Johannesburg* 13 B2
Seletar, Pulau *Singapore* 28 A3
Seletar Hills *Singapore* 28 A3
Seletar Res. *Singapore* 28 A2
Selhurst *London* 15 B3
Sembawang *Singapore* 28 A2
Senago *Milan* 19 A1
Sendling *Munich* 21 B2
Senju *Tokyo* 30 A3
Senriyama *Osaka* 23 A2
Sentosa *Singapore* 28 B2
Seobinggo *Seoul* 27 B1
Seocho *Seoul* 27 C1
Seodaemun *Seoul* 27 B1
Seokkwan *Seoul* 27 B2
Seongbuk *Seoul* 27 B2
Seongdong *Seoul* 27 B2
Seongsu *Seoul* 27 B2
Seoul *Seoul* 27 B2
Seoul National University *Seoul* 27 C1
Seoul Tower *Seoul* 27 B1
Sepolia *Athens* 2 A2
Sepulveda Dam Rec. Area ⌂ *Los Angeles* 16 A2
Serangoon *Singapore* 28 A3
Serangoon, Pulau *Singapore* 28 A3
Serangoon, Sungei → *Singapore* 28 A3
Serangoon Harbour *Singapore* 28 A3
Seraya, Pulau *Singapore* 28 B2
Serebryanka → *Moscow* 19 B3
Serramonte *San Francisco* 26 C2
Sesto San Giovanni *Milan* 19 A2
Sesto Ulteriano *Milan* 19 B2
Setagaya *Tokyo* 30 B2
Seter *Oslo* 23 A3
Setia Budi *Jakarta* 12 B1
Settebagni *Rome* 26 A2
Settecamini *Rome* 26 B2
Séttimo Milanese *Milan* 19 B1
Settsu *Osaka* 23 A2
Seutula *Helsinki* 11 A2
Seven Corners *Washington* 33 B2
Seven Kings *London* 15 A4
Sévesco → *Milan* 19 A1
Sevran *Paris* 24 A4
Sewri *Mumbai* 20 B2
Sforzesco, Castello *Milan* 19 B2
Sha Kok Mei *Hong Kong* 12 A2
Sha Tin *Hong Kong* 12 A2
Sha Tin Wai *Hong Kong* 12 A2
Sha'ar Binyamin *Jerusalem* 13 A2
Shabrâmant *Cairo* 7 B2
Shah Mosque *Tehran* 31 A2
Shahdara *Delhi* 10 A2
Shahe *Guangzhou* 11 B2
Shahr-e Rey *Tehran* 31 B2
Shahrak-e Golshahr *Tehran* 31 B1
Shahrak-e Qods *Tehran* 31 A2
Shaikh Aomar *Baghdad* 3 A2
Shakurbasti *Delhi* 10 A1
Shalimar *Kolkata* 14 B2
Sham Shui Po *Hong Kong* 12 B1
Shamapur *Delhi* 10 A1
Shamian *Guangzhou* 11 B2
Shan Mei *Hong Kong* 12 A2
Shanghai *Shanghai* 28 B2
Shanghai Hongqiao ✈ (SHA) *Shanghai* 28 B1
Shanghai Pudong ✈ (PVG) *Shanghai* 28 B2
Shankill *Dublin* 10 B3
Sharp I. *Hong Kong* 12 A2
Shastrinagar *Delhi* 10 A2
Shau Kei Wan *Hong Kong* 12 B2
Shawocun *Beijing* 4 B1
Shayuan *Guangzhou* 11 B2
Sheen, L. *Orlando* 23 B1
Sheepshead Bay *New York* 22 C2
Shek O *Hong Kong* 12 B2
Shelter I. *Hong Kong* 12 B2
Shepherds Bush *London* 15 A2
Shepperton *London* 15 B1
Sheremetyevo ✈ (SVO) *Moscow* 19 A2
Sherman Oaks *Los Angeles* 16 B
Sherman Park *Chicago* 9 C2
Sherwood, L. *Orlando* 23 A2
Shet Bandar *Mumbai* 20 B2
Sheung Fa Shan *Hong Kong* 12
Sheung Lau Wan *Hong Kong* 12 B2
Sheung Wan *Hong Kong* 12 B1
Sheva *Mumbai* 20 B2
Sheva Nhava *Mumbai* 20 B2
Shiba *Tokyo* 30 B3
Shibpur *Kolkata* 14 B1
Shibuya *Tokyo* 30 B3
Shimogawara *Tokyo* 30 B1
Shimosalo *Tokyo* 30 A2
Shimoshakujii *Tokyo* 30 A2
Shinagawa *Tokyo* 30 B3
Shing Mun Res. *Hong Kong* 12
Shinjuku *Tokyo* 30 A3
Shinjuku National Garden *Tokyo* 30 A3
Shinkoiwa *Tokyo* 30 A4
Shinnakano *Tokyo* 30 A3
Shipai *Guangzhou* 11 B3
Shirinashi → *Osaka* 23 B1
Shirogane *Tokyo* 30 B3
Shitennoji Temple *Osaka* 23 B2
Shiweitang *Guangzhou* 11 B2
Shogunle *Lagos* 14 A2
Shomolu *Lagos* 14 A2
Shooters Hill *London* 15 B4
Shoreditch *London* 15 A3
Shortlands *London* 15 B4
Shu'afat *Jerusalem* 13 B2
Shubrâ *Cairo* 7 A2
Shubrâ el Kheima *Cairo* 7 A2
Shuikou *Guangzhou* 11 A2
Sidcup *London* 15 B4
Siebenhirten *Vienna* 32 B1
Siedlung *Berlin* 5 A1
Siekierki *Warsaw* 32 B2
Sielce *Warsaw* 32 B2
Siemensstadt *Berlin* 5 A2
Sierra Madre *Los Angeles* 16 B4
Sievering *Vienna* 32 A2
Sighthill *Edinburgh* 11 B2
Signal Hill *Cape Town* 8 A1
Siheung *Seoul* 27 C1
Sikátorpuszta *Budapest* 7 A3
Silampur *Delhi* 10 B2
Sillim *Seoul* 27 C1
Silver, L. *Orlando* 23 A2
Silver Hill *Washington* 33 C4
Silver Spring *Washington* 33 A3
Silvermine Nature Reserve *Cape Town* 8 B1
Silvolantekojärvi *Helsinki* 11 B
Simei *Singapore* 28 A3
Simla *Kolkata* 14 B2
Simmering *Vienna* 32 A2
Simmering Heide *Vienna* 32 A
Simonkylä *Helsinki* 11 B3
Sinchon *Seoul* 27 B1
Sindang *Seoul* 27 B2
Singapore ■ *Singapore* 28 B3
Singapore, Univ. of *Singapore* 28 B2
Singapore Changi ✈ (SIN) *Singapore* 28 A3
Sinki, Selat *Singapore* 28 B2
Sinsa *Seoul* 27 B2
Sint-Genesius-Rode *Brussels*
Sion *Mumbai* 20 A2
Sipson *London* 15 B1
Siqeil *Cairo* 7 A1
Şişli *Istanbul* 12 B1
Site of Former World Trade Center = Ground Zero *New York* 22 B1
Skansen *Stockholm* 29 B2
Skärholmen *Stockholm* 29 B1
Skarpäng *Stockholm* 29 A2
Skarpnäck *Stockholm* 29 B2
Skaryszewski, Park *Warsaw* 32 B2
Skokie *Chicago* 9 A2
Skokie → *Chicago* 9 A2
Skokie Heritage Museum *Chicago* 9 A2
Skøklefald *Oslo* 23 A3
Sköndal *Stockholm* 29 B2
Skovlunde *Copenhagen* 8 A2
Skovshoved *Copenhagen* 8 A3
Skuru *Stockholm* 29 B3
Sky Lake *Orlando* 23 B2
Skyland *Atlanta* 3 A3
Slade Green *London* 15 B5
Slemmestad *Oslo* 23 B1
Slependen *Oslo* 23 A2
Slipi *Jakarta* 12 B1
Slivenec *Prague* 25 B2
Sloten *Amsterdam* 2 A1
Sloterdijk *Amsterdam* 2 A1
Sloterpark *Amsterdam* 2 A1
Sluhy *Prague* 25 A3
Służew *Warsaw* 32 B2
Służewiec *Warsaw* 32 B2
Smichov *Prague* 25 B2
Smith Forest Preserve *Chicago* 9 A2
Smolny *St. Petersburg* 27 B2
Smolny Cathedral *St. Petersburg* 27 B2
Snake Creek Canal *Miami* 18
Snakeden Branch → *Washington* 33 B1
Snarøya *Oslo* 23 A2
Snättringe *Stockholm* 29 B1
Søborg *Copenhagen* 8 A2
Sobreda *Lisbon* 16 B1
Söderby *Stockholm* 29 A3
Södermalm *Stockholm* 29 B2
Sodpur *Kolkata* 14 A2
Soeurs, Î. des *Montreal* 20 B2
Sognsvatn *Oslo* 23 A3
Soignes, Forêt de *Brussels* 6
Sok Kwu Wan *Hong Kong* 12
Sokolniki *Moscow* 19 B3
Sokolniki Park *Moscow* 19 B
Sokołów *Warsaw* 32 C1
Solalinden *Munich* 21 B3
Sollentuna *Stockholm* 29 A1
Solln *Munich* 21 B2
Solna *Stockholm* 29 A1
Somerset *Washington* 33 B3
Somerville *Boston* 6 A2
Somes I. *Wellington* 33 B2
Sonari *Mumbai* 20 B2
Søndersø *Copenhagen* 8 A2
Songpa *Seoul* 27 B2
Sony Picture Studio *Los Angeles* 16 B2

Soroksár Budapest 7 B2
Soroksari Duna → Budapest 7 B2
Sosenka → Moscow 19 B3
Sosnovka St. Petersburg 27 B2
Sŏul = Seoul Seoul 27 B2
Soundview New York 22 B2
South Beach New York 22 C1
South Bend Park Atlanta 3 B2
South Boston Boston 6 A2
South Decatur Atlanta 3 B3
South Deering Chicago 9 C3
South El Monte Los Angeles 16 B4
South Gate Los Angeles 16 C3
South Harbor Manila 17 B1
South Harrow London 15 A1
South Hd. Sydney 29 B2
South Hills Johannesburg 13 B2
South Hornchurch London 15 A5
South Lawn Washington 33 C3
South Miami Miami 18 B1
South Norwood London 15 B3
South of Market San Francisco 26 B2
South Ozone Park New York 22 B3
South Pasadena Los Angeles 16 B4
South Res. Boston 6 A2
South Ruislip London 15 A1
South San Francisco San Francisco 26 C2
South San Gabriel Los Angeles 16 B4
South Shore Chicago 9 C3
Southall London 15 A1
Southborough London 15 B4
Southend London 15 B3
Southern California, University of Los Angeles 16 B3
Southfields London 15 B2
Southwark □ London 15 B3
Southwest Museum Los Angeles 16 B3
Søvang Copenhagen 8 B3
Soweto Johannesburg 13 B1
Sowhānak Tehran 31 A3
Soya Tokyo 30 A4
Spandau Berlin 5 A1
Spånga Stockholm 29 A1
Spanish Monastery Miami 18 A2
Spectacle I. Boston 6 A3
Speicher-See Munich 21 A3
Speising Vienna 32 B1
Sphinx Cairo 7 B1
Spinaceto Rome 26 C1
Spit Junction Sydney 29 A2
Spořilov Prague 25 B3
Spot Pond Boston 6 A2
Spotswood Melbourne 18 B1
Springeberg Berlin 5 B5
Springfield Washington 33 C2
Squantum Boston 6 B2
Srednaya Rogatka St. Petersburg 27 C2
Śródmieście Warsaw 32 B2
Staaken Berlin 5 A1
Stabekk Oslo 23 A2
Stadlau Vienna 32 A2
Stadshuset Stockholm 29 B2
Stains Paris 24 A3
Stamford Hill London 15 A3
Stammersdorf Vienna 32 A2
Stanley Hong Kong 12 B2
Stanley Pen. Hong Kong 12 B2
Stanmore London 15 A2
Stapleton New York 22 C1
Staraya Derevnya St. Petersburg 27 B1
Staré Město Prague 25 B2
Stare Miasto Warsaw 32 B2
Starke, L. Orlando 23 A1
Staten Island Zoo New York 22 C1
Staten Islands Ferry Terminal New York 22 C1
Statenice Prague 25 B1
Stedelijk Museum Amsterdam 2 A2
Steele Creek Melbourne 18 A1
Steenokkerzeel Brussels 6 A2
Steer, L. Orlando 23 A2
Steglitz Berlin 5 B2
Stepaside Dublin 10 B2
Stephansdom Vienna 32 A2
Stepney London 15 A3
Sterling Park San Francisco 26 B2
Sticklinge udde Stockholm 29 A2
Stickney Chicago 9 C2
Stillorgan Dublin 10 B2
Stockholm Stockholm 29 B2
Stocksund Stockholm 29 A2
Stodůlky Prague 25 B1
Stoke Newington London 15 A3
Stokes Valley Wellington 33 B2
Stone Canyon Res. Los Angeles 16 B2
Stone Park Chicago 9 B1
Stonebridge London 15 A2
Stoneham Boston 6 A2
Stony Brook Res. Boston 6 B2
Stony Creek → Chicago 9 C2
Stora Värtan Stockholm 29 A2
Store Hareskov Copenhagen 8 A2
Store Magleby Copenhagen 8 B3
Storholmen Stockholm 29 A2
Stoyka St. Petersburg 27 B2
Straiton Edinburgh 11 B3
Strandfontein Cape Town 8 B2
Strašnice Prague 25 B2
Strasstrudering Munich 21 B3
Stratford London 15 A4
Strathfield Sydney 29 B1
Streatham London 15 B3
Streatham Vale London 15 B3
Strebersdorf Vienna 32 A2
Střešovice Prague 25 B2
Střížkov Prague 25 B2
Strombeek-Bever Brussels 6 A2
Stromovka Prague 25 B2
Studio City Los Angeles 16 B2
Stureby Stockholm 29 B2
Stuvsta Stockholm 29 B2
Subhepur Delhi 10 A2
Sucat Manila 17 C2
Suchdol Prague 25 B2
Sucy-en-Brie Paris 24 B4
Sue, L. Orlando 23 A2
Sugamo Tokyo 30 A3
Sugar Loaf Mt. = Açúcar, Pão de Rio de Janeiro 25 B2
Suge Tokyo 30 B2
Suginami Tokyo 30 A2
Sugō Tokyo 30 B2
Sui Sai Wan Hong Kong 12 B1
Suita Osaka 23 A2
Suitland Washington 33 B4
Sukchar Kolkata 14 A2
Sultanahme Camii Istanbul 12 B1
Sumida Tokyo 30 A3
Sumida → Tokyo 30 A3
Sumiyoshi Osaka 23 B2
Sumiyoshi Shrine Osaka 23 B1
Summerville Toronto 31 B1
Summit Chicago 9 C2
Sunamachi Tokyo 30 A4
Sunbury-on-Thames London 15 B1
Sundbyberg Stockholm 29 A1
Sundbyerne Copenhagen 8 B3
Sung Kong Hong Kong 12 B2
Sungei Kadut Industrial Estate Singapore 28 A2
Sungei Selatar Res. Singapore 28 A3
Sunset Park New York 22 C2
Sunter Jakarta 12 A2
Sunter, Kali → Jakarta 12 B2
Suomenlinna Helsinki 11 C2
Sur Bahr Jerusalem 13 B2
Sura Kolkata 14 B2
Suraksan Seoul 27 A2
Surbiton London 15 B2
Suresnes Paris 24 A2
Surfside Miami 18 A2
Surquillo Lima 14 B2
Surrey Hills Sydney 29 B2
Susaek Seoul 27 B1
Süssenbrunn Vienna 32 A2
Sutton Dublin 10 A3
Sutton London 15 B2
Suyu Seoul 27 B2
Suzukishinden Tokyo 30 A2
Svanemøllen Copenhagen 8 A3
Sveaborg = Suomenlinna Helsinki 11 C2
Sverdlov Moscow 19 B2
Svestad Oslo 23 B2
Svinö Helsinki 11 C1
Swanley London 15 B4
Swansea Toronto 31 B2
Swinburne I. New York 22 C1
Swords Dublin 10 A2
Sydenham Johannesburg 13 A2
Sydney Sydney 29 B2
Sydney, Univ. of Sydney 29 B2
Sydney Harbour Bridge Sydney 29 B2
Sydney Kingsford Smith ✕ (SYD) Sydney 29 B2
Sydstranden Copenhagen 8 B3
Sylvania Sydney 29 C1
Syon Park London 15 B2
Szczęśliwice Warsaw 32 B1
Széchnenyi-hegy Budapest 7 B1
Széphalom Budapest 7 A1

T

Taastrup Copenhagen 8 B1
Tabata Tokyo 30 A3
Tablada Buenos Aires 7 C1
Table B. Cape Town 8 A1
Table Mt. Cape Town 8 A1
Taboão da Serra São Paulo 27 B1
Täby Stockholm 29 A2
Tacuba Mexico City 18 B1
Tacubaya Mexico City 18 B1
Tafelbaai = Table B. Cape Town 8 A1
Taft Orlando 23 B2
Tagig → Manila 17 B2
Taguig Manila 17 B2
Tai Hang Hong Kong 12 B2
Tai Lo Shan Hong Kong 12 A2
Tai Po Tsai Hong Kong 12 A2
Tai Seng Singapore 28 A3
Tai Shui Hang Hong Kong 12 A2
Tai Tam B. Hong Kong 12 B2
Tai Tam Tuk Res. Hong Kong 12 B2
Tai Wai Hong Kong 12 A2
Tai Wan Tau Hong Kong 12 B2
Tai Wo Hau Hong Kong 12 A1
Tainaka Osaka 23 B2
Taishō Osaka 23 B1
Taita Wellington 33 B2
Tajrīsh Tehran 31 A2
Takaido Tokyo 30 A2
Takaishi Tokyo 30 B2
Takarazuka Osaka 23 A1
Takasago Tokyo 30 A4
Takatsu Tokyo 30 B2
Takeshita Tokyo 30 B2
Takinegawa Tokyo 30 A3
Takoma Park Washington 33 B3
Taksim Istanbul 12 B1
Talaide Lisbon 16 A1
Taliganga Kolkata 14 B2
Talipapa Manila 17 A2
Tallaght Dublin 10 B1
Tallkrogen Stockholm 29 B2
Tama Tokyo 30 B1
Tama → Tokyo 30 B2
Tama Kyūryō Tokyo 30 B2
Tamaden Tokyo 30 B2
Tamagawa-josui → Tokyo 30 A1
Taman Sari Jakarta 12 A1
Tamanduateí → São Paulo 27 B2
Tamboerskloof Cape Town 8 A1
Tambora Jakarta 12 A1
Tammisalo Helsinki 11 B3
Tammūh Cairo 7 B2
Tampines Singapore 28 A3
Tanah Abang Jakarta 12 B1
Tanah Kusir Jakarta 12 B1
Tangelo Park Orlando 23 B2
Tanjung Duren Jakarta 12 B1
Tanjung Priok Jakarta 12 A2
Tanum Oslo 23 A1
Tapada Lisbon 16 A1
Tapanila Helsinki 11 B3
Tapiales Buenos Aires 7 C1
Tapiola Helsinki 11 B1
Tapsia Kolkata 14 B2
Tara Mumbai 20 A1
Tarabya Istanbul 12 B2
Tårbæk Copenhagen 8 A3
Tarchomin Warsaw 32 B1
Tardeo Mumbai 20 B1
Targówek Warsaw 32 B2
Tårnby Copenhagen 8 B3
Tarqua Bay Lagos 14 B2
Tathong Channel Hong Kong 12 B2
Tathong Pt. Hong Kong 12 B2
Tatuapé São Paulo 27 B2
Taufkirchen Munich 21 B2
Tavares, I. dos Rio de Janeiro 25 A2
Tavros Athens 2 B2
Tawa Wellington 33 A1
Te Papa Museum Wellington 33 B1
Teaneck New York 22 A1
Tebet Jakarta 12 B2
Tecamachalco Mexico City 18 B1
Ted Williams Tunnel Boston 6 A2
Teddington London 15 B1
Tegel Berlin 5 A2
Tegel, Berlin ✕ (TXL) Berlin 5 A2
Tegeler See Berlin 5 A2
Tegelort Berlin 5 A2
Teheran = Tehrān Tehran 31 A2
Tehrān Tehran 31 A2
Tehrān Pārs Tehran 31 A3
Tei Tong Tsui Hong Kong 12 B2
Tejo, Rio → Lisbon 16 A2
Tekstilyshchik Moscow 19 B3
Telhal Lisbon 16 A1
Telok Blangah Singapore 28 B2
Teltow Berlin 5 B2
Teltow kanal Berlin 5 B3
Tempelhof Berlin 5 B3
Tempelhof, Berlin ✕ (THF) Berlin 5 A3
Temple City Los Angeles 16 B4
Temple Hills Washington 33 C4
Templeogue Dublin 10 B2
Temppeliaukio Church Helsinki 11 B2
Tenafly New York 22 A2
Tenayuca, Piramide de Mexico City 18 A1
Tengah → Singapore 28 A2
Tennoji Osaka 23 B2
Tepalcates Mexico City 18 B2
Tepeyac, Parque Nacional △ Mexico City 18 B2
Terrazzano Milan 19 A1
Terre des Hommes Montreal 20 A2
Terrugem Lisbon 16 A1
Tervuren Brussels 6 B3
Tervuren, Park van Brussels 6 B3
Tetuán Madrid 17 B1
Teufelsberg Berlin 5 B2
Thalkirchen Munich 21 B2
Thames Ditton London 15 B1
Thamesmead London 15 A4
Thana Cr. → Mumbai 20 A2
Thiais Paris 24 B3
Thisio Athens 2 B2
Thistletown Toronto 31 A1
Thomastown Melbourne 18 A2
Thompson I. Boston 6 B3
Thon Buri Bangkok 3 B1
Thornbury Melbourne 18 A2
Thorncliffe Toronto 31 A2
Thornhill Toronto 31 A2
Thornton Cape Town 8 A2
Thornton Heath London 15 B3
Threipmuir Res. Edinburgh 11 B2
Throgs Neck New York 22 B3
Tian'anmen Square Beijing 4 B2
Tiancun Beijing 4 B1
Tibet, L. Orlando 23 B1
Tibidabo Barcelona 4 A1
Tibradden Mt. Dublin 10 B2
Tiburon San Francisco 26 A2
Tiburtino Rome 26 B2
Ticomán Mexico City 18 A2
Tiefersee Berlin 5 B1
Tiejiangyin Beijing 4 C2
Tiergarten Berlin 5 A3
Tijgerhof Cape Town 8 A2
Tijuca Rio de Janeiro 25 B1
Tijuca, Pico da Rio de Janeiro 25 B1
Tijuca △ Rio de Janeiro 25 B1
Tikkurila Helsinki 11 B3
Tilak Nagar Delhi 10 B1
Tilanqiao Shanghai 28 B1
Timah, Bukit Singapore 28 A2
Timiryazev Park Moscow 19 B2
Ting Kau Hong Kong 12 A1
Tira Jerusalem 13 A1
Tirsa Cairo 7 B2
Tishrīyaa Baghdad 3 B2
Tiu Keng Leng Hong Kong 12 B2
Tizapán Mexico City 18 C1
Tlalnepantla → Mexico City 18 A1
Tlalpan Mexico City 18 C2
To Kwai Wan Hong Kong 12 B2
Toa Payoh Singapore 28 A3
Točná Prague 25 C2
Toco Hills Atlanta 3 B2
Todt Hill New York 22 C1
Tōkagi Tokyo 30 A4
Tokai Plantation Cape Town 8 B1
Tōkaichiba Tokyo 30 B2
Tōkyō Tokyo 30 B3
Tōkyō B. = Tōkyō-Wan Tokyo 30 B4
Tōkyō Disneyland Tokyo 30 B4
Tōkyō Haneda ✕ (HND) Tokyo 30 B3
Tōkyō Harbour Tokyo 30 B3
Tōkyō-Wan Tokyo 30 B4
Tolka → Dublin 10 A1
Tollygunge = Taliganga Kolkata 14 B2
Tolworth London 15 B2
Tomba di Nerone Rome 26 B1
Tommy Thompson Park Toronto 31 B3
Tondo Manila 17 B1
Tongbinggo Seoul 27 B1
Tongqiao Shanghai 28 A1
Toorak Melbourne 18 B2
Topanga State Park ⌂ Los Angeles 16 B1
Topkapı Istanbul 12 B1
Topkapı Palaca Istanbul 12 B1
Tor di Quinto Rome 26 B1
Tor Pignattara Rome 26 B2
Tor Sapienza Rome 26 B2
Torcy Paris 24 A4
Toronto Toronto 31 B2
Toronto, Univ. of Toronto 31 B2
Toronto City Centre ✕ (YTZ) Toronto 31 B2
Toronto Harbour Toronto 31 B2
Toronto I. Toronto 31 B2
Toronto Lester B. Pearson Int. ✕ (YYZ) Toronto 31 A1
Torre Lupara Rome 26 B2
Torre Nova Rome 26 B2
Torrellas → Barcelona 4 A1
Torrevécchia Rome 26 B1
Toshima Tokyo 30 A3
Toshimaen Tokyo 30 A2
Tottenham London 15 A3
Tottenham Melbourne 18 A1
Toussus-le-Noble Paris 24 B1
Toussus-le-Noble ✕ Paris 24 B1
Towchāl Cable Car Tehran 31 A2
Tower Hamlets □ London 15 A3
Tower of London London 15 A3
Towra Pt. Sydney 29 C2
Tøyen Oslo 23 A3
Toyonaka Osaka 23 A1
Trafaria Lisbon 16 A1
Traição, Cor. → São Paulo 27 B2
Tranegilde Copenhagen 8 B2
Trångsund Stockholm 29 B2
Trappenfelde Berlin 5 A4
Trastévere Rome 26 B1
Treasure I. San Francisco 26 B2
Třeboradice Prague 25 B3
Třebotov Prague 25 C1
Tremblay-en-France Paris 24 A4
Tremembe → São Paulo 27 A2
Tremont New York 22 A2
Trenno Milan 19 B1
Treptow Berlin 5 B3
Três Rios, Sa. dos Rio de Janeiro 25 B1
Trevi, Fontana di Rome 26 B1
Trezzano sul Naviglio Milan 19 B1
Trieste Rome 26 B2
Trinidad Washington 33 B4
Trinity Edinburgh 11 B2
Trinity College Dublin 10 A2
Trionfale Rome 26 B1
Triulzo Milan 19 B2
Troja Prague 25 B2
Trollbäcken Stockholm 29 B3
Trombay Mumbai 20 A2
Troparevo Moscow 19 C1
Trudeau, Montréal ✕ (YUL) Montreal 20 B1
Trudyashchikhsya, Ostrov St. Petersburg 27 B1
Tryvasshøgda Oslo 23 A3
Tseng Lan Shue Hong Kong 12 A2
Tseung Kwan Hong Kong 12 B2
Tsim Sha Tsui Hong Kong 12 B2
Tsing Yi Hong Kong 12 A1
Tsova Jerusalem 13 B1
Tsuen Wan Hong Kong 12 A1
Tsur Hadassa Jerusalem 13 B1
Tsurumi → Tokyo 30 B3
Tsz Wan Shan Hong Kong 12 A2
Tuas Singapore 28 B1
Tuchoměřice Prague 25 B1
Tuckahoe New York 22 A3
Tucuruvi São Paulo 27 A2
Tufello Rome 26 B2
Tufnell Park London 15 A3
Tufts University Boston 6 A2
Tughlakabad Delhi 10 B2
Tuindorp Amsterdam 2 A2
Tullamarine Melbourne 18 A1
Tulse Hill London 15 B3
Tung Lung Chau Hong Kong 12 B2
Tung O Hong Kong 12 B1
Tunis Baghdad 3 A2
Tuomarila Helsinki 11 B1
Tureberg Stockholm 29 A1
Turffontein Johannesburg 13 B2
Turkey L. Orlando 23 A2
Turkey Lake Park Orlando 23 A2
Turner Field Atlanta 3 B2
Turnham Green London 15 B2
Turnhouse Edinburgh 11 B1
Tuscolana, Via Rome 26 B2
Twelve Apostles Cape Town 8 A1
Twickenham London 15 B1
Twickenham Rugby Ground London 15 B1
Twin Peaks San Francisco 26 B2
Two Rock Mt. Dublin 10 B2
Tymon North Dublin 10 B1
Tysons Corner Washington 33 B2

U

U.S. Capitol Washington 33 B3
U.S. Cellular Field Chicago 9 C3
Ubeidiya Jerusalem 13 B2
Uberaba → São Paulo 27 B2
Ubin, Pulau Singapore 28 A3
Uccle Brussels 6 B2
Udelnaya St. Petersburg 27 A2
Udelnoe St. Petersburg 27 B1
Udlding Munich 21 A1
Ueno Tokyo 30 A3
Úholičky Prague 25 B1
Uhříněves Prague 25 B3
Uithoorn Amsterdam 2 B1
Ujazdów Warsaw 32 B2
Újpalota Budapest 7 A2
Újpest Budapest 7 A2
Ukita Tokyo 30 A4
Ullerup Copenhagen 8 B3
Ullevål Oslo 23 A3
Ulriksdal Stockholm 29 A1
Ulyanka St. Petersburg 27 B1
Um Al-Khanazir Island Baghdad 3 B2
Umeda Osaka 23 A1
Ümraniye Istanbul 12 B2
Underground Atlanta Atlanta 3 B2
Underhill, L. Orlando 23 A3
Unětický potok → Prague 25 B2
Unhos Lisbon 16 A2
Unidad Santa Fe Mexico City 18 B1
Union City New York 22 B1
Union Port New York 22 B2
Union Station Toronto 31 B2
United Center Chicago 9 B2
United Nations Headquarters New York 22 B2
Universal Studios Los Angeles 16 B2
Universal Studios Orlando 23 B2
Universidad Madrid 17 B1
Universidad de Chile Santiago 27 B2
University Park Washington 33 B4
Unterbiberg Munich 21 B2
Unterföhring Munich 21 A3
Unterhaching Munich 21 B2
Unterlaa Vienna 32 B2
Untermenzing Munich 21 A1
Upper B. New York 22 C1
Upper Elmers End London 15 B3
Upper New York B. = Upper B. New York 22 C1
Upper Norwood London 15 B3
Upper Peirce Res. Singapore 28 A2
Upper Sydenham London 15 B3
Upper Tooting London 15 B3
Upton London 15 A4
Uptown Chicago 9 B2
Uran Mumbai 20 B2
Urayasu Tokyo 30 B4
Urbe ✕ Rome 26 B2
Urca Rio de Janeiro 25 B2
Uritsk St. Petersburg 27 C1
Üröm Budapest 7 A2
Ursus Warsaw 32 B1
Ursvik Stockholm 29 A1
Usera Madrid 17 B1
Ushigome Tokyo 30 A3
Usina Rio de Janeiro 25 B1
Üsküdar Istanbul 12 B2
Ust-Slavyanka St. Petersburg 27 C3
Uteke Stockholm 29 A3
Utrata Warsaw 32 B2
Uttarpara Kolkata 14 B1
Utterslev Mose Copenhagen 8 A2

V

Vaclavské náměstí Prague 25 B2
Vadaul Mumbai 20 A2
Vaires-sur-Marne Paris 24 A4
Valby Copenhagen 8 B2
Valcannuta Rome 26 B1
Valdelatas Madrid 17 A1
Vale Washington 33 B1
Valenton Paris 24 B3
Valera Milan 19 A1
Vallcarca Barcelona 4 A1
Valldoreix Barcelona 4 A1
Vallecas Madrid 17 B2
Vallensbæk Copenhagen 8 B2
Vallensbæk Strand Copenhagen 8 B2
Vallentunasjön Stockholm 29 A2
Valleranello Rome 26 C1
Vallisaari Helsinki 11 C3
Vallvidrera Barcelona 4 A1
Valvidrera → Barcelona 4 A1
Van Gogh-museum Amsterdam 2 A2
Vanak Tehran 31 A2
Vanda = Vantaa Helsinki 11 B2
Vangede Copenhagen 8 A3
Vaniköy Istanbul 12 B2
Vanløse Copenhagen 8 A2
Vantaa Helsinki 11 B2
Vantaankoski Helsinki 11 B2
Vantaanpuisto Helsinki 11 B2
Vanves Paris 24 B2
Varedo Milan 19 A1
Varkiza Athens 2 C2
Vartiokylä Helsinki 11 B3
Vartiosaari Helsinki 11 B3
Vasamuseet Stockholm 29 B2
Vasco Cape Town 8 A2
Vasfanārd Tehran 31 B2
Vashi Mumbai 20 A2
Vasilyevskiy, Ostrov St. Petersburg 27 B1
Vatican City ■ Rome 26 B1
Vaucluse Sydney 29 B2
Vaucresson Paris 24 A1
Vaughan Toronto 31 A1
Vauhallan Paris 24 B2
Vaujours Paris 24 A4
Vauxhall London 15 B3
Vecsés Budapest 7 B3
Veleň Prague 25 A3
Veleslavín Prague 25 B2
Vélizy-Villacoublay Paris 24 B2
Velka-Chuchle Prague 25 B2
Velké Přílepy Prague 25 B1
Venda Seca Lisbon 16 A1
Venetian Islands Miami 18 B2
Venice Los Angeles 16 C2
Ventas Madrid 17 B1
Ventorro del Cano Madrid 17 B1
Venustiano Carranza Mexico City 18 B2
Verde → São Paulo 27 A1
Verdi Athens 2 A2
Verdugo Mts. Los Angeles 16 A2
Verdun Montreal 20 B2
Vérhalom Budapest 7 A2
Vermelho → São Paulo 27 B1
Vernon Los Angeles 16 B3
Verrières-le-Buisson Paris 24 B2
Versailles Buenos Aires 7 B1
Versailles Paris 24 B1
Veshnyaki Moscow 19 B3
Vesolyy Posolok St. Petersburg 27 B2
Vestra Helsinki 11 B1
Vestskoven Copenhagen 8 A2
Vicálvaro Madrid 17 B2
Vicente Lopez Buenos Aires 7 B2
Victoria Hong Kong 12 B2
Victoria, Mt. Wellington 33 B1
Victoria, Pont Montreal 20 B2
Victoria and Alfred Waterfront Cape Town 8 A1
Victoria Gardens Mumbai 20 B2
Victoria Harbour Hong Kong 12 B1
Victoria Island Lagos 14 B2
Victoria L. Johannesburg 13 B2
Victoria Lawn Tennis Courts Melbourne 18 B2
Victoria Park Singapore 28 B2
Victoria Peak Hong Kong 12 B1
Vienna = Wien Vienna 32 A2
Vienna Washington 33 B2
Vietnam Veterans Memorial Washington 33 B3
Vietnam War Museum Chicago 9 B3
View Park Los Angeles 16 B3
Vigário Geral Rio de Janeiro 25 A1
Vigentino Milan 19 B2
Viggbyholm Stockholm 29 A2
Vighignolo Milan 19 B1
Viikki Helsinki 11 B3
Vikhroli Mumbai 20 A2
Vila Guilherme São Paulo 27 B2
Vila Isabel Rio de Janeiro 25 B1
Vila Jaguára São Paulo 27 B1
Vila Madalena São Paulo 27 B1
Vila Maria São Paulo 27 B2
Vila Mariana São Paulo 27 B2
Vila Prudente São Paulo 27 B2
Viladecans Barcelona 4 B1
Vile Parle Mumbai 20 A2
Villa Adelina Buenos Aires 7 B1
Villa Ballester Buenos Aires 7 B1
Villa Barilari Buenos Aires 7 C2
Villa Bosch Buenos Aires 7 B1
Villa C. Colon Buenos Aires 7 C2
Villa Ciudadela Buenos Aires 7 B1
Villa de Guadalupe Mexico City 18 B2
Villa Devoto Buenos Aires 7 B1
Villa Diamante Buenos Aires 7 C2
Villa Dominico Buenos Aires 7 C3
Villa Lugano Buenos Aires 7 C2
Villa Lynch Buenos Aires 7 B1
Villa Madero Buenos Aires 7 C1
Villa Sáenz Pena Buenos Aires 7 B1
Villa Urquiza Buenos Aires 7 B2
Villaverde Madrid 17 B1
Villaverde Bajo Madrid 17 B1
Ville-d'Avray Paris 24 B2
Villecresnes Paris 24 B4
Villejuif Paris 24 B3
Villemomble Paris 24 A4
Villeneuve-la-Garenne Paris 24 A2
Villeneuve-le-Roi Paris 24 B3
Villeneuve-St-Georges Paris 24 B3
Villeparisis Paris 24 A4
Villevaudé Paris 24 A4
Villiers-le-Bâcle Paris 24 B1
Villiers-sur-Marne Paris 24 B4
Villinki Helsinki 11 C3
Villoresi, Canale Milan 19 A1
Vilvoorde Brussels 6 A2
Vimodrone Milan 19 A2
Vimont Montreal 20 A1
Vincennes Paris 24 A3
Vincennes, Bois de Paris 24 B3
Vineland Orlando 23 B1
Vinings Atlanta 3 A2
Vinohrady Prague 25 B2
Vinoř Prague 25 B3
Violet Hill Hong Kong 12 B2
Virányos Budapest 7 A1
Virgen del San Cristóbal Santiago 27 B2
Virginia, L. Orlando 23 A2
Virginia Gardens Miami 18 B1
Virginia Key Miami 18 B2
Viroflay Paris 24 B2
Vironas Athens 2 B2
Virum Copenhagen 8 A2
Visitacion Valley San Francisco 26 B2
Vista Alegre Lima 14 B3
Vista Alegre Santiago 27 C1
Vista Grove Atlanta 3 A3
Vitacura Santiago 27 B2
Vitinia Rome 26 C1
Vitry-sur-Seine Paris 24 B3
Vizcaya Museum and Gardens Miami 18 B2
Vladykino Moscow 19 A2
Vlezenbeek Brussels 6 B1
Vokovice Prague 25 B2
Volgelsdorf Berlin 5 B5
Volkhonka-Zil Moscow 19 C2
Vollen Oslo 23 B1
Volodarskoye St. Petersburg 27 B2
Volynkina-Derevnya St. Petersburg 27 B1
Vondelpark Amsterdam 2 A2
Vösendorf Vienna 32 B2
Voula Athens 2 C2
Vouliagmeni Athens 2 C2
Vredehoek Cape Town 8 A1
Vršovice Prague 25 B2
Vyborgskaya Storona St. Petersburg 27 B2
Vykhino Moscow 19 B3
Vyšehrad Prague 25 B2

W

Wachterhof Munich 21 B3
Wadala Mumbai 20 A2
Wadestown Wellington 33 B1
Wadi al-Arayis Jerusalem 13 B2
Wadi Fukin Jerusalem 13 B1
Waduk Pluit Jakarta 12 A1
Wah Fu Hong Kong 12 B1
Wahda Baghdad 3 B2
Währing Vienna 32 A2
Waidmannslust Berlin 5 A3
Wainuiomata Wellington 33 B2
Wainuiomata → Wellington 33 B2
Wakefield Boston 6 A2
Waldesruh Berlin 5 B4
Waldperlach Munich 21 B3
Waldtrudering Munich 21 B3
Walkinstown Dublin 10 B1
Wall Street New York 22 B1
Walt Disney World Orlando 23 B1
Walter D. Stone Memorial Zoo Boston 6 A2
Waltham Boston 6 A1
Waltham Forest □ London 15 A3
Walthamstow London 15 A3
Walton-on-Thames London 15 B1
Wambeek Brussels 6 A3
Wan Chai Hong Kong 12 B2
Wandsworth □ London 15 B2
Wannsee Berlin 5 B1
Wansdorf Berlin 5 A1
Wanstead London 15 A4
Wapping London 15 A3
Ward Dublin 10 A1
Ward I. Wellington 33 B2
Wards I. New York 22 B2
Warnberg Munich 21 B2
Warner Brothers Studios Los Angeles 16 B2
Warrâq el 'Arab Cairo 7 A2
Warringal Park Melbourne 18 A2
Warriston Edinburgh 11 B2
Warsaw = Warszawa Warsaw 32 B2
Warszawa Warsaw 32 B2
Warszawa ✕ (WAW) Warsaw 32 B1
Wartenberg Berlin 5 A4
Washington Washington 33 B3
Washington Heights New York 22 A2
Washington Park Chicago 9 C3
Washington Ronald Reagan National ✕ (DCA) Washington 33 B3
Wat Pho Bangkok 3 B1
Water of Leith → Edinburgh 11 B1
Watergraafsmeer Amsterdam 2 A2
Waterland Amsterdam 2 A2
Waterloo Brussels 6 B2
Waterloo Wellington 33 B2
Watermeal-Boitsfort Brussels 6 B2
Watertown Boston 6 A1
Watsonia Melbourne 18 A2
Waverley Boston 6 A1
Waverley Johannesburg 13 A2
Waverley Sydney 29 B2
Wawer Warsaw 32 B2
Wawrzyszew Warsaw 32 B1
Wazirabad Delhi 10 A2
Wazīrīya Baghdad 3 A2
Wazirpur Delhi 10 A2
Wealdstone London 15 A1
Wedding Berlin 5 A3
Weehawken New York 22 B1
Weesp Amsterdam 2 B3
Weidling Vienna 32 A1
Weidlingbach Vienna 32 A1
Weigongcun Beijing 4 B1
Weissensee Berlin 5 A3
Wellesley Hills Boston 6 B1
Welling London 15 B4
Wellington Boston 6 A2
Wellington Wellington 33 B1
Wellington Int. ✕ (WLE) Wellington 33 B1
Weltevreden Park Johannesburg 13 A1
Wembley London 15 A2
Wemmel Brussels 6 A1
Wemmer Pan Johannesburg 13 B2
Wenceslas Square = Vaclavské náměstí Prague 25 B2
Wendenschloss Berlin 5 B4
Wennington London 15 A5
Werneuchen Berlin 5 A5
West Don → Toronto 31 A2
West Drayton London 15 A1
West Ham London 15 A4
West Harrow London 15 A1
West Heath London 15 B4
West Hill Toronto 31 A3
West Hollywood Los Angeles 16 B2
West Lamma Channel Hong Kong 12 B1
West Los Angeles, University of Los Angeles 16 C2
West Medford Boston 6 A2
West Miami Miami 18 B1
West Molesey London 15 B1
West New York New York 22 B1
West of Twin Peaks San Francisco 26 B2
West Park Johannesburg 13 A1
West Rouge Toronto 31 A4
West Roxbury Boston 6 B2
West Springfield Washington 33 C2
West Town Chicago 9 B2
West Wharf Karachi 13 B1
Westchester Chicago 9 B1
Westchester Los Angeles 16 C2
Westchester New York 22 A2
Westcliff Johannesburg 13 B2
Westdene Johannesburg 13 B1
Westend Helsinki 11 C1
Wester Hailes Edinburgh 11 B2
Westerham Munich 21 B2
Western Addition San Francisco 26 B2
Westgate Washington 33 B3
Westlake Cape Town 8 B1
Westlake San Francisco 26 B2
Westminster London 15 A3
Westmount Montreal 20 B2
Weston Toronto 31 A1
Westwood Village Los Angeles 16 B2
Westzaan Amsterdam 2 A1
Wetton Cape Town 8 B2
Wexford Toronto 31 A3
Weybridge London 15 B1
Wezembeek-Oppem Brussels 6 A2
White Cloud Hill = Baiyun Hill Guangzhou 11 B2
White House, The Washington 33 B3
Whitechapel London 15 A3
Whitehall Dublin 10 A2
Whittier Los Angeles 16 C4
Whitton London 15 B1
Wieden Vienna 32 A2
Wien Vienna 32 A2
Wien-Schwechat ✕ (VIE) Vienna 32 B3
Wienerberg Vienna 32 B2
Wierzbno Warsaw 32 B2
Wijde Wormer Amsterdam 2 A2
Wilanów Warsaw 32 B2
Wilanówka → Warsaw 32 C2
Wilds, The Johannesburg 13 B2
Wilhelmshagen Berlin 5 B5
Wilket Creek Park Toronto 31 A2
Wilkieston Edinburgh 11 B1
Will Rogers State Historical Park ⌂ Los Angeles 16 B1
Willbrook Dublin 10 B2
Willesden London 15 A2
Willesden Green London 15 A2
Williamsbridge New York 22 A2
Williamsburg New York 22 B2
Williamsburg Orlando 23 B2
Williamstown Melbourne 18 B1
Willis, L. Orlando 23 B2
Willoughby Sydney 29 A2
Willow Springs Chicago 9 C1
Willowdale Toronto 31 A2
Wilmersdorf Berlin 5 B2
Wilmette Chicago 9 A2
Wilmington London 15 B5
Wimbledon London 15 B2
Wimbledon Common London 15 B2
Wimbledon Park London 15 B2
Wimbledon Tennis Ground London 15 B2
Winchester Boston 6 A2
Windermere Cape Town 8 A2
Windermere Orlando 23 B1
Windsor Johannesburg 13 A1
Windsor, Gare Montreal 20 B2
Windsor Hills Los Angeles 16 C2
Windy Arbour Dublin 10 B2
Winning Munich 21 B2
Wissous Paris 24 B2
Wittenau Berlin 5 A3
Witwatersrand, Univ. of Johannesburg 13 B2
Włochy Warsaw 32 B1
Wo Mei Hong Kong 12 B2
Wo Yi Hop Hong Kong 12 A1
Woburn Boston 6 A2
Woburn Toronto 31 A3
Wola Warsaw 32 B1
Wolf Trap Farm Park Washington 33 B2
Wolgok Seoul 27 B2
Wolica Warsaw 32 C1
Wólka Węglowa Warsaw 32 B1
Wollaston Boston 6 B2
Woltersdorf Berlin 5 B5
Woluwe-St-Lambert Brussels 6 A2
Woluwe-St-Pierre Brussels 6 A2
Wong Chuk Hang Hong Kong 12 B2
Wong Chuk Wan Hong Kong 12 A2
Wong Chuk Yeung Hong Kong 12 A2
Wong Tai Sin Hong Kong 12 A2
Wood Green London 15 A3
Wood Ridge New York 22 A1
Woodbine Race Track Toronto 31 A1
Woodbridge Toronto 31 A1
Woodford London 15 A4
Woodford Bridge London 15 A4
Woodford Green London 15 A4
Woodhaven New York 22 B2
Woodhouselee Edinburgh 11 B2
Woodlands Singapore 28 A2
Woodmont Washington 33 B3
Woodside London 15 B3
Woodside New York 22 B2
Woodstock Cape Town 8 A1
Woollahra Sydney 29 B2
Woolooware B. Sydney 29 C1
Woolwich London 15 B4
World Trade Center, site of former New York 22 B1
Worli Mumbai 20 A1
Worth Chicago 9 C2
Wren's Nest Atlanta 3 B2
Wrigley Field Chicago 9 B3
Wuhlgarten Berlin 5 A4
Wujiaochang Shanghai 28 B2
Würm → Munich 21 B1
Würm-kanal Munich 21 A1
Wusong Shanghai 28 A1
Wyczólki Warsaw 32 C1
Wygoda Warsaw 32 B2
Wynberg Cape Town 8 B1

Xabregas Lisbon 16 A2
Xianggang = Hong Kong Hong Kong 12 B1
Xiaogang Park Guangzhou 11 B2
Xiaoping Guangzhou 11 A2
Xiasha chong Guangzhou 11 B1
Xichang Guangzhou 11 B2
Xicheng Beijing 4 B1
Xidan Beijing 4 B2
Xizhimen Beijing 4 B1
Xochimilco, Parque Ecológico Mexico City 18 C2
Xuanwu Beijing 4 B1
Xuhui Shanghai 28 B1

Yaba Lagos 14 A2
Yaftābād Tehran 31 B1
Yahara Tokyo 30 A2
Yaho Tokyo 30 A1
Yakire Tokyo 30 A4
Yaksu Seoul 27 B2
Yamada Osaka 23 A2
Yamada Tokyo 30 B2
Yamato → Osaka 23 B1
Yan Kit Singapore 28 A3
Yanbu Guangzhou 11 B1
Yangcheon Seoul 27 B1
Yanghuayuan Beijing 4 C1
Yangjae Seoul 27 C2
Yangjiazhuang Shanghai 28 A1
Yangjing Shanghai 28 B2
Yangpu Shanghai 28 B2
Yangpu Park Shanghai 28 B2
Yannawa Bangkok 3 B2
Yarmūk Baghdad 3 B1
Yarra Bend Park Melbourne 18 A2
Yarraville Melbourne 18 A1
Yau Tong Hong Kong 12 B2
Yauza → Moscow 19 A3
Yeading London 15 A1
Yedikule Istanbul 12 C1
Yenikapı Istanbul 12 B1
Yeniköy Istanbul 12 B2
Yeongdeungpo Seoul 27 B1
Yeongdong Seoul 27 B2
Yeouido Seoul 27 B1
Yerba Buena I. San Francisco 26 B2
Yerres Paris 24 B4
Yerushalayim = Jerusalem Jerusalem 13 B2
Yiheyuan Beijing 4 A1
Yıldız Park Istanbul 12 B2
Yinhangzhen Shanghai 28 A2
Yishun Singapore 28 A3
Ylästö Helsinki 11 B2
Yodo → Osaka 23 A2
Yongdingman Beijing 4 B2
Yongfucun Guangzhou 11 B2
Yongsan Seoul 27 B1
Yonkers New York 22 A2
York Toronto 31 A2
York Mills Toronto 31 A2
York University Toronto 31 A1
You'anmen Beijing 4 B1
Youngsfield Cape Town 8 B1
Yuanxiatian Guangzhou 11 A2
Yuexiu Park Guangzhou 11 B2
Yugo-Zarad Moscow 19 B2
Yuhalixqui, Volcan Mexico City 18 C2
Yung Shue Wan Hong Kong 12 B1
Yūsofābād Tehran 31 A2

Zaandam Amsterdam 2 A1
Zaandijk Amsterdam 2 A1
Zaanstad Amsterdam 2 A1
Zaběhlice Prague 25 B2
Ząbki Warsaw 32 B2
Żacisze Warsaw 32 B2
Zahrā Baghdad 3 A1
Žalov Prague 25 A2
Załuski Warsaw 32 C1
Zamdorf Munich 21 B2
Zanevka St. Petersburg 27 B3
Zapote Manila 17 C1
Zaventem Brussels 6 A2
Zawady Warsaw 32 B2
Zāwiyet Abû Musallam Cairo 7 B1
Zawrā' Park Baghdad 3 B2
Zbraslav Prague 25 C2
Zbuzany Prague 25 B1
Zdiby Prague 25 B2
Zeekoevlei Cape Town 8 B2
Zehlendorf Berlin 5 B2
Zenne → Brussels 6 B1
Żerań Warsaw 32 B2
Zerzeń Warsaw 32 B2
Zeytinburnu Istanbul 12 C1
Zhabei Shanghai 28 B1
Zhdanov Moscow 19 B3
Zhenru Shanghai 28 B1
Zhernovka St. Petersburg 27 B2
Zhicun Guangzhou 11 B2
Zhongshan Park Shanghai 28 B1
Zhoucun Guangzhou 11 A2
Zhoujiadu Shanghai 28 B1
Zhoujiazhen Shanghai 28 B2
Zhulebino Moscow 19 B4
Zhushadi Guangzhou 11 A3
Zielona Warsaw 32 B3
Zielonka Warsaw 32 B2
Žižkov Prague 25 B2
Zličín Prague 25 B1
Zografou Athens 2 B2
Żoliborz Warsaw 32 B1
Zonnebloem Cape Town 8 A1
Zugliget Budapest 7 B1
Zugló Budapest 7 A2
Zuiderwoude Amsterdam 2 A3
Zumbi Rio de Janeiro 25 A1
Zunderdorp Amsterdam 2 A2
Zuvuvu → São Paulo 27 C1
Zwanenburg Amsterdam 2 A1
Zwölfaxing Vienna 32 B2

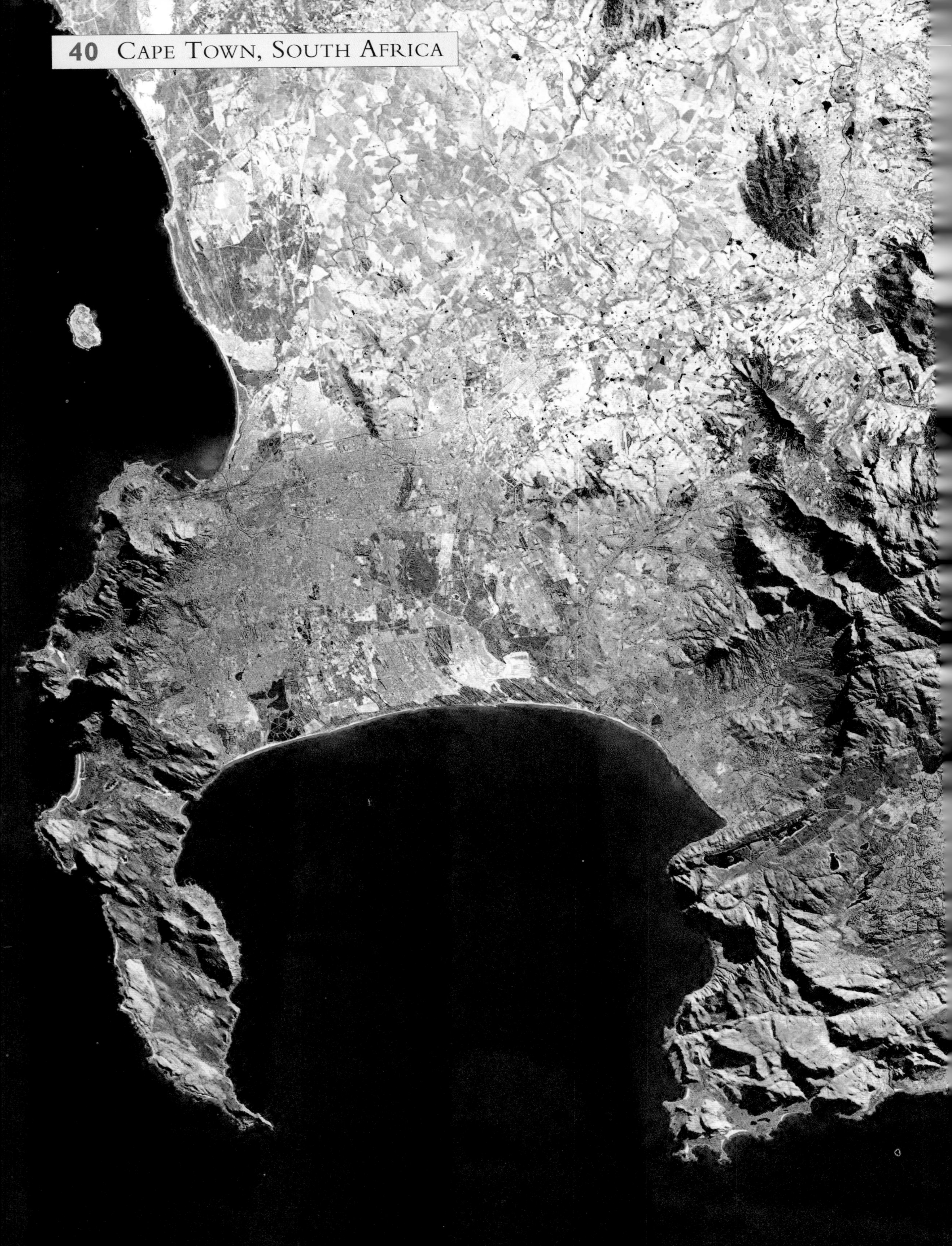

40 Cape Town, South Africa

42 Karachi, Pakistan

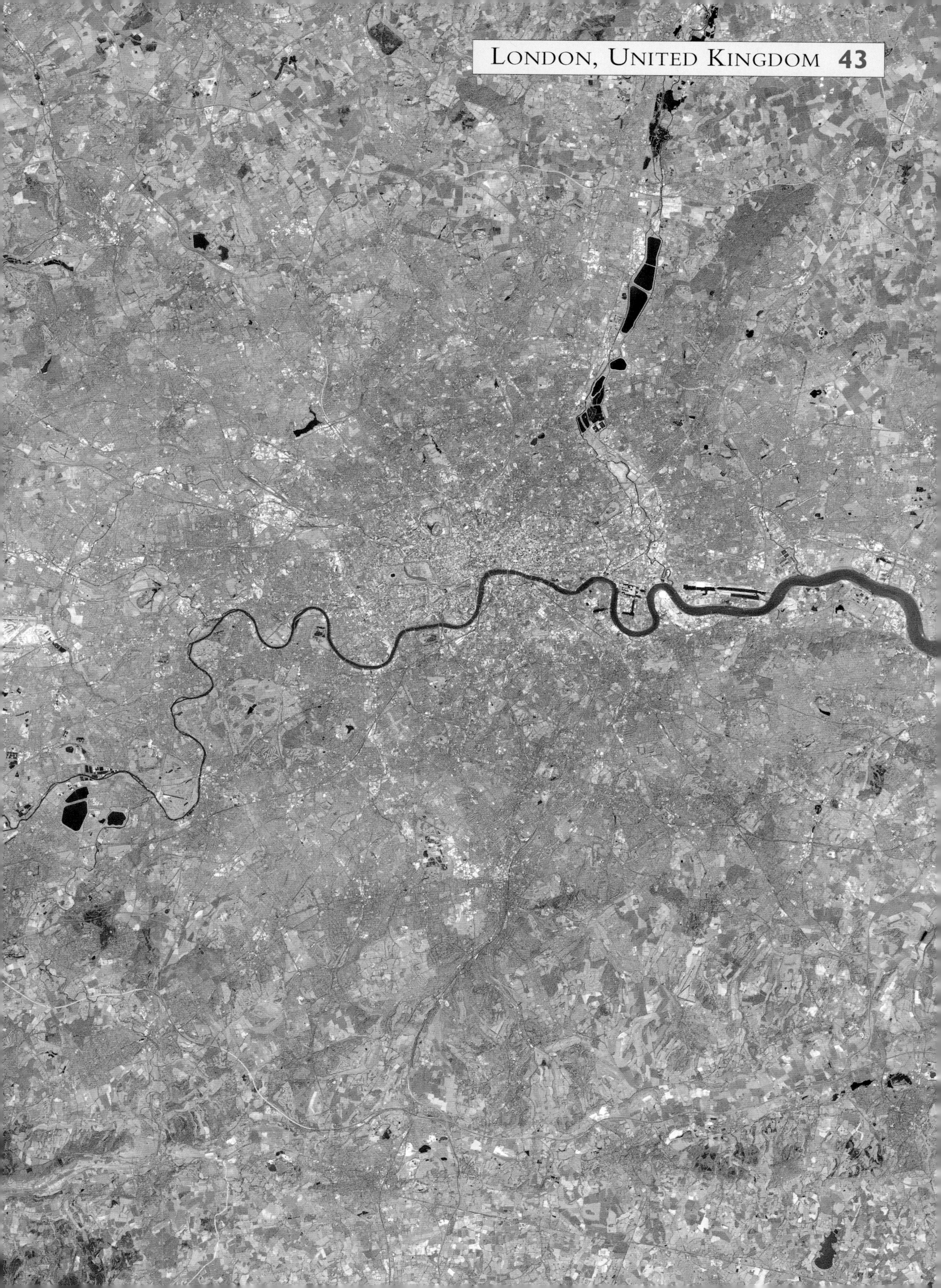

44 NEW YORK, NY, USA

46 SANTIAGO, CHILE

48 TOKYO, JAPAN

WORLD MAPS

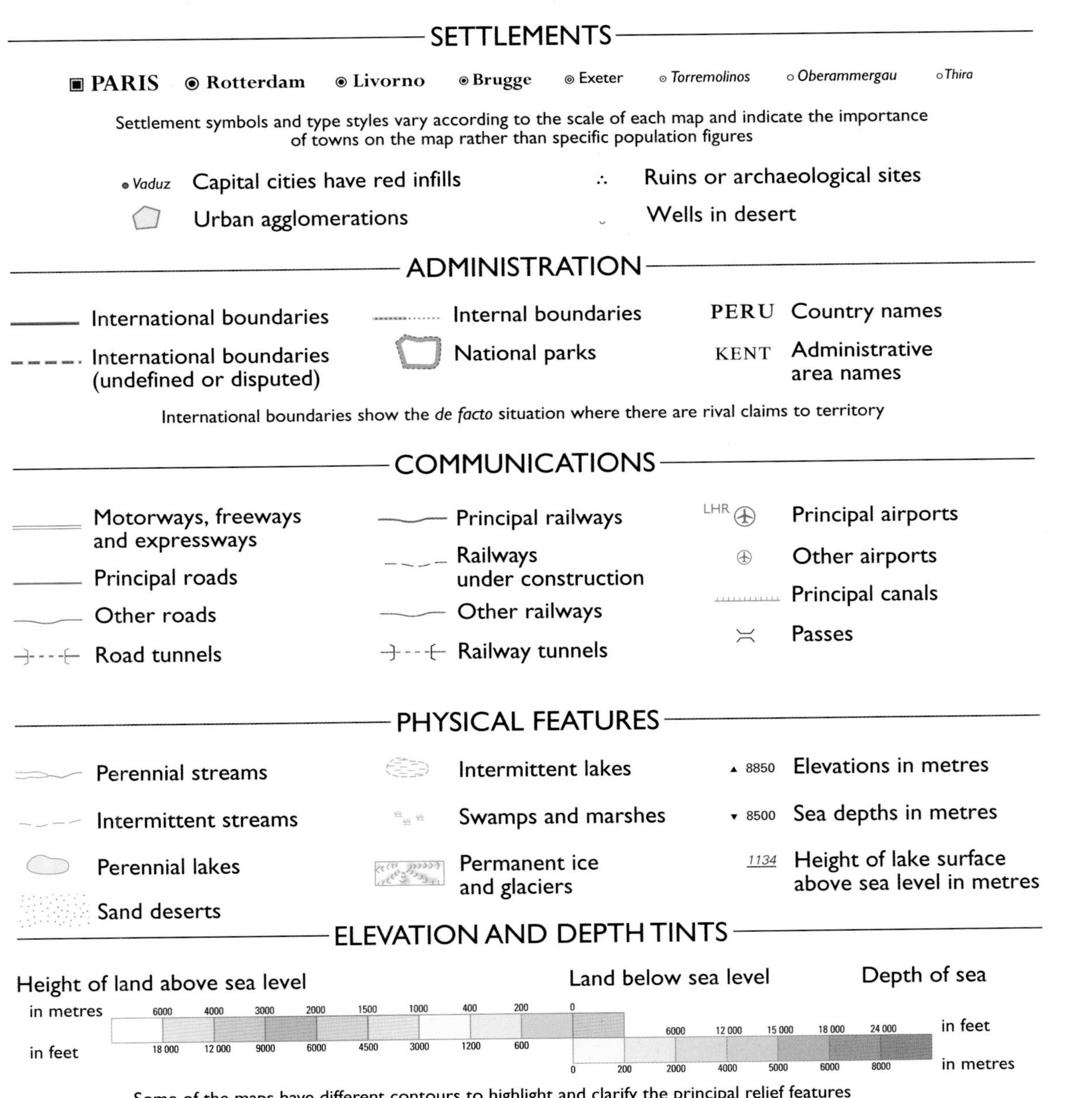
SETTLEMENTS
PARIS
Rotterdam
Livorno
Brugge
Exeter
Torremolinos
Oberammergau
Thira
Settlement symbols and type styles vary according to the scale of each map and indicate the importance of towns on the map rather than specific population figures
Vaduz
Capital cities have red infills
Urban agglomerations
Ruins or archaeological sites
Wells in desert
ADMINISTRATION
International boundaries
International boundaries (undefined or disputed)
Internal boundaries
National parks
PERU
Country names
KENT
Administrative area names
International boundaries show the de facto situation where there are rival claims to territory
COMMUNICATIONS
Motorways, freeways and expressways
Principal roads
Other roads
Road tunnels
Principal railways
Railways under construction
Other railways
Railway tunnels
LHR
Principal airports
Other airports
Principal canals
Passes
PHYSICAL FEATURES
Perennial streams
Intermittent streams
Perennial lakes
Sand deserts
Intermittent lakes
Swamps and marshes
Permanent ice and glaciers
8850
Elevations in metres
8500
Sea depths in metres
1134
Height of lake surface above sea level in metres
ELEVATION AND DEPTH TINTS
Height of land above sea level
Land below sea level
Depth of sea
in metres
6000
4000
3000
2000
1500
1000
400
200
0
in feet
18 000
12 000
9000
6000
4500
3000
1200
600
6000
12 000
15 000
18 000
24 000
in feet
0
200
2000
4000
5000
6000
8000
in metres
Some of the maps have different contours to highlight and clarify the principal relief features

THE WORLD : Political

Equatorial Scale 1:95 000 000

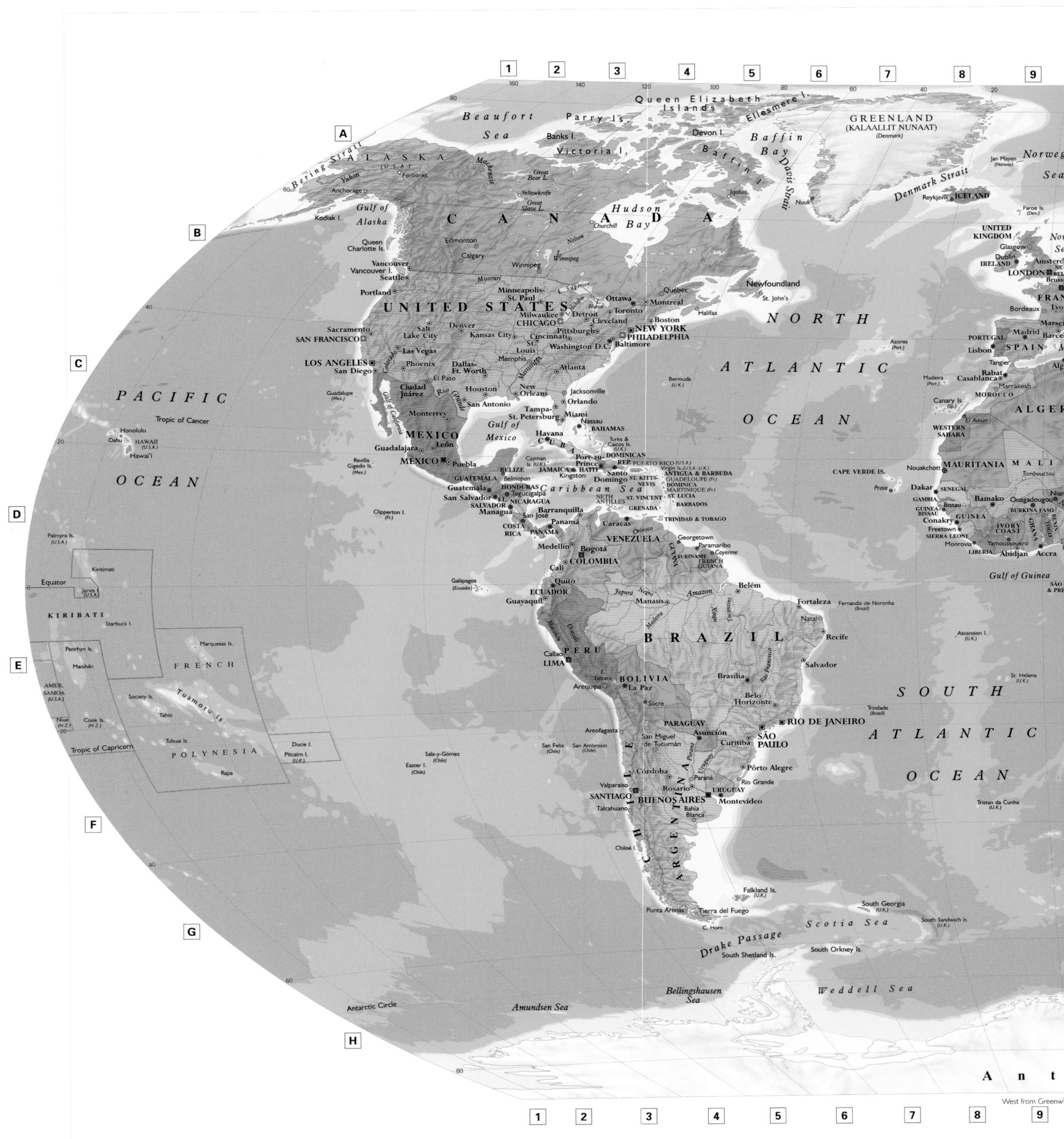

Projection: Winkel III

ARCTIC OCEAN
Barents Sea
Kara Sea
Laptev Sea
East Siberian Sea
Sea of Okhotsk
Bering Sea
R U S S I A
KAZAKHSTAN
MONGOLIA
CHINA
PACIFIC OCEAN
INDIAN OCEAN
SOUTHERN OCEAN
AUSTRALIA
INDONESIA
JAPAN
INDIA
IRAN
PAKISTAN
SAUDI ARABIA
PHILIPPINES
MALAYSIA
PAPUA NEW GUINEA
NEW ZEALAND
Tasman Sea
Bay of Bengal
Tropic of Cancer
Tropic of Capricorn
Equator
Arctic Circle
Antarctic Circle
International Date Line
Ross Sea
MOSCOW
BEIJING
TŌKYŌ
SHANGHAI
DELHI
MUMBAI (Bombay)
KOLKATA (Calcutta)
JAKARTA
MANILA
BANGKOK
SINGAPORE
Sydney
Melbourne
Perth
ft m
0 0
600 200
6 000 2000
12 000 4000
15 000 5000
18 000 6000
24 000 8000
11 12 13 14 15 16 17 18 19
A B C D E F G H
East from Greenwich

4 ARCTIC OCEAN

100 0 200 400 600 800 1000 1200 1400 km

1:35 000 000

100 0 200 400 600 800 1000 miles

18 17 16 15

6 7 8 9

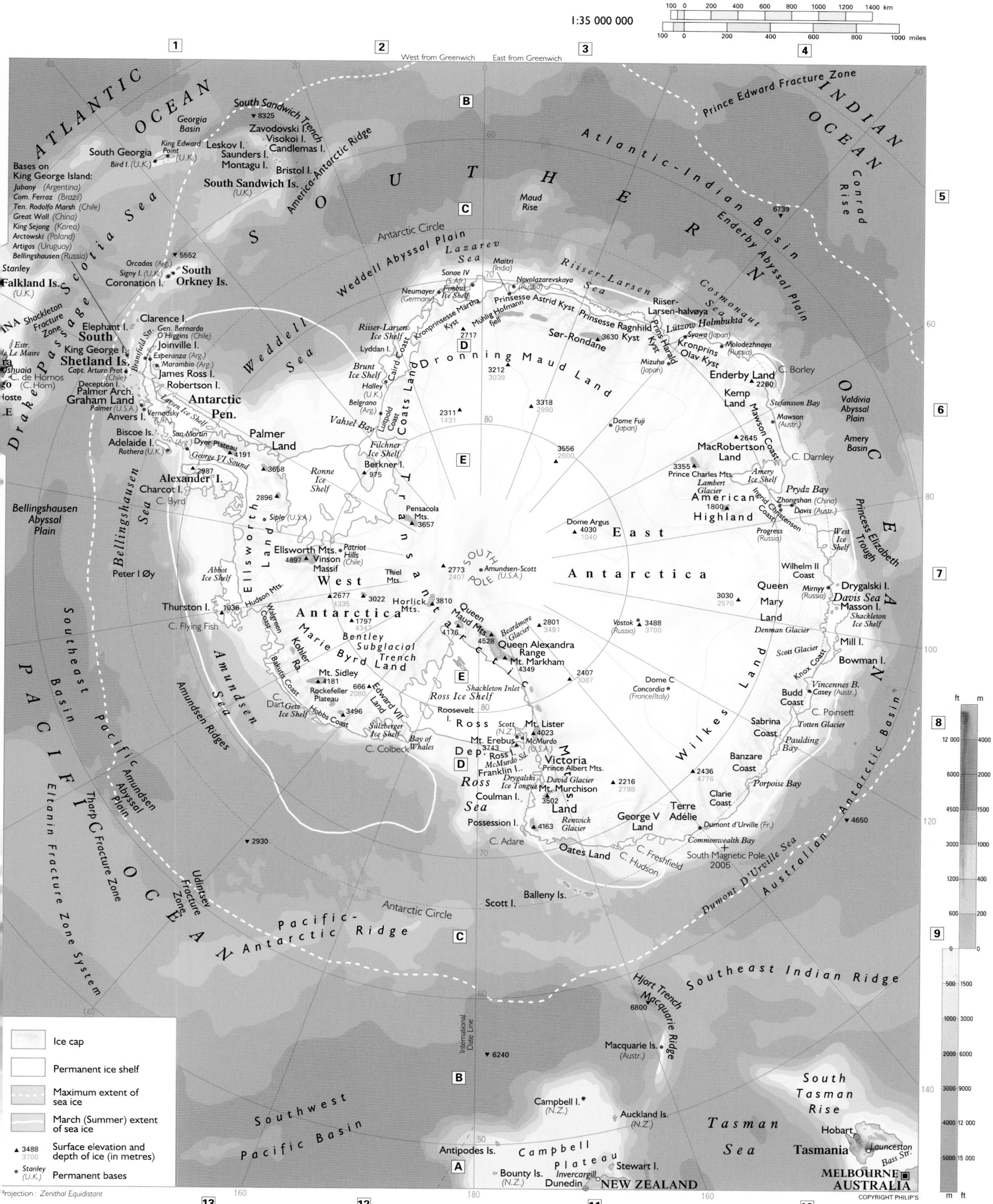

1:35 000 000

100 0 200 400 600 800 1000 1200 1400 km

100 0 200 400 600 800 1000 miles

Ice cap

Permanent ice shelf

Maximum extent of sea ice

March (Summer) extent of sea ice

▲ 3488 / 3700 Surface elevation and depth of ice (in metres)

• Stanley (U.K.) Permanent bases

Projection : Zenithal Equidistant

The Antarctic Treaty was signed in Washington in 1959 so that scientific and technical research could continue unhampered by international politics.

All territorial claims covering land areas south of latitude 60°S have been suspended. Those claims were:

Norwegian claim (Dronning Maud Land)	45°E - 20°W
Australian claims	45°E - 136°E 142°E - 160°E
French claim (Terre Adélie)	136°E - 142°E
New Zealand claim (Ross Dependency)	160°E - 150°W
British claim	80°W - 20°W
Argentine claim	74°W - 53°W
Chilean claim	90°W - 53°W

EUROPE : Physical

1:20 000 000

1:20 000 000

100 0 100 200 300 400 500 600 700 800 km

100 0 100 200 300 400 500 miles

■ LONDON Capital Cities

Projection: Bonne West from Greenwich East from Greenwich

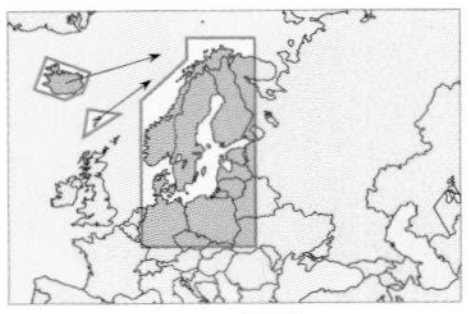

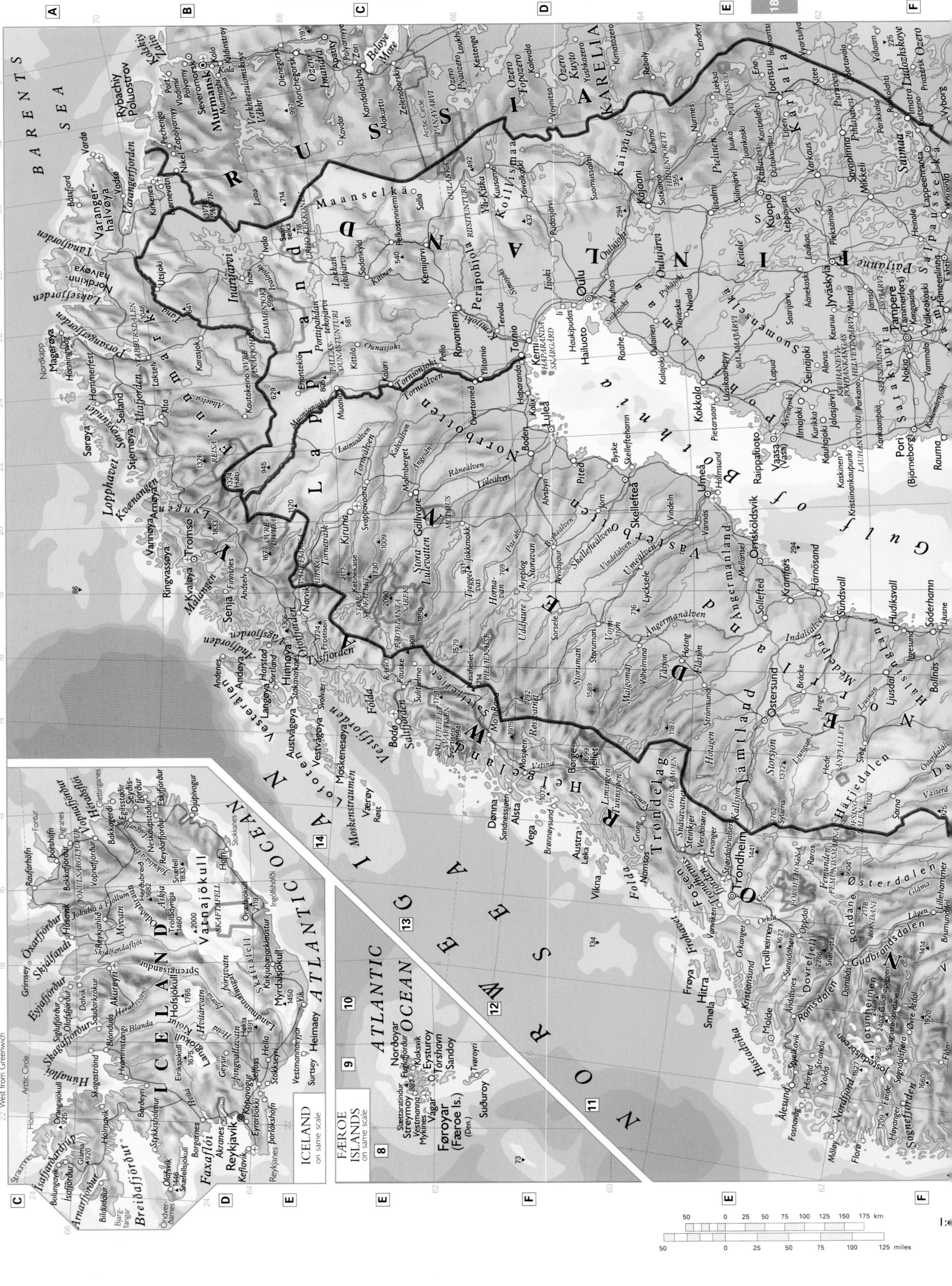
BARENTS SEA
NORWEGIAN SEA
ATLANTIC OCEAN
Gulf of Bothnia
ICELAND on same scale
FÆROE ISLANDS on same scale
ICELAND
FINLAND
SWEDEN
NORWAY
RUSSIA
KARELIA
Lappland
Finnmark
Norrbotten
Västerbotten
Jämtland
Trøndelag
Lofoten
Vesterålen
Vestfjorden
Maanselkä
Suomenselkä
Reykjavík
Vatnajökull
Akureyri
Tórshavn
Tromsø
Narvik
Bodø
Kiruna
Luleå
Umeå
Oulu
Kemi
Tornio
Rovaniemi
Vaasa (Vasa)
Kokkola
Kuopio
Tampere (Tammerfors)
Pori (Björneborg)
Trondheim
Östersund
Sundsvall
Ålesund
Murmansk
Vyborg
West from Greenwich
Arctic Circle
50 0 25 50 75 100 125 150 175 km
50 0 25 50 75 100 125 miles

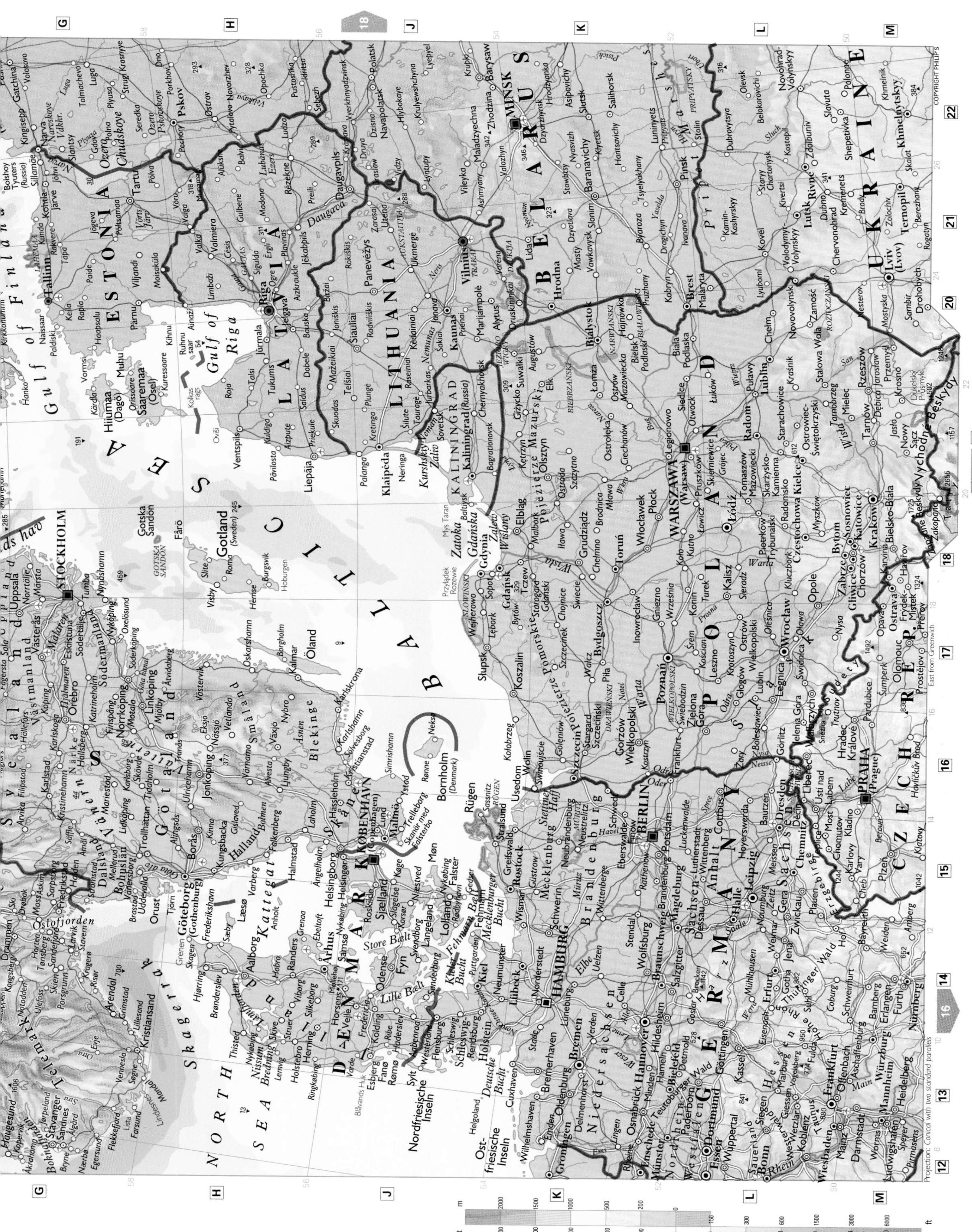
ESTONIA
LATVIA
LITHUANIA
BELARUS
POLAND
GERMANY
DENMARK
CZECH REP.
UKRAINE
KALININGRAD (Russia)
BALTIC SEA
NORTH SEA
Gulf of Finland
Gulf of Riga
Skagerrak
Kattegat
STOCKHOLM
KØBENHAVN (Copenhagen)
WARSZAWA (Warsaw)
BERLIN
PRAHA (Prague)
MINSK
Vilnius
Riga
Tallinn
HAMBURG
Projection: Conical with two standard parallels
COPYRIGHT PHILIP'S
East from Greenwich
m
ft
2000
1500
1000
500
200
0
6000
4500
3000
1500
600
0
50
100
200
500
1000
2000
150
300
600
1500
3000
6000

IRELAND

10 0 10 20 30 40 50 60 70 80 km

10 0 10 20 30 40 50 miles

1:2 000 000

1 2 3 4 5 6

A B C D E

ft	m
1500	500
600	200
300	100
0	0
50	150
100	300
200	600
500	1500
1000	3000
2000	6000
m	ft

ATLANTIC OCEAN

CELTIC SEA

IRISH SEA

North Channel

St. George's Channel

NORTHERN IRELAND

IRELAND

Ulster

Connacht

Leinster

Munster

DONEGAL, LONDONDERRY, ANTRIM, TYRONE, FERMANAGH, ARMAGH, DOWN, MONAGHAN, SLIGO, LEITRIM, CAVAN, LOUTH, MAYO, ROSCOMMON, LONGFORD, MEATH, WESTMEATH, GALWAY, OFFALY, KILDARE, DUBLIN, WICKLOW, LAOIS, CLARE, TIPPERARY, CARLOW, KILKENNY, LIMERICK, WEXFORD, KERRY, CORK, WATERFORD

Dublin, Belfast, Londonderry, Cork, Limerick, Galway, Waterford

Projection : Lambert's Conformal Conic

West from Greenwich

National Parks

1:2 000 000

National Parks and Forest Parks in Scotland

10
12

ENGLAND AND WALES

1:2 000 000

10 0 10 20 30 40 50 60 70 80 km

10 0 10 20 30 40 50 miles

Key to English unitary authorities on map

25 HARTLEPOOL
26 DARLINGTON
27 STOCKTON-ON-TEES
28 MIDDLESBROUGH
29 REDCAR AND CLEVELAND
30 BLACKPOOL
31 BLACKBURN WITH DARWEN
32 HALTON
33 WARRINGTON
34 KINGSTON UPON HULL
35 NORTH EAST LINCOLNSHIRE
36 STOKE-ON-TRENT
37 TELFORD AND WREKIN
38 DERBY CITY
39 CITY OF NOTTINGHAM
40 LEICESTER CITY
41 RUTLAND
42 PETERBOROUGH
43 MILTON KEYNES
44 LUTON
45 NORTH SOMERSET
46 CITY OF BRISTOL
47 BATH AND NORTH EAST SOMERSET
48 SWINDON
49 READING
50 WOKINGHAM
51 WINDSOR AND MAIDENHEAD
52 SLOUGH
53 BRACKNELL FOREST
54 THURROCK
55 SOUTHEND-ON-SEA
56 MEDWAY
57 PLYMOUTH
58 TORBAY
59 POOLE
60 BOURNEMOUTH
61 SOUTHAMPTON
62 PORTSMOUTH
63 BRIGHTON AND HOVE

Key to Welsh unitary authorities on map

15 SWANSEA
16 NEATH PORT TALBOT
17 BRIDGEND
18 RHONDDA CYNON TAFF
19 MERTHYR TYDFIL
20 CAERPHILLY
21 BLAENAU GWENT
22 TORFAEN
23 CARDIFF
24 NEWPORT

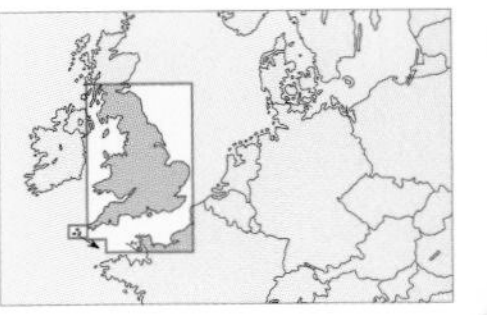

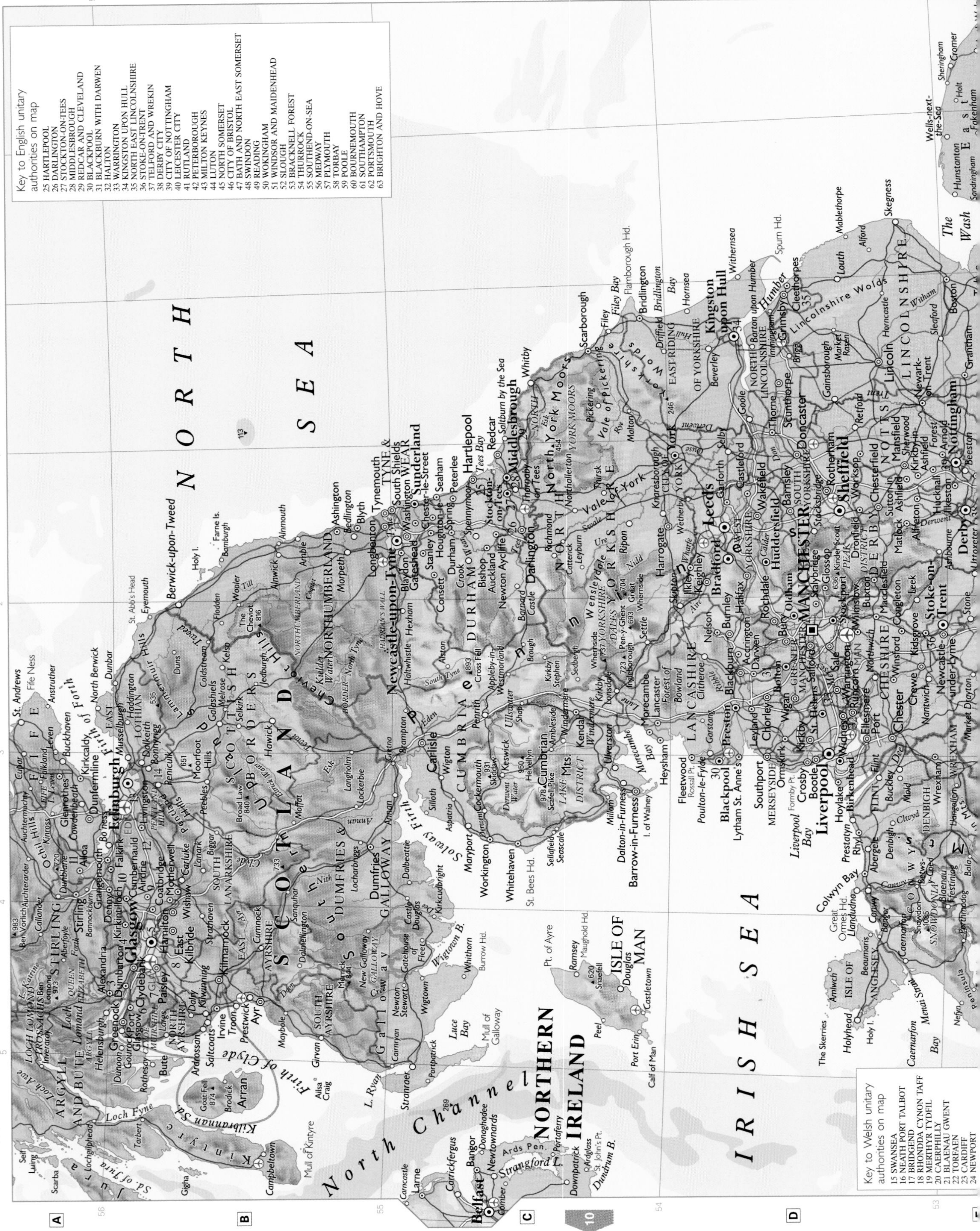

ENGLAND
WALES
FRANCE
ENGLISH CHANNEL
Bristol Channel
Strait of Dover
Thames Estuary
Baie de la Seine
Baie de la Somme
Lyme Bay
Carmarthen Bay
Milford Haven
Cardigan Bay
CHANNEL ISLANDS (U.K.)
Jersey
Guernsey
Alderney
Sark
Herm
ISLE OF WIGHT
ISLES OF SCILLY on same scale
LONDON
BIRMINGHAM
Bristol
Cardiff
Southampton
Portsmouth
Plymouth
Brighton
Bournemouth
Swansea
Newport
Oxford
Cambridge
Ipswich
Coventry
Northampton
Reading
Gloucester
Exeter
Le Havre
Rouen
Caen
Cherbourg
Calais
Boulogne-sur-Mer
Dieppe
NORMANDIE
HAUTE-NORMANDIE
SEINE-MARITIME
CALVADOS
MANCHE
National Parks in England and Wales
Forest Parks in Scotland
East from Greenwich
West from Greenwich
Projection : Lambert's Conformal Conic
COPYRIGHT PHILIP'S
20

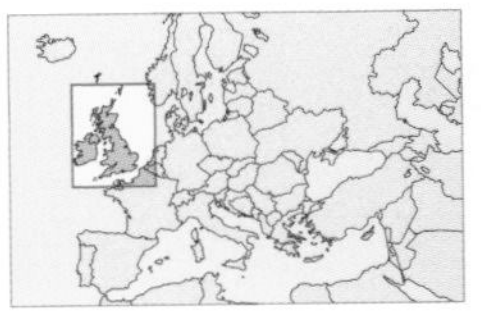

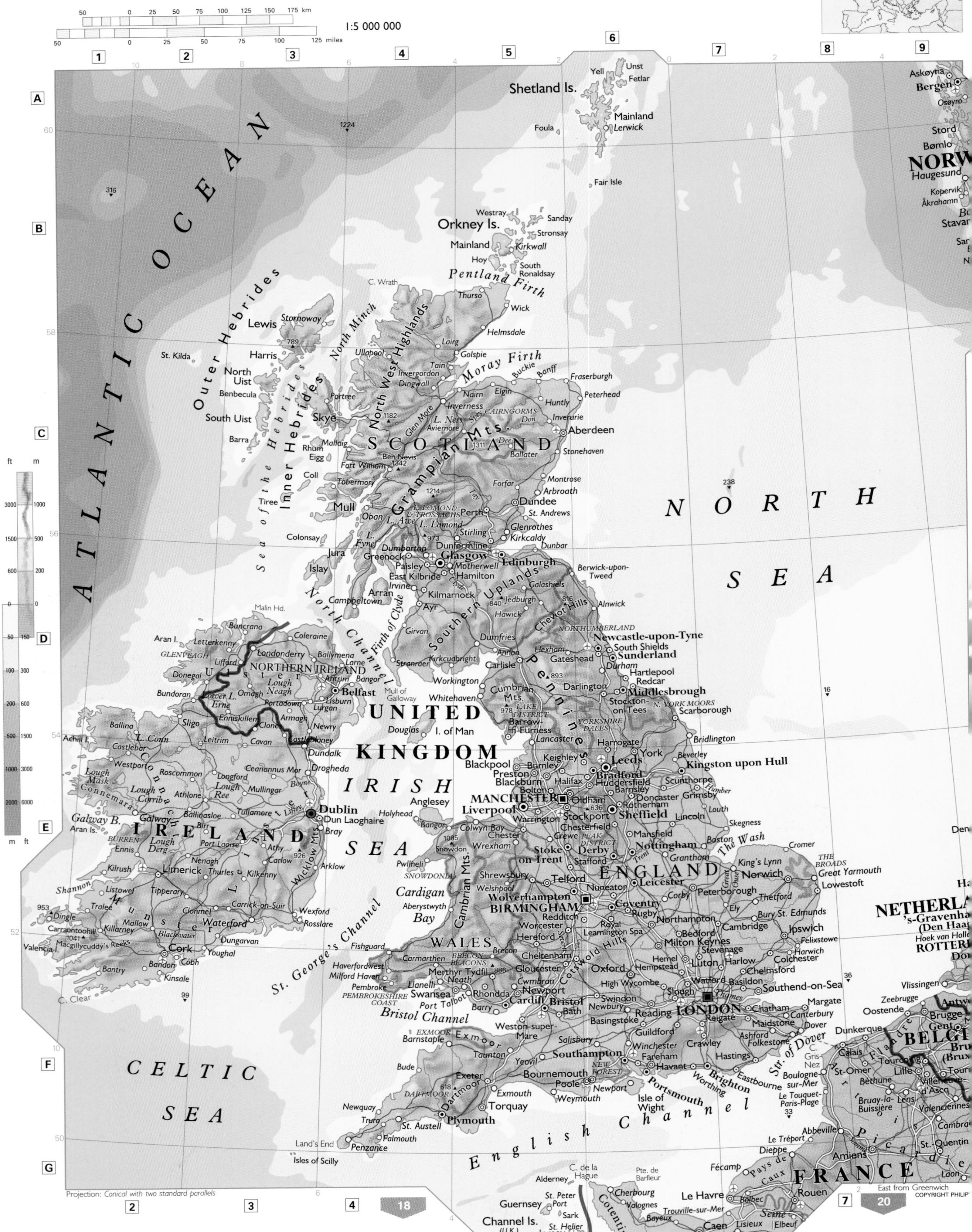

50 0 25 50 75 100 125 150 175 km
50 0 25 50 75 100 125 miles
1:5 000 000
ATLANTIC OCEAN
NORTH SEA
IRISH SEA
CELTIC SEA
English Channel
Bristol Channel
St. George's Channel
North Channel
Sea of the Hebrides
North Minch
Pentland Firth
Moray Firth
Firth of Clyde
Str. of Dover
The Wash
Shetland Is.
Yell
Unst
Fetlar
Mainland
Lerwick
Foula
Fair Isle
Orkney Is.
Westray
Sanday
Stronsay
Mainland
Kirkwall
Hoy
South Ronaldsay
C. Wrath
Thurso
Wick
Helmsdale
Outer Hebrides
Inner Hebrides
Lewis
Stornoway
Harris
St. Kilda
North Uist
Benbecula
South Uist
Barra
Skye
Portree
Rhum
Eigg
Coll
Tiree
Mull
Colonsay
Jura
Islay
Arran
North West Highlands
Ullapool
Lairg
Golspie
Tain
Invergordon
Dingwall
Inverness
Nairn
Elgin
Buckie
Banff
Fraserburgh
Peterhead
Huntly
Inverurie
Aberdeen
Stonehaven
CAIRNGORMS
Don
Dee
Glen More
L. Ness
Spey
Aviemore
Mallaig
Fort William
Ben Nevis
Tobermory
Oban
L. Awe
L. Lomond
LOMOND & TROSSACHS
Grampian Mts.
SCOTLAND
Ballater
Forfar
Montrose
Arbroath
Dundee
Perth
Tay
St. Andrews
Glenrothes
Kirkcaldy
Stirling
Dunfermline
Dunbar
Edinburgh
L. Fyne
Dumbarton
Greenock
Glasgow
Paisley
Motherwell
East Kilbride
Hamilton
Irvine
Clyde
Kilmarnock
Ayr
Campbeltown
Girvan
Southern Uplands
Galashiels
Jedburgh
Hawick
Cheviot Hills
Berwick-upon-Tweed
Alnwick
Tweed
Dumfries
Kirkcudbright
Stranraer
Malin Hd.
Buncrana
Aran I.
Letterkenny
GLENVEAGH
Lifford
Londonderry
Coleraine
Ballymena
Larne
NORTHERN IRELAND
Antrim
Bangor
Belfast
Lough Neagh
Omagh
Donegal
Ulster
Bundoran
Lower L. Erne
Enniskillen
Portadown
Lisburn
Lurgan
Armagh
Newry
Clones
Sligo
Ballina
Achill I.
L. Conn
Castlebar
Westport
Leitrim
Cavan
Castleblaney
Dundalk
Drogheda
Boyne
Ceanannus Mor
Longford
Roscommon
Connacht
Lough Mask
Connemara
Lough Corrib
Lough Ree
Athlone
Mullingar
Galway
Galway B.
Aran Is.
Ballinasloe
Tullamore
Liffey
Dublin
Dun Laoghaire
Bray
IRELAND
Birr
BURREN
Ennis
Lough Derg
Port Laoise
Athy
Carlow
Leinster
Wicklow Mts.
Arklow
Nenagh
Limerick
Thurles
Kilkenny
Kilrush
Shannon
Listowel
Tipperary
Munster
Carrick-on-Suir
Tralee
Clonmel
Waterford
Wexford
Rosslare
Dingle
Carrauntoohill
Killarney
Mallow
Blackwater
Dungarvan
Valencia I.
Macgillycuddy's Reeks
Cork
Cobh
Youghal
Bantry
Bandon
Kinsale
C. Clear
UNITED KINGDOM
I. of Man
Douglas
Mull of Galloway
Workington
Whitehaven
Carlisle
Annan
Hexham
Cumbrian Mts.
LAKE DISTRICT
Barrow-in-Furness
Lancaster
NORTHUMBERLAND
Newcastle-upon-Tyne
South Shields
Sunderland
Gateshead
Durham
Pennines
Hartlepool
Darlington
Middlesbrough
Redcar
Stockton-on-Tees
N. YORK MOORS
Scarborough
YORKSHIRE DALES
Harrogate
York
Bridlington
Beverley
Kingston upon Hull
Humber
Blackpool
Keighley
Leeds
Burnley
Bradford
Preston
Blackburn
Halifax
Huddersfield
Scunthorpe
Grimsby
Bolton
Barnsley
MANCHESTER
Oldham
Doncaster
Rotherham
Liverpool
Stockport
Sheffield
Lincoln
Louth
Warrington
Chesterfield
PEAK DISTRICT
Skegness
Anglesey
Holyhead
Bangor
Colwyn Bay
Chester
Crewe
Mansfield
Boston
Snowdon
Wrexham
Stoke on Trent
Derby
Nottingham
Trent
Cromer
Stafford
Grantham
King's Lynn
THE BROADS
Great Yarmouth
Pwllheli
SNOWDONIA
Shrewsbury
Telford
ENGLAND
Leicester
Norwich
Lowestoft
Cardigan Bay
Aberystwyth
Cambrian Mts.
Welshpool
Nuneaton
Great Ouse
Peterborough
Wolverhampton
BIRMINGHAM
Coventry
Corby
Thetford
Redditch
Rugby
Ely
Bury St. Edmunds
WALES
Worcester
Royal Leamington Spa
Northampton
Cambridge
Ipswich
Hereford
Severn
Bedford
Felixstowe
Fishguard
Milton Keynes
Stevenage
Harwich
Brecon
BRECON BEACONS
Cheltenham
Cotswold Hills
Colchester
Carmarthen
Hemel Hempstead
Luton
Harlow
Haverfordwest
Milford Haven
Merthyr Tydfil
Gloucester
Oxford
Chelmsford
Pembroke
Llanelli
Neath
Cwmbran
High Wycombe
Watford
Basildon
PEMBROKESHIRE COAST
Swansea
Port Talbot
Rhondda
Newport
Southend-on-Sea
Cardiff
Bristol
Swindon
Slough
LONDON
Thames
Barry
Bath
Newbury
Reading
Chatham
Margate
Basingstoke
Reigate
Maidstone
Canterbury
Dover
Weston-super-Mare
Guildford
Ashford
Folkestone
EXMOOR
Exmoor
Barnstaple
Salisbury
Crawley
Taunton
Southampton
Winchester
Hastings
Yeovil
Fareham
Havant
Bude
Bournemouth
NEW FOREST
Eastbourne
Brighton
Worthing
Exeter
Poole
Portsmouth
Newport
Exmouth
Weymouth
Isle of Wight
DARTMOOR
Dartmoor
Torquay
Newquay
Truro
St. Austell
Plymouth
Falmouth
Penzance
Land's End
Isles of Scilly
Alderney
C. de la Hague
Pte. de Barfleur
Cherbourg
Valognes
Cotentin
Guernsey
St. Peter Port
Sark
Channel Is. (U.K.)
St. Helier
Jersey
Fécamp
Le Havre
Bolbec
Trouville-sur-Mer
Seine
Bayeux
Caen
Lisieux
Elbeuf
Rouen
Pays de Caux
FRANCE
Dieppe
Le Tréport
Abbeville
Somme
Amiens
Picardie
St.-Quentin
Laon
Cambrai
Valenciennes
Lens
Bruay-la-Buissière
Béthune
Le Touquet-Paris-Plage
Boulogne-sur-Mer
St.-Omer
Calais
C. Gris-Nez
Dunkerque
Lille
Tourcoing
Villeneuve-d'Ascq
Tourn
Oostende
Zeebrugge
Brugge
Gent
BELGI
Bru (Brux
Antw
Vlissingen
NETHERLA
's-Gravenha (Den Haag
Hoek van Holl
ROTTER
Do
Ha
Den
Askøyna
Bergen
Osøyro
Stord
Bømlo
NORW
Haugesund
Kopervik
Åkrahamn
Stavar
1224
316
789
1182
1311
1342
1214
973
840
816
893
978
636
1085
886
926
1041
953
618
238
16
36
99
33
10
8
6
4
2
0
60
58
56
54
52
50
ft m
3000 1000
1500 500
600 200
0 0
50 150
100 300
200 600
500 1500
1000 3000
2000 6000
m ft
East from Greenwich
West from Greenwich
Projection: Conical with two standard parallels
COPYRIGHT PHILIP
A B C D E F G
1 2 3 4 5 6 7 8 9
18
20

1:2 500 000

10 0 10 20 30 40 50 60 70 80 90 km

10 0 10 20 30 40 50 60 miles

National Parks

Underlined towns give their name to the administrative area in which they stand.

16

20

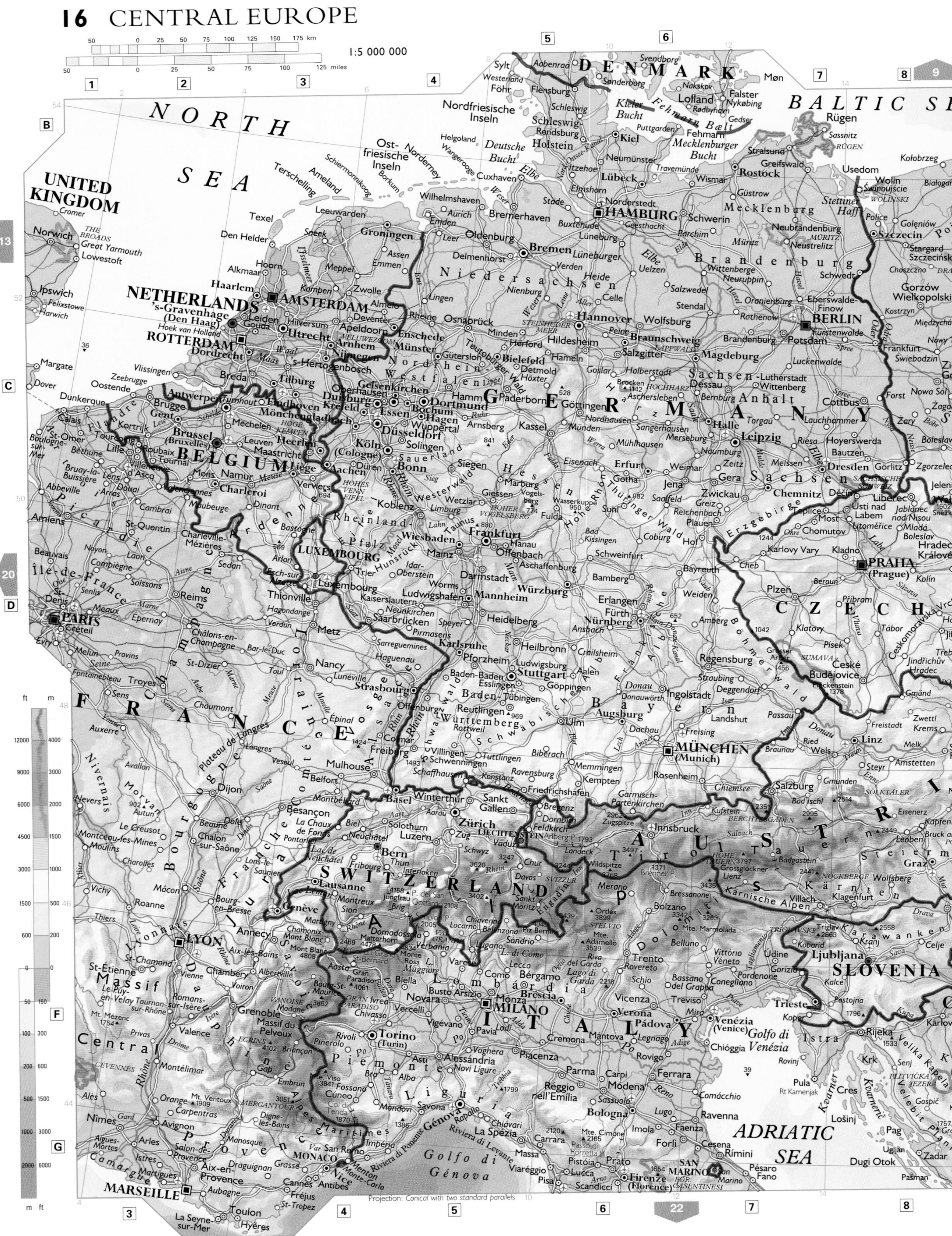
1:5 000 000
km
miles
NORTH SEA
BALTIC SEA
UNITED KINGDOM
NETHERLANDS
BELGIUM
LUXEMBOURG
DENMARK
GERMANY
CZECH
AUSTRIA
SWITZERLAND
LIECHTENSTEIN
FRANCE
ITALY
SLOVENIA
MONACO
SAN MARINO
ADRIATIC SEA
Golfo di Génova
Golfo di Venézia
AMSTERDAM
's-Gravenhage (Den Haag)
ROTTERDAM
Brussel (Bruxelles)
Antwerpen
LUXEMBOURG
PARIS
LYON
MARSEILLE
HAMBURG
BERLIN
Bremen
Hannover
Düsseldorf
Köln (Cologne)
Frankfurt
Stuttgart
MÜNCHEN (Munich)
Nürnberg
Leipzig
Dresden
PRAHA (Prague)
Zürich
Bern
Genève
MILANO
Torino (Turin)
Venézia (Venice)
Génova
Ljubljana
Strasbourg
Salzburg
Innsbruck
Sachsen
Niedersachsen
Nordrhein-Westfalen
Rheinland-Pfalz
Bayern
Baden-Württemberg
Brandenburg
Mecklenburg
Sachsen-Anhalt
Piemonte
Lombárdia
Liguria
Provence
Picardie
Champagne
Lorraine
Alsace
Bourgogne
Franche-Comté
Dauphiné
Massif Central
Île-de-France
Projection: Conical with two standard parallels

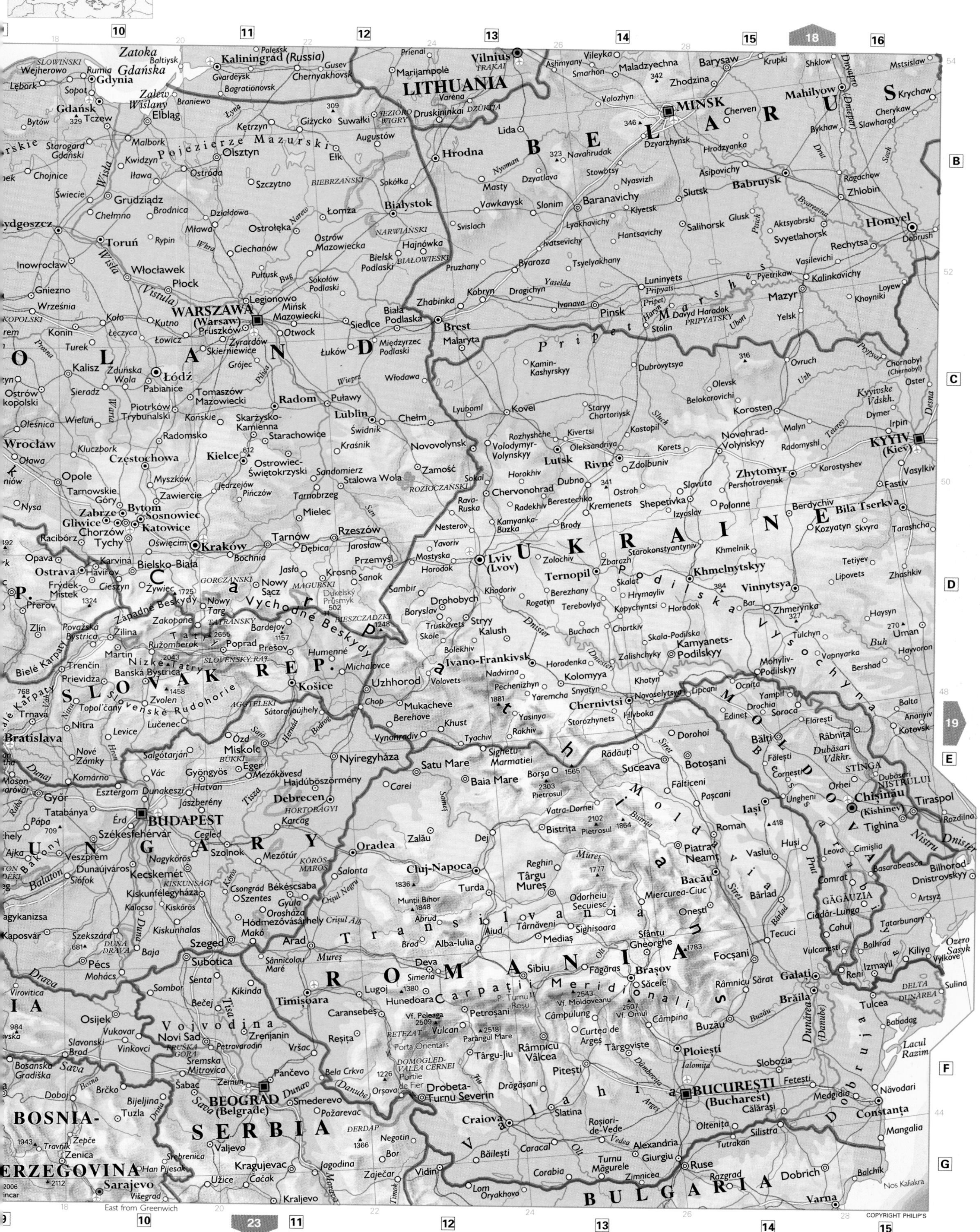
LITHUANIA
BELARUS
POLAND
UKRAINE
SLOVAK REP.
HUNGARY
ROMANIA
SERBIA
BOSNIA-
ERZEGOVINA
MOLDOVA
BULGARIA
Carpathians
Transilvania
Vojvodina
Moldavia
Dobruja
Podilska Vysochyna
Pripet Marshes
Pojezierze Mazurskie
Západné Beskydy
Východné Beskydy
Nízke Tatry
Slovenské Rudohorie
Carpaţii Meridionali
Zatoka Gdańska
Zalew Wiślany
Kaliningrad (Russia)
Vilnius
MINSK
WARSZAWA (Warsaw)
KYYIV (Kiev)
BUDAPEST
BUCUREŞTI (Bucharest)
BEOGRAD (Belgrade)
Chişinău (Kishinev)
Sarajevo
Gdańsk
Gdynia
Elbląg
Olsztyn
Białystok
Hrodna
Brest
Pinsk
Homyel
Mahilyow
Babruysk
Baranavichy
Łódź
Kraków
Katowice
Lublin
Radom
Kielce
Częstochowa
Wrocław
Opole
Rzeszów
Lviv (Lvov)
Lutsk
Rivne
Ternopil
Khmelnytskyy
Vinnytsya
Zhytomyr
Ivano-Frankivsk
Chernivtsi
Uzhhorod
Košice
Bratislava
Banská Bystrica
Miskolc
Debrecen
Szeged
Győr
Pécs
Cluj-Napoca
Oradea
Timişoara
Iaşi
Braşov
Sibiu
Galaţi
Brăila
Constanţa
Craiova
Ploieşti
Novi Sad
Osijek
Ruse
Varna
Dobrich
Danube
Vistula
Dnister
Dnipro (Dnieper)
Tisza
Drava
Sava
Prut
Siret
Mureş
Olt
East from Greenwich
COPYRIGHT PHILIP'S

50 0 100 200 300 400 km

1:10 000 000

50 0 50 100 150 200 250 miles

CASPIAN SEA
BLACK SEA
MEDITERRANEAN SEA
Sea of Azov
KAZAKHSTAN
Caspian Depression
UKRAINE
ROMANIA
BULGARIA
MOLDOVA
GEORGIA
ARMENIA
AZERBAIJAN
TURKEY
SYRIA
IRAQ
IRAN
CYPRUS
LEBANON
TURKMENISTAN
Caucasus Mountains
Ustyurt Plateau
Garabogazköl Aylagy (Kara Bogaz Gol)
CRIMEA
İSTANBUL
ANKARA
TBILISI
YEREVAN
BAKI (Baku)
TEHRĀN
BUCUREŞTI (Bucharest)
Chişinău
ODESA
VOLGOGRAD
ROSTOV
KHARKIV
DNIPROPETROVSK
DONETSK
HALAB (Aleppo)
AL MAWṢIL (Mosul)
DIMASHQ
BAYRŪT (Beirut)
Bādiyat ash Shām
Kuzey Anadolu Dağları
Toros Dağları
Reshteh-ye Kūhhā-ye Alborz
Projection: Conical with two standard parallels
East from Greenwich
COPYRIGHT PHILIP'S
Intermittent lakes
ft
m

1:5 000 000

50 0 25 50 75 100 125 150 175 km

50 0 25 50 75 100 125 miles

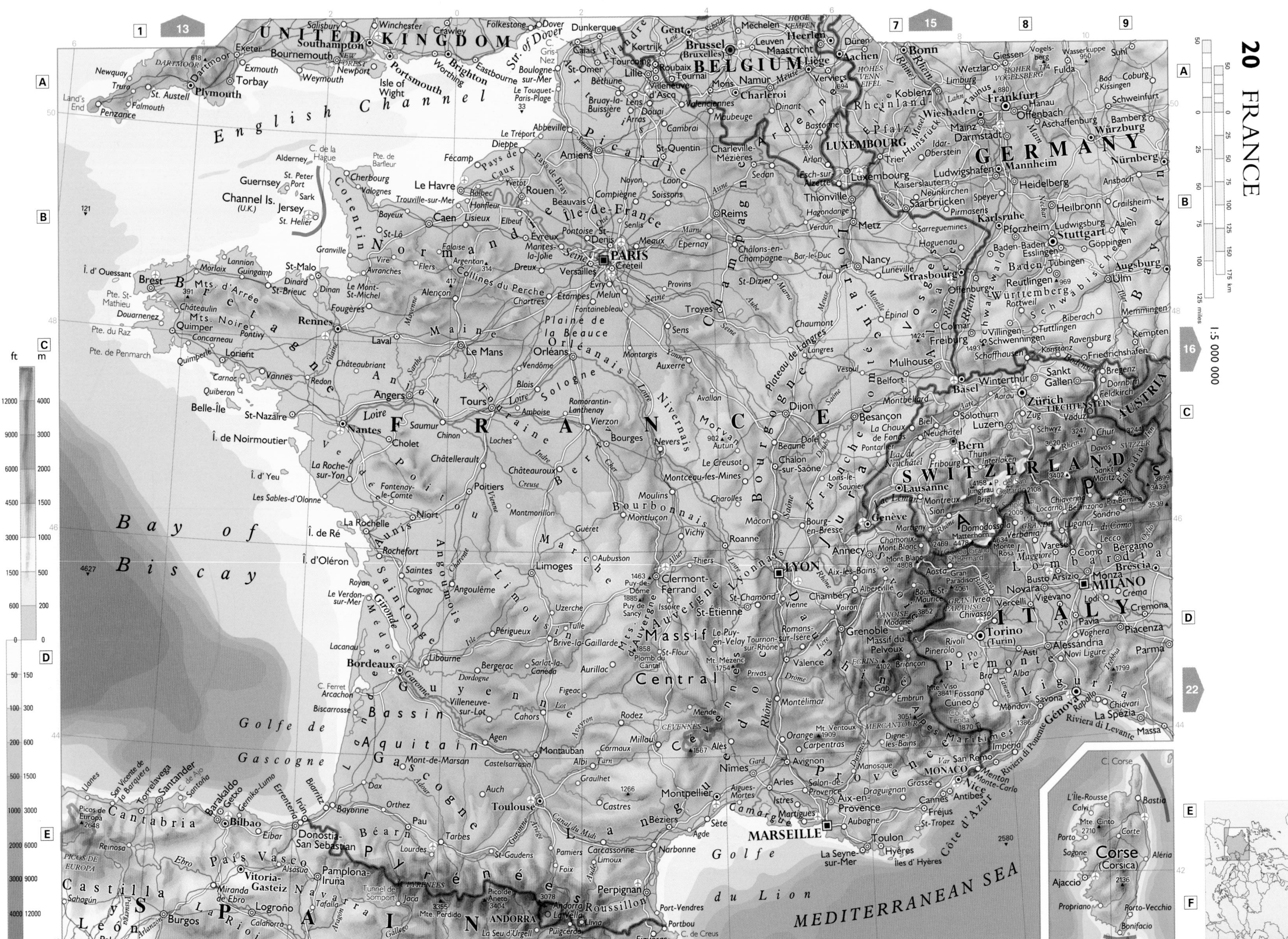

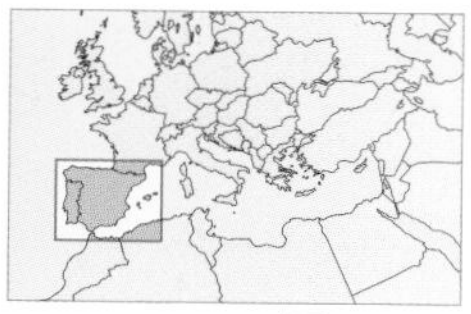

1:5 000 000

50 0 25 50 75 100 125 150 175 km

50 0 25 50 75 100 125 miles

Projection: Conical with two standard parallels

m ft
4000 12000
3000 9000
2000 6000
1000 3000
500 1500
200 600
100 300
50
0

ft m
6000 2000
4500 1500
3000 1000
1500 500
600 200
0 0

West from Greenwich 0 East from Greenwich

SWITZERLAND
AUSTRIA
SLOVENIA
CROATIA
FRANCE
ITALIA
ALGERIA
TUNISIA
MALTA
LIGURIAN SEA
TYRRHENIAN SEA
ADRIATIC SEA
MEDITERRANEAN
Golfo di Génova
Golfo di Venézia
Str. of Sicily
Corse (Corsica)
Sardegna (Sardinia)
Sicilia
Ísole Eólie
Ísole Égadi
Ísole Pelagie (Italy)
Pantelleria (Italy)
Bouches de Bonifacio
Str. di Messina
LYON
MARSEILLE
MONACO
MILANO
Torino (Turin)
Génova
Venézia (Venice)
Firenze (Florence)
ROMA
VATICAN CITY
SAN MARINO
Nápoli
Palermo
Cágliari
Ljubljana
ZAGREB
TUNIS
Valletta
Projection: Conical with two standard parallels

HUNGARY
ROMANIA
Transilvania
Carpații Meridionali
Vojvodina
Valahia
SERBIA
BEOGRAD (Belgrade)
BUCUREȘTI (Bucharest)
Timișoara
Szeged
Subotica
Novi Sad
Craiova
Ploiești
Brașov
Sibiu
Constanța
Dobrogea
UKRAINE
Ozero Sasyk
Sarajevo
Stara Planina
BULGARIA
SOFIYA
Plovdiv
Varna
Burgas
Ruse
Pleven
BLACK SEA
Rhodopi Planina
KOSOVO
Priština
MONTENEGRO
Podgorica
Skopje
MACEDONIA
ALBANIA
Tiranë
Makedonia
Thessaloniki (Salonica)
Thraki
İSTANBUL
Marmara Denizi
BURSA
TURKEY
İZMIR (Smyrna)
Sea of Thrace
AEGEAN SEA
Limnos
Lesbos
Northern Sporades
Evia
ATHINA (Athens)
Peloponnese
GREECE
Pindos Oros
Kerkyra (Corfu)
Kefalonia (Cephalonia)
Zakynthos (Zante)
Cyclades
Dodecanese
Rhodes
Mirtoo Sea
Sea of Crete
Kriti (Crete)
Iraklio
Karpathos
IONIAN SEA
MEDITERRANEAN SEA
Str. of Otranto
Brindisi
Lecce
East from Greenwich
COPYRIGHT PHILIP'S

Madeira
Balearic Islands
Canary Islands

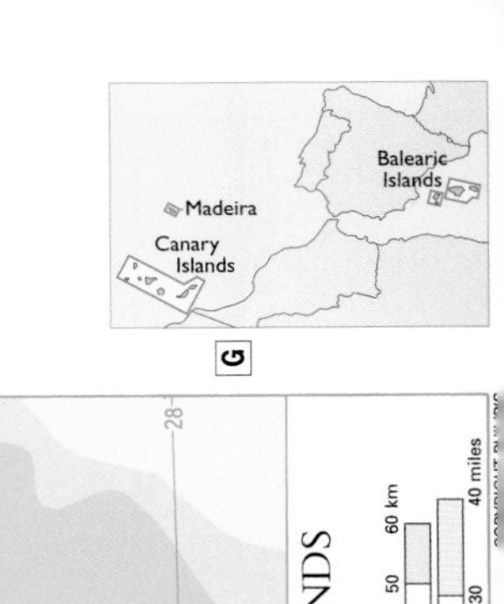

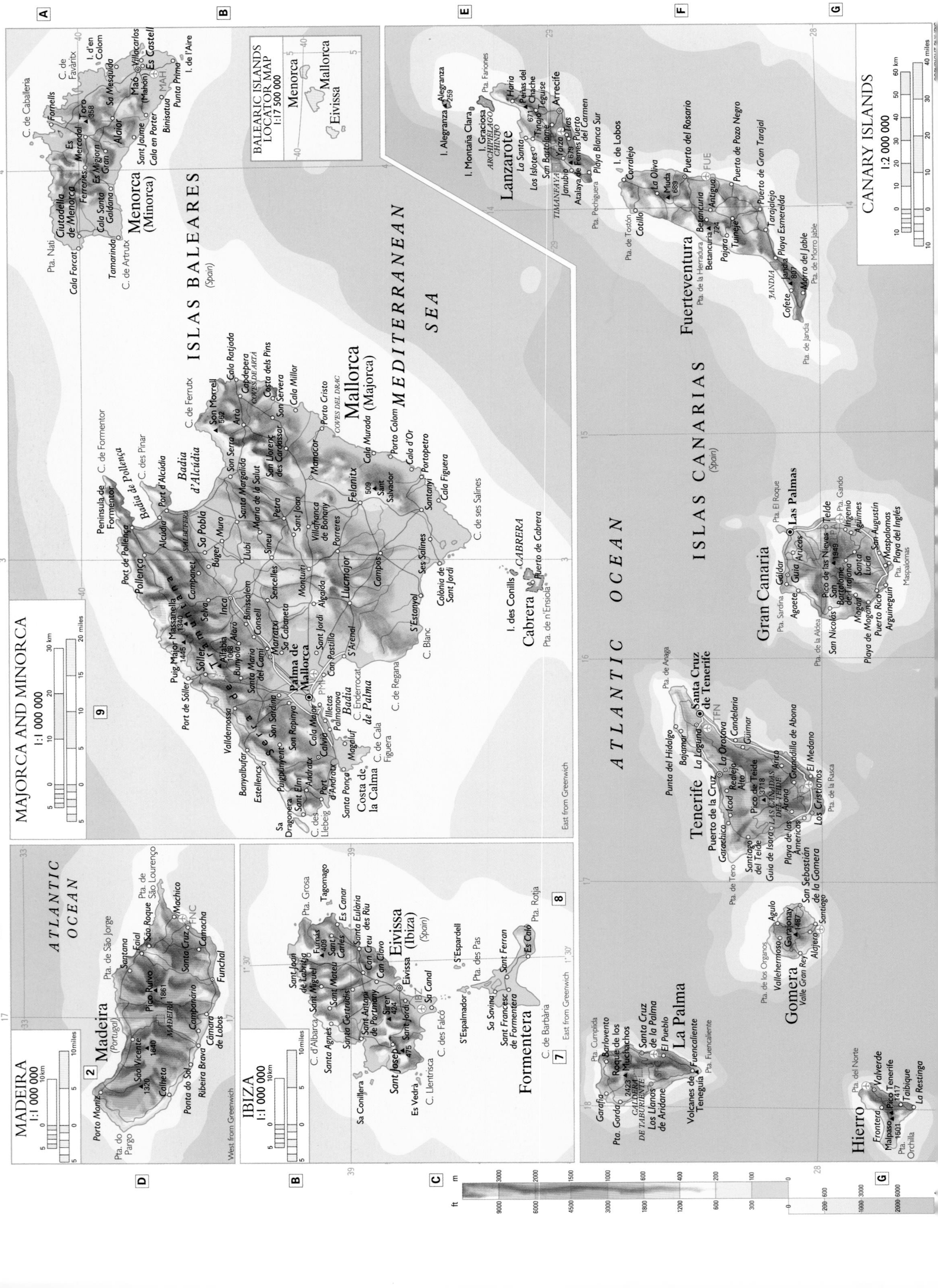

MAJORCA AND MINORCA
1:1 000 000
ISLAS BALEARES
(Spain)
Menorca (Minorca)
Mallorca (Majorca)
Palma de Mallorca
Cabrera
BALEARIC ISLANDS LOCATOR MAP
1:17 500 000
Menorca
Mallorca
Eivissa
MEDITERRANEAN SEA
IBIZA
1:1 000 000
Eivissa (Ibiza)
(Spain)
Formentera
MADEIRA
1:1 000 000
Madeira
(Portugal)
Funchal
Pico Ruivo
1861
ATLANTIC OCEAN
CANARY ISLANDS
1:2 000 000
ISLAS CANARIAS
(Spain)
Lanzarote
Arrecife
Fuerteventura
Puerto del Rosario
Gran Canaria
Las Palmas
Tenerife
Santa Cruz de Tenerife
Pico de Teide
3718
Gomera
San Sebastián de la Gomera
La Palma
Santa Cruz de la Palma
Hierro
Valverde
East from Greenwich
West from Greenwich

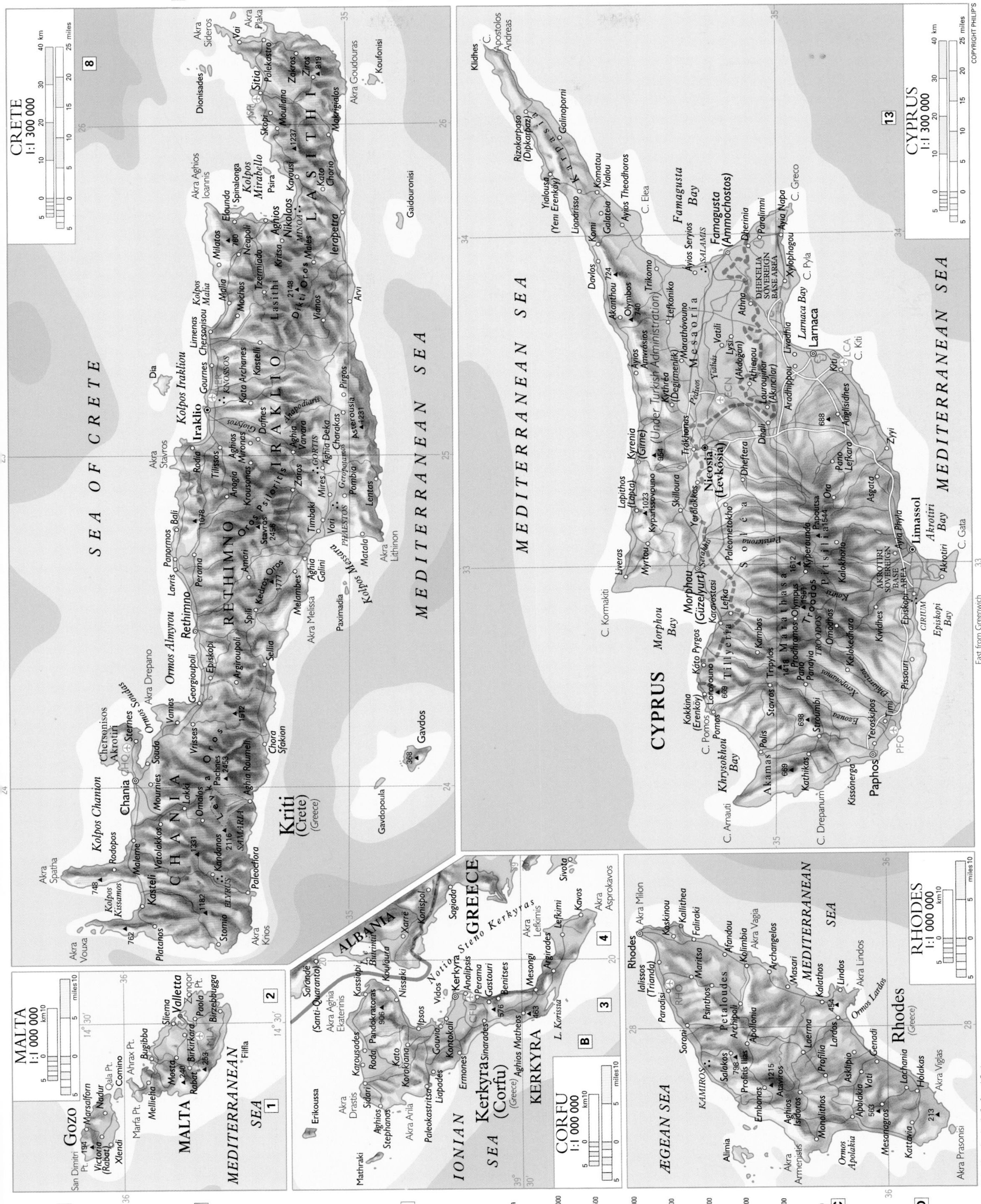

CRETE
1:1 300 000

SEA OF CRETE

MEDITERRANEAN SEA

Kriti (Crete) (Greece)

CHANIA · RETHIMNO · IRAKLIO · LASITHI

Akra Spatha · Kolpos Kissamos · Kolpos Chanion · Akra Vouxa · Kasteli · Platanos · Maleme · Rodopos · Chania · Chersonisos Akrotiri · Ormos Soudas · Souda · Akra Drepano · Georgioupoli · Vamos · Vrisses · Ormos Almyrou · Rethimno · Episkopi · Panormos · Bali · Perama · Spili · Amari · Kedros Oros · Lefka Ori · Pachnes 2453 · Omalos · Lakki · Kandanos · Paleochora · Sougia · Chora Sfakion · Agia Roumeli · Stomio · Akra Krios · Gavdos · Gavdopoula · Akra Stavros · Iraklio · Kolpos Iraklio · Gournes · Limenas Chersonisou · Kolpos Malia · Malia · Dia · Knossos · Tilissos · Anogia · Psiloritis · Timbaki · Mires · Phaestos · Gortis · Matala · Kolpos Messara · Akra Lithinon · Akra Melissa · Paximadia · Lentas · Pigros · Arvi · Dikti Oros 2148 · Ierapetra · Agios Nikolaos · Kolpos Mirabello · Elounda · Spinalonga · Neapoli · Kritsa · Sitia · Palekastro · Zakros · Makrigialos · Dionisades · Akra Sideros · Vai · Akra Plaka · Koufonisi · Akra Goudouras · Gaidouronisi · Kato Chorio

CYPRUS
1:1 300 000

MEDITERRANEAN SEA

CYPRUS

Kliclhes · C. Apostolos Andreas · Rizokarpaso (Dipkarpaz) · Galinoporni · Yialousa (Yeni Erenköy) · Komatou Yialou · Ayios Theodhoros · Liondrisso · Galateia · Kom · C. Elea · Famagusta Bay · Famagusta (Ammochostos) · Salamis · Dherinia · Paralimni · Ayia Napa · C. Greco · Xylophagou · C. Pyla · Dhekelia Sovereign Base Area · Larnaca Bay · Larnaca · Kiti · C. Kiti · Davlos · Akanthou · Olymbos · Trikomo · Lefkoniko · Mesaoria · Kyrenia (Girne) · Lapithos (Lapta) · Nicosia (Levkosia) · Morphou (Guzelyurt) · Morphou Bay · C. Kormakiti · Troodos · Olympus · Limassol · Akrotiri Bay · Akrotiri · C. Gata · Akrotiri Sovereign Base Area · Episkopi Bay · Episkopi · Curium · Pissouri · Paphos · Yeroskipos · Polis · Khrysokhou Bay · C. Arnauti · Akamas · C. Drepanum · Kissonerga · Pomos · C. Pomos · Kokkina (Erenköy) · Stavros · Palekhori · Lefkara · Dhali · Athienou

MALTA
1:1 000 000

Gozo · Victoria (Rabat) · Xlendi · Nadur · Marsalforn · Qala Pt. · Comino · San Dimitri Pt. · Marfa Pt. · Ahrax Pt. · Mellieha · Bugibba · Mosta · Rabat · Birkirkara · Sliema · Valletta · Zonqor Pt. · Paola · Birzebbuga · Filfla

MALTA

MEDITERRANEAN SEA

CORFU
1:1 000 000

IONIAN SEA

Kerkyra (Corfu) (Greece) · KERKYRA · Kerkyra · Sidari · Roda · Kassiopi · Pantokrator 906 · Paleokastritsa · Gouvia · Ipsos · Benitses · Perama · Agios Stephanos · Akra Drastis · Erikoussa · Mathraki · Agios Matheos · Mesongi · Argirades · Lefkimi · Kavos · Akra Asprokavos · L. Korissia · Notio Steno Kerkyras · ALBANIA · Butrint · Sarande (Santi-Quaranta) · GREECE · Konispol · Sagiada · Sivota

RHODES
1:1 000 000

AEGEAN SEA

MEDITERRANEAN SEA

Rhodes (Greece)

Rhodes · Akra Milon · Ialisos (Trianda) · Paradisi · Kalithea · Faliraki · Afandou · Kolimbia · Akra Vagia · Archangelos · Masari · Kalathos · Lindos · Akra Lindos · Ormos Lindos · Lardos · Gennadi · Lachania · Akra Viglas · Akra Prasonisi · Kattavia · Mesanagros · Apolakia · Ormos Apolakia · Monolithos · Embonas · Profitis Ilias 798 · Attaviros 1215 · Kamiros · Salakos · Soroni · Petaloudes · Psinthos · Archipoli · Apollona · Laerma · Asklipio · Alimia · Akra Armenistis

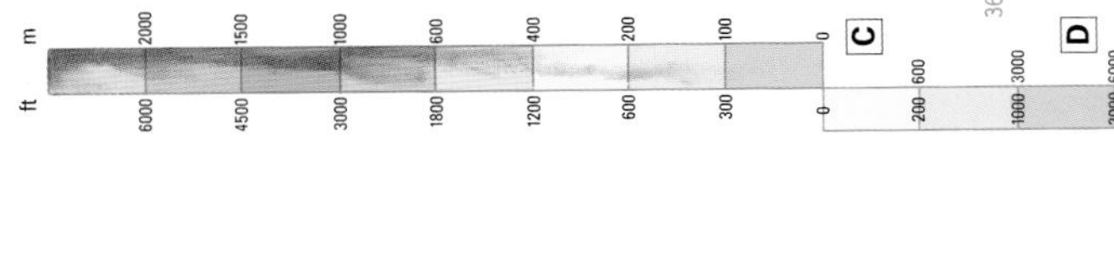

Projection: Lambert's Conformal Conic

East from Greenwich

1:47 000 000

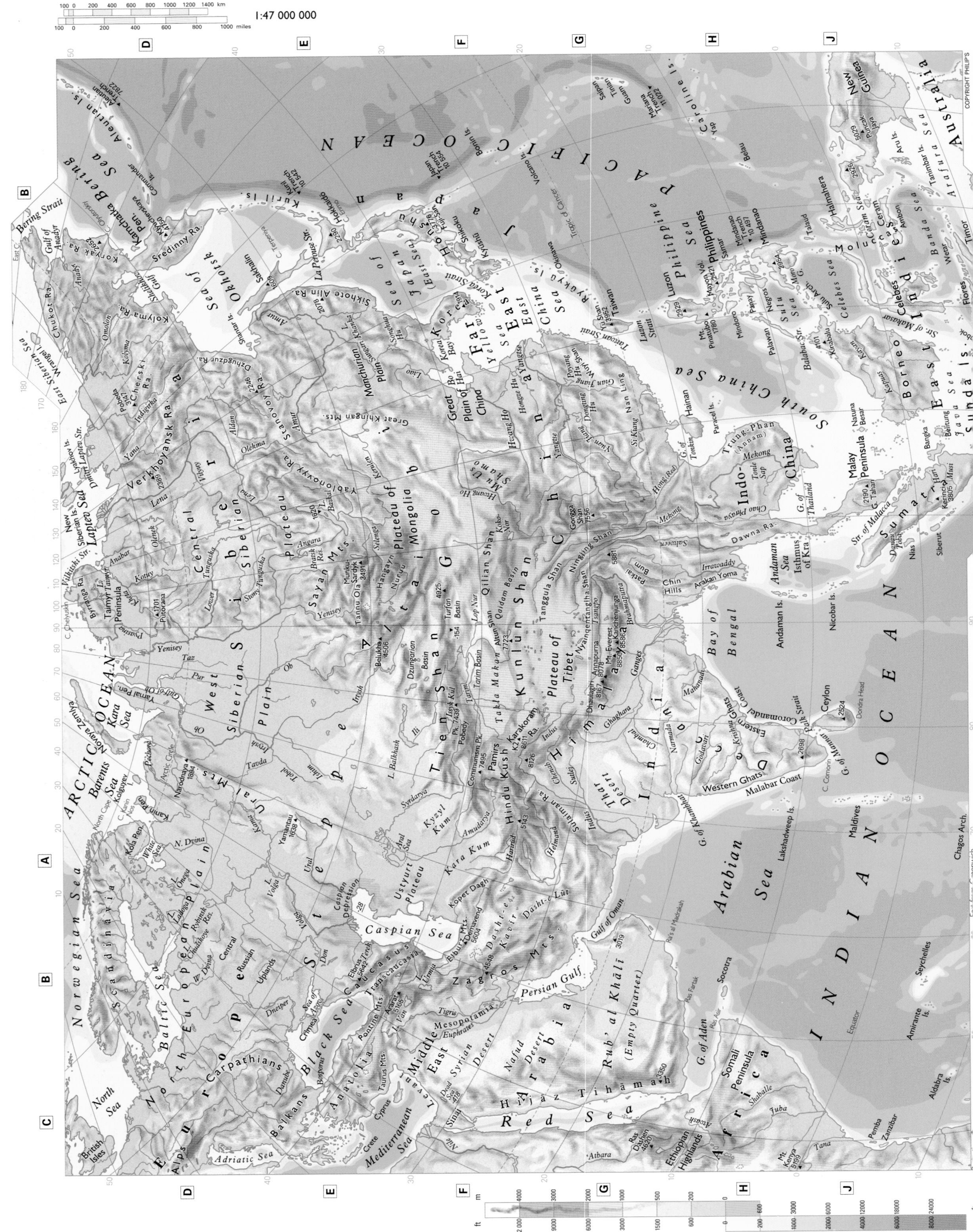
PACIFIC OCEAN
INDIAN OCEAN
ARCTIC OCEAN
Sea of Okhotsk
Sea of Japan (East Sea)
East China Sea
South China Sea
Philippine Sea
Bay of Bengal
Arabian Sea
Caspian Sea
Black Sea
Mediterranean Sea
Red Sea
Persian Gulf
Barents Sea
Kara Sea
Laptev Sea
Bering Sea
Norwegian Sea
North Sea
Baltic Sea
Central Siberian Plateau
West Siberian Plain
North European Plain
Plateau of Tibet
Plateau of Mongolia
Ural Mts
Himalaya
Kunlun Shan
Tien Shan
Altai
Hindu Kush
Karakoram Ra.
Zagros Mts.
Caucasus
Verkhoyansk Ra.
Gobi
Takla Makan
Arabia
India
China
Indo-China
Borneo
Sumatra
Celebes
Philippines
Japan
Mt. Everest 8850
Kamchatka Pen.
Malay Peninsula
Anatolia
Ceylon
Australia
Africa
COPYRIGHT PHILIP'S

1:47 000 000

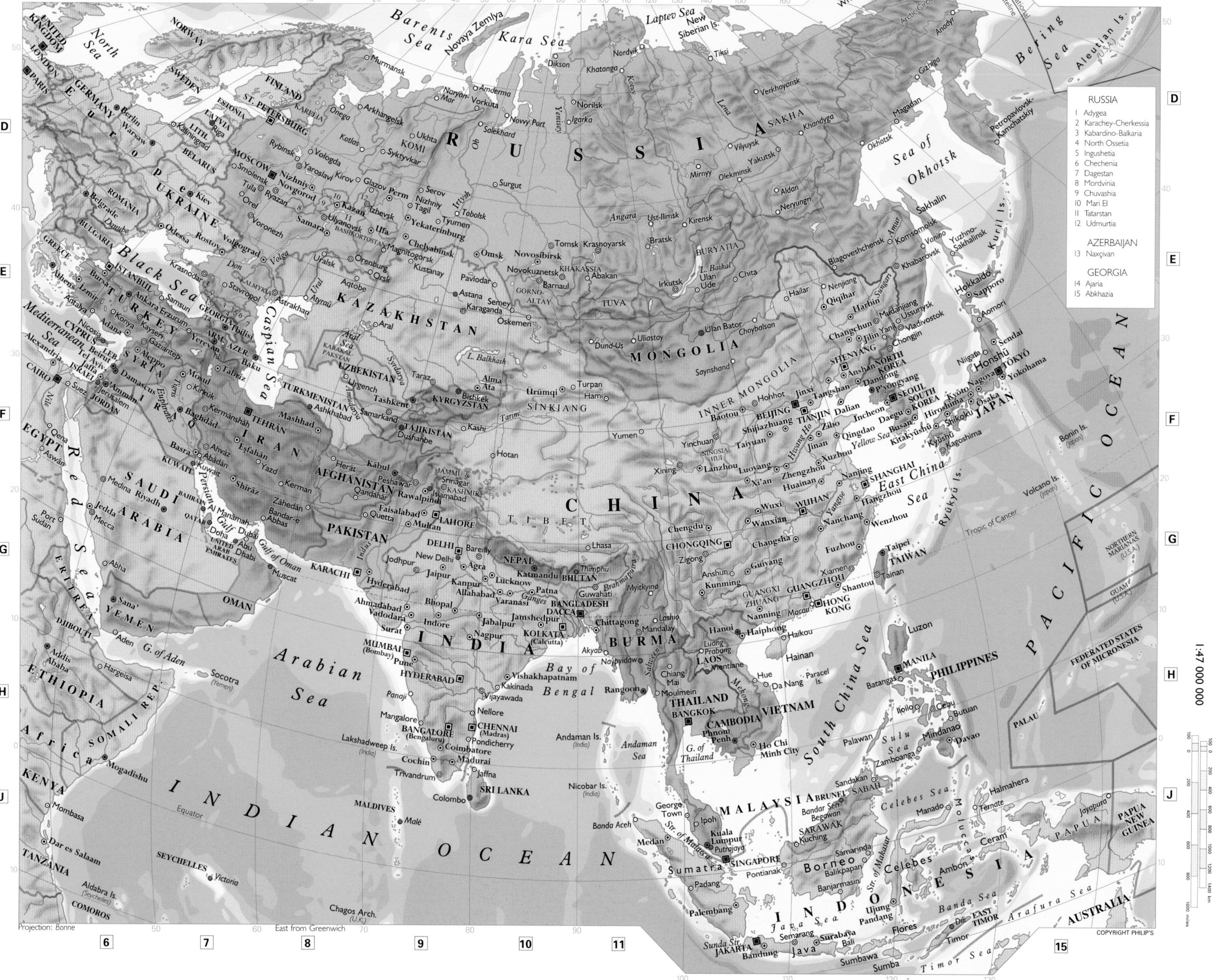
RUSSIA
1 Adygea
2 Karachey-Cherkessia
3 Kabardino-Balkaria
4 North Ossetia
5 Ingushetia
6 Chechenia
7 Dagestan
8 Mordvinia
9 Chuvashia
10 Mari El
11 Tatarstan
12 Udmurtia
AZERBAIJAN
13 Naxçivan
GEORGIA
14 Ajaria
15 Abkhazia
RUSSIA
KAZAKHSTAN
MONGOLIA
CHINA
INDIA
PACIFIC OCEAN
INDIAN OCEAN
Arabian Sea
Bay of Bengal
South China Sea
East China Sea
Sea of Okhotsk
Bering Sea
Barents Sea
Kara Sea
Laptev Sea
Caspian Sea
Black Sea
Red Sea
Mediterranean Sea
North Sea
Projection: Bonne
East from Greenwich

1:20 000 000

45
32

4

33

1:5 000 000
50 0 25 50 75 100 125 150 175 km
50 0 25 50 75 100 125 miles
SEA OF OKHOTSK
SEA OF JAPAN
(EAST SEA)
Yamato Rise
Sakhalin
(Russia)
Ostrov Moneron
(Russia)
La Perouse Strait
(Sōya-Kaikyō)
HOKKAIDŌ
Hokkaidō
SAPPORO
Hakodate
Asahikawa
Kushiro
Obihiro
Muroran
Otaru
Abashiri
Wakkanai
Nemuro
Tsugaru-Kaikyō
Honshū
TŌHOKU
Aomori
Hachinohe
Morioka
Akita
SENDAI
Yamagata
Fukushima
Niigata
Sado
Ostrov Kunashir
RUSSIA
PRIMORSKIY KRAY
Khrebet Sikhote-Alin'
Vladivostok
Nakhodka
Ussuriysk
Lake Khanka
Zaliv Petra Velikogo
CHINA
HEILONG-JIANG
Dongbei (Manchuria)
JILIN
NORTH KOREA
Ch'ŏngjin
Najin

RYUKYU ISLANDS
on same scale
EAST CHINA SEA
PACIFIC OCEAN
JAPAN
Nansei-Shotō (Ryukyu Is.)
Okinawa-Jima
Naha
Amami-Ō-Shima
Miyako-Jima
Ishigaki-Shima
Iriomote-Jima
Senkaku-Shotō
Sakishima-Guntō
Yaeyama-Rettō
Miyako-Rettō
Okinawa-Guntō
Amami-Guntō
Izu-Shotō
Hachijō-Jima
Miyake-Jima
Satsunan-Shotō
Tokara-Rettō
Ōsumi-Shotō
Ōsumi-Kaikyō
Yaku-Shima
Tane-ga-Shima
Korea Strait
Tsushima
SOUTH KOREA
ULSAN
Pohang
Yeongdeok
Ulleungdo (S. Korea)
Tokdo (Takeshima)
Oki-Shotō
KYŪSHŪ
SHIKOKU
CHŪGOKU
KINKI
KANTŌ
TOKYO
YOKOHAMA
KAWASAKI
Chiba
NAGOYA
KYŌTO
ŌSAKA
KOBE
HIROSHIMA
Okayama
FUKUOKA
KITAKYŪSHŪ
Nagasaki
Kumamoto
Kagoshima
Miyazaki
Ōita
Kōchi
Matsuyama
Tokushima
Takamatsu
Wakayama
Kii-Suidō
Bungo-Suidō
Ise-Wan
Suruga-Wan
Wakasa-Wan
Tosa-Wan
Projection: Conical with two standard parallels
East from Greenwich
COPYRIGHT PHILIP'S
m ft

1:15 000 000
100 0 100 200 300 400 500 600 km
100 0 100 200 300 400 miles
KAZAKHSTAN
Astana
Qaraghandy
Temirtau
Karsakpay
Zhezqazghan
Moyynty
Balqash
Balqash Köli
Betpaqdala
Moyynqum
Taldyqorghan
Qapshaghay
Bishkek
ALMATY
Taraz
Kirghiz Ra.
KYRGYZSTAN
Balykchy
Karakol
Naryn
Namangan
Andijon
UZBEK.
Osh
TAJIK.
AFG.
Hindu Kush
Semey
Rubtsovsk
Öskemen
Leninogorsk
Zyryan
Gorno-Altaysk
Belukha 4506
Tavan Bogd Uul 4374
Zaysan
Ayaköz
Khrebet Tarbagatay
Tacheng
Karamay
Ala Tau
Dzungarian Gate
Bole
Yining
Borohoro Shan
Gurbantünggüt Shamo
Junggar Pendi
Shihezi
Manas
Changji
ÜRÜMQI
Bogda Shan
Turpan
Turpan Pendi
Hami
Barkol Kazak Zizhixian
Tian Shan
Pik Pobedy 7439
Pik Khan-Tengri 6995
Aksu
Kuqa
Korla
Bosten Hu
Kuruktag
Kashi
Shule
Kongur Shan 7719
Muztagh-Ata 7546
Taxkorgan Tajik Zizhixian
Shache
Yecheng
Pishan
Hotan
Lop
Qira
Yutian
Minfeng
Qiemo
Ruoqiang
Tarim Pendi
Taklamakan Shamo
XINJIANG UYGUR ZIZHIQU (SINKIANG)
Lop Nur
Kumtag Shamo
Dunhuang
Anxi
Yumen
Jiayuguan
Jiuquan
Zhangye
Qilian Shan
Altun Shan
Mangnai Zhen
Qaidam Pendi
Golmud
Dulan
Qinghai Hu
Xining
LANZHOU
QINGHAI
Kunlun Shan
Hoh Xil Shan
Muz Tag 7723
Karakoram
K2 8611
Nanga Parbat 8126
JAMMU & KASHMIR
Aksai Chin
Srinagar
Leh
Rutog
Zaskar Mts.
XIZANG ZIZHIQU (TIBET)
Gangdisê Shan
Tanggula (Dangla) Shan
Siling Co
Nam Co
Nyainqêntanglha Shan
Lhasa
Xigazê
Yarlung Zangbo Jiang
Namcha Barwa 7756
Bayan Har Shan
Yushu
Qamdo
Nagqu
Amdo
HIMACHAL PRADESH
Shimla
Chandigarh
Dehra Dun
UTTARAKHAND
Saharanpur
MEERUT
DELHI
New Delhi
Moradabad
Bareilly
Aligarh
AGRA
Shahjahanpur
UTTAR PRADESH
LUCKNOW
KANPUR
Gwalior
Jhansi
ALLAHABAD
VARANASI
PATNA
BIHAR
Gorakhpur
Himalaya
NEPAL
KATHMANDU
Dhaulagiri 8167
Annapurna 8078
Manaslu 8156
Mt. Everest 8850
Kanchenjunga 8598
Makalu 8481
SIKKIM
Thimphu
BHUTAN
ARUNACHAL PRADESH
ASSAM
Brahmaputra
Guwahati
Dibrugarh
NAGALAND
MEGHALAYA
MANIPUR
Imphal
MIZORAM
Aizawl
BANGLADESH
DHAKA
Chittagong
KOLKATA (Calcutta)
WEST BENGAL
Khulna
Ranchi
JHARKHAND
JAMSHEDPUR
DHANBAD
ASANSOL
MADHYA PRADESH
JABALPUR
Bilaspur
BHILAINAGAR-DURG
NAGPUR
CHHATTISGARH
ORISSA
Cuttack
Bhubaneshwar
Brahmapur
Vishakhapatnam
BAY OF BENGAL
Tropic of Cancer
INDIA
BURMA (MYANMAR)
Kachin
Myitkyina
Mandalay
Sittwe (Akyab)
Arakan Yoma
Pegu Yoma
Shan
Taunggyi
Naypyidaw
Toungoo
THAILAND (SIAM)
LAOS
Luang Prabang
VIETNAM
HANOI
Mekong
Salween
Irrawaddy
YUNNAN
KUNMING
Dali
Lijiang
Panzhihua
Xichang
Zhaotong
CHENGDU
SICHUAN
LESHAN
ZIGONG
Ya'an
Gongga Shan 7556
Daxue Shan
Shaluli Shan
Ningjing Shan
Hengduan Shan
RUSSIA
Zapadnyy Sayan
Tannu Ola
Kyzyl
Irkutsk
Angarsk
Munku-Sardyk 3491
Hövsgöl Nuur
Uvs Nuur
Ulaangom
Ölgiy
Khovd
Har Us Nuur
Hyargas Nuur
Uliastay
Hangayn Nuruu
MONGOLIA
Aerhtai Shan (Altai)
Altay
Mörön
Erdenet
Bulgan
Tsetserleg
Bayanhongor
Arvayheer
Mandalgovĭ
Gurvan Sayhan Uul
Dalandzadgad
Gobi
Bei Shan
Badain Jaran Shamo
Tengger Shamo
Wuwei
Jinchang
Yinchuan
TIANSHUI
MIANYANG
Guangyuan
Projection: Bonne
East from Greenwich

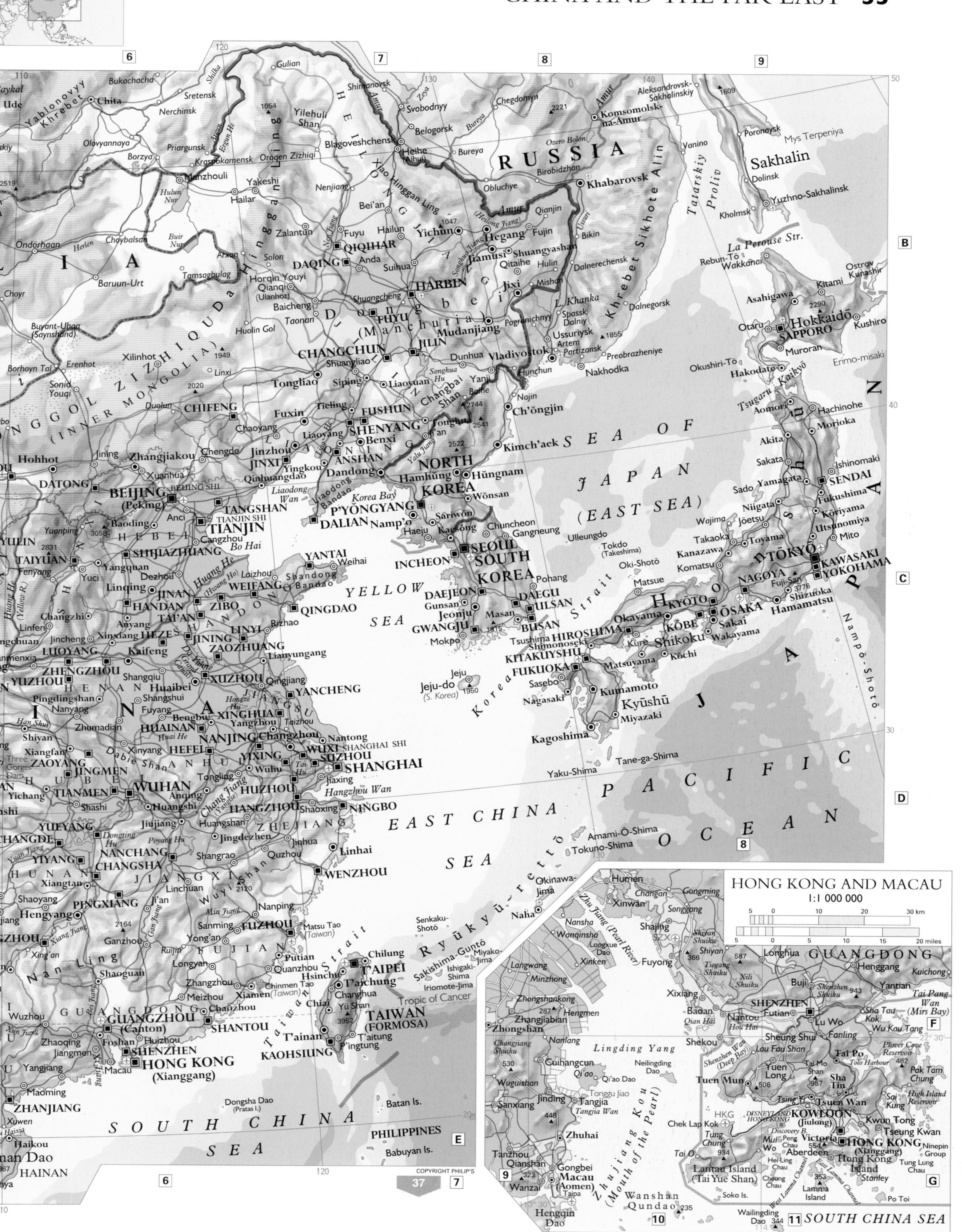
RUSSIA
SEA OF JAPAN (EAST SEA)
YELLOW SEA
EAST CHINA SEA
SOUTH CHINA SEA
PACIFIC OCEAN
NORTH KOREA
SOUTH KOREA
TAIWAN (FORMOSA)
PHILIPPINES
Sakhalin
Hokkaidō
Honshu
Shikoku
Kyūshū
Korea Strait
Taiwan Strait
La Perouse Str.
Tatarskiy Proliv
Tropic of Cancer
Ryūkyū-rettō
Nampō-Shotō
Amur
Heilong Jiang
Huang He (Yellow R.)
Chang Jiang (Yangtze)
Bo Hai
Korea Bay
Liaodong Wan
Hangzhou Wan
HARBIN
CHANGCHUN
SHENYANG
DALIAN
BEIJING (Peking)
TIANJIN
SHIJIAZHUANG
TAIYUAN
JINAN
QINGDAO
ZHENGZHOU
NANJING
SHANGHAI
HANGZHOU
NINGBO
WUHAN
CHANGSHA
NANCHANG
FUZHOU
XIAMEN
GUANGZHOU (Canton)
SHENZHEN
HONG KONG (Xianggang)
Macau
SHANTOU
T'AIPEI
KAOHSIUNG
P'YŎNGYANG
SEOUL
BUSAN
DAEGU
DAEJEON
GWANGJU
INCHEON
TŌKYŌ
YOKOHAMA
KAWASAKI
NAGOYA
ŌSAKA
KYŌTO
KŌBE
HIROSHIMA
FUKUOKA
KITAKYUSHU
SAPPORO
SENDAI
Vladivostok
Khabarovsk
Blagoveshchensk
Chita
HONG KONG AND MACAU
1:1 000 000
GUANGDONG
KOWLOON (Jiulong)
Lantau Island (Tai Yue Shan)
Zhuhai
Macau (Aomen)
SOUTH CHINA SEA
COPYRIGHT PHILIP'S

1:6 000 000

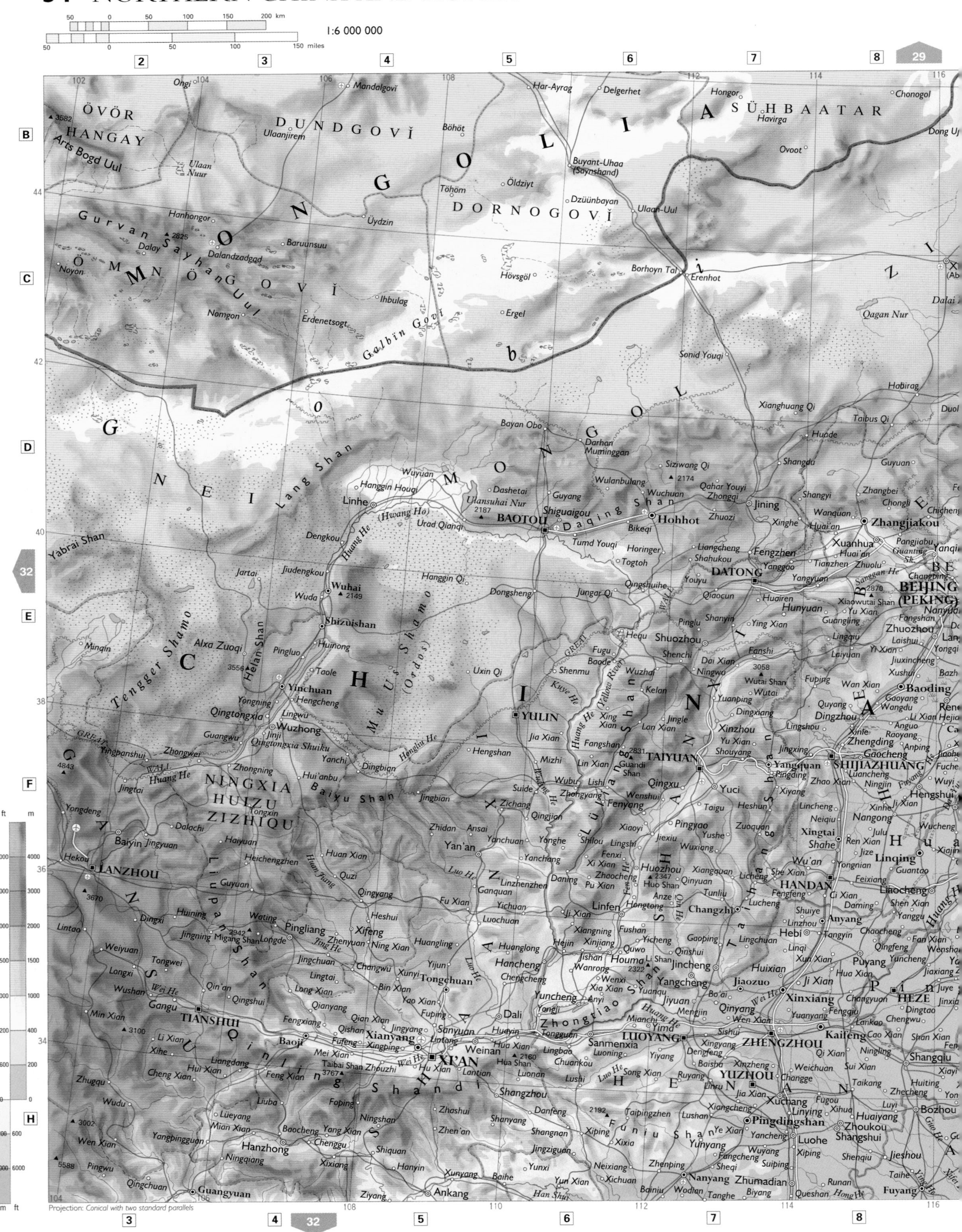

Projection: Conical with two standard parallels

Sand deserts

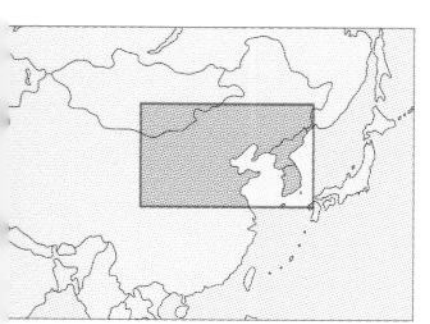

10
11
12
13
14
15
16
B
C
D
E
F
G
H
HARBIN
CHANGCHUN
JILIN
SHENYANG
FUSHUN
ANSHAN
DALIAN
(Lüda)
P'YŎNGYANG
SEOUL
INCHEON
SUWON
DAEJEON
DAEGU
BUSAN
GWANGJU
QINGDAO
YANTAI
WEIFANG
ZIBO
XINTAI
LINYI
ZAOZHUANG
HUAI'AN
YANCHENG
XINGHUA
CHIFENG
JINXI
Vladivostok
Ussuriysk
NORTH KOREA
SOUTH KOREA
RUSSIA
JAPAN
HEILONGJIANG
JILIN
LIAONING
SEA OF JAPAN
(EAST SEA)
YELLOW SEA
(Huang Hai)
Bo Hai
Korea Bay
Liaodong Wan
Korea Strait
Shandong Bandao
Changbai Shan
Paektu-san
Tongjosŏn Man
Jeju-do (S. Korea)
Tsushima (Japan)
East from Greenwich
30
31
33

INDONESIA AND THE PHILIPPINES

1:12 500 000

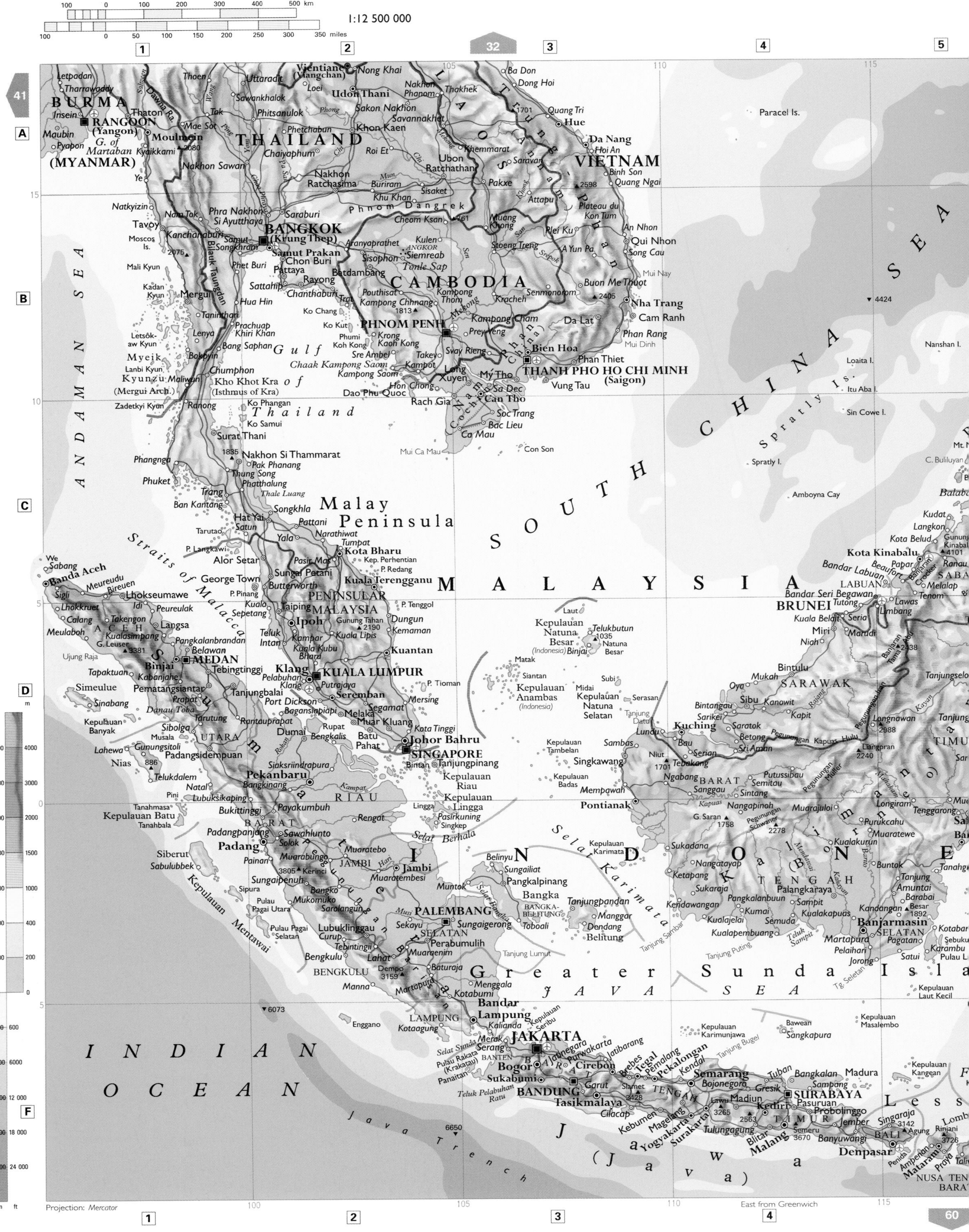

JAVA AND MADURA
1:7 500 000
50 0 50 100 150 200 250 300 km
50 0 50 100 150 200 miles
BALI
1:2 000 000
10 0 10 20 30 km
10 0 10 20 miles
JAKARTA
Bogor
Bandung
Tasikmalaya
Cirebon
Tegal
Pekalongan
Semarang
Surakarta
Yogyakarta
Madiun
Kediri
Malang
SURABAYA
Madura
Probolinggo
Jember
Banyuwangi
Kepulauan Karimunjawa
Bawean
Nusa Barung
BANTEN
B A R A T
T E N G A H
T I M U R
Selat Sunda
Selat Madura
Singaraja
Denpasar
Kuta
Nusa Dua
Nusa Penida
Bali
Jawa
Lombok
Mataram
Selat Lombok
Selat Badung
Selat Bali
BALI SEA
INDIAN OCEAN
Luzon
MANILA
Quezon City
Mindoro
Samar
Leyte
Cebu
Negros
Panay
Bohol
Mindanao
DAVAO
Zamboanga
Mindanao Trench
Sulu Arch.
CELEBES SEA
PACIFIC OCEAN
Halmahera
Ternate
Morotai
MOLUCCA SEA
Sulawesi (Celebes)
Manado
Gorontalo
Kendari
Buton
Seram (Ceram)
Buru
Ambon
MALUKU
BANDA SEA
Kepulauan Aru
Kepulauan Tanimbar
Kepulauan Kai
Jazirah Doberai
IRIAN JAYA
PAPUA
Pegunungan Maoke
Puncak Jaya 5029
Jayapura
Merauke
PAPUA NEW GUINEA
Equator
Flores
Sumba
Timor
Kupang
Dili
EAST TIMOR
NUSA TENGGARA TIMUR
Sawu Sea
ARAFURA SEA
FLORES SEA
Sunda Is.

50 0 50 100 150 200 km

1:6 000 000

50 0 50 100 150 miles

KO PHUKET
1:1 000 000
KO SAMUI
1:1 000 000
PINANG
1:1 000 000
SINGAPORE
1:1 000 000
1:1 000 000
SOUTH CHINA SEA
Gulf of Thailand
ANDAMAN SEA
Straits of Malacca
Straits of Singapore
PENINSULAR MALAYSIA
MALAYSIA
INDONESIA
Kho Khot Kra (Isthmus of Kra)
Myeik Kyunzu (Mergui Archipelago)
KUALA LUMPUR
PHNOM PENH
THANH PHO HO CHI MINH (Saigon)
SINGAPORE
Johor Bahru
MEDAN
Pulau Pinang
George Town
Ipoh
Kota Bharu
Kuala Terengganu
Kuantan
Melaka
Hat Yai
Phuket
Ko Samui
Surat Thani
Can Tho
Vung Tau
Projection: Conical with two standard parallels
East from Greenwich
COPYRIGHT PHILIP'S

Sand deserts

Intermittent lakes

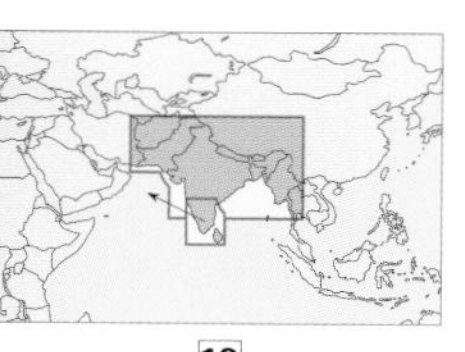

13 14 32 15 16 17 18 19 20 21 22

XINJIANG UYGUR ZIZHIQU (SINKIANG)
Kun Lun Shan
Hoh Xil Shan
QINGHAI
Bayan Har Shan
Muz Tag 7723
Gyaring Hu
Ngoring Hu
4237
6094
Huang He
Dogai Coring
Tanggula Shan (Dangla Shan)
CHINA
XIZANG ZIZHIQU (TIBET)
Gangdisê Shan (Kangri)
Nyainqentanglha Shan
Tanggula Shankou 5180
Amdo
Yushu
Dainkog
Nangqên
Garzê
Gamtog
Baqên
Dêngqên
Qamdo
Baiyü
Xinlong
Siling Co 4495
Dongco
Nagqu
SICHUAN
Ombu
Tangra Yumco
Gyaring Co
Nam Co 4627
Xainza
Coqên
Lhari
Lhorong
Nu Jiang
Salween
Zhaxizê
Yidun
Litang
Yajiang
Kangrinboqe Feng (Kailash) 6714
Mapam Yumco
Lhünzub
7088
Gongbo'gyamda
Ningjing
Lancang Jiang (Mekong)
Namcha Barwa 7756
Riga
Gogên
Lhasa
Namse Shankou 4944
Mugu
7059
Zhongba
Saga
Maquan He (Tsangpo)
Xigazê
Gyangzê
Lhazê
Yarlung Zangbo Jiang
Nang Xian
Brahmaputra
Jido
Muli Zangzu Zizhixian
Mainkung
Jinsha Jiang
Doti
Jumla
Mustang
Muktinath
Gyala Shankou 5602
Dhaulagiri 8167
Annapurna 8078
Xixabangma Feng 8012
Gamba
Dinggyê
Kula Kangri 7554
Lhünzê
Subansiri
Dihang
Nizamghat
Minutang
Hkakabo Razi 5881 (Thala La)
Zhongdian
Zhizhixian
NEPAL
Nepalganj
Nuwakot
Gurkha
Pokhara
Nyalam
Mt. Everest 8850
Nawakot
7314
Cona
7090
Kangto
ARUNACHAL PRADESH
Murkongselek
Saikhoa Ghat
Hpunan Pass 3072
Putao
Konglu
Weixi
5590
Lijiang
Siwalik Range
KATHMANDU
Bhaktapur
Kanchenjunga 8598
SIKKIM
Punakha
Tongsa Dzong
Thunkar
Rupa
Dum Duma
Dibrugarh
Tinsukia
North Lakhimpur
Sibsagar
Chaukan Pass 2432
Bumhpa Bum
Jianchuan
Jarwa
Nautanwa
Ramechhap
Gangtok
Thimphu
BHUTAN
Taga Dzong
Patkai Bum
Hukawng Valley
3411
Kumon Bum
Bahraich
Balrampur
Gonda
Birganj
Raxaul
Sun Kosi
Dhankuta
Darjiling
Jorhat
Basti
Bettiah
Udaipur Garhi
Shiliguri
Jayanti
Bongaigaon
Tezpur
Rangia
Silghat
Nowgong
ASSAM
Mokokchung
Maingkwan
KACHIN
Yunlong
Faizabad
Gorakhpur
Motihari
Deoria
Darbhanga
Biratnagar
Jalpaiguri
Alipur Duar
Koch Bihar
Goalpara
Barpeta
Mairabari
Guwahati
NAGALAND
Kohima 3824
Singkaling Hkamti
Mali
Nmai
YUNNAN
Bareli
Ghaghara
Sultanpur
Azamgarh
Siwan
Muzaffarpur
Supaul
Kishanganj
Saidpur
Dhuburi
Brahmaputra
Dimapur
2424
Myitkyina
Baoshan
Jaunpur
Bela
Chhapra
BIHAR
Bankipore
Beharigani
Katihar
Purnia
Barsoi
Rangpur
Shillong
Mogaung
Tengchong
Ara
1412
MEGHALAYA 1961
Cherrapunji
Tura
Barail Range
Ukhrul
Haflong
Tamenglong
Homalin
Longling
Changning
VARANASI
Ghazipur
PATNA
Mokoma
Munger
Ganga (Ganges)
Dinajpur
Jamalpur
Mohanganj
SYLHET
Sylhet
Silchar
Imphal
Chindwin
Mirzapur
Sasaram
Jahanabad
Dehri
Bihar
Jamalpur
Bhagalpur
Ingraj Bazar
Bogra
Sirajganj
Mymensingh
MANIPUR
Churachandpur
Thaungdut
Katha
Bhamo
Mauganj
Aurangabad
Gaya
Deoghar
Tinpahar
RAJSHAHI
East Bengal
Lalaghat
Kolosib
Tamu
Wuntho
Indaw
Shwegu
Rewa
Dudhi
Rampur Hat
Pabna
DHAKA
Brahmanbaria
TRIPURA
Agartala
Sairang
Aizawl
SAGAING
Tigyaing
Man Na
Kunlong
Tropic of Cancer
Pang-Long
Bharatpur
Hazaribag
Barhi
Giridih
Gomoh
DHANBAD
Siuri
Baharampur
Kushtia
Amarpur
Tiddim
Mawlaik
Kyunhla
Hsenwi
Namtu
Lashio
JHARKHAND
Lohardaga
Ramgarh
1366
ASANSOL
Raniganj
Krishnanagar
Narayanganj
Comilla
MIZORAM
Dighinala
Kennedy Mt. 2704
Kalewa
Bawdwin
Mogok
Salween
Ranchi
Puruliya
WEST BENGAL
Durgapur
Ranaghat
Jessore
Chandpur
Madaripur
Belonia
Lunglei
Mingin
Shwebo
2299
Mong Yai
Munar
1225
Chirmiri
Ambikapur
JAMSHEDPUR
Bankura
Barddhaman
Bhatpara
KHULNA
Barisal
Noakhali
Falam
Chin Hills
Budalin
Madaya
Gokteik
Pang-Yang
2698
Mong Pawk
1127
Chakradharpur
Shrirampur
Haora
KOLKATA (CALCUTTA)
BARISAL
Bhola
Hatia
CHITTAGONG
Raptai
Gangaw
Alon
Monywa
Mandalay
Mong Hsu
Korba
Birmitrapur
Raurkela
Chaibasa
Medinipur
Gua
Kharagpur
Diamond Harbour
Port Canning
Patuakhali
Dohazari
CHIN
Yinmabin
Sagaing
Kyaukse
Mong Kung
SHAN
Mong Wa
Keng Tung
Bilaspur
Sundargarh
Badampahar
Lakshmikantapur
Haldia
The Sundarbans
Haringhata
Kaladan
Pauk
Myingyan
Kawardha
Raigarh
CHHATTISGARH
Jharsuguda
Baleshwar
Contai
Hugli
Mouths of the Ganges
Cox's Bazar
Paletwa
3053
Kanpetlet
Pakokku
Meiktila
Taunggyi
Heho
2519
Keng Tawng
Raipur
Sarangarh
Hirakud Dam
Sambalpur
Keonjhargarh
1187
Subarnarekha
BURMA (MYANMAR)
Kyaukpadaung
Yenangyaung
Thazi
Yamethin
Inle L.
Mong Nai
Mong Ton
BHILAINAGAR-DURG
Sonepur
Talcher
Brahmani
Bhadrakh
St. Martin's I.
Mawk Mai
Mong Pan
2256
Muang Chiang Rai
Balangir
Mahanadi
Dhenkanal
Kendrapara
Sittwe (Akyab)
Minbu
Magwe
MAGWE
Taungdwingyi
Loi-kaw
2163
Kanker
Titlagarh
1001
ORISSA
Cuttack
Mahanadi
Paradip
Bhubaneshwar
Russellkonda
ARAKAN
Naypyidaw
Pyinmana
Thayetmyo
KAYAH
Mae Hong Son
Bhawanipatna
Puri
Kyaukpyu
Arakan Coast
Arakan Yoma
Irrawaddy
Bawlake
Toungoo
Chiang Mai
THAILAND
Brahmapur
Chilka L.
Chatrapur
Ichchapuram
Ramree I.
Letpan
Prome
Pegu Yoma
KAYIN
2620
Muang Lamphun
Bastar
Rayagada
1501
Taungup
Cheduba I.
2565
Lampang
Jagdalpur
Jeypore
Parvatipuram
BAY OF BENGAL
Pyu
Papun
Salur
Bobbili
Tekkali
Sandoway
Myanaung
Sittang Myit
Madauk
Srikakulam
Eastern Ghats
Letpadan
Tharrawaddy
1680
Vizianagaram
Gwa
Henzada
Pegu
Tak
Northern Circars
Anakapalle
VISHAKHAPATNAM
Kyonpyaw
Yandoon
PEGU
Thaton
Pa-an
Dawna Range
Insein
Bassein
Maubin
RANGOON
Martaban
Moulmein
Pithapuram
Godavari Point
Myaungmya
IRRAWADDY
Pyapon
Rangoon
MON
2080
Kakinada
Yanam
G. of Martaban
Amherst
Mai Klong
Narasapur
Maudin Sun
Mouths of the Irrawaddy
Kalegauk
Lamaing
Machilipatnam
Ye
Sangkhla Buri
Natkyizin
INDIAN OCEAN
Preparis North Channel
Sangkhla
Pariparit Kyun (Burma)
Nam Tok
Preparis South Channel
Moscos Is.
Maungmagan Is.
Yebyu
Tavoy
Koko Kyunzu (Burma)
Launglon Bok

B C D E F G H J K L M

82 84 86 88 90 92 94 96 98 100 102
34 32 30 28 26 24 22 20 18 16 14

38

82 East from Greenwich 84 86 88 90 92 94 96

13 14 15 16 17 18 19 20 39 21

NORTHERN INDIA, PAKISTAN AND NEPAL

50 0 50 100 150 200 km

1:6 000 000

50 0 50 100 150 miles

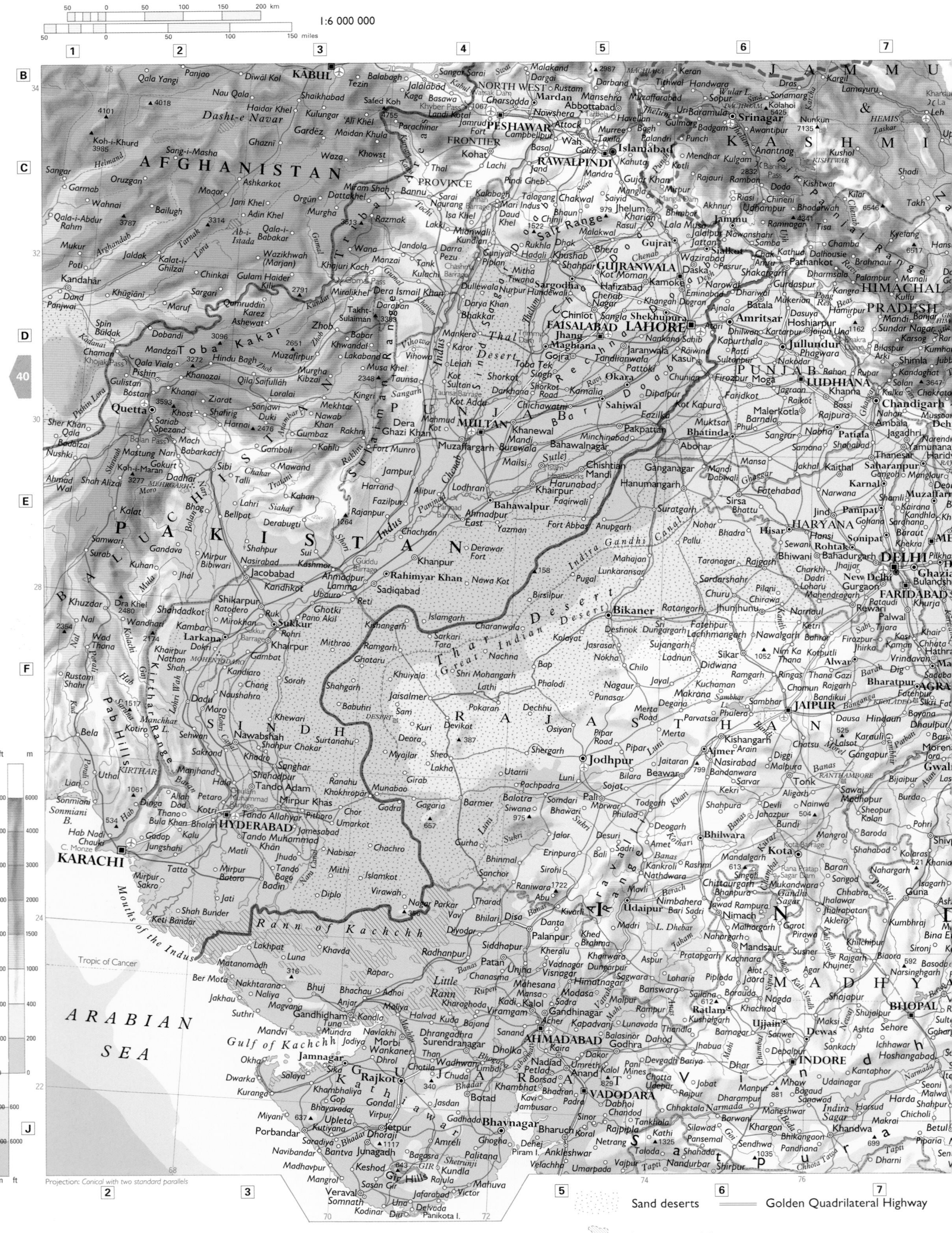

Sand deserts

Golden Quadrilateral Highway

Intermittent lakes

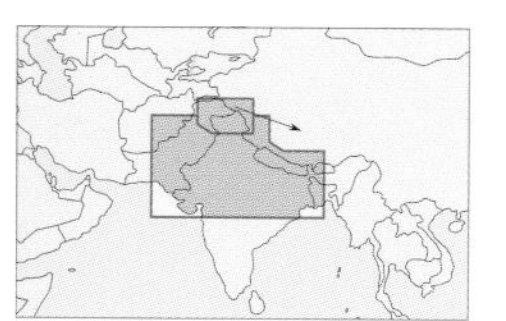

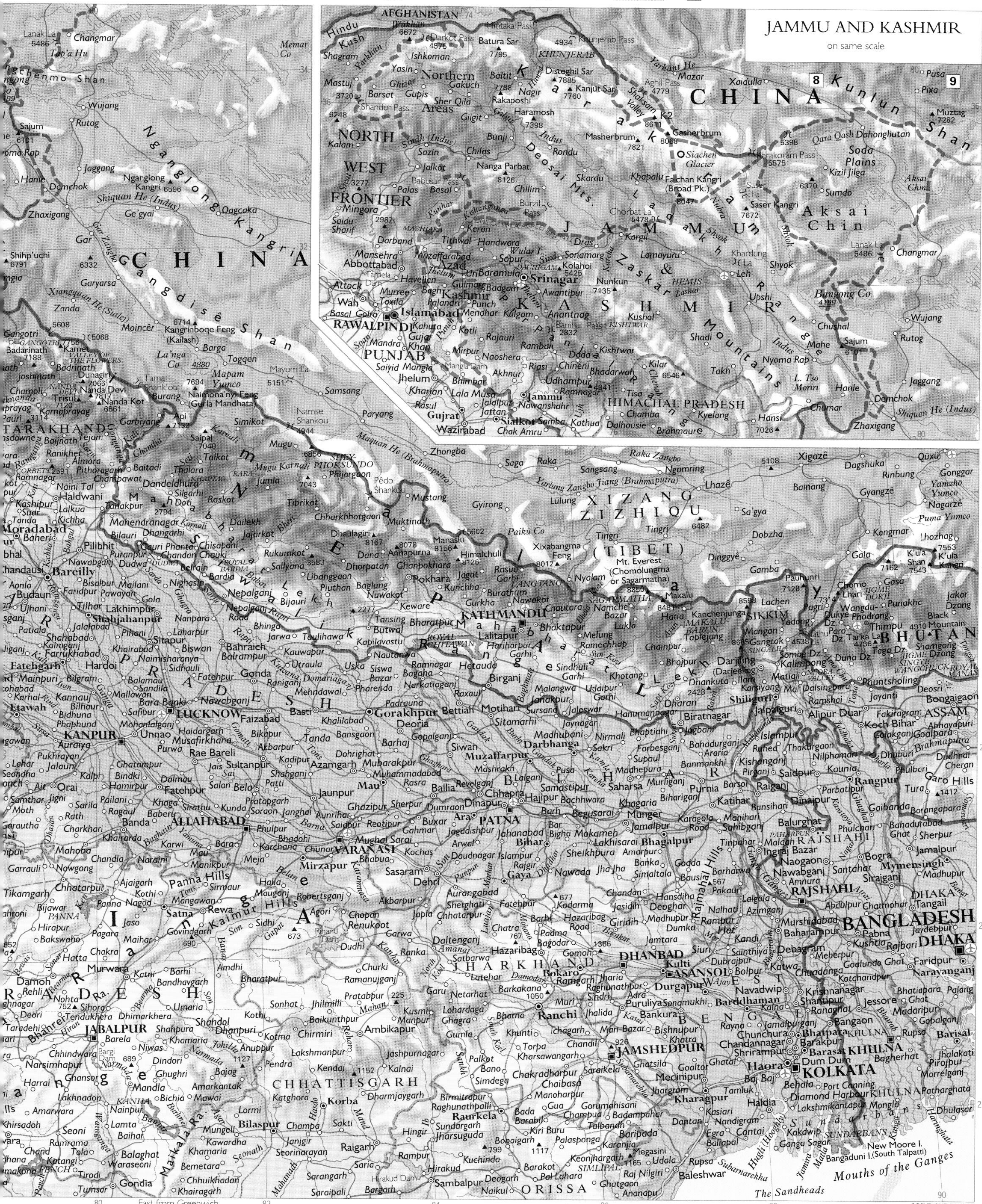

JAMMU AND KASHMIR
on same scale
AFGHANISTAN
CHINA
NORTH WEST FRONTIER
Northern Areas
JAMMU & KASHMIR
PUNJAB
HIMACHAL PRADESH
Aksai Chin
Karakoram Range
Ladakh Range
Zaskar Mountains
Kunlun Shan
Gangdisê Shan
XIZANG ZIZHIQU (TIBET)
NEPAL
BHUTAN
SIKKIM
BANGLADESH
UTTAR PRADESH
MADHYA PRADESH
BIHAR
JHARKHAND
CHHATTISGARH
ORISSA
WEST BENGAL
ASSAM
Mt. Everest (Chomolungma or Sagarmatha) 8850
KATHMANDU
ISLAMABAD
RAWALPINDI
LUCKNOW
KANPUR
ALLAHABAD
VARANASI
PATNA
DHAKA
KOLKATA
KHULNA
RAJSHAHI
JAMSHEDPUR
DHANBAD
ASANSOL
JABALPUR
Mouths of the Ganges
The Sandheads
East from Greenwich

50 0 50 100 150 200 250 300 km

50 0 50 100 150 200 miles

1:7 000 000

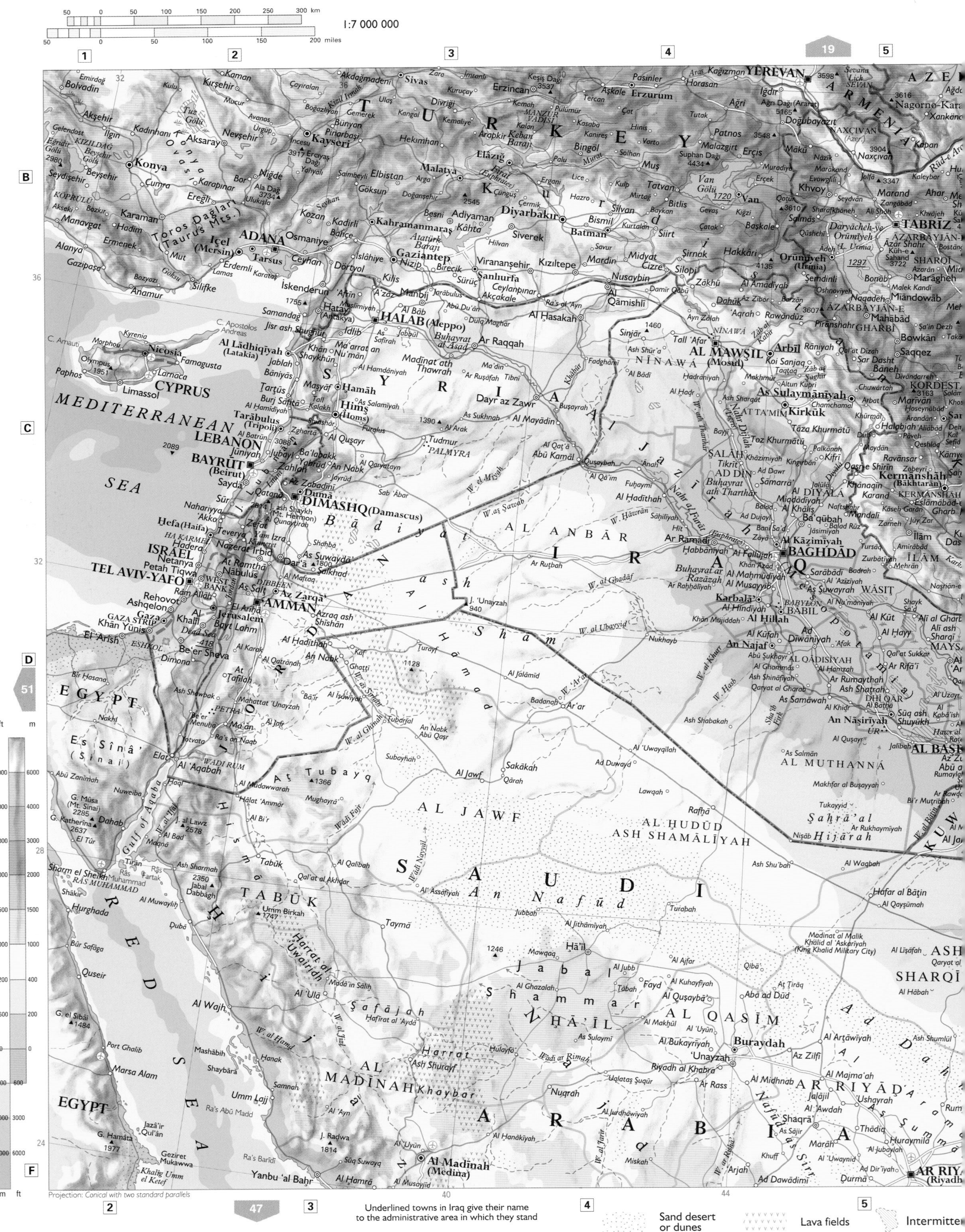

Projection: Conical with two standard parallels

2 3 4 5

Underlined towns in Iraq give their name to the administrative area in which they stand

Sand desert or dunes

Lava fields

Intermitte

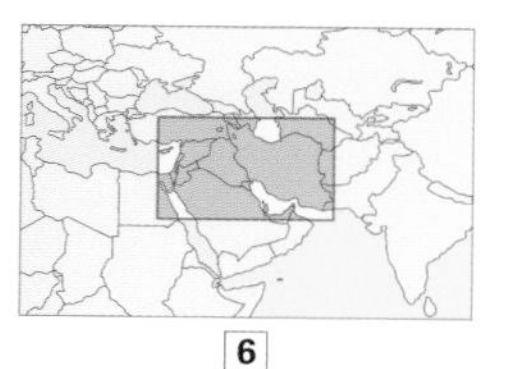

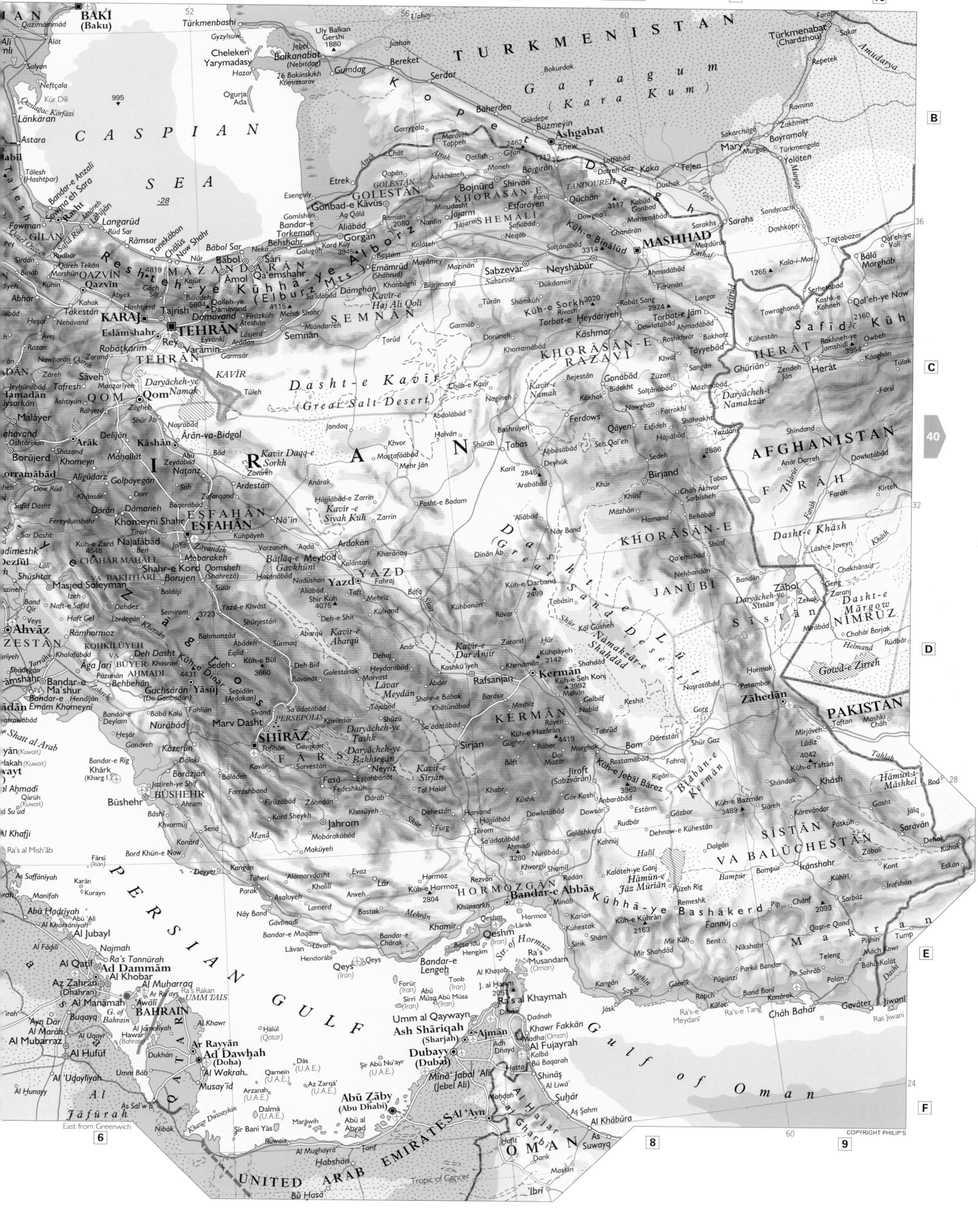

6 7 8 28 9 10

TURKMENISTAN
Garagum (Kara Kum)
Kopet Dagh
Türkmenbashi
Balkanabat (Nebitdag)
Gumdag
Serdar
Bereket
Ashgabat
Tejen
Mary
Türkmenabat (Chardzhou)
Amudarya
Sarahs

BAKI (Baku)
Länkäran
Astara
CASPIAN SEA
-28
Cheleken Yarymadasy
Ogurja Ada
995

IRAN
Reshteh-ye Kūhhā-ye Alborz (Elburz Mts.)
TEHRĀN
Karaj
Qazvīn
Rasht
GĪLĀN
MĀZANDARĀN
Sārī
Bābol
Āmol
Qā'emshahr
Gorgan
GOLESTĀN
Gonbad-e Kāvūs
Bojnūrd
KHORĀSĀN-E SHEMĀLĪ
Qūchān
MASHHAD
Neyshābūr
Sabzevār
SEMNĀN
Semnān
Dāmghān
Shāhrūd
Qom
QOM
Arāk
Kāshān
Dasht-e Kavīr (Great Salt Desert)
KHORĀSĀN-E RAZAVĪ
Torbat-e Heydārīyeh
Torbat-e Jām
Tabas
Birjand
KHORĀSĀN-E JANŪBĪ
Dasht-e Lūt (Great Sand Desert)
ESFAHĀN
Eşfahān
Najafābād
Khomeynī Shahr
CHAHĀR MAHALL VA BAKHTIĀRĪ
Shahr-e Kord
Yazd
YAZD
Kermān
KERMĀN
Rafsanjān
Sīrjān
Bam
Zāhedān
SĪSTĀN VA BALŪCHESTĀN
Zābol
Īrānshahr
Chāh Bahār
Shīrāz
FĀRS
Persepolis
Zagros Mts.
Kūh-e Dīnār 4431
KOHKĪLŪYEH VA BŪYER AHMADĪ
Yāsūj
Būshehr
BŪSHEHR
Ahvāz
Dezfūl
Bandar-e Emām Khomeynī
HORMOZGĀN
Bandar-e 'Abbās
Qeshm
Str. of Hormuz
Kūhhā-ye Bashākerd
Makran
Jāsk

AFGHANISTAN
Herāt
HERĀT
FARĀH
Farāh
Dasht-e Khāsh
NĪMRŪZ
Dasht-e Mārgow
Safīd Kūh
Shīndand

PAKISTAN
Hāmūn-i-Māshkel

PERSIAN GULF
Gulf of Oman
Shatt al Arab
Al Kuwayt
Ad Dammām
Al Khobar
Al Jubayl
Al Hufūf
BAHRAIN
Al Manāmah
QATAR
Ad Dawḩah (Doha)
UNITED ARAB EMIRATES
Abū Zāby (Abu Dhabi)
Dubayy (Dubai)
Ash Shāriqah (Sharjah)
Ra's al Khaymah
Al Fujayrah
Musandam (Oman)
Al 'Ayn
OMAN
Al Ḩajar al Gharbī
Şuḩār
Tropic of Cancer
Al Jāfūrah

B C D E F

East from Greenwich

40

THE NEAR EAST

10 0 10 20 30 40 50 60 70 80 100 km

1:2 500 000

10 0 10 20 30 40 50 60 miles

1 2 3 4 44 5 6

A B C D F

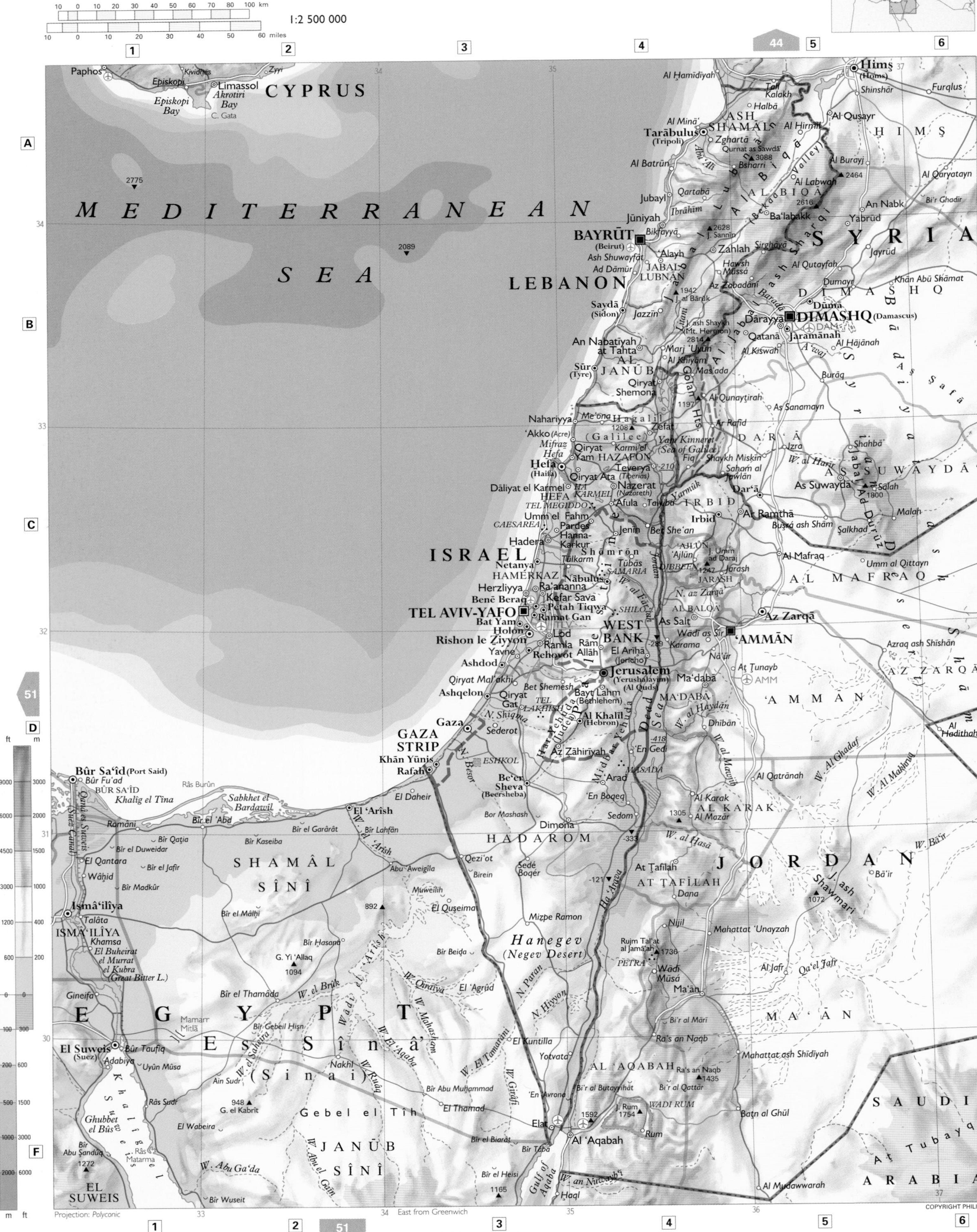

1 2 51 3 4 5 6

1974 Cease Fire Lines

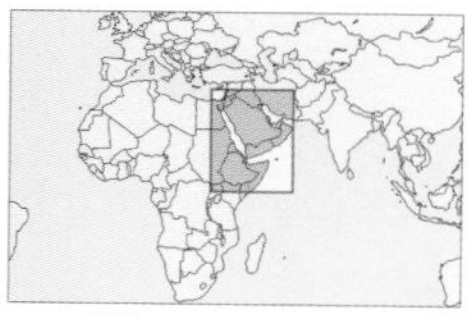

1:15 000 000

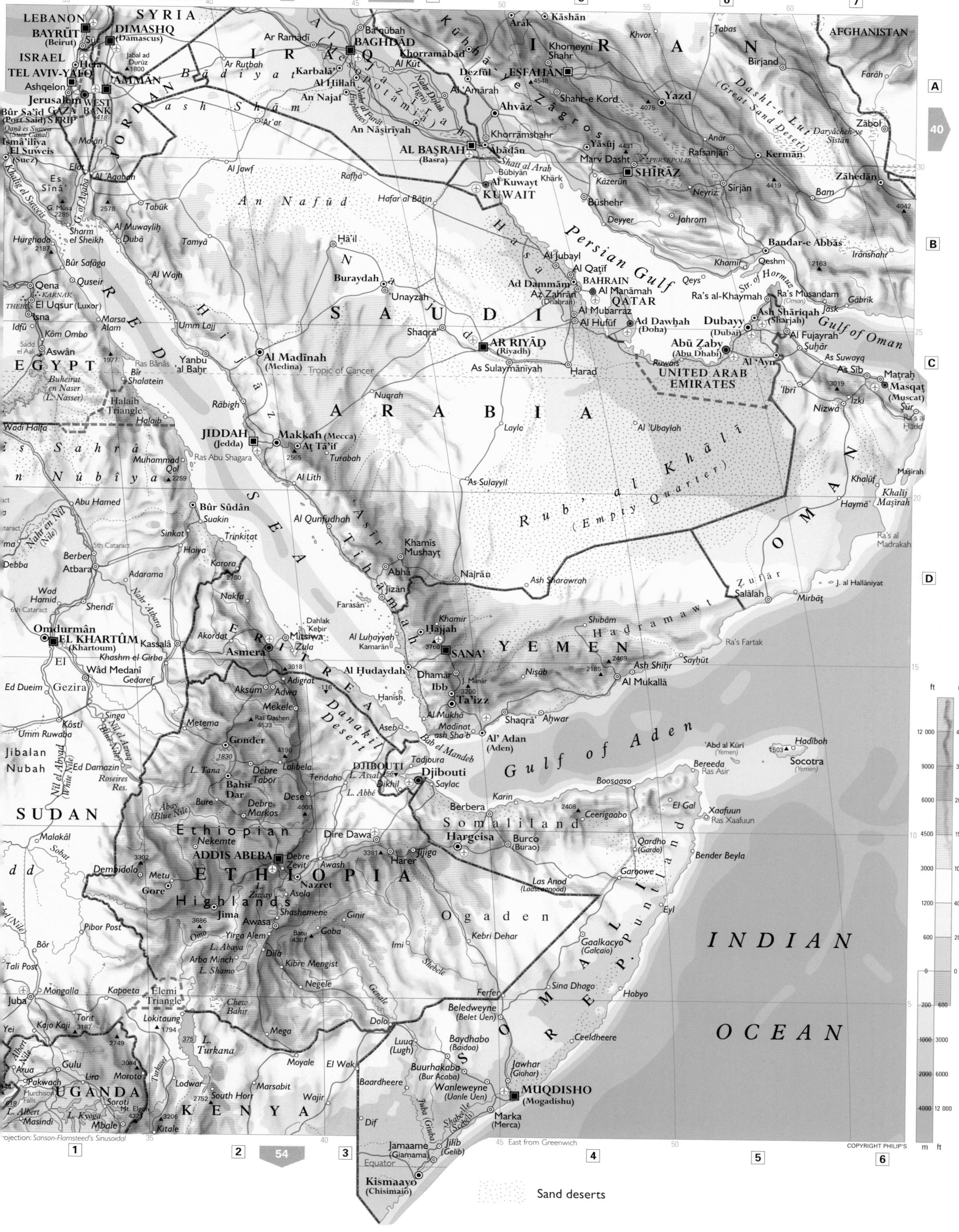

100 0 100 200 300 400 500 600 km
100 0 100 200 300 400 miles

SYRIA
LEBANON
BAYRŪT (Beirut)
DIMASHQ (Damascus)
ISRAEL
TEL AVIV-YAFO
Ashqelon
Jerusalem
WEST BANK
GAZA STRIP
'AMMĀN
JORDAN
Bûr Sa'îd (Port Said)
Ismâ'ilîya
El Suweis (Suez)
Es Sînâ'
Elat
Al 'Aqabah
Ar Ramādī
Ar Ruṭbah
Bādiyat ash Shām
IRAQ
BAGHDĀD
Ba'qūbah
Karbalā'
Al Ḥillah
An Najaf
Al Kūt
Al 'Amārah
An Nāṣirīyah
AL BAṢRAH (Basra)
Ar'ar
Rafḥā
KUWAIT
Al Kuwayt
Bubiyan
Khārk
IRAN
Kāshān
Arāk
Khorramābād
Dezfūl
Khomeynī Shahr
EṢFAHĀN
Shahr-e Kord
Ahvāz
Khorramshahr
Ābādān
Yāsūj
Marv Dasht
PERSEPOLIS
SHĪRĀZ
Kāzerūn
Būshehr
Jahrom
Yazd
Dasht-e Lut (Great Sand Desert)
Tabas
Khvor
Bīrjand
Farāh
AFGHANISTAN
Zābol
Daryācheh-ye Sīstān
Anār
Rafsanjān
Kermān
Sīrjān
Zāhedān
Bam
Neyrīz
Bandar-e 'Abbās
Qeshm
Īrānshahr
Gābrīk
Jāsk
Al Jawf
An Nafūd
Hafar al Bāṭin
Tabūk
Al Muwaylih
Ḍubā
Tamyā
Ḥā'il
Buraydah
'Unayzah
Al Wajh
Umm Lajj
Ḥijāz
SAUDI ARABIA
Shaqrā'
AR RIYĀḌ (Riyadh)
Al Madīnah (Medina)
Yanbu 'al Baḥr
Tropic of Cancer
As Sulaymānīyah
Harad
Rābigh
JIDDAH (Jedda)
Makkah (Mecca)
Aṭ Ṭā'if
Turabah
Al Līth
Layla
As Sulayyil
Al Qunfudhah
'Asīr
Tihāmah
Khamīs Mushayṭ
Abhā
Najrān
Jīzān
Farasān
Ash Sharawrah
Al Jubayl
Al Qaṭīf
Ad Dammām
Az Zahrān (Dhahran)
BAHRAIN
Al Manāmah
QATAR
Al Mubarraz
Al Hufūf
Ad Dawḥah (Doha)
Persian Gulf
Qeys
Str. of Hormuz
Ra's Musandam (Oman)
Ra's al-Khaymah
Ash Shāriqah (Sharjah)
Dubayy (Dubai)
Abū Ẓaby (Abu Dhabi)
Al Fujayrah
Ṣuḥār
Gulf of Oman
Al 'Ayn
Ruwais
UNITED ARAB EMIRATES
As Suwayq
As Sīb
Maṭraḥ
Masqaṭ (Muscat)
'Ibrī
Izkī
Nizwá
Ṣūr
Ra's al Hadd
Al 'Ubaylah
Rub' al Khālī (Empty Quarter)
OMAN
Maṣīrah
Khalūf
Khalīj Maṣīrah
Haymā'
Ra's al Madrakah
Ẓufār
Ṣalālah
Mirbāṭ
J. al Hallāniyat
Ḥaḍramawt
Shibām
Ra's Fartak
Sayḥūt
Ash Shiḥr
Al Mukallā
YEMEN
Ḥajjah
SANA'
Khamir
Al Luḥayyah
Kamarān
Al Ḥudaydah
Dhamār
Ibb
J. Mānār
Ta'izz
Al Mukhā
Niṣāb
Shaqrā'
Aḥwar
Al 'Adan (Aden)
Madinat ash Sha'b
Bab el Mandeb
Gulf of Aden
Socotra (Yemen)
Ḥadiboh
'Abd al Kūrī (Yemen)
EGYPT
Hurghada
Bûr Safâga
Quseir
Qena
KARNAK
THEBES
El Uqsur (Luxor)
Isna
Idfû
Kôm Ombo
Aswân
Sadd el Aali
Marsa Alam
Ras Bânâs
Bir Shalatein
Buheirat en Naser (L. Nasser)
Halaib Triangle
Halaib
Wadi Halfa
Sahrâ Nûbîya
Muhammad Qol
Ras Abu Shagara
RED SEA
G. Mûsa
Sharm el Sheikh
G. of Aqaba
Khalig el Suweis
Abu Hamed
Nahr en Nil (Nile)
5th Cataract
6th Cataract
Bûr Sûdân
Suakin
Sinkat
Trinkitat
Haiya
Karora
Berber
Atbara
Adarama
Nahr 'Atbara
Wad Hamid
Shendi
Debba
Omdurmân
EL KHARTÛM (Khartoum)
Kassalâ
Khashm el Girba
Wâd Medanî
Gedaref
Gezira
Ed Dueim
Kôstî
Singa
Umm Ruwaba
Jibalan Nubah
Nil el Azraq (Blue Nile)
Nil el Abyad (White Nile)
Ed Damazin
Roseires Res.
SUDAN
Malakâl
Sobat
Dembidolo
Pibor Post
Bôr
Tali Post
Mongalla
Juba
Kapoeta
Elemi Triangle
Torit
Kajo Kaji
Yei
ERITREA
Nakfa
Akordat
Asmera
Mitsiwa
Zula
Dahlak Kebir
Danakil Desert
Adigrat
Aksum
Adwa
Mekele
Metema
Ras Dashen
Gonder
L. Tana
Bahir Dar
Debre Tabor
Lalibela
Dese
Debre Markos
Abay (Blue Nile)
Bure
Ethiopian Highlands
Nekemte
ADDIS ABEBA
Debre Zeyit
Awash
Nazret
Asela
Ziway
ETHIOPIA
Metu
Gore
Jima
Awasa
Shashemene
Ginir
Goba
Yirga Alem
L. Abaya
Arba Minch
L. Shamo
Dila
Kibre Mengist
Negele
Omo
Chew Bahir
Lokitaung
L. Turkana
Mega
Moyale
El Wak
Dolo
Genale
Shebele
Imi
Kebri Dehar
Ogaden
Asseb
Hanish
DJIBOUTI
Djibouti
Tadjoura
L. Assal
L. Abbé
Dikhil
Tendaho
Saylac
Dire Dawa
Harer
Jijiga
Berbera
Somaliland
Hargeisa
Burco (Burao)
Karin
Boosaaso
Ceerigaabo
El Gal
Xaafuun
Ras Xaafuun
Bereeda
Ras Asir
Qardho (Gardo)
Bender Beyla
Garoowe
Las Anod (Laascaanood)
Eyl
Puntland
Gaalkacyo (Galcaio)
Hobyo
Sina Dhago
SOMALI REPUBLIC
Ferfer
Beledweyne (Belet Uen)
Ceeldheere
Baydhabo (Baidoa)
Luuq (Lugh)
Jawhar (Giohar)
Buurhakaba (Bur Acaba)
Wanleweyne (Uanle Uen)
MUQDISHO (Mogadishu)
Marka (Merca)
Baardheere
Juba (Giuba)
Shabeelle (Scebeli)
Dif
Jamaame (Giamama)
Jilib (Gelib)
Equator
Kismaayo (Chisimaio)
INDIAN OCEAN
Wajir
Marsabit
South Horr
Lodwar
Turkwel
KENYA
Kitale
UGANDA
Gulu
Lira
Moroto
Soroti
Mt. Elgon
Mbale
Masindi
L. Kyoga
L. Albert
Arua
Pakwach
Murchison Falls
Albert Nile

Projection: Sanson-Flamsteed's Sinusoidal
45 East from Greenwich
COPYRIGHT PHILIP'S

Sand deserts

ft m
12 000 4000
9000 3000
6000 2000
4500 1500
3000 1000
1200 400
600 200
0 0
200 600
1000 3000
2000 6000
4000 12 000
m ft

1:42 000 000

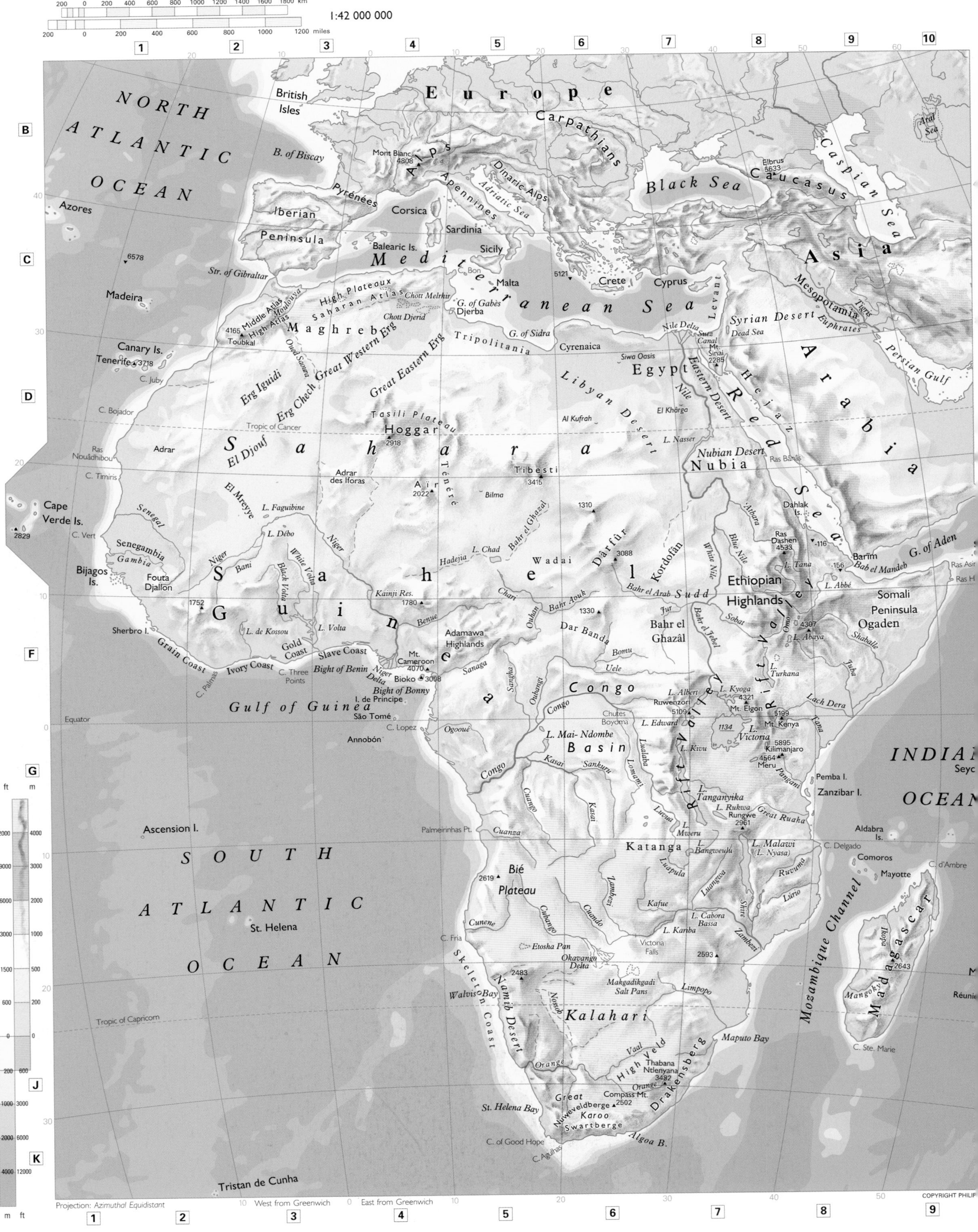

NORTH ATLANTIC OCEAN
British Isles
Europe
Carpathians
B. of Biscay
Mont Blanc 4808
Alps
Dinaric Alps
Apennines
Adriatic Sea
Black Sea
Elbrus 5633
Caucasus
Caspian Sea
Aral Sea
Azores
Pyrénées
Iberian Peninsula
Corsica
Sardinia
Balearic Is.
Sicily
6578
Mediterranean Sea
C. Bon
Malta
5121
Crete
Cyprus
Levant
Asia
Mesopotamia
Tigris
Euphrates
Str. of Gibraltar
Madeira
High Plateaux
Saharan Atlas
Chott Melrhir
G. of Gabès
Djerba
Chott Djerid
Middle Atlas
High Atlas
Moulouya
4165 Toubkal
Maghreb
Great Western Erg
Tripolitania
G. of Sidra
Cyrenaica
Nile Delta
Suez Canal
Mt. Sinai 2285
Syrian Desert
Dead Sea
Persian Gulf
Canary Is.
Tenerife 3718
C. Juby
Oued Saoura
Erg Iguidi
Erg Chech
Great Eastern Erg
Siwa Oasis
Egypt
Libyan Desert
Eastern Desert
Nile
Hejaz
Red Sea
Arabia
C. Bojador
Tropic of Cancer
Tasili Plateau
Hoggar 2918
El Khârga
Al Kufrah
L. Nasser
Adrar
El Djouf
Sahara
Tibesti 3415
Ras Nouâdhibou
Nubian Desert
Nubia
Ras Banâs
C. Timiris
Adrar des Iforas
Aïr 2022
Ténéré
Bilma
Cape Verde Is.
2829
C. Vert
Senegal
El Mreyyé
L. Faguibine
1310
Atbara
Dahlak Is.
L. Débo
Niger
Bahr el Ghazal
Ras Dashen 4533
-116
Barim
G. of Aden
Bab el Mandeb
Senegambia
Gambia
Bani
White Volta
Black Volta
Hadejia
L. Chad
Dârfûr 3088
Wadai
Sahel
Kordofân
White Nile
Blue Nile
L. Tana
-156
Ras Asir
Ras Hafun
Bijagos Is.
Fouta Djallon
Kainji Res.
1780
Chari
Bahr Aouk
Bahr el Arab
Sudd
Ethiopian Highlands
L. Abbé
Somali Peninsula
1752
Guinea
Benue
1330
Jur
Bahr el Ghazâl
Sobat
Omo
4307
L. Abaya
Ogaden
Shabelle
Sherbro I.
L. de Kossou
L. Volta
Gold Coast
Slave Coast
Ouham
Dar Banda
Bahr el Jebel
Rift Valley
Grain Coast
Ivory Coast
C. Palmas
C. Three Points
Bight of Benin
Niger Delta
Mt. Cameroon 4070
Bioko 3008
Adamawa Highlands
Sanaga
Sangha
Oubangi
Bomu
Uele
L. Turkana
Juba
Bight of Bonny
I. de Principe
São Tomé
Gulf of Guinea
Congo
L. Albert
Ruwenzori 5109
L. Kyoga 4321
Mt. Elgon
Lach Dera
Tana
Equator
C. Lopez
Annobón
Ogooué
Chutes Boyoma
L. Edward
1134
L. Victoria
5199 Mt. Kenya
L. Mai-Ndombe Basin
Lualaba
L. Kivu
5895 Kilimanjaro
4564 Meru
Kasai
Sankuru
Lomami
Pangani
INDIAN OCEAN
Seychelles
Pemba I.
Zanzibar I.
L. Tanganyika
L. Rukwa
Rungwe 2961
Great Ruaha
Cuango
Lueua
L. Mweru
Ascension I.
Palmeirinhas Pt.
Cuanza
Katanga
L. Bangweulu
L. Malawi (L. Nyasa)
C. Delgado
Aldabra Is.
Comoros
Mayotte
C. d'Ambre
SOUTH ATLANTIC OCEAN
Bié Plateau
2619
Luapula
Zambezi
Ruvuma
Lurio
Kafue
Luangwa
Shire
Cubango
Cuando
L. Cabora Bassa
L. Kariba
Cunene
St. Helena
C. Fria
Etosha Pan
Okavango Delta
Victoria Falls
2593
Mozambique Channel
Madagascar
Ihosy
2643
Skeleton Coast
2483
Walvis Bay
Makgadikgadi Salt Pans
Limpopo
Mangoky
Réunion
Tropic of Capricorn
Namib Desert
Nossob
Kalahari
Maputo Bay
C. Ste. Marie
Vaal
High Veld
Thabana Ntlenyana 3482
Orange
Drakensberg
Great Karoo
Compass Mt. 2502
St. Helena Bay
Nuweveldberge
Swartberge
Algoa B.
C. of Good Hope
C. Agulhas
Tristan de Cunha
Projection: Azimuthal Equidistant
West from Greenwich
East from Greenwich

1:42 000 000

200 0 200 400 600 800 1000 1200 1400 1600 1800 km

200 0 200 400 600 800 1000 1200 miles

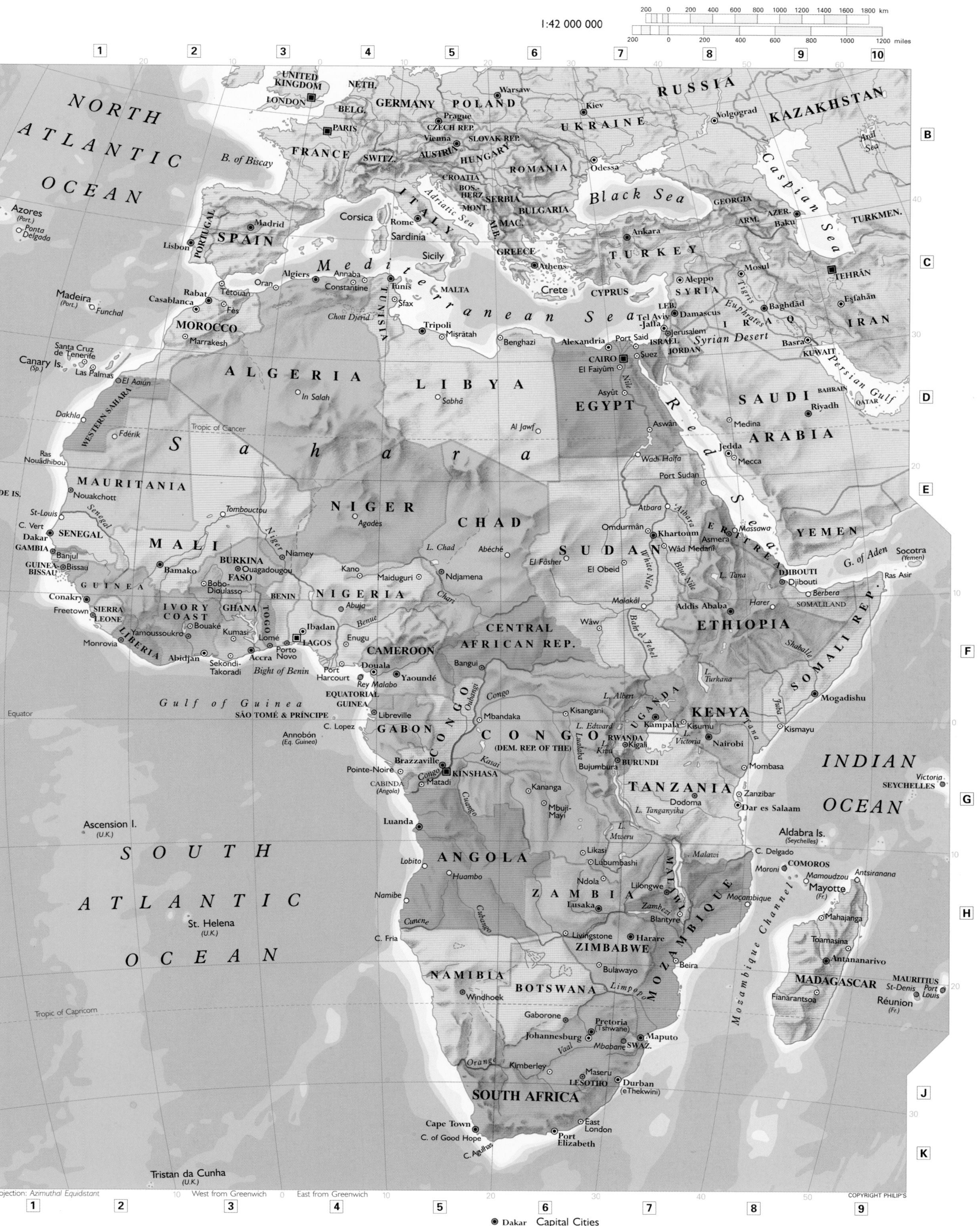

Dakar Capital Cities

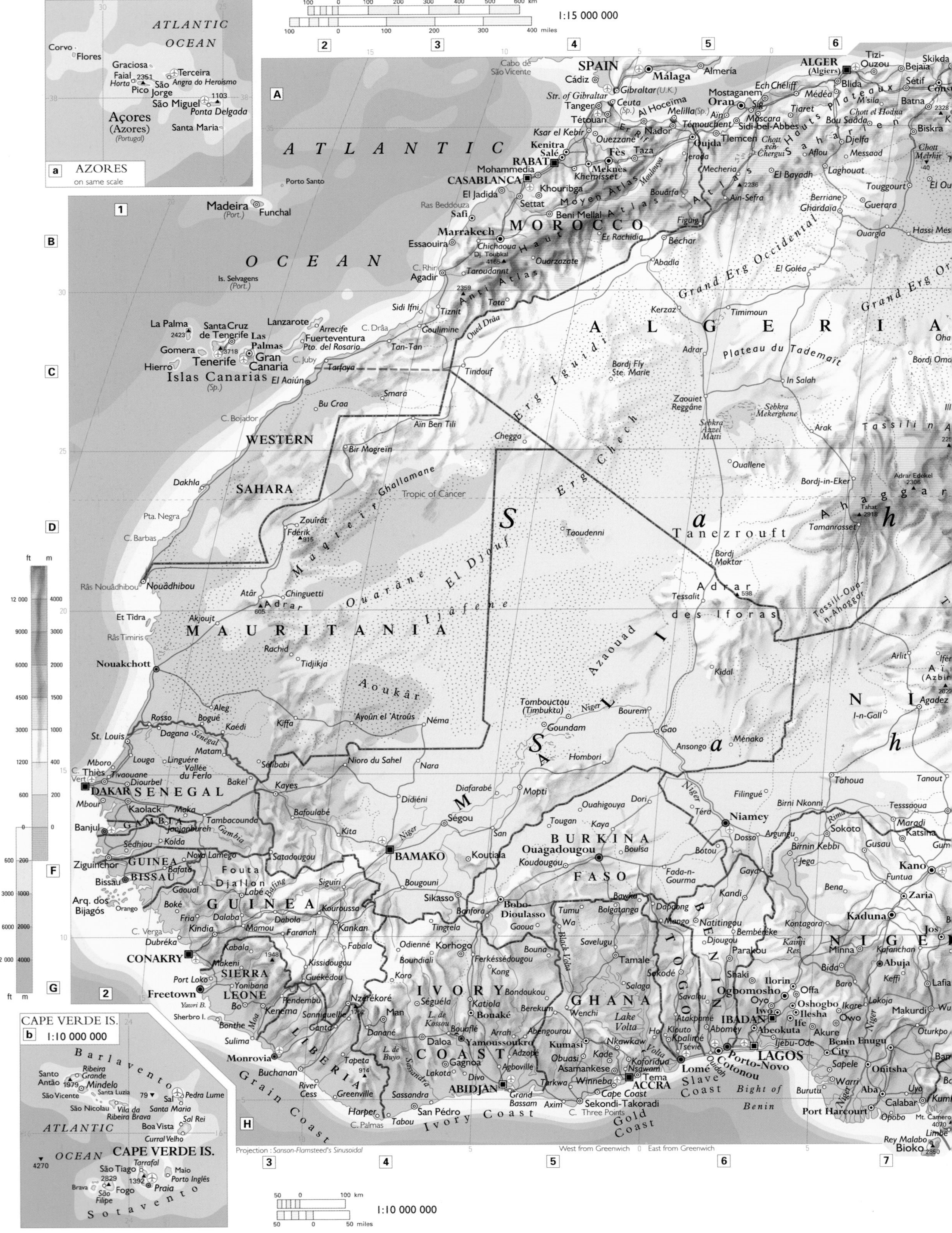
1:15 000 000
ATLANTIC OCEAN
Corvo
Flores
Graciosa
Faial
Horta
Terceira
Angra do Heroísmo
Pico
São Jorge
São Miguel
Ponta Delgada
Açores
(Azores)
(Portugal)
Santa Maria
AZORES
on same scale
Porto Santo
Madeira
(Port.)
Funchal
Is. Selvagens
(Port.)
La Palma
Santa Cruz de Tenerife
Las Palmas
Lanzarote
Arrecife
Fuerteventura
Pto. del Rosario
Gomera
Tenerife
Gran Canaria
Hierro
Islas Canarias
(Sp.)
SPAIN
Cádiz
Málaga
Almería
Gibraltar (U.K.)
Str. of Gibraltar
Tanger
Ceuta
(Sp.)
Tétouan
Al Hoceima
Melilla (Sp.)
Nador
Ksar el Kebir
Ouezzane
Kenitra
Salé
RABAT
Mohammedia
CASABLANCA
Meknès
Fès
Taza
Khemisset
El Jadida
Khouribga
Settat
Safi
Ras Beddouza
Beni Mellal
Marrakech
Essaouira
Chichaoua
Dj. Toubkal
4165
Ouarzazate
Taroudannt
Agadir
C. Rhir
Moyen Atlas
Haut Atlas
Anti Atlas
MOROCCO
Er Rachidia
Bouârfa
Figuig
Oujda
Tlemcen
Sidi-bel-Abbès
Oran
Mostaganem
Mascara
Tiaret
Ech Chéliff
Médéa
Blida
ALGER
(Algiers)
Tizi-Ouzou
Bejaïa
Skikda
Sétif
Batna
M'sila
Bou Saâda
Chott el Hodna
Biskra
Djelfa
Aflou
Messaad
Laghouat
El Bayadh
Mecheria
Aïn-Sefra
Chott ech Chergui
Hauts Plateaux
Saharien Atlas
Touggourt
El Oued
Ghardaïa
Berriane
Guerara
Ouargla
Hassi Messaoud
Béchar
Abadla
Grand Erg Occidental
Grand Erg Oriental
El Goléa
Sidi Ifni
Tiznit
Goulimine
Tata
Oued Drâa
C. Drâa
Tan-Tan
C. Juby
Tarfaya
El Aaiún
Tindouf
Smara
Bu Craa
C. Bojador
WESTERN SAHARA
Aïn Ben Tili
Bir Mogrein
Dakhla
Pta. Negra
C. Barbas
Tropic of Cancer
Zouîrât
Fdérik
915
Chegga
Erg Iguidi
Erg Chech
Kerzaz
Timimoun
Adrar
ALGERIA
Plateau du Tademaït
Bordj Fly Ste. Marie
In Salah
Zaouiet Reggâne
Sebkra Mekerghene
Sebkra Azzel Matti
Arak
Tassili n Ajjer
Ouallene
Bordj-in-Eker
Adrar Edekel
Ahaggar
Tahat
2918
Tamanrasset
Tanezrouft
Bordj Moktar
Taoudenni
Tessalit
Adrar des Iforas
Tassili-Oua-n-Ahaggar
Râs Nouâdhibou
Nouâdhibou
Atâr
Chinguetti
Adrar
El Djouf
Ouarâne
Majâbat al Koubrâ
Ijâfene
Et Tidra
Akjoujt
Râs Timiris
MAURITANIA
Rachid
Tidjikja
Nouakchott
Aoukâr
Aleg
Rosso
Bogué
Kaédi
Kiffa
'Ayoûn el 'Atroûs
Néma
St. Louis
Dagana
Sénégal
Matam
Louga
Linguére
Vallée du Ferlo
Mboro
Thiès
Tivaouane
C. Vert
Diourbel
DAKAR
SENEGAL
Bakel
Mbour
Kaolack
Kayes
Sélibabi
Nioro du Sahel
Nara
Banjul
GAMBIA
Tambacounda
Sédhiou
Kolda
Ziguinchor
GUINEA-BISSAU
Bissau
Bafatá
Arq. dos Bijagós
Orango
Gaoual
Fouta Djallon
Labé
Boké
GUINEA
Fria
Dalaba
Kindia
Mamou
Dabola
Faranah
Kouroussa
Kankan
C. Verga
Dubréka
CONAKRY
Kabala
Makeni
SIERRA LEONE
Port Loko
Freetown
Yonibana
Bo
Kenema
Sherbro I.
Bonthe
Sulima
Monrovia
LIBERIA
Buchanan
River Cess
Greenville
Harper
C. Palmas
Grain Coast
MALI
Tombouctou
(Timbuktu)
Niger
Goundam
Bourem
Gao
Ansongo
Ménako
Kidal
Azaouad
Hombori
Mopti
Diafarabé
Ségou
San
Kita
Bafoulabé
Didiéni
BAMAKO
Koutiala
Sikasso
Bougouni
Siguiri
Satadougou
Kolokani
Banfora
Bobo-Dioulasso
Gaoua
BURKINA FASO
Ouagadougou
Koudougou
Ouahigouya
Kaya
Tougan
Dori
Boulsa
Fada-n-Gourma
Tingréla
Odienné
Korhogo
Boundiali
Ferkéssédougou
Kong
Bouna
IVORY COAST
Séguéla
Katiola
Bouaké
Bondoukou
Man
Daloa
Bouaflé
Yamoussoukro
Gagnoa
Danané
Lakota
Divo
Agboville
Adzopé
ABIDJAN
Grand Bassam
Sassandra
San Pédro
Tabou
Ivory Coast
Guékédou
Kissidougou
Nzérékoré
Koro
Tapeta
Sanniquellie
Ganta
GHANA
Tumu
Wa
Bolgatanga
Bawku
Tamale
Salaga
Wenchi
Kumasi
Obuasi
Asamankese
Nkawkaw
Koforidua
Tarkwa
Axim
Winneba
Cape Coast
Sekondi-Takoradi
C. Three Points
ACCRA
Tema
Lake Volta
Gold Coast
Black Volta
TOGO
Dapaong
Mango
Sokodé
Atakpamé
Kpalimé
Tsévié
Lomé
BENIN
Natitingou
Djougou
Parakou
Abomey
Ouidah
Porto-Novo
Cotonou
Slave Coast
Bight of Benin
NIGER
Niamey
Téra
Filingué
Dosso
Gaya
Tahoua
Tanout
Birni Nkonni
Tessaoua
Maradi
Agadez
Arlit
Aïr
I-n-Gall
NIGERIA
Sokoto
Argungu
Birnin Kebbi
Jega
Gusau
Katsina
Kano
Funtua
Zaria
Kandi
Bembéréké
Kainji Res.
Kontagora
Kaduna
Minna
Bida
Abuja
Kafanchan
Keffi
Jos
Shaki
Ilorin
Ogbomosho
Offa
Oyo
Oshogbo
Iwo
Ilesha
IBADAN
Ife
Abeokuta
Akure
Owo
Ikare
Lokoja
Makurdi
Ijebu-Ode
LAGOS
Benin City
Enugu
Sapele
Onitsha
Warri
Aba
Uyo
Burutu
Port Harcourt
Opobo
Calabar
Mt. Cameroon
4070
Limbe
Bioko
Rey Malabo
2850
Projection : Sanson-Flamsteed's Sinusoidal
West from Greenwich
East from Greenwich
CAPE VERDE IS.
1:10 000 000
Barlavento
Santo Antão
Ribeira Grande
1979
Mindelo
São Vicente
Santa Luzia
Sal
Pedra Lume
São Nicolau
Vila da Ribeira Brava
Santa Maria
Sal Rei
Boa Vista
Curral Velho
ATLANTIC OCEAN
CAPE VERDE IS.
Tarrafal
São Tiago
2829
Maio
Porto Inglês
Brava
São Filipe
Fogo
Praia
Sotavento
4270
1:10 000 000

MEDITERRANEAN SEA
GREECE
TURKEY
CYPRUS
SYRIA
LEBANON
ISRAEL
JORDAN
IRAQ
LIBYA
EGYPT
SAUDI ARABIA
RED SEA
SUDAN
CHAD
CENTRAL AFRICAN REPUBLIC
ERITREA
ETHIOPIA
ITALY
MALTA
TUNIS
TARĀBULUS (Tripoli)
Banghāzī
EL ISKANDARÎYA (Alexandria)
EL QÂHIRA (Cairo)
EL KHARTÛM (Khartoum)
Omdurmân
Ndjamena
Bangui
BAYRŪT (Beirut)
DIMASHQ (Damascus)
'AMMĀN
TEL AVIV-YAFO
Jerusalem
HALAB (Aleppo)
ADANA
Antalya
Sahrâ' Rebiana
Sarîr Calanscio
Es Sahrâ el Gharbîya
Es Sahrâ en Nûbîya
Tibesti
Aozou Strip
Borkou
Ennedi
Dâr Fûr
Kordofân
Bahr el Ghazâl
Es Sûdd
El Istwa'iya
Lac Tchad
Fezzan
Barqa (Cyrenaica)
Tarābulus (Tripolitania)
Hadabat el Gilf el Kebîr
Halaib Triangle
Elemi Triangle
COPYRIGHT PHILIPS

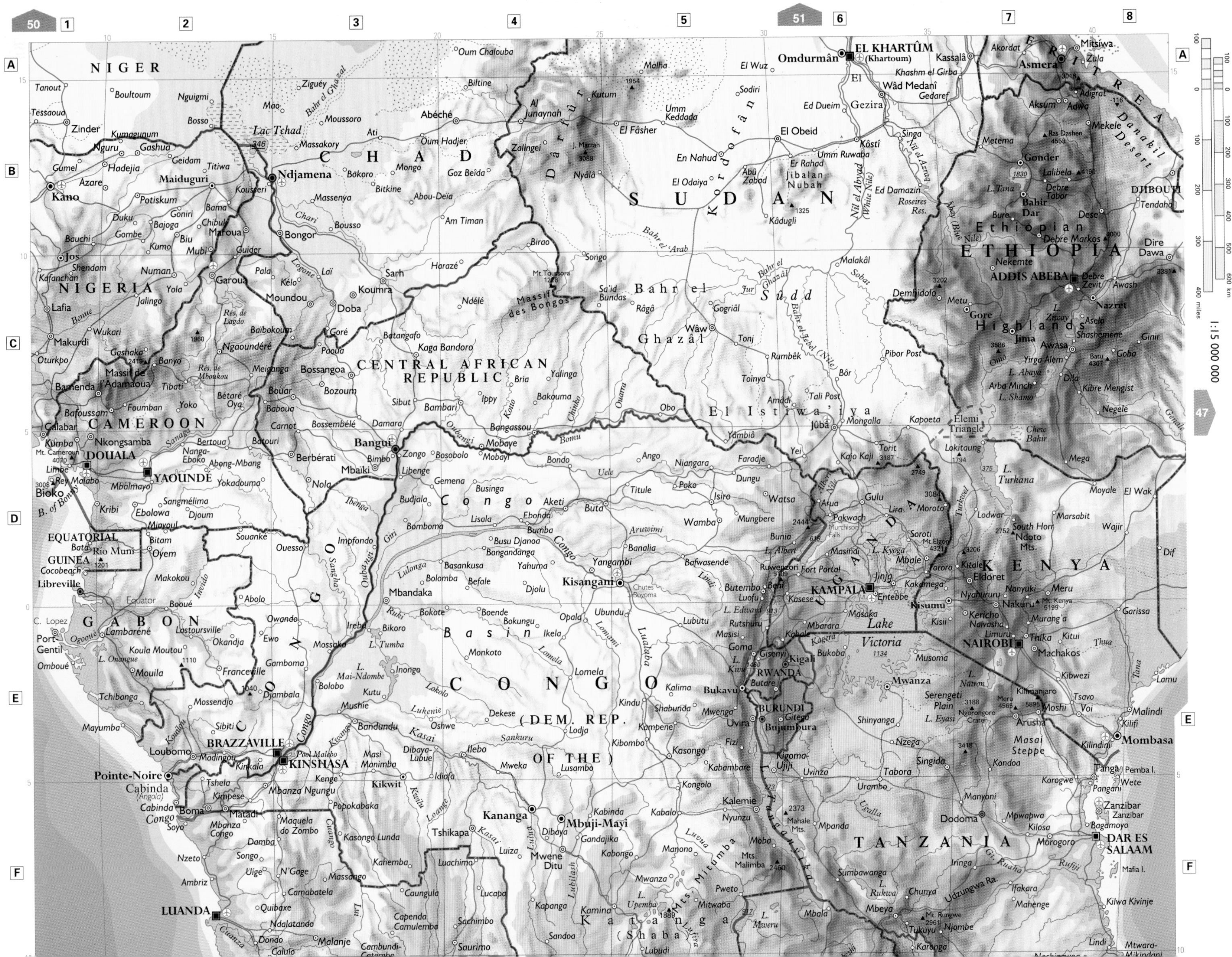

100 0 100 200 300 400 500 600 km
100 0 100 200 300 400 miles
1:15 000 000
47
51
50
NIGER
NIGERIA
CHAD
SUDAN
ERITREA
DJIBOUTI
ETHIOPIA
CAMEROON
CENTRAL AFRICAN REPUBLIC
EQUATORIAL GUINEA
GABON
CONGO
CONGO (DEM. REP. OF THE)
UGANDA
KENYA
RWANDA
BURUNDI
TANZANIA
EL KHARTÛM (Khartoum)
Omdurmân
ADDIS ABEBA
Ndjamena
Bangui
YAOUNDÉ
DOUALA
Libreville
BRAZZAVILLE
KINSHASA
LUANDA
KAMPALA
NAIROBI
DAR ES SALAAM
Mombasa
Kisangani
Lac Tchad
Lake Victoria
Ethiopian Highlands
Congo Basin
Massif des Bongos
Sudd
Bahr el Ghazâl
El Istiwa'iya
Kordofân
Dârfûr
Danakil Desert
Serengeti Plain
Masai Steppe
Katanga (Shaba)
Elemi Triangle
Asmera
Kano
Maiduguri
Garoua
Kisumu
Bujumbura
Kigali
Dodoma
Zanzibar
Pointe-Noire
Mbuji-Mayi
Kananga

COMOROS
1:8 000 000

MADAGASCAR
on same scale as main map

1:8 000 000

1:2 500 000

MAURITIUS
1:2 500 000

RÉUNION
1:2 500 000

SEYCHELLES
1:2 500 000

Projection: Sanson-Flamsteed's Sinusoidal

50 0 50 100 150 200 250 300 km

1:8 000 000

50 0 50 100 150 200 miles

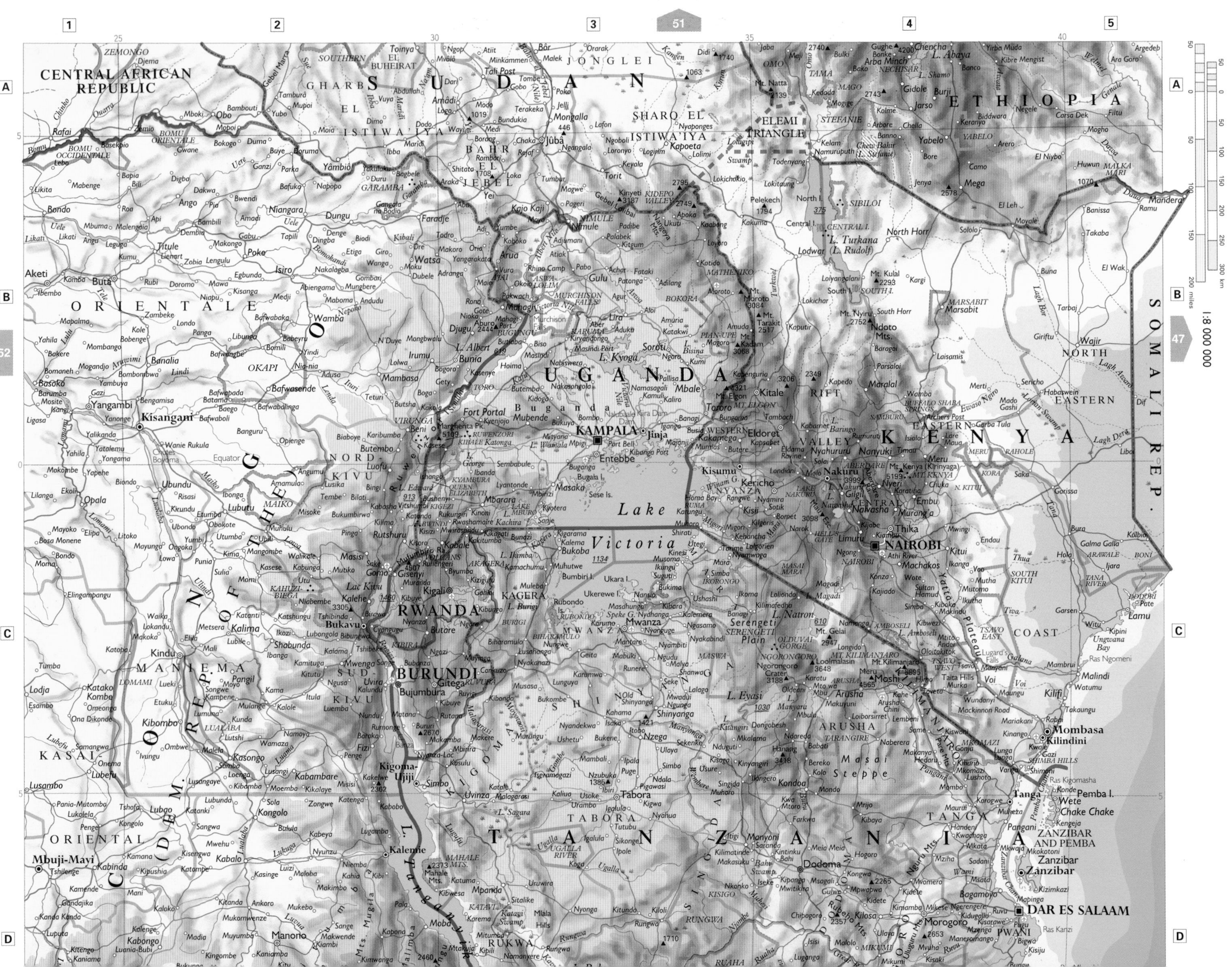

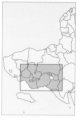

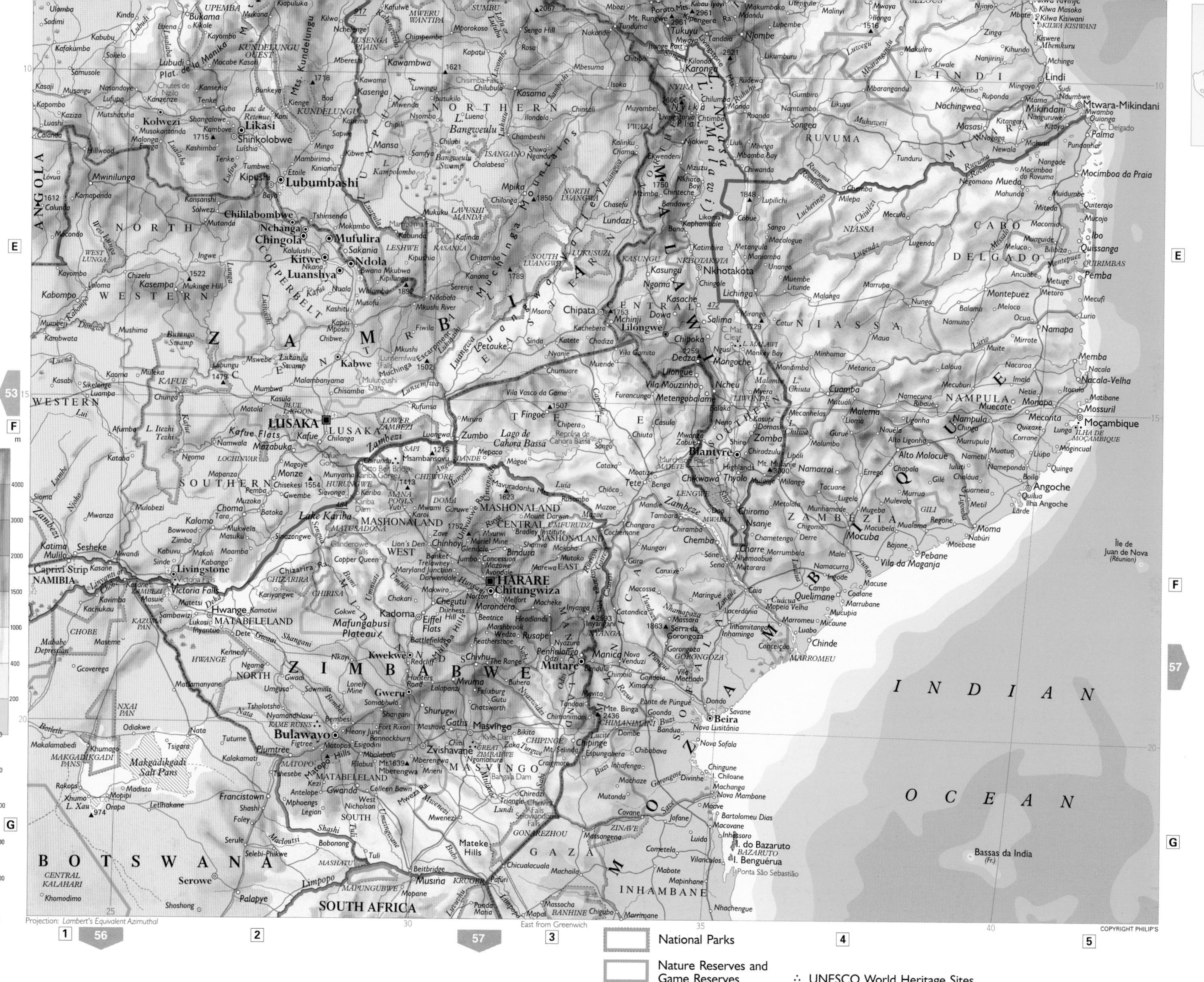
National Parks
Nature Reserves and Game Reserves
UNESCO World Heritage Sites
INDIAN OCEAN
Projection: Lambert's Equivalent Azimuthal
COPYRIGHT PHILIP'S

1:8 000 000

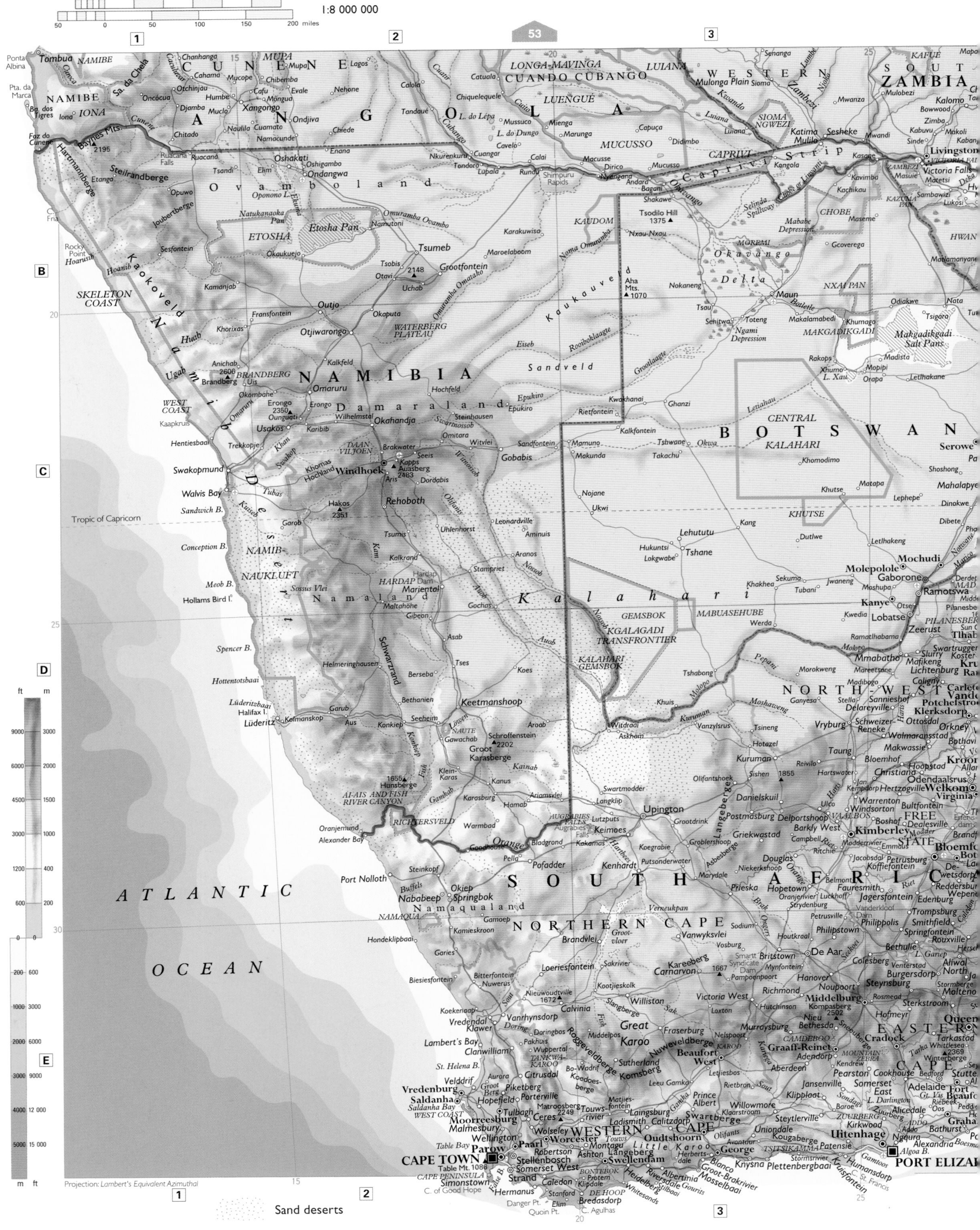

Sand deserts

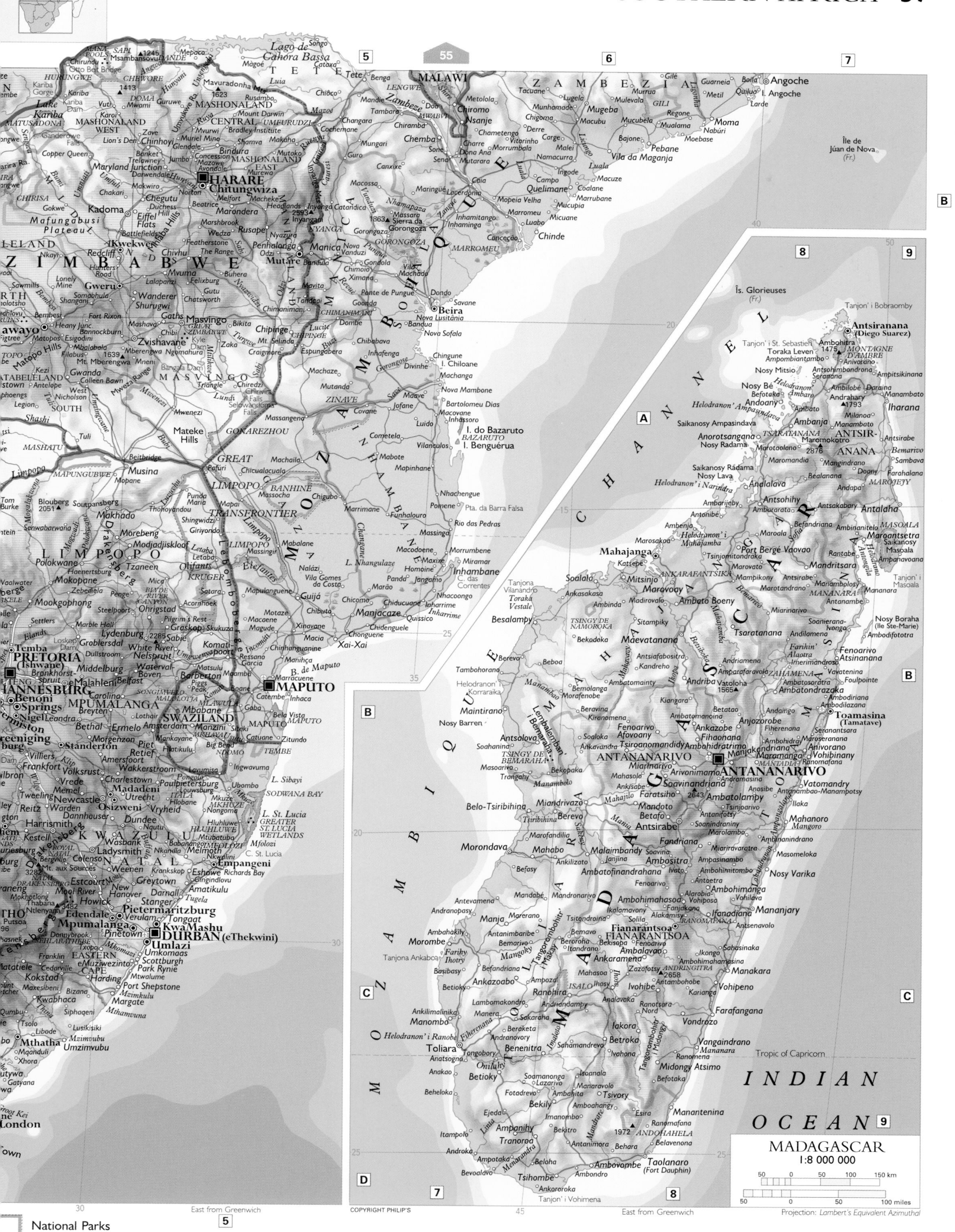

National Parks

Nature Reserves and Game Reserves

∴ UNESCO World Heritage Sites

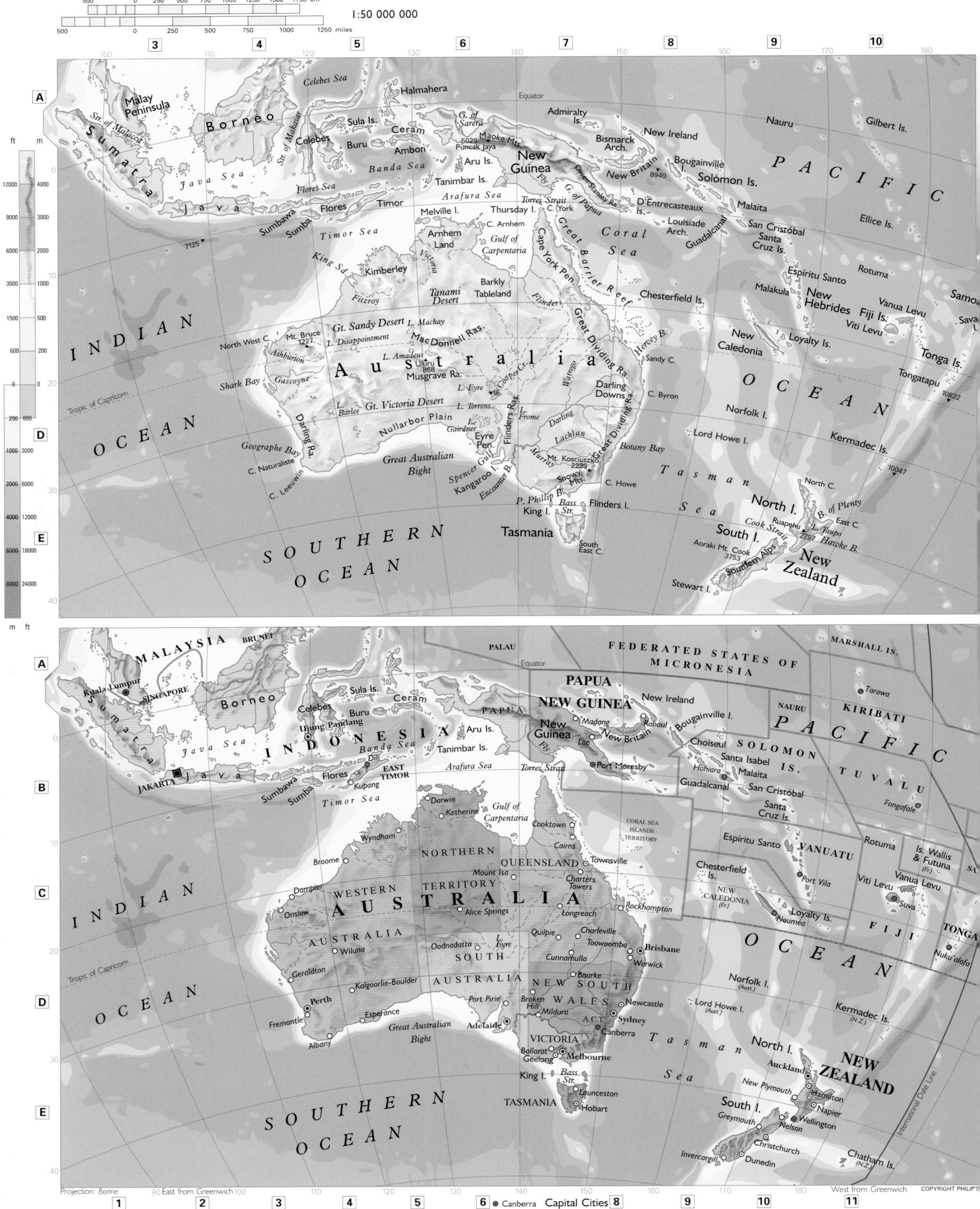
1:50 000 000
500 0 250 500 750 1000 1250 1500 1750 km
500 0 250 500 750 1000 1250 miles
Malay Peninsula
Str. of Malacca
Sumatra
Borneo
Celebes Sea
Str. of Makasar
Celebes
Halmahera
Sula Is.
Ceram
Buru
Ambon
Banda Sea
G. of Sarera
Maoke Mts.
5029 Puncak Jaya
Aru Is.
Tanimbar Is.
New Guinea
Fly
Owen Stanley Ra.
G. of Papua
Equator
Admiralty Is.
Bismarck Arch.
New Ireland
New Britain
8940
Bougainville I.
Solomon Is.
Nauru
Gilbert Is.
PACIFIC
Java Sea
Java
Flores Sea
Flores
Timor
Sumbawa
Sumba
7125
Arafura Sea
Torres Strait
Thursday I.
C. York
Melville I.
C. Arnhem
Arnhem Land
Gulf of Carpentaria
Cape York Pen.
Great Barrier Reef
Coral Sea
D'Entrecasteaux Is.
Louisiade Arch.
Guadalcanal
Malaita
San Cristóbal
Santa Cruz Is.
Ellice Is.
Timor Sea
King Sd.
Kimberley
Victoria
Barkly Tableland
Tanami Desert
Fitzroy
Flinders
Espíritu Santo
Rotuma
Malakula
New Hebrides
Vanua Levu
Fiji Is.
Viti Levu
Samoa
Sava
Chesterfield Is.
Gt. Sandy Desert
L. Mackay
Mt. Bruce 1227
L. Disappointment
North West C.
MacDonnell Ras.
Ashburton
L. Amadeus
Uluru 868
Musgrave Ra.
Australia
Great Dividing Ra.
Hervey B.
Sandy C.
New Caledonia
Loyalty Is.
Tonga Is.
Tongatapu
INDIAN OCEAN
Shark Bay
Gascoyne
Cooper Cr.
Warrego
L. Eyre
-16
Darling Downs
C. Byron
10822
Tropic of Capricorn
L. Barlee
Gt. Victoria Desert
L. Torrens
L. Frome
Darling
Norfolk I.
Nullarbor Plain
L. Gairdner
Darling Ra.
Eyre Pen.
Flinders Ras.
Lachlan
Lord Howe I.
Kermadec Is.
Geographe Bay
C. Naturaliste
C. Leeuwin
Great Australian Bight
Spencer Gulf
Kangaroo I.
Encounter B.
Murray
Mt. Kosciuszko 2230
Great Dividing Ra.
Snowy Mts.
Botany Bay
C. Howe
Tasman Sea
10047
North C.
North I.
B. of Plenty
East C.
Ruapehu 2797
L. Taupo
Hawke B.
Cook Strait
P. Phillip B.
Bass Str.
Flinders I.
King I.
Tasmania
South East C.
South I.
Aoraki Mt. Cook 3753
Southern Alps
New Zealand
Stewart I.
SOUTHERN OCEAN
OCEAN
ft m
12000 4000
9000 3000
6000 2000
3000 1000
1500 500
600 200
0 0
200 600
1000 3000
2000 6000
4000 12000
6000 18000
8000 24000
m ft
MALAYSIA
BRUNEI
Kuala Lumpur
SINGAPORE
PALAU
FEDERATED STATES OF MICRONESIA
MARSHALL IS.
PAPUA
PAPUA NEW GUINEA
Tarawa
NAURU
KIRIBATI
Ujung Pandang
INDONESIA
Madang
Lae
Rabaul
Port Moresby
Choiseul
SOLOMON IS.
Santa Isabel
Honiara
TUVALU
Fongafale
JAKARTA
Dili
EAST TIMOR
Kupang
Darwin
Katherine
CORAL SEA ISLANDS TERRITORY
Cooktown
Cairns
Wyndham
NORTHERN TERRITORY
QUEENSLAND
Townsville
Broome
Mount Isa
Charters Towers
VANUATU
Port Vila
Is. Wallis & Futuna (Fr.)
Dampier
WESTERN AUSTRALIA
AUSTRALIA
Alice Springs
Longreach
Rockhampton
Onslow
NEW CALEDONIA (Fr.)
Nouméa
Suva
FIJI
TONGA
Nuku'alofa
Wiluna
Oodnadatta
Quilpie
Charleville
Toowoomba
Brisbane
Cunnamulla
Warwick
SOUTH AUSTRALIA
Geraldton
Kalgoorlie-Boulder
Bourke
NEW SOUTH WALES
Norfolk I. (Aust.)
Port Pirie
Broken Hill
Newcastle
Lord Howe I. (Aust.)
Perth
Fremantle
Esperance
Mildura
Sydney
A.C.T.
Canberra
Kermadec Is. (N.Z.)
Adelaide
Albany
VICTORIA
Ballarat
Geelong
Melbourne
Auckland
NEW ZEALAND
New Plymouth
Hamilton
Napier
Launceston
Hobart
TASMANIA
Wellington
Greymouth
Nelson
Christchurch
Invercargill
Dunedin
Chatham Is. (N.Z.)
International Date Line
Projection: Bonne
East from Greenwich
West from Greenwich
Canberra Capital Cities
COPYRIGHT PHILIP'S

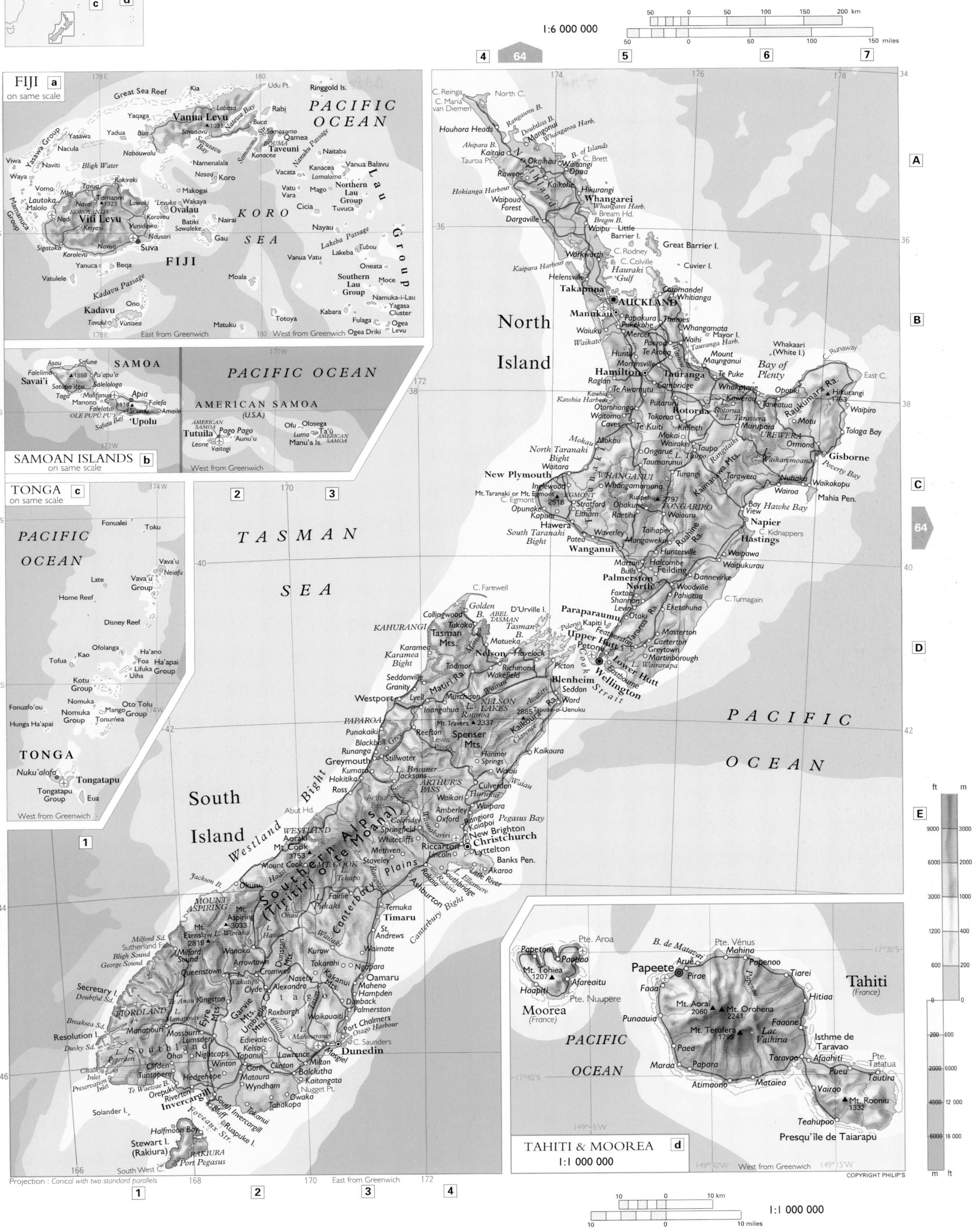

1:6 000 000

50 0 50 100 150 200 km

50 0 50 100 150 miles

4 64 5 6 7

FIJI a
on same scale

Great Sea Reef
Kia
Udu Pt.
Ringgold Is.
PACIFIC OCEAN
Vanua Levu
Labasa
Natewa Bay
Rabi
Yaqaga
Yasawa
Yadua
Bua
Savusavu
Buca
Somosomo
Qamea
Taveuni
Nabouwalu
Nacula
Yasawa Group
BOUMA
Kanacea
Naitaba
Viwa
Naviti
Bligh Water
Namenalala
Vanua Balavu
Waya
Nasau
Koro
Vacata
Kanacea
Lomaloma
Vomo
Rakiraki
Tavua
Makogai
Vatu Vara
Mago
Northern Lau Group
Lautoka
Malolo
Mba
Tomanivi 1323
Navai
Lowaki
Levuka
Wakaya
Ovalau
Cicia
Tuvuca
Mamanuca Group
Nadi
Viti Levu
KOROYANITU
Keiyasi
Vunidawa
Korovou
Batiki
Sawaleke
Nairai
KORO
Nayau
Lau Group
Navua
Nausori
Suva
Gau
SEA
Lakeba Passage
Tubou
Lakeba
Sigatoka
Korolevu
Vanua Vatu
Yanuca
Beqa
FIJI
Oneata
Vatulele
Moala
Southern Lau Group
Moce
Kadavu Passage
Namuka-i-Lau
Yagasa Cluster
Ono
Kabara
Kadavu
Tavuki
Vunisea
Matuku
Totoya
Fulaga
Ogea Levu
Ogea Driki
178 E 180
East from Greenwich
West from Greenwich

SAMOAN ISLANDS b
on same scale

Asau
Safune
SAMOA
Falelima
1858
Pu'apu'a
Savai'i
Salelologa
Satupa'itea
Apia
Mulifanua
Falefa
Taga
Manono
Faleolo
Si'umu
1113
Amaile
OLE PUPU PU'E
Safata Bay
'Upolu
172W
170W
PACIFIC OCEAN
AMERICAN SAMOA (U.S.A.)
AMERICAN SAMOA
Tutuila
Pago Pago
'Aunu'u
Leone
Vaitogi
Ofu
Olosega
Ta'u
Luma
AMERICAN SAMOA
Manu'a Is.
West from Greenwich

TONGA c
on same scale

174 W
PACIFIC OCEAN
Fonualei
Toku
Vava'u
Neiafu
Late
Vava'u Group
Home Reef
Disney Reef
Ofolanga
Kao
Ha'ano
Tofua
Foa
Lifuka
Uiha
Ha'apai Group
Kotu Group
Nomuka
Oto Tolu Group
Fonuafo'ou
Nomuka Group
Mango
Tonumea
Hunga Ha'apai
TONGA
Nuku'alofa
Tongatapu
Tongatapu Group
Eua
West from Greenwich

North Island

C. Reinga
C. Maria van Diemen
North C.
Rangaunu B.
Doubtless B.
Mangonui
Whangaroa Harb.
Houhora Heads
Ahipara B.
Kaitaia
Northland
B. of Islands
C. Brett
Tauroa Pt.
Okaihau
Waitangi
Opua
Rawene
Kaikohe
Hikurangi
Hokianga Harbour
Whangarei
Whangarei Harb.
Waipoua Forest
Bream Hd.
Bream B.
Dargaville
Waipu
Little Barrier I.
Great Barrier I.
Warkworth
C. Rodney
C. Colville
Kaipara Harbour
Hauraki Gulf
Cuvier I.
Helensville
Takapuna
Coromandel
AUCKLAND
Whitianga
Manukau
Papakura
Thames
Pukekohe
Whangamata
Waiuku
Mercer
Waihi
Mayor I.
Waikato
Tauranga Harb.
Whakaari (White I.)
Huntly
Paeroa
Mount Maunganui
C. Runaway
Morrinsville
Te Aroha
Hamilton
Tauranga
Te Puke
Bay of Plenty
East C.
Raglan
Cambridge
Whakatane
Opotiki
Hikurangi 1753
Kawhia
Te Awamutu
Kawerau
Raukumara Ra.
Kawhia Harbour
Otorohanga
Putaruru
Rotorua
L. Rotorua
L. Tarawera
Te Aroha
Waipiro
Waitomo Caves
Tokoroa
Kinleith
Murupara
Te Kuiti
Ruatoria
Mokai
UREWERA
Motu
Tolaga Bay
Mokau
Wairakei
Taupo
Ormond
North Taranaki Bight
Ongarue
L. Taupo
Rangitaiki
L. Waikaremoana
Gisborne
Waitara
Taumarunui
Poverty Bay
New Plymouth
WHANGANUI
Turangi
Tarawera
Nuhaka
Inglewood
Whangamomona
Kaimanawa Mts.
Wairoa
Waikokopu
Mt. Taranaki or Mt. Egmont
EGMONT
Ruapehu
2797
C. Egmont
2518
Stratford
Ohakune
TONGARIRO
Mahia Pen.
Opunake
Eltham
Raetihi
Waiouru
Bay View
Hawke Bay
Kaponga
Hawera
Napier
South Taranaki Bight
Patea
Waverley
Taihape
Ruahine Ra.
Hastings
C. Kidnappers
Wanganui
Mangaweka
Waipawa
Hunterville
Waipukurau
Marton
Bulls
Halcombe
Feilding
Palmerston North
Dannevirke
Foxton
Woodville
Shannon
Pahiatua
C. Turnagain
Levin
Eketahuna
Otaki
Paraparaumu
Kapiti I.
Featherston
Tararua Ra.
Masterton
Upper Hutt
Carterton
Petone
Greytown
Lower Hutt
Martinborough
Eastbourne
L. Wairarapa
Wellington
Cook Strait

South Island

C. Farewell
Golden B.
ABEL TASMAN
D'Urville I.
Collingwood
Takaka
Tasman B.
KAHURANGI
Tasman Mts.
Pelorus Sd.
Karamea
Motueka
Karamea Bight
Nelson
Havelock
Picton
Tadmor
Richmond
Wakefield
Blenheim
Seddonville
Matiri Ra.
Wairau
Seddon
Granity
Murchison
NELSON LAKES
Awatere
Ward
Westport
Lyell
L. Rotoroa
Tapuae-o-Uenuku
Inangahua
2885
Kaikoura Ra.
PAPAROA
Mt. Travers 2337
Reefton
Clarence
Punakaiki
Lewis Pass
Spenser Mts.
Blackball
Kaikoura
Grey
Runanga
Hanmer Springs
Greymouth
Stillwater
L. Brunner
Kumara
Jacksons
Waiau
Hokitika
ARTHUR'S PASS
Culverden
Ross
Arthur's Pass
Hurunui
Waikari
Amberley
Waipara
Abut Hd.
Oxford
Rangiora
Pegasus Bay
WESTLAND
Coleridge
Kaiapoi
Aoraki Mt. Cook 3753
Springfield
New Brighton
Westland Bight
Whitecliffs
Riccarton
Christchurch
Lyttelton
Southern Alps (Tiritiri o te Moana)
Methven
Lincoln
Banks Pen.
Mount Cook
MT. COOK
Staveley
Plains
Akaroa
Jackson B.
Tekapo
Rangitata
L. Ellesmere
Rakaia
Southbridge
Little River
Okuru
Haast
Ashburton
Canterbury
MOUNT ASPIRING
Fairlie
Temuka
Mt. Aspiring 3033
L. Pukaki
Canterbury Bight
L. Ohau
Timaru
Mt. Earnslaw 2819
L. Wanaka
St. Andrews
Milford Sd.
Sutherland Falls
L. Hawea
Waitaki
Waimate
Bligh Sound
Milford Sound
Dunstan Mts.
George Sound
Wanaka
Kurow
Arrowtown
Tokarahi
Ngapara
Queenstown
Cromwell
Naseby
Kakanui Mts.
Oamaru
Secretary I.
Wakatipu
Alexandra
Maheno
Doubtful Sd.
Clyde
Otago
Hampden
Te Anau
Kingston
Garvie Mts.
Dunback
FIORDLAND
L. Manapouri
Eyre Mts.
Palmerston
Breaksea Sd.
Roxburgh
Waikouaiti
Manapouri
Umbrella Mts.
Port Chalmers
Resolution I.
Mossburn
Clutha
Otago Harbour
Lumsden
Edievale
Mahinerangi
Dusky Sd.
Ohai
Nightcaps
Kelso
C. Saunders
Southland
Tapanui
Lawrence
Dunedin
L. Poteriteri
Clifden
Winton
Gore
Clinton
Mosgiel
Chalky Inlet
Tuatapere
Milton
Preservation Inlet
Hedgehope
Mataura
Balclutha
Te Waewae B.
Wyndham
Kaitangata
Riverton
Nugget Pt.
Orepuki
Invercargill
Owaka
Tahakopa
Solander I.
Bluff
Foveaux Str.
South Invercargill
Tokanui
Ruapuke I.
Halfmoon Bay
Stewart I. (Rakiura)
RAKIURA
Port Pegasus
South West C.

TASMAN SEA

PACIFIC OCEAN

TAHITI & MOOREA d
1:1 000 000

Pte. Aroa
Papetoai
Paopao
Mt. Tohiea 1207
Afareaitu
Haapiti
Pte. Nuupere
Moorea (France)
PACIFIC OCEAN
B. de Matavai
Pte. Vénus
Mahina
Papenoo
Arue
Papeete
Pirae
Tiarei
Faaa
Tahiti (France)
Mt. Aorai 2060
Mt. Orohena 2241
Hitiaa
Punaauia
Faaone
Mt. Tetufera 1799
Lac Vaihiria
Isthme de Taravao
Paea
Taravao
Afaahiti
Pte. Tatatua
Maraa
Papara
Pueu
Tautira
Atimaono
Mataiea
Vairao
Mt. Rooniu 1332
Teahupoo
Presqu'île de Taiarapu
17°30'S
17°45'S
149°45'W
149°30'W
149°15'W
West from Greenwich

ft m
9000 3000
6000 2000
3000 1000
1200 400
600 200
0 0
200 600
2000 6000
4000 12 000
6000 18 000
m ft

Projection : Conical with two standard parallels

166 168 170 172
East from Greenwich

1 2 3 4

10 0 10 km
10 0 10 miles
1:1 000 000

1:8 000 000

0 50 100 150 200 250 300 km

0 50 100 150 200 miles

INDIAN OCEAN
SOUTHERN OCEAN
Great Australian Bight
Nullarbor Plain
Great Victoria Desert
SOUTH AUSTRALIA
Hampton Tableland
PERTH
Fremantle
Rockingham
Mandurah
Bunbury
Busselton
Albany
Esperance
Kalgoorlie-Boulder
Geraldton
Carnarvon
Norseman
Merredin
Northam
Narrogin
Katanning
Eucla
GREAT NORTHERN HWY
EYRE HWY
NORTH WEST COASTAL HWY
Shark Bay
Dirk Hartog I.
Houtman Abrolhos
L. Barlee
L. Moore
L. Austin
L. Carnegie
L. Wells
L. Dundas
L. Cowan
Archipelago of the Recherche
C. Leeuwin
C. Naturaliste
Robinson Ra.
Musgrave Ranges
Petermann Ranges
Everard Ranges
Aboriginal lands
Sand desert
East from Greenwich
Projection: Bonne
COPYRIGHT PHILIP'S
1. NGALIWURRU / NUNGALI
2. WANIMIYN
3. WAMBARDI
4. LIYALATUMA
5. RODNA
6. NTARIA
7. ROULPMAULPMA
8. URUNA

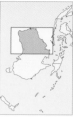

1:8 000 000

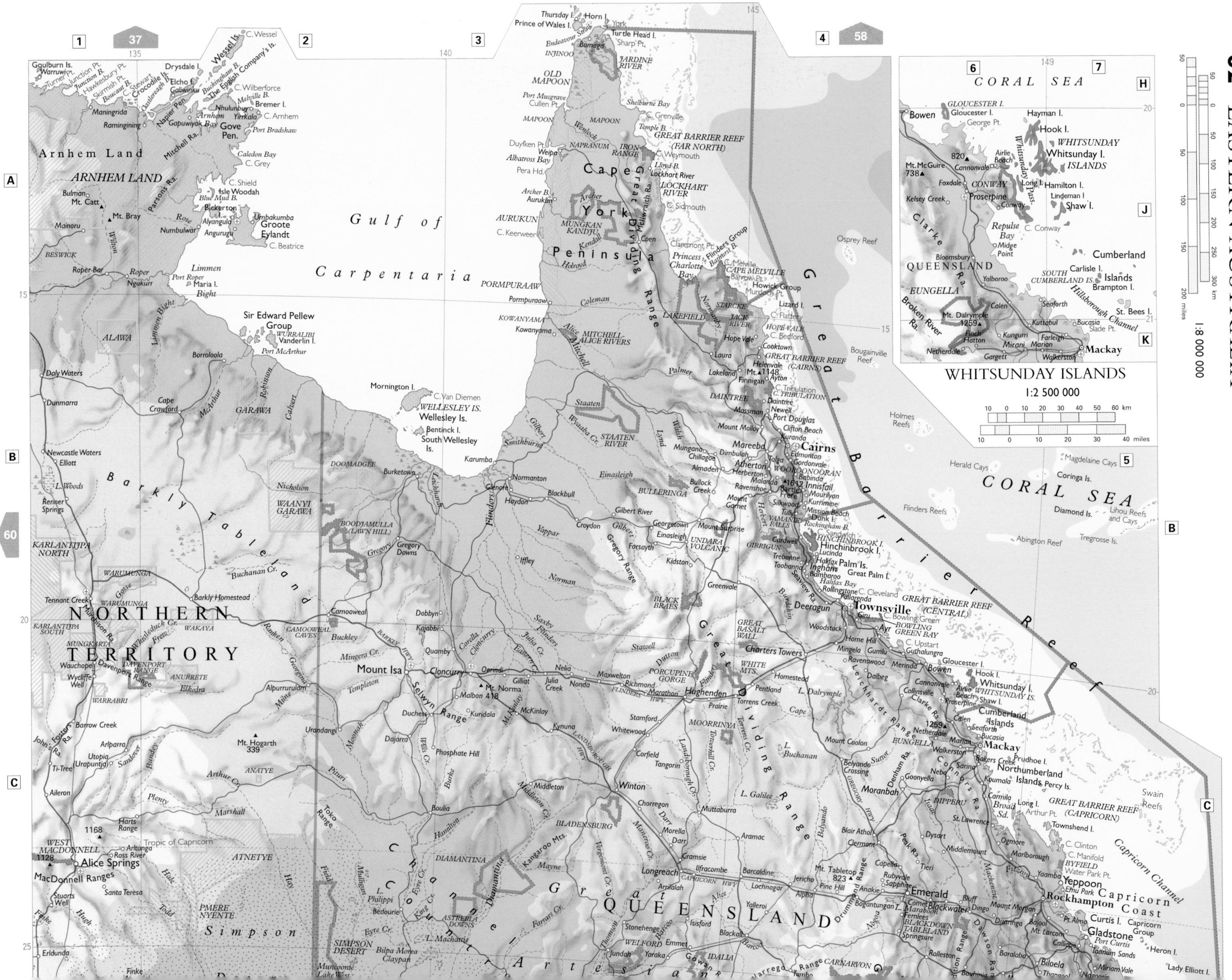

WHITSUNDAY ISLANDS
1:2 500 000
CORAL SEA
Whitsunday I.
Hook I.
Hayman I.
Bowen
Proserpine
Cumberland Islands
Mackay
Great Barrier Reef
Gulf of Carpentaria
Cape York Peninsula
Great Dividing Range
Arnhem Land
ARNHEM LAND
NORTHERN TERRITORY
QUEENSLAND
Barkly Tableland
Simpson
Channel Country
Cairns
Townsville
Rockhampton
Gladstone
Emerald
Longreach
Mount Isa
Cloncurry
Alice Springs
Tennant Creek
Groote Eylandt
Gove Pen.
Wellesley Is.
Mornington I.
Sir Edward Pellew Group
Capricorn Coast
Capricorn Channel
Tropic of Capricorn

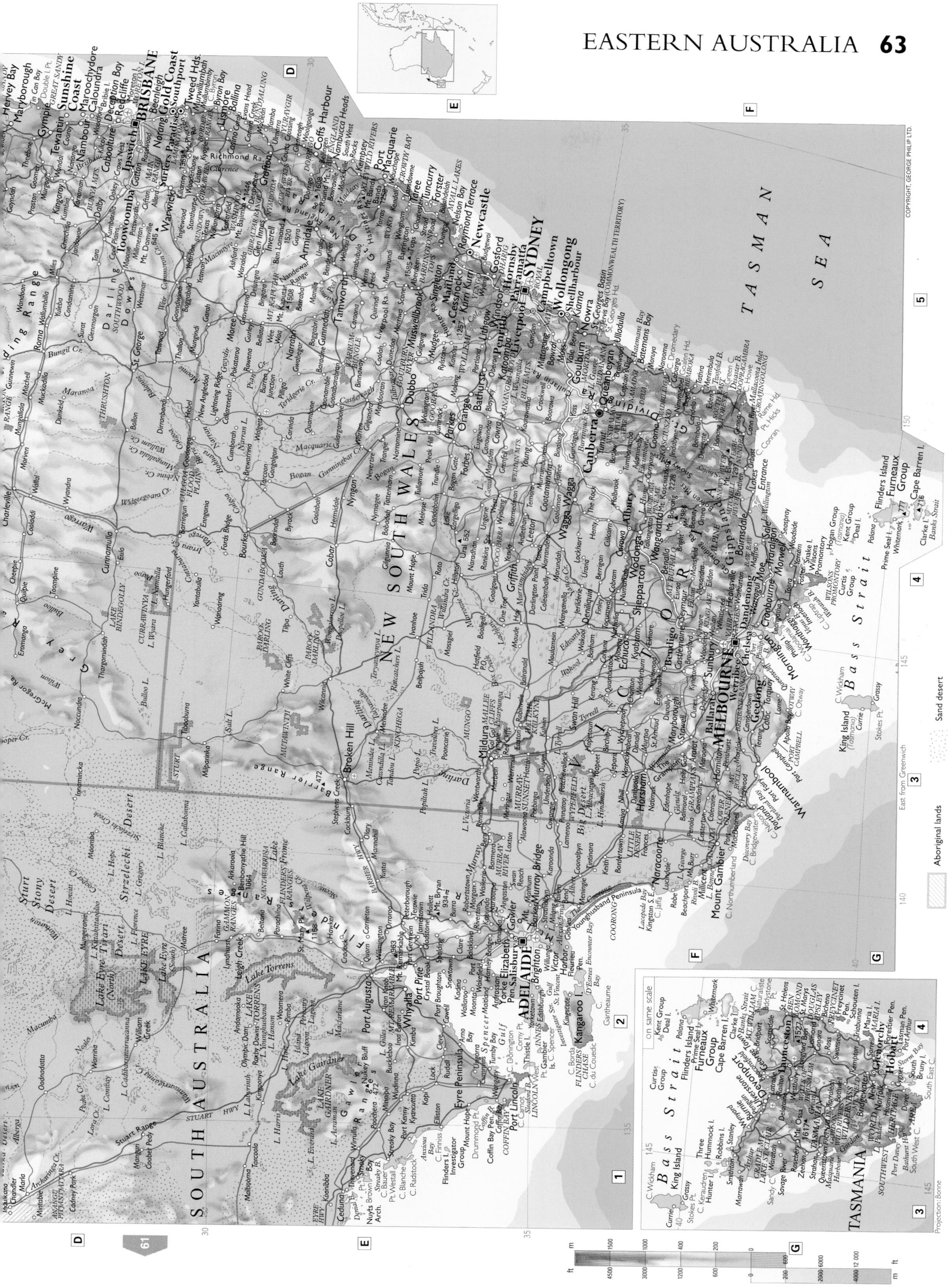

NEW SOUTH WALES

VICTORIA

SOUTH AUSTRALIA

TASMANIA

TASMAN SEA

Bass Strait

Aboriginal lands

Sand desert

East from Greenwich

Projection: Bonne

61

Equatorial Scale 1:54 000 000

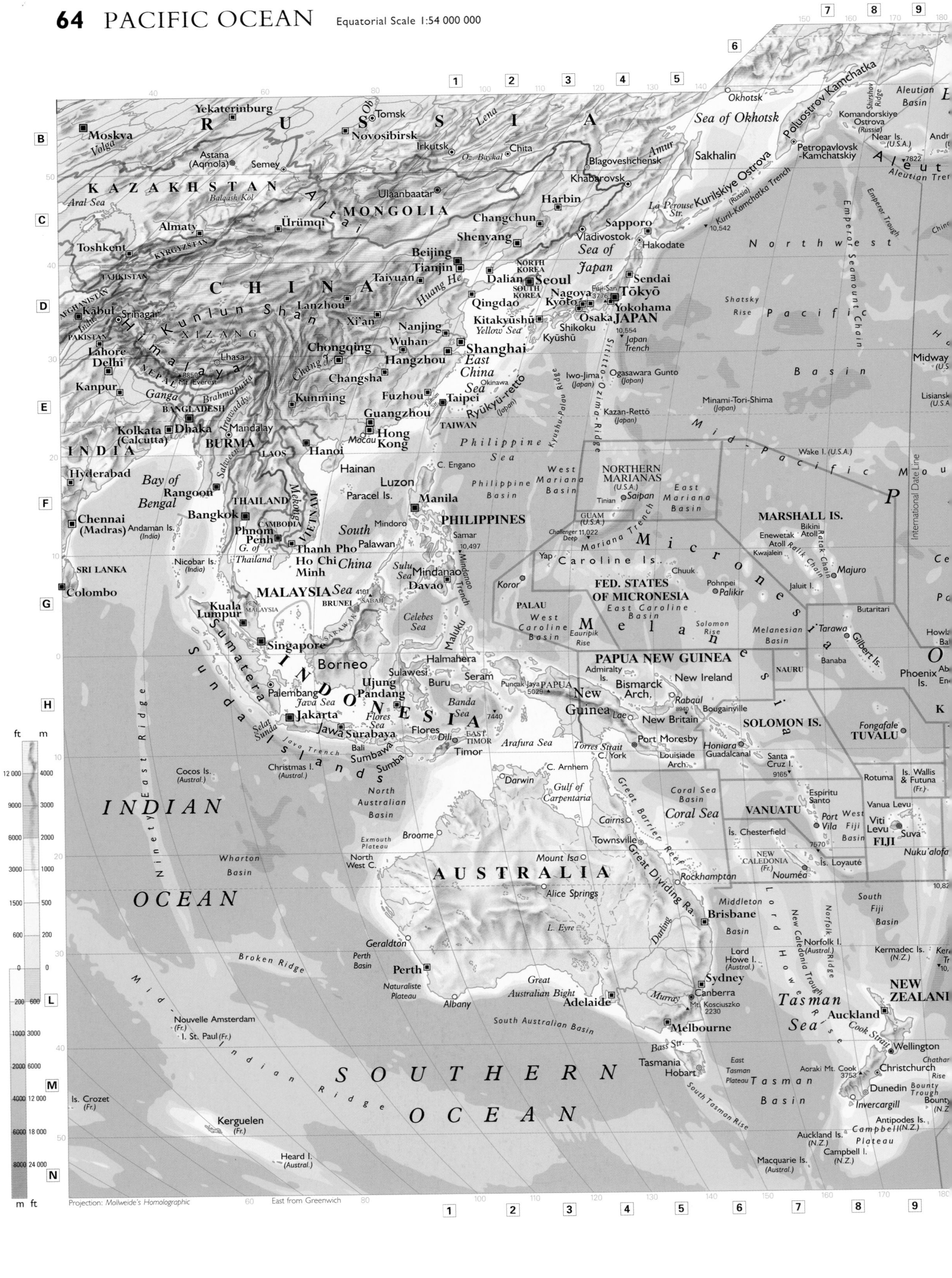

RUSSIA, KAZAKHSTAN, MONGOLIA, CHINA, JAPAN, INDIA, BURMA, THAILAND, VIETNAM, PHILIPPINES, MALAYSIA, INDONESIA, PAPUA NEW GUINEA, AUSTRALIA, NEW ZEALAND

Moskva, Yekaterinburg, Tomsk, Novosibirsk, Irkutsk, Chita, Astana (Aqmola), Semey, Almaty, Toshkent, Ürümqi, Ulaanbaatar, Blagoveshchensk, Khabarovsk, Harbin, Changchun, Shenyang, Vladivostok, Sapporo, Hakodate, Beijing, Tianjin, Dalian, Seoul, Taiyuan, Lanzhou, Xi'an, Qingdao, Nagoya, Kyōto, Ōsaka, Tōkyō, Yokohama, Sendai, Kitakyūshū, Nanjing, Wuhan, Shanghai, Chongqing, Hangzhou, Changsha, Kunming, Fuzhou, Taipei, Guangzhou, Hong Kong, Macau, Hanoi, Lhasa, Kābul, Srinagar, Lahore, Delhi, Kanpur, Kolkata (Calcutta), Dhaka, Mandalay, Hyderabad, Rangoon, Bangkok, Phnom Penh, Thanh Pho Ho Chi Minh, Chennai (Madras), Colombo, Kuala Lumpur, Singapore, Manila, Davao, Palembang, Jakarta, Surabaya, Ujung Pandang, Dili, Koror, Palikir, Majuro, Port Moresby, Honiara, Darwin, Broome, Cairns, Townsville, Mount Isa, Alice Springs, Rockhampton, Brisbane, Geraldton, Perth, Albany, Adelaide, Sydney, Canberra, Melbourne, Hobart, Auckland, Wellington, Christchurch, Dunedin, Invercargill, Nouméa, Port Vila, Suva, Fongafale, Okhotsk, Petropavlovsk-Kamchatskiy

Pacific Ocean, Indian Ocean, Southern Ocean, Sea of Okhotsk, Sea of Japan, Yellow Sea, East China Sea, Philippine Sea, South China Sea, Sulu Sea, Celebes Sea, Java Sea, Flores Sea, Banda Sea, Arafura Sea, Coral Sea, Tasman Sea, Bay of Bengal, G. of Thailand, Gulf of Carpentaria, Great Australian Bight, Bass Str., Torres Strait, Cook Strait, La Perouse Str., Selat Sunda

Himalaya, Kunlun Shan, Altai, Great Dividing Ra., Great Barrier Reef, Mt. Everest 8850, Fuji-San 3776, Mt. Kosciuszko 2230, Aoraki Mt. Cook 3753, Puncak Jaya 5029

Mariana Trench, Challenger Deep 11,022, Japan Trench 10,554, Kuril-Kamchatka Trench 10,542, Philippine Trench 10,497, Java Trench, Aleutian Trench, Emperor Seamount Chain, Shatsky Rise, Mid-Pacific Mountains, Ninety East Ridge, Broken Ridge, Mid-Indian Ridge, South Tasman Rise, Campbell Plateau, Lord Howe Rise, Norfolk Ridge, New Caledonia Trough, Northwest Pacific Basin, Philippine Basin, West Mariana Basin, East Mariana Basin, West Caroline Basin, East Caroline Basin, Melanesian Basin, Coral Sea Basin, North Australian Basin, Wharton Basin, Perth Basin, South Australian Basin, Tasman Basin, South Fiji Basin

ft / m: 12 000 / 4000, 9000 / 3000, 6000 / 2000, 3000 / 1000, 1500 / 500, 600 / 200, 0 / 0, 200 / 600, 1000 / 3000, 2000 / 6000, 4000 / 12 000, 6000 / 18 000, 8000 / 24 000

Projection: Mollweide's Homolographic

East from Greenwich

International Date Line

Arctic Circle
ALASKA
(U.S.A.)
Anchorage
5959
Juneau
Gulf of Alaska
Prince of Wales I.
(U.S.A.) Prince Rupert
Queen Charlotte Is.
(Canada)
R o c k y M t s
C A N A D A
Edmonton
Calgary
Regina
L. Winnipeg
Winnipeg
Tufts
Abyssal
Plain
Vancouver
Vancouver I.
Victoria
Seattle
Portland
Snake
Boise
Newfoundland
St. Lawrence
N O R T H
St. John's
L. Superior
Québec
Montréal
Ottawa
L. Huron
L. Michigan
Toronto
L. Ontario
Minneapolis
Missouri
Detroit
Buffalo
Boston
L. Erie
Chicago
Pittsburgh
New York
Philadelphia
Baltimore
Washington D.C.
Salt Lake City
Denver
Colorado
Kansas City
St. Louis
Cincinnati
Appalachian Mts.
o r t h e a s t
Mendocino Fracture Zone
C. Mendocino
Sacramento
San Francisco
4418
UNITED STATES
A T L A N T I C
6741
Murray Fracture Zone
Oklahoma City
Memphis
Mississippi
Atlanta
C. Hatteras
Los Angeles
Phoenix
Dallas
San Diego
P a c i f i c
Bermuda
(U.K.)
Ciudad Juárez
Houston
Jacksonville
Guadalupe
(Mex.)
Baja California
Golfo de California
San Antonio
New Orleans
Tampa
S a r g a s s o S e a
Molokai Fracture Zone
Gulf of Mexico
Miami
BAHAMAS
Florida Str.
O C E A N
M E X I C O
Monterrey
Tropic of Cancer
La Habana
C U B A
West Indies
Honolulu
Kauai
Maui
Oahu
HAWAIIAN IS.
(U.S.A.)
4205
Hilo
Hawaii
B a s i n
C. San Lucas
Canal de Yucatan
Guadalajara
Mexico
5610
Puebla
Mérida
9200
7680
JAMAICA
HAITI
DOMINICAN REP.
Kingston
Leeward Is.
Clarion Fracture Zone
Is. Revilla Gigedo
(Mex.)
BELIZE
PUERTO RICO
(U.S.A.)
Acapulco
GUATEMALA
HONDURAS
Caribbean Sea
I F I C
Middle America Trench
6662
Guatemala
BARBADOS
NICARAGUA
Windward Is.
San Salvador
EL SALVADOR
Managua
Barranquilla
Maracaibo
I. Clipperton
(Fr.)
Clipperton Fracture Zone
Guatemala Basin
San José
COSTA RICA
Colón
Panamá
PANAMA
Caracas
Orinoco
Cooper Ridge
Cocos Ridge
Panama Basin
VENEZUELA
I. del Coco
(Costa Rica)
Medellín
Bogotá
Teraina
Tabuaeran
Kiritimati
I. de Malpelo
(Colombia)
Cali
COLOMBIA
Galápagos Fracture Zone
Equator
Jarvis I.
(U.S.A.)
E A N
Galápagos
(Ecuador)
Carnegie Ridge
Quito
ECUADOR
Malden I.
Starbuck I.
Line Islands
Guayaquil
Iquitos
Amazonas
C. Paliñas
BRAZIL
Penrhyn
(Tongareva)
Îs. Marquises
Nuku Hiva
Hiva Oa
Marquesas Fracture Zone
East Pacific Ridge
Galápagos Rise
Trujillo
Manihiki
Vostok I.
Caroline I.
(Millennium I.)
Flint I.
Yupanqui Basin
6369
PERU
Lima
Suwarrow Is.
Îs. de la Société
Bora Bora
Huahine
Raiatéa
Tahiti
Papeete
Rangiroa
Îs. Tuamotu
Mendaña Fracture Zone
Peru Basin
Cuzco
L. Titicaca
Arequipa
Nevado Ancohuma
6550
La Paz
BOLIVIA
Cook Is.
(N.Z.)
Aitutaki
Atiu
Mangaia
FRENCH POLYNESIA
Austral Seamount Chain
Îs. Gambier
Mururoa
Tuamotu Ridge
6866
Peru-
Arica
Iquique
Chile
Nazca Ridge
Îs. Tubuaï
Tropic of Capricorn
Oeno I.
Henderson I.
Pitcairn I.
(U.K.)
Ducie I.
Sala y Gómez Ridge
Antofagasta
8050
Trench
PARAGUAY
Asunción
Rapa
Easter Fracture Zone
Sala-y-Gómez
(Chile)
I. de Pascua
(Chile)
San Felix
(Chile)
San Ambrosio
(Chile)
San Miguel de Tucumán
Pôrto Alegre
Roggeveen Basin
Córdoba
Aconcagua
6962
Rosario
Arch. de Juan Fernández
(Chile)
Valparaíso
Santiago
Buenos Aires
URUGUAY
Montevideo
Río de la Plata
Challenger Fracture Zone
Chile Rise
Concepción
ARGENTINA
S o u t h w e s t
P a c i f i c
B a s i n
SOUTH
ATLANTIC
OCEAN
6212
Menard Fracture Zone
East Pacific Ridge
Patagonia
Falkland Is.
(U.K.)
Pacific-Antarctic Ridge
Punta Arenas
Est. de Magallanes
Tierra del Fuego
South Georgia
(U.K.)
Southeast Pacific Basin
C. de Hornos
Drake Passage
West from Greenwich

1:35 000 000
ARCTIC OCEAN
Beaufort Sea
Lincoln Sea
Greenland
Baffin Bay
Baffin Island
Hudson Bay
Labrador Sea
Canadian Shield
Great Plains
Rocky Mountains
Mackenzie Mts.
Alaska Range
Brooks Ra.
Chukchi Sea
Bering Sea
Gulf of Alaska
Queen Elizabeth Is.
Ellesmere I.
Victoria I.
Banks I.
Great Bear L.
Great Slave L.
Great Lakes
Great Basin
Colorado Plateau
Columbia Plateau
Mexican Plateau
Western Sierra Madre
Eastern Sierra Madre
Gulf of Mexico
Gulf of California
PACIFIC OCEAN
NORTH ATLANTIC OCEAN
Sargasso Sea
Caribbean Sea
Central America
Greater Antilles
West Indies
Cuba
Hispaniola
Jamaica
Yucatán Peninsula
Isthmus of Tehuantepec
Appalachian Mts.
Laurentian Plateau
Newfoundland
Nova Scotia
Florida
Mississippi River Delta
Mt. McKinley 6194
Mt. Logan 5959
Mt. Elbert 4399
Mt. Whitney 4418
Popocatepetl 5452
Pico de Orizaba 5610
Mt. Washington 1917
Death Valley -86
Clarion Fracture Zone
Guatemala Trench
Tropic of Cancer
Arctic Circle
Projection: Bonne
West from Greenwich
COPYRIGHT PHILIP'S

1:35 000 000

100 0 200 400 600 800 1000 1200 1400 km

100 0 200 400 600 800 1000 miles

■ MÉXICO Capital Cities

100 0 100 200 300 400 500 600 km

100 0 100 200 300 400 miles

1:15 000 000

4 5 74 6 7 8 9 4

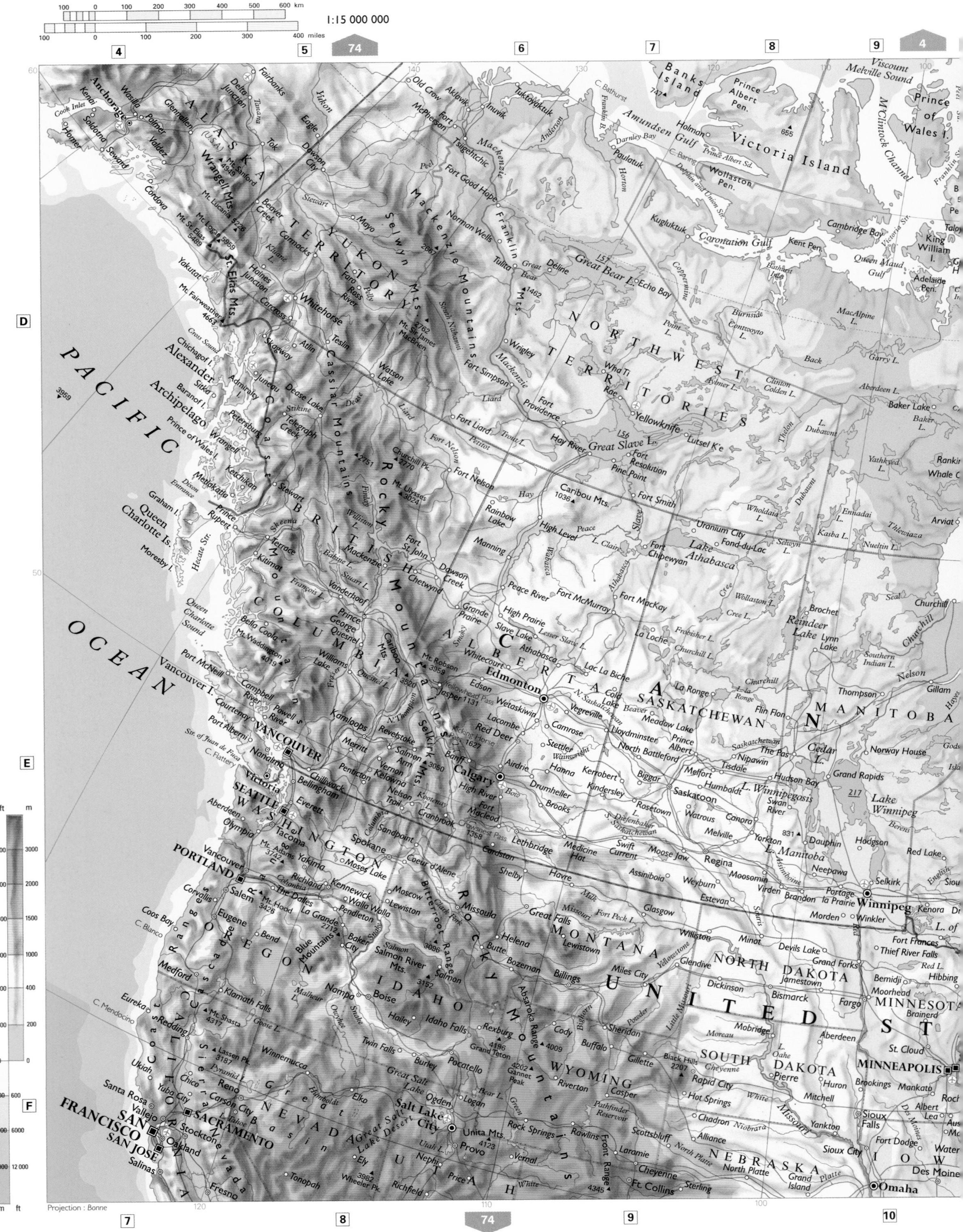

Projection : Bonne

NORTHERN CANADA
continuation northwards on same scale as main map
ARCTIC OCEAN
Queen Elizabeth Is.
Sverdrup Islands
Parry Islands
Ellesmere Island
Devon Island
Banks Island
Victoria Island
Prince of Wales Island
Somerset Island
Baffin Island
NUNAVUT
NORTHWEST TERRITORIES
GREENLAND (Denmark)
Baffin Bay
Baffin Island
Foxe Basin
Hudson Strait
Labrador Sea
Ungava Bay
Péninsule d'Ungava
Hudson Bay
James Bay
ATLANTIC OCEAN
NEWFOUNDLAND & LABRADOR
Newfoundland
Labrador
QUÉBEC
NEW BRUNSWICK
NOVA SCOTIA
PR. EDWARD I.
Gulf of St. Lawrence
Grand Banks
Québec
MONTRÉAL
OTTAWA
TORONTO
Hamilton
Halifax
BOSTON
PROVIDENCE
NEW YORK
DETROIT
CHICAGO
CLEVELAND
Buffalo
Rochester
Lake Huron
L. Ontario
L. Erie
L. Michigan
MAINE
VERMONT
NEW HAMPSHIRE
MASS.
CONN.
R.I.
NEW YORK
PENNSYLVANIA
OHIO
INDIANA
MICHIGAN
ST.-PIERRE et MIQUELON (Fr.)
St. John's
Iqaluit
Resolute
Alert
West from Greenwich
COPYRIGHT PHILIP'S

WESTERN CANADA

1:7 000 000

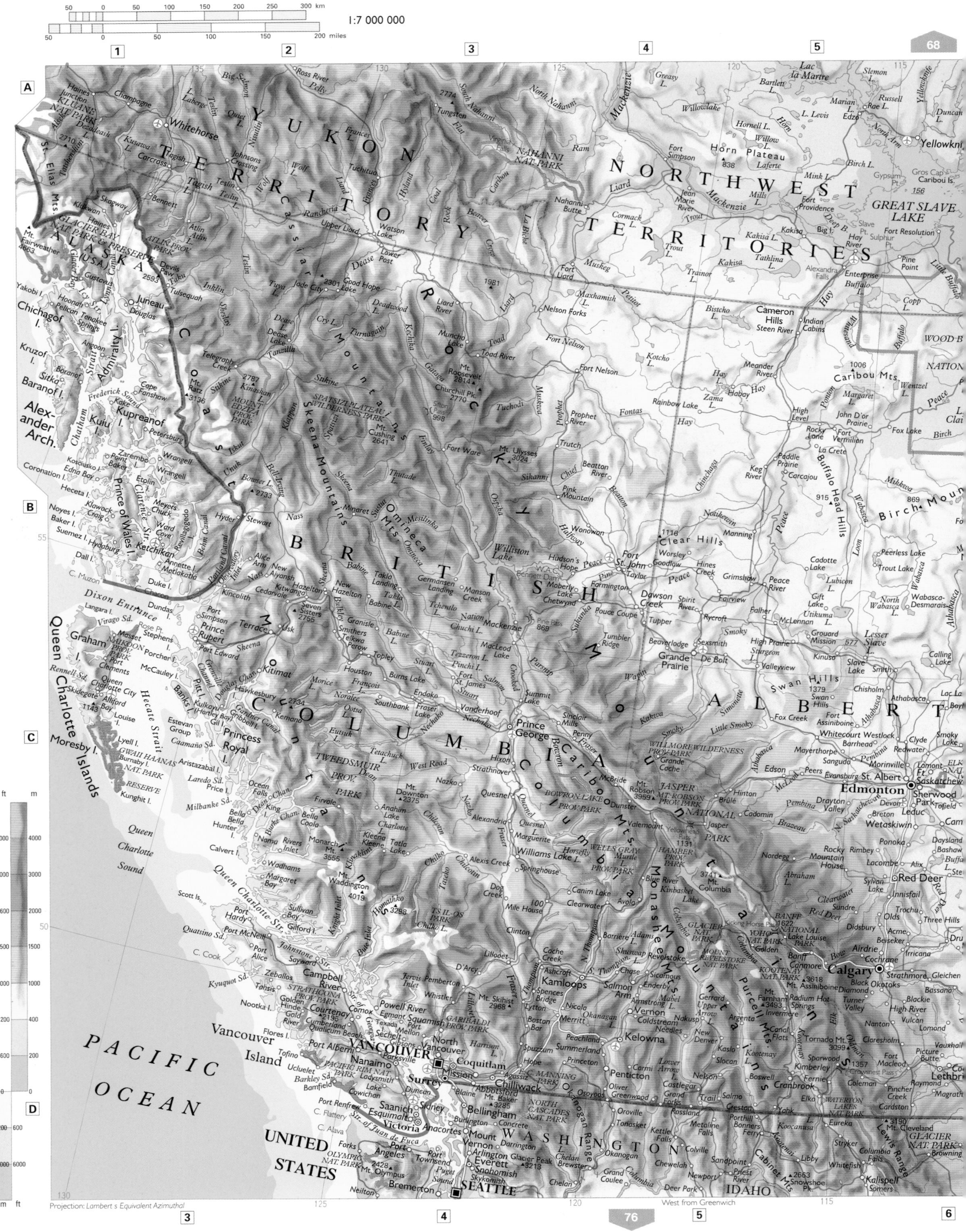

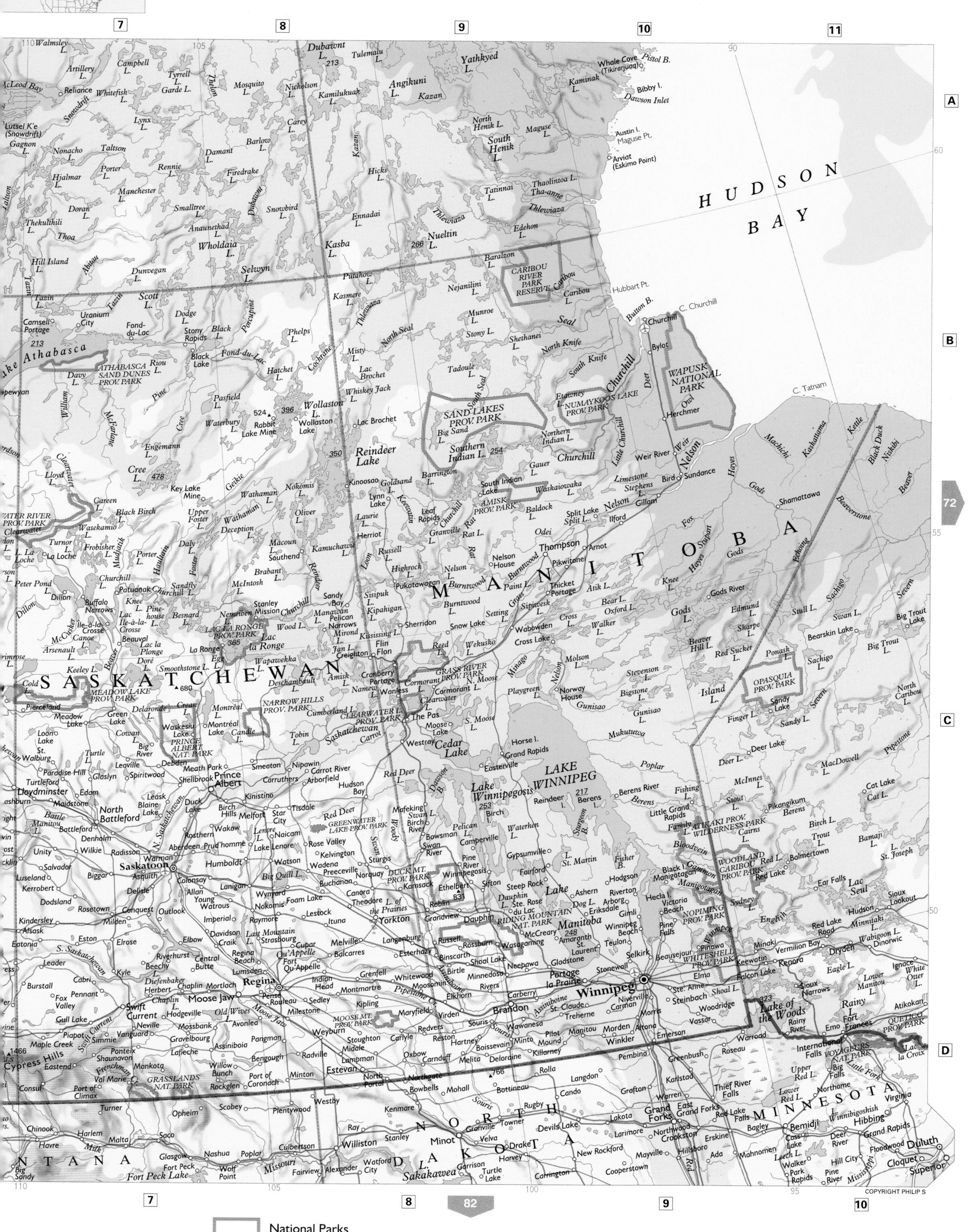

National Parks

50 0 50 100 150 200 250 300 km

1:7 000 000

50 0 50 100 150 200 miles

Projection: Lambert's Equivalent Azimuthal

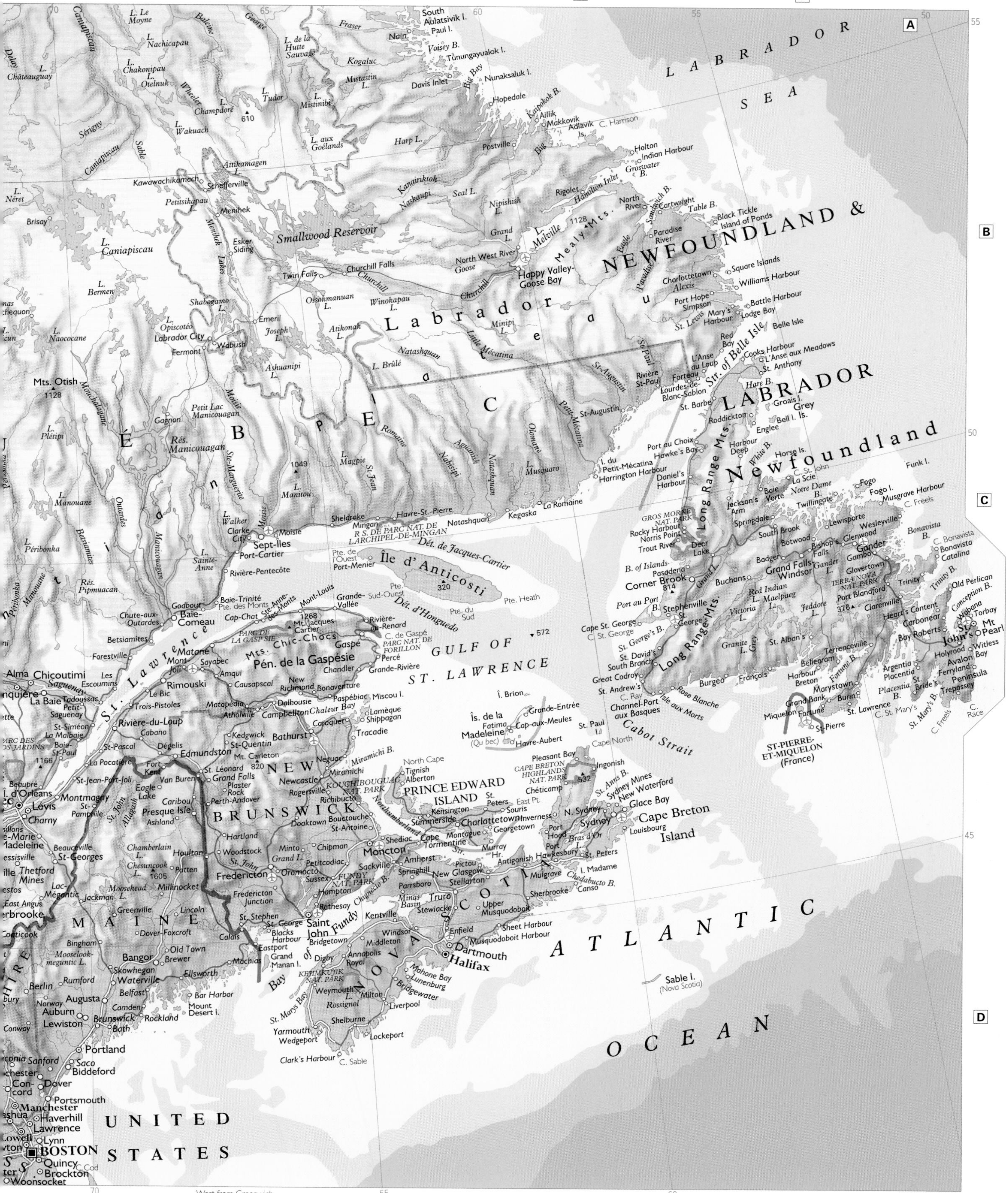

6 69 7 8 9

A B C D

LABRADOR SEA
NEWFOUNDLAND & LABRADOR
Labrador
Newfoundland
Q U É B E C
GULF OF ST. LAWRENCE
ATLANTIC OCEAN
UNITED STATES
NEW BRUNSWICK
NOVA SCOTIA
PRINCE EDWARD ISLAND
MAINE
ST-PIERRE-ET-MIQUELON (France)
Cape Breton Island
Île d'Anticosti
Pén. de la Gaspésie
Smallwood Reservoir
Cabot Strait
Str. of Belle Isle
Bay of Fundy
Nain
Hopedale
Postville
Cartwright
Happy Valley-Goose Bay
North West River
Churchill Falls
Labrador City
Wabush
Schefferville
Fermont
Sept-Îles
Port-Cartier
Havre-St.-Pierre
Baie-Comeau
Rimouski
Matane
Gaspé
Chicoutimi
Rivière-du-Loup
Lévis
Edmundston
Bathurst
Campbellton
Miramichi
Moncton
Fredericton
Saint John
Charlottetown
Summerside
Halifax
Dartmouth
Truro
New Glasgow
Sydney
Glace Bay
Yarmouth
Corner Brook
Stephenville
Deer Lake
Grand Falls-Windsor
Gander
St. John's
Clarenville
Port aux Basques
Bangor
Augusta
Portland
Lewiston
BOSTON
Manchester
Sable I. (Nova Scotia)

70 65 60 55 50 45

West from Greenwich

1:12 000 000

Projection: Albers' Equal Area with two standard parallels

West from Greenwich

86

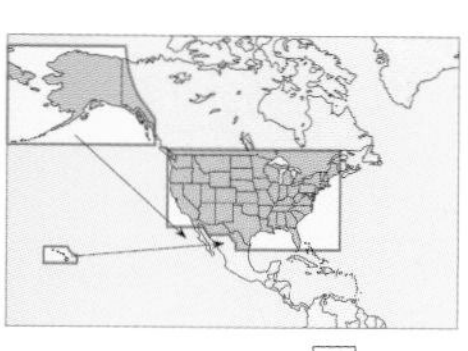

Tallahassee ⊛ U.S. state capitals

50 0 50 100 150 200 250 300 km

50 0 50 100 150 200 miles

1:6 700 000

Sand desert or dunes

Lava fields

Projection: Albers' Equal Area with two standard parallels

West from Greenwich

78 CENTRAL AND SOUTHERN CALIFORNIA AND WESTERN WASHINGTON

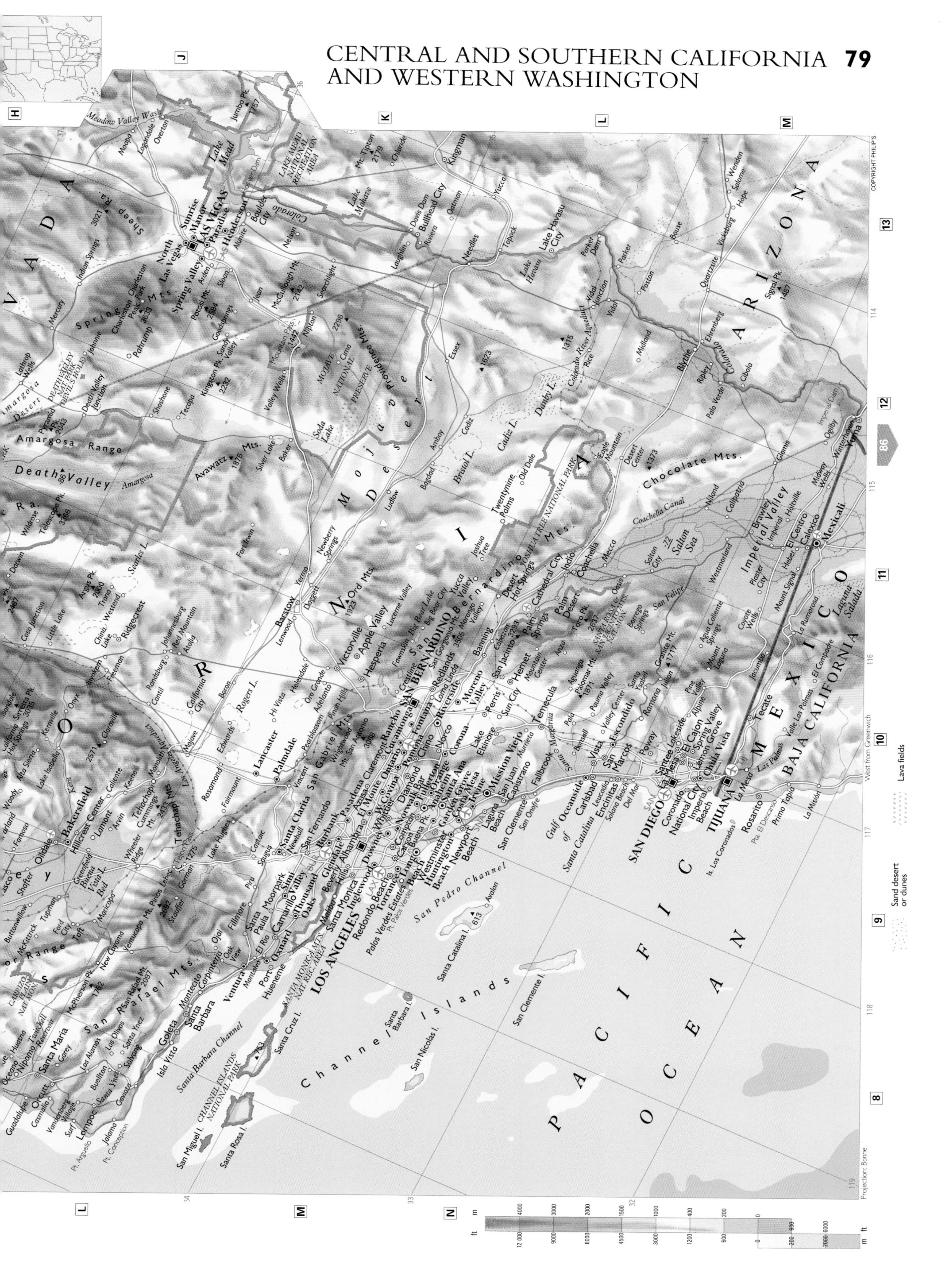
NEVADA
ARIZONA
CALIFORNIA
MEXICO
BAJA CALIFORNIA
PACIFIC OCEAN
Mojave Desert
LAS VEGAS
North Las Vegas
Henderson
Boulder City
Lake Mead
LAKE MEAD NATIONAL RECREATION AREA
Lake Mohave
Bullhead City
Laughlin
Kingman
Needles
Lake Havasu City
Parker
Blythe
Yuma
Mexicali
Calexico
El Centro
Brawley
Imperial Valley
Salton Sea
Chocolate Mts.
Coachella Canal
Indio
Coachella
Palm Springs
Palm Desert
Cathedral City
Desert Hot Springs
Twentynine Palms
JOSHUA TREE NATIONAL PARK
San Bernardino Mts.
SAN BERNARDINO
Riverside
Redlands
Moreno Valley
Hemet
Temecula
Escondido
SAN DIEGO
Chula Vista
National City
El Cajon
Oceanside
Carlsbad
TIJUANA
Tecate
Rosarito
Ensenada
LOS ANGELES
Long Beach
Santa Ana
Anaheim
Irvine
Huntington Beach
Newport Beach
Torrance
Pasadena
Glendale
Burbank
Santa Monica
Pomona
Ontario
Santa Clarita
Palmdale
Lancaster
Victorville
Hesperia
Apple Valley
Barstow
Mojave
Bakersfield
Tehachapi Mts.
Ventura
Oxnard
Thousand Oaks
Simi Valley
Santa Barbara
Goleta
Santa Maria
Lompoc
San Rafael Mts.
Santa Barbara Channel
CHANNEL ISLANDS NATIONAL PARK
Channel Islands
San Pedro Channel
Santa Catalina I.
San Clemente I.
San Nicolas I.
Santa Cruz I.
Santa Rosa I.
San Miguel I.
Gulf of Santa Catalina
Death Valley
Amargosa Range
Spring Mts.
Avawatz Mts.
Ord Mts.
Providence Mts.
MOJAVE NATIONAL PRESERVE
Soda Lake
Bristol L.
Cadiz L.
Danby L.
Colorado River Aqueduct
Lava fields
Sand desert or dunes
West from Greenwich
Projection: Bonne
COPYRIGHT PHILIP'S
86

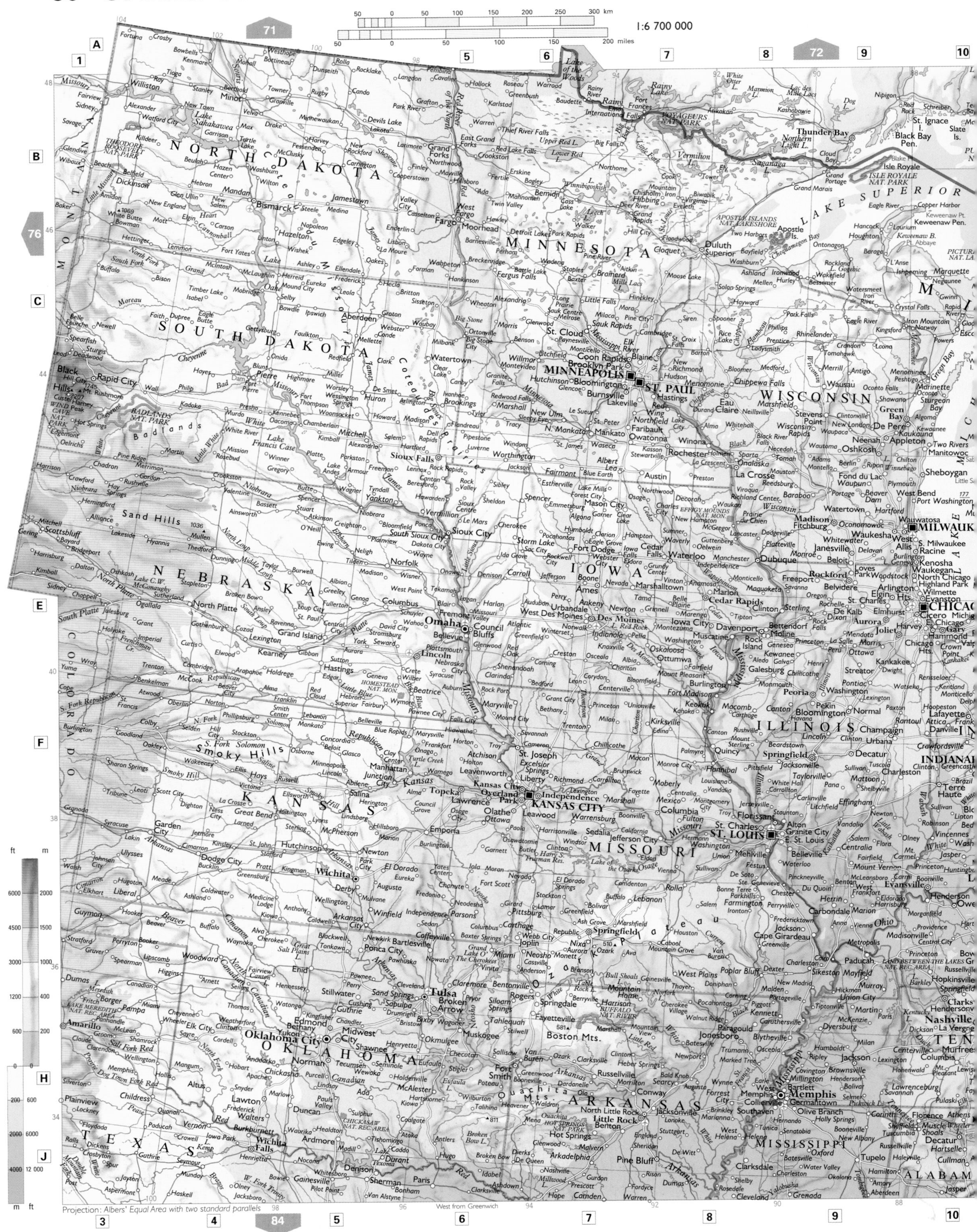

1:6 700 000
50 0 50 100 150 200 250 300 km
50 0 50 100 150 200 miles
NORTH DAKOTA
SOUTH DAKOTA
NEBRASKA
KANSAS
OKLAHOMA
MINNESOTA
IOWA
MISSOURI
ARKANSAS
WISCONSIN
ILLINOIS
MONTANA
COLORADO
TEXAS
MISSISSIPPI
LAKE SUPERIOR
MINNEAPOLIS
ST. PAUL
KANSAS CITY
ST. LOUIS
Omaha
Des Moines
Bismarck
Pierre
Lincoln
Topeka
Oklahoma City
Little Rock
Memphis
Tulsa
Wichita
Sioux Falls
Fargo
Duluth
Milwaukee
Springfield
Sand Hills
Smoky Hills
Badlands
Ozark Plateau
Ouachita Mts.
Boston Mts.
Projection: Albers' Equal Area with two standard parallels
West from Greenwich

ONTARIO
QUÉBEC
CANADA
L. St-Jean
Chicoutimi
Saguenay
Québec
Lévis
Trois-Rivières
Sherbrooke
MONTRÉAL
Laval
OTTAWA
Gatineau
Hull
Kingston
Sudbury
North Bay
Sault Ste. Marie
Timmins
Rouyn-Noranda
Val-d'Or
Georgian Bay
LAKE HURON
Manitoulin I.
North Channel
Saginaw Bay
LAKE ONTARIO
LAKE ERIE
TORONTO
Hamilton
London
Windsor
DETROIT
Toledo
CLEVELAND
Akron
Buffalo
Rochester
Syracuse
Albany
NEW YORK
Allegheny Plateau
PENNSYLVANIA
PITTSBURGH
PHILADELPHIA
Harrisburg
NEW JERSEY
OHIO
COLUMBUS
CINCINNATI
Dayton
MARYLAND
BALTIMORE
WASHINGTON D.C.
DELAWARE
Delaware Bay
Chesapeake Bay
WEST VIRGINIA
Charleston
VIRGINIA
Richmond
NORFOLK
Virginia Beach
NORTH CAROLINA
Raleigh
Charlotte
Greensboro
Durham
Pamlico Sound
C. Hatteras
Wilmington
SOUTH CAROLINA
Columbia
GEORGIA
VERMONT
NEW HAMPSHIRE
MAINE
MASSACHUSETTS
BOSTON
PROVIDENCE
R.I.
CT.
Hartford
Gulf of Maine
NEW BRUNS.
ATLANTIC OCEAN

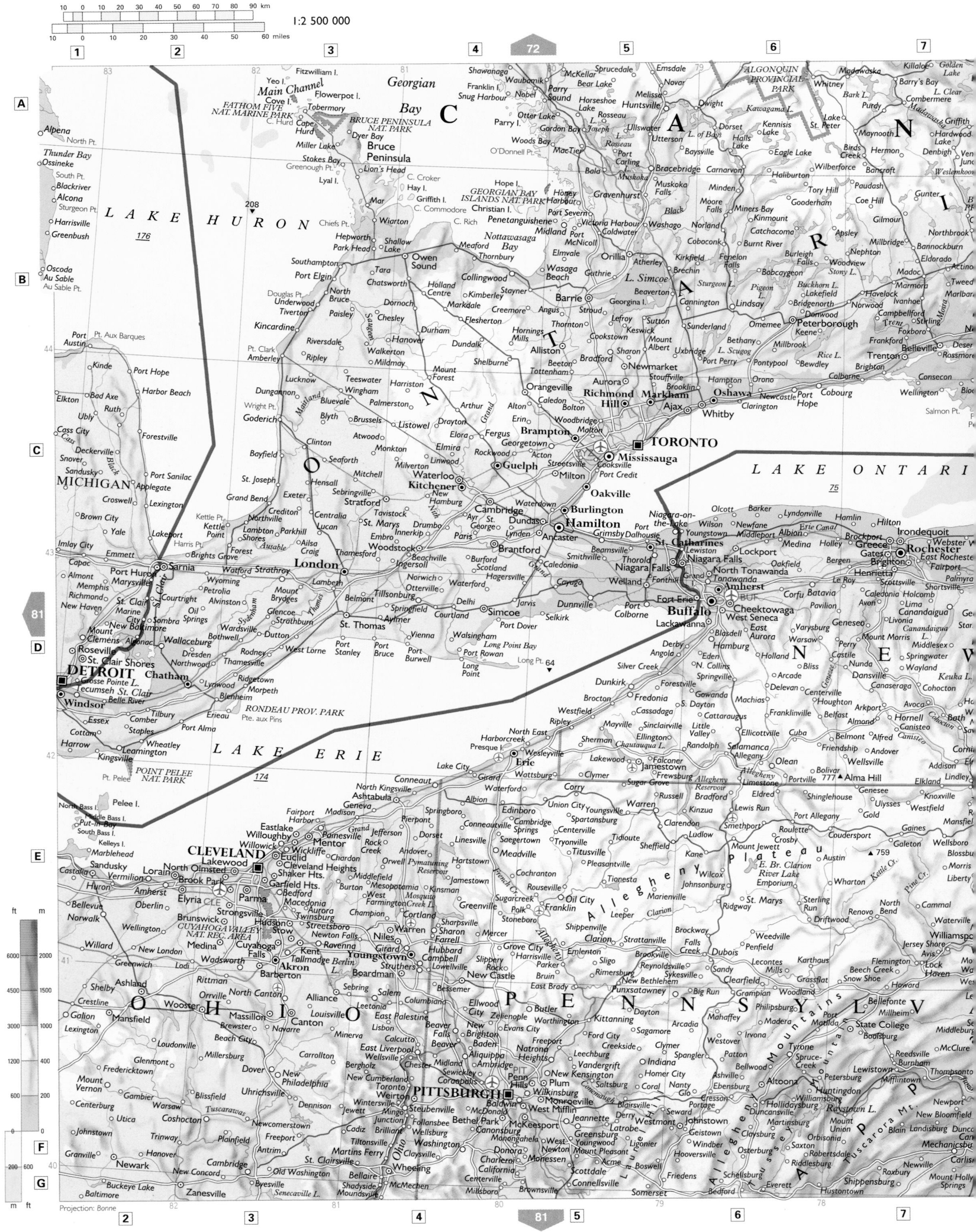

1:2 500 000
km
miles
Projection: Bonne
72
81
Georgian Bay
LAKE HURON
LAKE ONTARIO
LAKE ERIE
MICHIGAN
CANADA
ONTARIO
NEW YORK
OHIO
PENNSYLVANIA
Allegheny Plateau
Allegheny Mountains
Tussey Mountains
Tuscarora Mt.
Bruce Peninsula
BRUCE PENINSULA NAT. PARK
FATHOM FIVE NAT. MARINE PARK
GEORGIAN BAY ISLANDS NAT. PARK
ALGONQUIN PROVINCIAL PARK
POINT PELEE NAT. PARK
RONDEAU PROV. PARK
CUYAHOGA VALLEY NAT. REC. AREA
Nottawasaga Bay
L. Simcoe
TORONTO
Mississauga
Hamilton
Burlington
Oakville
Brampton
Kitchener
Waterloo
Guelph
Cambridge
Brantford
London
Sarnia
Windsor
DETROIT
St. Catharines
Niagara Falls
Buffalo
Rochester
Erie
CLEVELAND
Akron
Youngstown
Canton
PITTSBURGH
Barrie
Orillia
Owen Sound
Peterborough
Oshawa
Whitby
Chatham
St. Thomas
Alma Hill
Erie Canal

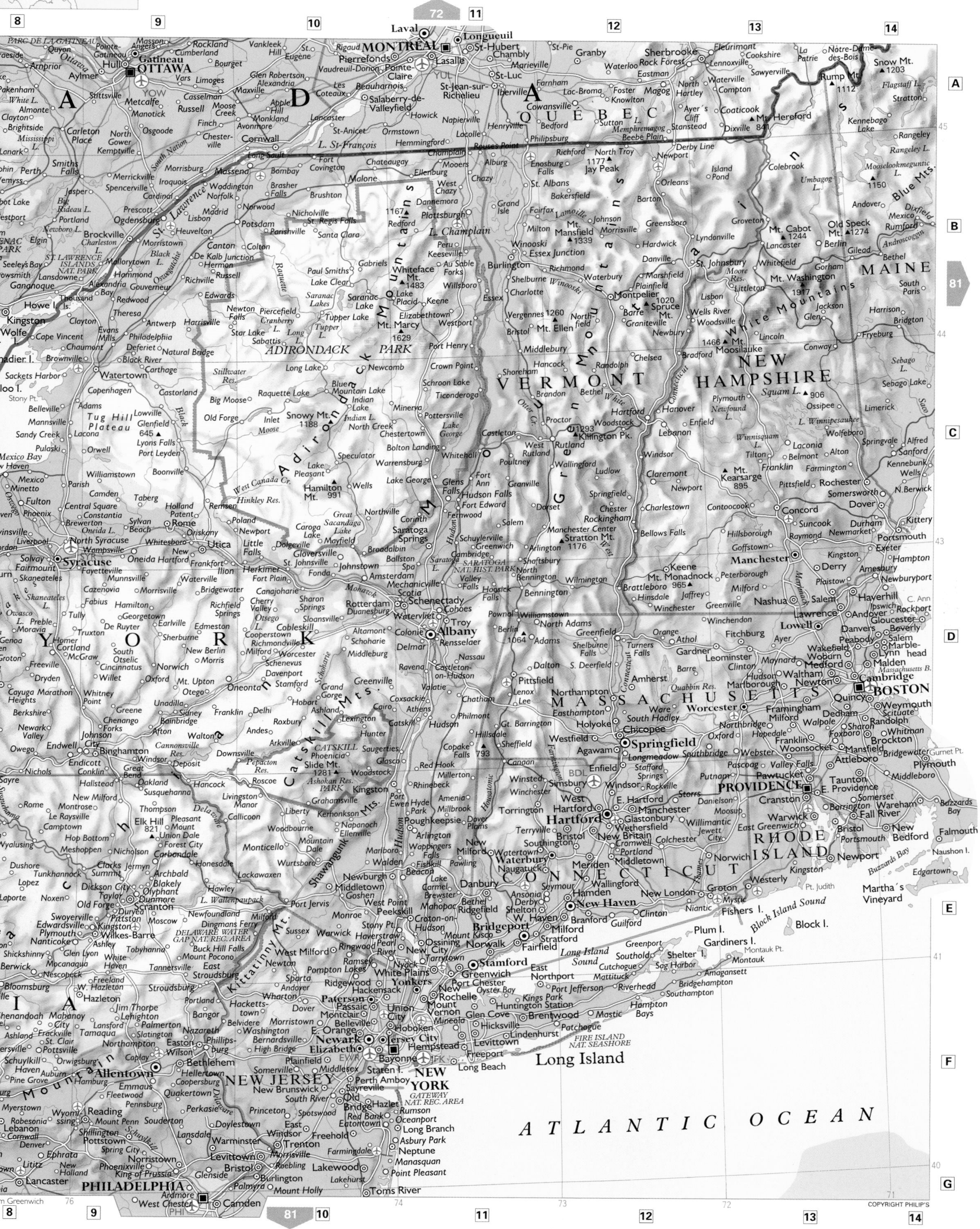
ATLANTIC OCEAN
NEW YORK
VERMONT
NEW HAMPSHIRE
MAINE
MASSACHUSETTS
CONNECTICUT
RHODE ISLAND
NEW JERSEY
QUÉBEC
Long Island
BOSTON
PHILADELPHIA
ALBANY
HARTFORD
PROVIDENCE
MONTREAL
OTTAWA
Adirondack Mountains
Green Mountains
White Mountains
Catskill Mts.
COPYRIGHT PHILIP'S

1:6 700 000

77
80
86

10
11
12
81
13
14
15
16
17
B
C
D
E
F
G
H
J
88
ILLINOIS
INDIANA
OHIO
PENNSYLVANIA
MARYLAND
DELAWARE
WEST VIRGINIA
VIRGINIA
KENTUCKY
TENNESSEE
NORTH CAROLINA
SOUTH CAROLINA
GEORGIA
ALABAMA
MISSISSIPPI
FLORIDA
BAHAMAS
ATLANTIC OCEAN
OF MEXICO
PITTSBURGH
PHILADELPHIA
BALTIMORE
WASHINGTON D.C.
INDIANAPOLIS
COLUMBUS
CINCINNATI
Dayton
Louisville
Lexington
Nashville
Memphis
Knoxville
Chattanooga
Birmingham
Huntsville
Montgomery
ATLANTA
Augusta
Columbia
Charleston
Savannah
Jacksonville
Tallahassee
ORLANDO
TAMPA
St. Petersburg
MIAMI
NEW ORLEANS
Mobile
Pensacola
Jackson
Richmond
NORFOLK
Virginia Beach
Chesapeake
Charlotte
Greensboro
Raleigh
Durham
Winston-Salem
Wilmington
Fort Lauderdale
West Palm Beach
Hialeah
Nassau
Cumberland Plateau
Appalachian Mts.
Chesapeake Bay
Delaware Bay
Pamlico Sound
Albemarle Sd.
Onslow Bay
Long Bay
Lake Okeechobee
Florida Bay
Florida Keys
Str. of Florida
Mississippi River Delta
Sea Islands
C. Hatteras
C. Fear
C. Canaveral
C. Lookout
Key West
Dry Tortugas
Andros I.
Grand Bahama
Abaco I.
Northwest Providence Channel
Northeast Providence Channel
EVERGLADES NAT. PARK
BIG CYPRESS NAT. PRESERVE
GREAT SMOKY MTS. NAT. PARK
MAMMOTH CAVE NATIONAL PARK
SHENANDOAH NAT. PARK

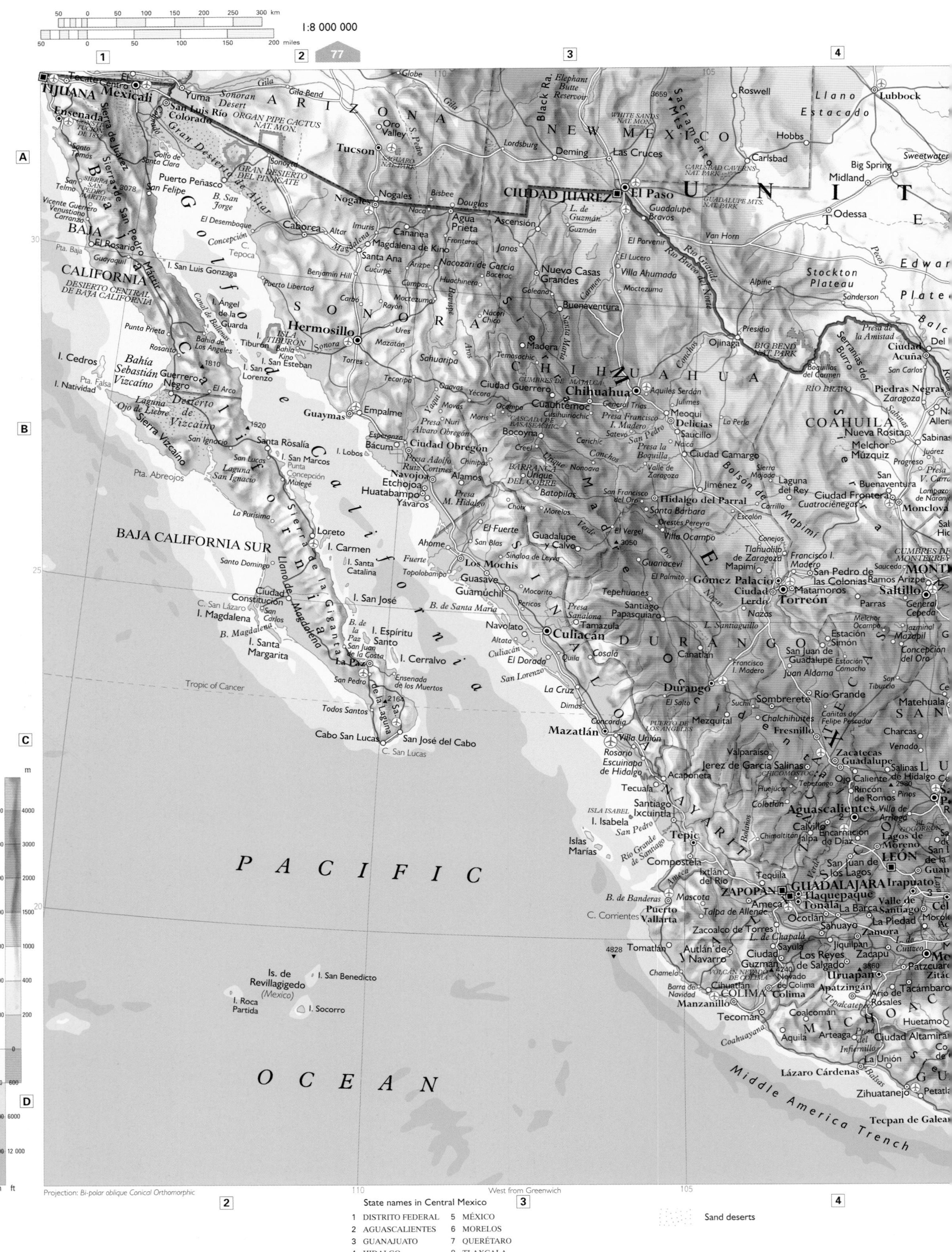

State names in Central Mexico

1	DISTRITO FEDERAL	5	MÉXICO
2	AGUASCALIENTES	6	MORELOS
3	GUANAJUATO	7	QUERÉTARO
4	HIDALGO	8	TLAXCALA

Sand deserts

Projection: Bi-polar oblique Conical Orthomorphic

West from Greenwich

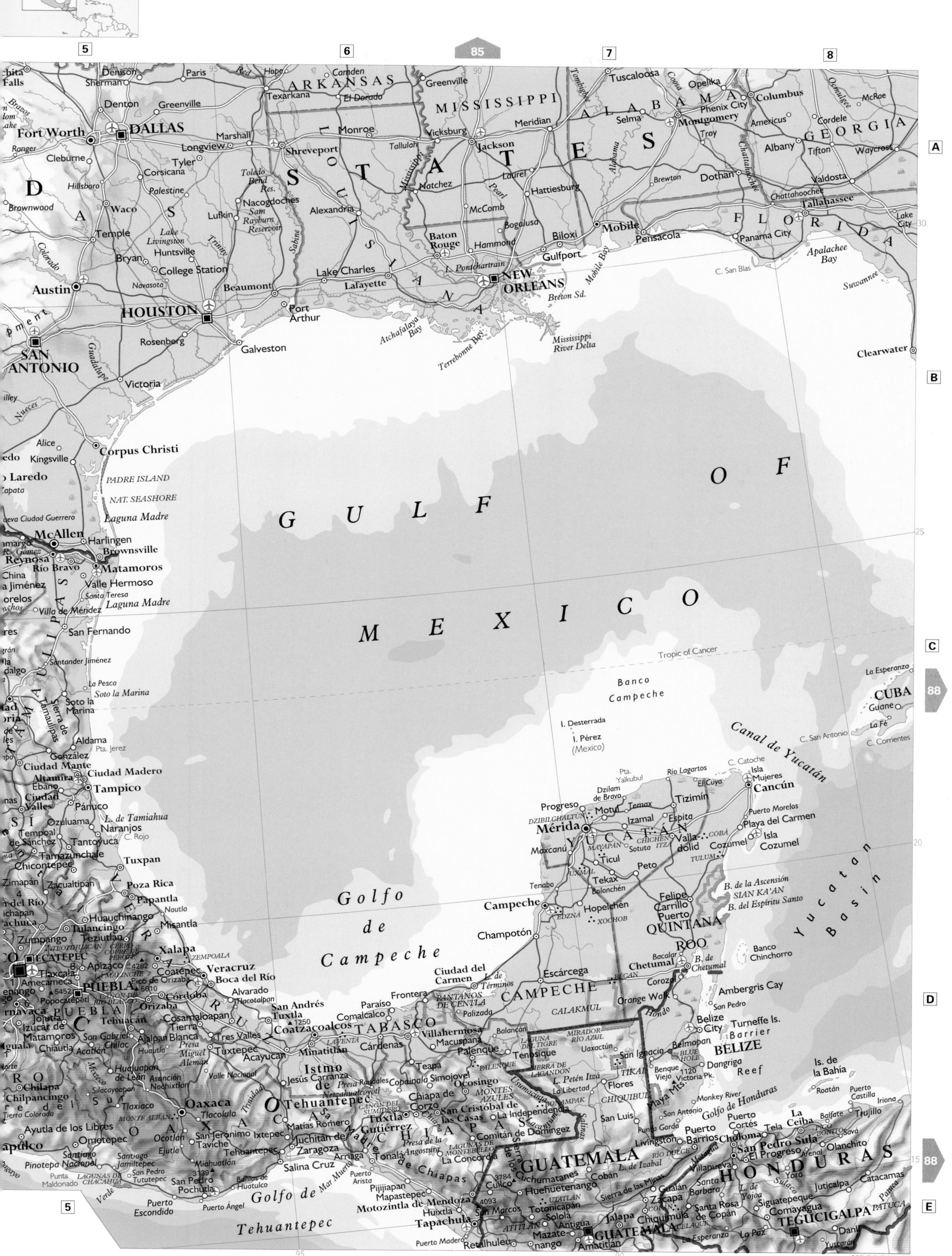
GULF OF MEXICO
Golfo de Campeche
Banco Campeche
Canal de Yucatán
Yucatan Basin
Tropic of Cancer
UNITED STATES
MISSISSIPPI
ALABAMA
GEORGIA
FLORIDA
LOUISIANA
ARKANSAS
TEXAS
HOUSTON
DALLAS
SAN ANTONIO
NEW ORLEANS
Corpus Christi
Mobile
Tallahassee
Mérida
Campeche
Cancún
Veracruz
Tampico
BELIZE
GUATEMALA
HONDURAS
TEGUCIGALPA
CUBA
Gulf of Tehuantepec
Istmo de Tehuantepec
YUCATÁN
CAMPECHE
TABASCO
QUINTANA ROO
CHIAPAS
OAXACA
PUEBLA
COPYRIGHT PHILIP'S

Projection: Bi-polar oblique Conical Orthomorphic

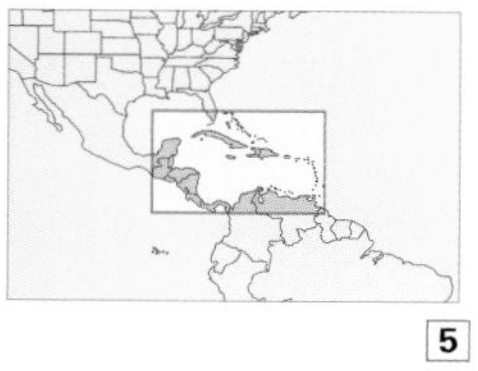

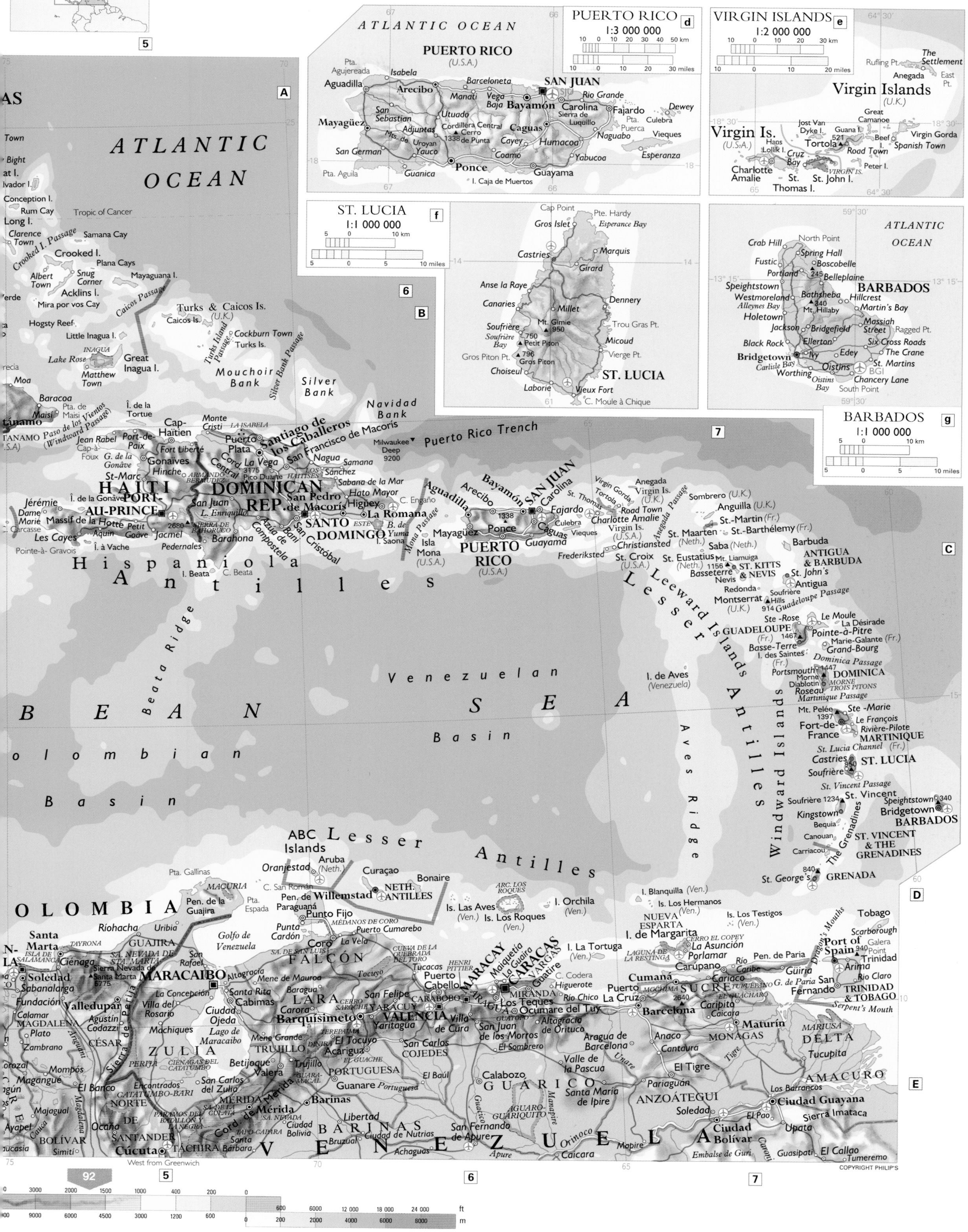

PUERTO RICO d

1:3 000 000

ATLANTIC OCEAN

PUERTO RICO (U.S.A.)

Aguadilla, Isabela, Arecibo, Barceloneta, SAN JUAN, Rio Grande, Mayagüez, Manatí, Vega Baja, Bayamón, Carolina, Fajardo, Dewey, San Sebastian, Utuado, Cordillera Central, Sierra de Luquillo, Culebra, Adjuntas, Cerro de Punta 1338, Caguas, Cayey, Humacao, Naguabo, Vieques, San Germán, Mts. de Uroyan, Yauco, Coamo, Yabucoa, Esperanza, Ponce, Guanica, Guayama, Pta. Aguila, I. Caja de Muertos

VIRGIN ISLANDS e

1:2 000 000

Virgin Islands (U.K.), Virgin Is. (U.S.A.), Anegada, The Settlement, East Pt., Great Camanoe, Jost Van Dyke I., Guana I., Beef I., Virgin Gorda, Spanish Town, Tortola, Road Town, Cruz Bay, Charlotte Amalie, St. Thomas I., St. John I., Peter I.

ST. LUCIA f

1:1 000 000

Cap Point, Pte. Hardy, Gros Islet, Esperance Bay, Castries, Marquis, Girard, Anse la Raye, Canaries, Millet, Dennery, Soufrière, Mt. Gimie 950, Petit Piton 750, Gros Piton 796, Micoud, Choiseul, Laborie, Vieux Fort, C. Moule à Chique, ST. LUCIA

BARBADOS g

1:1 000 000

ATLANTIC OCEAN

North Point, Crab Hill, Spring Hall, Fustic, Boscobelle, Portland, Belleplaine, Speightstown, Bathsheba, Hillcrest, Westmoreland, Mt. Hillaby 340, Martin's Bay, Holetown, Jackson, Bridgefield, Massiah Street, Ragged Pt., Black Rock, Ellerton, Six Cross Roads, Bridgetown, Ivy, Edey, The Crane, St. Martins, Oistins, Worthing, Chancery Lane, South Point, BARBADOS

Main map

ATLANTIC OCEAN

Tropic of Cancer

Turks & Caicos Is. (U.K.), Mouchoir Bank, Silver Bank, Navidad Bank, Puerto Rico Trench, Milwaukee Deep 9200

HAITI, PORT-AU-PRINCE, Cap-Haïtien, Gonaïves, Jérémie, Les Cayes, Jacmel

DOMINICAN REP., SANTO DOMINGO, Santiago de los Caballeros, San Francisco de Macorís, Puerto Plata, La Vega, San Pedro de Macorís, La Romana, Barahona

Hispaniola, Antilles, Beata Ridge, Venezuelan Basin, Colombian Basin, CARIBBEAN SEA

Leeward Islands, Lesser Antilles, Aves Ridge, Windward Islands, I. de Aves (Venezuela)

Anguilla (U.K.), St.-Martin (Fr.), St.-Barthélemy (Fr.), Saba (Neth.), St. Eustatius (Neth.), ST. KITTS & NEVIS, ANTIGUA & BARBUDA, Montserrat (U.K.), GUADELOUPE (Fr.), DOMINICA, MARTINIQUE (Fr.), ST. LUCIA, ST. VINCENT & THE GRENADINES, BARBADOS, GRENADA

ABC Islands, Aruba (Neth.), Curaçao, Bonaire, NETH. ANTILLES, Willemstad

COLOMBIA, VENEZUELA, TRINIDAD & TOBAGO

MARACAIBO, CARACAS, VALENCIA, MARACAY, Barquisimeto, Cumaná, Barcelona, Maturín, Ciudad Bolívar, Ciudad Guayana, Cúcuta, Mérida, Barinas

West from Greenwich

92

ft: 0, 600, 6000, 12 000, 18 000, 24 000

m: 0, 200, 2000, 4000, 6000, 8000

1:35 000 000

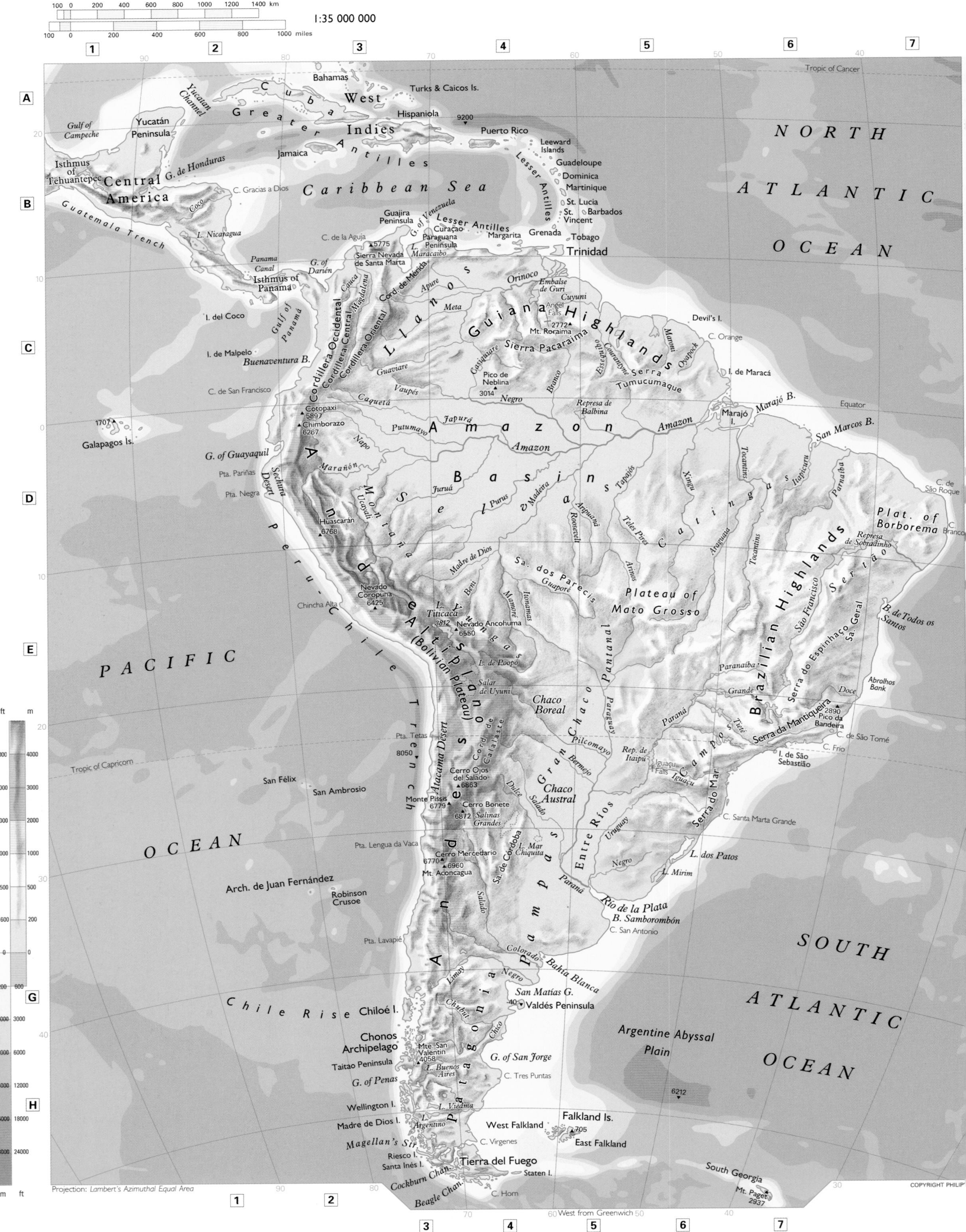

NORTH ATLANTIC OCEAN
SOUTH ATLANTIC OCEAN
PACIFIC OCEAN
Caribbean Sea
Tropic of Cancer
Tropic of Capricorn
Equator
Bahamas
Turks & Caicos Is.
Cuba
West Indies
Greater Antilles
Hispaniola
9200
Puerto Rico
Jamaica
Leeward Islands
Guadeloupe
Dominica
Martinique
St. Lucia
St. Vincent
Barbados
Grenada
Tobago
Trinidad
Lesser Antilles
Yucatan Channel
Gulf of Campeche
Yucatán Peninsula
Isthmus of Tehuantepec
G. de Honduras
Central America
C. Gracias a Dios
Coco
Guatemala Trench
L. Nicaragua
Guajira Peninsula
G. of Venezuela
Curaçao
Paraguana Peninsula
Margarita
C. de la Aguja
5775
Sierra Nevada de Santa Marta
L. Maracaibo
Panama Canal
G. of Darién
Isthmus of Panama
Gulf of Panamá
I. del Coco
I. de Malpelo
Buenaventura B.
C. de San Francisco
Cauca
Magdalena
Cord. de Merida
Cordillera Occidental
Cordillera Central
Cordillera Oriental
Apure
Orinoco
Llanos
Meta
Embalse de Guri
Cuyuni
Angel Falls
Guiana Highlands
2772
Mt. Roraima
Sierra Pacaraima
Essequibo
Courantyne
Maroni
Oyapock
Devil's I.
C. Orange
Serra Tumucumaque
I. de Maracá
Guaviare
Casiquiare
Pico de Neblina
3014
Negro
Branco
Represa de Balbina
Vaupés
Caquetá
Marajó I.
Marajó B.
Cotopaxi 5897
Chimborazo 6267
1707
Galapagos Is.
Japurá
Putumayo
Amazon
Amazon Basin
San Marcos B.
G. of Guayaquil
Napo
Marañón
Pta. Pariñas
Pta. Negra
Sechura Desert
Juruá
Purus
Madeira
Tapajós
Xingu
Tocantins
Itapicuru
Parnaíba
C. de São Roque
Montaña
Ucayali
Aripuanã
Roosevelt
Teles Pires
Caatinga
Plat. of Borborema
C. Branco
Represa de Sobradinho
Huascarán 6768
Peru-Chile Trench
Madre de Dios
Sa. dos Parecis
Guaporé
Arinos
Araguaia
Tocantins
Sertão
Brazilian Highlands
São Francisco
Beni
Mamoré
Itonamas
Plateau of Mato Grosso
B. de Todos os Santos
Nevado Coropuna 6425
Chincha Alta
L. Titicaca 3812
Nevado Ancohuma 6550
Yungas
Altiplano (Bolivian Plateau)
L. de Poopó
Salar de Uyuni
Pantanal
Chaco Boreal
Paraguay
Gran Chaco
Paranaíba
Grande
Serra do Espinhaço
Sa. Geral
Abrolhos Bank
Doce
2890 Pico da Bandeira
Serra da Mantiqueira
C. de São Tomé
C. Frio
I. de São Sebastião
Pta. Tetas
8050
Atacama Desert
Cord. de Calalaste
Pilcomayo
Bermejo
Rep. de Itaipú
Iguaçu Falls
Iguaçu
Paraná
Tietê
Campos
San Félix
San Ambrosio
Cerro Ojos del Salado 6863
Monte Pissis 6779
Cerro Bonete 6872
Salinas Grandes
Dulce
Salado
Chaco Austral
Entre Ríos
Uruguay
Serra do Mar
C. Santa Marta Grande
Pta. Lengua da Vaca
Cerro Mercedario 6770
6960 Mt. Aconcagua
Sa. de Córdoba
L. Mar Chiquita
Negro
L. dos Patos
L. Mirim
Arch. de Juan Fernández
Robinson Crusoe
Pampas
Río de la Plata
B. Samborombón
C. San Antonio
Andes
Pta. Lavapié
Colorado
Bahía Blanca
Limay
Negro
San Matías G.
Valdés Peninsula
40
Chile Rise
Chiloé I.
Chubut
Patagonia
Chico
Chonos Archipelago
Mte San Valentin 4058
Taitao Peninsula
L. Buenos Aires
G. of San Jorge
C. Tres Puntas
Argentine Abyssal Plain
G. of Penas
6212
Wellington I.
L. Viedma
L. Argentino
Madre de Dios I.
Falkland Is.
West Falkland
East Falkland
705
C. Virgenes
Magellan's Str.
Riesco I.
Santa Inés I.
Tierra del Fuego
Staten I.
Cockburn Chan.
Beagle Chan.
C. Horn
South Georgia
Mt. Paget 2937
Projection: Lambert's Azimuthal Equal Area
West from Greenwich
COPYRIGHT PHILIP

1:35 000 000

■ LIMA Capital Cities

100 0 200 400 600 800 1000 1200 1400 km

100 0 200 400 600 800 1000 miles

1 2 3 4 5 6 7

90 80 70 60 50 40

Tropic of Cancer

A

20

Havana

BAHAMAS

C U B A

Turks & Caicos Is.
(U.K.)

NORTH

Cayman Is.
(U.K.)

HAITI

DOMINICAN
REP.

San Juan

Virgin Is. (U.S.A. - U.K.)

Anguilla (U.K.)

St. Martin (Fr. - Neth.)

ATLANTIC

JAMAICA

Kingston

Port-au-
Prince

Santo
Domingo

PUERTO
RICO
(U.S.A.)

ANTIGUA &
BARBUDA

St. Kitts
& Nevis

GUADELOUPE
(Fr.)

B

MEXICO

BELIZE

GUATEMALA

HONDURAS

Tegucigalpa

Guatemala

San Salvador

EL SALVADOR

NICARAGUA

Managua

COSTA
RICA

San José

Panamá

P A N A M A

Caribbean Sea

Basse-Terre

DOMINICA

Fort-de-France

Castries

St. Vincent

Kingstown

GRENADA

St. George's

MARTINIQUE
(Fr.)

ST. LUCIA

BARBADOS

Bridgetown

Port of
Spain

TRINIDAD &
TOBAGO

OCEAN

I. del Coco
(Costa Rica)

Gulf of Panamá

G. of
Darién

Barranquilla

Cartagena

Maracaibo

Aruba
(Neth.)

Oranjestad

Willemstad

NETH.
ANTILLES

Caracas

Barquisimeto

Valencia

Orinoco

Ciudad Guayana

Georgetown

Paramaribo

Cayenne

C. Orange

10

C

I. de Malpelo

PERNAMBUCO

PARAÍBA

Campina Grande

Recife

Callao

LIMA

Cuzco

PERU

BRAZIL

MATO GROSSO

ALAGOAS

SERGIPE

Maceió

Aracaju

E

20

L.
Titicaca

La Paz

BOLIVIA

Cochabamba

Santa Cruz

Sucre

Arequipa

Mamoré

Cuiabá

BAHÍA

São Francisco

Salvador

GOIÁS

DIS. FED.

Brasília

Goiânia

MINAS GERAIS

PACIFIC

Iquique

MATO GROSSO
DO SUL

Paraguay

Ribeirão
Prêto

Belo
Horizonte

Juiz
de Fora

ESPÍRITO
SANTO

Vitória

Campos

F

30

San Félix
(Chile)

San Ambrosio
(Chile)

Antofagasta

Salta

PARAGUAY

Pilcomayo

Asunción

PARANÁ

SÃO
PAULO

Campinas

SANTA CATARINA

Uruguay

R. DE J.

Niterói

RIO DE
JANEIRO

Santos

Curitiba

RIO GRANDE
DO SUL

Pôrto Alegre

O C E A N

Tropic of Capricorn

San Miguel
de Tucumán

Salado

Resistencia

Corrientes

Paraná

Pelotas

G

40

A R G E N T I N A

Córdoba

San Juan

Mendoza

Santa Fé

Rosario

URUGUAY

Montevideo

Mar del Plata

SOUTH

Viña del Mar

Valparaiso

SANTIAGO

Talca

BUENOS AIRES

La Plata

Río de la Plata

C H I L E

Arch. de Juan Fernández
(Chile)

Robinson
Crusoe

Concepción

Bahía
Blanca

Colorado

ATLANTIC

Valdivia

Viedma

Negro

H

Puerto Montt

Chubut

OCEAN

Gulf of Penas

Comodoro Rivadavia

Gulf of San Jorge

West Falkland

FALKLAND IS.
(U.K.)

Stanley

East Falkland

South Georgia
(U.K.)

Magellan's Str.

Punta Arenas

Tierra del Fuego

C. Horn

Projection: Lambert's Azimuthal Equal Area

90 80 70 60 West from Greenwich 50 40 30

COPYRIGHT PHILIP'S

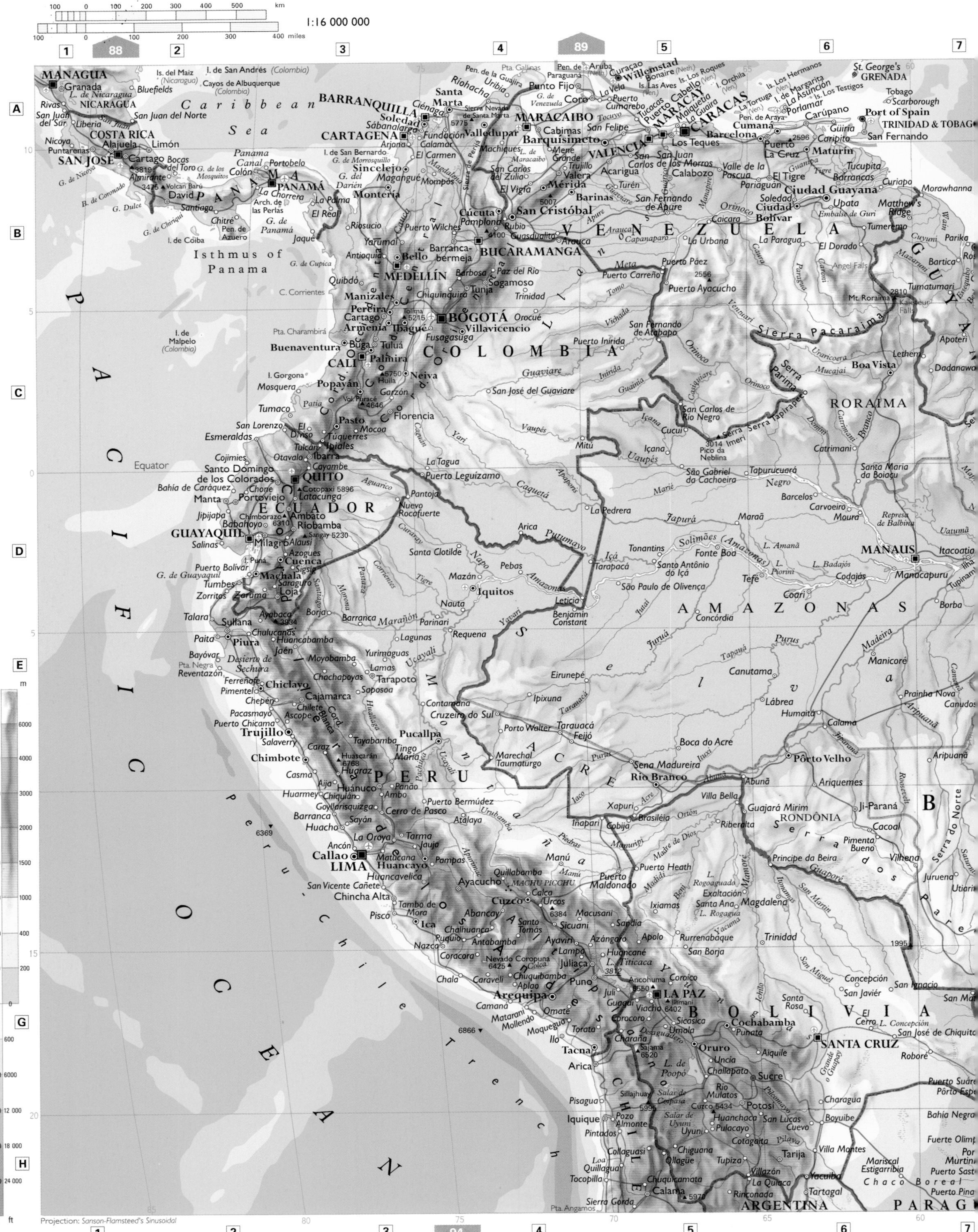

1:16 000 000
km
miles
88
89
94
Projection: Sanson-Flamsteed's Sinusoidal
MANAGUA
NICARAGUA
COSTA RICA
SAN JOSÉ
Limón
Caribbean Sea
Isthmus of Panama
PANAMÁ
Colón
BARRANQUILLA
CARTAGENA
Santa Marta
MARACAIBO
Barquisimeto
VALENCIA
MARACAY
CARACAS
Barcelona
Cumaná
Port of Spain
TRINIDAD & TOBAGO
St. George's
GRENADA
Ciudad Guayana
Ciudad Bolívar
VENEZUELA
San Cristóbal
Cúcuta
BUCARAMANGA
MEDELLÍN
Manizales
Pereira
BOGOTÁ
Villavicencio
Ibagué
CALI
Buenaventura
Popayán
Neiva
COLOMBIA
Pasto
Florencia
Mitú
Puerto Carreño
Puerto Ayacucho
Sierra Pacaraima
Boa Vista
RORAIMA
Mt. Roraima
Angel Falls
Esmeraldas
QUITO
Equator
Cotopaxi 5896
Chimborazo 6310
ECUADOR
GUAYAQUIL
Cuenca
Machala
Loja
Iquitos
Leticia
AMAZONAS
MANAUS
Manacapuru
Tefé
Coari
Piura
Sullana
Chiclayo
Cajamarca
Trujillo
Chimbote
Huaraz
Huascarán 6768
PERU
Pucallpa
Huánuco
Cerro de Pasco
Callao
LIMA
Huancayo
Ayacucho
Cuzco
Ica
Nazca
Juliaca
Puno
Arequipa
Tacna
Arica
L. Titicaca
LA PAZ
BOLIVIA
Cochabamba
Oruro
Sucre
Potosí
SANTA CRUZ
Tarija
Iquique
Calama
Rio Branco
ACRE
Porto Velho
RONDÔNIA
Trinidad
CHILE
ARGENTINA
PACIFIC OCEAN
Peru-Chile Trench

TRINIDAD AND TOBAGO
1:2 500 000
West from Greenwich
Tobago
Charlotteville
North Pt.
Little Tobago
Castara
Main Ridge
Roxborough
Plymouth
Buccoo Reef
Crown Pt.
Scarborough
Rockly Bay
Trinidad
ATLANTIC OCEAN
Golfo de Paria
Serpent's Mouth
Dragon's Mouths
VENEZUELA
Pen. de Paria
Macuro
Güiria
Corozal Pt.
Monos I.
Maraval
Blanchisseuse
Chupara Pt.
La Vache Pt.
Maracas Bay Village
Matelot
Sans Souci
Toco
Galera Pt.
Redhead
Salybia
Northern Range
Mt. Aripo
Port of Spain
San Juan
Tunapuna
Valencia
Arima
Caroni
Guaico
Matura Bay
Sangre Grande
Chaguanas
Talparo
Upper Manzanilla
Nariva Swamp
Cocos Bay
Couva
Point Lisas
Otaheite Bay
San Fernando
Gasparillo
Rio Claro
Guatuaro Pt.
Brighton
Guapo Bay
La Brea
Pitch Lake
Princes Town
Pierreville
Mayaro Bay
Point Fortin
Penal
Basse Terre
Guayaguayare
Cedros Bay
Bonasse
Palo Seco
Siparia
Trinity Hills
Galeota Pt.
Icacos Pt.
Erin Pt.
La Lune
Moruga
Pta. Bombedor
ATLANTIC OCEAN
Equator
Paramaribo
Nieuw Amsterdam
Moengo
Albina
St-Laurent du Maroni
Iracoubo
Sinnamary
Kourou
Cayenne
Kaw
Approuague
C. Orange
St-Georges
Oiapoque
FRENCH GUIANA
Camopi
Amapá
I. de Maracá
AMAPÁ
Tumucumaque
Merirumã
Serra do Navio
Macapá
I. Caviana
I. Mexiana
C. Maguarinho
Mazagão
Afuá
I. Grande de Gurupá
I. de Marajó
Soure
Curuçá
Salinópolis
Bragança
Vigia
BELÉM
Almeirim
Monte Alegre
Prainha
Gurupá
Breves
Castanhal
Viseu
Turiaçu
Cururupu
Porto de Moz
Curralinho
Abaetetuba
Cametá
Amazonas (Amazon)
Santarém
Belterra
Altamira
Aveiro
Baião
Alcântara
B. de São Marcos
São Luís
Barreirinhas
Tutóia
Luís Correia
Camocim
Pinheiro
Rosário
Viana
Itapecuru-Mirim
Parnaíba
Granja
Itapipoca
Caucaia
FORTALEZA
Santa Inês
Bacabal
Brejo
Piracuruca
Sobral
Maranguape
Cascavel
PARÁ
Tucuruí
Represa de Tucuruí
Coroatá
Codó
Piripiri
Baturité
Aracati
Rocas
Fernando de Noronha (Braz.)
Açailândia
Pedreiras
Caxias
Campo Maior
Oiticica
Ipu
Quixadá
Russas
Areia Branca
Mossoró
Macau
Ceará-Mirim
C. de São Roque
Marabá
MARANHÃO
Imperatriz
Teresina
Crateús
CEARÁ
RIO GRANDE DO NORTE
NATAL
São João do Araguaia
Barra do Corda
Senador Pompeu
Caraúbas
Currais Novos
Canguaretama
Mamanguape
Carajás
Grajaú
Tocantinópolis
Porto Franco
Colinas
Amarante
Valença do Piauí
Iguatu
Caicó
Estreito
Carolina
Floriano
Oeiras
Picos
Cedro
Sousa
Patos
Alagoa Grande
Cabedelo
João Pessoa
Araguaína
Riachão
Loreto
Nova Iorque
Uruçuí
PIAUÍ
Cajazeiras
Crato
Juàzeiro do Norte
Ouricuri
PARAÍBA
Campina Grande
Olinda
RECIFE
Jaboatão
Conceição do Araguaia
Paulistana
Salgueiro
Caruaru
PERNAMBUCO
Pesqueira
Vitória de Santo Antão
Araguacema
Pedro Afonso
Santa Filomena
São João do Piauí
Petrolina
Garanhuns
Palmares
Rio Largo
MACEIÓ
Caracol
Remanso
Casa Nova
Juàzeiro
Paulo Afonso
Palmeira dos Índios
Arapiraca
ALAGOAS
Penedo
Palmas
Porto Nacional
TOCANTINS
Parnaguá
Represa de Sobradinho
Senhor-do-Bonfim
Propriá
SERGIPE
Capela
Aracaju
Barra
Xique-Xique
Jacobina
Queimadas
Serrinha
Estância
São Cristóvão
Santa Isabel do Morro
Gurupi
Peixe
Taguatinga
Barreiras
Ibotirama
BAHIA
Mundo Novo
Feira de Santana
Alagoinhas
Santo Amaro
Cachoeira
Itaberaba
Paraná
Campos Belos
São Domingos
Bom Jesus da Lapa
Santa Maria da Vitória
Castro Alves
Valença
Nazaré
SALVADOR
B. de Todos os Santos
Jequié
Serra do Sincorá
Caetité
Brumado
Carinhanha
Posse
Niquelândia
Uruaçu
Aruanã
Ubaitaba
Vitória da Conquista
Itabuna
Ilhéus
Canavieiras
Condeúba
Monte Azul
Januária
São Francisco
Janaúba
Pedra Azul
Belmonte
Porto Seguro
DIST. FED.
Formosa
BRASÍLIA
Goiás
Anápolis
Luziânia
GOIÂNIA
Rondonópolis
Barra do Garças
Montes Claros
Salinas
Jequitinhonha
Araçuaí
Itamaraju
Prado
Caravelas
Teófilo Otoni
Nanuque
Pirapora
Paracatu
Vianópolis
GOIÁS
Morrinhos
Alto Araguaia
Jataí
Rio Verde
Ipameri
Catalão
Patos de Minas
Itumbiara
Quirinópolis
Corinto
Diamantina
Governador Valadares
Mucuri
Conceição da Barra
São Mateus
Banco dos Abrolhos
Araguari
MINAS GERAIS
Uberlândia
Patrocínio
Curvelo
Ipatinga
Nova Venécia
Colatina
Linhares
Ituiutaba
Araxá
Sete Lagoas
Itabira
Uberaba
BELO HORIZONTE
Caratinga
Sabará
Ponte Nova
Cariacica
VITÓRIA
Vila Velha
Campo Grande
Paranaíba
Santa Fé do Sul
Água Clara
São José do Rio Preto
Franca
Divinópolis
Conselheiro Lafaiete
Ouro Prêto
Três Lagoas
Andradina
Barretos
Passos
Ribeirão Prêto
Ubá
Cachoeiro de Itapemirim
Araçatuba
Penápolis
Catanduva
Guaxupé
São João del Rei
Barbacena
Itaperuna
Presidente Epitácio
Presidente Prudente
Marília
SÃO PAULO
Araraquara
Poços de Caldas
Juiz de Fora
Campos
São Carlos
Três Rios
Bauru
Jaú
Nova Friburgo
Assis
Piracicaba
Limeira
Petrópolis
Botucatu
CAMPINAS
Volta Redonda
RIO DE JANEIRO
Niterói
Cabo Frio
São Pedro & São Paulo (Braz.)
Trindade (Braz.)
Planalto do Mato Grosso
Trinidad

1:8 000 000

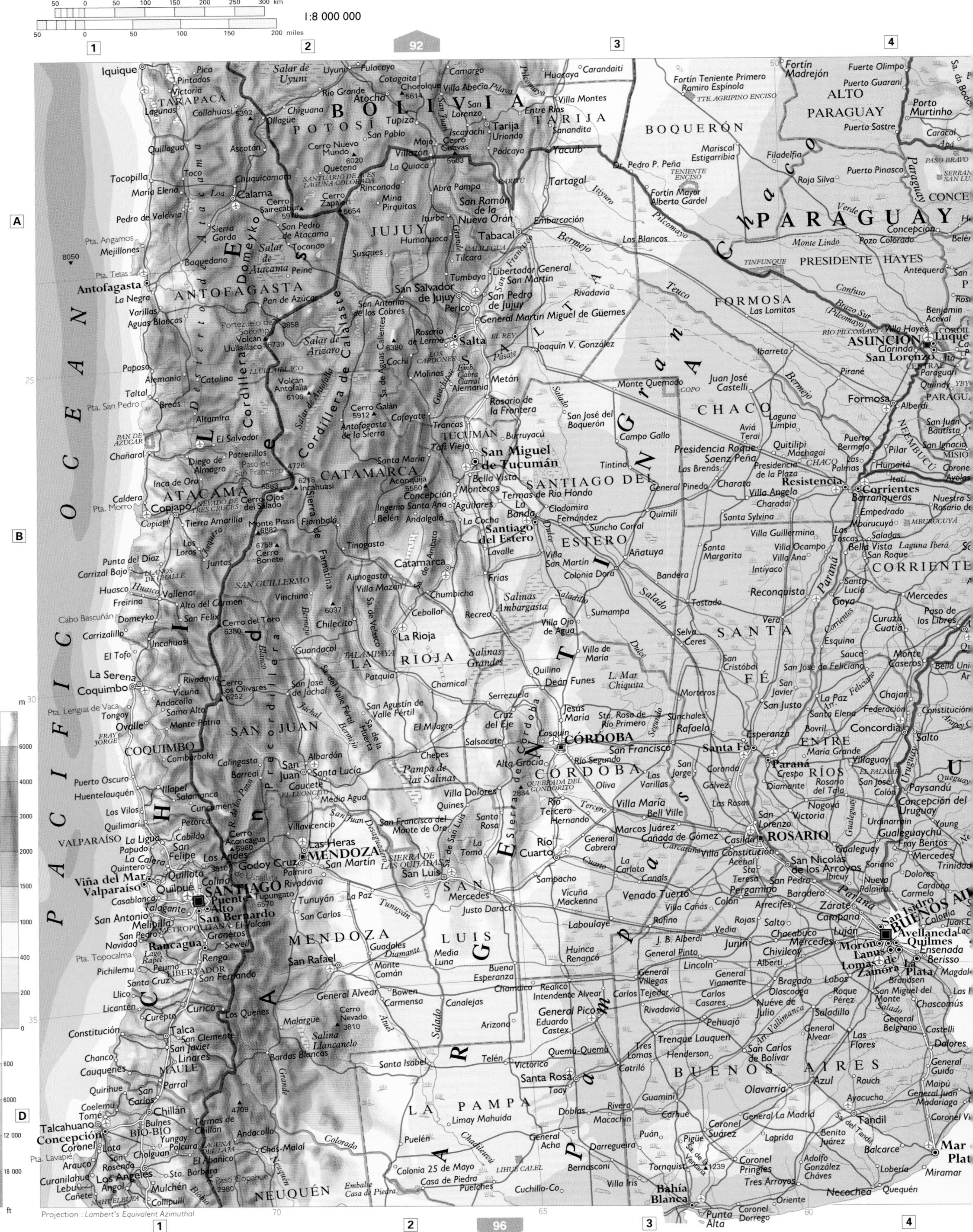

92
96

BRAZIL
ATLANTIC OCEAN
SÃO PAULO
RIO DE JANEIRO
BELO HORIZONTE
CURITIBA
PÔRTO ALEGRE
Florianópolis
SANTOS
CAMPINAS
VITÓRIA
Tropic of Capricorn
West from Greenwich

1:16 000 000

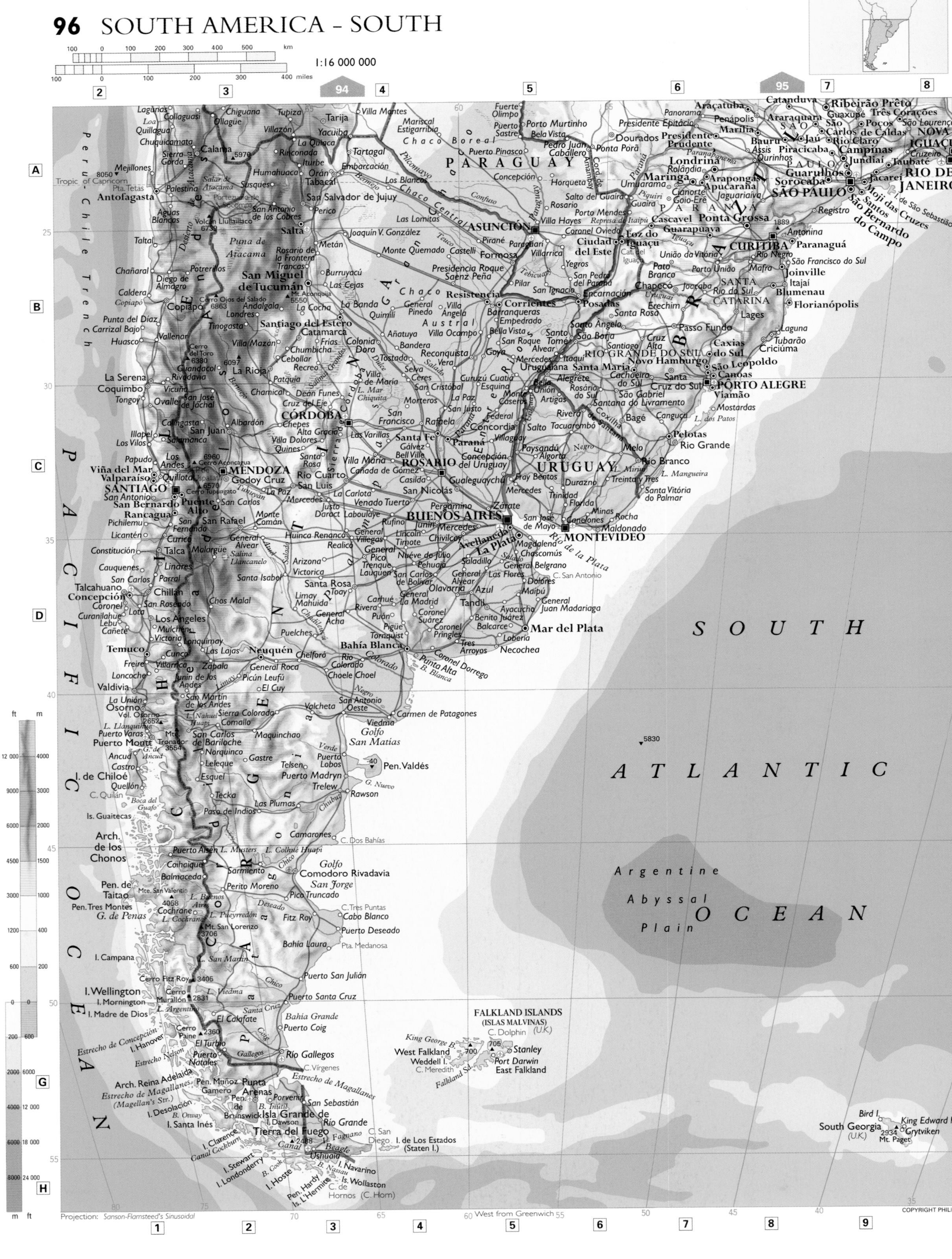

100 0 100 200 300 400 500 km
100 0 100 200 300 400 miles
94
95
1 2 3 4 5 6 7 8 9
A B C D E F G H
PACIFIC OCEAN
Peru-Chile Trench
SOUTH ATLANTIC OCEAN
Argentine Abyssal Plain
5830
Tropic of Capricorn
PARAGUAY
URUGUAY
Chaco Boreal
Chaco Central
Chaco Austral
Puna de Atacama
Desierto de Atacama
ANDES
PATAGONIA
PAMPAS
ASUNCIÓN
BUENOS AIRES
MONTEVIDEO
SANTIAGO
SÃO PAULO
RIO DE JANEIRO
CURITIBA
PORTO ALEGRE
Córdoba
Rosario
Mendoza
San Miguel de Tucumán
Salta
San Salvador de Jujuy
Antofagasta
Calama
Copiapó
La Serena
Coquimbo
Valparaíso
Viña del Mar
Rancagua
Talca
Chillán
Concepción
Talcahuano
Los Angeles
Temuco
Valdivia
Osorno
Puerto Montt
I. de Chiloé
Arch. de los Chonos
Pen. de Taitao
I. Wellington
Puerto Natales
Punta Arenas
Isla Grande de Tierra del Fuego
Ushuaia
C. de Hornos (C. Horn)
I. de Los Estados (Staten I.)
Estrecho de Magallanes
Río Gallegos
Puerto Santa Cruz
Puerto San Julián
Puerto Deseado
Comodoro Rivadavia
Golfo San Jorge
Trelew
Rawson
Puerto Madryn
Pen. Valdés
Golfo San Matías
Viedma
Carmen de Patagones
Bahía Blanca
Mar del Plata
Necochea
Tandil
La Plata
Santa Rosa
Neuquén
San Carlos de Bariloche
Santa Fe
Paraná
Corrientes
Resistencia
Formosa
Posadas
Encarnación
Ciudad del Este
Foz do Iguaçu
Santiago del Estero
La Rioja
San Juan
San Luis
Río Cuarto
Concordia
Salto
Paysandú
Rivera
Pelotas
Rio Grande
Florianópolis
Blumenau
Joinville
Ponta Grossa
Londrina
Maringá
Campinas
Santos
Ribeirão Prêto
Mt. Aconcagua 6960
Cerro Ojos del Salado 6863
Mt. Fitz Roy 3405
Mt. San Lorenzo 3706
FALKLAND ISLANDS (ISLAS MALVINAS) (U.K.)
West Falkland
East Falkland
Stanley
Port Darwin
South Georgia (U.K.)
Grytviken
King Edward Pt
Mt. Paget 2934
ft m
12 000 4000
9000 3000
6000 2000
4500 1500
3000 1000
1200 400
600 200
0 0
200 600
2000 6000
4000 12 000
6000 18 000
8000 24 000
m ft
Projection: Sanson-Flamsteed's Sinusoidal
West from Greenwich
COPYRIGHT PHILIP'S

INDEX TO WORLD MAPS

The index contains the names of all the principal places and features shown on the World Maps. Each name is followed by an additional entry in italics giving the country or region within which it is located. The alphabetical order of names composed of two or more words is governed primarily by the first word, then by the second, and then by the country or region name that follows. This is an example of the rule:

Mīr Kūh *Iran*	26°22N 58°55E **45** E8
Mīr Shahdād *Iran*	26°15N 58°29E **45** E8
Mira *Italy*	45°26N 12°8E **22** B5
Mira por vos Cay *Bahamas*	22°9N 74°30W **89** B5

Physical features composed of a proper name (Erie) and a description (Lake) are positioned alphabetically by the proper name. The description is positioned after the proper name and is usually abbreviated:

Erie, L. *N. Amer.*	42°15N 81°0W **82** D4

Where a description forms part of a settlement or administrative name, however, it is always written in full and put in its true alphabetical position:

Mount Morris *U.S.A.*	42°44N 77°52W **82** D7

Names beginning with M' and Mc are indexed as if they were spelled Mac. Names beginning St. are alphabetized under Saint, but Sankt, Sint, Sant', Santa and San are all spelt in full and are alphabetized accordingly. If the same place name occurs two or more times in the index and all are in the same country, each is followed by the name of the administrative subdivision in which it is located.

The geographical co-ordinates which follow each name in the index give the latitude and longitude of each place. The first co-ordinate indicates latitude – the distance north or south of the Equator. The second co-ordinate indicates longitude – the distance east or west of the Greenwich Meridian. Both latitude and longitude are measured in degrees and minutes (there are 60 minutes in a degree).

The latitude is followed by N(orth) or S(outh) and the longitude by E(ast) or W(est).

The number in bold type which follows the geographical co-ordinates refers to the number of the map page where that feature or place will be found. This is usually the largest scale at which the place or feature appears.

The letter and figure that are immediately after the page number give the grid square on the map page, within which the feature is situated. The letter represents the latitude and the figure the longitude. A lower-case letter immediately after the page number refers to an inset map on that page.

In some cases the feature itself may fall within the specified square, while the name is outside. This is usually the case only with features that are larger than a grid square.

Rivers are indexed to their mouths or confluences, and carry the symbol → after their names. The following symbols are also used in the index: ■ country, ⊘ overseas territory or dependency, □ first-order administrative area, △ national park, ⌓ other park (provincial park, nature reserve or game reserve), ✈ (LHR) principal airport (and location identifier).

Abbreviations used in the index

A.C.T. – Australian Capital Territory
A.R. – Autonomous Region
Afghan. – Afghanistan
Afr. – Africa
Ala. – Alabama
Alta. – Alberta
Amer. – America(n)
Ant. – Antilles
Arch. – Archipelago
Ariz. – Arizona
Ark. – Arkansas
Atl. Oc. – Atlantic Ocean
B. – Baie, Bahía, Bay, Bucht, Bugt
B.C. – British Columbia
Bangla. – Bangladesh
Barr. – Barrage
Bos.-H. – Bosnia-Herzegovina
C. – Cabo, Cap, Cape, Coast
C.A.R. – Central African Republic
C. Prov. – Cape Province
Calif. – California
Cat. – Catarata
Cent. – Central
Chan. – Channel
Colo. – Colorado
Conn. – Connecticut
Cord. – Cordillera
Cr. – Creek
Czech. – Czech Republic
D.C. – District of Columbia
Del. – Delaware
Dem. – Democratic
Dep. – Dependency
Des. – Desert
Dét. – Détroit
Dist. – District
Dj. – Djebel
Dom. Rep. – Dominican Republic
E. – East
El Salv. – El Salvador
Eq. Guin. – Equatorial Guinea
Est. – Estrecho
Falk. Is. – Falkland Is.
Fd. – Fjord
Fla. – Florida
Fr. – French
G. – Golfe, Golfo, Gulf, Guba, Gebel
Ga. – Georgia
Gt. – Great, Greater
Guinea-Biss. – Guinea-Bissau
H.K. – Hong Kong
H.P. – Himachal Pradesh
Hants. – Hampshire
Harb. – Harbor, Harbour
Hd. – Head
Hts. – Heights
I.(s). – Île, Ilha, Insel, Isla, Island, Isle
Ill. – Illinois
Ind. – Indiana
Ind. Oc. – Indian Ocean
Ivory C. – Ivory Coast
J. – Jabal, Jebel
Jaz. – Jazīrah
Junc. – Junction
K. – Kap, Kapp
Kans. – Kansas
Kep. – Kepulauan
Ky. – Kentucky
L. – Lac, Lacul, Lago, Lagoa, Lake, Limni, Loch, Lough
La. – Louisiana
Ld. – Land
Liech. – Liechtenstein
Lux. – Luxembourg
Mad. P. – Madhya Pradesh
Madag. – Madagascar
Man. – Manitoba
Mass. – Massachusetts
Md. – Maryland
Me. – Maine
Medit. S. – Mediterranean Sea
Mich. – Michigan
Minn. – Minnesota
Miss. – Mississippi
Mo. – Missouri
Mont. – Montana
Mozam. – Mozambique
Mt.(s) – Mont, Montaña, Mountain
Mte. – Monte
Mti. – Monti
N. – Nord, Norte, North, Northern, Nouveau, Nahal, Nahr
N.B. – New Brunswick
N.C. – North Carolina
N. Cal. – New Caledonia
N. Dak. – North Dakota
N.H. – New Hampshire
N.I. – North Island
N.J. – New Jersey
N. Mex. – New Mexico
N.S. – Nova Scotia
N.S.W. – New South Wales
N.W.T. – North West Territory
N.Y. – New York
N.Z. – New Zealand
Nac. – Nacional
Nat. – National
Nebr. – Nebraska
Neths. – Netherlands
Nev. – Nevada
Nfld & L. – Newfoundland and Labrador
Nic. – Nicaragua
O. – Oued, Ouadi
Occ. – Occidentale
Okla. – Oklahoma
Ont. – Ontario
Or. – Orientale
Oreg. – Oregon
Os. – Ostrov
Oz. – Ozero
P. – Pass, Passo, Pasul, Pulau
P.E.I. – Prince Edward Island
Pa. – Pennsylvania
Pac. Oc. – Pacific Ocean
Papua N.G. – Papua New Guinea
Pass. – Passage
Peg. – Pegunungan
Pen. – Peninsula, Péninsule
Phil. – Philippines
Pk. – Peak
Plat. – Plateau
Prov. – Province, Provincial
Pt. – Point
Pta. – Ponta, Punta
Pte. – Pointe
Qué. – Québec
Queens. – Queensland
R. – Rio, River
R.I. – Rhode Island
Ra. – Range
Raj. – Rajasthan
Recr. – Recreational, Récréatif
Reg. – Region
Rep. – Republic
Res. – Reserve, Reservoir
Rhld-Pfz. – Rheinland-Pfalz
S. – South, Southern, Sur
Si. Arabia – Saudi Arabia
S.C. – South Carolina
S. Dak. – South Dakota
S.I. – South Island
S. Leone – Sierra Leone
Sa. – Serra, Sierra
Sask. – Saskatchewan
Scot. – Scotland
Sd. – Sound
Sev. – Severnaya
Sib. – Siberia
Sprs. – Springs
St. – Saint
Sta. – Santa
Ste. – Sainte
Sto. – Santo
Str. – Strait, Stretto
Switz. – Switzerland
Tas. – Tasmania
Tenn. – Tennessee
Terr. – Territory, Territoire
Tex. – Texas
Tg. – Tanjung
Trin. & Tob. – Trinidad & Tobago
U.A.E. – United Arab Emirates
U.K. – United Kingdom
U.S.A. – United States of America
Ut. P. – Uttar Pradesh
Va. – Virginia
Vdkhr. – Vodokhranilishche
Vdskh. – Vodoskhovyshche
Vf. – Vírful
Vic. – Victoria
Vol. – Volcano
Vt. – Vermont
W. – Wadi, West
W. Va. – West Virginia
Wall. & F. Is. – Wallis and Futuna Is.
Wash. – Washington
Wis. – Wisconsin
Wlkp. – Wielkopolski
Wyo. – Wyoming
Yorks. – Yorkshire

A

A Coruña *Spain* 43°20N 8°25W **21** A1
A Estrada *Spain* 42°43N 8°27W **21** A1
A Fonsagrada *Spain* 43°8N 7°4W **21** A2
Aabenraa *Denmark* 55°3N 9°25E **9** J13
Aachen *Germany* 50°45N 6°6E **16** C4
Aalborg *Denmark* 57°2N 9°54E **9** H13
Aalen *Germany* 48°51N 10°6E **16** D6
Aalst *Belgium* 50°56N 4°2E **15** D4
Aalten *Neths.* 51°56N 6°35E **15** C6
Aalter *Belgium* 51°5N 3°28E **15** C3
Äänekoski *Finland* 62°36N 25°44E **8** E21
Aarau *Switz.* 47°23N 8°4E **20** C8
Aare → *Switz.* 47°33N 8°14E **20** C8
Aarhus = Århus *Denmark* 56°8N 10°11E **9** H14
Aarschot *Belgium* 50°59N 4°49E **15** D4
Aba *Dem. Rep. of the Congo* 3°58N 30°17E **54** B3
Aba *Nigeria* 5°10N 7°19E **50** G7
Abaco I. *Bahamas* 26°25N 77°10W **88** A4
Ābādān *Iran* 30°22N 48°20E **45** D6
Ābādeh *Iran* 31°8N 52°40E **45** D7
Abadla *Algeria* 31°2N 2°45W **50** B5
Abaetetuba *Brazil* 1°40S 48°50W **93** D9
Abagnar Qi = Xilinhot *China* 43°52N 116°2E **34** C9
Abah, Tanjung *Indonesia* 8°46S 115°38E **37** K18
Abai *Paraguay* 25°58S 55°54W **95** B4
Abakan *Russia* 53°40N 91°10E **29** D10
Abancay *Peru* 13°35S 72°55W **92** F4
Abariringa *Kiribati* 2°50S 171°40W **64** H10
Abarqū *Iran* 31°10N 53°20E **45** D7
Abashiri *Japan* 44°0N 144°15E **30** B12
Abashiri-Wan *Japan* 44°0N 144°30E **30** C12
Ābay = Nîl el Azraq → *Sudan* 15°38N 32°31E **51** E12
Abay *Kazakhstan* 49°38N 72°53E **28** E8
Abaya, L. *Ethiopia* 6°30N 37°50E **47** F2
Abaza *Russia* 52°39N 90°6E **28** D9
'Abbāsābād *Iran* 33°34N 58°23E **45** C8
Abbay = Nîl el Azraq → *Sudan* 15°38N 32°31E **51** E12
Abbaye, Pt. *U.S.A.* 46°58N 88°8W **80** B9
Abbé, L. *Ethiopia* 11°8N 41°47E **47** E3
Abbeville *France* 50°6N 1°49E **20** A4
Abbeville *Ala., U.S.A.* 31°34N 85°15W **85** F12
Abbeville *La., U.S.A.* 29°58N 92°8W **84** G8
Abbeville *S.C., U.S.A.* 34°11N 82°23W **85** D13
Abbeyfeale *Ireland* 52°23N 9°18W **10** D2
Abbot Ice Shelf *Antarctica* 73°0S 92°0W **5** D16
Abbotsford *Canada* 49°5N 122°20W **70** D4
Abbottabad *Pakistan* 34°10N 73°15E **42** B5
ABC Islands = Netherlands Antilles ⊠ *W. Indies* 12°15N 69°0W **92** A5
Abd al Kūrī *Yemen* 12°5N 52°20E **47** E5
Ābdar *Iran* 30°16N 55°19E **45** D7
'Abdolābād *Iran* 34°12N 56°30E **45** C8
Abdulpur *Bangla.* 24°15N 88°59E **43** G13
Abéché *Chad* 13°50N 20°35E **51** F10
Abel Tasman △ *N.Z.* 40°59S 173°3E **59** D4
Abengourou *Ivory C.* 6°42N 3°27W **50** G5
Åbenrå = Aabenraa *Denmark* 55°3N 9°25E **9** J13
Abeokuta *Nigeria* 7°3N 3°19E **50** G6
Aber *Uganda* 2°12N 32°25E **54** B3
Aberaeron *U.K.* 52°15N 4°15W **13** E3
Aberayron = Aberaeron *U.K.* 52°15N 4°15W **13** E3
Aberchirder *U.K.* 57°34N 2°37W **11** D6
Abercorn *Australia* 25°12S 151°5E **63** D5
Aberdare *U.K.* 51°43N 3°27W **13** F4
Aberdare △ *Kenya* 0°22S 36°44E **54** C4
Aberdare Ra. *Kenya* 0°15S 36°50E **54** C4
Aberdeen *Australia* 32°9S 150°56E **63** E5
Aberdeen *Canada* 52°20N 106°8W **71** C7
Aberdeen *China* 22°14N 114°8E **33** G11
Aberdeen *S. Africa* 32°28S 24°2E **56** E3
Aberdeen *U.K.* 57°9N 2°5W **11** D6
Aberdeen *Idaho, U.S.A.* 42°57N 112°50W **76** E7
Aberdeen *Md., U.S.A.* 39°31N 76°10W **81** F15
Aberdeen *Miss., U.S.A.* 33°49N 88°33W **85** E10
Aberdeen *S. Dak., U.S.A.* 45°28N 98°29W **80** C4
Aberdeen *Wash., U.S.A.* 46°59N 123°50W **78** D3
Aberdeen, City of □ *U.K.* 57°10N 2°10W **11** D6
Aberdeenshire □ *U.K.* 57°17N 2°36W **11** D6
Aberdovey = Aberdyfi *U.K.* 52°33N 4°3W **13** E3
Aberdyfi *U.K.* 52°33N 4°3W **13** E3
Aberfeldy *U.K.* 56°37N 3°51W **11** E5
Aberfoyle *U.K.* 56°11N 4°23W **11** E4
Abergavenny *U.K.* 51°49N 3°1W **13** F4
Abergele *U.K.* 53°17N 3°35W **12** D4
Abernathy *U.S.A.* 33°50N 101°51W **84** E4
Abert, L. *U.S.A.* 42°38N 120°14W **76** E3
Aberystwyth *U.K.* 52°25N 4°5W **13** E3
Abhā *Si. Arabia* 18°0N 42°34E **47** D3
Abhar *Iran* 36°9N 49°13E **45** B6
Abhayapuri *India* 26°24N 90°38E **43** F14
Abidjan *Ivory C.* 5°26N 3°58W **50** G5
Abilene *Kans., U.S.A.* 38°55N 97°13W **80** F5
Abilene *Tex., U.S.A.* 32°28N 99°43W **84** E5
Abingdon *U.K.* 51°40N 1°17W **13** F6
Abingdon *U.S.A.* 36°43N 81°59W **81** G13
Abington Reef *Australia* 18°0S 149°35E **62** B4
Abitau → *Canada* 59°53N 109°3W **71** B7
Abitibi → *Canada* 51°3N 80°55W **72** B3
Abitibi, L. *Canada* 48°40N 79°40W **72** C4
Abkhaz Republic = Abkhazia □ *Georgia* 43°12N 41°5E **19** F7
Abkhazia □ *Georgia* 43°12N 41°5E **19** F7
Abminga *Australia* 26°8S 134°51E **63** D1
Åbo = Turku *Finland* 60°30N 22°19E **9** F20
Abohar *India* 30°10N 74°10E **42** D6
Abomey *Benin* 7°10N 2°5E **50** G6
Abong-Mbang *Cameroon* 4°0N 13°8E **52** D2
Abou-Deïa *Chad* 11°20N 19°20E **51** F9
Aboyne *U.K.* 57°4N 2°47W **11** D6
Abra Pampa *Argentina* 22°43S 65°42W **94** A2
Abraham L. *Canada* 52°15N 116°35W **70** C5
Abreojos, Pta. *Mexico* 26°50N 113°40W **86** B2
Abrolhos, Banco dos *Brazil* 18°0S 38°0W **93** F11
Abrud *Romania* 46°19N 23°5E **17** E12
Absaroka Range *U.S.A.* 44°45N 109°50W **76** D9
Abu *India* 24°41N 72°50E **42** G5
Abū al Abyad *U.A.E.* 24°11N 53°50E **45** E7
Abū al Khaṣīb *Iraq* 30°25N 48°0E **44** D5
Abū 'Alī *Si. Arabia* 27°20N 49°27E **45** E6
Abū 'Alī → *Lebanon* 34°25N 35°50E **46** A4
Abu Dhabi = Abū Ẓāby *U.A.E.* 24°28N 54°22E **45** E7
Abū Du'ān *Syria* 36°25N 38°15E **44** B3
Abu el Gaīn, W. → *Egypt* 29°35N 33°30E **46** F2
Abu Ga'da, W. → *Egypt* 29°15N 32°53E **46** F1
Abū Ḥadrīyah *Si. Arabia* 27°20N 48°58E **45** E6
Abu Hamed *Sudan* 19°32N 33°13E **51** E12
Abū Kamāl *Syria* 34°30N 41°0E **44** C4
Abū Madd, Ra's *Si. Arabia* 24°50N 37°7E **44** E3
Abū Mūsā *U.A.E.* 25°52N 55°3E **45** E7
Abū Qaṣr *Si. Arabia* 30°21N 38°34E **44** D3
Abu Shagara, Ras *Sudan* 21°4N 37°19E **51** D13
Abu Simbel *Egypt* 22°18N 31°40E **51** D12
Abū Şukhayr *Iraq* 31°54N 44°30E **44** D5
Abu Zabad *Sudan* 12°25N 29°10E **51** F11
Abū Ẓāby *U.A.E.* 24°28N 54°22E **45** E7
Abū Zeydābād *Iran* 33°54N 51°45E **45** C6
Abuja *Nigeria* 9°5N 7°32E **50** G7
Abukuma-Gawa → *Japan* 38°6N 140°52E **30** E10
Abukuma-Sammyaku *Japan* 37°30N 140°45E **30** F10
Abunã *Brazil* 9°40S 65°20W **92** E5
Abunã → *Brazil* 9°41S 65°20W **92** E5
Aburo *Dem. Rep. of the Congo* 2°4N 30°53E **54** B3
Abut Hd. *N.Z.* 43°7S 170°15E **59** E3
Ābyek *Iran* 36°4N 50°33E **45** B6
Acadia △ *U.S.A.* 44°20N 68°13W **81** C19
Açailândia *Brazil* 4°57S 47°0W **93** D9
Acajutla *El Salv.* 13°36N 89°50W **88** D2
Acámbaro *Mexico* 20°2N 100°44W **86** D4
Acaponeta *Mexico* 22°30N 105°22W **86** C3
Acapulco *Mexico* 16°51N 99°55W **87** D5
Acaraí, Serra *Brazil* 1°50N 57°50W **92** C7
Acarigua *Venezuela* 9°33N 69°12W **92** B5
Acatlán *Mexico* 18°12N 98°3W **87** D5
Acayucán *Mexico* 17°57N 94°55W **87** D6
Accomac *U.S.A.* 37°43N 75°40W **81** G16
Accra *Ghana* 5°35N 0°6W **50** G5
Accrington *U.K.* 53°45N 2°22W **12** D5
Acebal *Argentina* 33°20S 60°50W **94** C3
Aceh □ *Indonesia* 4°15N 97°30E **36** D1
Achalpur *India* 21°22N 77°32E **40** J10
Acharnes *Greece* 38°5N 23°44E **23** E10
Acheloos → *Greece* 38°19N 21°7E **23** E9
Acheng *China* 45°30N 126°58E **35** B14
Acher *India* 23°10N 72°32E **42** H5
Achill Hd. *Ireland* 53°58N 10°15W **10** C1
Achill I. *Ireland* 53°58N 10°1W **10** C1
Achinsk *Russia* 56°20N 90°20E **29** D10
Acireale *Italy* 37°37N 15°10E **22** F6
Ackerman *U.S.A.* 33°19N 89°11W **85** E10
Acklins I. *Bahamas* 22°30N 74°0W **89** B5
Acme *Canada* 51°33N 113°30W **70** C6
Acme *U.S.A.* 40°8N 79°26W **82** F5
Aconcagua, Cerro *Argentina* 32°39S 70°0W **94** C2
Aconquija, Mt. *Argentina* 27°0S 66°0W **94** B2
Açores, Is. dos *Atl. Oc.* 38°0N 27°0W **50** a
Acornhoek *S. Africa* 24°37S 31°2E **57** C5
Acraman, L. *Australia* 32°2S 135°23E **63** E2
Acre = 'Akko *Israel* 32°55N 35°4E **46** C4
Acre □ *Brazil* 9°1S 71°0W **92** E4
Acre → *Brazil* 8°45S 67°22W **92** E5
Actinolite *Canada* 44°32N 77°19W **82** B7
Acton *Canada* 43°38N 80°3W **82** C4
Ad Dammām *Si. Arabia* 26°20N 50°5E **45** E6
Ad Dāmūr *Lebanon* 33°43N 35°27E **46** B4
Ad Dawādimī *Si. Arabia* 24°35N 44°15E **44** E5
Ad Dawḥah *Qatar* 25°15N 51°35E **45** E6
Ad Dawr *Iraq* 34°27N 43°47E **44** C4
Ad Dir'īyah *Si. Arabia* 24°44N 46°35E **44** E5
Ad Dīwānīyah *Iraq* 32°0N 45°0E **44** D5
Ad Dujayl *Iraq* 33°51N 44°14E **44** C5
Ad Duwayd *Si. Arabia* 30°15N 42°17E **44** D4
Ada *Minn., U.S.A.* 47°18N 96°31W **80** B5
Ada *Okla., U.S.A.* 34°46N 96°41W **84** D6
Adabiya *Egypt* 29°53N 32°28E **46** F1
Adair, C. *Canada* 71°30N 71°34W **69** B12
Adaja → *Spain* 41°32N 4°52W **21** B3
Adak I. *U.S.A.* 51°45N 176°45W **74** a
Adamaoua, Massif de l' *Cameroon* 7°20N 12°20E **51** G8
Adamawa Highlands = Adamaoua, Massif de l' *Cameroon* 7°20N 12°20E **51** G8
Adamello, Mte. *Italy* 46°9N 10°30E **20** C9
Adaminaby *Australia* 36°0S 148°45E **63** F4
Adams *Mass., U.S.A.* 42°38N 73°7W **83** D11
Adams *N.Y., U.S.A.* 43°49N 76°1W **83** C8
Adams *Wis., U.S.A.* 43°57N 89°49W **80** D9
Adams, Mt. *U.S.A.* 46°12N 121°30W **78** D5
Adam's Bridge *Sri Lanka* 9°15N 79°40E **40** Q11
Adams L. *Canada* 51°10N 119°40W **70** C5
Adam's Peak *Sri Lanka* 6°48N 80°30E **40** R12
Adana *Turkey* 37°0N 35°16E **44** B2
Adapazarı = Sakarya *Turkey* 40°48N 30°25E **19** F5
Adarama *Sudan* 17°10N 34°52E **51** E12
Adare, C. *Antarctica* 71°0S 171°0E **5** D11
Adaut *Indonesia* 8°8S 131°7E **37** F8
Adavale *Australia* 25°52S 144°32E **63** D3
Adda → *Italy* 45°8N 9°53E **20** D8
Addis Ababa = Addis Abeba *Ethiopia* 9°2N 38°42E **47** F2
Addis Abeba *Ethiopia* 9°2N 38°42E **47** F2
Addison *U.S.A.* 42°1N 77°14W **82** D7
Addo *S. Africa* 33°32S 25°45E **56** E4
Addo △ *S. Africa* 33°30S 25°50E **56** E4
Ādeh *Iran* 37°42N 45°11E **44** B5
Adel *U.S.A.* 31°8N 83°25W **85** F13
Adelaide *Australia* 34°52S 138°30E **63** E2
Adelaide *S. Africa* 32°42S 26°20E **56** E4
Adelaide I. *Antarctica* 67°15S 68°30W **5** C17
Adelaide Pen. *Canada* 68°15N 97°30W **68** C10
Adelaide River *Australia* 13°15S 131°7E **60** B5
Adelaide Village *Bahamas* 25°0N 77°31W **88** A4
Adelanto *U.S.A.* 34°35N 117°22W **79** L9
Adele I. *Australia* 15°32S 123°9E **60** C3
Adélie, Terre *Antarctica* 68°0S 140°0E **5** C10
Adelie Land = Adélie, Terre *Antarctica* 68°0S 140°0E **5** C10
Aden = Al 'Adan *Yemen* 12°45N 45°0E **47** E4
Aden, G. of *Ind. Oc.* 12°30N 47°30E **47** E4
Adendorp *S. Africa* 32°15S 24°30E **56** E3
Adh Dhayd *U.A.E.* 25°17N 55°53E **45** E7
Adhoi *India* 23°26N 70°32E **42** H4
Adi *Indonesia* 4°15S 133°30E **37** E8
Adieu, C. *Australia* 32°0S 132°10E **61** F5
Adieu Pt. *Australia* 15°14S 124°35E **60** C3
Adige → *Italy* 45°9N 12°20E **22** B5
Adigrat *Ethiopia* 14°20N 39°26E **47** E2
Adilabad *India* 19°33N 78°20E **40** K11
Adirondack ⌂ *U.S.A.* 44°0N 74°20W **83** C10
Adirondack Mts. *U.S.A.* 44°0N 74°0W **83** C10
Adis Abeba = Addis Abeba *Ethiopia* 9°2N 38°42E **47** F2
Adjumani *Uganda* 3°20N 31°50E **54** B3
Adjuntas *Puerto Rico* 18°10N 66°43W **89** d
Adlavik Is. *Canada* 55°0N 58°40W **73** B8
Admiralty G. *Australia* 14°20S 125°55E **60** B4
Admiralty I. *U.S.A.* 57°30N 134°30W **70** B2
Admiralty Is. *Papua N. G.* 2°0S 147°0E **58** B7
Adolfo González Chaves *Argentina* 38°2S 60°5W **94** D3
Adolfo Ruiz Cortines, Presa *Mexico* 27°15N 109°6W **86** B3
Adonara *Indonesia* 8°15S 123°5E **37** F6
Adoni *India* 15°33N 77°18E **40** M10
Adour → *France* 43°32N 1°32W **20** E3
Adra *India* 23°30N 86°42E **43** H12
Adra *Spain* 36°43N 3°3W **21** D4
Adrano *Italy* 37°40N 14°50E **22** F6
Adrar *Algeria* 27°51N 0°11E **50** C6
Adrar *Mauritania* 20°30N 7°30W **50** D3
Adrar des Iforas *Africa* 19°40N 1°40E **50** E6
Adrian *Mich., U.S.A.* 41°54N 84°2W **81** E11
Adrian *Tex., U.S.A.* 35°16N 102°40W **84** D3
Adriatic Sea *Medit. S.* 43°0N 16°0E **22** C6
Adua *Indonesia* 1°45S 129°50E **37** E7
Adwa *Ethiopia* 14°15N 38°52E **47** E2
Adygea □ *Russia* 45°0N 40°0E **19** F7
Adzhar Republic = Ajaria □ *Georgia* 41°30N 42°0E **19** F7
Adzopé *Ivory C.* 6°7N 3°49W **50** G5
Ægean Sea *Medit. S.* 38°30N 25°0E **23** E11
Aerhtai Shan *Mongolia* 46°40N 92°45E **32** B4
Afaahiti *Tahiti* 17°45S 149°17W **59** d
'Afak *Iraq* 32°4N 45°15E **44** C5
Afandou *Greece* 36°18N 28°12E **25** C10
Afareaitu *Moorea* 17°33S 149°47W **59** d
Afghanistan ■ *Asia* 33°0N 65°0E **40** C4
Aflou *Algeria* 34°7N 2°3E **50** B6
Africa 10°0N 20°0E **48** E6
'Afrīn *Syria* 36°32N 36°50E **44** B3
Afton *N.Y., U.S.A.* 42°14N 75°32W **83** D9
Afton *Wyo., U.S.A.* 42°44N 110°56W **76** E8
Afuá *Brazil* 0°15S 50°20W **93** D8
'Afula *Israel* 32°37N 35°17E **46** C4
Afyon *Turkey* 38°45N 30°33E **19** G5
Afyonkarahisar = Afyon *Turkey* 38°45N 30°33E **19** G5
Āgā Jarī *Iran* 30°42N 49°50E **45** D6
Agadès = Agadez *Niger* 16°58N 7°59E **50** E7
Agadez *Niger* 16°58N 7°59E **50** E7
Agadir *Morocco* 30°28N 9°55W **50** B4
Agaete *Canary Is.* 28°6N 15°43W **24** F4
Agalega Is. *Mauritius* 11°0S 57°0E **3** E12
Agar *India* 23°40N 76°2E **42** H7
Agartala *India* 23°50N 91°23E **41** H17
Agassiz *Canada* 49°14N 121°46W **70** D4
Agats *Indonesia* 5°33S 138°0E **37** F9
Agawam *U.S.A.* 42°5N 72°37W **83** D12
Agboville *Ivory C.* 5°55N 4°15W **50** G5
Ağdam *Azerbaijan* 40°0N 46°58E **44** B5
Agde *France* 43°19N 3°28E **20** E5
Agen *France* 44°12N 0°38E **20** D4
Āgh Kand *Iran* 37°15N 48°4E **45** B6
Aghia Deka *Greece* 35°3N 24°58E **25** D6
Aghia Ekaterinis, Akra *Greece* 39°50N 19°50E **25** A3
Aghia Galini *Greece* 35°6N 24°41E **25** D6
Aghia Varvara *Greece* 35°8N 25°1E **25** D7
Aghios Efstratios *Greece* 39°34N 24°58E **23** E11
Aghios Ioannis, Akra *Greece* 35°20N 25°40E **25** D7
Aghios Isidoros *Greece* 36°9N 27°51E **25** C9
Aghios Matheos *Greece* 39°30N 19°47E **25** B3
Aghios Nikolaos *Greece* 35°11N 25°41E **25** D7
Aghios Stephanos *Greece* 39°46N 19°39E **25** A3
Aghiou Orous, Kolpos *Greece* 40°6N 24°0E **23** D11
Aginskoye *Russia* 51°6N 114°32E **29** D12
Agnew *Australia* 28°1S 120°31E **61** E3
Agori *India* 24°33N 82°57E **43** G10
Agra *India* 27°17N 77°58E **42** F7
Ağri *Turkey* 39°44N 43°3E **19** G7
Agri → *Italy* 40°13N 16°44E **22** D7
Ağrı Dağı *Turkey* 39°50N 44°15E **44** B5
Ağri Karakose = Ağri *Turkey* 39°44N 43°3E **19** G7
Agrigento *Italy* 37°19N 13°34E **22** F5
Agrinio *Greece* 38°37N 21°27E **23** E9
Agua Caliente *Mexico* 32°29N 116°59W **79** N10
Agua Caliente Springs *U.S.A.* 32°56N 116°19W **79** N10
Água Clara *Brazil* 20°25S 52°45W **93** H8
Agua Fria ⌂ *U.S.A.* 34°14N 112°0W **77** J8
Agua Hechicera *Mexico* 32°28N 116°15W **79** N10
Agua Prieta *Mexico* 31°18N 109°34W **86** A3
Aguadilla *Puerto Rico* 18°26N 67°10W **89** d
Aguadulce *Panama* 8°15N 80°32W **88** E3
Aguanga *U.S.A.* 33°27N 116°51W **79** M10
Aguanish *Canada* 50°14N 62°2W **73** B7
Aguanish → *Canada* 50°13N 62°5W **73** B7
Aguapey → *Argentina* 29°7S 56°36W **94** B4
Aguaray Guazú → *Paraguay* 24°47S 57°19W **94** A4
Aguarico → *Ecuador* 0°59S 75°11W **92** D3
Aguaro-Guariquito △ *Venezuela* 8°20N 66°35W **89** E6
Aguas Blancas *Chile* 24°15S 69°55W **94** A2
Aguas Calientes, Sierra de *Argentina* 25°26S 66°40W **94** B2
Aguascalientes *Mexico* 21°53N 102°18W **86** C4
Aguascalientes □ *Mexico* 22°0N 102°20W **86** C4
Aguila, Punta *Puerto Rico* 17°57N 67°13W **89** d
Aguilares *Argentina* 27°26S 65°35W **94** B2
Águilas *Spain* 37°23N 1°35W **21** D5
Agüimes *Canary Is.* 27°58N 15°27W **24** G4
Aguja, C. de la *Colombia* 11°18N 74°12W **90** B3
Agujereada, Pta. *Puerto Rico* 18°30N 67°8W **89** d
Agulhas, C. *S. Africa* 34°52S 20°0E **56** E3
Agulo *Canary Is.* 28°11N 17°12W **24** F2
Agung, Gunung *Indonesia* 8°20S 115°28E **37** J18
Agur *Uganda* 2°28N 32°55E **54** B3
Agusan → *Phil.* 9°0N 125°30E **37** C7
Aha Mts. *Botswana* 19°45S 21°0E **56** B3
Ahaggar *Algeria* 23°0N 6°30E **50** D7
Ahar *Iran* 38°35N 47°0E **44** B5
Ahipara B. *N.Z.* 35°5S 173°5E **59** A4
Ahiri *India* 19°30N 80°0E **40** K12
Ahmad Wal *Pakistan* 29°18N 65°58E **42** E1
Ahmadabad *India* 23°0N 72°40E **42** H5
Aḥmadābād *Khorāsān, Iran* 35°3N 60°50E **45** C9
Aḥmadābād *Khorāsān, Iran* 35°49N 59°42E **45** C8
Aḥmadī *Iran* 27°56N 56°42E **45** E8
Ahmadnagar *India* 19°7N 74°46E **40** K9
Ahmadpur East *Pakistan* 29°12N 71°10E **42** E4
Ahmadpur Lamma *Pakistan* 28°19N 70°3E **42** E4
Ahmedabad = Ahmadabad *India* 23°0N 72°40E **42** H5
Ahmednagar = Ahmadnagar *India* 19°7N 74°46E **40** K9
Ahome *Mexico* 25°55N 109°11W **86** B3
Ahoskie *U.S.A.* 36°17N 76°59W **85** C16
Ahram *Iran* 28°52N 51°16E **45** D6
Ahrax Pt. *Malta* 36°0N 14°22E **25** D1
Ahuachapán *El Salv.* 13°54N 89°52W **88** D2
Ahvāz *Iran* 31°20N 48°40E **45** D6
Ahvenanmaa = Åland *Finland* 60°15N 20°0E **9** F19
Aḥwar *Yemen* 13°30N 46°40E **47** E4
Ai → *India* 26°26N 90°44E **43** F14
Ai-Ais *Namibia* 27°54S 17°59E **56** D2
Ai-Ais and Fish River Canyon △ *Namibia* 24°45S 17°15E **56** C2
Aichi □ *Japan* 35°0N 137°15E **31** G8
Aigrettes, Pte. des *Réunion* 21°3S 55°13E **53** c
Aiguá *Uruguay* 34°13S 54°46W **95** C5
Aigues-Mortes *France* 43°35N 4°12E **20** E6
Aihui = Heihe *China* 50°10N 127°30E **33** A7
Aija *Peru* 9°50S 77°45W **92** E3
Aikawa *Japan* 38°2N 138°15E **30** E9
Aiken *U.S.A.* 33°34N 81°43W **85** E14
Aileron *Australia* 22°39S 133°20E **62** C1
Aillik *Canada* 55°11N 59°18W **73** A8
Ailsa Craig *Canada* 43°8N 81°33W **82** C3
Ailsa Craig *U.K.* 55°15N 5°6W **11** F3
Aim *Russia* 59°0N 133°55E **29** D14
Aimere *Indonesia* 8°45S 121°3E **37** F6
Aimogasta *Argentina* 28°33S 66°50W **94** B2
Aïn Ben Tili *Mauritania* 25°59N 9°27W **50** C4
Aïn Sefra *Algeria* 32°47N 0°37W **50** B5
Ain Sudr *Egypt* 29°50N 33°6E **46** F2
Aïn Témouchent *Algeria* 35°16N 1°8W **50** A5
Ainaži *Latvia* 57°50N 24°24E **9** H21
Ainsworth *U.S.A.* 42°33N 99°52W **80** D4
Aiquile *Bolivia* 18°10S 65°10W **92** G5
Aïr *Niger* 18°30N 8°0E **50** E7
Air Force I. *Canada* 67°58N 74°5W **69** C12
Air Hitam *Malaysia* 1°55N 103°11E **39** M4
Airdrie *Canada* 51°18N 114°2W **70** C6
Airdrie *U.K.* 55°52N 3°57W **11** F5
Aire → *U.K.* 53°43N 0°55W **12** D7
Aire, I. de l' *Spain* 39°48N 4°16E **24** B11
Airlie Beach *Australia* 20°16S 148°43E **62** J6
Aisne → *France* 49°26N 2°50E **20** B5
Ait *India* 25°54N 79°14E **43** G8
Aitkin *U.S.A.* 46°32N 93°42W **80** B7
Aitutaki *Cook Is.* 18°52S 159°45W **65** J12
Aiud *Romania* 46°19N 23°44E **17** E12
Aix-en-Provence *France* 43°32N 5°27E **20** E6
Aix-la-Chapelle = Aachen *Germany* 50°45N 6°6E **16** C4
Aix-les-Bains *France* 45°41N 5°53E **20** D6
Aizawl *India* 23°40N 92°44E **41** H
Aizkraukle *Latvia* 56°36N 25°11E **9** H
Aizpute *Latvia* 56°43N 21°40E **9** H
Aizuwakamatsu *Japan* 37°30N 139°56E **30**
Ajaccio *France* 41°55N 8°40E **20**
Ajai ⌂ *Uganda* 2°52N 31°16E **54**
Ajaigarh *India* 24°52N 80°16E **43**
Ajalpan *Mexico* 18°22N 97°15W **87**
Ajanta Ra. *India* 20°28N 75°50E **40**
Ajari Rep. = Ajaria □ *Georgia* 41°30N 42°0E **19**
Ajaria □ *Georgia* 41°30N 42°0E **19**
Ajax *Canada* 43°50N 79°1W **82**
Ajdābiyā *Libya* 30°54N 20°4E **51** B
Ajka *Hungary* 47°4N 17°31E **17**
'Ajlūn *Jordan* 32°18N 35°47E **46**
'Ajlūn □ *Jordan* 32°18N 35°47E **46**
'Ajmān *U.A.E.* 25°25N 55°30E **45**
Ajmer *India* 26°28N 74°37E **42**
Ajnala *India* 31°50N 74°48E **42**
Ajo *U.S.A.* 32°22N 112°52W **77**
Ajo, C. de *Spain* 43°31N 3°35W **21**
Akabira *Japan* 43°33N 142°5E **30** C
Akagera △ *Rwanda* 1°31S 30°33E **54**
Akamas *Cyprus* 35°3N 32°18E **25** D
Akan △ *Japan* 43°20N 144°20E **30** C
Akanthou *Cyprus* 35°22N 33°45E **25** D
Akaroa *N.Z.* 43°49S 172°59E **59**
Akashi *Japan* 34°45N 134°58E **31**
Akbarpur *Bihar, India* 24°39N 83°58E **43** C
Akbarpur *Ut. P., India* 26°25N 82°32E **43**
Akçakale *Turkey* 36°41N 38°56E **44**
Akdoğan = Lysi *Cyprus* 35°6N 33°41E **25**
Akelamo *Indonesia* 1°35N 129°40E **37**
Aketi *Dem. Rep. of the Congo* 2°38N 23°47E **52**
Akhisar *Turkey* 38°56N 27°48E **23**
Akhnur *India* 32°52N 74°45E **43**
Akhtyrka = Okhtyrka *Ukraine* 50°25N 35°0E **19**
Aki *Japan* 33°30N 133°54E **31**
Akimiski I. *Canada* 52°50N 81°30W **72**
Akincilar = Louroujina *Cyprus* 35°0N 33°28E **25**
Akita *Japan* 39°45N 140°7E **30**
Akita □ *Japan* 39°40N 140°30E **30**
Akjoujt *Mauritania* 19°45N 14°15W **50**
Akkeshi *Japan* 43°2N 144°51E **30**
'Akko *Israel* 32°55N 35°4E **46**
Aklavik *Canada* 68°12N 135°0W **68**
Aklera *India* 24°26N 76°32E **42**
Akō *Japan* 34°45N 134°24E **31**
Akola *India* 20°42N 77°2E **40**
Akordat *Eritrea* 15°30N 37°40E **47**
Akpatok I. *Canada* 60°25N 68°8W **69**
Åkrahamn *Norway* 59°15N 5°10E **9**
Akranes *Iceland* 64°19N 22°5W **8**
Akron *Colo., U.S.A.* 40°10N 103°13W **76**
Akron *Ohio, U.S.A.* 41°5N 81°31W **82**
Akrotiri *Cyprus* 34°36N 32°57E **25**
Akrotiri Bay *Cyprus* 34°35N 33°10E **25**
Aksai Chin *China* 35°15N 79°55E **43**
Aksaray *Turkey* 38°25N 34°2E **44**
Aksay = Aqsay *Kazakhstan* 51°11N 53°0E **19**
Akşehir *Turkey* 38°18N 31°30E **44**
Akşehir Gölü *Turkey* 38°30N 31°25E **19**
Aksu *China* 41°5N 80°10E **32**
Aksum *Ethiopia* 14°5N 38°40E **47**
Aktsyabrski *Belarus* 52°38N 28°53E **17**
Aktyubinsk = Aqtöbe *Kazakhstan* 50°17N 57°10E **19**
Akure *Nigeria* 7°15N 5°5E **50**
Akureyri *Iceland* 65°40N 18°6W
Akuseki-Shima *Japan* 29°27N 129°37E **31**
Akyab = Sittwe *Burma* 20°18N 92°45E **41**
Al 'Adan *Yemen* 12°45N 45°0E
Al Aḥsā = Hasa *Si. Arabia* 25°50N 49°0E
Al Ajfar *Si. Arabia* 27°26N 43°0E
Al Amādīyah *Iraq* 37°5N 43°30E
Al 'Amārah *Iraq* 31°55N 47°15E
Al Anbār □ *Iraq* 33°25N 42°0E
Al 'Aqabah *Jordan* 29°31N 35°0E
Al 'Aqabah □ *Jordan* 29°30N 35°0E
Al Arak *Syria* 34°38N 38°35E
Al 'Aramah *Si. Arabia* 25°30N 46°0E
Al Arṭāwīyah *Si. Arabia* 26°31N 45°20E
Al 'Āṣimah = 'Ammān □ *Jordan* 31°40N 36°30E
Al 'Assāfīyah *Si. Arabia* 28°17N 38°59E
Al 'Awdah *Si. Arabia* 25°32N 45°41E
Al 'Ayn *Si. Arabia* 25°4N 38°6E
Al 'Ayn *U.A.E.* 24°15N 55°45E
Al 'Azīzīyah *Iraq* 32°54N 45°4E
Al Bāb *Syria* 36°23N 37°29E
Al Bad' *Si. Arabia* 28°28N 35°1E
Al Bādī *Iraq* 35°56N 41°32E
Al Baḥrah *Kuwait* 29°40N 47°52E
Al Baḥral Mayyit = Dead Sea *Asia* 31°30N 35°30E
Al Balqā' □ *Jordan* 32°5N 35°45E
Al Bārūk, J. *Lebanon* 33°39N 35°40E
Al Baṣrah *Iraq* 30°30N 47°50E
Al Baṭḥā *Iraq* 31°6N 45°53E
Al Batrūn *Lebanon* 34°15N 35°40E
Al Bayḍā *Libya* 32°50N 21°44E **5**
Al Biqā *Lebanon* 34°10N 36°10E
Al Bi'r *Si. Arabia* 28°51N 36°16E
Al Bukayrīyah *Si. Arabia* 26°9N 43°40E
Al Burayj *Syria* 34°15N 36°46E
Al Faḍilī *Si. Arabia* 26°58N 49°10E
Al Fallūjah *Iraq* 33°20N 43°55E
Al Fāw *Iraq* 30°0N 48°30E
Al Fujayrah *U.A.E.* 25°7N 56°18E
Al Ghadaf, W. → *Jordan* 31°26N 36°43E
Al Ghammās *Iraq* 31°45N 44°37E
Al Ghazālah *Si. Arabia* 26°48N 41°19E

Ḩadīthah Iraq 34°0N 41°13E 44 C4
Ḩadīthah Si. Arabia 31°28N 37°8E 46 D6
Ḩaḍr Iraq 35°35N 42°44E 44 C4
Ḩājānah Syria 33°20N 36°33E 46 B5
Ḩajar al Gharbī Oman 24°10N 56°15E 45 E8
Ḩāmad Si. Arabia 31°30N 39°30E 44 D3
Ḩamdānīyah Syria 35°25N 36°50E 44 C3
Ḩamīdīyah Syria 34°42N 35°57E 46 A4
Ḩammār Iraq 30°57N 46°51E 44 D5
Ḩamrā' Si. Arabia 24°2N 38°55E 44 E3
Ḩamzah Iraq 31°43N 44°58E 44 D5
Ḩanākīyah Si. Arabia 24°51N 40°31E 44 E4
Harūj al Aswad Libya 27°0N 17°10E 51 C9
Ḩasakah Syria 36°35N 40°45E 44 B4
Ḩayy Iraq 32°5N 46°5E 44 C5
Ḩijarah Asia 30°0N 44°0E 44 D4
Ḩillah Iraq 32°30N 44°25E 44 C5
Ḩillah Si. Arabia 23°35N 46°50E 47 B4
Hindīyah Iraq 32°30N 44°10E 44 C5
Hirmil Lebanon 34°26N 36°24E 46 A5
Hoceïma Morocco 35°8N 3°58W 50 A5
Ḩudaydah Yemen 14°50N 43°0E 47 E3
Ḩudūd ash Shamālīyah □
Si. Arabia 29°10N 42°30E 44 D4
Hufūf Si. Arabia 25°25N 49°45E 45 E6
Ḩumaydah Si. Arabia 29°14N 34°56E 44 D2
Ḩunayy Si. Arabia 25°58N 48°45E 45 E6
Īsāwīyah Si. Arabia 30°43N 37°59E 44 D3
Jafr Jordan 30°18N 36°14E 46 E5
Jāfūrah Si. Arabia 25°0N 50°15E 45 E7
Jaghbūb Libya 29°42N 24°38E 51 C10
Jahrah Kuwait 29°25N 47°40E 44 D5
Jalāmīd Si. Arabia 31°20N 40°6E 44 D3
Jamalīyah Qatar 25°37N 51°5E 45 E6
Janūb □ Lebanon 33°20N 35°20E 46 B4
Jawf Libya 24°10N 23°24E 51 D10
Jawf Si. Arabia 29°55N 39°40E 44 D3
Jawf □ Si. Arabia 29°30N 39°30E 44 D3
Jazair = Algeria ■
Africa 28°30N 2°0E 50 C6
Jazirah Iraq 33°30N 44°0E 44 C5
Jithāmīyah Si. Arabia 27°41N 41°43E 44 E4
Jubayl Si. Arabia 27°0N 49°50E 45 E6
Jubaylah Si. Arabia 24°55N 46°25E 44 E5
Jubb Si. Arabia 27°11N 42°17E 44 E4
Junaynah Sudan 13°27N 22°45E 51 F10
Kabā'ish Iraq 30°58N 47°0E 44 D5
Karak Jordan 31°11N 35°42E 46 D4
Karak □ Jordan 31°0N 36°0E 46 E5
Kāẓimīyah Iraq 33°22N 44°18E 44 C5
Khābūrah Oman 23°57N 57°5E 45 F8
Khafji Si. Arabia 28°24N 48°29E 45 E6
Khalīl West Bank 31°32N 35°6E 46 D4
Khāliş Iraq 33°49N 44°32E 44 C5
Kharsānīyah
i. Arabia 27°13N 49°18E 45 E6
Khaşab Oman 26°14N 56°15E 45 E8
Khawr Qatar 25°41N 51°30E 45 E6
Khiḑr Iraq 31°12N 45°33E 44 D5
Khiyām Lebanon 33°20N 35°36E 46 B4
Khobar Si. Arabia 26°17N 50°12E 45 E6
Khums Libya 32°40N 14°17E 51 B8
Kiswah Syria 33°23N 36°14E 46 B5
Kūfah Iraq 32°2N 44°24E 44 C5
Kufrah Libya 24°17N 23°15E 51 D10
Kuhayfiyah Si. Arabia 27°12N 43°3E 44 E4
Kūt Iraq 32°30N 46°0E 44 C5
Kuwayt Kuwait 29°30N 48°0E 44 D5
abwah Lebanon 34°11N 36°20E 46 A5
adhiqīyah Syria 35°30N 35°45E 44 C2
īth Si. Arabia 20°9N 40°15E 47 C3
iwā' Oman 24°31N 56°36E 45 E8
uḩayyah Yemen 15°45N 42°40E 47 D3
Madīnah Iraq 30°57N 47°16E 44 D5
Madīnah Si. Arabia 24°35N 39°52E 44 E3
Mafraq Jordan 32°17N 36°14E 46 C5
Mafraq □ Jordan 32°17N 36°15E 46 C5
Maghreb = Morocco ■
. Afr. 32°0N 5°50W 50 B4
Maḩmūdīyah Iraq 33°3N 44°21E 44 C5
Majma'ah Si. Arabia 25°57N 45°22E 44 E5
Makhruq, W. →
rdan 31°28N 37°0E 46 D6
Makḩūl Si. Arabia 26°37N 42°39E 44 E4
Manāmah Bahrain 26°10N 50°30E 45 E6
Maqwa' Kuwait 29°10N 47°59E 44 D5
Marāḩ Si. Arabia 25°35N 49°35E 45 E6
Marj Libya 32°25N 20°30E 51 B10
Maţlā Kuwait 29°24N 47°40E 44 D5
Mawşil Iraq 36°15N 43°5E 44 B4
Mayādin Syria 35°1N 40°27E 44 C4
Mazār Jordan 31°4N 35°41E 46 D4
Midhnab Si. Arabia 25°50N 44°18E 44 E5
Minā' Lebanon 34°24N 35°49E 46 A4
Miqdādīyah Iraq 34°0N 45°0E 44 C5
Mubarraz Si. Arabia 25°30N 49°40E 45 E6
Mudawwarah Jordan 29°19N 36°0E 46 F5
Mughayrā' U.A.E. 24°5N 53°32E 45 E7
Muḩarraq Bahrain 26°15N 50°40E 45 E6
Mukallā Yemen 14°33N 49°2E 47 E4
Mukhā Yemen 13°18N 43°15E 47 E3
Musayjīd Si. Arabia 24°5N 39°5E 44 E3
Musayyib Iraq 32°49N 44°20E 44 C5
Muthannā □ Iraq 30°30N 45°15E 44 D5
Muwayliḩ Si. Arabia 27°40N 35°30E 44 E2
ādisīyah □ Iraq 32°0N 45°0E 44 D5
ā'im Iraq 34°21N 41°7E 44 C4
alībah Si. Arabia 28°24N 37°42E 44 D3
āmishlī Syria 37°2N 41°14E 44 B4
aryatayn Syria 34°12N 37°13E 46 A6
aşīm □ Si. Arabia 26°0N 43°0E 44 E4
aţ'ā Syria 34°40N 40°48E 44 C4
aţīf Si. Arabia 26°35N 50°0E 45 E6
aţrānah Jordan 31°12N 36°6E 46 D5
aţrūn Libya 24°56N 15°3E 51 D9
ayşūmah Si. Arabia 28°20N 46°7E 44 D5
uds = Jerusalem
rael/West Bank 31°47N 35°10E 46 D4

Al Qunayţirah Syria 32°55N 35°45E 46 C4
Al Qunfudhah Si. Arabia 19°3N 41°4E 47 D3
Al Qurnah Iraq 31°1N 47°25E 44 D5
Al Quşayr Iraq 30°39N 45°50E 44 D5
Al Quşayr Syria 34°31N 36°34E 46 A5
Al Quţayfah Syria 33°44N 36°36E 46 B5
Al 'Ubaylah Si. Arabia 21°59N 50°57E 47 C5
Al 'Uḑaylīyah Si. Arabia 25°8N 49°18E 45 E6
Al 'Ulā Si. Arabia 26°35N 38°0E 44 E3
Al 'Uqayr Si. Arabia 25°40N 50°15E 45 E6
Al 'Uwaynid Si. Arabia 24°50N 46°0E 44 E5
Al 'Uwayqīlah Si. Arabia 30°30N 42°10E 44 D4
Al 'Uyūn Ḩijāz, Si. Arabia 24°33N 39°35E 44 E3
Al 'Uyūn Najd, Si. Arabia 26°30N 43°50E 44 E4
Al 'Uzayr Iraq 31°19N 47°25E 44 D5
Al Wajh Si. Arabia 26°10N 36°30E 44 E3
Al Wakrah Qatar 25°10N 51°40E 45 E6
Al Waqbah Si. Arabia 28°48N 45°33E 44 D5
Al Wari'āh Si. Arabia 27°51N 47°25E 44 E5
Al Yaman = Yemen ■
Asia 15°0N 44°0E 47 E3
Ala Dağ Turkey 37°44N 35°9E 44 B2
Ala Tau Asia 45°30N 80°40E 28 E9
Ala Tau Shankou = Dzungarian
Gate Asia 45°10N 82°0E 32 B3
Alabama □ U.S.A. 33°0N 87°0W 85 E11
Alabama → U.S.A. 31°8N 87°57W 85 F11
Alabaster U.S.A. 33°15N 86°49W 85 E11
Alaçam Dağları Turkey 39°18N 28°49E 23 E13
Alacant = Alicante Spain 38°23N 0°30W 21 C5
Alachua U.S.A. 29°47N 82°30W 85 G13
Alagoa Grande Brazil 7°3S 35°35W 93 E11
Alagoas □ Brazil 9°0S 36°0W 93 E11
Alagoinhas Brazil 12°7S 38°20W 93 F11
Alaior Spain 39°57N 4°8E 24 B11
Alajero Canary Is. 28°3N 17°13W 24 F2
Alajuela Costa Rica 10°2N 84°8W 88 D3
Alakamisy Madag. 21°19S 47°14E 57 C8
Alakananda → India 30°8N 78°36E 43 D8
Alakurtti Russia 66°58N 30°25E 8 C24
Alamarvdasht Iran 27°37N 52°59E 45 E7
Alameda Calif., U.S.A. 37°46N 122°15W 78 H4
Alameda N. Mex.,
U.S.A. 35°11N 106°37W 77 J10
Alamo U.S.A. 37°22N 115°10W 79 H11
Alamogordo U.S.A. 32°54N 105°57W 77 K11
Alamos Mexico 27°1N 108°56W 86 B3
Alamosa U.S.A. 37°28N 105°52W 77 H11
Åland Finland 60°15N 20°0E 9 F19
Ålands hav Europe 60°0N 19°30E 9 G18
Alania = North Ossetia □
Russia 43°30N 44°30E 19 F7
Alanya Turkey 36°38N 32°0E 44 B1
Alaotra, Farihin' Madag. 17°30S 48°30E 57 B8
Alapayevsk Russia 57°52N 61°42E 28 D7
Alappuzha = Alleppey
India 9°30N 76°28E 40 Q10
Alaró Spain 39°42N 2°47E 24 B9
Alarobia-Vohiposa
Madag. 20°59S 47°9E 57 C8
Alaşehir Turkey 38°23N 28°30E 23 E13
Alaska □ U.S.A. 64°0N 154°0W 74 a
Alaska, G. of Pac. Oc. 58°0N 145°0W 74 a
Alaska Peninsula U.S.A. 56°0N 159°0W 74 a
Alaska Range U.S.A. 62°50N 151°0W 74 a
Älät Azerbaijan 39°58N 49°25E 45 B6
Alatau Shan = Ala Tau
Asia 45°30N 80°40E 28 E9
Alatyr Russia 54°55N 46°35E 18 D8
Alausi Ecuador 2°0S 78°50W 92 D3
Alava, C. U.S.A. 48°10N 124°44W 76 B1
Alavo = Alavus Finland 62°35N 23°36E 8 E20
Alavus Finland 62°35N 23°36E 8 E20
Alawoona Australia 34°45S 140°30E 63 E3
'Alayh Lebanon 33°46N 35°33E 46 B4
Alba Italy 44°42N 8°2E 20 D8
Alba-Iulia Romania 46°8N 23°39E 17 E12
Albacete Spain 39°0N 1°50W 21 C5
Albacutya, L. Australia 35°45S 141°58E 63 F3
Albanel, L. Canada 50°55N 73°12W 72 B5
Albania ■ Europe 41°0N 20°0E 23 D9
Albany Australia 35°1S 117°58E 61 G2
Albany Ga., U.S.A. 31°35N 84°10W 85 F12
Albany N.Y., U.S.A. 42°39N 73°45W 83 D11
Albany Oreg., U.S.A. 44°38N 123°6W 76 D2
Albany Tex., U.S.A. 32°44N 99°18W 84 E5
Albany → Canada 52°17N 81°31W 72 B3
Albarca, C. d' Spain 39°4N 1°22E 24 B7
Albardón Argentina 31°20S 68°30W 94 C2
Albatross B. Australia 12°45S 141°30E 62 A3
Albemarle U.S.A. 35°21N 80°12W 85 D14
Albemarle Sd. U.S.A. 36°5N 76°0W 85 C16
Alberche → Spain 39°58N 4°46W 21 C3
Alberdi Paraguay 26°14S 58°20W 94 B4
Alberga → Australia 27°6S 135°33E 63 D2
Albert, L. Africa 1°30N 31°0E 54 B3
Albert, L. Australia 35°30S 139°10E 63 F2
Albert Edward Ra.
Australia 18°17S 127°57E 60 C4
Albert Lea U.S.A. 43°39N 93°22W 80 D7
Albert Nile → Uganda 3°36N 32°2E 54 B3
Albert Town Bahamas 22°37N 74°33W 89 B5
Alberta □ Canada 54°40N 115°0W 70 C6
Alberti Argentina 35°1S 60°16W 94 D3
Albertinia S. Africa 34°11S 21°34E 56 E3
Alberton Canada 46°50N 64°0W 73 C7
Albertville France 45°40N 6°22E 20 D7
Albertville U.S.A. 34°16N 86°13W 85 D11
Albi France 43°56N 2°9E 20 E5
Albia U.S.A. 41°2N 92°48W 80 E7
Albina Suriname 5°37N 54°15W 93 B8
Albina, Ponta Angola 15°52S 11°44E 56 B1
Albion Mich., U.S.A. 42°15N 84°45W 81 D11
Albion Nebr., U.S.A. 41°42N 98°0W 80 E4
Albion Pa., U.S.A. 41°53N 80°22W 82 E4
Alborán Medit. S. 35°57N 3°0W 21 E4
Ålborg = Aalborg Denmark 57°2N 9°54E 9 H13

Alborz, Reshteh-ye Kūhhā-ye
Iran 36°0N 52°0E 45 C7
Albufeira Portugal 37°5N 8°15W 21 D1
Albuquerque U.S.A. 35°5N 106°39W 77 J10
Albuquerque, Cayos de
Caribbean 12°10N 81°50W 88 D3
Alburg U.S.A. 44°59N 73°18W 83 B11
Albury Australia 36°3S 146°56E 63 F4
Alcalá de Henares Spain 40°28N 3°22W 21 B4
Alcalá la Real Spain 37°27N 3°57W 21 D4
Álcamo Italy 37°59N 12°55E 22 F5
Alcañiz Spain 41°2N 0°8W 21 B5
Alcântara Brazil 2°20S 44°30W 93 D10
Alcántara, Embalse de
Spain 39°44N 6°50W 21 C2
Alcantarilla Spain 37°59N 1°12W 21 D5
Alcaraz, Sierra de Spain 38°40N 2°20W 21 C4
Alcaudete Spain 37°35N 4°5W 21 D3
Alcázar de San Juan
Spain 39°24N 3°12W 21 C4
Alchevsk Ukraine 48°30N 38°45E 19 E6
Alcira = Alzira Spain 39°9N 0°30W 21 C5
Alcova U.S.A. 42°34N 106°43W 76 E10
Alcoy Spain 38°43N 0°30W 21 C5
Alcúdia Spain 39°51N 3°7E 24 B10
Alcúdia, B. d' Spain 39°47N 3°15E 24 B10
Aldabra Is. Seychelles 9°22S 46°28E 49 G8
Aldama Mexico 22°55N 98°4W 87 C5
Aldan Russia 58°40N 125°30E 29 D13
Aldan → Russia 63°28N 129°35E 29 C13
Aldea, Pta. de la
Canary Is. 28°0N 15°50W 24 G4
Aldeburgh U.K. 52°10N 1°37E 13 E9
Alder Pk. U.S.A. 35°53N 121°22W 78 K5
Alderney U.K. 49°42N 2°11W 13 H5
Aldershot U.K. 51°15N 0°44W 13 F7
Aledo U.S.A. 41°12N 90°45W 80 E8
Aleg Mauritania 17°3N 13°55W 50 E3
Alegranza Canary Is. 29°23N 13°32W 24 E6
Alegranza, I. Canary Is. 29°23N 13°32W 24 E6
Alegre Brazil 20°50S 41°30W 95 A7
Alegrete Brazil 29°40S 56°0W 95 B4
Aleksandriya = Oleksandriya
Ukraine 50°37N 26°19E 17 C14
Aleksandrov Gay Russia 50°9N 48°34E 19 D8
Aleksandrovsk-Sakhalinskiy
Russia 50°50N 142°20E 29 D15
Aleksandry, Zemlya
Russia 80°25N 48°0E 28 A5
Além Paraíba Brazil 21°52S 42°41W 95 A7
Alemania Argentina 25°40S 65°30W 94 B2
Alemania Chile 25°10S 69°55W 94 B2
Alençon France 48°27N 0°4E 20 B4
Alenquer Brazil 1°56S 54°46W 93 D8
'Alenuihähä Channel
U.S.A. 20°30N 156°0W 74 b
Aleppo = Ḩalab Syria 36°10N 37°15E 44 B3
Aléria France 42°5N 9°26E 20 E9
Alert Canada 83°2N 60°0W 69 A13
Alès France 44°9N 4°5E 20 D6
Alessándria Italy 44°54N 8°37E 20 D8
Ålesund Norway 62°28N 6°12E 8 E12
Aleutian Basin Pac. Oc. 57°0N 177°0E 64 B9
Aleutian Is. Pac. Oc. 52°0N 175°0W 74 a
Aleutian Trench Pac. Oc. 48°0N 180°0E 4 D17
Alexander U.S.A. 47°51N 103°39W 80 B2
Alexander, Mt.
Australia 28°58S 120°16E 61 E3
Alexander Arch. U.S.A. 56°0N 136°0W 68 D6
Alexander Bay S. Africa 28°40S 16°30E 56 D2
Alexander City U.S.A. 32°56N 85°58W 85 E12
Alexander I. Antarctica 69°0S 70°0W 5 C17
Alexandra Australia 37°8S 145°40E 63 F4
Alexandra N.Z. 45°14S 169°25E 59 F2
Alexandra Falls Canada 60°29N 116°18W 70 A5
Alexandria = El Iskandarîya
Egypt 31°13N 29°58E 51 B11
Alexandria B.C.,
Canada 52°35N 122°27W 70 C4
Alexandria Ont.,
Canada 45°19N 74°38W 83 A10
Alexandria Romania 43°57N 25°24E 17 G13
Alexandria S. Africa 33°38S 26°28E 56 E4
Alexandria U.K. 55°59N 4°35W 11 F4
Alexandria La., U.S.A. 31°18N 92°27W 84 F8
Alexandria Minn.,
U.S.A. 45°53N 95°22W 80 C6
Alexandria S. Dak.,
U.S.A. 43°39N 97°47W 80 D5
Alexandria Va., U.S.A. 38°49N 77°5W 81 F15
Alexandria Bay U.S.A. 44°20N 75°55W 83 B9
Alexandrina, L.
Australia 35°25S 139°10E 63 F2
Alexandroupoli Greece 40°50N 25°54E 23 D11
Alexis → Canada 52°33N 56°8W 73 B8
Alexis Creek Canada 52°10N 123°20W 70 C4
Aleysk Russia 52°40N 83°0E 28 D9
Alfabia Spain 39°44N 2°44E 24 B9
Alfenas Brazil 21°20S 46°10W 95 A6
Alford Aberds., U.K. 57°14N 2°41W 11 D6
Alford Lincs., U.K. 53°15N 0°10E 12 D8
Alfred Maine, U.S.A. 43°29N 70°43W 83 C14
Alfred N.Y., U.S.A. 42°16N 77°48W 82 D7
Alfreton U.K. 53°6N 1°24W 12 D6
Algaida Spain 39°33N 2°53E 24 B9
Ålgård Norway 58°46N 5°53E 9 G11
Algarve Portugal 36°58N 8°20W 21 D1
Algeciras Spain 36°9N 5°28W 21 D3
Algemesí Spain 39°11N 0°27W 21 C5
Alger Algeria 36°42N 3°8E 50 A6
Algeria ■ Africa 28°30N 2°0E 50 C6
Algha Kazakhstan 49°53N 57°20E 19 E10
Alghero Italy 40°33N 8°19E 22 D3
Algiers = Alger Algeria 36°42N 3°8E 50 A6
Algoa B. S. Africa 33°50S 25°45E 56 E4
Algoma U.S.A. 44°36N 87°26W 80 C10
Algona U.S.A. 43°4N 94°14W 80 D6

Algonac U.S.A. 42°37N 82°32W 82 D2
Algonquin △ Canada 45°50N 78°30W 72 C4
Algorta Uruguay 32°25S 57°23W 96 C5
Alhambra U.S.A. 34°5N 118°7W 79 L8
Alhucemas = Al Hoceïma
Morocco 35°8N 3°58W 50 A5
'Alī al Gharbī Iraq 32°30N 46°45E 44 C5
'Alī ash Sharqī Iraq 32°7N 46°44E 44 C5
Äli Bayramlı Azerbaijan 39°59N 48°52E 45 B6
'Alī Khēl Afghan. 33°57N 69°43E 42 C3
Alī Shāh Iran 38°9N 45°50E 44 B5
'Alīābād Iran 36°40N 54°33E 45 B7
'Alīābād Khorāsān, Iran 32°30N 57°30E 45 C8
'Alīābād Kordestān, Iran 35°4N 46°58E 44 C5
'Alīābād Yazd, Iran 31°41N 53°49E 45 D7
Aliağa Turkey 38°47N 26°59E 23 E12
Aliakmonas → Greece 40°30N 22°36E 23 D10
Alicante Spain 38°23N 0°30W 21 C5
Alice S. Africa 32°48S 26°55E 56 E4
Alice U.S.A. 27°45N 98°5W 84 H5
Alice → Queens.,
Australia 24°2S 144°50E 62 C3
Alice → Queens.,
Australia 15°35S 142°20E 62 B3
Alice Arm Canada 55°29N 129°31W 70 B3
Alice Springs Australia 23°40S 133°50E 62 C1
Alicedale S. Africa 33°15S 26°4E 56 E4
Aliceville U.S.A. 33°8N 88°9W 85 E10
Aliganj India 27°30N 79°10E 43 F8
Aligarh Raj., India 25°55N 76°15E 42 G7
Aligarh Ut. P., India 27°55N 78°10E 42 F8
Alīgūdarz Iran 33°25N 49°45E 45 C6
Alimia Greece 36°16N 27°43E 25 C9
Alingsås Sweden 57°56N 12°31E 9 H15
Alipur Pakistan 29°25N 70°55E 42 E4
Alipur Duar India 26°30N 89°35E 41 F16
Aliquippa U.S.A. 40°37N 80°15W 82 F4
Alitus = Alytus Lithuania 54°24N 24°3E 9 J21
Aliwal North S. Africa 30°45S 26°45E 56 E4
Alix Canada 52°24N 113°11W 70 C6
Aljustrel Portugal 37°55N 8°10W 21 D1
Alkmaar Neths. 52°37N 4°45E 15 B4
All American Canal
U.S.A. 32°45N 115°15W 77 K6
Allagash → U.S.A. 47°5N 69°3W 81 B19
Allah Dad Pakistan 25°38N 67°34E 42 G2
Allahabad India 25°25N 81°58E 43 G9
Allan Canada 51°53N 106°4W 71 C7
Allanridge S. Africa 27°45S 26°40E 56 D4
Allegany U.S.A. 42°6N 78°30W 82 D6
Allegheny → U.S.A. 40°27N 80°1W 82 F5
Allegheny Mts. U.S.A. 38°15N 80°10W 81 F13
Allegheny Plateau
U.S.A. 41°30N 78°30W 81 E14
Allegheny Res. U.S.A. 41°50N 79°0W 82 E6
Allègre, Pte. Guadeloupe 16°22N 61°46W 88 b
Allen, Bog of Ireland 53°15N 7°0W 10 C5
Allen, L. Ireland 54°8N 8°4W 10 B3
Allendale U.S.A. 33°1N 81°18W 85 E14
Allende Mexico 28°20N 100°51W 86 B4
Allentown U.S.A. 40°37N 75°29W 83 F9
Alleppey India 9°30N 76°28E 40 Q10
Aller → Germany 52°56N 9°12E 16 B5
Alleynes B. Barbados 13°13N 59°39W 89 g
Alliance Nebr., U.S.A. 42°6N 102°52W 80 D2
Alliance Ohio, U.S.A. 40°55N 81°6W 82 F3
Allier → France 46°57N 3°4E 20 C5
Alliford Bay Canada 53°12N 131°58W 70 C2
Alligator Pond Jamaica 17°52N 77°34W 88 a
Alliston Canada 44°9N 79°52W 82 B5
Alloa U.K. 56°7N 3°47W 11 E5
Allora Australia 28°2S 152°0E 63 D5
Alluitsup Paa Greenland 60°30N 45°35W 4 C5
Alma Canada 48°35N 71°40W 73 C5
Alma Ga., U.S.A. 31°33N 82°28W 85 F13
Alma Kans., U.S.A. 39°1N 96°17W 80 F5
Alma Mich., U.S.A. 43°23N 84°39W 81 D11
Alma Nebr., U.S.A. 40°6N 99°22W 80 E4
Alma Wis., U.S.A. 44°20N 91°55W 80 C8
Alma Ata = Almaty
Kazakhstan 43°15N 76°57E 28 E8
Alma Hill U.S.A. 42°2N 78°0W 82 D7
Almada Portugal 38°41N 9°8W 21 C1
Almaden Australia 17°22S 144°40E 62 B3
Almadén Spain 38°49N 4°52W 21 C3
Almalyk = Olmaliq
Uzbekistan 40°50N 69°35E 28 E7
Almanor, L. U.S.A. 40°14N 121°9W 76 F3
Almansa Spain 38°51N 1°5W 21 C5
Almanzor, Pico Spain 40°15N 5°18W 21 B3
Almanzora → Spain 37°14N 1°46W 21 D5
Almaty Kazakhstan 43°15N 76°57E 28 E8
Almazán Spain 41°30N 2°30W 21 B4
Almeirim Brazil 1°30S 52°34W 93 D8
Almelo Neths. 52°22N 6°42E 15 B6
Almendralejo Spain 38°41N 6°26W 21 C2
Almere-Stad Neths. 52°20N 5°15E 15 B5
Almería Spain 36°52N 2°27W 21 D4
Almirante Panama 9°10N 82°30W 88 E3
Almond U.S.A. 42°19N 77°44W 82 D7
Almont U.S.A. 42°55N 83°3W 82 D1
Almonte Canada 45°14N 76°12W 83 A8
Almora India 29°38N 79°40E 43 E8
Almyrou, Ormos Greece 35°23N 24°20E 25 D6
Alness U.K. 57°41N 4°16W 11 D4
Alnmouth U.K. 55°24N 1°37W 12 B6
Alnwick U.K. 55°24N 1°42W 12 B6
Aloi Uganda 2°16N 33°10E 54 B3
Alon Burma 22°12N 95°5E 41 H19
Alor Indonesia 8°15S 124°30E 37 F6
Alor Setar Malaysia 6°7N 100°22E 39 J3
Alot India 23°56N 75°40E 42 H6
Aloysius, Mt. Australia 26°0S 128°38E 61 E4
Alpaugh U.S.A. 35°53N 119°29W 78 K7
Alpena U.S.A. 45°4N 83°27W 81 C12
Alpha Australia 23°39S 146°37E 62 C4
Alpha Ridge Arctic 84°0N 118°0W 4 A2

Alphen aan den Rijn
Neths. 52°7N 4°40E 15 B4
Alpine Ariz., U.S.A. 33°51N 109°9W 77 K9
Alpine Calif., U.S.A. 32°50N 116°46W 79 N10
Alpine Tex., U.S.A. 30°22N 103°40W 84 F3
Alps Europe 46°30N 9°30E 20 C8
Alpurrurulam Australia 20°59S 137°50E 62 C2
Alsace □ France 48°15N 7°25E 20 B7
Alsask Canada 51°21N 109°59W 71 C7
Alsasua Spain 42°54N 2°10W 21 A4
Alsek → U.S.A. 59°10N 138°12W 70 B1
Alsta Norway 65°58N 12°40E 8 D15
Alston U.K. 54°49N 2°25W 12 C5
Alta Norway 69°57N 23°10E 8 B20
Alta Gracia Argentina 31°40S 64°30W 94 C3
Alta Sierra U.S.A. 35°42N 118°33W 79 K8
Altaelva → Norway 69°54N 23°17E 8 B20
Altafjorden Norway 70°5N 23°5E 8 A20
Altai = Aerhtai Shan
Mongolia 46°40N 92°45E 32 B4
Altai = Gorno-Altay □
Russia 51°0N 86°0E 28 D9
Altamaha → U.S.A. 31°20N 81°20W 85 F14
Altamira Brazil 3°12S 52°10W 93 D8
Altamira Chile 25°47S 69°51W 94 B2
Altamira Mexico 22°24N 97°55W 87 C5
Altamont U.S.A. 42°42N 74°2W 83 D10
Altamura Italy 40°49N 16°33E 22 D7
Altanbulag Mongolia 50°16N 106°30E 32 A5
Altar Mexico 30°43N 111°44W 86 A2
Altar, Gran Desierto de
Mexico 31°50N 114°10W 86 B2
Altata Mexico 24°40N 107°55W 86 C3
Altavista U.S.A. 37°6N 79°17W 81 G14
Altay China 47°48N 88°10E 32 B3
Altea Spain 38°38N 0°2W 21 C5
Altiplano Bolivia 17°0S 68°0W 92 G5
Alto Araguaia Brazil 17°15S 53°20W 93 G8
Alto Cuchumatanes =
Cuchumatanes, Sierra de los
Guatemala 15°35N 91°25W 88 C1
Alto del Carmen Chile 28°46S 70°30W 94 B1
Alto Ligonha Mozam. 15°30S 38°11E 55 F4
Alto Molocue Mozam. 15°50S 37°35E 55 F4
Alto Paraguay □
Paraguay 21°0S 58°30W 94 A4
Alto Paraná □ Paraguay 25°30S 54°50W 95 B5
Alton Canada 43°54N 80°5W 82 C4
Alton U.K. 51°9N 0°59W 13 F7
Alton Ill., U.S.A. 38°53N 90°11W 80 F8
Alton N.H., U.S.A. 43°27N 71°13W 83 C13
Altona Canada 49°6N 97°33W 71 D9
Altoona U.S.A. 40°31N 78°24W 82 F6
Altun Kupri Iraq 35°45N 44°9E 44 C5
Altun Shan China 38°30N 88°0E 32 C3
Alturas U.S.A. 41°29N 120°32W 76 F3
Altus U.S.A. 34°38N 99°20W 84 D5
Alucra Turkey 40°22N 38°47E 19 F6
Alūksne Latvia 57°24N 27°3E 9 H22
Alunite U.S.A. 35°59N 114°55W 79 K12
Alusi Indonesia 7°35S 131°40E 37 F8
Alva U.S.A. 36°48N 98°40W 84 C5
Alvarado Mexico 18°46N 95°46W 87 D5
Alvarado U.S.A. 32°24N 97°13W 84 E6
Alvaro Obregón, Presa
Mexico 27°52N 109°52W 86 B3
Alvear Argentina 29°5S 56°30W 94 B4
Alvesta Sweden 56°54N 14°35E 9 H16
Alvin U.S.A. 29°26N 95°15W 84 G7
Alvinston Canada 42°49N 81°52W 82 D3
Älvkarleby Sweden 60°34N 17°26E 9 F17
Alvord Desert U.S.A. 42°30N 118°25W 76 E4
Älvsbyn Sweden 65°40N 21°0E 8 D19
Alwar India 27°38N 76°34E 42 F7
Alxa Zuoqi China 38°50N 105°40E 34 E3
Alyangula Australia 13°55S 136°30E 62 A2
Alyata = Älät Azerbaijan 39°58N 49°25E 45 B6
Alyth U.K. 56°38N 3°13W 11 E5
Alytus Lithuania 54°24N 24°3E 9 J21
Alzada U.S.A. 45°2N 104°25W 76 D11
Alzamay Russia 55°33N 98°39E 29 D10
Alzira Spain 39°9N 0°30W 21 C5
Am Timan Chad 11°0N 20°10E 51 F10
Amadeus, L. Australia 24°54S 131°0E 61 D5
Amadi
Dem. Rep. of the Congo 3°40N 26°40E 54 B2
Amâdi Sudan 5°29N 30°25E 51 G12
Amadjuak L. Canada 65°0N 71°8W 69 C12
Amagansett U.S.A. 40°59N 72°9W 83 F12
Amagasaki Japan 34°42N 135°23E 31 G7
Amahai Indonesia 3°20S 128°55E 37 E7
Amaile Samoa 13°59S 171°22W 59 b
Amakusa-Shotō Japan 32°15N 130°10E 31 H5
Åmål Sweden 59°3N 12°42E 9 G15
Amaliada Greece 37°47N 21°22E 23 F9
Amalner India 21°5N 75°5E 40 J9
Amamapare Indonesia 4°53S 136°38E 37 E9
Amambaí Brazil 23°5S 55°13W 95 A4
Amambaí → Brazil 23°22S 53°56W 95 A5
Amambay □ Paraguay 23°0S 56°0W 95 A4
Amambay, Cordillera de
S. Amer. 23°0S 55°45W 95 A4
Amami-Guntō Japan 27°16N 129°21E 31 L4
Amami-Ō-Shima Japan 28°16N 129°21E 31 K4
Aman, Pulau Malaysia 5°16N 100°24E 39 c
Amaná, L. Brazil 2°35S 64°40W 92 D6
Amanat → India 24°7N 84°4E 43 G11
Amanda Park U.S.A. 47°28N 123°55W 78 C3
Amankeldi Kazakhstan 50°10N 65°10E 28 D7
Amapá Brazil 2°5N 50°50W 93 C8
Amapá □ Brazil 1°40N 52°0W 93 C8
Amarante Brazil 6°14S 42°50W 93 E10
Amaranth Canada 50°36N 98°43W 71 C9
Amargosa → U.S.A. 36°14N 116°51W 79 J10
Amargosa Desert
U.S.A. 36°40N 116°30W 79 J10
Amargosa Range
U.S.A. 36°20N 116°45W 79 J10

Amari Greece 35°13N 24°40E 25 D6
Amarillo U.S.A. 35°13N 101°50W 84 D4
Amarkantak India 22°40N 81°45E 43 H9
Amaro, Mte. Italy 42°5N 14°5E 22 C6
Amarpur India 25°5N 87°0E 43 G12
Amarwara India 22°18N 79°10E 43 H8
Amasya Turkey 40°40N 35°50E 19 F6
Amata Australia 26°9S 131°9E 61 E5
Amatikulu S. Africa 29°3S 31°33E 57 D5
Amatitlán Guatemala 14°29N 90°38W 88 D1
Amay Belgium 50°33N 5°19E 15 D5
Amazon = Amazonas → S. Amer. 0°5S 50°0W 93 D8
Amazonas □ Brazil 5°0S 65°0W 92 E6
Amazonas → S. Amer. 0°5S 50°0W 93 D8
Ambah India 26°43N 78°13E 42 F8
Ambahakily Madag. 21°36S 43°41E 57 C7
Ambahita Madag. 24°1S 45°16E 57 C8
Ambala India 30°23N 76°56E 42 D7
Ambalavao Madag. 21°50S 46°56E 57 C8
Ambanja Madag. 13°40S 48°27E 57 A8
Ambararata Madag. 15°3S 48°33E 57 B8
Ambarchik Russia 69°40N 162°20E 29 C17
Ambarijeby Madag. 14°56S 47°41E 57 A8
Ambaro, Helodranon' Madag. 13°23S 48°38E 57 A8
Ambato Ecuador 1°5S 78°42W 92 D3
Ambato Madag. 13°24S 48°29E 57 A8
Ambato, Sierra de Argentina 28°25S 66°10W 94 B2
Ambato Boeny Madag. 16°28S 46°43E 57 B8
Ambatofinandrahana Madag. 20°33S 46°48E 57 C8
Ambatolampy Madag. 19°20S 47°35E 57 B8
Ambatomainty Madag. 17°41S 45°40E 57 B8
Ambatomanoina Madag. 18°18S 47°37E 57 B8
Ambatondrazaka Madag. 17°55S 48°28E 57 B8
Ambatosoratra Madag. 17°37S 48°31E 57 B8
Ambenja Madag. 15°17S 46°58E 57 B8
Amberg Germany 49°26N 11°52E 16 D6
Ambergris Cay Belize 18°0N 87°55W 87 D7
Amberley Canada 44°2N 81°42W 82 B3
Amberley N.Z. 43°9S 172°44E 59 E4
Ambikapur India 23°15N 83°15E 43 H10
Ambilobé Madag. 13°10S 49°3E 57 A8
Ambinanindrano Madag. 20°5S 48°23E 57 C8
Ambinanitelo Madag. 15°21S 49°35E 57 B8
Ambinda Madag. 16°25S 45°52E 57 B8
Amble U.K. 55°20N 1°36W 12 B6
Ambleside U.K. 54°26N 2°58W 12 C5
Ambo Peru 10°5S 76°10W 92 F3
Amboahangy Madag. 24°15S 46°22E 57 C8
Ambodifototra Madag. 16°59S 49°52E 57 B8
Ambodilazana Madag. 18°6S 49°10E 57 B8
Ambodiriana Madag. 17°55S 49°18E 57 B8
Ambohidratrimo Madag. 18°50S 47°26E 57 B8
Ambohidray Madag. 18°36S 48°18E 57 B8
Ambohimahamasina Madag. 21°56S 47°11E 57 C8
Ambohimahasoa Madag. 21°7S 47°13E 57 C8
Ambohimanga Madag. 20°52S 47°36E 57 C8
Ambohimitombo Madag. 20°43S 47°26E 57 C8
Ambohitra Madag. 12°30S 49°10E 57 A8
Amboise France 47°24N 1°2E 20 C4
Ambon Indonesia 3°43S 128°12E 37 E7
Ambondro Madag. 25°13S 45°44E 57 D8
Amboseli, L. Kenya 2°40S 37°10E 54 C4
Amboseli △ Kenya 2°37S 37°13E 54 C4
Ambositra Madag. 20°31S 47°25E 57 C8
Ambovombe Madag. 25°11S 46°5E 57 D8
Amboy U.S.A. 34°33N 115°45W 79 L11
Amboyna Cay S. China Sea 7°50N 112°50E 36 C4
Ambridge U.S.A. 40°36N 80°14W 82 F4
Ambriz Angola 7°48S 13°8E 52 F2
Amchitka I. U.S.A. 51°32N 179°0E 74 a
Amderma Russia 69°45N 61°30E 28 C7
Amdhi India 23°51N 81°27E 43 H9
Amdo China 32°20N 91°40E 41 C17
Ameca Mexico 20°33N 104°2W 86 C4
Ameca → Mexico 20°41N 105°18W 86 C3
Amecameca de Juárez Mexico 19°8N 98°46W 87 D5
Ameland Neths. 53°27N 5°45E 15 A5
Amenia U.S.A. 41°51N 73°33W 83 E11
America-Antarctica Ridge S. Ocean 59°0S 16°0W 5 B2
American Falls U.S.A. 42°47N 112°51W 76 E7
American Falls Res. U.S.A. 42°47N 112°52W 76 E7
American Fork U.S.A. 40°23N 111°48W 76 F8
American Highland Antarctica 73°0S 75°0E 5 D6
American Samoa ⊠ Pac. Oc. 14°20S 170°0W 59 b
American Samoa △ Amer. Samoa 14°15S 170°28W 59 b
Americana Brazil 22°45S 47°20W 95 A6
Americus U.S.A. 32°4N 84°14W 85 E12
Amersfoort Neths. 52°9N 5°23E 15 B5
Amersfoort S. Africa 26°59S 29°53E 57 D4
Amery Basin S. Ocean 68°15S 74°30E 5 C6
Amery Ice Shelf Antarctica 69°30S 72°0E 5 C6
Ames U.S.A. 42°2N 93°37W 80 D7
Amesbury U.S.A. 42°51N 70°56W 83 D14
Amet India 25°18N 73°56E 42 G5
Amga Russia 60°50N 132°0E 29 C14
Amga → Russia 62°38N 134°32E 29 C14
Amgu Russia 45°45N 137°15E 30 B8
Amgun → Russia 52°56N 139°38E 29 D14
Amherst Canada 45°48N 64°8W 73 C7
Amherst Mass., U.S.A. 42°23N 72°31W 83 D12
Amherst N.Y., U.S.A. 42°59N 78°48W 82 D6
Amherst Ohio, U.S.A. 41°24N 82°14W 82 E2
Amherst I. Canada 44°8N 76°43W 83 B8
Amherstburg Canada 42°6N 83°6W 72 D3
Amiata, Mte. Italy 42°53N 11°37E 22 C4
Amidon U.S.A. 46°29N 103°19W 80 B2
Amiens France 49°54N 2°16E 20 B5
Aminuis Namibia 23°43S 19°21E 56 C2
Amīrābād Iran 33°20N 46°16E 44 C5
Amirante Is. Seychelles 6°0S 53°0E 26 J7
Amisk ⌓ Canada 56°43N 98°0W 71 B9
Amisk L. Canada 54°35N 102°15W 71 C8
Amistad, Presa de la Mexico 29°26N 101°3W 86 B4
Amistad ⌓ U.S.A. 29°32N 101°12W 84 G4
Amite U.S.A. 30°44N 90°30W 85 F9
Amla India 21°56N 78°7E 42 J8
Amlapura = Karangasem Indonesia 8°27S 115°37E 37 J18
Amlia I. U.S.A. 52°4N 173°30W 74 a
Amlwch U.K. 53°24N 4°20W 12 D3
'Ammān Jordan 31°57N 35°52E 46 D4
'Ammān □ Jordan 31°40N 36°30E 46 D5
'Ammān ✈ (AMM) Jordan 31°45N 36°2E 46 D5
Ammanford U.K. 51°48N 3°59W 13 F4
Ammassalik = Tasiilaq Greenland 65°40N 37°20W 4 C6
Ammochostos = Famagusta Cyprus 35°8N 33°55E 25 D12
Ammon U.S.A. 43°28N 111°58W 76 E8
Amnat Charoen Thailand 15°51N 104°38E 38 E5
Amnura Bangla. 24°37N 88°25E 43 G13
Āmol Iran 36°23N 52°20E 45 B7
Amorgos Greece 36°50N 25°57E 23 F11
Amory U.S.A. 33°59N 88°29W 85 E10
Amos Canada 48°35N 78°5W 72 C4
Åmot Norway 59°57N 9°54E 9 G13
Amoy = Xiamen China 24°25N 118°4E 33 D6
Ampanavoana Madag. 15°41S 50°22E 57 B9
Ampang Malaysia 3°8N 101°45E 39 L3
Ampangalana, Lakandranon' Madag. 22°48S 47°50E 57 C8
Ampanihy Madag. 24°40S 44°45E 57 C7
Amparafaravola Madag. 17°35S 48°13E 57 B8
Ampasinambo Madag. 20°31S 48°0E 57 C8
Ampasindava, Helodranon' Madag. 13°40S 48°15E 57 A8
Ampasindava, Saikanosy Madag. 13°42S 47°55E 57 A8
Ampenan Indonesia 8°34S 116°4E 37 K18
Amper → Germany 48°29N 11°55E 16 D6
Amphoe Kathu Thailand 7°55N 98°21E 39 a
Amphoe Thalang Thailand 8°1N 98°20E 39 a
Ampitsikinana Madag. 12°57S 49°49E 57 A8
Ampombiantambo Madag. 12°42S 48°57E 57 A8
Ampotaka Madag. 25°3S 44°41E 57 D7
Ampoza Madag. 22°20S 44°44E 57 C7
Amqui Canada 48°28N 67°27W 73 C6
Amravati India 20°55N 77°45E 40 J10
Amreli India 21°35N 71°17E 42 J4
Amritsar India 31°35N 74°57E 42 D6
Amroha India 28°53N 78°30E 43 E8
Amsterdam Neths. 52°23N 4°54E 15 B4
Amsterdam U.S.A. 42°56N 74°11W 83 D10
Amsterdam ✈ (AMS) Neths. 52°18N 4°45E 15 B4
Amsterdam, I. = Nouvelle Amsterdam, Î. Ind. Oc. 38°30S 77°30E 3 F13
Amstetten Austria 48°7N 14°51E 16 D8
Amudarya → Uzbekistan 43°58N 59°34E 28 E6
Amund Ringnes I. Canada 78°20N 96°25W 69 B10
Amundsen Abyssal Plain S. Ocean 65°0S 125°0W 5 C14
Amundsen Basin Arctic 87°30N 80°0E 4 A
Amundsen Gulf Canada 71°0N 124°0W 68 B7
Amundsen Ridges S. Ocean 69°15S 123°0W 5 C14
Amundsen-Scott Antarctica 90°0S 166°0E 5 E
Amundsen Sea Antarctica 72°0S 115°0W 5 D15
Amuntai Indonesia 2°28S 115°25E 36 E5
Amur → Russia 52°56N 141°10E 29 D15
Amurang Indonesia 1°5N 124°40E 37 D6
Amursk Russia 50°14N 136°54E 29 D14
Amyderya = Amudarya → Uzbekistan 43°58N 59°34E 28 E6
An Bien Vietnam 9°45N 105°0E 39 H5
An Hoa Vietnam 15°40N 108°5E 38 E7
An Nabatīyah at Tahta Lebanon 33°23N 35°27E 46 B4
An Nabk Si. Arabia 31°20N 37°20E 44 D3
An Nabk Syria 34°2N 36°44E 46 A5
An Nafūd Si. Arabia 28°15N 41°0E 44 D4
An Najaf Iraq 32°3N 44°15E 44 C5
An Nāṣirīyah Iraq 31°0N 46°15E 44 D5
An Nhon Vietnam 13°55N 109°7E 38 F7
An Nu'ayrīyah Si. Arabia 27°30N 48°30E 45 E6
An Thoi, Dao Vietnam 9°58N 104°0E 39 H5
An Uaimh Ireland 53°39N 6°41W 10 C5
Anabar → Russia 73°8N 113°36E 29 B12
'Anabtā West Bank 32°19N 35°7E 46 C4
Anaconda U.S.A. 46°8N 112°57W 76 C7
Anacortes U.S.A. 48°30N 122°37W 78 B4
Anadarko U.S.A. 35°4N 98°15W 84 D5
Anadolu Turkey 39°0N 30°0E 19 G5
Anadyr Russia 64°35N 177°20E 29 C18
Anadyr → Russia 64°55N 176°5E 29 C18
Anadyrskiy Zaliv Russia 64°0N 180°0E 29 C19
Anaga, Pta. de Canary Is. 28°34N 16°9W 24 F3
'Ānah Iraq 34°25N 42°0E 44 C4
Anaheim U.S.A. 33°50N 117°55W 79 M9
Anahim Lake Canada 52°28N 125°18W 70 C3
Anakapalle India 17°42N 83°6E 41 L13
Anakie Australia 23°32S 147°45E 62 C4
Analalava Madag. 14°35S 48°0E 57 A8
Analavoka Madag. 22°23S 46°30E 57 C8
Analipsis Greece 39°36N 19°55E 25 A3
Anambar → Pakistan 30°15N 68°50E 42 D3
Anambas, Kepulauan Indonesia 3°20N 106°30E 36 D3
Anambas Is. = Anambas, Kepulauan Indonesia 3°20N 106°30E 36 D3
Anamosa U.S.A. 42°7N 91°17W 80 D8
Anamur Turkey 36°8N 32°58E 44 B2
Anan Japan 33°54N 134°40E 31 H7
Anand India 22°32N 72°59E 42 H5
Anantapur India 14°39N 77°42E 40 M10
Anantnag India 33°45N 75°10E 43 C6
Ananyiv Ukraine 47°44N 29°58E 17 E15
Anapodiaris → Greece 34°59N 25°20E 25 E7
Anápolis Brazil 16°15S 48°50W 93 G9
Anapu → Brazil 1°53S 50°53W 93 D8
Anār Iran 30°55N 55°13E 45 D7
Anārak Iran 33°25N 53°40E 45 C7
Anas → India 23°26N 74°0E 42 H5
Anatolia = Anadolu Turkey 39°0N 30°0E 19 G5
Anatsogno Madag. 23°33S 43°46E 57 C7
Añatuya Argentina 28°20S 62°50W 94 B3
Anaunethad L. Canada 60°55N 104°25W 71 A8
Anbyŏn N. Korea 39°1N 127°35E 35 E14
Ancaster Canada 43°13N 79°59W 82 C5
Anchor Bay U.S.A. 38°48N 123°34W 78 G3
Anchorage U.S.A. 61°13N 149°54W 68 C5
Anci China 39°20N 116°40E 34 E9
Ancohuma, Nevado Bolivia 16°0S 68°50W 92 G5
Ancón Peru 11°50S 77°10W 92 F3
Ancona Italy 43°38N 13°30E 22 C5
Ancud Chile 42°0S 73°50W 96 E2
Ancud, G. de Chile 42°0S 73°0W 96 E2
Anda China 46°24N 125°19E 33 B7
Andacollo Argentina 37°10S 70°42W 94 D1
Andacollo Chile 30°14S 71°6W 94 C1
Andaingo Madag. 18°12S 48°17E 57 B8
Andalgalá Argentina 27°40S 66°30W 94 B2
Åndalsnes Norway 62°35N 7°43E 8 E12
Andalucía □ Spain 37°35N 5°0W 21 D3
Andalusia = Andalucía □ Spain 37°35N 5°0W 21 D3
Andalusia U.S.A. 31°18N 86°29W 85 F11
Andaman Is. Ind. Oc. 12°30N 92°45E 27 G11
Andaman Sea Ind. Oc. 13°0N 96°0E 36 B1
Andamooka Australia 30°27S 137°9E 63 E2
Andapa Madag. 14°39S 49°39E 57 A8
Andara Namibia 18°2S 21°9E 56 B3
Andenes Norway 69°19N 16°18E 8 B17
Andenne Belgium 50°28N 5°5E 15 D5
Anderson Alaska, U.S.A. 64°25N 149°15W 74 a
Anderson Calif., U.S.A. 40°27N 122°18W 76 F2
Anderson Ind., U.S.A. 40°10N 85°41W 81 E11
Anderson Mo., U.S.A. 36°39N 94°27W 80 G6
Anderson S.C., U.S.A. 34°31N 82°39W 85 D13
Anderson → Canada 69°42N 129°0W 68 C7
Andes U.S.A. 42°12N 74°47W 83 D10
Andes, Cord. de los S. Amer. 20°0S 68°0W 92 H5
Andfjorden Norway 69°10N 16°20E 8 B17
Andhra Pradesh □ India 18°0N 79°0E 40 L11
Andijon Uzbekistan 41°10N 72°15E 28 E8
Andikíthira = Antikythira Greece 35°52N 23°15E 23 G10
Andilamena Madag. 17°1S 48°35E 57 B8
Andīmeshk Iran 32°27N 48°21E 45 C6
Andizhan = Andijon Uzbekistan 41°10N 72°15E 28 E8
Andoany Madag. 13°25S 48°16E 57 A8
Andohahela ⌓ Madag. 24°4S 46°44E 57 C8
Andong S. Korea 36°40N 128°43E 35 F15
Andongwei China 35°6N 119°20E 35 G10
Andorra ■ Europe 42°30N 1°30E 20 E4
Andorra La Vella Andorra 42°31N 1°32E 20 E4
Andover U.K. 51°12N 1°29W 13 F6
Andover Maine, U.S.A. 44°38N 70°45W 83 B14
Andover Mass., U.S.A. 42°40N 71°8W 83 D13
Andover N.J., U.S.A. 40°59N 74°45W 83 F10
Andover N.Y., U.S.A. 42°10N 77°48W 82 D7
Andover Ohio, U.S.A. 41°36N 80°34W 82 E4
Andøya Norway 69°10N 15°50E 8 B16
Andradina Brazil 20°54S 51°23W 93 H8
Andrahary Madag. 13°37S 49°17E 57 A8
Andramasina Madag. 19°11S 47°35E 57 B8
Andranopasy Madag. 21°17S 43°44E 57 C7
Andranovory Madag. 23°8S 44°10E 57 C7
Andratx Spain 39°39N 2°25E 24 B9
Andreanof Is. U.S.A. 51°30N 176°0W 74 a
Andrews S.C., U.S.A. 33°27N 79°34W 85 E15
Andrews Tex., U.S.A. 32°19N 102°33W 84 E3
Ándria Italy 41°13N 16°17E 22 D7
Andriamena Madag. 17°26S 47°30E 57 B8
Andriandampy Madag. 22°45S 45°41E 57 C8
Andriba Madag. 17°30S 46°58E 57 B8
Andringitra ⌓ Madag. 22°13S 46°55E 57 C8
Androka Madag. 24°58S 44°2E 57 C7
Andros Greece 37°50N 24°57E 23 F11
Andros I. Bahamas 24°30N 78°0W 88 B4
Andros Town Bahamas 24°43N 77°47W 88 B4
Androscoggin → U.S.A. 43°58N 69°52W 83 C14
Andselv Norway 69°4N 18°34E 8 B18
Andújar Spain 38°3N 4°5W 21 C3
Andulo Angola 11°25S 16°45E 52 G3
Anegada Br. Virgin Is. 18°45N 64°20W 89 e
Anegada Passage W. Indies 18°15N 63°45W 89 C7
Aneto, Pico de Spain 42°37N 0°40E 21 A6
Ang Mo Kio Singapore 1°23N 103°50E 39 d
Ang Thong Thailand 14°35N 100°31E 38 E3
Ang Thong, Ko Thailand 9°37N 99°41E 39 b
Ang Thong △ Thailand 9°40N 99°43E 39 H2
Angamos, Punta Chile 23°1S 70°32W 94 A1
Angara → Russia 58°5N 94°20E 29 D10
Angarsk Russia 52°30N 104°0E 29 D11
Angas Hills Australia 23°0S 127°50E 60 D4
Angaston Australia 34°30S 139°8E 63 E2
Ånge Sweden 62°31N 15°35E 8 E16
Ángel, Salto = Angel Falls Venezuela 5°57N 62°30W 92 B6
Ángel de la Guarda, I. Mexico 29°20N 113°25W 86 B2
Angel Falls Venezuela 5°57N 62°30W 92 B6
Angeles Phil. 15°9N 120°33E 37 A6
Ängelholm Sweden 56°15N 12°58E 9 H15
Angels Camp U.S.A. 38°4N 120°32W 78 G6
Ångermanälven → Sweden 64°0N 17°20E 8 E17
Ångermanland Sweden 63°36N 17°45E 8 E17
Angers Canada 45°31N 75°29W 83 A9
Angers France 47°30N 0°35W 20 C3
Ängesån → Sweden 66°16N 22°47E 8 C20
Angikuni L. Canada 62°12N 99°59W 71 A9
Angkor Cambodia 13°22N 103°50E 38 F4
Anglesey U.K. 53°17N 4°20W 12 D3
Anglesey, Isle of □ U.K. 53°16N 4°18W 12 D3
Angleton U.S.A. 29°10N 95°26W 84 G7
Anglisidhes Cyprus 34°51N 33°27E 25 E12
Angmagssalik = Tasiilaq Greenland 65°40N 37°20W 4 C6
Ango Dem. Rep. of the Congo 4°10N 26°5E 54 B2
Angoche Mozam. 16°8S 39°55E 55 F4
Angoche, I. Mozam. 16°20S 39°50E 55 F4
Angol Chile 37°56S 72°45W 94 D1
Angola Ind., U.S.A. 41°38N 85°0W 81 E11
Angola N.Y., U.S.A. 42°38N 79°2W 82 D5
Angola ■ Africa 12°0S 18°0E 53 G3
Angoulême France 45°39N 0°10E 20 D4
Angoumois France 45°50N 0°25E 20 D3
Angra do Heroismo Azores 38°39N 27°13W 50 a
Angra dos Reis Brazil 23°0S 44°10W 95 A7
Angtassom Cambodia 11°1N 104°41E 39 G5
Angu Dem. Rep. of the Congo 3°23N 24°30E 54 B1
Anguang China 45°15N 123°45E 35 B12
Anguilla ⊠ W. Indies 18°14N 63°5W 89 C7
Anguo China 38°28N 115°15E 34 E8
Angurugu Australia 14°0S 136°25E 62 A2
Angus Canada 44°19N 79°53W 82 B5
Angus □ U.K. 56°46N 2°56W 11 E6
Angwa → Zimbabwe 16°0S 30°23E 57 B5
Anhanduí → Brazil 21°46S 52°9W 95 A5
Anholt Denmark 56°42N 11°33E 9 H14
Anhui □ China 32°0N 117°0E 33 C6
Anhwei = Anhui □ China 32°0N 117°0E 33 C6
Anichab Namibia 21°0S 14°46E 56 C1
Animas → U.S.A. 36°43N 108°13W 77 H9
Anivorano Madag. 18°44S 48°58E 57 B8
Anjalankoski Finland 60°45N 26°51E 8 F22
Anjar India 23°6N 70°10E 42 H4
Anjou France 47°20N 0°15W 20 C3
Anjouan Comoros Is. 12°15S 44°20E 53 a
Anjozorobe Madag. 18°22S 47°52E 57 B8
Anju N. Korea 39°36N 125°40E 35 E13
Ankaboa, Tanjona Madag. 21°58S 43°20E 57 C7
Ankang China 32°40N 109°1E 34 H5
Ankara Turkey 39°57N 32°54E 19 G5
Ankarafantsika ⌓ Madag. 16°8S 47°5E 57 B8
Ankaramena Madag. 21°57S 46°39E 57 C8
Ankaratra Madag. 19°25S 47°12E 53 H9
Ankasakasa Madag. 16°21S 44°52E 57 B7
Ankavandra Madag. 18°46S 45°18E 57 B8
Ankazoabo Madag. 22°18S 44°31E 57 C7
Ankazobe Madag. 18°20S 47°10E 57 B8
Ankeny U.S.A. 41°44N 93°36W 80 E7
Ankilimalinika Madag. 22°58S 43°45E 57 C7
Ankilizato Madag. 20°25S 45°1E 57 C8
Ankisabe Madag. 19°17S 46°29E 57 B8
Ankoro Dem. Rep. of the Congo 6°45S 26°55E 54 D2
Ankororoka Madag. 25°30S 45°11E 57 D8
Anlong Veng Cambodia 14°14N 104°5E 38 E5
Anmyeondo S. Korea 36°25N 126°25E 35 F14
Ann, C. U.S.A. 42°38N 70°35W 83 D14
Ann Arbor U.S.A. 42°17N 83°45W 81 D12
Anna U.S.A. 37°28N 89°15W 80 G9
Annaba Algeria 36°50N 7°46E 50 A7
Annalee → Ireland 54°2N 7°24W 10 B4
Annam Vietnam 16°0N 108°0E 38 E7
Annamitique, Chaîne Asia 17°0N 106°0E 38 D6
Annan U.K. 54°59N 3°16W 11 G5
Annan → U.K. 54°58N 3°16W 11 G5
Annapolis U.S.A. 38°59N 76°30W 81 F15
Annapolis Royal Canada 44°44N 65°32W 73 D6
Annapurna Nepal 28°34N 83°50E 43 E10
Annean, L. Australia 26°54S 118°14E 61 E2
Annecy France 45°55N 6°8E 20 D7
Annette I. U.S.A. 55°9N 131°28W 70 B2
Anning China 24°55N 102°26E 32 D5
Anniston U.S.A. 33°39N 85°50W 85 E12
Annobón Atl. Oc. 1°25S 5°36E 49 G4
Annotto B. Jamaica 18°17N 76°45W 88 a
Annville U.S.A. 40°20N 76°31W 83 F8
Anogia Greece 35°16N 24°52E 25 D6
Anorotsangana Madag. 13°56S 47°55E 57 A8
Anosibe Madag. 19°26S 48°13E 57 B8
Anping Hebei, China 38°15N 115°30E 34 E8
Anping Liaoning, China 41°5N 123°30E 35 D12
Anqing China 30°30N 117°3E 33 C6
Anqiu China 36°25N 119°10E 35 F10
Ansai China 36°50N 109°20E 34 F5
Ansan S. Korea 37°21N 126°52E 35 F14
Ansbach Germany 49°28N 10°34E 16 D6
Anse Boileau Seychelles 4°43S 55°29E 53 b
Anse Royale Seychelles 4°44S 55°31E 53 b
Anshan China 41°5N 122°58E 35 D12
Anshun China 26°18N 105°57E 32 D5
Ansley U.S.A. 41°18N 99°23W 80 E4
Anson U.S.A. 32°45N 99°54W 84 E5
Anson B. Australia 13°20S 130°6E 60 B5
Ansongo Mali 15°25N 0°35E 50 E6
Ansonia U.S.A. 41°21N 73°5W 83 E1
Anstruther U.K. 56°14N 2°41W 11 E
Ansudu Indonesia 2°11S 139°22E 37 E
Antabamba Peru 14°40S 73°0W 92 F
Antakya = Hatay Turkey 36°14N 36°10E 44 B
Antalaha Madag. 14°57S 50°20E 57 A
Antalya Turkey 36°52N 30°45E 19 G
Antalya Körfezi Turkey 36°15N 31°30E 19 G
Antambohobe Madag. 22°20S 46°47E 57 C
Antanambao-Manampotsy Madag. 19°29S 48°34E 57 B
Antanambe Madag. 16°26S 49°52E 57 B
Antananarivo Madag. 18°55S 47°31E 57 B
Antananarivo □ Madag. 19°0S 47°0E 57 B
Antanifotsy Madag. 19°39S 47°19E 57 B
Antanimbaribe Madag. 21°30S 44°48E 57 C
Antanimora Madag. 24°49S 45°40E 57 C
Antarctic Pen. Antarctica 67°0S 60°0W 5 C
Antarctica 90°0S 0°0 5
Antelope Zimbabwe 21°2S 28°31E 55
Antequera Paraguay 24°8S 57°7W 94
Antequera Spain 37°5N 4°33W 21
Antero, Mt. U.S.A. 38°41N 106°15W 76 G
Antevamena Madag. 21°2S 44°8E 57
Anthony Kans., U.S.A. 37°9N 98°2W 80
Anthony N. Mex., U.S.A. 32°0N 106°36W 77 K
Anti Atlas Morocco 30°0N 8°30W 50
Anti-Lebanon = Sharqi, Al Jabal ash Lebanon 33°40N 36°10E 46
Antibes France 43°34N 7°6E 20
Anticosti, Î. d' Canada 49°30N 63°0W 73
Antigo U.S.A. 45°9N 89°9W 80
Antigonish Canada 45°38N 61°58W 73
Antigua Canary Is. 28°24N 14°1W 24
Antigua Guatemala 14°34N 90°41W 88
Antigua W. Indies 17°0N 61°50W 89
Antigua & Barbuda ■ W. Indies 17°20N 61°48W 89
Antikythira Greece 35°52N 23°15E 23 G
Antilla Cuba 20°40N 75°50W 88
Antilles = West Indies Cent. Amer. 15°0N 65°0W 89
Antioch U.S.A. 38°1N 121°48W 78
Antioquia Colombia 6°40N 75°55W 92
Antipodes Is. Pac. Oc. 49°45S 178°40E 64
Antlers U.S.A. 34°14N 95°37W 84
Antoetra Madag. 20°46S 47°20E 57
Antofagasta Chile 23°50S 70°30W 94
Antofagasta □ Chile 24°0S 69°0W 94
Antofagasta de la Sierra Argentina 26°5S 67°20W 94
Antofalla Argentina 25°30S 68°5W 94
Antofalla, Salar de Argentina 25°40S 67°45W 94
Anton U.S.A. 33°49N 102°10W 84
Antongila, Helodrano Madag. 15°30S 49°50E 57
Antonibé Madag. 15°7S 47°24E 57
Antonibé, Presqu'île d' Madag. 14°55S 47°20E 57
Antonina Brazil 25°26S 48°42W 95
Antrim U.K. 54°43N 6°14W 10
Antrim U.S.A. 40°7N 81°21W 82
Antrim □ U.K. 54°56N 6°25W 10
Antrim, Mts. of U.K. 55°3N 6°14W 10
Antrim Plateau Australia 18°8S 128°20E 60
Antsakabary Madag. 15°3S 48°56E 57
Antsalova Madag. 18°40S 44°37E 57
Antsenavolo Madag. 21°24S 48°3E 57
Antsiafabositra Madag. 17°18S 46°57E 57
Antsirabe Antananarivo, Madag. 19°55S 47°2E 57
Antsirabe Antsiranana, Madag. 14°0S 49°59E 57
Antsirabe Mahajanga, Madag. 15°57S 48°58E 57
Antsiranana Madag. 12°25S 49°20E 57
Antsiranana □ Madag. 12°16S 49°17E 57
Antsohihy Madag. 14°50S 47°59E 57
Antsohimbondrona Seranana Madag. 13°7S 48°48E 57
Antu China 42°30N 128°20E 35
Antwerp = Antwerpen Belgium 51°13N 4°25E 15
Antwerp U.S.A. 44°12N 75°37W 83
Antwerpen Belgium 51°13N 4°25E 15
Antwerpen □ Belgium 51°15N 4°40E 15
Anupgarh India 29°10N 73°10E 42
Anuppur India 23°6N 81°41E 43
Anuradhapura Sri Lanka 8°22N 80°28E 40
Anveh Iran 27°23N 54°11E 45
Anvers = Antwerpen Belgium 51°13N 4°25E 15
Anvers I. Antarctica 64°30S 63°40W 5
Anxi China 40°30N 95°43E 32
Anxious B. Australia 33°24S 134°45E 63
Anyang China 36°5N 114°21E 34
Anyang S. Korea 37°23N 126°55E 35
Anyer Indonesia 6°4S 105°53E 37
Anyi China 35°2N 111°2E 34
Anza U.S.A. 33°35N 116°39W 79
Anze China 36°10N 112°12E 34
Anzhero-Sudzhensk Russia 56°10N 86°0E 28
Ánzio Italy 41°27N 12°37E 22
Ao Makham Thailand 7°50N 98°24E
Ao Phangnga △ Thailand 8°10N 98°32E
Aoga-Shima Japan 32°28N 139°46E 31
Aoji N. Korea 42°31N 130°23E 35
Aomen = Macau China 22°12N 113°33E 33
Aomori Japan 40°45N 140°45E 30
Aomori □ Japan 40°45N 140°40E 30
Aonla India 28°16N 79°11E 4
Aorai, Mt. Tahiti 17°34S 149°30W
Aoraki Mount Cook N.Z. 43°36S 170°9E 5

oral, Phnum Cambodia 12°0N 104°15E 39 G5
osta Italy 45°45N 7°20E 20 D7
otearoa = New Zealand ■
Oceania 40°0S 176°0E 59 D6
oukâr Mauritania 17°40N 10°0W 50 E4
ozou Strip Chad 22°0N 19°0E 51 D9
pá → S. Amer. 22°6S 58°2W 94 A4
pache U.S.A. 34°54N 98°22W 84 D5
pache Junction
U.S.A. 33°25N 111°33W 77 K8
palachee B. U.S.A. 30°0N 84°0W 85 G13
palachicola U.S.A. 29°43N 84°59W 85 G12
palachicola →
U.S.A. 29°43N 84°58W 85 G12
paporis → Colombia 1°23S 69°25W 92 D5
parados da Serra △
Brazil 29°10S 50°8W 95 B5
parri Phil. 18°22N 121°38E 37 A6
patity Russia 67°34N 33°22E 8 C25
patula = Finke
Australia 25°34S 134°35E 62 D1
patzingán Mexico 19°5N 102°21W 86 D4
peldoorn Neths. 52°13N 5°57E 15 B5
pennines = Appennini
Italy 44°30N 10°0E 22 B4
i Nepal 30°0N 80°57E 32 C3
ia Samoa 13°50S 171°50W 59 b
iacás, Serra dos Brazil 9°50S 57°0W 92 E7
ies → S. Africa 25°15S 28°8E 57 D4
izaco Mexico 19°25N 98°8W 87 D5
lao Peru 16°0S 72°40W 92 G4
o, Mt. Phil. 6°53N 125°14E 37 C7
olakia Greece 36°5N 27°48E 25 C9
olakia, Ormos Greece 36°5N 27°45E 25 C9
ollonia = Marsá Susah
ibya 32°52N 21°59E 51 B10
ollonia Greece 36°15N 27°58E 25 C9
olo Bolivia 14°30S 68°30W 92 F5
opa El Salv. 13°48N 89°10W 88 D2
oré → Brazil 19°27S 50°57W 93 G8
ostle Is. U.S.A. 47°0N 90°40W 80 B8
ostle Islands ⌂ U.S.A. 46°55N 91°0W 80 B8
óstoles Argentina 28°0S 56°0W 95 B4
ostolos Andreas, C.
yprus 35°42N 34°35E 25 D13
oteri Guyana 4°2N 58°32W 92 C7
palachian Mts. U.S.A. 38°0N 80°0W 81 G14
pennini Italy 44°30N 10°0E 22 B4
ple Hill Canada 45°13N 74°46W 83 A10
ple Valley U.S.A. 34°32N 117°14W 79 L9
pleby-in-Westmorland
.K. 54°35N 2°29W 12 C5
pledore U.K. 51°3N 4°13W 13 F3
pleton U.S.A. 44°16N 88°25W 80 C9
prouague →
r. Guiana 4°30N 51°57W 93 C8
rilia Italy 41°36N 12°39E 22 D5
sley Canada 44°45N 78°6W 82 B6
ucarana Brazil 23°55S 51°33W 95 A5
ure → Venezuela 7°37N 66°25W 92 B5
urimac → Peru 12°17S 73°56W 92 F4
Qālā Iran 37°10N 54°30E 45 B7
aba = Al 'Aqabah
rdan 29°31N 35°0E 46 F4
aba, G. of Red Sea 29°0N 34°40E 44 D2
abah, Khalīj al = Aqaba, G. of
ed Sea 29°0N 34°40E 44 D2
dā Iran 32°26N 53°37E 45 C7
rah Iraq 36°46N 43°45E 44 B4
ay Kazakhstan 51°11N 53°0E 19 D9
aū Kazakhstan 43°39N 51°12E 19 F9
öbe Kazakhstan 50°17N 57°10E 19 D10
oghay Kazakhstan 46°57N 79°40E 28 E8
idauana Brazil 20°30S 55°50W 93 H7
ila Mexico 18°36N 103°30W 86 D4
iles Serdán Mexico 28°36N 105°53W 86 B3
in Haiti 18°16N 73°24W 89 C5
itain, Bassin France 44°0N 0°30W 20 D3
Rachidiya = Er Rachidia
orocco 31°58N 4°20W 50 B5
Rafid Syria 32°57N 35°52E 46 C4
Raḩḩālīyah Iraq 32°44N 43°23E 44 C4
Ramādī Iraq 33°25N 43°20E 44 C4
Ramthā Jordan 32°34N 36°0E 46 C5
Raqqah Syria 35°59N 39°8E 44 C3
Rass Si. Arabia 25°50N 43°40E 44 E4
Rayyān Qatar 25°17N 51°25E 45 E6
Rifā'ī Iraq 31°50N 46°10E 44 D5
Riyāḍ Si. Arabia 24°41N 46°42E 44 E5
Ru'ays Qatar 26°8N 51°12E 45 E6
Rukhaymīyah Iraq 29°22N 45°38E 44 D5
Rumaythah Iraq 31°31N 45°12E 44 D5
Ruṣāfah Syria 35°45N 38°49E 44 C3
Ruṭbah Iraq 33°0N 40°15E 44 C4
India 25°35N 84°32E 43 G11
U.S.A. 34°19N 86°30W 85 D11
b, Bahr el → Sudan 9°0N 29°30E 51 G11
, Shatt al → Asia 29°57N 48°34E 45 D6
bābād Iran 33°2N 57°41E 45 C8
ia Asia 25°0N 45°0E 26 F6
ian Desert = Es Sahrâ' Esh
Sharqîya Egypt 27°30N 32°30E 51 C12
ian Gulf = Persian Gulf
ia 27°0N 50°0E 45 E6
ian Sea Ind. Oc. 16°0N 65°0E 26 G8
aju Brazil 10°55S 37°4W 93 F11
ati Brazil 4°30S 37°44W 93 D11
atuba Brazil 21°10S 50°30W 95 A5
ena Spain 37°53N 6°38W 21 D2
uai Brazil 16°52S 42°4W 93 G10
d Israel 31°15N 35°12E 46 D4
Romania 46°10N 21°20E 17 E11
ān Iran 35°21N 52°30E 45 C7
hippou Cyprus 34°57N 33°36E 25 E12
ura Sea E. Indies 9°0S 135°0E 58 B6
ón □ Spain 41°25N 0°40W 21 B5
ón → Spain 42°13N 1°44W 21 A5
Araguacema Brazil 8°50S 49°20W 93 E9
Araguaia → Brazil 5°21S 48°41W 93 E9
Araguaína Brazil 7°12S 48°12W 93 E9
Araguari Brazil 18°38S 48°11W 93 G9
Araguari → Brazil 1°15N 49°55W 93 C9
Arain India 26°27N 75°2E 42 F6
Arak Algeria 25°20N 3°45E 50 C6
Arāk Iran 34°0N 49°40E 45 C6
Arakan Coast Burma 19°0N 94°0E 41 K19
Arakan Yoma Burma 20°0N 94°40E 41 K19
Araks = Aras, Rūd-e →
Asia 40°5N 48°29E 44 B5
Aral Kazakhstan 46°41N 61°45E 28 E7
Aral Sea Asia 44°30N 60°0E 28 E7
Aral Tengizi = Aral Sea
Asia 44°30N 60°0E 28 E7
Aralsk = Aral Kazakhstan 46°41N 61°45E 28 E7
Aralskoye More = Aral Sea
Asia 44°30N 60°0E 28 E7
Aramac Australia 22°58S 145°14E 62 C4
Aran I. Ireland 55°0N 8°30W 10 A3
Aran Is. Ireland 53°6N 9°38W 10 C2
Aranda de Duero Spain 41°39N 3°42W 21 B4
Arandān Iran 35°23N 46°55E 44 C5
Aranjuez Spain 40°1N 3°40W 21 B4
Aranos Namibia 24°9S 19°7E 56 C2
Aransas Pass U.S.A. 27°55N 97°9W 84 H6
Aranyaprathet Thailand 13°41N 102°30E 38 F4
Arapahoe U.S.A. 40°18N 99°54W 80 E4
Arapey Grande →
Uruguay 30°55S 57°49W 94 C4
Arapgir Turkey 39°5N 38°30E 44 B3
Arapiraca Brazil 9°45S 36°39W 93 E11
Arapongas Brazil 23°29S 51°28W 95 A5
Ar'ar Si. Arabia 30°59N 41°2E 44 D4
Araranguá Brazil 29°0S 49°30W 95 B6
Araraquara Brazil 21°50S 48°0W 93 H9
Ararás, Serra das Brazil 25°0S 53°10W 95 B5
Ararat Australia 37°16S 142°58E 63 F3
Ararat, Mt. = Ağrı Dağı
Turkey 39°50N 44°15E 44 B5
Araria India 26°9N 87°33E 43 F12
Araripe, Chapada do
Brazil 7°20S 40°0W 93 E11
Araruama, L. de Brazil 22°53S 42°12W 95 A7
Aras, Rūd-e → Asia 40°5N 48°29E 44 B5
Arauca Colombia 7°0N 70°40W 92 B4
Arauca → Venezuela 7°24N 66°35W 92 B5
Arauco Chile 37°16S 73°25W 94 D1
Aravalli Range India 25°0N 73°30E 42 G5
Arawale ⌂ Kenya 1°24S 40°9E 54 C5
Araxá Brazil 19°35S 46°55W 93 G9
Araya, Pen. de Venezuela 10°40N 64°0W 92 A6
Arba Minch Ethiopia 6°0N 37°30E 47 F2
Arbat Iraq 35°25N 45°35E 44 C5
Árbatax Italy 39°56N 9°42E 22 E3
Arbīl Iraq 36°15N 44°5E 44 B5
Arborfield Canada 53°6N 103°39W 71 C8
Arborg Canada 50°54N 97°13W 71 C9
Arbroath U.K. 56°34N 2°35W 11 E6
Arbuckle U.S.A. 39°1N 122°3W 78 F4
Arcachon France 44°40N 1°10W 20 D3
Arcade U.S.A. 42°32N 78°25W 82 D6
Arcadia Fla., U.S.A. 27°13N 81°52W 85 H14
Arcadia La., U.S.A. 32°33N 92°55W 84 E8
Arcadia Pa., U.S.A. 40°47N 78°51W 82 F6
Arcata U.S.A. 40°52N 124°5W 76 F1
Archangel = Arkhangelsk
Russia 64°38N 40°36E 18 B7
Archangelos Greece 36°13N 28°7E 25 C10
Archbald U.S.A. 41°30N 75°32W 83 E9
Archer → Australia 13°28S 141°41E 62 A3
Archer B. Australia 13°20S 141°30E 62 A3
Archer Bend = Mungkan
Kandju △ Australia 13°35S 142°52E 62 A3
Archers Post Kenya 0°35N 37°35E 54 B4
Arches △ U.S.A. 38°45N 109°25W 76 G9
Archipel-de-Mingan △
Canada 50°13N 63°10W 73 B7
Archipiélago Chinijo △
Canary Is. 29°20N 13°30W 24 E6
Archipiélago Los Roques △
Venezuela 11°50N 66°44W 89 D6
Arckaringa Cr. →
Australia 28°10S 135°22E 63 D2
Arco U.S.A. 43°38N 113°18W 76 E7
Arcos de la Frontera
Spain 36°45N 5°49W 21 D3
Arcot India 12°53N 79°20E 40 N11
Arctic Bay Canada 73°1N 85°7W 69 B11
Arctic Mid-Ocean Ridge
Arctic 87°0N 90°0E 4 A
Arctic Ocean Arctic 78°0N 160°0W 4 B18
Arctic Red River = Tsiigehtchic
Canada 67°15N 134°0W 68 C6
Arctowski Antarctica 62°30S 58°0W 5 C18
Arda → Bulgaria 41°40N 26°30E 23 D12
Ardabīl Iran 38°15N 48°18E 45 B6
Ardabīl □ Iran 38°15N 48°20E 45 B6
Ardakān = Sepīdān Iran 30°20N 52°5E 45 D7
Ardakān Iran 32°19N 53°59E 45 C7
Ardara Ireland 54°46N 8°25W 10 B3
Ardee Ireland 53°52N 6°33W 10 C5
Arden Canada 44°43N 76°56W 82 B8
Arden Calif., U.S.A. 38°36N 121°33W 78 G5
Arden Nev., U.S.A. 36°1N 115°14W 79 J11
Ardenne Belgium 49°50N 5°5E 15 E5
Ardennes = Ardenne
Belgium 49°50N 5°5E 15 E5
Arderin Ireland 53°2N 7°39W 10 C4
Ardestān Iran 33°20N 52°25E 45 C7
Ardfert Ireland 52°20N 9°47W 10 D2
Ardglass U.K. 54°17N 5°36W 10 B6
Ardivachar Pt. U.K. 57°23N 7°26W 11 D1
Ardlethan Australia 34°22S 146°53E 63 E4
Ardmore Okla., U.S.A. 34°10N 97°8W 84 D6
Ardmore Pa., U.S.A. 40°2N 75°17W 83 F9
Ardnamurchan, Pt. of
U.K. 56°43N 6°14W 11 E2
Ardnave Pt. U.K. 55°53N 6°20W 11 F2
Ardrossan Australia 34°26S 137°53E 63 E2
Ardrossan U.K. 55°39N 4°49W 11 F4
Ards Pen. U.K. 54°33N 5°34W 10 B6
Arecibo Puerto Rico 18°29N 66°43W 89 d
Areia Branca Brazil 5°0S 37°0W 93 E11
Arena, Pt. U.S.A. 38°57N 123°44W 78 G3
Arenal Honduras 15°21N 86°50W 88 C2
Arendal Norway 58°28N 8°46E 9 G13
Arequipa Peru 16°20S 71°30W 92 G4
Arévalo Spain 41°3N 4°43W 21 B3
Arezzo Italy 43°25N 11°53E 22 C4
Arga Turkey 38°21N 37°59E 44 B3
Arganda del Rey Spain 40°19N 3°26W 21 B4
Argenta Canada 50°11N 116°56W 70 C5
Argentan France 48°45N 0°1W 20 B3
Argentário, Mte. Italy 42°24N 11°9E 22 C4
Argentia Canada 47°18N 53°58W 73 C9
Argentina ■ S. Amer. 35°0S 66°0W 96 D3
Argentine Basin Atl. Oc. 45°0S 45°0W 96 F6
Argentino, L. Argentina 50°10S 73°0W 96 G2
Argeș → Romania 44°5N 26°38E 17 F14
Arghandab → Afghan. 31°30N 64°15E 42 D1
Argirades Greece 39°27N 19°58E 25 B3
Argiroupoli Greece 35°17N 24°20E 25 D6
Argolikos Kolpos Greece 37°20N 22°52E 23 F10
Argos Greece 37°40N 22°43E 23 F10
Argostoli Greece 38°11N 20°29E 23 E9
Arguello, Pt. U.S.A. 34°35N 120°39W 79 L6
Arguineguín Canary Is. 27°46N 15°41W 24 G4
Argun → Russia 53°20N 121°28E 29 D13
Argungu Nigeria 12°40N 4°31E 50 F6
Argus Pk. U.S.A. 35°52N 117°26W 79 K9
Argyle, L. Australia 16°20S 128°40E 60 C4
Argyll ⌂ U.K. 56°6N 5°0W 11 E4
Argyll & Bute □ U.K. 56°13N 5°28W 11 E3
Århus Denmark 56°8N 10°11E 9 H14
Ariadnoye Russia 45°8N 134°25E 30 B7
Ariamsvlei Namibia 28°9S 19°51E 56 D2
Ariana Tunisia 36°52N 10°12E 51 A8
Arica Chile 18°32S 70°20W 92 G4
Arica Colombia 2°0S 71°50W 92 D4
Arico Canary Is. 28°9N 16°29W 24 F3
Arid, C. Australia 34°1S 123°10E 61 F3
Arida Japan 34°5N 135°8E 31 G7
Aride Seychelles 4°13S 55°40E 53 b
Ariège → France 43°30N 1°25E 20 E4
Arila, Akra Greece 39°43N 19°39E 25 A3
Arima Trin. & Tob. 10°38N 61°17W 89 D7
Arinos → Brazil 10°25S 58°20W 92 F7
Ario de Rosales Mexico 19°12N 101°43W 86 D4
Aripo, Mt. Trin. & Tob. 10°45N 61°15W 93 K15
Aripuanā Brazil 9°25S 60°30W 92 E6
Aripuanā → Brazil 5°7S 60°25W 92 E6
Ariquemes Brazil 9°55S 63°6W 92 E6
Arisaig U.K. 56°55N 5°51W 11 E3
Aristazabal I. Canada 52°40N 129°10W 70 C3
Arivonimamo Madag. 19°1S 47°11E 57 B8
Arizaro, Salar de
Argentina 24°40S 67°50W 94 A2
Arizona Argentina 35°45S 65°25W 94 D2
Arizona □ U.S.A. 34°0N 112°0W 77 J8
Arizpe Mexico 30°20N 110°10W 86 A2
'Arjah Si. Arabia 24°43N 44°17E 44 E5
Arjeplog Sweden 66°3N 17°54E 8 C17
Arjepluovve = Arjeplog
Sweden 66°3N 17°54E 8 C17
Arjona Colombia 10°14N 75°22W 92 A3
Arjuna Indonesia 7°49S 112°34E 37 G15
Arka Russia 60°15N 142°0E 29 C15
Arkadelphia U.S.A. 34°7N 93°4W 84 D8
Arkaig, L. U.K. 56°59N 5°10W 11 E3
Arkalyk = Arqalyk
Kazakhstan 50°13N 66°50E 28 D7
Arkansas □ U.S.A. 35°0N 92°30W 84 D8
Arkansas → U.S.A. 33°47N 91°4W 84 E9
Arkansas City U.S.A. 37°4N 97°2W 80 G5
Arkaroola Australia 30°20S 139°22E 63 E2
Arkhangelsk Russia 64°38N 40°36E 18 B7
Arki India 31°9N 76°58E 42 D7
Arklow Ireland 52°48N 6°10W 10 D5
Arkport U.S.A. 42°24N 77°42W 82 D7
Arkticheskiy, Mys
Russia 81°10N 95°0E 29 A10
Arkville U.S.A. 42°9N 74°37W 83 D10
Arlanzón → Spain 42°3N 4°17W 21 A3
Arlbergpass Austria 47°9N 10°12E 16 E6
Arles France 43°41N 4°40E 20 E6
Arlington S. Africa 28°1S 27°53E 57 D4
Arlington N.Y., U.S.A. 41°42N 73°54W 83 E11
Arlington Oreg., U.S.A. 45°43N 120°12W 76 D3
Arlington S. Dak., U.S.A. 44°22N 97°8W 80 C5
Arlington Tex., U.S.A. 32°44N 97°6W 84 E6
Arlington Va., U.S.A. 38°53N 77°7W 81 F15
Arlington Vt., U.S.A. 43°5N 73°9W 83 C11
Arlington Wash., U.S.A. 48°12N 122°8W 78 B4
Arlington Heights
U.S.A. 42°5N 87°59W 80 D10
Arlit Niger 19°0N 7°38E 50 E7
Arlon Belgium 49°42N 5°49E 15 E5
Arlparra Australia 22°11S 134°30E 62 C1
Arltunga Australia 23°26S 134°41E 62 C1
Armadale Australia 32°9S 116°0E 61 F2
Armagh U.K. 54°21N 6°39W 10 B5
Armagh □ U.K. 54°18N 6°37W 10 B5
Armando Bermudez △
Dom. Rep. 19°3N 71°0W 89 C5
Armavir Russia 45°2N 41°7E 19 E7
Armenia Colombia 4°35N 75°45W 92 C3
Armenia ■ Asia 40°20N 45°0E 19 F7
Armenistis, Akra Greece 36°8N 27°42E 25 C9
Armidale Australia 30°30S 151°40E 63 E5
Armour U.S.A. 43°19N 98°21W 80 D4
Armstrong B.C.,
Canada 50°25N 119°10W 70 C5
Armstrong Ont., Canada 50°18N 89°4W 72 B2
Arnarfjörður Iceland 65°48N 23°40W 8 D2
Arnaud → Canada 59°59N 69°46W 69 D13
Arnauti, C. Cyprus 35°6N 32°17E 25 D11
Arnett U.S.A. 36°8N 99°46W 84 C5
Arnhem Neths. 51°58N 5°55E 15 C5
Arnhem, C. Australia 12°20S 137°30E 62 A2
Arnhem B. Australia 12°20S 136°10E 62 A2
Arnhem Land Australia 13°10S 134°30E 62 A1
Arno → Italy 43°41N 10°17E 22 C4
Arno Bay Australia 33°54S 136°34E 63 E2
Arnold U.K. 53°1N 1°7W 12 D6
Arnold U.S.A. 38°15N 120°21W 78 G6
Arnot Canada 55°56N 96°41W 71 B9
Arnøya Norway 70°9N 20°40E 8 A19
Arnprior Canada 45°26N 76°21W 83 A8
Arnsberg Germany 51°24N 8°5E 16 C5
Aroa, Pte. Moorea 17°28S 149°46W 59 d
Aroab Namibia 26°41S 19°39E 56 D2
Aron India 25°57N 77°56E 42 G6
Arona Canary Is. 28°6N 16°40W 24 F3
Aros → Mexico 29°9N 107°57W 86 B3
Arqalyk Kazakhstan 50°13N 66°50E 28 D7
Arrah = Ara India 25°35N 84°32E 43 G11
Arrah Ivory C. 6°40N 3°58W 50 G5
Arran U.K. 55°34N 5°12W 11 F3
Arras France 50°17N 2°46E 20 A5
Arrecife Canary Is. 28°57N 13°37W 24 F6
Arrecifes Argentina 34°6S 60°9W 94 C3
Arrée, Mts. d' France 48°26N 3°55W 20 B2
Arriaga Mexico 16°14N 93°54W 87 D6
Arrilalah Australia 23°43S 143°54E 62 C3
Arrino Australia 29°30S 115°40E 61 E2
Arrow, L. Ireland 54°3N 8°19W 10 B3
Arrowtown N.Z. 44°57S 168°50E 59 F2
Arroyo Grande U.S.A. 35°7N 120°35W 79 K6
Ars Iran 37°9N 47°46E 44 B5
Arsenault L. Canada 55°6N 108°32W 71 B7
Arsenev Russia 44°10N 133°15E 30 B6
Arta Greece 39°8N 21°2E 23 E9
Artà Spain 39°41N 3°21E 24 B10
Artà, Coves de Spain 39°40N 3°24E 24 B10
Arteaga Mexico 18°28N 102°25W 86 D4
Artem Russia 43°22N 132°13E 30 C6
Artemovsk Russia 54°45N 93°35E 29 D10
Artemovsk Ukraine 48°35N 38°0E 19 E6
Artesia = Mosomane
Botswana 24°2S 26°19E 56 C4
Artesia U.S.A. 32°51N 104°24W 77 K11
Arthur Canada 43°50N 80°32W 82 C4
Arthur → Australia 41°2S 144°40E 63 G3
Arthur Cr. → Australia 22°30S 136°25E 62 C2
Arthur Pt. Australia 22°7S 150°3E 62 C5
Arthur River Australia 33°20S 117°2E 61 F2
Arthur's Pass N.Z. 42°54S 171°35E 59 E3
Arthur's Pass △ N.Z. 42°53S 171°42E 59 E3
Arthur's Town Bahamas 24°38N 75°42W 89 B4
Artigas Antarctica 62°30S 58°0W 5 C18
Artigas Uruguay 30°20S 56°30W 94 C4
Artillery L. Canada 63°9N 107°52W 71 A7
Artois France 50°20N 2°30E 20 A5
Artrutx, C. de Spain 39°55N 3°49E 24 B10
Artsyz Ukraine 46°4N 29°26E 17 E15
Artux China 39°40N 76°10E 32 C2
Artvin Turkey 41°14N 41°44E 19 F7
Artyk Russia 64°12N 145°6E 29 C15
Aru, Kepulauan Indonesia 6°0S 134°30E 37 F8
Aru Is. = Aru, Kepulauan
Indonesia 6°0S 134°30E 37 F8
Arua Uganda 3°1N 30°58E 54 B3
Aruanã Brazil 14°54S 51°10W 93 F8
Aruba ☒ W. Indies 12°30N 70°0W 89 D6
Arucas Canary Is. 28°7N 15°32W 24 F4
Arué Tahiti 17°31S 149°30W 59 d
Arun → Nepal 26°55N 87°10E 43 F12
Arun → U.K. 50°49N 0°33W 13 G7
Arunachal Pradesh □
India 28°0N 95°0E 41 F19
Arusha Tanzania 3°20S 36°40E 54 C4
Arusha □ Tanzania 4°0S 36°30E 54 C4
Arusha △ Tanzania 3°16S 36°47E 54 C4
Arusha Chini Tanzania 3°32S 37°20E 54 C4
Aruwimi →
Dem. Rep. of the Congo 1°13N 23°36E 54 B1
Arvada Colo., U.S.A. 39°48N 105°5W 76 G11
Arvada Wyo., U.S.A. 44°39N 106°8W 76 D10
Arvayheer Mongolia 46°15N 102°48E 32 B5
Arvi Greece 34°59N 25°28E 25 E7
Arviat Canada 61°6N 93°59W 71 A10
Arvidsjaur Sweden 65°35N 19°10E 8 D18
Arvika Sweden 59°40N 12°36E 9 G15
Arvin U.S.A. 35°12N 118°50W 79 K8
Arwal India 25°15N 84°41E 43 G11
Arxan China 47°11N 119°57E 33 B6
Arys Kazakhstan 42°26N 68°48E 28 E7
Arzamas Russia 55°27N 43°55E 18 C7
Arzanah U.A.E. 24°47N 52°34E 45 E7
Aş Şafā Syria 33°10N 37°0E 46 B6
As Saffānīyah Si. Arabia 27°55N 48°50E 45 E6
As Safīrah Syria 36°5N 37°21E 44 B3
Aş Şahm Oman 24°10N 56°53E 45 E8
As Sājir Si. Arabia 25°11N 44°36E 44 E5
As Salamīyah Syria 35°1N 37°2E 44 C3
As Salmān Iraq 30°30N 44°32E 44 D5
As Salṭ Jordan 32°2N 35°43E 46 C4
As Sal'w'a Qatar 24°23N 50°50E 45 E6
As Samāwah Iraq 31°15N 45°15E 44 D5
As Sanamayn Syria 33°3N 36°10E 46 B5
As Sohar = Şuḩār Oman 24°20N 56°40E 45 E8
As Sukhnah Syria 34°52N 38°52E 44 C3
As Sulaymānīyah Iraq 35°35N 45°29E 44 C5
As Sulaymī Si. Arabia 26°17N 41°21E 44 E4
As Sulayyil Si. Arabia 20°27N 45°34E 47 C4
As Summān Si. Arabia 25°0N 47°0E 44 E5
As Suwaydā' Syria 32°40N 36°30E 46 C5
As Suwaydā' □ Syria 32°45N 36°45E 46 C5
As Suwayq Oman 23°51N 57°26E 45 F8
Aş Şuwayrah Iraq 32°55N 45°0E 44 C5
Asab Namibia 25°30S 18°0E 56 D2
Asad, Buḩayrat al Syria 36°0N 38°15E 44 C3
Asahi-Gawa → Japan 34°36N 133°58E 31 G6
Asahigawa Japan 43°46N 142°22E 30 C11
Asaluyeh Iran 27°29N 52°37E 45 E7
Asamankese Ghana 5°50N 0°40W 50 G5
Asan → India 26°37N 78°24E 43 F8
Asansol India 23°40N 87°1E 43 H12
Asau Samoa 13°27S 172°33W 59 b
Asbesberge S. Africa 29°0S 23°0E 56 D3
Asbestos Canada 45°47N 71°58W 73 C5
Asbury Park U.S.A. 40°13N 74°1W 83 F10
Ascensión Mexico 31°6N 107°59W 86 A3
Ascensión, B. de la
Mexico 19°40N 87°30W 87 D7
Ascension I. Atl. Oc. 7°57S 14°23W 49 G2
Aschaffenburg Germany 49°58N 9°6E 16 D5
Aschersleben Germany 51°45N 11°29E 16 C6
Áscoli Piceno Italy 42°51N 13°34E 22 C5
Ascope Peru 7°46S 79°8W 92 E3
Ascotán Chile 21°45S 68°17W 94 A2
Aseb Eritrea 13°0N 42°40E 47 E3
Asela Ethiopia 8°0N 39°0E 47 F2
Asenovgrad Bulgaria 42°1N 24°51E 23 C11
Aşgabat = Ashgabat
Turkmenistan 38°0N 57°50E 45 B8
Asgata Cyprus 34°46N 33°15E 25 E12
Ash Fork U.S.A. 35°13N 112°29W 77 J7
Ash Grove U.S.A. 37°19N 93°35W 80 G7
Ash Shabakah Iraq 30°49N 43°39E 44 D4
Ash Shamāl □ Lebanon 34°25N 36°0E 46 A5
Ash Shāmīyah Iraq 31°55N 44°35E 44 D5
Ash Shāriqah U.A.E. 25°23N 55°26E 45 E7
Ash Sharmah Si. Arabia 28°1N 35°16E 44 D2
Ash Sharqāt Iraq 35°27N 43°16E 44 C4
Ash Shaṭrah Iraq 31°30N 46°10E 44 D5
Ash Shawbak Jordan 30°32N 35°34E 44 D2
Ash Shiḩr Yemen 14°45N 49°36E 47 E4
Ash Shināfīyah Iraq 31°35N 44°39E 44 D5
Ash Shu'bah Si. Arabia 28°54N 44°44E 44 D5
Ash Shumlūl Si. Arabia 26°31N 47°20E 44 E5
Ash Shūr'a Iraq 35°58N 43°13E 44 C4
Ash Shurayf Si. Arabia 25°43N 39°14E 44 E3
Ash Shuwayfāt Lebanon 33°45N 35°30E 46 B4
Asha Russia 55°0N 57°16E 18 D10
Ashau Vietnam 16°6N 107°22E 38 D6
Ashbourne U.K. 53°2N 1°43W 12 D6
Ashburn U.S.A. 31°43N 83°39W 85 F13
Ashburton N.Z. 43°53S 171°48E 59 E3
Ashburton → Australia 21°40S 114°56E 60 D1
Ashcroft Canada 50°40N 121°20W 70 C4
Ashdod Israel 31°49N 34°35E 46 D3
Ashdown U.S.A. 33°40N 94°8W 84 E7
Asheboro U.S.A. 35°43N 79°49W 85 D15
Ashern Canada 51°11N 98°21W 71 C9
Asherton U.S.A. 28°27N 99°46W 84 G5
Asheville U.S.A. 35°36N 82°33W 85 D13
Ashewat Pakistan 31°22N 68°32E 42 D3
Asheweig → Canada 54°17N 87°12W 72 B2
Ashford Australia 29°15S 151°3E 63 D5
Ashford U.K. 51°8N 0°53E 13 F8
Ashgabat Turkmenistan 38°0N 57°50E 45 B8
Ashibetsu Japan 43°31N 142°11E 30 C11
Ashikaga Japan 36°28N 139°29E 31 F9
Ashington U.K. 55°11N 1°33W 12 B6
Ashizuri-Uwakai △
Japan 32°56N 132°32E 31 H6
Ashizuri-Zaki Japan 32°44N 133°0E 31 H6
Ashkarkot Afghan. 33°3N 67°58E 42 C2
Ashkhabad = Ashgabat
Turkmenistan 38°0N 57°50E 45 B8
Āshkhāneh Iran 37°26N 56°55E 45 B8
Ashland Kans., U.S.A. 37°11N 99°46W 80 G4
Ashland Ky., U.S.A. 38°28N 82°38W 81 F12
Ashland Maine, U.S.A. 46°38N 68°24W 81 B19
Ashland Mont., U.S.A. 45°36N 106°16W 76 D10
Ashland Ohio, U.S.A. 40°52N 82°19W 82 F2
Ashland Oreg., U.S.A. 42°12N 122°43W 76 E2
Ashland Pa., U.S.A. 40°45N 76°22W 83 F8
Ashland Va., U.S.A. 37°46N 77°29W 81 G15
Ashland Wis., U.S.A. 46°35N 90°53W 80 B8
Ashley N. Dak., U.S.A. 46°2N 99°22W 80 B4
Ashley Pa., U.S.A. 41°12N 75°55W 83 E9
Ashmore and Cartier Is.
Ind. Oc. 12°15S 123°0E 60 B3
Ashmore Reef Australia 12°14S 123°5E 60 B3
Ashmyany Belarus 54°26N 25°52E 17 A13
Ashokan Res. U.S.A. 41°56N 74°13W 83 E10
Ashoknagar India 24°34N 77°43E 42 G7
Ashqelon Israel 31°42N 34°35E 46 D3
Ashta India 23°1N 76°43E 42 H7
Ashtabula U.S.A. 41°52N 80°47W 82 E4
Āshtiyān Iran 34°31N 50°0E 45 C6
Ashton S. Africa 33°50S 20°5E 56 E3
Ashton U.S.A. 44°4N 111°27W 76 D8
Ashuanipi, L. Canada 52°45N 66°15W 73 B6
Ashuapmushuan →
Canada 48°37N 72°20W 72 C5
Ashville U.S.A. 40°34N 78°33W 82 F6
Asia 45°0N 75°0E 26 E9
Asia, Kepulauan
Indonesia 1°0N 131°13E 37 D8
Asifabad India 19°20N 79°24E 40 K11
Asinara Italy 41°4N 8°16E 22 D3
Asinara, G. dell' Italy 41°0N 8°30E 22 D3
Asino Russia 57°0N 86°0E 28 D9
Asipovichy Belarus 53°19N 28°33E 17 B15
'Asīr Si. Arabia 18°40N 42°30E 47 D3
Asir, Ras Somali Rep. 11°55N 51°10E 47 E5
Askham S. Africa 26°59S 20°47E 56 D3
Askim Norway 59°35N 11°10E 9 G14
Askja Iceland 65°3N 16°48W 8 D5
Asklipio Greece 36°4N 27°56E 25 C9
Askøyna Norway 60°29N 5°10E 8 F11
Asmara = Asmera
Eritrea 15°19N 38°55E 47 D2

Asmera Eritrea 15°19N 38°55E 47 D2
Åsnen Sweden 56°37N 14°45E 9 H16
Aso Kuju △ Japan 32°53N 131°6E 31 H5
Aspatria U.K. 54°47N 3°19W 12 C4
Aspen U.S.A. 39°11N 106°49W 76 G10
Aspermont U.S.A. 33°8N 100°14W 84 E4
Aspiring, Mt. N.Z. 44°23S 168°46E 59 F2
Asprokavos, Akra Greece 39°21N 20°6E 25 B4
Aspur India 23°58N 74°7E 42 H6
Asquith Canada 52°8N 107°13W 71 C7
Assab = Aseb Eritrea 13°0N 42°40E 47 E3
Assal, L. Djibouti 11°40N 42°26E 47 E3
Assam □ India 26°0N 93°0E 41 G18
Assateague Island ⌓ U.S.A. 38°15N 75°10W 81 F16
Asse Belgium 50°24N 4°10E 15 D4
Assen Neths. 53°0N 6°35E 15 A6
Assiniboia Canada 49°40N 105°59W 71 D7
Assiniboine → Canada 49°53N 97°8W 71 D9
Assiniboine, Mt. Canada 50°52N 115°39W 70 C5
Assis Brazil 22°40S 50°20W 95 A5
Assisi Italy 43°4N 12°37E 22 C5
Assynt, L. U.K. 58°10N 5°3W 11 C3
Astana Kazakhstan 51°10N 71°30E 32 A2
Āstāneh Iran 37°17N 49°59E 45 B6
Astara Azerbaijan 38°30N 48°50E 45 B6
Astarabad = Gorgān Iran 36°55N 54°30E 45 B7
Asterousia Greece 34°59N 25°3E 25 E7
Asti Italy 44°54N 8°12E 20 D8
Astipalea Greece 36°32N 26°22E 23 F12
Astorga Spain 42°29N 6°8W 21 A2
Astoria U.S.A. 46°11N 123°50W 78 D3
Astrakhan Russia 46°25N 48°5E 19 E8
Astrebla Downs Australia 24°12S 140°34E 62 C3
Asturias □ Spain 43°15N 6°0W 21 A3
Asunción Paraguay 25°10S 57°30W 94 B4
Asunción Nochixtlán Mexico 17°28N 97°14W 87 D5
Aswa → Uganda 3°43N 31°55E 54 B3
Aswa-Lolim ⌓ Uganda 2°43N 31°35E 54 B3
Aswân Egypt 24°4N 32°57E 51 D12
Aswan High Dam = Sadd el Aali Egypt 23°54N 32°54E 51 D12
Asyût Egypt 27°11N 31°4E 51 C12
At Ṭafilah Jordan 30°45N 35°30E 46 E4
At Ṭafilah □ Jordan 30°45N 35°30E 46 E4
Aṭ Ṭā'if Si. Arabia 21°5N 40°27E 47 C3
At Ta'mīm □ Iraq 35°30N 44°20E 44 C5
Aṭ Ṭirāq Si. Arabia 27°19N 44°33E 44 E5
Aṭ Ṭubayq Si. Arabia 29°30N 37°0E 44 D3
Aṭ Ṭunayb Jordan 31°48N 35°57E 46 D4
Atacama □ Chile 27°30S 70°0W 94 B2
Atacama, Desierto de Chile 24°0S 69°20W 94 A2
Atacama, Salar de Chile 23°30S 68°20W 94 A2
Atakpamé Togo 7°31N 1°13E 50 G6
Atalaya Peru 10°45S 73°50W 92 F4
Atalaya de Femes Canary Is. 28°56N 13°47W 24 F6
Atami Japan 35°5N 139°4E 31 G9
Atamyrat Turkmenistan 37°50N 65°12E 28 F7
Atapupu Indonesia 9°0S 124°51E 37 F6
Atâr Mauritania 20°30N 13°5W 50 D3
Atari Pakistan 30°56N 74°2E 42 D6
Atascadero U.S.A. 35°29N 120°40W 78 K6
Atasū Kazakhstan 48°30N 71°0E 28 E8
Atatürk Barajı Turkey 37°28N 38°30E 19 G6
Atauro E. Timor 8°10S 125°30E 37 F7
Ataviros Greece 36°12N 27°50E 25 C9
Atbara Sudan 17°42N 33°59E 51 E12
'Atbara, Nahr → Sudan 17°40N 33°56E 51 E12
Atbasar Kazakhstan 51°48N 68°20E 28 D7
Atchafalaya B. U.S.A. 29°25N 91°25W 84 G9
Atchison U.S.A. 39°34N 95°7W 80 F6
Āteshān Iran 35°35N 52°37E 45 C7
Ath Belgium 50°38N 3°47E 15 D3
Athabasca Canada 54°45N 113°20W 70 C6
Athabasca → Canada 58°40N 110°50W 71 B6
Athabasca, L. Canada 59°15N 109°15W 71 B7
Athabasca Sand Dunes ⌓ Canada 59°4N 108°43W 71 B7
Athboy Ireland 53°37N 6°56W 10 C5
Athenry Ireland 53°18N 8°44W 10 C3
Athens = Athina Greece 37°58N 23°43E 23 F10
Athens Ala., U.S.A. 34°48N 86°58W 85 D11
Athens Ga., U.S.A. 33°57N 83°23W 85 E13
Athens N.Y., U.S.A. 42°16N 73°49W 83 D11
Athens Ohio, U.S.A. 39°20N 82°6W 81 F12
Athens Pa., U.S.A. 41°57N 76°31W 83 E8
Athens Tenn., U.S.A. 35°27N 84°36W 85 D12
Athens Tex., U.S.A. 32°12N 95°51W 84 E7
Atherley Canada 44°37N 79°20W 82 B5
Atherton Australia 17°17S 145°30E 62 B4
Athi River Kenya 1°28S 36°58E 54 C4
Athienou Cyprus 35°3N 33°32E 25 D12
Athina Greece 37°58N 23°43E 23 F10
Athínai = Athina Greece 37°58N 23°43E 23 F10
Athlone Ireland 53°25N 7°56W 10 C4
Athna Cyprus 35°3N 33°47E 25 D12
Athol U.S.A. 42°36N 72°14W 83 D12
Atholl, Forest of U.K. 56°51N 3°50W 11 E5
Atholville Canada 47°59N 66°43W 73 C6
Athos Greece 40°9N 24°22E 23 D11
Athy Ireland 53°0N 7°0W 10 C5
Ati Chad 13°13N 18°20E 51 F9
Atiak Uganda 3°12N 32°2E 54 B3
Atik L. Canada 55°15N 96°0W 71 B9
Atikaki ⌓ Canada 51°30N 95°31W 71 C9
Atikameg → Canada 52°30N 82°46W 72 B3
Atikokan Canada 48°45N 91°37W 72 C1
Atikonak L. Canada 52°40N 64°32W 73 B7
Atimaono Tahiti 17°46S 149°28W 59 d
Atitlán △ Cent. Amer. 14°38N 91°10W 87 E6
Atiu Cook Is. 20°0S 158°10W 65 J12
Atka Russia 60°50N 151°48E 29 C16
Atka I. U.S.A. 52°7N 174°30W 74 a
Atkinson U.S.A. 42°32N 98°59W 80 D4
Atlanta Ga., U.S.A. 33°45N 84°23W 85 E12
Atlanta Tex., U.S.A. 33°7N 94°10W 84 E7
Atlantic U.S.A. 41°24N 95°1W 80 E6
Atlantic City U.S.A. 39°21N 74°27W 81 F16
Atlantic-Indian Basin Antarctica 60°0S 30°0E 5 B4
Atlantic Ocean 0°0 20°0W 2 D8
Atlas Mts. = Haut Atlas Morocco 32°30N 5°0W 50 B4
Atlin Canada 59°31N 133°41W 70 B2
Atlin, L. Canada 59°26N 133°45W 70 B2
Atlin ⌓ Canada 59°10N 134°30W 70 B2
Atmore U.S.A. 31°2N 87°29W 85 F11
Atoka U.S.A. 34°23N 96°8W 84 D6
Atolia U.S.A. 35°19N 117°37W 79 K9
Atrai → Bangla. 24°7N 89°22E 43 G13
Atrak = Atrek → Turkmenistan 37°35N 53°58E 45 B8
Atrauli India 28°2N 78°20E 42 E8
Atrek → Turkmenistan 37°35N 53°58E 45 B8
Atsuta Japan 43°24N 141°26E 30 C10
Attalla U.S.A. 34°1N 86°6W 85 D11
Attapu Laos 14°48N 106°50E 38 E6
Attawapiskat Canada 52°56N 82°24W 72 B3
Attawapiskat → Canada 52°57N 82°18W 72 B3
Attawapiskat L. Canada 52°18N 87°54W 72 B2
Attica Ind., U.S.A. 40°18N 87°15W 80 E10
Attica Ohio, U.S.A. 41°4N 82°53W 82 E2
Attikamagen L. Canada 55°0N 66°30W 73 B6
Attleboro U.S.A. 41°57N 71°17W 83 E13
Attock Pakistan 33°52N 72°20E 42 C5
Attopeu = Attapu Laos 14°48N 106°50E 38 E6
Attu I. U.S.A. 52°55N 172°55E 74 a
Attur India 11°35N 78°30E 40 P11
Atuel → Argentina 36°17S 66°50W 94 D2
Åtvidaberg Sweden 58°12N 16°0E 9 G17
Atwater U.S.A. 37°21N 120°37W 78 H6
Atwood Canada 43°40N 81°1W 82 C3
Atwood U.S.A. 39°48N 101°3W 80 F3
Atyraū Kazakhstan 47°5N 52°0E 19 E9
Au Sable U.S.A. 44°25N 83°20W 82 B1
Au Sable → U.S.A. 44°25N 83°20W 81 C12
Au Sable Forks U.S.A. 44°27N 73°41W 83 B11
Au Sable Pt. U.S.A. 44°20N 83°20W 82 B1
Auas Honduras 15°29N 84°20W 88 C3
Auasberg Namibia 22°37S 17°13E 56 C2
Aubagne France 43°17N 5°37E 20 E6
Aube → France 48°34N 3°43E 20 B5
Auberry U.S.A. 37°7N 119°29W 78 H7
Auburn Ala., U.S.A. 32°36N 85°29W 85 E12
Auburn Calif., U.S.A. 38°54N 121°4W 78 G5
Auburn Ind., U.S.A. 41°22N 85°4W 81 E11
Auburn Maine, U.S.A. 44°6N 70°14W 81 C18
Auburn N.Y., U.S.A. 42°56N 76°34W 83 D8
Auburn Nebr., U.S.A. 40°23N 95°51W 80 E6
Auburn Pa., U.S.A. 40°36N 76°6W 83 F8
Auburn Wash., U.S.A. 47°18N 122°14W 78 C4
Auburn Ra. Australia 25°15S 150°30E 63 D5
Auburndale U.S.A. 28°4N 81°48W 85 G14
Aubusson France 45°57N 2°11E 20 D5
Auch France 43°39N 0°36E 20 E4
Auchterarder U.K. 56°18N 3°41W 11 E5
Auchtermuchty U.K. 56°18N 3°13W 11 E5
Auckland N.Z. 36°52S 174°46E 59 B5
Auckland Is. Pac. Oc. 50°40S 166°5E 64 N8
Aude → France 43°13N 3°14E 20 E5
Auden Canada 50°14N 87°53W 72 B2
Audubon U.S.A. 41°43N 94°56W 80 E6
Augathella Australia 25°48S 146°35E 63 D4
Aughnacloy U.K. 54°25N 6°59W 10 B5
Aughrim Ireland 53°18N 8°19W 10 C3
Augrabies Falls S. Africa 28°35S 20°20E 56 D3
Augrabies Falls △ S. Africa 28°40S 20°22E 56 D3
Augsburg Germany 48°25N 10°52E 16 D6
Augusta Australia 34°19S 115°9E 61 F2
Augusta Italy 37°13N 15°13E 22 F6
Augusta Ark., U.S.A. 35°17N 91°22W 84 D9
Augusta Ga., U.S.A. 33°28N 81°58W 85 E14
Augusta Kans., U.S.A. 37°41N 96°59W 80 G5
Augusta Maine, U.S.A. 44°19N 69°47W 81 C19
Augusta Mont., U.S.A. 47°30N 112°24W 76 C7
Augustów Poland 53°51N 23°0E 17 B12
Augustus, Mt. Australia 24°20S 116°50E 61 D2
Augustus I. Australia 15°20S 124°30E 60 C3
Aujuittuq = Grise Fiord Canada 76°25N 82°57W 69 B11
Aukštaitija △ Lithuania 55°15N 26°0E 9 J22
Aukum U.S.A. 38°34N 120°43W 78 G6
Auld, L. Australia 22°25S 123°50E 60 D3
Ault U.S.A. 40°35N 104°44W 76 F11
Aunis France 46°5N 0°50W 20 C3
Aunu'u Amer. Samoa 14°20S 170°31W 59 b
Auponhia Indonesia 1°58S 125°27E 37 E7
Aur, Pulau Malaysia 2°35N 104°10E 39 L5
Auraiya India 26°28N 79°33E 43 F8
Aurangabad Bihar, India 24°45N 84°18E 43 G11
Aurangabad Maharashtra, India 19°50N 75°23E 40 K9
Aurich Germany 53°28N 7°28E 16 B4
Aurillac France 44°55N 2°26E 20 D5
Aurora Canada 44°0N 79°28W 82 C5
Aurora S. Africa 32°40S 18°29E 56 E2
Aurora Colo., U.S.A. 39°43N 104°49W 76 G11
Aurora Ill., U.S.A. 41°45N 88°19W 80 E9
Aurora Mo., U.S.A. 36°58N 93°43W 80 G7
Aurora N.Y., U.S.A. 42°45N 76°42W 83 D8
Aurora Nebr., U.S.A. 40°52N 98°0W 80 E5
Aurora Ohio, U.S.A. 41°21N 81°20W 82 E3
Aurukun Australia 13°20S 141°45E 62 A3
Aus Namibia 26°35S 16°12E 56 D2
Ausable → Canada 43°19N 81°46W 82 C3
Auschwitz = Oświęcim Poland 50°2N 19°11E 17 C10
Austin Minn., U.S.A. 43°40N 92°58W 80 D7
Austin Nev., U.S.A. 39°30N 117°4W 76 G5
Austin Pa., U.S.A. 41°38N 78°6W 82 E6
Austin Tex., U.S.A. 30°17N 97°45W 84 F6
Austin, L. Australia 27°40S 118°0E 61 E2
Austin I. Canada 61°10N 94°0W 71 A10
Austra Norway 65°8N 11°55E 8 D14
Austral Is. = Tubuaï, Îs. French Polynesia 25°0S 150°0W 65 K13
Austral Seamount Chain Pac. Oc. 24°0S 150°0W 65 K13
Australia ■ Oceania 23°0S 135°0E 58 D6
Australian-Antarctic Basin S. Ocean 60°0S 120°0E 5 C9
Australian Capital Territory □ Australia 35°30S 149°0E 63 F4
Australind Australia 33°17S 115°42E 61 F2
Austria ■ Europe 47°0N 14°0E 16 E8
Austvågøya Norway 68°20N 14°40E 8 B16
Autlán de Navarro Mexico 19°46N 104°22W 86 D4
Autun France 46°58N 4°17E 20 C6
Auvergne □ France 45°20N 3°15E 20 D5
Auvergne, Mts. d' France 45°20N 2°55E 20 D5
Auxerre France 47°48N 3°32E 20 C5
Av-Dovurak Russia 51°17N 91°35E 29 D10
Ava U.S.A. 36°57N 92°40W 80 G7
Avallon France 47°30N 3°53E 20 C5
Avalon U.S.A. 33°21N 118°20W 79 M8
Avalon Pen. Canada 47°30N 53°20W 73 C9
Avanos Turkey 38°43N 34°51E 44 B2
Avaré Brazil 23°4S 48°58W 95 A6
Avawatz Mts. U.S.A. 35°40N 116°30W 79 K10
Aveiro Brazil 3°10S 55°5W 93 D7
Aveiro Portugal 40°37N 8°38W 21 B1
Āvej Iran 35°40N 49°15E 45 C6
Avellaneda Argentina 34°40S 58°22W 94 C4
Avellino Italy 40°54N 14°47E 22 D6
Avenal U.S.A. 36°0N 120°8W 78 K6
Aversa Italy 40°58N 14°12E 22 D6
Avery U.S.A. 47°15N 115°49W 76 C6
Aves, I. de W. Indies 15°45N 63°55W 89 C7
Aves, Is. las Venezuela 12°0N 67°30W 89 D6
Avesta Sweden 60°9N 16°10E 9 F17
Aveyron → France 44°5N 1°16E 20 D4
Avezzano Italy 42°2N 13°25E 22 C5
Aviá Terai Argentina 26°45S 60°50W 94 B3
Aviemore U.K. 57°12N 3°50W 11 D5
Avignon France 43°57N 4°50E 20 E6
Ávila Spain 40°39N 4°43W 21 B3
Avila Beach U.S.A. 35°11N 120°44W 79 K6
Avilés Spain 43°35N 5°57W 21 A3
Avis U.S.A. 41°11N 77°19W 82 E7
Avoca U.S.A. 42°25N 77°25W 82 D7
Avoca → Australia 35°40S 143°43E 63 F3
Avoca → Ireland 52°48N 6°10W 10 D5
Avola Canada 51°45N 119°19W 70 C5
Avola Italy 36°56N 15°7E 22 F6
Avon U.S.A. 42°55N 77°45W 82 D7
Avon → Australia 31°40S 116°7E 61 F2
Avon → Bristol, U.K. 51°29N 2°41W 13 F5
Avon → Dorset, U.K. 50°44N 1°46W 13 G6
Avon → Warks., U.K. 52°0N 2°8W 13 E5
Avon Park U.S.A. 27°36N 81°31W 85 H14
Avondale Zimbabwe 17°43S 30°58E 55 F3
Avonlea Canada 50°0N 105°0W 71 D8
Avonmore Canada 45°10N 74°58W 83 A10
Avonmouth U.K. 51°30N 2°42W 13 F5
Avranches France 48°40N 1°20W 20 B3
Awa-Shima Japan 38°27N 139°14E 30 E9
A'waj → Syria 33°23N 36°20E 46 B5
Awaji-Shima Japan 34°30N 134°50E 31 G7
'Awālī Bahrain 26°0N 50°30E 45 E6
Awantipur India 33°55N 75°3E 43 C6
Awasa Ethiopia 7°2N 38°28E 47 F2
Awash Ethiopia 9°1N 40°10E 47 F3
Awatere → N.Z. 41°37S 174°10E 59 D5
Awbārī Libya 26°46N 12°57E 51 C8
Awbārī, Idehan Libya 27°10N 11°30E 51 C8
Awe, L. U.K. 56°17N 5°16W 11 E3
Awjilah Libya 29°8N 21°7E 51 C10
Axe → U.K. 50°42N 3°4W 13 F5
Axel Heiberg I. Canada 80°0N 90°0W 69 B11
Axim Ghana 4°51N 2°15W 50 H5
Axios → Greece 40°57N 22°35E 23 D10
Axminster U.K. 50°46N 3°0W 13 G4
Ayabaca Peru 4°40S 79°53W 92 D3
Ayabe Japan 35°20N 135°20E 31 G7
Ayacucho Argentina 37°5S 58°20W 94 D4
Ayacucho Peru 13°0S 74°0W 92 F4
Ayaguz = Ayaköz Kazakhstan 48°10N 80°10E 32 B3
Ayaköz Kazakhstan 48°10N 80°10E 32 B3
Ayamonte Spain 37°12N 7°24W 21 D2
Ayan Russia 56°30N 138°16E 29 D14
Ayaviri Peru 14°50S 70°35W 92 F4
Aydın Turkey 37°51N 27°51E 23 F12
Aydingkol Hu China 42°40N 89°15E 32 B3
Ayer U.S.A. 42°34N 71°35W 83 D13
Ayer Hitam Malaysia 5°24N 100°16E 39 c
Ayer's Cliff Canada 45°10N 72°3W 83 A12
Ayers Rock = Uluru Australia 25°23S 131°5E 61 E5
Ayeyarwady = Irrawaddy → Burma 15°50N 95°6E 41 M19
Áyia Napa Cyprus 34°59N 34°0E 25 E13
Áyia Phyla Cyprus 34°43N 33°1E 25 E12
Áyios Amvrósios Cyprus 35°20N 33°35E 25 D12
Áyios Seryios Cyprus 35°12N 33°53E 25 D12
Áyios Theodhoros Cyprus 35°22N 34°1E 25 D13
Aykhal Russia 66°0N 111°30E 29 C12
Aykino Russia 62°15N 49°56E 18 B8
Aylesbury U.K. 51°49N 0°49W 13 F7
Aylmer Canada 42°46N 80°59W 83 D4
Aylmer, L. Canada 64°5N 108°30W 68 C9
'Ayn, Wādī al Oman 22°15N 55°28E 45 F7
Ayn Dār Si. Arabia 25°55N 49°10E 45 E7
Ayn Zālah Iraq 36°45N 42°35E 44 B4
Ayolas Paraguay 27°10S 56°59W 94 B4
Ayon, Ostrov Russia 69°50N 169°0E 29 C17
'Ayoûn el 'Atroûs Mauritania 16°38N 9°37W 50 E4
Ayr Australia 19°35S 147°25E 62 B4
Ayr Canada 43°17N 80°27W 82 C4
Ayr U.K. 55°28N 4°38W 11 F4
Ayr → U.K. 55°28N 4°38W 11 F4
Ayre, Pt. of I. of Man 54°25N 4°21W 12 C3
Ayton Australia 15°56S 145°22E 62 B4
Aytos Bulgaria 42°42N 27°16E 23 C12
Ayu, Kepulauan Indonesia 0°35N 131°5E 37 D8
Ayutla Guatemala 14°40N 92°10W 88 D1
Ayutla de los Libres Mexico 16°54N 99°13W 87 D5
Ayvacık Turkey 39°36N 26°24E 23 E12
Ayvalık Turkey 39°20N 26°46E 23 E12
Az Zabadānī Syria 33°43N 36°5E 46 B5
Aẓ Ẓāhirīyah West Bank 31°25N 34°58E 46 D3
Aẓ Ẓahrān Si. Arabia 26°10N 50°7E 45 E6
Az Zarqā Jordan 32°5N 36°4E 46 C5
Az Zarqā' U.A.E. 24°53N 53°4E 45 E7
Az Zarqā □ Jordan 32°5N 36°4E 46 C5
Az Zāwiyah Libya 32°52N 12°56E 51 B8
Az Zībār Iraq 36°52N 44°4E 44 B5
Az Zilfī Si. Arabia 26°12N 44°52E 44 E5
Az Zubayr Iraq 30°26N 47°40E 44 D5
Azad Kashmir □ Pakistan 33°50N 73°50E 43 C5
Azamgarh India 26°5N 83°13E 43 F10
Azangaro Peru 14°55S 70°13W 92 F4
Azaouad Mali 19°0N 3°0W 50 E5
Āzār Shahr Iran 37°45N 45°59E 44 B5
Azarān Iran 37°25N 47°16E 44 B5
Azärbayjan = Azerbaijan ■ Asia 40°20N 48°0E 19 F8
Āzarbāyjān-e Gharbī □ Iran 37°0N 44°30E 44 B5
Āzarbāyjān-e Sharqī □ Iran 37°20N 47°0E 44 B5
Azare Nigeria 11°55N 10°10E 50 F8
A'zāz Syria 36°36N 37°4E 44 B3
Azbine = Aïr Niger 18°30N 8°0E 50 E7
Azerbaijan ■ Asia 40°20N 48°0E 19 F8
Azimganj India 24°14N 88°16E 43 G13
Azogues Ecuador 2°35S 78°0W 92 D3
Azores = Açores, Is. dos Atl. Oc. 38°0N 27°0W 50 a
Azov Russia 47°3N 39°25E 19 E6
Azov, Sea of Europe 46°0N 36°30E 19 E6
Azovskoye More = Azov, Sea of Europe 46°0N 36°30E 19 E6
Azraq ash Shīshān Jordan 31°50N 36°49E 46 D5
Aztec U.S.A. 36°49N 107°59W 77 H10
Azúa de Compostela Dom. Rep. 18°25N 70°44W 89 C5
Azuaga Spain 38°16N 5°39W 21 C3
Azuero, Pen. de Panama 7°30N 80°30W 88 E3
Azul Argentina 36°42S 59°43W 94 D4
Azusa U.S.A. 34°8N 117°52W 79 L9
Azzel Matti, Sebkra Algeria 26°10N 0°43E 50 C6

B

Ba Be △ Vietnam 22°25N 105°37E 38 A5
Ba Don Vietnam 17°45N 106°26E 38 D6
Ba Dong Vietnam 9°40N 106°33E 39 H6
Ba Ngoi = Cam Lam Vietnam 11°54N 109°10E 39 G7
Ba Tri Vietnam 10°2N 106°36E 39 G6
Ba Vi △ Vietnam 21°1N 105°22E 38 B5
Ba Xian = Bazhou China 39°8N 116°22E 34 E9
Baa Indonesia 10°50S 123°0E 37 F6
Baardheere Somali Rep. 2°20N 42°27E 47 G3
Baarle-Nassau Belgium 51°27N 4°56E 15 C4
Bab el Mandeb Red Sea 12°35N 43°25E 47 E3
Bābā, Koh-i- Afghan. 34°30N 67°0E 40 B5
Baba Burnu Turkey 39°29N 26°2E 23 E12
Bābā Kalū Iran 30°7N 50°49E 45 D6
Babadag Romania 44°53N 28°44E 17 F15
Babaeski Turkey 41°26N 27°6E 23 D12
Babahoyo Ecuador 1°40S 79°30W 92 D3
Babai = Sarju → India 27°21N 81°23E 43 F9
Babar Indonesia 8°0S 129°30E 37 F7
Babar Pakistan 31°7N 69°32E 42 D3
Babarkach Pakistan 29°45N 68°0E 42 E3
Babb U.S.A. 48°51N 113°27W 76 B7
Baberu India 25°33N 80°43E 43 G9
Babi Besar, Pulau Malaysia 2°25N 103°59E 39 L4
Bābil □ Iraq 32°30N 44°30E 44 C5
Babinda Australia 17°20S 145°56E 62 B4
Babine Canada 55°22N 126°37W 70 B3
Babine → Canada 55°45N 127°44W 70 B3
Babine L. Canada 54°48N 126°0W 70 C3
Babo Indonesia 2°30S 133°30E 37 E8
Bābol Iran 36°40N 52°50E 45 B7
Bābol Sar Iran 36°45N 52°45E 45 B7
Baboua C.A.R. 5°49N 14°58E 52 C2
Babruysk Belarus 53°10N 29°15E 17 B15
Babuhri India 26°49N 69°43E 42 F3
Babusar Pass Pakistan 35°12N 73°59E 43 B5
Babuyan Chan. Phil. 18°40N 121°30E 37 A6
Babylon Iraq 32°34N 44°22E 44 C5
Bac Can Vietnam 22°8N 105°49E 38 A5
Bac Giang Vietnam 21°16N 106°11E 38 B6
Bac Lieu Vietnam 9°17N 105°43E 39 H5
Bac Ninh Vietnam 21°13N 106°4E 38 B
Bac Phan Vietnam 22°0N 105°0E 38 B
Bac Quang Vietnam 22°30N 104°48E 38 A
Bacabal Brazil 4°15S 44°45W 93 D1
Bacalar Mexico 18°43N 88°27W 87 D
Bacan, Kepulauan Indonesia 0°35S 127°30E 37 E
Bacarra Phil. 18°15N 120°37E 37 A
Bacău Romania 46°35N 26°55E 17 E1
Bacerac Mexico 30°18N 108°50W 86 A
Bach Long Vi, Dao Vietnam 20°10N 107°40E 38 B
Bach Ma △ Vietnam 16°11N 107°49E 38 D
Bachhwara India 25°35N 85°54E 43 G1
Back → Canada 65°10N 104°0W 68 C
Bacolod Phil. 10°40N 122°57E 37 B
Bacuk Malaysia 6°4N 102°25E 39 J
Bácum Mexico 27°33N 110°5W 86 B
Bād Iran 33°41N 52°1E 45 C
Bad → U.S.A. 44°21N 100°22W 80 C
Bad Axe U.S.A. 43°48N 83°0W 82 C
Bad Ischl Austria 47°44N 13°38E 16 E
Bad Kissingen Germany 50°11N 10°4E 16 C
Bada Barabil India 22°7N 85°24E 43 H1
Badagara India 11°35N 75°40E 40 P
Badain Jaran Shamo China 40°23N 102°0E 32 B
Badajós, L. Brazil 3°15S 62°50W 92 D
Badajoz Spain 38°50N 6°59W 21 C
Badakhshān □ Afghan. 36°30N 71°0E 40 A
Badalona Spain 41°26N 2°15E 21 B
Badalzai Afghan. 29°50N 65°35E 42 E
Badampahar India 22°10N 86°10E 41 H1
Badanah Si. Arabia 30°58N 41°30E 44 D
Badarinath India 30°45N 79°30E 43 D
Badas, Kepulauan Indonesia 0°45N 107°5E 36 D
Baddo → Pakistan 28°0N 64°20E 40
Bade Indonesia 7°10S 139°35E 37 F
Baden Austria 48°1N 16°13E 16 D
Baden U.S.A. 40°38N 80°14W 82 F
Baden-Baden Germany 48°44N 8°13E 16 D
Baden-Württemberg □ Germany 48°20N 8°40E 16 D
Badgam India 34°1N 74°45E 43
Badgastein Austria 47°7N 13°9E 16
Badger Canada 49°0N 56°4W 73 C
Badger U.S.A. 36°38N 119°1W 78
Bādghīs □ Afghan. 35°0N 63°0E 40
Badgingarra △ Australia 30°23S 115°22E 61
Badin Pakistan 24°38N 68°54E 42
Badlands U.S.A. 43°55N 102°30W 80
Badlands △ U.S.A. 43°38N 102°56W 80
Badrah Iraq 33°6N 45°58E 44
Badrinath India 30°44N 79°29E 43
Badulla Sri Lanka 7°1N 81°7E 40 R
Badung, Selat Indonesia 8°40S 115°22E 37 K
Baena Spain 37°37N 4°20W 21
Baengnyeongdo S. Korea 37°57N 124°40E 35 F
Baeza Spain 37°57N 3°25W 21
Bafatá Guinea-Biss. 12°8N 14°40W 50
Baffin B. N. Amer. 72°0N 64°0W 69 B
Baffin I. Canada 68°0N 75°0W 69 C
Bafing → Mali 13°49N 10°50W 50
Bafliyūn Syria 36°37N 36°59E 44
Bafoulabé Mali 13°50N 10°55W 50
Bafoussam Cameroon 5°28N 10°25E 52
Bāfq Iran 31°40N 55°25E 45
Bafra Turkey 41°34N 35°54E 19
Bāft Iran 29°15N 56°38E 45
Bafwasende Dem. Rep. of the Congo 1°3N 27°5E 54
Bagaha India 27°6N 84°5E 43 F
Bagamoyo Tanzania 6°28S 38°55E 54
Bagan Datoh Malaysia 3°59N 100°47E 39
Bagan Serai Malaysia 5°1N 100°32E 39
Baganga Phil. 7°34N 126°33E 37
Bagani Namibia 18°7S 21°41E 56
Bagansiapiapi Indonesia 2°12N 100°50E 36
Bagasra India 21°30N 71°0E 42
Bagaud India 22°19N 75°53E 42
Bagdad U.S.A. 34°35N 115°53W 79 L
Bagdarin Russia 54°26N 113°36E 29 D
Bagé Brazil 31°20S 54°15W 95
Bagenalstown = Muine Bheag Ireland 52°42N 6°58W 10
Baggs U.S.A. 41°2N 107°39W 76 F
Bagh Pakistan 33°59N 73°45E 43
Baghain → India 25°32N 81°1E 43
Baghdād Iraq 33°20N 44°23E 44
Bagheria Italy 38°5N 13°30E 22
Baghlān Afghan. 32°12N 68°46E 40
Baghlān □ Afghan. 36°0N 68°30E 40
Bagley U.S.A. 47°32N 95°24W 80
Bago = Pegu Burma 17°20N 96°29E 41
Bagodar India 24°5N 85°52E 43
Bagrationovsk Russia 54°23N 20°39E 9
Baguio Phil. 16°26N 120°34E 37
Bah India 26°53N 78°36E 43
Bahadurganj India 26°16N 87°49E 43
Bahadurgarh India 28°40N 76°57E 42
Bahama, Canal Viejo de W. Indies 22°10N 77°30W 88
Bahamas ■ N. Amer. 24°0N 75°0W 89
Bahār Iran 34°54N 48°26E 45
Baharampur India 24°2N 88°27E 43
Baharu Pandan = Pandan Malaysia 1°32N 103°46E 3
Bahawalnagar Pakistan 30°0N 73°15E 42
Bahawalpur Pakistan 29°24N 71°40E 42
Bäherden Turkmenistan 38°25N 57°26E 45
Baheri India 28°45N 79°34E 43
Bahgul → India 27°45N 79°36E 43
Bahi Tanzania 5°58S 35°21E 54
Bahi Swamp Tanzania 6°10S 35°0E 54

hía = Salvador *Brazil* 13°0S 38°30W **93** F11
hía □ *Brazil* 12°0S 42°0W **93** F10
hía, Is. de la *Honduras* 16°45N 86°15W **88** C2
hía Blanca *Argentina* 38°35S 62°13W **94** D3
hía de Caráquez
Ecuador 0°40S 80°27W **92** D2
hía Kino *Mexico* 28°47N 111°58W **86** B2
hía Laura *Argentina* 48°10S 66°30W **96** F3
hía Negra *Paraguay* 20°5S 58°5W **92** H7
hir Dar *Ethiopia* 11°37N 37°10E **47** E2
hmanzād *Iran* 31°15N 51°47E **45** D6
hraich *India* 27°38N 81°37E **43** F9
hrain ■ *Asia* 26°0N 50°35E **45** E6
hror *India* 27°51N 76°20E **42** F7
hū Kalāt *Iran* 25°43N 61°25E **45** E9
i Bung, Mui = Ca Mau, Mui
Vietnam 8°38N 104°44E **39** H5
i Duc *Vietnam* 18°3N 105°49E **38** C5
i Thuong *Vietnam* 19°54N 105°23E **38** C5
ia Mare *Romania* 47°40N 23°35E **17** E12
ião *Brazil* 2°40S 49°40W **93** D9
ïbokoum *Chad* 7°46N 15°43E **51** G9
icheng *China* 45°38N 122°42E **35** B12
idoa = Baydhabo
Somali Rep. 3°8N 43°30E **47** G3
ie-Comeau *Canada* 49°12N 68°10W **73** C6
ie-St-Paul *Canada* 47°28N 70°32W **73** C5
ie Ste-Anne *Seychelles* 4°18S 55°45E **53** b
ie-Trinité *Canada* 49°25N 67°20W **73** C6
ie Verte *Canada* 49°55N 56°12W **73** C8
ihar *India* 22°6N 80°33E **43** H9
ihe *China* 32°50N 110°5E **34** H6
'ījī *Iraq* 35°0N 43°30E **44** C4
ijnath *India* 29°55N 79°37E **43** E8
ikal, L. = Baykal, Oz.
Russia 53°0N 108°0E **29** D11
ikonur = Bayqongyr
Kazakhstan 45°40N 63°20E **28** E7
ikunthpur *India* 23°15N 82°33E **43** H10
ile Atha Cliath = Dublin
Ireland 53°21N 6°15W **10** C5
ileşti *Romania* 44°1N 23°20E **17** F12
inbridge *Ga., U.S.A.* 30°55N 84°35W **85** F12
inbridge *N.Y., U.S.A.* 42°18N 75°29W **83** D9
inbridge Island
U.S.A. 47°38N 122°32W **78** C4
ing *Indonesia* 10°14S 120°34E **37** F6
iniu *China* 32°50N 112°15E **34** H7
ir *Jordan* 30°45N 36°55E **46** E5
iriki = Tarawa *Kiribati* 1°30N 173°0E **64** G9
irin Youqi *China* 43°30N 118°35E **35** C10
irin Zuoqi *China* 43°58N 119°15E **35** C10
irnsdale *Australia* 37°48S 147°36E **63** F4
isha *China* 34°20N 112°32E **34** G7
itadi *Nepal* 29°35N 80°25E **43** E9
iyin *China* 36°45N 104°14E **34** F3
iyu Shan *China* 37°15N 107°30E **34** F4
i Baj *India* 22°30N 88°5E **43** H13
a *Hungary* 46°12N 18°59E **17** E10
a, Pta. *Mexico* 29°58N 115°49W **86** B1
a California *Mexico* 31°10N 115°12W **86** A1
a California □ *Mexico* 30°0N 115°0W **86** B2
a California Sur □
Mexico 25°50N 111°50W **86** B2
ag *India* 22°40N 81°21E **43** H9
amar *Canary Is.* 28°33N 16°20W **24** F3
ana *India* 23°7N 71°49E **42** H4
atrejo *Indonesia* 8°29S 114°19E **37** J17
era *Indonesia* 8°31S 115°2E **37** J18
gīrān *Iran* 37°36N 58°24E **45** B8
imba, Mt. *Australia* 29°17S 152°6E **63** D5
o Boquete *Panama* 8°46N 82°27W **88** E3
o Nuevo *Caribbean* 15°40N 78°50W **88** C4
oga *Nigeria* 10°57N 11°20E **51** F8
ool *Australia* 23°40S 150°35E **62** C5
kel *Senegal* 14°56N 12°20W **50** F3
ker *Calif., U.S.A.* 35°16N 116°4W **79** K10
ker *Mont., U.S.A.* 46°22N 104°17W **76** C11
ker, L. *Canada* 64°0N 96°0W **68** C10
ker, Mt. *U.S.A.* 48°50N 121°49W **76** B3
ker City *U.S.A.* 44°47N 117°50W **76** D5
ker I. *Pac. Oc.* 0°10N 176°35W **64** G10
ker I. *U.S.A.* 55°20N 133°40W **70** B2
ker L. *Australia* 26°54S 126°5E **61** E4
ker Lake *Canada* 64°20N 96°3W **68** C10
kers Creek *Australia* 21°13S 149°7E **62** C4
kers Dozen Is. *Canada* 56°45N 78°45W **72** A4
kersfield *Calif., U.S.A.* 35°23N 119°1W **79** K8
kersfield *Vt., U.S.A.* 44°45N 72°48W **83** B12
kharden = Bäherden
Turkmenistan 38°25N 57°26E **45** B8
khtarān = Kermānshāh
Iran 34°23N 47°0E **44** C5
khtarān = Kermānshāh □
Iran 34°0N 46°30E **44** C5
u *Azerbaijan* 40°29N 49°56E **45** A6
kafjörður *Iceland* 66°2N 14°48W **8** C6
kouma *C.A.R.* 5°40N 22°56E **52** C4
kswaho *India* 24°15N 79°18E **43** G8
ku = Bakı *Azerbaijan* 40°29N 49°56E **45** A6
kutis Coast *Antarctica* 74°0S 120°0W **5** D15
y = Bakı *Azerbaijan* 40°29N 49°56E **45** A6
a *Canada* 45°1N 79°37W **82** A5
a *U.K.* 52°54N 3°36W **12** E4
a, L. *U.K.* 52°53N 3°37W **12** E4
abac I. *Phil.* 8°0N 117°0E **36** C5
abac Str. *E. Indies* 7°53N 117°5E **36** C5
abagh *Afghan.* 34°25N 70°12E **42** B4
abakk *Lebanon* 34°0N 36°10E **46** B5
abalangan, Kepulauan
ndonesia 2°20S 117°30E **36** E5
ad *Iraq* 34°0N 44°9E **44** C5
ad Rūz *Iraq* 33°42N 45°5E **44** C5
ideh *Fārs, Iran* 29°17N 51°56E **45** D6
ideh *Māzandaran, Iran* 36°12N 51°48E **45** B6
aghat *India* 21°49N 80°12E **40** J12
aghat Ra. *India* 18°50N 76°30E **40** K10
Balaguer *Spain* 41°50N 0°50E **21** B6
Balaklava *Ukraine* 44°30N 33°30E **19** F5
Balakovo *Russia* 52°4N 47°55E **18** D8
Balamau *India* 27°10N 80°21E **43** F9
Balancán *Mexico* 17°48N 91°32W **87** D6
Balashov *Russia* 51°30N 43°10E **19** D7
Balasinor *India* 22°57N 73°23E **42** H5
Balasore = Baleshwar
India 21°35N 87°3E **41** J15
Balaton *Hungary* 46°50N 17°40E **17** E9
Balbina, Represa de *Brazil* 2°0S 59°30W **92** D7
Balboa *Panama* 8°57N 79°34W **88** E4
Balbriggan *Ireland* 53°37N 6°11W **10** C5
Balcarce *Argentina* 38°0S 58°10W **94** D4
Balcarres *Canada* 50°50N 103°35W **71** C8
Balchik *Bulgaria* 43°28N 28°11E **23** C13
Balclutha *N.Z.* 46°15S 169°45E **59** G2
Balcones Escarpment
U.S.A. 29°30N 99°15W **84** G5
Bald I. *Australia* 34°57S 118°27E **61** F2
Bald Knob *U.S.A.* 35°19N 91°34W **84** D9
Baldock L. *Canada* 56°33N 97°57W **71** B9
Baldwin *Mich., U.S.A.* 43°54N 85°51W **81** D11
Baldwin *Pa., U.S.A.* 40°21N 79°58W **82** F5
Baldwinsville *U.S.A.* 43°10N 76°20W **83** C8
Baldy Peak *U.S.A.* 33°54N 109°34W **77** K9
Baleares, Is. *Spain* 39°30N 3°0E **24** B10
Balearic Is. = Baleares, Is.
Spain 39°30N 3°0E **24** B10
Baleine = Whale →
Canada 58°15N 67°40W **73** A6
Baleine, Petite R. de la →
Canada 56°0N 76°45W **72** A4
Baler *Phil.* 15°46N 121°34E **37** A6
Baleshare *U.K.* 57°31N 7°22W **11** D1
Baleshwar *India* 21°35N 87°3E **41** J15
Baley *Russia* 51°36N 116°37E **29** D12
Balfate *Honduras* 15°48N 86°25W **88** C2
Balgo *Australia* 20°9S 127°58E **60** D4
Bali *Greece* 35°25N 24°47E **25** D6
Bali *India* 25°11N 73°17E **42** G5
Bali *Indonesia* 8°20S 115°0E **37** J18
Bali □ *Indonesia* 8°20S 115°0E **37** J18
Bali, Selat *Indonesia* 8°18S 114°25E **37** J17
Bali Sea *Indonesia* 8°0S 115°0E **37** J17
Baliapal *India* 21°40N 87°17E **43** J12
Balige *Indonesia* 2°14N 99°7E **39** L2
Balik Pulau *Malaysia* 5°21N 100°14E **39** c
Balikeşir *Turkey* 39°39N 27°53E **23** E12
Balikpapan *Indonesia* 1°10S 116°55E **36** E5
Balimbing *Phil.* 5°5N 119°58E **37** C5
Baling *Malaysia* 5°41N 100°55E **39** K3
Balkan Mts. = Stara Planina
Bulgaria 43°15N 23°0E **23** C10
Balkanabat *Turkmenistan* 39°30N 54°22E **45** B7
Balkhash = Balqash
Kazakhstan 46°50N 74°50E **28** E8
Balkhash, Ozero = Balqash Köli
Kazakhstan 46°0N 74°50E **28** E8
Ballachulish *U.K.* 56°41N 5°8W **11** E3
Balladonia *Australia* 32°27S 123°51E **61** F3
Ballaghaderreen *Ireland* 53°55N 8°34W **10** C3
Ballarat *Australia* 37°33S 143°50E **63** F3
Ballard, L. *Australia* 29°20S 120°40E **61** E3
Ballater *U.K.* 57°3N 3°3W **11** D5
Ballenas, Canal de
Mexico 29°10N 113°29W **86** B2
Balleny Is. *Antarctica* 66°30S 163°0E **5** C11
Ballia *India* 25°46N 84°12E **43** G11
Ballina *Australia* 28°50S 153°31E **63** D5
Ballina *Ireland* 54°7N 9°9W **10** B2
Ballinasloe *Ireland* 53°20N 8°13W **10** C3
Ballinger *U.S.A.* 31°45N 99°57W **84** F5
Ballinrobe *Ireland* 53°38N 9°13W **10** C2
Ballinskelligs B. *Ireland* 51°48N 10°13W **10** E1
Ballston Spa *U.S.A.* 43°0N 73°51W **83** D11
Ballyboghil *Ireland* 53°32N 6°16W **10** C5
Ballybunion *Ireland* 52°31N 9°40W **10** D2
Ballycanew *Ireland* 52°37N 6°19W **10** D5
Ballycastle *U.K.* 55°12N 6°15W **10** A5
Ballyclare *U.K.* 54°46N 6°0W **10** B5
Ballydehob *Ireland* 51°34N 9°28W **10** E2
Ballygawley *U.K.* 54°27N 7°2W **10** B4
Ballyhaunis *Ireland* 53°46N 8°46W **10** C3
Ballyheige *Ireland* 52°23N 9°49W **10** D2
Ballymena *U.K.* 54°52N 6°17W **10** B5
Ballymoney *U.K.* 55°5N 6°31W **10** A5
Ballymote *Ireland* 54°5N 8°31W **10** B3
Ballynahinch *U.K.* 54°24N 5°54W **10** B6
Ballyquintin Pt. *U.K.* 54°20N 5°30W **10** B6
Ballyshannon *Ireland* 54°30N 8°11W **10** B3
Balmaceda *Chile* 46°0S 71°50W **96** F2
Balmertown *Canada* 51°4N 93°41W **71** C10
Balmoral *Australia* 37°15S 141°48E **63** F3
Balmorhea *U.S.A.* 30°59N 103°45W **84** F3
Balochistan = Baluchistan □
Pakistan 27°30N 65°0E **40** F4
Balonne → *Australia* 28°47S 147°56E **63** D4
Balotra *India* 25°50N 72°14E **42** G5
Balqash *Kazakhstan* 46°50N 74°50E **28** E8
Balqash Köli *Kazakhstan* 46°0N 74°50E **28** E8
Balrampur *India* 27°30N 82°20E **43** F10
Balranald *Australia* 34°38S 143°33E **63** E3
Balsas → *Brazil* 7°15S 44°35W **93** E9
Balsas → *Mexico* 17°55N 102°10W **86** D4
Balsas del Norte *Mexico* 18°0N 99°46W **87** D5
Balta *Ukraine* 48°2N 29°45E **17** D15
Bălţi *Moldova* 47°48N 27°58E **17** E14
Baltic Sea *Europe* 57°0N 19°0E **9** H18
Baltimore *Ireland* 51°29N 9°22W **10** E2
Baltimore *Md., U.S.A.* 39°17N 76°36W **81** F15
Baltimore *Ohio, U.S.A.* 39°51N 82°36W **82** G2
Baltinglass *Ireland* 52°56N 6°43W **10** D5
Baltit *Pakistan* 36°15N 74°40E **43** A6
Baltiysk *Russia* 54°41N 19°58E **9** J18
Baluchistan □ *Pakistan* 27°30N 65°0E **40** F4
Balurghat *India* 25°15N 88°44E **43** G13
Balvi *Latvia* 57°8N 27°15E **9** H22
Balya *Turkey* 39°44N 27°35E **23** E12
Balykchy *Kyrgyzstan* 42°26N 76°12E **32** B2
Bam *Iran* 29°7N 58°14E **45** D8
Bama *Nigeria* 11°33N 13°41E **51** F8
Bamaga *Australia* 10°50S 142°25E **62** A3
Bamaji L. *Canada* 51°9N 91°25W **72** B1
Bamako *Mali* 12°34N 7°55W **50** F4
Bambari *C.A.R.* 5°40N 20°35E **52** C4
Bambaroo *Australia* 18°50S 146°10E **62** B4
Bamberg *Germany* 49°54N 10°54E **16** D6
Bamberg *U.S.A.* 33°18N 81°2W **85** E14
Bambili
Dem. Rep. of the Congo 3°40N 26°0E **54** B2
Bamburgh *U.K.* 55°37N 1°43W **12** B6
Bamenda *Cameroon* 5°57N 10°11E **52** C2
Bamfield *Canada* 48°45N 125°10W **70** D3
Bāmīān □ *Afghan.* 35°0N 67°0E **40** B5
Bamiancheng *China* 43°15N 124°2E **35** C13
Bampūr *Iran* 27°15N 60°21E **45** E9
Bampūr → *Iran* 27°24N 59°0E **45** E8
Ban Ao Tu Khun *Thailand* 8°9N 98°20E **39** a
Ban Ban *Laos* 19°31N 103°30E **38** C4
Ban Bang Hin *Thailand* 9°32N 98°35E **39** H2
Ban Bang Khu *Thailand* 7°57N 98°23E **39** a
Ban Bang Rong *Thailand* 8°3N 98°25E **39** a
Ban Bo Phut *Thailand* 9°33N 100°2E **39** b
Ban Chaweng *Thailand* 9°32N 100°3E **39** b
Ban Chiang Klang
Thailand 19°25N 100°55E **38** C3
Ban Choho *Thailand* 15°2N 102°9E **38** E4
Ban Dan Lan Hoi *Thailand* 17°0N 99°35E **38** D2
Ban Don = Surat Thani
Thailand 9°6N 99°20E **39** H2
Ban Don *Vietnam* 12°53N 107°48E **38** F6
Ban Don, Ao → *Thailand* 9°20N 99°25E **39** H2
Ban Dong *Thailand* 19°30N 100°59E **38** C3
Ban Hong *Thailand* 18°18N 98°50E **38** C2
Ban Hua Thanon *Thailand* 9°26N 100°1E **39** b
Ban Kantang *Thailand* 7°25N 99°31E **39** J2
Ban Karon *Thailand* 7°51N 98°18E **39** a
Ban Kata *Thailand* 7°50N 98°18E **39** a
Ban Keun *Laos* 18°22N 102°35E **38** C4
Ban Khai *Thailand* 12°46N 101°18E **38** F3
Ban Kheun *Laos* 20°13N 101°7E **38** B3
Ban Khlong Khian
Thailand 8°10N 98°26E **39** a
Ban Khlong Kua *Thailand* 6°57N 100°8E **39** J3
Ban Khuan *Thailand* 8°20N 98°25E **39** a
Ban Khuan Mao *Thailand* 7°50N 99°37E **39** J2
Ban Ko Yai Chim
Thailand 11°17N 99°26E **39** G2
Ban Laem *Thailand* 13°13N 99°59E **38** F2
Ban Lamai *Thailand* 9°28N 100°3E **39** b
Ban Lao Ngam *Laos* 15°28N 106°10E **38** E6
Ban Le Kathe *Thailand* 15°49N 98°53E **38** E2
Ban Lo Po Noi *Thailand* 8°1N 98°34E **39** a
Ban Mae Chedi *Thailand* 19°11N 99°31E **38** C2
Ban Mae Nam *Thailand* 9°34N 100°0E **39** b
Ban Mae Sariang
Thailand 18°10N 97°56E **38** C1
Ban Mê Thuôt = Buon Ma Thuot
Vietnam 12°40N 108°3E **38** F7
Ban Mi *Thailand* 15°3N 100°32E **38** E3
Ban Muong Mo *Laos* 19°4N 103°58E **38** C4
Ban Na Bo *Thailand* 9°19N 99°41E **39** b
Ban Na Mo *Laos* 17°7N 105°40E **38** D5
Ban Na San *Thailand* 8°53N 99°52E **39** H2
Ban Na Tong *Laos* 20°56N 101°47E **38** B3
Ban Nam Bac *Laos* 20°38N 102°20E **38** B4
Ban Nam Ma *Laos* 22°2N 101°37E **38** A3
Ban Ngang *Laos* 15°59N 106°11E **38** E6
Ban Nong Bok *Laos* 17°5N 104°48E **38** D5
Ban Nong Boua *Laos* 15°40N 106°33E **38** E6
Ban Nong Pling
Thailand 15°40N 100°10E **38** E3
Ban Pak Chan *Thailand* 10°32N 98°51E **39** G2
Ban Patong *Thailand* 7°54N 98°18E **39** a
Ban Phai *Thailand* 16°4N 102°44E **38** D4
Ban Phak Chit *Thailand* 8°0N 98°24E **39** a
Ban Pong *Thailand* 13°50N 99°55E **38** F2
Ban Rawai *Thailand* 7°47N 98°20E **39** a
Ban Ron Phibun *Thailand* 8°9N 99°51E **39** H2
Ban Sakhu *Thailand* 8°4N 98°18E **39** a
Ban Sanam Chai
Thailand 7°33N 100°25E **39** J3
Ban Sangkha *Thailand* 14°37N 103°52E **38** E4
Ban Tak *Thailand* 17°2N 99°4E **38** D2
Ban Tako *Thailand* 14°5N 102°40E **38** E4
Ban Tha Dua *Thailand* 17°59N 98°39E **38** D2
Ban Tha Nun *Thailand* 8°12N 98°18E **39** a
Ban Tha Rua *Thailand* 7°59N 98°22E **39** a
Ban Tha Yu *Thailand* 8°17N 98°22E **39** a
Ban Thahine *Laos* 14°12N 105°33E **38** E5
Ban Thong Krut *Thailand* 9°25N 99°57E **39** b
Ban Xien Kok *Laos* 20°54N 100°39E **38** B3
Ban Yen Nhan *Vietnam* 20°57N 106°2E **38** B6
Banaba *Kiribati* 0°45S 169°50E **64** H8
Banalia
Dem. Rep. of the Congo 1°32N 25°5E **54** B2
Banam *Cambodia* 11°20N 105°17E **39** G5
Bananal, I. do *Brazil* 11°30S 50°30W **93** F8
Banaras = Varanasi
India 25°22N 83°0E **43** G10
Banas → *Gujarat, India* 23°45N 71°25E **42** H4
Banas → *Mad. P., India* 24°15N 81°30E **43** G9
Bânâs, Ras *Egypt* 23°57N 35°59E **51** D13
Banbridge *U.K.* 54°22N 6°16W **10** B5
Banbury *U.K.* 52°4N 1°20W **13** E6
Banchory *U.K.* 57°3N 2°29W **11** D6
Bancroft *Canada* 45°3N 77°51W **82** A7
Band Bonī *Iran* 25°30N 59°33E **45** E8
Band Qīr *Iran* 31°39N 48°53E **45** D6
Banda *Mad. P., India* 24°3N 78°57E **43** G8
Banda *Ut. P., India* 25°30N 80°26E **43** G9
Banda, Kepulauan
Indonesia 4°37S 129°50E **37** E7
Banda Aceh *Indonesia* 5°35N 95°20E **36** C1
Banda Banda, Mt.
Australia 31°10S 152°28E **63** E5
Banda Elat *Indonesia* 5°40S 133°5E **37** F8
Banda Is. = Banda, Kepulauan
Indonesia 4°37S 129°50E **37** E7
Banda Sea *Indonesia* 6°0S 130°0E **37** F8
Bandai-Asahi △ *Japan* 37°38N 140°5E **30** F10
Bandai-San *Japan* 37°36N 140°4E **30** F10
Bandān *Iran* 31°23N 60°44E **45** D9
Bandanaira *Indonesia* 4°32S 129°54E **37** E7
Bandanwara *India* 26°9N 74°38E **42** F6
Bandar = Machilipatnam
India 16°12N 81°8E **41** L12
Bandar-e Abbās *Iran* 27°15N 56°15E **45** E8
Bandar-e Anzalī *Iran* 37°30N 49°30E **45** B6
Bandar-e Bushehr = Būshehr
Iran 28°55N 50°55E **45** D6
Bandar-e Chārak *Iran* 26°45N 54°20E **45** E7
Bandar-e Deylam *Iran* 30°5N 50°10E **45** D6
Bandar-e Emām Khomeyni
Iran 30°30N 49°5E **45** D6
Bandar-e Lengeh *Iran* 26°35N 54°58E **45** E7
Bandar-e Maqām *Iran* 26°56N 53°29E **45** E7
Bandar-e Ma'shur *Iran* 30°35N 49°10E **45** D6
Bandar-e Rīg *Iran* 29°29N 50°38E **45** D6
Bandar-e Torkeman *Iran* 37°0N 54°10E **45** B7
Bandar Lampung
Indonesia 5°20S 105°10E **36** F3
Bandar Maharani = Muar
Malaysia 2°3N 102°34E **39** L4
Bandar Penggaram = Batu Pahat
Malaysia 1°50N 102°56E **39** M4
Bandar Seri Begawan
Brunei 4°52N 115°0E **36** D5
Bandar Sri Aman = Sri Aman
Malaysia 1°15N 111°32E **36** D4
Bandawe *Malawi* 11°58S 34°5E **55** E3
Bandeira, Pico da *Brazil* 20°26S 41°47W **95** A7
Bandera *Argentina* 28°55S 62°20W **94** B3
Banderas, B. de *Mexico* 20°40N 105°25W **86** C3
Bandhavgarh *India* 23°40N 81°2E **43** H9
Bandi → *India* 26°12N 75°47E **42** F6
Bandikui *India* 27°3N 76°34E **42** F7
Bandırma *Turkey* 40°20N 28°0E **23** D13
Bandjarmasin = Banjarmasin
Indonesia 3°20S 114°35E **36** E4
Bandon *Ireland* 51°44N 8°44W **10** E3
Bandon → *Ireland* 51°43N 8°37W **10** E3
Bandula *Mozam.* 19°0S 33°7E **55** F3
Bandundu
Dem. Rep. of the Congo 3°15S 17°22E **52** E3
Bandung *Indonesia* 6°54S 107°36E **37** G12
Bāneh *Iran* 35°59N 45°53E **44** C5
Banes *Cuba* 21°0N 75°42W **89** B4
Banff *Canada* 51°10N 115°34W **70** C5
Banff *U.K.* 57°40N 2°33W **11** D6
Banff △ *Canada* 51°30N 116°15W **70** C5
Bang Fai → *Laos* 16°57N 104°45E **38** D5
Bang Hieng → *Laos* 16°10N 105°10E **38** D5
Bang Krathum *Thailand* 16°34N 100°18E **38** D3
Bang Lamung *Thailand* 13°3N 100°56E **38** F3
Bang Mun Nak *Thailand* 16°2N 100°23E **38** D3
Bang Pa In *Thailand* 14°14N 100°35E **38** E3
Bang Rakam *Thailand* 16°45N 100°7E **38** D3
Bang Saphan *Thailand* 11°14N 99°28E **39** G2
Bang Thao *Thailand* 7°59N 98°18E **39** a
Bangaduni I. *India* 21°34N 88°52E **43** J13
Bangala Dam *Zimbabwe* 21°7S 31°25E **55** G3
Bangalore *India* 12°59N 77°40E **40** N10
Banganga → *India* 27°6N 77°25E **42** F6
Bangaon *India* 23°0N 88°47E **43** H13
Bangassou *C.A.R.* 4°55N 23°7E **52** D4
Banggai *Indonesia* 1°34S 123°30E **37** E6
Banggai, Kepulauan
Indonesia 1°40S 123°30E **37** E6
Banggai Arch. = Banggai,
Kepulauan *Indonesia* 1°40S 123°30E **37** E6
Banggi, Pulau *Malaysia* 7°17N 117°12E **36** C5
Banghāzī *Libya* 32°11N 20°3E **51** B10
Bangka *Sulawesi, Indonesia* 1°50N 125°5E **37** D7
Bangka *Sumatera,*
Indonesia 2°0S 105°50E **36** E3
Bangka, Selat *Indonesia* 2°30S 105°30E **36** E3
Bangka-Belitung □
Indonesia 2°30S 107°0E **36** E3
Bangkalan *Indonesia* 7°2S 112°46E **37** G15
Bangkinang *Indonesia* 0°18N 101°5E **36** D2
Bangko *Indonesia* 2°5S 102°9E **36** E2
Bangkok *Thailand* 13°45N 100°35E **38** F3
Bangladesh ■ *Asia* 24°0N 90°0E **41** H17
Bangli *Indonesia* 8°27S 115°21E **37** J18
Bangong Co *China* 33°45N 78°43E **43** C8
Bangor *Down, U.K.* 54°40N 5°40W **10** B6
Bangor *Gwynedd, U.K.* 53°14N 4°8W **12** D3
Bangor *Maine, U.S.A.* 44°48N 68°46W **81** C19
Bangor *Pa., U.S.A.* 40°52N 75°13W **83** F9
Bangued *Phil.* 17°40N 120°37E **37** A6
Bangui *C.A.R.* 4°23N 18°35E **52** D3
Banguru
Dem. Rep. of the Congo 0°30N 27°10E **54** B2
Bangweulu, L. *Zambia* 11°0S 30°0E **55** E3
Bangweulu Swamp
Zambia 11°20S 30°15E **55** E3
Banhine △ *Mozam.* 22°49S 32°55E **57** C5
Baní *Dom. Rep.* 18°16N 70°22W **89** C5
Banī Sa'd *Iraq* 33°34N 44°32E **44** C5
Banihal Pass *India* 33°30N 75°12E **43** C6
Banissa *Kenya* 3°55N 40°19E **54** B4
Bāniyās *Syria* 35°10N 36°0E **44** C3
Banja Luka *Bos.-H.* 44°49N 17°11E **22** B7
Banjar *India* 31°38N 77°21E **42** D7
Banjar → *India* 22°36N 80°22E **43** H9
Banjarmasin *Indonesia* 3°20S 114°35E **36** E4
Banjul *Gambia* 13°28N 16°40W **50** F2
Banka *India* 24°53N 86°55E **43** G12
Banket *Zimbabwe* 17°27S 30°19E **55** F3
Bankipore *India* 25°35N 85°10E **41** G14
Banks I. *B.C., Canada* 53°20N 130°0W **70** C3
Banks I. *N.W.T., Canada* 73°15N 121°30W **68** B7
Banks Pen. *N.Z.* 43°45S 173°15E **59** E4
Banks Str. *Australia* 40°40S 148°10E **63** G4
Bankura *India* 23°11N 87°18E **43** H12
Banmankhi *India* 25°53N 87°11E **43** G12
Bann → *Armagh, U.K.* 54°30N 6°31W **10** B5
Bann → *L'derry., U.K.* 55°8N 6°41W **10** A5
Bannang Sata *Thailand* 6°16N 101°16E **39** J3
Banning *U.S.A.* 33°56N 116°53W **79** M10
Bannockburn *Canada* 44°39N 77°33W **82** B7
Bannockburn *U.K.* 56°5N 3°55W **11** E5
Bannockburn *Zimbabwe* 20°17S 29°48E **55** G2
Bannu *Pakistan* 33°0N 70°18E **40** C7
Bano *India* 22°40N 84°55E **43** H11
Bansgaon *India* 26°33N 83°21E **43** F10
Banská Bystrica
Slovak Rep. 48°46N 19°14E **17** D10
Banswara *India* 23°32N 74°24E **42** H6
Bantaeng *Indonesia* 5°32S 119°56E **37** F5
Banten □ *Indonesia* 6°30S 106°0E **37** G11
Bantry *Ireland* 51°41N 9°27W **10** E2
Bantry B. *Ireland* 51°37N 9°44W **10** E2
Bantul *Indonesia* 7°55S 110°19E **37** G14
Bantva *India* 21°29N 70°12E **42** J4
Banyak, Kepulauan
Indonesia 2°10N 97°10E **36** D1
Banyalbufar *Spain* 39°42N 2°31E **24** B9
Banyo *Cameroon* 6°52N 11°45E **52** C2
Banyumas *Indonesia* 7°32S 109°18E **37** G13
Banyuwangi *Indonesia* 8°13S 114°21E **37** J17
Banzare Coast *Antarctica* 68°0S 125°0E **5** C9
Bao Ha *Vietnam* 22°11N 104°21E **38** A5
Bao Lac *Vietnam* 22°57N 105°40E **38** A5
Bao Loc *Vietnam* 11°32N 107°48E **39** G6
Bao'an = Shenzhen
China 22°32N 114°5E **33** F10
Baocheng *China* 33°12N 106°56E **34** H4
Baode *China* 39°1N 111°5E **34** E6
Baodi *China* 39°38N 117°20E **35** E9
Baoding *China* 38°50N 115°28E **34** E8
Baoji *China* 34°20N 107°5E **34** G4
Baoshan *China* 25°10N 99°5E **32** D4
Baotou *China* 40°32N 110°2E **34** D6
Baoying *China* 33°17N 119°20E **35** H10
Baoyou = Ledong *China* 18°41N 109°5E **38** C7
Bap *India* 27°23N 72°18E **42** F5
Bapatla *India* 15°55N 80°30E **41** M12
Bāqerābād *Iran* 33°2N 51°58E **45** C6
Ba'qūbah *Iraq* 33°45N 44°50E **44** C5
Baquedano *Chile* 23°20S 69°52W **94** A2
Bar *Montenegro* 42°8N 19°6E **23** C8
Bar *Ukraine* 49°4N 27°40E **17** D14
Bar Bigha *India* 25°21N 85°47E **43** G11
Bar Harbor *U.S.A.* 44°23N 68°13W **81** C19
Bar-le-Duc *France* 48°47N 5°10E **20** B6
Bara *India* 25°16N 81°43E **43** G9
Bara Banki *India* 26°55N 81°12E **43** F9
Barabai *Indonesia* 2°32S 115°34E **36** E5
Baraboo *U.S.A.* 43°28N 89°45W **80** D9
Baracoa *Cuba* 20°20N 74°30W **89** B5
Baradā → *Syria* 33°33N 36°34E **46** B5
Baradero *Argentina* 33°52S 59°29W **94** C4
Baraga *U.S.A.* 46°47N 88°30W **80** B9
Baragoi *Kenya* 1°47N 36°47E **54** B4
Barah → *India* 27°42N 77°5E **42** F6
Barahona *Dom. Rep.* 18°13N 71°7W **89** C5
Barail Range *India* 25°15N 93°20E **41** G18
Barakaldo *Spain* 43°18N 2°59W **21** A4
Barakar → *India* 24°7N 86°14E **43** G12
Barakot *India* 21°33N 84°59E **43** J11
Barakpur *India* 22°47N 88°21E **43** H13
Baralaba *Australia* 24°13S 149°50E **62** C4
Baralzon L. *Canada* 60°0N 98°3W **71** B9
Baramula *India* 34°15N 74°20E **43** B6
Baran *India* 25°9N 76°40E **42** G7
Baran → *Pakistan* 25°13N 68°17E **42** G3
Baranavichy *Belarus* 53°10N 26°0E **17** B14
Baranof *U.S.A.* 57°5N 134°50W **70** B2
Baranof I. *U.S.A.* 57°0N 135°0W **68** D6
Barapasi *Indonesia* 2°15S 137°5E **37** E9
Barasat *India* 22°46N 88°31E **43** H13
Barat Daya, Kepulauan
Indonesia 7°30S 128°0E **37** F7
Barataria B. *U.S.A.* 29°20N 89°55W **85** G10
Barauda *India* 23°33N 75°15E **42** H6
Baraut *India* 29°13N 77°7E **42** E7
Barbacena *Brazil* 21°15S 43°56W **95** A7
Barbados ■ *W. Indies* 13°10N 59°30W **89** g
Barbària, C. de *Spain* 38°39N 1°24E **24** C7
Barbas, C. *W. Sahara* 22°20N 16°42W **50** D2
Barbastro *Spain* 42°2N 0°5E **21** A6
Barberton *S. Africa* 25°42S 31°2E **57** D5
Barberton *U.S.A.* 41°1N 81°39W **82** E3
Barbosa *Colombia* 5°57N 73°37W **92** B4
Barbourville *U.S.A.* 36°52N 83°53W **81** G12
Barbuda *W. Indies* 17°30N 61°40W **89** C7
Barcaldine *Australia* 23°43S 145°6E **62** C4
Barcellona Pozzo di Gotto
Italy 38°9N 15°13E **22** E6
Barcelona *Spain* 41°22N 2°10E **21** B7
Barcelona *Venezuela* 10°10N 64°40W **92** A6
Barceloneta *Puerto Rico* 18°27N 66°32W **89** d
Barcelos *Brazil* 1°0S 63°0W **92** D6
Barcoo → *Australia* 25°30S 142°50E **62** D3
Bardaï *Chad* 21°25N 17°0E **51** D9
Bardas Blancas
Argentina 35°49S 69°45W **94** D2
Bardawīl, Sabkhet el
Egypt 31°10N 33°15E **46** D2
Barddhaman *India* 23°14N 87°39E **43** H12
Bardejov *Slovak Rep.* 49°18N 21°15E **17** D11
Bardera = Baardheere
Somali Rep. 2°20N 42°27E **47** G3
Bardīyah *Libya* 31°45N 25°5E **51** B10
Bardsey I. *U.K.* 52°45N 4°47W **12** E3

Bardstown U.S.A. 37°49N 85°28W 81 G11
Bareilly India 28°22N 79°27E 43 E8
Barela India 23°6N 80°3E 43 H9
Barents Sea Arctic 73°0N 39°0E 4 B9
Barfleur, Pte. de France 49°42N 1°16W 20 B3
Bargara Australia 24°50S 152°25E 62 C5
Bargi Dam India 22°50N 80°0E 43 H9
Barguzin Russia 53°37N 109°37E 29 D11
Barh India 25°29N 85°46E 43 G11
Barhaj India 26°18N 83°44E 43 F10
Barharwa India 24°52N 87°47E 43 G12
Barhi India 24°15N 85°25E 43 G11
Bari India 26°39N 77°39E 42 F7
Bari Italy 41°8N 16°51E 22 D7
Bari Doab Pakistan 30°20N 73°0E 42 D5
Bari Sadri India 24°28N 74°30E 42 G6
Barīdī, Ra's Si. Arabia 24°17N 37°31E 44 E3
Barīm Yemen 12°39N 43°25E 48 E8
Barinas Venezuela 8°36N 70°15W 92 B4
Baring, C. Canada 70°0N 117°30W 68 C8
Baringo, L. Kenya 0°47N 36°16E 54 B4
Barisal Bangla. 22°45N 90°20E 41 H17
Barisal □ Bangla. 22°45N 90°20E 41 H17
Barisan, Pegunungan Indonesia 3°30S 102°15E 36 E2
Barito → Indonesia 4°0S 114°50E 36 E4
Baritú △ Argentina 23°43S 64°40W 94 A3
Barjūj, Wadi → Libya 25°26N 12°12E 51 C8
Bark L. Canada 45°27N 77°51W 82 A7
Barkakana India 23°37N 85°29E 43 H11
Barker U.S.A. 43°20N 78°33W 82 C6
Barkley, L. U.S.A. 37°1N 88°14W 85 C10
Barkley Sound Canada 48°50N 125°10W 70 D3
Barkly East S. Africa 30°58S 27°33E 56 E4
Barkly Homestead Australia 19°52S 135°50E 62 B2
Barkly Tableland Australia 17°50S 136°40E 62 B2
Barkly West S. Africa 28°5S 24°31E 56 D3
Barkol Kazak Zizhixian China 43°37N 93°2E 32 B4
Bârlad Romania 46°15N 27°38E 17 E14
Bârlad → Romania 45°38N 27°32E 17 F14
Barlee, L. Australia 29°15S 119°30E 61 E2
Barlee, Mt. Australia 24°38S 128°13E 61 D4
Barletta Italy 41°19N 16°17E 22 D7
Barlovento Canary Is. 28°48N 17°48W 24 F2
Barlovento C. Verde Is. 17°0N 25°0W 50 b
Barlow L. Canada 62°0N 103°0W 71 A8
Barmedman Australia 34°9S 147°21E 63 E4
Barmer India 25°45N 71°20E 42 G4
Barmera Australia 34°15S 140°28E 63 E3
Barmouth U.K. 52°44N 4°4W 12 E3
Barna → India 25°21N 83°3E 43 G10
Barnagar India 23°7N 75°19E 42 H6
Barnala India 30°23N 75°33E 42 D6
Barnard Castle U.K. 54°33N 1°55W 12 C6
Barnaul Russia 53°20N 83°40E 28 D9
Barnesville Ga., U.S.A. 33°3N 84°9W 85 E12
Barnesville Minn., U.S.A. 46°43N 96°28W 80 B5
Barnet □ U.K. 51°38N 0°9W 13 F7
Barneveld Neths. 52°7N 5°36E 15 B5
Barnhart U.S.A. 31°8N 101°10W 84 F4
Barnsley U.K. 53°34N 1°27W 12 D6
Barnstable U.S.A. 41°42N 70°18W 81 E18
Barnstaple U.K. 51°5N 4°4W 13 F3
Barnstaple Bay = Bideford Bay U.K. 51°5N 4°20W 13 F3
Barnwell U.S.A. 33°15N 81°23W 85 E14
Baro Nigeria 8°35N 6°18E 50 G7
Baroda = Vadodara India 22°20N 73°10E 42 H5
Baroda India 25°29N 76°35E 42 G7
Baroe S. Africa 33°13S 24°33E 56 E3
Baron Ra. Australia 23°30S 127°45E 60 D4
Barotseland Zambia 15°0S 24°0E 53 H4
Barpeta India 26°20N 91°10E 41 F17
Barqa Libya 27°0N 23°0E 51 C10
Barques, Pt. Aux U.S.A. 44°4N 82°58W 82 B2
Barquísimeto Venezuela 10°4N 69°19W 92 A5
Barr Smith Range Australia 27°4S 120°20E 61 E3
Barra Brazil 11°5S 43°10W 93 F10
Barra U.K. 57°0N 7°29W 11 E1
Barra, Sd. of U.K. 57°4N 7°25W 11 D1
Barra de Navidad Mexico 19°12N 104°41W 86 D4
Barra do Corda Brazil 5°30S 45°10W 93 E9
Barra do Garças Brazil 15°54S 52°16W 93 G8
Barra do Piraí Brazil 22°30S 43°50W 95 A7
Barra Falsa, Pta. da Mozam. 22°58S 35°37E 57 C6
Barra Hd. U.K. 56°47N 7°40W 11 E1
Barra Mansa Brazil 22°35S 44°12W 95 A7
Barraba Australia 30°21S 150°35E 63 E5
Barrackpur = Barakpur India 22°47N 88°21E 43 H13
Barradale Australia 22°42S 114°58E 60 D1
Barraigh = Barra U.K. 57°0N 7°29W 11 E1
Barranca Lima, Peru 10°45S 77°50W 92 F3
Barranca Loreto, Peru 4°50S 76°50W 92 D3
Barranca del Cobre △ Mexico 27°18N 107°40W 86 B3
Barrancabermeja Colombia 7°0N 73°50W 92 B4
Barrancas Venezuela 8°55N 62°5W 92 B6
Barrancos Portugal 38°10N 6°58W 21 C2
Barranqueras Argentina 27°30S 59°0W 94 B4
Barranquilla Colombia 11°0N 74°50W 92 A4
Barraute Canada 48°26N 77°38W 72 C4
Barre Mass., U.S.A. 42°25N 72°6W 83 D12
Barre Vt., U.S.A. 44°12N 72°30W 83 B12
Barreal Argentina 31°33S 69°28W 94 C2
Barreiras Brazil 12°8S 45°0W 93 F10
Barreirinhas Brazil 2°30S 42°50W 93 D10
Barreiro Portugal 38°39N 9°5W 21 C1
Barren, Nosy Madag. 18°25S 43°40E 57 B7
Barretos Brazil 20°30S 48°35W 93 H9
Barrhead Canada 54°10N 114°24W 70 C6
Barrie Canada 44°24N 79°40W 82 B5
Barrier Ra. Australia 31°0S 141°30E 63 E3
Barrier Reef Belize 17°9N 88°3W 87 D7
Barrière Canada 51°12N 120°7W 70 C4
Barrington U.S.A. 41°44N 71°18W 83 E13
Barrington L. Canada 56°55N 100°15W 71 B8
Barrington Tops Australia 32°6S 151°28E 63 E5
Barringun Australia 29°1S 145°41E 63 D4
Barron U.S.A. 45°24N 91°51W 80 C8
Barrow U.S.A. 71°18N 156°47W 74 a
Barrow → Ireland 52°25N 6°58W 10 D5
Barrow, Pt. U.S.A. 71°23N 156°29W 66 B4
Barrow Creek Australia 21°30S 133°55E 62 C1
Barrow I. Australia 20°45S 115°20E 60 D2
Barrow-in-Furness U.K. 54°7N 3°14W 12 C4
Barrow Pt. Australia 14°20S 144°40E 62 A3
Barrow Ra. Australia 26°0S 127°40E 61 E4
Barrow Str. Canada 74°20N 95°0W 4 B3
Barry U.K. 51°24N 3°16W 13 F4
Barry's Bay Canada 45°29N 77°41W 82 A7
Barsat Pakistan 36°10N 72°45E 43 A5
Barsi India 18°10N 75°50E 40 K9
Barsoi India 25°48N 87°57E 41 G15
Barstow U.S.A. 34°54N 117°1W 79 L9
Barthélemy, Col Vietnam 19°26N 104°6E 38 C5
Bartica Guyana 6°25N 58°40W 92 B7
Bartle Frere Australia 17°27S 145°50E 62 B4
Bartlesville U.S.A. 36°45N 95°59W 84 C7
Bartlett Calif., U.S.A. 36°29N 118°2W 78 J8
Bartlett Tenn., U.S.A. 35°12N 89°52W 85 D10
Bartlett, L. Canada 63°5N 118°20W 70 A5
Bartolomeu Dias Mozam. 21°10S 35°8E 55 G4
Barton U.S.A. 44°45N 72°11W 83 B12
Barton upon Humber U.K. 53°41N 0°25W 12 D7
Bartow U.S.A. 27°54N 81°50W 85 H14
Barú, Volcan Panama 8°55N 82°35W 88 E3
Barumba Dem. Rep. of the Congo 1°3N 23°37E 54 B1
Baruun Urt Mongolia 46°46N 113°15E 29 E12
Baruunsuu Mongolia 43°43N 105°35E 34 C3
Barwani India 22°2N 74°57E 42 H6
Barysaw Belarus 54°17N 28°28E 17 A15
Barzān Iraq 36°55N 44°3E 44 B5
Bāsa'idū Iran 26°35N 55°20E 45 E7
Basal Pakistan 33°33N 72°13E 42 C5
Basankusa Dem. Rep. of the Congo 1°5N 19°50E 52 D3
Basarabeasca Moldova 46°21N 28°58E 17 E15
Basarabia = Bessarabiya Moldova 47°0N 28°10E 17 E15
Basawa Afghan. 34°15N 70°50E 42 B4
Bascuñán, C. Chile 28°52S 71°35W 94 B1
Basel Switz. 47°35N 7°35E 20 C7
Bashākerd, Kūhhā-ye Iran 26°42N 58°35E 45 E8
Bashaw Canada 52°35N 112°58W 70 C6
Bāshī Iran 28°41N 51°4E 45 D6
Bashkir Republic = Bashkortostan □ Russia 54°0N 57°0E 18 D10
Bashkortostan □ Russia 54°0N 57°0E 18 D10
Basibasy Madag. 22°10S 43°40E 57 C7
Basilan Phil. 6°35N 122°0E 37 C6
Basilan Str. Phil. 6°50N 122°0E 37 C6
Basildon U.K. 51°34N 0°28E 13 F8
Basim = Washim India 20°3N 77°0E 40 J10
Basin U.S.A. 44°23N 108°2W 76 D9
Basingstoke U.K. 51°15N 1°5W 13 F6
Baskatong, Rés. Canada 46°46N 75°50W 72 C4
Basle = Basel Switz. 47°35N 7°35E 20 C7
Basoda India 23°52N 77°54E 42 H7
Basoko Dem. Rep. of the Congo 1°16N 23°40E 54 B1
Basque Provinces = País Vasco □ Spain 42°50N 2°45W 21 A4
Basra = Al Başrah Iraq 30°30N 47°50E 44 D5
Bass Str. Australia 39°15S 146°30E 63 F4
Bassano Canada 50°48N 112°20W 70 C6
Bassano del Grappa Italy 45°46N 11°44E 22 B4
Bassas da India Ind. Oc. 22°0S 39°0E 55 G4
Basse-Pointe Martinique 14°52N 61°8W 88 c
Basse-Terre Guadeloupe 16°0N 61°44W 88 b
Basse Terre Trin. & Tob. 10°7N 61°19W 93 K15
Bassein Burma 16°45N 94°30E 41 L19
Basses, Pte. des Guadeloupe 15°52N 61°17W 88 b
Basseterre St. Kitts & Nevis 17°17N 62°43W 89 C7
Bassett U.S.A. 42°35N 99°32W 80 D4
Bassi India 30°44N 76°21E 42 D7
Bastak Iran 27°15N 54°25E 45 E7
Baştām Iran 36°29N 55°4E 45 B7
Bastar India 19°15N 81°40E 41 K12
Basti India 26°52N 82°55E 43 F10
Bastia France 42°40N 9°30E 20 E8
Bastogne Belgium 50°1N 5°43E 15 D5
Bastrop La., U.S.A. 32°47N 91°55W 84 E9
Bastrop Tex., U.S.A. 30°7N 97°19W 84 F6
Basuo = Dongfang China 18°50N 108°33E 38 C7
Bat Yam Israel 32°2N 34°44E 46 C3
Bata Eq. Guin. 1°57N 9°50E 52 D1
Bataan □ Phil. 14°40N 120°25E 37 B6
Batabanó Cuba 22°41N 82°18W 88 B3
Batabanó, G. de Cuba 22°30N 82°30W 88 B3
Batac Phil. 18°3N 120°34E 37 A6
Batagai Russia 67°38N 134°38E 29 C14
Batala India 31°48N 75°12E 42 D6
Batama Dem. Rep. of the Congo 0°58N 26°33E 54 B2
Batamay Russia 63°30N 129°15E 29 C13
Batang Indonesia 6°55S 109°45E 37 G13
Batangafo C.A.R. 7°25N 18°20E 52 C3
Batangas Phil. 13°35N 121°10E 37 B6
Batanta Indonesia 0°55S 130°40E 37 E8
Batatais Brazil 20°54S 47°37W 95 A6
Batavia U.S.A. 43°0N 78°11W 82 D6
Batchelor Australia 13°4S 131°1E 60 B5
Batdambang Cambodia 13°7N 103°12E 38 F4
Batemans B. Australia 35°40S 150°12E 63 F5
Batemans Bay Australia 35°44S 150°11E 63 F5
Bates Ra. Australia 27°27S 121°5E 61 E3
Batesburg-Leesville U.S.A. 33°54N 81°33W 85 E14
Batesville Ark., U.S.A. 35°46N 91°39W 84 D9
Batesville Miss., U.S.A. 34°19N 89°57W 85 D10
Batesville Tex., U.S.A. 28°58N 99°37W 84 G5
Bath Canada 44°11N 76°47W 83 B8
Bath U.K. 51°23N 2°22W 13 F5
Bath Maine, U.S.A. 43°55N 69°49W 81 D19
Bath N.Y., U.S.A. 42°20N 77°19W 82 D7
Bath & North East Somerset □ U.K. 51°21N 2°27W 13 F5
Batheay Cambodia 11°59N 104°57E 39 G5
Bathsheba Barbados 13°13N 59°32W 89 g
Bathurst Australia 33°25S 149°31E 63 E4
Bathurst Canada 47°37N 65°43W 73 C6
Bathurst S. Africa 33°30S 26°50E 56 E4
Bathurst, C. Canada 70°34N 128°0W 68 B7
Bathurst B. Australia 14°16S 144°25E 62 A3
Bathurst Harb. Australia 43°15S 146°10E 63 G4
Bathurst I. Australia 11°30S 130°10E 60 B5
Bathurst I. Canada 76°0N 100°30W 69 B11
Bathurst Inlet Canada 66°50N 108°1W 68 C9
Batiki Fiji 17°48S 179°10E 59 a
Batlow Australia 35°31S 148°9E 63 F4
Batman Turkey 37°55N 41°5E 44 B4
Baţn al Ghūl Jordan 29°36N 35°56E 46 F4
Batna Algeria 35°34N 6°15E 50 A7
Batoka Zambia 16°45S 27°15E 55 F2
Baton Rouge U.S.A. 30°27N 91°11W 84 F9
Batong, Ko Thailand 6°32N 99°12E 39 J2
Batopilas Mexico 27°1N 107°44W 86 B3
Batouri Cameroon 4°30N 14°25E 52 D2
Båtsfjord Norway 70°38N 29°39E 8 A23
Battambang = Batdambang Cambodia 13°7N 103°12E 38 F4
Batticaloa Sri Lanka 7°43N 81°45E 40 R12
Battipáglia Italy 40°37N 14°58E 22 D6
Battle U.K. 50°55N 0°30E 13 G8
Battle → Canada 52°43N 108°15W 71 C7
Battle Creek U.S.A. 42°19N 85°11W 81 D11
Battle Ground U.S.A. 45°47N 122°32W 78 E4
Battle Harbour Canada 52°16N 55°35W 73 B8
Battle Lake U.S.A. 46°17N 95°43W 80 B6
Battle Mountain U.S.A. 40°38N 116°56W 76 F5
Battlefields Zimbabwe 18°37S 29°47E 55 F2
Battleford Canada 52°45N 108°15W 71 C7
Batu Ethiopia 6°55N 39°45E 47 F2
Batu Malaysia 3°15N 101°40E 39 L3
Batu, Kepulauan Indonesia 0°30S 98°25E 36 E1
Batu Ferringhi Malaysia 5°28N 100°15E 39 c
Batu Gajah Malaysia 4°28N 101°3E 39 K3
Batu Is. = Batu, Kepulauan Indonesia 0°30S 98°25E 36 E1
Batu Pahat Malaysia 1°50N 102°56E 39 M4
Batuata Indonesia 6°12S 122°42E 37 F6
Batugondang, Tanjung Indonesia 8°6S 114°29E 37 J17
Batukau, Gunung Indonesia 8°20S 115°5E 37 J18
Batumi Georgia 41°39N 41°44E 19 F7
Batur Indonesia 8°15S 115°20E 37 J18
Batur, Danau Indonesia 8°15S 115°24E 37 J18
Batur, Gunung Indonesia 8°14S 115°23E 37 J18
Batura Sar Pakistan 36°30N 74°31E 43 A6
Baturaja Indonesia 4°11S 104°15E 36 E2
Baturité Brazil 4°28S 38°45W 93 D11
Baturiti Indonesia 8°19S 115°11E 37 J18
Bau Malaysia 1°25N 110°9E 36 D4
Baubau Indonesia 5°25S 122°38E 37 F6
Baucau E. Timor 8°27S 126°27E 37 F7
Bauchi Nigeria 10°22N 9°48E 50 F7
Baudette U.S.A. 48°43N 94°36W 80 A6
Bauer, C. Australia 32°44S 134°4E 63 E1
Bauhinia Australia 24°35S 149°18E 62 C4
Baukau = Baucau E. Timor 8°27S 126°27E 37 F7
Bauld, C. Canada 51°38N 55°26W 69 D14
Bauru Brazil 22°10S 49°0W 95 A6
Bausi India 24°48N 87°1E 43 G12
Bauska Latvia 56°24N 24°15E 9 H21
Bautzen Germany 51°10N 14°26E 16 C8
Bavānāt Iran 30°28N 53°27E 45 D7
Bavaria = Bayern □ Germany 48°50N 12°0E 16 D6
Bavispe → Mexico 29°15N 109°11W 86 B3
Bawdwin Burma 23°5N 97°20E 41 H20
Bawean Indonesia 5°46S 112°35E 36 F4
Bawku Ghana 11°3N 0°19W 50 F5
Bawlake Burma 19°11N 97°21E 41 K20
Baxley U.S.A. 31°47N 82°21W 85 F13
Baxter U.S.A. 46°21N 94°17W 80 B6
Baxter Springs U.S.A. 37°2N 94°44W 80 G6
Baxter State △ U.S.A. 46°5N 68°57W 81 B19
Bay City Mich., U.S.A. 43°36N 83°54W 81 D12
Bay City Tex., U.S.A. 28°59N 95°58W 84 G7
Bay Minette U.S.A. 30°53N 87°46W 85 F11
Bay Roberts Canada 47°36N 53°16W 73 C9
Bay St. Louis U.S.A. 30°19N 89°20W 85 F10
Bay Springs U.S.A. 31°59N 89°17W 85 F10
Bay View N.Z. 39°25S 176°50E 59 C6
Baya Dem. Rep. of the Congo 11°53S 27°25E 55 E2
Bayamo Cuba 20°20N 76°40W 88 B4
Bayamón Puerto Rico 18°24N 66°9W 89 d
Bayan Har Shan China 34°0N 98°0E 32 C4
Bayan Hot = Alxa Zuoqi China 38°50N 105°40E 34 E3
Bayan Lepas Malaysia 5°17N 100°16E 39 c
Bayan Obo China 41°52N 109°59E 34 D5
Bayan-Ovoo = Erdenetsogt Mongolia 42°55N 106°5E 34 C4
Bayana India 26°55N 77°18E 42 F7
Bayanaūyl Kazakhstan 50°45N 75°45E 28 D8
Bayandalay Mongolia 43°30N 103°29E 34 C2
Bayanhongor Mongolia 46°8N 102°43E 32 B5
Bayard N. Mex., U.S.A. 32°46N 108°8W 77 K9
Bayard Nebr., U.S.A. 41°45N 103°20W 80 E2
Baybay Phil. 10°40N 124°55E 37 B6
Baydaratskaya Guba Russia 69°0N 67°30E 28 C7
Baydhabo Somali Rep. 3°8N 43°30E 47 G3
Bayern □ Germany 48°50N 12°0E 16 D6
Bayeux France 49°17N 0°42W 20 B3
Bayfield Canada 43°34N 81°42W 82 C3
Bayfield U.S.A. 46°49N 90°49W 80 B8
Bayındır Turkey 38°13N 27°39E 23 E12
Baykal, Oz. Russia 53°0N 108°0E 29 D11
Baykan Turkey 38°7N 41°44E 44 B4
Baykonur = Bayqongyr Kazakhstan 47°48N 65°50E 28 E7
Baykonyr Russia 52°36N 58°19E 18 D10
Baynes Mts. Namibia 17°15S 13°0E 56 B1
Bayombong Phil. 16°30N 121°10E 37 A6
Bayonne France 43°30N 1°28W 20 E3
Bayonne U.S.A. 40°40N 74°6W 83 F10
Bayovar Peru 5°50S 81°0W 92 E2
Bayqongyr Kazakhstan 45°40N 63°20E 28 E7
Bayram-Ali = Baýramaly Turkmenistan 37°37N 62°10E 45 B9
Baýramaly Turkmenistan 37°37N 62°10E 45 B9
Bayramiç Turkey 39°48N 26°36E 23 E12
Bayreuth Germany 49°56N 11°35E 16 D6
Bayrūt Lebanon 33°53N 35°31E 46 B4
Bays, L. of Canada 45°15N 79°4W 82 A5
Baysville Canada 45°9N 79°7W 82 A5
Bayt Lahm West Bank 31°43N 35°12E 46 D4
Baytown U.S.A. 29°43N 94°59W 84 G7
Bayun Indonesia 8°11S 115°16E 37 J18
Baza Spain 37°30N 2°47W 21 D4
Bazaruto, I. do Mozam. 21°40S 35°28E 57 C6
Bazaruto △ Mozam. 21°42S 35°26E 57 C6
Bazhou China 39°8N 116°22E 34 E9
Bazmān, Kūh-e Iran 28°4N 60°1E 45 D9
Beach U.S.A. 46°58N 104°0W 80 B2
Beach City U.S.A. 40°39N 81°35W 82 F3
Beachport Australia 37°29S 140°0E 63 F3
Beachville Canada 43°5N 80°49W 82 C4
Beachy Hd. U.K. 50°44N 0°15E 13 G8
Beacon Australia 30°26S 117°52E 61 F2
Beacon U.S.A. 41°30N 73°58W 83 E11
Beaconsfield Australia 41°11S 146°48E 63 G4
Beagle, Canal S. Amer. 55°0S 68°30W 96 H3
Beagle Bay Australia 16°58S 122°40E 60 C3
Beagle G. Australia 12°15S 130°25E 60 B5
Bealanana Madag. 14°33S 48°44E 57 A8
Beals Cr. → U.S.A. 32°10N 100°51W 84 E4
Beamsville Canada 43°12N 79°28W 82 C5
Bear → Calif., U.S.A. 38°56N 121°36W 78 G5
Bear → Utah, U.S.A. 41°30N 112°8W 74 B4
Bear I. Ireland 51°38N 9°50W 10 E2
Bear L. Canada 55°8N 96°0W 71 B9
Bear L. U.S.A. 41°59N 111°21W 76 F8
Bear Lake Canada 45°27N 79°35W 82 A5
Beardmore Canada 49°36N 87°57W 72 C2
Beardmore Glacier Antarctica 84°30S 170°0E 5 E11
Beardstown U.S.A. 40°1N 90°26W 80 E8
Bearma → India 24°20N 79°51E 43 G8
Béarn France 43°20N 0°30W 20 E3
Bearpaw Mts. U.S.A. 48°12N 109°30W 76 B9
Bearskin Lake Canada 53°58N 91°2W 72 B1
Beas → India 31°10N 74°59E 42 D6
Beata, C. Dom. Rep. 17°40N 71°30W 89 C5
Beata, I. Dom. Rep. 17°34N 71°31W 89 C5
Beatrice U.S.A. 40°16N 96°45W 80 E5
Beatrice Zimbabwe 18°15S 30°55E 55 F3
Beatrice, C. Australia 14°20S 136°55E 62 A2
Beatton → Canada 56°15N 120°45W 70 B4
Beatton River Canada 57°26N 121°20W 70 B4
Beatty U.S.A. 36°54N 116°46W 78 J10
Beau Bassin Mauritius 20°13S 57°27E 53 d
Beauce, Plaine de la France 48°10N 1°45E 20 B4
Beauceville Canada 46°13N 70°46W 73 C5
Beaudesert Australia 27°59S 153°0E 63 D5
Beaufort Malaysia 5°30N 115°40E 36 C5
Beaufort N.C., U.S.A. 34°43N 76°40W 85 D16
Beaufort S.C., U.S.A. 32°26N 80°40W 85 E14
Beaufort Sea Arctic 72°0N 140°0W 66 B5
Beaufort West S. Africa 32°18S 22°36E 56 E3
Beauharnois Canada 45°20N 73°52W 83 A11
Beaulieu → Canada 62°3N 113°11W 70 A6
Beauly U.K. 57°30N 4°28W 11 D4
Beauly → U.K. 57°29N 4°27W 11 D4
Beaumaris U.K. 53°16N 4°6W 12 D3
Beaumont Belgium 50°15N 4°14E 15 D4
Beaumont U.S.A. 30°5N 94°6W 84 F7
Beaune France 47°2N 4°50E 20 C6
Beaupré Canada 47°3N 70°54W 73 C5
Beauraing Belgium 50°7N 4°57E 15 D4
Beausejour Canada 50°5N 96°35W 71 C9
Beauvais France 49°25N 2°8E 20 B5
Beauval Canada 55°9N 107°37W 71 B7
Beaver Okla., U.S.A. 36°49N 100°31W 84 C4
Beaver Pa., U.S.A. 40°42N 80°19W 82 F4
Beaver Utah, U.S.A. 38°17N 112°38W 76 G7
Beaver → B.C., Canada 59°52N 124°20W 70 B4
Beaver → Ont., Canada 55°55N 87°48W 72 A2
Beaver → Sask., Canada 55°26N 107°45W 71 B7
Beaver → U.S.A. 36°35N 99°30W 84 C5
Beaver City U.S.A. 40°8N 99°50W 80 E4
Beaver Creek Canada 63°0N 141°0W 68 C5
Beaver Dam U.S.A. 43°28N 88°50W 80 D
Beaver Falls U.S.A. 40°46N 80°20W 82 F
Beaver Hill L. Canada 54°5N 94°50W 71 C
Beaver I. U.S.A. 45°40N 85°33W 81 C1
Beavercreek U.S.A. 39°43N 84°11W 81 F1
Beaverhill L. Canada 53°27N 112°32W 70 C
Beaverlodge Canada 55°11N 119°29W 70 B
Beaverstone → Canada 54°59N 89°25W 72 B
Beaverton Canada 44°26N 79°9W 82 B
Beaverton U.S.A. 45°29N 122°48W 78 E
Beawar India 26°3N 74°18E 42 F
Bebedouro Brazil 21°0S 48°25W 95 A
Bebera, Tanjung Indonesia 8°44S 115°51E 37 K1
Beboa Madag. 17°22S 44°33E 57 B
Becán Mexico 18°34N 89°31W 87 D
Bécancour Canada 46°20N 72°26W 81 B1
Beccles U.K. 52°27N 1°35E 13 E
Bečej Serbia 45°36N 20°3E 23 B
Béchar Algeria 31°38N 2°18W 50 B
Beckley U.S.A. 37°47N 81°11W 81 G1
Beddouza, Ras Morocco 32°33N 9°9W 50 B
Bedford Canada 45°7N 72°59W 83 A1
Bedford S. Africa 32°40S 26°10E 56 E
Bedford U.K. 52°8N 0°28W 13 E
Bedford Ind., U.S.A. 38°52N 86°29W 80 F1
Bedford Iowa, U.S.A. 40°40N 94°44W 80 E
Bedford Ohio, U.S.A. 41°23N 81°32W 82 E
Bedford Pa., U.S.A. 40°1N 78°30W 82 F
Bedford Va., U.S.A. 37°20N 79°31W 81 G
Bedford, C. Australia 15°14S 145°21E 62 B
Bedfordshire □ U.K. 52°4N 0°28W 13 E
Bedok Singapore 1°19N 103°56E 39
Bedourie Australia 24°30S 139°30E 62 C
Bedum Neths. 53°18N 6°36E 15 A
Beebe Plain Canada 45°1N 72°9W 83 A
Beech Creek U.S.A. 41°5N 77°36W 82 E
Beechy Canada 50°53N 107°24W 71 C
Beef I. Br. Virgin Is. 18°26N 64°30W 89
Beenleigh Australia 27°43S 153°10E 63 D
Be'er Menuha Israel 30°19N 35°8E 44 D
Be'er Sheva Israel 31°15N 34°48E 46 D
Beersheba = Be'er Sheva Israel 31°15N 34°48E 46 D
Beestekraal S. Africa 25°23S 27°38E 57 D
Beeston U.K. 52°56N 1°14W 12 E
Beeton Canada 44°5N 79°47W 82 B
Beeville U.S.A. 28°24N 97°45W 84 G
Befale Dem. Rep. of the Congo 0°25N 20°45E 52 D
Befandriana Mahajanga, Madag. 15°16S 48°32E 57 B
Befandriana Toliara, Madag. 21°55S 44°0E 57 C
Befasy Madag. 20°33S 44°23E 57 C
Befotaka Antsiranana, Madag. 13°15S 48°16E 57 A
Befotaka Fianarantsoa, Madag. 23°49S 47°0E 57 C
Bega Australia 36°41S 149°51E 63
Begusarai India 25°24N 86°9E 43 G
Behābād Iran 32°24N 59°47E 45
Behala India 22°30N 88°18E 43 H
Behara Madag. 24°55S 46°20E 57
Behbehān Iran 30°30N 50°15E 45
Behm Canal U.S.A. 55°10N 131°0W 70
Behshahr Iran 36°45N 53°35E 45
Bei Jiang → China 23°2N 112°58E 33
Bei Shan China 41°30N 96°0E 32
Bei'an China 48°10N 126°20E 33
Beihai China 21°28N 109°6E 33
Beijing China 39°53N 116°21E 34
Beijing □ China 39°55N 116°20E 34
Beilen Neths. 52°52N 6°27E 15
Beilpajah Australia 32°54S 143°52E 63
Beinn na Faoghla = Benbecula U.K. 57°26N 7°21W 11
Beipiao China 41°52N 120°32E 35 D
Beira Mozam. 19°50S 34°52E 55
Beirut = Bayrūt Lebanon 33°53N 35°31E 46
Beiseker Canada 51°23N 113°32W 70
Beit Lekhem = Bayt Lahm West Bank 31°43N 35°12E 46
Beitaolaizhao China 44°58N 125°58E 35 B
Beitbridge Zimbabwe 22°12S 30°0E 55
Beizhen = Binzhou China 37°20N 118°2E 35 F
Beizhen China 41°38N 121°54E 35 D
Beizhengzhen China 44°31N 123°30E 35 B
Beja Portugal 38°2N 7°53W 21
Béja Tunisia 36°43N 9°12E 51
Bejaïa Algeria 36°42N 5°2E 50
Béjar Spain 40°23N 5°46W 21
Bejestān Iran 34°30N 58°5E 45
Bekaa Valley = Al Biqā Lebanon 34°10N 36°10E 46
Békéscsaba Hungary 46°40N 21°5E 17 E
Bekily Madag. 24°13S 45°19E 57
Bekisopa Madag. 21°40S 45°54E 57
Bekitro Madag. 24°33S 45°18E 57
Bekodoka Madag. 16°58S 45°7E 57
Bekok Malaysia 2°20N 103°7E 39
Bekopaka Madag. 19°9S 44°48E 57
Bekuli Indonesia 8°22S 114°13E 37 J
Bela India 25°50N 82°0E 43 G
Bela Pakistan 26°12N 66°20E 42 F
Bela Bela S. Africa 24°51S 28°19E 57
Bela Crkva Serbia 44°55N 21°27E 23
Bela Vista Brazil 22°12S 56°20W 94
Bela Vista Mozam. 26°10S 32°44E 57
Belan → India 24°2N 81°45E 43
Belarus ■ Europe 53°30N 27°0E 17 B
Belau = Palau ■ Palau 7°30N 134°30E 58
Belavenona Madag. 24°50S 47°4E 57
Belawan Indonesia 3°33N 98°32E 36
Belaya → Russia 54°40N 56°0E 18
Belaya Tserkov = Bila Tserkva Ukraine 49°45N 30°10E 17 D

laya Zemlya, Ostrova
Russia 81°36N 62°18E 28 A7
lcher Chan. Canada 77°15N 95°0W 69 B10
lcher Is. Canada 56°15N 78°45W 72 A3
lden U.S.A. 40°2N 121°17W 78 E5
lebey Russia 54°7N 54°7E 18 D9
ledweyne Somali Rep. 4°30N 45°5E 47 G4
lém Brazil 1°20S 48°30W 93 D9
lén Argentina 27°40S 67°5W 94 B2
lén Paraguay 23°30S 57°6W 94 A4
len U.S.A. 34°40N 106°46W 77 J10
let Uen = Beledweyne
Somali Rep. 4°30N 45°5E 47 G4
lev Russia 53°50N 36°5E 18 D6
lfair U.S.A. 47°27N 122°50W 78 C4
lfast S. Africa 25°42S 30°2E 57 D5
lfast U.K. 54°37N 5°56W 10 B6
lfast Maine, U.S.A. 44°26N 69°1W 81 C19
lfast N.Y., U.S.A. 42°21N 78°7W 82 D6
lfast L. U.K. 54°40N 5°50W 10 B6
lfield U.S.A. 46°53N 103°12W 80 B2
lfort France 47°38N 6°50E 20 C7
lfry U.S.A. 45°9N 109°1W 76 D9
lgaum India 15°55N 74°35E 40 M9
lgium ■ Europe 50°30N 5°0E 15 D4
lgorod Russia 50°35N 36°35E 19 D6
lgorod-Dnestrovskiy =
Bilhorod-Dnistrovskyy
Ukraine 46°11N 30°23E 19 E5
lgrade = Beograd
Serbia 44°50N 20°37E 23 B9
lgrade U.S.A. 45°47N 111°11W 76 D8
lgrano Antarctica 77°52S 34°37W 5 D1
lhaven U.S.A. 35°33N 76°37W 85 D16
li Drim → Europe 42°6N 20°25E 23 C9
limbing Indonesia 8°24S 115°2E 37 J18
linyu Indonesia 1°35S 105°50E 36 E3
liton Is. = Belitung
Indonesia 3°10S 107°50E 36 E3
litung Indonesia 3°10S 107°50E 36 E3
lize ■ Cent. Amer. 17°0N 88°30W 87 D7
lize City Belize 17°25N 88°10W 87 D7
kovskiy, Ostrov
Russia 75°32N 135°44E 29 B14
l → Canada 49°48N 77°38W 72 C4
l I. Canada 50°46N 55°35W 73 B8
l-Irving → Canada 56°12N 129°5W 70 B3
l Peninsula Canada 63°50N 82°0W 69 C11
l Ville Argentina 32°40S 62°40W 94 C3
la Bella Canada 52°10N 128°10W 70 C3
la Coola Canada 52°25N 126°40W 70 C3
la Unión Uruguay 30°15S 57°40W 94 C4
la Vista Corrientes,
Argentina 28°33S 59°0W 94 B4
la Vista Tucuman,
Argentina 27°10S 65°25W 94 B2
laire U.S.A. 40°1N 80°45W 82 F4
lary India 15°10N 76°56E 40 M10
lata Australia 29°53S 149°46E 63 D4
le Fourche U.S.A. 44°40N 103°51W 80 C2
le Fourche →
U.S.A. 44°26N 102°18W 74 B6
le Glade U.S.A. 26°41N 80°40W 85 H14
le-Île France 47°20N 3°10W 20 C2
le Isle Canada 51°57N 55°25W 73 B8
le Isle, Str. of Canada 51°30N 56°30W 73 B8
le Plaine U.S.A. 41°54N 92°17W 80 E7
le River Canada 42°18N 82°43W 82 D2
lefontaine U.S.A. 40°22N 83°46W 81 E12
lefonte U.S.A. 40°55N 77°47W 82 F7
eoram Canada 47°31N 55°25W 73 C8
eplaine Barbados 13°15N 59°34W 89 g
eville Canada 44°10N 77°23W 82 B7
eville Ill., U.S.A. 38°31N 89°59W 80 F9
eville Kans., U.S.A. 39°50N 97°38W 80 F5
eville N.J., U.S.A. 40°47N 74°9W 83 F10
eville N.Y., U.S.A. 43°46N 76°10W 83 C8
evue Idaho, U.S.A. 43°28N 114°16W 76 E6
evue Nebr., U.S.A. 41°9N 95°54W 80 E6
evue Ohio, U.S.A. 41°17N 82°51W 82 E2
evue Wash., U.S.A. 47°37N 122°12W 78 C4
in = Kangirsuk
Canada 60°0N 70°0W 69 D13
ingen Australia 30°25S 152°50E 63 E5
ingham U.S.A. 48°46N 122°29W 78 B4
ingshausen Abyssal Plain
Ocean 64°0S 90°0W 5 C16
ingshausen Sea
Antarctica 66°0S 80°0W 5 C17
inzona Switz. 46°11N 9°1E 20 C8
o Colombia 6°20N 75°33W 92 B3
ows Falls U.S.A. 43°8N 72°27W 83 C12
pat Pakistan 29°0N 68°5E 42 E3
uno Italy 46°9N 12°13E 22 A5
wood U.S.A. 40°36N 78°20W 82 F6
mont Canada 42°53N 81°5W 82 D3
mont S. Africa 29°28S 24°22E 56 D3
mont U.S.A. 42°14N 78°2W 82 D6
monte Brazil 16°0S 39°0W 93 G11
nopan Belize 17°18N 88°30W 87 D7
nullet Ireland 54°14N 9°58W 10 B2
Horizonte Brazil 19°55S 43°56W 93 G10
-sur-Mer Madag. 20°42S 44°0E 57 C7
-Tsiribihina Madag. 19°40S 44°30E 57 B7
gorsk Russia 51°0N 128°20E 29 D13
ha Madag. 25°10S 45°3E 57 D8
it Kans., U.S.A. 39°28N 98°6W 80 F4
it Wis., U.S.A. 42°31N 89°2W 80 D9
korovichi Ukraine 51°7N 28°2E 17 C15
morsk Russia 64°35N 34°54E 18 B5
nia India 23°15N 91°30E 41 H17
retsk Russia 53°58N 58°24E 18 D10
russia = Belarus ■
urope 53°30N 27°0E 17 B14
vo Russia 54°30N 86°0E 28 D9
yarskiy Russia 63°42N 66°40E 28 C7
ye, Ozero Russia 60°10N 37°35E 18 B6
Beloye More Russia 66°30N 38°0E 8 C25
Belozersk Russia 60°1N 37°45E 18 B6
Belpre U.S.A. 39°17N 81°34W 81 F13
Belrain India 28°23N 80°55E 43 E9
Belt U.S.A. 47°23N 110°55W 76 C8
Beltana Australia 30°48S 138°25E 63 E2
Belterra Brazil 2°45S 55°0W 93 D8
Belton U.S.A. 31°3N 97°28W 84 F6
Belton L. U.S.A. 31°6N 97°28W 84 F6
Beltsy = Bălţi Moldova 47°48N 27°58E 17 E14
Belturbet Ireland 54°6N 7°26W 10 B4
Belukha Russia 49°50N 86°50E 28 E9
Beluran Malaysia 5°48N 117°35E 36 C5
Belvidere Ill., U.S.A. 42°15N 88°50W 80 D9
Belvidere N.J., U.S.A. 40°50N 75°5W 83 F9
Belyando → Australia 21°38S 146°50E 62 C4
Belyando Crossing
Australia 21°32S 146°51E 62 C4
Belyy, Ostrov Russia 73°30N 71°0E 28 B8
Belyy Yar Russia 58°26N 84°39E 28 D9
Belzoni U.S.A. 33°11N 90°29W 85 E9
Bemaraha, Lembalemban' i
Madag. 18°40S 44°45E 57 B7
Bemarivo Madag. 21°45S 44°45E 57 C7
Bemarivo → Antsiranana,
Madag. 14°9S 50°9E 57 A9
Bemarivo → Mahajanga,
Madag. 15°27S 47°40E 57 B8
Bemavo Madag. 21°33S 45°25E 57 C8
Bembéréke Benin 10°11N 2°43E 50 F6
Bembesi Zimbabwe 20°0S 28°58E 55 G2
Bembesi → Zimbabwe 18°57S 27°47E 55 F2
Bemetara India 21°42N 81°32E 43 J9
Bemidji U.S.A. 47°28N 94°53W 80 B6
Bemolanga Madag. 17°44S 45°6E 57 B8
Ben Iran 32°32N 50°45E 45 C6
Ben Cruachan U.K. 56°26N 5°8W 11 E3
Ben Dearg U.K. 57°47N 4°56W 11 D4
Ben En △ Vietnam 19°37N 105°30E 38 C5
Ben Gardane Tunisia 33°11N 11°11E 51 B8
Ben Hope U.K. 58°25N 4°36W 11 C4
Ben Lawers U.K. 56°32N 4°14W 11 E4
Ben Lomond N.S.W.,
Australia 30°1S 151°43E 63 E5
Ben Lomond Tas.,
Australia 41°38S 147°42E 63 G4
Ben Lomond U.K. 56°11N 4°38W 11 E4
Ben Lomond △
Australia 41°33S 147°39E 63 G4
Ben Luc Vietnam 10°39N 106°29E 39 G6
Ben Macdhui U.K. 57°4N 3°40W 11 D5
Ben Mhor U.K. 57°15N 7°18W 11 D1
Ben More Argyll & Bute,
U.K. 56°26N 6°1W 11 E2
Ben More Stirling, U.K. 56°23N 4°32W 11 E4
Ben More Assynt U.K. 58°8N 4°52W 11 C4
Ben Nevis U.K. 56°48N 5°1W 11 E3
Ben Quang Vietnam 17°3N 106°55E 38 D6
Ben Tre Vietnam 10°14N 106°23E 39 G6
Ben Vorlich U.K. 56°21N 4°14W 11 E4
Ben Wyvis U.K. 57°40N 4°35W 11 D4
Bena Nigeria 11°20N 5°50E 50 F7
Benalla Australia 36°30S 146°0E 63 F4
Benares = Varanasi
India 25°22N 83°0E 43 G10
Benavente Spain 42°2N 5°43W 21 A3
Benavides U.S.A. 27°36N 98°25W 84 H5
Benbecula U.K. 57°26N 7°21W 11 D1
Benbonyathe Hill
Australia 30°25S 139°11E 63 E2
Bend U.S.A. 44°4N 121°19W 76 D3
Bender Beyla Somali Rep. 9°30N 50°48E 47 F5
Bendery = Tighina
Moldova 46°50N 29°30E 17 E15
Bendigo Australia 36°40S 144°15E 63 F3
Benē Beraq Israel 32°6N 34°51E 46 C3
Benenitra Madag. 23°27S 45°5E 57 C8
Benevento Italy 41°8N 14°45E 22 D6
Benga Mozam. 16°11S 33°40E 55 F3
Bengal, Bay of Ind. Oc. 15°0N 90°0E 41 M17
Bengalūru = Bangalore
India 12°59N 77°40E 40 N10
Bengbu China 32°58N 117°20E 35 H9
Benghazi = Banghāzī
Libya 32°11N 20°3E 51 B10
Bengkalis Indonesia 1°30N 102°10E 39 M4
Bengkulu Indonesia 3°50S 102°12E 36 E2
Bengkulu □ Indonesia 3°48S 102°16E 36 E2
Bengough Canada 49°25N 105°10W 71 D7
Benguela Angola 12°37S 13°25E 53 G2
Benguérua, I. Mozam. 21°58S 35°28E 57 C6
Beni Dem. Rep. of the Congo 0°30N 29°27E 54 B2
Beni → Bolivia 10°23S 65°24W 92 F5
Beni Mellal Morocco 32°21N 6°21W 50 B4
Beni Suef Egypt 29°5N 31°6E 51 C12
Beniah L. Canada 63°23N 112°17W 70 A6
Benidorm Spain 38°33N 0°9W 21 C5
Benin ■ Africa 10°0N 2°0E 50 G6
Benin, Bight of W. Afr. 5°0N 3°0E 50 H6
Benin City Nigeria 6°20N 5°31E 50 G7
Benito Juárez Argentina 37°40S 59°43W 94 D4
Benitses Greece 39°32N 19°55E 25 A3
Benjamin Aceval
Paraguay 24°58S 57°34W 94 A4
Benjamin Constant
Brazil 4°40S 70°15W 92 D4
Benjamín Hill Mexico 30°9N 111°7W 86 A2
Benkelman U.S.A. 40°3N 101°32W 80 E3
Bennett Canada 59°51N 135°0W 70 B2
Bennett, L. Australia 22°50S 131°2E 60 D5
Bennetta, Ostrov
Russia 76°21N 148°56E 29 B15
Bennettsville U.S.A. 34°37N 79°41W 85 D15
Bennington N.H., U.S.A. 43°0N 71°55W 83 D11
Bennington Vt., U.S.A. 42°53N 73°12W 83 D11
Benom Malaysia 3°50N 102°6E 39 L4
Benoni S. Africa 26°11S 28°18E 57 D4
Benque Viejo Belize 17°5N 89°8W 87 D7
Benson Ariz., U.S.A. 31°58N 110°18W 77 L8
Benson Minn., U.S.A. 45°19N 95°36W 80 C6
Bent Iran 26°20N 59°31E 45 E8
Benteng Indonesia 6°10S 120°30E 37 F6
Bentinck I. Australia 17°3S 139°35E 62 B2
Bentley Subglacial Trench
Antarctica 80°0S 115°0W 5 E15
Bento Gonçalves Brazil 29°10S 51°31W 95 B5
Benton Ark., U.S.A. 34°34N 92°35W 84 D8
Benton Calif., U.S.A. 37°48N 118°32W 78 H8
Benton Ill., U.S.A. 38°0N 88°55W 80 F9
Benton Pa., U.S.A. 41°12N 76°23W 83 E8
Benton Harbor U.S.A. 42°6N 86°27W 80 D10
Bentong Malaysia 3°31N 101°55E 39 L3
Bentonville U.S.A. 36°22N 94°13W 84 C7
Benue → Nigeria 7°48N 6°46E 50 G7
Benxi China 41°20N 123°48E 35 D12
Beo Indonesia 4°25N 126°50E 37 D7
Beograd Serbia 44°50N 20°37E 23 B9
Beolgyo S. Korea 34°51N 127°21E 35 G14
Beppu Japan 33°15N 131°30E 31 H5
Beqa Fiji 18°23S 178°8E 59 a
Beqaa Valley = Al Biqā
Lebanon 34°10N 36°10E 46 A5
Ber Mota India 23°27N 68°34E 42 H3
Bera, Tasik Malaysia 3°5N 102°38E 39 L4
Berach → India 25°15N 75°2E 42 G6
Beraketa Madag. 23°7S 44°25E 57 C7
Berastagi Indonesia 3°11N 98°31E 39 L2
Berat Albania 40°43N 19°59E 23 D8
Berau, Teluk Indonesia 2°30S 132°30E 37 E8
Beravina Madag. 18°10S 45°14E 57 B8
Berber Sudan 18°0N 34°0E 51 E12
Berbera Somali Rep. 10°30N 45°2E 47 E4
Berbérati C.A.R. 4°15N 15°40E 52 D3
Berbice → Guyana 6°20N 57°32W 92 B7
Berdichev = Berdychiv
Ukraine 49°57N 28°30E 17 D15
Berdsk Russia 54°47N 83°2E 28 D9
Berdyansk Ukraine 46°45N 36°50E 19 E6
Berdychiv Ukraine 49°57N 28°30E 17 D15
Berea U.S.A. 37°34N 84°17W 81 G11
Berebere Indonesia 2°25N 128°45E 37 D7
Bereeda Somali Rep. 11°45N 51°0E 47 E5
Berehove Ukraine 48°15N 22°35E 17 D12
Bereket Turkmenistan 39°16N 55°32E 45 B7
Berekum Ghana 7°29N 2°34W 50 G5
Berens → Canada 52°25N 97°2W 71 C9
Berens I. Canada 52°18N 97°18W 71 C9
Berens River Canada 52°25N 97°0W 71 C9
Beresford U.S.A. 43°5N 96°47W 80 D5
Berestechko Ukraine 50°22N 25°5E 17 C13
Berevo Mahajanga,
Madag. 17°14S 44°17E 57 B7
Berevo Toliara, Madag. 19°44S 44°58E 57 B7
Berezhany Ukraine 49°26N 24°58E 17 D13
Berezina = Byarezina →
Belarus 52°33N 30°14E 17 B16
Bereznik Russia 62°51N 42°40E 18 B7
Berezniki Russia 59°24N 56°46E 18 C10
Berezovo Russia 64°0N 65°0E 28 C7
Berga Spain 42°6N 1°48E 21 A6
Bergama Turkey 39°8N 27°11E 23 E12
Bérgamo Italy 45°41N 9°43E 20 D8
Bergen Neths. 52°40N 4°43E 15 B4
Bergen Norway 60°20N 5°20E 8 F11
Bergen U.S.A. 43°5N 77°57W 82 C7
Bergen op Zoom Neths. 51°28N 4°18E 15 C4
Bergerac France 44°51N 0°30E 20 D4
Bergholz U.S.A. 40°31N 80°53W 82 F4
Bergisch Gladbach
Germany 50°59N 7°8E 15 D7
Bergville S. Africa 28°52S 29°18E 57 D4
Berhala, Selat Indonesia 1°0S 104°15E 36 E2
Berhampore = Baharampur
India 24°2N 88°27E 43 G13
Berhampur = Brahmapur
India 19°15N 84°54E 41 K14
Bering Sea Pac. Oc. 58°0N 171°0W 74 a
Bering Strait Pac. Oc. 65°30N 169°0W 74 a
Beringovskiy Russia 63°3N 179°19E 29 C18
Berisso Argentina 34°56S 57°50W 94 C4
Berja Spain 36°50N 2°56W 21 D4
Berkeley U.S.A. 37°51N 122°16W 78 H4
Berkner I. Antarctica 79°30S 50°0W 5 D18
Berkshire U.S.A. 42°19N 76°11W 83 D8
Berkshire Downs U.K. 51°33N 1°29W 13 F6
Berlin Germany 52°31N 13°23E 16 B7
Berlin Md., U.S.A. 38°20N 75°13W 81 F16
Berlin N.H., U.S.A. 44°28N 71°11W 83 B13
Berlin N.Y., U.S.A. 42°42N 73°23W 83 D11
Berlin Wis., U.S.A. 43°58N 88°57W 80 D9
Berlin L. U.S.A. 41°3N 81°0W 82 E4
Bermejo → Formosa,
Argentina 26°51S 58°23W 94 B4
Bermejo → San Juan,
Argentina 32°30S 67°30W 94 C2
Bermejo, Paso = Uspallata, P. de
Argentina 32°37S 69°22W 94 C2
Bermen, L. Canada 53°35N 68°55W 73 B6
Bermuda ☑ Atl. Oc. 32°18N 64°45W 67 F13
Bern Switz. 46°57N 7°28E 20 C7
Bernalillo U.S.A. 35°18N 106°33W 77 J10
Bernardo de Irigoyen
Argentina 26°15S 53°40W 95 B5
Bernardsville U.S.A. 40°43N 74°34W 83 F10
Bernasconi Argentina 37°55S 63°44W 94 D3
Bernburg Germany 51°47N 11°44E 16 C6
Berne = Bern Switz. 46°57N 7°28E 20 C7
Berneray U.K. 57°43N 7°11W 11 D1
Bernier I. Australia 24°50S 113°12E 61 D1
Bernina, Piz Switz. 46°20N 9°54E 20 C8
Beroroha Madag. 21°40S 45°10E 57 C8
Beroun Czech Rep. 49°57N 14°5E 16 D8
Berri Australia 34°14S 140°35E 63 E3
Berriane Algeria 32°50N 3°46E 50 B6
Berry Australia 34°46S 150°43E 63 E5
Berry France 46°50N 2°0E 20 C5
Berry Is. Bahamas 25°40N 77°50W 88 A4
Berryessa, L. U.S.A. 38°31N 122°6W 78 G4
Berryville U.S.A. 36°22N 93°34W 84 C8
Berseba Namibia 26°0S 17°46E 56 D2
Bershad Ukraine 48°22N 29°31E 17 D15
Berthold U.S.A. 48°19N 101°44W 80 A3
Berthoud U.S.A. 40°19N 105°5W 76 F11
Bertoua Cameroon 4°30N 13°45E 52 D2
Bertraghboy B. Ireland 53°22N 9°54W 10 C2
Berwick U.S.A. 41°3N 76°14W 83 E8
Berwick-upon-Tweed
U.K. 55°46N 2°0W 12 B6
Berwyn Mts. U.K. 52°54N 3°26W 12 E4
Besal Pakistan 35°4N 73°56E 43 B5
Besalampy Madag. 16°43S 44°29E 57 B7
Besançon France 47°15N 6°2E 20 C7
Besar Indonesia 2°40S 116°0E 36 E5
Besnard L. Canada 55°25N 106°0W 71 B7
Besni Turkey 37°41N 37°52E 44 B3
Besor, N. → Egypt 31°28N 34°22E 46 D3
Bessarabiya Moldova 47°0N 28°10E 17 E15
Bessarabka = Basarabeasca
Moldova 46°21N 28°58E 17 E15
Bessemer Ala., U.S.A. 33°24N 86°58W 85 E11
Bessemer Mich., U.S.A. 46°29N 90°3W 80 B8
Bessemer Pa., U.S.A. 40°59N 80°30W 82 F4
Beswick Australia 14°34S 132°53E 60 B5
Bet She'an Israel 32°30N 35°30E 46 C4
Bet Shemesh Israel 31°44N 35°0E 46 D4
Betafo Madag. 19°50S 46°51E 57 B8
Betancuria Canary Is. 28°25N 14°3W 24 F5
Betanzos Spain 43°15N 8°12W 21 A1
Bétaré Oya Cameroon 5°40N 14°5E 52 C2
Betatao Madag. 18°11S 47°52E 57 B8
Bethal S. Africa 26°27S 29°28E 57 D4
Bethanien Namibia 26°31S 17°8E 56 D2
Bethany Canada 44°11N 78°34W 82 B6
Bethany Mo., U.S.A. 40°16N 94°2W 80 E6
Bethany Okla., U.S.A. 35°31N 97°38W 84 D6
Bethel Alaska, U.S.A. 60°48N 161°45W 74 a
Bethel Conn., U.S.A. 41°22N 73°25W 83 E11
Bethel Maine, U.S.A. 44°25N 70°47W 83 B14
Bethel Vt., U.S.A. 43°50N 72°38W 83 C12
Bethel Park U.S.A. 40°19N 80°2W 82 F4
Bethlehem = Bayt Lahm
West Bank 31°43N 35°12E 46 D4
Bethlehem S. Africa 28°14S 28°18E 57 D4
Bethlehem U.S.A. 40°37N 75°23W 83 F9
Bethulie S. Africa 30°30S 25°59E 56 E4
Béthune France 50°30N 2°38E 20 A5
Betioky Madag. 23°48S 44°20E 57 C7
Betong Malaysia 1°24N 111°31E 36 D4
Betong Thailand 5°45N 101°5E 39 K3
Betoota Australia 25°45S 140°42E 62 D3
Betpaqdala Kazakhstan 45°45N 70°30E 32 B2
Betroka Madag. 23°16S 46°0E 57 C8
Betsiamites Canada 48°56N 68°40W 73 C6
Betsiamites → Canada 48°56N 68°38W 73 C6
Betsiboka → Madag. 16°3S 46°36E 57 B8
Bettendorf U.S.A. 41°32N 90°30W 80 E8
Bettiah India 26°48N 84°33E 43 F11
Betul India 21°58N 77°59E 40 J10
Betws-y-Coed U.K. 53°5N 3°48W 12 D4
Beulah Mich., U.S.A. 44°38N 86°6W 80 C10
Beulah N. Dak., U.S.A. 47°16N 101°47W 80 B3
Beveren Belgium 51°12N 4°16E 15 C4
Beverley Australia 32°9S 116°56E 61 F2
Beverley U.K. 53°51N 0°26W 12 D7
Beverly U.S.A. 42°33N 70°53W 83 D14
Beverly Hills Calif.,
U.S.A. 34°5N 118°24W 79 L8
Beverly Hills Fla.,
U.S.A. 28°55N 82°28W 85 G13
Bevoalavo Madag. 25°13S 45°26E 57 D7
Bewas → India 23°59N 79°21E 43 H8
Bewdley Canada 44°5N 78°19W 82 B6
Bexhill U.K. 50°51N 0°29E 13 G8
Beyānlū Iran 36°0N 47°51E 44 C5
Beyneu Kazakhstan 45°18N 55°9E 19 E10
Beypazarı Turkey 40°10N 31°56E 19 F5
Beyşehir Gölü Turkey 37°41N 31°33E 44 B1
Béziers France 43°20N 3°12E 20 E5
Bezwada = Vijayawada
India 16°31N 80°39E 41 L12
Bhabua India 25°3N 83°37E 43 G10
Bhachau India 23°20N 70°16E 40 H7
Bhadar → Gujarat, India 22°17N 72°20E 42 H5
Bhadar → Gujarat, India 21°27N 69°47E 42 J3
Bhadarwah India 32°58N 75°46E 43 C6
Bhadgaon = Bhaktapur
Nepal 27°38N 85°24E 43 F11
Bhadohi India 25°25N 82°34E 43 G10
Bhadra India 29°8N 75°14E 42 E6
Bhadrakh India 21°10N 86°30E 41 J15
Bhadran India 22°19N 72°6E 42 H5
Bhadravati India 13°49N 75°40E 40 N9
Bhag Pakistan 29°2N 67°49E 42 E2
Bhagalpur India 25°10N 87°0E 43 G12
Bhagirathi → Uttarakhand,
India 30°8N 78°35E 43 D8
Bhagirathi → W. Bengal,
India 23°25N 88°23E 43 H13
Bhakkar Pakistan 31°40N 71°5E 42 D4
Bhakra Dam India 31°30N 76°45E 42 D7
Bhaktapur Nepal 27°38N 85°24E 43 F11
Bhamo Burma 24°15N 97°15E 41 G20
Bhandara India 21°5N 79°42E 40 J11
Bhanpura India 24°31N 75°44E 42 G6
Bhanrer Ra. India 23°40N 79°45E 43 H8
Bhaptiahi India 26°19N 86°44E 43 F12
Bharat = India ■ Asia 20°0N 78°0E 40 K11
Bharatpur Chhattisgarh,
India 23°44N 81°46E 43 H9
Bharatpur Raj., India 27°15N 77°30E 42 F7
Bharatpur Nepal 27°34N 84°10E 43 F11
Bharno India 23°14N 84°53E 43 H11
Bharuch India 21°47N 73°0E 40 J8
Bhatinda India 30°15N 74°57E 42 D6
Bhatpara India 22°50N 88°25E 43 H13
Bhattu India 29°36N 75°19E 42 E6
Bhaun Pakistan 32°55N 72°40E 42 C5
Bhaunagar = Bhavnagar
India 21°45N 72°10E 40 J8
Bhavnagar India 21°45N 72°10E 40 J8
Bhawari India 25°42N 73°4E 42 G5
Bhayavadar India 21°51N 70°15E 42 J4
Bhera Pakistan 32°29N 72°57E 42 C5
Bhikangaon India 21°52N 75°57E 42 J6
Bhilai = Bhilainagar-Durg
India 21°13N 81°26E 41 J12
Bhilainagar-Durg India 21°13N 81°26E 41 J12
Bhilsa = Vidisha India 23°28N 77°53E 42 H7
Bhilwara India 25°25N 74°38E 42 G6
Bhima → India 16°25N 77°17E 40 L10
Bhimbar Pakistan 32°59N 74°3E 43 C6
Bhind India 26°30N 78°46E 43 F8
Bhinga India 27°43N 81°56E 43 F9
Bhinmal India 25°0N 72°15E 42 G5
Bhisho S. Africa 32°50S 27°23E 57 E4
Bhiwandi India 19°20N 73°0E 40 K8
Bhiwani India 28°50N 76°9E 42 E7
Bhogava → India 22°26N 72°20E 42 H5
Bhola Bangla. 22°45N 90°35E 41 H17
Bholari Pakistan 25°19N 68°13E 42 G3
Bhopal India 23°20N 77°30E 42 H7
Bhubaneshwar India 20°15N 85°50E 41 J14
Bhuj India 23°15N 69°49E 42 H3
Bhumiphol Res. Thailand 17°20N 98°40E 38 D2
Bhusawal India 21°3N 75°46E 40 J9
Bhutan ■ Asia 27°25N 90°30E 41 F17
Biafra, B. of = Bonny, Bight of
Africa 3°30N 9°20E 52 D1
Biak Indonesia 1°10S 136°6E 37 E9
Biała Podlaska Poland 52°4N 23°6E 17 B12
Białogard Poland 54°2N 15°58E 16 A8
Białystok Poland 53°10N 23°10E 17 B12
Biaora India 23°56N 76°56E 42 H7
Bīārjmand Iran 36°6N 55°53E 45 B7
Biaro Indonesia 2°5N 125°26E 37 D7
Biarritz France 43°29N 1°33W 20 E3
Bias Indonesia 8°24S 115°36E 37 J18
Bibai Japan 43°19N 141°52E 30 C10
Bibby I. Canada 61°55N 93°0W 71 A10
Biberach Germany 48°5N 9°47E 16 D5
Bibungwa
Dem. Rep. of the Congo 2°40S 28°15E 54 C2
Bicester U.K. 51°54N 1°9W 13 F6
Bicheno Australia 41°52S 148°18E 63 G4
Bichia India 22°27N 80°42E 43 H9
Bickerton I. Australia 13°45S 136°10E 62 A2
Bida Nigeria 9°3N 5°58E 50 G7
Bidar India 17°55N 77°35E 40 L10
Biddeford U.S.A. 43°30N 70°28W 81 D18
Bideford U.K. 51°1N 4°13W 13 F3
Bideford Bay U.K. 51°5N 4°20W 13 F3
Bidhuna India 26°49N 79°31E 43 F8
Bīdokht Iran 34°20N 58°46E 45 C8
Bidor Malaysia 4°6N 101°15E 39 K3
Bidyadanga Australia 18°45S 121°43E 60 C3
Bié, Planalto de Angola 12°0S 16°0E 53 G3
Bieber U.S.A. 41°7N 121°8W 76 F3
Biel Switz. 47°8N 7°14E 20 C7
Bielefeld Germany 52°1N 8°33E 16 B5
Biella Italy 45°34N 8°3E 20 D8
Bielsk Podlaski Poland 52°47N 23°12E 17 B12
Bielsko-Biała Poland 49°50N 19°2E 17 D10
Bien Hoa Vietnam 10°57N 106°49E 39 G6
Bienne = Biel Switz. 47°8N 7°14E 20 C7
Bienville, L. Canada 55°5N 72°40W 72 A5
Biesiesfontein S. Africa 30°57S 17°58E 56 E2
Big → Canada 54°50N 58°55W 73 B8
Big B. Canada 55°43N 60°35W 73 A7
Big Bear City U.S.A. 34°16N 116°51W 79 L10
Big Bear Lake U.S.A. 34°15N 116°56W 79 L10
Big Belt Mts. U.S.A. 46°30N 111°25W 76 C8
Big Bend Swaziland 26°50S 31°58E 57 D5
Big Bend △ U.S.A. 29°20N 103°5W 84 G3
Big Black → U.S.A. 32°3N 91°4W 85 E9
Big Blue → U.S.A. 39°35N 96°34W 80 F5
Big Creek U.S.A. 37°11N 119°14W 78 H7
Big Cypress ⌂ U.S.A. 26°0N 81°10W 85 H14
Big Desert Australia 35°45S 141°10E 63 F3
Big Falls U.S.A. 48°12N 93°48W 80 A7
Big Fork → U.S.A. 48°31N 93°43W 80 A7
Big Horn Mts. = Bighorn Mts.
U.S.A. 44°25N 107°0W 76 D10
Big I. Canada 61°7N 116°45W 70 A5
Big Lake U.S.A. 31°12N 101°28W 84 F4
Big Moose U.S.A. 43°49N 74°58W 83 C10
Big Muddy Cr. →
U.S.A. 48°8N 104°36W 76 B11
Big Pine U.S.A. 37°10N 118°17W 78 H8
Big Piney U.S.A. 42°32N 110°7W 76 E8
Big Quill L. Canada 51°55N 104°13W 71 C8
Big Rapids U.S.A. 43°42N 85°29W 81 D11
Big Rideau L. Canada 44°40N 76°15W 83 B8
Big River Canada 53°50N 107°0W 71 C7
Big Run U.S.A. 40°57N 78°55W 82 F6
Big Sable Pt. U.S.A. 44°3N 86°1W 80 C10
Big Salmon → Canada 61°52N 134°55W 70 A2
Big Sand L. Canada 57°45N 99°45W 71 B9
Big Sandy U.S.A. 48°11N 110°7W 76 B8
Big Sandy → U.S.A. 38°25N 82°36W 81 F12
Big Sandy Cr. = Sandy Cr. →
U.S.A. 41°51N 109°47W 76 F9
Big Sandy Cr. →
U.S.A. 38°7N 102°29W 76 G12
Big Sioux → U.S.A. 42°29N 96°27W 80 D5
Big South Fork ⌂
U.S.A. 36°27N 84°47W 85 C12
Big Spring U.S.A. 32°15N 101°28W 84 E4
Big Stone City U.S.A. 45°18N 96°28W 80 C5

Big Stone Gap U.S.A. 36°52N 82°47W 81 G12
Big Stone L. U.S.A. 45°18N 96°27W 80 C5
Big Sur U.S.A. 36°15N 121°48W 78 J5
Big Timber U.S.A. 45°50N 109°57W 76 D9
Big Trout L. Canada 53°40N 90°0W 72 B2
Big Trout Lake Canada 53°45N 90°0W 72 B2
Biğa Turkey 40°13N 27°14E 23 D12
Bigadiç Turkey 39°22N 28°7E 23 E13
Biggar Canada 52°4N 108°0W 71 C7
Biggar U.K. 55°38N 3°32W 11 F5
Bigge I. Australia 14°35S 125°10E 60 B4
Biggenden Australia 25°31S 152°4E 63 D5
Biggleswade U.K. 52°5N 0°14W 13 E7
Biggs U.S.A. 39°25N 121°43W 78 F5
Bighorn U.S.A. 46°10N 107°27W 76 C10
Bighorn → U.S.A. 46°10N 107°28W 76 C10
Bighorn Canyon ⌓ U.S.A. 45°10N 108°0W 76 D10
Bighorn L. U.S.A. 44°55N 108°15W 76 D9
Bighorn Mts. U.S.A. 44°25N 107°0W 76 D10
Bigstone L. Canada 53°42N 95°44W 71 C9
Bigwa Tanzania 7°10S 39°10E 54 D4
Bihać Bos.-H. 44°49N 15°57E 16 F8
Bihar India 25°5N 85°40E 43 G11
Bihar □ India 25°0N 86°0E 43 G12
Biharamulo Tanzania 2°25S 31°25E 54 C3
Biharamulo ⌓ Tanzania 2°24S 31°26E 54 C3
Bihariganj India 25°44N 86°59E 43 G12
Bihor, Munţii Romania 46°29N 22°47E 17 E12
Bijagós, Arquipélago dos Guinea-Biss. 11°15N 16°10W 50 F2
Bijaipur India 26°2N 77°20E 42 F7
Bijapur Chhattisgarh, India 18°50N 80°50E 41 K12
Bijapur Karnataka, India 16°50N 75°55E 40 L9
Bījār Iran 35°52N 47°35E 44 C5
Bijawar India 24°38N 79°30E 43 G8
Bijeljina Bos.-H. 44°46N 19°14E 23 B8
Bijnor India 29°27N 78°11E 42 E8
Bikaner India 28°2N 73°18E 42 E5
Bikapur India 26°30N 82°7E 43 F10
Bikeqi China 40°43N 111°20E 34 D6
Bikfayyā Lebanon 33°55N 35°41E 46 B4
Bikin Russia 46°50N 134°20E 30 A7
Bikin → Russia 46°51N 134°2E 30 A7
Bikini Atoll Marshall Is. 12°0N 167°30E 64 F8
Bikita Zimbabwe 20°6S 31°41E 57 C5
Bīkkū Bīttī Libya 22°0N 19°12E 51 D9
Bila Tserkva Ukraine 49°45N 30°10E 17 D16
Bilara India 26°14N 73°53E 42 F5
Bilaspur Chhattisgarh, India 22°2N 82°15E 43 H10
Bilaspur Punjab, India 31°19N 76°50E 42 D7
Bilauk Taungdan Thailand 13°0N 99°0E 38 F2
Bilbao Spain 43°16N 2°56W 21 A4
Bilbo = Bilbao Spain 43°16N 2°56W 21 A4
Bíldudalur Iceland 65°41N 23°36W 8 D2
Bílé Karpaty Europe 49°5N 18°0E 17 D9
Bilecik Turkey 40°5N 30°5E 19 F5
Bilgram India 27°11N 80°2E 43 F9
Bilhaur India 26°51N 80°5E 43 F9
Bilhorod-Dnistrovskyy Ukraine 46°11N 30°23E 19 E5
Bilibino Russia 68°3N 166°20E 29 C17
Bilibiza Mozam. 12°30S 40°20E 55 E5
Billabong Roadhouse Australia 27°25S 115°49E 61 E2
Billiluna Australia 19°37S 127°41E 60 C4
Billings U.S.A. 45°47N 108°30W 76 D9
Billiton Is. = Belitung Indonesia 3°10S 107°50E 36 E3
Bilma Niger 18°50N 13°30E 51 E8
Biloela Australia 24°24S 150°31E 62 C5
Biloxi U.S.A. 30°24N 88°53W 85 F10
Bilpa Morea Claypan Australia 25°0S 140°0E 62 D3
Biltine Chad 14°40N 20°50E 51 F10
Bima Indonesia 8°22S 118°49E 37 F5
Bimbo C.A.R. 4°15N 18°33E 52 D3
Bimini Is. Bahamas 25°42N 79°25W 88 A4
Bin Xian Heilongjiang, China 45°42N 127°32E 35 B14
Bin Xian Shaanxi, China 35°2N 108°4E 34 G5
Bina-Etawah India 24°13N 78°14E 42 G8
Binalbagan Phil. 10°12N 122°50E 37 B6
Binalong Australia 34°40S 148°39E 63 E4
Bīnālūd, Kūh-e Iran 36°30N 58°30E 45 B8
Binatang = Bintangau Malaysia 2°10N 111°40E 36 D4
Binche Belgium 50°26N 4°10E 15 D4
Bindki India 26°2N 80°36E 43 F9
Bindura Zimbabwe 17°18S 31°18E 55 F3
Bingara Australia 29°52S 150°36E 63 D5
Bingham U.S.A. 45°3N 69°53W 81 C19
Binghamton U.S.A. 42°6N 75°55W 83 D9
Bingöl Turkey 38°53N 40°29E 44 B4
Binh Dinh = An Nhon Vietnam 13°55N 109°7E 38 F7
Binh Khe Vietnam 13°57N 108°51E 38 F7
Binh Son Vietnam 15°20N 108°40E 38 E7
Binhai China 34°2N 119°49E 35 G10
Binisatua Spain 39°50N 4°11E 24 B11
Binissalem Spain 39°41N 2°50E 24 B9
Binjai Indonesia 3°20N 98°30E 36 D3
Binnaway Australia 31°28S 149°24E 63 E4
Binongko Indonesia 5°57S 124°2E 37 F6
Binscarth Canada 50°37N 101°17W 71 C8
Bintan Indonesia 1°0N 104°0E 36 D2
Bintangau Malaysia 2°10N 111°40E 36 D4
Bintulu Malaysia 3°10N 113°0E 36 D4
Bintuni Indonesia 2°7S 133°32E 37 E8
Binzert = Bizerte Tunisia 37°15N 9°50E 51 A7
Binzhou China 37°20N 118°2E 35 F10
Bío Bío □ Chile 37°35S 72°0W 94 D1
Bíobío → Chile 36°49S 73°10W 94 D1
Bioko Eq. Guin. 3°30N 8°40E 52 D1
Bir India 19°4N 75°46E 40 K9
Bîr Abu Muḥammad Egypt 29°44N 34°14E 46 F3
Bi'r ad Dabbāghāt Jordan 30°26N 35°32E 46 E4
Bi'r al Butayyihāt Jordan 29°47N 35°20E 46 F4
Bi'r al Mārī Jordan 30°4N 35°33E 46 E4
Bi'r al Qattār Jordan 29°47N 35°32E 46 F4
Bîr Atrun Sudan 18°15N 26°40E 51 E11
Bîr Beida Egypt 30°25N 34°29E 46 E3
Bîr el 'Abd Egypt 31°2N 33°0E 46 D2
Bîr el Biarât Egypt 29°30N 34°43E 46 F3
Bîr el Duweidar Egypt 30°56N 32°32E 46 E1
Bîr el Garârât Egypt 31°3N 33°34E 46 D2
Bîr el Heisi Egypt 29°22N 34°36E 46 F3
Bîr el Jafir Egypt 30°50N 32°41E 46 E1
Bîr el Mâlḥi Egypt 30°38N 33°19E 46 E2
Bîr el Thamâda Egypt 30°12N 33°27E 46 E2
Bîr Gebeil Ḥiṣn Egypt 30°2N 33°18E 46 E2
Bi'r Ghadīr Syria 34°6N 37°3E 46 A6
Bîr Ḥasana Egypt 30°29N 33°46E 46 E2
Bîr Kaseiba Egypt 31°0N 33°17E 46 E2
Bîr Lahfân Egypt 31°0N 33°51E 46 E2
Bîr Madkûr Egypt 30°44N 32°33E 46 E1
Bîr Mogreïn Mauritania 25°10N 11°25W 50 C3
Bi'r Muṭribah Kuwait 29°54N 47°17E 44 D5
Bîr Qaṭia Egypt 30°58N 32°45E 46 E1
Bîr Shalatein Egypt 23°5N 35°25E 51 D13
Birāk Libya 27°31N 14°20E 51 C8
Biratnagar Nepal 26°27N 87°17E 43 F12
Birawa Dem. Rep. of the Congo 2°20S 28°48E 54 C2
Birch → Canada 58°28N 112°17W 70 B6
Birch Hills Canada 52°59N 105°25W 71 C7
Birch I. Canada 52°26N 99°54W 71 C9
Birch L. N.W.T., Canada 62°4N 116°33W 70 A5
Birch L. Ont., Canada 51°23N 92°18W 72 B1
Birch Mts. Canada 57°30N 113°10W 70 B6
Birch River Canada 52°24N 101°6W 71 C8
Birchip Australia 35°56S 142°55E 63 F3
Bird Canada 56°30N 94°13W 71 B10
Bird I. = Aves, I. de W. Indies 15°45N 63°55W 89 C7
Bird I. S. Georgia 54°0S 38°3W 96 G9
Birds Creek Canada 45°6N 77°52W 82 A7
Birdsville Australia 25°51S 139°20E 62 D2
Birdum Cr. → Australia 15°14S 133°0E 60 C5
Birecik Turkey 37°2N 38°0E 44 B3
Birein Israel 30°50N 34°28E 46 E3
Bireuen Indonesia 5°14N 96°39E 36 C1
Birigüi Brazil 21°18S 50°16W 95 A5
Bīrjand Iran 32°53N 59°13E 45 C8
Birkenhead U.K. 53°23N 3°2W 12 D4
Bîrlad = Bârlad Romania 46°15N 27°38E 17 E14
Birmingham U.K. 52°29N 1°52W 13 E6
Birmingham U.S.A. 33°31N 86°48W 85 E11
Birmingham Int. ✕ (BHX) U.K. 52°26N 1°45W 13 E6
Birmitrapur India 22°24N 84°46E 41 H14
Birni Nkonni Niger 13°55N 5°15E 50 F7
Birnin Kebbi Nigeria 12°32N 4°12E 50 F6
Birobidzhan Russia 48°50N 132°50E 29 E14
Birr Ireland 53°6N 7°54W 10 C4
Birrie → Australia 29°43S 146°37E 63 D4
Birsilpur India 28°11N 72°15E 42 E5
Birsk Russia 55°25N 55°30E 18 C10
Birtle Canada 50°30N 101°5W 71 C8
Birur India 13°30N 75°55E 40 N9
Biržai Lithuania 56°11N 24°45E 9 H21
Birzebbugga Malta 35°50N 14°32E 25 D2
Bisa Indonesia 1°15S 127°28E 37 E7
Bisalpur India 28°14N 79°48E 43 E8
Bisbee U.S.A. 31°27N 109°55W 77 L9
Biscarrosse France 44°22N 1°20W 20 D3
Biscay, B. of Atl. Oc. 45°0N 2°0W 20 D1
Biscayne B. U.S.A. 25°40N 80°12W 85 J14
Biscoe Is. Antarctica 66°0S 67°0W 5 C17
Biscotasing Canada 47°18N 82°9W 72 C3
Bishkek Kyrgyzstan 42°54N 74°46E 28 E8
Bishnupur India 23°8N 87°20E 43 H12
Bisho = Bhisho S. Africa 32°50S 27°23E 57 E4
Bishop Calif., U.S.A. 37°22N 118°24W 78 H8
Bishop Tex., U.S.A. 27°35N 97°48W 84 H6
Bishop Auckland U.K. 54°39N 1°40W 12 C6
Bishop's Falls Canada 49°2N 55°30W 73 C8
Bishop's Stortford U.K. 51°52N 0°10E 13 F8
Bisina, L. Uganda 1°38N 33°56E 54 B3
Biskra Algeria 34°50N 5°44E 50 B7
Bismarck U.S.A. 46°48N 100°47W 80 B3
Bismarck Arch. Papua N. G. 2°30S 150°0E 58 B7
Biso Uganda 1°44N 31°26E 54 B3
Bison U.S.A. 45°31N 102°28W 80 C2
Bīsotūn Iran 34°23N 47°26E 44 C5
Bissagos = Bijagós, Arquipélago dos Guinea-Biss. 11°15N 16°10W 50 F2
Bissau Guinea-Biss. 11°45N 15°45W 50 F2
Bistcho L. Canada 59°45N 118°50W 70 B5
Bistriţa Romania 47°9N 24°35E 17 E13
Bistriţa → Romania 46°30N 26°57E 17 E14
Biswan India 27°29N 81°2E 43 F9
Bitam Gabon 2°5N 11°25E 52 D2
Bitkine Chad 11°59N 18°13E 51 F9
Bitlis Turkey 38°20N 42°3E 44 B4
Bitola Macedonia 41°1N 21°20E 23 D9
Bitolj = Bitola Macedonia 41°1N 21°20E 23 D9
Bitter Creek U.S.A. 41°33N 108°33W 76 F9
Bitterfontein S. Africa 31°1S 18°32E 56 E2
Bitterroot → U.S.A. 46°52N 114°7W 76 C6
Bitterroot Range U.S.A. 46°0N 114°20W 76 D6
Bitterwater U.S.A. 36°23N 121°0W 78 J6
Biu Nigeria 10°40N 12°3E 51 F8
Biwa-Ko Japan 35°15N 136°10E 31 G8
Biwabik U.S.A. 47°32N 92°21W 80 B7
Bixby U.S.A. 35°57N 95°53W 84 D7
Biyang China 32°38N 113°21E 34 H7
Biysk Russia 52°40N 85°0E 28 D9
Bizana S. Africa 30°50S 29°52E 57 E4
Bizen Japan 34°43N 134°8E 31 G7
Bizerte Tunisia 37°15N 9°50E 51 A7
Bjargtangar Iceland 65°30N 24°30W 8 D1
Bjelovar Croatia 45°56N 16°49E 22 B7
Björneborg = Pori Finland 61°29N 21°48E 8 F19
Bjørnevatn Norway 69°40N 30°0E 8 B24
Bjørnøya Arctic 74°30N 19°0E 4 B8
Black = Da → Vietnam 21°15N 105°20E 38 B5
Black → Canada 44°42N 79°19W 82 B5
Black → Ariz., U.S.A. 33°44N 110°13W 77 K8
Black → Ark., U.S.A. 35°38N 91°20W 84 D9
Black → La., U.S.A. 31°16N 91°50W 84 F9
Black → Mich., U.S.A. 42°59N 82°27W 82 D2
Black → N.Y., U.S.A. 43°59N 76°4W 83 C8
Black → Wis., U.S.A. 43°57N 91°22W 80 D8
Black Bay Pen. Canada 48°38N 88°21W 72 C2
Black Birch L. Canada 56°53N 107°45W 71 B7
Black Braes △ Australia 19°10S 144°10E 62 B3
Black Canyon of the Gunnison ⌓ U.S.A. 38°40N 107°35W 76 G10
Black Diamond Canada 50°45N 114°14W 70 C6
Black Duck → Canada 56°51N 89°2W 72 A2
Black Forest = Schwarzwald Germany 48°30N 8°20E 16 D5
Black Forest U.S.A. 39°0N 104°43W 76 G11
Black Hd. Ireland 53°9N 9°16W 10 C2
Black Hills U.S.A. 44°0N 103°45W 80 D2
Black I. Canada 51°12N 96°30W 71 C9
Black L. Canada 59°12N 105°15W 71 B7
Black L. Mich., U.S.A. 45°28N 84°16W 81 C11
Black L. N.Y., U.S.A. 44°31N 75°36W 83 B9
Black Lake Canada 59°11N 105°20W 71 B7
Black Mesa U.S.A. 36°58N 102°58W 84 C3
Black Mt. = Mynydd Du U.K. 51°52N 3°50W 13 F4
Black Mts. U.K. 51°55N 3°7W 13 F4
Black Range U.S.A. 33°15N 107°50W 77 K10
Black River Jamaica 18°0N 77°50W 88 a
Black River U.S.A. 44°0N 75°47W 83 C9
Black River Falls U.S.A. 44°18N 90°51W 80 C8
Black Rock Barbados 13°7N 59°37W 89 g
Black Rock Desert U.S.A. 41°10N 118°50W 76 F4
Black Sea Eurasia 43°30N 35°0E 19 F6
Black Tickle Canada 53°28N 55°45W 73 B8
Black Volta → Africa 8°41N 1°33W 50 G5
Black Warrior → U.S.A. 32°32N 87°51W 85 E11
Blackall Australia 24°25S 145°45E 62 C4
Blackball N.Z. 42°22S 171°26E 59 E3
Blackbull Australia 17°55S 141°45E 62 B3
Blackburn U.K. 53°45N 2°29W 12 D5
Blackburn with Darwen □ U.K. 53°45N 2°29W 12 D5
Blackdown Tableland △ Australia 23°52S 149°8E 62 C4
Blackfoot U.S.A. 43°11N 112°21W 76 E7
Blackfoot → U.S.A. 46°52N 113°53W 76 C7
Blackfoot Res. U.S.A. 42°55N 111°39W 76 E8
Blackpool U.K. 53°49N 3°3W 12 D4
Blackpool □ U.K. 53°49N 3°3W 12 D4
Blackriver U.S.A. 44°46N 83°17W 82 B1
Blacks Harbour Canada 45°3N 66°49W 73 C6
Blacksburg U.S.A. 37°14N 80°25W 81 G13
Blacksod B. Ireland 54°6N 10°0W 10 B1
Blackstairs Mt. Ireland 52°33N 6°48W 10 D5
Blackstone U.S.A. 37°5N 78°0W 81 G14
Blackstone Ra. Australia 26°0S 128°30E 61 E4
Blacktown Australia 33°48S 150°55E 63 E5
Blackwater = West Road → Canada 53°18N 122°53W 70 C4
Blackwater Australia 23°35S 148°53E 62 C4
Blackwater → Meath, Ireland 53°39N 6°41W 10 C4
Blackwater → Waterford, Ireland 52°4N 7°52W 10 D4
Blackwater → U.K. 54°31N 6°35W 10 B5
Blackwell U.S.A. 36°48N 97°17W 84 C6
Blackwells Corner U.S.A. 35°37N 119°47W 79 K7
Bladensburg △ Australia 22°30S 142°59E 62 C3
Blaenau Ffestiniog U.K. 53°0N 3°56W 12 E4
Blaenau Gwent □ U.K. 51°48N 3°12W 13 F4
Blagodarnoye = Blagodarnyy Russia 45°7N 43°37E 19 E7
Blagodarnyy Russia 45°7N 43°37E 19 E7
Blagoevgrad Bulgaria 42°2N 23°5E 23 C10
Blagoveshchensk Russia 50°20N 127°30E 29 D13
Blahkiuh Indonesia 8°31S 115°12E 37 J18
Blain U.S.A. 40°20N 77°31W 82 F7
Blaine Minn., U.S.A. 45°10N 93°13W 80 C7
Blaine Wash., U.S.A. 48°59N 122°45W 78 B4
Blaine Lake Canada 52°51N 106°52W 71 C7
Blair U.S.A. 41°33N 96°8W 80 E5
Blair Athol Australia 22°42S 147°31E 62 C4
Blair Atholl U.K. 56°46N 3°50W 11 E5
Blairgowrie U.K. 56°35N 3°21W 11 E5
Blairsden U.S.A. 39°47N 120°37W 78 F6
Blairsville U.S.A. 40°26N 79°16W 82 F5
Blakang Mati, Pulau Singapore 1°15N 103°50E 39 d
Blake Pt. U.S.A. 48°11N 88°25W 80 A9
Blakely Ga., U.S.A. 31°23N 84°56W 85 F12
Blakely Pa., U.S.A. 41°28N 75°37W 83 E9
Blanc, C. Spain 39°21N 2°51E 24 B9
Blanc, Mont Europe 45°48N 6°50E 20 D7
Blanca, B. Argentina 39°10S 61°30W 96 D4
Blanca, Cord. Peru 9°10S 77°35W 92 E3
Blanca Peak U.S.A. 37°35N 105°29W 77 H11
Blanche, C. Australia 33°1S 134°9E 63 E1
Blanche, L. S. Austral., Australia 29°15S 139°40E 63 D2
Blanche, L. W. Austral., Australia 22°25S 123°17E 60 D3
Blanchisseuse Trin. & Tob. 10°48N 61°18W 93 K15
Blanco S. Africa 33°55S 22°23E 56 E3
Blanco U.S.A. 30°6N 98°25W 84 F5
Blanco → Argentina 30°20S 68°42W 94 C2
Blanco, C. Costa Rica 9°34N 85°8W 88 E2
Blanco, C. U.S.A. 42°51N 124°34W 76 E1
Blanda → Iceland 65°37N 20°9W 8 D3
Blandford Forum U.K. 50°51N 2°9W 13 G5
Blanding U.S.A. 37°37N 109°29W 77 H9
Blanes Spain 41°40N 2°48E 21 B7
Blankenberge Belgium 51°20N 3°9E 15 C3
Blanquilla Venezuela 11°51N 64°37W 89 D7
Blanquillo Uruguay 32°53S 55°37W 95 C4
Blantyre Malawi 15°45S 35°0E 55 F4
Blarney Ireland 51°56N 8°33W 10 E3
Blasdell U.S.A. 42°48N 78°50W 82 D6
Blåvands Huk Denmark 55°33N 8°4E 9 J13
Blaydon U.K. 54°58N 1°42W 12 C6
Blayney Australia 33°32S 149°14E 63 E4
Blaze, Pt. Australia 12°56S 130°11E 60 B5
Blekinge Sweden 56°25N 15°20E 9 H16
Blenheim Canada 42°20N 82°0W 82 D3
Blenheim N.Z. 41°38S 173°57E 59 D4
Bletchley U.K. 51°59N 0°44W 13 F7
Blida Algeria 36°30N 2°49E 50 A6
Bligh Sound N.Z. 44°47S 167°32E 59 F1
Bligh Water Fiji 17°0S 178°0E 59 a
Blind River Canada 46°10N 82°58W 72 C3
Bliss Idaho, U.S.A. 42°56N 114°57W 76 E6
Bliss N.Y., U.S.A. 42°34N 78°15W 82 D6
Blissfield U.S.A. 40°24N 81°58W 82 F3
Blitar Indonesia 8°5S 112°11E 37 H15
Block I. U.S.A. 41°11N 71°35W 83 E13
Block Island Sd. U.S.A. 41°15N 71°40W 83 E13
Bloemfontein S. Africa 29°6S 26°7E 56 D4
Bloemhof S. Africa 27°38S 25°32E 56 D4
Blois France 47°35N 1°20E 20 C4
Blönduós Iceland 65°40N 20°12W 8 D3
Blongas Indonesia 8°53S 116°2E 37 K19
Bloodvein → Canada 51°47N 96°43W 71 C9
Bloody Foreland Ireland 55°10N 8°17W 10 A3
Bloomer U.S.A. 45°6N 91°29W 80 C8
Bloomfield Canada 43°59N 77°14W 82 C7
Bloomfield Iowa, U.S.A. 40°45N 92°25W 80 E7
Bloomfield N. Mex., U.S.A. 36°43N 107°59W 77 H10
Bloomfield Nebr., U.S.A. 42°36N 97°39W 80 D5
Bloomington Ill., U.S.A. 40°28N 89°0W 80 E9
Bloomington Ind., U.S.A. 39°10N 86°32W 80 F10
Bloomington Minn., U.S.A. 44°50N 93°17W 80 C7
Bloomsburg U.S.A. 41°0N 76°27W 83 F8
Bloomsbury Australia 20°48S 148°38E 62 J6
Blora Indonesia 6°57S 111°25E 37 G14
Blossburg U.S.A. 41°41N 77°4W 82 E7
Blouberg S. Africa 23°8S 28°59E 57 C4
Blountstown U.S.A. 30°27N 85°3W 85 F12
Blue Earth U.S.A. 43°38N 94°6W 80 D6
Blue Hole △ Belize 17°24N 88°30W 88 C2
Blue Lagoon △ Zambia 15°28S 27°26E 55 F2
Blue Mesa Res. U.S.A. 38°28N 107°20W 76 G10
Blue Mountain Lake U.S.A. 43°51N 74°27W 83 C10
Blue Mountain Pk. Jamaica 18°3N 76°36W 88 a
Blue Mt. U.S.A. 40°30N 76°30W 83 F8
Blue Mts. Jamaica 18°3N 76°36W 88 a
Blue Mts. Maine, U.S.A. 44°50N 70°35W 83 B14
Blue Mts. Oreg., U.S.A. 45°0N 118°20W 76 D4
Blue Mud B. Australia 13°30S 136°0E 62 A2
Blue Nile = Nîl el Azraq → Sudan 15°38N 32°31E 51 E12
Blue Rapids U.S.A. 39°41N 96°39W 80 F5
Blue Ridge U.S.A. 36°40N 80°50W 81 G13
Blue River Canada 52°6N 119°18W 70 C5
Bluefield U.S.A. 37°15N 81°17W 81 G13
Bluefields Nic. 12°20N 83°50W 88 D3
Bluevale Canada 43°51N 81°15W 82 C3
Bluff Australia 23°35S 149°4E 62 C4
Bluff N.Z. 46°37S 168°20E 59 G2
Bluff U.S.A. 37°17N 109°33W 77 H9
Bluff Knoll Australia 34°24S 118°15E 61 F2
Bluff Pt. Australia 27°50S 114°5E 61 E1
Bluffton U.S.A. 40°44N 85°11W 81 E11
Blumenau Brazil 27°0S 49°0W 95 B6
Blunt U.S.A. 44°31N 99°59W 80 C4
Bly U.S.A. 42°24N 121°3W 76 E3
Blyde River Canyon ⌓ S. Africa 24°37S 31°2E 57 C5
Blyth Canada 43°44N 81°26W 82 C3
Blyth U.K. 55°8N 1°31W 12 B6
Blythe U.S.A. 33°37N 114°36W 79 M12
Blytheville U.S.A. 35°56N 89°55W 85 D10
Bo S. Leone 7°55N 11°50W 50 G3
Bo Duc Vietnam 11°58N 106°50E 39 G6
Bo Hai China 39°0N 119°0E 35 E10
Bo Xian = Bozhou China 33°55N 115°41E 34 H8
Boa Vista Brazil 2°48N 60°30W 92 C6
Boa Vista C. Verde Is. 16°0N 22°49W 50 b
Boaco Nic. 12°29N 85°35W 88 D2
Bo'ai China 35°10N 113°3E 34 G7
Boalsburg U.S.A. 40°47N 77°49W 82 F7
Boane Mozam. 26°6S 32°19E 57 D5
Boardman U.S.A. 41°2N 80°40W 82 E4
Bobadah Australia 32°19S 146°41E 63 E4
Bobbili India 18°35N 83°30E 41 K13
Bobcaygeon Canada 44°33N 78°33W 82 B6
Bobo-Dioulasso Burkina Faso 11°8N 4°13W 50 F5
Bóbr → Poland 52°4N 15°4E 16 B8
Bobraomby, Tanjon' i Madag. 12°40S 49°10E 57 A8
Bobruysk = Babruysk Belarus 53°10N 29°15E 17 B15
Boby, Pic Madag. 22°12S 46°55E 53 J
Boca del Río Mexico 19°5N 96°4W 87 D
Boca do Acre Brazil 8°50S 67°27W 92
Boca Raton U.S.A. 26°21N 80°5W 85 H1
Bocas del Dragón Venezuela 11°0N 61°50W 93 K1
Bocas del Toro Panama 9°15N 82°20W 88
Bochnia Poland 49°58N 20°27E 17 D1
Bochum Germany 51°28N 7°13E 16 C
Bocoyna Mexico 27°52N 107°35W 86 B
Bodaybo Russia 57°50N 114°0E 29 D1
Boddam U.K. 59°56N 1°17W 11 B
Boddington Australia 32°50S 116°30E 61
Bodega Bay U.S.A. 38°20N 123°3W 78 G
Boden Sweden 65°50N 21°42E 8 D1
Bodensee Europe 47°35N 9°25E 20 C
Bodhan India 18°40N 77°44E 40 K1
Bodmin U.K. 50°28N 4°43W 13 G
Bodmin Moor U.K. 50°33N 4°36W 13 G
Bodø Norway 67°17N 14°24E 8 C1
Bodrog → Hungary 48°11N 21°22E 17 D1
Bodrum Turkey 37°3N 27°30E 23 F1
Boende Dem. Rep. of the Congo 0°24S 21°12E 52
Boerne U.S.A. 29°47N 98°44W 84
Boesmans → S. Africa 33°42S 26°39E 56
Bogalusa U.S.A. 30°47N 89°52W 85 F
Bogan → Australia 30°20S 146°55E 63
Bogan Gate Australia 33°7S 147°49E 63
Bogantungan Australia 23°41S 147°17E 62
Bogata U.S.A. 33°28N 95°13W 84
Bogda Shan China 43°35N 89°40E 32
Boggabilla Australia 28°36S 150°24E 63
Boggabri Australia 30°45S 150°5E 63
Boggeragh Mts. Ireland 52°2N 8°55W 10
Boglan = Solhan Turkey 38°57N 41°3E 44
Bognor Regis U.K. 50°47N 0°40W 13
Bogo Phil. 11°3N 124°0E 37
Bogong, Mt. Australia 36°47S 147°17E 63
Bogor Indonesia 6°36S 106°48E 37 G
Bogotá Colombia 4°34N 74°0W 92
Bogotol Russia 56°15N 89°50E 28
Bogra Bangla. 24°51N 89°22E 41 G
Boguchany Russia 58°40N 97°30E 29 D
Bogué Mauritania 16°45N 14°10W 50
Bohemian Forest = Böhmerwald Germany 49°8N 13°14E 16
Böhmerwald Germany 49°8N 13°14E 16
Bohol □ Phil. 9°50N 124°10E 37
Bohol Sea Phil. 9°0N 124°0E 37
Bohorok Indonesia 3°30N 98°12E 39
Bohuslän Sweden 58°25N 12°0E 9 G
Boi, Pta. do Brazil 23°55S 45°15W 95
Boiaçu Brazil 0°27S 61°46W 92
Boileau, C. Australia 17°40S 122°7E 60
Boise U.S.A. 43°37N 116°13W 76
Boise City U.S.A. 36°44N 102°31W 84
Boissevain Canada 49°15N 100°5W 71
Bojador, C. W. Sahara 26°0N 14°30W 50
Bojana → Albania 41°52N 19°22E 23
Bojnūrd Iran 37°30N 57°20E 45
Bojonegoro Indonesia 7°11S 111°54E 37 G
Bokaro India 23°46N 85°55E 43 H
Boké Guinea 10°56N 14°17W 50
Bokhara → Australia 29°55S 146°42E 63
Boknafjorden Norway 59°14N 5°40E 9 G
Bokor △ Cambodia 10°50N 104°1E 39
Bokora ⌓ Uganda 2°12N 31°32E 54
Bokoro Chad 12°25N 17°14E 51
Bokpyin Burma 11°18N 98°42E 39
Bokungu Dem. Rep. of the Congo 0°35S 22°50E 52
Bolan → Pakistan 28°38N 67°42E 42
Bolan Pass Pakistan 29°50N 67°20E 40
Bolaños → Mexico 21°12N 104°5W 86
Bolbec France 49°30N 0°30E 20
Boldājī Iran 31°56N 51°3E 45
Bole China 45°11N 81°37E 32
Bolekhiv Ukraine 49°0N 23°57E 17 D
Bolesławiec Poland 51°17N 15°37E 16
Bolgatanga Ghana 10°44N 0°53W 50
Bolgrad = Bolhrad Ukraine 45°40N 28°32E 17
Bolhrad Ukraine 45°40N 28°32E 17
Bolivar Mo., U.S.A. 37°37N 93°25W 80
Bolivar N.Y., U.S.A. 42°4N 78°10W 82
Bolivar Tenn., U.S.A. 35°12N 89°0W 85 D
Bolivia ■ S. Amer. 17°6S 64°0W 92
Bolivian Plateau = Altiplano Bolivia 17°0S 68°0W 92
Bollnäs Sweden 61°21N 16°24E 8
Bollon Australia 28°2S 147°29E 63
Bolmen Sweden 56°55N 13°40E 9
Bolobo Dem. Rep. of the Congo 2°6S 16°20E 52
Bologna Italy 44°29N 11°20E 22
Bologoye Russia 57°55N 34°5E 18
Bolomba Dem. Rep. of the Congo 0°35N 19°0E 52
Bolonchén Mexico 20°1N 89°45W 87
Boloven, Cao Nguyen Laos 15°10N 106°30E 38
Bolpur India 23°40N 87°45E 43
Bolsena, L. di Italy 42°36N 11°56E 22
Bolshevik, Ostrov Russia 78°30N 102°0E 29
Bolshoy Anyuy → Russia 68°30N 160°49E 29
Bolshoy Begichev, Ostrov Russia 74°20N 112°30E 29
Bolshoy Kamen Russia 43°7N 132°19E 30
Bolshoy Kavkas = Caucasus Mountains Eurasia 42°50N 44°0E 19
Bolshoy Lyakhovskiy, Ostrov Russia 73°35N 142°0E 29
Bolshoy Tyuters, Ostrov Russia 59°51N 27°13E 9

sward Neths. 53°3N 5°32E 15 A5
t Head U.K. 50°12N 3°48W 13 G4
ton Canada 43°54N 79°45W 82 C5
ton U.K. 53°35N 2°26W 12 D5
ton Landing U.S.A. 43°32N 73°35W 83 C11
u Turkey 40°45N 31°35E 19 F5
ungavík Iceland 66°9N 23°15W 8 C2
vadin Turkey 38°45N 31°4E 44 B1
zano Italy 46°31N 11°22E 22 A4
n Jesus da Lapa
Brazil 13°15S 43°25W 93 F10
na Dem. Rep. of the Congo 5°50S 13°4E 52 F2
nbala Australia 36°56S 149°15E 63 F4
nbay = Mumbai
ndia 18°56N 72°50E 40 K8
nbay U.S.A. 44°56N 74°34W 83 B10
nbedor, Pta.
'enezuela 9°53N 61°37W 93 L15
nboma
Dem. Rep. of the Congo 2°25N 18°55E 52 D3
nbombwa
Dem. Rep. of the Congo 1°40N 25°40E 54 B2
nili
Dem. Rep. of the Congo 1°45N 27°5E 54 B2
nlo Norway 59°37N 5°13E 9 G11
nokandi →
Dem. Rep. of the Congo 3°39N 26°8E 54 B2
nu → C.A.R. 4°40N 22°30E 52 D4
ı, C. = Ra's at Tib
unisia 37°1N 11°2E 22 F4
ı Acceuil Mauritius 20°10S 57°39E 53 d
ı Echo ⌂ Canada 44°55N 77°16W 82 B7
ı Sar Pa Vietnam 12°24N 107°35E 38 F6
ıāb Iran 36°35N 48°41E 45 B6
ıaigarh India 21°50N 84°57E 43 J11
ıaire Neth. Ant. 12°10N 68°15W 89 D6
ıampak Mexico 16°44N 91°5W 87 D6
ıang Australia 37°11S 148°41E 63 F4
ıanza Nic. 13°54N 84°35W 88 D3
ıaparte Arch.
ustralia 14°0S 124°30E 60 B3
ıar Bridge U.K. 57°54N 4°20W 11 D4
ıasse Trin. & Tob. 10°5N 61°54W 93 K15
ıaventure Canada 48°5N 65°32W 73 C6
ıavista Canada 48°40N 53°5W 73 C9
ıavista, C. Canada 48°42N 53°5W 73 C9
ıavista B. Canada 48°45N 53°25W 73 C9
ıdo
em. Rep. of the Congo 3°55N 23°53E 54 B1
ıdoukou Ivory C. 8°2N 2°47W 50 G5
ıdowoso Indonesia 7°55S 113°49E 37 G15
ıe, Teluk Indonesia 4°10S 120°50E 37 E6
ıerate Indonesia 7°25S 121°5E 37 F6
ıerate, Kepulauan
ndonesia 6°30S 121°10E 37 F6
ness U.K. 56°1N 3°37W 11 E5
ıete, Cerro Argentina 27°55S 68°40W 94 B2
ıg Son = Hoai Nhon
ietnam 14°28N 109°1E 38 E7
ıgaigaon India 26°28N 90°34E 32 D4
ıgandanga
em. Rep. of the Congo 1°24N 21°3E 52 D4
ıgor Chad 10°35N 15°20E 51 F9
ıgos, Massif des C.A.R. 8°40N 22°25E 52 C4
ham U.S.A. 33°35N 96°11W 84 E6
ıi ⌂ Kenya 1°35S 41°18E 54 C5
ıifacio France 41°24N 9°10E 20 F8
ıifacio, Bouches de
Medit. S. 41°12N 9°15E 22 D3
ıin Is. = Ogasawara Gunto
ac. Oc. 27°0N 142°0E 27 F16
ın Germany 50°46N 7°6E 16 C4
ıne Terre U.S.A. 37°55N 90°33W 80 G8
ıners Ferry U.S.A. 48°42N 116°19W 76 B5
ıney, L. Australia 37°50S 140°20E 63 F3
ınie Rock Australia 30°29S 118°22E 61 F2
ıny, Bight of Africa 3°30N 9°20E 52 D1
ınyrigg U.K. 55°53N 3°6W 11 F5
ınyville Canada 54°20N 110°45W 71 C6
oi Indonesia 1°45S 137°41E 37 E9
sall U.S.A. 33°16N 117°14W 79 M9
tang Indonesia 0°10N 117°30E 36 D5
tebok △ S. Africa 34°5S 20°28E 56 E3
the S. Leone 7°30N 12°33W 50 G3
toc Phil. 17°7N 120°58E 37 A6
ython Ra. Australia 23°40S 128°45E 60 D4
djamulla △ Australia 18°15S 138°6E 62 B2
kabie Australia 31°50S 132°41E 61 F5
ker U.S.A. 36°27N 100°32W 84 C4
ligal Australia 33°58S 144°53E 63 E3
n Tsagaan Nuur
Mongolia 45°35N 99°9E 32 B4
nah Australia 27°58S 152°41E 63 D5
ne Iowa, U.S.A. 42°4N 93°53W 80 D7
ne N.C., U.S.A. 36°13N 81°41W 85 C14
neville Ark., U.S.A. 35°8N 93°55W 84 D8
neville Miss., U.S.A. 34°39N 88°34W 85 D10
nville Calif., U.S.A. 39°1N 123°22W 78 F3
nville Ind., U.S.A. 38°3N 87°16W 80 F10
nville Mo., U.S.A. 38°58N 92°44W 80 F7
nville N.Y., U.S.A. 43°29N 75°20W 83 C9
rabbin △ Australia 31°30S 120°10E 61 F3
rindal Australia 30°22S 146°11E 63 E4
rowa Australia 34°28S 148°44E 63 E4
saaso Somali Rep. 11°12N 49°18E 47 E4
thia, Gulf of Canada 71°0N 90°0W 69 B11
thia Pen. Canada 71°0N 94°0W 68 B10
tle U.K. 53°28N 3°1W 12 D4
ué Gabon 0°5S 11°55E 52 E2
uilla, Presa de la
Mexico 27°31N 105°30W 86 B3
uillas del Carmen
exico 29°11N 102°58W 86 B4
Serbia 44°5N 22°7E 23 B10
Sudan 6°10N 31°40E 51 G12
Mashash Israel 31°7N 34°50E 46 D3
ı Bora
ench Polynesia 16°30S 151°45W 65 J12

Borah Peak U.S.A. 44°8N 113°47W 76 D7
Borås Sweden 57°43N 12°56E 9 H15
Borāzjān Iran 29°22N 51°10E 45 D6
Borba Brazil 4°12S 59°34W 92 D7
Borborema, Planalto da
Brazil 7°0S 37°0W 90 D7
Bord Khūn-e Now Iran 28°3N 51°28E 45 D6
Borda, C. Australia 35°45S 136°34E 63 F2
Bordeaux France 44°50N 0°36W 20 D3
Borden Australia 34°3S 118°12E 61 F2
Borden-Carleton Canada 46°18N 63°47W 73 C7
Borden I. Canada 78°30N 111°30W 69 B8
Borden Pen. Canada 73°0N 83°0W 69 B11
Border Ranges △
Australia 28°24S 152°56E 63 D5
Borders = Scottish Borders □
U.K. 55°35N 2°50W 11 F6
Bordertown Australia 36°19S 140°45E 63 F3
Borðeyri Iceland 65°12N 21°6W 8 D3
Bordj Fly Ste. Marie
Algeria 27°19N 2°32W 50 C5
Bordj-in-Eker Algeria 24°9N 5°3E 50 D7
Bordj Moktar Algeria 21°20N 0°56E 50 D6
Bordj Omar Driss Algeria 28°10N 6°40E 50 C7
Borehamwood U.K. 51°40N 0°15W 13 F7
Borgarfjörður Iceland 65°33N 13°47W 8 D7
Borgarnes Iceland 64°32N 21°55W 8 D3
Børgefjellet Norway 65°20N 13°45E 8 D15
Borger Neths. 52°54N 6°44E 15 B6
Borger U.S.A. 35°39N 101°24W 84 D4
Borgholm Sweden 56°52N 16°39E 9 H17
Borhoyn Tal Mongolia 43°50N 111°58E 34 C6
Borikhane Laos 18°33N 103°43E 38 C4
Borisoglebsk Russia 51°27N 42°5E 19 D7
Borisov = Barysaw
Belarus 54°17N 28°28E 17 A15
Borja Peru 4°20S 77°40W 92 D3
Borkou Chad 18°15N 18°50E 51 E9
Borkum Germany 53°34N 6°40E 16 B4
Borlänge Sweden 60°29N 15°26E 9 F16
Borley, C. Antarctica 66°15S 52°30E 5 C5
Borneo E. Indies 1°0N 115°0E 36 D5
Bornholm Denmark 55°10N 15°0E 9 J16
Borogontsy Russia 62°42N 131°8E 29 C14
Borohoro Shan China 44°6N 83°10E 32 B3
Boron U.S.A. 35°0N 117°39W 79 L9
Borongan Phil. 11°37N 125°26E 37 B7
Borovichi Russia 58°25N 33°55E 18 C5
Borrego Springs
U.S.A. 33°15N 116°23W 79 M10
Borrisokane Ireland 53°0N 8°7W 10 D3
Borroloola Australia 16°4S 136°17E 62 B2
Borşa Romania 47°41N 24°50E 17 E13
Borsad India 22°25N 72°54E 42 H5
Borth U.K. 52°29N 4°2W 13 E3
Borūjerd Iran 33°55N 48°50E 45 C6
Boryeong S. Korea 36°21N 126°36E 35 F14
Boryslav Ukraine 49°18N 23°28E 17 D12
Borzya Russia 50°24N 116°31E 29 D12
Bosa Italy 40°18N 8°30E 22 D3
Bosanska Gradiška
Bos.-H. 45°10N 17°15E 22 B7
Boscastle U.K. 50°41N 4°42W 13 G3
Boscobelle Barbados 13°17N 59°35W 89 g
Bose China 23°53N 106°35E 32 D5
Boseong S. Korea 34°46N 127°5E 35 G14
Boshan China 36°28N 117°49E 35 F9
Boshof S. Africa 28°31S 25°13E 56 D4
Boshrūyeh Iran 33°50N 57°30E 45 C8
Bosna → Bos.-H. 45°4N 18°29E 23 B8
Bosna i Hercegovina = Bosnia-
Herzegovina ■ Europe 44°0N 18°0E 22 B7
Bosnia-Herzegovina ■
Europe 44°0N 18°0E 22 B7
Bosnik Indonesia 1°5S 136°10E 37 E9
Bosobolo
Dem. Rep. of the Congo 4°15N 19°50E 52 D3
Bosporus = İstanbul Boğazı
Turkey 41°5N 29°3E 23 D13
Bosque Farms U.S.A. 35°51N 106°42W 77 J10
Bossangoa C.A.R. 6°35N 17°30E 52 C3
Bossier City U.S.A. 32°31N 93°44W 84 E8
Bosso Niger 13°43N 13°19E 51 F8
Bostan Pakistan 30°26N 67°2E 42 D2
Bostānābād Iran 37°50N 46°50E 44 B5
Bosten Hu China 41°55N 87°40E 32 B3
Boston U.K. 52°59N 0°2W 12 E7
Boston U.S.A. 42°22N 71°3W 83 D13
Boston Bar Canada 49°52N 121°30W 70 D4
Boston Mts. U.S.A. 35°42N 93°15W 84 D8
Boswell Canada 49°28N 116°45W 70 D5
Boswell U.S.A. 40°10N 79°2W 82 F5
Botad India 22°15N 71°40E 42 H4
Botany B. Australia 33°58S 151°11E 58 E8
Botene Laos 17°35N 101°12E 38 D3
Bothaville S. Africa 27°23S 26°34E 56 D4
Bothnia, G. of Europe 62°0N 20°0E 8 F19
Bothwell Australia 42°20S 147°1E 63 G4
Bothwell Canada 42°38N 81°52W 82 D3
Botlette → Botswana 20°10S 23°15E 56 C3
Botoşani Romania 47°42N 26°41E 17 E14
Botou Burkina Faso 12°42N 1°59E 50 F6
Botshabelo S. Africa 29°14S 26°44E 56 D4
Botswana ■ Africa 22°0S 24°0E 56 C3
Bottineau U.S.A. 48°50N 100°27W 80 A3
Bottrop Germany 51°31N 6°58E 15 C6
Botucatu Brazil 22°55S 48°30W 95 A6
Botum Sakor △
Cambodia 11°5N 103°15E 39 G4
Botwood Canada 49°6N 55°23W 73 C8
Bou Saâda Algeria 35°11N 4°9E 50 A6
Bouaflé Ivory C. 7°1N 5°47W 50 G4
Bouaké Ivory C. 7°40N 5°2W 50 G4
Bouar C.A.R. 6°0N 15°40E 52 C3
Bouârfa Morocco 32°32N 1°58W 50 B5
Boucaut B. Australia 12°0S 134°25E 62 A1
Bouctouche Canada 46°30N 64°45W 73 C7

Bougainville, C. Australia 13°57S 126°4E 60 B4
Bougainville I. Papua N. G. 6°0S 155°0E 58 B8
Bougainville Reef
Australia 15°30S 147°5E 62 B4
Bougie = Bejaïa Algeria 36°42N 5°2E 50 A7
Bougouni Mali 11°30N 7°20W 50 F4
Bouillon Belgium 49°44N 5°3E 15 E5
Boulder Colo., U.S.A. 40°1N 105°17W 76 F11
Boulder Mont., U.S.A. 46°14N 112°7W 76 C7
Boulder City U.S.A. 35°58N 114°49W 79 K12
Boulder Creek U.S.A. 37°7N 122°7W 78 H4
Boulder Dam = Hoover Dam
U.S.A. 36°1N 114°44W 79 K12
Boulia Australia 22°52S 139°51E 62 C2
Boulogne-sur-Mer France 50°42N 1°36E 20 A4
Boulsa Burkina Faso 12°39N 0°34W 50 F5
Boultoum Niger 14°45N 10°25E 51 F8
Bouma △ Fiji 16°50S 179°52E 59 a
Boun Neua Laos 21°38N 101°54E 38 B3
Boun Tai Laos 21°23N 101°58E 38 B3
Bouna Ivory C. 9°10N 3°0W 50 G5
Boundary Peak U.S.A. 37°51N 118°21W 78 H8
Boundiali Ivory C. 9°30N 6°20W 50 G4
Bountiful U.S.A. 40°53N 111°52W 76 F8
Bounty Is. Pac. Oc. 48°0S 178°30E 64 M9
Bounty Trough Pac. Oc. 46°0S 178°0E 64 M9
Bourbonnais France 46°28N 3°0E 20 C5
Bourdel L. Canada 56°43N 74°10W 72 A5
Bourem Mali 17°0N 0°24W 50 E5
Bourg-en-Bresse France 46°13N 5°12E 20 C6
Bourg-St-Maurice France 45°35N 6°46E 20 D7
Bourgas = Burgas
Bulgaria 42°33N 27°29E 23 C12
Bourges France 47°9N 2°25E 20 C5
Bourget Canada 45°26N 75°9W 83 A9
Bourgogne □ France 47°0N 4°50E 20 C6
Bourke Australia 30°8S 145°55E 63 E4
Bourne U.K. 52°47N 0°22W 12 E7
Bournemouth U.K. 50°43N 1°52W 13 G6
Bournemouth □ U.K. 50°43N 1°52W 13 G6
Bouse U.S.A. 33°56N 114°0W 79 M13
Bousso Chad 10°34N 16°52E 51 F9
Bouvet I. = Bouvetøya
Antarctica 54°26S 3°24E 2 G10
Bouvetøya Antarctica 54°26S 3°24E 2 G10
Bovill U.S.A. 46°51N 116°24W 76 C5
Bovril Argentina 31°21S 59°26W 94 C4
Bow → Canada 49°57N 111°41W 70 C6
Bow Island Canada 49°50N 111°23W 76 B8
Bowbells U.S.A. 48°48N 102°15W 80 A2
Bowdle U.S.A. 45°27N 99°39W 80 C4
Bowelling Australia 33°25S 116°30E 61 F2
Bowen Argentina 35°0S 67°31W 94 D2
Bowen Australia 20°0S 148°16E 62 J6
Bowen Mts. Australia 37°0S 147°50E 63 F4
Bowers Basin Pac. Oc. 53°45N 176°0E 4 D16
Bowers Ridge Pac. Oc. 54°0N 180°0E 4 D17
Bowie Ariz., U.S.A. 32°19N 109°29W 77 K9
Bowie Tex., U.S.A. 33°34N 97°51W 84 E6
Bowkān Iran 36°31N 46°12E 44 B5
Bowland, Forest of U.K. 54°0N 2°30W 12 D5
Bowling Green Ky.,
U.S.A. 36°59N 86°27W 80 G10
Bowling Green Ohio,
U.S.A. 41°23N 83°39W 81 E12
Bowling Green, C.
Australia 19°19S 147°25E 62 B4
Bowling Green Bay △
Australia 19°26S 146°57E 62 B4
Bowman U.S.A. 46°11N 103°24W 80 B2
Bowman I. Antarctica 65°0S 104°0E 5 C8
Bowmanville = Clarington
Canada 43°55N 78°41W 82 C6
Bowmore U.K. 55°45N 6°17W 11 F2
Bowral Australia 34°26S 150°27E 63 E5
Bowraville Australia 30°37S 152°52E 63 E5
Bowron → Canada 54°3N 121°50W 70 C4
Bowron Lake ⌂ Canada 53°10N 121°5W 70 C4
Bowser L. Canada 56°30N 129°30W 70 B3
Bowsman Canada 52°14N 101°12W 71 C8
Bowwood Zambia 17°5S 26°20E 55 F2
Box Cr. → Australia 34°10S 143°50E 63 E3
Boxmeer Neths. 51°38N 5°56E 15 C5
Boxtel Neths. 51°36N 5°20E 15 C5
Boyce U.S.A. 31°23N 92°40W 84 F8
Boyd L. Canada 52°46N 76°42W 72 B4
Boyle Canada 54°35N 112°49W 70 C6
Boyle Ireland 53°59N 8°18W 10 C3
Boyne → Ireland 53°43N 6°15W 10 C5
Boyne City U.S.A. 45°13N 85°1W 81 C11
Boynton Beach U.S.A. 26°32N 80°4W 85 H14
Boyolali Indonesia 7°32S 110°35E 37 G14
Boyoma, Chutes
Dem. Rep. of the Congo 0°35N 25°23E 54 B2
Boysen Res. U.S.A. 43°25N 108°11W 76 E9
Boyuibe Bolivia 20°25S 63°17W 92 G6
Boyup Brook Australia 33°50S 116°23E 61 F2
Boz Dağları Turkey 38°20N 28°0E 23 E13
Bozburun Turkey 36°43N 28°4E 23 F13
Bozcaada Turkey 39°49N 26°3E 23 E12
Bozdoğan Turkey 37°40N 28°17E 23 F13
Bozeman U.S.A. 45°41N 111°2W 76 D8
Bozen = Bolzano Italy 46°31N 11°22E 22 A4
Bozhou China 33°55N 115°41E 34 H8
Bozoum C.A.R. 6°25N 16°35E 52 C3
Bozyazi Turkey 36°6N 33°0E 44 B2
Bra Italy 44°42N 7°51E 20 D7
Brabant □ Belgium 50°46N 4°30E 15 D4
Brabant L. Canada 55°58N 103°43W 71 B8
Brač Croatia 43°20N 16°40E 22 C7
Bracadale, L. U.K. 57°20N 6°30W 11 D2
Bracciano, L. di Italy 42°7N 12°14E 22 C5
Bracebridge Canada 45°2N 79°19W 82 A5
Bräcke Sweden 62°45N 15°26E 8 E16
Brackettville U.S.A. 29°19N 100°25W 84 G4
Bracknell U.K. 51°25N 0°43W 13 F7
Bracknell Forest □ U.K. 51°25N 0°44W 13 F7

Brad Romania 46°10N 22°50E 17 E12
Bradenton U.S.A. 27°30N 82°34W 85 H13
Bradford Canada 44°7N 79°34W 82 B5
Bradford U.K. 53°47N 1°45W 12 D6
Bradford Pa., U.S.A. 41°58N 78°38W 82 E6
Bradford Vt., U.S.A. 43°59N 72°9W 83 C12
Bradley Ark., U.S.A. 33°6N 93°39W 84 E8
Bradley Calif., U.S.A. 35°52N 120°48W 78 K6
Bradley Institute
Zimbabwe 17°7S 31°25E 55 F3
Brady U.S.A. 31°9N 99°20W 84 F5
Braeside Canada 45°28N 76°24W 83 A8
Braga Portugal 41°35N 8°25W 21 B1
Bragado Argentina 35°2S 60°27W 94 D3
Bragança Brazil 1°0S 47°2W 93 D9
Bragança Portugal 41°48N 6°50W 21 B2
Bragança Paulista
Brazil 22°55S 46°32W 95 A6
Brahestad = Raahe
Finland 64°40N 24°28E 8 D21
Brahmanbaria Bangla. 23°58N 91°15E 41 H17
Brahmani → India 20°39N 86°46E 41 J15
Brahmapur India 19°15N 84°54E 41 K14
Brahmaputra → Asia 23°40N 90°35E 43 H13
Braich-y-pwll U.K. 52°47N 4°46W 12 E3
Braidwood Australia 35°27S 149°49E 63 F4
Brăila Romania 45°19N 27°59E 17 F14
Brainerd U.S.A. 46°22N 94°12W 80 B6
Braintree U.K. 51°53N 0°34E 13 F8
Braintree U.S.A. 42°13N 71°0W 83 D14
Brak → S. Africa 29°35S 22°55E 56 D3
Brakwater Namibia 22°28S 17°3E 56 C2
Brampton Canada 43°45N 79°45W 82 C5
Brampton U.K. 54°57N 2°44W 12 C5
Bramton I. Australia 20°50S 149°17E 62 J7
Branco → Brazil 1°20S 61°50W 92 D6
Brandberg Namibia 21°10S 14°33E 56 C1
Brandberg ⌂ Namibia 21°10S 14°30E 56 C1
Brandenburg = Neubrandenburg
Germany 53°33N 13°15E 16 B7
Brandenburg Germany 52°25N 12°33E 16 B7
Brandenburg □ Germany 52°50N 13°0E 16 B6
Brandfort S. Africa 28°40S 26°30E 56 D4
Brandon Canada 49°50N 99°57W 71 D9
Brandon U.S.A. 43°48N 73°6W 83 C11
Brandon B. Ireland 52°17N 10°8W 10 D1
Brandon Mt. Ireland 52°15N 10°15W 10 D1
Brandsen Argentina 35°10S 58°15W 94 D4
Brandvlei S. Africa 30°25S 20°30E 56 E3
Branford U.S.A. 41°17N 72°49W 83 E12
Braniewo Poland 54°25N 19°50E 17 A10
Bransfield Str. Antarctica 63°0S 59°0W 5 C18
Branson U.S.A. 36°39N 93°13W 80 G7
Brantford Canada 43°10N 80°15W 82 C4
Bras d'Or L. Canada 45°50N 60°50W 73 C7
Brasher Falls U.S.A. 44°49N 74°47W 83 B10
Brasil = Brazil ■ S. Amer. 12°0S 50°0W 93 F9
Brasil, Planalto Brazil 18°0S 46°30W 90 E6
Brasiléia Brazil 11°0S 68°45W 92 F5
Brasília Brazil 15°47S 47°55W 93 G9
Brasília Legal Brazil 3°49S 55°36W 93 D7
Braslaw Belarus 55°38N 27°0E 9 J22
Braşov Romania 45°38N 25°35E 17 F13
Brasschaat Belgium 51°19N 4°27E 15 C4
Brassey, Banjaran
Malaysia 5°0N 117°15E 36 D5
Brassey Ra. Australia 25°8S 122°15E 61 E3
Brasstown Bald U.S.A. 34°53N 83°49W 85 D13
Brastad Sweden 58°23N 11°30E 9 G14
Bratislava Slovak Rep. 48°10N 17°7E 17 D9
Bratsk Russia 56°10N 101°30E 29 D11
Brattleboro U.S.A. 42°51N 72°34W 83 D12
Braunau Austria 48°15N 13°3E 16 D7
Braunschweig Germany 52°15N 10°31E 16 B6
Braunton U.K. 51°7N 4°10W 13 F3
Brava C. Verde Is. 15°0N 24°40W 50 b
Bravo del Norte, Rio = Grande,
Rio → N. Amer. 25°58N 97°9W 84 J6
Brawley U.S.A. 32°59N 115°31W 79 N11
Bray Ireland 53°13N 6°7W 10 C5
Bray, Mt. Australia 14°0S 134°30E 62 A1
Bray, Pays de France 49°46N 1°26E 20 B4
Brazeau → Canada 52°55N 115°14W 70 C5
Brazil U.S.A. 39°32N 87°8W 80 F10
Brazil ■ S. Amer. 12°0S 50°0W 93 F9
Brazilian Highlands = Brasil,
Planalto Brazil 18°0S 46°30W 90 E6
Brazo Sur → S. Amer. 25°21S 57°42W 94 B4
Brazos → U.S.A. 28°53N 95°23W 84 G7
Brazzaville Congo 4°9S 15°12E 52 E3
Brčko Bos.-H. 44°54N 18°46E 23 B8
Breaden, L. Australia 25°51S 125°28E 61 E4
Breaksea Sd. N.Z. 45°35S 166°35E 59 F1
Bream B. N.Z. 35°56S 174°28E 59 A5
Bream Hd. N.Z. 35°51S 174°36E 59 A5
Breas Chile 25°29S 70°24W 94 B1
Brebes Indonesia 6°52S 109°3E 37 G13
Brechin Canada 44°32N 79°10W 82 B5
Brechin U.K. 56°44N 2°39W 11 E6
Brecht Belgium 51°21N 4°38E 15 C4
Breckenridge Colo.,
U.S.A. 39°29N 106°3W 76 G10
Breckenridge Minn.,
U.S.A. 46°16N 96°35W 80 B5
Breckenridge Tex.,
U.S.A. 32°45N 98°54W 84 E5
Breckland U.K. 52°30N 0°40E 13 E8
Brecon U.K. 51°57N 3°23W 13 F4
Brecon Beacons U.K. 51°53N 3°26W 13 F4
Brecon Beacons △ U.K. 51°50N 3°30W 13 F4
Breda Neths. 51°35N 4°45E 15 C4
Bredasdorp S. Africa 34°33S 20°2E 56 E3
Bree Belgium 51°8N 5°35E 15 C5
Bregenz Austria 47°30N 9°45E 16 E5
Breiðafjörður Iceland 65°15N 23°15W 8 D2
Brejo Brazil 3°41S 42°47W 93 D10
Bremen Germany 53°4N 8°47E 16 B5

Bremer Bay Australia 34°21S 119°20E 61 F2
Bremer I. Australia 12°5S 136°45E 62 A2
Bremerhaven Germany 53°33N 8°36E 16 B5
Bremerton U.S.A. 47°34N 122°37W 78 C4
Brenham U.S.A. 30°10N 96°24W 84 F6
Brennerpass Austria 47°2N 11°30E 16 E6
Brent U.S.A. 32°56N 87°10W 85 E11
Brentwood U.K. 51°37N 0°19E 13 F8
Brentwood Calif.,
U.S.A. 37°56N 121°42W 78 H5
Brentwood N.Y., U.S.A. 40°47N 73°15W 83 F11
Bréscia Italy 45°33N 10°15E 20 D9
Breskens Neths. 51°23N 3°33E 15 C3
Breslau = Wrocław Poland 51°5N 17°5E 17 C9
Bressanone Italy 46°43N 11°39E 22 A4
Bressay U.K. 60°9N 1°6W 11 A7
Brest Belarus 52°10N 23°40E 17 B12
Brest France 48°24N 4°31W 20 B1
Brest-Litovsk = Brest
Belarus 52°10N 23°40E 17 B12
Bretagne □ France 48°10N 3°0W 20 B2
Breton Canada 53°7N 114°28W 70 C6
Breton Sd. U.S.A. 29°35N 89°15W 85 G10
Brett, C. N.Z. 35°10S 174°20E 59 A5
Brevard U.S.A. 35°14N 82°44W 85 D13
Breves Brazil 1°40S 50°29W 93 D8
Brewarrina Australia 30°0S 146°51E 63 E4
Brewer U.S.A. 44°48N 68°46W 81 C19
Brewer, Mt. U.S.A. 36°44N 118°28W 78 J8
Brewster N.Y., U.S.A. 41°24N 73°36W 83 E11
Brewster Ohio, U.S.A. 40°43N 81°36W 82 F3
Brewster Wash., U.S.A. 48°6N 119°47W 76 B4
Brewster, Kap = Kangikajik
Greenland 70°7N 22°0W 4 B6
Brewton U.S.A. 31°7N 87°4W 85 F11
Breyten S. Africa 26°16S 30°0E 57 D5
Bria C.A.R. 6°30N 21°58E 52 C4
Briançon France 44°54N 6°39E 20 D7
Bribie I. Australia 27°0S 153°10E 63 D5
Bribri Costa Rica 9°38N 82°50W 88 E3
Bridgefield Barbados 13°9N 59°36W 89 g
Bridgehampton U.S.A. 40°56N 72°19W 83 F12
Bridgend U.K. 51°30N 3°34W 13 F4
Bridgend □ U.K. 51°36N 3°36W 13 F4
Bridgenorth Canada 44°23N 78°23W 82 B6
Bridgeport Calif., U.S.A. 38°15N 119°14W 78 G7
Bridgeport Conn.,
U.S.A. 41°11N 73°12W 83 E11
Bridgeport N.Y., U.S.A. 43°9N 75°58W 83 C9
Bridgeport Nebr., U.S.A. 41°40N 103°6W 80 E2
Bridgeport Tex., U.S.A. 33°13N 97°45W 84 E6
Bridger U.S.A. 45°18N 108°55W 76 D9
Bridgeton U.S.A. 39°26N 75°14W 81 F16
Bridgetown Australia 33°58S 116°7E 61 F2
Bridgetown Barbados 13°6N 59°37W 89 g
Bridgetown Canada 44°55N 65°18W 73 D6
Bridgewater Australia 42°44S 147°14E 63 G4
Bridgewater Canada 44°25N 64°31W 73 D7
Bridgewater Mass.,
U.S.A. 41°59N 70°58W 83 E14
Bridgewater N.Y.,
U.S.A. 42°53N 75°15W 83 D9
Bridgewater, C.
Australia 38°23S 141°23E 63 F3
Bridgnorth U.K. 52°32N 2°25W 13 E5
Bridgton U.S.A. 44°3N 70°42W 83 B14
Bridgwater U.K. 51°8N 2°59W 13 F5
Bridgwater B. U.K. 51°15N 3°15W 13 F4
Bridlington U.K. 54°5N 0°12W 12 C7
Bridlington B. U.K. 54°4N 0°10W 12 C7
Bridport Australia 40°59S 147°23E 63 G4
Bridport U.K. 50°44N 2°45W 13 G5
Brig Switz. 46°18N 7°59E 20 C7
Brigg U.K. 53°34N 0°28W 12 D7
Brigham City U.S.A. 41°31N 112°1W 76 F7
Bright Australia 36°42S 146°56E 63 F4
Brighton Australia 35°5S 138°30E 63 F2
Brighton Canada 44°2N 77°44W 82 B7
Brighton Trin. & Tob. 10°13N 61°39W 93 K15
Brighton U.K. 50°49N 0°7W 13 G7
Brighton U.S.A. 43°8N 77°34W 82 C7
Brightside Canada 45°7N 76°29W 83 A8
Brilliant U.S.A. 40°15N 80°39W 82 F4
Bríndisi Italy 40°39N 17°55E 23 D7
Brinkley U.S.A. 34°53N 91°12W 84 D9
Brinnon U.S.A. 47°41N 122°54W 78 C4
Brion, Î. Canada 47°46N 61°26W 73 C7
Brisay Canada 54°26N 70°31W 73 B5
Brisbane Australia 27°25S 153°2E 63 D5
Brisbane → Australia 27°24S 153°9E 63 D5
Bristol U.K. 51°26N 2°35W 13 F5
Bristol Conn., U.S.A. 41°40N 72°57W 83 E12
Bristol Pa., U.S.A. 40°6N 74°51W 83 F10
Bristol R.I., U.S.A. 41°40N 71°16W 83 E13
Bristol Tenn., U.S.A. 36°36N 82°11W 85 C13
Bristol Vt., U.S.A. 44°8N 73°4W 83 B11
Bristol, City of □ U.K. 51°27N 2°36W 13 F5
Bristol B. U.S.A. 58°0N 160°0W 74 a
Bristol Channel U.K. 51°18N 4°30W 13 F3
Bristol I. Antarctica 58°45S 28°0W 5 B1
Bristol L. U.S.A. 34°28N 115°41W 77 J6
Bristow U.S.A. 35°50N 96°23W 84 D6
Britain = Great Britain
Europe 54°0N 2°15W 6 E5
British Columbia □
Canada 55°0N 125°15W 70 C3
British Indian Ocean Terr. =
Chagos Arch. ☒ Ind. Oc. 6°0S 72°0E 26 J9
British Isles Europe 54°0N 4°0W 14 D5
British Virgin Is. ☒
W. Indies 18°30N 64°30W 89 e
Brits S. Africa 25°37S 27°48E 57 D4
Britstown S. Africa 30°37S 23°30E 56 E3
Britt Canada 45°46N 80°34W 72 C3
Brittany = Bretagne □
France 48°10N 3°0W 20 B2
Britton U.S.A. 45°48N 97°45W 80 C5

Brive-la-Gaillarde France 45°10N 1°32E 20 D4
Brixen = Bressanone Italy 46°43N 11°39E 22 A4
Brixham U.K. 50°23N 3°31W 13 G4
Brno Czech Rep. 49°10N 16°35E 17 D9
Broach = Bharuch India 21°47N 73°0E 40 J8
Broad → U.S.A. 34°1N 81°4W 85 D14
Broad Arrow Australia 30°23S 121°15E 61 F3
Broad B. U.K. 58°14N 6°18W 11 C2
Broad Haven Ireland 54°20N 9°55W 10 B2
Broad Law U.K. 55°30N 3°21W 11 F5
Broad Pk. = Faichan Kangri India 35°48N 76°34E 43 B7
Broad Sd. Australia 22°0S 149°45E 62 C4
Broadalbin U.S.A. 43°4N 74°12W 83 C10
Broadback → Canada 51°21N 78°52W 72 B4
Broadhurst Ra. Australia 22°30S 122°30E 60 D3
Broads, The U.K. 52°45N 1°30E 12 E9
Broadus U.S.A. 45°27N 105°25W 76 D11
Brochet, L. Canada 58°36N 101°35W 71 B8
Brock I. Canada 77°52N 114°19W 69 B8
Brocken Germany 51°47N 10°37E 16 C6
Brockport U.S.A. 43°13N 77°56W 82 C7
Brockton U.S.A. 42°5N 71°1W 83 D13
Brockville Canada 44°35N 75°41W 83 B9
Brockway Mont., U.S.A. 47°18N 105°45W 76 C11
Brockway Pa., U.S.A. 41°15N 78°47W 82 E6
Brocton U.S.A. 42°23N 79°26W 82 D5
Brodeur Pen. Canada 72°30N 88°10W 69 B11
Brodick U.K. 55°35N 5°9W 11 F3
Brodnica Poland 53°15N 19°25E 17 B10
Brody Ukraine 50°5N 25°10E 17 C13
Brogan U.S.A. 44°15N 117°31W 76 D5
Broken Arrow U.S.A. 36°3N 95°48W 84 C7
Broken Bow Nebr., U.S.A. 41°24N 99°38W 80 E4
Broken Bow Okla., U.S.A. 34°2N 94°44W 84 D7
Broken Bow Lake U.S.A. 34°9N 94°40W 84 D7
Broken Hill Australia 31°58S 141°29E 63 E3
Broken Ridge Ind. Oc. 30°0S 94°0E 64 L1
Broken River Ra. Australia 21°0S 148°22E 62 K6
Bromley □ U.K. 51°24N 0°2E 13 F8
Bromo Indonesia 7°55S 112°55E 37 G15
Bromsgrove U.K. 52°21N 2°2W 13 E5
Brønderslev Denmark 57°16N 9°57E 9 H13
Bronkhorstspruit S. Africa 25°46S 28°45E 57 D4
Brønnøysund Norway 65°28N 12°14E 8 D15
Brook Park U.S.A. 41°23N 81°48W 82 E4
Brookhaven U.S.A. 31°35N 90°26W 85 F9
Brookings Oreg., U.S.A. 42°3N 124°17W 76 E1
Brookings S. Dak., U.S.A. 44°19N 96°48W 80 C5
Brooklin Canada 43°55N 78°55W 82 C6
Brooklyn Park U.S.A. 45°6N 93°23W 80 C7
Brooks Canada 50°35N 111°55W 70 C6
Brooks Range U.S.A. 68°0N 152°0W 74 a
Brooksville U.S.A. 28°33N 82°23W 85 G13
Brookton Australia 32°22S 117°0E 61 F2
Brookville U.S.A. 41°10N 79°5W 82 E5
Broom, L. U.K. 57°55N 5°15W 11 D3
Broome Australia 18°0S 122°15E 60 C3
Brora U.K. 58°0N 3°52W 11 C5
Brora → U.K. 58°0N 3°51W 11 C5
Brosna → Ireland 53°14N 7°58W 10 C4
Brothers U.S.A. 43°49N 120°36W 76 E3
Brough U.K. 54°32N 2°18W 12 C5
Brough Hd. U.K. 59°8N 3°20W 11 B5
Broughton Island = Qikiqtarjuaq Canada 67°33N 63°0W 69 C13
Brown, L. Australia 31°5S 118°15E 61 F2
Brown, Pt. Australia 32°32S 133°50E 63 E1
Brown City U.S.A. 43°13N 82°59W 82 C2
Brown Willy U.K. 50°35N 4°37W 13 G3
Brownfield U.S.A. 33°11N 102°17W 84 E3
Browning U.S.A. 48°34N 113°1W 76 B7
Brownsville Oreg., U.S.A. 44°24N 122°59W 76 D2
Brownsville Pa., U.S.A. 40°1N 79°53W 82 F5
Brownsville Tenn., U.S.A. 35°36N 89°16W 85 D10
Brownsville Tex., U.S.A. 25°54N 97°30W 84 J6
Brownville U.S.A. 44°0N 75°59W 83 C9
Brownwood U.S.A. 31°43N 98°59W 84 F5
Browse I. Australia 14°7S 123°33E 60 B3
Bruas Malaysia 4°30N 100°47E 39 K3
Bruay-la-Buissière France 50°29N 2°33E 20 A5
Bruce, Mt. Australia 22°37S 118°8E 60 D2
Bruce Pen. Canada 45°0N 81°30W 82 B3
Bruce Peninsula △ Canada 45°14N 81°36W 82 A3
Bruce Rock Australia 31°52S 118°8E 61 F2
Bruck an der Leitha Austria 48°1N 16°47E 17 D9
Bruck an der Mur Austria 47°24N 15°16E 16 E8
Brue → U.K. 51°13N 2°59W 13 F5
Bruges = Brugge Belgium 51°13N 3°13E 15 C3
Brugge Belgium 51°13N 3°13E 15 C3
Bruin U.S.A. 41°3N 79°43W 82 E5
Brûk, W. el → Egypt 30°15N 33°50E 46 E2
Brûlé Canada 53°15N 117°58W 70 C5
Brûlé, L. Canada 53°35N 64°4W 73 B7
Brumado Brazil 14°14S 41°40W 93 F10
Brumunddal Norway 60°53N 10°56E 8 F14
Bruneau U.S.A. 42°53N 115°48W 76 E6
Bruneau → U.S.A. 42°56N 115°57W 76 E6
Brunei = Bandar Seri Begawan Brunei 4°52N 115°0E 36 D5
Brunei ■ Asia 4°50N 115°0E 36 D5
Brunner, L. N.Z. 42°37S 171°27E 59 E3
Brunssum Neths. 50°57N 5°59E 15 D5
Brunswick = Braunschweig Germany 52°15N 10°31E 16 B6
Brunswick Ga., U.S.A. 31°10N 81°30W 85 F14
Brunswick Maine, U.S.A. 43°55N 69°58W 81 D19
Brunswick Md., U.S.A. 39°19N 77°38W 81 F15
Brunswick Mo., U.S.A. 39°26N 93°8W 80 F7
Brunswick Ohio, U.S.A. 41°14N 81°51W 82 E3
Brunswick, Pen. de Chile 53°30S 71°30W 96 G2
Brunswick B. Australia 15°15S 124°50E 60 C3
Brunswick Junction Australia 33°15S 115°50E 61 F2
Brunt Ice Shelf Antarctica 75°30S 25°0W 5 D2
Brus Laguna Honduras 15°47N 84°35W 88 C3
Brush U.S.A. 40°15N 103°37W 76 F12
Brushton U.S.A. 44°50N 74°31W 83 B10
Brusque Brazil 27°5S 49°0W 95 B6
Brussel Belgium 50°51N 4°21E 15 D4
Brussel ✕ (BRU) Belgium 50°54N 4°29E 15 D5
Brussels = Brussel Belgium 50°51N 4°21E 15 D4
Brussels Canada 43°44N 81°15W 82 C3
Bruthen Australia 37°42S 147°50E 63 F4
Bruxelles = Brussel Belgium 50°51N 4°21E 15 D4
Bryan Ohio, U.S.A. 41°28N 84°33W 81 E11
Bryan Tex., U.S.A. 30°40N 96°22W 84 F6
Bryan, Mt. Australia 33°30S 139°5E 63 E2
Bryansk Russia 53°13N 34°25E 18 D4
Bryce Canyon △ U.S.A. 37°30N 112°10W 77 H7
Bryne Norway 58°44N 5°38E 9 G11
Bryson City U.S.A. 35°26N 83°27W 85 D13
Bsharri Lebanon 34°15N 36°0E 46 A5
Bū Baqarah U.A.E. 25°35N 56°25E 45 E8
Bu Craa W. Sahara 26°45N 12°50W 50 C3
Bū Ḩasā U.A.E. 23°30N 53°20E 45 F7
Bua Fiji 16°48S 178°37E 59 a
Bua Yai Thailand 15°33N 102°26E 38 E4
Buan S. Korea 35°44N 126°44E 35 G14
Buapinang Indonesia 4°40S 121°30E 37 E6
Bubanza Burundi 3°6S 29°23E 54 C2
Bubi → Zimbabwe 22°20S 31°7E 55 G3
Būbiyān Kuwait 29°45N 48°15E 45 D6
Buca Fiji 16°38S 179°52E 59 a
Bucaramanga Colombia 7°0N 73°0W 92 B4
Bucasia Australia 21°2S 149°10E 62 K7
Buccaneer Arch. Australia 16°7S 123°20E 60 C3
Buccoo Reef Trin. & Tob. 11°10N 60°51W 93 J16
Buchach Ukraine 49°5N 25°25E 17 D13
Buchan U.K. 57°32N 2°21W 11 D6
Buchan Ness U.K. 57°29N 1°46W 11 D7
Buchanan Canada 51°40N 102°45W 71 C8
Buchanan Liberia 5°57N 10°2W 50 G3
Buchanan, L. Queens., Australia 21°35S 145°52E 62 C4
Buchanan, L. W. Austral., Australia 25°33S 123°2E 61 E3
Buchanan, L. U.S.A. 30°45N 98°25W 84 F5
Buchanan Cr. → Australia 19°13S 136°33E 62 B2
Buchans Canada 48°50N 56°52W 73 C8
Bucharest = Bucureşti Romania 44°27N 26°10E 17 F14
Bucheon S. Korea 37°28N 126°45E 35 F14
Buchon, Pt. U.S.A. 35°15N 120°54W 78 K6
Buck Hill Falls U.S.A. 41°11N 75°16W 83 E9
Buckeye Lake U.S.A. 39°55N 82°29W 82 G2
Buckhannon U.S.A. 39°0N 80°8W 81 F13
Buckhaven U.K. 56°11N 3°3W 11 E5
Buckhorn L. Canada 44°29N 78°23W 82 B6
Buckie U.K. 57°41N 2°58W 11 D6
Buckingham Canada 45°37N 75°24W 72 C4
Buckingham U.K. 51°59N 0°57W 13 F7
Buckingham B. Australia 12°10S 135°40E 62 A2
Buckinghamshire □ U.K. 51°53N 0°55W 13 F7
Buckle Hd. Australia 14°26S 127°52E 60 B4
Buckleboo Australia 32°54S 136°12E 63 E2
Buckley U.K. 53°10N 3°5W 12 D4
Buckley → Australia 20°10S 138°49E 62 C2
Bucklin U.S.A. 37°33N 99°38W 80 G4
Bucks L. U.S.A. 39°54N 121°12W 78 F5
Bucureşti Romania 44°27N 26°10E 17 F14
Bucyrus U.S.A. 40°48N 82°59W 81 E12
Budalin Burma 22°20N 95°10E 41 H19
Budapest Hungary 47°29N 19°3E 17 E10
Budaun India 28°5N 79°10E 43 E8
Budd Coast Antarctica 68°0S 112°0E 5 C8
Bude U.K. 50°49N 4°34W 13 G3
Budennovsk Russia 44°50N 44°10E 19 F7
Budge Budge = Baj Baj India 22°30N 88°5E 43 H13
Budgewoi Australia 33°13S 151°34E 63 E5
Budjala Dem. Rep. of the Congo 2°50N 19°40E 52 D3
Buellton U.S.A. 34°37N 120°12W 79 L6
Buena Esperanza Argentina 34°45S 65°15W 94 C2
Buena Park U.S.A. 33°52N 117°59W 79 M9
Buena Vista Colo., U.S.A. 38°51N 106°8W 76 G10
Buena Vista Va., U.S.A. 37°44N 79°21W 81 G14
Buena Vista Lake Bed U.S.A. 35°12N 119°18W 79 K7
Buenaventura Colombia 3°53N 77°4W 92 C3
Buenaventura Mexico 29°51N 107°29W 86 B3
Buenos Aires Argentina 34°36S 58°22W 94 C4
Buenos Aires Costa Rica 9°10N 83°20W 88 E3
Buenos Aires □ Argentina 36°30S 60°0W 94 D4
Buenos Aires, L. Argentina 46°35S 72°30W 96 F2
Buffalo Mo., U.S.A. 37°39N 93°6W 80 G7
Buffalo N.Y., U.S.A. 42°53N 78°53W 82 D6
Buffalo Okla., U.S.A. 36°50N 99°38W 84 C5
Buffalo S. Dak., U.S.A. 45°35N 103°33W 80 C2
Buffalo Wyo., U.S.A. 44°21N 106°42W 76 D10
Buffalo → Canada 60°5N 115°5W 70 A5
Buffalo → S. Africa 28°43S 30°37E 57 D5
Buffalo ⌓ U.S.A. 36°14N 92°36W 84 C8
Buffalo Head Hills Canada 57°25N 115°55W 70 B5
Buffalo L. Alta., Canada 52°27N 112°54W 70 C6
Buffalo L. N.W.T., Canada 60°12N 115°25W 70 A5
Buffalo Narrows Canada 55°51N 108°29W 71 B7
Buffalo Springs ⌓ Kenya 0°32N 37°35E 54 B4
Buffels → S. Africa 29°36S 17°3E 56 D2
Buford U.S.A. 34°10N 84°0W 85 D12
Bug = Buh → Ukraine 46°59N 31°58E 19 E5
Bug → Poland 52°31N 21°5E 17 B11
Buga Colombia 4°0N 76°15W 92 C3
Bugala I. Uganda 0°40S 32°20E 54 C3
Buganda Uganda 0°0 31°30E 54 C3
Buganga Uganda 0°3S 32°0E 54 C3
Bugel, Tanjung Indonesia 6°26S 111°3E 37 G14
Búger Spain 39°45N 2°59E 24 B9
Bugibba Malta 35°57N 14°25E 25 D1
Bugsuk I. Phil. 8°12N 117°18E 36 C5
Bugulma Russia 54°33N 52°48E 18 D9
Bugungu ⌓ Uganda 2°17N 31°50E 54 B3
Buguruslan Russia 53°39N 52°26E 18 D9
Buh → Ukraine 46°59N 31°58E 19 E5
Buhera Zimbabwe 19°18S 31°29E 57 B5
Buhl U.S.A. 42°36N 114°46W 76 E6
Builth Wells U.K. 52°9N 3°25W 13 E4
Buir Nur Mongolia 47°50N 117°42E 33 B6
Buji China 22°37N 114°5E 33 F11
Bujumbura Burundi 3°16S 29°18E 54 C2
Bukachacha Russia 52°55N 116°50E 29 D12
Bukama Dem. Rep. of the Congo 9°10S 25°50E 55 D2
Bukavu Dem. Rep. of the Congo 2°20S 28°52E 54 C2
Bukene Tanzania 4°15S 32°48E 54 C3
Bukhara = Buxoro Uzbekistan 39°48N 64°25E 28 F7
Bukhoro = Buxoro Uzbekistan 39°48N 64°25E 28 F7
Bukima Tanzania 1°50S 33°25E 54 C3
Bukit Badung Indonesia 8°49S 115°10E 37 K18
Bukit Kerajaan Malaysia 5°25N 100°15E 39 c
Bukit Mertajam Malaysia 5°22N 100°28E 39 c
Bukit Ni Malaysia 1°22N 104°12E 39 d
Bukit Panjang Singapore 1°23N 103°46E 39 d
Bukit Tengah Malaysia 5°22N 100°25E 39 c
Bukittinggi Indonesia 0°20S 100°20E 36 E2
Bukoba Tanzania 1°20S 31°49E 54 C3
Bukum, Pulau Singapore 1°14N 103°46E 39 d
Bukuya Uganda 0°40N 31°52E 54 B3
Būl, Kuh-e Iran 30°48N 52°45E 45 D7
Bula Indonesia 3°6S 130°30E 37 E8
Bulahdelah Australia 32°23S 152°13E 63 E5
Bulan Phil. 12°40N 123°52E 37 B6
Bulandshahr India 28°28N 77°51E 42 E7
Bulawayo Zimbabwe 20°7S 28°32E 55 G2
Buldan Turkey 38°2N 28°50E 23 E13
Bulgan Mongolia 48°45N 103°34E 32 B5
Bulgar Russia 54°57N 49°4E 18 D8
Bulgaria ■ Europe 42°35N 25°30E 23 C11
Buli, Teluk Indonesia 0°48N 128°25E 37 D7
Bulilyan, C. Phil. 8°20N 117°15E 36 C5
Bulim Singapore 1°22N 103°43E 39 d
Bulkley → Canada 55°15N 127°40W 70 B3
Bull Shoals L. U.S.A. 36°22N 92°35W 84 C8
Bulleringa △ Australia 17°39S 143°56E 62 B3
Bullhead City U.S.A. 35°8N 114°32W 79 K12
Büllingen Belgium 50°25N 6°16E 15 D6
Bullock Creek Australia 17°43S 144°31E 62 B3
Bulloo → Australia 28°43S 142°30E 63 D3
Bulloo L. Australia 28°43S 142°25E 63 D3
Bulls N.Z. 40°10S 175°24E 59 D5
Bulman Australia 13°39S 134°20E 62 A1
Bulnes Chile 36°42S 72°19W 94 D1
Bulsar = Valsad India 20°40N 72°58E 40 J8
Bultfontein S. Africa 28°18S 26°10E 56 D4
Bulukumba Indonesia 5°33S 120°11E 37 F6
Bulun Russia 70°37N 127°30E 29 B13
Bumba Dem. Rep. of the Congo 2°13N 22°30E 52 D4
Bumbah, Khalīj Libya 32°20N 23°15E 51 B10
Bumbiri I. Tanzania 1°40S 31°55E 54 C3
Bumhpa Bum Burma 26°51N 97°14E 41 F20
Bumi → Zimbabwe 17°0S 28°20E 55 F2
Buna Kenya 2°58N 39°30E 54 B4
Bunaken Indonesia 1°37N 124°46E 37 D6
Bunazi Tanzania 1°3S 31°23E 54 C3
Bunbury Australia 33°20S 115°35E 61 F2
Bunclody Ireland 52°39N 6°40W 10 D5
Buncrana Ireland 55°8N 7°27W 10 A4
Bundaberg Australia 24°54S 152°22E 63 C5
Bundey → Australia 21°46S 135°37E 62 C2
Bundi India 25°30N 75°35E 42 G6
Bundjalung △ Australia 29°16S 153°21E 63 D5
Bundoran Ireland 54°28N 8°16W 10 B3
Bung Kan Thailand 18°23N 103°37E 38 C4
Bungay U.K. 52°27N 1°28E 13 E9
Bungil Cr. → Australia 27°5S 149°5E 63 D4
Bungle Bungle = Purnululu △ Australia 17°20S 128°20E 60 C4
Bungo-Suidō Japan 33°0N 132°15E 31 H6
Bungoma Kenya 0°34N 34°34E 54 B3
Bungotakada Japan 33°35N 131°25E 31 H5
Bungu Tanzania 7°35S 39°0E 54 D4
Bunia Dem. Rep. of the Congo 1°35N 30°20E 54 B3
Bunji Pakistan 35°45N 74°40E 43 B6
Bunkie U.S.A. 30°57N 92°11W 84 F8
Bunnell U.S.A. 29°28N 81°16W 85 G14
Buntok Indonesia 1°40S 114°58E 36 E4
Bunya Mts. △ Australia 26°51S 151°34E 63 D5
Bunyola Spain 39°41N 2°42E 24 B9
Bunyu Indonesia 3°35N 117°50E 36 D5
Buol Indonesia 1°15N 121°32E 37 D6
Buon Brieng Vietnam 13°9N 108°12E 38 F7
Buon Ma Thuot Vietnam 12°40N 108°3E 38 F7
Buong Long Cambodia 13°44N 106°59E 38 F6
Buorkhaya, Mys Russia 71°50N 132°40E 29 B14
Buqayq Si. Arabia 26°0N 49°45E 45 E6
Bur Acaba = Buurhakaba Somali Rep. 3°12N 44°20E 47 G3
Bûr Safâga Egypt 26°43N 33°57E 44 E2
Bûr Sa'îd Egypt 31°16N 32°18E 51 B12
Bûr Sûdân Sudan 19°32N 37°9E 51 E13
Bura Kenya 1°4S 39°58E 54 C4
Burakin Australia 30°31S 117°10E 61 F2
Burao = Burco Somali Rep. 9°32N 45°32E 47 F4
Burāq Syria 33°11N 36°29E 46 B5
Buraydah Si. Arabia 26°20N 43°59E 44 E4
Burbank U.S.A. 34°12N 118°18W 79 L8
Burco Somali Rep. 9°32N 45°32E 47 F4
Burda India 25°50N 77°35E 42 G6
Burdekin → Australia 19°38S 147°25E 62 B4
Burdur Turkey 37°45N 30°17E 19 G5
Burdwan = Barddhaman India 23°14N 87°39E 43 H12
Bure Ethiopia 10°40N 37°4E 47 E2
Bure → U.K. 52°38N 1°43E 12 E9
Bureya → Russia 49°27N 129°30E 29 E13
Burford Canada 43°7N 80°27W 82 C4
Burgas Bulgaria 42°33N 27°29E 23 C12
Burgeo Canada 47°37N 57°38W 73 C8
Burgersdorp S. Africa 31°0S 26°20E 56 E4
Burgess, Mt. Australia 30°50S 121°5E 61 F3
Burghead U.K. 57°43N 3°30W 11 D5
Burgos Spain 42°21N 3°41W 21 A4
Burgsvik Sweden 57°3N 18°19E 9 H18
Burgundy = Bourgogne □ France 47°0N 4°50E 20 C6
Burhaniye Turkey 39°30N 26°58E 23 E12
Burhanpur India 21°18N 76°14E 40 J10
Burhi Gandak → India 25°20N 86°37E 43 G12
Burhner → India 22°43N 80°31E 43 H9
Burias I. Phil. 12°55N 123°5E 37 B6
Burica, Pta. Costa Rica 8°3N 82°51W 88 E3
Burien U.S.A. 47°28N 122°20W 78 C4
Burigi, L. Tanzania 2°2S 31°22E 54 C3
Burigi ⌓ Tanzania 2°20S 31°6E 54 C3
Burin Canada 47°1N 55°14W 73 C8
Buriram Thailand 15°0N 103°0E 38 E4
Burkburnett U.S.A. 34°6N 98°34W 84 D5
Burke → Australia 23°12S 139°33E 62 C2
Burke Chan. Canada 52°10N 127°30W 70 C3
Burketown Australia 17°45S 139°33E 62 B2
Burkina Faso ■ Africa 12°0N 1°0W 50 F5
Burk's Falls Canada 45°37N 79°24W 72 C4
Burleigh Falls Canada 44°33N 78°12W 82 B6
Burley U.S.A. 42°32N 113°48W 76 E7
Burlingame U.S.A. 37°35N 122°21W 78 H4
Burlington Canada 43°18N 79°45W 82 C5
Burlington Colo., U.S.A. 39°18N 102°16W 76 G12
Burlington Iowa, U.S.A. 40°49N 91°14W 80 E8
Burlington Kans., U.S.A. 38°12N 95°45W 80 F6
Burlington N.C., U.S.A. 36°6N 79°26W 85 C15
Burlington N.J., U.S.A. 40°4N 74°51W 83 F10
Burlington Vt., U.S.A. 44°29N 73°12W 83 B11
Burlington Wash., U.S.A. 48°28N 122°20W 78 B4
Burlington Wis., U.S.A. 42°41N 88°17W 80 D9
Burma ■ Asia 21°0N 96°30E 41 J20
Burnaby I. Canada 52°25N 131°19W 70 C2
Burnet U.S.A. 30°45N 98°14W 84 F5
Burney U.S.A. 40°53N 121°40W 76 F3
Burnham U.S.A. 40°38N 77°34W 82 F7
Burnham-on-Sea U.K. 51°14N 3°0W 13 F5
Burnie Australia 41°4S 145°56E 63 G4
Burnley U.K. 53°47N 2°14W 12 D5
Burns U.S.A. 43°35N 119°3W 76 E4
Burns Junction U.S.A. 42°47N 117°51W 76 E5
Burns Lake Canada 54°14N 125°45W 70 C3
Burnside → Canada 66°51N 108°4W 68 C9
Burnside, L. Australia 25°22S 123°0E 61 E3
Burnsville U.S.A. 44°47N 93°17W 80 C7
Burnt River Canada 44°41N 78°42W 82 B6
Burntwood → Canada 56°8N 96°34W 71 B9
Burntwood L. Canada 55°22N 100°26W 71 B8
Burqān Kuwait 29°0N 47°57E 44 D5
Burqin China 47°43N 87°0E 32 B3
Burra Australia 33°40S 138°55E 63 E2
Burray U.K. 58°51N 2°54W 11 C6
Burren Ireland 53°9N 9°5W 10 C2
Burren △ Ireland 53°1N 8°58W 10 C3
Burren Junction Australia 30°7S 148°58E 63 E4
Burrinjuck Res. Australia 35°0S 148°36E 63 F4
Burro, Serranías del Mexico 28°56N 102°5W 86 B4
Burrow Hd. U.K. 54°41N 4°24W 11 G4
Burrum Coast △ Australia 25°13S 152°36E 63 D5
Burruyacú Argentina 26°30S 64°40W 94 B3
Burry Port U.K. 51°41N 4°15W 13 F3
Bursa Turkey 40°15N 29°5E 23 D13
Burstall Canada 50°39N 109°54W 71 C7
Burton Ohio, U.S.A. 41°28N 81°8W 82 E3
Burton S.C., U.S.A. 32°26N 80°43W 85 E14
Burton, L. Canada 54°45N 78°20W 72 B4
Burton upon Trent U.K. 52°48N 1°38W 12 E6
Buru Indonesia 3°30S 126°30E 37 E7
Burûn, Râs Egypt 31°14N 33°7E 46 D2
Burundi ■ Africa 3°15S 30°0E 54 C3
Bururi Burundi 3°57S 29°37E 54 C2
Burutu Nigeria 5°20N 5°29E 50 G7
Burwell U.S.A. 41°47N 99°8W 80 E4
Burwick U.K. 58°45N 2°58W 11 C5
Bury U.K. 53°35N 2°17W 12 D5
Bury St. Edmunds U.K. 52°15N 0°43E 13
Buryatia □ Russia 53°0N 110°0E 29 D
Busan S. Korea 35°5N 129°0E 35 G
Busango Swamp Zambia 14°15S 25°45E 55
Buşayrah Syria 35°9N 40°26E 44
Būshehr Iran 28°55N 50°55E 45
Būshehr □ Iran 28°20N 51°45E 45
Bushenyi Uganda 0°35S 30°10E 54
Bushire = Būshehr Iran 28°55N 50°55E 45
Businga Dem. Rep. of the Congo 3°16N 20°59E 52
Buşra ash Shām Syria 32°30N 36°25E 46
Busselton Australia 33°42S 115°15E 61
Bussum Neths. 52°16N 5°10E 15
Busto Arsízio Italy 45°37N 8°51E 20
Busu Djanoa Dem. Rep. of the Congo 1°43N 21°23E 52
Busuanga I. Phil. 12°10N 120°0E 37
Busungbiu Indonesia 8°16S 114°58E 37 J
Buta Dem. Rep. of the Congo 2°50N 24°53E 54
Butare Rwanda 2°31S 29°52E 54
Butaritari Kiribati 3°30N 174°0E 64
Bute U.K. 55°48N 5°2W 11
Bute Inlet Canada 50°40N 124°53W 70
Butemba Uganda 1°9N 31°37E 54
Butembo Dem. Rep. of the Congo 0°9N 29°18E 54
Butere Kenya 0°13N 34°30E 54
Butha Qi China 48°0N 122°32E 33
Butiaba Uganda 1°50N 31°20E 54
Butler Mo., U.S.A. 38°16N 94°20W 80
Butler Pa., U.S.A. 40°52N 79°54W 82
Buton Indonesia 5°0S 122°45E 37
Butte Mont., U.S.A. 46°0N 112°32W 76
Butte Nebr., U.S.A. 42°58N 98°51W 80
Butte Creek → U.S.A. 39°12N 121°56W 78
Butterworth = Gcuwa S. Africa 32°20S 28°11E 57
Butterworth Malaysia 5°24N 100°23E 39
Buttevant Ireland 52°14N 8°40W 10
Buttfield, Mt. Australia 24°45S 128°9E 61
Button B. Canada 58°45N 94°23W 71 B
Buttonwillow U.S.A. 35°24N 119°28W 79
Butty Hd. Australia 33°54S 121°39E 61
Butuan Phil. 8°57N 125°33E 37
Butung = Buton Indonesia 5°0S 122°45E 37
Buturlinovka Russia 50°50N 40°35E 19
Buurhakaba Somali Rep. 3°12N 44°20E 47
Buxa Duar India 27°45N 89°35E 43 F
Buxar India 25°34N 83°58E 43 G
Buxoro Uzbekistan 39°48N 64°25E 28
Buxtehude Germany 53°28N 9°39E 16
Buxton U.K. 53°16N 1°54W 12
Buy Russia 58°28N 41°28E 18
Buyant-Uhaa Mongolia 44°55N 110°11E 33
Buyo, L. de Ivory C. 6°16N 7°10W 50
Büyük Menderes → Turkey 37°28N 27°11E 23 F
Büyükçekmece Turkey 41°2N 28°35E 23 D
Buzău Romania 45°10N 26°50E 17 F
Buzău → Romania 45°26N 27°44E 17 F
Buzen Japan 33°35N 131°5E 31
Buzi → Mozam. 19°50S 34°43E 55
Büzmeÿin Turkmenistan 38°3N 58°12E 45
Buzuluk Russia 52°48N 52°12E 18
Buzzards Bay U.S.A. 41°45N 70°37W 83 E
Bwana Mkubwe Dem. Rep. of the Congo 13°8S 28°38E 55
Bwindi △ Uganda 1°2S 29°42E 54
Byarezina → Belarus 52°33N 30°14E 17 B
Bydgoszcz Poland 53°10N 18°0E 17
Byelorussia = Belarus ■ Europe 53°30N 27°0E 17 B
Byers U.S.A. 39°43N 104°14W 76 G
Byesville U.S.A. 39°58N 81°32W 82
Byfield △ Australia 22°52S 150°45E 62
Bykhaw Belarus 53°31N 30°14E 17 B
Bykhov = Bykhaw Belarus 53°31N 30°14E 17 B
Bylas U.S.A. 33°8N 110°7W 77
Bylot Canada 58°25N 94°8W 71 B
Bylot I. Canada 73°13N 78°34W 69 B
Byrd, C. Antarctica 69°38S 76°7W 5 C
Byrock Australia 30°40S 146°27E 63
Byron, C. Australia 28°43S 153°38E 63
Byron Bay Australia 28°43S 153°37E 63
Byrranga, Gory Russia 75°0N 100°0E 29 B
Byrranga Mts. = Byrranga, Gory Russia 75°0N 100°0E 29 B
Byske Sweden 64°57N 21°11E 8 D
Byskeälven → Sweden 64°57N 21°13E 8 D
Bytom Poland 50°25N 18°54E 17 C
Bytów Poland 54°10N 17°30E 17
Byumba Rwanda 1°35S 30°4E 54

C

C.W. McConaughy, L. U.S.A. 41°14N 101°40W 80
Ca → Vietnam 18°45N 105°45E 38
Ca Mau Vietnam 9°7N 105°8E 39
Ca Mau, Mui Vietnam 8°38N 104°44E 39
Ca Na Vietnam 11°20N 108°54E 39
Caacupé Paraguay 25°23S 57°5W 94
Caaguazú △ Paraguay 26°5S 55°31W 95
Caála Angola 12°46S 15°30E 53
Caamaño Sd. Canada 52°55N 129°25W 70
Caazapá Paraguay 26°8S 56°19W 94
Caazapá □ Paraguay 26°10S 56°0W 95
Caballeria, C. de Spain 40°5N 4°5E 24 A
Cabanatuan Phil. 15°30N 120°58E 37
Cabano Canada 47°40N 68°56W 73
Cabazon U.S.A. 33°55N 116°47W 79 M
Cabedelo Brazil 7°0S 34°50W 93 E
Cabildo Chile 32°30S 71°5W 94
Cabimas Venezuela 10°23N 71°25W 92

binda Angola 5°33S 12°11E 52 F2
binda □ Angola 5°0S 12°30E 52 F2
binet Mts. U.S.A. 48°10N 115°50W 76 B6
bo Blanco Argentina 47°15S 65°47W 96 F3
bo Frio Brazil 22°51S 42°3W 95 A7
bo Pantoja Peru 1°0S 75°10W 92 D3
bo San Lucas Mexico 22°53N 109°54W 86 C3
bo Verde = Cape Verde Is. ■
Atl. Oc. 16°0N 24°0W 50 b
bonga, Réservoir
Canada 47°20N 76°40W 72 C4
bool U.S.A. 37°7N 92°6W 80 G7
boolture Australia 27°5S 152°58E 63 D5
bora Bassa Dam = Cahora
Bassa, Lago de Mozam. 15°20S 32°50E 55 F3
borca Mexico 30°37N 112°6W 86 A2
bot, Mt. U.S.A. 44°30N 71°25W 83 B13
bot Hd. Canada 45°14N 81°17W 82 A3
bot Str. Canada 47°15N 59°40W 73 C8
bra Spain 37°30N 4°28W 21 D3
brera Spain 39°8N 2°57E 24 B9
bri Canada 50°35N 108°25W 71 C7
briel → Spain 39°14N 1°3W 21 C5
ador Brazil 26°47S 51°0W 95 B5
ak Serbia 43°54N 20°20E 23 C9
apava do Sul Brazil 30°30S 53°30W 95 C5
eres Brazil 16°5S 57°40W 92 G7
eres Spain 39°26N 6°23W 21 C2
he Bay Canada 46°22N 80°0W 72 C4
he Cr. → U.S.A. 38°42N 121°42W 78 G5
he Creek Canada 50°48N 121°19W 70 C4
hi Argentina 25°5S 66°10W 94 B2
himbo, Serra do
razil 9°30S 55°30W 93 E7
hinal de la Sierra
hile 24°58S 69°32W 94 A2
hoeira Brazil 12°30S 39°0W 93 F11
hoeira do Sul Brazil 30°3S 52°53W 95 C5
hoeiro de Itapemirim
razil 20°51S 41°7W 95 A7
oal Brazil 11°32S 61°18W 92 F6
ólo Angola 10°9S 19°21E 52 G3
onda Angola 13°48S 15°8E 53 G3
do U.S.A. 34°7N 96°16W 84 D6
er Idris U.K. 52°42N 3°53W 13 E4
ereyta de Jiménez
exico 25°36N 100°0W 86 B5
barrawirracanna, L.
ustralia 28°52S 135°27E 63 D2
llac U.S.A. 44°15N 85°24W 81 C11
iz Phil. 10°57N 123°15E 37 B6
iz Spain 36°30N 6°20W 21 D2
iz Calif., U.S.A. 34°30N 115°28W 79 L11
iz Ohio, U.S.A. 40°22N 81°0W 82 F4
z, G. de Spain 36°40N 7°0W 21 D2
z L. U.S.A. 34°18N 115°24W 77 J6
ney Park Australia 27°55S 134°3E 63 D1
omin Canada 53°2N 117°20W 70 C5
otte Lake Canada 56°26N 116°23W 70 B5
oux Australia 30°46S 117°7E 61 F2
n France 49°10N 0°22W 20 B3
narfon U.K. 53°8N 4°16W 12 D3
narfon B. U.K. 53°4N 4°40W 12 D3
narvon = Caernarfon
K. 53°8N 4°16W 12 D3
philly U.K. 51°35N 3°13W 13 F4
philly □ U.K. 51°37N 3°12W 13 F4
area Israel 32°30N 34°53E 46 C3
ité Brazil 13°50S 42°32W 93 F10
yate Argentina 26°2S 66°0W 94 B2
Angola 16°30S 15°8E 56 B2
ayan de Oro Phil. 8°30N 124°40E 37 C6
ayan Is. Phil. 9°40N 121°16E 37 C5
iari Italy 39°13N 9°7E 22 E3
iari, G. di Italy 39°8N 9°11E 22 E3
hán → Colombia 0°8S 74°18W 92 D4
as Puerto Rico 18°14N 66°2W 89 d
n Mts. Ireland 51°45N 9°40W 10 E2
ama Angola 16°17S 14°19E 56 B1
er Ireland 52°22N 7°56W 10 D4
rsiveen Ireland 51°56N 10°14W 10 E1
ra Bassa, L. de
ozam. 15°35S 32°0E 55 F3
ra Bassa, Lago de
ozam. 15°20S 32°50E 55 F3
re Pt. Ireland 52°33N 6°12W 10 D5
rs France 44°27N 1°27E 20 D4
l Moldova 45°50N 28°15E 17 F15
au, Dao Vietnam 21°10N 107°27E 38 B6
uoc Vietnam 8°56N 105°1E 39 H5
Mozam. 17°51S 35°24E 55 F4
nda Angola 11°2S 23°31E 55 E1
arién Cuba 22°30N 79°30W 88 B4
ara Venezuela 7°38N 66°10W 92 B5
Brazil 6°20S 37°0W 93 E11
os Is. Turks & Caicos 21°40N 71°40W 89 B5
os Passage W. Indies 22°45N 72°45W 89 B5
una Australia 32°16S 125°29E 61 F4
Coast Antarctica 75°0S 25°0W 5 D1
Gorm U.K. 57°7N 3°39W 11 D5
gorm Mts. U.K. 57°6N 3°42W 11 D5
gorms △ U.K. 57°10N 3°50W 11 D5
ryan U.K. 54°59N 5°1W 11 G3
ns Australia 16°57S 145°45E 62 B4
ns L. Canada 51°42N 94°30W 71 C10
= El Qâhira Egypt 30°2N 31°13E 51 B12
Ga., U.S.A. 30°52N 84°13W 85 F12
Ill., U.S.A. 37°0N 89°11W 80 G9
N.Y., U.S.A. 42°18N 74°0W 83 D10
ness U.K. 58°25N 3°35W 11 C5
ness, Ord of U.K. 58°8N 3°36W 11 C5
de Muertos, I.
rto Rico 17°54N 66°32W 89 d
narca Peru 7°5S 78°28W 92 E3
eiras Brazil 6°52S 38°30W 93 E11
d'Or Spain 39°23N 3°14E 24 B10
en Porter Spain 39°52N 4°8E 24 B11
Cala Figuera Spain 39°20N 3°10E 24 B10
Cala Figuera, C. de Spain 39°27N 2°31E 24 B9
Cala Forcat Spain 40°0N 3°47E 24 B10
Cala Major Spain 39°33N 2°37E 24 B9
Cala Mezquida = Sa Mesquida
Spain 39°55N 4°16E 24 B11
Cala Millor Spain 39°35N 3°22E 24 B10
Cala Murada Spain 39°27N 3°17E 24 B10
Cala Ratjada Spain 39°43N 3°27E 24 B10
Cala Santa Galdana
Spain 39°56N 3°58E 24 B10
Calabar Nigeria 4°57N 8°20E 50 H7
Calabogie Canada 45°18N 76°43W 83 A8
Calabozo Venezuela 9°0N 67°28W 92 B5
Calábria □ Italy 39°0N 16°30E 22 E7
Calahorra Spain 42°18N 1°59W 21 A5
Calais France 50°57N 1°56E 20 A4
Calais U.S.A. 45°11N 67°17W 81 C20
Calakmul △ Mexico 18°14N 89°48W 87 D7
Calalaste, Cord. de
Argentina 25°0S 67°0W 94 B2
Calama Brazil 8°0S 62°50W 92 E6
Calama Chile 22°30S 68°55W 94 A2
Calamar Colombia 10°15N 74°55W 92 A4
Calamian Group Phil. 11°50N 119°55E 37 B5
Calamocha Spain 40°50N 1°17W 21 B5
Calang Indonesia 4°37N 95°37E 36 D1
Calanscio, Sarīr Libya 27°30N 21°30E 51 C10
Calapan Phil. 13°25N 121°7E 37 B6
Călăraşi Romania 44°12N 27°20E 17 F14
Calatayud Spain 41°20N 1°40W 21 B5
Calauag Phil. 13°55N 122°15E 37 B6
Calavite, C. Phil. 13°26N 120°20E 37 B6
Calbayog Phil. 12°4N 124°38E 37 B6
Calca Peru 13°22S 72°0W 92 F4
Calcasieu L. U.S.A. 29°55N 93°18W 84 G8
Calcium U.S.A. 44°1N 75°50W 83 B9
Calcutta = Kolkata
India 22°34N 88°21E 43 H13
Calcutta U.S.A. 40°40N 80°34W 82 F4
Caldas da Rainha Portugal 39°24N 9°8W 21 C1
Calder → U.K. 53°44N 1°22W 12 D6
Caldera Chile 27°5S 70°55W 94 B1
Caldera de Taburiente △
Canary Is. 28°43N 17°52W 24 F2
Caldwell Idaho, U.S.A. 43°40N 116°41W 76 E5
Caldwell Kans., U.S.A. 37°2N 97°37W 80 G5
Caldwell Tex., U.S.A. 30°32N 96°42W 84 F6
Caledon Canada 43°51N 79°51W 82 C5
Caledon S. Africa 34°14S 19°26E 56 E2
Caledon → S. Africa 30°31S 26°5E 56 E4
Caledon B. Australia 12°45S 137°0E 62 A2
Caledonia Canada 43°7N 79°58W 82 C5
Caledonia U.S.A. 42°58N 77°51W 82 D7
Calemba Angola 16°0S 15°44E 56 B2
Calen Australia 20°56S 148°48E 62 J6
Caletones Chile 34°6S 70°27W 94 C1
Calexico U.S.A. 32°40N 115°30W 79 N11
Calf of Man I. of Man 54°3N 4°48W 12 C3
Calgary Canada 51°0N 114°10W 70 C6
Calheta Madeira 32°44N 17°11W 24 D2
Calhoun U.S.A. 34°30N 84°57W 85 D12
Cali Colombia 3°25N 76°35W 92 C3
Calicut India 11°15N 75°43E 40 P9
Caliente U.S.A. 37°37N 114°31W 77 H6
California Mo., U.S.A. 38°38N 92°34W 80 F7
California Pa., U.S.A. 40°4N 79°54W 82 F5
California □ U.S.A. 37°30N 119°30W 78 H7
California, Baja, T.N. = Baja
California □ Mexico 30°0N 115°0W 86 B2
California, Baja, T.S. = Baja
California Sur □
Mexico 25°50N 111°50W 86 B2
California, G. de Mexico 27°0N 111°0W 86 B2
California City U.S.A. 35°10N 117°55W 79 K9
California Hot Springs
U.S.A. 35°51N 118°41W 79 K8
Calilegua △ Argentina 25°36S 64°50W 94 B3
Calingasta Argentina 31°15S 69°30W 94 C2
Calipatria U.S.A. 33°8N 115°31W 79 M11
Calistoga U.S.A. 38°35N 122°35W 78 G4
Calitzdorp S. Africa 33°33S 21°42E 56 E3
Callabonna, L. Australia 29°40S 140°5E 63 D3
Callan Ireland 52°32N 7°24W 10 D4
Callander U.K. 56°15N 4°13W 11 E4
Callao Peru 12°3S 77°8W 92 F3
Callicoon U.S.A. 41°46N 75°3W 83 E9
Calling Lake Canada 55°15N 113°12W 70 B6
Calliope Australia 24°0S 151°16E 62 C5
Calma, Costa de la Spain 39°28N 2°26E 24 B9
Calne U.K. 51°26N 2°0W 13 F6
Calola Angola 16°25S 17°48E 56 B2
Caloundra Australia 26°45S 153°10E 63 D5
Calpella U.S.A. 39°14N 123°12W 78 F3
Calpine U.S.A. 39°40N 120°27W 78 F6
Calstock Canada 49°47N 84°9W 72 C3
Caltagirone Italy 37°14N 14°31E 22 F6
Caltanissetta Italy 37°29N 14°4E 22 F6
Calulo Angola 10°1S 14°56E 52 G2
Calvert → Australia 16°17S 137°44E 62 B2
Calvert I. Canada 51°30N 128°0W 70 C3
Calvert Ra. Australia 24°0S 122°30E 60 D3
Calvi France 42°34N 8°45E 20 E8
Calvià Spain 39°34N 2°31E 24 B9
Calvillo Mexico 21°51N 102°43W 86 C4
Calvinia S. Africa 31°28S 19°45E 56 E2
Calwa U.S.A. 36°42N 119°46W 78 J7
Cam → U.K. 52°21N 0°16E 13 E8
Cam Lam Vietnam 11°54N 109°10E 39 G7
Cam Pha Vietnam 21°7N 107°18E 38 B6
Cam Ranh Vietnam 11°54N 109°12E 39 G7
Cam Xuyen Vietnam 18°15N 106°0E 38 C6
Camabatela Angola 8°20S 15°26E 52 F3
Camacha Madeira 32°41N 16°49W 24 D3
Camacupa Angola 11°58S 17°22E 53 G3
Camagüey Cuba 21°20N 77°55W 88 B4
Camaná Peru 16°30S 72°50W 92 G4
Camanche Res. U.S.A. 38°14N 121°1W 78 G6
Camaquã Brazil 30°51S 51°49W 95 C5
Camaquã → Brazil 31°17S 51°47W 95 C5
Câmara de Lobos
Madeira 32°39N 16°59W 24 D3
Camargo Mexico 26°19N 98°50W 87 B5
Camarillo U.S.A. 34°13N 119°2W 79 L7
Camarón, C. Honduras 16°0N 85°5W 88 C2
Camarones Argentina 44°50S 65°40W 96 E3
Camas U.S.A. 45°35N 122°24W 78 E4
Camas Valley U.S.A. 43°2N 123°40W 76 E2
Camballin Australia 17°59S 124°12E 60 C3
Cambará Brazil 23°2S 50°5W 95 A5
Cambay = Khambhat
India 22°23N 72°33E 42 H5
Cambay, G. of = Khambhat, G. of
India 20°45N 72°30E 40 J8
Cambodia ■ Asia 12°15N 105°0E 38 F5
Camborne U.K. 50°12N 5°19W 13 G2
Cambrai France 50°11N 3°14E 20 A5
Cambria U.S.A. 35°34N 121°5W 78 K5
Cambrian Mts. U.K. 52°3N 3°57W 13 E4
Cambridge Canada 43°23N 80°15W 82 C4
Cambridge Jamaica 18°18N 77°54W 88 a
Cambridge N.Z. 37°54S 175°29E 59 B5
Cambridge U.K. 52°12N 0°8E 13 E8
Cambridge Mass., U.S.A. 42°23N 71°7W 83 D13
Cambridge Minn., U.S.A. 45°34N 93°13W 80 C7
Cambridge N.Y., U.S.A. 43°2N 73°22W 83 C11
Cambridge Nebr.,
U.S.A. 40°17N 100°10W 80 E3
Cambridge Ohio, U.S.A. 40°2N 81°35W 82 F3
Cambridge Bay = Ikaluktutiak
Canada 69°10N 105°0W 68 C9
Cambridge G. Australia 14°55S 128°15E 60 B4
Cambridge Springs
U.S.A. 41°48N 80°4W 82 E4
Cambridgeshire □ U.K. 52°25N 0°7W 13 E7
Cambuci Brazil 21°35S 41°55W 95 A7
Cambundi-Catembo
Angola 10°10S 17°35E 52 G3
Camden Australia 34°1S 150°43E 63 B5
Camden Ala., U.S.A. 31°59N 87°17W 85 F11
Camden Ark., U.S.A. 33°35N 92°50W 84 E8
Camden Maine, U.S.A. 44°13N 69°4W 81 C19
Camden N.J., U.S.A. 39°55N 75°7W 83 G9
Camden N.Y., U.S.A. 43°20N 75°45W 83 C9
Camden S.C., U.S.A. 34°16N 80°36W 85 D14
Camden Sd. Australia 15°27S 124°25E 60 C3
Camdenton U.S.A. 38°1N 92°45W 80 F7
Camelford U.K. 50°37N 4°42W 13 G3
Cameron Ariz., U.S.A. 35°53N 111°25W 77 J8
Cameron La., U.S.A. 29°48N 93°20W 84 G8
Cameron Mo., U.S.A. 39°44N 94°14W 80 F6
Cameron Tex., U.S.A. 30°51N 96°59W 84 F6
Cameron Highlands
Malaysia 4°27N 101°22E 39 K3
Cameron Hills Canada 59°48N 118°0W 70 B5
Cameroon ■ Africa 6°0N 12°30E 51 G7
Cameroun, Mt. Cameroon 4°13N 9°10E 52 D1
Cametá Brazil 2°12S 49°30W 93 D9
Camiguin I. Phil. 18°56N 121°55E 37 C6
Camilla U.S.A. 31°14N 84°12W 85 F12
Caminha Portugal 41°50N 8°50W 21 B1
Camino U.S.A. 38°44N 120°41W 78 G6
Camira Creek Australia 29°15S 152°58E 63 D5
Cammal U.S.A. 41°24N 77°28W 82 E7
Camocim Brazil 2°55S 40°50W 93 D10
Camooweal Australia 19°56S 138°7E 62 B2
Camooweal Caves △
Australia 20°1S 138°11E 62 C2
Camopi Fr. Guiana 3°12N 52°17W 93 C8
Camp Hill U.S.A. 40°14N 76°55W 82 F8
Camp Nelson U.S.A. 36°8N 118°39W 79 J8
Camp Pendleton
U.S.A. 33°13N 117°24W 79 M9
Camp Verde U.S.A. 34°34N 111°51W 77 J8
Camp Wood U.S.A. 29°40N 100°1W 84 G4
Campana Argentina 34°10S 58°55W 94 C4
Campana, I. Chile 48°20S 75°20W 96 F1
Campanário Madeira 32°39N 17°2W 24 D2
Campanet Spain 39°46N 2°58E 24 B9
Campánia □ Italy 41°0N 14°30E 22 D6
Campbell S. Africa 28°48S 23°44E 56 D3
Campbell Calif., U.S.A. 37°17N 121°57W 78 H5
Campbell Ohio, U.S.A. 41°5N 80°37W 82 E4
Campbell I. Pac. Oc. 52°30S 169°0E 64 N8
Campbell L. Canada 63°14N 106°55W 71 A7
Campbell Plateau S. Ocean 50°0S 170°0E 5 A11
Campbell River Canada 50°5N 125°20W 70 C3
Campbell Town
Australia 41°52S 147°30E 63 G4
Campbellford Canada 44°18N 77°48W 82 B7
Campbellpur Pakistan 33°46N 72°26E 42 C5
Campbellsville U.S.A. 37°21N 85°20W 81 G11
Campbellton Canada 47°57N 66°43W 73 C6
Campbelltown Australia 34°4S 150°49E 63 E5
Campbeltown U.K. 55°26N 5°36W 11 F3
Campeche Mexico 19°51N 90°32W 87 D6
Campeche □ Mexico 19°0N 90°30W 87 D6
Campeche, Golfo de
Mexico 19°30N 93°0W 87 D6
Camperdown Australia 38°14S 143°9E 63 F3
Camperville Canada 51°59N 100°9W 71 C8
Câmpina Romania 45°10N 25°45E 17 F13
Campina Grande Brazil 7°20S 35°47W 93 E11
Campinas Brazil 22°50S 47°0W 95 A6
Campo Grande Brazil 20°25S 54°40W 93 H8
Campo Maior Brazil 4°50S 42°12W 93 D10
Campo Mourão Brazil 24°3S 52°22W 95 A5
Campobasso Italy 41°34N 14°39E 22 D6
Campos Brazil 21°50S 41°20W 95 A7
Campos Spain 39°26N 3°1E 24 B10
Campos Belos Brazil 13°10S 47°3W 93 F9
Campos Novos Brazil 27°21S 51°50W 95 B5
Camptonville U.S.A. 39°27N 121°3W 78 F5
Camptown U.S.A. 41°44N 76°14W 83 E8
Câmpulung Romania 45°17N 25°3E 17 F13
Camrose Canada 53°0N 112°50W 70 C6
Camsell Portage
Canada 59°37N 109°15W 71 B7
Çan Turkey 40°2N 27°3E 23 D12
Can Clavo Spain 38°57N 1°27E 24 C7
Can Creu Spain 38°58N 1°28E 24 C7
Can Gio Vietnam 10°25N 106°58E 39 G6
Can Pastilla Spain 39°32N 2°42E 24 B9
Can Tho Vietnam 10°2N 105°46E 39 G5
Canaan U.S.A. 42°2N 73°20W 83 D11
Canada ■ N. Amer. 60°0N 100°0W 68 D10
Canada Abyssal Plain
Arctic 80°0N 140°0W 4 B18
Canada Basin Arctic 80°0N 145°0W 4 B18
Cañada de Gómez
Argentina 32°40S 61°30W 94 C3
Canadian U.S.A. 35°55N 100°23W 84 D4
Canadian → U.S.A. 35°28N 95°3W 84 D7
Canadian Shield Canada 53°0N 75°0W 66 D12
Canajoharie U.S.A. 42°54N 74°35W 83 D10
Çanakkale Turkey 40°8N 26°24E 23 D12
Çanakkale Boğazı
Turkey 40°17N 26°32E 23 D12
Canal Flats Canada 50°10N 115°48W 70 C5
Canalejas Argentina 35°15S 66°34W 94 D2
Canals Argentina 33°35S 62°53W 94 C3
Canandaigua U.S.A. 42°54N 77°17W 82 D7
Canandaigua L. U.S.A. 42°47N 77°19W 82 D7
Cananea Mexico 31°0N 110°18W 86 A2
Canarias, Is. Atl. Oc. 28°30N 16°0W 24 F4
Canaries St. Lucia 13°55N 61°4W 89 f
Canarreos, Arch. de los
Cuba 21°35N 81°40W 88 B3
Canary Is. = Canarias, Is.
Atl. Oc. 28°30N 16°0W 24 F4
Canaseraga U.S.A. 42°27N 77°45W 82 D7
Canatlán Mexico 24°31N 104°47W 86 C4
Canaveral, C. U.S.A. 28°27N 80°32W 85 G14
Canaveral △ U.S.A. 28°28N 80°34W 85 G14
Canavieiras Brazil 15°39S 39°0W 93 G11
Canberra Australia 35°15S 149°8E 63 F4
Canby Calif., U.S.A. 41°27N 120°52W 76 F3
Canby Minn., U.S.A. 44°43N 96°16W 80 C5
Canby Oreg., U.S.A. 45°16N 122°42W 78 E4
Cancún Mexico 21°8N 86°44W 87 C7
Candelaria Argentina 27°29S 55°44W 95 B4
Candelaria Canary Is. 28°22N 16°22W 24 F3
Candelo Australia 36°47S 149°43E 63 F4
Candi Dasa Indonesia 8°30S 115°34E 37 J18
Candia = Iraklio Greece 35°20N 25°12E 25 D7
Candle L. Canada 53°50N 105°18W 71 C7
Candlemas I. Antarctica 57°3S 26°40W 5 B1
Cando U.S.A. 48°32N 99°12W 80 A4
Canea = Chania Greece 35°30N 24°4E 25 D6
Canelones Uruguay 34°32S 56°17W 95 C4
Cañete Chile 37°50S 73°30W 94 D1
Cangas del Narcea Spain 43°10N 6°32W 21 A2
Canguaretama Brazil 6°20S 35°5W 93 E11
Canguçu Brazil 31°22S 52°43W 95 C5
Canguçu, Serra do
Brazil 31°20S 52°40W 95 C5
Cangzhou China 38°19N 116°52E 34 E9
Caniapiscau → Canada 56°40N 69°30W 73 A6
Caniapiscau, L. Canada 54°10N 69°55W 73 B6
Canicattì Italy 37°21N 13°51E 22 F5
Canim Lake Canada 51°47N 120°54W 70 C4
Canindeyu □ Paraguay 24°10S 55°0W 95 A5
Canisteo U.S.A. 42°16N 77°36W 82 D7
Canisteo → U.S.A. 42°7N 77°8W 82 D7
Cañitas de Felipe Pescador
Mexico 23°36N 102°43W 86 C4
Çankırı Turkey 40°40N 33°37E 19 F5
Cankuzo Burundi 3°10S 30°31E 54 C3
Canmore Canada 51°7N 115°18W 70 C5
Cann River Australia 37°35S 149°7E 63 F4
Canna U.K. 57°3N 6°33W 11 D2
Cannanore India 11°53N 75°27E 40 P9
Cannes France 43°32N 7°1E 20 E7
Canning Town = Port Canning
India 22°23N 88°40E 43 H13
Cannington Canada 44°20N 79°2W 82 B5
Cannock U.K. 52°41N 2°1W 13 E5
Cannonball → U.S.A. 46°26N 100°35W 80 B3
Cannondale Mt.
Australia 25°13S 148°57E 62 D4
Cannonsville Res. U.S.A. 42°4N 75°22W 83 D9
Cannonvale Australia 20°17S 148°43E 62 J6
Canoas Brazil 29°56S 51°11W 95 B5
Canoe L. Canada 55°10N 108°15W 71 B7
Cañon City U.S.A. 38°27N 105°14W 76 G11
Cañón de Río Blanco △
Mexico 18°43N 97°15W 87 D5
Cañón del Sumidero △
Mexico 19°22N 96°24W 87 D5
Canonniers Pt. Mauritius 20°2S 57°32E 53 d
Canora Canada 51°40N 102°30W 71 C8
Canowindra Australia 33°35S 148°38E 63 E4
Canso Canada 45°20N 61°0W 73 C7
Cantabria □ Spain 43°10N 4°0W 21 A4
Cantabrian Mts. = Cantábrica,
Cordillera Spain 43°0N 5°10W 21 A3
Cantábrica, Cordillera
Spain 43°0N 5°10W 21 A3
Cantal, Plomb du France 45°3N 2°45E 20 D5
Canterbury Australia 25°23S 141°53E 62 D3
Canterbury U.K. 51°16N 1°6E 13 F9
Canterbury Bight N.Z. 44°16S 171°55E 59 F3
Canterbury Plains N.Z. 43°55S 171°22E 59 E3
Cantil U.S.A. 35°18N 117°58W 79 K9
Canton = Guangzhou
China 23°6N 113°13E 33 D6
Canton Ga., U.S.A. 34°14N 84°29W 85 D12
Canton Ill., U.S.A. 40°33N 90°2W 80 E8
Canton Miss., U.S.A. 32°37N 90°2W 85 E9
Canton Mo., U.S.A. 40°8N 91°32W 80 E8
Canton N.Y., U.S.A. 44°36N 75°10W 83 B9
Canton Ohio, U.S.A. 40°48N 81°23W 82 F3
Canton Pa., U.S.A. 41°39N 76°51W 82 E8
Canton S. Dak., U.S.A. 43°18N 96°35W 80 D5
Canton L. U.S.A. 36°6N 98°35W 84 C5
Canudos Brazil 7°13S 58°5W 92 E7
Canumã → Brazil 3°55S 59°10W 92 D7
Canutama Brazil 6°30S 64°20W 92 E6
Canutillo U.S.A. 31°55N 106°36W 84 F1
Canvey U.K. 51°31N 0°37E 13 F8
Canyon U.S.A. 34°59N 101°55W 84 D4
Canyon De Chelly △
U.S.A. 36°10N 109°20W 77 H9
Canyonlands △ U.S.A. 38°15N 110°0W 77 G9
Canyons of the Ancients △
U.S.A. 37°30N 108°55W 77 H9
Canyonville U.S.A. 42°56N 123°17W 76 E2
Cao Bang Vietnam 22°40N 106°15E 38 A6
Cao He → China 40°10N 124°32E 35 D13
Cao Lanh Vietnam 10°27N 105°38E 39 G5
Cao Xian China 34°50N 115°35E 34 G8
Cap-aux-Meules Canada 47°23N 61°52W 73 C7
Cap-Chat Canada 49°6N 66°40W 73 C6
Cap-de-la-Madeleine
Canada 46°22N 72°31W 72 C5
Cap-Haïtien Haiti 19°40N 72°20W 89 C5
Cap Pt. St. Lucia 14°7N 60°57W 89 f
Capac U.S.A. 43°1N 82°56W 82 C2
Capanaparo → Venezuela 7°1N 67°7W 92 B5
Cape → Australia 20°59S 146°51E 62 C4
Cape Arid △ Australia 33°58S 123°13E 61 F3
Cape Barren I. Australia 40°25S 148°15E 63 G4
Cape Breton Highlands △
Canada 46°50N 60°40W 73 C7
Cape Breton I. Canada 46°0N 60°30W 73 C7
Cape Charles U.S.A. 37°16N 76°1W 81 G15
Cape Coast Ghana 5°5N 1°15W 50 G5
Cape Cod △ U.S.A. 41°56N 70°6W 81 E18
Cape Coral U.S.A. 26°33N 81°57W 85 H14
Cape Crawford Australia 16°41S 135°43E 62 B2
Cape Dorset = Kingait
Canada 64°14N 76°32W 69 C12
Cape Fear → U.S.A. 33°53N 78°1W 85 E15
Cape Girardeau U.S.A. 37°19N 89°32W 80 G9
Cape Hatteras △
U.S.A. 35°30N 75°28W 85 D17
Cape Le Grand △
Australia 33°54S 122°26E 61 F3
Cape Lookout △
U.S.A. 35°45N 76°25W 85 D16
Cape May U.S.A. 38°56N 74°56W 81 F16
Cape May Point U.S.A. 38°56N 74°58W 81 F16
Cape Melville △
Australia 14°26S 144°28E 62 A3
Cape Peninsula △
S. Africa 34°20S 18°28E 56 E2
Cape Range △ Australia 22°3S 114°0E 60 D1
Cape St. George Canada 48°28N 59°14W 73 C8
Cape Tormentine Canada 46°8N 63°47W 73 C7
Cape Town S. Africa 33°55S 18°22E 56 E2
Cape Tribulation △
Australia 16°5S 145°25E 62 B4
Cape Verde Is. ■ Atl. Oc. 16°0N 24°0W 50 b
Cape Vincent U.S.A. 44°8N 76°20W 83 B8
Cape York Peninsula
Australia 12°0S 142°30E 62 A3
Capela Brazil 10°30S 37°0W 93 F11
Capella Australia 23°2S 148°1E 62 C4
Capesterre-Belle-Eau
Guadeloupe 16°4N 61°36W 88 b
Capesterre-de-Marie-Galante
Guadeloupe 15°53N 61°14W 88 b
Capim → Brazil 1°40S 47°47W 93 D9
Capitan U.S.A. 33°35N 105°35W 77 K11
Capitán Arturo Prat
Antarctica 63°0S 61°0W 5 C17
Capitol Reef △ U.S.A. 38°15N 111°10W 77 G8
Capitola U.S.A. 36°59N 121°57W 78 J5
Capoche → Mozam. 15°35S 33°0E 55 F3
Capraia Italy 43°2N 9°50E 20 E8
Capreol Canada 46°43N 80°56W 72 C3
Capri Italy 40°33N 14°14E 22 D6
Capricorn Coast
Australia 23°16S 150°49E 62 C5
Capricorn Group
Australia 23°30S 151°55E 62 C5
Capricorn Ra. Australia 23°20S 116°50E 60 D2
Caprivi Game △ Namibia 17°55S 22°37E 56 B3
Caprivi Strip Namibia 18°0S 23°0E 56 B3
Captain's Flat Australia 35°35S 149°27E 63 F4
Capulin Volcano △
U.S.A. 36°47N 103°58W 84 C3
Caquetá → Colombia 1°15S 69°15W 92 D5
Caracal Romania 44°8N 24°22E 17 F13
Caracas Venezuela 10°30N 66°55W 92 A5
Caracol Belize 16°45N 89°6E 88 C2
Caracol Mato Grosso do Sul,
Brazil 22°18S 57°1W 94 A4
Caracol Piauí, Brazil 9°15S 43°22W 93 E10
Carajas Brazil 6°5S 50°23W 93 E8
Carajás, Serra dos Brazil 6°0S 51°30W 93 E8
Carangola Brazil 20°44S 42°5W 95 A7
Caransebeş Romania 45°28N 22°18E 17 F12
Caraquet Canada 47°48N 64°57W 73 C6
Caratasca, L. de
Honduras 15°20N 83°40W 88 C3
Caratinga Brazil 19°50S 42°10W 93 G10
Caraúbas Brazil 5°43S 37°33W 93 E11
Caravaca de la Cruz Spain 38°8N 1°52W 21 C5
Caravelas Brazil 17°45S 39°15W 93 G11
Caraveli Peru 15°45S 73°25W 92 G4
Caravelle, Presqu'île de la
Martinique 14°46N 60°48W 88 c
Caraz Peru 9°3S 77°47W 92 E3
Carazinho Brazil 28°16S 52°46W 95 B5
Carballo Spain 43°13N 8°41W 21 A1
Carberry Canada 49°50N 99°25W 71 D9
Carbó Mexico 29°42N 110°58W 86 B2

Carbonara, C. *Italy* 39°6N 9°31E **22** E3
Carbondale *Colo., U.S.A.* 39°24N 107°13W **76** G10
Carbondale *Ill., U.S.A.* 37°44N 89°13W **80** G9
Carbondale *Pa., U.S.A.* 41°35N 75°30W **83** E9
Carbonear *Canada* 47°42N 53°13W **73** C9
Carbónia *Italy* 39°10N 8°30E **22** E3
Carcajou *Canada* 57°47N 117°6W **70** B5
Carcarana → *Argentina* 32°27S 60°48W **94** C3
Carcasse, C. *Haiti* 18°30N 74°28W **89** C5
Carcassonne *France* 43°13N 2°20E **20** E5
Carcross *Canada* 60°13N 134°45W **70** A2
Cardamon Hills *India* 9°30N 77°15E **40** Q10
Cardamon Mts. = Kravanh, Chuor Phnum *Cambodia* 12°0N 103°32E **39** G4
Cárdenas *Cuba* 23°0N 81°30W **88** B3
Cárdenas *San Luis Potosí, Mexico* 22°0N 99°38W **87** C5
Cárdenas *Tabasco, Mexico* 17°59N 93°22W **87** D6
Cardiff *U.K.* 51°29N 3°10W **13** F4
Cardiff □ *U.K.* 51°31N 3°12W **13** F4
Cardiff-by-the-Sea *U.S.A.* 33°1N 117°17W **79** M9
Cardigan *U.K.* 52°5N 4°40W **13** E3
Cardigan B. *U.K.* 52°30N 4°30W **13** E3
Cardinal *Canada* 44°47N 75°23W **83** B9
Cardona *Uruguay* 33°53S 57°18W **94** C4
Cardoso, Ilha do *Brazil* 25°8S 47°58W **95** B5
Cardston *Canada* 49°15N 113°20W **70** D6
Cardwell *Australia* 18°14S 146°2E **62** B4
Careen L. *Canada* 57°0N 108°11W **71** B7
Carei *Romania* 47°40N 22°29E **17** E12
Careme = Ciremay *Indonesia* 6°55S 108°27E **37** G13
Carey *U.S.A.* 43°19N 113°57W **76** E7
Carey, L. *Australia* 29°0S 122°15E **61** E3
Carey L. *Canada* 62°12N 102°55W **71** A8
Carhué *Argentina* 37°10S 62°50W **94** D3
Caria *Turkey* 37°20N 28°10E **23** F13
Cariacica *Brazil* 20°16S 40°25W **93** H10
Caribbean Sea *W. Indies* 15°0N 75°0W **89** D5
Cariboo Mts. *Canada* 53°0N 121°0W **70** C4
Caribou *U.S.A.* 46°52N 68°1W **81** B19
Caribou → *Man., Canada* 59°20N 94°44W **71** B10
Caribou → *N.W.T., Canada* 61°27N 125°45W **70** A3
Caribou I. *Canada* 47°22N 85°49W **72** C2
Caribou Is. *Canada* 61°55N 113°15W **70** A6
Caribou L. *Man., Canada* 59°21N 96°10W **71** B9
Caribou L. *Ont., Canada* 50°25N 89°5W **72** B2
Caribou Mts. *Canada* 59°12N 115°40W **70** B5
Caribou River ⌓ *Canada* 59°35N 96°35W **71** B9
Carichíc *Mexico* 27°56N 107°3W **86** B3
Carinda *Australia* 30°28S 147°41E **63** E4
Carinhanha *Brazil* 14°15S 44°46W **93** F10
Carinhanha → *Brazil* 14°20S 43°47W **93** F10
Carinthia = Kärnten □ *Austria* 46°52N 13°30E **16** E8
Caripito *Venezuela* 10°8N 63°6W **92** A6
Carleton, Mt. *Canada* 47°23N 66°53W **73** C6
Carleton Place *Canada* 45°8N 76°9W **83** A8
Carletonville *S. Africa* 26°23S 27°22E **56** D4
Carlin *U.S.A.* 40°43N 116°7W **76** F5
Carlingford L. *U.K.* 54°3N 6°9W **10** B5
Carlinville *U.S.A.* 39°17N 89°53W **80** F9
Carlisle *U.K.* 54°54N 2°56W **12** C5
Carlisle *U.S.A.* 40°12N 77°12W **82** F7
Carlisle B. *Barbados* 13°5N 59°37W **89** g
Carlisle I. *Australia* 20°49S 149°18E **62** J7
Carlos Casares *Argentina* 35°32S 61°20W **94** D3
Carlos Tejedor *Argentina* 35°25S 62°25W **94** D3
Carlow *Ireland* 52°50N 6°56W **10** D5
Carlow □ *Ireland* 52°43N 6°50W **10** D5
Carlsbad *Calif., U.S.A.* 33°10N 117°21W **79** M9
Carlsbad *N. Mex., U.S.A.* 32°25N 104°14W **77** K11
Carlsbad Caverns △ *U.S.A.* 32°10N 104°35W **77** K11
Carluke *U.K.* 55°45N 3°50W **11** F5
Carlyle *Canada* 49°40N 102°20W **71** D8
Carmacks *Canada* 62°5N 136°16W **68** C6
Carman *Canada* 49°30N 98°0W **71** D9
Carmarthen *U.K.* 51°52N 4°19W **13** F3
Carmarthen B. *U.K.* 51°40N 4°30W **13** F3
Carmarthenshire □ *U.K.* 51°55N 4°13W **13** F3
Carmaux *France* 44°3N 2°10E **20** D5
Carmel *U.S.A.* 41°26N 73°41W **83** E11
Carmel-by-the-Sea *U.S.A.* 36°33N 121°55W **78** J5
Carmel Valley *U.S.A.* 36°29N 121°43W **78** J5
Carmelo *Uruguay* 34°0S 58°20W **94** C4
Carmen *Paraguay* 27°13S 56°12W **95** B4
Carmen → *Mexico* 30°42N 106°29W **86** A3
Carmen, I. *Mexico* 25°57N 111°12W **86** B2
Carmen de Patagones *Argentina* 40°50S 63°0W **96** E4
Carmensa *Argentina* 35°15S 67°40W **94** D2
Carmi *Canada* 49°36N 119°8W **70** D5
Carmi *U.S.A.* 38°5N 88°10W **80** F9
Carmichael *U.S.A.* 38°38N 121°19W **78** G5
Carmila *Australia* 21°55S 149°24E **62** C4
Carmona *Costa Rica* 10°0N 85°15W **88** E2
Carmona *Spain* 37°28N 5°42W **21** D3
Carn Ban *U.K.* 57°7N 4°15W **11** D4
Carn Eige *U.K.* 57°17N 5°8W **11** D3
Carnamah *Australia* 29°41S 115°53E **61** E2
Carnarvon *Australia* 24°51S 113°42E **61** D1
Carnarvon *Canada* 45°3N 78°41W **82** A6
Carnarvon *S. Africa* 30°56S 22°8E **56** E3
Carnarvon △ *Australia* 24°54S 148°2E **62** C4
Carnarvon Ra. *Queens., Australia* 25°15S 148°30E **62** D4
Carnarvon Ra. *W. Austral., Australia* 25°20S 120°45E **61** E3
Carnation *U.S.A.* 47°39N 121°55W **78** C5
Carncastle *U.K.* 54°54N 5°53W **10** B6
Carndonagh *Ireland* 55°16N 7°15W **10** A4
Carnduff *Canada* 49°10N 101°50W **71** D8
Carnegie *U.S.A.* 40°24N 80°5W **82** F4
Carnegie, L. *Australia* 26°5S 122°30E **61** E3
Carnegie Ridge *Pac. Oc.* 1°0S 87°0W **65** H19
Carnic Alps = Karnische Alpen *Europe* 46°36N 13°0E **16** E7
Carniche Alpi = Karnische Alpen *Europe* 46°36N 13°0E **16** E7
Carnot *C.A.R.* 4°59N 15°56E **52** D3
Carnot, C. *Australia* 34°57S 135°38E **63** E2
Carnot B. *Australia* 17°20S 122°15E **60** C3
Carnoustie *U.K.* 56°30N 2°42W **11** E6
Carnsore Pt. *Ireland* 52°10N 6°22W **10** D5
Caro *U.S.A.* 43°29N 83°24W **81** D12
Caroga Lake *U.S.A.* 43°8N 74°28W **83** C10
Carol City *U.S.A.* 25°56N 80°14W **85** J14
Carolina *Brazil* 7°10S 47°30W **93** E9
Carolina *Puerto Rico* 18°23N 65°58W **89** d
Carolina *S. Africa* 26°5S 30°6E **57** D5
Caroline I. *Kiribati* 9°58S 150°13W **65** H12
Caroline Is. *Micronesia* 8°0N 150°0E **64** G6
Caroni *Trin. & Tob.* 10°34N 61°23W **93** K15
Caroní → *Venezuela* 8°21N 62°43W **92** B6
Caronie = Nébrodi, Monti *Italy* 37°54N 14°35E **22** F6
Caroona *Australia* 31°24S 150°26E **63** E5
Carpathians *Europe* 49°30N 21°0E **17** D11
Carpații Meridionali *Romania* 45°30N 25°0E **17** F13
Carpentaria, G. of *Australia* 14°0S 139°0E **62** A2
Carpentras *France* 44°3N 5°2E **20** D6
Carpi *Italy* 44°47N 10°53E **22** B4
Carpinteria *U.S.A.* 34°24N 119°31W **79** L7
Carr Boyd Ra. *Australia* 16°15S 128°35E **60** C4
Carra, L. *Ireland* 53°41N 9°14W **10** C2
Carrabelle *U.S.A.* 29°51N 84°40W **85** G12
Carranza, Presa V. *Mexico* 27°20N 100°50W **86** B4
Carrara *Italy* 44°5N 10°6E **20** D9
Carrauntoohill *Ireland* 52°0N 9°45W **10** D2
Carrick-on-Shannon *Ireland* 53°57N 8°5W **10** C3
Carrick-on-Suir *Ireland* 52°21N 7°24W **10** D4
Carrickfergus *U.K.* 54°43N 5°49W **10** B6
Carrickmacross *Ireland* 53°59N 6°43W **10** C5
Carrieton *Australia* 32°25S 138°31E **63** E2
Carrillo *Mexico* 26°54N 103°55W **86** B4
Carrington *U.S.A.* 47°27N 99°8W **80** B4
Carrizal Bajo *Chile* 28°5S 71°20W **94** B1
Carrizalillo *Chile* 29°5S 71°30W **94** B1
Carrizo Cr. → *U.S.A.* 36°55N 103°55W **77** H12
Carrizo Plain ⌓ *U.S.A.* 35°11N 119°47W **78** K7
Carrizo Springs *U.S.A.* 28°31N 99°52W **84** G5
Carrizozo *U.S.A.* 33°38N 105°53W **77** K11
Carroll *U.S.A.* 42°4N 94°52W **80** D6
Carrollton *Ga., U.S.A.* 33°35N 85°5W **85** E12
Carrollton *Ill., U.S.A.* 39°18N 90°24W **80** F8
Carrollton *Ky., U.S.A.* 38°41N 85°11W **81** F11
Carrollton *Mo., U.S.A.* 39°22N 93°30W **80** F7
Carrollton *Ohio, U.S.A.* 40°34N 81°5W **82** F3
Carron → *U.K.* 57°53N 4°22W **11** D4
Carron, L. *U.K.* 57°22N 5°35W **11** D3
Carrot → *Canada* 53°50N 101°17W **71** C8
Carrot River *Canada* 53°17N 103°35W **71** C8
Carruthers *Canada* 52°52N 109°16W **71** C7
Carson *Calif., U.S.A.* 33°49N 118°16W **79** M8
Carson *N. Dak., U.S.A.* 46°25N 101°34W **80** B3
Carson → *U.S.A.* 39°45N 118°40W **78** F8
Carson City *U.S.A.* 39°10N 119°46W **78** F7
Carson Sink *U.S.A.* 39°50N 118°25W **76** G4
Cartagena *Colombia* 10°25N 75°33W **92** A3
Cartagena *Spain* 37°38N 0°59W **21** D5
Cartago *Colombia* 4°45N 75°55W **92** C3
Cartago *Costa Rica* 9°50N 83°55W **88** E3
Cartersville *U.S.A.* 34°10N 84°48W **85** D12
Carterton *N.Z.* 41°2S 175°31E **59** D5
Carthage *Tunisia* 36°52N 10°20E **22** F4
Carthage *Ill., U.S.A.* 40°25N 91°8W **80** E8
Carthage *Mo., U.S.A.* 37°11N 94°19W **80** G6
Carthage *N.Y., U.S.A.* 43°59N 75°37W **81** D16
Carthage *Tex., U.S.A.* 32°9N 94°20W **84** E7
Cartier I. *Australia* 12°31S 123°29E **60** B3
Cartwright *Canada* 53°41N 56°58W **73** B8
Caruaru *Brazil* 8°15S 35°55W **93** E11
Carúpano *Venezuela* 10°39N 63°15W **92** A6
Caruthersville *U.S.A.* 36°11N 89°39W **80** G9
Carvoeiro *Brazil* 1°30S 61°59W **92** D6
Carvoeiro, C. *Portugal* 39°21N 9°24W **21** C1
Cary *U.S.A.* 35°47N 78°46W **85** D15
Casa de Piedra *Argentina* 38°5S 67°28W **94** D2
Casa de Piedra, Embalse *Argentina* 38°5S 67°32W **94** D2
Casa Grande *U.S.A.* 32°53N 111°45W **77** K8
Casa Nova *Brazil* 9°25S 41°5W **93** E10
Casablanca *Chile* 33°20S 71°25W **94** C1
Casablanca *Morocco* 33°36N 7°36W **50** B4
Cascada de Basaseachic △ *Mexico* 28°9N 108°15W **86** B3
Cascade *Seychelles* 4°39S 55°29E **53** b
Cascade *Idaho, U.S.A.* 44°31N 116°2W **76** D5
Cascade *Mont., U.S.A.* 47°16N 111°42W **76** C8
Cascade Locks *U.S.A.* 45°40N 121°54W **78** E5
Cascade Ra. *U.S.A.* 47°0N 121°30W **78** D5
Cascade Res. *U.S.A.* 44°32N 116°3W **76** D5
Cascades, Pte. des *Réunion* 21°9S 55°51E **53** c
Cascais *Portugal* 38°41N 9°25W **21** C1
Cascavel *Brazil* 24°57S 53°28W **95** A5
Cáscina *Italy* 43°41N 10°33E **22** C4
Casco B. *U.S.A.* 43°45N 70°0W **81** D19
Caserta *Italy* 41°4N 14°20E **22** D6
Casey *Antarctica* 66°0S 76°0E **5** C8
Caseyr, Raas = Asir, Ras *Somali Rep.* 11°55N 51°10E **47** E5
Cashel *Ireland* 52°30N 7°53W **10** D4
Casiguran *Phil.* 16°22N 122°7E **37** A6
Casilda *Argentina* 33°10S 61°10W **94** C3
Casino *Australia* 28°52S 153°3E **63** D5
Casiquiare → *Venezuela* 2°1N 67°7W **92** C5
Casma *Peru* 9°30S 78°20W **92** E3
Casmalia *U.S.A.* 34°50N 120°32W **79** L6
Caspe *Spain* 41°14N 0°1W **21** B5
Casper *U.S.A.* 42°51N 106°19W **76** E10
Caspian Depression *Eurasia* 47°0N 48°0E **19** E8
Caspian Sea *Eurasia* 43°0N 50°0E **19** F9
Cass City *U.S.A.* 43°36N 83°10W **82** C1
Cass Lake *U.S.A.* 47°23N 94°37W **80** B6
Cassadaga *U.S.A.* 42°20N 79°19W **82** D5
Casselman *Canada* 45°19N 75°5W **83** A9
Casselton *U.S.A.* 46°54N 97°13W **80** B5
Cassiar Mts. *Canada* 59°30N 130°30W **70** B2
Cassino *Italy* 41°30N 13°49E **22** D5
Cassville *U.S.A.* 36°41N 93°52W **80** G7
Castaic *U.S.A.* 34°30N 118°38W **79** L8
Castalia *U.S.A.* 41°24N 82°49W **82** E2
Castanhal *Brazil* 1°18S 47°55W **93** D9
Castara *Trin. & Tob.* 11°17N 60°42W **93** J16
Castellammare di Stábia *Italy* 40°42N 14°29E **22** D6
Castelli *Argentina* 36°7S 57°47W **94** D4
Castelló de la Plana *Spain* 39°58N 0°3W **21** C5
Castelo *Brazil* 20°33S 41°14W **95** A7
Castelo Branco *Portugal* 39°50N 7°31W **21** C2
Castelsarrasin *France* 44°2N 1°7E **20** E4
Castelvetrano *Italy* 37°41N 12°47E **22** F5
Casterton *Australia* 37°30S 141°30E **63** F3
Castile *U.S.A.* 42°38N 78°3W **82** D6
Castilla-La Mancha □ *Spain* 39°30N 3°30W **21** C4
Castilla y Leon □ *Spain* 42°0N 5°0W **21** B3
Castillos *Uruguay* 34°12S 53°52W **95** C5
Castle Dale *U.S.A.* 39°13N 111°1W **76** G8
Castle Douglas *U.K.* 54°56N 3°56W **11** G5
Castle Rock *Colo., U.S.A.* 39°22N 104°51W **76** G11
Castle Rock *Wash., U.S.A.* 46°17N 122°54W **78** D4
Castlebar *Ireland* 53°52N 9°18W **10** C2
Castlebay *U.K.* 56°57N 7°31W **11** E1
Castleblaney *Ireland* 54°7N 6°44W **10** B5
Castlederg *U.K.* 54°42N 7°35W **10** B4
Castleford *U.K.* 53°43N 1°21W **12** D6
Castlegar *Canada* 49°20N 117°40W **70** D5
Castlemaine *Australia* 37°2S 144°12E **63** F3
Castlemaine *Ireland* 52°10N 9°42W **10** D2
Castlepollard *Ireland* 53°41N 7°19W **10** C4
Castlerea *Ireland* 53°46N 8°29W **10** C3
Castlereagh → *Australia* 30°12S 147°32E **63** E4
Castlereagh B. *Australia* 12°10S 135°10E **62** A2
Castleton *U.S.A.* 43°37N 73°11W **83** C11
Castleton-on-Hudson *U.S.A.* 42°31N 73°45W **83** D11
Castletown *I. of Man* 54°5N 4°38W **12** C3
Castletown Bearhaven *Ireland* 51°39N 9°55W **10** E2
Castor *Canada* 52°15N 111°50W **70** C6
Castor → *Canada* 53°24N 78°58W **72** B4
Castorland *U.S.A.* 43°53N 75°31W **83** C9
Castres *France* 43°37N 2°13E **20** E5
Castricum *Neths.* 52°33N 4°40E **15** B4
Castries *St. Lucia* 14°2N 60°58W **89** f
Castro *Brazil* 24°45S 50°0W **95** A6
Castro *Chile* 42°30S 73°50W **96** E2
Castro Alves *Brazil* 12°46S 39°33W **93** F11
Castro Valley *U.S.A.* 37°41N 122°5W **78** H4
Castroville *U.S.A.* 36°46N 121°45W **78** J5
Castuera *Spain* 38°43N 5°37W **21** C3
Cat Ba, Dao *Vietnam* 20°50N 107°0E **38** B6
Cat Ba △ *Vietnam* 20°47N 107°3E **38** B6
Cat I. *Bahamas* 24°30N 75°30W **89** B4
Cat L. *Canada* 51°40N 91°50W **72** B1
Cat Lake *Canada* 51°40N 91°50W **72** B1
Cat Tien △ *Vietnam* 11°25N 107°17E **39** G6
Catacamas *Honduras* 14°54N 85°56W **88** D2
Cataguases *Brazil* 21°23S 42°39W **95** A7
Catalão *Brazil* 18°10S 47°57W **93** G9
Çatalca *Turkey* 41°8N 28°27E **23** D13
Catalina *Canada* 48°31N 53°4W **73** C9
Catalina *Chile* 25°13S 69°43W **94** B2
Catalina *U.S.A.* 32°30N 110°50W **77** K8
Catalonia = Cataluña □ *Spain* 41°40N 1°15E **21** B6
Cataluña □ *Spain* 41°40N 1°15E **21** B6
Catamarca *Argentina* 28°30S 65°50W **94** B2
Catamarca □ *Argentina* 27°0S 65°50W **94** B2
Catanduanes □ *Phil.* 13°50N 124°20E **37** B6
Catanduva *Brazil* 21°5S 48°58W **95** A6
Catánia *Italy* 37°30N 15°6E **22** F6
Catanzaro *Italy* 38°54N 16°35E **22** E7
Catarman *Phil.* 12°28N 124°35E **37** B6
Catatumbo-Bari △ *Colombia* 9°3N 73°12W **89** E5
Catchacoma *Canada* 44°44N 78°19W **82** B6
Cateel *Phil.* 7°47N 126°24E **37** C7
Catembe *Mozam.* 26°0S 32°33E **57** D5
Caterham *U.K.* 51°15N 0°4W **13** F7
Cathcart *S. Africa* 32°18S 27°10E **56** E4
Cathedral City *U.S.A.* 33°47N 116°28W **79** M10
Cathlamet *U.S.A.* 46°12N 123°23W **78** D3
Catlettsburg *U.S.A.* 38°25N 82°36W **81** F12
Catoche, C. *Mexico* 21°35N 87°5W **87** C7
Catriló *Argentina* 36°26S 63°24W **94** D3
Catrimani *Brazil* 0°27N 61°41W **92** C6
Catrimani → *Brazil* 0°28N 61°44W **92** C6
Catskill *U.S.A.* 42°14N 73°52W **83** D11
Catskill ⌓ *U.S.A.* 42°8N 74°39W **83** D10
Catskill Mts. *U.S.A.* 42°10N 74°25W **83** D10
Catt, Mt. *Australia* 13°49S 134°23E **62** A1
Cattaraugus *U.S.A.* 42°20N 78°52W **82** D6
Catterick *U.K.* 54°23N 1°37W **12** C6
Catuala *Angola* 16°25S 19°2E **56** B2
Catuane *Mozam.* 26°48S 32°18E **57** D5
Catur *Mozam.* 13°45S 35°30E **55** E4
Cauca → *Colombia* 8°54N 74°28W **92** B4
Caucaia *Brazil* 3°40S 38°35W **93** D11
Caucasus Mountains *Eurasia* 42°50N 44°0E **19** F7
Caucete *Argentina* 31°38S 68°20W **94** C2
Caungula *Angola* 8°26S 18°38E **52** F3
Cauquenes *Chile* 36°0S 72°22W **94** D1
Caura → *Venezuela* 7°38N 64°53W **92** B6
Cauresi → *Mozam.* 17°8S 33°0E **55** F3
Causapscal *Canada* 48°19N 67°12W **73** C6
Cauvery → *India* 11°9N 78°52E **40** P11
Caux, Pays de *France* 49°38N 0°35E **20** B4
Cavalier *U.S.A.* 48°48N 97°37W **80** A5
Cavan *Ireland* 54°0N 7°22W **10** B4
Cavan □ *Ireland* 54°1N 7°16W **10** C4
Cave Creek *U.S.A.* 33°50N 111°57W **77** K8
Cavenagh Ra. *Australia* 26°12S 127°55E **61** E4
Cavendish *Australia* 37°31S 142°2E **63** F3
Caviana, I. *Brazil* 0°10N 50°10W **93** C8
Cavite *Phil.* 14°29N 120°54E **37** B6
Cawndilla L. *Australia* 32°30S 142°15E **63** E3
Cawnpore = Kanpur *India* 26°28N 80°20E **43** F9
Caxias *Brazil* 4°55S 43°20W **93** D10
Caxias do Sul *Brazil* 29°10S 51°10W **95** B5
Cay Sal Bank *Bahamas* 23°45N 80°0W **88** B4
Cayambe *Ecuador* 0°3N 78°8W **92** C3
Cayenne *Fr. Guiana* 5°5N 52°18W **93** B8
Cayey *Puerto Rico* 18°7N 66°10W **89** d
Cayman Brac *Cayman Is.* 19°43N 79°49W **88** C4
Cayman Is. ☒ *W. Indies* 19°40N 80°30W **88** C3
Cayman Trough *Caribbean* 19°0N 81°0W **66** H11
Cayuga *Canada* 42°59N 79°50W **82** D5
Cayuga *U.S.A.* 42°54N 76°44W **83** D8
Cayuga Heights *U.S.A.* 42°27N 76°29W **83** D8
Cayuga L. *U.S.A.* 42°41N 76°41W **83** D8
Cazenovia *U.S.A.* 42°56N 75°51W **83** D9
Cazombo *Angola* 11°54S 22°56E **53** G4
Ceanannus Mor *Ireland* 53°44N 6°53W **10** C5
Ceará = Fortaleza *Brazil* 3°45S 38°35W **93** D11
Ceará □ *Brazil* 5°0S 40°0W **93** E11
Ceará-Mirim *Brazil* 5°38S 35°25W **93** E11
Cébaco, I. de *Panama* 7°33N 81°9W **88** E3
Cebollar *Argentina* 29°10S 66°35W **94** B2
Cebu *Phil.* 10°18N 123°54E **37** B6
Cecil Plains *Australia* 27°30S 151°11E **63** D5
Cedar → *U.S.A.* 41°17N 91°21W **80** E8
Cedar City *U.S.A.* 37°41N 113°4W **77** H7
Cedar Creek Res. *U.S.A.* 32°11N 96°4W **84** E6
Cedar Falls *Iowa, U.S.A.* 42°32N 92°27W **80** D7
Cedar Falls *Wash., U.S.A.* 47°25N 121°45W **78** C5
Cedar Key *U.S.A.* 29°8N 83°2W **85** G13
Cedar L. *Canada* 53°10N 100°0W **71** C9
Cedar Park *U.S.A.* 30°30N 97°49W **84** F6
Cedar Rapids *U.S.A.* 41°59N 91°40W **80** E8
Cedartown *U.S.A.* 34°1N 85°15W **85** D12
Cedarvale *Canada* 55°1N 128°22W **70** B3
Cedarville *S. Africa* 30°23S 29°3E **57** E4
Cedral *Mexico* 23°50N 100°45W **86** C4
Cedro *Brazil* 6°34S 39°3W **93** E11
Cedros, I. *Mexico* 28°12N 115°15W **86** B1
Cedros B. *Trin. & Tob.* 10°16N 61°54W **93** K15
Ceduna *Australia* 32°7S 133°46E **63** E1
Ceeldheere *Somali Rep.* 3°50N 47°8E **47** G4
Ceerigaabo *Somali Rep.* 10°35N 47°20E **47** E4
Cefalù *Italy* 38°2N 14°1E **22** E6
Cegléd *Hungary* 47°11N 19°47E **17** E10
Cekik *Indonesia* 8°12S 114°27E **37** J17
Celaque △ *Honduras* 14°30N 88°43W **88** D2
Celaya *Mexico* 20°31N 100°37W **86** C4
Celebes = Sulawesi *Indonesia* 2°0S 120°0E **37** E6
Celebes Sea *Indonesia* 3°0N 123°0E **37** D6
Celina *U.S.A.* 40°33N 84°35W **81** E11
Celje *Slovenia* 46°16N 15°18E **16** E8
Celle *Germany* 52°37N 10°4E **16** B6
Celtic Sea *Atl. Oc.* 50°9N 9°34W **14** F2
Cenderwasih, Teluk *Indonesia* 3°0S 135°20E **37** E9
Center *N. Dak., U.S.A.* 47°7N 101°18W **80** B3
Center *Tex., U.S.A.* 31°48N 94°11W **84** F7
Centerburg *U.S.A.* 40°18N 82°42W **82** F2
Centerville *Calif., U.S.A.* 36°44N 119°30W **78** J7
Centerville *Iowa, U.S.A.* 40°44N 92°52W **80** E7
Centerville *Pa., U.S.A.* 40°3N 79°59W **82** F5
Centerville *Tenn., U.S.A.* 35°47N 87°28W **85** D11
Centerville *Tex., U.S.A.* 31°16N 95°59W **84** F7
Central = Tsentralnyy □ *Russia* 52°0N 40°0E **28** D4
Central □ *Kenya* 0°30S 37°30E **54** C4
Central □ *Malawi* 13°30S 33°30E **55** E3
Central □ *Zambia* 14°25S 28°50E **55** E2
Central, Cordillera *Colombia* 5°0N 75°0W **92** C4
Central, Cordillera *Costa Rica* 10°10N 84°5W **88** D3
Central, Cordillera *Dom. Rep.* 19°15N 71°0W **89** C5
Central, Cordillera *Puerto Rico* 18°8N 66°35W **89** d
Central African Rep. ■ *Africa* 7°0N 20°0E **51** G9
Central America *America* 12°0N 85°0W **66** H11
Central Butte *Canada* 50°48N 106°31W **71** C7
Central City *Colo., U.S.A.* 39°48N 105°31W **76** G11
Central City *Ky., U.S.A.* 37°18N 87°7W **80** G10
Central City *Nebr., U.S.A.* 41°7N 98°0W **80** E4
Central I. *Kenya* 3°30N 36°0E **54** B4
Central Island △ *Kenya* 2°33N 36°1E **54**
Central Kalahari ⌓ *Botswana* 22°36S 23°58E **56**
Central Makran Range *Pakistan* 26°30N 64°15E **40**
Central Pacific Basin *Pac. Oc.* 8°0N 175°0W **64** G
Central Patricia *Canada* 51°30N 90°9W **72**
Central Point *U.S.A.* 42°23N 122°55W **76**
Central Russian Uplands *Europe* 54°0N 36°0E **6** E
Central Siberian Plateau *Russia* 65°0N 105°0E **26** B
Central Square *U.S.A.* 43°17N 76°9W **83**
Centralia *Canada* 43°17N 81°28W **82**
Centralia *Ill., U.S.A.* 38°32N 89°8W **80**
Centralia *Mo., U.S.A.* 39°13N 92°8W **80**
Centralia *Wash., U.S.A.* 46°43N 122°58W **78**
Centre de Flacq *Mauritius* 20°12S 57°43E **5**
Centreville *N.Y., U.S.A.* 42°28N 78°14W **82**
Centreville *Pa., U.S.A.* 41°44N 79°45W **82**
Cephalonia = Kefalonia *Greece* 38°15N 20°30E **23**
Cepu *Indonesia* 7°9S 111°35E **37** G
Ceram = Seram *Indonesia* 3°10S 129°0E **37**
Ceram Sea = Seram Sea *Indonesia* 2°30S 128°30E **37**
Ceredigion □ *U.K.* 52°16N 4°15W **13**
Ceres *Argentina* 29°55S 61°55W **94**
Ceres *S. Africa* 33°21S 19°18E **56**
Ceres *U.S.A.* 37°35N 120°57W **78**
Cerf *Seychelles* 4°38S 55°40E **5**
Cerignola *Italy* 41°17N 15°53E **22**
Cerigo = Kythira *Greece* 36°8N 23°0E **23**
Çerkezköy *Turkey* 41°17N 28°0E **23** D
Cerralvo, I. *Mexico* 24°15N 109°55W **86**
Cerritos *Mexico* 22°25N 100°16W **86**
Cerro Chato *Uruguay* 33°6S 55°8W **95**
Cerro Cofre de Perote △ *Mexico* 19°29N 97°8W **87**
Cerro Corá △ *Paraguay* 22°35S 56°2W **95**
Cerro el Copey △ *Venezuela* 10°59N 63°53W **89**
Cerro Hoya △ *Panama* 7°17N 80°45W **88**
Cerro Saroche △ *Venezuela* 10°8N 69°38W **89**
Cerventes *Australia* 30°31S 115°3E **61**
Cervera *Spain* 41°40N 1°16E **21**
Cesena *Italy* 44°8N 12°15E **22**
Cēsis *Latvia* 57°18N 25°15E **9**
Česká Rep. = Czech Rep. ■ *Europe* 50°0N 15°0E **16**
České Budějovice *Czech Rep.* 48°55N 14°25E **16**
Českomoravská Vrchovina *Czech Rep.* 49°30N 15°40E **16**
Çeşme *Turkey* 38°20N 26°23E **23**
Cessnock *Australia* 32°50S 151°21E **63**
Cetinje *Montenegro* 42°23N 18°59E **23**
Cetraro *Italy* 39°31N 15°55E **22**
Ceuta *N. Afr.* 35°52N 5°18W **21**
Cévennes *France* 44°10N 3°50E **20**
Ceyhan *Turkey* 37°4N 35°47E **44**
Ceylanpınar *Turkey* 36°50N 40°2E **44**
Ceylon = Sri Lanka ■ *Asia* 7°30N 80°50E **40**
Cha-am *Thailand* 12°48N 99°58E **38**
Chacabuco *Argentina* 34°40S 60°27W **94**
Chachapoyas *Peru* 6°15S 77°50W **92**
Chachoengsao *Thailand* 13°42N 101°5E **38**
Chachran *Pakistan* 28°55N 70°30E **42**
Chachro *Pakistan* 25°5N 70°15E **42**
Chaco □ *Argentina* 26°30S 61°0W **94**
Chaco □ *Paraguay* 26°0S 60°0W **94**
Chaco → *U.S.A.* 36°46N 108°39W **77**
Chaco △ *Argentina* 27°0S 59°30W **94**
Chaco Austral *S. Amer.* 27°0S 61°30W **96**
Chaco Boreal *S. Amer.* 22°0S 60°0W **92**
Chaco Central *S. Amer.* 24°0S 61°0W **96**
Chaco Culture ⌓ *U.S.A.* 36°3N 107°58W **77**
Chacon, C. *U.S.A.* 54°42N 132°0W **70**
Chad ■ *Africa* 15°0N 17°15E **5**
Chad, L. = Tchad, L. *Chad* 13°30N 14°30E **5**
Chadileuvú → *Argentina* 37°46S 66°0W **94**
Chadiza *Zambia* 14°45S 32°27E **5**
Chadron *U.S.A.* 42°50N 103°0W **80**
Chadyr-Lunga = Ciadâr-Lunga *Moldova* 46°3N 28°51E **17**
Chae Hom *Thailand* 18°43N 99°35E **3**
Chae Son △ *Thailand* 18°42N 99°20E **3**
Chaem → *Thailand* 18°11N 98°38E **3**
Chaeryŏng *N. Korea* 38°24N 125°36E **35**
Chagai Hills = Chāh Gay Hills *Afghan.* 29°30N 64°0E **4**
Chagda *Russia* 58°45N 130°38E **29**
Chaghcharān *Afghan.* 34°31N 65°15E **4**
Chagos Arch. ☒ *Ind. Oc.* 6°0S 72°0E **2**
Chagres △ *Panama* 9°33N 79°37W **8**
Chaguanas *Trin. & Tob.* 10°30N 61°26W **93**
Chāh Ākhvor *Iran* 32°41N 59°40E **4**
Chāh Bahar *Iran* 25°20N 60°40E **4**
Chāh-e Kavīr *Iran* 34°29N 56°52E **4**
Chāh Gay Hills *Afghan.* 29°30N 64°0E **4**
Chahār Borjak *Afghan.* 30°17N 62°3E **4**
Chahār Mahāll va Bakhtīarī □ *Iran* 32°0N 49°0E **4**
Chai Badan *Thailand* 15°12N 101°8E **3**
Chai Wan *China* 22°16N 114°14E **33**
Chaibasa *India* 22°42N 85°49E **43**
Chainat *Thailand* 15°11N 100°8E **3**
Chaiya *Thailand* 9°23N 99°14E **3**
Chaiyaphum *Thailand* 15°48N 102°2E **3**
Chaj Doab *Pakistan* 32°15N 73°0E **4**
Chajari *Argentina* 30°42S 58°0W **9**
Chak Amru *Pakistan* 32°22N 75°11E **4**

akar → Pakistan 29°29N 68°2E 42 E3
akari Zimbabwe 18°5S 29°51E 57 B4
ake Chake Tanzania 5°15S 39°45E 54 D4
akhānsūr Afghan. 31°10N 62°0E 40 D3
akonipau, L. Canada 56°18N 68°30W 73 A6
akradharpur India 22°45N 85°40E 43 H11
akrata India 30°42N 77°51E 42 D7
akwal Pakistan 32°56N 72°53E 42 C5
ala Peru 15°48S 74°20W 92 G4
alchihuites Mexico 23°29N 103°53W 86 C4
alcis = Halkida
Greece 38°27N 23°42E 23 E10
aleur B. Canada 47°55N 65°30W 73 C6
alfant U.S.A. 37°32N 118°21W 78 H8
alhuanca Peru 14°15S 73°15W 92 F4
alisgaon India 20°30N 75°10E 40 J9
alk River Canada 46°1N 77°27W 72 C4
alky Inlet N.Z. 46°3S 166°31E 59 G1
allapata Bolivia 18°53S 66°50W 92 G5
allenger Deep Pac. Oc. 11°30N 142°0E 64 F6
allenger Fracture Zone
Pac. Oc. 35°0S 105°0W 65 L17
allis U.S.A. 44°30N 114°14W 76 D6
almette U.S.A. 29°56N 89°57W 85 G10
alon-sur-Saône France 46°48N 4°50E 20 C6
along Thailand 7°50N 98°22E 39 a
âlons-en-Champagne
France 48°58N 4°20E 20 B6
ilten, Cerro = Fitz Roy, Cerro
Argentina 49°17S 73°5W 96 F2
ālūs Iran 36°38N 51°26E 45 B6
am, Cu Lao Vietnam 15°57N 108°30E 38 E7
ama U.S.A. 36°54N 106°35W 77 H10
amaicó Argentina 35°3S 64°58W 94 D3
aman Pakistan 30°58N 66°25E 40 D5
amba India 32°35N 76°10E 42 C7
amba Tanzania 11°37S 37°0E 55 E4
ambal → India 26°29N 79°15E 43 F8
amberlain U.S.A. 43°49N 99°20W 80 D4
amberlain →
Australia 15°30S 127°54E 60 C4
amberlain L. U.S.A. 46°14N 69°19W 81 B19
ambers U.S.A. 35°11N 109°26W 77 J9
ambersburg U.S.A. 39°56N 77°40W 81 F15
ambéry France 45°34N 5°55E 20 D6
ambeshi → Zambia 11°53S 29°48E 52 G6
ambly Canada 45°27N 73°17W 83 A11
ambord Canada 48°25N 72°6W 73 C5
amchamal Iraq 35°32N 44°50E 44 C5
amela Mexico 19°32N 105°5W 86 D3
amical Argentina 30°22S 66°27W 94 C2
amkar Luong
Cambodia 11°0N 103°45E 39 G4
amoli India 30°24N 79°21E 43 D8
amonix-Mont Blanc
France 45°55N 6°51E 20 D7
amouchuane =
Ashuapmushuan →
Canada 48°37N 72°20W 72 C5
ampa India 22°2N 82°43E 43 H10
ampagne Canada 60°49N 136°30W 70 A1
ampagne France 48°40N 4°20E 20 B6
ampaign U.S.A. 40°7N 88°15W 80 E9
ampassak Laos 14°53N 105°52E 38 E5
ampawat India 29°20N 80°6E 43 E9
ampdoré, L. Canada 55°55N 65°49W 73 A6
ampion U.S.A. 41°19N 80°51W 82 E4
amplain U.S.A. 44°59N 73°27W 83 B11
amplain, L. U.S.A. 44°40N 73°20W 83 B11
ampotón Mexico 19°21N 90°43W 87 D6
ampua India 22°5N 85°40E 43 H11
ana Thailand 6°55N 100°44E 39 J3
añaral Chile 26°23S 70°40W 94 B1
anārān Iran 36°39N 59°6E 45 B8
anasma India 23°44N 72°5E 42 H5
ancery Lane Barbados 13°3N 59°30W 89 g
anco Chile 35°44S 72°32W 94 D1
and India 21°57N 79°7E 43 J8
andan India 24°38N 86°40E 43 G12
andan Chauki India 28°33N 80°47E 43 E9
andannagar India 22°52N 88°24E 43 H13
andausi India 28°27N 78°49E 43 E8
andeleur Is. U.S.A. 29°55N 88°57W 85 G10
andeleur Sd. U.S.A. 29°55N 89°0W 85 G10
andigarh India 30°43N 76°47E 42 D7
andil India 22°58N 86°3E 43 H12
andler Australia 27°0S 133°19E 63 D1
andler Canada 48°18N 64°46W 73 C7
andler Ariz., U.S.A. 33°18N 111°50W 77 K8
andler Okla., U.S.A. 35°42N 96°53W 84 D6
andod India 21°59N 73°28E 42 J5
andpur Bangla. 23°8N 90°45E 41 H17
andrapur India 19°57N 79°25E 40 K11
anf Iran 26°38N 60°29E 45 E9
ang Pakistan 26°59N 68°30E 42 F3
ang, Ko Thailand 12°0N 102°23E 39 G4
ang Chiang = Chang Jiang →
China 31°48N 121°10E 33 C7
ang Jiang → China 31°48N 121°10E 33 C7
ang-won S. Korea 35°16N 128°37E 35 G15
anga India 33°53N 77°35E 43 C7
angan China 22°48N 113°48E 33 F10
anganacheri India 9°25N 76°31E 40 Q10
angane → Mozam. 24°30S 33°30E 57 C5
angbai China 41°25N 128°5E 35 D15
angbai Shan China 42°20N 129°0E 35 C15
angchiak'ou = Zhangjiakou
China 40°48N 114°55E 34 D8
angchou = Changzhou
China 31°47N 119°58E 33 C6
angchun China 43°57N 125°17E 35 C13
angchunling China 45°18N 125°27E 35 B13
angde China 29°4N 111°35E 33 D6
angdo-ri N. Korea 38°30N 127°40E 35 E14
anghai = Shanghai
China 31°15N 121°26E 33 C7
anghua Taiwan 24°2N 120°30E 33 D7

Changhŭngni
N. Korea 40°24N 128°19E 35 D15
Changi Singapore 1°23N 103°59E 39 d
Changi, Singapore ✕ (SIN)
Singapore 1°23N 103°59E 39 M4
Changji China 44°1N 87°19E 32 B3
Changjiang China 19°20N 108°55E 38 C7
Changjiang Shuiku
China 22°29N 113°27E 33 G10
Changjin N. Korea 40°23N 127°15E 35 D14
Changjin-ho N. Korea 40°30N 127°15E 35 D14
Changli China 39°40N 119°13E 35 E10
Changling China 44°20N 123°58E 35 B12
Changlun Malaysia 6°25N 100°26E 39 J3
Changping China 40°14N 116°12E 34 D9
Changsha China 28°12N 113°0E 33 D6
Changshan Qundao
China 39°11N 122°32E 35 E12
Changuinola Panama 9°26N 82°31W 88 E3
Changwu China 35°10N 107°45E 34 G4
Changyi China 36°40N 119°30E 35 F10
Changyŏn N. Korea 38°15N 125°6E 35 E13
Changyuan China 35°15N 114°42E 34 G8
Changzhi China 36°10N 113°6E 34 F7
Changzhou China 31°47N 119°58E 33 C6
Chanhanga Angola 16°0S 14°8E 56 B1
Chania Greece 35°30N 24°4E 25 D6
Chania ☐ Greece 35°30N 24°0E 25 D6
Chanion, Kolpos Greece 35°33N 23°55E 25 D5
Channapatna India 12°40N 77°15E 40 N10
Channel Is. U.K. 49°19N 2°24W 13 H5
Channel Is. U.S.A. 33°40N 119°15W 79 M7
Channel Islands △
U.S.A. 34°0N 119°24W 79 L7
Channel-Port aux Basques
Canada 47°30N 59°9W 73 C8
Channel Tunnel Europe 51°0N 1°30E 13 F9
Channing U.S.A. 35°41N 102°20W 84 D3
Chantada Spain 42°36N 7°46W 21 A2
Chanthaburi Thailand 12°38N 102°12E 38 F4
Chantrey Inlet Canada 67°48N 96°20W 68 C10
Chanute U.S.A. 37°41N 95°27W 80 G6
Chao Phraya →
Thailand 13°40N 100°31E 38 F3
Chao Phraya Lowlands
Thailand 15°30N 100°0E 38 E3
Chaocheng China 36°4N 115°37E 34 F8
Chaoyang China 41°35N 120°22E 35 D11
Chaozhou China 23°42N 116°32E 33 D6
Chapaev Kazakhstan 50°25N 51°10E 19 D9
Chapais Canada 49°47N 74°51W 72 C5
Chapala Mozam. 15°50S 37°35E 55 F4
Chapala, L. de Mexico 20°15N 103°0W 86 C4
Chapayevsk Russia 53°0N 49°40E 18 D8
Chapecó Brazil 27°14S 52°41W 95 B5
Chapel Hill U.S.A. 35°55N 79°4W 85 D15
Chapleau Canada 47°50N 83°24W 72 C3
Chaplin Canada 50°28N 106°40W 71 C7
Chaplin L. Canada 50°22N 106°36W 71 C7
Chappell U.S.A. 41°6N 102°28W 80 E2
Chapra = Chhapra
India 25°48N 84°44E 43 G11
Chara Russia 56°54N 118°20E 29 D12
Charadai Argentina 27°35S 59°55W 94 B4
Charagua Bolivia 19°45S 63°10W 92 G6
Charakas Greece 35°1N 25°7E 25 D7
Charambirá, Punta
Colombia 4°16N 77°32W 92 C3
Charaña Bolivia 17°30S 69°25W 92 G5
Charanwala India 27°51N 72°10E 42 F5
Charata Argentina 27°13S 61°14W 94 B3
Charcas Mexico 23°8N 101°7W 86 C4
Charcot I. Antarctica 70°0S 70°0W 5 C17
Chard U.K. 50°52N 2°58W 13 G5
Chardon U.S.A. 41°35N 81°12W 82 E3
Chardzhou = Türkmenabat
Turkmenistan 39°6N 63°34E 45 B9
Charente → France 45°57N 1°5W 20 D3
Chari → Chad 12°58N 14°31E 51 F8
Chārīkār Afghan. 35°0N 69°10E 40 B6
Chariton U.S.A. 41°1N 93°19W 80 E7
Chariton → U.S.A. 39°19N 92°58W 80 F7
Chärjew = Türkmenabat
Turkmenistan 39°6N 63°34E 45 B9
Charkhari India 25°24N 79°45E 43 G8
Charkhi Dadri India 28°37N 76°17E 42 E7
Charleroi Belgium 50°24N 4°27E 15 D4
Charleroi U.S.A. 40°9N 79°57W 82 F5
Charles, C. U.S.A. 37°7N 75°58W 81 G16
Charles, Peak Australia 32°52S 121°11E 61 F3
Charles City U.S.A. 43°4N 92°41W 80 D7
Charles L. Canada 59°50N 110°33W 71 B6
Charles Town U.S.A. 39°17N 77°52W 81 F15
Charlesbourg Canada 46°51N 71°16W 81 B18
Charleston Ill., U.S.A. 39°30N 88°10W 80 F9
Charleston Miss., U.S.A. 34°1N 90°4W 85 D9
Charleston Mo., U.S.A. 36°55N 89°21W 80 G9
Charleston S.C., U.S.A. 32°46N 79°56W 85 E15
Charleston W. Va.,
U.S.A. 38°21N 81°38W 81 F13
Charleston L. Canada 44°32N 76°0W 83 B9
Charleston Peak
U.S.A. 36°16N 115°42W 79 J11
Charlestown Ireland 53°58N 8°48W 10 C3
Charlestown S. Africa 27°26S 29°53E 57 D4
Charlestown Ind.,
U.S.A. 38°27N 85°40W 81 F11
Charlestown N.H.,
U.S.A. 43°14N 72°25W 83 C12
Charlestown of Aberlour
U.K. 57°28N 3°14W 11 D5
Charleville = Rath Luirc
Ireland 52°21N 8°40W 10 D3
Charleville Australia 26°24S 146°15E 63 D4
Charleville-Mézières
France 49°44N 4°40E 20 B6
Charlevoix U.S.A. 45°19N 85°16W 81 C11

Charlotte Mich., U.S.A. 42°34N 84°50W 81 D11
Charlotte N.C., U.S.A. 35°13N 80°50W 85 D14
Charlotte Vt., U.S.A. 44°19N 73°16W 83 B11
Charlotte Amalie
U.S. Virgin Is. 18°21N 64°56W 89 e
Charlotte Harbor U.S.A. 26°57N 82°4W 85 H13
Charlotte L. Canada 52°12N 125°19W 70 C3
Charlottesville U.S.A. 38°2N 78°30W 81 F14
Charlottetown Nfld. & L.,
Canada 52°46N 56°7W 73 B8
Charlottetown P.E.I.,
Canada 46°14N 63°8W 73 C7
Charlotteville
Trin. & Tob. 11°20N 60°33W 93 J16
Charlton Australia 36°16S 143°24E 63 F3
Charlton I. Canada 52°0N 79°20W 72 B4
Charny Canada 46°43N 71°15W 73 C5
Charolles France 46°27N 4°16E 20 C6
Charre Mozam. 17°13S 35°10E 55 F4
Charsadda Pakistan 34°7N 71°45E 42 B4
Charters Towers
Australia 20°5S 146°13E 62 C4
Chartres France 48°29N 1°30E 20 B4
Chascomús Argentina 35°30S 58°0W 94 D4
Chase Canada 50°50N 119°41W 70 C5
Chasefu Zambia 11°55S 33°8E 55 E3
Chashma Barrage
Pakistan 32°27N 71°20E 42 C4
Chāt Iran 37°59N 55°16E 45 B7
Châteaubriant France 47°43N 1°23W 20 C3
Chateaugay U.S.A. 44°56N 74°5W 83 B10
Châteauguay, L. Canada 56°26N 70°3W 73 A5
Châteaulin France 48°11N 4°8W 20 B1
Châteauroux France 46°50N 1°40E 20 C4
Châteaux, Pte. des
Guadeloupe 16°15N 61°10W 88 b
Châtellerault France 46°50N 0°30E 20 C4
Chatham = Miramichi
Canada 47°2N 65°28W 73 C6
Chatham Canada 42°24N 82°11W 82 D2
Chatham U.K. 51°22N 0°32E 13 F8
Chatham U.S.A. 42°21N 73°36W 83 D11
Chatham Is. Pac. Oc. 44°0S 176°40W 64 M10
Chatham Rise Pac. Oc. 43°30S 180°0E 64 M10
Chatmohar Bangla. 24°15N 89°15E 43 G13
Chatra India 24°12N 84°56E 43 G11
Chatrapur India 19°22N 85°2E 41 K14
Chats, L. des Canada 45°30N 76°20W 83 A8
Chatsu India 26°36N 75°57E 42 F6
Chatsworth Canada 44°27N 80°54W 82 B4
Chatsworth Zimbabwe 19°38S 31°13E 55 F3
Chãttagâm = Chittagong
Bangla. 22°19N 91°48E 41 H17
Chattahoochee U.S.A. 30°42N 84°51W 85 F12
Chattahoochee →
U.S.A. 30°54N 84°57W 85 F12
Chattanooga U.S.A. 35°3N 85°19W 85 D12
Chatteris U.K. 52°28N 0°2E 13 E8
Chatturat Thailand 15°40N 101°51E 38 E3
Chau Doc Vietnam 10°42N 105°7E 39 G5
Chaukan Pass Burma 27°8N 97°10E 41 F20
Chaumont France 48°7N 5°8E 20 B6
Chaumont U.S.A. 44°4N 76°8W 83 B8
Chaunskaya G. Russia 69°0N 169°0E 29 C17
Chautauqua L. U.S.A. 42°10N 79°24W 82 D5
Chauvin Canada 52°45N 110°10W 71 C6
Chaves Brazil 0°15S 49°55W 93 D9
Chaves Portugal 41°45N 7°32W 21 B2
Chawang Thailand 8°25N 99°30E 39 H2
Chaykovskiy Russia 56°47N 54°9E 18 C9
Chazy U.S.A. 44°53N 73°26W 83 B11
Cheb Czech Rep. 50°9N 12°28E 16 C7
Cheboksary Russia 56°8N 47°12E 18 C8
Cheboygan U.S.A. 45°39N 84°29W 81 C11
Chech, Erg Africa 25°0N 2°15W 50 D5
Chechenia ☐ Russia 43°30N 45°29E 19 F8
Checheno-Ingush Republic =
Chechenia ☐ Russia 43°30N 45°29E 19 F8
Chechnya = Chechenia ☐
Russia 43°30N 45°29E 19 F8
Checotah U.S.A. 35°28N 95°31W 84 D7
Chedabucto B. Canada 45°25N 61°8W 73 C7
Cheduba I. Burma 18°45N 93°40E 41 K18
Cheektowaga U.S.A. 42°54N 78°45W 82 D6
Cheepie Australia 26°33S 145°1E 63 D4
Chegdomyn Russia 51°7N 133°1E 29 D14
Chegga Mauritania 25°27N 5°40W 50 C4
Chegutu Zimbabwe 18°10S 30°14E 55 F3
Chehalis U.S.A. 46°40N 122°58W 78 D4
Chehalis → U.S.A. 46°57N 123°50W 78 D3
Cheju = Jeju S. Korea 33°31N 126°32E 35 H14
Cheju-do = Jeju-do
S. Korea 33°29N 126°34E 35 H14
Chekiang = Zhejiang ☐
China 29°0N 120°0E 33 D7
Chela, Sa. da Angola 16°20S 13°20E 56 B1
Chelan U.S.A. 47°51N 120°1W 76 C3
Chelan, L. U.S.A. 48°11N 120°30W 76 B3
Cheleken = Hazar
Turkmenistan 39°34N 53°16E 19 G9
Cheleken Yarymadasy
Turkmenistan 39°30N 53°15E 45 B7
Chelforó Argentina 39°0S 66°33W 96 D3
Chelkar = Shalqar
Kazakhstan 47°48N 59°39E 28 E6
Chelm Poland 51°8N 23°30E 17 C12
Chelmno Poland 53°20N 18°30E 17 B10
Chelmsford U.K. 51°44N 0°29E 13 F8
Chelsea Australia 38°5S 145°8E 63 F4
Chelsea U.S.A. 43°59N 72°27W 83 C12
Cheltenham U.K. 51°54N 2°4W 13 F5
Chelyabinsk Russia 55°10N 61°24E 28 D7
Chelyuskin, C. = Chelyuskin, Mys
Russia 77°30N 103°0E 29 B11
Chelyuskin, Mys Russia 77°30N 103°0E 29 B11
Chemainus Canada 48°55N 123°42W 78 B3
Chemba Mozam. 17°9S 34°53E 53 H6

Chemin Grenier Mauritius 20°29S 57°28E 53 d
Chemnitz Germany 50°51N 12°54E 16 C7
Chemult U.S.A. 43°14N 121°47W 76 E3
Chen, Gora Russia 65°16N 141°50E 29 C15
Chenab → Pakistan 30°23N 71°2E 42 D4
Chenab Nagar Pakistan 31°45N 72°55E 42 D5
Chenango Forks U.S.A. 42°15N 75°51W 83 D9
Cheney U.S.A. 47°30N 117°35W 76 C5
Cheng Xian China 33°43N 105°42E 34 H3
Chengcheng China 35°8N 109°56E 34 G5
Chengchou = Zhengzhou
China 34°45N 113°34E 34 G7
Chengde China 40°59N 117°58E 35 D9
Chengdu China 30°38N 104°2E 32 C5
Chenggu China 33°10N 107°21E 34 H4
Chengjiang China 24°39N 103°0E 32 D5
Chengmai China 19°50N 109°58E 38 C7
Ch'engtu = Chengdu
China 30°38N 104°2E 32 C5
Chengwu China 34°58N 115°50E 34 G8
Chengyang China 36°18N 120°21E 35 F11
Chenjiagang China 34°23N 119°47E 35 G10
Chennai India 13°8N 80°19E 40 N12
Cheò, Eilean a' = Skye
U.K. 57°15N 6°10W 11 D2
Cheom Ksan Cambodia 14°13N 104°56E 38 E5
Cheonan S. Korea 36°48N 127°9E 35 F14
Cheongdo S. Korea 35°38N 128°42E 35 G15
Cheongju S. Korea 36°39N 127°27E 35 F14
Cheorwon S. Korea 38°15N 127°10E 35 E14
Chepén Peru 7°15S 79°23W 92 E3
Chepes Argentina 31°20S 66°35W 94 C2
Chepo Panama 9°10N 79°6W 88 E4
Chepstow U.K. 51°38N 2°41W 13 F5
Chequamegon B. U.S.A. 46°39N 90°51W 80 B8
Cher → France 47°21N 0°29E 20 C4
Cheraw U.S.A. 34°42N 79°53W 85 D15
Cherbourg France 49°39N 1°40W 20 B3
Cherdyn Russia 60°24N 56°29E 18 B10
Cheremkhovo Russia 53°8N 103°1E 29 D11
Cherepovets Russia 59°5N 37°55E 18 C6
Chergui, Chott ech
Algeria 34°21N 0°25E 50 B6
Cherikov = Cherykaw
Belarus 53°32N 31°20E 17 B16
Cherkasy Ukraine 49°27N 32°4E 19 E5
Cherkessk Russia 44°15N 42°5E 19 F7
Cherlak Russia 54°15N 74°55E 28 D8
Chernaya Russia 70°30N 89°10E 29 B9
Chernigov = Chernihiv
Ukraine 51°28N 31°20E 18 D5
Chernigovka Russia 44°19N 132°34E 30 B6
Chernihiv Ukraine 51°28N 31°20E 18 D5
Chernivtsi Ukraine 48°15N 25°52E 17 D13
Chernobyl = Chornobyl
Ukraine 51°20N 30°15E 17 C16
Chernogorsk Russia 53°49N 91°18E 29 D10
Chernovtsy = Chernivtsi
Ukraine 48°15N 25°52E 17 D13
Chernyakhovsk Russia 54°36N 21°48E 9 J19
Chernysheyskiy Russia 63°0N 112°30E 29 C12
Cherokee Iowa, U.S.A. 42°45N 95°33W 80 D6
Cherokee Okla., U.S.A. 36°45N 98°21W 84 C5
Cherokee Village U.S.A. 36°18N 91°31W 84 C9
Cherokees, Grand Lake O' The
U.S.A. 36°28N 94°55W 84 C7
Cherrapunji India 25°17N 91°47E 41 G17
Cherry Valley U.S.A. 42°48N 74°45W 83 D10
Cherskiy Russia 68°45N 161°18E 29 C17
Cherskogo Khrebet
Russia 65°0N 143°0E 29 C15
Chersonisos Greece 35°18N 25°22E 25 D7
Chersonisos Akrotiri
Greece 35°30N 24°10E 25 D6
Cherven Belarus 53°45N 28°28E 17 B15
Chervonohrad Ukraine 50°25N 24°10E 17 C13
Cherwell → U.K. 51°44N 1°14W 13 F6
Cherykaw Belarus 53°32N 31°20E 17 B16
Chesapeake U.S.A. 36°49N 76°16W 81 G15
Chesapeake B. U.S.A. 38°0N 76°10W 81 F14
Cheshire ☐ U.K. 53°14N 2°30W 12 D5
Cheshskaya Guba Russia 67°20N 47°0E 18 A8
Cheshunt U.K. 51°43N 0°1W 13 F7
Chesil Beach U.K. 50°37N 2°33W 13 G5
Chesley Canada 44°17N 81°5W 82 B3
Chester U.K. 53°12N 2°53W 12 D5
Chester Calif., U.S.A. 40°19N 121°14W 76 F3
Chester Ill., U.S.A. 37°55N 89°49W 80 G9
Chester Mont., U.S.A. 48°31N 110°58W 76 B8
Chester Pa., U.S.A. 39°51N 75°22W 81 F16
Chester S.C., U.S.A. 34°43N 81°12W 85 D14
Chester Vt., U.S.A. 43°16N 72°36W 83 C12
Chester W. Va., U.S.A. 40°37N 80°34W 82 F4
Chester-le-Street U.K. 54°51N 1°34W 12 C6
Chesterfield U.K. 53°15N 1°25W 12 D6
Chesterfield, Îs. N. Cal. 19°52S 158°15E 58 C8
Chesterfield Inlet
Canada 63°30N 90°45W 68 C10
Chesterton Ra.
Australia 25°30S 147°27E 63 D4
Chesterton Range △
Australia 26°16S 147°22E 63 D4
Chestertown U.S.A. 43°40N 73°48W 83 C11
Chesterville Canada 45°6N 75°14W 83 A9
Chesuncook L. U.S.A. 46°0N 69°21W 81 C19
Chéticamp Canada 46°37N 60°59W 73 C7
Chetumal Mexico 18°30N 88°20W 87 D7
Chetumal, B. de
Cent. Amer. 18°40N 88°10W 87 D7
Chetwynd Canada 55°45N 121°36W 70 B4
Cheviot, The U.K. 55°29N 2°9W 12 B5
Cheviot Hills U.K. 55°20N 2°30W 12 B5
Cheviot Ra. Australia 25°20S 143°45E 62 D3
Chew Bahir Ethiopia 4°40N 36°50E 47 G2
Chewelah U.S.A. 48°17N 117°43W 76 B5
Chewore ⌂ Zimbabwe 16°0S 29°52E 55 F2
Cheyenne Okla., U.S.A. 35°37N 99°40W 84 D5

Cheyenne Wyo., U.S.A. 41°8N 104°49W 76 F11
Cheyenne → U.S.A. 44°41N 101°18W 80 C3
Cheyenne Wells
U.S.A. 38°49N 102°21W 76 G12
Cheyne B. Australia 34°35S 118°50E 61 F2
Chhabra India 24°40N 76°54E 42 G7
Chhaktala India 22°6N 74°11E 42 H6
Chhapra India 25°48N 84°44E 43 G11
Chhata India 27°42N 77°30E 42 F7
Chhatarpur Jharkhand,
India 24°23N 84°11E 43 G11
Chhatarpur Mad. P.,
India 24°55N 79°35E 43 G8
Chhattisgarh ☐ India 22°0N 82°0E 43 J10
Chhep Cambodia 13°45N 105°24E 38 F5
Chhindwara Mad. P.,
India 23°3N 79°29E 43 H8
Chhindwara Mad. P.,
India 22°2N 78°59E 43 H8
Chhlong Cambodia 12°15N 105°58E 39 F5
Chhota Tawa → India 22°14N 76°36E 42 H7
Chhoti Kali Sindh →
India 24°2N 75°31E 42 G6
Chhuikhadan India 21°32N 80°59E 43 J9
Chhuk Cambodia 10°46N 104°28E 39 G5
Chi → Thailand 15°11N 104°43E 38 E5
Chiai Taiwan 23°29N 120°25E 33 D7
Chiamboni Somali Rep. 1°39S 41°35E 52 E8
Chiang Dao Thailand 19°22N 98°58E 38 C2
Chiang Kham Thailand 19°32N 100°18E 38 C3
Chiang Khan Thailand 17°52N 101°36E 38 D3
Chiang Khong Thailand 20°17N 100°24E 38 B3
Chiang Mai Thailand 18°47N 98°59E 38 C2
Chiang Rai Thailand 19°52N 99°50E 38 C2
Chiang Saen Thailand 20°16N 100°5E 38 B3
Chiapa → Mexico 16°42N 93°0W 87 D6
Chiapa de Corzo Mexico 16°42N 93°0W 87 D6
Chiapas ☐ Mexico 16°30N 92°30W 87 D6
Chiapas, Sa. Madre de
Mexico 15°40N 93°0W 87 D6
Chiautla de Tapia
Mexico 18°18N 98°36W 87 D5
Chiávari Italy 44°19N 9°19E 20 D8
Chiavenna Italy 46°19N 9°24E 20 C8
Chiba Japan 35°30N 140°7E 31 G10
Chiba ☐ Japan 35°30N 140°20E 31 G10
Chibabava Mozam. 20°17S 33°35E 57 C5
Chibemba Cunene, Angola 15°48S 14°8E 53 H2
Chibemba Huila, Angola 16°20S 15°20E 56 B2
Chibi Zimbabwe 20°18S 30°25E 57 C5
Chibia Angola 15°10S 13°42E 53 H2
Chibougamau Canada 49°56N 74°24W 72 C5
Chibougamau, L.
Canada 49°50N 74°20W 72 C5
Chibuk Nigeria 10°52N 12°50E 51 F8
Chibuto Mozam. 24°40S 33°33E 57 C5
Chic-Chocs, Mts. Canada 48°55N 66°0W 73 C6
Chicacole = Srikakulam
India 18°14N 83°58E 41 K13
Chicago U.S.A. 41°52N 87°38W 80 E10
Chicago Heights U.S.A. 41°30N 87°38W 80 E10
Chichagof I. U.S.A. 57°30N 135°30W 68 D6
Chichaoua Morocco 31°32N 8°44W 50 B4
Chichawatni Pakistan 30°32N 72°42E 42 D5
Chichén-Itzá Mexico 20°37N 88°35W 87 C7
Chicheng China 40°55N 115°55E 34 D8
Chichester U.K. 50°50N 0°47W 13 G7
Chichester Ra. Australia 22°12S 119°15E 60 D2
Chichibu Japan 35°59N 139°10E 31 F9
Chichibu-Tama △
Japan 35°52N 138°42E 31 G9
Ch'ich'ihaerh = Qiqihar
China 47°26N 124°0E 33 B7
Chicholi India 22°1N 77°40E 42 H8
Chickasaw ⌂ U.S.A. 34°26N 97°0W 84 D6
Chickasha U.S.A. 35°3N 97°58W 84 D6
Chiclana de la Frontera
Spain 36°26N 6°9W 21 D2
Chiclayo Peru 6°42S 79°50W 92 E3
Chico U.S.A. 39°44N 121°50W 78 F5
Chico → Chubut, Argentina 44°0S 67°0W 96 E3
Chico → Santa Cruz,
Argentina 50°0S 68°30W 96 G3
Chicomo Mozam. 24°31S 34°6E 57 C5
Chicomostoc Mexico 22°28N 102°46W 86 C4
Chicontepec Mexico 20°58N 98°10W 87 C5
Chicopee U.S.A. 42°9N 72°37W 83 D12
Chicoutimi Canada 48°28N 71°5W 73 C5
Chicualacuala Mozam. 22°6S 31°42E 57 C5
Chidambaram India 11°20N 79°45E 40 P11
Chidenguele Mozam. 24°55S 34°11E 57 C5
Chidley, C. Canada 60°23N 64°26W 69 C13
Chiducuane Mozam. 24°35S 34°25E 57 C5
Chiede Angola 17°15S 16°22E 56 B2
Chiefs Pt. Canada 44°41N 81°18W 82 B3
Chiem Hoa Vietnam 22°12N 105°17E 38 A5
Chiemsee Germany 47°53N 12°28E 16 E7
Chiengi Zambia 8°45S 29°10E 55 D2
Chiengmai = Chiang Mai
Thailand 18°47N 98°59E 38 C2
Chiese → Italy 45°8N 10°25E 20 D9
Chieti Italy 42°21N 14°10E 22 C6
Chifeng China 42°18N 118°58E 35 C10
Chignecto B. Canada 45°30N 64°40W 73 C7
Chiguana Bolivia 21°0S 67°58W 94 A2
Chigwell U.K. 51°37N 0°6E 13 F8
Chihli, G. of = Bo Hai
China 39°0N 119°0E 35 E10
Chihuahua Mexico 28°38N 106°5W 86 B3
Chihuahua ☐ Mexico 28°30N 106°0W 86 B3
Chiili = Shīeli Kazakhstan 44°20N 66°15E 28 E7
Chik Bollapur India 13°25N 77°45E 40 N10
Chikmagalur India 13°15N 75°45E 40 N9
Chikwawa Malawi 16°2S 34°50E 55 F3
Chilanga Zambia 15°33S 28°16E 55 F2
Chilapa Mexico 17°36N 99°10W 87 D5
Chilas Pakistan 35°25N 74°5E 43 B6

Chilaw *Sri Lanka* 7°30N 79°50E **40** R11
Chilcotin → *Canada* 51°44N 122°23W **70** C4
Childers *Australia* 25°15S 152°17E **63** D5
Childress *U.S.A.* 34°25N 100°13W **84** D4
Chile ■ *S. Amer.* 35°0S 72°0W **96** D2
Chile Rise *Pac. Oc.* 38°0S 92°0W **65** L18
Chilecito *Argentina* 29°10S 67°30W **94** B2
Chilete *Peru* 7°10S 78°50W **92** E3
Chililabombwe *Zambia* 12°18S 27°43E **55** E2
Chilim *Pakistan* 35°5N 75°5E **43** B6
Chilin = Jilin *China* 43°44N 126°30E **35** C14
Chilka L. *India* 19°40N 85°25E **41** K14
Chilko → *Canada* 52°0N 123°40W **70** C4
Chilko L. *Canada* 51°20N 124°10W **70** C4
Chillagoe *Australia* 17°7S 144°33E **62** B3
Chillán *Chile* 36°40S 72°10W **94** D1
Chillicothe *Ill., U.S.A.* 40°55N 89°29W **80** E9
Chillicothe *Mo., U.S.A.* 39°48N 93°33W **80** F7
Chillicothe *Ohio, U.S.A.* 39°20N 82°59W **81** F12
Chilliwack *Canada* 49°10N 121°54W **70** D4
Chilo *India* 27°25N 73°32E **42** F5
Chiloane, I. *Mozam.* 20°40S 34°55E **57** C5
Chiloé, I. de *Chile* 42°30S 73°50W **96** E2
Chilpancingo *Mexico* 17°33N 99°30W **87** D5
Chiltern Hills *U.K.* 51°40N 0°53W **13** F7
Chilton *U.S.A.* 44°2N 88°10W **80** C9
Chilubi *Zambia* 11°5S 29°58E **55** E2
Chilubula *Zambia* 10°14S 30°51E **55** E3
Chilumba *Malawi* 10°28S 34°12E **55** E3
Chilung *Taiwan* 25°3N 121°45E **33** D7
Chilwa, L. *Malawi* 15°15S 35°40E **55** F4
Chimaltitán *Mexico* 21°35N 103°50W **86** C4
Chimán *Panama* 8°45N 78°40W **88** E4
Chimanimani *Zimbabwe* 19°48S 32°52E **57** B5
Chimay *Belgium* 50°3N 4°20E **15** D4
Chimayo *U.S.A.* 36°0N 105°56W **77** J11
Chimbay *Uzbekistan* 42°57N 59°47E **28** E6
Chimborazo *Ecuador* 1°29S 78°55W **92** D3
Chimbote *Peru* 9°0S 78°35W **92** E3
Chimkent = Shymkent *Kazakhstan* 42°18N 69°36E **28** E7
Chimoio *Mozam.* 19°4S 33°30E **55** F3
Chimpembe *Zambia* 9°31S 29°33E **55** D2
Chin □ *Burma* 22°0N 93°0E **41** J18
Chin Hills *Burma* 22°30N 93°30E **41** H18
Chin Ling Shan = Qinling Shandi *China* 33°50N 108°10E **34** H5
China *Mexico* 25°42N 99°14W **87** B5
China ■ *Asia* 30°0N 110°0E **33** C6
China, Great Plain of *Asia* 35°0N 115°0E **26** E13
China Lake *U.S.A.* 35°44N 117°37W **79** K9
Chinan = Jinan *China* 36°38N 117°1E **34** F9
Chinandega *Nic.* 12°35N 87°12W **88** D2
Chinati Peak *U.S.A.* 29°57N 104°29W **84** G2
Chincha Alta *Peru* 13°25S 76°7W **92** F3
Chinchaga → *Canada* 58°53N 118°20W **70** B5
Chinchilla *Australia* 26°45S 150°38E **63** D5
Chinchorro, Banco *Mexico* 18°35N 87°22W **87** D7
Chinchou = Jinzhou *China* 41°5N 121°3E **35** D11
Chincoteague *U.S.A.* 37°56N 75°23W **81** G16
Chinde *Mozam.* 18°35S 36°30E **55** F4
Chindwin → *Burma* 21°26N 95°15E **41** J19
Chineni *India* 33°2N 75°15E **43** C6
Chinga *Mozam.* 15°13S 38°35E **55** F4
Chingola *Zambia* 12°31S 27°53E **55** E2
Chingole *Malawi* 13°4S 34°17E **55** E3
Ch'ingtao = Qingdao *China* 36°5N 120°20E **35** F11
Chinguetti *Mauritania* 20°25N 12°24W **50** D3
Chingune *Mozam.* 20°33S 34°58E **57** C5
Chinhanguanine *Mozam.* 25°21S 32°30E **57** D5
Chinhoyi *Zimbabwe* 17°20S 30°8E **55** F3
Chini *India* 31°32N 78°15E **42** D8
Chiniot *Pakistan* 31°45N 73°0E **42** D5
Chínipas *Mexico* 27°23N 108°32W **86** B3
Chinji *Pakistan* 32°42N 72°22E **42** C5
Chinju = Jinju *S. Korea* 35°12N 128°2E **35** G15
Chinko → *C.A.R.* 4°50N 23°53E **52** D4
Chinle *U.S.A.* 36°9N 109°33W **77** H9
Chinnampo = Namp'o *N. Korea* 38°52N 125°10E **35** E13
Chino *Japan* 35°59N 138°9E **31** G9
Chino *U.S.A.* 34°1N 117°41W **79** L9
Chino Valley *U.S.A.* 34°45N 112°27W **77** J7
Chinon *France* 47°10N 0°15E **20** C4
Chinook *U.S.A.* 48°35N 109°14W **76** B9
Chinook Trough *Pac. Oc.* 44°0N 175°0W **64** C10
Chinsali *Zambia* 10°30S 32°2E **55** E3
Chióggia *Italy* 45°13N 12°17E **22** B5
Chíos = Hios *Greece* 38°27N 26°9E **23** E12
Chipata *Zambia* 13°38S 32°28E **55** E3
Chipindo *Angola* 13°49S 15°48E **53** G3
Chipinge *Zimbabwe* 20°13S 32°28E **55** G3
Chipinge △ *Zimbabwe* 20°14S 33°0E **55** G3
Chipley *U.S.A.* 30°47N 85°32W **85** F12
Chipman *Canada* 46°6N 65°53W **73** C6
Chipoka *Malawi* 13°57S 34°28E **55** E3
Chippenham *U.K.* 51°27N 2°6W **13** F5
Chippewa → *U.S.A.* 44°25N 92°5W **80** C7
Chippewa Falls *U.S.A.* 44°56N 91°24W **80** C8
Chipping Norton *U.K.* 51°56N 1°32W **13** F6
Chiputneticook Lakes *N. Amer.* 45°35N 67°35W **81** C20
Chiquián *Peru* 10°10S 77°0W **92** F3
Chiquibul △ *Belize* 16°49N 88°52W **88** C2
Chiquimula *Guatemala* 14°51N 89°37W **88** D2
Chiquinquira *Colombia* 5°37N 73°50W **92** B4
Chirala *India* 15°50N 80°26E **40** M12
Chiramba *Mozam.* 16°55S 34°39E **55** F3
Chirawa *India* 28°14N 75°42E **42** E6
Chirchiq *Uzbekistan* 41°29N 69°35E **28** E7
Chiredzi *Zimbabwe* 21°0S 31°38E **57** C5
Chiricahua △ *U.S.A.* 32°0N 109°20W **77** K9
Chiricahua Peak *U.S.A.* 31°51N 109°18W **77** L9
Chiriquí, G. de *Panama* 8°0N 82°10W **88** E3
Chiriquí, L. de *Panama* 9°10N 82°0W **88** E3
Chirisa △ *Zimbabwe* 17°53S 28°15E **55** F2
Chirivira Falls *Zimbabwe* 21°10S 32°12E **55** G3
Chirmiri *India* 23°15N 82°20E **43** H10
Chirripó Grande, Cerro *Costa Rica* 9°29N 83°29W **88** E3
Chirundu *Zimbabwe* 16°3S 28°50E **57** B4
Chisamba *Zambia* 14°55S 28°20E **55** E2
Chisapani *Nepal* 28°37N 81°16E **43** E9
Chisasibi *Canada* 53°50N 79°0W **72** B4
Chisholm *Canada* 54°55N 114°10W **70** C6
Chisholm *U.S.A.* 47°29N 92°53W **80** B7
Chishtian Mandi *Pakistan* 29°50N 72°55E **42** E5
Chisimaio = Kismaayo *Somali Rep.* 0°22S 42°32E **47** H3
Chisimba Falls *Zambia* 10°12S 30°56E **55** E3
Chişinău *Moldova* 47°2N 28°50E **17** E15
Chisos Mts. *U.S.A.* 29°5N 103°15W **84** G3
Chistopol *Russia* 55°25N 50°38E **18** C9
Chita *Russia* 52°0N 113°35E **29** D12
Chitipa *Malawi* 9°41S 33°19E **55** D3
Chitose *Japan* 42°49N 141°39E **30** C10
Chitral *Pakistan* 35°50N 71°56E **40** B7
Chitré *Panama* 7°59N 80°27W **88** E3
Chittagong *Bangla.* 22°19N 91°48E **41** H17
Chittagong □ *Bangla.* 24°5N 91°0E **41** G17
Chittaurgarh *India* 24°52N 74°38E **42** G6
Chittoor *India* 13°15N 79°5E **40** N11
Chitungwiza *Zimbabwe* 18°0S 31°6E **55** F3
Chiusi *Italy* 43°1N 11°57E **22** C4
Chivasso *Italy* 45°11N 7°53E **20** D7
Chivhu *Zimbabwe* 19°2S 30°52E **55** F3
Chivilcoy *Argentina* 34°55S 60°0W **94** C4
Chiwanda *Tanzania* 11°23S 34°55E **55** E3
Chizarira *Zimbabwe* 17°36S 27°45E **55** F2
Chizarira △ *Zimbabwe* 17°44S 27°52E **55** F2
Chizela *Zambia* 13°8S 25°0E **55** E2
Chkalov = Orenburg *Russia* 51°45N 55°6E **18** D10
Chloride *U.S.A.* 35°25N 114°12W **79** K12
Cho Bo *Vietnam* 20°46N 105°10E **38** B5
Cho-do *N. Korea* 38°30N 124°40E **35** E13
Cho Phuoc Hai *Vietnam* 10°26N 107°18E **39** G6
Choa Chu Kang *Singapore* 1°22N 103°41E **39** d
Choba *Kenya* 2°30N 38°5E **54** B4
Chobe △ *Botswana* 18°37S 24°23E **56** B4
Chocolate Mts. *U.S.A.* 33°15N 115°15W **79** M11
Choctawhatchee → *U.S.A.* 30°25N 86°8W **85** F11
Choele Choel *Argentina* 39°11S 65°40W **96** D3
Choiseul *St. Lucia* 13°47N 61°3W **89** f
Choiseul *Solomon Is.* 7°0S 156°40E **58** B8
Choix *Mexico* 26°43N 108°17W **86** B3
Chojnice *Poland* 53°42N 17°32E **17** B9
Chok Chai *Thailand* 14°44N 102°10E **38** E4
Chōkai-San *Japan* 39°6N 140°3E **30** E10
Choke Canyon Res. *U.S.A.* 28°30N 98°20W **84** G5
Chokurdakh *Russia* 70°38N 147°55E **29** B15
Cholame *U.S.A.* 35°44N 120°18W **78** K6
Cholet *France* 47°4N 0°52W **20** C3
Cholguan *Chile* 37°10S 72°3W **94** D1
Choloma *Honduras* 15°37N 87°57W **88** C2
Choluteca *Honduras* 13°20N 87°14W **88** D2
Choluteca → *Honduras* 13°0N 87°20W **88** D2
Chom Bung *Thailand* 13°37N 99°36E **38** F2
Chom Thong *Thailand* 18°25N 98°41E **38** C2
Choma *Zambia* 16°48S 26°59E **55** F2
Chomolungma = Everest, Mt. *Nepal* 28°5N 86°58E **43** E12
Chomun *India* 27°15N 75°40E **42** F6
Chomutov *Czech Rep.* 50°28N 13°23E **16** C7
Chon Buri *Thailand* 13°21N 101°1E **38** F3
Chon Thanh *Vietnam* 11°24N 106°36E **39** G6
Chone *Ecuador* 0°40S 80°0W **92** D3
Chong Kai *Cambodia* 13°57N 103°35E **38** F4
Chong Mek *Thailand* 15°10N 105°27E **38** E5
Chong Phangan *Thailand* 9°39N 100°0E **39** b
Chong Samui *Thailand* 9°21N 99°50E **39** b
Ch'ŏngjin *N. Korea* 41°47N 129°50E **35** D15
Chŏngju *N. Korea* 39°40N 125°5E **35** E13
Chongli *China* 40°58N 115°15E **34** D8
Chongqing *China* 29°35N 106°25E **32** D5
Chongqing Shi □ *China* 30°0N 108°0E **32** C5
Chonguene *Mozam.* 25°3S 33°49E **57** C5
Chonos, Arch. de los *Chile* 45°0S 75°0W **96** F2
Chop *Ukraine* 48°26N 22°12E **17** D12
Chopim → *Brazil* 25°35S 53°5W **95** B5
Chor *Pakistan* 25°31N 69°46E **42** G3
Chora Sfakion *Greece* 35°15N 24°9E **25** D6
Chorbat La *India* 34°42N 76°37E **43** B7
Chorley *U.K.* 53°39N 2°38W **12** D5
Chornobyl *Ukraine* 51°20N 30°15E **17** C16
Chorolque, Cerro *Bolivia* 20°59S 66°5W **94** A2
Chorregon *Australia* 22°40S 143°32E **62** C3
Chorro el Indio △ *Venezuela* 7°43N 72°9W **89** E5
Chortkiv *Ukraine* 49°2N 25°46E **17** D13
Chorzów *Poland* 50°18N 18°57E **17** C10
Chos-Malal *Argentina* 37°20S 70°15W **94** D1
Ch'osan *N. Korea* 40°50N 125°47E **35** D13
Choszczno *Poland* 53°7N 15°25E **16** B8
Choteau *U.S.A.* 47°49N 112°11W **76** C7
Chotila *India* 22°23N 71°15E **42** H4
Chotta Udepur *India* 22°19N 74°1E **42** H6
Chowchilla *U.S.A.* 37°7N 120°16W **78** H6
Choybalsan *Mongolia* 48°4N 114°30E **33** B6
Choyr *Mongolia* 46°24N 108°30E **29** E11
Christchurch *N.Z.* 43°33S 172°47E **59** E4
Christchurch *U.K.* 50°44N 1°47W **13** G6
Christian I. *Canada* 44°50N 80°12W **82** B4
Christiana *S. Africa* 27°52S 25°8E **56** D4
Christiansted *U.S. Virgin Is.* 17°45N 64°42W **89** C7
Christie B. *Canada* 62°32N 111°10W **71** A6
Christina → *Canada* 56°40N 111°3W **71** B6
Christmas Cr. → *Australia* 18°29S 125°23E **60** C4
Christmas I. = Kiritimati *Kiribati* 1°58N 157°27W **65** G12
Christmas I. *Ind. Oc.* 10°30S 105°40E **64** J2
Christopher, L. *Australia* 24°49S 127°42E **61** D4
Chtimba *Malawi* 10°35S 34°13E **55** E3
Chū = Shū *Kazakhstan* 43°36N 73°42E **28** E8
Chu → *Vietnam* 19°53N 105°45E **38** C5
Chu Lai *Vietnam* 15°28N 108°45E **38** E7
Chuadanga *Bangla.* 23°38N 88°51E **43** H13
Chuak, Ko *Thailand* 9°28N 99°41E **39** b
Ch'uanchou = Quanzhou *China* 24°55N 118°34E **33** D6
Chuankou *China* 34°20N 110°59E **34** G6
Chubbuck *U.S.A.* 42°55N 112°28W **76** E7
Chūbu □ *Japan* 36°45N 137°30E **31** F8
Chubu-Sangaku △ *Japan* 36°30N 137°40E **31** F8
Chubut → *Argentina* 43°20S 65°5W **96** E3
Chuchi L. *Canada* 55°12N 124°30W **70** B4
Chuda *India* 22°29N 71°41E **42** H4
Chudskoye, Ozero *Russia* 58°13N 27°30E **9** G22
Chūgoku □ *Japan* 35°0N 133°0E **31** G6
Chūgoku-Sanchi *Japan* 35°0N 133°0E **31** G6
Chugwater *U.S.A.* 41°46N 104°50W **76** F11
Chuka *Kenya* 0°20S 37°39E **54** C4
Chukchi Plateau *Arctic* 78°0N 165°0W **4** B17
Chukchi Sea *Russia* 68°0N 175°0W **29** C19
Chukotskoye Nagorye *Russia* 68°0N 175°0E **29** C18
Chula Vista *U.S.A.* 32°38N 117°5W **79** N9
Chulucanas *Peru* 5°8S 80°10W **92** E2
Chulym → *Russia* 57°43N 83°51E **28** D9
Chum Phae *Thailand* 16°40N 102°6E **38** D4
Chum Saeng *Thailand* 15°55N 100°15E **38** E3
Chumar *India* 32°40N 78°35E **43** C8
Chumbicha *Argentina* 29°0S 66°10W **94** B2
Chumikan *Russia* 54°40N 135°10E **29** D14
Chumphon *Thailand* 10°35N 99°14E **39** G2
Chumuare *Mozam.* 14°31S 31°50E **55** E3
Chuna → *Russia* 57°47N 94°37E **29** D10
Chuncheon *S. Korea* 37°58N 127°44E **35** F14
Chunchura *India* 22°53N 88°27E **43** H13
Chunga *Zambia* 15°0S 26°2E **55** F2
Chunggang-ŭp *N. Korea* 41°48N 126°48E **35** D14
Chunghwa *N. Korea* 38°52N 125°47E **35** E13
Chungju *S. Korea* 36°58N 127°58E **35** F14
Chungking = Chongqing *China* 29°35N 106°25E **32** D5
Chungt'iaoshan = Zhongtiao Shan *China* 35°0N 111°10E **34** G6
Chunian *Pakistan* 30°57N 74°0E **42** D6
Chunya *Tanzania* 8°30S 33°27E **55** D3
Chunyang *China* 43°38N 129°23E **35** C15
Chupara Pt. *Trin. & Tob.* 10°49N 61°22W **93** K15
Chuquibamba *Peru* 15°47S 72°44W **92** G4
Chuquicamata *Chile* 22°15S 69°0W **94** A2
Chur *Switz.* 46°52N 9°32E **20** C8
Churachandpur *India* 24°20N 93°40E **41** G18
Church Stretton *U.K.* 52°32N 2°48W **13** E5
Churchill *Canada* 58°47N 94°11W **71** B10
Churchill → *Man., Canada* 58°47N 94°12W **71** B10
Churchill → *Nfld. & L., Canada* 53°19N 60°10W **73** B7
Churchill, C. *Canada* 58°46N 93°12W **71** B10
Churchill Falls *Canada* 53°36N 64°19W **73** B7
Churchill L. *Canada* 55°55N 108°20W **71** B7
Churchill Pk. *Canada* 58°10N 125°10W **70** B3
Churki *India* 23°50N 83°12E **43** H10
Churu *India* 28°20N 74°50E **42** E6
Churún Merú = Angel Falls *Venezuela* 5°57N 62°30W **92** B6
Chushal *India* 33°40N 78°40E **43** C8
Chuska Mts. *U.S.A.* 36°15N 108°50W **77** H9
Chusovoy *Russia* 58°22N 57°50E **18** C10
Chute-aux-Outardes *Canada* 49°7N 68°24W **73** C6
Chuuk = Truk *Micronesia* 7°25N 151°46E **64** G7
Chuvash Republic = Chuvashia □ *Russia* 55°30N 47°0E **18** C8
Chuvashia □ *Russia* 55°30N 47°0E **18** C8
Chuwārtah *Iraq* 35°43N 45°34E **44** C5
Chuy *Uruguay* 33°41S 53°27W **95** C5
Ci Xian *China* 36°20N 114°25E **34** F8
Ciadâr-Lunga *Moldova* 46°3N 28°51E **17** E15
Ciamis *Indonesia* 7°20S 108°21E **37** G13
Cianjur *Indonesia* 6°49S 107°8E **37** G12
Cianorte *Brazil* 23°37S 52°37W **95** A5
Cibola *U.S.A.* 33°17N 114°42W **79** M12
Cicero *U.S.A.* 41°51N 87°44W **80** E10
Cicia *Fiji* 17°45S 179°18W **59** a
Ciéagas del Cataumbo △ *Venezuela* 9°25N 71°54W **89** E5
Ciechanów *Poland* 52°52N 20°38E **17** B11
Ciego de Ávila *Cuba* 21°50N 78°50W **88** B4
Ciénaga *Colombia* 11°1N 74°15W **92** A4
Cienfuegos *Cuba* 22°10N 80°30W **88** B3
Cieszyn *Poland* 49°45N 18°35E **17** D10
Cieza *Spain* 38°17N 1°23W **21** C5
Cihuatlán *Mexico* 19°14N 104°35W **86** D4
Cijara, Embalse de *Spain* 39°18N 4°52W **21** C3
Cijulang *Indonesia* 7°42S 108°27E **37** G13
Cilacap *Indonesia* 7°43S 109°0E **37** G13
Cill Chainnigh = Kilkenny *Ireland* 52°39N 7°15W **10** D4
Cilo Dağı *Turkey* 37°28N 43°55E **19** G7
Cima *U.S.A.* 35°14N 115°30W **79** K11
Cimarron *Kans., U.S.A.* 37°48N 100°21W **80** G3
Cimarron *N. Mex., U.S.A.* 36°31N 104°55W **77** H11
Cimarron → *U.S.A.* 36°10N 96°16W **84** C6
Cimişlia *Moldova* 46°34N 28°44E **17** E15
Cimone, Mte. *Italy* 44°12N 10°42E **22** B4
Cinca → *Spain* 41°26N 0°21E **21** B6
Cincar *Bos.-H.* 43°55N 17°5E **22** C7
Cincinnati *U.S.A.* 39°9N 84°27W **81** F11
Cincinnatus *U.S.A.* 42°33N 75°54W **83** D9
Çine *Turkey* 37°37N 28°2E **23** F13
Ciney *Belgium* 50°18N 5°5E **15** D5
Cinto, Mte. *France* 42°24N 8°54E **20** E8
Circle *Alaska, U.S.A.* 65°50N 144°4W **74** a
Circle *Mont., U.S.A.* 47°25N 105°35W **76** C11
Circleville *U.S.A.* 39°36N 82°57W **81** F12
Cirebon *Indonesia* 6°45S 108°32E **37** G13
Ciremay *Indonesia* 6°55S 108°27E **37** G13
Cirencester *U.K.* 51°43N 1°57W **13** F6
Cirium *Cyprus* 34°40N 32°53E **25** E11
Cisco *U.S.A.* 32°23N 98°59W **84** E5
Citlaltépetl = Orizaba, Pico de *Mexico* 18°58N 97°15W **87** D5
Citrus Heights *U.S.A.* 38°42N 121°17W **78** G5
Citrusdal *S. Africa* 32°35S 19°0E **56** E2
Città del Vaticano = Vatican City ■ *Europe* 41°54N 12°27E **22** D5
Città di Castello *Italy* 43°27N 12°14E **22** C5
Ciudad Acuña *Mexico* 29°18N 100°55W **86** B4
Ciudad Altamirano *Mexico* 18°20N 100°40W **86** D4
Ciudad Anáhuac *Mexico* 27°14N 100°7W **86** B4
Ciudad Bolívar *Venezuela* 8°5N 63°36W **92** B6
Ciudad Camargo *Mexico* 27°40N 105°10W **86** B3
Ciudad Cortés *Costa Rica* 8°55N 84°0W **88** E3
Ciudad de México *Mexico* 19°24N 99°9W **87** D5
Ciudad de Valles *Mexico* 22°0N 99°0W **87** C5
Ciudad del Carmen *Mexico* 18°38N 91°50W **87** D6
Ciudad del Este *Paraguay* 25°30S 54°50W **95** B5
Ciudad Delicias = Delicias *Mexico* 28°13N 105°28W **86** B3
Ciudad Frontera *Mexico* 26°56N 101°27W **86** B4
Ciudad Guayana *Venezuela* 8°0N 62°30W **92** B6
Ciudad Guerrero *Mexico* 28°33N 107°30W **86** B3
Ciudad Guzmán *Mexico* 19°41N 103°29W **86** D4
Ciudad Juárez *Mexico* 31°44N 106°29W **86** A3
Ciudad Lerdo *Mexico* 25°32N 103°32W **86** B4
Ciudad Madero *Mexico* 22°19N 97°50W **87** C5
Ciudad Mante *Mexico* 22°44N 98°59W **87** C5
Ciudad Obregón *Mexico* 27°29N 109°56W **86** B3
Ciudad Real *Spain* 38°59N 3°55W **21** C4
Ciudad Rodrigo *Spain* 40°35N 6°32W **21** B2
Ciudad Victoria *Mexico* 23°44N 99°8W **87** C5
Ciudadela *Spain* 40°0N 3°50E **24** B10
Civitanova Marche *Italy* 43°18N 13°44E **22** C5
Civitavécchia *Italy* 42°6N 11°48E **22** C4
Cizre *Turkey* 37°19N 42°10E **44** B4
Clackmannanshire □ *U.K.* 56°10N 3°43W **11** E5
Clacton-on-Sea *U.K.* 51°47N 1°11E **13** F9
Claire, L. *Canada* 58°35N 112°5W **70** B6
Clairton *U.S.A.* 40°18N 79°53W **82** F5
Clallam Bay *U.S.A.* 48°15N 124°16W **78** B2
Clanton *U.S.A.* 32°51N 86°38W **85** E11
Clanwilliam *S. Africa* 32°11S 18°52E **56** E2
Clara *Ireland* 53°21N 7°37W **10** C4
Claraville *U.S.A.* 35°24N 118°20W **79** K8
Clare *Australia* 33°50S 138°37E **63** E2
Clare *U.S.A.* 43°49N 84°46W **81** D11
Clare □ *Ireland* 52°45N 9°0W **10** D3
Clare → *Ireland* 53°20N 9°2W **10** C2
Clare I. *Ireland* 53°49N 10°0W **10** C1
Claremont *Calif., U.S.A.* 34°6N 117°43W **79** L9
Claremont *N.H., U.S.A.* 43°23N 72°20W **83** C12
Claremont Pt. *Australia* 14°1S 143°41E **62** A3
Claremore *U.S.A.* 36°19N 95°36W **84** C7
Claremorris *Ireland* 53°45N 9°0W **10** C3
Clarence → *Australia* 29°25S 153°22E **63** D5
Clarence → *N.Z.* 42°10S 173°56E **59** E4
Clarence, I. *Chile* 54°0S 72°0W **96** G2
Clarence I. *Antarctica* 61°10S 54°0W **5** C18
Clarence Str. *Australia* 12°0S 131°0E **60** B5
Clarence Town *Bahamas* 23°6N 74°59W **89** B5
Clarendon *Pa., U.S.A.* 41°47N 79°6W **82** E5
Clarendon *Tex., U.S.A.* 34°56N 100°53W **84** D4
Clarenville *Canada* 48°10N 54°1W **73** C9
Claresholm *Canada* 50°2N 113°33W **70** D6
Clarie Coast *Antarctica* 68°0S 135°0E **5** C9
Clarinda *U.S.A.* 40°44N 95°2W **80** E6
Clarington *Canada* 43°55N 78°41W **82** C6
Clarion *Iowa, U.S.A.* 42°44N 93°44W **80** D7
Clarion *Pa., U.S.A.* 41°13N 79°23W **82** E5
Clarion → *U.S.A.* 41°7N 79°41W **82** E5
Clarion Fracture Zone *Pac. Oc.* 20°0N 120°0W **66** H7
Clark *U.S.A.* 44°53N 97°44W **80** C5
Clark, Pt. *Canada* 44°4N 81°45W **82** B3
Clark Fork *U.S.A.* 48°9N 116°11W **76** B5
Clark Fork → *U.S.A.* 48°9N 116°15W **76** B5
Clarkdale *U.S.A.* 34°46N 112°3W **77** J7
Clarke City *Canada* 50°12N 66°38W **73** B6
Clarke I. *Australia* 40°32S 148°10E **63** G4
Clarke Ra. *Australia* 20°40S 148°30E **62** J6
Clarks Fork Yellowstone → *U.S.A.* 45°32N 108°50W **76** D9
Clark's Harbour *Canada* 43°25N 65°38W **73** D6
Clarks Hill L. = J. Strom Thurmond L. *U.S.A.* 33°40N 82°12W **85** E13
Clarks Summit *U.S.A.* 41°30N 75°42W **83**
Clarksburg *U.S.A.* 39°17N 80°30W **81** F
Clarksdale *U.S.A.* 34°12N 90°35W **85**
Clarkston *U.S.A.* 46°25N 117°3W **76**
Clarksville *Ark., U.S.A.* 35°28N 93°28W **84**
Clarksville *Tenn., U.S.A.* 36°32N 87°21W **85** C
Clarksville *Tex., U.S.A.* 33°37N 95°3W **84**
Clatskanie *U.S.A.* 46°6N 123°12W **78**
Claude *U.S.A.* 35°7N 101°22W **84**
Claveria *Phil.* 18°37N 121°4E **37**
Clay *U.S.A.* 38°17N 121°10W **78**
Clay Center *U.S.A.* 39°23N 97°8W **80**
Claypool *U.S.A.* 33°25N 110°51W **77**
Claysburg *U.S.A.* 40°17N 78°27W **82**
Claysville *U.S.A.* 40°7N 80°25W **82**
Clayton *Canada* 45°11N 76°19W **83**
Clayton *N. Mex., U.S.A.* 36°27N 103°11W **77** H
Clayton *N.Y., U.S.A.* 44°14N 76°5W **83**
Clear, C. *Ireland* 51°25N 9°32W **10**
Clear, L. *Canada* 45°26N 77°12W **82**
Clear Hills *Canada* 56°40N 119°30W **70**
Clear I. *Ireland* 51°26N 9°30W **10**
Clear L. *U.S.A.* 39°2N 122°47W **78**
Clear Lake *Iowa, U.S.A.* 43°8N 93°23W **80**
Clear Lake *S. Dak., U.S.A.* 44°45N 96°41W **80**
Clear Lake Res. *U.S.A.* 41°56N 121°5W **76**
Clearfield *Pa., U.S.A.* 41°2N 78°27W **82**
Clearfield *Utah, U.S.A.* 41°7N 112°2W **76**
Clearlake *U.S.A.* 38°57N 122°38W **78**
Clearwater *Canada* 51°38N 120°2W **70**
Clearwater *U.S.A.* 27°59N 82°48W **85** H
Clearwater → *Alta., Canada* 52°22N 114°57W **70**
Clearwater → *Alta., Canada* 56°44N 111°23W **71**
Clearwater L. *Canada* 53°34N 99°49W **71**
Clearwater Lake ⌓ *Canada* 54°0N 101°0W **71**
Clearwater Mts. *U.S.A.* 46°5N 115°20W **76**
Clearwater River ⌓ *Canada* 56°55N 109°10W **71**
Cleburne *U.S.A.* 32°21N 97°23W **84**
Clee Hills *U.K.* 52°26N 2°35W **13**
Cleethorpes *U.K.* 53°33N 0°3W **12**
Cleeve Cloud *U.K.* 51°56N 2°0W **13**
Clemson *U.S.A.* 34°41N 82°50W **85** D
Clerke Reef *Australia* 17°22S 119°20E **60**
Clermont *Australia* 22°49S 147°39E **62**
Clermont *U.S.A.* 28°33N 81°46W **85** G
Clermont-Ferrand *France* 45°46N 3°4E **20**
Clervaux *Lux.* 50°4N 6°2E **15**
Clevedon *U.K.* 51°26N 2°52W **13**
Cleveland *Miss., U.S.A.* 33°45N 90°43W **85**
Cleveland *Ohio, U.S.A.* 41°29N 81°41W **82**
Cleveland *Okla., U.S.A.* 36°19N 96°28W **84**
Cleveland *Tenn., U.S.A.* 35°10N 84°53W **85**
Cleveland *Tex., U.S.A.* 30°21N 95°5W **84**
Cleveland, C. *Australia* 19°11S 147°1E **62**
Cleveland, Mt. *U.S.A.* 48°56N 113°51W **76**
Cleveland Heights *U.S.A.* 41°31N 81°33W **82**
Clevelândia *Brazil* 26°24S 52°23W **95**
Clew B. *Ireland* 53°50N 9°49W **10**
Clewiston *U.S.A.* 26°45N 80°56W **85** H
Clifden *Ireland* 53°29N 10°1W **10**
Clifden *N.Z.* 46°1S 167°42E **59**
Cliffdell *U.S.A.* 46°56N 121°5W **78**
Cliffy Hd. *Australia* 35°1S 116°29E **61**
Clifton *Australia* 27°59S 151°53E **63**
Clifton *Ariz., U.S.A.* 33°3N 109°18W **77**
Clifton *Colo., U.S.A.* 39°7N 108°25W **76**
Clifton *Tex., U.S.A.* 31°47N 97°35W **84**
Clifton Beach *Australia* 16°46S 145°39E **62**
Clinch → *U.S.A.* 35°53N 84°29W **85**
Clingmans Dome *U.S.A.* 35°34N 83°30W **85**
Clint *U.S.A.* 31°35N 106°14W **84**
Clinton *B.C., Canada* 51°6N 121°35W **70**
Clinton *Ont., Canada* 43°37N 81°32W **82**
Clinton *N.Z.* 46°12S 169°23E **59**
Clinton *Ark., U.S.A.* 35°36N 92°28W **84**
Clinton *Conn., U.S.A.* 41°17N 72°32W **83**
Clinton *Ill., U.S.A.* 40°9N 88°57W **80**
Clinton *Ind., U.S.A.* 39°40N 87°24W **80**
Clinton *Iowa, U.S.A.* 41°51N 90°12W **80**
Clinton *Mass., U.S.A.* 42°25N 71°41W **83**
Clinton *Miss., U.S.A.* 32°20N 90°20W **85**
Clinton *Mo., U.S.A.* 38°22N 93°46W **80**
Clinton *N.C., U.S.A.* 35°0N 78°22W **85**
Clinton *Okla., U.S.A.* 35°31N 98°58W **84**
Clinton *S.C., U.S.A.* 34°29N 81°53W **85**
Clinton *Tenn., U.S.A.* 36°6N 84°8W **85**
Clinton *Wash., U.S.A.* 47°59N 122°21W **78**
Clinton C. *Australia* 22°30S 150°45E **62**
Clinton Colden L. *Canada* 63°58N 107°27W **68**
Clintonville *U.S.A.* 44°37N 88°46W **80**
Clipperton, I. *Pac. Oc.* 10°18N 109°13W **65**
Clipperton Fracture Zone *Pac. Oc.* 19°0N 122°0W **65**
Clisham *U.K.* 57°58N 6°49W **11**
Clitheroe *U.K.* 53°53N 2°22W **12**
Clo-oose *Canada* 48°39N 124°49W **78**
Cloates, Pt. *Australia* 22°43S 113°40E **60**
Clocolan *S. Africa* 28°55S 27°34E **57**
Clodomira *Argentina* 27°35S 64°14W **94**
Clogher Hd. *Ireland* 53°48N 6°14W **10**
Clonakilty *Ireland* 51°37N 8°53W **10**
Clonakilty B. *Ireland* 51°35N 8°51W **10**
Cloncurry *Australia* 20°40S 140°28E **62**
Cloncurry *Ireland* 53°25N 6°48W **10**
Cloncurry → *Australia* 18°37S 140°40E **62**
Clondalkin *Ireland* 53°19N 6°25W **10**
Clones *Ireland* 54°11N 7°15W **10**

nmel *Ireland* 52°21N 7°42W **10** D4
quet *U.S.A.* 46°43N 92°28W **80** B7
rinda *Argentina* 25°16S 57°45W **94** B4
ud Bay *Canada* 48°5N 89°26W **72** C2
ud Peak *U.S.A.* 44°23N 107°11W **76** D10
udcroft *U.S.A.* 32°58N 105°45W **77** K11
verdale *U.S.A.* 38°48N 123°1W **78** G4
vis *Calif., U.S.A.* 36°49N 119°42W **78** J7
vis *N. Mex., U.S.A.* 34°24N 103°12W **77** J12
yne *Canada* 44°49N 77°11W **82** B7
j-Napoca *Romania* 46°47N 23°38E **17** E12
nes *Australia* 37°20S 143°45E **63** F3
tha → *N.Z.* 46°20S 169°49E **59** G2
yd → *U.K.* 53°19N 3°31W **12** D4
de *Canada* 54°9N 113°39W **70** C6
de *N.Z.* 45°12S 169°20E **59** F2
de *U.S.A.* 43°5N 76°52W **82** C8
de → *U.K.* 55°55N 4°30W **11** F4
de, Firth of *U.K.* 55°22N 5°1W **11** F3
de Muirshiel ⌂ *U.K.* 55°50N 4°40W **11** F4
de River *Canada* 70°30N 68°30W **69** B13
debank *U.K.* 55°54N 4°23W **11** F4
mer *N.Y., U.S.A.* 42°1N 79°37W **82** D5
mer *Pa., U.S.A.* 40°40N 79°1W **82** D5
chella *U.S.A.* 33°41N 116°10W **79** M10
chella Canal
.S.A. 32°43N 114°57W **79** N12
homa *U.S.A.* 32°18N 101°18W **84** E4
huayana →
lexico 18°41N 103°45W **86** D4
huila □ *Mexico* 27°20N 102°0W **86** B4
l → *Canada* 59°39N 126°57W **70** B3
lane *Mozam.* 17°48S 37°2E **55** F4
lcomán *Mexico* 18°47N 103°9W **86** D4
dale *Canada* 49°45N 112°35W **70** D6
gate *U.S.A.* 34°32N 96°13W **84** D6
linga *U.S.A.* 36°9N 120°21W **78** J6
lisland *U.K.* 54°33N 6°42W **10** B5
lville *U.K.* 52°44N 1°23W **12** E6
lville *U.S.A.* 40°55N 111°24W **76** F8
mo *Puerto Rico* 18°5N 66°22W **89** d
ri *Brazil* 4°8S 63°7W **92** D6
st □ *Kenya* 2°40S 39°45E **54** C4
st Mts. *Canada* 55°0N 129°20W **70** C3
st Ranges *U.S.A.* 39°0N 123°0W **78** G4
tbridge *U.K.* 55°52N 4°6W **11** F4
tepec *Mexico* 19°27N 96°58W **87** D5
tepeque *Guatemala* 14°46N 91°55W **88** D1
tesville *U.S.A.* 39°59N 75°50W **81** F16
ticook *Canada* 45°10N 71°46W **83** A13
ts I. *Canada* 62°30N 83°0W **69** C11
ts Land *Antarctica* 77°0S 25°0W **5** D1
tzacoalcos *Mexico* 18°7N 94°25W **87** D6
ti *Mexico* 20°31N 87°45W **87** C7
alt *Canada* 47°25N 79°42W **72** C4
an *Guatemala* 15°30N 90°21W **88** C1
ar *Australia* 31°27S 145°48E **63** E4
a *Ireland* 51°51N 8°17W **10** E3
ia *Bolivia* 11°0S 68°50W **92** F5
eskill *U.S.A.* 42°41N 74°29W **83** D10
conk *Canada* 44°39N 78°48W **82** B6
ourg *Canada* 43°58N 78°10W **82** C6
ourg Pen. *Australia* 11°20S 132°15E **60** B5
am *Australia* 35°54S 145°40E **63** F4
ué *Mozam.* 12°0S 34°58E **55** E3
rg *Germany* 50°15N 10°58E **16** C6
nada = Kakinada
dia 16°57N 82°11E **41** L13
ababamba *Bolivia* 17°26S 66°10W **92** G5
emane *Mozam.* 17°0S 32°54E **55** F3
in *India* 9°58N 76°20E **40** Q10
in China = Nam-Phan
tnam 10°30N 106°0E **39** G6
ran *U.S.A.* 32°23N 83°21W **85** E13
rane *Alta., Canada* 51°11N 114°30W **70** C6
rane *Ont., Canada* 49°0N 81°0W **72** C3
rane *Chile* 47°15S 72°33W **96** F2
rane → *Canada* 59°0N 103°40W **71** B8
rane, L. *Chile* 47°10S 72°0W **96** F2
ranton *U.S.A.* 41°31N 80°3W **82** E4
burn *Australia* 32°5S 141°0E **63** E3
burn, Canal *Chile* 54°30S 72°0W **96** G2
burn I. *Canada* 45°55N 83°22W **72** C3
burn Ra. *Australia* 15°46S 128°0E **60** C4
ermouth *U.K.* 54°40N 3°22W **12** C4
debiddy *Australia* 32°0S 126°3E **61** F4
pit Country, The
aica 18°15N 77°45W **88** a
→ *Cent. Amer.* 15°0N 83°8W **88** D3
I. del *Pac. Oc.* 5°25N 87°55W **65** G19
U.S.A. 28°21N 80°44W **85** G14
beach *Gabon* 0°59N 9°34E **52** D1
B. *Trin. & Tob.* 10°25N 61°2W **93** K15
Is. *Ind. Oc.* 12°10S 96°55E **64** J1
Ridge *Pac. Oc.* 4°0N 88°0W **65** G19
. *U.S.A.* 42°5N 70°10W **81** D18
ás *Brazil* 3°55S 62°0W **92** D6
Brazil 4°30S 43°55W **93** D10
U.S.A. 44°32N 109°3W **76** D9
ill *Canada* 44°52N 77°50W **82** B7
mu *Chile* 36°30S 72°48W **94** D1
Australia 13°52S 143°12E **62** A3
d'Alene *U.S.A.* 47°41N 116°46W **76** C5
d'Alene L.
.A. 47°32N 116°49W **76** C5
rden *Neths.* 52°40N 6°44E **15** B6
Canary Is. 28°6N 14°23W **24** F5
ville *U.S.A.* 37°2N 95°37W **80** G6
B. *Australia* 34°38S 135°28E **63** E2
Bay *Australia* 34°37S 135°29E **63** E2
Bay △ *Australia* 34°34S 135°19E **63** E2
Bay Peninsula
ralia 34°32S 135°15E **63** E2
Harbour *Australia* 30°16S 153°5E **63** E5
ac *France* 45°41N 0°20W **20** D3
ton *U.S.A.* 42°30N 77°30W **82** D7
ton → *U.S.A.* 42°9N 77°6W **82** D7
Cohoes *U.S.A.* 42°46N 73°42W **83** D11
Cohuna *Australia* 35°45S 144°15E **63** F3
Coiba, I. de *Panama* 7°30N 81°40W **88** E3
Coig → *Argentina* 51°0S 69°10W **96** G3
Coigeach, Rubha *U.K.* 58°6N 5°26W **11** C3
Coihaique *Chile* 45°30S 71°45W **96** F2
Coimbatore *India* 11°2N 76°59E **40** P10
Coimbra *Brazil* 19°55S 57°48W **92** G7
Coimbra *Portugal* 40°15N 8°27W **21** B1
Coín *Spain* 36°40N 4°48W **21** D3
Coipasa, Salar de *Bolivia* 19°26S 68°9W **92** G5
Cojimies *Ecuador* 0°20N 80°0W **92** C3
Cojutepequé *El Salv.* 13°41N 88°54W **88** D2
Cokeville *U.S.A.* 42°5N 110°57W **76** E8
Colac *Australia* 38°21S 143°35E **63** F3
Colatina *Brazil* 19°32S 40°37W **93** G10
Colbeck, C. *Antarctica* 77°6S 157°48W **5** D13
Colborne *Canada* 44°0N 77°53W **82** C7
Colby *U.S.A.* 39°24N 101°3W **80** F3
Colca → *Peru* 15°55S 72°43W **92** G4
Colchester *U.K.* 51°54N 0°55E **13** F8
Colchester *U.S.A.* 41°35N 72°20W **83** E12
Cold L. *Canada* 54°33N 110°5W **71** C7
Cold Lake *Canada* 54°27N 110°10W **71** C6
Coldstream *Canada* 50°13N 119°11W **70** C5
Coldstream *U.K.* 55°39N 2°15W **11** F6
Coldwater *Canada* 44°42N 79°40W **82** B5
Coldwater *Kans., U.S.A.* 37°16N 99°20W **80** G4
Coldwater *Mich., U.S.A.* 41°57N 85°0W **81** E11
Colebrook *U.S.A.* 44°54N 71°30W **83** B13
Coleman *Canada* 49°40N 114°30W **70** D6
Coleman *U.S.A.* 31°50N 99°26W **84** F5
Coleman → *Australia* 15°6S 141°38E **62** B3
Colenso *S. Africa* 28°44S 29°50E **57** D4
Coleraine *Australia* 37°36S 141°40E **63** F3
Coleraine *U.K.* 55°8N 6°41W **10** A5
Coleridge, L. *N.Z.* 43°17S 171°30E **59** E3
Colesberg *S. Africa* 30°45S 25°5E **56** E4
Coleville *U.S.A.* 38°34N 119°30W **78** G7
Colfax *Calif., U.S.A.* 39°6N 120°57W **78** F6
Colfax *La., U.S.A.* 31°31N 92°42W **84** F8
Colfax *Wash., U.S.A.* 46°53N 117°22W **76** C5
Colhué Huapi, L.
Argentina 45°30S 69°0W **96** F3
Coligny *S. Africa* 26°17S 26°15E **57** D4
Colima *Mexico* 19°14N 103°43W **86** D4
Colima □ *Mexico* 19°10N 104°0W **86** D4
Colima, Nevado de
Mexico 19°33N 103°38W **86** D4
Colina *Chile* 33°13S 70°45W **94** C1
Colinas *Brazil* 6°0S 44°10W **93** E10
Coll *U.K.* 56°39N 6°34W **11** E2
Collahuasi *Chile* 21°5S 68°45W **94** A2
Collarenebri *Australia* 29°33S 148°34E **63** D4
Colleen Bawn *Zimbabwe* 21°0S 29°12E **55** G2
College Park *U.S.A.* 33°39N 84°27W **85** E12
College Station *U.S.A.* 30°37N 96°21W **84** F6
Collie *Australia* 33°22S 116°8E **61** F2
Collier B. *Australia* 16°10S 124°15E **60** C3
Collier Ra. *Australia* 24°45S 119°10E **61** D2
Collier Range △
Australia 24°39S 119°7E **61** D2
Collierville *U.S.A.* 35°3N 89°40W **85** D10
Collina, Passo di *Italy* 44°2N 10°56E **22** B4
Collingwood *Canada* 44°29N 80°13W **82** B4
Collingwood *N.Z.* 40°41S 172°40E **59** D4
Collins *Canada* 50°17N 89°27W **72** B2
Collins Bay *Canada* 44°14N 76°36W **83** B8
Collinsville *Australia* 20°30S 147°56E **62** C4
Collipulli *Chile* 37°55S 72°30W **94** D1
Collooney *Ireland* 54°11N 8°29W **10** B3
Colmar *France* 48°5N 7°20E **20** B7
Colo → *Australia* 33°25S 150°52E **63** E5
Cologne = Köln *Germany* 50°56N 6°57E **16** C4
Colom, I. d'en *Spain* 39°58N 4°16E **24** B11
Coloma *U.S.A.* 38°48N 120°53W **78** G6
Colomb-Béchar = Béchar
Algeria 31°38N 2°18W **50** B5
Colombia ■ *S. Amer.* 3°45N 73°0W **92** C4
Colombian Basin
S. Amer. 14°0N 76°0W **66** H12
Colombo *Sri Lanka* 6°56N 79°58E **40** R11
Colón *B. Aires, Argentina* 33°53S 61°7W **94** C3
Colón *Entre Ríos,*
Argentina 32°12S 58°10W **94** C4
Colón *Cuba* 22°42N 80°54W **88** B3
Colón *Panama* 9°20N 79°54W **88** E4
Colón, Arch. de *Ecuador* 0°0 91°0W **90** D1
Colònia de Sant Jordi
Spain 39°19N 2°59E **24** B9
Colonia del Sacramento
Uruguay 34°25S 57°50W **94** C4
Colonia Dora *Argentina* 28°34S 62°59W **94** B3
Colonial Beach *U.S.A.* 38°15N 76°58W **81** F15
Colonie *U.S.A.* 42°43N 73°50W **83** D11
Colonsay *Canada* 51°59N 105°52W **71** C7
Colonsay *U.K.* 56°5N 6°12W **11** E2
Colorado □ *U.S.A.* 39°30N 105°30W **76** G11
Colorado → *Argentina* 39°50S 62°8W **96** D4
Colorado → *N. Amer.* 31°45N 114°40W **77** L6
Colorado → *U.S.A.* 28°36N 95°59W **84** G7
Colorado City *U.S.A.* 32°24N 100°52W **84** E4
Colorado Plateau *U.S.A.* 37°0N 111°0W **77** H8
Colorado River Aqueduct
U.S.A. 33°50N 117°23W **79** L12
Colorado Springs
U.S.A. 38°50N 104°49W **76** G11
Colotlán *Mexico* 22°6N 103°16W **86** C4
Colstrip *U.S.A.* 45°53N 106°38W **76** D10
Colton *U.S.A.* 44°33N 74°56W **83** B10
Columbia *Ky., U.S.A.* 37°6N 85°18W **81** G11
Columbia *La., U.S.A.* 32°6N 92°5W **84** E8
Columbia *Miss., U.S.A.* 31°15N 89°50W **85** F10
Columbia *Mo., U.S.A.* 38°57N 92°20W **80** F7
Columbia *Pa., U.S.A.* 40°2N 76°30W **83** F8
Columbia *S.C., U.S.A.* 34°0N 81°2W **85** D14
Columbia *Tenn., U.S.A.* 35°37N 87°2W **85** D11
Columbia → *N. Amer.* 46°15N 124°5W **78** D2
Columbia, C. *Canada* 83°6N 69°57W **69** A11
Columbia, District of □
U.S.A. 38°55N 77°0W **81** F15
Columbia, Mt. *Canada* 52°8N 117°20W **70** C5
Columbia Basin *U.S.A.* 46°45N 119°5W **76** C4
Columbia Falls *U.S.A.* 48°23N 114°11W **76** B6
Columbia Mts. *Canada* 52°0N 119°0W **70** C5
Columbia Plateau
U.S.A. 44°0N 117°30W **76** E5
Columbiana *U.S.A.* 40°53N 80°42W **82** F4
Columbretes, Is. *Spain* 39°50N 0°50E **21** C6
Columbus *Ga., U.S.A.* 32°28N 84°59W **85** E12
Columbus *Ind., U.S.A.* 39°13N 85°55W **81** F11
Columbus *Kans., U.S.A.* 37°10N 94°50W **80** G6
Columbus *Miss., U.S.A.* 33°30N 88°25W **85** E10
Columbus *Mont.,*
U.S.A. 45°38N 109°15W **76** D9
Columbus *N. Mex.,*
U.S.A. 31°50N 107°38W **77** L10
Columbus *Nebr., U.S.A.* 41°26N 97°22W **80** E5
Columbus *Ohio, U.S.A.* 39°58N 83°0W **81** F12
Columbus *Tex., U.S.A.* 29°42N 96°33W **84** G6
Colusa *U.S.A.* 39°13N 122°1W **78** F4
Colville *U.S.A.* 48°33N 117°54W **76** B5
Colville → *U.S.A.* 70°25N 150°30W **74** a
Colville, C. *N.Z.* 36°29S 175°21E **59** B5
Colwood *Canada* 48°26N 123°29W **78** B3
Colwyn Bay *U.K.* 53°18N 3°44W **12** D4
Comácchio *Italy* 44°42N 12°11E **22** B5
Comalcalco *Mexico* 18°16N 93°13W **87** D6
Comallo *Argentina* 41°0S 70°5W **96** E2
Comanche *U.S.A.* 31°54N 98°36W **84** F5
Comandante Ferraz
Antarctica 62°30S 58°0W **5** C18
Comayagua *Honduras* 14°25N 87°37W **88** D2
Combahee → *U.S.A.* 32°31N 80°31W **85** E14
Combarbalá *Chile* 31°11S 71°2W **94** C1
Combe Martin *U.K.* 51°12N 4°3W **13** F3
Comber *Canada* 42°14N 82°33W **82** D2
Comber *U.K.* 54°33N 5°45W **10** B6
Combermere *Canada* 45°22N 77°37W **82** A7
Comblain-au-Pont
Belgium 50°29N 5°35E **15** D5
Comeragh Mts. *Ireland* 52°18N 7°34W **10** D4
Comet *Australia* 23°36S 148°38E **62** C4
Comilla *Bangla.* 23°28N 91°10E **41** H17
Comino *Malta* 36°1N 14°20E **25** C1
Comino, C. *Italy* 40°32N 9°49E **22** D3
Comitán de Domínguez
Mexico 16°15N 92°8W **87** D6
Commerce *Ga., U.S.A.* 34°12N 83°28W **85** D13
Commerce *Tex., U.S.A.* 33°15N 95°54W **84** E7
Committee B. *Canada* 68°30N 86°30W **69** C11
Commodore, C. *Canada* 44°47N 80°54W **82** B4
Commonwealth B.
Antarctica 67°0S 144°0E **5** C10
Commoron Cr. →
Australia 28°22S 150°8E **63** D5
Communism Pk. = imeni Ismail
Samani, Pik *Tajikistan* 39°0N 72°2E **28** F8
Como *Italy* 45°47N 9°5E **20** D8
Como, Lago di *Italy* 46°0N 9°11E **20** D8
Comodoro Rivadavia
Argentina 45°50S 67°40W **96** F3
Comorin, C. = Kanyakumari
India 8°3N 77°40E **40** Q10
Comoros ■ *Ind. Oc.* 12°10S 44°15E **53** a
Comox *Canada* 49°42N 124°55W **70** D4
Compiègne *France* 49°24N 2°50E **20** B5
Compostela *Mexico* 21°14N 104°55W **86** C4
Comprida, I. *Brazil* 24°50S 47°42W **95** A6
Compton *Canada* 45°14N 71°49W **83** A13
Compton *U.S.A.* 33°53N 118°13W **79** M8
Comrat *Moldova* 46°18N 28°40E **17** E15
Con Cuong *Vietnam* 19°2N 104°54E **38** C5
Con Dao △ *Vietnam* 8°42N 106°35E **39** H6
Con Son *Vietnam* 8°41N 106°37E **39** H6
Conakry *Guinea* 9°29N 13°49W **50** G3
Conara *Australia* 41°50S 147°26E **63** G4
Concarneau *France* 47°52N 3°56W **20** C2
Conceição *Mozam.* 18°47S 36°7E **55** F4
Conceição da Barra
Brazil 18°35S 39°45W **93** G11
Conceição do Araguaia
Brazil 8°0S 49°2W **93** E9
Concepción *Argentina* 27°20S 65°35W **94** B2
Concepción *Bolivia* 16°15S 62°8W **92** G6
Concepción *Chile* 36°50S 73°0W **94** D1
Concepción *Mexico* 18°15N 90°5W **87** D6
Concepción *Paraguay* 23°22S 57°26W **94** A4
Concepción □ *Chile* 37°0S 72°30W **94** D1
Concepción → *Mexico* 30°32N 113°2W **86** A2
Concepción, Est. de
Chile 50°30S 74°55W **96** G2
Concepción, L. *Bolivia* 17°20S 61°20W **92** G6
Concepción, Pta.
Mexico 26°53N 111°50W **86** B2
Concepción del Oro
Mexico 24°38N 101°25W **86** C4
Concepción del Uruguay
Argentina 32°35S 58°20W **94** C4
Conception, Pt. *U.S.A.* 34°27N 120°28W **79** L6
Conception B. *Canada* 47°45N 53°0W **73** C9
Conception B. *Namibia* 23°55S 14°22E **56** C1
Conception I. *Bahamas* 23°52N 75°9W **89** B4
Concession *Zimbabwe* 17°27S 30°56E **55** F3
Conchas Dam *U.S.A.* 35°22N 104°11W **77** J11
Concho *U.S.A.* 34°28N 109°36W **77** J9
Concho → *U.S.A.* 31°34N 99°43W **84** F5
Conchos → *Chihuahua,*
Mexico 29°35N 104°25W **86** B4
Conchos → *Chihuahua,*
Mexico 27°29N 106°45W **86** B3
Conchos → *Tamaulipas,*
Mexico 24°55N 97°38W **87** B5
Concord *Calif., U.S.A.* 37°59N 122°2W **78** H4
Concord *N.C., U.S.A.* 35°25N 80°35W **85** D14
Concord *N.H., U.S.A.* 43°12N 71°32W **83** C13
Concordia *Antarctica* 75°6S 123°23E **5** D17
Concordia *Argentina* 31°20S 58°2W **94** C4
Concórdia *Amazonas,*
Brazil 4°36S 66°36W **92** D5
Concórdia *Sta. Catarina,*
Brazil 27°14S 52°1W **95** B5
Concordia *Mexico* 23°17N 106°4W **86** C3
Concordia *U.S.A.* 39°34N 97°40W **80** F5
Concrete *U.S.A.* 48°32N 121°45W **76** B3
Condamine *Australia* 26°56S 150°9E **63** D5
Conde *U.S.A.* 45°9N 98°6W **80** C4
Condeúba *Brazil* 14°52S 42°0W **93** F10
Condobolin *Australia* 33°4S 147°6E **63** E4
Condon *U.S.A.* 45°14N 120°11W **76** D3
Conegliano *Italy* 45°53N 12°18E **22** B5
Conejera, I. = Conills, I. des
Spain 39°11N 2°58E **24** B9
Conejos *Mexico* 26°14N 103°53W **86** B4
Conemaugh → *U.S.A.* 40°28N 79°19W **82** F5
Confuso → *Paraguay* 25°9S 57°34W **94** B4
Congleton *U.K.* 53°10N 2°13W **12** D5
Congo (Brazzaville) = Congo ■
Africa 1°0S 16°0E **52** E3
Congo (Kinshasa) = Congo, Dem.
Rep. of the ■ *Africa* 3°0S 23°0E **52** E4
Congo ■ *Africa* 1°0S 16°0E **52** E3
Congo → *Africa* 6°4S 12°24E **52** F2
Congo, Dem. Rep. of the ■
Africa 3°0S 23°0E **52** E4
Congo Basin *Africa* 0°10S 24°30E **52** E4
Congonhas *Brazil* 20°30S 43°52W **95** A7
Congress *U.S.A.* 34°9N 112°51W **77** J7
Conills, I. des *Spain* 39°11N 2°58E **24** B9
Coniston *Canada* 46°29N 80°51W **72** C3
Conjeeveram = Kanchipuram
India 12°52N 79°45E **40** N11
Conklin *Canada* 55°38N 111°5W **71** B6
Conklin *U.S.A.* 42°2N 75°49W **83** D9
Conn, L. *Ireland* 54°3N 9°15W **10** B2
Connacht □ *Ireland* 53°43N 9°12W **10** C2
Conneaut *U.S.A.* 41°57N 80°34W **82** E4
Conneautville *U.S.A.* 41°45N 80°22W **82** E4
Connecticut □ *U.S.A.* 41°30N 72°45W **83** E12
Connecticut → *U.S.A.* 41°16N 72°20W **83** E12
Connell *U.S.A.* 46°40N 118°52W **76** C4
Connellsville *U.S.A.* 40°1N 79°35W **82** F5
Connemara *Ireland* 53°29N 9°45W **10** C2
Connemara △ *Ireland* 53°32N 9°52W **10** C2
Connersville *U.S.A.* 39°39N 85°8W **81** F11
Connors Ra. *Australia* 21°40S 149°10E **62** C4
Conoename → *Suriname* 5°48N 55°55W **93** B7
Conquest *Canada* 51°32N 107°14W **71** C7
Conrad *U.S.A.* 48°10N 111°57W **76** B8
Conrad Rise *S. Ocean* 53°0S 41°0E **5** B5
Conran, C. *Australia* 37°49S 148°44E **63** F4
Conroe *U.S.A.* 30°19N 95°27W **84** F7
Consecon *Canada* 44°0N 77°31W **82** C7
Conselheiro Lafaiete
Brazil 20°40S 43°48W **95** A7
Consell *Spain* 39°40N 2°49E **24** B9
Consett *U.K.* 54°51N 1°50W **12** C6
Consort *Canada* 52°1N 110°46W **71** C6
Constance = Konstanz
Germany 47°40N 9°10E **16** E5
Constance, L. = Bodensee
Europe 47°35N 9°25E **20** C8
Constanța *Romania* 44°14N 28°38E **17** F15
Constantine *Algeria* 36°25N 6°42E **50** A7
Constitución *Chile* 35°20S 72°30W **94** D1
Constitución *Uruguay* 31°0S 57°50W **94** C4
Constitución de 1857 △
Mexico 32°4N 115°55W **86** A1
Consul *Canada* 49°20N 109°30W **71** D7
Contact *U.S.A.* 41°46N 114°45W **76** F6
Contai *India* 21°54N 87°46E **43** J12
Contamana *Peru* 7°19S 74°55W **92** E4
Contas → *Brazil* 14°17S 39°1W **93** F11
Contoocook *U.S.A.* 43°13N 71°45W **83** C13
Contra Costa *Mozam.* 25°9S 33°30E **57** D5
Contwoyto L. *Canada* 65°42N 110°50W **68** C8
Conway = Conwy *U.K.* 53°17N 3°50W **12** D4
Conway = Conwy →
U.K. 53°17N 3°50W **12** D4
Conway *Australia* 20°24S 148°41E **62** J6
Conway *Canada* 44°6N 76°54W **82** B8
Conway *Ark., U.S.A.* 35°5N 92°26W **84** D8
Conway *N.H., U.S.A.* 43°59N 71°7W **83** C13
Conway *S.C., U.S.A.* 33°51N 79°3W **85** E15
Conway, C. *Australia* 20°34S 148°46E **62** J6
Conway, L. *Australia* 28°17S 135°35E **63** D2
Conwy *U.K.* 53°17N 3°50W **12** D4
Conwy □ *U.K.* 53°10N 3°44W **12** D4
Conwy → *U.K.* 53°17N 3°50W **12** D4
Coober Pedy *Australia* 29°1S 134°43E **63** D1
Cooch Behar = Koch Bihar
India 26°22N 89°29E **41** F16
Cooinda *Australia* 13°15S 130°5E **60** B5
Cook *Australia* 30°37S 130°25E **61** F5
Cook *U.S.A.* 47°51N 92°41W **80** B7
Cook, B. *Chile* 55°10S 70°0W **96** H3
Cook, C. *Canada* 50°8N 127°55W **70** C3
Cook, Mt. = Aoraki Mount Cook
N.Z. 43°36S 170°9E **59** E3
Cook Inlet *U.S.A.* 60°0N 152°0W **68** D4
Cook Is. *Pac. Oc.* 17°0S 160°0W **65** J12
Cook Strait *N.Z.* 41°15S 174°29E **59** D5
Cookeville *U.S.A.* 36°10N 85°30W **85** C12
Cookhouse *S. Africa* 32°44S 25°47E **56** E4
Cooks Harbour *Canada* 51°36N 55°52W **73** B8
Cookshire *Canada* 45°25N 71°38W **83** A13
Cookstown *Canada* 44°11N 79°42W **82** B5
Cookstown *U.K.* 54°39N 6°45W **10** B5
Cooksville *Canada* 43°35N 79°38W **82** C5
Cooktown *Australia* 15°30S 145°16E **62** B4
Coolabah *Australia* 31°1S 146°43E **63** E4
Cooladdi *Australia* 26°37S 145°23E **63** D4
Coolah *Australia* 31°48S 149°41E **63** E4
Coolamon *Australia* 34°46S 147°8E **63** E4
Coolgardie *Australia* 30°55S 121°8E **61** F3
Coolidge *U.S.A.* 32°59N 111°31W **77** K8
Coolidge Dam *U.S.A.* 33°10N 110°32W **77** K8
Cooma *Australia* 36°12S 149°8E **63** F4
Coon Rapids *U.S.A.* 45°9N 93°19W **80** C7
Coonabarabran
Australia 31°14S 149°18E **63** E4
Coonamble *Australia* 30°56S 148°27E **63** E4
Coonana *Australia* 31°0S 123°0E **61** F3
Coondapoor *India* 13°42N 74°40E **40** N9
Cooninnie, L. *Australia* 26°4S 139°59E **63** D2
Cooper *U.S.A.* 33°23N 95°42W **84** E7
Cooper Cr. → *Australia* 28°29S 137°46E **63** D2
Cooper Ridge *Pac. Oc.* 10°0N 150°30W **65** G12
Cooperstown *N. Dak.,*
U.S.A. 47°27N 98°8W **80** B4
Cooperstown *N.Y.,*
U.S.A. 42°42N 74°56W **83** D10
Coorabie *Australia* 31°54S 132°18E **61** F5
Coorong, The *Australia* 35°50S 139°20E **63** F2
Coorow *Australia* 29°53S 116°2E **61** E2
Cooroy *Australia* 26°22S 152°54E **63** D5
Coos Bay *U.S.A.* 43°22N 124°13W **76** E1
Coosa → *U.S.A.* 32°30N 86°16W **85** E11
Cootamundra *Australia* 34°36S 148°1E **63** E4
Cootehill *Ireland* 54°4N 7°5W **10** B4
Copahue Paso *Argentina* 37°49S 71°8W **94** D1
Copainalá *Mexico* 17°4N 93°18W **87** D6
Copake *U.S.A.* 42°7N 73°31W **83** D11
Copán *Honduras* 14°50N 89°9W **88** D2
Cope *U.S.A.* 39°40N 102°51W **76** G12
Copenhagen = København
Denmark 55°40N 12°26E **9** J15
Copenhagen *U.S.A.* 43°54N 75°41W **83** C9
Copiapó *Chile* 27°30S 70°20W **94** B1
Copiapó → *Chile* 27°19S 70°56W **94** B1
Coplay *U.S.A.* 40°44N 75°29W **83** F9
Copo △ *Argentina* 25°53S 61°41W **94** B3
Copp L. *Canada* 60°14N 114°40W **70** A6
Copper Canyon = Barranca del
Cobre ⌂ *Mexico* 27°18N 107°40W **86** B3
Copper Harbor *U.S.A.* 47°28N 87°53W **80** B10
Copper Queen *Zimbabwe* 17°29S 29°18E **55** F2
Copperas Cove *U.S.A.* 31°8N 97°54W **84** F6
Copperbelt □ *Zambia* 13°15S 27°30E **55** E2
Coppermine = Kugluktuk
Canada 67°50N 115°5W **68** C8
Coppermine → *Canada* 67°49N 116°4W **68** C8
Copperopolis *U.S.A.* 37°58N 120°38W **78** H6
Coquet → *U.K.* 55°20N 1°32W **12** B6
Coquille *U.S.A.* 43°11N 124°11W **76** E1
Coquimbo *Chile* 30°0S 71°20W **94** C1
Coquimbo □ *Chile* 31°0S 71°0W **94** C1
Coquitlam *Canada* 49°17N 122°45W **70** D4
Corabia *Romania* 43°48N 24°30E **17** G13
Coracora *Peru* 15°5S 73°45W **92** G4
Coraki *Australia* 28°59S 153°17E **63** D5
Coral *U.S.A.* 40°29N 79°10W **82** F5
Coral Bay *Australia* 23°8S 113°46E **60** D1
Coral Gables *U.S.A.* 25°43N 80°16W **85** J14
Coral Harbour *Canada* 64°8N 83°10W **69** C11
Coral Sea *Pac. Oc.* 15°0S 150°0E **58** C8
Coral Sea Basin *Pac. Oc.* 14°0S 152°0E **64** J7
Coral Sea Islands Terr. □
Australia 20°0S 155°0E **58** C8
Coral Springs *U.S.A.* 26°16N 80°16W **85** H14
Coraopolis *U.S.A.* 40°31N 80°10W **82** F4
Corato *Italy* 41°9N 16°25E **22** D7
Corbett △ *India* 29°20N 79°0E **43** E8
Corbin *U.S.A.* 36°57N 84°6W **81** G11
Corby *U.K.* 52°30N 0°41W **13** E7
Corcaigh = Cork *Ireland* 51°54N 8°29W **10** E3
Corcoran *U.S.A.* 36°6N 119°33W **78** J7
Corcovado △ *Costa Rica* 8°33N 83°35W **88** E3
Corcubión *Spain* 42°56N 9°12W **21** A1
Cordele *U.S.A.* 31°58N 83°47W **85** F13
Cordell *U.S.A.* 35°17N 98°59W **84** D5
Córdoba *Argentina* 31°20S 64°10W **94** C3
Córdoba *Mexico* 18°53N 96°56W **87** D5
Córdoba *Spain* 37°50N 4°50W **21** D3
Córdoba □ *Argentina* 31°22S 64°15W **94** C3
Córdoba, Sierra de
Argentina 31°10S 64°25W **94** C3
Cordova *U.S.A.* 60°33N 145°45W **68** C5
Corella → *Australia* 19°34S 140°47E **62** B3
Corfield *Australia* 21°40S 143°21E **62** C3
Corfu = Kerkyra *Greece* 39°38N 19°50E **25** A3
Corfu *U.S.A.* 42°57N 78°24W **82** D6
Corfu, Str. of = Kerkyras, Notio
Steno *Greece* 39°34N 20°0E **25** A4
Coria *Spain* 39°58N 6°33W **21** C2
Corigliano Cálabro *Italy* 39°36N 16°31E **22** E7
Coringa Is. *Australia* 16°58S 149°58E **62** B4
Corinth = Korinthos
Greece 37°56N 22°55E **23** F10
Corinth *Miss., U.S.A.* 34°56N 88°31W **85** D10
Corinth *N.Y., U.S.A.* 43°15N 73°49W **83** C11
Corinth, G. of = Korinthiakos
Kolpos *Greece* 38°16N 22°30E **23** E10
Corinto *Brazil* 18°20S 44°30W **93** G10
Corinto *Nic.* 12°30N 87°10W **88** D2
Cork *Ireland* 51°54N 8°29W **10** E3
Cork □ *Ireland* 51°57N 8°40W **10** E3
Cork Harbour *Ireland* 51°47N 8°16W **10** E3
Çorlu *Turkey* 41°11N 27°49E **23** D12
Cormack L. *Canada* 60°56N 121°37W **70** A4
Cormorant *Canada* 54°14N 100°35W **71** C8
Cormorant L. *Canada* 54°15N 100°50W **71** C8
Corn Is. = Maíz, Is. del
Nic. 12°15N 83°4W **88** D3
Cornélio Procópio *Brazil* 23°7S 50°40W **95** A5
Corner Brook *Canada* 48°57N 57°58W **73** C8
Cornești *Moldova* 47°21N 28°1E **17** E15
Corning *Ark., U.S.A.* 36°25N 90°35W **85** C9

Corning Calif., U.S.A. 39°56N 122°11W 76 G2
Corning Iowa, U.S.A. 40°59N 94°44W 80 E6
Corning N.Y., U.S.A. 42°9N 77°3W 82 D7
Cornwall Canada 45°2N 74°44W 83 A10
Cornwall U.S.A. 40°17N 76°25W 83 F8
Cornwall □ U.K. 50°26N 4°40W 13 G3
Cornwall I. Canada 77°37N 94°38W 69 B10
Cornwallis I. Canada 75°8N 95°0W 69 B10
Corny Pt. Australia 34°55S 137°0E 63 E2
Coro Venezuela 11°25N 69°41W 92 A5
Coroatá Brazil 4°8S 44°0W 93 D10
Corocoro Bolivia 17°15S 68°28W 92 G5
Coroico Bolivia 16°0S 67°50W 92 G5
Coromandel N.Z. 36°45S 175°31E 59 B5
Coromandel Coast India 12°30N 81°0E 40 N12
Corona Calif., U.S.A. 33°53N 117°34W 79 M9
Corona N. Mex., U.S.A. 34°15N 105°36W 77 J11
Coronado U.S.A. 32°41N 117°10W 79 N9
Coronado, B. de Costa Rica 9°0N 83°40W 88 E3
Coronados, Is. Los Mexico 32°26N 117°19W 79 N9
Coronation Canada 52°5N 111°27W 70 C6
Coronation Gulf Canada 68°25N 110°0W 68 C9
Coronation I. Antarctica 60°45S 46°0W 5 C18
Coronation Is. Australia 14°57S 124°55E 60 B3
Coronda Argentina 31°58S 60°56W 94 C3
Coronel Chile 37°0S 73°10W 94 D1
Coronel Bogado Paraguay 27°11S 56°18W 94 B4
Coronel Dorrego Argentina 38°40S 61°10W 94 D3
Coronel Oviedo Paraguay 25°24S 56°30W 94 B4
Coronel Pringles Argentina 38°0S 61°30W 94 D3
Coronel Suárez Argentina 37°30S 61°52W 94 D3
Coronel Vidal Argentina 37°28S 57°45W 94 D4
Coropuna, Nevado Peru 15°30S 72°41W 92 G4
Corowa Australia 35°58S 146°21E 63 F4
Corozal □ Belize 18°23N 88°23W 87 D7
Corozal Pt. Trin. & Tob. 10°45N 61°37W 93 K15
Corpus Argentina 27°10S 55°30W 95 B4
Corpus Christi U.S.A. 27°47N 97°24W 84 H6
Corpus Christi, L. U.S.A. 28°2N 97°52W 84 G6
Corralejo Canary Is. 28°43N 13°53W 24 F6
Corraun Pen. Ireland 53°54N 9°54W 10 C2
Correntes, C. das Mozam. 24°6S 35°34E 57 C6
Corrib, L. Ireland 53°27N 9°16W 10 C2
Corrientes Argentina 27°30S 58°45W 94 B4
Corrientes □ Argentina 28°0S 57°0W 94 B4
Corrientes → Argentina 30°42S 59°38W 94 C4
Corrientes → Peru 3°43S 74°35W 92 D4
Corrientes, C. Colombia 5°30N 77°34W 92 B3
Corrientes, C. Cuba 21°43N 84°30W 88 B3
Corrientes, C. Mexico 20°25N 105°42W 86 C3
Corrigan U.S.A. 31°0N 94°52W 84 F7
Corrigin Australia 32°20S 117°53E 61 F2
Corriverton Guyana 5°55N 57°20W 92 B7
Corry U.S.A. 41°55N 79°39W 82 E5
Corse □ France 42°0N 9°0E 20 F8
Corse, C. France 43°1N 9°25E 20 E8
Corsica = Corse □ France 42°0N 9°0E 20 F8
Corsicana U.S.A. 32°6N 96°28W 84 E6
Corte France 42°19N 9°11E 20 E8
Cortés, Mar de = California, G. de Mexico 27°0N 111°0W 86 B2
Cortez U.S.A. 37°21N 108°35W 77 H9
Cortland N.Y., U.S.A. 42°36N 76°11W 83 D8
Cortland Ohio, U.S.A. 41°20N 80°44W 82 E4
Çorum Turkey 40°30N 34°57E 19 F5
Corumbá Brazil 19°0S 57°30W 92 G7
Corunna = A Coruña Spain 43°20N 8°25W 21 A1
Corvallis U.S.A. 44°34N 123°16W 76 D2
Corvette, L. de la Canada 53°25N 74°3W 72 B5
Corvo Azores 39°43N 31°8W 50 a
Corydon U.S.A. 40°46N 93°19W 80 E7
Cosalá Mexico 24°23N 106°41W 86 C3
Cosamaloapan de Carpio Mexico 18°22N 95°48W 87 D5
Cosenza Italy 39°18N 16°15E 22 E7
Coshocton U.S.A. 40°16N 81°51W 82 F3
Cosmo Newberry Australia 28°0S 122°54E 61 E3
Cosmonaut Sea S. Ocean 66°30S 40°0E 5 C5
Coso Junction U.S.A. 36°3N 117°57W 79 J9
Coso Pk. U.S.A. 36°13N 117°44W 79 J9
Cosquín Argentina 31°15S 64°30W 94 C3
Costa Blanca Spain 38°25N 0°10W 21 C5
Costa Brava Spain 41°30N 3°0E 21 B7
Costa Daurada Spain 41°12N 1°15E 21 B6
Costa del Sol Spain 36°30N 4°30W 21 D3
Costa dels Pins Spain 39°38N 3°26E 24 B10
Costa Mesa U.S.A. 33°38N 117°55W 79 M9
Costa Rica ■ Cent. Amer. 10°0N 84°0W 88 E3
Costa Smeralda Italy 41°5N 9°35E 22 D3
Cosumnes → U.S.A. 38°16N 121°26W 78 G5
Cotabato Phil. 7°14N 124°15E 37 C6
Cotagaita Bolivia 20°45S 65°40W 94 A2
Côte d'Azur France 43°25N 7°10E 20 E7
Côte-d'Ivoire = Ivory Coast ■ Africa 7°30N 5°0W 50 G4
Coteau des Prairies U.S.A. 45°20N 97°50W 80 C5
Coteau du Missouri U.S.A. 47°0N 100°0W 80 B4
Cotentin France 49°15N 1°30W 20 B3
Cotillo Canary Is. 28°41N 14°1W 24 F5
Cotonou Benin 6°20N 2°25E 50 G6
Cotopaxi Ecuador 0°40S 78°30W 92 D3
Cotswold Hills U.K. 51°42N 2°10W 13 F5
Cottage Grove U.S.A. 43°48N 123°3W 76 E2
Cottam Canada 42°8N 82°45W 82 D2
Cottbus Germany 51°45N 14°20E 16 C8
Cottonwood U.S.A. 34°45N 112°1W 77 J7
Cotulla U.S.A. 28°26N 99°14W 84 G5
Coudersport U.S.A. 41°46N 78°1W 82 E6
Couedic, C. du Australia 36°5S 136°40E 63 F2
Coulee City U.S.A. 47°37N 119°17W 76 C4
Coulee Dam Nat. Recr. Area = Lake Roosevelt ⌓ U.S.A. 48°5N 118°14W 76 B4
Coulman I. Antarctica 73°35S 170°0E 5 D11
Coulonge → Canada 45°52N 76°46W 72 C4
Coulterville U.S.A. 37°43N 120°12W 78 H6
Council U.S.A. 44°44N 116°26W 76 D5
Council Bluffs U.S.A. 41°16N 95°52W 80 E6
Council Grove U.S.A. 38°40N 96°29W 80 F5
Coupeville U.S.A. 48°13N 122°41W 78 B4
Courantyne → S. Amer. 5°55N 57°5W 92 B7
Courcelles Belgium 50°28N 4°22E 15 D4
Courtenay Canada 49°45N 125°0W 70 D4
Courtland Canada 42°51N 80°38W 82 D4
Courtland U.S.A. 38°20N 121°34W 78 G5
Courtrai = Kortrijk Belgium 50°50N 3°17E 15 D3
Courtright Canada 42°49N 82°28W 82 D2
Coushatta U.S.A. 32°1N 93°21W 84 E8
Coutts Crossing Australia 29°49S 152°55E 63 D5
Couva Trin. & Tob. 10°25N 61°27W 93 K15
Couvin Belgium 50°3N 4°29E 15 D4
Cove I. Canada 45°17N 81°44W 82 A3
Coventry U.K. 52°25N 1°28W 13 E6
Covilhã Portugal 40°17N 7°31W 21 B2
Covington Ga., U.S.A. 33°36N 83°51W 85 E13
Covington Ky., U.S.A. 39°5N 84°30W 81 F11
Covington Tenn., U.S.A. 35°34N 89°39W 85 D10
Covington Va., U.S.A. 37°47N 79°59W 81 G14
Cowal, L. Australia 33°40S 147°25E 63 E4
Cowan, L. Australia 31°45S 121°45E 61 F3
Cowan L. Canada 54°0N 107°15W 71 C7
Cowangie Australia 35°12S 141°26E 63 F3
Cowansville Canada 45°14N 72°46W 83 A12
Coward Springs Australia 29°24S 136°49E 63 D2
Cowcowing Lakes Australia 30°55S 117°20E 61 F2
Cowdenbeath U.K. 56°7N 3°21W 11 E5
Cowell Australia 33°39S 136°56E 63 E2
Cowes U.K. 50°45N 1°18W 13 G6
Cowichan L. Canada 48°53N 124°17W 78 B2
Cowlitz → U.S.A. 46°6N 122°55W 78 D4
Cowra Australia 33°49S 148°42E 63 E4
Coxilha Grande Brazil 28°18S 51°30W 95 B5
Coxim Brazil 18°30S 54°55W 93 G8
Cox's Bazar Bangla. 21°26N 91°59E 41 J17
Coyote Wells U.S.A. 32°44N 115°58W 79 N11
Coyuca de Benítez Mexico 17°2N 100°4W 87 D4
Coyuca de Catalán Mexico 18°20N 100°39W 86 D4
Cozad U.S.A. 40°52N 99°59W 80 E4
Cozumel Mexico 20°31N 86°55W 87 C7
Cozumel, Isla Mexico 20°30N 86°40W 87 C7
Crab Hill Barbados 13°19N 59°38W 89 g
Cracow = Kraków Poland 50°4N 19°57E 17 C10
Cracow Australia 25°17S 150°17E 63 D5
Cradle Mt.-Lake St. Clair △ Australia 41°49S 147°56E 63 G4
Cradock Australia 32°6S 138°31E 63 E2
Cradock S. Africa 32°8S 25°36E 56 E4
Craig U.S.A. 40°31N 107°33W 76 F10
Craigavon U.K. 54°27N 6°23W 10 B5
Craigmore Zimbabwe 20°28S 32°50E 55 G3
Craik Canada 51°3N 105°49W 71 C7
Crailsheim Germany 49°8N 10°5E 16 D6
Craiova Romania 44°21N 23°48E 17 F12
Cramsie Australia 23°20S 144°15E 62 C3
Cranberry L. U.S.A. 44°11N 74°50W 83 B10
Cranberry Portage Canada 54°35N 101°23W 71 C8
Cranbrook Australia 34°18S 117°33E 61 F2
Cranbrook Canada 49°30N 115°46W 70 D5
Crandon U.S.A. 45°34N 88°54W 80 C9
Crane Oreg., U.S.A. 43°25N 118°35W 76 E4
Crane Tex., U.S.A. 31°24N 102°21W 84 F3
Crane, The Barbados 13°6N 59°27W 89 g
Cranston U.S.A. 41°47N 71°26W 83 E13
Crater L. U.S.A. 42°56N 122°6W 76 E2
Crater Lake △ U.S.A. 42°55N 122°10W 76 E2
Craters of the Moon ⌓ U.S.A. 43°25N 113°30W 76 E7
Crateús Brazil 5°10S 40°39W 93 E10
Crato Brazil 7°10S 39°25W 93 E11
Craven, L. Canada 54°20N 76°56W 72 B4
Crawford U.S.A. 42°41N 103°25W 80 D2
Crawfordsville U.S.A. 40°2N 86°54W 80 E10
Crawley U.K. 51°7N 0°11W 13 F7
Crazy Mts. U.S.A. 46°12N 110°20W 76 C8
Crean L. Canada 54°5N 106°9W 71 C7
Crediton Canada 43°17N 81°33W 82 C3
Crediton U.K. 50°47N 3°40W 13 G4
Cree → Canada 58°57N 105°47W 71 B7
Cree → U.K. 54°55N 4°25W 11 G4
Cree L. Canada 57°30N 106°30W 71 B7
Creede U.S.A. 37°51N 106°56W 77 H10
Creekside U.S.A. 40°40N 79°11W 82 F5
Creel Mexico 27°45N 107°38W 86 B3
Creemore Canada 44°19N 80°6W 82 B4
Creighton Canada 54°45N 101°54W 71 C8
Creighton U.S.A. 42°28N 97°54W 80 D5
Crema Italy 45°22N 9°41E 20 D8
Cremona Italy 45°7N 10°2E 20 D9
Cres Croatia 44°58N 14°25E 16 F8
Crescent City U.S.A. 41°45N 124°12W 76 F1
Crespo Argentina 32°2S 60°19W 94 C3
Cresson U.S.A. 40°28N 78°36W 82 F6
Crestline Calif., U.S.A. 34°14N 117°18W 79 L9
Crestline Ohio, U.S.A. 40°47N 82°44W 82 F2
Creston Canada 49°10N 116°31W 70 D5
Creston Calif., U.S.A. 35°32N 120°33W 78 K6
Creston Iowa, U.S.A. 41°4N 94°22W 80 E6
Crestview Calif., U.S.A. 37°46N 118°58W 78 H8
Crestview Fla., U.S.A. 30°46N 86°34W 85 F11
Crete = Kriti Greece 35°15N 25°0E 25 D7
Crete U.S.A. 40°38N 96°58W 80 E5
Créteil France 48°47N 2°27E 20 B5
Creus, C. de Spain 42°20N 3°19E 21 A7
Creuse → France 47°0N 0°34E 20 C4
Crewe U.K. 53°6N 2°26W 12 D5
Crewkerne U.K. 50°53N 2°48W 13 G5
Crianlarich U.K. 56°24N 4°37W 11 E4
Criciúma Brazil 28°40S 49°23W 95 B6
Crieff U.K. 56°22N 3°50W 11 E5
Crimea □ Ukraine 45°30N 33°10E 19 E5
Crimean Pen. = Krymskyy Pivostriv Ukraine 45°0N 34°0E 19 F5
Crişul Alb → Romania 46°42N 21°17E 17 E11
Crişul Negru → Romania 46°42N 21°16E 17 E11
Crna → Macedonia 41°33N 21°59E 23 D9
Crna Gora = Montenegro ■ Europe 42°40N 19°20E 23 C8
Crna Gora Macedonia 42°10N 21°30E 23 C9
Crna Reka = Crna → Macedonia 41°33N 21°59E 23 D9
Croagh Patrick Ireland 53°46N 9°40W 10 C2
Croatia ■ Europe 45°20N 16°0E 16 F9
Crocker, Banjaran Malaysia 5°40N 116°30E 36 C5
Crockett U.S.A. 31°19N 95°27W 84 F7
Crocodile = Umgwenya → Mozam. 25°14S 32°18E 57 D5
Crocodile Is. Australia 12°3S 134°58E 62 A1
Crohy Hd. Ireland 54°55N 8°26W 10 B3
Croix, L. la Canada 48°20N 92°15W 72 C1
Croker, C. Australia 10°58S 132°35E 60 B5
Croker, C. Canada 44°58N 80°59W 82 B4
Croker I. Australia 11°12S 132°32E 60 B5
Cromarty U.K. 57°40N 4°2W 11 D4
Cromer U.K. 52°56N 1°17E 12 E9
Cromwell N.Z. 45°3S 169°14E 59 F2
Cromwell U.S.A. 41°36N 72°39W 83 E12
Crook U.K. 54°43N 1°45W 12 C6
Crooked → Canada 54°50N 122°54W 70 C4
Crooked → U.S.A. 44°32N 121°16W 76 D3
Crooked I. Bahamas 22°50N 74°10W 89 B5
Crooked Island Passage Bahamas 22°55N 74°35W 89 B5
Crookston Minn., U.S.A. 47°47N 96°37W 80 B5
Crookston Nebr., U.S.A. 42°56N 100°45W 80 D3
Crookwell Australia 34°28S 149°24E 63 E4
Crosby U.K. 53°30N 3°3W 12 D4
Crosby N. Dak., U.S.A. 48°55N 103°18W 80 A2
Crosby Pa., U.S.A. 41°45N 78°23W 82 E6
Crosbyton U.S.A. 33°40N 101°14W 84 E4
Cross City U.S.A. 29°38N 83°7W 85 G13
Cross Fell U.K. 54°43N 2°28W 12 C5
Cross L. Canada 54°45N 97°30W 71 C9
Cross Lake Canada 54°37N 97°47W 71 C9
Cross Sound U.S.A. 58°0N 135°0W 68 D6
Crossett U.S.A. 33°8N 91°58W 84 E9
Crosshaven Ireland 51°47N 8°17W 10 E3
Crossmaglen U.K. 54°5N 6°36W 10 B5
Crossmolina Ireland 54°6N 9°20W 10 B2
Crossville U.S.A. 35°57N 85°2W 85 D12
Croswell U.S.A. 43°16N 82°37W 82 C2
Croton-on-Hudson U.S.A. 41°12N 73°55W 83 E11
Crotone Italy 39°5N 17°8E 22 E7
Crow → Canada 59°41N 124°20W 70 B4
Crow Agency U.S.A. 45°36N 107°28W 76 D10
Crow Hd. Ireland 51°35N 10°9W 10 E1
Crowell U.S.A. 33°59N 99°43W 84 E5
Crowley U.S.A. 30°13N 92°22W 84 F8
Crowley, L. U.S.A. 37°35N 118°42W 78 H8
Crown Point Ind., U.S.A. 41°25N 87°22W 80 E10
Crown Point N.Y., U.S.A. 43°57N 73°26W 83 C11
Crown Pt. Trin. & Tob. 11°18N 60°51W 93 J16
Crownpoint U.S.A. 35°41N 108°9W 77 J9
Crows Landing U.S.A. 37°23N 121°6W 78 H5
Crows Nest Australia 27°16S 152°4E 63 D5
Crowsnest Pass Canada 49°40N 114°40W 70 D6
Croydon Australia 18°13S 142°14E 62 B3
Croydon □ U.K. 51°22N 0°5W 13 F7
Crozet, Is. Ind. Oc. 46°27S 52°0E 3 G12
Crusheen Ireland 52°57N 8°53W 10 D3
Cruz, C. Cuba 19°50N 77°50W 88 C4
Cruz Alta Brazil 28°45S 53°40W 95 B5
Cruz Bay U.S. Virgin Is. 18°20N 64°48W 89 e
Cruz del Eje Argentina 30°45S 64°50W 94 C3
Cruzeiro Brazil 22°33S 45°0W 95 A7
Cruzeiro do Oeste Brazil 23°46S 53°4W 95 A5
Cruzeiro do Sul Brazil 7°35S 72°35W 92 E4
Cry L. Canada 58°45N 129°0W 70 B3
Crystal Bay U.S.A. 39°15N 120°0W 78 F7
Crystal Brook Australia 33°21S 138°12E 63 E2
Crystal City U.S.A. 28°41N 99°50W 84 G5
Crystal Falls U.S.A. 46°5N 88°20W 80 B9
Crystal River U.S.A. 28°54N 82°35W 85 G13
Crystal Springs U.S.A. 31°59N 90°21W 85 F9
Csongrád Hungary 46°43N 20°12E 17 E11
Cu Lao Hon Vietnam 10°54N 108°18E 39 G7
Cua Rao Vietnam 19°16N 104°27E 38 C5
Cuácua → Mozam. 17°54S 37°0E 55 F4
Cuamato Angola 17°2S 15°7E 56 B2
Cuamba Mozam. 14°45S 36°22E 55 E4
Cuando → Angola 17°30S 23°15E 53 H4
Cuando Cubango □ Angola 16°25S 20°0E 56 B3
Cuangar Angola 17°36S 18°39E 56 B2
Cuango = Kwango → Dem. Rep. of the Congo 3°14S 17°22E 52 E3
Cuanza → Angola 9°21S 13°9E 52 F2
Cuarto → Argentina 33°25S 63°2W 94 C3
Cuatrociénegas Mexico 26°59N 102°5W 86 B4
Cuauhtémoc Mexico 28°25N 106°52W 86 B3
Cuba N. Mex., U.S.A. 36°1N 107°4W 77 H10
Cuba N.Y., U.S.A. 42°13N 78°17W 82 D6
Cuba ■ W. Indies 22°0N 79°0W 88 B4
Cubango → Africa 18°50S 22°25E 56 B3
Cuc Phuong △ Vietnam 20°17N 105°38E 38 B5
Cuchumatanes, Sierra de los Guatemala 15°35N 91°25W 88 C1
Cuckfield U.K. 51°1N 0°8W 13 F7
Cucuí Brazil 1°12N 66°50W 92 C5
Cucurpé Mexico 30°20N 110°43W 86 A2
Cúcuta Colombia 7°54N 72°31W 92 B4
Cuddalore India 11°46N 79°45E 40 P11
Cuddapah India 14°30N 78°47E 40 M11
Cuddapan, L. Australia 25°45S 141°26E 62 D3
Cue Australia 27°25S 117°54E 61 E2
Cuenca Ecuador 2°50S 79°9W 92 D3
Cuenca Spain 40°5N 2°10W 21 B4
Cuenca, Serranía de Spain 39°55N 1°50W 21 C5
Cuernavaca Mexico 18°55N 99°15W 87 D5
Cuero U.S.A. 29°6N 97°17W 84 G6
Cueva de la Quebrada del Toro △ Venezuela 10°46N 69°3W 89 D6
Cuevas del Almanzora Spain 37°18N 1°58W 21 D5
Cuevo Bolivia 20°15S 63°30W 92 H6
Cuiabá Brazil 15°30S 56°0W 93 G7
Cuiabá → Brazil 17°5S 56°36W 93 G7
Cuihangcun China 22°27N 113°32E 33 G10
Cuijk Neths. 51°44N 5°50E 15 C5
Cuilco Guatemala 15°24N 91°58W 88 C1
Cuillin Hills U.K. 57°13N 6°15W 11 D2
Cuillin Sd. U.K. 57°4N 6°20W 11 D2
Cuilo = Kwilu → Dem. Rep. of the Congo 3°22S 17°22E 52 E3
Cuito → Angola 18°1S 20°48E 56 B3
Cuitzeo, L. de Mexico 19°55N 101°5W 86 D4
Cukai Malaysia 4°13N 103°25E 39 K4
Culbertson U.S.A. 48°9N 104°31W 76 B11
Culcairn Australia 35°41S 147°3E 63 F4
Culebra Puerto Rico 18°19N 65°18W 89 d
Culgoa → Australia 29°56S 146°20E 63 D4
Culgoa Flood Plain △ Australia 28°58S 147°5E 63 D4
Culiacán Mexico 24°50N 107°23W 86 C3
Culiacán → Mexico 24°30N 107°42W 86 C3
Culik Indonesia 8°21S 115°37E 37 J18
Culion Phil. 11°54N 119°58E 37 B6
Cullarin Ra. Australia 34°30S 149°30E 63 E4
Cullen U.K. 57°42N 2°49W 11 D6
Cullen Pt. Australia 11°57S 141°54E 62 A3
Cullera Spain 39°9N 0°17W 21 C5
Cullman U.S.A. 34°11N 86°51W 85 D11
Cullompton U.K. 50°51N 3°24W 13 G4
Culpeper U.S.A. 38°30N 78°0W 81 F14
Culuene → Brazil 12°56S 52°51W 93 F8
Culver, Pt. Australia 32°54S 124°43E 61 F3
Culverden N.Z. 42°47S 172°49E 59 E4
Cumaná Venezuela 10°30N 64°5W 92 A6
Cumberland B.C., Canada 49°40N 125°0W 70 D4
Cumberland Ont., Canada 45°29N 75°24W 83 A9
Cumberland U.S.A. 39°39N 78°46W 81 F14
Cumberland → U.S.A. 37°9N 88°25W 80 G9
Cumberland, L. U.S.A. 36°52N 85°9W 81 G11
Cumberland Gap ⌓ U.S.A. 36°36N 83°40W 81 G12
Cumberland I. U.S.A. 30°50N 81°25W 85 F14
Cumberland Is. Australia 20°35S 149°10E 62 J7
Cumberland Island ⌓ U.S.A. 30°12N 81°24W 85 F14
Cumberland L. Canada 54°3N 102°18W 71 C8
Cumberland Pen. Canada 67°0N 64°0W 69 C13
Cumberland Plateau U.S.A. 36°0N 85°0W 85 D12
Cumberland Sd. Canada 65°30N 66°0W 69 C13
Cumbernauld U.K. 55°57N 3°58W 11 F5
Cumborah Australia 29°40S 147°45E 63 D4
Cumbres de Majalca △ Mexico 28°48N 106°30W 86 B3
Cumbres de Monterrey △ Mexico 25°26N 100°25W 86 B4
Cumbria □ U.K. 54°42N 2°52W 12 C5
Cumbrian Mts. U.K. 54°30N 3°0W 12 C5
Cumbum India 15°40N 79°10E 40 M11
Cuminá → Brazil 1°30S 56°0W 93 D7
Cummings Mt. U.S.A. 35°2N 118°34W 79 K8
Cummins Australia 34°16S 135°43E 63 E2
Cumnock Australia 32°59S 148°46E 63 E4
Cumnock U.K. 55°28N 4°17W 11 F4
Cumpas Mexico 30°2N 109°48W 86 B3
Cumplida, Pta. Canary Is. 28°50N 17°48W 24 F2
Cunco Chile 38°55S 72°2W 96 D2
Cuncumén Chile 31°53S 70°38W 94 C1
Cunderdin Australia 31°37S 117°12E 61 F2
Cunene → Angola 17°20S 11°50E 56 B1
Cúneo Italy 44°23N 7°32E 20 D7
Çüngüş Turkey 38°13N 39°17E 44 B3
Cunillera, I. = Sa Conillera Spain 38°59N 1°13E 24 C7
Cunnamulla Australia 28°2S 145°38E 63 D4
Cupar Canada 50°57N 104°10W 71 C8
Cupar U.K. 56°19N 3°1W 11 E5
Cupertino U.S.A. 37°19N 122°2W 78 H4
Cupica, G. de Colombia 6°25N 77°30W 92 B3
Curaçao Neth. Ant. 12°10N 69°0W 89 D6
Curanilahue Chile 37°29S 73°28W 94 D1
Curaray → Peru 2°20S 74°5W 92 D4
Curepipe Mauritius 20°19S 57°31E 53 d
Curepto Chile 35°8S 72°1W 94 D1
Curiapo Venezuela 8°33N 61°5W 92 B6
Curicó Chile 34°55S 71°20W 94 C1
Curieuse Seychelles 4°15S 55°44E 53 b
Curitiba Brazil 25°20S 49°10W 95
Curitibanos Brazil 27°18S 50°36W 95
Currabubula Australia 31°16S 150°44E 63
Currais Novos Brazil 6°13S 36°30W 93 E
Curral Velho C. Verde Is. 16°8N 22°48W 50
Curralinho Brazil 1°45S 49°46W 93
Currane, L. Ireland 51°49N 10°4W 10
Currant U.S.A. 38°44N 115°28W 76
Currawinya △ Australia 28°55S 144°27E 63
Current → U.S.A. 36°15N 90°55W 84
Currie Australia 39°56S 143°53E 63
Currie U.S.A. 40°16N 114°45W 76
Curtea de Argeş Romania 45°12N 24°42E 17 F
Curtin Springs Australia 25°20S 131°45E 61
Curtis U.S.A. 40°38N 100°31W 80
Curtis Group Australia 39°30S 146°37E 63
Curtis I. Australia 23°35S 151°10E 62
Curuápanema → Brazil 2°25S 55°2W 93
Curuçá Brazil 0°43S 47°50W 93
Curuguaty Paraguay 24°31S 55°42W 95
Curup Indonesia 4°26S 102°13E 36
Cururupu Brazil 1°50S 44°50W 93 D
Curuzú Cuatiá Argentina 29°50S 58°5W 94
Curvelo Brazil 18°45S 44°27W 93 G
Cusco = Cuzco Peru 13°32S 72°0W 92
Cushendall U.K. 55°5N 6°4W 10
Cushing U.S.A. 35°59N 96°46W 84
Cushing, Mt. Canada 57°35N 126°57W 70
Cusihuiriáchic Mexico 28°14N 106°50W 86
Custer U.S.A. 43°46N 103°36W 80
Cut Bank U.S.A. 48°38N 112°20W 76
Cutchogue U.S.A. 41°1N 72°30W 83
Cuthbert U.S.A. 31°46N 84°48W 85
Cutler U.S.A. 36°31N 119°17W 78
Cuttaburra → Australia 29°43S 144°22E 63
Cuttack India 20°25N 85°57E 41
Cuvier, C. Australia 23°14S 113°22E 61
Cuvier I. N.Z. 36°27S 175°50E 59
Cuxhaven Germany 53°51N 8°41E 16
Cuyahoga Falls U.S.A. 41°8N 81°29W 82
Cuyahoga Valley △ U.S.A. 41°14N 81°33W 82
Cuyo Phil. 10°51N 121°2E 37
Cuyuni → Guyana 6°23N 58°41W 92
Cuzco Bolivia 20°0S 66°50W 92
Cuzco Peru 13°32S 72°0W 92
Cwmbran U.K. 51°39N 3°2W 13
Cyangugu Rwanda 2°29S 28°54E 54
Cyclades Greece 37°0N 24°30E 23
Cygnet Australia 43°8S 147°1E 63
Cynthiana U.S.A. 38°23N 84°18W 81
Cypress Hills Canada 49°40N 109°30W 71
Cypress Hills ⌓ Canada 49°40N 109°30W 71
Cyprus ■ Asia 35°0N 33°0E 25
Cyrenaica = Barqa Libya 27°0N 23°0E 51
Cyrene Libya 32°53N 21°52E 51
Czar Canada 52°27N 110°50W 71
Czech Rep. ■ Europe 50°0N 15°0E 16
Częstochowa Poland 50°49N 19°7E 17

D

Da → Vietnam 21°15N 105°20E 3
Da Hinggan Ling China 48°0N 121°0E 3
Da Lat Vietnam 11°56N 108°25E 3
Da Nang Vietnam 16°4N 108°13E 3
Da Qaidam China 37°50N 95°15E 3
Da Yunhe → Hopei, China 39°10N 117°10E 3
Da Yunhe → Jiangsu, China 34°25N 120°5E 35
Da'an China 45°30N 124°7E 35
Daan Viljoen ⌓ Namibia 22°2S 16°45E
Daba Shan China 32°0N 109°0E 3
Dabbagh, Jabal Si. Arabia 27°52N 35°45E 4
Dabhoi India 22°10N 73°20E 4
Dabo = Pasirkuning Indonesia 0°30S 104°33E 3
Dabola Guinea 10°50N 11°5W 5
Dabung Malaysia 5°23N 102°1E 3
Dacca = Dhaka Bangla. 23°43N 90°26E 43
Dacca = Dhaka □ Bangla. 24°25N 90°25E 43
Dachau Germany 48°15N 11°26E 1
Dachigam △ India 34°10N 75°0E 4
Dacre Canada 45°22N 76°57W 8
Dadanawa Guyana 2°50N 59°30W 9
Dade City U.S.A. 28°22N 82°11W 85
Dadhar Pakistan 29°28N 67°39E 4
Ḑadnah U.A.E. 25°32N 56°22E 4
Dadra & Nagar Haveli □ India 20°5N 73°0E 4
Dadri = Charkhi Dadri India 28°37N 76°17E 4
Dadu Pakistan 26°45N 67°45E 4
Daegu S. Korea 35°50N 128°37E 3
Daejeon S. Korea 36°20N 127°28E 3
Daejeong S. Korea 33°8N 126°17E 3
Daet Phil. 14°2N 122°55E 3
Dafnes Greece 35°13N 25°3E 2
Dagana Senegal 16°30N 15°35W 5
Dagestan □ Russia 42°30N 47°0E
Daggett U.S.A. 34°52N 116°52W 7
Daghestan Republic = Dagestan □ Russia 42°30N 47°0E
Dağlıq Qarabağ = Nagorno-Karabakh □ Azerbaijan 39°55N 46°45E
Dagö = Hiiumaa Estonia 58°50N 22°45E
Dagu China 38°59N 117°40E
Dagupan Phil. 16°3N 120°20E
Daguragu Australia 17°33S 130°30E
Dahab Egypt 28°31N 34°31E
Dahlak Kebir Eritrea 15°50N 40°10E
Dahlonega U.S.A. 34°32N 83°59W 8

ahod India 22°50N 74°15E 42 H6
ahongliutan China 35°45N 79°20E 43 B8
ahra Libya 29°30N 17°50E 51 C9
ahūk Iraq 36°50N 43°1E 44 B3
ai Hao Vietnam 18°1N 106°25E 38 C6
ai-Sen Japan 35°22N 133°32E 31 G6
ai Xian China 39°4N 112°58E 34 E7
aicheng China 38°42N 116°38E 34 E9
aikondi = Day Kundī □ Afghan. 34°0N 66°0E 40 C5
aingean Ireland 53°18N 7°17W 10 C4
aintree Australia 16°20S 145°20E 62 B4
aintree △ Australia 16°8S 145°2E 62 B4
aiō-Misaki Japan 34°15N 136°45E 31 G8
isen-Oki △ Japan 35°23N 133°34E 31 G6
isetsu-Zan Japan 43°30N 142°57E 30 C11
isetsu-Zan △ Japan 43°30N 142°55E 30 C11
jarra Australia 21°42S 139°30E 62 C2
jiawa China 37°9N 119°0E 35 F10
k Dam Cambodia 12°20N 107°21E 38 F6
k Nhe Vietnam 15°28N 107°48E 38 E6
k Pek Vietnam 15°4N 107°44E 38 E6
k Song Vietnam 12°19N 107°35E 39 F6
k Sui Vietnam 14°55N 107°43E 38 E6
kar Senegal 14°34N 17°29W 50 F2
khla W. Sahara 23°50N 15°53W 50 D2
khla, El Wâhât el Egypt 25°30N 28°50E 51 C11
kor India 22°45N 73°11E 42 H5
kota City U.S.A. 42°25N 96°25W 80 D5
kovica Serbia 42°22N 20°26E 23 C9
achi China 36°48N 105°0E 34 F3
ai Nur China 43°20N 116°45E 34 C9
akī Iran 29°26N 51°17E 45 D6
älven → Sweden 60°12N 16°43E 9 F17
aman → Turkey 36°41N 28°43E 23 F13
andzadgad Mongolia 43°27N 104°30E 34 C3
ap-Uliga-Darrit = Majuro Marshall Is. 7°9N 171°12E 64 G9
arna Sweden 61°0N 14°0E 8 F16
bandīn Pakistan 29°0N 64°23E 40 E4
beattie U.K. 54°56N 3°50W 11 G5
beg Australia 20°16S 147°18E 62 C4
by Australia 27°10S 151°17E 63 D5
e City U.S.A. 38°38N 77°19W 81 F15
e Hollow L. U.S.A. 36°32N 85°27W 85 C12
gān Iran 27°31N 59°19E 45 E8
hart U.S.A. 36°4N 102°31W 84 C3
housie Canada 48°5N 66°26W 73 C6
housie India 32°38N 75°58E 42 C6
Shaanxi, China 34°48N 109°58E 34 G5
Yunnan, China 25°40N 100°10E 32 D5
an China 38°50N 121°40E 35 E11
ang Shan China 28°0N 102°45E 32 D5
ng He → China 40°55N 121°40E 35 D11
yat el Karmel Israel 32°43N 35°2E 46 C4
keith U.K. 55°54N 3°4W 11 F5
as Oreg., U.S.A. 44°55N 123°19W 76 D2
as Tex., U.S.A. 32°47N 96°48W 84 E6
es, The U.S.A. 45°36N 121°10W 76 D3
nā U.A.E. 24°30N 52°20E 45 E7
nacija Croatia 43°20N 17°0E 22 C7
nas, L. Canada 53°30N 71°50W 73 B5
natia = Dalmacija Croatia 43°20N 17°0E 22 C7
nau India 26°4N 81°2E 43 F9
nellington U.K. 55°19N 4°23W 11 F4
negorsk Russia 44°32N 135°33E 30 B7
nerechensk Russia 45°50N 133°40E 30 B6
nevostochnyy □ Russia 67°0N 140°0E 29 C14
a Ivory C. 7°0N 6°30W 50 G4
y U.K. 55°42N 4°43W 11 F4
ymple, L. Australia 20°40S 147°0E 62 C4
ymple, Mt. Australia 21°1S 148°39E 62 K6
land Sweden 58°50N 12°15E 9 G15
enganj India 24°0N 84°4E 43 H11
on Ga., U.S.A. 34°46N 84°58W 85 D12
on Mass., U.S.A. 42°28N 73°11W 83 D11
on Nebr., U.S.A. 41°25N 102°58W 80 E2
on-in-Furness U.K. 54°10N 3°11W 12 C4
ik Iceland 65°58N 18°32W 8 D4
vadis = Jokkmokk Sweden 66°35N 19°50E 8 C18
vallinu Australia 30°17S 116°40E 61 F2
→ Australia 13°35S 130°19E 60 B5
City U.S.A. 37°42N 122°27W 78 H4
L. Canada 56°32N 105°39W 71 B7
River Australia 13°46S 130°42E 60 B5
Waters Australia 16°15S 133°24E 62 B1
Doi Vietnam 8°50N 105°12E 39 H5
Ha Vietnam 21°21N 107°36E 38 B6
an India 20°25N 72°57E 40 J8
aneh Iran 33°1N 50°29E 45 C6
anhûr Egypt 31°0N 30°30E 51 B12
ant L. Canada 61°45N 105°5W 71 A7
anzhuang China 38°5N 116°35E 34 E9
ar Indonesia 7°7S 128°40E 37 F7
ara C.A.R. 4°58N 18°42E 52 D3
araland Namibia 20°0S 15°0E 56 C2
ascus = Dimashq Syria 33°30N 36°18E 46 B5
ivand Iran 35°47N 52°0E 45 C7
ivand, Qolleh-ye Iran 35°56N 52°10E 45 C7
a Angola 6°44S 15°20E 52 F3
ovița → Romania 44°12N 26°26E 17 F14
Marie Haiti 18°36N 74°26W 89 C5
ghān Iran 36°10N 54°17E 45 B7
el Spain 39°4N 3°37W 21 C4
etta = Dumyât Egypt 31°24N 31°48E 51 B12
ng China 36°15N 115°6E 34 F8
r Qābū Syria 36°58N 41°51E 44 B4
nam = Ad Dammām Si. Arabia 26°20N 50°5E 45 E6
dar → India 23°17N 87°35E 43 H12
Damoh India 23°50N 79°28E 43 H8
Dampier Australia 20°41S 116°42E 60 D2
Dampier, Selat Indonesia 0°40S 131°0E 37 E8
Dampier Arch. Australia 20°38S 116°32E 60 D2
Damrei, Chuor Phnum Cambodia 11°30N 103°0E 39 G4
Damyang S. Korea 35°19N 126°59E 35 G14
Dana Indonesia 11°0S 122°52E 37 F6
Dana Jordan 30°41N 35°37E 46 E4
Dana, L. Canada 50°53N 77°20W 72 B4
Dana, Mt. U.S.A. 37°54N 119°12W 78 H7
Danakil Desert Ethiopia 12°45N 41°0E 47 E3
Danané Ivory C. 7°16N 8°9W 50 G4
Danau Poso Indonesia 1°52S 120°35E 37 E6
Danbury U.S.A. 41°24N 73°28W 83 E11
Danby L. U.S.A. 34°13N 115°5W 77 J6
Dand Afghan. 31°28N 65°32E 42 D1
Dande ⌂ Zimbabwe 15°56S 30°16E 55 F3
Dandeldhura Nepal 29°20N 80°35E 43 E9
Dandeli India 15°5N 74°30E 40 M9
Dandenong Australia 38°0S 145°15E 63 F4
Dandong China 40°10N 124°20E 35 D13
Danfeng China 33°45N 110°25E 34 H6
Danger Is. = Pukapuka Cook Is. 10°53S 165°49W 65 J11
Danger Pt. S. Africa 34°40S 19°17E 56 E2
Danginpuri Indonesia 8°40S 115°13E 37 K18
Dangla Shan = Tanggula Shan China 32°40N 92°10E 32 C4
Dangrek, Phnom Thailand 14°15N 105°0E 38 E5
Dangriga Belize 17°0N 88°13W 87 D7
Dangshan China 34°27N 116°22E 34 G9
Daniel U.S.A. 42°52N 110°4W 76 E8
Daniel's Harbour Canada 50°13N 57°35W 73 B8
Danielskuil S. Africa 28°11S 23°33E 56 D3
Danielson U.S.A. 41°48N 71°53W 83 E13
Danilov Russia 58°16N 40°13E 18 C7
Daning China 36°28N 110°45E 34 F6
Ḑank Oman 23°33N 56°16E 45 F8
Dankhar Gompa India 32°10N 78°10E 42 C8
Danlí Honduras 14°4N 86°35W 88 D2
Danmark = Denmark ■ Europe 55°45N 10°0E 9 J14
Dannemora U.S.A. 44°43N 73°44W 83 B11
Dannevirke N.Z. 40°12S 176°8E 59 D6
Dannhauser S. Africa 28°0S 30°3E 57 D5
Dansville U.S.A. 42°34N 77°42W 82 D7
Danta India 24°11N 72°46E 42 G5
Dantan India 21°57N 87°20E 43 J12
Danube = Dunărea → Europe 45°20N 29°40E 17 F15
Danvers U.S.A. 42°34N 70°56W 83 D14
Danville Ill., U.S.A. 40°8N 87°37W 80 E10
Danville Ky., U.S.A. 37°39N 84°46W 81 G11
Danville Pa., U.S.A. 40°58N 76°37W 83 F8
Danville Va., U.S.A. 36°36N 79°23W 81 G14
Danville Vt., U.S.A. 44°25N 72°9W 83 B12
Danzhou China 19°31N 109°33E 38 C7
Danzig = Gdańsk Poland 54°22N 18°40E 17 A10
Dapaong Togo 10°55N 0°16E 50 F6
Daqing Shan China 40°40N 111°0E 34 D6
Daqq-e Sorkh, Kavīr Iran 33°45N 52°50E 45 C7
Dar Banda Africa 8°0N 23°0E 48 F6
Dar el Beida = Casablanca Morocco 33°36N 7°36W 50 B4
Dar es Salaam Tanzania 6°50S 39°12E 54 D4
Dar Mazār Iran 29°14N 57°20E 45 D8
Dar'ā Syria 32°36N 36°7E 46 C5
Dar'ā □ Syria 32°55N 36°10E 46 C5
Dārāb Iran 28°50N 54°30E 45 D7
Daraban Pakistan 31°44N 70°20E 42 D4
Daraina Madag. 13°12S 49°40E 57 A8
Daraj Libya 30°10N 10°28E 51 B8
Dārān Iran 32°59N 50°24E 45 C6
Dārayyā Syria 33°28N 36°15E 46 B5
Darband Pakistan 34°20N 72°50E 42 B5
Darband, Kūh-e Iran 31°34N 57°8E 45 D8
Darbhanga India 26°15N 85°55E 43 F11
D'Arcy Canada 50°33N 122°29W 70 C4
Dardanelle Ark., U.S.A. 35°13N 93°9W 84 D8
Dardanelle Calif., U.S.A. 38°20N 119°50W 78 G7
Dardanelles = Çanakkale Boğazı Turkey 40°17N 26°32E 23 D12
Dārestān Iran 29°9N 58°42E 45 D8
Dârfûr Sudan 13°40N 24°0E 51 F10
Dargai Pakistan 34°25N 71°55E 42 B4
Dargaville N.Z. 35°57S 173°52E 59 A4
Darhan Mongolia 49°37N 106°21E 32 B5
Darhan Muminggan Lianheqi China 41°40N 110°28E 34 D6
Darıca Turkey 40°45N 29°23E 23 D13
Darién, G. del Colombia 9°0N 77°0W 92 B3
Darién △ Panama 7°36N 77°57W 88 E4
Dariganga = Ovoot Mongolia 45°21N 113°45E 34 B7
Darjeeling = Darjiling India 27°3N 88°18E 43 F13
Darjiling India 27°3N 88°18E 43 F13
Darkan Australia 33°20S 116°43E 61 F2
Darkhana Pakistan 30°39N 72°11E 42 D5
Darkhazīneh Iran 31°54N 48°39E 45 D6
Darkot Pass Pakistan 36°45N 73°26E 43 A5
Darling → Australia 34°4S 141°54E 63 E3
Darling Downs Australia 27°30S 150°30E 63 D5
Darling Ra. Australia 32°30S 116°20E 61 F2
Darlington U.K. 54°32N 1°33W 12 C6
Darlington U.S.A. 34°18N 79°52W 85 D15
Darlington □ U.K. 54°32N 1°33W 12 C6
Darlington, L. S. Africa 33°10S 25°9E 56 E4
Darlot, L. Australia 27°48S 121°35E 61 E3
Darłowo Poland 54°25N 16°25E 16 A9
Darmstadt Germany 49°51N 8°39E 16 D5
Darnah Libya 32°45N 22°45E 51 B10
Darnall S. Africa 29°23S 31°18E 57 D5
Darnley, C. Antarctica 68°0S 69°0E 5 C6
Darnley B. Canada 69°30N 123°30W 68 C7
Darr → Australia 23°39S 143°50E 62 C3
Darra Pezu Pakistan 32°19N 70°44E 42 C4
Darrequeira Argentina 37°42S 63°10W 94 D3
Darrington U.S.A. 48°15N 121°36W 76 B3
Dart → U.K. 50°24N 3°39W 13 G4
Dart, C. Antarctica 73°6S 126°20W 5 D14
Dartford U.K. 51°26N 0°13E 13 F8
Dartmoor U.K. 50°38N 3°57W 13 G4
Dartmoor △ U.K. 50°37N 3°59W 13 G4
Dartmouth Canada 44°40N 63°30W 73 D7
Dartmouth U.K. 50°21N 3°36W 13 G4
Dartmouth Res. Australia 26°4S 145°18E 63 D4
Dartuch, C. = Artrutx, C. de Spain 39°55N 3°49E 24 B10
Darvaza Turkmenistan 40°11N 58°24E 28 E6
Darvel, Teluk = Lahad Datu, Telok Malaysia 4°50N 118°20E 37 D5
Darwen U.K. 53°42N 2°29W 12 D5
Darwendale Zimbabwe 17°41S 30°33E 57 B5
Darwha India 20°15N 77°45E 40 J10
Darwin Australia 12°25S 130°51E 60 B5
Darwin U.S.A. 36°15N 117°35W 79 J9
Darya Khan Pakistan 31°48N 71°6E 42 D4
Daryācheh-ye Bakhtegān Iran 29°40N 53°50E 45 D7
Daryoi Amu = Amudarya → Uzbekistan 43°58N 59°34E 28 E6
Dās U.A.E. 25°20N 53°30E 45 E7
Dashen, Ras Ethiopia 13°8N 38°26E 47 E2
Dashetai China 41°0N 109°5E 34 D5
Dashköpri Turkmenistan 36°16N 62°8E 45 B9
Dashoguz Turkmenistan 41°49N 59°58E 28 E6
Dasht → Pakistan 25°10N 61°40E 40 G2
Daska Pakistan 32°20N 74°20E 42 C6
Dasuya India 31°49N 75°38E 42 D6
Datça Turkey 36°46N 27°40E 23 F12
Datia India 25°39N 78°27E 43 G8
Datong China 40°6N 113°18E 34 D7
Dattakhel Pakistan 32°54N 69°46E 42 C3
Datu, Tanjung Indonesia 2°5N 109°39E 36 D3
Datu Piang Phil. 7°2N 124°30E 37 C6
Datuk, Tanjong = Datu, Tanjung Indonesia 2°5N 109°39E 36 D3
Daud Khel Pakistan 32°53N 71°34E 42 C4
Daudnagar India 25°2N 84°24E 43 G11
Daugava → Latvia 57°4N 24°3E 9 H21
Daugavpils Latvia 55°53N 26°32E 9 J22
Daulpur India 26°45N 77°59E 42 F7
Dauphin Canada 51°9N 100°5W 71 C8
Dauphin U.S.A. 40°22N 76°56W 82 F8
Dauphin L. Canada 51°20N 99°45W 71 C9
Dauphiné France 45°15N 5°25E 20 D6
Dausa India 26°52N 76°20E 42 F7
Davangere India 14°25N 75°55E 40 M9
Davao Phil. 7°0N 125°40E 37 C7
Davao G. Phil. 6°30N 125°48E 37 C7
Dāvar Panāh = Sarāvān Iran 27°25N 62°15E 45 E9
Davenport Calif., U.S.A. 37°1N 122°12W 78 H4
Davenport Iowa, U.S.A. 41°32N 90°35W 80 E8
Davenport Wash., U.S.A. 47°39N 118°9W 76 C4
Davenport Ra. Australia 20°28S 134°0E 62 C1
Davenport Range △ Australia 20°36S 134°22E 62 C1
Daventry U.K. 52°16N 1°10W 13 E6
David Panama 8°30N 82°30W 88 E3
David City U.S.A. 41°15N 97°8W 80 E5
David Glacier Antarctica 75°20S 162°0E 5 D21
David Gorodok = Davyd Haradok Belarus 52°4N 27°8E 17 B14
Davidson Canada 51°16N 105°59W 71 C7
Davis Antarctica 68°34S 77°55E 5 C6
Davis U.S.A. 38°33N 121°44W 78 G5
Davis Dam U.S.A. 35°12N 114°34W 79 K12
Davis Inlet Canada 55°50N 60°59W 73 A7
Davis Mts. U.S.A. 30°50N 103°55W 84 F3
Davis Sea Antarctica 66°0S 92°0E 5 C7
Davis Str. N. Amer. 65°0N 58°0W 66 C14
Davlos Cyprus 35°25N 33°54E 25 D12
Davos Switz. 46°48N 9°49E 20 C8
Davy L. Canada 58°53N 108°18W 71 B7
Davyd Haradok Belarus 52°4N 27°8E 17 B14
Dawei = Tavoy Burma 14°2N 98°12E 38 E2
Dawes Ra. Australia 24°40S 150°40E 62 C5
Dawlish U.K. 50°35N 3°28W 13 G4
Dawna Ra. Burma 16°30N 98°30E 38 D2
Dawros Hd. Ireland 54°50N 8°33W 10 B3
Dawson U.S.A. 31°46N 84°27W 85 F12
Dawson, I. Chile 53°50S 70°50W 96 G2
Dawson B. Canada 52°53N 100°49W 71 C8
Dawson City Canada 64°10N 139°30W 68 C6
Dawson Creek Canada 55°45N 120°15W 70 B4
Dawson Inlet Canada 61°50N 93°25W 71 A10
Dawson Ra. Australia 24°30S 149°48E 62 C4
Dax France 43°44N 1°3W 20 E3
Daxian China 31°15N 107°23E 32 C5
Daxindian China 37°30N 120°50E 35 F11
Daxinggou China 43°25N 129°40E 35 C15
Daxue Shan China 30°30N 101°30E 32 C5
Day Kundī □ Afghan. 34°0N 66°0E 40 C5
Daylesford Australia 37°21S 144°9E 63 F3
Dayr az Zawr Syria 35°20N 40°5E 44 C4
Daysland Canada 52°50N 112°20W 70 C6
Dayton Nev., U.S.A. 39°14N 119°36W 78 F7
Dayton Ohio, U.S.A. 39°45N 84°12W 81 F11
Dayton Pa., U.S.A. 40°53N 79°15W 82 F5
Dayton Tenn., U.S.A. 35°30N 85°1W 85 D12
Dayton Wash., U.S.A. 46°19N 117°59W 76 C5
Dayton Wyo., U.S.A. 44°53N 107°16W 76 D10
Daytona Beach U.S.A. 29°13N 81°1W 85 G14
Dayville U.S.A. 44°28N 119°32W 76 D4
De Aar S. Africa 30°39S 24°0E 56 E3
De Biesbosch △ Neths. 51°45N 4°48E 15 C4
De Funiak Springs U.S.A. 30°43N 86°7W 85 F11
De Grey → Australia 20°12S 119°13E 60 D2
De Haan Belgium 51°16N 3°2E 15 C3
De Hoge Veluwe △ Neths. 52°5N 5°46E 15 B5
De Hoop ⌂ S. Africa 34°30S 20°28E 56 E3
De Kalb Junction U.S.A. 44°30N 75°16W 83 B9
De Kennemerduinen △ Neths. 52°27N 4°33E 15 B4
De Land U.S.A. 29°2N 81°18W 85 G14
De Leon U.S.A. 32°7N 98°32W 84 E5
De Panne Belgium 51°6N 2°34E 15 C2
De Pere U.S.A. 44°27N 88°4W 80 C9
De Queen U.S.A. 34°2N 94°21W 84 D7
De Quincy U.S.A. 30°27N 93°26W 84 F8
De Ruyters U.S.A. 42°45N 75°53W 83 D9
De Smet U.S.A. 44°23N 97°33W 80 C5
De Soto U.S.A. 38°8N 90°34W 80 F8
De Tour Village U.S.A. 46°0N 83°56W 81 B12
De Witt U.S.A. 34°18N 91°20W 84 D9
Dead Sea Asia 31°30N 35°30E 46 D4
Deadwood U.S.A. 44°23N 103°44W 80 C2
Deadwood L. Canada 59°10N 128°30W 70 B3
Deal U.K. 51°13N 1°25E 13 F9
Deal I. Australia 39°30S 147°20E 63 F4
Dealesville S. Africa 28°41S 25°44E 56 D4
Dean → Canada 52°49N 126°58W 70 C3
Dean, Forest of U.K. 51°45N 2°33W 13 F5
Dean Chan. Canada 52°30N 127°15W 70 C3
Deán Funes Argentina 30°20S 64°20W 94 C3
Dease → Canada 59°56N 128°32W 70 B3
Dease L. Canada 58°40N 130°5W 70 B2
Dease Lake Canada 58°25N 130°6W 70 B2
Death Valley U.S.A. 36°15N 116°50W 79 J10
Death Valley △ U.S.A. 36°29N 117°6W 79 J9
Death Valley Junction U.S.A. 36°20N 116°25W 79 J10
Debagram India 23°51N 90°33E 43 H14
Debar Macedonia 41°31N 20°30E 23 D9
Debden Canada 53°30N 106°50W 71 C7
Dębica Poland 50°2N 21°25E 17 C11
DeBolt Canada 55°12N 118°1W 70 B5
Deborah East, L. Australia 30°45S 119°30E 61 F2
Deborah West, L. Australia 30°45S 119°5E 61 F2
Debre Markos Ethiopia 10°20N 37°40E 47 E2
Debre Tabor Ethiopia 11°50N 38°26E 47 E2
Debre Zebit Ethiopia 11°48N 38°30E 47 E2
Debrecen Hungary 47°33N 21°42E 17 E11
Decatur Ala., U.S.A. 34°36N 86°59W 85 D11
Decatur Ga., U.S.A. 33°46N 84°16W 85 E12
Decatur Ill., U.S.A. 39°51N 88°57W 80 F9
Decatur Ind., U.S.A. 40°50N 84°56W 81 E11
Decatur Tex., U.S.A. 33°14N 97°35W 84 E6
Deccan India 18°0N 79°0E 40 L11
Deception Bay Australia 27°10S 153°5E 63 D5
Deception I. Antarctica 63°0S 60°15W 5 C17
Deception L. Canada 56°33N 104°13W 71 B8
Dechhu India 26°46N 72°20E 42 F5
Děčín Czech Rep. 50°47N 14°12E 16 C8
Deckerville U.S.A. 43°32N 82°44W 82 C2
Decorah U.S.A. 43°18N 91°48W 80 D8
Dedéagach = Alexandroupoli Greece 40°50N 25°54E 23 D11
Dedham U.S.A. 42°15N 71°10W 83 D13
Dedza Malawi 14°20S 34°20E 55 E3
Dee → Aberds., U.K. 57°9N 2°5W 11 D6
Dee → Dumf. & Gall., U.K. 54°51N 4°3W 11 G4
Dee → Wales, U.K. 53°22N 3°17W 12 D4
Deep B. Canada 61°15N 116°35W 70 A5
Deep Bay = Shenzhen Wan China 22°27N 113°55E 33 G10
Deepwater Australia 29°25S 151°51E 63 D5
Deer → Canada 58°23N 94°13W 71 B10
Deer L. Canada 52°40N 94°20W 71 C10
Deer Lake Nfld. & L., Canada 49°11N 57°27W 73 C8
Deer Lake Ont., Canada 52°36N 94°20W 71 C10
Deer Lodge U.S.A. 46°24N 112°44W 76 C7
Deer Park U.S.A. 47°57N 117°28W 76 C5
Deer River U.S.A. 47°20N 93°48W 80 B7
Deeragun Australia 19°16S 146°33E 62 B4
Deerdepoort S. Africa 24°37S 26°27E 56 C4
Defiance U.S.A. 41°17N 84°22W 81 E11
Degana India 26°50N 74°20E 42 F6
Dégelis Canada 47°30N 68°35W 73 C6
Deggendorf Germany 48°50N 12°57E 16 D7
Degh → Pakistan 31°3N 73°21E 42 D5
Değirmenlik = Kythréa Cyprus 35°15N 33°29E 25 D12
Deh Bīd Iran 30°39N 53°11E 45 D7
Deh Dasht Iran 30°47N 50°33E 45 D6
Deh-e Shīr Iran 31°29N 53°45E 45 D7
Dehaj Iran 30°42N 54°53E 45 D7
Dehak Iran 27°11N 62°37E 45 E9
Dehdez Iran 31°43N 50°17E 45 D6
Dehej India 21°44N 72°40E 42 J5
Dehestān Iran 28°30N 55°35E 45 D7
Dehgolān Iran 35°17N 47°25E 44 C5
Dehibat Tunisia 32°0N 10°47E 51 B8
Dehlorān Iran 32°41N 47°16E 44 C5
Dehnow-e Kūhestān Iran 27°58N 58°32E 45 E8
Dehra Dun India 30°20N 78°4E 42 D8
Dehri India 24°50N 84°15E 43 G11
Dehui China 44°30N 125°40E 35 B13
Deinze Belgium 50°59N 3°32E 15 D3
Dej Romania 47°10N 23°52E 17 E12
Deka → Zimbabwe 18°4S 26°42E 56 B4
DeKalb U.S.A. 41°56N 88°46W 80 E9
Dekese Dem. Rep. of the Congo 3°24S 21°24E 52 E4
Del Mar U.S.A. 32°58N 117°16W 79 N9
Del Norte U.S.A. 37°41N 106°21W 77 H10
Del Rio U.S.A. 29°22N 100°54W 84 G4
Delambre I. Australia 20°26S 117°5E 60 D2
Delano U.S.A. 35°46N 119°15W 79 K7
Delano Peak U.S.A. 38°22N 112°22W 76 G7
Delareyville S. Africa 26°41S 25°26E 56 D4
Delaronde L. Canada 54°3N 107°3W 71 C7
Delavan U.S.A. 42°38N 88°39W 80 D9
Delaware U.S.A. 40°18N 83°4W 81 E12
Delaware □ U.S.A. 39°0N 75°20W 81 F16
Delaware → U.S.A. 39°15N 75°20W 83 G9
Delaware B. U.S.A. 39°0N 75°10W 81 F16
Delaware Water Gap ⌂ U.S.A. 41°10N 74°55W 83 E10
Delay → Canada 56°56N 71°28W 73 A5
Delegate Australia 37°4S 148°56E 63 F4
Delevan U.S.A. 42°29N 78°29W 82 D6
Delft Neths. 52°1N 4°22E 15 B4
Delfzijl Neths. 53°20N 6°55E 15 A6
Delgado, C. Mozam. 10°45S 40°40E 55 E5
Delgerhet Mongolia 45°50N 110°30E 34 B6
Delgo Sudan 20°6N 30°40E 51 D12
Delhi Canada 42°51N 80°30W 82 D4
Delhi India 28°39N 77°13E 42 E7
Delhi La., U.S.A. 32°28N 91°30W 84 E9
Delhi N.Y., U.S.A. 42°17N 74°55W 83 D10
Delia Canada 51°38N 112°23W 70 C6
Delice Turkey 39°54N 34°2E 19 G5
Delicias Mexico 28°13N 105°28W 86 B3
Delījān Iran 33°59N 50°40E 45 C6
Déline Canada 65°11N 123°25W 68 C7
Delisle Canada 51°55N 107°8W 71 C7
Dell City U.S.A. 31°56N 105°12W 84 F2
Dell Rapids U.S.A. 43°50N 96°43W 80 D5
Delmar U.S.A. 42°37N 73°47W 83 D11
Delmenhorst Germany 53°3N 8°37E 16 B5
Delonga, Ostrova Russia 76°40N 149°20E 29 B15
Deloraine Australia 41°30S 146°40E 63 G4
Deloraine Canada 49°15N 100°29W 71 D8
Delphi U.S.A. 40°36N 86°41W 80 E10
Delphos U.S.A. 40°51N 84°21W 81 E11
Delportshoop S. Africa 28°22S 24°20E 56 D3
Delray Beach U.S.A. 26°28N 80°4W 85 H14
Delta Colo., U.S.A. 38°44N 108°4W 76 G9
Delta Utah, U.S.A. 39°21N 112°35W 76 G7
Delta Dunării ⌂ Romania 45°15N 29°25E 17 F15
Delta Junction U.S.A. 64°2N 145°44W 68 C5
Deltona U.S.A. 28°54N 81°16W 85 G14
Delungra Australia 29°39S 150°51E 63 D5
Delvada India 20°46N 71°2E 42 J4
Delvinë Albania 39°59N 20°6E 23 E9
Demak Indonesia 6°53S 110°38E 37 G14
Demanda, Sierra de la Spain 42°15N 3°0W 21 A4
Demavend = Damāvand, Qolleh-ye Iran 35°56N 52°10E 45 C7
Dembia Dem. Rep. of the Congo 3°33N 25°48E 54 B2
Dembidolo Ethiopia 8°34N 34°50E 47 F1
Demchok India 32°42N 79°29E 43 C8
Demer → Belgium 50°57N 4°42E 15 D4
Deming N. Mex., U.S.A. 32°16N 107°46W 77 K10
Deming Wash., U.S.A. 48°50N 122°13W 78 B4
Demini → Brazil 0°46S 62°56W 92 D6
Demirci Turkey 39°2N 28°38E 23 E13
Demirköy Turkey 41°49N 27°45E 23 D12
Demopolis U.S.A. 32°31N 87°50W 85 E11
Dempo Indonesia 4°2S 103°15E 36 E2
Den Bosch = 's-Hertogenbosch Neths. 51°42N 5°17E 15 C5
Den Burg Neths. 53°3N 4°47E 15 A4
Den Chai Thailand 17°59N 100°4E 38 D3
Den Haag = 's-Gravenhage Neths. 52°7N 4°17E 15 B4
Den Helder Neths. 52°57N 4°45E 15 B4
Den Oever Neths. 52°56N 5°2E 15 B5
Denair U.S.A. 37°32N 120°48W 78 H6
Denali = McKinley, Mt. U.S.A. 63°4N 151°0W 74 a
Denau Uzbekistan 38°16N 67°54E 28 F7
Denbigh Canada 45°8N 77°15W 82 A7
Denbigh U.K. 53°12N 3°25W 12 D4
Denbighshire □ U.K. 53°8N 3°22W 12 D4
Dendang Indonesia 3°7S 107°56E 36 E3
Dendermonde Belgium 51°2N 4°5E 15 C4
Dengfeng China 34°25N 113°2E 34 G7
Dengkou China 40°18N 106°55E 34 D4
Denham Australia 25°56S 113°31E 61 E1
Denham, Mt. Jamaica 18°13N 77°32W 88 a
Denham Ra. Australia 21°55S 147°46E 62 C4
Denham Sd. Australia 25°45S 113°15E 61 E1
Denholm Canada 52°39N 108°1W 71 C7
Denia Spain 38°49N 0°8E 21 C6
Denial B. Australia 32°14S 133°32E 63 E1
Deniliquin Australia 35°30S 144°58E 63 F3
Denison Iowa, U.S.A. 42°1N 95°21W 80 D6
Denison Tex., U.S.A. 33°45N 96°33W 84 E6
Denison Plains Australia 18°35S 128°0E 60 C4
Denizli Turkey 37°42N 29°2E 19 G4
Denman Glacier Antarctica 66°45S 99°25E 5 C7
Denmark Australia 34°59S 117°25E 61 F2
Denmark ■ Europe 55°45N 10°0E 9 J14
Denmark Str. Atl. Oc. 66°0N 30°0W 66 C17
Dennery St. Lucia 13°55N 60°54W 89 f
Dennison U.S.A. 40°24N 81°19W 82 F3
Denny U.K. 56°1N 3°55W 11 E5
Denpasar Indonesia 8°39S 115°13E 37 K18
Denpasar ✕ (DPS) Indonesia 8°44S 115°10E 37 K18
Denton Mont., U.S.A. 47°19N 109°57W 76 C9
Denton Tex., U.S.A. 33°13N 97°8W 84 E6
D'Entrecasteaux, Pt. Australia 34°50S 115°57E 61 F2

D'Entrecasteaux △ Australia 34°20S 115°33E 61 F2
D'Entrecasteaux Is. Papua N. G. 9°0S 151°0E 58 B8
Denver Colo., U.S.A. 39°42N 104°59W 76 G11
Denver Pa., U.S.A. 40°14N 76°8W 83 F8
Denver City U.S.A. 32°58N 102°50W 84 E3
Deoband India 29°42N 77°43E 42 E7
Deogarh India 25°32N 73°54E 42 G5
Deoghar India 24°30N 86°42E 43 G12
Deolali India 19°58N 73°50E 40 K8
Deoli = Devli India 25°50N 75°20E 42 G6
Deora India 26°22N 70°55E 42 F4
Deori India 23°24N 79°1E 43 H8
Deoria India 26°31N 83°48E 43 F10
Deosai Mts. Pakistan 35°40N 75°0E 43 B6
Deosri India 26°46N 90°29E 43 F14
Depalpur India 22°51N 75°33E 42 H6
Deping China 37°25N 116°58E 35 F9
Deposit U.S.A. 42°4N 75°25W 83 D9
Depuch I. Australia 20°37S 117°44E 60 D2
Deputatskiy Russia 69°18N 139°54E 29 C14
Dera Ghazi Khan Pakistan 30°5N 70°43E 42 D4
Dera Ismail Khan Pakistan 31°50N 70°50E 42 D4
Derabugti Pakistan 29°2N 69°9E 42 E3
Derawar Fort Pakistan 28°46N 71°20E 42 E4
Derbent Russia 42°5N 48°15E 19 F8
Derby Australia 17°18S 123°38E 60 C3
Derby U.K. 52°56N 1°28W 12 E6
Derby Conn., U.S.A. 41°19N 73°5W 83 E11
Derby Kans., U.S.A. 37°33N 97°16W 80 G5
Derby N.Y., U.S.A. 42°41N 78°58W 82 D6
Derby City □ U.K. 52°56N 1°28W 12 E6
Derby Line U.S.A. 45°0N 72°6W 83 B12
Derbyshire □ U.K. 53°11N 1°38W 12 D6
Derdepoort S. Africa 24°38S 26°24E 56 C4
Dereham U.K. 52°41N 0°57E 13 E8
Derg → U.K. 54°44N 7°26W 10 B4
Derg, L. Ireland 53°0N 8°20W 10 D3
Deridder U.S.A. 30°51N 93°17W 84 F8
Dermott U.S.A. 33°32N 91°26W 84 E9
Derry = Londonderry U.K. 55°0N 7°20W 10 B4
Derry = Londonderry □ U.K. 55°0N 7°20W 10 B4
Derry N.H., U.S.A. 42°53N 71°19W 83 D13
Derry Pa., U.S.A. 40°20N 79°18W 82 F5
Derryveagh Mts. Ireland 54°56N 8°11W 10 B3
Derwent → Cumb., U.K. 54°39N 3°33W 12 C4
Derwent → Derby, U.K. 52°57N 1°28W 12 E6
Derwent → N. Yorks., U.K. 53°45N 0°58W 12 D7
Derwent Water U.K. 54°35N 3°9W 12 C4
Des Moines Iowa, U.S.A. 41°35N 93°37W 80 E7
Des Moines N. Mex., U.S.A. 36°46N 103°50W 77 H12
Des Moines Wash., U.S.A. 47°24N 122°19W 78 C4
Des Moines → U.S.A. 40°23N 91°25W 80 E8
Desaguadero → Argentina 34°30S 66°46W 94 C2
Desaguadero → Bolivia 16°35S 69°5W 92 G5
Desar Malaysia 1°31N 104°17E 39 d
Descanso, Pta. Mexico 32°21N 117°3W 79 N9
Deschaillons-sur-St-Laurent Canada 46°32N 72°7W 73 C5
Deschambault L. Canada 54°50N 103°30W 71 C8
Deschutes → U.S.A. 45°38N 120°55W 76 D3
Dese Ethiopia 11°5N 39°40E 47 E2
Deseado → Argentina 47°45S 65°54W 96 F3
Deseronto Canada 44°12N 77°3W 82 B7
Desert Center U.S.A. 33°43N 115°24W 79 M11
Desert Hot Springs U.S.A. 33°58N 116°30W 79 M10
Deshnok India 27°48N 73°21E 42 F5
Desierto Central de Baja California ⌂ Mexico 29°40N 114°50W 86 B2
Desna → Ukraine 50°33N 30°32E 17 C16
Desolación, I. Chile 53°0S 74°0W 96 G2
Despeñaperros, Paso Spain 38°24N 3°30W 21 C4
Dessau Germany 51°51N 12°14E 16 C7
Dessye = Dese Ethiopia 11°5N 39°40E 47 E2
D'Estrees B. Australia 35°55S 137°45E 63 F2
Desuri India 25°18N 73°35E 42 G5
Det Udom Thailand 14°54N 105°5E 38 E5
Dete Zimbabwe 18°38S 26°50E 56 B4
Detmold Germany 51°56N 8°52E 16 C5
Detour, Pt. U.S.A. 45°40N 86°40W 80 C10
Detroit U.S.A. 42°19N 83°12W 82 D1
Detroit Lakes U.S.A. 46°49N 95°51W 80 B6
Deua △ Australia 35°32S 149°46E 63 F4
Deurne Neths. 51°27N 5°49E 15 C5
Deutsche Bucht Germany 54°15N 8°0E 16 A5
Deutschland = Germany ■ Europe 51°0N 10°0E 16 C6
Deva Romania 45°53N 22°55E 17 F12
Devakottai India 9°55N 78°45E 40 Q11
Devaprayag India 30°13N 78°35E 43 D8
Deventer Neths. 52°15N 6°10E 15 B6
Deveron → U.K. 57°41N 2°32W 11 D6
Devgadh Bariya India 22°40N 73°55E 42 H5
Devikot India 26°42N 71°12E 42 F4
Devils Den U.S.A. 35°46N 119°58W 78 K7
Devils Hole = Death Valley △ U.S.A. 36°29N 117°6W 79 J9
Devils Lake U.S.A. 48°7N 98°52W 80 A4
Devils Paw Canada 58°47N 134°0W 70 B2
Devils Postpile ⌂ U.S.A. 37°37N 119°5W 78 H7
Devils Tower U.S.A. 44°35N 104°42W 76 D11
Devils Tower △ U.S.A. 44°48N 104°55W 76 D11
Devine U.S.A. 29°8N 98°54W 84 G5
Devizes U.K. 51°22N 1°58W 13 F6
Devli India 25°50N 75°20E 42 G6
Devon Canada 53°24N 113°44W 70 C6
Devon □ U.K. 50°50N 3°40W 13 G4
Devon I. Canada 75°10N 85°0W 69 B11
Devonport Australia 41°10S 146°22E 63 G4
Devonport N.Z. 36°49S 174°49E 59 B5
Dewas India 22°59N 76°3E 42 H7
Dewetsdorp S. Africa 29°33S 26°39E 56 D4
Dewey Puerto Rico 18°18N 65°18W 89 d
Dexter Maine, U.S.A. 45°1N 69°18W 81 C19
Dexter Mo., U.S.A. 36°48N 89°57W 80 G9
Dexter N. Mex., U.S.A. 33°12N 104°22W 77 K11
Dey-Dey, L. Australia 29°12S 131°4E 61 E5
Deyang China 31°3N 104°27E 32 C5
Deyhūk Iran 33°15N 57°30E 45 C8
Deyyer Iran 27°55N 51°55E 45 E6
Dez → Iran 31°39N 48°52E 45 D6
Dezadeash L. Canada 60°28N 136°58W 70 A1
Dezfūl Iran 32°20N 48°30E 45 C6
Dezhneva, Mys Russia 66°5N 169°40W 29 C19
Dezhou China 37°26N 116°18E 34 F9
Dhadhar → India 24°56N 85°24E 43 G11
Dhahiriya = Aẓ Ẓāhirīyah West Bank 31°25N 34°58E 46 D3
Dhahran = Aẓ Ẓahrān Si. Arabia 26°10N 50°7E 45 E6
Dhak Pakistan 32°25N 72°33E 42 C5
Dhaka Bangla. 23°43N 90°26E 43 H14
Dhaka □ Bangla. 24°25N 90°25E 43 G14
Dhali Cyprus 35°1N 33°25E 25 D12
Dhamār Yemen 14°30N 44°20E 47 E3
Dhampur India 29°19N 78°33E 43 E8
Dhamtari India 20°42N 81°35E 41 J12
Dhanbad India 23°50N 86°30E 43 H12
Dhangarhi Nepal 28°55N 80°40E 43 E9
Dhankuta Nepal 26°55N 87°40E 43 F12
Dhanpuri India 23°13N 81°30E 43 H9
Dhar India 22°35N 75°26E 42 H6
Dharampur India 22°13N 75°18E 42 H6
Dharamsala = Dharmsala India 32°16N 76°23E 42 C7
Dharan Nepal 26°49N 87°17E 43 F12
Dhariwal India 31°57N 75°19E 42 D6
Dharla → Bangla. 25°46N 89°42E 43 G13
Dharmapuri India 12°10N 78°10E 40 N11
Dharmjaygarh India 22°28N 83°13E 43 H10
Dharmsala India 32°16N 76°23E 42 C7
Dharni India 21°33N 76°53E 42 J7
Dharwad India 15°30N 75°4E 40 M9
Dhasan → India 25°48N 79°24E 43 G8
Dhaulagiri Nepal 28°39N 83°28E 43 E10
Dhebar, L. India 24°10N 74°0E 42 G6
Dheftera Cyprus 35°5N 33°16E 25 D12
Dhenkanal India 20°45N 85°35E 41 J14
Dherinia Cyprus 35°3N 33°57E 25 D12
Dhī Qār □ Iraq 31°0N 46°15E 44 D5
Dhiarrizos → Cyprus 34°41N 32°34E 25 E11
Dhībān Jordan 31°30N 35°46E 46 D4
Dhilwan India 31°31N 75°21E 42 D6
Dhimarkhera India 23°28N 80°22E 43 H9
Dhodhekánisos = Dodecanese Greece 36°35N 27°0E 23 F12
Dholka India 22°44N 72°29E 42 H5
Dhoraji India 21°45N 70°37E 42 J4
Dhrangadhra India 22°59N 71°31E 42 H4
Dhrol India 22°33N 70°25E 42 H4
Dhuburi India 26°2N 89°59E 41 F16
Dhule India 20°58N 74°50E 40 J9
Di Linh Vietnam 11°35N 108°4E 39 G7
Di Linh, Cao Nguyen Vietnam 11°30N 108°0E 39 G7
Dia Greece 35°28N 25°14E 25 D7
Diablo Range U.S.A. 37°20N 121°25W 78 J5
Diafarabé Mali 14°9N 4°57W 50 F5
Diamante Argentina 32°5S 60°40W 94 C3
Diamante → Argentina 34°30S 66°46W 94 C2
Diamantina Brazil 18°17S 43°40W 93 G10
Diamantina → Australia 26°45S 139°10E 63 D2
Diamantina △ Australia 23°33S 141°23E 62 C3
Diamantino Brazil 14°30S 56°30W 93 F7
Diamond Bar U.S.A. 34°1N 117°48W 79 L9
Diamond Harbour India 22°11N 88°14E 43 H13
Diamond Is. Australia 17°25S 151°5E 62 B5
Diamond Mts. U.S.A. 39°40N 115°50W 76 G6
Diamond Springs U.S.A. 38°42N 120°49W 78 G6
Diaoyu Tai = Senkaku-Shotō E. China Sea 25°45N 123°30E 31 M1
Dībā U.A.E. 25°45N 56°16E 45 E8
Dibai India 28°13N 78°15E 42 E8
Dibaya Dem. Rep. of the Congo 6°30S 22°57E 52 F4
Dibaya-Lubue Dem. Rep. of the Congo 4°12S 19°54E 52 E3
Dibbeen △ Jordan 32°20N 35°45E 46 C4
D'Iberville, Lac Canada 55°55N 73°15W 72 A5
Dibete Botswana 23°45S 26°32E 56 C4
Dibrugarh India 27°29N 94°55E 41 F19
Dickens U.S.A. 33°37N 100°50W 84 E4
Dickinson U.S.A. 46°53N 102°47W 80 B2
Dickson U.S.A. 36°5N 87°23W 85 C11
Dickson City U.S.A. 41°28N 75°36W 83 E9
Didiéni Mali 13°53N 8°6W 50 F4
Didsbury Canada 51°35N 114°10W 70 C6
Didwana India 27°23N 74°36E 42 F6
Diefenbaker, L. Canada 51°0N 106°55W 71 C7
Diego de Almagro Chile 26°22S 70°3W 94 B1
Diego Suarez = Antsiranana Madag. 12°25S 49°20E 57 A8
Diekirch Lux. 49°52N 6°10E 15 E6
Dien Ban Vietnam 15°53N 108°16E 38 E7
Dien Bien Vietnam 21°20N 103°0E 38 B4
Dien Khanh Vietnam 12°15N 109°6E 39 F7
Dieppe France 49°54N 1°4E 20 B4
Dierks U.S.A. 34°7N 94°1W 84 D7
Diest Belgium 50°58N 5°4E 15 D5
Dif Somali Rep. 0°59N 40°58E 47 G3
Differdange Lux. 49°31N 5°54E 15 E5
Dig India 27°28N 77°20E 42 F7
Digba Dem. Rep. of the Congo 4°25N 25°48E 54 B2
Digby Canada 44°38N 65°50W 73 D6
Diggi India 26°22N 75°26E 42 F6
Dighinala Bangla. 23°15N 92°5E 41 H18
Dighton U.S.A. 38°29N 100°28W 80 F3
Digne-les-Bains France 44°5N 6°12E 20 D7
Digos Phil. 6°45N 125°20E 37 C7
Digranes Iceland 66°4N 14°44W 8 C6
Digul → Indonesia 7°7S 138°42E 37 F9
Dihang = Brahmaputra → Asia 23°40N 90°35E 43 H13
Dijlah, Nahr → Asia 31°0N 47°25E 44 D5
Dijon France 47°20N 5°3E 20 C6
Dikhil Djibouti 11°8N 42°20E 47 E3
Dikkil = Dikhil Djibouti 11°8N 42°20E 47 E3
Diksmuide Belgium 51°2N 2°52E 15 C2
Dikson Russia 73°40N 80°5E 28 B9
Dikti Oros Greece 35°8N 25°30E 25 D7
Dila Ethiopia 6°21N 38°22E 47 F2
Dili E. Timor 8°39S 125°34E 37 F7
Dilley U.S.A. 28°40N 99°10W 84 G5
Dilli = Delhi India 28°39N 77°13E 42 E7
Dillingham U.S.A. 59°3N 158°28W 74 a
Dillon Canada 55°56N 108°35W 71 B7
Dillon Mont., U.S.A. 45°13N 112°38W 76 D7
Dillon S.C., U.S.A. 34°25N 79°22W 85 D15
Dillon → Canada 55°56N 108°56W 71 B7
Dillsburg U.S.A. 40°7N 77°2W 82 F7
Dilolo Dem. Rep. of the Congo 10°28S 22°18E 52 G4
Dimapur India 25°54N 93°45E 32 D4
Dimas Mexico 23°43N 106°47W 86 C3
Dimashq Syria 33°30N 36°18E 46 B5
Dimashq □ Syria 33°30N 36°30E 46 B5
Dimbaza S. Africa 32°50S 27°14E 57 E4
Dimboola Australia 36°28S 142°7E 63 F3
Dîmboviţa = Dâmboviţa → Romania 44°12N 26°26E 17 F14
Dimbulah Australia 17°8S 145°4E 62 B4
Dimitrovgrad Bulgaria 42°5N 25°35E 23 C11
Dimitrovgrad Russia 54°14N 49°39E 18 D8
Dimitrovo = Pernik Bulgaria 42°35N 23°2E 23 C10
Dimmitt U.S.A. 34°33N 102°19W 84 D3
Dimona Israel 31°2N 35°1E 46 D4
Dinagat Phil. 10°10N 125°40E 37 B7
Dinajpur Bangla. 25°33N 88°43E 41 G16
Dinan France 48°28N 2°2W 20 B2
Dīnān Āb Iran 32°4N 56°49E 45 C8
Dinant Belgium 50°16N 4°55E 15 D4
Dinapur India 25°38N 85°5E 43 G11
Dīnār, Kūh-e Iran 30°42N 51°46E 45 D6
Dinara Planina Croatia 44°0N 16°30E 22 C7
Dinard France 48°38N 2°6W 20 B2
Dinaric Alps = Dinara Planina Croatia 44°0N 16°30E 22 C7
Dindigul India 10°25N 78°0E 40 P11
Dindori India 22°57N 81°5E 43 H9
Ding Xian = Dingzhou China 38°30N 114°59E 34 E8
Dinga Pakistan 25°26N 67°10E 42 G2
Ding'an China 19°42N 110°19E 38 C8
Dingbian China 37°35N 107°32E 34 F4
Dingle Ireland 52°9N 10°17W 10 D1
Dingle B. Ireland 52°3N 10°20W 10 D1
Dingmans Ferry U.S.A. 41°13N 74°55W 83 E10
Dingo Australia 23°38S 149°19E 62 C4
Dingtao China 35°5N 115°35E 34 G8
Dingwall U.K. 57°36N 4°26W 11 D4
Dingxi China 35°30N 104°33E 34 G3
Dingxiang China 38°30N 112°58E 34 E7
Dingzhou China 38°30N 114°59E 34 E8
Dinh, Mui Vietnam 11°22N 109°1E 39 G7
Dinh Lap Vietnam 21°33N 107°6E 38 B6
Dinin → Ireland 52°43N 7°18W 10 D4
Dinira △ Venezuela 9°57N 70°6W 89 E6
Dinokwe Botswana 23°29S 26°37E 56 C4
Dinorwic Canada 49°41N 92°30W 71 D10
Dinosaur ⌂ Canada 50°47N 111°30W 70 C6
Dinosaur ⌂ U.S.A. 40°30N 108°45W 76 F9
Dinuba U.S.A. 36°32N 119°23W 78 J7
Dionisades Greece 35°20N 26°10E 25 D8
Diourbel Senegal 14°39N 16°12W 50 F2
Dipalpur Pakistan 30°40N 73°39E 42 D5
Dipkarpaz = Rizokarpaso Cyprus 35°36N 34°23E 25 D13
Diplo Pakistan 24°35N 69°35E 42 G3
Dipolog Phil. 8°36N 123°20E 37 C6
Dipperu △ Australia 21°56S 148°42E 62 C4
Dir Pakistan 35°8N 71°59E 40 B7
Dire Dawa Ethiopia 9°35N 41°45E 47 F3
Dirfis Oros Greece 38°40N 23°54E 23 E10
Diriamba Nic. 11°51N 86°19W 88 D2
Dirk Hartog I. Australia 25°50S 113°5E 61 E1
Dirranbandi Australia 28°33S 148°17E 63 D4
Disa India 24°18N 72°10E 42 G5
Disappointment, C. U.S.A. 46°18N 124°5W 76 C1
Disappointment, L. Australia 23°20S 122°40E 60 D3
Disaster B. Australia 37°15S 149°58E 63 F4
Discovery B. Australia 38°10S 140°40E 63 F3
Discovery B. China 22°18N 114°1E 33 G11
Disko = Qeqertarsuaq Greenland 69°45N 53°30W 66 C14
Disney Reef Tonga 19°17S 174°7W 59 c
Diss U.K. 52°23N 1°7E 13 E9
Disteghil Sar Pakistan 36°20N 75°12E 43 A6
District of Columbia □ U.S.A. 38°55N 77°0W 81 F15
Distrito Federal □ Brazil 15°45S 47°45W 93 G9
Distrito Federal □ Mexico 19°15N 99°10W 87 D5
Diu India 20°45N 70°58E 42 J4
Dīvāndarreh Iran 35°55N 47°2E 44 C5
Divide U.S.A. 45°45N 112°45W 76 D7
Dividing Ra. Australia 27°45S 116°0E 61 E2
Divinópolis Brazil 20°10S 44°54W 93 H10
Divnoye Russia 45°55N 43°21E 19 E7
Divo Ivory C. 5°48N 5°15W 50 G4
Dīwāl Kol Afghan. 34°23N 67°52E 42 B2
Dixie Mt. U.S.A. 39°55N 120°16W 78 F6
Dixon Calif., U.S.A. 38°27N 121°49W 78 G5
Dixon Ill., U.S.A. 41°50N 89°29W 80 E9
Dixon Entrance U.S.A. 54°30N 132°0W 68 D6
Dixville Canada 45°4N 71°46W 83 A13
Diyālā □ Iraq 33°45N 44°50E 44 C5
Diyālā → Iraq 33°13N 44°30E 44 C5
Diyarbakır Turkey 37°55N 40°18E 44 B4
Diyodar India 24°8N 71°50E 42 G4
Djakarta = Jakarta Indonesia 6°9S 106°52E 37 G12
Djamba Angola 16°45S 13°58E 56 B1
Djambala Congo 2°32S 14°30E 52 E2
Djanet Algeria 24°35N 9°32E 50 D7
Djawa = Jawa Indonesia 7°0S 110°0E 36 F3
Djelfa Algeria 34°40N 3°15E 50 B6
Djema C.A.R. 6°3N 25°15E 54 A2
Djerba, Î. de Tunisia 33°50N 10°48E 51 B8
Djerid, Chott Tunisia 33°42N 8°30E 50 B7
Djibouti Djibouti 11°30N 43°5E 47 E3
Djibouti ■ Africa 12°0N 43°0E 47 E3
Djolu Dem. Rep. of the Congo 0°35N 22°5E 52 D4
Djougou Benin 9°40N 1°45E 50 G6
Djoum Cameroon 2°41N 12°35E 52 D2
Djourab, Erg du Chad 16°40N 18°50E 51 E9
Djugu Dem. Rep. of the Congo 1°55N 30°35E 54 B3
Djukbinj △ Australia 12°11S 131°2E 60 B5
Djúpivogur Iceland 64°39N 14°17W 8 D6
Dmitriya Lapteva, Proliv Russia 73°0N 140°0E 29 B15
Dnepr = Dnipro → Ukraine 46°30N 32°18E 19 E5
Dneprodzerzhinsk = Dniprodzerzhynsk Ukraine 48°32N 34°37E 19 E5
Dnepropetrovsk = Dnipropetrovsk Ukraine 48°30N 35°0E 19 E6
Dnestr = Dnister → Europe 46°18N 30°17E 17 E16
Dnieper = Dnipro → Ukraine 46°30N 32°18E 19 E5
Dniester = Dnister → Europe 46°18N 30°17E 17 E16
Dnipro → Ukraine 46°30N 32°18E 19 E5
Dniprodzerzhynsk Ukraine 48°32N 34°37E 19 E5
Dnipropetrovsk Ukraine 48°30N 35°0E 19 E6
Dnister → Europe 46°18N 30°17E 17 E16
Dno Russia 57°50N 29°58E 9 H23
Dnyapro = Dnipro → Ukraine 46°30N 32°18E 19 E5
Do Gonbadān = Gachsārān Iran 30°15N 50°45E 45 D6
Doaktown Canada 46°33N 66°8W 73 C6
Doan Hung Vietnam 21°30N 105°10E 38 B5
Doany Madag. 14°21S 49°30E 57 A8
Doba Chad 8°40N 16°50E 51 G9
Dobandi Pakistan 31°13N 66°50E 42 D2
Dobbyn Australia 19°44S 140°2E 62 B3
Dobele Latvia 56°37N 23°16E 9 H20
Doberai, Jazirah Indonesia 1°25S 133°0E 37 E8
Doblas Argentina 37°5S 64°0W 94 D3
Dobo Indonesia 5°45S 134°15E 37 F8
Doboj Bos.-H. 44°46N 18°4E 23 B8
Dobrich Bulgaria 43°37N 27°49E 23 C12
Dobruja Europe 44°30N 28°15E 17 F15
Dobrush Belarus 52°25N 31°22E 17 B16
Doc, Mui Vietnam 17°58N 106°30E 38 D6
Docker River = Kaltukatjara Australia 24°52S 129°5E 61 D4
Doctor Arroyo Mexico 23°40N 100°11W 86 C4
Doctor Pedro P. Peña Paraguay 22°27S 62°21W 94 A3
Doda India 33°10N 75°34E 43 C6
Doda, L. Canada 49°25N 75°13W 72 C4
Dodecanese Greece 36°35N 27°0E 23 F12
Dodekanisa = Dodecanese Greece 36°35N 27°0E 23 F12
Dodge City U.S.A. 37°45N 100°1W 80 G3
Dodge L. Canada 59°50N 105°36W 71 B7
Dodgeville U.S.A. 42°58N 90°8W 80 D8
Dodoma Tanzania 6°8S 35°45E 54 D4
Dodoma □ Tanzania 6°0S 36°0E 54 D4
Dodori ⌂ Kenya 1°55S 41°7E 54 C5
Dodsland Canada 51°50N 108°45W 71 C7
Dodson U.S.A. 48°24N 108°15W 76 B9
Doesburg Neths. 52°1N 6°9E 15 B6
Doetinchem Neths. 51°59N 6°18E 15 C6
Dog Creek Canada 51°35N 122°14W 70 C4
Dog L. Man., Canada 51°2N 98°31W 71 C9
Dog L. Ont., Canada 48°48N 89°30W 72 C2
Dogran Pakistan 31°48N 73°35E 42 D5
Doğubayazıt Turkey 39°31N 44°5E 44 B5
Doha = Ad Dawḥah Qatar 25°15N 51°35E 45 E6
Dohazari Bangla. 22°10N 92°5E 41 H18
Dohrighat India 26°16N 83°31E 43 F10
Doi Indonesia 2°14N 127°49E 37 D7
Doi Inthanon △ Thailand 18°33N 98°34E 38 C2
Doi Khuntan △ Thailand 18°33N 99°14E 38 C2
Doi Luang Thailand 18°30N 101°0E 38 C3
Doi Luang △ Thailand 19°22N 99°35E 38 C2
Doi Saket Thailand 18°52N 99°9E 38 C2
Doi Suthep △ Thailand 18°49N 98°53E 38 C2
Dois Irmãos, Sa. Brazil 9°0S 42°30W 93 E10
Dokkum Neths. 53°20N 5°59E 15 A5
Dokri Pakistan 27°25N 68°7E 42 F3
Dolak, Pulau Indonesia 8°0S 138°30E 37
Dolbeau Canada 48°53N 72°14W 73 C
Dole France 47°7N 5°31E 20 C
Dolgellau U.K. 52°45N 3°53W 12 E
Dolgelley = Dolgellau U.K. 52°45N 3°53W 12 E
Dolinsk Russia 47°21N 142°48E 29 E
Dollard Neths. 53°20N 7°10E 15 A
Dolo Ethiopia 4°11N 42°3E 47 G
Dolomites = Dolomiti Italy 46°23N 11°51E 22 A
Dolomiti Italy 46°23N 11°51E 22 A
Dolores Argentina 36°20S 57°40W 94 D
Dolores Uruguay 33°34S 58°15W 94 C
Dolores U.S.A. 37°28N 108°30W 77 H
Dolores → U.S.A. 38°49N 109°17W 76 G
Dolphin, C. Falk. Is. 51°10S 59°0W 96 G
Dolphin and Union Str. Canada 69°5N 114°45W 68
Dom Pedrito Brazil 31°0S 54°40W 95 C
Doma ⌂ Zimbabwe 16°28S 30°12E 55
Domariaganj → India 26°17N 83°44E 43 F
Domasi Malawi 15°15S 35°22E 55
Dombarovskiy Russia 50°46N 59°32E 28
Dombås Norway 62°4N 9°8E 8 E
Dome Argus Antarctica 80°50S 76°30E 5 E
Dome C. Antarctica 75°12S 123°37E 5 D
Dome Fuji Antarctica 77°20S 39°45E 5
Domel I. = Letsôk-aw Kyun Burma 11°30N 98°25E 39
Domeyko Chile 29°0S 71°0W 94
Domeyko, Cordillera Chile 24°30S 69°0W 94
Dominador Chile 24°21S 69°20W 94
Dominica ■ W. Indies 15°20N 61°20W 89
Dominica Passage W. Indies 15°10N 61°20W 89
Dominican Rep. ■ W. Indies 19°0N 70°30W 89
Domodóssola Italy 46°7N 8°17E 20
Domville, Mt. Australia 28°1S 151°15E 63
Don → Russia 47°4N 39°18E 19
Don → Aberds., U.K. 57°11N 2°5W 11
Don → S. Yorks., U.K. 53°41N 0°52W 12
Don, C. Australia 11°18S 131°46E 60
Don Benito Spain 38°53N 5°51W 21
Don Figuerero Mts. Jamaica 18°5N 77°36W 8
Don Sak Thailand 9°18N 99°41E 3
Dona Ana = Nhamaabué Mozam. 17°25S 35°5E 55
Donaghadee U.K. 54°39N 5°33W 10
Donaghmore Ireland 52°52N 7°36W 10
Donald Australia 36°23S 143°0E 63
Donaldsonville U.S.A. 30°6N 90°59W 84
Donalsonville U.S.A. 31°3N 84°53W 85
Donau = Dunărea → Europe 45°20N 29°40E 17
Donauwörth Germany 48°43N 10°47E 16
Doncaster U.K. 53°32N 1°6W 12
Dondo Angola 9°45S 14°25E 52
Dondo Mozam. 19°33S 34°46E 55
Dondo, Teluk Indonesia 0°50N 120°30E 37
Dondra Head Sri Lanka 5°55N 80°40E 40
Donegal Ireland 54°39N 8°5W 10
Donegal □ Ireland 54°53N 8°0W 10
Donegal B. Ireland 54°31N 8°49W 10
Donets → Russia 47°33N 40°55E 19
Donets Basin Ukraine 49°0N 38°0E 6
Donetsk Ukraine 48°0N 37°45E 19
Dong Ba Thin Vietnam 12°8N 109°13E 39
Dong Dang Vietnam 21°54N 106°42E 38
Dong Giam Vietnam 19°25N 105°31E 38
Dong Ha Vietnam 16°55N 107°8E 38
Dong Hene Laos 16°40N 105°18E 38
Dong Hoi Vietnam 17°29N 106°36E 38
Dong Khe Vietnam 22°26N 106°27E 38
Dong Ujimqin Qi China 45°32N 116°55E 3
Dong Van Vietnam 23°16N 105°22E 38
Dong Xoai Vietnam 11°32N 106°55E 39
Dongara Australia 29°14S 114°57E 6
Dongbei China 45°0N 125°0E 3
Dongchuan China 26°8N 103°1E 32
Dongco China 32°8N 84°50E 41
Dongfang China 18°50N 108°33E 3
Dongfeng China 42°40N 125°34E 35
Donggala Indonesia 0°30S 119°40E 3
Donggang China 39°52N 124°10E 35
Dongguang China 37°50N 116°30E 3
Donghae S. Korea 37°29N 129°7E 35
Dongjingcheng China 44°5N 129°10E 35
Dongnae S. Korea 35°12N 129°5E 35
Dongning China 44°2N 131°5E 35
Dongola Sudan 19°9N 30°22E 51
Dongping China 35°55N 116°20E 3
Dongsheng China 39°50N 110°0E 3
Dongtai China 32°51N 120°21E 35
Dongting Hu China 29°18N 112°45E 3
Donington, C. Australia 34°45S 136°0E 6
Doniphan U.S.A. 36°37N 90°50W 8
Dønna Norway 66°6N 12°30E 8
Donna U.S.A. 26°9N 98°4W 8
Donnacona Canada 46°41N 71°41W 7
Donnelly's Crossing N.Z. 35°42S 173°38E 5
Donnybrook Australia 33°34S 115°48E 6
Donnybrook S. Africa 29°59S 29°48E 5
Donora U.S.A. 40°11N 79°52W 8
Donostia = Donostia-San Sebastián Spain 43°17N 1°58W 2
Donostia-San Sebastián Spain 43°17N 1°58W 2
Donwood Canada 44°19N 78°16W 8
Doon → U.K. 55°27N 4°39W 1
Dora, L. Australia 22°0S 123°0E 6
Dora Báltea → Italy 45°11N 8°3E 2
Doran L. Canada 61°13N 108°6W 7

rchester U.K. 50°42N 2°27W 13 G5
rchester, C. Canada 65°27N 77°27W 69 C12
rdabis Namibia 22°52S 17°38E 56 C2
rdogne → France 45°2N 0°36W 20 D3
rdrecht Neths. 51°48N 4°39E 15 C4
rdrecht S. Africa 31°20S 27°3E 56 E4
ré L. Canada 54°46N 107°17W 71 C7
ri Burkina Faso 14°3N 0°2W 50 F5
ring → S. Africa 31°54S 18°39E 56 E2
ringbos S. Africa 31°59S 19°16E 56 E2
rking U.K. 51°14N 0°19W 13 F7
rnbirn Austria 47°25N 9°45E 16 E5
rnie U.K. 57°17N 5°31W 11 D3
rnoch Canada 44°18N 80°51W 82 B4
rnoch U.K. 57°53N 4°2W 11 D4
rnoch Firth U.K. 57°51N 4°4W 11 D4
rnogovĭ □ Mongolia 44°0N 110°0E 34 C6
ro, Kavo Greece 38°9N 24°38E 23 E11
rohoi Romania 47°56N 26°23E 17 E14
röö Nuur Mongolia 48°0N 93°0E 32 B4
rr Iran 33°17N 50°38E 45 C6
rre I. Australia 25°13S 113°12E 61 E1
rrigo Australia 30°20S 152°44E 63 E5
rris U.S.A. 41°58N 121°55W 76 F3
rset Canada 45°14N 78°54W 82 A6
rset Ohio, U.S.A. 41°40N 80°40W 82 E4
rset Vt., U.S.A. 43°15N 73°5W 83 C11
rset □ U.K. 50°45N 2°26W 13 G5
rtmund Germany 51°30N 7°28E 16 C4
rtyol Turkey 36°50N 36°13E 44 B3
ruma
Dem. Rep. of the Congo 4°42N 27°33E 54 B2
rūneh Iran 35°10N 57°18E 45 C8
s Bahías, C. Argentina 44°58S 65°32W 96 E3
s Hermanas Spain 37°16N 5°55W 21 D3
s Palos U.S.A. 36°59N 120°37W 78 J6
sso Niger 13°0N 3°13E 50 F6
han U.S.A. 31°13N 85°24W 85 F12
y U.S.A. 46°38N 123°17W 78 D3
uai France 50°21N 3°4E 20 A5
uala Cameroon 4°0N 9°45E 52 D1
uarnenez France 48°6N 4°21W 20 B1
uble Island Pt.
ustralia 25°56S 153°11E 63 D5
uble Mountain Fork →
.S.A. 33°16N 100°0W 84 E4
ubs → France 46°53N 5°1E 20 C6
ubtful Sd. N.Z. 45°20S 166°49E 59 F1
ubtless B. N.Z. 34°55S 173°26E 59 A4
uglas Canada 45°31N 76°56W 82 A8
uglas I. of Man 54°10N 4°28W 12 C3
uglas S. Africa 29°4S 23°46E 56 D3
uglas Ariz., U.S.A. 31°21N 109°33W 77 L9
uglas Ga., U.S.A. 31°31N 82°51W 85 F13
uglas Wyo., U.S.A. 42°45N 105°24W 76 E11
uglas Apsley △
ustralia 41°45S 148°11E 63 G4
uglas Chan. Canada 53°40N 129°20W 70 C3
uglas Pt. Canada 44°19N 81°37W 82 B3
uglasville U.S.A. 33°45N 84°45W 85 E12
unreay U.K. 58°35N 3°44W 11 C5
urada, Serra Brazil 13°10S 48°45W 93 F9
urados Brazil 22°9S 54°50W 95 A5
urados → Brazil 21°58S 54°18W 95 A5
urados, Serra dos
razil 23°30S 53°30W 95 A5
ro → Europe 41°8N 8°40W 21 B1
e → U.K. 52°51N 1°36W 12 E6
e Creek U.S.A. 37°46N 108°54W 77 H9
er Australia 43°18S 147°2E 63 G4
er U.K. 51°7N 1°19E 13 F9
er Del., U.S.A. 39°10N 75°32W 81 F16
er N.H., U.S.A. 43°12N 70°56W 83 C14
er N.J., U.S.A. 40°53N 74°34W 83 F10
er Ohio, U.S.A. 40°32N 81°29W 82 F3
er, Pt. Australia 32°32S 125°32E 61 F4
er, Str. of Europe 51°0N 1°30E 13 G9
er-Foxcroft U.S.A. 45°11N 69°13W 81 C19
er Plains U.S.A. 41°43N 73°35W 83 E11
ey = Dyfi → U.K. 52°32N 4°3W 13 E3
refjell Norway 62°15N 9°33E 8 E13
Rūd Iran 33°28N 49°4E 45 C6
a Malawi 13°38S 33°58E 55 E3
agiac U.S.A. 41°59N 86°6W 80 E10
erin Australia 31°12S 117°2E 61 F2
gha'i Iran 36°54N 58°32E 45 B8
latābād Kermān,
n 28°20N 56°40E 45 D8
latābād Khorāsān,
n 35°16N 59°29E 45 C8
n □ U.K. 54°23N 6°2W 10 B5
ney Calif., U.S.A. 33°56N 118°9W 79 M8
ney Idaho, U.S.A. 42°26N 112°7W 76 E7
nham Market U.K. 52°37N 0°23E 13 E8
nieville U.S.A. 39°34N 120°50W 78 F6
npatrick U.K. 54°20N 5°43W 10 B6
npatrick Hd. Ireland 54°20N 9°21W 10 B2
nsville U.S.A. 42°5N 75°0W 83 D10
nton, Mt. Canada 52°42N 124°52W 70 C4
sārī Iran 28°25N 57°59E 45 D8
e U.S.A. 40°2N 120°6W 78 E6
estown U.S.A. 40°21N 75°10W 83 F9
is, Rés. Canada 47°30N 77°5W 72 C4
Khel Pakistan 27°58N 66°45E 42 F2
, C. Morocco 28°47N 11°0W 50 C3
, Oued → Morocco 28°40N 11°10W 50 C3
, Coves del Spain 39°31N 3°19E 24 B10
hten Neths. 53°7N 6°5E 15 A6
ăşani Romania 44°39N 24°17E 17 F13
ichyn Belarus 52°15N 25°8E 17 B13
oman, Prokhod
lgaria 42°58N 22°53E 23 C10
on's Mouths = Bocas del
agón Venezuela 11°0N 61°50W 93 K15
uignan France 43°32N 6°27E 20 E7
n U.S.A. 43°40N 123°19W 76 E2
e U.S.A. 47°55N 100°23W 80 B3
Drake Passage S. Ocean 58°0S 68°0W 5 B17
Drakensberg S. Africa 31°0S 28°0E 57 D4
Drama Greece 41°9N 24°10E 23 D11
Drammen Norway 59°42N 10°12E 9 G14
Drangajökull Iceland 66°9N 22°15W 8 C2
Dras India 34°25N 75°48E 43 B6
Drastis, Akra Greece 39°48N 19°40E 25 A3
Drau = Drava →
Croatia 45°33N 18°55E 23 B8
Drava → Croatia 45°33N 18°55E 23 B8
Drayton Canada 43°46N 80°40W 82 C4
Drayton Valley Canada 53°12N 114°58W 70 C6
Drenthe □ Neths. 52°52N 6°40E 15 B6
Drepano, Akra Greece 35°28N 24°14E 25 D6
Drepanum, C. Cyprus 34°54N 32°19E 25 E11
Dresden Canada 42°35N 82°11W 82 D2
Dresden Germany 51°3N 13°44E 16 C7
Dresden U.S.A. 42°41N 76°57W 82 D8
Dreux France 48°44N 1°23E 20 B4
Driffield U.K. 54°0N 0°26W 12 C7
Driftwood U.S.A. 41°20N 78°8W 82 E6
Driggs U.S.A. 43°44N 111°6W 76 E8
Drin → Albania 42°1N 19°38E 23 C8
Drina → Bos.-H. 44°53N 19°21E 23 B8
Drøbak Norway 59°39N 10°39E 9 G14
Drobeta-Turnu Severin
Romania 44°39N 22°41E 17 F12
Drochia Moldova 48°2N 27°48E 17 D14
Drogheda Ireland 53°43N 6°22W 10 C5
Drogichin = Dragichyn
Belarus 52°15N 25°8E 17 B13
Drogobych = Drohobych
Ukraine 49°20N 23°30E 17 D12
Drohobych Ukraine 49°20N 23°30E 17 D12
Droichead Atha = Drogheda
Ireland 53°43N 6°22W 10 C5
Droichead Nua Ireland 53°11N 6°48W 10 C5
Droitwich U.K. 52°16N 2°8W 13 E5
Drôme → France 44°46N 4°46E 20 D6
Dromedary, C. Australia 36°17S 150°10E 63 F5
Dromore U.K. 54°31N 7°28W 10 B4
Dromore West Ireland 54°15N 8°52W 10 B3
Dronfield U.K. 53°19N 1°27W 12 D6
Dronning Maud Land
Antarctica 72°30S 12°0E 5 D3
Dronten Neths. 52°32N 5°43E 15 B5
Druk Yul = Bhutan ■
Asia 27°25N 90°30E 41 F17
Drumbo Canada 43°16N 80°35W 82 C4
Drumcliff Ireland 54°20N 8°29W 10 B3
Drumheller Canada 51°25N 112°40W 70 C6
Drummond U.S.A. 46°40N 113°9W 76 C7
Drummond I. U.S.A. 46°1N 83°39W 81 B12
Drummond Pt. Australia 34°9S 135°16E 63 E2
Drummond Ra.
Australia 23°45S 147°10E 62 C4
Drummondville Canada 45°55N 72°25W 72 C5
Drumright U.S.A. 35°59N 96°36W 84 D6
Druskininkai Lithuania 54°3N 23°58E 9 J20
Drut → Belarus 53°8N 30°5E 17 B16
Druzhina Russia 68°14N 145°18E 29 C15
Dry Harbour Mts.
Jamaica 18°19N 77°24W 88 a
Dry Tortugas U.S.A. 24°38N 82°55W 85 F13
Dryden Canada 49°47N 92°50W 71 D10
Dryden U.S.A. 42°30N 76°18W 83 D8
Drygalski I. Antarctica 66°0S 92°0E 5 C7
Drygalski Ice Tongue
Antarctica 75°24S 163°30E 5 D21
Drysdale → Australia 13°59S 126°51E 60 B4
Drysdale I. Australia 11°41S 136°0E 62 A2
Drysdale River △
Australia 14°56S 127°2E 60 B4
Du Gué → Canada 57°21N 70°45W 72 A5
Du Quoin U.S.A. 38°1N 89°14W 80 F9
Duanesburg U.S.A. 42°45N 74°11W 83 D10
Duaringa Australia 23°42S 149°42E 62 C4
Duarte, Pico Dom. Rep. 19°2N 70°59W 89 D5
Dubai = Dubayy U.A.E. 25°18N 55°20E 45 E7
Dubăsari Moldova 47°15N 29°10E 17 E15
Dubăsari Vdkhr.
Moldova 47°30N 29°0E 17 E15
Dubawnt → Canada 64°33N 100°6W 71 A8
Dubawnt L. Canada 63°8N 101°28W 71 A8
Dubayy U.A.E. 25°18N 55°20E 45 E7
Dubbo Australia 32°11S 148°35E 63 E4
Dubele
Dem. Rep. of the Congo 2°56N 29°35E 54 B2
Dublin Ireland 53°21N 6°15W 10 C5
Dublin Ga., U.S.A. 32°32N 82°54W 85 E13
Dublin Tex., U.S.A. 32°5N 98°21W 84 E5
Dublin □ Ireland 53°24N 6°20W 10 C5
Dublin ✕ (DUB) Ireland 53°26N 6°15W 10 C5
Dubno Ukraine 50°25N 25°45E 17 C13
Dubois Idaho, U.S.A. 44°10N 112°14W 76 D7
Dubois Pa., U.S.A. 41°7N 78°46W 82 E6
Dubossary = Dubăsari
Moldova 47°15N 29°10E 17 E15
Dubossary Vdkhr. = Dubăsari
Vdkhr. Moldova 47°30N 29°0E 17 E15
Dubovka Russia 49°5N 44°50E 19 E7
Dubrajpur India 23°48N 87°25E 43 H12
Dubréka Guinea 9°46N 13°31W 50 G3
Dubrovitsa = Dubrovytsya
Ukraine 51°31N 26°35E 17 C14
Dubrovnik Croatia 42°39N 18°6E 23 C8
Dubrovytsya Ukraine 51°31N 26°35E 17 C14
Dubuque U.S.A. 42°30N 90°41W 80 D8
Duchesne U.S.A. 40°10N 110°24W 76 F8
Duchess Australia 21°20S 139°50E 62 C2
Ducie I. Pac. Oc. 24°40S 124°48W 65 K15
Duck → U.S.A. 36°2N 87°52W 85 C11
Duck Cr. → Australia 22°37S 116°53E 60 D2
Duck Lake Canada 52°50N 106°16W 71 C7
Duck Mountain △
Canada 51°45N 101°0W 71 C8
Duckwall, Mt. U.S.A. 37°58N 120°7W 78 H6
Dudhi India 24°15N 83°10E 43 G10
Dudinka Russia 69°30N 86°13E 29 C9
Dudley U.K. 52°31N 2°5W 13 E5
Dudwa India 28°30N 80°41E 43 E9
Dudwa △ India 28°30N 80°40E 43 E9
Duero = Douro → Europe 41°8N 8°40W 21 B1
Dufftown U.K. 57°27N 3°8W 11 D5
Dugi Otok Croatia 44°0N 15°3E 16 G8
Duisburg Germany 51°26N 6°45E 16 C4
Duiwelskloof = Modjadjiskloof
S. Africa 23°42S 30°10E 57 C5
Dūkdamīn Iran 35°59N 57°43E 45 C8
Dukelský Průsmyk
Slovak Rep. 49°25N 21°42E 17 D11
Dukhān Qatar 25°25N 50°50E 45 E6
Duki Pakistan 30°14N 68°25E 40 D6
Duku Nigeria 10°43N 10°43E 51 F8
Dulce U.S.A. 36°56N 107°0W 77 H10
Dulce → Argentina 30°32S 62°33W 94 C3
Dulce, G. Costa Rica 8°40N 83°20W 88 E3
Dulf Iraq 35°7N 45°51E 44 C5
Duliu China 39°2N 116°55E 34 E9
Dullewala Pakistan 31°50N 71°25E 42 D4
Dullstroom S. Africa 25°27S 30°7E 57 D5
Dulq Maghār Syria 36°22N 38°39E 44 B3
Duluth U.S.A. 46°47N 92°6W 80 B7
Dum Dum India 22°39N 88°26E 43 H13
Dum Duma India 27°40N 95°40E 41 F19
Dūmā Syria 33°34N 36°24E 46 B5
Dumaguete Phil. 9°17N 123°15E 37 C6
Dumai Indonesia 1°35N 101°28E 36 D2
Dumaran Phil. 10°33N 119°50E 37 B5
Dumas Ark., U.S.A. 33°53N 91°29W 84 E9
Dumas Tex., U.S.A. 35°52N 101°58W 84 D4
Dumayr Syria 33°39N 36°42E 46 B5
Dumbarton U.K. 55°57N 4°33W 11 F4
Dumbleyung Australia 33°17S 117°42E 61 F2
Dumfries U.K. 55°4N 3°37W 11 F5
Dumfries & Galloway □
U.K. 55°9N 3°58W 11 F5
Dumka India 24°12N 87°15E 43 G12
Dumoine → Canada 46°13N 77°51W 72 C4
Dumoine, L. Canada 46°55N 77°55W 72 C4
Dumont d'Urville
Antarctica 67°0S 110°0E 5 C10
Dumont d'Urville Sea
S. Ocean 63°30S 138°0E 5 C9
Dumraon India 25°33N 84°8E 43 G11
Dumyât Egypt 31°24N 31°48E 51 B12
Dún Dealgan = Dundalk
Ireland 54°1N 6°24W 10 B5
Dún Laoghaire Ireland 53°17N 6°8W 10 C5
Duna = Dunărea →
Europe 45°20N 29°40E 17 F15
Dunagiri India 30°31N 79°52E 43 D8
Dunaj = Dunărea →
Europe 45°20N 29°40E 17 F15
Dunakeszi Hungary 47°37N 19°8E 17 E10
Dunărea → Europe 45°20N 29°40E 17 F15
Dunaújváros Hungary 46°58N 18°57E 17 E10
Dunav = Dunărea →
Europe 45°20N 29°40E 17 F15
Dunay Russia 42°52N 132°22E 30 C6
Dunback N.Z. 45°23S 170°36E 59 F3
Dunbar U.K. 56°0N 2°31W 11 E6
Dunblane U.K. 56°11N 3°58W 11 E5
Duncan Canada 48°45N 123°40W 78 B3
Duncan Ariz., U.S.A. 32°43N 109°6W 77 K9
Duncan Okla., U.S.A. 34°30N 97°57W 84 D6
Duncan, L. Canada 53°29N 77°58W 72 B4
Duncan L. Canada 62°51N 113°58W 70 A6
Duncan Town Bahamas 22°15N 75°45W 88 B4
Duncannon U.S.A. 40°23N 77°2W 82 F7
Duncansby Head U.K. 58°38N 3°1W 11 C5
Duncansville U.S.A. 40°25N 78°26W 82 F6
Dundalk Canada 44°10N 80°24W 82 B4
Dundalk Ireland 54°1N 6°24W 10 B5
Dundalk U.S.A. 39°15N 76°31W 81 F15
Dundalk Bay Ireland 53°55N 6°15W 10 C5
Dundas = Uummannaq
Greenland 77°28N 69°13W 4 B4
Dundas Canada 43°17N 79°59W 82 C5
Dundas, L. Australia 32°35S 121°50E 61 F3
Dundas I. Canada 54°30N 130°50W 70 C2
Dundas Str. Australia 11°15S 131°35E 60 B5
Dundee S. Africa 28°11S 30°15E 57 D5
Dundee U.K. 56°28N 2°59W 11 E6
Dundee U.S.A. 42°32N 76°59W 82 D8
Dundee City □ U.K. 56°30N 2°58W 11 E6
Dundgovĭ □ Mongolia 45°10N 106°0E 34 B4
Dundrum U.K. 54°16N 5°52W 10 B6
Dundrum B. U.K. 54°13N 5°47W 10 B6
Dunedin N.Z. 45°50S 170°33E 59 F3
Dunedin U.S.A. 28°1N 82°46W 85 G13
Dunfanaghy Ireland 55°11N 7°58W 10 A4
Dunfermline U.K. 56°5N 3°27W 11 E5
Dungannon Canada 43°51N 81°36W 82 C3
Dungannon U.K. 54°31N 6°46W 10 B5
Dungarpur India 23°52N 73°45E 42 H5
Dungarvan Ireland 52°5N 7°37W 10 D4
Dungarvan Harbour
Ireland 52°4N 7°35W 10 D4
Dungeness U.K. 50°54N 0°59E 13 G8
Dunglow Ireland 54°57N 8°21W 10 B3
Dungo, L. do Angola 17°15S 19°0E 56 B2
Dungog Australia 32°22S 151°46E 63 E5
Dungu
Dem. Rep. of the Congo 3°40N 28°32E 54 B2
Dungun Malaysia 4°45N 103°25E 39 K4
Dunhua China 43°20N 128°14E 35 C15
Dunhuang China 40°8N 94°36E 32 B4
Dunk I. Australia 17°59S 146°29E 62 B4
Dunkeld Australia 33°25S 149°29E 63 E4
Dunkeld U.K. 56°34N 3°35W 11 E5
Dunkerque France 51°2N 2°20E 20 A5
Dunkery Beacon U.K. 51°9N 3°36W 13 F4
Dunkirk = Dunkerque
France 51°2N 2°20E 20 A5
Dunkirk U.S.A. 42°29N 79°20W 82 D5
Dúnleary = Dún Laoghaire
Ireland 53°17N 6°8W 10 C5
Dunleer Ireland 53°50N 6°24W 10 C5
Dunmanus B. Ireland 51°31N 9°50W 10 E2
Dunmanway Ireland 51°43N 9°6W 10 E2
Dunmarra Australia 16°42S 133°25E 62 B1
Dunmore U.S.A. 41°25N 75°38W 83 E9
Dunmore East Ireland 52°9N 7°0W 10 D5
Dunmore Hd. Ireland 52°10N 10°35W 10 D1
Dunmore Town
Bahamas 25°30N 76°39W 88 A4
Dunn U.S.A. 35°19N 78°37W 85 D15
Dunnellon U.S.A. 29°3N 82°28W 85 G13
Dunnet Hd. U.K. 58°40N 3°21W 11 C5
Dunning U.S.A. 41°50N 100°6W 80 E3
Dunnville Canada 42°54N 79°36W 82 D5
Dunolly Australia 36°51S 143°44E 63 F3
Dunoon U.K. 55°57N 4°56W 11 F4
Duns U.K. 55°47N 2°20W 11 F6
Dunseith U.S.A. 48°50N 100°3W 80 A3
Dunshaughlin Ireland 53°31N 6°33W 10 C5
Dunsmuir U.S.A. 41°13N 122°16W 76 F2
Dunstable U.K. 51°53N 0°32W 13 F7
Dunstan Mts. N.Z. 44°53S 169°35E 59 F2
Dunster Canada 53°8N 119°50W 70 C5
Dunvegan U.K. 57°27N 6°35W 11 D2
Dunvegan L. Canada 60°8N 107°10W 71 A7
Duolun China 42°12N 116°28E 34 C9
Duong Dong Vietnam 10°13N 103°58E 39 G4
Dupree U.S.A. 45°4N 101°35W 80 C3
Dupuyer U.S.A. 48°13N 112°30W 76 B7
Duque de Caxias Brazil 22°46S 43°18W 95 A7
Durack → Australia 15°33S 127°52E 60 C4
Durack Ra. Australia 16°50S 127°40E 60 C4
Durance → France 43°55N 4°45E 20 E6
Durand U.S.A. 44°38N 91°58W 80 C8
Durango Mexico 24°3N 104°39W 86 C4
Durango U.S.A. 37°16N 107°53W 77 H10
Durango □ Mexico 24°50N 105°20W 86 C4
Durant Miss., U.S.A. 33°4N 89°51W 85 E10
Durant Okla., U.S.A. 33°59N 96°25W 84 E6
Durazno Uruguay 33°25S 56°31W 94 C4
Durazzo = Durrës
Albania 41°19N 19°28E 23 D8
Durban S. Africa 29°49S 31°1E 57 D5
Durbuy Belgium 50°21N 5°28E 15 D5
Düren Germany 50°48N 6°29E 16 C4
Durg = Bhilainagar-Durg
India 21°13N 81°26E 41 J12
Durgapur India 23°30N 87°20E 43 H12
Durham Canada 44°10N 80°49W 82 B4
Durham U.K. 54°47N 1°34W 12 C6
Durham Calif., U.S.A. 39°39N 121°48W 78 F5
Durham N.C., U.S.A. 35°59N 78°54W 85 D15
Durham N.H., U.S.A. 43°8N 70°56W 83 C14
Durham □ U.K. 54°42N 1°45W 12 C6
Ḑurmā Si. Arabia 24°37N 46°8E 44 E5
Durmitor Montenegro 43°10N 19°0E 23 C8
Durness U.K. 58°34N 4°45W 11 C4
Durrës Albania 41°19N 19°28E 23 D8
Durrow Ireland 52°51N 7°24W 10 D4
Dursey I. Ireland 51°36N 10°12W 10 E1
Dursley U.K. 51°40N 2°21W 13 F5
Dursunbey Turkey 39°35N 28°37E 23 E13
Duru
Dem. Rep. of the Congo 4°14N 28°50E 54 B2
Durūz, Jabal ad Jordan 32°35N 36°40E 46 C5
D'Urville, Tanjung
Indonesia 1°28S 137°54E 37 E9
D'Urville I. N.Z. 40°50S 173°55E 59 D4
Duryea U.S.A. 41°20N 75°45W 83 E9
Dushak Turkmenistan 37°13N 60°1E 45 B9
Dushanbe Tajikistan 38°33N 68°48E 28 F7
Dushore U.S.A. 41°31N 76°24W 83 E8
Dusky Sd. N.Z. 45°47S 166°30E 59 F1
Dussejour, C. Australia 14°45S 128°13E 60 B4
Düsseldorf Germany 51°14N 6°47E 16 C4
Dutch Harbor U.S.A. 53°53N 166°32W 74 a
Dutlwe Botswana 23°58S 23°46E 56 C3
Dutton Canada 42°39N 81°30W 82 D3
Dutton → Australia 20°44S 143°10E 62 C3
Dutywa S. Africa 32°8S 28°18E 57 E4
Duwayhin, Khawr
U.A.E. 24°20N 51°25E 45 E6
Duyfken Pt. Australia 12°33S 141°38E 62 A3
Duyun China 26°18N 107°29E 32 D5
Dvina, Severnaya →
Russia 64°32N 40°30E 18 B7
Dvinsk = Daugavpils
Latvia 55°53N 26°32E 9 J22
Dvinskaya Guba Russia 65°0N 39°0E 18 B6
Dwarka India 22°18N 69°8E 42 H3
Dwellingup Australia 32°43S 116°4E 61 F2
Dwight Canada 45°20N 79°1W 82 A5
Dwight U.S.A. 41°5N 88°26W 80 E9
Dyatlovo = Dzyatlava
Belarus 53°28N 25°28E 17 B13
Dyce U.K. 57°13N 2°12W 11 D6
Dyer, C. Canada 66°37N 61°16W 69 C13
Dyer Bay Canada 45°10N 81°20W 82 A3
Dyer Plateau Antarctica 70°45S 65°30W 5 D17
Dyersburg U.S.A. 36°3N 89°23W 85 C10
Dyfi → U.K. 52°32N 4°3W 13 E3
Dymer Ukraine 50°47N 30°18E 17 C16
Dysart Australia 22°32S 148°23E 62 C4
Dzaoudzi Mayotte 12°47S 45°16E 53 a
Dzavhan Gol Mongolia 48°54N 93°23E 32 B4
Dzerzhinsk Russia 56°14N 43°30E 18 C7
Dzhalinda Russia 53°26N 124°0E 29 D13
Dzhambul = Taraz
Kazakhstan 42°54N 71°22E 28 E8
Dzhankoy Ukraine 45°40N 34°20E 19 E5
Dzhezkazgan = Zhezqazghan
Kazakhstan 47°44N 67°40E 28 E7
Dzhizak = Jizzax
Uzbekistan 40°6N 67°50E 28 E7
Dzhugdzur, Khrebet
Russia 57°30N 138°0E 29 D14
Dzhungarskiye Vorota =
Dzungarian Gate Asia 45°10N 82°0E 32 B3
Działdowo Poland 53°15N 20°15E 17 B11
Dzibilchaltún Mexico 21°10N 89°35W 87 C7
Dzierżoniów Poland 50°45N 16°39E 17 C9
Dzilam de Bravo Mexico 21°24N 88°53W 87 C7
Dzūkija △ Lithuania 54°10N 24°30E 9 J21
Dzungarian Basin = Junggar
Pendi China 44°30N 86°0E 32 B3
Dzungarian Gate Asia 45°10N 82°0E 32 B3
Dzüünharaa Mongolia 48°52N 106°28E 32 B5
Dzüünmod Mongolia 47°45N 106°58E 32 B5
Dzyarzhynsk Belarus 53°40N 27°1E 17 B14
Dzyatlava Belarus 53°28N 25°28E 17 B13

E

E.C. Manning △ Canada 49°5N 120°45W 70 D4
Eabamet L. Canada 51°30N 87°46W 72 B2
Eabametoong Canada 51°30N 88°0W 72 B2
Eads U.S.A. 38°29N 102°47W 76 G12
Eagar U.S.A. 34°6N 109°17W 77 J9
Eagle Alaska, U.S.A. 64°47N 141°12W 68 C5
Eagle Colo., U.S.A. 39°39N 106°50W 76 G10
Eagle → Canada 53°36N 57°26W 73 B8
Eagle Butte U.S.A. 45°0N 101°10W 80 C3
Eagle Grove U.S.A. 42°40N 93°54W 80 D7
Eagle L. Canada 49°42N 93°13W 71 D10
Eagle L. Calif., U.S.A. 40°39N 120°45W 76 F3
Eagle L. Maine, U.S.A. 46°20N 69°22W 81 B19
Eagle Lake Canada 45°8N 78°29W 82 A6
Eagle Lake Maine, U.S.A. 47°3N 68°36W 81 B19
Eagle Lake Tex., U.S.A. 29°35N 96°20W 84 G6
Eagle Mountain
U.S.A. 33°49N 115°27W 79 M11
Eagle Nest U.S.A. 36°33N 105°16W 77 H11
Eagle Pass U.S.A. 28°43N 100°30W 84 G4
Eagle Pk. U.S.A. 38°10N 119°25W 78 G7
Eagle Pt. Australia 16°11S 124°23E 60 C3
Eagle River Mich., U.S.A. 47°25N 88°18W 80 B9
Eagle River Wis., U.S.A. 45°55N 89°15W 80 C9
Eaglehawk Australia 36°44S 144°15E 63 F3
Eagles Mere U.S.A. 41°25N 76°33W 83 E8
Ealing □ U.K. 51°31N 0°20W 13 F7
Ear Falls Canada 50°38N 93°13W 71 C10
Earle U.S.A. 35°16N 90°28W 85 D9
Earlimart U.S.A. 35°53N 119°16W 79 K7
Earlville U.S.A. 42°44N 75°32W 83 D9
Earn → U.K. 56°21N 3°18W 11 E5
Earn, L. U.K. 56°23N 4°13W 11 E4
Earnslaw, Mt. N.Z. 44°32S 168°27E 59 F2
Earth U.S.A. 34°14N 102°24W 84 D3
Easley U.S.A. 34°50N 82°36W 85 D13
East Anglia U.K. 52°30N 1°0E 12 E9
East Angus Canada 45°30N 71°40W 73 C5
East Antarctica Antarctica 80°0S 90°0E 5 D7
East Aurora U.S.A. 42°46N 78°37W 82 D6
East Ayrshire □ U.K. 55°26N 4°11W 11 F4
East Bengal Bangla. 24°0N 90°0E 41 G17
East Beskids = Vychodné Beskydy
Europe 49°20N 22°0E 17 D11
East Brady U.S.A. 40°59N 79°37W 82 F5
East Branch Clarion River L.
U.S.A. 41°35N 78°35W 82 E6
East C. = Dezhneva, Mys
Russia 66°5N 169°40W 29 C19
East C. N.Z. 37°42S 178°35E 59 B7
East Caroline Basin
Pac. Oc. 4°0N 146°45E 64 G6
East Chicago U.S.A. 41°38N 87°27W 80 E10
East China Sea Asia 30°0N 126°0E 33 D7
East Coulee Canada 51°23N 112°27W 70 C6
East Dereham = Dereham
U.K. 52°41N 0°57E 13 E8
East Dunbartonshire □
U.K. 55°57N 4°13W 11 F4
East Falkland Falk. Is. 51°30S 58°30W 96 G5
East Grand Forks U.S.A. 47°56N 97°1W 80 B5
East Greenwich U.S.A. 41°40N 71°27W 83 E13
East Grinstead U.K. 51°7N 0°0 13 F8
East Hartford U.S.A. 41°46N 72°39W 83 E12
East Helena U.S.A. 46°35N 111°56W 76 C8
East Indies Asia 0°0 120°0E 26 J14
East Kilbride U.K. 55°47N 4°11W 11 F4
East Lamma Channel
China 22°14N 114°9E 33 G11
East Lansing U.S.A. 42°44N 84°29W 81 D11
East Liverpool U.S.A. 40°37N 80°35W 82 F4
East London S. Africa 33°0S 27°55E 57 E4
East Lothian □ U.K. 55°58N 2°44W 11 F6
East Main = Eastmain
Canada 52°10N 78°30W 72 B4
East Mariana Basin
Pac. Oc. 12°0N 153°0E 64 F7
East Northport U.S.A. 40°53N 73°20W 83 F11
East Orange U.S.A. 40°46N 74°12W 83 F10
East Pacific Rise Pac. Oc. 15°0S 110°0W 65 J17
East Palestine U.S.A. 40°50N 80°33W 82 F4
East Pine Canada 55°48N 120°12W 70 B4
East Point U.S.A. 33°41N 84°25W 85 E12
East Providence U.S.A. 41°49N 71°23W 83 E13
East Pt. Br. Virgin Is. 18°40N 64°18W 89 e
East Pt. Canada 46°27N 61°58W 73 C7
East Renfrewshire □
U.K. 55°46N 4°21W 11 F4
East Retford = Retford
U.K. 53°19N 0°56W 12 D7
East Riding of Yorkshire □
U.K. 53°55N 0°30W 12 D7
East Rochester U.S.A. 43°7N 77°29W 82 C7
East St. Louis U.S.A. 38°37N 90°9W 80 F8
East Schelde = Oosterschelde →
Neths. 51°33N 4°0E 15 C4
East Sea = Japan, Sea of
Asia 40°0N 135°0E 30 E7

East Siberian Sea *Russia* 73°0N 160°0E **29** B17
East Stroudsburg *U.S.A.* 41°1N 75°11W **83** E9
East Sussex □ *U.K.* 50°56N 0°19E **13** G8
East Tasman Plateau *Pac. Oc.* 43°30S 152°0E **64** M7
East Tawas *U.S.A.* 44°17N 83°29W **81** C12
East Timor ■ *Asia* 8°50S 126°0E **37** F7
East Toorale *Australia* 30°27S 145°28E **63** E4
East Walker → *U.S.A.* 38°52N 119°10W **78** G7
East Windsor *U.S.A.* 40°17N 74°34W **83** F10
Eastbourne *N.Z.* 41°19S 174°55E **59** D5
Eastbourne *U.K.* 50°46N 0°18E **13** G8
Eastend *Canada* 49°32N 108°50W **71** D7
Easter Fracture Zone *Pac. Oc.* 25°0S 115°0W **65** K16
Easter I. = Pascua, I. de *Chile* 27°7S 109°23W **65** K17
Eastern □ *Kenya* 0°0 38°30E **54** C4
Eastern Cape □ *S. Africa* 32°0S 26°0E **56** E4
Eastern Cr. → *Australia* 20°40S 141°35E **62** C3
Eastern Desert = Es Sahrâ' Esh Sharqîya *Egypt* 27°30N 32°30E **51** C12
Eastern Ghats *India* 14°0N 78°50E **40** N11
Eastern Group = Lau Group *Fiji* 17°0S 178°30W **59** a
Eastern Group *Australia* 33°30S 124°30E **61** F3
Eastern Transvaal = Mpumalanga □ *S. Africa* 26°0S 30°0E **57** D5
Easterville *Canada* 53°8N 99°49W **71** C9
Easthampton *U.S.A.* 42°16N 72°40W **83** D12
Eastlake *U.S.A.* 41°40N 81°26W **82** E3
Eastland *U.S.A.* 32°24N 98°49W **84** E5
Eastleigh *U.K.* 50°58N 1°21W **13** G6
Eastmain *Canada* 52°10N 78°30W **72** B4
Eastmain → *Canada* 52°27N 78°26W **72** B4
Eastman *Canada* 45°18N 72°19W **83** A12
Eastman *U.S.A.* 32°12N 83°11W **85** E13
Easton *Md., U.S.A.* 38°47N 76°5W **81** F15
Easton *Pa., U.S.A.* 40°41N 75°13W **83** F9
Easton *Wash., U.S.A.* 47°14N 121°11W **78** C5
Eastport *U.S.A.* 44°56N 67°0W **81** C20
Eastsound *U.S.A.* 48°42N 122°55W **78** B4
Eaton *U.S.A.* 40°32N 104°42W **76** F11
Eatonia *Canada* 51°13N 109°25W **71** C7
Eatonton *U.S.A.* 33°20N 83°23W **85** E13
Eatontown *U.S.A.* 40°19N 74°4W **83** F10
Eatonville *U.S.A.* 46°52N 122°16W **78** D4
Eau Claire *U.S.A.* 44°49N 91°30W **80** C8
Eau Claire, L. à l' *Canada* 56°10N 74°25W **72** A5
Eauripik Rise *Pac. Oc.* 2°0N 142°0E **64** G6
Ebano *Mexico* 22°13N 98°24W **87** C5
Ebbw Vale *U.K.* 51°46N 3°12W **13** F4
Ebeltoft *Denmark* 56°12N 10°41E **9** H14
Ebenezer, Mt. *Australia* 25°6S 132°34E **61** E5
Ebensburg *U.S.A.* 40°29N 78°44W **82** F6
Eberswalde-Finow *Germany* 52°50N 13°49E **16** B7
Ebetsu *Japan* 43°7N 141°34E **30** C10
Ebey's Landing ⌂ *U.S.A.* 48°12N 122°41W **78** B4
Ebinur Hu *China* 44°55N 82°55E **32** B3
Ebolowa *Cameroon* 2°55N 11°10E **52** D2
Ebonda *Dem. Rep. of the Congo* 2°12N 22°21E **52** D4
Ebre = Ebro → *Spain* 40°43N 0°54E **21** B6
Ebro → *Spain* 40°43N 0°54E **21** B6
Ecatepec de Morelos *Mexico* 19°36N 99°3W **87** D5
Ecbatana = Hamadān *Iran* 34°52N 48°32E **45** C6
Eceabat *Turkey* 40°11N 26°21E **23** D12
Ech Chéliff *Algeria* 36°10N 1°20E **50** A6
Echigo-Sammyaku *Japan* 36°50N 139°50E **31** F9
Echizen-Misaki *Japan* 35°59N 135°57E **31** G7
Echo Bay *N.W.T., Canada* 66°5N 117°55W **68** C8
Echo Bay *Ont., Canada* 46°29N 84°4W **72** C3
Echoing → *Canada* 55°51N 92°5W **72** B1
Echternach *Lux.* 49°49N 6°25E **15** E6
Echuca *Australia* 36°10S 144°45E **63** F3
Écija *Spain* 37°30N 5°10W **21** D3
Eclipse I. *Australia* 35°5S 117°58E **61** G2
Eclipse Is. *Australia* 13°54S 126°19E **60** B4
Eclipse Sd. *Canada* 72°38N 79°0W **69** B12
Ecuador ■ *S. Amer.* 2°0S 78°0W **92** D3
Ed Damazin *Sudan* 11°46N 34°21E **51** F12
Ed Dar el Beida = Casablanca *Morocco* 33°36N 7°36W **50** B4
Ed Debba *Sudan* 18°0N 30°51E **51** E12
Ed Déffa *Egypt* 30°40N 26°30E **51** B11
Ed Dueim *Sudan* 14°0N 32°10E **51** F12
Edam *Canada* 53°11N 108°46W **71** C7
Edam *Neths.* 52°31N 5°3E **15** B5
Eday *U.K.* 59°11N 2°47W **11** B6
Eddrachillis B. *U.K.* 58°17N 5°14W **11** C3
Eddystone *U.K.* 50°11N 4°16W **13** G3
Eddystone Pt. *Australia* 40°59S 148°20E **63** G4
Ede *Neths.* 52°4N 5°40E **15** B5
Edehon L. *Canada* 60°25N 97°15W **71** A9
Edekel, Adrar *Algeria* 23°56N 6°47E **50** D7
Eden *Australia* 37°3S 149°55E **63** F4
Eden *N.C., U.S.A.* 36°29N 79°53W **85** C15
Eden *N.Y., U.S.A.* 42°39N 78°55W **82** D6
Eden *Tex., U.S.A.* 31°13N 99°51W **84** F5
Eden → *U.K.* 54°57N 3°1W **12** C4
Edenburg *S. Africa* 29°43S 25°58E **56** D4
Edendale *S. Africa* 29°39S 30°18E **57** D5
Edenderry *Ireland* 53°21N 7°4W **10** C4
Edenton *U.S.A.* 36°4N 76°39W **85** C16
Edenville *S. Africa* 27°37S 27°34E **57** D4
Eder → *Germany* 51°12N 9°28E **16** C5
Edessa *Greece* 40°48N 22°5E **23** D10
Edfu = Idfû *Egypt* 24°55N 32°49E **51** D12
Edgar *U.S.A.* 40°22N 97°58W **80** E5
Edgartown *U.S.A.* 41°23N 70°31W **83** E14
Edge Hill *U.K.* 52°8N 1°26W **13** E6
Edgefield *U.S.A.* 33°47N 81°56W **85** E14
Edgeley *U.S.A.* 46°22N 98°43W **80** B4
Edgemont *U.S.A.* 43°18N 103°50W **80** D2
Edgeøya *Svalbard* 77°45N 22°30E **4** B9
Édhessa = Edessa *Greece* 40°48N 22°5E **23** D10
Edievale *N.Z.* 45°49S 169°22E **59** F2
Edina *U.S.A.* 40°10N 92°11W **80** E7
Edinboro *U.S.A.* 41°52N 80°8W **82** E4
Edinburg *U.S.A.* 26°18N 98°10W **84** H5
Edinburgh *U.K.* 55°57N 3°13W **11** F5
Edinburgh ✕ (EDI) *U.K.* 55°54N 3°22W **11** F5
Edinburgh, City of □ *U.K.* 55°57N 3°17W **11** F5
Edineţ *Moldova* 48°9N 27°18E **17** D14
Edirne *Turkey* 41°40N 26°34E **23** D12
Edison *U.S.A.* 48°33N 122°27W **78** B4
Edithburgh *Australia* 35°5S 137°43E **63** F2
Edmeston *U.S.A.* 42°42N 75°15W **83** D9
Edmond *U.S.A.* 35°39N 97°29W **84** D6
Edmonds *U.S.A.* 47°48N 122°22W **78** C4
Edmonton *Australia* 17°2S 145°46E **62** B4
Edmonton *Canada* 53°30N 113°30W **70** C6
Edmund L. *Canada* 54°45N 93°17W **72** B1
Edmundston *Canada* 47°23N 68°20W **73** C6
Edna *U.S.A.* 28°59N 96°39W **84** G6
Edremit *Turkey* 39°34N 27°0E **23** E12
Edremit Körfezi *Turkey* 39°30N 26°45E **23** E12
Edson *Canada* 53°35N 116°28W **70** C5
Eduardo Castex *Argentina* 35°50S 64°18W **94** D3
Edward → *Australia* 35°5S 143°30E **63** F3
Edward, L. *Africa* 0°25S 29°40E **54** C2
Edward VII Land *Antarctica* 80°0S 150°0W **5** E13
Edwards *Calif., U.S.A.* 34°50N 117°40W **79** L9
Edwards *N.Y., U.S.A.* 44°20N 75°15W **83** B9
Edwards Plateau *U.S.A.* 30°45N 101°20W **84** F4
Edwardsville *U.S.A.* 41°15N 75°56W **83** E9
Edzná *Mexico* 19°39N 90°19W **87** D6
Edzo *Canada* 62°49N 116°4W **70** A5
Eeklo *Belgium* 51°11N 3°33E **15** C3
Eesti = Estonia ■ *Europe* 58°30N 25°30E **9** G21
Effigy Mounds ⌂ *U.S.A.* 43°5N 91°11W **80** D8
Effingham *U.S.A.* 39°7N 88°33W **80** F9
Égadi, Ísole *Italy* 37°55N 12°16E **22** F5
Egan Range *U.S.A.* 39°35N 114°55W **76** G6
Eganville *Canada* 45°32N 77°5W **82** A7
Eger = Cheb *Czech Rep.* 50°9N 12°28E **16** C7
Eger *Hungary* 47°53N 20°27E **17** E11
Egersund *Norway* 58°26N 6°1E **9** G12
Egg L. *Canada* 55°5N 105°30W **71** B7
Eghezée *Belgium* 50°35N 4°55E **15** D4
Egio *Greece* 38°15N 22°5E **23** E10
Eglinton I. *Canada* 75°48N 118°30W **69** B8
Egmont *Canada* 49°45N 123°56W **70** D4
Egmont, C. *N.Z.* 39°16S 173°45E **59** C4
Egmont, Mt. = Taranaki, Mt. *N.Z.* 39°17S 174°5E **59** C5
Egmont △ *N.Z.* 39°17S 174°4E **59** C5
Egra *India* 21°54N 87°32E **43** J12
Eğridir *Turkey* 37°52N 30°51E **19** G5
Eğridir Gölü *Turkey* 37°53N 30°50E **44** B1
Egvekinot *Russia* 66°19N 179°50W **29** C19
Egypt ■ *Africa* 28°0N 31°0E **51** C12
Ehime □ *Japan* 33°30N 132°40E **31** H6
Ehrenberg *U.S.A.* 33°36N 114°31W **79** M12
Eibar *Spain* 43°11N 2°28W **21** A4
Eidsvold *Australia* 25°25S 151°12E **63** D5
Eidsvoll *Norway* 60°19N 11°14E **9** F14
Eifel *Germany* 50°15N 6°50E **16** C4
Eiffel Flats *Zimbabwe* 18°20S 30°0E **55** F3
Eigg *U.K.* 56°54N 6°10W **11** E2
Eighty Mile Beach *Australia* 19°30S 120°40E **60** C3
Eil, L. *U.K.* 56°51N 5°16W **11** E3
Eildon, L. *Australia* 37°10S 146°0E **63** F4
Eilean Sar = Western Isles □ *U.K.* 57°30N 7°10W **11** D1
Einasleigh *Australia* 18°32S 144°5E **62** B3
Einasleigh → *Australia* 17°30S 142°17E **62** B3
Eindhoven *Neths.* 51°26N 5°28E **15** C5
Eire = Ireland ■ *Europe* 53°50N 7°52W **10** C4
Eiríksjökull *Iceland* 64°46N 20°24W **8** D3
Eirunepé *Brazil* 6°35S 69°53W **92** E5
Eiseb → *Namibia* 20°33S 20°59E **56** C2
Eisenach *Germany* 50°58N 10°19E **16** C6
Eisenerz *Austria* 47°32N 14°54E **16** E8
Eivissa *Spain* 38°54N 1°26E **24** C7
Ejeda *Madag.* 24°20S 44°31E **57** C7
Ejutla *Mexico* 16°34N 96°44W **87** D5
Ekalaka *U.S.A.* 45°53N 104°33W **76** D11
Ekaterinburg = Yekaterinburg *Russia* 56°50N 60°30E **28** D7
Ekenäs = Tammisaari *Finland* 60°0N 23°26E **9** G20
Eketahuna *N.Z.* 40°38S 175°43E **59** D5
Ekibastuz *Kazakhstan* 51°50N 75°10E **28** D8
Ekoli *Dem. Rep. of the Congo* 0°23S 24°13E **54** C1
Eksjö *Sweden* 57°40N 14°58E **9** H16
Ekuma → *Namibia* 18°40S 16°2E **56** B2
Ekwan → *Canada* 53°12N 82°15W **72** B3
Ekwan Pt. *Canada* 53°16N 82°7W **72** B3
El Aaiún *W. Sahara* 27°9N 13°12W **50** C3
El Abanico *Chile* 37°20S 71°31W **94** D1
El 'Agrûd *Egypt* 30°14N 34°24E **46** E3
El 'Alamein *Egypt* 30°48N 28°58E **51** B11
El 'Aqaba, W. → *Egypt* 30°7N 33°54E **46** E2
El Arīḥā *West Bank* 31°52N 35°27E **46** D4
El 'Arîsh *Egypt* 31°8N 33°50E **46** D2
El 'Arîsh, W. → *Egypt* 31°8N 33°47E **46** D2
El Asnam = Ech Chéliff *Algeria* 36°10N 1°20E **50** A6
El Bayadh *Algeria* 33°40N 1°1E **50** B6
El Bluff *Nic.* 11°59N 83°40W **88** D3
El Cajon *U.S.A.* 32°48N 116°58W **79** N10
El Calafate *Argentina* 50°19S 72°15W **96** G2
El Campo *U.S.A.* 29°12N 96°16W **84** G6
El Capitan *U.S.A.* 37°44N 119°38E **78** H7
El Carbón *Honduras* 15°25N 85°32W **88** C2
El Carmen *Colombia* 9°43N 75°8W **92** B3
El Centro *U.S.A.* 32°48N 115°34W **79** N11
El Cerro *Bolivia* 17°30S 61°40W **92** G6
El Compadre *Mexico* 32°20N 116°14W **79** N10
El Cuy *Argentina* 39°55S 68°25W **96** D3
El Cuyo *Mexico* 21°31N 87°41W **87** C7
El Daheir *Egypt* 31°13N 34°10E **46** D3
El Descanso *Mexico* 32°12N 116°58W **79** N10
El Desemboque *Mexico* 30°33N 113°1W **86** A2
El Diviso *Colombia* 1°22N 78°14W **92** C3
El Djouf *Mauritania* 20°0N 9°0W **50** D4
El Dorado *Mexico* 24°17N 107°21W **86** C3
El Dorado *Ark., U.S.A.* 33°12N 92°40W **84** E8
El Dorado *Kans., U.S.A.* 37°49N 96°52W **80** G5
El Dorado *Venezuela* 6°55N 61°37W **92** B6
El Dorado Springs *U.S.A.* 37°52N 94°1W **80** G6
El Escorial *Spain* 40°35N 4°7W **21** B3
El Faiyûm *Egypt* 29°19N 30°50E **51** C12
El Fâsher *Sudan* 13°33N 25°26E **51** F11
El Ferrol = Ferrol *Spain* 43°29N 8°15W **21** A1
El Fuerte *Mexico* 26°25N 108°39W **86** B3
El Gal *Somali Rep.* 10°58N 50°20E **47** E5
El Geneina = Al Junaynah *Sudan* 13°27N 22°45E **51** F10
El Gezira □ *Sudan* 15°0N 33°0E **51** F12
El Gîza *Egypt* 30°0N 31°12E **51** C12
El Gogorrón △ *Mexico* 21°49N 100°57W **86** C4
El Goléa *Algeria* 30°30N 2°50E **50** B6
El Golfo de Santa Clara *Mexico* 31°42N 114°30W **86** A2
El Guácharo △ *Venezuela* 10°8N 63°21W **89** D7
El Guache △ *Venezuela* 9°45N 69°30W **89** E6
El Iskandarîya *Egypt* 31°13N 29°58E **51** B11
El Istiwa'iya *Sudan* 5°0N 28°0E **51** G11
El Jadida *Morocco* 33°11N 8°17W **50** B4
El Jardal *Honduras* 14°54N 88°50W **88** D2
El Kef □ *Tunisia* 36°0N 9°0E **51** A7
El Khârga *Egypt* 25°30N 30°33E **51** C12
El Khartûm *Sudan* 15°31N 32°35E **51** E12
El Khartûm Bahrî *Sudan* 15°40N 32°31E **51** E12
El Kuntilla *Egypt* 30°1N 34°45E **46** E3
El Leoncito △ *Argentina* 31°58S 69°10W **94** C2
El Lucero *Mexico* 30°37N 106°31W **86** A3
El Maestrazgo *Spain* 40°30N 0°25W **21** B5
El Mahalla el Kubra *Egypt* 31°0N 31°0E **51** B12
El Malpais ⌂ *U.S.A.* 34°53N 108°0W **77** J10
El Mansûra *Egypt* 31°0N 31°19E **51** B12
El Medano *Canary Is.* 28°3N 16°32W **24** F3
El Milagro *Argentina* 30°59S 65°59W **94** C2
El Minyâ *Egypt* 28°7N 30°33E **51** C12
El Monte *U.S.A.* 34°4N 118°1W **79** L8
El Obeid *Sudan* 13°8N 30°10E **51** F12
El Odaiya *Sudan* 12°8N 28°12E **51** F11
El Oro *Mexico* 19°51N 100°7W **87** D4
El Oued *Algeria* 33°20N 6°58E **50** B7
El Palmar △ *Argentina* 32°10S 58°31W **94** C4
El Palmito, Presa *Mexico* 25°40N 105°30W **86** B3
El Paso *U.S.A.* 31°45N 106°29W **84** F1
El Pinacate y Gran Desierto de Altar = Gran Desierto del Pinacate ⌂ *Mexico* 31°51N 113°32W **86** A2
El Portal *U.S.A.* 37°41N 119°47W **78** H7
El Porvenir *Mexico* 31°15N 105°51W **86** A3
El Prat de Llobregat *Spain* 41°19N 2°5E **21** B7
El Progreso *Honduras* 15°26N 87°51W **88** C2
El Pueblito *Mexico* 29°6N 105°7W **86** B3
El Pueblo *Canary Is.* 28°36N 17°47W **24** F2
El Puerto de Santa María *Spain* 36°36N 6°13W **21** D2
El Qâhira *Egypt* 30°2N 31°13E **51** B12
El Qantara *Egypt* 30°51N 32°20E **46** E1
El Quseima *Egypt* 30°40N 34°15E **46** E3
El Real de Santa María *Panama* 8°0N 77°40W **92** B3
El Reno *U.S.A.* 35°32N 97°57W **74** C7
El Rey △ *Argentina* 24°40S 64°34W **94** A3
El Rio *U.S.A.* 34°14N 119°10W **79** L7
El Roque, Pta. *Canary Is.* 28°10N 15°25W **24** F4
El Rosarito *Mexico* 28°38N 114°4W **86** B2
El Salto *Mexico* 23°47N 105°22W **86** C3
El Salvador ■ *Cent. Amer.* 13°50N 89°0W **88** D2
El Sauce *Nic.* 13°0N 86°40W **88** D2
El Sueco *Mexico* 29°54N 106°24W **86** B3
El Suweis *Egypt* 29°58N 32°31E **51** C12
El Tamarâni, W. → *Egypt* 30°7N 34°43E **46** E3
El Thamad *Egypt* 29°40N 34°28E **46** F3
El Tigre *Venezuela* 8°44N 64°15W **92** B6
El Tîh, Gebel *Egypt* 29°40N 33°50E **46** F2
El Tofo *Chile* 29°22S 71°18W **94** B1
El Tránsito *Chile* 28°52S 70°17W **94** B1
El Tûr *Egypt* 28°14N 33°36E **44** D2
El Turbio *Argentina* 51°45S 72°5W **96** G2
El Uqsur *Egypt* 25°41N 32°38E **51** C12
El Vergel *Mexico* 26°28N 106°22W **86** B3
El Vigía *Venezuela* 8°38N 71°39W **92** B4
El Wabeira *Egypt* 29°34N 33°6E **46** F2
El Wak *Kenya* 2°49N 40°56E **54** B5
El Wuz *Sudan* 15°5N 30°7E **51** E12
Elat *Israel* 29°30N 34°56E **46** F3
Elâzığ *Turkey* 38°37N 39°14E **44** B3
Elba *Italy* 42°46N 10°17E **22** C4
Elba *U.S.A.* 31°25N 86°4W **85** F11
Elbasan *Albania* 41°9N 20°9E **23** D9
Elbe *U.S.A.* 46°45N 122°10W **78** D4
Elbe → *Europe* 53°50N 9°0E **16** B5
Elbert, Mt. *U.S.A.* 39°7N 106°27W **76** G10
Elberton *U.S.A.* 34°7N 82°52W **85** D13
Elbeuf *France* 49°17N 1°2E **20** B4
Elbing = Elbląg *Poland* 54°10N 19°25E **17** A10
Elbistan *Turkey* 38°13N 37°15E **44** B3
Elbląg *Poland* 54°10N 19°25E **17** A10
Elbow *Canada* 51°7N 106°35W **71** C7
Elbrus *Russia* 43°21N 42°30E **19** F7
Elburz Mts. = Alborz, Reshteh-ye Kūhhā-ye *Iran* 36°0N 52°0E **45** C7
Elche *Spain* 38°15N 0°42W **21** C5
Elcho I. *Australia* 11°55S 135°45E **62** A2
Elda *Spain* 38°29N 0°47W **21** C5
Eldama Ravine *Kenya* 0°3N 35°43E **54** B4
Elde → *Germany* 53°7N 11°15E **16** B6
Eldon *Mo., U.S.A.* 38°21N 92°35W **80** F7
Eldon *Wash., U.S.A.* 47°33N 123°3W **78** C3
Eldora *U.S.A.* 42°22N 93°5W **80** D7
Eldorado *Argentina* 26°28S 54°43W **95** B5
Eldorado *Canada* 44°35N 77°31W **82** B7
Eldorado *Ill., U.S.A.* 37°49N 88°26W **80** G9
Eldorado *Tex., U.S.A.* 30°52N 100°36W **84** F4
Eldoret *Kenya* 0°30N 35°17E **54** B4
Eldred *U.S.A.* 41°58N 78°23W **82** E6
Elea, C. *Cyprus* 35°19N 34°4E **25** D13
Eleanora, Pk. *Australia* 32°57S 121°9E **61** F3
Elefantes → *Africa* 24°10S 32°40E **57** C5
Elektrostal *Russia* 55°41N 38°32E **18** C6
Elemi Triangle *Africa* 5°0N 35°20E **54** B4
Elephant Butte Res. *U.S.A.* 33°9N 107°11W **77** K10
Elephant I. *Antarctica* 61°0S 55°0W **5** C18
Eleuthera *Bahamas* 25°0N 76°20W **88** B4
Elgin *Canada* 44°36N 76°13W **83** B8
Elgin *U.K.* 57°39N 3°19W **11** D5
Elgin *Ill., U.S.A.* 42°2N 88°17W **80** D9
Elgin *N. Dak., U.S.A.* 46°24N 101°51W **80** B3
Elgin *Oreg., U.S.A.* 45°34N 117°55W **76** D5
Elgin *Tex., U.S.A.* 30°21N 97°22W **84** F6
Elgon, Mt. *Africa* 1°10N 34°30E **54** B3
Eliase *Indonesia* 8°21S 130°48E **37** F8
Elim *Namibia* 17°48S 15°31E **56** B2
Elim *S. Africa* 34°35S 19°45E **56** E2
Elista *Russia* 46°16N 44°14E **19** E7
Elizabeth *Australia* 34°42S 138°41E **63** E2
Elizabeth *U.S.A.* 40°39N 74°12W **83** F10
Elizabeth City *U.S.A.* 36°18N 76°14W **85** C16
Elizabethton *U.S.A.* 36°21N 82°13W **85** C13
Elizabethtown *Ky., U.S.A.* 37°42N 85°52W **81** G11
Elizabethtown *N.Y., U.S.A.* 44°13N 73°36W **83** B11
Elizabethtown *Pa., U.S.A.* 40°9N 76°36W **83** F8
Ełk *Poland* 53°50N 22°21E **17** B12
Elk → *Canada* 49°11N 115°14W **70** C5
Elk → *U.S.A.* 34°46N 87°16W **85** D11
Elk City *U.S.A.* 35°25N 99°25W **84** D5
Elk Creek *U.S.A.* 39°36N 122°32W **78** F4
Elk Grove *U.S.A.* 38°25N 121°22W **78** G5
Elk Island △ *Canada* 53°35N 112°59W **70** C6
Elk Lake *Canada* 47°40N 80°25W **72** C3
Elk Point *Canada* 53°54N 110°55W **71** C6
Elk River *Idaho, U.S.A.* 46°47N 116°11W **76** C5
Elk River *Minn., U.S.A.* 45°18N 93°35W **80** C7
Elkedra → *Australia* 21°8S 136°22E **62** C2
Elkhart *Ind., U.S.A.* 41°41N 85°58W **81** E11
Elkhart *Kans., U.S.A.* 37°0N 101°54W **80** G3
Elkhorn *Canada* 49°59N 101°14W **71** D8
Elkhorn → *U.S.A.* 41°8N 96°19W **80** E5
Elkhovo *Bulgaria* 42°10N 26°35E **23** C12
Elkin *U.S.A.* 36°15N 80°51W **85** C14
Elkins *U.S.A.* 38°55N 79°51W **81** F14
Elkland *U.S.A.* 41°59N 77°19W **82** E7
Elko *Canada* 49°20N 115°10W **70** D5
Elko *U.S.A.* 40°50N 115°46W **76** F6
Elkton *U.S.A.* 43°49N 83°11W **82** C1
Ellas = Greece ■ *Europe* 40°0N 23°0E **23** E9
Ellef Ringnes I. *Canada* 78°30N 102°2W **69** B9
Ellen, Mt. *U.S.A.* 44°9N 72°56W **83** B12
Ellenburg *U.S.A.* 44°54N 73°48W **83** B11
Ellendale *U.S.A.* 46°0N 98°32W **80** B4
Ellensburg *U.S.A.* 46°59N 120°34W **76** C3
Ellenville *U.S.A.* 41°43N 74°24W **83** E10
Ellerton *Barbados* 13°7N 59°33W **89** g
Ellery, Mt. *Australia* 37°28S 148°47E **63** F4
Ellesmere, L. *N.Z.* 43°47S 172°28E **59** G4
Ellesmere I. *Canada* 79°30N 80°0W **69** B12
Ellesmere Port *U.K.* 53°17N 2°54W **12** D5
Ellice Is. = Tuvalu ■ *Pac. Oc.* 8°0S 178°0E **58** B10
Ellicottville *U.S.A.* 42°17N 78°40W **82** D6
Ellington *U.S.A.* 42°13N 79°6W **82** D5
Elliot *Australia* 17°33S 133°32E **62** B1
Elliot *S. Africa* 31°22S 27°48E **57** E4
Elliot Lake *Canada* 46°25N 82°35W **72** C3
Elliotdale = Xhora *S. Africa* 31°55S 28°38E **57** E4
Ellis *U.S.A.* 38°56N 99°34W **80** F4
Elliston *Australia* 33°39S 134°53E **63** E1
Ellisville *U.S.A.* 31°36N 89°12W **85** F10
Ellon *U.K.* 57°22N 2°4W **11** D6
Ellore = Eluru *India* 16°48N 81°8E **41** L12
Ellsworth *Kans., U.S.A.* 38°44N 98°14W **80** F4
Ellsworth *Maine, U.S.A.* 44°33N 68°25W **81** C19
Ellsworth Land *Antarctica* 76°0S 89°0W **5** D16
Ellsworth Mts. *Antarctica* 78°30S 85°0W **5** D16
Ellwood City *U.S.A.* 40°52N 80°17W **82** F4
Elma *Canada* 49°52N 95°55W **71** D9
Elma *U.S.A.* 47°0N 123°25W **78** D3
Elmalı *Turkey* 36°44N 29°56E **19** G4
Elmhurst *U.S.A.* 41°53N 87°56W **80** E10
Elmira *Canada* 43°36N 80°33W **82** C4
Elmira *U.S.A.* 42°6N 76°48W **82** D8
Elmira Heights *U.S.A.* 42°8N 76°50W **82** D8
Elmore *Australia* 36°30S 144°37E **63** F3
Elmshorn *Germany* 53°43N 9°40E **16** B5
Elmvale *Canada* 44°35N 79°52W **82** B5
Elora *Canada* 43°41N 80°26W **82** C4
Elounda *Greece* 35°16N 25°42E **25** D7
Eloy *U.S.A.* 32°45N 111°33W **77** K8
Elphin *Canada* 44°55N 76°37W **83** B8
Elrose *Canada* 51°12N 108°0W **71** C7
Elsie *U.S.A.* 45°52N 123°36W **78** E3
Elsinore = Helsingør *Denmark* 56°2N 12°35E **9** H1
Eltanin Fracture Zone System *S. Ocean* 54°0S 130°0W **5** B1
Eltham *N.Z.* 39°26S 174°19E **59** C
Eluru *India* 16°48N 81°8E **41** L1
Elvas *Portugal* 38°50N 7°10W **21** C
Elverum *Norway* 60°53N 11°34E **8** F1
Elvire → *Australia* 17°51S 128°11E **60** C
Elvire, Mt. *Australia* 29°22S 119°36E **61** E
Elwell, L. = Tiber Res. *U.S.A.* 48°19N 111°6W **76** B
Elwood *Ind., U.S.A.* 40°17N 85°50W **81** E1
Elwood *Nebr., U.S.A.* 40°36N 99°52W **80** E
Elx = Elche *Spain* 38°15N 0°42W **21** C
Ely *U.K.* 52°24N 0°16E **13** E
Ely *Minn., U.S.A.* 47°55N 91°51W **80** B
Ely *Nev., U.S.A.* 39°15N 114°54W **76** G
Elyria *U.S.A.* 41°22N 82°7W **82** E
eMalahleni *S. Africa* 25°51S 29°14E **57** D
Emāmrūd *Iran* 36°30N 55°0E **45** B
Embarcación *Argentina* 23°10S 64°0W **94**
Embetsu *Japan* 44°44N 141°47E **30** B1
Embi *Kazakhstan* 48°50N 58°8E **28**
Embi → *Kazakhstan* 46°55N 53°28E **19**
Embonas *Greece* 36°13N 27°51E **25**
Embro *Canada* 43°9N 80°54W **82**
Embrun *France* 44°34N 6°30E **20**
Embu *Kenya* 0°32S 37°38E **54**
Emden *Germany* 53°21N 7°12E **16**
Emerald *Australia* 23°32S 148°10E **62**
Emerson *Canada* 49°0N 97°10W **71**
Emet *Turkey* 39°20N 29°15E **23** E
Emi Koussi *Chad* 19°45N 18°55E **51**
Eminabad *Pakistan* 32°2N 74°8E **42**
Emine, Nos *Bulgaria* 42°40N 27°56E **23** C
Emissi, Tarso *Chad* 21°27N 18°36E **51**
Emlenton *U.S.A.* 41°11N 79°43W **82**
Emmaus *S. Africa* 29°2S 25°15E **56**
Emmaus *U.S.A.* 40°32N 75°30W **83**
Emmeloord *Neths.* 52°44N 5°46E **15**
Emmen *Neths.* 52°48N 6°57E **15**
Emmet *Australia* 24°45S 144°30E **62**
Emmetsburg *U.S.A.* 43°7N 94°41W **80**
Emmett *Idaho, U.S.A.* 43°52N 116°30W **76**
Emmett *Mich., U.S.A.* 42°59N 82°46W **82**
Emmonak *U.S.A.* 62°47N 164°31W **7**
Emo *Canada* 48°38N 93°50W **71** D
Empalme *Mexico* 27°58N 110°51W **86**
Empangeni *S. Africa* 28°50S 31°52E **57**
Empedrado *Argentina* 28°0S 58°46W **94**
Emperor Seamount Chain *Pac. Oc.* 40°0N 170°0E **64**
Emperor Trough *Pac. Oc.* 43°0N 175°30E **64**
Emporia *Kans., U.S.A.* 38°25N 96°11W **80**
Emporia *Va., U.S.A.* 36°42N 77°32W **81** G
Emporium *U.S.A.* 41°31N 78°14W **82**
Empress *Canada* 50°57N 110°0W **71**
Empty Quarter = Rub' al Khālī *Si. Arabia* 19°0N 48°0E **47**
Ems → *Germany* 53°20N 7°12E **16**
Emsdale *Canada* 45°32N 79°19W **82**
Emu *China* 43°40N 128°6E **35** C
Emu Park *Australia* 23°13S 150°50E **62**
eMuziwezinto *S. Africa* 30°15S 30°45E **57**
'En 'Avrona *Israel* 29°43N 35°0E **46**
'En Boqeq *Israel* 31°12N 35°21E **45**
'En Gedi *Israel* 31°28N 35°25E **45**
En Nahud *Sudan* 12°45N 28°25E **51**
Ena *Japan* 35°25N 137°25E **31**
Enana *Namibia* 17°30S 16°23E **56**
Enard B. *U.K.* 58°5N 5°20W **11**
Enare = Inarijärvi *Finland* 69°0N 28°0E **8**
Enarotali *Indonesia* 3°55S 136°21E **37**
Encampment *U.S.A.* 41°12N 106°47W **76**
Encantadas, Serra *Brazil* 30°40S 53°0W **95**
Encarnación *Paraguay* 27°15S 55°50W **95**
Encarnación de Díaz *Mexico* 21°31N 102°14W **86**
Encinitas *U.S.A.* 33°3N 117°17W **79**
Encino *U.S.A.* 34°39N 105°28W **77**
Encounter B. *Australia* 35°45S 138°45E **63**
Endako *Canada* 54°6N 125°2W **70**
Endau *Kenya* 1°18S 38°31E **54**
Endau Rompin △ *Malaysia* 2°40N 103°15E **39**
Ende *Indonesia* 8°45S 121°40E **37**
Endeavour Str. *Australia* 10°45S 142°0E **62**
Enderbury I. *Kiribati* 3°8S 171°5W **64**
Enderby *Canada* 50°35N 119°10W **70**
Enderby Abyssal Plain *S. Ocean* 60°0S 40°0E **5**
Enderby I. *Australia* 20°35S 116°30E **60**
Enderby Land *Antarctica* 66°0S 53°0E **5**
Enderlin *U.S.A.* 46°38N 97°36W **80**
Enderrocat, C. *Spain* 39°28N 2°43E **2**
Endicott *U.S.A.* 42°6N 76°4W **83**
Endwell *U.S.A.* 42°6N 76°2W **83**
Endyalgout I. *Australia* 11°40S 132°35E **6**
Eneabba *Australia* 29°49S 115°16E **6**
Enewetak Atoll *Marshall Is.* 11°30N 162°15E **6**
Enez *Turkey* 40°45N 26°5E **23**
Enfer, Pte. d' *Martinique* 14°22N 60°54W
Enfield *Canada* 44°56N 63°32W **73**
Enfield *Conn., U.S.A.* 41°58N 72°36W **83**
Enfield *N.C., U.S.A.* 36°11N 77°41W **85**
Enfield *N.H., U.S.A.* 43°39N 72°9W **83**
Engadin *Switz.* 46°45N 10°10E **2**
Engaño, C. *Dom. Rep.* 18°30N 68°20W **8**
Engaño, C. *Phil.* 18°35N 122°23E **3**
Engaru *Japan* 44°3N 143°31E **30**
Engcobo = Ngcobo *S. Africa* 31°37S 28°0E **5**
Engels *Russia* 51°28N 46°6E **1**
Engemann L. *Canada* 58°0N 106°55W **7**
Enggano *Indonesia* 5°20S 102°40E **3**

gland U.S.A. 34°33N 91°58W 84 D9
gland □ U.K. 53°0N 2°0W 13 E5
glee Canada 50°45N 56°5W 73 B8
glehart Canada 47°49N 79°52W 72 C4
glewood U.S.A. 39°38N 104°59W 76 G11
glish → Canada 49°12N 91°5W 71 C10
glish Bazar = Ingraj Bazar
India 24°58N 88°10E 43 G13
glish Channel Europe 50°0N 2°0W 13 G6
glish Company's Is., The
Australia 11°50S 136°32E 62 A2
glish River Canada 49°14N 91°0W 72 C1
id U.S.A. 36°24N 97°53W 84 C6
khuizen Neths. 52°42N 5°17E 15 B5
na Italy 37°34N 14°16E 22 F6
nadai L. Canada 60°58N 101°20W 71 A8
nedi Chad 17°15N 22°0E 51 E10
ngonia Australia 29°21S 145°50E 63 D4
nis Ireland 52°51N 8°59W 10 D3
nis Mont., U.S.A. 45°21N 111°44W 76 D8
nis Tex., U.S.A. 32°20N 96°38W 84 E6
niscorthy Ireland 52°30N 6°34W 10 D5
niskillen U.K. 54°21N 7°39W 10 B4
nistimon Ireland 52°57N 9°17W 10 D2
ns → Austria 48°14N 14°32E 16 D8
) Finland 62°47N 30°10E 8 E24
ntekiö Finland 68°23N 23°37E 8 B20
osburg Falls U.S.A. 44°55N 72°48W 83 B12
riquillo, L. Dom. Rep. 18°20N 72°5W 89 C5
schede Neths. 52°13N 6°53E 15 B6
senada Argentina 34°55S 57°55W 94 C4
senada Mexico 31°52N 116°37W 86 A1
senada de los Muertos
Mexico 23°59N 109°51W 86 C2
siola, Pta. de n' Spain 39°7N 2°55E 24 B9
ebbe Uganda 0°4N 32°28E 54 B3
erprise Canada 60°47N 115°45W 70 A5
erprise Ala., U.S.A. 31°19N 85°51W 85 F12
erprise Oreg., U.S.A. 45°25N 117°17W 76 D5
re Ríos Bolivia 21°30S 64°25W 94 A3
re Ríos □ Argentina 30°30S 58°30W 94 C4
roncamento Portugal 39°28N 8°28W 21 C1
ugu Nigeria 6°30N 7°30E 50 G7
umclaw U.S.A. 47°12N 121°59W 78 C5
e, Ís. Italy 38°30N 14°57E 22 E6
Neths. 52°21N 5°59E 15 B5
rnay France 49°3N 3°56E 20 B5
esus Turkey 37°55N 27°22E 23 F12
raim U.S.A. 39°22N 111°35W 76 G8
rata Pa., U.S.A. 40°11N 76°11W 83 F8
rata Wash., U.S.A. 47°19N 119°33W 76 C4
nal France 48°10N 6°27E 20 B7
skopi Cyprus 34°40N 32°54E 25 E11
skopi Greece 35°20N 24°20E 25 D6
skopi Bay Cyprus 34°35N 32°50E 25 E11
om U.K. 51°19N 0°16W 13 F7
kiro Namibia 21°40S 19°9E 56 C2
atoria = El Istiwa'iya
udan 5°0N 28°0E 51 G11
atorial Guinea ■ Africa 2°0N 8°0E 52 D1
rachidia Morocco 31°58N 4°20W 50 B5
ahad Sudan 12°45N 30°32E 51 F12
fif Morocco 35°1N 4°1W 50 A5
wadī Myit = Irrawaddy →
urma 15°50N 95°6E 41 M19
wadī Myitwanya = Irrawaddy,
Mouths of the Burma 15°30N 95°0E 41 M19
wan △ Thailand 14°25N 98°58E 38 E2
l = Arbīl Iraq 36°15N 44°5E 44 B5
k Turkey 38°39N 43°36E 44 B4
yaş Dağı Turkey 38°30N 35°30E 44 B2
Hungary 47°22N 18°56E 17 E10
o Jiang → China 42°37N 128°0E 35 C14
ek Turkey 40°23N 27°47E 23 D12
ene = Ulaan-Uul
Mongolia 44°13N 111°10E 34 B6
enet Mongolia 49°2N 104°5E 32 B5
enetsogt Mongolia 42°55N 106°5E 34 C4
us, Mt. Antarctica 77°35S 167°0E 5 D11
him Brazil 27°35S 52°15W 95 B5
li Konya, Turkey 37°31N 34°4E 44 B2
li Zonguldak, Turkey 41°15N 31°24E 19 F5
hot China 43°48N 112°2E 34 C7
ma → Spain 41°26N 4°45W 21 B3
nisdam S. Africa 28°30S 26°50E 56 D4
rt Germany 50°58N 11°2E 16 C6
ni Turkey 38°17N 39°49E 44 B3
l Mongolia 43°8N 109°5E 34 C5
ni Vozvyshennost
ussia 47°0N 44°0E 19 E7
Latvia 56°54N 25°38E 9 H21
oll, L. U.K. 58°30N 4°42W 11 C4
e Italy 38°2N 12°35E 22 E5
U.S.A. 42°8N 80°5W 82 D4
L. N. Amer. 42°15N 81°0W 82 D4
Canal U.S.A. 43°5N 78°43W 82 C7
u Canada 42°16N 81°57W 82 D3
oussa Greece 39°53N 19°34E 25 A3
sdale Canada 50°52N 98°7W 71 C9
s Greece 37°57N 21°50E 23 F9
o-misaki Japan 41°50N 143°15E 30 D11
Canada 43°45N 80°7W 82 C4
Pt. Trin. & Tob. 10°3N 61°39W 93 K15
pura India 25°9N 73°3E 42 G5
kay U.K. 57°4N 7°18W 11 D1
ea ■ Africa 14°0N 38°30E 47 D2
ngen Germany 49°36N 11°0E 16 D6
unda Australia 25°14S 133°12E 62 D1
elo Neths. 52°18N 5°35E 15 B5
elo S. Africa 26°31S 29°59E 57 D4
enek Turkey 36°38N 33°0E 44 B2
ones Greece 39°37N 19°46E 25 A3
kulam India 9°59N 76°22E 40 Q10
→ Ireland 54°30N 8°16W 10 B3
, Lower L. U.K. 54°28N 7°47W 10 B4
, Upper L. U.K. 54°14N 7°32W 10 B4
st Giles Ra. Australia 27°0S 123°45E 61 E3
Erode India 11°24N 77°45E 40 P10
Eromanga Australia 26°40S 143°11E 63 D3
Erongo Namibia 21°39S 15°58E 56 C2
Erramala Hills India 15°30N 78°15E 40 M11
Errentería Spain 43°19N 1°54W 21 A5
Erri-Nundra △ Australia 37°28S 148°5E 63 F4
Errigal Ireland 55°2N 8°6W 10 A3
Erris Hd. Ireland 54°19N 10°0W 10 B1
Erskine U.S.A. 47°40N 96°0W 80 B6
Ertis = Irtysh → Russia 61°4N 68°52E 28 C7
Erwin U.S.A. 36°9N 82°25W 85 C13
Erzgebirge Germany 50°27N 12°55E 16 C7
Erzin Russia 50°15N 95°10E 29 D10
Erzincan Turkey 39°46N 39°30E 44 B3
Erzurum Turkey 39°57N 41°15E 44 B4
Es Caló Spain 38°40N 1°30E 24 C8
Es Canar Spain 39°2N 1°36E 24 B8
Es Mercadal Spain 39°59N 4°5E 24 B11
Es Migjorn Gran Spain 39°57N 4°3E 24 B11
Es Sahrâ' Esh Sharqîya
Egypt 27°30N 32°30E 51 C12
Es Sînâ' Egypt 29°0N 34°0E 46 F3
Es Vedrà Spain 38°52N 1°12E 24 C7
Esambo
Dem. Rep. of the Congo 3°48S 23°30E 54 C1
Esan-Misaki Japan 41°40N 141°10E 30 D10
Esashi Hokkaidō, Japan 44°56N 142°35E 30 B11
Esashi Hokkaidō, Japan 41°52N 140°7E 30 D10
Esbjerg Denmark 55°29N 8°29E 9 J13
Esbo = Espoo Finland 60°12N 24°40E 9 F21
Escalante U.S.A. 37°47N 111°36W 77 H8
Escalante → U.S.A. 37°24N 110°57W 77 H8
Escalón Mexico 26°45N 104°20W 86 B4
Escambia → U.S.A. 30°32N 87°11W 85 F11
Escanaba U.S.A. 45°45N 87°4W 80 C10
Esch-sur-Alzette Lux. 49°32N 6°0E 15 E6
Escondido U.S.A. 33°7N 117°5W 79 M9
Escuinapa de Hidalgo
Mexico 22°50N 105°50W 86 C3
Escuintla Guatemala 14°20N 90°48W 88 D1
Esenguly Turkmenistan 37°37N 53°59E 28 F6
Eşfahān Iran 32°39N 51°43E 45 C6
Eşfahān □ Iran 32°50N 51°50E 45 C6
Esfarāyen Iran 37°4N 57°30E 45 B8
Esfideh Iran 33°39N 59°46E 45 C8
Esh Sham = Dimashq
Syria 33°30N 36°18E 46 B5
Esha Ness U.K. 60°29N 1°38W 11 A7
Esher U.K. 51°21N 0°20W 13 F7
Eshkol △ Israel 31°20N 34°30E 46 D3
Eshowe S. Africa 28°50S 31°30E 57 D5
Esigodini Zimbabwe 20°18S 28°56E 57 C4
Esil = Ishim → Russia 57°45N 71°10E 28 D8
Esira Madag. 24°20S 46°42E 57 C8
Esk → Dumf. & Gall., U.K. 54°58N 3°2W 11 G5
Esk → N. Yorks., U.K. 54°30N 0°37W 12 C7
Eskān Iran 26°48N 63°9E 45 E9
Esker Siding Canada 53°53N 66°25W 73 B6
Eskifjörður Iceland 65°3N 13°55W 8 D7
Eskilstuna Sweden 59°22N 16°32E 9 G17
Eskimo Point = Arviat
Canada 61°6N 93°59W 71 A10
Eskişehir Turkey 39°50N 30°30E 19 G5
Esla → Spain 41°29N 6°3W 21 B2
Eslāmābād-e Gharb Iran 34°10N 46°30E 44 C5
Eslāmshahr Iran 35°40N 51°10E 45 C6
Eşme Turkey 38°23N 28°58E 23 E13
Esmeraldas Ecuador 1°0N 79°40W 92 C3
Esna = Isna Egypt 25°17N 32°30E 51 C12
Esnagi L. Canada 48°36N 84°33W 72 C3
España = Spain ■ Europe 39°0N 4°0W 21 B4
Espanola Canada 46°15N 81°46W 72 C3
Espanola U.S.A. 35°59N 106°5W 77 J10
Esparza Costa Rica 9°59N 84°40W 88 E3
Esperance Australia 33°45S 121°55E 61 F3
Esperance B. Australia 33°48S 121°55E 61 F3
Esperance Harbour
St. Lucia 14°4N 60°55W 89 f
Esperanza Antarctica 65°0S 55°0W 5 C18
Esperanza Argentina 31°29S 61°3W 94 C3
Esperanza Puerto Rico 18°6N 65°28W 89 d
Espichel, C. Portugal 38°22N 9°16W 21 C1
Espigão, Serra do Brazil 26°35S 50°30W 95 B5
Espinazo, Sierra del = Espinhaço,
Serra do Brazil 17°30S 43°30W 93 G10
Espinhaço, Serra do
Brazil 17°30S 43°30W 93 G10
Espinilho, Serra do Brazil 28°30S 55°0W 95 B5
Espírito Santo □ Brazil 20°0S 40°45W 93 H10
Espíritu Santo Vanuatu 15°15S 166°50E 58 C9
Espíritu Santo, B. del
Mexico 19°20N 87°35W 87 D7
Espíritu Santo, I.
Mexico 24°30N 110°22W 86 C2
Espita Mexico 21°1N 88°19W 87 C7
Espoo Finland 60°12N 24°40E 9 F21
Espungabera Mozam. 20°29S 32°45E 57 C5
Esquel Argentina 42°55S 71°20W 96 E2
Esquimalt Canada 48°26N 123°25W 78 B3
Esquina Argentina 30°0S 59°30W 94 C4
Essaouira Morocco 31°32N 9°42W 50 B4
Essebie
Dem. Rep. of the Congo 2°58N 30°40E 54 B3
Essen Belgium 51°28N 4°28E 15 C4
Essen Germany 51°28N 7°2E 16 C4
Essendon, Mt. Australia 25°0S 120°29E 61 E3
Essequibo → Guyana 6°50N 58°30W 92 B7
Essex Canada 42°10N 82°49W 82 D2
Essex Calif., U.S.A. 34°44N 115°15W 79 L11
Essex N.Y., U.S.A. 44°19N 73°21W 83 B11
Essex □ U.K. 51°54N 0°27E 13 F8
Essex Junction U.S.A. 44°29N 73°7W 83 B11
Esslingen Germany 48°44N 9°18E 16 D5
Estación Camacho
Mexico 24°25N 102°18W 86 C4
Estación Simón Mexico 24°42N 102°35W 86 C4
Estados, I. de Los
Argentina 54°40S 64°30W 96 G4
Eşţahbānāt Iran 29°8N 54°4E 45 D7
Estância Brazil 11°16S 37°26W 93 F11
Estancia U.S.A. 34°46N 106°4W 77 J10
Estārm Iran 28°21N 58°21E 45 D8
Estcourt S. Africa 29°0S 29°53E 57 D4
Este △ Dom. Rep. 18°14N 68°42W 89 C6
Estelí Nic. 13°9N 86°22W 88 D2
Estellencs Spain 39°39N 2°29E 24 B9
Esterhazy Canada 50°37N 102°5W 71 C8
Estevan Canada 49°10N 102°59W 71 D8
Estevan Group Canada 53°3N 129°38W 70 C3
Estherville U.S.A. 43°24N 94°50W 80 D6
Eston Canada 51°8N 108°40W 71 C7
Estonia ■ Europe 58°30N 25°30E 9 G21
Estreito Brazil 6°32S 47°25W 93 E9
Estrela, Serra da Portugal 40°10N 7°45W 21 B2
Estremoz Portugal 38°51N 7°39W 21 C2
Estrondo, Serra do Brazil 7°20S 48°0W 93 E9
Esztergom Hungary 47°47N 18°44E 17 E10
Et Tîdra Mauritania 19°45N 16°20W 50 E2
Etah India 27°35N 78°40E 43 F8
Étampes France 48°26N 2°10E 20 B5
Etanga Namibia 17°55S 13°0E 56 B1
Etawah India 26°48N 79°6E 43 F8
Etawney L. Canada 57°50N 96°50W 71 B9
Etchojoa Mexico 26°55N 109°38W 86 B3
eThekwini = Durban
S. Africa 29°49S 31°1E 57 D5
Ethel U.S.A. 46°32N 122°46W 78 D4
Ethelbert Canada 51°32N 100°25W 71 C8
Ethiopia ■ Africa 8°0N 40°0E 47 F3
Ethiopian Highlands
Ethiopia 10°0N 37°0E 47 F2
Etive, L. U.K. 56°29N 5°10W 11 E3
Etna Italy 37°50N 14°55E 22 F6
Etoile
Dem. Rep. of the Congo 11°33S 27°30E 55 E2
Etosha △ Namibia 19°0S 16°0E 56 B2
Etosha Pan Namibia 18°40S 16°30E 56 B2
Etowah U.S.A. 35°20N 84°32W 85 D12
Etrek Turkmenistan 37°36N 54°46E 45 B7
Ettelbruck Lux. 49°51N 6°5E 15 E6
Ettrick Water → U.K. 55°31N 2°55W 11 F6
Etuku
Dem. Rep. of the Congo 3°42S 25°45E 54 C2
Etzná-Tixmucuy = Edzná
Mexico 19°39N 90°19W 87 D6
Eua Tonga 21°22S 174°56W 59 c
Euboea = Evia Greece 38°30N 24°0E 23 E11
Eucla Australia 31°41S 128°52E 61 F4
Euclid U.S.A. 41°34N 81°32W 82 E3
Eucumbene, L. Australia 36°2S 148°40E 63 F4
Eudora U.S.A. 33°7N 91°16W 84 E9
Eufaula Ala., U.S.A. 31°54N 85°9W 85 F12
Eufaula Okla., U.S.A. 35°17N 95°35W 84 D7
Eufaula L. U.S.A. 35°18N 95°21W 84 D7
Eugene U.S.A. 44°5N 123°4W 76 D2
Eugowra Australia 33°22S 148°24E 63 E4
Eulo Australia 28°10S 145°3E 63 D4
Eungella △ Australia 20°57S 148°40E 62 C4
Eunice La., U.S.A. 30°30N 92°25W 84 F8
Eunice N. Mex., U.S.A. 32°26N 103°10W 77 K12
Eupen Belgium 50°37N 6°3E 15 D6
Euphrates = Furāt, Nahr al →
Asia 31°0N 47°25E 44 D5
Eureka Canada 80°0N 85°56W 69 B11
Eureka Calif., U.S.A. 40°47N 124°9W 76 F1
Eureka Kans., U.S.A. 37°49N 96°17W 80 G5
Eureka Mont., U.S.A. 48°53N 115°3W 76 B6
Eureka Nev., U.S.A. 39°31N 115°58W 76 G6
Eureka S. Dak., U.S.A. 45°46N 99°38W 80 C4
Eureka, Mt. Australia 26°35S 121°35E 61 E3
Euroa Australia 36°44S 145°35E 63 F4
Europa, Île Ind. Oc. 22°20S 40°22E 53 J8
Europa, Picos de Spain 43°10N 4°49W 21 A3
Europa, Pt. Gib. 36°3N 5°21W 21 D3
Europe 50°0N 20°0E 6 E10
Europoort Neths. 51°57N 4°10E 15 C4
Eustis U.S.A. 28°51N 81°41W 85 G14
Eutsuk L. Canada 53°20N 126°45W 70 C3
Evale Angola 16°33S 15°44E 56 B2
Evans U.S.A. 40°23N 104°41W 76 F11
Evans, L. Canada 50°50N 77°0W 72 B4
Evans City U.S.A. 40°46N 80°4W 82 F4
Evans Head Australia 29°7S 153°27E 63 D5
Evansburg Canada 53°36N 114°59W 70 C5
Evanston Ill., U.S.A. 42°3N 87°40W 80 D10
Evanston Wyo., U.S.A. 41°16N 110°58W 76 F8
Evansville U.S.A. 37°58N 87°35W 80 G10
Evaz Iran 27°46N 53°59E 45 E7
Eveleth U.S.A. 47°28N 92°32W 80 B7
Evensk Russia 62°12N 159°30E 29 C16
Everard, L. Australia 31°30S 135°0E 63 E2
Everard Ranges Australia 27°5S 132°28E 61 E5
Everest, Mt. Nepal 28°5N 86°58E 43 E12
Everett Pa., U.S.A. 40°1N 78°23W 82 F6
Everett Wash., U.S.A. 47°59N 122°12W 78 C4
Everglades, The U.S.A. 25°50N 81°0W 85 J14
Everglades △ U.S.A. 25°30N 81°0W 85 J14
Everglades City U.S.A. 25°52N 81°23W 85 J14
Evergreen Ala., U.S.A. 31°26N 86°57W 85 F11
Evergreen Mont.,
U.S.A. 48°14N 114°17W 76 B6
Evesham U.K. 52°6N 1°56W 13 E6
Evia Greece 38°30N 24°0E 23 E11
Evje Norway 58°36N 7°51E 9 G12
Évora Portugal 38°33N 7°57W 21 C2
Evowghlī Iran 38°43N 45°13E 44 B5
Évreux France 49°3N 1°8E 20 B4
Evros → Greece 41°40N 26°34E 23 D12
Évry France 48°38N 2°27E 20 B5
Évvoia = Evia Greece 38°30N 24°0E 23 E11
Ewe, L. U.K. 57°49N 5°38W 11 D3
Ewing U.S.A. 42°16N 98°21W 80 D4
Ewo Congo 0°48S 14°45E 52 E2
Exaltación Bolivia 13°10S 65°20W 92 F5
Excelsior Springs U.S.A. 39°20N 94°13W 80 F6
Exe → U.K. 50°41N 3°29W 13 G4
Exeter Canada 43°21N 81°29W 82 C3
Exeter U.K. 50°43N 3°31W 13 G4
Exeter Calif., U.S.A. 36°18N 119°9W 78 J7
Exeter N.H., U.S.A. 42°59N 70°57W 83 D14
Exmoor U.K. 51°12N 3°45W 13 F4
Exmoor △ U.K. 51°8N 3°42W 13 F4
Exmouth Australia 21°54S 114°10E 60 D1
Exmouth U.K. 50°37N 3°25W 13 G4
Exmouth G. Australia 22°15S 114°15E 60 D1
Exmouth Plateau Ind. Oc. 19°0S 114°0E 64 J3
Expedition △ Australia 25°41S 149°7E 63 D4
Expedition Ra. Australia 24°30S 149°12E 62 C4
Extremadura □ Spain 39°30N 6°5W 21 C2
Exuma Sound Bahamas 24°30N 76°20W 88 B4
Eyasi, L. Tanzania 3°30S 35°0E 54 C4
Eye Pen. U.K. 58°13N 6°10W 11 C2
Eyemouth U.K. 55°52N 2°5W 11 F6
Eyjafjörður Iceland 66°15N 18°30W 8 C4
Eyl Somali Rep. 8°0N 49°50E 47 F4
Eyre (North), L.
Australia 28°30S 137°20E 63 D2
Eyre (South), L.
Australia 29°18S 137°25E 63 D2
Eyre, L. Australia 29°30S 137°26E 58 D6
Eyre Mts. N.Z. 45°25S 168°25E 59 F2
Eyre Pen. Australia 33°30S 136°17E 63 E2
Eysturoy Færoe Is. 62°13N 6°54W 8 E9
Eyvān = Jūy Zar Iran 33°50N 46°18E 44 C5
Eyvānkī Iran 35°24N 51°56E 45 C6
Ezine Turkey 39°48N 26°20E 23 E12
Ezouza → Cyprus 34°44N 32°27E 25 E11

F

F.Y.R.O.M. = Macedonia ■
Europe 41°53N 21°40E 23 D9
Faaa Tahiti 17°34S 149°35W 59 d
Faaone Tahiti 17°40S 149°21W 59 d
Fabala Guinea 9°44N 9°5W 50 G4
Fabens U.S.A. 31°30N 106°10W 84 F1
Fabius U.S.A. 42°50N 75°59W 83 D9
Fabriano Italy 43°20N 12°54E 22 C5
Fachi Niger 18°6N 11°34E 51 E8
Fada Chad 17°13N 21°34E 51 E10
Fada-n-Gourma
Burkina Faso 12°10N 0°30E 50 F6
Faddeyevskiy, Ostrov
Russia 76°0N 144°0E 29 B15
Fadghāmī Syria 35°53N 40°52E 44 C4
Faenza Italy 44°17N 11°53E 22 B4
Færoe Is. = Føroyar ☑
Atl. Oc. 62°0N 7°0W 8 F9
Făgăras Romania 45°48N 24°58E 17 F13
Fagersta Sweden 60°1N 15°46E 9 F16
Fagnano, L. Argentina 54°30S 68°0W 96 G3
Fahlīān Iran 30°11N 51°28E 45 D6
Fahraj Kermān, Iran 29°0N 59°0E 45 D8
Fahraj Yazd, Iran 31°46N 54°36E 45 D7
Faial Azores 38°34N 28°42W 50 a
Faial Madeira 32°47N 16°53W 24 D3
Faichan Kangri India 35°48N 76°34E 43 B7
Fair Haven N.Y., U.S.A. 43°18N 76°42W 83 C8
Fair Haven Vt., U.S.A. 43°36N 73°16W 81 D17
Fair Hd. U.K. 55°14N 6°9W 10 A5
Fair Isle U.K. 59°32N 1°38W 14 B6
Fair Oaks U.S.A. 38°39N 121°16W 78 G5
Fairbanks U.S.A. 64°51N 147°43W 68 C5
Fairbury U.S.A. 40°8N 97°11W 80 E5
Fairfax U.S.A. 44°40N 73°1W 83 B11
Fairfield Ala., U.S.A. 33°29N 86°55W 85 E11
Fairfield Calif., U.S.A. 38°15N 122°3W 78 G4
Fairfield Conn., U.S.A. 41°9N 73°16W 83 E11
Fairfield Idaho, U.S.A. 43°21N 114°44W 76 E6
Fairfield Ill., U.S.A. 38°23N 88°22W 80 F9
Fairfield Iowa, U.S.A. 40°56N 91°57W 80 E8
Fairfield Tex., U.S.A. 31°44N 96°10W 84 F6
Fairford Canada 51°37N 98°38W 71 C9
Fairhope U.S.A. 30°31N 87°54W 85 F11
Fairlie N.Z. 44°5S 170°49E 59 F3
Fairmead U.S.A. 37°5N 120°10W 78 H6
Fairmont Minn., U.S.A. 43°39N 94°28W 80 D6
Fairmont W. Va., U.S.A. 39°29N 80°9W 81 F13
Fairmount Calif., U.S.A. 34°45N 118°26W 79 L8
Fairmount N.Y., U.S.A. 43°5N 76°12W 83 C8
Fairplay U.S.A. 39°15N 106°2W 76 G10
Fairport U.S.A. 43°6N 77°27W 82 C7
Fairport Harbor U.S.A. 41°45N 81°17W 82 E3
Fairview Canada 56°5N 118°25W 70 B5
Fairview Mont., U.S.A. 47°51N 104°3W 76 C11
Fairview Okla., U.S.A. 36°16N 98°29W 84 C5
Fairweather, Mt.
U.S.A. 58°55N 137°32W 70 B1
Faisalabad Pakistan 31°30N 73°5E 42 D5
Faith U.S.A. 45°2N 102°2W 80 C2
Faizabad India 26°45N 82°10E 43 F10
Fajardo Puerto Rico 18°20N 65°39W 89 d
Fajr, W. → Si. Arabia 29°10N 38°10E 44 D3
Fakenham U.K. 52°51N 0°51E 12 E8
Fakfak Indonesia 2°55S 132°18E 37 E8
Faku China 42°32N 123°21E 35 C12
Falaise France 48°54N 0°12W 20 B3
Falaise, Mui Vietnam 19°6N 105°45E 38 C5
Falam Burma 23°0N 93°45E 41 H18
Falcó, C. des Spain 38°50N 1°23E 24 C7
Falcón, Presa Mexico 26°35N 99°10W 87 B5
Falcon Lake Canada 49°42N 95°15W 71 D9
Falcon Res. U.S.A. 26°34N 99°10W 84 H5
Falconara Marittima
Italy 43°37N 13°24E 22 C5
Falcone, C. del Italy 40°58N 8°12E 22 D3
Falconer U.S.A. 42°7N 79°12W 82 D5
Falefa Samoa 13°54S 171°31W 59 b
Falelatai Samoa 13°55S 171°59W 59 b
Falelima Samoa 13°32S 172°41W 59 b
Faleshty = Fălești
Moldova 47°32N 27°44E 17 E14
Fălești Moldova 47°32N 27°44E 17 E14
Falfurrias U.S.A. 27°14N 98°9W 84 H5
Falher Canada 55°44N 117°15W 70 B5
Faliraki Greece 36°22N 28°12E 25 C10
Falkenberg Sweden 56°54N 12°30E 9 H15
Falkirk U.K. 56°0N 3°47W 11 F5
Falkirk □ U.K. 55°58N 3°49W 11 F5
Falkland U.K. 56°16N 3°12W 11 E5
Falkland Is. ☑ Atl. Oc. 51°30S 59°0W 96 G5
Falkland Sd. Falk. Is. 52°0S 60°0W 96 G5
Fall River U.S.A. 41°43N 71°10W 83 E13
Fallbrook U.S.A. 33°23N 117°15W 79 M9
Fallon U.S.A. 39°28N 118°47W 76 G4
Falls City U.S.A. 40°3N 95°36W 80 E6
Falls Creek U.S.A. 41°9N 78°48W 82 E6
Falmouth Jamaica 18°30N 77°40W 88 a
Falmouth U.K. 50°9N 5°5W 13 G2
Falmouth U.S.A. 41°33N 70°37W 83 E14
Falsa, Pta. Mexico 27°51N 115°3W 86 B1
False B. S. Africa 34°15S 18°40E 56 E2
Falso, C. Honduras 15°12N 83°21W 88 C3
Falster Denmark 54°45N 11°55E 9 J14
Falsterbo Sweden 55°23N 12°50E 9 J15
Fălticeni Romania 47°21N 26°20E 17 E14
Falun Sweden 60°37N 15°37E 8 F16
Famagusta Cyprus 35°8N 33°55E 25 D12
Famagusta Bay Cyprus 35°15N 34°0E 25 D13
Famatina, Sierra de
Argentina 27°30S 68°0W 94 B2
Family L. Canada 51°54N 95°27W 71 C9
Famoso U.S.A. 35°37N 119°12W 79 K7
Fan Xian China 35°55N 115°38E 34 G8
Fanad Hd. Ireland 55°17N 7°38W 10 A4
Fandriana Madag. 20°14S 47°21E 57 C8
Fang Thailand 19°55N 99°13E 38 C2
Fangcheng China 33°18N 112°59E 34 H7
Fangshan China 38°3N 111°25E 34 E6
Fangzi China 36°33N 119°10E 35 F10
Fanjakana Madag. 21°10S 46°53E 57 C8
Fanjiatun China 43°40N 125°15E 35 C13
Fanling China 22°30N 114°8E 33 F11
Fannich, L. U.K. 57°38N 4°59W 11 D4
Fannūj Iran 26°35N 59°38E 45 E8
Fanø Denmark 55°25N 8°25E 9 J13
Fano Italy 43°50N 13°1E 22 C5
Fanshi China 39°12N 113°20E 34 E7
Fao = Al Fāw Iraq 30°0N 48°30E 45 D6
Faqirwali Pakistan 29°27N 73°0E 42 E5
Far East = Dalnevostochnyy □
Russia 67°0N 140°0E 29 C14
Far East Asia 40°0N 130°0E 26 E14
Faradje
Dem. Rep. of the Congo 3°50N 29°45E 54 B2
Farafangana Madag. 22°49S 47°50E 57 C8
Farāh Afghan. 32°20N 62°7E 40 C3
Farāh □ Afghan. 32°25N 62°10E 40 C3
Farahalana Madag. 14°26S 50°10E 57 A9
Faranah Guinea 10°3N 10°45W 50 F3
Farasān, Jazā'ir
Si. Arabia 16°45N 41°55E 47 D3
Farasan Is. = Farasān, Jazā'ir
Si. Arabia 16°45N 41°55E 47 D3
Faratsiho Madag. 19°24S 46°57E 57 B8
Fareham U.K. 50°51N 1°11W 13 G6
Farewell, C. N.Z. 40°29S 172°43E 59 D4
Farewell C. = Nunap Isua
Greenland 59°48N 43°55W 66 D15
Farghona Uzbekistan 40°23N 71°19E 28 E8
Fargo U.S.A. 46°53N 96°48W 80 B5
Fār'iah, W. al →
West Bank 32°12N 35°27E 46 C4
Faribault U.S.A. 44°18N 93°16W 80 C7
Faridabad India 28°26N 77°19E 42 E6
Faridkot India 30°44N 74°45E 42 D6
Faridpur Bangla. 23°15N 89°55E 43 H13
Faridpur India 28°13N 79°33E 43 E8
Farīmān Iran 35°40N 59°49E 45 C8
Farina Australia 30°3S 138°15E 63 E2
Fariones, Pta. Canary Is. 29°13N 13°28W 24 E6
Farleigh Australia 21°4S 149°8E 62 K7
Farmerville U.S.A. 32°47N 92°24W 84 E8
Farmingdale U.S.A. 40°12N 74°10W 83 F10
Farmington Canada 55°54N 120°30W 70 B4
Farmington Calif.,
U.S.A. 37°55N 120°59W 78 H6
Farmington Maine,
U.S.A. 44°40N 70°9W 81 C18
Farmington Mo., U.S.A. 37°47N 90°25W 80 G8
Farmington N.H., U.S.A. 43°24N 71°4W 83 C13
Farmington N. Mex.,
U.S.A. 36°44N 108°12W 77 H9
Farmington Utah,
U.S.A. 40°59N 111°53W 76 F8
Farmington → U.S.A. 41°51N 72°38W 83 E12
Farmville U.S.A. 37°18N 78°24W 81 G14
Farne Is. U.K. 55°38N 1°37W 12 B6
Farnham Canada 45°17N 72°59W 83 A12
Farnham, Mt. Canada 50°29N 116°30W 70 C5
Faro Brazil 2°10S 56°39W 93 D7
Faro Canada 62°11N 133°22W 68 C6
Faro Portugal 37°2N 7°55W 21 D2
Fårö Sweden 57°55N 19°5E 9 H18
Farquhar, C. Australia 23°50S 113°36E 61 D1
Farrars Cr. → Australia 25°35S 140°43E 62 D3
Farrāshband Iran 28°57N 52°5E 45 D7
Farrell U.S.A. 41°13N 80°30W 82 E4
Farrokhī Iran 33°50N 59°31E 45 C8
Farruch, C. = Ferrutx, C. de
Spain 39°47N 3°21E 24 B10
Farrukhabad India 27°24N 79°34E 43 F8
Fārs □ Iran 29°30N 55°0E 45 D7
Fársala Greece 39°17N 22°23E 23 E10
Fārsī Iran 27°58N 50°11E 45 E6
Farson U.S.A. 42°7N 109°26W 76 E9
Farsund Norway 58°5N 6°55E 9 G12
Fartak, Râs Si. Arabia 28°5N 34°34E 44 D2
Fartak, Ra's Yemen 15°38N 52°15E 47 D5

Fartura, Serra da *Brazil* 26°21S 52°52W **95** B5
Fārūj *Iran* 37°14N 58°14E **45** B8
Farvel, Kap = Nunap Isua *Greenland* 59°48N 43°55W **66** D15
Farwell *U.S.A.* 34°23N 103°2W **84** D3
Fāryāb □ *Afghan.* 36°0N 65°0E **40** B4
Fasā *Iran* 29°0N 53°39E **45** D7
Fasano *Italy* 40°50N 17°22E **22** D7
Fastiv *Ukraine* 50°7N 29°57E **17** C15
Fastnet Rock *Ireland* 51°22N 9°37W **10** E2
Fastov = Fastiv *Ukraine* 50°7N 29°57E **17** C15
Fatagar, Tanjung *Indonesia* 2°46S 131°57E **37** E8
Fatehabad *Haryana, India* 29°31N 75°27E **42** E6
Fatehabad *Ut. P., India* 27°1N 78°19E **42** F8
Fatehgarh *India* 27°25N 79°35E **43** F8
Fatehpur *Bihar, India* 24°38N 85°14E **43** G11
Fatehpur *Raj., India* 28°0N 74°40E **42** F6
Fatehpur *Ut. P., India* 25°56N 81°13E **43** G9
Fatehpur *Ut. P., India* 27°10N 81°13E **43** F9
Fatehpur Sikri *India* 27°6N 77°40E **42** F6
Fathom Five ⌓ *Canada* 45°17N 81°40W **82** A3
Fatima *Canada* 47°24N 61°53W **73** C7
Faulkton *U.S.A.* 45°2N 99°8W **80** C4
Faure I. *Australia* 25°52S 113°50E **61** E1
Fauresmith *S. Africa* 29°44S 25°17E **56** D4
Fauske *Norway* 67°17N 15°25E **8** C16
Favara *Italy* 37°19N 13°39E **22** F5
Favàritx, C. de *Spain* 40°0N 4°15E **24** B11
Favignana *Italy* 37°56N 12°20E **22** F5
Fawcett, Pt. *Australia* 11°46S 130°2E **60** B5
Fawn → *Canada* 55°20N 87°35W **72** A2
Fawnskin *U.S.A.* 34°16N 116°56W **79** L10
Faxaflói *Iceland* 64°29N 23°0W **8** D2
Faya-Largeau *Chad* 17°58N 19°6E **51** E9
Fayd *Si. Arabia* 27°1N 42°52E **44** E4
Fayette *Ala., U.S.A.* 33°41N 87°50W **85** E11
Fayette *Mo., U.S.A.* 39°9N 92°41W **80** F7
Fayette *N.Y., U.S.A.* 42°48N 76°48W **83** D8
Fayetteville *Ark., U.S.A.* 36°4N 94°10W **84** C7
Fayetteville *N.C., U.S.A.* 35°3N 78°53W **85** D15
Fayetteville *N.Y., U.S.A.* 43°1N 76°0W **83** C9
Fayetteville *Tenn., U.S.A.* 35°9N 86°34W **85** D11
Faylakah *Kuwait* 29°27N 48°20E **45** D6
Fazilka *India* 30°27N 74°2E **42** D6
Fazilpur *Pakistan* 29°18N 70°29E **42** E4
Fdérik *Mauritania* 22°40N 12°45W **50** D3
Feakle *Ireland* 52°56N 8°40W **10** D3
Feale → *Ireland* 52°27N 9°37W **10** D2
Fear, C. *U.S.A.* 33°50N 77°58W **85** E16
Feather → *U.S.A.* 38°47N 121°36W **76** G3
Feather Falls *U.S.A.* 39°36N 121°16W **78** F5
Featherston *N.Z.* 41°6S 175°20E **59** D5
Featherstone *Zimbabwe* 18°42S 30°55E **55** F3
Fécamp *France* 49°45N 0°22E **20** B4
Fedala = Mohammedia *Morocco* 33°44N 7°21W **50** B4
Federación *Argentina* 31°0S 57°55W **94** C4
Féderal *Argentina* 30°57S 58°48W **96** C5
Federal Way *U.S.A.* 47°18N 122°19W **78** C4
Fedeshkūh *Iran* 28°49N 53°50E **45** D7
Fehmarn *Germany* 54°27N 11°7E **16** A6
Fehmarn Bælt *Europe* 54°35N 11°20E **9** J14
Fehmarn Belt = Fehmarn Bælt *Europe* 54°35N 11°20E **9** J14
Fei Xian *China* 35°18N 117°59E **35** G9
Feijó *Brazil* 8°9S 70°21W **92** E4
Feilding *N.Z.* 40°13S 175°35E **59** D5
Feira de Santana *Brazil* 12°15S 38°57W **93** F11
Feixiang *China* 36°30N 114°45E **34** F8
Felanitx *Spain* 39°28N 3°9E **24** B10
Feldkirch *Austria* 47°15N 9°37E **16** E5
Félicité *Seychelles* 4°19S 55°52E **53** b
Felipe Carrillo Puerto *Mexico* 19°38N 88°3W **87** D7
Felixburg *Zimbabwe* 19°29S 30°51E **57** B5
Felixstowe *U.K.* 51°58N 1°23E **13** F9
Felton *U.S.A.* 37°3N 122°4W **78** H4
Femer Bælt = Fehmarn Bælt *Europe* 54°35N 11°20E **9** J14
Femunden *Norway* 62°10N 11°53E **8** E14
Fen He → *China* 35°36N 110°42E **34** G6
Fenelon Falls *Canada* 44°32N 78°45W **82** B6
Feng Xian *Jiangsu, China* 34°43N 116°35E **34** G9
Feng Xian *Shaanxi, China* 33°54N 106°40E **34** H4
Fengcheng *China* 40°28N 124°5E **35** D13
Fengfeng *China* 36°28N 114°8E **34** F8
Fengning *China* 41°10N 116°33E **34** D9
Fengqiu *China* 35°2N 114°25E **34** G8
Fengrun *China* 39°48N 118°8E **35** E10
Fengtai *China* 39°49N 116°14E **34** E9
Fengxiang *China* 34°29N 107°25E **34** G4
Fengyang *China* 32°51N 117°29E **35** H9
Fengzhen *China* 40°25N 113°2E **34** D7
Fenoarivo *Fianarantsoa, Madag.* 21°43S 46°24E **57** C8
Fenoarivo *Fianarantsoa, Madag.* 20°52S 46°53E **57** C8
Fenoarivo Afovoany *Madag.* 18°26S 46°34E **57** B8
Fenoarivo Atsinanana *Madag.* 17°22S 49°25E **57** B8
Fens, The *U.K.* 52°38N 0°2W **12** E7
Fenton *U.S.A.* 42°48N 83°42W **81** D12
Fenxi *China* 36°40N 111°31E **34** F6
Fenyang *China* 37°18N 111°48E **34** F6
Feodosiya *Ukraine* 45°2N 35°16E **19** E6
Ferbane *Ireland* 53°16N 7°50W **10** C4
Ferdows *Iran* 33°58N 58°2E **45** C8
Ferfer *Somali Rep.* 5°4N 45°9E **47** F4
Fergana = Farghona *Uzbekistan* 40°23N 71°19E **28** E8
Fergus *Canada* 43°43N 80°24W **82** C4
Fergus Falls *U.S.A.* 46°17N 96°4W **80** B5
Ferkéssédougou *Ivory C.* 9°35N 5°6W **50** G4
Ferland *Canada* 50°19N 88°27W **72** B2
Ferlo, Vallée du *Senegal* 15°15N 14°15W **50** E3
Fermanagh □ *U.K.* 54°21N 7°40W **10** B4
Fermo *Italy* 43°9N 13°43E **22** C5
Fermont *Canada* 52°47N 67°5W **73** B6
Fermoy *Ireland* 52°9N 8°16W **10** D3
Fernández *Argentina* 27°55S 63°50W **94** B3
Fernandina Beach *U.S.A.* 30°40N 81°27W **85** F14
Fernando de Noronha *Brazil* 4°0S 33°10W **93** D12
Fernando Póo = Bioko *Eq. Guin.* 3°30N 8°40E **52** D1
Ferndale *Canada* 44°58N 81°17W **82** B3
Ferndale *U.S.A.* 48°51N 122°36W **78** B4
Fernie *Canada* 49°30N 115°5W **70** D5
Fernlees *Australia* 23°51S 148°7E **62** C4
Fernley *U.S.A.* 39°36N 119°15W **76** G4
Fernwood *U.S.A.* 43°16N 73°38W **83** C11
Ferozepore = Firozpur *India* 30°55N 74°40E **42** D6
Ferrara *Italy* 44°50N 11°35E **22** B4
Ferreñafe *Peru* 6°42S 79°50W **92** E3
Ferrerías *Spain* 39°59N 4°1E **24** B11
Ferret, C. *France* 44°38N 1°15W **20** D3
Ferriday *U.S.A.* 31°38N 91°33W **84** F9
Ferrol *Spain* 43°29N 8°15W **21** A1
Ferron *U.S.A.* 39°5N 111°8W **76** G8
Ferrutx, C. de *Spain* 39°47N 3°21E **24** B10
Ferryland *Canada* 47°2N 52°53W **73** C9
Fertile *U.S.A.* 47°32N 96°17W **80** B5
Fès *Morocco* 34°0N 5°0W **50** B5
Fessenden *U.S.A.* 47°39N 99°38W **80** B4
Festus *U.S.A.* 38°13N 90°24W **80** F8
Feteşti *Romania* 44°22N 27°51E **17** F14
Fethiye *Turkey* 36°36N 29°6E **19** G4
Fetlar *U.K.* 60°36N 0°52W **11** A8
Feuilles → *Canada* 58°47N 70°4W **69** D12
Fez = Fès *Morocco* 34°0N 5°0W **50** B5
Fezzan *Libya* 27°0N 13°0E **51** C8
Fiambalá *Argentina* 27°45S 67°37W **94** B2
Fianarantsoa *Madag.* 21°26S 47°5E **57** C8
Fianarantsoa □ *Madag.* 19°30S 47°0E **57** B8
Ficksburg *S. Africa* 28°51S 27°53E **57** D4
Field → *Australia* 23°48S 138°0E **62** C2
Field I. *Australia* 12°5S 132°23E **60** B5
Fier *Albania* 40°43N 19°33E **23** D8
Fife □ *U.K.* 56°16N 3°1W **11** E5
Fife ⌓ *U.K.* 56°15N 3°15W **11** E5
Fife Ness *U.K.* 56°17N 2°35W **11** E6
Fifth Cataract *Sudan* 18°22N 33°50E **51** E12
Figeac *France* 44°37N 2°2E **20** D5
Figtree *Zimbabwe* 20°22S 28°20E **55** G2
Figueira da Foz *Portugal* 40°7N 8°54W **21** B1
Figueres *Spain* 42°18N 2°58E **21** A7
Figuig *Morocco* 32°5N 1°11W **50** B5
Fihaonana *Madag.* 18°36S 47°12E **57** B8
Fiherenana *Madag.* 18°29S 48°24E **57** B8
Fiherenana → *Madag.* 23°19S 43°37E **57** C7
Fiji ■ *Pac. Oc.* 17°20S 179°0E **59** a
Filabusi *Zimbabwe* 20°34S 29°20E **57** C4
Filadelfia *Paraguay* 22°21S 60°2W **94** A3
Filchner Ice Shelf *Antarctica* 79°0S 40°0W **5** D1
Filey *U.K.* 54°12N 0°18W **12** C7
Filey B. *U.K.* 54°12N 0°15W **12** C7
Filfla *Malta* 35°47N 14°24E **25** D1
Filiatra *Greece* 37°9N 21°35E **23** F9
Filingué *Niger* 14°21N 3°22E **50** F6
Filipstad *Sweden* 59°43N 14°9E **9** G16
Fillmore *Calif., U.S.A.* 34°24N 118°55W **79** L8
Fillmore *Utah, U.S.A.* 38°58N 112°20W **76** G7
Fimbul Ice Shelf *S. Ocean* 69°30S 1°0W **5** C2
Finch *Canada* 45°11N 75°7W **83** A9
Finch Hatton *Australia* 20°25S 148°39E **62** K6
Findhorn → *U.K.* 57°38N 3°38W **11** D5
Findlay *U.S.A.* 41°2N 83°39W **81** E12
Fine *U.S.A.* 44°14N 75°8W **83** B9
Finger L. *Canada* 53°33N 93°30W **72** B1
Finger Lakes *U.S.A.* 42°40N 76°30W **83** D8
Fíngoè *Mozam.* 14°55S 31°50E **55** E3
Finisterre, C. = Fisterra, C. *Spain* 42°50N 9°19W **21** A1
Finke *Australia* 25°34S 134°35E **62** D1
Finke Gorge △ *Australia* 24°8S 132°49E **60** D5
Finland ■ *Europe* 63°0N 27°0E **8** E22
Finland, G. of *Europe* 60°0N 26°0E **9** G22
Finlay → *Canada* 57°0N 125°10W **70** B3
Finley *Australia* 35°38S 145°35E **63** F4
Finley *U.S.A.* 47°31N 97°50W **80** B5
Finn → *Ireland* 54°51N 7°28W **10** B4
Finnigan, Mt. *Australia* 15°49S 145°17E **62** B4
Finniss, C. *Australia* 33°8S 134°51E **63** E1
Finnmark *Norway* 69°37N 23°57E **8** B20
Finnsnes *Norway* 69°14N 18°0E **8** B18
Finspång *Sweden* 58°43N 15°47E **9** G16
Fiora → *Italy* 42°20N 11°34E **22** C4
Fiordland △ *N.Z.* 45°46S 167°0E **59** F1
Fīq *Syria* 32°46N 35°41E **46** C4
Firat = Furāt, Nahr al → *Asia* 31°0N 47°25E **44** D5
Fire Island ⌓ *U.S.A.* 40°38N 73°8W **83** F11
Firebag → *Canada* 57°45N 111°21W **71** B6
Firebaugh *U.S.A.* 36°52N 120°27W **78** J6
Firedrake L. *Canada* 61°25N 104°30W **71** A8
Firenze *Italy* 43°46N 11°15E **22** C4
Firk, Sha'ib → *Iraq* 30°59N 44°34E **44** D5
Firozabad *India* 27°10N 78°25E **43** F8
Firozpur *India* 30°55N 74°40E **42** D6
Firozpur-Jhirka *India* 27°48N 76°57E **42** F7
Fīrūzābād *Iran* 28°52N 52°35E **45** D7
Fīrūzkūh *Iran* 35°50N 52°50E **45** C7
Firvale *Canada* 52°27N 126°13W **70** C3
Fish → *Namibia* 28°7S 17°10E **56** D2
Fish → *S. Africa* 31°30S 20°16E **56** E3
Fish River Canyon *Namibia* 27°40S 17°35E **56** D2
Fisher B. *Canada* 51°35N 97°13W **71** C9
Fishers I. *U.S.A.* 41°15N 72°0W **83** E13
Fishguard *U.K.* 52°0N 4°58W **13** E3
Fishing L. *Canada* 52°10N 95°24W **71** C9
Fishkill *U.S.A.* 41°32N 73°54W **83** E11
Fisterra, C. *Spain* 42°50N 9°19W **21** A1
Fitchburg *Mass., U.S.A.* 42°35N 71°48W **83** D13
Fitchburg *Wis., U.S.A.* 42°58N 89°28W **80** D9
Fitz Roy *Argentina* 47°0S 67°0W **96** F3
Fitz Roy, Cerro *Argentina* 49°17S 73°5W **96** F2
Fitzgerald *Canada* 59°51N 111°36W **70** B6
Fitzgerald *U.S.A.* 31°43N 83°15W **85** F13
Fitzgerald River △ *Australia* 33°53S 119°55E **61** F3
Fitzmaurice → *Australia* 14°45S 130°5E **60** B5
Fitzroy → *Queens., Australia* 23°32S 150°52E **62** C5
Fitzroy → *W. Austral., Australia* 17°31S 123°35E **60** C3
Fitzroy Crossing *Australia* 18°9S 125°38E **60** C4
Fitzwilliam I. *Canada* 45°30N 81°45W **82** A3
Fiume = Rijeka *Croatia* 45°20N 14°21E **16** F8
Five Points *U.S.A.* 36°26N 120°6W **78** J6
Fizi *Dem. Rep. of the Congo* 4°17S 28°55E **54** C2
Flagstaff *U.S.A.* 35°12N 111°39W **77** J8
Flagstaff L. *U.S.A.* 45°12N 70°18W **83** A14
Flaherty I. *Canada* 56°15N 79°15W **72** A4
Flåm *Norway* 60°50N 7°7E **8** F12
Flambeau → *U.S.A.* 45°18N 91°14W **80** C8
Flamborough Hd. *U.K.* 54°7N 0°5W **12** C7
Flaming Gorge ⌓ *U.S.A.* 41°10N 109°25W **76** F9
Flaming Gorge Res. *U.S.A.* 41°10N 109°25W **76** F9
Flamingo, Teluk *Indonesia* 5°30S 138°0E **37** F9
Flanders = Flandre *Europe* 50°50N 2°30E **15** B9
Flandre *Europe* 50°50N 2°30E **15** B9
Flandre-Occidentale = West-Vlaanderen □ *Belgium* 51°0N 3°0E **15** D2
Flandre-Orientale = Oost-Vlaanderen □ *Belgium* 51°5N 3°50E **15** C3
Flandreau *U.S.A.* 44°3N 96°36W **80** C5
Flanigan *U.S.A.* 40°10N 119°53W **78** E7
Flannan Is. *U.K.* 58°9N 7°52W **11** C1
Flåsjön *Sweden* 64°5N 15°40E **8** D16
Flat → *Canada* 61°33N 125°18W **70** A3
Flat I. *Mauritius* 19°53S 57°35E **53** d
Flathead L. *U.S.A.* 47°51N 114°8W **76** C6
Flattery, C. *Australia* 14°58S 145°21E **62** A4
Flattery, C. *U.S.A.* 48°23N 124°29W **78** B2
Flatwoods *U.S.A.* 38°31N 82°43W **81** F12
Fleetwood *U.K.* 53°55N 3°1W **12** D4
Fleetwood *U.S.A.* 40°27N 75°49W **83** F9
Flekkefjord *Norway* 58°18N 6°39E **9** G12
Flemington *U.S.A.* 41°7N 77°28W **82** E7
Flensburg *Germany* 54°47N 9°27E **16** A5
Flers *France* 48°47N 0°33W **20** B3
Flesherton *Canada* 44°16N 80°33W **82** B4
Flesko, Tanjung *Indonesia* 0°29N 124°30E **37** D6
Fleurieu Pen. *Australia* 35°40S 138°5E **63** F2
Flevoland □ *Neths.* 52°30N 5°30E **15** B5
Flin Flon *Canada* 54°46N 101°53W **71** C8
Flinders → *Australia* 17°36S 140°36E **62** B3
Flinders B. *Australia* 34°19S 115°19E **61** F2
Flinders Group *Australia* 14°11S 144°15E **62** A3
Flinders I. *S. Austral., Australia* 33°44S 134°41E **63** E1
Flinders I. *Tas., Australia* 40°0S 148°0E **63** G4
Flinders Ranges *Australia* 31°30S 138°30E **63** E2
Flinders Reefs *Australia* 17°37S 148°31E **62** B4
Flint *U.K.* 53°15N 3°8W **12** D4
Flint *U.S.A.* 43°1N 83°41W **81** D12
Flint → *U.S.A.* 30°57N 84°34W **85** F12
Flint I. *Kiribati* 11°26S 151°48W **65** J12
Flintshire □ *U.K.* 53°17N 3°17W **12** D4
Flodden *U.K.* 55°37N 2°8W **12** B5
Floodwood *U.S.A.* 46°56N 92°55W **80** B7
Flora *U.S.A.* 38°40N 88°29W **80** F9
Florala *U.S.A.* 31°0N 86°20W **85** F11
Florence = Firenze *Italy* 43°46N 11°15E **22** C4
Florence *Ala., U.S.A.* 34°48N 87°41W **85** D11
Florence *Ariz., U.S.A.* 33°2N 111°23W **77** K8
Florence *Colo., U.S.A.* 38°23N 105°8W **76** G11
Florence *Oreg., U.S.A.* 43°58N 124°7W **76** D1
Florence *S.C., U.S.A.* 34°12N 79°46W **85** D15
Florence, L. *Australia* 28°53S 138°9E **63** D2
Florencia *Colombia* 1°36N 75°36W **92** C3
Florennes *Belgium* 50°15N 4°35E **15** D4
Florenville *Belgium* 49°40N 5°19E **15** E5
Flores *Azores* 39°26N 31°13W **50** a
Flores *Guatemala* 16°59N 89°50W **88** C2
Flores *Indonesia* 8°35S 121°0E **37** F6
Flores I. *Canada* 49°20N 126°10W **70** D3
Flores Sea *Indonesia* 6°30S 120°0E **37** F6
Floreşti *Moldova* 47°53N 28°17E **17** E15
Floresville *U.S.A.* 29°8N 98°10W **84** G5
Floriano *Brazil* 6°50S 43°0W **93** E10
Florianópolis *Brazil* 27°30S 48°30W **95** B6
Florida *Cuba* 21°32N 78°14W **88** B4
Florida *Uruguay* 34°7S 56°10W **95** C4
Florida □ *U.S.A.* 28°0N 82°0W **85** G14
Florida, Straits of *U.S.A.* 25°0N 80°0W **88** B4
Florida B. *U.S.A.* 25°0N 80°45W **88** B3
Florida Keys *U.S.A.* 24°40N 81°0W **85** J14
Florin *U.S.A.* 38°30N 121°24W **78** G5
Florina *Greece* 40°48N 21°26E **23** D9
Florissant *U.S.A.* 38°47N 90°19W **80** F8
Florø *Norway* 61°35N 5°1E **8** F11
Flower Station *Canada* 45°10N 76°41W **83** A8
Flowerpot I. *Canada* 45°18N 81°38W **82** A3
Floydada *U.S.A.* 33°59N 101°20W **84** E4
Fluk *Indonesia* 1°42S 127°44E **37** E7
Flushing = Vlissingen *Neths.* 51°26N 3°34E **15** C3
Fly → *Papua N. G.* 8°25S 143°0E **58** B7
Flying Fish, C. *Antarctica* 72°6S 102°29W **5** D15
Foa *Tonga* 19°45S 174°18W **59** c
Foam Lake *Canada* 51°40N 103°32W **71** C8
Foça *Turkey* 38°39N 26°46E **23** E12
Fochabers *U.K.* 57°37N 3°6W **11** D5
Focşani *Romania* 45°41N 27°15E **17** F14
Fóggia *Italy* 41°27N 15°34E **22** D6
Fogo *Canada* 49°43N 54°17W **73** C9
Fogo *C. Verde Is.* 15°5N 24°20W **50** b
Fogo I. *Canada* 49°40N 54°5W **73** C9
Föhr *Germany* 54°43N 8°30E **16** A5
Foix *France* 42°58N 1°38E **20** E4
Folda *Nord-Trøndelag, Norway* 64°32N 10°30E **8** D14
Folda *Nordland, Norway* 67°38N 14°50E **8** C16
Foley *Botswana* 21°34S 27°21E **56** C4
Foley *U.S.A.* 30°24N 87°41W **85** F11
Foleyet *Canada* 48°15N 82°25W **72** C3
Folgefonna *Norway* 60°3N 6°23E **9** F12
Foligno *Italy* 42°57N 12°42E **22** C5
Folkestone *U.K.* 51°5N 1°12E **13** F9
Folkston *U.S.A.* 30°50N 82°0W **85** F13
Follansbee *U.S.A.* 40°19N 80°35W **82** F4
Folsom L. *U.S.A.* 38°42N 121°9W **78** G5
Fomboni *Comoros Is.* 12°18S 43°46E **53** a
Fond-du-Lac *Canada* 59°19N 107°12W **71** B7
Fond du Lac *U.S.A.* 43°47N 88°27W **80** D9
Fond-du-Lac → *Canada* 59°17N 106°0W **71** B7
Fonda *U.S.A.* 42°57N 74°22W **83** D10
Fondi *Italy* 41°21N 13°25E **22** D5
Fongafale *Tuvalu* 8°31S 179°13E **58** B10
Fonsagrada = A Fonsagrada *Spain* 43°8N 7°4W **21** A2
Fonseca, G. de *Cent. Amer.* 13°10N 87°40W **88** D2
Fontainebleau *France* 48°24N 2°40E **20** B5
Fontana *U.S.A.* 34°6N 117°26W **79** L9
Fontas → *Canada* 58°14N 121°48W **70** B4
Fonte Boa *Brazil* 2°33S 66°0W **92** D5
Fontenay-le-Comte *France* 46°28N 0°48W **20** C3
Fontenelle Res. *U.S.A.* 42°1N 110°3W **76** E8
Fontur *Iceland* 66°23N 14°32W **8** C6
Fonuafo'ou *Tonga* 20°19S 175°25W **59** c
Fonualei *Tonga* 18°1S 174°19W **59** c
Foochow = Fuzhou *China* 26°5N 119°16E **33** D6
Foping *China* 33°41N 108°0E **34** H5
Forbes *Australia* 33°22S 148°5E **63** E4
Forbesganj *India* 26°17N 87°18E **43** F12
Ford City *Calif., U.S.A.* 35°9N 119°27W **79** K7
Ford City *Pa., U.S.A.* 40°46N 79°32W **82** F5
Førde *Norway* 61°27N 5°53E **8** F11
Fords Bridge *Australia* 29°41S 145°29E **63** D4
Fordyce *U.S.A.* 33°49N 92°25W **84** E8
Forel, Mt. *Greenland* 66°52N 36°55W **66** C16
Foremost *Canada* 49°26N 111°34W **70** D6
Forest *Canada* 43°6N 82°0W **82** C3
Forest *U.S.A.* 32°22N 89°29W **85** E10
Forest City *Iowa, U.S.A.* 43°16N 93°39W **80** D7
Forest City *N.C., U.S.A.* 35°20N 81°52W **85** D14
Forest City *Pa., U.S.A.* 41°39N 75°28W **83** E9
Forest Grove *U.S.A.* 45°31N 123°7W **78** E3
Forestburg *Canada* 52°35N 112°1W **70** C6
Foresthill *U.S.A.* 39°1N 120°49W **78** F6
Forestier Pen. *Australia* 43°0S 148°0E **63** G4
Forestville *Canada* 48°48N 69°2W **73** C6
Forestville *Calif., U.S.A.* 38°28N 122°54W **78** G4
Forestville *N.Y., U.S.A.* 42°28N 79°10W **82** D5
Forfar *U.K.* 56°39N 2°53W **11** E6
Forillon △ *Canada* 48°46N 64°12W **73** C7
Forks *U.S.A.* 47°57N 124°23W **78** C2
Forksville *U.S.A.* 41°29N 76°35W **83** E8
Forlì *Italy* 44°13N 12°3E **22** B5
Forman *U.S.A.* 46°7N 97°38W **80** B5
Formby Pt. *U.K.* 53°33N 3°6W **12** D4
Formentera *Spain* 38°43N 1°27E **24** C7
Formentor, C. de *Spain* 39°58N 3°13E **24** B10
Formentor, Pen. de *Spain* 39°56N 3°11E **24** B10
Former Yugoslav Republic of Macedonia = Macedonia ■ *Europe* 41°53N 21°40E **23** D9
Fórmia *Italy* 41°15N 13°37E **22** D5
Formosa = Taiwan ■ *Asia* 23°30N 121°0E **33** D7
Formosa *Argentina* 26°15S 58°10W **94** B4
Formosa *Brazil* 15°32S 47°20W **93** G9
Formosa □ *Argentina* 25°0S 60°0W **94** B4
Formosa, Serra *Brazil* 12°0S 55°0W **93** F8
Formosa B. = Ungwana B. *Kenya* 2°45S 40°20E **54** C5
Fornells *Spain* 40°3N 4°7E **24** A11
Føroyar ⊠ *Atl. Oc.* 62°0N 7°0W **8** F9
Forres *U.K.* 57°37N 3°37W **11** D5
Forrest *Australia* 30°51S 128°6E **61** F4
Forrest, Mt. *Australia* 24°48S 127°45E **61** D4
Forrest City *U.S.A.* 35°1N 90°47W **85** D9
Forsayth *Australia* 18°33S 143°34E **62** B3
Forssa *Finland* 60°49N 23°38E **8** F20
Forst *Germany* 51°45N 14°37E **16** C8
Forster *Australia* 32°12S 152°31E **63** E5
Forsyth *U.S.A.* 46°16N 106°41W **76** C10
Fort Abbas *Pakistan* 29°12N 72°52E **42** E5
Fort Albany *Canada* 52°15N 81°35W **72** B3
Fort Assiniboine *Canada* 54°20N 114°45W **70** C6
Fort Augustus *U.K.* 57°9N 4°42W **11** D4
Fort Beaufort *S. Africa* 32°46S 26°40E **56** E4
Fort Benton *U.S.A.* 47°49N 110°40W **76** C8
Fort Bragg *U.S.A.* 39°26N 123°48W **76** G2
Fort Bridger *U.S.A.* 41°19N 110°23W **76** F8
Fort Chipewyan *Canada* 58°42N 111°8W **71** B6
Fort Clatsop ⌓ *U.S.A.* 46°8N 123°53W **78** D3
Fort Collins *U.S.A.* 40°35N 105°5W **76** F11
Fort-Coulonge *Canada* 45°50N 76°45W **72** C4
Fort Covington *U.S.A.* 44°59N 74°29W **83** B10
Fort Dauphin = Taolanaro *Madag.* 25°2S 47°0E **57** D
Fort Davis *U.S.A.* 30°35N 103°54W **84**
Fort-de-France *Martinique* 14°36N 61°2W **88**
Fort Defiance *U.S.A.* 35°45N 109°5W **77**
Fort Dodge *U.S.A.* 42°30N 94°11W **80** D
Fort Edward *U.S.A.* 43°16N 73°35W **83** C1
Fort Erie *Canada* 42°54N 78°56W **82** D
Fort Fairfield *U.S.A.* 46°46N 67°50W **81** B2
Fort Frances *Canada* 48°36N 93°24W **71** D1
Fort Franklin = Déline *Canada* 65°11N 123°25W **68** C
Fort Garland *U.S.A.* 37°26N 105°26W **77** H1
Fort George = Chisasibi *Canada* 53°50N 79°0W **72** B
Fort Good Hope *Canada* 66°14N 128°40W **68** C
Fort Hancock *U.S.A.* 31°18N 105°51W **84**
Fort Hope = Eabametoong *Canada* 51°30N 88°0W **72** B
Fort Irwin *U.S.A.* 35°16N 116°41W **79** K1
Fort Kent *U.S.A.* 47°15N 68°36W **81** B
Fort Klamath *U.S.A.* 42°42N 122°0W **76** D
Fort Laramie *U.S.A.* 42°13N 104°31W **76** E1
Fort Lauderdale *U.S.A.* 26°7N 80°8W **85** H1
Fort Liard *Canada* 60°14N 123°30W **70** A
Fort Liberté *Haiti* 19°42N 71°51W **89** C
Fort Lupton *U.S.A.* 40°5N 104°49W **76** F
Fort MacKay *Canada* 57°12N 111°41W **70**
Fort Macleod *Canada* 49°45N 113°30W **70**
Fort McMurray *Canada* 56°44N 111°7W **70**
Fort McPherson *Canada* 67°30N 134°55W **68** C
Fort Madison *U.S.A.* 40°38N 91°27W **80**
Fort Meade *U.S.A.* 27°45N 81°48W **85** H
Fort Morgan *U.S.A.* 40°15N 103°48W **76** F
Fort Myers *U.S.A.* 26°39N 81°52W **85** H
Fort Nelson *Canada* 58°50N 122°44W **70**
Fort Nelson → *Canada* 59°32N 124°0W **70**
Fort Norman = Tulita *Canada* 64°57N 125°30W **68**
Fort Payne *U.S.A.* 34°26N 85°43W **85** D
Fort Peck *U.S.A.* 48°1N 106°27W **76** B
Fort Peck Dam *U.S.A.* 48°0N 106°26W **76** C
Fort Peck L. *U.S.A.* 48°0N 106°26W **76** C
Fort Pierce *U.S.A.* 27°27N 80°20W **85** H
Fort Pierre *U.S.A.* 44°21N 100°22W **80**
Fort Plain *U.S.A.* 42°56N 74°37W **83** D
Fort Portal *Uganda* 0°40N 30°20E **54**
Fort Providence *Canada* 61°3N 117°40W **70**
Fort Qu'Appelle *Canada* 50°45N 103°50W **71**
Fort Resolution *Canada* 61°10N 113°40W **70**
Fort Rixon *Zimbabwe* 20°2S 29°17E **55**
Fort Ross *U.S.A.* 38°32N 123°13W **78**
Fort Rupert = Waskaganish *Canada* 51°30N 78°40W **72**
Fort St. James *Canada* 54°30N 124°10W **70**
Fort St. John *Canada* 56°15N 120°50W **70**
Fort Saskatchewan *Canada* 53°40N 113°15W **70**
Fort Scott *U.S.A.* 37°50N 94°42W **80**
Fort Severn *Canada* 56°0N 87°40W **72**
Fort Shevchenko *Kazakhstan* 44°35N 50°23E **19**
Fort Simpson *Canada* 61°45N 121°15W **70**
Fort Smith *Canada* 60°0N 111°51W **70**
Fort Smith *U.S.A.* 35°23N 94°25W **84**
Fort Stockton *U.S.A.* 30°53N 102°53W **84**
Fort Sumner *U.S.A.* 34°28N 104°15W **77**
Fort Thompson *U.S.A.* 44°3N 99°26W **80**
Fort Union ⌓ *U.S.A.* 35°54N 105°1W **77**
Fort Valley *U.S.A.* 32°33N 83°53W **85**
Fort Vermilion *Canada* 58°24N 116°0W **70**
Fort Walton Beach *U.S.A.* 30°25N 86°36W **85** F
Fort Ware *Canada* 57°26N 125°41W **70**
Fort Wayne *U.S.A.* 41°4N 85°9W **81**
Fort William *U.K.* 56°49N 5°7W **11**
Fort Worth *U.S.A.* 32°43N 97°19W **84**
Fort Yates *U.S.A.* 46°5N 100°38W **80**
Fort Yukon *U.S.A.* 66°34N 145°16W **7**
Fortaleza *Brazil* 3°45S 38°35W **93**
Forteau *Canada* 51°28N 56°58W **73**
Fortescue → *Australia* 21°0S 116°4E **60**
Forth → *U.K.* 56°9N 3°50W **11**
Forth, Firth of *U.K.* 56°5N 2°55W **11**
Fortrose *U.K.* 57°35N 4°9W **11**
Fortuna *Calif., U.S.A.* 40°36N 124°9W **76**
Fortuna *N. Dak., U.S.A.* 48°55N 103°47W **80**
Fortune *Canada* 47°4N 55°50W **73**
Fortune B. *Canada* 47°30N 55°22W **73**
Forūr *Iran* 26°17N 54°32E **45**
Fosen *Norway* 63°50N 10°20E **8**
Foshan *China* 23°4N 113°5E **33**
Fosnavåg *Norway* 62°22N 5°38E **8**
Fossano *Italy* 44°33N 7°43E **20**
Fossil *U.S.A.* 45°0N 120°9W **76**
Fossil Butte ⌓ *U.S.A.* 41°50N 110°27W **76**
Foster *Canada* 45°17N 72°30W **83**
Foster → *Canada* 55°47N 105°49W **71**
Fosters Ra. *Australia* 21°35S 133°48E **62**
Fostoria *U.S.A.* 41°10N 83°25W **81**
Fotadrevo *Madag.* 24°3S 45°1E **57**
Fougères *France* 48°21N 1°14W **20**
Foul Pt. *Sri Lanka* 8°35N 81°18E **40**
Foula *U.K.* 60°10N 2°5W **11**
Foulness I. *U.K.* 51°36N 0°55E **13**
Foulpointe *Madag.* 17°41S 49°31E **57**
Foumban *Cameroon* 5°45N 10°50E **52**
Foumbouni *Comoros Is.* 11°51S 43°29E **5**
Fountain *U.S.A.* 38°41N 104°42W **76**
Fountain Hills *U.S.A.* 33°37N 111°43W **77**
Fountain Springs *U.S.A.* 35°54N 118°51W **79**
Fouriesburg *S. Africa* 28°38S 28°14E **56**
Fourni *Greece* 37°36N 26°32E **23**
Fourth Cataract *Sudan* 18°47N 32°3E **51**

outa Djallon Guinea 11°20N 12°10W 50 F3
oux, Cap-à- Haiti 19°43N 73°27W 89 C5
oveaux Str. N.Z. 46°42S 168°10E 59 G2
owey U.K. 50°20N 4°39W 13 G3
owler Calif., U.S.A. 36°38N 119°41W 78 J7
owler Colo., U.S.A. 38°8N 104°2W 76 G11
owler, Pt. Australia 32°2S 132°3E 61 F5
owlers B. Australia 31°59S 132°34E 61 F5
owman Iran 37°13N 49°19E 45 B6
ox → Canada 56°3N 93°18W 71 B10
ox Creek Canada 54°24N 116°48W 70 C5
ox Lake Canada 58°28N 114°31W 70 B6
ox Valley Canada 50°30N 109°25W 71 C7
oxboro Canada 44°14N 77°26W 82 B7
oxboro U.S.A. 42°4N 71°16W 83 D13
oxdale Australia 20°22S 148°35E 62 J6
oxe Basin Canada 66°0N 77°0W 69 C12
oxe Chan. Canada 65°0N 80°0W 69 C12
oxe Pen. Canada 65°0N 76°0W 69 C12
oxford Ireland 53°59N 9°7W 10 C2
oxton N.Z. 40°29S 175°18E 59 D5
oyle, Lough U.K. 55°7N 7°4W 10 A4
oynes Ireland 52°37N 9°7W 10 D2
oz do Cunene Angola 17°15S 11°48E 56 B1
oz do Iguaçu Brazil 25°30S 54°30W 95 B5
rackville U.S.A. 40°47N 76°14W 83 F8
raile Muerto Uruguay 32°31S 54°32W 95 C5
ramingham U.S.A. 42°18N 71°24W 83 D13
ranca Brazil 20°33S 47°30W 93 H9
rancavilla Fontana Italy 40°32N 17°35E 23 D7
rance ■ Europe 47°0N 3°0E 20 C5
rances Australia 36°41S 140°55E 63 F3
rances → Canada 60°16N 129°10W 70 A3
rances L. Canada 61°23N 129°30W 70 A3
ranceville Gabon 1°40S 13°32E 52 E2
ranche-Comté □ France 46°50N 5°55E 20 C6
rancis Case, L. U.S.A. 43°4N 98°34W 80 D4
rancisco Beltrão Brazil 26°5S 53°4W 95 B5
rancisco Ignacio Madero Coahuila, Mexico 25°48N 103°18W 86 B4
rancisco Ignacio Madero Durango, Mexico 24°26N 104°18W 86 C4
rancisco Ignacio Madero, Presa Mexico 28°10N 105°37W 86 B3
rancistown Botswana 21°7S 27°33E 57 C4
rançois Canada 47°35N 56°45W 73 C8
rançois L. Canada 54°0N 125°30W 70 C3
rancois Peron △ Australia 25°42S 113°33E 61 E1
rancs Pk. U.S.A. 43°58N 109°20W 76 E9
raneker Neths. 53°12N 5°33E 15 A5
rank Hann △ Australia 32°52S 120°19E 61 F3
rankford Canada 44°12N 77°36W 82 B7
rankfort S. Africa 27°17S 28°30E 57 D4
Frankfort Ind., U.S.A. 40°17N 86°31W 80 E10
Frankfort Kans., U.S.A. 39°42N 96°25W 80 F5
Frankfort Ky., U.S.A. 38°12N 84°52W 81 F11
Frankfort N.Y., U.S.A. 43°2N 75°4W 83 C9
Frankfurt Brandenburg, Germany 52°20N 14°32E 16 B8
Frankfurt Hessen, Germany 50°7N 8°41E 16 C5
Fränkische Alb Germany 49°10N 11°23E 16 D6
Frankland → Australia 35°0S 116°48E 61 G2
Franklin Ky., U.S.A. 36°43N 86°35W 80 G10
Franklin La., U.S.A. 29°48N 91°30W 84 G9
Franklin Mass., U.S.A. 42°5N 71°24W 83 D13
Franklin N.H., U.S.A. 43°27N 71°39W 83 C13
Franklin N.Y., U.S.A. 42°20N 75°9W 83 D9
Franklin Nebr., U.S.A. 40°6N 98°57W 80 E4
Franklin Pa., U.S.A. 41°24N 79°50W 82 E5
Franklin Va., U.S.A. 36°41N 76°56W 81 G15
Franklin W. Va., U.S.A. 38°39N 79°20W 81 F14
Franklin B. Canada 69°45N 126°0W 68 C7
Franklin D. Roosevelt L. U.S.A. 48°18N 118°9W 76 B4
Franklin-Gordon Wild Rivers △ Australia 42°19S 145°51E 63 G4
Franklin I. Antarctica 76°10S 168°30E 5 D11
Franklin I. Canada 45°24N 80°20W 82 A4
Franklin L. U.S.A. 40°25N 115°22W 76 F6
Franklin Mts. Canada 65°0N 125°0W 68 C7
Franklin Str. Canada 72°0N 96°0W 68 B10
Franklinton U.S.A. 30°51N 90°9W 85 F9
Franklinville U.S.A. 42°20N 78°27W 82 D6
Frankston Australia 38°8S 145°8E 63 F4
Fransfontein Namibia 20°12S 15°1E 56 C2
Frantsa Iosifa, Zemlya Russia 82°0N 55°0E 28 A6
Franz Canada 48°25N 84°30W 72 C3
Franz Josef Land = Frantsa Iosifa, Zemlya Russia 82°0N 55°0E 28 A6
Fraser U.S.A. 42°32N 82°57W 82 D2
Fraser → B.C., Canada 49°7N 123°11W 78 A3
Fraser → Nfld. & L., Canada 56°39N 62°10W 73 A7
Fraser, Mt. Australia 25°35S 118°20E 61 E2
Fraser I. Australia 25°15S 153°10E 63 D5
Fraser Lake Canada 54°0N 124°50W 70 C4
Fraserburg S. Africa 31°55S 21°30E 56 E3
Fraserburgh U.K. 57°42N 2°1W 11 D6
Fraserdale Canada 49°55N 81°37W 72 C3
Fray Bentos Uruguay 33°10S 58°15W 94 C4
Fray Jorge △ Chile 30°42S 71°40W 94 C1
Fredericia Denmark 55°34N 9°45E 9 J13
Frederick Md., U.S.A. 39°25N 77°25W 81 F15
Frederick Okla., U.S.A. 34°23N 99°1W 84 D5
Frederick S. Dak., U.S.A. 45°50N 98°31W 80 C4
Fredericksburg Pa., U.S.A. 40°27N 76°26W 83 F8
Fredericksburg Tex., U.S.A. 30°16N 98°52W 84 F5
Fredericksburg Va., U.S.A. 38°18N 77°28W 81 F15
Fredericktown Mo., U.S.A. 37°34N 90°18W 80 G8
Fredericktown Ohio, U.S.A. 40°29N 82°33W 82 F2
Frederico Westphalen Brazil 27°22S 53°24W 95 B5
Fredericton Canada 45°57N 66°40W 73 C6
Fredericton Junction Canada 45°41N 66°40W 73 C6
Frederikshåb = Paamiut Greenland 62°0N 49°43W 4 C5
Frederikshamn = Hamina Finland 60°34N 27°12E 8 F22
Frederikshavn Denmark 57°28N 10°31E 9 H14
Frederiksted U.S. Virgin Is. 17°43N 64°53W 89 C7
Fredonia Ariz., U.S.A. 36°57N 112°32W 77 H7
Fredonia Kans., U.S.A. 37°32N 95°49W 80 G6
Fredonia N.Y., U.S.A. 42°26N 79°20W 82 D5
Fredrikstad Norway 59°13N 10°57E 9 G14
Free State □ S. Africa 28°30S 27°0E 56 D4
Freehold U.S.A. 40°16N 74°17W 83 F10
Freeland U.S.A. 41°1N 75°54W 83 E9
Freels, C. Nfld. & L., Canada 49°15N 53°30W 73 C9
Freels, C. Nfld. & L., Canada 46°37N 53°32W 73 C9
Freeman Calif., U.S.A. 35°35N 117°53W 79 K9
Freeman S. Dak., U.S.A. 43°21N 97°26W 80 D5
Freeport Bahamas 26°30N 78°47W 88 A4
Freeport Ill., U.S.A. 42°17N 89°36W 80 D9
Freeport N.Y., U.S.A. 40°39N 73°35W 83 F11
Freeport Ohio, U.S.A. 40°12N 81°15W 82 F3
Freeport Pa., U.S.A. 40°41N 79°41W 82 F5
Freeport Tex., U.S.A. 28°57N 95°21W 84 G7
Freetown S. Leone 8°30N 13°17W 50 G3
Freeville U.S.A. 42°30N 76°20W 83 D8
Frégate, L. de la Canada 53°15N 74°45W 72 B5
Fregenal de la Sierra Spain 38°10N 6°39W 21 C2
Freibourg = Fribourg Switz. 46°49N 7°9E 20 C7
Freiburg Germany 47°59N 7°51E 16 E4
Freire Chile 38°54S 72°38W 96 D2
Freirina Chile 28°30S 71°10W 94 B1
Freising Germany 48°24N 11°45E 16 D6
Freistadt Austria 48°30N 14°30E 16 D8
Fréjus France 43°25N 6°44E 20 E7
Fremantle Australia 32°7S 115°47E 61 F2
Fremont Calif., U.S.A. 37°32N 121°57W 78 H4
Fremont Mich., U.S.A. 43°28N 85°57W 81 D11
Fremont Nebr., U.S.A. 41°26N 96°30W 80 E5
Fremont Ohio, U.S.A. 41°21N 83°7W 81 E12
Fremont → U.S.A. 38°24N 110°42W 76 G8
French Camp U.S.A. 37°53N 121°16W 78 H5
French Cays = Plana Cays Bahamas 22°38N 73°30W 89 B5
French Creek → U.S.A. 41°24N 79°50W 82 E5
French Guiana ☒ S. Amer. 4°0N 53°0W 93 C8
French Polynesia ☒ Pac. Oc. 20°0S 145°0W 65 J13
Frenchman Cr. → N. Amer. 48°31N 107°10W 76 B10
Frenchman Cr. → U.S.A. 40°14N 100°50W 80 E3
Fresco → Brazil 7°15S 51°30W 93 E8
Freshfield, C. Antarctica 68°25S 151°10E 5 C10
Fresnillo Mexico 23°10N 102°53W 86 C4
Fresno U.S.A. 36°44N 119°47W 78 J7
Fresno Res. U.S.A. 48°36N 109°57W 76 B9
Frew → Australia 20°0S 135°38E 62 C2
Frewsburg U.S.A. 42°3N 79°10W 82 D5
Freycinet △ Australia 42°11S 148°19E 63 G4
Freycinet Pen. Australia 42°10S 148°25E 63 G4
Fria Guinea 10°27N 13°38W 50 F3
Fria, C. Namibia 18°0S 12°0E 56 B1
Friant U.S.A. 36°59N 119°43W 78 J7
Frías Argentina 28°40S 65°5W 94 B2
Fribourg Switz. 46°49N 7°9E 20 C7
Friday Harbor U.S.A. 48°32N 123°1W 78 B3
Friedens U.S.A. 40°3N 78°59W 82 F6
Friedrichshafen Germany 47°39N 9°30E 16 E5
Friendship U.S.A. 42°12N 78°8W 82 D6
Friesland □ Neths. 53°5N 5°50E 15 A5
Frigate Seychelles 4°35S 55°56E 53 b
Frio → U.S.A. 28°26N 98°11W 84 G5
Frio, C. Brazil 22°50S 41°50W 90 F6
Friona U.S.A. 34°38N 102°43W 84 D3
Fritch U.S.A. 35°38N 101°36W 84 D4
Frobisher B. Canada 62°30N 66°0W 69 C13
Frobisher Bay = Iqaluit Canada 63°44N 68°31W 69 C13
Frobisher L. Canada 56°20N 108°15W 71 B7
Frohavet Norway 64°0N 9°30E 8 E13
Frome U.K. 51°14N 2°19W 13 F5
Frome → U.K. 50°41N 2°6W 13 G5
Frome, L. Australia 30°45S 139°45E 63 E2
Front Range U.S.A. 40°25N 105°45W 74 C5
Front Royal U.S.A. 38°55N 78°12W 81 F14
Frontenac ⌂ Canada 44°32N 76°30W 83 B8
Frontera Canary Is. 27°47N 17°59W 24 G2
Frontera Mexico 18°32N 92°38W 87 D6
Fronteras Mexico 30°56N 109°31W 86 A3
Frosinone Italy 41°38N 13°19E 22 D5
Frostburg U.S.A. 39°39N 78°56W 81 F14
Frostisen Norway 68°14N 17°10E 8 B17
Frøya Norway 63°43N 8°40E 8 E13
Frunze = Bishkek Kyrgyzstan 42°54N 74°46E 28 E8
Frutal Brazil 20°0S 49°0W 93 H9
Frýdek-Místek Czech Rep. 49°40N 18°20E 17 D10
Fryeburg U.S.A. 44°1N 70°59W 83 B14
Fu Xian = Wafangdian China 39°38N 121°58E 35 E11
Fu Xian China 36°0N 109°20E 34 G5
Fucheng China 37°50N 116°10E 34 F9
Fuchou = Fuzhou China 26°5N 119°16E 33 D6
Fuchū Japan 34°34N 133°14E 31 G6
Fuencaliente Canary Is. 28°28N 17°50W 24 F2
Fuencaliente, Pta. Canary Is. 28°27N 17°51W 24 F2
Fuengirola Spain 36°32N 4°41W 21 D3
Fuentes de Oñoro Spain 40°33N 6°52W 21 B2
Fuerte → Mexico 25°54N 109°22W 86 B3
Fuerte Olimpo Paraguay 21°0S 57°51W 94 A4
Fuerteventura Canary Is. 28°30N 14°0W 24 F6
Fuerteventura ✕ (FUE) Canary Is. 28°24N 13°52W 24 F6
Fufeng China 34°22N 108°0E 34 G5
Fugou China 34°3N 114°25E 34 G8
Fugu China 39°2N 111°3E 34 E6
Fuhai China 47°2N 87°25E 32 B3
Fuḩaymī Iraq 34°16N 42°10E 44 C4
Fuji Japan 35°9N 138°39E 31 G9
Fuji-Hakone-Izu △ Japan 35°15N 138°45E 31 G9
Fuji-San Japan 35°22N 138°44E 31 G9
Fuji-Yoshida Japan 35°30N 138°46E 31 G9
Fujian □ China 26°0N 118°0E 33 D6
Fujinomiya Japan 35°10N 138°40E 31 G9
Fujisawa Japan 35°22N 139°29E 31 G9
Fujiyama, Mt. = Fuji-San Japan 35°22N 138°44E 31 G9
Fukagawa Japan 43°43N 142°2E 30 C11
Fukien = Fujian □ China 26°0N 118°0E 33 D6
Fukuchiyama Japan 35°19N 135°9E 31 G7
Fukue-Shima Japan 32°40N 128°45E 31 H4
Fukui Japan 36°5N 136°10E 31 F8
Fukui □ Japan 36°0N 136°12E 31 G8
Fukuoka Japan 33°39N 130°21E 31 H5
Fukuoka □ Japan 33°30N 131°0E 31 H5
Fukushima Japan 37°44N 140°28E 30 F10
Fukushima □ Japan 37°30N 140°15E 30 F10
Fukuyama Japan 34°35N 133°20E 31 G6
Fulaga Fiji 19°8S 178°33W 59 a
Fulda Germany 50°32N 9°40E 16 C5
Fulda → Germany 51°25N 9°39E 16 C5
Fulford Harbour Canada 48°47N 123°27W 78 B3
Fullerton Calif., U.S.A. 33°53N 117°56W 79 M9
Fullerton Nebr., U.S.A. 41°22N 97°58W 80 E5
Fulongquan China 44°20N 124°42E 35 B13
Fulton Mo., U.S.A. 38°52N 91°57W 80 F8
Fulton N.Y., U.S.A. 43°19N 76°25W 83 C8
Funabashi Japan 35°45N 140°0E 31 G10
Funafuti = Fongafale Tuvalu 8°31S 179°13E 58 B10
Funchal Madeira 32°38N 16°54W 24 D3
Funchal ✕ (FNC) Madeira 32°42N 16°45W 24 D3
Fundación Colombia 10°31N 74°11W 92 A4
Fundão Portugal 40°8N 7°30W 21 B2
Fundy, B. of Canada 45°0N 66°0W 73 D6
Fundy △ Canada 45°35N 65°10W 73 C6
Funhalouro Mozam. 23°3S 34°25E 57 C5
Funing Hebei, China 39°53N 119°12E 35 E10
Funing Jiangsu, China 33°45N 119°50E 35 H10
Funiu Shan China 33°30N 112°20E 34 H7
Funtua Nigeria 11°30N 7°18E 50 F7
Fuping Hebei, China 38°48N 114°12E 34 E8
Fuping Shaanxi, China 34°42N 109°10E 34 G5
Furano Japan 43°21N 142°23E 30 C11
Furāt, Nahr al → Asia 31°0N 47°25E 44 D5
Fūrg Iran 28°18N 55°13E 45 D7
Furnás Spain 39°3N 1°32E 24 B8
Furnas, Represa de Brazil 20°50S 45°30W 95 A6
Furneaux Group Australia 40°10S 147°50E 63 G4
Furqlus Syria 34°36N 37°8E 46 A6
Fürstenwalde Germany 52°22N 14°3E 16 B8
Fürth Germany 49°28N 10°59E 16 D6
Furukawa Japan 38°34N 140°58E 30 E10
Fury and Hecla Str. Canada 69°56N 84°0W 69 C11
Fusagasugá Colombia 4°21N 74°22W 92 C4
Fushan Shandong, China 37°30N 121°15E 35 F11
Fushan Shanxi, China 35°58N 111°51E 34 G6
Fushun China 41°50N 123°56E 35 D12
Fusong China 42°20N 127°15E 35 C14
Fustic Barbados 13°16N 59°38W 89 g
Futian China 22°32N 114°4E 33 F11
Fuxin China 42°5N 121°48E 35 C11
Fuyang China 33°0N 115°48E 34 H8
Fuyang He → China 38°12N 117°0E 34 E9
Fuyong China 22°40N 113°49E 33 F10
Fuyu Heilongjiang, China 47°49N 124°27E 33 B7
Fuyu Jilin, China 45°12N 124°43E 35 B13
Fuyun China 47°0N 89°28E 32 B3
Fuzhou China 26°5N 119°16E 33 D6
Fylde U.K. 53°50N 2°58W 12 D5
Fyn Denmark 55°20N 10°30E 9 J14
Fyne, L. U.K. 55°59N 5°23W 11 F3

G

Gaalkacyo Somali Rep. 6°30N 47°30E 47 F4
Gabela Angola 11°0S 14°24E 52 G2
Gabès Tunisia 33°53N 10°2E 51 B8
Gabès, G. de Tunisia 34°0N 10°30E 51 B8
Gabon ■ Africa 0°10S 10°0E 52 E2
Gaborone Botswana 24°45S 25°57E 56 C4
Gabriels U.S.A. 44°26N 74°12W 83 B10
Gābrīk Iran 25°44N 58°28E 45 E8
Gabrovo Bulgaria 42°52N 25°19E 23 C11
Gāch Sār Iran 36°7N 51°19E 45 B6
Gachsārān Iran 30°15N 50°45E 45 D6
Gadag India 15°30N 75°45E 40 M9
Gadap Pakistan 25°5N 67°28E 42 G2
Gadarwara India 22°50N 78°50E 43 H8
Gadhada India 22°0N 71°35E 42 J4
Gadra Pakistan 25°40N 70°38E 42 G4
Gadsden U.S.A. 34°1N 86°1W 85 D11
Gadwal India 16°10N 77°50E 40 L10
Gaffney U.S.A. 35°5N 81°39W 85 D14
Gafsa Tunisia 34°24N 8°43E 50 B7
Gagaria India 25°43N 70°46E 42 G4
Găgăuzia □ Moldova 46°10N 28°40E 17 E15
Gagnoa Ivory C. 6°56N 5°16W 50 G4
Gagnon Canada 51°50N 68°5W 73 B6
Gagnon, L. Canada 62°3N 110°27W 71 A6
Gahini Rwanda 1°50S 30°30E 54 C3
Gahmar India 25°27N 83°49E 43 G10
Gai Xian = Gaizhou China 40°22N 122°20E 35 D12
Gaidouronisi Greece 34°53N 25°41E 25 E7
Gail U.S.A. 32°46N 101°27W 84 E4
Gaillimh = Galway Ireland 53°17N 9°3W 10 C2
Gaines U.S.A. 41°46N 77°35W 82 E7
Gainesville Fla., U.S.A. 29°40N 82°20W 85 G13
Gainesville Ga., U.S.A. 34°18N 83°50W 85 D13
Gainesville Mo., U.S.A. 36°36N 92°26W 80 G7
Gainesville Tex., U.S.A. 33°38N 97°8W 84 E6
Gainsborough U.K. 53°24N 0°46W 12 D7
Gairdner, L. Australia 31°30S 136°0E 63 E2
Gairloch U.K. 57°43N 5°41W 11 D3
Gairloch, L. U.K. 57°43N 5°45W 11 D3
Gaizhou China 40°22N 122°20E 35 D12
Gaj → Pakistan 26°26N 67°21E 42 F2
Gakuch Pakistan 36°7N 73°45E 43 A5
Galán, Cerro Argentina 25°55S 66°52W 94 B2
Galana → Kenya 3°9S 40°8E 54 C5
Galápagos = Colón, Arch. de Ecuador 0°0 91°0W 90 D1
Galapagos Fracture Zone Pac. Oc. 3°0N 110°0W 65 G17
Galapagos Rise Pac. Oc. 15°0S 95°0W 65 J18
Galashiels U.K. 55°37N 2°49W 11 F6
Galateia Cyprus 35°25N 34°4E 25 D13
Galaţi Romania 45°27N 28°2E 17 F15
Galatina Italy 40°10N 18°10E 23 D8
Galax U.S.A. 36°40N 80°56W 81 G13
Galcaio = Gaalkacyo Somali Rep. 6°30N 47°30E 47 F4
Galdhøpiggen Norway 61°38N 8°18E 8 F13
Galeana Chihuahua, Mexico 30°7N 107°38W 86 A3
Galeana Nuevo León, Mexico 24°50N 100°4W 86 A3
Galela Indonesia 1°50N 127°49E 37 D7
Galena U.S.A. 64°44N 156°56W 74 a
Galeota Pt. Trin. & Tob. 10°8N 60°59W 93 K16
Galera Pt. Trin. & Tob. 10°49N 60°54W 89 D7
Galesburg U.S.A. 40°57N 90°22W 80 E8
Galestan △ Iran 37°30N 56°0E 45 B8
Galeton U.S.A. 41°44N 77°39W 82 E7
Galich Russia 58°22N 42°24E 18 C7
Galicia □ Spain 42°43N 7°45W 21 A2
Galilee = Hagalil Israel 32°53N 35°18E 46 C4
Galilee, L. Australia 22°20S 145°50E 62 C4
Galilee, Sea of = Yam Kinneret Israel 32°45N 35°35E 46 C4
Galina Pt. Jamaica 18°24N 76°58W 88 a
Galinoporni Cyprus 35°31N 34°18E 25 D13
Galion U.S.A. 40°44N 82°47W 82 F2
Galiuro Mts. U.S.A. 32°30N 110°20W 77 K8
Galiwinku Australia 12°2S 135°34E 62 A2
Gallan Hd. U.K. 58°15N 7°2W 11 C1
Gallatin U.S.A. 36°24N 86°27W 85 C11
Galle Sri Lanka 6°5N 80°10E 40 R12
Gállego → Spain 41°39N 0°51W 21 B5
Gallegos → Argentina 51°35S 69°0W 96 G3
Galley Hd. Ireland 51°32N 8°55W 10 E3
Gallinas, Pta. Colombia 12°28N 71°40W 92 A4
Gallipoli = Gelibolu Turkey 40°28N 26°43E 23 D12
Gallípoli Italy 40°3N 17°58E 23 D8
Gallipolis U.S.A. 38°49N 82°12W 81 F12
Gällivare Sweden 67°9N 20°40E 8 C19
Galloo I. U.S.A. 43°55N 76°25W 83 C8
Galloway U.K. 55°1N 4°29W 11 F4
Galloway, Mull of U.K. 54°39N 4°52W 11 G4
Galloway ⌂ U.K. 55°3N 4°20W 11 F4
Gallup U.S.A. 35°32N 108°45W 77 J9
Galoya Sri Lanka 8°10N 80°55E 40 Q12
Galt U.S.A. 38°15N 121°18W 78 G5
Galty Mts. Ireland 52°22N 8°10W 10 D3
Galtymore Ireland 52°21N 8°11W 10 D3
Galugāh Iran 36°43N 53°48E 45 B7
Galva U.S.A. 41°10N 90°3W 80 E8
Galveston U.S.A. 29°18N 94°48W 84 G7
Galveston B. U.S.A. 29°36N 94°50W 84 G7
Gálvez Argentina 32°0S 61°14W 94 C3
Galway Ireland 53°17N 9°3W 10 C2
Galway □ Ireland 53°22N 9°1W 10 C2
Galway B. Ireland 53°13N 9°10W 10 C2
Gam → Vietnam 21°55N 105°12E 38 B5
Gamagōri Japan 34°50N 137°14E 31 G8
Gambat Pakistan 27°17N 68°26E 42 F3
Gambhir → India 26°58N 77°27E 42 F6
Gambia ■ W. Afr. 13°25N 16°0W 50 F2
Gambia → W. Afr. 13°28N 16°34W 50 F2
Gambier U.S.A. 40°22N 82°23W 82 F2
Gambier, C. Australia 11°56S 130°57E 60 B5
Gambier, Îs. French Polynesia 23°8S 134°58W 65 K14
Gambier Is. Australia 35°3S 136°30E 63 F2
Gambo Canada 48°47N 54°13W 73 C9
Gamboli Pakistan 29°53N 68°24E 42 E3
Gamboma Congo 1°55S 15°52E 52 E3
Gamka → S. Africa 33°18S 21°39E 56 E3
Gamkab → Namibia 28°4S 17°54E 56 D2
Gamlakarleby = Kokkola Finland 63°50N 23°8E 8 E20
Gammon → Canada 51°24N 95°44W 71 C9
Gammon Ranges △ Australia 30°38S 139°8E 63 E2
Gamtoos → S. Africa 33°58S 25°1E 56 E4
Gan Jiang → China 29°15N 116°0E 33 D6
Ganado U.S.A. 35°43N 109°33W 77 J9
Gananoque Canada 44°20N 76°10W 83 B8
Ganāveh Iran 29°35N 50°35E 45 D6
Gäncä Azerbaijan 40°45N 46°20E 19 F8
Gancheng China 18°51N 108°37E 38 C7
Gand = Gent Belgium 51°2N 3°42E 15 C3
Ganda Angola 13°3S 14°35E 53 G2
Gandajika Dem. Rep. of the Congo 6°46S 23°58E 52 F4
Gandak → India 25°39N 85°13E 43 G11
Gandava Pakistan 28°32N 67°32E 42 E2
Gander Canada 48°58N 54°35W 73 C9
Gander L. Canada 48°58N 54°35W 73 C9
Ganderowe Falls Zimbabwe 17°20S 29°10E 55 F2
Gandhi Sagar India 24°40N 75°40E 42 G6
Gandhinagar India 23°15N 72°45E 42 H5
Gandia Spain 38°58N 0°9W 21 C5
Gando, Pta. Canary Is. 27°55N 15°22W 24 G4
Ganedidalem = Gani Indonesia 0°48S 128°14E 37 E7
Ganga → India 23°20N 90°30E 43 H14
Ganga Sagar India 21°38N 88°5E 43 J13
Gangan → India 28°38N 78°58E 43 E8
Ganganagar India 29°56N 73°56E 42 E5
Gangapur India 26°32N 76°49E 42 F7
Gangaw Burma 22°5N 94°5E 41 H19
Gangdisê Shan China 31°20N 81°0E 43 D9
Ganges = Ganga → India 23°20N 90°30E 43 H14
Ganges Canada 48°51N 123°31W 70 D4
Ganges, Mouths of the India 21°30N 90°0E 43 J14
Ganggyeong S. Korea 36°10N 127°0E 35 F14
Ganghwa S. Korea 37°45N 126°30E 35 F14
Gangneung S. Korea 37°45N 128°54E 35 F15
Gangoh India 29°46N 77°18E 42 E7
Gangotri India 30°50N 79°10E 43 D8
Gangotri △ India 30°50N 79°10E 43 D8
Gangseong S. Korea 38°24N 128°30E 35 E15
Gangtok India 27°20N 88°37E 41 F16
Gangu China 34°40N 105°15E 34 G3
Gangyao China 44°12N 126°37E 35 B14
Gani Indonesia 0°48S 128°14E 37 E7
Ganj India 27°45N 78°57E 43 F8
Gannett Peak U.S.A. 43°11N 109°39W 76 E9
Ganquan China 36°20N 109°20E 34 F5
Gansu □ China 36°0N 104°0E 34 G3
Ganta Liberia 7°15N 8°59W 50 G4
Gantheaume, C. Australia 36°4S 137°32E 63 F2
Gantheaume B. Australia 27°40S 114°10E 61 E1
Gantsevichi = Hantsavichy Belarus 52°49N 26°30E 17 B14
Ganyem = Genyem Indonesia 2°46S 140°12E 37 E10
Ganyu China 34°50N 119°8E 35 G10
Ganzhou China 25°51N 114°56E 33 D6
Gao Mali 16°15N 0°5W 50 E5
Gaomi China 36°20N 119°42E 35 F10
Gaoping China 35°45N 112°55E 34 G7
Gaotang China 36°50N 116°15E 34 F9
Gaoua Burkina Faso 10°20N 3°8W 50 F5
Gaoual Guinea 11°45N 13°25W 50 F3
Gaoxiong = Kaohsiung Taiwan 22°35N 120°16E 33 D7
Gaoyang China 38°40N 115°45E 34 E8
Gaoyou Hu China 32°45N 119°20E 35 H10
Gaoyuan China 37°8N 117°58E 35 F9
Gap France 44°33N 6°5E 20 D7
Gapat → India 24°30N 82°28E 43 G10
Gapuwiyak Australia 12°25S 135°43E 62 A2
Gar China 32°10N 79°58E 32 C2
Gara, L. Ireland 53°57N 8°26W 10 C3
Garabogazköl Aylagy Turkmenistan 41°0N 53°30E 19 F9
Garachico Canary Is. 28°22N 16°46W 24 F3
Garachiné Panama 8°0N 78°12W 88 E4
Garafia Canary Is. 28°48N 17°57W 24 F2
Garagum Turkmenistan 39°30N 60°0E 45 B8
Garah Australia 29°5S 149°38E 63 D4
Garajonay Canary Is. 28°7N 17°14W 24 F2
Garamba △ Dem. Rep. of the Congo 4°10N 29°40E 54 B2
Garanhuns Brazil 8°50S 36°30W 93 E11
Garautha India 25°34N 79°18E 43 G8
Garba Tula Kenya 0°30N 38°32E 54 B4
Garberville U.S.A. 40°6N 123°48W 76 F2
Garbiyang India 30°8N 80°54E 43 D9
Gard → France 43°51N 4°37E 20 E6
Garda, L. di Italy 45°40N 10°41E 22 B4
Garde L. Canada 62°50N 106°13W 71 A7
Garden City Ga., U.S.A. 32°6N 81°9W 85 E14
Garden City Kans., U.S.A. 37°58N 100°53W 80 G3
Garden City Tex., U.S.A. 31°52N 101°29W 84 F4
Garden Grove U.S.A. 33°47N 117°55W 79 M9
Gardēz Afghan. 33°37N 69°9E 42 C3
Gardiner Maine, U.S.A. 44°14N 69°47W 81 C19
Gardiner Mont., U.S.A. 45°2N 110°22W 76 D8
Gardiners I. U.S.A. 41°6N 72°6W 83 E12
Gardner U.S.A. 42°34N 71°59W 83 D13
Gardner Canal Canada 53°27N 128°8W 70 C3
Gardnerville U.S.A. 38°56N 119°45W 78 G7
Gardo = Qardho Somali Rep. 9°30N 49°6E 47 F4
Garey U.S.A. 34°53N 120°19W 79 L6
Garfield U.S.A. 47°1N 117°9W 76 C5
Garforth U.K. 53°47N 1°24W 12 D6
Gargantua, C. Canada 47°36N 85°2W 81 B11
Gargett Australia 21°9S 148°46E 62 K6
Garibaldi ⌂ Canada 49°50N 122°40W 70 D4
Gariep, L. S. Africa 30°40S 25°40E 56 E4
Garies S. Africa 30°32S 17°59E 56 E2
Garig Gunak Barlu △ Australia 11°26S 131°58E 60 B5
Garigliano → Italy 41°13N 13°45E 22 D5
Garissa Kenya 0°25S 39°40E 54 C4
Garland Tex., U.S.A. 32°54N 96°38W 84 E6

Garland Utah, U.S.A. 41°45N 112°10W 76 F7
Garmāb Iran 35°25N 56°45E 45 C8
Garmisch-Partenkirchen Germany 47°30N 11°6E 16 E6
Garmsār Iran 35°20N 52°25E 45 C7
Garner U.S.A. 43°6N 93°36W 80 D7
Garnett U.S.A. 38°17N 95°14W 80 F6
Garo Hills India 25°30N 90°30E 43 G14
Garoe = Garoowe Somali Rep. 8°25N 48°33E 47 F4
Garonne → France 45°2N 0°36W 20 D3
Garoowe Somali Rep. 8°25N 48°33E 47 F4
Garot India 24°19N 75°41E 42 G6
Garoua Cameroon 9°19N 13°21E 51 G8
Garrauli India 25°5N 79°22E 43 G8
Garrison Mont., U.S.A. 46°31N 112°49W 76 C7
Garrison N. Dak., U.S.A. 47°40N 101°25W 80 B3
Garrison Res. = Sakakawea, L. U.S.A. 47°30N 101°25W 80 B3
Garron Pt. U.K. 55°3N 5°59W 10 A6
Garry → U.K. 56°44N 3°47W 11 E5
Garry, L. Canada 65°58N 100°18W 68 C9
Garrygala Turkmenistan 38°31N 56°29E 45 B8
Garsen Kenya 2°20S 40°5E 54 C5
Garson L. Canada 56°19N 110°2W 71 B6
Garstang U.K. 53°55N 2°46W 12 D5
Garu India 23°40N 84°14E 43 H11
Garub Namibia 26°37S 16°0E 56 D2
Garut Indonesia 7°14S 107°53E 37 G12
Garvie Mts. N.Z. 45°30S 168°50E 59 F2
Garwa = Garoua Cameroon 9°19N 13°21E 51 G8
Garwa India 24°11N 83°47E 43 G10
Gary U.S.A. 41°36N 87°20W 80 E10
Garzê China 31°38N 100°1E 32 C5
Garzón Colombia 2°10N 75°40W 92 C3
Gas-San Japan 38°32N 140°1E 30 E10
Gasan Kuli = Esenguly Turkmenistan 37°37N 53°59E 28 F6
Gascogne France 43°45N 0°20E 20 E4
Gascogne, G. de Europe 44°0N 2°0W 20 D2
Gascony = Gascogne France 43°45N 0°20E 20 E4
Gascoyne → Australia 24°52S 113°37E 61 D1
Gascoyne Junction Australia 25°2S 115°17E 61 E2
Gashaka Nigeria 7°20N 11°29E 51 G8
Gasherbrum Pakistan 35°40N 76°40E 43 B7
Gashua Nigeria 12°54N 11°0E 51 F8
Gasparillo Trin. & Tob. 10°18N 61°26W 93 K15
Gaspé Canada 48°52N 64°30W 73 C7
Gaspé, C. de Canada 48°48N 64°7W 73 C7
Gaspé Pen. = Gaspésie, Pén. de la Canada 48°45N 65°40W 73 C6
Gaspésie, Pén. de la Canada 48°45N 65°40W 73 C6
Gaspésie ⌓ Canada 48°55N 66°10W 73 C6
Gasteiz = Vitoria-Gasteiz Spain 42°50N 2°41W 21 A4
Gastonia U.S.A. 35°16N 81°11W 85 D14
Gastre Argentina 42°20S 69°15W 96 E3
Gata, C. Cyprus 34°34N 33°2E 25 E12
Gata, C. de Spain 36°41N 2°13W 21 D4
Gata, Sierra de Spain 40°20N 6°45W 21 B2
Gataga → Canada 58°35N 126°59W 70 B3
Gatchina Russia 59°35N 30°9E 9 G24
Gatehouse of Fleet U.K. 54°53N 4°12W 11 G4
Gates U.S.A. 43°9N 77°42W 82 C7
Gateshead U.K. 54°57N 1°35W 12 C6
Gatesville U.S.A. 31°26N 97°45W 84 F6
Gateway ⌓ U.S.A. 40°38N 73°51W 83 F11
Gaths Zimbabwe 20°2S 30°32E 55 G3
Gatineau Canada 45°29N 75°39W 83 A9
Gatineau → Canada 45°27N 75°42W 72 C4
Gatineau △ Canada 45°40N 76°0W 72 C4
Gatton Australia 27°32S 152°17E 63 D5
Gatún, L. Panama 9°7N 79°56W 88 E4
Gatwick, London ✕ (LGW) U.K. 51°10N 0°11W 13 F7
Gatyana S. Africa 32°16S 28°31E 57 E4
Gau Fiji 18°2S 179°18E 59 a
Gauer L. Canada 57°0N 97°50W 71 B9
Gauhati = Guwahati India 26°10N 91°45E 41 F17
Gauja → Latvia 57°10N 24°16E 9 H21
Gaujas △ Latvia 57°10N 24°50E 9 H21
Gaula → Norway 63°21N 10°14E 8 E14
Gauri Phanta India 28°41N 80°36E 43 E9
Gaustatoppen Norway 59°48N 8°40E 9 G13
Gauteng □ S. Africa 26°0S 28°0E 57 D4
Gāv Koshī Iran 28°38N 57°12E 45 D8
Gāvakān Iran 29°37N 53°10E 45 D7
Gavāter Iran 25°10N 61°31E 45 E9
Gāvbandī Iran 27°12N 53°4E 45 E7
Gavdopoula Greece 34°56N 24°0E 25 E6
Gavdos Greece 34°50N 24°5E 25 E6
Gaviota U.S.A. 34°29N 120°13W 79 L6
Gāvkhūnī, Bāţlāq-e Iran 32°6N 52°52E 45 C7
Gävle Sweden 60°40N 17°9E 8 F17
Gawachab Namibia 27°4S 17°55E 56 D2
Gawilgarh Hills India 21°15N 76°45E 40 J10
Gawler Australia 34°30S 138°42E 63 E2
Gawler Ranges Australia 32°30S 135°45E 63 E2
Gaxun Nur China 42°22N 100°30E 32 B5
Gay Russia 51°27N 58°27E 18 D10
Gaya India 24°47N 85°4E 43 G11
Gaya Niger 11°52N 3°28E 50 F6
Gaylord U.S.A. 45°2N 84°41W 81 C11
Gayndah Australia 25°35S 151°32E 63 D5
Gaysin = Haysyn Ukraine 48°57N 29°25E 17 D15
Gayvoron = Hayvoron Ukraine 48°22N 29°52E 17 D15
Gaza Gaza Strip 31°30N 34°28E 46 D3
Gaza □ Mozam. 23°10S 32°45E 57 C5
Gaza Strip ■ Asia 31°29N 34°25E 46 D3
Gazanjyk = Bereket Turkmenistan 39°16N 55°32E 45 B7
Gāzbor Iran 28°5N 58°51E 45 D8
Gazi Dem. Rep. of the Congo 1°3N 24°30E 54 B1
Gaziantep Turkey 37°6N 37°23E 44 B3
Gazimağusa = Famagusta Cyprus 35°8N 33°55E 25 D12
Gcoverega Botswana 19°8S 24°18E 56 B3
Gcuwa S. Africa 32°20S 28°11E 57 E4
Gdańsk Poland 54°22N 18°40E 17 A10
Gdańska, Zatoka Poland 54°30N 19°20E 17 A10
Gdov Russia 58°48N 27°55E 9 G22
Gdynia Poland 54°35N 18°33E 17 A10
Gebe Indonesia 0°5N 129°25E 37 D7
Gebze Turkey 40°47N 29°25E 23 D13
Gedaref Sudan 14°2N 35°28E 51 F13
Gediz → Turkey 38°35N 26°48E 23 E12
Gedser Denmark 54°35N 11°55E 9 J14
Gedung, Pulau Malaysia 5°17N 100°23E 39 c
Geegully Cr. → Australia 18°32S 123°41E 60 C3
Geel Belgium 51°10N 4°59E 15 C4
Geelong Australia 38°10S 144°22E 63 F3
Geelvink B. = Cenderwasih, Teluk Indonesia 3°0S 135°20E 37 E9
Geelvink Chan. Australia 28°30S 114°0E 61 E1
Geesthacht Germany 53°26N 10°22E 16 B6
Geidam Nigeria 12°57N 11°57E 51 F8
Geikie → Canada 57°45N 103°52W 71 B8
Geikie Gorge △ Australia 18°3S 125°41E 60 C4
Geistown U.S.A. 40°18N 78°52W 82 F6
Geita Tanzania 2°48S 32°12E 54 C3
Gejiu China 23°20N 103°10E 32 D5
Gel, Meydān-e Iran 29°4N 54°50E 45 D7
Gela Italy 37°4N 14°15E 22 F6
Gelang Patah Malaysia 1°27N 103°35E 39 d
Gelderland □ Neths. 52°5N 6°10E 15 B6
Geldrop Neths. 51°25N 5°32E 15 C5
Geleen Neths. 50°57N 5°49E 15 D5
Gelib = Jilib Somali Rep. 0°29N 42°46E 47 G3
Gelibolu Turkey 40°28N 26°43E 23 D12
Gelsenkirchen Germany 51°32N 7°6E 16 C4
Gelugur Malaysia 5°22N 100°18E 39 c
Gemas Malaysia 2°37N 102°36E 39 L4
Gembloux Belgium 50°34N 4°43E 15 D4
Gemena Dem. Rep. of the Congo 3°13N 19°48E 52 D3
Gemerek Turkey 39°15N 36°10E 44 B3
Gemlik Turkey 40°26N 29°9E 23 D13
Gemsbok △ Botswana 25°5S 21°1E 56 D3
Genadi Greece 36°2N 27°56E 25 C9
Genale → Ethiopia 6°2N 39°1E 47 F2
General Acha Argentina 37°20S 64°38W 94 D3
General Alvear B. Aires, Argentina 36°0S 60°0W 94 D4
General Alvear Mendoza, Argentina 35°0S 67°40W 94 D2
General Artigas Paraguay 26°52S 56°16W 94 B4
General Belgrano Argentina 36°35S 58°47W 94 D4
General Bernardo O'Higgins Antarctica 63°0S 58°3W 5 C18
General Cabrera Argentina 32°53S 63°52W 94 C3
General Cepeda Mexico 25°21N 101°22W 86 B4
General Guido Argentina 36°40S 57°50W 94 D4
General Juan Madariaga Argentina 37°0S 57°0W 94 D4
General La Madrid Argentina 37°17S 61°20W 94 D3
General MacArthur Phil. 11°18N 125°28E 37 B7
General Martin Miguel de Güemes Argentina 24°50S 65°0W 94 A3
General Pico Argentina 35°45S 63°50W 94 D3
General Pinedo Argentina 27°15S 61°20W 94 B3
General Pinto Argentina 34°45S 61°50W 94 C3
General Roca Argentina 39°2S 67°35W 96 D3
General Santos Phil. 6°5N 125°14E 37 C7
General Treviño Mexico 26°14N 99°29W 87 B5
General Trías Mexico 28°21N 106°22W 86 B3
General Viamonte Argentina 35°1S 61°3W 94 D3
General Villegas Argentina 35°5S 63°0W 94 D3
Genesee Idaho, U.S.A. 46°33N 116°56W 76 C5
Genesee Pa., U.S.A. 41°59N 77°54W 82 E7
Genesee → U.S.A. 43°16N 77°36W 82 C7
Geneseo Ill., U.S.A. 41°27N 90°9W 80 E8
Geneseo N.Y., U.S.A. 42°48N 77°49W 82 D7
Geneva = Genève Switz. 46°12N 6°9E 20 C7
Geneva Ala., U.S.A. 31°2N 85°52W 85 F12
Geneva N.Y., U.S.A. 42°52N 76°59W 82 D8
Geneva Nebr., U.S.A. 40°32N 97°36W 80 E5
Geneva Ohio, U.S.A. 41°48N 80°57W 82 E4
Geneva, L. = Léman, L. Europe 46°26N 6°30E 20 C7
Genève Switz. 46°12N 6°9E 20 C7
Genil → Spain 37°42N 5°19W 21 D3
Genk Belgium 50°58N 5°32E 15 D5
Gennargentu, Mti. del Italy 40°1N 9°19E 22 D3
Genoa = Génova Italy 44°25N 8°57E 20 D8
Genoa Australia 37°29S 149°35E 63 F4
Genoa N.Y., U.S.A. 42°40N 76°32W 83 D8
Genoa Nebr., U.S.A. 41°27N 97°44W 80 E5
Genoa Nev., U.S.A. 39°2N 119°50W 78 F7
Génova Italy 44°25N 8°57E 20 D8
Génova, G. di Italy 44°0N 9°0E 22 C3
Genriyetty, Ostrov Russia 77°6N 156°30E 29 B16
Gent Belgium 51°2N 3°42E 15 C3
Genteng Bali, Indonesia 8°22S 114°9E 37 J17
Genteng Jawa Barat, Indonesia 7°22S 106°24E 37 G12
Genyem Indonesia 2°46S 140°12E 37 E10
Geochang S. Korea 35°41N 127°55E 35 G14
Geographe B. Australia 33°30S 115°15E 61 F2
Geographe Chan. Australia 24°30S 113°0E 61 D1
Georga, Zemlya Russia 80°30N 49°0E 28 A5
George S. Africa 33°58S 22°29E 56 E3
George → Canada 58°49N 66°10W 73 A6
George, L. N.S.W., Australia 35°10S 149°25E 63 F4
George, L. S. Austral., Australia 37°25S 140°0E 63 F3
George, L. W. Austral., Australia 22°45S 123°40E 60 D3
George, L. Uganda 0°5N 30°10E 54 B3
George, L. Fla., U.S.A. 29°17N 81°36W 85 G14
George, L. N.Y., U.S.A. 43°37N 73°33W 83 C11
George Gill Ra. Australia 24°22S 131°45E 60 D5
George Pt. Australia 20°6S 148°36E 62 J6
George River = Kangiqsualujjuaq Canada 58°30N 65°59W 69 D13
George Sound N.Z. 44°52S 167°25E 59 F1
George Town Australia 41°6S 146°49E 63 G4
George Town Bahamas 23°33N 75°47W 88 B4
George Town Cayman Is. 19°20N 81°24W 88 C3
George Town Malaysia 5°25N 100°20E 39 c
George V Land Antarctica 69°0S 148°0E 5 C10
George VI Sound Antarctica 71°0S 68°0W 5 D17
George West U.S.A. 28°20N 98°7W 84 G5
Georgetown = Janjanbureh Gambia 13°30N 14°47W 50 F3
Georgetown Australia 18°17S 143°33E 62 B3
Georgetown Ont., Canada 43°40N 79°56W 82 C5
Georgetown P.E.I., Canada 46°13N 62°24W 73 C7
Georgetown Guyana 6°50N 58°12W 92 B7
Georgetown Calif., U.S.A. 38°54N 120°50W 78 G6
Georgetown Colo., U.S.A. 39°42N 105°42W 76 G11
Georgetown Ky., U.S.A. 38°13N 84°33W 81 F11
Georgetown N.Y., U.S.A. 42°46N 75°44W 83 D9
Georgetown Ohio, U.S.A. 38°52N 83°54W 81 F12
Georgetown S.C., U.S.A. 33°23N 79°17W 85 E15
Georgetown Tex., U.S.A. 30°38N 97°41W 84 F6
Georgia □ U.S.A. 32°50N 83°15W 85 E13
Georgia ■ Asia 42°0N 43°0E 19 F7
Georgia, Str. of N. Amer. 49°25N 124°0W 78 A3
Georgia Basin S. Ocean 50°45S 35°30W 5 B1
Georgian B. Canada 45°15N 81°0W 82 A4
Georgian Bay Islands △ Canada 44°53N 79°52W 82 B5
Georgīevka Kazakhstan 49°19N 84°34E 28 E9
Georgina → Australia 23°30S 139°47E 62 C2
Georgina I. Canada 44°22N 79°17W 82 B5
Georgioupoli Greece 35°20N 24°15E 25 D6
Georgiyevsk Russia 44°12N 43°28E 19 F7
Gera Germany 50°53N 12°4E 16 C7
Geraardsbergen Belgium 50°45N 3°53E 15 D3
Geral, Serra Brazil 26°25S 50°0W 95 B6
Geral de Goiás, Serra Brazil 12°0S 46°0W 93 F9
Geraldine U.S.A. 47°36N 110°16W 76 C8
Geraldton Australia 28°48S 114°32E 61 E1
Geraldton Canada 49°44N 86°59W 72 C2
Gereshk Afghan. 31°47N 64°35E 40 D4
Gerik Malaysia 5°50N 101°15E 39 K3
Gering U.S.A. 41°50N 103°40W 80 E2
Gerlach U.S.A. 40°39N 119°21W 76 F4
German Bight = Deutsche Bucht Germany 54°15N 8°0E 16 A5
Germansen Landing Canada 55°43N 124°40W 70 B4
Germantown U.S.A. 35°5N 89°49W 85 D10
Germany ■ Europe 51°0N 10°0E 16 C6
Germī Iran 39°1N 48°3E 45 B6
Germiston S. Africa 26°13S 28°10E 57 D4
Gernika-Lumo Spain 43°19N 2°40W 21 A4
Gero Japan 35°48N 137°14E 31 G8
Gerokgak Indonesia 8°11S 114°27E 37 J17
Gerona = Girona Spain 41°58N 2°46E 21 B7
Geropotamos → Greece 35°3N 24°50E 25 D6
Gerrard Canada 50°30N 117°17W 70 C5
Gertak Sanggul Malaysia 5°17N 100°12E 39 c
Gertak Sanggul, Tanjung Malaysia 5°16N 100°11E 39 c
Gerung Indonesia 8°43S 116°7E 37 K19
Geser Indonesia 3°50S 130°54E 37 E8
Getafe Spain 40°18N 3°43W 21 B4
Gettysburg Pa., U.S.A. 39°50N 77°14W 81 F15
Gettysburg S. Dak., U.S.A. 45°1N 99°57W 80 C4
Getxo Spain 43°21N 2°59W 21 A4
Getz Ice Shelf Antarctica 75°0S 130°0W 5 D14
Geyser U.S.A. 47°16N 110°30W 76 C8
Geyserville U.S.A. 38°42N 122°54W 78 G4
Ghadāf, W. al → Iraq 32°56N 43°30E 44 C4
Ghadāmis Libya 30°11N 9°29E 51 B8
Ghaggar → India 29°30N 74°53E 42 E6
Ghaghara → India 25°45N 84°40E 43 G11
Ghaghat → Bangla. 25°19N 89°38E 43 G13
Ghagra India 23°17N 84°33E 43 H11
Ghagra → India 27°29N 81°9E 43 F9
Ghallamane Mauritania 23°15N 10°0W 50 D4
Ghana ■ W. Afr. 8°0N 1°0W 50 G5
Ghansor India 22°39N 80°1E 43 H9
Ghanzi Botswana 21°50S 21°34E 56 C3
Gharb Bahr el Ghazâl □ Sudan 7°30N 27°30E 48 F6
Ghardaïa Algeria 32°20N 3°37E 50 B6
Gharm Tajikistan 39°0N 70°20E 28 F8
Gharyān Libya 32°10N 13°0E 51 B8
Ghat Libya 24°59N 10°11E 51 D8
Ghatal India 22°40N 87°46E 43 H12
Ghatampur India 26°8N 80°13E 43 F9
Ghats, Eastern India 14°0N 78°50E 40 N11
Ghats, Western India 14°0N 75°0E 40 N9
Ghatsila India 22°36N 86°29E 43 H12
Ghaţţī Si. Arabia 31°16N 37°31E 44 D3
Ghawdex = Gozo Malta 36°3N 14°15E 25 C1
Ghazal, Bahr el → Chad 13°0N 15°47E 51 F9
Ghazâl, Bahr el → Sudan 9°31N 30°25E 51 G12
Ghaziabad India 28°42N 77°26E 42 E7
Ghazipur India 25°38N 83°35E 43 G10
Ghaznī Afghan. 33°30N 68°28E 42 C3
Ghaznī □ Afghan. 32°10N 68°20E 40 C6
Ghent = Gent Belgium 51°2N 3°42E 15 C3
Gheorghe Gheorghiu-Dej = Oneşti Romania 46°17N 26°47E 17 E14
Ghīnah, Wādī al → Si. Arabia 30°27N 38°14E 44 D3
Ghizar → Pakistan 36°15N 73°43E 43 A5
Ghotaru India 27°20N 70°1E 42 F4
Ghotki Pakistan 28°5N 69°21E 42 E3
Ghowr □ Afghan. 34°0N 64°20E 40 C4
Ghughri India 22°39N 80°41E 43 H9
Ghugus India 19°58N 79°12E 40 K11
Ghulam Mohammad Barrage Pakistan 25°30N 68°20E 42 G3
Ghūrīān Afghan. 34°17N 61°25E 40 B2
Gia Dinh Vietnam 10°49N 106°42E 39 G6
Gia Lai = Plei Ku Vietnam 13°57N 108°0E 38 F7
Gia Nghia Vietnam 11°58N 107°42E 39 G6
Gia Ngoc Vietnam 14°50N 108°58E 38 E7
Gia Vuc Vietnam 14°42N 108°34E 38 E7
Giamama = Jamaame Somali Rep. 0°4N 42°44E 47 G3
Gianitsa Greece 40°46N 22°24E 23 D10
Giant Forest U.S.A. 36°36N 118°43W 78 J8
Giant Sequoia ⌓ U.S.A. 36°10N 118°35W 78 K8
Giants Causeway U.K. 55°16N 6°29W 10 A5
Gianyar Indonesia 8°32S 115°20E 37 K18
Giarabub = Al Jaghbūb Libya 29°42N 24°38E 51 C10
Giarre Italy 37°43N 15°11E 22 F6
Gibara Cuba 21°9N 76°11W 88 B4
Gibb River Australia 16°26S 126°26E 60 C4
Gibbon U.S.A. 40°45N 98°51W 80 E4
Gibeon Namibia 25°9S 17°43E 56 D2
Gibraltar ☒ Europe 36°7N 5°22W 21 D3
Gibraltar, Str. of Medit. S. 35°55N 5°40W 21 E3
Gibraltar Range △ Australia 29°31S 152°19E 63 D5
Gibson Desert Australia 24°0S 126°0E 60 D4
Gibsons Canada 49°24N 123°32W 70 D4
Gibsonville U.S.A. 39°46N 120°54W 78 F6
Giddings U.S.A. 30°11N 96°56W 84 F6
Giebnegáisi = Kebnekaise Sweden 67°53N 18°33E 8 C18
Giessen Germany 50°34N 8°41E 16 C5
Gīfān Iran 37°54N 57°28E 45 B8
Gift Lake Canada 55°53N 115°49W 70 B5
Gifu Japan 35°30N 136°45E 31 G8
Gifu □ Japan 35°40N 137°0E 31 G8
Giganta, Sa. de la Mexico 26°0N 111°39W 86 B2
Gigha U.K. 55°42N 5°44W 11 F3
Giglio Italy 42°20N 10°52E 22 C4
Gijón Spain 43°32N 5°42W 21 A3
Gil I. Canada 53°12N 129°15W 70 C3
Gila → U.S.A. 32°43N 114°33W 77 K6
Gila Bend U.S.A. 32°57N 112°43W 77 K7
Gila Bend Mts. U.S.A. 33°10N 113°0W 77 K7
Gila Cliff Dwellings ⌓ U.S.A. 33°12N 108°16W 77 K9
Gīlān □ Iran 37°0N 50°0E 45 B6
Gilbert → Australia 16°35S 141°15E 62 B3
Gilbert Is. Kiribati 1°0N 172°0E 58 A10
Gilbert River Australia 18°9S 142°52E 62 B3
Gilbert Seamounts Pac. Oc. 52°50N 150°10W 4 D18
Gilead U.S.A. 44°24N 70°59W 83 B14
Gilf el Kebîr, Hadabat el Egypt 23°50N 25°50E 51 D11
Gilford I. Canada 50°40N 126°30W 70 C3
Gilgandra Australia 31°43S 148°39E 63 E4
Gilgil Kenya 0°30S 36°20E 54 C4
Gilgit India 35°50N 74°15E 43 B6
Gilgit → Pakistan 35°44N 74°37E 43 B6
Gili ⌓ Mozam. 16°39S 38°27E 55 F4
Gilimanuk Indonesia 8°10S 114°26E 37 J17
Gillam Canada 56°20N 94°40W 71 B10
Gillen, L. Australia 26°11S 124°38E 61 E3
Gilles, L. Australia 32°50S 136°45E 63 E2
Gillette U.S.A. 44°18N 105°30W 76 D11
Gilliat Australia 20°40S 141°28E 62 C3
Gillingham U.K. 51°23N 0°33E 13 F8
Gilmer U.S.A. 32°44N 94°57W 84 E7
Gilmore, L. Australia 32°29S 121°37E 61 F3
Gilmour Canada 44°48N 77°37W 82 B7
Gilroy U.S.A. 37°1N 121°34W 78 H5
Gimcheon S. Korea 36°11N 128°4E 35 F15
Gimhae S. Korea 35°14N 128°53E 35 G15
Gimhwa S. Korea 38°17N 127°28E 35 E14
Gimie, Mt St. Lucia 13°54N 61°0W 89 f
Gimje S. Korea 35°48N 126°45E 35 G14
Gimli Canada 50°40N 97°0W 71 C9
Gin Gin Australia 25°0S 151°58E 63 D5
Gingin Australia 31°22S 115°54E 61 F2
Gingindlovu S. Africa 29°2S 31°30E 57 D5
Ginir Ethiopia 7°6N 40°40E 47 F3
Giofyros → Greece 35°20N 25°6E 25 D7
Giohar = Jawhar Somali Rep. 2°48N 45°30E 47 G4
Giona, Oros Greece 38°38N 22°14E 23 E10
Gir △ India 21°0N 71°0E 42 J4
Gir Hills India 21°0N 71°0E 42 J
Girab India 26°2N 70°38E 42 F
Girâfi, W. → Egypt 29°58N 34°39E 46 F
Girard St. Lucia 13°59N 60°57W 89 D
Girard Kans., U.S.A. 37°31N 94°51W 80 G
Girard Ohio, U.S.A. 41°9N 80°42W 82 E
Girard Pa., U.S.A. 42°0N 80°19W 82 E
Girdle Ness U.K. 57°9N 2°3W 11 D
Giresun Turkey 40°55N 38°30E 19 F
Girga Egypt 26°17N 31°55E 51 C1
Giri → India 30°28N 77°41E 42 D
Giridih India 24°10N 86°21E 43 G1
Giriftu Kenya 1°59N 39°46E 54 B
Giriyondo S. Africa 23°15S 31°40E 57 C
Girne = Kyrenia Cyprus 35°20N 33°20E 25 D1
Giron = Kiruna Sweden 67°52N 20°15E 8 C1
Girona Spain 41°58N 2°46E 21 B
Gironde → France 45°32N 1°7W 20 D
Girraween △ Australia 28°46S 151°54E 63 D
Girrigun △ Australia 18°15S 145°32E 62 B
Giru Australia 19°30S 147°5E 62 B
Girvan U.K. 55°14N 4°51W 11 F
Gisborne N.Z. 38°39S 178°5E 59 C
Gisenyi Rwanda 1°41S 29°15E 54 C
Gislaved Sweden 57°19N 13°32E 9 H1
Gitega Burundi 3°26S 29°56E 54 C
Githio Greece 36°46N 22°34E 23 F1
Giuba = Juba → Somali Rep. 1°30N 42°35E 47 G
Giurgiu Romania 43°52N 25°57E 17 G1
Giza = El Gîza Egypt 30°0N 31°12E 51 C1
Giza Pyramids Egypt 29°58N 31°9E 51 C1
Gizab Afghan. 33°22N 66°17E 42 C
Gizhiga Russia 62°3N 160°30E 29 C1
Gizhiginskaya Guba Russia 61°0N 158°0E 29 C1
Giżycko Poland 54°2N 21°48E 17 A1
Gjirokastër Albania 40°7N 20°10E 23 D
Gjoa Haven Canada 68°38N 95°53W 68 C1
Gjøvik Norway 60°47N 10°43E 8 F1
Glace Bay Canada 46°11N 59°58W 73 C
Glacier △ Canada 51°15N 117°30W 70 C
Glacier △ U.S.A. 48°42N 113°48W 76 B
Glacier Bay ⌓ U.S.A. 58°45N 136°30W 70 B
Glacier Peak U.S.A. 48°7N 121°7W 76 B
Gladewater U.S.A. 32°33N 94°56W 84 E
Gladstone Queens., Australia 23°52S 151°16E 62 C
Gladstone S. Austral., Australia 33°15S 138°22E 63 E
Gladstone Canada 50°13N 98°57W 71 C
Gladstone U.S.A. 45°51N 87°1W 80 C1
Gladwin U.S.A. 43°59N 84°29W 81 D1
Glagah Indonesia 8°13S 114°18E 37 J1
Glåma = Glomma → Norway 59°12N 10°57E 9 G1
Gláma Iceland 65°48N 23°0W 8 D
Glamis U.S.A. 32°55N 115°5W 79 N1
Glamorgan, Vale of □ U.K. 51°28N 3°25W 13 F
Glasco Kans., U.S.A. 39°22N 97°50W 80 F
Glasco N.Y., U.S.A. 42°3N 73°57W 83 D1
Glasgow U.K. 55°51N 4°15W 11 F
Glasgow Ky., U.S.A. 37°0N 85°55W 81 G1
Glasgow Mont., U.S.A. 48°12N 106°38W 76 B1
Glasgow, City of □ U.K. 55°51N 4°12W 11 F
Glasgow Int. ✕ (GLA) U.K. 55°51N 4°21W 11 F
Glaslyn Canada 53°22N 108°21W 71 C
Glastonbury U.K. 51°9N 2°43W 13 F
Glastonbury U.S.A. 41°43N 72°37W 83 E1
Glazov Russia 58°9N 52°40E 18 C
Gleichen Canada 50°52N 113°3W 70 C
Gleiwitz = Gliwice Poland 50°22N 18°41E 17 C1
Glen U.S.A. 44°7N 71°11W 83 B1
Glen Affric U.K. 57°17N 5°1W 11 D
Glen Canyon U.S.A. 37°30N 110°40W 77 H
Glen Canyon ⌓ U.S.A. 37°15N 111°0W 77 H
Glen Canyon Dam U.S.A. 36°57N 111°29W 77 H
Glen Coe U.K. 56°40N 5°0W 11 E
Glen Cove U.S.A. 40°51N 73°38W 83 F1
Glen Garry U.K. 57°3N 5°7W 11 D
Glen Innes Australia 29°44S 151°44E 63 D
Glen Lyon U.S.A. 41°10N 76°5W 83 E
Glen Mor U.K. 57°9N 4°37W 11 D
Glen More ⌓ U.K. 57°8N 3°40W 11 D
Glen Moriston U.K. 57°11N 4°52W 11 D
Glen Robertson Canada 45°22N 74°30W 83 A1
Glen Spean U.K. 56°53N 4°40W 11 E
Glen Ullin U.S.A. 46°49N 101°50W 80 B
Glenallen U.S.A. 62°7N 145°33W 68 C
Glenariff △ Ireland 55°2N 6°10W 10 A
Glenbeigh Ireland 52°3N 9°58W 10 D
Glencoe Canada 42°45N 81°43W 82 D
Glencoe S. Africa 28°11S 30°11E 57 D
Glencoe U.S.A. 44°46N 94°9W 80 C
Glencolumbkille Ireland 54°43N 8°42W 10 B
Glendale Ariz., U.S.A. 33°32N 112°11W 77 K
Glendale Calif., U.S.A. 34°9N 118°15W 79 L
Glendale Zimbabwe 17°22S 31°5E 55 F
Glendive U.S.A. 47°7N 104°43W 76 C1
Glendo U.S.A. 42°30N 105°2W 76 E1
Glenelg → Australia 38°4S 140°59E 63 F
Glenfield U.S.A. 43°43N 75°24W 83 C
Glengad Hd. Ireland 55°20N 7°10W 10 A
Glengarriff Ireland 51°45N 9°34W 10 E
Glenmont U.S.A. 40°31N 82°6W 82 F
Glenmorgan Australia 27°14S 149°42E 63 D
Glenn U.S.A. 39°31N 122°1W 78 F
Glennamaddy Ireland 53°37N 8°33W 10 C
Glenns Ferry U.S.A. 42°57N 115°18W 76 E
Glenora Canada 44°2N 77°3W 82 B
Glenorchy Australia 42°49S 147°18E 63 G
Glenore Australia 17°50S 141°12E 62 B
Glenreagh Australia 30°2S 153°1E 63 E

enrock U.S.A. 42°52N 105°52W 76 E11
enrothes U.K. 56°12N 3°10W 11 E5
ens Falls U.S.A. 43°19N 73°39W 83 C11
enside U.S.A. 40°6N 75°9W 83 F9
enties Ireland 54°49N 8°16W 10 B3
enveagh △ Ireland 55°3N 8°1W 10 A3
enville U.S.A. 38°56N 80°50W 81 F13
enwood Canada 49°0N 54°58W 73 C9
enwood Ark., U.S.A. 34°20N 93°33W 84 D8
enwood Iowa, U.S.A. 41°3N 95°45W 80 E6
enwood Minn., U.S.A. 45°39N 95°23W 80 C6
nwood Wash., U.S.A. 46°1N 121°17W 78 D5
enwood Springs
U.S.A. 39°33N 107°19W 76 G10
ettinganes Iceland 65°30N 13°37W 8 D7
n Ireland 52°34N 9°17W 10 D2
wice Poland 50°22N 18°41E 17 C10
be U.S.A. 33°24N 110°47W 77 K8
gów Poland 51°37N 16°5E 16 C9
mma → Norway 59°12N 10°57E 9 G14
rieuses, Îs. Ind. Oc. 11°30S 47°20E 57 A8
ssop U.K. 53°27N 1°56W 12 D6
ucester Australia 32°0S 151°59E 63 E5
ucester U.K. 51°53N 2°15W 13 F5
ucester U.S.A. 42°37N 70°40W 83 D14
ucester I. Australia 20°0S 148°30E 62 J6
ucester Island △
Australia 20°2S 148°30E 62 J6
ucester Point
U.S.A. 37°15N 76°30W 81 G15
ucestershire □ U.K. 51°46N 2°15W 13 F5
versville U.S.A. 43°3N 74°21W 83 C10
vertown Canada 48°40N 54°3W 73 C9
sk Belarus 52°53N 28°41E 17 B15
ünd Austria 48°45N 15°0E 16 D8
unden Austria 47°55N 13°48E 16 E7
iezno Poland 52°30N 17°35E 17 B9
owangerup Australia 33°58S 117°59E 61 F2
Cong Vietnam 10°22N 106°40E 39 G6
-no-ura Japan 33°44N 129°40E 31 H4
a India 15°33N 73°59E 40 M8
a □ India 15°33N 73°59E 40 M8
alen Hd. Australia 36°33S 150°4E 63 F5
alpara India 26°10N 90°40E 41 F17
altor India 22°43N 87°10E 43 H12
alundo Ghat Bangla. 23°50N 89°47E 43 H13
at Fell U.K. 55°38N 5°11W 11 F3
ba Ethiopia 7°1N 39°59E 47 F2
ba Mozam. 26°15S 32°13E 57 D5
babis Namibia 22°30S 19°0E 56 C2
bi Asia 44°0N 110°0E 34 C6
bō Japan 33°53N 135°10E 31 H7
chas Namibia 24°59S 18°55E 56 C2
dalming U.K. 51°11N 0°36W 13 F7
davari → India 16°25N 82°18E 41 L13
davari Pt. India 17°0N 82°20E 41 L13
dbout Canada 49°20N 67°38W 73 C6
dda India 24°50N 87°13E 43 G12
derich Canada 43°45N 81°41W 82 C3
dfrey Ra. Australia 24°0S 117°0E 61 D2
dhavn = Qeqertarsuaq
Greenland 69°15N 53°38W 4 C5
dhra India 22°49N 73°40E 42 H5
doy Cruz Argentina 32°56S 68°52W 94 C2
ds → Canada 56°22N 92°51W 72 A1
ds L. Canada 54°40N 94°15W 72 B1
ds River Canada 54°50N 94°50W 71 C10
dthåb = Nuuk
Greenland 64°10N 51°35W 67 C14
ie Hoop, Kaap die = Good
Hope, C. of S. Africa 34°24S 18°30E 56 E2
eland, L. au Canada 49°50N 76°48W 72 C4
elands, L. aux Canada 55°27N 64°17W 73 A7
ree Neths. 51°50N 4°0E 15 C3
es Neths. 51°30N 3°55E 15 C3
estown U.S.A. 43°1N 71°36W 83 C13
gama Canada 47°35N 81°43W 72 C3
gebic, L. U.S.A. 46°30N 89°35W 80 B9
gra = Ghaghara →
India 25°45N 84°40E 43 G11
grîal Sudan 8°30N 28°8E 51 G11
hana India 29°8N 76°42E 42 E7
harganj India 23°1N 77°41E 42 H7
i → India 22°4N 74°46E 42 H6
iânia Brazil 16°43S 49°20W 93 G9
iás Brazil 15°55S 50°10W 93 G8
iás □ Brazil 12°10S 48°0W 93 F9
o-Erê Brazil 24°12S 53°1W 95 A5
ō Japan 34°21N 135°42E 31 G7
ra Pakistan 31°10N 72°40E 42 D5
kçeada Turkey 40°10N 25°50E 23 D11
kova Körfezi Turkey 36°55N 27°50E 23 F12
ksu → Turkey 36°19N 34°5E 44 B2
kteik Burma 22°26N 97°0E 41 H20
kurt Pakistan 29°40N 67°26E 42 E2
kwe Zimbabwe 18°7S 28°58E 57 B4
a India 28°3N 80°32E 43 E9
akganj India 26°8N 89°52E 43 F13
lan Heights = Hagolan
Syria 33°0N 35°45E 46 C4
lshkerd Iran 27°59N 57°16E 45 E8
chikha Russia 71°45N 83°30E 4 B12
conda U.S.A. 40°58N 117°30W 76 F5
d U.S.A. 41°52N 77°50W 82 E7
d Beach U.S.A. 42°25N 124°25W 76 E1
d Coast W. Afr. 4°0N 1°40W 50 H5
d Hill U.S.A. 42°26N 123°3W 76 E2
d River Canada 49°46N 126°3W 70 D3
den Canada 51°20N 116°59W 70 C5
den B. N.Z. 40°40S 172°50E 59 D4
den Gate U.S.A. 37°48N 122°29W 77 H2
den Gate Highlands △
Africa 28°40S 28°40E 57 D4
den Hinde Canada 49°40N 125°44W 70 D3
den Lake Canada 45°34N 77°21W 82 A7
den Spike ⌂ U.S.A. 41°37N 112°33W 76 F7
den Vale Ireland 52°33N 8°17W 10 D3
Goldendale U.S.A. 45°49N 120°50W 76 D3
Goldfield U.S.A. 37°42N 117°14W 77 H5
Goldsand L. Canada 57°2N 101°8W 71 B8
Goldsboro U.S.A. 35°23N 77°59W 85 D16
Goldsmith U.S.A. 31°59N 102°37W 84 F3
Goldthwaite U.S.A. 31°27N 98°34W 84 F5
Goleniów Poland 53°35N 14°50E 16 B8
Golestān □ Iran 37°20N 55°25E 45 B7
Golestānak Iran 30°36N 54°14E 45 D7
Goleta U.S.A. 34°27N 119°50W 79 L7
Golfito Costa Rica 8°41N 83°5W 88 E3
Golfo Aranci Italy 40°59N 9°38E 22 D3
Goliad U.S.A. 28°40N 97°23W 84 G6
Golpāyegān Iran 33°27N 50°18E 45 C6
Golra Pakistan 33°37N 72°56E 42 C5
Golspie U.K. 57°58N 3°59W 11 D5
Goma
Dem. Rep. of the Congo 1°37S 29°10E 54 C2
Gomal Pass Pakistan 31°56N 69°20E 42 D3
Gomati → India 25°32N 83°11E 43 G10
Gombari
Dem. Rep. of the Congo 2°45N 29°3E 54 B2
Gombe Nigeria 10°19N 11°2E 51 F8
Gombe → Tanzania 4°38S 31°40E 54 C3
Gomel = Homyel Belarus 52°28N 31°0E 17 B16
Gomera Canary Is. 28°7N 17°14W 24 F2
Gómez Palacio Mexico 25°34N 103°30W 86 B4
Gomīshān Iran 37°4N 54°6E 45 B7
Gomogomo Indonesia 6°39S 134°43E 37 F8
Gomoh India 23°52N 86°10E 43 H12
Gompa = Ganta Liberia 7°15N 8°59W 50 G4
Gonābād Iran 34°15N 58°45E 45 C8
Gonaïves Haiti 19°20N 72°42W 89 C5
Gonarezhou △ Zimbabwe 21°32S 31°55E 55 G3
Gonâve, G. de la Haiti 19°29N 72°42W 89 C5
Gonâve, Île de la Haiti 18°51N 73°3W 89 C5
Gonbad-e Kāvūs Iran 37°20N 55°25E 45 B7
Gonda India 27°9N 81°58E 43 F9
Gondal India 21°58N 70°52E 42 J4
Gonder Ethiopia 12°39N 37°30E 47 E2
Gondia India 21°23N 80°10E 40 J12
Gondola Mozam. 19°10S 33°37E 55 F3
Gönen Turkey 40°6N 27°39E 23 D12
Gongbei China 22°12N 113°32E 33 G10
Gonghe China 36°18N 100°32E 32 C5
Gongju S. Korea 36°27N 127°7E 35 F14
Gongming China 22°47N 113°53E 33 F10
Gongolgon Australia 30°21S 146°54E 63 E4
Gongzhuling China 43°30N 124°40E 35 C13
Goniri Nigeria 11°30N 12°15E 51 F8
Gonzales Calif., U.S.A. 36°30N 121°26W 78 J5
Gonzales Tex., U.S.A. 29°30N 97°27W 84 G6
González Mexico 22°48N 98°25W 87 C5
Good Hope, C. of S. Africa 34°24S 18°30E 56 E2
Good Hope Lake
Canada 59°16N 129°18W 70 B3
Gooderham Canada 44°54N 78°21W 82 B6
Goodhouse S. Africa 28°57S 18°13E 56 D2
Gooding U.S.A. 42°56N 114°43W 76 E6
Goodland U.S.A. 39°21N 101°43W 80 F3
Goodlands Mauritius 20°2S 57°39E 53 d
Goodlow Canada 56°20N 120°8W 70 B4
Goodooga Australia 29°3S 147°28E 63 D4
Goodsprings U.S.A. 35°49N 115°27W 79 K11
Goole U.K. 53°42N 0°53W 12 D7
Goolgowi Australia 33°58S 145°41E 63 E4
Goomalling Australia 31°15S 116°49E 61 F2
Goomeri Australia 26°12S 152°6E 63 D5
Goonda Mozam. 19°48S 33°57E 55 F3
Goondiwindi Australia 28°30S 150°21E 63 D5
Goongarrie, L. Australia 30°3S 121°9E 61 F3
Goongarrie △ Australia 30°7S 121°30E 61 F3
Goonyella Australia 21°47S 147°58E 62 C4
Goose → Canada 53°20N 60°35W 73 B7
Goose Creek U.S.A. 32°59N 80°2W 85 E14
Goose L. U.S.A. 41°56N 120°26W 76 F3
Gop India 22°5N 69°50E 42 H3
Gopalganj India 26°28N 84°30E 43 F11
Göppingen Germany 48°42N 9°39E 16 D5
Gorakhpur India 26°47N 83°23E 43 F10
Goražde Bos.-H. 43°38N 18°58E 23 C8
Gorda, Pta. Canary Is. 28°45N 18°0W 24 F2
Gorda, Pta. Nic. 14°20N 83°10W 88 D3
Gordan B. Australia 11°35S 130°10E 60 B5
Gordon U.S.A. 42°48N 102°12W 80 D2
Gordon → Australia 42°27S 145°30E 63 G4
Gordon Bay Canada 45°12N 79°47W 82 A5
Gordon L. Alta., Canada 56°30N 110°25W 71 B6
Gordon L. N.W.T.,
Canada 63°5N 113°11W 70 A6
Gordonvale Australia 17°5S 145°50E 62 B4
Goré Chad 7°59N 16°31E 51 G9
Gore Ethiopia 8°12N 35°32E 47 F2
Gore N.Z. 46°5S 168°58E 59 G2
Gore Bay Canada 45°57N 82°28W 72 C3
Gorey Ireland 52°41N 6°18W 10 D5
Gorg Iran 29°29N 59°43E 45 D8
Gorgān Iran 36°55N 54°30E 45 B7
Gorgona, I. Colombia 3°0N 78°10W 92 C3
Gorham U.S.A. 44°23N 71°10W 83 B13
Goriganga → India 29°45N 80°23E 43 E9
Gorinchem Neths. 51°50N 4°59E 15 C4
Goris Armenia 39°31N 46°22E 19 G8
Gorízia Italy 45°56N 13°37E 22 B5
Gorkiy = Nizhniy Novgorod
Russia 56°20N 44°0E 18 C7
Gorkovskoye Vdkhr.
Russia 57°2N 43°4E 18 C7
Gorleston U.K. 52°35N 1°44E 13 E9
Görlitz Germany 51°9N 14°58E 16 C8
Gorlovka = Horlivka
Ukraine 48°19N 38°5E 19 E6
Gorman U.S.A. 34°47N 118°51W 79 L8
Gorna Dzhumayo = Blagoevgrad
Bulgaria 42°2N 23°5E 23 C10
Gorna Oryakhovitsa
Bulgaria 43°7N 25°40E 23 C11
Gorno-Altay □ Russia 51°0N 86°0E 28 D9
Gorno-Altaysk Russia 51°50N 86°5E 28 D9
Gornozavodsk Russia 46°33N 141°50E 29 E15
Gornyatski Russia 67°32N 64°3E 18 A11
Gornyy Russia 44°57N 133°59E 30 B6
Gorodenka = Horodenka
Ukraine 48°41N 25°29E 17 D13
Gorodok = Horodok
Ukraine 49°46N 23°32E 17 D12
Gorokhov = Horokhiv
Ukraine 50°30N 24°45E 17 C13
Goromonzi Zimbabwe 17°52S 31°22E 55 F3
Gorong, Kepulauan
Indonesia 3°59S 131°25E 37 E8
Gorongosa △ Mozam. 18°50S 34°29E 57 B5
Gorongose → Mozam. 20°30S 34°40E 57 C5
Gorongoza Mozam. 18°44S 34°2E 55 F3
Gorongoza, Sa. da Mozam. 18°27S 34°2E 55 F3
Gorontalo Indonesia 0°35N 123°5E 37 D6
Gorontalo □ Indonesia 0°50N 122°20E 37 D6
Gort Ireland 53°3N 8°49W 10 C3
Gortis Greece 35°4N 24°58E 25 D6
Goryeong S. Korea 35°44N 128°15E 35 G15
Gorzów Wielkopolski
Poland 52°43N 15°15E 16 B8
Gosford Australia 33°23S 151°18E 63 E5
Goshen Calif., U.S.A. 36°21N 119°25W 78 J7
Goshen Ind., U.S.A. 41°35N 85°50W 81 E11
Goshen N.Y., U.S.A. 41°24N 74°20W 83 E10
Goshogawara Japan 40°48N 140°27E 30 D10
Goslar Germany 51°54N 10°25E 16 C6
Gospič Croatia 44°35N 15°23E 16 F8
Gosport U.K. 50°48N 1°9W 13 G6
Gosse → Australia 19°32S 134°37E 62 B1
Göta älv → Sweden 57°42N 11°54E 9 H14
Göta kanal Sweden 58°30N 15°58E 9 G16
Götaland Sweden 57°30N 14°30E 9 H16
Göteborg Sweden 57°43N 11°59E 9 H14
Gotha Germany 50°56N 10°42E 16 C6
Gothenburg = Göteborg
Sweden 57°43N 11°59E 9 H14
Gothenburg U.S.A. 40°56N 100°10W 80 E3
Gotland Sweden 57°30N 18°33E 9 H18
Gotō-Rettō Japan 32°55N 129°5E 31 H4
Gotska Sandön Sweden 58°24N 19°15E 9 G18
Gōtsu Japan 35°0N 132°14E 31 G6
Göttingen Germany 51°31N 9°55E 16 C5
Gottwaldov = Zlín
Czech Rep. 49°14N 17°40E 17 D9
Goubangzi China 41°20N 121°52E 35 D11
Gouda Neths. 52°1N 4°42E 15 B4
Goudouras, Akra Greece 34°59N 26°6E 25 E8
Gouin, Rés. Canada 48°35N 74°40W 72 C5
Goulburn Australia 34°44S 149°44E 63 E4
Goulburn Is. Australia 11°40S 133°20E 62 A1
Goulimine Morocco 28°56N 10°0W 50 C3
Goundam Mali 16°27N 3°40W 50 E5
Gourits → S. Africa 34°21S 21°52E 56 E3
Gournes Greece 35°19N 25°16E 25 D7
Gourock U.K. 55°57N 4°49W 11 F4
Gouverneur U.S.A. 44°20N 75°28W 83 B9
Gouvia Greece 39°39N 19°50E 25 A3
Gove Peninsula
Australia 12°17S 136°49E 62 A2
Governador Valadares
Brazil 18°15S 41°57W 93 G10
Governor's Harbour
Bahamas 25°10N 76°14W 88 A4
Govindgarh India 24°23N 81°18E 43 G9
Gowan Ra. Australia 25°0S 145°0E 62 D4
Gowanda U.S.A. 42°28N 78°56W 82 D6
Gower U.K. 51°35N 4°10W 13 F3
Gowna, L. Ireland 53°51N 7°34W 10 C4
Goya Argentina 29°10S 59°10W 94 B4
Goyder Lagoon Australia 27°3S 138°58E 63 D2
Goyllarisquizga Peru 10°31S 76°24W 92 F3
Goz Beïda Chad 12°10N 21°20E 51 F10
Gozo Malta 36°3N 14°15E 25 C1
Graaff-Reinet S. Africa 32°13S 24°32E 56 E3
Gračac Croatia 44°18N 15°57E 16 F8
Gracias a Dios, C.
Honduras 15°0N 83°10W 88 D3
Graciosa Azores 39°4N 28°0W 50 a
Graciosa, I. Canary Is. 29°15N 13°32W 24 E6
Grado Spain 43°23N 6°4W 21 A2
Grady U.S.A. 34°49N 103°19W 77 J12
Grafham Water U.K. 52°19N 0°18W 13 E7
Grafton Australia 29°38S 152°58E 63 D5
Grafton N. Dak., U.S.A. 48°25N 97°25W 80 A5
Grafton W. Va., U.S.A. 39°21N 80°2W 81 F13
Graham Canada 49°20N 90°30W 72 C1
Graham U.S.A. 33°6N 98°35W 84 E5
Graham, Mt. U.S.A. 32°42N 109°52W 77 K9
Graham Bell, Ostrov = Greem-
Bell, Ostrov Russia 81°0N 62°0E 28 A7
Graham I. Canada 53°40N 132°30W 70 C2
Graham Land Antarctica 65°0S 64°0W 5 C17
Grahamstown S. Africa 33°19S 26°31E 56 E4
Grahamsville U.S.A. 41°51N 74°33W 83 E10
Grain Coast W. Afr. 4°20N 10°0W 50 H3
Grajagan Indonesia 8°35S 114°13E 37 K17
Grajagan, Teluk
Indonesia 8°40S 114°18E 37 K17
Grajaú Brazil 5°50S 46°4W 93 E9
Grajaú → Brazil 3°41S 44°48W 93 D10
Grampian U.S.A. 40°58N 78°37W 82 F6
Grampian Highlands = Grampian
Mts. U.K. 56°50N 4°0W 11 E5
Grampian Mts. U.K. 56°50N 4°0W 11 E5
Grampians, The
Australia 37°15S 142°20E 63 F3
Gran Canaria Canary Is. 27°55N 15°35W 24 G4
Gran Chaco S. Amer. 25°0S 61°0W 94 B3
Gran Desierto del Pinacate ⌂
Mexico 31°51N 113°32W 86 A2
Gran Paradiso Italy 45°33N 7°17E 20 D7
Gran Sasso d'Itália Italy 42°27N 13°42E 22 C5
Granada Nic. 11°58N 86°0W 88 D2
Granada Spain 37°10N 3°35W 21 D4
Granada U.S.A. 38°4N 102°19W 76 G12
Granadilla de Abona
Canary Is. 28°7N 16°33W 24 F3
Granard Ireland 53°47N 7°30W 10 C4
Granbury U.S.A. 32°27N 97°47W 84 E6
Granby Canada 45°25N 72°45W 83 A12
Granby U.S.A. 40°5N 105°56W 76 F11
Grand → Canada 42°51N 79°34W 82 D5
Grand → Mo., U.S.A. 39°23N 93°7W 80 F7
Grand → S. Dak.,
U.S.A. 45°40N 100°45W 80 C3
Grand Bahama I.
Bahamas 26°40N 78°30W 88 A4
Grand Baie Mauritius 20°0S 57°35E 53 d
Grand Bank Canada 47°6N 55°48W 73 C8
Grand Bassam Ivory C. 5°10N 3°49W 50 G5
Grand Bend Canada 43°18N 81°45W 82 C3
Grand-Bourg Guadeloupe 15°53N 61°19W 88 b
Grand Canal = Da Yunhe →
China 39°10N 117°10E 35 E9
Grand Canyon U.S.A. 36°3N 112°9W 77 H7
Grand Canyon △
U.S.A. 36°15N 112°30W 77 H7
Grand Canyon-Parashant ⌂
U.S.A. 36°30N 113°45W 77 H7
Grand Cayman
Cayman Is. 19°20N 81°20W 88 C3
Grand Coulee U.S.A. 47°57N 119°0W 76 C4
Grand Coulee Dam
U.S.A. 47°57N 118°59W 76 C4
Grand Erg de Bilma Niger 18°30N 14°0E 51 E8
Grand Falls Canada 47°3N 67°44W 73 C6
Grand Falls-Windsor
Canada 48°56N 55°40W 73 C8
Grand Forks Canada 49°0N 118°30W 70 D5
Grand Forks U.S.A. 47°55N 97°3W 80 B5
Grand Gorge U.S.A. 42°21N 74°29W 83 D10
Grand Haven U.S.A. 43°4N 86°13W 80 D10
Grand I. Mich., U.S.A. 46°31N 86°40W 80 B10
Grand I. N.Y., U.S.A. 43°0N 78°58W 82 D6
Grand Island U.S.A. 40°55N 98°21W 80 E4
Grand Isle La., U.S.A. 29°14N 90°0W 85 G9
Grand Isle Vt., U.S.A. 44°43N 73°18W 83 B11
Grand Junction U.S.A. 39°4N 108°33W 76 G9
Grand L. N.B., Canada 45°57N 66°7W 73 C6
Grand L. Nfld. & L.,
Canada 49°0N 57°30W 73 C8
Grand L. Nfld. & L.,
Canada 53°40N 60°30W 73 B7
Grand L. U.S.A. 29°55N 92°47W 84 G8
Grand Lake U.S.A. 40°15N 105°49W 76 F11
Grand Manan I. Canada 44°45N 66°52W 73 D6
Grand Marais Mich.,
U.S.A. 46°40N 85°59W 81 B11
Grand Marais Minn.,
U.S.A. 47°45N 90°25W 72 C1
Grand-Mère Canada 46°36N 72°40W 72 C5
Grand Portage U.S.A. 47°58N 89°41W 80 B9
Grand Prairie U.S.A. 32°44N 96°59W 84 E6
Grand Rapids Canada 53°12N 99°19W 71 C9
Grand Rapids Mich.,
U.S.A. 42°58N 85°40W 81 D11
Grand Rapids Minn.,
U.S.A. 47°14N 93°31W 80 B7
Grand St-Bernard, Col du
Europe 45°50N 7°10E 20 D7
Grand Staircase-Escalante ⌂
U.S.A. 37°25N 111°33W 77 H8
Grand Teton U.S.A. 43°54N 110°50W 76 E8
Grand Teton △ U.S.A. 43°50N 110°50W 76 E8
Grand Union Canal U.K. 52°7N 0°53W 13 E7
Grande → Jujuy,
Argentina 24°20S 65°2W 94 A2
Grande → Mendoza,
Argentina 36°52S 69°45W 94 D2
Grande → Bolivia 15°51S 64°39W 92 G6
Grande → Bahia, Brazil 11°30S 44°30W 93 F10
Grande → Minas Gerais,
Brazil 20°6S 51°4W 93 H8
Grande, B. Argentina 50°30S 68°20W 96 G3
Grande, Rio → N. Amer. 25°58N 97°9W 84 J6
Grande Anse Seychelles 4°18S 55°45E 53 b
Grande Baleine, R. de la →
Canada 55°16N 77°47W 72 A4
Grande Cache Canada 53°53N 119°8W 70 C5
Grande Comore
Comoros Is. 11°35S 43°20E 53 a
Grande-Entrée Canada 47°30N 61°40W 73 C7
Grande Prairie Canada 55°10N 118°50W 70 B5
Grande-Rivière Canada 48°26N 64°30W 73 C7
Grande-Terre Guadeloupe 16°20N 61°25W 88 b
Grande-Vallée Canada 49°14N 65°8W 73 C6
Grande Vigie, Pte. de la
Guadeloupe 16°32N 61°27W 88 b
Grandfalls U.S.A. 31°20N 102°51W 84 F3
Grands-Jardins ⌂
Canada 47°41N 70°51W 73 C5
Grandview Canada 51°10N 100°42W 71 C8
Grandview U.S.A. 46°15N 119°54W 76 C4
Graneros Chile 34°5S 70°45W 94 C1
Grangemouth U.K. 56°1N 3°42W 11 E5
Granger U.S.A. 41°35N 109°58W 76 F9
Grangeville U.S.A. 45°56N 116°7W 76 D5
Granisle Canada 54°53N 126°13W 70 C3
Granite City U.S.A. 38°42N 90°8W 80 F8
Granite Falls U.S.A. 44°49N 95°33W 80 C6
Granite L. Canada 48°8N 57°5W 73 C8
Granite Mt. U.S.A. 33°5N 116°28W 79 M10
Granite Pk. U.S.A. 45°10N 109°48W 76 D9
Graniteville U.S.A. 44°8N 72°29W 83 B12
Granity N.Z. 41°39S 171°51E 59 D3
Granja Brazil 3°7S 40°50W 93 D10
Granollers Spain 41°39N 2°18E 21 B7
Grant U.S.A. 40°50N 101°43W 80 E3
Grant, Mt. U.S.A. 38°34N 118°48W 76 G4
Grant City U.S.A. 40°29N 94°25W 80 E6
Grant I. Australia 11°10S 132°52E 60 B5
Grant Range U.S.A. 38°30N 115°25W 76 G6
Grantham U.K. 52°55N 0°38W 12 E7
Grantown-on-Spey U.K. 57°20N 3°36W 11 D5
Grants U.S.A. 35°9N 107°52W 77 J10
Grants Pass U.S.A. 42°26N 123°19W 76 E2
Grantsville U.S.A. 40°36N 112°28W 76 F7
Granville France 48°50N 1°35W 20 B3
Granville N. Dak.,
U.S.A. 48°16N 100°47W 80 A3
Granville N.Y., U.S.A. 43°24N 73°16W 83 C11
Granville Ohio, U.S.A. 40°4N 82°31W 82 F2
Granville L. Canada 56°18N 100°30W 71 B8
Graskop S. Africa 24°56S 30°49E 57 C5
Grass → Canada 56°3N 96°33W 71 B9
Grass Range U.S.A. 47°2N 108°48W 76 C9
Grass River ⌂ Canada 54°40N 100°50W 71 C8
Grass Valley Calif.,
U.S.A. 39°13N 121°4W 78 F6
Grass Valley Oreg.,
U.S.A. 45°22N 120°47W 76 D3
Grasse France 43°38N 6°56E 20 E7
Grassflat U.S.A. 41°0N 78°6W 82 E6
Grasslands △ Canada 49°11N 107°38W 71 D7
Grassy Australia 40°3S 144°5E 63 G3
Graulhet France 43°45N 1°59E 20 E4
Gravelbourg Canada 49°50N 106°35W 71 D7
's-Gravenhage Neths. 52°7N 4°17E 15 B4
Gravenhurst Canada 44°52N 79°20W 82 B5
Gravesend Australia 29°35S 150°20E 63 D5
Gravesend U.K. 51°26N 0°22E 13 F8
Gravois, Pointe-à- Haiti 18°15N 73°56W 89 C5
Grayling U.S.A. 44°40N 84°43W 81 C11
Grays U.K. 51°28N 0°21E 13 F8
Grays Harbor U.S.A. 46°59N 124°1W 76 C1
Grays L. U.S.A. 43°4N 111°26W 76 E8
Grays River U.S.A. 46°21N 123°37W 78 D3
Graz Austria 47°4N 15°27E 16 E8
Greasy L. Canada 62°55N 122°12W 70 A4
Great Abaco I. = Abaco I.
Bahamas 26°25N 77°10W 88 A4
Great Artesian Basin
Australia 23°0S 144°0E 62 C3
Great Australian Bight
Australia 33°30S 130°0E 61 F5
Great Bahama Bank
Bahamas 23°15N 78°0W 88 B4
Great Barrier I. N.Z. 36°11S 175°25E 59 B5
Great Barrier Reef
Australia 18°0S 146°50E 62 B4
Great Barrier Reef ⌂
Australia 20°0S 150°0E 62 B4
Great Barrington
U.S.A. 42°12N 73°22W 83 D11
Great Basalt Wall △
Australia 19°52S 145°43E 62 B4
Great Basin U.S.A. 40°0N 117°0W 76 G5
Great Basin △ U.S.A. 38°56N 114°15W 76 G6
Great Bear → Canada 65°0N 124°0W 68 C7
Great Bear L. Canada 65°30N 120°0W 68 C8
Great Belt = Store Bælt
Denmark 55°20N 11°0E 9 J14
Great Bend Kans., U.S.A. 38°22N 98°46W 80 F4
Great Bend Pa., U.S.A. 41°58N 75°45W 83 E9
Great Blasket I. Ireland 52°6N 10°32W 10 D1
Great Britain Europe 54°0N 2°15W 6 E5
Great Camanoe
Br. Virgin Is. 18°30N 64°35W 89 e
Great Codroy Canada 47°51N 59°16W 73 C8
Great Divide, The = Great
Dividing Ra. Australia 23°0S 146°0E 62 C4
Great Divide Basin
U.S.A. 42°0N 108°0W 76 E9
Great Dividing Ra.
Australia 23°0S 146°0E 62 C4
Great Driffield = Driffield
U.K. 54°0N 0°26W 12 C7
Great Exuma I. Bahamas 23°30N 75°50W 88 B4
Great Falls U.S.A. 47°30N 111°17W 76 C8
Great Fish = Groot-Vis →
S. Africa 33°28S 27°5E 56 E4
Great Guana Cay
Bahamas 24°0N 76°20W 88 B4
Great Himalayan △
India 31°30N 77°30E 42 D7
Great Inagua I. Bahamas 21°0N 73°20W 89 B5
Great Indian Desert = Thar Desert
India 28°0N 72°0E 42 F5
Great Karoo S. Africa 31°55S 21°0E 56 E3
Great Khingan Mts. = Da
Hinggan Ling China 48°0N 121°0E 33 B7
Great Lake Australia 41°50S 146°40E 63 G4
Great Lakes N. Amer. 46°0N 84°0W 66 E11
Great Limpopo Transfrontier △
Africa 23°0S 31°45E 57 C5
Great Malvern U.K. 52°7N 2°18W 13 E5
Great Miami → U.S.A. 39°7N 84°49W 81 F11
Great Ormes Head U.K. 53°20N 3°52W 12 D4
Great Ouse → U.K. 52°48N 0°21E 12 E8
Great Palm I. Australia 18°45S 146°40E 62 B4
Great Pedro Bluff Jamaica 17°51N 77°44W 88 a
Great Pee Dee →
U.S.A. 33°21N 79°10W 85 E15
Great Plains N. Amer. 47°0N 105°0W 66 E9
Great Ruaha → Tanzania 7°56S 37°52E 54 D4
Great Sacandaga L.
U.S.A. 43°6N 74°16W 83 C10
Great Saint Bernard Pass = Grand
St-Bernard, Col du
Europe 45°50N 7°10E 20 D7
Great Salt Desert = Kavīr, Dasht-e
Iran 34°30N 55°0E 45 C7
Great Salt L. U.S.A. 41°15N 112°40W 76 F7
Great Salt Lake Desert
U.S.A. 40°50N 113°30W 76 F7
Great Salt Plains L.
U.S.A. 36°45N 98°8W 84 C5

Great Sand Dunes ⌂ U.S.A. 37°48N 105°45W 77 H11
Great Sandy △ Australia 26°13S 153°2E 63 D5
Great Sandy Desert Australia 21°0S 124°0E 60 D3
Great Sandy Desert U.S.A. 43°35N 120°15W 74 B2
Great Sangi = Sangihe, Pulau Indonesia 3°35N 125°30E 37 D7
Great Sea Reef Fiji 16°15S 179°0E 59 a
Great Skellig Ireland 51°47N 10°33W 10 E1
Great Slave L. Canada 61°23N 115°38W 70 A5
Great Smoky Mts. △ U.S.A. 35°40N 83°40W 85 D13
Great Stour = Stour → U.K. 51°18N 1°22E 13 F9
Great Victoria Desert Australia 29°30S 126°30E 61 E4
Great Wall Antarctica 62°30S 58°0W 5 C18
Great Wall China 38°30N 109°30E 34 E5
Great Whernside U.K. 54°10N 1°58W 12 C6
Great Yarmouth U.K. 52°37N 1°44E 13 E9
Great Zab = Zāb al Kabīr → Iraq 36°1N 43°24E 44 B4
Great Zimbabwe Zimbabwe 20°16S 30°54E 55 G3
Greater Antilles W. Indies 17°40N 74°0W 89 C5
Greater London □ U.K. 51°31N 0°6W 13 F7
Greater Manchester □ U.K. 53°30N 2°15W 12 D5
Greater St. Lucia Wetlands ⌂ S. Africa 28°6S 32°27E 57 D5
Greater Sudbury = Sudbury Canada 46°30N 81°0W 72 C3
Greater Sunda Is. Indonesia 7°0S 112°0E 36 F4
Greco, C. Cyprus 34°57N 34°5E 25 E13
Gredos, Sierra de Spain 40°20N 5°0W 21 B3
Greece U.S.A. 43°13N 77°41W 82 C7
Greece ■ Europe 40°0N 23°0E 23 E9
Greeley Colo., U.S.A. 40°25N 104°42W 76 F11
Greeley Nebr., U.S.A. 41°33N 98°32W 80 E4
Greely Fd. Canada 80°30N 85°0W 69 A11
Greem-Bell, Ostrov Russia 81°0N 62°0E 28 A7
Green → Ky., U.S.A. 37°54N 87°30W 80 G10
Green → Utah, U.S.A. 38°11N 109°53W 76 G9
Green B. U.S.A. 45°0N 87°30W 80 C10
Green Bay U.S.A. 44°31N 88°0W 80 C9
Green C. Australia 37°13S 150°1E 63 F5
Green Cove Springs U.S.A. 29°59N 81°42W 85 G14
Green Lake Canada 54°17N 107°47W 71 C7
Green Mts. U.S.A. 43°45N 72°45W 83 C12
Green River Utah, U.S.A. 38°59N 110°10W 76 G8
Green River Wyo., U.S.A. 41°32N 109°28W 76 F9
Green Valley U.S.A. 31°52N 110°56W 77 L8
Greenbank U.S.A. 48°6N 122°34W 78 B4
Greenbush Mich., U.S.A. 44°35N 83°19W 82 B1
Greenbush Minn., U.S.A. 48°42N 96°11W 80 A5
Greencastle U.S.A. 39°38N 86°52W 80 F10
Greene U.S.A. 42°20N 75°46W 83 D9
Greeneville U.S.A. 36°10N 82°50W 85 C13
Greenfield Calif., U.S.A. 36°19N 121°15W 78 J5
Greenfield Calif., U.S.A. 35°15N 119°0W 79 K8
Greenfield Ind., U.S.A. 39°47N 85°46W 81 F11
Greenfield Iowa, U.S.A. 41°18N 94°28W 80 E6
Greenfield Mass., U.S.A. 42°35N 72°36W 83 D12
Greenfield Mo., U.S.A. 37°25N 93°51W 80 G7
Greenfield Park Canada 45°29N 73°28W 83 A11
Greenland ⊠ N. Amer. 66°0N 45°0W 67 C15
Greenland Sea Arctic 73°0N 10°0W 4 B7
Greenock U.K. 55°57N 4°46W 11 F4
Greenore Ireland 54°2N 6°8W 10 B5
Greenore Pt. Ireland 52°14N 6°19W 10 D5
Greenough Australia 28°58S 114°43E 61 E1
Greenough → Australia 28°51S 114°38E 61 E1
Greenough Pt. Canada 44°58N 81°26W 82 B3
Greenport U.S.A. 41°6N 72°22W 83 E12
Greensboro Ga., U.S.A. 33°35N 83°11W 85 E13
Greensboro N.C., U.S.A. 36°4N 79°48W 85 C15
Greensboro Vt., U.S.A. 44°36N 72°18W 83 B12
Greensburg Ind., U.S.A. 39°20N 85°29W 81 F11
Greensburg Kans., U.S.A. 37°36N 99°18W 80 G4
Greensburg Pa., U.S.A. 40°18N 79°33W 82 F5
Greenstone Pt. U.K. 57°55N 5°37W 11 D3
Greenvale Australia 18°59S 145°7E 62 B4
Greenville Liberia 5°1N 9°6W 50 G4
Greenville Ala., U.S.A. 31°50N 86°38W 85 F11
Greenville Calif., U.S.A. 40°8N 120°57W 78 E6
Greenville Maine, U.S.A. 45°28N 69°35W 81 C19
Greenville Mich., U.S.A. 43°11N 85°15W 81 D11
Greenville Miss., U.S.A. 33°24N 91°4W 85 E9
Greenville Mo., U.S.A. 37°8N 90°27W 80 G8
Greenville N.C., U.S.A. 35°37N 77°23W 85 D16
Greenville N.H., U.S.A. 42°46N 71°49W 83 D13
Greenville N.Y., U.S.A. 42°25N 74°1W 83 D10
Greenville Ohio, U.S.A. 40°6N 84°38W 81 E11
Greenville Pa., U.S.A. 41°24N 80°23W 82 E4
Greenville S.C., U.S.A. 34°51N 82°24W 85 D13
Greenville Tex., U.S.A. 33°8N 96°7W 84 E6
Greenwater Lake ⌂ Canada 52°32N 103°30W 71 C8
Greenwich Conn., U.S.A. 41°2N 73°38W 83 E11
Greenwich N.Y., U.S.A. 43°5N 73°30W 83 C11
Greenwich Ohio, U.S.A. 41°2N 82°31W 82 E2
Greenwich □ U.K. 51°29N 0°1E 13 F8
Greenwood Canada 49°10N 118°40W 70 D5
Greenwood Ark., U.S.A. 35°13N 94°16W 84 D7
Greenwood Ind., U.S.A. 39°37N 86°7W 80 F10
Greenwood Miss., U.S.A. 33°31N 90°11W 85 E9
Greenwood S.C., U.S.A. 34°12N 82°10W 85 D13
Greenwood, Mt. Australia 13°48S 130°4E 60 B5
Gregory U.S.A. 43°14N 99°26W 80 D4
Gregory → Australia 17°53S 139°17E 62 B2
Gregory, L. S. Austral., Australia 28°55S 139°0E 63 D2
Gregory, L. W. Austral., Australia 20°0S 127°40E 60 D4
Gregory, L. W. Austral., Australia 25°38S 119°58E 61 E2
Gregory △ Australia 15°38S 131°15E 60 C5
Gregory Downs Australia 18°35S 138°45E 62 B2
Gregory Ra. Queens., Australia 19°30S 143°40E 62 B3
Gregory Ra. W. Austral., Australia 21°20S 121°12E 60 D3
Greifswald Germany 54°5N 13°23E 16 A7
Greiz Germany 50°39N 12°10E 16 C7
Gremikha Russia 67°59N 39°47E 18 A6
Grenaa Denmark 56°25N 10°53E 9 H14
Grenada U.S.A. 33°47N 89°49W 85 E10
Grenada ■ W. Indies 12°10N 61°40W 89 D7
Grenadier I. U.S.A. 44°3N 76°22W 83 B8
Grenadines, The St. Vincent 12°40N 61°20W 89 D7
Grenen Denmark 57°44N 10°40E 9 H14
Grenfell Australia 33°52S 148°8E 63 E4
Grenfell Canada 50°30N 102°56W 71 C8
Grenoble France 45°12N 5°42E 20 D6
Grenville, C. Australia 12°0S 143°13E 62 A3
Grenville Chan. Canada 53°40N 129°46W 70 C3
Gresham U.S.A. 45°30N 122°25W 78 E4
Gresik Indonesia 7°13S 112°38E 37 G15
Gretna U.K. 55°0N 3°3W 11 F5
Gretna U.S.A. 29°54N 90°3W 85 G9
Grevenmacher Lux. 49°41N 6°26E 15 E6
Grey → Canada 47°34N 57°6W 73 C8
Grey → N.Z. 42°27S 171°12E 59 E3
Grey, C. Australia 13°0S 136°35E 62 A2
Grey Ra. Australia 27°0S 143°30E 63 D3
Greybull U.S.A. 44°30N 108°3W 76 D9
Greymouth N.Z. 42°29S 171°13E 59 E3
Greystones Ireland 53°9N 6°5W 10 C5
Greytown N.Z. 41°5S 175°29E 59 D5
Greytown S. Africa 29°1S 30°36E 57 D5
Gribbell I. Canada 53°23N 129°0W 70 C3
Gridley U.S.A. 39°22N 121°42W 78 F5
Griekwastad S. Africa 28°49S 23°15E 56 D3
Griffin U.S.A. 33°15N 84°16W 85 E12
Griffith Australia 34°18S 146°2E 63 E4
Griffith Canada 45°15N 77°10W 82 A7
Griffith I. Canada 44°50N 80°55W 82 B4
Grimaylov = Hrymayliv Ukraine 49°20N 26°5E 17 D14
Grimes U.S.A. 39°4N 121°54W 78 F5
Grimsay U.K. 57°29N 7°14W 11 D1
Grimsby Canada 43°12N 79°34W 82 C5
Grimsby U.K. 53°34N 0°5W 12 D7
Grímsey Iceland 66°33N 17°58W 8 C5
Grimshaw Canada 56°10N 117°40W 70 B5
Grimstad Norway 58°20N 8°35E 9 G13
Grinnell U.S.A. 41°45N 92°43W 80 E7
Gris-Nez, C. France 50°52N 1°35E 20 A4
Grise Fiord Canada 76°25N 82°57W 69 B11
Groais I. Canada 50°55N 55°35W 73 B8
Groblersdal S. Africa 25°15S 29°25E 57 D4
Grodno = Hrodna Belarus 53°42N 23°52E 17 B12
Grodzyanka = Hrodzyanka Belarus 53°31N 28°42E 17 B15
Groesbeck U.S.A. 31°31N 96°32W 84 F6
Grójec Poland 51°50N 20°58E 17 C11
Grong Norway 64°25N 12°8E 8 D15
Groningen Neths. 53°15N 6°35E 15 A6
Groningen □ Neths. 53°16N 6°40E 15 A6
Groom U.S.A. 35°12N 101°6W 84 D4
Groot → S. Africa 33°45S 24°36E 56 E3
Groot-Berg → S. Africa 32°47S 18°8E 56 E2
Groot-Brakrivier S. Africa 34°2S 22°18E 56 E3
Groot Karasberge Namibia 27°20S 18°40E 56 D2
Groot-Kei → S. Africa 32°41S 28°22E 57 E4
Groot-Vis → S. Africa 33°28S 27°5E 56 E4
Grootdrink S. Africa 28°33S 21°42E 56 D3
Groote Eylandt Australia 14°0S 136°40E 62 A2
Grootfontein Namibia 19°31S 18°6E 56 B2
Grootlaagte → Africa 20°55S 21°27E 56 C3
Grootvloer → S. Africa 30°0S 20°40E 56 E3
Gros C. Canada 61°59N 113°32W 70 A6
Gros Islet St. Lucia 14°5N 60°58W 89 f
Gros Morne △ Canada 49°40N 57°50W 73 C8
Gros Piton St. Lucia 13°49N 61°5W 89 f
Gros Piton Pt. St. Lucia 13°49N 61°5W 89 f
Grossa, Pta. Spain 39°6N 1°36E 24 B8
Grosse Point U.S.A. 42°23N 82°54W 82 D2
Grosser Arber Germany 49°6N 13°8E 16 D7
Grosseto Italy 42°46N 11°8E 22 C4
Grossglockner Austria 47°5N 12°40E 16 E7
Groswater B. Canada 54°20N 57°40W 73 B8
Groton Conn., U.S.A. 41°21N 72°5W 83 E12
Groton N.Y., U.S.A. 42°36N 76°22W 83 D8
Groton S. Dak., U.S.A. 45°27N 98°6W 80 C4
Grouard Mission Canada 55°33N 116°9W 70 B5
Groundhog → Canada 48°45N 82°58W 72 C3
Grouw Neths. 53°5N 5°51E 15 A5
Grove City U.S.A. 41°10N 80°5W 82 E4
Grove Hill U.S.A. 31°42N 87°47W 85 F11
Groveland U.S.A. 37°50N 120°14W 78 H6
Grover Beach U.S.A. 35°7N 120°37W 79 K6
Groves U.S.A. 29°57N 93°54W 84 G8
Groveton U.S.A. 44°36N 71°31W 83 B13
Groznyy Russia 43°20N 45°45E 19 F8
Grudziądz Poland 53°30N 18°47E 17 B10
Gruinard B. U.K. 57°56N 5°35W 11 D3
Grundy Center U.S.A. 42°22N 92°47W 80 D7
Gruver U.S.A. 36°16N 101°24W 84 C4
Gryazi Russia 52°30N 39°58E 18 D6
Gryazovets Russia 58°50N 40°10E 18 C7
Grytviken S. Georgia 54°19S 36°33W 96 G9
Gua India 22°18N 85°20E 43 H11
Gua Musang Malaysia 4°53N 101°58E 39 K3
Guacanayabo, G. de Cuba 20°40N 77°20W 88 B4
Guachípas → Argentina 25°40S 65°30W 94 B2
Guadalajara Mexico 20°40N 103°20W 86 C4
Guadalajara Spain 40°37N 3°12W 21 B4
Guadalcanal Solomon Is. 9°32S 160°12E 58 B9
Guadales Argentina 34°30S 67°55W 94 C2
Guadalete → Spain 36°35N 6°13W 21 D2
Guadalquivir → Spain 36°47N 6°22W 21 D2
Guadalupe = Guadeloupe ⊠ W. Indies 16°20N 61°40W 88 b
Guadalupe Mexico 32°4N 116°32W 79 N10
Guadalupe Zacatecas, Mexico 22°45N 102°31W 86 C4
Guadalupe U.S.A. 34°58N 120°34W 79 L6
Guadalupe → U.S.A. 28°27N 96°47W 84 G6
Guadalupe, Sierra de Spain 39°28N 5°30W 21 C3
Guadalupe Bravos Mexico 31°20N 106°10W 86 A3
Guadalupe I. Pac. Oc. 29°0N 118°50W 66 G8
Guadalupe Mts. △ U.S.A. 31°40N 104°30W 84 F2
Guadalupe Peak U.S.A. 31°50N 104°52W 84 F2
Guadalupe y Calvo Mexico 26°6N 106°58W 86 B3
Guadarrama, Sierra de Spain 41°0N 4°0W 21 B4
Guadeloupe ⊠ W. Indies 16°20N 61°40W 88 b
Guadeloupe △ Guadeloupe 16°10N 61°40W 88 b
Guadeloupe Passage W. Indies 16°50N 62°15W 89 C7
Guadiana → Portugal 37°14N 7°22W 21 D2
Guadix Spain 37°18N 3°11W 21 D4
Guafo, Boca del Chile 43°35S 74°0W 96 E2
Guaico Trin. & Tob. 10°35N 61°9W 93 K15
Guainía → Colombia 2°1N 67°7W 92 C5
Guaíra Brazil 24°5S 54°10W 95 A5
Guaíra □ Paraguay 25°45S 56°30W 94 B4
Guaitecas, Is. Chile 44°0S 74°30W 96 E2
Guajará-Mirim Brazil 10°50S 65°20W 92 F5
Guajira, Pen. de la Colombia 12°0N 72°0W 92 A4
Gualán Guatemala 15°8N 89°22W 88 C2
Gualeguay Argentina 33°10S 59°14W 94 C4
Gualeguaychú Argentina 33°3S 59°31W 94 C4
Gualequay → Argentina 33°19S 59°39W 94 C4
Guam ⊠ Pac. Oc. 13°27N 144°45E 64 F6
Guaminí Argentina 37°1S 62°28W 94 D3
Guamúchil Mexico 25°28N 108°6W 86 B3
Guana I. Br. Virgin Is. 18°30N 64°30W 89 e
Guanabacoa Cuba 23°8N 82°18W 88 B3
Guanacaste, Cordillera de Costa Rica 10°40N 85°4W 88 D2
Guanacaste △ Costa Rica 10°57N 85°30W 88 D2
Guanaceví Mexico 25°56N 105°57W 86 B3
Guanahani = San Salvador I. Bahamas 24°0N 74°40W 89 B5
Guanaja Honduras 16°30N 85°55W 88 C2
Guanajay Cuba 22°56N 82°42W 88 B3
Guanajuato Mexico 21°1N 101°15W 86 C4
Guanajuato □ Mexico 21°0N 101°0W 86 C4
Guandacol Argentina 29°30S 68°40W 94 B2
Guane Cuba 22°10N 84°7W 88 B3
Guangdong □ China 23°0N 113°0E 33 D6
Guangling China 39°47N 114°22E 34 E8
Guangrao China 37°5N 118°25E 35 F10
Guangwu China 37°48N 105°57E 34 F3
Guangxi Zhuangzu Zizhiqu □ China 24°0N 109°0E 33 D5
Guangzhou China 23°6N 113°13E 33 D6
Guanica Puerto Rico 17°58N 66°55W 89 d
Guanipa → Venezuela 9°56N 62°26W 92 B6
Guannan China 34°8N 119°21E 35 G10
Guantánamo Cuba 20°10N 75°14W 89 B4
Guantánamo B. Cuba 19°59N 75°10W 89 C4
Guantao China 36°42N 115°25E 34 F8
Guanyun China 34°20N 119°18E 35 G10
Guapay = Grande → Bolivia 15°51S 64°39W 92 G6
Guápiles Costa Rica 10°10N 83°46W 88 D3
Guapo B. Trin. & Tob. 10°12N 61°41W 93 K15
Guaporé Brazil 28°51S 51°54W 95 B5
Guaporé → Brazil 11°55S 65°4W 92 F5
Guaqui Bolivia 16°41S 68°54W 92 G5
Guaramacal △ Venezuela 9°13N 70°12W 89 E5
Guarapari Brazil 20°40S 40°30W 95 A7
Guarapuava Brazil 25°20S 51°30W 95 B5
Guaratinguetá Brazil 22°49S 45°9W 95 A6
Guaratuba Brazil 25°53S 48°38W 95 B6
Guarda Portugal 40°32N 7°20W 21 B2
Guardafui, C. = Asir, Ras Somali Rep. 11°55N 51°10E 47 E5
Guárico □ Venezuela 8°40N 66°35W 92 B5
Guarujá Brazil 24°2S 46°25W 95 A6
Guarulhos Brazil 23°29S 46°33W 95 A6
Guasave Mexico 25°34N 108°27W 86 B3
Guasdualito Venezuela 7°15N 70°44W 92 B4
Guatemala Guatemala 14°40N 90°22W 88 D1
Guatemala ■ Cent. Amer. 15°40N 90°30W 88 C1
Guatemala Basin Pac. Oc. 11°0N 95°0W 65 F18
Guatemala Trench Pac. Oc. 14°0N 95°0W 66 H10
Guatopo △ Venezuela 10°5N 66°30W 89 D6
Guatuaro Pt. Trin. & Tob. 10°19N 60°59W 93 K16
Guaviare → Colombia 4°3N 67°44W 92 C5
Guaxupé Brazil 21°10S 47°5W 95 A6
Guayaguayare Trin. & Tob. 10°8N 61°2W 93 K15
Guayama Puerto Rico 17°59N 66°7W 89 d
Guayaquil Ecuador 2°15S 79°52W 92 D3
Guayaquil Mexico 29°59N 115°4W 86 B1
Guayaquil, G. de Ecuador 3°10S 81°0W 92 D2
Guaymas Mexico 27°56N 110°54W 86 B2
Guba Dem. Rep. of the Congo 10°38S 26°27E 55 E2
Gubkin Russia 51°17N 37°32E 19 D6
Gubkinskiy Russia 64°27N 76°36E 28 C8
Gudbrandsdalen Norway 61°33N 10°10E 8 F14
Guddu Barrage Pakistan 28°30N 69°50E 42 E3
Gudur India 14°12N 79°55E 40 M11
Guecho = Getxo Spain 43°21N 2°59W 21 A4
Guékédou Guinea 8°40N 10°5W 50 G3
Guelmine = Goulimine Morocco 28°56N 10°0W 50 C3
Guelph Canada 43°35N 80°20W 82 C4
Guerara Algeria 32°51N 4°22E 50 B6
Guéret France 46°11N 1°51E 20 C4
Guerneville U.S.A. 38°30N 123°0W 78 G4
Guernica = Gernika-Lumo Spain 43°19N 2°40W 21 A4
Guernsey U.K. 49°26N 2°35W 13 H5
Guernsey U.S.A. 42°16N 104°45W 76 E11
Guerrero □ Mexico 17°40N 100°0W 87 D5
Gügher Iran 29°28N 56°27E 45 D8
Guhakolak, Tanjung Indonesia 6°50S 105°14E 37 G11
Guia Canary Is. 28°8N 15°38W 24 F4
Guia de Isora Canary Is. 28°12N 16°46W 24 F3
Guia Lopes da Laguna Brazil 21°26S 56°7W 95 A4
Guiana Highlands S. Amer. 5°10N 60°40W 90 C4
Guidónia-Montecélio Italy 42°1N 12°45E 22 C5
Guijá Mozam. 24°27S 33°0E 57 C5
Guildford U.K. 51°14N 0°34W 13 F7
Guilford U.S.A. 41°17N 72°41W 83 E12
Guilin China 25°18N 110°15E 33 D6
Guillaume-Delisle, L. Canada 56°15N 76°17W 72 A4
Güimar Canary Is. 28°18N 16°24W 24 F3
Guimarães Portugal 41°28N 8°24W 21 B1
Guimaras □ Phil. 10°35N 122°37E 37 B6
Guinda U.S.A. 38°50N 122°12W 78 G4
Guinea Africa 8°0N 8°0E 48 F4
Guinea ■ W. Afr. 10°20N 11°30W 50 F3
Guinea, Gulf of Atl. Oc. 3°0N 2°30E 49 F4
Guinea-Bissau ■ Africa 12°0N 15°0W 50 F3
Güines Cuba 22°50N 82°0W 88 B3
Guingamp France 48°34N 3°10W 20 B2
Güiria Venezuela 10°32N 62°18W 92 A6
Guiuan Phil. 11°5N 125°55E 37 B7
Guiyang China 26°32N 106°40E 32 D5
Guizhou □ China 27°0N 107°0E 32 D5
Gujar Khan Pakistan 33°16N 73°19E 42 C5
Gujarat □ India 23°20N 71°0E 42 H4
Gujranwala Pakistan 32°10N 74°12E 42 C6
Gujrat Pakistan 32°40N 74°2E 42 C6
Gulbarga India 17°20N 76°50E 40 L10
Gulbene Latvia 57°8N 26°52E 9 H22
Gulf, The = Persian Gulf Asia 27°0N 50°0E 45 E6
Gulf Islands ⌂ U.S.A. 30°10N 87°10W 85 F11
Gulfport U.S.A. 30°22N 89°6W 85 F10
Gulgong Australia 32°20S 149°49E 63 E4
Gulistan Pakistan 30°30N 66°35E 42 D2
Gulja = Yining China 43°58N 81°10E 32 B3
Gull Lake Canada 50°10N 108°29W 71 C7
Güllük Turkey 37°14N 27°35E 23 F12
Gulmarg India 34°3N 74°25E 43 B6
Gülshat Kazakhstan 46°38N 74°21E 28 C8
Gulu Uganda 2°48N 32°17E 54 B3
Gulwe Tanzania 6°30S 36°25E 54 D4
Gumal → Pakistan 31°40N 71°50E 42 D4
Gumbaz Pakistan 30°2N 69°0E 42 D3
Gumel Nigeria 12°39N 9°22E 50 F7
Gumi S. Korea 36°10N 128°12E 35 F15
Gumla India 23°3N 84°33E 43 H11
Gumlu Australia 19°53S 147°41E 62 B4
Gumma □ Japan 36°30N 138°20E 31 F9
Gumzai Indonesia 5°28S 134°42E 37 F8
Guna India 24°40N 77°19E 42 G7
Gunbalanya Australia 12°20S 133°4E 60 B5
Gundabooka △ Australia 30°30S 145°20E 63 E4
Gunisao → Canada 53°56N 97°53W 71 C9
Gunisao L. Canada 53°33N 96°15W 71 C9
Gunjyal Pakistan 32°20N 71°55E 42 C4
Gunnbjørn Fjeld Greenland 68°55N 29°47W 4 C6
Gunnedah Australia 30°59S 150°15E 63 E5
Gunnewin Australia 25°59S 148°33E 63 D4
Gunningbar Cr. → Australia 31°14S 147°6E 63 E4
Gunnison Colo., U.S.A. 38°33N 106°56W 76 G10
Gunnison Utah, U.S.A. 39°9N 111°49W 76 G8
Gunnison → U.S.A. 39°4N 108°35W 76 G9
Gunpowder Australia 19°42S 139°22E 62 B2
Gunsan S. Korea 35°59N 126°45E 35 G14
Guntakal India 15°11N 77°27E 40 M10
Gunter Canada 44°52N 77°32W 82 B7
Guntersville U.S.A. 34°21N 86°18W 85 D11
Guntong Malaysia 4°36N 101°3E 39 K3
Guntur India 16°23N 80°30E 41 L12
Gunungapi Indonesia 6°45S 126°30E 37 F7
Gunungsitoli Indonesia 1°15N 97°30E 36 D1
Gunza Angola 10°50S 13°50E 52 G2
Guo He → China 32°59N 117°10E 35 H9
Guoyang China 33°32N 116°12E 34 H9
Gupis Pakistan 36°15N 73°20E 43 A5
Gurbantünggüt Shamo China 45°8N 87°20E 32 B3
Gurdaspur India 32°5N 75°31E 42 C6
Gurdon U.S.A. 33°55N 93°9W 84 E8
Gurgaon India 28°27N 77°1E 42 E7
Gurgueia → Brazil 6°50S 43°24W 93 E10
Gurha India 25°12N 71°39E 42
Guri, Embalse de Venezuela 7°50N 62°52W 92
Gurkha Nepal 28°5N 84°40E 43 E
Gurla Mandhata = Naimona'nyi Feng Nepal 30°26N 81°18E 43 D
Gurley Australia 29°45S 149°48E 63 D
Gurnet Point U.S.A. 42°1N 70°34W 83 D
Guro Mozam. 17°26S 32°30E 55
Gurué Mozam. 15°25S 36°58E 55
Gurun Malaysia 5°49N 100°27E 39
Gürün Turkey 38°43N 37°15E 19
Gurupá Brazil 1°25S 51°35W 93 D
Gurupá, I. Grande de Brazil 1°25S 51°45W 93 D
Gurupi Brazil 11°43S 49°4W 93
Gurupi → Brazil 1°13S 46°6W 93 D
Guruwe Zimbabwe 16°40S 30°42E 57
Gurvan Sayhan Uul Mongolia 43°50N 104°0E 32
Guryev = Atyraū Kazakhstan 47°5N 52°0E 19
Gusau Nigeria 12°12N 6°40E 50
Gushan China 39°50N 123°35E 35 E
Gushgy = Serhetabat Turkmenistan 35°20N 62°18E 45
Gusinoozersk Russia 51°16N 106°27E 29 D
Gustavus U.S.A. 58°25N 135°44W 70
Gustine U.S.A. 37°16N 121°0W 78
Güstrow Germany 53°47N 12°10E 16
Gütersloh Germany 51°54N 8°24E 16
Gutha Australia 28°58S 115°55E 61
Guthalungra Australia 19°52S 147°50E 62
Guthrie Canada 44°28N 79°32W 82
Guthrie Okla., U.S.A. 35°53N 97°25W 84 D
Guthrie Tex., U.S.A. 33°37N 100°19W 84
Guttenberg U.S.A. 42°47N 91°6W 80
Gutu Zimbabwe 19°41S 31°9E 57
Guwahati India 26°10N 91°45E 41 F
Guy Fawkes River △ Australia 30°0S 152°20E 63 D
Guyana ■ S. Amer. 5°0N 59°0W 92
Guyane française = French Guiana ⊠ S. Amer. 4°0N 53°0W 93
Guyang China 41°0N 110°5E 34
Guyenne France 44°30N 0°40E 20
Guymon U.S.A. 36°41N 101°29W 84
Guyra Australia 30°15S 151°40E 63
Guyuan Hebei, China 41°37N 115°40E 34
Guyuan Ningxia Huizu, China 36°0N 106°20E 34
Güzelyurt = Morphou Cyprus 35°12N 32°59E 25 D
Guzhen China 33°22N 117°18E 35
Guzmán, L. de Mexico 31°20N 107°30W 86
Gwa Burma 17°36N 94°34E 41 L
Gwaai Zimbabwe 19°15S 27°45E 55
Gwaai → Zimbabwe 17°59S 26°52E 55
Gwabegar Australia 30°37S 148°59E 63
Gwādar Pakistan 25°10N 62°18E 40
Gwaii Haanas △ Canada 52°21N 131°26W 70
Gwalior India 26°12N 78°10E 42
Gwanda Zimbabwe 20°55S 29°0E 55
Gwane Dem. Rep. of the Congo 4°45N 25°48E 54
Gwangju S. Korea 35°9N 126°54E 35 G
Gwanju = Gwangju S. Korea 35°9N 126°54E 35 G
Gweebarra B. Ireland 54°51N 8°23W 10
Gweedore Ireland 55°3N 8°13W 10
Gweru Zimbabwe 19°28S 29°45E 55
Gwinn U.S.A. 46°19N 87°27W 80 B
Gwydir → Australia 29°27S 149°48E 63
Gwynedd □ U.K. 52°52N 4°10W 12
Gyandzha = Gäncä Azerbaijan 40°45N 46°20E 19
Gyaring Hu China 34°50N 97°40E 32
Gydanskiy Poluostrov Russia 70°0N 78°0E 28
Gyeongju S. Korea 35°51N 129°14E 35 G
Gympie Australia 26°11S 152°38E 63
Gyöngyös Hungary 47°48N 19°56E 17 E
Győr Hungary 47°41N 17°40E 17
Gypsum Pt. Canada 61°53N 114°35W 70
Gypsumville Canada 51°45N 98°40W 71
Gyula Hungary 46°38N 21°17E 17 E
Gyumri Armenia 40°47N 43°50E 19
Gyzylarbat = Serdar Turkmenistan 39°4N 56°23E 45
Gyzyletrek = Etrek Turkmenistan 37°36N 54°46E 45

H

Ha 'Arava → Israel 30°50N 35°20E 46
Ha Coi Vietnam 21°26N 107°46E 38
Ha Dong Vietnam 20°58N 105°46E 38
Ha Giang Vietnam 22°50N 104°59E 38
Ha Karmel △ Israel 32°45N 35°5E 46
Ha Long, Vinh Vietnam 20°56N 107°3E 38
Ha Tien Vietnam 10°23N 104°29E 39
Ha Tinh Vietnam 18°20N 105°54E 38
Ha Trung Vietnam 19°58N 105°50E 38
Haaksbergen Neths. 52°9N 6°45E 15
Ha'ano Tonga 19°41S 174°18W 59
Ha'apai Group Tonga 19°47S 174°27W 59
Haapiti Moorea 17°34S 149°52W 59
Haapsalu Estonia 58°56N 23°30E 9 G
Haarlem Neths. 52°23N 4°39E 15
Haast → N.Z. 43°50S 169°2E 59
Haast Bluff Australia 23°22S 132°0E 60
Hab → Pakistan 24°53N 66°41E 42
Hab Nadi Chauki Pakistan 25°0N 66°50E 42
Habahe China 48°3N 86°23E 32

baswein Kenya 1°2N 39°30E 54 B4
bay Canada 58°50N 118°44W 70 B5
bbānīyah Iraq 33°17N 43°29E 44 C4
boro Japan 44°22N 141°42E 30 B10
bshān U.A.E. 23°50N 53°37E 45 F7
chijō-Jima Japan 33°5N 139°45E 31 H9
chinohe Japan 40°30N 141°29E 30 D10
chiōji Japan 35°40N 139°20E 31 G9
ckensack U.S.A. 40°52N 74°4W 83 F10
ckettstown U.S.A. 40°51N 74°50W 83 F10
dali Pakistan 32°16N 72°11E 42 C5
darba, Ras Sudan 22°4N 36°51E 51 D13
darom □ Israel 31°0N 35°0E 46 E4
dd, Ra's al Oman 22°35N 59°50E 47 C6
ddington U.K. 55°57N 2°47W 11 F6
dejia Nigeria 12°30N 10°5E 50 F7
dera Israel 32°27N 34°55E 46 C3
dera, N. → Israel 32°28N 34°52E 46 C3
derslev Denmark 55°15N 9°30E 9 J13
dhramaut = Haḍramawt
'emen 15°30N 49°30E 47 D4
dīboh Yemen 12°39N 54°2E 47 E5
dong S. Korea 35°5N 127°44E 35 G14
ḍramawt Yemen 15°30N 49°30E 47 D4
drānīyah Iraq 35°38N 43°14E 44 C4
drian's Wall U.K. 55°0N 2°30W 12 B5
e, Ko Thailand 7°44N 98°22E 39 a
eju N. Korea 38°3N 125°45E 35 E13
enam S. Korea 34°34N 126°35E 35 G14
enertsburg S. Africa 24°0S 29°50E 57 C4
erhpin = Harbin
hina 45°48N 126°40E 35 B14
far al Bāṭin Si. Arabia 28°32N 45°52E 44 D5
fīrat al 'Aydā
i. Arabia 26°26N 39°12E 44 E3
fīt Oman 23°59N 55°49E 45 F7
fizabad Pakistan 32°5N 73°40E 42 C5
flong India 25°10N 93°5E 41 G18
ft Gel Iran 31°30N 49°32E 45 D6
galil Israel 32°53N 35°18E 46 C4
gen Germany 51°21N 7°27E 16 C4
german U.S.A. 33°7N 104°20W 77 K11
german Fossil Beds ⌂
.S.A. 42°48N 114°57W 76 E6
gerstown U.S.A. 39°39N 77°43W 81 F15
gersville Canada 42°58N 80°3W 82 D4
gfors Sweden 60°3N 13°45E 9 F15
gi Japan 34°30N 131°22E 31 G5
golan Syria 33°0N 35°45E 46 C4
gondange France 49°16N 6°11E 20 B7
gs Hd. Ireland 52°57N 9°28W 10 D2
gue, C. de la France 49°44N 1°56W 20 B3
gue, The = 's-Gravenhage
leths. 52°7N 4°17E 15 B4
guenau France 48°49N 7°47E 20 B7
Duong Vietnam 20°56N 106°19E 38 B6
cheng China 40°50N 122°45E 35 D12
dar Khel Afghan. 33°58N 68°38E 42 C3
darâbâd = Hyderabad
ndia 17°22N 78°29E 40 L11
dargarh India 26°37N 81°22E 43 F9
fa = Ḥefa Israel 32°46N 35°0E 46 C4
kou China 20°1N 110°16E 38 B8
īl □ Si. Arabia 26°40N 41°40E 44 E4
lar China 49°10N 119°38E 33 B6
ley U.S.A. 43°31N 114°19W 76 E6
leybury Canada 47°30N 79°38W 72 C4
lin China 44°37N 129°30E 35 B15
luoto Finland 65°3N 24°45E 8 D21
nan □ China 19°0N 109°30E 38 C7
nan Dao China 19°0N 109°30E 38 C7
nan Str. = Qiongzhou Haixia
hina 20°10N 110°15E 38 B8
naut □ Belgium 50°30N 4°0E 15 D4
nes Alaska, U.S.A. 59°14N 135°26W 70 B1
nes Oreg., U.S.A. 44°55N 117°56W 76 D5
nes City U.S.A. 28°7N 81°38W 85 G14
nes Junction
anada 60°45N 137°30W 70 A1
phong Vietnam 20°47N 106°41E 38 B6
ti ■ W. Indies 19°0N 72°30W 89 C5
ya Sudan 18°20N 36°21E 51 E13
yan China 36°53N 100°59E 32 C5
yang China 36°47N 121°9E 35 F11
yuan China 36°35N 105°52E 34 F3
zhou China 34°37N 119°7E 35 G10
zhou Wan China 34°50N 119°20E 35 G10
Ali Qoli, Kavīr Iran 35°55N 54°50E 45 C7
dúböszörmény
ungary 47°40N 21°30E 17 E11
Ibrahim Iraq 36°40N 44°30E 44 B5
ābād Iran 33°37N 60°0E 45 C9
pur India 25°45N 85°13E 43 G11
ah Yemen 15°42N 43°36E 47 D3
ābād Iran 28°19N 55°55E 45 D7
ābād-e Zarrīn Iran 33°9N 54°51E 45 C7
nówka Poland 52°47N 23°35E 17 B12
ansson, Mts.
em. Rep. of the Congo 8°40S 25°45E 55 D2
kâri Turkey 37°34N 43°44E 44 B4
ken-Zan Japan 34°10N 135°54E 31 G7
odate Japan 41°45N 140°44E 30 D10
os Namibia 23°13S 16°21E 56 C2
u-San Japan 36°9N 136°46E 31 F8
u-San △ Japan 36°15N 136°45E 31 F8
ui Japan 36°53N 136°47E 31 F8
a Pakistan 25°43N 68°20E 40 G6
ab Syria 36°10N 37°15E 44 B3
abjah Iraq 35°10N 45°58E 44 C5
aib Sudan 22°12N 36°30E 51 D13
aib Triangle Africa 22°30N 35°20E 51 D13
at 'Ammār Si. Arabia 29°10N 36°4E 44 D3
bā Lebanon 34°34N 36°6E 46 A5
berstadt Germany 51°54N 11°3E 16 C6
combe N.Z. 40°8S 175°30E 59 D5
con Phil. 13°0N 121°30E 37 B6
de Fjäll = Haltiatunturi
nland 69°17N 21°18E 8 B19
Halden Norway 59°9N 11°23E 9 G14
Haldia Bangla. 22°1N 88°3E 43 H13
Haldwani India 29°31N 79°30E 43 E8
Hale → Australia 24°56S 135°53E 62 C2
Halesowen U.K. 52°27N 2°3W 13 E5
Halesworth U.K. 52°20N 1°31E 13 E9
Haleyville U.S.A. 34°14N 87°37W 85 D11
Half Dome U.S.A. 37°44N 119°32W 78 H7
Halfmoon Bay N.Z. 46°50S 168°5E 59 G2
Halfway → Canada 56°12N 121°32W 70 B4
Halia India 24°50N 82°19E 43 G10
Haliburton Canada 45°3N 78°30W 82 A6
Halifax Australia 18°32S 146°22E 62 B4
Halifax Canada 44°38N 63°35W 73 D7
Halifax U.K. 53°43N 1°52W 12 D6
Halifax U.S.A. 40°25N 76°55W 82 F8
Halifax B. Australia 18°50S 147°0E 62 B4
Halifax I. Namibia 26°38S 15°4E 56 D2
Halīl → Iran 27°40N 58°30E 45 E8
Halkida Greece 38°27N 23°42E 23 E10
Halkirk U.K. 58°30N 3°29W 11 C5
Hall Beach = Sanirajak
Canada 68°46N 81°12W 69 C11
Hall Pen. Canada 63°30N 66°0W 69 C13
Hall Pt. Australia 15°40S 124°23E 60 C3
Halland Sweden 57°8N 12°47E 9 H15
Hallāniyat, Jazā'ir al
Oman 17°30N 55°58E 47 D6
Hallasan S. Korea 33°22N 126°32E 35 H14
Halle Belgium 50°44N 4°13E 15 D4
Halle Germany 51°30N 11°56E 16 C6
Hällefors Sweden 59°47N 14°31E 9 G16
Hallett Australia 33°25S 138°55E 63 E2
Hallettsville U.S.A. 29°27N 96°57W 84 G6
Halley Antarctica 75°35S 26°39W 5 D1
Hallim S. Korea 33°24N 126°15E 35 H14
Hallingdalselva →
Norway 60°23N 9°35E 8 F13
Hallock U.S.A. 48°47N 96°57W 80 A5
Halls Creek Australia 18°16S 127°38E 60 C4
Halls Gap Australia 37°8S 142°34E 63 F3
Halls Lake Canada 45°7N 78°45W 82 A6
Hallsberg Sweden 59°5N 15°7E 9 G16
Hallstead U.S.A. 41°58N 75°45W 83 E9
Halmahera Indonesia 0°40N 128°0E 37 D7
Halmstad Sweden 56°41N 12°52E 9 H15
Hälsingborg = Helsingborg
Sweden 56°3N 12°42E 9 H15
Hälsingland Sweden 61°40N 16°5E 8 F17
Halstead U.K. 51°57N 0°40E 13 F8
Haltiatunturi Finland 69°17N 21°18E 8 B19
Halton □ U.K. 53°22N 2°45W 12 D5
Haltwhistle U.K. 54°58N 2°26W 12 C5
Ḥālūl Qatar 25°40N 52°40E 45 E7
Halvad India 23°1N 71°11E 42 H4
Ḥalvān Iran 33°57N 56°15E 45 C8
Ham Tan Vietnam 10°40N 107°45E 39 G6
Ham Yen Vietnam 22°4N 105°3E 38 A5
Hamab Namibia 28°7S 19°16E 56 D2
Hamada Japan 34°56N 132°4E 31 G6
Hamadān Iran 34°52N 48°32E 45 C6
Hamadān □ Iran 35°0N 49°0E 45 C6
Ḥamāh Syria 35°5N 36°40E 44 C3
Hamamatsu Japan 34°45N 137°45E 31 G8
Hamar Norway 60°48N 11°7E 8 F14
Hamâta, Gebel Egypt 24°17N 35°0E 44 E2
Hambantota Sri Lanka 6°10N 81°10E 40 R12
Hamber ⌂ Canada 52°20N 118°0W 70 C5
Hamburg Germany 53°33N 9°59E 16 B5
Hamburg Ark., U.S.A. 33°14N 91°48W 84 E9
Hamburg N.Y., U.S.A. 42°43N 78°50W 82 D6
Hamburg Pa., U.S.A. 40°33N 75°59W 83 F9
Ḥamḍ, W. al →
Si. Arabia 24°55N 36°20E 44 E3
Hamden U.S.A. 41°23N 72°54W 83 E12
Häme Finland 61°38N 25°10E 8 F21
Hämeenlinna Finland 61°0N 24°28E 8 F21
Hamelin Pool Australia 26°22S 114°20E 61 E1
Hameln Germany 52°6N 9°21E 16 B5
Hamerkaz □ Israel 32°15N 34°55E 46 C3
Hamersley Ra. Australia 22°0S 117°45E 60 D2
Hamhŭng N. Korea 39°54N 127°30E 35 E14
Hami China 42°55N 93°25E 32 B4
Hamilton Australia 37°45S 142°2E 63 F3
Hamilton Canada 43°15N 79°50W 82 C5
Hamilton N.Z. 37°47S 175°19E 59 B5
Hamilton U.K. 55°46N 4°2W 11 F4
Hamilton Ala., U.S.A. 34°9N 87°59W 85 D11
Hamilton Mont., U.S.A. 46°15N 114°10W 76 C6
Hamilton N.Y., U.S.A. 42°50N 75°33W 83 D9
Hamilton Ohio, U.S.A. 39°24N 84°34W 81 F11
Hamilton Tex., U.S.A. 31°42N 98°7W 84 F5
Hamilton → Queens.,
Australia 23°30S 139°47E 62 C2
Hamilton → S. Austral.,
Australia 26°40S 135°19E 63 D2
Hamilton City U.S.A. 39°45N 122°1W 78 F4
Hamilton I. Australia 20°21S 148°56E 62 J6
Hamilton Inlet Canada 54°0N 57°30W 73 B8
Hamilton Mt. U.S.A. 43°25N 74°22W 83 C10
Hamina Finland 60°34N 27°12E 8 F22
Hamirpur H.P., India 31°41N 76°31E 42 D7
Hamirpur Ut. P., India 25°57N 80°9E 43 G9
Hamju N. Korea 39°51N 127°26E 35 E14
Hamlet U.S.A. 34°53N 79°42W 85 D15
Hamley Bridge Australia 34°17S 138°35E 63 E2
Hamlin = Hameln
Germany 52°6N 9°21E 16 B5
Hamlin N.Y., U.S.A. 43°17N 77°55W 82 C7
Hamlin Tex., U.S.A. 32°53N 100°8W 84 E4
Hamm Germany 51°40N 7°50E 16 C4
Ḥammār, Hawr al Iraq 30°50N 47°10E 44 D5
Hammerfest Norway 70°39N 23°41E 8 A20
Hammond Ind., U.S.A. 41°38N 87°30W 80 E10
Hammond La., U.S.A. 30°30N 90°28W 85 F9
Hammond N.Y., U.S.A. 44°27N 75°42W 83 B9
Hammondsport U.S.A. 42°25N 77°13W 82 D7
Hammonton U.S.A. 39°39N 74°48W 81 F16
Hampden N.Z. 45°18S 170°50E 59 F3
Hampshire □ U.K. 51°7N 1°23W 13 F6
Hampshire Downs U.K. 51°15N 1°10W 13 F6
Hampton N.B., Canada 45°32N 65°51W 73 C6
Hampton Ont., Canada 43°58N 78°45W 82 C6
Hampton Ark., U.S.A. 33°32N 92°28W 84 E8
Hampton Iowa, U.S.A. 42°45N 93°13W 80 D7
Hampton N.H., U.S.A. 42°57N 70°50W 83 D14
Hampton S.C., U.S.A. 32°52N 81°7W 85 E14
Hampton Va., U.S.A. 37°2N 76°21W 81 G15
Hampton Bays U.S.A. 40°53N 72°30W 83 F12
Hampton Tableland
Australia 32°0S 127°0E 61 F4
Hamyang S. Korea 35°32N 127°42E 35 G14
Han Pijesak Bos.-H. 44°5N 18°57E 23 B8
Hanak Si. Arabia 25°32N 37°0E 44 E3
Hanamaki Japan 39°23N 141°7E 30 E10
Hanang Tanzania 4°30S 35°25E 54 C4
Hanau Germany 50°7N 8°56E 16 C5
Hanbogd = Ihbulag
Mongolia 43°11N 107°10E 34 C4
Hancheng China 35°31N 110°25E 34 G6
Hancock Mich., U.S.A. 47°8N 88°35W 80 B9
Hancock N.Y., U.S.A. 41°57N 75°17W 83 E9
Hancock Vt., U.S.A. 43°55N 72°50W 83 C12
Handa Japan 34°53N 136°55E 31 G8
Handa I. U.K. 58°23N 5°11W 11 C3
Handan China 36°35N 114°28E 34 F8
Handeni Tanzania 5°25S 38°2E 54 D4
Handwara India 34°21N 74°20E 43 B6
Hanegev Israel 30°50N 35°0E 46 E4
Hanford U.S.A. 36°20N 119°39W 78 J7
Hanford Reach ⌂
U.S.A. 46°40N 119°30W 76 C4
Hang Chat Thailand 18°20N 99°21E 38 C2
Hang Dong Thailand 18°41N 98°55E 38 C2
Hangang → S. Korea 37°50N 126°30E 35 F14
Hangayn Nuruu Mongolia 47°30N 99°0E 32 B4
Hangchou = Hangzhou
China 30°18N 120°11E 33 C7
Hanggin Houqi China 40°58N 107°4E 34 D4
Hanggin Qi China 39°52N 108°50E 34 E5
Hangu China 39°18N 117°53E 35 E9
Hangzhou China 30°18N 120°11E 33 C7
Hangzhou Wan China 30°15N 120°45E 33 C7
Hanh Mongolia 51°32N 100°35E 32 A5
Hanhongor Mongolia 43°55N 104°28E 34 C3
Hania = Chania Greece 35°30N 24°4E 25 D6
Ḥanīdh Si. Arabia 26°35N 48°38E 45 E6
Ḥanīsh Yemen 13°45N 42°46E 47 E3
Hankinson U.S.A. 46°4N 96°54W 80 B5
Hankö Finland 59°50N 22°57E 9 G20
Hanksville U.S.A. 38°22N 110°43W 76 G8
Hanle India 32°42N 79°4E 43 C8
Hanmer Springs N.Z. 42°32S 172°50E 59 E4
Hann → Australia 17°26S 126°17E 60 C4
Hann, Mt. Australia 15°45S 126°0E 60 C4
Hanna Canada 51°40N 111°54W 70 C6
Hanna U.S.A. 41°52N 106°34W 76 F10
Hannah B. Canada 51°40N 80°0W 72 B4
Hannibal Mo., U.S.A. 39°42N 91°22W 80 F8
Hannibal N.Y., U.S.A. 43°19N 76°35W 83 C8
Hannover Germany 52°22N 9°46E 16 B5
Hanoi Vietnam 21°5N 105°55E 38 B5
Hanover = Hannover
Germany 52°22N 9°46E 16 B5
Hanover Canada 44°9N 81°2W 82 B3
Hanover S. Africa 31°4S 24°29E 56 E3
Hanover N.H., U.S.A. 43°42N 72°17W 83 C12
Hanover Ohio, U.S.A. 40°4N 82°16W 82 F2
Hanover Pa., U.S.A. 39°48N 76°59W 81 F15
Hanover, I. Chile 51°0S 74°50W 96 G2
Hans Lollik I.
U.S. Virgin Is. 18°24N 64°53W 89 e
Hansdiha India 24°36N 87°5E 43 G12
Hansi H.P., India 32°27N 77°50E 42 C7
Hansi Haryana, India 29°10N 75°57E 42 E6
Hanson, L. Australia 31°0S 136°15E 63 E2
Hantsavichy Belarus 52°49N 26°30E 17 B14
Hanumangarh India 29°35N 74°19E 42 E6
Hanzhong China 33°10N 107°1E 34 H4
Hanzhuang China 34°33N 117°23E 35 G9
Haora India 22°34N 88°18E 43 H13
Haparanda Sweden 65°52N 24°8E 8 D21
Happy U.S.A. 34°45N 101°52W 84 D4
Happy Camp U.S.A. 41°48N 123°23W 76 F2
Happy Valley-Goose Bay
Canada 53°15N 60°20W 73 B7
Hapsu N. Korea 41°13N 128°51E 35 D15
Hapur India 28°45N 77°45E 42 E7
Ḥaql Si. Arabia 29°10N 34°58E 46 F3
Har Indonesia 5°16S 133°14E 37 F8
Har-Ayrag Mongolia 45°47N 109°16E 34 B5
Har Hu China 38°20N 97°38E 32 C4
Har Us Nuur Mongolia 48°0N 92°0E 32 B4
Har Yehuda Israel 31°35N 34°57E 46 D3
Ḥaraḍ Si. Arabia 24°22N 49°0E 47 C4
Haramosh Pakistan 35°50N 74°54E 43 B6
Haranomachi Japan 37°38N 140°58E 30 F10
Harare Zimbabwe 17°43S 31°2E 55 F3
Harazé Chad 9°57N 20°48E 51 G10
Harbin China 45°48N 126°40E 35 B14
Harbor Beach U.S.A. 43°51N 82°39W 82 C2
Harborcreek U.S.A. 42°9N 79°57W 82 D5
Harbour Breton Canada 47°29N 55°50W 73 C8
Harbour Deep Canada 50°25N 56°32W 73 B8
Harda India 22°27N 77°5E 42 H7
Hardangerfjorden Norway 60°5N 6°0E 9 F12
Hardangervidda Norway 60°7N 7°20E 8 F12
Hardap ⌂ Namibia 24°29S 17°45E 56 C2
Hardap Dam Namibia 24°32S 17°50E 56 C2
Hardenberg Neths. 52°34N 6°37E 15 B6
Harderwijk Neths. 52°21N 5°38E 15 B5
Hardey → Australia 22°45S 116°8E 60 D2
Hardin U.S.A. 45°44N 107°37W 76 D10
Harding S. Africa 30°35S 29°55E 57 E4
Harding Ra. Australia 16°17S 124°55E 60 C3
Hardisty Canada 52°40N 111°18W 70 C6
Hardoi India 27°26N 80°6E 43 F9
Hardwar = Haridwar
India 29°58N 78°9E 42 E8
Hardwick U.S.A. 44°30N 72°22W 83 B12
Hardwood Lake Canada 45°12N 77°26W 82 A7
Hardy, Pen. Chile 55°30S 68°20W 96 H3
Hardy, Pte. St. Lucia 14°6N 60°56W 89 f
Hare B. Canada 51°15N 55°45W 73 B8
Hareid Norway 62°22N 6°1E 8 E12
Harer Ethiopia 9°20N 42°8E 47 F3
Hargeisa Somali Rep. 9°30N 44°2E 47 F3
Hari → Indonesia 1°16S 104°5E 36 E2
Haria Canary Is. 29°8N 13°32W 24 E6
Haridwar India 29°58N 78°9E 42 E8
Harim, Jabal al Oman 25°58N 56°14E 45 E8
Haringhata → Bangla. 22°0N 89°58E 41 J16
Harīr, W. al → Syria 32°44N 35°59E 46 C4
Harīrūd → Asia 37°24N 60°38E 45 B9
Härjedalen Sweden 62°22N 13°5E 8 E15
Harlan Iowa, U.S.A. 41°39N 95°19W 80 E6
Harlan Ky., U.S.A. 36°51N 83°19W 81 G12
Harlech U.K. 52°52N 4°6W 12 E3
Harlem U.S.A. 48°32N 108°47W 76 B9
Harlingen Neths. 53°11N 5°25E 15 A5
Harlingen U.S.A. 26°12N 97°42W 84 H6
Harlow U.K. 51°46N 0°8E 13 F8
Harlowton U.S.A. 46°26N 109°50W 76 C9
Harnai Pakistan 30°6N 67°56E 42 D2
Harney Basin U.S.A. 43°0N 119°30W 76 E4
Harney L. U.S.A. 43°14N 119°8W 76 E4
Harney Peak U.S.A. 43°52N 103°32W 80 D2
Härnösand Sweden 62°38N 17°55E 8 E17
Haroldswick U.K. 60°48N 0°50W 11 A8
Harp L. Canada 55°5N 61°50W 73 A7
Harper Liberia 4°25N 7°43W 50 H4
Harrai India 22°37N 79°13E 43 H8
Harrand Pakistan 29°28N 70°3E 42 E4
Harricana → Canada 50°56N 79°32W 72 B4
Harriman U.S.A. 35°56N 84°33W 85 D12
Harrington Harbour
Canada 50°31N 59°30W 73 B8
Harris U.K. 57°50N 6°55W 11 D2
Harris, L. Australia 31°10S 135°10E 63 E2
Harris, Sd. of U.K. 57°44N 7°6W 11 D1
Harris Pt. Canada 43°6N 82°9W 82 C2
Harrisburg Ill., U.S.A. 37°44N 88°32W 80 G9
Harrisburg Nebr.,
U.S.A. 41°33N 103°44W 80 E2
Harrisburg Pa., U.S.A. 40°16N 76°53W 82 F8
Harrismith S. Africa 28°15S 29°8E 57 D4
Harrison Ark., U.S.A. 36°14N 93°7W 84 C8
Harrison Maine, U.S.A. 44°7N 70°39W 83 B14
Harrison Nebr., U.S.A. 42°41N 103°53W 80 D2
Harrison, C. Canada 54°55N 57°55W 73 B8
Harrison L. Canada 49°33N 121°50W 70 D4
Harrisonburg U.S.A. 38°27N 78°52W 81 F14
Harrisonville U.S.A. 38°39N 94°21W 80 F6
Harriston Canada 43°57N 80°53W 82 C4
Harrisville Mich., U.S.A. 44°39N 83°17W 82 B1
Harrisville N.Y., U.S.A. 44°9N 75°19W 83 B9
Harrisville Pa., U.S.A. 41°8N 80°0W 82 E5
Harrodsburg U.S.A. 37°46N 84°51W 81 G11
Harrogate U.K. 54°0N 1°33W 12 C6
Harrow Canada 42°2N 82°55W 82 D2
Harrow □ U.K. 51°35N 0°21W 13 F7
Harrowsmith Canada 44°24N 76°40W 83 B8
Harry S. Truman Res.
U.S.A. 38°16N 93°24W 80 F7
Harsīn Iran 34°18N 47°33E 44 C5
Harstad Norway 68°48N 16°30E 8 B17
Harsud India 22°6N 76°44E 42 H7
Hart U.S.A. 43°42N 86°22W 80 D10
Hart, L. Australia 31°10S 136°25E 63 E2
Hartbees → S. Africa 28°45S 20°32E 56 D3
Hartford Conn., U.S.A. 41°46N 72°41W 83 E12
Hartford Ky., U.S.A. 37°27N 86°55W 80 G10
Hartford S. Dak., U.S.A. 43°38N 96°57W 80 D5
Hartford Vt., U.S.A. 43°40N 72°20W 83 C12
Hartford Wis., U.S.A. 43°19N 88°22W 80 D9
Hartford City U.S.A. 40°27N 85°22W 81 E11
Hartland Canada 46°20N 67°32W 73 C6
Hartland Pt. U.K. 51°1N 4°32W 13 F3
Hartlepool U.K. 54°42N 1°13W 12 C6
Hartlepool □ U.K. 54°42N 1°17W 12 C6
Hartley Bay Canada 53°25N 129°15W 70 C3
Hartmannberge Namibia 17°0S 13°0E 56 B1
Hartney Canada 49°30N 100°35W 71 D8
Harts → S. Africa 28°24S 24°17E 56 D3
Harts Range Australia 23°6S 134°55E 62 C1
Hartselle U.S.A. 34°27N 86°56W 85 D11
Hartshorne U.S.A. 34°51N 95°34W 84 D7
Hartstown U.S.A. 41°33N 80°23W 82 E4
Hartsville U.S.A. 34°23N 80°4W 85 D14
Hartswater S. Africa 27°34S 24°43E 56 D3
Hartwell U.S.A. 34°21N 82°56W 85 D13
Harunabad Pakistan 29°35N 73°8E 42 E5
Harvand Iran 28°25N 55°43E 45 D7
Harvey Australia 33°5S 115°54E 61 F2
Harvey Ill., U.S.A. 41°36N 87°50W 80 E10
Harvey N. Dak., U.S.A. 47°47N 99°56W 80 B4
Harwich U.K. 51°56N 1°17E 13 F9
Haryana □ India 29°0N 76°10E 42 E7
Haryn → Belarus 52°7N 27°17E 17 B14
Harz Germany 51°38N 10°44E 16 C6
Hasa Si. Arabia 25°50N 49°0E 45 E6
Ḥasā, W. al → Jordan 31°4N 35°29E 46 D4
Ḥasanābād Iran 32°8N 52°44E 45 C7
Ḥasb, W. → Iraq 31°45N 44°17E 44 D5
Hasdo → India 21°44N 82°44E 43 J10
Hashimoto Japan 34°19N 135°37E 31 G7
Hashtjerd Iran 35°52N 50°40E 45 C6
Hashtpur = Tālesh Iran 37°58N 48°58E 45 B6
Haskell U.S.A. 33°10N 99°44W 84 E5
Haskovo = Khaskovo
Bulgaria 41°56N 25°30E 23 D11
Haslemere U.K. 51°5N 0°43W 13 F7
Hasselt Belgium 50°56N 5°21E 15 D5
Hassi Messaoud Algeria 31°51N 6°1E 50 B7
Hässleholm Sweden 56°10N 13°46E 9 H15
Hastings N.Z. 39°39S 176°52E 59 C6
Hastings U.K. 50°51N 0°35E 13 G8
Hastings Mich., U.S.A. 42°39N 85°17W 81 D11
Hastings Minn., U.S.A. 44°44N 92°51W 80 C7
Hastings Nebr., U.S.A. 40°35N 98°23W 80 E4
Hastings Ra. Australia 31°15S 152°14E 63 E5
Hat Yai Thailand 7°1N 100°27E 39 J3
Hatanbulag = Ergel
Mongolia 43°8N 109°5E 34 C5
Hatay Turkey 36°14N 36°10E 44 B3
Hatch U.S.A. 32°40N 107°9W 77 K10
Hatchet L. Canada 58°36N 103°40W 71 B8
Hateruma-Shima Japan 24°3N 123°47E 31 M1
Hatfield P.O. Australia 33°54S 143°49E 63 E3
Hatgal Mongolia 50°26N 100°9E 32 A5
Hathras India 27°36N 78°6E 42 F8
Hatia Bangla. 22°30N 91°5E 41 H17
Hato Mayor Dom. Rep. 18°46N 69°15W 89 C6
Hatta India 24°7N 79°36E 43 G8
Hatta U.A.E. 24°45N 56°4E 45 E8
Hattah Australia 34°48S 142°17E 63 E3
Hattah Kulkyne △
Australia 34°16S 142°33E 63 E3
Hatteras, C. U.S.A. 35°14N 75°32W 85 D17
Hattiesburg U.S.A. 31°20N 89°17W 85 F10
Hatvan Hungary 47°40N 19°45E 17 E10
Hau Duc Vietnam 15°20N 108°13E 38 E7
Haugesund Norway 59°23N 5°13E 9 G11
Haukipudas Finland 65°12N 25°20E 8 D21
Haultain → Canada 55°51N 106°46W 71 B7
Hauraki G. N.Z. 36°35S 175°5E 59 B5
Haut Atlas Morocco 32°30N 5°0W 50 B4
Hautes Fagnes = Hohes Venn
Belgium 50°30N 6°5E 15 D6
Hauts Plateaux Algeria 35°0N 1°0E 50 B6
Havana = La Habana
Cuba 23°8N 82°22W 88 B3
Havana U.S.A. 40°18N 90°4W 80 E8
Havant U.K. 50°51N 0°58W 13 G7
Havasor = Kığzı Turkey 38°18N 43°25E 44 B4
Havasu, L. U.S.A. 34°18N 114°28W 79 L12
Havel → Germany 52°50N 12°3E 16 B7
Havelian Pakistan 34°2N 73°10E 42 B5
Havelock Canada 44°26N 77°53W 82 B7
Havelock N.Z. 41°17S 173°48E 59 D4
Havelock U.S.A. 34°53N 76°54W 85 D16
Haverfordwest U.K. 51°48N 4°58W 13 F3
Haverhill U.K. 52°5N 0°28E 13 E8
Haverhill U.S.A. 42°47N 71°5W 83 D13
Haverstraw U.S.A. 41°12N 73°58W 83 E11
Havirga Mongolia 45°41N 113°5E 34 B7
Havířov Czech Rep. 49°46N 18°20E 17 D10
Havlíčkův Brod
Czech Rep. 49°36N 15°33E 16 D8
Havre U.S.A. 48°33N 109°41W 76 B9
Havre-Aubert Canada 47°12N 61°56W 73 C7
Havre-St.-Pierre Canada 50°18N 63°33W 73 B7
Haw → U.S.A. 35°36N 79°3W 85 D15
Hawai'i U.S.A. 19°30N 155°30W 74 b
Hawai'i □ U.S.A. 19°30N 156°30W 74 b
Hawaiian Is. Pac. Oc. 20°30N 156°0W 74 b
Hawaiian Ridge Pac. Oc. 24°0N 165°0W 65 E11
Hawarden U.S.A. 43°0N 96°29W 80 D5
Hawea, L. N.Z. 44°28S 169°19E 59 F2
Hawera N.Z. 39°35S 174°19E 59 C5
Hawick U.K. 55°26N 2°47W 11 F6
Hawk Junction Canada 48°5N 84°38W 72 C3
Hawke B. N.Z. 39°25S 177°20E 59 C6
Hawker Australia 31°59S 138°22E 63 E2
Hawke's Bay Canada 50°36N 57°10W 73 B8
Hawkesbury Canada 45°37N 74°37W 72 C5
Hawkesbury I. Canada 53°37N 129°3W 70 C3
Hawkesbury Pt.
Australia 11°55S 134°5E 62 A1
Hawkinsville U.S.A. 32°17N 83°28W 85 E13
Hawley Minn., U.S.A. 46°53N 96°19W 80 B5
Hawley Pa., U.S.A. 41°28N 75°11W 83 E9
Ḥawrān, W. → Iraq 33°58N 42°34E 44 C4
Hawsh Mūssá Lebanon 33°45N 35°55E 46 B4
Hawthorne U.S.A. 38°32N 118°38W 76 G4
Hay Australia 34°30S 144°51E 63 E3
Hay → Australia 24°50S 138°0E 62 C2
Hay → Canada 60°50N 116°26W 70 A5
Hay, C. Australia 14°5S 129°29E 60 B4
Hay I. Canada 44°53N 80°58W 82 B4
Hay L. Canada 58°50N 118°50W 70 B5
Hay-on-Wye U.K. 52°5N 3°8W 13 E4
Hay River Canada 60°51N 115°44W 70 A5
Hay Springs U.S.A. 42°41N 102°41W 80 D2
Haya = Tehoru Indonesia 3°23S 129°30E 37 E7
Hayachine-San Japan 39°34N 141°29E 30 E10
Hayastan = Armenia ■
Asia 40°20N 45°0E 19 F7
Haydān, W. al → Jordan 31°29N 35°34E 46 D4
Hayden U.S.A. 40°30N 107°16W 76 F10
Haydon Australia 18°0S 141°30E 62 B3
Hayes U.S.A. 44°23N 101°1W 80 C3
Hayes → Canada 57°3N 92°12W 72 A1
Hayes Creek Australia 13°43S 131°22E 60 B5
Hayle U.K. 50°11N 5°26W 13 G2
Hayling I. U.K. 50°48N 0°59W 13 G7
Haymen I. Australia 20°3S 148°52E 62 J6
Hayrabolu Turkey 41°12N 27°5E 23 D12
Hays Canada 50°6N 111°48W 70 C6
Hays U.S.A. 38°53N 99°20W 80 F4
Haysyn Ukraine 48°57N 29°25E 17 D15
Hayvoron Ukraine 48°22N 29°52E 17 D15
Hayward Calif., U.S.A. 37°40N 122°4W 78 H4
Hayward Wis., U.S.A. 46°1N 91°29W 80 B8
Haywards Heath U.K. 51°0N 0°5W 13 G7
Hazafon □ Israel 32°40N 35°20E 46 C4
Hazar Turkmenistan 39°34N 53°16E 19 G9
Hazārān, Kūh-e Iran 29°35N 57°20E 45 D8

Hazard U.S.A. 37°15N 83°12W 81 G12
Hazaribag India 23°58N 85°26E 43 H11
Hazaribag Road India 24°12N 85°57E 43 G11
Hazelton Canada 55°20N 127°42W 70 B3
Hazelton U.S.A. 46°29N 100°17W 80 B3
Hazen U.S.A. 47°18N 101°38W 80 B3
Hazlehurst Ga., U.S.A. 31°52N 82°36W 85 F13
Hazlehurst Miss., U.S.A. 31°52N 90°24W 85 F9
Hazlet U.S.A. 40°25N 74°12W 83 F10
Hazleton U.S.A. 40°57N 75°59W 83 F9
Hazlett, L. Australia 21°30S 128°48E 60 D4
Hazro Turkey 38°15N 40°47E 44 B4
Head of Bight Australia 31°30S 131°25E 61 F5
Headlands Zimbabwe 18°15S 32°2E 55 F3
Healdsburg U.S.A. 38°37N 122°52W 78 G4
Healdton U.S.A. 34°14N 97°29W 84 D6
Healesville Australia 37°35S 145°30E 63 F4
Heany Junction Zimbabwe 20°6S 28°54E 57 C4
Heard I. Ind. Oc. 53°0S 74°0E 3 G13
Hearne U.S.A. 30°53N 96°36W 84 F6
Hearst Canada 49°40N 83°41W 72 C3
Heart ➛ U.S.A. 46°46N 100°50W 80 B3
Heart's Content Canada 47°54N 53°27W 73 C9
Heath, Pte. Canada 49°8N 61°40W 73 C7
Heathrow, London ✈ (LHR) U.K. 51°28N 0°27W 13 F7
Heavener U.S.A. 34°53N 94°36W 84 D7
Hebbronville U.S.A. 27°18N 98°41W 84 H5
Hebei □ China 39°0N 116°0E 34 E9
Hebel Australia 28°58S 147°47E 63 D4
Heber U.S.A. 32°44N 115°32W 79 N11
Heber Springs U.S.A. 35°30N 92°2W 84 D8
Hebgen L. U.S.A. 44°52N 111°20W 76 D8
Hebi China 35°57N 114°7E 34 G8
Hebrides U.K. 57°30N 7°0W 6 D4
Hebrides, Sea of the U.K. 57°5N 7°0W 11 D2
Hebron = Al Khalīl West Bank 31°32N 35°6E 46 D4
Hebron Canada 58°5N 62°30W 69 D13
Hebron N. Dak., U.S.A. 46°54N 102°3W 80 B2
Hebron Nebr., U.S.A. 40°10N 97°35W 80 E5
Hecate Str. Canada 53°10N 130°30W 70 C2
Heceta I. U.S.A. 55°46N 133°40W 70 B2
Hechi China 24°40N 108°2E 32 D5
Hechuan China 30°2N 106°12E 32 C5
Hecla U.S.A. 45°53N 98°9W 80 C4
Hecla I. Canada 51°10N 96°43W 71 C9
Hede Sweden 62°23N 13°30E 8 E15
Hedemora Sweden 60°18N 15°58E 9 F16
Heerde Neths. 52°24N 6°2E 15 B6
Heerenveen Neths. 52°57N 5°55E 15 B5
Heerhugowaard Neths. 52°40N 4°51E 15 B4
Heerlen Neths. 50°55N 5°58E 15 D5
Ḥefa Israel 32°46N 35°0E 46 C4
Ḥefa □ Israel 32°40N 35°0E 46 C4
Hefei China 31°52N 117°18E 33 C6
Hegang China 47°20N 130°19E 33 B8
Hei Ling Chau China 22°15N 114°2E 33 G11
Heichengzhen China 36°24N 106°3E 34 F4
Heidelberg Germany 49°24N 8°42E 16 D5
Heidelberg S. Africa 34°6S 20°59E 56 E3
Heihe China 50°10N 127°30E 33 A7
Heilbron S. Africa 27°16S 27°59E 57 D4
Heilbronn Germany 49°9N 9°13E 16 D5
Heilongjiang □ China 48°0N 126°0E 33 B7
Heilunkiang = Heilongjiang □ China 48°0N 126°0E 33 B7
Heimaey Iceland 63°26N 20°17W 8 E3
Heinola Finland 61°13N 26°2E 8 F22
Heinze Kyun Burma 14°25N 97°45E 38 E1
Heishan China 41°40N 122°5E 35 D12
Heishui China 42°8N 119°30E 35 C10
Hejaz = Ḥijāz Si. Arabia 24°0N 40°0E 44 E3
Hejian China 38°25N 116°5E 34 E9
Hejin China 35°35N 110°42E 34 G6
Hekımhan Turkey 38°50N 37°55E 44 B3
Hekla Iceland 63°56N 19°35W 8 E4
Hekou China 22°30N 103°59E 32 D5
Helan Shan China 38°30N 105°55E 34 E3
Helen Atoll Pac. Oc. 2°40N 132°0E 37 D8
Helena Ark., U.S.A. 34°32N 90°36W 85 D9
Helena Mont., U.S.A. 46°36N 112°2W 76 C7
Helendale U.S.A. 34°44N 117°19W 79 L9
Helensburgh U.K. 56°1N 4°43W 11 E4
Helensville N.Z. 36°41S 174°29E 59 B5
Helenvale Australia 15°43S 145°14E 62 B4
Helgeland Norway 66°7N 13°29E 8 C15
Helgoland Germany 54°10N 7°53E 16 A4
Heligoland = Helgoland Germany 54°10N 7°53E 16 A4
Heligoland B. = Deutsche Bucht Germany 54°15N 8°0E 16 A5
Hell Hole Gorge △ Australia 25°31S 144°12E 62 D3
Hella Iceland 63°50N 20°24W 8 E3
Hellas = Greece ■ Europe 40°0N 23°0E 23 E9
Hellertown U.S.A. 40°35N 75°21W 83 F9
Hellespont = Çanakkale Boğazı Turkey 40°17N 26°32E 23 D12
Hellevoetsluis Neths. 51°50N 4°8E 15 C4
Hellín Spain 38°31N 1°40W 21 C5
Hells Canyon ⌂ U.S.A. 45°30N 117°45W 76 D5
Hell's Gate △ Kenya 0°54S 36°19E 54 C4
Helmand □ Afghan. 31°20N 64°0E 40 D4
Helmand ➛ Afghan. 31°12N 61°34E 40 D2
Helmeringhausen Namibia 25°54S 16°57E 56 D2
Helmond Neths. 51°29N 5°41E 15 C5
Helmsdale U.K. 58°7N 3°39W 11 C5
Helmsdale ➛ U.K. 58°8N 3°43W 11 C5
Helong China 42°40N 129°0E 35 C15
Helper U.S.A. 39°41N 110°51W 76 G8
Helsingborg Sweden 56°3N 12°42E 9 H15
Helsingfors = Helsinki Finland 60°10N 24°55E 9 F21
Helsingør Denmark 56°2N 12°35E 9 H15
Helsinki Finland 60°10N 24°55E 9 F21
Helston U.K. 50°6N 5°17W 13 G2
Helvellyn U.K. 54°32N 3°1W 12 C4
Helwân Egypt 29°50N 31°20E 51 C12
Hemel Hempstead U.K. 51°44N 0°28W 13 F7
Hemet U.S.A. 33°45N 116°58W 79 M10
Hemingford U.S.A. 42°19N 103°4W 80 D2
Hemis △ India 34°10N 77°15E 42 B7
Hemmingford Canada 45°3N 73°35W 83 A11
Hempstead N.Y., U.S.A. 40°42N 73°37W 83 F11
Hempstead Tex., U.S.A. 30°6N 96°5W 84 F6
Hemse Sweden 57°15N 18°22E 9 H18
Henan □ China 34°0N 114°0E 34 H8
Henares ➛ Spain 40°24N 3°30W 21 B4
Henashi-Misaki Japan 40°37N 139°51E 30 D9
Henderson Argentina 36°18S 61°43W 94 D3
Henderson Ky., U.S.A. 37°50N 87°35W 80 G10
Henderson N.C., U.S.A. 36°20N 78°25W 85 C15
Henderson N.Y., U.S.A. 43°50N 76°10W 83 C8
Henderson Nev., U.S.A. 36°2N 114°58W 79 J12
Henderson Tenn., U.S.A. 35°26N 88°38W 85 D10
Henderson Tex., U.S.A. 32°9N 94°48W 84 E7
Henderson I. Pac. Oc. 24°22S 128°19W 65 K15
Hendersonville N.C., U.S.A. 35°19N 82°28W 85 D13
Hendersonville Tenn., U.S.A. 36°18N 86°37W 85 C11
Hendījān Iran 30°14N 49°43E 45 D6
Hendorābī Iran 26°40N 53°37E 45 E7
Hengcheng China 38°18N 106°28E 34 E4
Hengdaohezi China 44°52N 129°0E 35 B15
Hengduan Shan China 27°30N 99°0E 32 D4
Hengelo Neths. 52°16N 6°48E 15 B6
Henggang China 22°39N 114°12E 33 F11
Hengmen China 22°33N 113°35E 33 F10
Hengqin Dao China 22°7N 113°34E 33 G10
Hengshan China 37°58N 109°5E 34 F5
Hengshui China 37°41N 115°40E 34 F8
Hengyang China 26°59N 112°22E 33 D6
Henley-on-Thames U.K. 51°32N 0°54W 13 F7
Henlopen, C. U.S.A. 38°48N 75°6W 81 F16
Hennenman S. Africa 27°59S 27°1E 56 D4
Hennessey U.S.A. 36°6N 97°54W 84 C6
Henri Pittier △ Venezuela 10°26N 67°37W 89 D6
Henrietta N.Y., U.S.A. 43°4N 77°37W 82 C7
Henrietta Tex., U.S.A. 33°49N 98°12W 84 E5
Henrietta, Ostrov = Genriyetty, Ostrov Russia 77°6N 156°30E 29 B16
Henrietta Maria, C. Canada 55°9N 82°20W 72 A3
Henry U.S.A. 41°7N 89°22W 80 E9
Henryetta U.S.A. 35°27N 95°59W 84 D7
Henryville Canada 45°8N 73°11W 83 A11
Hensall Canada 43°26N 81°30W 82 C3
Hentiesbaai Namibia 22°8S 14°18E 56 C1
Hentiyn Nuruu Mongolia 48°30N 108°30E 33 B5
Henty Australia 35°30S 147°3E 63 F4
Henzada Burma 17°38N 95°26E 41 L19
Heppner U.S.A. 45°21N 119°33W 76 D4
Hepworth Canada 44°37N 81°9W 82 B3
Hequ China 39°20N 111°15E 34 E6
Héraðsflói Iceland 65°42N 14°12W 8 D6
Héraðsvötn ➛ Iceland 65°45N 19°25W 8 D4
Heraklion = Iraklio Greece 35°20N 25°12E 25 D7
Herald Cays Australia 16°58S 149°9E 62 B4
Herāt Afghan. 34°20N 62°7E 40 B3
Herāt □ Afghan. 35°0N 62°0E 40 B3
Herbert Canada 50°30N 107°10W 71 C7
Herbert ➛ Australia 18°31S 146°17E 62 B4
Herberton Australia 17°20S 145°25E 62 B4
Herbertsdale S. Africa 34°1S 21°46E 56 E3
Herceg-Novi Montenegro 42°30N 18°33E 23 C8
Herchmer Canada 57°22N 94°10W 71 B10
Herðubreið Iceland 65°11N 16°21W 8 D5
Hereford U.K. 52°4N 2°43W 13 E5
Hereford U.S.A. 34°49N 102°24W 84 D3
Herefordshire □ U.K. 52°8N 2°40W 13 E5
Herentals Belgium 51°12N 4°51E 15 C4
Herford Germany 52°7N 8°39E 16 B5
Herington U.S.A. 38°40N 96°57W 80 F5
Herkimer U.S.A. 43°2N 74°59W 83 D10
Herlong U.S.A. 40°8N 120°8W 78 E6
Herm U.K. 49°30N 2°28W 13 H5
Hermann U.S.A. 38°42N 91°27W 80 F8
Hermannsburg Australia 23°57S 132°45E 60 D5
Hermanus S. Africa 34°27S 19°12E 56 E2
Hermidale Australia 31°30S 146°42E 63 E4
Hermiston U.S.A. 45°51N 119°17W 76 D4
Hermon Canada 45°6N 77°37W 82 A7
Hermon U.S.A. 44°28N 75°14W 83 B9
Hermon, Mt. = Shaykh, J. ash Lebanon 33°25N 35°50E 46 B4
Hermosillo Mexico 29°10N 111°0W 86 B2
Hernád ➛ Hungary 47°56N 21°8E 17 D11
Hernandarias Paraguay 25°20S 54°40W 95 B5
Hernandez U.S.A. 36°24N 120°46W 78 J6
Hernando Argentina 32°28S 63°40W 94 C3
Hernando U.S.A. 34°50N 90°0W 85 D10
Herndon U.S.A. 40°43N 76°51W 82 F8
Herne Germany 51°32N 7°14E 15 C7
Herne Bay U.K. 51°21N 1°8E 13 F9
Herning Denmark 56°8N 8°58E 9 H13
Heroica Caborca = Caborca Mexico 30°37N 112°6W 86 A2
Heroica Nogales = Nogales Mexico 31°19N 110°56W 86 A2
Heron Bay Canada 48°40N 86°25W 72 C2
Heron I. Australia 23°27S 151°55E 62 C5
Herradura, Pta. de la Canary Is. 28°26N 14°8W 24 F5
Herreid U.S.A. 45°50N 100°4W 80 C3
Herrin U.S.A. 37°48N 89°2W 80 G9
Herriot Canada 56°22N 101°16W 71 B8
Herschel I. Canada 69°35N 139°5W 4 C1
Hershey U.S.A. 40°17N 76°39W 83 F8
Herstal Belgium 50°40N 5°38E 15 D5
Hertford U.K. 51°48N 0°4W 13 F7
Hertfordshire □ U.K. 51°51N 0°5W 13 F7
's-Hertogenbosch Neths. 51°42N 5°17E 15 C5
Hertzogville S. Africa 28°9S 25°30E 56 D4
Hervey B. Australia 25°0S 152°52E 62 C5
Herzliyya Israel 32°10N 34°50E 46 C3
Ḥeşār Fārs, Iran 29°52N 50°16E 45 D6
Ḥeşār Markazī, Iran 35°50N 49°12E 45 C6
Heshui China 35°48N 108°0E 34 G5
Heshun China 37°22N 113°32E 34 F7
Hesperia U.S.A. 34°25N 117°18W 79 L9
Hesse = Hessen □ Germany 50°30N 9°0E 16 C5
Hessen □ Germany 50°30N 9°0E 16 C5
Hetauda Nepal 27°25N 85°2E 42 F11
Hetch Hetchy Aqueduct U.S.A. 37°29N 122°19W 78 H5
Hettinger U.S.A. 46°0N 102°42W 80 B2
Heuksando S. Korea 34°40N 125°30E 35 G13
Heunghae S. Korea 36°12N 129°21E 35 F15
Heuvelton U.S.A. 44°37N 75°25W 83 B9
Hewitt U.S.A. 31°28N 97°12W 84 F6
Hexham U.K. 54°58N 2°4W 12 C5
Hexigten Qi China 43°18N 117°30E 35 C9
Ḥeydarābād Iran 30°33N 55°38E 45 D7
Heysham U.K. 54°3N 2°53W 12 C5
Heywood Australia 38°8S 141°37E 63 F3
Heze China 35°14N 115°20E 34 G8
Hi Vista U.S.A. 34°45N 117°46W 79 L9
Hialeah U.S.A. 25°51N 80°16W 85 J14
Hiawatha U.S.A. 39°51N 95°32W 80 F6
Hibbing U.S.A. 47°25N 92°56W 80 B7
Hibbs B. Australia 42°35S 145°15E 63 G4
Hibernia Reef Australia 12°0S 123°23E 60 B3
Hickman U.S.A. 36°34N 89°11W 80 G9
Hickory U.S.A. 35°44N 81°21W 85 D14
Hicks, Pt. Australia 37°49S 149°17E 63 F4
Hicks L. Canada 61°25N 100°0W 71 A9
Hicksville U.S.A. 40°46N 73°32W 83 F11
Hida-Gawa ➛ Japan 35°26N 137°3E 31 G8
Hida-Sammyaku Japan 36°30N 137°40E 31 F8
Hidaka-Sammyaku Japan 42°35N 142°45E 30 C11
Hidalgo □ Mexico 20°30N 99°0W 87 C5
Hidalgo, Presa M. Mexico 26°30N 108°35W 86 B3
Hidalgo del Parral Mexico 26°56N 105°40W 86 B3
Hierro Canary Is. 27°44N 18°0W 24 G1
Higashiajima-San Japan 37°40N 140°10E 30 F10
Higashiōsaka Japan 34°39N 135°37E 31 G7
Higgins U.S.A. 36°7N 100°2W 84 C4
Higgins Corner U.S.A. 39°2N 121°5W 78 F5
High Bridge U.S.A. 40°40N 74°54W 83 F10
High Island Res. China 22°22N 114°21E 33 G11
High Level Canada 58°31N 117°8W 70 B5
High Point U.S.A. 35°57N 80°0W 85 D15
High Prairie Canada 55°30N 116°30W 70 B5
High River Canada 50°30N 113°50W 70 C6
High Tatra = Tatry Slovak Rep. 49°20N 20°0E 17 D11
High Veld Africa 27°0S 27°0E 48 J6
High Wycombe U.K. 51°37N 0°45W 13 F7
Highland □ U.K. 57°17N 4°21W 11 D4
Highland Park U.S.A. 42°11N 87°48W 80 D10
Highmore U.S.A. 44°31N 99°27W 80 C4
Highrock L. Canada 55°45N 100°30W 71 B8
Higüey Dom. Rep. 18°37N 68°42W 89 C6
Hiiumaa Estonia 58°50N 22°45E 9 G20
Ḥijāz Si. Arabia 24°0N 40°0E 44 E3
Hijo = Tagum Phil. 7°33N 125°53E 37 C7
Hikari Japan 33°58N 131°58E 31 H5
Hiko U.S.A. 37°32N 115°14W 78 H11
Hikone Japan 35°15N 136°10E 31 G8
Hikurangi Gisborne, N.Z. 37°55S 178°4E 59 C6
Hikurangi Northland, N.Z. 35°36S 174°17E 59 A5
Hildesheim Germany 52°9N 9°56E 16 B5
Hill ➛ Australia 30°23S 115°3E 61 F2
Hill City Idaho, U.S.A. 43°18N 115°3W 76 E6
Hill City Kans., U.S.A. 39°22N 99°51W 80 F4
Hill City Minn., U.S.A. 46°59N 93°36W 80 B7
Hill City S. Dak., U.S.A. 43°56N 103°35W 80 D2
Hill Island L. Canada 60°30N 109°50W 71 A7
Hillaby, Mt. Barbados 13°12N 59°35W 89 g
Hillcrest Barbados 13°13N 59°31W 89 g
Hillcrest Center U.S.A. 35°23N 118°57W 79 K8
Hillegom Neths. 52°18N 4°35E 15 B4
Hillsboro Kans., U.S.A. 38°21N 97°12W 80 F5
Hillsboro N. Dak., U.S.A. 47°26N 97°3W 80 B5
Hillsboro Ohio, U.S.A. 39°12N 83°37W 81 F12
Hillsboro Oreg., U.S.A. 45°31N 122°59W 78 E4
Hillsboro Tex., U.S.A. 32°1N 97°8W 84 E6
Hillsborough Grenada 12°28N 61°28W 89 D7
Hillsborough U.S.A. 43°7N 71°54W 83 C13
Hillsborough Channel Australia 20°56S 149°15E 62 J7
Hillsdale Mich., U.S.A. 41°56N 84°38W 81 E11
Hillsdale N.Y., U.S.A. 42°11N 73°32W 83 D11
Hillsport Canada 49°27N 85°34W 72 C2
Hillston Australia 33°30S 145°31E 63 E4
Hilo U.S.A. 19°44N 155°5W 74 b
Hilton U.S.A. 43°17N 77°48W 82 C7
Hilton Head Island U.S.A. 32°13N 80°45W 85 E14
Hilversum Neths. 52°14N 5°10E 15 B5
Himachal Pradesh □ India 31°30N 77°0E 42 D7
Himalaya Asia 29°0N 84°0E 43 E11
Himalchuli Nepal 28°27N 84°38E 43 E11
Himatnagar India 23°37N 72°57E 42 H5
Himeji Japan 34°50N 134°40E 31 G7
Himi Japan 36°50N 136°55E 31 F8
Ḥimş Syria 34°40N 36°45E 46 A5
Ḥimş □ Syria 34°30N 37°0E 46 A6
Hinche Haiti 19°9N 72°1W 89 C5
Hinchinbrook I. Australia 18°20S 146°15E 62 B4
Hinchinbrook Island △ Australia 18°14S 146°6E 62 B4
Hinckley U.K. 52°33N 1°22W 13 E6
Hinckley U.S.A. 46°1N 92°56W 80 B7
Hindaun India 26°44N 77°5E 42 F7
Hindmarsh, L. Australia 36°5S 141°55E 63 F3
Hindu Bagh Pakistan 30°56N 67°50E 42 D2
Hindu Kush Asia 36°0N 71°0E 40 B7
Hindupur India 13°49N 77°32E 40 N10
Hines Creek Canada 56°20N 118°40W 70 B5
Hinesville U.S.A. 31°51N 81°36W 85 F14
Hinganghat India 20°30N 78°52E 40 J11
Hingham U.S.A. 48°33N 110°25W 76 B8
Hingir India 21°57N 83°41E 43 J10
Hingoli India 19°41N 77°15E 40 K10
Hinna = Imi Ethiopia 6°28N 42°10E 47 F3
Hinnøya Norway 68°35N 15°50E 8 B16
Hinojosa del Duque Spain 38°30N 5°9W 21 C3
Hinsdale U.S.A. 42°47N 72°29W 83 D12
Hinthada = Henzada Burma 17°38N 95°26E 41 L19
Hinton Canada 53°26N 117°34W 70 C5
Hinton U.S.A. 37°40N 80°54W 81 G13
Hios Greece 38°27N 26°9E 23 E12
Hirado Japan 33°22N 129°33E 31 H4
Hirakud Dam India 21°32N 83°45E 41 J13
Hiran ➛ India 23°6N 79°21E 43 H8
Hirapur India 24°22N 79°13E 43 G8
Hirara Japan 24°48N 125°17E 31 M2
Hiratsuka Japan 35°19N 139°21E 31 G9
Hiroo Japan 42°17N 143°19E 30 C11
Hirosaki Japan 40°34N 140°28E 30 D10
Hiroshima Japan 34°24N 132°30E 31 G6
Hiroshima □ Japan 34°50N 133°0E 31 G6
Hisar India 29°12N 75°45E 42 E6
Hisb, Sha'ib = Ḥasb, W. ➛ Iraq 31°45N 44°17E 44 D5
Ḥismá Si. Arabia 28°30N 36°0E 44 D3
Hispaniola W. Indies 19°0N 71°0W 89 C5
Hīt Iraq 33°38N 42°49E 44 C4
Hita Japan 33°20N 130°58E 31 H5
Hitachi Japan 36°36N 140°39E 31 F10
Hitchin U.K. 51°58N 0°16W 13 F7
Hitiaa Tahiti 17°36S 149°18W 59 d
Hitoyoshi Japan 32°13N 130°45E 31 H5
Hitra Norway 63°30N 8°45E 8 E13
Hiva Oa French Polynesia 9°45S 139°0W 65 H14
Hixon Canada 53°25N 122°35W 70 C4
Ḥiyyon, N. ➛ Israel 30°25N 35°10E 46 E4
Hjalmar L. Canada 61°33N 109°25W 71 A7
Hjälmaren Sweden 59°18N 15°40E 9 G16
Hjørring Denmark 57°29N 9°59E 9 H13
Hjort Trench S. Ocean 58°0S 157°30E 5 B10
Hkakabo Razi Burma 28°25N 97°23E 41 E20
Hlobane S. Africa 27°42S 31°0E 57 D5
Hluhluwe S. Africa 28°1S 32°15E 57 D5
Hluhluwe ⌂ S. Africa 22°10S 32°5E 57 C5
Hlyboka Ukraine 48°5N 25°56E 17 D13
Ho Ghana 6°37N 0°27E 50 G6
Ho Chi Minh City = Thanh Pho Ho Chi Minh Vietnam 10°58N 106°40E 39 G6
Ho Thuong Vietnam 19°32N 105°48E 38 C5
Hoa Binh Vietnam 20°50N 105°20E 38 B5
Hoa Da Vietnam 11°16N 108°40E 39 G7
Hoa Hiep Vietnam 11°34N 105°51E 39 G5
Hoai Nhon Vietnam 14°28N 109°1E 38 E7
Hoang Lien Son Vietnam 22°0N 104°0E 38 A4
Hoanib ➛ Namibia 19°27S 12°46E 56 B2
Hoare B. Canada 65°17N 62°30W 69 C13
Hoarusib ➛ Namibia 19°3S 12°36E 56 B2
Hobart Australia 42°50S 147°21E 63 G4
Hobart U.S.A. 35°1N 99°6W 84 D5
Hobbs U.S.A. 32°42N 103°8W 77 K12
Hobbs Coast Antarctica 74°50S 131°0W 5 D14
Hobe Sound U.S.A. 27°4N 80°8W 85 H14
Hoboken U.S.A. 40°44N 74°3W 83 F10
Hobro Denmark 56°39N 9°46E 9 H13
Hoburgen Sweden 56°55N 18°7E 9 H18
Hobyo Somali Rep. 5°25N 48°30E 47 F4
Hochfeld Namibia 21°28S 17°58E 56 C2
Hodaka-Dake Japan 36°17N 137°39E 31 F8
Hodeida = Al Ḥudaydah Yemen 14°50N 43°0E 47 E3
Hodgeville Canada 50°7N 106°58W 71 C7
Hodgson Canada 51°13N 97°36W 71 C9
Hódmezővásárhely Hungary 46°28N 20°22E 17 E11
Hodna, Chott el Algeria 35°26N 4°43E 50 A6
Hodonín Czech Rep. 48°50N 17°10E 17 D9
Hoek van Holland Neths. 52°0N 4°7E 15 C4
Hoengseong S. Korea 37°29N 127°59E 35 F14
Hoeryong N. Korea 42°30N 129°45E 35 C15
Hoeyang N. Korea 38°43N 127°36E 35 E14
Hof Germany 50°19N 11°55E 16 C6
Hofmeyr S. Africa 31°39S 25°50E 56 E4
Höfn Iceland 64°15N 15°13W 8 D6
Hofors Sweden 60°31N 16°15E 9 F17
Hofsjökull Iceland 64°49N 18°48W 8 D4
Hōfu Japan 34°3N 131°34E 31 G5
Hogan Group Australia 39°13S 147°1E 63 F4
Hogarth, Mt. Australia 21°48S 136°58E 62 C2
Hoge Kempen △ Belgium 51°6N 5°35E 15 C5
Hoggar = Ahaggar Algeria 23°0N 6°30E 50 D7
Hogsty Reef Bahamas 21°41N 73°48W 89 B5
Hoh ➛ U.S.A. 47°45N 124°29W 78 C2
Hoh Xil Shan China 35°0N 89°0E 32 C3
Hohenwald U.S.A. 35°33N 87°33W 85 D11
Hoher Rhön = Rhön Germany 50°24N 9°58E 16 C5
Hohes Venn Belgium 50°30N 6°5E 15 D6
Hohhot China 40°52N 111°40E 34 D6
Hoi An Vietnam 15°30N 108°19E 38 E7
Hoi Xuan Vietnam 20°25N 105°9E 38 B5
Hoisington U.S.A. 38°31N 98°47W 80 F4
Hōjō Japan 33°58N 132°46E 31 H6
Hokianga Harbour N.Z. 35°31S 173°22E 59
Hokitika N.Z. 42°42S 171°0E 59
Hokkaidō □ Japan 43°30N 143°0E 30 C
Hola Kenya 1°29S 40°2E 54
Holakas Greece 35°57N 27°53E 25
Holbrook Australia 35°42S 147°18E 63
Holbrook U.S.A. 34°54N 110°10W 77
Holcomb U.S.A. 42°54N 77°25W 82
Holden U.S.A. 39°6N 112°16W 76
Holdenville U.S.A. 35°5N 96°24W 84
Holdrege U.S.A. 40°26N 99°23W 80
Holetown Barbados 13°11N 59°38W 89
Holguín Cuba 20°50N 76°20W 88
Hollams Bird I. Namibia 24°40S 14°30E 56
Holland = Netherlands ■ Europe 52°0N 5°30E 15
Holland Mich., U.S.A. 42°47N 86°7W 80 D
Holland N.Y., U.S.A. 42°38N 78°32W 82
Holland Centre Canada 44°23N 80°47W 82
Holland Patent U.S.A. 43°14N 75°15W 83
Hollandale U.S.A. 33°10N 90°51W 85
Holley U.S.A. 43°14N 78°2W 82
Hollidaysburg U.S.A. 40°26N 78°24W 82
Hollis U.S.A. 34°41N 99°55W 84
Hollister Calif., U.S.A. 36°51N 121°24W 78
Hollister Idaho, U.S.A. 42°21N 114°35W 76
Holly Hill U.S.A. 29°16N 81°3W 85 G
Holly Springs U.S.A. 34°46N 89°27W 85 D
Hollywood U.S.A. 26°0N 80°8W 85 J
Holman Canada 70°44N 117°44W 68
Hólmavík Iceland 65°42N 21°40W 8
Holmen U.S.A. 43°58N 91°15W 80
Holmes Reefs Australia 16°27S 148°0E 62
Holmsund Sweden 63°41N 20°20E 8 E
Holroyd ➛ Australia 14°10S 141°36E 62
Holstebro Denmark 56°22N 8°37E 9 H
Holsworthy U.K. 50°48N 4°22W 13
Holton Canada 54°31N 57°12W 73
Holton U.S.A. 39°28N 95°44W 80
Holtville U.S.A. 32°49N 115°23W 79 N
Holwerd Neths. 53°22N 5°54E 15
Holy I. Anglesey, U.K. 53°17N 4°37W 12
Holy I. Northumberland, U.K. 55°40N 1°47W 12
Holyhead U.K. 53°18N 4°38W 12
Holyoke Colo., U.S.A. 40°35N 102°18W 76 F
Holyoke Mass., U.S.A. 42°12N 72°37W 83 D
Holyrood Canada 47°27N 53°8W 73
Homa Bay Kenya 0°36S 34°30E 54
Homalin Burma 24°55N 95°0E 41 G
Homand Iran 32°28N 59°37E 45
Homathko ➛ Canada 51°0N 124°56W 70
Hombori Mali 15°20N 1°38W 50
Home B. Canada 68°40N 67°10W 69 C
Home Hill Australia 19°43S 147°25E 62
Home Reef Tonga 18°59S 174°47W 5
Homedale U.S.A. 43°37N 116°56W 76
Homer Alaska, U.S.A. 59°39N 151°33W 68
Homer La., U.S.A. 32°48N 93°4W 84
Homer N.Y., U.S.A. 42°38N 76°10W 83
Homer City U.S.A. 40°32N 79°10W 82
Homestead Australia 20°20S 145°40E 62
Homestead U.S.A. 25°28N 80°29W 85 J
Homestead ⌂ U.S.A. 40°17N 96°50W 80
Homoine Mozam. 23°55S 35°8E 57
Homs = Ḥimş Syria 34°40N 36°45E 46
Homyel Belarus 52°28N 31°0E 17 B
Hon Chong Vietnam 10°25N 104°30E 39
Hon Hai Vietnam 10°0N 109°0E 39
Hon Me Vietnam 19°23N 105°56E 38
Honan = Henan □ China 34°0N 114°0E 34
Honbetsu Japan 43°7N 143°37E 30 C
Honcut U.S.A. 39°20N 121°32W 78
Honda, Bahía Cuba 22°54N 83°10W 88
Hondeklipbaai S. Africa 30°19S 17°17E 56
Hondo Japan 32°27N 130°12E 31
Hondo U.S.A. 29°21N 99°9W 84
Hondo, Río ➛ Belize 18°25N 88°21W 87
Honduras ■ Cent. Amer. 14°40N 86°30W 88
Honduras, G. de Caribbean 16°50N 87°0W 88
Hønefoss Norway 60°10N 10°18E 9
Honesdale U.S.A. 41°34N 75°16W 83
Honey Harbour Canada 44°52N 79°49W 82
Honey L. U.S.A. 40°15N 120°19W 78
Honfleur France 49°25N 0°13E 20
Hong Gai Vietnam 20°57N 107°5E 38
Hong He ➛ China 32°25N 115°35E 34
Hong Kong □ China 22°11N 114°14E 33
Hong Kong I. China 22°16N 114°12E 33
Hong Kong Int. ✈ (HKG) China 22°19N 113°57E 33
Hongcheon S. Korea 37°44N 127°53E 35
Hongjiang China 27°7N 109°59E 33
Hongliu He ➛ China 38°0N 109°50E 34
Hongor Mongolia 45°45N 112°50E 34
Hongsa Laos 19°43N 101°20E 38
Hongseong S. Korea 36°37N 126°38E 35
Hongshui He ➛ China 23°48N 109°30E 33
Hongtong China 36°16N 111°40E 34
Honguedo, Détroit d' Canada 49°15N 64°0W 73
Hongwon N. Korea 40°0N 127°56E 35
Hongze Hu China 33°15N 118°35E 35
Honiara Solomon Is. 9°27S 159°57E 58
Honiton U.K. 50°47N 3°11W 13
Honjō Japan 39°23N 140°3E 30
Honningsvåg Norway 70°59N 25°59E 8
Honolulu U.S.A. 21°19N 157°52W 74
Honshū Japan 36°0N 138°0E 30
Hood, Mt. U.S.A. 45°23N 121°42W 76
Hood, Pt. Australia 34°23S 119°34E 61
Hood River U.S.A. 45°43N 121°31W 76
Hoodsport U.S.A. 47°24N 123°9W 78
Hoogeveen Neths. 52°44N 6°28E 15
Hoogezand-Sappemeer Neths. 53°9N 6°45E 15

oghly = Hugli →
India 21°56N 88°4E 43 J13
oghly-Chinsura = Chunchura
India 22°53N 88°27E 43 H13
ok Hd. Ireland 52°7N 6°56W 10 D5
ok I. Australia 20°4S 149°0E 62 J6
ok of Holland = Hoek van
Holland Neths. 52°0N 4°7E 15 C4
oker U.S.A. 36°52N 101°13W 84 C4
oker Creek = Lajamanu
Australia 18°23S 130°38E 60 C5
onah U.S.A. 58°7N 135°27W 70 B1
oper Bay U.S.A. 61°32N 166°6W 74 a
opeston U.S.A. 40°28N 87°40W 80 E10
opstad S. Africa 27°50S 25°55E 56 D4
orn Neths. 52°38N 5°4E 15 B5
over U.S.A. 33°24N 86°49W 85 E11
over Dam U.S.A. 36°1N 114°44W 79 K12
oversville U.S.A. 40°9N 78°55W 82 F6
p Bottom U.S.A. 41°42N 75°46W 83 E9
pe Canada 49°25N 121°25W 70 D4
pe Ariz., U.S.A. 33°43N 113°42W 79 M13
pe Ark., U.S.A. 33°40N 93°36W 84 E8
pe, L. S. Austral.,
Australia 28°24S 139°18E 63 D2
pe, L. W. Austral.,
Australia 32°35S 120°15E 61 F3
pe, Pt. U.S.A. 68°21N 166°47W 66 C3
pe I. Canada 44°55N 80°11W 82 B4
pe Town Bahamas 26°35N 76°57W 88 A4
pe Vale Australia 15°16S 145°20E 62 B4
pedale Canada 55°28N 60°13W 73 A7
pedale U.S.A. 42°8N 71°33W 83 D13
pefield S. Africa 33°3S 18°22E 56 E2
pei = Hebei □ China 39°0N 116°0E 34 E9
pelchén Mexico 19°46N 89°51W 87 D7
petoun Vic., Australia 35°42S 142°22E 63 F3
petoun W. Austral.,
Australia 33°57S 120°7E 61 F3
petown S. Africa 29°34S 24°3E 56 D3
pewell U.S.A. 37°18N 77°17W 81 G15
pkins, L. Australia 24°15S 128°35E 60 D4
pkinsville U.S.A. 36°52N 87°29W 80 G10
pland U.S.A. 38°58N 123°7W 78 G3
quiam U.S.A. 46°59N 123°53W 78 D3
rdern Hills Australia 20°15S 130°0E 60 D5
inger China 40°28N 111°48E 34 D6
izontina Brazil 27°37S 54°19W 95 B5
lick Mts. Antarctica 84°0S 102°0W 5 E15
livka Ukraine 48°19N 38°5E 19 E6
mak Iran 29°58N 60°51E 45 D9
moz Iran 27°35N 55°0E 45 E7
moz, Jaz.-ye Iran 27°8N 56°28E 45 E8
mozgān □ Iran 27°30N 56°0E 45 E8
muz, Kūh-e Iran 27°27N 55°10E 45 E7
muz, Str. of The Gulf 26°30N 56°30E 45 E8
n Austria 48°39N 15°40E 16 D8
n → Canada 61°30N 118°1W 70 A5
n, Cape = Hornos, C. de
Chile 55°50S 67°30W 96 H3
n Head Ireland 55°14N 8°0W 10 A3
n I. Australia 10°37S 142°17E 62 A3
n Plateau Canada 62°15N 119°15W 70 A5
navan Sweden 66°15N 17°30E 8 C17
nbeck U.S.A. 31°20N 93°24W 84 F8
nbrook U.S.A. 41°55N 122°33W 76 F2
ncastle U.K. 53°13N 0°7W 12 D7
nell U.S.A. 42°20N 77°40W 82 D7
nell L. Canada 62°20N 119°25W 70 A5
nepayne Canada 49°14N 84°48W 72 C3
nings Mills Canada 44°9N 80°12W 82 B4
nitos U.S.A. 37°30N 120°14W 78 H6
nos, C. de Chile 55°50S 67°30W 96 H3
nsby Australia 33°42S 151°2E 63 B5
nsea U.K. 53°55N 0°11W 12 D7
obetsu = Noboribetsu
pan 42°24N 141°6E 30 C10
odenka Ukraine 48°41N 25°29E 17 D13
odok Khmelnytskyy,
kraine 49°10N 26°34E 17 D14
odok Lviv, Ukraine 49°46N 23°32E 17 D12
okhiv Ukraine 50°30N 24°45E 17 C13
qin Youyi Qianqi
ina 46°5N 122°3E 35 A12
queta Paraguay 23°15S 56°55W 94 A4
se Cr. → U.S.A. 41°57N 103°58W 76 F12
se I. Canada 53°20N 99°6W 71 C9
se Is. Canada 50°15N 55°50W 73 B8
sefly L. Canada 52°25N 121°0W 70 C4
seheads U.S.A. 42°10N 76°49W 82 D8
sens Denmark 55°52N 9°51E 9 J13
seshoe Lake Canada 45°17N 79°51W 82 A5
sham Australia 36°44S 142°13E 63 F3
sham U.K. 51°4N 0°20W 13 F7
ta Azores 38°32N 28°38W 50 a
ten Norway 59°25N 10°32E 9 G14
ton U.S.A. 39°40N 95°32W 80 F6
ton → Canada 69°56N 126°52W 68 C7
wood L. Canada 48°5N 82°20W 72 C3
eynābād Khuzestān,
an 32°45N 48°20E 45 C6
eynābād Kordestān,
an 35°33N 47°8E 44 C5
hangabad India 22°45N 77°45E 42 H7
hiarpur India 31°30N 75°58E 42 D6
pet India 15°15N 76°20E 40 M10
e, I. Chile 55°0S 69°0W 96 H3
Thailand 18°8N 98°29E 38 C2
Creek Range
S.A. 38°40N 116°20W 76 G5
Springs Ark., U.S.A. 34°31N 93°3W 84 D8
Springs S. Dak.,
S.A. 43°26N 103°29W 80 D2
Springs △ U.S.A. 34°31N 93°3W 84 D8
agen Sweden 63°59N 14°12E 8 E16
an China 37°25N 79°55E 32 C2
an He → China 40°22N 80°56E 32 B3
azel S. Africa 27°17S 22°58E 56 D3

Hotchkiss U.S.A. 38°48N 107°43W 76 G10
Hotham, C. Australia 12°2S 131°18E 60 B5
Hoting Sweden 64°8N 16°15E 8 D17
Hotte, Massif de la Haiti 18°30N 73°45W 89 C5
Hottentotsbaai Namibia 26°8S 14°59E 56 D1
Hou Hai China 22°32N 113°56E 33 F10
Houei Sai Laos 20°18N 100°26E 38 B3
Houffalize Belgium 50°8N 5°48E 15 D5
Houghton Mich., U.S.A. 47°7N 88°34W 80 B9
Houghton N.Y., U.S.A. 42°25N 78°10W 82 D6
Houghton L. U.S.A. 44°21N 84°44W 81 C11
Houghton-le-Spring
U.K. 54°51N 1°28W 12 C6
Houhora Heads N.Z. 34°49S 173°9E 59 A4
Houlton U.S.A. 46°8N 67°51W 81 B20
Houma U.S.A. 29°36N 90°43W 85 G9
Housatonic → U.S.A. 41°10N 73°7W 83 E11
Houston Canada 54°25N 126°39W 70 C3
Houston Mo., U.S.A. 37°22N 91°58W 80 G8
Houston Tex., U.S.A. 29°45N 95°21W 84 G7
Hout = Mogwadi →
S. Africa 23°4S 29°36E 57 C4
Houtkraal S. Africa 30°23S 24°5E 56 E3
Houtman Abrolhos
Australia 28°43S 113°48E 61 E1
Hovd □ Mongolia 48°2N 91°37E 32 B4
Hove U.K. 50°50N 0°10W 13 G7
Hovenweep ⌂ U.S.A. 37°20N 109°0W 77 H9
Hoveyzeh Iran 31°27N 48°4E 45 D6
Hövsgöl Mongolia 43°37N 109°39E 34 C5
Hövsgöl Nuur Mongolia 51°0N 100°30E 32 A5
Howar, Wadi → Sudan 17°30N 27°8E 51 E11
Howard Australia 25°16S 152°32E 63 D5
Howard Pa., U.S.A. 41°1N 77°40W 82 F7
Howard S. Dak., U.S.A. 44°1N 97°32W 80 C5
Howe U.S.A. 43°48N 113°0W 76 E7
Howe, C. Australia 37°30S 150°0E 63 F5
Howe, West Cape
Australia 35°8S 117°36E 61 G2
Howe I. Canada 44°16N 76°17W 83 B8
Howell U.S.A. 42°36N 83°56W 81 D12
Howick Canada 45°11N 73°51W 83 A11
Howick S. Africa 29°28S 30°14E 57 D5
Howick Group Australia 14°20S 145°30E 62 A4
Howitt, L. Australia 27°40S 138°40E 63 D2
Howland I. Pac. Oc. 0°48N 176°38W 64 G10
Howrah = Haora India 22°34N 88°18E 43 H13
Howth Ireland 53°23N 6°6W 10 C5
Howth Hd. Ireland 53°22N 6°4W 10 C5
Höxter Germany 51°46N 9°22E 16 C5
Hoy U.K. 58°50N 3°15W 11 C5
Høyanger Norway 61°13N 6°4E 8 F12
Hoyerswerda Germany 51°26N 14°14E 16 C8
Hoylake U.K. 53°24N 3°10W 12 D4
Hpa-an = Pa-an Burma 16°51N 97°40E 41 L20
Hpunan Pass Burma 27°30N 96°55E 41 F20
Hradec Králové
Czech Rep. 50°15N 15°50E 16 C8
Hrodna Belarus 53°42N 23°52E 17 B12
Hrodzyanka Belarus 53°31N 28°42E 17 B15
Hron → Slovak Rep. 47°49N 18°45E 17 E10
Hrvatska = Croatia ■
Europe 45°20N 16°0E 16 F9
Hrymayliv Ukraine 49°20N 26°5E 17 D14
Hsenwi Burma 23°22N 97°55E 41 H20
Hsiamen = Xiamen
China 24°25N 118°4E 33 D6
Hsian = Xi'an China 34°15N 109°0E 34 G5
Hsinchu Taiwan 24°48N 120°58E 33 D7
Hsinhailien = Lianyungang
China 34°40N 119°11E 35 G10
Hsüchou = Xuzhou
China 34°18N 117°10E 35 G9
Hu Xian China 34°8N 108°42E 34 G5
Hua Hin Thailand 12°34N 99°58E 38 F2
Hua Xian Henan, China 35°30N 114°30E 34 G8
Hua Xian Shaanxi, China 34°30N 109°48E 34 G5
Huab → Namibia 20°52S 13°25E 56 B2
Huachinera Mexico 30°9N 108°55W 86 A3
Huacho Peru 11°10S 77°35W 92 F3
Huade China 41°55N 113°59E 34 D7
Huadian China 43°0N 126°40E 35 C14
Huahine, Î.
French Polynesia 16°46S 150°58W 65 J12
Huai Hat △ Thailand 16°52N 104°17E 38 D5
Huai He → China 33°0N 118°30E 33 C6
Huai Nam Dang △
Thailand 19°30N 98°30E 38 C2
Huai Yot Thailand 7°45N 99°37E 39 J2
Huai'an Hebei, China 40°30N 114°20E 34 D8
Huai'an Jiangsu, China 33°30N 119°10E 35 H10
Huaibei China 34°0N 116°48E 34 G9
Huaide = Gongzhuling
China 43°30N 124°40E 35 C13
Huaidezhen China 43°48N 124°50E 35 C13
Huainan China 32°38N 116°58E 33 C6
Huairen China 39°48N 113°20E 34 E7
Huairou China 40°20N 116°35E 34 D9
Huaiyang China 33°40N 114°52E 34 H8
Huaiyin China 33°30N 119°2E 35 H10
Huaiyuan China 32°55N 117°10E 35 H9
Huajuapán de León
Mexico 17°48N 97°46W 87 D5
Hualapai Peak U.S.A. 35°5N 113°54W 77 J7
Huallaga → Peru 5°15S 75°30W 92 E3
Huambo Angola 12°42S 15°54E 53 G3
Huan Jiang → China 34°28N 109°0E 34 G5
Huan Xian China 36°33N 107°7E 34 F4
Huancabamba Peru 5°10S 79°15W 92 E3
Huancane Peru 15°10S 69°44W 92 G5
Huancavelica Peru 12°50S 75°5W 92 F3
Huancayo Peru 12°5S 75°12W 92 F3
Huanchaca Bolivia 20°15S 66°40W 92 H5
Huang Hai = Yellow Sea
China 35°0N 123°0E 35 G12
Huang He → China 37°55N 118°50E 35 F10
Huang Xian China 37°38N 120°30E 35 F11
Huangling China 35°34N 109°15E 34 G5

Huanglong China 35°30N 109°59E 34 G5
Huangshan China 29°42N 118°25E 33 D6
Huangshi China 30°10N 115°3E 33 C6
Huangsongdian China 43°45N 127°25E 35 C14
Huanren China 41°23N 125°20E 35 D13
Huantai China 36°58N 117°56E 35 F9
Huánuco Peru 9°55S 76°15W 92 E3
Huaraz Peru 9°30S 77°32W 92 E3
Huarmey Peru 10°5S 78°5W 92 F3
Huascarán, Nevado Peru 9°7S 77°37W 92 E3
Huasco Chile 28°30S 71°15W 94 B1
Huasco → Chile 28°27S 71°13W 94 B1
Huasna U.S.A. 35°6N 120°24W 79 K6
Huatabampo Mexico 26°50N 109°38W 86 B3
Huauchinango Mexico 20°12N 98°3W 87 C5
Huautla de Jiménez
Mexico 18°8N 96°51W 87 D5
Huayin China 34°35N 110°5E 34 G6
Hubbard Ohio, U.S.A. 41°9N 80°34W 82 E4
Hubbard Tex., U.S.A. 31°51N 96°48W 84 F6
Hubbart Pt. Canada 59°21N 94°41W 71 B10
Hubei □ China 31°0N 112°0E 33 C6
Hubli India 15°22N 75°15E 40 M9
Huch'ang N. Korea 41°25N 127°2E 35 D14
Hucknall U.K. 53°3N 1°13W 12 D6
Huddersfield U.K. 53°39N 1°47W 12 D6
Hudiksvall Sweden 61°43N 17°10E 8 F17
Hudson Canada 50°6N 92°9W 72 B1
Hudson Mass., U.S.A. 42°23N 71°34W 83 D13
Hudson N.Y., U.S.A. 42°15N 73°46W 83 D11
Hudson Wis., U.S.A. 44°58N 92°45W 80 C7
Hudson Wyo., U.S.A. 42°54N 108°35W 76 E9
Hudson → U.S.A. 40°42N 74°2W 83 F10
Hudson, C. Antarctica 68°21S 153°45E 5 C20
Hudson Bay Nunavut,
Canada 60°0N 86°0W 69 D11
Hudson Bay Sask.,
Canada 52°51N 102°23W 71 C8
Hudson Falls U.S.A. 43°18N 73°35W 83 C11
Hudson Mts. Antarctica 74°32S 99°20W 5 D16
Hudson Str. Canada 62°0N 70°0W 69 C13
Hudson's Hope Canada 56°0N 121°54W 70 B4
Hue Vietnam 16°30N 107°35E 38 D6
Huehuetenango
Guatemala 15°20N 91°28W 88 C1
Huejúcar Mexico 22°21N 103°13W 86 C4
Huelva Spain 37°18N 6°57W 21 D2
Huentelauquén Chile 31°38S 71°33W 94 C1
Huerta, Sa. de la
Argentina 31°10S 67°30W 94 C2
Huesca Spain 42°8N 0°25W 21 A5
Huetamo Mexico 18°35N 100°53W 86 D4
Hugh → Australia 25°1S 134°1E 62 D1
Hughenden Australia 20°52S 144°10E 62 C3
Hughesville U.S.A. 41°14N 76°44W 83 E8
Hugli → India 21°56N 88°4E 43 J13
Hugo Colo., U.S.A. 39°8N 103°28W 76 G12
Hugo Okla., U.S.A. 34°1N 95°31W 84 D7
Hugoton U.S.A. 37°11N 101°21W 80 G3
Hui Xian = Huixian
China 35°27N 113°12E 34 G7
Hui Xian China 33°50N 106°4E 34 H4
Hui'anbu China 37°28N 106°38E 34 F4
Huichapan Mexico 20°23N 99°39W 87 C5
Huichon N. Korea 40°10N 126°16E 35 D14
Huifa He → China 43°0N 127°50E 35 C14
Huila, Nevado del Colombia 3°0N 76°0W 92 C3
Huimin China 37°27N 117°28E 35 F9
Huinan China 42°40N 126°2E 35 C14
Huinca Renancó
Argentina 34°51S 64°22W 94 C3
Huining China 35°38N 105°0E 34 G3
Huinong China 39°5N 106°35E 34 E4
Huiting China 34°5N 116°5E 34 G9
Huixian China 35°27N 113°12E 34 G7
Huixtla Mexico 15°9N 92°28W 87 D6
Huize China 26°24N 103°15E 32 D5
Hukawng Valley
Burma 26°30N 96°30E 41 F20
Hukuntsi Botswana 23°58S 21°45E 56 C3
Ḩulayfā' Si. Arabia 25°58N 40°45E 44 E4
Hulin He → China 45°0N 122°10E 35 B12
Hull = Kingston upon Hull
U.K. 53°45N 0°21W 12 D7
Hull Canada 45°26N 75°43W 83 A9
Hull → U.K. 53°44N 0°20W 12 D7
Hulst Neths. 51°17N 4°2E 15 C4
Hulun Nur China 49°0N 117°30E 33 B6
Huma, Tanjung Malaysia 5°29N 100°16E 39 c
Humacao Puerto Rico 18°9N 65°50W 89 d
Humahuaca Argentina 23°10S 65°25W 94 A2
Humaitá Brazil 7°35S 63°1W 92 E6
Humaitá Paraguay 27°2S 58°31W 94 B4
Humansdorp S. Africa 34°2S 24°46E 56 E3
Humbe Angola 16°40S 14°55E 56 B1
Humber → U.K. 53°42N 0°27W 12 D7
Humboldt Canada 52°15N 105°9W 71 C7
Humboldt Iowa, U.S.A. 42°44N 94°13W 80 D6
Humboldt Tenn., U.S.A. 35°50N 88°55W 85 D10
Humboldt → U.S.A. 39°59N 118°36W 76 G4
Humboldt Gletscher =
Sermersuaq Greenland 79°30N 62°0W 4 B4
Hume U.S.A. 36°48N 118°54W 78 J8
Hume, L. Australia 36°0S 147°5E 63 F4
Humen China 22°50N 113°40E 33 F10
Humenné Slovak Rep. 48°55N 21°50E 17 D11
Humphreys, Mt.
U.S.A. 37°17N 118°40W 78 H8
Humphreys Peak
U.S.A. 35°21N 111°41W 77 J8
Humptulips U.S.A. 47°14N 123°57W 78 C3
Hūn Libya 29°2N 16°0E 51 C9
Hun Jiang → China 40°50N 125°38E 35 D13
Húnaflói Iceland 65°50N 20°50W 8 D3
Hunan □ China 27°30N 112°0E 33 D6
Hunchun China 42°52N 130°28E 35 C16
Hundewali Pakistan 31°55N 72°38E 42 D5

Hundred Mile House
Canada 51°38N 121°18W 70 C4
Hunedoara Romania 45°40N 22°50E 17 F12
Hung Yen Vietnam 20°39N 106°4E 38 B6
Hunga Ha'apai Tonga 20°41S 175°7W 59 c
Hungary ■ Europe 47°20N 19°20E 17 E10
Hungary, Plain of Europe 47°0N 20°0E 6 F10
Hungerford Australia 28°58S 144°24E 63 D3
Hŭngnam N. Korea 39°49N 127°45E 35 E14
Hunjiang China 41°54N 126°26E 35 D14
Hunsberge Namibia 27°45S 17°12E 56 D2
Hunsrück Germany 49°56N 7°27E 16 D4
Hunstanton U.K. 52°56N 0°29E 12 E8
Hunter U.S.A. 42°13N 74°13W 83 D10
Hunter I. Australia 40°30S 144°45E 63 G3
Hunter I. Canada 51°55N 128°0W 70 C3
Hunter Ra. Australia 32°45S 150°15E 63 E5
Hunters Road Zimbabwe 19°9S 29°49E 55 F2
Hunterville N.Z. 39°56S 175°35E 59 C5
Huntingburg U.S.A. 38°18N 86°57W 80 F10
Huntingdon U.K. 52°20N 0°11W 13 E7
Huntingdon U.S.A. 40°30N 78°1W 82 F6
Huntington Ind., U.S.A. 40°53N 85°30W 81 E11
Huntington N.Y.,
U.S.A. 40°52N 73°26W 83 F11
Huntington Oreg.,
U.S.A. 44°21N 117°16W 76 D5
Huntington Utah,
U.S.A. 39°20N 110°58W 76 G8
Huntington W. Va.,
U.S.A. 38°25N 82°27W 81 F12
Huntington Beach
U.S.A. 33°40N 118°5W 79 M9
Huntly N.Z. 37°34S 175°11E 59 B5
Huntly U.K. 57°27N 2°47W 11 D6
Huntsville Canada 45°20N 79°14W 82 A5
Huntsville Ala., U.S.A. 34°44N 86°35W 85 D11
Huntsville Tex., U.S.A. 30°43N 95°33W 84 F7
Hunyani → Zimbabwe 15°57S 30°39E 55 F3
Hunyuan China 39°42N 113°42E 34 E7
Hunza → India 35°54N 74°20E 43 B6
Huo Xian = Huozhou
China 36°36N 111°42E 34 F6
Huong Khe Vietnam 18°13N 105°41E 38 C5
Huonville Australia 43°0S 147°5E 63 G4
Huozhou China 36°36N 111°42E 34 F6
Hupeh = Hubei □ China 31°0N 112°0E 33 C6
Ḩūr Iran 30°50N 57°7E 45 D8
Hurānd Iran 38°51N 47°22E 44 B5
Ḩuraymīla Si. Arabia 25°8N 46°8E 44 E5
Hurd, C. Canada 45°13N 81°44W 82 A3
Hure Qi China 42°45N 121°45E 35 C11
Hurghada Egypt 27°15N 33°50E 51 C12
Hurley N. Mex., U.S.A. 32°42N 108°8W 77 K9
Hurley Wis., U.S.A. 46°27N 90°11W 80 B8
Huron Calif., U.S.A. 36°12N 120°6W 78 J6
Huron Ohio, U.S.A. 41°24N 82°33W 82 E2
Huron S. Dak., U.S.A. 44°22N 98°13W 80 C4
Huron, L. U.S.A. 44°30N 82°40W 82 B2
Huron East Canada 43°37N 81°18W 82 C3
Hurricane U.S.A. 37°11N 113°17W 77 H7
Hurungwe ⌂ Zimbabwe 16°7S 29°5E 55 F2
Hurunui → N.Z. 42°54S 173°18E 59 E4
Húsavík Iceland 66°3N 17°21W 8 C5
Huşi Romania 46°41N 28°7E 17 E15
Hustadvika Norway 63°0N 7°0E 8 E12
Hustontown U.S.A. 40°3N 78°2W 82 F6
Hutchinson Kans., U.S.A. 38°5N 97°56W 80 F5
Hutchinson Minn.,
U.S.A. 44°54N 94°22W 80 C6
Hutte Sauvage, L. de la
Canada 56°15N 64°45W 73 A7
Hutton, Mt. Australia 25°51S 148°20E 63 D4
Huy Belgium 50°31N 5°15E 15 D5
Huzhou China 30°51N 120°8E 33 C7
Hvammstangi Iceland 65°24N 20°57W 8 D3
Hvar Croatia 43°11N 16°28E 22 C7
Hvítá → Iceland 64°30N 21°58W 8 D3
Hwacheon-Cheosuji
S. Korea 38°5N 127°50E 35 E14
Hwang Ho = Huang He →
China 37°55N 118°50E 35 F10
Hwange Zimbabwe 18°18S 26°30E 55 F2
Hwange △ Zimbabwe 19°0S 26°30E 56 B4
Hyannis Mass., U.S.A. 41°39N 70°17W 81 E18
Hyannis Nebr., U.S.A. 42°0N 101°46W 80 E3
Hyargas Nuur Mongolia 49°0N 93°0E 32 B4
Hydaburg U.S.A. 55°15N 132°50W 70 B2
Hyde Park U.S.A. 41°47N 73°56W 83 E11
Hyden Australia 32°24S 118°53E 61 F2
Hyder U.S.A. 55°55N 130°5W 70 B2
Hyderabad India 17°22N 78°29E 40 L11
Hyderabad Pakistan 25°23N 68°24E 42 G3
Hydra Greece 37°20N 23°28E 23 F10
Hyères France 43°8N 6°9E 20 E7
Hyères, Îs. d' France 43°0N 6°20E 20 E7
Hyesan N. Korea 41°20N 128°10E 35 D15
Hyland → Canada 59°52N 128°12W 70 B3
Hymia India 33°40N 78°2E 43 C8
Hyndman Peak U.S.A. 43°45N 114°8W 76 E6
Hyōgo □ Japan 35°15N 134°50E 31 G7
Hyrum U.S.A. 41°38N 111°51W 76 F8
Hysham U.S.A. 46°18N 107°14W 76 C10
Hythe U.K. 51°4N 1°5E 13 F9
Hyūga Japan 32°25N 131°35E 31 H5
Hyvinge = Hyvinkää
Finland 60°38N 24°50E 8 F21
Hyvinkää Finland 60°38N 24°50E 8 F21

I

I-n-Gall Niger 16°51N 7°1E 50 E7
Iaco → Brazil 9°3S 68°34W 92 E5
Iakora Madag. 23°6S 46°40E 57 C8
Ialissos Greece 36°24N 28°10E 25 C10
Ialomiţa → Romania 44°42N 27°51E 17 F14
Iaşi Romania 47°10N 27°40E 17 E14

Ib → India 21°34N 83°48E 43 J10
Iba Phil. 15°22N 120°0E 37 A6
Ibadan Nigeria 7°22N 3°58E 50 G6
Ibagué Colombia 4°20N 75°20W 92 C3
Ibar → Serbia 43°43N 20°45E 23 C9
Ibaraki □ Japan 36°10N 140°10E 31 F10
Ibarra Ecuador 0°21N 78°7W 92 C3
Ibb Yemen 14°2N 44°10E 47 E3
Ibembo
Dem. Rep. of the Congo 2°35N 23°35E 54 B1
Ibenga → Congo 2°19N 18°9E 52 D3
Ibera, L. Argentina 28°30S 57°9W 94 B4
Iberian Peninsula Europe 40°0N 5°0W 6 H5
Iberville Canada 45°19N 73°17W 83 A11
Ibiá Brazil 19°30S 46°30W 93 G9
Ibiapaba, Sa. da Brazil 4°0S 41°30W 93 D10
Ibicuí → Brazil 29°25S 56°47W 95 B4
Ibicuy Argentina 33°55S 59°10W 94 C4
Ibiza = Eivissa Spain 38°54N 1°26E 24 C7
Ibo Mozam. 12°22S 40°40E 55 E5
Ibonma Indonesia 3°29S 133°31E 37 E8
Ibotirama Brazil 12°13S 43°12W 93 F10
Ibrāhīm → Lebanon 34°4N 35°38E 46 A4
'Ibrī Oman 23°14N 56°30E 45 F8
Ibu Indonesia 1°35N 127°33E 37 D7
Ibusuki Japan 31°12N 130°40E 31 J5
Ica Peru 14°0S 75°48W 92 F3
Iça → Brazil 2°55S 67°58W 92 D5
Icacos Pt. Trin. & Tob. 10°3N 61°57W 93 K15
Içana Brazil 0°21N 67°19W 92 C5
Içana → Brazil 0°26N 67°19W 92 C5
İçel Turkey 36°51N 34°36E 44 B2
Iceland ■ Europe 64°45N 19°0W 8 D4
Iceland Basin Atl. Oc. 61°0N 19°0W 4 C7
Icelandic Plateau Arctic 64°0N 10°0W 4 C7
Ich'ang = Yichang
China 30°40N 111°20E 33 C6
Ichchapuram India 19°10N 84°40E 41 K14
Icheon S. Korea 37°17N 127°27E 35 F14
Ichhawar India 23°1N 77°1E 42 H7
Ichihara Japan 35°28N 140°5E 31 G10
Ichikawa Japan 35°43N 139°54E 31 G9
Ichilo → Bolivia 15°57S 64°50W 92 G6
Ichinohe Japan 40°13N 141°17E 30 D10
Ichinomiya Japan 35°18N 136°48E 31 G8
Ichinoseki Japan 38°55N 141°8E 30 E10
Icod Canary Is. 28°22N 16°43W 24 F3
Icy C. U.S.A. 70°20N 161°52W 66 B3
Ida Grove U.S.A. 42°21N 95°28W 80 D6
Idabel U.S.A. 33°54N 94°50W 84 E7
Idaho □ U.S.A. 45°0N 115°0W 76 D6
Idaho City U.S.A. 43°50N 115°50W 76 E6
Idaho Falls U.S.A. 43°30N 112°2W 76 E7
Idalia △ Australia 24°49S 144°36E 62 C3
Idar-Oberstein Germany 49°43N 7°16E 16 D4
Idensalmi = Iisalmi
Finland 63°32N 27°10E 8 E22
Idfû Egypt 24°55N 32°49E 51 D12
Ídhra = Hydra Greece 37°20N 23°28E 23 F10
Idi Indonesia 5°2N 97°37E 36 C1
Idi, Oros = Psiloritis, Oros
Greece 35°15N 24°45E 25 D6
Idiofa
Dem. Rep. of the Congo 4°55S 19°42E 52 E3
Idlib Syria 35°55N 36°36E 44 C3
Idria U.S.A. 36°25N 120°41W 78 J6
Idutywa = Dutywa
S. Africa 32°8S 28°18E 57 E4
Ieper Belgium 50°51N 2°53E 15 D2
Ierapetra Greece 35°1N 25°44E 25 E7
Iesi Italy 43°31N 13°14E 22 C5
Ifakara Tanzania 8°8S 36°41E 52 F7
'Ifāl, W. al → Si. Arabia 28°7N 35°3E 44 D2
Ifanadiana Madag. 21°19S 47°39E 57 C8
Ife Nigeria 7°30N 4°31E 50 G6
Iffley Australia 18°53S 141°12E 62 B3
Iforas, Adrar des Africa 19°40N 1°40E 50 E6
Ifould, L. Australia 30°52S 132°6E 61 F5
Iganga Uganda 0°37N 33°28E 54 B3
Igarapava Brazil 20°3S 47°47W 93 H9
Igarka Russia 67°30N 86°33E 28 C9
Iggesund Sweden 61°39N 17°10E 8 F17
Iglésias Italy 39°19N 8°32E 22 E3
Igloolik = Iglulik
Canada 69°20N 81°49W 69 C11
Igluligaarjuk = Chesterfield Inlet
Canada 63°30N 90°45W 68 C10
Iglulik Canada 69°20N 81°49W 69 C11
Ignace Canada 49°30N 91°40W 72 C1
İğneada Burnu Turkey 41°53N 28°2E 23 D13
Igoumenitsa Greece 39°32N 20°18E 23 E9
Igrim Russia 63°12N 64°30E 28 C7
Iguaçu → Brazil 25°36S 54°36W 95 B5
Iguaçu, Cat. del Brazil 25°41S 54°26W 95 B5
Iguaçu △ Brazil 25°30S 54°0W 95 B5
Iguaçu Falls = Iguaçu, Cat. del
Brazil 25°41S 54°26W 95 B5
Iguala Mexico 18°21N 99°32W 87 D5
Igualada Spain 41°37N 1°37E 21 B6
Iguassu = Iguaçu →
Brazil 25°36S 54°36W 95 B5
Iguatu Brazil 6°20S 39°18W 93 E11
Iguazú △ Argentina 25°42S 54°22W 95 B5
Iguidi, Erg Africa 27°0N 7°0W 50 C4
Iharana Madag. 13°25S 50°0E 57 A9
Ihbulag Mongolia 43°11N 107°10E 34 C4
Iheya-Shima Japan 27°4N 127°58E 31 L3
Ihosy Madag. 22°24S 46°8E 57 C8
Ihotry, Farihy Madag. 21°56S 43°41E 57 C7
Ii Finland 65°19N 25°22E 8 D21
Ii-Shima Japan 26°43N 127°47E 31 L3
Iida Japan 35°35N 137°50E 31 G8
Iijoki → Finland 65°20N 25°20E 8 D21
Iisalmi Finland 63°32N 27°10E 8 E22
Iiyama Japan 36°51N 138°22E 31 F9
Iizuka Japan 33°38N 130°42E 31 H5
Ijâfene Mauritania 20°40N 8°0W 50 D4

Ijebu-Ode Nigeria 6°47N 3°58E 50 G6
IJmuiden Neths. 52°28N 4°35E 15 B4
Ijo älv = Iijoki → Finland 65°20N 25°20E 8 D21
IJssel → Neths. 52°35N 5°50E 15 B5
IJsselmeer Neths. 52°45N 5°20E 15 B5
Ijuí Brazil 28°23S 53°55W 95 B5
Ijuí → Brazil 27°58S 55°20W 95 B4
Ikalamavony Madag. 21°9S 46°35E 57 C8
Ikaluktutiak Canada 69°10N 105°0W 68 C9
Ikanga Kenya 1°42S 38°4E 54 C4
Ikare Nigeria 7°32N 5°40E 50 G7
Ikaria Greece 37°35N 26°10E 23 F12
Ikeda Japan 34°1N 133°48E 31 G6
Ikela Dem. Rep. of the Congo 1°6S 23°6E 52 E4
Iki Japan 33°45N 129°42E 31 H4
Ikimba L. Tanzania 1°30S 31°20E 54 C3
Ikongo Madag. 21°52S 47°27E 57 C8
Ikopa → Madag. 16°45S 46°40E 57 B8
Ikorongo ⌂ Tanzania 1°50S 34°53E 54 C3
Ikparjuk = Arctic Bay Canada 73°1N 85°7W 69 B11
Iksan S. Korea 35°59N 127°0E 35 G14
Ikungu Tanzania 1°33S 33°42E 54 C3
Ikuntji = Haast Bluff Australia 23°22S 132°0E 60 D5
Ilagan Phil. 17°7N 121°53E 37 A6
Ilaka Madag. 19°33S 48°52E 57 B8
Īlām Iran 33°36N 46°36E 44 C5
Ilam Nepal 26°58N 87°58E 43 F12
Īlām □ Iran 33°0N 47°0E 44 C5
Ilanskiy Russia 56°14N 96°3E 29 D10
Iława Poland 53°36N 19°34E 17 B10
Ile → Kazakhstan 45°53N 77°10E 28 E8
Île-à-la-Crosse Canada 55°27N 107°53W 71 B7
Île-à-la-Crosse, Lac Canada 55°40N 107°45W 71 B7
Île-de-France □ France 49°0N 2°20E 20 B5
Ilebo Dem. Rep. of the Congo 4°17S 20°55E 52 E4
Ilek Russia 51°32N 53°21E 28 D6
Ilek → Russia 51°30N 53°22E 18 D9
Ilesha Nigeria 7°37N 4°40E 50 G6
Ilford Canada 56°4N 95°35W 71 B9
Ilfracombe Australia 23°30S 144°30E 62 C3
Ilfracombe U.K. 51°12N 4°8W 13 F3
Ilha de Moçambique Mozam. 15°4S 40°52E 55 F5
Ilha Grande, Represa Brazil 23°10S 53°5W 95 A5
Ilha Grande △ Brazil 23°10S 53°20W 95 A5
Ilhéus Brazil 14°49S 39°2W 93 F11
Ili = Ile → Kazakhstan 45°53N 77°10E 28 E8
Iliamna L. U.S.A. 59°30N 155°0W 74 a
Ilias, Profitis Greece 36°17N 27°56E 25 C9
Iligan Phil. 8°12N 124°13E 37 C6
Ilion U.S.A. 43°1N 75°2W 83 D9
Ilkeston U.K. 52°58N 1°19W 12 E6
Ilkley U.K. 53°56N 1°48W 12 D6
Illampu = Ancohuma, Nevado Bolivia 16°0S 68°50W 92 G5
Illana B. Phil. 7°35N 123°45E 37 C6
Illapel Chile 32°0S 71°10W 94 C1
Iller → Germany 48°23N 9°58E 16 D6
Illetas Spain 39°32N 2°35E 24 B9
Illimani, Nevado Bolivia 16°30S 67°50W 92 G5
Illinois □ U.S.A. 40°15N 89°30W 80 E9
Illinois → U.S.A. 38°58N 90°28W 80 F8
Illizi Algeria 26°31N 8°32E 50 C7
Ilma, L. Australia 29°13S 127°46E 61 E4
Ilmajoki Finland 62°44N 22°34E 8 E20
Ilmen, Ozero Russia 58°15N 31°10E 18 C5
Ilo Peru 17°40S 71°20W 92 G4
Iloilo Phil. 10°45N 122°33E 37 B6
Ilomantsi Finland 62°38N 30°57E 8 E24
Ilorin Nigeria 8°30N 4°35E 50 G6
Ilwaco U.S.A. 46°19N 124°3W 78 D2
Ilwaki Indonesia 7°55S 126°30E 37 F7
Imabari Japan 34°4N 133°0E 31 G6
Imaloto → Madag. 23°27S 45°13E 57 C8
Imandra, Ozero Russia 67°30N 33°0E 8 C25
Imanombo Madag. 24°26S 45°49E 57 C8
Imari Japan 33°15N 129°52E 31 H4
Imatra Finland 61°12N 28°48E 8 F23
imeni 26 Bakinskikh Komissarov = Neftçala Azerbaijan 39°19N 49°12E 45 B6
imeni 26 Bakinskikh Komissarov Turkmenistan 39°22N 54°10E 45 B7
imeni Ismail Samani, Pik Tajikistan 39°0N 72°2E 28 F8
Imeri, Serra Brazil 0°50N 65°25W 92 C5
Imerimandroso Madag. 17°26S 48°35E 57 B8
Imfolozi ⌂ S. Africa 28°18S 31°50E 57 D5
Imi Ethiopia 6°28N 42°10E 47 F3
Imlay U.S.A. 40°40N 118°9W 76 F4
Imlay City U.S.A. 43°2N 83°5W 82 D1
Immingham U.K. 53°37N 0°13W 12 D7
Immokalee U.S.A. 26°25N 81°25W 85 H14
Ímola Italy 44°20N 11°42E 22 B4
Imperatriz Brazil 5°30S 47°29W 93 E9
Impéria Italy 43°53N 8°3E 20 E8
Imperial Canada 51°21N 105°28W 71 C7
Imperial Calif., U.S.A. 32°51N 115°34W 79 N11
Imperial Nebr., U.S.A. 40°31N 101°39W 80 E3
Imperial Beach U.S.A. 32°35N 117°6W 79 N9
Imperial Dam U.S.A. 32°55N 114°25W 79 N12
Imperial Res. U.S.A. 32°53N 114°28W 79 N12
Imperial Valley U.S.A. 33°0N 115°30W 79 N11
Imperieuse Reef Australia 17°36S 118°50E 60 C2
Impfondo Congo 1°40N 18°0E 52 D3
Imphal India 24°48N 93°56E 41 G18
İmroz = Gökçeada Turkey 40°10N 25°50E 23 D11
Imuris Mexico 30°47N 110°52W 86 A2
Imuruan B. Phil. 10°40N 119°10E 37 B5
In Salah Algeria 27°10N 2°32E 50 C6
Ina Japan 35°50N 137°55E 31 G8
Inagua △ Bahamas 21°5N 73°24W 89 B5
Inangahua N.Z. 41°52S 171°59E 59 D3
Inanwatan Indonesia 2°8S 132°10E 37 E8
Iñapari Peru 11°0S 69°40W 92 F5
Inari Finland 68°54N 27°1E 8 B22
Inarijärvi Finland 69°0N 28°0E 8 B23
Inawashiro-Ko Japan 37°29N 140°6E 30 F10
Inca Spain 39°43N 2°54E 24 B9
Inca de Oro Chile 26°45S 69°54W 94 B2
Incahuasi Argentina 27°2S 68°18W 94 B2
Incahuasi Chile 29°12S 71°5W 94 B1
İnce Burun Turkey 42°7N 34°56E 19 F5
İncesu Turkey 38°38N 35°11E 44 B2
Incheon S. Korea 37°27N 126°40E 35 F14
İncirliova Turkey 37°50N 27°41E 23 F12
Incline Village U.S.A. 39°10N 119°58W 76 G4
Incomáti → Mozam. 25°46S 32°43E 57 D5
Indalsälven → Sweden 62°36N 17°30E 8 E17
Indaw Burma 24°15N 96°5E 41 G20
Independence Calif., U.S.A. 36°48N 118°12W 78 J8
Independence Iowa, U.S.A. 42°28N 91°54W 80 D8
Independence Kans., U.S.A. 37°14N 95°42W 80 G6
Independence Ky., U.S.A. 38°57N 84°33W 81 F11
Independence Mo., U.S.A. 39°6N 94°25W 80 F6
Independence Fjord Greenland 82°10N 29°0W 4 A6
Independence Mts. U.S.A. 41°20N 116°0W 76 F5
Index U.S.A. 47°50N 121°33W 78 C5
India ■ Asia 20°0N 78°0E 40 K11
Indian → U.S.A. 27°59N 80°34W 85 H14
Indian Cabins Canada 59°52N 117°40W 70 B5
Indian Harbour Canada 54°27N 57°13W 73 B8
Indian Head Canada 50°30N 103°41W 71 C8
Indian L. U.S.A. 43°46N 74°16W 83 C10
Indian Lake U.S.A. 43°47N 74°16W 83 C10
Indian Springs U.S.A. 36°35N 115°40W 79 J11
Indiana U.S.A. 40°37N 79°9W 82 F5
Indiana □ U.S.A. 40°0N 86°0W 81 F11
Indianapolis U.S.A. 39°46N 86°9W 80 F10
Indianola Iowa, U.S.A. 41°22N 93°34W 80 E7
Indianola Miss., U.S.A. 33°27N 90°39W 85 E9
Indiga Russia 67°38N 49°9E 18 A8
Indigirka → Russia 70°48N 148°54E 29 B15
Indio U.S.A. 33°43N 116°13W 79 M10
Indira Gandhi Canal India 28°0N 72°0E 42 F5
Indira Sagar India 22°15N 76°40E 42 H7
Indo-China Asia 15°0N 102°0E 26 G12
Indonesia ■ Asia 5°0S 115°0E 36 F5
Indore India 22°42N 75°53E 42 H6
Indramayu Indonesia 6°20S 108°19E 37 G13
Indravati → India 19°20N 80°20E 41 K12
Indre → France 47°16N 0°11E 20 C4
Indulkana Australia 26°58S 133°5E 63 D1
Indus → Pakistan 24°20N 67°47E 42 G2
Indus, Mouths of the Pakistan 24°0N 68°0E 42 H3
İnebolu Turkey 41°55N 33°40E 19 F5
Infiernillo, Presa del Mexico 18°35N 101°50W 86 D4
Ingenio Canary Is. 27°55N 15°26W 24 G4
Ingenio Santa Ana Argentina 27°25S 65°40W 94 B2
Ingersoll Canada 43°4N 80°55W 82 C4
Ingham Australia 18°43S 146°10E 62 B4
Ingleborough U.K. 54°10N 2°22W 12 C5
Inglewood Queens., Australia 28°25S 151°2E 63 D5
Inglewood Vic., Australia 36°29S 143°53E 63 F3
Inglewood N.Z. 39°9S 174°14E 59 C5
Inglewood U.S.A. 33°58N 118°21W 79 M8
Ingólfshöfði Iceland 63°48N 16°39W 8 E5
Ingolstadt Germany 48°46N 11°26E 16 D6
Ingomar U.S.A. 46°35N 107°23W 76 C10
Ingonish Canada 46°42N 60°18W 73 C7
Ingraj Bazar India 24°58N 88°10E 43 G13
Ingrid Christensen Coast Antarctica 69°30S 76°0E 5 C6
Ingulec = Inhulec Ukraine 47°42N 33°14E 19 E5
Ingushetia □ Russia 43°20N 44°50E 19 F8
Ingwavuma S. Africa 27°9S 31°59E 57 D5
Inhaca Mozam. 26°1S 32°57E 57 D5
Inhafenga Mozam. 20°36S 33°53E 57 C5
Inhambane Mozam. 23°54S 35°30E 57 C6
Inhambane □ Mozam. 22°30S 34°20E 57 C5
Inhaminga Mozam. 18°26S 35°0E 55 F4
Inharrime Mozam. 24°30S 35°0E 57 C6
Inharrime → Mozam. 24°30S 35°0E 57 C6
Inhulec Ukraine 47°42N 33°14E 19 E5
Ining = Yining China 43°58N 81°10E 32 B3
Inírida → Colombia 3°55N 67°52W 92 C5
Inishbofin Ireland 53°37N 10°13W 10 C1
Inisheer Ireland 53°3N 9°32W 10 C2
Inishfree B. Ireland 55°4N 8°23W 10 A3
Inishkea North Ireland 54°9N 10°11W 10 B1
Inishkea South Ireland 54°7N 10°12W 10 B1
Inishmaan Ireland 53°5N 9°35W 10 C2
Inishmore Ireland 53°8N 9°45W 10 C2
Inishmurray I. Ireland 54°26N 8°39W 10 B3
Inishowen Pen. Ireland 55°14N 7°15W 10 A4
Inishshark Ireland 53°37N 10°16W 10 C1
Inishturk Ireland 53°42N 10°7W 10 C1
Inishvickillane Ireland 52°3N 10°37W 10 D1
Injune Australia 25°53S 148°32E 63 D4
Inklin → N. Amer. 58°50N 133°10W 70 B2
Inland Kaikoura Ra. N.Z. 41°59S 173°41E 59 D4
Inland Sea = Setonaikai Japan 34°20N 133°30E 31 G6
Inle L. Burma 20°30N 96°58E 41 J20
Inlet U.S.A. 43°45N 74°48W 83 C10
Inn → Austria 48°35N 13°28E 16 D7
Innamincka Australia 27°44S 140°46E 63 D3
Inner Hebrides U.K. 57°0N 6°30W 11 E2
Inner Mongolia = Nei Monggol Zizhiqu □ China 42°0N 112°0E 34 D7
Inner Sound U.K. 57°30N 5°55W 11 D3
Innerkip Canada 43°13N 80°42W 82 C4
Innetalling I. Canada 56°0N 79°0W 72 A4
Innisfail Australia 17°33S 146°5E 62 B4
Innisfail Canada 52°2N 113°57W 70 C6
In'noshima Japan 34°19N 133°10E 31 G6
Innsbruck Austria 47°16N 11°23E 16 E6
Inny → Ireland 53°30N 7°50W 10 C4
Inongo Dem. Rep. of the Congo 1°55S 18°30E 52 E3
Inoucdjouac = Inukjuak Canada 58°25N 78°15W 69 D12
Inowrocław Poland 52°50N 18°12E 17 B10
Inscription, C. Australia 25°29S 112°59E 61 E1
Insein Burma 16°50N 96°5E 41 L20
Inta Russia 66°5N 60°8E 18 A11
Intendente Alvear Argentina 35°12S 63°32W 94 D3
Interlaken Switz. 46°41N 7°50E 20 C7
Interlaken U.S.A. 42°37N 76°44W 83 D8
International Falls U.S.A. 48°36N 93°25W 80 A7
Intiyaco Argentina 28°43S 60°5W 94 B3
Inukjuak Canada 58°25N 78°15W 69 D12
Inútil, B. Chile 53°30S 70°15W 96 G2
Inuvik Canada 68°16N 133°40W 68 C6
Inveraray U.K. 56°14N 5°5W 11 E3
Inverbervie U.K. 56°51N 2°17W 11 E6
Invercargill N.Z. 46°24S 168°24E 59 G2
Inverclyde □ U.K. 55°55N 4°49W 11 F4
Inverell Australia 29°45S 151°8E 63 D5
Invergordon U.K. 57°41N 4°10W 11 D4
Inverloch Australia 38°38S 145°45E 63 F4
Invermere Canada 50°30N 116°2W 70 C5
Inverness Canada 46°15N 61°19W 73 C7
Inverness U.K. 57°29N 4°13W 11 D4
Inverness U.S.A. 28°50N 82°20W 85 G13
Inverurie U.K. 57°17N 2°23W 11 D6
Investigator Group Australia 34°45S 134°20E 63 E1
Investigator Str. Australia 35°30S 137°0E 63 F2
Inya Russia 50°28N 86°37E 28 D9
Inyanga Zimbabwe 18°12S 32°40E 55 F3
Inyangani Zimbabwe 18°5S 32°50E 55 F3
Inyantue Zimbabwe 18°33S 26°39E 56 B4
Inyo Mts. U.S.A. 36°40N 118°0W 78 J9
Inyokern U.S.A. 35°39N 117°49W 79 K9
Inza Russia 53°55N 46°25E 18 D8
Iō-Jima Japan 30°48N 130°18E 31 J5
Ioannina Greece 39°42N 20°47E 23 E9
Iola U.S.A. 37°55N 95°24W 80 G6
Iona U.K. 56°20N 6°25W 11 E2
Ione U.S.A. 38°21N 120°56W 78 G6
Ionia U.S.A. 42°59N 85°4W 81 D11
Ionian Is. = Ionioi Nisoi Greece 38°40N 20°0E 23 E9
Ionian Sea Medit. S. 37°30N 17°30E 23 E7
Ionioi Nisoi Greece 38°40N 20°0E 23 E9
Ios Greece 36°41N 25°20E 23 F11
Iowa □ U.S.A. 42°18N 93°30W 80 D7
Iowa → U.S.A. 41°10N 91°1W 80 E8
Iowa City U.S.A. 41°40N 91°32W 80 E8
Iowa Falls U.S.A. 42°31N 93°16W 80 D7
Iowa Park U.S.A. 33°57N 98°40W 84 E5
Ipala Tanzania 4°30S 32°52E 54 C3
Ipameri Brazil 17°44S 48°9W 93 G9
Ipatinga Brazil 19°32S 42°30W 93 G10
Ipiales Colombia 0°50N 77°37W 92 C3
Ipin = Yibin China 28°45N 104°32E 32 D5
Ipixuna Brazil 7°0S 71°40W 92 E4
Ipoh Malaysia 4°35N 101°5E 39 K3
Ippy C.A.R. 6°5N 21°7E 52 C4
Ipsala Turkey 40°55N 26°23E 23 D12
Ipswich Australia 27°35S 152°40E 63 D5
Ipswich U.K. 52°4N 1°10E 13 E9
Ipswich Mass., U.S.A. 42°41N 70°50W 83 D14
Ipswich S. Dak., U.S.A. 45°27N 99°2W 80 C4
Ipu Brazil 4°23S 40°44W 93 D10
Iqaluit Canada 63°44N 68°31W 69 C13
Iquique Chile 20°19S 70°5W 92 H4
Iquitos Peru 3°45S 73°10W 92 D4
Irabu-Jima Japan 24°50N 125°10E 31 M2
Iracoubo Fr. Guiana 5°30N 53°10W 93 B8
Īrafshān Iran 26°42N 61°56E 45 E9
Iraklio Greece 35°20N 25°12E 25 D7
Iraklio □ Greece 35°10N 25°10E 25 D7
Iráklion = Iraklio Greece 35°20N 25°12E 25 D7
Irakliou, Kolpos Greece 35°23N 25°8E 25 D7
Irala Paraguay 25°55S 54°35W 95 B5
Iran ■ Asia 33°0N 53°0E 45 C7
Iran, Pegunungan Malaysia 2°20N 114°50E 36 D4
Iran Ra. = Iran, Pegunungan Malaysia 2°20N 114°50E 36 D4
Īrānshahr Iran 27°15N 60°40E 45 E9
Irapuato Mexico 20°41N 101°28W 86 C4
Iraq ■ Asia 33°0N 44°0E 44 C5
Irati Brazil 25°25S 50°38W 95 B5
Irbid Jordan 32°35N 35°48E 46 C4
Irbid □ Jordan 32°30N 35°50E 46 C5
Irebu Dem. Rep. of the Congo 0°40S 17°46E 52 E3
Ireland ■ Europe 53°50N 7°52W 10 C4
Iri = Iksan S. Korea 35°59N 127°0E 35 G14
Irian Jaya = Papua □ Indonesia 4°0S 137°0E 37 E9
Irian Jaya Barat □ Indonesia 2°5S 132°50E 37 E8
Iringa Tanzania 7°48S 35°43E 54 D4
Iringa □ Tanzania 7°48S 35°43E 54 D4
Iriomote △ Japan 24°29N 123°53E 31 M1
Iriomote-Jima Japan 24°19N 123°48E 31 M1
Iriona Honduras 15°57N 85°11W 88 C2
Iriri → Brazil 3°52S 52°37W 93 D8
Irish Republic ■ Europe 53°50N 7°52W 10 C4
Irish Sea Europe 53°38N 4°48W 12 D3
Irkutsk Russia 52°18N 104°20E 29 D11
Irma Canada 52°55N 111°14W 71 C6
Irō-Zaki Japan 34°36N 138°51E 31 G9
Iron Baron Australia 32°58S 137°11E 63 E2
Iron Gate = Portile de Fier Europe 44°44N 22°30E 17 F12
Iron Knob Australia 32°46S 137°8E 63 E2
Iron Mountain U.S.A. 45°49N 88°4W 80 C9
Iron Range △ Australia 12°34S 143°18E 62 A3
Iron River U.S.A. 46°6N 88°39W 80 B9
Irondequoit U.S.A. 43°13N 77°35W 82 C7
Ironton Mo., U.S.A. 37°36N 90°38W 80 G8
Ironton Ohio, U.S.A. 38°32N 82°41W 81 F12
Ironwood U.S.A. 46°27N 90°9W 80 B8
Ironwood Forest ⌂ U.S.A. 32°32N 111°28W 77 K8
Iroquois Canada 44°51N 75°19W 83 B9
Iroquois Falls Canada 48°46N 80°41W 72 C3
Irpin Ukraine 50°30N 30°15E 17 C16
Irrara Cr. → Australia 29°35S 145°31E 63 D4
Irrawaddy □ Burma 17°0N 95°0E 41 L19
Irrawaddy → Burma 15°50N 95°6E 41 M19
Irrawaddy, Mouths of the Burma 15°30N 95°0E 41 M19
Irricana Canada 51°19N 113°37W 70 C6
Irtysh → Russia 61°4N 68°52E 28 C7
Irumu Dem. Rep. of the Congo 1°32N 29°53E 54 B2
Irún Spain 43°20N 1°52W 21 A5
Irunea = Pamplona-Iruña Spain 42°48N 1°38W 21 A5
Irvine Canada 49°57N 110°16W 71 D6
Irvine U.K. 55°37N 4°41W 11 F4
Irvine Calif., U.S.A. 33°41N 117°46W 79 M9
Irvine Ky., U.S.A. 37°42N 83°58W 81 G12
Irvinestown U.K. 54°28N 7°39W 10 B4
Irving U.S.A. 32°48N 96°56W 84 E6
Irvona U.S.A. 40°46N 78°33W 82 F6
Irwin → Australia 29°15S 114°54E 61 E1
Irymple Australia 34°14S 142°8E 63 E3
Isa Khel Pakistan 32°41N 71°17E 42 C4
Isaac → Australia 22°55S 149°20E 62 C4
Isabel U.S.A. 45°24N 101°26W 80 C3
Isabel, I. Mexico 21°51N 105°55W 86 C3
Isabela Phil. 6°40N 121°59E 37 C6
Isabela Puerto Rico 18°30N 67°2W 89 d
Isabella, Cord. Nic. 13°30N 85°25W 88 D2
Isabella Ra. Australia 21°0S 121°4E 60 D3
Isachenko, Ostrov Russia 77°13N 89°27E 29 B9
Ísafjarðardjúp Iceland 66°10N 23°0W 8 C2
Ísafjörður Iceland 66°5N 23°9W 8 C2
Isagarh India 24°48N 77°51E 42 G7
Isahaya Japan 32°52N 130°2E 31 H5
Isaka Tanzania 3°56S 32°59E 54 C3
Isalo △ Madag. 22°23S 45°16E 57 C8
Isan → India 26°51N 80°7E 43 F9
Isana = Içana → Brazil 0°26N 67°19W 92 C5
Isangano △ Zambia 11°8S 30°35E 55 E3
Isar → Germany 48°48N 12°57E 16 D7
Íschia Italy 40°44N 13°57E 22 D5
Isdell → Australia 16°27S 124°51E 60 C3
Ise Japan 34°25N 136°45E 31 G8
Ise-Shima △ Japan 34°25N 136°48E 31 G8
Ise-Wan Japan 34°43N 136°43E 31 G8
Iseramagazi Tanzania 4°37S 32°10E 54 C3
Isère → France 44°59N 4°51E 20 D6
Isérnia Italy 41°36N 14°14E 22 D6
Isfahan = Eşfahān Iran 32°39N 51°43E 45 C6
Ishigaki Japan 24°26N 124°10E 31 M2
Ishigaki-Shima Japan 24°20N 124°10E 31 M2
Ishikari-Gawa → Japan 43°15N 141°23E 30 C10
Ishikari-Sammyaku Japan 43°30N 143°0E 30 C11
Ishikari-Wan Japan 43°25N 141°1E 30 C10
Ishikawa Japan 26°25N 127°49E 31 L3
Ishikawa □ Japan 36°30N 136°30E 31 F8
Ishim Russia 56°10N 69°30E 28 D7
Ishim → Russia 57°45N 71°10E 28 D8
Ishinomaki Japan 38°32N 141°20E 30 E10
Ishioka Japan 36°11N 140°16E 31 F10
Ishkoman Pakistan 36°30N 73°50E 43 A5
Ishpeming U.S.A. 46°29N 87°40W 80 B10
Isil Kul Russia 54°55N 71°16E 28 D8
Isiolo Kenya 0°24N 37°33E 54 B4
Isiro Dem. Rep. of the Congo 2°53N 27°40E 54 B2
Isisford Australia 24°15S 144°21E 62 C3
İskenderun Turkey 36°32N 36°10E 44 B3
İskenderun Körfezi Turkey 36°40N 35°50E 19 G6
Iskŭr → Bulgaria 43°45N 24°25E 23 C11
Iskut → Canada 56°45N 131°49W 70 B2
Isla → U.K. 56°32N 3°20W 11 E5
Isla Coiba △ Panama 7°33N 81°36W 88 E3
Isla de Salamanca △ Colombia 10°59N 74°40W 89 D5
Isla Gorge △ Australia 25°10S 149°57E 62 D4
Isla Isabel △ Mexico 21°54N 105°58W 86 C3
Isla Tiburón y San Esteban ⌂ Mexico 29°0N 112°27W 86 B2
Isla Vista U.S.A. 34°25N 119°53W 79 L7
Islam Headworks Pakistan 29°49N 72°33E 42 E5
Islamabad Pakistan 33°40N 73°10E 42 C5
Islamgarh Pakistan 27°51N 70°48E 42 F4
Islamkot Pakistan 24°42N 70°13E 42 G4
Islampur India 26°16N 88°12E 43 F13
Islampur Bihar, India 25°9N 85°12E 43 G11
Island = Iceland ■ Europe 64°45N 19°0W 8 D4
Island L. Canada 53°47N 94°25W 71 C10
Island Lagoon Australia 31°30S 136°40E 63 E2
Island Pond U.S.A. 44°49N 71°53W 83 B13
Islands, B. of Canada 49°11N 58°15W 73 C8
Islands, B. of N.Z. 35°15S 174°6E 59
Islay U.K. 55°46N 6°10W 11
Isle → France 44°55N 0°15W 20
Isle aux Morts Canada 47°35N 59°0W 73
Isle of Wight □ U.K. 50°41N 1°17W 13
Isle Royale △ U.S.A. 48°0N 88°55W 80
Isleton U.S.A. 38°10N 121°37W 78
Ismail = Izmayil Ukraine 45°22N 28°46E 17 F
Ismâ'ilîya Egypt 30°37N 32°18E 51 B
Isna Egypt 25°17N 32°30E 51 C
Isoanala Madag. 23°50S 45°44E 57
Isogstalo India 34°15N 78°46E 43
Isparta Turkey 37°47N 30°30E 19
Ispica Italy 36°47N 14°55E 22
Israel ■ Asia 32°0N 34°50E 46
Issoire France 45°32N 3°15E 20
Issyk-Kul = Balykchy Kyrgyzstan 42°26N 76°12E 32
Issyk-Kul, Ozero = Ysyk-Köl Kyrgyzstan 42°25N 77°15E 28
İstanbul Turkey 41°0N 28°58E 23 D
İstanbul Boğazı Turkey 41°5N 29°3E 23 D
Istiea Greece 38°57N 23°9E 23 E
Istokpoga, L. U.S.A. 27°23N 81°17W 85 H
Istra Croatia 45°10N 14°0E 16
Istres France 43°31N 4°59E 20
Istria = Istra Croatia 45°10N 14°0E 16
Itá Paraguay 25°29S 57°21W 94
Itaberaba Brazil 12°32S 40°18W 93 F
Itabira Brazil 19°37S 43°13W 93 G
Itabirito Brazil 20°15S 43°48W 95
Itabuna Brazil 14°48S 39°16W 93 F
Itacaunas → Brazil 5°21S 49°8W 93
Itacoatiara Brazil 3°8S 58°25W 92
Itaipú, Represa de Brazil 25°30S 54°30W 95
Itaituba Brazil 4°10S 55°50W 93
Itajaí Brazil 27°50S 48°39W 95
Itajubá Brazil 22°24S 45°30W 95
Itaka Tanzania 8°50S 32°49E 55
Itala ⌂ S. Africa 27°30S 31°7E 57
Italy ■ Europe 42°0N 13°0E 22
Itamaraju Brazil 17°4S 39°32W 93 G
Itampolo Madag. 24°41S 43°57E 57
Itandrano Madag. 21°47S 45°17E 57
Itapecuru Mirim Brazil 3°24S 44°20W 93 D
Itaperuna Brazil 21°10S 41°54W 95
Itapetininga Brazil 23°36S 48°7W 95
Itapeva Brazil 23°59S 48°59W 95
Itapicuru → Bahia, Brazil 11°47S 37°32W 93 F
Itapicuru → Maranhão, Brazil 2°52S 44°12W 93 D
Itapipoca Brazil 3°30S 39°35W 93 D
Itapuá □ Paraguay 26°40S 55°40W 95
Itaquari Brazil 20°20S 40°25W 95
Itaquí Brazil 29°8S 56°30W 94
Itararé Brazil 24°6S 49°23W 95
Itarsi India 22°36N 77°51E 42
Itatí Argentina 27°16S 58°15W 94
Itatiaia △ Brazil 22°22S 44°38W 95
Itchen → U.K. 50°55N 1°22W 13
Itezhi Tezhi, L. Zambia 15°30S 25°30E 55
Ithaca = Ithaki Greece 38°25N 20°40E 23
Ithaca U.S.A. 42°27N 76°30W 83
Ithaki Greece 38°25N 20°40E 23
Itiquira → Brazil 17°18S 56°44W 93
Itiyuro → Argentina 22°40S 63°50W 94
Itō Japan 34°58N 139°5E 31
Itoigawa Japan 37°2N 137°51E 31
Itonamas → Bolivia 12°28S 64°24W 92
Ittoqqortoormiit Greenland 70°20N 23°0W 4
Itu Brazil 23°17S 47°15W 95
Itu Aba I. S. China Sea 10°23N 114°21E 36
Ituiutaba Brazil 19°0S 49°25W 93
Itumbiara Brazil 18°20S 49°10W 93
Ituna Canada 51°10N 103°24W 71
Itunge Port Tanzania 9°40S 33°55E 55
Iturbe Argentina 23°0S 65°25W 94
Ituri → Dem. Rep. of the Congo 1°40N 27°1E 54
Iturup, Ostrov Russia 45°0N 148°0E 29
Ituxi → Brazil 7°18S 64°51W 92
Itzehoe Germany 53°55N 9°31E 16
Ivahona Madag. 23°27S 46°10E 57
Ivaí → Brazil 23°18S 53°42W 95
Ivalo Finland 68°38N 27°35E 8 B
Ivalojoki → Finland 68°40N 27°40E 8 B
Ivanava Belarus 52°7N 25°29E 17 B
Ivanhoe Australia 32°56S 144°20E 63
Ivanhoe Canada 44°23N 77°28W 82
Ivanhoe Calif., U.S.A. 36°23N 119°13W 78
Ivanhoe Minn., U.S.A. 44°28N 96°15W 80
Ivano-Frankivsk Ukraine 48°40N 24°40E 17 D
Ivanovo = Ivanava Belarus 52°7N 25°29E 17 B
Ivanovo Russia 57°5N 41°0E 18
Ivato Madag. 20°37S 47°10E 57
Ivatsevichy Belarus 52°43N 25°21E 17 B
Ivdel Russia 60°42N 60°24E 18 B
Ivinheima → Brazil 23°14S 53°42W 95
Ivinhema Brazil 22°10S 53°37W 95
Ivohibe Madag. 22°31S 46°57E 57
Ivory Coast W. Afr. 4°20N 5°0W 50
Ivory Coast ■ Africa 7°30N 5°0W 50
Ivrea Italy 45°28N 7°52E 20
Ivujivik Canada 62°24N 77°55W 69
Ivybridge U.K. 50°23N 3°56W 13
Iwaizumi Japan 39°50N 141°45E 30
Iwaki Japan 37°3N 140°55E 31
Iwakuni Japan 34°15N 132°8E 31
Iwamizawa Japan 43°12N 141°46E 30
Iwanai Japan 42°58N 140°30E 30
Iwata Japan 34°42N 137°51E 31
Iwate □ Japan 39°30N 141°30E 30
Iwate-San Japan 39°51N 141°0E 30

) Nigeria 7°39N 4°9E 50 G6
ŏn N. Korea 40°19N 128°39E 35 D15
amas Bolivia 13°50S 68°5W 92 F5
po S. Africa 30°11S 30°5E 57 E5
epec Mexico 16°34N 95°6W 87 D5
án del Río Mexico 21°2N 104°22W 86 C4
Japan 33°45N 132°45E 31 H6
oal, L. de Guatemala 15°30N 89°10W 88 C2
mal Mexico 20°56N 89°1W 87 C7
ia-Shima Japan 26°56N 127°56E 31 L3
evsk Russia 56°51N 53°14E 18 C9
ma → Russia 65°19N 52°54E 18 A9
ayil Ukraine 45°22N 28°46E 17 F15
ir Turkey 38°25N 27°8E 23 E12
it = Kocaeli Turkey 40°45N 29°50E 19 F4
k Gölü Turkey 40°27N 29°30E 23 D13
Syria 32°51N 36°15E 46 C5
Shotō Japan 34°30N 140°0E 31 G10
car de Matamoros
Mexico 18°36N 98°28W 87 D5
ni-Sano Japan 34°23N 135°18E 31 G7
no Japan 35°20N 132°46E 31 G6
aslav Ukraine 50°5N 26°50E 17 C14

K. Int. ✕ (JFK)
S.A. 40°38N 73°47W 83 F11
rom Thurmond L.
S.A. 33°40N 82°12W 85 E13
alpur India 23°9N 79°58E 43 H8
ūl Syria 36°4N 37°30E 44 B3
ru Australia 12°40S 132°53E 60 B5
ah Syria 35°20N 36°0E 44 C3
onec nad Nisou
zech Rep. 50°43N 15°10E 16 C8
atão Brazil 8°7S 35°1W 93 E11
ticabal Brazil 21°15S 48°17W 95 A6
Spain 42°35N 0°33W 21 A5
reí Brazil 23°20S 46°0W 95 A6
rèzinho Brazil 23°5S 49°58W 95 A6
River △ Australia 14°58S 144°19E 62 A3
man U.S.A. 45°37N 70°15W 81 C18
sboro U.S.A. 33°13N 98°10W 84 E5
son Barbados 13°7N 59°36W 89 g
son Ala., U.S.A. 31°31N 87°53W 85 F11
son Calif., U.S.A. 38°21N 120°46W 78 G6
son Ky., U.S.A. 37°33N 83°23W 81 G12
son Mich., U.S.A. 42°15N 84°24W 81 D11
son Minn., U.S.A. 43°37N 95°1W 80 D6
son Miss., U.S.A. 32°18N 90°12W 85 E9
son Mo., U.S.A. 37°23N 89°40W 80 G9
son N.H., U.S.A. 44°10N 71°11W 83 B13
son Ohio, U.S.A. 39°3N 82°39W 81 F12
son Tenn., U.S.A. 35°37N 88°49W 85 D10
son Wyo., U.S.A. 43°29N 110°46W 76 E8
son B. N.Z. 43°58S 168°42E 59 E2
son L. U.S.A. 43°52N 110°36W 76 E8
sons N.Z. 42°46S 171°32E 59 E3
son's Arm Canada 49°52N 56°47W 73 C8
sonville Ala.,
S.A. 33°49N 85°46W 85 E12
sonville Ark., U.S.A. 34°52N 92°7W 84 D8
sonville Calif.,
S.A. 37°52N 120°24W 78 H6
sonville Fla.,
S.A. 30°20N 81°39W 85 F14
sonville Ill., U.S.A. 39°44N 90°14W 80 F8
sonville N.C.,
S.A. 34°45N 77°26W 85 D16
sonville Tex., U.S.A. 31°58N 95°17W 84 F7
sonville Beach
S.A. 30°17N 81°24W 85 F14
el Haiti 18°14N 72°32W 89 C5
Lake U.S.A. 36°43N 112°13W 77 H7
abad Pakistan 28°20N 68°29E 42 E3
bina Brazil 11°11S 40°30W 93 F10
ues-Cartier, Dét. de
nada 50°0N 63°30W 73 C7
ues-Cartier, Mt.
nada 48°57N 66°0W 73 C6
ues-Cartier △
nada 47°15N 71°33W 73 C5
→ Brazil 30°2S 51°15W 95 C5
mba U.S.A. 32°37N 116°11W 79 N10
ndá → Brazil 1°57S 50°26W 93 D8
City Canada 59°15N 129°37W 70 B3
Peru 5°25S 78°40W 92 E3
Spain 37°44N 3°43W 21 D4
abad India 20°52N 71°22E 42 J4
= Tel Aviv-Yafo
ael 32°4N 34°48E 46 C3
C. Australia 36°58S 139°40E 63 F2
a Sri Lanka 9°45N 80°2E 40 Q12
y U.S.A. 42°49N 72°2W 83 D12
hri India 30°10N 77°20E 42 D7
lishpur India 25°30N 84°21E 43 G11
alpur India 19°3N 82°0E 41 K13
sfontein S. Africa 29°44S 25°27E 56 D4
n → Iran 27°17N 57°13E 45 E8
ina Serbia 44°5N 21°15E 23 C9
on India 30°50N 75°25E 42 D6
l India 18°50N 79°0E 40 K11
riaíva Brazil 24°10S 49°50W 95 A6
ribe → Brazil 4°25S 37°45W 93 D11
y Grande Cuba 22°35N 81°7W 88 B3
abad India 25°13N 84°59E 43 G11
pur India 25°37N 75°17E 42 G6
m Iran 28°30N 53°31E 45 D7
India 31°21N 76°9E 42 D7
) Indonesia 1°5N 127°30E 37 D7
, Selat Indonesia 0°5N 129°5E 37 D7
India 27°0N 75°50E 42 F6
dia 26°15N 81°32E 43 F9
mer India 26°55N 70°54E 42 F4
ghnagar India 23°38N 78°34E 43 H8

Jaitaran India 26°12N 73°56E 42 F5
Jaithari India 23°14N 78°37E 43 H8
Jājarm Iran 36°58N 56°27E 45 B8
Jakam → India 23°54N 74°13E 42 H6
Jakarta Indonesia 6°9S 106°52E 37 G12
Jakhal India 29°48N 75°50E 42 E6
Jakhau India 23°13N 68°43E 42 H3
Jakobstad = Pietarsaari
Finland 63°40N 22°43E 8 E20
Jal U.S.A. 32°7N 103°12W 77 K12
Jalājil Si. Arabia 25°40N 45°27E 44 E5
Jalālābād Afghan. 34°30N 70°29E 42 B4
Jalalabad India 27°41N 79°42E 43 F8
Jalalpur Jattan Pakistan 32°38N 74°11E 42 C6
Jalama U.S.A. 34°29N 120°29W 79 L6
Jalapa Guatemala 14°39N 89°59W 88 D2
Jalapa Enríquez = Xalapa
Mexico 19°32N 96°55W 87 D5
Jalasjärvi Finland 62°29N 22°47E 8 E20
Jalaun India 26°8N 79°25E 43 F8
Jaldhaka → Bangla. 26°16N 89°16E 43 F13
Jalesar India 27°29N 78°19E 42 F8
Jaleswar Nepal 26°38N 85°48E 43 F11
Jalgaon India 21°0N 75°42E 40 J9
Jalībah Iraq 30°35N 46°32E 44 D5
Jalingo Nigeria 8°55N 11°25E 51 G8
Jalisco □ Mexico 20°20N 103°40W 86 D4
Jalkot Pakistan 35°14N 73°24E 43 B5
Jalna India 19°48N 75°38E 40 K9
Jalón → Spain 41°47N 1°4W 21 B5
Jalor India 25°21N 72°37E 42 G5
Jalpa Mexico 21°38N 102°58W 86 C4
Jalpaiguri India 26°32N 88°46E 41 F16
Jalpan Mexico 21°14N 99°29W 87 C5
Jaluit I. Marshall Is. 6°0N 169°30E 64 G8
Jalūlā Iraq 34°16N 45°10E 44 C5
Jamaame Somali Rep. 0°4N 42°44E 47 G3
Jamaica ■ W. Indies 18°10N 77°30W 88 a
Jamalpur Bangla. 24°52N 89°56E 41 G16
Jamalpur India 25°18N 86°28E 43 G12
Jamalpurganj India 23°2N 87°59E 43 H13
Jamanxim → Brazil 4°43S 56°18W 93 D7
Jambewangi Indonesia 8°17S 114°7E 37 J17
Jambi Indonesia 1°38S 103°30E 36 E2
Jambi □ Indonesia 1°30S 102°30E 36 E2
Jambongan, Pulau
Malaysia 6°45N 117°20E 36 C5
Jambusar India 22°3N 72°51E 42 H5
James → S. Dak., U.S.A. 42°52N 97°18W 80 D5
James → Va., U.S.A. 36°56N 76°27W 81 G15
James B. Canada 54°0N 80°0W 72 B3
James Ranges Australia 24°10S 132°30E 60 D5
James Ross I. Antarctica 63°58S 57°50W 5 C18
Jamesabad Pakistan 25°17N 69°15E 42 G3
Jamestown Australia 33°10S 138°32E 63 E2
Jamestown S. Africa 31°6S 26°45E 56 E4
Jamestown N. Dak.,
U.S.A. 46°54N 98°42W 80 B4
Jamestown N.Y., U.S.A. 42°6N 79°14W 82 D5
Jamestown Pa., U.S.A. 41°29N 80°27W 82 E4
Jamīlābād Iran 34°24N 48°28E 45 C6
Jamira → India 21°35N 88°28E 43 J13
Jamkhandi India 16°30N 75°15E 40 L9
Jammu India 32°43N 74°54E 42 C6
Jammu & Kashmir □
India 34°25N 77°0E 43 B7
Jamnagar India 22°30N 70°6E 42 H4
Jamni → India 25°13N 78°35E 43 G8
Jampur Pakistan 29°39N 70°40E 42 E4
Jamrud Pakistan 33°59N 71°24E 42 C4
Jämsä Finland 61°53N 25°10E 8 F21
Jamshedpur India 22°44N 86°12E 43 H12
Jamtara India 23°59N 86°49E 43 H12
Jämtland Sweden 63°31N 14°0E 8 E16
Jan L. Canada 54°56N 102°55W 71 C8
Jan Mayen Arctic 71°0N 9°0W 4 B7
Janakpur India 26°42N 85°55E 43 F11
Janaúba Brazil 15°48S 43°19W 93 G10
Jand Pakistan 33°30N 72°6E 42 C5
Jandaq Iran 34°3N 54°22E 45 C7
Jandía Canary Is. 28°6N 14°21W 24 F5
Jandía, Pta. de Canary Is. 28°3N 14°31W 24 F5
Jandía △ Canary Is. 28°4N 14°19W 24 F5
Jandola Pakistan 32°20N 70°9E 42 C4
Jandowae Australia 26°45S 151°7E 63 D5
Janesville U.S.A. 42°41N 89°1W 80 D9
Jangamo Mozam. 24°6S 35°21E 57 C6
Janghai India 25°33N 82°19E 43 G10
Jangheung S. Korea 34°41N 126°52E 35 G14
Janjanbureh Gambia 13°30N 14°47W 50 F3
Janjgir India 22°1N 82°34E 43 J10
Janjina Madag. 20°30S 45°50E 57 C8
Janos Mexico 30°54N 108°10W 86 A3
Januária Brazil 15°25S 44°25W 93 G10
Janûb Sînî □ Egypt 29°30N 33°50E 46 F2
Janubio Canary Is. 28°56N 13°50W 24 F6
Jaora India 23°40N 75°10E 42 H6
Japan ■ Asia 36°0N 136°0E 31 G8
Japan, Sea of Asia 40°0N 135°0E 30 E7
Japan Trench Pac. Oc. 32°0N 142°0E 64 D6
Japen = Yapen Indonesia 1°50S 136°0E 37 E9
Japla India 24°33N 84°1E 43 G11
Japurá → Brazil 3°8S 65°46W 92 D5
Jaquarão Brazil 32°34S 53°23W 95 C5
Jaqué Panama 7°27N 78°8W 88 E4
Jarābulus Syria 36°49N 38°1E 44 B3
Jarama → Spain 40°24N 3°32W 21 B4
Jaranwala Pakistan 31°15N 73°26E 42 D5
Jarash Jordan 32°17N 35°54E 46 C4
Jarash □ Jordan 32°17N 35°54E 46 C4
Jardim Brazil 21°28S 56°2W 94 A4
Jardín América Argentina 27°3S 55°14W 95 B4
Jardine River △ Australia 11°9S 142°21E 62 A3
Jardines de la Reina, Arch. de los
Cuba 20°50N 78°50W 88 B4
Jargalang China 43°5N 122°55E 35 C12
Jari → Brazil 1°9S 51°54W 93 D8

Jarīr, W. al → Si. Arabia 25°38N 42°30E 44 E4
Jarosław Poland 50°2N 22°42E 17 C12
Jarrahdale Australia 32°24S 116°5E 61 F2
Jarrahi → Iran 30°49N 48°48E 45 D6
Jarres, Plaine des Laos 19°27N 103°10E 38 C4
Jartai China 39°45N 105°48E 34 E3
Jarud Qi China 44°28N 120°50E 35 B11
Järvenpää Finland 60°29N 25°5E 8 F21
Jarvis Canada 42°53N 80°6W 82 D4
Jarvis I. Pac. Oc. 0°15S 160°5W 65 H12
Jarwa India 27°38N 82°30E 43 F10
Jasdan India 22°2N 71°12E 42 H4
Jashpurnagar India 22°54N 84°9E 43 H11
Jasidih India 24°31N 86°39E 43 G12
Jāsimīyah Iraq 33°45N 44°41E 44 C5
Jasin Malaysia 2°20N 102°26E 39 L4
Jāsk Iran 25°38N 57°45E 45 E8
Jasło Poland 49°45N 21°30E 17 D11
Jaso India 24°30N 80°29E 43 G9
Jasper Alta., Canada 52°55N 118°5W 70 C5
Jasper Ont., Canada 44°52N 75°57W 83 B9
Jasper Ala., U.S.A. 33°50N 87°17W 85 E11
Jasper Fla., U.S.A. 30°31N 82°57W 85 F13
Jasper Ind., U.S.A. 38°24N 86°56W 80 F10
Jasper Tex., U.S.A. 30°56N 94°1W 84 F7
Jasper △ Canada 52°50N 118°8W 70 C5
Jasrasar India 27°43N 73°49E 42 F5
Jászberény Hungary 47°30N 19°55E 17 E10
Jataí Brazil 17°58S 51°48W 93 G8
Jati Pakistan 24°20N 68°19E 42 G3
Jatibarang Indonesia 6°28S 108°18E 37 G13
Jatiluwih Indonesia 8°23S 115°8E 37 J18
Jatinegara Indonesia 6°13S 106°52E 37 G12
Játiva = Xátiva Spain 38°59N 0°32W 21 C5
Jaú Brazil 22°10S 48°30W 95 A6
Jauja Peru 11°45S 75°15W 92 F3
Jaunpur India 25°46N 82°44E 43 G10
Java = Jawa Indonesia 7°0S 110°0E 36 F3
Java Sea Indonesia 4°35S 107°15E 36 E3
Java Trench Ind. Oc. 9°0S 105°0E 36 F3
Jawa Indonesia 7°0S 110°0E 36 F3
Jawa Barat □ Indonesia 7°0S 107°0E 37 G12
Jawa Tengah □ Indonesia 7°0S 110°0E 37 G14
Jawa Timur □ Indonesia 8°0S 113°0E 37 G15
Jawad India 24°36N 74°51E 42 G6
Jawhar Somali Rep. 2°48N 45°30E 47 G4
Jay Peak U.S.A. 44°55N 72°32W 83 B12
Jaya, Puncak Indonesia 3°57S 137°17E 37 E9
Jayanti India 26°45N 89°40E 41 F16
Jayapura Indonesia 2°28S 140°38E 37 E10
Jayawijaya, Pegunungan
Indonesia 5°0S 139°0E 37 F9
Jaynagar India 26°43N 86°9E 43 F12
Jayrūd Syria 33°49N 36°44E 44 C3
Jayton U.S.A. 33°15N 100°34W 84 E4
Jāz Mūrīān, Hāmūn-e
Iran 27°20N 58°55E 45 E8
Jazīreh-ye Shīf Iran 29°4N 50°54E 45 D6
Jazminal Mexico 24°52N 101°24W 86 C4
Jazzīn Lebanon 33°31N 35°35E 46 B4
Jean U.S.A. 35°47N 115°20W 79 K11
Jean Marie River
Canada 61°32N 120°38W 70 A4
Jean-Rabel Haiti 19°50N 73°5W 89 C5
Jeanerette U.S.A. 29°55N 91°40W 84 G9
Jeanette, Ostrov = Zhannetty,
Ostrov Russia 76°43N 158°0E 29 B16
Jeannette U.S.A. 40°20N 79°36W 82 F5
Jebāl Bārez, Kūh-e Iran 28°30N 58°20E 45 D8
Jebel, Bahr el → Sudan 9°30N 30°25E 51 G12
Jebel Ali = Minā' Jabal 'Alī
U.A.E. 25°2N 55°8E 45 E7
Jecheon S. Korea 37°8N 128°12E 35 F15
Jedburgh U.K. 55°29N 2°33W 11 F6
Jedda = Jiddah Si. Arabia 21°29N 39°10E 47 C2
Jeddore L. Canada 48°3N 55°55W 73 C8
Jędrzejów Poland 50°35N 20°15E 17 C11
Jefferson Iowa, U.S.A. 42°1N 94°23W 80 D6
Jefferson Ohio, U.S.A. 41°44N 80°46W 82 E4
Jefferson Tex., U.S.A. 32°46N 94°21W 84 E7
Jefferson, Mt. Nev.,
U.S.A. 38°47N 116°56W 76 G5
Jefferson, Mt. Oreg.,
U.S.A. 44°41N 121°48W 76 D3
Jefferson City Mo.,
U.S.A. 38°34N 92°10W 80 F7
Jefferson City Tenn.,
U.S.A. 36°7N 83°30W 85 C13
Jeffersontown U.S.A. 38°12N 85°35W 81 F11
Jeffersonville U.S.A. 38°17N 85°44W 81 F11
Jeffrey City U.S.A. 42°30N 107°49W 76 E10
Jega Nigeria 12°15N 4°23E 50 F6
Jeju S. Korea 33°31N 126°32E 35 H14
Jeju-do S. Korea 33°29N 126°34E 35 H14
Jēkabpils Latvia 56°29N 25°57E 9 H21
Jekyll I. U.S.A. 31°4N 81°25W 85 F14
Jelenia Góra Poland 50°50N 15°45E 16 C8
Jelgava Latvia 56°41N 23°49E 9 H20
Jemaja Indonesia 3°5N 105°45E 39 L5
Jemaluang Malaysia 2°16N 103°52E 39 L4
Jember Indonesia 8°11S 113°41E 37 H15
Jena Germany 50°54N 11°35E 16 C6
Jena U.S.A. 31°41N 92°8W 84 F8
Jenīn West Bank 32°28N 35°18E 46 C4
Jenkins U.S.A. 37°10N 82°38W 81 G12
Jenner U.S.A. 38°27N 123°7W 78 G3
Jennings U.S.A. 30°13N 92°40W 84 F8
Jeong-eup S. Korea 35°35N 126°50E 35 G14
Jeonju S. Korea 35°50N 127°4E 35 G14
Jepara Indonesia 7°40S 109°14E 37 G14
Jeparit Australia 36°8S 142°1E 63 F3
Jequié Brazil 13°51S 40°5W 93 F10
Jequitinhonha Brazil 16°30S 41°0W 93 G10
Jequitinhonha →
Brazil 15°51S 38°53W 93 G11
Jerada Morocco 34°17N 2°10W 50 B5
Jerantut Malaysia 3°56N 102°22E 39 L4

Jerejak, Pulau Malaysia 5°19N 100°19E 39 c
Jérémie Haiti 18°40N 74°10W 89 C5
Jerez, Pta. Mexico 22°58N 97°40W 87 C5
Jerez de García Salinas
Mexico 22°39N 103°0W 86 C4
Jerez de la Frontera Spain 36°41N 6°7W 21 D2
Jerez de los Caballeros
Spain 38°20N 6°45W 21 C2
Jericho = El Arīḥā
West Bank 31°52N 35°27E 46 D4
Jericho Australia 23°38S 146°6E 62 C4
Jerid, Chott el = Djerid, Chott
Tunisia 33°42N 8°30E 50 B7
Jerilderie Australia 35°20S 145°41E 63 F4
Jermyn U.S.A. 41°32N 75°33W 83 E9
Jerome U.S.A. 42°44N 114°31W 76 E6
Jerramungup Australia 33°55S 118°55E 61 F2
Jersey U.K. 49°11N 2°7W 13 H5
Jersey City U.S.A. 40°42N 74°4W 83 F10
Jersey Shore U.S.A. 41°12N 77°15W 82 E7
Jerseyville U.S.A. 39°7N 90°20W 80 F8
Jerusalem
Israel/West Bank 31°47N 35°10E 46 D4
Jervis B. Australia 35°8S 150°46E 63 F5
Jervis Inlet Canada 50°0N 123°57W 70 C4
Jesi = Iesi Italy 43°31N 13°14E 22 C5
Jessore Bangla. 23°10N 89°10E 41 H16
Jesup U.S.A. 31°36N 81°53W 85 F14
Jesús Carranza Mexico 17°26N 95°2W 87 D5
Jesús María Argentina 30°59S 64°5W 94 C3
Jetmore U.S.A. 38°4N 99°54W 80 F4
Jetpur India 21°45N 70°10E 42 J4
Jevnaker Norway 60°15N 10°26E 9 F14
Jewett U.S.A. 40°22N 81°2W 82 F3
Jewett City U.S.A. 41°36N 71°59W 83 E13
Jeyḥūnābād Iran 34°58N 48°59E 45 C6
Jeypore India 18°50N 82°38E 41 K13
Jha Jha India 24°46N 86°22E 43 G12
Jhaarkand = Jharkhand □
India 24°0N 85°50E 43 H11
Jhabua India 22°46N 74°36E 42 H6
Jhajjar India 28°37N 76°42E 42 E7
Jhal Pakistan 28°17N 67°27E 42 E2
Jhal Jhao Pakistan 26°20N 65°35E 40 F4
Jhalawar India 24°40N 76°10E 42 G7
Jhalida India 23°22N 85°58E 43 H11
Jhalrapatan India 24°33N 76°10E 42 G7
Jhang Maghiana
Pakistan 31°15N 72°22E 42 D5
Jhansi India 25°30N 78°36E 43 G8
Jhargram India 22°27N 86°59E 43 H12
Jharia India 23°45N 86°26E 43 H12
Jharkhand □ India 24°0N 85°50E 43 H11
Jharsuguda India 21°56N 84°5E 41 J14
Jhelum Pakistan 33°0N 73°45E 42 C5
Jhelum → Pakistan 31°20N 72°10E 42 D5
Jhilmilli India 23°24N 82°51E 43 H10
Jhudo Pakistan 24°58N 69°18E 42 G3
Jhunjhunu India 28°10N 75°30E 42 E6
Ji-Paraná Brazil 10°52S 62°57W 92 F6
Ji Xian Hebei, China 37°35N 115°30E 34 F8
Ji Xian Henan, China 35°22N 114°5E 34 G8
Ji Xian Shanxi, China 36°7N 110°40E 34 F6
Jia Xian Henan, China 33°59N 113°12E 34 H7
Jia Xian Shaanxi, China 38°12N 110°28E 34 E6
Jiaji = Qionghai China 19°15N 110°26E 38 C8
Jiamusi China 46°40N 130°26E 33 B8
Ji'an Jiangxi, China 27°6N 114°59E 33 D6
Ji'an Jilin, China 41°5N 126°10E 35 D14
Jianchang China 40°55N 120°35E 35 D11
Jianchangying China 40°10N 118°50E 35 D10
Jiangcheng China 22°36N 101°52E 32 D5
Jiangmen China 22°32N 113°0E 33 D6
Jiangsu □ China 33°0N 120°0E 35 H11
Jiangxi □ China 27°30N 116°0E 33 D6
Jiao Xian = Jiaozhou
China 36°18N 120°1E 35 F11
Jiaohe Hebei, China 38°2N 116°20E 34 E9
Jiaohe Jilin, China 43°40N 127°22E 35 C14
Jiaozhou China 36°18N 120°1E 35 F11
Jiaozhou Wan China 36°5N 120°10E 35 F11
Jiaozuo China 35°16N 113°12E 34 G7
Jiawang China 34°28N 117°26E 35 G9
Jiaxiang China 35°25N 116°20E 34 G9
Jiaxing China 30°49N 120°45E 33 C7
Jiayi = Chiai Taiwan 23°29N 120°25E 33 D7
Jibuti = Djibouti ■ Africa 12°0N 43°0E 47 E3
Jicarón, I. Panama 7°10N 81°50W 88 E3
Jiddah Si. Arabia 21°29N 39°10E 47 C2
Jido India 29°2N 94°58E 41 E19
Jieshou China 33°18N 115°22E 34 H8
Jiexiu China 37°2N 111°55E 34 F6
Jigalong Australia 23°21S 120°47E 60 D3
Jigni India 25°45N 79°25E 43 G8
Jihlava Czech Rep. 49°28N 15°35E 16 D8
Jihlava → Czech Rep. 48°55N 16°36E 17 D9
Jijiga Ethiopia 9°20N 42°50E 47 F3
Jilib Somali Rep. 0°29N 42°46E 47 G3
Jilin China 43°44N 126°30E 35 C14
Jilin □ China 44°0N 127°0E 35 C14
Jilong = Chilung Taiwan 25°3N 121°45E 33 D7
Jim Thorpe U.S.A. 40°52N 75°44W 83 F9
Jima Ethiopia 7°40N 36°47E 47 F2
Jimbaran, Teluk
Indonesia 8°46S 115°9E 37 K18
Jiménez Mexico 27°8N 104°54W 86 B4
Jimo China 36°23N 120°30E 35 F11
Jin Xian = Jinzhou Hebei,
China 38°2N 115°2E 34 E8
Jin Xian = Jinzhou Liaoning,
China 38°55N 121°42E 35 E11
Jinan China 36°38N 117°1E 34 F9
Jinchang China 38°30N 102°10E 32 C5
Jincheng China 35°29N 112°50E 34 G7
Jind India 29°19N 76°22E 42 E7
Jindabyne Australia 36°25S 148°35E 63 F4
Jinding China 22°22N 113°33E 33 G10

Jindo S. Korea 34°28N 126°15E 35 G14
Jindřichův Hradec
Czech Rep. 49°10N 15°2E 16 D8
Jing He → China 34°27N 109°4E 34 G5
Jingbian China 37°20N 108°30E 34 F5
Jingchuan China 35°20N 107°20E 34 G4
Jingdezhen China 29°20N 117°11E 33 D6
Jinggu China 23°35N 100°41E 32 D5
Jinghai China 38°55N 116°55E 34 E9
Jingle China 38°20N 111°55E 34 E6
Jingning China 35°30N 105°43E 34 G3
Jingpo Hu China 43°55N 128°55E 35 C15
Jingtai China 37°10N 104°6E 34 F3
Jingxing China 38°2N 114°8E 34 E8
Jingyang China 34°30N 108°50E 34 G5
Jingyu China 42°25N 126°45E 35 C14
Jingyuan China 36°30N 104°40E 34 F3
Jingziguan China 33°15N 111°0E 34 H6
Jinhua China 29°8N 119°38E 33 D6
Jining Nei Monggol Zizhiqu,
China 41°5N 113°0E 34 D7
Jining Shandong, China 35°22N 116°34E 34 G9
Jinja Uganda 0°25N 33°12E 54 B3
Jinjang Malaysia 3°13N 101°39E 39 L3
Jinji China 37°58N 106°8E 34 F4
Jinju S. Korea 35°12N 128°2E 35 G15
Jinnah Barrage Pakistan 32°58N 71°33E 42 C4
Jinotega Nic. 13°6N 85°59W 88 D2
Jinotepe Nic. 11°50N 86°10W 88 D2
Jinsha Jiang → China 28°50N 104°36E 32 D5
Jinxi China 40°52N 120°50E 35 D11
Jinxiang China 35°5N 116°22E 34 G9
Jinzhou Hebei, China 38°2N 115°2E 34 E8
Jinzhou Liaoning, China 38°55N 121°42E 35 E11
Jinzhou Liaoning, China 41°5N 121°3E 35 D11
Jiparaná → Brazil 8°3S 62°52W 92 E6
Jipijapa Ecuador 1°0S 80°40W 92 D2
Jiquilpan Mexico 19°59N 102°43W 86 D4
Jirisan S. Korea 35°20N 127°44E 35 G14
Jishan China 35°34N 110°58E 34 G6
Jisr ash Shughūr Syria 35°49N 36°18E 44 C3
Jitarning Australia 32°48S 117°57E 61 F2
Jitra Malaysia 6°16N 100°25E 39 J3
Jiu → Romania 43°47N 23°48E 17 F12
Jiudengkou China 39°56N 106°40E 34 E4
Jiujiang China 29°42N 115°58E 33 D6
Jiulong = Kowloon
China 22°19N 114°11E 33 G11
Jiuquan China 39°50N 98°20E 32 C4
Jiutai China 44°10N 125°50E 35 B13
Jiuxincheng China 39°17N 115°59E 34 E8
Jiwani Pakistan 25°1N 61°44E 40 G2
Jixi China 45°20N 130°50E 35 B16
Jiyang China 37°0N 117°12E 35 F9
Jiyuan China 35°7N 112°57E 34 G7
Jīzān Si. Arabia 17°0N 42°20E 47 D3
Jize China 36°54N 114°56E 34 F8
Jizl, Wādī al → Si. Arabia 25°39N 38°25E 44 E3
Jizō-Zaki Japan 35°34N 133°20E 31 G6
Jizzax Uzbekistan 40°6N 67°50E 28 E7
Joaçaba Brazil 27°5S 51°31W 95 B5
João Pessoa Brazil 7°10S 34°52W 93 E12
Joaquín V. González
Argentina 25°10S 64°0W 94 B3
Jobat India 22°25N 74°34E 42 H6
Jodhpur India 26°23N 73°8E 42 F5
Jodiya India 22°42N 70°18E 42 H4
Joensuu Finland 62°37N 29°49E 8 E23
Jōetsu Japan 37°12N 138°10E 31 F9
Jofane Mozam. 21°15S 34°18E 57 C5
Jogbani India 26°25N 87°15E 43 F12
Jõgeva Estonia 58°45N 26°24E 9 G22
Jogjakarta = Yogyakarta
Indonesia 7°49S 110°22E 37 G14
Johannesburg S. Africa 26°11S 28°2E 57 D4
Johannesburg U.S.A. 35°22N 117°38W 79 K9
Johilla → India 23°37N 81°14E 43 H9
John Crow Mts. Jamaica 18°5N 76°25W 88 a
John Day U.S.A. 44°25N 118°57W 76 D4
John Day → U.S.A. 45°44N 120°39W 76 D3
John Day Fossil Beds △
U.S.A. 44°33N 119°38W 76 D4
John D'or Prairie
Canada 58°30N 115°8W 70 B5
John H. Kerr Res.
U.S.A. 36°36N 78°18W 85 C15
John o' Groats U.K. 58°38N 3°4W 11 C5
Johnnie U.S.A. 36°25N 116°5W 79 J10
John's Ra. Australia 21°55S 133°23E 62 C1
Johnson U.S.A. 44°38N 72°41W 83 B12
Johnson City Kans.,
U.S.A. 37°34N 101°45W 80 G3
Johnson City N.Y., U.S.A. 42°7N 75°58W 83 D9
Johnson City Tenn.,
U.S.A. 36°19N 82°21W 85 C13
Johnson City Tex., U.S.A. 30°17N 98°25W 84 F5
Johnsonburg U.S.A. 41°29N 78°41W 82 E6
Johnsondale U.S.A. 35°58N 118°32W 79 K8
Johnsons Crossing
Canada 60°29N 133°18W 70 A2
Johnston, L. Australia 32°25S 120°30E 61 F3
Johnston Falls = Mambilima Falls
Zambia 10°31S 28°45E 55 E2
Johnston I. Pac. Oc. 17°10N 169°8W 65 F11
Johnstone Str. Canada 50°28N 126°0W 70 C3
Johnstown Ireland 52°45N 7°33W 10 D4
Johnstown N.Y., U.S.A. 43°0N 74°22W 83 C10
Johnstown Ohio, U.S.A. 40°9N 82°41W 82 F2
Johnstown Pa., U.S.A. 40°20N 78°55W 82 F6
Johor, Selat Asia 1°28N 103°47E 39 d
Johor Bahru Malaysia 1°28N 103°46E 39 d
Jōhvi Estonia 59°22N 27°27E 9 G22
Joinville Brazil 26°15S 48°55W 95 B6
Joinville I. Antarctica 65°0S 55°30W 5 C18
Jojutla Mexico 18°37N 99°11W 87 D5
Jokkmokk Sweden 66°35N 19°50E 8 C18
Jökulsá á Bru → Iceland 65°40N 14°16W 8 D6

Jökulsá á Fjöllum → *Iceland* 66°10N 16°30W **8** C5
Jolfā *Āzarbājān-e Sharqī, Iran* 38°57N 45°38E **44** B5
Jolfā *Eşfahan, Iran* 32°58N 51°37E **45** C6
Joliet *U.S.A.* 41°32N 88°5W **80** E9
Joliette *Canada* 46°3N 73°24W **72** C5
Jolo *Phil.* 6°0N 121°0E **37** C6
Jolon *U.S.A.* 35°58N 121°9W **78** K5
Jombang *Indonesia* 7°33S 112°14E **37** G15
Jonava *Lithuania* 55°8N 24°12E **9** J21
Jones Sound *Canada* 76°0N 85°0W **69** B11
Jonesboro *Ark., U.S.A.* 35°50N 90°42W **85** D9
Jonesboro *La., U.S.A.* 32°15N 92°43W **84** E8
Joniškis *Lithuania* 56°13N 23°35E **9** H20
Jönköping *Sweden* 57°45N 14°8E **9** H16
Jonquière *Canada* 48°27N 71°14W **73** C5
Joplin *U.S.A.* 37°6N 94°31W **80** G6
Jora *India* 26°20N 77°49E **42** F6
Jordan *Mont., U.S.A.* 47°19N 106°55W **76** C10
Jordan *N.Y., U.S.A.* 43°4N 76°29W **83** C8
Jordan ■ *Asia* 31°0N 36°0E **46** E5
Jordan → *Asia* 31°48N 35°32E **46** D4
Jordan Valley *U.S.A.* 42°59N 117°3W **76** E5
Jorhat *India* 26°45N 94°12E **41** F19
Jörn *Sweden* 65°4N 20°1E **8** D19
Jorong *Indonesia* 3°58S 114°56E **36** E4
Jørpeland *Norway* 59°3N 6°1E **9** G12
Jorquera → *Chile* 28°3S 69°58W **94** B2
Jos *Nigeria* 9°53N 8°51E **50** G7
José Batlle y Ordóñez *Uruguay* 33°20S 55°10W **95** C4
Joseph, L. *Canada* 45°10N 79°44W **82** A5
Joseph Bonaparte G. *Australia* 14°35S 128°50E **60** B4
Joseph L. *Canada* 52°45N 65°18W **73** B6
Joshinath *India* 30°34N 79°34E **43** D8
Joshinetsu-Kōgen △ *Japan* 36°42N 138°32E **31** F9
Joshua Tree *U.S.A.* 34°8N 116°19W **79** L10
Joshua Tree △ *U.S.A.* 33°55N 116°0W **79** M10
Jost Van Dyke I. *Br. Virgin Is.* 18°29N 64°47W **89** e
Jostedalsbreen *Norway* 61°40N 6°59E **8** F12
Jotunheimen *Norway* 61°35N 8°25E **8** F13
Joubertberge *Namibia* 18°30S 14°0E **56** B1
Jourdanton *U.S.A.* 28°55N 98°33W **84** G5
Jovellanos *Cuba* 22°40N 81°10W **88** B3
Ju Xian *China* 36°35N 118°20E **35** F10
Juan Aldama *Mexico* 24°19N 103°21W **86** C4
Juan Bautista Alberdi *Argentina* 34°26S 61°48W **94** C3
Juan de Fuca, Str of. *N. Amer.* 48°15N 124°0W **78** B3
Juán de Nova *Ind. Oc.* 17°3S 43°45E **57** B7
Juan Fernández, Arch. de *Pac. Oc.* 33°50S 80°0W **90** G2
Juan José Castelli *Argentina* 25°27S 60°57W **94** B3
Juan L. Lacaze *Uruguay* 34°26S 57°25W **94** C4
Juankoski *Finland* 63°3N 28°19E **8** E23
Juárez *Mexico* 32°20N 115°57W **79** N11
Juárez *Coahuila, Mexico* 27°37N 100°44W **86** B4
Juárez, Sierra de *Mexico* 32°0N 116°0W **86** A1
Juàzeiro *Brazil* 9°30S 40°30W **93** E10
Juàzeiro do Norte *Brazil* 7°10S 39°18W **93** E11
Jûbâ *Sudan* 4°50N 31°35E **51** H12
Juba → *Somali Rep.* 1°30N 42°35E **47** G3
Jubany *Antarctica* 62°30S 58°0W **5** C18
Jubayl *Lebanon* 34°5N 35°39E **46** A4
Jubbah *Si. Arabia* 28°2N 40°56E **44** D4
Jubbal *India* 31°5N 77°40E **42** D7
Jubbulpore = Jabalpur *India* 23°9N 79°58E **43** H8
Jubilee L. *Australia* 29°0S 126°50E **61** E4
Juby, C. *Morocco* 28°0N 12°59W **50** C3
Júcar = Xúquer → *Spain* 39°5N 0°10W **21** C5
Júcaro *Cuba* 21°37N 78°51W **88** B4
Juchitán de Zaragoza *Mexico* 16°26N 95°1W **87** D5
Judea = Har Yehuda *Israel* 31°35N 34°57E **46** D3
Judith → *U.S.A.* 47°44N 109°39W **76** C9
Judith, Pt. *U.S.A.* 41°22N 71°29W **83** E13
Judith Gap *U.S.A.* 46°41N 109°45W **76** C9
Jugoslavia = Serbia ■ *Europe* 43°20N 20°0E **23** B9
Juigalpa *Nic.* 12°6N 85°26W **88** D2
Juiz de Fora *Brazil* 21°43S 43°19W **95** A7
Jujuy □ *Argentina* 23°20S 65°40W **94** A2
Julesburg *U.S.A.* 40°59N 102°16W **76** F12
Juli *Peru* 16°10S 69°25W **92** G5
Julia Cr. → *Australia* 20°0S 141°11E **62** C3
Julia Creek *Australia* 20°39S 141°44E **62** C3
Juliaca *Peru* 15°25S 70°10W **92** G4
Julian *U.S.A.* 33°4N 116°38W **79** M10
Julian, L. *Canada* 54°25N 77°57W **72** B4
Julianatop *Suriname* 3°40N 56°30W **93** C7
Julianehåb = Qaqortoq *Greenland* 60°43N 46°0W **4** C5
Julimes *Mexico* 28°25N 105°27W **86** B3
Jullundur *India* 31°20N 75°40E **42** D6
Julu *China* 37°15N 115°2E **34** F8
Jumbo *Zimbabwe* 17°30S 30°58E **55** F3
Jumbo Pk. *U.S.A.* 36°12N 114°11W **79** J12
Jumentos Cays *Bahamas* 23°0N 75°40W **88** B4
Jumilla *Spain* 38°28N 1°19W **21** C5
Jumla *Nepal* 29°15N 82°13E **43** E10
Jumna = Yamuna → *India* 25°30N 81°53E **43** G9
Jumunjin *S. Korea* 37°55N 128°54E **35** F15
Junagadh *India* 21°30N 70°30E **42** J4
Junction *Tex., U.S.A.* 30°29N 99°46W **84** F5
Junction *Utah, U.S.A.* 38°14N 112°13W **77** G7
Junction B. *Australia* 11°52S 133°55E **62** A1
Junction City *Kans., U.S.A.* 39°2N 96°50W **80** F5
Junction City *Oreg., U.S.A.* 44°13N 123°12W **76** D2
Junction Pt. *Australia* 11°45S 133°50E **62** A1
Jundah *Australia* 24°46S 143°2E **62** C3
Jundiaí *Brazil* 24°30S 47°0W **95** A6
Juneau *U.S.A.* 58°18N 134°25W **70** B2
Junee *Australia* 34°53S 147°35E **63** E4
Jungfrau *Switz.* 46°32N 7°58E **20** C7
Junggar Pendi *China* 44°30N 86°0E **32** B3
Jungshahi *Pakistan* 24°52N 67°44E **42** G2
Juniata → *U.S.A.* 40°24N 77°1W **82** F7
Junín *Argentina* 34°33S 60°57W **94** C3
Junín de los Andes *Argentina* 39°45S 71°0W **96** D2
Jūniyah *Lebanon* 33°59N 35°38E **46** B4
Juntas *Chile* 28°24S 69°58W **94** B2
Juntura *U.S.A.* 43°45N 118°5W **76** E4
Jur, Nahr el → *Sudan* 8°45N 29°15E **51** G11
Jura = Jura, Mts. du *Europe* 46°40N 6°5E **20** C7
Jura = Schwäbische Alb *Germany* 48°20N 9°30E **16** D5
Jura *U.K.* 56°0N 5°50W **11** F3
Jura, Mts. du *Europe* 46°40N 6°5E **20** C7
Jura, Sd. of *U.K.* 55°57N 5°45W **11** F3
Jurbarkas *Lithuania* 55°4N 22°46E **9** J20
Jurien Bay *Australia* 30°18S 115°2E **61** F2
Jūrmala *Latvia* 56°58N 23°34E **9** H20
Jurong *Singapore* 1°19N 103°42E **39** d
Juruá → *Brazil* 2°37S 65°44W **92** D5
Juruena *Brazil* 13°0S 58°10W **92** F7
Juruena → *Brazil* 7°20S 58°3W **92** E7
Juruti *Brazil* 2°9S 56°4W **93** D7
Justo Daract *Argentina* 33°52S 65°12W **94** C2
Jutaí → *Brazil* 2°43S 66°57W **92** D5
Juticalpa *Honduras* 14°40N 86°12W **88** D2
Jutland = Jylland *Denmark* 56°25N 9°30E **9** H13
Juuka *Finland* 63°13N 29°17E **8** E23
Juventud, I. de la *Cuba* 21°40N 82°40W **88** B3
Jūy Zar *Iran* 33°50N 46°18E **44** C5
Juye *China* 35°22N 116°5E **34** G9
Jwaneng *Botswana* 24°45S 24°50E **53** J4
Jylland *Denmark* 56°25N 9°30E **9** H13
Jyväskylä *Finland* 62°14N 25°50E **8** E21

K

K2 *Pakistan* 35°58N 76°32E **43** B7
Kaakha = Kaka *Turkmenistan* 37°21N 59°36E **45** B8
Kaap Plateau *S. Africa* 28°30S 24°0E **56** D3
Kaapkruis *Namibia* 21°55S 13°57E **56** C1
Kaapstad = Cape Town *S. Africa* 33°55S 18°22E **56** E2
Kabaena *Indonesia* 5°15S 122°0E **37** F6
Kabala *S. Leone* 9°38N 11°37W **50** G3
Kabale *Uganda* 1°15S 30°0E **54** C3
Kabalo *Dem. Rep. of the Congo* 6°0S 27°0E **54** D2
Kabambare *Dem. Rep. of the Congo* 4°41S 27°39E **54** C2
Kabango *Dem. Rep. of the Congo* 8°35S 28°30E **55** D2
Kabanjahe *Indonesia* 3°6N 98°30E **36** D1
Kabara *Fiji* 18°59S 178°56W **59** a
Kabardino-Balkaria □ *Russia* 43°30N 43°30E **19** F7
Kabarega Falls = Murchison Falls *Uganda* 2°15N 31°30E **54** B3
Kabarnet *Kenya* 0°30N 35°45E **54** B4
Kabasalan *Phil.* 7°47N 122°44E **37** C6
Kabat *Indonesia* 8°16S 114°19E **37** J17
Kabin Buri *Thailand* 13°57N 101°43E **38** F3
Kabinakagami L. *Canada* 48°54N 84°25W **72** C3
Kabinda *Dem. Rep. of the Congo* 6°19S 24°20E **52** F4
Kabompo *Zambia* 13°36S 24°14E **55** E1
Kabompo → *Zambia* 14°11S 23°11E **53** G4
Kabondo *Dem. Rep. of the Congo* 8°58S 25°40E **55** D2
Kabongo *Dem. Rep. of the Congo* 7°22S 25°33E **54** D2
Kabrît, G. el *Egypt* 29°42N 33°16E **46** F2
Kabūd Gonbad *Iran* 37°5N 59°45E **45** B8
Kābul *Afghan.* 34°28N 69°11E **42** B3
Kābul □ *Afghan.* 34°30N 69°0E **40** B6
Kābul → *Pakistan* 33°55N 72°14E **42** C5
Kabunga *Dem. Rep. of the Congo* 1°38S 28°3E **54** C2
Kaburuang *Indonesia* 3°50N 126°30E **37** D7
Kabwe *Zambia* 14°30S 28°29E **55** E2
Kachchh, Gulf of *India* 22°50N 69°15E **42** H3
Kachchh, Rann of *India* 24°0N 70°0E **42** H4
Kachchhidhana *India* 21°44N 78°46E **43** J8
Kachebera *Zambia* 13°50S 32°50E **55** E3
Kachikau *Botswana* 18°8S 24°26E **56** B3
Kachin □ *Burma* 26°0N 97°30E **41** G20
Kachira, L. *Uganda* 0°40S 31°7E **54** C3
Kachīry *Kazakhstan* 53°10N 75°50E **28** D8
Kachnara *India* 23°50N 75°6E **42** H6
Kachot *Cambodia* 11°30N 103°3E **39** G4
Kaçkar *Turkey* 40°45N 41°10E **19** F7
Kadam, Mt. *Uganda* 1°45N 34°45E **54** B3
Kadan Kyun *Burma* 12°30N 98°20E **38** F2
Kadanai → *Afghan.* 31°22N 65°45E **42** D1
Kadavu *Fiji* 19°0S 178°15E **59** a
Kadavu Passage *Fiji* 18°45S 178°0E **59** a
Kade *Ghana* 6°7N 0°56W **50** G5
Kadhimain = Al Kāẓimīyah *Iraq* 33°22N 44°18E **44** C5
Kadi *India* 23°18N 72°23E **42** H5
Kadina *Australia* 33°55S 137°43E **63** E2
Kadipur *India* 26°10N 82°23E **43** F10
Kadirli *Turkey* 37°23N 36°5E **44** B3
Kadiyevka = Stakhanov *Ukraine* 48°35N 38°40E **19** E6
Kadoka *U.S.A.* 43°50N 101°31W **80** D3
Kadoma *Zimbabwe* 18°20S 29°52E **55** F2
Kâdugli *Sudan* 11°0N 29°45E **51** F11
Kaduna *Nigeria* 10°30N 7°21E **50** F7
Kaédi *Mauritania* 16°9N 13°28W **50** E3
Kaeng Khoï *Thailand* 14°35N 101°0E **38** E3
Kaeng Krachan △ *Thailand* 12°57N 99°23E **38** F2
Kaeng Tana △ *Thailand* 15°25N 105°32E **38** E5
Kaesŏng *N. Korea* 37°58N 126°35E **35** F14
Kāf *Si. Arabia* 31°25N 37°29E **44** D3
Kafan = Kapan *Armenia* 39°18N 46°27E **44** B5
Kafanchan *Nigeria* 9°40N 8°20E **50** G7
Kafinda *Zambia* 12°32S 30°20E **55** E3
Kafue *Zambia* 15°46S 28°9E **55** F2
Kafue → *Zambia* 15°30S 29°0E **53** H5
Kafue △ *Zambia* 15°12S 25°38E **55** F2
Kafue Flats *Zambia* 15°40S 27°25E **55** F2
Kafulwe *Zambia* 9°0S 29°1E **55** D2
Kaga *Afghan.* 34°14N 70°10E **42** B4
Kaga Bandoro *C.A.R.* 7°0N 19°10E **52** C3
Kagawa □ *Japan* 34°15N 134°0E **31** G7
Kagera □ *Tanzania* 2°0S 31°30E **54** C3
Kagera → *Uganda* 0°57S 31°47E **54** C3
Kağızman *Turkey* 40°5N 43°10E **44** B4
Kagoshima *Japan* 31°35N 130°33E **31** J5
Kagoshima □ *Japan* 31°30N 130°30E **31** J5
Kagul = Cahul *Moldova* 45°50N 28°15E **17** F15
Kahak *Iran* 36°6N 49°46E **45** B6
Kahama *Tanzania* 4°8S 32°30E **54** C3
Kahan *Pakistan* 29°18N 68°54E **42** E3
Kahang *Malaysia* 2°12N 103°32E **39** L4
Kahayan → *Indonesia* 3°40S 114°0E **36** E4
Kahe *Tanzania* 3°30S 37°25E **54** C4
Kahemba *Dem. Rep. of the Congo* 7°18S 18°55E **52** F3
Kahnūj *Iran* 27°55N 57°40E **45** E8
Kahoka *U.S.A.* 40°25N 91°44W **80** E8
Kaho'olawe *U.S.A.* 20°33N 156°37W **74** b
Kahramanmaraş *Turkey* 37°37N 36°53E **44** B3
Kâhta *Turkey* 37°46N 38°36E **44** B3
Kahului *U.S.A.* 20°54N 156°28W **74** b
Kahurangi △ *N.Z.* 41°10S 172°32E **59** D4
Kahuta *Pakistan* 33°35N 73°24E **42** C5
Kahuzi-Biega △ *Dem. Rep. of the Congo* 1°50S 27°55E **54** C2
Kai, Kepulauan *Indonesia* 5°55S 132°45E **37** F8
Kai Besar *Indonesia* 5°35S 133°0E **37** F8
Kai Is. = Kai, Kepulauan *Indonesia* 5°55S 132°45E **37** F8
Kai Kecil *Indonesia* 5°45S 132°40E **37** F8
Kaiapoi *N.Z.* 43°24S 172°40E **59** E4
Kaidu He → *China* 41°46N 86°31E **32** B3
Kaieteur Falls *Guyana* 5°1N 59°10W **92** B7
Kaifeng *China* 34°48N 114°21E **34** G8
Kaikohe *N.Z.* 35°25S 173°49E **59** A4
Kaikoura *N.Z.* 42°25S 173°43E **59** E4
Kailash = Kangrinboqe Feng *China* 31°0N 81°25E **43** D9
Kailu *China* 43°38N 121°18E **35** C11
Kailua *U.S.A.* 19°39N 155°59W **74** b
Kaimana *Indonesia* 3°39S 133°45E **37** E8
Kaimanawa Mts. *N.Z.* 39°15S 175°56E **59** C5
Kaimganj *India* 27°33N 79°24E **43** F8
Kaimur Hills *India* 24°30N 82°0E **43** G10
Kainab → *Namibia* 28°32S 19°34E **56** D2
Kainji Res. *Nigeria* 10°1N 4°40E **50** F6
Kainuu *Finland* 64°30N 29°7E **8** D23
Kaipara Harbour *N.Z.* 36°25S 174°14E **59** B5
Kaipokok B. *Canada* 54°54N 59°47W **73** B8
Kaira *India* 22°45N 72°50E **42** H5
Kairana *India* 29°24N 77°15E **42** E7
Kaironi *Indonesia* 0°47S 133°40E **37** E8
Kairouan *Tunisia* 35°45N 10°5E **51** A8
Kaiserslautern *Germany* 49°26N 7°45E **16** D4
Kaitaia *N.Z.* 35°8S 173°17E **59** A4
Kaitangata *N.Z.* 46°17S 169°51E **59** G2
Kaithal *India* 29°48N 76°26E **42** E7
Kaitu → *Pakistan* 33°10N 70°30E **42** C4
Kaiyuan *Liaoning, China* 42°28N 124°1E **35** C13
Kaiyuan *Yunnan, China* 23°40N 103°12E **32** D5
Kajaani *Finland* 64°17N 27°46E **8** D22
Kajabbi *Australia* 20°0S 140°1E **62** C3
Kajana = Kajaani *Finland* 64°17N 27°46E **8** D22
Kajang *Malaysia* 2°59N 101°48E **39** L3
Kajiado *Kenya* 1°53S 36°48E **54** C4
Kajo Kaji *Sudan* 3°58N 31°40E **51** H12
Kaka *Turkmenistan* 37°21N 59°36E **45** B8
Kakabeka Falls *Canada* 48°24N 89°37W **72** C2
Kakadu △ *Australia* 12°0S 132°3E **60** B5
Kakamas *S. Africa* 28°45S 20°33E **56** D3
Kakamega *Kenya* 0°20N 34°46E **54** B3
Kakanui Mts. *N.Z.* 45°10S 170°30E **59** F3
Kakdwip *India* 21°53N 88°11E **43** J13
Kake *Japan* 34°36N 132°19E **31** G6
Kake *U.S.A.* 56°59N 133°57W **70** B2
Kakegawa *Japan* 34°45N 138°1E **31** G9
Kakeroma-Jima *Japan* 28°8N 129°14E **31** K4
Kākhak *Iran* 34°9N 58°38E **45** C8
Kakhovka *Ukraine* 46°45N 33°30E **19** E5
Kakhovske Vdskh. *Ukraine* 47°5N 34°0E **19** E5
Kakinada *India* 16°57N 82°11E **41** L13
Kakisa *Canada* 60°56N 117°25W **70** A5
Kakisa → *Canada* 61°3N 118°10W **70** A5
Kakisa L. *Canada* 60°56N 117°43W **70** A5
Kakogawa *Japan* 34°46N 134°51E **31** G7
Kakuma *Kenya* 3°43N 34°52E **54** B3
Kakwa → *Canada* 54°37N 118°28W **70** C5
Kāl Gūsheh *Iran* 30°59N 58°12E **45** D8
Kal Sefid *Iran* 34°52N 47°23E **44** C5
Kalaallit Nunaat = Greenland ☑ *N. Amer.* 66°0N 45°0W **67** C15
Kalabagh *Pakistan* 33°0N 71°28E **42** C4
Kalabahi *Indonesia* 8°13S 124°31E **37** F6
Kalach *Russia* 50°22N 41°0E **19** D7
Kaladan → *Burma* 20°20N 93°5E **41** J18
Kaladar *Canada* 44°37N 77°5W **82** B7
Kalahari *Africa* 24°0S 21°30E **56** C3
Kalahari Gemsbok △ *S. Africa* 25°30S 20°30E **56** D3
Kalajoki *Finland* 64°12N 24°10E **8** D21
Kalakamati *Botswana* 20°40S 27°25E **57** C4
Kalakan *Russia* 55°15N 116°45E **29** D12
K'alak'unlun Shank'ou = Karakoram Pass *Asia* 35°33N 77°50E **43** B7
Kalam *Pakistan* 35°34N 72°30E **43** B5
Kalama *Dem. Rep. of the Congo* 2°52S 28°35E **54** C2
Kalama *U.S.A.* 46°1N 122°51W **78** E4
Kalamata *Greece* 37°3N 22°10E **23** F10
Kalamazoo *U.S.A.* 42°17N 85°35W **81** D11
Kalamazoo → *U.S.A.* 42°40N 86°10W **80** D10
Kalambo Falls *Tanzania* 8°37S 31°35E **55** D3
Kalan *Turkey* 39°7N 39°32E **44** B3
Kalannie *Australia* 30°22S 117°5E **61** F2
Kalāntarī *Iran* 32°10N 54°8E **45** C7
Kalao *Indonesia* 7°21S 121°0E **37** F6
Kalaotoa *Indonesia* 7°20S 121°50E **37** F6
Kalasin *Thailand* 16°26N 103°30E **38** D4
Kalat *Iran* 25°29N 59°22E **45** E8
Kalat *Pakistan* 29°8N 66°31E **40** E5
Kalāteh *Iran* 36°33N 55°41E **45** B7
Kalāteh-ye Ganj *Iran* 27°31N 57°55E **45** E8
Kalbā *U.A.E.* 25°5N 56°22E **45** E8
Kalbarri *Australia* 27°40S 114°10E **61** E1
Kalbarri △ *Australia* 27°51S 114°30E **61** E1
Kalce *Slovenia* 45°54N 14°13E **16** F8
Kale *Turkey* 37°27N 28°49E **23** F13
Kalegauk Kyun *Burma* 15°33N 97°35E **38** E1
Kalehe *Dem. Rep. of the Congo* 2°6S 28°50E **54** C2
Kalema *Tanzania* 1°12S 31°55E **54** C3
Kalemie *Dem. Rep. of the Congo* 5°55S 29°9E **54** D2
Kalewa *Burma* 23°10N 94°15E **41** H19
Kaleybar *Iran* 38°47N 47°2E **44** B5
Kalgoorlie-Boulder *Australia* 30°40S 121°22E **61** F3
Kali → *India* 27°6N 79°55E **43** F8
Kali Sindh → *India* 25°32N 76°17E **42** G6
Kaliakra, Nos *Bulgaria* 43°21N 28°30E **23** C13
Kalianda *Indonesia* 5°50S 105°45E **36** F3
Kalibo *Phil.* 11°43N 122°22E **37** B6
Kalima *Dem. Rep. of the Congo* 2°33S 26°32E **54** C2
Kalimantan *Indonesia* 0°0 114°0E **36** E4
Kalimantan Barat □ *Indonesia* 0°0 110°30E **36** E4
Kalimantan Selatan □ *Indonesia* 2°30S 115°30E **36** E5
Kalimantan Tengah □ *Indonesia* 2°0S 113°30E **36** E4
Kalimantan Timur □ *Indonesia* 1°30N 116°30E **36** D5
Kálimnos *Greece* 37°0N 27°0E **23** F12
Kalimpong *India* 27°4N 88°35E **43** F13
Kaliningrad *Russia* 54°42N 20°32E **9** J19
Kalinkavichy *Belarus* 52°12N 29°20E **17** B15
Kalinkovichi = Kalinkavichy *Belarus* 52°12N 29°20E **17** B15
Kaliro *Uganda* 0°56N 33°30E **54** B3
Kalispell *U.S.A.* 48°12N 114°19W **76** B6
Kalisz *Poland* 51°45N 18°8E **17** C10
Kaliua *Tanzania* 5°5S 31°48E **54** D3
Kalix = Kalixälven → *Sweden* 65°50N 23°11E **8** D20
Kalix *Sweden* 65°53N 23°12E **8** D20
Kalixälven → *Sweden* 65°50N 23°11E **8** D20
Kalka *India* 30°46N 76°57E **42** D7
Kalkarindji *Australia* 17°30S 130°47E **60** C5
Kalkaska *U.S.A.* 44°44N 85°11W **81** C11
Kalkfeld *Namibia* 20°57S 16°14E **56** C2
Kalkfontein *Botswana* 22°4S 20°57E **56** C3
Kalkrand *Namibia* 24°1S 17°35E **56** C2
Kallavesi *Finland* 62°58N 27°30E **8** E22
Kallsjön *Sweden* 63°38N 13°0E **8** E15
Kalmar *Sweden* 56°40N 16°20E **9** H17
Kalmykia □ *Russia* 46°5N 46°1E **19** E8
Kalmykovo *Kazakhstan* 49°0N 51°47E **19** E9
Kalna *India* 23°13N 88°25E **43** H13
Kalnai *India* 22°46N 83°30E **43** H10
Kalocsa *Hungary* 46°32N 19°0E **17** E10
Kalokhorio *Cyprus* 34°51N 33°2E **25** E12
Kaloko *Dem. Rep. of the Congo* 6°47S 25°48E **54** D2
Kalol *Gujarat, India* 22°37N 73°31E **42** H5
Kalol *Gujarat, India* 23°15N 72°33E **42** H5
Kalomo *Zambia* 17°0S 26°30E **55** F2
Kalpi *India* 26°8N 79°47E **43** F8
Kaltukatjara *Australia* 24°52S 129°5E **61** D4
Kalu *Pakistan* 25°5N 67°39E **42** G2
Kaluga *Russia* 54°35N 36°10E **18** D6
Kalulushi *Zambia* 12°50S 28°3E **55** E2
Kalumburu *Australia* 13°55S 126°35E **60** B4
Kalush *Ukraine* 49°3N 24°23E **17** D13
Kalutara *Sri Lanka* 6°35N 80°0E **40** R12
Kalya *Russia* 60°15N 59°59E **18** B10
Kalyan *India* 19°15N 73°9E **40** K8
Kama *Dem. Rep. of the Congo* 3°30S 27°5E **54** C2
Kama → *Russia* 55°45N 52°0E **18** C9
Kamachumu *Tanzania* 1°37S 31°37E **54** C3
Kamaishi *Japan* 39°16N 141°53E **30** E10
Kamalia *Pakistan* 30°44N 72°42E **42** D5
Kaman *India* 27°39N 77°16E **42** F6
Kamanjab *Namibia* 19°35S 14°51E **56** B2
Kamapanda *Zambia* 12°5S 24°0E **55** E1
Kamarān *Yemen* 15°21N 42°35E **47** D3
Kamativi *Zimbabwe* 18°20S 27°6E **56** B4
Kambalda West *Australia* 31°10S 121°37E **61** F3
Kambar *Pakistan* 27°37N 68°1E **42** F3
Kambarka *Russia* 56°15N 54°11E **18** C9
Kambolé *Zambia* 8°47S 30°48E 55
Kambos *Cyprus* 35°2N 32°44E 25 D
Kambove *Dem. Rep. of the Congo* 10°51S 26°33E 55
Kamchatka, Poluostrov *Russia* 57°0N 160°0E 29 D
Kamchatka Pen. = Kamchatka, Poluostrov *Russia* 57°0N 160°0E 29 D
Kamchiya → *Bulgaria* 43°4N 27°44E 23 C
Kame Ruins *Zimbabwe* 20°7S 28°25E 55
Kamen *Russia* 53°50N 81°30E 28
Kamen-Rybolov *Russia* 44°46N 132°2E 30
Kamenjak, Rt *Croatia* 44°47N 13°55E 16
Kamenka *Russia* 65°58N 44°0E 18
Kamenka Bugskaya = Kamyanka-Buzka *Ukraine* 50°8N 24°16E 17 C
Kamensk Uralskiy *Russia* 56°25N 62°2E 28
Kamenskoye *Russia* 62°45N 165°30E 29 C
Kameoka *Japan* 35°0N 135°35E 31
Kamet *India* 30°55N 79°35E 43
Kamiah *U.S.A.* 46°14N 116°2W 76
Kamieskroon *S. Africa* 30°9S 17°56E 56
Kamilukuak L. *Canada* 62°22N 101°40W 71
Kamin-Kashyrskyy *Ukraine* 51°39N 24°56E 17 C
Kamina *Dem. Rep. of the Congo* 8°45S 25°0E 55
Kaminak L. *Canada* 62°10N 95°0W 71 A
Kaministiquia *Canada* 48°32N 89°35W 72
Kaminoyama *Japan* 38°9N 140°17E 30
Kamiros *Greece* 36°20N 27°56E 25
Kamituga *Dem. Rep. of the Congo* 3°2S 28°10E 54
Kamla → *India* 25°35N 86°36E 43
Kamloops *Canada* 50°40N 120°20W 70
Kamo *Japan* 37°39N 139°3E 30
Kamoke *Pakistan* 32°4N 74°4E 42
Kampala *Uganda* 0°20N 32°30E 54
Kampar *Malaysia* 4°18N 101°9E 39
Kampar → *Indonesia* 0°30N 103°8E 36
Kampen *Neths.* 52°33N 5°53E 15
Kampene *Dem. Rep. of the Congo* 3°36S 26°40E 52
Kamphaeng Phet *Thailand* 16°28N 99°30E 38
Kampolombo, L. *Zambia* 11°37S 29°42E 5
Kampong Chhnang *Cambodia* 12°20N 104°35E 39
Kampong Pengerang *Malaysia* 1°22N 104°7E
Kampong Punggai *Malaysia* 1°27N 104°18E
Kampong Saom *Cambodia* 10°38N 103°30E 39
Kampong Saom, Chaak *Cambodia* 10°50N 103°32E 39
Kampong Tanjong Langsat *Malaysia* 1°28N 104°1E
Kampong Telok Ramunia *Malaysia* 1°22N 104°15E
Kampot *Cambodia* 10°36N 104°10E 3
Kampuchea = Cambodia ■ *Asia* 12°15N 105°0E 3
Kampung Air Putih *Malaysia* 4°15N 103°10E 3
Kampung Jerangau *Malaysia* 4°50N 103°10E 3
Kampung Raja *Malaysia* 5°45N 102°35E 3
Kampungbaru = Tolitoli *Indonesia* 1°5N 120°50E 3
Kamrau, Teluk *Indonesia* 3°30S 133°36E 3
Kamsack *Canada* 51°34N 101°54W 7
Kamskoye Vdkhr. *Russia* 58°41N 56°7E 18
Kamuchawie L. *Canada* 56°18N 101°59W 7
Kamuela *U.S.A.* 20°1N 155°41W
Kamui-Misaki *Japan* 43°20N 140°21E 30
Kamyanets-Podilskyy *Ukraine* 48°45N 26°40E 17
Kamyanka-Buzka *Ukraine* 50°8N 24°16E 17
Kāmyārān *Iran* 34°47N 46°56E 4
Kamyshin *Russia* 50°10N 45°24E 1
Kanaaupscow *Canada* 53°39N 77°9W 69
Kanaaupscow → *Canada* 54°2N 76°30W 7
Kanab *U.S.A.* 37°3N 112°32W 7
Kanab Cr. → *U.S.A.* 36°24N 112°38W 7
Kanacea *Lau Group, Fiji* 17°15S 179°6W
Kanacea *Taveuni, Fiji* 16°59S 179°56E
Kanagi *Japan* 40°54N 140°27E 30
Kanairiktok → *Canada* 55°2N 60°18W 7
Kananga *Dem. Rep. of the Congo* 5°55S 22°18E 5
Kanash *Russia* 55°30N 47°32E 1
Kanaskat *U.S.A.* 47°19N 121°54W 7
Kanastraíon, Ákra = Palioúri, Akra *Greece* 39°57N 23°45E 2
Kanawha → *U.S.A.* 38°50N 82°9W 8
Kanazawa *Japan* 36°30N 136°38E
Kanchanaburi *Thailand* 14°2N 99°31E
Kanchenjunga *Nepal* 27°50N 88°10E 4
Kanchipuram *India* 12°52N 79°45E 4
Kandaghat *India* 30°59N 77°7E 4
Kandahār *Afghan.* 31°32N 65°43E
Kandahār □ *Afghan.* 31°0N 65°0E
Kandalaksha *Russia* 67°9N 32°30E
Kandalakshkiy Zaliv *Russia* 66°0N 35°0E
Kandangan *Indonesia* 2°50S 115°20E
Kandanghaur *Indonesia* 6°21S 108°6E
Kandanos *Greece* 35°19N 23°44E 2
Kandavu = Kadavu *Fiji* 19°0S 178°15E
Kandavu Passage = Kadavu Passage *Fiji* 18°45S 178°0E
Kandhkot *Pakistan* 28°16N 69°8E

adhla India 29°18N 77°19E 42 E7
adi Benin 11°7N 2°55E 50 F6
adi India 23°58N 88°5E 43 H13
adiaro Pakistan 27°4N 68°13E 42 F3
adla India 23°0N 70°10E 42 H4
ados Australia 32°45S 149°58E 63 E4
adreho Madag. 17°29S 46°6E 57 B8
ady Sri Lanka 7°18N 80°43E 40 R12
ae U.S.A. 41°40N 78°49W 82 E6
ae Basin Greenland 79°1N 70°0W 66 B12
e'ohe U.S.A. 21°25N 157°48W 74 b
g Botswana 23°41S 22°50E 56 C3
g Krung △ Thailand 9°30N 98°50E 39 H2
gān Fārs, Iran 27°50N 52°3E 45 E7
gān Hormozgān, Iran 25°48N 57°28E 45 E8
gar Malaysia 6°27N 100°12E 39 J3
garoo I. Australia 35°45S 137°0E 63 F2
garoo Mts.
ıstralia 23°29S 141°51E 62 C3
gasala Finland 61°28N 24°4E 8 F21
gāvar Iran 34°40N 48°0E 45 C6
gdong N. Korea 39°9N 126°5E 35 E14
gean, Kepulauan
donesia 6°55S 115°23E 36 F5
gean Is. = Kangean,
epulauan Indonesia 6°55S 115°23E 36 F5
ggye N. Korea 41°0N 126°35E 35 D14
gikajik Greenland 70°7N 22°0W 4 B6
giqliniq = Rankin Inlet
nada 62°30N 93°0W 68 C10
giqsualujjuaq
nada 58°30N 65°59W 69 D13
giqsujuaq Canada 61°30N 72°0W 69 C12
giqtugaapik = Clyde River
nada 70°30N 68°30W 69 B13
girsuk Canada 60°0N 70°0W 69 D13
gkar Chemaran
alaysia 1°34N 104°12E 39 d
gkar Sungai Tiram
alaysia 1°35N 103°55E 39 d
gkar Teberau
alaysia 1°32N 103°51E 39 d
gping China 42°43N 123°18E 35 C12
gra India 32°6N 76°16E 42 C7
grinboqe Feng China 31°0N 81°25E 43 D9
gto China 27°50N 92°35E 41 F18
na △ India 22°15N 80°40E 43 H9
nar → India 24°28N 83°8E 43 G10
ama
n. Rep. of the Congo 7°30S 24°12E 54 D1
apiskau = Caniapiscau →
nada 56°40N 69°30W 73 A6
apiskau, L. = Caniapiscau, L.
nada 54°10N 69°55W 73 B6
n, Poluostrov Russia 68°0N 45°0E 18 A8
n Nos, Mys Russia 68°39N 43°32E 18 A7
n Pen. = Kanin, Poluostrov
ssia 68°0N 45°0E 18 A8
va Australia 36°22S 141°18E 63 F3
ut Sar Pakistan 36°7N 75°25E 43 A6
aanpää Finland 61°44N 22°50E 8 F20
akee U.S.A. 41°7N 87°52W 80 E10
akee → U.S.A. 41°23N 88°15W 80 E9
an Guinea 10°23N 9°15W 50 F4
endy = Xankändi
rbaijan 39°52N 46°49E 44 B5
er India 20°10N 81°40E 41 J12
roli India 25°4N 73°53E 42 G5
apolis U.S.A. 35°30N 80°37W 85 D14
auj India 27°3N 79°56E 43 F8
od India 22°45N 76°40E 40 H10
Nigeria 12°2N 8°30E 50 F7
onji Japan 34°7N 133°39E 31 G6
wit Malaysia 2°14N 112°20E 36 D4
ya Japan 31°25N 130°50E 31 J5
etlet Burma 21°10N 93°59E 41 J18
ur India 26°28N 80°20E 43 F9
as □ U.S.A. 38°30N 99°0W 80 F4
as → U.S.A. 39°7N 94°37W 80 F6
as City Kans., U.S.A. 39°7N 94°38W 80 F6
as City Mo., U.S.A. 39°6N 94°35W 80 F6
enia
. Rep. of the Congo 10°20S 26°0E 55 E2
k Russia 56°20N 95°37E 29 D10
u = Gansu □ China 36°0N 104°0E 34 G3
aphor India 22°35N 76°34E 42 H7
naralak Thailand 14°39N 104°39E 38 E5
i → India 28°20N 75°30E 42 E6
5 □ Japan 36°15N 139°30E 31 F9
5-Sanchi Japan 35°59N 138°50E 31 G9
urk Ireland 52°11N 8°54W 10 D3
ma Japan 36°34N 139°42E 31 F9
s Namibia 27°50S 18°39E 56 D2
akumari India 8°3N 77°40E 40 Q10
e Botswana 24°55S 25°28E 56 C4
enze
. Rep. of the Congo 10°30S 25°12E 55 E2
, Ras Tanzania 7°1S 39°33E 54 D4
'onga 19°40S 175°1W 59 c
hara Thailand 8°3N 98°22E 39 a
siung Taiwan 22°35N 120°16E 33 D7
oveld Namibia 19°15S 14°30E 56 B1
ck Senegal 14°5N 16°8W 50 F2
an China 44°38N 124°50E 35 B13
ı U.S.A. 22°5N 159°19W 74 b
dvanj India 23°5N 73°0E 42 H5
ı Armenia 39°18N 46°27E 44 B5
ıga
. Rep. of the Congo 8°30S 22°40E 52 F4
ıagai = Qapshaghay
kstan 43°51N 77°14E 28 E8
lo Kenya 1°10N 36°6E 54 B4
a = Velika Kapela
atia 45°10N 15°50E 16 F8
na
. Rep. of the Congo 10°45S 28°22E 55 E2
guria Kenya 1°14N 35°7E 54 B4
Kapfenberg Austria 47°26N 15°18E 16 E8
Kapiri Mposhi Zambia 13°59S 28°43E 55 E2
Kāpīsā □ Afghan. 35°0N 69°20E 40 B6
Kapiskau → Canada 52°47N 81°55W 72 B3
Kapit Malaysia 2°0N 112°55E 36 D4
Kapiti I. N.Z. 40°50S 174°56E 59 D5
Kaplan U.S.A. 30°0N 92°17W 84 F8
Kapoe Thailand 9°34N 98°32E 39 H2
Kapoeta Sudan 4°50N 33°35E 51 H12
Kaposvár Hungary 46°25N 17°47E 17 E9
Kapowsin U.S.A. 46°59N 122°13W 78 D4
Kapps Namibia 22°32S 17°18E 56 C2
Kapsabet Kenya 0°12N 35°6E 54 B4
Kapsan N. Korea 41°4N 128°19E 35 D15
Kapsukas = Marijampolė
Lithuania 54°33N 23°19E 9 J20
Kaptai L. Bangla. 22°40N 92°20E 41 H18
Kapuas → Indonesia 0°25S 109°20E 36 E3
Kapuas Hulu, Pegunungan
Malaysia 1°30N 113°30E 36 D4
Kapuas Hulu Ra. = Kapuas Hulu,
Pegunungan Malaysia 1°30N 113°30E 36 D4
Kapulo
Dem. Rep. of the Congo 8°18S 29°15E 55 D2
Kapunda Australia 34°20S 138°56E 63 E2
Kapuni N.Z. 39°29S 174°8E 59 C5
Kapurthala India 31°23N 75°25E 42 D6
Kapuskasing Canada 49°25N 82°30W 72 C3
Kapuskasing → Canada 49°49N 82°0W 72 C3
Kaputar, Mt. Australia 30°15S 150°10E 63 E5
Kaputir Kenya 2°5N 35°28E 54 B4
Kara Russia 69°10N 65°0E 28 C7
Kara Bogaz Gol, Zaliv =
Garabogazköl Aylagy
Turkmenistan 41°0N 53°30E 19 F9
Kara-Kala = Garrygala
Turkmenistan 38°31N 56°29E 45 B8
Kara Kalpak Republic =
Qoraqalpoghistan □
Uzbekistan 43°0N 58°0E 28 E6
Kara Kum = Garagum
Turkmenistan 39°30N 60°0E 45 B8
Kara Sea Russia 75°0N 70°0E 28 B8
Karabiğa Turkey 40°23N 27°17E 23 D12
Karabük Turkey 41°12N 32°37E 19 F5
Karaburun Turkey 38°41N 26°28E 23 E12
Karabutak = Qarabutaq
Kazakhstan 49°59N 60°14E 28 E7
Karacabey Turkey 40°12N 28°21E 23 D13
Karacasu Turkey 37°43N 28°35E 23 F13
Karachey-Cherkessia □
Russia 43°40N 41°30E 19 F7
Karachi Pakistan 24°50N 67°0E 42 G2
Karad India 17°15N 74°10E 40 L9
Karaganda = Qaraghandy
Kazakhstan 49°50N 73°10E 28 E8
Karagayly = Qaraghayly
Kazakhstan 49°26N 76°0E 28 E8
Karaginskiy, Ostrov
Russia 58°45N 164°0E 29 D17
Karagiye, Vpadina
Kazakhstan 43°27N 51°45E 19 F9
Karagiye Depression = Karagiye,
Vpadina Kazakhstan 43°27N 51°45E 19 F9
Karagola Road India 25°29N 87°23E 43 G12
Karaikal India 10°59N 79°50E 40 P11
Karaikkudi India 10°5N 78°45E 40 P11
Karaj Iran 35°48N 51°0E 45 C6
Karak Malaysia 3°25N 102°2E 39 L4
Karakalpakstan =
Qoraqalpoghistan □
Uzbekistan 43°0N 58°0E 28 E6
Karakelong Indonesia 4°35N 126°50E 37 D7
Karakitang Indonesia 3°14N 125°28E 37 D7
Karakol Kyrgyzstan 42°30N 78°20E 32 B2
Karakoram Pass Asia 35°33N 77°50E 43 B7
Karakoram Ra. Pakistan 35°30N 77°0E 43 B7
Karakuwisa Namibia 18°56S 19°40E 56 B2
Karalon Russia 57°5N 115°50E 29 D12
Karama Jordan 31°57N 35°35E 46 D4
Karaman Turkey 37°14N 33°13E 44 B2
Karamay China 45°30N 84°58E 32 B3
Karambu Indonesia 3°53S 116°6E 36 E5
Karamea Bight N.Z. 41°22S 171°40E 59 D3
Karamnasa → India 25°31N 83°52E 43 G10
Karān Si. Arabia 27°43N 49°49E 45 E6
Karand Iran 34°16N 46°15E 44 C5
Karanganyar Indonesia 7°38S 109°37E 37 G13
Karangasem Indonesia 8°27S 115°37E 37 J18
Karanjia India 21°47N 85°58E 43 J11
Karasburg Namibia 28°0S 18°44E 56 D2
Karasino Russia 66°50N 86°50E 28 C9
Karasjok Norway 69°27N 25°30E 8 B21
Karasuk Russia 53°44N 78°2E 28 D8
Karasuyama Japan 36°39N 140°9E 31 F10
Karatau, Khrebet = Qarataū
Kazakhstan 43°30N 69°30E 28 E7
Karatax Shan China 35°57N 81°0E 32 C3
Karatsu Japan 33°26N 129°58E 31 H5
Karaul Russia 70°6N 82°15E 28 B9
Karauli India 26°30N 77°4E 42 F7
Karavostasi Cyprus 35°8N 32°50E 25 D11
Karawang Indonesia 6°30S 107°15E 37 G12
Karawanken Europe 46°30N 14°40E 16 E8
Karayazı Turkey 39°41N 42°9E 19 G7
Karazhal = Qarazhal
Kazakhstan 48°2N 70°49E 28 E8
Karbalā' Iraq 32°36N 44°3E 44 C5
Karcag Hungary 47°19N 20°57E 17 E11
Karcha → Pakistan 34°45N 76°10E 43 B7
Karchana India 25°17N 81°56E 43 G9
Karditsa Greece 39°23N 21°54E 23 E9
Kärdla Estonia 59°0N 22°45E 9 G20
Kareeberge S. Africa 30°59S 21°50E 56 E3
Kareha → India 25°44N 86°21E 43 G12
Kareima Sudan 18°30N 31°49E 51 E12
Karelia □ Russia 65°30N 32°30E 8 D25
Karelian Republic = Karelia □
Russia 65°30N 32°30E 8 D25
Karera India 25°32N 78°9E 42 G8
Kārevāndar Iran 27°53N 60°44E 45 E9
Kargasok Russia 59°3N 80°53E 28 D9
Kargat Russia 55°10N 80°15E 28 D9
Kargi Kenya 2°31N 37°34E 54 B4
Kargil India 34°32N 76°12E 43 B7
Kargopol Russia 61°30N 38°58E 18 B6
Karhal India 27°1N 78°57E 43 F8
Karīān Iran 26°57N 57°14E 45 E8
Karianga Madag. 22°25S 47°22E 57 C8
Kariba Zimbabwe 16°28S 28°50E 55 F2
Kariba, L. Zimbabwe 16°40S 28°25E 55 F2
Kariba Dam Zimbabwe 16°30S 28°35E 55 F2
Kariba Gorge Zambia 16°30S 28°50E 55 F2
Karibib Namibia 22°0S 15°56E 56 C2
Karijini △ Australia 23°8S 118°15E 60 D2
Karimata, Kepulauan
Indonesia 1°25S 109°0E 36 E3
Karimata, Selat Indonesia 2°0S 108°40E 36 E3
Karimata Is. = Karimata,
Kepulauan Indonesia 1°25S 109°0E 36 E3
Karimnagar India 18°26N 79°10E 40 K11
Karimun Kecil, Pulau
Indonesia 1°8N 103°22E 39 d
Karimunjawa, Kepulauan
Indonesia 5°50S 110°30E 36 F4
Karin Somali Rep. 10°50N 45°52E 47 E4
Karīt Iran 33°29N 56°55E 45 C8
Kariya Japan 34°58N 137°1E 31 G8
Kariyangwe Zimbabwe 18°0S 27°38E 57 B4
Karjala Finland 62°0N 30°25E 8 F24
Karkaralinsk = Qarqaraly
Kazakhstan 49°26N 75°30E 28 E8
Karkheh → Iran 31°2N 47°29E 44 D5
Karkinitska Zatoka
Ukraine 45°56N 33°0E 19 E5
Karkinitskiy Zaliv = Karkinitska
Zatoka Ukraine 45°56N 33°0E 19 E5
Karkuk = Kirkūk Iraq 35°30N 44°21E 44 C5
Karleby = Kokkola
Finland 63°50N 23°8E 8 E20
Karlovac Croatia 45°31N 15°36E 16 F8
Karlovo Bulgaria 42°38N 24°47E 23 C11
Karlovy Vary Czech Rep. 50°13N 12°51E 16 C7
Karlsbad = Karlovy Vary
Czech Rep. 50°13N 12°51E 16 C7
Karlsena, Mys Russia 77°0N 67°42E 28 B7
Karlshamn Sweden 56°10N 14°51E 9 H16
Karlskoga Sweden 59°28N 14°33E 9 G16
Karlskrona Sweden 56°10N 15°35E 9 H16
Karlsruhe Germany 49°0N 8°23E 16 D5
Karlstad Sweden 59°23N 13°30E 9 G15
Karlstad U.S.A. 48°35N 96°31W 80 A5
Karmi'el Israel 32°55N 35°18E 46 C4
Karnak Egypt 25°43N 32°39E 51 C12
Karnal India 29°42N 77°2E 42 E7
Karnali → Nepal 28°45N 81°16E 43 E9
Karnaphuli Res. = Kaptai L.
Bangla. 22°40N 92°20E 41 H18
Karnaprayag India 30°16N 79°15E 43 D8
Karnataka □ India 13°15N 77°0E 40 N10
Karnes City U.S.A. 28°53N 97°54W 84 G6
Karnische Alpen Europe 46°36N 13°0E 16 E7
Kärnten □ Austria 46°52N 13°30E 16 E8
Karoi Zimbabwe 16°48S 29°45E 55 F2
Karon, Ao Thailand 7°51N 98°17E 39 a
Karonga Malawi 9°57S 33°55E 55 D3
Karoo △ S. Africa 32°18S 22°27E 56 E3
Karoonda Australia 35°1S 139°59E 63 F2
Karor Pakistan 31°15N 70°59E 42 D4
Karora Sudan 17°44N 38°15E 51 E13
Karpasia Cyprus 35°32N 34°15E 25 D13
Karpathos Greece 35°37N 27°10E 23 G12
Karpinsk Russia 59°45N 60°1E 18 C11
Karpogory Russia 64°0N 44°27E 18 B7
Karpuz Burnu = Apostolos
Andreas, C. Cyprus 35°42N 34°35E 25 D13
Karratha Australia 20°53S 116°40E 60 D2
Kars Turkey 40°40N 43°5E 19 F7
Karsakpay Kazakhstan 47°55N 66°40E 28 E7
Karshi = Qarshi
Uzbekistan 38°53N 65°48E 28 F7
Karsiyang India 26°56N 88°18E 43 F13
Karsog India 31°23N 77°12E 42 D7
Kartala Comoros Is. 11°45S 43°21E 53 a
Kartaly Russia 53°3N 60°40E 28 D7
Kartapur India 31°27N 75°32E 42 D6
Karthaus U.S.A. 41°8N 78°9W 82 E6
Karufa Indonesia 3°50S 133°20E 37 E8
Karuma △ Uganda 2°5N 32°15E 54 B3
Karumba Australia 17°31S 140°50E 62 B3
Karumo Tanzania 2°25S 32°50E 54 C3
Karumwa Tanzania 3°12S 32°38E 54 C3
Kārūn → Iran 30°26N 48°10E 45 D6
Karungu Kenya 0°50S 34°10E 54 C3
Karviná Czech Rep. 49°53N 18°31E 17 D10
Karwan → India 27°26N 78°4E 42 F8
Karwar India 14°55N 74°13E 40 M9
Karwi India 25°12N 80°57E 43 G9
Karymskoye Russia 51°36N 114°21E 29 D12
Kasache Malawi 13°25S 34°20E 55 E3
Kasai →
Dem. Rep. of the Congo 3°30S 16°10E 52 E3
Kasai-Oriental □
Dem. Rep. of the Congo 5°0S 24°30E 54 D1
Kasaji
Dem. Rep. of the Congo 10°25S 23°27E 55 E1
Kasama Zambia 10°16S 31°9E 55 E3
Kasan N. Korea 41°18N 126°55E 35 D14
Kasandra Kolpos Greece 40°5N 23°30E 23 D10
Kasane Namibia 17°34S 24°50E 56 B3
Kasanga Tanzania 8°30S 31°10E 55 D3
Kasanka △ Zambia 11°34S 30°15E 55 E3
Kasaragod India 12°30N 74°58E 40 N9
Kasba L. Canada 60°20N 102°10W 71 A8
Kāsh Garān Iran 34°5N 46°2E 44 C5
Kasempa Zambia 13°30S 25°44E 55 E2
Kasenga
Dem. Rep. of the Congo 10°20S 28°45E 55 E2
Kasese Uganda 0°13N 30°3E 54 B3
Kasewa Zambia 14°28S 28°53E 55 E2
Kasganj India 27°48N 78°42E 43 F8
Kashabowie Canada 48°40N 90°26W 72 C1
Kashaf Iran 35°58N 61°7E 45 C9
Kāshān Iran 34°5N 51°30E 45 C6
Kashechewan Canada 52°18N 81°37W 72 B3
Kashgar = Kashi China 39°30N 76°2E 32 C2
Kashi China 39°30N 76°2E 32 C2
Kashimbo
Dem. Rep. of the Congo 11°12S 26°19E 55 E2
Kashipur India 29°15N 79°0E 43 E8
Kashiwazaki Japan 37°22N 138°33E 31 F9
Kashk-e Kohneh
Afghan. 34°55N 62°30E 40 B3
Kashkū'īyeh Iran 30°31N 55°40E 45 D7
Kāshmar Iran 35°16N 58°26E 45 C8
Kashmir Asia 34°0N 76°0E 43 C7
Kashmor Pakistan 28°28N 69°32E 42 E3
Kashun Noerh = Gaxun Nur
China 42°22N 100°30E 32 B5
Kasiari India 22°8N 87°14E 43 H12
Kasimov Russia 54°55N 41°20E 18 D7
Kasinge
Dem. Rep. of the Congo 6°15S 26°58E 54 D2
Kasiruta Indonesia 0°25S 127°12E 37 E7
Kaskaskia → U.S.A. 37°58N 89°57W 80 G9
Kaskattama → Canada 57°3N 90°4W 71 B10
Kaskinen Finland 62°22N 21°15E 8 E19
Kaskö = Kaskinen
Finland 62°22N 21°15E 8 E19
Kaslo Canada 49°55N 116°55W 70 D5
Kasmere L. Canada 59°34N 101°10W 71 B8
Kasongo
Dem. Rep. of the Congo 4°30S 26°33E 54 C2
Kasongo Lunda
Dem. Rep. of the Congo 6°35S 16°49E 52 F3
Kasos Greece 35°20N 26°55E 23 G12
Kassalâ Sudan 15°30N 36°0E 51 E13
Kassel Germany 51°18N 9°26E 16 C5
Kassiopi Greece 39°48N 19°53E 25 A3
Kasson U.S.A. 44°2N 92°45W 80 C7
Kastamonu Turkey 41°25N 33°43E 19 F5
Kasteli Greece 35°29N 23°38E 25 D5
Kastelli Greece 35°12N 25°20E 25 D7
Kasterlee Belgium 51°15N 4°59E 15 C4
Kastoria Greece 40°30N 21°19E 23 D9
Kasulu Tanzania 4°37S 30°5E 54 C3
Kasumi Japan 35°38N 134°38E 31 G7
Kasungu Malawi 13°0S 33°29E 55 E3
Kasungu △ Malawi 12°53S 33°9E 55 E3
Kasur Pakistan 31°5N 74°25E 42 D6
Kata, Ao Thailand 7°48N 98°18E 39 J2
Kata Archanes Greece 35°15N 25°10E 25 D7
Kata Tjuta Australia 25°20S 130°50E 61 E5
Kataba Zambia 16°5S 25°10E 55 F2
Katahdin, Mt. U.S.A. 45°54N 68°56W 81 C19
Katako Kombe
Dem. Rep. of the Congo 3°25S 24°20E 54 C1
Katale Tanzania 4°52S 31°7E 54 C3
Katanda Katanga,
Dem. Rep. of the Congo 7°52S 24°13E 54 D1
Katanda Nord-Kivu,
Dem. Rep. of the Congo 0°55S 29°21E 54 C2
Katanga □
Dem. Rep. of the Congo 8°0S 25°0E 54 D2
Katangi India 21°56N 79°50E 40 J11
Katanning Australia 33°40S 117°33E 61 F2
Katavi △ Tanzania 6°51S 31°3E 54 D3
Katavi Swamp Tanzania 6°50S 31°10E 54 D3
Katerini Greece 40°18N 22°37E 23 D10
Katghora India 22°30N 82°33E 43 H10
Katha Burma 24°10N 96°30E 41 G20
Katherîna, Gebel Egypt 28°30N 33°57E 44 D2
Katherine Australia 14°27S 132°20E 60 B5
Katherine Gorge
Australia 14°18S 132°28E 60 B5
Kathi India 21°47N 74°3E 42 J6
Kathiawar India 22°20N 71°0E 42 H4
Kathikas Cyprus 34°55N 32°25E 25 E11
Kathmandu Nepal 27°45N 85°20E 43 F11
Kathua India 32°23N 75°34E 42 C6
Katihar India 25°34N 87°36E 43 G12
Katima Mulilo Namibia 17°28S 24°13E 56 B3
Katimbira Malawi 12°40S 34°0E 55 E3
Katingan = Mendawai →
Indonesia 3°30S 113°0E 36 E4
Katiola Ivory C. 8°10N 5°10W 50 G4
Katmandu = Kathmandu
Nepal 27°45N 85°20E 43 F11
Katni India 23°51N 80°24E 43 H9
Kato Chorio Greece 35°3N 25°47E 25 D7
Kato Korakiana Greece 39°42N 19°45E 25 A3
Káto Pyrgos Cyprus 35°11N 32°41E 25 D11
Katompe
Dem. Rep. of the Congo 6°2S 26°23E 54 D2
Katong Singapore 1°18N 103°53E 39 d
Katonga → Uganda 0°34N 31°50E 54 B3
Katoomba Australia 33°41S 150°19E 63 E5
Katowice Poland 50°17N 19°5E 17 C10
Katrine, L. U.K. 56°15N 4°30W 11 E4
Katrineholm Sweden 59°9N 16°12E 9 G17
Katsepe Madag. 15°45S 46°15E 57 B8
Katsina Nigeria 13°0N 7°32E 50 F7
Katsumoto Japan 33°51N 129°42E 31 H4
Katsuura Japan 35°10N 140°20E 31 G10
Katsuyama Japan 36°3N 136°30E 31 F8
Kattavia Greece 35°57N 27°46E 25 D9
Kattegat Denmark 56°40N 11°20E 9 H14
Katumba
Dem. Rep. of the Congo 7°40S 25°17E 54 D2
Katwa India 23°30N 88°5E 43 H13
Katwijk Neths. 52°12N 4°24E 15 B4
Kaua'i U.S.A. 22°3N 159°30W 74 b
Kauai Channel U.S.A. 21°45N 158°50W 74 b
Kaudom △ Namibia 18°45S 20°51E 56 B3
Kaufman U.S.A. 32°35N 96°19W 84 E6
Kauhajoki Finland 62°25N 22°10E 8 E20
Kaukauna U.S.A. 44°17N 88°17W 80 C9
Kaukauveld Namibia 20°0S 20°15E 56 C3
Kaunakakai U.S.A. 21°6N 157°1W 74 b
Kaunas Lithuania 54°54N 23°54E 9 J20
Kaunia Bangla. 25°46N 89°26E 43 G13
Kautokeino Norway 69°0N 23°4E 8 B20
Kauwapur India 27°31N 82°18E 43 F10
Kavacha Russia 60°16N 169°51E 29 C17
Kavala Greece 40°57N 24°28E 23 D11
Kavalerovo Russia 44°15N 135°4E 30 B7
Kavali India 14°55N 80°1E 40 M12
Kavār Iran 29°11N 52°44E 45 D7
Kavi India 22°12N 72°38E 42 H5
Kavimba Botswana 18°2S 24°38E 56 B3
Kavīr, Dasht-e Iran 34°30N 55°0E 45 C7
Kavīr △ Iran 34°40N 52°0E 45 C7
Kavos Greece 39°23N 20°3E 25 B4
Kaw Fr. Guiana 4°30N 52°15W 93 C8
Kawagama L. Canada 45°18N 78°45W 82 A6
Kawagoe Japan 35°55N 139°29E 31 G9
Kawaguchi Japan 35°52N 139°45E 31 G9
Kawambwa Zambia 9°48S 29°3E 55 D2
Kawanoe Japan 34°1N 133°34E 31 G6
Kawardha India 22°0N 81°17E 43 J9
Kawasaki Japan 35°31N 139°43E 31 G9
Kawasi Indonesia 1°38S 127°28E 37 E7
Kawawachikamach
Canada 54°48N 66°50W 73 B6
Kawerau N.Z. 38°7S 176°42E 59 C6
Kawhia N.Z. 38°4S 174°49E 59 C5
Kawhia Harbour N.Z. 38°5S 174°51E 59 C5
Kawio, Kepulauan
Indonesia 4°30N 125°30E 37 D7
Kawthaung Burma 10°5N 98°36E 39 H2
Kawthoolei = Kayin □
Burma 18°0N 97°30E 41 L20
Kawthule = Kayin □
Burma 18°0N 97°30E 41 L20
Kaya Burkina Faso 13°4N 1°10W 50 F5
Kayah □ Burma 19°15N 97°15E 41 K20
Kayan → Indonesia 2°55N 117°35E 36 D5
Kaycee U.S.A. 43°43N 106°38W 76 E10
Kayeli Indonesia 3°20S 127°10E 37 E7
Kayenta U.S.A. 36°44N 110°15W 77 H8
Kayes Mali 14°25N 11°30W 50 F3
Kayin □ Burma 18°0N 97°30E 41 L20
Kayoa Indonesia 0°1N 127°28E 37 D7
Kayomba Zambia 13°11S 24°2E 55 E1
Kayseri Turkey 38°45N 35°30E 44 B2
Kaysville U.S.A. 41°2N 111°56W 76 F8
Kazachye Russia 70°52N 135°58E 29 B14
Kazakhstan ■ Asia 50°0N 70°0E 28 E8
Kazan Russia 55°50N 49°10E 18 C8
Kazan → Canada 64°2N 95°29W 71 A9
Kazan-Rettō Pac. Oc. 25°0N 141°0E 64 E6
Kazanlŭk Bulgaria 42°38N 25°20E 23 C11
Kazatin = Kozyatyn
Ukraine 49°45N 28°50E 17 D15
Kāzerūn Iran 29°38N 51°40E 45 D6
Kazi Magomed = Qazımämmäd
Azerbaijan 40°3N 49°0E 45 A6
Kazuma Pan △
Zimbabwe 18°20S 25°48E 55 F2
Kazuno Japan 40°10N 140°45E 30 D10
Kazym → Russia 63°54N 65°50E 28 C7
Kea Greece 37°35N 24°22E 23 F11
Keady U.K. 54°15N 6°42W 10 B5
Kearney U.S.A. 40°42N 99°5W 80 E4
Kearny U.S.A. 33°3N 110°55W 77 K8
Kearsarge, Mt. U.S.A. 43°22N 71°50W 83 C13
Keban Turkey 38°50N 38°50E 19 G6
Keban Barajı Turkey 38°41N 38°33E 44 B3
Kebnekaise Sweden 67°53N 18°33E 8 C18
Kebri Dehar Ethiopia 6°45N 44°17E 47 F3
Kebumen Indonesia 7°42S 109°40E 37 G13
Kechika → Canada 59°41N 127°12W 70 B3
Kecskemét Hungary 46°57N 19°42E 17 E10
Kėdainiai Lithuania 55°15N 24°2E 9 J21
Kedarnath India 30°44N 79°4E 43 D8
Kedgwick Canada 47°40N 67°20W 73 C6
Kediri Indonesia 7°51S 112°1E 37 G15
Kedros Oros Greece 35°11N 24°37E 25 D6
Keeler U.S.A. 36°29N 117°52W 78 J9
Keeley L. Canada 54°54N 108°8W 71 C7
Keeling Is. = Cocos Is.
Ind. Oc. 12°10S 96°55E 64 J1
Keelung = Chilung
Taiwan 25°3N 121°45E 33 D7
Keene Canada 44°15N 78°10W 82 B6
Keene Calif., U.S.A. 35°13N 118°33W 79 K8
Keene N.H., U.S.A. 42°56N 72°17W 83 D12
Keene N.Y., U.S.A. 44°16N 73°46W 83 B11
Keep River △ Australia 15°49S 129°8E 60 C4
Keeper Hill Ireland 52°45N 8°16W 10 D3
Keerweer, C. Australia 14°0S 141°32E 62 A3
Keeseville U.S.A. 44°29N 73°30W 83 B11
Keetmanshoop Namibia 26°35S 18°8E 56 D2
Keewatin Canada 49°46N 94°34W 71 D10
Keewatin → Canada 56°29N 100°46W 71 B8
Kefalonia Greece 38°15N 20°30E 23 E9
Kefamenanu Indonesia 9°28S 124°29E 37 F6
Kefar Sava Israel 32°11N 34°54E 46 C3
Keffi Nigeria 8°55N 7°43E 50 G7
Keflavík Iceland 64°2N 22°35W 8 D2
Keg River Canada 57°54N 117°55W 70 B5
Kegaska Canada 50°9N 61°18W 73 B7
Kehancha Kenya 1°11S 34°37E 54 C3
Keighley U.K. 53°52N 1°54W 12 D6
Keila Estonia 59°18N 24°25E 9 G21
Keimoes S. Africa 28°41S 20°59E 56 D3
Keitele Finland 63°10N 26°20E 8 E22
Keith Australia 36°6S 140°20E 63 F3

Keith *U.K.* 57°32N 2°57W **11** D6
Keiyasi *Fiji* 17°53S 177°46E **59** a
Keizer *U.S.A.* 44°57N 123°1W **76** D2
Kejimkujik △ *Canada* 44°25N 65°25W **73** D6
Kejserr Franz Joseph Fd. *Greenland* 73°30N 24°30W **4** B6
Kekri *India* 26°0N 75°10E **42** G6
Kelan *China* 38°43N 111°31E **34** E6
Kelang = Klang *Malaysia* 3°2N 101°26E **39** L3
Kelantan → *Malaysia* 6°13N 102°14E **39** J4
Kelkit → *Turkey* 40°45N 36°32E **19** F6
Kellerberrin *Australia* 31°36S 117°38E **61** F2
Kellett, C. *Canada* 72°0N 126°0W **69** B7
Kelleys I. *U.S.A.* 41°36N 82°42W **82** E2
Kellogg *U.S.A.* 47°32N 116°7W **76** C5
Kells = Ceanannus Mor *Ireland* 53°44N 6°53W **10** C5
Kélo *Chad* 9°10N 15°45E **51** G9
Kelokedhara *Cyprus* 34°48N 32°39E **25** E11
Kelowna *Canada* 49°50N 119°25W **70** D5
Kelsey Creek *Australia* 20°26S 148°31E **62** J6
Kelseyville *U.S.A.* 38°59N 122°50W **78** G4
Kelso *N.Z.* 45°54S 169°15E **59** F2
Kelso *U.K.* 55°36N 2°26W **11** F6
Kelso *U.S.A.* 46°9N 122°54W **78** D4
Keluang = Kluang *Malaysia* 2°3N 103°18E **39** L4
Kelvington *Canada* 52°10N 103°30W **71** C8
Kem *Russia* 65°0N 34°38E **18** B5
Kem → *Russia* 64°57N 34°41E **18** B5
Kema *Indonesia* 1°22N 125°8E **37** D7
Kemah *Turkey* 39°32N 39°5E **44** B3
Kemaman *Malaysia* 4°12N 103°18E **39** K4
Kemano *Canada* 53°35N 128°0W **70** C3
Kemasik *Malaysia* 4°25N 103°27E **39** K4
Kemerovo *Russia* 55°20N 86°5E **28** D9
Kemi *Finland* 65°44N 24°34E **8** D21
Kemi älv = Kemijoki → *Finland* 65°47N 24°32E **8** D21
Kemi träsk = Kemijärvi *Finland* 66°43N 27°22E **8** C22
Kemijärvi *Finland* 66°43N 27°22E **8** C22
Kemijoki → *Finland* 65°47N 24°32E **8** D21
Kemmerer *U.S.A.* 41°48N 110°32W **76** F8
Kemmuna = Comino *Malta* 36°1N 14°20E **25** C1
Kemp, L. *U.S.A.* 33°46N 99°9W **84** E5
Kemp Land *Antarctica* 69°0S 55°0E **5** C5
Kempas *Malaysia* 1°33N 103°42E **39** d
Kempsey *Australia* 31°1S 152°50E **63** E5
Kempt, L. *Canada* 47°25N 74°22W **72** C5
Kempten *Germany* 47°45N 10°17E **16** E6
Kempton *Australia* 42°31S 147°12E **63** G4
Kemptville *Canada* 45°0N 75°38W **83** B9
Ken → *India* 25°13N 80°27E **43** G9
Kenai *U.S.A.* 60°33N 151°16W **68** C4
Kendai *India* 22°45N 82°37E **43** H10
Kendal *Indonesia* 6°56S 110°14E **37** G14
Kendal *U.K.* 54°20N 2°44W **12** C5
Kendall *Australia* 31°35S 152°44E **63** E5
Kendall *U.S.A.* 25°40N 80°19W **85** J14
Kendall → *Australia* 14°4S 141°35E **62** A3
Kendallville *U.S.A.* 41°27N 85°16W **81** E11
Kendari *Indonesia* 3°50S 122°30E **37** E6
Kendawangan *Indonesia* 2°32S 110°17E **36** E4
Kendi, Pulau *Malaysia* 5°13N 100°11E **39** c
Kendrapara *India* 20°35N 86°30E **41** J15
Kendrew *S. Africa* 32°32S 24°30E **56** E3
Kene Thao *Laos* 17°44N 101°10E **38** D3
Kenedy *U.S.A.* 28°49N 97°51W **84** G6
Kenema *S. Leone* 7°50N 11°14W **50** G3
Keng Kok *Laos* 16°26N 105°12E **38** D5
Keng Tawng *Burma* 20°45N 98°18E **41** J21
Keng Tung *Burma* 21°0N 99°30E **41** J21
Kengeja *Tanzania* 5°26S 39°45E **54** D4
Kenhardt *S. Africa* 29°19S 21°12E **56** D3
Kenitra *Morocco* 34°15N 6°40W **50** B4
Kenli *China* 37°30N 118°20E **35** F10
Kenmare *Ireland* 51°53N 9°36W **10** E2
Kenmare *U.S.A.* 48°41N 102°5W **80** A2
Kenmare River *Ireland* 51°48N 9°51W **10** E2
Kennebago Lake *U.S.A.* 45°4N 70°40W **83** A14
Kennebec *U.S.A.* 43°54N 99°52W **80** D4
Kennebec → *U.S.A.* 43°45N 69°46W **81** D19
Kennebunk *U.S.A.* 43°23N 70°33W **83** C14
Kennedy *Zimbabwe* 18°52S 27°10E **56** B4
Kennedy Ra. *Australia* 24°45S 115°10E **61** D2
Kennedy Range △ *Australia* 24°34S 115°2E **61** D2
Kenner *U.S.A.* 29°59N 90°14W **85** G9
Kennet → *U.K.* 51°27N 0°57W **13** F7
Kenneth Ra. *Australia* 23°50S 117°8E **61** D2
Kennett *U.S.A.* 36°14N 90°3W **80** G8
Kennewick *U.S.A.* 46°12N 119°7W **76** C4
Kennisis Lake *Canada* 45°13N 78°36W **82** A6
Kenogami → *Canada* 51°6N 84°28W **72** B3
Kenora *Canada* 49°47N 94°29W **71** D10
Kenosha *U.S.A.* 42°35N 87°49W **80** D10
Kensington *Canada* 46°28N 63°34W **73** C7
Kent *Ohio, U.S.A.* 41°9N 81°22W **82** E3
Kent *Tex., U.S.A.* 31°4N 104°13W **84** F2
Kent *Wash., U.S.A.* 47°22N 122°14W **78** C4
Kent □ *U.K.* 51°12N 0°40E **13** F8
Kent Group *Australia* 39°30S 147°20E **63** F4
Kent Pen. *Canada* 68°30N 107°0W **68** C9
Kentaū *Kazakhstan* 43°32N 68°36E **28** E7
Kentland *U.S.A.* 40°46N 87°27W **80** E10
Kenton *U.S.A.* 40°39N 83°37W **81** E12
Kentucky □ *U.S.A.* 37°0N 84°0W **81** G11
Kentucky → *U.S.A.* 38°41N 85°11W **81** F11
Kentucky L. *U.S.A.* 37°1N 88°16W **80** G9
Kentville *Canada* 45°6N 64°29W **73** C7
Kentwood *U.S.A.* 30°56N 90°31W **85** F9
Kenya ■ *Africa* 1°0N 38°0E **54** B4
Kenya, Mt. *Kenya* 0°10S 37°18E **54** C4
Kenyir, Tasik *Malaysia* 5°1N 102°54E **39** K4
Keo Neua, Deo *Vietnam* 18°23N 105°10E **38** C5
Keokuk *U.S.A.* 40°24N 91°24W **80** E8
Keoladeo △ *India* 27°0N 77°20E **42** F7
Keonjhargarh *India* 21°28N 85°35E **43** J11
Kep *Cambodia* 10°29N 104°19E **39** G5
Kep *Vietnam* 21°24N 106°16E **38** B6
Kepala Batas *Malaysia* 5°31N 100°26E **39** c
Kepi *Indonesia* 6°32S 139°19E **37** F9
Kerala □ *India* 11°0N 76°15E **40** P10
Kerama-Rettō *Japan* 26°5N 127°15E **31** L3
Keran *Pakistan* 34°35N 73°59E **43** B5
Kerang *Australia* 35°40S 143°55E **63** F3
Keraudren, C. *Australia* 19°58S 119°45E **60** C2
Kerch *Ukraine* 45°20N 36°20E **19** E6
Kerguelen *Ind. Oc.* 49°15S 69°10E **3** G13
Kericho *Kenya* 0°22S 35°15E **54** C4
Kerinci *Indonesia* 1°40S 101°15E **36** E2
Kerki = Atamyrat *Turkmenistan* 37°50N 65°12E **28** F7
Kerkrade *Neths.* 50°53N 6°4E **15** D6
Kerkyra *Greece* 39°38N 19°50E **25** A3
Kerkyras, Notio Steno *Greece* 39°34N 20°0E **25** A4
Kermadec Is. *Pac. Oc.* 30°0S 178°15W **58** E11
Kermadec Trench *Pac. Oc.* 30°30S 176°0W **64** L10
Kermān *Iran* 30°15N 57°1E **45** D8
Kerman *U.S.A.* 36°43N 120°4W **78** J6
Kermān □ *Iran* 30°0N 57°0E **45** D8
Kermān, Bīābān-e *Iran* 28°45N 59°45E **45** D8
Kermānshāh *Iran* 34°23N 47°0E **44** C5
Kermānshāh □ *Iran* 34°0N 46°30E **44** C5
Kermit *U.S.A.* 31°52N 103°6W **84** F3
Kern → *U.S.A.* 35°16N 119°18W **79** K7
Kernow = Cornwall □ *U.K.* 50°26N 4°40W **13** G3
Kernville *U.S.A.* 35°45N 118°26W **79** K8
Keroh *Malaysia* 5°43N 101°1E **39** K3
Kerrera *U.K.* 56°24N 5°33W **11** E3
Kerrobert *Canada* 51°56N 109°8W **71** C7
Kerrville *U.S.A.* 30°3N 99°8W **84** F5
Kerry □ *Ireland* 52°7N 9°35W **10** D2
Kerry Hd. *Ireland* 52°25N 9°56W **10** D2
Kerulen → *Asia* 48°48N 117°0E **33** B6
Kerzaz *Algeria* 29°29N 1°37W **50** C5
Kesagami → *Canada* 51°40N 79°45W **72** B4
Kesagami L. *Canada* 50°23N 80°15W **72** B3
Keşan *Turkey* 40°49N 26°38E **23** D12
Kesennuma *Japan* 38°54N 141°35E **30** E10
Keshit *Iran* 29°43N 58°17E **45** D8
Kestell *S. Africa* 28°17S 28°42E **57** D4
Kestenga *Russia* 65°50N 31°45E **8** D24
Keswick *U.K.* 54°36N 3°8W **12** C4
Ket → *Russia* 58°55N 81°32E **28** D9
Ketapang *Bali, Indonesia* 8°9S 114°23E **37** J17
Ketapang *Kalimantan, Indonesia* 1°55S 110°0E **36** E4
Ketchikan *U.S.A.* 55°21N 131°39W **70** B2
Ketchum *U.S.A.* 43°41N 114°22W **76** E6
Ketef, Khalig Umm el *Egypt* 23°40N 35°35E **44** F2
Keti Bandar *Pakistan* 24°8N 67°27E **42** G2
Ketri *India* 28°1N 75°50E **42** E6
Kętrzyn *Poland* 54°7N 21°22E **17** A11
Kettering *U.K.* 52°24N 0°43W **13** E7
Kettering *U.S.A.* 39°41N 84°10W **81** F11
Kettle → *Canada* 56°40N 89°34W **71** B11
Kettle Falls *U.S.A.* 48°37N 118°3W **76** B4
Kettle Point *Canada* 43°10N 82°1W **82** C2
Kettle Pt. *Canada* 43°13N 82°1W **82** C2
Kettleman City *U.S.A.* 36°1N 119°58W **78** J7
Keuka L. *U.S.A.* 42°30N 77°9W **82** D7
Keuruu *Finland* 62°16N 24°41E **8** E21
Kewanee *U.S.A.* 41°14N 89°56W **80** E9
Kewaunee *U.S.A.* 44°27N 87°31W **80** C10
Keweenaw B. *U.S.A.* 47°0N 88°15W **80** B9
Keweenaw Pen. *U.S.A.* 47°15N 88°15W **80** B9
Keweenaw Pt. *U.S.A.* 47°25N 87°43W **80** B10
Key, L. *Ireland* 54°0N 8°15W **10** C3
Key Lake Mine *Canada* 57°5N 105°32W **71** B7
Key Largo *U.S.A.* 25°5N 80°27W **85** J14
Key West *U.S.A.* 24°33N 81°48W **88** B3
Keynsham *U.K.* 51°24N 2°29W **13** F5
Keyser *U.S.A.* 39°26N 78°59W **81** F14
Kezhma *Russia* 58°59N 101°9E **29** D11
Kezi *Zimbabwe* 20°58S 28°32E **57** C4
Kgalagadi Transfrontier ⌂ *Africa* 25°10S 21°0E **56** D3
Khabarovsk *Russia* 48°30N 135°5E **29** E14
Khabr *Iran* 28°51N 56°22E **45** D8
Khābūr → *Syria* 35°17N 40°35E **44** C4
Khachmas = Xaçmaz *Azerbaijan* 41°31N 48°42E **19** F8
Khachrod *India* 23°25N 75°20E **42** H6
Khadro *Pakistan* 26°11N 68°50E **42** F3
Khadzhilyangar = Dahongliutan *China* 35°45N 79°20E **43** B8
Khaga *India* 25°47N 81°7E **43** G9
Khagaria *India* 25°30N 86°32E **43** G12
Khaipur *Pakistan* 29°34N 72°17E **42** E5
Khair *India* 27°57N 77°46E **42** F7
Khairabad *India* 27°33N 80°47E **43** F9
Khairagarh *India* 21°27N 81°2E **43** J9
Khairpur *Pakistan* 27°32N 68°49E **42** F3
Khairpur Nathan Shah *Pakistan* 27°6N 67°44E **42** F2
Khairwara *India* 23°58N 73°38E **42** H5
Khaisor → *Pakistan* 31°17N 68°59E **42** D3
Khajuri Kach *Pakistan* 32°4N 69°51E **42** C3
Khakassia □ *Russia* 53°0N 90°0E **28** D9
Khakhea *Botswana* 24°48S 23°22E **56** C3
Khalafābād *Iran* 30°54N 49°24E **45** D6
Khalilabad *India* 26°48N 83°5E **43** F10
Khalīlī *Iran* 27°38N 53°17E **45** E7
Khalkhāl *Iran* 37°37N 48°32E **45** B6
Khalkís = Halkida *Greece* 38°27N 23°42E **23** E10
Khalmer Yu *Russia* 67°58N 65°1E **28** C7
Khalturin *Russia* 58°40N 48°50E **18** C8
Khalūf *Oman* 20°30N 58°13E **47** C6
Kham Keut *Laos* 18°15N 104°43E **38** C5
Khamaria *India* 23°5N 80°48E **43** H9
Khambhaliya *India* 22°14N 69°41E **42** H3
Khambhat *India* 22°23N 72°33E **42** H5
Khambhat, G. of *India* 20°45N 72°30E **40** J8
Khamīr *Iran* 26°57N 55°36E **45** E7
Khamir *Yemen* 16°2N 44°0E **47** D3
Khamīs Mushayṭ *Si. Arabia* 18°18N 42°44E **47** D3
Khamsa *Egypt* 30°27N 32°23E **46** E1
Khan → *Namibia* 22°37S 14°56E **56** C2
Khān Abū Shāmat *Syria* 33°39N 36°53E **46** B5
Khān Azād *Iraq* 33°7N 44°22E **44** C5
Khān Mujiddah *Iraq* 32°21N 43°48E **44** C4
Khān Shaykhūn *Syria* 35°26N 36°38E **44** C3
Khan Tengri, Pik *Asia* 42°12N 80°10E **32** B3
Khān Yūnis *Gaza Strip* 31°21N 34°18E **46** D3
Khanai *Pakistan* 30°30N 67°8E **42** D2
Khānaqīn *Iraq* 34°23N 45°25E **44** C5
Khānbāghī *Iran* 36°10N 55°25E **45** B7
Khandwa *India* 21°49N 76°22E **40** J10
Khandyga *Russia* 62°42N 135°35E **29** C14
Khanewal *Pakistan* 30°20N 71°55E **42** D4
Khangah Dogran *Pakistan* 31°50N 73°37E **42** D5
Khanh Duong *Vietnam* 12°44N 108°44E **38** F7
Khaniá = Chania *Greece* 35°30N 24°4E **25** D6
Khaniadhana *India* 25°1N 78°8E **42** G8
Khanka, L. *Asia* 45°0N 132°24E **30** B6
Khankendy = Xankändi *Azerbaijan* 39°52N 46°49E **44** B5
Khanna *India* 30°42N 76°16E **42** D7
Khanozai *Pakistan* 30°37N 67°19E **42** D2
Khanpur *Pakistan* 28°42N 70°35E **42** E4
Khanty-Mansiysk *Russia* 61°0N 69°0E **28** C7
Khao Laem △ *Thailand* 14°56N 98°31E **38** E2
Khao Laem Res. *Thailand* 14°50N 98°30E **38** E2
Khao Lak △ *Malaysia* 8°38N 98°18E **39** H2
Khao Luang △ *Thailand* 8°34N 99°42E **39** H2
Khao Phlu *Thailand* 9°29N 99°59E **39** b
Khao Pu-Khao Ya △ *Thailand* 7°26N 99°57E **39** J2
Khao Sam Roi Yot △ *Thailand* 12°13N 99°57E **39** F2
Khao Sok △ *Thailand* 8°55N 98°38E **39** H2
Khao Yai △ *Thailand* 14°21N 101°29E **38** E3
Khaoen Si Nakarin △ *Thailand* 14°47N 99°0E **38** E2
Khapalu *Pakistan* 35°10N 76°20E **43** B7
Khapcheranga *Russia* 49°42N 112°24E **29** E12
Khaptao △ *Nepal* 29°20N 81°10E **43** E9
Kharaghoda *India* 23°11N 71°46E **42** H4
Kharagpur *India* 22°20N 87°25E **43** H12
Kharan Kalat *Pakistan* 28°34N 65°21E **40** E4
Kharānaq *Iran* 32°20N 54°45E **45** C7
Kharda *India* 18°40N 75°34E **40** K9
Khardung La *India* 34°20N 77°43E **43** B7
Kharg = Khārk, Jazīreh-ye *Iran* 29°15N 50°28E **45** D6
Khârga, El Wâhât el *Egypt* 25°10N 30°35E **51** C12
Khargon *India* 21°45N 75°40E **40** J9
Khari → *India* 25°54N 74°31E **42** G6
Kharian *Pakistan* 32°49N 73°52E **42** C5
Khārk, Jazīreh-ye *Iran* 29°15N 50°28E **45** D6
Kharkiv *Ukraine* 49°58N 36°20E **19** E6
Kharkov = Kharkiv *Ukraine* 49°58N 36°20E **19** E6
Kharovsk *Russia* 59°56N 40°13E **18** C7
Kharsawangarh *India* 22°48N 85°50E **43** H11
Kharta *Turkey* 40°55N 29°7E **23** D13
Khartoum = El Khartûm *Sudan* 15°31N 32°35E **51** E12
Khartum *Canada* 45°15N 77°5W **82** A7
Khasan *Russia* 42°25N 130°40E **30** C5
Khāsh *Iran* 28°15N 61°15E **45** D9
Khashm el Girba *Sudan* 14°59N 35°58E **51** F13
Khaskovo *Bulgaria* 41°56N 25°30E **23** D11
Khatanga *Russia* 72°0N 102°20E **29** B11
Khatanga → *Russia* 72°55N 106°0E **29** B11
Khatauli *India* 29°17N 77°43E **42** E7
Khatra *India* 22°59N 86°51E **43** H12
Khātūnābād *Iran* 30°1N 55°25E **45** D7
Khatyrka *Russia* 62°3N 175°15E **29** C18
Khavda *India* 23°51N 69°43E **42** H3
Khawr Fakkān *U.A.E.* 25°21N 56°22E **45** E8
Khaybar, Ḥarrat *Si. Arabia* 25°45N 40°0E **44** E4
Khāzimiyah *Iraq* 34°46N 43°37E **44** C4
Khe Bo *Vietnam* 19°8N 104°41E **38** C5
Khe Long *Vietnam* 21°29N 104°46E **38** B5
Khe Sanh *Vietnam* 16°37N 106°45E **38** D6
Khed Brahma *India* 24°7N 73°5E **42** G5
Khekra *India* 28°52N 77°20E **42** E7
Khemarak Phouminville = Krong Kaoh Kong *Cambodia* 11°37N 102°59E **39** G4
Khemisset *Morocco* 33°50N 6°1W **50** B4
Khemmarat *Thailand* 16°10N 105°15E **38** D5
Khenāmān *Iran* 30°27N 56°29E **45** D8
Khenchela *Algeria* 35°28N 7°11E **50** A7
Khersān → *Iran* 31°33N 50°22E **45** D6
Kherson *Ukraine* 46°35N 32°35E **19** E5
Kheta → *Russia* 71°54N 102°6E **29** B11
Khewari *Pakistan* 26°36N 68°52E **42** F3
Khilchipur *India* 24°2N 76°34E **42** G7
Khilok *Russia* 51°30N 110°45E **29** D12
Khíos = Hios *Greece* 38°27N 26°9E **23** E12
Khirsadoh *India* 22°11N 78°47E **43** H8
Khiuma = Hiiumaa *Estonia* 58°50N 22°45E **9** G20
Khiva *Uzbekistan* 41°30N 60°18E **28** E7
Khlong Khlung *Thailand* 16°12N 99°43E **38** D2
Khmelnik *Ukraine* 49°33N 27°58E **17** D14
Khmelnytskyy *Ukraine* 49°23N 27°0E **17** D14
Khmer Rep. = Cambodia ■ *Asia* 12°15N 105°0E **38** F5
Khoai, Hon *Vietnam* 8°26N 104°50E **39** H5
Khodoriv *Ukraine* 49°24N 24°19E **17** D13
Khodzent = Khŭjand *Tajikistan* 40°17N 69°37E **28** E7
Khojak Pass *Afghan.* 30°51N 66°34E **42** D2
Khok Kloi *Thailand* 8°17N 98°19E **39** a
Khok Pho *Thailand* 6°43N 101°6E **39** J3
Khok Samrong *Thailand* 15°3N 100°43E **38** E3
Kholm *Russia* 57°10N 31°15E **18** C5
Kholmsk *Russia* 47°40N 142°5E **29** E15
Khomas Hochland *Namibia* 22°40S 16°0E **56** C2
Khomeyn *Iran* 33°40N 50°7E **45** C6
Khomeynī Shahr *Iran* 32°41N 51°31E **45** C6
Khomodino *Botswana* 22°46S 23°52E **56** C3
Khon Kaen *Thailand* 16°30N 102°47E **38** D4
Khong → *Cambodia* 13°32N 105°58E **38** F5
Khong Sedone *Laos* 15°34N 105°49E **38** E5
Khonuu *Russia* 66°30N 143°12E **29** C15
Khoper → *Russia* 49°30N 42°20E **19** D6
Khorāsān □ *Iran* 34°0N 58°0E **45** C8
Khorat = Nakhon Ratchasima *Thailand* 14°59N 102°12E **38** E4
Khorat, Cao Nguyen *Thailand* 15°30N 102°50E **38** E4
Khorixas *Namibia* 20°16S 14°59E **56** C1
Khorramābād *Khorāsān, Iran* 35°6N 57°57E **45** C8
Khorramābād *Lorestān, Iran* 33°30N 48°25E **45** C6
Khorrāmshahr *Iran* 30°29N 48°15E **45** D6
Khorugh *Tajikistan* 37°30N 71°36E **28** F8
Khosravī *Iran* 30°48N 51°28E **45** D6
Khosrowābād *Khuzestān, Iran* 30°10N 48°25E **45** D6
Khosrowābād *Kordestān, Iran* 35°31N 47°38E **44** C5
Khost *Pakistan* 30°13N 67°35E **42** D2
Khosūyeh *Iran* 28°32N 54°26E **45** D7
Khotyn *Ukraine* 48°31N 26°27E **17** D14
Khouribga *Morocco* 32°58N 6°57W **50** B4
Khowst *Afghan.* 33°22N 69°58E **42** C3
Khowst □ *Afghan.* 33°20N 70°0E **40** C6
Khoyniki *Belarus* 51°54N 29°55E **17** C15
Khrysokhou B. *Cyprus* 35°6N 32°25E **25** D11
Khu Khan *Thailand* 14°42N 104°12E **38** E5
Khuan Wa *Thailand* 7°53N 98°17E **39** a
Khudzhand = Khŭjand *Tajikistan* 40°17N 69°37E **28** E7
Khuff *Si. Arabia* 24°55N 44°53E **44** E5
Khūgīānī *Afghan.* 31°34N 66°32E **42** D2
Khuis *Botswana* 26°40S 21°49E **56** D3
Khuiyala *India* 27°9N 70°25E **42** F4
Khŭjand *Tajikistan* 40°17N 69°37E **28** E7
Khujner *India* 23°47N 76°36E **42** H7
Khulna *Bangla.* 22°45N 89°34E **41** H16
Khulna □ *Bangla.* 22°25N 89°35E **41** H16
Khumago *Botswana* 20°26S 24°32E **56** C3
Khunjerab △ *Pakistan* 36°40N 75°30E **43** A6
Khunjerab Pass = Kinjirap Daban *Asia* 36°40N 75°25E **40** A9
Khūnsorkh *Iran* 27°9N 56°7E **45** E8
Khunti *India* 23°5N 85°17E **43** H11
Khūr *Iran* 32°55N 58°18E **45** C8
Khurai *India* 24°3N 78°23E **42** G8
Khurayṣ *Si. Arabia* 25°6N 48°2E **45** E6
Khurja *India* 28°15N 77°58E **42** E7
Khūrmāl *Iraq* 35°18N 46°2E **44** C5
Khurr, Wādī al *Iraq* 32°3N 43°52E **44** C4
Khūsf *Iran* 32°46N 58°53E **45** C8
Khushab *Pakistan* 32°20N 72°20E **42** C5
Khust *Ukraine* 48°10N 23°18E **17** D12
Khutse ⌂ *Botswana* 23°31S 24°12E **56** C3
Khuzdar *Pakistan* 27°52N 66°30E **42** F2
Khūzestān □ *Iran* 31°0N 49°0E **45** D6
Khvāf *Iran* 34°33N 60°8E **45** C9
Khvājeh *Iran* 38°9N 46°35E **44** B5
Khvānsār *Iran* 29°56N 54°8E **45** D7
Khvor *Iran* 33°45N 55°0E **45** C7
Khvorgū *Iran* 27°34N 56°27E **45** E8
Khvormūj *Iran* 28°40N 51°30E **45** D6
Khvoy *Iran* 38°35N 45°0E **44** B5
Khyber Pass *Afghan.* 34°10N 71°8E **42** B4
Kia *Fiji* 16°16S 179°8E **59** a
Kiabukwa *Dem. Rep. of the Congo* 8°40S 24°48E **55** D1
Kiama *Australia* 34°40S 150°50E **63** E5
Kiamba *Phil.* 6°2N 124°46E **37** C6
Kiambi *Dem. Rep. of the Congo* 7°15S 28°0E **54** D2
Kiambu *Kenya* 1°8S 36°50E **54** C4
Kiangara *Madag.* 17°58S 47°2E **57** B8
Kiangsi = Jiangxi □ *China* 27°30N 116°0E **33** D6
Kiangsu = Jiangsu □ *China* 33°0N 120°0E **35** H11
Kibale △ *Uganda* 0°16N 30°18E **54** B3
Kibanga Port *Uganda* 0°10N 32°58E **54** B3
Kibara *Tanzania* 2°8S 33°30E **54** C3
Kibare, Mts. *Dem. Rep. of the Congo* 8°25S 27°10E **54** D2
Kibira △ *Burundi* 3°6S 30°24E **54** C3
Kibombo *Dem. Rep. of the Congo* 3°57S 25°53E **54** C2
Kibondo *Tanzania* 3°35S 30°45E **54** C3
Kibre Mengist *Ethiopia* 5°54N 38°59E **47** F2
Kıbrıs = Cyprus ■ *Asia* 35°0N 33°0E **25** E12
Kibumbu *Burundi* 3°32S 29°45E **54** C2
Kibungo *Rwanda* 2°10S 30°32E **54** C3
Kibuye *Burundi* 3°39S 29°59E **54** C2
Kibuye *Rwanda* 2°3S 29°21E **54** C2
Kibwesa *Tanzania* 6°30S 29°58E **54** D2
Kibwezi *Kenya* 2°27S 37°57E **54** C4
Kichha *India* 28°53N 79°30E **43** E8
Kichha → *India* 28°41N 79°18E **43** E8
Kichmengskiy Gorodok *Russia* 59°59N 45°48E **18** B8
Kicking Horse Pass *Canada* 51°28N 116°16W
Kidal *Mali* 18°26N 1°22E
Kidderminster *U.K.* 52°24N 2°15W
Kidepo Valley △ *Uganda* 3°52N 33°50E
Kidete *Tanzania* 6°25S 37°17E
Kidnappers, C. *N.Z.* 39°38S 177°5E
Kidsgrove *U.K.* 53°5N 2°14W
Kidston *Australia* 18°52S 144°8E
Kidugallo *Tanzania* 6°49S 38°15E
Kiel *Germany* 54°19N 10°8E
Kiel Canal = Nord-Ostsee-Kanal *Germany* 54°12N 9°32E
Kielce *Poland* 50°52N 20°42E
Kielder Water *U.K.* 55°11N 2°31W
Kieler Bucht *Germany* 54°35N 10°25E
Kien Binh *Vietnam* 9°55N 105°19E
Kien Tan *Vietnam* 10°7N 105°17E
Kienge *Dem. Rep. of the Congo* 10°30S 27°30E
Kiev = Kyyiv *Ukraine* 50°30N 30°28E
Kiffa *Mauritania* 16°37N 11°24W
Kifrī *Iraq* 34°45N 45°0E
Kigali *Rwanda* 1°59S 30°4E
Kigarama *Tanzania* 1°1S 31°50E
Kigezi ⌂ *Uganda* 0°34S 29°55E
Kigoma □ *Tanzania* 5°0S 30°0E
Kigoma-Ujiji *Tanzania* 4°55S 29°36E
Kigomasha, Ras *Tanzania* 4°58S 38°58E
Kığzı *Turkey* 38°18N 43°25E
Kihnu *Estonia* 58°9N 24°1E
Kii-Sanchi *Japan* 34°20N 136°0E
Kii-Suidō *Japan* 33°40N 134°45E
Kiira Dam *Uganda* 0°25N 33°0E
Kikaiga-Shima *Japan* 28°19N 129°59E
Kikinda *Serbia* 45°50N 20°30E
Kikládhes = Cyclades *Greece* 37°0N 24°30E
Kikwit *Dem. Rep. of the Congo* 5°0S 18°45E
Kilar *India* 33°6N 76°25E
Kīlauea Caldera *U.S.A.* 19°25N 155°17W
Kilbeggan *Ireland* 53°22N 7°30W
Kilbrannan Sd. *U.K.* 55°37N 5°26W
Kilchu *N. Korea* 40°57N 129°25E
Kilcoy *Australia* 26°59S 152°30E
Kildare *Ireland* 53°9N 6°55W
Kildare □ *Ireland* 53°10N 6°50W
Kildinstroy *Russia* 68°48N 33°6E
Kilfinnane *Ireland* 52°21N 8°28W
Kilgarvan *Ireland* 51°54N 9°27W
Kilgore *U.S.A.* 32°23N 94°53W
Kilgoris *Kenya* 1°0S 34°53E
Kilifi *Kenya* 3°40S 39°48E
Kilimanjaro *Tanzania* 3°7S 37°20E
Kilimanjaro □ *Tanzania* 4°0S 38°0E
Kilindini *Kenya* 4°4S 39°40E
Kilis *Turkey* 36°42N 37°6E
Kiliya *Ukraine* 45°28N 29°16E
Kilkee *Ireland* 52°41N 9°39W
Kilkeel *U.K.* 54°4N 6°0W
Kilkenny *Ireland* 52°39N 7°15W
Kilkenny □ *Ireland* 52°35N 7°15W
Kilkieran B. *Ireland* 53°20N 9°41W
Kilkis *Greece* 40°58N 22°57E
Killala *Ireland* 54°13N 9°12W
Killala B. *Ireland* 54°16N 9°8W
Killaloe *Canada* 45°33N 77°25W
Killaloe *Ireland* 52°48N 8°28W
Killarney *Australia* 28°20S 152°18E
Killarney *Canada* 49°10N 99°40W
Killarney *Ireland* 52°4N 9°30W
Killarney △ *Ireland* 52°0N 9°33W
Killary Harbour *Ireland* 53°38N 9°52W
Killdeer *U.S.A.* 47°22N 102°45W
Killeen *U.S.A.* 31°7N 97°44W
Killin *U.K.* 56°28N 4°19W
Killiney *Ireland* 53°15N 6°7W
Killington Pk. *U.S.A.* 43°36N 72°49W
Killini *Greece* 37°54N 22°25E
Killorglin *Ireland* 52°6N 9°47W
Killybegs *Ireland* 54°38N 8°26W
Kilmarnock *U.K.* 55°37N 4°29W
Kilmore *Australia* 37°25S 144°53E
Kilmore Quay *Ireland* 52°10N 6°36W
Kilondo *Tanzania* 9°45S 34°20E
Kilosa *Tanzania* 6°48S 37°0E
Kilrush *Ireland* 52°38N 9°29W
Kilwa Kisiwani *Tanzania* 8°58S 39°32E
Kilwa Kivinje *Tanzania* 8°45S 39°25E
Kilwa Masoko *Tanzania* 8°55S 39°30E
Kilwinning *U.K.* 55°39N 4°43W
Kim *U.S.A.* 37°15N 103°21W
Kimaam *Indonesia* 7°58S 138°53E
Kimamba *Tanzania* 6°45S 37°10E
Kimba *Australia* 33°8S 136°23E
Kimball *Nebr., U.S.A.* 41°14N 103°40W
Kimball *S. Dak., U.S.A.* 43°45N 98°57W
Kimberley *Australia* 16°20S 127°0E
Kimberley *B.C., Canada* 49°40N 115°59W
Kimberley *Ont., Canada* 44°23N 80°32W
Kimberley *S. Africa* 28°43S 24°46E
Kimberly *U.S.A.* 42°32N 114°22W
Kimch'aek *N. Korea* 40°40N 129°10E
Kimhae = Gimhae *S. Korea* 35°14N 128°53E
Kimmirut *Canada* 62°50N 69°50W
Kimpese *Dem. Rep. of the Congo* 5°35S 14°26E
Kimry *Russia* 56°55N 37°15E
Kinabalu, Gunung *Malaysia* 6°3N 116°14E
Kinango *Kenya* 4°8S 39°19E
Kinaskan L. *Canada* 57°38N 130°8W
Kinbasket L. *Canada* 52°0N 118°10W
Kincardine *Canada* 44°10N 81°40W
Kincolith *Canada* 55°0N 129°57W

da Dem. Rep. of the Congo 9°18S 25°4E 55 D2
de U.S.A. 43°56N 83°0W 82 C2
der Scout U.K. 53°24N 1°52W 12 D6
dersley Canada 51°30N 109°10W 71 C7
dia Guinea 10°0N 12°52W 50 F3
du
em. Rep. of the Congo 2°55S 25°50E 54 C2
eshma Russia 57°30N 42°5E 18 C7
esi Tanzania 1°25S 33°50E 54 C3
g, L. Australia 33°10S 119°35E 61 F2
g, Mt. Australia 25°10S 147°30E 62 D4
g City U.S.A. 36°13N 121°8W 78 J5
g Cr. → Australia 24°35S 139°30E 62 C2
g Edward →
ustralia 14°14S 126°35E 60 B4
g Edward Point
Georgia 54°17S 36°30W 96 G9
g Frederick VI Land = Kong
ederik VI Kyst
eenland 63°0N 43°0W 4 C5
g George B. Falk. Is. 51°30S 60°30W 96 G4
g George I. Antarctica 60°0S 60°0W 5 C18
g George Is. Canada 57°20N 80°30W 69 D11
g George Sd. Australia 35°5S 118°0E 61 G2
g I. = Kadan Kyun
urma 12°30N 98°20E 38 F2
g I. Australia 39°50S 144°0E 63 F3
g I. Canada 52°10N 127°40W 70 C3
g Khalid Military City =
adinat al Malik Khālid al
skarīyah Si. Arabia 27°54N 45°31E 44 E5
g Leopold Ranges
ustralia 17°30S 125°45E 60 C4
, of Prussia U.S.A. 40°5N 75°23W 83 F9
, Sd. Australia 16°50S 123°20E 60 C3
, Sejong Antarctica 62°30S 58°0W 5 C18
, William I. Canada 69°10N 97°25W 68 C10
, William's Town
Africa 32°51S 27°22E 56 E4
ait Canada 64°14N 76°32W 69 C12
aok = Bathurst Inlet
nada 66°50N 108°1W 68 C9
aroy Australia 26°32S 151°51E 63 D5
fisher U.S.A. 35°52N 97°56W 84 D6
irbān Iraq 34°40N 44°54E 44 C5
isepp = Kuressaare
onia 58°15N 22°30E 9 G20
isepp Russia 59°25N 28°40E 9 G23
man Ariz., U.S.A. 35°12N 114°4W 79 K12
man Kans., U.S.A. 37°39N 98°7W 80 G4
oonya Australia 30°55S 135°19E 63 E2
ri Pakistan 30°27N 69°49E 42 D3
s → U.S.A. 36°3N 119°50W 78 J7
s Canyon Australia 24°15S 131°34E 60 D5
s Canyon △
.A. 36°50N 118°40W 78 J8
's Lynn U.K. 52°45N 0°24E 12 E8
s Park U.S.A. 40°53N 73°16W 83 F11
s Peak U.S.A. 40°46N 110°23W 76 F8
sbridge U.K. 50°17N 3°47W 13 G4
sburg U.S.A. 36°31N 119°33W 78 J7
scote Australia 35°40S 137°38E 63 F2
scourt Ireland 53°55N 6°48W 10 C5
sford U.S.A. 45°48N 88°4W 80 C9
sland U.S.A. 30°48N 81°41W 85 F14
sport U.S.A. 36°33N 82°33W 85 C13
ston Canada 44°14N 76°30W 83 B8
ston Jamaica 18°0N 76°50W 88 a
ston N.Z. 45°20S 168°43E 59 F2
ston N.H., U.S.A. 42°56N 71°3W 83 D13
ston N.Y., U.S.A. 41°56N 73°59W 83 E11
ston Pa., U.S.A. 41°16N 75°54W 83 E9
ston R.I., U.S.A. 41°29N 71°30W 83 E13
ston Pk. U.S.A. 35°44N 115°55W 79 K11
ston South East
stralia 36°51S 139°55E 63 F2
ston upon Hull U.K. 53°45N 0°21W 12 D7
ston upon Hull □
. 53°45N 0°21W 12 D7
ston-upon-Thames □
. 51°24N 0°17W 13 F7
stown St. Vincent 13°10N 61°10W 89 D7
stree U.S.A. 33°40N 79°50W 85 E15
sville Canada 42°2N 82°45W 82 D2
sville U.S.A. 27°31N 97°52W 84 H6
ussie U.K. 57°6N 4°2W 11 D4
vood U.S.A. 30°2N 95°16W 84 F7
Turkey 39°6N 27°24E 23 E12
ino Canada 52°57N 105°2W 71 C7
ap Daban Asia 36°40N 75°25E 40 A9
ala Congo 4°18S 14°49E 52 E2
□ Japan 33°45N 136°0E 31 H8
ith N.Z. 38°20S 175°56E 59 C5
chleven U.K. 56°43N 5°0W 11 E4
ount Canada 44°48N 78°45W 82 B6
a Sweden 57°32N 12°42E 9 H15
airds Hd. U.K. 57°43N 2°1W 11 D6
Nuevo Mexico 28°52N 112°3W 86 B2
e → Canada 52°8N 81°25W 72 B3
moto Japan 35°30N 136°13E 31 G8
ai Uganda 0°41S 30°28E 54 D3
sao Canada 57°5N 102°1W 71 B8
ss U.K. 56°13N 3°25W 11 E5
le Ireland 51°42N 8°31W 10 E3
le, Old Hd. of
nd 51°37N 8°33W 10 E3
a = Chang Jiang →
a 31°48N 121°10E 33 C7
asa
. Rep. of the Congo 4°20S 15°15E 52 E3
y U.S.A. 37°55N 99°25W 80 G4
an U.S.A. 41°26N 80°35W 82 E4
on U.S.A. 35°16N 77°35W 85 D16
mani Indonesia 8°14S 115°19E 37 J18
e U.K. 57°14N 2°20W 11 D6
re Ra. Australia 23°15S 128°47E 60 D4
e U.K. 55°30N 5°35W 11 F3
Kintyre, Mull of U.K. 55°17N 5°47W 11 F3
Kinushseo → Canada 55°15N 83°45W 72 A3
Kinuso Canada 55°20N 115°25W 70 B5
Kinvarra Ireland 53°8N 8°56W 10 C3
Kinyangiri Tanzania 4°25S 34°37E 54 C3
Kinyeti Sudan 3°57N 32°54E 54 B3
Kinzua U.S.A. 41°52N 78°58W 82 E6
Kiosk Canada 46°6N 78°53W 72 C4
Kiowa Kans., U.S.A. 37°1N 98°29W 80 G4
Kiowa Okla., U.S.A. 34°43N 95°54W 84 D7
Kipahigan L. Canada 55°20N 101°55W 71 B8
Kipanga Tanzania 6°15S 35°20E 54 D4
Kiparissia Greece 37°15N 21°40E 23 F9
Kiparissiakos Kolpos
Greece 37°25N 21°25E 23 F9
Kipawa, L. Canada 46°50N 79°0W 72 C4
Kipembawe Tanzania 7°38S 33°27E 54 D3
Kipengere Ra. Tanzania 9°12S 34°15E 55 D3
Kipili Tanzania 7°28S 30°32E 54 D3
Kipini Kenya 2°30S 40°32E 54 C5
Kipling Canada 50°6N 102°38W 71 C8
Kippure Ireland 53°11N 6°21W 10 C5
Kipushi
Dem. Rep. of the Congo 11°48S 27°12E 55 E2
Kiranomena Madag. 18°17S 46°2E 57 B8
Kirensk Russia 57°50N 107°55E 29 D11
Kirghiz Range Asia 42°40N 73°40E 32 B2
Kirghizia = Kyrgyzstan ■
Asia 42°0N 75°0E 28 E8
Kirgiziya Steppe Eurasia 50°0N 55°0E 19 E10
Kiribati ■ Pac. Oc. 3°0S 180°0E 58 B10
Kırıkkale Turkey 39°51N 33°32E 19 G5
Kirillov Russia 59°49N 38°24E 18 C6
Kirin = Jilin China 43°44N 126°30E 35 C14
Kirinyaga = Kenya, Mt.
Kenya 0°10S 37°18E 54 C4
Kirirom △ Cambodia 11°18N 104°5E 39 G5
Kirishima Yaku △
Japan 31°24N 130°50E 31 J5
Kiritimati Kiribati 1°58N 157°27W 65 G12
Kirkby U.K. 53°30N 2°54W 12 D5
Kirkby-in-Ashfield U.K. 53°6N 1°14W 12 D6
Kirkby Lonsdale U.K. 54°12N 2°36W 12 C5
Kirkby Stephen U.K. 54°29N 2°21W 12 C5
Kirkcaldy U.K. 56°7N 3°9W 11 E5
Kirkcudbright U.K. 54°50N 4°2W 11 G4
Kirkee India 18°34N 73°56E 40 K8
Kirkenes Norway 69°40N 30°5E 8 B24
Kirkfield Canada 44°34N 78°59W 82 B6
Kirkintilloch U.K. 55°56N 4°8W 11 F4
Kirkjubæjarklaustur
Iceland 63°47N 18°4W 8 E4
Kirkkonummi Finland 60°8N 24°26E 9 F21
Kirkland U.S.A. 47°40N 122°12W 78 C4
Kirkland Lake Canada 48°9N 80°2W 72 C3
Kırklareli Turkey 41°44N 27°15E 23 D12
Kirksville U.S.A. 40°12N 92°35W 80 E7
Kirkūk Iraq 35°30N 44°21E 44 C5
Kirkwall U.K. 58°59N 2°58W 11 C6
Kirkwood S. Africa 33°22S 25°15E 56 E4
Kirov Russia 58°35N 49°40E 18 C8
Kirovabad = Gäncä
Azerbaijan 40°45N 46°20E 19 F8
Kirovograd = Kirovohrad
Ukraine 48°35N 32°20E 19 E5
Kirovohrad Ukraine 48°35N 32°20E 19 E5
Kirovsk Russia 67°32N 33°41E 18 A5
Kirovskiy Kamchatka,
Russia 54°27N 155°42E 29 D16
Kirovskiy Primorsk,
Russia 45°7N 133°30E 30 B6
Kirriemuir U.K. 56°41N 3°1W 11 E5
Kirsanov Russia 52°35N 42°40E 18 D7
Kırşehir Turkey 39°14N 34°5E 44 B2
Kirthar △ Pakistan 25°45N 67°30E 42 F2
Kirthar Range Pakistan 27°0N 67°0E 42 F2
Kirtland U.S.A. 36°44N 108°21W 77 H9
Kiruna Sweden 67°52N 20°15E 8 C19
Kirundu
Dem. Rep. of the Congo 0°50S 25°35E 54 C2
Kiryū Japan 36°24N 139°20E 31 F9
Kisaga Tanzania 4°30S 34°23E 54 C3
Kisanga
Dem. Rep. of the Congo 2°30N 26°35E 54 B2
Kisangani
Dem. Rep. of the Congo 0°35N 25°15E 54 B2
Kisar Indonesia 8°5S 127°10E 37 F7
Kisarawe Tanzania 6°53S 39°0E 54 D4
Kisarazu Japan 35°23N 139°55E 31 G9
Kiselevsk Russia 54°0N 86°39E 28 D9
Kishanganga →
Pakistan 34°18N 73°28E 43 B5
Kishanganj India 26°3N 88°14E 43 F13
Kishangarh Raj., India 26°34N 74°52E 42 F6
Kishangarh Raj., India 27°50N 70°30E 42 F4
Kishinev = Chişinău
Moldova 47°2N 28°50E 17 E15
Kishiwada Japan 34°28N 135°22E 31 G7
Kishtwar India 33°20N 75°48E 42 C6
Kisigo ⌂ Tanzania 6°27S 34°17E 54 D3
Kisii Kenya 0°40S 34°45E 54 C3
Kisiju Tanzania 7°23S 39°19E 54 D4
Kisizi Uganda 1°0S 29°58E 54 C2
Kiskőrös Hungary 46°37N 19°20E 17 E10
Kiskunfélegyháza
Hungary 46°42N 19°53E 17 E10
Kiskunhalas Hungary 46°28N 19°37E 17 E10
Kislovodsk Russia 43°50N 42°45E 19 F7
Kismaayo Somali Rep. 0°22S 42°32E 47 H3
Kiso-Gawa → Japan 35°20N 136°45E 31 G8
Kiso-Sammyaku Japan 35°45N 137°45E 31 G8
Kisofukushima Japan 35°52N 137°43E 31 G8
Kisoro Uganda 1°17S 29°48E 54 C2
Kissamos = Kasteli
Greece 35°29N 23°38E 25 D5
Kissamos, Kolpos Greece 35°30N 23°38E 25 D5
Kissidougou Guinea 9°5N 10°5W 50 G3
Kissimmee U.S.A. 28°18N 81°24W 85 G14
Kissimmee → U.S.A. 27°9N 80°52W 85 H14
Kississing L. Canada 55°10N 101°20W 71 B8
Kissónerga Cyprus 34°49N 32°24E 25 E11
Kisumu Kenya 0°3S 34°45E 54 C3
Kiswani Tanzania 4°5S 37°57E 54 C4
Kiswere Tanzania 9°27S 39°30E 55 D4
Kit Carson U.S.A. 38°46N 102°48W 76 G12
Kita Mali 13°5N 9°25W 50 F4
Kitaibaraki Japan 36°50N 140°45E 31 F10
Kitakami Japan 39°20N 141°10E 30 E10
Kitakami-Gawa →
Japan 38°25N 141°19E 30 E10
Kitakami-Sammyaku
Japan 39°30N 141°30E 30 E10
Kitakata Japan 37°39N 139°52E 30 F9
Kitakyūshū Japan 33°50N 130°50E 31 H5
Kitale Kenya 1°0N 35°0E 54 B4
Kitami Japan 43°48N 143°54E 30 C11
Kitami-Sammyaku
Japan 44°22N 142°43E 30 B11
Kitangiri, L. Tanzania 4°5S 34°20E 54 C3
Kitaya Tanzania 10°38S 40°8E 55 E5
Kitchener Canada 43°27N 80°29W 82 C4
Kitee Finland 62°5N 30°8E 8 E24
Kitega = Gitega Burundi 3°26S 29°56E 54 C2
Kitengo
Dem. Rep. of the Congo 7°26S 24°8E 54 D1
Kitgum Uganda 3°17N 32°52E 54 B3
Kíthira = Kythira Greece 36°8N 23°0E 23 F10
Kíthnos Greece 37°26N 24°27E 23 F11
Kiti Cyprus 34°50N 33°34E 25 E12
Kiti, C. Cyprus 34°48N 33°36E 25 E12
Kitimat Canada 54°3N 128°38W 70 C3
Kitinen → Finland 67°14N 27°27E 8 C22
Kitsuki Japan 33°25N 131°37E 31 H5
Kittakittaooloo, L.
Australia 28°3S 138°14E 63 D2
Kittanning U.S.A. 40°49N 79°31W 82 F5
Kittatinny Mt. U.S.A. 41°19N 74°39W 83 F10
Kittery U.S.A. 43°5N 70°45W 83 C14
Kittilä Finland 67°40N 24°51E 8 C21
Kitui Kenya 1°17S 38°0E 54 C4
Kitwanga Canada 55°6N 128°4W 70 B3
Kitwe Zambia 12°54S 28°13E 55 E2
Kivarli India 24°33N 72°46E 42 G5
Kivertsi Ukraine 50°50N 25°28E 17 C13
Kividhes Cyprus 34°46N 32°51E 25 E11
Kivu, L.
Dem. Rep. of the Congo 1°48S 29°0E 54 C2
Kiwirrkurra Australia 22°49S 127°45E 60 D4
Kiyev = Kyyiv Ukraine 50°30N 30°28E 17 C16
Kiyevskoye Vdkhr. = Kyyivske
Vdskh. Ukraine 51°0N 30°25E 17 C16
Kizel Russia 59°3N 57°40E 18 C10
Kiziguru Rwanda 1°46S 30°23E 54 C3
Kızıl Irmak → Turkey 41°44N 35°58E 19 F6
Kizil Jilga China 35°26N 78°50E 43 B8
Kızıldağ △ Turkey 38°5N 31°20E 44 B1
Kızıltepe Turkey 37°12N 40°35E 44 B4
Kizimkazi Tanzania 6°28S 39°30E 54 D4
Kizlyar Russia 43°51N 46°40E 19 F8
Kizyl-Arvat = Serdar
Turkmenistan 39°4N 56°23E 45 B8
Kjölur Iceland 64°50N 19°25W 8 D4
Kladno Czech Rep. 50°10N 14°7E 16 C8
Klaeng Thailand 12°47N 101°39E 38 F3
Klagenfurt Austria 46°38N 14°20E 16 E8
Klaipėda Lithuania 55°43N 21°10E 9 J19
Klaksvík Færoe Is. 62°14N 6°35W 8 E9
Klamath → U.S.A. 41°33N 124°5W 76 F1
Klamath Falls U.S.A. 42°13N 121°46W 76 E3
Klamath Mts. U.S.A. 41°50N 123°20W 76 F2
Klamono Indonesia 1°8S 131°30E 37 E8
Klang Malaysia 3°2N 101°26E 39 L3
Klappan → Canada 58°0N 129°43W 70 B3
Klarälven → Sweden 59°23N 13°32E 9 G15
Klatovy Czech Rep. 49°23N 13°18E 16 D7
Klawer S. Africa 31°44S 18°36E 56 E2
Klazienaveen Neths. 52°44N 7°0E 15 B6
Kleena Kleene Canada 52°0N 124°59W 70 C4
Klein-Karas Namibia 27°33S 18°7E 56 D2
Klerksdorp S. Africa 26°53S 26°38E 56 D4
Kletsk = Klyetsk Belarus 53°5N 26°45E 17 B14
Kletskiy Russia 49°16N 43°11E 19 E7
Klickitat U.S.A. 45°49N 121°9W 76 D3
Klickitat → U.S.A. 45°42N 121°17W 78 E5
Klidhes Cyprus 35°42N 34°36E 25 D13
Klinaklini → Canada 51°21N 125°40W 70 C3
Klip → S. Africa 27°3S 29°3E 57 D4
Klipdale S. Africa 34°19S 19°57E 56 E2
Klipplaat S. Africa 33°1S 24°22E 56 E3
Kłodzko Poland 50°28N 16°38E 17 C9
Klong Wang Chao △
Thailand 16°20N 99°9E 38 D2
Klouto Togo 6°57N 0°44E 50 G6
Kluane △ Canada 60°45N 139°30W 70 A1
Kluane L. Canada 61°15N 138°40W 68 C6
Kluang Malaysia 2°3N 103°18E 39 L4
Kluczbork Poland 50°58N 18°12E 17 C10
Klukwan U.S.A. 59°24N 135°54W 70 B1
Klungkung Indonesia 8°32S 115°24E 37 K18
Klyetsk Belarus 53°5N 26°45E 17 B14
Klyuchevskaya, Gora
Russia 55°50N 160°30E 29 D17
Klyuchi Russia 56°18N 160°51E 29 D17
Knaresborough U.K. 54°1N 1°28W 12 C6
Knee L. Man., Canada 55°3N 94°45W 72 A1
Knee L. Sask., Canada 55°51N 107°0W 71 B7
Knight Inlet Canada 50°45N 125°40W 70 C3
Knighton U.K. 52°21N 3°3W 13 E4
Knights Ferry U.S.A. 37°50N 120°40W 78 H6
Knights Landing
U.S.A. 38°48N 121°43W 78 G5
Knob, C. Australia 34°32S 119°16E 61 F2
Knock Ireland 53°48N 8°55W 10 C3
Knockmealdown Mts.
Ireland 52°14N 7°56W 10 D4
Knokke-Heist Belgium 51°21N 3°17E 15 C3
Knossos Greece 35°16N 25°10E 25 D7
Knowlton Canada 45°13N 72°31W 83 A12
Knox U.S.A. 41°18N 86°37W 80 E10
Knox Coast Antarctica 66°30S 108°0E 5 C8
Knoxville Iowa, U.S.A. 41°19N 93°6W 80 E7
Knoxville Pa., U.S.A. 41°57N 77°27W 82 E7
Knoxville Tenn., U.S.A. 35°58N 83°55W 85 D13
Knud Rasmussen Land
Greenland 78°0N 60°0W 4 A5
Knysna S. Africa 34°2S 23°2E 56 E3
Ko Kha Thailand 18°11N 99°24E 38 C2
Ko Tarutao △ Thailand 6°31N 99°26E 39 J2
Ko Yao Thailand 8°7N 98°35E 39 a
Koartac = Quaqtaq
Canada 60°55N 69°40W 69 C13
Koba Indonesia 6°37S 134°37E 37 F8
Kobarid Slovenia 46°15N 13°30E 16 E7
Kobayashi Japan 31°56N 130°59E 31 J5
Kōbe Japan 34°41N 135°13E 31 G7
København Denmark 55°40N 12°26E 9 J15
Kōbi-Sho Japan 25°56N 123°41E 31 M1
Koblenz Germany 50°21N 7°36E 16 C4
Kobryn Belarus 52°15N 24°22E 17 B13
Kocaeli Turkey 40°45N 29°50E 19 F4
Kočani Macedonia 41°55N 22°25E 23 D10
Koch Bihar India 26°22N 89°29E 41 F16
Kochas India 25°15N 83°56E 43 G10
Kochi = Cochin India 9°58N 76°20E 40 Q10
Kōchi Japan 33°30N 133°35E 31 H6
Kōchi □ Japan 33°40N 133°30E 31 H6
Kochiu = Gejiu China 23°20N 103°10E 32 D5
Kodarma India 24°28N 85°36E 43 G11
Kodiak U.S.A. 57°47N 152°24W 74 a
Kodiak I. U.S.A. 57°30N 152°45W 74 a
Kodinar India 20°46N 70°46E 42 J4
Kodinsk Russia 58°40N 99°10E 29 D10
Koedoesberge S. Africa 32°40S 20°11E 56 E3
Koes Namibia 26°0S 19°15E 56 D2
Koffiefontein S. Africa 29°30S 25°0E 56 D4
Kofiau Indonesia 1°11S 129°50E 37 E7
Koforidua Ghana 6°3N 0°17W 50 G5
Kōfu Japan 35°40N 138°30E 31 G9
Koga Japan 36°11N 139°43E 31 F9
Kogaluc → Canada 56°12N 61°44W 73 A7
Køge Denmark 55°27N 12°11E 9 J15
Kogon Uzbekistan 39°43N 64°33E 28 F7
Koh-i-Khurd Afghan. 33°30N 65°59E 42 C1
Koh-i-Maran Pakistan 29°18N 66°50E 42 E2
Kohat Pakistan 33°40N 71°29E 42 C4
Kohima India 25°35N 94°10E 41 G19
Kohkīlūyeh va Būyer Aḥmadi □
Iran 31°30N 50°30E 45 D6
Kohler Ra. Antarctica 77°0S 110°0W 5 D15
Kohlu Pakistan 29°54N 69°15E 42 E3
Kohtla-Järve Estonia 59°20N 27°20E 9 G22
Koi Sanjaq Iraq 36°5N 44°38E 44 B5
Koillismaa Finland 65°44N 28°36E 8 D23
Koin N. Korea 40°28N 126°18E 35 D14
Kojŏ N. Korea 38°58N 127°58E 35 E14
Kojonup Australia 33°48S 117°10E 61 F2
Kojūr Iran 36°23N 51°43E 45 B6
Kokand = Qŭqon
Uzbekistan 40°31N 70°56E 28 E8
Kokas Indonesia 2°42S 132°26E 37 E8
Kokchetav = Kökshetaū
Kazakhstan 53°20N 69°25E 28 D7
Kokemäenjoki →
Finland 61°32N 21°44E 8 F19
Kokkola Finland 63°50N 23°8E 8 E20
Koko Kyunzu Burma 14°10N 93°25E 41 M18
Kokomo U.S.A. 40°29N 86°8W 80 E10
Koksan N. Korea 38°46N 126°40E 35 E14
Kökshetaū Kazakhstan 53°20N 69°25E 28 D7
Koksoak → Canada 58°30N 68°10W 69 D13
Kokstad S. Africa 30°32S 29°29E 57 E4
Kokubu Japan 31°44N 130°46E 31 J5
Kola Indonesia 5°35S 134°30E 37 F8
Kola Russia 68°45N 33°8E 8 B25
Kola Pen. = Kolskiy Poluostrov
Russia 67°30N 38°0E 18 A6
Kolachi → Pakistan 27°8N 67°2E 42 F2
Kolahoi India 34°12N 75°22E 43 B6
Kolaka Indonesia 4°3S 121°46E 37 E6
Kolar India 13°12N 78°15E 40 N11
Kolar Gold Fields India 12°58N 78°16E 40 N11
Kolaras India 25°14N 77°36E 42 G6
Kolari Finland 67°20N 23°48E 8 C20
Kolayat India 27°50N 72°50E 42 F5
Kolda Senegal 12°55N 14°57W 50 F3
Kolding Denmark 55°30N 9°29E 9 J13
Kolepom = Dolak, Pulau
Indonesia 8°0S 138°30E 37 F9
Kolguyev, Ostrov Russia 69°20N 48°30E 18 A8
Kolhapur India 16°43N 74°15E 40 L9
Kolimbia Greece 36°15N 28°10E 25 C10
Kolín Czech Rep. 50°2N 15°9E 16 C8
Kolkas rags Latvia 57°46N 22°37E 9 H20
Kolkata India 22°34N 88°21E 43 H13
Kollam = Quilon India 8°50N 76°38E 40 Q10
Kollum Neths. 53°17N 6°10E 15 A6
Kolmanskop Namibia 26°45S 15°14E 56 D2
Köln Germany 50°56N 6°57E 16 C4
Kolo Poland 52°14N 18°40E 17 B10
Kołobrzeg Poland 54°10N 15°35E 16 A8
Kolomna Russia 55°8N 38°45E 18 C6
Kolomyya Ukraine 48°31N 25°2E 17 D13
Kolonodale Indonesia 2°0S 121°19E 37 E6
Kolosib India 24°15N 92°45E 41 G18
Kolpashevo Russia 58°20N 83°5E 28 D9
Kolpino Russia 59°44N 30°39E 18 C5
Kolskiy Poluostrov
Russia 67°30N 38°0E 18 A6
Kolskiy Zaliv Russia 69°23N 34°0E 8 B26
Kolwezi
Dem. Rep. of the Congo 10°40S 25°25E 55 E2
Kolyma → Russia 69°30N 161°0E 29 C17
Kolymskoye Nagorye
Russia 63°0N 157°0E 29 C16
Kôm Ombo Egypt 24°25N 32°52E 51 D12
Komandorskiye Is. =
Komandorskiye Ostrova
Russia 55°0N 167°0E 29 D17
Komandorskiye Ostrova
Russia 55°0N 167°0E 29 D17
Komárno Slovak Rep. 47°49N 18°5E 17 E10
Komatipoort S. Africa 25°25S 31°55E 57 D5
Komatou Yialou Cyprus 35°25N 34°8E 25 D13
Komatsu Japan 36°25N 136°30E 31 F8
Komatsushima Japan 34°0N 134°35E 31 H7
Komi Cyprus 35°24N 34°0E 25 D13
Komi □ Russia 64°0N 55°0E 18 B10
Kommunarsk = Alchevsk
Ukraine 48°30N 38°45E 19 E6
Kommunizma, Pik = imeni Ismail
Samani, Pik Tajikistan 39°0N 72°2E 28 F8
Komodo Indonesia 8°37S 119°20E 37 F5
Komoran, Pulau
Indonesia 8°18S 138°45E 37 F9
Komoro Japan 36°19N 138°26E 31 F9
Komotini Greece 41°9N 25°26E 23 D11
Kompasberg S. Africa 31°45S 24°32E 56 E3
Kompong Cham
Cambodia 12°0N 105°30E 39 G5
Kompong Chhnang = Kampong
Chhnang Cambodia 12°20N 104°35E 39 F5
Kompong Chikreng
Cambodia 13°5N 104°18E 38 F5
Kompong Kleang
Cambodia 13°6N 104°8E 38 F5
Kompong Luong
Cambodia 11°49N 104°48E 39 G5
Kompong Pranak
Cambodia 13°35N 104°55E 38 F5
Kompong Som = Kampong Saom
Cambodia 10°38N 103°30E 39 G4
Kompong Som, Chhung =
Kampong Saom, Chaak
Cambodia 10°50N 103°32E 39 G4
Kompong Speu
Cambodia 11°26N 104°32E 39 G5
Kompong Sralau
Cambodia 14°5N 105°46E 38 E5
Kompong Thom
Cambodia 12°35N 104°51E 38 F5
Kompong Trabeck
Cambodia 13°6N 105°14E 38 F5
Kompong Trabeck
Cambodia 11°9N 105°28E 39 G5
Kompong Trach
Cambodia 11°25N 105°48E 39 G5
Kompong Tralach
Cambodia 11°54N 104°47E 39 G5
Komrat = Comrat
Moldova 46°18N 28°40E 17 E15
Komsberg S. Africa 32°40S 20°45E 56 E3
Komsomolets, Ostrov
Russia 80°30N 95°0E 29 A10
Komsomolsk-na-Amure
Russia 50°30N 137°0E 33 A8
Kon Tum Vietnam 14°24N 108°0E 38 E7
Kon Tum, Plateau du
Vietnam 14°30N 108°30E 38 E7
Konar □ Afghan. 34°30N 71°3E 40 B7
Konārī Iran 28°13N 51°36E 45 D6
Konch India 26°0N 79°10E 43 G8
Konde Tanzania 4°57S 39°45E 54 C4
Kondinin Australia 32°34S 118°8E 61 F2
Kondoa Tanzania 4°55S 35°50E 54 C4
Kondopaga Russia 62°12N 34°17E 18 B5
Kondratyevo Russia 57°22N 98°15E 29 D10
Köneürgench
Turkmenistan 42°19N 59°10E 28 E6
Konevo Russia 62°8N 39°20E 18 B6
Kong = Khong →
Cambodia 13°32N 105°58E 38 F5
Kong Ivory C. 8°54N 4°36W 50 G5
Kong, Koh Cambodia 11°20N 103°0E 39 G4
Kong Christian IX Land
Greenland 68°0N 36°0W 4 C6
Kong Christian X Land
Greenland 74°0N 29°0W 4 B6
Kong Frederik IX Land
Greenland 67°0N 52°0W 4 C5
Kong Frederik VI Kyst
Greenland 63°0N 43°0W 4 C5
Kong Frederik VIII Land
Greenland 78°30N 26°0W 4 B6
Kong Oscar Fjord
Greenland 72°20N 24°0W 4 B6
Konglu Burma 27°13N 97°57E 41 F20
Kongola Namibia 17°45S 23°20E 56 B3
Kongolo Kasai-Or.,
Dem. Rep. of the Congo 5°26S 24°49E 54 D1
Kongolo Katanga,
Dem. Rep. of the Congo 5°22S 27°0E 54 D2
Kongsberg Norway 59°39N 9°39E 9 G13
Kongsvinger Norway 60°12N 12°2E 9 F15
Kongur Shan China 38°34N 75°18E 32 C2
Kongwa Tanzania 6°11S 36°26E 54 D4
Koni
Dem. Rep. of the Congo 10°40S 27°11E 55 E2
Koni, Mts.
Dem. Rep. of the Congo 10°36S 27°10E 55 E2
Konin Poland 52°12N 18°15E 17 B10
Konjic Bos.-H. 43°42N 17°58E 23 C7
Konkiep Namibia 26°49S 17°15E 56 D2
Konosha Russia 61°0N 40°5E 18 B7
Kōnosu Japan 36°3N 139°31E 31 F9
Konotop Ukraine 51°12N 33°7E 19 D5
Konqi He → China 41°0N 86°0E 32 B3
Końskie Poland 51°15N 20°23E 17 C11
Konstanz Germany 47°40N 9°10E 16 E5
Kont Iran 26°55N 61°50E 45 E9

Kontagora Nigeria 10°23N 5°27E 50 F7
Kontiolahti Finland 62°46N 29°50E 8 E23
Kontokali Greece 39°38N 19°51E 25 A3
Konya Turkey 37°52N 32°35E 44 B2
Konza Kenya 1°45S 37°7E 54 C4
Koocanusa, L. Canada 49°20N 115°15W 76 B6
Kookynie Australia 29°17S 121°22E 61 E3
Koolyanobbing Australia 30°48S 119°36E 61 F2
Koonibba Australia 31°54S 133°25E 63 E1
Koorawatha Australia 34°2S 148°33E 63 E4
Koorda Australia 30°48S 117°35E 61 F2
Kooskia U.S.A. 46°9N 115°59W 76 C6
Kootenay → U.S.A. 49°19N 117°39W 70 D5
Kootenay △ Canada 51°0N 116°0W 70 C5
Kootenay L. Canada 49°45N 116°50W 76 B5
Kootjieskolk S. Africa 31°15S 20°21E 56 E3
Kopaonik Serbia 43°10N 20°50E 23 C9
Kópavogur Iceland 64°6N 21°55W 8 D3
Koper Slovenia 45°31N 13°44E 16 F7
Kopervik Norway 59°17N 5°17E 9 G11
Kopet Dagh Asia 38°0N 58°0E 45 B8
Kopi Australia 33°24S 135°40E 63 E2
Köping Sweden 59°31N 16°3E 9 G17
Koppeh Dāgh = Kopet Dagh Asia 38°0N 58°0E 45 B8
Koppies S. Africa 27°20S 27°30E 57 D4
Koprivnica Croatia 46°12N 16°45E 22 A7
Köprülü △ Turkey 37°20N 31°5E 44 B1
Kopychyntsi Ukraine 49°7N 25°58E 17 D13
Kora △ Kenya 0°14S 38°44E 54 C4
Korab Macedonia 41°44N 20°40E 23 D9
Koral India 21°50N 73°12E 42 J5
Korba India 22°20N 82°45E 43 H10
Korbu, G. Malaysia 4°41N 101°18E 39 K3
Korçë Albania 40°37N 20°50E 23 D9
Korčula Croatia 42°56N 16°57E 22 C7
Kord Küy Iran 36°48N 54°7E 45 B7
Kord Sheykh Iran 28°31N 52°53E 45 D7
Kordestān □ Iran 36°0N 47°0E 44 C5
Kordofân Sudan 13°0N 29°0E 51 F11
Korea, North ■ Asia 40°0N 127°0E 35 E14
Korea, South ■ Asia 36°0N 128°0E 35 G15
Korea Bay Korea 39°0N 124°0E 35 E13
Korea Strait Asia 34°0N 129°30E 35 H15
Korets Ukraine 50°40N 27°5E 17 C14
Korhogo Ivory C. 9°29N 5°28W 50 G4
Korinthiakos Kolpos Greece 38°16N 22°30E 23 E10
Korinthos Greece 37°56N 22°55E 23 F10
Korissia, L. Greece 39°27N 19°53E 25 B3
Kōriyama Japan 37°24N 140°23E 30 F10
Korla China 41°45N 86°4E 32 B3
Kormakiti, C. Cyprus 35°23N 32°56E 25 D11
Korneshty = Corneşti Moldova 47°21N 28°1E 17 E15
Koro Fiji 17°19S 179°23E 59 a
Koro Ivory C. 8°32N 7°30W 50 G4
Koro Sea Fiji 17°30S 179°45W 59 a
Korogwe Tanzania 5°5S 38°25E 54 D4
Korolevu Fiji 18°12S 177°46E 59 a
Koronadal Phil. 6°12N 125°1E 37 C6
Koror Palau 7°20N 134°28E 64 G5
Körös → Hungary 46°43N 20°12E 17 E11
Korosten Ukraine 50°54N 28°36E 17 C15
Korostyshev Ukraine 50°19N 29°4E 17 C15
Korovou Fiji 17°47S 178°32E 59 a
Koroyanitu △ Fiji 17°40S 177°35E 59 a
Korraraika, Helodranon' i Madag. 17°45S 43°57E 57 B7
Korsakov Russia 46°36N 142°42E 29 E15
Korshunovo Russia 58°37N 110°10E 29 D12
Korsør Denmark 55°20N 11°9E 9 J14
Kortrijk Belgium 50°50N 3°17E 15 D3
Korwai India 24°7N 78°5E 42 G8
Koryakskoye Nagorye Russia 61°0N 171°0E 29 C18
Kos Greece 36°50N 27°15E 23 F12
Kosan N. Korea 38°52N 127°25E 35 E14
Koschagyl Kazakhstan 46°40N 54°0E 19 E9
Kościan Poland 52°5N 16°40E 17 B9
Kosciusko U.S.A. 33°4N 89°35W 85 E10
Kosciuszko, Mt. Australia 36°27S 148°16E 63 F4
Kosha Sudan 20°50N 30°30E 51 D12
K'oshih = Kashi China 39°30N 76°2E 32 C2
Koshiki-Rettō Japan 31°45N 129°49E 31 J4
Kosi India 27°48N 77°29E 42 F7
Kosi → India 28°41N 78°57E 43 E8
Košice Slovak Rep. 48°42N 21°15E 17 D11
Koskinou Greece 36°23N 28°13E 25 C10
Koslan Russia 63°34N 49°14E 18 B8
Kosŏng N. Korea 38°40N 128°22E 35 E15
Kosovo □ Serbia 42°30N 21°0E 23 C9
Kosovska Mitrovica Serbia 42°54N 20°52E 23 C9
Kossou, L. de Ivory C. 6°59N 5°31W 50 G4
Koster S. Africa 25°52S 26°54E 56 D4
Kôstî Sudan 13°8N 32°43E 51 F12
Kostopil Ukraine 50°51N 26°22E 17 C14
Kostroma Russia 57°50N 40°58E 18 C7
Kostrzyn Poland 52°35N 14°39E 16 B8
Koszalin Poland 54°11N 16°8E 16 A9
Kot Addu Pakistan 30°30N 71°0E 42 D4
Kot Kapura India 30°35N 74°50E 42 D6
Kot Moman Pakistan 32°13N 73°0E 42 C5
Kot Sultan Pakistan 30°46N 70°56E 42 D4
Kota India 25°14N 75°49E 42 G6
Kota Barrage India 25°6N 75°51E 42 G6
Kota Belud Malaysia 6°21N 116°26E 36 C5
Kota Bharu Malaysia 6°7N 102°14E 39 J4
Kota Kinabalu Malaysia 6°0N 116°4E 36 C5
Kota Tinggi Malaysia 1°44N 103°53E 39 M4
Kotaagung Indonesia 5°38S 104°29E 36 F2
Kotabaru Indonesia 3°20S 116°20E 36 E5
Kotabumi Indonesia 4°49S 104°54E 36 E2
Kotamobagu Indonesia 0°57N 124°31E 37 D6
Kotapinang Indonesia 1°53N 100°5E 39 M3
Kotcho L. Canada 59°7N 121°12W 70 B4
Kotdwara India 29°45N 78°32E 43 E8
Kotelnich Russia 58°22N 48°24E 18 C8
Kotelnikovo Russia 47°38N 43°8E 19 E7
Kotelnyy, Ostrov Russia 75°10N 139°0E 29 B14
Kothari → India 25°20N 75°4E 42 G6
Kothi Chhattisgarh, India 23°21N 82°3E 43 H10
Kothi Mad. P., India 24°45N 80°40E 43 G9
Kotiro Pakistan 26°17N 67°13E 42 F2
Kotka Finland 60°28N 26°58E 8 F22
Kotlas Russia 61°17N 46°43E 18 B8
Kotli Pakistan 33°30N 73°55E 42 C5
Kotma India 23°12N 81°58E 43 H9
Kotor Montenegro 42°25N 18°47E 23 C8
Kotovsk Ukraine 47°45N 29°35E 17 E15
Kotputli India 27°43N 76°12E 42 F7
Kotri Pakistan 25°22N 68°22E 42 G3
Kotto → C.A.R. 4°14N 22°2E 52 D4
Kotturu India 14°45N 76°10E 40 M10
Kotu Group Tonga 20°0S 174°45W 59 c
Kotuy → Russia 71°54N 102°6E 29 B11
Kotzebue U.S.A. 66°53N 162°39W 74 a
Kotzebue Sound U.S.A. 66°20N 163°0W 66 C3
Kouchibouguac △ Canada 46°50N 65°0W 73 C6
Koudougou Burkina Faso 12°10N 2°20W 50 F5
Koufonisi Greece 34°56N 26°8E 25 E8
Kougaberge S. Africa 33°48S 23°50E 56 E3
Kouilou → Congo 4°10S 12°5E 52 E2
Koula Moutou Gabon 1°15S 12°25E 52 E2
Koulen = Kulen Cambodia 13°50N 104°40E 38 F5
Kouloura Greece 39°42N 19°54E 25 A3
Koumala Australia 21°38S 149°15E 62 C4
Koumra Chad 8°50N 17°35E 51 G9
Kountze U.S.A. 30°22N 94°19W 84 F7
Kouris → Cyprus 34°38N 32°54E 25 E11
Kourou Fr. Guiana 5°9N 52°39W 93 B8
Kouroussa Guinea 10°45N 9°45W 50 F4
Kousseri Cameroon 12°0N 14°55E 51 F8
Koutiala Mali 12°25N 5°23W 50 F4
Kouvola Finland 60°52N 26°43E 8 F22
Kovdor Russia 67°34N 30°24E 8 C24
Kovel Ukraine 51°11N 24°38E 17 C13
Kovrov Russia 56°25N 41°25E 18 C7
Kowanyama Australia 15°29S 141°44E 62 B3
Kowloon China 22°19N 114°11E 33 G11
Kowŏn N. Korea 39°26N 127°14E 35 E14
Koyampattur = Coimbatore India 11°2N 76°59E 40 P10
Köyceğiz Turkey 36°57N 28°40E 23 F13
Koyukuk → U.S.A. 64°55N 157°32W 66 C4
Koza = Okinawa Japan 26°19N 127°46E 31 L3
Kozan Turkey 37°26N 35°50E 44 B2
Kozani Greece 40°19N 21°47E 23 D9
Kozhikode = Calicut India 11°15N 75°43E 40 P9
Kozhva Russia 65°10N 57°0E 18 A10
Kozyatyn Ukraine 49°45N 28°50E 17 D15
Kozyrevsk Russia 56°3N 159°51E 29 D16
Kpalimé Togo 6°57N 0°44E 50 G6
Kra, Isthmus of = Kra, Kho Khot Thailand 10°15N 99°30E 39 G2
Kra, Kho Khot Thailand 10°15N 99°30E 39 G2
Kra Buri Thailand 10°22N 98°46E 39 G2
Kraai → S. Africa 30°40S 26°45E 56 E4
Krabi Thailand 8°4N 98°55E 39 H2
Kracheh Cambodia 12°32N 106°10E 38 F6
Kragan Indonesia 6°43S 111°38E 37 G14
Kragerø Norway 58°52N 9°25E 9 G13
Kragujevac Serbia 44°2N 20°56E 23 B9
Krakatau = Rakata, Pulau Indonesia 6°10S 105°20E 36 F3
Krakatoa = Rakata, Pulau Indonesia 6°10S 105°20E 36 F3
Krakor Cambodia 12°32N 104°12E 38 F5
Kraków Poland 50°4N 19°57E 17 C10
Kralanh Cambodia 13°35N 103°25E 38 F4
Kraljevo Serbia 43°44N 20°41E 23 C9
Kramatorsk Ukraine 48°50N 37°30E 19 E6
Kramfors Sweden 62°55N 17°48E 8 E17
Kranj Slovenia 46°16N 14°22E 16 E8
Krankskop S. Africa 28°0S 30°47E 57 D5
Krasavino Russia 60°58N 46°29E 18 B8
Kraskino Russia 42°44N 130°48E 30 C5
Kraśnik Poland 50°55N 22°15E 17 C12
Krasnoarmeysk Russia 51°0N 45°42E 28 D5
Krasnodar Russia 45°5N 39°0E 19 E6
Krasnokamensk Russia 50°3N 118°0E 29 D12
Krasnokamsk Russia 58°4N 55°48E 18 C10
Krasnoperekopsk Ukraine 46°0N 33°54E 19 E5
Krasnorechenskiy Russia 44°41N 135°14E 30 B7
Krasnoselkup Russia 65°20N 82°10E 28 C9
Krasnoturinsk Russia 59°46N 60°12E 18 C11
Krasnoufimsk Russia 56°36N 57°38E 18 C10
Krasnouralsk Russia 58°21N 60°3E 18 C11
Krasnovishersk Russia 60°23N 57°3E 18 B10
Krasnoyarsk Russia 56°8N 93°0E 29 D10
Krasnyy Kut Russia 50°50N 47°0E 19 D8
Krasnyy Luch Ukraine 48°13N 39°0E 19 E6
Krasnyy Yar Russia 46°43N 48°23E 19 E8
Kratie = Kracheh Cambodia 12°32N 106°10E 38 F6
Krau Indonesia 3°19S 140°5E 37 E10
Kravanh, Chuor Phnum Cambodia 12°0N 103°32E 39 G4
Krefeld Germany 51°20N 6°33E 16 C4
Kremen Croatia 44°28N 15°53E 16 F8
Kremenchuk Ukraine 49°5N 33°25E 19 E5
Kremenchuksk Vdskh. Ukraine 49°20N 32°30E 19 E5
Kremenets Ukraine 50°8N 25°43E 17 C13
Kremmling U.S.A. 40°4N 106°24W 76 F10
Krems Austria 48°25N 15°36E 16 D8
Kretinga Lithuania 55°53N 21°15E 9 J19
Kribi Cameroon 2°57N 9°56E 52 D1
Krichev = Krychaw Belarus 53°40N 31°41E 17 B16
Kril'on, Mys Russia 45°53N 142°5E 30 B11
Krios, Akra Greece 35°13N 23°34E 25 D5
Krishna → India 15°57N 80°59E 41 M12
Krishnanagar India 23°24N 88°33E 43 H13
Kristiansand Norway 58°8N 8°1E 9 G13
Kristianstad Sweden 56°2N 14°9E 9 H16
Kristiansund Norway 63°7N 7°45E 8 E12
Kristiinankaupunki Finland 62°16N 21°21E 8 E19
Kristinehamn Sweden 59°18N 14°7E 9 G16
Kristinestad = Kristiinankaupunki Finland 62°16N 21°21E 8 E19
Kriti Greece 35°15N 25°0E 25 D7
Kritsa Greece 35°10N 25°41E 25 D7
Krivoy Rog = Kryvyy Rih Ukraine 47°51N 33°20E 19 E5
Krk Croatia 45°8N 14°40E 16 F8
Krokodil = Umgwenya → Mozam. 25°14S 32°18E 57 D5
Krong Kaoh Kong Cambodia 11°37N 102°59E 39 G4
Kronprins Olav Kyst Antarctica 69°0S 42°0E 5 C5
Kronprinsesse Märtha Kyst Antarctica 73°30S 10°0W 5 D2
Kronshtadt Russia 59°57N 29°51E 18 B4
Kroonstad S. Africa 27°43S 27°19E 56 D4
Kropotkin Russia 45°28N 40°28E 19 E7
Krosno Poland 49°42N 21°46E 17 D11
Krotoszyn Poland 51°42N 17°23E 17 C9
Krousonas Greece 35°13N 24°59E 25 D6
Kruger △ S. Africa 24°50S 26°10E 57 C5
Krugersdorp S. Africa 26°5S 27°46E 57 D4
Kruisfontein S. Africa 33°59S 24°43E 56 E3
Krung Thep = Bangkok Thailand 13°45N 100°35E 38 F3
Krupki Belarus 54°19N 29°8E 17 A15
Kruševac Serbia 43°35N 21°28E 23 C9
Krychaw Belarus 53°40N 31°41E 17 B16
Krymskiy Poluostrov = Krymskyy Pivostriv Ukraine 45°0N 34°0E 19 F5
Krymskyy Pivostriv Ukraine 45°0N 34°0E 19 F5
Kryvyy Rih Ukraine 47°51N 33°20E 19 E5
Ksar el Kebir Morocco 35°0N 6°0W 50 B4
Ksar es Souk = Er Rachidia Morocco 31°58N 4°20W 50 B5
Kuah Malaysia 6°19N 99°51E 39 J2
Kuala Belait Malaysia 4°35N 114°11E 36 D4
Kuala Berang Malaysia 5°5N 103°1E 39 K4
Kuala Dungun = Dungun Malaysia 4°45N 103°25E 39 K4
Kuala Kangsar Malaysia 4°46N 100°56E 39 K3
Kuala Kelawang Malaysia 2°56N 102°5E 39 L4
Kuala Kerai Malaysia 5°30N 102°12E 39 K4
Kuala Kerian Malaysia 5°10N 100°25E 39 c
Kuala Kubu Bharu Malaysia 3°34N 101°39E 39 L3
Kuala Lipis Malaysia 4°10N 102°3E 39 K4
Kuala Lumpur Malaysia 3°9N 101°41E 39 L3
Kuala Nerang Malaysia 6°16N 100°37E 39 J3
Kuala Pilah Malaysia 2°45N 102°15E 39 L4
Kuala Rompin Malaysia 2°49N 103°29E 39 L4
Kuala Selangor Malaysia 3°20N 101°15E 39 L3
Kuala Sepetang Malaysia 4°49N 100°28E 39 K3
Kuala Terengganu Malaysia 5°20N 103°8E 39 K4
Kualajelai Indonesia 2°58S 110°46E 36 E4
Kualakapuas Indonesia 2°55S 114°20E 36 E4
Kualakurun Indonesia 1°10S 113°50E 36 E4
Kualapembuang Indonesia 3°14S 112°38E 36 E4
Kualasimpang Indonesia 4°17N 98°3E 36 D1
Kuancheng China 40°37N 118°30E 35 D10
Kuandang Indonesia 0°56N 123°1E 37 D6
Kuandian China 40°45N 124°45E 35 D13
Kuangchou = Guangzhou China 23°6N 113°13E 33 D6
Kuantan Malaysia 3°49N 103°20E 39 L4
Kuba = Quba Azerbaijan 41°21N 48°32E 19 F8
Kuban → Russia 45°20N 37°30E 19 E6
Kubokawa Japan 33°12N 133°8E 31 H6
Kubu Indonesia 8°16S 115°35E 37 J18
Kubutambahan Indonesia 8°5S 115°10E 37 J18
Kucar, Tanjung Indonesia 8°39S 114°34E 37 K18
Kuchaman India 27°13N 74°47E 42 F6
Kuchinda India 21°44N 84°21E 43 J11
Kuching Malaysia 1°33N 110°25E 36 D4
Kuchino-eruba-Jima Japan 30°28N 130°12E 31 J5
Kuchino-Shima Japan 29°57N 129°55E 31 K4
Kuchinotsu Japan 32°36N 130°11E 31 H5
Kucing = Kuching Malaysia 1°33N 110°25E 36 D4
Kud → Pakistan 26°5N 66°20E 42 F2
Kuda India 23°10N 71°15E 42 H4
Kudat Malaysia 6°55N 116°55E 36 C5
Kudus Indonesia 6°48S 110°51E 37 G14
Kudymkar Russia 59°1N 54°39E 18 C9
Kueiyang = Guiyang China 26°32N 106°40E 32 D5
Kufra Oasis = Al Kufrah Libya 24°17N 23°15E 51 D10
Kufstein Austria 47°35N 12°11E 16 E7
Kugaaruk = Pelly Bay Canada 68°38N 89°50W 69 C11
Kugluktuk Canada 67°50N 115°5W 68 C8
Kugong I. Canada 56°18N 79°50W 72 A4
Kūh Dasht Iran 33°32N 47°36E 44 C5
Kūh-e-Jebāl Bārez Iran 29°0N 58°0E 45 D8
Kūhak Iran 27°12N 63°10E 45 E9
Kuhan Pakistan 28°19N 67°14E 42 E2
Kūhbonān Iran 31°23N 56°19E 45 D8
Kūhestak Iran 26°47N 57°2E 45 E8
Kuhin Iran 36°22N 49°40E 45 B6
Kūhīrī Iran 26°55N 61°2E 45 E9
Kuhmo Finland 64°7N 29°31E 8 D23
Kūhpāyeh Eşfahan, Iran 32°44N 52°20E 45 C7
Kūhpāyeh Kermān, Iran 30°35N 57°15E 45 D8
Kūhrān, Kūh-e Iran 26°46N 58°12E 45 E8
Kui Buri Thailand 12°3N 99°52E 39 F2
Kuichong China 22°38N 114°25E 33 F11
Kuiseb → Namibia 22°59S 14°31E 56 C1
Kuito Angola 12°22S 16°55E 53 G3
Kuiu I. U.S.A. 57°45N 134°10W 70 B2
Kujang N. Korea 39°57N 126°1E 35 E14
Kuji Japan 40°11N 141°46E 30 D10
Kujū-San Japan 33°5N 131°15E 31 H5
Kukës Albania 42°5N 20°27E 23 C9
Kukup Malaysia 1°20N 103°27E 39 d
Kukup, Pulau Malaysia 1°18N 103°25E 39 d
Kula Turkey 38°32N 28°40E 23 E13
K'ula Shan Bhutan 28°14N 90°36E 32 C4
Kulachi Pakistan 31°56N 70°27E 42 D4
Kulai Malaysia 1°44N 103°35E 39 M4
Kulasekarappattinam India 8°20N 78°5E 40 Q11
Kuldīga Latvia 56°58N 21°59E 9 H19
Kulen Cambodia 13°50N 104°40E 38 F5
Kulgam India 33°36N 75°2E 43 C6
Kulgera Australia 25°50S 133°18E 62 D1
Kulim Malaysia 5°22N 100°34E 39 K3
Kulin Australia 32°40S 118°2E 61 F2
Kulkayu = Hartley Bay Canada 53°25N 129°15W 70 C3
Kullu India 31°58N 77°6E 42 D7
Kŭlob Tajikistan 37°55N 69°50E 28 F7
Kulsary = Qulsary Kazakhstan 46°59N 54°1E 19 E9
Kulti India 23°43N 86°50E 43 H12
Kulunda Russia 52°35N 78°57E 28 D8
Kulungar Afghan. 34°0N 69°2E 42 C3
Kūlvand Iran 31°21N 54°35E 45 D7
Kulwin Australia 35°2S 142°42E 63 F3
Kulyab = Kŭlob Tajikistan 37°55N 69°50E 28 F7
Kuma → Russia 44°55N 47°0E 19 F8
Kumaganum Nigeria 13°8N 10°38E 51 F8
Kumagaya Japan 36°9N 139°22E 31 F9
Kumai Indonesia 2°44S 111°43E 36 E4
Kumamba, Kepulauan Indonesia 1°36S 138°45E 37 E9
Kumamoto Japan 32°45N 130°45E 31 H5
Kumamoto □ Japan 32°55N 130°55E 31 H5
Kumanovo Macedonia 42°9N 21°42E 23 C9
Kumara N.Z. 42°37S 171°12E 59 E3
Kumarina Roadhouse Australia 24°41S 119°32E 61 D2
Kumasi Ghana 6°41N 1°38W 50 G5
Kumba Cameroon 4°36N 9°24E 52 D1
Kumbakonam India 10°58N 79°25E 40 P11
Kumbarilla Australia 27°15S 150°55E 63 D5
Kumbhraj India 24°22N 77°3E 42 G7
Kumbia Australia 26°41S 151°39E 63 D5
Kŭmch'ŏn N. Korea 38°10N 126°29E 35 E14
Kumdok India 33°32N 78°10E 43 C8
Kume-Shima Japan 26°20N 126°47E 31 L3
Kumertau Russia 52°45N 55°57E 18 D10
Kumharsain India 31°19N 77°27E 42 D7
Kumi Uganda 1°30N 33°58E 54 B3
Kumo Nigeria 10°1N 11°12E 51 F8
Kumo älv = Kokemäenjoki → Finland 61°32N 21°44E 8 F19
Kumon Bum Burma 26°30N 97°15E 41 F20
Kumtag Shamo China 39°40N 92°0E 32 C4
Kunashir, Ostrov Russia 44°0N 146°0E 29 E15
Kunda Estonia 59°30N 26°34E 9 G22
Kunda India 25°43N 81°31E 43 G9
Kundar → Pakistan 31°56N 69°19E 42 D3
Kundelungu △ Dem. Rep. of the Congo 10°30S 27°40E 55 E2
Kundelungu Ouest △ Dem. Rep. of the Congo 9°55S 27°17E 55 D2
Kundian Pakistan 32°27N 71°28E 42 C4
Kundla India 21°21N 71°25E 42 J4
Kung, Ao Thailand 8°5N 98°24E 39 a
Kunga → Bangla. 21°46N 89°30E 43 J13
Kunghit I. Canada 52°6N 131°3W 70 C2
Kungrad = Qŭnghirot Uzbekistan 43°2N 58°50E 28 E6
Kungsbacka Sweden 57°30N 12°5E 9 H15
Kungur Russia 57°25N 56°57E 18 C10
Kungurri Australia 21°4S 148°45E 62 K6
Kunhar → Pakistan 34°20N 73°30E 43 B5
Kuningan Indonesia 6°59S 108°29E 37 G13
Kunlong Burma 23°20N 98°50E 41 H21
Kunlun Shan Asia 36°0N 86°30E 32 C3
Kunming China 25°1N 102°41E 32 D5
Kununurra Australia 15°40S 128°50E 60 C4
Kunwari → India 26°26N 79°11E 43 F8
Kunya-Urgench = Köneürgench Turkmenistan 42°19N 59°10E 28 E6
Kuopio Finland 62°53N 27°35E 8 E22
Kupa → Croatia 45°28N 16°24E 16 F9
Kupang Indonesia 10°19S 123°39E 37 F6
Kupreanof I. U.S.A. 56°50N 133°30W 70 B2
Kupyansk-Uzlovoi Ukraine 49°40N 37°43E 19 E6
Kuqa China 41°35N 82°30E 32 B3
Kür → Azerbaijan 39°29N 49°15E 19 G8
Kür Dili Azerbaijan 39°3N 49°13E 45 B6
Kura = Kür → Azerbaijan 39°29N 49°15E 19 G8
Kuranda Australia 16°48S 145°35E 62 B4
Kuranga India 22°4N 69°10E 42 H3
Kurashiki Japan 34°40N 133°50E 31 G6
Kurayn Si. Arabia 27°39N 49°50E 45
Kurayoshi Japan 35°26N 133°50E 31
Kŭrchatov Kazakhstan 50°45N 78°32E 28
Kŭrdzhali Bulgaria 41°38N 25°21E 23
Kure Japan 34°14N 132°32E 31
Kuressaare Estonia 58°15N 22°30E 9
Kurgan Russia 55°26N 65°18E 28
Kuri India 26°37N 70°43E 42
Kuria Maria Is. = Hallāniyat, Jazā'ir al Oman 17°30N 55°58E 47
Kuridala Australia 21°16S 140°29E 62
Kurigram Bangla. 25°49N 89°39E 41
Kurikka Finland 62°36N 22°24E 8
Kuril Basin Pac. Oc. 47°0N 150°0E 4
Kuril Is. = Kurilskiye Ostrova Russia 45°0N 150°0E 29
Kuril-Kamchatka Trench Pac. Oc. 44°0N 153°0E 64
Kurilsk Russia 45°14N 147°53E 29
Kurilskiye Ostrova Russia 45°0N 150°0E 29
Kurino Japan 31°57N 130°43E 3
Kurinskaya Kosa = Kür Dili Azerbaijan 39°3N 49°13E 45
Kurnool India 15°45N 78°0E 40
Kuro-Shima Kagoshima, Japan 30°50N 129°57E 3
Kuro-Shima Okinawa, Japan 24°14N 124°1E 31
Kurow N.Z. 44°44S 170°29E 5
Kurram → Pakistan 32°36N 71°20E 4
Kurri Kurri Australia 32°50S 151°28E 6
Kurrimine Australia 17°47S 146°6E 6
Kurshskiy Zaliv Russia 55°9N 21°6E 9
Kursk Russia 51°42N 36°11E 1
Kuruçay Turkey 39°39N 38°29E 4
Kuruktag China 41°0N 89°0E 3
Kuruman S. Africa 27°28S 23°28E 5
Kuruman → S. Africa 26°56S 20°39E 5
Kurume Japan 33°15N 130°30E 3
Kurunegala Sri Lanka 7°30N 80°23E 40
Kurya Russia 61°42N 57°9E 18
Kus Gölü Turkey 40°10N 27°55E 23
Kuşadası Turkey 37°52N 27°15E 23
Kusamba Indonesia 8°34S 115°27E 37
Kusatsu Japan 36°37N 138°36E 3
Kusawa L. Canada 60°20N 136°13W 7
Kushalgarh India 23°10N 74°27E 4
Kushikino Japan 31°44N 130°16E 3
Kushima Japan 31°29N 131°14E 3
Kushimoto Japan 33°28N 135°47E 3
Kushiro Japan 43°0N 144°25E 30
Kushiro-Gawa → Japan 42°59N 144°23E 30
Kushiro Shitsugen △ Japan 43°9N 144°26E 30
Kūshk Iran 28°46N 56°51E 4
Kushka = Serhetabat Turkmenistan 35°20N 62°18E 4
Kushol India 33°40N 76°36E 4
Kushtia Bangla. 23°55N 89°5E 41
Kushva Russia 58°18N 59°45E 18
Kuskokwim → U.S.A. 60°5N 162°25W 6
Kuskokwim B. U.S.A. 59°45N 162°25W
Kusmi India 23°17N 83°55E 43
Kusŏng N. Korea 39°59N 125°15E 35
Kussharo-Ko Japan 43°38N 144°21E 30
Kustanay = Qostanay Kazakhstan 53°10N 63°35E 2
Kut, Ko Thailand 11°40N 102°35E 3
Kuta Indonesia 8°43S 115°11E 37
Kütahya Turkey 39°30N 30°2E 1
Kutaisi Georgia 42°19N 42°40E 1
Kutaraja = Banda Aceh Indonesia 5°35N 95°20E 3
Kutch, Gulf of = Kachchh, Gulf of India 22°50N 69°15E 4
Kutch, Rann of = Kachchh, Rann of India 24°0N 70°0E 4
Kutiyana India 21°36N 70°2E
Kutno Poland 52°15N 19°23E 1
Kutse Botswana 21°7S 22°16E 5
Kuttabul Australia 21°1S 148°54E 6
Kutu Dem. Rep. of the Congo 2°40S 18°11E 5
Kutum Sudan 14°10N 24°40E 5
Kuujjuaq Canada 58°6N 68°15W 6
Kuujjuarapik Canada 55°20N 77°35W
Kuusamo Finland 65°57N 29°8E 8
Kuusankoski Finland 60°55N 26°38E
Kuwait = Al Kuwayt Kuwait 29°30N 48°0E 4
Kuwait ■ Asia 29°30N 47°30E 4
Kuwana Japan 35°5N 136°43E
Kuwana → India 26°25N 83°15E 4
Kuybyshev = Samara Russia 53°8N 50°6E
Kuybyshev Russia 55°27N 78°19E
Kuybyshevskoye Vdkhr. Russia 55°2N 49°30E
Kuye He → China 38°23N 110°46E
Kūyeh Iran 38°45N 47°57E
Kuyto, Ozero Russia 65°6N 31°20E
Kuyumba Russia 60°58N 96°59E 2
Kuzey Anadolu Dağları Turkey 41°0N 36°45E
Kuznetsk Russia 53°12N 46°40E
Kuzomen Russia 66°22N 36°50E
Kvænangen Norway 70°5N 21°15E
Kvaløya Norway 69°40N 18°30E
Kvarner Croatia 44°50N 14°10E
Kvarnerič Croatia 44°43N 14°37E
Kwabhaca S. Africa 30°51S 29°0E
Kwajalein Marshall Is. 9°5N 167°20E
Kwakhanai Botswana 21°39S 21°16E
Kwakoegron Suriname 5°12N 55°25W
Kwale Kenya 4°15S 39°31E
KwaMashu S. Africa 29°45S 30°58E

vando → Africa 18°27S 23°32E 56 B3
vangchow = Guangzhou
China 23°6N 113°13E 33 D6
vango →
Dem. Rep. of the Congo 3°14S 17°22E 52 E3
vangsi-Chuang = Guangxi
Zhuangzu Zizhiqu □
China 24°0N 109°0E 33 D5
vangtung = Guangdong □
China 23°0N 113°0E 33 D6
vataboahegan →
Canada 51°9N 80°50W 72 B3
vatisore Indonesia 3°18S 134°50E 37 E8
vaZulu Natal □ S. Africa 29°0S 30°0E 57 D5
veichow = Guizhou □
China 27°0N 107°0E 32 D5
vekwe Zimbabwe 18°58S 29°48E 55 F2
vidzyn Poland 53°44N 18°55E 17 B10
vilu →
Dem. Rep. of the Congo 3°22S 17°22E 52 E3
vinana Australia 32°15S 115°47E 61 F2
voka Indonesia 0°31S 132°27E 37 E8
vun Tong China 22°19N 114°13E 33 G11
abra Cr. → Australia 25°36S 142°55E 63 D3
abram Australia 36°19S 145°4E 63 F4
aikto Burma 17°20N 97°3E 38 D1
akhta Russia 50°30N 106°25E 29 D11
ambura ⌂ Uganda 0°7S 30°9E 54 C3
ancutta Australia 33°8S 135°33E 63 E2
aukpadaung Burma 20°52N 95°8E 41 J19
aukpyu Burma 19°28N 93°30E 41 K18
aukse Burma 21°36N 96°10E 41 J20
burz U.S.A. 38°47N 120°18W 78 G6
elang India 32°35N 77°2E 42 C7
enjojo Uganda 0°40N 30°37E 54 B3
le Canada 50°50N 108°2W 71 C7
le Dam Zimbabwe 20°15S 31°0E 55 G3
le of Lochalsh U.K. 57°17N 5°44W 11 D3
mijoki → Finland 60°30N 26°55E 8 F22
mmene älv = Kymijoki →
Finland 60°30N 26°55E 8 F22
neton Australia 37°10S 144°29E 63 F3
nuna Australia 21°37S 141°55E 62 C3
ō-ga-Saki Japan 35°45N 135°15E 31 G7
oga, L. Uganda 1°35N 33°0E 54 B3
ogle Australia 28°40S 153°0E 63 D5
ŏngju = Gyeongju
S. Korea 35°51N 129°14E 35 G15
ŏngsŏng N. Korea 41°35N 129°36E 35 D15
onpyaw Burma 17°12N 95°10E 41 L19
ōto Japan 35°0N 135°45E 31 G7
ōto □ Japan 35°15N 135°45E 31 G7
parissovouno Cyprus 35°19N 33°10E 25 D12
perounda Cyprus 34°56N 32°58E 25 E11
pros = Cyprus ■ Asia 35°0N 33°0E 25 E12
renia Cyprus 35°20N 33°20E 25 D12
rgyzstan ■ Asia 42°0N 75°0E 28 E8
ro älv = Kyrönjoki →
Finland 63°14N 21°45E 8 E19
rönjoki → Finland 63°14N 21°45E 8 E19
statyam Russia 67°20N 123°10E 29 C13
thira Greece 36°8N 23°0E 23 F10
thréa Cyprus 35°15N 33°29E 25 D12
unhla Burma 23°25N 95°15E 41 H19
uquot Sound Canada 50°2N 127°22W 70 D3
ūshū Japan 33°0N 131°0E 31 H5
ūshū □ Japan 33°0N 131°0E 31 H5
ushu-Palau Ridge
Pac. Oc. 20°0N 136°0E 64 E5
ūshū-Sanchi Japan 32°35N 131°17E 31 H5
ustendil Bulgaria 42°16N 22°41E 23 C10
usyur Russia 70°19N 127°30E 29 B13
yiv Ukraine 50°30N 30°28E 17 C16
yivske Vdskh.
Ukraine 51°0N 30°25E 17 C16
yl Russia 51°50N 94°30E 32 A4
yl Kum Uzbekistan 42°30N 65°0E 28 E7
yl Kyya Kyrgyzstan 40°16N 72°8E 28 E8
yl Orda = Qyzylorda
Kazakhstan 44°48N 65°28E 28 E7

Alcarria Spain 40°31N 2°45W 21 B4
Amistad △ Cent. Amer. 9°28N 83°18W 88 E3
Asunción Venezuela 11°2N 63°53W 92 A6
Baie Canada 48°19N 70°53W 73 C5
Banda Argentina 27°45S 64°10W 94 B3
Barca Mexico 20°17N 102°34W 86 C4
Barge U.S.A. 42°16N 110°12W 76 E8
Barra Nic. 12°54N 83°33W 88 D3
Belle U.S.A. 26°46N 81°26W 85 H14
Biche → Canada 59°57N 123°50W 70 B4
Biche, L. Canada 54°50N 112°3W 70 C6
Brea Trin. & Tob. 10°15N 61°37W 93 K15
Calera Chile 32°50S 71°10W 94 C1
Campana △ Chile 32°58S 71°14W 94 C1
Canal = Sa Canal
Spain 38°51N 1°23E 24 C7
Carlota Argentina 33°30S 63°20W 94 C3
Ceiba Honduras 15°40N 86°50W 88 C2
Chaux-de-Fonds Switz. 47°7N 6°50E 20 C7
Chorrera Panama 8°53N 79°47W 88 E4
Cocha Argentina 27°50S 65°40W 94 B2
Concepción Panama 8°31N 82°37W 88 E3
Concordia Mexico 16°5N 92°38W 87 D6
Coruña = A Coruña
Spain 43°20N 8°25W 21 A1
Crescent U.S.A. 43°50N 91°18W 80 D8
Crete Canada 58°11N 116°24W 70 B5
Crosse Kans., U.S.A. 38°32N 99°18W 80 F4
Crosse Wis., U.S.A. 43°48N 91°15W 80 D8
Cruz Costa Rica 11°4N 85°39W 88 D2
Cruz Mexico 23°55N 106°54W 86 C3
Désirade Guadeloupe 16°18N 61°3W 88 b
Digue Seychelles 4°20S 55°51E 53 b

La Esperanza Cuba 22°46N 83°44W 88 B3
La Esperanza Honduras 14°15N 88°10W 88 D2
La Estrada = A Estrada
Spain 42°43N 8°27W 21 A1
La Fayette U.S.A. 34°42N 85°17W 85 D12
La Fé Cuba 22°2N 84°15W 88 B3
La Follette U.S.A. 36°23N 84°7W 85 C12
La Grande U.S.A. 45°20N 118°5W 76 D4
La Grande → Canada 53°50N 79°0W 72 B5
La Grande 3, Rés.
Canada 53°40N 75°10W 72 B4
La Grande 4, Rés. Canada 54°0N 73°15W 72 B5
La Grange Calif., U.S.A. 37°42N 120°27W 78 H6
La Grange Ga., U.S.A. 33°2N 85°2W 85 E12
La Grange Ky., U.S.A. 38°24N 85°22W 81 F11
La Grange Tex., U.S.A. 29°54N 96°52W 84 G6
La Guaira Venezuela 10°36N 66°56W 92 A5
La Habana Cuba 23°8N 82°22W 88 B3
La Independencia Mexico 16°15N 92°1W 87 D6
La Isabela Dom. Rep. 19°58N 71°2W 89 C5
La Junta U.S.A. 37°59N 103°33W 76 H12
La Laguna Canary Is. 28°28N 16°18W 24 F3
La Libertad = Puerto Libertad
Mexico 29°55N 112°43W 86 B2
La Libertad Guatemala 16°47N 90°7W 88 C1
La Ligua Chile 32°30S 71°16W 94 C1
La Línea de la Concepción
Spain 36°15N 5°23W 21 D3
La Loche Canada 56°29N 109°26W 71 B7
La Louvière Belgium 50°27N 4°10E 15 D4
La Lune Trin. & Tob. 10°3N 61°22W 93 K15
La Malbaie Canada 47°40N 70°10W 73 C5
La Malinche △ Mexico 19°15N 98°3W 87 D5
La Mancha Spain 39°10N 2°54W 21 C4
La Martre, L. Canada 63°15N 117°55W 70 A5
La Mesa Mexico 32°30N 116°57W 79 N10
La Mesa U.S.A. 32°46N 117°1W 79 N9
La Mesilla U.S.A. 32°16N 106°48W 77 K10
La Misión Mexico 32°6N 116°53W 86 A1
La Moure U.S.A. 46°21N 98°18W 80 B4
La Negra Chile 23°46S 70°18W 94 A1
La Oliva Canary Is. 28°36N 13°57W 24 F6
La Orotava Canary Is. 28°22N 16°31W 24 F3
La Oroya Peru 11°32S 75°54W 92 F3
La Palma Canary Is. 28°40N 17°50W 24 F2
La Palma Panama 8°15N 78°0W 88 E4
La Palma del Condado
Spain 37°21N 6°38W 21 D2
La Paloma Chile 30°35S 71°0W 94 C1
La Pampa □ Argentina 36°50S 66°0W 94 D2
La Paragua Venezuela 6°50N 63°20W 92 B6
La Paz Entre Ríos,
Argentina 30°50S 59°45W 94 C4
La Paz San Luis,
Argentina 33°30S 67°20W 94 C2
La Paz Bolivia 16°20S 68°10W 92 G5
La Paz Honduras 14°20N 87°47W 88 D2
La Paz Mexico 24°10N 110°18W 86 C2
La Paz Centro Nic. 12°20N 86°41W 88 D2
La Pedrera Colombia 1°18S 69°43W 92 D5
La Pérade Canada 46°35N 72°12W 73 C5
La Perla Mexico 28°18N 104°32W 86 B4
La Perouse Str. Asia 45°40N 142°0E 30 B11
La Pesca Mexico 23°46N 97°47W 87 C5
La Piedad Mexico 20°21N 102°0W 86 C4
La Pine U.S.A. 43°40N 121°30W 76 E3
La Plata Argentina 35°0S 57°55W 94 D4
La Pocatière Canada 47°22N 70°2W 73 C5
La Porte U.S.A. 29°40N 95°1W 84 G7
La Purísima Mexico 26°10N 112°4W 86 B2
La Push U.S.A. 47°55N 124°38W 78 C2
La Quiaca Argentina 22°5S 65°35W 94 A2
La Restinga Canary Is. 27°38N 17°59W 24 G2
La Rioja Argentina 29°20S 67°0W 94 B2
La Rioja □ Argentina 29°30S 67°0W 94 B2
La Rioja □ Spain 42°20N 2°20W 21 A4
La Robla Spain 42°50N 5°41W 21 A3
La Roche-en-Ardenne
Belgium 50°11N 5°35E 15 D5
La Roche-sur-Yon France 46°40N 1°25W 20 C3
La Rochelle France 46°10N 1°9W 20 C3
La Roda Spain 39°13N 2°15W 21 C4
La Romaine Canada 50°13N 60°40W 73 B7
La Romana Dom. Rep. 18°27N 68°57W 89 C6
La Ronge Canada 55°5N 105°20W 71 B7
La Rumorosa Mexico 32°34N 116°6W 79 N10
La Sabina = Sa Savina
Spain 38°44N 1°25E 24 C7
La Salle U.S.A. 41°20N 89°6W 80 E9
La Santa Canary Is. 29°5N 13°40W 24 E6
La Sarre Canada 48°45N 79°15W 72 C4
La Scie Canada 49°57N 55°36W 73 C8
La Selva Beach U.S.A. 36°56N 121°51W 78 J5
La Serena Chile 29°55S 71°10W 94 B1
La Seu d'Urgell Spain 42°22N 1°23E 21 A6
La Seyne-sur-Mer France 43°7N 5°52E 20 E6
La Soufrière St. Vincent 13°20N 61°11W 89 D7
La Spézia Italy 44°7N 9°50E 20 D8
La Tagua Colombia 0°3N 74°40W 92 C4
La Tortuga Venezuela 11°0N 65°22W 89 D6
La Trinité Martinique 14°43N 60°58W 88 c
La Tuque Canada 47°30N 72°50W 72 C5
La Unión Chile 40°10S 73°0W 96 E2
La Unión El Salv. 13°20N 87°50W 88 D2
La Unión Mexico 17°58N 101°49W 86 D4
La Urbana Venezuela 7°8N 66°56W 92 B5
La Vache Pt.
Trin. & Tob. 10°47N 61°28W 93 K15
La Vall d'Uixó Spain 39°49N 0°15W 21 C5
La Vega Dom. Rep. 19°20N 70°30W 89 C5
La Vela de Coro
Venezuela 11°27N 69°34W 92 A5
La Venta Mexico 18°5N 94°3W 87 D6
La Vergne U.S.A. 36°1N 86°35W 85 C11
La Villa Joiosa = Villajoyosa
Spain 38°30N 0°12W 21 C5
Laascaanood Somali Rep. 8°26N 47°19E 47 F4

Labasa Fiji 16°30S 179°27E 59 a
Labdah = Leptis Magna
Libya 32°40N 14°12E 51 B8
Labe = Elbe → Europe 53°50N 9°0E 16 B5
Labé Guinea 11°24N 12°16W 50 F3
Laberge, L. Canada 61°11N 135°12W 70 A1
Labinsk Russia 44°40N 40°48E 19 F7
Labis Malaysia 2°22N 103°2E 39 L4
Laborie St. Lucia 13°45N 61°2W 89 f
Laboulaye Argentina 34°10S 63°30W 94 C3
Labrador Canada 53°20N 61°0W 73 B7
Labrador City Canada 52°57N 66°55W 73 B6
Labrador Sea Atl. Oc. 57°0N 54°0W 69 D14
Lábrea Brazil 7°15S 64°51W 92 E6
Labuan Malaysia 5°20N 115°14E 36 C5
Labuan, Pulau Malaysia 5°21N 115°13E 36 C5
Labuha Indonesia 0°30S 127°30E 37 E7
Labuhan Indonesia 6°22S 105°50E 37 G11
Labuhanbajo Indonesia 8°28S 119°54E 37 F6
Labuhanbilik Indonesia 2°31N 100°10E 39 L3
Labuk, Telok Malaysia 6°10N 117°50E 36 C5
Labyrinth, L. Australia 30°40S 135°11E 63 E2
Labytnangi Russia 66°39N 66°21E 28 C7
Lac-Bouchette Canada 48°16N 72°11W 73 C5
Lac Brochet Canada 57°53N 101°40W 71 B8
Lac Édouard Canada 47°40N 72°16W 72 C5
Lac La Biche Canada 54°45N 111°58W 70 C6
Lac la Martre = Wha Ti
Canada 63°8N 117°16W 68 C8
Lac La Ronge ⌂ Canada 55°9N 104°41W 71 B7
Lac-Mégantic Canada 45°35N 70°53W 73 C5
Lac Thien Vietnam 12°25N 108°11E 38 F7
Lacanau France 44°58N 1°5W 20 D3
Lacantún → Mexico 16°36N 90°39W 87 D6
Laccadive Is. = Lakshadweep Is.
India 10°0N 72°30E 3 D13
Lacepede B. Australia 36°40S 139°40E 63 F2
Lacepede Is. Australia 16°55S 122°0E 60 C3
Lacerdónia Mozam. 18°3S 35°35E 55 F4
Lacey U.S.A. 47°7N 122°49W 78 C4
Lachania Greece 35°58N 27°54E 25 D9
Lachhmangarh India 27°50N 75°4E 42 F6
Lachi Pakistan 33°25N 71°20E 42 C4
Lachine Canada 45°26N 73°42W 72 C5
Lachlan → Australia 34°22S 143°55E 63 E3
Lachute Canada 45°39N 74°21W 72 C5
Lackagh Hills Ireland 54°16N 8°10W 10 B3
Lackawanna U.S.A. 42°50N 78°50W 82 D6
Lackawaxen U.S.A. 41°29N 74°59W 83 E10
Lacolle Canada 45°5N 73°22W 83 A11
Lacombe Canada 52°30N 113°44W 70 C6
Lacona U.S.A. 43°39N 76°10W 83 C8
Laconia U.S.A. 43°32N 71°28W 83 C13
Ladakh Ra. India 34°0N 78°0E 43 C8
Ladismith S. Africa 33°28S 21°15E 56 E3
Lādīz Iran 28°55N 61°15E 45 D9
Ladnun India 27°38N 74°25E 42 F6
Ladoga, L. = Ladozhskoye Ozero
Russia 61°15N 30°30E 8 F24
Ladozhskoye Ozero
Russia 61°15N 30°30E 8 F24
Lady Elliott I. Australia 24°7S 152°42E 62 C5
Lady Grey S. Africa 30°43S 27°13E 56 E4
Ladybrand S. Africa 29°9S 27°29E 56 D4
Ladysmith Canada 49°0N 123°49W 78 B3
Ladysmith S. Africa 28°32S 29°46E 57 D4
Ladysmith U.S.A. 45°28N 91°12W 80 C8
Lae Papua N. G. 6°40S 147°2E 58 B7
Laem Hin Khom Thailand 9°25N 99°56E 39 b
Laem Khat Thailand 8°6N 98°26E 39 a
Laem Nga Thailand 7°55N 98°27E 39 a
Laem Ngop Thailand 12°10N 102°26E 39 F4
Laem Phan Wa Thailand 7°47N 98°25E 39 a
Laem Pho Thailand 6°55N 101°19E 39 J3
Laem Phrom Thep Thailand 7°45N 98°19E 39 a
Laem Riang Thailand 8°7N 98°27E 39 a
Laem Sam Rong Thailand 9°35N 100°4E 39 b
Laem Son Thailand 7°59N 98°16E 39 a
Laem Yamu Thailand 7°59N 98°26E 39 a
Laerma Greece 36°9N 27°57E 25 C9
Læsø Denmark 57°15N 11°5E 9 H14
Lafayette Ind., U.S.A. 40°25N 86°54W 80 E10
Lafayette La., U.S.A. 30°14N 92°1W 84 F8
Lafayette Tenn., U.S.A. 36°31N 86°2W 85 C11
Laferte → Canada 61°53N 117°44W 70 A5
Lafia Nigeria 8°30N 8°34E 50 G7
Lafleche Canada 49°45N 106°40W 71 D7
Lagan → U.K. 54°36N 5°55W 10 B6
Lagarfljót → Iceland 65°40N 14°18W 8 D6
Lagdo, Rés. de Cameroon 8°40N 14°0E 51 G8
Lågen → Oppland, Norway 61°8N 10°25E 8 F14
Lågen → Vestfold, Norway 59°3N 10°3E 9 G14
Lages Brazil 27°48S 50°20W 95 B5
Laghouat Algeria 33°50N 2°59E 50 B6
Lagoa do Peixe △ Brazil 31°12S 50°55W 95 C5
Lagoa Vermelha Brazil 28°13S 51°32W 95 B5
Lagonoy G. Phil. 13°35N 123°50E 37 B6
Lagos Nigeria 6°25N 3°27E 50 G6
Lagos Portugal 37°5N 8°41W 21 D1
Lagos de Moreno
Mexico 21°21N 101°55W 86 C4
Lagrange = Bidyadanga
Australia 18°45S 121°43E 60 C3
Lagrange B. Australia 18°38S 121°42E 60 C3
Laguna Brazil 28°30S 48°50W 95 B6
Laguna U.S.A. 35°2N 107°25W 77 J10
Laguna, Sa. de la
Mexico 23°35N 109°55W 86 C3
Laguna Beach U.S.A. 33°33N 117°47W 79 M9
Laguna de la Restinga △
Venezuela 10°58N 64°0W 89 D6
Laguna de Lachuá △
Guatemala 15°55N 90°40W 88 C1
Laguna del Laja △ Chile 37°27S 71°20W 94 D1
Laguna del Tigre △
Guatemala 17°32N 90°56W 88 C1
Laguna Limpia
Argentina 26°32S 59°45W 94 B4

Lagunas Chile 21°0S 69°45W 94 A2
Lagunas Peru 5°10S 75°35W 92 E3
Lagunas de Chacahua △
Mexico 16°0N 97°43W 87 D5
Lagunas de Montebello △
Mexico 16°4N 91°42W 87 D6
Lahad Datu Malaysia 5°0N 118°20E 37 D5
Lahad Datu, Telok
Malaysia 4°50N 118°20E 37 D5
Lahan Sai Thailand 14°25N 102°52E 38 E4
Lahanam Laos 16°16N 105°16E 38 D5
Lahar India 26°12N 78°57E 43 F8
Laharpur India 27°43N 80°56E 43 F9
Lahat Indonesia 3°45S 103°30E 36 E2
Lahewa Indonesia 1°22N 97°12E 36 D1
Lāhījān Iran 37°10N 50°6E 45 B6
Lahn → Germany 50°19N 7°37E 16 C4
Laholm Sweden 56°30N 13°2E 9 H15
Lahore Pakistan 31°32N 74°22E 42 D6
Lahri Pakistan 29°11N 68°13E 42 E3
Lāhrūd Iran 38°30N 47°52E 44 B5
Lahti Finland 60°58N 25°40E 8 F21
Lahtis = Lahti Finland 60°58N 25°40E 8 F21
Laï Chad 9°25N 16°18E 51 G9
Lai Chau Vietnam 22°5N 103°3E 38 A4
Laila = Layla Si. Arabia 22°10N 46°40E 47 C4
Laingsburg S. Africa 33°9S 20°52E 56 E3
Lainioälven → Sweden 67°35N 22°40E 8 C20
Lairg U.K. 58°2N 4°24W 11 C4
Laisamis Kenya 1°36N 37°48E 54 B4
Laishui China 39°23N 115°45E 34 E8
Laiwu China 36°15N 117°40E 35 F9
Laixi China 36°50N 120°31E 35 F11
Laiyang China 36°59N 120°45E 35 F11
Laiyuan China 39°20N 114°40E 34 E8
Laizhou China 37°8N 119°57E 35 F10
Laizhou Wan China 37°30N 119°30E 35 F10
Laja → Mexico 20°55N 100°46W 86 C4
Lajamanu Australia 18°23S 130°38E 60 C5
Lak Sao Laos 18°11N 104°59E 38 C5
Lakaband Pakistan 31°2N 69°15E 42 D3
Lake U.S.A. 44°33N 110°24W 76 D8
Lake Alpine U.S.A. 38°29N 120°0W 78 G7
Lake Andes U.S.A. 43°9N 98°32W 80 D4
Lake Arthur U.S.A. 30°5N 92°41W 84 F8
Lake Bindegolly △
Australia 28°0S 144°12E 63 D3
Lake Cargelligo
Australia 33°15S 146°22E 63 E4
Lake Charles U.S.A. 30°14N 93°13W 84 F8
Lake City Colo., U.S.A. 38°2N 107°19W 76 G10
Lake City Fla., U.S.A. 30°11N 82°38W 85 F13
Lake City Mich., U.S.A. 44°20N 85°13W 81 C11
Lake City Minn., U.S.A. 44°27N 92°16W 80 C7
Lake City Pa., U.S.A. 42°1N 80°21W 82 D4
Lake City S.C., U.S.A. 33°52N 79°45W 85 E15
Lake Cowichan Canada 48°49N 124°3W 70 D4
Lake District △ U.K. 54°30N 3°21W 12 C4
Lake Elsinore U.S.A. 33°38N 117°20W 79 M9
Lake Eyre △ Australia 28°40S 137°31E 63 D2
Lake Gairdner △
Australia 31°41S 135°51E 63 E2
Lake George U.S.A. 43°26N 73°43W 83 C11
Lake Grace Australia 33°7S 118°28E 61 F2
Lake Harbour = Kimmirut
Canada 62°50N 69°50W 69 C13
Lake Havasu City
U.S.A. 34°27N 114°22W 79 L12
Lake Hughes U.S.A. 34°41N 118°26W 79 L8
Lake Isabella U.S.A. 35°38N 118°28W 79 K8
Lake Jackson U.S.A. 29°3N 95°27W 84 G7
Lake King Australia 33°5S 119°45E 61 F2
Lake Lenore Canada 52°24N 104°59W 71 C8
Lake Louise Canada 51°30N 116°10W 70 C5
Lake Malawi △ Malawi 14°2S 34°53E 55 E3
Lake Mburo △ Uganda 0°33S 30°56E 54 C3
Lake Mead ⌂ U.S.A. 36°30N 114°22W 79 K12
Lake Meredith ⌂
U.S.A. 35°50N 101°50W 84 D4
Lake Mills U.S.A. 43°25N 93°32W 80 D7
Lake Nakura △ Kenya 0°21S 36°8E 54 C4
Lake Placid U.S.A. 44°17N 73°59W 83 B11
Lake Pleasant U.S.A. 43°28N 74°25W 83 C10
Lake Providence U.S.A. 32°48N 91°10W 84 E9
Lake Roosevelt ⌂
U.S.A. 48°5N 118°14W 76 B4
Lake St. Peter Canada 45°18N 78°2W 82 A6
Lake Superior ⌂ Canada 47°45N 84°45W 72 C3
Lake Torrens △
Australia 30°55S 137°40E 63 E2
Lake Village U.S.A. 33°20N 91°17W 84 E9
Lake Wales U.S.A. 27°54N 81°35W 85 H14
Lake Worth U.S.A. 26°37N 80°3W 85 H14
Lakeba Fiji 18°13S 178°47W 59 a
Lakeba Passage Fiji 18°0S 178°45W 59 a
Lakefield Canada 44°25N 78°16W 82 B6
Lakefield △ Australia 15°24S 144°26E 62 B3
Lakehurst U.S.A. 40°1N 74°19W 83 F10
Lakeland Australia 15°49S 144°57E 62 B3
Lakeland U.S.A. 28°3N 81°57W 85 G14
Lakemba = Lakeba Fiji 18°13S 178°47W 59 a
Lakeport Calif., U.S.A. 39°3N 122°55W 78 F4
Lakeport Mich., U.S.A. 43°7N 82°30W 82 C2
Lakes Entrance Australia 37°50S 148°0E 63 F4
Lakeside Calif., U.S.A. 32°52N 116°55W 79 N10
Lakeside Nebr., U.S.A. 42°3N 102°26W 80 D2
Lakeview U.S.A. 42°11N 120°21W 76 E3
Lakeville U.S.A. 44°39N 93°14W 80 C7
Lakewood Colo., U.S.A. 39°42N 105°4W 76 G11
Lakewood N.J., U.S.A. 40°6N 74°13W 83 F10
Lakewood N.Y., U.S.A. 42°6N 79°19W 82 D5
Lakewood Ohio, U.S.A. 41°28N 81°47W 82 E3
Lakewood Wash.,
U.S.A. 47°11N 122°32W 78 C4
Lakha India 26°9N 70°54E 42 F4
Lakhimpur India 27°57N 80°46E 43 F9
Lakhisarai India 25°11N 86°5E 43 G12

Lakhnadon India 22°36N 79°36E 43 H8
Lakhnau = Lucknow
India 26°50N 81°0E 43 F9
Lakhonpheng Laos 15°54N 105°34E 38 E5
Lakhpat India 23°48N 68°47E 42 H3
Lakin U.S.A. 37°57N 101°15W 80 G3
Lakitusaki → Canada 54°21N 82°25W 72 B3
Lakki Greece 35°24N 23°57E 25 D5
Lakki Pakistan 32°36N 70°55E 42 C4
Lakonikos Kolpos
Greece 36°40N 22°40E 23 F10
Lakor Indonesia 8°15S 128°17E 37 F7
Lakota Ivory C. 5°50N 5°30W 50 G4
Lakota U.S.A. 48°2N 98°21W 80 A4
Laksar India 29°46N 78°3E 42 E8
Laksefjorden Norway 70°45N 26°50E 8 A22
Lakselv Norway 70°2N 25°0E 8 A21
Lakshadweep Is. India 10°0N 72°30E 3 D13
Lakshmanpur India 22°58N 83°3E 43 H10
Lakshmikantapur India 22°5N 88°20E 43 H13
Lala Musa Pakistan 32°40N 73°57E 42 C5
Lalaghat India 24°30N 92°40E 41 G18
Lalago Tanzania 3°28S 33°58E 54 C3
Lalapanzi Zimbabwe 19°20S 30°15E 55 F3
L'Albufera Spain 39°20N 0°27W 21 C5
Lalganj India 25°52N 85°13E 43 G11
Lalgola India 24°25N 88°15E 43 G13
Lālī Iran 32°21N 49°6E 45 C6
Lalibela Ethiopia 12°3N 39°0E 47 E2
Lalin China 45°12N 127°0E 35 B14
Lalín Spain 42°40N 8°5W 21 A1
Lalin He → China 45°32N 125°40E 35 B13
Lalitapur Nepal 27°40N 85°20E 43 F11
Lalitpur India 24°42N 78°28E 43 G8
Lalkua India 29°5N 79°31E 43 E8
Lalsot India 26°34N 76°20E 42 F7
Lam Pao Res. Thailand 16°50N 103°15E 38 D4
Lamae Malaysia 9°51N 99°5E 39 H2
Lamaing Burma 15°25N 97°53E 38 E1
Lamar Colo., U.S.A. 38°5N 102°37W 76 G12
Lamar Mo., U.S.A. 37°30N 94°16W 80 G6
Lamas Peru 6°28S 76°31W 92 E3
Lamayuru India 34°18N 76°46E 43 B7
Lamayuru Jammu & Kashmir,
India 34°25N 76°56E 43 B7
Lambaréné Gabon 0°41S 10°12E 52 E2
Lambasa = Labasa Fiji 16°30S 179°27E 59 a
Lambay I. Ireland 53°29N 6°1W 10 C5
Lambert's Bay S. Africa 32°5S 18°17E 56 E2
Lambeth Canada 42°54N 81°18W 82 D3
Lambomakondro
Madag. 22°41S 44°44E 57 C7
Lambton Shores Canada 43°10N 81°56W 82 C3
Lame Deer U.S.A. 45°37N 106°40W 76 D10
Lamego Portugal 41°5N 7°52W 21 B2
Lamèque Canada 47°45N 64°38W 73 C7
Lameroo Australia 35°19S 140°33E 63 F3
Lamesa U.S.A. 32°44N 101°58W 84 E4
Lamia Greece 38°55N 22°26E 23 E10
Lamington △ Australia 28°13S 153°12E 63 D5
Lamma I. China 22°12N 114°7E 33 G11
Lammermuir Hills U.K. 55°50N 2°40W 11 F6
Lamoille → U.S.A. 44°38N 73°13W 83 B11
Lamon B. Phil. 14°30N 122°20E 37 B6
Lamont Canada 53°46N 112°50W 70 C6
Lamont Calif., U.S.A. 35°15N 118°55W 79 K8
Lamont Wyo., U.S.A. 42°13N 107°29W 76 E10
Lampa Peru 15°22S 70°22W 92 G4
Lampang Thailand 18°16N 99°32E 38 C2
Lampasas U.S.A. 31°4N 98°11W 84 F5
Lampazos de Naranjo
Mexico 27°1N 100°31W 86 B4
Lampedusa Medit. S. 35°36N 12°40E 22 G5
Lampeter U.K. 52°7N 4°4W 13 E3
Lampione Medit. S. 35°33N 12°20E 22 G5
Lampman Canada 49°25N 102°50W 71 D8
Lampung □ Indonesia 5°30S 104°30E 36 F2
Lamta India 22°8N 80°7E 43 H9
Lamu Kenya 2°16S 40°55E 54 C5
Lamy U.S.A. 35°29N 105°53W 77 J11
Lan Xian China 38°15N 111°35E 34 E6
Lāna'i U.S.A. 20°50N 156°55W 74 b
Lanak La China 34°27N 79°32E 43 B8
Lanak'o Shank'ou = Lanak La
China 34°27N 79°32E 43 B8
Lanark Canada 45°1N 76°22W 83 A8
Lanark U.K. 55°40N 3°47W 11 F5
Lanbi Kyun Burma 10°50N 98°20E 39 G2
Lancang Jiang →
China 21°40N 101°10E 32 D5
Lancashire □ U.K. 53°50N 2°48W 12 D5
Lancaster Canada 45°10N 74°30W 83 A10
Lancaster U.K. 54°3N 2°48W 12 C5
Lancaster Calif., U.S.A. 34°42N 118°8W 79 L8
Lancaster Ky., U.S.A. 37°37N 84°35W 81 G11
Lancaster N.H., U.S.A. 44°29N 71°34W 83 B13
Lancaster Ohio, U.S.A. 39°43N 82°36W 81 F12
Lancaster Pa., U.S.A. 40°2N 76°19W 83 F8
Lancaster S.C., U.S.A. 34°43N 80°46W 85 D14
Lancaster Wis., U.S.A. 42°51N 90°43W 80 D8
Lancaster Sd. Canada 74°13N 84°0W 69 B11
Lancelin Australia 31°0S 115°18E 61 F2
Lanchow = Lanzhou
China 36°1N 103°52E 34 F2
Lanciano Italy 42°14N 14°23E 22 C6
Lancun China 36°25N 120°10E 35 F11
Land Between the Lakes ⌂
U.S.A. 36°25N 88°0W 85 C11
Landeck Austria 47°9N 10°34E 16 E6
Lander U.S.A. 42°50N 108°44W 76 E9
Lander → Australia 22°0S 132°0E 60 D5
Landes France 44°0N 1°0W 20 D3
Landi Kotal Pakistan 34°7N 71°6E 42 B4
Landisburg U.S.A. 40°21N 77°19W 82 F7
Landmannalaugar Iceland 63°59N 19°4W 8 E4
Land's End U.K. 50°4N 5°44W 13 G2
Landsborough Cr. →
Australia 22°28S 144°35E 62 C3

Landshut Germany 48°34N 12°8E 16 D7
Lanesboro U.S.A. 41°57N 75°34W 83 E9
Lanett U.S.A. 32°52N 85°12W 85 E12
Lang Shan China 41°0N 106°30E 34 D4
Lang Son Vietnam 21°52N 106°42E 38 B6
Lang Suan Thailand 9°57N 99°4E 39 H2
La'nga Co China 30°45N 81°15E 43 D9
Langar Iran 35°23N 60°25E 45 C9
Langara I. Canada 54°14N 133°1W 70 C2
Langarūd Iran 37°11N 50°8E 45 B6
Langdon U.S.A. 48°45N 98°22W 80 A4
Langeberg S. Africa 33°55S 21°0E 56 E3
Langeberge S. Africa 28°15S 22°33E 56 D3
Langeland Denmark 54°56N 10°48E 9 J14
Langenburg Canada 50°51N 101°43W 71 C8
Langholm U.K. 55°9N 3°0W 11 F5
Langjökull Iceland 64°39N 20°12W 8 D3
Langkawi, Pulau Malaysia 6°25N 99°45E 39 J2
Langklip S. Africa 28°12S 20°20E 56 D3
Langkon Malaysia 6°30N 116°40E 36 C5
Langley Canada 49°7N 122°39W 78 A4
Langøya Norway 68°45N 14°50E 8 B16
Langreo Spain 43°18N 5°40W 21 A3
Langres France 47°52N 5°20E 20 C6
Langres, Plateau de France 47°45N 5°3E 20 C6
Langsa Indonesia 4°30N 97°57E 36 D1
Langtang △ Nepal 28°10N 85°30E 43 E11
Langtry U.S.A. 29°49N 101°34W 84 G4
Langu Thailand 6°53N 99°47E 39 J2
Languedoc France 43°58N 3°55E 20 E5
Langwang China 22°38N 113°27E 33 F9
Langxiangzhen China 39°43N 116°8E 34 E9
Lanigan Canada 51°51N 105°2W 71 C7
Lankao China 34°48N 114°50E 34 G8
Länkäran Azerbaijan 38°48N 48°52E 45 B6
Lannion France 48°46N 3°29W 20 B2
L'Annonciation Canada 46°25N 74°55W 72 C5
Lansdale U.S.A. 40°14N 75°17W 83 F9
Lansdowne Australia 31°48S 152°30E 63 E5
Lansdowne Canada 44°24N 76°1W 83 B8
Lansdowne India 29°50N 78°41E 43 E8
Lansdowne House = Neskantaga Canada 52°14N 87°53W 72 B2
L'Anse U.S.A. 46°45N 88°27W 80 B9
L'Anse au Loup Canada 51°32N 56°50W 73 B8
L'Anse aux Meadows Canada 51°36N 55°32W 73 B8
L'Anse la Raye St. Lucia 13°55N 61°3W 89 f
Lansford U.S.A. 40°50N 75°53W 83 F9
Lansing U.S.A. 42°44N 84°33W 81 D11
Lanta Yai, Ko Thailand 7°35N 99°3E 39 J2
Lantau I. China 22°15N 113°56E 33 G10
Lantian China 34°11N 109°20E 34 G5
Lanus Argentina 34°42S 58°23W 94 C4
Lanusei Italy 39°52N 9°34E 22 E3
Lanzarote Canary Is. 29°0N 13°40W 24 F6
Lanzarote ✕ (ACE) Canary Is. 28°57N 13°40W 24 F6
Lanzhou China 36°1N 103°52E 34 F2
Lao Bao Laos 16°35N 106°30E 38 D6
Lao Cai Vietnam 22°30N 103°57E 38 A4
Laoag Phil. 18°7N 120°34E 37 A6
Laoang Phil. 12°32N 125°8E 37 B7
Laoha He → China 43°25N 120°35E 35 C11
Laois □ Ireland 52°57N 7°36W 10 D4
Laon France 49°33N 3°35E 20 B5
Laona U.S.A. 45°34N 88°40W 80 C9
Laos ■ Asia 17°45N 105°0E 38 D5
Lapa Brazil 25°46S 49°44W 95 B6
Lapeer U.S.A. 43°3N 83°19W 81 D12
Lapithos Cyprus 35°21N 33°11E 25 D12
Lapland = Lappland Europe 68°7N 24°0E 8 B21
LaPorte Ind., U.S.A. 41°36N 86°43W 80 E10
Laporte Pa., U.S.A. 41°25N 76°30W 83 E8
Lappeenranta Finland 61°3N 28°12E 8 F23
Lappland Europe 68°7N 24°0E 8 B21
Lappo = Lapua Finland 62°58N 23°0E 8 E20
Laprida Argentina 37°34S 60°45W 94 D3
Lâpseki Turkey 40°20N 26°41E 23 D12
Laptev Sea Russia 76°0N 125°0E 29 B13
Lapua Finland 62°58N 23°0E 8 E20
L'Áquila Italy 42°22N 13°22E 22 C5
Lār Iran 27°40N 54°14E 45 E7
Laramie U.S.A. 41°19N 105°35W 76 F11
Laramie Mts. U.S.A. 42°0N 105°30W 76 F11
Laranjeiras do Sul Brazil 25°23S 52°23W 95 B5
Larantuka Indonesia 8°21S 122°55E 37 F6
Larat Indonesia 7°0S 132°0E 37 F8
Larde Mozam. 16°28S 39°43E 55 F4
Larder Lake Canada 48°5N 79°40W 72 C4
Lardos Greece 36°6N 28°1E 25 C10
Lardos, Akra = Lindos, Akra Greece 36°4N 28°10E 25 C10
Lardos, Ormos Greece 36°4N 28°2E 25 C10
Lare Kenya 0°20N 37°56E 54 C4
Laredo U.S.A. 27°30N 99°30W 84 H5
Laredo Sd. Canada 52°30N 128°53W 70 C3
Largo U.S.A. 27°54N 82°47W 85 H13
Largs U.K. 55°47N 4°52W 11 F4
Lariang Indonesia 1°26S 119°17E 37 E5
Larimore U.S.A. 47°54N 97°38W 80 B5
Larisa Greece 39°36N 22°27E 23 E10
Larkana Pakistan 27°32N 68°18E 42 F3
Larnaca Cyprus 34°55N 33°38E 25 E12
Larnaca Bay Cyprus 34°53N 33°45E 25 E12
Larne U.K. 54°51N 5°51W 10 B6
Larned U.S.A. 38°11N 99°6W 80 F4
Larose U.S.A. 29°34N 90°23W 85 G9
Larrimah Australia 15°35S 133°12E 60 C5
Larsen Ice Shelf Antarctica 67°0S 62°0W 5 C17
Larvik Norway 59°4N 10°2E 9 G14
Las Animas U.S.A. 38°4N 103°13W 76 G12
Las Anod = Laascaanood Somali Rep. 8°26N 47°19E 47 F4
Las Brenãs Argentina 27°5S 61°7W 94 B3
Las Cañadas del Teide △ Canary Is. 28°15N 16°37W 24 F3
Las Cejas Argentina 26°53S 64°44W 96 B4
Las Chimeneas Mexico 32°8N 116°5W 79 N10
Las Cruces U.S.A. 32°19N 106°47W 77 K10
Las Flores Argentina 36°10S 59°7W 94 D4
Las Heras Argentina 32°51S 68°49W 94 C2
Las Lajas Argentina 38°30S 70°25W 96 D2
Las Lomitas Argentina 24°43S 60°35W 94 A3
Las Palmas Argentina 27°8S 58°45W 94 B4
Las Palmas Canary Is. 28°7N 15°26W 24 F4
Las Palmas → Mexico 32°31N 116°58W 79 N10
Las Palmas ✕ (LPA) Canary Is. 27°55N 15°25W 24 G4
Las Piedras Uruguay 34°44S 56°14W 95 C4
Las Pipinas Argentina 35°30S 57°19W 94 D4
Las Plumas Argentina 43°40S 67°15W 96 E3
Las Rosas Argentina 32°30S 61°35W 94 C3
Las Tablas Panama 7°49N 80°14W 88 E3
Las Toscas Argentina 28°21S 59°18W 94 B4
Las Truchas Mexico 17°57N 102°13W 86 D4
Las Tunas Cuba 20°58N 76°59W 88 B4
Las Varillas Argentina 31°50S 62°50W 94 C3
Las Vegas N. Mex., U.S.A. 35°36N 105°13W 77 J11
Las Vegas Nev., U.S.A. 36°10N 115°8W 79 J11
Las Vegas McCarran Int. ✕ (LAS) U.S.A. 36°5N 115°9W 79 J11
Lascano Uruguay 33°35S 54°12W 95 C5
Lash-e Joveyn Afghan. 31°45N 61°30E 40 D2
Lashburn Canada 53°10N 109°40W 71 C7
Lashio Burma 22°56N 97°45E 41 H20
Lashkar India 26°10N 78°10E 42 F8
Lasithi Greece 35°11N 25°31E 25 D7
Lasithi □ Greece 35°5N 25°50E 25 D7
Lāsjerd Iran 35°24N 53°4E 45 C7
Lassen Pk. U.S.A. 40°29N 121°30W 76 F3
Lassen Volcanic △ U.S.A. 40°30N 121°20W 76 F3
Last Mountain L. Canada 51°5N 105°14W 71 C7
Lastchance Cr. → U.S.A. 40°2N 121°15W 78 E5
Lastoursville Gabon 0°55S 12°38E 52 E2
Lastovo Croatia 42°46N 16°55E 22 C7
Lat Yao Thailand 15°45N 99°48E 38 E2
Latacunga Ecuador 0°50S 78°35W 92 D3
Latakia = Al Lādhiqīyah Syria 35°30N 35°45E 44 C2
Latchford Canada 47°20N 79°50W 72 C4
Late Tonga 18°48S 174°39W 59 c
Latehar India 23°45N 84°30E 43 H11
Latham Australia 29°44S 116°20E 61 E2
Lathi India 27°43N 71°23E 42 F4
Lathrop Wells U.S.A. 36°39N 116°24W 79 J10
Latina Italy 41°28N 12°52E 22 D5
Latium = Lazio □ Italy 42°10N 12°30E 22 C5
Laton U.S.A. 36°26N 119°41W 78 J7
Latouche Treville, C. Australia 18°27S 121°49E 60 C3
Latrobe Australia 41°14S 146°30E 63 G4
Latrobe U.S.A. 40°19N 79°23W 82 F5
Latvia ■ Europe 56°50N 24°0E 9 H21
Lau Fau Shan China 22°28N 113°59E 33 G10
Lau Group Fiji 17°0S 178°30W 59 a
Lauchhammer Germany 51°29N 13°47E 16 C7
Laughlin U.S.A. 35°10N 114°34W 77 J6
Laukaa Finland 62°24N 25°56E 8 E21
Launceston Australia 41°24S 147°8E 63 G4
Launceston U.K. 50°38N 4°22W 13 G3
Laune → Ireland 52°7N 9°47W 10 D2
Launglon Bok Burma 13°50N 97°54E 38 F1
Laura Australia 15°32S 144°32E 62 B3
Laurel Miss., U.S.A. 31°41N 89°8W 85 F10
Laurel Mont., U.S.A. 45°40N 108°46W 76 D9
Laurel Hill U.S.A. 40°14N 79°6W 82 F5
Laurencekirk U.K. 56°50N 2°28W 11 E6
Laurens U.S.A. 34°30N 82°1W 85 D13
Laurentian Plateau Canada 52°0N 70°0W 73 B6
Lauria Italy 40°2N 15°50E 22 E6
Laurie L. Canada 56°35N 101°57W 71 B8
Laurinburg U.S.A. 34°47N 79°28W 85 D15
Laurium U.S.A. 47°14N 88°27W 80 B9
Lausanne Switz. 46°32N 6°38E 20 C7
Laut Indonesia 4°45N 108°0E 36 D3
Laut, Pulau Indonesia 3°40S 116°10E 36 E5
Laut Kecil, Kepulauan Indonesia 4°45S 115°40E 36 E5
Lautoka Fiji 17°37S 177°27E 59 a
Lava Beds ⌂ U.S.A. 41°40N 121°30W 76 F3
Lavagh More Ireland 54°46N 8°6W 10 B3
Laval France 48°4N 0°48W 20 B3
Laval-des-Rapides Canada 45°33N 73°42W 72 C5
Lavalle Argentina 28°15S 65°15W 94 B2
Lāvān Iran 26°48N 53°22E 45 E7
Lavant Canada 45°3N 76°42W 83 A8
Lāvar Meydān Iran 30°20N 54°30E 45 D7
Laverton Australia 28°44S 122°29E 61 E3
Lavras Brazil 21°20S 45°0W 95 A7
Lavrio Greece 37°40N 24°4E 23 F11
Lavris Greece 35°25N 24°40E 25 D6
Lavumisa Swaziland 27°20S 31°55E 57 D5
Lavushi Manda △ Zambia 12°46S 31°0E 55 E3
Lawaki Fiji 17°40S 178°35E 59 a
Lawas Malaysia 4°55N 115°25E 36 D5
Lawele Indonesia 5°13S 122°57E 37 F6
Lawn Hill = Boodjamulla △ Australia 18°15S 138°6E 62 B2
Lawqah Si. Arabia 29°49N 42°45E 44 D4
Lawrence N.Z. 45°55S 169°41E 59 F2
Lawrence Ind., U.S.A. 39°50N 86°2W 80 F10
Lawrence Kans., U.S.A. 38°58N 95°14W 80 F6
Lawrence Mass., U.S.A. 42°43N 71°10W 83 D13
Lawrenceburg Ind., U.S.A. 39°6N 84°52W 81 F11
Lawrenceburg Tenn., U.S.A. 35°14N 87°20W 85 D11
Lawrenceville Ga., U.S.A. 33°57N 83°59W 85 E13
Lawrenceville Pa., U.S.A. 41°59N 77°8W 82 E7
Laws U.S.A. 37°24N 118°20W 78 H8
Lawton U.S.A. 34°37N 98°25W 84 D5
Lawu Indonesia 7°40S 111°13E 37 G14
Laxford, L. U.K. 58°24N 5°6W 11 C3
Layla Si. Arabia 22°10N 46°40E 47 C4
Laylān Iraq 35°18N 44°31E 44 C5
Layton U.S.A. 41°4N 111°58W 76 F8
Laytonville U.S.A. 39°41N 123°29W 76 G2
Lazarev Russia 52°13N 141°30E 29 D15
Lazarev Sea S. Ocean 67°30S 3°0W 5 C2
Lazarivo Madag. 23°54S 44°59E 57 C8
Lázaro Cárdenas Mexico 17°55N 102°11W 86 D4
Lazio □ Italy 42°10N 12°30E 22 C5
Lazo Russia 43°25N 133°55E 30 C6
Le Bic Canada 48°20N 68°41W 73 C6
Le Creusot France 46°48N 4°24E 20 C6
Le François Martinique 14°38N 60°57W 88 c
Le Gosier Guadeloupe 16°14N 61°29W 88 b
Le Gris Gris Mauritius 20°31S 57°32E 53 d
Le Havre France 49°30N 0°5E 20 B4
Le Lamentin Martinique 14°35N 61°2W 88 c
Le Mans France 48°0N 0°10E 20 C4
Le Marin Martinique 14°27N 60°55W 88 c
Le Mars U.S.A. 42°47N 96°10W 80 D5
Le Mont-St-Michel France 48°40N 1°30W 20 B3
Le Moule Guadeloupe 16°20N 61°22W 88 b
Le Moyne, L. Canada 56°45N 68°47W 73 A6
Le Port Réunion 20°56S 55°18E 53 c
Le Prêcheur Martinique 14°50N 61°12W 88 c
Le Puy-en-Velay France 45°3N 3°52E 20 D5
Le Raysville U.S.A. 41°50N 76°10W 83 E8
Le Robert Martinique 14°40N 60°56W 88 c
Le Roy U.S.A. 42°58N 77°59W 82 D7
Le St-Esprit Martinique 14°34N 60°56W 88 c
Le Sueur U.S.A. 44°28N 93°55W 80 C7
Le Tampon Réunion 21°16S 55°32E 53 c
Le Thuy Vietnam 17°14N 106°49E 38 D6
Le Touquet-Paris-Plage France 50°30N 1°36E 20 A4
Le Tréport France 50°3N 1°20E 20 A4
Le Verdon-sur-Mer France 45°33N 1°4W 20 D3
Lea → U.K. 51°31N 0°1E 13 F8
Leach Cambodia 12°21N 103°46E 39 F4
Lead U.S.A. 44°21N 103°46W 80 C2
Leader Canada 50°50N 109°30W 71 C7
Leadville U.S.A. 39°15N 106°18W 76 G10
Leaf → U.S.A. 30°59N 88°44W 85 F10
Leaf Rapids Canada 56°30N 99°59W 71 B9
Leamington Canada 42°3N 82°36W 82 D2
Leamington U.S.A. 39°32N 112°17W 76 G7
Leamington Spa = Royal Leamington Spa U.K. 52°18N 1°31W 13 E6
Leandro Norte Alem Argentina 27°34S 55°15W 95 B4
Leane, L. Ireland 52°2N 9°32W 10 D2
Learmonth Australia 22°13S 114°10E 60 D1
Leask Canada 53°5N 106°45W 71 C7
Leatherhead U.K. 51°18N 0°20W 13 F7
Leavenworth Kans., U.S.A. 39°19N 94°55W 80 F6
Leavenworth Wash., U.S.A. 47°36N 120°40W 76 C3
Leawood U.S.A. 38°58N 94°37W 80 F6
Lebak Phil. 6°32N 124°5E 37 C6
Lebam U.S.A. 46°34N 123°33W 78 D3
Lebanon Ind., U.S.A. 40°3N 86°28W 80 E10
Lebanon Kans., U.S.A. 39°49N 98°33W 80 F4
Lebanon Ky., U.S.A. 37°34N 85°15W 81 G11
Lebanon Mo., U.S.A. 37°41N 92°40W 80 G7
Lebanon N.H., U.S.A. 43°39N 72°15W 83 C12
Lebanon Oreg., U.S.A. 44°32N 122°55W 76 D2
Lebanon Pa., U.S.A. 40°20N 76°26W 83 F8
Lebanon Tenn., U.S.A. 36°12N 86°18W 85 C11
Lebanon ■ Asia 34°0N 36°0E 46 B5
Lebec U.S.A. 34°51N 118°52W 79 L8
Lebel-sur-Quévillon Canada 49°3N 76°59W 72 C4
Lebomboberge S. Africa 24°30S 32°0E 57 C5
Lębork Poland 54°33N 17°46E 17 A9
Lebrija Spain 36°53N 6°5W 21 D2
Lebu Chile 37°40S 73°47W 94 D1
Lecce Italy 40°23N 18°11E 23 D8
Lecco Italy 45°51N 9°23E 20 D8
Lech → Germany 48°43N 10°56E 16 D6
Lecontes Mills U.S.A. 41°5N 78°17W 82 E6
Łęczyca Poland 52°5N 19°15E 17 B10
Ledong China 18°41N 109°5E 38 C7
Leduc Canada 53°15N 113°30W 70 C6
Lee U.S.A. 42°19N 73°15W 83 D11
Lee → Ireland 51°53N 8°56W 10 E3
Lee Vining U.S.A. 37°58N 119°7W 78 H7
Leech L. U.S.A. 47°10N 94°24W 80 B6
Leechburg U.S.A. 40°37N 79°36W 82 F5
Leeds U.K. 53°48N 1°33W 12 D6
Leeds U.S.A. 33°33N 86°33W 85 E11
Leek Neths. 53°10N 6°24E 15 A6
Leek U.K. 53°7N 2°1W 12 D5
Leeman Australia 29°57S 114°58E 61 E1
Leeper U.S.A. 41°22N 79°18W 82 E5
Leer Germany 53°13N 7°26E 16 B4
Leesburg U.S.A. 28°49N 81°53W 85 G14
Leesville U.S.A. 31°8N 93°16W 84 F8
Leeton Australia 34°33S 146°23E 63 E4
Leetonia U.S.A. 40°53N 80°45W 82 F4
Leeu Gamka S. Africa 32°47S 21°59E 56 E3
Leeuwarden Neths. 53°15N 5°48E 15 A5
Leeuwin, C. Australia 34°20S 115°9E 61 F2
Leeuwin Naturaliste △ Australia 34°6S 115°3E 61 F2
Leeward Is. Atl. Oc. 16°30N 63°30W 89 C7
Lefka Cyprus 35°6N 32°51E 25 D11
Lefkada Greece 38°40N 20°43E 23 E9
Lefkimi Greece 39°25N 20°3E 25 B4
Lefkimis, Akra Greece 39°29N 20°4E 25 B4
Lefkoniko Cyprus 35°18N 33°44E 25 D12
Lefroy Canada 44°16N 79°34W 82 B5
Lefroy, L. Australia 31°21S 121°40E 61 F3
Leganés Spain 40°19N 3°45W 21 B4
Legazpi Phil. 13°10N 123°45E 37 B6
Legendre I. Australia 20°22S 116°55E 60 D2
Leghorn = Livorno Italy 43°33N 10°19E 22 C4
Legionowo Poland 52°25N 20°50E 17 B11
Legnago Italy 45°11N 11°18E 22 B4
Legnica Poland 51°12N 16°10E 16 C9
Leh India 34°9N 77°35E 43 B7
Lehigh Acres U.S.A. 26°36N 81°39W 85 H14
Lehighton U.S.A. 40°50N 75°43W 83 F9
Lehututu Botswana 23°54S 21°55E 56 C3
Leiah Pakistan 30°58N 70°58E 42 D4
Leicester U.K. 52°38N 1°8W 13 E6
Leicester City □ U.K. 52°38N 1°8W 13 E6
Leicestershire □ U.K. 52°41N 1°17W 13 E6
Leichhardt → Australia 17°35S 139°48E 62 B2
Leichhardt Ra. Australia 20°46S 147°40E 62 C4
Leiden Neths. 52°9N 4°30E 15 B4
Leie → Belgium 51°2N 3°45E 15 C3
Leimus Nic. 14°40N 84°3W 88 D3
Leine → Germany 52°43N 9°36E 16 B5
Leinster Australia 27°51S 120°36E 61 E3
Leinster □ Ireland 53°3N 7°8W 10 C4
Leinster, Mt. Ireland 52°37N 6°46W 10 D5
Leipzig Germany 51°18N 12°22E 16 C7
Leiria Portugal 39°46N 8°53W 21 C1
Leirvik Norway 59°47N 5°28E 9 G11
Leisler, Mt. Australia 23°23S 129°20E 60 D4
Leith U.K. 55°59N 3°11W 11 F5
Leith Hill U.K. 51°11N 0°22W 13 F7
Leitrim Ireland 54°0N 8°5W 10 B3
Leitrim □ Ireland 54°8N 8°0W 10 B4
Leizhou Bandao China 21°0N 110°0E 33 D6
Lek → Neths. 51°54N 4°35E 15 C4
Leka Norway 65°5N 11°35E 8 D14
Leland Mich., U.S.A. 45°1N 85°45W 81 C11
Leland Miss., U.S.A. 33°24N 90°54W 85 E9
Leleque Argentina 42°28S 71°0W 96 E2
Lelystad Neths. 52°30N 5°25E 15 B5
Léman, L. Europe 46°26N 6°30E 20 C7
Lembar Indonesia 8°45S 116°4E 37 K19
Lembuak Indonesia 8°36S 116°11E 37 K19
Lemera Dem. Rep. of the Congo 3°0S 28°55E 54 C2
Lemhi Ra. U.S.A. 44°0N 113°0W 76 D7
Lemmer Neths. 52°51N 5°43E 15 B5
Lemmon U.S.A. 45°57N 102°10W 80 C2
Lemon Grove U.S.A. 32°44N 117°1W 79 N9
Lemoore U.S.A. 36°18N 119°46W 78 J7
Lemvig Denmark 56°33N 8°20E 9 H13
Lena → Russia 72°52N 126°40E 29 B13
Lenadoon Pt. Ireland 54°18N 9°3W 10 B2
Lenggong Malaysia 5°6N 100°58E 39 K3
Lengua de Vaca, Pta. Chile 30°14S 71°38W 94 C1
Lengwe △ Malawi 16°14S 34°45E 55 F3
Leninogorsk Kazakhstan 50°20N 83°30E 28 D9
Leninsk Russia 48°40N 45°15E 19 E8
Leninsk-Kuznetskiy Russia 54°44N 86°10E 28 D9
Lenkoran = Länkäran Azerbaijan 38°48N 48°52E 45 B6
Lenmalu Indonesia 1°45S 130°15E 37 E8
Lennox U.S.A. 43°21N 96°53W 80 D5
Lennoxville Canada 45°22N 71°51W 83 A13
Lenoir U.S.A. 35°55N 81°32W 85 D14
Lenoir City U.S.A. 35°48N 84°16W 85 D12
Lenore L. Canada 52°30N 104°59W 71 C8
Lenox U.S.A. 42°22N 73°17W 83 D11
Lens France 50°26N 2°50E 20 A5
Lensk Russia 60°48N 114°55E 29 C12
Lentas Greece 34°56N 24°56E 25 E6
Lentini Italy 37°17N 15°0E 22 F6
Lenwood U.S.A. 34°53N 117°7W 79 L9
Lenya Burma 11°33N 98°57E 39 G2
Leoben Austria 47°22N 15°5E 16 E8
Leodhas = Lewis U.K. 58°9N 6°40W 11 C2
Leola U.S.A. 45°43N 98°56W 80 C4
Leominster U.K. 52°14N 2°43W 13 E5
Leominster U.S.A. 42°32N 71°46W 83 D13
León Mexico 21°6N 101°41W 86 C4
León Nic. 12°20N 86°51W 88 D2
León Spain 42°38N 5°34W 21 A3
Leon U.S.A. 40°44N 93°45W 80 E7
Leon → U.S.A. 31°14N 97°28W 84 F6
León, Montes de Spain 42°30N 6°18W 21 A2
Leonardtown U.S.A. 38°17N 76°38W 81 F15
Leonardville Namibia 23°29S 18°49E 56 C2
Leone Amer. Samoa 14°23S 170°48W 59 b
Leongatha Australia 38°30S 145°58E 63 F4
Leonora Australia 28°49S 121°19E 61 E3
Leopoldina Brazil 21°28S 42°40W 95 A7
Leopoldsburg Belgium 51°7N 5°13E 15 C5
Leoti U.S.A. 38°29N 101°21W 80 F3
Leova Moldova 46°28N 28°15E 17 E15
Leoville Canada 53°39N 107°33W 71 C7
Lepel = Lyepyel Belarus 54°50N 28°40E 9 J23
Lépo, L. do Angola 17°0S 19°0E 56 B2
Leppävirta Finland 62°29N 27°46E 8 E22
Leptis Magna Libya 32°40N 14°12E 51 B8
Leribe Lesotho 28°51S 28°3E 57 D4
Lérida = Lleida Spain 41°37N 0°39E 21 B6
Lerwick U.K. 60°9N 1°9W 11 A7
Les Cayes Haiti 18°15N 73°46W 89 C5
Les Coteaux Canada 45°15N 74°13W 83 A10
Les Escoumins Canada 48°21N 69°24W 73 C6
Les Sables-d'Olonne France 46°30N 1°45W 20 C3
Lesbos Greece 39°10N 26°20E 23 E12
Leshan China 29°33N 103°41E 32 D5
Leshukonskoye Russia 64°54N 45°46E 18 B
Leshwe ⌂ Dem. Rep. of the Congo 12°45S 29°30E 55 E
Leskov I. Antarctica 56°0S 28°0W 5 B
Leskovac Serbia 43°0N 21°58E 23 C
Lesopilnoye Russia 46°44N 134°20E 30 A
Lesotho ■ Africa 29°40S 28°0E 57 D
Lesozavodsk Russia 45°30N 133°29E 30 B
Lesse → Belgium 50°15N 4°54E 15 D
Lesse et Lomme ⌂ Belgium 50°8N 5°9E 15 D
Lesser Antilles W. Indies 15°0N 61°0W 89 D
Lesser Slave L. Canada 55°30N 115°25W 70 B
Lesser Sunda Is. Indonesia 8°0S 120°0E 37
Lessines Belgium 50°42N 3°50E 15 D
Lester B. Pearson Int., Toronto ✕ (YYZ) Canada 43°46N 79°35W 82
Lestock Canada 51°19N 103°59W 71
Lesuer I. Australia 13°50S 127°17E 60
Lesueur △ Australia 30°11S 115°10E 61
Lésvos = Lesbos Greece 39°10N 26°20E 23 E
Leszno Poland 51°50N 16°30E 17 C
Letaba S. Africa 23°59S 31°50E 57 C
Letchworth U.K. 51°59N 0°13W 13
Lethbridge Canada 49°45N 112°45W 70 D
Lethem Guyana 3°20N 59°50W 92 C
Leti, Kepulauan Indonesia 8°10S 128°0E 37
Leti Is. = Leti, Kepulauan Indonesia 8°10S 128°0E 37
Letiahau → Botswana 21°16S 24°0E 56
Leticia Colombia 4°9S 70°0W 92 D
Leting China 39°23N 118°55E 35 E
Letjiesbos S. Africa 32°34S 22°16E 56
Letlhakane Botswana 21°27S 25°30E 56
Letlhakeng Botswana 24°0S 24°59E 56
Letpadan Burma 17°45N 95°45E 41 L
Letpan Burma 19°28N 94°10E 41 K
Letsôk-aw Kyun Burma 11°30N 98°25E 39
Letterkenny Ireland 54°57N 7°45W 10
Leucadia U.S.A. 33°4N 117°18W 79
Leuchars U.K. 56°24N 2°53W 11
Leuser, G. Indonesia 3°46N 97°12E 36
Leuven Belgium 50°52N 4°42E 15 D
Leuze-en-Hainaut Belgium 50°36N 3°37E 15
Levanger Norway 63°45N 11°19E 8 E
Levelland U.S.A. 33°35N 102°23W 84
Leven U.K. 56°12N 3°0W 11
Leven, L. U.K. 56°12N 3°22W 11
Leven, Toraka Madag. 12°30S 47°45E 57
Leveque C. Australia 16°20S 123°0E 60
Levice Slovak Rep. 48°13N 18°35E 17 D
Levin N.Z. 40°37S 175°18E 59 D
Lévis Canada 46°48N 71°9W 73 C
Levis, L. Canada 62°37N 117°58W 70
Levittown N.Y., U.S.A. 40°44N 73°31W 83 F
Levittown Pa., U.S.A. 40°9N 74°51W 83 F
Levka Oros Greece 35°18N 24°3E 25
Levkás = Lefkada Greece 38°40N 20°43E 23
Levkôsia = Nicosia Cyprus 35°10N 33°25E 25 D
Levskigrad = Karlovo Bulgaria 42°38N 24°47E 23 C
Levuka Fiji 17°34S 179°0E 59
Lewes U.K. 50°52N 0°1E 13
Lewes U.S.A. 38°46N 75°9W 81 F
Lewis U.K. 58°9N 6°40W 11
Lewis → U.S.A. 45°51N 122°48W 78
Lewis, Butt of U.K. 58°31N 6°16W 11
Lewis Ra. Australia 20°3S 128°50E 60
Lewis Range U.S.A. 48°5N 113°5W 76
Lewis Run U.S.A. 41°52N 78°40W 82
Lewisburg Pa., U.S.A. 40°58N 76°54W 82
Lewisburg Tenn., U.S.A. 35°27N 86°48W 85 D
Lewisburg W. Va., U.S.A. 37°48N 80°27W 81 G
Lewisporte Canada 49°15N 55°3W 73
Lewiston Idaho, U.S.A. 46°25N 117°1W 76
Lewiston Maine, U.S.A. 44°6N 70°13W 81 C
Lewiston N.Y., U.S.A. 43°11N 79°3W 82
Lewistown Mont., U.S.A. 47°4N 109°26W 76
Lewistown Pa., U.S.A. 40°36N 77°34W 82
Lexington Ill., U.S.A. 40°39N 88°47W 80
Lexington Ky., U.S.A. 38°3N 84°30W 81 F
Lexington Mich., U.S.A. 43°16N 82°32W 82
Lexington Mo., U.S.A. 39°11N 93°52W 80
Lexington N.C., U.S.A. 35°49N 80°15W 85 D
Lexington N.Y., U.S.A. 42°15N 74°22W 83 D
Lexington Nebr., U.S.A. 40°47N 99°45W 80
Lexington Ohio, U.S.A. 40°41N 82°35W 82
Lexington Tenn., U.S.A. 35°39N 88°24W 85 D
Lexington Va., U.S.A. 37°47N 79°27W 81 G
Lexington Park U.S.A. 38°16N 76°27W 81 F
Leyburn U.K. 54°19N 1°48W 12
Leyland U.K. 53°42N 2°43W 12
Leyte □ Phil. 11°0N 125°0E 37
Lezhë Albania 41°47N 19°39E 23
Lhasa China 29°25N 90°58E 32
Lhazê China 29°5N 87°38E 32
L'Hermite, I. Chile 55°50S 68°0W 96
Lhokkruet Indonesia 4°55N 95°24E 36
Lhokseumawe Indonesia 5°10N 97°10E 36
L'Hospitalet de Llobregat Spain 41°21N 2°6E 21
Li Thailand 17°48N 98°57E 38
Li Xian Gansu, China 34°10N 105°5E 34
Li Xian Hebei, China 38°30N 115°35E 34
Liancourt Rocks = Tokdo Asia 37°15N 131°52E 31
Lianga Phil. 8°38N 126°6E 37
Liangcheng Nei Monggol Zizhiqu, China 40°28N 112°25E 34
Liangcheng Shandong, China 35°32N 119°37E 35 G
Liangdang China 33°56N 106°18E 34
Liangpran Indonesia 1°4N 114°23E 36
Lianshanguan China 40°53N 123°43E 35 D
Lianshui China 33°42N 119°20E 35 H

anyungang China 34°40N 119°11E 35 G10
ao He → China 41°0N 121°50E 35 D11
aocheng China 36°28N 115°58E 34 F8
aodong Bandao China 40°20N 122°30E 35 E12
aodong Wan China 40°20N 121°10E 35 D11
aoning □ China 41°40N 122°30E 35 D12
aotung, G. of = Liaodong Wan
China 40°20N 121°10E 35 D11
aoyang China 41°15N 122°58E 35 D12
aoyuan China 42°58N 125°2E 35 C13
aozhong China 41°23N 122°50E 35 D12
apades Greece 39°42N 19°40E 25 A3
ard → Canada 61°51N 121°18W 70 A4
ard River Canada 59°25N 126°5W 70 B3
ari Pakistan 25°37N 66°30E 42 G2
oau = Liepāja Latvia 56°30N 21°0E 9 H19
oby U.S.A. 48°23N 115°33W 76 B6
oenge
Dem. Rep. of the Congo 3°40N 18°55E 52 D3
oeral U.S.A. 37°3N 100°55W 80 G3
oerec Czech Rep. 50°47N 15°7E 16 C8
oeria Costa Rica 10°40N 85°30W 88 D2
oeria ■ W. Afr. 6°30N 9°30W 50 G4
oertador □ Chile 34°15S 70°45W 94 C1
oerty Mo., U.S.A. 39°15N 94°25W 80 F6
oerty N.Y., U.S.A. 41°48N 74°45W 83 E10
oerty Pa., U.S.A. 41°34N 77°6W 82 E7
oerty Tex., U.S.A. 30°3N 94°48W 84 F7
erty-Newark Int. ✕ (EWR)
U.S.A. 40°42N 74°10W 83 F10
iya, Sahrâ' Africa 25°0N 25°0E 51 C10
obo, Tanjung
Indonesia 0°54S 128°28E 37 E7
ode S. Africa 31°33S 29°2E 57 E4
ong, Ko Thailand 7°15N 99°23E 39 J2
ourne France 44°55N 0°14W 20 D3
ramont Belgium 49°55N 5°23E 15 E5
reville Gabon 0°25N 9°26E 52 D1
ya ■ N. Afr. 27°0N 17°0E 51 C9
yan Desert = Lîbîya, Sahrâ'
Africa 25°0N 25°0E 51 C10
yan Plateau = Ed Déffa
Egypt 30°40N 26°30E 51 B11
antén Chile 35°55S 72°0W 94 D1
ata Italy 37°6N 13°56E 22 F5
heng China 36°28N 113°20E 34 F7
hfield U.K. 52°41N 1°49W 13 E6
hinga Mozam. 13°13S 35°11E 55 E4
htenburg S. Africa 26°8S 26°8E 56 D4
king → U.S.A. 39°6N 84°30W 81 F11
ungo → Mozam. 17°40S 37°15E 55 F4
a Belarus 53°53N 25°15E 17 B13
köping Sweden 58°31N 13°7E 9 G15
big, Mt. Australia 23°18S 131°22E 60 D5
chtenstein ■ Europe 47°8N 9°35E 20 C8
ge Belgium 50°38N 5°35E 15 D5
ge □ Belgium 50°32N 5°35E 15 D5
gnitz = Legnica
Poland 51°12N 16°10E 16 C9
ksa Finland 63°18N 30°2E 8 E24
nart
Dem. Rep. of the Congo 3°3N 25°31E 54 B2
nyünchiangshih =
ianyungang China 34°40N 119°11E 35 G10
nz Austria 46°50N 12°46E 16 E7
pāja Latvia 56°30N 21°0E 9 H19
r Belgium 51°7N 4°34E 15 C4
tuva = Lithuania ■
Europe 55°30N 24°0E 9 J21
vre → Canada 45°31N 75°26W 72 C4
ey → Ireland 53°21N 6°13W 10 C5
ord Ireland 54°51N 7°29W 10 B4
dzin Russia 44°21N 134°58E 30 B7
ntning Ridge
Australia 29°22S 148°0E 63 D4
onha → Mozam. 16°54S 39°9E 55 F4
onier U.S.A. 40°15N 79°14W 82 F5
uria □ Italy 44°30N 8°50E 20 D8
urian Sea Medit. S. 43°20N 9°0E 22 C3
ou Reefs and Cays
Australia 17°25S 151°40E 62 B5
ue U.S.A. 21°59N 159°23W 74 b
ué Calel △ Argentina 38°0S 65°10W 94 D2
ang China 26°55N 100°20E 32 D5
asi
Dem. Rep. of the Congo 10°55S 26°48E 55 E2
oma I. Malawi 12°3S 34°45E 55 E3
umburu Tanzania 9°43S 35°8E 55 D4
-Rousse France 42°38N 8°57E 20 E8
France 50°38N 3°3E 20 A5
Bælt Denmark 55°20N 9°45E 9 J13
hammer Norway 61°8N 10°30E 8 F14
sand Norway 58°15N 8°23E 9 G13
an Pt. Australia 27°40S 126°6E 61 E4
oet Canada 50°44N 121°57W 70 C4
oet → Canada 49°15N 121°57W 70 D4
ngwe Malawi 14°0S 33°48E 55 E3
y Phil. 8°4N 122°39E 37 C6
→ Europe 43°45N 19°15E 23 C8
Chu Kang Singapore 1°26N 103°43E 39 d
a Indonesia 3°39S 127°58E 37 E7
a Peru 12°3S 77°2W 92 F3
a Mont., U.S.A. 44°38N 112°36W 76 D7
a N.Y., U.S.A. 42°54N 77°36W 82 D7
a Ohio, U.S.A. 40°44N 84°6W 81 E11
a → Portugal 41°41N 8°50W 21 B1
an Indonesia 7°48S 111°45E 37 G14
assol Cyprus 34°42N 33°1E 25 E12
avady U.K. 55°3N 6°56W 10 A5
ay → Argentina 39°0S 68°0W 96 D3
ay Mahuida
Argentina 37°10S 66°45W 94 D2
oang Brunei 4°42N 115°6E 36 D5
baži Latvia 57°31N 24°42E 9 H21
odi India 22°34N 71°51E 42 H4
oe Cameroon 4°1N 9°10E 52 D1
ourg Germany 50°22N 8°4E 16 C5
Limburg □ Belgium 51°2N 5°25E 15 C5
Limburg □ Neths. 51°20N 5°55E 15 C5
Limeira Brazil 22°35S 47°28W 95 A6
Limerick Ireland 52°40N 8°37W 10 D3
Limerick U.S.A. 43°41N 70°48W 83 C14
Limerick □ Ireland 52°30N 8°50W 10 D3
Limestone U.S.A. 42°2N 78°38W 82 D6
Limestone → Canada 56°31N 94°7W 71 B10
Limfjorden Denmark 56°55N 9°0E 9 H13
Limia = Lima → Portugal 41°41N 8°50W 21 B1
Limingen Norway 64°48N 13°35E 8 D15
Limmen Bight Australia 14°40S 135°35E 62 A2
Limmen Bight →
Australia 15°7S 135°44E 62 B2
Limnos Greece 39°50N 25°5E 23 E11
Limoges Canada 45°20N 75°16W 83 A9
Limoges France 45°50N 1°15E 20 D4
Limón Costa Rica 10°0N 83°2W 88 E3
Limon U.S.A. 39°16N 103°41W 76 G12
Limousin □ France 45°30N 1°30E 20 D4
Limoux France 43°4N 2°12E 20 E5
Limpopo □ S. Africa 24°5S 29°0E 57 C4
Limpopo → Africa 25°5S 33°30E 57 D5
Limuru Kenya 1°2S 36°35E 54 C4
Lin Xian China 37°57N 110°58E 34 F6
Linares Chile 35°50S 71°40W 94 D1
Linares Mexico 24°52N 99°34W 87 C5
Linares Spain 38°10N 3°40W 21 C4
Lincang China 23°58N 100°1E 32 D5
Lincheng China 37°25N 114°30E 34 F8
Lincoln = Beamsville
Canada 43°12N 79°28W 82 C5
Lincoln Argentina 34°55S 61°30W 94 C3
Lincoln N.Z. 43°38S 172°30E 59 E4
Lincoln U.K. 53°14N 0°32W 12 D7
Lincoln Calif., U.S.A. 38°54N 121°17W 78 G5
Lincoln Ill., U.S.A. 40°9N 89°22W 80 E9
Lincoln Kans., U.S.A. 39°3N 98°9W 80 F4
Lincoln Maine, U.S.A. 45°22N 68°30W 81 C19
Lincoln N.H., U.S.A. 44°3N 71°40W 83 B13
Lincoln N. Mex.,
U.S.A. 33°30N 105°23W 77 K11
Lincoln Nebr., U.S.A. 40°49N 96°41W 80 E5
Lincoln City U.S.A. 44°57N 124°1W 76 D1
Lincoln Hav = Lincoln Sea
Arctic 84°0N 55°0W 66 A14
Lincoln Sea Arctic 84°0N 55°0W 66 A14
Lincolnshire □ U.K. 53°14N 0°32W 12 D7
Lincolnshire Wolds U.K. 53°26N 0°13W 12 D7
Lincolnton U.S.A. 35°29N 81°16W 85 D14
Lind U.S.A. 46°58N 118°37W 76 C4
Linda U.S.A. 39°8N 121°34W 78 F5
Lindeman I. Australia 20°27S 149°3E 62 J7
Linden Guyana 6°0N 58°10W 92 B7
Linden Ala., U.S.A. 32°18N 87°48W 85 E11
Linden Calif., U.S.A. 38°1N 121°5W 78 G5
Linden Tex., U.S.A. 33°1N 94°22W 84 E7
Lindenhurst U.S.A. 40°41N 73°23W 83 F11
Lindesnes Norway 57°58N 7°3E 9 H12
Lindi Tanzania 9°58S 39°38E 55 D4
Lindi □ Tanzania 9°40S 38°30E 55 D4
Lindi →
Dem. Rep. of the Congo 0°33N 25°5E 54 B2
Lindley U.S.A. 42°1N 77°8W 82 D7
Lindos Greece 36°6N 28°4E 25 C10
Lindos, Akra Greece 36°4N 28°10E 25 C10
Lindsay Canada 44°22N 78°43W 82 B6
Lindsay Calif., U.S.A. 36°12N 119°5W 78 J7
Lindsay Okla., U.S.A. 34°50N 97°38W 84 D6
Lindsborg U.S.A. 38°35N 97°40W 80 F5
Line Islands Pac. Oc. 7°0N 160°0W 65 H12
Linesville U.S.A. 41°39N 80°26W 82 E4
Linfen China 36°3N 111°30E 34 F6
Ling Xian China 37°22N 116°30E 34 F9
Lingao China 19°56N 109°42E 38 C7
Lingayen Phil. 16°1N 120°14E 37 A6
Lingayen G. Phil. 16°10N 120°15E 37 A6
Lingbi China 33°33N 117°33E 35 H9
Lingchuan China 35°45N 113°12E 34 G7
Lingding Yang China 22°25N 113°44E 33 G10
Lingen Germany 52°31N 7°19E 16 B4
Lingga Indonesia 0°12S 104°37E 36 E2
Lingga, Kepulauan
Indonesia 0°10S 104°30E 36 E2
Lingga Arch. = Lingga,
Kepulauan Indonesia 0°10S 104°30E 36 E2
Lingle U.S.A. 42°8N 104°21W 76 E11
Lingqiu China 39°28N 114°22E 34 E8
Lingshi China 36°48N 111°48E 34 F6
Lingshou China 38°20N 114°20E 34 E8
Lingshui China 18°27N 110°0E 38 C8
Lingtai China 35°0N 107°40E 34 G4
Linguère Senegal 15°25N 15°5W 50 E2
Lingwu China 38°6N 106°20E 34 E4
Lingyuan China 41°10N 119°15E 35 D10
Linhai China 28°50N 121°8E 33 D7
Linhares Brazil 19°25S 40°4W 93 G10
Linhe China 40°48N 107°20E 34 D4
Linjiang China 41°50N 127°0E 35 D14
Linköping Sweden 58°28N 15°36E 9 G16
Linkou China 45°15N 130°18E 35 B16
Linnhe, L. U.K. 56°36N 5°25W 11 E3
Linosa Medit. S. 35°51N 12°50E 22 G5
Linqi China 35°45N 113°52E 34 G7
Linqing China 36°50N 115°42E 34 F8
Linqu China 36°25N 118°30E 35 F10
Linru China 34°11N 112°52E 34 G7
Lins Brazil 21°40S 49°44W 95 A6
Linstead Jamaica 18°8N 77°2W 88 a
Linta → Madag. 25°2S 44°5E 57 D7
Linton Ind., U.S.A. 39°2N 87°10W 80 F10
Linton N. Dak., U.S.A. 46°16N 100°14W 80 B3
Lintong China 34°20N 109°10E 34 G5
Linwood Canada 43°35N 80°43W 82 C4
Linxi China 43°36N 118°2E 35 C10
Linxia China 35°36N 103°10E 32 C5
Linyanti → Africa 17°50S 25°5E 56 B4
Linyi China 35°5N 118°21E 35 G10
Linz Austria 48°18N 14°18E 16 D8
Linzhenzhen China 36°30N 109°59E 34 F5
Linzi China 36°50N 118°20E 35 F10
Lion, G. du France 43°10N 4°0E 20 E6
Lionárisso Cyprus 35°28N 34°8E 25 D13
Lions, G. of = Lion, G. du
France 43°10N 4°0E 20 E6
Lion's Den Zimbabwe 17°15S 30°5E 55 F3
Lion's Head Canada 44°58N 81°15W 82 B3
Lipa Phil. 13°57N 121°10E 37 B6
Lipali Mozam. 15°50S 35°50E 55 F4
Lípari Italy 38°26N 14°58E 22 E6
Lípari, Is. = Eólie, Ís.
Italy 38°30N 14°57E 22 E6
Lipcani Moldova 48°14N 26°48E 17 D14
Liperi Finland 62°31N 29°24E 8 E23
Lipetsk Russia 52°37N 39°35E 18 D6
Lipkany = Lipcani
Moldova 48°14N 26°48E 17 D14
Lipovets Ukraine 49°12N 29°1E 17 D15
Lippe → Germany 51°39N 6°36E 16 C4
Lipscomb U.S.A. 36°14N 100°16W 84 C4
Liptrap, C. Australia 38°50S 145°55E 63 F4
Lira Uganda 2°17N 32°57E 54 B3
Liria = Lliria Spain 39°37N 0°35W 21 C5
Lisala
Dem. Rep. of the Congo 2°12N 21°38E 52 D4
Lisboa Portugal 38°42N 9°8W 21 C1
Lisbon = Lisboa Portugal 38°42N 9°8W 21 C1
Lisbon N. Dak., U.S.A. 46°27N 97°41W 80 B5
Lisbon N.H., U.S.A. 44°13N 71°55W 83 B13
Lisbon N.Y., U.S.A. 44°43N 75°19W 83 B9
Lisbon Ohio, U.S.A. 40°46N 80°46W 82 F4
Lisbon Falls U.S.A. 44°0N 70°4W 81 D18
Lisburn U.K. 54°31N 6°3W 10 B5
Lisburne, C. U.S.A. 68°53N 166°13W 4 C17
Liscannor B. Ireland 52°55N 9°24W 10 D2
Lisdoonvarna Ireland 53°2N 9°18W 10 C2
Lishi China 37°31N 111°8E 34 F6
Lishu China 43°20N 124°18E 35 C13
Lisianski I. U.S.A. 26°2N 174°0W 64 E10
Lisichansk = Lysychansk
Ukraine 48°55N 38°30E 19 E6
Lisieux France 49°10N 0°12E 20 B4
Liski Russia 51°3N 39°30E 19 D6
Lismore Australia 28°44S 153°21E 63 D5
Lismore Ireland 52°8N 7°55W 10 D4
Lista Norway 58°7N 6°39E 9 G12
Lister, Mt. Antarctica 78°0S 162°0E 5 D11
Liston Australia 28°39S 152°6E 63 D5
Listowel Canada 43°44N 80°58W 82 C4
Listowel Ireland 52°27N 9°29W 10 D2
Litani → Lebanon 33°20N 35°15E 46 B4
Litchfield Calif., U.S.A. 40°24N 120°23W 78 E6
Litchfield Conn., U.S.A. 41°45N 73°11W 83 E11
Litchfield Ill., U.S.A. 39°11N 89°39W 80 F9
Litchfield Minn., U.S.A. 45°8N 94°32W 80 C6
Litchfield △ Australia 13°14S 131°1E 60 B5
Lithgow Australia 33°25S 150°8E 63 E5
Lithino, Akra Greece 34°55N 24°44E 25 E6
Lithuania ■ Europe 55°30N 24°0E 9 J21
Lititz U.S.A. 40°9N 76°18W 83 F8
Litoměřice Czech Rep. 50°33N 14°10E 16 C8
Little Abaco Bahamas 26°50N 77°30W 88 A4
Little Barrier I. N.Z. 36°12S 175°8E 59 B5
Little Belt Mts. U.S.A. 46°40N 110°45W 76 C8
Little Bighorn Battlefield ⌂
U.S.A. 45°34N 107°25W 76 D10
Little Blue → U.S.A. 39°42N 96°41W 80 F5
Little Buffalo → Canada 61°0N 113°46W 70 A6
Little Cayman Cayman Is. 19°41N 80°3W 88 C3
Little Churchill →
Canada 57°30N 95°22W 71 B9
Little Colorado →
U.S.A. 36°12N 111°48W 77 H8
Little Current Canada 45°55N 82°0W 72 C3
Little Current → Canada 50°57N 84°36W 72 B3
Little Falls Minn., U.S.A. 45°59N 94°22W 80 C6
Little Falls N.Y., U.S.A. 43°3N 74°51W 83 C10
Little Fork → U.S.A. 48°31N 93°35W 80 A7
Little Grand Rapids
Canada 52°0N 95°29W 71 C9
Little Humboldt →
U.S.A. 41°1N 117°43W 76 F5
Little Inagua I. Bahamas 21°40N 73°50W 89 B5
Little Karoo S. Africa 33°45S 21°0E 56 E3
Little Khingan Mts. = Xiao
Hinggan Ling China 49°0N 127°0E 33 B7
Little Lake U.S.A. 35°56N 117°55W 79 K9
Little Laut Is. = Laut Kecil,
Kepulauan Indonesia 4°45S 115°40E 36 E5
Little Mecatina = Petit-
Mécatina → Canada 50°40N 59°30W 73 B8
Little Minch U.K. 57°35N 6°45W 11 D2
Little Missouri →
U.S.A. 47°36N 102°25W 80 B2
Little Ouse → U.K. 52°22N 1°12E 13 E9
Little Rann India 23°25N 71°25E 42 H4
Little Red → U.S.A. 35°11N 91°27W 84 D9
Little River N.Z. 43°45S 172°49E 59 E4
Little Rock U.S.A. 34°45N 92°17W 84 D8
Little Ruaha → Tanzania 7°57S 37°53E 54 D4
Little Sable Pt. U.S.A. 43°38N 86°33W 80 D10
Little Sioux → U.S.A. 41°48N 96°4W 80 E5
Little Smoky →
Canada 54°44N 117°11W 70 C5
Little Snake → U.S.A. 40°27N 108°26W 76 F9
Little Tobago
Trin. & Tob. 11°18N 60°30W 93 J16
Little Valley U.S.A. 42°15N 78°48W 82 D6
Little Wabash → U.S.A. 37°55N 88°5W 80 G9
Little White → U.S.A. 43°40N 100°40W 80 D3
Little Zab = Zāb aş Şaghīr →
Iraq 35°17N 43°29E 44 C4
Littlefield U.S.A. 33°55N 102°20W 84 E3
Littlehampton U.K. 50°49N 0°32W 13 G7
Littleton U.S.A. 44°18N 71°46W 83 B13
Liu He → China 40°55N 121°35E 35 D11
Liuba China 33°38N 106°55E 34 H4
Liugou China 40°57N 118°15E 35 D10
Liuhe China 42°17N 125°43E 35 C13
Liukang Tenggaja = Sabalana,
Kepulauan Indonesia 6°45S 118°50E 37 F5
Liuli Tanzania 11°3S 34°38E 55 E3
Liupanshui China 26°38N 104°48E 32 D5
Liuwa Plain Zambia 14°20S 22°30E 53 G4
Liuzhou China 24°22N 109°22E 33 D5
Liuzhuang China 33°12N 120°18E 35 H11
Livadhia Cyprus 34°57N 33°38E 25 E12
Livadia Greece 38°27N 22°54E 23 E10
Live Oak Calif., U.S.A. 39°17N 121°40W 78 F5
Live Oak Fla., U.S.A. 30°18N 82°59W 85 F13
Lively Canada 46°26N 81°9W 81 B13
Liveras Cyprus 35°23N 32°57E 25 D11
Livermore U.S.A. 37°41N 121°47W 78 H5
Livermore, Mt. U.S.A. 30°38N 104°11W 84 F2
Livermore Falls U.S.A. 44°29N 70°11W 81 C18
Liverpool Australia 33°54S 150°58E 63 B5
Liverpool Canada 44°5N 64°41W 73 D7
Liverpool U.K. 53°25N 3°0W 12 D4
Liverpool U.S.A. 43°6N 76°13W 83 C8
Liverpool Bay U.K. 53°30N 3°20W 12 D4
Liverpool Ra. Australia 31°50S 150°30E 63 E5
Livingston Guatemala 15°50N 88°50W 88 C2
Livingston U.K. 55°54N 3°30W 11 F5
Livingston Ala., U.S.A. 32°35N 88°11W 85 E10
Livingston Calif., U.S.A. 37°23N 120°43W 78 H6
Livingston Mont.,
U.S.A. 45°40N 110°34W 76 D8
Livingston S.C., U.S.A. 33°38N 81°7W 85 E14
Livingston Tenn.,
U.S.A. 36°23N 85°19W 85 C12
Livingston Tex., U.S.A. 30°43N 94°56W 84 F7
Livingston, L. U.S.A. 30°50N 95°10W 84 F7
Livingston Manor
U.S.A. 41°54N 74°50W 83 E10
Livingstone Zambia 17°46S 25°52E 55 F2
Livingstone Mts. Tanzania 9°40S 34°20E 55 D3
Livingstonia Malawi 10°38S 34°5E 55 E3
Livny Russia 52°30N 37°30E 18 D6
Livonia Mich., U.S.A. 42°23N 83°23W 81 D12
Livonia N.Y., U.S.A. 42°49N 77°40W 82 D7
Livorno Italy 43°33N 10°19E 22 C4
Livramento Brazil 30°55S 55°30W 95 C4
Liwale Tanzania 9°48S 37°58E 55 D4
Liwonde △ Malawi 14°48S 35°20E 55 E4
Lizard I. Australia 14°42S 145°30E 62 A4
Lizard Pt. U.K. 49°57N 5°13W 13 H2
Ljubljana Slovenia 46°4N 14°33E 16 E8
Ljungan → Sweden 62°18N 17°23E 8 E17
Ljungby Sweden 56°49N 13°55E 9 H15
Ljusdal Sweden 61°46N 16°3E 8 F17
Ljusnan → Sweden 61°12N 17°8E 8 F17
Ljusne Sweden 61°13N 17°7E 8 F17
Llancanelo, Salina
Argentina 35°40S 69°8W 94 D2
Llandeilo U.K. 51°53N 3°59W 13 F4
Llandovery U.K. 51°59N 3°48W 13 F4
Llandrindod Wells U.K. 52°14N 3°22W 13 E4
Llandudno U.K. 53°19N 3°50W 12 D4
Llanelli U.K. 51°41N 4°10W 13 F3
Llanes Spain 43°25N 4°50W 21 A3
Llangollen U.K. 52°58N 3°11W 12 E4
Llanidloes U.K. 52°27N 3°31W 13 E4
Llano U.S.A. 30°45N 98°41W 84 F5
Llano → U.S.A. 30°39N 98°26W 84 F5
Llano Estacado U.S.A. 33°30N 103°0W 84 E3
Llanos S. Amer. 5°0N 71°35W 92 C4
Llanos de Challe △ Chile 28°8S 71°1W 94 B1
Llanquihue, L. Chile 41°10S 72°50W 96 E1
Llanwrtyd Wells U.K. 52°7N 3°38W 13 E4
Llebeig, C. des Spain 39°33N 2°18E 24 B9
Lleida Spain 41°37N 0°39E 21 B6
Llentrisca, C. Spain 38°52N 1°15E 24 C7
Llera de Canales Mexico 23°19N 99°1W 87 C5
Lleyn Peninsula U.K. 52°51N 4°36W 12 E3
Llico Chile 34°46S 72°5W 94 C1
Lliria Spain 39°37N 0°35W 21 C5
Llobregat → Spain 41°19N 2°5E 21 B7
Lloret de Mar Spain 41°41N 2°53E 21 B7
Lloseta Spain 39°43N 2°52E 24 B9
Lloyd B. Australia 12°45S 143°27E 62 A3
Lloyd L. Canada 57°22N 108°57W 71 B7
Lloydminster Canada 53°17N 110°0W 71 C7
Llubí Spain 39°42N 3°0E 24 B10
Llucmajor Spain 39°29N 2°53E 24 B9
Llullaillaco, Volcán
S. Amer. 24°43S 68°30W 94 A2
Llullaillaco △ Chile 24°50S 68°51W 94 A2
Lo → Vietnam 21°18N 105°25E 38 B5
Loa U.S.A. 38°24N 111°39W 76 G8
Loa → Chile 21°26S 70°41W 94 A1
Loaita I. S. China Sea 10°41N 114°25E 36 B4
Loange →
Dem. Rep. of the Congo 4°17S 20°2E 52 E4
Lobatse Botswana 25°12S 25°40E 56 D4
Lobería Argentina 38°10S 58°40W 94 D4
Lobito Angola 12°18S 13°35E 53 G2
Lobos Argentina 35°10S 59°0W 94 D4
Lobos, I. Mexico 27°20N 110°36W 86 B2
Lobos, I. de Canary Is. 28°45N 13°50W 24 F6
Loc Binh Vietnam 21°46N 106°54E 38 B6
Loc Ninh Vietnam 11°50N 106°34E 39 G6
Locarno Switz. 46°10N 8°47E 20 C8
Loch Baghasdail = Lochboisdale
U.K. 57°9N 7°20W 11 D1
Loch Garman = Wexford
Ireland 52°20N 6°28W 10 D5
Loch Lomond and the
Trossachs △ U.K. 56°10N 4°40W 11 E4
Loch Nam Madadh = Lochmaddy
U.K. 57°36N 7°10W 11 D1
Lochaber U.K. 56°59N 5°1W 11 E3
Locharbriggs U.K. 55°7N 3°35W 11 F5
Lochboisdale U.K. 57°9N 7°20W 11 D1
Loche, L. La Canada 56°30N 109°30W 71 B7
Lochem Neths. 52°9N 6°26E 15 B6
Loches France 47°7N 1°0E 20 C4
Lochgilphead U.K. 56°2N 5°26W 11 E3
Lochinvar △ Zambia 15°55S 27°15E 55 F2
Lochinver U.K. 58°9N 5°14W 11 C3
Lochmaddy U.K. 57°36N 7°10W 11 D1
Lochnagar Australia 23°33S 145°38E 62 C4
Lochnagar U.K. 56°57N 3°15W 11 E5
Lochy, L. U.K. 57°0N 4°53W 11 E4
Lock Australia 33°34S 135°46E 63 E2
Lock Haven U.S.A. 41°8N 77°28W 82 E7
Lockeford U.S.A. 38°10N 121°9W 78 G5
Lockeport Canada 43°47N 65°4W 73 D6
Lockerbie U.K. 55°7N 3°21W 11 F5
Lockhart U.S.A. 29°53N 97°40W 84 G6
Lockhart, L. Australia 33°15S 119°3E 61 F2
Lockhart River
Australia 12°58S 143°30E 62 A3
Lockney U.S.A. 34°7N 101°27W 84 D4
Lockport U.S.A. 43°10N 78°42W 82 C6
Lod Israel 31°57N 34°54E 46 D3
Lodeinoye Pole Russia 60°44N 33°33E 18 B5
Lodge Bay Canada 52°14N 55°51W 73 B8
Lodge Grass U.S.A. 45°19N 107°22W 76 D10
Lodhran Pakistan 29°32N 71°30E 42 E4
Lodi Italy 45°19N 9°30E 20 D8
Lodi Calif., U.S.A. 38°8N 121°16W 78 G5
Lodi Ohio, U.S.A. 41°2N 82°1W 82 E3
Lodja
Dem. Rep. of the Congo 3°30S 23°23E 54 C1
Lodwar Kenya 3°7N 35°36E 54 B4
Łódź Poland 51°45N 19°27E 17 C10
Loei Thailand 17°29N 101°35E 38 D3
Loengo
Dem. Rep. of the Congo 4°48S 26°30E 54 C2
Loeriesfontein S. Africa 31°0S 19°26E 56 E2
Lofoten Norway 68°30N 14°0E 8 B16
Logan Iowa, U.S.A. 41°39N 95°47W 80 E6
Logan Ohio, U.S.A. 39°32N 82°25W 81 F12
Logan Utah, U.S.A. 41°44N 111°50W 76 F8
Logan W. Va., U.S.A. 37°51N 81°59W 81 G13
Logan, Mt. Canada 60°34N 140°23W 68 C5
Logandale U.S.A. 36°36N 114°29W 79 J12
Logansport Ind., U.S.A. 40°45N 86°22W 80 E10
Logansport La., U.S.A. 31°58N 94°0W 84 F8
Logone → Chad 12°6N 15°2E 51 F9
Logroño Spain 42°28N 2°27W 21 A4
Lohardaga India 23°27N 84°45E 43 H11
Loharia India 23°45N 74°14E 42 H6
Loharu India 28°27N 75°49E 42 E6
Lohri Wah → Pakistan 27°27N 67°37E 42 F2
Loi-kaw Burma 19°40N 97°17E 41 K20
Loimaa Finland 60°50N 23°5E 8 F20
Loir → France 47°33N 0°32W 20 C3
Loire → France 47°16N 2°10W 20 C2
Loja Ecuador 3°59S 79°16W 92 D3
Loja Spain 37°10N 4°10W 21 D3
Loji = Kawasi Indonesia 1°38S 127°28E 37 E7
Lokandu
Dem. Rep. of the Congo 2°30S 25°45E 54 C2
Lokeren Belgium 51°6N 3°59E 15 C3
Lokgwabe Botswana 24°10S 21°50E 56 C3
Lokichar Kenya 2°23N 35°39E 54 B4
Lokichokio Kenya 4°19N 34°13E 54 B3
Lokitaung Kenya 4°12N 35°48E 54 B4
Lokkan tekojärvi
Finland 67°55N 27°35E 8 C22
Lokoja Nigeria 7°47N 6°45E 50 G7
Lokolo →
Dem. Rep. of the Congo 1°43S 18°23E 52 E3
Lola, Mt. U.S.A. 39°26N 120°22W 78 F6
Lolgorien Kenya 1°14S 34°48E 54 C3
Loliondo Tanzania 2°2S 35°39E 54 C4
Lolland Denmark 54°45N 11°30E 9 J14
Lolo U.S.A. 46°45N 114°5W 76 C6
Lom Bulgaria 43°48N 23°12E 23 C10
Lom Kao Thailand 16°53N 101°14E 38 D3
Lom Sak Thailand 16°47N 101°15E 38 D3
Loma U.S.A. 47°56N 110°30W 76 C8
Loma Linda U.S.A. 34°3N 117°16W 79 L9
Lomaloma Fiji 17°17S 178°59W 59 a
Lomami →
Dem. Rep. of the Congo 0°46N 24°16E 54 B1
Lomas de Zamora
Argentina 34°45S 58°24W 94 C4
Lombadina Australia 16°31S 122°54E 60 C3
Lombárdia □ Italy 45°40N 9°30E 20 D8
Lombardy = Lombárdia □
Italy 45°40N 9°30E 20 D8
Lomblen Indonesia 8°30S 123°32E 37 F6
Lombok Indonesia 8°45S 116°30E 36 F5
Lombok, Selat Indonesia 8°30S 115°50E 37 K18
Lomé Togo 6°9N 1°20E 50 G6
Lomela
Dem. Rep. of the Congo 2°19S 23°15E 52 E4
Lomela →
Dem. Rep. of the Congo 0°15S 20°40E 52 E4
Lommel Belgium 51°14N 5°19E 15 C5
Lomond Canada 50°24N 112°36W 70 C6
Lomond, L. U.K. 56°8N 4°38W 11 E4
Lomonosov Ridge Arctic 88°0N 140°0E 4 A
Lomphat Cambodia 13°30N 106°59E 38 F6
Lompobatang Indonesia 5°24S 119°56E 37 F5
Lompoc U.S.A. 34°38N 120°28W 79 L6
Łomża Poland 53°10N 22°2E 17 B12
Lon, Ko Thailand 7°47N 98°23E 39 a
Loncoche Chile 39°20S 72°50W 96 D2
Londa India 15°30N 74°30E 40 M9
Londiani Kenya 0°10S 35°33E 54 C4
London Canada 42°59N 81°15W 82 D3
London U.K. 51°30N 0°3W 13 F7
London Ky., U.S.A. 37°8N 84°5W 81 G11
London Ohio, U.S.A. 39°53N 83°27W 81 F12
London, Greater □ U.K. 51°36N 0°5W 13 F7

London Gatwick ✈ (LGW) *U.K.* 51°10N 0°11W **13** F7
London Heathrow ✈ (LHR) *U.K.* 51°28N 0°27W **13** F7
London Stansted ✈ (STN) *U.K.* 51°54N 0°14E **13** F8
Londonderry *U.K.* 55°0N 7°20W **10** B4
Londonderry □ *U.K.* 55°0N 7°20W **10** B4
Londonderry, C. *Australia* 13°45S 126°55E **60** B4
Londonderry, I. *Chile* 55°0S 71°0W **96** H2
Londres *Argentina* 27°43S 67°7W **96** B3
Londrina *Brazil* 23°18S 51°10W **95** A5
Lone Pine *U.S.A.* 36°36N 118°4W **78** J8
Lonely Mine *Zimbabwe* 19°30S 28°49E **57** B4
Long B. *U.S.A.* 33°35N 78°45W **85** E15
Long Beach *Calif., U.S.A.* 33°46N 118°11W **79** M8
Long Beach *N.Y., U.S.A.* 40°35N 73°39W **83** F11
Long Beach *Wash., U.S.A.* 46°21N 124°3W **78** D2
Long Branch *U.S.A.* 40°18N 74°0W **83** F11
Long Creek *U.S.A.* 44°43N 119°6W **76** D4
Long Eaton *U.K.* 52°53N 1°15W **12** E6
Long I. *Australia* 20°22S 148°51E **62** J6
Long I. *Bahamas* 23°20N 75°10W **89** B4
Long I. *Canada* 54°50N 79°20W **72** B4
Long I. *Ireland* 51°30N 9°34W **10** E2
Long I. *U.S.A.* 40°45N 73°30W **83** F11
Long Island Sd. *U.S.A.* 41°10N 73°0W **83** E12
Long L. *Canada* 49°30N 86°50W **72** C2
Long L. *U.S.A.* 44°0N 74°23W **83** C10
Long Lake *U.S.A.* 43°58N 74°25W **83** C10
Long Point *Canada* 42°34N 80°25W **82** D4
Long Point B. *Canada* 42°40N 80°10W **82** D4
Long Prairie *U.S.A.* 45°59N 94°52W **80** C6
Long Prairie → *U.S.A.* 46°20N 94°36W **80** B6
Long Pt. *Ont., Canada* 42°35N 80°2W **82** D4
Long Pt. *Ont., Canada* 43°56N 76°53W **83** C8
Long Range Mts. *Canada* 49°30N 57°30W **73** C8
Long Reef *Australia* 14°1S 125°48E **60** B4
Long Sault *Canada* 45°2N 74°53W **83** A10
Long Str. = Longa, Proliv *Russia* 70°0N 175°0E **29** C18
Long Thanh *Vietnam* 10°47N 106°57E **39** G6
Long Xian *China* 34°55N 106°55E **34** G4
Long Xuyen *Vietnam* 10°19N 105°28E **39** G5
Longa, Proliv *Russia* 70°0N 175°0E **29** C18
Longbenton *U.K.* 55°1N 1°31W **12** B6
Longboat Key *U.S.A.* 27°23N 82°39W **85** H13
Longde *China* 35°30N 106°20E **34** G4
Longford *Australia* 41°32S 147°3E **63** G4
Longford *Ireland* 53°43N 7°49W **10** C4
Longford □ *Ireland* 53°42N 7°45W **10** C4
Longhua *Guangdong, China* 22°39N 114°0E **33** F11
Longhua *Hebei, China* 41°18N 117°45E **35** D9
Longido *Tanzania* 2°43S 36°42E **54** C4
Longiram *Indonesia* 0°5S 115°45E **36** E5
Longkou *China* 37°40N 120°18E **35** F11
Longlac *Canada* 49°45N 86°25W **72** C2
Longmeadow *U.S.A.* 42°3N 72°34W **83** D12
Longmont *U.S.A.* 40°10N 105°6W **76** F11
Longnawan *Indonesia* 1°51N 114°55E **36** D4
Longreach *Australia* 23°28S 144°14E **62** C3
Longueuil *Canada* 45°31N 73°29W **83** A11
Longview *Tex., U.S.A.* 32°30N 94°44W **84** E7
Longview *Wash., U.S.A.* 46°8N 122°57W **78** D4
Longxi *China* 34°53N 104°40E **34** G3
Longxue Dao *China* 22°41N 113°38E **33** F10
Longyearbyen *Svalbard* 78°13N 15°40E **4** B8
Lonoke *U.S.A.* 34°47N 91°54W **84** D9
Lonquimay *Chile* 38°26S 71°14W **96** D2
Lons-le-Saunier *France* 46°40N 5°31E **20** C6
Looe *U.K.* 50°22N 4°28W **13** G3
Lookout, C. *Canada* 55°18N 83°56W **72** A3
Lookout, C. *U.S.A.* 34°35N 76°32W **85** D16
Loolmalasin *Tanzania* 3°0S 35°53E **54** C4
Loon → *Alta., Canada* 57°8N 115°3W **70** B5
Loon → *Man., Canada* 55°53N 101°59W **71** B8
Loon Lake *Canada* 54°2N 109°10W **71** C7
Loongana *Australia* 30°52S 127°5E **61** F4
Loop Hd. *Ireland* 52°34N 9°56W **10** D2
Lop *China* 37°3N 80°11E **32** C3
Lop Buri *Thailand* 14°48N 100°37E **38** E3
Lop Nor = Lop Nur *China* 40°20N 90°10E **32** B4
Lop Nur *China* 40°20N 90°10E **32** B4
Lopatina, Gora *Russia* 50°47N 143°10E **29** D15
Lopatka, Mys *Russia* 50°52N 156°40E **29** D16
Lopez *U.S.A.* 41°27N 76°20W **83** E8
Lopez, C. *Gabon* 0°47S 8°40E **52** E1
Lopphavet *Norway* 70°27N 21°15E **8** A19
Lora → *Afghan.* 31°35N 66°32E **40** D4
Lora, Hāmūn-i- *Pakistan* 29°38N 64°58E **40** E4
Lora Cr. → *Australia* 28°10S 135°22E **63** D2
Lora del Río *Spain* 37°39N 5°33W **21** D3
Lorain *U.S.A.* 41°28N 82°11W **82** E2
Loralai *Pakistan* 30°20N 68°41E **42** D3
Lorca *Spain* 37°41N 1°42W **21** D5
Lord Howe I. *Pac. Oc.* 31°33S 159°6E **58** E8
Lord Howe Rise *Pac. Oc.* 30°0S 162°30E **64** L8
Lordsburg *U.S.A.* 32°21N 108°43W **77** K9
Lorestān □ *Iran* 33°30N 48°40E **45** C6
Loreto *Brazil* 7°5S 45°10W **93** E9
Loreto *Mexico* 26°0N 111°21W **86** B2
Lorient *France* 47°45N 3°23W **20** C2
Lormi *India* 22°17N 81°41E **43** H9
Lorn *U.K.* 56°26N 5°10W **11** E3
Lorn, Firth of *U.K.* 56°20N 5°40W **11** E3
Lorne *Australia* 38°33S 143°59E **63** F3
Lorovouno *Cyprus* 35°8N 32°36E **25** D11
Lorraine □ *France* 48°53N 6°0E **20** B7
Los Alamos *Calif., U.S.A.* 34°44N 120°17W **79** L6
Los Alamos *N. Mex., U.S.A.* 35°53N 106°19W **77** J10
Los Altos *U.S.A.* 37°23N 122°7W **78** H4
Los Andes *Chile* 32°50S 70°40W **94** C1
Los Angeles *Chile* 37°28S 72°23W **94** D1
Los Angeles *U.S.A.* 34°4N 118°15W **79** M8
Los Angeles, Bahia de *Mexico* 28°56N 113°34W **86** B2
Los Angeles Aqueduct *U.S.A.* 35°22N 118°5W **79** K9
Los Angeles Int. ✈ (LAX) *U.S.A.* 33°57N 118°25W **79** M8
Los Banos *U.S.A.* 37°4N 120°51W **78** H6
Los Blancos *Argentina* 23°40S 62°30W **94** A3
Los Cardones △ *Argentina* 25°8S 65°55W **94** B2
Los Chiles *Costa Rica* 11°2N 84°43W **88** D3
Los Cristianos *Canary Is.* 28°3N 16°42W **24** F3
Los Gatos *U.S.A.* 37°14N 121°59W **78** H5
Los Haïtises △ *Dom. Rep.* 19°4N 69°36W **89** C6
Los Hermanos Is. *Venezuela* 11°45N 64°25W **89** D7
Los Islotes *Canary Is.* 29°4N 13°44W **24** E6
Los Llanos de Aridane *Canary Is.* 28°38N 17°54W **24** F2
Los Loros *Chile* 27°50S 70°6W **94** B1
Los Lunas *U.S.A.* 34°48N 106°44W **77** J10
Los Mochis *Mexico* 25°45N 108°57W **86** B3
Los Olivos *U.S.A.* 34°40N 120°7W **79** L6
Los Palacios *Cuba* 22°35N 83°15W **88** B3
Los Queñes *Chile* 35°1S 70°48W **94** D1
Los Reyes de Salgado *Mexico* 19°35N 102°29W **86** D4
Los Roques Is. *Venezuela* 11°50N 66°45W **89** D6
Los Teques *Venezuela* 10°21N 67°2W **92** A5
Los Testigos, Is. *Venezuela* 11°23N 63°6W **92** A6
Los Vilos *Chile* 32°10S 71°30W **94** C1
Lošinj *Croatia* 44°30N 14°30E **16** F8
Loskop Dam *S. Africa* 25°23S 29°20E **57** D4
Lossiemouth *U.K.* 57°42N 3°17W **11** D5
Lostwithiel *U.K.* 50°24N 4°41W **13** G3
Lot → *France* 44°18N 0°20E **20** D4
Lota *Chile* 37°5S 73°10W **94** D1
Loṭfābād *Iran* 37°32N 59°20E **45** B8
Lothair *S. Africa* 26°22S 30°27E **57** D5
Lotta → *Europe* 68°42N 31°6E **8** B24
Loubomo *Congo* 4°9S 12°47E **52** E2
Loudonville *U.S.A.* 40°38N 82°14W **82** F2
Louga *Senegal* 15°45N 16°5W **50** E2
Loughborough *U.K.* 52°47N 1°11W **12** E6
Lougheed I. *Canada* 77°26N 105°6W **69** B9
Loughrea *Ireland* 53°12N 8°33W **10** C3
Loughros More B. *Ireland* 54°48N 8°32W **10** B3
Louis Trichardt *S. Africa* 23°1S 29°43E **57** C4
Louis XIV, Pte. *Canada* 54°37N 79°45W **72** B4
Louisa *U.S.A.* 38°7N 82°36W **81** F12
Louisbourg *Canada* 45°55N 60°0W **73** C8
Louisburgh *Ireland* 53°46N 9°49W **10** C2
Louise I. *Canada* 52°55N 131°50W **70** C2
Louiseville *Canada* 46°20N 72°56W **72** C5
Louisiade Arch. *Papua N. G.* 11°10S 153°0E **58** C8
Louisiana *U.S.A.* 39°27N 91°3W **80** F8
Louisiana □ *U.S.A.* 30°50N 92°0W **84** F9
Louisville *Ky., U.S.A.* 38°15N 85°46W **81** F11
Louisville *Miss., U.S.A.* 33°7N 89°3W **85** E10
Louisville *Ohio, U.S.A.* 40°50N 81°16W **82** F3
Louisville Ridge *Pac. Oc.* 31°0S 172°30W **64** L10
Loulé *Portugal* 37°9N 8°0W **21** D1
Loup City *U.S.A.* 41°17N 98°58W **80** E4
Loups Marins, Lacs des *Canada* 56°30N 73°45W **72** A5
Lourdes *France* 43°6N 0°3W **20** E3
Lourdes-de-Blanc-Sablon *Canada* 51°24N 57°12W **73** B8
Louroujina *Cyprus* 35°0N 33°28E **25** E12
Louth *Australia* 30°30S 145°8E **63** E4
Louth *Ireland* 53°58N 6°32W **10** C5
Louth *U.K.* 53°22N 0°1W **12** D7
Louth □ *Ireland* 53°56N 6°34W **10** C5
Louvain = Leuven *Belgium* 50°52N 4°42E **15** D4
Louwsburg *S. Africa* 27°37S 31°7E **57** D5
Lovech *Bulgaria* 43°8N 24°42E **23** C11
Loveland *U.S.A.* 40°24N 105°5W **76** F11
Lovell *U.S.A.* 44°50N 108°24W **76** D9
Lovelock *U.S.A.* 40°11N 118°28W **76** F4
Loviisa *Finland* 60°28N 26°12E **8** F22
Loving *U.S.A.* 32°17N 104°6W **77** K11
Lovington *U.S.A.* 32°57N 103°21W **77** K12
Lovisa = Loviisa *Finland* 60°28N 26°12E **8** F22
Low, L. *Canada* 52°29N 76°17W **72** B4
Low Pt. *Australia* 32°25S 127°25E **61** F4
Low Tatra = Nízké Tatry *Slovak Rep.* 48°55N 19°30E **17** D10
Lowa *Dem. Rep. of the Congo* 1°25S 25°47E **54** C2
Lowa → *Dem. Rep. of the Congo* 1°24S 25°51E **54** C2
Lowell *U.S.A.* 42°38N 71°19W **83** D13
Lowellville *U.S.A.* 41°2N 80°32W **82** E4
Löwen → *Namibia* 26°51S 18°17E **56** D2
Lower Alkali L. *U.S.A.* 41°16N 120°2W **76** F3
Lower Arrow L. *Canada* 49°40N 118°5W **70** D5
Lower California = Baja California *Mexico* 31°10N 115°12W **86** A1
Lower Hutt *N.Z.* 41°10S 174°55E **59** D5
Lower Lake *U.S.A.* 38°55N 122°37W **78** G4
Lower Manitou L. *Canada* 49°15N 93°0W **71** D10
Lower Post *Canada* 59°58N 128°30W **70** B3
Lower Red L. *U.S.A.* 47°58N 95°0W **80** B6
Lower Saxony = Niedersachsen □ *Germany* 52°50N 9°0E **16** B5
Lower Tunguska = Tunguska, Nizhnyaya → *Russia* 65°48N 88°4E **29** C9
Lower Zambezi △ *Zambia* 15°25S 29°40E **55** F2
Lowestoft *U.K.* 52°29N 1°45E **13** E9
Lowgar □ *Afghan.* 34°0N 69°0E **40** B6
Łowicz *Poland* 52°6N 19°55E **17** B10
Lowville *U.S.A.* 43°47N 75°29W **83** C9
Loxton *Australia* 34°28S 140°31E **63** E3
Loxton *S. Africa* 31°30S 22°22E **56** E3
Loyalton *U.S.A.* 39°41N 120°14W **78** F6
Loyalty Is. = Loyauté, Îs. *N. Cal.* 20°50S 166°30E **58** D9
Loyang = Luoyang *China* 34°40N 112°26E **34** G7
Loyauté, Îs. *N. Cal.* 20°50S 166°30E **58** D9
Loyev = Loyew *Belarus* 51°56N 30°46E **17** C16
Loyew *Belarus* 51°56N 30°46E **17** C16
Loyoro *Uganda* 3°22N 34°14E **54** B3
Lu Wo *China* 22°33N 114°6E **33** F11
Luachimo *Angola* 7°23S 20°48E **52** F4
Luajan → *India* 24°44N 85°1E **43** G11
Lualaba → *Dem. Rep. of the Congo* 0°26N 25°20E **54** B2
Luampa *Zambia* 15°4S 24°20E **55** F1
Luan Chau *Vietnam* 21°38N 103°24E **38** B4
Luan He → *China* 39°20N 119°5E **35** E10
Luan Xian *China* 39°40N 118°40E **35** E10
Luancheng *China* 37°53N 114°40E **34** F8
Luanda *Angola* 8°50S 13°15E **52** F2
Luang, Thale *Thailand* 7°30N 100°15E **39** J3
Luang Prabang *Laos* 19°52N 102°10E **38** C4
Luangwa *Zambia* 15°35S 30°16E **55** F3
Luangwa → *Zambia* 14°25S 30°25E **55** E3
Luangwa Valley *Zambia* 13°30S 31°30E **55** E3
Luanne *China* 40°55N 117°40E **35** D9
Luanping *China* 40°53N 117°23E **35** D9
Luanshya *Zambia* 13°3S 28°28E **55** E2
Luapula □ *Zambia* 11°0S 29°0E **55** E2
Luapula → *Africa* 9°26S 28°33E **55** D2
Luarca *Spain* 43°32N 6°32W **21** A2
Luashi *Dem. Rep. of the Congo* 10°50S 23°36E **55** E1
Luau *Angola* 10°40S 22°10E **52** G4
Lubana, Ozero = Lubānas Ezers *Latvia* 56°45N 27°0E **9** H22
Lubānas Ezers *Latvia* 56°45N 27°0E **9** H22
Lubang Is. *Phil.* 13°50N 120°12E **37** B6
Lubango *Angola* 14°55S 13°30E **53** G2
Lubao *Dem. Rep. of the Congo* 5°17S 25°42E **54** D2
Lubbock *U.S.A.* 33°35N 101°51W **84** E4
Lübeck *Germany* 53°52N 10°40E **16** B6
Lubefu *Dem. Rep. of the Congo* 4°47S 24°27E **54** C1
Lubefu → *Dem. Rep. of the Congo* 4°10S 23°0E **54** C1
Lubero = Luofu *Dem. Rep. of the Congo* 0°10S 29°15E **54** C2
Lubicon L. *Canada* 56°23N 115°56W **70** B5
Lubilash → *Dem. Rep. of the Congo* 6°2S 23°45E **52** F4
Lubin *Poland* 51°24N 16°11E **16** C9
Lublin *Poland* 51°12N 22°38E **17** C12
Lubnān = Lebanon ■ *Asia* 34°0N 36°0E **46** B5
Lubnān, Jabal *Lebanon* 33°45N 35°40E **46** B4
Lubny *Ukraine* 50°3N 32°58E **28** D4
Lubongola *Dem. Rep. of the Congo* 2°35S 27°50E **54** C2
Lubudi *Dem. Rep. of the Congo* 9°57S 25°58E **52** F5
Lubudi → *Dem. Rep. of the Congo* 9°0S 25°35E **55** D2
Lubuklinggau *Indonesia* 3°15S 102°55E **36** E2
Lubuksikaping *Indonesia* 0°10N 100°15E **36** D2
Lubumbashi *Dem. Rep. of the Congo* 11°40S 27°28E **55** E2
Lubunda *Dem. Rep. of the Congo* 5°12S 26°41E **54** D2
Lubungu *Zambia* 14°35S 26°24E **55** E2
Lubutu *Dem. Rep. of the Congo* 0°45S 26°30E **54** C2
Luc An Chau *Vietnam* 22°6N 104°43E **38** A5
Lucan *Canada* 43°11N 81°24W **82** C3
Lucania, Mt. *Canada* 61°1N 140°27W **68** C5
Lucas Channel = Main Channel *Canada* 45°21N 81°45W **82** A3
Lucca *Italy* 43°50N 10°29E **22** C4
Luce Bay *U.K.* 54°45N 4°48W **11** G4
Lucea *Jamaica* 18°27N 78°10W **88** a
Lucedale *U.S.A.* 30°56N 88°35W **85** F10
Lucena *Phil.* 13°56N 121°37E **37** B6
Lucena *Spain* 37°27N 4°31W **21** D3
Lučenec *Slovak Rep.* 48°18N 19°42E **17** D10
Lucerne = Luzern *Switz.* 47°3N 8°18E **20** C8
Lucerne *U.S.A.* 39°6N 122°48W **78** F4
Lucerne Valley *U.S.A.* 34°27N 116°57W **79** L10
Lucero *Mexico* 30°49N 106°30W **86** A3
Lucheng *China* 36°20N 113°11E **34** F7
Lucheringo → *Mozam.* 11°43S 36°17E **55** E4
Lucia *U.S.A.* 36°2N 121°33W **78** J5
Lucinda *Australia* 18°32S 146°20E **62** B4
Luckenwalde *Germany* 52°5N 13°10E **16** B7
Luckhoff *S. Africa* 29°44S 24°43E **56** D3
Lucknow *Canada* 43°57N 81°31W **82** C3
Lucknow *India* 26°50N 81°0E **43** F9
Lüda = Dalian *China* 38°50N 121°40E **35** E11
Lüderitz *Namibia* 26°41S 15°8E **56** D2
Lüderitzbaai *Namibia* 26°36S 15°8E **56** D2
Ludhiana *India* 30°57N 75°56E **42** D6
Ludington *U.S.A.* 43°57N 86°27W **80** D10
Ludlow *U.K.* 52°22N 2°42W **13** E5
Ludlow *Calif., U.S.A.* 34°43N 116°10W **79** L10
Ludlow *Pa., U.S.A.* 41°43N 78°56W **82** E6
Ludlow *Vt., U.S.A.* 43°24N 72°42W **83** C12
Ludvika *Sweden* 60°8N 15°14E **9** F16
Ludwigsburg *Germany* 48°53N 9°11E **16** D5
Ludwigshafen *Germany* 49°29N 8°26E **16** D5
Lueki *Dem. Rep. of the Congo* 3°20S 25°48E **54** C2
Luena *Dem. Rep. of the Congo* 9°28S 25°43E **55** D2
Luena *Zambia* 10°40S 30°25E **55** E3
Luena Flats *Zambia* 14°47S 23°17E **53** G4
Luenha = Ruenya → *Africa* 16°24S 33°48E **55** F3
Lüeyang *China* 33°22N 106°10E **34** H4
Lufira → *Dem. Rep. of the Congo* 9°30S 27°0E **55** D2
Lufkin *U.S.A.* 31°21N 94°44W **84** F7
Lufupa *Dem. Rep. of the Congo* 10°37S 24°56E **55** E1
Luga *Russia* 58°40N 29°55E **9** G23
Lugano *Switz.* 46°1N 8°57E **20** C8
Lugansk = Luhansk *Ukraine* 48°38N 39°15E **19** E6
Lugard's Falls *Kenya* 3°6S 38°41E **54** C4
Lugela *Mozam.* 16°25S 36°43E **55** F4
Lugenda → *Mozam.* 11°25S 38°33E **55** E4
Lugh Ganana = Luuq *Somali Rep.* 3°48N 42°34E **47** G3
Lugnaquillia *Ireland* 52°58N 6°28W **10** D5
Lugo *Italy* 44°25N 11°54E **22** B4
Lugo *Spain* 43°2N 7°35W **21** A2
Lugoj *Romania* 45°42N 21°57E **17** F11
Lugovoy = Qulan *Kazakhstan* 42°55N 72°43E **28** E8
Luhansk *Ukraine* 48°38N 39°15E **19** E6
Lui → *Angola* 8°21S 17°33E **52** F3
Luiana *Angola* 17°25S 22°59E **56** B3
Luiana → *Angola* 17°24S 23°3E **53** H4
Luichow Pen. = Leizhou Bandao *China* 21°0N 110°0E **33** D6
Luimneach = Limerick *Ireland* 52°40N 8°37W **10** D3
Luing *U.K.* 56°14N 5°39W **11** E3
Luís Correia *Brazil* 3°0S 41°35W **93** D10
Luitpold Coast *Antarctica* 78°30S 32°0W **5** D1
Luiza *Dem. Rep. of the Congo* 7°40S 22°30E **52** F4
Luizi *Dem. Rep. of the Congo* 6°0S 27°25E **54** D2
Luján *Argentina* 34°45S 59°5W **94** C4
Lukanga Swamp *Zambia* 14°30S 27°40E **55** E2
Lukenie → *Dem. Rep. of the Congo* 3°0S 18°50E **52** E3
Lukolela *Dem. Rep. of the Congo* 5°23S 24°32E **54** D1
Lukosi *Zimbabwe* 18°30S 26°30E **55** F2
Łuków *Poland* 51°55N 22°23E **17** C12
Lukusuzi △ *Zambia* 12°43S 32°36E **55** E3
Luleå *Sweden* 65°35N 22°10E **8** D20
Luleälven → *Sweden* 65°35N 22°10E **8** D20
Lüleburgaz *Turkey* 41°23N 27°22E **23** D12
Luling *U.S.A.* 29°41N 97°39W **84** G6
Lulong *China* 39°53N 118°51E **35** E10
Lulonga → *Dem. Rep. of the Congo* 1°0N 18°10E **52** D3
Lulua → *Dem. Rep. of the Congo* 4°30S 20°30E **52** E4
Luma *Amer. Samoa* 14°16S 169°33W **59** b
Lumajang *Indonesia* 8°8S 113°13E **37** H15
Lumbala N'guimbo *Angola* 14°18S 21°18E **53** G4
Lumberton *U.S.A.* 34°37N 79°0W **85** D15
Lumsden *Canada* 50°39N 104°52W **71** C8
Lumsden *N.Z.* 45°44S 168°27E **59** F2
Lumut *Malaysia* 4°13N 100°37E **39** K3
Lumut, Tanjung *Indonesia* 3°50S 105°58E **36** E3
Luna *India* 23°43N 69°16E **42** H3
Lunavada *India* 23°8N 73°37E **42** H5
Lund *Sweden* 55°44N 13°12E **9** J15
Lundazi *Zambia* 12°20S 33°7E **55** E3
Lundi → *Zimbabwe* 21°43S 32°34E **55** G3
Lundu *Malaysia* 1°40N 109°50E **36** D3
Lundy *U.K.* 51°10N 4°41W **13** F3
Lune → *U.K.* 54°0N 2°51W **12** C5
Lüneburg *Germany* 53°15N 10°24E **16** B6
Lüneburg Heath = Lüneburger Heide *Germany* 53°10N 10°12E **16** B6
Lüneburger Heide *Germany* 53°10N 10°12E **16** B6
Lunenburg *Canada* 44°22N 64°18W **73** D7
Lunéville *France* 48°36N 6°30E **20** B7
Lunga → *Zambia* 14°34S 26°25E **55** E2
Lunga Lunga *Kenya* 4°33S 39°7E **54** C4
Lunglei *India* 22°55N 92°45E **41** H18
Luni *India* 26°0N 73°6E **42** G5
Luni → *India* 24°41N 71°14E **42** G4
Luninets = Luninyets *Belarus* 52°15N 26°50E **17** B14
Luning *U.S.A.* 38°30N 118°11W **76** G4
Luninyets *Belarus* 52°15N 26°50E **17** B14
Lunkaransar *India* 28°29N 73°44E **42** E5
Lunsemfwa → *Zambia* 14°54S 30°12E **55** E3
Lunsemfwa Falls *Zambia* 14°30S 29°6E **55** E2
Luo He → *China* 34°35N 110°20E **34** G6
Luochuan *China* 35°45N 109°26E **34** G5
Luofu *Dem. Rep. of the Congo* 0°10S 29°15E **54** C2
Luohe *China* 33°32N 114°2E **34** H8
Luonan *China* 34°5N 110°10E **34** G6
Luoning *China* 34°35N 111°40E **34** G6
Luoyang *China* 34°40N 112°26E **34** G7
Luozigou *China* 43°42N 130°18E **35** C16
Lupilichi *Mozam.* 11°47S 35°13E **55** E4
Luque *Paraguay* 25°19S 57°25W **94** B4
Luquillo, Sierra de *Puerto Rico* 18°20N 65°47W **89** d
Luray *U.S.A.* 38°40N 78°28W **81** F14
Lurgan *U.K.* 54°28N 6°19W **10** B5
Lusaka *Zambia* 15°28S 28°16E **55** F2
Lusaka □ *Zambia* 15°30S 29°0E **55** F2
Lusambo *Dem. Rep. of the Congo* 4°58S 23°28E **54** C1
Lusangaye *Dem. Rep. of the Congo* 4°54S 26°0E **54** C2
Luseland *Canada* 52°5N 109°24W **71** C7
Lusenga Plain △ *Zambia* 9°22S 29°14E **55** D2
Lushan *China* 33°45N 112°55E **34** H7
Lushi *China* 34°3N 111°3E **34** G
Lushnjë *Albania* 40°55N 19°41E **23** D
Lushoto *Tanzania* 4°47S 38°20E **54** C
Lüshun *China* 38°45N 121°15E **35** E1
Lusk *U.S.A.* 42°46N 104°27W **76** E1
Lūt, Dasht-e *Iran* 31°30N 58°0E **45** D
Luta = Dalian *China* 38°50N 121°40E **35** E1
Lutherstadt Wittenberg *Germany* 51°53N 12°39E **16** C
Luton *U.K.* 51°53N 0°24W **13** F
Luton □ *U.K.* 51°53N 0°24W **13** F
Łutselk'e *Canada* 62°24N 110°44W **71** A
Lutsk *Ukraine* 50°50N 25°15E **17** C1
Lutto = Lotta → *Europe* 68°42N 31°6E **8** B2
Lützow Holmbukta *Antarctica* 69°10S 37°30E **5** C
Lutzputs *S. Africa* 28°3S 20°40E **56** D
Luuq *Somali Rep.* 3°48N 42°34E **47** G
Luverne *Ala., U.S.A.* 31°43N 86°16W **85** F
Luverne *Minn., U.S.A.* 43°39N 96°13W **80** D
Luvua *Dem. Rep. of the Congo* 8°48S 25°17E **55** D
Luvua → *Dem. Rep. of the Congo* 6°50S 27°30E **54** D
Luvuvhu → *S. Africa* 22°25S 31°18E **57** C
Luwegu → *Tanzania* 8°31S 37°23E **55** D
Luwuk *Indonesia* 0°56S 122°47E **37** E
Luxembourg *Lux.* 49°37N 6°9E **15**
Luxembourg □ *Belgium* 49°58N 5°30E **15**
Luxembourg ■ *Europe* 49°45N 6°0E **15**
Luxembourg ✈ (LUX) *Lux.* 49°37N 6°10E **15**
Luxi *China* 24°27N 98°36E **32** D
Luxor = El Uqsur *Egypt* 25°41N 32°38E **51** C
Luyi *China* 33°50N 115°35E **34** H
Luza *Russia* 60°39N 47°10E **18** B
Luzern *Switz.* 47°3N 8°18E **20** C
Luzhou *China* 28°52N 105°20E **32**
Luziânia *Brazil* 16°20S 48°0W **93** G
Luzon *Phil.* 16°0N 121°0E **37** A
Lviv *Ukraine* 49°50N 24°0E **17** D
Lvov = Lviv *Ukraine* 49°50N 24°0E **17** D
Lyakhavichy *Belarus* 53°2N 26°32E **17** B
Lyakhovskiye, Ostrova *Russia* 73°40N 141°0E **29** B
Lyal I. *Canada* 44°57N 81°24W **82**
Lybster *U.K.* 58°18N 3°15W **11**
Lycksele *Sweden* 64°38N 18°40E **8** D
Lydda = Lod *Israel* 31°57N 34°54E **46**
Lyddan I. *Antarctica* 74°0S 21°0W **5**
Lydenburg *S. Africa* 25°10S 30°29E **57**
Lydia *Turkey* 38°48N 28°19E **23** E
Lyell *N.Z.* 41°48S 172°4E **59**
Lyell I. *Canada* 52°40N 131°35W **70**
Lyepyel *Belarus* 54°50N 28°40E **9** J
Lykens *U.S.A.* 40°34N 76°42W **83**
Lyman *U.S.A.* 41°20N 110°18W **76**
Lyme B. *U.K.* 50°42N 2°53W **13**
Lyme Regis *U.K.* 50°43N 2°57W **13**
Lymington *U.K.* 50°45N 1°32W **13**
Łyna → *Poland* 54°37N 21°14E **17** A
Lynchburg *U.S.A.* 37°25N 79°9W **81** G
Lynd → *Australia* 16°28S 143°18E **62**
Lynd Ra. *Australia* 25°30S 149°20E **63**
Lynden *Canada* 43°14N 80°9W **82**
Lynden *U.S.A.* 48°57N 122°27W **78**
Lyndhurst *Australia* 30°15S 138°18E **63**
Lyndon → *Australia* 23°29S 114°6E **61**
Lyndonville *N.Y., U.S.A.* 43°20N 78°23W **82**
Lyndonville *Vt., U.S.A.* 44°31N 72°1W **83** B
Lyngen *Norway* 69°45N 20°30E **8** B
Lynher Reef *Australia* 15°27S 121°55E **60**
Lynn *U.S.A.* 42°28N 70°57W **83** D
Lynn Haven *U.S.A.* 30°15N 85°39W **85** F
Lynn Lake *Canada* 56°51N 101°3W **71**
Lynnwood *U.S.A.* 47°49N 122°18W **78**
Lynton *U.K.* 51°13N 3°50W **13**
Lyntupy *Belarus* 55°4N 26°23E **9** J
Lynx L. *Canada* 62°25N 106°15W **71**
Lyon *France* 45°46N 4°50E **20**
Lyonnais *France* 45°45N 4°15E **20**
Lyons = Lyon *France* 45°46N 4°50E **20**
Lyons *Ga., U.S.A.* 32°12N 82°19W **85** E
Lyons *Kans., U.S.A.* 38°21N 98°12W **80**
Lyons *N.Y., U.S.A.* 43°5N 77°0W **82**
Lyons → *Australia* 25°2S 115°9E **61**
Lyons Falls *U.S.A.* 43°37N 75°22W **83**
Lys = Leie → *Belgium* 51°2N 3°45E **15**
Lysi *Cyprus* 35°6N 33°41E **25** D
Lysva *Russia* 58°7N 57°49E **18** C
Lysychansk *Ukraine* 48°55N 38°30E **19**
Lytham St. Anne's *U.K.* 53°45N 3°0W **12**
Lyttelton *N.Z.* 43°35S 172°44E **59**
Lytton *Canada* 50°13N 121°31W **70**
Lyubertsy *Russia* 55°40N 37°51E **18**
Lyuboml *Ukraine* 51°11N 24°4E **17** C

M

Ma → *Vietnam* 19°47N 105°56E **38**
Ma'adaba *Jordan* 30°43N 35°47E **46**
Maamba *Zambia* 17°17S 26°28E **56**
Ma'ān *Jordan* 30°12N 35°44E **46**
Ma'ān □ *Jordan* 30°0N 36°0E **46**
Maanselkä *Finland* 63°52N 28°32E **8**
Ma'anshan *China* 31°44N 118°29E **33**
Maarianhamina = Mariehamn *Finland* 60°5N 19°55E **9** F
Ma'arrat an Nu'mān *Syria* 35°43N 36°43E **44**
Maas → *Neths.* 51°45N 4°32E **15**
Maaseik *Belgium* 51°6N 5°45E **15**
Maasin *Phil.* 10°8N 124°50E **37**
Maastricht *Neths.* 50°50N 5°40E **15**
Maave *Mozam.* 21°4S 34°47E **57**
Mababe Depression *Botswana* 18°50S 24°15E **56**

Mabalane Mozam. 23°37S 32°31E 57 C5
Mabel L. Canada 50°35N 118°43W 70 C5
Mabenge Dem. Rep. of the Congo 4°15N 24°12E 54 B1
Maberly Canada 44°50N 76°32W 83 B8
Mablethorpe U.K. 53°20N 0°15E 12 D8
Maboma Dem. Rep. of the Congo 2°30N 28°10E 54 B2
Mabuasehube ⌓ Botswana 25°5S 21°10E 56 D3
Mac Bac Vietnam 9°46N 106°7E 39 H6
Macachín Argentina 37°10S 63°43W 94 D3
Macaé Brazil 22°20S 41°43W 95 A7
McAlester U.S.A. 34°56N 95°46W 84 D7
McAllen U.S.A. 26°12N 98°14W 84 H5
MacAlpine L. Canada 66°32N 102°45W 68 C9
Macamic Canada 48°45N 79°0W 72 C4
Macao = Macau China 22°12N 113°33E 33 G10
Macapá Brazil 0°5N 51°4W 93 C8
Macarao △ Venezuela 10°22N 67°7W 89 D6
McArthur → Australia 15°54S 136°40E 62 B2
McArthur, Port Australia 16°4S 136°23E 62 B2
Macau Brazil 5°15S 36°40W 93 E11
Macau China 22°12N 113°33E 33 G10
McBride Canada 53°20N 120°19W 70 C4
McCall U.S.A. 44°55N 116°6W 76 D5
McCamey U.S.A. 31°8N 102°14W 84 F3
McCammon U.S.A. 42°39N 112°12W 76 E7
McCarran Int., Las Vegas ✕ (LAS) U.S.A. 36°5N 115°9W 79 J11
McCauley I. Canada 53°40N 130°15W 70 C2
McCleary U.S.A. 47°3N 123°16W 78 C3
Macclenny U.S.A. 30°17N 82°7W 85 F13
Macclesfield U.K. 53°15N 2°8W 12 D5
M'Clintock Chan. Canada 72°0N 102°0W 68 B9
McClintock Ra. Australia 18°44S 127°38E 60 C4
McCloud U.S.A. 41°15N 122°8W 76 F2
McCluer I. Australia 11°5S 133°0E 60 B5
McClure U.S.A. 40°42N 77°19W 82 F7
McClure, L. U.S.A. 37°35N 120°16W 78 H6
M'Clure Str. Canada 75°0N 119°0W 69 B8
McClusky U.S.A. 47°29N 100°27W 80 B3
McComb U.S.A. 31°15N 90°27W 85 F9
McCook U.S.A. 40°12N 100°38W 80 E3
McCreary Canada 50°47N 99°29W 71 C9
McCullough Mt. U.S.A. 35°35N 115°13W 79 K11
McCusker → Canada 55°32N 108°39W 71 B7
McDermitt U.S.A. 41°59N 117°43W 76 F5
McDonald U.S.A. 40°22N 80°14W 82 F4
Macdonald, L. Australia 23°30S 129°0E 60 D4
McDonald Is. Ind. Oc. 53°0S 73°0E 3 G13
MacDonnell Ranges Australia 23°40S 133°0E 60 D5
MacDowell L. Canada 52°15N 92°45W 72 B1
Macduff U.K. 57°40N 2°31W 11 D6
Macedonia U.S.A. 41°19N 81°31W 82 E3
Macedonia □ Greece 40°39N 22°0E 23 D10
Macedonia ■ Europe 41°53N 21°40E 23 D9
Maceió Brazil 9°40S 35°41W 93 E11
Macerata Italy 43°18N 13°27E 22 C5
McFarland U.S.A. 35°41N 119°14W 79 K7
McFarlane → Canada 59°12N 107°58W 71 B7
Macfarlane, L. Australia 32°0S 136°40E 63 E2
McGehee U.S.A. 33°38N 91°24W 84 E9
McGill U.S.A. 39°23N 114°47W 76 G6
Macgillycuddy's Reeks Ireland 51°58N 9°45W 10 E2
McGraw U.S.A. 42°36N 76°8W 83 D8
McGregor U.S.A. 43°1N 91°11W 80 D8
McGregor Ra. Australia 27°0S 142°45E 63 D3
McGuire, Mt. Australia 20°18S 148°23E 62 J6
Mach Pakistan 29°50N 67°20E 42 E2
Māch Kowr Iran 25°48N 61°28E 45 E9
Machado = Jiparaná → Brazil 8°3S 62°52W 92 E6
Machagai Argentina 26°56S 60°2W 94 B3
Machakos Kenya 1°30S 37°15E 54 C4
Machala Ecuador 3°20S 79°57W 92 D3
Machanga Mozam. 20°59S 35°0E 57 C6
Machattie, L. Australia 24°50S 139°48E 62 C2
Machava Mozam. 25°54S 32°28E 57 D5
Machece Mozam. 19°15S 35°32E 55 F4
Macheke Zimbabwe 18°5S 31°51E 57 B5
Machhu → India 23°6N 70°46E 42 H4
Machiara △ Pakistan 34°40N 73°30E 42 B5
Machias Maine, U.S.A. 44°43N 67°28W 81 C20
Machias N.Y., U.S.A. 42°25N 78°29W 82 D6
Machichi → Canada 57°3N 92°6W 71 B10
Machico Madeira 32°43N 16°44W 24 D3
Machilipatnam India 16°12N 81°8E 41 L12
Machiques Venezuela 10°4N 72°34W 92 A4
Machu Picchu Peru 13°8S 72°30W 92 F4
Machynlleth U.K. 52°35N 3°50W 13 E4
Macia Mozam. 25°2S 33°8E 57 D5
McIlwraith Ra. Australia 13°50S 143°20E 62 A3
McInnes L. Canada 52°13N 93°45W 71 C10
McIntosh U.S.A. 45°55N 101°21W 80 C3
McIntosh L. Canada 55°45N 105°0W 71 B8
Macintosh Ra. Australia 27°39S 125°32E 61 E4
Macintyre → Australia 28°37S 150°47E 63 D5
Mackay Australia 21°8S 149°11E 62 K7
Mackay U.S.A. 43°55N 113°37W 76 E7
MacKay → Canada 57°10N 111°38W 70 B6
Mackay, L. Australia 22°30S 129°0E 60 D4
McKay Ra. Australia 23°0S 122°30E 60 D3
McKeesport U.S.A. 40°20N 79°51W 82 F5
McKellar Canada 45°30N 79°55W 82 A5
McKenna U.S.A. 46°56N 122°33W 78 D4
Mackenzie Canada 55°20N 123°5W 70 B4
McKenzie U.S.A. 36°8N 88°31W 85 C10
Mackenzie → Australia 23°38S 149°46E 62 C4
Mackenzie → Canada 69°10N 134°20W 68 D6
McKenzie → U.S.A. 44°7N 123°6W 76 D2
Mackenzie Bay Canada 69°0N 137°30W 66 C6
Mackenzie City = Linden Guyana 6°0N 58°10W 92 B7
Mackenzie King I. Canada 77°45N 111°0W 69 B8
Mackenzie Mts. Canada 64°0N 130°0W 68 C7
Mackinaw City U.S.A. 45°47N 84°44W 81 C11
McKinlay Australia 21°16S 141°18E 62 C3
McKinlay → Australia 20°50S 141°28E 62 C3
McKinley, Mt. U.S.A. 63°4N 151°0W 74 a
McKinley Sea Arctic 82°0N 0°0 4 A7
McKinney U.S.A. 33°12N 96°37W 84 E6
Mackinnon Road Kenya 3°40S 39°1E 54 C4
McKittrick U.S.A. 35°18N 119°37W 79 K7
Macklin Canada 52°20N 109°56W 71 C7
Macksville Australia 30°40S 152°56E 63 E5
McLaughlin U.S.A. 45°49N 100°49W 80 C3
Maclean Australia 29°26S 153°16E 63 D5
McLean U.S.A. 35°14N 100°36W 84 D4
McLeansboro U.S.A. 38°6N 88°32W 80 F9
Maclear S. Africa 31°2S 28°23E 57 E4
Maclear, C. Malawi 13°58S 34°49E 55 E3
Macleay → Australia 30°56S 153°0E 63 E5
McLennan Canada 55°42N 116°50W 70 B5
McLeod → Canada 54°9N 115°44W 70 C5
McLeod, L. Australia 24°9S 113°47E 61 D1
MacLeod B. Canada 62°53N 110°0W 71 A7
MacLeod Lake Canada 54°58N 123°0W 70 C4
McLoughlin, Mt. U.S.A. 42°27N 122°19W 76 E2
McMechen U.S.A. 39°57N 80°44W 82 G4
McMinnville Oreg., U.S.A. 45°13N 123°12W 76 D2
McMinnville Tenn., U.S.A. 35°41N 85°46W 85 D12
McMurdo Antarctica 77°0S 140°0E 5 D11
McMurdo Sd. Antarctica 77°0S 170°0E 5 D11
McMurray = Fort McMurray Canada 56°44N 111°7W 70 B6
McMurray U.S.A. 48°19N 122°14W 78 B4
Macodoene Mozam. 23°32S 35°5E 57 C6
Macomb U.S.A. 40°27N 90°40W 80 E8
Mâcon France 46°19N 4°50E 20 C6
Macon Ga., U.S.A. 32°51N 83°38W 85 E13
Macon Miss., U.S.A. 33°7N 88°34W 85 E10
Macon Mo., U.S.A. 39°44N 92°28W 80 F7
Macossa Mozam. 17°55S 33°56E 55 F3
Macoun L. Canada 56°32N 103°40W 71 B8
Macovane Mozam. 21°30S 35°2E 57 C6
McPherson U.S.A. 38°22N 97°40W 80 F5
McPherson Pk. U.S.A. 34°53N 119°53W 79 L7
McPherson Ra. Australia 28°15S 153°15E 63 D5
Macquarie → Australia 30°7S 147°24E 63 E4
Macquarie Harbour Australia 42°15S 145°23E 63 G4
Macquarie Is. Pac. Oc. 54°36S 158°55E 64 N7
Macquarie Ridge S. Ocean 57°0S 159°0E 5 B10
MacRobertson Land Antarctica 71°0S 64°0E 5 D6
Macroom Ireland 51°54N 8°57W 10 E3
MacTier Canada 45°8N 79°47W 82 A5
Macubela Mozam. 16°53S 37°49E 55 F4
Macuira △ Colombia 12°9N 71°21W 89 D5
Macuiza Mozam. 18°7S 34°29E 55 F3
Macumba → Australia 27°52S 137°12E 63 D2
Macuro Venezuela 10°42N 61°55W 93 K15
Macusani Peru 14°4S 70°29W 92 F4
Macuse Mozam. 17°45S 37°10E 55 F4
Macuspana Mexico 17°46N 92°36W 87 D6
Macusse Angola 17°48S 20°23E 56 B3
Ma'dabā □ Jordan 31°43N 35°47E 46 D4
Madadeni S. Africa 27°43S 30°3E 57 D5
Madagascar ■ Africa 20°0S 47°0E 57 C8
Madā'in Sālih Si. Arabia 26°46N 37°57E 44 E3
Madama Niger 22°0N 13°40E 51 D8
Madame, I. Canada 45°30N 60°58W 73 C7
Madang Papua N. G. 5°12S 145°49E 58 B7
Madaripur Bangla. 23°19N 90°15E 41 H17
Madauk Burma 17°56N 96°52E 41 L20
Madawaska Canada 45°30N 78°0W 82 A7
Madawaska → Canada 45°27N 76°21W 82 A7
Madaya Burma 22°12N 96°10E 41 H20
Maddalena Italy 41°16N 9°23E 22 D3
Madeira Atl. Oc. 32°50N 17°0W 24 D3
Madeira → Brazil 3°22S 58°45W 92 D7
Madeleine, Îs. de la Canada 47°30N 61°40W 73 C7
Madera Mexico 29°12N 108°7W 86 B3
Madera Calif., U.S.A. 36°57N 120°3W 78 J6
Madera Pa., U.S.A. 40°49N 78°26W 82 F6
Madha India 18°0N 75°30E 40 L9
Madhavpur India 21°15N 69°58E 42 J3
Madhepura India 26°11N 86°23E 43 F12
Madhubani India 26°21N 86°7E 43 F12
Madhupur India 24°16N 86°39E 43 G12
Madhya Pradesh □ India 22°50N 78°0E 42 J8
Madidi → Bolivia 12°32S 66°52W 92 F5
Madikeri India 12°30N 75°45E 40 N9
Madikwe ⌓ S. Africa 27°38S 32°15E 57 D5
Madill U.S.A. 34°6N 96°46W 84 D6
Madimba Dem. Rep. of the Congo 4°58S 15°5E 52 E3
Ma'din Syria 35°45N 39°36E 44 C3
Madinat al Malik Khālid al Askarīyah Si. Arabia 27°54N 45°31E 44 E5
Madingou Congo 4°10S 13°33E 52 E2
Madirovalo Madag. 16°26S 46°32E 57 B8
Madison Calif., U.S.A. 38°41N 121°59W 78 G5
Madison Fla., U.S.A. 30°28N 83°25W 85 F13
Madison Ind., U.S.A. 38°44N 85°23W 81 F11
Madison Nebr., U.S.A. 41°50N 97°27W 80 E5
Madison Ohio, U.S.A. 41°46N 81°3W 82 E3
Madison S. Dak., U.S.A. 44°0N 97°7W 80 C5
Madison Wis., U.S.A. 43°4N 89°24W 80 D9
Madison → U.S.A. 45°56N 111°31W 76 D8
Madison Heights U.S.A. 37°25N 79°8W 81 G14
Madisonville Ky., U.S.A. 37°20N 87°30W 80 G10
Madisonville Tex., U.S.A. 30°57N 95°55W 84 F7
Madista Botswana 21°15S 25°6E 56 C4
Madiun Indonesia 7°38S 111°32E 37 G14
Mado Gashi Kenya 0°44N 39°10E 54 B4
Madoc Canada 44°30N 77°28W 82 B7
Madona Latvia 56°53N 26°5E 9 H22
Madrakah, Ra's al Oman 19°0N 57°50E 47 D6
Madras = Chennai India 13°8N 80°19E 40 N12
Madras = Tamil Nadu □ India 11°0N 77°0E 40 P10
Madras U.S.A. 44°38N 121°8W 76 D3
Madre, L. U.S.A. 25°15N 97°30W 84 J6
Madre, Sierra Phil. 17°0N 122°0E 37 A6
Madre de Dios → Bolivia 10°59S 66°8W 92 F5
Madre de Dios, I. Chile 50°20S 75°10W 96 G1
Madre del Sur, Sierra Mexico 17°30N 100°0W 87 D5
Madre Occidental, Sierra Mexico 27°0N 107°0W 86 B3
Madre Oriental, Sierra Mexico 25°0N 100°0W 86 C5
Madri India 24°16N 73°32E 42 G5
Madrid Spain 40°24N 3°42W 21 B4
Madrid U.S.A. 44°45N 75°8W 83 B9
Madura Australia 31°55S 127°0E 61 F4
Madura Indonesia 7°30S 114°0E 37 G15
Madura, Selat Indonesia 7°30S 113°20E 37 G15
Madurai India 9°55N 78°10E 40 Q11
Madurantakam India 12°30N 79°50E 40 N11
Mae Chan Thailand 20°9N 99°52E 38 B2
Mae Hong Son Thailand 19°16N 97°56E 38 C2
Mae Khlong → Thailand 13°24N 100°0E 38 F3
Mae Phrik Thailand 17°27N 99°7E 38 D2
Mae Ping △ Thailand 17°37N 98°51E 38 D2
Mae Ramat Thailand 16°58N 98°31E 38 D2
Mae Rim Thailand 18°54N 98°57E 38 C2
Mae Sai Thailand 20°20N 99°55E 38 B2
Mae Sot Thailand 16°43N 98°34E 38 D2
Mae Suai Thailand 19°39N 99°33E 38 C2
Mae Tha Thailand 18°28N 99°8E 38 C2
Mae Wong △ Thailand 15°54N 99°12E 38 E2
Mae Yom △ Thailand 18°43N 100°15E 38 C3
Maebashi Japan 36°24N 139°4E 31 F9
Maesteg U.K. 51°36N 3°40W 13 F4
Maestra, Sierra Cuba 20°15N 77°0W 88 B4
Maevatanana Madag. 16°56S 46°49E 57 B8
Mafeking = Mafikeng S. Africa 25°50S 25°38E 56 D4
Mafeking Canada 52°40N 101°10W 71 C8
Mafeteng Lesotho 29°51S 27°15E 56 D4
Maffra Australia 37°53S 146°58E 63 F4
Mafia I. Tanzania 7°45S 39°50E 54 D4
Mafikeng S. Africa 25°50S 25°38E 56 D4
Mafra Brazil 26°10S 49°55W 95 B6
Mafra Portugal 38°55N 9°20W 21 C1
Mafungabusi Plateau Zimbabwe 18°30S 29°8E 55 F2
Magadan Russia 59°38N 150°50E 29 D16
Magadi Kenya 1°54S 36°19E 54 C4
Magadi, L. Kenya 1°54S 36°19E 54 C4
Magaliesburg S. Africa 26°0S 27°32E 57 D4
Magallanes, Estrecho de Chile 52°30S 75°0W 96 G2
Magangué Colombia 9°14N 74°45W 92 B4
Magdagachi Russia 53°27N 125°48E 29 D13
Magdalen Is. = Madeleine, Îs. de la Canada 47°30N 61°40W 73 C7
Magdalena Argentina 35°5S 57°30W 94 D4
Magdalena Bolivia 13°13S 63°57W 92 F6
Magdalena U.S.A. 34°7N 107°15W 77 J10
Magdalena → Colombia 11°6N 74°51W 92 A4
Magdalena → Mexico 30°40N 112°25W 86 A2
Magdalena, B. Mexico 24°35N 112°0W 86 C2
Magdalena, I. Mexico 24°40N 112°15W 86 C2
Magdalena, Llano de Mexico 25°0N 111°25W 86 C2
Magdalena de Kino Mexico 30°38N 110°57W 86 A2
Magdeburg Germany 52°7N 11°38E 16 B6
Magdelaine Cays Australia 16°33S 150°18E 62 B5
Magee U.S.A. 31°52N 89°44W 85 F10
Magelang Indonesia 7°29S 110°13E 37 G14
Magellan's Str. = Magallanes, Estrecho de Chile 52°30S 75°0W 96 G2
Magenta, L. Australia 33°30S 119°2E 61 F2
Magerøya Norway 71°3N 25°40E 8 A21
Maggiore, Lago Italy 45°57N 8°39E 20 D8
Maggotty Jamaica 18°9N 77°46W 88 a
Maghâgha Egypt 28°38N 30°50E 51 C12
Magherafelt U.K. 54°45N 6°37W 10 B5
Maghreb N. Afr. 32°0N 4°0W 50 B5
Magistralnyy Russia 56°16N 107°36E 29 D11
Magnetic Pole (North) Canada 82°42N 114°24W 69 B9
Magnetic Pole (South) Antarctica 64°8S 138°8E 5 C9
Magnitogorsk Russia 53°27N 59°4E 18 D10
Magnolia Ark., U.S.A. 33°16N 93°14W 84 E8
Magnolia Miss., U.S.A. 31°9N 90°28W 85 F9
Mago Fiji 17°26S 179°8W 59 a
Magog Canada 45°18N 72°9W 83 A12
Magoro Uganda 1°45N 34°12E 54 B3
Magoša = Famagusta Cyprus 35°8N 33°55E 25 D12
Magoulades Greece 39°45N 19°42E 25 A3
Magoye Zambia 16°1S 27°30E 55 F2
Magpie, L. Canada 51°0N 64°41W 73 B7
Magrath Canada 49°25N 112°50W 70 D6
Maguarinho, C. Brazil 0°15S 48°30W 93 D9
Magude Mozam. 25°2S 32°40E 57 D5
Mağusa = Famagusta Cyprus 35°8N 33°55E 25 D12
Maguse L. Canada 61°37N 95°10W 71 A9
Maguse Pt. Canada 61°20N 93°50W 71 A10
Magvana India 23°13N 69°22E 42 H3
Magwe Burma 20°10N 95°0E 41 J19
Magyarorszag = Hungary ■ Europe 47°20N 19°20E 17 E10
Maha Sarakham Thailand 16°12N 103°16E 38 D4
Mahābād Iran 36°50N 45°45E 44 B5
Mahabharat Lekh Nepal 28°30N 82°0E 43 E10
Mahabo Madag. 20°23S 44°40E 57 C7
Mahadeo Hills India 22°20N 78°30E 43 H8
Mahaffey U.S.A. 40°53N 78°44W 82 F6
Mahagi Dem. Rep. of the Congo 2°20N 31°0E 54 B3
Mahajamba → Madag. 15°33S 47°8E 57 B8
Mahajamba, Helodranon' i Madag. 15°24S 47°5E 57 B8
Mahajan India 28°48N 73°56E 42 E5
Mahajanga Madag. 15°40S 46°25E 57 B8
Mahajanga □ Madag. 17°0S 47°0E 57 B8
Mahajilo → Madag. 19°42S 45°22E 57 B8
Mahakam → Indonesia 0°35S 117°17E 36 E5
Mahalapye Botswana 23°1S 26°51E 56 C4
Mahale Mts. Tanzania 6°20S 30°0E 54 D3
Mahale Mts. △ Tanzania 6°10S 29°50E 54 D2
Maḥallāt Iran 33°55N 50°30E 45 C6
Māhān Iran 30°5N 57°18E 45 D8
Mahan → India 23°30N 82°50E 43 H10
Mahanadi → India 20°20N 86°25E 41 J15
Mahananda → India 25°12N 87°52E 43 G12
Mahanoro Madag. 19°54S 48°48E 57 B8
Mahanoy City U.S.A. 40°49N 76°9W 83 F8
Maharashtra □ India 20°30N 75°30E 40 J9
Mahasham, W. → Egypt 30°15N 34°10E 46 E3
Mahasoa Madag. 22°12S 46°6E 57 C8
Mahasolo Madag. 19°7S 46°22E 57 B8
Mahattat ash Shīdīyah Jordan 29°55N 35°55E 46 F4
Mahattat 'Unayzah Jordan 30°30N 35°47E 46 E4
Mahavavy → Madag. 15°57S 45°54E 57 B8
Mahaxay Laos 17°22N 105°12E 38 D5
Mahbubnagar India 16°45N 77°59E 40 L10
Maḥḍah Oman 24°24N 55°59E 45 E7
Mahdia Tunisia 35°28N 11°0E 51 A8
Mahe India 33°10N 78°32E 43 C8
Mahé Seychelles 5°0S 55°30E 53 b
Mahé ✕ (SEZ) Seychelles 4°40S 55°31E 53 b
Mahébourg Mauritius 20°24S 57°42E 53 d
Mahendragarh India 28°17N 76°14E 42 E7
Mahendranagar Nepal 28°55N 80°20E 43 E9
Mahenge Tanzania 8°45S 36°41E 55 D4
Maheno N.Z. 45°10S 170°50E 59 F3
Mahesana India 23°39N 72°26E 42 H5
Maheshwar India 22°11N 75°35E 42 H6
Mahgawan India 26°29N 78°37E 43 F8
Mahi → India 22°15N 72°55E 42 H5
Mahia Pen. N.Z. 39°9S 177°55E 59 C6
Mahilyow Belarus 53°55N 30°18E 17 B16
Mahina Tahiti 17°30S 149°27W 59 d
Mahinerangi, L. N.Z. 45°50S 169°56E 59 F2
Mahmud Kot Pakistan 30°16N 71°0E 42 D4
Mahnomen U.S.A. 47°19N 95°58W 80 B6
Mahoba India 25°15N 79°55E 43 G8
Mahón = Maó Spain 39°53N 4°16E 24 B11
Mahone Bay Canada 44°27N 64°23W 73 D7
Mahopac U.S.A. 41°22N 73°45W 83 E11
Mahuva India 21°5N 71°48E 42 J4
Mai-Ndombe, L. Dem. Rep. of the Congo 2°0S 18°20E 52 E3
Mai Thon, Ko Thailand 7°40N 98°28E 39 a
Maicuru → Brazil 2°14S 54°17W 93 D8
Maidan Khula Afghan. 33°36N 69°50E 42 C3
Maidenhead U.K. 51°31N 0°42W 13 F7
Maidstone Canada 53°5N 109°20W 71 C7
Maidstone U.K. 51°16N 0°32E 13 F8
Maiduguri Nigeria 12°0N 13°20E 51 F8
Maihar India 24°16N 80°45E 43 G9
Maijdi Bangla. 22°48N 91°10E 41 H17
Maikala Ra. India 22°0N 81°0E 41 J12
Maiko △ Dem. Rep. of the Congo 0°30S 27°50E 54 C2
Mailani India 28°17N 80°21E 43 E9
Mailsi Pakistan 29°48N 72°15E 42 E5
Main → Germany 50°0N 8°18E 16 C5
Main → U.K. 54°48N 6°18W 10 B5
Main Channel Canada 45°21N 81°45W 82 A3
Main Range △ Australia 28°11S 152°27E 63 D5
Main Ridge Trin. & Tob. 11°16N 60°40W 93 J16
Maine France 48°20N 0°15W 20 C3
Maine □ U.S.A. 45°20N 69°0W 81 C19
Maine → Ireland 52°9N 9°45W 10 D2
Maine, G. of U.S.A. 43°0N 68°30W 81 D19
Maingkwan Burma 26°15N 96°37E 41 F20
Mainit, L. Phil. 9°31N 125°30E 37 C7
Mainland Orkney, U.K. 58°59N 3°8W 11 C5
Mainland Shet., U.K. 60°15N 1°22W 11 A7
Mainoru Australia 14°0S 134°6E 62 A1
Mainpuri India 27°18N 79°4E 43 F8
Maintirano Madag. 18°3S 44°1E 57 B7
Mainz Germany 50°1N 8°14E 16 C5
Maio C. Verde Is. 15°10N 23°10W 50 b
Maipú Argentina 36°52S 57°50W 94 D4
Maiquetía Venezuela 10°36N 66°57W 92 A5
Mairabari India 26°30N 92°22E 41 F18
Maisi Cuba 20°17N 74°9W 89 B5
Maisí, Pta. de Cuba 20°10N 74°10W 89 B5
Maitland N.S.W., Australia 32°33S 151°36E 63 E5
Maitland S. Austral., Australia 34°23S 137°40E 63 E2
Maitland → Canada 43°45N 81°43W 82 C3
Maitri Antarctica 70°0S 3°0W 5 D3
Maíz, Is. del Nic. 12°15N 83°4W 88 D3
Maizuru Japan 35°25N 135°22E 31 G7
Majalengka Indonesia 6°50S 108°13E 37 G13
Majene Indonesia 3°38S 118°57E 37 E5
Majete ⌓ Malawi 15°54S 34°34E 55 F3
Majorca = Mallorca Spain 39°30N 3°0E 24 B10
Majuro Marshall Is. 7°9N 171°12E 64 G9
Maka Senegal 13°40N 14°10W 50 F3
Makaha Zimbabwe 17°20S 32°39E 57 B5
Makalamabedi Botswana 20°19S 23°51E 56 C3
Makale Indonesia 3°6S 119°51E 37 E5
Makalu-Barun △ Nepal 27°45N 87°10E 43 F12
Makamba Burundi 4°8S 29°49E 54 C2
Makarikari = Makgadikgadi Salt Pans Botswana 20°40S 25°45E 56 C4
Makarov Basin Arctic 87°0N 150°0W 4 A
Makarovo Russia 57°40N 107°45E 29 D11
Makasar = Ujung Pandang Indonesia 5°10S 119°20E 37 F5
Makasar, Selat Indonesia 1°0S 118°20E 37 E5
Makasar, Str. of = Makasar, Selat Indonesia 1°0S 118°20E 37 E5
Makat = Maqat Kazakhstan 47°39N 53°19E 19 E9
Makedonija = Macedonia ■ Europe 41°53N 21°40E 23 D9
Makeni S. Leone 8°55N 12°5W 50 G3
Makeyevka = Makiyivka Ukraine 48°0N 38°0E 19 E6
Makgadikgadi △ Botswana 20°27S 24°47E 56 C3
Makgadikgadi Salt Pans Botswana 20°40S 25°45E 56 C4
Makhachkala Russia 43°0N 47°30E 19 F8
Makhado = Louis Trichardt S. Africa 23°1S 29°43E 57 C4
Makham, Ao Thailand 7°51N 98°25E 39 a
Makhfar al Buşayyah Iraq 30°0N 46°10E 44 D5
Makhmūr Iraq 35°46N 43°35E 44 C4
Makian Indonesia 0°20N 127°20E 37 D7
Makindu Kenya 2°18S 37°50E 54 C4
Makīnsk Kazakhstan 52°37N 70°26E 28 D8
Makira = San Cristóbal Solomon Is. 10°30S 161°0E 58 C9
Makiyivka Ukraine 48°0N 38°0E 19 E6
Makkah Si. Arabia 21°30N 39°54E 47 C2
Makkovik Canada 55°10N 59°10W 73 A8
Makó Hungary 46°14N 20°33E 17 E11
Makogai Fiji 17°28S 179°0E 59 a
Makokou Gabon 0°40N 12°50E 52 D2
Makongo Dem. Rep. of the Congo 3°25N 26°17E 54 B2
Makoro Dem. Rep. of the Congo 3°10N 29°59E 54 B2
Makrai India 22°2N 77°0E 42 H7
Makran Coast Range Pakistan 25°40N 64°0E 40 G4
Makrana India 27°2N 74°46E 42 F6
Makrigialos Greece 35°2N 25°59E 25 D7
Mākū Iran 39°15N 44°31E 44 B5
Makunda Botswana 22°30S 20°7E 56 C3
Makurazaki Japan 31°15N 130°20E 31 J5
Makurdi Nigeria 7°43N 8°35E 50 G7
Makūyeh Iran 28°7N 53°9E 45 D7
Makwassie S. Africa 27°17S 26°0E 56 D4
Makwiro Zimbabwe 17°58S 30°25E 57 B5
Mal B. Ireland 52°50N 9°30W 10 D2
Mala, Pta. Panama 7°28N 80°2W 88 E3
Malabar Coast India 11°0N 75°0E 40 P9
Malacca, Straits of Indonesia 3°0N 101°0E 39 L3
Malad City U.S.A. 42°12N 112°15W 76 E7
Maladzyechna Belarus 54°20N 26°50E 17 A14
Málaga Spain 36°43N 4°23W 21 D3
Malagarasi Tanzania 5°5S 30°50E 54 D3
Malagarasi → Tanzania 5°12S 29°47E 54 D2
Malagasy Rep. = Madagascar ■ Africa 20°0S 47°0E 57 C8
Malahide Ireland 53°26N 6°9W 10 C5
Malaimbandy Madag. 20°20S 45°36E 57 C8
Malaita Solomon Is. 9°0S 161°0E 58 B9
Malakâl Sudan 9°33N 31°40E 51 G12
Malakand Pakistan 34°40N 71°55E 42 B4
Malakula Vanuatu 16°15S 167°30E 58 C9
Malakwal Pakistan 32°34N 73°13E 42 C5
Malamala Indonesia 3°21S 120°55E 37 E6
Malanda Australia 17°22S 145°35E 62 B4
Malang Indonesia 7°59S 112°45E 37 G15
Malanga Mozam. 13°28S 36°7E 55 E4
Malangen Norway 69°24N 18°37E 8 B18
Malanje Angola 9°36S 16°17E 52 F3
Mälaren Sweden 59°30N 17°10E 9 G17
Malargüe Argentina 35°32S 69°30W 94 D2
Malartic Canada 48°9N 78°9W 72 C4
Malaryta Belarus 51°50N 24°3E 17 C13
Malatya Turkey 38°25N 38°20E 44 B3
Malawi ■ Africa 11°55S 34°0E 55 E3
Malawi, L. Africa 12°30S 34°30E 55 E3
Malay Pen. Asia 7°25N 100°0E 39 J3
Malaya Vishera Russia 58°55N 32°25E 18 C5
Malaybalay Phil. 8°5N 125°7E 37 C7
Malāyer Iran 34°19N 48°51E 45 C6
Malaysia ■ Asia 5°0N 110°0E 39 K4
Malazgirt Turkey 39°10N 42°33E 44 B4
Malbon Australia 21°5S 140°17E 62 C3
Malbooma Australia 30°41S 134°11E 63 E1
Malbork Poland 54°3N 19°1E 17 B10
Malcolm Australia 28°51S 121°25E 61 E3
Malcolm, Pt. Australia 33°48S 123°45E 61 F3
Maldah India 25°2N 88°9E 43 G13
Maldegem Belgium 51°14N 3°26E 15 C3
Malden Mass., U.S.A. 42°26N 71°3W 83 D13
Malden Mo., U.S.A. 36°34N 89°57W 80 G9
Malden I. Kiribati 4°3S 155°1W 65 H12
Maldives ■ Ind. Oc. 5°0N 73°0E 26 H9
Maldon U.K. 51°44N 0°42E 13 F8
Maldonado Uruguay 34°59S 55°0W 95 C5
Maldonado, Pta. Mexico 16°20N 98°33W 87 D5
Malé Karpaty Slovak Rep. 48°30N 17°20E 17 D9

Maleas, Akra *Greece* 36°28N 23°7E **23** F10
Malebo, Pool *Africa* 4°17S 15°20E **52** E3
Malegaon *India* 20°30N 74°38E **40** J9
Malei *Mozam.* 17°12S 36°58E **55** F4
Malek Kandī *Iran* 37°9N 46°6E **44** B5
Malela
Dem. Rep. of the Congo 4°22S 26°8E **54** C2
Malema *Mozam.* 14°57S 37°20E **55** E4
Maleme *Greece* 35°31N 23°49E **25** D5
Malerkotla *India* 30°32N 75°58E **42** D6
Males *Greece* 35°6N 25°35E **25** D7
Malgomaj *Sweden* 64°40N 16°30E **8** D17
Malha *Sudan* 15°8N 25°10E **51** E11
Malhargarh *India* 24°17N 74°59E **42** G6
Malheur → *U.S.A.* 44°4N 116°59W **76** D5
Malheur L. *U.S.A.* 43°20N 118°48W **76** E4
Mali ■ *Africa* 17°0N 3°0W **50** E5
Mali → *Burma* 25°42N 97°30E **41** G20
Mali Kyun *Burma* 13°0N 98°20E **38** F2
Malia *Greece* 35°17N 25°32E **25** D7
Malia, Kolpos *Greece* 35°19N 25°27E **25** D7
Malibu *U.S.A.* 34°2N 118°41W **79** L8
Maliku *Indonesia* 0°39S 123°16E **37** E6
Malili *Indonesia* 2°42S 121°6E **37** E6
Malimba, Mts.
Dem. Rep. of the Congo 7°30S 29°30E **54** D2
Malin Hd. *Ireland* 55°23N 7°23W **10** A4
Malin Pen. *Ireland* 55°20N 7°17W **10** A4
Malindi *Kenya* 3°12S 40°5E **54** C5
Malines = Mechelen
Belgium 51°2N 4°29E **15** C4
Malino *Indonesia* 1°0N 121°0E **37** D6
Malinyi *Tanzania* 8°56S 36°0E **55** D4
Malita *Phil.* 6°19N 125°39E **37** C7
Maliwun *Burma* 10°17N 98°40E **39** G2
Maliya *India* 23°5N 70°46E **42** H4
Malka Mari △ *Kenya* 4°11N 40°46E **54** B5
Malkara *Turkey* 40°53N 26°53E **23** D12
Mallacoota Inlet
Australia 37°34S 149°40E **63** F4
Mallaig *U.K.* 57°0N 5°50W **11** D3
Mallawan *India* 27°4N 80°12E **43** F9
Mallawi *Egypt* 27°44N 30°44E **51** C12
Mallicolo = Malakula
Vanuatu 16°15S 167°30E **58** C9
Mallorca *Spain* 39°30N 3°0E **24** B10
Mallorytown *Canada* 44°29N 75°53W **83** B9
Mallow *Ireland* 52°8N 8°39W **10** D3
Malmberget *Sweden* 67°11N 20°40E **8** C19
Malmédy *Belgium* 50°25N 6°2E **15** D6
Malmesbury *S. Africa* 33°28S 18°41E **56** E2
Malmivaara = Malmberget
Sweden 67°11N 20°40E **8** C19
Malmö *Sweden* 55°36N 12°59E **9** J15
Malolo *Fiji* 17°45S 177°11E **59** a
Malolos *Phil.* 14°50N 120°49E **37** B6
Malolotja ⌓ *Swaziland* 26°4S 31°6E **57** D5
Malombe L. *Malawi* 14°40S 35°15E **55** E4
Malone *U.S.A.* 44°51N 74°18W **83** B10
Måløy *Norway* 61°57N 5°6E **8** F11
Malpaso *Canary Is.* 27°43N 18°3W **24** G1
Malpaso, Presa =
Netzahualcóyotl, Presa
Mexico 17°8N 93°35W **87** D6
Malpelo, I. de *Colombia* 4°3N 81°35W **92** C2
Malpur *India* 23°21N 73°27E **42** H5
Malpura *India* 26°17N 75°23E **42** F6
Malta *Idaho, U.S.A.* 42°18N 113°22W **76** E7
Malta *Mont., U.S.A.* 48°21N 107°52W **76** B10
Malta ■ *Europe* 35°55N 14°26E **25** D2
Maltahöhe *Namibia* 24°55S 17°0E **56** C2
Malton *Canada* 43°42N 79°38W **82** C5
Malton *U.K.* 54°8N 0°49W **12** C7
Maluku *Indonesia* 1°0S 127°0E **37** E7
Maluku □ *Indonesia* 3°0S 128°0E **37** E7
Maluku Sea = Molucca Sea
Indonesia 0°0 125°0E **37** E6
Malvan *India* 16°2N 73°30E **40** L8
Malvern *U.S.A.* 34°22N 92°49W **84** D8
Malvern Hills *U.K.* 52°0N 2°19W **13** E5
Malvinas, Is. = Falkland Is. ☒
Atl. Oc. 51°30S 59°0W **96** G5
Malya *Tanzania* 3°5S 33°38E **54** C3
Malyn *Ukraine* 50°46N 29°3E **17** C15
Malyy Lyakhovskiy, Ostrov
Russia 74°7N 140°36E **29** B15
Malyy Taymyr, Ostrov
Russia 78°6N 107°15E **29** B11
Mama *Russia* 58°18N 112°54E **29** D12
Mamanguape *Brazil* 6°50S 35°4W **93** E11
Mamanuca Group *Fiji* 17°35S 177°5E **59** a
Mamarr Mitlā *Egypt* 30°2N 32°54E **46** E1
Mamasa *Indonesia* 2°55S 119°20E **37** E5
Mambasa
Dem. Rep. of the Congo 1°22N 29°3E **54** B2
Mamberamo → *Indonesia* 2°0S 137°50E **37** E9
Mambilima Falls *Zambia* 10°31S 28°45E **55** E2
Mambirima
Dem. Rep. of the Congo 11°25S 27°33E **55** E2
Mambo *Tanzania* 4°52S 38°22E **54** C4
Mambrui *Kenya* 3°5S 40°5E **54** C5
Mamburao *Phil.* 13°13N 120°39E **37** B6
Mameigwess L. *Canada* 52°35N 87°50W **72** B2
Mammoth *U.S.A.* 32°43N 110°39W **77** K8
Mammoth Cave △
U.S.A. 37°8N 86°13W **80** G10
Mamoré → *Bolivia* 10°23S 65°53W **92** F5
Mamou *Guinea* 10°15N 12°0W **50** F3
Mamoudzou *Mayotte* 12°48S 45°14E **53** a
Mampikony *Madag.* 16°6S 47°38E **57** B8
Mamuju *Indonesia* 2°41S 118°50E **37** E5
Mamuno *Botswana* 22°16S 20°1E **56** C3
Man *Ivory C.* 7°30N 7°40W **50** G4
Man, I. of *U.K.* 54°15N 4°30W **12** C3
Man-Bazar *India* 23°4N 86°39E **43** H12
Man Na *Burma* 23°27N 97°19E **41** H20
Mana → *Fr. Guiana* 5°45N 53°55W **93** B8
Mana Pools △ *Zimbabwe* 15°56S 29°25E **55** F2
Manaar, G. of = Mannar, G. of
Asia 8°30N 79°0E **40** Q11
Manacapuru *Brazil* 3°16S 60°37W **92** D6
Manacor *Spain* 39°34N 3°13E **24** B10
Manado *Indonesia* 1°29N 124°51E **37** D6
Managua *Nic.* 12°6N 86°20W **88** D2
Managua, L. de *Nic.* 12°20N 86°30W **88** D2
Manakara *Madag.* 22°8S 48°1E **57** C8
Manali *India* 32°16N 77°10E **42** C7
Manama = Al Manāmah
Bahrain 26°10N 50°30E **45** E6
Manambao → *Madag.* 17°35S 44°0E **57** B7
Manambato *Madag.* 13°43S 49°7E **57** A8
Manambolo → *Madag.* 19°18S 44°22E **57** B7
Manambolosy *Madag.* 16°2S 49°40E **57** B8
Mananara *Madag.* 16°10S 49°46E **57** B8
Mananara → *Madag.* 23°21S 47°42E **57** C8
Mananara ⌓ *Madag.* 16°14S 49°45E **57** B8
Mananjary *Madag.* 21°13S 48°20E **57** C8
Manantenina *Madag.* 24°17S 47°19E **57** C8
Manaos = Manaus *Brazil* 3°0S 60°0W **92** D7
Manapire → *Venezuela* 7°42N 66°7W **92** B5
Manapouri *N.Z.* 45°34S 167°39E **59** F1
Manapouri, L. *N.Z.* 45°32S 167°32E **59** F1
Manār, Jabal *Yemen* 14°2N 44°17E **47** E3
Manaravolo *Madag.* 23°59S 45°39E **57** C8
Manas *China* 44°17N 85°56E **32** B3
Manas → *India* 26°12N 90°40E **41** F17
Manas He → *China* 45°38N 85°12E **32** B3
Manaslu *Nepal* 28°33N 84°33E **43** E11
Manasquan *U.S.A.* 40°8N 74°3W **83** F10
Manassa *U.S.A.* 37°11N 105°56W **77** H11
Manatí *Puerto Rico* 18°26N 66°29W **89** d
Manaung *Burma* 18°45N 93°40E **41** K18
Manaus *Brazil* 3°0S 60°0W **92** D7
Manawan L. *Canada* 55°24N 103°14W **71** B8
Manbij *Syria* 36°31N 37°57E **44** B3
Manchegorsk *Russia* 67°54N 32°58E **28** C4
Manchester *U.K.* 53°29N 2°12W **12** D5
Manchester *Calif.,*
U.S.A. 38°58N 123°41W **78** G3
Manchester *Conn.,*
U.S.A. 41°47N 72°31W **83** E12
Manchester *Ga., U.S.A.* 32°51N 84°37W **85** E12
Manchester *Iowa, U.S.A.* 42°29N 91°27W **80** D8
Manchester *Ky., U.S.A.* 37°9N 83°46W **81** G12
Manchester *N.H.,*
U.S.A. 42°59N 71°28W **83** D13
Manchester *N.Y., U.S.A.* 42°56N 77°16W **82** D7
Manchester *Pa., U.S.A.* 40°4N 76°43W **83** F8
Manchester *Tenn.,*
U.S.A. 35°29N 86°5W **85** D11
Manchester *Vt., U.S.A.* 43°10N 73°5W **83** C11
Manchester Int. ✈ **(MAN)**
U.K. 53°21N 2°17W **12** D5
Manchester L. *Canada* 61°28N 107°29W **71** A7
Manchhar L. *Pakistan* 26°25N 67°39E **42** F2
Manchuria = Dongbei
China 45°0N 125°0E **30** A5
Manchurian Plain *China* 47°0N 124°0E **26** D14
Mand → *India* 21°42N 83°15E **43** J10
Mand → *Iran* 28°20N 52°30E **45** D7
Manda *Ludewe, Tanzania* 10°30S 34°40E **55** E3
Manda *Mbeya, Tanzania* 7°58S 32°29E **54** D3
Manda *Mbeya, Tanzania* 8°30S 32°49E **55** D3
Mandabé *Madag.* 21°0S 44°55E **57** C7
Mandaguari *Brazil* 23°32S 51°42W **95** A5
Mandah = Töhöm
Mongolia 44°27N 108°2E **34** B5
Mandal *Norway* 58°2N 7°25E **9** G12
Mandala, Puncak
Indonesia 4°44S 140°20E **37** E10
Mandalay *Burma* 22°0N 96°4E **41** J20
Mandale = Mandalay
Burma 22°0N 96°4E **41** J20
Mandalgarh *India* 25°12N 75°6E **42** G6
Mandalgovĭ *Mongolia* 45°45N 106°10E **34** B4
Mandalī *Iraq* 33°43N 45°28E **44** C5
Mandan *U.S.A.* 46°50N 100°54W **80** B3
Mandar, Teluk *Indonesia* 3°35S 119°15E **37** E5
Mandaue *Phil.* 10°20N 123°56E **37** B6
Mandera *Kenya* 3°55N 41°53E **54** B5
Mandeville *Jamaica* 18°2N 77°31W **88** a
Mandi *India* 31°39N 76°58E **42** D7
Mandi Burewala *Pakistan* 30°9N 72°41E **42** D5
Mandi Dabwali *India* 29°58N 74°42E **42** E6
Mandimba *Mozam.* 14°20S 35°40E **55** E4
Mandioli *Indonesia* 0°40S 127°20E **37** E7
Mandla *India* 22°39N 80°30E **43** H9
Mandorah *Australia* 12°32S 130°42E **60** B5
Mandoto *Madag.* 19°34S 46°17E **57** B8
Mandra *Pakistan* 33°23N 73°12E **42** C5
Mandrare → *Madag.* 25°10S 46°30E **57** D8
Mandritsara *Madag.* 15°50S 48°49E **57** B8
Mandronarivo *Madag.* 21°7S 45°38E **57** C8
Mandsaur *India* 24°3N 75°8E **42** G6
Mandurah *Australia* 32°36S 115°48E **61** F2
Mandvi *India* 22°51N 69°22E **42** H3
Mandya *India* 12°30N 77°0E **40** N10
Mandzai *Pakistan* 30°55N 67°6E **42** D2
Maneh *Iran* 37°39N 57°7E **45** B8
Manera *Madag.* 22°55S 44°20E **57** C7
Maneroo Cr. →
Australia 23°21S 143°53E **62** C3
Manfalût *Egypt* 27°20N 30°52E **51** C12
Manfredónia *Italy* 41°38N 15°55E **22** D6
Mangabeiras, Chapada das
Brazil 10°0S 46°30W **93** F9
Mangaia *Cook Is.* 21°55S 157°55W **65** K12
Mangalia *Romania* 43°50N 28°35E **17** G15
Mangalore *India* 12°55N 74°47E **40** N9
Mangan *India* 27°31N 88°32E **43** F13
Mangawan *India* 24°41N 81°33E **43** G9
Mangaweka *N.Z.* 39°48S 175°47E **59** C5
Manggar *Indonesia* 2°50S 108°10E **36** E3
Manggawitu *Indonesia* 4°8S 133°32E **37** E8
Mangghystaū Tübegi
Kazakhstan 44°30N 52°30E **28** E6
Manggis *Indonesia* 8°29S 115°31E **37** J18
Mangindrano *Madag.* 14°17S 48°58E **57** A8
Mangkalihat, Tanjung
Indonesia 1°2N 118°59E **37** D5
Mangla *Pakistan* 33°7N 73°39E **42** C5
Mangla Dam *Pakistan* 33°9N 73°44E **43** C5
Manglaur *India* 29°44N 77°49E **42** E7
Mangnai *China* 37°52N 91°43E **32** C4
Mangnai Zhen *China* 38°24N 90°14E **32** C4
Mango *Togo* 10°20N 0°30E **50** F6
Mango *Tonga* 20°17S 174°29W **59** c
Mangoche *Malawi* 14°25S 35°16E **55** E4
Mangoky → *Madag.* 21°29S 43°41E **57** C7
Mangole *Indonesia* 1°50S 125°55E **37** E6
Mangombe
Dem. Rep. of the Congo 1°20S 26°48E **54** C2
Mangonui *N.Z.* 35°1S 173°32E **59** A4
Mangoro → *Madag.* 20°0S 48°45E **57** B8
Mangrol *Mad. P., India* 21°7N 70°7E **42** J4
Mangrol *Raj., India* 25°20N 76°31E **42** G6
Mangueira, L. da *Brazil* 33°0S 52°50W **95** C5
Mangum *U.S.A.* 34°53N 99°30W **84** D5
Manguri *Australia* 28°58S 134°22E **63** A1
Mangyshlak, Poluostrov =
Mangghystaū Tübegi
Kazakhstan 44°30N 52°30E **28** E6
Manhattan *U.S.A.* 39°11N 96°35W **80** F5
Manhiça *Mozam.* 25°23S 32°49E **57** D5
Mania → *Madag.* 19°42S 45°22E **57** B8
Manica *Mozam.* 18°58S 32°59E **57** B5
Manica □ *Mozam.* 19°10S 33°45E **57** B5
Manicaland □ *Zimbabwe* 19°0S 32°30E **55** F3
Manicoré *Brazil* 5°48S 61°16W **92** E6
Manicouagan →
Canada 49°30N 68°30W **73** C6
Manicouagan, Rés.
Canada 51°5N 68°40W **73** B6
Maniema □
Dem. Rep. of the Congo 3°0S 26°0E **54** C2
Manīfah *Si. Arabia* 27°44N 49°0E **45** E6
Manifold, C. *Australia* 22°41S 150°50E **62** C5
Manigotagan *Canada* 51°6N 96°18W **71** C9
Manigotagan → *Canada* 51°7N 96°20W **71** C9
Manihari *India* 25°21N 87°38E **43** G12
Manihiki *Cook Is.* 10°24S 161°1W **65** J11
Manihiki Plateau
Pac. Oc. 11°0S 164°0W **65** J11
Manika, Plateau de la
Dem. Rep. of the Congo 10°0S 25°5E **55** E2
Manikpur *India* 25°4N 81°7E **43** G9
Manila *Phil.* 14°35N 120°58E **37** B6
Manila *U.S.A.* 40°59N 109°43W **76** F9
Manila B. *Phil.* 14°40N 120°35E **37** B6
Manilla *Australia* 30°45S 150°43E **63** E5
Maningrida *Australia* 12°3S 134°13E **62** A1
Manipur □ *India* 25°0N 94°0E **41** G19
Manipur → *Burma* 23°45N 94°20E **41** H19
Manisa *Turkey* 38°38N 27°30E **23** E12
Manistee *U.S.A.* 44°15N 86°19W **80** C10
Manistee → *U.S.A.* 44°15N 86°21W **80** C10
Manistique *U.S.A.* 45°57N 86°15W **80** C10
Manitoba □ *Canada* 53°30N 97°0W **71** B9
Manitoba, L. *Canada* 51°0N 98°45W **71** C9
Manitou *Canada* 49°15N 98°32W **71** D9
Manitou, L. *Canada* 50°55N 65°17W **73** B6
Manitou Is. *U.S.A.* 45°8N 86°0W **81** C10
Manitou L. *Canada* 52°43N 109°43W **71** C7
Manitou Springs
U.S.A. 38°52N 104°55W **76** G11
Manitoulin I. *Canada* 45°40N 82°30W **72** C3
Manitouwadge *Canada* 49°8N 85°48W **72** C2
Manitowoc *U.S.A.* 44°5N 87°40W **80** C10
Manizales *Colombia* 5°5N 75°32W **92** B3
Manja *Madag.* 21°26S 44°20E **57** C7
Manjacaze *Mozam.* 24°45S 34°0E **57** C5
Manjakandriana *Madag.* 18°55S 47°47E **57** B8
Manjhand *Pakistan* 25°50N 68°10E **42** G3
Manjimup *Australia* 34°15S 116°6E **61** F2
Manjra → *India* 18°49N 77°52E **40** K10
Mankato *Kans., U.S.A.* 39°47N 98°13W **80** F4
Mankato *Minn., U.S.A.* 44°10N 94°0W **80** C6
Mankayane *Swaziland* 26°40S 31°4E **57** D5
Mankera *Pakistan* 31°23N 71°26E **42** D4
Mankota *Canada* 49°25N 107°5W **71** D7
Manlay = Üydzin
Mongolia 44°9N 107°0E **34** B4
Manmad *India* 20°18N 74°28E **40** J9
Mann Ranges *Australia* 26°6S 130°5E **61** E5
Manna *Indonesia* 4°25S 102°55E **36** E2
Mannahill *Australia* 32°25S 140°0E **63** E3
Mannar *Sri Lanka* 9°1N 79°54E **40** Q11
Mannar, G. of *Asia* 8°30N 79°0E **40** Q11
Mannar I. *Sri Lanka* 9°5N 79°45E **40** Q11
Mannheim *Germany* 49°29N 8°29E **16** D5
Manning *Canada* 56°53N 117°39W **70** B5
Manning *Oreg., U.S.A.* 45°45N 123°13W **78** E3
Manning *S.C., U.S.A.* 33°42N 80°13W **85** E14
Mannum *Australia* 34°50S 139°20E **63** E2
Manoharpur *India* 22°23N 85°12E **43** H11
Manokwari *Indonesia* 0°54S 134°0E **37** E8
Manombo *Madag.* 22°57S 43°28E **57** C7
Manono
Dem. Rep. of the Congo 7°15S 27°25E **54** D2
Manono *Samoa* 13°50S 172°5W **59** b
Manorhamilton *Ireland* 54°18N 8°9W **10** B3
Manosque *France* 43°49N 5°47E **20** E6
Manotick *Canada* 45°13N 75°41W **83** A9
Manouane → *Canada* 49°30N 71°10W **73** C5
Manouane, L. *Canada* 50°45N 70°45W **73** B5
Manp'o *N. Korea* 41°6N 126°24E **35** D14
Manpojin = Manp'o
N. Korea 41°6N 126°24E **35** D14
Manpur *Chhattisgarh,*
India 23°17N 83°35E **43** H10
Manpur *Mad. P., India* 22°26N 75°37E **42** H6
Manresa *Spain* 41°48N 1°50E **21** B6
Mansa *Gujarat, India* 23°27N 72°45E **42** H5
Mansa *Punjab, India* 30°0N 75°27E **42** E6
Mansa *Zambia* 11°13S 28°55E **55** E2
Mansehra *Pakistan* 34°20N 73°15E **42** B5
Mansel I. *Canada* 62°0N 80°0W **69** C12
Mansfield *Australia* 37°4S 146°6E **63** F4
Mansfield *U.K.* 53°9N 1°11W **12** D6
Mansfield *La., U.S.A.* 32°2N 93°43W **84** E8
Mansfield *Mass., U.S.A.* 42°2N 71°13W **83** D13
Mansfield *Ohio, U.S.A.* 40°45N 82°31W **82** F2
Mansfield *Pa., U.S.A.* 41°48N 77°5W **82** E7
Mansfield *Tex., U.S.A.* 32°33N 97°8W **84** E6
Mansfield, Mt. *U.S.A.* 44°33N 72°49W **83** B12
Manson Creek *Canada* 55°37N 124°32W **70** B4
Manta *Ecuador* 1°0S 80°40W **92** D2
Mantadia △ *Madag.* 18°54S 48°21E **57** B8
Mantalingajan, Mt.
Phil. 8°55N 117°45E **36** C5
Mantare *Tanzania* 2°42S 33°13E **54** C3
Manteca *U.S.A.* 37°48N 121°13W **78** H5
Manteo *U.S.A.* 35°55N 75°40W **85** D17
Mantes-la-Jolie *France* 48°58N 1°41E **20** B4
Manthani *India* 18°40N 79°35E **40** K11
Manti *U.S.A.* 39°16N 111°38W **76** G8
Mantiqueira, Serra da
Brazil 22°0S 44°0W **95** A7
Manton *U.S.A.* 44°25N 85°24W **81** C11
Mántova *Italy* 45°9N 10°48E **22** B4
Mänttä *Finland* 62°3N 24°40E **8** E21
Mantua = Mántova *Italy* 45°9N 10°48E **22** B4
Manú *Peru* 12°10S 70°51W **92** F4
Manú → *Peru* 12°16S 70°55W **92** F4
Manu'a Is. *Amer. Samoa* 14°13S 169°35W **59** b
Manuel Alves → *Brazil* 11°19S 48°28W **93** F9
Manui *Indonesia* 3°35S 123°5E **37** E6
Manukau *N.Z.* 37°0S 174°52E **59** B5
Manuripi → *Bolivia* 11°6S 67°36W **92** F5
Many *U.S.A.* 31°34N 93°29W **84** F8
Manyara *Kenya* 3°5S 38°30E **54** C4
Manyara, L. *Tanzania* 3°40S 35°50E **54** C4
Manych-Gudilo, Ozero
Russia 46°24N 42°38E **19** E7
Manyonga → *Tanzania* 4°10S 34°15E **54** C3
Manyoni *Tanzania* 5°45S 34°55E **54** D3
Manzai *Pakistan* 32°12N 70°15E **42** C4
Manzanar ⌓ *U.S.A.* 36°44N 118°9W **78** J7
Manzanares *Spain* 39°2N 3°22W **21** C4
Manzanillo *Cuba* 20°20N 77°31W **88** B4
Manzanillo *Mexico* 19°3N 104°20W **86** D4
Manzanillo, Pta. *Panama* 9°30N 79°40W **88** E4
Manzano Mts. *U.S.A.* 34°40N 106°20W **77** J10
Manzarīyeh *Iran* 34°53N 50°50E **45** C6
Manzhouli *China* 49°35N 117°25E **33** B6
Manzini *Swaziland* 26°30S 31°25E **57** D5
Manzur Vadisi △ *Turkey* 39°10N 39°30E **44** B3
Mao *Chad* 14°4N 15°19E **51** F9
Maó *Spain* 39°53N 4°16E **24** B11
Maoke, Pegunungan
Indonesia 3°40S 137°30E **37** E9
Maolin *China* 43°58N 123°30E **35** C12
Maoming *China* 21°50N 110°54E **33** D6
Maoxing *China* 45°28N 124°40E **35** B13
Mapam Yumco *China* 30°45N 81°28E **43** D9
Mapastepec *Mexico* 15°26N 92°54W **87** D6
Maphrao, Ko *Thailand* 7°56N 98°26E **39** a
Mapia, Kepulauan
Indonesia 0°50N 134°20E **37** D8
Mapimí *Mexico* 25°49N 103°51W **86** B4
Mapimí, Bolsón de
Mexico 27°0N 104°15W **86** B4
Mapinga *Tanzania* 6°40S 39°12E **54** D4
Mapinhane *Mozam.* 22°20S 35°0E **57** C6
Maple Creek *Canada* 49°55N 109°29W **71** D7
Maple Valley *U.S.A.* 47°25N 122°3W **78** C4
Mapleton *U.S.A.* 44°2N 123°52W **76** D2
Mapuera → *Brazil* 1°5S 57°2W **92** D7
Mapulanguene *Mozam.* 24°29S 32°6E **57** C5
Mapungubwe △
S. Africa 22°12S 29°22E **55** G2
Maputo *Mozam.* 25°58S 32°32E **57** D5
Maputo □ *Mozam.* 26°0S 32°25E **57** D5
Maputo, B. de *Mozam.* 25°50S 32°45E **57** D5
Maputo ⌓ *Mozam.* 26°23S 32°48E **57** D5
Maqat *Kazakhstan* 47°39N 53°19E **19** E9
Maqên *China* 34°24N 100°6E **32** C5
Maqiaohe *China* 44°40N 130°30E **35** B16
Maqnā *Si. Arabia* 28°25N 34°50E **44** D2
Maqteïr *Mauritania* 21°50N 11°40W **50** D3
Maquan He = Brahmaputra →
Asia 23°40N 90°35E **43** H13
Maquela do Zombo *Angola* 6°0S 15°15E **52** F3
Maquinchao *Argentina* 41°15S 68°50W **96** E3
Maquoketa *U.S.A.* 42°4N 90°40W **80** D8
Mar *Canada* 44°49N 81°12W **82** B3
Mar, Serra do *Brazil* 25°30S 49°0W **95** B6
Mar Chiquita, L.
Argentina 30°40S 62°50W **94** C3
Mar del Plata *Argentina* 38°0S 57°30W **94** D4
Mar Menor *Spain* 37°40N 0°45W **21** D5
Mara *Tanzania* 1°30S 34°32E **54** C3
Mara □ *Tanzania* 1°45S 34°20E **54** C3
Maraã *Brazil* 1°52S 65°25W **92** D5
Maraa *Tahiti* 17°46S 149°34W **59** d
Marabá *Brazil* 5°20S 49°5W **93** E9
Maraboon, L. *Australia* 23°41S 148°0E **62** C4
Maracá, I. de *Brazil* 2°10N 50°30W **93** C8
Maracaibo *Venezuela* 10°40N 71°37W **92** A4
Maracaibo, L. de
Venezuela 9°40N 71°30W **92** B4
Maracaju *Brazil* 21°38S 55°9W **95** A4
Maracas Bay Village
Trin. & Tob. 10°46N 61°28W **93** K15
Maracay *Venezuela* 10°15N 67°28W **92** A5
Marādah *Libya* 29°15N 19°15E **51** C9
Maradi *Niger* 13°29N 7°20E **50** F7
Marāgheh *Iran* 37°30N 46°12E **44** B5
Marāh *Si. Arabia* 25°0N 45°35E **44** E5
Marajó, I. de *Brazil* 1°0S 49°30W **93** D9
Marākand *Iran* 38°51N 45°16E **44** B5
Marakele △ *S. Africa* 32°14S 25°27E **57** E4
Maralal *Kenya* 1°0N 36°38E **54** B4
Maralinga *Australia* 30°13S 131°32E **61** F5
Marambio *Antarctica* 64°0S 56°0W **5** C18
Maran *Malaysia* 3°35N 102°45E **39** L4
Marana *U.S.A.* 32°27N 111°13W **77** K8
Maranboy *Australia* 14°40S 132°39E **60** B5
Marand *Iran* 38°30N 45°45E **44** B5
Marang *Malaysia* 5°12N 103°13E **39** K4
Maranguape *Brazil* 3°55S 38°50W **93** D11
Maranhão = São Luís
Brazil 2°39S 44°15W **93** D10
Maranhão □ *Brazil* 5°0S 46°0W **93** E9
Maranoa → *Australia* 27°50S 148°37E **63** D4
Marañón → *Peru* 4°30S 73°35W **92** D4
Marão *Mozam.* 24°18S 34°2E **57** C5
Maraş = Kahramanmaraş
Turkey 37°37N 36°53E **44** B3
Marathasa *Cyprus* 34°59N 32°51E **25** E11
Marathon *Australia* 20°51S 143°32E **62** C3
Marathon *Canada* 48°44N 86°23W **72** C2
Marathon *N.Y., U.S.A.* 42°27N 76°2W **83** D8
Marathon *Tex., U.S.A.* 30°12N 103°15W **84** F3
Marathóvouno *Cyprus* 35°13N 33°37E **25** D12
Maratua *Indonesia* 2°10N 118°35E **37** D5
Maraval *Trin. & Tob.* 10°42N 61°31W **93** K15
Maravatío *Mexico* 19°54N 100°27W **86** D4
Marāwih *U.A.E.* 24°18N 53°18E **45** E7
Marbella *Spain* 36°30N 4°57W **21** D3
Marble Bar *Australia* 21°9S 119°44E **60** D2
Marble Falls *U.S.A.* 30°35N 98°16W **84** F5
Marblehead *Mass.,*
U.S.A. 42°29N 70°51W **83** D14
Marblehead *Ohio, U.S.A.* 41°32N 82°44W **82** E2
Marburg *Germany* 50°47N 8°46E **16** C5
Marca, Pta. Da *Angola* 16°31S 11°43E **53** H2
March *U.K.* 52°33N 0°5E **13** E8
Marche *France* 46°5N 1°20E **20** C4
Marche-en-Famenne
Belgium 50°14N 5°19E **15** D5
Marchena *Spain* 37°18N 5°23W **21** D3
Marco Island *U.S.A.* 25°58N 81°44W **85** J14
Marcos Juárez *Argentina* 32°42S 62°5W **94** C3
Marcus I. = Minami-Tori-Shima
Pac. Oc. 24°20N 153°58E **64** E7
Marcy, Mt. *U.S.A.* 44°7N 73°56W **83** B11
Mardan *Pakistan* 34°20N 72°0E **42** B5
Mardin *Turkey* 37°20N 40°43E **44** B4
Maree, L. *U.K.* 57°40N 5°26W **11** D3
Mareeba *Australia* 16°59S 145°28E **62** B4
Mareetsane *S. Africa* 26°9S 25°25E **56** D4
Marek = Stanke Dimitrov
Bulgaria 42°17N 23°9E **23** C10
Marengo *U.S.A.* 41°48N 92°4W **80** E7
Marerano *Madag.* 21°23S 44°52E **57** C7
Marfa *U.S.A.* 30°19N 104°1W **84** F2
Marfa Pt. *Malta* 35°59N 14°19E **25** D1
Margaret → *Australia* 18°9S 125°41E **60** C4
Margaret Bay *Canada* 51°20N 127°35W **70** C3
Margaret L. *Canada* 58°56N 115°25W **70** B5
Margaret River *Australia* 33°57S 115°4E **61** F
Margarita, I. de *Venezuela* 11°0N 64°0W **92** A
Margaritovo *Russia* 43°25N 134°45E **30** C
Margate *S. Africa* 30°50S 30°20E **57** E5
Margate *U.K.* 51°23N 1°23E **13** F
Margherita Pk. *Uganda* 0°22N 29°51E **54** B
Marghilon *Uzbekistan* 40°27N 71°42E **28** E
Mārgow, Dasht-e
Afghan. 30°40N 62°30E **40** D
Marguerite *Canada* 52°30N 122°25W **70** C
Mari El □ *Russia* 56°30N 48°0E **18** C
Mari Indus *Pakistan* 32°57N 71°34E **42** C
Mari Republic = Mari El □
Russia 56°30N 48°0E **18** C8
María de la Salut *Spain* 39°40N 3°5E **24** B1
María Elena *Chile* 22°18S 69°40W **94** A
María Grande *Argentina* 31°45S 59°55W **94** C
Maria I. *N. Terr.,*
Australia 14°52S 135°45E **62** A
Maria I. *Tas., Australia* 42°35S 148°0E **63** G
Maria Island △ *Australia* 42°38S 148°5E **63** G
Maria van Diemen, C.
N.Z. 34°29S 172°40E **59** A
Mariakani *Kenya* 3°50S 39°27E **54** C
Mariala △ *Australia* 25°57S 145°2E **63** D
Marian *Australia* 21°9S 148°57E **62** K
Marian L. *Canada* 63°0N 116°15W **70** A
Mariana Trench *Pac. Oc.* 13°0N 145°0E **64** F
Marianna *Ark., U.S.A.* 34°46N 90°46W **85** D
Marianna *Fla., U.S.A.* 30°46N 85°14W **85** F1
Marias → *U.S.A.* 47°56N 110°30W **76** C
Marías, Islas *Mexico* 21°25N 106°28W **86** C
Mariato, Punta *Panama* 7°12N 80°52W **88** E
Maribor *Slovenia* 46°36N 15°40E **16** E
Marico → *Africa* 23°35S 26°57E **56** C
Maricopa *Ariz., U.S.A.* 33°4N 112°3W **77** K
Maricopa *Calif., U.S.A.* 35°4N 119°24W **79** K
Marié → *Brazil* 0°27S 66°26W **92** D
Marie Byrd Land
Antarctica 79°30S 125°0W **5** D1
Marie-Galante
Guadeloupe 15°56N 61°16W **88**
Mariecourt = Kangiqsujuaq
Canada 61°30N 72°0W **69** C1
Mariehamn *Finland* 60°5N 19°55E **9** F1
Mariembourg *Belgium* 50°6N 4°31E **15** D
Mariental *Namibia* 24°36S 18°0E **56** C
Marienville *U.S.A.* 41°28N 79°8W **82** E
Mariestad *Sweden* 58°43N 13°50E **9** G1
Marietta *Ga., U.S.A.* 33°57N 84°33W **85** E1
Marietta *Ohio, U.S.A.* 39°25N 81°27W **81** F1
Marieville *Canada* 45°26N 73°10W **83** A1
Mariinsk *Russia* 56°10N 87°20E **28** D
Marijampolė *Lithuania* 54°33N 23°19E **9** J2

arília *Brazil* 22°13S 50°0W **95** A6
arín *Spain* 42°23N 8°42W **21** A1
arina *U.S.A.* 36°41N 121°48W **78** J5
arinduque *Phil.* 13°25N 122°0E **37** B6
arine City *U.S.A.* 42°43N 82°30W **82** D2
arinette *U.S.A.* 45°6N 87°38W **80** C10
aringá *Brazil* 23°26S 52°2W **95** A5
arion *Ala., U.S.A.* 32°38N 87°19W **85** E11
arion *Ill., U.S.A.* 37°44N 88°56W **80** G9
arion *Ind., U.S.A.* 40°32N 85°40W **81** E11
arion *Iowa, U.S.A.* 42°2N 91°36W **80** D8
arion *Kans., U.S.A.* 38°21N 97°1W **80** F5
arion *N.C., U.S.A.* 35°41N 82°1W **85** D13
arion *Ohio, U.S.A.* 40°35N 83°8W **81** E12
arion *S.C., U.S.A.* 34°11N 79°24W **85** D15
arion *Va., U.S.A.* 36°50N 81°31W **81** G13
arion, L. *U.S.A.* 33°28N 80°10W **85** E14
ariposa *U.S.A.* 37°29N 119°58W **78** H7
ariscal Estigarribia
Paraguay 22°3S 60°40W **94** A3
aritime Alps = Maritimes, Alpes
Europe 44°10N 7°10E **20** D7
aritimes, Alpes *Europe* 44°10N 7°10E **20** D7
aritsa = Evros →
Greece 41°40N 26°34E **23** D12
aritsa *Greece* 36°22N 28°8E **25** C10
ariupol *Ukraine* 47°5N 37°31E **19** E6
ariusa △ *Venezuela* 9°24N 61°27W **89** E7
arīvān *Iran* 35°30N 46°25E **44** C5
arj 'Uyūn *Lebanon* 33°21N 35°34E **46** B4
arka *Somali Rep.* 1°48N 44°50E **47** G3
arkam *China* 29°42N 98°38E **32** D4
arkdale *Canada* 44°19N 80°39W **82** B4
arked Tree *U.S.A.* 35°32N 90°25W **85** D9
arket Drayton *U.K.* 52°54N 2°29W **12** E5
arket Harborough
U.K. 52°29N 0°55W **13** E7
arket Rasen *U.K.* 53°24N 0°20W **12** D7
arkham *Canada* 43°52N 79°16W **82** C5
arkham, Mt. *Antarctica* 83°0S 164°0E **5** E11
arkleeville *U.S.A.* 38°42N 119°47W **78** G7
arkovo *Russia* 64°40N 170°24E **29** C17
arks *Russia* 51°45N 46°50E **18** D8
arksville *U.S.A.* 31°8N 92°4W **84** F8
arla *Australia* 27°19S 133°33E **63** D1
arlbank *Canada* 44°26N 77°6W **82** B7
arlboro *U.S.A.* 41°36N 73°59W **83** E11
arlborough *Australia* 22°46S 149°52E **62** C4
arlborough *U.K.* 51°25N 1°43W **13** F6
arlborough *U.S.A.* 42°21N 71°33W **83** D13
arlborough Downs
U.K. 51°27N 1°53W **13** F6
arlin *U.S.A.* 31°18N 96°54W **84** F6
arlow *U.K.* 51°34N 0°46W **13** F7
arlow *U.S.A.* 34°39N 97°58W **84** D6
armagao *India* 15°25N 73°56E **40** M8
armara *Turkey* 40°35N 27°34E **23** D12
armara, Sea of = Marmara
Denizi *Turkey* 40°45N 28°15E **23** D13
armara Denizi *Turkey* 40°45N 28°15E **23** D13
armaris *Turkey* 36°50N 28°14E **23** F13
armion, Mt. *Australia* 29°16S 119°50E **61** E2
armion L. *Canada* 48°55N 91°20W **72** C1
armolada, Mte. *Italy* 46°26N 11°51E **22** A4
armora *Canada* 44°28N 77°41W **82** B7
arne → *France* 48°47N 2°29E **20** B5
aroala *Madag.* 15°23S 47°59E **57** B8
aroantsetra *Madag.* 15°26S 49°44E **57** B8
aroelaboom *Namibia* 19°15S 18°53E **56** B2
arofandilia *Madag.* 20°7S 44°34E **57** C7
arojejy △ *Madag.* 14°26S 49°21E **57** A8
arolambo *Madag.* 20°2S 48°7E **57** C8
aromandia *Madag.* 14°13S 48°5E **57** A8
aromokotro *Madag.* 14°0S 49°0E **57** A8
arondera *Zimbabwe* 18°5S 31°42E **55** F3
aroni → *Fr. Guiana* 5°30N 54°0W **93** B8
aroochydore *Australia* 26°29S 153°5E **63** D5
aroona *Australia* 37°27S 142°54E **63** F3
arosakoa *Madag.* 15°26S 46°38E **57** B8
aroseranana *Madag.* 18°32S 48°51E **57** B8
arotandrano *Madag.* 16°10S 48°50E **57** B8
arotaolano *Madag.* 12°47S 49°15E **57** A8
aroua *Cameroon* 10°40N 14°20E **51** F8
arovato *Madag.* 15°48S 48°5E **57** B8
arovoay *Madag.* 16°6S 46°39E **57** B8
arquard *S. Africa* 28°40S 27°28E **56** D4
arquesas Fracture Zone
Pac. Oc. 9°0S 125°0W **65** H15
arquesas Is. = Marquises, Îs.
French Polynesia 9°30S 140°0W **65** H14
arquette *U.S.A.* 46°33N 87°24W **80** B10
arquis *St. Lucia* 14°2N 60°54W **89** f
arquises, Îs.
French Polynesia 9°30S 140°0W **65** H14
arra, Djebel *Sudan* 13°10N 24°22E **51** F10
arracuene *Mozam.* 25°45S 32°35E **57** D5
arrakech *Morocco* 31°9N 8°0W **50** B4
arrawah *Australia* 40°55S 144°42E **63** G3
arree *Australia* 29°39S 138°1E **63** D2
arrero *U.S.A.* 29°53N 90°6W **85** G9
arrimane *Mozam.* 22°58S 33°34E **57** C5
arromeu *Mozam.* 18°15S 36°25E **57** B6
arromeu △ *Mozam.* 19°0S 36°0E **57** B6
arrowie Cr. →
Australia 33°23S 145°40E **63** E4
arrubane *Mozam.* 18°0S 37°0E **55** F4
arrupa *Mozam.* 13°8S 37°30E **55** E4
ars Hill *U.S.A.* 46°31N 67°52W **81** B20
arsá 'Alam *Egypt* 25°5N 34°54E **47** B1
arsá Matrûh *Egypt* 31°19N 27°9E **51** B11
arsá Susah *Libya* 32°52N 21°59E **51** B10
arsabit *Kenya* 2°18N 38°0E **54** B4
arsabit △ *Kenya* 2°23N 37°56E **54** B4
arsala *Italy* 37°48N 12°26E **22** F5
arsalforn *Malta* 36°4N 14°16E **25** C1
arsden *Australia* 33°47S 147°32E **63** E4
arseille *France* 43°18N 5°23E **20** E6

Marseilles = Marseille
France 43°18N 5°23E **20** E6
Marsh I. *U.S.A.* 29°34N 91°53W **84** G9
Marshall *Ark., U.S.A.* 35°55N 92°38W **84** D8
Marshall *Mich., U.S.A.* 42°16N 84°58W **81** D11
Marshall *Minn., U.S.A.* 44°27N 95°47W **80** C6
Marshall *Mo., U.S.A.* 39°7N 93°12W **80** F7
Marshall *Tex., U.S.A.* 32°33N 94°23W **84** E7
Marshall → *Australia* 22°59S 136°59E **62** C2
Marshall Is. ■ *Pac. Oc.* 9°0N 171°0E **58** A10
Marshalltown *U.S.A.* 42°3N 92°55W **80** D7
Marshbrook *Zimbabwe* 18°33S 31°9E **57** B5
Marshfield *Mo., U.S.A.* 37°15N 92°54W **80** G7
Marshfield *Vt., U.S.A.* 44°20N 72°20W **83** B12
Marshfield *Wis., U.S.A.* 44°40N 90°10W **80** C8
Marshūn *Iran* 36°19N 49°23E **45** B6
Märsta *Sweden* 59°37N 17°52E **9** G17
Mart *U.S.A.* 31°33N 96°50W **84** F6
Martaban *Burma* 16°30N 97°35E **41** L20
Martaban, G. of *Burma* 16°5N 96°30E **41** L20
Martapura *Kalimantan,*
Indonesia 3°22S 114°47E **36** E4
Martapura *Sumatera,*
Indonesia 4°19S 104°22E **36** E2
Marte R. Gómez, Presa
Mexico 26°10N 99°0W **87** B5
Martelange *Belgium* 49°49N 5°43E **15** E5
Martha's Vineyard
U.S.A. 41°25N 70°38W **83** E14
Martigny *Switz.* 46°6N 7°3E **20** C7
Martigues *France* 43°24N 5°4E **20** E6
Martin *Slovak Rep.* 49°6N 18°58E **17** D10
Martin *S. Dak., U.S.A.* 43°11N 101°44W **80** D3
Martin *Tenn., U.S.A.* 36°21N 88°51W **85** C10
Martin L. *U.S.A.* 32°41N 85°55W **85** E12
Martina Franca *Italy* 40°42N 17°20E **22** D7
Martinborough *N.Z.* 41°14S 175°29E **59** D5
Martinez *Calif., U.S.A.* 38°1N 122°8W **78** G4
Martinez *Ga., U.S.A.* 33°31N 82°5W **85** E13
Martinique ☑ *W. Indies* 14°40N 61°0W **88** c
Martinique Passage
W. Indies 15°15N 61°0W **89** C7
Martinópolis *Brazil* 22°11S 51°12W **95** A5
Martin's Bay *Barbados* 13°12N 59°29W **89** g
Martins Ferry *U.S.A.* 40°6N 80°44W **82** F4
Martinsburg *Pa., U.S.A.* 40°19N 78°20W **82** F6
Martinsburg *W. Va.,*
U.S.A. 39°27N 77°58W **81** F15
Martinsville *Ind.,*
U.S.A. 39°26N 86°25W **80** F10
Martinsville *Va., U.S.A.* 36°41N 79°52W **81** G14
Marton *N.Z.* 40°4S 175°23E **59** D5
Martos *Spain* 37°44N 3°58W **21** D4
Marudi *Malaysia* 4°11N 114°19E **36** D4
Maruf *Afghan.* 31°30N 67°6E **40** D5
Marugame *Japan* 34°15N 133°40E **31** G6
Marunga *Angola* 17°28S 20°2E **56** B3
Marungu, Mts.
Dem. Rep. of the Congo 7°30S 30°0E **54** D3
Marv Dasht *Iran* 29°50N 52°40E **45** D7
Marvast *Iran* 30°30N 54°15E **45** D7
Marvel Loch *Australia* 31°28S 119°29E **61** F2
Marwar *India* 25°43N 73°45E **42** G5
Mary *Turkmenistan* 37°40N 61°50E **45** B9
Maryborough = Port Laoise
Ireland 53°2N 7°18W **10** C4
Maryborough *Queens.,*
Australia 25°31S 152°37E **63** D5
Maryborough *Vic.,*
Australia 37°3S 143°44E **63** F3
Maryfield *Canada* 49°50N 101°35W **71** D8
Maryland ☐ *U.S.A.* 39°0N 76°30W **81** F15
Maryland Junction
Zimbabwe 17°45S 30°31E **55** F3
Maryport *U.K.* 54°44N 3°28W **12** C4
Mary's Harbour *Canada* 52°18N 55°51W **73** B8
Marystown *Canada* 47°10N 55°10W **73** C8
Marysville *Calif., U.S.A.* 39°9N 121°35W **78** F5
Marysville *Kans., U.S.A.* 39°51N 96°39W **80** F5
Marysville *Mich., U.S.A.* 42°54N 82°29W **82** D2
Marysville *Ohio, U.S.A.* 40°14N 83°22W **81** E12
Marysville *Wash., U.S.A.* 48°3N 122°11W **78** B4
Maryville *Mo., U.S.A.* 40°21N 94°52W **80** E6
Maryville *Tenn., U.S.A.* 35°46N 83°58W **85** D13
Marzūq *Libya* 25°53N 13°57E **51** C8
Marzūq, Idehān *Libya* 24°50N 13°51E **51** D8
Masada *Israel* 31°15N 35°20E **46** D4
Masahunga *Tanzania* 2°6S 33°18E **54** C3
Masai *Malaysia* 1°29N 103°55E **39** d
Masai Mara △ *Kenya* 1°25S 35°5E **54** C4
Masai Steppe *Tanzania* 4°30S 36°30E **54** C4
Masaka *Uganda* 0°21S 31°45E **54** C3
Masalembo, Kepulauan
Indonesia 5°35S 114°30E **36** F4
Masalima, Kepulauan
Indonesia 5°4S 117°5E **36** F5
Masamba *Indonesia* 2°30S 120°15E **37** E6
Masan *S. Korea* 35°11N 128°32E **35** G15
Masandam, Ra's *Oman* 26°30N 56°30E **45** E8
Masasi *Tanzania* 10°45S 38°52E **55** E4
Masaya *Nic.* 12°0N 86°7W **88** D2
Masbate *Phil.* 12°21N 123°36E **37** B6
Mascara *Algeria* 35°26N 0°6E **50** A6
Mascota *Mexico* 20°32N 104°49W **86** C4
Masela *Indonesia* 8°9S 129°51E **37** F7
Maseru *Lesotho* 29°18S 27°30E **56** D4
Mashaba *Zimbabwe* 20°2S 30°29E **55** G3
Mashābih *Si. Arabia* 25°35N 36°30E **44** E3
Mashatu △ *Botswana* 22°45S 29°5E **57** C4
Masherbrum *Pakistan* 35°38N 76°18E **43** B7
Mashhad *Iran* 36°20N 59°35E **45** B8
Mashīz *Iran* 29°56N 56°37E **45** D8
Māshkel, Hāmūn-i-
Pakistan 28°20N 62°56E **45** D9
Mashki Chāh *Pakistan* 29°5N 62°30E **40** E3
Mashonaland *Zimbabwe* 16°30S 31°0E **53** H6
Mashonaland Central ☐
Zimbabwe 17°30S 31°0E **57** B5

Mashonaland East ☐
Zimbabwe 18°0S 32°0E **57** B5
Mashonaland West ☐
Zimbabwe 17°30S 29°30E **57** B4
Mashrakh *India* 26°7N 84°48E **43** F11
Masi Manimba
Dem. Rep. of the Congo 4°40S 17°54E **52** E3
Masindi *Uganda* 1°40N 31°43E **54** B3
Masindi Port *Uganda* 1°43N 32°2E **54** B3
Maşīrah *Oman* 21°0N 58°50E **47** C6
Maşīrah, Khalīj *Oman* 20°10N 58°10E **47** C6
Masisi
Dem. Rep. of the Congo 1°23S 28°49E **54** C2
Masjed Soleyman *Iran* 31°55N 49°18E **45** D6
Mask, L. *Ireland* 53°36N 9°22W **10** C2
Maskin *Oman* 23°44N 56°52E **45** F8
Masoala, Tanjon' i
Madag. 15°59S 50°13E **57** B9
Masoala △ *Madag.* 15°30S 50°12E **57** B9
Masoarivo *Madag.* 19°3S 44°19E **57** B7
Masohi = Amahai
Indonesia 3°20S 128°55E **37** E7
Masomeloka *Madag.* 20°17S 48°37E **57** C8
Mason *Nev., U.S.A.* 38°56N 119°8W **78** G7
Mason *Tex., U.S.A.* 30°45N 99°14W **84** F5
Mason City *U.S.A.* 43°9N 93°12W **80** D7
Maspalomas *Canary Is.* 27°46N 15°35W **24** G4
Maspalomas, Pta.
Canary Is. 27°43N 15°36W **24** G4
Masqat *Oman* 23°37N 58°36E **47** C6
Massa *Italy* 44°1N 10°9E **20** D9
Massachusetts ☐ *U.S.A.* 42°30N 72°0W **83** D13
Massachusetts B.
U.S.A. 42°25N 70°50W **83** D14
Massakory *Chad* 13°0N 15°49E **51** F9
Massanella *Spain* 39°48N 2°51E **24** B9
Massangena *Mozam.* 21°34S 33°0E **57** C5
Massango *Angola* 8°2S 16°21E **52** F3
Massawa = Mitsiwa
Eritrea 15°35N 39°25E **47** D2
Massena *U.S.A.* 44°56N 74°54W **83** B10
Massénya *Chad* 11°21N 16°9E **51** F9
Masset *Canada* 54°2N 132°10W **70** C2
Massiah Street *Barbados* 13°9N 59°29W **89** g
Massif Central *France* 44°55N 3°0E **20** D5
Massillon *U.S.A.* 40°48N 81°32W **82** F3
Massinga *Mozam.* 23°15S 35°22E **57** C6
Massingir *Mozam.* 23°51S 32°4E **57** C5
Masson-Angers *Canada* 45°32N 75°25W **83** A9
Masson I. *Antarctica* 66°10S 93°20E **5** C7
Mastanli = Momchilgrad
Bulgaria 41°33N 25°23E **23** D11
Masterton *N.Z.* 40°56S 175°39E **59** D5
Mastic *U.S.A.* 40°47N 72°54W **83** F12
Mastuj *Pakistan* 36°20N 72°36E **43** A5
Mastung *Pakistan* 29°50N 66°56E **40** E5
Masty *Belarus* 53°27N 24°38E **17** B13
Masuda *Japan* 34°40N 131°51E **31** G5
Masurian Lakes = Mazurski,
Pojezierze *Poland* 53°50N 21°0E **17** B11
Masvingo *Zimbabwe* 20°8S 30°49E **55** G3
Masvingo ☐ *Zimbabwe* 21°0S 31°30E **55** G3
Maswa △ *Tanzania* 2°58S 34°19E **54** C3
Maşyāf *Syria* 35°4N 36°20E **44** C3
Mata-au = Clutha →
N.Z. 46°20S 169°49E **59** G2
Matabeleland *Zimbabwe* 18°0S 27°0E **53** H5
Matabeleland North ☐
Zimbabwe 19°0S 28°0E **55** F2
Matabeleland South ☐
Zimbabwe 21°0S 29°0E **55** G2
Matachewan *Canada* 47°56N 80°39W **72** C3
Matadi
Dem. Rep. of the Congo 5°52S 13°31E **52** F2
Matagalpa *Nic.* 13°0N 85°58W **88** D2
Matagami *Canada* 49°45N 77°34W **72** C4
Matagami, L. *Canada* 49°50N 77°40W **72** C4
Matagorda B. *U.S.A.* 28°40N 96°12W **84** G6
Matagorda I. *U.S.A.* 28°15N 96°30W **84** G6
Mataiea *Tahiti* 17°46S 149°25W **59** d
Matak *Indonesia* 3°18N 106°16E **36** D3
Matala *Greece* 34°59N 24°45E **25** E6
Matam *Senegal* 15°34N 13°17W **50** E3
Matamoros *Campeche,*
Mexico 18°50N 90°50W **87** D6
Matamoros *Coahuila,*
Mexico 25°32N 103°15W **86** B4
Matamoros *Tamaulipas,*
Mexico 25°53N 97°30W **87** B5
Ma'tan as Sarra *Libya* 21°45N 22°0E **51** D10
Matandu → *Tanzania* 8°45S 34°19E **55** D3
Matane *Canada* 48°50N 67°33W **73** C6
Matanomadh *India* 23°33N 68°57E **42** H3
Matanzas *Cuba* 23°0N 81°40W **88** B3
Matapa *Botswana* 23°11S 24°39E **56** C3
Matapan, C. = Tenaro, Akra
Greece 36°22N 22°27E **23** F10
Matapédia *Canada* 48°0N 66°59W **73** C6
Matapo △ *Zimbabwe* 20°30S 29°40E **55** G2
Matara *Sri Lanka* 5°58N 80°30E **40** S12
Mataram *Indonesia* 8°35S 116°7E **37** K19
Matarani *Peru* 17°0S 72°10W **92** G4
Mataranka *Australia* 14°55S 133°4E **60** B5
Matarma, Râs *Egypt* 30°27N 32°44E **46** E1
Mataró *Spain* 41°32N 2°29E **21** B7
Matatiele *S. Africa* 30°20S 28°49E **57** E4
Mataura *N.Z.* 46°11S 168°51E **59** G2
Matavai, B. de *Tahiti* 17°30S 149°23W **59** d
Matehuala *Mexico* 23°39N 100°39W **86** C4
Mateke Hills *Zimbabwe* 21°48S 31°0E **55** G3
Matelot *Trin. & Tob.* 10°50N 61°7W **93** K15
Matera *Italy* 40°40N 16°36E **22** D7
Matetsi *Zimbabwe* 18°12S 26°0E **55** F2
Matheniko △ *Uganda* 2°49N 34°27E **54** B3
Mathis *U.S.A.* 28°6N 97°50W **84** G6
Mathraki *Greece* 39°48N 19°31E **25** A3
Mathura *India* 27°30N 77°40E **42** F7

Mati *Phil.* 6°55N 126°15E **37** C7
Matiali *India* 26°56N 88°49E **43** F13
Matías Romero *Mexico* 16°53N 95°2W **87** D5
Matibane *Mozam.* 14°49S 40°45E **55** E5
Matiri Ra. *N.Z.* 41°38S 172°20E **59** D4
Matjiesfontein *S. Africa* 33°14S 20°35E **56** E3
Matla → *India* 21°40N 88°40E **43** J13
Matlamanyane
Botswana 19°33S 25°57E **56** B4
Matli *Pakistan* 25°2N 68°39E **42** G3
Matlock *U.K.* 53°9N 1°33W **12** D6
Mato Grosso ☐ *Brazil* 14°0S 55°0W **93** F8
Mato Grosso, Planalto do
Brazil 15°0S 55°0W **93** G8
Mato Grosso do Sul ☐
Brazil 18°0S 55°0W **93** G8
Matobo = Matapo △
Zimbabwe 20°30S 29°40E **55** G2
Matochkin Shar, Proliv
Russia 73°23N 55°12E **28** B6
Matopo Hills *Zimbabwe* 20°36S 28°20E **55** G2
Matopos *Zimbabwe* 20°20S 28°29E **55** G2
Matosinhos *Portugal* 41°11N 8°42W **21** B1
Matroosberg *S. Africa* 33°23S 19°40E **56** E2
Maţruḩ *Oman* 23°37N 58°30E **47** C6
Matsue *Japan* 35°25N 133°10E **31** G6
Matsum, Ko *Thailand* 9°22N 99°59E **39** b
Matsumae *Japan* 41°26N 140°7E **30** D10
Matsumoto *Japan* 36°15N 138°0E **31** F9
Matsusaka *Japan* 34°34N 136°32E **31** G8
Matsuura *Japan* 33°20N 129°49E **31** H4
Matsuyama *Japan* 33°45N 132°45E **31** H6
Mattagami → *Canada* 50°43N 81°29W **72** B3
Mattancheri *India* 9°50N 76°15E **40** Q10
Mattawa *Canada* 46°20N 78°45W **72** C4
Matterhorn *Switz.* 45°58N 7°39E **20** D7
Matthew Town
Bahamas 20°57N 73°40W **89** B5
Matthews Ridge *Guyana* 7°37N 60°10W **92** B6
Mattice *Canada* 49°40N 83°20W **72** C3
Mattituck *U.S.A.* 40°59N 72°32W **83** F12
Mattō *Japan* 36°31N 136°34E **31** F8
Mattoon *U.S.A.* 39°29N 88°23W **80** F9
Matuba *Mozam.* 24°28S 32°49E **57** C5
Matucana *Peru* 11°55S 76°25W **92** F3
Matuku *Fiji* 19°10S 179°44E **59** a
Matūn = Khowst
Afghan. 33°22N 69°58E **42** C3
Matura B. *Trin. & Tob.* 10°39N 61°1W **93** K15
Maturín *Venezuela* 9°45N 63°11W **92** B6
Matusadona △ *Zimbabwe* 16°58S 28°42E **55** F2
Mau *Mad. P., India* 26°17N 78°41E **43** F8
Mau *Ut. P., India* 25°56N 83°33E **43** G10
Mau *Ut. P., India* 25°17N 81°23E **43** G9
Mau Escarpment *Kenya* 0°40S 36°0E **54** C4
Mau Ranipur *India* 25°16N 79°8E **43** G8
Maua *Kenya* 0°14N 37°56E **54** C4
Maubeuge *France* 50°17N 3°57E **20** A6
Maubin *Burma* 16°44N 95°39E **41** L19
Maud, Pt. *Australia* 23°6S 113°45E **60** D1
Maud Rise *S. Ocean* 66°0S 3°0E **5** C3
Maude *Australia* 34°29S 144°18E **63** E3
Maudin Sun *Burma* 16°0N 94°30E **41** M19
Maués *Brazil* 3°20S 57°45W **92** D7
Mauganj *India* 24°50N 81°55E **43** G9
Maughold Hd. *I. of Man* 54°18N 4°18W **12** C3
Maui *U.S.A.* 20°48N 156°20W **74** b
Maulamyaing = Moulmein
Burma 16°30N 97°40E **41** L20
Maule ☐ *Chile* 36°5S 72°30W **94** D1
Maumee *U.S.A.* 41°34N 83°39W **81** E12
Maumee → *U.S.A.* 41°42N 83°28W **81** E12
Maumere *Indonesia* 8°38S 122°13E **37** F6
Maun *Botswana* 20°0S 23°26E **56** C3
Mauna Kea *U.S.A.* 19°50N 155°28W **74** b
Mauna Loa *U.S.A.* 19°30N 155°35W **74** b
Maungmagan Kyunzu
Burma 14°0N 97°48E **38** E1
Maungu *Kenya* 3°33S 38°45E **54** C4
Maupin *U.S.A.* 45°11N 121°5W **76** D3
Maurepas, L. *U.S.A.* 30°15N 90°30W **85** F9
Maurice, L. *Australia* 29°30S 131°0E **61** E5
Mauricie △ *Canada* 46°45N 73°0W **72** C5
Mauritania ■ *Africa* 20°50N 10°0W **50** E3
Mauritius ■ *Ind. Oc.* 20°0S 57°0E **53** d
Mauston *U.S.A.* 43°48N 90°5W **80** D8
Mavli *India* 24°45N 73°55E **42** G5
Mavuradonha Mts.
Zimbabwe 16°30S 31°30E **55** F3
Mawa
Dem. Rep. of the Congo 2°45N 26°40E **54** B2
Mawai *India* 22°30N 81°4E **43** H9
Mawana *India* 29°6N 77°58E **42** E7
Mawand *Pakistan* 29°33N 68°38E **42** E3
Mawjib, W. al → *Jordan* 31°28N 35°36E **46** D4
Mawk Mai *Burma* 20°14N 97°37E **41** J20
Mawlaik *Burma* 23°40N 94°26E **41** H19
Mawlamyine = Moulmein
Burma 16°30N 97°40E **41** L20
Mawqaq *Si. Arabia* 27°25N 41°8E **44** E4
Mawson Base *Antarctica* 67°30S 62°53E **5** C6
Mawson Coast *Antarctica* 68°30S 63°0E **5** C6
Max *U.S.A.* 47°49N 101°18W **80** B3
Maxcanú *Mexico* 20°35N 90°0W **87** C6
Maxesibeni *S. Africa* 30°49S 29°23E **57** E4
Maxhamish L. *Canada* 59°50N 123°17W **70** B4
Maxixe *Mozam.* 23°54S 35°17E **57** C6
Maxville *Canada* 45°17N 74°51W **83** A10
Maxwell *U.S.A.* 39°17N 122°11W **78** F4
Maxwelton *Australia* 20°43S 142°41E **62** C3
May, C. *U.S.A.* 38°56N 74°58W **81** F16
May Pen *Jamaica* 17°58N 77°15W **88** a
Maya → *Russia* 60°28N 134°28E **29** D14
Maya Mts. *Belize* 16°30N 89°0W **87** D7
Mayaguana *Bahamas* 22°30N 72°44W **89** B5
Mayagüez *Puerto Rico* 18°12N 67°9W **89** d
Mayāmey *Iran* 36°24N 55°42E **45** B7

Mayanup *Australia* 33°57S 116°27E **61** F2
Mayapán *Mexico* 20°29N 89°11W **87** C7
Mayarí *Cuba* 20°40N 75°41W **89** B4
Mayaro B. *Trin. & Tob.* 10°14N 60°59W **93** K16
Maybell *U.S.A.* 40°31N 108°5W **76** F9
Maybole *U.K.* 55°21N 4°42W **11** F4
Maydān *Iraq* 34°55N 45°37E **44** C5
Maydena *Australia* 42°45S 146°30E **63** G4
Mayenne → *France* 47°30N 0°32W **20** C3
Mayer *U.S.A.* 34°24N 112°14W **77** J7
Mayerthorpe *Canada* 53°57N 115°8W **70** C5
Mayfield *Ky., U.S.A.* 36°44N 88°38W **80** G9
Mayfield *N.Y., U.S.A.* 43°6N 74°16W **83** C10
Mayhill *U.S.A.* 32°53N 105°29W **77** K11
Maykop *Russia* 44°35N 40°10E **19** F7
Maymyo *Burma* 22°2N 96°28E **38** A1
Maynard *Mass., U.S.A.* 42°26N 71°27W **83** D13
Maynard *Wash., U.S.A.* 47°59N 122°55W **78** C4
Maynard Hills *Australia* 28°28S 119°49E **61** E2
Mayne → *Australia* 23°40S 141°55E **62** C3
Maynooth *Canada* 45°13N 77°56W **82** A7
Maynooth *Ireland* 53°23N 6°34W **10** C5
Mayo *Canada* 63°38N 135°57W **68** C6
Mayo ☐ *Ireland* 53°53N 9°3W **10** C2
Mayon Volcano *Phil.* 13°15N 123°41E **37** B6
Mayor I. *N.Z.* 37°16S 176°17E **59** B6
Mayotte ☑ *Ind. Oc.* 12°50S 45°10E **53** a
Maysān ☐ *Iraq* 31°55N 47°15E **44** D5
Maysville *U.S.A.* 38°39N 83°46W **81** F12
Mayu *Indonesia* 1°30N 126°30E **37** D7
Mayville *N. Dak., U.S.A.* 47°30N 97°20W **80** B5
Mayville *N.Y., U.S.A.* 42°15N 79°30W **82** D5
Mazabuka *Zambia* 15°52S 27°44E **55** F2
Mazagán = El Jadida
Morocco 33°11N 8°17W **50** B4
Mazagão *Brazil* 0°7S 51°16W **93** D8
Mazán *Peru* 3°30S 73°0W **92** D4
Māzandarān ☐ *Iran* 36°30N 52°0E **45** B7
Mazapil *Mexico* 24°39N 101°34W **86** C4
Mazar *China* 36°32N 77°1E **32** C2
Mazara del Vallo *Italy* 37°39N 12°35E **22** F5
Mazarrón *Spain* 37°38N 1°19W **21** D5
Mazaruni → *Guyana* 6°25N 58°35W **92** B7
Mazatán *Mexico* 29°0N 110°8W **86** B2
Mazatenango *Guatemala* 14°35N 91°30W **88** D1
Mazatlán *Mexico* 23°13N 106°25W **86** C3
Mažeikiai *Lithuania* 56°20N 22°20E **9** H20
Māzhān *Iran* 32°30N 59°0E **45** C8
Mazīnān *Iran* 36°19N 56°56E **45** B8
Mazoe *Mozam.* 16°42S 33°7E **55** F3
Mazoe → *Mozam.* 16°20S 33°30E **55** F3
Mazowe *Zimbabwe* 17°28S 30°58E **55** F3
Mazurski, Pojezierze
Poland 53°50N 21°0E **17** B11
Mazyr *Belarus* 51°59N 29°15E **17** B15
Mba *Fiji* 17°33S 177°41E **59** a
Mbabane *Swaziland* 26°18S 31°6E **57** D5
Mbaïki *C.A.R.* 3°53N 18°1E **52** D3
Mbala *Zambia* 8°46S 31°24E **55** D3
Mbalabala *Zimbabwe* 20°27S 29°3E **57** C4
Mbale *Uganda* 1°8N 34°12E **54** B3
Mbalmayo *Cameroon* 3°33N 11°33E **52** D2
Mbamba Bay *Tanzania* 11°13S 34°49E **55** E3
Mbandaka
Dem. Rep. of the Congo 0°1N 18°18E **52** D3
Mbanza Congo *Angola* 6°18S 14°16E **52** F2
Mbanza Ngungu
Dem. Rep. of the Congo 5°12S 14°53E **52** F2
Mbarangandu *Tanzania* 10°11S 36°48E **55** D4
Mbarara *Uganda* 0°35S 30°40E **54** C3
Mbengga = Beqa *Fiji* 18°23S 178°8E **59** a
Mbenkuru → *Tanzania* 9°25S 39°50E **55** D4
Mberengwa *Zimbabwe* 20°29S 29°57E **55** G2
Mberengwa, Mt.
Zimbabwe 20°37S 29°55E **55** G2
Mbesuma *Zambia* 10°0S 32°2E **55** E3
Mbeya *Tanzania* 8°54S 33°29E **55** D3
Mbeya ☐ *Tanzania* 8°15S 33°30E **54** D3
Mbhashe → *S. Africa* 32°15S 28°54E **57** E4
Mbinga *Tanzania* 10°50S 35°0E **55** E4
Mbini = Río Muni ☐
Eq. Guin. 1°30N 10°0E **52** D2
Mbour *Senegal* 14°22N 16°54W **50** F2
Mbuji-Mayi
Dem. Rep. of the Congo 6°9S 23°40E **54** D1
Mbulu *Tanzania* 3°45S 35°30E **54** C4
Mburucuyá *Argentina* 28°1S 58°14W **94** B4
Mburucuyá △ *Argentina* 28°1S 58°12W **94** B4
Mchinja *Tanzania* 9°44S 39°45E **55** D4
Mchinji *Malawi* 13°47S 32°58E **55** E3
Mdantsane *S. Africa* 32°56S 27°46E **57** E4
Mead, L. *U.S.A.* 36°0N 114°44W **79** J12
Meade *U.S.A.* 37°17N 100°20W **80** G3
Meadow Lake *Canada* 54°10N 108°26W **71** C7
Meadow Lake △ *Canada* 54°27N 109°0W **71** C7
Meadow Valley Wash →
U.S.A. 36°40N 114°34W **79** J12
Meadville *U.S.A.* 41°39N 80°9W **82** E4
Meaford *Canada* 44°36N 80°35W **82** B4
Mealpaeg L. *Canada* 48°20N 56°30W **73** C8
Mealy Mts. *Canada* 53°10N 58°0W **73** B8
Meander River *Canada* 59°2N 117°42W **70** B5
Meares, C. *U.S.A.* 45°37N 124°0W **76** D1
Mearim → *Brazil* 3°4S 44°35W **93** D10
Meath ☐ *Ireland* 53°40N 6°57W **10** C5
Meath Park *Canada* 53°27N 105°22W **71** C7
Meaux *France* 48°58N 2°50E **20** B5
Mebechi-Gawa →
Japan 40°31N 141°31E **30** D10
Mebulu, Tanjung
Indonesia 8°50S 115°5E **37** K18
Mecanhelas *Mozam.* 15°12S 35°54E **55** F4
Mecca = Makkah
Si. Arabia 21°30N 39°54E **47** C2
Mecca *U.S.A.* 33°34N 116°5W **79** M10
Mechanicsburg *U.S.A.* 40°13N 77°1W **82** F8
Mechanicville *U.S.A.* 42°54N 73°41W **83** D11

Mechelen Belgium 51°2N 4°29E 15 C4
Mecheria Algeria 33°35N 0°18W 50 B5
Mecklenburg Germany 53°33N 11°40E 16 B7
Mecklenburger Bucht Germany 54°20N 11°40E 16 A6
Meconta Mozam. 14°59S 39°50E 55 E4
Medan Indonesia 3°40N 98°38E 36 D1
Médanos de Coro △ Venezuela 11°35N 69°44W 89 D6
Medanosa, Pta. Argentina 48°8S 66°0W 96 F3
Médéa Algeria 36°12N 2°50E 50 A6
Medellín Colombia 6°15N 75°35W 92 B3
Medelpad Sweden 62°33N 16°30E 8 E17
Medemblik Neths. 52°46N 5°8E 15 B5
Medford Mass., U.S.A. 42°25N 71°7W 83 D13
Medford Oreg., U.S.A. 42°19N 122°52W 76 E2
Medford Wis., U.S.A. 45°9N 90°20W 80 C8
Medgidia Romania 44°15N 28°19E 17 F15
Media Agua Argentina 31°58S 68°25W 94 C2
Media Luna Argentina 34°45S 66°44W 94 C2
Medianeira Brazil 25°17S 54°5W 95 B5
Mediaş Romania 46°9N 24°22E 17 E13
Medicine Bow U.S.A. 41°54N 106°12W 76 F10
Medicine Bow Mts. U.S.A. 40°40N 106°0W 76 F10
Medicine Bow Pk. U.S.A. 41°21N 106°19W 76 F10
Medicine Hat Canada 50°0N 110°45W 71 D6
Medicine Lake U.S.A. 48°30N 104°30W 76 B11
Medicine Lodge U.S.A. 37°17N 98°35W 80 G4
Medina = Al Madīnah Si. Arabia 24°35N 39°52E 44 E3
Medina N. Dak., U.S.A. 46°54N 99°18W 80 B4
Medina N.Y., U.S.A. 43°13N 78°23W 82 C6
Medina Ohio, U.S.A. 41°8N 81°52W 82 E3
Medina → U.S.A. 29°16N 98°29W 84 G5
Medina del Campo Spain 41°18N 4°55W 21 B3
Medina L. U.S.A. 29°32N 98°56W 84 G5
Medina Sidonia Spain 36°28N 5°57W 21 D3
Medinipur India 22°25N 87°21E 43 H12
Mediterranean Sea Europe 35°0N 15°0E 6 H7
Médoc France 45°10N 0°50W 20 D3
Medveditsa → Russia 49°35N 42°41E 19 E7
Medvezhi, Ostrava Russia 71°0N 161°0E 29 B17
Medvezhyegorsk Russia 63°0N 34°25E 18 B5
Medway □ U.K. 51°25N 0°32E 13 F8
Medway → U.K. 51°27N 0°46E 13 F8
Meekatharra Australia 26°32S 118°29E 61 E2
Meeker U.S.A. 40°2N 107°55W 76 F10
Meerut India 29°1N 77°42E 42 E7
Meeteetse U.S.A. 44°9N 108°52W 76 D9
Mega Ethiopia 3°57N 38°19E 47 G2
Megara Greece 37°58N 23°22E 23 F10
Megasini India 21°38N 86°21E 43 J12
Meghalaya □ India 25°50N 91°0E 41 G17
Meghna → Bangla. 22°50N 90°50E 41 H17
Megion Russia 61°3N 76°6E 28 C8
Mégiscane, L. Canada 48°35N 75°55W 72 C4
Meharry, Mt. Australia 22°59S 118°35E 60 D2
Mehlville U.S.A. 38°31N 90°19W 80 F8
Mehndawal India 26°58N 83°5E 43 F10
Mehr Jān Iran 33°50N 55°6E 45 C7
Mehrābād Iran 36°53N 47°55E 44 B5
Mehrān Iran 33°7N 46°10E 44 C5
Mehrān → Iran 26°45N 55°26E 45 E7
Mehrgarh Pakistan 29°30N 67°30E 42 E2
Mehrīz Iran 31°35N 54°28E 45 D7
Mei Xian China 34°18N 107°55E 34 G4
Meighen I. Canada 80°0N 99°30W 69 B10
Meihekou China 42°32N 125°40E 35 C13
Meiktila Burma 20°53N 95°54E 41 J19
Meissen Germany 51°9N 13°29E 16 C7
Meizhou China 24°16N 116°6E 33 D6
Meja India 25°9N 82°7E 43 G10
Mejillones Chile 23°10S 70°30W 94 A1
Mekele Ethiopia 13°33N 39°30E 47 E2
Mekerghene, Sebkra Algeria 26°21N 1°30E 50 C6
Mekhtar Pakistan 30°30N 69°15E 40 D6
Meknès Morocco 33°57N 5°33W 50 B4
Mekong → Asia 9°30N 106°15E 39 H6
Mekongga Indonesia 3°39S 121°15E 37 E6
Mekvari = Kür → Azerbaijan 39°29N 49°15E 19 G8
Melagiri Hills India 12°20N 77°30E 40 N10
Melaka Malaysia 2°15N 102°15E 39 L4
Melalap Malaysia 5°10N 116°5E 36 C5
Melambes Greece 35°8N 24°40E 25 D6
Melanesia Pac. Oc. 4°0S 155°0E 64 H7
Melanesian Basin Pac. Oc. 0°5N 160°35E 64 G8
Melaya Indonesia 8°17S 114°30E 37 J17
Melbourne Australia 37°48S 144°58E 63 F4
Melbourne U.S.A. 28°5N 80°37W 85 G14
Melchor Múzquiz Mexico 27°53N 101°31W 86 B4
Melchor Ocampo Mexico 24°51N 101°39W 86 C4
Mélèzes → Canada 57°40N 69°29W 72 A5
Melfort Canada 52°50N 104°37W 71 C8
Melfort Zimbabwe 18°0S 31°25E 55 F3
Melhus Norway 63°17N 10°18E 8 E14
Melilla N. Afr. 35°21N 2°57W 21 E4
Melipilla Chile 33°42S 71°15W 94 C1
Melissa Canada 45°24N 79°14W 82 A5
Melissa, Akra Greece 35°6N 24°33E 25 D6
Melita Canada 49°15N 101°0W 71 D8
Melitopol Ukraine 46°50N 35°22E 19 E6
Melk Austria 48°13N 15°20E 16 D8
Mellansel Sweden 63°26N 18°19E 8 E18
Mellen U.S.A. 46°20N 90°40W 80 B8
Mellerud Sweden 58°41N 12°28E 9 G15
Mellette U.S.A. 45°9N 98°30W 80 C4
Mellieha Malta 35°57N 14°22E 25 D1
Melo Uruguay 32°20S 54°10W 95 C5
Melolo Indonesia 9°53S 120°40E 37 F6
Melouprey Cambodia 13°48N 105°16E 38 F5
Melrhir, Chott Algeria 34°13N 6°30E 50 B7
Melrose Australia 32°42S 146°57E 63 E4
Melrose U.K. 55°36N 2°43W 11 F6
Melrose Minn., U.S.A. 45°40N 94°49W 80 C6
Melrose N. Mex., U.S.A. 34°26N 103°38W 77 J12
Melstone U.S.A. 46°36N 107°52W 76 C10
Melton Mowbray U.K. 52°47N 0°54W 12 E7
Melun France 48°32N 2°39E 20 B5
Melville Canada 50°55N 102°50W 71 C8
Melville, C. Australia 14°11S 144°30E 62 A3
Melville, L. Canada 53°30N 60°0W 73 B8
Melville B. Australia 12°0S 136°45E 62 A2
Melville I. Australia 11°30S 131°0E 60 B5
Melville I. Canada 75°30N 112°0W 69 B8
Melville Pen. Canada 68°0N 84°0W 69 C11
Melvin, Lough Ireland 54°26N 8°10W 10 B3
Memba Mozam. 14°11S 40°30E 55 E5
Memboro Indonesia 9°30S 119°30E 37 F5
Memel = Klaipėda Lithuania 55°43N 21°10E 9 J19
Memel S. Africa 27°38S 29°36E 57 D4
Memmingen Germany 47°58N 10°10E 16 E6
Mempawah Indonesia 0°30N 109°5E 36 D3
Memphis Mich., U.S.A. 42°54N 82°46W 82 D2
Memphis Tenn., U.S.A. 35°8N 90°2W 85 D9
Memphis Tex., U.S.A. 34°44N 100°33W 84 D4
Memphrémagog, L. N. Amer. 45°8N 72°17W 83 B12
Mena U.S.A. 34°35N 94°15W 84 D7
Menai Strait U.K. 53°11N 4°13W 12 D3
Ménaka Mali 15°59N 2°18E 50 E6
Menan = Chao Phraya → Thailand 13°40N 100°31E 38 F3
Menarandra → Madag. 25°17S 44°30E 57 D7
Menard U.S.A. 30°55N 99°47W 84 F5
Menard Fracture Zone Pac. Oc. 43°0S 97°0W 65 M18
Mendaña Fracture Zone Pac. Oc. 16°0S 91°0W 65 J18
Mendawai → Indonesia 3°30S 113°0E 36 E4
Mende France 44°31N 3°30E 20 D5
Mendeleyev Ridge Arctic 80°0N 178°0W 4 B17
Mendhar India 33°35N 74°10E 43 C6
Mendip Hills U.K. 51°17N 2°40W 13 F5
Mendocino U.S.A. 39°19N 123°48W 76 G2
Mendocino, C. U.S.A. 40°26N 124°25W 76 F1
Mendocino Fracture Zone Pac. Oc. 40°0N 142°0W 65 D13
Mendota Calif., U.S.A. 36°45N 120°23W 78 J6
Mendota Ill., U.S.A. 41°33N 89°7W 80 E9
Mendoyo Indonesia 8°23S 114°42E 37 J17
Mendoza Argentina 32°50S 68°52W 94 C2
Mendoza □ Argentina 33°0S 69°0W 94 C2
Mene Grande Venezuela 9°49N 70°56W 92 B4
Menemen Turkey 38°34N 27°3E 23 E12
Menen Belgium 50°47N 3°7E 15 D3
Menggala Indonesia 4°30S 105°15E 36 E3
Mengjin China 34°55N 112°45E 34 G7
Mengyin China 35°40N 117°58E 35 G9
Mengzi China 23°20N 103°22E 32 D5
Menihek Canada 54°28N 56°36W 73 B6
Menihek L. Canada 54°0N 67°0W 73 B6
Menin = Menen Belgium 50°47N 3°7E 15 D3
Menindee Australia 32°20S 142°25E 63 E3
Menindee L. Australia 32°20S 142°25E 63 E3
Meningie Australia 35°50S 139°18E 63 F2
Menjangan, Pulau Indonesia 8°7S 114°31E 37 J17
Menlo Park U.S.A. 37°27N 122°12W 78 H4
Menominee U.S.A. 45°6N 87°37W 80 C10
Menominee → U.S.A. 45°6N 87°35W 80 C10
Menomonie U.S.A. 44°53N 91°55W 80 C8
Menongue Angola 14°48S 17°52E 53 G3
Menorca Spain 40°0N 4°0E 24 B11
Mentakab Malaysia 3°29N 102°21E 39 L4
Mentawai, Kepulauan Indonesia 2°0S 99°0E 36 E1
Menton France 43°50N 7°29E 20 E7
Mentor U.S.A. 41°40N 81°21W 82 E3
Menzelinsk Russia 55°47N 53°11E 18 C9
Menzies Australia 29°40S 121°2E 61 E3
Meob B. Namibia 24°25S 14°34E 56 C1
Me'ona Israel 33°1N 35°15E 46 B4
Meoqui Mexico 28°17N 105°29W 86 B3
Mepaco Mozam. 15°57S 30°48E 55 F3
Meppel Neths. 52°42N 6°12E 15 B6
Merak Indonesia 6°10N 106°26E 37 F12
Meramangye, L. Australia 28°25S 132°13E 61 E5
Meran = Merano Italy 46°40N 11°9E 22 A4
Merano Italy 46°40N 11°9E 22 A4
Merauke Indonesia 8°29S 140°24E 37 F10
Merbein Australia 34°10S 142°2E 63 E3
Merbuk, Gunung Indonesia 8°13S 114°39E 37 J17
Merca = Marka Somali Rep. 1°48N 44°50E 47 G3
Merced U.S.A. 37°18N 120°29W 78 H6
Merced → U.S.A. 37°21N 120°59W 78 H6
Merced Pk. U.S.A. 37°36N 119°24W 78 H7
Mercedes B. Aires, Argentina 34°40S 59°30W 94 C4
Mercedes Corrientes, Argentina 29°10S 58°5W 94 B4
Mercedes San Luis, Argentina 33°40S 65°21W 94 C2
Mercedes Uruguay 33°12S 58°0W 94 C4
Merceditas Chile 28°20S 70°35W 94 B1
Mercer N.Z. 37°16S 175°5E 59 B5
Mercer U.S.A. 41°14N 80°15W 82 E4
Mercer Island U.S.A. 47°34N 122°13W 78 C4
Mercury U.S.A. 36°40N 115°59W 79 J11
Mercy, C. Canada 65°0N 63°30W 69 C13
Mere U.K. 51°6N 2°16W 13 F5
Meredith, C. Falk. Is. 52°15S 60°40W 96 G4
Meredith, L. U.S.A. 35°43N 101°33W 84 D4
Mergui Burma 12°26N 98°34E 38 F2
Mergui Arch. = Myeik Kyunzu Burma 11°30N 97°30E 39 G1
Mérida Mexico 20°58N 89°37W 87 C7
Mérida Spain 38°55N 6°25W 21 C2
Mérida Venezuela 8°24N 71°8W 92 B4
Mérida, Cord. de Venezuela 9°0N 71°0W 92 B4
Meriden U.K. 52°26N 1°38W 13 E6
Meriden U.S.A. 41°32N 72°48W 83 E12
Meridian Calif., U.S.A. 39°9N 121°55W 78 F5
Meridian Idaho, U.S.A. 43°37N 116°24W 76 E5
Meridian Miss., U.S.A. 32°22N 88°42W 85 E10
Merinda Australia 20°2S 148°11E 62 C4
Merir Pac. Oc. 4°10N 132°30E 37 D8
Merirumã Brazil 1°15N 54°50W 93 C8
Merkel U.S.A. 32°28N 100°1W 84 E4
Mermaid Reef Australia 17°6S 119°36E 60 C2
Merredin Australia 31°28S 118°18E 61 F2
Merrick U.K. 55°8N 4°28W 11 F4
Merrickville Canada 44°55N 75°50W 83 B9
Merrill Oreg., U.S.A. 42°1N 121°36W 76 E3
Merrill Wis., U.S.A. 45°11N 89°41W 80 C9
Merrimack → U.S.A. 42°49N 70°49W 83 D14
Merriman U.S.A. 42°55N 101°42W 80 D3
Merritt Canada 50°10N 120°45W 70 C4
Merritt Island U.S.A. 28°21N 80°42W 85 G14
Merriwa Australia 32°6S 150°22E 63 E5
Merry I. Canada 55°29N 77°31W 72 A4
Merryville U.S.A. 30°45N 93°33W 84 F8
Mersch Lux. 49°44N 6°7E 15 E6
Mersea I. U.K. 51°47N 0°58E 13 F8
Merseburg Germany 51°22N 11°59E 16 C6
Mersey → U.K. 53°25N 3°1W 12 D4
Merseyside □ U.K. 53°31N 3°2W 12 D4
Mersin = İçel Turkey 36°51N 34°36E 44 B2
Mersing Malaysia 2°25N 103°50E 39 L4
Merta India 26°39N 74°4E 42 F6
Merta Road India 26°43N 73°55E 42 F5
Merthyr Tydfil U.K. 51°45N 3°22W 13 F4
Merthyr Tydfil □ U.K. 51°46N 3°21W 13 F4
Merti Kenya 1°4N 38°40E 54 B4
Mértola Portugal 37°40N 7°40W 21 D2
Mertzon U.S.A. 31°16N 100°49W 84 F4
Meru Kenya 0°3N 37°40E 54 B4
Meru Tanzania 3°15S 36°46E 54 C4
Meru △ Kenya 0°5N 38°10E 54 B4
Mesa U.S.A. 33°25N 111°50W 77 K8
Mesa Verde △ U.S.A. 37°11N 108°29W 77 H9
Mesanagros Greece 36°1N 27°49E 25 C9
Mesaoría Cyprus 35°12N 33°14E 25 D12
Mesgouez, L. Canada 51°20N 75°0W 72 B5
Meshed = Mashhad Iran 36°20N 59°35E 45 B8
Meshgīn Shahr Iran 38°30N 47°45E 44 B5
Meshoppen U.S.A. 41°36N 76°3W 83 E8
Mesilinka → Canada 56°6N 124°30W 70 B4
Mesologi Greece 38°21N 21°28E 23 E9
Mesongi Greece 39°29N 19°56E 25 B3
Mesopotamia = Al Jazirah Iraq 33°30N 44°0E 44 C5
Mesopotamia U.S.A. 41°27N 80°57W 82 E4
Mesquite U.S.A. 36°48N 114°4W 77 H6
Messaad Algeria 34°8N 3°30E 50 B6
Messalo → Mozam. 12°25S 39°15E 55 E4
Messara, Kolpos Greece 35°6N 24°47E 25 D6
Messina = Musina S. Africa 22°20S 30°5E 57 C5
Messina Italy 38°11N 15°34E 22 E6
Messina, Str. di Italy 38°15N 15°35E 22 F6
Messini Greece 37°4N 22°1E 23 F10
Messiniakos Kolpos Greece 36°45N 22°5E 23 F10
Mesta → Bulgaria 40°54N 24°49E 23 D11
Meta → S. Amer. 6°12N 67°28W 92 B5
Meta Incognita Pen. Canada 62°45N 68°30W 69 C13
Metabetchouan Canada 48°26N 71°52W 73 C5
Metairie U.S.A. 29°59N 90°9W 85 G9
Metaline Falls U.S.A. 48°52N 117°22W 76 B5
Metán Argentina 25°30S 65°0W 94 B3
Metangula Mozam. 12°40S 34°50E 55 E3
Metcalfe Canada 45°14N 75°28W 83 A9
Metema Ethiopia 12°58N 36°12E 47 E2
Metengobalame Mozam. 14°49S 34°30E 55 E3
Methven N.Z. 43°38S 171°40E 59 E3
Metil Mozam. 16°24S 39°0E 55 F4
Metlakatla U.S.A. 55°8N 131°35W 68 D6
Metropolis U.S.A. 37°9N 88°44W 80 G9
Metropolitana □ Chile 33°30S 70°50W 94 C1
Metu Ethiopia 8°18N 35°35E 47 F2
Metz France 49°8N 6°10E 20 B7
Meulaboh Indonesia 4°11N 96°3E 36 D1
Meureudu Indonesia 5°19N 96°10E 36 C1
Meuse → Europe 50°45N 5°41E 15 D5
Mexia U.S.A. 31°41N 96°29W 84 F6
Mexiana, I. Brazil 0°0 49°30W 93 D9
Mexicali Mexico 32°40N 115°30W 79 N11
Mexican Plateau Mexico 25°0N 104°0W 66 G9
Mexican Water U.S.A. 36°57N 109°32W 77 H9
México Mexico 19°24N 99°9W 87 D5
Mexico Maine, U.S.A. 44°34N 70°33W 83 B14
Mexico Mo., U.S.A. 39°10N 91°53W 80 F8
Mexico N.Y., U.S.A. 43°28N 76°14W 83 C8
México □ Mexico 19°20N 99°30W 87 D5
Mexico ■ Cent. Amer. 25°0N 105°0W 86 C4
México, Ciudad de Mexico 19°24N 99°9W 87 D5
Mexico, G. of Cent. Amer. 25°0N 90°0W 87 C7
Mexico B. U.S.A. 43°35N 76°20W 83 C8
Meydān-e Naftūn Iran 31°56N 49°18E 45 D6
Meydani, Ra's-e Iran 25°24N 59°6E 45 E8
Meyers Chuck U.S.A. 55°45N 132°15W 70 B2
Meymaneh Afghan. 35°53N 64°38E 40 B4
Mezen Russia 65°50N 44°20E 18 A7
Mezen → Russia 65°44N 44°22E 18 A7
Mézenc, Mt. France 44°54N 4°11E 20 D6
Mezhdurechensk Russia 53°41N 88°3E 28 D9
Mezhdurechenskiy Russia 59°36N 65°56E 28 D7
Mezőkövesd Hungary 47°49N 20°35E 17 E11
Mezőtúr Hungary 47°1N 20°41E 17 E11
Mezquital Mexico 23°29N 104°23W 86 C4
Mfolozi → S. Africa 28°25S 32°26E 57 D5
Mgeta Tanzania 8°22S 36°6E 55 D4
Mhlaba Hills Zimbabwe 18°30S 30°30E 55 F3
Mhow India 22°33N 75°50E 42 H6
Miahuatlán Mexico 16°20N 96°36W 87 D5
Miami Fla., U.S.A. 25°46N 80°11W 85 J14
Miami Okla., U.S.A. 36°53N 94°53W 84 C7
Miami Tex., U.S.A. 35°42N 100°38W 84 D4
Miami Beach U.S.A. 25°47N 80°7W 85 J14
Mian Xian China 33°10N 106°32E 34 H4
Mianchi China 34°48N 111°48E 34 G6
Mīāndarreh Iran 35°37N 53°39E 45 C7
Mīāndowāb Iran 37°0N 46°5E 44 B5
Miandrivazo Madag. 19°31S 45°29E 57 B8
Mīāneh Iran 37°30N 47°40E 44 B5
Mianwali Pakistan 32°38N 71°28E 42 C4
Mianyang China 31°22N 104°47E 32 C5
Miarinarivo Antananarivo, Madag. 18°57S 46°55E 57 B8
Miarinarivo Toamasina, Madag. 16°38S 48°15E 57 B8
Miariravaratra Madag. 20°13S 47°31E 57 C8
Miass Russia 54°59N 60°6E 18 D11
Mica S. Africa 24°10S 30°48E 57 C5
Michalovce Slovak Rep. 48°47N 21°58E 17 D11
Michigan □ U.S.A. 44°0N 85°0W 81 C11
Michigan, L. U.S.A. 44°0N 87°0W 80 D10
Michigan City U.S.A. 41°43N 86°54W 80 E10
Michipicoten I. Canada 47°40N 85°40W 72 C2
Michoacán □ Mexico 19°10N 101°50W 86 D4
Michurin Bulgaria 42°9N 27°51E 23 C12
Michurinsk Russia 52°58N 40°27E 18 D7
Micoud St. Lucia 13°49N 60°54W 89 f
Micronesia Pac. Oc. 11°0N 160°0E 64 G7
Micronesia, Federated States of ■ Pac. Oc. 9°0N 150°0E 58 A8
Mid-Pacific Seamounts Pac. Oc. 18°0N 177°0W 64 F10
Midai Indonesia 3°0N 107°47E 36 D3
Midale Canada 49°25N 103°20W 71 D8
Middelburg Neths. 51°30N 3°36E 15 C3
Middelburg Eastern Cape, S. Africa 31°30S 25°0E 56 E4
Middelburg Mpumalanga, S. Africa 25°49S 29°28E 57 D4
Middelpos S. Africa 31°55S 20°13E 56 E3
Middelwit S. Africa 24°51S 27°3E 56 C4
Middle Alkali L. U.S.A. 41°27N 120°5W 76 F3
Middle America Trench = Guatemala Trench Pac. Oc. 14°0N 95°0W 66 H10
Middle Bass I. U.S.A. 41°41N 82°48W 82 E2
Middle East Asia 35°0N 40°0E 26 E5
Middle Fork Feather → U.S.A. 38°33N 121°30W 78 F5
Middle I. Australia 34°6S 123°11E 61 F3
Middle Loup → U.S.A. 41°17N 98°24W 80 E4
Middleboro U.S.A. 41°54N 70°55W 83 E14
Middleburg Fla., U.S.A. 30°4N 81°52W 85 F14
Middleburg Pa., U.S.A. 40°47N 77°3W 82 F7
Middleburgh U.S.A. 42°36N 74°20W 83 D10
Middlebury U.S.A. 44°1N 73°10W 83 B11
Middlefield U.S.A. 41°27N 81°4W 82 E3
Middlemount Australia 22°50S 148°40E 62 C4
Middleport N.Y., U.S.A. 43°13N 78°29W 82 C6
Middleport Ohio, U.S.A. 39°0N 82°3W 81 F12
Middlesboro U.S.A. 36°36N 83°43W 81 G12
Middlesbrough U.K. 54°35N 1°13W 12 C6
Middlesbrough □ U.K. 54°28N 1°13W 12 C6
Middlesex Belize 17°2N 88°31W 88 C2
Middlesex N.J., U.S.A. 40°36N 74°30W 83 F10
Middlesex N.Y., U.S.A. 42°42N 77°16W 82 D7
Middleton Australia 22°22S 141°32E 62 C3
Middleton Canada 44°57N 65°4W 73 D6
Middleton Cr. → Australia 22°35S 141°51E 62 C3
Middletown U.K. 54°17N 6°51W 10 B5
Middletown Calif., U.S.A. 38°45N 122°37W 78 G4
Middletown Conn., U.S.A. 41°34N 72°39W 83 E12
Middletown N.Y., U.S.A. 41°27N 74°25W 83 E10
Middletown Ohio, U.S.A. 39°31N 84°24W 81 F11
Middletown Pa., U.S.A. 40°12N 76°44W 83 F8
Midge Point Australia 20°39S 148°43E 62 J6
Midhurst Canada 44°26N 79°43W 82 B5
Midhurst U.K. 50°59N 0°44W 13 G7
Midi, Canal du → France 43°45N 1°21E 20 E4
Midland Australia 31°54S 116°1E 61 F2
Midland Canada 44°45N 79°50W 82 B5
Midland Calif., U.S.A. 33°52N 114°48W 79 M12
Midland Mich., U.S.A. 43°37N 84°14W 81 D11
Midland Pa., U.S.A. 40°39N 80°27W 82 F4
Midland Tex., U.S.A. 32°0N 102°3W 84 F3
Midlands □ Zimbabwe 19°40S 29°0E 55 F2
Midleton Ireland 51°55N 8°10W 10 E3
Midlothian □ U.K. 55°51N 3°5W 11 F5
Midongy, Tangorombohitr' i Madag. 23°30S 47°0E 57 C8
Midongy Atsimo Madag. 23°35S 47°1E 57 C8
Midway Is. Pac. Oc. 28°13N 177°22W 64 E10
Midway Wells U.S.A. 32°41N 115°7W 79 N11
Midwest U.S.A. 42°0N 90°0W 75 B9
Midwest Wyo., U.S.A. 43°25N 106°16W 76 E10
Midwest City U.S.A. 35°27N 97°24W 84 D6
Midyat Turkey 37°25N 41°23E 44 B4
Midžor Bulgaria 43°24N 22°40E 23 C10
Mie □ Japan 34°30N 136°10E 31 G8
Międzychód Poland 52°35N 15°53E 16 B8
Międzyrzec Podlaski Poland 51°58N 22°45E 17 C12
Mielec Poland 50°15N 21°25E 17 C11
Mienga Angola 17°12S 19°48E 56 B2
Miercurea-Ciuc Romania 46°21N 25°48E 17 E13
Mieres Spain 43°18N 5°48W 21 A3
Mifflintown U.S.A. 40°34N 77°24W 82 F7
Mifraz Hefa Israel 32°52N 35°0E 46 C4
Migori Kenya 1°4S 34°28E 54 C3
Miguel Alemán, Presa Mexico 18°15N 96°32W 87 D5
Mihara Japan 34°24N 133°5E 31 G6
Mikese Tanzania 6°48S 37°55E 54 D4
Mikhaylovgrad = Montana Bulgaria 43°27N 23°16E 23 C10
Mikhaylovka Russia 50°3N 43°5E 19 D7
Mikines Greece 37°43N 22°46E 23 F10
Mikkeli Finland 61°43N 27°15E 8 F22
Mikkwa → Canada 58°25N 114°46W 70 B6
Míkonos = Mykonos Greece 37°30N 25°25E 23 F11
Mikumi Tanzania 7°26S 37°0E 54 D4
Mikumi △ Tanzania 7°35S 37°15E 54 D4
Mikun Russia 62°20N 50°0E 18 B9
Milaca U.S.A. 45°45N 93°39W 80 C7
Milagro Ecuador 2°11S 79°36W 92 D3
Milan = Milano Italy 45°28N 9°10E 20 D8
Milan Mo., U.S.A. 40°12N 93°7W 80 E7
Milan Tenn., U.S.A. 35°55N 88°46W 85 D10
Milange Mozam. 16°3S 35°45E 55 F4
Milano Italy 45°28N 9°10E 20 D8
Milanoa Madag. 13°35S 49°47E 57 A8
Milâs Turkey 37°20N 27°50E 23 F12
Milatos Greece 35°18N 25°34E 25 D7
Milazzo Italy 38°13N 15°15E 22 E6
Milbank U.S.A. 45°13N 96°38W 80 C6
Milbanke Sd. Canada 52°19N 128°33W 70 C3
Milden Canada 51°29N 107°32W 71 C7
Mildenhall U.K. 52°21N 0°32E 13 E8
Mildmay Canada 44°3N 81°7W 82 B3
Mildura Australia 34°13S 142°9E 63 E3
Miles Australia 26°40S 150°9E 63 D5
Miles City U.S.A. 46°25N 105°51W 76 C11
Milestone Canada 49°59N 104°31W 71 D8
Miletus Turkey 37°30N 27°18E 23 F12
Milford Calif., U.S.A. 40°10N 120°22W 78 E6
Milford Conn., U.S.A. 41°14N 73°3W 83 E11
Milford Del., U.S.A. 38°55N 75°26W 81 F16
Milford Mass., U.S.A. 42°8N 71°31W 83 D13
Milford N.H., U.S.A. 42°50N 71°39W 83 D13
Milford N.Y., U.S.A. 42°35N 74°56W 83 D10
Milford Pa., U.S.A. 41°19N 74°48W 83 E10
Milford Utah, U.S.A. 38°24N 113°1W 76 G7
Milford Haven U.K. 51°42N 5°7W 13 F2
Milford Sd. N.Z. 44°41S 167°47E 59 F1
Milford Sound N.Z. 44°41S 167°55E 59 F1
Milḥ, Baḥr al = Razāzah, Buḥayrat ar Iraq 32°40N 43°35E 44 C4
Milikapiti Australia 11°26S 130°40E 60 B5
Miling Australia 30°30S 116°17E 61 F2
Milk River Canada 49°10N 112°5W 70 D6
Mill → U.S.A. 42°57N 83°23W 82 D1
Mill I. Antarctica 66°0S 101°30E 5 C8
Mill Valley U.S.A. 37°54N 122°32W 78 H4
Millau France 44°8N 3°4E 20 D5
Millbridge Canada 44°41N 77°36W 82 B7
Millbrook Canada 44°10N 78°29W 82 B6
Millbrook Ala., U.S.A. 32°29N 86°22W 85 E11
Millbrook N.Y., U.S.A. 41°47N 73°42W 83 E11
Mille Lacs, L. des Canada 48°45N 90°35W 72 C1
Mille Lacs L. U.S.A. 46°15N 93°39W 80 B7
Milledgeville U.S.A. 33°5N 83°14W 85 E13
Millen U.S.A. 32°48N 81°57W 85 E14
Millennium I. = Caroline I. Kiribati 9°58S 150°13W 65 H12
Miller U.S.A. 44°31N 98°59W 80 C4
Miller Lake Canada 45°6N 81°26W 82 A3
Millersburg Ohio, U.S.A. 40°33N 81°55W 82 F3
Millersburg Pa., U.S.A. 40°32N 76°58W 82 F8
Millerton U.S.A. 41°57N 73°31W 83 E11
Millerton L. U.S.A. 37°1N 119°41W 78 J7
Millet St. Lucia 13°55N 60°59W 89 f
Millheim U.S.A. 40°54N 77°29W 82 F7
Millicent Australia 37°34S 140°21E 63 F3
Millington U.S.A. 35°20N 89°53W 85 D10
Millinocket U.S.A. 45°39N 68°43W 81 C19
Millmerran Australia 27°53S 151°16E 63 D5
Millom U.K. 54°13N 3°16W 12 C4
Mills L. Canada 61°30N 118°20W 70 A5
Millsboro U.S.A. 40°0N 80°0W 82 G5
Millstream Chichester △ Australia 21°35S 117°6E 60 D2
Millstreet Ireland 52°4N 9°4W 10 D2
Milltown Malbay Ireland 52°52N 9°24W 10 D2
Millville N.J., U.S.A. 39°24N 75°2W 81 F16
Millville Pa., U.S.A. 41°7N 76°32W 83 E8
Millwood L. U.S.A. 33°42N 93°58W 84 E8
Milne → Australia 21°10S 137°33E 62 C2
Milo U.S.A. 45°15N 68°59W 81 C19
Milon, Akra Greece 36°15N 28°11E 25 C9
Milos Greece 36°44N 24°25E 23 F11
Milparinka Australia 29°46S 141°57E 63 D3
Milpitas U.S.A. 37°26N 121°55W 78 H5
Milton N.S., Canada 44°4N 64°45W 73 D7
Milton Ont., Canada 43°31N 79°53W 82 C5
Milton N.Z. 46°7S 169°59E 59 G2
Milton Calif., U.S.A. 38°3N 120°51W 78 G6
Milton Fla., U.S.A. 30°38N 87°3W 85 F11
Milton Pa., U.S.A. 41°1N 76°51W 82 E8
Milton Vt., U.S.A. 44°38N 73°7W 83 B11
Milton-Freewater U.S.A. 45°56N 118°23W 76 D4
Milton Keynes U.K. 52°1N 0°44W 13 E7
Milton Keynes □ U.K. 52°1N 0°44W 13 E7
Milverton Canada 43°34N 80°55W 82 C4
Milwaukee U.S.A. 43°2N 87°54W 80 D10
Milwaukee Deep Atl. Oc. 19°50N 68°0W 89 C6
Milwaukie U.S.A. 45°26N 122°38W 78 E4
Min Jiang → Fujian, China 26°0N 119°35E 33 D6

n Jiang → Sichuan,
China 28°45N 104°40E 32 D5
n Xian China 34°25N 104°5E 34 G3
nā' Jabal 'Alī U.A.E. 25°2N 55°8E 45 E7
na Pirquitas
Argentina 22°40S 66°30W 94 A2
nā Su'ud Si. Arabia 28°45N 48°28E 45 D6
nā'al Aḥmadī Kuwait 29°5N 48°10E 45 D6
nago → Canada 54°33N 98°59W 71 C9
naki Canada 49°59N 94°40W 71 D10
namata Japan 32°10N 130°30E 31 H5
nami-Arapusa △
Japan 35°30N 138°9E 31 G9
nami-Tori-Shima
Pac. Oc. 24°20N 153°58E 64 E7
nas Uruguay 34°20S 55°10W 95 C4
nas, Sierra de las
Guatemala 15°9N 89°31W 88 C2
nas Basin Canada 45°20N 64°12W 73 C7
nas Gerais □ Brazil 18°50S 46°0W 93 G9
natitlán Mexico 17°59N 94°31W 87 D6
nbu Burma 20°10N 94°52E 41 J19
nchinabad Pakistan 30°10N 73°34E 42 D5
ndanao Phil. 8°0N 125°0E 37 C7
ndanao Sea = Bohol Sea
Phil. 9°0N 124°0E 37 C6
ndanao Trench
Pac. Oc. 12°0N 126°6E 37 B7
ndelo C. Verde Is. 16°24N 25°0W 50 b
nden Canada 44°55N 78°43W 82 B6
nden Germany 52°17N 8°55E 16 B5
nden La., U.S.A. 32°37N 93°17W 84 E8
nden Nev., U.S.A. 38°57N 119°46W 78 G7
ndibungu = Billiluna
Australia 19°37S 127°41E 60 C4
ndiptana Indonesia 5°55S 140°22E 37 F10
ndoro Phil. 13°0N 121°0E 37 B6
ndoro Str. Phil. 12°30N 120°30E 37 B6
ne Japan 34°12N 131°7E 31 G5
nehead U.K. 51°12N 3°29W 13 F4
neola N.Y., U.S.A. 40°44N 73°38W 83 F11
neola Tex., U.S.A. 32°40N 95°29W 84 E7
neral King U.S.A. 36°27N 118°36W 78 J8
neral Wells U.S.A. 32°48N 98°7W 84 E5
ners Bay Canada 44°49N 78°46W 82 B6
nersville U.S.A. 40°41N 76°16W 83 F8
nerva N.Y., U.S.A. 43°47N 73°59W 83 C11
nerva Ohio, U.S.A. 40°44N 81°6W 82 F3
netto U.S.A. 43°24N 76°28W 83 C8
nfeng China 37°4N 82°46E 32 C3
ngäçevir Su Anbarı
Azerbaijan 40°57N 46°50E 19 F8
ngan Canada 50°20N 64°0W 73 B7
ngechaurskoye Vdkhr. =
Mingäçevir Su Anbarı
Azerbaijan 40°57N 46°50E 19 F8
ngela Australia 19°52S 146°38E 62 B4
ngenew Australia 29°12S 115°21E 61 E2
ngera Cr. →
Australia 20°38S 137°45E 62 C2
ngin Burma 22°50N 94°30E 41 H19
ngo Junction U.S.A. 40°19N 80°37W 82 F4
ngora Pakistan 34°48N 72°22E 43 B5
ngteke Daban = Mintaka Pass
Pakistan 37°0N 74°58E 43 A6
ngyuegue China 43°2N 128°50E 35 C15
nho = Miño → Spain 41°52N 8°40W 21 A2
nho Portugal 41°25N 8°20W 21 B1
nidoka U.S.A. 42°45N 113°29W 76 E7
nigwal, L. Australia 29°31S 123°14E 61 E3
nilya → Australia 23°45S 114°0E 61 D1
nilya Roadhouse
Australia 23°55S 114°0E 61 D1
nipi L. Canada 52°25N 60°45W 73 B7
nk L. Canada 61°54N 117°40W 70 A5
nna Nigeria 9°37N 6°30E 50 G7
nneapolis Kans., U.S.A. 39°8N 97°42W 80 F5
nneapolis Minn.,
U.S.A. 44°57N 93°16W 80 C7
nnedosa Canada 50°14N 99°50W 71 C9
nnesota □ U.S.A. 46°0N 94°15W 80 B6
nnesota → U.S.A. 44°54N 93°9W 80 C7
nnewaukan U.S.A. 48°4N 99°15W 80 A4
nnipa Australia 32°51S 135°9E 63 E2
nnitaki L. Canada 49°57N 92°10W 72 C1
no Japan 35°32N 136°55E 31 G8
ño → Spain 41°52N 8°40W 21 A2
norca = Menorca Spain 40°0N 4°0E 24 B11
not U.S.A. 48°14N 101°18W 80 A3
nqin China 38°38N 103°20E 34 E2
nsk Belarus 53°52N 27°30E 17 B14
nsk Mazowiecki
Poland 52°10N 21°33E 17 B11
ntabie Australia 27°15S 133°7E 63 D1
ntaka Pass Pakistan 37°0N 74°58E 43 A6
nto Canada 46°5N 66°5W 73 C6
nto, L. Canada 57°13N 75°0W 72 A5
nton Canada 49°10N 104°35W 71 D8
nturn U.S.A. 39°35N 106°26W 76 G10
nudasht Iran 37°17N 56°7E 45 B8
nusinsk Russia 53°43N 91°20E 29 D10
nutang India 28°15N 96°30E 41 E20
nvoul Gabon 2°9N 12°8E 52 D2
nzhong China 22°37N 113°30E 33 F10
quelon Canada 49°25N 76°27W 72 C4
quelon St-P. & M. 47°8N 56°22W 73 C8
Kūh Iran 26°22N 58°55E 45 E8
Shahdād Iran 26°15N 58°29E 45 E8
a Italy 45°26N 12°8E 22 B5
a por vos Cay
Bahamas 22°9N 74°30W 89 B5
abello, Kolpos Greece 35°10N 25°50E 25 D7
ador-Río Azul △
Guatemala 17°45N 89°50W 88 C2
aj India 16°50N 74°45E 40 L9
am Shah Pakistan 33°0N 70°2E 42 C4
amar Argentina 38°15S 57°50W 94 D4
Miramar Mozam. 23°50S 35°35E 57 C6
Miramichi Canada 47°2N 65°28W 73 C6
Miramichi B. Canada 47°15N 65°0W 73 C7
Miranda Brazil 20°10S 56°15W 93 H7
Miranda → Brazil 19°25S 57°20W 92 G7
Miranda de Ebro Spain 42°41N 2°57W 21 A4
Miranda do Douro
Portugal 41°30N 6°16W 21 B2
Mirandópolis Brazil 21°9S 51°6W 95 A5
Mirango Malawi 13°32S 34°58E 55 E3
Mirani Australia 21°8S 148°53E 62 K6
Mirassol Brazil 20°46S 49°28W 95 A6
Mirbāṭ Oman 17°0N 54°45E 47 D5
Mires Greece 35°4N 24°56E 25 D6
Miri Malaysia 4°23N 113°59E 36 D4
Miriam Vale Australia 24°20S 151°33E 62 C5
Mirim, L. S. Amer. 32°45S 52°50W 95 C5
Mīrjāveh Iran 29°1N 61°30E 45 D9
Mirnyy Antarctica 66°50S 92°30E 5 C14
Mirnyy Russia 62°33N 113°53E 29 C12
Mirokhan Pakistan 27°46N 68°6E 42 F3
Mirond L. Canada 55°6N 102°47W 71 B8
Mirpur Pakistan 33°32N 73°56E 43 C5
Mirpur Batoro Pakistan 24°44N 68°16E 42 G3
Mirpur Bibiwari Pakistan 28°33N 67°44E 42 E2
Mirpur Khas Pakistan 25°30N 69°0E 42 G3
Mirpur Sakro Pakistan 24°33N 67°41E 42 G2
Mirs Bay = Tai Pang Wan
China 22°33N 114°24E 33 F11
Mirtağ Turkey 38°23N 41°56E 44 B4
Mirtoo Sea Greece 37°0N 23°20E 23 F10
Miryang S. Korea 35°31N 128°44E 35 G15
Mirzapur India 25°10N 82°34E 43 G10
Mirzapur-cum-Vindhyachal =
Mirzapur India 25°10N 82°34E 43 G10
Misantla Mexico 19°56N 96°50W 87 D5
Misawa Japan 40°41N 141°24E 30 D10
Miscou I. Canada 47°57N 64°31W 73 C7
Mish'āb, Ra's al
Si. Arabia 28°15N 48°43E 45 D6
Mishan China 45°37N 131°48E 30 B5
Mishawaka U.S.A. 41°40N 86°11W 80 E10
Mishima Japan 35°10N 138°52E 31 G9
Misión Mexico 32°6N 116°53W 79 N10
Misiones □ Argentina 27°0S 55°0W 95 B5
Misiones □ Paraguay 27°0S 56°0W 94 B4
Miskah Si. Arabia 24°49N 42°56E 44 E4
Miskitos, Cayos Nic. 14°26N 82°50W 88 D3
Miskolc Hungary 48°7N 20°50E 17 D11
Misoke
Dem. Rep. of the Congo 0°42S 28°2E 54 C2
Misool Indonesia 1°52S 130°10E 37 E8
Miṣr = Egypt ■ Africa 28°0N 31°0E 51 C12
Miṣrātah Libya 32°24N 15°3E 51 B9
Missanabie Canada 48°20N 84°6W 72 C3
Missinaibi → Canada 50°43N 81°29W 72 B3
Missinaibi L. Canada 48°23N 83°40W 72 C3
Mission Canada 49°10N 122°15W 70 D4
Mission S. Dak., U.S.A. 43°18N 100°39W 80 D3
Mission Tex., U.S.A. 26°13N 98°20W 84 H5
Mission Beach Australia 17°53S 146°6E 62 B4
Mission Viejo U.S.A. 33°36N 117°40W 79 M9
Missisa L. Canada 52°20N 85°7W 72 B2
Missisicabi → Canada 51°14N 79°31W 72 B4
Mississagi → Canada 46°15N 83°9W 72 C3
Mississauga Canada 43°32N 79°35W 82 C5
Mississippi □ U.S.A. 33°0N 90°0W 85 E10
Mississippi → U.S.A. 29°9N 89°15W 85 G10
Mississippi L. Canada 45°5N 76°10W 83 A8
Mississippi River Delta
U.S.A. 29°10N 89°15W 85 G10
Mississippi Sd. U.S.A. 30°20N 89°0W 85 F10
Missoula U.S.A. 46°52N 114°1W 76 C6
Missouri □ U.S.A. 38°25N 92°30W 80 F7
Missouri → U.S.A. 38°49N 90°7W 80 F8
Missouri City U.S.A. 29°37N 95°32W 84 G7
Missouri Valley U.S.A. 41°34N 95°53W 80 E6
Mist U.S.A. 45°59N 123°15W 78 E3
Mistassibi → Canada 48°53N 72°13W 73 B5
Mistassini Canada 48°53N 72°12W 73 C5
Mistassini → Canada 48°42N 72°20W 73 C5
Mistassini, L. Canada 51°0N 73°30W 72 B5
Mistastin L. Canada 55°57N 63°20W 73 A7
Mistinibi, L. Canada 55°56N 64°17W 73 A7
Mistissini Canada 48°53N 72°12W 73 C5
Misty L. Canada 58°53N 101°40W 71 B8
Misurata = Miṣrātah
Libya 32°24N 15°3E 51 B9
Mitchell Australia 26°29S 147°58E 63 D4
Mitchell Canada 43°28N 81°12W 82 C3
Mitchell Nebr., U.S.A. 41°57N 103°49W 80 E2
Mitchell Oreg., U.S.A. 44°34N 120°9W 76 D3
Mitchell S. Dak., U.S.A. 43°43N 98°2W 80 D4
Mitchell → Australia 15°12S 141°35E 62 B3
Mitchell, Mt. U.S.A. 35°46N 82°16W 85 D13
Mitchell-Alice Rivers △
Australia 15°28S 142°5E 62 B3
Mitchell Ra. Australia 12°49S 135°36E 62 A2
Mitchelstown Ireland 52°15N 8°16W 10 D3
Mitha Tiwana Pakistan 32°13N 72°6E 42 C5
Mithi Pakistan 24°44N 69°48E 42 G3
Mithrao Pakistan 27°28N 69°40E 42 F3
Mitilini Greece 39°6N 26°35E 23 E12
Mitla Pass = Mamarr Mitlā
Egypt 30°2N 32°54E 46 E1
Mito Japan 36°20N 140°30E 31 F10
Mitrovica = Kosovska Mitrovica
Serbia 42°54N 20°52E 23 C9
Mitsamiouli Comoros Is. 11°20S 43°16E 53 a
Mitsinjo Madag. 16°1S 45°52E 57 B8
Mitsiwa Eritrea 15°35N 39°25E 47 D2
Mitsukaidō Japan 36°1N 139°59E 31 F9
Mittagong Australia 34°28S 150°29E 63 E5
Mittimatalik = Pond Inlet
Canada 72°40N 77°0W 69 B12
Mitú Colombia 1°15N 70°13W 92 C4
Mitumba Tanzania 7°8S 31°2E 54 D3
Mitumba, Mts.
Dem. Rep. of the Congo 7°0S 27°30E 54 D2
Mitwaba
Dem. Rep. of the Congo 8°2S 27°17E 55 D2
Mityana Uganda 0°23N 32°2E 54 B3
Mixteco → Mexico 18°11N 98°30W 87 D5
Miyagi □ Japan 38°15N 140°45E 30 E10
Miyāh, W. el → Syria 34°44N 39°57E 44 C3
Miyake-Jima Japan 34°5N 139°30E 31 G9
Miyako Japan 39°40N 141°59E 30 E10
Miyako-Jima Japan 24°45N 125°20E 31 M2
Miyako-Rettō Japan 24°24N 125°0E 31 M2
Miyakonojō Japan 31°40N 131°5E 31 J5
Miyani India 21°50N 69°26E 42 J3
Miyanoura-Dake Japan 30°20N 130°31E 31 J5
Miyazaki Japan 31°56N 131°30E 31 J5
Miyazaki □ Japan 32°30N 131°30E 31 H5
Miyazu Japan 35°35N 135°10E 31 G7
Miyet, Bahr el = Dead Sea
Asia 31°30N 35°30E 46 D4
Miyoshi Japan 34°48N 132°51E 31 G6
Miyun China 40°28N 116°50E 34 D9
Miyun Shuiku China 40°30N 117°0E 35 D9
Mizdah Libya 31°30N 13°0E 51 B8
Mizen Hd. Cork, Ireland 51°27N 9°50W 10 E2
Mizen Hd. Wicklow, Ireland 52°51N 6°4W 10 D5
Mizhi China 37°47N 110°12E 34 F6
Mizoram □ India 23°30N 92°40E 41 H18
Mizpe Ramon Israel 30°34N 34°49E 46 E3
Mizuho Antarctica 70°30S 41°0E 5 D5
Mizusawa Japan 39°8N 141°8E 30 E10
Mjölby Sweden 58°20N 15°10E 9 G16
Mjøsa Norway 60°40N 11°0E 8 F14
Mkata Tanzania 5°45S 38°20E 54 D4
Mkhaya ⌂ Swaziland 26°34S 31°45E 57 D5
Mkhuze ⌂ S. Africa 29°27S 29°30E 57 D4
Mkokotoni Tanzania 5°55S 39°15E 54 D4
Mkomazi Tanzania 4°40S 38°7E 54 C4
Mkomazi → S. Africa 30°12S 30°50E 57 E5
Mkomazi ⌂ Tanzania 4°4S 30°2E 54 C3
Mkulwe Tanzania 8°37S 32°20E 55 D3
Mkumbi, Ras Tanzania 7°38S 39°55E 54 D4
Mkushi Zambia 14°25S 29°15E 55 E2
Mkushi River Zambia 13°32S 29°45E 55 E2
Mkuze S. Africa 27°10S 32°0E 57 D5
Mladá Boleslav
Czech Rep. 50°27N 14°53E 16 C8
Mlala Hills Tanzania 6°50S 31°40E 54 D3
Mlange = Mulanje, Mt.
Malawi 16°2S 35°33E 55 F4
Mława Poland 53°9N 20°25E 17 B11
Mlawula ⌂ Swaziland 26°12S 32°2E 57 D5
Mljet Croatia 42°43N 17°30E 22 C7
Mmabatho S. Africa 25°49S 25°30E 56 D4
Mo i Rana Norway 66°20N 14°7E 8 C16
Moa Cuba 20°40N 74°56W 89 B4
Moa Indonesia 8°0S 128°0E 37 F7
Moa → S. Leone 6°59N 11°36W 50 G3
Moab U.S.A. 38°35N 109°33W 76 G9
Moala Fiji 18°36S 179°53E 59 a
Moama Australia 36°7S 144°46E 63 F3
Moamba Mozam. 25°36S 32°15E 57 D5
Moapa U.S.A. 36°40N 114°37W 79 J12
Moate Ireland 53°24N 7°44W 10 C4
Moba Dem. Rep. of the Congo 7°0S 29°48E 54 D2
Mobārakābād Iran 28°24N 53°20E 45 D7
Mobaye C.A.R. 4°25N 21°5E 52 D4
Mobayi
Dem. Rep. of the Congo 4°15N 21°8E 52 D4
Moberly U.S.A. 39°25N 92°26W 80 F7
Moberly Lake Canada 55°50N 121°44W 70 B4
Mobile U.S.A. 30°41N 88°3W 85 F10
Mobile B. U.S.A. 30°30N 88°0W 85 F11
Mobridge U.S.A. 45°32N 100°26W 80 C3
Moc Chau Vietnam 20°50N 104°38E 38 B5
Moc Hoa Vietnam 10°46N 105°56E 39 G5
Mocabe Kasari
Dem. Rep. of the Congo 9°58S 26°12E 55 D2
Moçambique = Mozambique ■
Africa 19°0S 35°0E 55 F4
Moçambique Mozam. 15°3S 40°42E 55 F5
Mocanaqua U.S.A. 41°9N 76°8W 83 E8
Moce Fiji 18°40S 178°29W 59 a
Mochima △ Venezuela 10°30N 64°5W 89 D7
Mochos Greece 35°16N 25°27E 25 D7
Mochudi Botswana 24°27S 26°7E 56 C4
Mocimboa da Praia
Mozam. 11°25S 40°20E 55 E5
Moclips U.S.A. 47°14N 124°13W 78 C2
Mocoa Colombia 1°7N 76°35W 92 C3
Mococa Brazil 21°28S 47°0W 95 A6
Mocorito Mexico 25°29N 107°55W 86 B3
Moctezuma Mexico 29°48N 109°42W 86 B3
Moctezuma → Mexico 21°59N 98°34W 87 C5
Mocuba Mozam. 16°54S 36°57E 55 F4
Modane France 45°12N 6°40E 20 D7
Modasa India 23°30N 73°21E 42 H5
Modder → S. Africa 29°2S 24°37E 56 D3
Modderrivier S. Africa 29°2S 24°38E 56 D3
Módena Italy 44°40N 10°55E 22 B4
Modena U.S.A. 37°48N 113°56W 77 H7
Modesto U.S.A. 37°39N 121°0W 78 H6
Módica Italy 36°52N 14°46E 22 F6
Modimolle S. Africa 24°42S 28°22E 57 C4
Modjadjiskloof S. Africa 23°42S 30°10E 57 C5
Moe Australia 38°12S 146°19E 63 F4
Moebase Mozam. 17°3S 38°41E 55 F4
Moengo Suriname 5°45N 54°20W 93 B8
Moffat U.K. 55°21N 3°27W 11 F5
Moga India 30°48N 75°8E 42 D6
Mogadishu = Muqdisho
Somali Rep. 2°2N 45°25E 47 G4
Mogador = Essaouira
Morocco 31°32N 9°42W 50 B4
Mogalakwena →
S. Africa 22°38S 28°40E 57 C4
Mogami-Gawa →
Japan 38°45N 140°0E 30 E10
Mogán Canary Is. 27°53N 15°43W 24 G4
Mogaung Burma 25°20N 97°0E 41 G20
Mogi das Cruzes Brazil 23°31S 46°11W 95 A6
Mogi-Guaçu → Brazil 20°53S 48°10W 95 A6
Mogi-Mirim Brazil 22°29S 47°0W 93 H9
Mogilev = Mahilyow
Belarus 53°55N 30°18E 17 B16
Mogilev-Podolskiy = Mohyliv-
Podilskyy Ukraine 48°26N 27°48E 17 D14
Mogincual Mozam. 15°35S 40°25E 55 F5
Mogocha Russia 53°40N 119°50E 29 D12
Mogok Burma 23°0N 96°40E 41 H20
Mogollon Rim U.S.A. 34°10N 110°50W 77 J8
Mogumber Australia 31°2S 116°3E 61 F2
Mogwadi → S. Africa 23°4S 29°36E 57 C4
Mohács Hungary 45°58N 18°41E 17 F10
Mohales Hoek Lesotho 30°7S 27°26E 56 E4
Mohall U.S.A. 48°46N 101°31W 80 A3
Moḥammadābād Iran 37°52N 59°5E 45 B8
Mohammedia Morocco 33°44N 7°21W 50 B4
Mohana → India 24°43N 85°0E 43 G11
Mohanlalganj India 26°41N 80°58E 43 F9
Mohave, L. U.S.A. 35°12N 114°34W 79 K12
Mohawk → U.S.A. 42°47N 73°41W 83 D11
Mohéli Comoros Is. 12°20S 43°40E 53 a
Mohenjodaro Pakistan 27°19N 68°7E 42 F3
Moher, Cliffs of Ireland 52°58N 9°27W 10 D2
Mohicanville Res. U.S.A. 40°45N 82°9W 82 F2
Mohns Ridge Arctic 72°30N 5°0W 4 B7
Mohoro Tanzania 8°6S 39°8E 54 D4
Mohsenābād Iran 36°40N 59°35E 45 B8
Mohyliv-Podilskyy
Ukraine 48°26N 27°48E 17 D14
Moidart, L. U.K. 56°47N 5°52W 11 E3
Moira → Canada 44°21N 77°24W 82 B7
Moisaküla Estonia 58°3N 25°12E 9 G21
Moisie Canada 50°12N 66°1W 73 B6
Moisie → Canada 50°14N 66°5W 73 B6
Mojave U.S.A. 35°3N 118°10W 79 K8
Mojave ⌂ U.S.A. 35°7N 115°32W 79 K11
Mojave Desert U.S.A. 35°0N 116°30W 79 L10
Mojo Bolivia 21°48S 65°33W 94 A2
Mojokerto Indonesia 7°28S 112°26E 37 G15
Mokai N.Z. 38°32S 175°56E 59 C5
Mokambo
Dem. Rep. of the Congo 12°25S 28°20E 55 E2
Mokameh India 25°24N 85°55E 43 G11
Mokau N.Z. 38°42S 174°39E 59 C5
Mokelumne → U.S.A. 38°13N 121°28W 78 G5
Mokelumne Hill
U.S.A. 38°18N 120°43W 78 G6
Mokhotlong Lesotho 29°22S 29°2E 57 D4
Mokokchung India 26°15N 94°30E 41 F19
Mokolo → S. Africa 23°14S 27°43E 57 C4
Mokopane S. Africa 24°10S 28°55E 57 C4
Mokpo S. Korea 34°50N 126°25E 35 G14
Mokra Gora Europe 42°50N 20°30E 23 C9
Mol Belgium 51°11N 5°5E 15 C5
Molchanovo Russia 57°40N 83°50E 28 D9
Mold U.K. 53°9N 3°8W 12 D4
Moldavia = Moldova ■
Europe 47°0N 28°0E 17 E15
Moldavia Romania 46°30N 27°0E 17 E14
Molde Norway 62°45N 7°9E 8 E12
Moldova ■ Europe 47°0N 28°0E 17 E15
Moldoveanu, Vf.
Romania 45°36N 24°45E 17 F13
Mole → U.K. 51°24N 0°21W 13 F7
Mole Creek Australia 41°34S 146°24E 63 G4
Molepolole Botswana 24°28S 25°28E 56 C4
Molfetta Italy 41°12N 16°36E 22 D7
Moline U.S.A. 41°30N 90°31W 80 E8
Molinos Argentina 25°28S 66°15W 94 B2
Moliro
Dem. Rep. of the Congo 8°12S 30°30E 54 D3
Mollendo Peru 17°0S 72°0W 92 G4
Mollerin, L. Australia 30°30S 117°35E 61 F2
Molo Kenya 0°15S 35°44E 54 C4
Molodechno = Maladzyechna
Belarus 54°20N 26°50E 17 A14
Molodezhnaya Antarctica 67°40S 45°51E 5 C9
Moloka'i U.S.A. 21°8N 157°0W 74 b
Molokai Fracture Zone
Pac. Oc. 28°0N 125°0W 65 E15
Molong Australia 33°5S 148°54E 63 E4
Molopo → Africa 28°30S 20°12E 56 D3
Molson L. Canada 54°22N 96°40W 71 C9
Molteno S. Africa 31°22S 26°22E 56 E4
Molu Indonesia 6°45S 131°40E 37 F8
Molucca Sea Indonesia 0°0 125°0E 37 E6
Moluccas = Maluku
Indonesia 1°0S 127°0E 37 E7
Moma
Dem. Rep. of the Congo 1°35S 23°52E 54 C1
Moma Mozam. 16°47S 39°4E 55 F4
Mombasa Kenya 4°3S 39°40E 54 C4
Mombetsu Japan 44°21N 143°22E 30 B11
Momchilgrad Bulgaria 41°33N 25°23E 23 D11
Momi Dem. Rep. of the Congo 1°42S 27°0E 54 C2
Mompós Colombia 9°14N 74°26W 92 B4
Møn Denmark 54°57N 12°20E 9 J15
Mon □ Burma 16°0N 97°30E 41 L20
Mona, Canal de la = Mona
Passage W. Indies 18°30N 67°45W 89 C6
Mona, Isla Puerto Rico 18°5N 67°54W 89 C6
Mona, Pta. Costa Rica 9°37N 82°36W 88 E3
Mona Passage W. Indies 18°30N 67°45W 89 C6
Monaca U.S.A. 40°41N 80°17W 82 F4
Monaco ■ Europe 43°46N 7°23E 20 E7
Monadhliath Mts. U.K. 57°10N 4°4W 11 D4
Monadnock, Mt. U.S.A. 42°52N 72°7W 83 D12
Monaghan Ireland 54°15N 6°57W 10 B5
Monaghan □ Ireland 54°11N 6°56W 10 B5
Monahans U.S.A. 31°36N 102°54W 84 F3
Monapo Mozam. 14°56S 40°19E 55 E5
Monar, L. U.K. 57°26N 5°8W 11 D3
Monarch Mt. Canada 51°55N 125°57W 70 C3
Monashee Mts. Canada 51°0N 118°43W 70 C5
Monasterevin Ireland 53°8N 7°4W 10 C4
Monastir = Bitola
Macedonia 41°1N 21°20E 23 D9
Monastir Tunisia 35°50N 10°49E 51 A8
Moncayo, Sierra del
Spain 41°48N 1°50W 21 B5
Monchegorsk Russia 67°54N 32°58E 8 C25
Mönchengladbach
Germany 51°11N 6°27E 16 C4
Monchique Portugal 37°19N 8°38W 21 D1
Moncks Corner U.S.A. 33°12N 80°1W 85 E14
Monclova Mexico 26°54N 101°25W 86 B4
Moncton Canada 46°7N 64°51W 73 C7
Mondego → Portugal 40°9N 8°52W 21 B1
Mondeodo Indonesia 3°34S 122°9E 37 E6
Mondovì Italy 44°23N 7°49E 20 D7
Mondrain I. Australia 34°9S 122°14E 61 F3
Moneague Jamaica 18°16N 77°7W 88 a
Moneron, Ostrov
Russia 46°15N 141°16E 30 A10
Monessen U.S.A. 40°9N 79°54W 82 F5
Monett U.S.A. 36°55N 93°55W 80 G7
Moneymore U.K. 54°41N 6°40W 10 B5
Monforte de Lemos Spain 42°31N 7°33W 21 A2
Mong Cai Vietnam 21°27N 107°54E 38 B6
Mong Hsu Burma 21°54N 98°30E 41 J21
Mong Kung Burma 21°35N 97°35E 41 J20
Mong Nai Burma 20°32N 97°46E 41 J20
Mong Pawk Burma 22°4N 99°16E 41 H21
Mong Ton Burma 20°17N 98°45E 41 J21
Mong Wa Burma 21°26N 100°27E 41 J22
Mong Yai Burma 22°21N 98°3E 41 H21
Mongalla Sudan 5°8N 31°42E 51 G12
Mongers, L. Australia 29°25S 117°5E 61 E2
Monghyr = Munger
India 25°23N 86°30E 43 G12
Mongibello = Etna Italy 37°50N 14°55E 22 F6
Mongo Chad 12°14N 18°43E 51 F9
Mongolia ■ Asia 47°0N 103°0E 32 B5
Mongolia, Plateau of
Asia 45°0N 105°0E 26 D12
Mongu Zambia 15°16S 23°12E 53 H4
Mônguа Angola 16°43S 15°20E 56 B2
Monifieth U.K. 56°30N 2°48W 11 E6
Monkey Bay Malawi 14°7S 35°1E 55 E4
Monkey Mia Australia 25°48S 113°43E 61 E1
Monkey River Belize 16°22N 88°29W 87 D7
Monkland Canada 45°11N 74°52W 83 A10
Monkoto
Dem. Rep. of the Congo 1°38S 20°35E 52 E4
Monkton Canada 43°35N 81°5W 82 C3
Monmouth U.K. 51°48N 2°42W 13 F5
Monmouth Ill., U.S.A. 40°55N 90°39W 80 E8
Monmouth Oreg.,
U.S.A. 44°51N 123°14W 76 D2
Monmouthshire □ U.K. 51°48N 2°54W 13 F5
Mono, Pta. Nic. 12°0N 83°30W 88 D3
Mono L. U.S.A. 38°1N 119°1W 78 H7
Monolith U.S.A. 35°7N 118°22W 79 K8
Monolithos Greece 36°7N 27°45E 25 C9
Monongahela U.S.A. 40°12N 79°56W 82 F5
Monópoli Italy 40°57N 17°18E 22 D7
Monos I. Trin. & Tob. 10°42N 61°44W 93 K15
Monroe Ga., U.S.A. 33°47N 83°43W 85 E13
Monroe La., U.S.A. 32°30N 92°7W 84 E8
Monroe Mich., U.S.A. 41°55N 83°24W 81 E12
Monroe N.C., U.S.A. 34°59N 80°33W 85 D14
Monroe N.Y., U.S.A. 41°20N 74°11W 83 E10
Monroe Utah, U.S.A. 38°38N 112°7W 76 G7
Monroe Wash., U.S.A. 47°51N 121°58W 78 C5
Monroe Wis., U.S.A. 42°36N 89°38W 80 D9
Monroe City U.S.A. 39°39N 91°44W 80 F8
Monroeton U.S.A. 41°43N 76°29W 83 E8
Monroeville Ala.,
U.S.A. 31°31N 87°20W 85 F11
Monroeville Pa., U.S.A. 40°26N 79°45W 82 F5
Monrovia Liberia 6°18N 10°47W 50 G3
Mons Belgium 50°27N 3°58E 15 D3
Monse Indonesia 4°7S 123°15E 37 E6
Mont-de-Marsan France 43°54N 0°31W 20 E3
Mont-Joli Canada 48°37N 68°10W 73 C6
Mont-Laurier Canada 46°35N 75°30W 72 C4
Mont-Louis Canada 49°15N 65°44W 73 C6
Mont-St-Michel, Le
France 48°40N 1°30W 20 B3
Mont-Tremblant ⌂
Canada 46°30N 74°30W 72 C5
Montagne d'Ambre △
Madag. 12°37S 49°8E 57 A8
Montagu S. Africa 33°45S 20°8E 56 E3
Montagu I. Antarctica 58°25S 26°20W 5 B1
Montague Canada 46°10N 62°39W 73 C7
Montague, I. Mexico 31°45N 114°48W 86 A2
Montague Ra. Australia 27°15S 119°30E 61 E2
Montague Sd. Australia 14°28S 125°20E 60 B4
Montalbán Spain 40°50N 0°45W 21 B5
Montalvo U.S.A. 34°15N 119°12W 79 L7
Montana Bulgaria 43°27N 23°16E 23 C10
Montaña Peru 6°0S 73°0W 92 E4
Montana □ U.S.A. 47°0N 110°0W 76 C9
Montaña Clara, I.
Canary Is. 29°17N 13°33W 24 E6
Montargis France 47°59N 2°43E 20 C5
Montauban France 44°2N 1°21E 20 D4
Montauk U.S.A. 41°3N 71°57W 83 E13
Montauk Pt. U.S.A. 41°4N 71°51W 83 E13
Montbéliard France 47°31N 6°48E 20 C7
Montceau-les-Mines
France 46°40N 4°23E 20 C6
Montclair U.S.A. 40°49N 74°12W 83 F10
Monte Albán Mexico 17°2N 96°46W 87 D5
Monte Alegre Brazil 2°0S 54°0W 93 D8
Monte Azul Brazil 15°9S 42°53W 93 G10
Monte-Carlo Monaco 43°44N 7°25E 20 E7
Monte Caseros
Argentina 30°10S 57°50W 94 C4

Monte Comán Argentina 34°40S 67°53W 94 C2
Monte Cristi Dom. Rep. 19°52N 71°39W 89 C5
Monte Lindo ➜ Paraguay 23°56S 57°12W 94 A4
Monte Patria Chile 30°42S 70°58W 94 C1
Monte Quemado Argentina 25°53S 62°41W 94 B3
Monte Rio U.S.A. 38°28N 123°0W 78 G4
Monte Santu, C. di Italy 40°5N 9°44E 22 D3
Monte Vista U.S.A. 37°35N 106°9W 77 H10
Monteagudo Argentina 27°14S 54°8W 95 B5
Montebello Canada 45°40N 74°55W 72 C5
Montebello Is. Australia 20°30S 115°45E 60 D2
Montecarlo Argentina 26°34S 54°47W 95 B5
Montecito U.S.A. 34°26N 119°40W 79 L7
Montecristo Italy 42°20N 10°19E 22 C4
Montego Bay Jamaica 18°28N 77°55W 88 a
Montélimar France 44°33N 4°45E 20 D6
Montello U.S.A. 43°48N 89°20W 80 D9
Montemorelos Mexico 25°12N 99°49W 87 B5
Montenegro Brazil 29°39S 51°29W 95 B5
Montenegro ■ Europe 42°40N 19°20E 23 C8
Montepuez Mozam. 13°8S 38°59E 55 E4
Montepuez ➜ Mozam. 12°32S 40°27E 55 E5
Monterey U.S.A. 36°37N 121°55W 78 J5
Monterey B. U.S.A. 36°45N 122°0W 78 J5
Montería Colombia 8°46N 75°53W 92 B3
Monteros Argentina 27°11S 65°30W 94 B2
Monterrey Mexico 25°40N 100°19W 86 B4
Montes Azules ⌂ Mexico 16°21N 91°3W 87 D6
Montes Claros Brazil 16°30S 43°50W 93 G10
Montesano U.S.A. 46°59N 123°36W 78 D3
Montesilvano Italy 42°29N 14°8E 22 C6
Montevideo Uruguay 34°50S 56°11W 95 C4
Montevideo U.S.A. 44°57N 95°43W 80 C6
Montezuma U.S.A. 41°35N 92°32W 80 E7
Montezuma Castle ⌂ U.S.A. 34°39N 111°45W 77 J8
Montgomery U.K. 52°34N 3°8W 13 E4
Montgomery Ala., U.S.A. 32°23N 86°19W 85 E11
Montgomery Pa., U.S.A. 41°10N 76°53W 82 E8
Montgomery W. Va., U.S.A. 38°11N 81°19W 81 F13
Montgomery City U.S.A. 38°59N 91°30W 80 F8
Monticello Ark., U.S.A. 33°38N 91°47W 84 E9
Monticello Fla., U.S.A. 30°33N 83°52W 85 F13
Monticello Ind., U.S.A. 40°45N 86°46W 80 E10
Monticello Iowa, U.S.A. 42°15N 91°12W 80 D8
Monticello Ky., U.S.A. 36°50N 84°51W 81 G11
Monticello Minn., U.S.A. 45°18N 93°48W 80 C7
Monticello Miss., U.S.A. 31°33N 90°7W 85 F9
Monticello N.Y., U.S.A. 41°39N 74°42W 83 E10
Monticello Utah, U.S.A. 37°52N 109°21W 77 H9
Montijo Portugal 38°41N 8°54W 21 C1
Montilla Spain 37°36N 4°40W 21 D3
Montluçon France 46°22N 2°36E 20 C5
Montmagny Canada 46°58N 70°34W 73 C5
Montmartre Canada 50°14N 103°27W 71 C8
Montmorillon France 46°26N 0°50E 20 C4
Monto Australia 24°52S 151°6E 62 C5
Montongbuwoh Indonesia 8°33S 116°4E 37 K19
Montoro Spain 38°1N 4°27W 21 C3
Montour Falls U.S.A. 42°21N 76°51W 82 D8
Montoursville U.S.A. 41°15N 76°55W 82 E8
Montpelier Idaho, U.S.A. 42°19N 111°18W 76 E8
Montpelier Vt., U.S.A. 44°16N 72°35W 83 B12
Montpellier France 43°37N 3°52E 20 E5
Montréal Canada 45°30N 73°33W 83 A11
Montreal ➜ Canada 47°14N 84°39W 72 C3
Montréal L. Canada 54°20N 105°45W 71 C7
Montreal Lake Canada 54°3N 105°46W 71 C7
Montreux Switz. 46°26N 6°55E 20 C7
Montrose U.K. 56°44N 2°27W 11 E6
Montrose Colo., U.S.A. 38°29N 107°53W 76 G10
Montrose Pa., U.S.A. 41°50N 75°53W 83 E9
Monts, Pte. des Canada 49°20N 67°12W 73 C6
Montserrat ☑ W. Indies 16°40N 62°10W 89 C7
Montuiri Spain 39°34N 2°59E 24 B9
Monywa Burma 22°7N 95°11E 41 H19
Monza Italy 45°35N 9°16E 20 D8
Monze Zambia 16°17S 27°29E 55 F2
Monze, C. Pakistan 24°47N 66°37E 42 G2
Monzón Spain 41°52N 0°10E 21 B6
Mooers U.S.A. 44°58N 73°35W 83 B11
Mooi ➜ S. Africa 28°45S 30°34E 57 D5
Mooi River S. Africa 29°13S 29°50E 57 D4
Moomba Australia 28°6S 140°12E 63 A3
Moonah ➜ Australia 22°3S 138°33E 62 C2
Moonda, L. Australia 25°52S 140°25E 62 D3
Moonie Australia 27°46S 150°20E 63 D5
Moonie ➜ Australia 29°19S 148°43E 63 D4
Moonta Australia 34°6S 137°32E 63 E2
Moora Australia 30°37S 115°58E 61 F2
Moorcroft U.S.A. 44°16N 104°57W 76 D11
Moore ➜ Australia 31°22S 115°30E 61 F2
Moore, L. Australia 29°50S 117°35E 61 E2
Moore Falls Canada 44°48N 78°48W 82 B6
Moore Park Australia 24°43S 152°17E 62 C5
Moore Res. U.S.A. 44°20N 71°53W 83 B13
Moore River △ Australia 31°7S 115°39E 61 F2
Moorea French Polynesia 17°30S 149°50W 59 d
Moorefield U.S.A. 39°4N 78°58W 81 F14
Moorfoot Hills U.K. 55°44N 3°8W 11 F5
Moorhead U.S.A. 46°53N 96°45W 80 B5
Moorpark U.S.A. 34°17N 118°53W 79 L8
Moorreesburg S. Africa 33°6S 18°38E 56 E2
Moorrinya △ Australia 21°42S 144°58E 62 C3
Moose ➜ Canada 51°20N 80°25W 72 B3
Moose ➜ U.S.A. 43°38N 75°24W 83 C9
Moose Creek Canada 45°15N 74°58W 83 A10
Moose Factory Canada 51°16N 80°32W 72 B3
Moose Jaw Canada 50°24N 105°30W 71 C7
Moose Jaw ➜ Canada 50°34N 105°18W 71 C7
Moose Lake Canada 53°46N 100°8W 71 C8
Moose Lake U.S.A. 46°27N 92°46W 80 B7
Moose Mountain ⌂ Canada 49°48N 102°25W 71 D8
Moosehead L. U.S.A. 45°38N 69°40W 81 C19
Mooselookmeguntic L. U.S.A. 44°55N 70°49W 83 B14
Moosilauke, Mt. U.S.A. 44°3N 71°40W 83 B13
Moosomin Canada 50°9N 101°40W 71 C8
Moosonee Canada 51°17N 80°39W 72 B3
Moosup U.S.A. 41°43N 71°53W 83 E13
Mopane S. Africa 22°37S 29°52E 57 C4
Mopeia Velha Mozam. 17°30S 35°40E 55 F4
Mopipi Botswana 21°6S 24°55E 56 C3
Mopoi C.A.R. 5°6N 26°54E 54 A2
Mopti Mali 14°30N 4°0W 50 F5
Moqor Afghan. 32°50N 67°42E 42 C2
Moquegua Peru 17°15S 70°46W 92 G4
Mora Sweden 61°2N 14°38E 8 F16
Mora Minn., U.S.A. 45°53N 93°18W 80 C7
Mora N. Mex., U.S.A. 35°58N 105°20W 77 J11
Moradabad India 28°50N 78°50E 43 E8
Morafenobe Madag. 17°50S 44°53E 57 B7
Moramanga Madag. 18°56S 48°12E 57 B8
Moran Kans., U.S.A. 37°55N 95°10W 80 G6
Moran Wyo., U.S.A. 43°50N 110°31W 76 E8
Moranbah Australia 22°1S 148°6E 62 C4
Morant Bay Jamaica 17°53N 76°25W 88 a
Morant Cays Jamaica 17°22N 76°0W 88 C4
Morant Pt. Jamaica 17°55N 76°12W 88 a
Morar India 26°14N 78°14E 42 F8
Morar, L. U.K. 56°57N 5°40W 11 E3
Moratuwa Sri Lanka 6°45N 79°55E 40 R11
Morava ➜ Serbia 44°36N 21°4E 23 B9
Morava ➜ Slovak Rep. 48°10N 16°59E 17 D9
Moravia U.S.A. 42°43N 76°25W 83 D8
Moravian Hts. = Českomoravská Vrchovina Czech Rep. 49°30N 15°40E 16 D8
Morawa Australia 29°13S 116°0E 61 E2
Morawhanna Guyana 8°30N 59°40W 92 B7
Moray ☐ U.K. 57°31N 3°18W 11 D5
Moray Firth U.K. 57°40N 3°52W 11 D5
Morbi India 22°50N 70°42E 42 H4
Morden Canada 49°15N 98°10W 71 D9
Mordovian Republic = Mordvinia ☐ Russia 54°20N 44°30E 18 D7
Mordvinia ☐ Russia 54°20N 44°30E 18 D7
Moreau ➜ U.S.A. 45°18N 100°43W 80 C3
Morebeng S. Africa 23°30S 29°55E 57 C4
Morecambe U.K. 54°5N 2°52W 12 C5
Morecambe B. U.K. 54°7N 3°0W 12 C5
Moree Australia 29°28S 149°54E 63 D4
Morehead U.S.A. 38°11N 83°26W 81 F12
Morehead City U.S.A. 34°43N 76°43W 85 D16
Morel ➜ India 26°13N 76°36E 42 F7
Morelia Mexico 19°42N 101°7W 86 D4
Morella Australia 23°0S 143°52E 62 C3
Morella Spain 40°35N 0°5W 21 B5
Morelos Mexico 26°42N 107°40W 86 B3
Morelos ☐ Mexico 18°45N 99°0W 87 D5
Moremi ⌂ Botswana 19°18S 23°10E 56 B3
Morena India 26°30N 78°4E 42 F8
Morena, Sierra Spain 38°20N 4°0W 21 C3
Moreno Valley U.S.A. 33°56N 117°14W 79 M10
Moresby I. Canada 52°30N 131°40W 70 C2
Moreton I. Australia 27°10S 153°25E 63 D5
Moreton Island △ Australia 27°2S 153°24E 63 D5
Morgan U.S.A. 41°2N 111°41W 76 F8
Morgan City U.S.A. 29°42N 91°12W 84 G9
Morgan Hill U.S.A. 37°8N 121°39W 78 H5
Morganfield U.S.A. 37°41N 87°55W 80 G10
Morganton U.S.A. 35°45N 81°41W 85 D14
Morgantown U.S.A. 39°38N 79°57W 81 F14
Morgenzon S. Africa 26°45S 29°36E 57 D4
Morghak Iran 29°7N 57°54E 45 D8
Morhar ➜ India 25°29N 85°11E 43 G11
Mori Japan 42°6N 140°35E 30 C10
Moriarty U.S.A. 34°59N 106°3W 77 J10
Morice L. Canada 53°50N 127°40W 70 C3
Morinville Canada 53°49N 113°41W 70 C6
Morioka Japan 39°45N 141°8E 30 E10
Moris Mexico 28°10N 108°32W 86 B3
Morlaix France 48°36N 3°52W 20 B2
Mornington Australia 38°15S 145°5E 63 F4
Mornington, I. Chile 49°50S 75°30W 96 F1
Mornington I. Australia 16°30S 139°30E 62 B2
Moro Pakistan 26°40N 68°0E 42 F2
Moro ➜ Pakistan 29°42N 67°22E 42 E2
Moro G. Phil. 6°30N 123°0E 37 C6
Morocco ■ N. Afr. 32°0N 5°50W 50 B4
Morogoro Tanzania 6°50S 37°40E 54 D4
Morogoro ☐ Tanzania 8°0S 37°0E 54 D4
Moroleón Mexico 20°8N 101°12W 86 C4
Morombe Madag. 21°45S 43°22E 57 C7
Moron Argentina 34°39S 58°37W 94 C4
Morón Cuba 22°8N 78°39W 88 B4
Mörön Mongolia 49°38N 100°9E 32 B4
Morón de la Frontera Spain 37°6N 5°28W 21 D3
Morona ➜ Peru 4°40S 77°10W 92 D3
Morondava Madag. 20°17S 44°17E 57 C7
Morongo Valley U.S.A. 34°3N 116°37W 79 L10
Moroni Comoros Is. 11°40S 43°16E 53 a
Moroni U.S.A. 39°32N 111°35W 76 G8
Morotai Indonesia 2°10N 128°30E 37 D7
Moroto Uganda 2°28N 34°42E 54 B3
Moroto, Mt. Uganda 2°30N 34°43E 54 B3
Morpeth Canada 42°23N 81°50W 82 D3
Morpeth U.K. 55°10N 1°41W 12 B6
Morphou Cyprus 35°12N 32°59E 25 D11
Morphou Bay Cyprus 35°15N 32°50E 25 D11
Morrilton U.S.A. 35°9N 92°44W 84 D8
Morrinhos Brazil 17°45S 49°10W 93 G9
Morrinsville N.Z. 37°40S 175°32E 59 B5
Morris Canada 49°25N 97°22W 71 D9
Morris Ill., U.S.A. 41°22N 88°26W 80 E9
Morris Minn., U.S.A. 45°35N 95°55W 80 C6
Morris N.Y., U.S.A. 42°33N 75°15W 83 D9
Morris Pa., U.S.A. 41°35N 77°17W 82 E7
Morris, Mt. Australia 26°9S 131°4E 61 E5
Morris Jesup, Kap Greenland 83°40N 34°0W 66 A16
Morrisburg Canada 44°55N 75°7W 83 B9
Morristown Ariz., U.S.A. 33°51N 112°37W 77 K7
Morristown N.J., U.S.A. 40°48N 74°29W 83 F10
Morristown N.Y., U.S.A. 44°35N 75°39W 83 B9
Morristown Tenn., U.S.A. 36°13N 83°18W 85 C13
Morrisville N.Y., U.S.A. 42°53N 75°35W 83 D9
Morrisville Pa., U.S.A. 40°13N 74°47W 83 F10
Morrisville Vt., U.S.A. 44°34N 72°36W 83 B12
Morro, Pta. Chile 27°6S 71°0W 94 B1
Morro Bay U.S.A. 35°22N 120°51W 78 K6
Morro del Jable Canary Is. 28°3N 14°23W 24 F5
Morro Jable, Pta. de Canary Is. 28°2N 14°20W 24 F5
Morrocoy △ Venezuela 10°48N 68°13W 89 D6
Morrosquillo, G. de Colombia 9°35N 75°40W 88 E4
Morrumbene Mozam. 23°31S 35°16E 57 C6
Morshansk Russia 53°28N 41°50E 18 D7
Morteros Argentina 30°50S 62°0W 94 C3
Mortlach Canada 50°27N 106°4W 71 C7
Mortlake Australia 38°5S 142°50E 63 F3
Morton Tex., U.S.A. 33°44N 102°46W 84 E3
Morton Wash., U.S.A. 46°34N 122°17W 78 D4
Moruga Trin. & Tob. 10°4N 61°16W 93 K15
Morundah Australia 34°57S 146°19E 63 E4
Moruya Australia 35°58S 150°3E 63 F5
Morvan France 47°5N 4°3E 20 C6
Morven Australia 26°22S 147°5E 63 D4
Morvern U.K. 56°38N 5°44W 11 E3
Morwell Australia 38°10S 146°22E 63 F4
Morzhovets, Ostrov Russia 66°44N 42°35E 18 A7
Moscos Is. Burma 14°0N 97°30E 38 F1
Moscow = Moskva Russia 55°45N 37°37E 18 C6
Moscow Idaho, U.S.A. 46°44N 117°0W 76 C5
Moscow Pa., U.S.A. 41°20N 75°31W 83 E9
Mosel ➜ Europe 50°22N 7°36E 20 A7
Moselle = Mosel ➜ Europe 50°22N 7°36E 20 A7
Moses Lake U.S.A. 47°8N 119°17W 76 C4
Mosgiel N.Z. 45°53S 170°21E 59 F3
Moshaweng ➜ S. Africa 26°35S 22°50E 56 D3
Moshchnyy, Ostrov Russia 60°1N 27°50E 9 F22
Moshi Tanzania 3°22S 37°18E 54 C4
Moshupa Botswana 24°46S 25°29E 56 C4
Mosjøen Norway 65°51N 13°12E 8 D15
Moskenesøya Norway 67°58N 13°0E 8 C15
Moskenstraumen Norway 67°47N 12°45E 8 C15
Moskva Russia 55°45N 37°37E 18 C6
Mosomane Botswana 24°2S 26°19E 56 C4
Mosonmagyaróvár Hungary 47°52N 17°18E 17 E9
Mosquera Colombia 2°35N 78°24W 92 C3
Mosquero U.S.A. 35°47N 103°58W 77 J12
Mosquitia Honduras 15°20N 84°10W 88 C3
Mosquito Coast = Mosquitia Honduras 15°20N 84°10W 88 C3
Mosquito Creek L. U.S.A. 41°18N 80°46W 82 E4
Mosquito L. Canada 62°35N 103°20W 71 A8
Mosquitos, G. de los Panama 9°15N 81°10W 88 E3
Moss Norway 59°27N 10°40E 9 G14
Moss Vale Australia 34°32S 150°25E 63 E5
Mossaka Congo 1°15S 16°45E 52 E3
Mossbank Canada 49°56N 105°56W 71 D7
Mossburn N.Z. 45°41S 168°15E 59 F2
Mosselbaai S. Africa 34°11S 22°8E 56 E3
Mossendjo Congo 2°55S 12°42E 52 E2
Mossgiel Australia 33°15S 144°5E 63 E3
Mossman Australia 16°21S 145°15E 62 B4
Mossoró Brazil 5°10S 37°15W 93 E11
Mossuril Mozam. 14°58S 40°42E 55 E5
Most Czech Rep. 50°31N 13°38E 16 C7
Mosta Malta 35°55N 14°26E 25 D1
Mostaganem Algeria 35°54N 0°5E 50 A6
Mostar Bos.-H. 43°22N 17°50E 23 C7
Mostardas Brazil 31°2S 50°51W 95 C5
Mostiska = Mostyska Ukraine 49°48N 23°4E 17 D12
Mosty = Masty Belarus 53°27N 24°38E 17 B13
Mostyska Ukraine 49°48N 23°4E 17 D12
Mosul = Al Mawşil Iraq 36°15N 43°5E 44 B4
Motagua ➜ Guatemala 15°44N 88°14W 88 C2
Motala Sweden 58°32N 15°1E 9 G16
Motaze Mozam. 24°48S 32°52E 57 C5
Moth India 25°43N 78°57E 43 G8
Motherwell U.K. 55°47N 3°58W 11 F5
Motihari India 26°30N 84°55E 43 F11
Motozintla de Mendoza Mexico 15°22N 92°14W 87 D6
Motril Spain 36°31N 3°37W 21 D4
Mott U.S.A. 46°23N 102°20W 80 B2
Motueka N.Z. 41°7S 173°1E 59 D4
Motueka ➜ N.Z. 41°5S 173°1E 59 D4
Motul Mexico 21°6N 89°17W 87 C7
Mouchalagane ➜ Canada 50°56N 68°41W 73 B6
Moudros Greece 39°50N 25°18E 23 E11
Mouila Gabon 1°50S 11°0E 52 E2
Moulamein Australia 35°3S 144°1E 63 F3
Moule à Chique, C. St. Lucia 13°43N 60°57W 89 f
Mouliana Greece 35°10N 25°59E 25 D7
Moulins France 46°35N 3°19E 20 C5
Moulmein Burma 16°30N 97°40E 41 L20
Moulouya, O. ➜ Morocco 35°5N 2°25W 50 B5
Moultrie U.S.A. 31°11N 83°47W 85 F13
Moultrie, L. U.S.A. 33°20N 80°5W 85 E14
Mound City Mo., U.S.A. 40°7N 95°14W 80 E6
Mound City S. Dak., U.S.A. 45°44N 100°4W 80 C3
Moundou Chad 8°40N 16°10E 51 G9
Moundsville U.S.A. 39°55N 80°44W 82 G4
Moung Cambodia 12°46N 103°27E 38 F4
Mount Airy U.S.A. 36°31N 80°37W 85 C14
Mount Albert Canada 44°8N 79°19W 82 B5
Mount Aspiring △ N.Z. 44°19S 168°47E 59 F2
Mount Barker S. Austral., Australia 35°5S 138°52E 63 F2
Mount Barker W. Austral., Australia 34°38S 117°40E 61 F2
Mount Bellew Bridge Ireland 53°28N 8°31W 10 C3
Mount Brydges Canada 42°54N 81°29W 82 D3
Mount Burr Australia 37°34S 140°26E 63 F3
Mount Carmel = Ha Karmel △ Israel 32°45N 35°5E 46 C4
Mount Carmel Ill., U.S.A. 38°25N 87°46W 80 F10
Mount Carmel Pa., U.S.A. 40°47N 76°26W 83 F8
Mount Clemens U.S.A. 42°35N 82°53W 82 D2
Mount Coolon Australia 21°25S 147°25E 62 C4
Mount Darwin Zimbabwe 16°47S 31°38E 55 F3
Mount Desert I. U.S.A. 44°21N 68°20W 81 C19
Mount Dora U.S.A. 28°48N 81°38W 85 G14
Mount Edziza ⌂ Canada 57°30N 130°45W 70 B2
Mount Elgon △ E. Afr. 1°4N 34°42E 54 B3
Mount Field △ Australia 42°39S 146°35E 63 G4
Mount Fletcher S. Africa 30°40S 28°30E 57 E4
Mount Forest Canada 43°59N 80°43W 82 C4
Mount Frankland △ Australia 31°47S 116°37E 60 F2
Mount Gambier Australia 37°50S 140°46E 63 F3
Mount Garnet Australia 17°37S 145°6E 62 B4
Mount Holly U.S.A. 39°59N 74°47W 83 G10
Mount Holly Springs U.S.A. 40°7N 77°12W 82 F7
Mount Hope N.S.W., Australia 32°51S 145°51E 63 E4
Mount Hope S. Austral., Australia 34°7S 135°23E 63 E2
Mount Isa Australia 20°42S 139°26E 62 C2
Mount Jewett U.S.A. 41°44N 78°39W 82 E6
Mount Kaputar △ Australia 30°16S 150°10E 63 E5
Mount Kenya △ Kenya 0°7S 37°21E 54 C4
Mount Kilimanjaro △ Tanzania 3°2S 37°19E 54 C4
Mount Kisco U.S.A. 41°12N 73°44W 83 E11
Mount Laguna U.S.A. 32°52N 116°25W 79 N10
Mount Larcom Australia 23°48S 150°59E 62 C5
Mount Lofty Ranges Australia 34°35S 139°5E 63 E2
Mount Magnet Australia 28°2S 117°47E 61 E2
Mount Maunganui N.Z. 37°40S 176°14E 59 B6
Mount Molloy Australia 16°42S 145°20E 62 B4
Mount Morgan Australia 23°40S 150°25E 62 C5
Mount Morris U.S.A. 42°44N 77°52W 82 D7
Mount Pearl Canada 47°31N 52°47W 73 C9
Mount Penn U.S.A. 40°20N 75°54W 83 F9
Mount Perry Australia 25°13S 151°42E 63 D5
Mount Pleasant Iowa, U.S.A. 40°58N 91°33W 80 E8
Mount Pleasant Mich., U.S.A. 43°36N 84°46W 81 D11
Mount Pleasant Pa., U.S.A. 40°9N 79°33W 82 F5
Mount Pleasant S.C., U.S.A. 32°47N 79°52W 85 E15
Mount Pleasant Tenn., U.S.A. 35°32N 87°12W 85 D11
Mount Pleasant Tex., U.S.A. 33°9N 94°58W 84 E7
Mount Pleasant Utah, U.S.A. 39°33N 111°27W 76 G8
Mount Pocono U.S.A. 41°7N 75°22W 83 E9
Mount Rainier △ U.S.A. 46°55N 121°50W 78 D5
Mount Revelstoke △ Canada 51°5N 118°30W 70 C5
Mount Robson ⌂ Canada 53°0N 119°0W 70 C5
Mount St. Helens ⌂ U.S.A. 46°14N 122°11W 78 D4
Mount Selinda Zimbabwe 20°24S 32°43E 57 C5
Mount Shasta U.S.A. 41°19N 122°19W 76 F2
Mount Signal U.S.A. 32°39N 115°37W 79 N11
Mount Sterling Ill., U.S.A. 39°59N 90°45W 80 F8
Mount Sterling Ky., U.S.A. 38°4N 83°56W 81 F12
Mount Surprise Australia 18°10S 144°17E 62 B3
Mount Union U.S.A. 40°23N 77°53W 82 F7
Mount Upton U.S.A. 42°26N 75°23W 83 D9
Mount Vernon Ill., U.S.A. 38°19N 88°55W 80 F9
Mount Vernon Ind., U.S.A. 37°56N 87°54W 80 G10
Mount Vernon N.Y., U.S.A. 40°54N 73°49W 83 F11
Mount Vernon Ohio, U.S.A. 40°23N 82°29W 82 F2
Mount Vernon Wash., U.S.A. 48°25N 122°20W 78 B4
Mount William △ Australia 40°56S 148°14E 63 G4
Mountain Ash U.K. 51°40N 3°23W 13
Mountain Center U.S.A. 33°42N 116°44W 79 M
Mountain City Nev., U.S.A. 41°50N 115°58W 76
Mountain City Tenn., U.S.A. 36°29N 81°48W 85 C
Mountain Dale U.S.A. 41°41N 74°32W 83 E
Mountain Grove U.S.A. 37°8N 92°16W 80
Mountain Home Ark., U.S.A. 36°20N 92°23W 84
Mountain Home Idaho, U.S.A. 43°8N 115°41W 76
Mountain Iron U.S.A. 47°32N 92°37W 80
Mountain Pass U.S.A. 35°29N 115°35W 79 K
Mountain View Ark., U.S.A. 35°52N 92°7W 84
Mountain View Calif., U.S.A. 37°23N 122°5W 78
Mountain View Hawai'i, U.S.A. 19°33N 155°7W 74
Mountain Zebra △ S. Africa 32°14S 25°27E 56
Mountainair U.S.A. 34°31N 106°15W 77 J
Mountlake Terrace U.S.A. 47°47N 122°18W 78
Mountmellick Ireland 53°7N 7°20W 10
Mountrath Ireland 53°0N 7°28W 10
Moura Australia 24°35S 149°58E 62
Moura Brazil 1°32S 61°38W 92
Moura Portugal 38°7N 7°30W 21
Mourdi, Dépression du Chad 18°10N 23°0E 51 E
Mourilyan Australia 17°35S 146°3E 62
Mourne ➜ U.K. 54°52N 7°26W 10
Mourne Mts. U.K. 54°10N 6°0W 10
Mournies Greece 35°29N 24°1E 25
Mouscron Belgium 50°45N 3°12E 15
Moussoro Chad 13°41N 16°35E 51
Moutong Indonesia 0°28N 121°13E 37
Movas Mexico 28°10N 109°25W 86
Moville Ireland 55°11N 7°3W 10
Mowandjum Australia 17°22S 123°40E 60
Moy ➜ Ireland 54°8N 9°8W 10
Moya Comoros Is. 12°18S 44°18E 5
Moyale Kenya 3°30N 39°0E 54
Moyen Atlas Morocco 33°0N 5°0W 50
Moyo Indonesia 8°10S 117°40E 36
Moyobamba Peru 6°0S 77°0W 92
Moyyero ➜ Russia 68°44N 103°42E 29 C
Moyynqum Kazakhstan 44°12N 71°0E 32
Moyynty Kazakhstan 47°10N 73°18E 28
Mozambique = Moçambique Mozam. 15°3S 40°42E 55
Mozambique ■ Africa 19°0S 35°0E 55
Mozambique Chan. Africa 17°30S 42°30E 57
Mozdok Russia 43°45N 44°48E 19
Mozdūrān Iran 36°9N 60°35E 45
Mozhnābād Iran 34°7N 60°6E 45
Mozyr = Mazyr Belarus 51°59N 29°15E 17 E
Mpanda Tanzania 6°23S 31°1E 54
Mphoengs Zimbabwe 21°10S 27°51E 57
Mpika Zambia 11°51S 31°25E 55
Mpulungu Zambia 8°51S 31°5E 55
Mpumalanga S. Africa 29°50S 30°33E 57
Mpumalanga ☐ S. Africa 26°0S 30°0E 57
Mpwapwa Tanzania 6°23S 36°30E 54
Mqanduli S. Africa 31°49S 28°45E 57
Msaken Tunisia 35°49N 10°33E 51
Msambansovu Zimbabwe 15°50S 30°3E 55
M'sila ➜ Algeria 35°30N 4°29E 50
Msoro Zambia 13°35S 31°50E 55
Mstislavl = Mstsislaw Belarus 54°0N 31°50E 17
Mstsislaw Belarus 54°0N 31°50E 17
Mtama Tanzania 10°17S 39°21E 55
Mtamvuna = Mthamvuna ➜ S. Africa 31°6S 30°12E 57
Mthamvuna ➜ S. Africa 31°6S 30°12E 57
Mthatha S. Africa 31°36S 28°49E 57
Mtilikwe ➜ Zimbabwe 21°9S 31°30E 55
Mtito Andei Kenya 2°41S 38°10E 54
Mtubatuba S. Africa 28°30S 32°8E 57
Mtwalume S. Africa 30°30S 30°38E 57
Mtwara-Mikindani Tanzania 10°20S 40°20E 55
Mu Gia, Deo Vietnam 17°40N 105°47E 38
Mu Ko Chang △ Thailand 11°59N 102°22E 39
Mu Us Shamo China 39°0N 109°0E 34
Muang Chiang Rai = Chiang Rai Thailand 19°52N 99°50E 38
Muang Khong Laos 14°7N 105°51E 38
Muang Lamphun Thailand 18°40N 99°2E 38
Muang Mai Thailand 8°5N 98°21E 3
Muang Pak Beng Laos 19°54N 101°8E 38
Muar Malaysia 2°3N 102°34E 39
Muarabungo Indonesia 1°28S 102°52E 36
Muaraenim Indonesia 3°40S 103°50E 36
Muarajuloi Indonesia 0°12S 114°3E 36
Muarakaman Indonesia 0°2S 116°45E 36
Muaratebo Indonesia 1°30S 102°26E 36
Muaratembesi Indonesia 1°42S 103°8E 36
Muaratewe Indonesia 0°58S 114°52E 36
Mubarakpur India 26°6N 83°18E 43
Mubarraz = Al Mubarraz Si. Arabia 25°30N 49°40E 45
Mubende Uganda 0°33N 31°22E 54
Mubi Nigeria 10°18N 13°16E 51
Mucajaí ➜ Brazil 2°25N 60°52W 92
Muchachos, Roque de los Canary Is. 28°44N 17°52W 24
Muchinga Mts. Zambia 11°30S 31°30E 5
Muck U.K. 56°50N 6°15W 11
Muckadilla Australia 26°35S 148°23E 63

ackle Flugga U.K. 60°51N 0°54W 11 A8
acuri Brazil 18°0S 39°36W 93 G11
acusso Angola 18°1S 21°25E 56 B3
ada Canary Is. 28°34N 13°57W 24 F6
adanjiang China 44°38N 129°30E 35 B15
adanya Turkey 40°25N 28°50E 23 D13
addy Cr. → U.S.A. 38°24N 110°42W 76 G8
adgee Australia 32°32S 149°31E 63 E4
adjatik → Canada 56°1N 107°36W 71 B7
ecate Mozam. 14°55S 39°40E 55 E4
eda Mozam. 11°36S 39°28E 55 E4
eller Ranges
ustralia 18°18S 126°46E 60 C4
ende Mozam. 14°28S 33°0E 55 E3
erto, Mar Mexico 16°10N 94°10W 87 D6
fulira Zambia 12°32S 28°15E 55 E2
fumbiro Range Africa 1°25S 29°30E 54 C2
ghal Sarai India 25°18N 83°7E 43 G10
ghayrā' Si. Arabia 29°17N 37°41E 44 D3
gi Japan 33°40N 134°25E 31 H7
gila, Mts.
em. Rep. of the Congo 7°0S 28°50E 54 D2
ğla Turkey 37°15N 28°22E 23 F13
gu Nepal 29°45N 82°30E 43 E10
hammad, Râs Egypt 27°44N 34°16E 44 E2
hammad Qol Sudan 20°53N 37°9E 51 D13
hammadabad India 26°4N 83°25E 43 F10
hesi → Tanzania 7°0S 35°20E 54 D4
hlhausen Germany 51°12N 10°27E 16 C6
hlig Hofmann fjell
ntarctica 72°30S 5°0E 5 D3
hos Finland 64°47N 25°59E 8 D21
hu Estonia 58°36N 23°11E 9 G20
hutwe Tanzania 1°35S 31°45E 54 C3
Wo China 22°16N 113°59E 33 G10
ne Bheag Ireland 52°42N 6°58W 10 D5
r, L. Australia 34°30S 116°40E 61 F2
r of Ord U.K. 57°32N 4°28W 11 D4
eres, I. Mexico 21°13N 86°43W 88 B2
nak = Muynak
zbekistan 43°44N 59°10E 28 E6
ka, Tanjung Malaysia 5°28N 100°11E 39 c
kacheve Ukraine 48°27N 22°45E 17 D12
kachevo = Mukacheve
kraine 48°27N 22°45E 17 D12
kah Malaysia 2°55N 112°5E 36 D4
kandwara India 24°49N 75°59E 42 G6
kawwa, Geziret
gypt 23°55N 35°53E 44 F2
kdahan Thailand 16°32N 104°43E 38 D5
kden = Shenyang
hina 41°48N 123°27E 35 D12
kerian India 31°57N 75°37E 42 D6
kinbudin Australia 30°55S 118°5E 61 F2
kishi
m. Rep. of the Congo 8°30S 24°44E 55 D1
komuko Indonesia 2°30S 101°10E 36 E2
komwenze
m. Rep. of the Congo 6°49S 27°15E 54 D2
tsar India 30°30N 74°30E 42 D6
ur = Moqor Afghan. 32°50N 67°42E 42 C2
utuwa → Canada 53°10N 97°24W 71 C9
wela Zambia 17°0S 26°40E 55 F2
a Spain 38°3N 1°33W 21 C5
a → Pakistan 27°57N 67°36E 42 F2
ange
m. Rep. of the Congo 3°40S 27°10E 54 C2
anje, Mt. Malawi 16°2S 35°33E 55 F4
chén Chile 37°45S 72°20W 94 D1
le → Germany 51°53N 12°15E 16 C7
e Creek Junction
S.A. 43°23N 104°13W 76 E11
eba Tanzania 1°50S 31°37E 54 C3
egé Mexico 26°53N 111°59W 86 B2
eshoe U.S.A. 34°13N 102°43W 84 D3
grave Canada 45°38N 61°31W 73 C7
nacén Spain 37°4N 3°20W 21 D4
house France 47°40N 7°20E 20 C7
fanua Samoa 13°50S 171°59W 59 b
ng China 44°35N 130°10E 35 B16
U.K. 56°25N 5°56W 11 E3
, Sound of U.K. 56°30N 5°50W 11 E3
aittivu Sri Lanka 9°15N 80°49E 40 Q12
en U.S.A. 42°3N 101°1W 80 D3
ens U.S.A. 37°35N 81°23W 81 G13
er, Pegunungan
onesia 0°30N 113°30E 36 D4
et Pen. Ireland 54°13N 10°2W 10 B1
ewa Australia 28°29S 115°30E 61 E2
gan → Australia 25°0S 139°0E 62 D2
ngar Ireland 53°31N 7°21W 10 C4
ins U.S.A. 34°12N 79°15W 85 D15
umbimby Australia 28°30S 153°30E 63 D5
bezi Zambia 16°45S 25°7E 55 F2
nga Plain Zambia 16°20S 22°40E 53 H4
oy B. Ireland 55°15N 7°46W 10 A4
an Pakistan 30°15N 71°36E 42 D4
mbe, Mts.
n. Rep. of the Congo 8°40S 27°30E 55 D2
ngushi Dam
mbia 14°48S 28°48E 55 E2
ane U.S.A. 37°29N 97°15W 80 G5
bai India 18°56N 72°50E 40 K8
bwa Zambia 15°0S 27°0E 55 F2
ias Kenya 0°20N 34°29E 54 C4
→ Thailand 15°19N 105°30E 38 E5
a Indonesia 5°0S 122°30E 37 F6
abao India 25°45N 70°17E 42 G4
amagi Estonia 57°43N 27°4E 9 H22
can Indonesia 8°34S 115°11E 37 K18
car Indonesia 8°26S 114°20E 37 J17
chen Germany 48°8N 11°34E 16 D6
chen-Gladbach =
nchengladbach
many 51°11N 6°27E 16 C4
cho Lake Canada 59°0N 125°50W 70 B3
ch'ŏn N. Korea 39°14N 127°19E 35 E14
Muncie U.S.A. 40°12N 85°23W 81 E11
Muncoonie L. West
Australia 25°12S 138°40E 62 D2
Mundabbera Australia 25°36S 151°18E 63 D5
Munday U.S.A. 33°27N 99°38W 84 E5
Münden Germany 51°25N 9°38E 16 C5
Mundiwindi Australia 23°47S 120°9E 60 D3
Mundo Novo Brazil 11°50S 40°29W 93 F10
Mundra India 22°54N 69°48E 42 H3
Mundrabilla Australia 31°52S 127°51E 61 F4
Mungallala Australia 26°28S 147°34E 63 D4
Mungallala Cr. →
Australia 28°53S 147°5E 63 D4
Mungana Australia 17°8S 144°27E 62 B3
Mungaoli India 24°24N 78°7E 42 G8
Mungari Mozam. 17°12S 33°30E 55 F3
Mungbere
Dem. Rep. of the Congo 2°36N 28°28E 54 B2
Mungeli India 22°4N 81°41E 43 H9
Munger India 25°23N 86°30E 43 G12
Mungeranie Australia 28°1S 138°39E 63 A2
Mungkan Kandju △
Australia 13°35S 142°52E 62 A3
Munich = München
Germany 48°8N 11°34E 16 D6
Munising U.S.A. 46°25N 86°40W 80 B10
Munku-Sardyk Russia 51°45N 100°20E 29 D11
Munnsville U.S.A. 42°58N 75°35W 83 D9
Muñoz Gamero, Pen.
Chile 52°30S 73°5W 96 G2
Munroe L. Canada 59°13N 98°35W 71 B9
Munsan S. Korea 37°51N 126°48E 35 F14
Münster Germany 51°58N 7°37E 16 C4
Munster □ Ireland 52°18N 8°44W 10 D3
Muntadgin Australia 31°45S 118°33E 61 F2
Muntok Indonesia 2°5S 105°10E 36 E3
Munyama Zambia 16°5S 28°31E 55 F2
Muong Beng Laos 20°23N 101°46E 38 B3
Muong Boum Vietnam 22°24N 102°49E 38 A4
Muong Et Laos 20°49N 104°1E 38 B5
Muong Hai Laos 21°3N 101°49E 38 B3
Muong Hiem Laos 20°5N 103°22E 38 B4
Muong Houn Laos 20°8N 101°23E 38 B3
Muong Hung Vietnam 20°56N 103°53E 38 B4
Muong Kau Laos 15°6N 105°47E 38 E5
Muong Khao Laos 19°38N 103°32E 38 C4
Muong Khoua Laos 21°5N 102°31E 38 B4
Muong Liep Laos 18°29N 101°40E 38 C3
Muong May Laos 14°49N 106°56E 38 E6
Muong Ngeun Laos 20°36N 101°3E 38 B3
Muong Ngoi Laos 20°43N 102°41E 38 B4
Muong Nhie Vietnam 22°12N 102°28E 38 A4
Muong Nong Laos 16°22N 106°30E 38 D6
Muong Ou Tay Laos 22°7N 101°48E 38 A3
Muong Oua Laos 18°18N 101°20E 38 C3
Muong Peun Laos 20°13N 103°52E 38 B4
Muong Phalane Laos 16°39N 105°34E 38 D5
Muong Phieng Laos 19°6N 101°32E 38 C3
Muong Phine Laos 16°32N 106°2E 38 D6
Muong Sai Laos 20°42N 101°59E 38 B3
Muong Saiapoun Laos 18°24N 101°31E 38 C3
Muong Sen Vietnam 19°24N 104°8E 38 C5
Muong Sing Laos 21°11N 101°9E 38 B3
Muong Son Laos 20°27N 103°19E 38 B4
Muong Soui Laos 19°33N 102°52E 38 C4
Muong Va Laos 21°53N 102°19E 38 B4
Muong Xia Vietnam 20°19N 104°50E 38 B5
Muonio Finland 67°57N 23°40E 8 C20
Muonio älv = Muonionjoki →
Finland 67°11N 23°34E 8 C20
Muonioälven = Muonionjoki →
Finland 67°11N 23°34E 8 C20
Muonionjoki → Finland 67°11N 23°34E 8 C20
Muping China 37°22N 121°36E 35 F11
Muqdisho Somali Rep. 2°2N 45°25E 47 G4
Mur → Austria 46°18N 16°52E 17 E9
Murakami Japan 38°14N 139°29E 30 E9
Murallón, Cerro Chile 49°48S 73°30W 96 F2
Muranda Rwanda 1°52S 29°20E 54 C2
Murang'a Kenya 0°45S 37°9E 54 C4
Murashi Russia 59°30N 49°0E 18 C8
Murat → Turkey 38°46N 40°0E 19 G7
Muratlı Turkey 41°10N 27°29E 23 D12
Murayama Japan 38°30N 140°25E 30 E10
Murchison → Australia 27°45S 114°0E 61 E1
Murchison, Mt.
Antarctica 73°25S 166°20E 5 D11
Murchison Falls Uganda 2°15N 31°30E 54 B3
Murchison Falls △
Uganda 2°17N 31°48E 54 B3
Murchison Ra. Australia 20°0S 134°10E 62 C1
Murchison Rapids
Malawi 15°55S 34°35E 55 F3
Murchison Roadhouse
Australia 27°39S 114°14E 61 E1
Murcia Spain 38°5N 1°10W 21 D5
Murcia □ Spain 37°50N 1°30W 21 D5
Murdo U.S.A. 43°53N 100°43W 80 D3
Murdoch Pt. Australia 14°37S 144°55E 62 A3
Mureş → Romania 46°15N 20°13E 17 E11
Mureşul = Mureş →
Romania 46°15N 20°13E 17 E11
Murewa Zimbabwe 17°39S 31°47E 57 B5
Murfreesboro N.C.,
U.S.A. 36°27N 77°6W 85 C16
Murfreesboro Tenn.,
U.S.A. 35°51N 86°24W 85 D11
Murgap Tajikistan 38°10N 74°2E 28 F8
Murgap → Turkmenistan 38°18N 61°12E 45 B9
Murgenella Australia 11°34S 132°56E 60 B5
Murgha Kibzai Pakistan 30°44N 69°25E 42 D3
Murghob = Murgap
Tajikistan 38°10N 74°2E 28 F8
Murgon Australia 26°15S 151°54E 63 D5
Muri India 23°22N 85°52E 43 H11
Muria Indonesia 6°36S 110°53E 37 G14
Muriaé Brazil 21°8S 42°23W 95 A7
Muriel Mine Zimbabwe 17°14S 30°40E 55 F3
Müritz Germany 53°25N 12°42E 16 B7
Murliganj India 25°54N 86°59E 43 G12
Murmansk Russia 68°57N 33°10E 8 B25
Murmashi Russia 68°47N 32°42E 8 B25
Muro Spain 39°44N 3°3E 24 B10
Murom Russia 55°35N 42°3E 18 C7
Muroran Japan 42°25N 141°0E 30 C10
Muroto Japan 33°18N 134°9E 31 H7
Muroto-Misaki Japan 33°15N 134°10E 31 H7
Murphy U.S.A. 43°13N 116°33W 76 E5
Murphys U.S.A. 38°8N 120°28W 78 G6
Murray Ky., U.S.A. 36°37N 88°19W 80 G9
Murray Utah, U.S.A. 40°40N 111°53W 76 F8
Murray → Australia 35°20S 139°22E 63 F2
Murray, L. U.S.A. 34°3N 81°13W 85 D14
Murray Bridge Australia 35°6S 139°14E 63 F2
Murray Fracture Zone
Pac. Oc. 35°0N 130°0W 65 D14
Murray Harbour Canada 46°0N 62°28W 73 C7
Murray River △
Australia 34°23S 140°32E 63 E3
Murraysburg S. Africa 31°58S 23°47E 56 E3
Murree Pakistan 33°56N 73°28E 42 C5
Murrieta U.S.A. 33°33N 117°13W 79 M9
Murrumbidgee →
Australia 34°43S 143°12E 63 E3
Murrumburrah
Australia 34°32S 148°22E 63 E4
Murrurundi Australia 31°42S 150°51E 63 E5
Murshidabad India 24°11N 88°19E 43 G13
Murtle L. Canada 52°8N 119°38W 70 C5
Murtoa Australia 36°35S 142°28E 63 F3
Murungu Tanzania 4°12S 31°10E 54 C3
Mururoa
French Polynesia 21°52S 138°55W 65 K14
Murwara India 23°46N 80°28E 43 H9
Murwillumbah
Australia 28°18S 153°27E 63 D5
Mürzzuschlag Austria 47°36N 15°41E 16 E8
Muş Turkey 38°45N 41°30E 44 B4
Mûsa, Gebel Egypt 28°33N 33°59E 44 D2
Musa Khel Pakistan 30°59N 69°52E 42 D3
Mūsa Qal'eh Afghan. 32°20N 64°50E 40 C4
Musafirkhana India 26°22N 81°48E 43 F9
Musala Bulgaria 42°13N 23°37E 23 C10
Musala Indonesia 1°41N 98°28E 36 D1
Musan N. Korea 42°12N 129°12E 35 C15
Musangu
Dem. Rep. of the Congo 10°28S 23°55E 55 E1
Musasa Tanzania 3°25S 31°30E 54 C3
Musay'īd Qatar 25°0N 51°33E 45 E6
Muscat = Masqat Oman 23°37N 58°36E 47 C6
Muscatine U.S.A. 41°25N 91°3W 80 E8
Muscle Shoals U.S.A. 34°45N 87°40W 85 D11
Musengezi = Unsengedsi →
Zimbabwe 15°43S 31°14E 55 F3
Musgrave Harbour
Canada 49°27N 53°58W 73 C9
Musgrave Ranges
Australia 26°0S 132°0E 61 E5
Mushie
Dem. Rep. of the Congo 2°56S 16°55E 52 E3
Musi → Indonesia 2°20S 104°56E 36 E2
Musina S. Africa 22°20S 30°5E 57 C5
Muskeg → Canada 60°20N 123°20W 70 A4
Muskegon U.S.A. 43°14N 86°16W 80 D10
Muskegon → U.S.A. 43°14N 86°21W 80 D10
Muskegon Heights
U.S.A. 43°12N 86°16W 80 D10
Muskogee U.S.A. 35°45N 95°22W 84 D7
Muskoka, L. Canada 45°0N 79°25W 82 B5
Muskoka Falls Canada 44°59N 79°17W 82 B5
Muskwa → Canada 58°47N 122°48W 70 B4
Muslīmiyah Syria 36°19N 37°12E 44 B3
Musofu Zambia 13°30S 29°0E 55 E2
Musoma Tanzania 1°30S 33°48E 54 C3
Musquaro, L. Canada 50°38N 61°5W 73 B7
Musquodoboit Harbour
Canada 44°50N 63°9W 73 D7
Musselburgh U.K. 55°57N 3°2W 11 F5
Musselshell → U.S.A. 47°21N 107°57W 76 C10
Mussende Angola 10°32S 16°5E 52 G3
Mussoorie India 30°27N 78°6E 42 D8
Mussuco Angola 17°2S 19°3E 56 B2
Mustafakemalpaşa
Turkey 40°2N 28°24E 23 D13
Mustang Nepal 29°10N 83°55E 43 E10
Musters, L. Argentina 45°20S 69°25W 96 F3
Musudan N. Korea 40°50N 129°43E 35 D15
Muswellbrook Australia 32°16S 150°56E 63 E5
Mût Egypt 25°28N 28°58E 51 C11
Mut Turkey 36°40N 33°28E 44 B2
Mutanda Mozam. 21°0S 33°34E 57 C5
Mutanda Zambia 12°24S 26°13E 55 E2
Mutare Zimbabwe 18°58S 32°38E 55 F3
Mutawintji △ Australia 31°10S 142°30E 63 E3
Mutha Kenya 1°48S 38°26E 54 C4
Muting Indonesia 7°23S 140°20E 37 F10
Mutki = Mirtağ Turkey 38°23N 41°56E 44 B4
Mutoko Zimbabwe 17°24S 32°13E 57 B5
Mutomo Kenya 1°51S 38°12E 54 C4
Mutoray Russia 60°56N 101°0E 29 C11
Mutsamudu Comoros Is. 12°10S 44°25E 53 a
Mutshatsha
Dem. Rep. of the Congo 10°35S 24°20E 55 E1
Mutsu Japan 41°5N 140°55E 30 D10
Mutsu-Wan Japan 41°5N 140°55E 30 D10
Muttaburra Australia 22°38S 144°29E 62 C3
Mutton I. Ireland 52°49N 9°32W 10 D2
Mutuáli Mozam. 14°55S 37°0E 55 E4
Muweilih Egypt 30°42N 34°19E 46 E3
Muy Muy Nic. 12°39N 85°36W 88 D2
Muyinga Burundi 3°14S 30°33E 54 C3
Muynak Uzbekistan 43°44N 59°10E 28 E6
Muyunkum, Peski = Moyynqum
Kazakhstan 44°12N 71°0E 32 B2
Muz Tag China 36°25N 87°25E 32 C3
Muzaffarabad Pakistan 34°25N 73°30E 43 B5
Muzaffargarh Pakistan 30°5N 71°14E 42 D4
Muzaffarnagar India 29°26N 77°40E 42 E7
Muzaffarpur India 26°7N 85°23E 43 F11
Muzafirpur Pakistan 30°58N 69°9E 42 D3
Muzhi Russia 65°25N 64°40E 18 A11
Muztagh-Ata China 38°17N 75°7E 32 C2
Mvuma Zimbabwe 19°16S 30°30E 55 F3
Mvurwi Zimbabwe 17°0S 30°57E 55 F3
Mwabvi △ Malawi 16°42S 35°0E 55 F3
Mwadui Tanzania 3°26S 33°32E 54 C3
Mwali = Mohéli
Comoros Is. 12°20S 43°40E 53 a
Mwambo Tanzania 10°30S 40°22E 55 E5
Mwandi Zambia 17°30S 24°51E 55 F1
Mwanza
Dem. Rep. of the Congo 7°55S 26°43E 54 D2
Mwanza Tanzania 2°30S 32°58E 54 C3
Mwanza Zambia 16°58S 24°28E 55 F1
Mwanza □ Tanzania 2°0S 33°0E 54 C3
Mwaya Tanzania 9°32S 33°55E 55 D3
Mweelrea Ireland 53°39N 9°49W 10 C2
Mweka
Dem. Rep. of the Congo 4°50S 21°34E 52 E4
Mwene-Ditu
Dem. Rep. of the Congo 6°35S 22°27E 52 F4
Mwenezi Zimbabwe 21°15S 30°48E 55 G3
Mwenezi → Mozam. 22°40S 31°50E 55 G3
Mwenga
Dem. Rep. of the Congo 3°1S 28°28E 54 C2
Mweru, L. Zambia 9°0S 28°40E 55 D2
Mweru Wantipa △
Zambia 8°39S 29°25E 55 D2
Mweza Range Zimbabwe 21°0S 30°0E 55 G3
Mwilambwe
Dem. Rep. of the Congo 8°7S 25°5E 54 D2
Mwimbi Tanzania 8°38S 31°39E 55 D3
Mwingi Kenya 0°56S 38°4E 54 C4
Mwinilunga Zambia 11°43S 24°25E 55 E1
My Tho Vietnam 10°29N 106°23E 39 G6
Myajlar India 26°15N 70°20E 42 F4
Myanaung Burma 18°18N 95°22E 41 K19
Myanmar = Burma ■
Asia 21°0N 96°30E 41 J20
Myaungmya Burma 16°30N 94°40E 41 L19
Mycenæ = Mikines
Greece 37°43N 22°46E 23 F10
Myeik Kyunzu Burma 11°30N 97°30E 39 G1
Myerstown U.S.A. 40°22N 76°19W 83 F8
Myingyan Burma 21°30N 95°20E 41 J19
Myitkyina Burma 25°24N 97°26E 41 G20
Mykines Færoe Is. 62°7N 7°35W 8 E9
Mykolayiv Ukraine 46°58N 32°0E 19 E5
Mykonos Greece 37°30N 25°25E 23 F11
Mymensingh Bangla. 24°45N 90°24E 41 G17
Mynydd Du U.K. 51°52N 3°50W 13 F4
Mýrdalsjökull Iceland 63°40N 19°6W 8 E4
Myrtle Beach U.S.A. 33°42N 78°53W 85 E15
Myrtle Creek U.S.A. 43°1N 123°17W 76 E2
Myrtle Point U.S.A. 43°4N 124°8W 76 E1
Myrtou Cyprus 35°18N 33°4E 25 D12
Mysia Turkey 39°50N 27°0E 23 E12
Mysore = Karnataka □
India 13°15N 77°0E 40 N10
Mysore India 12°17N 76°41E 40 N10
Mystic U.S.A. 41°21N 71°58W 83 E13
Myszków Poland 50°45N 19°22E 17 C10
Mytishchi Russia 55°50N 37°50E 18 C6
Mývatn Iceland 65°36N 17°0W 8 D5
Mzimba Malawi 11°55S 33°39E 55 E3
Mzimkulu → S. Africa 30°44S 30°28E 57 E5
Mzimvubu → S. Africa 31°38S 29°33E 57 E4
Mzuzu Malawi 11°30S 33°55E 55 E3

N

Na Hearadh = Harris
U.K. 57°50N 6°55W 11 D2
Na Noi Thailand 18°19N 100°43E 38 C3
Na Phao Laos 17°35N 105°44E 38 D5
Na Sam Vietnam 22°3N 106°37E 38 A6
Na San Vietnam 21°12N 104°2E 38 B5
Na Thon Thailand 9°32N 99°56E 39 b
Naab → Germany 49°1N 12°2E 16 D6
Naantali Finland 60°29N 22°2E 9 F20
Naas Ireland 53°12N 6°40W 10 C5
Nababeep S. Africa 29°36S 17°46E 56 D2
Nabadwip = Navadwip
India 23°34N 88°20E 43 H13
Nabawa Australia 28°30S 114°48E 61 E1
Nabberu, L. Australia 25°50S 120°30E 61 E3
Naberezhnyye Chelny
Russia 55°42N 52°19E 18 C9
Nabeul Tunisia 36°30N 10°44E 51 A8
Nabha India 30°26N 76°14E 42 D7
Nabīd Iran 29°40N 57°38E 45 D8
Nabire Indonesia 3°15S 135°26E 37 E9
Nabisar Pakistan 25°8N 69°40E 42 G3
Nabisipi → Canada 50°14N 62°13W 73 B7
Nabiswera Uganda 1°27N 32°15E 54 B3
Nāblus = Nābulus
West Bank 32°14N 35°15E 46 C4
Naboomspruit S. Africa 24°32S 28°40E 57 C4
Nabouwalu Fiji 17°0S 178°45E 59 a
Nābulus West Bank 32°14N 35°15E 46 C4
Nacala-Velha Mozam. 14°32S 40°34E 55 E5
Nacaome Honduras 13°31N 87°30W 88 D2
Nacaroa Mozam. 14°22S 39°56E 55 E4
Naches U.S.A. 46°44N 120°42W 76 C3
Naches → U.S.A. 46°38N 120°31W 78 D6
Nachicapau, L. Canada 56°40N 68°5W 73 A6
Nachingwea Tanzania 10°23S 38°49E 55 E4
Nachna India 27°34N 71°41E 42 F4
Nacimiento, L. U.S.A. 35°46N 120°53W 78 K6
Naco Mexico 31°19N 109°56W 86 A3
Nacogdoches U.S.A. 31°36N 94°39W 84 F7
Nácori Chico Mexico 29°40N 108°57W 86 B3
Nacozari de García
Mexico 30°25N 109°38W 86 A3
Nacula Fiji 16°54S 177°27E 59 a
Nådendal = Naantali
Finland 60°29N 22°2E 9 F20
Nadi Fiji 17°42S 177°20E 59 a
Nadiad India 22°41N 72°56E 42 H5
Nador Morocco 35°14N 2°58W 50 B5
Nadur Malta 36°2N 14°18E 25 C1
Nadūshan Iran 32°2N 53°35E 45 C7
Nadvirna Ukraine 48°37N 24°30E 17 D13
Nadvoitsy Russia 63°52N 34°14E 18 B5
Nadvornaya = Nadvirna
Ukraine 48°37N 24°30E 17 D13
Nadym Russia 65°35N 72°42E 28 C8
Nadym → Russia 66°12N 72°0E 28 C8
Nærbø Norway 58°40N 5°39E 9 G11
Næstved Denmark 55°13N 11°44E 9 J14
Nafpaktos Greece 38°24N 21°50E 23 E9
Nafplio Greece 37°33N 22°50E 23 F10
Naft-e Safīd Iran 31°40N 49°17E 45 D6
Naftshahr Iran 34°0N 45°30E 44 C5
Nafud Desert = An Nafūd
Si. Arabia 28°15N 41°0E 44 D4
Naga Phil. 13°38N 123°15E 37 B6
Nagagami Canada 50°23N 84°20W 72 B3
Nagahama Japan 35°23N 136°16E 31 G8
Nagai Japan 38°6N 140°2E 30 E10
Nagaland □ India 26°0N 94°30E 41 G19
Nagano Japan 36°40N 138°10E 31 F9
Nagano □ Japan 36°15N 138°0E 31 F9
Nagaoka Japan 37°27N 138°51E 31 F9
Nagappattinam India 10°46N 79°51E 40 P11
Nagar → Bangla. 24°27N 89°12E 43 G13
Nagar Parkar Pakistan 24°28N 70°46E 42 G4
Nagasaki Japan 32°47N 129°50E 31 H4
Nagasaki □ Japan 32°50N 129°40E 31 H4
Nagato Japan 34°19N 131°5E 31 G5
Nagaur India 27°15N 73°45E 42 F5
Nagda India 23°27N 75°25E 42 H6
Nagercoil India 8°12N 77°26E 40 Q10
Nagina India 29°30N 78°30E 43 E8
Nagīneh Iran 34°20N 57°15E 45 C8
Nagir Pakistan 36°12N 74°42E 43 A6
Nagles Mts. Ireland 52°8N 8°30W 10 D3
Nagod India 24°34N 80°36E 43 G9
Nagoorin Australia 24°17S 151°15E 62 C5
Nagorno-Karabakh □
Azerbaijan 39°55N 46°45E 44 B5
Nagornyy Russia 55°58N 124°57E 29 D13
Nagoya Japan 35°10N 136°50E 31 G8
Nagpur India 21°8N 79°10E 40 J11
Nagua Dom. Rep. 19°23N 69°50W 89 C6
Naguabo Puerto Rico 18°13N 65°44W 89 d
Nagykanizsa Hungary 46°28N 17°0E 17 E9
Nagykőrös Hungary 47°5N 19°48E 17 E10
Naha Japan 26°13N 127°42E 31 L3
Nahan India 30°33N 77°18E 42 D7
Nahanni △ Canada 61°36N 125°41W 70 A4
Nahanni Butte Canada 61°2N 123°31W 70 A4
Nahargarh Mad. P., India 24°10N 75°14E 42 G6
Nahargarh Raj., India 24°55N 76°50E 42 G7
Nahariyya Israel 33°1N 35°5E 44 C2
Nahāvand Iran 34°10N 48°22E 45 C6
Nahuel Huapi, L.
Argentina 41°0S 71°32W 96 E2
Nahuelbuta △ Chile 37°44S 72°57W 94 D1
Nai Yong Thailand 8°14N 98°22E 39 a
Naicá Mexico 27°53N 105°31W 86 B3
Naicam Canada 52°30N 104°30W 71 C8
Naikoon △ Canada 53°55N 131°55W 70 C2
Naimisharanya India 27°21N 80°30E 43 F9
Naimona'nyi Feng Nepal 30°26N 81°18E 43 D9
Nain Canada 56°34N 61°40W 73 A7
Nā'īn Iran 32°54N 53°0E 45 C7
Naini Tal India 29°30N 79°30E 43 E8
Nainpur India 22°30N 80°10E 43 H9
Nainwa India 25°46N 75°51E 42 G6
Nairai Fiji 17°49S 179°15E 59 a
Nairn U.K. 57°35N 3°53W 11 D5
Nairobi Kenya 1°17S 36°48E 54 C4
Nairobi △ Kenya 1°22S 36°50E 54 C4
Naissaar Estonia 59°34N 24°29E 9 G21
Naitaba Fiji 17°0S 179°16W 59 a
Naivasha Kenya 0°40S 36°30E 54 C4
Naivasha, L. Kenya 0°48S 36°20E 54 C4
Najaf = An Najaf Iraq 32°3N 44°15E 44 C5
Najafābād Iran 32°40N 51°15E 45 C6
Najd Si. Arabia 26°30N 42°0E 47 B3
Najibabad India 29°40N 78°20E 42 E8
Najin N. Korea 42°12N 130°15E 35 C16
Najmah Si. Arabia 26°42N 50°6E 45 E6
Najrān Si. Arabia 17°34N 44°18E 47 D3
Naju S. Korea 35°3N 126°43E 35 G14
Nakadōri-Shima Japan 32°57N 129°4E 31 H4
Nakalagba
Dem. Rep. of the Congo 2°50N 27°58E 54 B2
Nakaminato Japan 36°21N 140°36E 31 F10
Nakamura Japan 32°59N 132°56E 31 H6
Nakano Japan 36°45N 138°22E 31 F9
Nakano-Shima Japan 29°51N 129°52E 31 K4
Nakashibetsu Japan 43°33N 144°59E 30 C12
Nakfa Eritrea 16°40N 38°32E 47 D2
Nakha Yai, Ko Thailand 8°3N 98°28E 39 a
Nakhichevan = Naxçıvan
Azerbaijan 39°12N 45°15E 44 B5
Nakhichevan Rep. = Naxçıvan □
Azerbaijan 39°25N 45°26E 44 B5
Nakhl Egypt 29°55N 33°43E 46 F2
Nakhl-e Taqī Iran 27°28N 52°36E 45 E7
Nakhodka Russia 42°53N 132°54E 30 C6
Nakhon Nayok
Thailand 14°12N 101°13E 38 E3
Nakhon Pathom
Thailand 13°49N 100°3E 38 F3

Nakhon Phanom Thailand 17°23N 104°43E 38 D5
Nakhon Ratchasima Thailand 14°59N 102°12E 38 E4
Nakhon Sawan Thailand 15°35N 100°10E 38 E3
Nakhon Si Thammarat Thailand 8°29N 100°0E 39 H3
Nakhon Thai Thailand 17°5N 100°44E 38 D3
Nakhtarana India 23°20N 69°15E 42 H3
Nakina Canada 50°10N 86°40W 72 B2
Nakodar India 31°8N 75°31E 42 D6
Naktong → S. Korea 35°7N 128°57E 35 G15
Nakuru Kenya 0°15S 36°4E 54 C4
Nakuru, L. Kenya 0°23S 36°5E 54 C4
Nakusp Canada 50°20N 117°45W 70 C5
Nal Pakistan 27°40N 66°12E 42 F2
Nal → Pakistan 25°20N 65°30E 42 G1
Nalázi Mozam. 24°3S 33°20E 57 C5
Nalchik Russia 43°30N 43°33E 19 F7
Nalgonda India 17°6N 79°15E 40 L11
Nalhati India 24°17N 87°52E 43 G12
Naliya India 23°16N 68°50E 42 H3
Nallamalai Hills India 15°30N 78°50E 40 M11
Nalubaale Dam Uganda 0°30N 33°5E 54 B3
Nam Can Vietnam 8°46N 104°59E 39 H5
Nam-ch'on N. Korea 38°15N 126°26E 35 E14
Nam Co China 30°30N 90°45E 32 C4
Nam Dinh Vietnam 20°25N 106°5E 38 B6
Nam Du, Hon Vietnam 9°41N 104°21E 39 H5
Nam Nao △ Thailand 16°44N 101°32E 38 D3
Nam Ngum Res. Laos 18°35N 102°34E 38 C4
Nam-Phan Vietnam 10°30N 106°0E 39 G6
Nam Phong Thailand 16°42N 102°52E 38 D4
Nam Tha Laos 20°58N 101°30E 38 B3
Nam Tok Thailand 14°21N 99°4E 38 E2
Namacunde Angola 17°18S 15°50E 56 B2
Namacurra Mozam. 17°30S 36°50E 57 B6
Namak, Daryācheh-ye Iran 34°30N 52°0E 45 C7
Namak, Kavir-e Iran 34°30N 57°30E 45 C8
Namakzār, Daryācheh-ye Iran 34°0N 60°30E 45 C9
Namaland Namibia 26°0S 17°0E 56 C2
Namanga Kenya 2°33S 36°47E 54 C4
Namangan Uzbekistan 41°0N 71°40E 28 E8
Namapa Mozam. 13°43S 39°50E 55 E4
Namaqualand S. Africa 30°0S 17°25E 56 E2
Namasagali Uganda 1°2N 33°0E 54 B3
Namber Indonesia 1°2S 134°49E 37 E8
Nambour Australia 26°32S 152°58E 63 D5
Nambouwalu = Nabouwalu Fiji 17°0S 178°45E 59 a
Nambucca Heads Australia 30°37S 153°0E 63 E5
Nambung △ Australia 30°30S 115°5E 61 F2
Namcha Barwa China 29°40N 95°10E 32 D4
Namche Bazar Nepal 27°51N 86°47E 43 F12
Namchonjŏm = Nam-ch'on N. Korea 38°15N 126°26E 35 E14
Namecunda Mozam. 14°54S 37°37E 55 E4
Namenalala Fiji 17°8S 179°9E 59 a
Nameponda Mozam. 15°50S 39°50E 55 F4
Nametil Mozam. 15°40S 39°21E 55 F4
Namew L. Canada 54°14N 101°56W 71 C8
Namgia India 31°48N 78°40E 43 D8
Namib Desert Namibia 22°30S 15°0E 56 C2
Namib-Naukluft ⌓ Namibia 24°40S 15°16E 56 C2
Namibe Angola 15°7S 12°11E 53 H2
Namibe □ Angola 16°35S 12°30E 56 B1
Namibia ■ Africa 22°0S 18°9E 56 C2
Namibwoestyn = Namib Desert Namibia 22°30S 15°0E 56 C2
Namlea Indonesia 3°18S 127°5E 37 E7
Namoi → Australia 30°12S 149°30E 63 E4
Nampa U.S.A. 43°34N 116°34W 76 E5
Namp'o N. Korea 38°52N 125°10E 35 E13
Nampō-Shotō Japan 32°0N 140°0E 31 J10
Nampula Mozam. 15°6S 39°15E 55 F4
Namrole Indonesia 3°46S 126°46E 37 E7
Namse Shankou China 30°0N 82°25E 43 E10
Namsen → Norway 64°28N 11°37E 8 D14
Namsos Norway 64°29N 11°30E 8 D14
Namtok Chat Trakan △ Thailand 17°17N 100°40E 38 D3
Namtok Mae Surin △ Thailand 18°55N 98°2E 38 C2
Namtsy Russia 62°43N 129°37E 29 C13
Namtu Burma 23°5N 97°28E 41 H20
Namtumbo Tanzania 10°30S 36°4E 55 E4
Namu Canada 51°52N 127°50W 70 C3
Namuka-i-Lau Fiji 18°53S 178°37W 59 a
Namur Belgium 50°27N 4°52E 15 D4
Namur □ Belgium 50°17N 5°0E 15 D4
Namuruputh Kenya 4°34N 35°57E 54 B4
Namutoni Namibia 18°49S 16°55E 56 B2
Namwala Zambia 15°44S 26°30E 55 F2
Namwon S. Korea 35°23N 127°23E 35 G14
Namyang N. Korea 42°57N 129°52E 35 C15
Nan Thailand 18°48N 100°46E 38 C3
Nan → Thailand 15°42N 100°9E 38 E3
Nan-ch'ang = Nanchang China 28°42N 115°55E 33 D6
Nanaimo Canada 49°10N 124°0W 70 D4
Nanam N. Korea 41°44N 129°40E 35 D15
Nanango Australia 26°40S 152°0E 63 D5
Nanao Japan 37°0N 137°0E 31 F8
Nanchang China 28°42N 115°55E 33 D6
Nanching = Nanjing China 32°2N 118°47E 33 C6
Nanchong China 30°43N 106°2E 32 C5
Nancy France 48°42N 6°12E 20 B7
Nanda Devi India 30°23N 79°59E 43 D8
Nanda Devi △ India 30°30N 79°50E 43 D8
Nanda Kot India 30°17N 80°5E 43 D9
Nandan Japan 34°10N 134°42E 31 G7
Nanded India 19°10N 77°20E 40 K10
Nandewar Ra. Australia 30°15S 150°35E 63 E5
Nandi = Nadi Fiji 17°42S 177°20E 59 a
Nandigram India 22°1N 87°58E 43 H12
Nandurbar India 21°20N 74°15E 40 J9
Nandyal India 15°30N 78°30E 40 M11
Nang Rong Thailand 14°38N 102°48E 38 E4
Nanga-Eboko Cameroon 4°41N 12°22E 52 D2
Nanga Parbat Pakistan 35°10N 74°35E 43 B6
Nangade Mozam. 11°5S 39°36E 55 E4
Nangapinoh Indonesia 0°20S 111°44E 36 E4
Nangarhār □ Afghan. 34°20N 70°0E 40 B7
Nangatayap Indonesia 1°32S 110°34E 36 E4
Nangeya Mts. Uganda 3°30N 33°30E 54 B3
Nangong China 37°23N 115°22E 34 F8
Nanhuang China 36°58N 121°48E 35 F11
Nanjeko Zambia 15°31S 23°30E 55 F1
Nanjing China 32°2N 118°47E 33 C6
Nanjirinji Tanzania 9°41S 39°5E 55 D4
Nankana Sahib Pakistan 31°27N 73°38E 42 D5
Nanking = Nanjing China 32°2N 118°47E 33 C6
Nankoku Japan 33°39N 133°44E 31 H6
Nanlang China 22°30N 113°32E 33 G10
Nanning China 22°48N 108°20E 32 D5
Nannup Australia 33°59S 115°48E 61 F2
Nanpara India 27°52N 81°33E 43 F9
Nanpi China 38°2N 116°45E 34 E9
Nanping China 26°38N 118°10E 33 D6
Nanripe Mozam. 13°52S 38°52E 55 E4
Nansei-Shotō = Ryūkyū-rettō Japan 26°0N 126°0E 31 M3
Nansen Basin Arctic 84°0N 50°0E 4 A10
Nansen Sd. Canada 81°0N 91°0W 69 A10
Nansha China 22°45N 113°34E 33 F10
Nanshan I. S. China Sea 10°45N 115°49E 36 B5
Nansio Tanzania 2°3S 33°4E 54 C3
Nantes France 47°12N 1°33W 20 C3
Nanticoke U.S.A. 41°12N 76°0W 83 E8
Nanton Canada 50°21N 113°46W 70 C6
Nantong China 32°1N 120°52E 33 C7
Nantou China 22°32N 113°55E 33 F10
Nantucket U.S.A. 41°17N 70°6W 81 E18
Nantucket I. U.S.A. 41°16N 70°5W 81 E18
Nantwich U.K. 53°4N 2°31W 12 D5
Nanty Glo U.S.A. 40°28N 78°50W 82 F6
Nanuku Passage Fiji 16°45S 179°15W 59 a
Nanuque Brazil 17°50S 40°21W 93 G10
Nanusa, Kepulauan Indonesia 4°45N 127°1E 37 D7
Nanutarra Roadhouse Australia 22°32S 115°30E 60 D2
Nanyang China 33°11N 112°30E 34 H7
Nanyuki Kenya 0°2N 37°4E 54 B4
Nao, C. de la Spain 38°44N 0°14E 21 C6
Naococane, L. Canada 52°50N 70°45W 73 B5
Napa U.S.A. 38°18N 122°17W 78 G4
Napa → U.S.A. 38°10N 122°19W 78 G4
Napanee Canada 44°15N 77°0W 82 B8
Napanoch U.S.A. 41°44N 74°22W 83 E10
Nape Laos 18°18N 105°6E 38 C5
Nape Pass = Keo Neua, Deo Vietnam 18°23N 105°10E 38 C5
Napier N.Z. 39°30S 176°56E 59 C6
Napier Broome B. Australia 14°2S 126°37E 60 B4
Napier Pen. Australia 12°4S 135°43E 62 A2
Napierville Canada 45°11N 73°25W 83 A11
Naples = Nápoli Italy 40°50N 14°15E 22 D6
Naples U.S.A. 26°8N 81°48W 85 H14
Napo → Peru 3°20S 72°40W 92 D4
Napoleon N. Dak., U.S.A. 46°30N 99°46W 80 B4
Napoleon Ohio, U.S.A. 41°23N 84°8W 81 E11
Nápoli Italy 40°50N 14°15E 22 D6
Napopo Dem. Rep. of the Congo 4°15N 28°0E 54 B2
Naqadeh Iran 36°57N 45°23E 44 B5
Naqb, Ra's an Jordan 29°48N 35°44E 46 F4
Naqqāsh Iran 35°40N 49°6E 45 C6
Nara Japan 34°40N 135°49E 31 G7
Nara Mali 15°10N 7°20W 50 E4
Nara □ Japan 34°30N 136°0E 31 G8
Nara Canal Pakistan 24°30N 69°20E 42 G3
Nara Visa U.S.A. 35°37N 103°6W 77 J12
Naracoorte Australia 36°58S 140°45E 63 F3
Naradhan Australia 33°34S 146°17E 63 E4
Naraini India 25°11N 80°29E 43 G9
Naranjos Mexico 21°21N 97°41W 87 C5
Narasapur India 16°26N 81°40E 41 L12
Narathiwat Thailand 6°30N 101°48E 39 J3
Narayanganj Bangla. 23°40N 90°33E 41 H17
Narayanpet India 16°45N 77°30E 40 L10
Narberth U.K. 51°47N 4°44W 13 F3
Narbonne France 43°11N 3°0E 20 E5
Nardīn Iran 37°3N 55°59E 45 B7
Nardò Italy 40°11N 18°2E 23 D8
Narembeen Australia 32°7S 118°24E 61 F2
Narendranagar India 30°10N 78°18E 42 D8
Nares Str. Arctic 80°0N 70°0W 66 A13
Naretha Australia 31°0S 124°45E 61 F3
Narew → Poland 52°26N 20°41E 17 B11
Nari → Pakistan 28°0N 67°40E 42 F2
Narin Afghan. 36°5N 69°0E 40 A6
Narindra, Helodranon' i Madag. 14°55S 47°30E 57 A8
Narita Japan 35°47N 140°19E 31 G10
Nariva Swamp Trin. & Tob. 10°26N 61°4W 93 K15
Narmada → India 21°38N 72°36E 42 J5
Narnaul India 28°5N 76°11E 42 E7
Narodnaya Russia 65°5N 59°58E 18 A10
Narok Kenya 1°55S 35°52E 54 C4
Narooma Australia 36°14S 150°4E 63 F5
Narowal Pakistan 32°6N 74°52E 42 C6
Narrabri Australia 30°19S 149°46E 63 E4
Narran → Australia 28°37S 148°12E 63 D4
Narrandera Australia 34°42S 146°31E 63 E4
Narrogin Australia 32°58S 117°14E 61 F2
Narromine Australia 32°12S 148°12E 63 E4
Narrow Hills ⌓ Canada 54°0N 104°37W 71 C8
Narsimhapur India 22°54N 79°14E 43 H8
Narsinghgarh India 23°45N 76°40E 42 H7
Naruto Japan 34°11N 134°37E 31 G7
Narva Estonia 59°23N 28°12E 18 C4
Narva → Russia 59°27N 28°2E 9 G23
Narva Bay = Narva Laht Estonia 59°35N 27°35E 9 G22
Narva Laht Estonia 59°35N 27°35E 9 G22
Narvik Norway 68°28N 17°26E 8 B17
Narwana India 29°39N 76°6E 42 E7
Naryan-Mar Russia 67°42N 53°12E 18 A9
Narym Russia 59°0N 81°30E 28 D9
Naryn Kyrgyzstan 41°26N 75°58E 28 E8
Naryn Qum Kazakhstan 47°30N 49°0E 28 E5
Nasa Norway 66°29N 15°23E 8 C16
Nasau Fiji 17°19S 179°27E 59 a
Nasca = Nazca Peru 14°50S 74°57W 92 F4
Naseby N.Z. 45°1S 170°10E 59 F3
Naselle U.S.A. 46°22N 123°49W 78 D3
Naser, Buheirat en Egypt 23°0N 32°30E 51 D12
Nashua Mont., U.S.A. 48°8N 106°22W 76 B10
Nashua N.H., U.S.A. 42°45N 71°28W 83 D13
Nashville Ark., U.S.A. 33°57N 93°51W 84 E8
Nashville Ga., U.S.A. 31°12N 83°15W 85 F13
Nashville Tenn., U.S.A. 36°10N 86°47W 85 C11
Nasik India 19°58N 73°50E 40 K8
Nasirabad India 26°15N 74°45E 42 F6
Nasirabad Pakistan 28°23N 68°24E 42 E3
Nasiri = Ahvāz Iran 31°20N 48°40E 45 D6
Nasiriyah = An Nāṣirīyah Iraq 31°0N 46°15E 44 D5
Naskaupi → Canada 53°47N 60°51W 73 B7
Naṣrābād Iran 34°8N 51°26E 45 C6
Naṣriān-e Pā'īn Iran 32°52N 46°52E 44 C5
Nass → Canada 55°0N 129°40W 70 C3
Nassau Bahamas 25°5N 77°20W 88 A4
Nassau U.S.A. 42°31N 73°37W 83 D11
Nassau, B. Chile 55°20S 68°0W 96 H3
Nasser, L. = Naser, Buheirat en Egypt 23°0N 32°30E 51 D12
Nässjö Sweden 57°39N 14°42E 9 H16
Nastapoka → Canada 56°55N 76°33W 72 A4
Nastapoka, Is. Canada 56°55N 76°50W 72 A4
Nata Botswana 20°12S 26°12E 56 C4
Nata → Botswana 20°14S 26°10E 56 C4
Natal Brazil 5°47S 35°13W 93 E11
Natal Indonesia 0°35N 99°7E 36 D1
Natal Drakensberg ⌓ S. Africa 29°27S 29°30E 57 D4
Naṭanz Iran 33°30N 51°55E 45 C6
Natashquan Canada 50°14N 61°46W 73 B7
Natashquan → Canada 50°7N 61°50W 73 B7
Natchez U.S.A. 31°34N 91°24W 84 F9
Natchitoches U.S.A. 31°46N 93°5W 84 F8
Natewa B. Fiji 16°35S 179°40E 59 a
Nathalia Australia 36°1S 145°13E 63 F4
Nathdwara India 24°55N 73°50E 42 G5
Nati, Pta. Spain 40°3N 3°50E 24 A10
Natimuk Australia 36°42S 142°0E 63 F3
Nation → Canada 55°30N 123°32W 70 B4
National City U.S.A. 32°40N 117°5W 79 N9
Natitingou Benin 10°20N 1°26E 50 F6
Natividad, I. Mexico 27°52N 115°11W 86 B1
Natkyizin Burma 14°57N 97°59E 38 E1
Natron, L. Tanzania 2°20S 36°0E 54 C4
Natrona Heights U.S.A. 40°37N 79°44W 82 F5
Natukanaoka Pan Namibia 18°40S 15°45E 56 B2
Natuna Besar, Kepulauan Indonesia 4°0N 108°15E 36 D3
Natuna Is. = Natuna Besar, Kepulauan Indonesia 4°0N 108°15E 36 D3
Natuna Selatan, Kepulauan Indonesia 2°45N 109°0E 36 D3
Natural Bridge U.S.A. 44°5N 75°30W 83 B9
Natural Bridges ⌓ U.S.A. 37°36N 110°0W 77 H9
Naturaliste, C. Tas., Australia 40°50S 148°15E 63 G4
Naturaliste, C. W. Austral., Australia 33°32S 115°0E 61 F2
Naturaliste Plateau Ind. Oc. 34°0S 112°0E 64 L3
Nau Qala Afghan. 34°5N 68°5E 42 B3
Naugatuck U.S.A. 41°30N 73°3W 83 E11
Naujaat = Repulse Bay Canada 66°30N 86°30W 69 C11
Naumburg Germany 51°9N 11°47E 16 C6
Nauru ■ Pac. Oc. 1°0S 166°0E 58 B9
Naushahra = Nowshera Pakistan 34°0N 72°0E 40 C8
Naushahro Pakistan 26°50N 68°7E 42 F3
Naushon I. U.S.A. 41°29N 70°45W 83 E14
Nausori Fiji 18°2S 178°32E 59 a
Nauta Peru 4°31S 73°35W 92 D4
Nautanwa India 27°20N 83°25E 43 F10
Naute ⌓ Namibia 26°55S 17°57E 56 D2
Nautla Mexico 20°13N 96°47W 87 C5
Nava Mexico 28°25N 100°45W 86 B4
Navadwip India 23°34N 88°20E 43 H13
Navahrudak Belarus 53°40N 25°50E 17 B13
Navajo Res. U.S.A. 36°48N 107°36W 77 H10
Navalmoral de la Mata Spain 39°52N 5°33W 21 C3
Navan = An Uaimh Ireland 53°39N 6°41W 10 C5
Navarin, Mys Russia 62°15N 179°5E 29 C18
Navarino, I. Chile 55°0S 67°40W 96 H3
Navarra □ Spain 42°40N 1°40W 21 A5
Navarre U.S.A. 40°43N 81°31W 82 F3
Navarro → U.S.A. 39°11N 123°45W 78 F3
Navasota U.S.A. 30°23N 96°5W 84 F6
Navassa I. W. Indies 18°30N 75°0W 89 C5
Naver → U.K. 58°32N 4°14W 11 C4
Navibandar India 21°26N 69°48E 42 J3
Navidad Chile 33°57S 71°50W 94 C1
Naviraí Brazil 23°8S 54°13W 95 A5
Naviti Fiji 17°7S 177°15E 59 a
Navlakhi India 22°58N 70°28E 42 H4
Năvodari Romania 44°19N 28°36E 17 F15
Navoi Uzbekistan 40°9N 65°22E 28 E7
Navojoa Mexico 27°6N 109°26W 86 B3
Navolato Mexico 24°47N 107°42W 86 C3
Navsari India 20°57N 72°59E 40 J8
Navua Fiji 18°12S 178°11E 59 a
Nawa Kot Pakistan 28°21N 71°24E 42 E4
Nawab Khan Pakistan 30°17N 69°12E 42 D3
Nawabganj Ut. P., India 26°56N 81°14E 43 F9
Nawabganj Ut. P., India 28°32N 79°40E 43 E8
Nawabshah Pakistan 26°15N 68°25E 42 F3
Nawada India 24°50N 85°33E 43 G11
Nawakot Nepal 27°55N 85°10E 43 F11
Nawalgarh India 27°50N 75°15E 42 F6
Nawanshahr India 32°33N 74°48E 43 C6
Nawar, Dasht-i- Afghan. 33°52N 68°0E 42 C3
Nawoiy = Navoi Uzbekistan 40°9N 65°22E 28 E7
Naxçıvan Azerbaijan 39°12N 45°15E 44 B5
Naxçıvan □ Azerbaijan 39°25N 45°26E 44 B5
Naxos Greece 37°8N 25°25E 23 F11
Nay, Mui Vietnam 12°55N 109°23E 36 B3
Nāy Band Būshehr, Iran 27°20N 52°40E 45 E7
Nāy Band Khorāsān, Iran 32°20N 57°34E 45 C8
Nayakhan Russia 61°56N 159°0E 29 C16
Nayarit □ Mexico 22°0N 105°0W 86 C4
Nayau Fiji 18°6S 178°10E 59 a
Nayoro Japan 44°21N 142°28E 30 B11
Naypyidaw Burma 19°44N 96°12E 38 C1
Nayyāl, W. → Si. Arabia 28°35N 39°4E 44 D3
Nazaré Brazil 13°2S 39°0W 93 F11
Nazareth = Naẓerat Israel 32°42N 35°17E 46 C4
Nazareth U.S.A. 40°44N 75°19W 83 F9
Nazarovo Russia 57°2N 90°40E 29 D10
Nazas Mexico 25°14N 104°8W 86 B4
Nazas → Mexico 25°12N 104°12W 86 B4
Nazca Peru 14°50S 74°57W 92 F4
Nazca Ridge Pac. Oc. 20°0S 80°0W 65 K19
Naze Japan 28°22N 129°27E 31 K4
Naze, The U.K. 51°53N 1°18E 13 F9
Naẓerat Israel 32°42N 35°17E 46 C4
Nāzīk Iran 39°1N 45°4E 44 B5
Nazilli Turkey 37°55N 28°15E 23 F13
Nazko Canada 53°1N 123°37W 70 C4
Nazko → Canada 53°7N 123°34W 70 C4
Nazret Ethiopia 8°32N 39°22E 47 F2
Nchanga Zambia 12°30S 27°49E 55 E2
Ncheu Malawi 14°50S 34°47E 55 E3
Ndala Tanzania 4°45S 33°15E 54 C3
Ndalatando Angola 9°12S 14°48E 52 F2
Ndareda Tanzania 4°12S 35°30E 54 C4
Ndélé C.A.R. 8°25N 20°36E 52 C4
Ndjamena Chad 12°10N 14°59E 51 F8
Ndola Zambia 13°0S 28°34E 55 E2
Ndomo ⌓ S. Africa 26°52S 32°15E 57 D5
Ndoto Mts. Kenya 2°0N 37°0E 54 B4
Nduguti Tanzania 4°18S 34°41E 54 C3
Neagh, Lough U.K. 54°37N 6°25W 10 B5
Neah Bay U.S.A. 48°22N 124°37W 78 B2
Neale, L. Australia 24°15S 130°0E 60 D5
Neales → Australia 28°8S 136°47E 63 D2
Neapoli Greece 35°15N 25°37E 25 D7
Near Is. U.S.A. 52°30N 174°0E 74 E2
Neath U.K. 51°39N 3°48W 13 F4
Neath Port Talbot □ U.K. 51°42N 3°45W 13 F4
Nebine Cr. → Australia 29°27S 146°56E 63 D4
Nebitdag = Balkanabat Turkmenistan 39°30N 54°22E 45 B7
Nebo Australia 21°42S 148°42E 62 C4
Nebraska □ U.S.A. 41°30N 99°30W 80 E4
Nebraska City U.S.A. 40°41N 95°52W 80 E6
Nébrodi, Monti Italy 37°54N 14°35E 22 F6
Necedah U.S.A. 44°2N 90°4W 80 C8
Nechako → Canada 53°55N 122°42W 70 C4
Neches → U.S.A. 29°58N 93°51W 84 G8
Neckar → Germany 49°27N 8°29E 16 D5
Necochea Argentina 38°30S 58°50W 94 D4
Nederland = Netherlands ■ Europe 52°0N 5°30E 15 C5
Needles Canada 49°53N 118°7W 70 D5
Needles U.S.A. 34°51N 114°37W 79 L12
Needles, The U.K. 50°39N 1°35W 13 G6
Neembucú □ Paraguay 27°0S 58°0W 94 B4
Neemuch = Nimach India 24°30N 74°56E 42 G6
Neenah U.S.A. 44°11N 88°28W 80 C9
Neepawa Canada 50°15N 99°30W 71 C9
Neftçala Azerbaijan 39°19N 49°12E 45 B6
Neftegorsk Russia 53°1N 142°58E 29 D15
Neftekumsk Russia 44°46N 44°50E 19 F7
Nefteyugansk Russia 61°5N 72°42E 28 C8
Nefyn U.K. 52°56N 4°31W 12 E3
Negapatam = Nagappattinam India 10°46N 79°51E 40 P11
Negara Indonesia 8°22S 114°37E 37 J17
Negaunee U.S.A. 46°30N 87°36W 80 B10
Negele Ethiopia 5°20N 39°36E 47 F2
Negev Desert = Hanegev Israel 30°50N 35°0E 46 E4
Negombo Sri Lanka 7°12N 79°50E 40 R11
Negotin Serbia 44°16N 22°37E 23 B10
Negra, Pta. Mauritania 22°54N 16°18W 50 D2
Negra, Pta. Peru 6°6S 81°10W 92 E2
Negrais, C. = Maudin Sun Burma 16°0N 94°30E 41 M19
Negril Jamaica 18°22N 78°20W 88 a
Negro → Argentina 41°2S 62°47W 96 E4
Negro → Brazil 3°0S 60°0W 92 D7
Negro → Uruguay 33°24S 58°22W 94 C4
Negros Phil. 9°30N 122°40E 37
Neguac Canada 47°15N 65°5W 73
Nehalem → U.S.A. 45°40N 123°56W 78
Nehāvand Iran 35°56N 49°31E 45
Nehbandān Iran 31°35N 60°5E 45
Nei Monggol Zizhiqu □ China 42°0N 112°0E 34
Neiafu Tonga 18°39S 173°59W 59
Neiges, Piton des Réunion 21°5S 55°29E 53
Neijiang China 29°35N 104°55E 32
Neilingding Dao China 22°25N 113°48E 33 G
Neillsville U.S.A. 44°34N 90°36W 80
Neilton U.S.A. 47°25N 123°53W 76
Neiqiu China 37°15N 114°30E 34
Neiva Colombia 2°56N 75°18W 92
Neixiang China 33°10N 111°52E 34
Nejanilini L. Canada 59°33N 97°48W 71
Nejd = Najd Si. Arabia 26°30N 42°0E 47
Nekā Iran 36°39N 53°19E 45
Nekemte Ethiopia 9°4N 36°30E 47
Neksø Denmark 55°4N 15°8E 9
Nelia Australia 20°39S 142°12E 62
Neligh U.S.A. 42°8N 98°2W 80
Nelkan Russia 57°40N 136°4E 29 D
Nellore India 14°27N 79°59E 40 M
Nelson Canada 49°30N 117°20W 70
Nelson N.Z. 41°18S 173°16E 59
Nelson U.K. 53°50N 2°13W 12
Nelson Ariz., U.S.A. 35°31N 113°19W 77
Nelson Nev., U.S.A. 35°42N 114°49W 79 K
Nelson → Canada 54°33N 98°2W 71
Nelson, C. Australia 38°26S 141°32E 63
Nelson, Estrecho Chile 51°30S 75°0W 96
Nelson Forks Canada 59°30N 124°0W 70
Nelson House Canada 55°47N 98°51W 71
Nelson L. Canada 55°48N 100°7W 71
Nelson Lakes △ N.Z. 41°55S 172°44E 59
Nelspoort S. Africa 32°7S 23°0E 56
Nelspruit S. Africa 25°29S 30°59E 57
Néma Mauritania 16°40N 7°15W 50
Neman = Nemunas → Lithuania 55°25N 21°10E 9
Nemeiben L. Canada 55°20N 105°20W 71
Nemiscau Canada 51°18N 76°54W 72
Nemiscau, L. Canada 51°25N 76°40W 72
Nemunas → Lithuania 55°25N 21°10E 9
Nemuro Japan 43°20N 145°35E 30
Nemuro-Kaikyō Japan 43°30N 145°30E 30
Nen Jiang → China 45°28N 124°30E 35
Nenagh Ireland 52°52N 8°11W 10
Nenasi Malaysia 3°9N 103°23E 39
Nene → U.K. 52°49N 0°11E 13
Nenjiang China 49°10N 125°10E 33
Neno Malawi 15°25S 34°40E 55
Neodesha U.S.A. 37°25N 95°41W 80
Neora Valley △ India 27°0N 88°45E 43
Neosho U.S.A. 36°52N 94°22W 80
Neosho → U.S.A. 36°48N 95°18W 84
Nepal ■ Asia 28°0N 84°30E 43
Nepalganj Nepal 28°5N 81°40E 43
Nepalganj Road India 28°1N 81°41E 43
Nephi U.S.A. 39°43N 111°50W 76
Nephin Ireland 54°1N 9°22W 10
Nephin Beg Range Ireland 54°0N 9°40W 10
Neptune U.S.A. 40°13N 74°2W 83
Neqāb Iran 36°42N 57°25E 45
Nerang Australia 27°58S 153°20E 63
Nerastro, Sarīr Libya 24°20N 20°37E 51
Nerchinsk Russia 52°0N 116°39E 29
Néret, L. Canada 54°45N 70°44W 73
Neretva → Croatia 43°1N 17°27E 23
Neringa Lithuania 55°20N 21°5E 9
Neris → Lithuania 55°8N 24°16E 9
Neryungri Russia 57°38N 124°28E 29
Nescopeck U.S.A. 41°3N 76°12W 8
Neskantaga Canada 52°14N 87°53W 7
Ness, L. U.K. 57°15N 4°32W 11
Ness City U.S.A. 38°27N 99°54W 8
Nesterov Ukraine 50°4N 23°58E 17
Nesvizh = Nyasvizh Belarus 53°14N 26°38E 17
Netanya Israel 32°20N 34°51E 4
Netarhat India 23°29N 84°16E 43
Nete → Belgium 51°7N 4°14E 1
Netherdale Australia 21°10S 148°33E 6
Netherlands ■ Europe 52°0N 5°30E 1
Netherlands Antilles ☒ W. Indies 12°15N 69°0W 9
Netrang India 21°39N 73°21E 4
Nettilling L. Canada 66°30N 71°0W 69
Netzahualcóyotl, Presa Mexico 17°8N 93°35W 8
Neubrandenburg Germany 53°33N 13°15E 1
Neuchâtel Switz. 47°0N 6°55E 2
Neuchâtel, Lac de Switz. 46°53N 6°50E 2
Neufchâteau Belgium 49°50N 5°25E 1
Neumayer Antarctica 71°0S 68°30W 5
Neumünster Germany 54°4N 9°58E 1
Neunkirchen Germany 49°20N 7°9E 1
Neuquén Argentina 38°55S 68°0W 9
Neuquén □ Argentina 38°0S 69°50W 9
Neuruppin Germany 52°55N 12°48E 1
Neuse → U.S.A. 35°6N 76°29W 85
Neusiedler See Austria 47°50N 16°47E 1
Neustrelitz Germany 53°21N 13°4E 1
Neva → Russia 59°56N 30°20E 1
Nevada Iowa, U.S.A. 42°1N 93°27W 8
Nevada Mo., U.S.A. 37°51N 94°22W 8
Nevada □ U.S.A. 39°0N 117°0W 7
Nevada City U.S.A. 39°16N 121°1W 7
Nevado, Cerro Argentina 35°30S 68°32W 9
Nevado de Colima = Volcán de Colima △ Mexico 19°30N 103°40W 8
Nevado de Tres Cruces △ Chile 27°13S 69°5W 9
Nevel Russia 56°0N 29°55E 1

evelsk Russia 46°40N 141°51E 29 E15
evers France 47°0N 3°9E 20 C5
evertire Australia 31°50S 147°44E 63 E4
eville Canada 49°58N 107°39W 71 D7
evinnomyssk Russia 44°40N 42°0E 19 F7
evis St. Kitts & Nevis 17°0N 62°30W 89 C7
evşehir Turkey 38°33N 34°40E 44 B2
evyansk Russia 57°30N 60°13E 18 C11
ew → U.S.A. 38°10N 81°12W 81 F13
ew Aiyansh Canada 55°12N 129°4W 70 B3
ew Albany Ind., U.S.A. 38°18N 85°49W 81 F11
ew Albany Miss., U.S.A. 34°29N 89°0W 85 D10
ew Albany Pa., U.S.A. 41°36N 76°27W 83 E8
ew Amsterdam Guyana 6°15N 57°36W 92 B7
ew Angledool Australia 29°5S 147°55E 63 D4
ew Baltimore U.S.A. 42°41N 82°44W 82 D2
ew Bedford U.S.A. 41°38N 70°56W 83 E14
ew Berlin N.Y., U.S.A. 42°37N 75°20W 83 D9
ew Berlin Pa., U.S.A. 40°50N 76°57W 82 F8
w Bern U.S.A. 35°7N 77°3W 85 D16
w Bethlehem U.S.A. 41°0N 79°20W 82 F5
w Bight Bahamas 24°19N 75°24W 89 B4
w Bloomfield U.S.A. 40°25N 77°11W 82 F7
w Boston U.S.A. 33°28N 94°25W 84 E7
w Braunfels U.S.A. 29°42N 98°8W 84 G5
w Brighton N.Z. 43°29S 172°43E 59 E4
w Brighton U.S.A. 40°42N 80°19W 82 F4
w Britain Papua N. G. 5°50S 150°20E 58 B8
w Britain U.S.A. 41°40N 72°47W 83 E12
w Brunswick U.S.A. 40°30N 74°27W 83 F10
w Brunswick □ Canada 46°50N 66°30W 73 C6
w Caledonia ⊠ Pac. Oc. 21°0S 165°0E 58 D9
w Caledonia Trough Pac. Oc. 30°0S 165°0E 64 L8
w Castile = Castilla-La Mancha □ Spain 39°30N 3°30W 21 C4
w Castle Ind., U.S.A. 39°55N 85°22W 81 F11
w Castle Pa., U.S.A. 41°0N 80°21W 82 F4
w City U.S.A. 41°9N 73°59W 83 E11
w Concord U.S.A. 39°59N 81°54W 82 G3
w Cumberland U.S.A. 40°30N 80°36W 82 F4
w Cuyama U.S.A. 34°57N 119°38W 79 L7
w Delhi India 28°36N 77°11E 42 E7
w Denver Canada 50°0N 117°25W 70 D5
w Don Pedro Res. U.S.A. 37°43N 120°24W 78 H6
w England U.S.A. 43°0N 71°0W 75 B12
w England N. Dak., U.S.A. 46°32N 102°52W 80 B2
w England Ra. Australia 30°20S 151°45E 63 E5
w Forest △ U.K. 50°53N 1°34W 13 G6
w Galloway U.K. 55°5N 4°9W 11 F4
v Glasgow Canada 45°35N 62°36W 73 C7
v Guinea Oceania 4°0S 136°0E 58 B6
v Hamburg Canada 43°23N 80°42W 82 C4
v Hampshire □ U.S.A. 44°0N 71°30W 83 C13
v Hampton U.S.A. 43°3N 92°19W 80 D7
v Hanover S. Africa 29°22S 30°31E 57 D5
v Hartford U.S.A. 43°4N 75°18W 83 C9
v Haven Conn., U.S.A. 41°18N 72°55W 83 E12
v Haven Mich., U.S.A. 42°44N 82°48W 82 D2
v Haven N.Y., U.S.A. 43°28N 76°18W 83 C8
v Hazelton Canada 55°20N 127°30W 70 B3
v Hebrides = Vanuatu ■ Pac. Oc. 15°0S 168°0E 58 C9
v Holland U.S.A. 40°6N 76°5W 83 F8
v Iberia U.S.A. 30°1N 91°49W 84 F9
v Ireland Papua N. G. 3°20S 151°50E 58 B8
v Jersey □ U.S.A. 40°0N 74°30W 81 F16
v Kensington U.S.A. 40°34N 79°46W 82 F5
Lexington U.S.A. 39°43N 82°13W 81 F12
Liskeard Canada 47°31N 79°41W 72 C4
London Conn., U.S.A. 41°22N 72°6W 83 E12
London Ohio, U.S.A. 41°5N 82°24W 82 E2
London Wis., U.S.A. 44°23N 88°45W 80 C9
Madrid U.S.A. 36°36N 89°32W 80 G9
Martinsville U.S.A. 39°39N 80°52W 81 F13
Meadows U.S.A. 44°58N 116°18W 76 D5
Melones L. U.S.A. 37°57N 120°31W 78 H6
Mexico □ U.S.A. 34°30N 106°0W 77 J11
Milford Conn., U.S.A. 41°35N 73°25W 83 E11
Milford Pa., U.S.A. 41°52N 75°44W 83 E9
Moore I. Ind. Oc. 21°37N 89°10E 43 J13
Norcia Australia 30°57S 116°13E 61 F2
Norfolk Australia 42°46S 147°2E 63 G4
Orleans U.S.A. 29°57N 90°4W 85 G9
Philadelphia U.S.A. 40°30N 81°27W 82 F3
Plymouth N.Z. 39°4S 174°5E 59 C5
Plymouth U.S.A. 43°58N 116°49W 76 E5
Port Richey U.S.A. 28°16N 82°43W 85 G13
Providence Bahamas 25°25N 78°35W 88 A4
Quay U.K. 52°13N 4°21W 13 E3
Radnor U.K. 52°15N 3°9W 13 E4
Richmond Canada 48°15N 65°45W 73 C6
Richmond U.S.A. 45°7N 92°32W 80 C7
River Gorge ⌂ U.S.A. 37°53N 81°5W 81 G13
Roads U.S.A. 30°42N 91°26W 84 F9
Rochelle U.S.A. 40°55N 73°46W 83 F11
Rockford U.S.A. 47°41N 99°8W 80 B4
Romney U.K. 50°59N 0°57E 13 G8
Ross Ireland 52°23N 6°57W 10 D5
New Salem U.S.A. 46°51N 101°25W 80 B3
New Scone = Scone U.K. 56°25N 3°24W 11 E5
New Siberian I. = Novaya Sibir, Ostrov Russia 75°10N 150°0E 29 B16
New Siberian Is. = Novosibirskiye Ostrova Russia 75°0N 142°0E 29 B15
New Smyrna Beach U.S.A. 29°1N 80°56W 85 G14
New South Wales □ Australia 33°0S 146°0E 63 E4
New Tecumseth = Alliston Canada 44°9N 79°52W 82 B5
New Town U.S.A. 47°59N 102°30W 80 B2
New Tredegar U.K. 51°44N 3°16W 13 F4
New Ulm U.S.A. 44°19N 94°28W 80 C6
New Waterford Canada 46°13N 60°4W 73 C7
New Westminster Canada 49°13N 122°55W 78 A4
New York U.S.A. 40°43N 74°0W 83 F11
New York □ U.S.A. 43°0N 75°0W 83 D9
New York J.F. Kennedy Int. ✈ (JFK) U.S.A. 40°38N 73°47W 83 F11
New Zealand ■ Oceania 40°0S 176°0E 59 D6
Newaj → India 24°24N 76°49E 42 G7
Newala Tanzania 10°58S 39°18E 55 E4
Newark Del., U.S.A. 39°41N 75°46W 81 F16
Newark N.J., U.S.A. 40°44N 74°10W 83 F10
Newark N.Y., U.S.A. 43°3N 77°6W 82 C7
Newark Ohio, U.S.A. 40°3N 82°24W 82 F2
Newark Liberty Int. ✈ (EWR) U.S.A. 40°42N 74°10W 83 F10
Newark-on-Trent U.K. 53°5N 0°48W 12 D7
Newark Valley U.S.A. 42°14N 76°11W 83 D8
Newberg U.S.A. 45°18N 122°58W 76 D2
Newberry Mich., U.S.A. 46°21N 85°30W 80 B11
Newberry S.C., U.S.A. 34°17N 81°37W 85 D14
Newberry Springs U.S.A. 34°50N 116°41W 79 L10
Newboro L. Canada 44°38N 76°20W 83 B8
Newbridge = Droichead Nua Ireland 53°11N 6°48W 10 C5
Newburgh Canada 44°19N 76°52W 82 B8
Newburgh U.S.A. 41°30N 74°1W 83 E10
Newbury U.K. 51°24N 1°20W 13 F6
Newbury N.H., U.S.A. 43°19N 72°3W 83 B12
Newbury Vt., U.S.A. 44°5N 72°4W 83 B12
Newburyport U.S.A. 42°49N 70°53W 83 D14
Newcastle Australia 33°0S 151°46E 63 E5
Newcastle N.B., Canada 47°1N 65°38W 73 C6
Newcastle Ont., Canada 43°55N 78°35W 72 D4
Newcastle S. Africa 27°45S 29°58E 57 D4
Newcastle U.K. 54°13N 5°54W 10 B6
Newcastle Calif., U.S.A. 38°53N 121°8W 78 G5
Newcastle Wyo., U.S.A. 43°50N 104°11W 76 E11
Newcastle Emlyn U.K. 52°2N 4°28W 13 E3
Newcastle Ra. Australia 15°45S 130°15E 60 C5
Newcastle-under-Lyme U.K. 53°1N 2°14W 12 D5
Newcastle-upon-Tyne U.K. 54°58N 1°36W 12 C6
Newcastle Waters Australia 17°30S 133°28E 62 B1
Newcastle West Ireland 52°27N 9°3W 10 D2
Newcomb U.S.A. 43°58N 74°10W 83 C10
Newcomerstown U.S.A. 40°16N 81°36W 82 F3
Newdegate Australia 33°6S 119°0E 61 F2
Newell Australia 16°20S 145°16E 62 B4
Newell U.S.A. 44°43N 103°25W 80 C2
Newfane U.S.A. 43°17N 78°43W 82 C6
Newfield U.S.A. 42°18N 76°33W 83 D8
Newfound L. U.S.A. 43°40N 71°47W 83 C13
Newfoundland Canada 49°0N 55°0W 73 C8
Newfoundland U.S.A. 41°18N 75°19W 83 E9
Newfoundland & Labrador □ Canada 53°0N 58°0W 73 B8
Newhaven U.K. 50°47N 0°3E 13 G8
Newkirk U.S.A. 36°53N 97°3W 84 C6
Newlyn U.K. 50°6N 5°34W 13 G2
Newman Australia 23°18S 119°45E 60 D2
Newman U.S.A. 37°19N 121°1W 78 H5
Newmarket Canada 44°3N 79°28W 82 B5
Newmarket Ireland 52°13N 9°0W 10 D2
Newmarket U.K. 52°15N 0°25E 13 E8
Newmarket U.S.A. 43°5N 70°56W 83 C14
Newnan U.S.A. 33°23N 84°48W 85 E12
Newport Ireland 53°53N 9°33W 10 C2
Newport I. of W., U.K. 50°42N 1°17W 13 G6
Newport Newport, U.K. 51°35N 3°0W 13 F5
Newport Ark., U.S.A. 35°37N 91°16W 84 D9
Newport Ky., U.S.A. 39°5N 84°29W 81 F11
Newport N.H., U.S.A. 43°22N 72°10W 83 C12
Newport N.Y., U.S.A. 43°11N 75°1W 83 C9
Newport Oreg., U.S.A. 44°39N 124°3W 76 D1
Newport Pa., U.S.A. 40°29N 77°8W 82 F7
Newport R.I., U.S.A. 41°29N 71°19W 83 E13
Newport Tenn., U.S.A. 35°58N 83°11W 85 D13
Newport Vt., U.S.A. 44°56N 72°13W 83 B12
Newport Wash., U.S.A. 48°11N 117°3W 76 B5
Newport □ U.K. 51°33N 3°1W 13 F4
Newport Beach U.S.A. 33°37N 117°56W 79 M9
Newport News U.S.A. 36°58N 76°25W 81 G15
Newport Pagnell U.K. 52°5N 0°43W 13 E7
Newquay U.K. 50°25N 5°6W 13 G2
Newry U.K. 54°11N 6°21W 10 B5
Newton Ill., U.S.A. 38°59N 88°10W 80 F9
Newton Iowa, U.S.A. 41°42N 93°3W 80 E7
Newton Kans., U.S.A. 38°3N 97°21W 80 F5
Newton Mass., U.S.A. 42°21N 71°12W 83 D13
Newton Miss., U.S.A. 32°19N 89°10W 85 E10
Newton N.C., U.S.A. 35°40N 81°13W 85 D14
Newton N.J., U.S.A. 41°3N 74°45W 83 E10
Newton Tex., U.S.A. 30°51N 93°46W 84 F8
Newton Abbot U.K. 50°32N 3°37W 13 G4
Newton Aycliffe U.K. 54°37N 1°34W 12 C6
Newton Falls N.Y., U.S.A. 44°12N 74°59W 83 B10
Newton Falls Ohio, U.S.A. 41°11N 80°59W 82 E4
Newton Stewart U.K. 54°57N 4°30W 11 G4
Newtonmore U.K. 57°4N 4°8W 11 D4
Newtown U.K. 52°31N 3°19W 13 E4
Newtownabbey U.K. 54°40N 5°56W 10 B6
Newtownards U.K. 54°36N 5°42W 10 B6
Newtownbarry = Bunclody Ireland 52°39N 6°40W 10 D5
Newtownstewart U.K. 54°43N 7°23W 10 B4
Newville U.S.A. 40°10N 77°24W 82 F7
Neya Russia 58°21N 43°49E 18 C7
Neyrīz Iran 29°15N 54°19E 45 D7
Neyshābūr Iran 36°10N 58°50E 45 B8
Nezhin = Nizhyn Ukraine 51°5N 31°55E 19 D5
Nezperce U.S.A. 46°14N 116°14W 76 C5
Ngabang Indonesia 0°23N 109°55E 36 D3
Ngabordamlu, Tanjung Indonesia 6°56S 134°11E 37 F8
N'Gage Angola 7°46S 15°15E 52 F3
Ngami Depression Botswana 20°30S 22°46E 56 C3
Ngamo Zimbabwe 19°3S 27°32E 55 F2
Nganglong Kangri China 33°0N 81°0E 43 C9
Ngao Thailand 18°46N 99°59E 38 C2
Ngaoundéré Cameroon 7°15N 13°35E 52 C2
Ngapara N.Z. 44°57S 170°46E 59 F3
Ngara Tanzania 2°29S 30°40E 54 C3
Ngawi Indonesia 7°24S 111°26E 37 G14
Ngcobo S. Africa 31°37S 28°0E 57 E4
Nghia Lo Vietnam 21°33N 104°28E 38 B5
Ngoma Malawi 13°8S 33°45E 55 E3
Ngomahura Zimbabwe 20°26S 30°43E 55 G3
Ngomba Tanzania 8°20S 32°53E 55 D3
Ngomeni, Ras Kenya 2°59S 40°14E 54 C5
Ngong Kenya 1°22S 36°39E 54 C4
Ngoring Hu China 34°55N 97°5E 32 C4
Ngorongoro Tanzania 3°11S 35°32E 54 C4
Ngorongoro ⌂ Tanzania 2°40S 35°30E 54 C4
Ngozi Burundi 2°54S 29°50E 54 C2
Ngudu Tanzania 2°58S 33°25E 54 C3
Nguigmi Niger 14°20N 13°20E 51 F8
Nguiu Australia 11°46S 130°38E 60 B5
Ngukurr Australia 14°44S 134°44E 62 A1
Ngunga Tanzania 3°37S 33°37E 54 C3
Nguru Nigeria 12°56N 10°29E 51 F8
Nguru Mts. Tanzania 6°0S 37°30E 54 D4
Ngusi Malawi 14°0S 34°50E 55 E3
Nguyen Binh Vietnam 22°39N 105°56E 38 A5
Nha Trang Vietnam 12°16N 109°10E 39 F7
Nhacoongo Mozam. 24°18S 35°14E 57 C6
Nhamaabué Mozam. 17°25S 35°5E 55 F4
Nhamundá → Brazil 2°12S 56°41W 93 D7
Nhangulaze, L. Mozam. 24°0S 34°30E 57 C5
Nhill Australia 36°18S 141°40E 63 F3
Nho Quan Vietnam 20°18N 105°45E 38 B5
Nhulunbuy Australia 12°10S 137°20E 62 A2
Nia-nia Dem. Rep. of the Congo 1°30N 27°40E 54 B2
Niagara Falls Canada 43°7N 79°5W 82 C5
Niagara Falls U.S.A. 43°5N 79°4W 82 C6
Niagara-on-the-Lake Canada 43°15N 79°4W 82 C5
Niah Malaysia 3°58N 113°46E 36 D4
Niamey Niger 13°27N 2°6E 50 F6
Niangara Dem. Rep. of the Congo 3°42N 27°50E 54 B2
Niantic U.S.A. 41°20N 72°11W 83 E12
Nias Indonesia 1°0N 97°30E 36 D1
Niassa □ Mozam. 13°30S 36°0E 55 E4
Niassa ⌂ Mozam. 12°4S 36°57E 55 E4
Nibāk Si. Arabia 24°25N 50°50E 45 E7
Nicaragua ■ Cent. Amer. 11°40N 85°30W 88 D2
Nicaragua, L. de Nic. 12°0N 85°30W 88 D2
Nicastro Italy 38°59N 16°19E 22 E7
Nice France 43°42N 7°14E 20 E7
Niceville U.S.A. 30°31N 86°30W 85 F11
Nichicun, L. Canada 53°5N 71°0W 73 B5
Nichinan Japan 31°38N 131°23E 31 J5
Nicholás, Canal W. Indies 23°30N 80°5W 88 B3
Nicholasville U.S.A. 37°53N 84°34W 81 G11
Nichols U.S.A. 42°1N 76°22W 83 D8
Nicholson Australia 18°2S 128°54E 60 C4
Nicholson U.S.A. 41°37N 75°47W 83 E9
Nicholson → Australia 17°31S 139°36E 62 B2
Nicholson L. Canada 62°40N 102°40W 71 A8
Nicholson Ra. Australia 27°15S 116°45E 61 E2
Nicholville U.S.A. 44°41N 74°39W 83 B10
Nicobar Is. Ind. Oc. 8°0N 93°30E 27 H11
Nicola Canada 50°12N 120°40W 70 C4
Nicolls Town Bahamas 25°8N 78°0W 88 A4
Nicosia Cyprus 35°10N 33°25E 25 D12
Nicoya Costa Rica 10°9N 85°27W 88 D2
Nicoya, G. de Costa Rica 10°0N 85°0W 88 E3
Nicoya, Pen. de Costa Rica 9°45N 85°40W 88 E2
Nidd → U.K. 53°59N 1°23W 12 D6
Niedersachsen □ Germany 52°50N 9°0E 16 B5
Niekerkshoop S. Africa 29°19S 22°51E 56 D3
Niemba Dem. Rep. of the Congo 5°58S 28°24E 54 D2
Niemen = Nemunas → Lithuania 55°25N 21°10E 9 J19
Nienburg Germany 52°39N 9°13E 16 B5
Nieu Bethesda S. Africa 31°51S 24°34E 56 E3
Nieuw Amsterdam Suriname 5°53N 55°5W 93 B7
Nieuw Nickerie Suriname 6°0N 56°59W 93 B7
Nieuwoudtville S. Africa 31°23S 19°7E 56 E2
Nieuwpoort Belgium 51°8N 2°45E 15 C2
Nieves, Pico de las Canary Is. 27°57N 15°35W 24 G4
Niğde Turkey 37°58N 34°40E 44 B2
Nigel S. Africa 26°27S 28°25E 57 D4
Niger ■ W. Afr. 17°30N 10°0E 50 E7
Niger → W. Afr. 5°33N 6°33E 50 G7
Nigeria ■ W. Afr. 8°30N 8°0E 50 G7
Nighasin India 28°14N 80°52E 43 E9
Nightcaps N.Z. 45°57S 168°2E 59 F2
Nihon = Japan ■ Asia 36°0N 136°0E 31 G8
Nii-Jima Japan 34°20N 139°15E 31 G9
Niigata Japan 37°58N 139°0E 30 F9
Niigata □ Japan 37°15N 138°45E 31 F9
Niihama Japan 33°55N 133°16E 31 H6
Ni'ihau U.S.A. 21°54N 160°9W 74 b
Niimi Japan 34°59N 133°28E 31 G6
Niitsu Japan 37°48N 139°7E 30 F9
Nijil Jordan 30°32N 35°33E 46 E4
Nijkerk Neths. 52°13N 5°30E 15 B5
Nijmegen Neths. 51°50N 5°52E 15 C5
Nijverdal Neths. 52°22N 6°28E 15 B6
Nīk Pey Iran 36°50N 48°10E 45 B6
Nikel Russia 69°24N 30°13E 8 B24
Nikiniki Indonesia 9°49S 124°30E 37 F6
Nikkō Japan 36°45N 139°35E 31 F9
Nikkō △ Japan 36°56N 139°37E 31 F9
Nikolayev = Mykolayiv Ukraine 46°58N 32°0E 19 E5
Nikolayevsk Russia 50°0N 45°35E 19 E8
Nikolayevsk-na-Amur Russia 53°8N 140°44E 29 D15
Nikolskoye Russia 55°12N 166°0E 29 D17
Nikopol Ukraine 47°35N 34°25E 19 E5
Nīkshahr Iran 26°15N 60°10E 45 E9
Nikšić Montenegro 42°50N 18°57E 23 C8
Nîl, Nahr en → Africa 30°10N 31°6E 51 B12
Nîl el Abyad → Sudan 15°38N 32°31E 51 E12
Nîl el Azraq → Sudan 15°38N 32°31E 51 E12
Nila Indonesia 6°44S 129°31E 37 F7
Niland U.S.A. 33°14N 115°31W 79 M11
Nile = Nîl, Nahr en → Africa 30°10N 31°6E 51 B12
Niles Mich., U.S.A. 41°50N 86°15W 80 E10
Niles Ohio, U.S.A. 41°11N 80°46W 82 E4
Nim Ka Thana India 27°44N 75°48E 42 F6
Nimach India 24°30N 74°56E 42 G6
Nimbahera India 24°37N 74°45E 42 G6
Nîmes France 43°50N 4°23E 20 E6
Nimfaíon, Ákra = Pines, Akra Greece 40°5N 24°20E 23 D11
Nimmitabel Australia 36°29S 149°15E 63 F4
Nīnawá Iraq 36°25N 43°10E 44 B4
Nīnawá □ Iraq 36°15N 43°0E 44 B4
Nindigully Australia 28°21S 148°50E 63 D4
Ninepin Group China 22°16N 114°21E 33 G11
Nineveh = Nīnawá Iraq 36°25N 43°10E 44 B4
Ning Xian China 35°30N 107°58E 34 G4
Ningaloo ⌂ Australia 22°23S 113°32E 60 D1
Ning'an China 44°22N 129°20E 35 B15
Ningbo China 29°51N 121°28E 33 D7
Ningcheng China 41°32N 119°53E 35 D10
Ningjin China 37°35N 114°57E 34 F8
Ningjing Shan China 30°0N 98°20E 32 C4
Ningling China 34°25N 115°22E 34 G8
Ningpo = Ningbo China 29°51N 121°28E 33 D7
Ningqiang China 32°47N 106°15E 34 H4
Ningshan China 33°21N 108°21E 34 H5
Ningsia Hui A.R. = Ningxia Huizu Zizhiqu □ China 38°0N 106°0E 34 F4
Ningwu China 39°0N 112°18E 34 E7
Ningxia Huizu Zizhiqu □ China 38°0N 106°0E 34 F4
Ningyang China 35°47N 116°45E 34 G9
Ninh Binh Vietnam 20°15N 105°55E 38 B5
Ninh Giang Vietnam 20°44N 106°24E 38 B6
Ninh Hoa Vietnam 12°30N 109°7E 38 F7
Ninh Ma Vietnam 12°48N 109°21E 38 F7
Ninove Belgium 50°51N 4°2E 15 D4
Nioaque Brazil 21°5S 55°50W 95 A4
Niobrara U.S.A. 42°45N 98°2W 80 D4
Niobrara → U.S.A. 42°46N 98°3W 80 D4
Nioro du Sahel Mali 15°15N 9°30W 50 E4
Niort France 46°19N 0°29W 20 C3
Nipawin Canada 53°20N 104°0W 71 C8
Nipigon Canada 49°0N 88°17W 72 C2
Nipigon, L. Canada 49°50N 88°30W 72 C2
Nipishish L. Canada 54°12N 60°45W 73 B7
Nipissing, L. Canada 46°20N 80°0W 72 C4
Nipomo U.S.A. 35°3N 120°29W 79 K6
Nippon = Japan ■ Asia 36°0N 136°0E 31 G8
Nipton U.S.A. 35°28N 115°16W 79 K11
Niquelândia Brazil 14°33S 48°23W 93 F9
Nīr Iran 38°2N 47°59E 44 B5
Nirasaki Japan 35°42N 138°27E 31 G9
Nirmal India 19°3N 78°20E 40 K11
Nirmali India 26°20N 86°35E 43 F12
Niš Serbia 43°19N 21°58E 23 C9
Nişāb Si. Arabia 29°11N 44°43E 44 D5
Nişāb Yemen 14°25N 46°29E 47 E4
Nishinomiya Japan 34°45N 135°20E 31 G7
Nishino'omote Japan 30°43N 130°59E 31 J5
Nishiwaki Japan 34°59N 134°58E 31 G7
Niskibi → Canada 56°29N 88°9W 72 A2
Nisqually → U.S.A. 47°7N 122°42W 78 C4
Nissaki Greece 39°43N 19°52E 25 A3
Nissum Bredning Denmark 56°40N 8°20E 9 H13
Nistru = Dnister → Europe 46°18N 30°17E 17 E16
Nisutlin → Canada 60°14N 132°34W 70 A2
Nitchequon Canada 53°10N 70°58W 73 B5
Niterói Brazil 22°53S 43°7W 95 A7
Nith → Canada 43°12N 80°23W 82 C4
Nith → U.K. 55°14N 3°33W 11 F5
Nitmiluk △ Australia 14°6S 132°15E 60 B5
Nitra Slovak Rep. 48°19N 18°4E 17 D10
Nitra → Slovak Rep. 47°46N 18°10E 17 E10
Niue Pac. Oc. 19°2S 169°54W 65 J11
Niut Indonesia 0°55N 110°6E 36 D4
Niuzhuang China 40°58N 122°28E 35 D12
Nivala Finland 63°56N 24°57E 8 E21
Nivelles Belgium 50°35N 4°20E 15 D4
Nivernais France 47°15N 3°30E 20 C5
Niverville Canada 49°36N 97°3W 71 D9
Niwas India 23°3N 80°26E 43 H9
Nixa U.S.A. 37°3N 93°18W 80 G7
Nixon U.S.A. 29°16N 97°46W 84 G6
Nizamabad India 18°45N 78°7E 40 K11
Nizamghat India 28°20N 95°45E 41 E19
Nizhne Kolymsk Russia 68°34N 160°55E 29 C17
Nizhnekamsk Russia 55°38N 51°49E 18 C9
Nizhneudinsk Russia 54°54N 99°3E 29 D10
Nizhnevartovsk Russia 60°56N 76°38E 28 C8
Nizhniy Bestyakh Russia 61°57N 129°54E 29 C13
Nizhniy Novgorod Russia 56°20N 44°0E 18 C7
Nizhniy Tagil Russia 57°55N 59°57E 18 C10
Nizhyn Ukraine 51°5N 31°55E 19 D5
Nizip Turkey 37°5N 37°50E 44 B3
Nizké Tatry Slovak Rep. 48°55N 19°30E 17 D10
Nizwá Oman 22°56N 57°32E 47 C6
Njakwa Malawi 11°1S 33°56E 55 E3
Njanji Zambia 14°25S 31°46E 55 E3
Njazidja = Grande Comore Comoros Is. 11°35S 43°20E 53 a
Njinjo Tanzania 8°48S 38°54E 55 D4
Njombe Tanzania 9°20S 34°50E 55 D3
Njombe → Tanzania 6°56S 35°6E 54 D4
Nkana Zambia 12°50S 28°8E 55 E2
Nkandla S. Africa 28°37S 31°5E 57 D5
Nkawkaw Ghana 6°36N 0°49W 50 G5
Nkayi Zimbabwe 19°41S 29°20E 55 F2
Nkhotakota Malawi 12°56S 34°15E 55 E3
Nkhotakota ⌂ Malawi 12°50S 34°0E 55 E3
Nkongsamba Cameroon 4°55N 9°55E 52 D1
Nkurenkuru Namibia 17°42S 18°32E 56 B2
Nmai → Burma 25°30N 97°25E 41 G20
Noakhali = Maijdi Bangla. 22°48N 91°10E 41 H17
Nobel Canada 45°25N 80°6W 82 A4
Nobeoka Japan 32°36N 131°41E 31 H5
Noblesville U.S.A. 40°3N 86°1W 80 E10
Noboribetsu Japan 42°24N 141°6E 30 C10
Noccundra Australia 27°50S 142°36E 63 D3
Nocera Inferiore Italy 40°44N 14°38E 22 D6
Nocona U.S.A. 33°47N 97°44W 84 E6
Noda Japan 35°56N 139°52E 31 G9
Nogales Mexico 31°19N 110°56W 86 A2
Nogales U.S.A. 31°21N 110°56W 77 L8
Nōgata Japan 33°48N 130°44E 31 H5
Noggerup Australia 33°32S 116°5E 61 F2
Noginsk Russia 64°30N 90°50E 29 C10
Nogliki Russia 51°50N 143°10E 29 D15
Nogoa → Australia 23°40S 147°55E 62 C4
Nogoyá Argentina 32°24S 59°48W 94 C4
Nohar India 29°11N 74°49E 42 E6
Nohta India 23°40N 79°34E 43 H8
Noires, Mts. France 48°11N 3°40W 20 B2
Noirmoutier, Î. de France 46°58N 2°10W 20 C2
Nojane Botswana 23°15S 20°14E 56 C3
Nojima-Zaki Japan 34°54N 139°53E 31 G9
Nok Kundi Pakistan 28°50N 62°45E 40 E3
Nok Ta Phao, Ko Thailand 9°23N 99°40E 39 b
Nokaneng Botswana 19°40S 22°17E 56 B3
Nokia Finland 61°30N 23°30E 8 F20
Nokomis Canada 51°35N 105°0W 71 C8
Nokomis L. Canada 57°0N 103°0W 71 B8
Nola C.A.R. 3°35N 16°4E 52 D3
Noma Omuramba → Namibia 18°52S 20°53E 56 B3
Nombre de Dios Panama 9°34N 79°28W 88 E4
Nome U.S.A. 64°30N 165°25W 74 a
Nomo-Zaki Japan 32°35N 129°44E 31 H4
Nomuka Tonga 20°17S 174°48W 59 c
Nomuka Group Tonga 20°20S 174°48W 59 c
Nonacho L. Canada 61°42N 109°40W 71 A7
Nonda Australia 20°40S 142°28E 62 C3
Nong Chang Thailand 15°23N 99°51E 38 E2
Nong Het Laos 19°29N 103°59E 38 C4
Nong Khai Thailand 17°50N 102°46E 38 D4
Nong'an China 44°25N 125°5E 35 B13
Nongoma S. Africa 27°58S 31°35E 57 D5
Nongsa Indonesia 1°11N 104°8E 39 d
Nonoava Mexico 27°28N 106°44W 86 B3
Nonsan S. Korea 36°12N 127°5E 35 F14
Nonthaburi Thailand 13°50N 100°29E 38 F3
Noonamah Australia 12°40S 131°4E 60 B5
Noondie, L. Australia 28°30S 119°30E 61 E2
Noord Brabant □ Neths. 51°40N 5°0E 15 C5
Noord Holland □ Neths. 52°30N 4°45E 15 B4
Noordbeveland Neths. 51°35N 3°50E 15 C3
Noordoostpolder Neths. 52°45N 5°45E 15 B5
Noordwijk Neths. 52°14N 4°26E 15 B4
Noosa Heads Australia 26°25S 153°6E 63 D5
Nootka I. Canada 49°32N 126°42W 70 D3
Nopiming ⌂ Canada 50°30N 95°37W 71 C9
Noralee Canada 53°59N 126°26W 70 C3
Noranda = Rouyn-Noranda Canada 48°20N 79°0W 72 C4
Norco U.S.A. 33°56N 117°33W 79 M9
Nord-Kivu □ Dem. Rep. of the Congo 1°0S 29°0E 54 C2
Nord-Ostsee-Kanal Germany 54°12N 9°32E 16 A5
Nordaustlandet Svalbard 79°14N 23°0E 4 B9
Nordegg Canada 52°29N 116°5W 70 C5
Norderney Germany 53°42N 7°9E 16 B4
Norderstedt Germany 53°42N 10°1E 16 B5
Nordfjord Norway 61°55N 5°30E 8 F11
Nordfriesische Inseln Germany 54°40N 8°20E 16 A5
Nordhausen Germany 51°30N 10°47E 16 C6
Norðoyar Færoe Is. 62°17N 6°35W 8 E9
Nordkapp Norway 71°10N 25°50E 8 A21
Nordkapp Svalbard 80°31N 20°0E 4 A9
Nordkinnhalvøya Norway 70°55N 27°40E 8 A22
Nordrhein-Westfalen □ Germany 51°45N 7°30E 16 C4
Nordvik Russia 74°2N 111°32E 29 B12
Nore → Ireland 52°25N 6°58W 10 D4
Noreland Canada 44°43N 78°48W 82 B6

Norfolk = Simcoe Canada 42°50N 80°23W 82 D4
Norfolk N.Y., U.S.A. 44°48N 74°59W 83 B10
Norfolk Nebr., U.S.A. 42°2N 97°25W 80 D5
Norfolk Va., U.S.A. 36°50N 76°17W 81 G15
Norfolk □ U.K. 52°39N 0°54E 13 E8
Norfolk Broads △ U.K. 52°45N 1°30E 13 E9
Norfolk I. Pac. Oc. 28°58S 168°3E 58 D9
Norfolk Ridge Pac. Oc. 29°0S 168°0E 64 K8
Norfork L. U.S.A. 36°15N 92°14W 84 C8
Norge = Norway ■ Europe 63°0N 11°0E 8 E14
Norilsk Russia 69°20N 88°6E 29 C9
Norma, Mt. Australia 20°55S 140°42E 62 C3
Normal U.S.A. 40°31N 88°59W 80 E9
Norman U.S.A. 35°13N 97°26W 84 D6
Norman → Australia 19°18S 141°51E 62 B3
Norman Wells Canada 65°17N 126°51W 68 C7
Normanby → Australia 14°23S 144°10E 62 A3
Normandie France 48°45N 0°10E 20 B4
Normandin Canada 48°49N 72°31W 72 C5
Normandy = Normandie France 48°45N 0°10E 20 B4
Normanhurst, Mt. Australia 25°4S 122°30E 61 E3
Normanton Australia 17°40S 141°10E 62 B3
Normétal Canada 49°0N 79°22W 72 C4
Norquay Canada 51°53N 102°5W 71 C8
Norquinco Argentina 41°51S 70°55W 96 E2
Norrbottens län □ Sweden 66°50N 20°0E 8 C19
Norris Point Canada 49°31N 57°53W 73 C8
Norristown U.S.A. 40°7N 75°21W 83 F9
Norrköping Sweden 58°37N 16°11E 9 G17
Norrland Sweden 62°15N 15°45E 8 E16
Norrtälje Sweden 59°46N 18°42E 9 G18
Norseman Australia 32°8S 121°43E 61 F3
Norsk Russia 52°30N 130°5E 29 D14
Norte, Pta. del Canary Is. 27°51N 17°57W 24 G2
Norte, Serra do Brazil 11°20S 59°0W 92 F7
North, C. Canada 47°2N 60°20W 73 C7
North Adams U.S.A. 42°42N 73°7W 83 D11
North America 40°0N 100°0W 66 F10
North Arm Canada 62°0N 114°30W 70 A5
North Augusta U.S.A. 33°30N 81°59W 85 E14
North Australian Basin Ind. Oc. 14°30S 116°30E 64 J3
North Ayrshire □ U.K. 55°45N 4°44W 11 F4
North Bass I. U.S.A. 41°40N 82°56W 82 E2
North Battleford Canada 52°50N 108°17W 71 C7
North Bay Canada 46°20N 79°30W 72 C4
North Belcher Is. Canada 56°50N 79°50W 72 A4
North Bend Oreg., U.S.A. 43°24N 124°14W 76 E1
North Bend Pa., U.S.A. 41°20N 77°42W 82 E7
North Bend Wash., U.S.A. 47°30N 121°47W 78 C5
North Bennington U.S.A. 42°56N 73°15W 83 D11
North Berwick U.K. 56°4N 2°42W 11 E6
North Berwick U.S.A. 43°18N 70°44W 83 C14
North Bruce Canada 44°22N 81°26W 82 B3
North C. Canada 47°5N 64°0W 73 C7
North C. N.Z. 34°23S 173°4E 59 A4
North Canadian → U.S.A. 35°22N 95°37W 84 D7
North Canton U.S.A. 40°53N 81°24W 82 F3
North Cape = Nordkapp Norway 71°10N 25°50E 8 A21
North Caribou L. Canada 52°50N 90°40W 72 B1
North Carolina □ U.S.A. 35°30N 80°0W 85 D15
North Cascades △ U.S.A. 48°45N 121°10W 76 B3
North Channel Canada 46°0N 83°0W 72 C3
North Channel U.K. 55°13N 5°52W 11 F3
North Charleston U.S.A. 32°53N 79°58W 85 E15
North Chicago U.S.A. 42°19N 87°51W 80 D10
North Collins U.S.A. 42°35N 78°56W 82 D6
North Creek U.S.A. 43°42N 73°59W 83 C11
North Dakota □ U.S.A. 47°30N 100°15W 80 B3
North Downs U.K. 51°19N 0°21E 13 F8
North East U.S.A. 42°13N 79°50W 82 D5
North East Frontier Agency = Arunachal Pradesh □ India 28°0N 95°0E 41 F19
North East Lincolnshire □ U.K. 53°34N 0°2W 12 D7
North Eastern □ Kenya 1°30N 40°0E 54 B5
North Esk → U.K. 56°46N 2°24W 11 E6
North European Plain Europe 55°0N 25°0E 6 E10
North Foreland U.K. 51°22N 1°28E 13 F9
North Fork U.S.A. 37°14N 119°21W 78 H7
North Fork American → U.S.A. 38°57N 120°59W 78 G5
North Fork Feather → U.S.A. 38°33N 121°30W 78 F5
North Fork Grand → U.S.A. 45°47N 102°16W 80 C2
North Fork Red → U.S.A. 34°24N 99°14W 84 D5
North Frisian Is. = Nordfriesische Inseln Germany 54°40N 8°20E 16 A5
North Gower Canada 45°8N 75°43W 83 A9
North Hd. Australia 30°14S 114°59E 61 F1
North Henik L. Canada 61°45N 97°40W 71 A9
North Highlands U.S.A. 38°40N 121°23W 78 G5
North Horr Kenya 3°20N 37°8E 54 B4
North I. Kenya 4°5N 36°5E 54 B4
North I. N.Z. 38°0S 175°0E 59 C5
North I. Seychelles 4°25S 55°13E 53 b
North Kingsville U.S.A. 41°54N 80°42W 82 E4
North Kitui ⌓ Kenya 0°15S 38°29E 54 C4
North Knife → Canada 58°53N 94°45W 71 B10
North Koel → India 24°45N 83°50E 43 G10
North Korea ■ Asia 40°0N 127°0E 35 E14
North Lakhimpur India 27°14N 94°7E 41 F19
North Lanarkshire □ U.K. 55°52N 3°56W 11 F5
North Las Vegas U.S.A. 36°11N 115°7W 79 J11
North Lincolnshire □ U.K. 53°36N 0°30W 12 D7
North Little Rock U.S.A. 34°45N 92°16W 84 D8
North Loup → U.S.A. 41°17N 98°24W 80 E4
North Luangwa △ Zambia 11°49S 32°9E 55 E3
North Magnetic Pole Canada 82°42N 114°24W 69 B9
North Mankato U.S.A. 44°10N 94°2W 80 C6
North Minch U.K. 58°5N 5°55W 11 C3
North Moose L. Canada 54°4N 100°12W 71 C8
North Myrtle Beach U.S.A. 33°48N 78°42W 85 E15
North Nahanni → Canada 62°15N 123°20W 70 A4
North Olmsted U.S.A. 41°25N 81°56W 82 E3
North Ossetia □ Russia 43°30N 44°30E 19 F7
North Pagai, I. = Pagai Utara, Pulau Indonesia 2°35S 100°0E 36 E2
North Palisade U.S.A. 37°6N 118°31W 78 H8
North Platte U.S.A. 41°8N 100°46W 80 E3
North Platte → U.S.A. 41°7N 100°42W 80 E3
North Pole Arctic 90°0N 0°0 4 A
North Portal Canada 49°0N 102°33W 71 D8
North Powder U.S.A. 45°2N 117°55W 76 D5
North Pt. Barbados 13°20N 59°37W 89 g
North Pt. Trin. & Tob. 11°21N 60°31W 93 J16
North Pt. U.S.A. 45°2N 83°16W 82 A1
North Rhine Westphalia = Nordrhein-Westfalen □ Germany 51°45N 7°30E 16 C4
North River Canada 53°49N 57°6W 73 B8
North Ronaldsay U.K. 59°22N 2°26W 11 B6
North Saskatchewan → Canada 53°15N 105°5W 71 C7
North Sea Europe 56°0N 4°0E 6 D6
North Seal → Canada 58°50N 98°7W 71 B9
North Somerset □ U.K. 51°24N 2°45W 13 F5
North Sydney Canada 46°12N 60°15W 73 C7
North Syracuse U.S.A. 43°8N 76°7W 83 C8
North Taranaki Bight N.Z. 38°50S 174°15E 59 C5
North Thompson → Canada 50°40N 120°20W 70 C4
North Tonawanda U.S.A. 43°2N 78°53W 82 C6
North Troy U.S.A. 45°0N 72°24W 83 B12
North Twin I. Canada 53°20N 80°0W 72 B4
North Tyne → U.K. 55°0N 2°8W 12 B5
North Uist U.K. 57°40N 7°15W 11 D1
North Vancouver Canada 49°19N 123°4W 78 A3
North Vernon U.S.A. 39°0N 85°38W 81 F11
North Wabasca L. Canada 56°0N 113°55W 70 B6
North Walsham U.K. 52°50N 1°22E 12 E9
North West = Severo-Zapadnyy □ Russia 65°0N 40°0E 28 C4
North-West □ S. Africa 27°0S 25°0E 56 D4
North West C. Australia 21°45S 114°9E 60 D1
North West Frontier □ Pakistan 34°0N 72°0E 42 C4
North West Highlands U.K. 57°33N 4°58W 11 D4
North West River Canada 53°30N 60°10W 73 B7
North Western □ Zambia 13°30S 25°30E 55 E2
North Wildwood U.S.A. 39°0N 74°48W 81 F16
North York Moors U.K. 54°23N 0°53W 12 C7
North York Moors △ U.K. 54°27N 0°51W 12 C7
North Yorkshire □ U.K. 54°15N 1°25W 12 C6
Northallerton U.K. 54°20N 1°26W 12 C6
Northam Australia 31°35S 116°42E 61 F2
Northam S. Africa 24°56S 27°18E 56 C4
Northampton Australia 28°27S 114°33E 61 E1
Northampton U.K. 52°15N 0°53W 13 E7
Northampton Mass., U.S.A. 42°19N 72°38W 83 D12
Northampton Pa., U.S.A. 40°41N 75°30W 83 F9
Northamptonshire □ U.K. 52°16N 0°55W 13 E7
Northbridge U.S.A. 42°9N 71°39W 83 D13
Northbrook Canada 44°44N 77°9W 82 B7
Northcliffe Australia 34°39S 116°7E 61 F2
Northeast Pacific Basin Pac. Oc. 32°0N 145°0W 65 D13
Northeast Providence Chan. W. Indies 26°0N 76°0W 88 A4
Northern = Limpopo □ S. Africa 24°5S 29°0E 57 C4
Northern □ Malawi 11°0S 34°0E 55 E3
Northern □ Zambia 10°30S 31°0E 55 E3
Northern Areas □ Pakistan 36°30N 73°0E 43 A5
Northern Cape □ S. Africa 30°0S 20°0E 56 D3
Northern Circars India 17°30N 82°30E 41 L13
Northern Indian L. Canada 57°20N 97°20W 71 B9
Northern Ireland □ U.K. 54°45N 7°0W 10 B5
Northern Lau Group Fiji 17°30S 178°59W 59 a
Northern Light L. Canada 48°15N 90°39W 72 C1
Northern Marianas ⊿ Pac. Oc. 17°0N 145°0E 64 F6
Northern Province □ S. Africa 24°0S 29°0E 57 C4
Northern Range Trin. & Tob. 10°46N 61°15W 93 K15
Northern Sporades Greece 39°15N 23°30E 23 E10
Northern Territory □ Australia 20°0S 133°0E 60 D5
Northfield Minn., U.S.A. 44°27N 93°9W 80 C7
Northfield Vt., U.S.A. 44°9N 72°40W 83 B12
Northgate Canada 49°0N 102°16W 71 D8
Northland □ N.Z. 35°30S 173°30E 59 A4
Northome U.S.A. 47°52N 94°17W 80 B6
Northport Ala., U.S.A. 33°14N 87°35W 85 E11
Northport Wash., U.S.A. 48°55N 117°48W 76 B5
Northumberland □ U.K. 55°12N 2°0W 12 B6
Northumberland, C. Australia 38°5S 140°40E 63 F3
Northumberland Is. Australia 21°30S 149°50E 62 C4
Northumberland Str. Canada 46°20N 64°0W 73 C7
Northville U.S.A. 43°13N 74°11W 83 C10
Northwest Pacific Basin Pac. Oc. 32°0N 165°0E 64 D8
Northwest Providence Channel W. Indies 26°0N 78°0W 88 A4
Northwest Territories □ Canada 63°0N 118°0W 68 C8
Northwich U.K. 53°15N 2°31W 12 D5
Northwood Iowa, U.S.A. 43°27N 93°13W 80 D7
Northwood N. Dak., U.S.A. 47°44N 97°34W 80 B5
Norton U.S.A. 39°50N 99°53W 80 F4
Norton Zimbabwe 17°52S 30°40E 55 F3
Norton Sd. U.S.A. 63°50N 164°0W 74 a
Norwalk Calif., U.S.A. 33°54N 118°4W 79 M8
Norwalk Conn., U.S.A. 41°7N 73°22W 83 E11
Norwalk Iowa, U.S.A. 41°29N 93°41W 80 E7
Norwalk Ohio, U.S.A. 41°15N 82°37W 82 E2
Norway Maine, U.S.A. 44°13N 70°32W 81 C18
Norway Mich., U.S.A. 45°47N 87°55W 80 C10
Norway ■ Europe 63°0N 11°0E 8 E14
Norway House Canada 53°59N 97°50W 71 C9
Norwegian B. Canada 77°30N 90°0W 69 B11
Norwegian Basin Atl. Oc. 68°0N 2°0W 4 C7
Norwegian Sea Atl. Oc. 66°0N 1°0E 6 B6
Norwich Canada 42°59N 80°36W 82 D4
Norwich U.K. 52°38N 1°18E 13 E9
Norwich Conn., U.S.A. 41°31N 72°5W 83 E12
Norwich N.Y., U.S.A. 42°32N 75°32W 83 D9
Norwood Canada 44°23N 77°59W 82 B7
Norwood U.S.A. 44°45N 75°0W 83 B10
Nosappu-Misaki Japan 45°26N 141°39E 30 C12
Noshiro Japan 40°12N 140°0E 30 D10
Noşratābād Iran 29°55N 60°0E 45 D8
Noss Hd. U.K. 58°28N 3°3W 11 C5
Nossob → S. Africa 26°55S 20°45E 56 D3
Nosy Barren Madag. 18°25S 43°40E 53 H8
Nosy Bé Madag. 13°25S 48°15E 53 G9
Nosy Boraha Madag. 16°50S 49°55E 57 B8
Nosy Lava Madag. 14°33S 47°36E 57 A8
Nosy Varika Madag. 20°35S 48°32E 57 C8
Noteć → Poland 52°44N 15°26E 16 B8
Notikewin → Canada 57°2N 117°38W 70 B5
Notodden Norway 59°35N 9°17E 9 G13
Notre Dame B. Canada 49°45N 55°30W 73 C8
Notre-Dame-de-Koartac = Quaqtaq Canada 60°55N 69°40W 69 C13
Notre-Dame-des-Bois Canada 45°24N 71°4W 83 A13
Notre-Dame-d'Ivugivic = Ivujivik Canada 62°24N 77°55W 69 C12
Notre-Dame-du-Nord Canada 47°36N 79°30W 72 C4
Nottawasaga B. Canada 44°35N 80°15W 82 B4
Nottaway → Canada 51°22N 78°55W 72 B4
Nottingham U.K. 52°58N 1°10W 12 E6
Nottingham, City of □ U.K. 52°58N 1°10W 12 E6
Nottingham I. Canada 63°20N 77°55W 69 C12
Nottinghamshire □ U.K. 53°10N 1°3W 12 D6
Nottoway → U.S.A. 36°33N 76°55W 81 G15
Notwane → Botswana 23°35S 26°58E 56 C4
Nouâdhibou Mauritania 20°54N 17°0W 50 D2
Nouâdhibou, Râs Mauritania 20°50N 17°0W 50 D2
Nouakchott Mauritania 18°9N 15°58W 50 E2
Nouméa N. Cal. 22°17S 166°30E 58 D9
Noupoort S. Africa 31°10S 24°57E 56 E3
Nouveau Comptoir = Wemindji Canada 53°0N 78°49W 72 B4
Nouvelle Amsterdam, Î. Ind. Oc. 38°30S 77°30E 3 F13
Nouvelle-Calédonie = New Caledonia ⊿ Pac. Oc. 21°0S 165°0E 58 D9
Nova Esperança Brazil 23°8S 52°24W 95 A5
Nova Friburgo Brazil 22°16S 42°30W 95 A7
Nova Iguaçu Brazil 22°45S 43°28W 95 A7
Nova Iorque Brazil 7°0S 44°5W 93 E10
Nova Lamego Guinea-Biss. 12°19N 14°11W 50 F3
Nova Lima Brazil 19°59S 43°51W 93 G10
Nova Lusitânia Mozam. 19°50S 34°34E 55 F3
Nova Mambone Mozam. 21°0S 35°3E 57 C6
Nova Scotia □ Canada 45°10N 63°0W 73 C7
Nova Sofala Mozam. 20°7S 34°42E 57 C5
Nova Venécia Brazil 18°45S 40°24W 93 G10
Nova Zagora Bulgaria 42°32N 26°1E 23 C11
Novar Canada 45°27N 79°15W 82 A5
Novara Italy 45°28N 8°38E 20 D8
Novato U.S.A. 38°6N 122°35W 78 G4
Novaya Ladoga Russia 60°7N 32°16E 18 B5
Novaya Lyalya Russia 59°4N 60°45E 18 C11
Novaya Sibir, Ostrov Russia 75°10N 150°0E 29 B16
Novaya Zemlya Russia 75°0N 56°0E 28 B6
Nové Zámky Slovak Rep. 48°2N 18°8E 17 D10
Novgorod Russia 58°30N 31°25E 18 C5
Novgorod-Severskiy = Novhorod-Siverskyy Ukraine 52°2N 33°10E 18 D5
Novhorod-Siverskyy Ukraine 52°2N 33°10E 18 D5
Novi Lígure Italy 44°46N 8°47E 20 D8
Novi Pazar Serbia 43°12N 20°28E 23 C9
Novi Sad Serbia 45°18N 19°52E 23 B8
Novo Hamburgo Brazil 29°37S 51°7W 95 B5
Novo Mesto Slovenia 45°47N 15°12E 22 B6
Novoaltaysk Russia 53°30N 84°0E 28 D9
Novocherkassk Russia 47°27N 40°15E 19 E7
Novodvinsk Russia 64°25N 40°42E 28 C5
Novogrudok = Navahrudak Belarus 53°40N 25°50E 17 B13
Novohrad-Volynskyy Ukraine 50°34N 27°35E 17 C14
Novokachalinsk Russia 45°5N 132°0E 30 B5
Novokuybyshevsk Russia 53°7N 49°58E 18 D8
Novokuznetsk Russia 53°45N 87°10E 28 D9
Novolazarevskaya Antarctica 71°0S 12°0E 5 D3
Novomoskovsk Russia 54°5N 38°15E 18 D6
Novorossiysk Russia 44°43N 37°46E 19 F6
Novorybnoye Russia 72°50N 105°50E 29 B11
Novoselytsya Ukraine 48°14N 26°15E 17 D14
Novoshakhtinsk Russia 47°46N 39°58E 19 E6
Novosibirsk Russia 55°0N 83°5E 28 D9
Novosibirskiye Ostrova Russia 75°0N 142°0E 29 B15
Novotroitsk Russia 51°10N 58°15E 18 D10
Novouzensk Russia 50°32N 48°17E 19 D8
Novovolynsk Ukraine 50°45N 24°4E 17 C13
Novska Croatia 45°19N 17°0E 22 B7
Novvy Urengoy Russia 65°48N 76°52E 28 C8
Novyy Bor Russia 66°43N 52°19E 18 A9
Novyy Port Russia 67°40N 72°30E 28 C8
Nowa Sól Poland 51°48N 15°44E 16 C8
Nowata U.S.A. 36°42N 95°38W 84 C7
Nowbarān Iran 35°8N 49°42E 45 C6
Nowghāb Iran 33°53N 59°4E 45 C8
Nowgong Assam, India 26°20N 92°50E 41 F18
Nowgong Mad. P., India 25°4N 79°27E 43 G8
Nowra Australia 34°53S 150°35E 63 E5
Nowshera Pakistan 34°0N 72°0E 40 C8
Nowy Sącz Poland 49°40N 20°41E 17 D11
Nowy Targ Poland 49°29N 20°2E 17 D11
Nowy Tomyśl Poland 52°19N 16°10E 16 B9
Noxen U.S.A. 41°25N 76°4W 83 E8
Noyabr'sk Russia 64°34N 76°21E 28 C8
Noyon France 49°34N 2°59E 20 B5
Noyon Mongolia 43°2N 102°4E 34 C2
Nqutu S. Africa 28°13S 30°32E 57 D5
Nsanje Malawi 16°55S 35°12E 55 F4
Nsawam Ghana 5°50N 0°24W 50 G5
Nsomba Zambia 10°45S 29°51E 55 E2
Nu Jiang → China 29°58N 97°25E 32 D4
Nu Shan China 26°0N 99°20E 32 D4
Nuba Mts. = Nubah, Jibalan Sudan 12°0N 31°0E 51 F12
Nubah, Jibalan Sudan 12°0N 31°0E 51 F12
Nubia Africa 21°0N 32°0E 48 D7
Nubian Desert = Nûbîya, Es Sahrâ en Sudan 21°30N 33°30E 51 D12
Nûbîya, Es Sahrâ en Sudan 21°30N 33°30E 51 D12
Nuboai Indonesia 2°10S 136°30E 37 E9
Nubra → India 34°35N 77°35E 43 B7
Nueces → U.S.A. 27°51N 97°30W 84 H6
Nueltin L. Canada 60°30N 99°30W 71 A9
Nuestra Señora del Rosario de Caá-Catí Argentina 27°45S 57°36W 94 B4
Nueva Ciudad Guerrero Mexico 26°34N 99°12W 87 B5
Nueva Gerona Cuba 21°53N 82°49W 88 B3
Nueva Palmira Uruguay 33°52S 58°20W 94 C4
Nueva Rosita Mexico 27°57N 101°13W 86 B4
Nueva San Salvador El Salv. 13°40N 89°18W 88 D2
Nuéve de Julio Argentina 35°30S 61°0W 94 D3
Nuevitas Cuba 21°30N 77°20W 88 B4
Nuevo, G. Argentina 43°0S 64°30W 96 E4
Nuevo Casas Grandes Mexico 30°25N 107°55W 86 A3
Nuevo Laredo Mexico 27°30N 99°31W 87 B5
Nuevo León □ Mexico 25°20N 100°0W 86 C5
Nuevo Rocafuerte Ecuador 0°55S 75°27W 92 D3
Nugget Pt. N.Z. 46°27S 169°50E 59 G2
Nuhaka N.Z. 39°3S 177°45E 59 C6
Nukey Bluff Australia 32°26S 135°29E 63 E2
Nukhayb Iraq 32°4N 42°3E 44 C4
Nuku Hiva French Polynesia 8°54S 140°6W 65 H13
Nuku'alofa Tonga 21°10S 175°12W 59 c
Nukus Uzbekistan 42°27N 59°41E 28 E6
Nullagine Australia 21°53S 120°7E 60 D3
Nullagine → Australia 21°20S 120°20E 60 D3
Nullarbor Australia 31°28S 130°55E 61 F5
Nullarbor △ Australia 32°39S 130°0E 61 F2
Nullarbor Plain Australia 31°10S 129°0E 61 F4
Numalla, L. Australia 28°43S 144°20E 63 D3
Numan Nigeria 9°29N 12°3E 51 G8
Numata Japan 36°45N 139°4E 31 F9
Numaykoos Lake ⌓ Canada 57°52N 95°58W 71 B9
Numazu Japan 35°7N 138°51E 31 G9
Numbulwar Australia 14°15S 135°45E 62 A2
Numfoor Indonesia 1°0S 134°50E 37 E8
Numurkah Australia 36°5S 145°26E 63 F4
Nunaksaluk I. Canada 55°49N 60°20W 73 A7
Nunap Isua Greenland 59°48N 43°55W 66 D15
Nunavut □ Canada 66°0N 85°0W 69 D11
Nunda U.S.A. 42°35N 77°56W 82 D7
Nuneaton U.K. 52°32N 1°27W 13 E6
Nungarin Australia 31°12S 118°6E 61 F2
Nungo Mozam. 13°23S 37°43E 55 E4
Nungwe Tanzania 2°48S 32°2E 54 C3
Nunivak I. U.S.A. 60°10N 166°30W 74 a
Nunkun India 33°57N 76°2E 43 C7
Núoro Italy 40°20N 9°20E 22 D3
Nūr Iran 36°33N 52°1E 45 B
Nūrābād Hormozgān, Iran 27°47N 57°12E 45 E
Nūrābād Lorestān, Iran 34°4N 47°58E 44 C
Nuremberg = Nürnberg Germany 49°27N 11°3E 16 D
Nuri Mexico 28°5N 109°22W 86 B
Nuriootpa Australia 34°27S 139°0E 63 E
Nuristān □ Afghan. 35°20N 71°0E 40 B
Nurmes Finland 63°33N 29°10E 8 E2
Nürnberg Germany 49°27N 11°3E 16 D
Nurpur Pakistan 31°53N 71°54E 42 D
Nurran, L. = Terewah, L. Australia 29°52S 147°35E 63 D
Nurrari Lakes Australia 29°1S 130°5E 61 E
Nusa Barung Indonesia 8°30S 113°30E 37 H1
Nusa Dua Indonesia 8°48S 115°14E 37 K1
Nusa Kambangan Indonesia 7°40S 108°10E 37 G1
Nusa Tenggara Barat □ Indonesia 8°50S 117°30E 36 F
Nusa Tenggara Timur □ Indonesia 9°30S 122°0E 37 F
Nusaybin Turkey 37°3N 41°10E 19 G
Nushki Pakistan 29°35N 66°0E 42 E
Nuuk Greenland 64°10N 51°35W 67 C1
Nuupere, Pte. Moorea 17°36S 149°47W 59
Nuwakot Nepal 28°10N 83°55E 43 E
Nuwayb'ī, W. an → Si. Arabia 29°18N 34°57E 46 F
Nuweiba' Egypt 28°59N 34°39E 44 D
Nuwerus S. Africa 31°8S 18°24E 56 E
Nuweveldberge S. Africa 32°10S 21°45E 56
Nuyts, Pt. Australia 35°4S 116°38E 61
Nuyts Arch. Australia 32°35S 133°20E 63
Nxai Pan △ Botswana 19°50S 24°46E 56
Nxau-Nxau Botswana 18°57S 21°4E 56
Nyabing Australia 33°33S 118°9E 61
Nyack U.S.A. 41°5N 73°55W 83 E
Nyagan Russia 62°30N 65°38E 28
Nyahanga Tanzania 2°20S 33°37E 54
Nyahua Tanzania 5°25S 33°23E 54
Nyahururu Kenya 0°2N 36°27E 54
Nyainqêntanglha Shan China 30°0N 90°0E 32
Nyakanazi Tanzania 3°2S 31°10E 54
Nyâlâ Sudan 12°2N 24°58E 51 F
Nyamandhlovu Zimbabwe 19°55S 28°16E 55
Nyambiti Tanzania 2°48S 33°27E 54
Nyamira Kenya 0°36S 34°52E 54
Nyamwaga Tanzania 1°27S 34°33E 54
Nyandekwa Tanzania 3°57S 32°32E 54
Nyandoma Russia 61°40N 40°12E 18
Nyanga △ Zimbabwe 18°17S 32°46E 55
Nyangana Namibia 18°0S 20°40E 56
Nyanguge Tanzania 2°30S 33°12E 54
Nyanza Rwanda 2°20S 29°42E 54
Nyanza □ Kenya 0°10S 34°15E 54
Nyanza-Lac Burundi 4°21S 29°36E 54
Nyasa, L. = Malawi, L. Africa 12°30S 34°30E 55
Nyasvizh Belarus 53°14N 26°38E 17 B
Nyazepetrovsk Russia 56°3N 59°36E 18 C
Nyazura Zimbabwe 18°40S 32°16E 55
Nyazwidzi → Zimbabwe 20°0S 31°17E 55
Nybro Sweden 56°44N 15°55E 9 H
Nyda Russia 66°40N 72°58E 28
Nyeri Kenya 0°23S 36°56E 54
Nyika △ Malawi 10°30S 33°53E 55
Nyíregyháza Hungary 47°58N 21°47E 17 E
Nyiru, Mt. Kenya 2°8N 36°50E 54
Nykarleby = Uusikaarlepyy Finland 63°32N 22°31E 8
Nykøbing Nordjylland, Denmark 56°48N 8°51E 9 H
Nykøbing Sjælland, Denmark 54°56N 11°52E 9
Nykøbing Sjælland, Denmark 55°55N 11°40E 9
Nyköping Sweden 58°45N 17°1E 9
Nylstroom = Modimolle S. Africa 24°42S 28°22E 57
Nymagee Australia 32°7S 146°20E 63
Nymboida △ Australia 29°38S 152°26E 63
Nynäshamn Sweden 58°54N 17°57E 9
Nyngan Australia 31°30S 147°8E 63
Nyoma Rap India 33°10N 78°40E 43
Nyoman = Nemunas → Lithuania 55°25N 21°10E 9
Nysa Poland 50°30N 17°22E 17
Nysa → Europe 52°4N 14°46E 16
Nyslott = Savonlinna Finland 61°52N 28°53E 8
Nyssa U.S.A. 43°53N 117°0W 76
Nystad = Uusikaupunki Finland 60°47N 21°25E 8
Nyunzu Dem. Rep. of the Congo 5°57S 27°58E 54
Nyurba Russia 63°17N 118°28E 29
Nzega Tanzania 4°10S 33°12E 54
Nzérékoré Guinea 7°49N 8°48W 50
Nzeto Angola 7°10S 12°52E 52
Nzilo, Chutes de Dem. Rep. of the Congo 10°18S 25°27E 55
Nzubuka Tanzania 4°45S 32°50E 54
Nzwani = Anjouan Comoros Is. 12°15S 44°20E

O

O Le Pupū Pu'e △ Samoa 13°59S 171°43W
Ō-Shima Hokkaidō, Japan 41°30N 139°22E 30
Ō-Shima Shizuoka, Japan 34°44N 139°24E 3
Oa, Mull of U.K. 55°35N 6°20W 1

acoma U.S.A. 43°48N 99°24W 80 D4
ahe, L. U.S.A. 44°27N 100°24W 80 C3
ahe Dam U.S.A. 44°27N 100°24W 80 C3
'ahu U.S.A. 21°28N 157°58W 74 b
ak Harbor U.S.A. 48°18N 122°39W 78 B4
ak Hill U.S.A. 37°59N 81°9W 81 G13
ak Island U.S.A. 33°55N 78°10W 85 E15
ak Ridge U.S.A. 36°1N 84°16W 85 C12
ak View U.S.A. 34°24N 119°18W 79 L7
akan-Dake Japan 43°27N 144°10E 30 C12
akdale Calif., U.S.A. 37°46N 120°51W 78 H6
akdale La., U.S.A. 30°49N 92°40W 84 F8
akes U.S.A. 46°8N 98°6W 80 B4
akesdale U.S.A. 47°8N 117°15W 76 C5
akey Australia 27°25S 151°43E 63 D5
akfield U.S.A. 43°4N 78°16W 82 C6
akham U.K. 52°40N 0°43W 13 E7
akhurst U.S.A. 37°19N 119°40W 78 H7
akland Calif., U.S.A. 37°48N 122°18W 78 H4
akland Pa., U.S.A. 41°57N 75°36W 83 E9
akley Idaho, U.S.A. 42°15N 113°53W 76 E7
akley Kans., U.S.A. 39°8N 100°51W 80 F3
akover → Australia 21°0S 120°40E 60 D3
akridge U.S.A. 43°45N 122°28W 76 E2
akville Canada 43°27N 79°41W 82 C5
akville U.S.A. 46°51N 123°14W 78 D3
amaru N.Z. 45°5S 170°59E 59 F3
asis Calif., U.S.A. 37°29N 117°55W 78 H9
asis Calif., U.S.A. 33°28N 116°6W 79 M10
ates Land Antarctica 69°0S 160°0E 5 C11
atlands Australia 42°17S 147°21E 63 G4
atman U.S.A. 35°1N 114°19W 79 K12
axaca Mexico 17°3N 96°43W 87 D5
axaca □ Mexico 17°0N 96°30W 87 D5
→ Russia 66°45N 69°30E 28 C7
a Canada 49°4N 84°7W 72 C3
ama Japan 35°30N 135°45E 31 G7
an U.K. 56°25N 5°29W 11 E3
erá Argentina 27°21S 55°2W 95 B4
erhausen Germany 51°28N 6°51E 16 C4
erlin Kans., U.S.A. 39°49N 100°32W 80 F3
erlin La., U.S.A. 30°37N 92°46W 84 F8
erlin Ohio, U.S.A. 41°18N 82°13W 82 E2
eron Australia 33°45S 149°52E 63 E4
i, Kepulauan Indonesia 1°23S 127°45E 37 E7
idos Brazil 1°50S 55°30W 93 D7
ihiro Japan 42°56N 143°12E 30 C11
ilatu Indonesia 1°25S 127°20E 37 E7
luchye Russia 49°1N 131°4E 29 E14
o C.A.R. 5°20N 26°32E 54 A2
oyan Russia 51°15N 36°21E 28 D4
ozerskaya = Obozerskiy Russia 63°34N 40°21E 18 B7
ozerskiy Russia 63°34N 40°21E 18 B7
servatory Inlet Canada 55°10N 129°54W 70 B3
shchi Syrt Russia 52°0N 53°0E 6 E16
skaya Guba Russia 69°0N 73°0E 28 C8
uasi Ghana 6°17N 1°40W 50 G5
ala U.S.A. 29°11N 82°8W 85 G13
ampo Chihuahua, Mexico 28°11N 108°23W 86 B3
ampo Tamaulipas, Mexico 22°50N 99°20W 87 C5
aña Spain 39°55N 3°30W 21 C4
cidental, Cordillera Colombia 5°0N 76°0W 92 C3
cidental, Grand Erg Algeria 30°20N 1°0E 50 B6
ean City Md., U.S.A. 38°20N 75°5W 81 F16
ean City N.J., U.S.A. 39°17N 74°35W 81 F16
ean City Wash., U.S.A. 47°4N 124°10W 78 C2
ean Falls Canada 52°18N 127°48W 70 C3
ean I. = Banaba Kiribati 0°45S 169°50E 64 H8
ean Park U.S.A. 46°30N 124°3W 78 D2
eano U.S.A. 35°6N 120°37W 79 K6
eanport U.S.A. 40°19N 74°3W 83 F10
eanside U.S.A. 33°12N 117°23W 79 M9
hil Hills U.K. 56°14N 3°40W 11 E5
ho Rios Jamaica 18°24N 77°6W 88 a
lla U.S.A. 31°36N 83°15W 85 F13
mulgee → U.S.A. 31°58N 82°33W 85 F13
niţa Moldova 48°25N 27°30E 17 D14
onee → U.S.A. 31°58N 82°33W 85 F13
onomowoc U.S.A. 43°7N 88°30W 80 D9
onto U.S.A. 44°53N 87°52W 80 C10
onto Falls U.S.A. 44°52N 88°9W 80 C9
osingo Mexico 16°53N 92°6W 87 D6
otal Nic. 13°41N 86°31W 88 D2
otlán Jalisco, Mexico 20°21N 102°46W 86 C4
otlán Oaxaca, Mexico 16°48N 96°40W 87 D5
a Japan 35°11N 132°30E 31 G6
ðahraun Iceland 65°5N 17°0W 8 D5
aejin N. Korea 41°34N 129°40E 30 D4
ate Japan 40°16N 140°34E 30 D10
awara Japan 35°20N 139°6E 31 G9
da Norway 60°3N 6°35E 9 F12
ei → Canada 56°6N 96°54W 71 B9
emiş Turkey 38°15N 28°0E 23 E13
endaalsrus S. Africa 27°48S 26°45E 56 D4
ense Denmark 55°22N 10°23E 9 J14
er → Europe 53°33N 14°38E 16 B8
essa Ukraine 46°30N 30°45E 19 E5
essa = Odesa Ukraine 46°30N 30°45E 19 E5
essa Canada 44°17N 76°43W 83 B8
essa Tex., U.S.A. 31°52N 102°23W 84 F3
essa Wash., U.S.A. 47°20N 118°41W 76 C4
akwe Botswana 20°12S 25°17E 56 C4
enné Ivory C. 9°30N 7°34W 50 G4
ntsovo Russia 55°40N 37°16E 18 C6
onnell U.S.A. 32°58N 101°50W 84 E4
onnell Pt. Canada 45°5N 80°5W 82 A4
orheiu Secuiesc Romania 46°21N 25°21E 17 E13
a = Oder → Europe 53°33N 14°38E 16 B8
Odzi Zimbabwe 19°0S 32°20E 57 B5
Odzi → Zimbabwe 19°45S 32°23E 57 B5
Oeiras Brazil 7°0S 42°8W 93 E10
Oelrichs U.S.A. 43°11N 103°14W 80 D2
Oelwein U.S.A. 42°41N 91°55W 80 D8
Oeno I. Pac. Oc. 24°0S 131°0W 65 K14
Oenpelli = Gunbalanya Australia 12°20S 133°4E 60 B5
Ofanto → Italy 41°22N 16°13E 22 D7
Offa Nigeria 8°13N 4°42E 50 G6
Offaly □ Ireland 53°15N 7°30W 10 C4
Offenbach Germany 50°6N 8°44E 16 C5
Offenburg Germany 48°28N 7°56E 16 D4
Officer Cr. → Australia 27°46S 132°30E 61 E5
Ofolanga Tonga 19°38S 174°27W 59 c
Ofotfjorden Norway 68°27N 17°0E 8 B17
Ofu Amer. Samoa 14°11S 169°41W 59 b
Ōfunato Japan 39°4N 141°43E 30 E10
Oga Japan 39°55N 139°50E 30 E9
Oga-Hantō Japan 39°58N 139°47E 30 E9
Ogaden Ethiopia 7°30N 45°30E 47 F3
Ōgaki Japan 35°21N 136°37E 31 G8
Ogallala U.S.A. 41°8N 101°43W 80 E3
Ogasawara Gunto Pac. Oc. 27°0N 142°0E 27 F16
Ogbomosho Nigeria 8°1N 4°11E 50 G6
Ogden U.S.A. 41°13N 111°58W 76 F8
Ogdensburg U.S.A. 44°42N 75°30W 83 B9
Ogea Driki Fiji 19°12S 178°27W 59 a
Ogea Levu Fiji 19°8S 178°24W 59 a
Ogeechee → U.S.A. 31°50N 81°3W 85 F14
Ogilby U.S.A. 32°49N 114°50W 79 N12
Oglio → Italy 45°2N 10°39E 22 B4
Ogmore Australia 22°37S 149°35E 62 C4
Ogoki Canada 51°38N 85°58W 72 B2
Ogoki → Canada 51°38N 85°57W 72 B2
Ogoki L. Canada 50°50N 87°10W 72 B2
Ogoki Res. Canada 50°45N 88°15W 72 B2
Ogooué → Gabon 1°0S 9°0E 52 E1
Ogowe = Ogooué → Gabon 1°0S 9°0E 52 E1
Ogre Latvia 56°49N 24°36E 9 H21
Ogurchinskiy, Ostrov Turkmenistan 38°55N 53°2E 45 B7
Ohai N.Z. 45°55S 168°0E 59 F2
Ohakune N.Z. 39°24S 175°24E 59 C5
Ohata Japan 41°24N 141°10E 30 D10
Ohau, L. N.Z. 44°15S 169°53E 59 F2
Ohio □ U.S.A. 40°15N 82°45W 82 F2
Ohio → U.S.A. 36°59N 89°8W 80 G9
Ohře → Czech Rep. 50°30N 14°10E 16 C8
Ohrid Macedonia 41°8N 20°52E 23 D9
Ohridsko Jezero Macedonia 41°8N 20°52E 23 D9
Ohrigstad S. Africa 24°39S 30°36E 57 C5
Oiapoque Brazil 3°50N 51°50W 93
Oikou China 38°35N 117°42E 35 E9
Oil City U.S.A. 41°26N 79°42W 82 E5
Oil Springs Canada 42°47N 82°7W 82 D2
Oildale U.S.A. 35°25N 119°1W 79 K7
Oise → France 49°0N 2°4E 20 B5
Oistins Barbados 13°4N 59°33W 89 g
Oistins B. Barbados 13°4N 59°33W 89 g
Ōita Japan 33°14N 131°36E 31 H5
Ōita □ Japan 33°15N 131°30E 31 H5
Oiticica Brazil 5°3S 41°5W 93 E10
Ojai U.S.A. 34°27N 119°15W 79 L7
Ojinaga Mexico 29°34N 104°25W 86 B4
Ojiya Japan 37°18N 138°48E 31 F9
Ojo Caliente Mexico 21°53N 102°15W 86 C4
Ojos del Salado, Cerro Argentina 27°0S 68°40W 94 B2
Oka → Russia 56°20N 43°59E 18 C7
Okaba Indonesia 8°6S 139°42E 37 F9
Okahandja Namibia 22°0S 16°59E 56 C2
Okanagan L. Canada 50°0N 119°30W 70 D5
Okandja Gabon 0°35S 13°45E 52 E2
Okanogan U.S.A. 48°22N 119°35W 76 B4
Okanogan → U.S.A. 48°6N 119°44W 76 B4
Okanogan Range N. Amer. 49°0N 119°55W 70 D5
Okapi △ Dem. Rep. of the Congo 2°30N 27°20E 54 B2
Okaputa Namibia 20°5S 17°0E 56 C2
Okara Pakistan 30°50N 73°31E 42 D5
Okaukuejo Namibia 19°10S 16°0E 56 B2
Okavango Delta Botswana 18°45S 22°45E 56 B3
Okavango Swamp = Okavango Delta Botswana 18°45S 22°45E 56 B3
Okaya Japan 36°5N 138°10E 31 F9
Okayama Japan 34°40N 133°54E 31 G6
Okayama □ Japan 35°0N 133°50E 31 G6
Okazaki Japan 34°57N 137°10E 31 G8
Okeechobee U.S.A. 27°15N 80°50W 85 H14
Okeechobee, L. U.S.A. 27°0N 80°50W 85 H14
Okefenokee ⌂ U.S.A. 30°45N 82°18W 85 F13
Okefenokee Swamp U.S.A. 30°40N 82°20W 85 F13
Okehampton U.K. 50°44N 4°0W 13 G4
Okha India 22°27N 69°4E 42 H3
Okha Russia 53°40N 143°0E 29 D15
Okhotsk Russia 59°20N 143°10E 29 D15
Okhotsk, Sea of Asia 55°0N 145°0E 29 D15
Okhotskiy Perevoz Russia 61°52N 135°35E 29 C14
Okhtyrka Ukraine 50°25N 35°0E 19 D5
Oki-Shotō Japan 36°5N 133°15E 31 F6
Okiep S. Africa 29°39S 17°53E 56 D2
Okinawa Japan 26°19N 127°46E 31 L3
Okinawa □ Japan 26°40N 128°0E 31 L4
Okinawa-Guntō Japan 26°40N 128°0E 31 L4
Okinawa-Jima Japan 26°32N 128°0E 31 L4
Okino-erabu-Shima Japan 27°21N 128°33E 31 L4
Oklahoma □ U.S.A. 35°20N 97°30W 84 D6
Oklahoma City U.S.A. 35°30N 97°30W 84 D6
Okmulgee U.S.A. 35°37N 95°58W 84 D7
Oknitsa = Ocniţa Moldova 48°25N 27°30E 17 D14
Okolo Uganda 2°37N 31°8E 54 B3
Okolona U.S.A. 34°0N 88°45W 85 E10
Okombahe Namibia 21°23S 15°22E 56 C2
Okotoks Canada 50°43N 113°58W 70 C6
Oksibil Indonesia 4°59S 140°35E 37 E10
Oksovskiy Russia 62°33N 39°57E 18 B6
Oktyabrsk = Qandyaghash Kazakhstan 49°28N 57°25E 19 E10
Oktyabrskiy = Aktsyabrski Belarus 52°38N 28°53E 17 B15
Oktyabrskiy Bashkortostan, Russia 54°28N 53°28E 18 D9
Oktyabrskiy Kamchatka, Russia 52°39N 156°14E 29 D16
Oktyabrskoy Revolyutsii, Ostrov Russia 79°30N 97°0E 29 B10
Okuru N.Z. 43°55S 168°55E 59 E2
Okushiri-Tō Japan 42°15N 139°30E 30 C9
Okwa → Botswana 22°30S 23°0E 56 C3
Ola Russia 59°35N 151°17E 29 D16
Ola U.S.A. 35°2N 93°13W 84 D8
Ólafsfjörður Iceland 66°4N 18°39W 8 C4
Ólafsvík Iceland 64°53N 23°43W 8 D2
Olancha U.S.A. 36°17N 118°1W 79 J8
Olancha Pk. U.S.A. 36°16N 118°7W 79 J8
Olanchito Honduras 15°30N 86°30W 88 C2
Öland Sweden 56°45N 16°38E 9 H17
Olary Australia 32°18S 140°19E 63 E3
Olascoaga Argentina 35°15S 60°39W 94 D3
Olathe U.S.A. 38°53N 94°49W 80 F6
Olavarría Argentina 36°55S 60°20W 94 D3
Oława Poland 50°57N 17°20E 17 C9
Ólbia Italy 40°55N 9°31E 22 D3
Olcott U.S.A. 43°20N 78°42W 82 C6
Old Bahama Chan. = Bahama, Canal Viejo de W. Indies 22°10N 77°30W 88 B4
Old Baldy Pk. = San Antonio, Mt. U.S.A. 34°17N 117°38W 79 L9
Old Bridge U.S.A. 40°25N 74°22W 83 F10
Old Castile = Castilla y Leon □ Spain 42°0N 5°0W 21 B3
Old Crow Canada 67°30N 139°55W 68 C6
Old Dale U.S.A. 34°8N 115°47W 79 L11
Old Forge N.Y., U.S.A. 43°43N 74°58W 83 C10
Old Forge Pa., U.S.A. 41°22N 75°45W 83 E9
Old Perlican Canada 48°5N 53°1W 73 C9
Old Shinyanga Tanzania 3°33S 33°27E 54 C3
Old Speck Mt. U.S.A. 44°34N 70°57W 83 B14
Old Town U.S.A. 44°56N 68°39W 81 C19
Old Washington U.S.A. 40°2N 81°27W 82 F3
Old Wives L. Canada 50°5N 106°0W 71 C7
Oldbury U.K. 51°38N 2°33W 13 F5
Oldcastle Ireland 53°46N 7°10W 10 C4
Oldeani Tanzania 3°22S 35°35E 54 C4
Oldenburg Germany 53°9N 8°13E 16 B5
Oldenzaal Neths. 52°19N 6°53E 15 B6
Oldham U.K. 53°33N 2°7W 12 D5
Oldman → Canada 49°57N 111°42W 70 D6
Oldmeldrum U.K. 57°20N 2°19W 11 D6
Olds Canada 51°50N 114°10W 70 C6
Olduvai Gorge Tanzania 2°57S 35°23E 54 C4
Oldziyt Mongolia 44°40N 109°1E 34 B5
Olean U.S.A. 42°5N 78°26W 82 D6
Olekma → Russia 60°22N 120°42E 29 C13
Olekminsk Russia 60°25N 120°30E 29 C13
Oleksandriya Ukraine 50°37N 26°19E 17 C14
Olema U.S.A. 38°3N 122°47W 78 G4
Olenegorsk Russia 68°9N 33°18E 8 B25
Olenek Russia 68°28N 112°18E 29 C12
Olenek → Russia 73°0N 120°10E 29 B13
Oléron, Î. d' France 45°55N 1°15W 20 D3
Oleśnica Poland 51°13N 17°22E 17 C9
Olevsk Ukraine 51°12N 27°39E 17 C14
Olga, L. Canada 49°47N 77°15W 72 C4
Olgas, The = Kata Tjuta Australia 25°20S 130°50E 61 E5
Ölgiy Mongolia 48°56N 89°57E 32 B3
Olhão Portugal 37°3N 7°48W 21 D2
Olifants = Elefantes → Africa 24°10S 32°40E 57 C5
Olifants → Namibia 25°30S 19°30E 56 C2
Olifantshoek S. Africa 27°57S 22°42E 56 D3
Ólimbos, Óros = Olymbos Oros Greece 40°6N 22°23E 23 D10
Olímpia Brazil 20°44S 48°54W 95 A6
Olinda Brazil 8°1S 34°51W 93 E12
Oliva Argentina 32°0S 63°38W 94 C3
Olivares, Cerro los Argentina 30°18S 69°55W 94 C2
Olive Branch U.S.A. 34°57N 89°49W 85 D10
Olivehurst U.S.A. 39°6N 121°34W 78 F5
Olivenza Spain 38°41N 7°9W 21 C2
Oliver Canada 49°13N 119°37W 70 D5
Oliver L. Canada 56°56N 103°22W 71 B8
Ollagüe Chile 21°15S 68°10W 94 A2
Olmaliq Uzbekistan 40°50N 69°35E 28 E7
Olney Ill., U.S.A. 38°44N 88°5W 80 F9
Olney Tex., U.S.A. 33°22N 98°45W 84 E5
Oloitokitok Kenya 2°56S 37°30E 54 C4
Olomane → Canada 50°14N 60°37W 73 B7
Olomouc Czech Rep. 49°38N 17°12E 17 D9
Olonets Russia 61°0N 32°54E 18 B5
Olongapo Phil. 14°50N 120°18E 37 B6
Olosega Amer. Samoa 14°10S 169°37W 59 b
Olosenga = Swains I. Amer. Samoa 11°11S 171°4W 65 J11
Olot Spain 42°11N 2°30E 21 A7
Olovyannaya Russia 50°58N 115°35E 29 D12
Oloy → Russia 66°29N 159°29E 29 C16
Olsztyn Poland 53°48N 20°29E 17 B11
Olt → Romania 43°43N 24°51E 17 G13
Olteniţa Romania 44°7N 26°42E 17 F14
Olton U.S.A. 34°11N 102°8W 84 D3
Olymbos Cyprus 35°21N 33°45E 25 D12
Olymbos Oros Greece 40°6N 22°23E 23 D10
Olympia Greece 37°39N 21°39E 23 F9
Olympia U.S.A. 47°3N 122°53W 78 D4
Olympic △ U.S.A. 47°45N 123°43W 78 C3
Olympic Dam Australia 30°30S 136°55E 63 E2
Olympic Mts. U.S.A. 47°55N 123°45W 78 C3
Olympus Cyprus 34°56N 32°52E 25 E11
Olympus, Mt. = Olymbos Oros Greece 40°6N 22°23E 23 D10
Olympus, Mt. = Uludağ Turkey 40°4N 29°13E 23 D13
Olympus, Mt. U.S.A. 47°48N 123°43W 78 C3
Olyphant U.S.A. 41°27N 75°36W 83 E9
Olyutorskiy, Mys Russia 59°55N 170°27E 29 D18
Om → Russia 54°59N 73°22E 28 D8
Om Koi Thailand 17°48N 98°22E 38 D2
Ōma Japan 41°45N 141°5E 30 D10
Ōmachi Japan 36°30N 137°50E 31 F8
Ōmae-Zaki Japan 34°36N 138°14E 31 G9
Ōmagari Japan 39°27N 140°29E 30 E10
Omagh U.K. 54°36N 7°19W 10 B4
Omagh □ U.K. 54°35N 7°15W 10 B4
Omaha U.S.A. 41°17N 95°58W 80 E6
Omak U.S.A. 48°25N 119°31W 76 B4
Omalos Greece 35°19N 23°55E 25 D5
Oman ■ Asia 23°0N 58°0E 47 C6
Oman, G. of Asia 24°30N 58°30E 45 E8
Omaruru Namibia 21°26S 16°0E 56 C2
Omaruru → Namibia 22°7S 14°15E 56 C1
Omate Peru 16°45S 71°0W 92 G4
Ombai, Selat Indonesia 8°30S 124°50E 37 F6
Omboué Gabon 1°35S 9°15E 52 E1
Ombrone → Italy 42°42N 11°5E 22 C4
Omdurmân Sudan 15°40N 32°28E 51 E12
Omemee Canada 44°18N 78°33W 82 B6
Omeonga Dem. Rep. of the Congo 3°40S 24°22E 54 C1
Ometepe, I. de Nic. 11°32N 85°35W 88 D2
Ometepec Mexico 16°41N 98°25W 87 D5
Ominato Japan 41°17N 141°10E 30 D10
Omineca → Canada 56°3N 124°16W 70 B4
Omineca Mts. Canada 56°30N 125°30W 70 B3
Omitara Namibia 22°16S 18°2E 56 C2
Ōmiya = Saitama Japan 35°54N 139°38E 31 G9
Ommen Neths. 52°31N 6°26E 15 B6
Ömnögovĭ □ Mongolia 43°15N 104°0E 34 C3
Omo → Ethiopia 6°25N 36°10E 47 F2
Omodhos Cyprus 34°51N 32°48E 25 E11
Omolon → Russia 68°42N 158°36E 29 C16
Omono-Gawa → Japan 39°46N 140°3E 30 E10
Ompha Canada 45°0N 76°50W 83 B8
Omsk Russia 55°0N 73°12E 28 D8
Omsukchan Russia 62°32N 155°48E 29 C16
Ōmu Japan 44°34N 142°58E 30 B11
Omul, Vf. Romania 45°27N 25°29E 17 F13
Ōmura Japan 32°56N 129°57E 31 H4
Omuramba Omatako → Namibia 17°45S 20°25E 56 B2
Omuramba Ovambo → Namibia 18°45S 16°59E 56 B2
Ōmuta Japan 33°5N 130°26E 31 H5
Onaga U.S.A. 39°29N 96°10W 80 F5
Onalaska U.S.A. 43°53N 91°14W 80 D8
Onancock U.S.A. 37°43N 75°45W 81 G16
Onang Indonesia 3°2S 118°49E 37 E5
Onangue, L. Gabon 0°57S 10°4E 52 E2
Onaping L. Canada 47°3N 81°30W 72 C3
Onavas Mexico 28°31N 109°35W 86 B3
Onawa U.S.A. 42°2N 96°6W 80 D5
Oncócua Angola 16°30S 13°25E 56 B1
Onda Spain 39°55N 0°17W 21 C5
Ondangwa Namibia 17°57S 16°4E 56 B2
Ondjiva Angola 16°48S 15°50E 56 B2
Öndörshil Mongolia 45°13N 108°5E 34 B5
Öndverðarnes Iceland 64°52N 24°0W 8 D2
One Tree Australia 34°11S 144°43E 63 E3
Oneata Fiji 18°26S 178°25W 59 a
Onega Russia 64°0N 38°10E 18 B6
Onega → Russia 63°58N 38°2E 18 B6
Onega, G. of = Onezhskaya Guba Russia 64°24N 36°38E 18 B6
Onega, L. = Onezhskoye Ozero Russia 61°44N 35°22E 18 B6
Oneida U.S.A. 43°6N 75°39W 83 C9
Oneida L. U.S.A. 43°12N 75°54W 83 C9
O'Neill U.S.A. 42°27N 98°39W 80 D4
Onekotan, Ostrov Russia 49°25N 154°45E 29 E16
Onema Dem. Rep. of the Congo 4°35S 24°30E 54 C1
Oneonta U.S.A. 42°27N 75°4W 83 D9
Oneşti Romania 46°17N 26°47E 17 E14
Onezhskaya Guba Russia 64°24N 36°38E 18 B6
Onezhskoye Ozero Russia 61°44N 35°22E 18 B6
Ongarue N.Z. 38°42S 175°19E 59 C5
Ongea Levu = Ogea Levu Fiji 19°8S 178°24W 59 a
Ongers → S. Africa 31°4S 23°13E 56 E3
Ongerup Australia 33°58S 118°28E 61 F2
Ongjin N. Korea 37°56N 125°21E 35 F13
Ongkharak Thailand 14°8N 101°1E 38 E3
Ongniud Qi China 43°0N 118°38E 35 C10
Ongoka Dem. Rep. of the Congo 1°20S 26°0E 54 C2
Ongole India 15°33N 80°2E 40 M12
Ongon = Havirga Mongolia 45°41N 113°5E 34 B7
Onida U.S.A. 44°42N 100°4W 80 C3
Onilahy → Madag. 23°34S 43°45E 57 C7
Onitsha Nigeria 6°6N 6°42E 50 G7
Ono Fiji 18°55S 178°29E 59 a
Onoda Japan 33°59N 131°11E 31 G5
Onslow Australia 21°40S 115°12E 60 D2
Onslow B. U.S.A. 34°20N 77°15W 85 D16
Ontake-San Japan 35°53N 137°29E 31 G8
Ontario Calif., U.S.A. 34°4N 117°39W 79 L9
Ontario Oreg., U.S.A. 44°2N 116°58W 76 D5
Ontario □ Canada 48°0N 83°0W 72 B2
Ontario, L. N. Amer. 43°20N 78°0W 82 C7
Ontonagon U.S.A. 46°52N 89°19W 80 B9
Onyx U.S.A. 35°41N 118°14W 79 K8
Oodnadatta Australia 27°33S 135°30E 63 D2
Ooldea Australia 30°27S 131°50E 61 F5
Oombulgurri Australia 15°15S 127°45E 60 C4
Oorindi Australia 20°40S 141°1E 62 C3
Oost-Vlaanderen □ Belgium 51°5N 3°50E 15 C3
Oostende Belgium 51°15N 2°54E 15 C2
Oosterhout Neths. 51°39N 4°47E 15 C4
Oosterschelde → Neths. 51°33N 4°0E 15 C4
Oosterwolde Neths. 53°0N 6°17E 15 B6
Ootacamund = Udagamandalam India 11°30N 76°44E 40 P10
Ootsa L. Canada 53°50N 126°2W 70 C3
Op Luang △ Thailand 18°12N 98°32E 38 C2
Opala Dem. Rep. of the Congo 0°40S 24°20E 54 C1
Opanake Sri Lanka 6°35N 80°40E 40 R12
Opasatika Canada 49°30N 82°50W 72 C3
Opasquia ⌂ Canada 53°33N 93°5W 72 B1
Opava Czech Rep. 49°57N 17°58E 17 D9
Opelika U.S.A. 32°39N 85°23W 85 E12
Opelousas U.S.A. 30°32N 92°5W 84 F8
Opémisca, L. Canada 49°56N 74°52W 72 C5
Opheim U.S.A. 48°51N 106°24W 76 B10
Ophthalmia Ra. Australia 23°15S 119°30E 60 D2
Opinaca → Canada 52°15N 78°2W 72 B4
Opinaca, Rés. Canada 52°39N 76°20W 72 B4
Opinnagau → Canada 54°12N 82°25W 72 B3
Opiscotéo, L. Canada 53°10N 68°10W 73 B6
Opobo Nigeria 4°35N 7°34E 50 H7
Opole Poland 50°42N 17°58E 17 C9
Oponono L. Namibia 18°8S 15°45E 56 B2
Oporto = Porto Portugal 41°8N 8°40W 21 B1
Opotiki N.Z. 38°1S 177°19E 59 C6
Opp U.S.A. 31°17N 86°16W 85 F11
Oppdal Norway 62°35N 9°41E 8 E13
Opportunity U.S.A. 47°39N 117°15W 76 C5
Opua N.Z. 35°19S 174°9E 59 A5
Opunake N.Z. 39°26S 173°52E 59 C4
Opuwo Namibia 18°3S 13°45E 56 B1
Ora Cyprus 34°51N 33°12E 25 E12
Oracle U.S.A. 32°37N 110°46W 77 K8
Oradea Romania 47°2N 21°58E 17 E11
Öræfajökull Iceland 64°2N 16°39W 8 D5
Orai India 25°58N 79°30E 43 G8
Oral = Zhayyq → Kazakhstan 47°0N 51°48E 19 E9
Oral Kazakhstan 51°20N 51°20E 19 D9
Oran Algeria 35°45N 0°39W 50 A5
Orange Australia 33°15S 149°7E 63 E4
Orange France 44°8N 4°47E 20 D6
Orange Calif., U.S.A. 33°47N 117°51W 79 M9
Orange Mass., U.S.A. 42°35N 72°19W 83 D12
Orange Tex., U.S.A. 30°6N 93°44W 84 F8
Orange Va., U.S.A. 38°15N 78°7W 81 F14
Orange → S. Africa 28°41S 16°28E 56 D2
Orange, C. Brazil 4°20N 51°30W 93 C8
Orange Cove U.S.A. 36°38N 119°19W 78 J7
Orange Free State = Free State □ S. Africa 28°30S 27°0E 56 D4
Orange Grove U.S.A. 27°58N 97°56W 84 H6
Orange Walk Belize 18°6N 88°33W 87 D7
Orangeburg U.S.A. 33°30N 80°52W 85 E14
Orangeville Canada 43°55N 80°5W 82 C4
Orango Guinea-Biss. 11°5N 16°0W 50 F2
Oranienburg Germany 52°45N 13°14E 16 B7
Oranje = Orange → S. Africa 28°41S 16°28E 56 D2
Oranjemund Namibia 28°38S 16°29E 56 D2
Oranjerivier S. Africa 29°40S 24°12E 56 D3
Oranjestad Aruba 12°32N 70°2W 89 D5
Orapa Botswana 21°15S 25°30E 53 J5
Oras Phil. 12°9N 125°28E 37 B7
Orbetello Italy 42°27N 11°13E 22 C4
Orbisonia U.S.A. 40°15N 77°54W 82 F7
Orbost Australia 37°40S 148°29E 63 F4
Orcadas Antarctica 60°44S 44°37W 5 C18
Orcas I. U.S.A. 48°42N 122°56W 78 B4
Orchard City U.S.A. 38°50N 107°58W 76 G10
Orchard Homes U.S.A. 46°55N 114°4W 76 C6
Orchila, I. Venezuela 11°48N 66°10W 89 D6
Orchilla, Pta. Canary Is. 27°42N 18°10W 24 G1
Orcutt U.S.A. 34°52N 120°27W 79 L6
Ord U.S.A. 41°36N 98°56W 80 E4
Ord → Australia 15°33S 128°15E 60 C4
Ord, Mt. Australia 17°20S 125°34E 60 C4
Ord Mts. U.S.A. 34°39N 116°45W 79 L10
Orderville U.S.A. 37°17N 112°38W 77 H7
Ordos = Mu Us Shamo China 39°0N 109°0E 34 E5
Ordu Turkey 40°55N 37°53E 19 F6
Ordway U.S.A. 38°13N 103°46W 76 G12
Ore Dem. Rep. of the Congo 3°17N 29°30E 54 B2
Ore Mts. = Erzgebirge Germany 50°27N 12°55E 16 C7
Örebro Sweden 59°20N 15°18E 9 G16
Oregon U.S.A. 42°1N 89°20W 80 D9
Oregon □ U.S.A. 44°0N 121°0W 76 E3
Oregon City U.S.A. 45°21N 122°36W 78 E4
Oregon Dunes ⌂ U.S.A. 43°40N 124°10W 76 E1
Orekhovo-Zuyevo Russia 55°50N 38°55E 18 C6
Orel Russia 52°57N 36°3E 18 D6
Orem U.S.A. 40°19N 111°42W 76 F8
Ören Turkey 37°3N 27°57E 23 F12
Orenburg Russia 51°45N 55°6E 18 D10
Orense = Ourense Spain 42°19N 7°55W 21 A2
Orepuki N.Z. 46°19S 167°46E 59 G1

Orestes Pereyra Mexico 26°30N 105°39W 86 B3
Orestiada Greece 41°30N 26°33E 23 D12
Orfanos Kolpos Greece 40°33N 24°0E 23 D11
Orford Ness U.K. 52°5N 1°35E 13 E9
Organ Pipe Cactus △ U.S.A. 32°0N 112°52W 77 K7
Organos, Pta. de los Canary Is. 28°12N 17°17W 24 F2
Orgaz Spain 39°39N 3°53W 21 C4
Orgeyev = Orhei Moldova 47°24N 28°50E 17 E15
Orhaneli Turkey 39°54N 28°59E 23 E13
Orhangazi Turkey 40°29N 29°18E 23 D13
Orhei Moldova 47°24N 28°50E 17 E15
Orhon Gol → Mongolia 50°21N 106°0E 32 A5
Oriental, Cordillera Colombia 6°0N 73°0W 92 B4
Oriental, Grand Erg Algeria 30°0N 6°30E 50 B7
Orientale □ Dem. Rep. of the Congo 2°20N 26°0E 54 B2
Oriente Argentina 38°44S 60°37W 94 D3
Orihuela Spain 38°7N 0°55W 21 C5
Orillia Canada 44°40N 79°24W 82 B5
Orinoco → Venezuela 9°15N 61°30W 92 B6
Orion Canada 49°27N 110°49W 71 D6
Oriskany U.S.A. 43°10N 75°20W 83 C9
Orissa □ India 20°0N 84°0E 41 K14
Orissaare Estonia 58°34N 23°5E 9 G20
Oristano Italy 39°54N 8°36E 22 E3
Oristano, G. di Italy 39°50N 8°29E 22 E3
Orizaba Mexico 18°51N 97°6W 87 D5
Orizaba, Pico de Mexico 18°58N 97°15W 87 D5
Orkanger Norway 63°18N 9°52E 8 E13
Orkla → Norway 63°18N 9°51E 8 E13
Orkney S. Africa 26°58S 26°40E 56 D4
Orkney □ U.K. 59°2N 3°13W 11 B5
Orkney Is. U.K. 59°0N 3°0W 11 B6
Orland U.S.A. 39°45N 122°12W 78 F4
Orlando U.S.A. 28°32N 81°22W 85 G14
Orléanais France 48°0N 2°0E 20 C5
Orléans France 47°54N 1°52E 20 C4
Orleans U.S.A. 44°49N 72°12W 83 B12
Orléans, Î. d' Canada 46°54N 70°58W 73 C5
Ormara Pakistan 25°16N 64°33E 40 G4
Ormoc Phil. 11°0N 124°37E 37 B6
Ormond N.Z. 38°33S 177°56E 59 C6
Ormond Beach U.S.A. 29°17N 81°3W 85 G14
Ormskirk U.K. 53°35N 2°54W 12 D5
Ormstown Canada 45°8N 74°0W 83 A11
Örnsköldsvik Sweden 63°17N 18°40E 8 E18
Oro N. Korea 40°1N 127°27E 35 D14
Oro → Mexico 25°35N 105°2W 86 B3
Oro Grande U.S.A. 34°36N 117°20W 79 L9
Oro Valley U.S.A. 32°26N 110°58W 77 K8
Orocué Colombia 4°48N 71°20W 92 C4
Orofino U.S.A. 46°29N 116°15W 76 C5
Orohena, Mt. Tahiti 17°37S 149°28W 59 d
Orol Dengizi = Aral Sea Asia 44°30N 60°0E 28 E7
Oromocto Canada 45°54N 66°29W 73 C6
Orono Canada 43°59N 78°37W 82 C6
Orono U.S.A. 44°53N 68°40W 81 C19
Oronsay U.K. 56°1N 6°15W 11 E2
Oroqen Zizhiqi China 50°34N 123°43E 33 A7
Oroquieta Phil. 8°32N 123°44E 37 C6
Orosei Italy 40°23N 9°42E 22 D3
Orosháza Hungary 46°32N 20°42E 17 E11
Orotukan Russia 62°16N 151°42E 29 C16
Oroville Calif., U.S.A. 39°31N 121°33W 78 F5
Oroville Wash., U.S.A. 48°56N 119°26W 76 B4
Oroville, L. U.S.A. 39°33N 121°29W 78 F5
Orroroo Australia 32°43S 138°38E 63 E2
Orrville U.S.A. 40°50N 81°46W 82 F3
Orsha Belarus 54°30N 30°25E 18 D5
Orsk Russia 51°12N 58°34E 28 D6
Orşova Romania 44°41N 22°25E 17 F12
Ortaca Turkey 36°49N 28°45E 23 F13
Ortegal, C. Spain 43°43N 7°52W 21 A2
Orthez France 43°29N 0°48W 20 E3
Ortigueira Spain 43°40N 7°50W 21 A2
Orting U.S.A. 47°6N 122°12W 78 C4
Ortles Italy 46°31N 10°33E 20 C9
Ortón → Bolivia 10°50S 67°0W 92 F5
Ortonville U.S.A. 45°19N 96°27W 80 C5
Orūmīyeh Iran 37°40N 45°0E 44 B5
Orūmīyeh, Daryācheh-ye Iran 37°50N 45°30E 44 B5
Oruro Bolivia 18°0S 67°9W 92 G5
Orust Sweden 58°10N 11°40E 9 G14
Oruzgān □ Afghan. 33°0N 66°0E 40 C5
Orvieto Italy 42°43N 12°7E 22 C5
Orwell N.Y., U.S.A. 43°35N 75°50W 83 C9
Orwell Ohio, U.S.A. 41°32N 80°52W 82 E4
Orwell → U.K. 51°59N 1°18E 13 F9
Orwigsburg U.S.A. 40°38N 76°6W 83 F8
Oryakhovo Bulgaria 43°40N 23°57E 23 C10
Osa Russia 57°17N 55°26E 18 C10
Osa, Pen. de Costa Rica 8°0N 84°0W 88 E3
Osage U.S.A. 43°17N 92°49W 80 D7
Osage → U.S.A. 38°36N 91°57W 80 F8
Osage City U.S.A. 38°38N 95°50W 80 F6
Ōsaka Japan 34°42N 135°30E 31 G7
Osan S. Korea 37°11N 127°4E 35 F14
Osawatomie U.S.A. 38°31N 94°57W 80 F6
Osborne U.S.A. 39°26N 98°42W 80 F4
Osceola Ark., U.S.A. 35°42N 89°58W 85 D10
Osceola Iowa, U.S.A. 41°2N 93°46W 80 E7
Oscoda U.S.A. 44°26N 83°20W 82 B1
Ösel = Saaremaa Estonia 58°30N 22°30E 9 G20
Osgoode Canada 45°8N 75°36W 83 A9
Osh Kyrgyzstan 40°37N 72°49E 32 B2
Oshakati Namibia 17°45S 15°40E 53 H3
Oshawa Canada 43°50N 78°50W 82 C6
Oshigambo Namibia 17°45S 16°5E 56 B2
Oshkosh Nebr., U.S.A. 41°24N 102°21W 80 E2
Oshkosh Wis., U.S.A. 44°1N 88°33W 80 C9
Oshmyany = Ashmyany Belarus 54°26N 25°52E 17 A13
Oshnovīyeh Iran 37°2N 45°6E 44 B5
Oshogbo Nigeria 7°48N 4°37E 50 G6
Oshtorīnān Iran 34°1N 48°38E 45 C6
Oshwe Dem. Rep. of the Congo 3°25S 19°28E 52 E3
Osijek Croatia 45°34N 18°41E 23 B8
Osipovichi = Asipovichy Belarus 53°19N 28°33E 17 B15
Osiyan India 26°43N 72°55E 42 F5
Osizweni S. Africa 27°49S 30°7E 57 D5
Oskaloosa U.S.A. 41°18N 92°39W 80 E7
Oskarshamn Sweden 57°15N 16°27E 9 H17
Oskélanéo Canada 48°5N 75°15W 72 C4
Öskemen Kazakhstan 50°0N 82°36E 28 E9
Oslo Norway 59°54N 10°43E 9 G14
Oslofjorden Norway 59°20N 10°35E 9 G14
Osmanabad India 18°5N 76°10E 40 K10
Osmaniye Turkey 37°5N 36°10E 44 B3
Osnabrück Germany 52°17N 8°3E 16 B5
Osório Brazil 29°53S 50°17W 95 B5
Osorno Chile 40°25S 73°0W 96 E2
Osorno, Vol. Chile 41°0S 72°30W 96 D2
Osoyoos Canada 49°0N 119°30W 70 D5
Osøyro Norway 60°9N 5°30E 8 F11
Ospika → Canada 56°20N 124°0W 70 B4
Osprey Reef Australia 13°52S 146°36E 62 A4
Oss Neths. 51°46N 5°32E 15 C5
Ossa, Mt. Australia 41°52S 146°3E 63 G4
Ossa, Oros Greece 39°47N 22°42E 23 E10
Ossabaw I. U.S.A. 31°50N 81°5W 85 F14
Ossining U.S.A. 41°10N 73°55W 83 E11
Ossipee U.S.A. 43°41N 71°7W 83 C13
Ossokmanuan L. Canada 53°25N 65°0W 73 B7
Ossora Russia 59°20N 163°13E 29 D17
Ostend = Oostende Belgium 51°15N 2°54E 15 C2
Oster Ukraine 50°57N 30°53E 17 C16
Österbotten = Pohjanmaa Finland 62°58N 22°50E 8 E20
Osterburg U.S.A. 40°16N 78°31W 82 F6
Österdalälven Sweden 61°30N 13°45E 8 F15
Østerdalen Norway 61°40N 10°50E 8 F14
Östermyra = Seinäjoki Finland 62°40N 22°51E 8 E20
Österreich = Austria ■ Europe 47°0N 14°0E 16 E8
Östersund Sweden 63°10N 14°38E 8 E16
Ostfriesische Inseln Germany 53°42N 7°0E 16 B4
Ostrava Czech Rep. 49°51N 18°18E 17 D10
Ostróda Poland 53°42N 19°58E 17 B10
Ostroh Ukraine 50°20N 26°30E 17 C14
Ostrołęka Poland 53°4N 21°32E 17 B11
Ostrów Mazowiecka Poland 52°50N 21°51E 17 B11
Ostrów Wielkopolski Poland 51°36N 17°44E 17 C9
Ostrowiec-Świętokrzyski Poland 50°55N 21°22E 17 C11
Ostuni Italy 40°44N 17°35E 23 D7
Ōsumi-Kaikyō Japan 30°55N 131°0E 31 J5
Ōsumi-Shotō Japan 30°30N 130°0E 31 J5
Osuna Spain 37°14N 5°8W 21 D3
Oswegatchie → U.S.A. 44°42N 75°30W 83 B9
Oswego U.S.A. 43°27N 76°31W 83 C8
Oswego → U.S.A. 43°27N 76°30W 83 C8
Oswestry U.K. 52°52N 3°3W 12 E4
Oświęcim Poland 50°2N 19°11E 17 C10
Otago □ N.Z. 45°15S 170°0E 59 F2
Otago Harbour N.Z. 45°47S 170°42E 59 F3
Otaheite B. Trin. & Tob. 10°15N 61°30W 93 K15
Ōtake Japan 34°12N 132°13E 31 G6
Otaki N.Z. 40°45S 175°10E 59 D5
Otaru Japan 43°10N 141°0E 30 C10
Otaru-Wan = Ishikari-Wan Japan 43°25N 141°1E 30 C10
Otavalo Ecuador 0°13N 78°20W 92 C3
Otavi Namibia 19°40S 17°24E 56 B2
Otchinjau Angola 16°30S 13°56E 56 B1
Otego U.S.A. 42°23N 75°10W 83 D9
Otelnuk, L. Canada 56°9N 68°12W 73 A6
Othello U.S.A. 46°50N 119°10W 76 C4
Otish, Mts. Canada 52°18N 70°37W 73 B5
Otjiwarongo Namibia 20°30S 16°33E 56 C2
Oto Tolu Group Tonga 20°21S 174°32W 59 c
Otoineppu Japan 44°44N 142°16E 30 B11
Otorohanga N.Z. 38°12S 175°14E 59 C5
Otoskwin → Canada 52°13N 88°6W 72 B2
Otra → Norway 58°9N 8°1E 9 G13
Otranto Italy 40°9N 18°28E 23 D8
Otranto, C. d' Italy 40°7N 18°30E 23 D8
Otranto, Str. of Italy 40°15N 18°40E 23 D8
Otse S. Africa 25°2S 25°45E 56 D4
Otsego L. U.S.A. 42°45N 74°53W 83 D10
Ōtsu Japan 35°0N 135°50E 31 G7
Ōtsuki Japan 35°36N 138°57E 31 G9
Ottawa = Outaouais → Canada 45°27N 74°8W 72 C5
Ottawa Canada 45°26N 75°42W 83 A9
Ottawa Ill., U.S.A. 41°21N 88°51W 80 E9
Ottawa Kans., U.S.A. 38°37N 95°16W 80 F6
Ottawa Is. Canada 59°35N 80°10W 69 D11
Otter Cr. → U.S.A. 44°13N 73°17W 83 B11
Otter Lake Canada 45°17N 79°56W 82 A5
Otterville Canada 42°55N 80°36W 82 D4
Ottery St. Mary U.K. 50°44N 3°17W 13 G4
Otto Beit Bridge Zimbabwe 15°59S 28°56E 55 F2
Ottosdal S. Africa 26°46S 25°59E 56 D4
Ottumwa U.S.A. 41°1N 92°25W 80 E7
Oturkpo Nigeria 7°16N 8°8E 50 G7
Otway, B. Chile 53°30S 74°0W 96 G2
Otway, C. Australia 38°52S 143°30E 63 F3
Otwock Poland 52°5N 21°20E 17 B11
Ou → Laos 20°4N 102°13E 38 B4
Ou Neua Laos 22°18N 101°48E 38 A3
Ou-Sammyaku Japan 39°20N 140°35E 30 E10
Ouachita → U.S.A. 31°38N 91°49W 84 F9
Ouachita, L. U.S.A. 34°34N 93°12W 84 D8
Ouachita Mts. U.S.A. 34°30N 94°30W 84 D7
Ouagadougou Burkina Faso 12°25N 1°30W 50 F5
Ouahigouya Burkina Faso 13°31N 2°25W 50 F5
Ouahran = Oran Algeria 35°45N 0°39W 50 A5
Ouallene Algeria 24°41N 1°11E 50 D6
Ouarâne Mauritania 21°0N 10°30W 50 D3
Ouargla Algeria 31°59N 5°16E 50 B7
Ouarra → C.A.R. 5°5N 24°26E 52 C4
Ouarzazate Morocco 30°55N 6°50W 50 B4
Oubangi → Dem. Rep. of the Congo 0°30S 17°50E 52 E3
Ouddorp Neths. 51°50N 3°57E 15 C3
Oude Rijn → Neths. 52°12N 4°24E 15 B4
Oudenaarde Belgium 50°50N 3°37E 15 D3
Oudtshoorn S. Africa 33°35S 22°14E 56 E3
Ouessant, Î. d' France 48°28N 5°6W 20 B1
Ouesso Congo 1°37N 16°5E 52 D3
Ouest, Pte. de l' Canada 49°52N 64°40W 73 C7
Ouezzane Morocco 34°51N 5°35W 50 B4
Oughter, L. Ireland 54°1N 7°28W 10 B4
Oughterard Ireland 53°26N 9°18W 10 C2
Ouidah Benin 6°25N 2°0E 50 G6
Oujda Morocco 34°41N 1°55W 50 B5
Oulainen Finland 64°17N 24°47E 8 D21
Oulu Finland 65°1N 25°29E 8 D21
Oulujärvi Finland 64°25N 27°15E 8 D22
Oulujoki → Finland 65°1N 25°30E 8 D21
Oum Chalouba Chad 15°48N 20°46E 51 E10
Oum Hadjer Chad 13°18N 19°41E 51 F9
Ounasjoki → Finland 66°31N 25°40E 8 C21
Ounguati Namibia 22°0S 15°46E 56 C2
Ounianga Kébir Chad 19°4N 20°29E 51 E10
Our → Lux. 49°55N 6°5E 15 E6
Ouray U.S.A. 38°1N 107°40W 77 G10
Ourense Spain 42°19N 7°55W 21 A2
Ouricuri Brazil 7°53S 40°5W 93 E10
Ourinhos Brazil 23°0S 49°54W 95 A6
Ouro Fino Brazil 22°16S 46°25W 95 A6
Ouro Prêto Brazil 20°20S 43°30W 95 A7
Ourthe → Belgium 50°29N 5°35E 15 D5
Ouse → E. Sussex, U.K. 50°47N 0°4E 13 G8
Ouse → N. Yorks., U.K. 53°44N 0°55W 12 D7
Outaouais → Canada 45°27N 74°8W 72 C5
Outardes → Canada 49°24N 69°30W 73 C6
Outer Hebrides U.K. 57°30N 7°40W 11 D1
Outjo Namibia 20°5S 16°7E 56 C2
Outlook Canada 51°30N 107°0W 71 C7
Outokumpu Finland 62°43N 29°1E 8 E23
Ouyen Australia 35°1S 142°22E 63 F3
Ovalau Fiji 17°40S 178°48E 59 a
Ovalle Chile 30°33S 71°18W 94 C1
Ovamboland Namibia 18°30S 16°0E 56 B2
Overflakkee Neths. 51°44N 4°10E 15 C4
Overijssel □ Neths. 52°25N 6°35E 15 B6
Overland Park U.S.A. 38°58N 94°40W 80 F6
Overton U.S.A. 36°33N 114°27W 79 J12
Övertorneå Sweden 66°23N 23°38E 8 C20
Ovid U.S.A. 42°41N 76°49W 83 D8
Oviedo Spain 43°25N 5°50W 21 A3
Oviši Latvia 57°33N 21°44E 9 H19
Ovoot Mongolia 45°21N 113°45E 34 B7
Övör Hangay □ Mongolia 45°0N 102°30E 34 B2
Øvre Årdal Norway 61°19N 7°48E 8 F12
Ovruch Ukraine 51°25N 28°45E 17 C15
Owaka N.Z. 46°27S 169°40E 59 G2
Owambo = Ovamboland Namibia 18°30S 16°0E 56 B2
Owasco L. U.S.A. 42°50N 76°31W 83 D8
Owase Japan 34°7N 136°12E 31 G8
Owatonna U.S.A. 44°5N 93°14W 80 C7
Owbeh Afghan. 34°28N 63°10E 40 B3
Owego U.S.A. 42°6N 76°16W 83 D8
Owen Falls Dam = Nalubaale Dam Uganda 0°30N 33°5E 54 B3
Owen Sound Canada 44°35N 80°55W 82 B4
Owen Stanley Ra. Papua N. G. 8°30S 147°0E 58 B7
Oweniny → Ireland 54°8N 9°34W 10 B2
Owens → U.S.A. 36°32N 117°59W 78 J9
Owens L. U.S.A. 36°26N 117°57W 79 J9
Owensboro U.S.A. 37°46N 87°7W 80 G10
Owl → Canada 57°51N 92°44W 71 B10
Owo Nigeria 7°10N 5°39E 50 G7
Owosso U.S.A. 43°0N 84°10W 81 D11
Owyhee U.S.A. 41°57N 116°6W 76 F5
Owyhee → U.S.A. 43°49N 117°2W 76 E5
Owyhee, L. U.S.A. 43°38N 117°14W 76 E5
Ox Mts. = Slieve Gamph Ireland 54°6N 9°0W 10 B3
Öxarfjörður Iceland 66°15N 16°45W 8 C5
Oxbow Canada 49°14N 102°10W 71 D8
Oxelösund Sweden 58°43N 17°5E 9 G17
Oxford N.Z. 43°18S 172°11E 59 E4
Oxford U.K. 51°46N 1°15W 13 F6
Oxford Mass., U.S.A. 42°7N 71°52W 83 D13
Oxford Miss., U.S.A. 34°22N 89°31W 85 D10
Oxford N.C., U.S.A. 36°19N 78°35W 85 C15
Oxford N.Y., U.S.A. 42°27N 75°36W 83 D9
Oxford Ohio, U.S.A. 39°31N 84°45W 81 F11
Oxford L. Canada 54°51N 95°37W 71 C9
Oxfordshire □ U.K. 51°48N 1°16W 13 F6
Oxnard U.S.A. 34°12N 119°11W 79 L7
Oxus = Amudarya → Uzbekistan 43°58N 59°34E 28 E6
Oya Malaysia 2°55N 111°55E 36 D4
Oyama Japan 36°18N 139°48E 31 F9
Oyem Gabon 1°34N 11°31E 52 D2
Oyen Canada 51°22N 110°28W 71 C6
Oykel → U.K. 57°56N 4°26W 11 D4
Oymyakon Russia 63°25N 142°44E 29 C15
Oyo Nigeria 7°46N 3°56E 50 G6
Oyster Bay U.S.A. 40°52N 73°32W 83 F11
Ōyūbari Japan 43°1N 142°5E 30 C11
Ozamiz Phil. 8°15N 123°50E 37 C6
Ozark Ala., U.S.A. 31°28N 85°39W 85 F12
Ozark Ark., U.S.A. 35°29N 93°50W 84 D8
Ozark Mo., U.S.A. 37°1N 93°12W 80 G7
Ozark Plateau U.S.A. 37°20N 91°40W 80 G8
Ozarks, L. of the U.S.A. 38°12N 92°38W 80 F7
Ózd Hungary 48°14N 20°15E 17 D11
Ozernovskiy Russia 51°30N 156°31E 29 D16
Ozette, L. U.S.A. 48°6N 124°38W 78 B2
Ozieri Italy 40°35N 9°0E 22 D3
Ozona U.S.A. 30°43N 101°12W 84 F4
Ozuluama Mexico 21°40N 97°51W 87 C5

P

Pa-an Burma 16°51N 97°40E 41 L20
Pa Mong Dam Thailand 18°0N 102°22E 38 D4
Pa Sak → Thailand 15°30N 101°0E 38 E3
Paamiut Greenland 62°0N 49°43W 4 C5
Paarl S. Africa 33°45S 18°56E 56 E2
Pab Hills Pakistan 26°30N 66°45E 42 F2
Pabbay U.K. 57°46N 7°14W 11 D1
Pabianice Poland 51°40N 19°20E 17 C10
Pabna Bangla. 24°1N 89°18E 41 G16
Pabo Uganda 3°1N 32°10E 54 B3
Pacaja → Brazil 1°56S 50°50W 93 D8
Pacaraima, Sa. S. Amer. 4°0N 62°30W 92 C6
Pacasmayo Peru 7°20S 79°35W 92 E3
Pachitea → Peru 8°46S 74°33W 92 E4
Pachmarhi India 22°28N 78°26E 43 H8
Pachnes Greece 35°16N 24°4E 25 D6
Pachpadra India 25°58N 72°10E 42 G5
Pachuca Mexico 20°7N 98°44W 87 C5
Pacific Antarctic Ridge Pac. Oc. 43°0S 115°0W 5 B13
Pacific Grove U.S.A. 36°38N 121°56W 78 J5
Pacific Ocean 10°0N 140°0W 65 G14
Pacific Rim △ Canada 48°40N 124°45W 78 B2
Pacifica U.S.A. 37°37N 122°27W 78 H4
Pacitan Indonesia 8°12S 111°7E 37 H14
Packwood U.S.A. 46°36N 121°40W 78 D5
Padaido, Kepulauan Indonesia 1°15S 136°30E 37 E9
Padang Riau, Indonesia 1°30N 102°30E 39 M4
Padang Sumatera Barat, Indonesia 1°0S 100°20E 36 E2
Padang Endau Malaysia 2°40N 103°38E 39 L4
Padangpanjang Indonesia 0°40S 100°20E 36 E2
Padangsidempuan Indonesia 1°30N 99°15E 36 D1
Paddle Prairie Canada 57°57N 117°29W 70 B5
Paderborn Germany 51°42N 8°45E 16 C5
Padma India 24°12N 85°22E 43 G11
Pádova Italy 45°25N 11°53E 22 B4
Padra India 22°15N 73°7E 42 H5
Padrauna India 26°54N 83°59E 43 F10
Padre I. U.S.A. 27°10N 97°25W 84 H6
Padre Island △ U.S.A. 27°0N 97°25W 84 H6
Padstow U.K. 50°33N 4°58W 13 G3
Padua = Pádova Italy 45°25N 11°53E 22 B4
Paducah Ky., U.S.A. 37°5N 88°37W 80 G9
Paducah Tex., U.S.A. 34°1N 100°18W 84 D4
Paea Tahiti 17°41S 149°35W 59 d
Paeroa N.Z. 37°23S 175°41E 59 B5
Pafúri Mozam. 22°28S 31°17E 57 C5
Pag Croatia 44°25N 15°3E 16 F8
Pagadian Phil. 7°55N 123°30E 37 C6
Pagai Selatan, Pulau Indonesia 3°0S 100°15E 36 E2
Pagai Utara, Pulau Indonesia 2°35S 100°0E 36 E2
Pagalu = Annobón Atl. Oc. 1°25S 5°36E 49 G4
Pagara India 24°22N 80°1E 43 G9
Pagastikos Kolpos Greece 39°15N 23°0E 23 E10
Pagatan Indonesia 3°33S 115°59E 36 E5
Page U.S.A. 36°57N 111°27W 77 H8
Paget, Mt. S. Georgia 54°26S 36°31W 96 G9
Pago Pago Amer. Samoa 14°16S 170°43W 59 b
Pagosa Springs U.S.A. 37°16N 107°1W 77 H10
Pagwa River Canada 50°2N 85°14W 72 B2
Pāhala U.S.A. 19°12N 155°29W 74 b
Pahang → Malaysia 3°30N 103°9E 39 L4
Pahiatua N.Z. 40°27S 175°50E 59 D5
Pahokee U.S.A. 26°50N 80°40W 85 H14
Pahrump U.S.A. 36°12N 115°59W 79 J11
Pahute Mesa U.S.A. 37°20N 116°45W 78 H10
Pai Thailand 19°19N 98°27E 38 C2
Paicines U.S.A. 36°44N 121°17W 78 J5
Paide Estonia 58°53N 25°33E 9 G21
Paignton U.K. 50°26N 3°35W 13 G4
Päijänne Finland 61°30N 25°30E 8 F21
Pailani India 25°45N 80°26E 43 G9
Pailin Cambodia 12°46N 102°36E 38 F4
Painan Indonesia 1°21S 100°34E 36 E2
Painesville U.S.A. 41°43N 81°15W 82 E3
Paint Hills = Wemindji Canada 53°0N 78°49W 72 B4
Paint L. Canada 55°28N 97°57W 71 B9
Painted Desert U.S.A. 36°0N 111°0W 77 H8
Paintsville U.S.A. 37°49N 82°48W 81 G12
País Vasco □ Spain 42°50N 2°45W 21 A4
Paisley Canada 44°18N 81°16W 82 B3
Paisley U.K. 55°50N 4°25W 11 F4
Paisley U.S.A. 42°42N 120°32W 76 E3
Paita Peru 5°11S 81°9W 92 E2
Pajares, Puerto de Spain 42°58N 5°46W 21 A3
Pak Lay Laos 18°15N 101°27E 38 C3
Pak Phanang Thailand 8°21N 100°12E 39 H3
Pak Sane Laos 18°22N 103°39E 38 C4
Pak Song Laos 15°11N 106°14E 38 E6
Pak Suong Laos 19°58N 102°15E 38 C4
Pak Tam Chung China 22°24N 114°19E 33 G11
Pakaur India 24°38N 87°51E 43 G12
Pakch'ŏn N. Korea 39°44N 125°35E 35 E13
Pakenham Canada 45°18N 76°18W 83 A8
Pakhuis S. Africa 32°9S 19°5E 56 E
Pakistan ■ Asia 30°0N 70°0E 42 E
Pakkading Laos 18°19N 103°59E 38 C
Pakokku Burma 21°20N 95°0E 41 J1
Pakowki L. Canada 49°20N 111°0W 71 D
Pakpattan Pakistan 30°25N 73°27E 42 D
Paktīā □ Afghan. 33°30N 69°15E 40 C
Paktīkā □ Afghan. 32°30N 69°0E 40 C
Pakwach Uganda 2°28N 31°27E 54 B
Pakxe Laos 15°5N 105°52E 38 E
Pal Lahara India 21°27N 85°11E 43 J1
Pala Chad 9°25N 15°5E 51 G
Pala Dem. Rep. of the Congo 6°45S 29°30E 54 D
Pala U.S.A. 33°22N 117°5W 79 M
Palabek Uganda 3°22N 32°33E 54 B
Palacios U.S.A. 28°42N 96°13W 84 G
Palagruža Croatia 42°24N 16°15E 22 C
Palam India 19°0N 77°0E 40 K1
Palampur India 32°10N 76°30E 42 C
Palana Australia 39°45S 147°55E 63 F
Palana Russia 59°10N 159°59E 29 D1
Palanan Phil. 17°8N 122°29E 37 A
Palanan Pt. Phil. 17°17N 122°30E 37 A
Palandri Pakistan 33°42N 73°40E 43 C
Palanga Lithuania 55°58N 21°3E 9 J1
Palangkaraya Indonesia 2°16S 113°56E 36 E
Palani Hills India 10°14N 77°33E 40 P1
Palanpur India 24°10N 72°25E 42 G
Palapye Botswana 22°30S 27°7E 56 C
Palas Pakistan 35°4N 73°14E 43 B
Palasponga India 21°47N 85°34E 43 J1
Palatka Russia 60°6N 150°54E 29 C1
Palatka U.S.A. 29°39N 81°38W 85 G1
Palau ■ Palau 7°30N 134°30E 58 A
Palauk Burma 13°10N 98°40E 38 F
Palawan Phil. 9°30N 118°30E 36 C
Palayankottai India 8°45N 77°45E 40 Q1
Paldiski Estonia 59°23N 24°9E 9 G2
Palekastro Greece 35°12N 26°15E 25 D
Paleleh Indonesia 1°10N 121°50E 37 D
Palembang Indonesia 3°0S 104°50E 36 E
Palencia Spain 42°1N 4°34W 21 A
Palenque Mexico 17°29N 92°1W 87 D
Paleochora Greece 35°16N 23°39E 25 D
Paleokastritsa Greece 39°40N 19°41E 25 A
Paleometokho Cyprus 35°7N 33°11E 25 D1
Palermo Italy 38°7N 13°22E 22
Palermo U.S.A. 39°26N 121°33W 76 G
Palestina Chile 23°50S 69°47W 96 A
Palestine Asia 32°0N 35°0E 46 D
Palestine U.S.A. 31°46N 95°38W 84
Paletwa Burma 21°10N 92°50E 41 J
Palghat India 10°46N 76°42E 40 P
Palgrave, Mt. Australia 23°22S 115°58E 60
Pali India 25°50N 73°20E 42 G
Palikir Micronesia 6°55N 158°9E 64
Paliouri, Akra Greece 39°57N 23°45E 23 E
Palisades Res. U.S.A. 43°20N 111°12W 76
Paliseul Belgium 49°54N 5°8E 15
Palitana India 21°32N 71°49E 42 J
Palizada Mexico 18°15N 92°5W 87 D
Palk Bay Asia 9°30N 79°15E 40 Q1
Palk Strait Asia 10°0N 79°45E 40 Q1
Palkānah Iraq 35°49N 44°26E 44
Palkot India 22°53N 84°39E 43 H1
Pallanza = Verbánia Italy 45°56N 8°33E 20
Pallarenda Australia 19°12S 146°46E 62
Pallinup → Australia 34°27S 118°50E 61
Pallisa Uganda 1°12N 33°43E 54
Pallu India 28°59N 74°14E 42
Palm Bay U.S.A. 28°2N 80°35W 85 G1
Palm Beach U.S.A. 26°43N 80°2W 85 H1
Palm Coast U.S.A. 29°35N 81°12W 85 G1
Palm Desert U.S.A. 33°43N 116°22W 79 M1
Palm Is. Australia 18°40S 146°35E 62
Palm Springs U.S.A. 33°50N 116°33W 79 M1
Palma Mozam. 10°46S 40°29E 55
Palma, B. de Spain 39°30N 2°39E 24
Palma de Mallorca Spain 39°35N 2°39E 24
Palma Nova = Palmanova Spain 39°32N 2°34E 24
Palma Soriano Cuba 20°15N 76°0W 88
Palmanova Spain 39°32N 2°34E 24
Palmares Brazil 8°41S 35°28W 93 E1
Palmas Brazil 26°29S 52°0W 95
Palmas, C. Liberia 4°27N 7°46W 50
Pálmas, G. di Italy 39°0N 8°30E 22
Palmdale U.S.A. 34°35N 118°7W 79
Palmeira das Missões Brazil 27°55S 53°17W 95
Palmeira dos Índios Brazil 9°25S 36°37W 93 E1
Palmer Antarctica 64°35S 65°0W 5 C
Palmer U.S.A. 61°36N 149°7W 68
Palmer → Australia 16°0S 142°26E 62
Palmer Arch. Antarctica 64°15S 65°0W 5 C
Palmer Lake U.S.A. 39°7N 104°55W 76 G
Palmer Land Antarctica 73°0S 63°0W 5 D
Palmerston Australia 12°31S 130°59E 60
Palmerston Canada 43°50N 80°51W 82
Palmerston N.Z. 45°29S 170°43E 59
Palmerston North N.Z. 40°21S 175°39E 59
Palmerton U.S.A. 40°48N 75°37W 83
Palmetto U.S.A. 27°31N 82°34W 85 H
Palmi Italy 38°21N 15°51E 22
Palmira Argentina 32°59S 68°34W 94
Palmira Colombia 3°32N 76°16W 92
Palmyra = Tudmur Syria 34°36N 38°15E 44
Palmyra Mo., U.S.A. 39°48N 91°32W 80
Palmyra N.J., U.S.A. 40°0N 75°1W 83
Palmyra N.Y., U.S.A. 43°5N 77°18W 82
Palmyra Pa., U.S.A. 40°18N 76°36W 83
Palmyra Is. Pac. Oc. 5°52N 162°5W 65 G
Palo Alto U.S.A. 37°27N 122°10W 78
Palo Seco Trin. & Tob. 10°4N 61°36W 93 K
Palo Verde U.S.A. 33°26N 114°44W 79 M

lo Verde △ Costa Rica 10°21N 85°21W 88 D2
lomar Mt. U.S.A. 33°22N 116°50W 79 M10
lopo Indonesia 3°0S 120°16E 37 E6
los, C. de Spain 37°38N 0°40W 21 D5
los Verdes, Pt. U.S.A. 33°46N 118°25W 79 M8
los Verdes Estates U.S.A. 33°48N 118°23W 79 M8
lu Indonesia 1°0S 119°52E 37 E5
lu Turkey 38°45N 40°0E 44 B3
lwal India 28°8N 77°19E 42 E7
manukan Indonesia 6°16S 107°49E 37 G12
mekasan Indonesia 7°10S 113°28E 37 G15
menang Indonesia 8°24S 116°6E 37 J19
miers France 43°7N 1°39E 20 E4
mir Tajikistan 37°40N 73°0E 28 F8
mlico → U.S.A. 35°20N 76°28W 85 D16
mlico Sd. U.S.A. 35°20N 76°0W 85 D17
mpa U.S.A. 35°32N 100°58W 84 D4
mpa de las Salinas Argentina 32°1S 66°58W 94 C2
mpanua Indonesia 4°16S 120°8E 37 E6
mpas Argentina 35°0S 63°0W 94 D3
mpas Peru 12°20S 74°50W 92 F4
mplona Colombia 7°23N 72°39W 92 B4
mplona-Iruña Spain 42°48N 1°38W 21 A5
mpoenpoort S. Africa 31°3S 22°40E 56 E3
n de Azúcar Chile 24°5S 68°10W 94 A2
n de Azúcar △ Chile 26°0S 70°40W 94 B1
na U.S.A. 39°23N 89°5W 80 F9
naca U.S.A. 37°47N 114°23W 77 H6
naitan Indonesia 6°36S 105°12E 37 G11
naji India 15°25N 73°50E 40 M8
namá Panama 9°0N 79°25W 88 E4
nama ■ Cent. Amer. 8°48N 79°55W 88 E4
namá, G. de Panama 8°4N 79°20W 88 E4
nama, Isthmus of Cent. Amer. 9°0N 79°0W 66 J12
nama Basin Pac. Oc. 5°0N 83°30W 65 G19
nama Canal Panama 9°10N 79°37W 88 E4
nama City U.S.A. 30°10N 85°40W 85 F12
namint Range U.S.A. 36°20N 117°20W 79 J9
namint Springs U.S.A. 36°20N 117°28W 79 J9
não Peru 9°55S 75°55W 92 E3
nare Thailand 6°51N 101°30E 39 J3
nay Phil. 11°10N 122°30E 37 B6
nay G. Phil. 11°0N 122°30E 37 B6
nayarvi △ Russia 66°16N 30°10E 8 C24
nčevo Serbia 44°52N 20°41E 23 B9
nda Mozam. 24°2S 34°45E 57 C5
ndan Malaysia 1°32N 103°46E 39 d
ndan Phil. 11°45N 122°10E 37 B6
ndan, Selat Singapore 1°15N 103°44E 39 d
ndan Tampoi = Tampoi Malaysia 1°30N 103°39E 39 d
ndegelang Indonesia 6°25S 106°5E 37 G12
ndhana India 21°42N 76°13E 42 J7
ndharpur India 17°41N 75°20E 40 L9
ndo Uruguay 34°44S 56°0W 95 C4
ndo, L. = Hope, L. Australia 28°24S 139°18E 63 D2
ndokratoras Greece 39°45N 19°50E 25 A3
ndora Costa Rica 9°43N 83°3W 88 E3
nevėžys Lithuania 55°42N 24°25E 9 J21
ng-Long Burma 23°11N 98°45E 41 H21
ng Sida △ Thailand 14°5N 102°17E 38 E4
ng-Yang Burma 22°7N 98°48E 41 H21
nga Dem. Rep. of the Congo 1°52N 26°18E 54 B2
ngalanes, Canal des = Ampangalana, Lakandranon' Madag. 22°48S 47°50E 57 C8
ngani Tanzania 5°25S 38°58E 54 D4
ngani → Tanzania 5°26S 38°58E 54 D4
ngfou = Bengbu China 32°58N 117°20E 35 H9
ngil Dem. Rep. of the Congo 3°10S 26°35E 54 C2
ngkah, Tanjung Indonesia 6°51S 112°33E 37 G15
ngkajene Indonesia 4°46S 119°34E 37 E5
ngkalanbrandan Indonesia 4°1N 98°20E 36 D1
ngkalanbuun Indonesia 2°41S 111°37E 36 E4
ngkalpinang Indonesia 2°0S 106°0E 36 E3
ngkor, P. Malaysia 4°13N 100°34E 39 K3
ngnirtung Canada 66°8N 65°43W 69 C13
ngody Russia 65°52N 74°27E 28 C8
nguitch U.S.A. 37°50N 112°26W 77 H7
ngutaran Group Phil. 6°18N 120°34E 37 C6
nhandle U.S.A. 35°21N 101°23W 84 D4
ni Mines India 22°29N 73°50E 42 H5
nia-Mutombo Dem. Rep. of the Congo 5°11S 23°51E 54 D1
nikota I. India 20°46N 71°21E 42 J4
nipat India 29°25N 77°2E 42 E7
njal Range = Pir Panjal Range India 32°30N 76°50E 42 C7
njang, Hon Vietnam 9°20N 103°28E 39 H4
njgur Pakistan 27°0N 64°5E 40 F4
njim = Panaji India 15°25N 73°50E 40 M8
njin China 41°3N 122°2E 35 D12
njnad → Pakistan 28°57N 70°30E 42 E4
njnad Barrage Pakistan 29°22N 71°15E 42 E4
njwai Afghan. 31°26N 65°27E 42 D1
nmunjŏm N. Korea 37°59N 126°38E 35 F14
nna India 24°40N 80°15E 43 G9
nna △ India 24°40N 80°0E 43 G8
nna Hills India 24°40N 81°15E 43 G9
nnawonica Australia 21°39S 116°19E 60 D2
nnga, Tanjung Indonesia 8°54S 116°2E 37 K19
nnirtuuq = Pangnirtung Canada 66°8N 65°43W 69 C13
Pano Akil Pakistan 27°51N 69°7E 42 F3
Pano Lefkara Cyprus 34°53N 33°20E 25 E12
Pano Panayia Cyprus 34°55N 32°38E 25 E11
Panorama Brazil 21°21S 51°51W 95 A5
Panormos Greece 35°25N 24°41E 25 D6
Pansemal India 21°39N 74°42E 42 J6
Panshan = Panjin China 41°3N 122°2E 35 D12
Panshi China 42°58N 126°5E 35 C14
Pantanal Brazil 17°30S 57°40W 92 H7
Pantanos de Centla △ Mexico 18°25N 92°25W 87 D6
Pantar Indonesia 8°28S 124°10E 37 F6
Pante Macassar E. Timor 9°30S 123°58E 37 F6
Pantelleria Italy 36°50N 11°57E 22 F4
Pánuco Mexico 22°3N 98°10W 87 C5
Panzhihua China 26°33N 101°44E 32 D5
Paola Malta 35°52N 14°30E 25 D2
Paola U.S.A. 38°35N 94°53W 80 F6
Paonia U.S.A. 38°52N 107°36W 76 G10
Paopao Moorea 17°30S 149°49W 59 d
Paoting = Baoding China 38°50N 115°28E 34 E8
Paot'ou = Baotou China 40°32N 110°2E 34 D6
Paoua C.A.R. 7°9N 16°20E 52 C3
Pápa Hungary 47°22N 17°30E 17 E9
Papa Stour U.K. 60°20N 1°42W 11 A7
Papa Westray U.K. 59°20N 2°55W 11 B6
Papagayo → Mexico 16°46N 99°43W 87 D5
Papagayo, G. de Costa Rica 10°30N 85°50W 88 D2
Papakura N.Z. 37°4S 174°59E 59 B5
Papantla Mexico 20°27N 97°19W 87 C5
Papar Malaysia 5°45N 116°0E 36 C5
Papara Tahiti 17°43S 149°31W 59 d
Paparoa △ N.Z. 42°7S 171°26E 59 E3
Papeete Tahiti 17°32S 149°34W 59 d
Papenoo Tahiti 17°30S 149°25W 59 d
Papenoo → Tahiti 17°30S 149°25W 59 d
Papetoai Moorea 17°29S 149°52W 59 d
Paphos Cyprus 34°46N 32°25E 25 E11
Paposo Chile 25°0S 70°30W 94 B1
Papoutsa Cyprus 34°54N 33°4E 25 E12
Papua □ Indonesia 4°0S 137°0E 37 E9
Papua, G. of Papua N. G. 9°0S 144°50E 58 B7
Papua New Guinea ■ Oceania 8°0S 145°0E 58 B7
Papudo Chile 32°29S 71°27W 94 C1
Papun Burma 18°2N 97°30E 41 K20
Papunya Australia 23°15S 131°54E 60 D5
Pará = Belém Brazil 1°20S 48°30W 93 D9
Pará □ Brazil 3°20S 52°0W 93 D8
Paraburdoo Australia 23°14S 117°32E 60 D2
Paracatu Brazil 17°10S 46°50W 93 G9
Paracel Is. S. China Sea 15°50N 112°0E 36 A4
Parachilna Australia 31°10S 138°21E 63 E2
Parachinar Pakistan 33°55N 70°5E 42 C4
Paradip India 20°15N 86°35E 41 J15
Paradise Calif., U.S.A. 39°46N 121°37W 78 F5
Paradise Nev., U.S.A. 36°5N 115°8W 79 J11
Paradise → Canada 53°27N 57°19W 73 B8
Paradise Hill Canada 53°32N 109°28W 71 C7
Paradise River Canada 53°27N 57°17W 73 B8
Paradise Valley U.S.A. 41°30N 117°32W 76 F5
Paradisi Greece 36°18N 28°7E 25 C10
Parado Indonesia 8°42S 118°30E 37 F5
Paragould U.S.A. 36°3N 90°29W 85 C9
Paragua → Venezuela 6°55N 62°55W 92 B6
Paraguaçu → Brazil 12°45S 38°54W 93 F11
Paraguaçu Paulista Brazil 22°22S 50°35W 95 A5
Paraguaná, Pen. de Venezuela 12°0N 70°0W 92 A5
Paraguarí Paraguay 25°36S 57°0W 94 B4
Paraguarí □ Paraguay 26°0S 57°10W 94 B4
Paraguay ■ S. Amer. 23°0S 57°0W 94 A4
Paraguay → Paraguay 27°18S 58°38W 94 B4
Paraíba = João Pessoa Brazil 7°10S 34°52W 93 E12
Paraíba □ Brazil 7°0S 36°0W 93 E11
Paraíba do Sul → Brazil 21°37S 41°3W 95 A7
Parainen Finland 60°18N 22°18E 9 F20
Paraíso Mexico 18°24N 93°14W 87 D6
Parak Iran 27°38N 52°25E 45 E7
Parakou Benin 9°25N 2°40E 50 G6
Paralimni Cyprus 35°2N 33°58E 25 D12
Paramaribo Suriname 5°50N 55°10W 93 B7
Páramos del Batallón y La Negra △ Venezuela 8°2N 71°55W 89 E5
Paramushir, Ostrov Russia 50°24N 156°0E 29 D16
Paran → Israel 30°20N 35°10E 46 E4
Paraná Argentina 31°45S 60°30W 94 C3
Paraná Brazil 12°30S 47°48W 93 F9
Paraná □ Brazil 24°30S 51°0W 95 A5
Paraná → Argentina 33°43S 59°15W 94 C4
Paranaguá Brazil 25°30S 48°30W 95 B6
Paranaíba Brazil 19°40S 51°11W 93 G8
Paranaíba → Brazil 20°6S 51°4W 93 H8
Paranapanema → Brazil 22°40S 53°9W 95 A5
Paranapiacaba, Serra do Brazil 24°31S 48°35W 95 A6
Paranavaí Brazil 23°4S 52°56W 95 A5
Parang Maguindanao, Phil. 7°23N 124°16E 37 C6
Parang Sulu, Phil. 5°55N 120°54E 37 C6
Parângul Mare, Vf. Romania 45°20N 23°37E 17 F12
Paraparaumu N.Z. 40°57S 175°3E 59 D5
Parbati → Mad. P., India 25°50N 76°30E 42 G7
Parbati → Raj., India 26°54N 77°53E 42 F7
Parbhani India 19°8N 76°52E 40 K10
Parchim Germany 53°26N 11°52E 16 B6
Pardes Hanna-Karkur Israel 32°28N 34°57E 46 C3
Pardo → Bahia, Brazil 15°40S 39°0W 93 G11
Pardo → Mato Grosso, Brazil 21°46S 52°9W 95 A5
Pardoo Roadhouse Australia 20°6S 119°3E 60 D2
Pardubice Czech Rep. 50°3N 15°45E 16 C8
Pare Indonesia 7°43S 112°12E 37 G15
Pare Mts. Tanzania 4°0S 37°45E 54 C4
Parecis, Serra dos Brazil 13°0S 60°0W 92 F7
Paren Russia 62°30N 163°15E 29 C17
Parent Canada 47°55N 74°35W 72 C5
Parent, L. Canada 48°31N 77°1W 72 C4
Parepare Indonesia 4°0S 119°40E 37 E5
Parga Greece 39°15N 20°29E 23 E9
Pargas = Parainen Finland 60°18N 22°18E 9 F20
Pargo, Pta. do Madeira 32°49N 17°17W 24 D2
Parham Canada 44°39N 76°43W 83 B8
Paria → U.S.A. 36°52N 111°36W 77 H8
Paria, G. de Venezuela 10°20N 62°0W 93 K14
Pariaguán Venezuela 8°51N 64°34W 92 B6
Paricutín, Cerro Mexico 19°28N 102°15W 86 D4
Parigi Indonesia 0°50S 120°5E 37 E6
Parika Guyana 6°50N 58°20W 92 B7
Parikkala Finland 61°33N 29°31E 8 F23
Parima, Serra Brazil 2°30N 64°0W 92 C6
Parinari Peru 4°35S 74°25W 92 D4
Pariñas, Pta. S. Amer. 4°30S 82°0W 90 D2
Parintins Brazil 2°40S 56°50W 93 D7
Pariparit Kyun Burma 14°55N 93°45E 41 M18
Paris Canada 43°12N 80°25W 82 C4
Paris France 48°53N 2°20E 20 B5
Paris Idaho, U.S.A. 42°14N 111°24W 76 E8
Paris Ky., U.S.A. 38°13N 84°15W 81 F11
Paris Tenn., U.S.A. 36°18N 88°19W 85 C10
Paris Tex., U.S.A. 33°40N 95°33W 84 E7
Parish U.S.A. 43°25N 76°8W 83 C8
Parishville U.S.A. 44°38N 74°49W 83 B10
Park U.S.A. 48°45N 122°18W 78 B4
Park City U.S.A. 37°48N 97°20W 80 G5
Park Falls U.S.A. 45°56N 90°27W 80 C8
Park Head Canada 44°36N 81°9W 82 B3
Park Hills U.S.A. 37°51N 90°51W 80 G8
Park Range U.S.A. 40°41N 106°41W 76 F10
Park Rapids U.S.A. 46°55N 95°4W 80 B6
Park River U.S.A. 48°24N 97°45W 80 A5
Park Rynie S. Africa 30°25S 30°45E 57 E5
Parkā Bandar Iran 25°55N 59°35E 45 E8
Parkano Finland 62°1N 23°0E 8 E20
Parker Ariz., U.S.A. 34°9N 114°17W 79 L12
Parker Pa., U.S.A. 41°5N 79°41W 82 E5
Parker Dam U.S.A. 34°18N 114°8W 79 L12
Parkersburg U.S.A. 39°16N 81°34W 81 F13
Parkes Australia 33°9S 148°11E 63 E4
Parkfield U.S.A. 35°54N 120°26W 78 K6
Parkhill Canada 43°15N 81°38W 82 C3
Parkland U.S.A. 47°9N 122°26W 78 C4
Parkston U.S.A. 43°24N 97°59W 80 D5
Parksville Canada 49°20N 124°21W 70 D4
Parkway U.S.A. 38°32N 121°26W 78 G5
Parla Spain 40°14N 3°46W 21 B4
Parma Italy 44°48N 10°20E 20 D9
Parma Idaho, U.S.A. 43°47N 116°57W 76 E5
Parma Ohio, U.S.A. 41°24N 81°43W 82 E3
Parnaguá Brazil 10°10S 44°38W 93 F10
Parnaíba Brazil 2°54S 41°47W 93 D10
Parnaíba → Brazil 3°0S 41°50W 93 D10
Parnassos Greece 38°35N 22°30E 23 E10
Pärnu Estonia 58°28N 24°33E 9 G21
Paro Dzong Bhutan 27°32N 89°53E 43 F13
Paroo → Australia 31°28S 143°32E 63 E3
Paroo-Darling △ Australia 31°32S 144°0E 63 E3
Paros Greece 37°5N 25°12E 23 F11
Parowan U.S.A. 37°51N 112°50W 77 H7
Parral Chile 36°10S 71°52W 94 D1
Parramatta Australia 33°48S 151°1E 63 B5
Parras Mexico 25°25N 102°11W 86 B4
Parrett → U.K. 51°12N 3°1W 13 F4
Parris I. U.S.A. 32°20N 80°41W 85 E14
Parrsboro Canada 45°30N 64°25W 73 C7
Parry I. Canada 45°18N 80°10W 82 A4
Parry Is. Canada 77°0N 110°0W 69 B9
Parry Sound Canada 45°20N 80°0W 82 A5
Parsaloi Kenya 1°16N 36°51E 54 B4
Parsnip → Canada 55°10N 123°2W 70 B4
Parsons U.S.A. 37°20N 95°16W 80 G6
Parsons Ra. Australia 13°30S 135°15E 62 A2
Partinico Italy 38°3N 13°7E 22 E5
Partizansk Russia 43°8N 133°9E 30 C6
Partridge I. Canada 55°59N 87°37W 72 A2
Partry Mts. Ireland 53°40N 9°28W 10 C2
Paru → Brazil 1°33S 52°38W 93 D8
Parvān □ Afghan. 35°0N 69°0E 40 B6
Parvatipuram India 18°50N 83°25E 41 K13
Parvatsar India 26°52N 74°49E 42 F6
Parys S. Africa 26°52S 27°29E 56 D4
Pas, Pta. des Spain 38°46N 1°26E 24 C7
Pas, The Canada 53°45N 101°15W 71 C8
Pasadena Canada 49°1N 57°36W 73 C8
Pasadena Calif., U.S.A. 34°9N 118°8W 79 L8
Pasadena Tex., U.S.A. 29°43N 95°13W 84 G7
Pasaje → Argentina 25°39S 63°56W 94 B3
Pasar Indonesia 8°27S 114°54E 37 J17
Pascagoula U.S.A. 30°21N 88°33W 85 F10
Pascagoula → U.S.A. 30°23N 88°37W 85 F10
Paşcani Romania 47°14N 26°45E 17 E14
Pasco U.S.A. 46°14N 119°6W 76 C4
Pasco, Cerro de Peru 10°45S 76°10W 92 F3
Pasco I. Australia 20°57S 115°20E 60 D2
Pascoag U.S.A. 41°57N 71°42W 83 E13
Pascua, I. de Chile 27°7S 109°23W 65 K17
Pasfield L. Canada 58°24N 105°20W 71 B7
Pasir Mas Malaysia 6°2N 102°8E 39 J4
Pasir Panjang Singapore 1°18N 103°46E 39 d
Pasir Putih Malaysia 5°50N 102°24E 39 K4
Pasirian Indonesia 8°13S 113°8E 37 H15
Pasirkuning Indonesia 0°30S 104°33E 36 E2
Paskūh Iran 27°34N 61°39E 45 E9
Pasley, C. Australia 33°52S 123°35E 61 F3
Pašman Croatia 43°58N 15°20E 16 G8
Pasni Pakistan 25°15N 63°27E 40 G3
Paso Bravo △ Paraguay 22°32S 57°5W 94 A4
Paso Cantinela Mexico 32°33N 115°47W 79 N11
Paso de Indios Argentina 43°55S 69°0W 96 E3
Paso de los Libres Argentina 29°44S 57°10W 94 B4
Paso de los Toros Uruguay 32°45S 56°30W 94 C4
Paso Robles U.S.A. 35°38N 120°41W 78 K6
Paspébiac Canada 48°3N 65°17W 73 C6
Pasrur Pakistan 32°16N 74°43E 42 C6
Passage East Ireland 52°14N 7°0W 10 D5
Passage West Ireland 51°52N 8°21W 10 E3
Passaic U.S.A. 40°51N 74°7W 83 F10
Passau Germany 48°34N 13°28E 16 D7
Passero, C. Italy 36°41N 15°10E 22 F6
Passo Fundo Brazil 28°10S 52°20W 95 B5
Passos Brazil 20°45S 46°37W 93 H9
Pastavy Belarus 55°4N 26°50E 9 J22
Pastaza → Peru 4°50S 76°52W 92 D3
Pasto Colombia 1°13N 77°17W 92 C3
Pasuruan Indonesia 7°40S 112°44E 37 G15
Patagonia Argentina 45°0S 69°0W 96 F3
Patagonia U.S.A. 31°33N 110°45W 77 L8
Patambar Iran 29°45N 60°17E 45 D9
Patan = Lalitapur Nepal 27°40N 85°20E 43 F11
Patan India 23°54N 72°14E 42 H5
Patani Indonesia 0°20N 128°50E 37 D7
Pataudi India 28°18N 76°48E 42 E7
Patchewollock Australia 35°22S 142°12E 63 F3
Patchogue U.S.A. 40°46N 73°1W 83 F11
Pate Kenya 2°10S 41°0E 54 C5
Patea N.Z. 39°45S 174°30E 59 C5
Patensie S. Africa 33°46S 24°49E 56 E3
Paternò Italy 37°34N 14°54E 22 F6
Pateros U.S.A. 48°3N 119°54W 76 B4
Paterson U.S.A. 40°54N 74°9W 83 F10
Paterson Ra. Australia 21°45S 122°10E 60 D3
Pathankot India 32°18N 75°45E 42 C6
Pathein = Bassein Burma 16°45N 94°30E 41 L19
Pathfinder Res. U.S.A. 42°28N 106°51W 76 E10
Pathiu Thailand 10°42N 99°19E 39 G2
Pathum Thani Thailand 14°1N 100°32E 38 E3
Pati Indonesia 6°45S 111°1E 37 G14
Patía → Colombia 2°13N 78°40W 92 C3
Patiala Punjab, India 30°23N 76°26E 42 D7
Patiala Ut. P., India 27°43N 79°1E 43 F8
Patkai Bum India 27°0N 95°30E 41 F19
Patmos Greece 37°21N 26°36E 23 F12
Patna India 25°35N 85°12E 43 G11
Pato Branco Brazil 26°13S 52°40W 95 B5
Patong, Ao Thailand 7°54N 98°17E 39 a
Patonga Uganda 2°45N 33°15E 54 B3
Patos Brazil 6°55S 37°16W 93 E11
Patos, L. dos Brazil 31°20S 51°0W 95 C5
Patos, Río de los → Argentina 31°18S 69°25W 94 C2
Patos de Minas Brazil 18°35S 46°32W 93 G9
Patquía Argentina 30°2S 66°55W 94 C2
Patra Greece 38°14N 21°47E 23 E9
Patraikos Kolpos Greece 38°17N 21°30E 23 E9
Patras = Patra Greece 38°14N 21°47E 23 E9
Patriot Hills Antarctica 82°20S 81°25W 5 E16
Patrocínio Brazil 18°57S 47°0W 93 G9
Pattani Thailand 6°48N 101°15E 39 J3
Pattaya Thailand 12°52N 100°55E 38 F3
Patten U.S.A. 46°0N 68°38W 81 B19
Patterson Calif., U.S.A. 37°28N 121°8W 78 H5
Patterson La., U.S.A. 29°42N 91°18W 84 G9
Patterson, Mt. U.S.A. 38°29N 119°20W 78 G7
Patti Punjab, India 31°17N 74°54E 42 D6
Patti Ut. P., India 25°55N 82°12E 43 G10
Pattoki Pakistan 31°5N 73°52E 42 D5
Patton U.S.A. 40°38N 78°39W 82 F6
Patuakhali Bangla. 22°20N 90°25E 41 H17
Patuanak Canada 55°55N 107°43W 71 B7
Patuca → Honduras 15°50N 84°18W 88 C3
Patuca, Punta Honduras 15°49N 84°14W 88 C3
Patuca △ Honduras 14°30N 85°30W 88 D2
Patvinsuo △ Finland 63°7N 30°45E 8 E24
Pátzcuaro Mexico 19°31N 101°38W 86 D4
Pau France 43°19N 0°25W 20 E3
Paudash Canada 44°59N 77°58W 82 B7
Pauk Burma 21°27N 94°30E 41 J19
Paul I. Canada 56°30N 61°20W 73 A7
Paul Smiths U.S.A. 44°26N 74°15W 83 B10
Paulatuk Canada 69°25N 124°0W 68 C7
Paulding Bay S. Ocean 66°0S 118°0E 5 C8
Paulistana Brazil 8°9S 41°9W 93 E10
Paulo Afonso Brazil 9°21S 38°15W 93 E11
Paulpietersburg S. Africa 27°23S 30°50E 57 D5
Pauls Valley U.S.A. 34°44N 97°13W 84 D6
Pauma Valley U.S.A. 33°16N 116°58W 79 M10
Pauri India 30°9N 78°47E 43 D8
Pāveh Iran 35°3N 46°22E 44 C5
Pavia Italy 45°7N 9°8E 20 D8
Pavilion U.S.A. 42°52N 78°1W 82 D6
Pāvilosta Latvia 56°53N 21°14E 9 H19
Pavlodar Kazakhstan 52°33N 77°0E 28 D8
Pavlograd = Pavlohrad Ukraine 48°30N 35°52E 19 E6
Pavlohrad Ukraine 48°30N 35°52E 19 E6
Pavlovo Russia 55°58N 43°5E 18 C7
Pavlovsk Russia 50°26N 40°5E 19 D7
Pavlovskaya Russia 46°17N 39°47E 19 E6
Pawai, Pulau Singapore 1°11N 103°44E 39 d
Pawayan India 28°4N 80°6E 43 E9
Pawhuska U.S.A. 36°40N 96°20W 84 C6
Pawling U.S.A. 41°34N 73°36W 83 E11
Pawnee U.S.A. 36°20N 96°48W 84 C6
Pawnee City U.S.A. 40°7N 96°9W 80 E5
Pawtucket U.S.A. 41°53N 71°23W 83 E13
Paxi Greece 39°14N 20°12E 23 E9
Paximadia Greece 35°0N 24°35E 25 E6
Paxton U.S.A. 40°27N 88°6W 80 E9
Payakumbuh Indonesia 0°20S 100°35E 36 E2
Payette U.S.A. 44°5N 116°56W 76 D5
Payne Bay = Kangirsuk Canada 60°0N 70°0W 69 D13
Payne L. Canada 59°30N 74°30W 69 D12
Paynes Find Australia 29°15S 117°42E 61 E2
Paynesville U.S.A. 45°23N 94°43W 80 C6
Paysandú Uruguay 32°19S 58°8W 94 C4
Payson Ariz., U.S.A. 34°14N 111°20W 77 J8
Payson Utah, U.S.A. 40°3N 111°44W 76 F8
Paz → Guatemala 13°44N 90°10W 88 D1
Paz, B. de la Mexico 24°9N 110°25W 86 C2
Pāzanān Iran 30°35N 49°59E 45 D6
Pazardzhik Bulgaria 42°12N 24°20E 23 C11
Pe Ell U.S.A. 46°34N 123°18W 78 D3
Peabody U.S.A. 42°31N 70°56W 83 D14
Peace → Canada 59°0N 111°25W 70 B6
Peace Point Canada 59°7N 112°27W 70 B6
Peace River Canada 56°15N 117°18W 70 B5
Peach Springs U.S.A. 35°32N 113°25W 77 J7
Peachland Canada 49°47N 119°45W 70 D5
Peachtree City U.S.A. 33°25N 84°35W 85 E12
Peak, The = Kinder Scout U.K. 53°24N 1°52W 12 D6
Peak Charles △ Australia 32°42S 121°10E 61 F3
Peak District △ U.K. 53°24N 1°46W 12 D6
Peak Hill N.S.W., Australia 32°47S 148°11E 63 E4
Peak Hill W. Austral., Australia 25°35S 118°43E 61 E2
Peak Ra. Australia 22°50S 148°20E 62 C4
Peake Cr. → Australia 28°2S 136°7E 63 D2
Peale, Mt. U.S.A. 38°26N 109°14W 76 G9
Pearblossom U.S.A. 34°30N 117°55W 79 L9
Pearl → U.S.A. 30°11N 89°32W 85 F10
Pearl City U.S.A. 21°24N 157°59W 74 b
Pearl Harbor U.S.A. 21°21N 157°57W 74 b
Pearl River U.S.A. 41°4N 74°2W 83 E10
Pearsall U.S.A. 28°54N 99°6W 84 G5
Pearson Int. Toronto ✕ (YYZ) Canada 43°46N 79°35W 82 C5
Peary Land Greenland 82°40N 33°0W 4 A6
Pease → U.S.A. 34°12N 99°2W 84 D5
Peawanuck Canada 55°15N 85°12W 72 A2
Pebane Mozam. 17°10S 38°8E 55 F4
Pebas Peru 3°10S 71°46W 92 D4
Pebble Beach U.S.A. 36°34N 121°57W 78 J5
Peć Serbia 42°40N 20°17E 23 C9
Pechenga Russia 69°29N 31°4E 8 B24
Pechenizhyn Ukraine 48°30N 24°48E 17 D13
Pechiguera, Pta. Canary Is. 28°51N 13°53W 24 F6
Pechora Russia 65°10N 57°11E 18 A10
Pechora → Russia 68°13N 54°15E 18 A9
Pechorskaya Guba Russia 68°40N 54°0E 18 A9
Pechory Russia 57°48N 27°40E 9 H22
Pecos N. Mex., U.S.A. 35°35N 105°41W 77 J11
Pecos Tex., U.S.A. 31°26N 103°30W 84 F3
Pecos → U.S.A. 29°42N 101°22W 84 G4
Pécs Hungary 46°5N 18°15E 17 E10
Pedasí Panama 7°32N 80°2W 88 E3
Pedder, L. Australia 42°55S 146°10E 63 G4
Peddie S. Africa 33°14S 27°7E 57 E4
Pedernales Dom. Rep. 18°2N 71°44W 89 C5
Pedieos → Cyprus 35°10N 33°54E 25 D12
Pedirka Australia 26°40S 135°14E 63 D2
Pedirka Desert Australia 26°47S 134°11E 63 A1
Pedra Azul Brazil 16°2S 41°17W 93 G10
Pedra Lume C. Verde Is. 16°40N 22°52W 50 b
Pedreiras Brazil 4°32S 44°40W 93 D10
Pedro Afonso Brazil 9°0S 48°10W 93 E9
Pedro Cays Jamaica 17°5N 77°48W 88 C4
Pedro de Valdivia Chile 22°55S 69°38W 94 A2
Pedro Juan Caballero Paraguay 22°30S 55°40W 95 A4
Pee Dee = Great Pee Dee → U.S.A. 33°21N 79°10W 85 E15
Peebinga Australia 34°52S 140°57E 63 E3
Peebles U.K. 55°40N 3°11W 11 F5
Peekskill U.S.A. 41°17N 73°55W 83 E11
Peel I. of Man 54°13N 4°40W 12 C3
Peel → Australia 30°50S 150°29E 63 E5
Peel → Canada 67°0N 135°0W 68 C6
Peel Sd. Canada 73°0N 96°0W 68 B10
Peera Peera Poolanna L. Australia 26°30S 138°0E 63 D2
Peerless Lake Canada 56°37N 114°40W 70 B6
Peers Canada 53°40N 116°0W 70 C5
Pegasus Bay N.Z. 43°20S 173°10E 59 E4
Pegu Burma 17°20N 96°29E 41 L20
Pegu Yoma Burma 19°0N 96°0E 41 K20
Pehuajó Argentina 35°45S 62°0W 94 D3
Pei Xian = Pizhou China 34°44N 116°55E 34 G9
Peine Chile 23°45S 68°8W 94 A2
Peine Germany 52°19N 10°14E 16 B6
Peip'ing = Beijing China 39°53N 116°21E 34 E9
Peipus, L. = Chudskoye, Ozero Russia 58°13N 27°30E 9 G22
Peixe Brazil 12°0S 48°40W 93 F9
Peixe → Brazil 21°31S 51°58W 93 H8
Pekalongan Indonesia 6°53S 109°40E 37 G13
Pekan Malaysia 3°30N 103°25E 39 L4
Pekan Nenas Malaysia 1°31N 103°31E 39 d
Pekanbaru Indonesia 0°30N 101°15E 36 D2
Pekin U.S.A. 40°35N 89°40W 80 E9
Peking = Beijing China 39°53N 116°21E 34 E9
Pekutatan Indonesia 8°25S 114°49E 37 J17
Pelabuhan Klang Malaysia 3°0N 101°23E 39 L3
Pelabuhan Ratu, Teluk Indonesia 7°5S 106°30E 37 G12
Pelabuhanratu Indonesia 7°0S 106°32E 37 G12
Pelagie, Is. Italy 35°39N 12°33E 22 G5

Pelaihari *Indonesia* 3°55S 114°45E **36** E4
Peleaga, Vf. *Romania* 45°22N 22°55E **17** F12
Pelée, Mt. *Martinique* 14°48N 61°10W **88** c
Pelee, Pt. *Canada* 41°54N 82°31W **72** D3
Pelee I. *Canada* 41°47N 82°40W **82** E2
Pelekech *Kenya* 3°52N 35°8E **54** B4
Peleng *Indonesia* 1°20S 123°30E **37** E6
Pelentong *Malaysia* 1°32N 103°49E **39** d
Pelican *U.S.A.* 57°58N 136°14W **70** B1
Pelican L. *Canada* 52°28N 100°20W **71** C8
Pelican Narrows *Canada* 55°10N 102°56W **71** B8
Pelješac *Croatia* 42°55N 17°25E **22** C7
Pelkosenniemi *Finland* 67°6N 27°28E **8** C22
Pella *S. Africa* 29°1S 19°6E **56** D2
Pella *U.S.A.* 41°25N 92°55W **80** E7
Pello *Finland* 66°47N 23°59E **8** C20
Pelly → *Canada* 62°47N 137°19W **70** A1
Pelly Bay *Canada* 68°38N 89°50W **69** C11
Peloponnese □ *Greece* 37°10N 22°0E **23** F10
Pelorus Sd. *N.Z.* 40°59S 173°59E **59** D4
Pelotas *Brazil* 31°42S 52°23W **95** C5
Pelotas → *Brazil* 27°28S 51°55W **95** B5
Pelvoux, Massif du *France* 44°52N 6°20E **20** D7
Pemalang *Indonesia* 6°53S 109°23E **37** G13
Pemanggil, Pulau *Malaysia* 2°37N 104°21E **39** L5
Pematangsiantar *Indonesia* 2°57N 99°5E **36** D1
Pemba *Mozam.* 12°58S 40°30E **55** E5
Pemba *Zambia* 16°30S 27°28E **55** F2
Pemba Channel *Tanzania* 5°0S 39°37E **54** D4
Pemba I. *Tanzania* 5°0S 39°45E **54** D4
Pemberton *Australia* 34°30S 116°0E **61** F2
Pemberton *Canada* 50°25N 122°50W **70** C4
Pembina → *Canada* 54°45N 114°17W **70** C6
Pembroke *Canada* 45°50N 77°7W **72** C4
Pembroke *U.K.* 51°41N 4°55W **13** F3
Pembrokeshire □ *U.K.* 51°52N 4°56W **13** F3
Pembrokeshire Coast △ *U.K.* 51°50N 5°2W **13** F2
Pen-y-Ghent *U.K.* 54°10N 2°14W **12** C5
Penal *Trin. & Tob.* 10°9N 61°29W **93** K15
Penang = Pinang *Malaysia* 5°25N 100°15E **39** c
Penápolis *Brazil* 21°30S 50°0W **95** A6
Peñarroya-Pueblonuevo *Spain* 38°19N 5°16W **21** C3
Penarth *U.K.* 51°26N 3°11W **13** F4
Peñas, C. de *Spain* 43°42N 5°52W **21** A3
Peñas, G. de *Chile* 47°0S 75°0W **96** F2
Peñas del Chache *Canary Is.* 29°6N 13°33W **24** E6
Pench △ *India* 21°45N 79°20E **43** J8
Pench'i = Benxi *China* 41°20N 123°48E **35** D12
Pend Oreille → *U.S.A.* 49°4N 117°37W **76** B5
Pend Oreille, L. *U.S.A.* 48°10N 116°21W **76** B5
Pendembu *S. Leone* 9°7N 11°14W **50** G3
Pender B. *Australia* 16°45S 122°42E **60** C3
Pendleton *U.S.A.* 45°40N 118°47W **76** D4
Pendra *India* 22°46N 81°57E **43** H9
Penedo *Brazil* 10°15S 36°36W **93** F11
Penelokan *Indonesia* 8°17S 115°22E **37** J18
Penetanguishene *Canada* 44°50N 79°55W **82** B5
Penfield *U.S.A.* 41°13N 78°35W **82** E6
Peng Chau *China* 22°17N 114°2E **33** G11
Pengalengan *Indonesia* 7°9S 107°30E **37** G12
Penge *Kasai-Or., Dem. Rep. of the Congo* 5°30S 24°33E **54** D1
Penge *Sud-Kivu, Dem. Rep. of the Congo* 4°27S 28°25E **54** C2
Penglai *China* 37°48N 120°42E **35** F11
Penguin *Australia* 41°8S 146°6E **63** G4
Penhalonga *Zimbabwe* 18°52S 32°40E **55** F3
Peniche *Portugal* 39°19N 9°22W **21** C1
Penicuik *U.K.* 55°50N 3°13W **11** F5
Penida, Nusa *Indonesia* 8°45S 115°30E **37** K18
Peninsular Malaysia □ *Malaysia* 4°0N 102°0E **39** L4
Penitente, Serra do *Brazil* 8°45S 46°20W **93** E9
Penkridge *U.K.* 52°44N 2°6W **12** E5
Penmarch, Pte. de *France* 47°48N 4°22W **20** C1
Penn Hills *U.S.A.* 40°28N 79°52W **82** F5
Penn Yan *U.S.A.* 42°40N 77°3W **82** D7
Pennant *Canada* 50°32N 108°14W **71** C7
Penner → *India* 14°35N 80°10E **40** M12
Pennines *U.K.* 54°45N 2°27W **12** C5
Pennington *U.S.A.* 39°15N 121°47W **78** F5
Pennsburg *U.S.A.* 40°23N 75°29W **83** F9
Pennsylvania □ *U.S.A.* 40°45N 77°30W **81** E15
Penny *Canada* 53°51N 121°20W **70** C4
Penny Str. *Canada* 76°30N 97°0W **69** B8
Penobscot → *U.S.A.* 44°30N 68°48W **81** C19
Penobscot B. *U.S.A.* 44°35N 68°50W **81** C19
Penola *Australia* 37°25S 140°48E **63** F3
Penong *Australia* 31°56S 133°1E **61** F5
Penonomé *Panama* 8°31N 80°21W **88** E3
Penrhyn *Cook Is.* 9°0S 158°0W **65** H12
Penrith *Australia* 33°43S 150°38E **63** E5
Penrith *U.K.* 54°40N 2°45W **12** C5
Penryn *U.K.* 50°9N 5°7W **13** G2
Pensacola *U.S.A.* 30°25N 87°13W **85** F11
Pensacola Mts. *Antarctica* 84°0S 40°0W **5** E1
Pense *Canada* 50°25N 104°59W **71** C8
Penshurst *Australia* 37°49S 142°20E **63** F3
Penticton *Canada* 49°30N 119°38W **70** D5
Pentland *Australia* 20°32S 145°25E **62** C4
Pentland Firth *U.K.* 58°43N 3°10W **11** C5
Pentland Hills *U.K.* 55°48N 3°25W **11** F5
Pentland Hills ⌂ *U.K.* 55°50N 3°20W **11** F5
Penza *Russia* 53°15N 45°5E **18** D8
Penzance *U.K.* 50°7N 5°33W **13** G2
Penzhino *Russia* 63°30N 167°55E **29** C17
Penzhinskaya Guba *Russia* 61°30N 163°0E **29** C17
Peoria *Ariz., U.S.A.* 33°43N 112°14W **77** K7
Peoria *Ill., U.S.A.* 40°42N 89°36W **80** E9
Pepacton Res. *U.S.A.* 42°5N 74°58W **83** D10
Pepani → *S. Africa* 25°49S 22°47E **56** D3
Pera Hd. *Australia* 12°55S 141°37E **62** A3
Perabumulih *Indonesia* 3°27S 104°15E **36** E2
Perak → *Malaysia* 4°0N 100°50E **39** K3
Perama *Kerkyra, Greece* 39°34N 19°54E **25** A3
Perama *Kriti, Greece* 35°20N 24°40E **25** D6
Perancak *Indonesia* 8°24S 114°37E **37** J17
Peräpohjola *Finland* 66°16N 26°10E **8** C22
Percé *Canada* 48°31N 64°13W **73** C7
Perche, Collines du *France* 48°30N 0°40E **20** B4
Percival Lakes *Australia* 21°25S 125°0E **60** D4
Percy Is. *Australia* 21°39S 150°16E **62** C5
Perdido, Mte. *Spain* 42°40N 0°5E **21** A6
Perdu, Mt. = Perdido, Mte. *Spain* 42°40N 0°5E **21** A6
Pereira *Colombia* 4°49N 75°43W **92** C3
Perenjori *Australia* 29°26S 116°16E **61** E2
Pereyaslav-Khmelnytskyy *Ukraine* 50°3N 31°28E **19** D5
Pérez, I. *Mexico* 22°24N 89°42W **87** C7
Pergamino *Argentina* 33°52S 60°30W **94** C3
Pergau → *Malaysia* 5°23N 102°2E **39** K3
Perham *U.S.A.* 46°36N 95°34W **80** B6
Perhentian, Kepulauan *Malaysia* 5°54N 102°42E **39** K4
Péribonka → *Canada* 48°45N 72°5W **73** C5
Péribonka, L. *Canada* 50°1N 71°10W **73** B5
Perico *Argentina* 24°20S 65°5W **94** A2
Pericos *Mexico* 25°3N 107°42W **86** B3
Périgueux *France* 45°10N 0°42E **20** D4
Perijá, Sierra de *Colombia* 9°30N 73°3W **92** B4
Perijá △ *Venezuela* 9°30N 72°55W **89** E5
Peristerona → *Cyprus* 35°8N 33°5E **25** D12
Perito Moreno *Argentina* 46°36S 70°56W **96** F2
Perkasie *U.S.A.* 40°22N 75°18W **83** F9
Perlas, Arch. de las *Panama* 8°41N 79°7W **88** E4
Perlas, Punta de *Nic.* 12°30N 83°30W **88** D3
Perm *Russia* 58°0N 56°10E **18** C10
Pernambuco = Recife *Brazil* 8°0S 35°0W **93** E12
Pernambuco □ *Brazil* 8°0S 37°0W **93** E11
Pernatty Lagoon *Australia* 31°30S 137°12E **63** E2
Pernik *Bulgaria* 42°35N 23°2E **23** C10
Peron Is. *Australia* 13°9S 130°4E **60** B5
Peron Pen. *Australia* 26°0S 113°10E **61** E1
Perow *Canada* 54°35N 126°10W **70** C3
Perpignan *France* 42°42N 2°53E **20** E5
Perris *U.S.A.* 33°47N 117°14W **79** M9
Perry *Fla., U.S.A.* 30°7N 83°35W **85** F13
Perry *Ga., U.S.A.* 32°28N 83°44W **85** E13
Perry *Iowa, U.S.A.* 41°51N 94°6W **80** E6
Perry *N.Y., U.S.A.* 42°42N 78°0W **82** D7
Perry *Okla., U.S.A.* 36°17N 97°14W **84** C6
Perryton *U.S.A.* 36°24N 100°48W **84** C4
Perryville *U.S.A.* 37°43N 89°52W **80** G9
Persepolis *Iran* 29°55N 52°50E **45** D7
Pershotravensk *Ukraine* 50°13N 27°40E **17** C14
Persia = Iran ■ *Asia* 33°0N 53°0E **45** C7
Persian Gulf *Asia* 27°0N 50°0E **45** E6
Perth *Australia* 31°57S 115°52E **61** F2
Perth *Canada* 44°55N 76°15W **83** B8
Perth *U.K.* 56°24N 3°26W **11** E5
Perth & Kinross □ *U.K.* 56°45N 3°55W **11** E5
Perth Amboy *U.S.A.* 40°30N 74°15W **83** F10
Perth-Andover *Canada* 46°44N 67°42W **73** C6
Perth Basin *Ind. Oc.* 30°0S 108°0E **64** L2
Peru *Ind., U.S.A.* 40°45N 86°4W **80** E10
Peru *N.Y., U.S.A.* 44°35N 73°32W **83** B11
Peru ■ *S. Amer.* 4°0S 75°0W **92** D4
Peru Basin *Pac. Oc.* 20°0S 95°0W **65** J18
Peru-Chile Trench *Pac. Oc.* 20°0S 72°0W **92** G3
Perúgia *Italy* 43°7N 12°23E **22** C5
Pervomaysk *Ukraine* 48°10N 30°46E **19** E5
Pervouralsk *Russia* 56°59N 59°59E **18** C10
Pésaro *Italy* 43°54N 12°55E **22** C5
Pescara *Italy* 42°28N 14°13E **22** C6
Peshawar *Pakistan* 34°2N 71°37E **42** B4
Peshkopi *Albania* 41°41N 20°25E **23** D9
Peshtigo *U.S.A.* 45°3N 87°45W **80** C10
Pesqueira *Brazil* 8°20S 36°42W **93** E11
Petah Tiqwa *Israel* 32°6N 34°53E **46** C3
Petaling Jaya *Malaysia* 3°4N 101°42E **39** L3
Petaloudes *Greece* 36°18N 28°5E **25** C10
Petaluma *U.S.A.* 38°14N 122°39W **78** G4
Pétange *Lux.* 49°33N 5°55E **15** E5
Petaro *Pakistan* 25°31N 68°18E **42** G3
Petatlán *Mexico* 17°31N 101°16W **86** D4
Petauke *Zambia* 14°14S 31°20E **55** E3
Petawawa *Canada* 45°54N 77°17W **72** C4
Petén Itzá, L. *Guatemala* 16°58N 89°50W **88** C2
Peter I. *Br. Virgin Is.* 18°22N 64°35W **89** e
Peter I. Øy *Antarctica* 69°0S 91°0W **5** C16
Peter Pond L. *Canada* 55°55N 108°44W **71** B7
Peterbell *Canada* 48°36N 83°21W **72** C3
Peterborough *Australia* 32°58S 138°51E **63** E2
Peterborough *Canada* 44°20N 78°20W **82** B6
Peterborough *U.K.* 52°35N 0°15W **13** E7
Peterborough *U.S.A.* 42°53N 71°57W **83** D13
Peterborough □ *U.K.* 52°35N 0°15W **13** E7
Peterculter *U.K.* 57°6N 2°16W **11** D6
Peterhead *U.K.* 57°31N 1°48W **11** D7
Peterlee *U.K.* 54°47N 1°20W **12** C6
Petermann Ranges *Australia* 26°0S 130°30E **61** E5
Petersburg *Alaska, U.S.A.* 56°48N 132°58W **68** D6
Petersburg *Pa., U.S.A.* 40°34N 78°3W **82** F6
Petersburg *Va., U.S.A.* 37°14N 77°24W **81** G15
Petersburg *W. Va., U.S.A.* 39°1N 79°5W **81** F14
Petersfield *U.K.* 51°1N 0°56W **13** F7
Petit-Canal *Guadeloupe* 16°25N 61°31W **88** b
Petit Goâve *Haiti* 18°27N 72°51W **89** C5
Petit Lac Manicouagan *Canada* 51°25N 67°40W **73** B6
Petit-Mécatina → *Canada* 50°40N 59°30W **73** B8
Petit-Mécatina, Î. du *Canada* 50°30N 59°25W **73** B8
Petit Piton *St. Lucia* 13°51N 61°5W **89** f
Petit-Saguenay *Canada* 48°15N 70°4W **73** C5
Petitcodiac *Canada* 45°57N 65°11W **73** C6
Petite Terre, Îles de la *Guadeloupe* 16°13N 61°9W **88** b
Petitot → *Canada* 60°14N 123°29W **70** A4
Petitsikapau L. *Canada* 54°37N 66°25W **73** B6
Petlad *India* 22°30N 72°45E **42** H5
Peto *Mexico* 20°8N 88°55W **87** C7
Petone *N.Z.* 41°13S 174°53E **59** D5
Petorca *Chile* 32°15S 70°56W **94** C1
Petoskey *U.S.A.* 45°22N 84°57W **81** C11
Petra *Jordan* 30°20N 35°22E **46** E4
Petra *Spain* 39°37N 3°6E **24** B10
Petra, Ostrova *Russia* 76°15N 118°30E **29** B12
Petra Velikogo, Zaliv *Russia* 42°40N 132°0E **30** C6
Petre, Pt. *Canada* 43°50N 77°9W **82** C7
Petrich *Bulgaria* 41°24N 23°13E **23** D10
Petrified Forest △ *U.S.A.* 35°0N 109°30W **77** J9
Petrikov = Pyetrikaw *Belarus* 52°11N 28°29E **17** B15
Petrolândia *Brazil* 9°5S 38°20W **93** E11
Petrolia *Canada* 42°54N 82°9W **82** D2
Petrolina *Brazil* 9°24S 40°30W **93** E10
Petropavl *Kazakhstan* 54°53N 69°13E **28** D7
Petropavlovsk = Petropavl *Kazakhstan* 54°53N 69°13E **28** D7
Petropavlovsk-Kamchatskiy *Russia* 53°3N 158°43E **29** D16
Petrópolis *Brazil* 22°33S 43°9W **95** A7
Petroşani *Romania* 45°28N 23°20E **17** F12
Petrovaradin *Serbia* 45°16N 19°55E **23** B8
Petrovsk *Russia* 52°22N 45°19E **18** D8
Petrovsk-Zabaykalskiy *Russia* 51°20N 108°55E **29** D11
Petrozavodsk *Russia* 61°41N 34°20E **18** B5
Petrus Steyn *S. Africa* 27°38S 28°8E **57** D4
Petrusburg *S. Africa* 29°4S 25°26E **56** D4
Peumo *Chile* 34°21S 71°12W **94** C1
Peureulak *Indonesia* 4°48N 97°45E **36** D1
Pevek *Russia* 69°41N 171°19E **29** C18
Pforzheim *Germany* 48°52N 8°41E **16** D5
Pha Taem △ *Thailand* 15°32N 105°30E **38** E5
Phaestos *Greece* 35°2N 24°50E **25** D6
Phagwara *India* 31°10N 75°40E **42** D6
Phala *Botswana* 23°45S 26°50E **56** C4
Phalera = Phulera *India* 26°52N 75°16E **42** F6
Phalodi *India* 27°12N 72°24E **42** F5
Phaluai, Ko *Thailand* 9°32N 99°41E **39** b
Phan *Thailand* 19°28N 99°43E **38** C2
Phan Rang *Vietnam* 11°34N 109°0E **39** G7
Phan Ri = Hoa Da *Vietnam* 11°16N 108°40E **39** G7
Phan Si Pan *Vietnam* 22°18N 103°46E **38** A4
Phan Thiet *Vietnam* 11°1N 108°9E **39** G7
Phanat Nikhom *Thailand* 13°27N 101°11E **38** F3
Phangan, Ko *Thailand* 9°45N 100°0E **39** H3
Phangnga *Thailand* 8°28N 98°30E **39** H2
Phangnga, Ao *Thailand* 8°16N 98°33E **39** a
Phanom Sarakham *Thailand* 13°45N 101°21E **38** F3
Phaphund *India* 26°36N 79°28E **43** F8
Pharenda *India* 27°5N 83°17E **43** F10
Pharr *U.S.A.* 26°12N 98°11W **84** H5
Phatthalung *Thailand* 7°39N 100°6E **39** J3
Phayao *Thailand* 19°11N 99°55E **38** C2
Phelps *U.S.A.* 42°58N 77°3W **82** D7
Phelps L. *Canada* 59°15N 103°15W **71** B8
Phenix City *U.S.A.* 32°28N 85°0W **85** E12
Phet Buri *Thailand* 13°1N 99°55E **38** F2
Phetchabun *Thailand* 16°25N 101°8E **38** D3
Phetchabun, Thiu Khao *Thailand* 16°0N 101°20E **38** E3
Phetchaburi = Phet Buri *Thailand* 13°1N 99°55E **38** F2
Phi Phi, Ko *Thailand* 7°45N 98°46E **39** J2
Phiafay *Laos* 14°48N 106°0E **38** E6
Phibun Mangsahan *Thailand* 15°14N 105°14E **38** E5
Phichai *Thailand* 17°22N 100°10E **38** D3
Phichit *Thailand* 16°26N 100°22E **38** D3
Philadelphia *Miss., U.S.A.* 32°46N 89°7W **85** E10
Philadelphia *N.Y., U.S.A.* 44°9N 75°43W **83** B9
Philadelphia *Pa., U.S.A.* 39°57N 75°9W **83** G9
Philip *U.S.A.* 44°2N 101°40W **80** C3
Philippeville *Belgium* 50°12N 4°33E **15** D4
Philippi *U.S.A.* 39°9N 80°3W **81** F13
Philippi L. *Australia* 24°20S 138°55E **62** C2
Philippine Basin *Pac. Oc.* 17°0N 132°0E **64** F5
Philippine Sea *Pac. Oc.* 18°0N 125°0E **64** F4
Philippine Trench = Mindanao Trench *Pac. Oc.* 12°0N 126°6E **37** B7
Philippines ■ *Asia* 12°0N 123°0E **37** B6
Philippolis *S. Africa* 30°15S 25°16E **56** E4
Philippopolis = Plovdiv *Bulgaria* 42°8N 24°44E **23** C11
Philipsburg *Canada* 45°2N 73°5W **83** A11
Philipsburg *Mont., U.S.A.* 46°20N 113°18W **76** C7
Philipsburg *Pa., U.S.A.* 40°54N 78°13W **82** F6
Philipstown = Daingean *Ireland* 53°18N 7°17W **10** C4
Philipstown *S. Africa* 30°28S 24°30E **56** E3
Phillip I. *Australia* 38°30S 145°12E **63** F4
Phillips *U.S.A.* 45°42N 90°24W **80** C8
Phillipsburg *Kans., U.S.A.* 39°45N 99°19W **80** F4
Phillipsburg *N.J., U.S.A.* 40°42N 75°12W **83** F9
Philmont *U.S.A.* 42°15N 73°39W **83** D11
Philomath *U.S.A.* 44°32N 123°22W **76** D2
Phimai *Thailand* 15°13N 102°30E **38** E4
Phitsanulok *Thailand* 16°50N 100°12E **38** D3
Phnom Dangrek *Thailand* 14°20N 104°0E **38** E5
Phnom Kulen △ *Cambodia* 13°38N 104°15E **38** F5
Phnom Penh *Cambodia* 11°33N 104°55E **39** G5
Phnum Penh = Phnom Penh *Cambodia* 11°33N 104°55E **39** G5
Phoenicia *U.S.A.* 42°5N 74°14W **83** D10
Phoenix *Mauritius* 20°17S 57°30E **53** d
Phoenix *Ariz., U.S.A.* 33°26N 112°4W **77** K7
Phoenix *N.Y., U.S.A.* 43°14N 76°18W **83** C8
Phoenix Is. *Kiribati* 3°30S 172°0W **64** H10
Phoenixville *U.S.A.* 40°8N 75°31W **83** F9
Phon *Thailand* 15°49N 102°36E **38** E4
Phon Tiou *Laos* 17°53N 104°37E **38** D5
Phong → *Thailand* 16°23N 102°56E **38** D4
Phong Saly *Laos* 21°42N 102°9E **38** B4
Phong Tho *Vietnam* 22°32N 103°21E **38** A4
Phonhong *Laos* 18°30N 102°25E **38** C4
Phonum *Thailand* 8°49N 98°48E **39** H2
Phosphate Hill *Australia* 21°53S 139°58E **62** C2
Photharam *Thailand* 13°41N 99°51E **38** F2
Phra Nakhon Si Ayutthaya *Thailand* 14°25N 100°30E **38** E3
Phra Thong, Ko *Thailand* 9°5N 98°17E **39** H2
Phrae *Thailand* 18°7N 100°9E **38** C3
Phrom Phiram *Thailand* 17°2N 100°12E **38** D3
Phu Bia *Laos* 19°10N 103°0E **38** C4
Phu Chong-Na Yoi △ *Thailand* 14°25N 105°30E **38** E5
Phu Dien *Vietnam* 18°58N 105°31E **38** C5
Phu Hin Rang Kla △ *Thailand* 17°0N 100°59E **38** D3
Phu Kradung △ *Thailand* 17°2N 101°44E **38** D3
Phu Loi *Laos* 20°14N 103°14E **38** B4
Phu Luang △ *Thailand* 17°15N 101°29E **38** D3
Phu Ly *Vietnam* 20°35N 105°50E **38** B5
Phu Phan △ *Thailand* 17°0N 103°56E **38** D4
Phu Quoc, Dao *Vietnam* 10°20N 104°0E **39** G4
Phu Tho *Vietnam* 21°24N 105°13E **38** B5
Phu Wiang △ *Thailand* 16°39N 102°23E **38** D4
Phuc Yen *Vietnam* 21°16N 105°45E **38** B5
Phuket *Thailand* 7°53N 98°24E **39** a
Phuket, Ko *Thailand* 8°0N 98°22E **39** a
Phul *India* 30°19N 75°14E **42** D6
Phulad *India* 25°38N 73°49E **42** G5
Phulchari *Bangla.* 25°11N 89°37E **43** G13
Phulera *India* 26°52N 75°16E **42** F6
Phulpur *India* 25°31N 82°49E **43** G10
Phun Phin *Thailand* 9°7N 99°12E **39** H2
Phuntsholing *Bhutan* 26°51N 89°23E **43** F13
Piacenza *Italy* 45°1N 9°40E **20** D8
Piai, Tanjung *Malaysia* 1°17N 103°30E **39** d
Pian Cr. → *Australia* 30°2S 148°12E **63** E4
Pian-Upe ⌂ *Uganda* 1°44N 34°20E **54** B3
Pianosa *Italy* 42°35N 10°5E **22** C4
Piapot *Canada* 49°59N 109°8W **71** D7
Piatra Neamţ *Romania* 46°56N 26°21E **17** E14
Piauí □ *Brazil* 7°0S 43°0W **93** E10
Piauí → *Brazil* 6°38S 42°42W **93** E10
Piave → *Italy* 45°32N 12°44E **22** B5
Pibor Post *Sudan* 6°47N 33°3E **51** G12
Picardie □ *France* 49°50N 3°0E **20** B5
Picardy = Picardie □ *France* 49°50N 3°0E **20** B5
Picayune *U.S.A.* 30°32N 89°41W **85** F10
Pichhor *India* 25°58N 78°20E **43** G8
Pichilemu *Chile* 34°22S 72°0W **94** C1
Pichor *India* 25°11N 78°11E **42** G8
Pickerel L. *Canada* 48°40N 91°25W **72** C1
Pickering *U.K.* 54°15N 0°46W **12** C7
Pickering, Vale of *U.K.* 54°14N 0°45W **12** C7
Pickle Lake *Canada* 51°30N 90°12W **72** B1
Pickwick L. *U.S.A.* 35°4N 88°15W **85** D10
Pico *Azores* 38°28N 28°20W **50** a
Pico Bonito △ *Honduras* 15°34N 86°48W **88** C2
Pico Truncado *Argentina* 46°40S 68°0W **96** F3
Picos *Brazil* 7°5S 41°28W **93** E10
Picton *Australia* 34°12S 150°34E **63** E5
Picton *Canada* 44°1N 77°9W **82** B7
Picton *N.Z.* 41°18S 174°3E **59** D5
Pictou *Canada* 45°41N 62°42W **73** C7
Picture Butte *Canada* 49°55N 112°45W **70** D6
Pictured Rocks ⌂ *U.S.A.* 46°30N 86°30W **80** B10
Picún Leufú *Argentina* 39°30S 69°5W **96** D3
Pidurutalagala *Sri Lanka* 7°10N 80°50E **40** R12
Piedmont = Piemonte □ *Italy* 45°0N 8°0E **20** D7
Piedmont *Ala., U.S.A.* 33°55N 85°37W **85** E12
Piedmont *S.C., U.S.A.* 34°42N 82°28W **75** D10
Piedras Negras *Mexico* 28°42N 100°31W **86** B4
Pieksämäki *Finland* 62°18N 27°10E **8** E22
Pielinen *Finland* 63°15N 29°40E **8** E23
Piemonte □ *Italy* 45°0N 8°0E **20** D7
Pienaarsrivier *S. Africa* 25°15S 28°18E **57** D4
Piercefield *U.S.A.* 44°13N 74°35W **83** B10
Pierceland *Canada* 54°20N 109°46W **71** C7
Pierpont *U.S.A.* 41°45N 80°34W **82** E4
Pierre *U.S.A.* 44°22N 100°21W **80** C3
Pierrefonds *Canada* 45°29N 73°51W **83** A11
Pierreville *Trin. & Tob.* 10°16N 61°0W **93** K16
Piet Retief *S. Africa* 27°1S 30°50E **57** D5
Pietarsaari *Finland* 63°40N 22°43E **8** E20
Pietermaritzburg *S. Africa* 29°35S 30°25E **57** D5
Pietersburg = Polokwane *S. Africa* 23°54S 29°25E **57** C4
Pietrosul, Vf. *Maramureș, Romania* 47°35N 24°43E **17** E13
Pietrosul, Vf. *Suceava, Romania* 47°12N 25°18E **17** E13
Pigeon L. *Canada* 44°27N 78°30W **82** B
Piggott *U.S.A.* 36°23N 90°11W **85** C
Pigüe *Argentina* 37°36S 62°25W **94** D
Pihani *India* 27°36N 80°15E **43** F
Pihlajavesi *Finland* 61°45N 28°45E **8** F2
Pijijiapan *Mexico* 15°42N 93°14W **87** D
Pikangikum *Canada* 51°49N 94°0W **71** C
Pikes Peak *U.S.A.* 38°50N 105°3W **76** G
Piketberg *S. Africa* 32°55S 18°40E **56** E
Pikeville *U.S.A.* 37°29N 82°31W **81** G
Pikou *China* 39°18N 122°22E **35** E
Pikwitonei *Canada* 55°35N 97°9W **71** B
Piła *Poland* 53°10N 16°48E **17** B
Pilanesberg △ *S. Africa* 25°15S 27°4E **56** D
Pilani *India* 28°22N 75°33E **42** E
Pilar *Paraguay* 26°50S 58°20W **94** B
Pilaya → *Bolivia* 20°55S 64°4W **92**
Pilbara *Australia* 23°35S 117°25E **60** D
Pilcomayo → *Paraguay* 25°21S 57°42W **94**
Pilgrim's Rest *S. Africa* 24°55S 30°44E **57**
Pilibhit *India* 28°40N 79°50E **43** E
Pilica → *Poland* 51°52N 21°17E **17** C
Pilipinas = Philippines ■ *Asia* 12°0N 123°0E **37** B
Pilkhawa *India* 28°43N 77°42E **42**
Pilliga *Australia* 30°21S 148°54E **63**
Pilos *Greece* 36°55N 21°42E **23**
Pilot Mound *Canada* 49°15N 98°54W **71**
Pilot Point *U.S.A.* 33°24N 96°58W **84**
Pilot Rock *U.S.A.* 45°29N 118°50W **76**
Pima *U.S.A.* 32°54N 109°50W **77**
Pimba *Australia* 31°18S 136°46E **63**
Pimenta Bueno *Brazil* 11°35S 61°10W **92**
Pimentel *Peru* 6°45S 79°55W **92**
Pin Valley △ *India* 31°50N 77°50E **42**
Pinang *Malaysia* 5°25N 100°15E **39**
Pinar, C. des *Spain* 39°53N 3°12E **24** B
Pinar del Río *Cuba* 22°26N 83°40W **88**
Pınarhisar *Turkey* 41°37N 27°30E **23** D
Pinatubo, Mt. *Phil.* 15°8N 120°21E **37**
Pinawa *Canada* 50°9N 95°50W **71**
Pincher Creek *Canada* 49°30N 113°57W **70**
Pinchi L. *Canada* 54°38N 124°30W **70**
Pinckneyville *U.S.A.* 38°5N 89°23W **80**
Pińczów *Poland* 50°32N 20°32E **17** C
Pindar *Australia* 28°30S 115°47E **61**
Pindi Gheb *Pakistan* 33°14N 72°21E **42**
Pindos Oros *Greece* 40°0N 21°0E **23**
Pindus Mts. = Pindos Oros *Greece* 40°0N 21°0E **23**
Pine → *B.C., Canada* 56°8N 120°43W **70**
Pine → *Sask., Canada* 58°50N 105°38W **71**
Pine Bluff *U.S.A.* 34°13N 92°1W **84**
Pine Bluffs *U.S.A.* 41°11N 104°4W **76** F
Pine City *U.S.A.* 45°50N 92°59W **80**
Pine Cr. → *U.S.A.* 41°10N 77°16W **82**
Pine Creek *Australia* 13°50S 131°50E **60**
Pine Falls *Canada* 50°34N 96°11W **71**
Pine Flat L. *U.S.A.* 36°50N 119°20W **78**
Pine Grove *U.S.A.* 40°33N 76°23W **83**
Pine Hill *Australia* 23°38S 146°57E **62**
Pine Pass *Canada* 55°25N 122°42W **70**
Pine Point *Canada* 60°50N 114°28W **70**
Pine Ridge *U.S.A.* 43°2N 102°33W **80**
Pine River *Canada* 51°45N 100°30W **71**
Pine River *U.S.A.* 46°43N 94°24W **80**
Pine Valley *U.S.A.* 32°50N 116°32W **79** N
Pinecrest *U.S.A.* 38°12N 120°1W **78**
Pinedale *Calif., U.S.A.* 36°50N 119°48W **78**
Pinedale *Wyo., U.S.A.* 42°52N 109°52W **76**
Pinega → *Russia* 64°30N 44°19E **18**
Pinehouse L. *Canada* 55°32N 106°35W **71**
Pineimuta → *Canada* 52°8N 88°33W **72**
Pinerolo *Italy* 44°53N 7°21E **20**
Pines, Akra *Greece* 40°5N 24°20E **23** D
Pinetop-Lakeside *U.S.A.* 34°9N 109°58W **77**
Pinetown *S. Africa* 29°48S 30°54E **57**
Pineville *U.S.A.* 31°19N 92°26W **84**
Ping → *Thailand* 15°42N 100°9E **38**
Pingaring *Australia* 32°40S 118°32E **61**
Pingding *China* 37°47N 113°38E **34**
Pingdingshan *China* 33°43N 113°27E **34**
Pingdong *Taiwan* 22°39N 120°30E **33**
Pingdu *China* 36°42N 119°59E **35** F
Pingelly *Australia* 32°32S 117°5E **61**
Pingliang *China* 35°35N 106°31E **34**
Pinglu *China* 39°31N 112°30E **34**
Pingluo *China* 38°52N 106°30E **34**
Pingquan *China* 41°1N 118°37E **35** D
Pingrup *Australia* 33°32S 118°29E **61**
P'ingtung *Taiwan* 22°38N 120°30E **33**
Pingwu *China* 32°25N 104°30E **34**
Pingxiang *China* 22°6N 106°46E **32**
Pingyao *China* 37°12N 112°10E **34**
Pingyi *China* 35°30N 117°35E **35**
Pingyin *China* 36°20N 116°25E **34**
Pingyuan *China* 37°10N 116°22E **34**
Pinhal *Brazil* 22°10S 46°46W **95**
Pinheiro *Brazil* 2°31S 45°5W **93**
Pinheiro Machado *Brazil* 31°34S 53°23W **95**
Pinhel *Portugal* 40°50N 7°1W **21**
Pini *Indonesia* 0°10N 98°40E **36**
Piniós → *Greece* 39°55N 22°41E **23** B
Pinjarra *Australia* 32°37S 115°52E **61**
Pink Mountain *Canada* 57°3N 122°52W **70**
Pinnacles ⌂ *U.S.A.* 36°25N 121°12W **78**
Pinnaroo *Australia* 35°17S 140°53E **63**
Pinon Hills *U.S.A.* 34°26N 117°39W **79**
Pinos *Mexico* 22°18N 101°34W **86**
Pinos, Mt. *U.S.A.* 34°49N 119°8W **79**
Pinos Pt. *U.S.A.* 36°38N 121°57W **77**
Pinrang *Indonesia* 3°46S 119°41E **37**
Pins, Pte. aux *Canada* 42°15N 81°51W **82**
Pinsk *Belarus* 52°10N 26°1E **17** B
Pintados *Chile* 20°35S 69°40W **92**
Pinyug *Russia* 60°5N 48°0E **18**

oche U.S.A. 37°56N 114°27W 77 H6
ombino Italy 42°55N 10°32E 22 C4
oner, Ostrov Russia 79°50N 92°0E 29 B10
opiotaki = Milford Sd. N.Z. 44°41S 167°47E 59 F1
orini, L. Brazil 3°15S 62°35W 92 D6
otrków Trybunalski Poland 51°23N 19°43E 17 C10
p Iran 26°45N 60°10E 45 E9
par India 26°25N 73°31E 42 F5
par Road India 26°27N 73°27E 42 F5
paria Mad. P., India 22°45N 78°23E 42 H8
paria Mad. P., India 21°49N 77°37E 42 J7
pestone U.S.A. 44°0N 96°19W 80 D5
pestone → Canada 52°53N 89°23W 72 B2
pestone Cr. → Canada 49°38N 100°15W 71 D8
plan Pakistan 32°17N 71°21E 42 C4
ploda India 23°37N 74°56E 42 H6
pmuacan, Rés. Canada 49°45N 70°30W 73 C5
ppingarra Australia 20°27S 118°42E 60 D2
qua U.S.A. 40°9N 84°15W 81 E11
quiri → Brazil 24°3S 54°14W 95 A5
Panjal Range India 32°30N 76°50E 42 C7
r Sohrāb Iran 25°44N 60°54E 45 E9
racicaba Brazil 22°45S 47°40W 95 A6
racuruca Brazil 3°50S 41°50W 93 D10
rae Tahiti 17°31S 149°32W 59 d
ræus = Pireas Greece 37°57N 23°42E 23 F10
raiévs = Pireas Greece 37°57N 23°42E 23 F10
rajuí Brazil 21°59S 49°29W 95 A6
ram I. India 21°36N 72°21E 42 J5
rané Argentina 25°42S 59°6W 94 B4
rānshahr Iran 36°41N 45°8E 44 B5
rapora Brazil 17°20S 44°56W 93 G10
rawa India 24°10N 76°2E 42 G7
reas Greece 37°57N 23°42E 23 F10
rgos Greece 37°40N 21°27E 23 F9
ribebuy Paraguay 25°26S 57°2W 94 B4
rimapun Indonesia 6°20S 138°24E 37 F9
rin Planina Bulgaria 41°40N 23°30E 23 D10
rineos = Pyrénées Europe 42°45N 0°18E 20 E4
ripiri Brazil 4°15S 41°46W 93 D10
rlangimpi Australia 11°24S 130°26E 60 B5
rmasens Germany 49°12N 7°36E 16 D4
rot Serbia 43°9N 22°33E 23 C10
ru Indonesia 3°4S 128°12E 37 E7
ru U.S.A. 34°25N 118°48W 79 L8
sa Italy 43°43N 10°23E 22 C4
sagua Chile 19°40S 70°15W 92 G4
sco Peru 13°50S 76°12W 92 F3
sek Czech Rep. 49°19N 14°10E 16 D8
shan China 37°30N 78°33E 32 C2
shīn Iran 26°6N 61°47E 45 E9
shin Pakistan 30°35N 67°0E 42 D2
shin Lora → Pakistan 29°9N 64°5E 42 E1
sing Indonesia 5°8S 121°53E 37 F6
smo Beach U.S.A. 35°9N 120°38W 79 K6
ssis, Cerro Argentina 27°45S 68°48W 94 B2
ssouri Cyprus 34°40N 32°42E 25 E11
stóia Italy 43°55N 10°54E 22 C4
stol B. Canada 62°25N 92°37W 71 A10
suerga → Spain 41°33N 4°52W 21 B3
→ U.S.A. 40°47N 122°6W 76 F2
arpunga L. Australia 34°24S 143°30E 63 E3
cairn I. Pac. Oc. 25°5S 130°5W 65 K14
ch L. Trin. & Tob. 10°12N 61°39W 93 K15
eå Sweden 65°20N 21°25E 8 D19
eälven → Sweden 65°20N 21°25E 8 D19
ești Romania 44°52N 24°54E 17 F13
hapuram India 17°10N 82°15E 41 L13
hara Australia 30°20S 116°35E 61 F2
horagarh India 29°35N 80°13E 43 E9
horo Pakistan 25°31N 69°23E 42 G3
lochry U.K. 56°42N 3°44W 11 E5
silia Cyprus 34°55N 33°0E 25 E12
t I. Canada 53°30N 129°50W 70 C3
tsburg Calif., U.S.A. 38°2N 121°53W 78 G5
tsburg Kans., U.S.A. 37°25N 94°42W 80 G6
tsburg Tex., U.S.A. 33°0N 94°59W 84 E7
tsburgh U.S.A. 40°26N 79°58W 82 F5
tsfield Ill., U.S.A. 39°36N 90°49W 80 F8
tsfield Maine, U.S.A. 44°47N 69°23W 81 C19
tsfield Mass., U.S.A. 42°27N 73°15W 83 D11
tsfield N.H., U.S.A. 43°18N 71°20W 83 C13
tston U.S.A. 41°19N 75°47W 83 E9
tsworth Australia 27°41S 151°37E 63 D5
uri → Australia 22°35S 138°30E 62 C2
ura Peru 5°15S 80°38W 92 E2
xley U.S.A. 35°58N 119°18W 78 K7
hou China 34°44N 116°55E 34 G9
acentia Canada 47°20N 54°0W 73 C9
acentia B. Canada 47°0N 55°0W 73 C9
acerville U.S.A. 38°44N 120°48W 78 G6
acetas Cuba 22°15N 79°44W 88 B4
ainfield N.J., U.S.A. 40°37N 74°25W 83 F10
ainfield Ohio, U.S.A. 40°13N 81°43W 82 F3
ainfield Vt., U.S.A. 44°17N 72°26W 83 B12
ains Mont., U.S.A. 47°28N 114°53W 76 C6
ains Tex., U.S.A. 33°11N 102°50W 84 E3
ainview Nebr., U.S.A. 42°21N 97°47W 80 D5
ainview Tex., U.S.A. 34°11N 101°43W 84 D4
ainwell U.S.A. 42°27N 85°38W 81 D11
aistow U.S.A. 42°50N 71°6W 83 D13
aka, Akra Greece 35°11N 26°19E 25 D8
ana Cays Bahamas 22°38N 73°30W 89 B5
anada U.S.A. 37°16N 120°19W 78 H6
ano U.S.A. 33°1N 96°42W 84 E6
ant City U.S.A. 28°1N 82°7W 85 G13
aquemine U.S.A. 30°17N 91°14W 84 F9
asencia Spain 40°3N 6°8W 21 B2
aster City U.S.A. 32°47N 115°51W 79 N11
aster Rock Canada 46°53N 67°22W 73 C6
astun Russia 44°45N 136°19E 30 B8
ata, Río de la → S. Amer. 34°45S 57°30W 94 C4
Plátani → Italy 37°23N 13°16E 22 F5
Platanos Greece 35°28N 23°33E 25 D5
Platte U.S.A. 43°23N 98°51W 80 D4
Platte → Mo., U.S.A. 39°16N 94°50W 80 F6
Platte → Nebr., U.S.A. 41°4N 95°53W 80 E6
Platteville U.S.A. 42°44N 90°29W 80 D8
Plattsburgh U.S.A. 44°42N 73°28W 83 B11
Plattsmouth U.S.A. 41°1N 95°53W 80 E6
Plauen Germany 50°30N 12°8E 16 C7
Plavinas Latvia 56°35N 25°46E 9 H21
Playa Blanca Canary Is. 28°55N 13°37W 24 F6
Playa Blanca Sur Canary Is. 28°51N 13°50W 24 F6
Playa de las Americas Canary Is. 28°5N 16°43W 24 F3
Playa de Mogán Canary Is. 27°48N 15°47W 24 G4
Playa del Carmen Mexico 20°37N 87°4W 87 C7
Playa del Inglés Canary Is. 27°45N 15°33W 24 G4
Playa Esmerelda Canary Is. 28°8N 14°16W 24 F5
Playgreen L. Canada 54°0N 98°15W 71 C9
Pleasant Bay Canada 46°51N 60°48W 73 C7
Pleasant Hill U.S.A. 37°57N 122°4W 78 H4
Pleasant Mount U.S.A. 41°44N 75°26W 83 E9
Pleasanton Calif., U.S.A. 37°39N 121°52W 78 H5
Pleasanton Tex., U.S.A. 28°58N 98°29W 84 G5
Pleasantville N.J., U.S.A. 39°24N 74°32W 81 F16
Pleasantville Pa., U.S.A. 41°35N 79°34W 82 E5
Plei Ku Vietnam 13°57N 108°0E 38 F7
Plenty → Australia 23°25S 136°31E 62 C2
Plenty, B. of N.Z. 37°45S 177°0E 59 B6
Plentywood U.S.A. 48°47N 104°34W 76 B11
Plesetsk Russia 62°43N 40°20E 18 B7
Plessisville Canada 46°14N 71°47W 73 C5
Plétipi, L. Canada 51°44N 70°6W 73 B5
Pleven Bulgaria 43°26N 24°37E 23 C11
Plevlja Montenegro 43°21N 19°21E 23 C8
Plevna Canada 44°58N 76°59W 82 B8
Płock Poland 52°32N 19°40E 17 B10
Plöckenstein Germany 48°46N 13°51E 16 D7
Ploiești Romania 44°57N 26°5E 17 F14
Plonge, Lac la Canada 55°8N 107°20W 71 B7
Plovdiv Bulgaria 42°8N 24°44E 23 C11
Plover Cove Res. China 22°28N 114°15E 33 G11
Plum U.S.A. 40°29N 79°47W 82 F5
Plum I. U.S.A. 41°11N 72°12W 83 E12
Plumas U.S.A. 39°45N 120°4W 78 F6
Plummer U.S.A. 47°20N 116°53W 76 C5
Plumtree Zimbabwe 20°27S 27°55E 55 G2
Plungė Lithuania 55°53N 21°59E 9 J19
Plymouth Trin. & Tob. 11°14N 60°48W 93 J16
Plymouth U.K. 50°22N 4°10W 13 G3
Plymouth Calif., U.S.A. 38°29N 120°51W 78 G6
Plymouth Ind., U.S.A. 41°21N 86°19W 80 E10
Plymouth Mass., U.S.A. 41°57N 70°40W 83 E14
Plymouth N.C., U.S.A. 35°52N 76°43W 85 D16
Plymouth N.H., U.S.A. 43°46N 71°41W 83 C13
Plymouth Pa., U.S.A. 41°14N 75°57W 83 E9
Plymouth Wis., U.S.A. 43°45N 87°59W 80 D10
Plympton-Wyoming = Wyoming Canada 42°57N 82°7W 82 D2
Plynlimon = Pumlumon Fawr U.K. 52°28N 3°46W 13 E4
Plyusa Russia 58°28N 29°27E 9 G23
Plzeň Czech Rep. 49°45N 13°22E 16 D7
Po → Italy 44°57N 12°4E 22 B5
Po Hai = Bo Hai China 39°0N 119°0E 35 E10
Po Toi China 22°10N 114°16E 33 G11
Pobeda Russia 65°12N 146°12E 29 C15
Pobedy, Pik Kyrgyzstan 42°0N 79°58E 32 B2
Pocahontas Ark., U.S.A. 36°16N 90°58W 85 C9
Pocahontas Iowa, U.S.A. 42°44N 94°40W 80 D6
Pocatello U.S.A. 42°52N 112°27W 76 E7
Pocomoke City U.S.A. 38°5N 75°34W 81 F16
Poços de Caldas Brazil 21°50S 46°33W 95 A6
Podgorica Montenegro 42°30N 19°19E 23 C8
Podilska Vysochyna Ukraine 49°0N 28°0E 17 D14
Podolsk Russia 55°25N 37°30E 18 C6
Podporozhye Russia 60°55N 34°2E 18 B5
Pofadder S. Africa 29°10S 19°22E 56 D2
Pogranichnyy Russia 44°25N 131°24E 30 B5
Poh Indonesia 0°46S 122°51E 37 E6
Pohang S. Korea 36°1N 129°23E 35 F15
Pohjanmaa Finland 62°58N 22°50E 8 E20
Pohnpei Micronesia 6°55N 158°10E 64 G7
Pohri India 25°32N 77°22E 42 G6
Poinsett, C. Antarctica 65°42S 113°18E 5 C8
Point Arena U.S.A. 38°55N 123°41W 78 G3
Point Baker U.S.A. 56°21N 133°37W 70 B2
Point Fortin Trin. & Tob. 10°10N 61°42W 93 K15
Point Hope U.S.A. 68°21N 166°47W 74 a
Point L. Canada 65°15N 113°4W 68 C8
Point Lisas Industrial Estate Trin. & Tob. 10°24N 61°29W 93 K15
Point Pedro Sri Lanka 9°50N 80°15E 40 Q12
Point Pelee △ Canada 41°57N 82°31W 82 E2
Point Pleasant N.J., U.S.A. 40°5N 74°4W 83 F10
Point Pleasant W. Va., U.S.A. 38°51N 82°8W 81 F12
Point Reyes △ U.S.A. 38°10N 122°55W 78 G2
Pointe-à-Pitre Guadeloupe 16°10N 61°32W 88 b
Pointe-au-Pic = La Malbaie Canada 47°40N 70°10W 73 C5
Pointe-Claire Canada 45°26N 73°50W 83 A11
Pointe-Gatineau Canada 45°27N 75°41W 83 A9
Pointe-Noire Congo 4°48S 11°53E 52 E2
Pointe-Noire Guadeloupe 16°14N 61°47W 88 b
Poipet Cambodia 13°39N 102°33E 38 F4
Poisonbush Ra. Australia 22°30S 121°30E 60 D3
Poissonnier Pt. Australia 19°57S 119°10E 60 C2
Poitiers France 46°35N 0°20E 20 C4
Poitou France 46°40N 0°10W 20 C3
Pojoaque U.S.A. 35°54N 106°1W 77 J10
Pokaran India 27°0N 71°50E 42 F4
Pokataroo Australia 29°30S 148°36E 63 D4
Pokhara Nepal 28°14N 83°58E 43 E10
Poko Dem. Rep. of the Congo 3°7N 26°52E 54 B2
Pokrovsk Russia 61°29N 129°0E 29 C13
Pola = Pula Croatia 44°54N 13°57E 16 F7
Polacca U.S.A. 35°50N 110°23W 77 J8
Polan Iran 25°30N 61°10E 45 E9
Poland U.S.A. 43°13N 75°3W 83 C9
Poland ■ Europe 52°0N 20°0E 17 C10
Polar Bear △ Canada 55°0N 83°45W 72 A2
Polatsk Belarus 55°30N 28°50E 9 J23
Polcura Chile 37°17S 71°43W 94 D1
Polesye = Pripet Marshes Europe 52°10N 28°10E 17 B15
Polevskoy Russia 56°26N 60°11E 18 C11
Police Poland 53°33N 14°33E 16 B8
Police, Pte. Seychelles 4°51S 55°32E 53 b
Poligiros Greece 40°23N 23°25E 23 D10
Polillo Is. Phil. 14°56N 122°0E 37 B6
Polis Cyprus 35°2N 32°26E 25 D11
Polk U.S.A. 41°22N 79°56W 82 E5
Pollachi India 10°35N 77°0E 40 P10
Pollença Spain 39°54N 3°1E 24 B10
Pollença, B. de Spain 39°53N 3°8E 24 B10
Polnovat Russia 63°50N 65°54E 28 C7
Polokwane S. Africa 23°54S 29°25E 57 C4
Polokwane → S. Africa 22°25S 30°5E 57 C5
Polonne Ukraine 50°6N 27°30E 17 C14
Polonnoye = Polonne Ukraine 50°6N 27°30E 17 C14
Polson U.S.A. 47°41N 114°9W 76 C6
Poltava Ukraine 49°35N 34°35E 19 E5
Põltsamaa Estonia 58°39N 25°58E 9 G21
Polunochnoye Russia 60°52N 60°25E 28 C7
Põlva Estonia 58°3N 27°3E 9 G22
Polyarny Russia 69°8N 33°20E 8 B25
Polyarnyye Zori Russia 67°22N 32°30E 8 C25
Polynesia Pac. Oc. 10°0S 162°0W 65 F11
Polynésie française = French Polynesia ☒ Pac. Oc. 20°0S 145°0W 65 J13
Pombal Portugal 39°55N 8°40W 21 C1
Pombia Greece 35°0N 24°51E 25 E6
Pomene Mozam. 22°53S 35°33E 57 C6
Pomeroy Ohio, U.S.A. 39°2N 82°2W 81 F12
Pomeroy Wash., U.S.A. 46°28N 117°36W 76 C5
Pomézia Italy 41°40N 12°30E 22 D5
Pomona Australia 26°22S 152°52E 63 D5
Pomona U.S.A. 34°4N 117°45W 79 L9
Pomorskie, Pojezierze Poland 53°40N 16°37E 17 B9
Pomos Cyprus 35°9N 32°33E 25 D11
Pomos, C. Cyprus 35°10N 32°33E 25 D11
Pompano Beach U.S.A. 26°14N 80°7W 85 H14
Pompeys Pillar U.S.A. 45°59N 107°57W 76 D10
Pompeys Pillar △ U.S.A. 46°0N 108°0W 76 D10
Pompton Lakes U.S.A. 41°0N 74°17W 83 F10
Ponape = Pohnpei Micronesia 6°55N 158°10E 64 G7
Ponask L. Canada 54°0N 92°41W 72 B1
Ponca U.S.A. 42°34N 96°43W 80 D5
Ponca City U.S.A. 36°42N 97°5W 84 C6
Ponce Puerto Rico 18°1N 66°37W 89 d
Ponchatoula U.S.A. 30°26N 90°26W 85 F9
Poncheville, L. Canada 50°10N 76°55W 72 B4
Pond U.S.A. 35°43N 119°20W 79 K7
Pond Inlet Canada 72°40N 77°0W 69 B12
Pondicherry = Puducherry India 11°59N 79°50E 40 P11
Ponds, I. of Canada 53°27N 55°52W 73 B8
Ponferrada Spain 42°32N 6°35W 21 A2
Ponnani India 10°45N 75°59E 40 P9
Ponoka Canada 52°42N 113°40W 70 C6
Ponorogo Indonesia 7°52S 111°27E 37 G14
Ponoy Russia 67°0N 41°13E 18 A7
Ponoy → Russia 66°59N 41°17E 18 A7
Ponta Delgada Azores 37°44N 25°40W 50 a
Ponta do Sol Madeira 32°42N 17°7W 24 D2
Ponta Grossa Brazil 25°7S 50°10W 95 B5
Ponta Porã Brazil 22°20S 55°35W 95 A4
Pontarlier France 46°54N 6°20E 20 C7
Pontchartrain, L. U.S.A. 30°5N 90°5W 85 F9
Ponte do Pungué Mozam. 19°30S 34°33E 55 F3
Ponte Nova Brazil 20°25S 42°54W 95 A7
Ponteix Canada 49°46N 107°29W 71 D7
Pontevedra Spain 42°26N 8°40W 21 A1
Pontiac Ill., U.S.A. 40°53N 88°38W 80 E9
Pontiac Mich., U.S.A. 42°38N 83°18W 81 D12
Pontian Kechil Malaysia 1°29N 103°23E 39 d
Pontianak Indonesia 0°3S 109°15E 36 E3
Pontine Is. = Ponziane, Ísole Italy 40°55N 12°57E 22 D5
Pontine Mts. = Kuzey Anadolu Dağları Turkey 41°0N 36°45E 19 F6
Pontivy France 48°5N 2°58W 20 B2
Pontoise France 49°3N 2°5E 20 B5
Ponton → Canada 58°27N 116°11W 70 B5
Pontypool Canada 44°6N 78°38W 82 B6
Pontypool U.K. 51°42N 3°2W 13 F4
Ponziane, Ísole Italy 40°55N 12°57E 22 D5
Poochera Australia 32°43S 134°51E 63 E1
Poole U.K. 50°43N 1°59W 13 G6
Poole □ U.K. 50°43N 1°59W 13 G6
Poona = Pune India 18°29N 73°57E 40 K8
Pooncarie Australia 33°22S 142°31E 63 E3
Poopelloe L. Australia 31°40S 144°0E 63 E3
Poopó, L. de Bolivia 18°30S 67°35W 92 G5
Popayán Colombia 2°27N 76°36W 92 C3
Poperinge Belgium 50°51N 2°42E 15 D2
Popiltah L. Australia 33°10S 141°42E 63 E3
Popio L. Australia 33°10S 141°52E 63 E3
Poplar U.S.A. 48°7N 105°12W 76 B11
Poplar → Canada 53°0N 97°19W 71 C9
Poplar Bluff U.S.A. 36°46N 90°24W 80 G8
Poplarville U.S.A. 30°51N 89°32W 85 F10
Popocatépetl, Volcán Mexico 19°2N 98°38W 87 D5
Popokabaka Dem. Rep. of the Congo 5°41S 16°40E 52 F3
Poprad Slovak Rep. 49°3N 20°18E 17 D11
Porali → Pakistan 25°58N 66°26E 42 G2
Porbandar India 21°44N 69°43E 42 J3
Porcher I. Canada 53°50N 130°30W 70 C2
Porcupine → Canada 59°11N 104°46W 71 B8
Porcupine → U.S.A. 66°34N 145°19W 74 a
Porcupine Gorge △ Australia 20°22S 144°26E 62 C3
Pordenone Italy 45°57N 12°39E 22 B5
Pori Finland 61°29N 21°48E 8 F19
Porkhov Russia 57°45N 29°38E 9 H23
Porlamar Venezuela 10°57N 63°51W 92 A6
Pormpuraaw Australia 14°59S 141°26E 62 A3
Poronaysk Russia 49°13N 143°0E 29 E15
Poroshiri-Dake Japan 42°41N 142°52E 30 C11
Poroto Mts. Tanzania 9°0S 33°30E 55 D3
Porpoise B. Antarctica 66°0S 127°0E 5 C9
Porreres Spain 39°31N 3°2E 24 B10
Porsangerfjorden Norway 70°40N 25°40E 8 A21
Porsgrunn Norway 59°10N 9°40E 9 G13
Port Alberni Canada 49°14N 124°50W 70 D4
Port Alfred S. Africa 33°36S 26°55E 56 E4
Port Alice Canada 50°20N 127°25W 70 C3
Port Allegany U.S.A. 41°48N 78°17W 82 E6
Port Allen U.S.A. 30°27N 91°12W 84 F9
Port Alma Australia 23°38S 150°53E 62 C5
Port Alma Canada 42°10N 82°14W 82 D2
Port Angeles U.S.A. 48°7N 123°27W 78 B3
Port Antonio Jamaica 18°10N 76°26W 88 a
Port Aransas U.S.A. 27°50N 97°4W 84 H6
Port Arthur Australia 43°7S 147°50E 63 G4
Port Arthur U.S.A. 29°54N 93°56W 84 G8
Port au Choix Canada 50°43N 57°22W 73 B8
Port au Port B. Canada 48°40N 58°50W 73 C8
Port-au-Prince Haiti 18°40N 72°20W 89 C5
Port Augusta Australia 32°30S 137°50E 63 E2
Port Austin U.S.A. 44°3N 83°1W 82 B2
Port Bell Uganda 0°18N 32°35E 54 B3
Port Bergé Vaovao Madag. 15°33S 47°40E 57 B8
Port Blandford Canada 48°20N 54°10W 73 C9
Port Bradshaw Australia 12°30S 137°20E 62 A2
Port Broughton Australia 33°37S 137°56E 63 E2
Port Bruce Canada 42°39N 81°0W 82 D4
Port Burwell Canada 42°40N 80°48W 82 D4
Port Canning India 22°23N 88°40E 43 H13
Port Carling Canada 45°7N 79°35W 82 A5
Port-Cartier Canada 50°2N 66°50W 73 B6
Port Chalmers N.Z. 45°49S 170°30E 59 F3
Port Charlotte U.S.A. 26°59N 82°6W 85 H13
Port Chester U.S.A. 41°0N 73°40W 83 F11
Port Clements Canada 53°40N 132°10W 70 C2
Port Clinton U.S.A. 41°31N 82°56W 81 E12
Port Colborne Canada 42°50N 79°10W 82 D5
Port Coquitlam Canada 49°15N 122°45W 78 A4
Port Credit Canada 43°33N 79°35W 82 C5
Port Curtis Australia 23°57S 151°20E 62 C5
Port d'Alcúdia Spain 39°50N 3°7E 24 B10
Port Dalhousie Canada 43°13N 79°16W 82 C5
Port d'Andratx Spain 39°32N 2°23E 24 B9
Port Darwin Australia 12°24S 130°45E 60 B5
Port Darwin Falk. Is. 51°50S 59°0W 96 G5
Port Davey Australia 43°16S 145°55E 63 G4
Port-de-Paix Haiti 19°50N 72°50W 89 C5
Port de Pollença Spain 39°54N 3°4E 24 B10
Port de Sóller Spain 39°48N 2°42E 24 B9
Port Dickson Malaysia 2°30N 101°49E 39 L3
Port Douglas Australia 16°30S 145°30E 62 B4
Port Dover Canada 42°47N 80°12W 82 D4
Port Edward Canada 54°12N 130°10W 70 C2
Port Elgin Canada 44°25N 81°25W 82 B3
Port Elizabeth S. Africa 33°58S 25°40E 56 E4
Port Ellen U.K. 55°38N 6°11W 11 F2
Port Erin I. of Man 54°5N 4°45W 12 C3
Port Essington Australia 11°15S 132°10E 60 B5
Port Ewen U.S.A. 41°54N 73°59W 83 E11
Port Fairy Australia 38°22S 142°12E 63 F3
Port Gamble U.S.A. 47°51N 122°34W 78 C4
Port-Gentil Gabon 0°40S 8°50E 52 E1
Port Germein Australia 33°1S 138°1E 63 E2
Port Ghalib Egypt 25°20N 34°50E 44 E2
Port Gibson U.S.A. 31°58N 90°59W 84 F9
Port Glasgow U.K. 55°56N 4°41W 11 F4
Port Harcourt Nigeria 4°40N 7°10E 50 H7
Port Hardy Canada 50°41N 127°30W 70 C3
Port Harrison = Inukjuak Canada 58°25N 78°15W 69 D12
Port Hawkesbury Canada 45°36N 61°22W 73 C7
Port Hedland Australia 20°25S 118°35E 60 D2
Port Henry U.S.A. 44°3N 73°28W 83 B11
Port Hood Canada 46°0N 61°32W 73 C7
Port Hope Canada 43°56N 78°20W 82 C6
Port Hope U.S.A. 43°57N 82°43W 82 C2
Port Hope Simpson Canada 52°33N 56°18W 73 B8
Port Hueneme U.S.A. 34°7N 119°12W 79 L7
Port Huron U.S.A. 42°58N 82°26W 82 D2
Port Jefferson U.S.A. 40°57N 73°3W 83 F11
Port Jervis U.S.A. 41°22N 74°41W 83 E10
Port Kelang = Pelabuhan Klang Malaysia 3°0N 101°23E 39 L3
Port Kenny Australia 33°10S 134°41E 63 E1
Port Lairge = Waterford Ireland 52°15N 7°8W 10 D4
Port Laoise Ireland 53°2N 7°18W 10 C4
Port Lavaca U.S.A. 28°37N 96°38W 84 G6
Port Leyden U.S.A. 43°35N 75°21W 83 C9
Port Lincoln Australia 34°42S 135°52E 63 E2
Port Loko S. Leone 8°48N 12°46W 50 G3
Port-Louis Guadeloupe 16°28N 61°32W 88 b
Port Louis Mauritius 20°10S 57°30E 53 d
Port MacDonnell Australia 38°5S 140°48E 63 F3
Port McNeill Canada 50°35N 127°6W 70 C3
Port Macquarie Australia 31°25S 152°25E 63 E5
Port Maria Jamaica 18°22N 76°54W 88 a
Port Matilda U.S.A. 40°48N 78°3W 82 F6
Port McNicoll Canada 44°44N 79°48W 82 B5
Port Mellon Canada 49°32N 123°31W 70 D4
Port-Menier Canada 49°51N 64°15W 73 C7
Port Moody Canada 49°17N 122°51W 78 A4
Port Morant Jamaica 17°54N 76°19W 88 a
Port Moresby Papua N. G. 9°24S 147°8E 58 B7
Port Musgrave Australia 11°55S 141°50E 62 A3
Port Neches U.S.A. 30°0N 93°59W 84 G8
Port Nolloth S. Africa 29°17S 16°52E 56 D2
Port Nouveau-Québec = Kangiqsualujjuaq Canada 58°30N 65°59W 69 D13
Port of Climax Canada 49°10N 108°20W 71 D7
Port of Coronach Canada 49°7N 105°31W 71 D7
Port of Spain Trin. & Tob. 10°40N 61°31W 89 D7
Port Orange U.S.A. 29°9N 80°59W 85 G14
Port Orchard U.S.A. 47°32N 122°38W 78 C4
Port Orford U.S.A. 42°45N 124°30W 76 E1
Port Pegasus N.Z. 47°12S 167°41E 59 G1
Port Perry Canada 44°6N 78°56W 82 B6
Port Phillip B. Australia 38°10S 144°50E 63 F3
Port Pirie Australia 33°10S 138°1E 63 E2
Port Renfrew Canada 48°30N 124°20W 78 B2
Port Roper Australia 14°45S 135°25E 62 A2
Port Rowan Canada 42°40N 80°30W 82 D4
Port Safaga = Bûr Safâga Egypt 26°43N 33°57E 44 E2
Port Said = Bûr Sa'îd Egypt 31°16N 32°18E 51 B12
Port St. Joe U.S.A. 29°49N 85°18W 85 G12
Port St. Johns = Umzimvubu S. Africa 31°38S 29°33E 57 E4
Port St. Lucie U.S.A. 27°18N 80°21W 85 H14
Port Sanilac U.S.A. 43°26N 82°33W 82 C2
Port Severn Canada 44°48N 79°43W 82 B5
Port Shepstone S. Africa 30°44S 30°28E 57 E5
Port Simpson Canada 54°30N 130°20W 70 C2
Port Stanley = Stanley Falk. Is. 51°40S 59°51W 96 G5
Port Stanley Canada 42°40N 81°10W 82 D3
Port Sudan = Bûr Sûdân Sudan 19°32N 37°9E 51 E13
Port Sulphur U.S.A. 29°29N 89°42W 85 G10
Port Talbot U.K. 51°35N 3°47W 13 F4
Port Townsend U.S.A. 48°7N 122°45W 78 B4
Port-Vendres France 42°32N 3°8E 20 E5
Port Vila Vanuatu 17°45S 168°18E 58 C9
Port Vladimir Russia 69°25N 33°6E 8 B25
Port Wakefield Australia 34°12S 138°10E 63 E2
Port Washington U.S.A. 43°23N 87°53W 80 D10
Porta Orientalis Romania 45°6N 22°18E 17 F12
Portacloy Ireland 54°20N 9°46W 10 B2
Portadown U.K. 54°25N 6°27W 10 B5
Portaferry U.K. 54°23N 5°33W 10 B6
Portage Pa., U.S.A. 40°23N 78°41W 82 F6
Portage Wis., U.S.A. 43°33N 89°28W 80 D9
Portage la Prairie Canada 49°58N 98°18W 71 D9
Portageville U.S.A. 36°26N 89°42W 80 G9
Portalegre Portugal 39°19N 7°25W 21 C2
Portales U.S.A. 34°11N 103°20W 77 J12
Portarlington Ireland 53°9N 7°14W 10 C4
Portbou Spain 42°25N 3°9E 21 A7
Porter L. N.W.T., Canada 61°41N 108°5W 71 A7
Porter L. Sask., Canada 56°20N 107°20W 71 B7
Porterville S. Africa 33°0S 19°0E 56 E2
Porterville U.S.A. 36°4N 119°1W 78 J8
Porthcawl U.K. 51°29N 3°42W 13 F4
Porthill U.S.A. 48°59N 116°30W 76 B5
Porthmadog U.K. 52°55N 4°8W 12 E3
Portile de Fier Europe 44°44N 22°30E 17 F12
Portimão Portugal 37°8N 8°32W 21 D1
Portishead U.K. 51°29N 2°46W 13 F5
Portknockie U.K. 57°42N 2°51W 11 D6
Portland N.S.W., Australia 33°20S 150°0E 63 E5
Portland Vic., Australia 38°20S 141°35E 63 F3
Portland Canada 44°42N 76°12W 83 B8
Portland Conn., U.S.A. 41°34N 72°38W 83 E12
Portland Maine, U.S.A. 43°39N 70°16W 81 D18
Portland Mich., U.S.A. 42°52N 84°54W 81 D11
Portland Oreg., U.S.A. 45°32N 122°37W 78 E4
Portland Pa., U.S.A. 40°55N 75°6W 83 F9
Portland Tex., U.S.A. 27°53N 97°20W 84 H6
Portland, I. of U.K. 50°33N 2°26W 13 G5
Portland B. Australia 38°15S 141°45E 63 F3
Portland Bight Jamaica 17°52N 77°5W 88 a
Portland Bill U.K. 50°31N 2°28W 13 G5
Portland Canal U.S.A. 55°56N 130°0W 70 B2
Portland Int. ✕ (PDX) U.S.A. 45°35N 122°36W 78 E4
Portland Pt. Jamaica 17°42N 77°11W 88 a
Portmadoc = Porthmadog U.K. 52°55N 4°8W 12 E3
Portmore Jamaica 17°53N 76°53W 88 a
Porto France 42°16N 8°42E 20 E1
Porto Portugal 41°8N 8°40W 21 B1
Pôrto Alegre Brazil 30°5S 51°10W 95 C5
Porto Colom Spain 39°26N 3°15E 24 B10

Porto Cristo Spain 39°33N 3°20E 24 B10
Porto de Moz Brazil 1°41S 52°13W 93 D8
Porto Empédocle Italy 37°17N 13°32E 22 F5
Porto Esperança Brazil 19°37S 57°29W 92 G7
Porto Franco Brazil 6°20S 47°24W 93 E9
Porto Inglês C. Verde Is. 15°21N 23°10W 50 b
Porto Mendes Brazil 24°30S 54°15W 95 A5
Porto Moniz Madeira 32°52N 17°11W 24 D2
Porto Murtinho Brazil 21°45S 57°55W 92 H7
Porto Nacional Brazil 10°40S 48°30W 93 F9
Porto-Novo Benin 6°23N 2°42E 50 G6
Porto Primavera, Represa Brazil 22°10S 52°45W 95 A5
Porto Santo, I. de Madeira 33°45N 16°25W 50 B2
Porto São José Brazil 22°43S 53°10W 95 A5
Porto Seguro Brazil 16°26S 39°5W 93 G11
Porto Tórres Italy 40°50N 8°24E 22 D3
Porto União Brazil 26°10S 51°10W 95 B5
Porto-Vecchio France 41°35N 9°16E 20 F8
Pôrto Velho Brazil 8°46S 63°54W 92 E6
Porto Walter Brazil 8°15S 72°40W 92 E4
Portobelo Panama 9°35N 79°42W 88 E4
Portoferráio Italy 42°48N 10°20E 22 C4
Portola U.S.A. 39°49N 120°28W 78 F6
Portopetro Spain 39°22N 3°13E 24 B10
Portoscuso Italy 39°12N 8°24E 22 E3
Portoviejo Ecuador 1°7S 80°28W 92 D2
Portpatrick U.K. 54°51N 5°7W 11 G3
Portree U.K. 57°25N 6°12W 11 D2
Portrush U.K. 55°12N 6°40W 10 A5
Portsmouth Dominica 15°34N 61°27W 89 C7
Portsmouth U.K. 50°48N 1°6W 13 G6
Portsmouth N.H., U.S.A. 43°5N 70°45W 83 C14
Portsmouth Ohio, U.S.A. 38°44N 82°57W 81 F12
Portsmouth R.I., U.S.A. 41°36N 71°15W 83 E13
Portsmouth Va., U.S.A. 36°58N 76°23W 81 G15
Portsmouth □ U.K. 50°48N 1°6W 13 G6
Portsoy U.K. 57°41N 2°41W 11 D6
Portstewart U.K. 55°11N 6°43W 10 A5
Porttipahdan tekojärvi Finland 68°5N 26°40E 8 B22
Portugal ■ Europe 40°0N 8°0W 21 C1
Portumna Ireland 53°6N 8°14W 10 C3
Portville U.S.A. 42°3N 78°20W 82 D6
Porvenir Chile 53°10S 70°16W 96 G2
Posadas Argentina 27°30S 55°50W 95 B4
Posht-e Badam Iran 33°2N 55°23E 45 C7
Poso Indonesia 1°20S 120°55E 37 E6
Posse Brazil 14°4S 46°18W 93 F9
Possession I. Antarctica 72°4S 172°0E 5 D11
Possum Kingdom L. U.S.A. 32°52N 98°26W 84 E5
Post U.S.A. 33°12N 101°23W 84 E4
Post Falls U.S.A. 47°43N 116°57W 76 C5
Postavy = Pastavy Belarus 55°4N 26°50E 9 J22
Poste-de-la-Baleine = Kuujjuarapik Canada 55°20N 77°35W 72 A4
Postmasburg S. Africa 28°18S 23°5E 56 D3
Postojna Slovenia 45°46N 14°12E 16 F8
Poston U.S.A. 34°0N 114°24W 79 M12
Postville Canada 54°54N 59°47W 73 B8
Posyet Russia 42°39N 130°48E 30 C5
Potchefstroom S. Africa 26°41S 27°7E 56 D4
Poteau U.S.A. 35°3N 94°37W 84 D7
Poteet U.S.A. 29°2N 98°35W 84 G5
Potenza Italy 40°38N 15°48E 22 D6
Poteriteri, L. N.Z. 46°5S 167°10E 59 G1
Potgietersrus = Mokopane S. Africa 24°10S 28°55E 57 C4
Poti Georgia 42°10N 41°38E 19 F7
Potiskum Nigeria 11°39N 11°2E 51 F8
Potomac → U.S.A. 38°0N 76°23W 81 F14
Potosí Bolivia 19°38S 65°50W 92 G5
Potosi Mt. U.S.A. 35°57N 115°29W 79 K11
Pototan Phil. 10°54N 122°38E 37 B6
Potrerillos Chile 26°30S 69°30W 94 B2
Potsdam Germany 52°23N 13°3E 16 B7
Potsdam U.S.A. 44°40N 74°59W 83 B10
Pottersville U.S.A. 43°43N 73°50W 83 C11
Pottstown U.S.A. 40°15N 75°39W 83 F9
Pottsville U.S.A. 40°41N 76°12W 83 F8
Pottuvil Sri Lanka 6°55N 81°50E 40 R12
Pouce Coupé Canada 55°40N 120°10W 70 B4
Poughkeepsie U.S.A. 41°42N 73°56W 83 E11
Poulaphouca Res. Ireland 53°8N 6°30W 10 C5
Poulsbo U.S.A. 47°44N 122°38W 78 C4
Poultney U.S.A. 43°31N 73°14W 83 C11
Poulton-le-Fylde U.K. 53°51N 2°58W 12 D5
Pouso Alegre Brazil 22°14S 45°57W 95 A6
Pouthisat Cambodia 12°34N 103°50E 38 F4
Považská Bystrica Slovak Rep. 49°8N 18°27E 17 D10
Povenets Russia 62°50N 34°50E 18 B5
Poverty B. N.Z. 38°43S 178°2E 59 C7
Póvoa de Varzim Portugal 41°25N 8°46W 21 B1
Povorotnyy, Mys Russia 42°40N 133°2E 30 C6
Povungnituk = Puvirnituq Canada 60°2N 77°10W 69 C12
Powassan Canada 46°5N 79°25W 72 C4
Poway U.S.A. 32°58N 117°2W 79 N9
Powder → U.S.A. 46°45N 105°26W 76 C11
Powder River U.S.A. 43°2N 106°59W 76 E10
Powell U.S.A. 44°45N 108°46W 76 D9
Powell, L. U.S.A. 36°57N 111°29W 77 H8
Powell River Canada 49°50N 124°35W 70 D4
Powers U.S.A. 45°41N 87°32W 80 C10
Pownal U.S.A. 42°45N 73°14W 83 D11
Powys □ U.K. 52°20N 3°20W 13 E4
Poyang Hu China 29°5N 116°20E 33 D6
Poyarkovo Russia 49°36N 128°41E 29 E13
Poza Rica Mexico 20°33N 97°27W 87 C5
Požarevac Serbia 44°35N 21°18E 23 B9
Poznań Poland 52°25N 16°55E 17 B9
Pozo U.S.A. 35°20N 120°24W 79 K6
Pozo Almonte Chile 20°10S 69°50W 92 H5
Pozo Colorado Paraguay 23°30S 58°45W 94 A4
Pozoblanco Spain 38°23N 4°51W 21 C3
Pozzuoli Italy 40°49N 14°7E 22 D6
Prachin Buri Thailand 14°0N 101°25E 38 F3
Prachuap Khiri Khan Thailand 11°49N 99°48E 39 G2
Prado Brazil 17°20S 39°13W 93 G11
Prague = Praha Czech Rep. 50°4N 14°25E 16 C8
Praha Czech Rep. 50°4N 14°25E 16 C8
Praia C. Verde Is. 15°2N 23°34W 50 b
Prainha Brazil 1°45S 53°30W 93 D8
Prainha Nova Brazil 7°10S 60°30W 92 E6
Prairie Australia 20°50S 144°35E 62 C3
Prairie City U.S.A. 44°28N 118°43W 76 D4
Prairie Dog Town Fork Red → U.S.A. 34°34N 99°58W 84 D5
Prairie du Chien U.S.A. 43°3N 91°9W 80 D8
Prairies, L. of the Canada 51°16N 101°32W 71 C8
Pran Buri Thailand 12°23N 99°55E 38 F2
Prapat Indonesia 2°41N 98°58E 36 D1
Praslin Seychelles 4°18S 55°45E 53 b
Prasonisi, Akra Greece 35°42N 27°46E 25 D9
Prata Brazil 19°25S 48°54W 93 G9
Pratabpur India 23°28N 83°15E 43 H10
Pratapgarh Raj., India 24°2N 74°40E 42 G6
Pratapgarh Ut. P., India 25°56N 81°59E 43 G9
Prato Italy 43°53N 11°6E 22 C4
Pratt U.S.A. 37°39N 98°44W 80 G4
Prattville U.S.A. 32°28N 86°29W 85 E11
Pravia Spain 43°30N 6°12W 21 A2
Praya Indonesia 8°39S 116°17E 36 F5
Preble U.S.A. 42°44N 76°8W 83 D8
Precipice △ Australia 25°18S 150°5E 63 D5
Precordillera Argentina 30°0S 69°1W 94 C2
Preeceville Canada 51°57N 102°40W 71 C8
Preiļi Latvia 56°18N 26°43E 9 H22
Premont U.S.A. 27°22N 98°7W 84 H5
Prentice U.S.A. 45°33N 90°17W 80 C8
Preobrazheniye Russia 42°54N 133°54E 30 C6
Preparis North Channel Ind. Oc. 15°27N 94°5E 41 M18
Preparis South Channel Ind. Oc. 14°33N 93°30E 41 M18
Přerov Czech Rep. 49°28N 17°27E 17 D9
Prescott Canada 44°45N 75°30W 83 B9
Prescott Ariz., U.S.A. 34°33N 112°28W 77 J7
Prescott Ark., U.S.A. 33°48N 93°23W 84 E8
Prescott Valley U.S.A. 34°40N 112°18W 77 J7
Preservation Inlet N.Z. 46°8S 166°35E 59 G1
Presho U.S.A. 43°54N 100°3W 80 D3
Presidencia de la Plaza Argentina 27°0S 59°50W 94 B4
Presidencia Roque Saenz Peña Argentina 26°45S 60°30W 94 B3
Presidente Epitácio Brazil 21°56S 52°6W 93 H8
Presidente Hayes □ Paraguay 24°0S 59°0W 94 A4
Presidente Prudente Brazil 22°5S 51°25W 95 A5
Presidio Mexico 29°29N 104°23W 86 B4
Presidio U.S.A. 29°34N 104°22W 84 G2
Prešov Slovak Rep. 49°0N 21°15E 17 D11
Prespa, L. = Prespansko Jezero Macedonia 40°55N 21°0E 23 D9
Prespansko Jezero Macedonia 40°55N 21°0E 23 D9
Presque I. U.S.A. 42°10N 80°6W 82 D4
Presque Isle U.S.A. 46°41N 68°1W 81 B19
Prestatyn U.K. 53°20N 3°24W 12 D4
Presteigne U.K. 52°17N 3°0W 13 E5
Preston Canada 43°23N 80°21W 82 C4
Preston U.K. 53°46N 2°42W 12 D5
Preston Idaho, U.S.A. 42°6N 111°53W 76 E8
Preston Minn., U.S.A. 43°40N 92°5W 80 D7
Preston, C. Australia 20°51S 116°12E 60 D2
Prestonsburg U.S.A. 37°40N 82°47W 81 G12
Prestwick U.K. 55°29N 4°37W 11 F4
Pretoria S. Africa 25°44S 28°12E 57 D4
Preveza Greece 38°57N 20°45E 23 E9
Prey Veng Cambodia 11°35N 105°29E 39 G5
Pribilof Is. U.S.A. 57°0N 170°0W 74 a
Příbram Czech Rep. 49°41N 14°2E 16 D8
Price U.S.A. 39°36N 110°49W 76 G8
Price I. Canada 52°23N 128°41W 70 C3
Prichard U.S.A. 30°44N 88°5W 85 F10
Priekule Latvia 56°26N 21°35E 9 H19
Prienai Lithuania 54°38N 23°57E 9 J20
Prieska S. Africa 29°40S 22°42E 56 D3
Priest L. U.S.A. 48°35N 116°52W 76 B5
Priest River U.S.A. 48°11N 116°55W 76 B5
Priest Valley U.S.A. 36°10N 120°39W 78 J6
Prievidza Slovak Rep. 48°46N 18°36E 17 D10
Prikaspiyskaya Nizmennost = Caspian Depression Eurasia 47°0N 48°0E 19 E8
Prilep Macedonia 41°21N 21°32E 23 D9
Priluki = Pryluky Ukraine 50°30N 32°24E 19 D5
Prime Seal I. Australia 40°3S 147°43E 63 G4
Primo Tapia Mexico 32°16N 116°54W 79 N10
Primorskiy Kray □ Russia 45°0N 135°0E 30 B7
Primrose L. Canada 54°55N 109°45W 71 C7
Prince Albert Canada 53°15N 105°50W 71 C7
Prince Albert S. Africa 33°12S 22°2E 56 E3
Prince Albert △ Canada 54°0N 106°25W 71 C7
Prince Albert Mts. Antarctica 76°0S 161°30E 5 D11
Prince Albert Pen. Canada 72°30N 116°0W 68 B8
Prince Albert Sd. Canada 70°25N 115°0W 68 B8
Prince Alfred, C. Canada 74°20N 124°40W 69 B7
Prince Charles I. Canada 67°47N 76°12W 69 C12
Prince Charles Mts. Antarctica 72°0S 67°0E 5 D6
Prince Edward Fracture Zone Ind. Oc. 46°0S 35°0E 5 A4
Prince Edward I. □ Canada 46°20N 63°20W 73 C7
Prince Edward Is. Ind. Oc. 46°35S 38°0E 3 G11
Prince George Canada 53°55N 122°50W 70 C4
Prince Gustaf Adolf Sea Canada 78°30N 107°0W 69 B9
Prince of Wales, C. U.S.A. 65°36N 168°5W 66 C3
Prince of Wales I. Australia 10°40S 142°10E 62 A3
Prince of Wales I. Canada 73°0N 99°0W 68 B10
Prince of Wales I. U.S.A. 55°47N 132°50W 68 D6
Prince Patrick I. Canada 77°0N 120°0W 69 B8
Prince Regent Inlet Canada 73°0N 90°0W 4 B3
Prince Rupert Canada 54°20N 130°20W 70 C2
Princes Town Trin. & Tob. 10°16N 61°23W 93 K15
Princess Charlotte B. Australia 14°25S 144°0E 62 A3
Princess Elizabeth Trough S. Ocean 64°10S 83°0E 5 C7
Princess May Ranges Australia 15°30S 125°30E 60 C4
Princess Royal I. Canada 53°0N 128°40W 70 C3
Princeton Canada 49°27N 120°30W 70 D4
Princeton Calif., U.S.A. 39°24N 122°1W 78 F4
Princeton Ill., U.S.A. 41°23N 89°28W 80 E9
Princeton Ind., U.S.A. 38°21N 87°34W 80 F10
Princeton Ky., U.S.A. 37°7N 87°53W 80 G10
Princeton Mo., U.S.A. 40°24N 93°35W 80 E7
Princeton N.J., U.S.A. 40°21N 74°39W 83 F10
Princeton W. Va., U.S.A. 37°22N 81°6W 81 G13
Príncipe São Tomé & Principe 1°37N 7°25E 48 F4
Principe da Beira Brazil 12°20S 64°30W 92 F6
Prineville U.S.A. 44°18N 120°51W 76 D3
Prins Harald Kyst Antarctica 70°0S 35°1E 5 D4
Prinsesse Astrid Kyst Antarctica 70°45S 12°30E 5 D3
Prinsesse Ragnhild Kyst Antarctica 70°15S 27°30E 5 D4
Prinzapolca Nic. 13°20N 83°35W 88 D3
Priozersk Russia 61°2N 30°7E 8 F24
Pripet = Prypyat → Europe 51°20N 30°15E 17 C16
Pripet Marshes Europe 52°10N 28°10E 17 B15
Pripyat Marshes = Pripet Marshes Europe 52°10N 28°10E 17 B15
Pripyats = Prypyat → Europe 51°20N 30°15E 17 C16
Priština Serbia 42°40N 21°13E 23 C9
Privas France 44°45N 4°37E 20 D6
Privolzhskaya Vozvyshennost Russia 51°0N 46°0E 19 D8
Privolzhskiy □ Russia 56°0N 50°0E 28 D6
Prizren Serbia 42°13N 20°45E 23 C9
Probolinggo Indonesia 7°46S 113°13E 37 G15
Proctor U.S.A. 43°40N 73°2W 83 C11
Proddatur India 14°45N 78°30E 40 M11
Prodhromos Cyprus 34°57N 32°50E 25 E11
Profilia Greece 36°5N 27°51E 25 C9
Profondeville Belgium 50°23N 4°52E 15 D4
Progreso Coahuila, Mexico 27°28N 100°59W 86 B4
Progreso Yucatán, Mexico 21°20N 89°40W 87 C7
Progress Antarctica 66°22S 76°22E 5 C12
Progress Russia 49°45N 129°37E 29 E13
Prokopyevsk Russia 54°0N 86°45E 28 D9
Prokuplje Serbia 43°16N 21°36E 23 C9
Prome Burma 18°49N 95°13E 41 K19
Prophet → Canada 58°48N 122°40W 70 B4
Prophet River Canada 58°6N 122°43W 70 B4
Propriá Brazil 10°13S 36°51W 93 F11
Propriano France 41°41N 8°52E 20 F8
Proserpine Australia 20°21S 148°36E 62 J6
Prosna → Poland 52°6N 17°44E 17 B9
Prospect U.S.A. 43°18N 75°9W 83 C9
Prosser U.S.A. 46°12N 119°46W 76 C4
Prostějov Czech Rep. 49°30N 17°9E 17 D9
Proston Australia 26°8S 151°32E 63 D5
Provence France 43°40N 5°46E 20 E6
Providence Ky., U.S.A. 37°24N 87°46W 80 G10
Providence R.I., U.S.A. 41°49N 71°24W 83 E13
Providence Bay Canada 45°41N 82°15W 72 C3
Providence Mts. U.S.A. 35°10N 115°15W 79 K11
Providencia, I. de Colombia 13°25N 81°26W 88 D3
Provideniya Russia 64°23N 173°18W 29 C19
Provincetown U.S.A. 42°3N 70°11W 81 D18
Provins France 48°33N 3°15E 20 B5
Provo U.S.A. 40°14N 111°39W 76 F8
Provost Canada 52°25N 110°20W 71 C6
Prudhoe Bay U.S.A. 70°18N 148°22W 74 a
Prudhoe I. Australia 21°19S 149°41E 62 C4
Prud'homme Canada 52°20N 105°54W 71 C7
Pruszków Poland 52°9N 20°49E 17 B11
Prut → Romania 45°28N 28°10E 17 F15
Pruzhany Belarus 52°33N 24°28E 17 B13
Prydz B. Antarctica 69°0S 74°0E 5 C6
Pryluky Ukraine 50°30N 32°24E 19 D5
Pryor U.S.A. 36°19N 95°19W 84 C7
Prypyat → Europe 51°20N 30°15E 17 C16
Przemyśl Poland 49°50N 22°45E 17 D12
Przhevalsk = Karakol Kyrgyzstan 42°30N 78°20E 32 B2
Psara Greece 38°37N 25°38E 23 E11
Psiloritis, Oros Greece 35°15N 24°45E 25 D6
Psira Greece 35°12N 25°52E 25 D7
Pskov Russia 57°50N 28°25E 9 H23
Ptich = Ptsich → Belarus 52°9N 28°52E 17 B15
Ptichia = Vidos Greece 39°38N 19°55E 25 A3
Ptolemaida Greece 40°30N 21°43E 23 D9
Ptsich → Belarus 52°9N 28°52E 17 B15
Pu Xian China 36°24N 111°6E 34 F6
Pua Thailand 19°11N 100°55E 38 C3
Puán Argentina 37°30S 62°45W 94 D3
Pu'apu'a Samoa 13°34S 172°9W 59 b
Pucallpa Peru 8°25S 74°30W 92 E4
Puch'on = Bucheon S. Korea 37°28N 126°45E 35 F14
Pudasjärvi Finland 65°23N 26°53E 8 D22
Pudozh Russia 61°48N 36°32E 18 B6
Puducherry India 11°59N 79°50E 40 P11
Pudukkottai India 10°28N 78°47E 40 P11
Puebla Mexico 19°3N 98°12W 87 D5
Puebla □ Mexico 18°50N 98°0W 87 D5
Pueblo U.S.A. 38°16N 104°37W 76 G11
Puelches Argentina 38°5S 65°51W 94 D2
Puelén Argentina 37°32S 67°38W 94 D2
Puente Alto Chile 33°32S 70°35W 94 C1
Puente-Genil Spain 37°22N 4°47W 21 D3
Puerca, Pta. Puerto Rico 18°13N 65°36W 89 d
Puerco → U.S.A. 34°22N 107°50W 77 J10
Puerto Aisén Chile 45°27S 73°0W 96 F2
Puerto Ángel Mexico 15°40N 96°29W 87 D5
Puerto Arista Mexico 15°56N 93°48W 87 D6
Puerto Armuelles Panama 8°20N 82°51W 88 E3
Puerto Ayacucho Venezuela 5°40N 67°35W 92 B5
Puerto Barrios Guatemala 15°40N 88°32W 88 C2
Puerto Bermejo Argentina 26°55S 58°34W 94 B4
Puerto Bermúdez Peru 10°20S 74°58W 92 F4
Puerto Bolívar Ecuador 3°19S 79°55W 92 D3
Puerto Cabello Venezuela 10°28N 68°1W 92 A5
Puerto Cabezas Nic. 14°0N 83°30W 88 D3
Puerto Cabo Gracias á Dios Nic. 15°0N 83°10W 88 D3
Puerto Carreño Colombia 6°12N 67°22W 92 B5
Puerto Castilla Honduras 16°0N 86°0W 88 C2
Puerto Chicama Peru 7°45S 79°20W 92 E3
Puerto Coig Argentina 50°54S 69°15W 96 G3
Puerto Cortés Honduras 15°51N 88°0W 88 C2
Puerto Cumarebo Venezuela 11°29N 69°30W 92 A5
Puerto de Alcudia = Port d'Alcúdia Spain 39°50N 3°7E 24 B10
Puerto de Cabrera Spain 39°8N 2°56E 24 B9
Puerto de Gran Tarajal Canary Is. 28°13N 14°1W 24 F5
Puerto de la Cruz Canary Is. 28°24N 16°32W 24 F3
Puerto de los Angeles ⌂ Mexico 23°39N 105°45W 86 C3
Puerto de Pozo Negro Canary Is. 28°19N 13°55W 24 F6
Puerto de Sóller = Port de Sóller Spain 39°48N 2°42E 24 B9
Puerto del Carmen Canary Is. 28°55N 13°38W 24 F6
Puerto del Rosario Canary Is. 28°30N 13°52W 24 F6
Puerto Deseado Argentina 47°55S 66°0W 96 F3
Puerto Escondido Mexico 15°50N 97°3W 87 D5
Puerto Heath Bolivia 12°34S 68°39W 92 F5
Puerto Inírida Colombia 3°53N 67°52W 92 C5
Puerto Juárez Mexico 21°11N 86°49W 87 C7
Puerto La Cruz Venezuela 10°13N 64°38W 92 A6
Puerto Leguízamo Colombia 0°12S 74°46W 92 D4
Puerto Lempira Honduras 15°16N 83°46W 88 C3
Puerto Libertad Mexico 29°55N 112°43W 86 B2
Puerto Limón Colombia 3°23N 73°30W 92 C4
Puerto Lobos Argentina 42°0S 65°3W 96 E3
Puerto Madryn Argentina 42°48S 65°4W 96 E3
Puerto Maldonado Peru 12°30S 69°10W 92 F5
Puerto Manatí Cuba 21°22N 76°50W 88 B4
Puerto Montt Chile 41°28S 73°0W 96 E2
Puerto Morazán Nic. 12°51N 87°11W 88 D2
Puerto Morelos Mexico 20°50N 86°52W 87 C7
Puerto Natales Chile 51°45S 72°15W 96 G2
Puerto Oscuro Chile 31°24S 71°35W 94 C1
Puerto Padre Cuba 21°13N 76°35W 88 B4
Puerto Páez Venezuela 6°13N 67°28W 92 B5
Puerto Peñasco Mexico 31°20N 113°33W 86 A2
Puerto Pinasco Paraguay 22°36S 57°50W 94 A4
Puerto Plata Dom. Rep. 19°48N 70°45W 89 C5
Puerto Pollensa = Port de Pollença Spain 39°54N 3°4E 24 B10
Puerto Princesa Phil. 9°46N 118°45E 37 C5
Puerto Quepos Costa Rica 9°29N 84°6W 88 E3
Puerto Rico Canary Is. 27°47N 15°42W 24 G4
Puerto Rico ☑ W. Indies 18°15N 66°45W 89 d
Puerto Rico Trench Atl. Oc. 19°50N 66°0W 89 C6
Puerto San Julián Argentina 49°18S 67°43W 96 F3
Puerto Santa Cruz Argentina 50°0S 68°32W 96 G3
Puerto Sastre Paraguay 22°2S 57°55W 94 A4
Puerto Suárez Bolivia 18°58S 57°52W 92 G7
Puerto Vallarta Mexico 20°37N 105°15W 86 C3
Puerto Varas Chile 41°19S 72°59W 96 E2
Puerto Wilches Colombia 7°21N 73°54W 92 B4
Puertollano Spain 38°43N 4°7W 21 C3
Pueu Tahiti 17°44S 149°13W 59 d
Pueyrredón, L. Argentina 47°20S 72°0W 96 F2
Puffin I. Ireland 51°50N 10°24W 10 E1
Pugachev Russia 52°0N 48°49E 18 D8
Pugal India 28°30N 72°48E 42 E5
Puge Tanzania 4°45S 33°11E 54 C
Puget Sound U.S.A. 47°50N 122°30W 76 C
Pugŏdong N. Korea 42°5N 130°0E 35 C1
Pugu Tanzania 6°55S 39°4E 54 D
Pūgūnzī Iran 25°49N 59°10E 45 E
Puig Major Spain 39°48N 2°47E 24 B
Puigcerdà Spain 42°24N 1°50E 21 A
Puigpunyent Spain 39°38N 2°32E 24 B
Pujon-ho N. Korea 40°35N 127°35E 35 D1
Pukaki, L. N.Z. 44°4S 170°1E 59 F
Pukapuka Cook Is. 10°53S 165°49W 65 J1
Pukaskwa △ Canada 48°20N 86°0W 72 C
Pukatawagan Canada 55°45N 101°20W 71 B
Pukchin N. Korea 40°12N 125°45E 35 D1
Pukch'ŏng N. Korea 40°14N 128°10E 35 D1
Pukekohe N.Z. 37°12S 174°55E 59 B
Pukhrayan India 26°14N 79°51E 43 F
Pula Croatia 44°54N 13°57E 16 F
Pulacayo Bolivia 20°25S 66°41W 92 H
Pulai Malaysia 1°20N 103°31E 39
Pulandian China 39°25N 121°58E 35 E1
Pulaski N.Y., U.S.A. 43°34N 76°8W 83 C
Pulaski Tenn., U.S.A. 35°12N 87°2W 85 D1
Pulaski Va., U.S.A. 37°3N 80°47W 81 G1
Pulau → Indonesia 5°50S 138°15E 37 F
Puławy Poland 51°23N 21°59E 17 C1
Pulga U.S.A. 39°48N 121°29W 78 F
Pulicat L. India 13°40N 80°15E 40 N1
Pullman U.S.A. 46°44N 117°10W 76 C
Pulog, Mt. Phil. 16°40N 120°50E 37 A
Pułtusk Poland 52°43N 21°6E 17 B1
Pumlumon Fawr U.K. 52°28N 3°46W 13 E
Puná, I. Ecuador 2°55S 80°5W 92 D
Punaauia Tahiti 17°37S 149°34W 59
Punakaiki N.Z. 42°7S 171°20E 59 E
Punakha Dzong Bhutan 27°42N 89°52E 41 F1
Punasar India 27°6N 73°6E 42 F
Punata Bolivia 17°32S 65°50W 92 G
Punch India 33°48N 74°4E 43 C
Punch → Pakistan 33°12N 73°40E 42 C
Punda Maria S. Africa 22°40S 31°5E 57 C
Pune India 18°29N 73°57E 40 K
P'ungsan N. Korea 40°50N 128°9E 35 D1
Pungue, Ponte de Mozam. 19°0S 34°0E 55 F
Punjab □ India 31°0N 76°0E 42 D
Punjab □ Pakistan 32°0N 72°30E 42 E
Puno Peru 15°55S 70°3W 92 G
Punpun → India 25°31N 85°18E 43 G1
Punta, Cerro de Puerto Rico 18°10N 66°37W 89
Punta Alta Argentina 38°53S 62°4W 96 D
Punta Arenas Chile 53°10S 71°0W 96 G
Punta del Díaz Chile 28°0S 70°45W 94 B
Punta del Hidalgo Canary Is. 28°33N 16°19W 24 F
Punta Gorda Belize 16°10N 88°45W 87 D
Punta Gorda U.S.A. 26°56N 82°3W 85 H1
Punta Prieta Mexico 28°58N 114°17W 86 B
Punta Prima Spain 39°48N 4°16E 24 B1
Puntarenas Costa Rica 10°0N 84°50W 88 E
Puntland Somali Rep. 8°0N 49°0E 47 F
Punto Fijo Venezuela 11°50N 70°13W 92 A
Punxsatawney U.S.A. 40°57N 78°59W 82 F
Pupuan Indonesia 8°19S 115°0E 37 J1
Puquio Peru 14°45S 74°10W 92 F
Pur → Russia 67°31N 77°55E 28 C
Puracé, Vol. Colombia 2°21N 76°23W 92 C
Puralia = Puruliya India 23°17N 86°24E 43 H1
Puranpur India 28°31N 80°9E 43 E
Purbeck, Isle of U.K. 50°39N 1°59W 13 G
Purcell U.S.A. 35°1N 97°22W 84 D
Purcell Mts. Canada 49°55N 116°15W 70 D
Purdy Canada 45°19N 77°44W 82 A
Puri India 19°50N 85°58E 41 K1
Purmerend Neths. 52°32N 4°58E 15 B
Purnia India 25°45N 87°31E 43 G1
Purnululu △ Australia 17°20S 128°20E 60 C
Pursat = Pouthisat Cambodia 12°34N 103°50E 38 F
Purukcahu Indonesia 0°35S 114°35E 36 E
Puruliya India 23°17N 86°24E 43 H1
Purus → Brazil 3°42S 61°28W 92 D
Puruvesi Finland 61°50N 29°30E 8 F2
Purvis U.S.A. 31°9N 89°25W 85 F1
Purwa India 26°28N 80°47E 43 F
Purwakarta Indonesia 6°35S 107°29E 37 G1
Purwo, Tanjung Indonesia 8°44S 114°21E 37 K1
Purwodadi Indonesia 7°7S 110°55E 37 G1
Purwokerto Indonesia 7°25S 109°14E 37 G1
Puryŏng N. Korea 42°5N 129°43E 35 C1
Pusa India 25°59N 85°41E 43 G1
Pusan = Busan S. Korea 35°5N 129°0E 35 G1
Pushkin Russia 59°45N 30°25E 9 G2
Pushkino Russia 51°16N 47°0E 19 D
Put-in-Bay U.S.A. 41°39N 82°49W 82 E
Putahow L. Canada 59°54N 100°40W 71 B
Putao Burma 27°28N 97°30E 41 F2
Putaruru N.Z. 38°2S 175°50E 59 C
Putignano Italy 40°51N 17°7E 22 D
Puting, Tanjung Indonesia 3°31S 111°46E 36 E
Putnam U.S.A. 41°55N 71°55W 83 E1
Putorana, Gory Russia 69°0N 95°0E 29 C1
Putrajaya Malaysia 2°55N 101°40E 39 L
Puttalam Sri Lanka 8°1N 79°55E 40 Q1
Puttgarden Germany 54°30N 11°10E 16 A
Putumayo → S. Amer. 3°7S 67°58W 92 D
Putussibau Indonesia 0°50N 112°56E 36 D
Puvirnituq Canada 60°2N 77°10W 69 C1
Puy-de-Dôme France 45°46N 2°57E 20 D
Puyallup U.S.A. 47°12N 122°18W 78 C
Puyang China 35°40N 115°1E 34 G
Pūzeh Rīg Iran 27°20N 58°40E 45 E
Pwani □ Tanzania 7°0S 39°0E 54 D
Pweto Dem. Rep. of the Congo 8°25S 28°51E 55 D

llheli U.K. 52°53N 4°25W 12 E3
aozero, Ozero Russia 66°5N 30°58E 8 C24
apon Burma 16°20N 95°40E 41 L19
asina → Russia 73°30N 87°0E 29 B9
atigorsk Russia 44°2N 43°6E 19 F7
= Prome Burma 18°49N 95°13E 41 K19
eongtaek S. Korea 37°1N 127°4E 35 F14
etrikaw Belarus 52°11N 28°29E 17 B15
häjoki Finland 64°28N 24°14E 8 D21
nmana Burma 19°45N 96°12E 41 K20
a, C. Cyprus 34°56N 33°51E 25 E12
natuning Res. U.S.A. 41°30N 80°28W 82 E4
ŏktong N. Korea 40°50N 125°50E 35 D13
ŏnggang N. Korea 38°24N 127°17E 35 E14
ŏngsong N. Korea 39°14N 125°52E 35 E13
ŏngyang N. Korea 39°0N 125°30E 35 E13
ote U.S.A. 31°32N 103°8W 84 F3
amid L. U.S.A. 40°1N 119°35W 76 F4
amid Pk. U.S.A. 36°25N 116°37W 79 J10
amids Egypt 29°58N 31°9E 51 C12
énées Europe 42°45N 0°18E 20 E4
Burma 18°30N 96°28E 41 K20

Q

anaaq Greenland 77°40N 69°0W 4 B4
chasnek S. Africa 30°6S 28°42E 57 E4
el Jafr Jordan 30°20N 36°25E 46 E5
emābād Iran 31°44N 60°2E 45 D9
emshahr Iran 36°30N 52°53E 45 B7
gan Nur China 43°30N 114°55E 34 C8
har Youyi Zhongqi China 41°12N 112°40E 34 D7
hremānshahr = Kermānshāh Iran 34°23N 47°0E 44 C5
dam Pendi China 37°0N 95°0E 32 C4
arīyeh Iran 31°1N 48°22E 45 D6
a, Ras il Malta 36°2N 14°20E 25 C1
a-i-Jadid = Spīn Būldak Afghan. 31°1N 66°25E 42 D2
a Point = Qala, Ras il Malta 36°2N 14°20E 25 C1
a Viala Pakistan 30°49N 67°17E 42 D2
a Yangi Afghan. 34°20N 66°30E 42 B2
'at al Akhḑar Si. Arabia 28°4N 37°9E 44 E3
at Dīzah Iraq 36°11N 45°7E 44 B5
at Şāliḩ Iraq 31°31N 47°16E 44 D5
'at Sukkar Iraq 31°51N 46°5E 44 D5
nani'tuaq = Baker Lake Canada 64°20N 96°3W 68 C10
ndo China 31°15N 97°6E 32 C4
nea Fiji 16°45S 179°45W 59 a
nruddin Karez Pakistan 31°45N 68°20E 42 D3
dahār = Kandahār Afghan. 31°32N 65°43E 40 D4
dahār = Kandahār □ Afghan. 31°0N 65°0E 40 D4
dyaghash Kazakhstan 49°28N 57°25E 19 E10
ān Iran 37°40N 55°47E 45 B7
shaghay Kazakhstan 43°51N 77°14E 28 E8
ortoq Greenland 60°43N 46°0W 4 C5
a Qash → China 35°0N 78°30E 43 B8
abutaq Kazakhstan 49°59N 60°14E 28 E7
aghandy Kazakhstan 49°50N 73°10E 28 E8
aghayly Kazakhstan 49°26N 76°0E 28 E8
ah Si. Arabia 29°55N 40°3E 44 D4
ataū Kazakhstan 43°30N 69°30E 28 E7
ataū Zhambyl, Kazakhstan 43°10N 70°28E 28 E8
azhal Kazakhstan 48°2N 70°49E 28 E8
dho Somali Rep. 9°30N 49°6E 47 F4
eh → Iran 39°25N 47°22E 44 B5
eh Tekān Iran 36°38N 49°29E 45 B6
nein U.A.E. 24°56N 52°52E 45 E7
qan He → China 39°30N 88°30E 32 C3
qaraly Kazakhstan 49°26N 75°30E 28 E8
shi Uzbekistan 38°53N 65°48E 28 F7
abā Lebanon 34°4N 35°50E 46 A4
ūh Kuwait 28°49N 48°46E 45 D6
vat al Gharab Iraq 31°27N 44°48E 44 D5
vat al 'Ulyā Si. Arabia 27°33N 47°42E 44 E5
'Amra Jordan 31°48N 36°35E 44 D3
-e Qand Iran 26°15N 60°45E 45 E9
-e Shīrīn Iran 34°31N 45°35E 44 C5
Farâfra Egypt 27°0N 28°1E 51 C11
anā Syria 33°26N 36°4E 46 B5
ar ■ Asia 25°30N 51°15E 45 E6
īsh Iran 37°50N 57°19E 45 B8
âra, Munkhafed el Egypt 29°30N 27°30E 51 C11
âra Depression = Qattâra, Munkhafed el Egypt 29°30N 27°30E 51 C11
siuittuq = Resolute Canada 74°42N 94°54W 69 B10
'ām al Ḩamzah = Al Ḩamzah Iraq 31°43N 44°58E 44 D5
en Iran 33°40N 59°10E 45 C8
aqstan = Kazakhstan ■ Asia 50°0N 70°0E 28 E8
mämmäd Azerbaijan 40°3N 49°0E 45 A6
vīn Iran 36°15N 50°0E 45 B6
vīn □ Iran 36°20N 50°0E 45 B6
a Egypt 26°10N 32°43E 51 C12
ertarsuaq Greenland 69°15N 53°38W 4 C5
ertarsuaq Greenland 69°45N 53°30W 66 C14
alāq Iran 34°55N 46°28E 44 C5
am Iran 26°55N 56°10E 45 E8
Iran 26°32N 53°58E 45 E7
l Owzen → Iran 36°45N 49°22E 45 B6
'ot Israel 30°52N 34°26E 46 E3
an China 34°40N 114°48E 34 G8
Gorlos China 45°5N 124°42E 35 B13
Hai China 22°32N 113°54E 33 F10
Qian Xian China 34°31N 108°15E 34 G5
Qianshan China 22°15N 113°31E 33 G10
Qianyang China 34°40N 107°8E 34 G4
Qi'ao China 22°25N 113°39E 33 G10
Qi'ao Dao China 22°25N 113°38E 33 G10
Qiemo China 38°8N 85°32E 32 C3
Qijiaojing China 43°28N 91°36E 32 B4
Qikiqtarjuaq Canada 67°33N 63°0W 69 C13
Qila Saifullāh Pakistan 30°45N 68°17E 42 D3
Qilian Shan China 38°30N 96°0E 32 C4
Qin He → China 35°1N 113°22E 34 G7
Qin Ling = Qinling Shandi China 33°50N 108°10E 34 H5
Qin'an China 34°48N 105°40E 34 G3
Qing Xian China 38°35N 116°45E 34 E9
Qingcheng China 37°15N 117°40E 35 F9
Qingdao China 36°5N 120°20E 35 F11
Qingfeng China 35°52N 115°8E 34 G8
Qinghai □ China 36°0N 98°0E 32 C4
Qinghai Hu China 36°40N 100°10E 32 C5
Qinghecheng China 41°28N 124°15E 35 D13
Qinghemen China 41°48N 121°25E 35 D11
Qingjian China 37°8N 110°8E 34 F6
Qingjiang = Huaiyin China 33°30N 119°2E 35 H10
Qingshui China 34°48N 106°8E 34 G4
Qingshuihe China 39°55N 111°35E 34 E6
Qingtongxia Shuiku China 37°50N 105°58E 34 F3
Qingxu China 37°34N 112°22E 34 F7
Qingyang China 36°2N 107°55E 34 F4
Qingyuan China 42°10N 124°55E 35 C13
Qingyun China 37°45N 117°20E 35 F9
Qinhuangdao China 39°56N 119°30E 35 E10
Qinling Shandi China 33°50N 108°10E 34 H5
Qinshui China 35°40N 112°8E 34 G7
Qinyang = Jiyuan China 35°7N 112°57E 34 G7
Qinyuan China 36°29N 112°20E 34 F7
Qinzhou China 21°58N 108°38E 32 D5
Qionghai China 19°15N 110°26E 38 C8
Qiongzhou Haixia China 20°10N 110°15E 38 B8
Qiqihar China 47°26N 124°0E 33 B7
Qira China 37°0N 80°48E 32 C3
Qiraîya, W. → Egypt 30°27N 34°0E 46 E3
Qiryat Ata Israel 32°47N 35°6E 46 C4
Qiryat Gat Israel 31°32N 34°46E 46 D3
Qiryat Mal'akhi Israel 31°44N 34°44E 46 D3
Qiryat Shemona Israel 33°13N 35°35E 46 B4
Qiryat Yam Israel 32°51N 35°4E 46 C4
Qishan China 34°25N 107°38E 34 G4
Qitai China 44°2N 89°35E 32 B3
Qitaihe China 45°48N 130°51E 30 B5
Qixia China 37°17N 120°52E 35 F11
Qızılağac Körfäzi Azerbaijan 39°9N 49°0E 45 B6
Qojūr Iran 36°12N 47°55E 44 B5
Qom Iran 34°40N 51°0E 45 C6
Qom □ Iran 34°40N 51°0E 45 C6
Qomolangma Feng = Everest, Mt. Nepal 28°5N 86°58E 43 E12
Qomsheh Iran 32°0N 51°55E 45 D6
Qoqek = Tacheng China 46°40N 82°58E 32 B3
Qoqon = Qŭqon Uzbekistan 40°31N 70°56E 28 E8
Qoraqalpoghistan □ Uzbekistan 43°0N 58°0E 28 E6
Qorveh Iran 35°10N 47°48E 44 C5
Qostanay Kazakhstan 53°10N 63°35E 28 D7
Quabbin Res. U.S.A. 42°20N 72°20W 83 D12
Quairading Australia 32°0S 117°21E 61 F2
Quakertown U.S.A. 40°26N 75°21W 83 F9
Qualicum Beach Canada 49°22N 124°26W 70 D4
Quambatook Australia 35°49S 143°34E 63 F3
Quambone Australia 30°57S 147°53E 63 E4
Quamby Australia 20°22S 140°17E 62 C3
Quan Long = Ca Mau Vietnam 9°7N 105°8E 39 H5
Quanah U.S.A. 34°18N 99°44W 84 D5
Quang Ngai Vietnam 15°13N 108°58E 38 E7
Quang Tri Vietnam 16°45N 107°13E 38 D6
Quang Yen Vietnam 20°56N 106°52E 38 B6
Quantock Hills U.K. 51°8N 3°10W 13 F4
Quanzhou China 24°55N 118°34E 33 D6
Qu'Appelle → Canada 50°33N 103°53W 71 C8
Quaqtaq Canada 60°55N 69°40W 69 C13
Quaraí Brazil 30°15S 56°20W 94 C4
Quartu Sant'Élena Italy 39°15N 9°10E 22 E3
Quartzsite U.S.A. 33°40N 114°13W 79 M12
Quatre Bornes Mauritius 20°15S 57°28E 53 d
Quatsino Sd. Canada 50°25N 127°58W 70 C3
Quba Azerbaijan 41°21N 48°32E 19 F8
Qūchān Iran 37°10N 58°27E 45 B8
Queanbeyan Australia 35°17S 149°14E 63 F4
Québec Canada 46°52N 71°13W 73 C5
Québec □ Canada 48°0N 74°0W 73 C6
Quebrada del Condorito △ Argentina 31°49S 64°40W 94 C3
Queen Alexandra Ra. Antarctica 85°0S 170°0E 5 E11
Queen Charlotte City Canada 53°15N 132°2W 70 C2
Queen Charlotte Is. Canada 53°20N 132°10W 70 C2
Queen Charlotte Sd. Canada 51°0N 128°0W 70 C3
Queen Charlotte Strait Canada 50°45N 127°10W 70 C3
Queen Elizabeth △ Uganda 0°0 30°0E 54 C3
Queen Elizabeth ⌓ U.K. 56°7N 4°30W 11 E4
Queen Elizabeth Is. Canada 76°0N 95°0W 69 B10
Queen Mary Land Antarctica 70°0S 95°0E 5 D7
Queen Maud G. Canada 68°15N 102°30W 68 C9
Queen Maud Land = Dronning Maud Land Antarctica 72°30S 12°0E 5 D3
Queen Maud Mts. Antarctica 86°0S 160°0W 5 E13
Queens Channel Australia 15°0S 129°30E 60 C4
Queenscliff Australia 38°16S 144°39E 63 F3
Queensland □ Australia 22°0S 142°0E 62 C3
Queenstown Australia 42°4S 145°35E 63 G4
Queenstown N.Z. 45°1S 168°40E 59 F2
Queenstown Singapore 1°18N 103°48E 39 d
Queenstown S. Africa 31°52S 26°52E 56 E4
Queets U.S.A. 47°32N 124°19W 78 C2
Queguay Grande → Uruguay 32°9S 58°9W 94 C4
Queimadas Brazil 11°0S 39°38W 93 F11
Quelimane Mozam. 17°53S 36°58E 55 F4
Quellón Chile 43°7S 73°37W 96 E2
Quelpart = Jeju-do S. Korea 33°29N 126°34E 35 H14
Quemado N. Mex., U.S.A. 34°20N 108°30W 77 J9
Quemado Tex., U.S.A. 28°56N 100°37W 84 G4
Quemú-Quemú Argentina 36°3S 63°36W 94 D3
Quequén Argentina 38°30S 58°30W 94 D4
Querétaro Mexico 20°36N 100°23W 86 C4
Querétaro □ Mexico 21°0N 99°55W 86 C5
Queshan China 32°55N 114°2E 34 H8
Quesnel Canada 53°0N 122°30W 70 C4
Quesnel → Canada 52°58N 122°29W 70 C4
Quesnel L. Canada 52°30N 121°20W 70 C4
Questa U.S.A. 36°42N 105°36W 77 H11
Quetico ⌓ Canada 48°30N 91°45W 72 C1
Quetta Pakistan 30°15N 66°55E 42 D2
Quezaltenango Guatemala 14°50N 91°30W 88 D1
Quezon City Phil. 14°37N 121°2E 37 B6
Qufār Si. Arabia 27°26N 41°37E 44 E4
Qui Nhon Vietnam 13°40N 109°13E 38 F7
Quibala Angola 10°46S 14°59E 52 G2
Quibaxe Angola 8°24S 14°27E 52 F2
Quibdó Colombia 5°42N 76°40W 92 B3
Quiberon France 47°29N 3°9W 20 C2
Quiet L. Canada 61°5N 133°5W 70 A2
Quiindy Paraguay 25°58S 57°14W 94 B4
Quilá Mexico 24°23N 107°13W 86 C3
Quilán, C. Chile 43°15S 74°30W 96 E2
Quilcene U.S.A. 47°49N 122°53W 78 C4
Quilimarí Chile 32°5S 71°30W 94 C1
Quilino Argentina 30°14S 64°29W 94 C3
Quillabamba Peru 12°50S 72°50W 92 F4
Quillagua Chile 21°40S 69°40W 94 A2
Quillota Chile 32°54S 71°16W 94 C1
Quilmes Argentina 34°43S 58°15W 94 C4
Quilon India 8°50N 76°38E 40 Q10
Quilpie Australia 26°35S 144°11E 63 D3
Quilpué Chile 33°5S 71°33W 94 C1
Quilua Mozam. 16°17S 39°54E 55 F4
Quimilí Argentina 27°40S 62°30W 94 B3
Quimper France 48°0N 4°9W 20 B1
Quimperlé France 47°53N 3°33W 20 C2
Quinault → U.S.A. 47°21N 124°18W 78 C2
Quincy Calif., U.S.A. 39°56N 120°57W 78 F6
Quincy Fla., U.S.A. 30°35N 84°34W 85 F12
Quincy Ill., U.S.A. 39°56N 91°23W 80 F8
Quincy Mass., U.S.A. 42°14N 71°0W 83 D14
Quincy Wash., U.S.A. 47°14N 119°51W 76 C4
Quines Argentina 32°13S 65°48W 94 C2
Quinga Mozam. 15°49S 40°15E 55 F5
Quintana Roo □ Mexico 19°40N 88°30W 87 D7
Quintanar de la Orden Spain 39°36N 3°5W 21 C4
Quintero Chile 32°45S 71°30W 94 C1
Quirihue Chile 36°15S 72°35W 94 D1
Quirimbas △ Mozam. 12°30S 40°15E 55 E5
Quirindi Australia 31°28S 150°40E 63 E5
Quirinópolis Brazil 18°32S 50°30W 93 G8
Quissanga Mozam. 12°24S 40°28E 55 E5
Quissico Mozam. 24°42S 34°44E 57 C5
Quitilipi Argentina 26°50S 60°13W 94 B3
Quitman U.S.A. 30°47N 83°34W 85 F13
Quito Ecuador 0°15S 78°35W 92 D3
Quixadá Brazil 4°55S 39°0W 93 D11
Quixaxe Mozam. 15°17S 40°4E 55 F5
Qulan Kazakhstan 42°55N 72°43E 28 E8
Qul'ân, Jazâ'ir Egypt 24°22N 35°31E 44 E2
Qulsary Kazakhstan 46°59N 54°1E 19 E9
Qumbu S. Africa 31°10S 28°48E 57 E4
Quneitra Syria 33°7N 35°48E 46 B4
Qŭnghirot Uzbekistan 43°2N 58°50E 28 E6
Quoin I. Australia 14°54S 129°32E 60 B4
Quoin Pt. S. Africa 34°46S 19°37E 56 E2
Quorn Australia 32°25S 138°5E 63 E2
Qŭqon Uzbekistan 40°31N 70°56E 28 E8
Qurnat as Sawdā' Lebanon 34°18N 36°6E 46 A5
Quşaybā' Si. Arabia 26°53N 43°35E 44 E4
Qusaybah Iraq 34°24N 40°59E 44 C4
Quseir Egypt 26°7N 34°16E 44 E2
Qūshchī Iran 37°59N 45°3E 44 B5
Quthing Lesotho 30°25S 27°36E 57 E4
Qūţīābād Iran 35°47N 48°30E 45 C6
Quwo China 35°38N 111°25E 34 G6
Quyang China 38°35N 114°40E 34 E8
Quynh Nhai Vietnam 21°49N 103°33E 38 B4
Quyon Canada 45°31N 76°14W 83 A8
Quzhou China 28°57N 118°54E 33 D6
Quzi China 36°20N 107°20E 34 F4
Qyzylorda Kazakhstan 44°48N 65°28E 28 E7

R

Ra, Ko Thailand 9°13N 98°16E 39 H2
Raahe Finland 64°40N 24°28E 8 D21
Raalte Neths. 52°23N 6°16E 15 B6
Raasay U.K. 57°25N 6°4W 11 D2
Raasay, Sd. of U.K. 57°30N 6°8W 11 D2
Raba Indonesia 8°36S 118°55E 37 F5
Rába → Hungary 47°38N 17°38E 17 E9
Rabai Kenya 3°50S 39°31E 54 C4
Rabat = Victoria Malta 36°3N 14°14E 25 C1
Rabat Malta 35°53N 14°24E 25 D1
Rabat Morocco 34°2N 6°48W 50 B4
Rabaul Papua N. G. 4°24S 152°18E 58 B8
Rabbit Flat Australia 20°11S 130°1E 60 D5
Rabbit Lake Mine Canada 58°4N 104°5W 71 B8
Rabi Fiji 16°30S 179°59W 59 a
Rābigh Si. Arabia 22°50N 39°5E 47 C2
Râbniţa Moldova 47°45N 29°0E 17 E15
Rābor Iran 29°17N 56°55E 45 D8
Rabwah = Chenab Nagar Pakistan 31°45N 72°55E 42 D5
Race, C. Canada 46°40N 53°5W 73 C9
Rach Gia Vietnam 10°5N 105°5E 39 G5
Rachid Mauritania 18°45N 11°35W 50 E3
Racibórz Poland 50°7N 18°18E 17 C10
Racine U.S.A. 42°44N 87°47W 80 D10
Rackerby U.S.A. 39°26N 121°22W 78 F5
Radama, Nosy Madag. 14°0S 47°47E 57 A8
Radama, Saikanosy Madag. 14°16S 47°53E 57 A8
Rădăuţi Romania 47°50N 25°59E 17 E13
Radcliff U.S.A. 37°51N 85°57W 81 G11
Radekhiv Ukraine 50°25N 24°32E 17 C13
Radekhov = Radekhiv Ukraine 50°25N 24°32E 17 C13
Radford U.S.A. 37°8N 80°34W 81 G13
Radhanpur India 23°50N 71°38E 42 H4
Radhwa, Jabal Si. Arabia 24°34N 38°18E 44 E3
Radisson Qué., Canada 53°47N 77°37W 72 B4
Radisson Sask., Canada 52°30N 107°20W 71 C7
Radium Hot Springs Canada 50°35N 116°2W 70 C5
Radnor Forest U.K. 52°17N 3°10W 13 E4
Radom Poland 51°23N 21°12E 17 C11
Radomsko Poland 51°5N 19°28E 17 C10
Radomyshl Ukraine 50°30N 29°12E 17 C15
Radstock, C. Australia 33°12S 134°20E 63 E1
Raduzhnyy Russia 62°5N 77°28E 28 C8
Radviliškis Lithuania 55°49N 23°33E 9 J20
Radville Canada 49°30N 104°15W 71 D8
Rae Canada 62°50N 116°3W 70 A5
Rae Bareli India 26°18N 81°20E 43 F9
Rae Isthmus Canada 66°40N 87°30W 69 C11
Raeren Belgium 50°41N 6°7E 15 D6
Raeside, L. Australia 29°20S 122°0E 61 E3
Raetihi N.Z. 39°25S 175°17E 59 C5
Rafaela Argentina 31°10S 61°30W 94 C3
Rafah Gaza Strip 31°18N 34°14E 46 D3
Rafai C.A.R. 4°59N 23°58E 54 B1
Rafḩā Si. Arabia 29°35N 43°35E 44 D4
Rafsanjān Iran 30°30N 56°5E 45 D8
Raft Pt. Australia 16°4S 124°26E 60 C3
Râgâ Sudan 8°28N 25°41E 51 G11
Ragachow Belarus 53°8N 30°5E 17 B16
Ragama Sri Lanka 7°0N 79°50E 40 R11
Ragged, Mt. Australia 33°27S 123°25E 61 F3
Ragged Pt. Barbados 13°10N 59°26W 89 g
Raghunathpalli India 22°14N 84°48E 43 H11
Raghunathpur India 23°33N 86°40E 43 H12
Raglan N.Z. 37°55S 174°55E 59 B5
Ragusa Italy 36°55N 14°44E 22 F6
Raha Indonesia 4°55S 123°0E 37 E6
Rahaeng = Tak Thailand 16°52N 99°8E 38 D2
Rahatgarh India 23°47N 78°22E 43 H8
Rahimyar Khan Pakistan 28°30N 70°25E 42 E4
Rāhjerd Iran 34°22N 50°22E 45 C6
Rahole ⌓ Kenya 0°5N 38°57E 54 B4
Rahon India 31°3N 76°7E 42 D7
Raiatéa, Î. French Polynesia 16°50S 151°25W 65 J12
Raichur India 16°10N 77°20E 40 L10
Raiganj India 25°37N 88°10E 43 G13
Raigarh India 21°56N 83°25E 41 J13
Raijua Indonesia 10°37S 121°36E 37 F6
Raikot India 30°41N 75°42E 42 D6
Railton Australia 41°25S 146°28E 63 G4
Rainbow Bridge ⌓ U.S.A. 37°5N 110°58W 77 H8
Rainbow Lake Canada 58°30N 119°23W 70 B5
Rainier U.S.A. 46°53N 122°41W 78 D4
Rainier, Mt. U.S.A. 46°52N 121°46W 78 D5
Rainy L. Canada 48°42N 93°10W 71 D10
Rainy River Canada 48°43N 94°29W 71 D10
Raippaluoto Finland 63°13N 21°14E 8 E19
Raipur India 21°17N 81°45E 41 J12
Raisen India 23°20N 77°48E 42 H8
Raisio Finland 60°28N 22°11E 9 F20
Raj Nandgaon India 21°5N 81°5E 41 J12
Raj Nilgiri India 21°28N 86°46E 43 J12
Raja, Ujung Indonesia 3°40N 96°25E 36 D1
Raja Ampat, Kepulauan Indonesia 0°30S 130°0E 37 E8
Rajahmundry India 17°1N 81°48E 41 L12
Rajaji △ India 30°10N 78°20E 42 D8
Rajang → Malaysia 2°30N 112°0E 36 D4
Rajanpur Pakistan 29°6N 70°19E 42 E4
Rajapalaiyam India 9°25N 77°35E 40 Q10
Rajasthan □ India 26°45N 73°30E 42 F5
Rajasthan Canal = Indira Gandhi Canal India 28°0N 72°0E 42 F5
Rajauri India 33°25N 74°21E 43 C6
Rajgarh Mad. P., India 24°2N 76°45E 42 G7
Rajgarh Raj., India 27°14N 76°38E 42 F7
Rajgarh Raj., India 28°40N 75°25E 42 E6
Rajgir India 25°2N 85°25E 43 G11
Rajkot India 22°15N 70°56E 42 H4
Rajmahal Hills India 24°30N 87°30E 43 G12
Rajpipla India 21°50N 73°30E 40 J8
Rajpur India 22°18N 74°21E 42 H6
Rajpura India 30°25N 76°32E 42 D7
Rajshahi Bangla. 24°22N 88°39E 41 G16
Rajshahi □ Bangla. 25°0N 89°0E 43 G13
Rajula India 21°3N 71°26E 42 J4
Rakaia N.Z. 43°45S 172°1E 59 E4
Rakaia → N.Z. 43°36S 172°15E 59 E4
Rakan, Ra's Qatar 26°10N 51°20E 45 E6
Rakaposhi Pakistan 36°10N 74°25E 43 A6
Rakata, Pulau Indonesia 6°10S 105°20E 36 F3
Rakhiv Ukraine 48°3N 24°12E 17 D13
Rakhni Pakistan 30°4N 69°56E 42 D3
Rakhni → Pakistan 29°31N 69°36E 42 E3
Rakiraki Fiji 17°22S 178°11E 59 a
Rakitnoye Russia 45°36N 134°17E 30 B7
Rakiura △ N.Z. 47°0S 167°50E 59 G1
Rakops Botswana 21°1S 24°28E 56 C3
Rakvere Estonia 59°20N 26°25E 9 G22
Raleigh U.S.A. 35°47N 78°39W 85 D15
Ralik Chain Pac. Oc. 8°0N 168°0E 64 G8
Ralls U.S.A. 33°41N 101°24W 84 E4
Ralston U.S.A. 41°30N 76°57W 82 E8
Ram → Canada 62°1N 123°41W 70 A4
Rām Allāh West Bank 31°55N 35°10E 46 D4
Rama Nic. 12°9N 84°15W 88 D3
Ramakona India 21°43N 78°50E 43 J8
Rāmallāh = Rām Allāh West Bank 31°55N 35°10E 46 D4
Raman Thailand 6°29N 101°18E 39 J3
Ramanathapuram India 9°25N 78°55E 40 Q11
Ramanetaka, B. de Madag. 14°13S 47°52E 57 A8
Ramanujganj India 23°48N 83°42E 43 H10
Ramat Gan Israel 32°4N 34°48E 46 C3
Ramatlhabama S. Africa 25°37S 25°33E 56 D4
Ramban India 33°14N 75°12E 43 C6
Rambi = Rabi Fiji 16°30S 179°59W 59 a
Rambipuji Indonesia 8°12S 113°37E 37 H15
Rame Hd. Australia 37°47S 149°30E 63 F4
Ramechhap Nepal 27°25N 86°10E 43 F12
Ramganga → India 27°5N 79°58E 43 F8
Ramgarh Jharkhand, India 23°40N 85°35E 43 H11
Ramgarh Raj., India 27°16N 75°14E 42 F6
Ramgarh Raj., India 27°30N 70°36E 42 F4
Rāmhormoz Iran 31°15N 49°35E 45 D6
Ramīān Iran 37°3N 55°16E 45 B7
Ramingining Australia 12°19S 135°3E 62 A2
Ramla Israel 31°55N 34°52E 46 D3
Ramm = Rum Jordan 29°39N 35°26E 46 F4
Ramm, Jabal Jordan 29°35N 35°24E 46 F4
Ramnad = Ramanathapuram India 9°25N 78°55E 40 Q11
Ramnagar Jammu & Kashmir, India 32°47N 75°18E 43 C6
Ramnagar Uttarakhand, India 29°24N 79°7E 43 E8
Râmnicu Sărat Romania 45°26N 27°3E 17 F14
Râmnicu Vâlcea Romania 45°9N 24°21E 17 F13
Ramona U.S.A. 33°2N 116°52W 79 M10
Ramore Canada 48°30N 80°25W 72 C3
Ramotswa Botswana 24°50S 25°52E 56 C4
Rampur H.P., India 31°26N 77°43E 42 D7
Rampur Mad. P., India 23°25N 73°53E 42 H5
Rampur Ut. P., India 28°50N 79°5E 43 E8
Rampur Hat India 24°10N 87°50E 43 G12
Rampura India 24°30N 75°27E 42 G6
Ramrama Tola India 21°52N 79°55E 43 J8
Ramree I. Burma 19°0N 93°40E 41 K19
Rāmsar Iran 36°53N 50°41E 45 B6
Ramsey I. of Man 54°20N 4°22W 12 C3
Ramsey U.S.A. 41°4N 74°9W 83 E10
Ramsey L. Canada 47°13N 82°15W 72 C3
Ramsgate U.K. 51°20N 1°25E 13 F9
Ramtek India 21°20N 79°15E 40 J11
Ramu Kenya 3°55N 41°10E 54 B5
Rana Pratap Sagar Dam India 24°58N 75°38E 42 G6
Ranaghat India 23°15N 88°35E 43 H13
Ranahu Pakistan 25°55N 69°45E 42 G3
Ranau Malaysia 6°2N 116°40E 36 C5
Rancagua Chile 34°10S 70°50W 94 C1
Rancheria → Canada 60°13N 129°7W 70 A3
Ranchester U.S.A. 44°54N 107°10W 76 D10
Ranchi India 23°19N 85°27E 43 H11
Rancho Cordova U.S.A. 38°36N 121°18W 78 G5
Rancho Cucamonga U.S.A. 34°10N 117°30W 79 L9
Randalstown U.K. 54°45N 6°19W 10 B5
Randers Denmark 56°29N 10°1E 9 H14
Randfontein S. Africa 26°8S 27°45E 57 D4
Randle U.S.A. 46°32N 121°57W 78 D5
Randolph Mass., U.S.A. 42°10N 71°2W 83 D13
Randolph N.Y., U.S.A. 42°10N 78°59W 82 D6
Randolph Utah, U.S.A. 41°40N 111°11W 76 F8
Randolph Vt., U.S.A. 43°55N 72°40W 83 C12
Randsburg U.S.A. 35°22N 117°39W 79 K9
Råneälven → Sweden 65°50N 22°20E 8 D20
Rangae Thailand 6°19N 101°44E 39 J3
Rangaunu B. N.Z. 34°51S 173°15E 59 A4
Range, The Zimbabwe 19°2S 31°2E 55 F3
Rangeley U.S.A. 44°58N 70°39W 83 B14
Rangeley L. U.S.A. 44°55N 70°43W 83 B14
Rangely U.S.A. 40°5N 108°48W 76 F9
Ranger U.S.A. 32°28N 98°41W 84 E5
Rangia India 26°28N 91°38E 41 F17
Rangiora N.Z. 43°19S 172°36E 59 E4
Rangitaiki → N.Z. 37°54S 176°49E 59 B6
Rangitata → N.Z. 43°45S 171°15E 59 E3
Rangitoto ke te tonga = D'Urville I. N.Z. 40°50S 173°55E 59 D4
Rangkasbitung Indonesia 6°21S 106°15E 37 G12
Rangon → Burma 16°28N 96°40E 41 L20
Rangoon Burma 16°45N 96°20E 41 L20
Rangpur Bangla. 25°42N 89°22E 41 G16
Rangsang Indonesia 1°20N 103°30E 39 M4
Rangsit Thailand 13°59N 100°37E 38 F3
Ranibennur India 14°35N 75°30E 40 M9
Raniganj Ut. P., India 27°3N 82°13E 43 F9
Raniganj W. Bengal, India 23°40N 87°5E 41 H15

Ranikhet India 29°39N 79°25E 43 E8
Raniwara India 24°50N 72°10E 42 G5
Rāniyah Iraq 36°15N 44°53E 44 B5
Ranka India 23°59N 83°47E 43 H10
Ranken → Australia 20°31S 137°36E 62 C2
Rankin U.S.A. 31°13N 101°56W 84 F4
Rankin Inlet Canada 62°30N 93°0W 68 C10
Rankins Springs Australia 33°49S 146°14E 63 E4
Rannoch, L. U.K. 56°41N 4°20W 11 E4
Rannoch Moor U.K. 56°38N 4°48W 11 E4
Ranobe, Helodranon' i Madag. 23°3S 43°33E 57 C7
Ranohira Madag. 22°29S 45°24E 57 C8
Ranomafana Toamasina, Madag. 18°57S 48°50E 57 B8
Ranomafana Toliara, Madag. 24°34S 47°0E 57 C8
Ranomafana △ Madag. 21°16S 47°25E 57 C8
Ranomena Madag. 23°25S 47°17E 57 C8
Ranong Thailand 9°56N 98°40E 39 H2
Ranotsara Nord Madag. 22°48S 46°36E 57 C8
Rānsa Iran 33°39N 48°18E 45 C6
Ransiki Indonesia 1°30S 134°10E 37 E8
Rantabe Madag. 15°42S 49°39E 57 B8
Rantauprapat Indonesia 2°15N 99°50E 36 D1
Rantemario Indonesia 3°15S 119°57E 37 E5
Ranthambore △ India 26°10N 76°30E 42 F7
Rantoul U.S.A. 40°19N 88°9W 80 E9
Raohe China 46°47N 134°0E 30 A7
Raoyang China 38°15N 115°45E 34 E8
Rap, Ko Thailand 9°19N 99°58E 39 b
Rapa French Polynesia 27°35S 144°20W 65 K13
Rapa Nui = Pascua, I. de Chile 27°7S 109°23W 65 K17
Rapallo Italy 44°21N 9°14E 20 D8
Rapar India 23°34N 70°38E 42 H4
Rāpch Iran 25°40N 59°15E 45 E8
Rapel, Lago Chile 34°20S 71°14W 94 C1
Raper, C. Canada 69°44N 67°6W 69 C13
Rapid City U.S.A. 44°5N 103°14W 80 C2
Rapid River U.S.A. 45°55N 86°58W 80 C10
Rapla Estonia 59°1N 24°52E 9 G21
Rapti → India 26°18N 83°41E 43 F10
Raquette → U.S.A. 45°0N 74°42W 83 B10
Raquette Lake U.S.A. 43°49N 74°40W 83 C10
Rara △ Nepal 29°30N 82°10E 43 E10
Rarotonga Cook Is. 21°30S 160°0W 65 K12
Ra's al 'Ayn Syria 36°45N 40°12E 44 B4
Ra's al Khaymah U.A.E. 25°50N 55°59E 45 E7
Ra's at Tib Tunisia 37°1N 11°2E 22 F4
Rasa, Pta. Argentina 36°20S 56°41W 94 D4
Rasca, Pta. de la Canary Is. 27°59N 16°41W 24 G3
Raseiniai Lithuania 55°25N 23°5E 9 J20
Rashmi India 25°4N 74°22E 42 G6
Rasht Iran 37°20N 49°40E 45 B6
Rasi Salai Thailand 15°20N 104°9E 38 E5
Rason L. Australia 28°45S 124°25E 61 E3
Rasra India 25°50N 83°50E 43 G10
Rasul Pakistan 32°42N 73°34E 42 C5
Rat → Canada 49°35N 97°10W 71 D9
Rat Buri Thailand 13°30N 99°54E 38 F2
Rat Islands U.S.A. 52°0N 178°0E 74 a
Rat L. Canada 56°10N 99°40W 71 B9
Ratak Chain Pac. Oc. 1°0N 170°0E 64 G8
Ratangarh India 28°5N 74°35E 42 E6
Raṭāwī Iraq 30°38N 47°13E 44 D5
Rath India 25°36N 79°37E 43 G8
Rath Luirc Ireland 52°21N 8°40W 10 D3
Rathangan Ireland 53°13N 7°1W 10 C4
Rathdrum Ireland 52°56N 6°14W 10 D5
Rathenow Germany 52°37N 12°19E 16 B7
Rathkeale Ireland 52°32N 8°56W 10 D3
Rathlin I. U.K. 55°18N 6°14W 10 A5
Rathmelton Ireland 55°2N 7°38W 10 A4
Ratibor = Racibórz Poland 50°7N 18°18E 17 C10
Ratlam India 23°20N 75°0E 42 H6
Ratnagiri India 16°57N 73°18E 40 L8
Ratodero Pakistan 27°48N 68°18E 42 F3
Raton U.S.A. 36°54N 104°24W 77 H11
Rattaphum Thailand 7°8N 100°16E 39 J3
Rattray Hd. U.K. 57°38N 1°50W 11 D7
Ratz, Mt. Canada 57°23N 132°12W 70 B2
Raub Malaysia 3°47N 101°52E 39 L3
Rauch Argentina 36°45S 59°5W 94 D4
Raudales Mexico 17°27N 93°39W 87 D6
Raufarhöfn Iceland 66°27N 15°57W 8 C6
Raufoss Norway 60°44N 10°37E 8 F14
Raukumara Ra. N.Z. 38°5S 177°55E 59 C6
Rauma Finland 61°10N 21°30E 8 F19
Raumo = Rauma Finland 61°10N 21°30E 8 F19
Raung, Gunung Indonesia 8°8S 114°3E 37 J17
Raurkela India 22°14N 84°50E 43 H11
Rausu-Dake Japan 44°4N 145°7E 30 B12
Rava-Ruska Ukraine 50°15N 23°42E 17 C12
Rava Russkaya = Rava-Ruska Ukraine 50°15N 23°42E 17 C12
Ravalli U.S.A. 47°17N 114°11W 76 C6
Ravānsar Iran 34°43N 46°40E 44 C5
Rāvar Iran 31°20N 56°51E 45 D8
Ravena U.S.A. 42°28N 73°49W 83 D11
Ravenna Italy 44°25N 12°12E 22 B5
Ravenna Nebr., U.S.A. 41°1N 98°55W 80 E4
Ravenna Ohio, U.S.A. 41°9N 81°15W 82 E3
Ravensburg Germany 47°46N 9°36E 16 E5
Ravenshoe Australia 17°37S 145°29E 62 B4
Ravensthorpe Australia 33°35S 120°2E 61 F3
Ravenswood Australia 20°6S 146°54E 62 C4
Ravenswood U.S.A. 38°57N 81°46W 81 F13
Ravi → Pakistan 30°35N 71°49E 42 D4
Rawalpindi Pakistan 33°38N 73°8E 42 C5
Rawang Malaysia 3°20N 101°35E 39 L3
Rawene N.Z. 35°25S 173°32E 59 A4
Rawlinna Australia 30°58S 125°28E 61 F4
Rawlins U.S.A. 41°47N 107°14W 76 F10
Rawlinson Ra. Australia 24°40S 128°30E 61 D4
Rawson Argentina 43°15S 65°5W 96 E3
Raxaul India 26°59N 84°51E 43 F11
Ray U.S.A. 48°21N 103°10W 80 A2
Ray, C. Canada 47°33N 59°15W 73 C8
Raya Ring, Ko Thailand 8°18N 98°29E 39 a
Rayadurg India 14°40N 76°50E 40 M10
Rayagada India 19°15N 83°20E 41 K13
Raychikhinsk Russia 49°46N 129°25E 29 E13
Rāyen Iran 29°34N 57°26E 45 D8
Rayleigh U.K. 51°36N 0°37E 13 F8
Raymond Canada 49°30N 112°35W 70 D6
Raymond Calif., U.S.A. 37°13N 119°54W 78 H7
Raymond N.H., U.S.A. 43°2N 71°11W 83 C13
Raymond Wash., U.S.A. 46°41N 123°44W 78 D3
Raymondville U.S.A. 26°29N 97°47W 84 H6
Raymore Canada 51°25N 104°31W 71 C8
Rayón Mexico 29°43N 110°35W 86 B2
Rayong Thailand 12°40N 101°20E 38 F3
Raystown L. U.S.A. 40°25N 78°5W 82 F6
Rayville U.S.A. 32°29N 91°46W 84 E9
Raz, Pte. du France 48°2N 4°47W 20 C1
Razan Iran 35°23N 49°2E 45 C6
Razāzah, Buḥayrat ar Iraq 32°40N 43°35E 44 C4
Razazah, L. = Razāzah, Buḥayrat ar Iraq 32°40N 43°35E 44 C4
Razdel'naya = Rozdilna Ukraine 46°50N 30°2E 17 E16
Razdolnoye Russia 43°30N 131°52E 30 C5
Razeh Iran 32°47N 48°9E 45 C6
Razgrad Bulgaria 43°33N 26°34E 23 C12
Razim, Lacul Romania 44°50N 29°0E 17 F15
Razmak Pakistan 32°45N 69°50E 42 C3
Re, Cu Lao Vietnam 15°22N 109°8E 38 E7
Ré, Î. de France 46°12N 1°30W 20 C3
Reading U.K. 51°27N 0°58W 13 F7
Reading U.S.A. 40°20N 75°56W 83 F9
Reading ☐ U.K. 51°27N 0°58W 13 F7
Realicó Argentina 35°0S 64°15W 94 D3
Ream Cambodia 10°34N 103°39E 39 G4
Ream △ Cambodia 10°30N 103°45E 39 G4
Reay Forest U.K. 58°22N 4°55W 11 C4
Rebecca, L. Australia 30°0S 122°15E 61 F3
Rebi Indonesia 6°23S 134°7E 37 F8
Rebiana Libya 24°12N 22°10E 51 D10
Rebiana, Sahrâ' Libya 24°30N 21°0E 51 D10
Reboly Russia 63°49N 30°47E 8 E24
Rebun-Tō Japan 45°23N 141°2E 30 B10
Recherche, Arch. of the Australia 34°15S 122°50E 61 F3
Rechna Doab Pakistan 31°35N 73°30E 42 D5
Rechytsa Belarus 52°21N 30°24E 17 B16
Recife Brazil 8°0S 35°0W 93 E12
Recife Seychelles 4°36S 55°42E 53 b
Recklinghausen Germany 51°37N 7°12E 15 C7
Reconquista Argentina 29°10S 59°45W 94 B4
Recreo Argentina 29°25S 65°10W 94 B2
Red → U.S.A. 31°1N 91°45W 84 F9
Red Bank U.S.A. 40°21N 74°5W 83 F10
Red Bay Canada 51°44N 56°25W 73 B8
Red Bluff U.S.A. 40°11N 122°15W 76 F2
Red Bluff Res. U.S.A. 31°54N 103°55W 77 L12
Red Cliffs Australia 34°19S 142°11E 63 E3
Red Cloud U.S.A. 40°5N 98°32W 80 E4
Red Creek U.S.A. 43°14N 76°45W 83 C8
Red Deer Canada 52°20N 113°50W 70 C6
Red Deer → Alta., Canada 50°58N 110°0W 71 C7
Red Deer → Man., Canada 52°53N 101°1W 71 C8
Red Deer L. Canada 52°55N 101°20W 71 C8
Red Hook U.S.A. 41°55N 73°53W 83 E11
Red Indian L. Canada 48°35N 57°0W 73 C8
Red L. Canada 51°3N 93°49W 71 C10
Red Lake Canada 51°3N 93°49W 71 C10
Red Lake Falls U.S.A. 47°53N 96°16W 80 B5
Red Lake Road Canada 49°59N 93°25W 71 C10
Red Lodge U.S.A. 45°11N 109°15W 76 D9
Red Mountain U.S.A. 35°37N 117°38W 79 K9
Red Oak U.S.A. 41°1N 95°14W 80 E6
Red River of the North → N. Amer. 49°0N 97°15W 80 A5
Red Rock Canada 48°55N 88°15W 72 C2
Red Rock, L. U.S.A. 41°22N 92°59W 80 E7
Red Rocks Pt. Australia 32°13S 127°32E 61 F4
Red Sea Asia 25°0N 36°0E 47 C2
Red Slate Mt. U.S.A. 37°31N 118°52W 78 H8
Red Sucker L. Canada 54°9N 93°40W 72 B1
Red Tower Pass = Turnu Roşu, P. Romania 45°33N 24°17E 17 F13
Red Wing U.S.A. 44°34N 92°31W 80 C7
Redang Malaysia 5°49N 103°2E 39 K4
Redange Lux. 49°46N 5°52E 15 E5
Redcar U.K. 54°37N 1°4W 12 C6
Redcar & Cleveland ☐ U.K. 54°29N 1°0W 12 C7
Redcliff Canada 50°10N 110°50W 76 A8
Redcliffe Australia 27°12S 153°0E 63 D5
Redcliffe, Mt. Australia 28°30S 121°30E 61 E3
Reddersburg S. Africa 29°41S 26°10E 56 D4
Redding U.S.A. 40°35N 122°24W 76 F2
Redditch U.K. 52°18N 1°55W 13 E6
Redfield U.S.A. 44°53N 98°31W 80 C4
Redford U.S.A. 44°38N 73°48W 83 B11
Redhead Trin. & Tob. 10°44N 60°58W 93 K16
Redlands U.S.A. 34°4N 117°11W 79 M9
Redmond Oreg., U.S.A. 44°17N 121°11W 76 D3
Redmond Wash., U.S.A. 47°40N 122°7W 78 C4
Redon France 47°40N 2°6W 20 C2
Redonda Antigua & B. 16°58N 62°19W 89 C7
Redondela Spain 42°15N 8°38W 21 A1
Redondo Beach U.S.A. 33°50N 118°23W 79 M8
Redruth U.K. 50°14N 5°14W 13 G2
Redvers Canada 49°35N 101°40W 71 D8
Redwater Canada 53°55N 113°6W 70 C6
Redwood U.S.A. 44°18N 75°48W 83 B9
Redwood △ U.S.A. 41°40N 124°5W 76 F1
Redwood City U.S.A. 37°30N 122°15W 78 H4
Redwood Falls U.S.A. 44°32N 95°7W 80 C6
Ree, L. Ireland 53°35N 8°0W 10 C3
Reed City U.S.A. 43°53N 85°31W 81 D11
Reed L. Canada 54°38N 100°30W 71 C8
Reedley U.S.A. 36°36N 119°27W 78 J7
Reedsburg U.S.A. 43°32N 90°0W 80 D8
Reedsport U.S.A. 43°42N 124°6W 76 E1
Reedsville U.S.A. 40°39N 77°35W 82 F7
Reefton N.Z. 42°6S 171°51E 59 E3
Reese → U.S.A. 40°48N 117°4W 76 F5
Refugio U.S.A. 28°18N 97°17W 84 G6
Regana, C. de Spain 39°25N 2°43E 24 B9
Regensburg Germany 49°1N 12°6E 16 D7
Reggâne = Zaouiet Reggâne Algeria 26°32N 0°3E 50 C6
Réggio di Calábria Italy 38°6N 15°39E 22 E6
Réggio nell'Emília Italy 44°43N 10°36E 22 B4
Reghin Romania 46°46N 24°42E 17 E13
Regina Canada 50°27N 104°35W 71 C8
Regina Beach Canada 50°47N 105°0W 71 C8
Registro Brazil 24°29S 47°49W 95 A6
Rehar → India 23°55N 82°40E 43 H10
Rehli India 23°38N 79°5E 43 H8
Rehoboth Namibia 23°15S 17°4E 56 C2
Rehovot Israel 31°54N 34°48E 46 D3
Reichenbach Germany 50°37N 12°17E 16 C7
Reid Australia 30°49S 128°26E 61 F4
Reidsville U.S.A. 36°21N 79°40W 85 C15
Reigate U.K. 51°14N 0°12W 13 F7
Reims France 49°15N 4°1E 20 B6
Reina Adelaida, Arch. Chile 52°20S 74°0W 96 G2
Reina Sofia, Tenerife ✕ (TFS) Canary Is. 28°3N 16°33W 24 F3
Reindeer → Canada 55°36N 103°11W 71 B8
Reindeer I. Canada 52°30N 98°0W 71 C9
Reindeer L. Canada 57°15N 102°15W 71 B8
Reinga, C. N.Z. 34°25S 172°43E 59 A4
Reinosa Spain 43°2N 4°15W 21 A3
Reitz S. Africa 27°48S 28°29E 57 D4
Reivilo S. Africa 27°36S 24°8E 56 D3
Reliance Canada 63°0N 109°20W 71 A7
Remanso Brazil 9°41S 42°4W 93 E10
Remarkable, Mt. Australia 32°48S 138°10E 63 E2
Rembang Indonesia 6°42S 111°21E 37 G14
Remedios Panama 8°15N 81°50W 88 E3
Remeshk Iran 26°55N 58°50E 45 E8
Remich Lux. 49°32N 6°22E 15 E6
Remscheid Germany 51°11N 7°12E 15 C7
Ren Xian China 37°8N 114°40E 34 F8
Rendang Indonesia 8°26S 115°25E 37 J18
Rendsburg Germany 54°17N 9°39E 16 A5
Renfrew Canada 45°30N 76°40W 83 A8
Renfrewshire ☐ U.K. 55°49N 4°38W 11 F4
Rengat Indonesia 0°30S 102°45E 36 E2
Rengo Chile 34°24S 70°50W 94 C1
Reni Ukraine 45°28N 28°15E 17 F15
Renmark Australia 34°11S 140°43E 63 E3
Rennell Sd. Canada 53°23N 132°35W 70 C2
Renner Springs Australia 18°20S 133°47E 62 B1
Rennes France 48°7N 1°41W 20 B3
Rennick Glacier Antarctica 70°30S 161°45E 5 D21
Rennie L. Canada 61°32N 105°35W 71 A7
Reno U.S.A. 39°31N 119°48W 78 F7
Reno → Italy 44°38N 12°16E 22 B5
Renovo U.S.A. 41°20N 77°45W 82 E7
Renqiu China 38°43N 116°5E 34 E9
Rensselaer Ind., U.S.A. 40°57N 87°9W 80 E10
Rensselaer N.Y., U.S.A. 42°38N 73°45W 83 D11
Renton U.S.A. 47°28N 122°12W 78 C4
Reotipur India 25°33N 83°45E 43 G10
Republic Mo., U.S.A. 37°7N 93°29W 80 G7
Republic Wash., U.S.A. 48°39N 118°44W 76 B4
Republican → U.S.A. 39°4N 96°48W 80 F5
Repulse B. Australia 20°35S 148°46E 62 J6
Repulse Bay Canada 66°30N 86°30W 69 C11
Requena Peru 5°5S 73°52W 92 E4
Requena Spain 39°30N 1°4W 21 C5
Reserve U.S.A. 33°43N 108°45W 77 K9
Resht = Rasht Iran 37°20N 49°40E 45 B6
Resistencia Argentina 27°30S 59°0W 94 B4
Reşiţa Romania 45°18N 21°53E 17 F11
Reso = Raisio Finland 60°28N 22°11E 9 F20
Resolute Canada 74°42N 94°54W 69 B10
Resolution I. Canada 61°30N 65°0W 69 C13
Resolution I. N.Z. 45°40S 166°40E 59 F1
Ressano Garcia Mozam. 25°25S 32°0E 57 D5
Reston Canada 49°33N 101°6W 71 D8
Retalhuleu Guatemala 14°33N 91°46W 88 D1
Retenue, L. de Dem. Rep. of the Congo 11°0S 27°0E 55 E2
Retford U.K. 53°19N 0°56W 12 D7
Rethimno Greece 35°18N 24°30E 25 D6
Rethimno ☐ Greece 35°23N 24°28E 25 D6
Reti Pakistan 28°5N 69°48E 42 E3
Réunion ☐ Ind. Oc. 21°0S 56°0E 53 c
Reus Spain 41°10N 1°5E 21 B6
Reutlingen Germany 48°29N 9°12E 16 D5
Reval = Tallinn Estonia 59°22N 24°48E 9 G21
Revda Russia 56°48N 59°57E 18 C10
Revelganj India 25°50N 84°40E 43 G11
Revelstoke Canada 51°0N 118°10W 70 C5
Reventazón Peru 6°10S 80°58W 92 E2
Revillagigedo, Is. de Pac. Oc. 18°40N 112°0W 86 D2
Revuè → Mozam. 19°50S 34°0E 55 F3
Rewa India 24°33N 81°25E 43 G9
Rewari India 28°15N 76°40E 42 E7
Rexburg U.S.A. 43°49N 111°47W 76 E8
Rey Iran 35°35N 51°25E 45 C6
Rey, I. del Panama 8°20N 78°30W 88 E4
Rey, L. del Mexico 27°1N 103°26W 86 B4
Rey Malabo Eq. Guin. 3°45N 8°50E 52 D1
Reyðarfjörður Iceland 65°2N 14°13W 8 D6
Reyes, Pt. U.S.A. 38°0N 123°0W 78 H3
Reykjahlíð Iceland 65°40N 16°55W 8 D5
Reykjanes Iceland 63°48N 22°40W 8 E2
Reykjavík Iceland 64°10N 21°57W 8 D3
Reynolds Ra. Australia 22°30S 133°0E 60 D5
Reynoldsville U.S.A. 41°6N 78°53W 82 E6
Reynosa Mexico 26°7N 98°18W 87 B5
Rēzekne Latvia 56°30N 27°17E 9 H22
Rezvān Iran 27°34N 56°6E 45 E8
Rhayader U.K. 52°18N 3°29W 13 E4
Rhein → Europe 51°52N 6°2E 15 C6
Rhein-Main-Donau-Kanal Germany 49°1N 11°27E 16 D6
Rheine Germany 52°17N 7°26E 16 B4
Rheinland-Pfalz ☐ Germany 50°0N 7°0E 16 C4
Rhin = Rhein → Europe 51°52N 6°2E 15 C6
Rhine = Rhein → Europe 51°52N 6°2E 15 C6
Rhinebeck U.S.A. 41°56N 73°55W 83 E11
Rhineland-Palatinate = Rheinland-Pfalz ☐ Germany 50°0N 7°0E 16 C4
Rhinelander U.S.A. 45°38N 89°25W 80 C9
Rhinns Pt. U.K. 55°40N 6°29W 11 F2
Rhino Camp Uganda 3°0N 31°22E 54 B3
Rhir, Cap Morocco 30°38N 9°54W 50 B4
Rhode Island ☐ U.S.A. 41°40N 71°30W 83 E13
Rhodes Greece 36°15N 28°10E 25 C10
Rhodope Mts. = Rhodopi Planina Bulgaria 41°40N 24°20E 23 D11
Rhodopi Planina Bulgaria 41°40N 24°20E 23 D11
Rhön Germany 50°24N 9°58E 16 C5
Rhondda U.K. 51°39N 3°31W 13 F4
Rhondda Cynon Taff ☐ U.K. 51°42N 3°27W 13 F4
Rhône → France 43°28N 4°42E 20 E6
Rhum U.K. 57°0N 6°20W 11 E2
Rhyl U.K. 53°20N 3°29W 12 D4
Riachão Brazil 7°20S 46°37W 93 E9
Riasi India 33°10N 74°50E 43 C6
Riau ☐ Indonesia 0°0 102°35E 36 E2
Riau, Kepulauan Indonesia 0°30N 104°20E 36 D2
Riau Arch. = Riau, Kepulauan Indonesia 0°30N 104°20E 36 D2
Ribadeo Spain 43°35N 7°5W 21 A2
Ribas do Rio Pardo Brazil 20°27S 53°46W 93 H8
Ribauè Mozam. 14°57S 38°17E 55 E4
Ribble → U.K. 53°52N 2°25W 12 D5
Ribe Denmark 55°19N 8°44E 9 J13
Ribeira Brava Madeira 32°41N 17°4W 24 D2
Ribeira Grande C. Verde Is. 17°0N 25°4W 50 b
Ribeirão Prêto Brazil 21°10S 47°50W 95 A6
Riberalta Bolivia 11°0S 66°0W 92 F5
Riccarton N.Z. 43°32S 172°37E 59 E4
Rice U.S.A. 34°5N 114°51W 79 L12
Rice L. Canada 44°12N 78°10W 82 B6
Rice Lake U.S.A. 45°30N 91°44W 80 C8
Rich, C. Canada 44°43N 80°38W 82 B4
Richards Bay S. Africa 28°48S 32°6E 57 D5
Richardson → Canada 58°25N 111°14W 71 B6
Richardson Lakes U.S.A. 44°46N 70°58W 81 C18
Richardson Springs U.S.A. 39°51N 121°46W 78 F5
Riche, C. Australia 34°36S 118°47E 61 F2
Richey U.S.A. 47°39N 105°4W 76 C11
Richfield U.S.A. 38°46N 112°5W 76 G7
Richfield Springs U.S.A. 42°51N 74°59W 83 D10
Richford U.S.A. 45°0N 72°40W 83 B12
Richibucto Canada 46°42N 64°54W 73 C7
Richland Ga., U.S.A. 32°5N 84°40W 85 E12
Richland Wash., U.S.A. 46°17N 119°18W 76 C4
Richland Center U.S.A. 43°21N 90°23W 80 D8
Richlands U.S.A. 37°6N 81°48W 81 G13
Richmond Australia 20°43S 143°8E 62 C3
Richmond N.Z. 41°20S 173°12E 59 D4
Richmond U.K. 54°25N 1°43W 12 C6
Richmond Calif., U.S.A. 37°56N 122°21W 78 H4
Richmond Ind., U.S.A. 39°50N 84°53W 81 F11
Richmond Ky., U.S.A. 37°45N 84°18W 81 G11
Richmond Mich., U.S.A. 42°49N 82°45W 82 D2
Richmond Mo., U.S.A. 39°17N 93°58W 80 F7
Richmond Tex., U.S.A. 29°35N 95°46W 84 G7
Richmond Utah, U.S.A. 41°56N 111°48W 76 F8
Richmond Va., U.S.A. 37°33N 77°27W 81 G15
Richmond Vt., U.S.A. 44°24N 72°59W 83 B12
Richmond Hill Canada 43°52N 79°27W 82 C5
Richmond Ra. Australia 29°0S 152°45E 63 D5
Richmondville U.S.A. 42°38N 74°33W 83 D10
Richtersveld △ S. Africa 28°15S 17°10E 56 D2
Richville U.S.A. 44°25N 75°23W 83 B9
Richwood U.S.A. 38°14N 80°32W 81 F13
Ridder = Leninogorsk Kazakhstan 50°20N 83°30E 28 D9
Riddlesburg U.S.A. 40°9N 78°15W 82 F6
Ridgecrest U.S.A. 35°38N 117°40W 79 K9
Ridgefield Conn., U.S.A. 41°17N 73°30W 83 E11
Ridgefield Wash., U.S.A. 45°49N 122°45W 78 E4
Ridgeland Miss., U.S.A. 32°26N 90°8W 85 E9
Ridgeland S.C., U.S.A. 32°29N 80°59W 85 E14
Ridgetown Canada 42°26N 81°52W 82 D3
Ridgewood U.S.A. 40°59N 74°7W 83 F10
Ridgway U.S.A. 41°25N 78°44W 82 E6
Riding Mountain △ Canada 50°50N 100°0W 71 C9
Ridley, Mt. Australia 33°12S 122°7E 61 F3
Riebeek-Oos S. Africa 33°10S 26°10E 56 E4
Ried Austria 48°14N 13°30E 16 D7
Riesa Germany 51°17N 13°17E 16 C7
Riet → S. Africa 29°0S 23°54E 56
Rietbron S. Africa 32°54S 23°10E 56
Rietfontein Namibia 21°58S 20°58E 56
Rieti Italy 42°24N 12°51E 22
Rif = Er Rif Morocco 35°1N 4°1W 50
Riffe L. U.S.A. 46°32N 122°26W 78
Rifle U.S.A. 39°32N 107°47W 76 G
Rift Valley Africa 7°0N 30°0E 48
Rift Valley ☐ Kenya 0°20N 36°0E 54
Rīga Latvia 56°53N 24°8E 9 H
Riga, G. of Latvia 57°40N 23°45E 9 H
Rīgān Iran 28°37N 58°58E 45
Rīgas Jūras Līcis = Riga, G. of Latvia 57°40N 23°45E 9 H
Rigaud Canada 45°29N 74°18W 83 A
Rigby U.S.A. 43°40N 111°55W 76
Rīgestān Afghan. 30°15N 65°0E 40
Riggins U.S.A. 45°25N 116°19W 76
Rigolet Canada 54°10N 58°23W 73
Rihand Dam India 24°9N 83°2E 43 G
Riihimäki Finland 60°45N 24°48E 8 F
Riiser-Larsen-halvøya Antarctica 68°0S 35°0E 5
Riiser-Larsen Ice Shelf S. Ocean 74°0S 19°0W 5
Riiser-Larsen Sea S. Ocean 67°30S 22°0E 5
Rijeka Croatia 45°20N 14°21E 16
Rijssen Neths. 52°19N 6°31E 15
Rikuchū-Kaigan △ Japan 39°20N 142°0E 30 E
Rikuzentakada Japan 39°0N 141°40E 30 E
Riley U.S.A. 43°32N 119°28W 76
Rima → Nigeria 13°4N 5°10E 50
Rimah, Wadi ar → Si. Arabia 26°5N 41°30E 44
Rimau, Pulau Malaysia 5°15N 100°16E 3
Rimbey Canada 52°35N 114°15W 70
Rimersburg U.S.A. 41°3N 79°30W 82
Rímini Italy 44°3N 12°33E 22
Rimouski Canada 48°27N 68°30W 73
Rimrock U.S.A. 46°40N 121°7W 78
Rinca Indonesia 8°45S 119°35E 37
Rincón de Romos Mexico 22°14N 102°18W 86
Rinconada Argentina 22°26S 66°10W 94
Rind → India 25°53N 80°33E 43
Ringas India 27°21N 75°34E 42
Ringgold Is. Fiji 16°15S 179°25W 5
Ringkøbing Denmark 56°5N 8°15E 9 H
Ringvassøya Norway 69°56N 19°15E 8 B
Ringwood U.S.A. 41°7N 74°15W 83 E
Rinjani Indonesia 8°24S 116°28E 36
Rio Branco Brazil 9°58S 67°49W 92
Río Branco Uruguay 32°40S 53°40W 95
Río Bravo Mexico 25°59N 98°6W 87
Río Bravo △ N. Amer. 29°2N 102°45W 86
Río Bravo del Norte → Mexico 25°57N 97°9W 87
Rio Brilhante Brazil 21°48S 54°33W 95
Rio Claro Brazil 22°19S 47°35W 95
Rio Claro Trin. & Tob. 10°20N 61°25W 89
Río Colorado Argentina 39°0S 64°0W 96
Río Cuarto Argentina 33°10S 64°25W 94
Rio das Pedras Mozam. 23°8S 35°28E 57
Rio de Janeiro Brazil 22°54S 43°12W 95
Rio de Janeiro ☐ Brazil 22°50S 43°0W 95
Rio do Sul Brazil 27°13S 49°37W 95
Río Dulce △ Guatemala 15°43N 88°50W 88
Río Gallegos Argentina 51°35S 69°15W 96
Río Grande Argentina 53°50S 67°45W 96
Rio Grande Brazil 32°0S 52°20W 95
Río Grande Mexico 23°50N 103°2W 86
Río Grande Puerto Rico 18°23N 65°50W 8
Rio Grande → N. Amer. 25°58N 97°9W 84
Rio Grande City U.S.A. 26°23N 98°49W 84
Río Grande de Santiago → Mexico 21°36N 105°26W 86
Rio Grande do Norte ☐ Brazil 5°40S 36°0W 93 E
Rio Grande do Sul ☐ Brazil 30°0S 53°0W 95
Río Hato Panama 8°22N 80°10W 88
Río Lagartos Mexico 21°36N 88°10W 87
Rio Largo Brazil 9°28S 35°50W 93 E
Río Mulatos Bolivia 19°40S 66°50W 92
Río Muni ☐ Eq. Guin. 1°30N 10°0E 52
Rio Negro Brazil 26°0S 49°55W 95
Rio Pardo Brazil 30°0S 52°30W 95
Río Pilcomayo △ Argentina 25°5S 58°5W 94
Río Platano △ Honduras 15°45N 85°0W 88
Rio Rancho U.S.A. 35°14N 106°41W 77
Río Segundo Argentina 31°40S 63°59W 94
Río Tercero Argentina 32°15S 64°8W 94
Rio Verde Brazil 17°50S 51°0W 93
Río Verde Mexico 21°56N 99°59W 87
Rio Vista U.S.A. 38°10N 121°42W 78
Ríobamba Ecuador 1°50S 78°45W 92
Ríohacha Colombia 11°33N 72°55W 92
Ríosucio Colombia 7°27N 77°7W 92
Riou L. Canada 59°7N 106°25W 71
Ripley Canada 44°4N 81°35W 82
Ripley Calif., U.S.A. 33°32N 114°39W 79 M
Ripley N.Y., U.S.A. 42°16N 79°43W 82
Ripley Tenn., U.S.A. 35°45N 89°32W 85 D
Ripley W. Va., U.S.A. 38°49N 81°43W 81 I
Ripon U.K. 54°9N 1°31W 12
Ripon Calif., U.S.A. 37°44N 121°7W 78
Ripon Wis., U.S.A. 43°51N 88°50W 80
Rishā', W. ar → Si. Arabia 25°33N 44°5E 44
Rishiri-Rebun-Sarobetsu △ Japan 45°26N 141°30E 30
Rishiri-Tō Japan 45°11N 141°15E 30 E
Rishon le Ẕiyyon Israel 31°58N 34°48E 46
Rison U.S.A. 33°58N 92°11W 84
Risør Norway 58°43N 9°13E 9 C
Rita Blanca Cr. → U.S.A. 35°40N 102°29W 84

ter, Mt. U.S.A. 37°41N 119°12W 78 H7
tman U.S.A. 40°58N 81°47W 82 F3
zville U.S.A. 47°8N 118°23W 76 C4
a del Garda Italy 45°53N 10°50E 22 B4
adavia B. Aires, Argentina 35°29S 62°59W 94 D3
adavia Mendoza, Argentina 33°13S 68°30W 94 C2
adavia Salta, Argentina 24°5S 62°54W 94 A3
adavia Chile 29°57S 70°35W 94 B1
as Nic. 11°30N 85°50W 88 D2
ash Iran 35°28N 58°26E 45 C8
er Cess Liberia 5°30N 9°32W 50 G4
er Jordan Canada 48°26N 124°3W 78 B2
era Argentina 37°12S 63°14W 94 D3
era Uruguay 31°0S 55°50W 95 C4
erbank U.S.A. 37°44N 120°56W 78 H6
erdale U.S.A. 36°26N 119°52W 78 J7
erhead U.S.A. 40°55N 72°40W 83 F12
erhurst Canada 50°55N 106°50W 71 C7
ers Canada 50°2N 100°14W 71 C8
ers Inlet Canada 51°42N 127°15W 70 C3
ersdale Canada 44°5N 81°20W 82 B3
ersdale S. Africa 34°7S 21°15E 56 E3
erside U.S.A. 33°59N 117°22W 79 M9
erton Australia 34°10S 138°46E 63 E2
erton Canada 51°1N 97°0W 71 C9
erton N.Z. 46°21S 168°0E 59 G2
erton U.S.A. 43°2N 108°23W 76 E9
iera U.S.A. 35°4N 114°35W 79 K12
iera di Levante Italy 44°15N 9°30E 20 D8
iera di Ponente Italy 44°10N 8°20E 20 D8
ière-au-Renard Canada 48°59N 64°23W 73 C7
ière-du-Loup Canada 47°50N 69°30W 73 C6
ière-Pentecôte Canada 49°57N 67°1W 73 C6
ière-Pilote Martinique 14°26N 60°53W 88 c
ière St-Paul Canada 51°28N 57°45W 73 B8
ière-Salée Martinique 14°31N 61°0W 88 c
ne Ukraine 50°40N 26°10E 17 C14
oli Italy 45°3N 7°31E 20 D7
oli B. Australia 37°32S 140°3E 63 F3
adh = Ar Riyāḍ Si. Arabia 24°41N 46°42E 44 E5
adh al Khabrā' Si. Arabia 26°2N 43°33E 44 E4
Turkey 41°0N 40°30E 19 F7
hao China 35°25N 119°30E 35 G10
okarpaso Cyprus 35°36N 34°23E 25 D13
uto, C. Italy 38°53N 17°5E 22 E7
kan Norway 59°54N 8°33E 9 G13
d Town Br. Virgin Is. 18°27N 64°37W 89 e
n Plateau U.S.A. 39°20N 109°20W 76 G9
nne France 46°3N 4°4E 20 C6
noke Ala., U.S.A. 33°9N 85°22W 85 E12
noke Va., U.S.A. 37°16N 79°56W 81 G14
noke → U.S.A. 35°57N 76°42W 85 D16
noke I. U.S.A. 35°53N 75°39W 85 D17
noke Rapids U.S.A. 36°28N 77°40W 85 C16
tán Honduras 16°18N 86°35W 88 C2
āt Sang Iran 35°35N 59°10E 45 C8
āṭkarīm Iran 35°25N 50°59E 45 C6
bins I. Australia 40°42S 145°0E 63 G4
e → Australia 21°42S 116°15E 60 D2
ert Bourassa, Rés. Canada 53°40N 76°55W 72 B4
ert Lee U.S.A. 31°54N 100°29W 84 F4
ertsdale U.S.A. 40°11N 78°6W 82 F6
ertsganj India 24°44N 83°4E 43 G10
ertson S. Africa 33°46S 19°50E 56 E2
ertson I. Antarctica 65°15S 59°30W 5 C18
ertson Ra. Australia 23°15S 121°0E 60 D3
ertstown Australia 33°58S 139°5E 63 E2
erval Canada 48°32N 72°15W 73 C5
eson Chan. N. Amer. 82°0N 61°30W 4 A4
esonia U.S.A. 40°21N 76°8W 83 F8
inson U.S.A. 39°0N 87°44W 80 F10
inson → Australia 16°3S 137°16E 62 B2
inson Crusoe I. Pac. Oc. 33°38S 78°52W 90 F2
inson Ra. Australia 25°40S 119°0E 61 E2
invale Australia 34°40S 142°45E 63 E3
lin Canada 51°14N 101°21W 71 C8
oré Bolivia 18°10S 59°45W 92 G7
son, Mt. Canada 53°10N 119°10W 70 C5
stown U.S.A. 27°47N 97°40W 84 H6
a, C. da Portugal 38°40N 9°31W 21 C1
a Partida, I. Mexico 19°1N 112°2W 86 D2
as, I. Brazil 4°0S 34°1W 93 D12
ha Uruguay 34°30S 54°25W 95 C5
hdale U.K. 53°38N 2°9W 12 D5
hefort Belgium 50°9N 5°12E 15 D5
hefort France 45°56N 0°57W 20 D3
helle U.S.A. 41°56N 89°4W 80 E9
her River Canada 61°23N 112°44W 70 A6
hester U.K. 51°23N 0°31E 13 F8
hester Ind., U.S.A. 41°4N 86°13W 80 E10
hester Minn., U.S.A. 44°1N 92°28W 80 C7
hester N.H., U.S.A. 43°18N 70°59W 83 C14
hester N.Y., U.S.A. 43°10N 77°37W 82 C7
k → Canada 60°7N 127°7W 70 A3
k, The Australia 35°15S 147°2E 63 F4
k Creek U.S.A. 41°40N 80°52W 82 E4
k Falls U.S.A. 41°47N 89°41W 80 E9
k Hill U.S.A. 34°56N 81°1W 85 D14
k Island U.S.A. 41°30N 90°34W 80 E8
k Port U.S.A. 40°25N 95°31W 80 E6
k Rapids U.S.A. 43°26N 96°10W 80 D5
k Sound Bahamas 24°54N 76°12W 88 B4
k Springs Mont., U.S.A. 46°49N 106°15W 76 C10
k Springs Wyo., U.S.A. 41°35N 109°14W 76 F9
k Valley U.S.A. 43°12N 96°18W 80 D5
kall Atl. Oc. 57°37N 13°42W 6 D3
kdale Tex., U.S.A. 30°39N 97°0W 84 F6
kdale Wash., U.S.A. 47°22N 121°28W 78 C5
Rockeby = Mungkan Kandju △ Australia 13°35S 142°52E 62 A3
Rockefeller Plateau Antarctica 76°0S 130°0W 5 E14
Rockford U.S.A. 42°16N 89°6W 80 D9
Rockglen Canada 49°11N 105°57W 71 D7
Rockhampton Australia 23°22S 150°32E 62 C5
Rockingham Australia 32°15S 115°38E 61 F2
Rockingham N.C., U.S.A. 34°57N 79°46W 85 D15
Rockingham Vt., U.S.A. 43°11N 72°29W 83 C12
Rockingham B. Australia 18°5S 146°10E 62 B4
Rocklake U.S.A. 48°47N 99°15W 80 A4
Rockland Canada 45°33N 75°17W 83 A9
Rockland Idaho, U.S.A. 42°34N 112°53W 76 E7
Rockland Maine, U.S.A. 44°6N 69°7W 81 C19
Rockland Mich., U.S.A. 46°44N 89°11W 80 B9
Rocklin U.S.A. 38°48N 121°14W 78 G5
Rockly B. Trin. & Tob. 11°9N 60°46W 93 J16
Rockmart U.S.A. 34°0N 85°3W 85 D12
Rockport Mass., U.S.A. 42°39N 70°37W 83 D14
Rockport Tex., U.S.A. 28°2N 97°3W 84 G6
Rocksprings U.S.A. 30°1N 100°13W 84 F4
Rockville Conn., U.S.A. 41°52N 72°28W 83 E12
Rockville Md., U.S.A. 39°5N 77°9W 81 F15
Rockwall U.S.A. 32°56N 96°28W 84 E6
Rockwell City U.S.A. 42°24N 94°38W 80 D6
Rockwood Canada 43°37N 80°8W 82 C4
Rockwood Maine, U.S.A. 45°41N 69°45W 81 C19
Rockwood Tenn., U.S.A. 35°52N 84°41W 85 D12
Rocky Ford U.S.A. 38°3N 103°43W 76 G12
Rocky Gully Australia 34°30S 116°57E 61 F2
Rocky Harbour Canada 49°36N 57°55W 73 C8
Rocky Island L. Canada 46°55N 83°0W 72 C3
Rocky Lane Canada 58°31N 116°22W 70 B5
Rocky Mount U.S.A. 35°57N 77°48W 85 D16
Rocky Mountain △ U.S.A. 40°25N 105°45W 76 F11
Rocky Mountain House Canada 52°22N 114°55W 70 C6
Rocky Mts. N. Amer. 49°0N 115°0W 76 B6
Rocky Point Namibia 19°3S 12°30E 56 B2
Rod Pakistan 28°10N 63°5E 40 E3
Roda Greece 39°48N 19°46E 25 A3
Rødbyhavn Denmark 54°39N 11°22E 9 J14
Roddickton Canada 50°51N 56°8W 73 B8
Rodez France 44°21N 2°33E 20 D5
Ródhos = Rhodes Greece 36°15N 28°10E 25 C10
Rodia Greece 35°22N 25°1E 25 D7
Rodney Canada 42°34N 81°41W 82 D3
Rodney, C. N.Z. 36°17S 174°50E 59 B5
Rodopos Greece 35°34N 23°45E 25 D5
Rodriguez Ind. Oc. 19°45S 63°20E 3 E13
Roe → U.K. 55°6N 6°59W 10 A5
Roebling U.S.A. 40°7N 74°47W 83 F10
Roebourne Australia 20°44S 117°9E 60 D2
Roebuck B. Australia 18°5S 122°20E 60 C3
Roermond Neths. 51°12N 6°0E 15 C6
Roes Welcome Sd. Canada 65°0N 87°0W 69 C11
Roeselare Belgium 50°57N 3°7E 15 D3
Rogachev = Ragachow Belarus 53°8N 30°5E 17 B16
Rogagua, L. Bolivia 13°43S 66°50W 92 F5
Rogatyn Ukraine 49°24N 24°36E 17 D13
Rogers U.S.A. 36°20N 94°7W 84 C7
Rogers City U.S.A. 45°25N 83°49W 81 C12
Rogersville Canada 46°44N 65°26W 73 C6
Roggan → Canada 54°24N 79°25W 72 B4
Roggan L. Canada 54°8N 77°50W 72 B4
Roggeveen Basin Pac. Oc. 31°30S 95°30W 65 L18
Roggeveldberge S. Africa 32°10S 20°10E 56 E3
Rogoaguado, L. Bolivia 13°0S 65°30W 92 F5
Rogojampi Indonesia 8°19S 114°17E 37 J17
Rogue → U.S.A. 42°26N 124°26W 76 E1
Rohnert Park U.S.A. 38°16N 122°40W 78 G4
Rohri Pakistan 27°45N 68°51E 42 F3
Rohri Canal Pakistan 26°15N 68°27E 42 F3
Rohtak India 28°55N 76°43E 42 E7
Roi Et Thailand 16°4N 103°40E 38 D4
Roja Latvia 57°29N 22°43E 9 H20
Rojas Argentina 34°10S 60°45W 94 C3
Rojo, C. Mexico 21°33N 97°20W 87 C5
Rokan → Indonesia 2°0N 100°50E 36 D2
Rokiškis Lithuania 55°55N 25°35E 9 J21
Rolândia Brazil 23°18S 51°23W 95 A5
Rolla Mo., U.S.A. 37°57N 91°46W 80 G8
Rolla N. Dak., U.S.A. 48°52N 99°37W 80 A4
Rolleston Australia 24°28S 148°35E 62 C4
Rollingstone Australia 19°2S 146°24E 62 B4
Roma Australia 26°32S 148°49E 63 D4
Roma Italy 41°54N 12°28E 22 D5
Roma Sweden 57°32N 18°26E 9 H18
Roma-Los Saenz U.S.A. 26°24N 99°1W 84 H5
Romain, C. U.S.A. 33°0N 79°22W 85 E15
Romaine → Canada 50°18N 63°47W 73 B7
Roman Romania 46°57N 26°55E 17 E14
Romang Indonesia 7°30S 127°20E 37 F7
Romāni Egypt 30°59N 32°38E 46 E1
Romania ■ Europe 46°0N 25°0E 17 F12
Romano, Cayo Cuba 22°0N 77°30W 88 B4
Romans-sur-Isère France 45°3N 5°3E 20 D6
Romblon Phil. 12°33N 122°17E 37 B6
Rome = Roma Italy 41°54N 12°28E 22 D5
Rome Ga., U.S.A. 34°15N 85°10W 85 D12
Rome N.Y., U.S.A. 43°13N 75°27W 83 C9
Rome Pa., U.S.A. 41°51N 76°21W 83 E8
Romney U.S.A. 39°21N 78°45W 81 F14
Romney Marsh U.K. 51°2N 0°54E 13 F8
Rømø Denmark 55°10N 8°30E 9 J13
Romorantin-Lanthenay France 47°21N 1°45E 20 C4
Romsdalen Norway 62°25N 7°52E 8 E12
Romsey U.K. 51°0N 1°29W 13 G6
Ron Vietnam 17°53N 106°27E 38 D6
Rona U.K. 57°34N 5°59W 11 D3
Ronan U.S.A. 47°32N 114°6W 76 C6
Roncador, Cayos Colombia 13°32N 80°4W 88 D3
Roncador, Serra do Brazil 12°30S 52°30W 93 F8
Ronda Spain 36°46N 5°12W 21 D3
Rondane Norway 61°57N 9°50E 8 F13
Rondônia □ Brazil 11°0S 63°0W 92 F6
Rondonópolis Brazil 16°28S 54°38W 93 G8
Rondu Pakistan 35°32N 75°10E 43 B6
Rong, Koh Cambodia 10°45N 103°15E 39 G4
Ronge, L. la Canada 55°6N 105°17W 71 B7
Rønne Denmark 55°6N 14°43E 9 J16
Ronne Ice Shelf Antarctica 77°30S 60°0W 5 D18
Ronsard, C. Australia 24°46S 113°10E 61 D1
Ronse Belgium 50°45N 3°35E 15 D3
Roodepoort S. Africa 26°11S 27°54E 57 D4
Roof Butte U.S.A. 36°28N 109°5W 77 H9
Rooiboklaagte → Namibia 20°50S 21°0E 56 C3
Rooniu, Mt. Tahiti 17°49S 149°12W 59 d
Roorkee India 29°52N 77°59E 42 E7
Roosendaal Neths. 51°32N 4°29E 15 C4
Roosevelt U.S.A. 40°18N 109°59W 76 F9
Roosevelt → Brazil 7°35S 60°20W 92 E6
Roosevelt, Mt. Canada 58°26N 125°20W 70 B3
Roosevelt I. Antarctica 79°30S 162°0W 5 D12
Roper → Australia 14°43S 135°27E 62 A2
Roper Bar Australia 14°44S 134°44E 62 A1
Roque Pérez Argentina 35°25S 59°24W 94 D4
Roquetas de Mar Spain 36°46N 2°36W 21 D4
Roraima □ Brazil 2°0N 61°30W 92 C6
Roraima, Mt. Venezuela 5°10N 60°40W 92 B6
Røros Norway 62°35N 11°23E 8 E14
Rosa Zambia 9°33S 31°15E 55 D3
Rosa, Monte Europe 45°57N 7°53E 20 D7
Rosalia U.S.A. 47°14N 117°22W 76 C5
Rosamond U.S.A. 34°52N 118°10W 79 L8
Rosario Argentina 33°0S 60°40W 94 C3
Rosário Brazil 3°0S 44°15W 93 D10
Rosario Baja Calif., Mexico 30°0N 115°50W 86 B1
Rosario Sinaloa, Mexico 22°58N 105°53W 86 C3
Rosario Paraguay 24°30S 57°35W 94 A4
Rosario de la Frontera Argentina 25°50S 65°0W 94 B3
Rosario de Lerma Argentina 24°59S 65°35W 94 A2
Rosario del Tala Argentina 32°20S 59°10W 94 C4
Rosário do Sul Brazil 30°15S 54°55W 95 C5
Rosarito Mexico 32°20N 117°2W 79 N9
Roscoe U.S.A. 41°56N 74°55W 83 E10
Roscommon Ireland 53°38N 8°11W 10 C3
Roscommon □ Ireland 53°49N 8°23W 10 C3
Roscrea Ireland 52°57N 7°49W 10 D4
Rose → Australia 14°16S 135°45E 62 A2
Rose, L. Bahamas 21°0N 73°30W 89 B5
Rose Belle Mauritius 20°24S 57°36E 53 d
Rose Blanche Canada 47°38N 58°45W 73 C8
Rose Hill Mauritius 20°14S 57°27E 53 d
Rose Pt. Canada 54°11N 131°39W 70 C2
Rose Valley Canada 52°19N 103°49W 71 C8
Roseau Dominica 15°17N 61°24W 89 C7
Roseau U.S.A. 48°51N 95°46W 80 A6
Rosebery Australia 41°46S 145°33E 63 G4
Rosebud S. Dak., U.S.A. 43°14N 100°51W 80 D3
Rosebud Tex., U.S.A. 31°4N 96°59W 84 F6
Roseburg U.S.A. 43°13N 123°20W 76 E2
Rosedale U.S.A. 33°51N 91°2W 85 E9
Rosehearty U.K. 57°42N 2°7W 11 D6
Roseires Res. Sudan 11°51N 34°23E 51 F12
Roseland U.S.A. 38°25N 122°43W 78 G4
Rosemary Canada 50°46N 112°5W 70 C6
Rosenberg U.S.A. 29°34N 95°49W 84 G7
Rosenheim Germany 47°51N 12°7E 16 E7
Roses, G. de Spain 42°10N 3°15E 21 A7
Rosetown Canada 51°35N 107°59W 71 C7
Roseville Calif., U.S.A. 38°45N 121°17W 78 G5
Roseville Mich., U.S.A. 42°30N 82°56W 82 D2
Roseville Pa., U.S.A. 41°51N 76°57W 83 E8
Rosewood Australia 27°38S 152°36E 63 D5
Roshkhvār Iran 34°58N 59°37E 45 C8
Rosignano Maríttimo Italy 43°24N 10°28E 22 C4
Rosignol Guyana 6°15N 57°30W 92 B7
Roşiori de Vede Romania 44°9N 25°0E 17 F13
Roskilde Denmark 55°38N 12°3E 9 J15
Roslavl Russia 53°57N 32°55E 18 D5
Rosmead S. Africa 31°29S 25°8E 56 E4
Ross Australia 42°2S 147°30E 63 G4
Ross N.Z. 42°53S 170°49E 59 E3
Ross Dependency Antarctica 76°0S 170°0W 5 D12
Ross I. Antarctica 77°30S 168°0E 5 D11
Ross Ice Shelf Antarctica 80°0S 180°0E 5 E12
Ross L. U.S.A. 48°44N 121°4W 76 B3
Ross-on-Wye U.K. 51°54N 2°34W 13 F5
Ross River Australia 23°44S 134°30E 62 C1
Ross River Canada 62°30N 131°30W 70 A2
Ross Sea Antarctica 74°0S 178°0E 5 D11
Rossall Pt. U.K. 53°55N 3°3W 12 D4
Rossan Pt. Ireland 54°42N 8°47W 10 B3
Rossano Italy 39°36N 16°39E 22 E7
Rossburn Canada 50°40N 100°49W 71 C8
Rosseau Canada 45°16N 79°39W 82 A5
Rosseau, L. Canada 45°10N 79°35W 82 A5
Rosses, The Ireland 55°2N 8°20W 10 A3
Rossignol, L. Canada 52°43N 73°40W 72 B5
Rossignol L. Canada 44°12N 65°10W 73 D6
Rossiya = Russia ■ Eurasia 62°0N 105°0E 29 C11
Rossland Canada 49°6N 117°50W 70 D5
Rosslare Ireland 52°17N 6°24W 10 D5
Rosslare Harbour Ireland 52°15N 6°20W 10 D5
Rossmore Canada 44°8N 77°23W 82 B7
Rosso Mauritania 16°40N 15°45W 50 E2
Rossosh Russia 50°15N 39°28E 19 D6
Røssvatnet Norway 65°45N 14°5E 8 D16
Røst Norway 67°32N 12°0E 8 C15
Rosthern Canada 52°40N 106°20W 71 C7
Rostock Germany 54°5N 12°8E 16 A7
Rostov Don, Russia 47°15N 39°45E 19 E6
Rostov Yaroslavl, Russia 57°14N 39°25E 18 C6
Roswell Ga., U.S.A. 34°2N 84°22W 85 D12
Roswell N. Mex., U.S.A. 33°24N 104°32W 77 K11
Rotan U.S.A. 32°51N 100°28W 84 E4
Rother → U.K. 50°59N 0°45E 13 G8
Rothera Antarctica 67°34S 68°8W 5 C17
Rotherham U.K. 53°26N 1°20W 12 D6
Rothes U.K. 57°32N 3°13W 11 D5
Rothesay Canada 45°23N 66°0W 73 C6
Rothesay U.K. 55°50N 5°3W 11 F3
Roti Indonesia 10°50S 123°0E 37 F6
Roto Australia 33°0S 145°30E 63 E4
Rotondo, Mte. France 42°14N 9°8E 20 E8
Rotoroa, L. N.Z. 41°55S 172°39E 59 D4
Rotorua N.Z. 38°9S 176°16E 59 C6
Rotorua, L. N.Z. 38°5S 176°18E 59 C6
Rotterdam Neths. 51°55N 4°30E 15 C4
Rotterdam U.S.A. 42°48N 74°1W 83 D10
Rottnest I. Australia 32°0S 115°27E 61 F2
Rottumeroog Neths. 53°33N 6°34E 15 A6
Rottweil Germany 48°9N 8°37E 16 D5
Rotuma Fiji 12°25S 177°5E 58 C10
Roubaix France 50°40N 3°10E 20 A5
Rouen France 49°27N 1°4E 20 B4
Rouleau Canada 50°10N 104°56W 71 C8
Round I. Mauritius 19°51S 57°45E 53 d
Round Mountain U.S.A. 38°43N 117°4W 76 G5
Round Mt. Australia 30°26S 152°16E 63 E5
Round Rock U.S.A. 30°31N 97°41W 84 F6
Roundup U.S.A. 46°27N 108°33W 76 C9
Rousay U.K. 59°10N 3°2W 11 B5
Rouses Point U.S.A. 44°59N 73°22W 83 B11
Rouseville U.S.A. 41°28N 79°42W 82 E5
Rousse = Ruse Bulgaria 43°48N 25°59E 23 C12
Roussillon France 42°30N 2°35E 20 E5
Rouxville S. Africa 30°25S 26°50E 56 E4
Rouyn-Noranda Canada 48°20N 79°0W 72 C4
Rovaniemi Finland 66°29N 25°41E 8 C21
Rovereto Italy 45°53N 11°3E 22 B4
Rovigo Italy 45°4N 11°47E 22 B4
Rovinj Croatia 45°5N 13°40E 16 F7
Rovno = Rivne Ukraine 50°40N 26°10E 17 C14
Rovuma = Ruvuma → Tanzania 10°29S 40°28E 55 E5
Row'ān Iran 35°8N 48°51E 45 C6
Rowena Australia 29°48S 148°55E 63 D4
Rowley Shoals Australia 17°30S 119°0E 60 C2
Roxas Phil. 11°36N 122°49E 37 B6
Roxboro U.S.A. 36°24N 78°59W 85 C15
Roxborough Trin. & Tob. 11°15N 60°35W 93 J16
Roxburgh N.Z. 45°33S 169°19E 59 F2
Roxbury N.Y., U.S.A. 42°17N 74°33W 83 D10
Roxbury Pa., U.S.A. 40°6N 77°39W 82 F7
Roxby Downs Australia 30°43S 136°46E 63 E2
Roy Mont., U.S.A. 47°20N 108°58W 76 C9
Roy N. Mex., U.S.A. 35°57N 104°12W 77 J11
Roy Utah, U.S.A. 41°10N 112°2W 76 F7
Royal Bardia △ Nepal 28°20N 81°20E 43 E9
Royal Canal Ireland 53°30N 7°13W 10 C4
Royal Chitawan △ Nepal 26°30N 84°30E 43 F11
Royal Leamington Spa U.K. 52°18N 1°31W 13 E6
Royal Natal △ S. Africa 28°43S 28°51E 57 D4
Royal Tunbridge Wells U.K. 51°7N 0°16E 13 F8
Royale, Isle U.S.A. 48°0N 88°54W 80 B9
Royan France 45°37N 1°2W 20 D3
Royston U.K. 52°3N 0°0 13 E7
Rozdilna Ukraine 46°50N 30°2E 17 E16
Rozhyshche Ukraine 50°54N 25°15E 17 C13
Rtishchevo Russia 52°18N 43°46E 18 D7
Ruacaná Namibia 17°27S 14°21E 56 B1
Ruaha △ Tanzania 7°41S 34°30E 54 D3
Ruahine Ra. N.Z. 39°55S 176°2E 59 C6
Ruapehu N.Z. 39°17S 175°35E 59 C5
Ruapuke I. N.Z. 46°46S 168°31E 59 G2
Ruâq, W. → Egypt 30°0N 33°49E 46 F2
Rub' al Khālī Si. Arabia 19°0N 48°0E 47 D4
Rubeho Mts. Tanzania 6°50S 36°25E 54 D4
Rubh a' Mhail U.K. 55°56N 6°8W 11 F2
Rubha Hunish U.K. 57°42N 6°20W 11 D2
Rubha Robhanais = Lewis, Butt of U.K. 58°31N 6°16W 11 C2
Rubicon → U.S.A. 38°53N 121°4W 78 G5
Rubio Venezuela 7°43N 72°22W 92 B4
Rubondo △ Tanzania 2°18S 31°58E 54 C3
Rubtsovsk Russia 51°30N 81°10E 28 D9
Ruby L. U.S.A. 40°10N 115°28W 76 F6
Ruby Mts. U.S.A. 40°30N 115°20W 76 F6
Rubyvale Australia 23°25S 147°42E 62 C4
Rūd Sar Iran 37°8N 50°18E 45 B6
Rudall Australia 33°43S 136°17E 63 E2
Rudall → Australia 22°34S 122°13E 60 D3
Rudall River △ Australia 22°38S 122°30E 60 D3
Rudbar Iran 36°48N 49°23E 45 B6
Rudewa Tanzania 10°7S 34°40E 55 E3
Rudnyy Kazakhstan 52°57N 63°7E 28 D7
Rudolfa, Ostrov Russia 81°45N 58°30E 28 A6
Rudyard U.S.A. 46°14N 84°36W 81 B11
Ruenya → Africa 16°24S 33°48E 55 F3
Ruffling Pt. Br. Virgin Is. 18°44N 64°27W 89 e
Rufiji → Tanzania 7°50S 39°15E 54 D4
Rufino Argentina 34°20S 62°50W 94 C3
Rufunsa Zambia 15°4S 29°34E 55 F2
Rugby U.K. 52°23N 1°16W 13 E6
Rugby U.S.A. 48°22N 100°0W 80 A4
Rügen Germany 54°22N 13°24E 16 A7
Ruhengeri Rwanda 1°30S 29°36E 54 C2
Ruhnu Estonia 57°48N 23°15E 9 H20
Ruhr → Germany 51°27N 6°43E 16 C4
Ruhuhu → Tanzania 10°31S 34°34E 55 E3
Ruidoso U.S.A. 33°20N 105°41W 77 K11
Ruivo, Pico Madeira 32°45N 16°56W 24 D3
Rujm Tal'at al Jamā'ah Jordan 30°24N 35°30E 46 E4
Ruk Pakistan 27°50N 68°42E 42 F3
Rukhla Pakistan 32°27N 71°57E 42 C4
Ruki → Dem. Rep. of the Congo 0°5N 18°17E 52 E3
Rukwa □ Tanzania 7°0S 31°30E 54 D3
Rukwa, L. Tanzania 8°0S 32°20E 54 D3
Rulhieres, C. Australia 13°56S 127°22E 60 B4
Rum = Rhum U.K. 57°0N 6°20W 11 E2
Rum Jordan 29°39N 35°26E 46 F4
Rum Cay Bahamas 23°40N 74°58W 89 B5
Rum Jungle Australia 13°0S 130°59E 60 B5
Ruma △ Kenya 0°39S 34°18E 54 C3
Rumāḥ Si. Arabia 25°29N 47°10E 44 E5
Rumania = Romania ■ Europe 46°0N 25°0E 17 F12
Rumaylah Iraq 30°47N 47°37E 44 D5
Rumbêk Sudan 6°54N 29°37E 51 G11
Rumford U.S.A. 44°33N 70°33W 83 B14
Rumia Poland 54°37N 18°25E 17 A10
Rumoi Japan 43°56N 141°39E 30 C10
Rumonge Burundi 3°59S 29°26E 54 C2
Rumson U.S.A. 40°23N 74°0W 83 F11
Rumuruti Kenya 0°17N 36°32E 54 B4
Runan China 33°0N 114°30E 34 H8
Runanga N.Z. 42°25S 171°15E 59 E3
Runaway, C. N.Z. 37°32S 177°59E 59 B6
Runaway Bay Jamaica 18°27N 77°20W 88 a
Runcorn U.K. 53°21N 2°44W 12 D5
Rundu Namibia 17°52S 19°43E 56 B2
Rungwa Tanzania 6°55S 33°32E 54 D3
Rungwa → Tanzania 7°36S 31°50E 54 D3
Rungwa △ Tanzania 6°53S 34°2E 54 D3
Rungwe Tanzania 9°11S 33°32E 55 D3
Rungwe, Mt. Tanzania 9°8S 33°40E 52 F6
Runton Ra. Australia 23°31S 123°6E 60 D3
Ruo Shui → China 41°0N 100°16E 32 B5
Ruokolahti Finland 61°17N 28°50E 8 F23
Ruoqiang China 38°55N 88°10E 32 C3
Rupa India 27°15N 92°21E 41 F18
Rupar India 31°2N 76°38E 42 D7
Rupat Indonesia 1°45N 101°40E 36 D2
Rupen → India 23°28N 71°31E 42 H4
Rupert U.S.A. 42°37N 113°41W 76 E7
Rupert → Canada 51°29N 78°45W 72 B4
Rupert B. Canada 51°35N 79°0W 72 B4
Rupert House = Waskaganish Canada 51°30N 78°40W 72 B4
Rupsa India 21°37N 87°1E 43 J12
Rurrenabaque Bolivia 14°30S 67°32W 92 F5
Rusambo Zimbabwe 16°30S 32°4E 55 F3
Rusape Zimbabwe 18°35S 32°8E 55 F3
Ruschuk = Ruse Bulgaria 43°48N 25°59E 23 C12
Ruse Bulgaria 43°48N 25°59E 23 C12
Rush Ireland 53°31N 6°6W 10 C5
Rushan China 36°56N 121°30E 35 F11
Rushden U.K. 52°18N 0°35W 13 E7
Rushmore, Mt. U.S.A. 43°53N 103°28W 80 D2
Rushville Ill., U.S.A. 40°7N 90°34W 80 E8
Rushville Ind., U.S.A. 39°37N 85°27W 81 F11
Rushville Nebr., U.S.A. 42°43N 102°28W 80 D2
Russas Brazil 4°55S 37°50W 93 D11
Russell Canada 50°50N 101°20W 71 C8
Russell Kans., U.S.A. 38°54N 98°52W 80 F4
Russell N.Y., U.S.A. 44°27N 75°9W 83 B9
Russell Pa., U.S.A. 41°56N 79°8W 82 E5
Russell Cave △ U.S.A. 34°59N 85°49W 85 D12
Russell L. Man., Canada 56°15N 101°30W 71 B8
Russell L. N.W.T., Canada 63°5N 115°44W 70 A5
Russellkonda India 19°57N 84°42E 41 K14
Russellville Ala., U.S.A. 34°30N 87°44W 85 D11
Russellville Ark., U.S.A. 35°17N 93°8W 84 D8
Russellville Ky., U.S.A. 36°51N 86°53W 80 G10
Russia ■ Eurasia 62°0N 105°0E 29 C11
Russian → U.S.A. 38°27N 123°8W 78 G3
Russkoye Ustye Russia 71°0N 149°0E 4 B15
Rustam Pakistan 34°25N 72°13E 42 B5
Rustam Shahr Pakistan 26°58N 66°6E 42 F2
Rustavi Georgia 41°30N 45°0E 19 F8
Rustenburg S. Africa 25°41S 27°14E 56 D4
Ruston U.S.A. 32°32N 92°38W 84 E8
Rutana Burundi 3°55S 30°0E 54 C3
Ruteng Indonesia 8°35S 120°30E 37 F6
Ruth U.S.A. 43°42N 82°45W 82 C2
Rutherford U.S.A. 38°26N 122°24W 78 G4
Rutland U.S.A. 43°37N 72°58W 83 C12
Rutland □ U.K. 52°38N 0°40W 13 E7
Rutland Water U.K. 52°39N 0°38W 13 E7
Rutledge → Canada 61°4N 112°0W 71 A6
Rutledge L. Canada 61°33N 110°47W 71 A6
Rutog China 33°27N 79°42E 32 C2
Rutshuru Dem. Rep. of the Congo 1°13S 29°25E 54 C2
Ruvu Tanzania 6°49S 38°43E 54 D4
Ruvu → Tanzania 6°23S 38°52E 54 D4
Ruvuba △ Burundi 3°3S 29°33E 54 C2
Ruvuma □ Tanzania 10°20S 36°0E 55 E4
Ruvuma → Tanzania 10°29S 40°28E 55 E5
Ruwais U.A.E. 24°5N 52°50E 45 E7
Ruwenzori Africa 0°30N 29°55E 54 B2
Ruwenzori △ Uganda 0°20N 30°0E 54 B2
Ruya → Zimbabwe 16°27S 32°5E 57 B5

Ruyigi Burundi 3°29S 30°15E 54 C3
Ružomberok Slovak Rep. 49°3N 19°17E 17 D10
Rwanda ■ Africa 2°0S 30°0E 54 C3
Ryan, L. U.K. 55°0N 5°2W 11 G3
Ryazan Russia 54°40N 39°40E 18 D6
Ryazhsk Russia 53°45N 40°3E 18 D7
Rybachiy Poluostrov Russia 69°43N 32°0E 8 B25
Rybachye = Balykchy Kyrgyzstan 42°26N 76°12E 32 B2
Rybinsk Russia 58°5N 38°50E 18 C6
Rybinskoye Vdkhr. Russia 58°30N 38°25E 18 C6
Rybnitsa = Râbniţa Moldova 47°45N 29°0E 17 E15
Rycroft Canada 55°45N 118°40W 70 B5
Ryde U.K. 50°43N 1°9W 13 G6
Ryderwood U.S.A. 46°23N 123°3W 78 D3
Rye U.K. 50°57N 0°45E 13 G8
Rye → U.K. 54°11N 0°44W 12 C7
Rye Bay U.K. 50°52N 0°49E 13 G8
Rye Patch Res. U.S.A. 40°28N 118°19W 76 F4
Ryegate U.S.A. 46°18N 109°15W 76 C9
Ryley Canada 53°17N 112°26W 70 C6
Rylstone Australia 32°46S 149°58E 63 E4
Ryn Peski = Naryn Qum Kazakhstan 47°30N 49°0E 28 E5
Ryōtsu Japan 38°5N 138°26E 30 E9
Rypin Poland 53°3N 19°25E 17 B10
Ryūgasaki Japan 35°54N 140°11E 31 G10
Ryukyu Is. = Ryūkyū-rettō Japan 26°0N 126°0E 31 M3
Ryūkyū-rettō Japan 26°0N 126°0E 31 M3
Rzeszów Poland 50°5N 21°58E 17 C11
Rzhev Russia 56°20N 34°20E 18 C5

S

Sa Thailand 18°34N 100°45E 38 C3
Sa Cabaneta Spain 39°37N 2°45E 24 B9
Sa Canal Spain 38°51N 1°23E 24 C7
Sa Conillera Spain 38°59N 1°13E 24 C7
Sa Dec Vietnam 10°20N 105°46E 39 G5
Sa Dragonera Spain 39°35N 2°19E 24 B9
Sa Kaeo Thailand 13°49N 102°4E 38 F4
Sa Mesquida Spain 39°55N 4°16E 24 B11
Sa Pa Vietnam 22°20N 103°47E 38 A4
Sa Savina Spain 38°44N 1°25E 24 C7
Sa'ādatābād Fārs, Iran 30°10N 53°5E 45 D7
Sa'ādatābād Hormozgān, Iran 28°3N 55°53E 45 D7
Sa'ādatābād Kermān, Iran 29°40N 55°51E 45 D7
Saale → Germany 51°56N 11°54E 16 C6
Saalfeld Germany 50°38N 11°21E 16 C6
Saanich Canada 48°29N 123°26W 78 B3
Saar → Europe 49°41N 6°32E 15 E6
Saarbrücken Germany 49°14N 6°59E 16 D4
Saaremaa Estonia 58°30N 22°30E 9 G20
Saarijärvi Finland 62°43N 25°16E 8 E21
Saariselkä Finland 68°16N 28°15E 8 B23
Sab 'Ābar Syria 33°46N 37°41E 44 C3
Saba W. Indies 17°38N 63°14W 89 C7
Šabac Serbia 44°48N 19°42E 23 B8
Sabadell Spain 41°28N 2°7E 21 B7
Sabah □ Malaysia 6°0N 117°0E 36 C5
Sabak Malaysia 3°46N 100°58E 39 L3
Sabalān, Kūhhā-ye Iran 38°15N 47°45E 44 B5
Sabalana, Kepulauan Indonesia 6°45S 118°50E 37 F5
Sábana de la Mar Dom. Rep. 19°7N 69°24W 89 C6
Sábanalarga Colombia 10°38N 74°55W 92 A4
Sabang Indonesia 5°50N 95°15E 36 C1
Sabará Brazil 19°55S 43°46W 93 G10
Sabarmati → India 22°18N 72°22E 42 H5
Sabattis U.S.A. 44°6N 74°40W 83 B10
Saberania Indonesia 2°5S 138°18E 37 E9
Sabhā Libya 27°9N 14°29E 51 C8
Sabi → India 28°29N 76°44E 42 E7
Sabie S. Africa 25°10S 30°48E 57 D5
Sabinal Mexico 30°57N 107°30W 86 A3
Sabinal U.S.A. 29°19N 99°28W 84 G5
Sabinas Mexico 27°51N 101°7W 86 B4
Sabinas → Mexico 27°37N 100°42W 86 B4
Sabinas Hidalgo Mexico 26°30N 100°10W 86 B4
Sabine → U.S.A. 29°59N 93°47W 84 G8
Sabine L. U.S.A. 29°53N 93°51W 84 G8
Sabine Pass U.S.A. 29°44N 93°54W 84 G8
Sablayan Phil. 12°50N 120°50E 37 B6
Sable Canada 55°30N 68°21W 73 A6
Sable, C. Canada 43°29N 65°38W 73 D6
Sable, C. U.S.A. 25°9N 81°8W 88 A3
Sable I. Canada 44°0N 60°0W 73 D8
Sabrina Coast Antarctica 68°0S 120°0E 5 C9
Sabulubbek Indonesia 1°36S 98°40E 36 E1
Sabzevār Iran 36°15N 57°40E 45 B8
Sabzvārān Iran 28°45N 57°50E 45 D8
Sac City U.S.A. 42°25N 95°0W 80 D6
Săcele Romania 45°37N 25°41E 17 F13
Sacheon S. Korea 35°0N 128°6E 35 G15
Sachigo → Canada 55°6N 88°58W 72 A2
Sachigo, L. Canada 53°50N 92°12W 72 B1
Sachimbo Angola 9°14S 20°16E 52 F4
Sachsen □ Germany 50°55N 13°10E 16 C7
Sachsen-Anhalt □ Germany 52°0N 12°0E 16 C7
Sackets Harbor U.S.A. 43°57N 76°7W 83 C8
Sackville Canada 45°54N 64°22W 73 C7
Saco Maine, U.S.A. 43°30N 70°27W 83 C14
Saco Mont., U.S.A. 48°28N 107°21W 76 B10
Sacramento U.S.A. 38°35N 121°29W 78 G5
Sacramento → U.S.A. 38°3N 121°56W 78 G5
Sacramento Mts. U.S.A. 32°30N 105°30W 77 K11
Sacramento Valley U.S.A. 39°30N 122°0W 78 G5
Sada-Misaki Japan 33°20N 132°5E 31 H6
Sadabad India 27°27N 78°3E 42 F8
Sadani Tanzania 5°58S 38°35E 54 D4
Sadao Thailand 6°38N 100°26E 39 J3
Sadd el Aali Egypt 23°54N 32°54E 51 D12
Saddle Mt. U.S.A. 45°58N 123°41W 78 E3
Sadimi Dem. Rep. of the Congo 9°25S 23°32E 55 D1
Sado Japan 38°0N 138°25E 30 F9
Sadra India 23°21N 72°43E 42 H5
Sadri India 25°11N 73°26E 42 G5
Sæby Denmark 57°21N 10°30E 9 H14
Saegertown U.S.A. 41°43N 80°9W 82 E4
Ṣafājah Si. Arabia 26°25N 39°0E 44 E3
Safata B. Samoa 14°0S 171°50W 59 b
Säffle Sweden 59°8N 12°55E 9 G15
Safford U.S.A. 32°50N 109°43W 77 K9
Saffron Walden U.K. 52°1N 0°16E 13 E8
Safi Morocco 32°18N 9°20W 50 B4
Şafīābād Iran 36°45N 57°58E 45 B8
Safīd Dasht Iran 33°27N 48°11E 45 C6
Safīd Kūh Afghan. 34°45N 63°0E 40 B3
Safīd Rūd → Iran 37°23N 50°11E 45 B6
Safipur India 26°44N 80°21E 43 F9
Şāfītā Syria 34°48N 36°7E 44 C3
Safune Samoa 13°25S 172°21W 59 b
Şafwān Iraq 30°7N 47°43E 44 D5
Sag Harbor U.S.A. 41°0N 72°18W 83 F12
Saga Japan 33°15N 130°16E 31 H5
Saga □ Japan 33°15N 130°20E 31 H5
Sagae Japan 38°22N 140°17E 30 E10
Sagaing Burma 21°52N 95°59E 41 J19
Sagamore U.S.A. 40°46N 79°14W 82 F5
Saganaga L. Canada 48°14N 90°52W 80 A8
Sagar Karnataka, India 14°14N 75°6E 40 M9
Sagar Mad. P., India 23°50N 78°44E 43 H8
Sagara, L. Tanzania 5°20S 31°0E 54 D3
Sagarmatha = Everest, Mt. Nepal 28°5N 86°58E 43 E12
Sagarmatha △ Nepal 27°55N 86°45E 43 F12
Saginaw U.S.A. 43°26N 83°56W 81 D12
Saginaw B. U.S.A. 43°50N 83°40W 81 D12
Saglouc = Salluit Canada 62°14N 75°38W 69 C12
Sagone France 42°7N 8°42E 20 E8
Sagua la Grande Cuba 22°50N 80°10W 88 B3
Saguache U.S.A. 38°5N 106°8W 76 G10
Saguaro △ U.S.A. 32°12N 110°38W 77 K8
Saguenay → Canada 48°22N 71°0W 73 C5
Sagunt Spain 39°42N 0°18W 21 C5
Sagunto = Sagunt Spain 39°42N 0°18W 21 C5
Sagwara India 23°41N 74°1E 42 H6
Sahagún Spain 42°18N 5°2W 21 A3
Saḩam al Jawlān Syria 32°45N 35°55E 46 C4
Sahamandrevo Madag. 23°15S 45°35E 57 C8
Sahand, Kūh-e Iran 37°44N 46°27E 44 B5
Sahara Africa 23°0N 5°0E 50 D6
Saharan Atlas = Saharien, Atlas Algeria 33°30N 1°0E 50 B6
Saharanpur India 29°58N 77°33E 42 E7
Saharien, Atlas Algeria 33°30N 1°0E 50 B6
Saharsa India 25°53N 86°36E 43 G12
Sahasinaka Madag. 21°49S 47°49E 57 C8
Sahaswan India 28°5N 78°45E 43 E8
Saheira, W. el → Egypt 30°5N 33°25E 46 E2
Sahel Africa 16°0N 5°0E 50 E5
Sahibganj India 25°12N 87°40E 43 G12
Sāḩilīyah Iraq 33°43N 42°42E 44 C4
Sahiwal Pakistan 30°45N 73°8E 42 D5
Şahneh Iran 34°29N 47°41E 44 C5
Sahrawi = Western Sahara ■ Africa 25°0N 13°0W 50 D3
Sahuaripa Mexico 29°3N 109°14W 86 B3
Sahuarita U.S.A. 31°57N 110°58W 77 L8
Sahuayo de Díaz Mexico 20°4N 102°43W 86 C4
Sai → India 25°39N 82°47E 43 G10
Sai Buri Thailand 6°43N 101°45E 39 J3
Sai Kung China 22°23N 114°16E 33 G11
Sai Twong △ Thailand 15°56N 101°10E 38 E3
Sai Yok △ Thailand 14°25N 98°40E 38 E2
Sa'id Bundâs Sudan 8°24N 24°48E 51 G10
Sa'īdābād = Sīrjān Iran 29°30N 55°45E 45 D7
Sa'īdābād Iran 36°8N 54°11E 45 B7
Sa'īdīyeh Iran 36°20N 48°55E 45 B6
Saidpur Bangla. 25°48N 89°0E 41 G16
Saidpur India 25°33N 83°11E 43 G10
Saidu Sharif Pakistan 34°43N 72°24E 43 B5
Saigō Japan 36°12N 133°20E 31 F6
Saigon = Thanh Pho Ho Chi Minh Vietnam 10°58N 106°40E 39 G6
Saijō Japan 33°55N 133°11E 31 H6
Saikai △ Japan 33°12N 129°36E 31 H4
Saikanosy Masoala Madag. 15°45S 50°10E 57 B9
Saikhoa Ghat India 27°50N 95°40E 41 F19
Saiki Japan 32°58N 131°51E 31 H5
Şā'īl Si. Arabia 27°28N 41°45E 44 E4
Sailana India 23°28N 74°55E 42 H6
Sailolof Indonesia 1°15S 130°46E 37 E8
Saimaa Finland 61°15N 28°15E 8 F23
Saimen = Saimaa Finland 61°15N 28°15E 8 F23
Şa'in Dezh Iran 36°40N 46°25E 44 B5
St. Abb's Head U.K. 55°55N 2°8W 11 F6
St. Alban's Canada 47°51N 55°50W 73 C8
St. Albans U.K. 51°45N 0°19W 13 F7
St. Albans Vt., U.S.A. 44°49N 73°5W 83 B11
St. Albans W. Va., U.S.A. 38°23N 81°50W 81 F13
St. Alban's Head U.K. 50°34N 2°4W 13 G5
St. Albert Canada 53°37N 113°32W 70 C6
St-André Réunion 20°57S 55°39E 53 c
St. Andrew's Canada 47°45N 59°15W 73 C8
St. Andrews U.K. 56°20N 2°47W 11 E6
St-Anicet Canada 45°8N 74°22W 83 A10
St. Annes Canada 49°40N 96°39W 71 D9
St. Anns B. Canada 46°22N 60°25W 73 C7
St. Ann's Bay Jamaica 18°26N 77°12W 88 a
St. Anthony Canada 51°22N 55°35W 73 B8
St. Anthony U.S.A. 43°58N 111°41W 76 E8
St-Antoine Canada 46°22N 64°45W 73 C7
St. Arnaud Australia 36°40S 143°16E 63 F3
St-Augustin Canada 51°13N 58°38W 73 B8
St-Augustin → Canada 51°16N 58°40W 73 B8
St. Augustine U.S.A. 29°54N 81°19W 85 G14
St. Austell U.K. 50°20N 4°47W 13 G3
St. Barbe Canada 51°12N 56°46W 73 B8
St-Barthélemy W. Indies 17°50N 62°50W 89 C7
St. Bees Hd. U.K. 54°31N 3°38W 12 C4
St. Bees I. Australia 20°56S 149°26E 62 J7
St-Benoît Réunion 21°2S 55°43E 53 c
St. Bride's Canada 46°56N 54°10W 73 C9
St. Brides B. U.K. 51°49N 5°9W 13 F2
St-Brieuc France 48°30N 2°46W 20 B2
St. Catharines Canada 43°10N 79°15W 82 C5
St. Catherines I. U.S.A. 31°40N 81°10W 85 F14
St. Catherine's Pt. U.K. 50°34N 1°18W 13 G6
St-Chamond France 45°28N 4°31E 20 D6
St. Charles Ill., U.S.A. 41°54N 88°19W 80 E9
St. Charles Md., U.S.A. 38°36N 76°56W 81 F15
St. Charles Mo., U.S.A. 38°47N 90°29W 80 F8
St. Charles Va., U.S.A. 36°48N 83°4W 81 G12
St. Christopher-Nevis = St. Kitts & Nevis ■ W. Indies 17°20N 62°40W 89 C7
St. Clair Mich., U.S.A. 42°50N 82°30W 82 D2
St. Clair Pa., U.S.A. 40°43N 76°12W 83 F8
St. Clair → U.S.A. 42°38N 82°31W 82 D2
St. Clair, L. N. Amer. 42°27N 82°39W 82 D2
St. Clairsville U.S.A. 40°5N 80°54W 82 F4
St. Claude Canada 49°40N 98°20W 71 D9
St. Clears U.K. 51°49N 4°31W 13 F3
St-Clet Canada 45°21N 74°13W 83 A10
St. Cloud Fla., U.S.A. 28°15N 81°17W 85 G14
St. Cloud Minn., U.S.A. 45°34N 94°10W 80 C6
St. Cricq, C. Australia 25°17S 113°6E 61 E1
St. Croix U.S. Virgin Is. 17°45N 64°45W 89 C7
St. Croix → U.S.A. 44°45N 92°48W 80 C7
St. Croix Falls U.S.A. 45°24N 92°38W 80 C7
St. David's Canada 48°12N 58°52W 73 C8
St. David's U.K. 51°53N 5°16W 13 F2
St. David's Head U.K. 51°54N 5°19W 13 F2
St-Denis France 48°56N 2°20E 20 B5
St-Denis Réunion 20°52S 55°27E 53 c
St-Denis ✕ (RUN) Réunion 20°53S 55°32E 53 c
St-Dizier France 48°38N 4°56E 20 B6
St. Elias, Mt. U.S.A. 60°18N 140°56W 68 C5
St. Elias Mts. N. Amer. 60°33N 139°28W 70 A1
St-Étienne France 45°27N 4°22E 20 D6
St. Eugène Canada 45°30N 74°28W 83 A10
St. Eustatius W. Indies 17°20N 63°0W 89 C7
St-Félicien Canada 48°40N 72°25W 72 C5
St-Flour France 45°2N 3°6E 20 D5
St. Francis U.S.A. 39°47N 101°48W 80 F3
St. Francis → U.S.A. 34°38N 90°36W 85 D9
St. Francis, C. S. Africa 34°14S 24°49E 56 E3
St. Francisville U.S.A. 30°47N 91°23W 84 F9
St-François, L. Canada 45°10N 74°22W 83 A10
St-Gabriel Canada 46°17N 73°24W 72 C5
St. Gallen = Sankt Gallen Switz. 47°26N 9°22E 20 C8
St-Gaudens France 43°6N 0°44E 20 E4
St. George Australia 28°1S 148°30E 63 D4
St. George N.B., Canada 45°11N 66°50W 73 C6
St. George Ont., Canada 43°15N 80°15W 82 C4
St. George S.C., U.S.A. 33°11N 80°35W 85 E14
St. George Utah, U.S.A. 37°6N 113°35W 77 H7
St. George, C. Canada 48°30N 59°16W 73 C8
St. George, C. U.S.A. 29°40N 85°5W 85 G12
St. George Ra. Australia 18°40S 125°0E 60 C4
St. George's Canada 48°26N 58°31W 73 C8
St-Georges Canada 46°8N 70°40W 73 C5
St. George's Grenada 12°5N 61°43W 89 D7
St. George's B. Canada 48°24N 58°53W 73 C8
St. Georges Basin N.S.W., Australia 35°7S 150°36E 63 F5
St. Georges Basin W. Austral., Australia 15°23S 125°2E 60 C4
St. George's Channel Europe 52°0N 6°0W 10 E6
St. Georges Hd. Australia 35°12S 150°42E 63 F5
St. Gotthard P. = San Gottardo, P. del Switz. 46°33N 8°33E 20 C8
St. Helena Atl. Oc. 15°58S 5°42W 48 H3
St. Helena U.S.A. 38°30N 122°28W 76 G2
St. Helena, Mt. U.S.A. 38°40N 122°36W 78 G4
St. Helena B. S. Africa 32°40S 18°10E 56 E2
St. Helens Australia 41°20S 148°15E 63 G4
St. Helens U.K. 53°27N 2°44W 12 D5
St. Helens U.S.A. 45°52N 122°48W 78 E4
St. Helens, Mt. U.S.A. 46°12N 122°12W 78 D4
St. Helier U.K. 49°10N 2°7W 13 H5
St-Hubert Belgium 50°2N 5°23E 15 D5
St-Hubert Canada 45°29N 73°25W 83 A11
St-Hyacinthe Canada 45°40N 72°58W 72 C5
St. Ignace U.S.A. 45°52N 84°44W 81 C11
St. Ignace I. Canada 48°45N 88°0W 72 C2
St. Ignatius U.S.A. 47°19N 114°6W 76 C6
St. Ives Cambs., U.K. 52°20N 0°4W 13 E7
St. Ives Corn., U.K. 50°12N 5°30W 13 G2
St. James U.S.A. 43°59N 94°38W 80 D6
St-Jean → Canada 50°17N 64°20W 73 B7
St-Jean, L. Canada 48°40N 72°0W 73 C5
St-Jean-Port-Joli Canada 47°15N 70°13W 73 C5
St-Jean-sur-Richelieu Canada 45°20N 73°20W 83 A11
St-Jérôme Canada 45°47N 74°0W 72 C5
St. John Canada 45°20N 66°8W 73 C6
St. John U.S.A. 38°0N 98°46W 80 F4
St. John → N. Amer. 45°12N 66°5W 81 C20
St. John, C. Canada 50°0N 55°32W 73 C8
St. John I. U.S. Virgin Is. 18°20N 64°42W 89 e
St. John's Antigua & B. 17°6N 61°51W 89 C7
St. John's Canada 47°35N 52°40W 73 C9
St. Johns Ariz., U.S.A. 34°30N 109°22W 77 J9
St. Johns Mich., U.S.A. 43°0N 84°33W 81 D11
St. Johns → U.S.A. 30°24N 81°24W 85 F14
St. John's Pt. Ireland 54°34N 8°27W 10 B3
St. Johnsbury U.S.A. 44°25N 72°1W 83 B12
St. Johnsville U.S.A. 43°0N 74°43W 83 C10
St. Joseph Canada 43°24N 81°42W 82 C3
St-Joseph Martinique 14°39N 61°4W 88 c
St-Joseph Réunion 21°22S 55°37E 53 c
St. Joseph La., U.S.A. 31°55N 91°14W 84 F9
St. Joseph Mo., U.S.A. 39°46N 94°50W 80 F6
St. Joseph → U.S.A. 42°7N 86°29W 80 D10
St. Joseph, I. Canada 46°12N 83°58W 72 C3
St. Joseph, L. Canada 51°10N 90°35W 72 B1
St-Jovite Canada 46°8N 74°38W 72 C5
St. Kilda U.K. 57°49N 8°34W 14 C2
St. Kitts & Nevis ■ W. Indies 17°20N 62°40W 89 C7
St. Laurent Canada 50°25N 97°58W 71 C9
St. Lawrence Australia 22°16S 149°31E 62 C4
St. Lawrence Canada 46°54N 55°23W 73 C8
St. Lawrence → Canada 49°30N 66°0W 73 C6
St. Lawrence, Gulf of Canada 48°25N 62°0W 73 C7
St. Lawrence I. U.S.A. 63°30N 170°30W 74 a
St. Lawrence Islands △ Canada 44°27N 75°52W 83 B9
St. Léonard Canada 47°12N 67°58W 73 C6
St-Leu Réunion 21°9S 55°18E 53 c
St. Lewis → Canada 52°26N 56°11W 73 B8
St-Lô France 49°7N 1°5W 20 B3
St-Louis Guadeloupe 15°56N 61°19W 88 b
St-Louis Réunion 21°16S 55°25E 53 c
St. Louis Senegal 16°8N 16°27W 50 E2
St. Louis U.S.A. 38°37N 90°11W 80 F8
St. Louis → U.S.A. 46°44N 92°9W 80 B7
St-Luc Canada 45°22N 73°18W 83 A11
St. Lucia ■ W. Indies 14°0N 60°57W 89 f
St. Lucia, L. S. Africa 28°5S 32°30E 57 D5
St. Lucia Channel W. Indies 14°15N 61°0W 89 D7
St. Maarten ⊠ W. Indies 18°0N 63°5W 89 C7
St. Magnus B. U.K. 60°25N 1°35W 11 A7
St-Malo France 48°39N 2°1W 20 B2
St-Marc Haiti 19°10N 72°41W 89 C5
St. Maries U.S.A. 47°19N 116°35W 76 C5
St-Martin ⊠ W. Indies 18°0N 63°0W 89 C7
St-Martin, C. Martinique 14°52N 61°14W 88 c
St. Martin, L. Canada 51°40N 98°30W 71 C9
St. Martins Barbados 13°5N 59°28W 89 g
St. Mary Pk. Australia 31°32S 138°34E 63 E2
St. Marys Australia 41°35S 148°11E 63 G4
St. Marys Canada 43°20N 81°10W 82 C3
St. Mary's Corn., U.K. 49°55N 6°18W 13 H1
St. Mary's Orkney, U.K. 58°54N 2°54W 11 C6
St. Marys Ga., U.S.A. 30°44N 81°33W 85 F14
St. Marys Pa., U.S.A. 41°26N 78°34W 82 E6
St. Mary's, C. Canada 46°50N 54°12W 73 C9
St. Mary's B. Canada 46°50N 53°50W 73 C9
St. Marys Bay Canada 44°25N 66°10W 73 D6
St-Mathieu, Pte. France 48°20N 4°45W 20 B1
St. Matthew I. U.S.A. 60°24N 172°42W 74 a
St-Maurice → Canada 46°21N 72°31W 72 C5
St. Mawes U.K. 50°10N 5°2W 13 G2
St-Nazaire France 47°17N 2°12W 20 C2
St. Neots U.K. 52°14N 0°15W 13 E7
St-Niklaas Belgium 51°10N 4°8E 15 C4
St-Omer France 50°45N 2°15E 20 A5
St-Pamphile Canada 46°58N 69°48W 73 C6
St-Pascal Canada 47°32N 69°48W 73 C6
St. Paul Canada 54°0N 111°17W 70 C6
St-Paul Réunion 20°59S 55°17E 53 c
St. Paul Minn., U.S.A. 44°56N 93°5W 80 C7
St. Paul Nebr., U.S.A. 41°13N 98°27W 80 E4
St-Paul → Canada 51°27N 57°42W 73 B8
St. Paul, I. Ind. Oc. 38°55S 77°34E 3 F13
St. Paul I. Canada 47°12N 60°9W 73 C7
St. Peter U.S.A. 44°20N 93°57W 80 C7
St. Peter Port U.K. 49°26N 2°33W 13 H5
St. Peters N.S., Canada 45°40N 60°53W 73 C7
St. Peters P.E.I., Canada 46°25N 62°35W 73 C7
St. Petersburg = Sankt-Peterburg Russia 59°55N 30°20E 9 G24
St. Petersburg U.S.A. 27°46N 82°40W 85 H13
St-Phillippe Réunion 21°21S 55°44E 53 c
St-Pie Canada 45°30N 72°54W 83 A12
St-Pierre Martinique 14°45N 61°10W 88 c
St-Pierre Réunion 21°19S 55°28E 53 c
St-Pierre St-P. & M. 46°46N 56°12W 73 C8
St-Pierre, L. Canada 46°12N 72°52W 72 C5
St-Pierre-et-Miquelon ⊠ N. Amer. 46°55N 56°10W 73 C8
St-Quentin Canada 47°30N 67°23W 73 C6
St-Quentin France 49°50N 3°16E 20 B5
St. Regis U.S.A. 47°18N 115°6W 76 C6
St. Regis Falls U.S.A. 44°40N 74°32W 83 B10
St. Sebastien, Tanjon' i Madag. 12°26S 48°44E 57 A8
St-Siméon Canada 47°51N 69°54W 73 C6
St. Simons I. U.S.A. 31°12N 81°15W 85 F14
St. Simons Island U.S.A. 31°9N 81°22W 85 F14
St. Stephen Canada 45°16N 67°17W 73 C6
St. Thomas Canada 42°45N 81°10W 82 D3
St. Thomas I. U.S. Virgin Is. 18°20N 64°55W 89 e
St-Tite Canada 46°45N 72°34W 72 C5
St-Tropez France 43°17N 6°38E 20 E7
St-Troud = St. Truiden Belgium 50°48N 5°10E 15 D5
St. Truiden Belgium 50°48N 5°10E 15 D5
St. Vincent = São Vicente C. Verde Is. 17°0N 25°0W 50 b
St. Vincent, G. Australia 35°0S 138°0E 63 F2
St. Vincent & the Grenadines ■ W. Indies 13°0N 61°10W 89 D7
St. Vincent Passage W. Indies 13°30N 61°0W 89
St-Vith Belgium 50°17N 6°9E 15
St. Walburg Canada 53°39N 109°12W 71
Ste-Agathe-des-Monts Canada 46°3N 74°17W 72
Ste-Anne Guadeloupe 16°13N 61°24W 88
Ste-Anne Seychelles 4°36S 55°31E 53
Ste-Anne, L. Canada 50°0N 67°42W 73
Ste-Anne-des-Monts Canada 49°8N 66°30W 73
Ste. Genevieve U.S.A. 37°59N 90°2W 80
Ste-Marguerite → Canada 50°9N 66°36W 73
Ste-Marie Canada 46°26N 71°0W 73
Ste-Marie Martinique 14°48N 61°1W 88
Ste-Marie Réunion 20°53S 55°33E 53
Ste-Marie, Ile = Nosy Boraha Madag. 16°50S 49°55E 57
Ste-Rose Guadeloupe 16°20N 61°45W 88
Ste-Rose Réunion 21°8S 55°45E 53
Ste. Rose du Lac Canada 51°4N 99°30W 71
Saintes France 45°45N 0°37W 20
Saintes, Îs. des Guadeloupe 15°50N 61°35W 88
Saintfield U.K. 54°28N 5°49W 10
Saintonge France 45°40N 0°50W 20
Saipan N. Marianas 15°12N 145°45E 64
Sairang India 23°50N 92°45E 41 H
Sairecábur, Cerro Bolivia 22°43S 67°54W 94
Saitama Japan 35°54N 139°38E 31
Saitama □ Japan 36°25N 139°30E 31
Saiyid Pakistan 33°7N 73°2E 42
Sajama Bolivia 18°7S 69°0W 92
Sajószentpéter Hungary 48°12N 20°44E 17 D
Sajum India 33°20N 79°0E 43
Sak → S. Africa 30°52S 20°25E 56
Saka Kenya 0°9S 39°20E 54
Sakai Japan 34°34N 135°27E 31
Sakaide Japan 34°19N 133°50E 31
Sakaiminato Japan 35°38N 133°11E 31
Sakākah Si. Arabia 30°0N 40°8E 44
Sakakawea, L. U.S.A. 47°30N 101°25W 80
Sakami → Canada 53°40N 76°40W 72
Sakami, L. Canada 53°15N 77°0W 72
Sakania Dem. Rep. of the Congo 12°43S 28°30E 55
Sakaraha Madag. 22°55S 44°32E 57
Sakartvelo = Georgia ■ Asia 42°0N 43°0E 19
Sakarya Turkey 40°48N 30°25E 19
Sakashima-Guntō Japan 24°46N 124°0E 31
Sakata Japan 38°55N 139°50E 30
Sakchu N. Korea 40°23N 125°2E 35 D
Sakeny → Madag. 20°0S 45°25E 57
Sakha □ Russia 66°0N 130°0E 29 C
Sakhalin Russia 51°0N 143°0E 29 D
Sakhalinskiy Zaliv Russia 54°0N 141°0E 29 D
Šakiai Lithuania 54°59N 23°2E 9 J
Sakon Nakhon Thailand 17°10N 104°9E 38
Sakrand Pakistan 26°10N 68°15E 42
Sakri India 26°13N 86°5E 43 F
Sakrivier S. Africa 30°54S 20°28E 56
Sakti India 22°2N 82°58E 43 H
Sakuma Japan 35°3N 137°49E 31
Sakurai Japan 34°30N 135°51E 31
Sal C. Verde Is. 16°45N 22°55W 50
Sal Rei C. Verde Is. 16°11N 22°53W 50
Sala Sweden 59°58N 16°35E 9 G
Sala Consilina Italy 40°23N 15°36E 22
Sala-y-Gómez Pac. Oc. 26°28S 105°28W 65 K
Sala y Gómez Ridge Pac. Oc. 25°0S 98°0W 65 K
Salaberry-de-Valleyfield Canada 45°15N 74°8W 83 A
Salada, L. Mexico 32°20N 115°40W 77
Saladas Argentina 28°15S 58°40W 94
Saladillo Argentina 35°40S 59°55W 94
Salado → B. Aires, Argentina 35°44S 57°22W 94
Salado → La Pampa, Argentina 37°30S 67°0W 96
Salado → Santa Fe, Argentina 31°40S 60°41W 94
Salado → Mexico 26°52N 99°19W 84
Salaga Ghana 8°31N 0°31W 50
Sālah Syria 32°40N 36°45E 46
Şalāḩ ad Dīn □ Iraq 34°35N 43°35E 44
Salakos Greece 36°17N 27°57E 25
Salālah Oman 16°56N 53°59E 47
Salamanca Chile 31°46S 70°59W 94
Salamanca Spain 40°58N 5°39W 21
Salamanca U.S.A. 42°10N 78°43W 82
Salāmatābād Iran 35°39N 47°50E 44
Salamina Greece 37°56N 23°30E 23 F
Salamis Cyprus 35°11N 33°54E 25 D
Salar de Atacama Chile 23°30S 68°25W 94
Salar de Uyuni Bolivia 20°30S 67°45W 92
Salatiga Indonesia 7°19S 110°30E 37 G
Salavat Russia 53°21N 55°55E 18 D
Salaverry Peru 8°15S 79°0W 92
Salawati Indonesia 1°7S 130°52E 37
Salaya India 22°19N 69°35E 42
Salayar Indonesia 6°7S 120°30E 37
S'Albufera Spain 39°47N 3°7E 24 B
Salcombe U.K. 50°14N 3°47W 13
Saldanha S. Africa 33°0S 17°58E 56
Saldanha B. S. Africa 33°6S 18°0E 56
Saldus Latvia 56°38N 22°30E 9 H
Sale Australia 38°6S 147°6E 63
Salé Morocco 34°3N 6°48W 50
Sale U.K. 53°26N 2°19W 12
Salekhard Russia 66°30N 66°35E 28
Salelologa Samoa 13°41S 172°11W 59
Salem India 11°40N 78°11E 40 P
Salem Ill., U.S.A. 38°38N 88°57W 80

lem *Ind., U.S.A.* 38°36N 86°6W 80 F10
lem *Mass., U.S.A.* 42°31N 70°53W 83 D14
lem *Mo., U.S.A.* 37°39N 91°32W 80 G8
lem *N.H., U.S.A.* 42°45N 71°12W 83 D13
lem *N.J., U.S.A.* 39°34N 75°28W 81 F16
lem *N.Y., U.S.A.* 43°10N 73°20W 83 C11
lem *Ohio, U.S.A.* 40°54N 80°52W 82 F4
lem *Oreg., U.S.A.* 44°56N 123°2W 76 D2
lem *S. Dak., U.S.A.* 43°44N 97°23W 80 D5
lem *Va., U.S.A.* 37°18N 80°3W 81 G13
erno *Italy* 40°41N 14°47E 22 D6
ford *U.K.* 53°30N 2°18W 12 D5
gótarján *Hungary* 48°5N 19°47E 17 D10
gueiro *Brazil* 8°4S 39°6W 93 E11
ibabu *Indonesia* 3°51N 126°40E 37 D7
ibea = Salybia
rin. & Tob. 10°43N 61°2W 93 K15
ida *U.S.A.* 38°32N 106°0W 74 C5
ihli *Turkey* 38°28N 28°8E 23 E13
ihorsk *Belarus* 52°51N 27°27E 17 B14
ima *Malawi* 13°47S 34°28E 53 G6
ina *Italy* 38°34N 14°50E 22 E6
ina *Kans., U.S.A.* 38°50N 97°37W 80 F5
ina *Utah, U.S.A.* 38°58N 111°51W 76 G8
ina Cruz *Mexico* 16°10N 95°12W 87 D5
inas *Brazil* 16°10S 42°10W 93 G10
inas *Ecuador* 2°10S 80°58W 92 D2
inas *U.S.A.* 36°40N 121°39W 78 J5
inas → *Guatemala* 16°28N 90°31W 87 D6
inas → *U.S.A.* 36°45N 121°48W 78 J5
inas, B. de *Nic.* 11°4N 85°45W 88 D2
inas, Pampa de las
rgentina 31°58S 66°42W 94 C2
inas Ambargasta
rgentina 29°0S 65°0W 94 B3
inas de Hidalgo
Mexico 22°38N 101°43W 86 C4
inas Grandes *Argentina* 30°0S 65°0W 94 C3
inas Pueblo Missions △
U.S.A. 34°6N 106°4W 77 J10
inas Valley *U.S.A.* 36°15N 121°15W 78 J5
ine → *Ark., U.S.A.* 33°10N 92°8W 84 E8
ine → *Kans., U.S.A.* 38°52N 97°30W 80 F5
ines, C. de ses *Spain* 39°16N 3°4E 24 B10
inópolis *Brazil* 0°40S 47°20W 93 D9
isbury *Australia* 34°46S 138°38E 63 E2
isbury *U.K.* 51°4N 1°47W 13 F6
isbury *Md., U.S.A.* 38°22N 75°36W 81 F16
isbury *N.C., U.S.A.* 35°40N 80°29W 85 D14
isbury I. *Canada* 63°30N 77°0W 69 C12
isbury Plain *U.K.* 51°14N 1°55W 13 F6
khad *Syria* 32°29N 36°43E 46 C5
a *Finland* 66°50N 28°49E 8 C23
iq = Coral Harbour
anada 64°8N 83°10W 69 C11
isaw *U.S.A.* 35°28N 94°47W 84 D7
uit *Canada* 62°14N 75°38W 69 C12
nās *Iran* 38°11N 44°47E 44 B5
mo *Canada* 49°10N 117°20W 70 D5
mon *U.S.A.* 45°11N 113°54W 76 D7
mon → *Canada* 54°3N 122°40W 70 C4
mon → *U.S.A.* 45°51N 116°47W 76 D5
mon Arm *Canada* 50°40N 119°15W 70 C5
mon Gums *Australia* 32°59S 121°38E 61 F3
mon Pt. *Canada* 43°52N 77°15W 82 C7
mon River Mts.
.S.A. 44°50N 115°30W 76 D6
mon River Res.
.S.A. 43°32N 75°55W 83 C9
o *Finland* 60°22N 23°10E 9 F20
ome *U.S.A.* 33°47N 113°37W 79 M13
n *India* 26°2N 81°27E 43 F9
on-de-Provence *France* 43°39N 5°6E 20 E6
onica = Thessaloniki
reece 40°38N 22°58E 23 D10
nta *Romania* 46°49N 21°42E 17 E11
ausselkä *Finland* 61°3N 26°15E 8 F22
acate *Argentina* 31°20S 65°5W 94 C2
k *Russia* 46°28N 41°30E 19 E7
o → *Italy* 37°6N 13°57E 22 F5
→ *Canada* 60°0N 112°25W 70 B6
→ *U.S.A.* 33°23N 112°19W 77 K7
Fork Red → *U.S.A.* 34°27N 99°21W 84 D5
L. *Australia* 30°6S 142°8E 63 E3
Lake City *U.S.A.* 40°45N 111°53W 76 F8
Range *Pakistan* 32°30N 72°25E 42 C5
a *Argentina* 24°57S 65°25W 94 A2
a □ *Argentina* 24°48S 65°30W 94 A2
ash *U.K.* 50°24N 4°14W 13 G3
burn by the Sea *U.K.* 54°35N 0°58W 12 C7
coats *U.K.* 55°38N 4°47W 11 F4
ee Is. *Ireland* 52°7N 6°37W 10 D5
jellet *Norway* 66°40N 15°15E 8 C16
jorden *Norway* 67°15N 14°10E 8 C16
llo *Mexico* 25°25N 101°0W 86 B4
o *Argentina* 34°20S 60°15W 94 C3
o *Uruguay* 31°27S 57°50W 94 C4
o → *Italy* 42°26N 12°25E 22 C5
o del Guaíra *Paraguay* 24°3S 54°17W 95 A5
on City *U.S.A.* 33°18N 115°57W 79 M11
on Sea *U.S.A.* 33°15N 115°45W 79 M11
sburg *U.S.A.* 40°29N 79°27W 82 F5
da → *U.S.A.* 34°1N 81°4W 85 D14
m *Egypt* 31°31N 25°7E 51 B11
r *India* 18°27N 83°18E 41 K13
ador *Brazil* 13°0S 38°30W 93 F11
ador *Canada* 52°10N 109°32W 71 C7
ador, El ■
nt. Amer. 13°50N 89°0W 88 D2
ador, L. *U.S.A.* 29°43N 90°15W 85 G9
een → *Burma* 16°31N 97°37E 41 L20
an *Azerbaijan* 39°33N 48°59E 45 B6
bia *Trin. & Tob.* 10°43N 61°2W 93 K15
ach → *Austria* 48°12N 12°56E 16 D7
burg *Austria* 47°48N 13°2E 16 E7
gitter *Germany* 52°9N 10°19E 16 B6
wedel *Germany* 52°52N 11°10E 16 B6
Sam *India* 26°50N 70°31E 42 F4
Sam Neua *Laos* 20°29N 104°5E 38 B5
Sam Ngao *Thailand* 17°18N 99°0E 38 D2
Sam Rayburn Res. *U.S.A.* 31°4N 94°5W 84 F7
Sam Son *Vietnam* 19°44N 105°54E 38 C5
Sam Teu *Laos* 19°59N 104°38E 38 C5
Sama de Langreo = Langreo
Spain 43°18N 5°40W 21 A3
Samagaltay *Russia* 50°36N 95°3E 29 D10
Samales Group *Phil.* 6°0N 122°0E 37 C6
Samana *India* 30°10N 76°13E 42 D7
Samana Cay *Bahamas* 23°3N 73°45W 89 B5
Samanga *Tanzania* 8°20S 39°13E 55 D4
Samangān □ *Afghan.* 36°15N 68°3E 40 B5
Samangwa
Dem. Rep. of the Congo 4°23S 24°10E 54 C1
Samani *Japan* 42°7N 142°56E 30 C11
Samar *Phil.* 12°0N 125°0E 37 B7
Samara *Russia* 53°8N 50°6E 18 D9
Samaria = Shōmrōn
West Bank 32°15N 35°13E 46 C4
Samaria △ *Greece* 35°17N 23°58E 25 D5
Samarinda *Indonesia* 0°30S 117°9E 36 E5
Samarkand = Samarqand
Uzbekistan 39°40N 66°55E 28 F7
Samarqand *Uzbekistan* 39°40N 66°55E 28 F7
Sāmarrā' *Iraq* 34°12N 43°52E 44 C4
Samastipur *India* 25°50N 85°50E 43 G11
Samba
Dem. Rep. of the Congo 4°38S 26°22E 54 C2
Samba *India* 32°32N 75°10E 43 C6
Sambalpur *India* 21°28N 84°4E 41 J14
Sambar, Tanjung
Indonesia 2°59S 110°19E 36 E4
Sambas *Indonesia* 1°20N 109°20E 36 D3
Sambava *Madag.* 14°16S 50°10E 57 A9
Sambawizi *Zimbabwe* 18°24S 26°13E 55 F2
Sambhal *India* 28°35N 78°37E 43 E8
Sambhar *India* 26°52N 75°6E 42 F6
Sambhar L. *India* 26°55N 75°12E 42 F6
Sambiase *Italy* 38°58N 16°17E 22 E7
Sambir *Ukraine* 49°30N 23°10E 17 D12
Sambor *Cambodia* 12°46N 106°0E 38 F6
Samborombón, B.
Argentina 36°5S 57°20W 94 D4
Samburu △ *Kenya* 0°37N 37°31E 54 B4
Samcheok *S. Korea* 37°30N 129°10E 35 F15
Same *Tanzania* 4°2S 37°38E 54 C4
Samfya *Zambia* 11°22S 29°31E 55 E2
Samnah *Si. Arabia* 25°10N 37°15E 44 E3
Samo Alto *Chile* 30°22S 71°0W 94 C1
Samoa ■ *Pac. Oc.* 14°0S 172°0W 59 b
Samokov *Bulgaria* 42°18N 23°35E 23 C10
Samos *Greece* 37°45N 26°50E 23 F12
Samothráki = Mathraki
Greece 39°48N 19°31E 25 A3
Samothraki *Greece* 40°28N 25°28E 23 D11
Sampacho *Argentina* 33°20S 64°50W 94 C3
Sampalan *Indonesia* 8°41S 115°34E 37 K18
Sampang *Indonesia* 7°11S 113°13E 37 G15
Sampit *Indonesia* 2°34S 113°0E 36 E4
Sampit, Teluk *Indonesia* 3°5S 113°3E 36 E4
Samrong *Cambodia* 14°15N 103°30E 38 E4
Samrong *Thailand* 15°10N 100°40E 38 E3
Samsø *Denmark* 55°50N 10°35E 9 J14
Samsun *Turkey* 41°15N 36°22E 19 F6
Samui, Ko *Thailand* 9°30N 100°0E 39 b
Samusole
Dem. Rep. of the Congo 10°2S 24°0E 55 E1
Samut Prakan *Thailand* 13°32N 100°40E 38 F3
Samut Songkhram
Thailand 13°24N 100°1E 38 F3
Samwari *Pakistan* 28°30N 66°46E 42 E2
San *Mali* 13°15N 4°57W 50 F5
San → *Cambodia* 13°32N 105°57E 38 F5
San → *Poland* 50°45N 21°51E 17 C11
San Agustin, C. *Phil.* 6°20N 126°13E 37 C7
San Agustín de Valle Fértil
Argentina 30°35S 67°30W 94 C2
San Ambrosio *Pac. Oc.* 26°28S 79°53W 90 F3
San Andreas *U.S.A.* 38°12N 120°41W 78 G6
San Andrés, I. de
Caribbean 12°42N 81°46W 88 D3
San Andres Mts.
U.S.A. 33°0N 106°30W 77 K10
San Andrés Tuxtla
Mexico 18°27N 95°13W 87 D5
San Angelo *U.S.A.* 31°28N 100°26W 84 F4
San Anselmo *U.S.A.* 37°59N 122°34W 78 H4
San Antonio *Belize* 16°15N 89°2W 87 D7
San Antonio *Chile* 33°40S 71°40W 94 C1
San Antonio *N. Mex.,*
U.S.A. 33°55N 106°52W 77 K10
San Antonio *Tex.,*
U.S.A. 29°25N 98°29W 84 G5
San Antonio → *U.S.A.* 28°30N 96°54W 84 G6
San Antonio, C.
Argentina 36°15S 56°40W 94 D4
San Antonio, C. de *Cuba* 21°50N 84°57W 88 B3
San Antonio, Mt.
U.S.A. 34°17N 117°38W 79 L9
San Antonio de los Baños
Cuba 22°54N 82°31W 88 B3
San Antonio de los Cobres
Argentina 24°10S 66°17W 94 A2
San Antonio Oeste
Argentina 40°40S 65°0W 96 E4
San Ardo *U.S.A.* 36°1N 120°54W 78 J6
San Augustín *Canary Is.* 27°47N 15°32W 24 G4
San Augustine *U.S.A.* 31°32N 94°7W 84 F7
San Bartolomé
Canary Is. 28°59N 13°37W 24 F6
San Bartolomé de Tirajana
Canary Is. 27°54N 15°34W 24 G4
San Benedetto del Tronto
Italy 42°57N 13°53E 22 C5
San Benedicto, I.
Mexico 19°18N 110°49W 86 D2
San Benito *U.S.A.* 26°8N 97°38W 84 H6
San Benito → *U.S.A.* 36°53N 121°34W 78 J5
San Benito Mt. *U.S.A.* 36°22N 120°37W 78 J6
San Bernardino *U.S.A.* 34°7N 117°19W 79 L9
San Bernardino Mts.
U.S.A. 34°10N 116°45W 79 L10
San Bernardino Str. *Phil.* 13°0N 125°0E 37 B7
San Bernardo *Chile* 33°40S 70°50W 94 C1
San Bernardo, I. de
Colombia 9°45N 75°50W 92 B3
San Blas *Mexico* 26°5N 108°46W 86 B3
San Blas, Arch. de
Panama 9°50N 78°31W 88 E4
San Blas, C. *U.S.A.* 29°40N 85°21W 85 G12
San Borja *Bolivia* 14°50S 66°52W 92 F5
San Buenaventura = Ventura
U.S.A. 34°17N 119°18W 79 L7
San Buenaventura
Mexico 27°5N 101°32W 86 B4
San Carlos = Sant Carles
Spain 39°3N 1°34E 24 B8
San Carlos *Argentina* 33°50S 69°0W 94 C2
San Carlos *Chile* 36°10S 72°0W 94 D1
San Carlos *Baja Calif. S.,*
Mexico 24°47N 112°7W 86 C2
San Carlos *Coahuila,*
Mexico 29°1N 100°51W 86 B4
San Carlos *Nic.* 11°12N 84°50W 88 D3
San Carlos *Phil.* 10°29N 123°25E 37 B6
San Carlos *Uruguay* 34°46S 54°58W 95 C5
San Carlos *U.S.A.* 33°21N 110°27W 77 K8
San Carlos *Venezuela* 9°40N 68°36W 92 B5
San Carlos de Bariloche
Argentina 41°10S 71°25W 96 E2
San Carlos de Bolívar
Argentina 36°15S 61°6W 94 D3
San Carlos del Zulia
Venezuela 9°1N 71°55W 92 B4
San Carlos L. *U.S.A.* 33°11N 110°32W 77 K8
San Clemente *Chile* 35°30S 71°29W 94 D1
San Clemente *U.S.A.* 33°26N 117°37W 79 M9
San Clemente I. *U.S.A.* 32°53N 118°29W 79 N8
San Cristóbal = Es Migjorn Gran
Spain 39°57N 4°3E 24 B11
San Cristóbal *Argentina* 30°20S 61°10W 94 C3
San Cristóbal *Dom. Rep.* 18°25N 70°6W 89 C5
San Cristóbal *Solomon Is.* 10°30S 161°0E 58 C9
San Cristóbal *Venezuela* 7°46N 72°14W 92 B4
San Cristóbal de las Casas
Mexico 16°45N 92°38W 87 D6
San Diego *Calif., U.S.A.* 32°42N 117°9W 79 N9
San Diego *Tex., U.S.A.* 27°46N 98°14W 84 H5
San Diego, C. *Argentina* 54°40S 65°10W 96 G3
San Diego de la Unión
Mexico 21°28N 100°52W 86 C4
San Diego Int. ✕ (SAN)
U.S.A. 32°44N 117°11W 79 N9
San Dimitri, Ras *Malta* 36°4N 14°11E 25 C1
San Dimitri Point = San Dimitri,
Ras *Malta* 36°4N 14°11E 25 C1
San Estanislao *Paraguay* 24°39S 56°26W 94 A4
San Felipe *Chile* 32°43S 70°42W 94 C1
San Felipe *Mexico* 31°1N 114°52W 86 A2
San Felipe *Venezuela* 10°20N 68°44W 92 A5
San Felipe → *U.S.A.* 33°10N 115°49W 79 M11
San Félix *Chile* 28°56S 70°28W 94 B1
San Félix *Pac. Oc.* 26°23S 80°0W 90 F2
San Fernando = Sant Ferran
Spain 38°42N 1°28E 24 C7
San Fernando *Chile* 34°30S 71°0W 94 C1
San Fernando *Mexico* 24°51N 98°10W 87 C5
San Fernando *La Union,*
Phil. 16°40N 120°23E 37 A6
San Fernando *Pampanga,*
Phil. 15°5N 120°37E 37 A6
San Fernando *Spain* 36°28N 6°17W 21 D2
San Fernando
Trin. & Tob. 10°16N 61°28W 89 D7
San Fernando *U.S.A.* 34°17N 118°26W 79 L8
San Fernando de Apure
Venezuela 7°54N 67°15W 92 B5
San Fernando de Atabapo
Venezuela 4°3N 67°42W 92 C5
San Francisco *Argentina* 31°30S 62°5W 94 C3
San Francisco *U.S.A.* 37°46N 122°23W 78 H4
San Francisco →
U.S.A. 32°59N 109°22W 77 K9
San Francisco, C. de
Colombia 6°18N 77°29W 90 C3
San Francisco, Paso de
S. Amer. 27°0S 68°0W 94 B2
San Francisco de Macorís
Dom. Rep. 19°19N 70°15W 89 C5
San Francisco del Monte de Oro
Argentina 32°36S 66°8W 94 C2
San Francisco del Oro
Mexico 26°52N 105°51W 86 B3
San Francisco Int. ✕ (SFO)
U.S.A. 37°37N 122°22W 78 H4
San Francisco Javier = Sant
Francesc de Formentera
Spain 38°42N 1°26E 24 C7
San Gabriel *Chile* 33°47S 70°15W 94 C1
San Gabriel Chilac
Mexico 18°19N 97°21W 87 D5
San Gabriel Mts.
U.S.A. 34°17N 117°38W 79 L9
San Gavino Monreale
Italy 39°33N 8°47E 22 E3
San German *Puerto Rico* 18°4N 67°4W 89 d
San Gorgonio Mt.
U.S.A. 34°6N 116°50W 79 L10
San Gottardo, P. del
Switz. 46°33N 8°33E 20 C8
San Gregorio *Uruguay* 32°37S 55°40W 95 C4
San Gregorio *U.S.A.* 37°20N 122°23W 78 H4
San Guillermo △
Argentina 27°50S 69°45W 94 B2
San Ignacio *Belize* 17°10N 89°5W 87 D7
San Ignacio *Bolivia* 16°20S 60°55W 92 G6
San Ignacio *Mexico* 27°27N 112°51W 86 B2
San Ignacio *Paraguay* 26°52S 57°3W 94 B4
San Ignacio, L. *Mexico* 26°54N 113°13W 86 B2
San Ildefonso, C. *Phil.* 16°0N 122°1E 37 A6
San Isidro *Argentina* 34°29S 58°31W 94 C4
San Jacinto *U.S.A.* 33°47N 116°57W 79 M10
San Jaime = Sant Jaume
Spain 39°54N 4°4E 24 B11
San Javier *Misiones,*
Argentina 27°55S 55°5W 95 B4
San Javier *Santa Fe,*
Argentina 30°40S 59°55W 94 C4
San Javier *Bolivia* 16°18S 62°30W 92 G6
San Javier *Chile* 35°40S 71°45W 94 D1
San Jerónimo Taviche
Mexico 16°44N 96°35W 87 D5
San Joaquin *U.S.A.* 36°36N 120°11W 78 J6
San Joaquin → *U.S.A.* 38°4N 121°51W 78 G5
San Joaquin Valley
U.S.A. 37°20N 121°0W 78 J6
San Jon *U.S.A.* 35°6N 103°20W 77 J12
San Jordi = Sant Jordi
Spain 39°33N 2°46E 24 B9
San Jorge *Argentina* 31°54S 61°50W 94 C3
San Jorge, B. *Mexico* 31°20N 113°20W 86 A2
San Jorge, G. *Argentina* 46°0S 66°0W 96 F3
San José = San Josep
Spain 38°55N 1°18E 24 C7
San José *Argentina* 32°12S 58°15W 94 C4
San José *Costa Rica* 9°55N 84°2W 88 E3
San José *Guatemala* 14°0N 90°50W 88 D1
San Jose *Mind. Occ., Phil.* 12°27N 121°4E 37 B6
San Jose *Nueva Ecija,*
Phil. 15°45N 120°55E 37 A6
San Jose *U.S.A.* 37°20N 121°53W 78 H5
San Jose → *U.S.A.* 34°25N 106°45W 77 J10
San José, I. *Mexico* 25°0N 110°38W 86 C2
San Jose de Buenavista
Phil. 10°45N 121°56E 37 B6
San José de Chiquitos
Bolivia 17°53S 60°50W 92 G6
San José de Feliciano
Argentina 30°26S 58°46W 94 C4
San José de Jáchal
Argentina 30°15S 68°46W 94 C2
San José de Mayo
Uruguay 34°27S 56°40W 94 C4
San José del Cabo
Mexico 23°3N 109°41W 86 C3
San José del Guaviare
Colombia 2°35N 72°38W 92 C4
San Josep *Spain* 38°55N 1°18E 24 C7
San Juan *Argentina* 31°30S 68°30W 94 C2
San Juan *Puerto Rico* 18°28N 66°7W 89 d
San Juan *Trin. & Tob.* 10°39N 61°29W 93 K15
San Juan □ *Argentina* 31°9S 69°0W 94 C2
San Juan → *Argentina* 32°20S 67°25W 94 C2
San Juan → *Nic.* 10°56N 83°42W 88 D3
San Juan → *U.S.A.* 37°16N 110°26W 77 H8
San Juan Bautista = Sant Joan de
Labritja *Spain* 39°5N 1°31E 24 B8
San Juan Bautista
Paraguay 26°37S 57°6W 94 B4
San Juan Bautista
U.S.A. 36°51N 121°32W 78 J5
San Juan Capistrano
U.S.A. 33°30N 117°40W 79 M9
San Juan Cr. → *U.S.A.* 35°40N 120°22W 78 J5
San Juan de Guadelupe
Mexico 24°38N 102°44W 86 C4
San Juan de la Costa
Mexico 24°20N 110°41W 86 C2
San Juan de los Lagos
Mexico 21°15N 102°18W 86 C4
San Juan de los Morros
Venezuela 9°55N 67°21W 92 B5
San Juan del Norte *Nic.* 10°58N 83°40W 88 D3
San Juan del Norte, B. de
Nic. 11°0N 83°40W 88 D3
San Juan del Río *Mexico* 20°23N 100°0W 87 C5
San Juan del Sur *Nic.* 11°20N 85°51W 88 D2
San Juan I. *U.S.A.* 48°32N 123°5W 78 B3
San Juan Island △
U.S.A. 48°35N 123°8W 78 B4
San Juan Mts. *U.S.A.* 37°30N 107°0W 77 H10
San Justo *Argentina* 30°47S 60°30W 94 C3
San Kamphaeng *Thailand* 18°45N 99°8E 38 C2
San Lázaro, C. *Mexico* 24°50N 112°18W 86 C2
San Leandro *U.S.A.* 37°42N 122°9W 78 H4
San Lorenzo = Sant Llorenç des
Cardassar *Spain* 39°37N 3°17E 24 B10
San Lorenzo *Argentina* 32°45S 60°45W 94 C3
San Lorenzo *Ecuador* 1°15N 78°50W 92 C3
San Lorenzo *Paraguay* 25°20S 57°32W 94 B4
San Lorenzo → *Mexico* 24°15N 107°24W 86 C3
San Lorenzo, I. *Mexico* 28°38N 112°51W 86 B2
San Lorenzo, Mte.
Argentina 47°40S 72°20W 96 F2
San Lucas = Cabo San Lucas
Mexico 22°53N 109°54W 86 C3
San Lucas *Bolivia* 20°5S 65°7W 92 H5
San Lucas *Mexico* 27°10N 112°14W 86 B2
San Lucas *U.S.A.* 36°8N 121°1W 78 J5
San Lucas, C. *Mexico* 22°52N 109°53W 86 C3
San Luis *Argentina* 33°20S 66°20W 94 C2
San Luis *Cuba* 22°17N 83°46W 88 B3
San Luis *Guatemala* 16°14N 89°27W 88 C2
San Luis *Ariz., U.S.A.* 32°29N 114°47W 77 K6
San Luis *Colo., U.S.A.* 37°12N 105°25W 77 H11
San Luis □ *Argentina* 34°0S 66°0W 94 C2
San Luis, I. *Mexico* 29°58N 114°26W 86 B2
San Luis, Sierra de
Argentina 32°30S 66°10W 94 C2
San Luis de la Paz
Mexico 21°18N 100°31W 86 C4
San Luis Obispo *U.S.A.* 35°17N 120°40W 79 K6
San Luis Potosí *Mexico* 22°9N 100°59W 86 C4
San Luis Potosí □ *Mexico* 23°0N 101°0W 86 C4
San Luis Res. *U.S.A.* 37°4N 121°5W 78 H5
San Luis Río Colorado
Mexico 32°29N 114°58W 86 A2
San Manuel *U.S.A.* 32°36N 110°38W 77 K8
San Marcos *Guatemala* 14°59N 91°52W 88 D1
San Marcos *Calif.,*
U.S.A. 33°9N 117°10W 79 M9
San Marcos *Tex., U.S.A.* 29°53N 97°56W 84 G6
San Marcos, I. *Mexico* 27°13N 112°6W 86 B2
San Marino *San Marino* 43°55N 12°30E 16 G7
San Marino ■ *Europe* 43°56N 12°25E 22 C5
San Martín *Antarctica* 68°11S 67°0W 5 C17
San Martín *Argentina* 33°5S 68°28W 94 C2
San Martín → *Bolivia* 13°8S 63°43W 92 F6
San Martín, L. *Argentina* 48°50S 72°50W 96 F2
San Martín de los Andes
Argentina 40°10S 71°20W 96 E2
San Mateo = Sant Mateu
Spain 39°3N 1°23E 24 B7
San Mateo *U.S.A.* 37°34N 122°19W 78 H4
San Matías *Bolivia* 16°25S 58°20W 92 G7
San Matías, G. *Argentina* 41°30S 64°0W 96 E4
San Miguel = Sant Miquel
Spain 39°3N 1°26E 24 B7
San Miguel *El Salv.* 13°30N 88°12W 88 D2
San Miguel *Panama* 8°27N 78°55W 88 E4
San Miguel *U.S.A.* 35°45N 120°42W 78 K6
San Miguel → *Bolivia* 13°52S 63°56W 92 F6
San Miguel de Tucumán
Argentina 26°50S 65°20W 94 B2
San Miguel del Monte
Argentina 35°23S 58°50W 94 D4
San Miguel I. *U.S.A.* 34°2N 120°23W 79 L6
San Nicolás *Canary Is.* 27°58N 15°47W 24 G4
San Nicolás de los Arroyos
Argentina 33°25S 60°10W 94 C3
San Nicolas I. *U.S.A.* 33°15N 119°30W 79 M7
San Onofre *U.S.A.* 33°22N 117°34W 79 M9
San Pablo *Bolivia* 21°43S 66°38W 94 A2
San Pablo *U.S.A.* 37°58N 122°21W 78 H4
San Pedro *B. Aires,*
Argentina 33°40S 59°40W 94 C4
San Pedro *Misiones,*
Argentina 26°30S 54°10W 95 B5
San Pedro *Chile* 33°54S 71°28W 94 C1
San Pedro *Ivory C.* 4°50N 6°33W 50 H4
San Pedro *Mexico* 23°55N 110°17W 86 C2
San Pedro □ *Paraguay* 24°0S 57°0W 94 A4
San Pedro → *Chihuahua,*
Mexico 28°20N 106°10W 86 B3
San Pedro → *Nayarit,*
Mexico 21°45N 105°30W 86 C3
San Pedro → *U.S.A.* 32°59N 110°47W 77 K8
San Pedro, Pta. *Chile* 25°30S 70°38W 94 B1
San Pedro Channel
U.S.A. 33°30N 118°25W 79 M8
San Pedro de Atacama
Chile 22°55S 68°15W 94 A2
San Pedro de Jujuy
Argentina 24°12S 64°55W 94 A3
San Pedro de las Colonias
Mexico 25°45N 102°59W 86 B4
San Pedro de Macorís
Dom. Rep. 18°30N 69°18W 89 C6
San Pedro del Norte *Nic.* 13°4N 84°33W 88 D3
San Pedro del Paraná
Paraguay 26°43S 56°13W 94 B4
San Pedro Mártir, Sierra
Mexico 31°0N 115°30W 86 A1
San Pedro Mártir △
Mexico 31°0N 115°21W 86 A1
San Pedro Ocampo = Melchor
Ocampo *Mexico* 24°51N 101°39W 86 C4
San Pedro Pochutla
Mexico 15°44N 96°28W 87 D5
San Pedro Sula *Honduras* 15°30N 88°0W 88 C2
San Pedro Tututepec
Mexico 16°9N 97°38W 87 D5
San Pietro *Italy* 39°8N 8°17E 22 E3
San Rafael *Argentina* 34°40S 68°21W 94 C2
San Rafael *Calif., U.S.A.* 37°58N 122°32W 78 H4
San Rafael *N. Mex.,*
U.S.A. 35°7N 107°53W 77 J10
San Rafael Mt. *U.S.A.* 34°41N 119°52W 79 L7
San Rafael Mts. *U.S.A.* 34°40N 119°50W 79 L7
San Ramón de la Nueva Orán
Argentina 23°10S 64°20W 94 A3
San Remo *Italy* 43°49N 7°46E 20 E7
San Roque *Argentina* 28°25S 58°45W 94 B4
San Roque *Spain* 36°17N 5°21W 21 D3
San Rosendo *Chile* 37°16S 72°43W 94 D1
San Saba *U.S.A.* 31°12N 98°43W 84 F5
San Salvador *El Salv.* 13°40N 89°10W 88 D2
San Salvador de Jujuy
Argentina 24°10S 64°48W 94 A3
San Salvador I. *Bahamas* 24°0N 74°40W 89 B5
San Sebastián = Donostia-San
Sebastián *Spain* 43°17N 1°58W 21 A5
San Sebastián *Argentina* 53°10S 68°30W 96 G3
San Sebastián *Puerto Rico* 18°20N 66°59W 89 d
San Sebastián de la Gomera
Canary Is. 28°5N 17°7W 24 F2
San Serra = Son Serra
Spain 39°43N 3°13E 24 B10
San Severo *Italy* 41°41N 15°23E 22 D6
San Simeon *U.S.A.* 35°39N 121°11W 78 K5
San Simon *U.S.A.* 32°16N 109°14W 77 K9
San Telmo = Sant Elm
Spain 39°35N 2°21E 24 B9
San Telmo *Mexico* 30°58N 116°6W 86 A1
San Tiburcio *Mexico* 24°8N 101°32W 86 C4
San Valentín, Mte. *Chile* 46°30S 73°30W 96 F2
San Vicente de Cañete
Peru 13°8S 76°30W 92 F3

San Vicente de la Barquera
Spain 43°23N 4°29W 21 A3
San Vito *Costa Rica* 8°50N 82°58W 88 E3
Sana' *Yemen* 15°27N 44°12E 47 D3
Sana → *Bos.-H.* 45°3N 16°23E 16 F9
Sanae IV *Antarctica* 70°20S 9°0W 5 D2
Sanaga → *Cameroon* 3°35N 9°38E 52 D1
Sanaloa, Presa *Mexico* 24°50N 107°20W 86 C3
Sanana *Indonesia* 2°4S 125°58E 37 E7
Sanand *India* 22°59N 72°25E 42 H5
Sanandaj *Iran* 35°18N 47°1E 44 C5
Sanandita *Bolivia* 21°40S 63°45W 94 A3
Sanawad *India* 22°11N 76°5E 42 H7
Sancellas = Sencelles
Spain 39°39N 2°54E 24 B9
Sanchahe *China* 44°50N 126°2E 35 B14
Sánchez *Dom. Rep.* 19°15N 69°36W 89 C6
Sanchor *India* 24°45N 71°55E 42 G4
Sancti Spíritus *Cuba* 21°52N 79°33W 88 B4
Sancy, Puy de *France* 45°32N 2°50E 20 D5
Sand = Polokwane →
S. Africa 22°25S 30°5E 57 C5
Sand Hills *U.S.A.* 42°10N 101°30W 80 D3
Sand Lakes ⌂ *Canada* 57°51N 98°32W 71 B9
Sand Springs *U.S.A.* 36°9N 96°7W 84 C6
Sanda *Japan* 34°53N 135°14E 31 G7
Sandakan *Malaysia* 5°53N 118°4E 36 C5
Sandan = Sambor
Cambodia 12°46N 106°0E 38 F6
Sandanski *Bulgaria* 41°35N 23°16E 23 D10
Sanday *U.K.* 59°16N 2°31W 11 B6
Sandefjord *Norway* 59°10N 10°15E 9 G14
Sanders *U.S.A.* 35°13N 109°20W 77 J9
Sanderson *U.S.A.* 30°9N 102°24W 84 F3
Sandersville *U.S.A.* 32°59N 82°48W 85 E13
Sandfire Roadhouse
Australia 19°45S 121°15E 60 C3
Sandfly L. *Canada* 55°43N 106°6W 71 B7
Sandfontein *Namibia* 23°48S 19°1E 56 C2
Sandheads, The *India* 21°10N 88°20E 43 J13
Sandía *Peru* 14°10S 69°30W 92 F5
Sandila *India* 27°5N 80°31E 43 F9
Sandnes *Norway* 58°50N 5°45E 9 G11
Sandnessjøen *Norway* 66°2N 12°38E 8 C15
Sandoa
Dem. Rep. of the Congo 9°41S 23°0E 52 F4
Sandomierz *Poland* 50°40N 21°43E 17 C11
Sandover → *Australia* 21°43S 136°32E 62 C2
Sandoway = Thandwe
Burma 18°20N 94°30E 41 K19
Sandoy *Færoe Is.* 61°52N 6°46W 8 F9
Sandpoint *U.S.A.* 48°17N 116°33W 76 B5
Sandray *U.K.* 56°53N 7°31W 11 E1
Sandringham *U.K.* 52°51N 0°31E 12 E8
Sandstone *Australia* 27°59S 119°16E 61 E2
Sandusky *Mich., U.S.A.* 43°25N 82°50W 82 C2
Sandusky *Ohio, U.S.A.* 41°27N 82°42W 82 E2
Sandveld *Namibia* 21°25S 20°0E 56 C3
Sandviken *Sweden* 60°38N 16°46E 8 F17
Sandwich, C. *Australia* 18°14S 146°18E 62 B4
Sandwich B. *Canada* 53°40N 57°15W 73 B8
Sandwich B. *Namibia* 23°25S 14°20E 56 C1
Sandy *Oreg., U.S.A.* 45°24N 122°16W 78 E4
Sandy *Pa., U.S.A.* 41°6N 78°46W 82 E6
Sandy *Utah, U.S.A.* 40°32N 111°50W 76 F8
Sandy Bay *Canada* 55°31N 102°19W 71 B8
Sandy Bight *Australia* 33°50S 123°20E 61 F3
Sandy C. *Queens.,*
Australia 24°42S 153°15E 62 C5
Sandy C. *Tas., Australia* 41°25S 144°45E 63 G3
Sandy Cay *Bahamas* 23°13N 75°18W 89 B4
Sandy Cr. → *U.S.A.* 41°51N 109°47W 76 F9
Sandy Creek *U.S.A.* 43°38N 76°5W 83 C8
Sandy L. *Canada* 53°2N 93°0W 72 B1
Sandy Lake *Canada* 53°0N 93°15W 72 B1
Sandy Valley *U.S.A.* 35°49N 115°38W 79 K11
Sanford *Fla., U.S.A.* 28°48N 81°16W 85 G14
Sanford *Maine, U.S.A.* 43°27N 70°47W 83 C14
Sanford *N.C., U.S.A.* 35°29N 79°10W 85 D15
Sanford → *Australia* 27°22S 115°53E 61 E2
Sanford, Mt. *U.S.A.* 62°13N 144°8W 68 C5
Sang-i-Masha *Afghan.* 33°8N 67°27E 42 C2
Sanga *Mozam.* 12°22S 35°21E 55 E4
Sanga → *Congo* 1°5S 17°0E 52 E3
Sangamner *India* 19°37N 74°15E 40 K9
Sangān *Iran* 34°23N 60°15E 45 C9
Sangar *Afghan.* 32°56N 65°30E 42 C1
Sangar *Russia* 64°2N 127°31E 29 C13
Sangar Sarai *Afghan.* 34°27N 70°35E 42 B4
Sangarh → *Pakistan* 30°43N 70°44E 42 D4
Sangay *Ecuador* 2°0S 78°20W 92 D3
Sange
Dem. Rep. of the Congo 6°58S 28°21E 54 D2
Sangeang *Indonesia* 8°12S 119°6E 37 F5
Sanger *U.S.A.* 36°42N 119°33W 78 J7
Sangerhausen *Germany* 51°28N 11°18E 16 C6
Sanggan He → *China* 38°12N 117°15E 34 E9
Sanggau *Indonesia* 0°5N 110°30E 36 D4
Sanghar *Pakistan* 26°2N 68°57E 42 F3
Sangihe, Kepulauan
Indonesia 3°0N 125°30E 37 D7
Sangihe, Pulau *Indonesia* 3°35N 125°30E 37 D7
Sangju *S. Korea* 36°25N 128°10E 35 F15
Sangkapura *Indonesia* 5°52S 112°40E 36 F4
Sangkhla Buri *Thailand* 14°57N 98°28E 38 E2
Sangkulirang *Indonesia* 0°59N 117°58E 36 D5
Sangla *Pakistan* 31°43N 73°23E 42 D5
Sangli *India* 16°55N 74°33E 40 L9
Sangmélima *Cameroon* 2°57N 12°1E 52 D2
Sangod *India* 24°55N 76°17E 42 G7
Sangre de Cristo Mts.
U.S.A. 37°30N 105°20W 77 H11
Sangre Grande
Trin. & Tob. 10°35N 61°8W 93 K15
Sangrur *India* 30°14N 75°50E 42 D6
Sangudo *Canada* 53°50N 114°54W 70 C6
Sangue → *Brazil* 11°1S 58°39W 92 F7
Sanibel *U.S.A.* 26°27N 82°1W 85 H13
Sanikluaq *Canada* 56°32N 79°14W 72 A4
Sanin-Kaigan △ *Japan* 35°39N 134°37E 31 G7
Sanirajak *Canada* 68°46N 81°12W 69 C11
Sanjawi *Pakistan* 30°17N 68°21E 42 D3
Sanje *Uganda* 0°49S 31°30E 54 C3
Sanjo *Japan* 37°37N 138°57E 30 F9
Sankh → *India* 22°15N 84°48E 43 H11
Sankt Gallen *Switz.* 47°26N 9°22E 20 C8
Sankt Michel = Mikkeli
Finland 61°43N 27°15E 8 F22
Sankt Moritz *Switz.* 46°30N 9°51E 20 C8
Sankt-Peterburg *Russia* 59°55N 30°20E 9 G24
Sankt Pölten *Austria* 48°12N 15°38E 16 D8
Sankuru →
Dem. Rep. of the Congo 4°17S 20°25E 52 E4
Sanliurfa *Turkey* 37°12N 38°50E 44 B3
Sanlúcar de Barrameda
Spain 36°46N 6°21W 21 D2
Sanmenxia *China* 34°47N 111°12E 34 G6
Sanming *China* 26°15N 117°40E 33 D6
Sannicandro Gargánico
Italy 41°50N 15°34E 22 D6
Sânnicolau Mare
Romania 46°5N 20°39E 17 E11
Sannieshof *S. Africa* 26°30S 25°47E 56 D4
Sannīn, J. *Lebanon* 33°57N 35°52E 46 B4
Sanniquellie *Liberia* 7°19N 8°38W 50 G4
Sanok *Poland* 49°35N 22°10E 17 D12
Sanquhar *U.K.* 55°22N 3°54W 11 F5
Sans Souci *Trin. & Tob.* 10°50N 61°0W 93 K16
Sant Antoni de Portmany
Spain 38°59N 1°19E 24 C7
Sant Carles *Spain* 39°3N 1°34E 24 B8
Sant Elm *Spain* 39°35N 2°21E 24 B9
Sant Feliu de Guíxols *Spain* 41°45N 3°1E 21 B7
Sant Ferran *Spain* 38°42N 1°28E 24 C7
Sant Francesc de Formentera
Spain 38°42N 1°26E 24 C7
Sant Jaume *Spain* 39°54N 4°4E 24 B11
Sant Joan *Spain* 39°36N 3°4E 24 B10
Sant Joan de Labritja *Spain* 39°5N 1°31E 24 B8
Sant Jordi *Ibiza, Spain* 38°53N 1°24E 24 C7
Sant Jordi *Mallorca, Spain* 39°33N 2°46E 24 B9
Sant Jordi, G. de *Spain* 40°53N 1°2E 21 B6
Sant Llorenç des Cardassar
Spain 39°37N 3°17E 24 B10
Sant Mateu *Spain* 39°3N 1°23E 24 B7
Sant Miquel *Spain* 39°3N 1°26E 24 B7
Sant Salvador *Spain* 39°27N 3°11E 24 B10
Santa Agnés *Spain* 39°3N 1°21E 24 B7
Santa Ana *Bolivia* 13°50S 65°40W 92 F5
Santa Ana *El Salv.* 14°0N 89°31W 88 D2
Santa Ana *Mexico* 30°33N 111°7W 86 A2
Santa Ana *U.S.A.* 33°46N 117°52W 79 M9
Sant' Antíoco *Italy* 39°4N 8°27E 22 E3
Santa Bárbara *Chile* 37°40S 72°1W 94 D1
Santa Bárbara *Honduras* 14°53N 88°14W 88 D2
Santa Bárbara *Mexico* 26°48N 105°49W 86 B3
Santa Barbara *U.S.A.* 34°25N 119°42W 79 L7
Santa Barbara Channel
U.S.A. 34°15N 120°0W 79 L7
Santa Barbara I. *U.S.A.* 33°29N 119°2W 79 M7
Santa Catalina, Gulf of
U.S.A. 33°10N 117°50W 79 N9
Santa Catalina, I.
Mexico 25°40N 110°47W 86 B2
Santa Catalina I.
U.S.A. 33°23N 118°25W 79 M8
Santa Catarina □ *Brazil* 27°25S 48°30W 95 B6
Santa Catarina, I. de
Brazil 27°30S 48°40W 95 B6
Santa Cecília *Brazil* 26°56S 50°18W 95 B5
Santa Clara *Cuba* 22°20N 80°0W 88 B4
Santa Clara *Calif.,*
U.S.A. 37°21N 121°57W 78 H5
Santa Clara *N.Y.,*
U.S.A. 44°38N 74°27W 83 B10
Santa Clara *Utah, U.S.A.* 37°8N 113°39W 77 H7
Santa Clara de Olimar
Uruguay 32°50S 54°54W 95 C5
Santa Clara Valley
U.S.A. 36°50N 121°30W 78 J5
Santa Clarita *U.S.A.* 34°24N 118°33W 79 L8
Santa Clotilde *Peru* 2°33S 73°45W 92 D4
Santa Coloma de Gramenet
Spain 41°27N 2°13E 21 B7
Santa Cruz *Bolivia* 17°43S 63°10W 92 G6
Santa Cruz *Chile* 34°38S 71°27W 94 C1
Santa Cruz *Costa Rica* 10°15N 85°35W 88 D2
Santa Cruz *Madeira* 32°42N 16°46W 24 D3
Santa Cruz *Phil.* 14°20N 121°24E 37 B6
Santa Cruz *U.S.A.* 36°58N 122°1W 78 J4
Santa Cruz → *Argentina* 50°10S 68°20W 96 G3
Santa Cruz de la Palma
Canary Is. 28°41N 17°46W 24 F2
Santa Cruz de la Palma ✈ **(SPC)**
Canary Is. 28°40N 17°45W 24 F2
Santa Cruz de Tenerife
Canary Is. 28°28N 16°15W 24 F3
Santa Cruz del Norte
Cuba 23°9N 81°55W 88 B3
Santa Cruz del Sur *Cuba* 20°44N 78°0W 88 B4
Santa Cruz do Rio Pardo
Brazil 22°54S 49°37W 95 A6
Santa Cruz do Sul *Brazil* 29°42S 52°25W 95 B5
Santa Cruz I. *U.S.A.* 34°1N 119°43W 79 M7
Santa Cruz Is. *Solomon Is.* 10°30S 166°0E 58 C9
Santa Cruz Mts. *Jamaica* 17°58N 77°43W 88 a
Santa Domingo, Cay
Bahamas 21°25N 75°15W 88 B4
Santa Elena *Argentina* 30°58S 59°47W 94 C4
Santa Elena, C.
Costa Rica 10°54N 85°56W 88 D2
Santa Eulària des Riu
Spain 38°59N 1°32E 24 C8
Santa Fé *Argentina* 31°35S 60°41W 94 C3
Santa Fe *U.S.A.* 35°41N 105°57W 77 J11
Santa Fé □ *Argentina* 31°50S 60°55W 94 C3
Santa Fé do Sul *Brazil* 20°13S 50°56W 93 H8
Santa Filomena *Brazil* 9°6S 45°50W 93 E9
Santa Gertrudis *Spain* 39°0N 1°26E 24 C7
Santa Inês *Brazil* 13°17S 39°48W 93 F11
Santa Inés, I. *Chile* 54°0S 73°0W 96 G2
Santa Isabel *Argentina* 36°10S 66°54W 94 D2
Santa Isabel do Morro
Brazil 11°34S 50°40W 93 F8
Santa Lucía *Corrientes,*
Argentina 28°58S 59°5W 94 B4
Santa Lucía *San Juan,*
Argentina 31°30S 68°30W 94 C2
Santa Lucía *Uruguay* 34°27S 56°24W 94 C4
Santa Lucia Range
U.S.A. 36°0N 121°20W 78 K5
Santa Luzia *C. Verde Is.* 16°50N 24°35W 50 b
Santa Margalida *Spain* 39°42N 3°6E 24 B10
Santa Margarita
Argentina 38°28S 61°35W 94 D3
Santa Margarita
U.S.A. 35°23N 120°37W 78 K6
Santa Margarita →
U.S.A. 33°13N 117°23W 79 M9
Santa Margarita, I.
Mexico 24°27N 111°50W 86 C2
Santa María *Argentina* 26°40S 66°0W 94 B2
Santa Maria *Azores* 36°58N 25°6W 50 a
Santa Maria *Brazil* 29°40S 53°48W 95 B5
Santa Maria *C. Verde Is.* 16°31N 22°53W 50 b
Santa Maria *U.S.A.* 34°57N 120°26W 79 L6
Santa María → *Mexico* 31°0N 107°14W 86 A3
Santa María, B. de
Mexico 25°4N 108°6W 86 B3
Santa Maria da Vitória
Brazil 13°24S 44°12W 93 F10
Santa María del Camí
Spain 39°38N 2°47E 24 B9
Santa Maria di Léuca, C.
Italy 39°47N 18°22E 23 E8
Santa Marta *Colombia* 11°15N 74°13W 92 A4
Santa Marta, Sierra Nevada de
Colombia 10°55N 73°50W 92 A4
Santa Marta Grande, C.
Brazil 28°43S 48°50W 95 B6
Santa Maura = Lefkada
Greece 38°40N 20°43E 23 E9
Santa Monica *U.S.A.* 34°1N 118°29W 79 M8
Santa Monica Mts. ⌂
U.S.A. 34°4N 118°44W 79 L8
Santa Paula *U.S.A.* 34°21N 119°4W 79 L7
Santa Ponça *Spain* 39°30N 2°28E 24 B9
Santa Rosa *La Pampa,*
Argentina 36°40S 64°17W 94 D3
Santa Rosa *San Luis,*
Argentina 32°21S 65°10W 94 C2
Santa Rosa *Brazil* 27°52S 54°29W 95 B5
Santa Rosa *Calif.,*
U.S.A. 38°26N 122°43W 78 G4
Santa Rosa *N. Mex.,*
U.S.A. 34°57N 104°41W 77 J11
Santa Rosa and San Jacinto
Mts. ⌂ *U.S.A.* 33°28N 116°20W 79 M10
Santa Rosa de Copán
Honduras 14°47N 88°46W 88 D2
Santa Rosa de Río Primero
Argentina 31°8S 63°20W 94 C3
Santa Rosa del Sara
Bolivia 17°7S 63°35W 92 G6
Santa Rosa I. *Calif.,*
U.S.A. 33°58N 120°6W 79 M6
Santa Rosa I. *Fla.,*
U.S.A. 30°20N 86°50W 85 F11
Santa Rosa Range
U.S.A. 41°45N 117°40W 76 F5
Santa Rosalía *Mexico* 27°19N 112°17W 86 B2
Santa Sylvina *Argentina* 27°50S 61°10W 94 B3
Santa Tecla = Nueva San
Salvador *El Salv.* 13°40N 89°18W 88 D2
Santa Teresa *Argentina* 33°25S 60°47W 94 C3
Santa Teresa *Australia* 24°8S 134°22E 62 C1
Santa Teresa *Mexico* 25°17N 97°51W 87 B5
Santa Teresa △ *Uruguay* 33°57S 53°31W 95 C5
Santa Teresita *Argentina* 36°32S 56°41W 94 D4
Santa Vitória do Palmar
Brazil 33°32S 53°25W 95 C5
Santa Ynez → *U.S.A.* 34°41N 120°36W 79 L6
Santa Ynez Mts. *U.S.A.* 34°30N 120°0W 79 L6
Santa Ysabel *U.S.A.* 33°7N 116°40W 79 M10
Santai *China* 31°5N 104°58E 32 C5
Santana *Madeira* 32°48N 16°52W 24 D3
Santana, Coxilha de
Brazil 30°50S 55°35W 95 C4
Santana do Livramento
Brazil 30°55S 55°30W 95 C4
Santander *Spain* 43°27N 3°51W 21 A4
Santander Jiménez
Mexico 24°13N 98°28W 87 C5
Santanilla, Is. *Honduras* 17°22N 83°57W 88 C3
Santanyí *Spain* 39°20N 3°5E 24 B10
Santaquin *U.S.A.* 39°59N 111°47W 76 G8
Santarém *Brazil* 2°25S 54°42W 93 D8
Santarém *Portugal* 39°12N 8°42W 21 C1
Santaren Channel
W. Indies 24°0N 79°30W 88 B4
Santee *U.S.A.* 32°50N 116°58W 79 N10
Santee → *U.S.A.* 33°7N 79°17W 85 E15
Santiago = Río Grande de
Santiago → *Mexico* 21°36N 105°26W 86 C3
Santiago = São Tiago
C. Verde Is. 15°0N 23°40W 50 b
Santiago *Brazil* 29°11S 54°52W 95 B5
Santiago *Canary Is.* 28°2N 17°12W 24 F2
Santiago *Chile* 33°26S 70°40W 94 C1
Santiago *Panama* 8°0N 81°0W 88 E3
Santiago → *Peru* 4°27S 77°38W 92 D3
Santiago de Compostela
Spain 42°52N 8°37W 21 A1
Santiago de Cuba *Cuba* 20°0N 75°49W 88 C4
Santiago de los Caballeros
Dom. Rep. 19°30N 70°40W 89 C5
Santiago del Estero
Argentina 27°50S 64°15W 94 B3
Santiago del Estero □
Argentina 27°40S 63°15W 94 B3
Santiago del Teide
Canary Is. 28°17N 16°48W 24 F3
Santiago Ixcuintla
Mexico 21°49N 105°13W 86 C3
Santiago Jamiltepec
Mexico 16°17N 97°49W 87 D5
Santiago Papasquiaro
Mexico 25°3N 105°25W 86 C3
Santiago Pinotepa Nacional
Mexico 16°19N 98°1W 87 D5
Santiaguillo, L. de
Mexico 24°48N 104°48W 86 C4
Santo Amaro *Brazil* 12°30S 38°43W 93 F11
Santo Anastácio *Brazil* 21°58S 51°39W 95 A5
Santo André *Brazil* 23°39S 46°29W 95 A6
Santo Ângelo *Brazil* 28°15S 54°15W 95 B5
Santo Antão *C. Verde Is.* 16°52N 25°10W 50 b
Santo Antônio do Içá
Brazil 3°5S 67°57W 92 D5
Santo Antônio do Leverger
Brazil 15°52S 56°5W 93 G7
Santo Domingo
Dom. Rep. 18°30N 69°59W 89 C6
Santo Domingo *Baja Calif.,*
Mexico 30°43N 116°2W 86 A1
Santo Domingo *Baja Calif. S.,*
Mexico 25°29N 111°55W 86 B2
Santo Domingo *Nic.* 12°14N 84°59W 88 D3
Santo Domingo de los Colorados
Ecuador 0°15S 79°9W 92 D3
Santo Domingo Pueblo
U.S.A. 35°31N 106°22W 77 J10
Santo Tomás *Mexico* 31°33N 116°24W 86 A1
Santo Tomás *Peru* 14°26S 72°8W 92 F4
Santo Tomé *Argentina* 28°40S 56°5W 95 B4
Santo Tomé de Guayana = Ciudad
Guayana *Venezuela* 8°0N 62°30W 92 B6
Santoña *Spain* 43°29N 3°27W 21 A4
Santorini *Greece* 36°23N 25°27E 23 F11
Santos *Brazil* 24°0S 46°20W 95 A6
Santos Dumont *Brazil* 22°55S 43°10W 95 A7
Santuario de Aves Laguna
Colorada △ *Bolivia* 22°10S 67°45W 94 A2
Sanur *Indonesia* 8°41S 115°15E 37 K18
Sanwer *India* 22°59N 75°50E 42 H6
Sanxiang *China* 22°21N 113°25E 33 G9
Sanya *China* 18°14N 109°29E 38 C7
Sanyuan *China* 34°35N 108°58E 34 G5
São Bernardo do Campo
Brazil 23°45S 46°34W 95 A6
São Borja *Brazil* 28°39S 56°0W 95 B4
São Carlos *Brazil* 22°0S 47°50W 95 A6
São Cristóvão *Brazil* 11°1S 37°15W 93 F11
São Domingos *Brazil* 13°25S 46°19W 93 F9
São Filipe *C. Verde Is.* 15°2N 24°30W 50 b
São Francisco *Brazil* 16°0S 44°50W 93 G10
São Francisco →
Brazil 10°30S 36°24W 93 F11
São Francisco do Sul
Brazil 26°15S 48°36W 95 B6
São Gabriel *Brazil* 30°20S 54°20W 95 C5
São Gonçalo *Brazil* 22°48S 43°5W 95 A7
Sao Hill *Tanzania* 8°20S 35°12E 55 D4
São João da Boa Vista
Brazil 22°0S 46°52W 95 A6
São João da Madeira
Portugal 40°54N 8°30W 21 B1
São João del Rei *Brazil* 21°8S 44°15W 95 A7
São João do Araguaia
Brazil 5°23S 48°46W 93 E9
São João do Piauí *Brazil* 8°21S 42°15W 93 E10
São Joaquim *Brazil* 28°18S 49°56W 95 B6
São Joaquim △ *Brazil* 28°12S 49°37W 95 B6
São Jorge *Azores* 38°38N 28°3W 50 a
São Jorge, Pta. de
Madeira 32°50N 16°53W 24 D3
São José *Brazil* 27°38S 48°39W 95 B5
São José do Norte *Brazil* 32°1S 52°3W 95 C5
São José do Rio Preto
Brazil 20°50S 49°20W 95 A6
São José dos Campos
Brazil 23°7S 45°52W 95 A6
São Leopoldo *Brazil* 29°50S 51°10W 95 B5
São Lourenço *Brazil* 22°7S 45°3W 95 A6
São Lourenço → *Brazil* 17°53S 57°27W 93 G7
São Lourenço, Pta. de
Madeira 32°44N 16°39W 24 D3
São Lourenço do Sul
Brazil 31°22S 51°58W 95 C5
São Luís *Brazil* 2°39S 44°15W 93 D10
São Luís Gonzaga *Brazil* 28°25S 55°0W 95 B5
São Marcos → *Brazil* 18°15S 47°37W 93 G9
São Marcos, B. de *Brazil* 2°0S 44°0W 93 D10
São Mateus *Brazil* 18°44S 39°50W 93 G11
São Mateus do Sul
Brazil 25°52S 50°23W 95 B5
São Miguel *Azores* 37°47N 25°30W 50 a
São Miguel do Oeste
Brazil 26°45S 53°34W 95 B5
São Nicolau *C. Verde Is.* 16°20N 24°20W 50 b
São Paulo *Brazil* 23°32S 46°38W 95 A6
São Paulo □ *Brazil* 22°0S 49°0W 95 A6
São Paulo de Olivença
Brazil 3°27S 68°48W 92 D5
São Roque *Madeira* 32°46N 16°48W 24 D3
São Roque, C. de *Brazil* 5°30S 35°16W 93 E11
São Sebastião, I. de
Brazil 23°50S 45°18W 95 A6
São Sebastião do Paraíso
Brazil 20°54S 46°59W 95 A
São Tiago *C. Verde Is.* 15°0N 23°40W 50
São Tomé
São Tomé & Príncipe 0°10N 6°39E 48 F
São Tomé, C. de *Brazil* 22°0S 40°59W 95 A
São Tomé & Príncipe ■
Africa 0°12N 6°39E 49 F
São Vicente *Brazil* 23°57S 46°23W 95 A
São Vicente *C. Verde Is.* 17°0N 25°0W 50
São Vicente *Madeira* 32°48N 17°3W 24 D
São Vicente, C. de *Portugal* 37°0N 9°0W 21 D
Saona, I. *Dom. Rep.* 18°10N 68°40W 89 C
Saône → *France* 45°44N 4°50E 20 D
Saonek *Indonesia* 0°22S 130°55E 37 E
Sapam, Ao *Thailand* 8°0N 98°26E 39
Saparua *Indonesia* 3°33S 128°40E 37 E
Sapele *Nigeria* 5°50N 5°40E 50 G
Sapelo I. *U.S.A.* 31°25N 81°12W 85 F
Sapi ⌂ *Zimbabwe* 15°48S 29°42E 55 F
Saposoa *Peru* 6°55S 76°45W 92 E
Sapphire *Australia* 23°28S 147°43E 62 C
Sappho *U.S.A.* 48°4N 124°16W 78 B
Sapporo *Japan* 43°0N 141°21E 30 C
Sapulpa *U.S.A.* 35°59N 96°5W 84 D
Saqqez *Iran* 36°15N 46°20E 44 B
Sar Dasht *Āzarbāyjān-e Gharbī,*
Iran 36°9N 45°28E 44 B
Sar Dasht *Khuzestān, Iran* 32°32N 48°52E 45 C
Sar-e Pol □ *Afghan.* 36°20N 65°50E 40 B
Sar Gachīneh = Yāsūj
Iran 30°31N 51°31E 45 D
Sar Planina *Macedonia* 42°0N 21°0E 23 C
Sara Buri = Saraburi
Thailand 14°30N 100°55E 38 E
Sarāb *Iran* 37°55N 47°40E 44 B
Sarābādī *Iraq* 33°1N 44°48E 44 C
Saraburi *Thailand* 14°30N 100°55E 38
Saradiya *India* 21°34N 70°2E 42
Saragossa = Zaragoza
Spain 41°39N 0°53W 21 B
Saraguro *Ecuador* 3°35S 79°16W 92 D
Sarahs *Turkmenistan* 36°32N 61°13E 45 B
Sarai Naurang *Pakistan* 32°50N 70°47E 42
Saraikela *India* 22°42N 85°56E 43 H
Sarajevo *Bos.-H.* 43°52N 18°26E 23
Sarakhs = Sarahs
Turkmenistan 36°32N 61°13E 45 B
Saran, Gunung *Indonesia* 0°30S 111°25E 36
Saranac Lake *U.S.A.* 44°20N 74°10W 83 B
Saranac Lakes *U.S.A.* 44°20N 74°28W 83 B
Saranda *Tanzania* 5°45S 34°59E 54
Sarandí del Yí *Uruguay* 33°18S 55°38W 95
Sarandí Grande
Uruguay 33°44S 56°20W 94
Sarangani B. *Phil.* 6°0N 125°13E 37
Sarangani Is. *Phil.* 5°25N 125°25E 37
Sarangarh *India* 21°30N 83°5E 41 J
Saransk *Russia* 54°10N 45°10E 18
Sarapul *Russia* 56°28N 53°48E 18
Sarasota *U.S.A.* 27°20N 82°32W 85 H
Saratoga *Calif., U.S.A.* 37°16N 122°2W 78
Saratoga *Wyo., U.S.A.* 41°27N 106°49W 76 F
Saratoga ⌂ *U.S.A.* 43°0N 73°38W 83 D
Saratoga L. *U.S.A.* 43°1N 73°44W 83 C
Saratoga Springs *U.S.A.* 43°5N 73°47W 83 C
Saratok *Malaysia* 1°55N 111°17E 36
Saratov *Russia* 51°30N 46°2E 19
Sarāvān *Iran* 27°25N 62°15E 45
Saravane *Laos* 15°43N 106°25E 38
Sarawak □ *Malaysia* 2°0N 113°0E 36
Saray *Turkey* 41°26N 27°55E 23 D
Sarayköy *Turkey* 37°55N 28°54E 23 F
Sarbāz *Iran* 26°38N 61°19E 45
Sarbīsheh *Iran* 32°30N 59°40E 45
Sarda → *India* 27°21N 81°23E 43
Sardarshahr *India* 28°30N 74°29E 42
Sardegna □ *Italy* 40°0N 9°0E 22
Sardhana *India* 29°9N 77°39E 42
Sardina, Pta. *Canary Is.* 28°9N 15°44W 24
Sardinia = Sardegna □
Italy 40°0N 9°0E 22
Sardis *Turkey* 38°28N 27°58E 23 E
Sārdūīyeh = Dar Mazār
Iran 29°14N 57°20E 45
Saren *Indonesia* 8°26S 115°34E 37 J
S'Arenal *Spain* 39°30N 2°45E 24
Sarera, G. of *Indonesia* 2°0S 135°0E 58
Sargasso Sea *Atl. Oc.* 27°0N 72°0W 66 G
Sargodha *Pakistan* 32°10N 72°40E 42
Sarh *Chad* 9°5N 18°23E 51
Sārī *Iran* 36°30N 53°4E 45
Saria *India* 21°38N 83°22E 43 J
Sariab *Pakistan* 30°6N 66°59E 42
Sarıgöl *Turkey* 38°14N 28°41E 23 E
Sarikei *Malaysia* 2°8N 111°30E 36
Sarila *India* 25°46N 79°41E 43
Sarina *Australia* 21°22S 149°13E 62
Sarita *U.S.A.* 27°13N 97°47W 84
Sariwŏn *N. Korea* 38°31N 125°46E 35 E
Sarju → *India* 27°21N 81°23E 43
Sark *U.K.* 49°25N 2°22W 13
Sarkari Tala *India* 27°39N 70°52E 42
Şarköy *Turkey* 40°36N 27°6E 23 D
Sarlat-la-Canéda *France* 44°54N 1°13E 20
Sarmi *Indonesia* 1°49S 138°44E 37
Sarmiento *Argentina* 45°35S 69°5W 96
Särna *Sweden* 61°41N 13°8E 8
Sarnia *Canada* 42°58N 82°23W 82
Sarolangun *Indonesia* 2°19S 102°42E 36
Saronikos Kolpos
Greece 37°45N 23°45E 23 F
Saros Körfezi *Turkey* 40°30N 26°15E 23 D
Sarpsborg *Norway* 59°16N 11°7E 9 G
Sarqan *Kazakhstan* 45°24N 79°55E 32
Sarre = Saar → *Europe* 49°41N 6°32E 15
Sarreguemines *France* 49°5N 7°4E 20

ithe → France 47°33N 0°31W 20 C3
una → Pakistan 26°31N 67°7E 42 F2
var India 26°4N 75°0E 42 F6
vestān Iran 29°20N 53°10E 45 D7
y-Tash Kyrgyzstan 39°44N 73°15E 28 F8
yshaghan Kazakhstan 46°12N 73°38E 28 E8
an Gir India 21°10N 70°36E 42 J4
aram India 24°57N 84°5E 43 G11
ebo Japan 33°10N 129°43E 31 H4
er Kangri India 34°50N 77°50E 43 B7
katchewan □
anada 54°40N 106°0W 71 C7
katchewan →
anada 53°37N 100°40W 71 C8
katoon Canada 52°10N 106°38W 71 C7
kylakh Russia 71°55N 114°1E 29 B12
laya △ Nic. 13°45N 85°4W 88 D2
olburg S. Africa 26°46S 27°49E 57 D4
ovo Russia 54°25N 41°55E 18 D7
sandra Ivory C. 4°55N 6°8W 50 H4
sandra → Ivory C. 4°58N 6°5W 50 H4
sari Italy 40°43N 8°34E 22 D3
snitz Germany 54°29N 13°39E 16 A7
suolo Italy 44°33N 10°47E 22 B4
vk, Ozero Ukraine 45°45N 29°20E 17 F15
a-Misaki Japan 31°0N 130°40E 31 J5
adougou Mali 12°25N 11°25W 50 F3
akunda = Satakunta
inland 61°45N 23°0E 8 F20
akunta Finland 61°45N 23°0E 8 F20
ara India 17°44N 73°58E 40 L8
ara S. Africa 24°29S 31°47E 57 C5
arwa India 23°55N 84°16E 43 H11
evó Mexico 27°57N 106°7W 86 B3
illa → U.S.A. 30°59N 81°29W 85 F14
ka Russia 55°3N 59°1E 18 C10
nala Hills Andhra Pradesh,
dia 19°45N 78°45E 40 K11
nala Hills Maharashtra,
dia 20°15N 74°40E 40 J9
na India 24°35N 80°50E 43 G9
oraljaújhely
ungary 48°25N 21°41E 17 D11
ura △ India 22°40N 78°15E 42 H8
ura Ra. India 21°25N 76°10E 40 J10
una-Shotō Japan 30°0N 130°0E 31 K5
ahip Thailand 12°41N 100°54E 38 F3
i Mare Romania 47°46N 22°55E 17 E12
i Indonesia 3°50S 115°27E 36 E5
un Thailand 6°43N 100°2E 39 J3
pa'itea Samoa 13°45S 172°18W 59 b
rnina → Brazil 12°15S 58°10W 92 F7
ce Argentina 30°5S 58°46W 94 C4
ceda Mexico 25°46N 101°19W 86 B4
cillo Mexico 28°1N 105°17W 86 B3
la Norway 59°40N 6°20E 9 G12
Ðarkrókur Iceland 65°45N 19°40W 8 D4
di Arabia ■ Asia 26°0N 44°0E 44 B3
erland Germany 51°12N 7°59E 16 C4
geen → Canada 44°30N 81°22W 82 B3
gerties U.S.A. 42°5N 73°57W 83 D11
gus U.S.A. 34°25N 118°32W 79 L8
k Centre U.S.A. 45°44N 94°57W 80 C6
k Rapids U.S.A. 45°35N 94°10W 80 C6
t Ste. Marie Canada 46°30N 84°20W 72 C3
t Ste. Marie U.S.A. 46°30N 84°21W 81 B11
nlaki Indonesia 7°55S 131°20E 37 F8
mur France 47°15N 0°5W 20 C3
nders, C. N.Z. 45°53S 170°45E 59 F3
nders I. Antarctica 57°48S 26°28W 5 B1
nders Pt. Australia 27°52S 125°38E 61 E4
rimo Angola 9°40S 20°12E 52 F4
salito U.S.A. 37°51N 122°29W 78 H4
Honduras 15°32N 86°15W 88 C2
→ Serbia 44°50N 20°26E 23 B9
ge U.S.A. 47°27N 104°21W 76 C11
ge I. = Niue
c. Oc. 19°2S 169°54W 65 J11
ge River Australia 41°31S 145°14E 63 G4
i'i Samoa 13°28S 172°24W 59 b
llou Benin 7°57N 1°58E 50 G6
ne Mozam. 19°37S 35°8E 55 F4
na U.S.A. 42°5N 90°8W 80 D8
nna-la-Mar Jamaica 18°10N 78°10W 88 a
nnah Ga., U.S.A. 32°5N 81°6W 85 E14
nnah Mo., U.S.A. 39°56N 94°50W 80 F6
nnah Tenn., U.S.A. 35°14N 88°15W 85 D10
nnah → U.S.A. 32°2N 80°53W 85 E14
nnakhet Laos 16°30N 104°49E 38 D5
nt L. Canada 50°16N 90°44W 72 B1
nt Lake Canada 50°14N 90°40W 72 B1
→ Mozam. 21°16S 34°0E 57 C5
h Iran 35°2N 50°20E 45 C6
lugu Ghana 9°38N 0°54W 50 G5
Finland 62°45N 27°30E 8 E22
ie □ France 45°26N 6°25E 20 D7
lax = Savo Finland 62°45N 27°30E 8 E22
na Italy 44°17N 8°30E 20 D8
na U.S.A. 42°17N 77°13W 82 D7
onlinna Finland 61°52N 28°53E 8 F23
y = Savoie □ France 45°26N 6°25E 20 D7
r Turkey 37°34N 40°53E 44 B4
savu Fiji 16°34S 179°15E 59 a
savu B. Fiji 16°45S 179°15E 59 a
hlunto Indonesia 0°40S 100°52E 36 E2
i Indonesia 3°0S 129°5E 37 E7
i Madhopur India 26°0N 76°25E 42 G7
leke Fiji 17°59S 179°18E 59 a
ng Daen Din
ailand 17°28N 103°28E 38 D4
nkhalok Thailand 17°19N 99°50E 38 D2
ra Japan 35°55N 140°30E 31 G10
tch Range U.S.A. 39°0N 106°30W 76 G10
l Mt. U.K. 54°50N 7°2W 10 B4
Thailand 10°14N 99°5E 39 G2
hills Zimbabwe 19°30S 28°2E 55 F2
ooth ⌂ U.S.A. 44°0N 114°50W 76 D6
Sawtooth Range U.S.A. 44°3N 114°58W 76 D6
Sawu Indonesia 10°35S 121°50E 37 F6
Sawu Sea Indonesia 9°30S 121°50E 37 F6
Saxby → Australia 18°25S 140°53E 62 B3
Saxmundham U.K. 52°13N 1°30E 13 E9
Saxony = Sachsen □
Germany 50°55N 13°10E 16 C7
Saxony, Lower =
Niedersachsen □
Germany 52°50N 9°0E 16 B5
Saxton U.S.A. 40°13N 78°15W 82 F6
Sayabec Canada 48°35N 67°41W 73 C6
Sayaboury Laos 19°15N 101°45E 38 C3
Sayán Peru 11°8S 77°12W 92 F3
Sayan, Vostochnyy
Russia 54°0N 96°0E 29 D10
Sayan, Zapadnyy Russia 52°30N 94°0E 32 A4
Sayanogorsk Russia 53°5N 91°23E 29 D10
Saydā Lebanon 33°35N 35°25E 46 B4
Sayhandulaan = Oldziyt
Mongolia 44°40N 109°1E 34 B5
Sayḩūt Yemen 15°12N 51°10E 47 D5
Saylac Somali Rep. 11°21N 43°30E 47 E3
Saynshand = Buyant-Uhaa
Mongolia 44°55N 110°11E 33 B6
Sayre Okla., U.S.A. 35°18N 99°38W 84 D5
Sayre Pa., U.S.A. 41°59N 76°32W 83 E8
Sayreville U.S.A. 40°28N 74°22W 83 F10
Sayula Mexico 19°52N 103°36W 86 D4
Sayward Canada 50°21N 125°55W 70 C3
Sazanit Albania 40°30N 19°20E 23 D8
Sázava → Czech Rep. 49°53N 14°24E 16 D8
Sazin Pakistan 35°35N 73°30E 43 B5
Scafell Pike U.K. 54°27N 3°14W 12 C4
Scalloway U.K. 60°9N 1°17W 11 A7
Scalpay U.K. 57°18N 6°0W 11 D3
Scandia Canada 50°20N 112°2W 70 C6
Scandicci Italy 43°45N 11°11E 22 C4
Scandinavia Europe 64°0N 12°0E 8 E15
Scapa Flow U.K. 58°53N 3°3W 11 C5
Scappoose U.S.A. 45°45N 122°53W 78 E4
Scarba U.K. 56°11N 5°43W 11 E3
Scarborough
Trin. & Tob. 11°11N 60°42W 89 D7
Scarborough U.K. 54°17N 0°24W 12 C7
Scariff I. Ireland 51°44N 10°15W 10 E1
Scarp U.K. 58°1N 7°8W 11 C1
Scebeli = Shabeelle →
Somali Rep. 2°0N 44°0E 47 G3
Schaffhausen Switz. 47°42N 8°39E 20 C8
Schagen Neths. 52°49N 4°48E 15 B4
Schaghticoke U.S.A. 42°54N 73°35W 83 D11
Schefferville Canada 54°48N 66°50W 73 B6
Schelde → Belgium 51°15N 4°16E 15 C4
Schell Creek Ra. U.S.A. 39°25N 114°40W 76 G6
Schellsburg U.S.A. 40°3N 78°39W 82 F6
Schenectady U.S.A. 42°49N 73°57W 83 D11
Schenevus U.S.A. 42°33N 74°50W 83 D10
Schiedam Neths. 51°55N 4°25E 15 C4
Schiermonnikoog Neths. 53°30N 6°15E 15 A6
Schio Italy 45°43N 11°22E 22 B4
Schiphol, Amsterdam ✕ (AMS)
Neths. 52°18N 4°45E 15 B4
Schleswig Germany 54°31N 9°34E 16 A5
Schleswig-Holstein □
Germany 54°30N 9°30E 16 A5
Schœlcher Martinique 14°36N 61°7W 88 c
Schoharie U.S.A. 42°40N 74°19W 83 D10
Schoharie Cr. →
U.S.A. 42°57N 74°18W 83 D10
Scholls U.S.A. 45°24N 122°56W 78 E4
Schouten I. Australia 42°20S 148°20E 63 G4
Schouten Is. = Supiori
Indonesia 1°0S 136°0E 37 E9
Schouwen Neths. 51°43N 3°45E 15 C3
Schreiber Canada 48°45N 87°20W 72 C2
Schroffenstein Namibia 27°11S 18°42E 56 D2
Schroon Lake U.S.A. 43°50N 73°46W 83 C11
Schuler Canada 50°20N 110°6W 71 C6
Schumacher Canada 48°30N 81°16W 72 C3
Schurz U.S.A. 38°57N 118°49W 76 G4
Schuyler U.S.A. 41°27N 97°4W 80 E5
Schuylerville U.S.A. 43°6N 73°35W 83 C11
Schuylkill → U.S.A. 39°53N 75°12W 83 G9
Schuylkill Haven U.S.A. 40°37N 76°11W 83 F8
Schwäbische Alb
Germany 48°20N 9°30E 16 D5
Schwaner, Pegunungan
Indonesia 1°0S 112°30E 36 E4
Schwarzrand Namibia 25°37S 16°50E 56 D2
Schwarzwald Germany 48°30N 8°20E 16 D5
Schwedt Germany 53°3N 14°16E 16 B8
Schweinfurt Germany 50°3N 10°14E 16 C6
Schweiz = Switzerland ■
Europe 46°30N 8°0E 20 C8
Schweizer-Reneke
S. Africa 27°11S 25°18E 56 D4
Schwenningen = Villingen-
Schwenningen Germany 48°3N 8°26E 16 D5
Schwerin Germany 53°36N 11°22E 16 B6
Schwyz Switz. 47°2N 8°39E 20 C8
Sciacca Italy 37°31N 13°3E 22 F5
Scilla Italy 38°15N 15°43E 22 E6
Scilly, Isles of U.K. 49°56N 6°22W 13 H1
Scioto → U.S.A. 38°44N 83°1W 81 F12
Scituate U.S.A. 42°12N 70°44W 83 D14
Scobey U.S.A. 48°47N 105°25W 76 B11
Scone Australia 32°5S 150°52E 63 E5
Scone U.K. 56°25N 3°24W 11 E5
Scoresbysund = Ittoqqortoormiit
Greenland 70°20N 23°0W 4 B6
Scotia Calif., U.S.A. 40°29N 124°6W 76 F1
Scotia N.Y., U.S.A. 42°50N 73°58W 83 D11
Scotia Sea Antarctica 56°5S 56°0W 5 B18
Scotland Canada 43°1N 80°22W 82 C4
Scotland □ U.K. 57°0N 4°0W 11 E5
Scott Antarctica 77°0S 165°0E 5 D11
Scott, C. Australia 13°30S 129°49E 60 B4
Scott City U.S.A. 38°29N 100°54W 80 F3
Scott Glacier Antarctica 66°15S 100°5E 5 C8
Scott I. Antarctica 67°0S 179°0E 5 C11
Scott Is. Canada 50°48N 128°40W 70 C3
Scott L. Canada 59°55N 106°18W 71 B7
Scott Reef Australia 14°0S 121°50E 60 B3
Scottburgh S. Africa 30°15S 30°47E 57 E5
Scottdale U.S.A. 40°6N 79°35W 82 F5
Scottish Borders □ U.K. 55°35N 2°50W 11 F6
Scotts Valley U.S.A. 37°3N 122°1W 78 H4
Scottsbluff U.S.A. 41°52N 103°40W 80 E2
Scottsboro U.S.A. 34°40N 86°2W 85 D11
Scottsburg U.S.A. 38°41N 85°47W 81 F11
Scottsdale Australia 41°9S 147°31E 63 G4
Scottsdale U.S.A. 33°40N 111°53W 77 K8
Scottsville Ky., U.S.A. 36°45N 86°11W 80 G10
Scottsville N.Y., U.S.A. 43°2N 77°47W 82 C7
Scottville U.S.A. 43°58N 86°17W 80 D10
Scranton U.S.A. 41°25N 75°40W 83 E9
Scugog, L. Canada 44°10N 78°55W 82 B6
Scunthorpe U.K. 53°36N 0°39W 12 D7
Scutari = Shkodër
Albania 42°4N 19°32E 23 C8
Sea Is. U.S.A. 31°30N 81°7W 85 F14
Seabrook, L. Australia 30°55S 119°40E 61 F2
Seaford U.K. 50°47N 0°7E 13 G8
Seaford U.S.A. 38°39N 75°37W 81 F16
Seaforth Australia 20°55S 148°57E 62 J6
Seaforth Canada 43°35N 81°25W 82 C3
Seaforth, L. U.K. 57°52N 6°36W 11 D2
Seagraves U.S.A. 32°57N 102°34W 84 E3
Seaham U.K. 54°50N 1°20W 12 C6
Seal → Canada 59°4N 94°48W 71 B10
Seal L. Canada 54°20N 61°30W 73 B7
Sealy U.S.A. 29°47N 96°9W 84 G6
Searchlight U.S.A. 35°28N 114°55W 79 K12
Searcy U.S.A. 35°15N 91°44W 84 D9
Searles L. U.S.A. 35°44N 117°21W 79 K9
Seascale U.K. 54°24N 3°29W 12 C4
Seaside Calif., U.S.A. 36°37N 121°50W 78 J5
Seaside Oreg., U.S.A. 46°0N 123°56W 78 E3
Seaspray Australia 38°25S 147°15E 63 F4
Seattle U.S.A. 47°36N 122°19W 78 C4
Seattle-Tacoma Int. ✕ (SEA)
U.S.A. 47°27N 122°18W 78 C4
Seaview Ra. Australia 18°40S 145°45E 62 B4
Sebago L. U.S.A. 43°52N 70°34W 83 C14
Sebago Lake U.S.A. 43°51N 70°34W 83 C14
Sebastián Vizcaíno, B.
Mexico 28°0N 114°30W 86 B2
Sebastopol = Sevastopol
Ukraine 44°35N 33°30E 19 F5
Sebastopol U.S.A. 38°24N 122°49W 78 G4
Sebewaing U.S.A. 43°44N 83°27W 81 D12
Sebha = Sabhā Libya 27°9N 14°29E 51 C8
Şebinkarahisar Turkey 40°22N 38°28E 19 F6
Sebring Fla., U.S.A. 27°30N 81°27W 85 H14
Sebring Ohio, U.S.A. 40°55N 81°2W 82 F3
Sebringville Canada 43°24N 81°4W 82 C3
Sebta = Ceuta N. Afr. 35°52N 5°18W 21 E3
Sebuku Indonesia 3°30S 116°25E 36 E5
Sebuku, Teluk Malaysia 4°0N 118°10E 36 D5
Sechelt Canada 49°25N 123°42W 70 D4
Sechura, Desierto de Peru 6°0S 80°30W 92 E2
Secretary I. N.Z. 45°15S 166°56E 59 F1
Secunderabad India 17°28N 78°30E 40 L11
Security U.S.A. 38°45N 104°45W 76 G11
Sedalia U.S.A. 38°42N 93°14W 80 F7
Sedan France 49°43N 4°57E 20 B6
Sedan U.S.A. 37°8N 96°11W 80 G5
Sedbergh U.K. 54°20N 2°31W 12 C5
Seddon N.Z. 41°40S 174°7E 59 D5
Seddonville N.Z. 41°33S 172°1E 59 D4
Sedé Boqér Israel 30°52N 34°47E 46 E3
Sedeh Fārs, Iran 30°45N 52°11E 45 D7
Sedeh Khorāsān, Iran 33°20N 59°14E 45 C8
Sederot Israel 31°32N 34°37E 46 D3
Sédhiou Senegal 12°44N 15°30W 50 F2
Sedley Canada 50°10N 104°0W 71 C8
Sedona U.S.A. 34°52N 111°46W 77 J8
Sedova, Pik Russia 73°29N 54°58E 28 B6
Sedro-Woolley U.S.A. 48°30N 122°14W 78 B4
Seeheim Namibia 26°50S 17°45E 56 D2
Seeis Namibia 22°29S 17°39E 56 C2
Seekoei → S. Africa 30°18S 25°1E 56 E4
Seeley's Bay Canada 44°29N 76°14W 83 B8
Seferihisar Turkey 38°10N 26°50E 23 E12
Seg-ozero Russia 63°20N 33°46E 18 B5
Segamat Malaysia 2°30N 102°50E 39 L4
Segesta Italy 37°56N 12°50E 22 F5
Seget Indonesia 1°24S 130°58E 37 E8
Segezha Russia 63°44N 34°19E 18 B5
Ségou Mali 13°30N 6°16W 50 F4
Segovia = Coco →
Cent. Amer. 15°0N 83°8W 88 D3
Segovia Spain 40°57N 4°10W 21 B3
Segre → Spain 41°40N 0°43E 21 B6
Séguéla Ivory C. 7°55N 6°40W 50 G4
Seguin U.S.A. 29°34N 97°58W 84 G6
Segundo → Argentina 30°53S 62°44W 94 C3
Segura → Spain 38°3N 0°44W 21 C5
Seh Konj, Kūh-e Iran 30°6N 57°30E 45 D8
Seh Qal'eh Iran 33°40N 58°24E 45 C8
Sehitwa Botswana 20°30S 22°30E 56 C3
Sehlabathebe △ Lesotho 29°53S 29°7E 57 D4
Sehore India 23°10N 77°5E 42 H7
Sehwan Pakistan 26°28N 67°53E 42 F2
Seikan Tunnel Japan 41°28N 140°10E 30 D10
Seil U.K. 56°18N 5°38W 11 E3
Seiland Norway 70°25N 23°15E 8 A20
Seiling U.S.A. 36°9N 98°56W 84 C5
Seinäjoki Finland 62°40N 22°51E 8 E20
Seine → France 49°26N 0°26E 20 B4
Seistan = Sīstān Asia 30°50N 61°0E 45 D9
Seistan, Daryācheh-ye = Sīstān,
Daryācheh-ye Iran 31°0N 61°0E 45 D9
Sekayu Indonesia 2°51S 103°51E 36 E2
Seke Tanzania 3°20S 33°31E 54 C3
Sekenke Tanzania 4°18S 34°11E 54 C3
Sekondi-Takoradi Ghana 4°58N 1°45W 50 H5
Sekudai Malaysia 1°32N 103°39E 39 d
Sekuma Botswana 24°36S 23°50E 56 C3
Selah U.S.A. 46°39N 120°32W 76 C3
Selama Malaysia 5°12N 100°42E 39 K3
Selaru Indonesia 8°9S 131°0E 37 F8
Selatan, Selat Malaysia 5°15N 100°20E 39 c
Selby U.K. 53°47N 1°5W 12 D6
Selby U.S.A. 45°31N 100°2W 80 C3
Selçuk Turkey 37°56N 27°22E 23 F12
Selden U.S.A. 39°33N 100°34W 80 F3
Sele → Italy 40°29N 14°56E 22 D6
Selebi-Phikwe Botswana 21°58S 27°48E 57 C4
Selemdzha → Russia 51°42N 128°53E 29 D13
Selenga = Selenge Mörön →
Asia 52°16N 106°16E 32 A5
Selenge Mörön → Asia 52°16N 106°16E 32 A5
Seletan, Tanjung
Indonesia 4°10S 114°40E 36 E4
Sélibabi Mauritania 15°10N 12°15W 50 E3
Seligman U.S.A. 35°20N 112°53W 77 J7
Selîma, El Wâhât el
Sudan 21°22N 29°19E 51 D11
Selinda Spillway →
Botswana 18°35S 23°10E 56 B3
Selinsgrove U.S.A. 40°48N 76°52W 82 F8
Selkirk Man., Canada 50°10N 96°55W 71 C9
Selkirk Ont., Canada 42°49N 79°56W 82 D5
Selkirk U.K. 55°33N 2°50W 11 F6
Selkirk I. = Horse I.
Canada 53°20N 99°6W 71 C9
Selkirk Mts. Canada 51°15N 117°40W 68 D8
Sellafield U.K. 54°25N 3°29W 12 C4
Sellia Greece 35°12N 24°23E 25 D6
Sells U.S.A. 31°55N 111°53W 77 L8
Selma Ala., U.S.A. 32°25N 87°1W 85 E11
Selma Calif., U.S.A. 36°34N 119°37W 78 J7
Selma N.C., U.S.A. 35°32N 78°17W 85 D15
Selmer U.S.A. 35°10N 88°36W 85 D10
Selous ⌂ Tanzania 8°37S 37°42E 55 D4
Selowandoma Falls
Zimbabwe 21°15S 31°50E 55 G3
Selpele Indonesia 0°1S 130°5E 37 E8
Selsey Bill U.K. 50°43N 0°47W 13 G7
Seltso Russia 53°22N 34°4E 18 D5
Selu Indonesia 7°32S 130°55E 37 F8
Selva Argentina 29°50S 62°0W 94 B3
Selva Spain 39°46N 2°54E 24 B9
Selva Lancandona = Montes
Azules ⌂ Mexico 16°21N 91°3W 87 D6
Selvagens, Ilhas Madeira 30°5N 15°55W 50 B2
Selvas Brazil 6°30S 67°0W 92 E5
Selwyn L. Canada 60°0N 104°30W 71 B8
Selwyn Mts. Canada 63°0N 130°0W 68 C6
Selwyn Ra. Australia 21°10S 140°0E 62 C3
Seman → Albania 40°47N 19°30E 23 D8
Semarang Indonesia 7°0S 110°26E 37 G14
Sembabule Uganda 0°4S 31°25E 54 C3
Sembawang Singapore 1°27N 103°50E 39 d
Sembung Indonesia 8°28S 115°11E 37 J18
Semenanjung Blambangan
Indonesia 8°42S 114°29E 37 K17
Semeru Indonesia 8°4S 112°55E 37 H15
Semey Kazakhstan 50°30N 80°10E 28 D9
Seminoe Res. U.S.A. 42°9N 106°55W 76 E10
Seminole Okla., U.S.A. 35°14N 96°41W 84 D6
Seminole Tex., U.S.A. 32°43N 102°39W 84 E3
Seminole Draw →
U.S.A. 32°27N 102°20W 84 E3
Semipalatinsk = Semey
Kazakhstan 50°30N 80°10E 28 D9
Semirara Is. Phil. 12°0N 121°20E 37 B6
Semitau Indonesia 0°29N 111°57E 36 D4
Semmering P. Austria 47°41N 15°45E 16 E8
Semnān Iran 35°40N 53°23E 45 C7
Semnān □ Iran 36°0N 54°0E 45 C7
Semporna Malaysia 4°30N 118°33E 37 D5
Semuda Indonesia 2°51S 112°58E 36 E4
Sen → Cambodia 12°32N 104°28E 38 F5
Senā Iran 28°27N 51°36E 45 D6
Sena Mozam. 17°25S 35°0E 55 F4
Sena Madureira Brazil 9°5S 68°45W 92 E5
Senador Pompeu Brazil 5°40S 39°20W 93 E11
Senang, Pulau Singapore 1°11N 103°52E 39 d
Senanga Zambia 16°7S 23°16E 53 H4
Senatobia U.S.A. 34°37N 89°58W 85 D10
Sencelles Spain 39°39N 2°54E 24 B9
Sendai Kagoshima, Japan 31°50N 130°20E 31 J5
Sendai Miyagi, Japan 38°15N 140°53E 30 E10
Sendai-Wan Japan 38°15N 141°0E 30 E10
Sendhwa India 21°41N 75°6E 42 J6
Seneca U.S.A. 34°41N 82°57W 85 D13
Seneca Falls U.S.A. 42°55N 76°48W 83 D8
Seneca L. U.S.A. 42°40N 76°54W 82 D8
Senecaville L. U.S.A. 39°55N 81°25W 82 G3
Senegal ■ W. Afr. 14°30N 14°30W 50 F3
Sénégal → W. Afr. 15°48N 16°32W 50 E2
Senegambia Africa 12°45N 12°0W 48 E2
Senekal S. Africa 28°20S 27°36E 57 D4
Senga Hill Zambia 9°19S 31°11E 55 D3
Senge Khambab = Indus →
Pakistan 24°20N 67°47E 42 G2
Sengua → Zimbabwe 17°7S 28°5E 55 F2
Senhor-do-Bonfim
Brazil 10°30S 40°10W 93 F10
Senigállia Italy 43°43N 13°13E 22 C5
Senj Croatia 45°0N 14°58E 16 F8
Senja Norway 69°25N 17°30E 8 B17
Senkaku-Shotō
E. China Sea 25°45N 123°30E 31 M1
Senkuang Indonesia 1°11N 104°2E 39 d
Senlis France 49°13N 2°35E 20 B5
Senmonorom Cambodia 12°27N 107°12E 38 F6
Senneterre Canada 48°25N 77°15W 72 C4
Seno Laos 16°35N 104°50E 38 D5
Sens France 48°11N 3°15E 20 B5
Senta Serbia 45°55N 20°3E 23 B9
Sentani Indonesia 2°36S 140°37E 37 E10
Sentery = Lubao
Dem. Rep. of the Congo 5°17S 25°42E 54 D2
Sentinel U.S.A. 32°52N 113°13W 77 K7
Sentosa Singapore 1°16N 103°50E 39 d
Seo de Urgel = La Seu d'Urgell
Spain 42°22N 1°23E 21 A6
Seogwipo S. Korea 33°13N 126°34E 35 H14
Seohara India 29°15N 78°33E 43 E8
Seonath → India 21°44N 82°28E 43 J10
Seondha India 26°9N 78°48E 43 F8
Seongnam S. Korea 37°26N 127°8E 35 F14
Seoni India 22°5N 79°30E 43 H8
Seoni Malwa India 22°27N 77°28E 42 H8
Seonsan S. Korea 36°14N 128°17E 35 F15
Seosan S. Korea 36°47N 126°27E 35 F14
Seoul S. Korea 37°31N 126°58E 35 F14
Sepīdān Iran 30°20N 52°5E 45 D7
Sep'o N. Korea 38°57N 127°25E 35 E14
Sepone Laos 16°45N 106°13E 38 D6
Sept-Îles Canada 50°13N 66°22W 73 B6
Sequim U.S.A. 48°5N 123°6W 78 B3
Sequoia △ U.S.A. 36°30N 118°30W 78 J8
Seraing Belgium 50°35N 5°32E 15 D5
Serakhis → Cyprus 35°13N 32°55E 25 D11
Seram Indonesia 3°10S 129°0E 37 E7
Seram Sea Indonesia 2°30S 128°30E 37 E7
Seranantsara Madag. 18°30S 49°5E 57 B8
Serang Indonesia 6°8S 106°10E 37 G12
Serangoon Singapore 1°23N 103°54E 39 d
Serasan Indonesia 2°29N 109°4E 36 D3
Serbia □ Serbia 43°30N 21°0E 23 C9
Serbia ■ Europe 43°20N 20°0E 23 B9
Serdar Turkmenistan 39°4N 56°23E 45 B8
Serdobsk Russia 52°28N 44°10E 18 D7
Seremban Malaysia 2°43N 101°53E 39 L3
Serengeti △ Tanzania 2°11S 35°0E 54 C3
Serengeti Plain Tanzania 2°40S 35°0E 54 C4
Serenje Zambia 13°14S 30°15E 55 E3
Sereth = Siret →
Romania 45°24N 28°1E 17 F14
Sergeya Kirova, Ostrova
Russia 77°30N 90°0E 29 B10
Sergino Russia 62°25N 65°12E 28 C7
Sergipe □ Brazil 10°30S 37°30W 93 F11
Sergiyev Posad Russia 56°20N 38°10E 18 C6
Serhetabat Turkmenistan 35°20N 62°18E 45 C9
Seria Brunei 4°37N 114°23E 36 D4
Serian Malaysia 1°10N 110°31E 36 D4
Seribu, Kepulauan
Indonesia 5°36S 106°33E 36 F3
Sericho Kenya 1°5N 39°5E 54 B4
Serifos Greece 37°9N 24°30E 23 F11
Sérigny → Canada 56°47N 66°0W 73 A6
Seringapatam Reef
Australia 13°38S 122°5E 60 B3
Seririt Indonesia 8°12S 114°56E 37 J17
Sermata Indonesia 8°15S 128°50E 37 F7
Sermersuaq Greenland 79°30N 62°0W 4 B4
Serov Russia 59°29N 60°35E 18 C11
Serowe Botswana 22°25S 26°43E 56 C4
Serpentine Lakes
Australia 28°30S 129°10E 61 E4
Serpent's Mouth = Sierpe, Bocas
de la Venezuela 10°0N 61°30W 93 L15
Serpukhov Russia 54°55N 37°28E 18 D6
Serra do Navio Brazil 0°59N 52°3W 93 C8
Serranía San Luís △
Paraguay 22°35S 57°22W 94 A4
Serranía San Rafael △
Paraguay 26°30S 56°0W 95 B4
Serres Greece 41°5N 23°31E 23 D10
Serrezuela Argentina 30°40S 65°20W 94 C2
Serrinha Brazil 11°39S 39°0W 93 F11
Sertanópolis Brazil 23°4S 51°2W 95 A5
Serua Indonesia 6°18S 130°1E 37 F8
Serui Indonesia 1°53S 136°10E 37 E9
Serule Botswana 21°57S 27°20E 56 C4
Ses Salines Spain 39°21N 3°3E 24 B10
Sese Is. Uganda 0°20S 32°20E 54 C3
Sesepe Indonesia 1°30S 127°59E 37 E7
Sesfontein Namibia 19°7S 13°39E 56 B1
Sesheke Zambia 17°29S 24°13E 56 B3
S'Espalmador Spain 38°47N 1°26E 24 C7
S'Espardell Spain 38°48N 1°29E 24 C7
S'Estanyol Spain 39°22N 2°54E 24 B9
Setana Japan 42°26N 139°51E 30 C9
Sète France 43°25N 3°42E 20 E5
Sete Lagoas Brazil 19°27S 44°16W 93 G10
Sétif Algeria 36°9N 5°26E 50 A7
Seto Japan 35°14N 137°6E 31 G8
Setonaikai Japan 34°20N 133°30E 31 G6
Setonaikai △ Japan 34°15N 133°15E 31 G6
Settat Morocco 33°0N 7°40W 50 B4
Setting L. Canada 55°0N 98°38W 71 C9
Settle U.K. 54°5N 2°16W 12 C5
Settlement, The
Br. Virgin Is. 18°43N 64°22W 89 e
Settlers S. Africa 25°2S 28°30E 57 C4
Setúbal Portugal 38°30N 8°58W 21 C1
Setúbal, B. de Portugal 38°40N 8°56W 21 C1
Seul, Lac Canada 50°20N 92°30W 72 B1
Sevan, Ozero = Sevana Lich
Armenia 40°30N 45°20E 44 A5
Sevana Lich Armenia 40°30N 45°20E 44 A5
Sevastopol Ukraine 44°35N 33°30E 19 F5
Seven Sisters Canada 54°56N 128°10W 70 C3
Severn → Canada 56°2N 87°36W 72 A2
Severn → U.K. 51°35N 2°40W 13 F5
Severnaya Zemlya
Russia 79°0N 100°0E 29 B11
Severnyye Uvaly Russia 60°0N 50°0E 18 C8
Severo-Kurilsk Russia 50°40N 156°8E 29 D16
Severo-Yeniseyskiy
Russia 60°22N 93°1E 29 C10

Severo-Zapadnyy □ *Russia* 65°0N 40°0E **28** C4
Severobaykalsk *Russia* 55°39N 109°19E **29** D11
Severodvinsk *Russia* 64°27N 39°58E **18** B6
Severomorsk *Russia* 69°5N 33°27E **8** B25
Severouralsk *Russia* 60°9N 59°57E **18** B10
Seversk *Russia* 56°36N 84°49E **28** D9
Sevier → *U.S.A.* 39°4N 113°6W **76** G7
Sevier Desert *U.S.A.* 39°40N 112°45W **76** G7
Sevier L. *U.S.A.* 38°54N 113°9W **76** G7
Sevilla *Spain* 37°23N 5°58W **21** D2
Seville = Sevilla *Spain* 37°23N 5°58W **21** D2
Sevlievo *Bulgaria* 43°2N 25°6E **23** C11
Sewani *India* 28°58N 75°39E **42** E6
Seward *Alaska, U.S.A.* 60°7N 149°27W **68** C5
Seward *Nebr., U.S.A.* 40°55N 97°6W **80** E5
Seward *Pa., U.S.A.* 40°25N 79°1W **82** F5
Seward Peninsula *U.S.A.* 65°30N 166°0W **74** a
Sewell *Chile* 34°10S 70°23W **94** C1
Sewer *Indonesia* 5°53S 134°40E **37** F8
Sewickley *U.S.A.* 40°32N 80°12W **82** F4
Sexsmith *Canada* 55°21N 118°47W **70** B5
Seychelles ■ *Ind. Oc.* 5°0S 56°0E **53** b
Seyðisfjörður *Iceland* 65°16N 13°57W **8** D7
Seydişehir *Turkey* 37°25N 31°51E **19** G5
Seydvān *Iran* 38°34N 45°2E **44** B5
Seyhan → *Turkey* 36°43N 34°53E **44** B2
Seym → *Ukraine* 51°27N 32°34E **19** D5
Seymour *Australia* 37°2S 145°10E **63** F4
Seymour *S. Africa* 32°33S 26°46E **57** E4
Seymour *Conn., U.S.A.* 41°24N 73°4W **83** E11
Seymour *Ind., U.S.A.* 38°58N 85°53W **81** F11
Seymour *Tex., U.S.A.* 33°35N 99°16W **84** E5
Sfântu Gheorghe *Romania* 45°52N 25°48E **17** F13
Sfax *Tunisia* 34°49N 10°48E **51** B8
Sha Tau Kok *China* 22°33N 114°13E **33** F11
Sha Tin *China* 22°23N 114°12E **33** G11
Shaanxi □ *China* 35°0N 109°0E **34** G5
Shaba = Katanga □ *Dem. Rep. of the Congo* 8°0S 25°0E **54** D2
Shaba ⌂ *Kenya* 0°38N 37°48E **54** B4
Shabeelle → *Somali Rep.* 2°0N 44°0E **47** G3
Shabogamo L. *Canada* 53°15N 66°30W **73** B6
Shabunda *Dem. Rep. of the Congo* 2°40S 27°16E **54** C2
Shache *China* 38°20N 77°10E **32** C2
Shackleton Fracture Zone *S. Ocean* 60°0S 60°0W **5** B18
Shackleton Ice Shelf *Antarctica* 66°0S 100°0E **5** C8
Shackleton Inlet *Antarctica* 83°0S 160°0E **5** E11
Shādegān *Iran* 30°40N 48°38E **45** D6
Shadi *India* 33°24N 77°14E **43** C7
Shadrinsk *Russia* 56°5N 63°32E **28** D7
Shadyside *U.S.A.* 39°58N 80°45W **82** G4
Shafter *U.S.A.* 35°30N 119°16W **79** K7
Shaftesbury *U.K.* 51°0N 2°11W **13** F5
Shaftsbury *U.S.A.* 43°0N 73°11W **83** D11
Shagram *Pakistan* 36°24N 72°20E **43** A5
Shah Alam *Malaysia* 3°5N 101°32E **39** L3
Shah Alizai *Pakistan* 29°25N 66°33E **42** E2
Shah Bunder *Pakistan* 24°13N 67°56E **42** G2
Shahabad *Punjab, India* 30°10N 76°55E **42** D7
Shahabad *Raj., India* 25°15N 77°11E **42** G7
Shahabad *Ut. P., India* 27°36N 79°56E **43** F8
Shahadpur *Pakistan* 25°55N 68°35E **42** G3
Shahbā' *Syria* 32°52N 36°38E **46** C5
Shahdād *Iran* 30°30N 57°40E **45** D8
Shahdād, Namakzār-e *Iran* 30°20N 58°20E **45** D8
Shahdadkot *Pakistan* 27°50N 67°55E **42** F2
Shahdol *India* 23°19N 81°26E **43** H9
Shahe *China* 37°0N 114°32E **34** F8
Shahganj *India* 26°3N 82°44E **43** F10
Shahgarh *India* 27°15N 69°50E **42** F3
Shahjahanpur *India* 27°54N 79°57E **43** F8
Shahpur = Salmās *Iran* 38°11N 44°47E **44** B5
Shahpur *India* 22°12N 77°58E **42** H7
Shahpur *Baluchistan, Pakistan* 28°46N 68°27E **42** E3
Shahpur *Punjab, Pakistan* 32°17N 72°26E **42** C5
Shahpur Chakar *Pakistan* 26°9N 68°39E **42** F3
Shahpura *Mad. P., India* 23°10N 80°45E **43** H9
Shahpura *Raj., India* 25°38N 74°56E **42** G6
Shahr-e Bābak *Iran* 30°7N 55°9E **45** D7
Shahr-e Kord *Iran* 32°15N 50°55E **45** C6
Shāhrakht *Iran* 33°38N 60°16E **45** C9
Shahrezā = Qomsheh *Iran* 32°0N 51°55E **45** D6
Shahrig *Pakistan* 30°15N 67°40E **42** D2
Shāhrūd = Emāmrūd *Iran* 36°30N 55°0E **45** B7
Shahukou *China* 40°20N 112°18E **34** D7
Shaikhabad *Afghan.* 34°2N 68°45E **42** B3
Shajapur *India* 23°27N 76°21E **42** H7
Shajing *China* 22°44N 113°48E **33** F10
Shakargarh *Pakistan* 32°17N 75°10E **42** C6
Shakawe *Botswana* 18°28S 21°49E **56** B3
Shaker Heights *U.S.A.* 41°28N 81°32W **82** E3
Shakhtersk *Russia* 49°10N 142°8E **29** E15
Shakhty *Russia* 47°40N 40°16E **19** E7
Shakhunya *Russia* 57°40N 46°46E **18** C8
Shaki *Nigeria* 8°41N 3°21E **50** G6
Shaksam Valley *Asia* 36°0N 76°20E **43** A7
Shallow Lake *Canada* 44°36N 81°5W **82** B3
Shalqar *Kazakhstan* 47°48N 59°39E **28** E6
Shaluli Shan *China* 30°40N 99°55E **32** C4
Shām *Iran* 26°39N 57°21E **45** E8
Shām, Bādiyat ash *Asia* 32°0N 40°0E **44** C3
Shamâl Sînî □ *Egypt* 30°30N 33°30E **46** E2
Shamattawa *Canada* 55°51N 92°5W **72** A1
Shamattawa → *Canada* 55°1N 85°23W **72** A2
Shamīl *Iran* 27°30N 56°55E **45** E8
Shāmkūh *Iran* 35°47N 57°50E **45** C8
Shamli *India* 29°32N 77°18E **42** E7
Shammar, Jabal *Si. Arabia* 27°40N 41°0E **44** E4
Shamo = Gobi *Asia* 44°0N 110°0E **34** C6
Shamo, L. *Ethiopia* 5°45N 37°30E **47** F2
Shamokin *U.S.A.* 40°47N 76°34W **83** F8
Shamrock *Canada* 45°23N 76°50W **83** A8
Shamrock *U.S.A.* 35°13N 100°15W **84** D4
Shamva *Zimbabwe* 17°20S 31°32E **55** F3
Shan □ *Burma* 21°30N 98°30E **41** J21
Shan Xian *China* 34°50N 116°5E **34** G9
Shanchengzhen *China* 42°20N 125°20E **35** C13
Shāndak *Iran* 28°28N 60°27E **45** D9
Shandon *U.S.A.* 35°39N 120°23W **78** K6
Shandong □ *China* 36°0N 118°0E **35** G10
Shandong Bandao *China* 37°0N 121°0E **35** F11
Shandur Pass *Pakistan* 36°4N 72°31E **43** A5
Shang Xian = Shangzhou *China* 33°50N 109°58E **34** H5
Shangalowe *Dem. Rep. of the Congo* 10°50S 26°30E **55** E2
Shangani *Zimbabwe* 19°41S 29°20E **57** B4
Shangani → *Zimbabwe* 18°41S 27°10E **55** F2
Shangbancheng *China* 40°50N 118°1E **35** D10
Shangdu *China* 41°30N 113°30E **34** D7
Shanghai *China* 31°15N 121°26E **33** C7
Shanghe *China* 37°20N 117°10E **35** F9
Shangnan *China* 33°32N 110°50E **34** H6
Shangqiu *China* 34°26N 115°36E **34** G8
Shangrao *China* 28°25N 117°59E **33** D6
Shangshui *China* 33°42N 114°35E **34** H8
Shangzhi *China* 45°22N 127°56E **35** B14
Shangzhou *China* 33°50N 109°58E **34** H5
Shanhetun *China* 44°33N 127°15E **35** B14
Shanklin *U.K.* 50°38N 1°11W **13** G6
Shannon *N.Z.* 40°33S 175°25E **59** D5
Shannon → *Ireland* 52°35N 9°30W **10** D2
Shannon ✕ **(SNN)** *Ireland* 52°42N 8°57W **10** D3
Shannon, Mouth of the *Ireland* 52°30N 9°55W **10** D2
Shannon △ *Australia* 34°35S 116°25E **61** F2
Shannonbridge *Ireland* 53°17N 8°3W **10** C3
Shansi = Shanxi □ *China* 37°0N 112°0E **34** F7
Shantar, Ostrov Bolshoy *Russia* 55°9N 137°40E **29** D14
Shantipur *India* 23°17N 88°25E **43** H13
Shantou *China* 23°18N 116°40E **33** D6
Shantung = Shandong □ *China* 36°0N 118°0E **35** G10
Shanxi □ *China* 37°0N 112°0E **34** F7
Shanyang *China* 33°31N 109°55E **34** H5
Shanyin *China* 39°25N 112°56E **34** E7
Shaoguan *China* 24°48N 113°35E **33** D6
Shaoxing *China* 30°0N 120°35E **33** D7
Shaoyang *China* 27°14N 111°25E **33** D6
Shap *U.K.* 54°32N 2°40W **12** C5
Shapinsay *U.K.* 59°3N 2°51W **11** B6
Shaqra' *Si. Arabia* 25°15N 45°16E **44** E5
Shaqrā' *Yemen* 13°22N 45°44E **47** E4
Sharafkhāneh *Iran* 38°11N 45°29E **44** B5
Sharbot Lake *Canada* 44°46N 76°41W **83** B8
Shari *Japan* 43°55N 144°40E **30** C12
Sharjah = Ash Shāriqah *U.A.E.* 25°23N 55°26E **45** E7
Shark B. *Australia* 25°30S 113°32E **61** E1
Shark Bay △ *Australia* 25°30S 113°30E **61** E1
Sharm el Sheikh *Egypt* 27°53N 34°18E **51** C12
Sharon *Canada* 44°6N 79°26W **82** B5
Sharon *Mass., U.S.A.* 42°7N 71°11W **83** D13
Sharon *Pa., U.S.A.* 41°14N 80°31W **82** E4
Sharon Springs *Kans., U.S.A.* 38°54N 101°45W **80** F3
Sharon Springs *N.Y., U.S.A.* 42°48N 74°37W **83** D10
Sharp Pt. *Australia* 10°58S 142°43E **62** A3
Sharpe L. *Canada* 54°24N 93°40W **72** B1
Sharpsville *U.S.A.* 41°15N 80°29W **82** E4
Sharqi, Al Jabal ash *Lebanon* 33°40N 36°10E **46** B5
Sharya *Russia* 58°22N 45°20E **18** C8
Shashemene *Ethiopia* 7°13N 38°33E **47** F2
Shashi *Botswana* 21°15S 27°27E **57** C4
Shashi *China* 30°25N 112°14E **33** C6
Shashi → *Africa* 21°14S 29°20E **55** G2
Shasta, Mt. *U.S.A.* 41°25N 122°12W **76** F2
Shasta L. *U.S.A.* 40°43N 122°25W **76** F2
Shatsky Rise *Pac. Oc.* 34°0N 157°0E **64** D7
Shatt al Arab *Asia* 29°57N 48°34E **45** D6
Shaunavon *Canada* 49°35N 108°25W **71** D7
Shaver L. *U.S.A.* 37°9N 119°18W **78** H7
Shaw → *Australia* 20°21S 119°17E **60** D2
Shaw I. *Australia* 20°30S 149°2E **62** J7
Shawanaga *Canada* 45°31N 80°17W **82** A4
Shawangunk Mts. *U.S.A.* 41°35N 74°30W **83** E10
Shawano *U.S.A.* 44°47N 88°36W **80** C9
Shawinigan *Canada* 46°35N 72°50W **72** C5
Shawmari, J. ash *Jordan* 30°35N 36°35E **46** E5
Shawnee *U.S.A.* 35°20N 96°55W **84** D6
Shay Gap *Australia* 20°30S 120°10E **60** D3
Shaybārā *Si. Arabia* 25°26N 36°47E **44** E3
Shaykh, J. ash *Lebanon* 33°25N 35°50E **46** B4
Shaykh Miskīn *Syria* 32°49N 36°9E **46** C5
Shaykh Sa'īd *Iraq* 32°34N 46°17E **44** C5
Shāzand *Iran* 33°56N 49°24E **45** C6
Shchūchīnsk *Kazakhstan* 52°56N 70°12E **28** D8
She Xian *China* 36°30N 113°40E **34** F7
Shebele = Shabeelle → *Somali Rep.* 2°0N 44°0E **47** G3
Sheboygan *U.S.A.* 43°46N 87°45W **80** D10
Shediac *Canada* 46°14N 64°32W **73** C7
Sheelin, L. *Ireland* 53°48N 7°20W **10** C4
Sheep Haven *Ireland* 55°11N 7°52W **10** A4
Sheep Range *U.S.A.* 36°35N 115°15W **79** J11
Sheerness *U.K.* 51°26N 0°47E **13** F8
Sheet Harbour *Canada* 44°56N 62°31W **73** D7
Sheffield *U.K.* 53°23N 1°28W **12** D6
Sheffield *Ala., U.S.A.* 34°46N 87°41W **85** D11
Sheffield *Mass., U.S.A.* 42°5N 73°21W **83** D11
Sheffield *Pa., U.S.A.* 41°42N 79°3W **82** E5
Sheikhpura *India* 25°9N 85°53E **43** G11
Shekhupura *Pakistan* 31°42N 73°58E **42** D5
Shekou *China* 22°30N 113°55E **33** G10
Shelburne *N.S., Canada* 43°47N 65°20W **73** D6
Shelburne *Ont., Canada* 44°4N 80°15W **82** B4
Shelburne *U.S.A.* 44°23N 73°14W **83** B11
Shelburne B. *Australia* 11°50S 142°50E **62** A3
Shelburne Falls *U.S.A.* 42°36N 72°45W **83** D12
Shelby *Mich., U.S.A.* 43°37N 86°22W **80** D10
Shelby *Miss., U.S.A.* 33°57N 90°46W **85** E9
Shelby *Mont., U.S.A.* 48°30N 111°51W **76** B8
Shelby *N.C., U.S.A.* 35°17N 81°32W **85** D14
Shelby *Ohio, U.S.A.* 40°53N 82°40W **82** F2
Shelbyville *Ill., U.S.A.* 39°24N 88°48W **80** F9
Shelbyville *Ind., U.S.A.* 39°31N 85°47W **81** F11
Shelbyville *Ky., U.S.A.* 38°13N 85°14W **81** F11
Shelbyville *Tenn., U.S.A.* 35°29N 86°28W **85** D11
Sheldon *U.S.A.* 43°11N 95°51W **80** D6
Sheldrake *Canada* 50°20N 64°51W **73** B7
Shelikhova, Zaliv *Russia* 59°30N 157°0E **29** D16
Shell Lakes *Australia* 29°20S 127°30E **61** E4
Shellbrook *Canada* 53°13N 106°24W **71** C7
Shellharbour *Australia* 34°31S 150°51E **63** E5
Shelter I. *U.S.A.* 41°4N 72°20W **83** E12
Shelton *Conn., U.S.A.* 41°19N 73°5W **83** E11
Shelton *Wash., U.S.A.* 47°13N 123°6W **78** C3
Shen Xian *China* 36°15N 115°40E **34** F8
Shenandoah *Iowa, U.S.A.* 40°46N 95°22W **80** E6
Shenandoah *Pa., U.S.A.* 40°49N 76°12W **83** F8
Shenandoah *Va., U.S.A.* 38°29N 78°37W **81** F14
Shenandoah → *U.S.A.* 39°19N 77°44W **81** F15
Shenandoah △ *U.S.A.* 38°35N 78°22W **81** F14
Shenchi *China* 39°8N 112°10E **34** E7
Shendam *Nigeria* 8°49N 9°30E **50** G7
Shendî *Sudan* 16°46N 33°22E **51** E12
Shengfang *China* 39°3N 116°42E **34** E9
Shenjingzi *China* 44°40N 124°30E **35** B13
Shenmu *China* 38°50N 110°29E **34** E6
Shenqiu *China* 33°25N 115°5E **34** H8
Shensi = Shaanxi □ *China* 35°0N 109°0E **34** G5
Shenyang *China* 41°48N 123°27E **35** D12
Shenzhen *China* 22°32N 114°5E **33** F10
Shenzhen ✕ **(SZX)** *China* 22°41N 113°49E **33** F10
Shenzhen Shuiku *China* 22°34N 114°8E **33** F11
Shenzhen Wan *China* 22°27N 113°55E **33** G10
Sheo *India* 26°11N 71°15E **42** F4
Sheopur Kalan *India* 25°40N 76°40E **42** G7
Shepetivka *Ukraine* 50°10N 27°10E **17** C14
Shepparton *Australia* 36°23S 145°26E **63** F4
Sheppey, I. of *U.K.* 51°25N 0°48E **13** F8
Shepton Mallet *U.K.* 51°11N 2°33W **13** F5
Sheqi *China* 33°12N 112°57E **34** H7
Sher Qila *Pakistan* 36°7N 74°2E **43** A6
Sherborne *U.K.* 50°57N 2°31W **13** G5
Sherbro I. *S. Leone* 7°30N 12°40W **50** G3
Sherbrooke *N.S., Canada* 45°8N 61°59W **73** C7
Sherbrooke *Qué., Canada* 45°28N 71°57W **83** A13
Sherburne *U.S.A.* 42°41N 75°30W **83** D9
Shergarh *India* 26°20N 72°18E **42** F5
Sherghati *India* 24°34N 84°47E **43** G11
Sheridan *Ark., U.S.A.* 34°19N 92°24W **84** D8
Sheridan *Wyo., U.S.A.* 44°48N 106°58W **76** D10
Sheringham *U.K.* 52°56N 1°13E **12** E9
Sherkin I. *Ireland* 51°28N 9°26W **10** E2
Sherkot *India* 29°22N 78°35E **43** E8
Sherlovaya Gora *Russia* 50°34N 116°15E **29** D12
Sherman *N.Y., U.S.A.* 42°9N 79°35W **82** D5
Sherman *Tex., U.S.A.* 33°38N 96°36W **84** E6
Sherpur *India* 25°34N 83°47E **43** G10
Sherridon *Canada* 55°8N 101°5W **71** B8
Sherwood Forest *U.K.* 53°6N 1°7W **12** D6
Sherwood Park *Canada* 53°31N 113°19W **70** C6
Sheslay → *Canada* 58°48N 132°5W **70** B2
Shethanei L. *Canada* 58°48N 97°50W **71** B9
Shetland □ *U.K.* 60°30N 1°30W **11** A7
Shetland Is. *U.K.* 60°30N 1°30W **11** A7
Shetrunji → *India* 21°19N 72°7E **42** J5
Sheung Shui *China* 22°31N 114°7E **33** F11
Shey-Phoksundo △ *Nepal* 29°30N 82°45E **43** E10
Sheyenne → *U.S.A.* 47°2N 96°50W **80** B5
Shiashkotan, Ostrov *Russia* 48°49N 154°6E **29** E16
Shibām *Yemen* 15°59N 48°36E **47** D4
Shibata *Japan* 37°57N 139°20E **30** F9
Shibecha *Japan* 43°17N 144°36E **30** C12
Shibetsu *Japan* 44°10N 142°23E **30** B11
Shibogama L. *Canada* 53°35N 88°15W **72** B2
Shibushi *Japan* 31°25N 131°8E **31** J5
Shickshinny *U.S.A.* 41°9N 76°9W **83** E8
Shickshock Mts. = Chic-Chocs, Mts. *Canada* 48°55N 66°0W **73** C6
Shidao *China* 36°50N 122°25E **35** F12
Shido *Japan* 34°19N 134°10E **31** G7
Shiel, L. *U.K.* 56°48N 5°34W **11** E3
Shield, C. *Australia* 13°20S 136°20E **62** A2
Shīeli *Kazakhstan* 44°20N 66°15E **28** E7
Shiga □ *Japan* 35°20N 136°0E **31** G8
Shiguaigou *China* 40°52N 110°15E **34** D6
Shihchiachuangi = Shijiazhuang *China* 38°2N 114°28E **34** E8
Shihezi *China* 44°15N 86°2E **32** B3
Shijiazhuang *China* 38°2N 114°28E **34** E8
Shikarpur *India* 28°17N 78°7E **42** E8
Shikarpur *Pakistan* 27°57N 68°39E **42** F3
Shikohabad *India* 27°6N 78°36E **43** F8
Shikoku □ *Japan* 33°30N 133°30E **31** H6
Shikoku-Sanchi *Japan* 33°30N 133°30E **31** H6
Shikotan, Ostrov *Asia* 43°47N 146°44E **29** E15
Shikotsu-Ko *Japan* 42°45N 141°25E **30** C10
Shikotsu-Tōya △ *Japan* 44°4N 145°8E **30** C10
Shiliguri *India* 26°45N 88°25E **41** F16
Shiliu = Changjiang *China* 19°20N 108°55E **38** C7
Shilka *Russia* 52°0N 115°55E **29** D12
Shilka → *Russia* 53°20N 121°26E **29** D13
Shillelagh *Ireland* 52°45N 6°32W **10** D5
Shillington *U.S.A.* 40°18N 75°58W **83** F9
Shillong *India* 25°35N 91°53E **41** G17
Shilo *West Bank* 32°4N 35°18E **46** C4
Shilou *China* 37°0N 110°48E **34** F6
Shimabara *Japan* 32°48N 130°20E **31** H5
Shimada *Japan* 34°49N 138°10E **31** G9
Shimane □ *Japan* 35°0N 132°30E **31** G6
Shimanovsk *Russia* 52°15N 127°30E **29** D13
Shimba Hills ⌂ *Kenya* 4°14S 39°25E **54** C4
Shimizu *Japan* 35°0N 138°30E **31** G9
Shimla *India* 31°2N 77°9E **42** D7
Shimodate *Japan* 36°20N 139°55E **31** F9
Shimoga *India* 13°57N 75°32E **40** N9
Shimoni *Kenya* 4°38S 39°20E **54** C4
Shimonoseki *Japan* 33°58N 130°55E **31** H5
Shimpuru Rapids *Namibia* 17°45S 19°55E **56** B2
Shin, L. *U.K.* 58°5N 4°30W **11** C4
Shinano-Gawa → *Japan* 36°50N 138°30E **31** F9
Shināş *Oman* 24°46N 56°28E **45** E8
Shīndand *Afghan.* 33°12N 62°8E **40** C3
Shinglehouse *U.S.A.* 41°58N 78°12W **82** E6
Shingū *Japan* 33°40N 135°55E **31** H7
Shingwidzi *S. Africa* 23°5S 31°25E **57** C5
Shinjō *Japan* 38°46N 140°18E **30** E10
Shinkolobwe *Dem. Rep. of the Congo* 11°10S 26°40E **52** G5
Shinshār *Syria* 34°36N 36°43E **46** A5
Shinyanga *Tanzania* 3°45S 33°27E **54** C3
Shinyanga □ *Tanzania* 3°50S 34°0E **54** C3
Shio-no-Misaki *Japan* 33°25N 135°45E **31** H7
Shiogama *Japan* 38°19N 141°1E **30** E10
Shiojiri *Japan* 36°6N 137°58E **31** F8
Shipchenski Prokhod *Bulgaria* 42°45N 25°15E **23** C11
Shiping *China* 23°45N 102°23E **32** D5
Shippagan *Canada* 47°45N 64°45W **73** C7
Shippensburg *U.S.A.* 40°3N 77°31W **82** F7
Shippenville *U.S.A.* 41°15N 79°28W **82** E5
Shiprock *U.S.A.* 36°47N 108°41W **77** H9
Shiqma, N. → *Israel* 31°37N 34°30E **46** D3
Shiquan *China* 33°5N 108°15E **34** H5
Shiquan He = Indus → *Pakistan* 24°20N 67°47E **42** G2
Shīr Kūh *Iran* 31°39N 54°3E **45** D7
Shiragami-Misaki *Japan* 41°24N 140°12E **30** D10
Shirakawa *Fukushima, Japan* 37°7N 140°13E **31** F10
Shirakawa *Gifu, Japan* 36°17N 136°56E **31** F8
Shirane-San *Gumma, Japan* 36°48N 139°22E **31** F9
Shirane-San *Yamanashi, Japan* 35°42N 138°9E **31** G9
Shiraoi *Japan* 42°33N 141°21E **30** C10
Shīrāz *Iran* 29°42N 52°30E **45** D7
Shire → *Africa* 17°42S 35°19E **55** F4
Shiretoko-Misaki *Japan* 44°21N 145°20E **30** B12
Shirinab → *Pakistan* 30°15N 66°28E **42** D2
Shiriya-Zaki *Japan* 41°25N 141°30E **30** D10
Shiroishi *Japan* 38°0N 140°37E **30** F10
Shirshov Ridge *Pac. Oc.* 58°0N 170°0E **64** B8
Shīrvān *Iran* 37°30N 57°50E **45** B8
Shirwa, L. = Chilwa, L. *Malawi* 15°15S 35°40E **55** F4
Shivpuri *India* 25°26N 77°42E **42** G7
Shixian *China* 43°5N 129°50E **35** C15
Shiyan *China* 22°42N 113°56E **33** F10
Shiyan Shuiku *China* 22°42N 113°54E **33** F10
Shizuishan *China* 39°15N 106°50E **34** E4
Shizuoka *Japan* 34°57N 138°24E **31** G9
Shizuoka □ *Japan* 35°15N 138°40E **31** G9
Shklov = Shklow *Belarus* 54°16N 30°15E **17** A16
Shklow *Belarus* 54°16N 30°15E **17** A16
Shkodër *Albania* 42°4N 19°32E **23** C8
Shkumbini → *Albania* 41°2N 19°31E **23** D8
Shmidta, Ostrov *Russia* 81°0N 91°0E **29** A10
Shō-Gawa → *Japan* 36°47N 137°4E **31** F8
Shoal L. *Canada* 49°33N 95°1W **71** D9
Shoal Lake *Canada* 50°30N 100°35W **71** C8
Shōdo-Shima *Japan* 34°30N 134°15E **31** G7
Sholapur = Solapur *India* 17°43N 75°56E **40** L9
Shōmrōn *West Bank* 32°15N 35°13E **46** C4
Shoreham *U.S.A.* 43°53N 73°18W **83** C11
Shoreham by Sea *U.K.* 50°50N 0°16W **13** G7
Shori → *Pakistan* 28°29N 69°44E **42** E3
Shorkot *Pakistan* 30°50N 72°0E **42** D5
Shorkot Road *Pakistan* 30°47N 72°15E **42** D5
Shoshone *Calif., U.S.A.* 35°58N 116°16W **79** K10
Shoshone *Idaho, U.S.A.* 42°56N 114°25W **76** E6
Shoshone L. *U.S.A.* 44°22N 110°43W **76** D8
Shoshone Mts. *U.S.A.* 39°20N 117°25W **76** G5
Shoshong *Botswana* 22°56S 26°31E **56** C4
Shoshoni *U.S.A.* 43°14N 108°7W **76** E9
Shouguang *China* 37°52N 118°45E **35** F10
Shouyang *China* 37°54N 113°8E **34** F7
Show Low *U.S.A.* 34°15N 110°2W **77** J8
Shqipëria = Albania ■ *Europe* 41°0N 20°0E **23** D9
Shreveport *U.S.A.* 32°31N 93°45W **84** E8
Shrewsbury *U.K.* 52°43N 2°45W **13** E5
Shri Mohangarh *India* 27°17N 71°18E **42** F4
Shrirampur *India* 22°44N 88°21E **43** H
Shropshire □ *U.K.* 52°36N 2°45W **13**
Shū *Kazakhstan* 43°36N 73°42E **28**
Shuangcheng *China* 45°20N 126°15E **35** B
Shuanggou *China* 34°2N 117°30E **35**
Shuangliao *China* 43°29N 123°30E **35** C
Shuangshanzi *China* 40°20N 119°8E **35** D
Shuangyang *China* 43°28N 125°40E **35** C
Shuangyashan *China* 46°28N 131°5E **33**
Shuguri Falls *Tanzania* 8°33S 37°22E **55**
Shuiye *China* 36°7N 114°8E **34**
Shujalpur *India* 23°18N 76°46E **42**
Shukpa Kunzang *India* 34°22N 78°22E **43**
Shulan *China* 44°28N 127°0E **35** B
Shule *China* 39°25N 76°3E **32**
Shule He → *China* 40°20N 92°50E **32**
Shumagin Is. *U.S.A.* 55°7N 160°30W **74**
Shumen *Bulgaria* 43°18N 26°55E **23** C
Shumikha *Russia* 55°10N 63°15E **28**
Shuo Xian = Shuozhou *China* 39°20N 112°33E **34**
Shuozhou *China* 39°20N 112°33E **34**
Shūr → *Fārs, Iran* 28°30N 55°0E **45**
Shūr → *Kermān, Iran* 30°52N 57°37E **45**
Shūr → *Yazd, Iran* 31°45N 55°15E **45**
Shūr Āb *Iran* 34°23N 51°11E **45**
Shūr Gaz *Iran* 29°10N 59°20E **45**
Shūrāb *Iran* 33°43N 56°29E **45**
Shūrjestān *Iran* 31°24N 52°25E **45**
Shurugwi *Zimbabwe* 19°40S 30°0E **55**
Shūsf *Iran* 31°50N 60°5E **45**
Shūshtar *Iran* 32°0N 48°50E **45**
Shuswap L. *Canada* 50°55N 119°3W **70**
Shuyang *China* 34°10N 118°42E **35** G
Shūzū *Iran* 29°52N 54°30E **45**
Shwebo *Burma* 22°30N 95°45E **41** H
Shwegu *Burma* 24°15N 96°26E **41** G
Shweli → *Burma* 23°45N 96°45E **41** H
Shymkent *Kazakhstan* 42°18N 69°36E **28**
Shyok *India* 34°13N 78°12E **43**
Shyok → *Pakistan* 35°13N 75°53E **43**
Si Kiang = Xi Jiang → *China* 22°5N 113°20E **33**
Si Lanna △ *Thailand* 19°17N 99°12E **38**
Si Nakarin Res. *Thailand* 14°35N 99°0E **38**
Si-ngan = Xi'an *China* 34°15N 109°0E **34**
Si Prachan *Thailand* 14°37N 100°9E **38**
Si Racha *Thailand* 13°10N 100°48E **38**
Si Xian *China* 33°30N 117°50E **35**
Siachen Glacier *Asia* 35°20N 77°30E **43**
Siahaf → *Pakistan* 29°3N 68°57E **42**
Siahan Range *Pakistan* 27°30N 64°40E **40**
Siaksriindrapura *Indonesia* 0°51N 102°0E **36**
Sialkot *Pakistan* 32°32N 74°30E **42**
Siam = Thailand ■ *Asia* 16°0N 102°0E **38**
Sian = Xi'an *China* 34°15N 109°0E **34**
Sian Ka'an ⌂ *Mexico* 19°35N 87°40W **87**
Siantan *Indonesia* 3°10N 106°15E **36**
Sīāreh *Iran* 28°5N 60°14E **45**
Siargao I. *Phil.* 9°52N 126°3E **37**
Siari *Pakistan* 34°55N 76°40E **43**
Siasi *Phil.* 5°34N 120°50E **37**
Siau *Indonesia* 2°50N 125°25E **37**
Šiauliai *Lithuania* 55°56N 23°15E **9**
Sibâi, Gebel el *Egypt* 25°45N 34°10E **44**
Sibang *Indonesia* 8°34S 115°13E **37** K
Sibay *Russia* 52°42N 58°39E **18** D
Sibayi, L. *S. Africa* 27°20S 32°45E **57**
Šibenik *Croatia* 43°48N 15°54E **22**
Siberia = Sibirskiy □ *Russia* 58°0N 90°0E **29** D
Siberia *Russia* 60°0N 100°0E **4** D
Siberut *Indonesia* 1°30S 99°0E **36**
Sibi *Pakistan* 29°30N 67°54E **42**
Sibil = Oksibil *Indonesia* 4°59S 140°35E **37**
Sibiloi △ *Kenya* 4°0N 36°20E **54**
Sibirskiy □ *Russia* 58°0N 90°0E **29** D
Sibirtsevo *Russia* 44°12N 132°26E **30**
Sibiti *Congo* 3°38S 13°19E **52**
Sibiu *Romania* 45°45N 24°9E **17**
Sibley *U.S.A.* 43°24N 95°45W **80**
Sibolga *Indonesia* 1°42N 98°45E **36**
Siborongborong *Indonesia* 2°13N 98°59E **39**
Sibsagar *India* 27°0N 94°36E **41**
Sibu *Malaysia* 2°18N 111°49E **36**
Sibuco *Phil.* 7°20N 122°10E **37**
Sibuguey B. *Phil.* 7°50N 122°45E **37**
Sibut *C.A.R.* 5°46N 19°10E **52**
Sibutu *Phil.* 4°45N 119°30E **37**
Sibutu Passage *E. Indies* 4°50N 120°0E **37**
Sibuyan I. *Phil.* 12°25N 122°40E **37**
Sibuyan Sea *Phil.* 12°30N 122°20E **37**
Sicamous *Canada* 50°49N 119°0W **70**
Siccus → *Australia* 31°55S 139°17E **63**
Sichon *Thailand* 9°0N 99°54E **39**
Sichuan □ *China* 30°30N 103°0E **32**
Sicilia *Italy* 37°30N 14°30E **22**
Sicily = Sicilia *Italy* 37°30N 14°30E **22**
Sicily, Str. of *Medit. S.* 37°35N 11°56E **22**
Sico → *Honduras* 15°58N 84°58W **88**
Sicuani *Peru* 14°21S 71°10W **92**
Sidari *Greece* 39°47N 19°41E **25**
Siddhapur *India* 23°56N 72°25E **42**
Siddipet *India* 18°5N 78°51E **40**
Sideros, Akra *Greece* 35°19N 26°19E **25**
Sidhauli *India* 27°17N 80°50E **43**
Sidhi *India* 24°25N 81°53E **43**
Sidi-bel-Abbès *Algeria* 35°13N 0°39W **50**
Sidi Ifni *Morocco* 29°29N 10°12W **50**
Sidikalang *Indonesia* 2°45N 98°19E **39**
Sidlaw Hills *U.K.* 56°32N 3°2W **11**
Sidley, Mt. *Antarctica* 77°2S 126°2W **5**
Sidmouth *U.K.* 50°40N 3°15W **13**
Sidmouth, C. *Australia* 13°25S 143°36E **62**
Sidney *Canada* 48°39N 123°24W **78**
Sidney *Mont., U.S.A.* 47°43N 104°9W **76**

ney N.Y., U.S.A. 42°19N 75°24W 83 D9
ney Nebr., U.S.A. 41°8N 102°59W 80 E2
ney Ohio, U.S.A. 40°17N 84°9W 81 E11
ney Lanier, L. U.S.A. 34°10N 84°4W 85 D12
oarjo Indonesia 7°27S 112°43E 37 G15
on = Saydā Lebanon 33°35N 35°25E 46 B4
ra, G. of = Surt, Khalīj
ibya 31°40N 18°30E 51 B9
dlce Poland 52°10N 22°20E 17 B12
g → Germany 50°46N 7°6E 16 C4
gen Germany 50°51N 8°0E 16 C5
n Pang Cambodia 14°7N 106°23E 38 E6
n Reap = Siemreab
ambodia 13°20N 103°52E 38 F4
nreab Cambodia 13°20N 103°52E 38 F4
na Italy 43°19N 11°21E 22 C4
adz Poland 51°37N 18°41E 17 C10
pe, Bocas de la
enezuela 10°0N 61°30W 93 L15
ra Blanca U.S.A. 31°11N 105°22W 84 F2
ra Blanca Peak
.S.A. 33°23N 105°49W 77 K11
ra City U.S.A. 39°34N 120°38W 78 F6
ra Colorada
rgentina 40°35S 67°50W 96 E3
ra de Agalta △
onduras 15°1N 85°48W 88 C2
ra de Bahoruco △
om. Rep. 18°10N 71°25W 89 C5
ra de La Culata △
enezuela 8°45N 71°10W 89 E5
ra de Lancandón △
uatemala 16°59N 90°23W 88 C1
ra de las Quijadas △
rgentina 32°29S 67°5W 94 C2
ra de San Luis △
enezuela 11°20N 69°43W 89 D6
ra de San Pedro Mártir,
arque Nacional △
lexico 31°10N 115°30W 86 A1
ra Gorda Chile 22°50S 69°15W 94 A2
ra Leone ■ W. Afr. 9°0N 12°0W 50 G3
ra Madre Mexico 16°0N 93°0W 87 D6
ra Madre Occidental
lexico 27°0N 107°0W 86 B3
ra Madre Oriental
lexico 25°0N 100°0W 86 C5
ra Mojada Mexico 27°18N 103°41W 86 B4
ra Nevada Spain 37°3N 3°15W 21 D4
ra Nevada U.S.A. 39°0N 120°30W 78 H8
ra Nevada △
enezuela 8°35N 70°45W 89 E5
ra Nevada de Santa Marta △
olombia 10°56N 73°36W 89 D5
ra Vista U.S.A. 31°33N 110°18W 77 L8
raville U.S.A. 39°36N 120°22W 78 F6
os Greece 37°0N 24°45E 23 F11
n Canada 51°21N 100°8W 71 C8
n Pass Canada 57°52N 126°15W 70 B3
Algeria 35°32N 0°12W 50 A5
toka Fiji 18°8S 177°32E 59 a
etu-Marmaţiei
omania 47°57N 23°52E 17 E12
işoara Romania 46°12N 24°50E 17 E13
Indonesia 5°25N 96°0E 36 C1
ufjörður Iceland 66°12N 18°55W 8 C4
al de Botrang Belgium 50°29N 6°4E 15 D6
al Pk. U.S.A. 33°20N 114°2W 79 M12
y I. Antarctica 60°43S 45°36W 5 C18
g Ecuador 3°0S 78°50W 92 D3
enza Spain 41°3N 2°40W 21 B4
iri Guinea 11°31N 9°10W 50 F4
lda Latvia 57°10N 24°55E 9 H21
ra India 23°29N 80°6E 43 H9
ajoki → Finland 64°50N 24°43E 8 D21
njärvi Finland 63°4N 27°39E 8 E22
ira Ra. = Chizarira
mbabwe 17°36S 27°45E 55 F2
India 22°26N 69°47E 42 H3
nni Chief →
anada 57°47N 122°15W 70 B4
o Thailand 7°34N 99°21E 39 J2
r India 27°33N 75°10E 42 F6
sso Mali 11°18N 5°35W 50 F4
ston U.S.A. 36°53N 89°35W 80 G9
ote Alin, Khrebet
ussia 45°0N 136°0E 30 B8
ote Alin Ra. = Sikhote Alin,
hrebet Russia 45°0N 136°0E 30 B8
nos Greece 36°40N 25°8E 23 F11
im □ India 27°50N 88°30E 41 F16
→ Spain 42°27N 7°43W 21 A2
ayoapan Mexico 17°30N 98°9W 87 D5
wad India 21°54N 74°54E 42 J6
ar India 24°49N 92°48E 41 G18
City U.S.A. 35°44N 79°28W 85 D15
ia = Śląsk Poland 51°0N 16°30E 16 C9
rhi Doti Nepal 29°15N 81°0E 43 E9
at India 26°35N 93°0E 41 F18
ouette Seychelles 4°29S 55°12E 53 b
e Turkey 36°22N 33°58E 44 B2
uri = Shiliguri India 26°45N 88°25E 41 F16
g Co China 31°50N 89°20E 32 C3
tra Bulgaria 44°6N 27°19E 23 B12
ri Turkey 41°4N 28°14E 23 D13
n Sweden 60°55N 14°45E 8 F16
borg Denmark 56°10N 9°32E 9 H13
wood Australia 17°45S 146°2E 62 B4
huay, Cordillera
ile 19°46S 68°40W 92 G5
mäe Estonia 59°24N 27°45E 9 G22
th U.K. 54°52N 3°23W 12 C4
m Springs U.S.A. 36°11N 94°32W 84 C7
i Turkey 37°15N 42°27E 44 B4
ee U.S.A. 30°21N 94°11W 84 F7
ė Lithuania 55°21N 21°33E 9 J19
n Turkey 38°7N 41°2E 44 B4
Silvani India 23°18N 78°25E 43 H8
Silver City U.S.A. 32°46N 108°17W 77 K9
Silver Cr. → U.S.A. 43°16N 119°13W 76 E4
Silver Creek U.S.A. 42°33N 79°10W 82 D5
Silver L. U.S.A. 38°39N 120°6W 78 G6
Silver Lake Calif., U.S.A. 35°21N 116°7W 79 K10
Silver Lake Oreg., U.S.A. 43°8N 121°3W 76 E3
Silvermine Mts. Ireland 52°47N 8°15W 10 D3
Silverton Colo., U.S.A. 37°49N 107°40W 77 H10
Silverton Tex., U.S.A. 34°28N 101°19W 84 D4
Silvies → U.S.A. 43°34N 119°2W 76 E4
Simaltala India 24°43N 86°33E 43 G12
Simanggang = Sri Aman Malaysia 1°15N 111°32E 36 D4
Simard, L. Canada 47°40N 78°40W 72 C4
Simav Turkey 39°4N 28°58E 23 E13
Simba Tanzania 2°10S 37°36E 54 C4
Simbirsk = Ulyanovsk Russia 54°20N 48°25E 18 D8
Simbo Tanzania 4°51S 29°41E 54 C2
Simcoe Canada 42°50N 80°23W 82 D4
Simcoe, L. Canada 44°25N 79°20W 82 B5
Simdega India 22°37N 84°31E 43 H11
Simeria Romania 45°51N 23°1E 17 F12
Simeulue Indonesia 2°45N 95°45E 36 D1
Simferopol Ukraine 44°55N 34°3E 19 F5
Simi Greece 36°35N 27°50E 23 F12
Simi Valley U.S.A. 34°16N 118°47W 79 L8
Simikot Nepal 30°0N 81°50E 43 E9
Simla = Shimla India 31°2N 77°9E 42 D7
Simlipal △ India 21°45N 86°30E 43 J12
Simmie Canada 49°56N 108°6W 71 D7
Simmler U.S.A. 35°21N 119°59W 79 K7
Simo älv = Simojoki → Finland 65°35N 25°1E 8 D21
Simojoki → Finland 65°35N 25°1E 8 D21
Simojovel Mexico 17°12N 92°38W 87 D6
Simonette → Canada 55°9N 118°15W 70 B5
Simonstown S. Africa 34°14S 18°26E 56 E2
Simpang Empat Malaysia 5°27N 100°29E 39 c
Simplonpass Switz. 46°15N 8°3E 20 C8
Simpson Desert Australia 25°0S 137°0E 62 D2
Simpson Desert △ Australia 24°59S 138°21E 62 C2
Simpson Pen. Canada 68°34N 88°45W 69 C11
Simrishamn Sweden 55°33N 14°22E 9 J16
Simsbury U.S.A. 41°53N 72°48W 83 E12
Simushir, Ostrov Russia 46°50N 152°30E 29 E16
Sin Cowe I. S. China Sea 9°53N 114°19E 36 C4
Sina Dhago Somali Rep. 5°50N 47°0E 47 F4
Sinabang Indonesia 2°30N 96°24E 36 D1
Sinai = Es Sînâ' Egypt 29°0N 34°0E 46 F3
Sinai, Mt. = Mûsa, Gebel Egypt 28°33N 33°59E 44 D2
Sinaloa □ Mexico 25°0N 107°30W 86 C3
Sinaloa de Leyva Mexico 25°50N 108°14W 86 B3
Sinarades Greece 39°34N 19°51E 25 A3
Sincelejo Colombia 9°18N 75°24W 92 B3
Sinch'ang N. Korea 40°7N 128°28E 35 D15
Sinch'ŏn N. Korea 38°17N 125°21E 35 E13
Sinclair U.S.A. 41°47N 107°7W 76 F10
Sinclair Mills Canada 54°5N 121°40W 70 C4
Sinclair's B. U.K. 58°31N 3°5W 11 C5
Sinclairville U.S.A. 42°16N 79°16W 82 D5
Sincorá, Serra do Brazil 13°30S 41°0W 93 F10
Sind = Sindh □ Pakistan 26°0N 69°0E 42 G3
Sind → Jammu & Kashmir, India 34°18N 74°45E 43 B6
Sind → Mad. P., India 26°26N 79°13E 43 F8
Sind Sagar Doab Pakistan 32°0N 71°30E 42 D4
Sindangan Phil. 8°10N 123°5E 37 C6
Sindangbarang Indonesia 7°27S 107°1E 37 G12
Sinde Zambia 17°28S 25°51E 55 F2
Sindh = Indus → Pakistan 24°20N 67°47E 42 G2
Sindh □ Pakistan 26°0N 69°0E 42 G3
Sindri India 23°45N 86°42E 43 H12
Sines Portugal 37°56N 8°51W 21 D1
Sines, C. de Portugal 37°58N 8°53W 21 D1
Sineu Spain 39°38N 3°1E 24 B10
Sing Buri Thailand 14°53N 100°25E 38 E3
Singa Sudan 13°10N 33°57E 51 F12
Singalila △ India 27°10N 88°5E 43 F13
Singapore ■ Asia 1°17N 103°51E 39 d
Singapore, Straits of Asia 1°15N 104°0E 39 d
Singapore Changi ✕ (SIN) Singapore 1°23N 103°59E 39 M4
Singaraja Indonesia 8°7S 115°6E 37 J18
Singatoka = Sigatoka Fiji 18°8S 177°32E 59 a
Singida Tanzania 4°49S 34°48E 54 C3
Singida □ Tanzania 6°0S 34°30E 54 D3
Singkaling Hkamti Burma 26°0N 95°39E 41 G19
Singkang Indonesia 4°8S 120°1E 37 E6
Singkawang Indonesia 1°0N 108°57E 36 D3
Singkep Indonesia 0°30S 104°25E 36 E2
Singkil Indonesia 2°17N 97°49E 39 L1
Singleton Australia 32°33S 151°0E 63 E5
Singleton, Mt. N. Terr., Australia 22°0S 130°46E 60 D5
Singleton, Mt. W. Austral., Australia 29°27S 117°15E 61 E2
Singoli India 25°0N 75°22E 42 G6
Singora = Songkhla Thailand 7°13N 100°37E 39 J3
Sinhŭng N. Korea 40°11N 127°34E 35 D14
Siniscóla Italy 40°34N 9°41E 22 D3
Sinjai Indonesia 5°7S 120°20E 37 F6
Sinjār Iraq 36°19N 41°52E 44 B4
Sinkat Sudan 18°55N 36°49E 51 E13
Sinkiang = Xinjiang Uygur Zizhiqu □ China 42°0N 86°0E 32 C3
Sinmak N. Korea 38°25N 126°14E 35 E14
Sinmi-do N. Korea 39°33N 124°53E 35 E13
Sinnamary Fr. Guiana 5°25N 53°0W 93 B8
Sinni → Italy 40°8N 16°41E 22 D7
Sinop Turkey 42°1N 35°11E 19 F6
Sinor India 21°55N 73°20E 42 J5
Sinp'o N. Korea 40°0N 128°13E 35 E15
Sinsk Russia 61°8N 126°48E 29 C13
Sintang Indonesia 0°5N 111°35E 36 D4
Sinton U.S.A. 28°2N 97°31W 84 G6
Sintra Portugal 38°47N 9°25W 21 C1
Sinŭiju N. Korea 40°5N 124°24E 35 D13
Siocon Phil. 7°40N 122°10E 37 C6
Siófok Hungary 46°54N 18°3E 17 E10
Sion Switz. 46°14N 7°20E 20 C7
Sion Mills U.K. 54°48N 7°29W 10 B4
Sioux Center U.S.A. 43°5N 96°11W 80 D5
Sioux City U.S.A. 42°30N 96°24W 80 D5
Sioux Falls U.S.A. 43°33N 96°44W 80 D5
Sioux Lookout Canada 50°10N 91°50W 72 B1
Sioux Narrows Canada 49°25N 94°10W 71 D10
Sipadan Malaysia 7°6N 118°38E 37 D5
Siparia Trin. & Tob. 10°8N 61°31W 93 K15
Siping China 43°8N 124°21E 35 C13
Sipiwesk L. Canada 55°5N 97°35W 71 B9
Siple Antarctica 75°0S 74°0W 5 D7
Sipra → India 23°55N 75°28E 42 H6
Sipura Indonesia 2°18S 99°40E 36 E1
Siquia → Nic. 12°10N 84°20W 88 D3
Siquijor Phil. 9°12N 123°35E 37 C6
Siquirres Costa Rica 10°6N 83°30W 88 D3
Şīr Abu Nu'ayr U.A.E. 25°20N 54°20E 45 E7
Şīr Banī Yās U.A.E. 24°19N 52°37E 45 E7
Sir Edward Pellew Group Australia 15°40S 137°10E 62 B2
Sir Graham Moore Is. Australia 13°53S 126°34E 60 B4
Sir James MacBrien, Mt. Canada 62°7N 127°41W 68 C7
Sira → Norway 58°23N 6°34E 9 G12
Siracusa Italy 37°4N 15°17E 22 F6
Sirajganj Bangla. 24°25N 89°47E 43 G13
Sirathu India 25°39N 81°19E 43 G9
Sīrdān Iran 36°39N 49°12E 45 B6
Siren U.S.A. 45°47N 92°24W 80 C7
Sirer Spain 38°56N 1°22E 24 C7
Siret → Romania 45°24N 28°1E 17 F14
Sirghāyā Syria 33°51N 36°8E 46 B5
Sirinat △ Thailand 8°6N 98°17E 39 a
Sīrjān Iran 29°30N 55°45E 45 D7
Sirmaur India 24°51N 81°23E 43 G9
Sirohi India 24°52N 72°53E 42 G5
Sironj India 24°5N 77°39E 42 G7
Síros = Syros Greece 37°28N 24°57E 23 F11
Sirr, Nafud as Si. Arabia 25°33N 44°35E 44 E5
Sirretta Pk. U.S.A. 35°56N 118°19W 79 K8
Sīrrī Iran 25°55N 54°32E 45 E7
Sirsa India 29°33N 75°4E 42 E6
Sirsa → India 26°51N 79°4E 43 F8
Sisak Croatia 45°30N 16°21E 16 F9
Sisaket Thailand 15°8N 104°23E 38 E5
Sishen S. Africa 27°47S 22°59E 56 D3
Sishui Henan, China 34°48N 113°15E 34 G7
Sishui Shandong, China 35°42N 117°18E 35 G9
Sisipuk L. Canada 55°45N 101°50W 71 B8
Sisophon Cambodia 13°38N 102°59E 38 F4
Sisseton U.S.A. 45°40N 97°3W 80 C5
Sīstān Asia 30°50N 61°0E 45 D9
Sīstān, Daryācheh-ye Iran 31°0N 61°0E 45 D9
Sīstān va Balūchestān □ Iran 27°0N 62°0E 45 E9
Sisters U.S.A. 44°18N 121°33W 76 D3
Sisters, The Seychelles 4°16S 55°52E 53 b
Siswa Bazar India 27°9N 83°46E 43 F10
Sitamarhi India 26°37N 85°30E 43 F11
Sitampiky Madag. 16°41S 46°6E 57 B8
Sitapur India 27°38N 80°45E 43 F9
Siteki Swaziland 26°32S 31°58E 57 D5
Sitges Spain 41°17N 1°47E 21 B6
Sitia Greece 35°13N 26°6E 25 D8
Sitito-Ozima Ridge Pac. Oc. 23°0N 143°0E 64 E6
Sitka U.S.A. 57°3N 135°20W 70 B1
Sitoti Botswana 23°15S 23°40E 56 C3
Sittang Myit → Burma 17°20N 96°45E 41 L20
Sittard Neths. 51°0N 5°52E 15 C5
Sittingbourne U.K. 51°21N 0°45E 13 F8
Sittoung = Sittang Myit → Burma 17°20N 96°45E 41 L20
Sittwe Burma 20°18N 92°45E 41 J18
Situbondo Indonesia 7°42S 114°0E 37 G16
Si'umu Samoa 14°1S 171°48W 59 b
Siuna Nic. 13°37N 84°45W 88 D3
Siuri India 23°50N 87°34E 43 H12
Sīvand Iran 30°5N 52°55E 45 D7
Sivas Turkey 39°43N 36°58E 44 B3
Siverek Turkey 37°50N 39°19E 44 B3
Sivomaskinskiy Russia 66°40N 62°35E 18 A11
Sivrihisar Turkey 39°30N 31°35E 19 G5
Sîwa Egypt 29°11N 25°31E 51 C11
Sîwa, El Wâhât es Egypt 29°10N 25°30E 48 D6
Siwa Oasis = Sîwa, El Wâhât es Egypt 29°10N 25°30E 48 D6
Siwalik Range Nepal 28°0N 83°0E 43 F10
Siwan India 26°13N 84°21E 43 F11
Siwana India 25°38N 72°25E 42 G5
Six Cross Roads Barbados 13°7N 59°28W 89 g
Sixmilebridge Ireland 52°44N 8°46W 10 D3
Sixth Cataract Sudan 16°20N 32°42E 51 E12
Siyah Kuh, Kavīr-e Iran 32°55N 53°55E 45 C7
Siziwang Qi China 41°25N 111°40E 34 D6
Sjælland Denmark 55°30N 11°30E 9 J14
Sjumen = Shumen Bulgaria 43°18N 26°55E 23 C12
Skadarsko Jezero Europe 42°10N 19°20E 23 C8
Skaftafell Iceland 64°1N 17°0W 8 D5
Skaftafell △ Iceland 64°9N 16°50W 8 D5
Skagafjörður Iceland 65°54N 19°35W 8 D4
Skagastølstindane Norway 61°28N 7°52E 8 F12
Skagaströnd Iceland 65°50N 20°19W 8 D3
Skagen Denmark 57°43N 10°35E 9 H14
Skagerrak Denmark 57°30N 9°0E 9 H13
Skagit → U.S.A. 48°23N 122°22W 78 B4
Skagway U.S.A. 59°28N 135°19W 68 D6
Skala-Podilska Ukraine 48°50N 26°15E 17 D14
Skalat Ukraine 49°23N 25°55E 17 D13
Skåne Sweden 55°59N 13°30E 9 J15
Skaneateles U.S.A. 42°57N 76°26W 83 D8
Skaneateles L. U.S.A. 42°51N 76°22W 83 D8
Skardu Pakistan 35°20N 75°44E 43 B6
Skarżysko-Kamienna Poland 51°7N 20°52E 17 C11
Skeena → Canada 54°9N 130°5W 70 C2
Skeena Mts. Canada 56°40N 128°30W 70 B3
Skegness U.K. 53°9N 0°20E 12 D8
Skeldon = Corriverton Guyana 5°55N 57°20W 92 B7
Skeleton Coast Namibia 20°0S 13°0E 53 J2
Skeleton Coast ⌂ Namibia 20°0S 13°20E 56 C1
Skellefteå Sweden 64°45N 20°50E 8 D19
Skellefteälven → Sweden 64°45N 21°10E 8 D19
Skelleftehamn Sweden 64°40N 21°9E 8 D19
Skerries, The U.K. 53°25N 4°36W 12 D3
Ski Norway 59°43N 10°52E 9 G14
Skiathos Greece 39°12N 23°30E 23 E10
Skibbereen Ireland 51°33N 9°16W 10 E2
Skiddaw U.K. 54°39N 3°9W 12 C4
Skidegate Canada 53°15N 132°1W 70 C2
Skien Norway 59°12N 9°35E 9 G13
Skierniewice Poland 51°58N 20°10E 17 C11
Skihist, Mt. Canada 50°12N 121°54W 70 C4
Skikda Algeria 36°50N 6°58E 50 A7
Skilloura Cyprus 35°14N 33°10E 25 D12
Skipton U.K. 53°58N 2°3W 12 D5
Skirmish Pt. Australia 11°59S 134°17E 62 A1
Skiros Greece 38°55N 24°34E 23 E11
Skive Denmark 56°33N 9°2E 9 H13
Skjálfandafljót → Iceland 65°59N 17°25W 8 D5
Skjálfandi Iceland 66°5N 17°30W 8 C5
Skole Ukraine 49°3N 23°30E 17 D12
Skopelos Greece 39°9N 23°47E 23 E10
Skopi Greece 35°11N 26°2E 25 D8
Skopje Macedonia 42°1N 21°26E 23 C9
Skövde Sweden 58°24N 13°50E 9 G15
Skovorodino Russia 54°0N 124°0E 29 D13
Skowhegan U.S.A. 44°46N 69°43W 81 C19
Skull Ireland 51°32N 9°34W 10 E2
Skunk → U.S.A. 40°42N 91°7W 80 E8
Skuodas Lithuania 56°16N 21°33E 9 H19
Skvyra Ukraine 49°44N 29°40E 17 D15
Skye U.K. 57°15N 6°10W 11 D2
Skykomish U.S.A. 47°42N 121°22W 76 C3
Skyros = Skiros Greece 38°55N 24°34E 23 E11
Slade Pt. Australia 21°5S 149°13E 62 K7
Slættaratindur Færoe Is. 62°18N 7°1W 8 E9
Slagelse Denmark 55°23N 11°19E 9 J14
Slamet Indonesia 7°16S 109°8E 37 G13
Slane Ireland 53°42N 6°33W 10 C5
Slaney → Ireland 52°26N 6°33W 10 D5
Slangberge S. Africa 31°32S 20°48E 56 E3
Śląsk Poland 51°0N 16°30E 16 C9
Slate Is. Canada 48°40N 87°0W 72 C2
Slatina Romania 44°28N 24°22E 17 F13
Slatington U.S.A. 40°45N 75°37W 83 F9
Slaton U.S.A. 33°26N 101°39W 84 E4
Slave → Canada 61°18N 113°39W 70 A6
Slave Coast W. Afr. 6°0N 2°30E 50 G6
Slave Lake Canada 55°17N 114°43W 70 B6
Slave Pt. Canada 61°11N 115°56W 70 A5
Slavgorod Russia 53°1N 78°37E 28 D8
Slavonski Brod Croatia 45°11N 18°1E 23 B8
Slavuta Ukraine 50°15N 27°2E 17 C14
Slavyanka Russia 42°53N 131°21E 30 C5
Slavyansk = Slovyansk Ukraine 48°55N 37°36E 19 E6
Slawharad Belarus 53°27N 31°0E 17 B16
Sleaford U.K. 53°0N 0°24W 12 D7
Sleaford B. Australia 34°55S 135°45E 63 E2
Sleat, Sd. of U.K. 57°5N 5°47W 11 D3
Sleeper Is. Canada 58°30N 81°0W 69 D11
Sleeping Bear Dunes ⌂ U.S.A. 44°50N 86°5W 80 C10
Sleepy Eye U.S.A. 44°18N 94°43W 80 C6
Slemon L. Canada 63°13N 116°4W 70 A5
Slide Mt. U.S.A. 42°0N 74°25W 83 E10
Slidell U.S.A. 30°17N 89°47W 85 F10
Sliema Malta 35°55N 14°30E 25 D2
Slieve Aughty Ireland 53°4N 8°30W 10 C3
Slieve Bloom Ireland 53°4N 7°40W 10 C4
Slieve Donard U.K. 54°11N 5°55W 10 B6
Slieve Gamph Ireland 54°6N 9°0W 10 B3
Slieve Gullion U.K. 54°7N 6°26W 10 B5
Slieve League Ireland 54°40N 8°42W 10 B3
Slieve Mish Ireland 52°12N 9°50W 10 D2
Slievenamon Ireland 52°25N 7°34W 10 D4
Sligeach = Sligo Ireland 54°16N 8°28W 10 B3
Sligo Ireland 54°16N 8°28W 10 B3
Sligo U.S.A. 41°6N 79°29W 82 E5
Sligo □ Ireland 54°8N 8°42W 10 B3
Sligo B. Ireland 54°18N 8°40W 10 B3
Slippery Rock U.S.A. 41°4N 80°3W 82 E4
Slite Sweden 57°42N 18°48E 9 H18
Sliven Bulgaria 42°42N 26°19E 23 C12
Sloan U.S.A. 35°57N 115°13W 79 K11
Sloansville U.S.A. 42°45N 74°22W 83 D10
Slobodskoy Russia 58°40N 50°6E 18 C9
Slobozia Romania 44°34N 27°23E 17 F14
Slocan Canada 49°48N 117°28W 70 D5
Slonim Belarus 53°4N 25°19E 17 B13
Slough U.K. 51°30N 0°36W 13 F7
Slough □ U.K. 51°30N 0°36W 13 F7
Sloughhouse U.S.A. 38°26N 121°12W 78 G5
Slovak Rep. ■ Europe 48°30N 20°0E 17 D10
Slovakia = Slovak Rep. ■ Europe 48°30N 20°0E 17 D10
Slovakian Ore Mts. = Slovenské Rudohorie Slovak Rep. 48°45N 20°0E 17 D10
Slovenia ■ Europe 45°58N 14°30E 16 F8
Slovenija = Slovenia ■ Europe 45°58N 14°30E 16 F8
Slovenska = Slovak Rep. ■ Europe 48°30N 20°0E 17 D10
Slovenské Rudohorie Slovak Rep. 48°45N 20°0E 17 D10
Slovyansk Ukraine 48°55N 37°36E 19 E6
Sluch → Ukraine 51°37N 26°38E 17 C14
Sluis Neths. 51°18N 3°23E 15 C3
Słupsk Poland 54°30N 17°3E 17 A9
Slurry S. Africa 25°49S 25°42E 56 D4
Slutsk Belarus 53°2N 27°31E 17 B14
Slyne Hd. Ireland 53°25N 10°10W 10 C1
Slyudyanka Russia 51°40N 103°40E 29 D11
Småland Sweden 57°15N 15°25E 9 H16
Smalltree L. Canada 61°0N 105°0W 71 A8
Smallwood Res. Canada 54°5N 64°30W 73 B7
Smarhon Belarus 54°20N 26°24E 17 A14
Smartt Syndicate Dam S. Africa 30°45S 23°10E 56 E3
Smartville U.S.A. 39°13N 121°18W 78 F5
Smeaton Canada 53°30N 104°49W 71 C8
Smederevo Serbia 44°40N 20°57E 23 B9
Smerwick Harbour Ireland 52°12N 10°23W 10 D1
Smethport U.S.A. 41°49N 78°27W 82 E6
Smidovich Russia 48°36N 133°49E 29 E14
Smith Canada 55°10N 114°0W 70 B6
Smith Center U.S.A. 39°47N 98°47W 80 F4
Smith River ⌂ U.S.A. 41°55N 124°0W 76 F2
Smithburne → Australia 17°3S 140°57E 62 B3
Smithers Canada 54°45N 127°10W 70 C3
Smithfield S. Africa 30°9S 26°30E 57 E4
Smithfield N.C., U.S.A. 35°31N 78°21W 85 D15
Smithfield Utah, U.S.A. 41°50N 111°50W 76 F8
Smiths Falls Canada 44°55N 76°0W 83 B9
Smithton Australia 40°53S 145°6E 63 G4
Smithville Canada 43°6N 79°33W 82 C5
Smithville U.S.A. 30°1N 97°10W 84 F6
Smoke Creek Desert U.S.A. 40°30N 119°40W 76 F4
Smoky → Canada 56°10N 117°21W 70 B5
Smoky Bay Australia 32°22S 134°13E 63 E1
Smoky Hill → U.S.A. 39°4N 96°48W 80 F5
Smoky Hills U.S.A. 39°15N 99°30W 80 F4
Smoky Lake Canada 54°10N 112°30W 70 C6
Smøla Norway 63°23N 8°3E 8 E13
Smolensk Russia 54°45N 32°5E 18 D5
Smolikas, Oros Greece 40°9N 20°58E 23 D9
Smolyan Bulgaria 41°36N 24°38E 23 D11
Smooth Rock Falls Canada 49°17N 81°37W 72 C3
Smoothstone L. Canada 54°40N 106°50W 71 C7
Smorgon = Smarhon Belarus 54°20N 26°24E 17 A14
Smyrna = İzmir Turkey 38°25N 27°8E 23 E12
Smyrna U.S.A. 39°18N 75°36W 81 F16
Snæfell Iceland 64°48N 15°34W 8 D6
Snaefell I. of Man 54°16N 4°27W 12 C3
Snæfellsjökull Iceland 64°49N 23°46W 8 D2
Snake → U.S.A. 46°12N 119°2W 76 C4
Snake I. Australia 38°47S 146°33E 63 F4
Snake Range U.S.A. 39°0N 114°20W 76 G6
Snake River Plain U.S.A. 42°50N 114°0W 76 E7
Snåsavatnet Norway 64°12N 12°0E 8 D15
Sneek Neths. 53°2N 5°40E 15 A5
Sneem Ireland 51°50N 9°54W 10 E2
Sneeuberge S. Africa 31°46S 24°20E 56 E3
Snelling U.S.A. 37°31N 120°26W 78 H6
Sněžka Europe 50°41N 15°50E 16 C8
Snizort, L. U.K. 57°33N 6°28W 11 D2
Snøhetta Norway 62°19N 9°16E 8 E13
Snohomish U.S.A. 47°55N 122°6W 78 C4
Snoqualmie Pass U.S.A. 47°25N 121°25W 78 C5
Snoul Cambodia 12°4N 106°26E 39 F6
Snover U.S.A. 43°27N 82°58W 82 C2
Snow Hill U.S.A. 38°11N 75°24W 81 F16
Snow Lake Canada 54°52N 100°3W 71 C8
Snow Mt. Calif., U.S.A. 39°23N 122°45W 78 F4
Snow Mt. Maine, U.S.A. 45°18N 70°48W 83 A14
Snow Shoe U.S.A. 41°2N 77°57W 82 E7
Snowbird L. Canada 60°45N 103°0W 71 A8
Snowdon U.K. 53°4N 4°5W 12 D3
Snowdonia △ U.K. 53°7N 3°59W 12 D4
Snowdrift = Łutsel K'e Canada 62°24N 110°44W 71 A6
Snowdrift → Canada 62°24N 110°44W 71 A6
Snowflake U.S.A. 34°30N 110°5W 77 J8
Snowshoe Pk. U.S.A. 48°13N 115°41W 76 B6
Snowtown Australia 33°46S 138°14E 63 E2
Snowville U.S.A. 41°58N 112°43W 76 F7
Snowy → Australia 37°46S 148°30E 63 F4
Snowy Mt. U.S.A. 43°42N 74°23W 83 C10
Snowy Mts. Australia 36°30S 148°20E 63 F4
Snug Corner Bahamas 22°33N 73°52W 89 B5
Snug Harbour Canada 45°22N 80°17W 82 A4
Snyatyn Ukraine 48°27N 25°38E 17 D13
Snyder Okla., U.S.A. 34°40N 98°57W 84 D5
Snyder Tex., U.S.A. 32°44N 100°55W 84 E4
Soahanina Madag. 18°42S 44°13E 57 B7
Soalala Madag. 16°6S 45°20E 57 B8
Soaloka Madag. 18°32S 45°15E 57 B8
Soamanonga Madag. 23°52S 44°47E 57 C7
Soan → Pakistan 33°1N 71°44E 42 C4
Soanierana-Ivongo Madag. 16°55S 49°35E 57 B8
Soanindraniny Madag. 19°54S 47°14E 57 B8
Soavina Madag. 20°23S 46°56E 57 C8
Soavinandriana Madag. 19°9S 46°45E 57 B8
Sobat, Nahr → Sudan 9°22N 31°33E 51 G12
Sobhapur India 22°47N 78°17E 42 H8
Sobradinho, Represa de Brazil 9°30S 42°0W 93 E10

Sobral Brazil 3°50S 40°20W 93 D10
Soc Giang Vietnam 22°54N 106°1E 38 A6
Soc Trang Vietnam 9°37N 105°50E 39 H5
Socastee U.S.A. 33°41N 78°59W 85 E15
Soch'e = Shache China 38°20N 77°10E 32 C2
Sochi Russia 43°35N 39°40E 19 F6
Société, Îs. de la French Polynesia 17°0S 151°0W 65 J12
Society Is. = Société, Îs. de la French Polynesia 17°0S 151°0W 65 J12
Socompa, Portezuelo de Chile 24°27S 68°18W 94 A2
Socorro N. Mex., U.S.A. 34°4N 106°54W 77 J10
Socorro Tex., U.S.A. 31°39N 106°18W 84 F1
Socorro, I. Mexico 18°45N 110°58W 86 D2
Socotra Yemen 12°30N 54°0E 47 E5
Soda L. U.S.A. 35°10N 116°4W 77 J5
Soda Plains India 35°30N 79°0E 43 B8
Soda Springs U.S.A. 42°39N 111°36W 76 E8
Sodankylä Finland 67°29N 26°40E 8 C22
Soddy-Daisy U.S.A. 35°17N 85°10W 85 D12
Söderhamn Sweden 61°18N 17°10E 8 F17
Söderköping Sweden 58°31N 16°20E 9 G17
Södermanland Sweden 58°56N 16°55E 9 G17
Södertälje Sweden 59°12N 17°39E 9 G17
Sodiri Sudan 14°27N 29°0E 51 F11
Sodus U.S.A. 43°14N 77°4W 82 C7
Sodwana Bay △ S. Africa 27°35S 32°43E 57 D5
Soekmekaar = Morebeng S. Africa 23°30S 29°55E 57 C4
Soest Neths. 52°9N 5°19E 15 B5
Sofala □ Mozam. 19°30S 34°30E 57 B5
Sofia = Sofiya Bulgaria 42°45N 23°20E 23 C10
Sofia → Madag. 15°27S 47°23E 57 B8
Sofiya Bulgaria 42°45N 23°20E 23 C10
Sōfu-Gan Japan 29°49N 140°21E 31 K10
Sogamoso Colombia 5°43N 72°56W 92 B4
Sogār Iran 25°53N 58°6E 45 E8
Sogndalsfjøra Norway 61°14N 7°5E 8 F12
Søgne Norway 58°5N 7°48E 9 G12
Sognefjorden Norway 61°10N 5°50E 8 F11
Soh Iran 33°26N 51°27E 45 C6
Sohâg Egypt 26°33N 31°43E 51 C12
Sohagpur India 22°42N 78°12E 42 H8
Soignies Belgium 50°35N 4°5E 15 D4
Soissons France 49°25N 3°19E 20 B5
Sōja Japan 34°40N 133°45E 31 G6
Sojat India 25°55N 73°45E 42 G5
Sokal Ukraine 50°31N 24°15E 17 C13
Sokcho S. Korea 38°12N 128°36E 35 E15
Söke Turkey 37°48N 27°28E 23 F12
Sokelo Dem. Rep. of the Congo 9°55S 24°36E 55 D1
Sokhumi Georgia 43°0N 41°0E 19 F7
Soko Is. China 22°10N 113°54E 33 G10
Sokodé Togo 9°0N 1°11E 50 G6
Sokol Russia 59°30N 40°5E 18 C7
Sokółka Poland 53°25N 23°30E 17 B12
Sokołów Podlaski Poland 52°25N 22°15E 17 B12
Sokoto Nigeria 13°2N 5°16E 50 F7
Sol Iletsk Russia 51°10N 55°0E 18 D10
Solai Kenya 0°2N 36°12E 54 B4
Solan India 30°55N 77°7E 42 D7
Solana Beach U.S.A. 32°58N 117°16W 79 N9
Solander I. N.Z. 46°34S 166°54E 59 G1
Solano Phil. 16°31N 121°15E 37 A6
Solapur India 17°43N 75°56E 40 L9
Soldotna U.S.A. 60°29N 151°3W 68 C4
Soléa Cyprus 35°5N 33°4E 25 D12
Soledad Colombia 10°55N 74°46W 92 A4
Soledad U.S.A. 36°26N 121°20W 78 J5
Soledad Venezuela 8°10N 63°34W 92 B6
Solent, The U.K. 50°45N 1°25W 13 G6
Solfonntaggen Norway 60°2N 6°57E 9 F12
Solhan Turkey 38°57N 41°3E 44 B4
Soligalich Russia 59°5N 42°10E 18 C7
Soligorsk = Salihorsk Belarus 52°51N 27°27E 17 B14
Solihull U.K. 52°26N 1°47W 13 E6
Solikamsk Russia 59°38N 56°50E 18 C10
Solila Madag. 21°25S 46°37E 57 C8
Solimões = Amazonas → S. Amer. 0°5S 50°0W 93 D8
Solingen Germany 51°10N 7°5E 16 C4
Sollefteå Sweden 63°12N 17°20E 8 E17
Sóller Spain 39°46N 2°43E 24 B9
Solo → Indonesia 6°47S 112°22E 37 G15
Sologne France 47°40N 1°45E 20 C4
Solok Indonesia 0°45S 100°40E 36 E2
Sololá Guatemala 14°49N 91°10W 88 D1
Sololo Kenya 3°33N 38°39E 54 B4
Solomon, N. Fork → U.S.A. 39°29N 98°26W 80 F4
Solomon, S. Fork → U.S.A. 39°25N 99°12W 80 F4
Solomon Is. ■ Pac. Oc. 6°0S 155°0E 58 B8
Solomon Rise Pac. Oc. 1°0N 157°0E 64 G7
Solon China 46°32N 121°10E 33 B7
Solon Springs U.S.A. 46°22N 91°49W 80 B8
Solor Indonesia 8°27S 123°0E 37 F6
Solothurn Switz. 47°13N 7°32E 20 C7
Šolta Croatia 43°24N 16°15E 22 C7
Solṭānābād Khorāsān, Iran 34°13N 59°58E 45 C8
Solṭānābād Khorāsān, Iran 36°29N 58°5E 45 B8
Solunska Glava Macedonia 41°44N 21°31E 23 D9
Solvang U.S.A. 34°36N 120°8W 79 L6
Solvay U.S.A. 43°3N 76°13W 83 C8
Sölvesborg Sweden 56°5N 14°35E 9 H16
Solvychegodsk Russia 61°21N 46°56E 18 B8
Solway Firth U.K. 54°49N 3°35W 12 C4
Solwezi Zambia 12°11S 26°21E 55 E2
Sōma Japan 37°40N 140°50E 30 F10
Soma Turkey 39°10N 27°35E 23 E12
Somabhula Zimbabwe 19°42S 29°40E 57 B4
Somali Pen. Africa 7°0N 46°0E 48 F8
Somali Rep. ■ Africa 7°0N 47°0E 47 F4
Somalia = Somali Rep. ■ Africa 7°0N 47°0E 47 F4
Somaliland □ Somali Rep. 9°0N 46°0E 47 F4
Sombor Serbia 45°46N 19°9E 23 B8
Sombra Canada 42°43N 82°29W 82 D2
Sombrerete Mexico 23°38N 103°39W 86 C4
Sombrero Anguilla 18°37N 63°30W 89 C7
Somdari India 25°47N 72°38E 42 G5
Somers U.S.A. 48°5N 114°13W 76 B6
Somerset Ky., U.S.A. 37°5N 84°36W 81 G11
Somerset Mass., U.S.A. 41°47N 71°8W 83 E13
Somerset Pa., U.S.A. 40°1N 79°5W 82 F5
Somerset □ U.K. 51°9N 3°0W 13 F5
Somerset East S. Africa 32°42S 25°35E 56 E4
Somerset I. Canada 73°30N 93°0W 68 B10
Somerset West S. Africa 34°8S 18°50E 56 E2
Somersworth U.S.A. 43°16N 70°52W 83 C14
Somerton U.S.A. 32°36N 114°43W 77 K6
Somerville U.S.A. 40°35N 74°38W 83 F10
Someș → Romania 47°49N 22°43E 17 D12
Somme → France 50°11N 1°38E 20 A4
Somnath India 20°53N 70°22E 42 J4
Somosierra, Puerto de Spain 41°4N 3°35W 21 B4
Somosomo Fiji 16°47S 179°58W 59 a
Somosomo Str. Fiji 16°0S 180°0E 59 a
Somoto Nic. 13°28N 86°37W 88 D2
Somport, Tunnel de Spain 42°48N 0°31W 20 E3
Son → India 25°42N 84°52E 43 G11
Son Ha Vietnam 15°3N 108°34E 38 E7
Son Hoa Vietnam 13°2N 108°58E 38 F7
Son La Vietnam 21°20N 103°50E 38 B4
Son Morrell Spain 39°44N 3°20E 24 B10
Son Rapinya Spain 39°35N 2°37E 24 B9
Son Sardina Spain 39°37N 2°40E 24 B9
Son Serra Spain 39°43N 3°13E 24 B10
Son Tay Vietnam 21°8N 105°30E 38 B5
Soná Panama 8°0N 81°20W 88 E3
Sonamarg India 34°18N 75°21E 43 B6
Sonamukhi India 23°18N 87°27E 43 H12
Sonar → India 24°24N 79°56E 43 G8
Sŏnch'ŏn N. Korea 39°48N 124°55E 35 E13
Sondags → S. Africa 33°44S 25°51E 56 E4
Sondar India 33°28N 75°56E 43 C6
Sønderborg Denmark 54°55N 9°49E 9 J13
Sóndrio Italy 46°10N 9°52E 20 C8
Sone Mozam. 17°23S 34°55E 55 F3
Sonepur India 20°55N 83°50E 41 J13
Song Thailand 18°28N 100°11E 38 C3
Song Cau Vietnam 13°27N 109°18E 38 F7
Song Hong → Vietnam 22°0N 104°0E 32 D5
Song Xian China 34°12N 112°8E 34 G7
Songan Indonesia 8°13S 115°24E 37 J18
Songea Tanzania 10°40S 35°40E 55 E4
Songgang China 22°46N 113°50E 33 F10
Songhua Hu China 43°35N 126°50E 35 C14
Songhua Jiang → China 47°45N 132°30E 33 B8
Songimvelo △ S. Africa 25°50S 31°2E 57 D5
Sŏngjin = Kimch'aek N. Korea 40°40N 129°10E 35 D15
Songkhla Thailand 7°13N 100°37E 39 J3
Songnim N. Korea 38°45N 125°39E 35 E13
Songo Mozam. 15°34S 32°38E 55 F3
Songo Sudan 9°47N 24°21E 51 G10
Songpan China 32°40N 103°30E 32 C5
Songwe Dem. Rep. of the Congo 3°20S 26°16E 54 C2
Songwe → Africa 9°44S 33°58E 55 D3
Sonhat India 23°29N 82°31E 43 H10
Sonid Youqi China 42°45N 112°48E 34 C7
Sonipat India 29°0N 77°5E 42 E7
Sonkach India 22°59N 76°21E 42 H7
Sonmiani Pakistan 25°25N 66°40E 42 G2
Sonmiani B. Pakistan 25°15N 66°30E 42 G2
Sono → Brazil 9°58S 48°11W 93 E9
Sonoma U.S.A. 38°18N 122°28W 78 G4
Sonora Calif., U.S.A. 37°59N 120°23W 78 H6
Sonora Tex., U.S.A. 30°34N 100°39W 84 F4
Sonora □ Mexico 29°20N 110°40W 86 B2
Sonora → Mexico 29°5N 110°55W 86 B2
Sonoran Desert U.S.A. 33°40N 113°30W 79 L12
Sonoyta Mexico 31°51N 112°50W 86 A2
Sonsonate El Salv. 13°43N 89°44W 88 D2
Soochow = Suzhou China 31°19N 120°38E 33 C7
Sooke Canada 48°13N 123°43W 78 B3
Soomaaliya = Somali Rep. ■ Africa 7°0N 47°0E 47 F4
Sop Hao Laos 20°33N 104°27E 38 B5
Sop Prap Thailand 17°53N 99°20E 38 D2
Sopi Indonesia 2°34N 128°28E 37 D7
Sopot Poland 54°27N 18°31E 17 A10
Sopron Hungary 47°45N 16°32E 17 E9
Sopur India 34°18N 74°27E 43 B6
Sør-Rondane Antarctica 72°0S 25°0E 5 D4
Sorah Pakistan 27°13N 68°56E 42 F3
Soraon India 25°37N 81°51E 43 G9
Sorel Canada 46°0N 73°10W 72 C5
Sórgono Italy 40°1N 9°6E 22 D3
Soria Spain 41°43N 2°32W 21 B4
Soriano Uruguay 33°24S 58°19W 94 C4
Sorkh, Kuh-e Iran 35°40N 58°30E 45 C8
Soroca Moldova 48°8N 28°12E 17 D15
Sorocaba Brazil 23°31S 47°27W 95 A6
Sorochinsk Russia 52°26N 53°10E 18 D9
Soroki = Soroca Moldova 48°8N 28°12E 17 D15
Sorong Indonesia 0°55S 131°15E 37 E8
Soroni Greece 36°21N 28°1E 25 C10
Soroti Uganda 1°43N 33°35E 54 B3
Sørøya Norway 70°40N 22°30E 8 A20
Sørøysundet Norway 70°25N 23°0E 8 A20
Sorrell Australia 42°47S 147°34E 63 G4
Sorrento Italy 40°37N 14°22E 22 D6
Sorsele Sweden 65°31N 17°30E 8 D17
Sorsogon Phil. 13°0N 124°0E 37 B6
Sortavala Russia 61°42N 30°41E 8 F24
Sortland Norway 68°42N 15°25E 8 B16
Soscumica, L. Canada 50°15N 77°27W 72 B4
Sosnogorsk Russia 63°37N 53°51E 18 B9
Sosnowiec Poland 50°20N 19°10E 17 C10
Sossus Vlei Namibia 24°40S 15°23E 56 C2
Sŏsura N. Korea 42°16N 130°36E 35 C16
Sot → India 27°27N 79°37E 43 F8
Sotavento C. Verde Is. 15°0N 25°0W 50 b
Sotik Kenya 0°41S 35°7E 54 C4
Sotkamo Finland 64°8N 28°23E 8 D23
Soto la Marina Mexico 23°46N 98°13W 87 C5
Soto la Marina → Mexico 23°45N 97°45W 87 C5
Sotuta Mexico 20°36N 89°1W 87 C7
Souanké Congo 2°10N 14°3E 52 D2
Souda Greece 35°29N 24°4E 25 D6
Soudas, Ormos Greece 35°25N 24°10E 25 D6
Souderton U.S.A. 40°19N 75°19W 83 F9
Soufrière Guadeloupe 16°5N 61°40W 88 b
Soufrière St. Lucia 13°51N 61°3W 89 f
Soufrière Bay Dominica 15°13N 61°22W 89 f
Soukhouma Laos 14°38N 105°48E 38 E5
Sŏul = Seoul S. Korea 37°31N 126°58E 35 F14
Sound, The U.K. 50°20N 4°10W 13 G3
Sources, Mt. aux Lesotho 28°45S 28°50E 57 D4
Soure Brazil 0°35S 48°30W 93 D9
Souris Man., Canada 49°40N 100°20W 71 D8
Souris P.E.I., Canada 46°21N 62°15W 73 C7
Souris → N. Amer. 49°40N 99°34W 80 A4
Sousa Brazil 6°45S 38°10W 93 E11
Sousse Tunisia 35°50N 10°38E 51 A8
Sout → S. Africa 31°35S 18°24E 56 E2
South Africa ■ Africa 32°0S 23°0E 56 E3
South America 10°0S 60°0W 90 E5
South Aulatsivik I. Canada 56°45N 61°30W 73 A7
South Australia □ Australia 32°0S 139°0E 63 E2
South Australian Basin Ind. Oc. 38°0S 126°0E 64 L4
South Ayrshire □ U.K. 55°18N 4°41W 11 F4
South Baldy Pk. U.S.A. 34°6N 107°11W 77 J10
South Bass I. U.S.A. 41°39N 82°49W 82 E2
South Bend Ind., U.S.A. 41°41N 86°15W 80 E10
South Bend Wash., U.S.A. 46°40N 123°48W 78 D3
South Boston U.S.A. 36°42N 78°54W 81 G14
South Branch Canada 47°55N 59°2W 73 C8
South Brook Canada 49°26N 56°5W 73 C8
South Bruny I. Australia 43°20S 147°15E 63 G4
South Carolina □ U.S.A. 34°0N 81°0W 85 E14
South Charleston U.S.A. 38°22N 81°44W 81 F13
South China Sea Asia 10°0N 113°0E 36 C4
South Cumberland Is. △ Australia 20°42S 149°11E 62 J7
South Dakota □ U.S.A. 44°15N 100°0W 80 C4
South Dayton U.S.A. 42°21N 79°3W 82 D5
South Deerfield U.S.A. 42°29N 72°37W 83 D12
South Downs U.K. 50°52N 0°25W 13 G7
South East C. Australia 43°40S 146°50E 63 G4
South East Is. Australia 34°17S 123°30E 61 F3
South Esk → U.K. 56°43N 2°31W 11 E6
South Fiji Basin Pac. Oc. 26°0S 175°0E 64 K9
South Foreland U.K. 51°8N 1°24E 13 F9
South Fork American → U.S.A. 38°57N 120°59W 78 G5
South Fork Feather → U.S.A. 39°17N 121°36W 78 F5
South Fork Grand → U.S.A. 45°43N 102°17W 80 C2
South Fork Milk → U.S.A. 48°4N 106°19W 76 B10
South Fork Republican → U.S.A. 40°3N 101°31W 80 E3
South Georgia Antarctica 54°30S 37°0W 96 G9
South Gloucestershire □ U.K. 51°32N 2°28W 13 F5
South Hadley U.S.A. 42°16N 72°35W 83 D12
South Haven U.S.A. 42°24N 86°16W 80 D10
South Henik L. Canada 61°30N 97°20W 71 A9
South Horr Kenya 2°12N 36°56E 54 B4
South I. Kenya 2°35N 36°35E 54 B4
South I. N.Z. 44°0S 170°0E 59 F3
South Indian Lake Canada 56°47N 98°56W 71 B9
South Invercargill N.Z. 46°26S 168°23E 59 G2
South Island △ Kenya 2°39N 36°35E 54 B4
South Kitui △ Kenya 1°48S 38°46E 54 C4
South Knife → Canada 58°55N 94°37W 71 B10
South Koel → India 22°32N 85°14E 43 H11
South Korea ■ Asia 36°0N 128°0E 35 G15
South Lake Tahoe U.S.A. 38°57N 119°59W 78 G6
South Lanarkshire □ U.K. 55°37N 3°53W 11 F5
South Loup → U.S.A. 41°4N 98°39W 80 E4
South Luangwa △ Zambia 13°0S 31°20E 55 E3
South Magnetic Pole Antarctica 64°8S 138°8E 5 C9
South Milwaukee U.S.A. 42°55N 87°52W 80 D10
South Molton U.K. 51°1N 3°51W 13 F4
South Moose L. Canada 53°49N 100°1W 71 C8
South Nahanni → Canada 61°3N 123°21W 70 A4
South Nation → Canada 45°34N 75°6W 83 A9
South Natuna Is. = Natuna Selatan, Kepulauan Indonesia 2°45N 109°0E 36 D3
South Negril Pt. Jamaica 18°16N 78°22W 88 a
South Orkney Is. Antarctica 63°0S 45°0W 5 C18
South Ossetia □ Georgia 42°21N 44°2E 19 F7
South Otselic U.S.A. 42°38N 75°46W 83 D9
South Pagai, I. = Pagai Selatan, Pulau Indonesia 3°0S 100°15E 36 E2
South Paris U.S.A. 44°14N 70°31W 83 B14
South Pittsburg U.S.A. 35°1N 85°42W 85 D12
South Platte → U.S.A. 41°7N 100°42W 80 E3
South Pole Antarctica 90°0S 0°0 5 E
South Porcupine Canada 48°30N 81°12W 72 C3
South Portland U.S.A. 43°38N 70°15W 81 D18
South Pt. Barbados 13°2N 59°32W 89 g
South Pt. U.S.A. 44°52N 83°19W 82 B1
South River Canada 45°52N 79°23W 72 C4
South River U.S.A. 40°27N 74°23W 83 F10
South Ronaldsay U.K. 58°48N 2°58W 11 C6
South Sandwich Is. Antarctica 57°0S 27°0W 5 B1
South Sandwich Trench Atl. Oc. 56°0S 24°0W 5 B1
South Saskatchewan → Canada 53°15N 105°5W 71 C7
South Seal → Canada 58°48N 98°8W 71 B9
South Shetland Is. Antarctica 62°0S 59°0W 5 C18
South Shields U.K. 55°0N 1°25W 12 C6
South Sioux City U.S.A. 42°28N 96°24W 80 D5
South Sister U.S.A. 44°4N 121°51W 76 D3
South Talpatti = New Moore I. Ind. Oc. 21°37N 89°10E 43 J13
South Taranaki Bight N.Z. 39°40S 174°5E 59 C5
South Tasman Rise S. Ocean 48°0S 146°0E 5 A10
South Thompson → Canada 50°40N 120°20W 70 C4
South Twin I. Canada 53°7N 79°52W 72 B4
South Tyne → U.K. 54°59N 2°8W 12 C5
South Uist U.K. 57°20N 7°15W 11 D1
South Valley U.S.A. 35°1N 106°41W 77 J10
South Wellesley Is. Australia 16°58S 139°17E 62 B2
South West C. Australia 43°34S 146°3E 63 G4
South West C. N.Z. 47°17S 167°28E 59 G1
South Williamsport U.S.A. 41°13N 77°0W 82 E8
South Yorkshire □ U.K. 53°27N 1°36W 12 D6
Southampton Canada 44°30N 81°25W 82 B3
Southampton U.K. 50°54N 1°23W 13 G6
Southampton U.S.A. 40°53N 72°23W 83 F12
Southampton □ U.K. 50°54N 1°23W 13 G6
Southampton I. Canada 64°30N 84°0W 69 C11
Southaven U.S.A. 34°59N 90°0W 85 D9
Southbank Canada 54°2N 125°46W 70 C3
Southbridge N.Z. 43°48S 172°16E 59 E4
Southbridge U.S.A. 42°5N 72°2W 83 D12
Southend Canada 56°19N 103°22W 71 B8
Southend-on-Sea U.K. 51°32N 0°44E 13 F8
Southend-on-Sea □ U.K. 51°32N 0°44E 13 F8
Southern = Yuzhnyy □ Russia 44°0N 40°0E 28 E5
Southern □ Malawi 15°0S 35°0E 55 F4
Southern □ Zambia 16°20S 26°20E 55 F2
Southern Alps N.Z. 43°41S 170°11E 59 E3
Southern Cross Australia 31°12S 119°15E 61 F2
Southern Indian L. Canada 57°10N 98°30W 71 B9
Southern Lau Group Fiji 18°40S 178°40W 59 a
Southern Ocean Antarctica 62°0S 60°0E 5 C6
Southern Pines U.S.A. 35°11N 79°24W 85 D15
Southern Uplands U.K. 55°28N 3°52W 11 F5
Southington U.S.A. 41°36N 72°53W 83 E12
Southland □ N.Z. 45°30S 168°0E 59 F1
Southold U.S.A. 41°4N 72°26W 83 E12
Southport Australia 27°58S 153°25E 63 D5
Southport U.K. 53°39N 3°0W 12 D4
Southport U.S.A. 42°3N 76°49W 82 D8
Southwest △ Australia 43°8S 146°5E 63 G4
Southwest Pacific Basin Pac. Oc. 40°0S 140°0W 5 A12
Southwold U.K. 52°20N 1°41E 13 E9
Southwood △ Australia 27°48S 150°8E 63 D5
Soutpansberg S. Africa 23°0S 29°30E 57 C4
Sovetsk Kaliningrad, Russia 55°6N 21°50E 9 J19
Sovetsk Kirov, Russia 57°38N 48°53E 18 C8
Sovetskaya Gavan Russia 48°58N 140°18E 29 E15
Soweto S. Africa 26°14S 27°52E 57 D4
Sowma'eh Sarā Iran 37°17N 49°18E 45 B6
Sōya-Kaikyō = La Perouse Str. Asia 45°40N 142°0E 30 B11
Sōya-Misaki Japan 45°30N 141°55E 30 B10
Soyo Angola 6°13S 12°20E 52 F2
Sozh → Belarus 51°57N 30°48E 17 B16
Spa Belgium 50°29N 5°53E 15 D5
Spain ■ Europe 39°0N 4°0W 21 B4
Spalding Australia 33°30S 138°37E 63 E2
Spalding U.K. 52°48N 0°9W 12 E7
Spanaway U.S.A. 47°6N 122°26W 78 C4
Spangler U.S.A. 40°39N 78°48W 82 F6
Spanish Canada 46°12N 82°20W 72 C3
Spanish Fork U.S.A. 40°7N 111°39W 76 F8
Spanish Town Br. Virgin Is. 17°43N 64°26W 89 e
Spanish Town Jamaica 18°0N 76°57W 88 a
Sparks U.S.A. 39°32N 119°45W 78 F7
Sparta = Sparti Greece 37°5N 22°25E 23 F10
Sparta Mich., U.S.A. 43°10N 85°42W 81 D11
Sparta N.J., U.S.A. 41°2N 74°38W 83 E10
Sparta Wis., U.S.A. 43°56N 90°49W 80 D8
Spartanburg U.S.A. 34°56N 81°57W 85 D14
Sparti Greece 37°5N 22°25E 23 F10
Spartivento, C. Calabria, Italy 37°55N 16°4E 22 F7
Spartivento, C. Sard., Italy 38°53N 8°50E 22 E3
Sparwood Canada 49°44N 114°53W 70 D6
Spassk Dalniy Russia 44°40N 132°48E 30
Spatha, Akra Greece 35°42N 23°43E 25
Spatsizi → Canada 57°42N 128°7W 70
Spatsizi Plateau Wilderness △ Canada 57°40N 128°0W 70
Spean → U.K. 56°55N 4°59W 11
Spearfish U.S.A. 44°30N 103°52W 80
Spearman U.S.A. 36°12N 101°12W 84
Speculator U.S.A. 43°30N 74°22W 83 C
Speightstown Barbados 13°15N 59°39W 89
Speke Gulf Tanzania 2°20S 32°50E 54
Spence Bay = Taloyoak Canada 69°32N 93°32W 68 C
Spencer Idaho, U.S.A. 44°22N 112°11W 76
Spencer Iowa, U.S.A. 43°9N 95°9W 80
Spencer N.Y., U.S.A. 42°13N 76°30W 83
Spencer Nebr., U.S.A. 42°53N 98°42W 80
Spencer, C. Australia 35°20S 136°53E 63
Spencer B. Namibia 25°30S 14°47E 56
Spencer G. Australia 34°0S 137°20E 63
Spencerville Canada 44°51N 75°33W 83
Spences Bridge Canada 50°25N 121°20W 70
Spennymoor U.K. 54°42N 1°36W 12
Spenser Mts. N.Z. 42°15S 172°45E 59
Sperrin Mts. U.K. 54°50N 7°0W 10
Spey → U.K. 57°40N 3°6W 11
Speyer Germany 49°29N 8°25E 16
Spezand Pakistan 29°59N 67°0E 42
Spiddle Ireland 53°15N 9°18W 10
Spili Greece 35°13N 24°31E 25
Spīn Būldak Afghan. 31°1N 66°25E 42
Spinalonga Greece 35°18N 25°44E 25
Spirit Lake U.S.A. 46°15N 122°9W 78
Spirit River Canada 55°45N 118°50W 70
Spiritwood Canada 53°24N 107°33W 71
Spithead U.K. 50°45N 1°10W 13
Spitzbergen = Svalbard Arctic 78°0N 17°0E 4
Spjelkavik Norway 62°28N 6°22E 8 E
Split Croatia 43°31N 16°26E 22
Split L. Canada 56°8N 96°15W 71
Split Lake Canada 56°8N 96°15W 71
Spofford U.S.A. 29°10N 100°25W 84
Spokane U.S.A. 47°40N 117°24W 76
Spoleto Italy 42°44N 12°44E 22
Spooner U.S.A. 45°50N 91°53W 80
Sporyy Navolok, Mys Russia 75°50N 68°40E 28
Sprague U.S.A. 47°18N 117°59W 76
Spratly I. S. China Sea 8°38N 111°55E 36
Spratly Is. S. China Sea 8°20N 112°0E 36
Spray U.S.A. 44°50N 119°48W 76
Spree → Germany 52°32N 13°12E 16
Sprengisandur Iceland 64°52N 18°7W 8
Spring City U.S.A. 40°11N 75°33W 83
Spring Creek U.S.A. 40°44N 115°35W 76
Spring Garden U.S.A. 39°52N 120°47W 78
Spring Hall Barbados 13°18N 59°36W 8
Spring Hill U.S.A. 28°27N 82°41W 85
Spring Mts. U.S.A. 36°0N 115°45W 79
Spring Valley Calif., U.S.A. 32°44N 116°59W 79 N
Spring Valley Nev., U.S.A. 36°6N 115°14W 79
Springbok S. Africa 29°42S 17°54E 56
Springboro U.S.A. 41°48N 80°22W 82
Springdale Canada 49°30N 56°6W 73
Springdale U.S.A. 36°11N 94°8W 84
Springer U.S.A. 36°22N 104°36W 77 H
Springerville U.S.A. 34°8N 109°17W 77
Springfield Canada 42°50N 80°56W 82
Springfield N.Z. 43°19S 171°56E 59
Springfield Colo., U.S.A. 37°24N 102°37W 77 H
Springfield Ill., U.S.A. 39°48N 89°39W 80
Springfield Mass., U.S.A. 42°6N 72°35W 83 D
Springfield Mo., U.S.A. 37°13N 93°17W 80
Springfield Ohio, U.S.A. 39°55N 83°49W 81 F
Springfield Oreg., U.S.A. 44°3N 123°1W 76
Springfield Tenn., U.S.A. 36°31N 86°53W 85 C
Springfield Vt., U.S.A. 43°18N 72°29W 83 C
Springfontein S. Africa 30°15S 25°40E 56
Springhill Canada 45°40N 64°4W 73
Springhill U.S.A. 33°0N 93°28W 84
Springhouse Canada 51°56N 122°7W 70
Springs S. Africa 26°13S 28°25E 57
Springsure Australia 24°8S 148°6E 62
Springvale U.S.A. 43°28N 70°48W 83 C
Springville Calif., U.S.A. 36°8N 118°49W 78
Springville N.Y., U.S.A. 42°31N 78°40W 82
Springville Utah, U.S.A. 40°10N 111°37W 76
Springwater U.S.A. 42°38N 77°35W 82
Spruce-Creek U.S.A. 40°36N 78°9W 82
Spruce Knob-Seneca Rocks △ U.S.A. 38°50N 79°30W 81 F
Spruce Mt. U.S.A. 44°12N 72°19W 83 B
Sprucedale Canada 45°29N 79°28W 82
Spur U.S.A. 33°28N 100°52W 84
Spurn Hd. U.K. 53°35N 0°8E 12
Spuzzum Canada 49°37N 121°23W 70
Squam L. U.S.A. 43°45N 71°32W 83 C
Squamish Canada 49°45N 123°10W 70
Square Islands Canada 52°47N 55°47W 73
Squires, Mt. Australia 26°14S 127°28E 61
Srbija = Serbia ■ Europe 43°20N 20°0E 23
Sre Ambel Cambodia 11°8N 103°46E 39
Sre Khtum Cambodia 12°10N 106°52E 39
Sre Umbell = Sre Ambel Cambodia 11°8N 103°46E 39
Srebrenica Bos.-H. 44°6N 19°18E 23
Sredinny Ra. = Sredinnyy Khrebet Russia 57°0N 160°0E 29 D
Sredinnyy Khrebet Russia 57°0N 160°0E 29 C
Srednekolymsk Russia 67°27N 153°40E 29 C
Śrem Poland 52°6N 17°2E 17

mska Mitrovica Serbia 44°59N 19°38E 23 B8
pok ➔ Cambodia 13°33N 106°16E 38 F6
tensk Russia 52°10N 117°40E 29 D12
Aman Malaysia 1°15N 111°32E 36 D4
Lanka ■ Asia 7°30N 80°50E 40 R12
kakulam India 18°14N 83°58E 41 K13
nagar India 34°5N 74°50E 43 B6
no Indonesia 8°24S 114°16E 37 J17
aten ➔ Australia 16°24S 141°17E 62 B3
aten River △ Australia 16°15S 142°40E 62 B3
de Germany 53°35N 9°29E 16 B5
dskanaal Neths. 53°4N 6°55E 15 A6
ffa U.K. 56°27N 6°21W 11 E2
fford U.K. 52°49N 2°7W 12 E5
fford U.S.A. 37°58N 98°36W 80 G4
fford Springs U.S.A. 41°57N 72°18W 83 E12
ffordshire □ U.K. 52°53N 2°10W 12 E5
ines U.K. 51°26N 0°29W 13 F7
khanov Ukraine 48°35N 38°40E 19 E6
lida Greece 35°17N 25°25E 25 D7
lowa Wola Poland 50°34N 22°3E 17 C12
lybridge U.K. 53°28N 2°3W 12 D5
mford Australia 21°15S 143°46E 62 C3
mford U.K. 52°39N 0°29W 13 E7
mford Conn., U.S.A. 41°3N 73°32W 83 E11
mford N.Y., U.S.A. 42°25N 74°38W 83 D10
mford Tex., U.S.A. 32°57N 99°48W 84 E5
mpriet Namibia 24°20S 18°28E 56 C2
mps U.S.A. 33°22N 93°30W 84 E8
nderton S. Africa 26°55S 29°7E 57 D4
ndish U.S.A. 43°59N 83°57W 81 D12
nford S. Africa 34°26S 19°29E 56 E2
nford U.S.A. 47°9N 110°13W 76 C8
nger S. Africa 29°27S 31°14E 57 D5
ngselåsen = Salpausselkä Finland 61°3N 26°15E 8 F22
nislaus ➔ U.S.A. 37°40N 121°14W 78 H5
nke Dimitrov Bulgaria 42°17N 23°9E 23 C10
nley Australia 40°46S 145°19E 63 G4
nley China 22°13N 114°12E 33 G11
nley Falk. Is. 51°40S 59°51W 96 G5
nley U.K. 54°53N 1°41W 12 C6
nley Idaho, U.S.A. 44°13N 114°56W 76 D6
nley N. Dak., U.S.A. 48°19N 102°23W 80 A2
nley N.Y., U.S.A. 42°48N 77°6W 82 D7
nley Mission Canada 55°25N 104°33W 71 B8
nnards U.S.A. 42°5N 77°55W 82 D7
novoy Khrebet Russia 55°0N 130°0E 29 D14
novoy Ra. = Stanovoy Khrebet Russia 55°0N 130°0E 29 D14
nsmore Ra. Australia 21°23S 128°33E 60 D4
nsted, London ✕ (STN) U.K. 51°54N 0°14E 13 F8
nthorpe Australia 28°36S 151°59E 63 D5
nton U.S.A. 32°8N 101°48W 84 E4
nwood U.S.A. 48°15N 122°23W 78 B4
ples Canada 42°10N 82°35W 82 D2
ples U.S.A. 46°21N 94°48W 80 B6
pleton U.S.A. 41°29N 100°31W 80 E3
City Canada 52°50N 104°20W 71 C8
Lake U.S.A. 44°10N 75°2W 83 B9
a Planina Bulgaria 43°15N 23°0E 23 C10
a Zagora Bulgaria 42°26N 25°39E 23 C11
achowice Poland 51°3N 21°2E 17 C11
aya Russa Russia 57°58N 31°23E 18 C5
buck I. Kiribati 5°37S 155°55W 65 H12
cke △ Australia 14°56S 145°2E 62 A4
gard Szczeciński Poland 53°20N 15°0E 16 B8
itsa Russia 56°33N 34°55E 18 C5
ke U.S.A. 29°57N 82°7W 85 G13
kville U.S.A. 33°28N 88°49W 85 E10
ogard Gdański Poland 53°59N 18°30E 17 B10
okonstantinov = Starokonstyantyniv Ukraine 49°48N 27°10E 17 D14
okonstyantyniv Ukraine 49°48N 27°10E 17 D14
t Pt. U.K. 50°13N 3°39W 13 G4
yy Chartoriysk Ukraine 51°15N 25°54E 17 C13
yy Oskol Russia 51°19N 37°55E 19 D6
e College U.S.A. 40°48N 77°52W 82 F7
eline U.S.A. 38°57N 119°56W 78 G7
en, I. = Estados, I. de Los Argentina 54°40S 64°30W 96 G4
en I. U.S.A. 40°35N 74°9W 83 F10
esboro U.S.A. 32°27N 81°47W 85 E14
esville U.S.A. 35°47N 80°53W 85 D14
a = St. Eustatius W. Indies 17°20N 63°0W 89 C7
ffer U.S.A. 34°45N 119°3W 79 L7
nton Ill., U.S.A. 39°1N 89°47W 80 F9
nton Va., U.S.A. 38°9N 79°4W 81 F14
anger Norway 58°57N 5°40E 9 G11
eley N.Z. 43°40S 171°32E 59 E3
elot Belgium 50°23N 5°55E 15 D5
ern Norway 59°0N 10°1E 9 G14
oren Neths. 52°53N 5°22E 15 B5
ropol Russia 45°5N 42°0E 19 E7
ros Cyprus 35°1N 32°38E 25 D11
ros Greece 35°12N 24°45E 25 D6
ros, Akra Greece 35°26N 24°58E 25 D6
ell Australia 37°5S 142°47E 63 F3
ell ➔ Australia 20°20S 142°55E 62 C3
ner Canada 44°25N 80°5W 82 B4
on U.S.A. 44°48N 122°48W 76 D2
nboat Springs U.S.A. 40°29N 106°50W 76 F10
e U.S.A. 46°51N 99°55W 80 B4
ton U.S.A. 40°14N 76°50W 82 F8
Steen River Canada 59°40N 117°12W 70 B5
Steens Mt. U.S.A. 42°35N 118°40W 76 E4
Steenwijk Neths. 52°47N 6°7E 15 B6
Steep Pt. Australia 26°8S 113°8E 61 E1
Steep Rock Canada 51°30N 98°48W 71 C9
Stefanie L. = Chew Bahir Ethiopia 4°40N 36°50E 47 G2
Stefansson Bay Antarctica 67°20S 59°8E 5 C5
Steiermark □ Austria 47°26N 15°0E 16 E8
Steilacoom U.S.A. 47°10N 122°36W 78 C4
Steilrandberge Namibia 17°45S 13°20E 56 B1
Steinbach Canada 49°32N 96°40W 71 D9
Steinhausen Namibia 21°49S 18°20E 56 C2
Steinkjer Norway 64°1N 11°31E 8 D14
Steinkopf S. Africa 29°18S 17°43E 56 D2
Stellarton Canada 45°32N 62°30W 73 C7
Stellenbosch S. Africa 33°58S 18°50E 56 E2
Stendal Germany 52°36N 11°53E 16 B6
Steornabhaigh = Stornoway U.K. 58°13N 6°23W 11 C2
Stepanakert = Xankändi Azerbaijan 39°52N 46°49E 44 B5
Stephens Creek Australia 31°50S 141°30E 63 E3
Stephens I. Canada 54°10N 130°45W 70 C2
Stephens L. Canada 56°32N 95°0W 71 B9
Stephenville Canada 48°31N 58°35W 73 C8
Stephenville U.S.A. 32°13N 98°12W 84 E5
Steppe Asia 50°0N 50°0E 26 C7
Sterkstroom S. Africa 31°32S 26°32E 56 E4
Sterling Colo., U.S.A. 40°37N 103°13W 76 F12
Sterling Ill., U.S.A. 41°48N 89°42W 80 E9
Sterling Kans., U.S.A. 38°13N 98°12W 80 F4
Sterling City U.S.A. 31°51N 101°0W 84 F4
Sterling Heights U.S.A. 42°35N 83°2W 81 D12
Sterling Run U.S.A. 41°25N 78°12W 82 E6
Sterlitamak Russia 53°40N 56°0E 18 D10
Sternes Greece 35°30N 24°9E 25 D6
Stettin = Szczecin Poland 53°27N 14°27E 16 B8
Stettiner Haff Germany 53°47N 14°15E 16 B8
Stettler Canada 52°19N 112°40W 70 C6
Steubenville U.S.A. 40°22N 80°37W 82 F4
Stevenage U.K. 51°55N 0°13W 13 F7
Stevens Point U.S.A. 44°31N 89°34W 80 C9
Stevenson U.S.A. 45°42N 121°53W 78 E5
Stevenson ➔ Australia 27°6S 135°33E 63 D2
Stevenson L. Canada 53°55N 96°0W 71 C9
Stevensville U.S.A. 46°30N 114°5W 76 C6
Stewart Canada 55°56N 129°57W 70 B3
Stewart U.S.A. 39°5N 119°46W 78 F7
Stewart ➔ Canada 63°19N 139°26W 68 C6
Stewart, C. Australia 11°57S 134°56E 62 A1
Stewart, I. Chile 54°50S 71°15W 96 G2
Stewart I. N.Z. 46°58S 167°54E 59 G1
Stewarts Point U.S.A. 38°39N 123°24W 78 G3
Stewartville U.S.A. 43°51N 92°29W 80 D7
Stewiacke Canada 45°9N 63°22W 73 C7
Steynsburg S. Africa 31°15S 25°49E 56 E4
Steyr Austria 48°3N 14°25E 16 D8
Steytlerville S. Africa 33°17S 24°19E 56 E3
Stigler U.S.A. 35°15N 95°8W 84 D7
Stikine ➔ Canada 56°40N 132°30W 70 B2
Stilfontein S. Africa 26°51S 26°50E 56 D4
Stillwater N.Z. 42°27S 171°20E 59 E3
Stillwater N.Y., U.S.A. 42°55N 73°41W 83 D11
Stillwater Okla., U.S.A. 36°7N 97°4W 84 C6
Stillwater Range U.S.A. 39°50N 118°5W 76 G4
Stillwater Res. U.S.A. 43°54N 75°3W 83 C9
Stilwell U.S.A. 35°49N 94°38W 84 D7
Stînga Nistrului □ Moldova 47°20N 29°15E 17 E15
Štip Macedonia 41°42N 22°10E 23 D10
Stirling Canada 44°18N 77°33W 82 B7
Stirling U.K. 56°8N 3°57W 11 E5
Stirling □ U.K. 56°12N 4°18W 11 E4
Stirling Ra. Australia 34°23S 118°0E 61 F2
Stirling Range △ Australia 34°26S 118°20E 61 F2
Stittsville Canada 45°15N 75°55W 83 A9
Stjernøya Norway 70°20N 22°40E 8 A20
Stjørdalshalsen Norway 63°29N 10°51E 8 E14
Stockerau Austria 48°24N 16°12E 16 D9
Stockholm Sweden 59°19N 18°4E 9 G18
Stockport U.K. 53°25N 2°9W 12 D5
Stocksbridge U.K. 53°29N 1°35W 12 D6
Stockton Calif., U.S.A. 37°58N 121°17W 78 H5
Stockton Kans., U.S.A. 39°26N 99°16W 80 F4
Stockton Mo., U.S.A. 37°42N 93°48W 80 G7
Stockton-on-Tees U.K. 54°35N 1°19W 12 C6
Stockton-on-Tees □ U.K. 54°35N 1°19W 12 C6
Stockton Plateau U.S.A. 30°30N 102°30W 84 F3
Stoeng Treng Cambodia 13°31N 105°58E 38 F5
Stoer, Pt. of U.K. 58°16N 5°23W 11 C3
Stoke-on-Trent U.K. 53°1N 2°11W 12 D5
Stoke-on-Trent □ U.K. 53°1N 2°11W 12 D5
Stokes △ Australia 33°45S 121°11E 61 F3
Stokes Bay Canada 45°0N 81°28W 82 B3
Stokes Pt. Australia 40°10S 143°56E 63 G3
Stokes Ra. Australia 15°50S 130°50E 60 C5
Stokksnes Iceland 64°14N 14°58W 8 D6
Stokmarknes Norway 68°34N 14°54E 8 B16
Stolac Bos.-H. 43°5N 17°59E 23 C7
Stolbovoy, Ostrov Russia 74°44N 135°14E 29 B14
Stolbtsy = Stowbtsy Belarus 53°30N 26°43E 17 B14
Stolin Belarus 51°53N 26°50E 17 C14
Stomio Greece 35°21N 23°32E 25 D5
Stone U.K. 52°55N 2°9W 12 E5
Stoneboro U.S.A. 41°20N 80°7W 82 E4
Stonehaven U.K. 56°59N 2°12W 11 E6
Stonehenge Australia 24°22S 143°17E 62 C3
Stonehenge U.K. 51°9N 1°45W 13 F6
Stonewall Canada 50°10N 97°19W 71 C9
Stony I. U.S.A. 43°53N 76°19W 83 C8
Stony L. Man., Canada 58°51N 98°40W 71 B9
Stony L. Ont., Canada 44°30N 78°5W 82 B6
Stony Point U.S.A. 41°14N 73°59W 83 E11
Stony Pt. U.S.A. 43°50N 76°18W 83 C8
Stony Rapids Canada 59°16N 105°50W 71 B7
Stony Tunguska = Tunguska, Podkamennaya ➔ Russia 61°50N 90°13E 29 C10
Stonyford U.S.A. 39°23N 122°33W 78 F4
Stora Lulevatten Sweden 67°10N 19°30E 8 C18
Storavan Sweden 65°45N 18°10E 8 D18
Stord Norway 59°52N 5°23E 9 G11
Store Bælt Denmark 55°20N 11°0E 9 J14
Storm B. Australia 43°10S 147°30E 63 G4
Storm Lake U.S.A. 42°39N 95°13W 80 D6
Stormberge S. Africa 31°16S 26°17E 56 E4
Stormsrivier S. Africa 33°59S 23°52E 56 E3
Stornoway U.K. 58°13N 6°23W 11 C2
Storozhinets = Storozhynets Ukraine 48°14N 25°45E 17 D13
Storozhynets Ukraine 48°14N 25°45E 17 D13
Storrs U.S.A. 41°49N 72°15W 83 E12
Storsjön Sweden 63°9N 14°30E 8 E16
Storuman Sweden 65°5N 17°10E 8 D17
Storuman, L. Sweden 65°13N 16°50E 8 D17
Stouffville Canada 43°58N 79°15W 82 C5
Stoughton Canada 49°40N 103°0W 71 D8
Stour ➔ Dorset, U.K. 50°43N 1°47W 13 G6
Stour ➔ Kent, U.K. 51°18N 1°22E 13 F9
Stour ➔ Suffolk, U.K. 51°57N 1°4E 13 F9
Stourbridge U.K. 52°28N 2°8W 13 E5
Stout L. Canada 52°0N 94°40W 71 C10
Stove Pipe Wells Village U.S.A. 36°35N 117°11W 79 J9
Stow U.S.A. 41°10N 81°27W 82 E3
Stowbtsy Belarus 53°30N 26°43E 17 B14
Stowmarket U.K. 52°12N 1°0E 13 E9
Strabane U.K. 54°50N 7°27W 10 B4
Strahan Australia 42°9S 145°20E 63 G4
Stralsund Germany 54°18N 13°4E 16 A7
Strand S. Africa 34°9S 18°48E 56 E2
Stranda Møre og Romsdal, Norway 62°19N 6°58E 8 E12
Stranda Nord-Trøndelag, Norway 63°33N 10°14E 8 E14
Strangford L. U.K. 54°30N 5°37W 10 B6
Stranorlar Ireland 54°48N 7°46W 10 B4
Stranraer U.K. 54°54N 5°1W 11 G3
Strasbourg Canada 51°4N 104°55W 71 C8
Strasbourg France 48°35N 7°42E 20 B7
Stratford Canada 43°23N 81°0W 82 C4
Stratford N.Z. 39°20S 174°19E 59 C5
Stratford Calif., U.S.A. 36°11N 119°49W 78 J7
Stratford Conn., U.S.A. 41°12N 73°8W 83 E11
Stratford Tex., U.S.A. 36°20N 102°4W 84 C3
Stratford-upon-Avon U.K. 52°12N 1°42W 13 E6
Strath Spey U.K. 57°9N 3°49W 11 D5
Strathalbyn Australia 35°13S 138°53E 63 F2
Strathaven U.K. 55°40N 4°5W 11 F4
Strathcona ⌂ Canada 49°38N 125°40W 70 D3
Strathmore Canada 51°5N 113°18W 70 C6
Strathmore U.K. 56°37N 3°7W 11 E5
Strathmore U.S.A. 36°9N 119°4W 78 J7
Strathnaver Canada 53°20N 122°33W 70 C4
Strathpeffer U.K. 57°35N 4°32W 11 D4
Strathroy Canada 42°58N 81°38W 82 D3
Strathy Pt. U.K. 58°36N 4°1W 11 C4
Strattanville U.S.A. 41°12N 79°19W 82 E5
Stratton U.S.A. 45°8N 70°26W 83 A14
Stratton Mt. U.S.A. 43°4N 72°55W 83 C12
Straubing Germany 48°52N 12°34E 16 D7
Straumnes Iceland 66°26N 23°8W 8 C2
Strawberry ➔ U.S.A. 40°10N 110°24W 76 F8
Streaky B. Australia 32°48S 134°13E 63 E1
Streaky Bay Australia 32°51S 134°18E 63 E1
Streator U.S.A. 41°8N 88°50W 80 E9
Streetsboro U.S.A. 41°14N 81°21W 82 E3
Streetsville Canada 43°35N 79°42W 82 C5
Streng ➔ Cambodia 13°12N 103°37E 38 F4
Streymoy Færoe Is. 62°8N 7°5W 8 E9
Strezhevoy Russia 60°42N 77°34E 28 C8
Strimonas ➔ Greece 40°46N 23°51E 23 D10
Strokestown Ireland 53°46N 8°7W 10 C3
Stroma U.K. 58°41N 3°7W 11 C5
Strómboli Italy 38°47N 15°13E 22 E6
Stromeferry U.K. 57°21N 5°33W 11 D3
Stromness U.K. 58°58N 3°17W 11 C5
Stromsburg U.S.A. 41°7N 97°36W 80 E5
Strömstad Sweden 58°56N 11°10E 9 G14
Strömsund Sweden 63°51N 15°33E 8 E16
Strongsville U.S.A. 41°19N 81°50W 82 E3
Stronsay U.K. 59°7N 2°35W 11 B6
Stroud U.K. 51°45N 2°13W 13 F5
Stroud Road Australia 32°18S 151°57E 63 E5
Stroudsburg U.S.A. 40°59N 75°12W 83 F9
Stroumbi Cyprus 34°53N 32°29E 25 E11
Struer Denmark 56°30N 8°35E 9 H13
Strugi Krasnyye Russia 58°21N 29°1E 9 G23
Strumica Macedonia 41°28N 22°41E 23 D10
Struthers U.S.A. 41°4N 80°39W 82 E4
Stryker U.S.A. 48°41N 114°46W 76 B6
Stryy Ukraine 49°16N 23°48E 17 D12
Strzelecki Cr. ➔ Australia 29°37S 139°59E 63 D2
Strzelecki Desert Australia 29°30S 140°0E 63 D3
Stuart Fla., U.S.A. 27°12N 80°15W 85 H14
Stuart Nebr., U.S.A. 42°36N 99°8W 80 D4
Stuart ➔ Canada 54°0N 123°35W 70 C4
Stuart Bluff Ra. Australia 22°50S 131°52E 60 D5
Stuart L. Canada 54°30N 124°30W 70 C4
Stuart Ra. Australia 29°10S 134°56E 63 D1
Stull L. Canada 54°24N 92°34W 72 B1
Stung Treng = Stoeng Treng Cambodia 13°31N 105°58E 38 F5
Stupart ➔ Canada 56°0N 93°25W 72 A1
Sturgeon B. Canada 52°0N 97°50W 71 C9
Sturgeon Bay U.S.A. 44°50N 87°23W 80 C10
Sturgeon Falls Canada 46°25N 79°57W 72 C4
Sturgeon L. Alta., Canada 55°6N 117°32W 70 B5
Sturgeon L. Ont., Canada 50°0N 90°45W 72 C1
Sturgeon L. Ont., Canada 44°28N 78°43W 82 B6
Sturgis Canada 51°56N 102°36W 71 C8
Sturgis Mich., U.S.A. 41°48N 85°25W 81 E11
Sturgis S. Dak., U.S.A. 44°25N 103°31W 80 C2
Sturt △ Australia 27°17S 141°37E 63 D3
Sturt Cr. ➔ Australia 19°8S 127°50E 60 C4
Sturt Stony Desert Australia 28°30S 141°0E 63 D3
Stutterheim S. Africa 32°33S 27°28E 56 E4
Stuttgart Germany 48°48N 9°11E 16 D5
Stuttgart U.S.A. 34°30N 91°33W 84 D9
Stuyvesant U.S.A. 42°23N 73°45W 83 D11
Stykkishólmur Iceland 65°2N 22°40W 8 D2
Styria = Steiermark □ Austria 47°26N 15°0E 16 E8
Su Xian = Suzhou China 33°41N 116°59E 34 H9
Suakin Sudan 19°8N 37°20E 51 E13
Suan N. Korea 38°42N 126°22E 35 E14
Suar India 29°2N 79°3E 43 E8
Şubā Si. Arabia 27°10N 35°40E 44 E2
Subang Indonesia 6°34S 107°45E 37 G12
Subansiri ➔ India 26°48N 93°50E 41 F18
Subarnarekha ➔ India 22°34N 87°24E 43 H12
Subayhah Si. Arabia 30°2N 38°50E 44 D3
Subi Indonesia 2°58N 108°50E 36 D3
Subotica Serbia 46°6N 19°39E 23 A8
Suceava Romania 47°38N 26°16E 17 E14
Suchan = Partizansk Russia 43°8N 133°9E 30 C6
Suchil Mexico 23°38N 103°55W 86 C4
Suchou = Suzhou China 31°19N 120°38E 33 C7
Süchow = Xuzhou China 34°18N 117°10E 35 G9
Suck ➔ Ireland 53°17N 8°3W 10 C3
Sucre Bolivia 19°0S 65°15W 92 G5
Sucuriú ➔ Brazil 20°47S 51°38W 93 H8
Sud, Pte. du Canada 49°3N 62°14W 73 C7
Sud-Kivu □ Dem. Rep. of the Congo 3°0S 28°30E 54 C2
Sud-Ouest, Pte. Canada 49°23N 63°36W 73 C7
Sud Ouest, Pte. Mauritius 20°28S 57°18E 53 d
Sudan U.S.A. 34°4N 102°31W 84 D3
Sudan ■ Africa 15°0N 30°0E 51 E11
Sudbury Canada 46°30N 81°0W 72 C3
Sudbury U.K. 52°2N 0°45E 13 E8
Sûdd Sudan 8°20N 30°0E 51 G12
Sudeten Mts. = Sudety Europe 50°20N 16°45E 17 C9
Sudety Europe 50°20N 16°45E 17 C9
Suðuroy Færoe Is. 61°32N 6°50W 8 F9
Sudi Tanzania 10°11S 39°57E 55 E4
Sudirman, Pegunungan Indonesia 4°30S 137°0E 37 E9
Sudong, Pulau Singapore 1°13N 103°44E 39 d
Sueca Spain 39°12N 0°21W 21 C5
Suemez I. U.S.A. 55°15N 133°20W 70 B2
Suez = El Suweis Egypt 29°58N 32°31E 51 C12
Suez, G. of = Suweis, Khalîg el Egypt 28°40N 33°0E 51 C12
Suez Canal = Suweis, Qanâ es Egypt 31°0N 32°20E 51 B12
Suffield Canada 50°12N 111°10W 70 C6
Suffolk U.S.A. 36°44N 76°35W 81 G15
Suffolk □ U.K. 52°16N 1°0E 13 E9
Sugar Grove U.S.A. 41°59N 79°20W 82 E5
Sugarcreek U.S.A. 41°25N 79°52W 82 E5
Sugarive ➔ India 26°16N 86°24E 43 F12
Sugluk = Salluit Canada 62°14N 75°38W 69 C12
Şuḩār Oman 24°20N 56°40E 45 E8
Sühbaatar Mongolia 50°17N 106°10E 32 A5
Sühbaatar □ Mongolia 45°30N 114°0E 34 B8
Suhl Germany 50°36N 10°42E 16 C6
Sui Pakistan 28°37N 69°19E 42 E3
Sui Xian China 34°25N 115°2E 34 G8
Suide China 37°30N 110°12E 34 F6
Suifenhe China 44°25N 131°10E 35 B16
Suihua China 46°32N 126°55E 33 B7
Suining Jiangsu, China 33°56N 117°58E 35 H9
Suining Sichuan, China 30°26N 105°35E 32 C5
Suiping China 33°10N 113°59E 34 H7
Suir ➔ Ireland 52°16N 7°9W 10 D4
Suisse = Switzerland ■ Europe 46°30N 8°0E 20 C8
Suisun City U.S.A. 38°15N 122°2W 78 G4
Suiyang China 44°30N 130°56E 35 B16
Suizhong China 40°21N 120°20E 35 D11
Sujangarh India 27°42N 74°31E 42 F6
Sukabumi Indonesia 6°56S 106°50E 37 G12
Sukadana Indonesia 1°10S 110°0E 36 E4
Sukagawa Japan 37°17N 140°23E 31 F10
Sukaraja Indonesia 2°28S 110°25E 36 E4
Sukawati Indonesia 8°35S 115°17E 37 K18
Sukch'ŏn N. Korea 39°22N 125°35E 35 E13
Sukhona ➔ Russia 61°15N 46°39E 18 C6
Sukhothai Thailand 17°1N 99°49E 38 D2
Sukhumi = Sokhumi Georgia 43°0N 41°0E 19 F7
Sukkur Pakistan 27°42N 68°54E 42 F3
Sukkur Barrage Pakistan 27°40N 68°50E 42 F3
Sukri ➔ India 25°4N 71°43E 42 G4
Sukumo Japan 32°56N 132°44E 31 H6
Sukunka ➔ Canada 55°45N 121°15W 70 B4
Sula, Kepulauan Indonesia 1°45S 125°0E 37 E7
Sulaco ➔ Honduras 15°2N 87°44W 88 C2
Sulaiman Range Pakistan 30°30N 69°50E 42 D3
Sūlār Iran 31°53N 51°54E 45 D6
Sulawesi Indonesia 2°0S 120°0E 37 E6
Sulawesi Barat □ Indonesia 3°0S 119°0E 37 E5
Sulawesi Sea = Celebes Sea Indonesia 3°0N 123°0E 37 D6
Sulawesi Selatan □ Indonesia 2°30S 120°0E 37 E6
Sulawesi Tengah □ Indonesia 1°30S 121°0E 37 E6
Sulawesi Tenggara □ Indonesia 3°50S 122°0E 37 E6
Sulawesi Utara □ Indonesia 1°0N 124°0E 37 D6
Sulima S. Leone 6°58N 11°32W 50 G3
Sulina Romania 45°10N 29°40E 17 F15
Sulitjelma Norway 67°9N 16°3E 8 C17
Sullana Peru 4°52S 80°39W 92 D2
Sullivan Ill., U.S.A. 39°36N 88°37W 80 F9
Sullivan Ind., U.S.A. 39°6N 87°24W 80 F10
Sullivan Mo., U.S.A. 38°13N 91°10W 80 F8
Sullivan Bay Canada 50°55N 126°50W 70 C3
Sullivan I. = Lanbi Kyun Burma 10°50N 98°20E 39 G2
Sullom Voe U.K. 60°27N 1°20W 11 A7
Sulphur La., U.S.A. 30°14N 93°23W 84 F8
Sulphur Okla., U.S.A. 34°31N 96°58W 84 D6
Sulphur Pt. Canada 60°56N 114°48W 70 A6
Sulphur Springs U.S.A. 33°8N 95°36W 84 E7
Sultan Canada 47°36N 82°47W 72 C3
Sultan U.S.A. 47°52N 121°49W 78 C5
Sultan Hamud Kenya 2°1S 37°22E 54 C4
Sultanābād = Arāk Iran 34°0N 49°40E 45 C6
Sultanpur Mad. P., India 23°9N 77°56E 42 H8
Sultanpur Punjab, India 31°13N 75°11E 42 D6
Sultanpur Ut. P., India 26°18N 82°4E 43 F10
Sulu Arch. Phil. 6°0N 121°0E 37 C6
Sulu Sea E. Indies 8°0N 120°0E 37 C6
Suluq Libya 31°44N 20°14E 51 B10
Sulzberger Ice Shelf Antarctica 78°0S 150°0W 5 E13
Sumalata Indonesia 1°0N 122°31E 37 D6
Sumampa Argentina 29°25S 63°29W 94 B3
Sumatera Indonesia 0°40N 100°20E 36 D2
Sumatera Barat □ Indonesia 1°0S 101°0E 36 E2
Sumatera Utara □ Indonesia 2°30N 98°0E 36 D1
Sumatra = Sumatera Indonesia 0°40N 100°20E 36 D2
Sumba Indonesia 9°45S 119°35E 37 F5
Sumba, Selat Indonesia 9°0S 118°40E 37 F5
Sumbawa Indonesia 8°26S 117°30E 36 F5
Sumbawa Besar Indonesia 8°30S 117°26E 36 F5
Sumbawanga □ Tanzania 8°0S 31°30E 52 F6
Sumbe Angola 11°10S 13°48E 52 G2
Sumbu △ Zambia 8°43S 30°22E 55 D3
Sumburgh Hd. U.K. 59°52N 1°17W 11 B7
Sumdeo India 31°26N 78°44E 43 D8
Sumdo China 35°6N 78°41E 43 B8
Sumedang Indonesia 6°52S 107°55E 37 G12
Šumen = Shumen Bulgaria 43°18N 26°55E 23 C12
Sumenep Indonesia 7°1S 113°52E 37 G15
Sumgait = Sumqayıt Azerbaijan 40°34N 49°38E 19 F8
Summer L. U.S.A. 42°50N 120°45W 76 E3
Summerland Canada 49°32N 119°41W 70 D5
Summerside Canada 46°24N 63°47W 73 C7
Summersville U.S.A. 38°17N 80°51W 81 F13
Summerville Ga., U.S.A. 34°29N 85°21W 85 D12
Summerville S.C., U.S.A. 33°1N 80°11W 85 E14
Summit Lake Canada 54°20N 122°40W 70 C4
Summit Peak U.S.A. 37°21N 106°42W 77 H10
Sumner Iowa, U.S.A. 42°51N 92°6W 80 D7
Sumner Wash., U.S.A. 47°12N 122°14W 78 C4
Sumoto Japan 34°21N 134°54E 31 G7
Šumperk Czech Rep. 49°59N 16°59E 17 D9
Sumqayıt Azerbaijan 40°34N 49°38E 19 F8
Sumter U.S.A. 33°55N 80°21W 85 E14
Sumy Ukraine 50°57N 34°50E 19 D5
Sun City S. Africa 25°17S 27°3E 56 D4
Sun City Ariz., U.S.A. 33°35N 112°16W 77 K7
Sun City Calif., U.S.A. 33°42N 117°11W 79 M9
Sun City Center U.S.A. 27°43N 82°21W 85 H13
Sun Lakes U.S.A. 33°10N 111°52W 77 K8
Sun Valley U.S.A. 43°42N 114°21W 76 E6
Sunagawa Japan 43°29N 141°55E 30 C10
Sunan N. Korea 39°15N 125°40E 35 E13
Sunart, L. U.K. 56°42N 5°43W 11 E3
Sunburst U.S.A. 48°53N 111°55W 76 B8
Sunbury Australia 37°35S 144°44E 63 F3
Sunbury U.S.A. 40°52N 76°48W 83 F8
Sunchales Argentina 30°58S 61°35W 94 C3
Suncheon S. Korea 34°52N 127°31E 35 G14
Suncho Corral Argentina 27°55S 63°27W 94 B3
Sunch'on N. Korea 39°25N 125°56E 35 E13
Suncook U.S.A. 43°8N 71°27W 83 C13
Sunda, Selat Indonesia 6°20S 105°30E 36 F3
Sunda Is. Indonesia 5°0S 105°0E 64 H2
Sunda Str. = Sunda, Selat Indonesia 6°20S 105°30E 36 F3
Sunda Trench = Java Trench Ind. Oc. 9°0S 105°0E 36 F3
Sundance Canada 56°32N 94°4W 71 B10
Sundance U.S.A. 44°24N 104°23W 76 D11
Sundar Nagar India 31°32N 76°53E 42 D7
Sundarbans Asia 22°0N 89°0E 41 J16
Sundarbans △ India 22°0N 88°45E 43 J13
Sundargarh India 22°4N 84°5E 41 H14
Sundays = Sondags ➔ S. Africa 33°44S 25°51E 56 E4
Sunderland Canada 44°16N 79°4W 82 B5
Sunderland U.K. 54°55N 1°23W 12 C6
Sundown △ Australia 28°49S 151°38E 63 D5
Sundre Canada 51°49N 114°38W 70 C6
Sundsvall Sweden 62°23N 17°17E 8 E17
Sung Hei Vietnam 10°20N 106°2E 39 G6
Sungai Acheh Malaysia 5°8N 100°30E 39 c

Sungai Kolok *Thailand* 6°2N 101°58E **39** J3
Sungai Lembing *Malaysia* 3°55N 103°3E **39** L4
Sungai Petani *Malaysia* 5°37N 100°30E **39** K3
Sungaigerong *Indonesia* 2°59S 104°52E **36** E2
Sungailiat *Indonesia* 1°51S 106°8E **36** E3
Sungaipenuh *Indonesia* 2°1S 101°20E **36** E2
Sungari = Songhua Jiang → *China* 47°45N 132°30E **33** B8
Sunghua Chiang = Songhua Jiang → *China* 47°45N 132°30E **33** B8
Sunland Park *U.S.A.* 31°50N 106°40W **77** L10
Sunndalsøra *Norway* 62°40N 8°33E **8** E13
Sunnyside *U.S.A.* 46°20N 120°0W **76** C4
Sunnyvale *U.S.A.* 37°23N 122°2W **78** H4
Sunrise Manor *U.S.A.* 36°12N 115°4W **79** J11
Suntar *Russia* 62°15N 117°30E **29** C12
Suomenselkä *Finland* 62°52N 24°0E **8** E21
Suomi = Finland ■ *Europe* 63°0N 27°0E **8** E22
Suomussalmi *Finland* 64°54N 29°10E **8** D23
Suoyarvi *Russia* 62°3N 32°20E **18** B5
Supai *U.S.A.* 36°15N 112°41W **77** H7
Supaul *India* 26°10N 86°40E **43** F12
Superior *Ariz., U.S.A.* 33°18N 111°6W **77** K8
Superior *Mont., U.S.A.* 47°12N 114°53W **76** C6
Superior *Nebr., U.S.A.* 40°1N 98°4W **80** E4
Superior *Wis., U.S.A.* 46°44N 92°6W **80** B7
Superior, L. *N. Amer.* 47°0N 87°0W **72** C2
Suphan Buri *Thailand* 14°14N 100°10E **38** E3
Suphan Dağı *Turkey* 38°54N 42°48E **44** B4
Supiori *Indonesia* 1°0S 136°0E **37** E9
Supung Shuiku *China* 40°35N 124°50E **35** D13
Sūq ash Shuyūkh *Iraq* 30°53N 46°28E **44** D5
Sūq Suwayq *Si. Arabia* 24°23N 38°27E **44** E3
Suqian *China* 33°54N 118°8E **35** H10
Suquṭra = Socotra *Yemen* 12°30N 54°0E **47** E5
Sūr *Lebanon* 33°19N 35°16E **46** B4
Şūr *Oman* 22°34N 59°32E **47** C6
Sur, Pt. *U.S.A.* 36°18N 121°54W **78** J5
Sura → *Russia* 56°6N 46°0E **18** C8
Surab *Pakistan* 28°25N 66°15E **42** E2
Surabaja = Surabaya *Indonesia* 7°17S 112°45E **37** G15
Surabaya *Indonesia* 7°17S 112°45E **37** G15
Surakarta *Indonesia* 7°35S 110°48E **37** G14
Surat *Australia* 27°10S 149°6E **63** D4
Surat *India* 21°12N 72°55E **40** J8
Surat Thani *Thailand* 9°6N 99°20E **39** H2
Suratgarh *India* 29°18N 73°55E **42** E5
Şuraymilā *Si. Arabia* 25°7N 46°7E **44** E5
Surendranagar *India* 22°45N 71°40E **42** H4
Surf *U.S.A.* 34°41N 120°36W **79** L6
Surfers Paradise *Australia* 28°0S 153°25E **63** D5
Surgut *Russia* 61°14N 73°20E **28** C8
Suriapet *India* 17°10N 79°40E **40** L11
Surigao *Phil.* 9°47N 125°29E **37** C7
Surin *Thailand* 14°50N 103°34E **38** E4
Surin Nua, Ko *Thailand* 9°30N 97°55E **39** H1
Surinam = Suriname ■ *S. Amer.* 4°0N 56°0W **93** C7
Suriname ■ *S. Amer.* 4°0N 56°0W **93** C7
Suriname → *Suriname* 5°50N 55°15W **93** B7
Sürmaq *Iran* 31°3N 52°48E **45** D7
Surrey *Canada* 49°7N 122°45W **78** A4
Surrey □ *U.K.* 51°15N 0°31W **13** F7
Sursand *India* 26°39N 85°43E **43** F11
Sursar → *India* 26°14N 87°3E **43** F12
Surt *Libya* 31°11N 16°39E **51** B9
Surt, Khalīj *Libya* 31°40N 18°30E **51** B9
Surtanahu *Pakistan* 26°22N 70°0E **42** F4
Surtsey *Iceland* 63°20N 20°30W **8** E3
Suruga-Wan *Japan* 34°45N 138°30E **31** G9
Susaki *Japan* 33°22N 133°17E **31** H6
Sūsangerd *Iran* 31°35N 48°6E **45** D6
Susanville *U.S.A.* 40°25N 120°39W **76** F3
Susner *India* 23°57N 76°5E **42** H7
Susquehanna *U.S.A.* 41°57N 75°36W **83** E9
Susquehanna → *U.S.A.* 39°33N 76°5W **83** G8
Susques *Argentina* 23°35S 66°25W **94** A2
Sussex *Canada* 45°45N 65°37W **73** C6
Sussex *U.S.A.* 41°13N 74°37W **83** E10
Sussex, E. □ *U.K.* 51°0N 0°20E **13** G8
Sussex, W. □ *U.K.* 51°0N 0°30W **13** G7
Sustut → *Canada* 56°20N 127°30W **70** B3
Susuman *Russia* 62°47N 148°10E **29** C15
Susunu *Indonesia* 3°7S 133°39E **37** E8
Susurluk *Turkey* 39°54N 28°8E **23** E13
Sutay Uul *Asia* 46°35N 93°38E **32** B4
Sutherland *S. Africa* 32°24S 20°40E **56** E3
Sutherland *U.K.* 58°12N 4°50W **11** C4
Sutherland *U.S.A.* 41°10N 101°8W **80** E3
Sutherland Falls *N.Z.* 44°48S 167°46E **59** F1
Sutherlin *U.S.A.* 43°23N 123°19W **76** E2
Suthri *India* 23°3N 68°55E **42** H3
Sutlej → *Pakistan* 29°23N 71°3E **42** E4
Sutter *U.S.A.* 39°10N 121°45W **78** F5
Sutter Buttes *U.S.A.* 39°12N 121°49W **78** F5
Sutter Creek *U.S.A.* 38°24N 120°48W **78** G6
Sutton *Canada* 45°6N 72°37W **83** A12
Sutton *Nebr., U.S.A.* 40°36N 97°52W **80** E5
Sutton *W. Va., U.S.A.* 38°40N 80°43W **81** F13
Sutton → *Canada* 55°15N 83°45W **72** A3
Sutton Coldfield *U.K.* 52°35N 1°49W **13** E6
Sutton in Ashfield *U.K.* 53°8N 1°16W **12** D6
Sutton L. *Canada* 54°15N 84°42W **72** B3
Suttor → *Australia* 21°36S 147°2E **62** C4
Suttsu *Japan* 42°48N 140°14E **30** C10
Suva *Fiji* 18°6S 178°30E **59** a
Suva Planina *Serbia* 43°10N 22°5E **23** C10
Suvorov Is. = Suwarrow Is. *Cook Is.* 13°15S 163°5W **65** J11
Suwałki *Poland* 54°8N 22°59E **17** A12
Suwana *Indonesia* 8°44S 115°36E **37** K18
Suwannaphum *Thailand* 15°33N 103°47E **38** E4
Suwannee → *U.S.A.* 29°17N 83°10W **85** G13
Suwanose-Jima *Japan* 29°38N 129°43E **31** K4
Suwarrow Is. *Cook Is.* 13°15S 163°5W **65** J11
Suweis, Khalîg el *Egypt* 28°40N 33°0E **51** C12
Suweis, Qanâ es *Egypt* 31°0N 32°20E **51** B12
Suwon *S. Korea* 37°17N 127°1E **35** F14
Suzdal *Russia* 56°29N 40°26E **18** C7
Suzhou *Anhui, China* 33°41N 116°59E **34** H9
Suzhou *Jiangsu, China* 31°19N 120°38E **33** C7
Suzu *Japan* 37°25N 137°17E **31** F8
Suzu-Misaki *Japan* 37°31N 137°21E **31** F8
Suzuka *Japan* 34°55N 136°36E **31** G8
Svalbard *Arctic* 78°0N 17°0E **4** B8
Svalbard Radio = Longyearbyen *Svalbard* 78°13N 15°40E **4** B8
Svappavaara *Sweden* 67°40N 21°3E **8** C19
Svartisen *Norway* 66°40N 13°59E **8** C15
Svay Chek *Cambodia* 13°48N 102°58E **38** F4
Svay Rieng *Cambodia* 11°9N 105°45E **39** G5
Svealand □ *Sweden* 60°20N 15°0E **9** F16
Sveg *Sweden* 62°2N 14°21E **8** E16
Svendborg *Denmark* 55°4N 10°35E **9** J14
Sverdrup Chan. *Canada* 79°56N 96°25W **69** B10
Sverdrup Is. *Canada* 79°0N 97°0W **69** B10
Sverige = Sweden ■ *Europe* 57°0N 15°0E **9** H16
Svetlaya *Russia* 46°33N 138°18E **30** A9
Svetlogorsk = Svyetlahorsk *Belarus* 52°38N 29°46E **17** B15
Svir → *Russia* 60°30N 32°48E **18** B5
Svishtov *Bulgaria* 43°36N 25°23E **23** C11
Svislach *Belarus* 53°3N 24°2E **17** B13
Svizzera = Switzerland ■ *Europe* 46°30N 8°0E **20** C8
Svobodnyy *Russia* 51°20N 128°0E **29** D13
Svolvær *Norway* 68°15N 14°34E **8** B16
Svyetlahorsk *Belarus* 52°38N 29°46E **17** B15
Swabian Alps = Schwäbische Alb *Germany* 48°20N 9°30E **16** D5
Swaffham *U.K.* 52°39N 0°42E **13** E8
Swains I. *Amer. Samoa* 11°11S 171°4W **65** J11
Swainsboro *U.S.A.* 32°36N 82°20W **85** E13
Swakop → *Namibia* 22°38S 14°36E **56** C2
Swakopmund *Namibia* 22°37S 14°30E **56** C1
Swale → *U.K.* 54°5N 1°20W **12** C6
Swan → *Australia* 32°3S 115°45E **61** F2
Swan → *Canada* 52°30N 100°45W **71** C8
Swan Hill *Australia* 35°20S 143°33E **63** F3
Swan Hills *Canada* 54°43N 115°24W **70** C5
Swan Is. = Santanilla, Is. *Honduras* 17°22N 83°57W **88** C3
Swan L. *Man., Canada* 52°30N 100°40W **71** C8
Swan L. *Ont., Canada* 54°16N 91°11W **72** B1
Swan Ra. *U.S.A.* 48°0N 113°45W **76** C7
Swan River *Canada* 52°10N 101°16W **71** C8
Swanage *U.K.* 50°36N 1°58W **13** G6
Swansea *Australia* 42°8S 148°4E **63** G4
Swansea *Canada* 43°38N 79°28W **82** C5
Swansea *U.K.* 51°37N 3°57W **13** F4
Swansea □ *U.K.* 51°38N 4°3W **13** F3
Swartberge *S. Africa* 33°20S 22°0E **56** E3
Swartmodder *S. Africa* 28°1S 20°32E **56** D3
Swartnossob → *Namibia* 23°8S 18°42E **56** C2
Swartruggens *S. Africa* 25°39S 26°42E **56** D4
Swastika *Canada* 48°7N 80°6W **72** C3
Swat → *Pakistan* 34°40N 72°5E **43** B5
Swatow = Shantou *China* 23°18N 116°40E **33** D6
Swaziland ■ *Africa* 26°30S 31°30E **57** D5
Sweden ■ *Europe* 57°0N 15°0E **9** H16
Sweet Grass *U.S.A.* 48°59N 111°58W **76** B8
Sweet Home *U.S.A.* 44°24N 122°44W **76** D2
Sweetwater *Nev., U.S.A.* 38°27N 119°9W **78** G7
Sweetwater *Tenn., U.S.A.* 35°36N 84°28W **85** D12
Sweetwater *Tex., U.S.A.* 32°28N 100°25W **84** E4
Sweetwater → *U.S.A.* 42°31N 107°2W **76** E10
Swellendam *S. Africa* 34°1S 20°26E **56** E3
Świdnica *Poland* 50°50N 16°30E **17** C9
Świdnik *Poland* 51°13N 22°39E **17** C12
Świebodzin *Poland* 52°15N 15°31E **16** B8
Świecie *Poland* 53°25N 18°30E **17** B10
Swift Current *Canada* 50°20N 107°45W **71** C7
Swift Current → *Canada* 50°38N 107°44W **71** C7
Swilly, L. *Ireland* 55°12N 7°33W **10** A4
Swindon *U.K.* 51°34N 1°46W **13** F6
Swindon □ *U.K.* 51°34N 1°46W **13** F6
Swinemünde = Świnoujście *Poland* 53°54N 14°16E **16** B8
Swinford *Ireland* 53°57N 8°58W **10** C3
Świnoujście *Poland* 53°54N 14°16E **16** B8
Switzerland ■ *Europe* 46°30N 8°0E **20** C8
Swords *Ireland* 53°28N 6°13W **10** C5
Swoyerville *U.S.A.* 41°18N 75°53W **83** E9
Sydenham → *Canada* 42°33N 82°25W **82** D2
Sydney *Australia* 33°52S 151°12E **63** E5
Sydney *Canada* 46°7N 60°7W **73** C7
Sydney L. *Canada* 50°41N 94°25W **71** C10
Sydney Mines *Canada* 46°18N 60°15W **73** C7
Sydprøven = Alluitsup Paa *Greenland* 60°30N 45°35W **4** C5
Sydra, G. of = Surt, Khalīj *Libya* 31°40N 18°30E **51** B9
Sykesville *U.S.A.* 41°3N 78°50W **82** E6
Syktyvkar *Russia* 61°45N 50°40E **18** B9
Sylacauga *U.S.A.* 33°10N 86°15W **85** E11
Sylarna *Sweden* 63°2N 12°13E **8** E15
Sylhet *Bangla.* 24°54N 91°52E **41** G17
Sylhet □ *Bangla.* 24°50N 91°50E **41** G17
Sylt *Germany* 54°54N 8°22E **16** A5
Sylvan Beach *U.S.A.* 43°12N 75°44W **83** C9
Sylvan Lake *Canada* 52°20N 114°3W **70** C6
Sylvania *Ga., U.S.A.* 32°45N 81°38W **85** E14
Sylvania *Ohio, U.S.A.* 41°43N 83°42W **81** E12
Sylvester *U.S.A.* 31°32N 83°50W **85** F13
Sym *Russia* 60°20N 88°18E **28** C9
Synnot Ra. *Australia* 16°30S 125°20E **60** C4
Syowa *Antarctica* 68°50S 12°0E **5** C5
Syracuse *Kans., U.S.A.* 37°59N 101°45W **80** G3
Syracuse *N.Y., U.S.A.* 43°3N 76°9W **83** C8
Syracuse *Nebr., U.S.A.* 40°39N 96°11W **80** E5
Syrdarya → *Kazakhstan* 46°3N 61°0E **28** E7
Syria ■ *Asia* 35°0N 38°0E **44** C3
Syrian Desert = Shām, Bādiyat ash *Asia* 32°0N 40°0E **44** C3
Syros *Greece* 37°28N 24°57E **23** F11
Syzran *Russia* 53°12N 48°30E **18** D8
Szczecin *Poland* 53°27N 14°27E **16** B8
Szczecinek *Poland* 53°43N 16°41E **17** B9
Szczeciński, Zalew = Stettiner Haff *Germany* 53°47N 14°15E **16** B8
Szczytno *Poland* 53°33N 21°0E **17** B11
Szechwan = Sichuan □ *China* 30°30N 103°0E **32** C5
Szeged *Hungary* 46°16N 20°10E **17** E11
Székesfehérvár *Hungary* 47°15N 18°25E **17** E10
Szekszárd *Hungary* 46°22N 18°42E **17** E10
Szentes *Hungary* 46°39N 20°21E **17** E11
Szolnok *Hungary* 47°10N 20°15E **17** E11
Szombathely *Hungary* 47°14N 16°38E **17** E9

T

Ta Khli *Thailand* 15°15N 100°21E **38** E3
Ta Khli Khok *Thailand* 15°18N 100°20E **38** E3
Ta Lai *Vietnam* 11°24N 107°23E **39** G6
Tabacal *Argentina* 23°15S 64°15W **94** A3
Tabaco *Phil.* 13°22N 123°44E **37** B6
Ṭābah *Si. Arabia* 26°55N 42°38E **44** E4
Tabanan *Indonesia* 8°32S 115°8E **37** K18
Ṭabas *Khorāsān, Iran* 32°48N 60°12E **45** C9
Ṭabas *Yazd, Iran* 33°35N 56°55E **45** C8
Tabasará, Serranía de *Panama* 8°35N 81°40W **88** E3
Tabasco □ *Mexico* 18°0N 92°40W **87** D6
Tabāsīn *Iran* 31°12N 57°54E **45** D8
Tabatinga, Serra da *Brazil* 10°30S 44°0W **93** F10
Taber *Canada* 49°47N 112°8W **70** D6
Tablas *Phil.* 12°25N 122°2E **37** B6
Table, Pte. de la *Réunion* 21°14S 55°48E **53** c
Table B. *Canada* 53°40N 56°25W **73** B8
Table B. *S. Africa* 33°35S 18°25E **56** E2
Table Mt. *S. Africa* 33°58S 18°26E **56** E2
Table Rock L. *U.S.A.* 36°36N 93°19W **80** G7
Tabletop, Mt. *Australia* 23°24S 147°11E **62** C4
Tábor *Czech Rep.* 49°25N 14°39E **16** D8
Tabora *Tanzania* 5°2S 32°50E **54** D3
Tabora □ *Tanzania* 5°0S 33°0E **54** D3
Tabou *Ivory C.* 4°30N 7°20W **50** H4
Tabrīz *Iran* 38°7N 46°20E **44** B5
Tabuaeran *Kiribati* 3°51N 159°22W **65** G12
Tabūk *Si. Arabia* 28°23N 36°36E **44** D3
Tabūk □ *Si. Arabia* 27°40N 36°50E **44** E3
Tacámbaro de Codallos *Mexico* 19°14N 101°28W **86** D4
Tacheng *China* 46°40N 82°58E **32** B3
Tach'ing Shan = Daqing Shan *China* 40°40N 111°0E **34** D6
Tacloban *Phil.* 11°15N 124°58E **37** B6
Tacna *Peru* 18°0S 70°20W **92** G4
Tacoma *U.S.A.* 47°14N 122°26W **78** C4
Tacuarembó *Uruguay* 31°45S 56°0W **95** C4
Tademaït, Plateau du *Algeria* 28°30N 2°30E **50** C6
Tadjoura *Djibouti* 11°50N 42°55E **47** E3
Tadmor *N.Z.* 41°27S 172°45E **59** D4
Tadoule L. *Canada* 58°36N 98°20W **71** B9
Tadoussac *Canada* 48°11N 69°42W **73** C6
Tadzhikistan = Tajikistan ■ *Asia* 38°30N 70°0E **28** F8
Taegu = Daegu *S. Korea* 35°50N 128°37E **35** G15
Taegwan *N. Korea* 40°13N 125°12E **35** D13
Taejŏn = Daejeon *S. Korea* 36°20N 127°28E **35** F14
Taen, Ko *Thailand* 9°22N 99°57E **39** b
Tafalla *Spain* 42°30N 1°41W **21** A5
Tafelbaai = Table B. *S. Africa* 33°35S 18°25E **56** E2
Tafermaar *Indonesia* 6°47S 134°10E **37** F8
Tafí Viejo *Argentina* 26°43S 65°17W **94** B2
Tafīhān *Iran* 29°25N 52°39E **45** D7
Tafresh *Iran* 34°45N 49°57E **45** C6
Taft *Iran* 31°45N 54°14E **45** D7
Taft *Phil.* 11°57N 125°30E **37** B7
Taft *U.S.A.* 35°8N 119°28W **79** K7
Taftan *Pakistan* 29°0N 61°30E **40** E2
Taftān, Kūh-e *Iran* 28°40N 61°0E **45** D9
Taga *Samoa* 13°46S 172°28W **59** b
Taga Dzong *Bhutan* 27°5N 89°55E **41** F16
Taganrog *Russia* 47°12N 38°50E **19** E6
Tagbilaran *Phil.* 9°39N 123°51E **37** C6
Tagish *Canada* 60°19N 134°16W **70** A2
Tagish L. *Canada* 60°10N 134°20W **70** A2
Tagliamento → *Italy* 45°38N 13°6E **22** B5
Tagomago *Spain* 39°2N 1°39E **24** B8
Taguatinga *Brazil* 12°27S 46°22W **93** F10
Tagum *Phil.* 7°33N 125°53E **37** C7
Tagus = Tejo → *Europe* 38°40N 9°24W **21** C1
Tahakopa *N.Z.* 46°30S 169°23E **59** G2
Tahan, Gunung *Malaysia* 4°34N 102°17E **39** K4
Tahat *Algeria* 23°18N 5°33E **50** D7
Tāherī *Iran* 27°43N 52°20E **45** E7
Tahiti *French Polynesia* 17°37S 149°27W **59** d
Tahiti, I. *Tahiti* 17°37S 149°27W **59** d
Tahlequah *U.S.A.* 35°55N 94°58W **84** D7
Tahoe, L. *U.S.A.* 39°6N 120°2W **78** G6
Tahoe City *U.S.A.* 39°10N 120°9W **78** F6
Tahoka *U.S.A.* 33°10N 101°48W **84** E4
Taholah *U.S.A.* 47°21N 124°17W **78** C2
Tahoua *Niger* 14°57N 5°16E **50** F7
Tahrūd *Iran* 29°26N 57°49E **45** D8
Tahsis *Canada* 49°55N 126°40W **70** D3
Tahta *Egypt* 26°44N 31°32E **51** C12
Tahulandang *Indonesia* 2°27N 125°23E **37** D7
Tahuna *Indonesia* 3°38N 125°30E **37** D7
Tai Au Mun *China* 22°18N 114°17E **33** G11
Tai Mo Shan *China* 22°25N 114°7E **33** G11
Tai O *China* 22°15N 113°52E **33** G10
Tai Pang Wan *China* 22°33N 114°24E **33** F11
Tai Po *China* 22°27N 114°10E **33** G11
Tai Rom Yen △ *Thailand* 8°45N 99°30E **39** H2
Tai Shan *China* 36°25N 117°20E **35** F9
Tai Yue Shan = Lantau I. *China* 22°15N 113°56E **33** G10
Tai'an *China* 36°12N 117°8E **35** F9
Taiarapu, Presqu'île de *Tahiti* 17°47S 149°14W **59** d
Taibei = T'aipei *Taiwan* 25°4N 121°29E **33** D7
Taibique *Canary Is.* 27°42N 17°58W **24** G2
Taibus Qi *China* 41°54N 115°22E **34** D8
T'aichung *Taiwan* 24°9N 120°37E **33** D7
Taieri → *N.Z.* 46°3S 170°12E **59** G3
Taigu *China* 37°28N 112°30E **34** F7
Taihang Shan *China* 36°0N 113°30E **34** G7
Taihape *N.Z.* 39°41S 175°48E **59** C5
Taihe *China* 33°20N 115°42E **34** H8
Taikang *China* 34°5N 114°50E **34** G8
Tailem Bend *Australia* 35°12S 139°29E **63** F2
Taimyr Peninsula = Taymyr, Poluostrov *Russia* 75°0N 100°0E **29** B11
Tain *U.K.* 57°49N 4°4W **11** D4
T'ainan *Taiwan* 23°0N 120°10E **33** D7
Taipa *China* 22°10N 113°35E **33** G10
T'aipei *Taiwan* 25°4N 121°29E **33** D7
Taiping *Malaysia* 4°51N 100°44E **39** K3
Taipingzhen *China* 33°35N 111°42E **34** H6
Tairbeart = Tarbert *U.K.* 57°54N 6°49W **11** D2
Taita Hills *Kenya* 3°25S 38°15E **54** C4
Taitao, Pen. de *Chile* 46°30S 75°0W **96** F2
T'aitung *Taiwan* 22°43N 121°4E **33** D7
Taivalkoski *Finland* 65°33N 28°12E **8** D23
Taiwan ■ *Asia* 23°30N 121°0E **33** D7
Taiyiba *Israel* 32°36N 35°27E **46** C4
Taiyuan *China* 37°52N 112°33E **34** F7
Taizhong = T'aichung *Taiwan* 24°9N 120°37E **33** D7
Ta'izz *Yemen* 13°35N 44°2E **47** E3
Tājābād *Iran* 30°2N 54°24E **45** D7
Tajikistan ■ *Asia* 38°30N 70°0E **28** F8
Tajima *Japan* 37°12N 139°46E **31** F9
Tajo = Tejo → *Europe* 38°40N 9°24W **21** C1
Tajrīsh *Iran* 35°48N 51°25E **45** C6
Tak *Thailand* 16°52N 99°8E **38** D2
Takāb *Iran* 36°24N 47°7E **44** B5
Takachiho *Japan* 32°42N 131°18E **31** H5
Takachu *Botswana* 22°37S 21°58E **56** C3
Takada *Japan* 37°7N 138°15E **31** F9
Takahagi *Japan* 36°43N 140°45E **31** F10
Takaka *N.Z.* 40°51S 172°50E **59** D4
Takamaka *Seychelles* 4°50S 55°30E **53** b
Takamatsu *Japan* 34°20N 134°5E **31** G7
Takaoka *Japan* 36°47N 137°0E **31** F8
Takapuna *N.Z.* 36°47S 174°47E **59** B5
Takasaki *Japan* 36°20N 139°0E **31** F9
Takatsuki *Japan* 34°51N 135°37E **31** G7
Takaungu *Kenya* 3°38S 39°52E **54** C4
Takayama *Japan* 36°18N 137°11E **31** F8
Take-Shima *Japan* 30°49N 130°26E **31** J5
Takefu *Japan* 35°50N 136°10E **31** G8
Takengon *Indonesia* 4°45N 96°50E **36** D1
Takeo *Japan* 33°12N 130°1E **31** H5
Takeshima = Tokdo *Asia* 37°15N 131°52E **31** F5
Tākestān *Iran* 36°0N 49°40E **45** C6
Taketa *Japan* 32°58N 131°24E **31** H5
Takev *Cambodia* 10°59N 104°47E **39** G5
Takh *India* 33°6N 77°32E **43** C7
Takhmau *Cambodia* 11°29N 104°57E **39** G5
Takht-Sulaiman *Pakistan* 31°40N 69°58E **42** D3
Takikawa *Japan* 43°33N 141°54E **30** C10
Takla L. *Canada* 55°15N 125°45W **70** B3
Takla Landing *Canada* 55°30N 125°50W **70** B3
Takla Makan *China* 38°0N 83°0E **32** C3
Taklamakan Shamo = Takla Makan *China* 38°0N 83°0E **32** C3
Taksimo *Russia* 56°20N 114°52E **29** D12
Taku → *Canada* 58°30N 133°50W **70** B2
Takua Pa *Thailand* 8°52N 98°21E **39** H2
Takua Thung *Thailand* 8°24N 98°27E **39** a
Tal Halāl *Iran* 28°54N 55°1E **45** D7
Tala *Uruguay* 34°21S 55°46W **95** C4
Talagang *Pakistan* 32°55N 72°25E **42** C5
Talagante *Chile* 33°40S 70°50W **94** C1
Talamanca, Cordillera de *Cent. Amer.* 9°20N 83°20W **88** E3
Talampaya △ *Argentina* 29°43S 67°42W **94** B2
Talara *Peru* 4°38S 81°18W **92** D2
Talas *Kyrgyzstan* 42°30N 72°13E **28** E8
Talâta *Egypt* 30°36N 32°20E **46** E1
Talaud, Kepulauan *Indonesia* 4°30N 126°50E **37** D7
Talaud Is. = Talaud, Kepulauan *Indonesia* 4°30N 126°50E **37** D7
Talavera de la Reina *Spain* 39°55N 4°46W **21** C3
Talayan *Phil.* 6°52N 124°24E **37** C6
Talbandh *India* 22°3N 86°20E **43** H12
Talbot, C. *Australia* 13°48S 126°43E **60** B4
Talbragar → *Australia* 32°12S 148°37E **63** E4
Talca *Chile* 35°28S 71°40W **94** D1
Talcahuano *Chile* 36°40S 73°10W **94** D1
Talcher *India* 21°0N 85°18E **41** J14
Taldy Kurgan = Taldyqorghan *Kazakhstan* 45°10N 78°45E **28** E8
Taldyqorghan *Kazakhstan* 45°10N 78°45E **28** E8
Tālesh *Iran* 37°58N 48°58E **45**
Tālesh, Kūhhā-ye *Iran* 37°42N 48°55E **45**
Tali Post *Sudan* 5°55N 30°44E **51** G
Taliabu *Indonesia* 1°50S 125°0E **37**
Talibon *Phil.* 10°9N 124°20E **37**
Talihina *U.S.A.* 34°45N 95°3W **84**
Taliwang *Indonesia* 8°50S 116°55E **36**
Tall 'Afar *Iraq* 36°22N 42°27E **44**
Tall Kalakh *Syria* 34°41N 36°15E **46**
Talladega *U.S.A.* 33°26N 86°6W **85** E
Tallahassee *U.S.A.* 30°27N 84°17W **85** F
Tallangatta *Australia* 36°15S 147°19E **63**
Tallering Pk. *Australia* 28°6S 115°37E **61**
Talli *Pakistan* 29°32N 68°8E **42**
Tallinn *Estonia* 59°22N 24°48E **9** G
Tallmadge *U.S.A.* 41°6N 81°27W **82**
Tallulah *U.S.A.* 32°25N 91°11W **84**
Talnakh *Russia* 69°29N 88°22E **29**
Taloyoak *Canada* 69°32N 93°32W **68** C
Talpa de Allende *Mexico* 20°23N 104°51W **86**
Talparo *Trin. & Tob.* 10°30N 61°17W **93** K
Talsi *Latvia* 57°10N 22°30E **9** H
Taltal *Chile* 25°23S 70°33W **94**
Taltson → *Canada* 61°24N 112°46W **70**
Talwood *Australia* 28°29S 149°29E **63**
Talyawalka Cr. → *Australia* 32°28S 142°22E **63**
Tam Ky *Vietnam* 15°34N 108°29E **38**
Tam Quan *Vietnam* 14°35N 109°3E **38**
Tama *U.S.A.* 41°58N 92°35W **80**
Tamale *Ghana* 9°22N 0°50W **50**
Taman Negara △ *Malaysia* 4°38N 102°26E **39**
Tamano *Japan* 34°29N 133°59E **31**
Tamanrasset *Algeria* 22°50N 5°30E **50**
Tamaqua *U.S.A.* 40°48N 75°58W **83**
Tamar → *U.K.* 50°27N 4°15W **13**
Tamarin *Mauritius* 20°19S 57°20E **5**
Tamarinda *Spain* 39°55N 3°49E **24** B
Tamashima *Japan* 34°32N 133°40E **31**
Tamatave = Toamasina *Madag.* 18°10S 49°25E **57**
Tamaulipas □ *Mexico* 24°0N 98°45W **87**
Tamaulipas, Sierra de *Mexico* 23°30N 98°20W **87**
Tamazula *Mexico* 24°57N 106°57W **86**
Tamazunchale *Mexico* 21°16N 98°47W **87**
Tambach *Kenya* 0°36N 35°31E **54**
Tambacounda *Senegal* 13°45N 13°40W **50**
Tambelan, Kepulauan *Indonesia* 1°0N 107°30E **36**
Tambellup *Australia* 34°4S 117°37E **61**
Tambo *Australia* 24°54S 146°14E **62**
Tambo de Mora *Peru* 13°30S 76°8W **92**
Tambohorano *Madag.* 17°30S 43°58E **57**
Tambora *Indonesia* 8°12S 118°5E **36**
Tambov *Russia* 52°45N 41°28E **18**
Tambuku *Indonesia* 7°8S 113°40E **37** C
Tâmega → *Portugal* 41°5N 8°21W **21**
Tamenglong *India* 25°0N 93°35E **41** C
Tamiahua, L. de *Mexico* 21°35N 97°35W **87**
Tamil Nadu □ *India* 11°0N 77°0E **40**
Tamluk *India* 22°18N 87°58E **43**
Tammerfors = Tampere *Finland* 61°30N 23°50E **8** F
Tammisaari *Finland* 60°0N 23°26E **9**
Tamo Abu, Banjaran *Malaysia* 3°10N 115°5E **36**
Tampa *U.S.A.* 27°56N 82°27W **85**
Tampa, Tanjung *Indonesia* 8°55S 116°12E **37**
Tampa B. *U.S.A.* 27°50N 82°30W **85**
Tampere *Finland* 61°30N 23°50E **8**
Tampico *Mexico* 22°13N 97°51W **87**
Tampin *Malaysia* 2°28N 102°13E **39**
Tampoi *Malaysia* 1°30N 103°39E **3**
Tamu *Burma* 24°13N 94°12E **41**
Tamworth *Australia* 31°7S 150°58E **63**
Tamworth *Canada* 44°29N 77°0W **82**
Tamworth *U.K.* 52°39N 1°41W **13**
Tan An *Vietnam* 10°32N 106°25E **39**
Tan Chau *Vietnam* 10°48N 105°12E **39**
Tan-Tan *Morocco* 28°29N 11°1W **50**
Tana → *Kenya* 2°32S 40°31E **54**
Tana → *Norway* 70°30N 28°14E **8**
Tana, L. *Ethiopia* 13°5N 37°30E **47**
Tana River Primate ⌓ *Kenya* 1°55S 40°7E **54**
Tanabe *Japan* 33°44N 135°22E **31**
Tanafjorden *Norway* 70°45N 28°25E **8**
Tanahbala *Indonesia* 0°30S 98°30E **36**
Tanahgrogot *Indonesia* 1°55S 116°15E **36**
Tanahjampea *Indonesia* 7°10S 120°35E **37**
Tanahmasa *Indonesia* 0°12S 98°39E **36**
Tanahmerah *Indonesia* 6°5S 140°16E **37**
Tanakpur *India* 29°5N 80°7E **43**
Tanakura *Japan* 37°10N 140°20E **31**
Tanami Desert *Australia* 18°50S 132°0E **60**
Tanami Mine *Australia* 19°59S 129°43E **60**
Tananarive = Antananarivo *Madag.* 18°55S 47°31E **57**
Tánaro → *Italy* 44°55N 8°40E **20**
Tancheng *China* 34°25N 118°20E **35**
Tanch'ŏn *N. Korea* 40°27N 128°54E **35**
Tanda *Ut. P., India* 26°33N 82°35E **43**
Tanda *Ut. P., India* 28°57N 78°56E **43**
Tandag *Phil.* 9°4N 126°9E **37**
Tandaia *Tanzania* 9°25S 34°15E **55**
Tandaué *Angola* 16°58S 18°5E **56**
Tandil *Argentina* 37°15S 59°6W **94**
Tandil, Sa. del *Argentina* 37°30S 59°0W **94**
Tandlianwala *Pakistan* 31°3N 73°9E **42**
Tando Adam *Pakistan* 25°45N 68°40E **42**
Tando Allahyar *Pakistan* 25°28N 68°43E **42**
Tando Bago *Pakistan* 24°47N 68°58E **42**
Tando Mohommed Khan *Pakistan* 25°8N 68°32E **42**

ndou L. *Australia* 32°40S 142°5E **63** E3
ndoureh △ *Iran* 37°50N 59°0E **44** B8
ndragee *U.K.* 54°21N 6°24W **10** B5
ne-ga-Shima *Japan* 30°30N 131°0E **31** J5
neatua *N.Z.* 38°45S 177°1E **59** C6
nen Tong Dan = Dawna Ra.
Burma 16°30N 98°30E **38** D2
nezrouft *Algeria* 23°9N 0°11E **50** D6
ng, Koh *Cambodia* 10°16N 103°7E **39** G4
ng, Ra's-e *Iran* 25°21N 59°52E **45** E8
ng Krasang *Cambodia* 12°34N 105°3E **38** F5
nga *Tanzania* 5°5S 39°2E **54** D4
nga □ *Tanzania* 5°20S 38°0E **54** D4
nganyika, L. *Africa* 6°40S 30°0E **54** D3
nger *Morocco* 35°50N 5°49W **50** A4
ngerang *Indonesia* 6°11S 106°37E **37** G12
nggu *China* 39°2N 117°40E **35** E9
nggula Shan *China* 32°40N 92°10E **32** C4
nggula Shankou
China 32°42N 92°27E **32** C4
nghe *China* 32°47N 112°50E **34** H7
nghla Range = Tanggula Shan
China 32°40N 92°10E **32** C4
ngier = Tanger
Morocco 35°50N 5°49W **50** A4
ngjia *China* 22°22N 113°35E **33** G10
ngjia Wan *China* 22°21N 113°36E **33** G10
ngorin *Australia* 21°47S 144°12E **62** C3
ngorombohitr'i Makay
Madag. 21°0S 45°15E **57** C8
ngra Yumco *China* 31°0N 86°38E **32** C3
ngshan *China* 39°38N 118°10E **35** E10
ngtou *China* 35°28N 118°30E **35** G10
nimbar, Kepulauan
Indonesia 7°30S 131°30E **37** F8
nimbar Is. = Tanimbar,
Kepulauan *Indonesia* 7°30S 131°30E **37** F8
ninthari = Tenasserim
Burma 12°6N 99°3E **39** F2
njay *Phil.* 9°30N 123°5E **37** C6
njong Malim *Malaysia* 3°42N 101°31E **39** L3
njong Pelepas *Malaysia* 1°21N 103°33E **39** d
njore = Thanjavur
India 10°48N 79°12E **40** P11
njung *Indonesia* 8°21S 116°9E **37** J19
njung *Phil.* 2°10S 115°25E **36** E5
njung Tokong *Malaysia* 5°28N 100°18E **39** c
njungbalai *Indonesia* 2°55N 99°44E **36** D1
njungbatu *Indonesia* 2°23N 118°3E **36** D5
njungkarang Telukbetung =
Bandar Lampung
Indonesia 5°20S 105°10E **36** F3
njungpandan
Indonesia 2°43S 107°38E **36** E3
njungpinang *Indonesia* 1°5N 104°30E **36** D2
njungredeb *Indonesia* 2°9N 117°29E **36** D5
njungselor *Indonesia* 2°55N 117°25E **36** D5
nk *Pakistan* 32°14N 70°25E **42** C4
nkhala *India* 21°58N 73°47E **42** J5
nkwa-Karoo △
S. Africa 32°14S 19°50E **56** E2
nnersville *U.S.A.* 41°3N 75°18W **83** E9
nnu Ola *Asia* 51°0N 94°0E **29** D10
nnum Sands
Australia 23°57S 151°22E **62** C5
nout *Niger* 14°50N 8°55E **50** F7
nta *Egypt* 30°45N 30°57E **51** B12
ntoyuca *Mexico* 21°21N 98°14W **87** C5
ntung = Dandong
China 40°10N 124°20E **35** D13
nunda *Australia* 34°30S 139°0E **63** E2
nzania ■ *Africa* 6°0S 34°0E **54** D3
nzhou *China* 22°16N 113°28E **33** G9
nzilla → *Canada* 58°8N 130°43W **70** B2
o, Ko *Thailand* 10°5N 99°52E **39** G2
o'an = Taonan
China 45°22N 122°40E **35** B12
o'er He → *China* 45°45N 124°5E **35** B13
olanaro *Madag.* 25°2S 47°0E **57** D8
ole *China* 38°48N 106°40E **34** E4
onan *China* 45°22N 122°40E **35** B12
os *U.S.A.* 36°24N 105°35W **77** H11
oudenni *Mali* 22°40N 3°55W **50** D5
pa *Estonia* 59°15N 25°50E **9** G21
pa Shan = Daba Shan
China 32°0N 109°0E **33** C5
pachula *Mexico* 14°54N 92°17W **87** E6
pah *Malaysia* 4°12N 101°15E **39** K3
pajós → *Brazil* 2°24S 54°41W **93** D8
paktuan *Indonesia* 3°15N 97°10E **36** D1
panahoni → *Suriname* 4°20N 54°25W **93** C8
panui *N.Z.* 45°56S 169°18E **59** F2
pauá → *Brazil* 5°40S 64°21W **92** E6
pes *Brazil* 30°40S 51°23W **95** C5
peta *Liberia* 6°29N 8°52W **50** G4
phan Hin *Thailand* 16°13N 100°26E **38** D3
pirapecó, Serra
Venezuela 1°10N 65°0W **92** C6
po-Capara △ *Venezuela* 7°55N 71°15W **89** E5
pti → *India* 21°8N 72°41E **40** J8
puae-o-Uenuku *N.Z.* 42°0S 173°39E **59** E4
pul Group *Phil.* 5°35N 120°50E **37** C6
purucuará *Brazil* 0°24S 65°2W **92** D5
qtaq *Iraq* 35°53N 44°35E **44** C5
quara *Brazil* 29°36S 50°46W **95** B5
quari → *Brazil* 19°15S 57°17W **92** G7
ra *Australia* 27°17S 150°31E **63** D5
ra *Canada* 44°28N 81°9W **82** B3
ra *Russia* 56°55N 74°24E **28** D8
ra *Zambia* 16°58S 26°45E **55** F2
ra → *Montenegro* 43°21N 18°51E **23** C8
rābulus *Lebanon* 34°31N 35°50E **46** A4
rābulus *Libya* 32°49N 13°7E **51** B8
rābulus *N. Afr.* 31°0N 13°0E **51** B8
radehi *India* 23°18N 79°21E **43** H8
rajalejo *Canary Is.* 28°12N 14°7W **24** F5
rakan *Indonesia* 3°20N 117°35E **36** D5
Tarakit, Mt. *Kenya* 2°2N 35°10E **54** B4
Tarama-Jima *Japan* 24°39N 124°42E **31** M2
Taran, Mys *Russia* 54°56N 19°59E **9** J18
Taranagar *India* 28°43N 74°50E **42** E6
Taranaki □ *N.Z.* 39°25S 174°30E **59** C5
Taranaki, Mt. *N.Z.* 39°17S 174°5E **59** C5
Tarancón *Spain* 40°1N 3°1W **21** B4
Tarangire △ *Tanzania* 4°21S 36°7E **54** C4
Taransay *U.K.* 57°54N 7°0W **11** D1
Táranto *Italy* 40°28N 17°14E **22** D7
Táranto, G. di *Italy* 40°8N 17°20E **22** D7
Tarapacá *Colombia* 2°56S 69°46W **92** D5
Tarapacá □ *Chile* 20°45S 69°30W **94** A2
Tarapoto *Peru* 6°30S 76°20W **92** E3
Tararua Ra. *N.Z.* 40°45S 175°25E **59** D5
Tarashcha *Ukraine* 49°30N 30°31E **17** D16
Tarauacá *Brazil* 8°6S 70°48W **92** E4
Tarauacá → *Brazil* 6°42S 69°48W **92** E5
Taravao *Tahiti* 17°43S 149°18W **59** d
Taravao, Isthme de
Tahiti 17°43S 149°19W **59** d
Tarawa *Kiribati* 1°30N 173°0E **64** G9
Tarawera *N.Z.* 39°2S 176°36E **59** C6
Tarawera, L. *N.Z.* 38°13S 176°27E **59** C6
Taraz *Kazakhstan* 42°54N 71°22E **28** E8
Tarazona *Spain* 41°55N 1°43W **21** B5
Tarbagatay, Khrebet
Kazakhstan 48°0N 83°0E **28** E9
Tarbat Ness *U.K.* 57°52N 3°47W **11** D5
Tarbela Dam *Pakistan* 34°8N 72°52E **42** B5
Tarbert *Ireland* 52°34N 9°22W **10** D2
Tarbert *Argyll & Bute,*
U.K. 55°52N 5°25W **11** F3
Tarbert *W. Isles, U.K.* 57°54N 6°49W **11** D2
Tarbes *France* 43°15N 0°3E **20** E4
Tarboro *U.S.A.* 35°54N 77°32W **85** D16
Tarcoola *Australia* 30°44S 134°36E **63** E1
Tarcoon *Australia* 30°15S 146°43E **63** E4
Taree *Australia* 31°50S 152°30E **63** E5
Tarfaya *Morocco* 27°55N 12°55W **50** C3
Târgoviște *Romania* 44°55N 25°27E **17** F13
Târgu Jiu *Romania* 45°5N 23°19E **17** F12
Târgu Mureș *Romania* 46°31N 24°38E **17** E13
Ṭarif *U.A.E.* 24°3N 53°46E **45** E7
Tarifa *Spain* 36°1N 5°36W **21** D3
Tarija *Bolivia* 21°30S 64°40W **94** A3
Tarija □ *Bolivia* 21°30S 63°30W **94** A3
Tariku → *Indonesia* 2°55S 138°26E **37** E9
Tarim Basin = Tarim Pendi
China 40°0N 84°0E **32** B3
Tarim He → *China* 39°30N 88°30E **32** C3
Tarim Pendi *China* 40°0N 84°0E **32** B3
Taritatu → *Indonesia* 2°54S 138°27E **37** E9
Tarka → *S. Africa* 32°10S 26°0E **56** E4
Tarka La *Bhutan* 27°12N 89°44E **43** F13
Tarkastad *S. Africa* 32°0S 26°16E **56** E4
Tarkhankut, Mys
Ukraine 45°25N 32°30E **19** E5
Tarko Sale *Russia* 64°55N 77°50E **28** C8
Tarkwa *Ghana* 5°20N 2°0W **50** G5
Tarlac *Phil.* 15°29N 120°35E **37** A6
Tarma *Peru* 11°25S 75°45W **92** F3
Tarn → *France* 44°5N 1°6E **20** E4
Târnăveni *Romania* 46°19N 24°13E **17** E13
Tarnobrzeg *Poland* 50°35N 21°41E **17** C11
Tarnów *Poland* 50°3N 21°0E **17** C11
Tarnowskie Góry
Poland 50°27N 18°54E **17** C10
Ţārom *Iran* 28°11N 55°46E **45** D7
Taroom *Australia* 25°36S 149°48E **63** D4
Taroudannt *Morocco* 30°30N 8°52W **50** B4
Tarpon Springs *U.S.A.* 28°9N 82°45W **85** G13
Tarrafal *C. Verde Is.* 15°18N 23°39W **50** b
Tarragona *Spain* 41°5N 1°17E **21** B6
Tarraleah *Australia* 42°17S 146°26E **63** G4
Tarrasa = Terrassa *Spain* 41°34N 2°1E **21** B7
Tarrytown *U.S.A.* 41°4N 73°52W **83** E11
Tarshiha = Me'ona *Israel* 33°1N 35°15E **46** B4
Tarsus *Turkey* 36°58N 34°55E **44** B2
Tartagal *Argentina* 22°30S 63°50W **94** A3
Tartu *Estonia* 58°20N 26°44E **9** G22
Ţarţūs *Syria* 34°55N 35°55E **44** C2
Tarumizu *Japan* 31°29N 130°42E **31** J5
Tarutao = Ko Tarutao △
Thailand 6°31N 99°26E **39** J2
Tarutao, Ko *Thailand* 6°33N 99°40E **39** J2
Tarutung *Indonesia* 2°0N 98°54E **36** D1
Taseko → *Canada* 52°8N 123°45W **70** C4
Tash-Kömür *Kyrgyzstan* 41°40N 72°10E **28** E8
Tash-Kumyr = Tash-Kömür
Kyrgyzstan 41°40N 72°10E **28** E8
Tashauz = Dashoguz
Turkmenistan 41°49N 59°58E **28** E6
Tashi Chho Dzong = Thimphu
Bhutan 27°31N 89°45E **41** F16
Ţashk, Daryācheh-ye
Iran 29°45N 53°35E **45** D7
Tashkent = Toshkent
Uzbekistan 41°20N 69°10E **28** E7
Tashtagol *Russia* 52°47N 87°53E **28** D9
Tasiilaq *Greenland* 65°40N 37°20W **4** C6
Tasik Kenyir *Malaysia* 5°5N 102°45E **39** K4
Tasikmalaya *Indonesia* 7°18S 108°12E **37** G13
Tåsjön *Sweden* 64°15N 15°40E **8** D16
Taskan *Russia* 62°59N 150°20E **29** C16
Tasman B. *N.Z.* 40°59S 173°25E **59** D4
Tasman Basin *Pac. Oc.* 46°0S 158°0E **64** M7
Tasman Mts. *N.Z.* 41°3S 172°25E **59** D4
Tasman Pen. *Australia* 43°10S 148°0E **63** G4
Tasman Sea *Pac. Oc.* 36°0S 160°0E **58** E9
Tasmania □ *Australia* 42°0S 146°30E **63** G4
Tasmanian Wilderness World
Heritage Area △
Australia 43°0S 146°0E **63** G4
Tassili n'Ajjer *Algeria* 25°47N 8°1E **50** C7
Tassili-Oua-n-Ahaggar
Algeria 20°41N 5°30E **50** D7
Tat Ton △ *Thailand* 15°57N 102°2E **38** E4
Tata *Morocco* 29°46N 7°56W **50** C4
Tatabánya *Hungary* 47°32N 18°25E **17** E10
Tatahouine *Tunisia* 32°56N 10°27E **51** B8
Tataouine *Tunisia* 32°57N 10°29E **51** B8
Tatar Republic = Tatarstan □
Russia 55°30N 51°30E **18** C9
Tatarbunary *Ukraine* 45°50N 29°39E **17** F15
Tatarsk *Russia* 55°14N 76°0E **28** D8
Tatarskiy Proliv *Russia* 50°0N 141°0E **29** E15
Tatarstan □ *Russia* 55°30N 51°30E **18** C9
Tatatua, Pte. *Tahiti* 17°44S 149°8W **59** d
Tateyama *Japan* 35°0N 139°50E **31** G9
Tathlina L. *Canada* 60°33N 117°39W **70** A5
Tathra *Australia* 36°44S 149°59E **63** F4
Tatinnai L. *Canada* 60°55N 97°40W **71** A9
Tatla Lake *Canada* 52°0N 124°20W **70** C4
Tatnam, C. *Canada* 57°16N 91°0W **71** B10
Tatra = Tatry *Slovak Rep.* 49°20N 20°0E **17** D11
Tatry *Slovak Rep.* 49°20N 20°0E **17** D11
Tatshenshini →
Canada 59°28N 137°45W **70** B1
Tatsuno *Japan* 34°52N 134°33E **31** G7
Tatta *Pakistan* 24°42N 67°55E **42** G2
Tatuí *Brazil* 23°25S 47°53W **95** A6
Tatum *U.S.A.* 33°16N 103°19W **77** K12
Tat'ung = Datong *China* 40°6N 113°18E **34** D7
Tatvan *Turkey* 38°31N 42°15E **44** B4
Ta'ū *Amer. Samoa* 14°15S 169°30W **59** b
Taubaté *Brazil* 23°0S 45°36W **95** A6
Tauern *Austria* 47°15N 12°40E **16** E7
Taumarunui *N.Z.* 38°53S 175°15E **59** C5
Taumaturgo *Brazil* 8°54S 72°51W **92** E4
Taung *S. Africa* 27°33S 24°47E **56** D3
Taungdwingyi *Burma* 20°1N 95°40E **41** J19
Taunggyi *Burma* 20°50N 97°0E **41** J20
Taungup *Burma* 18°51N 94°14E **41** K19
Taunsa *Pakistan* 30°42N 70°39E **42** D4
Taunsa Barrage *Pakistan* 30°42N 70°50E **42** D4
Taunton *U.K.* 51°1N 3°5W **13** F4
Taunton *U.S.A.* 41°54N 71°6W **83** E13
Taunus *Germany* 50°13N 8°34E **16** C5
Taupo *N.Z.* 38°41S 176°7E **59** C6
Taupo, L. *N.Z.* 38°46S 175°55E **59** C5
Tauragė *Lithuania* 55°14N 22°16E **9** J20
Tauranga *N.Z.* 37°42S 176°11E **59** B6
Tauranga Harb. *N.Z.* 37°30S 176°5E **59** B6
Taureau, Rés. *Canada* 46°46N 73°50W **72** C5
Taurianova *Italy* 38°21N 16°1E **22** E7
Taurus Mts. = Toros Dağları
Turkey 37°0N 32°30E **44** B2
Tautira *Tahiti* 17°44S 149°9W **59** d
Tauyskaya Guba
Russia 59°20N 150°20E **29** D16
Tavan Bogd Uul
Mongolia 49°10N 87°49E **32** B3
Tavastehus = Hämeenlinna
Finland 61°0N 24°28E **8** F21
Tavda *Russia* 58°7N 65°8E **28** D7
Tavda → *Russia* 57°47N 67°18E **28** D7
Taveta *Kenya* 3°23S 37°37E **54** C4
Taveuni *Fiji* 16°51S 179°58W **59** a
Tavira *Portugal* 37°8N 7°40W **21** D2
Tavistock *Canada* 43°19N 80°50W **82** C4
Tavistock *U.K.* 50°33N 4°9W **13** G3
Tavoy *Burma* 14°2N 98°12E **38** E2
Tavrichanka *Russia* 43°18N 131°59E **30** C5
Tavua *Fiji* 17°37S 177°5E **59** a
Tavuki *Fiji* 19°7S 178°8E **59** a
Taw → *U.K.* 51°4N 4°4W **13** F3
Tawa → *India* 22°48N 77°48E **42** H8
Tawas City *U.S.A.* 44°16N 83°31W **81** C12
Tawau *Malaysia* 4°20N 117°55E **36** D5
Tawi-Tawi *Phil.* 5°10N 120°15E **37** C6
Taxco *Mexico* 18°33N 99°36W **87** D5
Taxila *Pakistan* 33°42N 72°52E **42** C5
Taxkorgan Tajik Zizhixian
China 37°49N 75°14E **32** C2
Tay → *U.K.* 56°37N 3°38W **11** E5
Tay, Firth of *U.K.* 56°25N 3°8W **11** E5
Tay, L. *Australia* 32°55S 120°48E **61** F3
Tay, L. *U.K.* 56°32N 4°8W **11** E4
Tay △ *U.K.* 56°43N 3°59W **11** E5
Tay Ninh *Vietnam* 11°20N 106°5E **39** G6
Tayabamba *Peru* 8°15S 77°16W **92** E3
Taygetos Oros *Greece* 37°0N 22°23E **23** F10
Taylakova *Russia* 59°13N 74°0E **28** D8
Taylor *Canada* 56°13N 120°40W **70** B4
Taylor *Nebr., U.S.A.* 41°46N 99°23W **80** E4
Taylor *Pa., U.S.A.* 41°23N 75°43W **83** E9
Taylor *Tex., U.S.A.* 30°34N 97°25W **84** F6
Taylor, Mt. *U.S.A.* 35°14N 107°37W **77** J10
Taylorville *U.S.A.* 39°33N 89°18W **80** F9
Taymā *Si. Arabia* 27°35N 38°45E **44** E3
Taymyr, Oz. *Russia* 74°20N 102°0E **29** B11
Taymyr, Poluostrov
Russia 75°0N 100°0E **29** B11
Tayport *U.K.* 56°27N 2°52W **11** E6
Tayrona △ *Colombia* 11°20N 74°2W **89** D5
Tayshet *Russia* 55°58N 98°1E **29** D10
Taytay *Phil.* 10°45N 119°30E **37** B5
Tāyyebād *Iran* 34°45N 60°45E **45** C9
Tāyyebād □ *Iran* 34°44N 60°44E **45** C9
Taz → *Russia* 67°32N 78°40E **28** C8
Taza *Morocco* 34°16N 4°6W **50** B5
Tāza Khurmātū *Iraq* 35°18N 44°20E **44** C5
Tazawa-Ko *Japan* 39°43N 140°40E **30** E10
Tazerbo *Libya* 25°45N 21°0E **51** C10
Tazin → *Canada* 59°48N 109°55W **71** B7
Tazin L. *Canada* 59°44N 108°42W **71** B7
Tazovskiy *Russia* 67°30N 78°44E **28** C8
Tbilisi *Georgia* 41°43N 44°50E **19** F7
Tchad = Chad ■ *Africa* 15°0N 17°15E **51** F8
Tchad, L. *Chad* 13°30N 14°30E **51** F8
Tch'eng-tou = Chengdu
China 30°38N 104°2E **32** C5
Tchentlo L. *Canada* 55°15N 125°0W **70** B4
Tchibanga *Gabon* 2°45S 11°0E **52** E2
Tch'ong-k'ing = Chongqing
China 29°35N 106°25E **32** D5
Tczew *Poland* 54°8N 18°50E **17** A10
Te Anau, L. *N.Z.* 45°15S 167°45E **59** F1
Te Aroha *N.Z.* 37°32S 175°44E **59** B5
Te Awamutu *N.Z.* 38°1S 175°20E **59** C5
Te Ika a Maui = North I.
N.Z. 38°0S 175°0E **59** C5
Te Kuiti *N.Z.* 38°20S 175°11E **59** C5
Te Puke *N.Z.* 37°46S 176°22E **59** B6
Te Waewae B. *N.Z.* 46°13S 167°33E **59** G1
Te Wai Pounamu = South I.
N.Z. 44°0S 170°0E **59** F3
Teague *U.S.A.* 31°38N 96°17W **84** F6
Teahupoo *Tahiti* 17°50S 149°16W **59** d
Teapa *Mexico* 17°33N 92°57W **87** D6
Tebakang *Malaysia* 1°6N 110°30E **36** D4
Teberu *Malaysia* 1°30N 103°42E **39** d
Tébessa *Algeria* 35°22N 8°8E **50** A7
Tebicuary → *Paraguay* 26°36S 58°16W **94** B4
Tebingtinggi *Riau,*
Indonesia 1°0N 102°45E **36** E2
Tebingtinggi *Sumatera Utara,*
Indonesia 3°20N 99°9E **36** D1
Tecate *Mexico* 32°34N 116°38W **79** N10
Tecka *Argentina* 43°29S 70°48W **96** E2
Tecomán *Mexico* 18°55N 103°53W **86** D4
Tecopa *U.S.A.* 35°51N 116°13W **79** K10
Tecoripa *Mexico* 28°37N 109°57W **86** B3
Tecuala *Mexico* 22°23N 105°27W **86** C3
Tecuci *Romania* 45°51N 27°27E **17** F14
Tecumseh *Canada* 42°19N 82°54W **82** D2
Tecumseh *Mich., U.S.A.* 42°0N 83°57W **81** D12
Tecumseh *Okla., U.S.A.* 35°15N 96°56W **84** D6
Tedzhen = Tejen
Turkmenistan 37°23N 60°31E **28** F7
Tees → *U.K.* 54°37N 1°10W **12** C6
Tees B. *U.K.* 54°40N 1°9W **12** C6
Teeswater *Canada* 43°59N 81°17W **82** C3
Tefé *Brazil* 3°25S 64°50W **92** D6
Tegal *Indonesia* 6°52S 109°8E **37** G13
Tegallalang *Indonesia* 8°27S 115°17E **37** J18
Tegalsari *Indonesia* 8°25S 114°8E **37** J17
Tegid, L. = Bala, L. *U.K.* 52°53N 3°37W **12** E4
Tegucigalpa *Honduras* 14°5N 87°14W **88** D2
Tehachapi *U.S.A.* 35°8N 118°27W **79** K8
Tehachapi Mts. *U.S.A.* 35°0N 118°30W **79** L8
Teheran = Tehrān *Iran* 35°41N 51°25E **45** C6
Tehoru *Indonesia* 3°23S 129°30E **37** E7
Tehrān *Iran* 35°41N 51°25E **45** C6
Tehrān □ *Iran* 35°30N 51°30E **45** C6
Tehri *India* 30°23N 78°29E **43** D8
Tehuacán *Mexico* 18°27N 97°23W **87** D5
Tehuantepec *Mexico* 16°21N 95°13W **87** D5
Tehuantepec, G. de
Mexico 15°50N 95°12W **87** D5
Tehuantepec, Istmo de
Mexico 17°15N 94°30W **87** D6
Teide, Pico de *Canary Is.* 28°15N 16°38W **24** F3
Teifi → *U.K.* 52°5N 4°41W **13** E3
Teign → *U.K.* 50°32N 3°32W **13** G4
Teignmouth *U.K.* 50°33N 3°31W **13** G4
Tejakula *Indonesia* 8°8S 115°20E **37** J18
Tejam *India* 29°57N 80°11E **43** E9
Tejen *Turkmenistan* 37°23N 60°31E **28** F7
Tejen → *Turkmenistan* 37°24N 60°38E **45** B9
Tejo → *Europe* 38°40N 9°24W **21** C1
Tejon Pass *U.S.A.* 34°49N 118°53W **79** L8
Tekamah *U.S.A.* 41°47N 96°13W **80** E5
Tekapo, L. *N.Z.* 43°53S 170°33E **59** E3
Tekax *Mexico* 20°12N 89°17W **87** C7
Tekeli *Kazakhstan* 44°50N 79°0E **28** E8
Tekirdağ *Turkey* 40°58N 27°30E **23** D12
Tekkali *India* 18°37N 84°15E **41** K14
Tekoa *U.S.A.* 47°14N 117°4W **76** C5
Tekong Besar, Pulau
Singapore 1°25N 104°3E **39** d
Tel Aviv ✈ (TLV) *Israel* 32°5N 34°49E **46** C3
Tel Aviv-Yafo *Israel* 32°4N 34°48E **46** C3
Tel Lakhish *Israel* 31°34N 34°51E **46** D3
Tel Megiddo *Israel* 32°35N 35°11E **46** C4
Tela *Honduras* 15°40N 87°28W **88** C2
Telanaipura = Jambi
Indonesia 1°38S 103°30E **36** E2
Telavi *Georgia* 42°0N 45°30E **19** F8
Telde *Canary Is.* 27°59N 15°25W **24** G4
Telegraph Creek *Canada* 58°0N 131°10W **70** B2
Telekhany = Tsyelyakhany
Belarus 52°30N 25°46E **17** B13
Telemark *Norway* 59°15N 7°40E **9** G12
Telén *Argentina* 36°15S 65°31W **94** D2
Teleng *Iran* 25°47N 61°3E **45** E9
Teles Pires → *Brazil* 7°21S 58°3W **92** E7
Telescope Pk. *U.S.A.* 36°10N 117°5W **79** J9
Telfer Mine *Australia* 21°40S 122°12E **60** C3
Telford *U.K.* 52°40N 2°27W **13** E5
Telford and Wrekin □
U.K. 52°45N 2°27W **12** E5
Telkwa *Canada* 54°41N 127°5W **70** C3
Tell City *U.S.A.* 37°57N 86°46W **80** G10
Tellicherry *India* 11°45N 75°30E **40** P9
Telluride *U.S.A.* 37°56N 107°49W **77** H10
Teloloapán *Mexico* 18°21N 99°51W **87** D5
Telpos Iz *Russia* 63°16N 59°13E **18** B10
Telsen *Argentina* 42°30S 66°50W **96** E3
Telšiai *Lithuania* 55°59N 22°14E **9** J20
Teluk Anson = Teluk Intan
Malaysia 4°3N 101°0E **39** K3
Teluk Bahang *Malaysia* 5°28N 100°13E **39** c
Teluk Betung = Bandar Lampung
Indonesia 5°20S 105°10E **36** F3
Teluk Intan *Malaysia* 4°3N 101°0E **39** K3
Teluk Kumbar *Malaysia* 5°18N 100°14E **39** c
Telukbutun *Indonesia* 4°13N 108°12E **36** D3
Telukdalem *Indonesia* 0°33N 97°50E **36** D1
Tema *Ghana* 5°41N 0°0 **50** G5
Temagami, L. *Canada* 47°0N 80°10W **72** C3
Temax *Mexico* 21°9N 88°56W **87** C7
Temba *S. Africa* 25°20S 28°17E **57** D4
Tembagapura *Indonesia* 4°20S 137°0E **37** E9
Tembe
Dem. Rep. of the Congo 0°16S 28°14E **54** C2
Tembe △ *S. Africa* 26°51S 32°24E **57** D5
Temblor Range *U.S.A.* 35°20N 119°50W **79** K7
Teme → *U.K.* 52°11N 2°13W **13** E5
Temecula *U.S.A.* 33°30N 117°9W **79** M9
Temengor, Tasik
Malaysia 5°24N 101°18E **39** K3
Temerloh *Malaysia* 3°27N 102°25E **39** L4
Teminabuan *Indonesia* 1°26S 132°1E **37** E8
Temir *Kazakhstan* 49°1N 57°14E **19** E10
Temirtau *Kazakhstan* 50°5N 72°56E **32** A2
Temirtau *Russia* 53°10N 87°30E **28** D9
Témiscamie → *Canada* 50°59N 73°5W **73** B5
Témiscaming *Canada* 46°44N 79°5W **72** C4
Témiscamingue, L.
Canada 47°10N 79°25W **72** C4
Temosachic *Mexico* 28°57N 107°51W **86** B3
Tempe *U.S.A.* 33°24N 111°54W **77** K8
Tempiute *U.S.A.* 37°39N 115°38W **78** H11
Temple *U.S.A.* 31°6N 97°21W **84** F6
Temple B. *Australia* 12°15S 143°3E **62** A3
Templemore *Ireland* 52°47N 7°51W **10** D4
Templeton *U.S.A.* 35°33N 120°42W **78** K6
Templeton → *Australia* 21°0S 138°40E **62** C2
Tempoal de Sánchez
Mexico 21°31N 98°23W **87** C5
Temuco *Chile* 38°45S 72°40W **96** D2
Temuka *N.Z.* 44°14S 171°17E **59** F3
Tenabo *Mexico* 20°3N 90°14W **87** C6
Tenaha *U.S.A.* 31°57N 94°15W **84** F7
Tenakee Springs
U.S.A. 57°47N 135°13W **70** B1
Tenali *India* 16°15N 80°35E **41** L12
Tenancingo de Degollado
Mexico 18°58N 99°36W **87** D5
Tenango del Valle
Mexico 19°7N 99°33W **87** D5
Tenaro, Akra *Greece* 36°22N 22°27E **23** F10
Tenasserim *Burma* 12°6N 99°3E **39** F2
Tenasserim □ *Burma* 14°0N 98°30E **38** F2
Tenby *U.K.* 51°40N 4°42W **13** F3
Tenda, Colle di *France* 44°7N 7°36E **20** D7
Tendaho *Ethiopia* 11°48N 40°54E **47** E3
Tendukhera *India* 23°24N 79°33E **43** H8
Teneguía, Volcanes de
Canary Is. 28°28N 17°51W **24** F2
Ténéré, Erg du *Niger* 17°35N 10°55E **51** E8
Tenerife *Canary Is.* 28°15N 16°35W **24** F3
Tenerife, Pico *Canary Is.* 27°43N 18°1W **24** G1
Tenerife Norte ✈ (TFN)
Canary Is. 28°28N 16°17W **24** F3
Tenerife Sur ✈ (TFS)
Canary Is. 28°3N 16°33W **24** F3
Teng Xian *China* 35°5N 117°10E **35** G9
Tengah, Kepulauan
Indonesia 7°5S 118°15E **36** F5
Tengchong *China* 25°0N 98°32E **32** D4
Tengchowfu = Penglai
China 37°48N 120°42E **35** F11
Tenggarong *Indonesia* 0°24S 116°58E **36** E5
Tengger Shamo *China* 38°0N 104°0E **32** C5
Tenggol, Pulau *Malaysia* 4°48N 103°41E **39** K4
Tengiz Köli *Kazakhstan* 50°30N 69°0E **32** A1
Teniente Enciso △
Paraguay 21°5S 61°8W **94** A3
Teniente Rodolfo Marsh
Antarctica 62°30S 58°0W **5** C18
Tenino *U.S.A.* 46°51N 122°51W **78** D4
Tenkasi *India* 8°55N 77°20E **40** Q10
Tenke *Katanga,*
Dem. Rep. of the Congo 11°22S 26°40E **55** E2
Tenke *Katanga,*
Dem. Rep. of the Congo 10°32S 26°7E **55** E2
Tennant Creek
Australia 19°30S 134°15E **62** B1
Tennessee □ *U.S.A.* 36°0N 86°30W **85** D11
Tennessee → *U.S.A.* 37°4N 88°34W **85** C10
Teno, Pta. de *Canary Is.* 28°21N 16°55W **24** F3
Tenom *Malaysia* 5°4N 115°57E **36** C5
Tenosique *Mexico* 17°29N 91°26W **87** D6
Tenryū-Gawa → *Japan* 35°39N 137°48E **31** G8
Tenterden *U.K.* 51°4N 0°42E **13** F8
Tenterfield *Australia* 29°0S 152°0E **63** D5
Teófilo Otoni *Brazil* 17°50S 41°30W **93** G10
Tepa *Indonesia* 7°52S 129°31E **37** F7
Tepalcatepec →
Mexico 18°35N 101°59W **86** D4
Tepehuanes *Mexico* 25°21N 105°44W **86** B3
Tepetongo *Mexico* 22°28N 103°9W **86** C4
Tepic *Mexico* 21°30N 104°54W **86** C4
Teplice *Czech Rep.* 50°40N 13°48E **16** C7
Tepoca, C. *Mexico* 30°20N 112°25W **86** A2
Tequila *Mexico* 20°54N 103°47W **86** C4
Ter → *Spain* 42°2N 3°12E **21** A7
Ter Apel *Neths.* 52°53N 7°5E **15** B7
Téra *Niger* 14°0N 0°45E **50** F6
Teraina *Kiribati* 4°43N 160°25W **65** G12
Téramo *Italy* 42°39N 13°42E **22** C5
Terang *Australia* 38°15S 142°55E **63** F3
Terang, Teluk *Indonesia* 8°44S 116°0E **37** K19
Terceira *Azores* 38°43N 27°13W **50** a
Tercero → *Argentina* 32°58S 61°47W **94** C3
Terebovlya *Ukraine* 49°18N 25°44E **17** D13
Terek → *Russia* 44°0N 47°30E **19** F8
Terepaima △ *Venezuela* 9°58N 69°17W **89** E6
Teresina *Brazil* 5°9S 42°45W **93** E10
Terewah, L. *Australia* 29°52S 147°35E **63** D4
Teridgerie Cr. →
Australia 30°25S 148°50E **63** E4
Termas de Río Hondo
Argentina 27°29S 64°52W **94** B3
Termez = Termiz
Uzbekistan 37°15N 67°15E **28** F7

Términi Imerese *Italy* 37°59N 13°42E **22** F5
Términos, L. de *Mexico* 18°37N 91°33W **87** D6
Termiz *Uzbekistan* 37°15N 67°15E **28** F7
Térmoli *Italy* 42°0N 15°0E **22** C6
Ternate *Indonesia* 0°45N 127°25E **37** D7
Terneuzen *Neths.* 51°20N 3°50E **15** C3
Terney *Russia* 45°3N 136°37E **30** B8
Terni *Italy* 42°34N 12°37E **22** C5
Ternopil *Ukraine* 49°30N 25°40E **17** D13
Ternopol = Ternopil *Ukraine* 49°30N 25°40E **17** D13
Terowie *Australia* 33°8S 138°55E **63** E2
Terra Bella *U.S.A.* 35°58N 119°3W **79** K7
Terra Nova △ *Canada* 48°33N 53°55W **73** C9
Terrace *Canada* 54°30N 128°35W **70** C3
Terrace Bay *Canada* 48°47N 87°5W **72** C2
Terracina *Italy* 41°17N 13°15E **22** D5
Terralba *Italy* 39°43N 8°39E **22** E3
Terrassa *Spain* 41°34N 2°1E **21** B7
Terre Haute *U.S.A.* 39°28N 87°25W **80** F10
Terrebonne B. *U.S.A.* 29°5N 90°35W **85** G9
Terrell *U.S.A.* 32°44N 96°17W **84** E6
Terrenceville *Canada* 47°40N 54°44W **73** C9
Terry *U.S.A.* 46°47N 105°19W **76** C11
Terryville *U.S.A.* 41°41N 73°3W **83** E11
Terschelling *Neths.* 53°25N 5°20E **15** A5
Teruel *Spain* 40°22N 1°8W **21** B5
Tervola *Finland* 66°6N 24°49E **8** C21
Teryaweynya L. *Australia* 32°18S 143°22E **63** E3
Teshio *Japan* 44°53N 141°44E **30** B10
Teshio-Gawa → *Japan* 44°53N 141°45E **30** B10
Tesiyn Gol → *Mongolia* 50°40N 93°20E **32** A4
Teslin *Canada* 60°10N 132°43W **70** A2
Teslin → *Canada* 61°34N 134°35W **70** A2
Teslin L. *Canada* 60°15N 132°57W **70** A2
Tessalit *Mali* 20°12N 1°0E **50** D6
Tessaoua *Niger* 13°47N 7°56E **50** F7
Test → *U.K.* 50°56N 1°29W **13** G6
Testigos, Is. Los *Venezuela* 11°23N 63°7W **89** D7
Tetachuck L. *Canada* 53°18N 125°55W **70** C3
Tetas, Pta. *Chile* 23°31S 70°38W **94** A1
Tete *Mozam.* 16°13S 33°33E **55** F3
Tete □ *Mozam.* 15°15S 32°40E **55** F3
Teterev → *Ukraine* 51°1N 30°5E **17** C16
Teteven *Bulgaria* 42°58N 24°17E **23** C11
Tethul → *Canada* 60°35N 112°12W **70** A6
Tetiyev *Ukraine* 49°22N 29°38E **17** D15
Teton → *U.S.A.* 47°56N 110°31W **76** C8
Tétouan *Morocco* 35°35N 5°21W **50** A4
Tetovo *Macedonia* 42°1N 20°59E **23** C9
Tetufera, Mt. *Tahiti* 17°40S 149°26W **59** d
Teuco → *Argentina* 25°35S 60°11W **94** B3
Teulon *Canada* 50°23N 97°16W **71** C9
Teun *Indonesia* 6°59S 129°8E **37** F7
Teuri-Tō *Japan* 44°26N 141°19E **30** B10
Teutoburger Wald *Germany* 52°5N 8°22E **16** B5
Tevere → *Italy* 41°44N 12°14E **22** D5
Teverya *Israel* 32°47N 35°32E **46** C4
Teviot → *U.K.* 55°29N 2°38W **11** F6
Tewantin *Australia* 26°27S 153°3E **63** D5
Tewkesbury *U.K.* 51°59N 2°9W **13** F5
Texada I. *Canada* 49°40N 124°25W **70** D4
Texarkana *Ark., U.S.A.* 33°26N 94°2W **84** E7
Texarkana *Tex., U.S.A.* 33°26N 94°3W **84** E7
Texas *Australia* 28°49S 151°9E **63** D5
Texas □ *U.S.A.* 31°40N 98°30W **84** F5
Texas City *U.S.A.* 29°24N 94°54W **84** G7
Texel *Neths.* 53°5N 4°50E **15** A4
Texline *U.S.A.* 36°23N 103°2W **84** C3
Texoma, L. *U.S.A.* 33°50N 96°34W **84** E6
Teyateyaneng *Lesotho* 29°7S 27°34E **53** K5
Tezin *Afghan.* 34°24N 69°30E **42** B3
Teziutlán *Mexico* 19°49N 97°21W **87** D5
Tezpur *India* 26°40N 92°45E **41** F18
Tezzeron L. *Canada* 54°43N 124°30W **70** C4
Tha-anne → *Canada* 60°31N 94°37W **71** A10
Tha Deua *Laos* 17°57N 102°53E **38** D4
Tha Deua *Laos* 19°26N 101°50E **38** C3
Tha Li *Thailand* 17°37N 101°25E **38** D3
Tha Pla *Thailand* 17°48N 100°32E **38** D3
Tha Rua *Thailand* 14°34N 100°44E **38** E3
Tha Sala *Thailand* 8°40N 99°56E **39** H2
Tha Song Yang *Thailand* 17°34N 97°55E **38** D1
Thaba Putsoa *Lesotho* 29°45S 28°0E **57** D4
Thabana Ntlenyana *Lesotho* 29°30S 29°16E **57** D4
Thabazimbi *S. Africa* 24°40S 27°21E **57** C4
Thādiq *Si. Arabia* 25°18N 45°52E **44** E5
Thai Binh *Vietnam* 20°35N 106°1E **38** B6
Thai Muang *Thailand* 8°24N 98°16E **39** H2
Thai Nguyen *Vietnam* 21°35N 105°55E **38** B5
Thailand ■ *Asia* 16°0N 102°0E **38** E4
Thailand, G. of *Asia* 11°30N 101°0E **39** G3
Thakhek *Laos* 17°25N 104°45E **38** D5
Thal *Pakistan* 33°28N 70°33E **42** C4
Thal Desert *Pakistan* 31°10N 71°30E **42** D4
Thala La = Hkakabo Razi *Burma* 28°25N 97°23E **41** E20
Thalabarivat *Cambodia* 13°33N 105°57E **38** F5
Thallon *Australia* 28°39S 148°49E **63** D4
Thalu, Ko *Thailand* 9°26N 99°54E **39** b
Thames *N.Z.* 37°7S 175°34E **59** B5
Thames → *Canada* 42°20N 82°25W **82** D2
Thames → *U.K.* 51°29N 0°34E **13** F8
Thames → *U.S.A.* 41°18N 72°5W **83** E12
Thames Estuary *U.K.* 51°29N 0°52E **13** F8
Thamesford *Canada* 43°4N 81°0W **82** C4
Thamesville *Canada* 42°33N 81°59W **82** D3
Than *India* 22°34N 71°11E **42** H4
Than Uyen *Vietnam* 22°0N 103°54E **38** B4
Thana Gazi *India* 27°25N 76°19E **42** F7
Thandla *India* 23°0N 74°34E **42** H6
Thandwe *Burma* 18°20N 94°30E **41** K19
Thane *India* 19°12N 72°59E **40** K8
Thanesar *India* 30°1N 76°52E **42** D7
Thanet, I. of *U.K.* 51°21N 1°20E **13** F9
Thangool *Australia* 24°38S 150°42E **62** C5
Thanh Hoa *Vietnam* 19°48N 105°46E **38** C5
Thanh Hung *Vietnam* 9°55N 105°43E **39** H5
Thanh Pho Ho Chi Minh *Vietnam* 10°58N 106°40E **39** G6
Thanh Thuy *Vietnam* 22°55N 104°51E **38** A5
Thanjavur *India* 10°48N 79°12E **40** P11
Thano Bula Khan *Pakistan* 25°22N 67°50E **42** G2
Thaolintoa L. *Canada* 61°30N 96°25W **71** A9
Thap Lan △ *Thailand* 14°15N 102°16E **38** E4
Thap Sakae *Thailand* 11°30N 99°37E **39** G2
Thap Than *Thailand* 15°27N 99°54E **38** E2
Thar Desert *India* 28°0N 72°0E **42** F5
Tharad *India* 24°30N 71°44E **42** G4
Thargomindah *Australia* 27°58S 143°46E **63** D3
Tharp Fracture Zone *S. Ocean* 54°0S 135°0W **5** B14
Tharrawaddy *Burma* 17°38N 95°48E **41** L19
Tharthār, Buḩayrat ath *Iraq* 34°0N 43°15E **44** C4
Tharthār, L. = Tharthār, Buḩayrat ath *Iraq* 34°0N 43°15E **44** C4
Tharthār, W. ath → *Iraq* 34°32N 43°4E **44** C4
Thasos *Greece* 40°40N 24°40E **23** D11
That Khe *Vietnam* 22°16N 106°28E **38** A6
Thatcher *Ariz., U.S.A.* 32°51N 109°46W **77** K9
Thatcher *Colo., U.S.A.* 37°33N 104°7W **77** H11
Thaton *Burma* 16°55N 97°22E **41** L20
Thaungdut *Burma* 24°30N 94°40E **41** G19
Thayer *U.S.A.* 36°31N 91°33W **80** G8
Thayetmyo *Burma* 19°20N 95°10E **41** K19
Thazi *Burma* 21°0N 96°5E **41** J20
Thbeng Meanchey *Cambodia* 13°49N 104°58E **38** F5
The Broads *U.K.* 52°45N 1°30E **12** E9
The Everglades *U.S.A.* 25°50N 81°0W **85** J14
The Gulf = Persian Gulf *Asia* 27°0N 50°0E **45** E6
The Hague = 's-Gravenhage *Neths.* 52°7N 4°17E **15** B4
The Pas *Canada* 53°45N 101°15W **71** C8
The Wash *U.K.* 52°58N 0°20E **12** E8
The Weald *U.K.* 51°4N 0°20E **13** F8
Thebes = Thiva *Greece* 38°19N 23°19E **23** E10
Thebes *Egypt* 25°40N 32°35E **51** C12
Thedford *U.S.A.* 41°59N 100°35W **80** E3
Theebine *Australia* 25°57S 152°34E **63** D5
Thekulthili L. *Canada* 61°3N 110°0W **71** A7
Thelon → *Canada* 64°16N 96°4W **71** A8
Theodore *Australia* 24°55S 150°3E **62** C5
Theodore *Canada* 51°26N 102°55W **71** C8
Theodore *U.S.A.* 30°33N 88°10W **85** F10
Theodore Roosevelt △ *U.S.A.* 47°0N 103°25W **80** B2
Theodore Roosevelt L. *U.S.A.* 33°40N 111°10W **77** K8
Thepha *Thailand* 6°52N 100°58E **39** J3
Theresa *U.S.A.* 44°13N 75°48W **83** B9
Thermopolis *U.S.A.* 43°39N 108°13W **76** E9
Thermopylae *Greece* 38°48N 22°35E **23** E10
Thessalon *Canada* 46°20N 83°30W **72** C3
Thessalonica, Gulf of = Thessaloniki Kolpos *Greece* 40°15N 22°45E **23** D10
Thessaloniki *Greece* 40°38N 22°58E **23** D10
Thessaloniki Kolpos *Greece* 40°15N 22°45E **23** D10
Thetford *U.K.* 52°25N 0°45E **13** E8
Thetford Mines *Canada* 46°8N 71°18W **73** C5
Theun → *Laos* 18°19N 104°0E **38** C5
Theunissen *S. Africa* 28°26S 26°43E **56** D4
Thevenard *Australia* 32°9S 133°38E **63** E1
Thibodaux *U.S.A.* 29°48N 90°49W **85** G9
Thicket Portage *Canada* 55°19N 97°42W **71** B9
Thief River Falls *U.S.A.* 48°7N 96°10W **80** A5
Thiel Mts. *Antarctica* 85°15S 91°0W **5** E16
Thiers *France* 45°52N 3°33E **20** D5
Thiès *Senegal* 14°50N 16°51W **50** F2
Thika *Kenya* 1°1S 37°5E **54** C4
Thimphu *Bhutan* 27°31N 89°45E **41** F16
Thina → *S. Africa* 31°18S 29°13E **57** E4
Þingvallavatn *Iceland* 64°11N 21°9W **8** D3
Thionville *France* 49°20N 6°10E **20** B7
Thira = Santorini *Greece* 36°23N 25°27E **23** F11
Third Cataract *Sudan* 19°42N 30°20E **51** E12
Thirsk *U.K.* 54°14N 1°19W **12** C6
Thiruvananthapuram = Trivandrum *India* 8°41N 77°0E **40** Q10
Thisted *Denmark* 56°58N 8°40E **9** H13
Thistle I. *Australia* 35°0S 136°8E **63** F2
Thithia = Cicia *Fiji* 17°45S 179°18W **59** a
Thiva *Greece* 38°19N 23°19E **23** E10
Þjórsá → *Iceland* 63°47N 20°48W **8** E3
Thlewiaza → *Canada* 60°29N 94°40W **71** A10
Thmar Puok *Cambodia* 13°57N 103°4E **38** F4
Tho Vinh *Vietnam* 19°16N 105°42E **38** C5
Thoa → *Canada* 60°31N 109°47W **71** A7
Thoen *Thailand* 17°43N 99°12E **38** D2
Thoeng *Thailand* 19°41N 100°12E **38** C3
Thohoyandou *S. Africa* 22°58S 30°29E **53** J6
Tholdi *Pakistan* 35°5N 76°6E **43** B7
Thomas *U.S.A.* 35°45N 98°45W **84** D5
Thomas, L. *Australia* 26°4S 137°58E **63** D2
Thomaston *U.S.A.* 32°53N 84°20W **85** E12
Thomasville *Ala., U.S.A.* 31°55N 87°44W **85** F11
Thomasville *Ga., U.S.A.* 30°50N 83°59W **85** F13
Thomasville *N.C., U.S.A.* 35°53N 80°5W **85** D14
Thompson *Canada* 55°45N 97°52W **71** B9
Thompson *U.S.A.* 41°52N 75°31W **83** E9
Thompson → *Canada* 50°15N 121°24W **70** C4
Thompson → *U.S.A.* 39°46N 93°37W **80** F7
Thompson Falls *U.S.A.* 47°36N 115°21W **76** C6
Thompson Pk. *U.S.A.* 41°0N 123°2W **76** F2
Thompson Springs *U.S.A.* 38°58N 109°43W **76** G9
Thompsontown *U.S.A.* 40°33N 77°14W **82** F7
Thomson *U.S.A.* 33°28N 82°30W **85** E13
Thomson → *Australia* 25°11S 142°53E **62** C3
Thong Yang *Thailand* 9°28N 99°56E **39** b
Þórisvatn *Iceland* 64°20N 18°55W **8** D4
Thornaby on Tees *U.K.* 54°33N 1°18W **12** C6
Thornbury *Canada* 44°34N 80°26W **82** B4
Thorne *U.K.* 53°37N 0°57W **12** D7
Thornton *Canada* 44°16N 79°43W **82** B5
Thornton *U.S.A.* 39°52N 104°58W **76** G11
Thorold *Canada* 43°7N 79°12W **82** C5
Þórshöfn *Iceland* 66°12N 15°20W **8** C6
Thouin, C. *Australia* 20°20S 118°10E **60** D2
Thousand Islands *U.S.A.* 44°20N 76°0W **83** B9
Thousand Oaks *U.S.A.* 34°10N 118°50W **79** L8
Thrace *Turkey* 41°0N 27°0E **23** D12
Three Forks *U.S.A.* 45°54N 111°33W **76** D8
Three Hills *Canada* 51°43N 113°15W **70** C6
Three Hummock I. *Australia* 40°25S 144°55E **63** G3
Three Pagodas Pass *Asia* 15°20N 98°30E **38** E2
Three Points, C. *Ghana* 4°42N 2°6W **50** H5
Three Rivers *Calif., U.S.A.* 36°26N 118°54W **78** J8
Three Rivers *Tex., U.S.A.* 28°28N 98°11W **84** G5
Three Springs *Australia* 29°32S 115°45E **61** E2
Throssell, L. *Australia* 27°33S 124°10E **61** E3
Throssell Ra. *Australia* 22°3S 121°43E **60** D3
Thrushton △ *Australia* 27°47S 147°40E **63** D4
Thua → *Kenya* 1°31S 39°30E **54** C4
Thuan Hoa *Vietnam* 8°58N 105°30E **39** H5
Thubun Lakes *Canada* 61°30N 112°0W **71** A6
Thuin *Belgium* 50°20N 4°17E **15** D4
Thule = Qaanaaq *Greenland* 77°40N 69°0W **4** B4
Thule Air Base = Uummannaq *Greenland* 77°28N 69°13W **4** B4
Thun *Switz.* 46°45N 7°38E **20** C7
Thunder B. *U.S.A.* 45°0N 83°20W **82** B1
Thunder Bay *Canada* 48°20N 89°15W **72** C2
Thung Salaeng Luang △ *Thailand* 16°43N 100°50E **38** D3
Thung Song *Thailand* 8°10N 99°40E **39** H2
Thunkar *Bhutan* 27°55N 91°0E **41** F17
Thuong Tra *Vietnam* 16°2N 107°42E **38** D6
Thüringer Wald *Germany* 50°35N 11°0E **16** C6
Thurles *Ireland* 52°41N 7°49W **10** D4
Thurrock □ *U.K.* 51°31N 0°23E **13** F8
Thursday I. *Australia* 10°30S 142°3E **62** A3
Thurso *Canada* 45°36N 75°15W **72** C4
Thurso *U.K.* 58°36N 3°32W **11** C5
Thurso → *U.K.* 58°36N 3°32W **11** C5
Thurston I. *Antarctica* 72°0S 100°0W **5** D16
Thutade L. *Canada* 57°0N 126°55W **70** B3
Thyolo *Malawi* 16°7S 35°5E **55** F4
Ti-Tree *Australia* 22°5S 133°22E **62** C1
Tian Shan *Asia* 40°30N 76°0E **32** B3
Tianjin *China* 39°7N 117°12E **35** E9
Tianshifu *China* 41°17N 124°22E **35** D13
Tianshui *China* 34°32N 105°40E **34** G3
Tianyar *Indonesia* 8°12S 115°30E **37** J18
Tianzhen *China* 40°24N 114°5E **34** D8
Tianzhuangtai *China* 40°43N 122°5E **35** D12
Tiarei *Tahiti* 17°32S 149°20W **59** d
Tiaret *Algeria* 35°20N 1°21E **50** A6
Tibagi *Brazil* 24°30S 50°24W **95** A5
Tibagi → *Brazil* 22°47S 51°1W **95** A5
Tībastī, Sarīr *Libya* 22°50N 18°30E **51** D9
Tibati *Cameroon* 6°22N 12°30E **52** C2
Tiber = Tevere → *Italy* 41°44N 12°14E **22** D5
Tiber Res. *U.S.A.* 48°19N 111°6W **76** B8
Tiberias = Teverya *Israel* 32°47N 35°32E **46** C4
Tiberias, L. = Yam Kinneret *Israel* 32°45N 35°35E **46** C4
Tibesti *Chad* 21°0N 17°30E **51** D9
Tibet = Xizang Zizhiqu □ *China* 32°0N 88°0E **32** C3
Tibet, Plateau of *Asia* 32°0N 86°0E **26** E10
Tibnī *Syria* 35°36N 39°50E **44** C3
Tibooburra *Australia* 29°26S 142°1E **63** D3
Tiburón, I. *Mexico* 29°0N 112°25W **86** B2
Ticino → *Italy* 45°9N 9°14E **20** D8
Ticonderoga *U.S.A.* 43°51N 73°26W **83** C11
Ticul *Mexico* 20°24N 89°32W **87** C7
Tidaholm *Sweden* 58°12N 13°58E **9** G15
Tiddim *Burma* 23°28N 93°45E **41** H18
Tidioute *U.S.A.* 41°41N 79°24W **82** E5
Tidjikja *Mauritania* 18°29N 11°35W **50** E3
Tidore *Indonesia* 0°40N 127°25E **37** D7
Tiefa *China* 42°28N 123°26E **35** C12
Tiegang Shuiku *China* 22°37N 113°53E **33** F10
Tiel *Neths.* 51°53N 5°26E **15** C5
Tieling *China* 42°20N 123°55E **35** C12
Tielt *Belgium* 51°0N 3°20E **15** C3
Tien Shan = Tian Shan *Asia* 40°30N 76°0E **32** B3
Tien-tsin = Tianjin *China* 39°7N 117°12E **35** E9
Tien Yen *Vietnam* 21°20N 107°24E **38** B6
T'ienching = Tianjin *China* 39°7N 117°12E **35** E9
Tienen *Belgium* 50°48N 4°57E **15** D4
Tientsin = Tianjin *China* 39°7N 117°12E **35** E9
Tieri *Australia* 23°2S 148°21E **62** C4
Tierra Amarilla *Chile* 27°28S 70°18W **94** B1
Tierra Amarilla *U.S.A.* 36°42N 106°33W **77** H10
Tierra Colorada *Mexico* 17°11N 99°32W **87** D5
Tierra de Campos *Spain* 42°10N 4°50W **21** A3
Tierra del Fuego, I. Grande de *Argentina* 54°0S 69°0W **96** G3
Tiétar → *Spain* 39°50N 6°1W **21** C3
Tieté → *Brazil* 20°40S 51°35W **95** A5
Tiffin *U.S.A.* 41°7N 83°11W **81** E12
Tifton *U.S.A.* 31°27N 83°31W **85** F13
Tifu *Indonesia* 3°39S 126°24E **37** E7
Tighina *Moldova* 46°50N 29°30E **17** E15
Tigil *Russia* 57°49N 158°40E **29** D16
Tignish *Canada* 46°58N 64°2W **73** C7
Tigre → *Peru* 4°30S 74°10W **92** D4
Tigre → *Venezuela* 9°20N 62°30W **92** B6
Tigris = Dijlah, Nahr → *Asia* 31°0N 47°25E **44** D5
Tigyaing *Burma* 23°45N 96°10E **41** H20
Tihāmah *Asia* 15°3N 41°55E **47** D3
Tijara *India* 27°56N 76°31E **42** F7
Tijuana *Mexico* 32°32N 117°1W **79** N9
Tikal *Guatemala* 17°13N 89°24W **88** C2
Tikal △ *Guatemala* 17°23N 89°34W **88** C2
Tikamgarh *India* 24°44N 78°50E **43** G8
Tikhoretsk *Russia* 45°56N 40°5E **19** E7
Tikhvin *Russia* 59°35N 33°30E **18** C5
Tikirarjuaq = Whale Cove *Canada* 62°10N 92°34W **71** A10
Tikrīt *Iraq* 34°35N 43°37E **44** C4
Tiksi *Russia* 71°40N 128°45E **29** B13
Tilamuta *Indonesia* 0°32N 122°23E **37** D6
Tilburg *Neths.* 51°31N 5°6E **15** C5
Tilbury *Canada* 42°17N 82°23W **82** D2
Tilbury *U.K.* 51°27N 0°22E **13** F8
Tilcara *Argentina* 23°36S 65°23W **94** A2
Tilden *U.S.A.* 42°3N 97°50W **80** D5
Tilhar *India* 28°0N 79°45E **43** F8
Tilichiki *Russia* 60°27N 166°5E **29** C17
Tilissos *Greece* 35°20N 25°1E **25** D7
Till → *U.K.* 55°41N 2°13W **12** B5
Tillamook *U.S.A.* 45°27N 123°51W **76** D2
Tillsonburg *Canada* 42°53N 80°44W **82** D4
Tillyeria *Cyprus* 35°6N 32°40E **25** D11
Tilos *Greece* 36°27N 27°27E **23** F12
Tilpa *Australia* 30°57S 144°24E **63** E3
Tilt → *U.K.* 56°46N 3°51W **11** E5
Tilton *U.S.A.* 43°27N 71°36W **83** C13
Tiltonsville *U.S.A.* 40°10N 80°41W **82** F4
Timanfaya △ *Canary Is.* 29°0N 13°46W **24** F6
Timanskiy Kryazh *Russia* 65°58N 50°5E **18** A9
Timaru *N.Z.* 44°23S 171°14E **59** F3
Timau *Kenya* 0°4N 37°15E **54** B4
Timbaki *Greece* 35°4N 24°45E **25** D6
Timber Creek *Australia* 15°40S 130°29E **60** C5
Timber Lake *U.S.A.* 45°26N 101°5W **80** C3
Timber Mt. *U.S.A.* 37°6N 116°28W **78** H10
Timbuktu = Tombouctou *Mali* 16°50N 3°0W **50** E5
Timi *Cyprus* 34°44N 32°31E **25** E11
Timimoun *Algeria* 29°14N 0°16E **50** C6
Timiris, Râs *Mauritania* 19°21N 16°30W **50** E2
Timiskaming, L. = Témiscamingue, L. *Canada* 47°10N 79°25W **72** C4
Timişoara *Romania* 45°43N 21°15E **17** F11
Timmins *Canada* 48°28N 81°25W **72** C3
Timok → *Serbia* 44°10N 22°40E **23** B10
Timoleague *Ireland* 51°39N 8°46W **10** E3
Timor *Asia* 9°0S 125°0E **37** F7
Timor Leste = East Timor ■ *Asia* 8°50S 126°0E **37** F7
Timor Sea *Ind. Oc.* 12°0S 127°0E **60** B4
Tin Can Bay *Australia* 25°56S 153°0E **63** D5
Tin Mt. *U.S.A.* 36°50N 117°10W **78** J9
Tina = Thina → *S. Africa* 31°18S 29°13E **57** E4
Tîna, Khalîg el *Egypt* 31°10N 32°40E **46** D1
Tinaca Pt. *Phil.* 5°30N 125°25E **37** C7
Tinajo *Canary Is.* 29°4N 13°42W **24** E6
Tindal *Australia* 14°31S 132°22E **60** B5
Tindouf *Algeria* 27°42N 8°10W **50** C4
Tinfunque △ *Paraguay* 23°55S 60°17W **94** A3
Tinggi, Pulau *Malaysia* 2°18N 104°7E **39** L5
Tingo María *Peru* 9°10S 75°54W **92** E3
Tingrela *Ivory C.* 10°27N 6°25W **50** F4
Tinh Bien *Vietnam* 10°36N 104°57E **39** G5
Tinian *N. Marianas* 15°0N 145°38E **64** F6
Tinnevelly = Tirunelveli *India* 8°45N 77°45E **40** Q10
Tinogasta *Argentina* 28°5S 67°32W **94** B2
Tinos *Greece* 37°33N 25°8E **23** F11
Tinpahar *India* 24°59N 87°44E **43** G12
Tintina *Argentina* 27°2S 62°45W **94** B3
Tintinara *Australia* 35°48S 140°2E **63** F3
Tioga *N. Dak., U.S.A.* 48°24N 102°56W **80** A2
Tioga *Pa., U.S.A.* 41°55N 77°8W **82** E7
Tioman, Pulau *Malaysia* 2°50N 104°10E **39** L5
Tionesta *U.S.A.* 41°30N 79°28W **82** E5
Tipperary *Ireland* 52°28N 8°10W **10** D3
Tipperary □ *Ireland* 52°37N 7°55W **10** D4
Tipton *Calif., U.S.A.* 36°4N 119°19W **78** J7
Tipton *Iowa, U.S.A.* 41°46N 91°8W **80** E8
Tipton Mt. *U.S.A.* 35°32N 114°12W **79** K12
Tiptonville *U.S.A.* 36°23N 89°29W **85** C10
Tīrān *Iran* 32°45N 51°8E **45** C6
Tiranë *Albania* 41°18N 19°49E **23** D8
Tirari Desert *Australia* 28°22S 138°7E **63** D2
Tiraspol *Moldova* 46°55N 29°35E **17** E15
Tire *Turkey* 38°5N 27°45E **23** E12
Tirebolu *Turkey* 40°58N 38°45E **19** F6
Tiree *U.K.* 56°31N 6°55W **11** E2
Tiree, Passage of *U.K.* 56°30N 6°30W **11** E2
Tîrgovişte = Târgovişte *Romania* 44°55N 25°27E **17** F13
Tîrgu Jiu = Târgu Jiu *Romania* 45°5N 23°19E **17** F12
Tîrgu Mureş = Târgu Mureş *Romania* 46°31N 24°38E **17** E13
Tirich Mir *Pakistan* 36°15N 71°55E **40** A7
Tiritiri o te Moana = Southern Alps *N.Z.* 43°41S 170°11E **59** E3
Tirnavos *Greece* 39°45N 22°18E **23** E10
Tirodi *India* 21°40N 79°44E **40** J11
Tirol □ *Austria* 47°3N 10°43E **16** E6
Tirso → *Italy* 39°53N 8°32E **22** E3
Tiruchchirappalli *India* 10°45N 78°45E **40** P
Tirunelveli *India* 8°45N 77°45E **40** Q
Tirupati *India* 13°39N 79°25E **40** N
Tiruppur *India* 11°5N 77°22E **40** P
Tiruvannamalai *India* 12°15N 79°5E **40** N
Tisa *India* 32°50N 76°9E **42**
Tisa → *Serbia* 45°15N 20°17E **23**
Tisdale *Canada* 52°50N 104°0W **71**
Tishomingo *U.S.A.* 34°14N 96°41W **84**
Tisza = Tisa → *Serbia* 45°15N 20°17E **23**
Tit-Ary *Russia* 71°55N 127°2E **29** B
Tithwal *Pakistan* 34°21N 73°50E **43**
Titicaca, L. *S. Amer.* 15°30S 69°30W **92**
Titiwa *Nigeria* 12°14N 12°53E **51**
Titule *Dem. Rep. of the Congo* 3°15N 25°31E **54**
Titusville *Fla., U.S.A.* 28°37N 80°49W **85** G
Titusville *Pa., U.S.A.* 41°38N 79°41W **82**
Tivaouane *Senegal* 14°56N 16°45W **50**
Tiverton *Canada* 44°16N 81°32W **82**
Tiverton *U.K.* 50°54N 3°29W **13**
Tívoli *Italy* 41°58N 12°45E **22**
Tizi-Ouzou *Algeria* 36°42N 4°3E **50**
Tizimín *Mexico* 21°9N 88°9W **87**
Tiznit *Morocco* 29°48N 9°45W **50**
Tjeggelvas *Sweden* 66°37N 17°45E **8** C
Tjieggelvas = Tjeggelvas *Sweden* 66°37N 17°45E **8** C
Tjirebon = Cirebon *Indonesia* 6°45S 108°32E **37** G
Tjluring *Indonesia* 8°25S 114°13E **37** J
Tjörn *Sweden* 58°0N 11°35E **9** H
Tlacotalpan *Mexico* 18°37N 95°40W **87**
Tlahualilo de Zaragoza *Mexico* 26°7N 103°27W **86**
Tlaquepaque *Mexico* 20°39N 103°19W **86**
Tlaxcala *Mexico* 19°19N 98°14W **87**
Tlaxcala □ *Mexico* 19°25N 98°10W **87**
Tlaxiaco *Mexico* 17°25N 97°35W **87**
Tlemcen *Algeria* 34°52N 1°21W **50**
To Bong *Vietnam* 12°45N 109°16E **38**
Toa Payoh *Singapore* 1°20N 103°51E **3**
Toad → *Canada* 59°25N 124°57W **70**
Toad River *Canada* 58°51N 125°14W **70**
Toamasina *Madag.* 18°10S 49°25E **57**
Toamasina □ *Madag.* 18°0S 49°0E **57**
Toay *Argentina* 36°43S 64°38W **94**
Toba *Japan* 34°30N 136°51E **31**
Toba, Danau *Indonesia* 2°30N 97°30E **36**
Toba Kakar *Pakistan* 31°30N 69°0E **42**
Toba Tek Singh *Pakistan* 30°55N 72°25E **42**
Tobago *Trin. & Tob.* 11°10N 60°30W **89**
Tobelo *Indonesia* 1°45N 127°56E **37**
Tobermory *Canada* 45°12N 81°40W **82**
Tobermory *U.K.* 56°38N 6°5W **11**
Tobi *Pac. Oc.* 2°40N 131°10E **37**
Tobi-Shima *Japan* 41°12N 139°34E **30**
Tobin, L. *Australia* 21°45S 125°49E **60**
Tobin L. *Canada* 53°35N 103°30W **71**
Toboali *Indonesia* 3°0S 106°25E **36**
Tobol → *Russia* 58°10N 68°12E **28**
Toboli *Indonesia* 0°38S 120°5E **37**
Tobolsk *Russia* 58°15N 68°10E **28**
Tobruk = Tubruq *Libya* 32°7N 23°55E **51** E
Tobyhanna *U.S.A.* 41°11N 75°25W **83**
Tobyl = Tobol → *Russia* 58°10N 68°12E **28**
Tocantinópolis *Brazil* 6°20S 47°25W **93**
Tocantins □ *Brazil* 10°0S 48°0W **93**
Tocantins → *Brazil* 1°45S 49°10W **93**
Toccoa *U.S.A.* 34°35N 83°19W **85** D
Tochi → *Pakistan* 32°49N 70°41E **42**
Tochigi *Japan* 36°25N 139°45E **31**
Tochigi □ *Japan* 36°45N 139°45E **31**
Toco *Trin. & Tob.* 10°49N 60°57W **93** K
Toconao *Chile* 23°11S 68°1W **94**
Tocopilla *Chile* 22°5S 70°10W **94**
Tocumwal *Australia* 35°51S 145°31E **63**
Tocuyo → *Venezuela* 11°3N 68°23W **92**
Todd → *Australia* 24°52S 135°48E **62**
Todeli *Indonesia* 1°40S 124°29E **37**
Todenyang *Kenya* 4°35N 35°56E **54**
Todgarh *India* 25°42N 73°58E **42**
Todos os Santos, B. de *Brazil* 12°48S 38°38W **93** F
Todos Santos *Mexico* 23°26N 110°13W **86**
Toe Hd. *U.K.* 57°50N 7°8W **11**
Tofield *Canada* 53°25N 112°40W **70**
Tofino *Canada* 49°11N 125°55W **70**
Tofua *Tonga* 19°45S 175°5W **5**
Tōgane *Japan* 35°33N 140°22E **31** G
Togian, Kepulauan *Indonesia* 0°20S 121°50E **37**
Togliatti *Russia* 53°32N 49°24E **18**
Togo ■ *W. Afr.* 8°30N 1°35E **50**
Togtoh *China* 40°15N 111°10E **34**
Tohiea, Mt. *Moorea* 17°33S 149°49W **5**
Tōhoku □ *Japan* 39°50N 141°45E **30** E
Töhöm *Mongolia* 44°27N 108°2E **34**
Toinya *Sudan* 6°17N 29°46E **51** G
Toiyabe Range *U.S.A.* 39°30N 117°0W **76**
Tojikiston = Tajikistan ■ *Asia* 38°30N 70°0E **28**
Tojo *Indonesia* 1°20S 121°15E **37**
Tōjō *Japan* 34°53N 133°16E **31**
Tok *U.S.A.* 63°20N 142°59W **68**
Tokachi-Dake *Japan* 43°17N 142°5E **30** C
Tokachi-Gawa → *Japan* 42°44N 143°42E **30** C
Tokala *Indonesia* 1°30S 121°40E **37**
Tōkamachi *Japan* 37°8N 138°43E **31**
Tokanui *N.Z.* 46°34S 168°56E **59**
Tokara-Rettō *Japan* 29°37N 129°43E **31**
Tokarahi *N.Z.* 44°56S 170°39E **59**
Tokashiki-Shima *Japan* 26°11N 127°21E **31**
Tokat *Turkey* 40°22N 36°35E **19**
Tŏkch'ŏn *N. Korea* 39°45N 126°18E **35** E
Tokdo *Asia* 37°15N 131°52E **31**

okeland U.S.A. 46°42N 123°59W 78 D3
okelau Is. Pac. Oc. 9°0S 171°45W 64 H10
okmak Kyrgyzstan 42°49N 75°15E 28 E8
oko Ra. Australia 23°5S 138°20E 62 C2
okoro-Gawa → Japan 44°7N 144°5E 30 B12
oku Tonga 18°10S 174°11W 59 c
okuno-Shima Japan 27°56N 128°55E 31 L4
okushima Japan 34°4N 134°34E 31 G7
okushima □ Japan 33°55N 134°0E 31 H7
okuyama Japan 34°3N 131°50E 31 G5
ōkyō Japan 35°43N 139°45E 31 G9
olaga Bay N.Z. 38°21S 178°20E 59 C7
olbukhin = Dobrich
Bulgaria 43°37N 27°49E 23 C12
oledo Brazil 24°44S 53°45W 95 A5
oledo Spain 39°50N 4°2W 21 C3
oledo Ohio, U.S.A. 41°39N 83°33W 81 E12
oledo Oreg., U.S.A. 44°37N 123°56W 76 D2
oledo Wash., U.S.A. 46°26N 122°51W 76 C2
oledo, Montes de Spain 39°33N 4°20W 21 C3
oledo Bend Res. U.S.A. 31°11N 93°34W 84 F8
olga Australia 17°15S 145°29E 62 B4
oliara Madag. 23°21S 43°40E 57 C7
oliara □ Madag. 21°0S 45°0E 57 C8
olima Colombia 4°40N 75°19W 92 C3
olitoli Indonesia 1°5N 120°50E 37 D6
ollhouse U.S.A. 37°1N 119°24W 78 H7
olmachevo Russia 58°56N 29°51E 9 G23
olo, Teluk Indonesia 2°20S 122°10E 37 E6
olo Harbour China 22°27N 114°12E 33 G11
oluca Mexico 19°17N 99°40W 87 D5
om Burke S. Africa 23°5S 28°0E 57 C4
om Price Australia 22°40S 117°48E 60 D2
omah U.S.A. 43°59N 90°30W 80 D8
omahawk U.S.A. 45°28N 89°44W 80 C9
omakomai Japan 42°38N 141°36E 30 C10
omales U.S.A. 38°15N 122°53W 78 G4
omales B. U.S.A. 38°15N 123°58W 78 G3
omanivi Fiji 17°37S 178°1E 59 a
omar Portugal 39°36N 8°25W 21 C1
omaszów Mazowiecki
Poland 51°30N 20°2E 17 C10
omatlán Mexico 19°56N 105°15W 86 D3
ombador, Serra do Brazil 12°0S 58°0W 92 F7
ombigbee → U.S.A. 31°8N 87°57W 85 F11
ombouctou Mali 16°50N 3°0W 50 E5
ombstone U.S.A. 31°43N 110°4W 77 L8
ombua Angola 15°55S 11°55E 56 B1
omé Chile 36°36S 72°57W 94 D1
omelloso Spain 39°10N 3°2W 21 C4
omini Indonesia 0°30N 120°30E 37 D6
omini, Teluk Indonesia 0°10S 121°0E 37 E6
omintoul U.K. 57°15N 3°23W 11 D5
omkinson Ranges
Australia 26°11S 129°5E 61 E4
ommot Russia 59°4N 126°20E 29 D13
omnop Ta Suos
Cambodia 11°20N 104°15E 39 G5
omo → Colombia 5°20N 67°48W 92 B5
oms Place U.S.A. 37°34N 118°41W 78 H8
oms River U.S.A. 39°58N 74°12W 83 G10
omsk Russia 56°30N 85°5E 28 D9
onalá Chiapas, Mexico 16°4N 93°45W 87 D6
onalá Jalisco, Mexico 20°37N 103°14W 86 C4
onantins Brazil 2°45S 67°45W 92 D5
onasket U.S.A. 48°42N 119°26W 76 B4
onawanda U.S.A. 43°1N 78°53W 82 D6
onb Iran 26°15N 55°15E 45 E7
onbridge U.K. 51°11N 0°17E 13 F8
ondano Indonesia 1°35N 124°54E 37 D6
ondoro Namibia 17°45S 18°50E 56 B2
one → Australia 34°25S 116°25E 61 F2
one-Gawa → Japan 35°44N 140°51E 31 F9
onekābon Iran 36°45N 51°12E 45 B6
ong Xian China 39°55N 116°35E 34 E9
ong-Yeong S. Korea 34°50N 128°20E 35 G15
onga ■ Pac. Oc. 19°50S 174°30W 59 c
onga Trench Pac. Oc. 18°0S 173°0W 64 J10
ongaat S. Africa 29°33S 31°9E 57 D5
ongareva = Penrhyn
Cook Is. 9°0S 158°0W 65 H12
ongariro △ N.Z. 39°8S 175°33E 59 C5
ongatapu Tonga 21°10S 175°10W 59 c
ongatapu Group Tonga 21°0S 175°0W 59 c
ongchuan China 35°6N 109°3E 34 G5
ongeren Belgium 50°47N 5°28E 15 D5
onggu Jiao China 22°22N 113°37E 33 G10
ongguan China 34°40N 110°25E 34 G6
onghua China 41°42N 125°58E 35 D13
ongjosŏn Man
N. Korea 39°30N 128°0E 35 E15
ongking, G. of = Tonkin, G. of
Asia 20°0N 108°0E 38 C7
ongliao China 43°38N 122°18E 35 C12
ongling China 30°55N 117°48E 33 C6
ongobory Madag. 23°32S 44°20E 57 C7
ongoy Chile 30°16S 71°31W 94 C1
ongres = Tongeren
Belgium 50°47N 5°28E 15 D5
ongsa Dzong Bhutan 27°31N 90°31E 41 F17
ongshi China 18°30N 109°20E 38 C7
ongue U.K. 58°29N 4°25W 11 C4
ongue → U.S.A. 46°25N 105°52W 76 C11
ongwei China 35°0N 105°5E 34 G3
ongxin China 36°59N 105°58E 34 F3
ongyang N. Korea 39°9N 126°53E 35 E14
ongyu China 44°45N 123°4E 35 B12
onj Sudan 7°20N 28°44E 51 G11
onk India 26°6N 75°54E 42 F6
onkawa U.S.A. 36°41N 97°18W 84 C6
onkin = Bac Phan
Vietnam 22°0N 105°0E 38 B5
onkin, G. of Asia 20°0N 108°0E 38 C7
onle Sap Cambodia 13°0N 104°0E 38 F5
ono Japan 39°19N 141°32E 30 E10
onopah U.S.A. 38°4N 117°14W 77 G5
onosí Panama 7°20N 80°20W 88 E3
Tons → Haryana, India 30°30N 77°39E 42 D7
Tons → Ut. P., India 26°1N 83°33E 43 F10
Tønsberg Norway 59°19N 10°25E 9 G14
Tonto △ U.S.A. 33°39N 111°7W 77 K8
Tonumea Tonga 20°30S 174°30W 59 c
Toobanna Australia 18°42S 146°9E 62 B4
Toodyay Australia 31°34S 116°28E 61 F2
Tooele U.S.A. 40°32N 112°18W 76 F7
Toompine Australia 27°15S 144°19E 63 D3
Toora Australia 38°39S 146°23E 63 F4
Toora-Khem Russia 52°28N 96°17E 29 D10
Toowoomba Australia 27°32S 151°56E 63 D5
Top Springs Australia 16°37S 131°51E 60 C5
Topaz U.S.A. 38°41N 119°30W 78 G7
Topeka U.S.A. 39°3N 95°40W 80 F6
Topley Canada 54°49N 126°18W 70 C3
Topocalma, Pta. Chile 34°10S 72°2W 94 C1
Topock U.S.A. 34°46N 114°29W 79 L12
Topoľčany Slovak Rep. 48°35N 18°12E 17 D10
Topolobampo Mexico 25°36N 109°3W 86 B3
Topozero, Ozero Russia 65°35N 32°0E 8 D25
Toppenish U.S.A. 46°23N 120°19W 76 C3
Toraka Vestale Madag. 16°20S 43°58E 57 B7
Torata Peru 17°23S 70°1W 92 G4
Torbalı Turkey 38°10N 27°21E 23 E12
Torbat-e Heydārīyeh
Iran 35°15N 59°12E 45 C8
Torbat-e Jām Iran 35°16N 60°35E 45 C9
Torbay Canada 47°40N 52°42W 73 C9
Torbay □ U.K. 50°26N 3°31W 13 G4
Tordesillas Spain 41°30N 5°0W 21 B3
Torfaen □ U.K. 51°43N 3°3W 13 F4
Torgau Germany 51°34N 13°0E 16 C7
Torhout Belgium 51°5N 3°7E 15 C3
Tori-Shima Japan 30°29N 140°19E 31 J10
Torino Italy 45°3N 7°40E 20 D7
Torit Sudan 4°27N 32°31E 51 H12
Torkamān Iran 37°35N 47°23E 44 B5
Tormes → Spain 41°18N 6°29W 21 B2
Tornado Mt. Canada 49°55N 114°40W 70 D6
Torneå = Tornio Finland 65°50N 24°12E 8 D21
Torneälven → Europe 65°50N 24°12E 8 D21
Torneträsk Sweden 68°24N 19°15E 8 B18
Tornio Finland 65°50N 24°12E 8 D21
Tornionjoki = Torneälven →
Europe 65°50N 24°12E 8 D21
Tornquist Argentina 38°8S 62°15W 94 D3
Toro Spain 41°35N 5°24W 21 B3
Toro, Cerro del Chile 29°10S 69°50W 94 B2
Toro ⌓ Uganda 1°5N 30°22E 54 C3
Toro Pk. U.S.A. 33°34N 116°24W 79 M10
Toronto Canada 43°39N 79°20W 82 C5
Toronto U.S.A. 40°28N 80°36W 82 F4
Toronto Lester B. Pearson Int. ✈
(YYZ) Canada 43°46N 79°35W 82 C5
Toropets Russia 56°30N 31°40E 18 C5
Tororo Uganda 0°45N 34°12E 54 B3
Toros Dağları Turkey 37°0N 32°30E 44 B2
Torpa India 22°57N 85°6E 43 H11
Torquay U.K. 50°27N 3°32W 13 G4
Torrance U.S.A. 33°50N 118°20W 79 M8
Torre de Moncorvo
Portugal 41°12N 7°8W 21 B2
Torre del Greco Italy 40°47N 14°22E 22 D6
Torrejón de Ardoz Spain 40°27N 3°29W 21 B4
Torrelavega Spain 43°20N 4°5W 21 A3
Torremolinos Spain 36°38N 4°30W 21 D3
Torrens, L. Australia 31°0S 137°50E 63 E2
Torrens Cr. → Australia 22°23S 145°9E 62 C4
Torrens Creek Australia 20°48S 145°3E 62 C4
Torrent Spain 39°27N 0°28W 21 C5
Torreón Mexico 25°33N 103°26W 86 B4
Torres Brazil 29°21S 49°44W 95 B5
Torres Mexico 28°46N 110°47W 86 B2
Torres Strait Australia 9°50S 142°20E 58 B7
Torres Vedras Portugal 39°5N 9°15W 21 C1
Torrevieja Spain 37°59N 0°42W 21 D5
Torrey U.S.A. 38°18N 111°25W 76 G8
Torridge → U.K. 51°0N 4°13W 13 G3
Torridon, L. U.K. 57°35N 5°50W 11 D3
Torrington Conn., U.S.A. 41°48N 73°7W 83 E11
Torrington Wyo.,
U.S.A. 42°4N 104°11W 76 E11
Tórshavn Færoe Is. 62°5N 6°56W 8 E9
Tortola Br. Virgin Is. 18°19N 64°45W 89 e
Tortosa Spain 40°49N 0°31E 21 B6
Tortosa, C. Spain 40°41N 0°52E 21 B6
Tortue, Î. de la Haiti 20°5N 72°57W 89 B5
Tortuguero △ Costa Rica 10°31N 83°29W 88 D3
Torūd Iran 35°25N 55°5E 45 C7
Toruń Poland 53°2N 18°39E 17 B10
Tory Hill Canada 44°58N 78°16W 82 B6
Tory I. Ireland 55°16N 8°14W 10 A3
Tosa Japan 33°24N 133°23E 31 H6
Tosa-Shimizu Japan 32°52N 132°58E 31 H6
Tosa-Wan Japan 33°15N 133°30E 31 H6
Toscana □ Italy 43°25N 11°0E 22 C4
Toshka Lakes Egypt 22°50N 31°0E 51 D12
Toshkent Uzbekistan 41°20N 69°10E 28 E7
Tostado Argentina 29°15S 61°50W 94 B3
Tostón, Pta. de Canary Is. 28°42N 14°2W 24 F5
Tosu Japan 33°22N 130°31E 31 H5
Toteng Botswana 20°22S 22°58E 56 C3
Totma Russia 60°0N 42°40E 18 C7
Totnes U.K. 50°26N 3°42W 13 G4
Totness Suriname 5°53N 56°19W 93 B7
Totonicapán Guatemala 14°58N 91°12W 88 D1
Totoya, I. Fiji 18°57S 179°50W 59 a
Totten Glacier Antarctica 66°45S 116°10E 5 C8
Tottenham Australia 32°14S 147°21E 63 E4
Tottenham Canada 44°1N 79°49W 82 B5
Tottori Japan 35°30N 134°15E 31 G7
Tottori □ Japan 35°30N 134°12E 31 G7
Toubkal, Djebel Morocco 31°0N 8°0W 50 B4
Tougan Burkina Faso 13°11N 2°58W 50 F5
Touggourt Algeria 33°6N 6°4E 50 B7
Toul France 48°40N 5°53E 20 B6
Toulon France 43°10N 5°55E 20 E6
Toulouse France 43°37N 1°27E 20 E4
Toummo Niger 22°45N 14°8E 51 D8
Toungoo Burma 19°0N 96°30E 41 K20
Touraine France 47°20N 0°30E 20 C4
Tourcoing France 50°42N 3°10E 20 A5
Touriñán, C. Spain 43°3N 9°18W 21 A1
Tournai Belgium 50°35N 3°25E 15 D3
Tournon-sur-Rhône
France 45°4N 4°50E 20 D6
Tours France 47°22N 0°40E 20 C4
Toussoro, Mt. C.A.R. 9°7N 23°14E 52 C4
Touws → S. Africa 33°45S 21°11E 56 E3
Touwsrivier S. Africa 33°20S 20°2E 56 E3
Towada Japan 40°37N 141°13E 30 D10
Towada-Hachimantai △
Japan 40°20N 140°55E 30 D10
Towada-Ko Japan 40°28N 140°55E 30 D10
Towanda U.S.A. 41°46N 76°27W 83 E8
Tower U.S.A. 47°48N 92°17W 80 B7
Towerhill Cr. →
Australia 22°28S 144°35E 62 C3
Towner U.S.A. 48°21N 100°25W 80 A3
Townsend U.S.A. 46°19N 111°31W 76 C8
Townshend I. Australia 22°10S 150°31E 62 C5
Townsville Australia 19°15S 146°45E 62 B4
Towraghondī Afghan. 35°13N 62°16E 40 B3
Towson U.S.A. 39°24N 76°36W 81 F15
Towuti, Danau Indonesia 2°45S 121°32E 37 E6
Toya-Ko Japan 42°35N 140°51E 30 C10
Toyama Japan 36°40N 137°15E 31 F8
Toyama □ Japan 36°45N 137°30E 31 F8
Toyama-Wan Japan 37°0N 137°30E 31 F8
Toyapakeh Indonesia 8°41S 115°29E 37 K18
Toyohashi Japan 34°45N 137°25E 31 G8
Toyokawa Japan 34°48N 137°27E 31 G8
Toyonaka Japan 34°46N 135°28E 31 G7
Toyooka Japan 35°35N 134°48E 31 G7
Toyota Japan 35°3N 137°7E 31 G8
Tozeur Tunisia 33°56N 8°8E 50 B7
Trá Li = Tralee Ireland 52°16N 9°42W 10 D2
Tra On Vietnam 9°58N 105°55E 39 H5
Trabzon Turkey 41°0N 39°45E 19 F6
Tracadie Canada 47°30N 64°55W 73 C7
Tracy Canada 46°1N 73°9W 72 C5
Tracy Calif., U.S.A. 37°44N 121°26W 78 H5
Tracy Minn., U.S.A. 44°14N 95°37W 80 C6
Trafalgar, C. Spain 36°10N 6°2W 21 D2
Trail Canada 49°5N 117°40W 70 D5
Trainor L. Canada 60°24N 120°17W 70 A4
Trakai △ Lithuania 54°30N 25°10E 9 J21
Trákhonas Cyprus 35°12N 33°21E 25 D12
Tralee Ireland 52°16N 9°42W 10 D2
Tralee B. Ireland 52°17N 9°55W 10 D2
Tramore Ireland 52°10N 7°10W 10 D4
Tramore B. Ireland 52°9N 7°10W 10 D4
Tramuntana, Serra de
Spain 39°48N 2°54E 24 B9
Tran Ninh, Cao Nguyen
Laos 19°30N 103°10E 38 C4
Tranås Sweden 58°3N 14°59E 9 G16
Trancas Argentina 26°11S 65°20W 94 B2
Trang Thailand 7°33N 99°38E 39 J2
Trangahy Madag. 19°7S 44°31E 57 B7
Trangan Indonesia 6°40S 134°20E 37 F8
Trangie Australia 32°4S 148°0E 63 E4
Trani Italy 41°17N 16°25E 22 D7
Tranoroa Madag. 24°42S 45°4E 57 C8
Tranqueras Uruguay 31°13S 55°45W 95 C4
Transantarctic Mts.
Antarctica 85°0S 170°0W 5 E12
Transilvania Romania 46°30N 24°0E 17 E12
Transilvanian Alps = Carpaţii
Meridionali Romania 45°30N 25°0E 17 F13
Transnistria = Stînga Nistrului □
Moldova 47°20N 29°15E 17 E15
Transylvania = Transilvania
Romania 46°30N 24°0E 17 E12
Trápani Italy 38°1N 12°29E 22 E5
Trapper Pk. U.S.A. 45°54N 114°18W 76 D6
Traralgon Australia 38°12S 146°34E 63 F4
Trasimeno, L. Italy 43°8N 12°6E 22 C5
Trat Thailand 12°14N 102°33E 39 F4
Tratani → Pakistan 29°19N 68°20E 42 E3
Traun Austria 48°14N 14°15E 16 D8
Travellers L. Australia 33°20S 142°0E 63 E3
Travemünde Germany 53°57N 10°52E 16 B6
Travers, Mt. N.Z. 42°1S 172°45E 59 E4
Traverse City U.S.A. 44°46N 85°38W 81 C11
Travis, L. U.S.A. 30°24N 97°55W 84 F6
Travnik Bos.-H. 44°17N 17°39E 23 B7
Trawbreaga B. Ireland 55°20N 7°25W 10 A4
Trébbia → Italy 45°4N 9°41E 20 D8
Třebíč Czech Rep. 49°14N 15°55E 16 D8
Trebinje Bos.-H. 42°44N 18°22E 23 C8
Trebonne Australia 18°37S 146°5E 62 B4
Tregaron U.K. 52°14N 3°56W 13 E4
Tregrosse Is. Australia 17°41S 150°43E 62 B5
Treherne Canada 49°38N 98°42W 71 D9
Treinta y Tres Uruguay 33°16S 54°17W 95 C5
Trelawney Zimbabwe 17°30S 30°30E 57 B5
Trelew Argentina 43°10S 65°20W 96 E3
Trelleborg Sweden 55°20N 13°10E 9 J15
Tremadog Bay U.K. 52°51N 4°18W 12 E3
Tremonton U.S.A. 41°43N 112°10W 76 F7
Tremp Spain 42°10N 0°52E 21 A6
Trenche → Canada 47°46N 72°53W 72 C5
Trenčín Slovak Rep. 48°52N 18°4E 17 D10
Trenggalek Indonesia 8°3S 111°43E 37 H14
Trenque Lauquen
Argentina 36°5S 62°45W 94 D3
Trent → Canada 44°6N 77°34W 82 B7
Trent → U.K. 53°41N 0°42W 12 D7
Trento Italy 46°4N 11°8E 22 A4
Trenton Canada 44°10N 77°34W 82 B7
Trenton Mo., U.S.A. 40°5N 93°37W 80 E7
Trenton N.J., U.S.A. 40°14N 74°46W 83 F10
Trenton Nebr., U.S.A. 40°11N 101°1W 80 E3
Trepassey Canada 46°43N 53°25W 73 C9
Tres Arroyos Argentina 38°26S 60°20W 94 D3
Três Corações Brazil 21°44S 45°15W 95 A6
Três Lagoas Brazil 20°50S 51°43W 93 H8
Tres Lomas Argentina 36°27S 62°51W 94 D3
Tres Montes, C. Chile 46°50S 75°30W 96 F1
Tres Pinos U.S.A. 36°48N 121°19W 78 J5
Três Pontas Brazil 21°23S 45°29W 95 A6
Tres Puentes Chile 27°50S 70°15W 94 B1
Tres Puntas, C. Argentina 47°0S 66°0W 96 F3
Três Rios Brazil 22°6S 43°15W 95 A7
Tres Valles Mexico 18°15N 96°8W 87 D5
Tresco U.K. 49°57N 6°20W 13 H1
Treviso Italy 45°40N 12°15E 22 B5
Triabunna Australia 42°30S 147°55E 63 G4
Trianda Greece 36°25N 28°10E 25 C10
Triangle Zimbabwe 21°2S 31°28E 57 C5
Tribal Areas □ Pakistan 33°0N 70°0E 42 C4
Tribulation, C. Australia 16°5S 145°29E 62 B4
Tribune U.S.A. 38°28N 101°45W 80 F3
Trichinopoly = Tiruchchirappalli
India 10°45N 78°45E 40 P11
Trichur India 10°30N 76°18E 40 P10
Trida Australia 33°1S 145°1E 63 E4
Trier Germany 49°45N 6°38E 16 D4
Trieste Italy 45°40N 13°46E 22 B5
Triglav Slovenia 46°21N 13°50E 16 E7
Trikala Greece 39°34N 21°47E 23 E9
Trikomo Cyprus 35°17N 33°52E 25 D12
Trikora, Puncak
Indonesia 4°15S 138°45E 37 E9
Trim Ireland 53°33N 6°48W 10 C5
Trimmu Dam Pakistan 31°10N 72°8E 42 D5
Trincomalee Sri Lanka 8°38N 81°15E 40 Q12
Trindade Brazil 16°40S 49°30W 93 G9
Trindade, I. Atl. Oc. 20°20S 29°50W 2 F8
Trinidad Bolivia 14°46S 64°50W 92 F6
Trinidad Cuba 21°48N 80°0W 88 B4
Trinidad Trin. & Tob. 10°30N 61°15W 89 D7
Trinidad Uruguay 33°30S 56°50W 94 C4
Trinidad U.S.A. 37°10N 104°31W 77 H11
Trinidad → Mexico 17°49N 95°9W 87 D5
Trinidad & Tobago ■
W. Indies 10°30N 61°20W 89 D7
Trinity Canada 48°59N 53°55W 73 C9
Trinity U.S.A. 30°57N 95°22W 84 F7
Trinity → Calif., U.S.A. 41°11N 123°42W 76 F2
Trinity → Tex., U.S.A. 29°45N 94°43W 84 G7
Trinity B. Canada 48°20N 53°10W 73 C9
Trinity Hills Trin. & Tob. 10°7N 61°7W 93 K15
Trinity Is. U.S.A. 56°33N 154°25W 74 a
Trinity Range U.S.A. 40°10N 118°40W 76 F4
Trinkitat Sudan 18°45N 37°51E 51 E13
Trinway U.S.A. 40°9N 82°1W 82 F2
Triolet Mauritius 20°4S 57°32E 53 d
Tripoli = Tarābulus
Lebanon 34°31N 35°50E 46 A4
Tripoli = Tarābulus Libya 32°49N 13°7E 51 B8
Tripoli Greece 37°31N 22°25E 23 F10
Tripolitania = Tarābulus
N. Afr. 31°0N 13°0E 51 B8
Tripura □ India 24°0N 92°0E 41 H18
Tripylos Cyprus 34°59N 32°41E 25 E11
Tristan da Cunha Atl. Oc. 37°6S 12°20W 49 K2
Trisul India 30°19N 79°47E 43 D8
Trivandrum India 8°41N 77°0E 40 Q10
Trnava Slovak Rep. 48°23N 17°35E 17 D9
Trochu Canada 51°50N 113°13W 70 C6
Trodely I. Canada 52°15N 79°26W 72 B4
Troglav Croatia 43°56N 16°36E 22 C7
Troilus, L. Canada 50°50N 74°35W 72 B5
Trois-Pistoles Canada 48°5N 69°10W 73 C6
Trois-Rivières Canada 46°25N 72°34W 72 C5
Trois-Rivières Guadeloupe 15°57N 61°40W 88 b
Troitsk Russia 54°10N 61°35E 28 D7
Troitsko Pechorsk
Russia 62°40N 56°10E 18 B10
Trölladyngja Iceland 64°54N 17°16W 8 D5
Trollhättan Sweden 58°17N 12°20E 9 G15
Trollheimen Norway 62°46N 9°1E 8 E13
Trombetas → Brazil 1°55S 55°35W 93 D7
Tromsø Norway 69°40N 18°56E 8 B18
Tron Thailand 17°28N 100°7E 38 D3
Trona U.S.A. 35°46N 117°23W 79 K9
Tronador, Mte.
Argentina 41°10S 71°50W 96 E2
Trøndelag Norway 64°17N 11°50E 8 D14
Trondheim Norway 63°36N 10°25E 8 E14
Trondheimsfjorden
Norway 63°35N 10°30E 8 E14
Troodos Cyprus 34°55N 32°52E 25 E11
Troon U.K. 55°33N 4°39W 11 F4
Tropic U.S.A. 37°37N 112°5W 77 H7
Trostan U.K. 55°3N 6°10W 10 A5
Trou Gras Pt. St. Lucia 13°51N 60°53W 89 f
Trout → Canada 61°19N 119°51W 70 A5
Trout L. N.W.T., Canada 60°40N 121°14W 70 A4
Trout L. Ont., Canada 51°20N 93°15W 71 C10
Trout Lake Canada 56°30N 114°32W 70 B6
Trout Lake U.S.A. 46°0N 121°32W 78 E5
Trout River Canada 49°29N 58°8W 73 C8
Trout Run U.S.A. 41°23N 77°3W 82 E7
Trouville-sur-Mer France 49°21N 0°5E 20 B4
Trowbridge U.K. 51°18N 2°12W 13 F5
Troy Turkey 39°57N 26°12E 23 E12
Troy Ala., U.S.A. 31°48N 85°58W 85 F12
Troy Kans., U.S.A. 39°47N 95°5W 80 F6
Troy Mo., U.S.A. 38°59N 90°59W 80 F8
Troy Mont., U.S.A. 48°28N 115°53W 76 B6
Troy N.Y., U.S.A. 42°44N 73°41W 83 D11
Troy Ohio, U.S.A. 40°2N 84°12W 81 E11
Troy Pa., U.S.A. 41°47N 76°47W 83 E8
Troyes France 48°19N 4°3E 20 B6
Truchas Pk. U.S.A. 35°58N 105°39W 77 J11
Trucial States = United Arab
Emirates ■ Asia 23°50N 54°0E 45 F7
Truckee U.S.A. 39°20N 120°11W 78 F6
Trudovoye Russia 43°17N 132°5E 30 C6
Trujillo Honduras 16°0N 86°0W 88 C2
Trujillo Peru 8°6S 79°0W 92 E3
Trujillo Spain 39°28N 5°55W 21 C3
Trujillo U.S.A. 35°32N 104°42W 77 J11
Trujillo Venezuela 9°22N 70°38W 92 B4
Truk Micronesia 7°25N 151°46E 64 G7
Trumann U.S.A. 35°41N 90°31W 85 D9
Trumansburg U.S.A. 42°33N 76°40W 83 D8
Trumbull, Mt. U.S.A. 36°25N 113°19W 77 H7
Trundle Australia 32°53S 147°35E 63 E4
Trung-Phan = Annam
Vietnam 16°0N 108°0E 38 E7
Truro Canada 45°21N 63°14W 73 C7
Truro U.K. 50°16N 5°4W 13 G2
Truskavets Ukraine 49°17N 23°30E 17 D12
Trutch Canada 57°44N 122°57W 70 B4
Truth or Consequences
U.S.A. 33°8N 107°15W 77 K10
Trutnov Czech Rep. 50°37N 15°54E 16 C8
Tryonville U.S.A. 41°42N 79°48W 82 E5
Tsandi Namibia 17°42S 14°50E 56 B1
Tsaratanana Madag. 16°47S 47°39E 57 B8
Tsaratanana, Mt. de =
Maromokotro Madag. 14°0S 49°0E 57 A8
Tsaratanana ⌓ Madag. 13°57S 48°52E 57 A8
Tsau Botswana 20°8S 22°22E 56 C3
Tsavo Kenya 2°59S 38°28E 54 C4
Tsavo East △ Kenya 2°44S 38°47E 54 C4
Tsavo West △ Kenya 3°19S 37°57E 54 C4
Tsentralnyy □ Russia 52°0N 40°0E 28 D4
Tses Namibia 25°58S 18°8E 56 D2
Tsetserleg Mongolia 47°36N 101°32E 32 B5
Tsévié Togo 6°25N 1°20E 50 G6
Tshabong Botswana 26°2S 22°29E 56 D3
Tshane Botswana 24°5S 21°54E 56 C3
Tshela
Dem. Rep. of the Congo 4°57S 13°4E 52 E2
Tshesebe Botswana 21°51S 27°32E 57 C4
Tshibeke
Dem. Rep. of the Congo 2°40S 28°35E 54 C2
Tshibinda
Dem. Rep. of the Congo 2°23S 28°43E 54 C2
Tshikapa
Dem. Rep. of the Congo 6°28S 20°48E 52 F4
Tshilenge
Dem. Rep. of the Congo 6°17S 23°48E 54 D1
Tshinsenda
Dem. Rep. of the Congo 12°20S 28°0E 55 E2
Tshofa
Dem. Rep. of the Congo 5°13S 25°16E 54 D2
Tshwane = Pretoria
S. Africa 25°44S 28°12E 57 D4
Tshwane Botswana 22°24S 22°1E 56 C3
Tsigara Botswana 20°22S 25°54E 56 C4
Tsihombe Madag. 25°10S 45°41E 57 D8
Tsiigehtchic Canada 67°15N 134°0W 68 C6
Ts'il-os ⌓ Canada 51°9N 123°59W 70 C4
Tsimlyansk Res. = Tsimlyanskoye
Vdkhr. Russia 48°0N 43°0E 19 E7
Tsimlyanskoye Vdkhr.
Russia 48°0N 43°0E 19 E7
Tsinan = Jinan China 36°38N 117°1E 34 F9
Tsineng S. Africa 27°5S 23°5E 56 D3
Tsing Yi China 22°21N 114°6E 33 G11
Tsinghai = Qinghai □
China 36°0N 98°0E 32 C4
Tsingtao = Qingdao
China 36°5N 120°20E 35 F11
Tsingy de Bemaraha ⌓
Madag. 18°35S 45°25E 57 B8
Tsingy de Namoroka ⌓
Madag. 16°29S 45°25E 57 B8
Tsinjoarivo Madag. 19°37S 47°40E 57 B8
Tsinjomitondraka Madag. 15°40S 47°8E 57 B8
Tsirigo = Kythira Greece 36°8N 23°0E 23 F10
Tsiroanomandidy Madag. 18°46S 46°2E 57 B8
Tsitondroina Madag. 21°19S 46°0E 57 C8
Tsitsikamma △ S. Africa 34°3S 23°40E 56 E3
Tsivory Madag. 24°4S 46°5E 57 C8
Tskhinvali Georgia 42°14N 44°1E 19 F7
Tsna → Russia 54°55N 41°58E 18 D7
Tso Moriri, L. India 32°50N 78°20E 43 C8
Tsobis Namibia 19°27S 17°30E 56 B2
Tsodilo Hill Botswana 18°49S 21°43E 56 B3
Tsogttsetsiy = Baruunsuu
Mongolia 43°43N 105°35E 34 C3
Tsolo S. Africa 31°18S 28°37E 57 E4
Tsomo S. Africa 32°0S 27°42E 57 E4
Tsu Japan 34°45N 136°25E 31 G8
Tsu L. Canada 60°40N 111°52W 70 A6
Tsuchiura Japan 36°5N 140°15E 31 F10
Tsuen Wan China 22°22N 114°6E 33 G11
Tsugaru-Kaikyō Japan 41°35N 141°0E 30 D10
Tsumeb Namibia 19°9S 17°44E 56 B2
Tsumis Namibia 23°39S 17°29E 56 C2
Tsuruga Japan 35°45N 136°2E 31 G8
Tsurugi-San Japan 33°51N 134°6E 31 H7
Tsuruoka Japan 38°44N 139°50E 30 E9
Tsushima Gifu, Japan 35°10N 136°43E 31 G8
Tsushima Nagasaki,
Japan 34°20N 129°20E 31 G4
Tsuyama Japan 35°3N 134°0E 31 G7
Tsyelyakhany Belarus 52°30N 25°46E 17 B13
Tual Indonesia 5°38S 132°44E 37 F8
Tualatin U.S.A. 45°23N 122°45W 78 E4
Tuam Ireland 53°31N 8°51W 10 C3
Tuamotu, Îs.
French Polynesia 17°0S 144°0W 65 J13
Tuamotu Arch. = Tuamotu, Îs.
French Polynesia 17°0S 144°0W 65 J13
Tuamotu Ridge Pac. Oc. 20°0S 138°0W 65 K14
Tuan Giao Vietnam 21°35N 103°25E 38 B4
Tuao Phil. 17°55N 121°22E 37 A6
Tuapse Russia 44°5N 39°10E 19 F6
Tuas Singapore 1°19N 103°39E 39 d

Tuatapere N.Z. 46°8S 167°41E 59 G1
Tuba City U.S.A. 36°8N 111°14W 77 H8
Tuban Indonesia 6°54S 112°3E 37 G15
Tubani Botswana 24°46S 24°18E 56 C3
Tubarão Brazil 28°30S 49°0W 95 B6
Tūbās West Bank 32°20N 35°22E 46 C4
Tubas → Namibia 22°54S 14°35E 56 C2
Tübingen Germany 48°31N 9°4E 16 D5
Tubou Fiji 18°13S 178°48W 59 a
Tubruq Libya 32°7N 23°55E 51 B10
Tubuaï, Îs. French Polynesia 25°0S 150°0W 65 K13
Tuc Trung Vietnam 11°1N 107°12E 39 G6
Tucacas Venezuela 10°48N 68°19W 92 A5
Tuchitua Canada 60°55N 129°13W 70 A3
Tuchodi → Canada 58°17N 123°42W 70 B4
Tuckanarra Australia 27°7S 118°5E 61 E2
Tucson U.S.A. 32°13N 110°58W 77 K8
Tucumán □ Argentina 26°48S 66°2W 94 B2
Tucumcari U.S.A. 35°10N 103°44W 77 J12
Tucupita Venezuela 9°2N 62°3W 92 B6
Tucuruí Brazil 3°42S 49°44W 93 D9
Tucuruí, Represa de Brazil 4°0S 49°30W 93 D9
Tudela Spain 42°4N 1°39W 21 A5
Tudmur Syria 34°36N 38°15E 44 C3
Tudor, L. Canada 55°50N 65°25W 73 A6
Tuen Mun China 22°24N 113°59E 33 G10
Tugela → S. Africa 29°14S 31°30E 57 D5
Tuguegarao Phil. 17°35N 121°42E 37 A6
Tugur Russia 53°44N 136°45E 29 D14
Tui Spain 42°3N 8°39W 21 A1
Tuineje Canary Is. 28°19N 14°3W 24 F5
Tukangbesi, Kepulauan Indonesia 6°0S 124°0E 37 F6
Tukarak I. Canada 56°15N 78°45W 72 A4
Tukayyid Iraq 29°47N 45°36E 44 D5
Tuktoyaktuk Canada 69°27N 133°2W 68 C6
Tukums Latvia 56°58N 23°10E 9 H20
Tukuyu Tanzania 9°17S 33°35E 55 D3
Tula Hidalgo, Mexico 20°3N 99°21W 87 C5
Tula Tamaulipas, Mexico 23°0N 99°43W 87 C5
Tula Russia 54°13N 37°38E 18 D6
Tulancingo Mexico 20°5N 98°22W 87 C5
Tulare U.S.A. 36°13N 119°21W 78 J7
Tulare Lake Bed U.S.A. 36°0N 119°48W 78 K7
Tularosa U.S.A. 33°5N 106°1W 77 K10
Tulbagh S. Africa 33°16S 19°6E 56 E2
Tulcán Ecuador 0°48N 77°43W 92 C3
Tulcea Romania 45°13N 28°46E 17 F15
Tulchyn Ukraine 48°41N 28°49E 17 D15
Tūleh Iran 34°35N 52°33E 45 C7
Tulemalu L. Canada 62°58N 99°25W 71 A9
Tuli Zimbabwe 21°58S 29°13E 55 G2
Tulia U.S.A. 34°32N 101°46W 84 D4
Tulita Canada 64°57N 125°30W 68 C7
Ţūlkarm West Bank 32°19N 35°2E 46 C4
Tulla Ireland 52°53N 8°46W 10 D3
Tullahoma U.S.A. 35°22N 86°13W 85 D11
Tullamore Australia 32°39S 147°36E 63 E4
Tullamore Ireland 53°16N 7°31W 10 C4
Tulle France 45°16N 1°46E 20 D4
Tullow Ireland 52°49N 6°45W 10 D5
Tully Australia 17°56S 145°55E 62 B4
Tully U.S.A. 42°48N 76°7W 83 D8
Tulsa U.S.A. 36°10N 95°55W 84 C7
Tulsequah Canada 58°39N 133°35W 70 B2
Tuluá Colombia 4°6N 76°11W 92 C3
Tulun Russia 54°32N 100°35E 29 D11
Tulungagung Indonesia 8°5S 111°54E 37 H14
Tuma → Nic. 13°6N 84°35W 88 D3
Tumacacori ⌓ U.S.A. 31°35N 111°6W 77 L8
Tumaco Colombia 1°50N 78°45W 92 C3
Tumatumari Guyana 5°20N 58°55W 92 B7
Tumba Sweden 59°12N 17°48E 9 G17
Tumba, L. Dem. Rep. of the Congo 0°50S 18°0E 52 E3
Tumbarumba Australia 35°44S 148°0E 63 F4
Tumbaya Argentina 23°50S 65°26W 94 A2
Tumbes Peru 3°37S 80°27W 92 D2
Tumbler Ridge Canada 55°8N 121°0W 70 B4
Tumbwe Dem. Rep. of the Congo 11°25S 27°15E 55 E2
Tumby Bay Australia 34°21S 136°8E 63 E2
Tumd Youqi China 40°30N 110°30E 34 D6
Tumen China 43°0N 129°50E 30 C4
Tumen Jiang → China 42°20N 130°35E 35 C16
Tumeremo Venezuela 7°18N 61°30W 92 B6
Tumkur India 13°18N 77°6E 40 N10
Tump Pakistan 26°7N 62°16E 40 F3
Tumpat Malaysia 6°11N 102°10E 39 J4
Tumu Ghana 10°56N 1°56W 50 F5
Tumucumaque, Serra Brazil 2°0N 55°0W 93 C8
Tumut Australia 35°16S 148°13E 63 F4
Tumwater U.S.A. 47°1N 122°54W 78 C4
Tuna India 22°59N 70°5E 42 H4
Tunapuna Trin. & Tob. 10°38N 61°24W 93 K15
Tunas de Zaza Cuba 21°39N 79°34W 88 B4
Tunbridge Wells = Royal Tunbridge Wells U.K. 51°7N 0°16E 13 F8
Tuncurry Australia 32°17S 152°29E 63 E5
Tundla India 27°12N 78°17E 42 F8
Tunduru Tanzania 11°8S 37°25E 55 E4
Tundzha → Bulgaria 41°40N 26°35E 23 C11
Tung Chung China 22°17N 113°57E 33 G10
Tung Lung Chau China 22°15N 114°17E 33 G11
Tungabhadra → India 15°57N 78°15E 40 M11
Tungla Nic. 13°24N 84°21W 88 D3
Tungsten Canada 61°57N 128°16W 70 A3
Tunguska, Nizhnyaya → Russia 65°48N 88°4E 29 C9
Tunguska, Podkamennaya → Russia 61°50N 90°13E 29 C10
Tunica U.S.A. 34°41N 90°23W 85 D9
Tunis Tunisia 36°50N 10°11E 50 A7
Tunisia ■ Africa 33°30N 9°10E 51 A7
Tunja Colombia 5°33N 73°25W 92 B4
Tunkhannock U.S.A. 41°32N 75°57W 83 E9
Tunliu China 36°13N 112°52E 34 F7
Tunnel Creek △ Australia 17°41S 125°18E 60 C4
Tunnsjøen Norway 64°45N 13°25E 8 D15
Tunungayualok I. Canada 56°0N 61°0W 73 A7
Tunuyán Argentina 33°35S 69°0W 94 C2
Tunuyán → Argentina 33°33S 67°30W 94 C2
Tuolumne U.S.A. 37°58N 120°15W 78 H6
Tuolumne → U.S.A. 37°36N 121°13W 78 H5
Tūp Āghāj Iran 36°3N 47°50E 44 B5
Tupã Brazil 21°57S 50°28W 95 A5
Tupelo U.S.A. 34°16N 88°43W 85 D10
Tupinambarana, Ilha Brazil 3°0S 58°0W 92 D7
Tupiza Bolivia 21°30S 65°40W 94 A2
Tupman U.S.A. 35°18N 119°21W 79 K7
Tupper Canada 55°32N 120°1W 70 B4
Tupper L. U.S.A. 44°10N 74°32W 83 B10
Tupper Lake U.S.A. 44°14N 74°28W 83 B10
Tupungato, Cerro S. Amer. 33°15S 69°50W 94 C2
Tuquan China 45°18N 121°38E 35 B11
Túquerres Colombia 1°5N 77°37W 92 C3
Tura Russia 64°20N 100°17E 29 C11
Turabah Si. Arabia 28°20N 43°15E 44 D4
Tūrān Iran 35°39N 56°42E 45 C8
Turan Russia 51°55N 94°0E 29 D10
Ţurayf Si. Arabia 31°41N 38°39E 44 D3
Turda Romania 46°34N 23°47E 17 E12
Turek Poland 52°3N 18°30E 17 B10
Turén Venezuela 9°17N 69°6W 92 B5
Turfan = Turpan China 43°58N 89°10E 32 B3
Turfan Basin = Turpan Pendi China 42°40N 89°25E 32 B3
Turfan Depression = Turpan Pendi China 42°40N 89°25E 32 B3
Turgeon → Canada 50°0N 78°56W 72 C4
Tŭrgovishte Bulgaria 43°17N 26°38E 23 C12
Turgutlu Turkey 38°30N 27°43E 23 E12
Turgwe → Zimbabwe 21°31S 32°15E 57 C5
Turia → Spain 39°27N 0°19W 21 C5
Turiaçu Brazil 1°40S 45°19W 93 D9
Turiaçu → Brazil 1°36S 45°19W 93 D9
Turin = Torino Italy 45°3N 7°40E 20 D7
Turkana, L. Africa 3°30N 36°5E 54 B4
Turkestan = Türkistan Kazakhstan 43°17N 68°16E 28 E7
Turkey ■ Eurasia 39°0N 36°0E 19 G6
Turkey Creek = Warmun Australia 17°2S 128°12E 60 C4
Türkistan Kazakhstan 43°17N 68°16E 28 E7
Türkmenabat Turkmenistan 39°6N 63°34E 45 B9
Türkmenbashi Turkmenistan 40°5N 53°5E 45 A7
Turkmenistan ■ Asia 39°0N 59°0E 28 F6
Turks Island Passage W. Indies 21°30N 71°30W 89 B5
Turku Finland 60°30N 22°19E 9 F20
Turkwel → Kenya 3°6N 36°6E 54 B4
Turlock U.S.A. 37°30N 120°51W 78 H6
Turnagain → Canada 59°12N 127°35W 70 B3
Turnagain, C. N.Z. 40°28S 176°38E 59 D6
Turneffe Is. Belize 17°20N 87°50W 87 D7
Turner U.S.A. 48°51N 108°24W 76 B9
Turner Pt. Australia 11°47S 133°32E 62 A1
Turner Valley Canada 50°40N 114°17W 70 C6
Turners Falls U.S.A. 42°36N 72°33W 83 D12
Turnhout Belgium 51°19N 4°57E 15 C4
Turnor L. Canada 56°35N 108°35W 71 B7
Tŭrnovo = Veliko Tŭrnovo Bulgaria 43°5N 25°41E 23 C11
Turnu Măgurele Romania 43°46N 24°56E 17 G13
Turnu Roşu, P. Romania 45°33N 24°17E 17 F13
Turpan China 43°58N 89°10E 32 B3
Turpan Pendi China 42°40N 89°25E 32 B3
Turriff U.K. 57°32N 2°27W 11 D6
Tursāq Iraq 33°27N 45°47E 44 C5
Turtle Head I. Australia 10°56S 142°37E 62 A3
Turtle L. Canada 53°36N 108°38W 71 C7
Turtle Lake U.S.A. 47°31N 100°53W 80 B3
Turtleford Canada 53°23N 108°57W 71 C7
Turuépano △ Venezuela 10°34N 62°43W 89 D7
Turukhansk Russia 65°21N 88°5E 29 C9
Tuscaloosa U.S.A. 33°12N 87°34W 85 E11
Tuscany = Toscana □ Italy 43°25N 11°0E 22 C4
Tuscarawas → U.S.A. 40°24N 81°25W 82 F3
Tuscarora Mt. U.S.A. 40°55N 77°55W 82 F7
Tuscola Ill., U.S.A. 39°48N 88°17W 80 F9
Tuscola Tex., U.S.A. 32°12N 99°48W 84 E5
Tuscumbia U.S.A. 34°44N 87°42W 85 D11
Tuskegee U.S.A. 32°25N 85°42W 85 E12
Tuticorin India 8°50N 78°12E 40 Q11
Tutóia Brazil 2°45S 42°20W 93 D10
Tutong Brunei 4°47N 114°40E 36 D4
Tutrakan Bulgaria 44°2N 26°40E 23 B12
Tuttle Creek L. U.S.A. 39°15N 96°36W 80 F5
Tuttlingen Germany 47°58N 8°48E 16 E5
Tutuala E. Timor 8°25S 127°15E 37 F7
Tutuila Amer. Samoa 14°19S 170°50W 59 b
Tutume Botswana 20°30S 27°5E 53 J5
Tuul Gol → Mongolia 48°30N 104°25E 32 B5
Tuva □ Russia 51°30N 95°0E 29 D10
Tuvalu ■ Pac. Oc. 8°0S 178°0E 58 B10
Tuvuca Fiji 17°40S 178°48W 59 a
Tuxpan Mexico 20°57N 97°24W 87 C5
Tuxtla Gutiérrez Mexico 16°45N 93°7W 87 D6
Tuy = Tui Spain 42°3N 8°39W 21 A1
Tuy An Vietnam 13°17N 109°16E 38 F7
Tuy Duc Vietnam 12°15N 107°27E 39 F6
Tuy Hoa Vietnam 13°5N 109°10E 38 F7
Tuy Phong Vietnam 11°14N 108°43E 39 G7
Tuya L. Canada 59°7N 130°35W 70 B2
Tuyen Hoa Vietnam 17°50N 106°10E 38 D6
Tuyen Quang Vietnam 21°50N 105°10E 38 B5
Tūysarkān Iran 34°33N 48°27E 45 C6
Tuz Gölü Turkey 38°42N 33°18E 19 G5
Ţūz Khurmātū Iraq 34°56N 44°38E 44 C5
Tuzigoot △ U.S.A. 34°46N 112°2W 77 J7
Tuzla Bos.-H. 44°34N 18°41E 23 B8
Tver Russia 56°55N 35°55E 18 C6
Twain U.S.A. 40°1N 121°3W 78 E5
Twain Harte U.S.A. 38°2N 120°14W 78 G6
Tweed Canada 44°29N 77°19W 82 B7
Tweed → U.K. 55°45N 2°0W 11 F6
Tweed Heads Australia 28°10S 153°31E 63 D5
Tweedsmuir ⌓ Canada 53°0N 126°20W 70 C3
Twentynine Palms U.S.A. 34°8N 116°3W 79 L10
Twillingate Canada 49°42N 54°45W 73 C9
Twin Bridges U.S.A. 45°33N 112°20W 76 D7
Twin Falls Canada 53°30N 64°32W 73 B7
Twin Falls U.S.A. 42°34N 114°28W 76 E6
Twin Valley U.S.A. 47°16N 96°16W 80 B5
Twinsburg U.S.A. 41°19N 81°26W 82 E3
Twitchell Res. U.S.A. 34°59N 120°19W 79 L6
Two Harbors U.S.A. 47°2N 91°40W 80 B8
Two Hills Canada 53°43N 111°52W 70 C6
Two Rivers U.S.A. 44°9N 87°34W 80 C10
Two Rocks Australia 31°30S 115°35E 61 F2
Twofold B. Australia 37°8S 149°59E 63 F4
Tyachiv Ukraine 48°1N 23°35E 17 D12
Tychy Poland 50°9N 18°59E 17 C10
Tyler Minn., U.S.A. 44°17N 96°8W 80 C5
Tyler Tex., U.S.A. 32°21N 95°18W 84 E7
Tynda Russia 55°10N 124°43E 29 D13
Tyndall U.S.A. 43°0N 97°50W 80 D5
Tyne → U.K. 54°59N 1°32W 12 C6
Tyne & Wear □ U.K. 55°6N 1°17W 12 B6
Tynemouth U.K. 55°1N 1°26W 12 B6
Tyre = Sūr Lebanon 33°19N 35°16E 46 B4
Tyrifjorden Norway 60°2N 10°8E 9 F14
Tyrol = Tirol □ Austria 47°3N 10°43E 16 E6
Tyrone U.S.A. 40°40N 78°14W 82 F6
Tyrone □ U.K. 54°38N 7°11W 10 B4
Tyrrell → Australia 35°26S 142°51E 63 F3
Tyrrell, L. Australia 35°20S 142°50E 63 F3
Tyrrell L. Canada 63°7N 105°27W 71 A7
Tyrrhenian Sea Medit. S. 40°0N 12°30E 22 E5
Tysfjorden Norway 68°7N 16°25E 8 B17
Tyulgan Russia 52°22N 56°12E 18 D10
Tyumen Russia 57°11N 65°29E 28 D7
Tywi → U.K. 51°48N 4°21W 13 F3
Tywyn U.K. 52°35N 4°5W 13 E3
Tzaneen S. Africa 23°47S 30°9E 57 C5
Tzermiado Greece 35°12N 25°29E 25 D7
Tzukong = Zigong China 29°15N 104°48E 32 D5

U

U.S.A. = United States of America ■ N. Amer. 37°0N 96°0W 74 C7
U.S. Virgin Is. ▨ W. Indies 18°20N 65°0W 89 e
Uanle Uen = Wanleweyne Somali Rep. 2°37N 44°54E 47 G3
Uatumã → Brazil 2°26S 57°37W 92 D7
Uaupés Brazil 0°8S 67°5W 92 D5
Uaupés → Brazil 0°2N 67°16W 92 C5
Uaxactún Guatemala 17°25N 89°29W 88 C2
Ubá Brazil 21°8S 43°0W 95 A7
Ubaitaba Brazil 14°18S 39°20W 93 F11
Ubangi = Oubangi → Dem. Rep. of the Congo 0°30S 17°50E 52 E3
Ubauro Pakistan 28°15N 69°45E 42 E3
Ubayyiḍ, W. al → Iraq 32°34N 43°48E 44 C4
Ube Japan 33°56N 131°15E 31 H5
Úbeda Spain 38°3N 3°23W 21 C4
Uberaba Brazil 19°50S 47°55W 93 G9
Uberlândia Brazil 19°0S 48°20W 93 G9
Ubin, Pulau Singapore 1°24N 103°57E 39 d
Ubly U.S.A. 43°42N 82°55W 82 C2
Ubolratna Res. Thailand 16°45N 102°30E 38 D4
Ubombo S. Africa 27°31S 32°4E 57 D5
Ubon Ratchathani Thailand 15°15N 104°50E 38 E5
Ubondo Dem. Rep. of the Congo 0°55S 25°42E 54 C2
Ubort → Belarus 52°6N 28°30E 17 B15
Ubud Indonesia 8°30S 115°16E 37 J18
Ubundu Dem. Rep. of the Congo 0°22S 25°30E 54 C2
Ucayali → Peru 4°30S 73°30W 92 D4
Uchab Namibia 19°47S 17°42E 56 B2
Uchiura-Wan Japan 42°25N 140°40E 30 C10
Uchquduq Uzbekistan 41°50N 62°50E 28 E7
Uchur → Russia 58°48N 130°35E 29 D14
Ucluelet Canada 48°57N 125°32W 70 D3
Uda → Russia 54°42N 135°14E 29 D14
Udachnyy Russia 66°25N 112°24E 29 C12
Udagamandalam India 11°30N 76°44E 40 P10
Udainagar India 22°33N 76°13E 42 H7
Udaipur India 24°36N 73°44E 42 G5
Udaipur Garhi Nepal 27°0N 86°35E 43 F12
Udala India 21°35N 86°34E 43 J12
Uddevalla Sweden 58°21N 11°55E 9 G14
Uddjaure Sweden 65°56N 17°49E 8 D17
Uden Neths. 51°40N 5°37E 15 C5
Udgir India 18°25N 77°5E 40 K10
Udhampur India 33°0N 75°5E 43 C6
Údine Italy 46°3N 13°14E 22 A5
Udintsev Fracture Zone S. Ocean 57°0S 145°0W 5 B13
Udmurtia □ Russia 57°30N 52°30E 18 C9
Udon Thani Thailand 17°29N 102°46E 38 D4
Udong Cambodia 11°48N 104°45E 39 G5
Udskaya Guba Russia 54°50N 135°45E 29 D14
Udu Pt. Fiji 16°9S 179°57W 59 a
Udupi India 13°25N 74°42E 40 N9
Udzungwa △ Tanzania 7°52S 36°35E 54 D4
Udzungwa Range Tanzania 9°30S 35°10E 55 D4
Ueda Japan 36°24N 138°16E 31 F9
Uedineniya, Os. Russia 78°0N 85°0E 4 B12
Uele → Dem. Rep. of the Congo 3°45N 24°45E 52 D4
Uelen Russia 66°10N 170°0W 29 C19
Uelzen Germany 52°57N 10°32E 16 B6
Ufa Russia 54°45N 55°55E 18 D10
Ufa → Russia 54°40N 56°0E 18 D10
Ugab → Namibia 20°55S 13°30E 56 C1
Ugalla → Tanzania 5°8S 30°42E 54 D3
Ugalla River ⌓ Tanzania 5°50S 31°54E 54 D3
Uganda ■ Africa 2°0N 32°0E 54 B3
Ugie S. Africa 31°10S 28°13E 57 E4
Uglegorsk Russia 49°5N 142°2E 29 E15
Ugljan Croatia 44°12N 15°10E 16 F8
Ugolnye Kopi Russia 64°44N 177°42E 29 C18
Uhlenhorst Namibia 23°45S 17°55E 56 C2
Uhrichsville U.S.A. 40°24N 81°21W 82 F3
Uibhist a Deas = South Uist U.K. 57°20N 7°15W 11 D1
Uibhist a Tuath = North Uist U.K. 57°40N 7°15W 11 D1
Uig U.K. 57°35N 6°21W 11 D2
Uíge Angola 7°30S 14°40E 52 F2
Uiha Tonga 19°54S 174°25W 59 c
Uijeongbu S. Korea 37°44N 127°2E 35 F14
Ŭiju N. Korea 40°15N 124°35E 35 D13
Uinta Mts. U.S.A. 40°45N 110°30W 76 F8
Uis Namibia 21°8S 14°49E 56 C1
Uiseong S. Korea 36°21N 128°45E 35 F15
Uitenhage S. Africa 33°40S 25°28E 56 E4
Uithuizen Neths. 53°24N 6°41E 15 A6
Ujh → India 32°10N 75°18E 42 C6
Ujhani India 28°0N 79°6E 43 F8
Uji-guntō Japan 31°15N 129°25E 31 J4
Ujjain India 23°9N 75°43E 42 H6
Ujung Pandang Indonesia 5°10S 119°20E 37 F5
Uka Russia 57°50N 162°0E 29 D17
Ukara I. Tanzania 1°50S 33°0E 54 C3
Uke-Shima Japan 28°2N 129°14E 31 K4
Ukerewe I. Tanzania 2°0S 33°0E 54 C3
Ukhrul India 25°10N 94°25E 41 G19
Ukhta Russia 63°34N 53°41E 18 B9
Ukiah U.S.A. 39°9N 123°13W 78 F3
Ukmergė Lithuania 55°15N 24°45E 9 J21
Ukraine ■ Europe 49°0N 32°0E 19 E5
Ukwi Botswana 23°29S 20°30E 56 C3
Ulaan-Uul Mongolia 44°13N 111°10E 34 B6
Ulaanbaatar Mongolia 47°55N 106°53E 32 B5
Ulaangom Mongolia 50°5N 92°10E 32 A4
Ulaanjirem Mongolia 45°5N 105°30E 34 B3
Ulamba Dem. Rep. of the Congo 9°3S 23°38E 55 D1
Ulan Bator = Ulaanbaatar Mongolia 47°55N 106°53E 32 B5
Ulan Ude Russia 51°45N 107°40E 29 D11
Ulaya Morogoro, Tanzania 7°3S 36°55E 54 D4
Ulaya Tabora, Tanzania 4°25S 33°30E 54 C3
Ulcinj Montenegro 41°58N 19°10E 23 D8
Ulco S. Africa 28°21S 24°15E 56 D3
Ule älv = Oulujoki → Finland 65°1N 25°30E 8 D21
Ule träsk = Oulujärvi Finland 64°25N 27°15E 8 D22
Uleåborg = Oulu Finland 65°1N 25°29E 8 D21
Ulefoss Norway 59°17N 9°16E 9 G13
Ulhasnagar India 19°15N 73°10E 40 K8
Uliastay Mongolia 47°56N 97°28E 32 B4
Uljin S. Korea 36°59N 129°24E 35 F15
Ulladulla Australia 35°21S 150°29E 63 F5
Ullapool U.K. 57°54N 5°9W 11 D3
Ulleungdo S. Korea 37°30N 130°30E 31 F5
Ullswater Canada 45°12N 79°29W 82 A5
Ullswater U.K. 54°34N 2°52W 12 C5
Ulm Germany 48°23N 9°58E 16 D5
Ulmarra Australia 29°37S 153°4E 63 D5
Ulonguè Mozam. 14°37S 34°19E 55 E3
Ulricehamn Sweden 57°46N 13°26E 9 H15
Ulsan S. Korea 35°20N 129°15E 35 G15
Ulsta U.K. 60°30N 1°9W 11 A7
Ulster □ U.K. 54°35N 6°30W 10 B5
Ulubat Gölü Turkey 40°9N 28°35E 23 D13
Uludağ Turkey 40°4N 29°13E 23 D13
Uluguru Mts. Tanzania 7°15S 37°40E 54 D4
Ulungur He → China 47°1N 87°24E 32 B3
Ulungur Hu China 47°20N 87°10E 32 B3
Uluru Australia 25°23S 131°5E 61 E5
Uluru-Kata Tjuta △ Australia 25°19S 131°1E 61 E5
Ulutau Kazakhstan 48°39N 67°1E 28 E7
Uluwatu Indonesia 8°50S 115°5E 37 K18
Ulva U.K. 56°29N 6°13W 11 E2
Ulverston U.K. 54°13N 3°5W 12 C4
Ulverstone Australia 41°11S 146°11E 63 G4
Ulya Russia 59°10N 142°0E 29 D15
Ulyanovsk Russia 54°20N 48°25E 18 D8
Ulyasutay = Uliastay Mongolia 47°56N 97°28E 32 B4
Ulysses Kans., U.S.A. 37°35N 101°22W 80 G3
Ulysses Pa., U.S.A. 41°54N 77°46W 82 E7
Ulysses, Mt. Canada 57°20N 124°5W 70 B4
Umala Bolivia 17°25S 68°5W 92 G5
'Umān = Oman ■ Asia 23°0N 58°0E 47 C6
Uman Ukraine 48°40N 30°12E 17 D16
Umaria India 23°35N 80°50E 43 H9
Umarkot Pakistan 25°15N 69°40E 42 G3
Umarpada India 21°27N 73°30E 42 J5
Umatilla U.S.A. 45°55N 119°21W 76 D4
Umba Russia 66°42N 34°11E 18 A5
Umbagog L. U.S.A. 44°46N 71°3W 83 B13
Umbakumba Australia 13°47S 136°50E 62 A2
Umbrella Mts. N.Z. 45°35S 169°5E 59 F2
Umeå Sweden 63°45N 20°20E 8 E
Umeälven → Sweden 63°45N 20°20E 8 E
Umera Indonesia 0°12S 129°37E 37
Umfuli → Zimbabwe 17°30S 29°23E 55
Umfurudzi ⌓ Zimbabwe 17°6S 31°40E 55
Umgusa Zimbabwe 19°29S 27°52E 55
Umgwenya → Mozam. 25°14S 32°18E 57
Umiujaq Canada 56°33N 76°33W 72
Umkomaas S. Africa 30°13S 30°48E 57
Umlazi S. Africa 29°59S 30°54E 53
Umm ad Daraj, J. Jordan 32°18N 35°48E 46
Umm al Qaywayn U.A.E. 25°30N 55°35E 45
Umm al Qittayn Jordan 32°18N 36°40E 46
Umm Bāb Qatar 25°12N 50°48E 45
Umm Durman = Omdurmân Sudan 15°40N 32°28E 51 E
Umm el Fahm Israel 32°31N 35°9E 46
Umm Keddada Sudan 13°33N 26°35E 51 F
Umm Lajj Si. Arabia 25°0N 37°23E 44
Umm Qasr Iraq 30°1N 47°58E 44
Umm Ruwaba Sudan 12°50N 31°20E 51 F
Umnak I. U.S.A. 53°15N 168°20W 74
Umniati → Zimbabwe 16°49S 28°45E 55
Umpqua → U.S.A. 43°40N 124°12W 76
Umreth India 22°41N 73°4E 42
Umtata = Mthatha S. Africa 31°36S 28°49E 57
Umuarama Brazil 23°45S 53°20W 95
Umvukwe Ra. Zimbabwe 16°45S 30°45E 55
Umzimvubu S. Africa 31°38S 29°33E 57
Umzingwane → Zimbabwe 22°12S 29°56E 55
Umzinto = eMuziwezinto S. Africa 30°15S 30°45E 57
Una India 20°46N 71°8E 42
Una → Bos.-H. 45°0N 16°20E 16
Unadilla U.S.A. 42°20N 75°19W 83
Unalakleet U.S.A. 63°52N 160°47W 74
Unalaska U.S.A. 53°53N 166°32W 74
Unalaska I. U.S.A. 53°35N 166°50W 74
'Unayzah Si. Arabia 26°6N 43°58E 44
'Unayzah, J. Asia 32°12N 39°18E 44
Uncía Bolivia 18°25S 66°40W 92
Uncompahgre Peak U.S.A. 38°4N 107°28W 76 G
Uncompahgre Plateau U.S.A. 38°20N 108°15W 76
Undara Volcanic △ Australia 18°14S 144°41E 62
Underbool Australia 35°10S 141°51E 63
Underwood Canada 44°18N 81°29W 82
Ungarie Australia 33°38S 146°56E 63
Ungarra Australia 34°12S 136°2E 63
Ungava, Pén. d' Canada 60°0N 74°0W 69 D
Ungava B. Canada 59°30N 67°30W 69 D
Ungeny = Ungheni Moldova 47°11N 27°51E 17 E
Unggi N. Korea 42°16N 130°28E 35 C
Ungheni Moldova 47°11N 27°51E 17 E
Ungwana B. Kenya 2°45S 40°20E 54
União da Vitória Brazil 26°13S 51°5W 95
Unimak I. U.S.A. 54°45N 164°0W 74
Union Miss., U.S.A. 32°34N 89°7W 85 E
Union Mo., U.S.A. 38°27N 91°0W 80
Union S.C., U.S.A. 34°43N 81°37W 85 D
Union City Calif., U.S.A. 37°36N 122°1W 78
Union City N.J., U.S.A. 40°45N 74°2W 83 F
Union City Pa., U.S.A. 41°54N 79°51W 82
Union City Tenn., U.S.A. 36°26N 89°3W 85 C
Union Dale U.S.A. 41°43N 75°29W 83
Union Gap U.S.A. 46°33N 120°28W 76
Union Springs Ala., U.S.A. 32°9N 85°43W 85 E
Union Springs N.Y., U.S.A. 42°50N 76°41W 83
Uniondale S. Africa 33°39S 23°7E 56
Uniontown U.S.A. 39°54N 79°44W 81 F
Unionville U.S.A. 40°29N 93°1W 80
United Arab Emirates ■ Asia 23°50N 54°0E 45
United Kingdom ■ Europe 53°0N 2°0W 14
United States of America ■ N. Amer. 37°0N 96°0W 74
Unity Canada 52°30N 109°5W 71
University Park U.S.A. 32°17N 106°45W 77 K
University Place U.S.A. 47°14N 122°33W 78
Unjha India 23°46N 72°24E 42
Unnao India 26°35N 80°30E 43
Unsengedsi → Zimbabwe 15°43S 31°14E 55
Unst U.K. 60°44N 0°53W 11
Unuk → Canada 56°5N 131°3W 70
Unzen-Amakusa △ Japan 32°15N 130°10E 31
Uozu Japan 36°48N 137°24E 31
Upata Venezuela 8°1N 62°24W 92
Upemba, L. Dem. Rep. of the Congo 8°30S 26°20E 55
Upemba △ Dem. Rep. of the Congo 9°0S 26°35E 55
Upernavik Greenland 72°49N 56°20W 4
Upington S. Africa 28°25S 21°15E 56
Upleta India 21°46N 70°16E 42
'Upolu Samoa 13°58S 172°0W 59
Upper Alkali L. U.S.A. 41°47N 120°8W 76
Upper Arrow L. Canada 50°30N 117°50W 70
Upper Darby U.S.A. 39°55N 75°16W 81 F
Upper Foster L. Canada 56°47N 105°20W 71
Upper Hutt N.Z. 41°8S 175°5E 59
Upper Klamath L. U.S.A. 42°25N 121°55W 76
Upper Lake U.S.A. 39°10N 122°54W 78
Upper Liard Canada 60°3N 128°54W 70
Upper Manzanilla Trin. & Tob. 10°31N 61°4W 93 K
Upper Missouri Breaks ⌓ U.S.A. 47°50N 109°55W 76

pper Musquodoboit Canada 45°10N 62°58W 73 C7
pper Red L. U.S.A. 48°8N 94°45W 80 A6
pper Sandusky U.S.A. 40°50N 83°17W 81 E12
pper Volta = Burkina Faso ■ Africa 12°0N 1°0W 50 F5
ppland Sweden 59°59N 17°48E 9 G17
ppsala Sweden 59°53N 17°38E 9 G17
pshi India 33°48N 77°52E 43 C7
pstart, C. Australia 19°41S 147°45E 62 B4
pton U.S.A. 44°6N 104°38W 76 D11
qsuqtuuq = Gjoa Haven Canada 68°38N 95°53W 68 C10
· Iraq 30°55N 46°25E 44 D5
ad Qianqi China 40°40N 108°30E 34 D5
akawa Japan 42°9N 142°47E 30 C11
al = Uralskiy □ Russia 64°0N 70°0E 28 C7
al = Zhayyq → Kazakhstan 47°0N 51°48E 19 E9
al Australia 33°21S 146°12E 63 E4
al Mts. = Uralskie Gory Eurasia 60°0N 59°0E 18 C10
alla Australia 30°37S 151°29E 63 E5
alsk = Oral Kazakhstan 51°20N 51°20E 19 D9
alskie Gory Eurasia 60°0N 59°0E 18 C10
alskiy □ Russia 64°0N 70°0E 28 C7
ambo Tanzania 5°4S 32°0E 54 D3
andangi Australia 21°32S 138°14E 62 C2
anium City Canada 59°34N 108°37W 71 B7
apuntja = Utopia Australia 22°14S 134°33E 62 C1
aricoera → Brazil 3°2N 60°30W 92 C6
asoe Japan 26°15N 127°43E 31 L3
awa = Saitama Japan 35°54N 139°38E 31 G9
ay Russia 60°5N 65°15E 28 C7
ray'irah Si. Arabia 25°57N 48°53E 45 E6
bana Ill., U.S.A. 40°7N 88°12W 80 E9
bana Ohio, U.S.A. 40°7N 83°45W 81 E12
bandale U.S.A. 41°38N 93°43W 80 E7
bino Italy 43°43N 12°38E 22 C5
bión, Picos de Spain 42°1N 2°52W 21 A4
cos Peru 13°40S 71°38W 92 F4
dinarrain Argentina 32°37S 58°52W 94 C4
e → U.K. 54°5N 1°20W 12 C6
engoy Russia 65°58N 78°22E 28 C8
es Mexico 29°26N 110°24W 86 B2
ewera △ N.Z. 38°29S 177°7E 59 C6
fa = Sanliurfa Turkey 37°12N 38°50E 44 B3
ganch Uzbekistan 41°40N 60°41E 28 E7
gench = Urganch Uzbekistan 41°40N 60°41E 28 E7
güp Turkey 38°38N 34°56E 44 B2
i India 34°8N 74°2E 43 B6
ibia Colombia 11°43N 72°16W 92 A4
iondo Bolivia 21°41S 64°41W 94 A3
ique Mexico 27°13N 107°55W 86 B3
ique → Mexico 26°29N 107°58W 86 B3
k Neths. 52°39N 5°36E 15 B5
la Turkey 38°20N 26°47E 23 E12
mia = Orūmīyeh Iran 37°40N 45°0E 44 B5
oševac Serbia 42°23N 21°10E 23 C9
oyan, Montanas de Puerto Rico 18°12N 67°0W 89 d
uaçu Brazil 14°30S 49°10W 93 F9
uapan Mexico 19°24N 102°3W 86 D4
ubamba → Peru 10°43S 73°48W 92 F4
ucará Brazil 2°32S 57°45W 92 D7
uçuí Brazil 7°20S 44°28W 93 E10
uguai → Brazil 26°0S 53°30W 95 B5
uguaiana Brazil 29°50S 57°0W 94 B4
uguay ■ S. Amer. 32°30S 56°30W 94 C4
uguay → S. Amer. 34°12S 58°18W 94 C4
umchi = Ürümqi China 43°45N 87°45E 32 B3
ümqi China 43°45N 87°45E 32 B3
up, Ostrov Russia 46°0N 151°0E 29 E16
zhar Kazakhstan 47°5N 81°38E 28 E9
a → Russia 66°16N 59°49E 18 A10
ak Turkey 38°43N 29°28E 19 G4
akos Namibia 21°54S 15°31E 56 C2
edom Germany 53°55N 14°2E 16 B8
eless Loop Australia 26°8S 113°23E 61 E1
hakova, Ostrov Russia 82°0N 80°0E 29 A8
hant = Ouessant, Î. d' France 48°28N 5°6W 20 B1
hashi Tanzania 1°59S 33°57E 54 C3
shayrah Si. Arabia 25°35N 45°47E 44 E5
hibuka Japan 32°11N 130°1E 31 H5
htöbe Kazakhstan 45°16N 78°0E 28 E8
huaia Argentina 54°50S 68°23W 96 G3
humun Russia 52°47N 126°32E 29 D13
insk Russia 65°57N 57°27E 28 C6
k Canada 54°38N 128°26W 70 C3
k → U.K. 51°33N 2°58W 13 F5
ka India 27°12N 83°7E 43 F10
man Russia 52°5N 39°48E 18 D6
oke Tanzania 5°8S 32°24E 54 D3
olye-Sibirskoye Russia 52°48N 103°40E 29 D11
pallata, P. de Argentina 32°37S 69°22W 94 C2
suriysk Russia 43°48N 131°59E 30 C5
surka Russia 45°12N 133°31E 30 B6
t-Chaun Russia 68°47N 170°30E 29 C18
t-Ilimsk Russia 58°3N 102°39E 29 D11
t-Ishim Russia 57°45N 71°10E 28 D8
t-Kamchatsk Russia 56°10N 162°28E 29 D17
t-Kamenogorsk = Öskemen Kazakhstan 50°0N 82°36E 28 E9
t-Khayryuzovo Russia 57°15N 156°45E 29 D16
t-Kut Russia 56°50N 105°42E 29 D11
t-Kuyga Russia 70°1N 135°43E 29 B14
t-Maya Russia 60°30N 134°28E 29 C14
t-Mil Russia 59°40N 133°11E 29 D14
t-Nera Russia 64°35N 143°15E 29 C15
Ust-Nyukzha Russia 56°34N 121°37E 29 D13
Ust-Olenek Russia 73°0N 120°5E 29 B12
Ust-Omchug Russia 61°9N 149°38E 29 C15
Ust-Port Russia 69°40N 84°26E 28 C9
Ust-Tsilma Russia 65°28N 52°11E 18 A9
Ust-Urt = Ustyurt Plateau Asia 44°0N 55°0E 28 E6
Ust-Usa Russia 66°2N 56°57E 18 A10
Ust-Vorkuta Russia 67°24N 64°0E 18 A11
Ústí nad Labem Czech Rep. 50°41N 14°3E 16 C8
Ústica Italy 38°42N 13°11E 22 E5
Ustinov = Izhevsk Russia 56°51N 53°14E 18 C9
Ustyurt Plateau Asia 44°0N 55°0E 28 E6
Usu China 44°27N 84°40E 32 B3
Usuki Japan 33°8N 131°49E 31 H5
Usulután El Salv. 13°25N 88°28W 88 D2
Usumacinta → Mexico 18°24N 92°38W 87 D6
Usumbura = Bujumbura Burundi 3°16S 29°18E 54 C2
Usure Tanzania 4°40S 34°22E 54 C3
Usutuo → Mozam. 26°48S 32°7E 57 D5
Uta Indonesia 4°33S 136°0E 37 E9
Utah □ U.S.A. 39°20N 111°30W 76 G8
Utah L. U.S.A. 40°12N 111°48W 76 F8
Utara, Selat Malaysia 5°28N 100°20E 39 c
Utarni India 26°5N 71°58E 42 F4
Utatlan Guatemala 15°2N 91°11W 88 C1
Ute Creek → U.S.A. 35°21N 103°50W 77 J12
Utena Lithuania 55°27N 25°40E 9 J21
Utete Tanzania 8°0S 38°45E 54 D4
Uthai Thani Thailand 15°22N 100°3E 38 E3
Uthal Pakistan 25°44N 66°40E 42 G2
Utiariti Brazil 13°0S 58°10W 92 F7
Utica N.Y., U.S.A. 43°6N 75°14W 83 C9
Utica Ohio, U.S.A. 40°14N 82°27W 82 F2
Utikuma L. Canada 55°50N 115°30W 70 B5
Utila Honduras 16°6N 86°56W 88 C2
Utopia Australia 22°14S 134°33E 62 C1
Utraula India 27°19N 82°25E 43 F10
Utrecht Neths. 52°5N 5°8E 15 B5
Utrecht S. Africa 27°38S 30°20E 57 D5
Utrecht □ Neths. 52°6N 5°7E 15 B5
Utrera Spain 37°12N 5°48W 21 D3
Utsjoki → Finland 69°51N 26°59E 8 B22
Utsunomiya Japan 36°30N 139°50E 31 F9
Uttar Pradesh □ India 27°0N 80°0E 43 F9
Uttaradit Thailand 17°36N 100°5E 38 D3
Uttarakhand □ India 30°0N 79°30E 43 D8
Utterson Canada 45°12N 79°19W 82 A5
Uttoxeter U.K. 52°54N 1°52W 12 E6
Utuado Puerto Rico 18°16N 66°42W 89 d
Uummannaq Avannaarsua, Greenland 77°28N 69°13W 4 B4
Uummannaq Kitaa, Greenland 70°58N 52°17W 4 B5
Uummannarsuaq = Nunap Isua Greenland 59°48N 43°55W 66 D15
Uusikaarlepyy Finland 63°32N 22°31E 8 E20
Uusikaupunki Finland 60°47N 21°25E 8 F19
Uva Russia 56°59N 52°13E 18 C9
Uvalde U.S.A. 29°13N 99°47W 84 G5
Uvat Russia 59°5N 68°50E 28 D7
Uvinza Tanzania 5°5S 30°24E 54 D3
Uvira Dem. Rep. of the Congo 3°22S 29°3E 54 C2
Uvs Nuur Mongolia 50°20N 92°30E 32 A4
'Uwairidh, Ḥarrat al Si. Arabia 26°50N 38°0E 44 E3
Uwajima Japan 33°10N 132°35E 31 H6
Uwanda △ Tanzania 7°46S 32°0E 54 D3
Uweinat, Jebel Sudan 21°54N 24°58E 51 D10
Uxbridge Canada 44°6N 79°7W 82 B5
Uxin Qi China 38°50N 109°5E 34 E5
Uxmal Mexico 20°22N 89°46W 87 C7
Üydzin Mongolia 44°9N 107°0E 34 B4
Uyo Nigeria 5°1N 7°53E 50 G7
Uyûn Mûsa Egypt 29°53N 32°40E 46 F1
Uyuni Bolivia 20°28S 66°47W 92 H5
Uzbekistan ■ Asia 41°30N 65°0E 28 E7
Uzboy → Turkmenistan 39°30N 55°0E 45 B7
Uzen Kazakhstan 43°29N 52°54E 19 F9
Uzen, Bolshoi = Uzen, Mal → Kazakhstan 49°4N 49°44E 19 E8
Uzen, Mal → Kazakhstan 49°4N 49°44E 19 E8
Uzerche France 45°25N 1°34E 20 D4
Uzh → Ukraine 51°15N 30°12E 17 C16
Uzhgorod = Uzhhorod Ukraine 48°36N 22°18E 17 D12
Uzhhorod Ukraine 48°36N 22°18E 17 D12
Užice Serbia 43°55N 19°50E 23 C8
Uzunköprü Turkey 41°16N 26°43E 23 D12

V

Vaal → S. Africa 29°4S 23°38E 56 D3
Vaal Dam S. Africa 27°0S 28°14E 57 D4
Vaalbos △ S. Africa 28°22S 24°20E 56 D3
Vaalwater S. Africa 24°15S 28°8E 57 C4
Vaasa Finland 63°6N 21°38E 8 E19
Vác Hungary 47°49N 19°10E 17 E10
Vacaria Brazil 28°31S 50°52W 95 B5
Vacata Fiji 17°15S 179°31W 59 a
Vacaville U.S.A. 38°21N 121°59W 78 G5
Vach = Vakh → Russia 60°45N 76°45E 28 C8
Vache, Î. à Haiti 18°2N 73°35W 89 C5
Vacoas Mauritius 20°18S 57°29E 53 d
Vadnagar India 23°47N 72°40E 42 H5
Vadodara India 22°20N 73°10E 42 H5
Vadsø Norway 70°3N 29°50E 8 A23
Vaduz Liech. 47°8N 9°31E 20 C8
Værøy Norway 67°40N 12°40E 8 C15
Vágar Færoe Is. 62°5N 7°15W 8 E9
Vagia, Akra Greece 36°15N 28°11E 25 C10
Vågsfjorden Norway 68°50N 16°50E 8 B17
Váh → Slovak Rep. 47°43N 18°7E 17 D9
Vahsel B. Antarctica 75°0S 35°0W 5 D1
Váhtjer = Gällivare Sweden 67°9N 20°40E 8 C19
Vaï Greece 35°15N 26°18E 25 D8
Vaihiria, L. Tahiti 17°40S 149°25W 59 d
Vail U.S.A. 39°40N 106°20W 74 C5
Vairao Tahiti 17°47S 149°17W 59 d
Vaisali → India 26°28N 78°53E 43 F8
Vaitogi Amer. Samoa 14°24S 170°44W 59 b
Vakh → Russia 60°45N 76°45E 28 C8
Val-d'Or Canada 48°7N 77°47W 72 C4
Val Marie Canada 49°15N 107°45W 71 D7
Valaam Russia 61°22N 30°57E 8 F24
Valahia Romania 44°35N 25°0E 17 F13
Valandovo Macedonia 41°19N 22°34E 23 D10
Valatie U.S.A. 42°24N 73°40W 83 D11
Valcheta Argentina 40°40S 66°8W 96 E3
Valdai Hills = Valdayskaya Vozvyshennost Russia 57°0N 33°30E 18 C5
Valdayskaya Vozvyshennost Russia 57°0N 33°30E 18 C5
Valdepeñas Spain 38°43N 3°25W 21 C4
Valdés, Pen. Argentina 42°30S 63°45W 96 E4
Valdez U.S.A. 61°7N 146°16W 68 C5
Valdivia Chile 39°50S 73°14W 96 D2
Valdivia Abyssal Plain S. Ocean 62°30S 70°0E 5 C6
Valdosta U.S.A. 30°50N 83°17W 85 F13
Valdres Norway 61°5N 9°5E 8 F13
Vale U.S.A. 43°59N 117°15W 76 E5
Vale of Glamorgan □ U.K. 51°28N 3°25W 13 F4
Valemount Canada 52°50N 119°15W 70 C5
Valença Brazil 13°20S 39°5W 93 F11
Valença do Piauí Brazil 6°20S 41°45W 93 E10
Valence France 44°57N 4°54E 20 D6
Valencia Spain 39°27N 0°23W 21 C5
Valencia Trin. & Tob. 10°39N 61°11W 93 K15
Valencia U.S.A. 34°48N 106°43W 77 J10
Valencia Venezuela 10°11N 68°0W 92 A5
Valencia □ Spain 39°20N 0°40W 21 C5
Valencia, G. de Spain 39°30N 0°20E 21 C6
Valencia de Alcántara Spain 39°25N 7°14W 21 C2
Valencia I. Ireland 51°54N 10°22W 10 E1
Valenciennes France 50°20N 3°34E 20 A5
Valentim, Sa. do Brazil 6°0S 43°30W 93 E10
Valentin Russia 43°8N 134°17E 30 C7
Valentine Nebr., U.S.A. 42°52N 100°33W 80 D3
Valentine Tex., U.S.A. 30°35N 104°30W 84 F2
Valera Venezuela 9°19N 70°37W 92 B4
Valga Estonia 57°47N 26°2E 9 H22
Valier U.S.A. 48°18N 112°16W 76 B7
Valjevo Serbia 44°18N 19°53E 23 B8
Valka Latvia 57°46N 26°3E 9 H22
Valkeakoski Finland 61°16N 24°2E 8 F21
Valkenswaard Neths. 51°21N 5°29E 15 C5
Vall de Uxó = La Vall d'Uixó Spain 39°49N 0°15W 21 C5
Valladolid Mexico 20°41N 88°12W 87 C7
Valladolid Spain 41°38N 4°43W 21 B3
Valldemossa Spain 39°43N 2°37E 24 B9
Valle de la Pascua Venezuela 9°13N 66°0W 92 B5
Valle de las Palmas Mexico 32°20N 116°43W 79 N10
Valle de Santiago Mexico 20°23N 101°12W 86 C4
Valle de Zaragoza Mexico 27°25N 105°50W 86 B3
Valle Fértil, Sierra del Argentina 30°20S 68°0W 94 C2
Valle Gran Rey Canary Is. 28°5N 17°20W 24 F2
Valle Hermoso Mexico 25°35N 97°40W 87 B5
Valle Nacional Mexico 17°47N 96°18W 87 D5
Valledupar Colombia 10°29N 73°15W 92 A4
Vallehermoso Canary Is. 28°10N 17°15W 24 F2
Vallejo U.S.A. 38°7N 122°14W 78 G4
Vallenar Chile 28°30S 70°50W 94 B1
Valletta Malta 35°54N 14°31E 25 D2
Valley Center U.S.A. 33°13N 117°2W 79 M9
Valley City U.S.A. 46°55N 98°0W 80 B5
Valley Falls Oreg., U.S.A. 42°29N 120°17W 76 E3
Valley Falls R.I., U.S.A. 41°54N 71°24W 83 E13
Valley of Flowers △ India 30°50N 79°40E 43 D8
Valley Springs U.S.A. 38°12N 120°50W 78 G6
Valley View U.S.A. 40°39N 76°33W 83 F8
Valley Wells U.S.A. 35°27N 115°46W 79 K11
Valleyview Canada 55°5N 117°17W 70 B5
Vallimanca, Arroyo Argentina 35°40S 59°10W 94 D4
Valls Spain 41°18N 1°15E 21 B6
Valmiera Latvia 57°37N 25°29E 9 H21
Valognes France 49°30N 1°28W 20 B3
Valona = Vlorë Albania 40°32N 19°28E 23 D8
Valozhyn Belarus 54°3N 26°30E 17 A14
Valparaíso Chile 33°2S 71°40W 94 C1
Valparaíso Mexico 22°46N 103°34W 86 C4
Valparaiso U.S.A. 41°28N 87°4W 80 E10
Valparaíso □ Chile 33°2S 71°40W 94 C1
Vals → S. Africa 27°23S 26°30E 56 D4
Vals, Tanjung Indonesia 8°26S 137°25E 37 F9
Valsad India 20°40N 72°58E 40 J8
Valverde Canary Is. 27°48N 17°55W 24 G2
Valverde del Camino Spain 37°35N 6°47W 21 D2
Vammala Finland 61°20N 22°54E 8 F20
Vamos Greece 35°24N 24°13E 25 D6
Van Turkey 38°30N 43°20E 44 B4
Van, L. = Van Gölü Turkey 38°30N 43°0E 44 B4
Van Alstyne U.S.A. 33°25N 96°35W 84 E6
Van Blommestein Meer Suriname 4°45N 55°5W 93 C7
Van Buren Canada 47°10N 67°55W 73 C6
Van Buren Ark., U.S.A. 35°26N 94°21W 84 D7
Van Buren Maine, U.S.A. 47°10N 67°58W 81 B20
Van Buren Mo., U.S.A. 37°0N 91°1W 80 G8
Van Canh Vietnam 13°37N 109°0E 38 F7
Van Diemen, C. N. Terr., Australia 11°9S 130°22E 60 B5
Van Diemen, C. Queens., Australia 16°30S 139°46E 62 B2
Van Diemen G. Australia 11°45S 132°0E 60 B5
Van Gölü Turkey 38°30N 43°0E 44 B4
Van Horn U.S.A. 31°3N 104°50W 84 F2
Van Ninh Vietnam 12°42N 109°14E 38 F7
Van Rees, Pegunungan Indonesia 2°35S 138°15E 37 E9
Van Wert U.S.A. 40°52N 84°35W 81 E11
Van Yen Vietnam 21°4N 104°42E 38 B5
Vanadzor Armenia 40°48N 44°30E 19 F7
Vanavara Russia 60°22N 102°16E 29 C11
Vancouver Canada 49°15N 123°7W 78 A3
Vancouver U.S.A. 45°38N 122°40W 78 E4
Vancouver, C. Australia 35°2S 118°11E 61 G2
Vancouver I. Canada 49°50N 126°0W 78 B2
Vancouver Int. ✕ (YVR) Canada 49°10N 123°10W 78 A3
Vanda = Vantaa Finland 60°18N 24°56E 9 F21
Vandalia Ill., U.S.A. 38°58N 89°6W 80 F9
Vandalia Mo., U.S.A. 39°19N 91°29W 80 F8
Vandenberg Village U.S.A. 34°43N 120°28W 79 L6
Vanderbijlpark S. Africa 26°42S 27°54E 57 D4
Vandergrift U.S.A. 40°36N 79°34W 82 F5
Vanderhoof Canada 54°0N 124°0W 70 C4
Vanderkloof Dam S. Africa 30°4S 24°40E 56 E3
Vanderlin I. Australia 15°44S 137°2E 62 B2
Vänern Sweden 58°47N 13°30E 9 G15
Vänersborg Sweden 58°26N 12°19E 9 G15
Vang Vieng Laos 18°58N 102°32E 38 C4
Vanga Kenya 4°35S 39°12E 54 C4
Vangaindrano Madag. 23°21S 47°36E 57 C8
Vanguard Canada 49°55N 107°20W 71 D7
Vanino Russia 48°50N 140°5E 29 E15
Vankleek Hill Canada 45°32N 74°40W 83 A10
Vännäs Sweden 63°58N 19°48E 8 E18
Vannes France 47°40N 2°47W 20 C2
Vannøya Norway 70°6N 19°50E 8 A18
Vanrhynsdorp S. Africa 31°36S 18°44E 56 E2
Vansbro Sweden 60°32N 14°15E 9 F16
Vansittart B. Australia 14°3S 126°17E 60 B4
Vantaa Finland 60°18N 24°56E 9 F21
Vanua Balavu Fiji 17°12S 178°55W 59 a
Vanua Levu Fiji 16°33S 179°15E 59 a
Vanua Vatu Fiji 18°22S 179°15W 59 a
Vanuatu ■ Pac. Oc. 15°0S 168°0E 58 C9
Vanwyksvlei S. Africa 30°18S 21°49E 56 E3
Vanzylsrus S. Africa 26°52S 22°4E 56 D3
Vapnyarka Ukraine 48°32N 28°45E 17 D15
Var → France 43°39N 7°12E 20 E7
Varāmīn Iran 35°20N 51°39E 45 C6
Varāmīn □ Iran 35°18N 51°35E 45 B6
Varanasi India 25°22N 83°0E 43 G10
Varangerfjorden Norway 70°3N 29°25E 8 A23
Varangerhalvøya Norway 70°25N 29°30E 8 A23
Varaždin Croatia 46°20N 16°20E 16 E9
Varberg Sweden 57°6N 12°20E 9 H15
Vardak □ Afghan. 34°0N 68°0E 40 B6
Vardar = Axios → Greece 40°57N 22°35E 23 D10
Varde Denmark 55°38N 8°29E 9 J13
Vardø Norway 70°23N 31°5E 8 A24
Varella, Mui Vietnam 12°54N 109°26E 38 F7
Varėna Lithuania 54°12N 24°30E 9 J21
Varese Italy 45°48N 8°50E 20 D8
Varginha Brazil 21°33S 45°25W 95 A6
Varillas Chile 24°0S 70°10W 94 A1
Varkaus Finland 62°19N 27°50E 8 E22
Varna Bulgaria 43°13N 27°56E 23 C12
Värnamo Sweden 57°10N 14°3E 9 H16
Vars Canada 45°21N 75°21W 83 A9
Varysburg U.S.A. 42°46N 78°19W 82 D6
Varzaneh Iran 32°25N 52°40E 45 C7
Vasa = Vaasa Finland 63°6N 21°38E 8 E19
Vasa Barris → Brazil 11°10S 37°10W 93 F11
Vascongadas = País Vasco □ Spain 42°50N 2°45W 21 A4
Vasht = Khāsh Iran 28°15N 61°15E 45 D9
Vasilevichi Belarus 52°15N 29°50E 17 B15
Vasilkov = Vasylkiv Ukraine 50°7N 30°15E 17 C16
Vaslui Romania 46°38N 27°42E 17 E14
Vassar Canada 49°10N 95°55W 71 D9
Vassar U.S.A. 43°22N 83°35W 81 D12
Västerås Sweden 59°37N 16°38E 9 G17
Västerbotten Sweden 64°36N 20°4E 8 D19
Västerdalälven → Sweden 60°30N 14°7E 8 F16
Västervik Sweden 57°43N 16°33E 9 H17
Västmanland Sweden 59°45N 16°20E 9 G17
Vasto Italy 42°8N 14°40E 22 C6
Vasylkiv Ukraine 50°7N 30°15E 17 C16
Vatersay U.K. 56°55N 7°32W 11 E1
Vati Greece 36°3N 27°53E 25 C9
Vatican City ■ Europe 41°54N 12°27E 22 D5
Vatili Cyprus 35°6N 33°40E 25 D12
Vatiu = Atiu Cook Is. 20°0S 158°10W 65 J12
Vatnajökull Iceland 64°30N 16°48W 8 D5
Vatolakkos Greece 35°27N 23°53E 25 D5
Vatoloha Madag. 17°52S 47°48E 57 B8
Vatomandry Madag. 19°20S 48°59E 57 B8
Vatra-Dornei Romania 47°22N 25°22E 17 E13
Vatrak → India 23°9N 73°2E 42 H5
Vättern Sweden 58°25N 14°30E 9 G16
Vatu Vara Fiji 17°26S 179°31W 59 a
Vatulele Fiji 18°33S 177°37E 59 a
Vaudreuil-Dorion Canada 45°23N 74°3W 83 A10
Vaughn Mont., U.S.A. 47°33N 111°33W 76 C8
Vaughn N. Mex., U.S.A. 34°36N 105°13W 77 J11
Vaujours L. Canada 55°27N 74°15W 72 A5
Vaupés = Uaupés → Brazil 0°2N 67°16W 92 C5
Vaupés □ Colombia 1°0N 71°0W 92 C4
Vauxhall Canada 50°5N 112°9W 70 C6
Vav India 24°22N 71°31E 42 G4
Vavatenina Madag. 17°28S 49°12E 57 B8
Vava'u Tonga 18°36S 174°0W 59 c
Vava'u Group Tonga 18°40S 174°0W 59 c
Vawkavysk Belarus 53°9N 24°30E 17 B13
Växjö Sweden 56°52N 14°50E 9 H16
Vaygach, Ostrov Russia 70°0N 60°0E 28 C7
Veaikevárri = Svappavaara Sweden 67°40N 21°3E 8 C19
Vechte → Neths. 52°34N 6°6E 15 B6
Vedea → Romania 43°42N 25°41E 17 G13
Vedia Argentina 34°30S 61°31W 94 C3
Veendam Neths. 53°5N 6°52E 15 A6
Veenendaal Neths. 52°2N 5°34E 15 B5
Vefsna → Norway 65°48N 13°10E 8 D15
Vega Norway 65°40N 11°55E 8 D14
Vega U.S.A. 35°15N 102°26W 84 D3
Vega Baja Puerto Rico 18°27N 66°23W 89 d
Vegreville Canada 53°30N 112°5W 70 C6
Vejer de la Frontera Spain 36°15N 5°59W 21 D3
Vejle Denmark 55°43N 9°30E 9 J13
Velas, C. Costa Rica 10°21N 85°52W 88 D2
Velasco, Sierra de Argentina 29°20S 67°10W 94 B2
Velddrif S. Africa 32°42S 18°11E 56 E2
Velebit Planina Croatia 44°50N 15°20E 16 F8
Veles Macedonia 41°46N 21°47E 23 D9
Vélez-Málaga Spain 36°48N 4°5W 21 D3
Vélez Rubio Spain 37°41N 2°5W 21 D4
Velhas → Brazil 17°13S 44°49W 93 G10
Velika Kapela Croatia 45°10N 15°5E 16 F8
Velikaya → Russia 57°48N 28°10E 18 C4
Velikaya Kema Russia 45°30N 137°12E 30 B8
Veliki Ustyug Russia 60°47N 46°20E 18 B8
Velikiye Luki Russia 56°25N 30°32E 18 C5
Veliko Tŭrnovo Bulgaria 43°5N 25°41E 23 C11
Velikonda Range India 14°45N 79°10E 40 M11
Velletri Italy 41°41N 12°47E 22 D5
Vellore India 12°57N 79°10E 40 N11
Velsk Russia 61°10N 42°5E 18 B7
Veluwezoom △ Neths. 52°5N 6°0E 15 B6
Velva U.S.A. 48°4N 100°56W 80 A3
Venado Mexico 22°56N 101°6W 86 C4
Venado Tuerto Argentina 33°50S 62°0W 94 C3
Vendée □ France 46°50N 1°35W 20 C3
Vendôme France 47°47N 1°3E 20 C4
Venézia Italy 45°27N 12°21E 22 B5
Venézia, G. di Italy 45°15N 13°0E 22 B5
Venezuela ■ S. Amer. 8°0N 66°0W 92 B5
Venezuela, G. de Venezuela 11°30N 71°0W 92 A4
Vengurla India 15°53N 73°45E 40 M8
Venice = Venézia Italy 45°27N 12°21E 22 B5
Venice U.S.A. 27°6N 82°27W 85 H13
Venkatapuram India 18°20N 80°30E 41 K12
Venlo Neths. 51°22N 6°11E 15 C6
Vennachar Junction Canada 45°5N 77°14W 82 A7
Vennesla Norway 58°15N 7°59E 9 G12
Venray Neths. 51°31N 6°0E 15 C6
Ventana, Punta de la Mexico 24°4N 109°48W 86 C3
Ventana, Sa. de la Argentina 38°0S 62°30W 94 D3
Ventersburg S. Africa 28°7S 27°9E 56 D4
Venterstad S. Africa 30°47S 25°48E 56 E4
Ventnor U.K. 50°36N 1°12W 13 G6
Ventoténe Italy 40°47N 13°25E 22 D5
Ventoux, Mt. France 44°10N 5°17E 20 D6
Ventspils Latvia 57°25N 21°32E 9 H19
Ventuarí → Venezuela 3°58N 67°2W 92 C5
Ventucopa U.S.A. 34°50N 119°29W 79 L7
Ventura U.S.A. 34°17N 119°18W 79 L7
Vénus, Pte. Tahiti 17°29S 149°29W 59 d
Venus B. Australia 38°40S 145°42E 63 F4
Venustiano Carranza Mexico 30°25N 115°53W 86 A1
Vera Argentina 29°30S 60°20W 94 B3
Vera Spain 37°15N 1°51W 21 D5
Veracruz Mexico 19°11N 96°8W 87 D5
Veracruz □ Mexico 19°0N 96°15W 87 D5
Veraval India 20°53N 70°27E 42 J4
Verbánia Italy 45°56N 8°33E 20 D8
Vercelli Italy 45°19N 8°25E 20 D8
Verdalsøra Norway 63°48N 11°30E 8 E14
Verde → Argentina 41°56S 65°5W 96 E3
Verde → Goiás, Brazil 18°1S 50°14W 93 G8
Verde → Mato Grosso do Sul, Brazil 21°25S 52°20W 93 H8
Verde → Chihuahua, Mexico 26°29N 107°58W 86 B3
Verde → Oaxaca, Mexico 15°59N 97°50W 87 D5
Verde → Veracruz, Mexico 21°10N 102°50W 86 C4
Verde → Paraguay 23°9S 57°37W 94 A4
Verde → U.S.A. 33°33N 111°40W 74 D4
Verde, Cay Bahamas 23°0N 75°5W 88 B4
Verden Germany 52°55N 9°14E 16 B5
Verdi U.S.A. 39°31N 119°59W 78 F7
Verdun France 49°9N 5°24E 20 B6
Vereeniging S. Africa 26°38S 27°57E 57 D4
Verga, C. Guinea 10°30N 14°10W 50 F3
Vergara Uruguay 32°56S 53°57W 95 C5
Vergemont Cr. → Australia 24°16S 143°16E 62 C3
Vergennes U.S.A. 44°10N 73°15W 83 B11
Veria Greece 40°34N 22°12E 23 D10
Verín Spain 41°57N 7°27W 21 B2
Verkhnetulomskoye Vdkhr. Russia 68°36N 31°12E 8 B24

Verkhnevilyuysk Russia 63°27N 120°18E 29 C13
Verkhniy Baskunchak Russia 48°14N 46°44E 19 E8
Verkhoyansk Russia 67°35N 133°25E 29 C14
Verkhoyansk Ra. = Verkhoyanskiy Khrebet Russia 66°0N 129°0E 29 C13
Verkhoyanskiy Khrebet Russia 66°0N 129°0E 29 C13
Vermilion Canada 53°20N 110°50W 71 C6
Vermilion U.S.A. 41°25N 82°22W 82 E2
Vermilion → Canada 53°22N 110°51W 71 C6
Vermilion B. U.S.A. 29°42N 92°0W 84 G9
Vermilion Bay Canada 49°51N 93°34W 71 D10
Vermilion L. U.S.A. 47°53N 92°26W 80 B7
Vermillion U.S.A. 42°47N 96°56W 80 D5
Vermillion → Canada 47°38N 72°56W 72 C5
Vermont □ U.S.A. 44°0N 73°0W 83 C12
Vernadsky Antarctica 65°0S 64°0W 5 C17
Vernal U.S.A. 40°27N 109°32W 76 F9
Vernalis U.S.A. 37°36N 121°17W 78 H5
Verner Canada 46°25N 80°8W 72 C3
Verneukpan S. Africa 30°0S 21°0E 56 E3
Vernon Canada 50°20N 119°15W 70 C5
Vernon U.S.A. 34°9N 99°17W 84 D5
Vernonia U.S.A. 45°52N 123°11W 78 E3
Vero Beach U.S.A. 27°38N 80°24W 85 H14
Véroia = Veria Greece 40°34N 22°12E 23 D10
Verona Canada 44°29N 76°42W 83 B8
Verona Italy 45°27N 10°59E 22 B4
Versailles France 48°48N 2°7E 20 B5
Vert, C. Senegal 14°45N 17°30W 50 F2
Verulam S. Africa 29°38S 31°2E 57 D5
Verviers Belgium 50°37N 5°52E 15 D5
Veselovskoye Vdkhr. Russia 46°58N 41°25E 19 E7
Vesoul France 47°40N 6°11E 20 C7
Vesterålen Norway 68°45N 15°0E 8 B16
Vestfjorden Norway 67°55N 14°0E 8 C16
Vestmannaeyjar Iceland 63°27N 20°15W 8 E3
Vestspitsbergen Svalbard 78°40N 17°0E 4 B8
Vestvågøya Norway 68°18N 13°50E 8 B15
Vesuvio Italy 40°49N 14°26E 22 D6
Vesuvius, Mt. = Vesuvio Italy 40°49N 14°26E 22 D6
Veszprém Hungary 47°8N 17°57E 17 E9
Vetlanda Sweden 57°24N 15°3E 9 H16
Vetlugu → Russia 56°36N 46°4E 18 C8
Vettore, Mte. Italy 42°49N 13°16E 22 C5
Veurne Belgium 51°5N 2°40E 15 C2
Veys Iran 31°30N 49°0E 45 D6
Vezhen Bulgaria 42°50N 24°20E 23 C11
Vi Thanh Vietnam 9°42N 105°26E 39 H5
Viacha Bolivia 16°39S 68°18W 92 G5
Viamão Brazil 30°5S 51°0W 95 C5
Viana Brazil 3°13S 44°55W 93 D10
Viana do Alentejo Portugal 38°17N 7°59W 21 C2
Viana do Castelo Portugal 41°42N 8°50W 21 B1
Vianden Lux. 49°56N 6°12E 15 E6
Viangchan = Vientiane Laos 17°58N 102°36E 38 D4
Vianópolis Brazil 16°40S 48°35W 93 G9
Vianos Greece 35°2N 25°21E 25 D7
Viaréggio Italy 43°52N 10°14E 22 C4
Vibo Valéntia Italy 38°40N 16°6E 22 E7
Viborg Denmark 56°27N 9°23E 9 H13
Vic Spain 41°58N 2°19E 21 B7
Vicenza Italy 45°33N 11°33E 22 B4
Vich = Vic Spain 41°58N 2°19E 21 B7
Vichada → Colombia 4°55N 67°50W 92 C5
Vichy France 46°9N 3°26E 20 C5
Vicksburg Ariz., U.S.A. 33°45N 113°45W 79 M13
Vicksburg Miss., U.S.A. 32°21N 90°53W 85 E9
Victor India 21°0N 71°30E 42 J4
Victor Harbor Australia 35°30S 138°37E 63 F2
Victoria Argentina 32°40S 60°10W 94 C3
Victoria Canada 48°30N 123°25W 78 B3
Victoria Chile 38°13S 72°20W 96 D2
Victoria China 22°17N 114°9E 33 G1
Victoria Malta 36°3N 14°14E 25 C1
Victoria Seychelles 4°38S 55°28E 53 b
Victoria Kans., U.S.A. 38°52N 99°9W 80 F4
Victoria Tex., U.S.A. 28°48N 97°0W 84 G6
Victoria □ Australia 37°0S 144°0E 63 F3
Victoria → Australia 15°10S 129°40E 60 C4
Victoria, Grand L. Canada 47°31N 77°30W 72 C4
Victoria, L. Africa 1°0S 33°0E 54 C3
Victoria, L. Australia 33°57S 141°15E 63 E3
Victoria, Mt. Burma 21°14N 93°55E 41 J18
Victoria Beach Canada 50°40N 96°35W 71 C9
Victoria de Durango = Durango Mexico 24°3N 104°39W 86 C4
Victoria de las Tunas = Las Tunas Cuba 20°58N 76°59W 88 B4
Victoria Falls Zimbabwe 17°58S 25°52E 55 F2
Victoria Harbour Canada 44°45N 79°45W 82 B5
Victoria I. Canada 71°0N 111°0W 68 B8
Victoria L. Canada 48°20N 57°27W 73 C8
Victoria Ld. Antarctica 75°0S 160°0E 5 D11
Victoria Nile → Uganda 2°14N 31°26E 54 B3
Victoria Pk. Belize 16°48N 88°37W 87 D7
Victoria River Australia 16°25S 131°0E 60 C5
Victoria Str. Canada 69°31N 100°30W 68 C9
Victoria West S. Africa 31°25S 23°4E 56 E3
Victoriaville Canada 46°4N 71°56W 73 C5
Victorica Argentina 36°20S 65°30W 94 D2
Victorville U.S.A. 34°32N 117°18W 79 L9
Vicuña Chile 30°0S 70°50W 94 C1
Vicuña Mackenna Argentina 33°53S 64°25W 94 C3
Vidal U.S.A. 34°7N 114°31W 79 L12
Vidal Junction U.S.A. 34°11N 114°34W 79 L12
Vidalia U.S.A. 32°13N 82°25W 85 E13
Vidin Bulgaria 43°59N 22°50E 23 C10
Vidisha India 23°28N 77°53E 42 H7
Vidos Greece 39°38N 19°55E 25 A3
Vidzy Belarus 55°23N 26°37E 9 J22
Viedma Argentina 40°50S 63°0W 96 E4
Viedma, L. Argentina 49°30S 72°30W 96 F2
Vielsalm Belgium 50°17N 5°54E 15 D5
Vieng Pou Kha Laos 20°41N 101°4E 38 B3
Vienna = Wien Austria 48°12N 16°22E 16 D9
Vienna Canada 42°41N 80°48W 82 D4
Vienna Ill., U.S.A. 37°25N 88°54W 80 G9
Vienna Mo., U.S.A. 38°11N 91°57W 80 F8
Vienne France 45°31N 4°53E 20 D6
Vienne → France 47°13N 0°5E 20 C4
Vientiane Laos 17°58N 102°36E 38 D4
Vientos, Paso de los Caribbean 20°0N 74°0W 89 C5
Vieques Puerto Rico 18°8N 65°25W 89 d
Vierge Pt. St. Lucia 13°49N 60°53W 89 f
Vierzon France 47°13N 2°5E 20 C5
Viet Tri Vietnam 21°18N 105°25E 38 B5
Vietnam ■ Asia 19°0N 106°0E 38 C6
Vieux Fort St. Lucia 13°46N 60°58W 89 f
Vigan Phil. 17°35N 120°28E 37 A6
Vigévano Italy 45°19N 8°51E 20 D8
Vigia Brazil 0°50S 48°5W 93 D9
Viglas, Akra Greece 35°54N 27°51E 25 D9
Vigo Spain 42°12N 8°41W 21 A1
Vihowa Pakistan 31°8N 70°30E 42 D4
Vihowa → Pakistan 31°8N 70°41E 42 D4
Vijayawada India 16°31N 80°39E 41 L12
Vijosë → Albania 40°37N 19°24E 23 D8
Vík Iceland 63°25N 19°1W 8 E4
Vikeke = Viqueque E. Timor 8°52S 126°23E 37 F7
Viking Canada 53°7N 111°50W 70 C6
Vikna Norway 64°55N 10°58E 8 D14
Vila da Maganja Mozam. 17°18S 37°30E 55 F4
Vila da Ribeira Brava C. Verde Is. 16°32N 24°25W 50 b
Vila do Bispo Portugal 37°5N 8°53W 21 D1
Vila Franca de Xira Portugal 38°57N 8°59W 21 C1
Vila Gamito Mozam. 14°12S 33°0E 55 E3
Vila Gomes da Costa Mozam. 24°20S 33°37E 57 C5
Vila Machado Mozam. 19°15S 34°14E 55 F3
Vila Mouzinho Mozam. 14°48S 34°25E 55 E3
Vila Nova de Gaia Portugal 41°8N 8°37W 21 B1
Vila Real Portugal 41°17N 7°48W 21 B2
Vila-Real Spain 39°55N 0°3W 21 C5
Vila Real de Santo António Portugal 37°10N 7°28W 21 D2
Vila Vasco da Gama Mozam. 14°54S 32°14E 55 E3
Vila Velha Brazil 20°20S 40°17W 95 A7
Vilagarcía de Arousa Spain 42°34N 8°46W 21 A1
Vilaine → France 47°30N 2°27W 20 C2
Vilanandro, Tanjona Madag. 16°11S 44°27E 57 B7
Vilanculos Mozam. 22°1S 35°17E 57 C6
Vilanova i la Geltrú Spain 41°13N 1°40E 21 B6
Vilcheka, Ostrov Russia 80°0N 58°31E 28 B6
Vilcheka, Zemlya Russia 80°30N 60°30E 4 A11
Vileyka Belarus 54°30N 26°53E 17 A14
Vilhelmina Sweden 64°35N 16°39E 8 D17
Vilhena Brazil 12°40S 60°5W 92 F6
Viliya = Neris → Lithuania 55°8N 24°16E 9 J21
Viljandi Estonia 58°28N 25°30E 9 G21
Vilkitskogo, Proliv Russia 78°0N 103°0E 29 B11
Vilkovo = Vylkove Ukraine 45°28N 29°32E 17 F15
Villa Abecia Bolivia 21°0S 68°18W 94 A2
Villa Ana Argentina 28°28S 59°40W 94 B4
Villa Angela Argentina 27°34S 60°45W 94 B3
Villa Bella Bolivia 10°25S 65°22W 92 F5
Villa Cañás Argentina 34°0S 61°35W 94 C3
Villa Constitución Argentina 33°15S 60°20W 94 C3
Villa de Arriaga Mexico 21°56N 101°20W 86 C4
Villa de María Argentina 29°55S 63°43W 94 B3
Villa de Méndez Mexico 25°7N 98°34W 87 B5
Villa Dolores Argentina 31°58S 65°15W 94 C2
Villa Frontera Mexico 26°56N 101°27W 86 B4
Villa Gesell Argentina 37°15S 56°55W 94 D4
Villa Guillermina Argentina 28°15S 59°29W 94 B4
Villa Hayes Paraguay 25°5S 57°20W 94 B4
Villa Hidalgo Mexico 24°15N 99°26W 87 C5
Villa Iris Argentina 38°12S 63°12W 94 D3
Villa María Argentina 32°20S 63°10W 94 C3
Villa Mazán Argentina 28°40S 66°30W 94 B2
Villa Montes Bolivia 21°10S 63°30W 94 A3
Villa Ocampo Argentina 28°30S 59°20W 94 B4
Villa Ocampo Mexico 26°27N 105°31W 86 B3
Villa Ojo de Agua Argentina 29°30S 63°44W 94 B3
Villa San Martín Argentina 28°15S 64°9W 94 B3
Villa Unión Mexico 23°12N 106°14W 86 C3
Villacarlos Spain 39°53N 4°17E 24 B11
Villacarrillo Spain 38°7N 3°3W 21 C4
Villach Austria 46°37N 13°51E 16 E7
Villafranca de Bonany Spain 39°34N 3°5E 24 B10
Villagrán Mexico 24°29N 99°29W 87 C5
Villaguay Argentina 32°0S 59°0W 94 C4
Villahermosa Mexico 17°59N 92°55W 87 D6
Villajoyosa Spain 38°30N 0°12W 21 C5
Villalba Spain 43°26N 7°40W 21 A2
Villanueva U.S.A. 35°16N 105°22W 77 J11
Villanueva de la Serena Spain 38°59N 5°50W 21 C3
Villanueva y Geltrú = Vilanova i la Geltrú Spain 41°13N 1°40E 21 B6
Villarreal = Vila-Real Spain 39°55N 0°3W 21 C5
Villarrica Chile 39°15S 72°15W 96 D2
Villarrica Paraguay 25°40S 56°30W 94 B4
Villarrobledo Spain 39°18N 2°36W 21 C4
Villavicencio Argentina 32°28S 69°0W 94 C2
Villavicencio Colombia 4°9N 73°37W 92 C4
Villaviciosa Spain 43°32N 5°27W 21 A3
Villazón Bolivia 22°0S 65°35W 94 A2
Ville-Marie Canada 47°20N 79°30W 72 C4
Ville Platte U.S.A. 30°41N 92°17W 84 F8
Villena Spain 38°39N 0°52W 21 C5
Villeneuve-d'Ascq France 50°38N 3°9E 20 A5
Villeneuve-sur-Lot France 44°24N 0°42E 20 D4
Villiers S. Africa 27°2S 28°36E 57 D4
Villingen-Schwenningen Germany 48°3N 8°26E 16 D5
Villmanstrand = Lappeenranta Finland 61°3N 28°12E 8 F23
Vilna Canada 54°7N 111°55W 70 C6
Vilnius Lithuania 54°38N 25°19E 9 J21
Vilvoorde Belgium 50°56N 4°26E 15 D4
Vilyuchinsk Russia 52°55N 158°24E 29 D16
Vilyuy → Russia 64°24N 126°26E 29 C13
Vilyuysk Russia 63°40N 121°35E 29 C13
Viña del Mar Chile 33°0S 71°30W 94 C1
Vinarós Spain 40°30N 0°27E 21 B6
Vincennes U.S.A. 38°41N 87°32W 80 F10
Vincennes Bay S. Ocean 66°0S 109°0E 5 C8
Vincent U.S.A. 34°33N 118°11W 79 L8
Vinchina Argentina 28°45S 68°15W 94 B2
Vindelälven → Sweden 63°55N 19°50E 8 E18
Vindeln Sweden 64°12N 19°43E 8 D18
Vindhya Ra. India 22°50N 77°0E 42 H7
Vineland U.S.A. 39°29N 75°2W 81 F16
Vinh Vietnam 18°45N 105°38E 38 C5
Vinh Linh Vietnam 17°4N 107°2E 38 D6
Vinh Long Vietnam 10°16N 105°57E 39 G5
Vinh Yen Vietnam 21°21N 105°35E 38 B5
Vinita U.S.A. 36°39N 95°9W 84 C7
Vinkovci Croatia 45°19N 18°48E 23 B8
Vinnitsa = Vinnytsya Ukraine 49°15N 28°30E 17 D15
Vinnytsya Ukraine 49°15N 28°30E 17 D15
Vinson Massif Antarctica 78°35S 85°25W 5 D16
Vinton Calif., U.S.A. 39°48N 120°10W 78 F6
Vinton Iowa, U.S.A. 42°10N 92°1W 80 D7
Vinton La., U.S.A. 30°11N 93°35W 84 F8
Viqueque E. Timor 8°52S 126°23E 37 F7
Virac Phil. 13°30N 124°20E 37 B6
Virachey Cambodia 13°59N 106°49E 38 F6
Virachey △ Cambodia 14°14N 106°55E 38 E6
Virago Sd. Canada 54°0N 132°30W 70 C2
Viramgam India 23°5N 72°0E 42 H5
Viranşehir Turkey 37°13N 39°45E 44 B3
Virawah Pakistan 24°31N 70°46E 42 G4
Virden Canada 49°50N 100°56W 71 D8
Vire France 48°50N 0°53W 20 B3
Vírgenes, C. Argentina 52°19S 68°21W 96 G3
Virgin → U.S.A. 36°28N 114°21W 77 H6
Virgin Gorda Br. Virgin Is. 18°30N 64°26W 89 e
Virgin Is. (British) ☑ W. Indies 18°30N 64°30W 89 e
Virgin Is. (U.S.) ☑ W. Indies 18°20N 65°0W 89 e
Virgin Islands △ U.S. Virgin Is. 18°21N 64°43W 89 C7
Virginia S. Africa 28°8S 26°55E 56 D4
Virginia U.S.A. 47°31N 92°32W 80 B7
Virginia □ U.S.A. 37°30N 78°45W 81 G14
Virginia Beach U.S.A. 36°49N 76°9W 81 F16
Virginia City Mont., U.S.A. 45°18N 111°56W 76 D8
Virginia City Nev., U.S.A. 39°19N 119°39W 78 F7
Virginia Falls Canada 61°38N 125°42W 70 A3
Virginiatown Canada 48°9N 79°36W 72 C4
Viroqua U.S.A. 43°34N 90°53W 80 D8
Virovitica Croatia 45°51N 17°21E 22 B7
Virpur India 21°51N 70°42E 42 J4
Virton Belgium 49°35N 5°32E 15 E5
Virudunagar India 9°30N 77°58E 40 Q10
Virunga △ Dem. Rep. of the Congo 0°5N 29°38E 54 B2
Vis Croatia 43°4N 16°10E 22 C7
Visalia U.S.A. 36°20N 119°18W 78 J7
Visayan Sea Phil. 11°30N 123°30E 37 B6
Visby Sweden 57°37N 18°18E 9 H18
Viscount Melville Sd. Canada 74°10N 108°0W 69 B9
Visé Belgium 50°44N 5°41E 15 D5
Vise, Ostrov Russia 79°33N 76°50E 28 B8
Višegrad Bos.-H. 43°47N 19°17E 23 C8
Viseu Brazil 1°10S 46°5W 93 D9
Viseu Portugal 40°40N 7°55W 21 B2
Vishakhapatnam India 17°45N 83°20E 41 L13
Visnagar India 23°45N 72°32E 42 H5
Viso, Mte. Italy 44°38N 7°5E 20 D7
Visokoi I. Antarctica 56°43S 27°15W 5 B1
Vista U.S.A. 33°12N 117°14W 79 M9
Vistula = Wisła → Poland 54°22N 18°55E 17 A10
Vitebsk = Vitsyebsk Belarus 55°10N 30°15E 18 C5
Viterbo Italy 42°25N 12°6E 22 C5
Viti Levu Fiji 17°30S 177°30E 59 a
Vitigudino Spain 41°1N 6°26W 21 B2
Vitim Russia 59°28N 112°35E 29 D12
Vitim → Russia 59°26N 112°34E 29 D12
Vitória Brazil 20°20S 40°22W 93 H10
Vitória da Conquista Brazil 14°51S 40°51W 93 F10
Vitória de São Antão Brazil 8°10S 35°20W 93 E11
Vitoria-Gasteiz Spain 42°50N 2°41W 21 A4
Vitsyebsk Belarus 55°10N 30°15E 18 C5
Vittória Italy 36°57N 14°32E 22 F6
Vittório Véneto Italy 45°59N 12°18E 22 B5
Viveiro Spain 43°39N 7°38W 21 A2
Vivian U.S.A. 32°53N 93°59W 84 E8
Viwa Fiji 17°10S 177°58E 59 a
Vizcaíno, Desierto de Mexico 27°30N 113°45W 86 B2
Vizcaíno, Sierra Mexico 27°30N 114°0W 86 B2
Vize Turkey 41°34N 27°45E 23 D12
Vizianagaram India 18°6N 83°30E 41 K13
Vlaardingen Neths. 51°55N 4°21E 15 C4
Vladikavkaz Russia 43°0N 44°35E 19 F7
Vladimir Russia 56°15N 40°30E 18 C7
Vladimir Volynskiy = Volodymyr-Volynskyy Ukraine 50°50N 24°18E 17 C13
Vladivostok Russia 43°10N 131°53E 30 C5
Vlieland Neths. 53°16N 4°55E 15 A4
Vlissingen Neths. 51°26N 3°34E 15 C3
Vlorë Albania 40°32N 19°28E 23 D8
Vltava → Czech Rep. 50°21N 14°30E 16 D8
Vo Dat Vietnam 11°9N 107°31E 39 G6
Voe U.K. 60°21N 1°16W 11 A7
Vogelkop = Doberai, Jazirah Indonesia 1°25S 133°0E 37 E8
Vogelsberg Germany 50°31N 9°12E 16 C5
Voghera Italy 44°59N 9°1E 20 D8
Vohibinany Madag. 18°49S 49°4E 57 B8
Vohilava Madag. 21°4S 48°0E 57 C8
Vohimarina = Iharana Madag. 13°25S 50°0E 57 A9
Vohimena, Tanjon' i Madag. 25°36S 45°8E 57 D8
Vohipeno Madag. 22°22S 47°51E 57 C8
Voi Kenya 3°25S 38°32E 54 C4
Voiron France 45°22N 5°35E 20 D6
Voisey B. Canada 56°15N 61°50W 73 A7
Vojmsjön Sweden 65°0N 16°24E 8 D17
Vojvodina □ Serbia 45°20N 20°0E 23 B9
Volborg U.S.A. 45°51N 105°41W 76 D11
Volcán de Colima △ Mexico 19°30N 103°40W 86 D4
Volcano Is. = Kazan-Rettō Pac. Oc. 25°0N 141°0E 64 E6
Volcans △ Rwanda 1°30S 29°26E 54 C2
Volda Norway 62°9N 6°5E 8 E12
Volga = Privolzhskiy □ Russia 56°0N 50°0E 28 D6
Volga → Russia 46°0N 48°30E 19 E8
Volga Hts. = Privolzhskaya Vozvyshennost Russia 51°0N 46°0E 19 D8
Volgodonsk Russia 47°33N 42°5E 19 E7
Volgograd Russia 48°40N 44°25E 19 E7
Volgogradskoye Vdkhr. Russia 50°0N 45°20E 19 D8
Volkhov → Russia 60°8N 32°20E 18 B5
Volkovysk = Vawkavysk Belarus 53°9N 24°30E 17 B13
Volksrust S. Africa 27°24S 29°53E 57 D4
Volochanka Russia 71°0N 94°28E 29 B10
Volodymyr-Volynskyy Ukraine 50°50N 24°18E 17 C13
Vologda Russia 59°10N 39°45E 18 C6
Volos Greece 39°24N 22°59E 23 E10
Volosovo Russia 59°27N 29°32E 9 G23
Volovets Ukraine 48°43N 23°11E 17 D12
Volozhin = Valozhyn Belarus 54°3N 26°30E 17 A14
Volsk Russia 52°5N 47°22E 18 D8
Volta → Ghana 5°46N 0°41E 48 F4
Volta, L. Ghana 7°30N 0°0 50 G6
Volta Redonda Brazil 22°31S 44°5W 95 A7
Voltaire, C. Australia 14°16S 125°35E 60 B4
Volterra Italy 43°24N 10°51E 22 C4
Volturno → Italy 41°1N 13°55E 22 D5
Volzhskiy Russia 48°56N 44°46E 19 E7
Vomo Fiji 17°30S 177°15E 59 a
Vondrozo Madag. 22°49S 47°20E 57 C8
Vopnafjörður Iceland 65°45N 14°50W 8 D6
Vorkuta Russia 67°48N 64°20E 18 A11
Vormsi Estonia 59°1N 23°13E 9 G20
Voronezh Russia 51°40N 39°10E 19 D6
Võrts Järv Estonia 58°16N 26°3E 9 G22
Võru Estonia 57°48N 26°54E 9 H22
Vosges France 48°20N 7°10E 20 B7
Voss Norway 60°38N 6°26E 8 F12
Vostok Antarctica 78°30S 106°50E 5 D8
Vostok I. Kiribati 10°5S 152°23W 65 J12
Votkinsk Russia 57°0N 53°55E 18 C9
Votkinskoye Vdkhr. Russia 57°22N 55°12E 18 C10
Votsuri-Shima Japan 25°45N 123°29E 31 M1
Vouga → Portugal 40°41N 8°40W 21 B1
Vouxa, Akra Greece 35°37N 23°32E 25 D5
Voyageurs △ U.S.A. 48°32N 93°0W 80 A7
Voynitsa Russia 65°10N 30°20E 8 D24
Voyvozh Russia 62°56N 54°56E 28 C6
Vozhe, Ozero Russia 60°45N 39°0E 18 B6
Voznesensk Ukraine 47°35N 31°21E 19 E5
Voznesenye Russia 61°0N 35°28E 18 B6
Vrangel Russia 42°43N 133°5E 30 C6
Vrangelya, Ostrov Russia 71°0N 180°0E 29 B18
Vranje Serbia 42°34N 21°54E 23 C9
Vratsa Bulgaria 43°15N 23°30E 23 C10
Vrbas → Bos.-H. 45°8N 17°29E 22 B7
Vrede S. Africa 27°24S 29°6E 57 D4
Vredefort S. Africa 27°0S 27°22E 56 D4
Vredenburg S. Africa 32°56S 18°0E 56 E2
Vredendal S. Africa 31°41S 18°35E 56 E2
Vrindavan India 27°37N 77°40E 42 F7
Vrisses Greece 35°23N 24°13E 25 D6
Vršac Serbia 45°8N 21°20E 23 B9
Vryburg S. Africa 26°55S 24°45E 56 D3
Vryheid S. Africa 27°45S 30°47E 57 D5
Vu Liet Vietnam 18°43N 105°23E 38 C5
Vukovar Croatia 45°21N 18°59E 23 B8
Vuktyl Russia 63°52N 57°20E 28 C
Vulcan Canada 50°25N 113°15W 70 C
Vulcan Romania 45°23N 23°17E 17 F
Vulcaneşti Moldova 45°41N 28°18E 17 F
Vulcano Italy 38°24N 14°58E 22 E
Vulkaneshty = Vulcaneşti Moldova 45°41N 28°18E 17 F1
Vunduzi → Mozam. 18°56S 34°1E 55 F
Vung Tau Vietnam 10°21N 107°4E 39 G
Vunidawa Fiji 17°50S 178°21E 59
Vunisea Fiji 19°3S 178°10E 59
Vwaza △ Malawi 10°58S 33°25E 55 E
Vyartsilya Russia 62°8N 30°45E 8 E2
Vyatka = Kirov Russia 58°35N 49°40E 18 C
Vyatka → Russia 55°37N 51°28E 18 C
Vyatskiye Polyany Russia 56°14N 51°5E 18 C
Vyazemskiy Russia 47°32N 134°45E 29 E1
Vyazma Russia 55°10N 34°15E 18 C
Vyborg Russia 60°43N 28°47E 8 F2
Vychegda → Russia 61°18N 46°36E 18 B
Vychodné Beskydy Europe 49°20N 22°0E 17 D1
Vyg-ozero Russia 63°47N 34°29E 18 B
Vylkove Ukraine 45°28N 29°32E 17 F1
Vynohradiv Ukraine 48°9N 23°2E 17 D1
Vyrnwy, L. U.K. 52°48N 3°31W 12 E
Vyshniy Volochek Russia 57°30N 34°30E 18 C
Vyshzha = imeni 26 Bakinskikh Komissarov Turkmenistan 39°22N 54°10E 45 B
Vyškov Czech Rep. 49°17N 17°0E 17 D
Vytegra Russia 61°0N 36°27E 18 B

W

W.A.C. Bennett Dam Canada 56°2N 122°6W 70 B
Wa Ghana 10°7N 2°25W 50 F
Waal → Neths. 51°37N 5°0E 15 C
Waalwijk Neths. 51°42N 5°4E 15 C
Wabakimi △ Canada 50°43N 89°29W 72 B
Wabana Canada 47°40N 53°0W 73 C
Wabasca → Canada 58°22N 115°20W 70 B
Wabasca-Desmarais Canada 55°57N 113°56W 70 B
Wabash U.S.A. 40°48N 85°49W 81 E
Wabash → U.S.A. 37°48N 88°2W 80 G
Wabigoon L. Canada 49°44N 92°44W 71 D
Wabowden Canada 54°55N 98°38W 71 C
Wabuk Pt. Canada 55°20N 85°5W 72 A
Wabush Canada 52°55N 66°52W 73 B
Waco U.S.A. 31°33N 97°9W 84 F
Waconichi, L. Canada 50°8N 74°0W 72 B
Wad Hamid Sudan 16°30N 32°45E 51 E
Wad Medanî Sudan 14°28N 33°30E 51 F
Wad Thana Pakistan 27°22N 66°23E 42 F
Wadai Africa 12°0N 19°0E 48 E
Wadayama Japan 35°19N 134°52E 31 G
Waddeneilanden Neths. 53°25N 5°10E 15 A
Waddenzee Neths. 53°6N 5°10E 15 A
Waddington U.S.A. 44°52N 75°12W 83 B
Waddington, Mt. Canada 51°23N 125°15W 70 C
Waddy Pt. Australia 24°58S 153°21E 63 C
Wadebridge U.K. 50°31N 4°51W 13 G
Wadena Canada 51°57N 103°47W 71 C
Wadena U.S.A. 46°26N 95°8W 80 B
Wadeye Australia 14°28S 129°52E 60 B
Wadhams Canada 51°30N 127°30W 70 C
Wadhwan India 22°42N 71°41E 42 H
Wādī as Sīr Jordan 31°56N 35°49E 46 D
Wadi Halfa Sudan 21°53N 31°19E 51 D
Wadi Rum △ Jordan 29°30N 35°20E 46 F
Wadsworth Nev., U.S.A. 39°38N 119°17W 76 G
Wadsworth Ohio, U.S.A. 41°2N 81°44W 82 E
Waegwan S. Korea 35°59N 128°23E 35 G
Wafangdian China 39°38N 121°58E 35 E
Wafrah Kuwait 28°33N 47°56E 44 D
Wageningen Neths. 51°58N 5°40E 15 C
Wager B. Canada 65°26N 88°40W 69 C
Wagga Wagga Australia 35°7S 147°24E 63 F
Waghete Indonesia 4°10S 135°50E 37 E
Wagin Australia 33°17S 117°25E 61 F
Wagner U.S.A. 43°5N 98°18W 80 D
Wagon Mound U.S.A. 36°1N 104°42W 77 H
Wagoner U.S.A. 35°58N 95°22W 84 D
Wah Pakistan 33°45N 72°40E 42 C
Wahai Indonesia 2°48S 129°35E 37 E
Wahiawā U.S.A. 21°30N 158°2W 74
Wâḥid Egypt 30°48N 32°21E 46 E
Wahnai Afghan. 32°40N 65°50E 42 C
Wahoo U.S.A. 41°13N 96°37W 80 E
Wahpeton U.S.A. 46°16N 96°36W 80 B
Waiau → N.Z. 42°47S 173°22E 59 E
Waibeem Indonesia 0°30S 132°59E 37 E
Waigeo Indonesia 0°20S 130°40E 37 E
Waihi N.Z. 37°23S 175°52E 59 B
Waihou → N.Z. 37°15S 175°40E 59 B
Waika Dem. Rep. of the Congo 2°22S 25°42E 54 C
Waikabubak Indonesia 9°45S 119°25E 37 F
Waikaremoana, L. N.Z. 38°49S 177°9E 59 C
Waikari N.Z. 42°58S 172°41E 59 E
Waikato → N.Z. 37°23S 174°43E 59 B
Waikerie Australia 34°9S 140°0E 63 E
Waikokopu N.Z. 39°3S 177°52E 59 C
Waikouaiti N.Z. 45°36S 170°41E 59 F
Wailingding Dao China 22°6N 114°2E 33 G
Wailuku U.S.A. 20°53N 156°30W 74
Waimakariri → N.Z. 43°24S 172°42E 59 E
Waimate N.Z. 44°45S 171°3E 59 F
Wainganga → India 18°50N 79°55E 40 K
Waingapu Indonesia 9°35S 120°11E 37 F
Waini → Guyana 8°20N 59°50W 92 B

ainwright Canada 52°50N 110°50W 71 C6
aiouru N.Z. 39°28S 175°41E 59 C5
aipara N.Z. 43°3S 172°46E 59 E4
aipawa N.Z. 39°56S 176°38E 59 C6
aipiro N.Z. 38°2S 178°22E 59 C7
aipoua Forest N.Z. 35°39S 173°33E 59 A4
aipu N.Z. 35°59S 174°29E 59 A5
aipukurau N.Z. 40°1S 176°33E 59 D6
airakei N.Z. 38°37S 176°6E 59 C6
airarapa, L. N.Z. 41°14S 175°15E 59 D5
airoa N.Z. 39°3S 177°25E 59 C6
aitaki → N.Z. 44°56S 171°7E 59 F3
aitangi N.Z. 35°16S 174°5E 59 A5
aitara N.Z. 38°59S 174°15E 59 C5
aitomo Caves N.Z. 38°16S 175°7E 59 C5
aitsburg U.S.A. 46°16N 118°9W 76 C4
aiuku N.Z. 37°15S 174°45E 59 B5
ajima Japan 37°30N 137°0E 31 F8
ajir Kenya 1°42N 40°5E 54 B5
akasa Japan 35°20N 134°24E 31 G7
akasa-Wan Japan 35°40N 135°30E 31 G7
akatipu, L. N.Z. 45°5S 168°33E 59 F2
akaw Canada 52°39N 105°44W 71 C7
akaya Fiji 17°37S 179°0E 59 a
akayama Japan 34°15N 135°15E 31 G7
akayama □ Japan 33°50N 135°30E 31 H7
ake Forest U.S.A. 35°59N 78°30W 85 D15
ke I. Pac. Oc. 19°18N 166°36E 64 F8
Keeney U.S.A. 39°1N 99°53W 80 F4
kefield Jamaica 18°26N 77°42W 88 a
kefield N.Z. 41°24S 173°5E 59 D4
kefield U.K. 53°41N 1°29W 12 D6
kefield Mass., U.S.A. 42°30N 71°5W 83 D13
kefield Mich., U.S.A. 46°29N 89°56W 80 B9
kkanai Japan 45°28N 141°35E 30 B10
kkerstroom S. Africa 27°24S 30°10E 57 D5
kool Australia 35°28S 144°23E 63 F3
kool → Australia 35°5S 143°33E 63 F3
kre Indonesia 0°19S 131°5E 37 E8
kuach, L. Canada 55°34N 67°32W 73 A6
lamba Zambia 13°30S 28°42E 55 E2
lbrzych Poland 50°45N 16°18E 16 C9
lbury Hill U.K. 51°21N 1°28W 13 F6
lcha Australia 30°55S 151°31E 63 E5
lcheren Neths. 51°30N 3°35E 15 C3
lcott U.S.A. 41°46N 106°51W 76 F10
lcz Poland 53°17N 16°27E 16 B9
ldburg Ra. Australia 24°40S 117°35E 61 D2
lden Colo., U.S.A. 40°44N 106°17W 76 F10
lden N.Y., U.S.A. 41°34N 74°11W 83 E10
ldport U.S.A. 44°26N 124°4W 76 D1
ldron U.S.A. 34°54N 94°5W 84 D7
lebing Australia 30°41S 116°13E 61 F2
les □ U.K. 52°19N 4°43W 13 E3
lgett Australia 30°0S 148°5E 63 E4
lgreen Coast ntarctica 75°15S 105°0W 5 D15
lker U.S.A. 47°6N 94°35W 80 B6
lker, L. Canada 50°20N 67°11W 73 B6
lker L. Canada 54°42N 95°57W 71 C9
lker L. U.S.A. 38°42N 118°43W 76 G4
lkerston Australia 21°11S 149°8E 62 K7
lkerton Canada 44°10N 81°10W 82 B3
ll U.S.A. 44°0N 102°8W 80 C2
lla Walla U.S.A. 46°4N 118°20W 76 C4
llace Idaho, U.S.A. 47°28N 115°56W 76 C6
llace N.C., U.S.A. 34°44N 77°59W 85 D16
llaceburg Canada 42°34N 82°23W 82 D2
llachia = Valahia omania 44°35N 25°0E 17 F13
llal Australia 26°32S 146°7E 63 D4
llam Cr. → ustralia 28°40S 147°20E 63 D4
llambin, L. Australia 30°57S 117°35E 61 F2
llangarra Australia 28°56S 151°58E 63 D5
llaroo Australia 33°56S 137°39E 63 E2
llenpaupack, L. .S.A. 41°25N 75°15W 83 E9
llingford Conn., .S.A. 41°27N 72°50W 83 E12
llingford Vt., U.S.A. 43°28N 72°58W 83 C12
llis & Futuna, Is. ac. Oc. 13°18S 176°10W 58 C11
llowa U.S.A. 45°34N 117°32W 76 D5
llowa Mts. U.S.A. 45°20N 117°30W 76 D5
lls U.K. 60°14N 1°33W 11 A7
lls of Jerusalem △ ustralia 41°56S 146°15E 63 G4
llula U.S.A. 46°5N 118°54W 76 C4
llumbilla Australia 26°33S 149°9E 63 D4
lmsley L. Canada 63°25N 108°36W 71 A7
lney, I. of U.K. 54°6N 3°15W 12 C4
lnut Canyon ⌂ .S.A. 35°15N 111°20W 77 J8
lnut Creek U.S.A. 37°54N 122°4W 78 H4
lnut Ridge U.S.A. 36°4N 90°57W 85 C9
lpole Australia 34°58S 116°44E 61 F2
lpole U.S.A. 42°9N 71°15W 83 D13
lpole-Nornalup △ ustralia 35°0S 116°45E 61 G2
lsall U.K. 52°35N 1°58W 13 E6
lsenburg U.S.A. 37°38N 104°47W 77 H11
sh U.S.A. 37°23N 102°17W 77 H12
sh → Australia 16°31S 143°42E 62 B3
singham Canada 42°40N 80°31W 82 D4
lter F. George Res. .S.A. 31°38N 85°4W 85 F12
terboro U.S.A. 32°55N 80°40W 85 E14
ters U.S.A. 34°22N 98°19W 84 D5
tham U.S.A. 42°23N 71°14W 83 D13
tman U.S.A. 43°4N 107°12W 76 E10
ton U.S.A. 42°10N 75°8W 83 D9
ton-on-the-Naze U.K. 51°51N 1°17E 13 F9
vis Bay Namibia 23°0S 14°28E 56 C1
visbaai = Walvis Bay amibia 23°0S 14°28E 56 C1
nba m. Rep. of the Congo 2°10N 27°57E 54 B2
Wamba Kenya 0°58N 37°19E 54 B4
Wamego U.S.A. 39°12N 96°18W 80 F5
Wamena Indonesia 4°4S 138°57E 37 E9
Wampsville U.S.A. 43°4N 75°42W 83 C9
Wamsutter U.S.A. 41°40N 107°58W 76 F10
Wamulan Indonesia 3°27S 126°7E 37 E7
Wan Xian China 38°47N 115°7E 34 E8
Wana Pakistan 32°20N 69°32E 42 C3
Wanaaring Australia 29°38S 144°9E 63 D3
Wanaka N.Z. 44°42S 169°9E 59 F2
Wanaka, L. N.Z. 44°33S 169°7E 59 F2
Wanapitei L. Canada 46°45N 80°40W 72 C3
Wandel Sea = McKinley Sea Arctic 82°0N 0°0 4 A7
Wanderer Zimbabwe 19°36S 30°1E 55 F3
Wandhari Pakistan 27°42N 66°48E 42 F2
Wandoan Australia 26°5S 149°55E 63 D4
Wanfu China 40°8N 122°38E 35 D12
Wang → Thailand 17°8N 99°2E 38 D2
Wang Noi Thailand 14°13N 100°44E 38 E3
Wang Saphung Thailand 17°18N 101°46E 38 D3
Wang Thong Thailand 16°50N 100°26E 38 D3
Wanga Dem. Rep. of the Congo 2°58N 29°12E 54 B2
Wangal Indonesia 6°8S 134°9E 37 F8
Wanganella Australia 35°6S 144°49E 63 F3
Wanganui N.Z. 39°56S 175°3E 59 C5
Wangaratta Australia 36°21S 146°19E 63 F4
Wangary Australia 34°35S 135°29E 63 E2
Wangdu China 38°40N 115°7E 34 E8
Wangerooge Germany 53°47N 7°54E 16 B4
Wangiwangi Indonesia 5°22S 123°37E 37 F6
Wangqing China 43°12N 129°42E 35 C15
Wankaner India 22°35N 71°0E 42 H4
Wanless Canada 54°11N 101°21W 71 C8
Wanleweyne Somali Rep. 2°37N 44°54E 47 G3
Wanneroo Australia 31°42S 115°46E 61 F2
Wanning China 18°48N 110°22E 38 C8
Wanon Niwat Thailand 17°38N 103°46E 38 D4
Wanqinsha China 22°43N 113°33E 33 F10
Wanquan China 40°50N 114°40E 34 D8
Wanrong China 35°25N 110°50E 34 G6
Wanshan Qundao China 21°57N 113°45E 33 G10
Wantage U.K. 51°35N 1°25W 13 F6
Wanxian China 30°42N 108°20E 32 C5
Wanzai China 22°12N 113°31E 33 G10
Wapakoneta U.S.A. 40°34N 84°12W 81 E11
Wapato U.S.A. 46°27N 120°25W 76 C3
Wapawekka L. Canada 54°55N 104°40W 71 C8
Wapikopa L. Canada 52°56N 87°53W 72 B2
Wapiti → Canada 55°5N 118°18W 70 B5
Wappingers Falls U.S.A. 41°36N 73°55W 83 E11
Wapsipinicon → U.S.A. 41°44N 90°19W 80 E8
Wapusk △ Canada 57°46N 93°22W 71 B10
Warangal India 17°58N 79°35E 40 L11
Waraseoni India 21°45N 80°2E 43 J9
Waratah Australia 41°30S 145°30E 63 G4
Waratah B. Australia 38°54S 146°5E 63 F4
Warburton Vic., Australia 37°47S 145°42E 63 F4
Warburton W. Austral., Australia 26°8S 126°35E 61 E4
Warburton → Australia 28°4S 137°28E 63 D2
Warburton Ra. Australia 25°55S 126°28E 61 E4
Ward N.Z. 41°49S 174°11E 59 D5
Ward → Australia 26°28S 146°6E 63 D4
Ward Mt. U.S.A. 37°12N 118°54W 78 H8
Warden S. Africa 27°50S 29°0E 57 D4
Wardha India 20°45N 78°39E 40 J11
Wardha → India 19°57N 79°11E 40 K11
Wardsville Canada 42°39N 81°45W 82 D3
Ware U.K. 51°49N 0°0 13 F8
Ware U.S.A. 42°16N 72°14W 83 D12
Waregem Belgium 50°53N 3°27E 15 D3
Wareham U.S.A. 41°46N 70°43W 83 E14
Waremme Belgium 50°43N 5°15E 15 D5
Warialda Australia 29°29S 150°33E 63 D5
Wariap Indonesia 1°30S 134°5E 37 E8
Warin Chamrap Thailand 15°12N 104°53E 38 E5
Warkopi Indonesia 1°12S 134°9E 37 E8
Warm Springs U.S.A. 38°10N 116°20W 77 G5
Warman Canada 52°19N 106°30W 71 C7
Warmbad = Bela Bela S. Africa 24°51S 28°19E 57 C4
Warmbad Namibia 28°25S 18°42E 56 D2
Warminster U.K. 51°12N 2°10W 13 F5
Warminster U.S.A. 40°12N 75°6W 83 F9
Warmun Australia 17°2S 128°12E 60 C4
Warner Mts. U.S.A. 41°40N 120°15W 76 F3
Warner Robins U.S.A. 32°37N 83°36W 85 E13
Waroona Australia 32°50S 115°58E 61 F2
Warracknabeal Australia 36°9S 142°26E 63 F3
Warragul Australia 38°10S 145°58E 63 F4
Warrego → Australia 30°24S 145°21E 63 E4
Warrego Ra. Australia 24°58S 146°0E 62 C4
Warren Australia 31°42S 147°51E 63 E4
Warren Ark., U.S.A. 33°37N 92°4W 84 E8
Warren Mich., U.S.A. 42°28N 83°1W 81 D12
Warren Minn., U.S.A. 48°12N 96°46W 80 A5
Warren Ohio, U.S.A. 41°14N 80°49W 82 E4
Warren Pa., U.S.A. 41°51N 79°9W 82 E5
Warrenpoint U.K. 54°6N 6°15W 10 B5
Warrensburg Mo., U.S.A. 38°46N 93°44W 80 F7
Warrensburg N.Y., U.S.A. 43°29N 73°46W 83 C11
Warrenton S. Africa 28°9S 24°47E 56 D3
Warrenton U.S.A. 46°10N 123°56W 78 D3
Warri Nigeria 5°30N 5°41E 50 G7
Warrina Australia 28°12S 135°50E 63 D2
Warrington U.K. 53°24N 2°35W 12 D5
Warrington U.S.A. 30°23N 87°17W 85 F11
Warrington □ U.K. 53°24N 2°35W 12 D5
Warrnambool Australia 38°25S 142°30E 63 F3
Warroad U.S.A. 48°54N 95°19W 80 A6
Warruwi Australia 11°36S 133°20E 62 A1
Warsa Indonesia 0°47S 135°55E 37 E9
Warsak Dam Pakistan 34°11N 71°19E 42 B4
Warsaw = Warszawa Poland 52°14N 21°0E 17 B11
Warsaw Ind., U.S.A. 41°14N 85°51W 81 E11
Warsaw N.Y., U.S.A. 42°45N 78°8W 82 D6
Warsaw Ohio, U.S.A. 40°20N 82°0W 82 F3
Warszawa Poland 52°14N 21°0E 17 B11
Warta → Poland 52°35N 14°39E 16 B8
Warthe = Warta → Poland 52°35N 14°39E 16 B8
Waru Indonesia 3°30S 130°36E 37 E8
Warwick Australia 28°10S 152°1E 63 D5
Warwick U.K. 52°18N 1°35W 13 E6
Warwick N.Y., U.S.A. 41°16N 74°22W 83 E10
Warwick R.I., U.S.A. 41°42N 71°28W 83 E13
Warwickshire □ U.K. 52°14N 1°38W 13 E6
Wasaga Beach Canada 44°31N 80°1W 82 B4
Wasagaming Canada 50°39N 99°58W 71 C9
Wasatch Ra. U.S.A. 40°0N 111°30W 76 F8
Wasbank S. Africa 28°15S 30°9E 57 D5
Wasco Calif., U.S.A. 35°36N 119°20W 79 K7
Wasco Oreg., U.S.A. 45°36N 120°42W 76 D3
Waseca U.S.A. 44°5N 93°30W 80 C7
Wasekamio L. Canada 56°45N 108°45W 71 B7
Wash, The U.K. 52°58N 0°20E 12 E8
Washago Canada 44°45N 79°20W 82 B5
Washburn N. Dak., U.S.A. 47°17N 101°2W 80 B3
Washburn Wis., U.S.A. 46°40N 90°54W 80 B8
Washim India 20°3N 77°0E 40 J10
Washington U.K. 54°55N 1°30W 12 C6
Washington D.C., U.S.A. 38°53N 77°2W 81 F15
Washington Ga., U.S.A. 33°44N 82°44W 85 E13
Washington Ind., U.S.A. 38°40N 87°10W 80 F10
Washington Iowa, U.S.A. 41°18N 91°42W 80 E8
Washington Mo., U.S.A. 38°33N 91°1W 80 F8
Washington N.C., U.S.A. 35°33N 77°3W 85 D16
Washington N.J., U.S.A. 40°46N 74°59W 83 F10
Washington Pa., U.S.A. 40°10N 80°15W 82 F4
Washington Utah, U.S.A. 37°8N 113°31W 77 H7
Washington □ U.S.A. 47°30N 120°30W 76 C3
Washington, Mt. U.S.A. 44°16N 71°18W 83 B13
Washington Court House U.S.A. 39°32N 83°26W 81 F12
Washington I. U.S.A. 45°23N 86°54W 80 C10
Washougal U.S.A. 45°35N 122°21W 78 E4
Washpool △ Australia 29°22S 152°20E 63 D5
Wasian Indonesia 1°47S 133°19E 37 E8
Wasilla U.S.A. 61°35N 149°26W 68 C5
Wasior Indonesia 2°43S 134°30E 37 E8
Wāsiṭ □ Iraq 32°50N 45°50E 44 C5
Waskaganish Canada 51°30N 78°40W 72 B4
Waskaiowaka L. Canada 56°33N 96°23W 71 B9
Waskesiu Lake Canada 53°55N 106°5W 71 C7
Wasserkuppe Germany 50°29N 9°55E 16 C5
Waswanipi Canada 49°40N 76°29W 72 C4
Waswanipi, L. Canada 49°35N 76°40W 72 C4
Watampone Indonesia 4°29S 120°25E 37 E6
Watamu Kenya 3°23S 40°0E 54 C5
Watarrka △ Australia 24°20S 131°30E 60 D5
Water Park Pt. Australia 22°56S 150°47E 62 C5
Water Valley U.S.A. 34°10N 89°38W 85 D10
Waterberg Plateau ⌂ Namibia 20°25S 17°18E 56 C2
Waterberge S. Africa 24°10S 28°0E 57 C4
Waterbury Conn., U.S.A. 41°33N 73°3W 83 E11
Waterbury Vt., U.S.A. 44°20N 72°46W 83 B12
Waterbury L. Canada 58°10N 104°22W 71 B8
Waterdown Canada 43°20N 79°53W 82 C5
Waterford Canada 42°56N 80°17W 82 D4
Waterford Ireland 52°15N 7°8W 10 D4
Waterford Calif., U.S.A. 37°38N 120°46W 78 H6
Waterford Pa., U.S.A. 41°57N 79°59W 82 E5
Waterford □ Ireland 52°10N 7°40W 10 D4
Waterford Harbour Ireland 52°8N 6°58W 10 D5
Waterhen L. Canada 52°10N 99°40W 71 C9
Waterloo Belgium 50°43N 4°25E 15 D4
Waterloo Ont., Canada 43°30N 80°32W 82 C4
Waterloo Qué., Canada 45°22N 72°32W 83 A12
Waterloo Ill., U.S.A. 38°20N 90°9W 80 F8
Waterloo Iowa, U.S.A. 42°30N 92°21W 80 D7
Waterloo N.Y., U.S.A. 42°54N 76°52W 82 D8
Watersmeet U.S.A. 46°16N 89°11W 80 B9
Waterton Lakes △ Canada 48°45N 115°0W 70 D6
Watertown Conn., U.S.A. 41°36N 73°7W 83 E11
Watertown N.Y., U.S.A. 43°59N 75°55W 83 C9
Watertown S. Dak., U.S.A. 44°54N 97°7W 80 C5
Watertown Wis., U.S.A. 43°12N 88°43W 80 D9
Waterval-Boven S. Africa 25°40S 30°18E 57 D5
Waterville Canada 45°16N 71°54W 83 A13
Waterville Maine, U.S.A. 44°33N 69°38W 81 C19
Waterville N.Y., U.S.A. 42°56N 75°23W 83 D9
Waterville Pa., U.S.A. 41°19N 77°21W 82 E7
Waterville Wash., U.S.A. 47°39N 120°4W 76 C3
Watervliet U.S.A. 42°44N 73°42W 83 D11
Wates Indonesia 7°51S 110°10E 37 G14
Watford Canada 42°57N 81°53W 82 D3
Watford U.K. 51°40N 0°24W 13 F7
Watford City U.S.A. 47°48N 103°17W 80 B2
Wathaman → Canada 57°16N 102°59W 71 B8
Wathaman L. Canada 56°58N 103°44W 71 B8
Watheroo Australia 30°15S 116°5E 61 F2
Watheroo △ Australia 30°19S 115°48E 61 F2
Wating China 35°40N 106°38E 34 G4
Watkins Glen U.S.A. 42°23N 76°52W 82 D8
Watling I. = San Salvador I. Bahamas 24°0N 74°40W 89 B5
Watonga U.S.A. 35°51N 98°25W 84 D5
Watrous Canada 51°40N 105°25W 71 C7
Watrous U.S.A. 35°48N 104°59W 77 J11
Watsa Dem. Rep. of the Congo 3°4N 29°30E 54 B2
Watseka U.S.A. 40°47N 87°44W 80 E10
Watson Canada 52°10N 104°30W 71 C8
Watson Lake Canada 60°6N 128°49W 70 A3
Watsontown U.S.A. 41°5N 76°52W 82 E8
Watsonville U.S.A. 36°55N 121°45W 78 J5
Wattiwarriganna Cr. → Australia 28°57S 136°10E 63 D2
Watuata = Batuata Indonesia 6°12S 122°42E 37 F6
Watubela, Kepulauan Indonesia 4°28S 131°35E 37 E8
Watubela Is. = Watubela, Kepulauan Indonesia 4°28S 131°35E 37 E8
Wau = Wâw Sudan 7°45N 28°1E 51 G11
Waubamik Canada 45°27N 80°1W 82 A4
Waubay U.S.A. 45°20N 97°18W 80 C5
Wauchope N.S.W., Australia 31°28S 152°45E 63 E5
Wauchope N. Terr., Australia 20°36S 134°15E 62 C1
Wauchula U.S.A. 27°33N 81°49W 85 H14
Waukarlycarly, L. Australia 21°18S 121°56E 60 D3
Waukegan U.S.A. 42°22N 87°50W 80 D10
Waukesha U.S.A. 43°1N 88°14W 80 D9
Waukon U.S.A. 43°16N 91°29W 80 D8
Waupaca U.S.A. 44°21N 89°5W 80 C9
Waupun U.S.A. 43°38N 88°44W 80 D9
Waurika U.S.A. 34°10N 98°0W 84 D6
Wausau U.S.A. 44°58N 89°38W 80 C9
Wautoma U.S.A. 44°4N 89°18W 80 C9
Wauwatosa U.S.A. 43°2N 88°0W 80 D9
Wave Hill = Kalkarindji Australia 17°30S 130°47E 60 C5
Wave Rock ⌂ Australia 32°26S 118°53E 61 F2
Waveney → U.K. 52°35N 1°39E 13 E9
Waverley N.Z. 39°46S 174°37E 59 C5
Waverly Iowa, U.S.A. 42°44N 92°29W 80 D7
Waverly N.Y., U.S.A. 42°1N 76°32W 83 E8
Wavre Belgium 50°43N 4°38E 15 D4
Wâw Sudan 7°45N 28°1E 51 G11
Wāw al Kabīr Libya 25°20N 16°43E 51 C9
Wawa Canada 47°59N 84°47W 72 C3
Wawanesa Canada 49°36N 99°40W 71 D9
Wawona U.S.A. 37°32N 119°39W 78 H7
Waxahachie U.S.A. 32°24N 96°51W 84 E6
Way, L. Australia 26°45S 120°16E 61 E3
Waya Fiji 17°19S 177°10E 59 a
Waycross U.S.A. 31°13N 82°21W 85 F13
Wayland U.S.A. 42°34N 77°35W 82 D7
Wayne Nebr., U.S.A. 42°14N 97°1W 80 D5
Wayne W. Va., U.S.A. 38°13N 82°27W 81 F12
Waynesboro Ga., U.S.A. 33°6N 82°1W 85 E13
Waynesboro Miss., U.S.A. 31°40N 88°39W 85 F10
Waynesboro Pa., U.S.A. 39°45N 77°35W 81 F15
Waynesboro Va., U.S.A. 38°4N 78°53W 81 F14
Waynesburg U.S.A. 39°54N 80°11W 81 F13
Waynesville U.S.A. 35°28N 82°58W 85 D13
Waynoka U.S.A. 36°35N 98°53W 84 C5
Wazirabad Pakistan 32°30N 74°8E 42 C6
We Indonesia 5°51N 95°18E 36 C1
Weald, The U.K. 51°4N 0°20E 13 F8
Wear → U.K. 54°55N 1°23W 12 C6
Weatherford Okla., U.S.A. 35°32N 98°43W 84 D5
Weatherford Tex., U.S.A. 32°46N 97°48W 84 E6
Weaverville U.S.A. 40°44N 122°56W 76 F2
Webb City U.S.A. 37°9N 94°28W 80 G6
Webequie Canada 52°59N 87°21W 72 B2
Webster Mass., U.S.A. 42°3N 71°53W 83 D13
Webster N.Y., U.S.A. 43°13N 77°26W 82 C7
Webster S. Dak., U.S.A. 45°20N 97°31W 80 C5
Webster City U.S.A. 42°28N 93°49W 80 D7
Webster Springs U.S.A. 38°29N 80°25W 81 F13
Weda Indonesia 0°21N 127°50E 37 D7
Weda, Teluk Indonesia 0°20N 128°0E 37 D7
Weddell Abyssal Plain S. Ocean 65°0S 20°0W 5 C2
Weddell I. Falk. Is. 51°50S 61°0W 96 G4
Weddell Sea Antarctica 72°30S 40°0W 5 D1
Wedderburn Australia 36°26S 143°33E 63 F3
Wedgeport Canada 43°44N 65°59W 73 D6
Wedza Zimbabwe 18°40S 31°33E 55 F3
Wee Waa Australia 30°11S 149°26E 63 E4
Weed U.S.A. 41°25N 122°23W 76 F2
Weed Heights U.S.A. 38°59N 119°13W 78 G7
Weedsport U.S.A. 43°2N 76°33W 83 C8
Weedville U.S.A. 41°17N 78°30W 82 E6
Weenen S. Africa 28°48S 30°7E 57 D5
Weert Neths. 51°15N 5°43E 15 C5
Wei He → Hebei, China 36°10N 115°45E 34 F8
Wei He → Shaanxi, China 34°38N 110°15E 34 G6
Weichang China 41°58N 117°49E 35 D9
Weichuan China 34°20N 113°59E 34 G7
Weiden Germany 49°41N 12°10E 16 D7
Weifang China 36°44N 119°7E 35 F10
Weihai China 37°30N 122°6E 35 F12
Weimar Germany 50°58N 11°19E 16 C6
Weinan China 34°31N 109°29E 34 G5
Weipa Australia 12°40S 141°50E 62 A3
Weir → Australia 28°20S 149°50E 63 D4
Weir → Canada 56°54N 93°21W 71 B10
Weir River Canada 56°49N 94°6W 71 B10
Weirton U.S.A. 40°24N 80°35W 82 F4
Weiser U.S.A. 44°15N 116°58W 76 D5
Weishan China 34°47N 117°5E 35 G9
Weiyuan China 35°7N 104°10E 34 G3
Wejherowo Poland 54°35N 18°12E 17 A10
Wekusko L. Canada 54°40N 99°50W 71 C9
Welch U.S.A. 37°26N 81°35W 81 G13
Welford △ Australia 25°5S 143°16E 62 D3
Welkom S. Africa 28°0S 26°46E 56 D4
Welland Canada 43°0N 79°15W 82 D5
Welland → U.K. 52°51N 0°5W 13 E7
Wellesley Is. Australia 16°42S 139°30E 62 B2
Wellingborough U.K. 52°19N 0°41W 13 E7
Wellington Australia 32°35S 148°59E 63 E4
Wellington Canada 43°57N 77°20W 82 C7
Wellington N.Z. 41°19S 174°46E 59 D5
Wellington S. Africa 33°38S 19°1E 56 E2
Wellington Somst., U.K. 50°58N 3°13W 13 G4
Wellington Telford & Wrekin, U.K. 52°42N 2°30W 13 E5
Wellington Colo., U.S.A. 40°42N 105°0W 76 F11
Wellington Kans., U.S.A. 37°16N 97°24W 80 G5
Wellington Nev., U.S.A. 38°45N 119°23W 78 G7
Wellington Ohio, U.S.A. 41°10N 82°13W 82 E2
Wellington Tex., U.S.A. 34°51N 100°13W 84 D4
Wellington, I. Chile 49°30S 75°0W 96 F2
Wellington, L. Australia 38°6S 147°20E 63 F4
Wellington Chan. Canada 75°0N 93°0W 69 B10
Wells U.K. 51°13N 2°39W 13 F5
Wells Maine, U.S.A. 43°20N 70°35W 83 C14
Wells N.Y., U.S.A. 43°24N 74°17W 83 C10
Wells Nev., U.S.A. 41°7N 114°58W 76 F6
Wells, L. Australia 26°44S 123°15E 61 E3
Wells, Mt. Australia 17°25S 127°8E 60 C4
Wells Gray ⌂ Canada 52°30N 120°15W 70 C4
Wells-next-the-Sea U.K. 52°57N 0°51E 12 E8
Wells River U.S.A. 44°9N 72°4W 83 B12
Wellsboro U.S.A. 41°45N 77°18W 82 E7
Wellsburg U.S.A. 40°16N 80°37W 82 F4
Wellsville N.Y., U.S.A. 42°7N 77°57W 82 D7
Wellsville Ohio, U.S.A. 40°36N 80°39W 82 F4
Wellsville Utah, U.S.A. 41°38N 111°56W 76 F8
Wellton U.S.A. 32°40N 114°8W 77 K6
Wels Austria 48°9N 14°1E 16 D8
Welshpool U.K. 52°39N 3°8W 13 E4
Welwyn Garden City U.K. 51°48N 0°12W 13 F7
Wem U.K. 52°52N 2°44W 12 E5
Wembere → Tanzania 4°10S 34°15E 54 C3
Wemindji Canada 53°0N 78°49W 72 B4
Wemyss Canada 44°52N 76°23W 83 B8
Wen Xian China 34°55N 113°5E 34 G7
Wenatchee U.S.A. 47°25N 120°19W 76 C3
Wenchang China 19°38N 110°42E 38 C8
Wenchi Ghana 7°46N 2°8W 50 G5
Wenchow = Wenzhou China 28°0N 120°38E 33 D7
Wenden U.S.A. 33°49N 113°33W 79 M13
Wendeng China 37°15N 122°5E 35 F12
Wendesi Indonesia 2°30S 134°17E 37 E8
Wendover U.S.A. 40°44N 114°2W 76 F6
Wenlock → Australia 12°2S 141°55E 62 A3
Wenshan China 23°20N 104°18E 32 D5
Wenshang China 35°45N 116°30E 34 G9
Wenshui China 37°26N 112°1E 34 F7
Wensleydale U.K. 54°17N 2°0W 12 C6
Wensu China 41°15N 80°10E 32 B3
Wensum → U.K. 52°40N 1°15E 12 E8
Wentworth Australia 34°2S 141°54E 63 E3
Wentzel L. Canada 59°2N 114°28W 70 B6
Wenut Indonesia 3°11S 133°19E 37 E8
Wenxi China 35°20N 111°10E 34 G6
Wenxian China 32°43N 104°36E 34 H3
Wenzhou China 28°0N 120°38E 33 D7
Weott U.S.A. 40°20N 123°55W 76 F2
Wepener S. Africa 29°42S 27°3E 56 D4
Werda Botswana 25°24S 23°15E 56 D3
Weri Indonesia 3°10S 132°38E 37 E8
Werra → Germany 51°24N 9°39E 16 C5
Werrimull Australia 34°25S 141°38E 63 E3
Werris Creek Australia 31°18S 150°38E 63 E5
Weser → Germany 53°36N 8°28E 16 B5
Wesiri Indonesia 7°30S 126°30E 37 F7
Weslaco U.S.A. 26°10N 97°58W 84 H6
Weslemkoon L. Canada 45°2N 77°25W 82 A7
Wesleyville Canada 49°9N 53°33W 73 C9
Wesleyville U.S.A. 42°9N 80°1W 82 D4
Wessel, C. Australia 10°59S 136°46E 62 A2
Wessel Is. Australia 11°10S 136°45E 62 A2
Wessington Springs U.S.A. 44°5N 98°34W 80 C4
West U.S.A. 31°48N 97°6W 84 F6
West → U.S.A. 42°52N 72°33W 83 D12
West Allis U.S.A. 43°1N 88°0W 80 D9
West Antarctica Antarctica 80°0S 90°0W 5 D15
West Baines → Australia 15°38S 129°59E 60 C4
West Bank ■ Asia 32°6N 35°13E 46 C4
West Bend U.S.A. 43°25N 88°11W 80 D9
West Bengal □ India 23°0N 88°0E 43 H13
West Berkshire □ U.K. 51°25N 1°17W 13 F6
West Beskids = Západné Beskydy Europe 49°30N 19°0E 17 D10
West Branch U.S.A. 44°17N 84°14W 81 C11
West Branch Susquehanna → U.S.A. 40°53N 76°48W 83 F8
West Bromwich U.K. 52°32N 1°59W 13 E6
West Burra U.K. 60°5N 1°21W 11 A7
West Canada Cr. → U.S.A. 43°1N 74°58W 83 C10
West Caroline Basin Pac. Oc. 4°0N 138°0E 64 G5

West Chazy U.S.A. 44°49N 73°28W 83 B11
West Chester U.S.A. 39°58N 75°36W 83 G9
West Coast ⌂ Namibia 21°53S 14°14E 56 C1
West Coast △ S. Africa 33°13S 18°0E 56 E2
West Columbia U.S.A. 29°9N 95°39W 84 G7
West Covina U.S.A. 34°4N 117°54W 79 L9
West Des Moines U.S.A. 41°35N 93°43W 80 E7
West Dunbartonshire □ U.K. 55°59N 4°30W 11 F4
West End Bahamas 26°41N 78°58W 88 A4
West Falkland Falk. Is. 51°40S 60°0W 96 G4
West Fargo U.S.A. 46°52N 96°54W 80 B5
West Fiji Basin Pac. Oc. 17°0S 173°0E 64 J9
West Fjord = Vestfjorden Norway 67°55N 14°0E 8 C16
West Fork Trinity → U.S.A. 32°48N 96°54W 84 E6
West Frankfort U.S.A. 37°54N 88°55W 80 G9
West Grand L. U.S.A. 45°14N 67°51W 81 C20
West Hartford U.S.A. 41°45N 72°44W 83 E12
West Haven U.S.A. 41°17N 72°57W 83 E12
West Hazleton U.S.A. 40°58N 76°0W 83 F9
West Helena U.S.A. 34°33N 90°38W 85 D9
West Hurley U.S.A. 41°59N 74°7W 83 E10
West Ice Shelf Antarctica 67°0S 85°0E 5 C7
West Indies Cent. Amer. 15°0N 65°0W 89 D7
West Jordan U.S.A. 40°36N 111°56W 76 F8
West Lamma Channel China 22°14N 114°4E 33 G11
West Linn U.S.A. 45°21N 122°36W 78 E4
West Lorne Canada 42°36N 81°36W 82 D3
West Lothian □ U.K. 55°54N 3°36W 11 F5
West Lunga → Zambia 13°6S 24°39E 55 E1
West MacDonnell △ Australia 23°38S 132°59E 60 D5
West Mariana Basin Pac. Oc. 15°0N 137°0E 64 F5
West Memphis U.S.A. 35°8N 90°10W 85 D9
West Midlands □ U.K. 52°26N 2°0W 13 E6
West Mifflin U.S.A. 40°21N 79°52W 82 F5
West Milford U.S.A. 41°8N 74°22W 83 E10
West Milton U.S.A. 41°1N 76°50W 82 E8
West Monroe U.S.A. 32°31N 92°9W 84 E8
West Newton U.S.A. 40°14N 79°46W 82 F5
West Nicholson Zimbabwe 21°2S 29°20E 55 G2
West Odessa U.S.A. 31°50N 102°30W 84 F3
West Palm Beach U.S.A. 26°43N 80°3W 85 H14
West Plains U.S.A. 36°44N 91°51W 80 G8
West Point Miss., U.S.A. 33°36N 88°39W 85 E10
West Point N.Y., U.S.A. 41°24N 73°58W 83 E11
West Point Nebr., U.S.A. 41°51N 96°43W 80 E5
West Point Va., U.S.A. 37°32N 76°48W 81 G15
West Point L. U.S.A. 33°8N 85°0W 85 E12
West Pt. = Ouest, Pte. de l' Canada 49°52N 64°40W 73 C7
West Pt. Australia 35°1S 135°56E 63 F2
West Road → Canada 53°18N 122°53W 70 C4
West Rutland U.S.A. 43°36N 73°3W 83 C11
West Schelde = Westerschelde → Neths. 51°25N 3°25E 15 C3
West Seneca U.S.A. 42°51N 78°48W 82 D6
West Siberian Plain Russia 62°0N 75°0E 26 B9
West Sussex □ U.K. 50°55N 0°30W 13 G7
West-Terschelling Neths. 53°22N 5°13E 15 A5
West Valley City U.S.A. 40°42N 111°58W 76 F8
West Virginia □ U.S.A. 38°45N 80°30W 81 F13
West-Vlaanderen □ Belgium 51°0N 3°0E 15 D2
West Walker → U.S.A. 38°54N 119°9W 78 G7
West Wyalong Australia 33°56S 147°10E 63 E4
West Yellowstone U.S.A. 44°40N 111°6W 76 D8
West Yorkshire □ U.K. 53°45N 1°40W 12 D6
Westall, Pt. Australia 32°55S 134°4E 63 E1
Westbrook U.S.A. 43°41N 70°22W 81 D18
Westbury Australia 41°30S 146°51E 63 G4
Westby U.S.A. 48°52N 104°3W 76 B11
Westend U.S.A. 35°42N 117°24W 79 K9
Westerland Germany 54°54N 8°17E 16 A5
Westerly U.S.A. 41°22N 71°50W 83 E13
Western □ Kenya 0°30N 34°30E 54 B3
Western □ Zambia 15°0S 24°4E 55 F1
Western Australia □ Australia 25°0S 118°0E 61 E2
Western Cape □ S. Africa 34°0S 20°0E 56 E3
Western Dvina = Daugava → Latvia 57°4N 24°3E 9 H21
Western Ghats India 14°0N 75°0E 40 N9
Western Isles □ U.K. 57°30N 7°10W 11 D1
Western Sahara ■ Africa 25°0N 13°0W 50 D3
Western Samoa = Samoa ■ Pac. Oc. 14°0S 172°0W 59 b
Western Sierra Madre = Madre Occidental, Sierra Mexico 27°0N 107°0W 86 B3
Westernport U.S.A. 39°29N 79°3W 81 F14
Westerschelde → Neths. 51°25N 3°25E 15 C3
Westerwald Germany 50°38N 7°56E 16 C4
Westfield Mass., U.S.A. 42°7N 72°45W 83 D12
Westfield N.Y., U.S.A. 42°20N 79°35W 82 D5
Westfield Pa., U.S.A. 41°55N 77°32W 82 E7
Westhill U.K. 57°9N 2°19W 11 D6
Westhope U.S.A. 48°55N 101°1W 80 A3
Westland △ N.Z. 43°16S 170°16E 59 E2
Westland Bight N.Z. 42°55S 170°5E 59 E3
Westlock Canada 54°9N 113°55W 70 C6
Westmar Australia 27°55S 149°44E 63 D4
Westmeath □ Ireland 53°33N 7°34W 10 C4
Westminster Calif., U.S.A. 33°45N 118°0W 79 M8
Westminster Colo., U.S.A. 39°50N 105°2W 76 G11
Westminster Md., U.S.A. 39°34N 76°59W 81 F15
Westmont U.S.A. 40°19N 78°58W 82 F6
Westmoreland Barbados 13°13N 59°37W 89 g
Westmorland U.S.A. 33°2N 115°37W 79 M11
Weston Oreg., U.S.A. 45°49N 118°26W 76 D4
Weston W. Va., U.S.A. 39°2N 80°28W 81 F13
Weston I. Canada 52°33N 79°36W 72 B4
Weston-super-Mare U.K. 51°21N 2°58W 13 F5
Westover U.S.A. 40°45N 78°40W 82 F6
Westport Canada 44°40N 76°25W 83 B8
Westport Ireland 53°48N 9°31W 10 C2
Westport N.Z. 41°46S 171°37E 59 D3
Westport N.Y., U.S.A. 44°11N 73°26W 83 B11
Westport Oreg., U.S.A. 46°8N 123°23W 78 D3
Westport Wash., U.S.A. 46°53N 124°6W 78 D2
Westray Canada 53°36N 101°24W 71 C8
Westray U.K. 59°18N 3°0W 11 B5
Westree Canada 47°26N 81°34W 72 C3
Westville U.S.A. 39°8N 120°42W 78 F6
Westwood U.S.A. 40°18N 121°0W 76 F3
Wetar Indonesia 7°48S 126°30E 37 F7
Wetaskiwin Canada 52°55N 113°24W 70 C6
Wete Tanzania 5°4S 39°43E 52 F7
Wetherby U.K. 53°56N 1°23W 12 D6
Wethersfield U.S.A. 41°42N 72°40W 83 E12
Wetteren Belgium 51°0N 3°53E 15 D3
Wetzlar Germany 50°32N 8°31E 16 C5
Wewoka U.S.A. 35°9N 96°30W 84 D6
Wexford Ireland 52°20N 6°28W 10 D5
Wexford □ Ireland 52°20N 6°25W 10 D5
Wexford Harbour Ireland 52°20N 6°25W 10 D5
Weyburn Canada 49°40N 103°50W 71 D8
Weymouth Canada 44°30N 66°1W 73 D6
Weymouth U.K. 50°37N 2°28W 13 G5
Weymouth U.S.A. 42°13N 70°58W 83 D14
Weymouth, C. Australia 12°37S 143°27E 62 A3
Wha Ti Canada 63°8N 117°16W 68 C8
Whakaari = White I. N.Z. 37°30S 177°13E 59 B6
Whakatane N.Z. 37°57S 177°1E 59 B6
Whale → Canada 58°15N 67°40W 73 A6
Whale Cove Canada 62°10N 92°34W 71 A10
Whales, B. of Antarctica 78°0S 160°0W 5 D12
Whalsay U.K. 60°22N 0°59W 11 A8
Whangamata N.Z. 37°12S 175°53E 59 B5
Whangamomona N.Z. 39°8S 174°44E 59 C5
Whanganui △ N.Z. 39°17S 174°53E 59 C5
Whangarei N.Z. 35°43S 174°21E 59 A5
Whangarei Harb. N.Z. 35°45S 174°28E 59 A5
Wharekauri = Chatham Is. Pac. Oc. 44°0S 176°40W 64 M10
Wharfe → U.K. 53°51N 1°9W 12 D6
Wharfedale U.K. 54°6N 2°1W 12 C5
Wharton N.J., U.S.A. 40°54N 74°35W 83 F10
Wharton Pa., U.S.A. 41°31N 78°1W 82 E6
Wharton Tex., U.S.A. 29°19N 96°6W 84 G6
Wharton Basin Ind. Oc. 22°0S 92°0E 64 K1
Wheatland Calif., U.S.A. 39°1N 121°25W 78 F5
Wheatland Wyo., U.S.A. 42°3N 104°58W 76 E11
Wheatley Canada 42°6N 82°27W 82 D2
Wheaton Md., U.S.A. 39°3N 77°3W 81 F15
Wheaton Minn., U.S.A. 45°48N 96°30W 80 C5
Wheelbarrow Pk. U.S.A. 37°26N 116°5W 78 H10
Wheeler Oreg., U.S.A. 45°41N 123°53W 76 D2
Wheeler Tex., U.S.A. 35°27N 100°16W 84 D4
Wheeler → Canada 57°2N 67°13W 73 A6
Wheeler L. U.S.A. 34°48N 87°23W 85 D11
Wheeler Pk. N. Mex., U.S.A. 36°34N 105°25W 77 H11
Wheeler Pk. Nev., U.S.A. 38°57N 114°15W 76 G6
Wheeler Ridge U.S.A. 35°0N 118°57W 79 L8
Wheelersburg U.S.A. 38°44N 82°51W 81 F12
Wheeling U.S.A. 40°4N 80°43W 82 F4
Whernside U.K. 54°14N 2°24W 12 C5
Whiddy I. Ireland 51°41N 9°31W 10 E2
Whim Creek Australia 20°50S 117°49E 60 D2
Whiskey Jack L. Canada 58°23N 101°55W 71 B8
Whiskeytown-Shasta-Trinity ⌂ U.S.A. 40°45N 122°15W 76 F2
Whistleduck Cr. → Australia 20°15S 135°18E 62 C2
Whistler Canada 50°7N 122°58W 70 C4
Whitby Canada 43°52N 78°56W 82 C6
Whitby U.K. 54°29N 0°37W 12 C7
White → Ark., U.S.A. 33°57N 91°5W 84 E9
White → Ind., U.S.A. 38°25N 87°45W 80 F10
White → S. Dak., U.S.A. 43°42N 99°27W 80 D4
White → Tex., U.S.A. 33°14N 100°56W 84 E4
White → Utah, U.S.A. 40°4N 109°41W 76 F9
White → Vt., U.S.A. 43°37N 72°20W 83 C12
White → Wash., U.S.A. 47°12N 122°15W 78 C4
White, L. Australia 21°9S 128°56E 60 D4
White B. Canada 50°0N 56°35W 73 C8
White Bird U.S.A. 45°46N 116°18W 76 D5
White Butte U.S.A. 46°23N 103°18W 80 B2
White City U.S.A. 42°26N 122°51W 76 E2
White Cliffs Australia 30°50S 143°10E 63 E3
White Hall U.S.A. 39°26N 90°24W 80 F8
White Haven U.S.A. 41°4N 75°47W 83 E9
White Horse, Vale of U.K. 51°37N 1°30W 13 F6
White I. N.Z. 37°30S 177°13E 59 B6
White L. Canada 45°18N 76°31W 83 A8
White L. U.S.A. 29°44N 92°30W 84 G8
White Lake Canada 45°21N 76°29W 83 A8
White Mountain Peak U.S.A. 37°38N 118°15W 77 H4
White Mts. Calif., U.S.A. 37°30N 118°15W 78 H8
White Mts. N.H., U.S.A. 44°15N 71°15W 83 B13
White Mts. △ Australia 20°43S 145°12E 62 C4
White Nile = Nil el Abyad → Sudan 15°38N 32°31E 51 E12
White Otter L. Canada 49°5N 91°55W 72 C1
White Pass U.S.A. 46°38N 121°24W 78 D5
White Plains U.S.A. 41°2N 73°46W 83 E11
White River Canada 48°35N 85°20W 72 C2
White River S. Africa 25°20S 31°0E 57 D5
White River U.S.A. 43°34N 100°45W 80 D3
White Rock Canada 49°2N 122°48W 78 A4
White Rock U.S.A. 35°50N 106°12W 77 J10
White Russia = Belarus ■ Europe 53°30N 27°0E 17 B14
White Sands ⌂ U.S.A. 32°46N 106°20W 77 K10
White Sea = Beloye More Russia 66°30N 38°0E 8 C25
White Sulphur Springs Mont., U.S.A. 46°33N 110°54W 76 C8
White Sulphur Springs W. Va., U.S.A. 37°48N 80°18W 81 G13
White Swan U.S.A. 46°23N 120°44W 78 D6
Whitecliffs N.Z. 43°26S 171°55E 59 E3
Whitecourt Canada 54°10N 115°45W 70 C5
Whiteface Mt. U.S.A. 44°22N 73°54W 83 B11
Whitefield U.S.A. 44°23N 71°37W 83 B13
Whitefish U.S.A. 48°25N 114°20W 76 B6
Whitefish B. U.S.A. 46°40N 84°55W 72 C3
Whitefish L. Canada 62°41N 106°48W 71 A7
Whitefish Pt. U.S.A. 46°45N 84°59W 81 B11
Whitegull, L. = Goélands, L. aux Canada 55°27N 64°17W 73 A7
Whitehall Mich., U.S.A. 43°24N 86°21W 80 D10
Whitehall Mont., U.S.A. 45°52N 112°6W 76 D7
Whitehall N.Y., U.S.A. 43°33N 73°24W 83 C11
Whitehall Wis., U.S.A. 44°22N 91°19W 80 C8
Whitehaven U.K. 54°33N 3°35W 12 C4
Whitehorse Canada 60°43N 135°3W 70 A1
Whitemark Australia 40°7S 148°3E 63 G4
Whiteriver U.S.A. 33°50N 109°58W 77 K9
Whitesand → Canada 60°9N 115°45W 70 A5
Whitesands S. Africa 34°23S 20°50E 56 E3
Whitesboro N.Y., U.S.A. 43°7N 75°18W 83 C9
Whitesboro Tex., U.S.A. 33°39N 96°54W 84 E6
Whiteshell ⌂ Canada 50°0N 95°40W 71 D9
Whiteville U.S.A. 34°20N 78°42W 85 D15
Whitewater U.S.A. 42°50N 88°44W 80 D9
Whitewater Baldy U.S.A. 33°20N 108°39W 77 K9
Whitewater L. Canada 50°50N 89°10W 72 B2
Whitewood Australia 21°28S 143°30E 62 C3
Whitewood Canada 50°20N 102°20W 71 C8
Whithorn U.K. 54°44N 4°26W 11 G4
Whitianga N.Z. 36°47S 175°41E 59 B5
Whitman U.S.A. 42°5N 70°56W 83 D14
Whitney Canada 45°31N 78°14W 82 A6
Whitney, Mt. U.S.A. 36°35N 118°18W 78 J8
Whitney Point U.S.A. 42°20N 75°58W 83 D9
Whitstable U.K. 51°21N 1°3E 13 F9
Whitsunday I. Australia 20°15S 149°4E 62 J7
Whitsunday Islands △ Australia 20°15S 149°0E 62 J7
Whitsunday Passage Australia 20°16S 148°51E 62 J6
Whittier U.S.A. 33°58N 118°2W 79 M8
Whittlesea Australia 37°27S 145°9E 63 F4
Wholdaia L. Canada 60°43N 104°20W 71 A8
Whyalla Australia 33°2S 137°30E 63 E2
Wiang Kosai △ Thailand 17°54N 99°29E 38 D2
Wiang Sa Thailand 18°34N 100°45E 38 C3
Wiarton Canada 44°40N 81°10W 82 B3
Wiay U.K. 57°24N 7°13W 11 D1
Wibaux U.S.A. 46°59N 104°11W 76 C11
Wichian Buri Thailand 15°39N 101°7E 38 E3
Wichita U.S.A. 37°42N 97°20W 80 G5
Wichita Falls U.S.A. 33°54N 98°30W 84 E5
Wick U.K. 58°26N 3°5W 11 C5
Wickenburg U.S.A. 33°58N 112°44W 77 K7
Wickepin Australia 32°50S 117°30E 61 F2
Wickham Australia 20°42S 117°11E 60 D2
Wickham, C. Australia 39°35S 143°57E 63 F3
Wickliffe U.S.A. 41°36N 81°28W 82 E3
Wicklow Ireland 52°59N 6°3W 10 D5
Wicklow □ Ireland 52°57N 6°25W 10 D5
Wicklow Hd. Ireland 52°58N 6°0W 10 D6
Wicklow Mts. Ireland 52°58N 6°26W 10 C5
Wicklow Mts. △ Ireland 53°6N 6°21W 10 C5
Widgeegoara Cr. → Australia 28°51S 146°34E 63 D4
Widgiemooltha Australia 31°30S 121°34E 61 F3
Widnes U.K. 53°23N 2°45W 12 D5
Wieluń Poland 51°15N 18°34E 17 C10
Wien Austria 48°12N 16°22E 16 D9
Wiener Neustadt Austria 47°49N 16°16E 16 E9
Wiesbaden Germany 50°4N 8°14E 16 C5
Wigan U.K. 53°33N 2°38W 12 D5
Wiggins Colo., U.S.A. 40°14N 104°4W 76 F11
Wiggins Miss., U.S.A. 30°51N 89°8W 85 F10
Wight, I. of U.K. 50°41N 1°17W 13 G6
Wigston U.K. 52°35N 1°6W 13 E6
Wigton U.K. 54°50N 3°10W 12 C4
Wigtown U.K. 54°53N 4°27W 11 G4
Wigtown B. U.K. 54°46N 4°15W 11 G4
Wilber U.S.A. 40°29N 96°58W 80 E5
Wilberforce Canada 45°2N 78°13W 82 A6
Wilberforce, C. Australia 11°54S 136°35E 62 A2
Wilburton U.S.A. 34°55N 95°19W 84 D7
Wilcannia Australia 31°30S 143°26E 63 E3
Wilcox U.S.A. 41°35N 78°41W 82 E6
Wildrose U.S.A. 36°14N 117°11W 79 J9
Wildspitze Austria 46°53N 10°53E 16 E6
Wilge → S. Africa 27°3S 28°20E 57 D4
Wilhelm II Coast Antarctica 68°0S 90°0E 5 C7
Wilhelmshaven Germany 53°31N 8°7E 16 B5
Wilhelmstal Namibia 21°58S 16°21E 56 C2
Wilkes-Barre U.S.A. 41°15N 75°53W 83 E9
Wilkes Land Antarctica 69°0S 120°0E 5 D9
Wilkie Canada 52°27N 108°42W 71 C7
Wilkinsburg U.S.A. 40°26N 79°52W 82 F5
Wilkinson Lakes Australia 29°40S 132°39E 61 E5
Willandra Creek → Australia 33°22S 145°52E 63 E4
Willapa B. U.S.A. 46°40N 124°0W 76 C1
Willapa Hills U.S.A. 46°35N 123°25W 78 D3
Willard U.S.A. 41°3N 82°44W 82 E2
Willcox U.S.A. 32°15N 109°50W 77 K9
Willemstad Neth. Ant. 12°5N 68°55W 89 D6
William → Canada 59°8N 109°19W 71 B7
William 'Bill' Dannelly Res. U.S.A. 32°6N 87°24W 85 E11
William Creek Australia 28°58S 136°22E 63 D2
Williams Australia 33°2S 116°52E 61 F2
Williams Ariz., U.S.A. 35°15N 112°11W 77 J7
Williams Calif., U.S.A. 39°9N 122°9W 78 F4
Williams Harbour Canada 52°33N 55°47W 73 B8
Williams Lake Canada 52°10N 122°10W 70 C4
Williamsburg Ky., U.S.A. 36°44N 84°10W 81 G11
Williamsburg Pa., U.S.A. 40°28N 78°12W 82 F6
Williamsburg Va., U.S.A. 37°16N 76°43W 81 G15
Williamson N.Y., U.S.A. 43°14N 77°11W 82 C7
Williamson W. Va., U.S.A. 37°41N 82°17W 81 G12
Williamsport U.S.A. 41°15N 77°1W 82 E7
Williamston U.S.A. 35°51N 77°4W 85 D16
Williamstown Australia 37°51S 144°52E 63 F3
Williamstown Ky., U.S.A. 38°38N 84°34W 81 F11
Williamstown Mass., U.S.A. 42°43N 73°12W 83 D11
Williamstown N.Y., U.S.A. 43°26N 75°53W 83 C9
Willimantic U.S.A. 41°43N 72°13W 83 E12
Willingboro U.S.A. 40°3N 74°54W 81 E16
Williston S. Africa 31°20S 20°53E 56 E3
Williston Fla., U.S.A. 29°23N 82°27W 85 G13
Williston N. Dak., U.S.A. 48°9N 103°37W 80 A2
Williston L. Canada 56°0N 124°0W 70 B4
Willits U.S.A. 39°25N 123°21W 76 G2
Willmar U.S.A. 45°7N 95°3W 80 C6
Willmore Wilderness ⌂ Canada 53°45N 119°30W 70 C5
Willoughby U.S.A. 41°39N 81°24W 82 E3
Willow Bunch Canada 49°20N 105°35W 71 D7
Willow L. Canada 62°10N 119°8W 70 A5
Willow Wall, The China 42°10N 122°0E 35 C12
Willowick U.S.A. 41°38N 81°28W 82 E3
Willowlake → Canada 62°42N 123°8W 70 A4
Willowmore S. Africa 33°15S 23°30E 56 E3
Willows U.S.A. 39°31N 122°12W 78 F4
Willowvale = Gatyana S. Africa 32°16S 28°31E 57 E4
Wills, L. Australia 21°25S 128°51E 60 D4
Wills Cr. → Australia 22°43S 140°2E 62 C3
Willsboro U.S.A. 44°21N 73°24W 83 B11
Willunga Australia 35°15S 138°30E 63 F2
Wilmette U.S.A. 42°4N 87°42W 80 D10
Wilmington Australia 32°39S 138°7E 63 E2
Wilmington Del., U.S.A. 39°45N 75°33W 81 F16
Wilmington N.C., U.S.A. 34°14N 77°55W 85 D16
Wilmington Ohio, U.S.A. 39°27N 83°50W 81 F12
Wilmington Vt., U.S.A. 42°52N 72°52W 83 D12
Wilmslow U.K. 53°19N 2°13W 12 D5
Wilpena Cr. → Australia 31°25S 139°29E 63 E2
Wilsall U.S.A. 45°59N 110°38W 76 D8
Wilson N.C., U.S.A. 35°44N 77°55W 85 D16
Wilson N.Y., U.S.A. 43°19N 78°50W 82 C6
Wilson Pa., U.S.A. 40°41N 75°15W 83 F9
Wilson → Australia 16°48S 128°16E 60 C4
Wilson Bluff Australia 31°41S 129°0E 61 F4
Wilson Inlet Australia 35°0S 117°22E 61 G2
Wilsons Promontory Australia 38°59S 146°23E 63 F4
Wilton U.S.A. 47°10N 100°47W 80 B3
Wilton → Australia 14°45S 134°33E 62 A1
Wiltshire □ U.K. 51°18N 1°53W 13 F6
Wiltz Lux. 49°57N 5°55E 15 E5
Wiluna Australia 26°36S 120°14E 61 E3
Wimborne Minster U.K. 50°48N 1°59W 13 G6
Wimmera → Australia 36°8S 141°56E 63 F3
Winam G. Kenya 0°20S 34°15E 54 C3
Winburg S. Africa 28°30S 27°2E 56 D4
Winchendon U.S.A. 42°41N 72°3W 83 D12
Winchester U.K. 51°4N 1°18W 13 F6
Winchester Conn., U.S.A. 41°53N 73°9W 83 E11
Winchester Idaho, U.S.A. 46°14N 116°38W 76 C5
Winchester Ind., U.S.A. 40°10N 84°59W 81 E11
Winchester Ky., U.S.A. 37°59N 84°11W 81 G11
Winchester N.H., U.S.A. 42°46N 72°23W 83 D12
Winchester Nev., U.S.A. 36°7N 115°7W 79 J11
Winchester Tenn., U.S.A. 35°11N 86°7W 85 D11
Winchester Va., U.S.A. 39°11N 78°10W 81 F14
Wind → U.S.A. 43°12N 108°12W 76 E9
Wind Cave △ U.S.A. 43°32N 103°17W 80 D2
Wind River Range U.S.A. 43°0N 109°30W 76 E9
Windau = Ventspils Latvia 57°25N 21°32E 9 H19
Windber U.S.A. 40°14N 78°50W 82 F6
Winder U.S.A. 34°0N 83°45W 85 D13
Windermere U.K. 54°23N 2°55W 12 C5
Windhoek Namibia 22°35S 17°4E 56 C2
Windjana Gorge △ Australia 17°51S 125°0E 60 C3
Windom U.S.A. 43°52N 95°7W 80 D6
Windorah Australia 25°24S 142°36E 62 D3
Window Rock U.S.A. 35°41N 109°3W 77
Windrush → U.K. 51°43N 1°24W 13 F
Windsor Australia 33°37S 150°50E 63
Windsor N.S., Canada 44°59N 64°5W 73 D
Windsor Ont., Canada 42°18N 83°0W 82 D
Windsor U.K. 51°29N 0°36W 13 F
Windsor Calif., U.S.A. 38°33N 122°49W 76 G
Windsor Colo., U.S.A. 40°29N 104°54W 76 F
Windsor Conn., U.S.A. 41°50N 72°39W 83 E
Windsor Mo., U.S.A. 38°32N 93°31W 80 F
Windsor N.Y., U.S.A. 42°5N 75°37W 83 D
Windsor Vt., U.S.A. 43°29N 72°24W 83 C
Windsor & Maidenhead □ U.K. 51°29N 0°40W 13 F
Windsorton S. Africa 28°16S 24°44E 56 D
Windward Is. W. Indies 13°0N 61°0W 89 D
Windward Passage = Vientos, Paso de los Caribbean 20°0N 74°0W 89 C
Winefred L. Canada 55°30N 110°30W 71 B
Winfield U.S.A. 37°15N 96°59W 80 G
Wingate Mts. Australia 14°25S 130°40E 60 B
Wingham Australia 31°48S 152°22E 63
Wingham Canada 43°55N 81°20W 82 C
Winisk → Canada 55°17N 85°5W 72 A
Winisk L. Canada 52°55N 87°22W 72 B
Wink U.S.A. 31°45N 103°9W 84 F
Winkler Canada 49°10N 97°56W 71 D
Winlock U.S.A. 46°30N 122°56W 78 D
Winneba Ghana 5°25N 0°36W 50 G
Winnebago, L. U.S.A. 44°0N 88°26W 80 D
Winnecke Cr. → Australia 18°35S 131°34E 60 C
Winnemucca U.S.A. 40°58N 117°44W 76 F
Winnemucca L. U.S.A. 40°7N 119°21W 76 F
Winner U.S.A. 43°22N 99°52W 80 D
Winnett U.S.A. 47°0N 108°21W 76 C
Winnfield U.S.A. 31°56N 92°38W 84
Winnibigoshish, L. U.S.A. 47°27N 94°13W 80 B
Winnipeg Canada 49°54N 97°9W 71 D
Winnipeg → Canada 50°38N 96°19W 71 C
Winnipeg, L. Canada 52°0N 97°0W 71 C
Winnipeg Beach Canada 50°30N 96°58W 71 C
Winnipegosis Canada 51°39N 99°55W 71
Winnipegosis L. Canada 52°30N 100°0W 71
Winnipesaukee, L. U.S.A. 43°38N 71°21W 83 C
Winnisquam L. U.S.A. 43°33N 71°31W 83 C
Winnsboro La., U.S.A. 32°10N 91°43W 84
Winnsboro S.C., U.S.A. 34°23N 81°5W 85 D
Winnsboro Tex., U.S.A. 32°58N 95°17W 84
Winokapau, L. Canada 53°15N 62°50W 73
Winona Minn., U.S.A. 44°3N 91°39W 80 C
Winona Miss., U.S.A. 33°29N 89°44W 85 E
Winooski U.S.A. 44°29N 73°11W 83 B
Winooski → U.S.A. 44°32N 73°17W 83 B
Winschoten Neths. 53°9N 7°3E 15 A
Winsford U.K. 53°12N 2°31W 12 D
Winslow = Bainbridge Island U.S.A. 47°38N 122°32W 78 C
Winslow U.S.A. 35°2N 110°42W 77
Winsted U.S.A. 41°55N 73°4W 83 E
Winston-Salem U.S.A. 36°6N 80°15W 85 C
Winter Garden U.S.A. 28°34N 81°35W 85 G
Winter Haven U.S.A. 28°1N 81°44W 85 G
Winter Park U.S.A. 28°36N 81°20W 85 G
Winterhaven U.S.A. 32°44N 114°38W 79 N
Winters U.S.A. 38°32N 121°58W 78
Winterset U.S.A. 41°20N 94°1W 80
Wintersville U.S.A. 40°23N 80°42W 82
Winterswijk Neths. 51°58N 6°43E 15
Winterthur Switz. 47°30N 8°44E 20
Winthrop U.S.A. 48°28N 120°10W 76
Winton Australia 22°24S 143°3E 62
Winton N.Z. 46°8S 168°20E 59
Wirrulla Australia 32°24S 134°31E 63
Wisbech U.K. 52°41N 0°9E 13
Wisconsin □ U.S.A. 44°45N 89°30W 80
Wisconsin → U.S.A. 43°0N 91°15W 80
Wisconsin Rapids U.S.A. 44°23N 89°49W 80
Wisdom U.S.A. 45°37N 113°27W 76
Wishaw U.K. 55°46N 3°54W 11
Wishek U.S.A. 46°16N 99°33W 80
Wisła → Poland 54°22N 18°55E 17 A
Wismar Germany 53°54N 11°29E 16
Wisner U.S.A. 41°59N 96°55W 80
Witbank = eMalahleni S. Africa 25°51S 29°14E 57
Witdraai S. Africa 26°58S 20°48E 56
Witham U.K. 51°48N 0°40E 13
Witham → U.K. 52°59N 0°2W 12
Withernsea U.K. 53°44N 0°1E 12
Witjira △ Australia 26°22S 135°37E 63
Witless Bay Canada 47°17N 52°50W 73
Witney U.K. 51°48N 1°28W 13
Witnossob → Namibia 23°55S 18°45E 56
Wittenberge Germany 53°0N 11°45E 16
Wittenoom Australia 22°15S 118°20E 60
Witu Kenya 2°23S 40°26E 54
Witvlei Namibia 22°23S 18°32E 56
Wiwon N. Korea 40°54N 126°3E 35 D
Wkra → Poland 52°27N 20°44E 17 B
Wlingi Indonesia 8°5S 112°25E 37 H
Włocławek Poland 52°40N 19°3E 17 B
Włodawa Poland 51°33N 23°31E 17 C
Woburn U.S.A. 42°29N 71°9W 83 D
Wodian China 32°50N 112°35E 34
Wodonga Australia 36°5S 146°50E 63
Wokam Indonesia 5°45S 134°28E 37
Woking U.K. 51°19N 0°34W 13
Wokingham U.K. 51°24N 0°49W 13
Wokingham □ U.K. 51°25N 0°51W 13
Wolf → Canada 60°17N 132°33W 70
Wolf Creek U.S.A. 47°0N 112°4W 76
Wolf L. Canada 60°24N 131°40W 70
Wolf Point U.S.A. 48°5N 105°39W 76 B

olfe I. Canada 44°7N 76°20W 83 B8
olfeboro U.S.A. 43°35N 71°13W 83 C13
olfsberg Austria 46°50N 14°52E 16 E8
olfsburg Germany 52°25N 10°48E 16 B6
olin Poland 53°50N 14°37E 16 B8
ollaston, Is. Chile 55°40S 67°30W 96 H3
ollaston L. Canada 58°7N 103°10W 71 B8
ollaston Lake Canada 58°3N 103°33W 71 B8
ollaston Pen. Canada 69°30N 115°0W 68 D8
ollongong Australia 34°25S 150°54E 63 E5
olmaransstad S. Africa 27°12S 25°59E 56 D4
olseley S. Africa 33°26S 19°7E 56 E2
olsey U.S.A. 44°25N 98°28W 80 C4
olstenholme, C.
Canada 62°35N 77°30W 66 C12
olvega Neths. 52°52N 6°0E 15 B6
olverhampton U.K. 52°35N 2°7W 13 E5
ondai Australia 26°20S 151°49E 63 D5
ongalarroo L. Australia 31°32S 144°0E 63 E3
ongan Hills Australia 30°51S 116°37E 61 F2
onju S. Korea 37°22N 127°58E 35 F14
onosari Indonesia 7°58S 110°36E 37 G14
onosobo Indonesia 7°22S 109°54E 37 G13
onowon Canada 56°44N 121°48W 70 B4
onsan N. Korea 39°11N 127°27E 35 E14
onthaggi Australia 38°37S 145°37E 63 F4
od Buffalo △ Canada 59°0N 113°41W 70 B6
od Is. Australia 16°24S 123°19E 60 C3
od L. Canada 55°17N 103°17W 71 B8
odah, I. Australia 13°27S 136°10E 62 A2
odbourne U.S.A. 41°46N 74°36W 83 E10
odbridge Canada 43°47N 79°36W 82 C5
odbridge U.K. 52°6N 1°20E 13 E9
odburn U.S.A. 45°9N 122°51W 76 D2
odenbong Australia 28°24S 152°39E 63 D5
odend Australia 37°20S 144°33E 63 F3
odford Australia 26°58S 152°47E 63 D5
odfords U.S.A. 38°47N 119°50W 78 G7
odlake U.S.A. 36°25N 119°6W 78 J7
odland Calif., U.S.A. 38°41N 121°46W 78 G5
odland Maine, U.S.A. 45°9N 67°25W 81 C20
odland Pa., U.S.A. 41°0N 78°21W 82 F6
odland Wash.,
.S.A. 45°54N 122°45W 78 E4
odland Caribou ⌂
anada 51°0N 94°45W 71 C10
odlands Singapore 1°26N 103°46E 39 d
odlands, The U.S.A. 30°9N 95°29W 84 F7
odonga Australia 36°10S 146°50E 63 F4
odridge Canada 49°20N 96°9W 71 D9
odroffe, Mt.
ustralia 26°20S 131°45E 61 E5
ods, L. Australia 17°50S 133°30E 62 B1
ods, L. of the
anada 49°15N 94°45W 71 D10
ods Bay Canada 45°8N 79°59W 82 A5
odstock Australia 19°35S 146°50E 62 B4
odstock N.B., Canada 46°11N 67°37W 73 C6
odstock Ont., Canada 43°10N 80°45W 82 C4
odstock U.K. 51°51N 1°20W 13 F6
odstock Ill., U.S.A. 42°19N 88°27W 80 D9
odstock N.Y., U.S.A. 42°2N 74°7W 83 D10
odstock Vt., U.S.A. 43°37N 72°31W 83 C12
odsville U.S.A. 44°9N 72°2W 83 B13
odview Canada 44°35N 78°8W 82 B6
odville N.Z. 40°20S 175°53E 59 D5
odville Miss., U.S.A. 31°6N 91°18W 84 F9
odville Tex., U.S.A. 30°47N 94°25W 84 F7
odward U.S.A. 36°26N 99°24W 84 C5
ody U.S.A. 35°42N 118°50W 79 K8
ody → Canada 52°31N 100°51W 71 C8
olacombe U.K. 51°10N 4°13W 13 F3
olamai, C. Australia 38°30S 145°23E 63 F4
oler U.K. 55°33N 2°1W 12 B5
olgoolga Australia 30°6S 153°11E 63 E5
omera Australia 31°5S 136°50E 63 E2
onsocket R.I., U.S.A. 42°0N 71°31W 83 E13
onsocket S. Dak.,
.S.A. 44°3N 98°17W 80 C4
oramel → Australia 25°47S 114°10E 61 E1
oramel Roadhouse
ustralia 25°45S 114°17E 61 E1
oroonooran △
ustralia 16°25S 146°1E 62 B4
oster U.S.A. 40°48N 81°56W 82 F3
rcester S. Africa 33°39S 19°27E 56 E2
rcester U.K. 52°11N 2°12W 13 E5
rcester Mass.,
.S.A. 42°16N 71°48W 83 D13
rcester N.Y., U.S.A. 42°36N 74°45W 83 D10
rcestershire □ U.K. 52°13N 2°10W 13 E5
rkington U.K. 54°39N 3°33W 12 C4
rksop U.K. 53°18N 1°7W 12 D6
rkum Neths. 52°59N 5°26E 15 B5
rland U.S.A. 44°1N 107°57W 76 D10
rms Germany 49°37N 8°21E 16 D5
rsley Canada 56°31N 119°8W 70 B5
rtham U.S.A. 31°47N 96°28W 84 F6
rthing Barbados 13°5N 59°35W 89 g
rthing U.K. 50°49N 0°21W 13 G7
rthington Minn.,
.S.A. 43°37N 95°36W 80 D6
rthington Pa., U.S.A. 40°50N 79°38W 82 F5
si Indonesia 0°15S 128°0E 37 E7
e Kenya 1°47S 37°38E 54 C4
ı-han = Wuhan
ina 30°31N 114°18E 33 C6
ısi = Wuxi China 31°33N 120°18E 33 C7
voni Indonesia 4°5S 123°5E 37 E6
ngel I. = Vrangelya, Ostrov
ıssia 71°0N 180°0E 29 B18
ngell U.S.A. 56°28N 132°23W 70 B2
ngell Mts. U.S.A. 61°30N 142°0W 68 C5
th, C. U.K. 58°38N 5°1W 11 C3
y U.S.A. 40°5N 102°13W 76 F12
kin, The U.K. 52°41N 2°32W 13 E5
ns U.S.A. 33°12N 82°23W 85 E13

Wrexham U.K. 53°3N 3°0W 12 D4
Wrexham □ U.K. 53°1N 2°58W 12 D5
Wright Fla., U.S.A. 30°27N 86°38W 85 F11
Wright Wyo., U.S.A. 43°45N 105°28W 76 E11
Wright Pt. Canada 43°48N 81°44W 82 C3
Wrightson, Mt. U.S.A. 31°42N 110°51W 77 L8
Wrightwood U.S.A. 34°22N 117°38W 79 L9
Wrigley Canada 63°16N 123°37W 68 C7
Wrocław Poland 51°5N 17°5E 17 C9
Września Poland 52°21N 17°36E 17 B9
Wu Jiang → China 29°40N 107°20E 32 D5
Wu Kau Tang China 22°30N 114°14E 33 F11
Wu'an China 36°40N 114°15E 34 F8
Wubin Australia 30°6S 116°37E 61 F2
Wubu China 37°28N 110°42E 34 F6
Wuchang China 44°55N 127°5E 35 B14
Wucheng China 37°12N 116°20E 34 F9
Wuchuan China 41°5N 111°28E 34 D6
Wudi China 37°40N 117°35E 35 F9
Wuding He → China 37°2N 110°23E 34 F6
Wudinna Australia 33°0S 135°22E 63 E2
Wudu China 33°22N 104°54E 34 H3
Wuguishan China 22°25N 113°25E 33 G9
Wugullar = Beswick
Australia 14°34S 132°53E 60 B5
Wuhai China 39°47N 106°52E 34 E4
Wuhan China 30°31N 114°18E 33 C6
Wuhe China 33°10N 117°50E 35 H9
Wuhsi = Wuxi China 31°33N 120°18E 33 C7
Wuhu China 31°22N 118°21E 33 C6
Wukari Nigeria 7°51N 9°42E 50 G7
Wulajie China 44°6N 126°33E 35 B14
Wulanbulang China 41°5N 110°55E 34 D6
Wular L. India 34°20N 74°30E 43 B6
Wulian China 35°40N 119°12E 35 G10
Wuliaru Indonesia 7°27S 131°0E 37 F8
Wulumuchi = Ürümqi
China 43°45N 87°45E 32 B3
Wundanyi Kenya 3°24S 38°22E 54 C4
Wunnummin L. Canada 52°55N 89°10W 72 B2
Wuntho Burma 23°55N 95°45E 41 H19
Wupatki ⌂ U.S.A. 35°35N 111°20W 77 J8
Wuppertal Germany 51°16N 7°12E 16 C4
Wuppertal S. Africa 32°13S 19°12E 56 E2
Wuqing China 39°23N 117°4E 35 E9
Wurtsboro U.S.A. 41°35N 74°29W 83 E10
Würzburg Germany 49°46N 9°55E 16 D5
Wushan China 34°43N 104°53E 34 G3
Wushi China 41°9N 79°13E 32 B2
Wutai China 38°40N 113°12E 34 E7
Wuting = Huimin
China 37°27N 117°28E 35 F9
Wutonghaolai China 42°50N 120°5E 35 C11
Wutongqiao China 29°22N 103°50E 32 D5
Wuwei China 37°57N 102°34E 32 C5
Wuxi China 31°33N 120°18E 33 C7
Wuxiang China 36°49N 112°50E 34 F7
Wuyang China 33°25N 113°35E 34 H7
Wuyi China 37°46N 115°56E 34 F8
Wuyi Shan China 27°0N 117°0E 33 D6
Wuyuan China 41°2N 108°20E 34 D5
Wuzhai China 38°54N 111°48E 34 E6
Wuzhi Shan China 18°45N 109°45E 38 C7
Wuzhong China 38°2N 106°12E 34 E4
Wuzhou China 23°30N 111°18E 33 D6
Wyaaba Cr. →
Australia 16°27S 141°35E 62 B3
Wyalkatchem Australia 31°8S 117°22E 61 F2
Wyalusing U.S.A. 41°40N 76°16W 83 E8
Wyandotte U.S.A. 42°12N 83°9W 81 D12
Wyandra Australia 27°12S 145°56E 63 D4
Wyangala, L. Australia 33°54S 149°0E 63 E4
Wyara, L. Australia 28°42S 144°14E 63 D3
Wycheproof Australia 36°5S 143°17E 63 F3
Wycliffe Well Australia 20°48S 134°14E 62 C1
Wye → U.K. 51°38N 2°40W 13 F5
Wyemandoo Australia 28°28S 118°29E 61 E2
Wymondham U.K. 52°35N 1°7E 13 E9
Wymore U.S.A. 40°7N 96°40W 80 E5
Wyndham Australia 15°33S 128°3E 60 C4
Wyndham N.Z. 46°20S 168°51E 59 G2
Wynne U.S.A. 35°14N 90°47W 85 D9
Wynyard Australia 41°5S 145°44E 63 G4
Wynyard Canada 51°45N 104°10W 71 C8
Wyola L. Australia 29°8S 130°17E 61 E5
Wyoming Canada 42°57N 82°7W 82 D2
Wyoming □ U.S.A. 43°0N 107°30W 76 E10
Wyomissing U.S.A. 40°20N 75°59W 83 F9
Wyong Australia 33°14S 151°24E 63 E5
Wytheville U.S.A. 36°57N 81°5W 81 G13

X

Xaafuun Somali Rep. 10°25N 51°16E 47 E5
Xaafuun, Ras Somali Rep. 10°27N 51°24E 47 E5
Xaçmaz Azerbaijan 41°31N 48°42E 19 F8
Xai-Xai Mozam. 25°6S 33°31E 57 D5
Xainza China 30°58N 88°35E 32 C3
Xalapa Mexico 19°32N 96°55W 87 D5
Xangongo Angola 16°45S 15°5E 56 B2
Xankändi Azerbaijan 39°52N 46°49E 44 B5
Xanthi Greece 41°10N 24°58E 21 D11
Xanxerê Brazil 26°53S 52°23W 95 B5
Xapuri Brazil 10°35S 68°35W 92 F5
Xar Moron He →
China 43°25N 120°35E 35 C11
Xátiva Spain 38°59N 0°32W 21 C5
Xau, L. Botswana 21°15S 24°44E 56 C3
Xavantina Brazil 21°15S 52°48W 95 A5
Xenia U.S.A. 39°41N 83°56W 81 F12
Xeropotamos →
Cyprus 34°42N 32°33E 25 E11
Xhora S. Africa 31°55S 28°38E 57 E4
Xhumo Botswana 21°7S 24°35E 56 C3
Xi Jiang → China 22°5N 113°20E 33 D6
Xi Xian China 36°41N 110°58E 34 F6
Xia Xian China 35°8N 111°12E 34 G6
Xiachengzi China 44°40N 130°18E 35 B16
Xiaguan China 25°32N 100°16E 32 D5
Xiajin China 36°56N 116°0E 34 F9
Xiamen China 24°25N 118°4E 33 D6
Xi'an China 34°15N 109°0E 34 G5
Xian Xian China 38°12N 116°6E 34 E9
Xiang Jiang → China 28°55N 112°50E 33 D6
Xiangcheng Henan,
China 33°29N 114°52E 34 H8
Xiangcheng Henan,
China 33°50N 113°27E 34 H7
Xiangfan China 32°2N 112°8E 33 C6
Xianggang = Hong Kong □
China 22°11N 114°14E 33 G11
Xianghuang Qi China 42°2N 113°50E 34 C7
Xiangning China 35°58N 110°50E 34 G6
Xiangquan China 36°30N 113°1E 34 F7
Xiangquan He = Sutlej →
Pakistan 29°23N 71°3E 42 E4
Xiangshui China 34°12N 119°33E 35 G10
Xiangtan China 27°51N 112°54E 33 D6
Xianyang China 34°20N 108°40E 34 G5
Xiao Hinggan Ling China 49°0N 127°0E 33 B7
Xiao Xian China 34°15N 116°55E 34 G9
Xiaoyi China 37°8N 111°48E 34 F6
Xiawa China 42°35N 120°38E 35 C11
Xiayi China 34°15N 116°10E 34 G9
Xichang China 27°51N 102°19E 32 D5
Xichuan China 33°0N 111°30E 34 H6
Xieng Khouang Laos 19°17N 103°25E 38 C4
Xifei He → China 32°45N 116°40E 34 H9
Xifeng Gansu, China 35°40N 107°40E 34 G4
Xifeng Liaoning, China 42°42N 124°45E 35 C13
Xifengzhen = Xifeng
China 35°40N 107°40E 34 G4
Xigazê China 29°5N 88°45E 32 D3
Xihe China 34°2N 105°20E 34 G3
Xihua China 33°45N 114°30E 34 H8
Xili Shuiku China 22°36N 113°57E 33 F10
Xiliao He → China 43°32N 123°35E 35 C12
Xilinhot China 43°52N 116°2E 34 C9
Ximana Mozam. 19°24S 33°58E 55 F3
Xin Xian = Xinzhou
China 38°22N 112°46E 34 E7
Xinavane Mozam. 25°2S 32°47E 57 D5
Xinbin China 41°40N 125°2E 35 D13
Xincun China 38°15N 117°45E 35 E9
Xing Xian China 38°27N 111°7E 34 E6
Xing'an China 25°38N 110°40E 33 D6
Xingcheng China 40°40N 120°45E 35 D11
Xinghe China 40°55N 113°55E 34 D7
Xinghua China 32°58N 119°48E 35 H10
Xinglong China 40°25N 117°30E 35 D9
Xingping China 34°20N 108°28E 34 G5
Xingtai China 37°3N 114°32E 34 F8
Xingu → Brazil 1°30S 51°53W 93 D8
Xingyang China 34°45N 112°52E 34 G7
Xinhe China 37°30N 115°15E 34 F8
Xining China 36°34N 101°40E 32 C5
Xinjiang China 35°34N 111°11E 34 G6
Xinjiang Uygur Zizhiqu □
China 42°0N 86°0E 32 C3
Xinjin = Pulandian
China 39°25N 121°58E 35 E11
Xinkai He → China 43°32N 123°35E 35 C12
Xinken China 22°39N 113°36E 33 F10
Xinle China 38°25N 114°40E 34 E8
Xinlitun China 42°0N 122°8E 35 D12
Xinmin China 41°59N 122°50E 35 D12
Xintai China 35°55N 117°45E 35 G9
Xinwan China 22°47N 113°40E 33 F10
Xinxiang China 35°18N 113°50E 34 G7
Xinzhan China 43°50N 127°18E 35 C14
Xinzheng China 34°20N 113°45E 34 G7
Xinzhou Hainan, China 19°43N 109°17E 38 C7
Xinzhou Shanxi, China 38°22N 112°46E 34 E7
Xiongyuecheng China 40°12N 122°5E 35 D12
Xiping Henan, China 33°22N 114°5E 34 H8
Xiping Henan, China 33°25N 111°8E 34 H6
Xique-Xique Brazil 10°50S 42°40W 93 F10
Xisha Qundao = Paracel Is.
S. China Sea 15°50N 112°0E 36 A4
Xiuyan China 40°18N 123°11E 35 D12
Xixabangma Feng
China 28°20N 85°40E 43 E11
Xixia China 33°25N 111°29E 34 H6
Xixiang China 33°0N 107°44E 33 F10
Xixón = Gijón Spain 43°32N 5°42W 21 A3
Xiyang China 37°38N 113°38E 34 F7
Xizang Zizhiqu □ China 32°0N 88°0E 32 C3
Xlendi Malta 36°1N 14°12E 25 C1
Xochob Mexico 19°21N 89°48W 87 D7
Xuan Loc Vietnam 10°56N 107°14E 39 G6
Xuanhua China 40°40N 115°2E 34 D8
Xuchang China 34°2N 113°48E 34 G7
Xun Xian China 35°42N 114°33E 34 G8
Xunyang China 32°48N 109°22E 34 H5
Xunyi China 35°8N 108°20E 34 G5
Xúquer → Spain 39°5N 0°10W 21 C5
Xushui China 39°2N 115°40E 34 E8
Xuyen Moc Vietnam 10°34N 107°25E 39 G6
Xuzhou China 34°18N 117°10E 35 G9
Xylophagou Cyprus 34°54N 33°51E 25 E12

Y

Ya Xian = Sanya China 18°14N 109°29E 38 C7
Yaamba Australia 23°8S 150°22E 62 C5
Yaapeet Australia 35°45S 142°3E 63 F3
Yablonovyy Khrebet
Russia 53°0N 114°0E 29 D12
Yablonovyy Ra. = Yablonovyy
Khrebet Russia 53°0N 114°0E 29 D12
Yabrai Shan China 39°40N 103°0E 34 E2
Yabrūd Syria 33°58N 36°39E 46 B5
Yabucoa Puerto Rico 18°3N 65°53W 89 d
Yacambú △ Venezuela 9°42N 69°27W 89 E6
Yacheng China 18°22N 109°6E 38 C7
Yacuiba Bolivia 22°0S 63°43W 94 A3
Yacuma → Bolivia 13°38S 65°23W 92 F5
Yadgir India 16°45N 77°5E 40 L10
Yadkin → U.S.A. 35°23N 80°4W 85 D14
Yadua Fiji 16°49S 178°18E 59 a
Yaeyama-Rettō Japan 24°30N 123°40E 31 M1
Yagasa Cluster Fiji 18°57S 178°28W 59 a
Yagodnoye Russia 62°33N 149°40E 29 C15
Yahila
Dem. Rep. of the Congo 0°13N 24°28E 54 B1
Yahk Canada 49°6N 116°10W 70 D5
Yahuma
Dem. Rep. of the Congo 1°0N 23°10E 52 D4
Yaita Japan 36°48N 139°56E 31 F9
Yaiza Canary Is. 28°57N 13°46W 24 F6
Yakima U.S.A. 46°36N 120°31W 76 C3
Yakima → U.S.A. 46°15N 119°14W 76 C4
Yakishiri-Jima Japan 44°26N 141°25E 30 B10
Yakobi I. U.S.A. 58°0N 136°30W 70 B1
Yakovlevka Russia 44°26N 133°28E 30 B6
Yaku-Shima Japan 30°20N 130°30E 31 J5
Yakumo Japan 42°15N 140°16E 30 C10
Yakutat U.S.A. 59°33N 139°44W 68 D6
Yakutia = Sakha □
Russia 66°0N 130°0E 29 C14
Yakutsk Russia 62°5N 129°50E 29 C13
Yala Thailand 6°33N 101°18E 39 J3
Yalboroo Australia 20°50S 148°40E 62 J6
Yale U.S.A. 43°8N 82°48W 82 C2
Yalgoo Australia 28°16S 116°39E 61 E2
Yalgorup △ Australia 32°39S 115°38E 61 F2
Yalinga C.A.R. 6°33N 23°10E 52 C4
Yalkabul, Pta. Mexico 21°32N 88°37W 87 C7
Yalleroi Australia 24°3S 145°42E 62 C4
Yalobusha → U.S.A. 33°33N 90°10W 85 E9
Yalong Jiang → China 26°40N 101°55E 32 D5
Yalova Turkey 40°41N 29°15E 23 D13
Yalta Ukraine 44°30N 34°10E 19 F5
Yalu Jiang → China 39°55N 124°19E 35 E13
Yam Ha Melah = Dead Sea
Asia 31°30N 35°30E 46 D4
Yam Kinneret Israel 32°45N 35°35E 46 C4
Yamada Japan 33°33N 130°49E 31 H5
Yamagata Japan 38°15N 140°15E 30 E10
Yamagata □ Japan 38°30N 140°0E 30 E10
Yamaguchi Japan 34°10N 131°32E 31 G5
Yamaguchi □ Japan 34°20N 131°40E 31 G5
Yamal, Poluostrov Russia 71°0N 70°0E 28 B8
Yamal Pen. = Yamal, Poluostrov
Russia 71°0N 70°0E 28 B8
Yamanashi □ Japan 35°40N 138°40E 31 G9
Yamanie Falls △
Australia 18°29S 146°9E 62 B4
Yamantau, Gora Russia 54°15N 58°6E 18 D10
Yamato Ridge
Sea of Japan 39°20N 135°0E 30 E7
Yamba Australia 29°26S 153°23E 63 D5
Yambarran Ra.
Australia 15°10S 130°25E 60 C5
Yâmbiô Sudan 4°35N 28°16E 51 H11
Yambol Bulgaria 42°30N 26°30E 23 C12
Yamburg Russia 68°21N 77°8E 28 C8
Yamdena Indonesia 7°45S 131°20E 37 F8
Yame Japan 33°13N 130°35E 31 H5
Yamethin Burma 20°29N 96°18E 41 J20
Yamma Yamma, L.
Australia 26°16S 141°20E 63 D3
Yamoussoukro Ivory C. 6°49N 5°17W 50 G4
Yampa → U.S.A. 40°32N 108°59W 76 F9
Yampi Sd. Australia 16°8S 123°38E 60 C3
Yampil Moldova 48°15N 28°15E 17 D15
Yampol = Yampil
Moldova 48°15N 28°15E 17 D15
Yamuna → India 25°30N 81°53E 43 G9
Yamunanagar India 30°7N 77°17E 42 D7
Yamzho Yumco China 28°48N 90°35E 32 D4
Yana → Russia 71°30N 136°0E 29 B14
Yanagawa Japan 33°10N 130°24E 31 H5
Yanai Japan 33°58N 132°7E 31 H6
Yan'an China 36°35N 109°26E 34 F5
Yanaul Russia 56°25N 55°0E 18 C10
Yanbu 'al Baḥr Si. Arabia 24°0N 38°5E 44 F3
Yanchang China 36°43N 110°1E 34 F6
Yancheng Henan, China 33°35N 114°0E 34 H8
Yancheng Jiangsu, China 33°23N 120°8E 35 H11
Yanchep Australia 31°33S 115°37E 61 F2
Yanchi China 37°48N 107°20E 34 F4
Yanchuan China 36°51N 110°10E 34 F6
Yanco Cr. → Australia 35°14S 145°35E 63 F4
Yandicoogina Australia 22°49S 119°12E 60 D2
Yandoon Burma 17°0N 95°40E 41 L19
Yang Xian China 33°15N 107°30E 34 H4
Yang-yang S. Korea 38°4N 128°38E 35 E15
Yangambi
Dem. Rep. of the Congo 0°47N 24°24E 54 B1
Yangcheng China 35°28N 112°22E 34 G7
Yangch'ü = Taiyuan
China 37°52N 112°33E 34 F7
Yanggao China 40°21N 113°55E 34 D7
Yanggu China 36°8N 115°43E 34 F8
Yangliuqing China 39°2N 117°5E 35 E9
Yangon = Rangoon
Burma 16°45N 96°20E 41 L20
Yangpingguan China 32°58N 106°5E 34 H4
Yangquan China 37°58N 113°31E 34 F7
Yangtse = Chang Jiang →
China 31°48N 121°10E 33 C7
Yangtze Kiang = Chang Jiang →
China 31°48N 121°10E 33 C7
Yangyuan China 40°1N 114°10E 34 D8
Yangzhou China 32°21N 119°26E 33 C6
Yanji China 42°59N 129°30E 35 C15
Yankton U.S.A. 42°53N 97°23W 80 D5
Yanonge
Dem. Rep. of the Congo 0°35N 24°38E 54 B1
Yanqi China 42°5N 86°35E 32 B3
Yanqing China 40°30N 115°58E 34 D8
Yanshan China 38°4N 117°22E 35 E9
Yanshou China 45°28N 128°22E 35 B15
Yantabulla Australia 29°21S 145°0E 63 D4
Yantai China 37°34N 121°22E 35 F11
Yantian China 22°35N 114°16E 33 F11
Yanuca Fiji 18°24S 178°0E 59 a
Yanzhou China 35°35N 116°49E 34 G9
Yao Noi, Ko Thailand 8°7N 98°37E 39 a
Yao Xian China 34°55N 108°59E 34 G5
Yao Yai, Ko Thailand 8°0N 98°35E 39 a
Yaoundé Cameroon 3°50N 11°35E 52 D2
Yaowan China 34°15N 118°3E 35 G10
Yap Pac. Oc. 9°30N 138°10E 64 G5
Yapen Indonesia 1°50S 136°0E 37 E9
Yapen, Selat Indonesia 1°20S 136°10E 37 E9
Yapero Indonesia 4°59S 137°11E 37 E9
Yappar → Australia 18°22S 141°16E 62 B3
Yaqaga Fiji 16°35S 178°36E 59 a
Yaqui → Mexico 27°37N 110°39W 86 B2
Yar-Sale Russia 66°50N 70°50E 28 C8
Yaraka Australia 24°53S 144°3E 62 C3
Yaransk Russia 57°22N 47°49E 18 C8
Yare → U.K. 52°35N 1°38E 13 E9
Yaremcha Ukraine 48°27N 24°33E 17 D13
Yarensk Russia 62°11N 49°15E 18 B8
Yarí → Colombia 0°20S 72°20W 92 D4
Yarkand = Shache
China 38°20N 77°10E 32 C2
Yarkant He → China 40°26N 80°59E 32 B3
Yarker Canada 44°23N 76°46W 83 B8
Yarkhun → Pakistan 36°17N 72°30E 43 A5
Yarlung Ziangbo Jiang =
Brahmaputra →
Asia 23°40N 90°35E 43 H13
Yarmouth Canada 43°50N 66°7W 73 D6
Yarmūk → Syria 32°42N 35°40E 46 C4
Yaroslavl Russia 57°35N 39°55E 18 C6
Yarqa, W. → Egypt 30°0N 33°49E 46 F2
Yarra Yarra Lakes
Australia 29°40S 115°45E 61 E2
Yarram Australia 38°29S 146°39E 63 F4
Yarraman Australia 26°50S 152°0E 63 D5
Yarras Australia 31°25S 152°20E 63 E5
Yarrie Australia 20°40S 120°12E 60 D3
Yartsevo Russia 60°20N 90°0E 29 C10
Yarumal Colombia 6°58N 75°24W 92 B3
Yasawa Fiji 16°47S 177°31E 59 a
Yasawa Group Fiji 17°0S 177°23E 59 a
Yaselda Belarus 52°7N 26°28E 17 B14
Yasin Pakistan 36°24N 73°23E 43 A5
Yasinski, L. Canada 53°16N 77°35W 72 B4
Yasinya Ukraine 48°16N 24°21E 17 D13
Yasothon Thailand 15°50N 104°10E 38 E5
Yass Australia 34°49S 148°54E 63 E4
Yāsūj Iran 30°31N 51°31E 45 D6
Yatağan Turkey 37°20N 28°10E 23 F13
Yates Center U.S.A. 37°53N 95°44W 80 G6
Yathkyed L. Canada 62°40N 98°0W 71 A9
Yatsushiro Japan 32°30N 130°40E 31 H5
Yatta Plateau Kenya 2°0S 38°0E 54 C4
Yauco Puerto Rico 18°2N 66°51W 89 d
Yavari → Peru 4°21S 70°2W 92 D4
Yávaros Mexico 26°42N 109°31W 86 B3
Yavatmal India 20°20N 78°15E 40 J11
Yavne Israel 31°52N 34°45E 46 D3
Yavoriv Ukraine 49°55N 23°20E 17 D12
Yavorov = Yavoriv
Ukraine 49°55N 23°20E 17 D12
Yawatahama Japan 33°27N 132°24E 31 H6
Yawri B. S. Leone 8°22N 13°0W 50 G3
Yaxian = Sanya China 18°14N 109°29E 38 C7
Yazd Iran 31°55N 54°27E 45 D7
Yazd □ Iran 32°0N 55°0E 45 D7
Yazd-e Khvāst Iran 31°31N 52°7E 45 D7
Yazman Pakistan 29°8N 71°45E 42 E4
Yazoo → U.S.A. 32°22N 90°54W 85 E9
Yazoo City U.S.A. 32°51N 90°25W 85 E9
Ybycuí △ Paraguay 26°5S 56°46W 94 B4
Ybytyruzú △ Paraguay 25°51S 56°11W 95 B4
Ye Burma 15°15N 97°15E 38 E1
Ye Xian China 33°35N 113°25E 34 H7
Yebyu Burma 14°15N 98°13E 38 E2
Yecheng China 37°54N 77°26E 32 C2
Yecheon S. Korea 36°39N 128°27E 35 F15
Yecla Spain 38°35N 1°5W 21 C5
Yécora Mexico 28°20N 108°58W 86 B3
Yedintsy = Edineț
Moldova 48°9N 27°18E 17 D14
Yegros Paraguay 26°20S 56°25W 94 B4
Yehbuah Indonesia 8°23S 114°45E 37 J17
Yehuda, Midbar Israel 31°35N 35°15E 46 D4
Yei Sudan 4°9N 30°40E 51 H12
Yekaterinburg Russia 56°50N 60°30E 28 D7
Yelarbon Australia 28°33S 150°38E 63 D5
Yelets Russia 52°40N 38°30E 18 D6
Yelizavetgrad = Kirovohrad
Ukraine 48°35N 32°20E 19 E5
Yelizovo Russia 53°11N 158°23E 29 D16
Yell U.K. 60°35N 1°5W 11 A7
Yell Sd. U.K. 60°33N 1°15W 11 A7
Yellow = Huang He →
China 37°55N 118°50E 35 F10
Yellow Sea China 35°0N 123°0E 35 G12
Yellowhead Pass
Canada 52°53N 118°25W 70 C5
Yellowknife Canada 62°27N 114°29W 70 A6
Yellowknife → Canada 62°31N 114°19W 70 A6
Yellowstone →
U.S.A. 47°59N 103°59W 76 C12
Yellowstone △ U.S.A. 44°40N 110°30W 76 D8
Yellowstone L. U.S.A. 44°27N 110°22W 76 D8
Yelsk Belarus 51°50N 29°10E 17 C15
Yemen ■ Asia 15°0N 44°0E 47 E3
Yen Bai Vietnam 21°42N 104°52E 38 B5
Yenangyaung Burma 20°30N 95°0E 41 J19

Yenbo = Yanbu 'al Baḥr Si. Arabia 24°0N 38°5E 44 F3
Yenda Australia 34°13S 146°14E 63 E4
Yeni Erenköy = Yialousa Cyprus 35°32N 34°10E 25 D13
Yenice Turkey 39°55N 27°17E 23 E12
Yenisey → Russia 71°50N 82°40E 28 B9
Yeniseysk Russia 58°27N 92°13E 29 D10
Yeniseyskiy Zaliv Russia 72°20N 81°0E 28 B9
Yenyuka Russia 57°57N 121°15E 29 D13
Yeo → U.K. 51°2N 2°49W 13 G5
Yeo, L. Australia 28°0S 124°30E 61 E3
Yeo I. Canada 45°24N 81°48W 82 A3
Yeoju S. Korea 37°20N 127°35E 35 F14
Yeola India 20°2N 74°30E 40 J9
Yeong-wol S. Korea 37°11N 128°28E 35 F15
Yeongcheon S. Korea 35°58N 128°56E 35 G15
Yeongdeok S. Korea 36°24N 129°22E 35 F15
Yeongdeungpo S. Korea 37°31N 126°54E 35 F14
Yeongdong S. Korea 36°10N 127°46E 35 F14
Yeongju S. Korea 36°50N 128°40E 35 F15
Yeosu S. Korea 34°47N 127°45E 35 G14
Yeovil U.K. 50°57N 2°38W 13 G5
Yeppoon Australia 23°5S 150°47E 62 C5
Yerbent Turkmenistan 39°30N 58°50E 28 F6
Yerbogachen Russia 61°16N 108°0E 29 C11
Yerevan Armenia 40°10N 44°31E 44 A5
Yerington U.S.A. 38°59N 119°10W 76 G4
Yermak Kazakhstan 52°2N 76°55E 28 D8
Yermo U.S.A. 34°54N 116°50W 79 L10
Yerólakkos Cyprus 35°11N 33°15E 25 D12
Yeropol Russia 65°15N 168°40E 29 C17
Yeroskipos Cyprus 34°46N 32°28E 25 E11
Yershov Russia 51°23N 48°27E 19 D8
Yerushalayim = Jerusalem Israel/West Bank 31°47N 35°10E 46 D4
Yes Tor U.K. 50°41N 4°0W 13 G4
Yesan S. Korea 36°41N 126°51E 35 F14
Yeso U.S.A. 34°26N 104°37W 77 J11
Yessey Russia 68°29N 102°10E 29 C11
Yetman Australia 28°56S 150°48E 63 D5
Yeu, Î. d' France 46°42N 2°20W 20 C2
Yevpatoriya Ukraine 45°15N 33°20E 19 E5
Yeysk Russia 46°40N 38°12E 19 E6
Yezd = Yazd Iran 31°55N 54°27E 45 D7
Ygatimi Paraguay 24°5S 55°40W 95 A4
Yhati Paraguay 25°45S 56°35W 94 B4
Yhú Paraguay 25°0S 56°0W 95 B4
Yí → Uruguay 33°7S 57°8W 94 C4
Yi 'Allaq, G. Egypt 30°21N 33°31E 46 E2
Yi He → China 34°10N 118°8E 35 G10
Yi Xian Hebei, China 39°20N 115°30E 34 E8
Yi Xian Liaoning, China 41°30N 121°22E 35 D11
Yialiás → Cyprus 35°9N 33°44E 25 D12
Yialousa Cyprus 35°32N 34°10E 25 D13
Yibin China 28°45N 104°32E 32 D5
Yichang China 30°40N 111°20E 33 C6
Yicheng China 35°42N 111°40E 34 G6
Yichuan China 36°2N 110°10E 34 F6
Yichun China 47°44N 128°52E 33 B7
Yidu China 36°43N 118°28E 35 F10
Yijun China 35°28N 109°8E 34 G5
Yıldız Dağları Turkey 41°48N 27°36E 23 D12
Yilehuli Shan China 51°20N 124°20E 33 A7
Yimianpo China 45°7N 128°2E 35 B15
Yinchuan China 38°30N 106°15E 34 E4
Yindarlgooda, L. Australia 30°40S 121°52E 61 F3
Ying He → China 32°30N 116°30E 34 H9
Ying Xian China 39°32N 113°10E 34 E7
Yingkou China 40°37N 122°18E 35 D12
Yining China 43°58N 81°10E 32 B3
Yinmabin Burma 22°10N 94°55E 41 H19
Yirga Alem Ethiopia 6°48N 38°22E 47 F2
Yirrkala Australia 12°14S 136°56E 62 A2
Yishan China 24°28N 108°38E 32 D5
Yishui China 35°47N 118°30E 35 G10
Yishun Singapore 1°26N 103°51E 39 d
Yitong China 43°13N 125°20E 35 C13
Yixing China 31°21N 119°48E 33 C6
Yiyang Henan, China 34°27N 112°10E 34 G7
Yiyang Hunan, China 28°35N 112°18E 33 D6
Yli-Kitka Finland 66°8N 28°30E 8 C23
Ylitornio Finland 66°19N 23°39E 8 C20
Ylivieska Finland 64°4N 24°28E 8 D21
Yoakum U.S.A. 29°17N 97°9W 84 G6
Yog Pt. Phil. 14°6N 124°12E 37 B6
Yogyakarta Indonesia 7°49S 110°22E 37 G14
Yogyakarta □ Indonesia 7°48S 110°22E 37 G14
Yoho △ Canada 51°25N 116°30W 70 C5
Yojoa, L. de Honduras 14°53N 88°0W 88 D2
Yok Don △ Vietnam 12°50N 107°40E 38 F6
Yokadouma Cameroon 3°26N 14°55E 52 D2
Yokkaichi Japan 34°55N 136°38E 31 G8
Yoko Cameroon 5°32N 12°20E 52 C2
Yokohama Japan 35°27N 139°28E 31 G9
Yokosuka Japan 35°20N 139°40E 31 G9
Yokote Japan 39°20N 140°30E 30 E10
Yola Nigeria 9°10N 12°29E 51 G8
Yolaina, Cordillera de Nic. 11°30N 84°0W 88 D3
Ýolöten Turkmenistan 37°18N 62°21E 45 B9
Yom → Thailand 15°35N 100°1E 38 E3
Yonago Japan 35°25N 133°19E 31 G6
Yonaguni-Jima Japan 24°27N 123°0E 31 M1
Yŏnan N. Korea 37°55N 126°11E 35 F14
Yonezawa Japan 37°57N 140°4E 30 F10
Yong Peng Malaysia 2°0N 103°3E 39 M4
Yong Sata Thailand 7°8N 99°41E 39 J2
Yongamp'o N. Korea 39°56N 124°23E 35 E13
Yongcheng China 33°55N 116°20E 34 H9
Yongdeng China 36°38N 103°25E 34 F2
Yonghe China 36°46N 110°38E 34 F6
Yŏnghŭng N. Korea 39°31N 127°18E 35 E14
Yongji China 34°52N 110°28E 34 G6
Yongnian China 36°47N 114°29E 34 F8
Yongning China 38°15N 106°14E 34 E4
Yongqing China 39°25N 116°28E 34 E9
Yonibana S. Leone 8°30N 12°19W 50 G3
Yonkers U.S.A. 40°56N 73°52W 83 F11
Yonne → France 48°23N 2°58E 20 B5
York Australia 31°52S 116°47E 61 F2
York U.K. 53°58N 1°6W 12 D6
York Ala., U.S.A. 32°29N 88°18W 85 E10
York Nebr., U.S.A. 40°52N 97°36W 80 E5
York Pa., U.S.A. 39°58N 76°44W 81 F15
York, C. Australia 10°42S 142°31E 62 A3
York, City of □ U.K. 53°58N 1°6W 12 D6
York, Kap Greenland 75°55N 66°25W 4 B4
York, Vale of U.K. 54°15N 1°25W 12 C6
York Sd. Australia 15°0S 125°5E 60 C4
Yorke Pen. Australia 34°50S 137°40E 63 E2
Yorkshire Dales △ U.K. 54°12N 2°10W 12 C5
Yorkshire Wolds U.K. 54°8N 0°31W 12 C7
Yorkton Canada 51°11N 102°28W 71 C8
Yorkville U.S.A. 38°52N 123°13W 78 G3
Yoro Honduras 15°9N 87°7W 88 C2
Yoron-Jima Japan 27°2N 128°26E 31 L4
Yos Sudarso, Pulau = Dolak, Pulau Indonesia 8°0S 138°30E 37 F9
Yosemite △ U.S.A. 37°45N 119°40W 78 H7
Yosemite Village U.S.A. 37°45N 119°35W 78 H7
Yoshino-Kumano △ Japan 34°12N 135°55E 31 H8
Yoshkar Ola Russia 56°38N 47°55E 18 C8
Yotvata Israel 29°55N 35°2E 46 F4
Youbou Canada 48°53N 124°13W 78 B2
Youghal Ireland 51°56N 7°52W 10 E4
Youghal B. Ireland 51°55N 7°49W 10 E4
Young Australia 34°19S 148°18E 63 E4
Young Canada 51°47N 105°45W 71 C7
Young Uruguay 32°44S 57°36W 94 C4
Younghusband, L. Australia 30°50S 136°5E 63 E2
Younghusband Pen. Australia 36°0S 139°25E 63 F2
Youngstown Canada 51°35N 111°10W 71 C6
Youngstown N.Y., U.S.A. 43°15N 79°3W 82 C5
Youngstown Ohio, U.S.A. 41°6N 80°39W 82 E4
Youngsville U.S.A. 41°51N 79°19W 82 E5
Youngwood U.S.A. 40°14N 79°34W 82 F5
Youyu China 40°10N 112°20E 34 D7
Yozgat Turkey 39°51N 34°47E 19 G5
Ypacaraí △ Paraguay 25°18S 57°19W 94 B4
Ypané → Paraguay 23°29S 57°19W 94 A4
Ypres = Ieper Belgium 50°51N 2°53E 15 D2
Yreka U.S.A. 41°44N 122°38W 76 F2
Ystad Sweden 55°26N 13°50E 9 J15
Ysyk-Köl = Balykchy Kyrgyzstan 42°26N 76°12E 32 B2
Ysyk-Köl Kyrgyzstan 42°25N 77°15E 28 E8
Ythan → U.K. 57°19N 1°59W 11 D7
Ytyk-Kyuyel Russia 62°30N 133°45E 29 C14
Yu Jiang → China 23°22N 110°3E 33 D6
Yu Xian = Yuzhou China 34°10N 113°28E 34 G7
Yu Xian Hebei, China 39°50N 114°35E 34 E8
Yu Xian Shanxi, China 38°5N 113°20E 34 E7
Yuan Jiang → China 28°55N 111°50E 33 D6
Yuanqu China 35°18N 111°40E 34 G6
Yuanyang China 35°3N 113°58E 34 G7
Yuba → U.S.A. 39°8N 121°36W 78 F5
Yuba City U.S.A. 39°8N 121°37W 78 F5
Yūbari Japan 43°4N 141°59E 30 C10
Yūbetsu Japan 44°13N 143°50E 30 B11
Yucatán □ Mexico 20°50N 89°0W 87 C7
Yucatán, Canal de Caribbean 22°0N 86°30W 88 B2
Yucatán, Península de Mexico 19°30N 89°0W 66 H11
Yucatan Basin Cent. Amer. 19°0N 86°0W 87 D7
Yucatan Channel = Yucatán, Canal de Caribbean 22°0N 86°30W 88 B2
Yucca U.S.A. 34°52N 114°9W 79 L12
Yucca Valley U.S.A. 34°8N 116°27W 79 L10
Yucheng China 36°55N 116°32E 34 F9
Yuci China 37°42N 112°46E 34 F7
Yuen Long China 22°26N 114°2E 33 G11
Yuendumu Australia 22°16S 131°49E 60 D5
Yugorenok Russia 59°47N 137°40E 29 D14
Yugoslavia = Serbia ■ Europe 43°20N 20°0E 23 B9
Yukon U.S.A. 35°31N 97°45W 84 D6
Yukon → U.S.A. 62°32N 163°54W 74 a
Yukon Territory □ Canada 63°0N 135°0W 68 C6
Yukta Russia 63°26N 105°42E 29 C11
Yukuhashi Japan 33°44N 130°59E 31 H5
Yulara Australia 25°10S 130°55E 61 E5
Yule → Australia 20°41S 118°17E 60 D2
Yuleba Australia 26°37S 149°24E 63 D4
Yulin Hainan, China 18°10N 109°31E 38 C7
Yulin Shaanxi, China 38°20N 109°30E 34 E5
Yuma Ariz., U.S.A. 32°43N 114°37W 79 N12
Yuma Colo., U.S.A. 40°8N 102°43W 76 F12
Yuma, B. de Dom. Rep. 18°20N 68°35W 89 C6
Yumbe Uganda 3°28N 31°15E 54 B3
Yumbi Dem. Rep. of the Congo 1°12S 26°15E 54 C2
Yumen China 39°50N 97°30E 32 C4
Yuna Australia 28°20S 115°0E 61 E2
Yuncheng Henan, China 35°36N 115°57E 34 G8
Yuncheng Shanxi, China 35°2N 111°0E 34 G6
Yungas Bolivia 17°0S 66°0W 92 G5
Yungay Chile 37°10S 72°5W 94 D1
Yunnan □ China 25°0N 102°0E 32 D5
Yunta Australia 32°34S 139°36E 63 E2
Yunxi China 33°0N 110°22E 34 H6
Yupanqui Basin Pac. Oc. 19°0S 101°0W 65 J17
Yuraygir △ Australia 29°45S 153°15E 63 D5
Yurga Russia 55°42N 84°51E 28 D9
Yurimaguas Peru 5°55S 76°7W 92 E3
Yurubí △ Venezuela 10°26N 68°42W 89 D6
Yuscarán Honduras 13°58N 86°45W 88 D2
Yushe China 37°4N 112°58E 34 F7
Yushu Jilin, China 44°43N 126°38E 35 B14
Yushu Qinghai, China 33°5N 96°55E 32 C4
Yutai China 35°0N 116°45E 34 G9
Yutian Hebei, China 39°53N 117°45E 35 E9
Yutian Sinkiang-Uigur, China 36°52N 81°42E 32 C3
Yuxarı Qarabağ = Nagorno-Karabakh □ Azerbaijan 39°55N 46°45E 44 B5
Yuxi China 24°30N 102°35E 32 D5
Yuzawa Japan 39°10N 140°30E 30 E10
Yuzhno-Kurilsk Russia 44°1N 145°51E 29 E15
Yuzhno-Sakhalinsk Russia 46°58N 142°45E 29 E15
Yuzhnyy □ Russia 44°0N 40°0E 28 E5
Yuzhou China 34°10N 113°28E 34 G7
Yvetot France 49°37N 0°44E 20 B4

Z

Zaanstad Neths. 52°27N 4°50E 15 B4
Zāb al Kabīr → Iraq 36°1N 43°24E 44 B4
Zāb aş Şaghīr → Iraq 35°17N 43°29E 44 C4
Zabaykalsk Russia 49°40N 117°25E 29 E12
Zābol Iran 31°0N 61°32E 45 D9
Zābol □ Afghan. 32°0N 67°0E 40 D5
Zābolī Iran 27°10N 61°35E 45 E9
Zabrze Poland 50°18N 18°50E 17 C10
Zacapa Guatemala 14°59N 89°31W 88 D2
Zacapu Mexico 19°50N 101°43W 86 D4
Zacatecas Mexico 22°47N 102°35W 86 C4
Zacatecas □ Mexico 23°0N 103°0W 86 C4
Zacatecoluca El Salv. 13°29N 88°51W 88 D2
Zachary U.S.A. 30°39N 91°9W 84 F9
Zacoalco de Torres Mexico 20°14N 103°35W 86 C4
Zacualtipán Mexico 20°39N 98°36W 87 C5
Zadar Croatia 44°8N 15°14E 16 F8
Zadetkyi Kyun Burma 10°0N 98°25E 39 G2
Zafarqand Iran 33°11N 52°29E 45 C7
Zafra Spain 38°26N 6°30W 21 C2
Żagań Poland 51°39N 15°22E 16 C8
Zagaoua Chad 15°30N 22°24E 51 E10
Zagazig Egypt 30°40N 31°30E 51 B12
Zāgheh Iran 33°30N 48°42E 45 C6
Zagreb Croatia 45°50N 15°58E 16 F9
Zāgros, Kūhhā-ye Iran 33°45N 48°5E 45 C6
Zagros Mts. = Zāgros, Kūhhā-ye Iran 33°45N 48°5E 45 C6
Zahamena △ Madag. 17°37S 48°49E 57 B8
Zāhedān Fārs, Iran 28°46N 53°52E 45 D7
Zāhedān Sīstān va Balūchestān, Iran 29°30N 60°50E 45 D9
Zahlah Lebanon 33°52N 35°50E 46 B4
Zaïre = Congo → Africa 6°4S 12°24E 52 F2
Zaječar Serbia 43°53N 22°18E 23 C10
Zaka Zimbabwe 20°20S 31°29E 57 C5
Zakamensk Russia 50°23N 103°17E 29 D11
Zakhodnaya Dzvina = Daugava → Latvia 57°4N 24°3E 9 H21
Zākhū Iraq 37°10N 42°50E 44 B4
Zakinthos = Zakynthos Greece 37°47N 20°54E 23 F9
Zakopane Poland 49°18N 19°57E 17 D10
Zakros Greece 35°6N 26°10E 25 D8
Zakynthos Greece 37°47N 20°54E 23 F9
Zalaegerszeg Hungary 46°53N 16°47E 17 E9
Zalari Russia 53°33N 102°30E 29 D11
Zalău Romania 47°12N 23°3E 17 E12
Zaleshchiki = Zalishchyky Ukraine 48°45N 25°45E 17 D13
Zalew Wiślany Poland 54°20N 19°50E 17 A10
Zalingei Sudan 12°51N 23°29E 51 F10
Zalishchyky Ukraine 48°45N 25°45E 17 D13
Zama L. Canada 58°45N 119°5W 70 B5
Zambeke Dem. Rep. of the Congo 2°8N 25°17E 54 B2
Zambeze → Africa 18°35S 36°20E 55 F4
Zambezi = Zambeze → Africa 18°35S 36°20E 55 F4
Zambezi Zambia 13°30S 23°15E 53 G4
Zambezi △ Zimbabwe 17°54S 25°41E 55 F2
Zambezia □ Mozam. 16°15S 37°30E 55 F4
Zambia ■ Africa 15°0S 28°0E 55 F2
Zamboanga Phil. 6°59N 122°3E 37 C6
Zamora Mexico 19°59N 102°16W 86 D4
Zamora Spain 41°30N 5°45W 21 B3
Zamość Poland 50°43N 23°15E 17 C12
Zanda China 31°32N 79°50E 32 C2
Zandvoort Neths. 52°22N 4°32E 15 B4
Zanesville U.S.A. 39°56N 82°1W 82 G2
Zangābād Iran 38°26N 46°44E 44 B5
Zangue → Mozam. 17°50S 35°21E 55 F4
Zanjān Iran 36°40N 48°35E 45 B6
Zanjān □ Iran 37°20N 49°30E 45 B6
Zanjān → Iran 37°8N 47°47E 45 B6
Zante = Zakynthos Greece 37°47N 20°54E 23 F9
Zanthus Australia 31°2S 123°34E 61 F3
Zanzibar Tanzania 6°12S 39°12E 54 D4
Zaouiet El-Kala = Bordj Omar Driss Algeria 28°10N 6°40E 50 C7
Zaouiet Reggâne Algeria 26°32N 0°3E 50 C6
Zaozhuang China 34°50N 117°35E 35 G9
Zap Suyu = Zāb al Kabīr → Iraq 36°1N 43°24E 44 B4
Zapadnaya Dvina = Daugava → Latvia 57°4N 24°3E 9 H21
Západné Beskydy Europe 49°30N 19°0E 17 D10
Zapala Argentina 39°0S 70°5W 96 D2
Zapaleri, Cerro Bolivia 22°49S 67°11W 94 A2
Zapata U.S.A. 26°55N 99°16W 84 H5
Zapolyarnyy Russia 69°26N 30°51E 8 B24
Zapopán Mexico 20°43N 103°24W 86 C4
Zaporizhzhya Ukraine 47°50N 35°10E 19 E6
Zaporozhye = Zaporizhzhya Ukraine 47°50N 35°10E 19 E6
Zara Turkey 39°58N 37°43E 44 B3
Zaragoza Coahuila, Mexico 28°29N 100°55W 86 B4
Zaragoza Nuevo León, Mexico 23°58N 99°46W 87 C5
Zaragoza Spain 41°39N 0°53W 21 B5
Zarand Kermān, Iran 30°46N 56°34E 45 D8
Zarand Markazī, Iran 35°18N 50°25E 45 C6
Zaranj Afghan. 30°55N 61°55E 40 D2
Zarasai Lithuania 55°40N 26°20E 9 J22
Zárate Argentina 34°7S 59°0W 94 C4
Zard, Kūh-e Iran 32°22N 50°4E 45 C6
Zāreh Iran 35°7N 49°9E 45 C6
Zaria Nigeria 11°0N 7°40E 50 F7
Zarneh Iran 33°55N 46°10E 44 C5
Zaros Greece 35°8N 24°54E 25 D6
Zarqā', Nahr az → Jordan 32°10N 35°37E 46 C4
Zarrīn Iran 32°46N 54°37E 45 C7
Zaruma Ecuador 3°40S 79°38W 92 D3
Żary Poland 51°37N 15°10E 16 C8
Zarzis Tunisia 33°31N 11°2E 51 B8
Zaskar → India 34°13N 77°20E 43 B7
Zaskar Mts. India 33°15N 77°30E 43 C7
Zastron S. Africa 30°18S 27°7E 56 E4
Zavāreh Iran 33°29N 52°28E 45 C7
Zave Zimbabwe 17°6S 30°1E 57 B5
Zavitinsk Russia 50°10N 129°20E 29 D13
Zavodovski, I. Antarctica 56°0S 27°45W 5 B1
Zawiercie Poland 50°30N 19°24E 17 C10
Zāwiyat al Bayḍā = Al Bayḍā Libya 32°50N 21°44E 51 B10
Zāyā Iraq 33°33N 44°13E 44 C5
Zāyandeh → Iran 32°35N 52°0E 45 C7
Zaysan Kazakhstan 47°28N 84°52E 32 B3
Zaysan Köli Kazakhstan 48°0N 83°0E 28 E9
Zayü China 28°48N 97°27E 32 D4
Zazafotsy Madag. 21°11S 46°21E 57 C8
Zbarazh Ukraine 49°43N 25°44E 17 D13
Zdolbuniv Ukraine 50°30N 26°15E 17 C14
Zduńska Wola Poland 51°37N 18°59E 17 C10
Zeballos Canada 49°59N 126°50W 70 D3
Zebediela S. Africa 24°20S 29°17E 57 C4
Zeebrugge Belgium 51°19N 3°12E 15 C3
Zeehan Australia 41°52S 145°25E 63 G4
Zeeland □ Neths. 51°30N 3°50E 15 C3
Zeerust S. Africa 25°31S 26°4E 56 D4
Zefat Israel 32°58N 35°29E 46 C4
Zehak Iran 30°53N 61°42E 45 D9
Zeil, Mt. Australia 23°30S 132°23E 60 D5
Zeila = Saylac Somali Rep. 11°21N 43°30E 47 E3
Zeist Neths. 52°5N 5°15E 15 B5
Zeitz Germany 51°2N 12°7E 16 C7
Zelenogorsk Russia 60°12N 29°43E 8 F23
Zelenograd Russia 56°1N 37°12E 18 C6
Zelienople U.S.A. 40°48N 80°8W 82 F4
Zémio C.A.R. 5°2N 25°5E 54 A2
Zempoala Mexico 19°27N 96°23W 87 D5
Zemun Serbia 44°51N 20°25E 23 B9
Zenica Bos.-H. 44°10N 17°57E 23 B7
Žepče Bos.-H. 44°28N 18°2E 23 B8
Zevenaar Neths. 51°56N 6°5E 15 C6
Zeya Russia 53°48N 127°14E 29 D13
Zeya → Russia 51°42N 128°53E 29 D13
Zêzere → Portugal 39°28N 8°20W 21 C1
Zghartā Lebanon 34°21N 35°53E 46 A4
Zgorzelec Poland 51°10N 15°0E 16 C8
Zhabinka Belarus 52°13N 24°2E 17 B13
Zhambyl = Taraz Kazakhstan 42°54N 71°22E 28 E8
Zhangaqazaly Kazakhstan 45°48N 62°6E 28 E7
Zhangbei China 41°10N 114°45E 34 D8
Zhangguangcai Ling China 45°0N 129°0E 35 B15
Zhangjiabian China 22°33N 113°28E 33 F9
Zhangjiagang China 31°55N 120°30E 37 B13
Zhangjiakou China 40°48N 114°55E 34 D8
Zhangwu China 42°43N 123°52E 35 C12
Zhangye China 38°50N 100°23E 32 C5
Zhangzhou China 24°30N 117°35E 33 D6
Zhanhua China 37°40N 118°8E 35 F10
Zhanjiang China 21°15N 110°20E 33 D6
Zhannetty, Ostrov Russia 76°43N 158°0E 29 B16
Zhanyi China 25°38N 103°48E 32 D5
Zhanyu China 44°30N 122°30E 35 B12
Zhao Xian China 37°43N 114°45E 34 F8
Zhaocheng China 36°22N 111°38E 34 F6
Zhaotong China 27°20N 103°44E 32 D5
Zhaoyuan Heilongjiang, China 45°27N 125°0E 35 B13
Zhaoyuan Shandong, China 37°20N 120°23E 35 F11
Zhari Namco China 31°6N 85°36E 32 C3
Zharkent Kazakhstan 44°10N 80°0E 28 E9
Zhashkiv Ukraine 49°15N 30°5E 17 D16
Zhashui China 33°40N 109°8E 34 H5
Zhayylma Kazakhstan 51°37N 61°33E 28 D7
Zhayyq → Kazakhstan 47°0N 51°48E 19 E9
Zhdanov = Mariupol Ukraine 47°5N 37°31E 19 E6
Zhecheng China 34°7N 115°20E 34 G8
Zhejiang □ China 29°0N 120°0E 33 D7
Zheleznodorozhnyy Russia 62°35N 50°55E 18 B9
Zheleznogorsk-Ilimskiy Russia 56°34N 104°8E 29 D11
Zhen'an China 33°27N 109°9E 34 H5
Zhengding China 38°8N 114°32E 34 E8
Zhengzhou China 34°45N 113°34E 34 G7
Zhenlai China 45°50N 123°5E 35 B12
Zhenping China 33°10N 112°16E 34 H7
Zhenyuan China 35°35N 107°30E 34 G4
Zhetiqara Kazakhstan 52°11N 61°12E 28 D7
Zhezqazghan Kazakhstan 47°44N 67°40E 28 E7
Zhidan China 36°48N 108°48E 34 F5
Zhigansk Russia 66°48N 123°27E 29 C13
Zhilinda Russia 70°0N 114°20E 29 C
Zhitomir = Zhytomyr Ukraine 50°20N 28°40E 17 C
Zhlobin Belarus 52°55N 30°0E 17 B
Zhmerynka Ukraine 49°2N 28°2E 17 D
Zhob Pakistan 31°20N 69°31E 42 D
Zhob → Pakistan 32°4N 69°50E 42
Zhodzina Belarus 54°5N 28°17E 17 A
Zhokhova, Ostrov Russia 76°4N 152°40E 29 B
Zhongdian China 27°48N 99°42E 32 D
Zhongning China 37°29N 105°40E 34
Zhongshan Antarctica 69°0S 39°50E 5
Zhongshan China 22°26N 113°20E 33
Zhongshankong China 22°35N 113°29E 33
Zhongtiao Shan China 35°0N 111°10E 34
Zhongwei China 37°30N 105°12E 34
Zhongyang China 37°20N 111°11E 34
Zhosaly Kazakhstan 45°29N 64°4E 28
Zhoucun China 36°47N 117°48E 35
Zhouzhi China 34°10N 108°12E 34
Zhuanghe China 39°40N 123°0E 35 E
Zhucheng China 36°0N 119°27E 35 G
Zhugqu China 33°40N 104°30E 34
Zhuhai China 22°17N 113°34E 33 G
Zhujiang Kou China 22°20N 113°45E 33 G
Zhumadian China 32°59N 114°2E 34
Zhuo Xian = Zhuozhou China 39°28N 115°58E 34
Zhuolu China 40°20N 115°12E 34
Zhuozhou China 39°28N 115°58E 34
Zhuozi China 41°0N 112°25E 34
Zhytomyr Ukraine 50°20N 28°40E 17 C
Ziarat Pakistan 30°25N 67°49E 42
Zibo China 36°47N 118°3E 35 F
Zichang China 37°18N 109°40E 34
Zidi = Wandhari Pakistan 27°42N 66°48E 42
Zielona Góra Poland 51°57N 15°31E 16
Zierikzee Neths. 51°40N 3°55E 15
Zigong China 29°15N 104°48E 32
Ziguéy Chad 14°43N 15°50E 51
Ziguinchor Senegal 12°35N 16°20W 50
Zihuatanejo Mexico 17°39N 101°33W 86
Žilina Slovak Rep. 49°12N 18°42E 17 D
Zillah Libya 28°30N 17°33E 51
Zima Russia 54°0N 102°5E 29 D
Zimapán Mexico 20°45N 99°21W 87
Zimba Zambia 17°20S 26°11E 55
Zimbabwe Zimbabwe 20°16S 30°54E 55
Zimbabwe ■ Africa 19°0S 30°0E 55
Zimnicea Romania 43°40N 25°22E 17 G
Zinave △ Mozam. 21°35S 33°40E 57
Zinder Niger 13°48N 9°0E 50
Zinga Tanzania 9°16S 38°49E 55
Zion △ U.S.A. 37°15N 113°5W 77
Ziros Greece 35°5N 26°8E 25
Zirreh, Gowd-e Afghan. 29°45N 62°0E 40
Zitácuaro Mexico 19°24N 100°22W 86
Zitundo Mozam. 26°48S 32°47E 57
Ziwa Maghariba = Kagera □ Tanzania 2°0S 31°30E 54
Ziway, L. Ethiopia 8°0N 38°50E 47
Ziyang China 32°32N 108°31E 34
Zlatograd Bulgaria 41°22N 25°7E 23 D
Zlatoust Russia 55°10N 59°40E 18 C
Zlín Czech Rep. 49°14N 17°40E 17
Zmeinogorsk Kazakhstan 51°10N 82°13E 28
Znojmo Czech Rep. 48°50N 16°2E 16
Zobeyrī Iran 34°10N 46°40E 44
Zobia Dem. Rep. of the Congo 3°0N 25°59E 54
Zoetermeer Neths. 52°3N 4°30E 15
Zohreh → Iran 30°16N 51°15E 45
Zolochiv Ukraine 49°45N 24°51E 17 D
Zomba Malawi 15°22S 35°19E 55
Zongo Dem. Rep. of the Congo 4°20N 18°35E 52
Zonguldak Turkey 41°28N 31°50E 19
Zonqor Pt. Malta 35°52N 14°34E 25
Zorritos Peru 3°43S 80°40W 92
Zou Xiang China 35°30N 116°58E 34
Zouar Chad 20°30N 16°32E 51
Zouérate = Zouîrât Mauritania 22°44N 12°21W 50
Zouîrât Mauritania 22°44N 12°21W 50
Zoutkamp Neths. 53°20N 6°18E 15
Zrenjanin Serbia 45°22N 20°23E 23
Zufār Oman 17°40N 54°0E 47
Zug Switz. 47°10N 8°31E 20
Zugspitze Germany 47°25N 10°59E 16
Zuid-Holland □ Neths. 52°0N 4°35E 15
Zuidbeveland Neths. 51°30N 3°50E 15
Zuidhorn Neths. 53°15N 6°23E 15
Zula Eritrea 15°17N 39°40E 47
Zumbo Mozam. 15°35S 30°26E 55
Zumpango Mexico 19°48N 99°6W 87
Zunhua China 40°18N 117°58E 35
Zuni Pueblo U.S.A. 35°4N 108°51W 77
Zunyi China 27°42N 106°53E 32
Zurbātīyah Iraq 33°9N 46°3E 44
Zürich Switz. 47°22N 8°32E 20
Zutphen Neths. 52°9N 6°12E 15
Zuurberg △ S. Africa 33°12S 25°32E 56
Zuwārah Libya 32°58N 12°1E 51
Zūzan Iran 34°22N 59°53E 45
Zvishavane Zimbabwe 20°17S 30°2E 55
Zvolen Slovak Rep. 48°33N 19°10E 17 D
Zwettl Austria 48°35N 15°9E 16
Zwickau Germany 50°44N 12°30E 16
Zwolle Neths. 52°31N 6°6E 15
Zwolle U.S.A. 31°38N 93°39W 84
Żyrardów Poland 52°3N 20°28E 17 B
Zyryan Kazakhstan 49°43N 84°20E 28
Zyryanka Russia 65°45N 150°51E 29
Zyryanovsk = Zyryan Kazakhstan 49°43N 84°20E 28
Żywiec Poland 49°42N 19°10E 17 D